THE WORLD BOOK ENCYCLOPEDIA

M

Volume 13

FIELD ENTERPRISES EDUCATIONAL CORPORATION

CHICAGO   LONDON   ROME   SYDNEY   TORONTO

THE WORLD BOOK ENCYCLOPEDIA

COPYRIGHT © 1971, U.S.A.

by FIELD ENTERPRISES EDUCATIONAL CORPORATION

M is the 13th letter of our alphabet. It was also the 13th letter in the alphabet used by the Semites, who once lived in Syria and Palestine. They named it *mem*, their word for *water*, and adapted an Egyptian *hieroglyphic*, or picture symbol, for water. The Greeks called it *mu*. See ALPHABET.

Uses. *M* or *m* ranks as the 14th most frequently used letter in books, newspapers, and other printed material in English. It stands for *mile* or *meter* in measurements of distance. In chemistry, *m* is the short form for *metal*. $\overline{M}$ in the Roman numeral system stands for 1,000, while $\overline{M}$ stands for 1,000,000. *M* is also the abbreviation for *Master* in college degrees, and *m* stands for *milli*, as in *millimeter*. In Germany, people use *M* to stand for the *mark*, the basic unit of their money. In French, *M* stands for *monsieur*, equal to our *mister*. It is the seventh letter of the Hawaiian alphabet.

Pronunciation. In English, a person pronounces *m* by closing both lips and making the sound through his nose. Double *m* usually has the same sound, as in *stammer*. But there are some words, like *immobile*, in which each *m* is often pronounced. These words come from a Latin prefix ending in *m* and a Latin stem beginning with *m*. The letter has almost exactly the same sound in French, German, Italian, and Spanish as it has in English. The Romans also gave it the same sound. The Portuguese nasalize the sound when it comes after a vowel. See PRONUNCIATION.   I. J. GELB and J. M. WELLS

The thirteenth letter took its shape from a symbol used in ancient Egypt to represent water. Its sound came from the Semitic *mem*, meaning *water*.

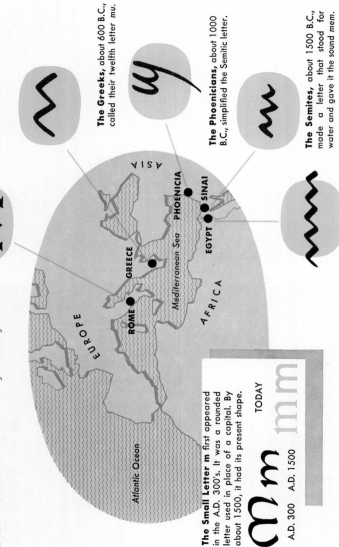

The Romans, about A.D. 114, used vertical lines for the M.

The Greeks, about 600 B.C., called their twelfth letter *mu*.

The Phoenicians, about 1000 B.C., simplified the Semitic letter.

The Semites, about 1500 B.C., made a letter that stood for water and gave it the sound *mem*.

The Egyptians, about 3000 B.C., drew a symbol for waves of water.

The Small Letter m first appeared in the A.D. 300's. It was a rounded letter used in place of a capital. By about 1500, it had its present shape.

A.D. 300   A.D. 1500   TODAY

MA YÜAN

MA YÜAN, *mah you ON,* was the most famous member of an honored family of painters. With his fellow painter Hsia Kuei, Ma Yüan produced some of the greatest landscape paintings in ink during the early 1200's in the Southern Sung period in China.

Ma Yüan's typical compositions are severely simple, with a framework of strong diagonal lines usually developed in one corner. His foregrounds may contain a few boldly silhouetted forms—rocks, a mountain path, a dramatically angular pine tree. The rest of the scene is largely mist, through which river banks or silhouetted faraway peaks can be seen.

Ma Yüan was born in Ho-Chung in Shansi province. His birth and death dates are unknown. ALEXANDER SOPER

MAAS RIVER. See MEUSE RIVER.

MAB, QUEEN. See FAIRY (Noble Fairies).

MABINOGION. See STORYTELLING (Europe).

MAC, Mc. Biographies of persons whose names begin with *Mac,* such as *MacDonald,* are listed alphabetically under *Mac.* Names which begin with *Mc,* such as *McKinley,* are listed alphabetically under *Mc,* following all names beginning *Ma* and *Mb.*

MACADAM. See ROADS AND HIGHWAYS (Surfacing).

MACADAMIA NUT, *mack uh DAY mih uh,* is a large, smooth, shiny seed that grows on a tropical evergreen tree. People sometimes call it the *Queensland nut.* The macadamia tree is a native of Australia. But the nut has been cultivated in Hawaii as a major commercial crop. The macadamia nut is rich in oil and has a sweet flavor, somewhat like that of the Brazil nut. The seeds can be eaten either raw or after roasting and salting.

Scientific Classification. The macadamia tree belongs to the protea family, *Proteaceae.* It is genus *Macadamia,* species *M. ternifolia.*
REID M. BROOKS

MACALESTER COLLEGE. See UNIVERSITIES AND COLLEGES (table).

MACAO, *muh KOW,* or MACAU is an overseas province of Portugal on the south coast of China. It lies at the mouth of the Canton (Pearl) River, about 40 miles west of Hong Kong. The province consists of the city of Macao and three small islands. Macao has a population of 268,000 and covers 6 square miles. Its coastline is 20 miles long (see Asia [political map]).

Fewer than 10 of every 100 persons in Macao are Portuguese. Most of the rest are Chinese. Large ships cannot dock at Macao's shallow harbor. But smaller ships carry goods from Macao to China. The province exports cement, firecrackers, fish, and matches. People often call Macao the *Monte Carlo of the Far East* because of its huge gambling business.

Portugal appoints a governor to administer Macao. The Portuguese first settled the province about 1557, and they paid China for use of the land until the 1850's. China recognized Macao as Portuguese territory in 1887. But in 1966 and 1967, Communist groups rioted against Portuguese rule in Macao.

MACARONI, *mack uh RO nih,* is a popular food made from *durum* (hard wheat) flour mixed with water. Macaroni products come in many different shapes and kinds. The best known are long, hollow tubes of dough, about ⅛ to ¼ of an inch in diameter. *Elbow* macaroni is made in the form of short, curved tubes. *Shell* macaroni has the shape of tiny sea shells.

Spaghetti is made from the same kind of dough as macaroni, but it is thinner and has solid tubes. *Vermicelli,* another macaroni product, consists of tiny strings. Manufacturers add 5 per cent or more of egg solids to macaroni dough to make *egg macaroni* or *egg noodles.* Other ingredients in macaroni may include milk, whole wheat, soy flour, vegetables, seasonings, and salt.

Macaroni contains about three-fourths carbohydrates. Manufacturers enrich most macaroni to supply from one-fourth to one-half of a person's daily requirements of the B vitamins. Macaroni is easily digested.

Macaroni products are made in modern factories. To make ordinary macaroni, the flour and water are thoroughly mixed and formed into dough. After the dough has been kneaded, it goes to a press where it is forced through holes. Steel pins in the center of the holes go through the dough and form it into hollow tubes. Forced air dries the dough in large, heated drying rooms. Other macaroni products are made in a similar way.

Macaroni has been a staple food in many European countries for hundreds of years. Because of macaroni's bland taste, it can be served with many other types of food. Common types of seasoning for macaroni include meat sauces, tomatoes, and mushrooms.

The invention of macaroni occurred long ago. Historians believe the Chinese probably developed the food, and they generally credit the Germans and Italians with introducing it into Europe. ROBERT M. GREEN

Macaroni Shapes vary from long solid rods to tiny egg rings. The United States has the largest macaroni industry in the world. It produces macaroni in more than 100 different shapes and sizes.
National Macaroni Institute

MACARTHUR, DOUGLAS (1880-1964), was one of the leading American generals of World War II. He gallantly defended Bataan Peninsula in the Philippine Islands in the early days of the war, and later led the Allied forces to victory in the Southwest Pacific. After the war, he proved his ability as a statesman in his administration of American-occupied Japan. He directed the changeover of Japan from dictatorship to democracy.

MacArthur became United Nations commander in Korea at the outbreak of the Korean War in 1950. He directed the invasion at Inchon, and the attack that carried UN troops to the northern border of North Korea. But he disagreed with President Harry S. Truman over the conduct of the war. When MacArthur defied Truman's orders in 1951, Truman recalled him from Korea.

Early Career. MacArthur was born in Little Rock, Ark., on Jan. 26, 1880. He was greatly influenced by his father, Arthur MacArthur, also a famous general. Arthur MacArthur joined the Union Army when he was 17 and fought in the Civil War. He won the Congressional Medal of Honor for heroism at Missionary Ridge in the Battle of Chattanooga. Douglas MacArthur was awarded the Medal of Honor in 1942. This marked the only time the son of a Medal of Honor winner also won the medal.

In 1898, the elder MacArthur was ordered to the Philippines. Douglas remained in the United States with his mother, the former Mary Pinkney Hardy of Norfolk, Va., to prepare for his entrance to the U.S. Military Academy.

Douglas MacArthur was graduated from the U.S. Military Academy in 1903 as the leading man in his class. He spent his first year after graduation as an engineer helping to map the Philippines. MacArthur served at various U.S. army posts from 1904 until 1914. In 1914, he performed a daring mission in Mexico under secret orders from the Army Chief of Staff. Relations between the U.S. and Mexico were strained at this time. MacArthur was sent there to find locomotives that could move U.S. troops in Mexico in case of war.

MacArthur held the rank of colonel when the United States entered World War I in 1917. He became chief of staff of the famous 42nd (Rainbow) Division. MacArthur rose to the rank of brigadier general in 1918. He won fame as a front-line general during the war in France in the battles of the Meuse-Argonne and Saint Mihiel. He was wounded 3 times, decorated 13 times, and cited for bravery in action 7 times.

MacArthur became Superintendent of the U.S. Military Academy in 1919. He is credited with broadening the academy's curriculum and raising its academic standards. MacArthur was transferred to the Philippines in 1922. In 1925, he returned to the United States as a major general. In 1930, he became a four-star general and was named Army Chief of Staff, the youngest in U.S. history.

At the height of the Great Depression, in 1932, several thousand unemployed World War I veterans gathered in Washington, D.C. The veterans, called the *Bonus Army,* demanded immediate payment of war bonuses. On orders from President Herbert Hoover, MacArthur and his armed troops drove the veterans out of Washington. This action brought MacArthur severe public criticism.

From 1935 to 1941, MacArthur worked as military adviser to the Philippine government. He helped pre-

United Press Int.

General Douglas MacArthur, an American soldier, won fame during World War II as the hero of Bataan and liberator of the Philippines. On Sept. 2 (Sept. 1 in U.S.), 1945, the Japanese surrendered to him on the U.S.S. *Missouri,* in Tokyo Bay.

pare the Philippines for an expected Japanese attack. He was named Grand Field Marshal of the Philippines.

Defense of the Philippines. President Franklin D. Roosevelt named MacArthur commander of all U.S. Army forces in the Far East in July, 1941. MacArthur held this position when the Japanese attacked the Philippines on Dec. 8, 1941. His forces were isolated, but they fought desperately. MacArthur withdrew his troops to Bataan Peninsula, where they resisted courageously for four months.

In March, 1942, President Roosevelt ordered MacArthur to Australia to become commander of the Allied forces in the Southwest Pacific. By night, a navy torpedo boat took MacArthur, his wife, and son from Corregidor to the southern Philippines. From there they flew to Australia, where he spoke of his reluctance to leave his men in the Philippines and made his famous promise, "I shall return." See BATAAN PENINSULA.

The Road Back. MacArthur spent several months assembling men and supplies. Late in 1942, he opened a three-year offensive against the Japanese. By early 1944, his troops had freed most of New Guinea, New Britain, the Solomons, and the Admiralty Islands. By autumn 1944, MacArthur was ready to make good his promise to return to the Philippines. On Oct. 20, 1944, his forces invaded Leyte Island, and six months later most of the Philippine Islands were free. During this period, MacArthur showed great military genius and personal bravery. His haughty manner aroused some resentment. But his heroism was seldom questioned.

MacArthur became a five-star general of the army in December, 1944. He took command of all American army forces in the Pacific in April, 1945. President Truman announced the Japanese acceptance of Allied surrender terms on Aug. 14, 1945. Truman made MacArthur supreme commander for the Allied Powers.

As supreme commander, it was MacArthur's job to receive the surrender and to rule Japan. He accepted the Japanese surrender aboard the battleship *Missouri* on Sept. 2 (Sept. 1 in the U.S.), 1945.

He set up headquarters in Tokyo and became the sole administrator of the military government in Japan. His firm, but fair, methods soon won him the respect of the Japanese, who had feared a harsh occupation. In keeping with Allied plans, MacArthur introduced reforms in government, education, and industry. These reforms were designed to turn Japan into a democracy.

War in Korea. In 1950, North Korean Communists invaded South Korea, and the United Nations authorized the United States to organize armed forces to fight the Communists. MacArthur, in addition to his occupation duties, became UN commander in Korea. After the Chinese Communists entered the war on the side of the North Koreans, MacArthur wanted to attack the Chinese mainland. But his superiors forbade this action, feeling it would increase the risk of a world war.

MacArthur made several public statements that did not agree with UN policies and those of the U.S. State and Defense departments. He also violated an order of public silence imposed on him by President Truman. In April, 1951, Truman relieved MacArthur of his Far Eastern commands, causing a nationwide controversy.

MacArthur returned home, received a hero's welcome, and defended his policies in a memorable address before a joint meeting of Congress. The speech included the famous reference to a line from a military ballad: "Old soldiers never die, they just fade away." In 1952, he became board chairman of Remington Rand, Inc. (now the Sperry Rand Corp.). He received many honors later in life. In 1962, he received a unanimous joint resolution of tribute from the U.S. Congress. In 1963, at the request of President John F. Kennedy, he helped settle a dispute between the National Collegiate Athletic Association and the Amateur Athletic Union that endangered the U.S. Olympic team.

MacArthur died on April 5, 1964, at the age of 84. President Lyndon B. Johnson called MacArthur "one of America's greatest heroes," and proclaimed a week of public mourning. MacArthur was buried in a crypt of the MacArthur Memorial in Norfolk, Va. JULES ARCHER

See also TRUMAN, HARRY S. (The Korean War); JAPAN (Allied Military Occupation); KOREAN WAR; WORLD WAR II.

MACASSAR. See MAKASAR.

MACAU. See MACAO.

MACAULAY, THOMAS BABINGTON (1800-1859), was an English statesman, historian, essayist, and poet. He was the most widely read essayist of his time. His *Lays of Ancient Rome*, ballads based on Roman legends, became popular. He wrote famous essays on John Milton, William Pitt, Lord Clive, and Francis Bacon.

Macaulay's greatest work, *The History of England from the Accession of James II*, in four volumes, is written in a clear and lively style. It is vivid and colorful, but sometimes inaccurate and generally unfair to the political opponents of the Whig party.

Macaulay was born in Rothley Temple, Leicestershire. He could read by the time he was 3, and he remembered without effort the words he had read. His biographer, Sir George Trevelyan, wrote that Macaulay could absorb the contents of a printed page at a glance. When Macaulay went to Trinity College, Cambridge, in 1818, his idea of education was to be able to get as many books as he could read. Thackeray said of him, "He reads 20 books to write a sentence; he travels a hundred miles to make a description."

In college Macaulay won prizes for his writing, and became a brilliant debater. Later, he was admitted to the bar, but did not practice long.

He became a member of Parliament in 1830, where he was a prominent Whig, and helped get the Reform Bill of 1832 adopted (see GREAT BRITAIN [The Era of Reform]). For a time, he was a member of the supreme council in India. Queen Victoria made him Baron Macaulay of Rothley in 1857. He died two years later, leaving a great history unfinished.

G. E. BENTLEY

See also FOURTH ESTATE; HORATIUS.

Thomas B. Macaulay

MACAW, *muth KAW*, is a long-tailed parrot that lives in South America and northwestern Mexico. It has long, pointed wings and a short, arched bill. Beautifully colored feathers of blue, red, yellow, and green cover the macaw's body. Macaws fly swiftly in pairs. They eat nuts, seeds, and fruit.

Macaws can be easily tamed, but do not readily learn to talk. Their loud screams and the danger of their biting make them rather undesirable pets.

Scientific Classification. Typical macaws are members of the parrot family, *Psittacidae*. They make up the genus *Ara*.

RODOLPHE MEYER DE SCHAUENSEE

See also BIRD (color picture: Birds of Other Lands); PARROT.

MACBETH, *muk BETH* (? -1057), seized the throne of Scotland in 1040 after defeating and killing Duncan I. He based his claim to the crown on his wife's royal descent. Malcolm III, son of Duncan I, and Earl Siward of Northumberland defeated Macbeth at Dunsinane in 1054, but they did not dethrone him. Three years later, Malcolm III killed Macbeth at Lumphanan. Macbeth's stepson Lulach reigned for a few months, and then Malcolm III succeeded him as king.

William Shakespeare based his play, *Macbeth*, one of his greatest tragedies, upon a distorted version of these events which he found in Raphael Holinshed's *Chronicle of Scottish History*. The only kernel of historical truth in the play is Duncan's death at the hand of Macbeth. From this fact, Shakespeare drew his portrait of ambition leading to a violent and tragic end. ROBERT S. HOYT

See also SHAKESPEARE, WILLIAM (Synopses of Plays).

MACCABAEUS, JUDAS. See JUDAS MACCABAEUS.

MACCABEES is the name of a line of Jewish rulers. The name comes from the title *Maccabaeus* (the hammerer) given to Judas, son of Mattathias. Judas led the Jews in their great revolt against the Syrians. It began in 167 B.C. The Syrian king, Antiochus IV (called Epiphanes), wanted to stamp out the Jewish religion and make the Jews worship Greek gods. The old Jewish priest Mattathias killed a renegade Jew and a Syrian who were leading a pagan celebration. Mattathias and his sons then fled to the Judean hills. Other Jews joined them. Judas led them to a series of victories against much larger forces. He had won back most of Jerusalem by the end of 164 B.C., but he was killed in 160 B.C. The leadership went to his brother Jonathan, and then to another brother, Simon, who, with his descendants, ruled for more than 100 years.   BRUCE M. METZGER

See also HASMONEANS.

MACCABEES, *MACK uh beez,* is the name of a fraternal and benevolent legal reserve society (see FRATERNAL SOCIETY). Families of deceased members receive benefits in the form of legal-reserve insurance. All white persons of sound health and good character, from birth to 70 years of age, are eligible for membership. The name comes from the Biblical Maccabees. The order was founded in London, Ont., in 1878, and reorganized in 1883. Before 1914, it was known as The Knights of the Maccabees. The headquarters of the order is at 5057 Woodward Ave., Detroit 2, Mich., and is known as the *Supreme Tent.*   D. A. TALUCCI

MACCOOL, FINN, was the leader of the Fenians, or Fianna, Irish warriors of the A.D. 100's or 200's. Stories about Finn are deeply colored by fancy. Finn studied poetry with a master named Finegas who had been trying to catch the "salmon of knowledge." Finegas caught the fish. He asked Finn to cook it, but not to taste it. In turning the fish, Finn burned his thumb and instinctively put it in his mouth. From that day on, Finn had only to put his thumb against a certain tooth to obtain supernatural knowledge.

A charm was laid on Finn to marry a deer, though he recognized the deer as a woman under a spell. Their child was named Oisin, or Little Fawn. Finn, as an old widower, wooed a beautiful lady, Grainne, but she eloped with Finn's friend, Diarmuid. In James Macpherson's Ossianic poems, Finn was called Fingal and Oisin was called Ossian.   KNOX WILSON

See also IRISH LITERATURE (The Finn or Ossianic Cycle).

MACCORMICK, AUSTIN H. (1893-   ), has been the United States Army's consultant on correctional problems since 1942. Earlier, in 1940, he became executive director of The Osborne Association, Inc., and made nationwide surveys of prisons and juvenile institutions. He was a professor of criminology at the University of California from 1951 to 1960. He also served as executive officer of the Portsmouth (N.H.) Naval Prison, as assistant director of the U.S. Bureau of Prisons, and as New York City Commissioner of Correction. He was born in Georgetown, Ont. O. W. WILSON

MACDONALD, FLORA (1722-1790). In 1746, Prince Charles Edward of the House of Stuart fought the English in an attempt to seize the English throne. He was defeated at Culloden and fled for his life. Flora Macdonald, daughter of a Scottish farmer, helped him escape to the island of Skye. She reportedly had the prince dress in woman's clothes and helped him escape detection by stating he was her maid. From the island of Skye, the prince went to France. Flora was imprisoned for a year in the Tower of London for her part in the escape.   W. M. SOUTHGATE

MACDONALD, JAMES E. H. (1874-1932), was a Canadian painter. He was an original member of the Group of Seven, an influential group of Toronto painters. His works stressed subjects of local interest such as farm pumps, picket fences, sunflowers, and old apple trees.

Macdonald was born at Durham, England, and came to Canada in 1887. He studied at the Hamilton Art School and the Ontario School of Art in Toronto. He was elected a member of the Ontario Society of Artists in 1909 and of the Royal Canadian Academy of Arts in 1929. Macdonald wrote a volume of poems, *West By East,* published in 1933.   W. R. WILLOUGHBY

MACDONALD, JAMES RAMSAY (1866-1937), led Great Britain's first Labour party government. He served as the first Labour party prime minister of Britain in 1924, and from 1929 to 1935. He was secretary of Britain's Labour party from the party's origin in 1900 until 1911.

He entered Parliament in 1906. As Labour party leader in 1914, he opposed England's entrance into World War I. His stand met considerable opposition within his own party. His pacifism resulted in his defeat for reelection to Parliament in 1918. However, he was elected in 1922, and became prime minister in 1924, with Liberal party support. MacDonald remained in office for a period of only 10 months. He was defeated, in part, because his government was considered too friendly toward Russia. He accepted, but did not wholeheartedly support, the 1926 general strike of workers on behalf of coal miners faced with reductions in wages and longer working hours.

Harris & Ewing

James Ramsay MacDonald

The Labour party won the general election of 1929, and MacDonald formed his second government as prime minister. It achieved considerable success in international affairs. Diplomatic relations with Russia were resumed. MacDonald visited the United States to discuss with President Herbert Hoover proposals for naval reduction. He became chairman of the London arms conference in 1930. But MacDonald was unable to deal effectively with rapidly rising unemployment and his government resigned in August, 1931. MacDonald continued as prime minister, heading a national coalition government of Labour, Conservative, and Liberal party members. A large majority of the Labourites in Parliament disapproved of his move. The Conservatives held an overwhelming majority in the government. They overshadowed MacDonald. Stanley Baldwin replaced him as prime minister in 1935.

MacDonald was born of farmer parents in the Scottish seaside village of Lossiemouth. He left school at the age of 13, to help support the family. Six years later, he went to London and worked as a clerk, accountant, and newspaper writer. He read widely in the fields of science, history, and economics. He became interested in socialism, joined the Fabian Society, and became one of its speakers.   ALFRED F. HAVIGHURST

See also FABIAN SOCIETY.

Canada had four provinces (*shown in black*) when Macdonald became Prime Minister at the time of confederation. During his first administration, three new provinces (*in white*) joined the dominion.

BRITISH COLUMBIA

MANITOBA

ONTARIO

QUEBEC

NEW BRUNSWICK

NOVA SCOTIA

PRINCE EDWARD ISLAND

SIR JOHN A. MACDONALD
Prime Minister of Canada
1867-1873, 1878-1891

Brown Bros.

ABBOTT 1891-1892

MACKENZIE 1873-1878

MACDONALD, SIR JOHN ALEXANDER (1815-1891), was the first Prime Minister of the Dominion of Canada. He is often called the father of present-day Canada because he played the leading role in establishing the dominion in 1867. Macdonald served as Prime Minister from 1867 until 1873, and from 1878 until his death in 1891. He held the office for nearly 19 years, longer than any other Canadian Prime Minister except W. L. Mackenzie King, who served for 21 years.

Macdonald, a Conservative, entered politics when he was only 28 years old. During his long public career, Canada grew from a group of colonies into a self-governing, united dominion extending across North America. Macdonald stood out as the greatest political figure of Canada's early years. He helped strengthen the new nation by promoting western expansion, railway construction, and economic development.

A man of great personal charm, Macdonald knew how to make people like him. He was naturally sociable, with a quick wit and a remarkable ability to remember faces. Macdonald was not a flowery-speaking orator as were most politicians of his day. He kept his speeches short and filled with funny stories. People preferred his talks to the long, dull speeches of others.

Early Life

Boyhood and Education. John Alexander Macdonald was born on Jan. 11, 1815, in Glasgow, Scotland. He was the son of Helen Shaw Macdonald and Hugh Macdonald, an easy-going and usually unsuccessful businessman. John had an older sister, Margaret, and a younger sister, Louisa. He was 5 years old when the family moved to Canada in 1820.

The Macdonalds settled in Kingston, Upper Canada (present-day Ontario). Hugh opened a small shop, and the family lived above it. The business did not prosper, so Hugh decided he would be more successful elsewhere. In 1824, the family moved westward to Hay Bay. They moved to Glenora in Prince Edward county in 1825, then back to Kingston. Hugh tried one business after another, but none brought him success.

As a boy, John developed an interest in books and was a bright student. He finished his formal schooling in 1829 when he was 14. The next year, John began to study law with George Mackenzie, a prominent Kingston lawyer.

Macdonald lived with the Mackenzie family and worked in the law office. In 1832, Mackenzie opened a branch office in nearby Napanee, and 17-year-old John became its manager. In 1833, John learned that a relative, a lawyer in Hallowell, Prince Edward county, was seriously ill. John agreed to take over his practice.

Lawyer. Macdonald returned to Kingston in 1835. He was admitted to the bar of Upper Canada in 1836. That same year, he took on his first apprentice-lawyer, Oliver Mowat, who became prime minister of Ontario.

During the Rebellion of 1837-1838, Macdonald served in the Frontenac county militia. In 1838, some of William Lyon Mackenzie's American supporters staged a raid into Canada. About 150 raiders were captured, and Macdonald defended some of them in court. Several Americans were hanged, but the case helped establish Macdonald's legal reputation. See REBELLION OF 1837-1838; MACKENZIE, WILLIAM LYON.

In 1841, Upper Canada (part of present-day Ontario) and Lower Canada (part of present-day Quebec) united to form the Province of Canada. The Province of Canada, sometimes called United Canada, had one legislative assembly, with an equal number of members from Upper and Lower Canada.

Kingston, in Upper Canada, became the capital of the Province of Canada. Both the city and Macdonald's law practice grew prosperous. In 1843, Macdonald began a law partnership with Alexander Campbell, who had been his second apprentice-lawyer.

Marriages. On the same day that he set up his law partnership, Macdonald married his cousin, Isabella Clark. The Macdonalds had two sons, John Jr., who died at the age of 1, and Hugh John, who became prime minister of Manitoba.

In 1845, Isabella was stricken by tuberculosis. Macdonald tried everything to cure her. He and his wife were separated for long periods while Isabella tried to restore her health in the southern United States or sought medical care in New Haven, Conn. But she died in 1857.

The years of his wife's illness were a strain on John Macdonald, both physically and financially. He remained at Isabella's bedside as much as possible. But he was also building a law practice and a political career. He often felt he was not giving enough attention to his wife, to his practice, or to politics.

Ten years after the death of Isabella, in 1867, Macdonald married Susan Agnes Bernard, a widow. The couple had a daughter, Mary.

Early Public Career

In 1843, at the age of 28, Macdonald was elected an alderman in Kingston. In 1844, he accepted the Conservative nomination in Kingston for the legislative assembly of the Province of Canada. He easily won election.

Macdonald took his seat in the assembly on Nov. 28, 1844. His associates soon recognized his abilities. In 1847, he was appointed receiver-general in the Conservative administration of William Henry Draper. But Draper's government was defeated later that year.

For the next few years, Macdonald helped rebuild the Conservative party. He wanted the party to include men of liberal and conservative views, French-Canadians and English-Canadians, Roman Catholics and Protestants, and rich and poor. A Liberal-Conservative coalition party was formed. It came to power in 1854 under Conservative leader Sir Allan McNab. Macdonald served as attorney general in this administration.

Associate Provincial Prime Minister. In 1856, Macdonald and Sir Étienne P. Taché became associate prime ministers of the Province of Canada. Taché was the senior prime minister in what was called the Taché-Macdonald government. The next year, Taché retired. Macdonald became senior prime minister with Georges É. Cartier as his associate prime minister. The Conservatives adopted a policy favoring confederation of all the British provinces in North America.

In 1858, the Macdonald-Cartier government was defeated. But Macdonald returned to power a week later when the governor-general asked Cartier to become senior prime minister and form a government. Cartier needed Macdonald's help in the task, and the new government became the Cartier-Macdonald government.

The formation of the Cartier-Macdonald government became known as the "double shuffle." The action was legal, but the opposition charged it was dishonest. Macdonald and Cartier simply took advantage of a provision in the law. This provision permitted a cabinet minister to resign and accept another cabinet position within a month without running for re-election. All the government ministers resigned. A few days later, they all returned to office with new titles. Then they quickly dropped the new titles and resumed their former offices.

The Conservative government was defeated in 1862, although Macdonald won re-election to the assembly from Kingston. Macdonald served as leader of the opposition party until 1864. The Conservatives won the election that year. Taché came out of retirement, and the second Taché-Macdonald government was formed.

Forming the Dominion. In the early 1860's, the northern half of North America was called British North America. It consisted of only a few provinces. Most of the people lived in the east. The Maritime Provinces—New Brunswick, Newfoundland, Nova Scotia, and Prince Edward Island—lay along the Atlantic coast. The Province of Canada was next to them on the west. Of these five provinces, Nova Scotia and the Province of Canada were older and more developed. The other three had only begun to govern themselves in the 1840's and 1850's. Farther west was an expanse of mainly unsettled territory owned by the Hudson's Bay Company (see HUDSON'S BAY COMPANY). On the west coast lay British Columbia, then a British colony.

For several years, the British provinces in North America had considered the idea of confederation. Several factors gave force to this idea. They included the frequent changes of provincial governments, the desire to expand to the west, and fear of U.S. expansion.

Nova Scotia and the Province of Canada took the lead in the confederation movement. In the Province of Canada, Macdonald joined forces with his opponent, Liberal leader George Brown, to achieve confederation.

From 1864 to 1867, Macdonald led in planning confederation. In September, 1864, he attended a conference in Charlottetown, P.E.I., to present the confederation plan to the Maritime Provinces. In October, delegates from all the provinces gathered at a second conference in Quebec. At this meeting, Macdonald was largely responsible for drawing up the Quebec Resolutions, the plan for confederation.

New Brunswick, Nova Scotia, and the Province of Canada approved the idea, but Newfoundland and Prince Edward Island rejected it. Final details were agreed upon at a conference in London, England, in 1866. In 1867, the British parliament passed the British North America Act, which brought the Dominion of Canada into being (see BRITISH NORTH AMERICA ACT). The new nation had four provinces: Ontario (previously Upper Canada), Quebec (previously Lower Canada), New Brunswick, and Nova Scotia. Governor-General Charles S. Monck asked Macdonald to lead the first dominion government as Prime Minister.

Confederation was largely Macdonald's achievement and Queen Victoria knighted him for it. The announce-

MACDONALD, SIR JOHN A.

ment of his knighthood came on July 1, 1867, the first day of the dominion's existence. A general election was held in August, and the new parliament assembled on Nov. 6, 1867.

First Term As Prime Minister (1867–1873)

Completing the Dominion. Sir John A. Macdonald took office as Prime Minister of the Dominion of Canada on July 1, 1867. His goal was to enlarge the dominion into a unified nation extending across the continent.

In 1869, the Canadian and British governments agreed with the Hudson's Bay Company to purchase the company's lands. The company was paid 300,000 pounds (about $1½ million) and 5 per cent of the land south of the North Saskatchewan River. But the *métis* (persons of mixed European and Indian descent) in the territory rebelled. They were led by Louis Riel. They feared that an onrush of settlers would deprive them of their lands. Many Canadians also thought the United States might annex this land. Parliament passed the Manitoba Act in 1870, and in July, 1870, the lands became the fifth Canadian province (see RED RIVER RE-

Fathers of Confederation, a painting by J. D. Kelly, represents the scene at the Quebec Conference of 1864. Macdonald is shown standing in the center of this group.

Houses of Parliament, *left,* looked like this in 1867 when Macdonald first became Prime Minister. The buildings were constructed in the early 1860's.

National Film Board, Toronto, Canada

IMPORTANT EVENTS DURING MACDONALD'S ADMINISTRATIONS

BELLION). British Columbia became the sixth province in 1871, and Prince Edward Island the seventh in 1873. In 1871, delegates from Great Britain and the United States held a conference in Washington, D.C. Mac-

IMPORTANT DATES IN MACDONALD'S LIFE

1815 (Jan. 11) Born in Glasgow, Scotland.
1820 Macdonald family moved to Kingston, Upper Canada.
1836 Admitted to the bar of Upper Canada.
1843 (Sept. 1) Married Isabella Clark.
1844 (Oct. 14) Elected to legislative assembly of the Province of Canada.
1856 Became associate prime minister of Province of Canada.
1857 (Dec. 28) Mrs. Isabella Macdonald died.
1867 British parliament passed the British North America Act.
(Feb. 16) Married Susan Agnes Bernard.
(July 1) Macdonald became the first Prime Minister of the Dominion of Canada and was knighted.
1869 Louis Riel led the Red River Rebellion.
1870 Manitoba became the fifth Canadian province.
1871 British Columbia became the sixth province.
1873 Prince Edward Island became the seventh province.
1878 (Oct. 17) Became Prime Minister for second time.
1885 Riel led the Saskatchewan Rebellion.
The Canadian Pacific Railway was completed.
1891 Macdonald and the Conservatives won re-election.
(June 6) Died in Ottawa, Ont.

MACDONALD, SIR JOHN A.

donald attended the meeting as the Canadian member of the British delegation. He tried to obtain a trade agreement with the United States, but failed. Nevertheless, Macdonald signed the Treaty of Washington. Among other points, this treaty granted the United States extensive fishing rights in Canadian waters. Macdonald felt that refusal to sign the treaty might encourage the United States to back its demands with force. He was always careful to do nothing that might endanger the young Canadian nation. See WASHINGTON, TREATY OF.

The Pacific Scandal. Next, Macdonald turned to the goal of building a transcontinental railroad to unify Canada. The completion of such a railroad had been one of the terms of British Columbia's entry into the confederation.

Two financial groups competed with each other to build the line. Then, in 1873, it was learned that Sir Hugh Allan, head of one of the groups, had contributed a large sum of money to help re-elect Macdonald's government in the 1872 election. Some Liberal members of parliament charged there had been an "understanding" between Allan and the government. They accused the government of giving Allan a charter to build the railroad because he had contributed to the Conservatives' election fund.

The incident became known as the Pacific Scandal. Macdonald was innocent, but some of his associates had received money from Allan. Macdonald resigned as Prime Minister. He offered to resign as head of the Conservative party, but his supporters persuaded him to remain in that post. The Conservatives lost the 1874 election, although Macdonald won re-election to parliament from Kingston. Alexander Mackenzie, the leader of the Liberal party, became Prime Minister of Canada.

The National Policy. For the next four years, Macdonald led the opposition party in the house of commons. During this period, he worked to rebuild the Conservative party. Macdonald formed a program of economic nationalism that he called the National Policy. This program called for developing Canada by protecting its industries against those of other countries.

The idea appealed to Canadians, especially because a depression had begun in 1873. On the strength of the National Policy, the Conservatives defeated the Liberals

by Tom Dorsett for WORLD BOOK

Pacific Scandal toppled Macdonald's government in 1873 when graft was charged in the building of a transcontinental railroad, above. In C. W. Jefferys' painting, below, Macdonald crosses the Rockies on the Canadian Pacific Railway, completed in 1885.

Public Archives of Canada, Toronto

Louis Riel led revolts against the Canadian government in 1869 and 1885. English-Canadians called him a traitor. But French-Canadians hailed Riel as a hero.

Macdonald Memorial stands on Parliament Hill in Ottawa, Ont. A memorial tablet in St. Paul's Cathedral in London, England, also honors the first Prime Minister of Canada.

Ottawa, Canada, National Film Board

in the 1878 election. They returned to power with an election victory in almost every province.

Second Term As Prime Minister (1878-1891)

National Prosperity. Macdonald began his second term as Prime Minister on Oct. 17, 1878. The government immediately put tariffs on a variety of goods to protect the manufacturing and mining industries. Macdonald again began to push for construction of a transcontinental railroad. With government support, a new company was formed. By November, 1885, the Canadian Pacific Railway had been completed to the Pacific Ocean. Macdonald had achieved his program of western expansion, railway construction, and economic nationalism. Canada was riding a wave of prosperity.

Threats to Canadian Unity. Macdonald had worked long and hard to build a unified Canadian nation. But beginning in 1885, a number of political developments seriously threatened this unity.

In 1885, the métis of northwest Canada rebelled for the second time. They were again led by Louis Riel. When Riel finally surrendered, the government found him guilty of treason and sentenced him to hang. The sentence caused severe bad feeling between French-Canadians and English-Canadians. For a time, the issue threatened to split the confederation. But Macdonald refused to give in to Riel's supporters. "He shall die though every dog in Quebec bark in his favour," Macdonald declared. Riel was hanged in November, 1885. See SASKATCHEWAN REBELLION.

MACDONALD, JOHN SANDFIELD (1812-1872), served as joint Prime Minister of the Province of Canada from 1862 to 1864, before the formation of the Canadian federation. He also served as first premier of Ontario from 1867 to 1871. He held office in both Liberal and Conservative governments. On most public issues, he voted as a member of the Reform, or Liberal, party. But he differed, on occasion, with the party leader, George Brown (see BROWN, GEORGE). Macdonald voted against the Liberal aim of "representation by population."

He opposed provincial union at first, but finally accepted Confederation.

He agreed in 1867 to Sir John A. Macdonald's request that he form a Liberal-Conservativecoalition government for Ontario (see MACDONALD, Sir John A.). The noncoalitionLiberalsdefeatedMacdonald in 1871, and he then retired from public life.

John S. Macdonald

John S. Macdonald, portrait by Samuel B. Waugh, Public Archives of Canada, Toronto

Related Articles in WORLD BOOK include:

Brown, George
Canada, Government of
Canada, History of
Cartier, Sir Georges-É.
Mackenzie, Alexander
Monck, Baron
Political Party (Political Parties in Canada)
Riel, Louis
Taché, Sir Étienne-Paschal

Macdonald next faced an attack by the provincial prime ministers on his program for a strong central government. In 1888, the prime ministers met at a conference in Quebec. They proposed changes in the British North America Act that would decentralize the government. Great Britain rejected their demands. But the conference showed the growing strength of provincial opinion against federal centralization.

Still another blow to Macdonald was the depression of 1883. The National Policy had not produced all the expected results. In 1886 and 1887, a demand arose for a change in Canada's financial policy. Some persons favored political federation with Great Britain. Others spoke of a commercial union with the United States. Macdonald opposed both proposals.

In the 1891 election, the Liberals adopted a party platform calling for unrestricted reciprocal trade with the United States (see RECIPROCAL TRADE AGREEMENT). The 75-year-old Macdonald fought this proposal with all the strength he could muster.

"Shall we endanger our possession of the great heritage bequeathed to us by our fathers," he asked the Canadian people, "and submit ourselves to direct taxation for the privilege of having our tariffs fixed at Washington, with the prospect of ultimately becoming a portion of the American Union? ... As for myself, my course is clear. A British subject I was born, a British subject I will die." With this appeal, Macdonald won his last election.

Death. The strain of campaigning proved severe for Macdonald. He caught cold after a long day of speaking, and suffered a stroke on May 29, 1891. He died on June 6 in Ottawa. Macdonald was buried near his mother in Kingston, Ont.

G. F. G. STANLEY

Macdonald was born in St. Raphael, Ont. He became a lawyer in 1840, and a member of the legislature for Glengarry County in 1841. Macdonald represented Cornwall County in the legislature from 1857 to 1867. In 1840, he married a daughter of George Waggaman, a U.S. Senator from Louisiana. Macdonald and his wife had three sons and four daughters. He died in Cornwall on June 1, 1872.   G. F. G. STANLEY

MACDONOUGH, *muck DAHN uh,* **THOMAS** (1783-1825), an American naval officer, became a hero of the War of 1812. In 1814, he defeated the British on Lake Champlain at Plattsburgh, N.Y., in one of the most decisive battles ever fought by the U.S. Navy.

When Macdonough took command of the Lake Champlain naval squadron in 1812, he found small, poorly armed vessels that lacked supplies and had untrained crews. After two years of preparations, he entered the harbor at Plattsburgh, carefully stationed his ships, and awaited the British. His victory there destroyed the British plan of invading New York state, and forced the British Army to retreat into Canada.

Macdonough was born in New Castle County, Delaware, on Dec. 31, 1783. He became a midshipman at 16. In 1804, he helped Stephen Decatur destroy the *Philadelphia,* which had been taken by Tripoli pirates. Macdonough became commander of the Mediterranean Squadron in 1824.   RICHARD S. WEST, JR.

See also WAR OF 1812 (Lake Champlain).

MACDOWELL, EDWARD ALEXANDER (1861-1908), was an American composer and pianist. He is best remembered for such short, descriptive piano pieces as "To a Wild Rose" and "To a Water Lily." Many of these pieces are grouped in sets, which the composer called *Fireside Tales, New England Idyls, Sea Pieces,* and *Woodland Sketches.* He also wrote an *Indian Suite* for orchestra, two concertos for piano and orchestra, four sonatas for piano, several symphonic poems, and some songs. "Thy Beaming Eyes," is typical of his songs.

MacDowell was born in New York City, where he studied piano under Teresa Carreño, a brilliant Venezuelan pianist. From the age of 15, he studied in France and Germany, where he lived for 12 years. He married his former pupil, Marian Nevins, in 1884. MacDowell served as head of the music department at Columbia University from 1896 to 1904. He was elected to the Hall of Fame in 1960.   GILBERT CHASE

MACE, *maps,* is a liquid tear gas that can be sprayed from a pressurized container. It causes a strong burning sensation and makes the eyes fill with tears. Mace disables a person temporarily but causes no lasting effects. *Chemical Mace* is a trade name, but the term *Mace* is often used for all hand-controlled liquid chemical irritants.

Many police departments in the United States use Mace to help control riots and violent demonstrations. It can be used on individual targets without affecting people nearby.

Some persons claim that Mace permanently harms the eyes or nervous system. But the U.S. Public Health Service reported in 1968 that its tests of Chemical Mace indicated no permanent effects. Nevertheless, all such substances should be used only by trained officers under careful control and regulation.   MARVIN E. WOLFGANG

MACE, *maps,* is a club-shaped staff used as a symbol of authority. It is most often seen in legislative assemblies where it is used chiefly to restore order. The mace originally was a weapon of the Middle Ages. It was a club with a long handle, heavily weighted at one end. As the science of war developed, the weighted end became a heavy iron ball. Archers and other unmounted warriors used the mace as a hand arm. Church officials who could not shed blood, also used it. Sergeants at arms, who were guards of kings and other high officials, carried a ceremonial mace. Gradually the mace gained a ceremonial character. The mace used in the U.S. House of Representatives is about 3 feet long. It is made up of ebony rods bound with a band of silver. A longer ebony rod in the center of the bundle has a silver globe mounted on it. A silver eagle with outspread wings is on top of the globe.   WILLIAM C. BARK

See also NORTHWEST TERRITORIES (picture).

Mace of the United States House of Representatives.

Mace of the British House of Commons

MACE is a highly flavored spice used on foods. It comes from the red covering of the nutmeg (see NUTMEG). Fresh mace is fleshy, and smells and tastes like nutmeg. Before it is sold, it is dried in the sun. When dry, it becomes orange-yellow and transparent. Then it is ground or used in its whole form.

MACEDONIA is a mountainous region in the central part of the Balkan Peninsula in southeastern Europe. It covers 25,636 square miles and has a population of about 3,605,000. Most of the people are farmers. They raise barley, corn, rice, rye, tobacco, wheat, and a variety of fruits and vegetables. The Macedonians also raise sheep and goats.

Macedonia is inhabited chiefly by Slavs in the north and Greeks in the south. The Balkan Wars in 1912-1913 divided Macedonia between Serbia (now Yugoslavia), Greece, and Bulgaria.

Greek Macedonia covers 13,206 square miles and has a population of about 1,896,000. Much of Greek Macedonia is a plain, watered by the Axiós, Strimón, and Néstos rivers. Its capital is Salonika.

Yugoslavian Macedonia is one of Yugoslavia's six "republics." It covers 9,928 square miles and has a population of about 1,406,000. Skopje is the capital.

Bulgarian Macedonia covers 2,502 square miles and has a population of about 303,000. Its capital is Blagoevgrad.

History. A savage and barbaric European people called the Thracians moved into the region about 2000 B.C. After 1100 B.C., the Macedonians came under the cultural influence of the Greeks. King Philip II of Macedonia unified the Greeks in 338 B.C., and prepared an expedition against the Persians. His son Alexander the Great succeeded in founding a vast new empire on the ruins of the Persian Empire. After his death in 323 B.C., his empire was divided among his generals.

Macedonia became a Roman province in 148 B.C. It was made part of the Byzantine Empire when the Roman Empire was divided in A.D. 395. Macedonia was included in the first Bulgarian empire in the 800's and in the Serbian empire in the 1300's. From 1389 until 1912, the Turks had possession of Macedonia.

The Bulgarian, Greek, and Serb inhabitants of Macedonia struggled against Turkey from the 1890's to 1912. The Balkan allies defeated Turkey in the First Balkan War in 1912, and Macedonia was divided among Greece, Serbia (Yugoslavia), and Bulgaria. Bulgaria started the Second Balkan War in 1913 to get more land but was defeated by the other Balkan countries. In attempts to gain more of Macedonia, Bulgaria invaded the region during both World Wars. Both times, the Greeks and Serbs fought on the victorious side and drove the Bulgarians from Macedonia.   G. G. ARNAKIS

See also ALEXANDER THE GREAT; BALKANS; GREECE, ANCIENT (The End of the Classical Period); PHILIP II; SALONIKA.

MACGREGOR, ROBERT. See ROB ROY.

MACH, *makh*, ERNST (1838-1916), was an Austrian physicist and psychologist. He studied the action of bodies moving at high speeds through gases, and developed an accurate method for measuring their speeds in terms of the speed of sound. This method is important in problems of supersonic flight.

Mach's work remained obscure until the speed of aircraft began to approach the speed of sound. Then the term *Mach number* came to be used as a measure of speed. *Mach 1* is the speed of sound, or *supersonic*. *Mach 0.5* is half the speed of sound, or *subsonic*. *Mach 2* is twice the speed of sound, or *transonic*, and so on (see AERODYNAMICS [Supersonic Flight]).

Mach was deeply interested in the historical development of the ideas on which the science of mechanics is based. He taught that all knowledge of the physical world comes to us by the five senses—sight, hearing, smell, taste, and feeling. He also taught that a scientific law was a correlation between observed data.

Mach was born at Turas, Moravia. He was graduated from the University of Vienna.   R. T. ELLICKSON

See also MACH NUMBER; MACH, ERNST.

MACH NUMBER. See AERODYNAMICS (Supersonic Flight); MACH, ERNST.

MACHADO, ANTONIO. See SPANISH LITERATURE (The 1900's).

MACHETE, *mah CHAY tay*, or *muh SHET*, is a large heavy knife with a blade shaped like a broadsword. It is used chiefly in South America and the West Indies. Machetes used as weapons have narrow blades often 2 or 3 feet long. Short-bladed machetes are used to cut sugar cane and to clear brush. See also KNIFE.

MACHIAVELLI, *MAH kyah VEL lee*, **NICCOLÒ** (1469-1527), was an Italian statesman and student of politics. His name has long stood for all that is deep, dark, and treacherous in statesmanship. In Elizabethan literature, for example, there are hundreds of references that connect him with the Evil One or the Devil.

He is best known for his book *The Prince*, written in 1513 and published in 1532. This book established Machiavelli as the father of the modern science of politics. It skillfully sets forth the idea that a ruler need not trouble himself about the means he uses to accomplish a purpose. He must use any means, no matter how wicked, to strike down his enemies and make his people obey. Machiavelli set down rules to be followed to keep power. The book also sets forth the idea of a united Italy. He also wrote a *History of Florence, The Art of War*, and *Discourses Upon the First Ten Books of Livy*, indicating in then his favor for a republican form of government.

Machiavelli was born in Florence. The son of a jurist, and a member of an old Tuscan family, Machiavelli was educated chiefly through private study. He became a leading figure in the Republic of Florence after the Medici family was driven out in 1498 (see MEDICI). For 14 years he served as first secretary of the council of the republic. His duties brought him in contact with the notorious Cesare Borgia (see BORGIA). He also became interested in reorganizing the militia.

The Medici family returned to power in 1512, and dismissed Machiavelli from his office. They arrested, tortured, and imprisoned him. They finally released him on order of Pope Leo X. He spent the last 14 years of his life in retirement near Florence. There he wrote his books on history and politics. He also wrote poetry and comedies. He became a leading literary figure of the Renaissance.   R. JOHN RATH

See also ITALIAN LITERATURE (The 1500's and 1600's).

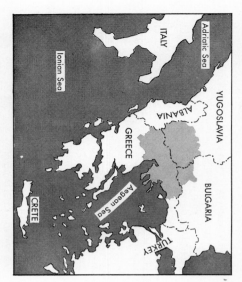

Location Map of Macedonia (Shaded Area)

Niccolò Machiavelli
Sculpture by Lorenzo Bartolini, Uffizi, Florence (Alinari from Art Reference Bureau)

MACHINE is a device that does work. Industries use giant drill presses, lathes, and presses to make the products we use. Businesses depend on typewriters, computers, and other office machines. Automobiles, buses, and airplanes transport people swiftly over great distances. Trucks, railroads, and ships are machines used to haul goods to and from markets. Without machines, the residents of our cities would find it more difficult to live, and farmers could not raise enough food to feed us. Almost every activity of our daily life depends in some way on machines.

Man has constructed a wide variety of machines to satisfy his needs. Early man made stone axes that served as weapons and tools. The machines that man gradually developed gave him great control over his *environment* (physical surroundings). To operate his improved machines, he harnessed the energy of falling water and of such fuels as coal, oil, and the atom. Today, we use so many machines that the age we live in is often called the *Machine Age*.

Principles of Machines

A machine produces force and controls the direction and the motion of force. But it cannot create energy. A machine can never do more work than the energy put into it. It only transforms one kind of energy, such as electrical energy, and passes it along as mechanical energy. Some machines, such as diesel engines or steam turbines, are called *prime movers*, because they change energy directly into mechanical motion. For example, the energy of falling water rushing through the wheel of a turbine produces rotary motion. This direct motion of the wheel can be used to turn a generator, a water pump, or a harvesting machine, are run by prime movers. These machines only control or produce certain forces and motions.

The ability of a machine to do work is measured by two factors. These factors are known as *efficiency* and *mechanical advantage*.

Efficiency. The efficiency of a machine is the ratio between the energy it supplies and the energy put into it. Machines that transmit only mechanical energy may have an efficiency of nearly 100 per cent. But some machines have an efficiency as low as 5 per cent. No machine can operate with 100 per cent efficiency, because the friction of its parts always uses up some of the energy that is supplied to the machine. All machines produce some friction. For this reason, a perpetual-motion machine is impossible (see PERPETUAL MOTION MACHINE).

A simple lever is a good example of a machine that has a high efficiency (see LEVER). The work it puts out is almost equal to the energy it receives, because the energy used up by friction is quite small. On the other hand, an automobile engine has an efficiency of only about 25 per cent, because much of the energy supplied by the fuel is lost in the form of heat that escapes into the surrounding air. See EFFICIENCY.

Mechanical Advantage. In machines that transmit only mechanical energy, the ratio of the force exerted by the machine to the force applied to the machine is known as *mechanical advantage*. Mechanical advantage can be demonstrated with a crowbar, which is a type of lever. When one end of the crowbar is directly under the weight, a part of the crowbar must rest on a *fulcrum* (support). The closer the fulcrum is to the load, the less the effort required to raise the load by pushing down on the handle of the crowbar, and the greater the mechanical advantage of the crowbar. For example, if the load is 400 pounds, and the distance from the load to the fulcrum is one fourth of the distance from the handle to the fulcrum, it will take 100 pounds of effort to raise the load. Therefore, the mechanical advantage

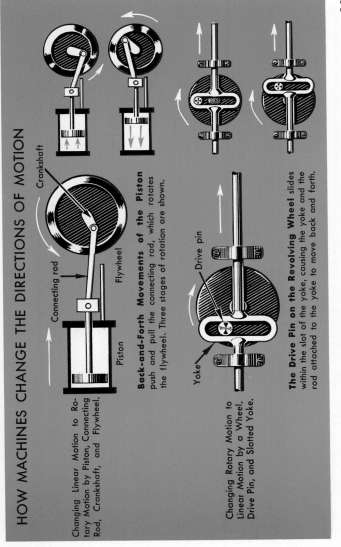

HOW MACHINES CHANGE THE DIRECTIONS OF MOTION

Changing Linear Motion to Rotary Motion by Piston, Connecting Rod, Crankshaft, and Flywheel.

Crankshaft

Connecting rod

Piston

Flywheel

Back-and-Forth Movements of the Piston push and pull the connecting rod, which rotates the flywheel. Three stages of rotation are shown.

Changing Rotary Motion to Linear Motion by a Wheel, Drive Pin, and Slotted Yoke.

Drive pin

Yoke

The Drive Pin on the Revolving Wheel slides within the slot of the yoke, causing the yoke and the rod attached to the yoke to move back and forth.

SIX SIMPLE MACHINES

The Lever is one of the earliest and simplest machines. Its advantage lies in the short distance between the fulcrum (pivotal point) and load, and in the long distance between the fulcrum and the point where effort is applied.

FIG. 1

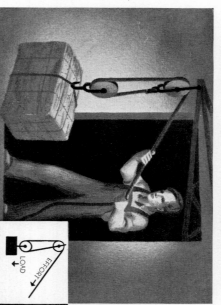

The Pulley consists of a wheel with a grooved rim over which a rope is passed. It is used to change the direction of the effort applied to the rope. A block and tackle uses two or more pulleys to reduce the amount of effort needed to lift a load.

FIG. 3

The Wheel and Axle has a rope attached to the axle to lift the load. The crank handle is the point where effort is applied. The effort is smaller than the load because it is at a greater distance from the axle which is the fulcrum.

FIG. 2

The Inclined Plane makes it easier to slide or skid a load upward than to lift it directly. The longer the slope, the smaller the effort required. The amount of work, however, is no less than if the load were lifted directly upward.

FIG. 4

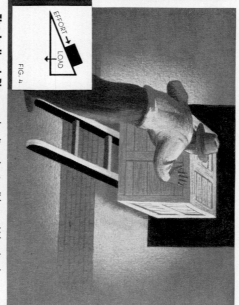

The Wedge, when struck with a mallet or sledge, exerts a large force on its sides. The gently tapering, or thin, wedge is more effective than the thick one which tapers sharply. Its mechanical advantage is of great importance.

FIG. 5

Shely

The Pulley consists of a wheel with a grooved rim over which a rope is passed. It is used to change the direction of the effort applied to the rope. A block and tackle uses two or more pulleys to reduce the amount of effort needed to lift a load.

The Screw is a spiral inclined plane. The jackscrew is a combination of the lever and the screw. It can lift a heavy load with relatively small effort. Therefore, it has a very high mechanical advantage for practical purposes.

FIG. 6

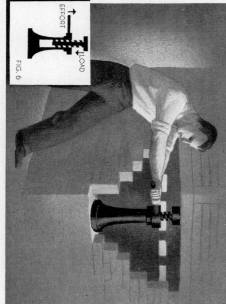

will be four to one. But the distance the 400-pound load will be moved will be only one-fourth of the distance through which that effort is applied.

Six Simple Machines

Most machines consist of a number of elements, such as gears and ball bearings, that work together in a complex way. But no matter how complex they are, all machines are based in some way on six types of simple machines: the lever, the wheel and axle, the pulley, the inclined plane, the wedge, and the screw.

Lever. There are three basic types of levers, depending on where the effort is applied, on the position of the load, and on the position of the fulcrum. In a first-class lever, such as a crowbar, the fulcrum is between the load and the applied force. In a second-class lever, such as a wheelbarrow, the load lies between the fulcrum and the applied force. In a third-class lever, the effort is applied between the load and the fulcrum. For example, when a person lifts a ball in the palm of his hand, the load is at the hand and the fulcrum is at the elbow. The forearm supplies the upward force that lifts the ball.

Wheel and Axle. The wheel and axle is essentially a modified lever, but it can move a load farther than a lever can. In a windlass used to raise water from a well, the rope that carries the load is wrapped around the axle of the wheel. The effort is applied to a crank handle on the side of the wheel. The center of the axle serves as a fulcrum. The mechanical advantage depends upon the ratio between the radius of the axle and the distance traveled by the crank handle. The wheel-and-axle machine has important applications when it is used to transport heavy goods by rolling rather than by sliding. The wheel itself is regarded as one of the most important inventions of all time. It is widely used in all types of machinery and motor vehicles. See WHEEL; WHEEL AND AXLE.

Pulley. A pulley is a wheel over which a rope or belt is passed. It is a form of the wheel and axle. The mechanical advantage of a single pulley is one, because the downward force exerted on the rope equals the weight lifted by the other end of the rope that passes over the pulley. The main advantage of the single pulley is that it changes the direction of the force. For example, to lift a load, a man can more conveniently pull down on a rope and also use the weight of his body. When one pulley is attached to a support and another is attached to the load and allowed to move freely, a definite mechanical advantage is obtained. See BLOCK AND TACKLE; PULLEY.

Inclined Plane. The inclined plane is such a simple device that it scarcely looks like a machine at all. The average person cannot raise a 200-pound box up 2 feet into the rear of a truck. But if he placed a 10-foot plank from the truck to the ground, he could raise the load easily. If there were no friction, the force required to move the box would be exactly 40 pounds. The mechanical advantage of an inclined plane is the length of the incline divided by the vertical rise. The mechanical advantage increases as the slope of the incline decreases. But the load will then have to be moved a greater distance. By adding rollers, it is possible to make a roller conveyor that will reduce friction and have great efficiency. See INCLINED PLANE.

Wedge. The wedge is an adaptation of the inclined plane. It can be used to raise a heavy load over a short distance or to split a log. The wedge is driven by blows from a mallet or sledge hammer. The effectiveness of the wedge depends on the angle of the thin end. The smaller the angle, the less the force required to raise a given load. See WEDGE.

Screw. The screw is actually an inclined plane cut in a spiral around a shaft. The mechanical advantage of a screw is approximately the ratio of the circumference of the screw to the distance the screw advances during each revolution.

A *jackscrew*, such as those sometimes used to raise homes and other structures, combines the usefulness of both the screw and the lever. The lever is used to turn the screw. The mechanical advantage of a jackscrew is quite high, and only a small effort will raise a heavy load. See SCREW.

Designing Machines

By combining the principles of simple machines, engineers develop new and specialized machines. The parts for many of these machines are often standardized so they can be used in a variety of machines that perform entirely different tasks. Some of the more common parts found in machines include ball bearings, gears, pistons, V-belt pulleys, connecting rods, valves, universal joints, and flexible shafts. There is an increasing demand in industry today for new machines to perform new tasks and for improvements that will increase the value of old machines.

ALLEN S. HALL, JR.

Related Articles in WORLD BOOK include:

SOME KINDS OF MACHINES

Archimedean Screw	Machine Tool
Battering-Ram	Pulley
Bell	Pump
Block and Tackle	Rolamite
Boiler	Screw
Building and	Slot Machine
Wrecking Machines	Steam Shovel
Catapult	Trip Hammer
Derricks and Cranes	Turbine
Die and Diemaking	Vacuum Cleaner
Electric Bell	Water Wheel
Electric Generator	Wedge
Gasoline Engine	Wheel and Axle
Inclined Plane	Windlass
Lever	Windmill

MACHINE PARTS

Bearing	Governor	Safety Valve
Gauge	Injector	Valve
Gear	Ratchet	

USES OF MACHINES

See these articles and their lists of Related Articles:

Atomic Energy	Business Machines	Printing
Automobile	Engine	Rocket
Aviation	Farm and Farming	Tool
	Instrument, Scientific	

OTHER RELATED ARTICLES

Efficiency	Mechanical Drawing
Industrial Revolution	Mechanics
Invention	Work

MACHINE AGE. See INDUSTRIAL REVOLUTION.

MACHINE GUN

U.S. Army Machine Gun M60 can be fired from the shoulder or hip, or on a support. It weighs 23 pounds, and is aircooled.

MACHINE GUN is an automatic weapon that can fire from 400 to 1,600 rounds of ammunition each minute. Machine gun barrels range in size from .22 caliber to 30 millimeters. Ammunition is fed into the gun from a cloth or metal belt, or from a cartridge holder called a *magazine*. Because machine guns fire so rapidly, they must be cooled by water or air. Machine guns are heavy weapons and are usually mounted on a support.

Operation. In all machine guns, extremely high gas pressure provides the operating energy for the firing cycle. The cycle begins when the propellant charge in the cartridge case burns. This combustion creates the gas pressure that is used in the *blowback, gas,* and *recoil* operating systems. All three systems fire the projectile through the *bore* of the barrel, eject the cartridge case, place a new cartridge in the firing chamber, and ready the mechanism to repeat the cycle.

In the *blowback system,* the operating energy comes from the cartridge case as the case is forced to the rear by the gas pressure. The case moves against the

bolt, driving the bolt backward against a spring. The case is ejected, and the compressed spring drives the bolt forward. As the bolt moves forward, it cocks the firing mechanism, picks up a new cartridge, carries it into the chamber, and the cycle begins again.

In the *gas system,* the gas pressure drives a piston against the bolt. The bolt is driven to the rear, providing energy for a cycle similar to the blowback system.

In the *recoil system,* the bolt locks to the barrel when the gun is fired. These parts remain locked together as they are forced to the rear by the gas pressure. This movement provides energy to operate the gun.

Ground Weapons. The 7.62-millimeter M60 machine gun is a major infantry weapon. It is air-cooled, gas operated, and fires about 600 rounds a minute. The M60 replaced the Browning machine gun, an important weapon in World Wars I and II. The standard U.S.

MACHINE GUNS OF WORLD WARS I AND II

Browning Automatic Rifle (BAR) was designed by John M. Browning. The U.S. Army adopted it in 1917.

Submachine Gun M3, first produced early in World War II, replaced the older Thompson submachine gun.

Carbine M2 became a standard U.S. Army weapon in the early 1940's, during World War II.

Light Machine Guns evolved from the original model that John M. Browning made after World War I.

Heavy Machine Guns were the most destructive weapons of World War I, firing 500 rounds a minute.

HEAVY
MACHINE GUN

AUTOMATIC RIFLE

SUBMACHINE GUN

CARBINE

LIGHT
MACHINE GUNS

U.S. Army

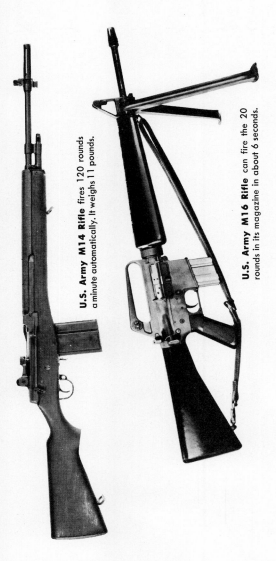

U.S. Army M14 Rifle fires 120 rounds a minute automatically. It weighs 11 pounds.

U.S. Army M16 Rifle can fire the 20 rounds in its magazine in about 6 seconds.

Army submachine gun is the .45-caliber M3, a short-range weapon weighing 9 pounds.

Aircraft Weapons. By the close of World War I, several types of machine guns were mounted on airplanes. These types included the Vickers, Maxim, Hotchkiss, Colt-Martin, and Lewis. Some of these guns were synchronized to fire in between the blades of propellers.

During World War II, fighters and bombers carried machine guns as armament. They also carried automatic cannon up to 20 millimeters in size. Today, most fighter planes carry rockets for air-to-air and air-to-ground use. Bombers use machine guns mounted in groups of two or four in power-driven turrets. The Vulcan 20-millimeter aircraft cannon has six rotating barrels. It can fire more than a ton of metal and explosives each minute.

Antiaircraft Weapons. The .50-caliber Browning machine gun was used as an antiaircraft weapon during World War II. It was used alone, or in groups of two or four. Large-caliber automatic cannon that fired explosive shells were also developed as antiaircraft weapons. The 20-millimeter Oerlikon gun was used on U.S. Navy ships. It was a self-fed, self-firing cannon that could fire 600 rounds a minute.

History. A type of machine gun appeared as early as the 1500's. It consisted of several guns bound together in a bundle or spread out in a row. A device that was fitted to the gun barrels caused them to fire simultaneously or in series. But little success was achieved until the Civil War, when many quick-fire guns appeared. Practical, rapid-fire, mechanical guns were used in the Franco-Prussian War, when soldiers operated them with a crank or lever. The French *Montigny mitrailleuse* and the American *Gatling* were among the more successful of these guns. In 1889, Hiram Maxim, an American-born inventor, developed the first entirely automatic weapon to gain wide acceptance. By the time of World War I, many different types of machine guns had come into use.

JOHN D. BILLINGSLEY

See also ANTIAIRCRAFT DEFENSE; GATLING, RICHARD JORDAN; LEWIS, ISAAC NEWTON; MAXIM (Sir Hiram Stevens).

EARLY MACHINE GUNS

Maxim Gun

Hiram Maxim invented the first fully automatic machine gun.

Gatling Gun

Richard Gatling produced a hand-cranked machine gun in 1862.

The Montigny Mitrailleuse was a quick-firing gun with 37 barrels.

Mitrailleuse

MACHINE TOOL

MACHINE TOOL is a piece of equipment used to shape metal. These important tools shape metal by cutting, shearing, hammering, or squeezing. Machine tools do to metal what a carpenter's tools do to wood. A carpenter cuts wood with a saw, drills holes with a brace and bit, and smooths surfaces with a plane. A *machinist* (worker who operates a machine tool) cuts, drills, planes, and grinds or shapes metals with power-driven machine tools.

Machine tools play an important part in the production of almost all metal products known to man. They make the working parts of telephones, television sets, radios, washing machines, and vacuum cleaners. Sewing machines are made with machine tools. Refrigerators could not operate without the ability of machine tools to make the precise parts they need to operate.

Machine tools are essential to the manufacture of automobiles. Chairs, tables, beds, bookcases, and other furniture are made by machines that consist of parts turned out by machine tools. Without machine tools, farmers would have no plows, cultivators, or tractors.

There are more than 400 kinds of machine tools, each designed to do a certain type of work. Each kind of tool comes in various sizes. Each size and type has many special attachments that make metalworking easier.

Kinds of Machine Tools

The variety and number of combinations of machine tools in use are almost unlimited. Some are so small that they are mounted on a workbench. Other machine tools are as large as a three-story house. They range in cost from a few hundred dollars to hundreds of thou-

sands of dollars. Some machine tools weigh several hundred tons and require a large area for their operation.

Whether large or small, machine tools can be classified into six major groups, according to the six basic operations in shaping metals. These basic operations are: (1) drilling and boring, which includes reaming and tapping; (2) turning; (3) milling; (4) planing, which includes shaping and broaching; (5) grinding, which includes lapping and honing; and (6) metal forming, which includes shearing, pressing, and forging.

Machinists may use many variations of these groupings to meet unusual situations. For example, a number of machines combine two or more of the six basic methods. Such equipment might be a combination boring, drilling, and milling machine, or a combination milling machine and planer.

In addition, many machine tools have been built to perform not one, but a whole series of operations once the metal to be worked on has been put in place. The operator of such a machine does not touch the work from the beginning to the end of the various machining steps. Machinists call such pieces of equipment *transfer machines*, because the work moves automatically from one tool to the next.

Drilling and Boring. The process of *drilling*, or cutting a round hole by means of a rotating drill, dates back to primitive man. *Boring* involves *finishing*, or smoothing, a hole already drilled.

In most machine shops, drills are mounted on large machines called *drill presses*. The metal part to be drilled is placed on a platform, and the operator lowers the drill to the metal. Machinists also use motor-driven hand drills. See DRILLING TOOLS.

An Engine Lathe peels rough surfaces off a huge steel part for a turbine. A housewife peeling an apple does the same type of job on a small scale.

National Machine Tool Builders' Assoc.

MACHINE TOOL

National Machine Tool Builders' Association

Boring is done with a rotating *tool*, a sharp-edged piece of metal that looks somewhat like a drill. But a borer has only one cutting edge, and a drill usually has several. On some boring machines, the tool is stationary and the work revolves. On other boring machines, the tool revolves and the work is stationary.

Drilling and boring also include two other operations, reaming and tapping. *Reaming* consists of finishing a hole already drilled to extremely close *tolerances* (almost exact dimensions). Tapping is the process of cutting a screw thread inside the hole (see SCREW).

Turning is one of the most important operations in a machine shop. It consists of rotating a piece of metal against a cutting tool in a machine called a *lathe*. Turning is used chiefly to shape round pieces of metal.

In the common lathe, a single cutting tool is mounted at the side of the turning piece of metal. As the metal rotates, the cutting edge of the tool is fed against the area to be cut. *Turret* lathes have six tools mounted on a toolholder or turret. This device makes it possible to bring several different cutting tools into use one after the other. The same operations can be repeated over and over again on different pieces of metal without changing the setting of the tools.

When the number of identical parts to be produced increases from a few to hundreds or thousands, machinists use an automatic *multiple spindle bar machine*. This machine is actually six lathes in one. It performs six different operations at one time on six parts. After the machinist sets up the machine, he has only to feed in long metal bars and remove the finished parts.

Milling consists of machining a piece of metal by bringing it in contact with a rotating cutting tool that has several cutting edges. The cutting tool on most milling machines looks like a wheel with sharp teeth sticking out of it. Milling is used to produce such simple shapes as slots and flat surfaces. Other shapes are more complicated. They may consist of a variety of flat and curved surfaces, depending on the shape of the tool's cutting edges. Special milling machines used to make gears are called *hobbing* machines.

Planing metal with a machine tool is similar to planing wood with a carpenter's hand plane. The chief differences are that a machine-tool planer (1) is larger than a carpenter's plane, and (2) is not portable. In the machine tool, the cutting part remains stationary while the pieces to be planed move beneath.

A machine called a *shaper* does a job similar to planing. But the cutting tool moves while the metal remains stationary. In a *slotter* (vertical shaper) the cutting tool moves up and down instead of back and forth. Slotters are used chiefly to cut certain types of gears.

Machinists also classify *broaches* as planing machines. Broaches are used when the metal to be removed is not too thick, and where many parts must be machined at one time. A broach looks like a long metal bar with a row of teeth on it. Each tooth cuts a little deeper than the one before. The broach is pulled or pushed over the surface to be finished, and the teeth cut the metal to the desired depth in one operation.

Grinding involves shaping a piece of metal by bringing it into contact with a rotating wheel covered with an abrasive material similar to that found on sandpaper (see ABRASIVE). Machinists use this process chiefly to finish a piece of work to close dimensions after it has

A Milling Machine shapes metal surfaces with revolving wheels. The wheels have cutting edges that are drawn across the metal surface like a hoe pulled across the ground.

National Machine Tool Builders' Association

been heat treated to make it hard. But some grinding equipment can remove metal as fast as cutting tools. This equipment is used for *abrasive machining*. Machinists can grind cylindrical surfaces, as well as holes, flat surfaces, and screw threads.

Grinding also includes two other operations, lapping and honing. *Lapping* involves the use of abrasive paste or other compounds to remove metal. It is limited to jobs where only a small amount of metal must be re-

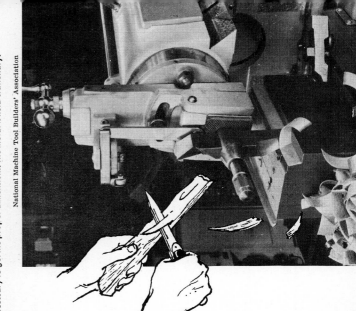

A Shaper cuts metal in much the same way a man with a knife whittles a piece of wood. It slices across the metal as many times as necessary to get the proper dimensions. The metal is held stationary.

moved and the machinist desires a high degree of precision and an extremely smooth surface. A lapping machine has a metal plate coated with the abrasive. *Honing* is used to finish holes accurately. In this process, the abrasive material is inserted in rotating cylindrical *heads* that are inserted in the hole. The head grinds the inside of the hole by rotating while it moves up and down.

Metal-Forming machine tools are the giant successors to the tools used by blacksmiths. There are several types of metal-forming machines. The most important of these include (1) presses, (2) shears, (3) press brakes, (4) drop hammers, and (5) forging machines.

Presses stamp a metal sheet into a desired shape, then squeeze the piece, called a *blank*, into the final shape with a die (see DIE AND DIEMAKING). There are two types of these huge machines, *mechanical* presses and *hydraulic* presses. Both do the same job. A *punch press* is a machine tool that punches holes in metal sheets.

Shears cut sheets of metal much as scissors cut sheets of paper. In a shearing machine, the metal is placed on a flat surface, and a sharp blade drops down to cut it into the desired shape.

Press Brakes are large machines that machinists use to bend sheets of metal.

Drop Hammers are operated mechanically by steam or by air. They are used to *forge* (hammer) white-hot metal on an anvil. The steam or air raises the hammer and controls its falling on the metal.

Forging Machines squeeze white-hot metal in a die under great pressure. The metal flows to every part of the die and takes the desired shape.

New Developments in Machine Tools include the electrical-discharge method and the ultrasonic method. Both are useful in working with extremely hard metals. They are chiefly used to make dies and tools. But machinists have hopes of developing them for uses on larger, more complicated jobs.

The Electrical-Discharge Method, also called the *disintegrator* method, uses electricity to cut metal. In an electrical-discharge machine, charges of electricity are directed from a negatively charged tool to a positively charged piece of work. Each charge of electricity removes a small amount of metal. An automatic device keeps the tool and the piece of work the same distance apart during the cutting.

The Ultrasonic Method drills hard materials, such as glass, quartz, and tungsten carbide. In this method, a rod of brass or soft steel is placed on the material to be drilled, and a mixture of abrasive and water is aimed at the place where the rod and piece of work touch. A magnetic field makes the rod vibrate at an ultrasonic frequency. This vibration drills the hole. See SOUND (Ultrasound).

Numerical Control brings automation to the machine-tool industry. In this system, punched or magnetic tape controls the machine tool. The tape, prepared by computers and programmers, guides the production of a part. Because the same tape is used over and over, the

A Planer smooths flat surfaces somewhat as a woman grates cheese. The planer remains stationary while the metal moves beneath it. A planer can also cut slots or grooves.

National Machine Tool Builders' Association

A Jig Borer drills holes quickly in a metal plate that will eventually be part of a jet engine. The borer resembles a carpenter's hand drill.

National Machine Tool Builders' Association

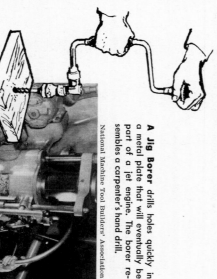

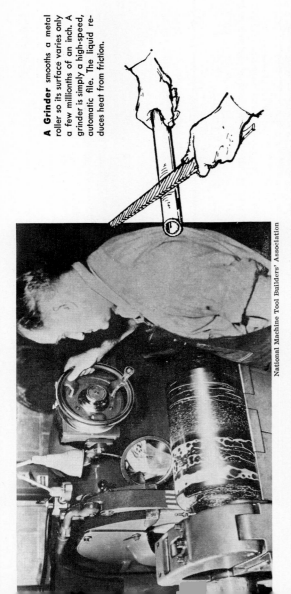

National Machine Tool Builders' Association

A Grinder smooths a metal roller so its surface varies only a few millionths of an inch. A grinder is simply a high-speed, automatic file. The liquid reduces heat from friction.

new parts are identical. This improves efficiency and uniformity of quality. The machine-tool industry is also testing many other new methods of forming metal.

The Machine-Tool Industry

In the United States, the machine-tool industry has a key part in the nation's production system. But the industry is small compared with the giant industries—such as steel, oil, and automobile—that use machine tools. It has seldom employed more than 60,000 workers.

The machine-tool industry consists of about 300 companies. A few of them employ as many as 5,000 workers. But the average is between 200 and 250 employees. Some companies make only machine tools. Others make different types of equipment as well.

A Boring Machine smooths holes that have been cut with other machines. A woman does the same type of job when she trims the inside of a cored apple.

National Machine Tool Builders' Association

The American machine-tool industry centers in the area north of the Ohio and Potomac rivers, and east of the Mississippi River. A few companies operate in the western part of the country.

In Other Countries. A number of other countries have developed large machine-tool industries of their own. In the late 1950's, West Germany ranked as the leading producer of machine tools among the noncommunist nations. Other countries with large machine-tool industries include Great Britain, Italy, Switzerland, Japan, France, Belgium, and The Netherlands.

Russia is known to be building an increasing quantity of machine tools. Some of these machines are being sold to South American countries and to a few European nations. Communist China, with the aid of Russia, has also built large machine-tool plants to help equip its other industries.

History

When James Watt began his experiments with the steam engine in 1763, he could not find anyone who could drill a perfect hole. As a result, his engines leaked steam until an Englishman, John Wilkinson, invented the boring machine in 1775. The planer, like the boring machine, was not developed until needed to make steam engines. Three Englishmen—Matthew Murray, Joseph Clement, and Richard Murray—took part in its development between 1800 and 1825.

The principle of the lathe has been known since ancient times. The idea probably originated with the potter's wheel (see POTTERY). Until 1800, lathes were crude machines that could not be used to cut screw threads accurately. That year, Henry Maudslay of England invented the first good screw-cutting lathe. James Nasmyth, an assistant to Maudslay, invented the shaper in 1836. Nasmyth also invented the steam hammer and other machine tools.   LUDLOW KING

Related Articles in WORLD BOOK include:

Brown, Joseph R.
Drilling Tools
Forging
Grinding and
Polishing
Nasmyth, James

Sound (picture:
Ultrasound)
Steam Hammer
Whitworth, Sir
Joseph

MACHINIST

MACHINIST. See DIE AND DIEMAKING; MACHINE TOOL; MACHINISTS AND AEROSPACE WORKERS.

MACHINISTS AND AEROSPACE WORKERS, INTERNATIONAL ASSOCIATION OF, formerly the INTERNATIONAL ASSOCIATION OF MACHINISTS, is a labor union affiliated with the American Federation of Labor and Congress of Industrial Organizations. It has locals throughout the U. S. and its territories, and Canada.

Membership is open to men and women who work in the metalworking industries, on production lines, in machine shops, garages, toolrooms, and everywhere that machinery and equipment are manufactured, installed, repaired, or operated.

Founded in Atlanta, Ga., in 1888, the International Association of Machinists and Aerospace Workers is one of the largest unions in the aircraft and guided-missile industry, as well as one of the largest among the railroad, automobile mechanics, airlines, machine tool, and business machine industry unions. Services include a research and statistical department, an educational department, a public relations department, and a department of health and welfare. The union has headquarters at 1300 Connecticut Ave. NW, Washington, D.C. 20036. It publishes a weekly newspaper, *The Machinist.* For membership, see LABOR (table); GORDON H. COLE

MACHU PICCHU, *MAH choo PEEK choo,* is the site of an ancient Inca city about 50 miles northwest of Cusco, Peru. The stone structures which are the ruins of Machu Picchu stand on a mountain about 8,000 feet high. In 1911, Hiram Bingham discovered the ruins. See also SOUTH AMERICA (color picture); INCA.

MACINTOSH, CHARLES (1766-1843), a British chemist and inventor, is best known as the inventor of waterproof fabrics. The *mackintosh,* a waterproof outer garment, is named after him. He also made many significant contributions to chemical technology. He opened a factory to manufacture alum and sal ammoniac before he was 20. He also introduced into Great Britain the manufacture of lead and aluminum acetates and contributed to the technology of dyeing. He was born in Glasgow.

MACK, ALEXANDER. See BRETHREN, CHURCH OF THE.

MACK, CONNIE (1862-1956), became one of the greatest managers in baseball history. He helped organize the American League, and served as owner-manager of the Philadelphia Athletics from 1901 until he retired in 1950. Mack spent more than 60 years in baseball, and led the Athletics in nine World Series. They won five of them. His sons later sold the team, and it was moved to Kansas City, Mo. Mack was born in Brookfield, Mass. See also BASEBALL (National Baseball Hall of Fame).

MACKAY was the family name of two American businessmen, father and son.

John William Mackay (1831-1902) and James Gordon Bennett, Jr., organized the Commercial Cable Company and the Postal Telegraph Company in 1883. They laid two cables under the Atlantic Ocean, and were beginning one under the Pacific when Mackay died. Mackay was born in Ireland, but came to New York City with his parents as a boy. In 1851 he went to California to seek gold. He made his fortune as one of the owners of the "Big Bonanza" gold and silver mine. This mine, discovered in 1873 at Virginia City, Nev., was the richest deposit of gold and silver ore ever found. The value of a share in it shot up from 15 cents to $1,850.

Clarence Hungerford Mackay (1874-1938) succeeded his father as a director of the telegraph and cable companies. He became vice-president of the Postal Telegraph Company at 23. Congress combined his cable and telegraph companies with the Western Union Telegraph Company in 1943. Mackay was born in San Francisco. DONALD L. KEMMERER

MACKENZIE (pop. 18,685) is a district of the Northwest Territories of Canada. It lies east of the Yukon Territory and west of the District of Keewatin. Mackenzie covers an area of 527,490 square miles, including 34,265 square miles of inland water. Fur trade opened the district to settlement. But today, minerals, notably gold, are more important. There also are rich deposits of tungsten, base metals, and petroleum. Fisheries operate on Great Slave Lake.

Mackenzie was made a district in 1895. It elects four members to the Council of the Northwest Territories, and one to the federal House of Commons. The federal and territorial governments provide civil administration. In 1962, the federal government announced plans to make the district Mackenzie Territory. All the Indians of the Northwest Territories live in Mackenzie.

See also NORTHWEST TERRITORIES.

MACKENZIE, ALEXANDER (1822-1892), served as prime minister of Canada from 1873 to 1878. He was a member of the legislature of the Province of Canada from 1861 to 1867, of the dominion parliament from 1867 to 1892, and of the legislature of Ontario from 1867 to 1872, when dual representation was abolished.

He was a follower of George Brown, and supported the union of Canada (see BROWN, GEORGE). But, like Brown, he would not continue in the coalition government of Sir John A. Macdonald. After Brown's defeat in 1867, Mackenzie became leader of the Liberal party. He welded differing groups into a strong political force.

Mackenzie became the first Liberal party prime minister of the Dominion when Macdonald resigned in 1873 over the Canadian Pacific Railway scandal (see MACDONALD, SIR JOHN A.). His government introduced the ballot into Canadian elections in 1874, and set up the Supreme Court in 1875. But it failed to solve the problems posed by the economic depression or the building of the Canadian Pacific Railway. Mackenzie was defeated by Macdonald in the election of 1878. After his defeat, he resigned the Liberal party leadership to Edward Blake. He continued in politics as a member of parliament until his death.

Mackenzie was born in Scotland and came to Canada in 1842. He was a stonemason by trade. He became a builder and contractor in Kingston and Sarnia before entering politics. G. F. G. STANLEY

Alexander Mackenzie
Public Archives of Canada, Ottawa

MACKENZIE, SIR ALEXANDER

MACKENZIE, SIR ALEXANDER (1764?-1820), was a Canadian trader and explorer. He discovered the Mackenzie River, and he was the first white man to cross the northern part of the North American continent to the Pacific Ocean.

In 1789, Mackenzie left Fort Chipewyan on Lake Athabasca with a small party of Canadians and Indian guides. He pushed his way north to Great Slave Lake, and then followed the river that now bears his name. It took him to the Arctic Ocean. He had hoped that the river would lead him to the Pacific Ocean, and was keenly disappointed. Because of this, Mackenzie called it the *River of Disappointment.*

Three years later, Mackenzie started on his trip to the west coast. He followed the Peace River, crossed the Rocky Mountains, and reached the Pacific Ocean in 1793. This trip convinced him that a search for a Northwest Passage to the Orient would be useless.

He wrote *Voyages on the River Saint Lawrence and Through the Continent of North America to the Frozen and Pacific Oceans in the Years 1789 and 1793* (1801). This book contains much valuable information on Indian tribes and Canadian history.

Mackenzie was born on the island of Lewis, off the coast of Scotland. He went to Canada in 1778. There, he entered the countinghouse of a Montreal fur-trading company. After his last trip, he settled down and made a large fortune as a fur trader. He spent his last years in Scotland.

W. R. WILLOUGHBY

MACKENZIE, RODERICK

MACKENZIE, RODERICK (1760?-1844), was a Canadian frontiersman and fur trader. He accompanied his cousin, Sir Alexander Mackenzie, on a trip to western Canada in 1786, and built Fort Chipewyan in northeastern Alberta in 1788. He commanded the fort from 1789 to 1793. He was a capable administrator rather than a trailbreaker. He returned to eastern Canada in 1797, and became a partner in the Northwest Company in 1799. Later, he served in the Legislative Council of Lower Canada. He was born in Scotland, and lived at Terrebonne, Canada.

THOMAS D. CLARK

MACKENZIE, WILLIAM LYON

MACKENZIE, WILLIAM LYON (1795-1861), a Canadian politician, led the unsuccessful December Rebellion of 1837 in Upper Canada. As a member of the Reform party, Mackenzie was elected to the Legislative Assembly in 1828. He was a busy agitator from the start. Although he was not an original thinker, he succeeded in popularizing the ideas of others. Mackenzie insisted that Canada have more self-government than Britain allowed, and urged more democratic govern-

ment within Canada itself. He wanted an independent judiciary, responsible government like that in Britain, less power for the governor-general, and more power for the legislature, especially control over taxation.

In 1837 the British Parliament rejected the demands of the Reform party, and Mackenzie and the party were defeated in the elections. Mackenzie, angry and bitter after his defeat, decided to revolt. But his plans were badly organized, and only about 800 of his followers gathered to march on Toronto. The Loyalist militia quickly defeated them.

Mackenzie escaped to the United States and established a temporary government on Navy Island in the Niagara River. After a month's stay, United States officials arrested him for breaking the neutrality laws. In 1849 he was permitted to return to Canada, where he was re-elected to the Legislative Assembly in 1851.

Mackenzie was born near Dundee, Scotland, and moved to Canada in 1820.

WILLARD M. WALLACE

See also CANADA, HISTORY OF (Struggle for Responsible Government); KING, WILLIAM LYON MACKENZIE.

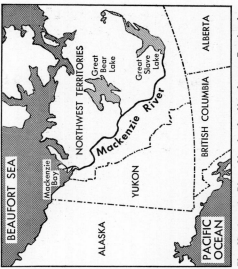

BEAUFORT SEA

Mackenzie Bay

ALASKA

YUKON

PACIFIC OCEAN

NORTHWEST TERRITORIES

Great Bear Lake

Great Slave Lake

Mackenzie River

BRITISH COLUMBIA

ALBERTA

The Mackenzie River Lies in the Northwest Territories.

Sir Alexander Mackenzie
Portrait by Sir Thomas Lawrence. The National Gallery of Canada, Canadian War Memorials Collection, Ottawa

William L. Mackenzie
Portrait by J. W. L. Forster. Public Archives of Canada, Ottawa

MACKENZIE RIVER, in the Northwest Territories, is the longest river in Canada. The Mackenzie flows north and west for about a thousand miles from Great Slave Lake to the Beaufort Sea, a part of the Arctic Ocean. Many parts of the Mackenzie are more than a mile wide. Every second, an average of about 500,000 cubic feet of water flows from its mouth. Water flows into the Mackenzie from many tributaries, including the Liard, Great Bear, Arctic Red, and Peel rivers. Water also enters the Mackenzie from Great Slave Lake. It reaches Great Slave Lake through the Slave River, which collects water from the Peace and Athabasca rivers. The Mackenzie River was named for the Canadian explorer Sir Alexander Mackenzie (see MACKENZIE, SIR ALEXANDER).

All the rivers mentioned above are part of the *Mackenzie River System,* Canada's largest river system. This vast system drains water from about 682,000 square miles, an area larger than Alaska. Its most distant water source is high in Alberta's Rocky Mountains, 2,635 miles from the Arctic mouth of the Mackenzie.

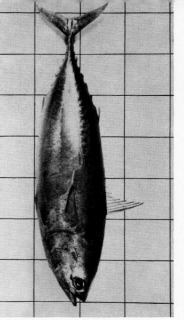

H. L. Moore, Fish and Wildlife Service

The Frigate Mackerel Lives in Most Warm Seas.

In North America, only the Mississippi-Missouri system is longer than the Mackenzie system.

A 1,700-mile stretch of the Mackenzie system, from Waterways, Alberta, to the Beaufort Sea, is almost completely navigable. Along this route, only a 7-mile rapids on the Slave River interferes with shipping.

The Mackenzie River basin is rich in natural resources. The Peace River area of Alberta and British Columbia includes millions of acres of farmland. It also has petroleum and natural gas deposits and abundant water for hydroelectric power. In the northern part of the basin, the delta at the mouth of the Mackenzie is a famous muskrat-trapping area. This region has little agriculture, but it is rich in petroleum, radium, and uranium deposits.

See also NORTHWEST TERRITORIES; RIVER (chart: Longest Rivers).

D. F. PUTNAM

MACKEREL, *MACK er ul,* is one of the most valuable food fishes. It lives in the North Atlantic Ocean. On the American side, it lives in waters from Cape Hatteras to the Strait of Belle Isle between Newfoundland and Labrador. In European waters, it can be found from Norway to the Mediterranean and Adriatic seas.

The mackerel is related to the tuna. Its shape and beautiful colors make it outstanding. Its body is of various shades of blue and green. The mackerel is silvery-white below, and has wavy black stripes on its back. *Mackerel,* or *mackerel-back,* clouds are so named because they resemble the markings on the back of this fish.

The mackerel has two large fins on its back and two smaller ones beneath. Its tail is large and shaped like a fork. Five tiny fins are on each side just in front of the tail. Mackerel grow 10 to 18 inches long, and weigh from one-half to three pounds.

In spring, schools of mackerel appear near Cape Hatteras and swim north into Canadian waters. In autumn, they return to deeper seas. Their spawning season on the North American coast is from May to July. June is the most active spawning month. Mackerel breed chiefly in shallow waters of New England and the Gulf of St. Lawrence. Mackerel flesh tastes best when the fish is caught just after the spawning period.

Sharks, bluefish, porpoises, and whales attack and eat mackerel. A sea bird, the gannet, eats small mackerel. Mackerel themselves eat crustaceans, herring, anchovies, menhaden, and other small fish.

The mackerel fisheries of Great Britain, Ireland, Norway, Canada, and the United States provide most of the world's supply of this fish.

Scientific Classification. Mackerel belong to three families, the *Scombridae, Cybiidae,* and *Katsuwonidae.* The common mackerel is in the family *Scombridae.* It is genus *Scomber,* species *S. scombrus.*

See also FISH (color picture: Salt-Water Fishes); FISHING INDUSTRY (table: Chief Kinds of Ocean Fish); KINGFISH; LIFE (table: Length of Life); TUNA.

LEONARD P. SCHULTZ

MACKINAC, *MACK ih naw,* **STRAITS OF,** is an important link in the water route that leads from Lake Michigan to the Atlantic Ocean. The straits connect Lake Michigan and Lake Huron. They are at the northern end of the Lower Peninsula of Michigan (see MICHIGAN [physical map]). Mackinac Island lies in the straits. The straits are about 40 miles long, and about 5 miles wide at the narrowest point. In 1957, engineers completed the Mackinac Bridge across the straits. It is one of the longest suspension bridges in the world. Its center span is 3,800 feet long. The bridge links Mackinaw City in the Lower Peninsula with the city of St. Ignace in the Upper Peninsula. See MICHIGAN (color picture).

WILLIS F. DUNBAR

MACKINAC ISLAND, *MACK ih naw,* or *MACH ih nack,* is a north Michigan island summer resort in the Straits of Mackinac (see MICHIGAN [political map]). The Chippewa Indians called the island *Michilimackinac,* usually defined as *Great Spirits* or *Great Turtle.* The city of Mackinac Island lies on the southeastern end of the island. No passenger cars are permitted on Mackinac. Ferries link the island with the mainland. The longest fresh-water yachting event in the world is the Chicago-to-Mackinac Island race, held each July.

In 1671, Father Jacques Marquette established a mission at nearby Point St. Ignace. The French built forts at St. Ignace and Mackinaw City, on the Michigan mainland. In 1761, the French surrendered the area to the British. The British built Fort Mackinac on the island in 1780. In 1796, the United States gained the island, but the British recaptured it in 1812. In 1815, the British returned it to the United States. The island became the headquarters of John Jacob Astor's American Fur Company. After the fort was abandoned in 1894, the federal government transferred about half of the island to the state of Michigan. It became Mackinac Island State Park.

WILLIS F. DUNBAR

MACKINDER, SIR HALFORD. See GEOPOLITICS.

MACLEISH, ARCHIBALD (1892-   ), is an American poet, dramatist, and critic. He also served as librarian of Congress from 1939 to 1944 and assistant secretary of state in 1944 and 1945.

MacLeish's early work is lyrical and thoughtful, using free verse and other technical methods of such older poets as Ezra Pound and T. S. Eliot. *Conquistador* (1932) is a strong, individual achievement, describing in epic terms the Spanish exploration of the New World. The work gained MacLeish the first of his three Pulitzer prizes. With the mounting problems of social unrest in America and the rise of fascism abroad, MacLeish turned to more direct expression of the issues of his day. He particularly explored these issues in *Public Speech* (1936) and his two radio dramas, *The Fall of the City* (1937) and *Air Raid* (1938).

MacLeish's later work became somewhat less topical

and more philosophic in tone. His successful verse drama, *J.B.*, raises the eternal problem of man's suffering, treating the Biblical story of Job in terms of modern American life. The play won the 1959 Pulitzer prize for drama. His *Collected Poems, 1917-1952* won the 1953 Pulitzer prize.

MacLeish's most mature reflections on the value of poetry as a means of knowledge are developed in *Poetry and Experience* (1961). He concludes, "To face the truth of the passing away of the world, and make song of it, make beauty of it, is not to solve the riddle of our mortal lives but perhaps to accomplish something more."

MacLeish was born in Glencoe, Ill. He earned a law degree, but gave up practice to devote himself to literature. He taught at Harvard from 1949 to 1962, and at Amherst from 1963 to 1967. ELMER W. BORKLUND

MACLENNAN, HUGH (1907-), a Canadian novelist and essayist, first won recognition in 1941 for *Barometer Rising*, a novel about the 1917 Halifax explosion. He won the Governor General's Award in 1946 for *Two Solitudes*, a novel about Anglo-French relations in Canada. He also wrote *The Precipice* (1948), a novel dealing with relations between Canada and the United States, *Each Man's Son* (1951), and *Return of the Sphinx* (1967). He also contributed many articles to magazines.

He was born in Glace Bay, Nova Scotia, and studied at the Halifax Academy, Dalhousie University in Halifax, and Oxford and Princeton universities. Later, he taught Latin at Lower Canada College and English at McGill University. DESMOND PACEY

See also CANADIAN LITERATURE (Fiction).

MACLEOD, *muk LOUD,* **JOHN JAMES RICKARD** (1876-1935), was a Scottish physiologist. He and Sir Frederick Banting won the 1923 Nobel prize in physiology and medicine for their discovery of insulin in 1921 (see BANTING, SIR FREDERICK G.). Macleod was born near Dunkeld, Scotland. He taught physiology in Cleveland, Toronto, and Aberdeen. A. M. WINCHESTER

MACLURE, WILLIAM. See NEW HARMONY.

MACMANUS, *muk MAN us,* **SEUMAS,** *SHAY mus* (1869-1960), was an Irish writer of stories, poems, and plays. He was born in County Donegal, and worked as a shepherd and farm hand. He listened to old Irish tales, and later retold them in his stories. MacManus' first book of poems was *Shuilers (Vagrants)* (1893). He described his childhood and youth in *The Rocky Road to Dublin* (1938). He also wrote *Top o' the Mornin'* (1920), *Well of the World's End* (1939), and *The Bold Heroes of Hungry Hill* (1951). He taught in a mountain school until he came to the United States in the 1890's to sell many of his stories. JOSEPH E. BAKER

MACMECHAN, ARCHIBALD McKELLAR (1862-1933), was a Canadian essayist, critic, and educator. He published about fifteen books, including essays such as *The Life of a Little College* (1914) and *The Book of Ultima Thule* (1927); historical works such as *The Winning of Responsible Government* (1915); such literary history and criticism as *Headwaters of Canadian Literature* (1924); and one book of poems, *Late Harvest* (1934). He was born in Berlin (now Kitchener), Ont., and was graduated from the University of Toronto. He received his Ph.D. degree from Johns Hopkins University. He served as a professor of English at Dalhousie University in Halifax, N.S., from 1889 to 1933. DESMOND PACEY

MACMILLAN, DONALD BAXTER (1874-), an American polar explorer, added much to our knowledge of Greenland and the Canadian Arctic. He advanced the belief that the glacier fields are pushing southward. He discovered coal deposits 9 degrees from the North Pole. These contained remains of 36 kinds of trees, showing that the climate there had once been milder. MacMillan's 1924 Arctic expedition used radio extensively. He established winter quarters in Etah, Greenland. MacMillan's 1925 expedition was one of the first to use airplanes in the Far North. His men made many special aerial photographs.

He received the Special Congressional Medal for surveying and charting Greenland and the Canadian Arctic for the United States Army during World War II. In 1957, at the age of 82, MacMillan went on his 31st trip to the Arctic. He wrote several books about his experiences, including *Four Years in the White North* (1918), *Etah and Beyond* (1927), and *How Peary Reached the Pole* (1932).

MacMillan was born in Provincetown, Mass. He studied at Bowdoin College and Harvard University. He taught school until 1908, when he made his first polar expedition as assistant to Commander Robert Peary. MacMillan helped train many younger explorers including Richard and E. Byrd. MacMillan served in the U.S. Navy during World War II, and retired with the rank of a rear admiral in the naval reserve. JOHN E. CASWELL

Donald B. MacMillan

BROWN BROS.

MacMillan's Ship was often greeted by crowds as he returned from exploring Arctic waters. The explorer and a team of scientists studied the movements of glaciers, and discovered coal deposits only 9 degrees from the North Pole.

United Press Int.

MACMILLAN, SIR ERNEST CAMPBELL (1893–   ), a Canadian musician, began his career as a concert organist at the age of 10. From 1926 to 1942, he served as principal of the Toronto Conservatory of Music. He was dean of music at the University of Toronto from 1927 to 1952. Macmillan served as conductor of the Toronto Symphony Orchestra from 1931 to 1956. He was born at Mimico, Ontario, and was graduated from the University of Toronto.   W. R. WILLOUGHBY

MACMILLAN, HAROLD (1894–   ), served as prime minister of Great Britain from January, 1957, until October, 1963. He was forced to resign because of illness. Macmillan succeeded Anthony Eden. Eden resigned after the failure of the attack on Egypt by Great Britain and France in October, 1956.

Macmillan was elected to the House of Commons in 1924, as a Conservative. In the 1930's he was a progressive back-bench member. He criticized Prime Minister Neville Chamberlain and the Munich settlement with Nazi Germany in 1938 (see MUNICH AGREEMENT). He also urged action to combat the depression.

He served in Winston Churchill's wartime coalition government as British resident minister at Allied Headquarters in Northwest Africa, from 1942 to 1945. He also served as Churchill's minister of housing and local government from 1951 to 1954, and as minister of defense in 1954. He became foreign secretary under Eden in April, 1955, and was named chancellor of the exchequer in December, 1955.

United Press Int.
Harold Macmillan

He was born in London, and named MAURICE HAROLD MACMILLAN. His father was a Scotsman and a member of the Macmillan publishing family. His mother was the former Helen Artie Belles of Spencer, Ind. He attended Eton College and was graduated from Balliol College, Oxford. An officer in the Grenadier Guards during World War I, he was wounded three times and received the Military Cross.   C. L. MOWAT

MACMURRAY COLLEGE. See UNIVERSITIES AND COLLEGES (table).

MACMURROUGH, DERMOT. See IRELAND (Norman Invaders).

MACON, *MĀY kun*, Ga. (pop. 122,876; met. area 180,403; alt. 434 ft.), serves as the market for many products raised on the rich dairy and general farms of central Georgia. The city is also an important manufacturing and processing center. Macon lies on the Ocmulgee River near the geographic center of the state. Because of this, people call the city the *Heart of Georgia*. For location, see GEORGIA (political map).

Macon is the home of Wesleyan College and Mercer University. The Georgia Academy for the Blind is also in Macon. Poet Sidney Lanier was born in Macon. Macon serves as the trading center for the famous peach region of Georgia, and produces a large part of Georgia's lumber output. Most central Georgia farmers

sell their livestock there. Peanuts, pecans, watermelons, and other crops are marketed or processed in Macon. One of the world's largest kaolin deposits lies near Macon. It provides about 80 per cent of the country's kaolin and clay. Macon has more than 170 manufacturing and processing plants. Cotton textile manufacturing is the most important of these. Other products include farm machinery, fertilizer, and fruits. Macon also has railroad shops, paper mills, and canned-food plants.

Five railroads, two airlines, and many bus and motor freight lines serve Macon. Robins Air Force Base lies about 20 miles south of the city.

Creek Indians first settled the Macon area. Thomas Jefferson established Fort Hawkins there in 1806. The city was chartered in 1823. Its founders named it for Nathaniel Macon, a North Carolina congressman. During the 1840's and 1850's, Macon became an important railroad center. Confederates repulsed a Union attack on Macon in 1864. The city has a mayor-council form of government.   ALBERT B. SAYE

MACON ACT. See WAR OF 1812 (American Reaction).

MACONN MEMORIAL GARDEN. See FLOWER (Famous Flower Gardens).

MACPHAIL, AGNES CAMPBELL (1890–1954), was the first woman ever elected to the Canadian House of Commons. She served in the federal parliament from 1921 to 1940, and in the Ontario legislature from 1943 to 1945 and from 1948 to 1951. She represented Canada in the Assembly of the League of Nations. Miss MacPhail was elected to Parliament as a United Farmers of Ontario candidate. She later supported the Cooperative Commonwealth Federation (C.C.F.). She was born in Grey County, Ontario, and taught in Canadian schools before she entered politics.   JOHN T. SAYWELL

MACQUARIE ISLAND is a Tasmanian dependency in the South Pacific. The island lies about 800 miles southeast of Tasmania. It is about 21 miles long and 2 miles wide. The island is a breeding ground for penguins, albatrosses, and fur seals. It is uninhabited, but the Australian National Antarctic Research Expeditions has a permanent research station there.

MAD ANTHONY WAYNE. See WAYNE, ANTHONY.
MADAGASCAR. See MALAGASY REPUBLIC.

The City of Macon lies on either side of the Ocmulgee River. Carl Vinson Bridge, *left*, leads to the downtown business area.

Chamber of Commerce, Macon, Ga.

The Harbor of Funchal, Madeira, presents a picturesque sight, with its old fortress and array of small boats. An ocean liner and freighters are anchored in the distance. The town is the main seaport and capital of the island group.

MADAME BOVARY. See FLAUBERT, GUSTAVE.

MADAME BUTTERFLY. See OPERA (Some of the Famous Operas).

MADDEN DAM. See PANAMA CANAL (The Canal Since 1920).

MADDER is a plant which is grown in Europe and Asia for use in making dyes. The madder has rough, prickly leaves and small greenish-yellow flowers. The fruit is black. The roots of the madder produce the coloring matter which manufacturers use to make dyes. A madder which grows in Levant and Italy produces Turkey-red dye. Many other colors can be obtained by chemical treatment. These colors vary from pink and red to yellow, purple, and brown. Madder also produces coloring extracts such as alizarin and purpurin. A closely related plant, called *white bedstraw,* grows in Europe and eastern North America.

Scientific Classification. Madder belongs to the madder family, *Rubiaceae.* The madder used by dyers is classified as genus *Rubia,* species *R. tinctorum.* White bedstraw is *Galium mollugo.*

FRED FORTESS

MADEIRA, *muh DEER uh,* is the name of an island group that belongs to Portugal. The islands, of volcanic origin, lie in the Atlantic Ocean off the northwest coast of Africa. For location, see ATLANTIC OCEAN (map).

The islands cover 308 square miles and have an 88-mile coastline. Most of the 268,900 residents live on Madeira, the larger of the two inhabited islands. The other inhabited island is Porto Santo. Noted for its sandy beaches, it lies about 26 miles northeast of Madeira. About 3,500 persons live there. The Desertas and Selvagens are groups of tiny, uninhabited isles.

The Island of Madeira, largest and most important of the group, is a great ocean mountain range rising to a height of 6,104 feet above sea level in the Pico Ruivo. Madeira is known as the *Rock Garden of the Atlantic* because its settlements and farms rise in terraces, covered with a profusion of exotic flowers and trees. There are lush growths of orchids, bougainvillaea, bignonia, hibiscus, camellias, hydrangeas, wisteria, and jacaranda. Trees include the mimosa, eucalyptus, Brazilian auracarian, Indian fig, West Indies coral, and Japanese camphor, bamboo, laurel, and palm.

The richness of the vegetation is remarkable because rain falls only in the winter months. In order to grow crops, water has to be rationed and distributed by stone aqueducts, called *levadas.* Water retained from the rainy season flows down the levadas from the mountains to the farms and villages.

Chief crops include sugar cane, corn and other vegetables, bananas, oranges, mangoes, pomegranates, and the grapes that have made Madeira famous for wine. Wine production is the principal industry of Madeira.

Next in importance are the making of willow wicker furniture and baskets, and embroidering. Most Madeiran women do embroidering in their own homes. The Madeirans are expert fishermen. Britons handle much of Madeira's trade.

Funchal is the capital of Funchal district, which includes the Madeira Islands. It ranks as the largest city and chief resort center of the group. Funchal has ship connections with Lisbon, Portugal, and English ports, and air links with European and North African cities. See FUNCHAL.

Madeira has several unusual kinds of local transportation. Oxen draw sleighs over the iceless steep streets and roads. Basket sleds for fast, downhill travel provide thrills. Visitors to remote places can also travel in hammocks carried on poles by two men.

History. The Romans called the Madeiras the *Purpuriarae*, or "Purple" islands. The Portuguese first sailed to the island of Madeira in 1419. They gave it that name —meaning *wood*—because it was heavily forested. They cleared much of the land by burning trees, the ashes from which gave the soil increased fertility. Funchal was founded in 1421. Porto Santo also was settled about that time. The Spaniards seized and held the islands from 1580 to 1640. The British occupied them twice in the early 1800's.

CHARLES EDWARD NOWELL

MADEIRA RIVER, or RIO MADEIRA, is the largest branch of the Amazon River and an important trade waterway of South America. Madeira is Portuguese for *wood* or *timber*. The river was named for the great amount of driftwood that floats on its waters.

The Madeira begins where several large streams meet on the boundary between Brazil and Bolivia. It flows northeast for about 2,000 miles before emptying into the Amazon River about 100 miles east of Manaus. For location, see BRAZIL (physical map).

The mouth of the Madeira is nearly 2 miles wide. Large ships can sail about 700 miles up the stream. Here a long series of rapids make steamboat navigation impossible. Twenty of these rapids extend for 230 miles, with a drop of 475 feet. A railroad runs on the banks of the river around the rapids. Traders bring rubber and other tropical products to the Amazon region by way of this railroad and the Madeira River.

One branch of the Madeira is the Rio Teodoro, once called Rio Duvida. This stream is 1,000 miles long. Few people outside the country knew about it until Theodore Roosevelt explored it in 1914.

See also RIVER (chart: Longest Rivers).

MARGUERITE UTTLEY

MADERO, FRANCISCO INDALECIO. See MEXICO (The Revolution of 1910).

MADĪNAT ASH SHA'B, *mah DEE naht ahsh shahb* (pop. 1,000; alt. 1 ft.), is the administrative capital of Southern Yemen. However, most government buildings and foreign embassies are in Aden, the national capital, 14 miles to the southeast. Madīnat was founded in 1959. It became the capital when Southern Yemen gained independence in 1967. Madīnat ash Sha'b means *People's City*. For location, see SOUTHERN YEMEN (map). See also ADEN.

MADISON, Ind. (pop. 11,857; alt. 497 ft.), is an Ohio River port and tobacco-auction center. It was once the largest city in Indiana. Madison is located in southeastern Indiana on the north bank of the Ohio River, 90 miles from Indianapolis. It is 46 miles from Louisville, Ky., and 88 miles from Cincinnati, Ohio. For location, see INDIANA (political map). Tobacco buyers from all parts of the United States attend the auctions that are held in Madison in December.

Indiana's first railroad ran from Madison to Indianapolis, the state capital, in 1847. During the Civil War, Madison was a banking center. In 1862, James F. Lanier, a Madison banker, loaned about $1 million to the state administration of Governor Oliver P. Morton, and kept Indiana from bankruptcy.

Madison's well-kept old mansions give the city an atmosphere of the middle 1800's. Among these old homes are the *Shrewsbury Home* and the *Lanier Home*. Francis Costigan, a famous architect of that period, built both houses. Clifty Falls, a state park, is situated on the bluff above Madison. Hanover College is 7 miles outside the city.

PAUL E. MILLION, JR.

MADISON, Wis. (pop. 157,844; met. area 222,095; alt. 860 ft.), is the state capital and home of the oldest campus of the University of Wisconsin, one of the largest universities in the United States. Madison serves as the trade center of a rich dairying and diversified farming area. Madison is an important manufacturing city. It was named for James Madison, fourth President of the United States.

Location, Size, and General Description. Downtown Madison lies between two lakes, Mendota and Monona. They are linked by the Yahara River with two other lakes, Waubesa and Kegonsa, south of the city. These lakes provide swimming and boating facilities, and Mendota has fishing. The lakes also make Madison one of the most beautiful capital cities in the United States. Madison lies 76 miles west of Milwaukee. For location, see WISCONSIN (political map).

Madison covers approximately 42 square miles. The residential districts embrace the West Side, the far East Side, and the lake shores, and the industrial section is on the near East Side. The white granite state Capitol towers 285.9 feet above the city in a park square from which streets lead in every direction. The Federal post office, city-county building, and other public buildings cluster around the Capitol. The University of Wisconsin's campus stretches for miles along the south shore of Lake Mendota from the west end of State Street (see WISCONSIN, UNIVERSITY OF). The university experimental farm and the U.S. Forest Products Laboratory are west of the university grounds. The State Historical Society building lies at the foot of Bascom Hill. The University Arboretum and Wildlife Refuge, a 1,200-acre forest experimental preserve, and Vilas Park zoo flank Lake Wingra. The Arboretum and some of the other parks in Madison have Indian mounds. Madison is the headquarters of the U.S. Armed Forces Institute, with an enrollment of 250,000 correspondence students in armed forces installations throughout the world. A large Veterans Administration hospital, a state mental hospital, and nine other hospitals, make Madison an important medical center. Madison has about 30 public schools. The city has eight public libraries, with a total of more than 2 million volumes.

Downtown Madison, Wis., Lies on a Narrow Isthmus Between Lakes Monona, foreground, and Mendota, background.

Industry and Trade. There are more than 170 manufacturing plants in Madison. Major manufactures include machine tools, batteries, flashlights, electrical appliances, hospital furniture, surgical supplies, gas and oil engines, pumps, die-casting products, road-building machinery, automobile parts, paints and varnishes, building materials, ceramics, and beer. Madison is an important center for meat-packing, and dairy and other food products. It is a wholesale lumber market, and a shipping point for the area's farm products and for lead, zinc, and other minerals from southwest Wisconsin.

Transportation and Communications. Three railway lines and many bus and truck lines serve Madison. Truax Field, 2,150 acres, is a municipal airport and a U.S. Air Force base. Madison has two daily newspapers, six radio stations and four television stations.

Government. Madison has a mayor-council form of government. It serves as the seat of Dane County.

History. In the 1830's, James D. Doty, a land speculator, and Stevens T. Mason, governor of Michigan Territory, purchased the uninhabited site of Madison. In 1836, Doty persuaded the first legislature of Wisconsin territory to make Madison the capital, even though it was still only a planned, or "paper," city. The first house was built in 1837. Madison became the state capital in 1848. It received a city charter in 1856. In the early 1900's, Madison was headquarters of the LaFollette-led Progressive political party, which pioneered in social reform legislation (see LaFollette [family]). The erection in 1956 of a well-planned prefabricated home designed by Frank Lloyd Wright was acclaimed as a pioneering effort in architecture.

JAMES I. CLARK

See also WISCONSIN (picture, The State Capitol).

MADISON, DOLLEY PAYNE (1768-1849), a famous Washington hostess, was the wife of President James Madison. She is best known for her flight from Washington in August, 1814, when the British invaded the city during the War of 1812. She saved many state papers and a portrait of George Washington.

She and Madison were married in 1794 when he was a Congressman. While Madison served as Secretary of State under President Thomas Jefferson, a widower, Mrs. Madison often helped Jefferson when he entertained guests. She also entertained frequently on her own. When Madison became President, official functions became more elaborate than Jefferson had permitted. Mrs. Madison was noted for her charm and tact. At her home, people of strongly differing views could meet at ease, and her good-humored laughter eased many awkward situations.

Mrs. Madison was born in Guilford County, North Carolina, the third child of Quaker parents. She did not spell her name "Dolly," as is done today. Tradition also says wrongly that her real name was "Dorothea." She spent her childhood in Scotchtown, Va. In 1783, the family moved to Philadelphia. Dolley and John Todd, Jr., a lawyer and a Quaker, were married in 1790. They had two sons. Todd and one of the sons died in 1793. After her marriage to Madison in 1794, she was expelled from the Society of Friends because of her marriage to a non-Quaker.

After Madison's two terms as President the couple retired to Montpelier, his Virginia plantation. In 1837, after his death, Mrs. Madison returned to Washington to live.

ROBERT J. TAYLOR

See also MADISON, JAMES (picture).

JAMES MADISON

James Madison

JOHN ADAMS
2nd President
1797—1801

JEFFERSON
3rd President
1801—1809

MONROE
5th President
1817—1825

J. Q. ADAMS
6th President
1825—1829

4TH PRESIDENT OF THE UNITED STATES 1809-1817

Sculpture by F. William Sievers, Rotunda of the Virginia
State Capitol, Richmond, Va. (Elliott Erwitt, Magnum)

MADISON, JAMES (1751-1836), is called "the Father of the Constitution." He planned the system of checks and balances that regulate the legislative, executive, and judicial branches of the United States government. Madison served his country in many public offices during a period of 40 years. As Secretary of State and as President, he kept the United States out of the Napoleonic Wars. But, reluctantly, he led the country into the War of 1812. After the war, Madison's wise policies encouraged national growth.

Madison was a close friend of Thomas Jefferson, whom he followed in the presidency. Together, these two Virginians made an unexcelled team in constructive statesmanship. Madison displayed skill at solving difficult problems of government. Jefferson contributed a fine ability to phrase political truths. Their close agreement on political matters led them to join in organizing the Democratic-Republican party.

Physically small and frail, Madison did as much as any American toward building a strong federal government. At the Constitutional Convention, he worked to strengthen the national union of states. He spoke out fearlessly for nationalism when most Americans put states' rights ahead of the national interest. But Madison was by nature a mediator. He resisted Alexander Hamilton's tendency to strengthen the federal government at the expense of the states. He also softened Jefferson's views favoring states' rights. Most Americans today accept Madison's view on the relationship between the states and the federal government, rather than the extreme views of either Hamilton or Jefferson.

Streams of settlers surged westward during Madison's administration. The lack of imported goods during the War of 1812 encouraged industries to expand, and set the country on the path to becoming an industrial nation. The war also gave the American people their national anthem. Early one morning, as British shells burst about Fort McHenry in Baltimore harbor, Francis Scott Key wrote "The Star-Spangled Banner."

Early Life

James Madison was born in the home of his mother's parents on March 16, 1751 (March 5 by the calendar then in use). They lived at Port Conway, Va., about 12 miles from Fredericksburg. James was the eldest of 12 children. His father, James Madison, and his mother, Nelly Conway Madison, both came from families that had settled in Virginia during the 1600's. Dozens of

—— IMPORTANT DATES IN MADISON'S LIFE ——

1751 (March 16) Born at Port Conway, Va.
1779 Elected to the Continental Congress.
1787 Served at the Constitutional Convention.
1789 Elected to the U.S. House of Representatives.
1794 (Sept. 15) Married Dolley Payne Todd.
1801 Appointed Secretary of State.
1808 Elected President of the United States.
1812 Recommended war with Great Britain.
Re-elected President.
1829 Served at the Virginia Constitutional Convention.
1836 (June 28) Died at Montpelier, his family estate.

MADISON, JAMES

slaves worked on the Madison plantation, Montpelier. James was a frail and sickly child. He studied with private tutors, and attended the Donald Robertson School in King and Queen County. At the age of 18, he entered the College of New Jersey (now Princeton University). He took an active interest in politics, and was an early member of the American Whig Society. Madison studied very hard, sometimes sleeping only five hours a night. He completed the regular course at Princeton in two years, and was graduated in 1771. Madison spent the next six months studying Hebrew, philosophy, and other subjects that showed his deep interest in religious questions. A weak speaking voice prevented him from taking up a career as a minister. He soon turned his attention to politics.

Political and Public Career

Entry into Politics. Madison entered politics in 1774, when he was elected to the Committee of Safety in

Orange County, Virginia. Committees of this kind provided local government in the days when the British colonial government was crumbling. In 1776, Madison served on a committee that drafted a new Virginia constitution and the Virginia Declaration of Rights. Other colonies later copied these documents.

Madison served in Virginia's first legislative assembly in 1776, where he met Thomas Jefferson. The two men soon began a lifetime friendship. Madison was defeated for re-election in 1777. Late in life, he said he lost because he did not provide enough refreshments for the electors. In 1778, the Virginia Assembly elected Madison to the Governor's Council, an advisory group. He held this post until December, 1779, when he was elected to the Continental Congress.

Madison took his seat in Congress in March, 1780. In those days, Congress had no power to raise taxes, and

Napoleon Bonaparte

THE WORLD OF PRESIDENT MADISON

U.S. population was 8,900,000 in 1817. Louisiana became a state in 1812, and Indiana in 1816. Congress organized the Missouri Territory in 1812, and the Alabama Territory in 1817.

WORLD EVENTS

1812 Napoleon invaded Russia, but had to retreat.
1814 Denmark gave Norway to Sweden.
1815 Belgium united with The Netherlands to form a single country.
1815 Napoleon was crushed at Waterloo.
1815 Switzerland became independent of France.

MISSOURI TER.

INDIANA

ALA. TER.

LOUISIANA

White House Was Burned by the British in 1814, during the War of 1812. Madison had to flee to avoid capture.

"The Star-Spangled Banner" was written in 1814 by Francis Scott Key. He wrote it during the British attack on Baltimore.

Treaty of Ghent, signed by Great Britain and the United States in 1814, ended the indecisive War of 1812.

Cumberland Road was started in 1811 as part of the federal program to improve canals, roads, and bridges.

First Savings Banks in the country were founded at Philadelphia and Boston in 1816.

found it difficult to pay national debts. Madison strongly favored increasing the powers of Congress in financial matters. He also advocated many other measures to stabilize and dignify the government.

Virginia Assemblyman. Madison returned to Virginia in 1783. By that time, Americans generally recognized him as the ablest member of Congress. He planned to study law, history, and the sciences. Jefferson sent books from France to further Madison's studies. These studies were partially interrupted when the people of Orange County elected him to the state assembly for three successive one-year terms.

In the assembly, Madison continued the struggle Jefferson had begun for separation of church and state in Virginia. His chief opponent was Patrick Henry, who favored state support for teachers of the Christian religion. In 1786, the assembly passed Virginia's Statute of Religious Freedom. Madison wrote to Jefferson that the convention finally adopted (see UNITED STATES CONSTITUTION [The Compromises]).

Constitutional Convention. Madison represented Virginia at the Constitutional Convention of 1787. Although only 36 years old, he took a leading part. Madison fought for strong central government, and drafted the Virginia plan for the union. This plan, also called the Randolph plan, foreshadowed the constitution that the convention finally adopted (see UNITED STATES CONSTITUTION [The Compromises]).

Madison proved valuable to the convention in many ways. He had a deep knowledge of confederacies of the past. He was well acquainted with the Articles of Confederation, and fully understood the problems of federalism. He also wrote his famous *Notes on the Federal Convention,* the only full record of the debates.

Madison's part in the adoption of the Constitution did not end at the convention. He served as a member of the Virginia Ratifying Convention. At the same time, he joined Alexander Hamilton and John Jay of New York in writing *The Federalist,* a series of letters to newspapers. Scholars still consider these letters the most authoritative explanation of the American constitutional system. See FEDERALIST, THE.

Congressman. Madison's support of the Constitution displeased many Virginians who supported states' rights. They united in the Virginia legislature to defeat him in 1788 for a seat in the first United States Senate. Early the next year, Madison defeated James Monroe in an election for the U.S. House of Representatives.

Madison, one of the ablest members of the House, proposed resolutions for organizing the Departments of State, Treasury, and War. He also drafted much of the first tariff act. Most important, he was largely responsible for drafting the first 10 amendments to the Constitution, the Bill of Rights (see BILL OF RIGHTS).

At first, Madison supported many policies of the Federalist party. But he soon decided that Alexander Hamilton's financial plans favored Eastern merchants at the expense of Western and Southern farmers. Madison then turned against the Federalists. After Jefferson returned from France in 1789, he and Madison joined in organizing the Democratic-Republican party, the forerunner of today's Democratic party. During this period in Philadelphia, Madison met Dolley Payne

Todd, a young widow to whom he was married in 1794 (see MADISON, DOLLEY PAYNE).

By 1797, Madison had become weary of politics, and retired to his estate. In 1798, Congress passed the Alien and Sedition Acts (see ALIEN AND SEDITION ACTS). Madison was outraged. He drafted the Virginia Resolutions of 1798, proposing joint action by the states in declaring these laws unconstitutional. He was elected to the Virginia legislature in 1799 and 1800, and led the fight against what he considered Federalist efforts to undermine basic human rights.

Secretary of State. Thomas Jefferson became President in 1801, and appointed Madison Secretary of State. The purchase of Louisiana was the most important success in foreign relations (see LOUISIANA PURCHASE). War with the Barbary pirates between 1801 and 1805 caused excitement throughout the country. The peace treaty signed with Tripoli brought only brief satisfaction. The pirates soon began preying on American shipping again (see BARBARY STATES).

Madison and Jefferson failed to force Great Britain and France to respect the rights of Americans on the high seas. The British and French were fighting each other in the Napoleonic Wars, and each had blockaded the other's coast. American ships that tried to trade with either country were stopped by warships of the other. Many American seamen were seized and forced

Dolley Payne Madison, the President's wife, dazzled Washington with her stylish clothes and brilliant manner of entertaining. She served as official White House hostess for 16 years, assuming the duties of First Lady for the widowed Thomas Jefferson, and continuing during the eight years her husband was in office.

Portrait by Ezra Ames, 1818. The New-York Historical Society, N.Y.C.

to serve on British or French warships. The Embargo Act of 1807 attempted to protect American ships by stopping all commerce with foreign countries. But the loss of trade brought widespread economic distress to the United States, and many Northern merchants evaded the embargo. In the end, the embargo hurt Americans more than it did the British or French.

The Embargo Act was repealed in 1809, just before Jefferson left office. In its place, Congress passed the Non-Intercourse Act, which opened trade with all countries except Great Britain and France. Congress hoped this law would force the British and French to recognize American commercial rights. See EMBARGO (The Embargo Act); NON-INTERCOURSE ACT.

Jefferson chose Madison to succeed him as President. Madison received 122 electoral votes to 47 for the Federalist candidate, former minister to France C. C. Pinckney. Madison's running mate, Vice-President George Clinton, polled 113 electoral votes.

Madison's Administration (1809-1817)

"Mr. Madison's War." Trade with Britain and France was still the government's greatest problem when Madison became President. British and French warships continued to stop American shipping, in spite of the Non-Intercourse Act. In 1810, Congress passed a bill that reopened trade with both Britain and France. This curious bill attempted to stop violations of American shipping by economic pressure. It provided that if Britain ended its attacks on American ships, the United States would stop trade with France—and vice versa. But this bait did not work. Napoleon blandly announced that he would revoke the French blockade against neutral trade with Great Britain. But, at the same time, he issued secret orders which maintained the French blockade against American shipping. Madison halted all trade with Great Britain, but the French continued to stop American ships.

Americans were angered by France's deceit. Reports that the British were stirring up the Western Indians also aroused feelings against the British. These reports seemed to be confirmed when Tecumseh, chief of the Shawnee tribe, tried to organize an Indian alliance to fight the Americans. Governor William Henry Harrison of the Indiana Territory shattered the Indian forces in the Battle of Tippecanoe on Nov. 7, 1811 (see HARRISON, WILLIAM HENRY [Entry into Politics]). But people throughout the West believed that the British as well as the Indians were their enemy.

Adding to the war feeling was a strongly nationalistic generation which had arisen in politics. This group included many persons who felt that a war would result in the annexation of Canada and Spanish Florida. Henry Clay of Kentucky, Felix Grundy of Tennessee, and John Calhoun of South Carolina acted as spokesmen in the House of Representatives for this group.

Madison knew that the United States was unprepared for war, and that New England merchants feared war would destroy trade. But he also knew that people outside New England wanted it, and that the nation could tolerate no more insults from Great Britain. He finally recommended war, and Congress approved it on June 18, 1812. The Federalists opposed the war, and called it "Mr. Madison's War."

A few months later, Madison was re-elected President by 128 electoral votes to 89 for Mayor DeWitt Clinton

VICE-PRESIDENTS AND CABINET

Vice-President.............	*George Clinton
	*Elbridge Gerry (1813)
Secretary of State.........	Robert Smith
	*James Monroe (1811)
Secretary of the Treasury...	*Albert Gallatin
	George W. Campbell (1814)
	Alexander J. Dallas (1814)
	*William H. Crawford (1816)
Secretary of War...........	*William Eustis
	John Armstrong (1813)
	*James Monroe (1814)
	*William H. Crawford (1815)
Attorney General...........	Caesar A. Rodney
	William Pinkney (1811)
	Richard Rush (1814)
Secretary of the Navy......	Paul Hamilton
	William Jones (1813)
	B. W. Crowninshield (1814)

*Has a separate biography in WORLD BOOK.

Virginia State Chamber of Commerce

Montpelier, the family estate of James Madison, stands in Orange County, Virginia. Madison and his wife retired there after he left the presidency.

of New York City, Madison's running mate, Governor Elbridge Gerry of Massachusetts, won 131 votes to 86 for Jared Ingersoll, Attorney General of Pennsylvania.

Progress of the War. American military forces had little success at the start of the war. The British Navy clamped on a blockade which the pitifully small U.S. Navy could not break. American land forces attacked Canada in 1812, but were defeated. The fight for Canada continued for two years, with no decisive victories on either side. In 1814, Napoleon was defeated in Europe. Great Britain then sent experienced troops to Canada, ending American hopes for conquest.

In the summer of 1814, General Winfield Scott fought the British to a standstill at Chippewa and Lundy's Lane in southern Ontario. British troops invaded Maryland and, on August 24, burned the Capitol and other public buildings in Washington. Dolley Madison fled the White House so late that British soldiers ate a hot meal she had prepared. Only heroic resistance at Fort McHenry kept the British from capturing Baltimore.

In September, 1814, American forces stopped an invasion down the west side of Lake Champlain. Early in 1815, Andrew Jackson won a stunning victory at New Orleans. The Treaty of Ghent was ratified in February, 1815. It settled none of the problems that had caused the war. But it did preserve American territorial integrity (see GHENT, TREATY OF; WAR OF 1812).

In 1814, before the end of the war, New England Federalists had held a secret meeting known as the *Hartford Convention.* None of the convention's activities was disloyal. But rumors sprang up that the members planned secession of the New England States. The Federalist party was branded as unpatriotic, and fell apart shortly after James Monroe was elected President in 1816. See HARTFORD CONVENTION.

The Growth of Nationalism. Albert Gallatin, Madison's first Secretary of the Treasury, believed that the War of 1812 had "renewed and reinstated the national feeling of character which the Revolution had given and which, was daily lessening. The people . . . are more American; they feel and act more as a nation." The end of the war ushered in "the era of good feeling." With the disappearance of the Federalist party, political conflicts were submerged within the Democratic-Republican party. During the two years after the war, the country experienced great domestic growth. The settlement of the West was hastened by improved roads and canals, and a land system that made it easier to claim frontier property. The tariff of 1816 continued the protection of American industries. Madison received the credit for this prosperity.

Life in the White House. Mrs. Madison began an extravagant round of parties as soon as her husband took office. She served elaborate dinners, and delighted in surprising her guests with delicacies. She was the first person to serve ice cream in the White House. Washington Irving wrote of the presidential couple: "Mrs. Madison is a fine, portly, buxom dame who has a smile and a pleasant word for everybody . . . as to Jeemy Madison—ah! poor Jeemy!—he is but a withered little apple-John."

The British invasion of the capital, and the burning of the White House, ended social gaiety. The Madisons fled Washington. When they returned, they established a new residence in the Octagon House, a private home just west of the White House. In 1815, they moved to a house on the corner of Pennsylvania Avenue and 19th Street. Dolley Madison resumed her busy social life, but longed to reoccupy the White House. Reconstruction work proceeded slowly, however, and the Executive Mansion was not ready for occupancy until nine months after Madison left office in 1817.

Later Years

In retirement at Montpelier, Madison busied himself with the affairs of his estate. After Jefferson's death in 1826, he became *rector* (president) of the University of Virginia. He also served as a member of the Virginia Constitutional Convention of 1829. Madison died at Montpelier on June 28, 1836. His wife returned to Washington, where she lived until her death in 1849. The Madisons are buried in a family plot near Montpelier. They had no children, but they reared the son of Mrs. Madison by her first husband. An authoritative work on the life of Madison is *James Madison* by Irving Brant.

RALPH L. KETCHAM

Related Articles in WORLD BOOK include:

BIOGRAPHIES

Clay, Henry	Jefferson, Thomas
Clinton, George	Key, Francis Scott
Gallatin, Albert	Madison, Dolley Payne
Gerry, Elbridge	Monroe, James
Hamilton, Alexander	Washington, George
Henry, Patrick	

OTHER RELATED ARTICLES

Alien and Sedition Acts	Kentucky and Virginia
Anti-Federalist	Resolutions
Bill of Rights	Non-Intercourse Act
Continental Congress	President of the United States
Democratic-Republican	States' Rights
Party	United States, Government of
Embargo	(Separation of Powers)
Federalist, The	United States, History of
Federalist Party	United States Constitution
Ghent, Treaty of	War of 1812
Hartford Convention	

Outline

I. Early Life
II. Political and Public Career
   A. Entry into Politics   D. Congressman
   B. Virginia Assemblyman   E. Secretary of
   C. Constitutional Convention   State
III. Madison's Administration (1809-1817)
   A. "Mr. Madison's War"
   B. Progress of the War
   C. The Growth of Nationalism
   D. Life in the White House
IV. Later Years

Questions

Why is Madison called "the Father of the Constitution"?
What were some important principles that Madison supported in the Continental Congress?
Who called Madison "a withered little apple-John"?
What effect did Madison have on the relationship of church and state in Virginia?
How did Madison prove valuable in the first Congress?
How did the War of 1812 affect American nationalism?
How did Madison explain his defeat for re-election to Virginia's Assembly in 1777?
What was Madison's relationship to *The Federalist?*
What was his approach to federal-state relations?
How did Dolley Madison shine as First Lady?

MADISON COLLEGE. See UNIVERSITIES AND COLLEGES (table).

MADISON RIVER. See MONTANA (physical map); YELLOWSTONE NATIONAL PARK.

MADISON SQUARE GARDEN is a famous indoor sports and entertainment arena in New York City. The Garden is one of seven facilities in the circular Madison Square Garden Center at 4 Pennsylvania Plaza, New York, N.Y., 10001. The 20,000-seat arena hosts a variety of events, including circuses, ice shows, political meetings, and sports contests. In addition to the main arena, the 5,000-seat Felt Forum provides space for smaller events. Madison Square Garden Center also has an exposition rotunda, a motion-picture theater, a 48-lane bowling center, a hall of fame honoring outstanding Garden performers, and a gallery of sports art.

The present Garden Center was completed in 1968. The first of three earlier Gardens received its name in 1879. It occupied an abandoned railroad station at Madison Square. The next Garden was built in 1890 on the same site. In 1925, another Garden was built on a new site. *Critically reviewed by* MADISON SQUARE GARDEN

MADONNA AND CHILD are the Virgin Mary and the infant Jesus in works of art. They rank among the most important art subjects that the Christian religion has inspired. Madonna means *my lady* in Italian. But the term has come to mean *the Virgin Mary*. Painters and sculptors produced their greatest works on the Madonna during the Renaissance (see RENAISSANCE). Michelangelo's *Medici Madonna* is one of the finest sculptures

MADONNA AND CHILD

grace art museums in all parts of the world. Raphael's Madonnas are lovely and gentle, and seem to glow with mother love.

Pitti Palace, Florence

The *Madonna of the Chair*, by the Italian artist Raphael, is one of his many paintings of the Holy Mother that today

Raphael's *Sistine Madonna* was the Italian artist's last painting of a Madonna. The Virgin Mother stands with her feet on earth, between Pope Sixtus II and St. Barbara. The painting gives the idea of a wonderful vision behind raised curtains.

Staatliche Kunstsammlungen Dresden

of the Madonna. Terra-cotta figures of the Madonna by Luca della Robbia are well known.

Painters of the Madonna. Saint Luke painted the first Madonna picture, according to legend. But the Virgin Mary and Child became symbols of the accepted Christian faith only after the Council of Ephesus, in present-day Turkey, in A.D. 431. Then the number of Madonna pictures began to increase. The oldest ones are those found in the catacombs of the early Christians. Portraits of the Madonna in the Byzantine period served as models until the 1200's. Then the painters of the early Renaissance introduced a new style, with more background scenery. Giovanni Cimabue, the first of these painters, tried to put natural life into his paintings instead of copying stiff Byzantine figures.

The Madonna and Child developed as a popular subject for painters in the later Renaissance period. Raphael produced some of the greatest paintings of the Madonna. His painting *Sistine Madonna*, completed in 1515, hangs in the Dresden Gallery in Germany. It shows the Virgin Mary carrying Jesus in her arms. On one side, Pope Sixtus II kneels in prayer. Saint Barbara kneels on the other side. Below, two cherubs lean forward. Raphael originally painted this work as an altarpiece for the Church of San Sisto in Piacenza. Raphael's other Madonnas include *The Beautiful Gardener*, *The Madonna of the Chair*, and *The Madonna of the Goldfinch*.

Other great painters who portrayed the Madonna included Alesso Baldovinetti, Giovanni Bellini, Giorgione, Fra Filippo Lippi, Andrea del Sarto, and Titian.

Types of Madonna Paintings. Paintings of the Madonna are usually divided into five classes, according to the general styles of treatment:

(1) *Portrait of the Madonna.* In this class, the Madonna usually appears as a half-length figure against a background of solid gold leaf, or with cherubs. She wears a blue robe, starred or marked with gold, often draped over her head. The first paintings of the Madonna, in the Greek or Byzantine period, belong to this group. Many old churches of Italy contain examples of portraits of the Madonna (see FRA ANGELICO [picture: *The Madonna of Humility*]). Baldovinetti's *Madonna*, in the Louvre, Paris, is an example of a Madonna portrait of the late Renaissance.

(2) *The Madonna Enthroned.* The Madonna sits on some sort of throne or platform in this largest class of paintings. The treatments vary widely. They represent every school of Italian art. To this group belong Bellini's *Madonna* in the Church of the Frari, Venice, Italy; Cimabue's *Madonna Enthroned* in the Uffizi Gallery in Florence; and Perugino's *Madonna and Saints* in the Vatican Gallery. See BELLINI (picture: *Madonna with Saints*); LIPPI (picture: *Madonna and Child*); PAINTING (color picture: *Enthroned Madonna and Child*).

(3) *The Madonna in Glory.* The Madonna and her attendants hover in the sky in paintings of this group. Heaven is suggested by a *halo* (circle of light), clouds, or cherubs, or by posing the figures in air just above the earth. The halo originally surrounded the entire figure, instead of only the head. It was generally oval in shape. Examples of this type include *The Sistine Madonna* by Raphael; and *Madonna of the Stars* by Fra Angelico, in the monastery of San Marco in Florence. See VIRGIN MARY (picture: *The Virgin with Saint Inez and Saint Tecla*).

(4) *The Madonna in Pastoral Scenes.* Paintings in this class have a landscape background. One of the best-known examples is *The Beautiful Gardener* by Raphael, in the Louvre, Paris. Also located in the Louvre is another example in this class, *The Madonna of the Rocks*, by Leonardo da Vinci. Raphael's *Alba Madonna* hangs in the National Gallery of Art in Washington, D.C. (see RAPHAEL [picture: *The Alba Madonna*]).

(5) *The Madonna in a Home Environment.* Only a small number of paintings come under this heading. The painters of northern Europe were fond of home life. So they painted the Madonna in settings that resemble their own homes. *Madonna* by Quentin Massys pictures a Flemish bedroom of the 1400's. In *Madonna of Chancellor Rolin*, Jan Van Eyck pictured the Madonna in Flemish scenery of the 1430's. Another work of this class is *In a Carpenter's Home* by Rembrandt.   THOMAS MUNRO

For other paintings of the Madonna, see the following articles: BOTTICELLI, SANDRO; BYZANTINE ART; CHERUB; DELLA ROBBIA; HALO; HOLY FAMILY; RUBENS, PETER PAUL; SCULPTURE.

MADONNA COLLEGE. See UNIVERSITIES AND COLLEGES (table).

MADONNA LILY. See LILY.

MADRAS, *muh DRAS* (pop. 1,927,431; alt. 30 ft.), is India's fourth largest city. Bombay, Calcutta, and Delhi are larger. Madras lies on the eastern coast, and is the capital of the state of Tamil Nadu (formerly Madras). Although it does not have a good harbor, the city carries on a large sea trade. Several canals and railroads center in Madras. Cotton, rice, coffee, hides, and skins are brought from the interior for shipment to other countries.

Madras' factories assemble automobiles, manufacture bicycles and cigarettes, and weave cotton cloth. Tanning hides for leather is also important. Madras is the site of Madras University, one of India's leading educational institutions. The Madras Institute of Technology is also located there.

Madras was founded in 1639, when an Indian rajah granted some land to a British subject. The first settlers built a fortified trading post, and a village soon grew up around it. Madras can claim an even earlier date of founding, for it now includes the old village of Saint Thomé, which the Portuguese established in 1504. The city received its municipal charter in 1687. French forces captured the city in 1746 during the War of the Austrian Succession. The French returned Madras to the British in 1749 as a result of the Treaty of Aix-la-Chapelle that ended the war.   ROBERT I. CRANE

MADRAS is a shirting fabric that is characterized by a woven design on a plain ground. It is usually made with colored yarns, and in many patterns, such as stripes or small figure effects. Madras is generally preshrunk and *mercerized* (see MERCERIZING).

Madras gingham is lighter in weight than the average gingham. It is made of fancy-weave, vat-dyed yarns. Curtain madras, or *grenadine*, has an all-over design made by an extra *filling* (crosswise) yarn that forms a decorative design on the sheer background. This extra filling yarn is cut, so the trimmed ends are shaggy, outlining the design.   HAZEL B. STRAHAN

MADRASAH. See ISLAMIC ART (Madrasahs).
MADRE. See RADAR (Recent Developments).

MADRID, *muh DRID* (pop. 2,443,152), is the capital and largest city of Spain. It stands on a plateau about 2,150 feet above sea level. This makes Madrid the highest capital in Europe. Madrid is the capital of the province of Madrid, which lies in the region of New Castile. The Spanish people call this area the *Heart of Spain.* Madrid is about equally distant from the Mediterranean Sea, the Atlantic Ocean, and the Bay of Biscay. See SPAIN (color map). Madrid is the railroad and airline center of Spain. It is also the most important Spanish city, in banking, insurance, and finance. Ernest Hemingway, the American author, described Madrid as the most "Spanish" of Spain's cities. Hemingway said the others were typical only of their own regions.

Description. Madrid withstood a two-and-a-half-year siege and suffered serious damage during the Spanish Civil War (1936-1939). But by the end of the 1950's, most of the damaged areas had been restored or rebuilt. Today, Madrid is a modern city with many tall new buildings amid its historic monuments and beautiful old churches.

The center of Madrid is the Puerta del Sol. From this spacious, crescent-shaped plaza, Madrid's principal streets branch out like the spokes of a wheel. The city's most important street, *Calle de Alcalá,* extends from Puerta del Sol to the bullring in the northeastern suburb of Las Ventas. This Moorish-style *Plaza de Toros* seats 13,000 spectators.

A few blocks east of Puerta del Sol, Calle de Alcalá crosses Madrid's most impressive street. This beautiful boulevard has three parts—Paseo del Prado, Paseo de Calvo Sotelo, and Avenida del Generalísimo. Stately trees line the broad avenue, and fountains, monuments, and statues stand in parkways and circles in its center.

Famous Buildings. The Prado, or National Museum of Painting and Sculpture, is a treasure house of art. The best of its 3,000 paintings represent artists of the 1500's, 1600's, and early 1800's. The Prado has more than 30 excellent works by the great painter El Greco. The Prado's 50 paintings by Diego Velázquez include *The Christ, The Surrender of Breda, The Spinners,* and *Las Meninas* (The Maids of Honor), which appears in the PAINTING article. The museum also houses an outstanding collection of the works of Francisco de Goya. They include paintings of Charles IV and his family; the two *Majas,* the tapestry factory pictures, and *The 3rd of May, 1808* (also in the PAINTING article). In another room, the museum exhibits Goya's etchings and drawings inspired by bullfighting and by incidents of the Napoleonic Wars. Other artists represented in the Prado include Murillo, Raphael, Ribera, Rubens, Titian, and Zurbarán.

The Galdiano Museum, now owned by the government, contains a splendid collection of paintings, antique jewelry, porcelain, brocades, armor, and tapestry. It is housed in the residence of the Galdiano family.

During the late 1950's, workers completed a new skyscraper office building in Madrid. Called "The Tower of Madrid," it is 38 stories high and ranks as one of the tallest buildings in Europe.

The National Palace lies to the west of Puerta del Sol. King Philip V planned this magnificent granite

Madrid's Gran Via, or main street, is the chief shopping area of the city. It also has many financial firms and theaters. The street's official name is Avenida de José Antonio. It was named for a young hero of the Spanish revolution led by Francisco Franco.

The National Palace, or Royal Palace, in Madrid was the home of Spanish kings from the 1700's until Alfonso XIII was forced to leave the country in 1931. Since that time, it has been used only for official social functions. It is open to the public.

El Escorial Building, erected near Madrid in the 1500's, is a combined convent, church, palace, and burial place for kings.

building in the 1700's. Vast grounds and gardens surround the palace, which houses many art treasures, and is now maintained as a public museum. The Royal Armory houses a priceless collection of old weapons and armor. The opera house of Madrid is famous throughout the world for its architectural beauty.

Climate. Madrid lies about as far north of the equator as New York City. But Madrid has a slightly warmer climate than New York City. Temperatures in Madrid average about 74° F. in July and 40° F. in January. San Sebastián serves as the official seat of Spain's government from July 20 to October 1, the hottest months in Madrid. Madrid usually has some rain about one day out of three from October to May, but little during July and August. An average of less than 17 inches of rain falls in a year. Snow rarely falls there.

Daily Life. There is almost no activity on Madrid streets before 8 A.M. Most stores and offices open about 9 A.M. They remain closed from 1 to 4 P.M. and close for the night at about 8 P.M. *Madrileños*, the residents of Madrid, eat dinner between 9:30 and 11:00 P.M.

Recreation. Many Madrileños enjoy soccer and *pelota* (similar to jai alai) more than other sports. But the largest crowds attend the bullfights. Spanish men with common interests generally meet at sidewalk cafés at certain hours to drink coffee and talk.

Industry. Madrid became Spain's capital in 1561. Since then, the most important work of the city's people has been government administration. However, since 1900, many factories have been built in Madrid. The chief products include chemicals, clothing, fans, jewelry, leather, paper, soap, and glass and pottery. Madrid's tapestry makers have done beautiful work for many years.

Publishing. Madrid has seven important daily newspapers. The three morning dailies do not publish on Monday. Instead, the Press Association of Madrid issues the weekly *Hoja del Lunes* each Monday. The Spanish government controls all newspapers in Madrid as well as in the rest of the country. *Arriba* of Madrid is one of the more than 30 Spanish newspapers owned and directed by the Falange party, the only political party permitted in Spain. Madrid's other daily newspapers include *El Pueblo, A B C, Ya, El Alcázar, Informaciones,* and *Madrid.* Madrid serves as the center of publishing

for Spain's books and periodicals. Ten research centers and institutes publish learned and technical materials.

Schools and Libraries. The Central University of Madrid occupies a spacious campus in an area called University City. With its more than 10,000 students, it is one of the largest universities in Europe, and the most important of the 12 national universities in Spain. It has schools of philosophy and letters, law, political economy, science, medicine, pharmacy, and veterinary science. Also located on the University City campus are the schools of engineering, architecture, dentistry, agriculture, fine arts, and journalism. Madrid also has an Academy of Music and Dramatic Arts.

The National Library and Museum in Madrid has more than 1,500,000 volumes. Madrid's excellent naval library and other libraries make the city a cultural center of interest for travelers and scholars.

History. Historians are not certain whether there was a settlement on the site of Madrid during the time of the Roman Empire. But, by the 900's, a Moorish outpost called Magerit had been established. This fortress changed hands, and was destroyed and rebuilt repeatedly during the reconquest of Moorish Spain by the Christians. The Christians finally occupied Madrid permanently in 1083 under King Alfonso VI of Castile. In 1561, King Philip II made Madrid the capital of Spain. He did this because of its central location and because he liked to hunt in its neighboring forests. The city grew slowly until modern times.

The French occupied Madrid from 1808 to 1813, during the Napoleonic Wars. British forces under the Duke of Wellington, with the help of Spanish guerrillas, drove the French out. In 1939, after the Spanish Civil War, General Francisco Franco entered Madrid and set up his government. Most of the city's suburbs became part of Madrid in 1950. In 1956, the Spanish government completed the Valley of the Fallen, a mausoleum near Madrid. The bodies of more than 150,000 men who died fighting for Franco's forces during the Spanish Civil War may be placed in it. WALTER C. LANGSAM

See also FOUNTAIN (picture); SPAIN (Moorish Control; Civil War).

L. Huish, Cushing

MADRIGAL, *MAD rīi gul,* is a pastoral song, usually contemplative in nature, in which two or more voices sing separate melodies to a simple text. It usually has no instrumental accompaniment, and amounts to vocal chamber music, with one voice to a part.

Italian composers began writing madrigals in the late 1200's. The form reached its high point in the early 1600's in the works of Luca Marenzio, Carlo Gesualdo, and Claudio Monteverdi. Outside of Italy, it developed chiefly in England. It had a number of names, including *songs, canzonets,* and *ayres.* English madrigal composers of the 1500's included William Byrd, Thomas Morley, Thomas Weelkes, and John Wilbye. The madrigal was usually a secular song, but such composers as Orlando di Lasso and Giovanni Palestrina wrote sacred madrigals. Some German and Spanish composers composed madrigals. But the movement never gained the significance it did in Italy and England. RAYMOND KENDALL

See also MUSIC (The Renaissance).

MADROÑA, *muh DROH nyuh,* is a small tree with white, urn-shaped flowers and leathery evergreen leaves. The rough, berrylike fruit has mealy flesh and hard seeds. It grows along the Pacific coast of the United States, from southern California to British Columbia, and in other parts of the world. The wood of the madroña tree may be used for fuel. See also HEATH.

Scientific Classification. Madroña belongs to the heath family, *Ericaceae.* It is classified as genus *Arbutus,* species *A. menziesii.*

MAE WEST JACKET. See LIFE JACKET.

MAELSTROM, *MAYL strum,* is a swift and dangerous current in the Arctic Ocean. This current sweeps back and forth between two islands of the Lofoten group off the northwestern coast of Norway. It has been a menace to sailors for hundreds of years. The Maelstrom becomes more dangerous when the wind blows against it between high and low tide. The waters then form immense whirlpools that destroy small ships.

Writers, including the Norwegian poet Peter Dass and the American author Edgar Allan Poe, have greatly exaggerated the Maelstrom's power. As a result, the word *maelstrom* has come to mean any kind of whirlpool or any turmoil of widespread influence. HENRY STOMMEL

See also WHIRLPOOL.

MAETERLINCK, *MAY tur lingk,* **MAURICE** (1862-1949), was a Belgian dramatist, poet, naturalist, and philosopher. Maeterlinck was born in Ghent. He became a lawyer, but spent his life writing. He won the 1911 Nobel prize for literature.

Maeterlinck's contribution to drama was his ability to express a world beyond reality. His most famous play is *The Blue Bird* (1909). It is a symbolic story of a child who searches for happiness and finds it in his own home. Maeterlinck's short plays *The Intruder* (1890) and *The Blind* (1890) treat the commonplaceness of death and the need for love in symbolic terms. These plays have little physical action and Maeterlinck called them *static drama.* In *Pelleas and Melisande* (1892), Maeterlinck dramatized the medieval story of Paolo and Francesca. The play symbolizes the inescapable bond between two persons in love and the necessity of their death. Maeterlinck's other plays include *Monna Vanna* (1902) and *The Mayor of Stilmonde* (1919).

Maeterlinck's mystical philosophy is most evident in his essays *The Treasure of the Humble* (1896) and *Wisdom and Destiny* (1898). His ideas about the mystery of life and death also appear in several nature studies, notably *The Life of the Bees* (1901) and *The Life of the Ants* (1930). Both works were basic to further discoveries about the social systems under which ants and bees live. His dreamy and melancholy poetry was published in *Hot Houses* (1889) and *Twelve Songs* (1896). FREDERICK J. HUNTER

MAFEKING, *MAFF ee KING* (pop. 8,362; alt. 4,217 ft.), is a railroad center in Cape of Good Hope Province in northeastern South Africa. It is also a dairy center and cattle-raising area. Mafeking was the administrative capital of the British protectorate of Bechuanaland (now Botswana) until 1965, when Gaberones became the capital. For location, see SOUTH AFRICA (color map).

During the Boer War, a Boer army surrounded British troops under Colonel Robert Baden-Powell in Mafeking. The British held out for 217 days, until help arrived. Mafeking was founded in 1885. HIBBERD V. B. KLINE, JR.

See also BADEN-POWELL, LORD.

MAFIA, *MAH fee ah,* is the name of a secret Sicilian terrorist society. *Mafia* comes from the Arabic word *maefisi,* meaning *union.* The Mafia began in the 1600's as an organization to combat corruption and tyranny in the Kingdom of the Two Sicilies. Later, lawless and criminal elements, who robbed, murdered, and waged bloody vendettas, gained control (see VENDETTA). The Mafia has been a power both in Italy and among Italians abroad. Its members, organized into cells of no more than five persons, are bound by an oath of fidelity. Authorities have had difficulty in gathering evidence against the Mafia. The society operates outside of the law, but some of its activities are legal. WILLIAM H. MAEHL.

MAGARAC, *MAG uh rak,* **JOE,** is the mythical strong man of the steel mills. He was reputed to be a 7-foot giant, born in an ore mountain and made of steel. He first became famous as the winner of a weight-lifting contest for the hand of Mary Mestrovich. Joe Magarac made so many steel rails, by squeezing the hot steel through his fingers, that his mill was ordered shut down. In protest he melted himself down in a ladle full of boiling metal. His stubborn self-sacrifice made the name *Magarac,* Croatian and Serbian for *jackass,* one to be proud of rather than laughed at.

Joe Magarac startled a crowd at a weight-lifting contest by lifting a contestant and an 850-pound weight at the same time.

Illustration by Richard Hook

Magazines reach billions of readers every year. Many persons buy magazines at newsstands. Millions of others receive theirs at home.

MAGAZINE

MAGAZINE. Millions of magazines are sold and read in the United States every week. They provide information and entertainment of many kinds. Some magazines are concerned with debating foreign policy and national defense. Some discuss the latest developments in science and mechanics. Some merely amuse us with stories about love and romance, cowboy days in the Far West, or detectives tracking down criminals.

A magazine is a collection of articles or stories and pictures on various topics. It appears at regular intervals. The magazine usually represents the work of several different authors or artists. Magazines differ from newspapers because they do not usually concentrate upon giving the reader a summary of the day's news. There is a special type of magazine, called a news magazine, which summarizes the weekly news.

The form of magazines differs from that of newspapers. Most magazines are printed on better paper. They are smaller, and stapled or stitched together so they last longer. Many of them have substantial covers. The largest magazines have pages which are about half the size of an average newspaper page.

The line between magazines and newspapers is not clearly drawn. Some weeklies that appear in newspaper form are really magazines. Many books are printed, some periodically, that contain collections of articles and stories. These are really a kind of magazine.

Kinds of Magazines

There are two ways of classifying magazines. One is by the intervals at which they are published. The other is by their purpose and form. Thus, some magazines appear every week (weeklies), others every other week (biweeklies), still others every month (monthlies). A small group of magazines is published every two months (bimonthlies), and another group is published every three months (quarterlies).

Magazines are edited to suit the interests of certain kinds of readers. For that reason, the kinds of topics covered in magazines are as wide as human interests and activities. Some magazines are intended to appeal to a fairly wide range of readers. Others are designed to interest only a special group. Those edited to appeal to a wide audience are called *mass* magazines. Those aimed at a special group are called *class* magazines.

The weekly magazines which have national circulation are examples of those with wide appeals, although the content of each magazine may differ. Some concentrate upon telling a story largely by means of pictures. Others provide more varied material, and contain articles as well as pictures on foreign affairs, interesting personalities, new developments in industry and science, and fiction designed for a wide range of tastes. The monthly magazines with general circulation are much like the general weekly magazines. Many of the monthly magazines with the largest circulations are addressed to an audience of women. They contain fiction, articles, and practical advice designed for women. Types of magazines also especially designed for women are those that have love stories and those that concentrate upon the lives and activities of motion-picture stars.

Men provide the largest audience for adventure, sports, and certain other types of magazines. The *pulps*, named for their cheap printing paper, limit themselves to a certain kind of story, such as western cowboy adventure, weird and fabulous stories, science

39

fiction, war, sports, and crime detection stories.

There are, of course, special magazines for boys and girls of various ages. These contain stories and articles of practical value. Comic books are really magazines, because they usually contain different types of comic strips and appear at regular intervals.

Certain monthly and weekly magazines do not aim at large circulations. They carry articles and stories of thoughtful quality for the discriminating reader. This class includes weekly magazines of opinion, a few serious monthly magazines, and periodicals devoted to the arts, economics, history, or science.

Another large and important group of magazines, although not so well known, are the *trade journals*. These are magazines for readers in a specific industry, such as producing and marketing seeds, selling jewelry, or brewing beer. Their articles tell of advances in manufacturing and selling, and their advertising columns are designed for the people in that industry.

Hobbyists of all sorts have magazines devoted to their interests. Magazines are published for many types of collectors, animal breeders, and camera fans.

Religious groups publish magazines containing articles and stories advancing their particular faith. Scientific and other scholarly groups often have their own journals in which they publish the results of research. Religious magazines and scholarly journals are usually supported by the organizations which publish them, rather than by income from circulation or advertising. There are also magazines which are not published primarily for profit. They are called *the little magazines*. They publish serious articles, poetry, and fiction, and their circulation is usually small.

Digest magazines specialize in reprinting material that has appeared in other magazines or books. They may appeal to the mass public, or they may cover a special field, such as science, or matters of interest to special groups, such as Negroes.

How Magazines Are Edited

Like newspapers, magazines must meet regular deadlines. That is, they must come out at certain times. A newspaper has one or more deadlines a day. But a magazine's deadlines are days or weeks apart.

Every issue of a magazine must be planned before it appears. Usually the editors have some sort of *formula*. In a general mass-circulation magazine, for example, the formula might include the following types of material: an article on a person prominent in the news; one on foreign affairs; one on national politics; one on a specific region or town; a short story stressing love interest, designed to appeal to women; one stressing historical romance; a detective story; and a story about modern business. There may also be regular departments, such as humor, cartoons, editorials, and various special features.

Not every issue of the magazine contains all parts of this formula. Many special stories and articles may not fall into any classification. But the formula is the backbone around which the editors build every issue.

Producing a Magazine, a board of editors decides basic policies and schedules, above. It may assign a writer to produce a feature story, top left, or buy one from an author. It may send a photographer to take pictures, left center, or have commercial artists prepare illustrations, left below.

Ollie Atkins, *Saturday Evening Post;* Famous Artists Schools

Torkel Korling

It contains all the elements that will appeal to the magazine's readers.

Formulas vary for various types of magazines. News magazines are almost completely departmentalized, and editing becomes the exacting task of filling in the departments. Picture magazines also have formulas.

The articles which appear in a magazine may be sent in directly by the authors or their agents. In some cases, however, the editors of a magazine may assign a special story to be written by a member of their staff. Or they may assign an article or story to a free-lance writer. Usually they plan the article with the writer.

If there are illustrations, they are planned at the same time. Photographs must be taken by staff photographers or bought from agencies. Special drawings may be made to illustrate certain kinds of articles.

After the articles are accepted, they are edited, set in type, proofread, and the art work is engraved. The text and the art work are put together on blank pages, called a *dummy*, which show how the completed magazine will look. Proofs are taken of the dummy. After these have been approved by the editors, the magazine is put on the presses and printed, and then is bound. Finally, copies of the magazines are distributed to readers from newsstands and through the mail.

The Magazine Business

Magazines receive their money from two sources. One is from subscriptions and individual sales of copies of the magazine. The other is from advertising.

In most magazines, advertising is the larger and by far the more important source of income. Only a few academic journals, pulps, and digests rely on subscriptions and sales for most of their income.

Many magazines that depend on advertising may be designed to appeal to certain groups that the adver-

After the Magazine Is Printed, pages are gathered, or assembled, and stapled together. Finished copies will be trimmed, addressed, wrapped (in some cases), and put in the mail.

tisers also appeal to. For example, the large-circulation women's magazines are designed to attract the attention of women who will read the magazine and shop from the advertising. Some magazines plan their editorial content to make the reader want to buy the goods that are advertised.

Other income comes from sales of the magazine itself. This is done by subscription or newsstand sales. The amount received from these sales will not even pay for the cost of the paper used in many of the large magazines which contain many pages and illustrations.

There are two ways of selling a magazine on a newsstand. In one system, the magazine goes directly to wholesalers in several cities, who sell the magazine directly to the retail dealers. The other system uses a national distributing company. The publisher ships the magazine to distributing branches in various cities. The branches send the magazine to the newsstands. The publisher is paid only for those copies that the news dealer sells. On a magazine that costs 25 cents, the publisher usually receives $12\frac{1}{2}$ cents from the national distributing company. The distributor sells the magazine to the wholesaler for $14\frac{1}{2}$ cents. The wholesaler delivers it to the newsstand for 19 cents.

Magazine subscriptions are usually obtained by sending out mailings to selected lists of prospects. Sometimes crews of magazine salesmen are used. In most

MAGAZINE

LEADING MAGAZINES

Name	Publication Period	Circulation
UNITED STATES		
Reader's Digest (all editions)	Monthly	17,585,611
TV Guide (all editions)	Weekly	13,790,347
McCall's Magazine	Monthly	8,554,899
Life	Weekly	8,535,874
Look	Biweekly	7,800,531
Better Homes and Gardens	Monthly	7,603,108
Ladies' Home Journal	Monthly	6,906,024
Woman's Day	Monthly	6,661,010
Family Circle	Monthly	6,505,106
National Geographic Magazine	Monthly	6,332,665
Good Housekeeping	Monthly	5,716,429
Playboy	Monthly	5,262,432
Redbook Magazine	Monthly	4,561,537
Time	Weekly	4,164,021
American Home	Monthly	3,669,781
Farm Journal	Monthly	2,944,726
Boys' Life	Monthly	2,655,498
American Legion Magazine	Monthly	2,623,826
Newsweek	Weekly	2,472,890
True	Monthly	2,400,813
Parents' Magazine and Better Family Living	Monthly	2,156,214
True Story Magazine	Monthly	2,153,862
Sports Illustrated	Weekly	1,777,454
U.S. News & World Report	Weekly	1,756,844
CANADA		
Reader's Digest*	Monthly	1,448,312
Chatelaine*	Monthly	1,224,991
Homemaker's Digest*	Bimonthly	1,006,937
Maclean's Magazine*	Monthly	906,745
Hostess*	Bimonthly	859,589
TV Guide (all editions)	Weekly	847,844

*Includes English and French editions
Source: 1970 Ayer Directory of Newspapers, Magazines and Trade Publications

general magazines, the cost of the subscription does not pay for the magazine.

The newsstand method of selling is somewhat wasteful. In periods when magazine sales are high, few magazines are returned unsold to the publishers. But in normal times, such returns may run as high as 20 to 50 per cent. Returned magazines are usually sold as waste paper.

History

The earliest magazines probably developed from newspapers or as regularly published pamphlets bearing a single article. But such pamphlets as those which made up *The Tatler* and *The Spectator* of the 1700's cannot properly be considered magazines because a magazine contains a group of different kinds of articles.

One of the first British magazines was *Gentleman's Magazine,* published between 1731 and 1914. It began as a collection of articles from books and pamphlets, like a modern digest. Later, it published original material. Dr. Samuel Johnson, a famous writer and critic, was once associated with this magazine.

The first magazine published in America was the *American Magazine, or A Monthly View,* which was published in 1741 in Philadelphia by Andrew Bradford. John Webb edited the magazine, which lasted only three months. A few days after the publication of this magazine, Benjamin Franklin began his *General Magazine.* Many other magazines were published in America shortly after that.

Around 1800, British literary magazines, such as the *Quarterly Review* and the *Edinburgh Review,* played an important part in forming the literary tastes of England. The *Quarterly Review* was supposed to have been partly responsible for the early death of John Keats because of its harsh criticism of his poetry.

Famous American magazine editors have included Edgar Allan Poe, who edited several magazines during his journalistic career; James Russell Lowell, who edited the *Atlantic Monthly* and *North American Review;* William Cullen Bryant, editor of the *New York Review* and *Athenaeum Magazine;* Walter Hines Page, who edited *The Atlantic* and later founded *The World's Work;* S. S. McClure, who founded and edited *McClure's Magazine;* Harold Ross, who founded and edited *The New Yorker* from 1925 until his death in 1951; and Frank Crowninshield, who edited *Vanity Fair* from 1914 until 1937, when the magazine merged with *Vogue.*

Many famous magazines have influenced American thought. Among the first of these was the *Dial,* published by the New England Transcendentalists and edited by Margaret Fuller. During the Civil War, many readers turned to *Harper's Weekly* for the pictures that were drawn of the battle front. In the early 1900's, the reformers who exposed conditions in American politics, business, and industry found an outlet in *Everybody's Magazine* and *McClure's Magazine.* *The New Yorker* published such writers as John O'Hara, Clarence Day, James Thurber, Dorothy Parker, and Dame Rebecca West. Many of the articles, stories, poems, and cartoons that appeared in *The New Yorker* were reprinted as books.

The circulation of magazines has grown tremendously since 1900. Many American magazines have established foreign language editions which are sold in other countries.

The number of magazines established and those that have died out has been large. It once cost little to launch a magazine. Two prominent American magazines, *Time* and *The New Yorker,* were started in the 1920's with little money and small circulations. Today, it costs a great deal to start a magazine. The magazine business is highly competitive, and chance plays a great role in success or failure.

EDWARD WEEKS

Related Articles in World Book include:

Biographies

Bok, Edward W.
Church, William C.
Curtis, Cyrus H. K.
Godey, Louis A.
Hale, Sarah J.
Johnson, John H.
Leslie, Frank
Lorimer, George H.
Luce (Henry R.)
Munsey, Frank A.
Ross, Harold W.
Steffens, Lincoln
Sullivan, Mark

Other Related Articles

Advertising
Audit Bureau of Circulations
Cartoon
Comics
Commercial Art
Editorial
Journalism
Periodical
Trade Publication
Writing
Yank

MAGAZINE is a military and naval term for a protected building or storage room for ammunition. The term comes from an Arabic word meaning *storehouse*. The ammunition supply chamber of a repeating rifle or machine gun is also called a magazine.

Shore magazines are usually concrete buildings shaped like beehives. They are half buried in the ground and are covered with several feet of earth. Some powder magazines are built in many compartments, each of which is covered with a light roof. If an explosion occurs, the damage will be confined to a small space and the force will move upward when the roof gives way.

On ships, magazines are placed as far as possible from the engines and firerooms, and far below the water line. They are made up of many watertight rooms with steel walls lined with asbestos. In the tropics, magazines are cooled by ventilators which pipe cool air from a refrigerator, while other pipes take away hot air.

All magazines are equipped with water pipes so they can be flooded in case of fire. No iron or steel tools are allowed inside a magazine, and the men who work in them must wear shoes without nails. These precautions are taken to avoid the danger of an explosion caused by sparks from metals. Ammunition is lifted out through openings.

JACK O'CONNOR (Land).

MAGAZINE MOUNTAIN. See ARKANSAS (Land).

MAGDALEN COLLEGE. See OXFORD UNIVERSITY (picture: The Tower of Magdalen College).

MAGDALEN ISLANDS, *MAG duh lun* (pop. 13,213), is a group of tiny islands in the Gulf of St. Lawrence. The islands make up one of the counties of Quebec. They cover an area of 88 square miles. They lie about 50 miles northwest of Cape Breton and about 100 miles southwest of Newfoundland. Most of the islanders are French Canadians. They make their living by fishing in the surrounding waters, which are rich in lobster, cod, herring, and seal. The islands contain large deposits of gypsum. The making of grindstones is a leading industry. The village of Cap-aux-Meules (pop. 972) is the islands' largest incorporated place.

ALFRED LEROY BURT

MAGDALENA RIVER, *MAG duh LEE nuh,* serves as the chief trade waterway of Colombia. The river rises in the Andes Mountains and flows northward for about 950 miles. Bogotá, the capital of Colombia, depends largely on the river for transportation to the coast. Steamers can sail up the Magdalena as far as Girardot. From there, trains carry products to Bogotá. For location, see COLOMBIA (color map).

MARGUERITE UTTLEY

MAGDALENE. See MARY MAGDALENE.

MAGDEBURG, *MAG duh boorg* (pop. 267,783; alt. 164 ft.), is a manufacturing city, inland port, and rail center in East Germany. It lies on the banks of the Elbe River. The city is commercially important because of its great machine shops, beet-sugar refining plants, and synthetic oil plant. Magdeburg was founded in the A.D. 800's.

JAMES K. POLLOCK

MAGEE, "SNAKE," is a legendary oil-well driller from West Virginia. Cable-tool drillers there were called "snakes" because they drilled formations that no one but a snake could get through. The story of "'Snake' Magee and the Rotary Boiler" described how a boiler blew up and hurled Magee 16 miles. His tool-dresser said, "You were blown back so fast you arrived before you started. You can't sue for injuries because you ain't been to work yet this morning."

B. A. BOTKIN

MAGELLAN, *muh JEL un,* **FERDINAND** (1480?-1521), a Portuguese navigator, commanded the first expedition that sailed around the earth. He did not live to complete the expedition, but he received most of the credit for it. He is considered by many to be the greatest navigator who ever lived. His voyage provided the first positive proof that the earth is round.

Early Life. Magellan was born of a noble family in northern Portugal. His name in Portuguese was FERNÃO DE MAGALHÃES. As a boy, he served as a page to the queen of Portugal. He was about 17 years old when the Portuguese explorer Vasco da Gama sailed around the Cape of Good Hope to India. When he was about 25 years old, he enlisted as a soldier for service in India. He fought in several campaigns, and traveled as far east as Malacca, near Singapore. Later, while fighting against the Moors in Morocco, he received a wound that made him lame for life.

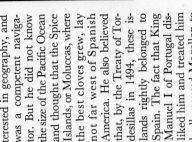

Real Academia de Bellas Artes de San Fernando, Madrid, Spain

Ferdinand Magellan

His Plans. Meanwhile, Magellan had become interested in geography, and was a competent navigator. But he did not know the size of the Pacific Ocean and thought that the Spice Islands, or Moluccas, where the best cloves grew, lay not far west of Spanish America. He also believed that, by the Treaty of Tordesillas in 1494, these islands rightly belonged to Spain. The fact that King Manuel I of Portugal disliked him and treated him badly caused Magellan to enter Spanish service in 1517. When he offered to discover a western route to the Spice Islands for Spain, King Charles V eagerly accepted his proposal.

The king agreed to supply Magellan with a fleet of ships for his voyage, and give him one-twentieth of the profits. With five ships, the *Concepción, San Antonio, Santiago, Trinidad,* and *Victoria,* and about 240 men, Magellan set sail from Sanlúcar de Barrameda on Sept. 20, 1519. He had no intention of sailing around the world, but intended to return by his outward-bound route.

His Voyage. Magellan arrived at the bay of Río de Janeiro early in December, 1519. He explored the South American coast, looking for a strait that would lead him through the continent. From March to October, 1520, he stayed in San Julián and Santa Cruz in what is now southern Argentina. The sailors called this region *Patagonia,* or *land of the big feet,* because they believed that the Indians there had big feet.

Magellan's men soon became dissatisfied because the food was running short and they were tired of the hardships that they had already endured. They were also jealous of Magellan. They started a mutiny, but Magellan suppressed the uprising, and put some of the leaders to death. He declared that he would push on southward even if they had "to eat the leather rigging."

Entering the Pacific. When he resumed the voyage, he discovered the Strait of Magellan leading from the

43

44

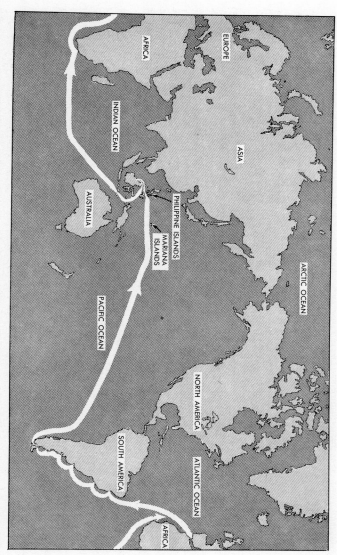

Magellan's Dangerous Voyage around the southern tip of South America opened a western sea route to the East. The engraving, above, is designed to show the difficulties, some real and some imagined, that the great navigator met on his voyage.

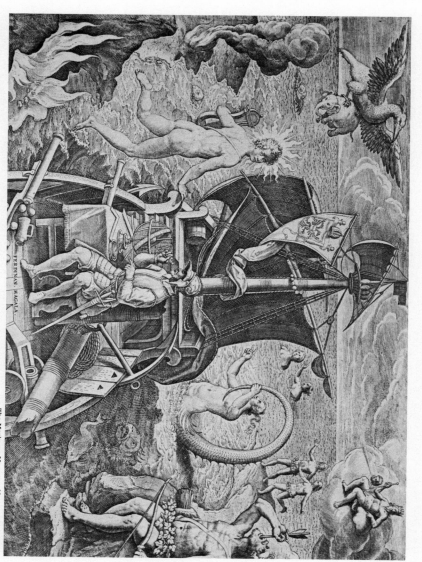

The Mariners Museum, Newport News, Va.

A Map of Magellan's Expedition, below, shows the route he followed. Starting from Sanlúcar de Barrameda, Spain, he traveled southward along the South American coast. After his death in the Philippines, his men sailed around Africa and back to Spain.

Atlantic to the Pacific around the southern end of South America. This proved to be the passage that Magellan had been seeking. As the seamen passed through the strait, they saw many Indian campfires at night on the land to their left. For this reason they called it *Tierra del Fuego* (Fireland). Magellan had searched for this strait for 38 days. He told his men that they had discovered the "nearest" route from Spain to the East Indies. He encouraged his men with the thought of the fame and riches they would gain by this discovery. Many of the men thought that they had done enough, and wanted to return home for new supplies. But Magellan was determined to finish the trip.

Soon he entered the smooth waters of the western ocean, with only three ships. The *Santiago* had been wrecked in a storm, and the *San Antonio* had sailed back secretly to Spain. Magellan named the new ocean the Pacific, because it seemed so calm compared with the stormy waters through which he had sailed. For 98 days he sailed westward and saw no land, except two desert islands. The provisions gave out or spoiled, and the water supply ran low. Hunger and disease made the condition of his men serious. They ate sawdust and rats. Many died from starvation. By the time the fleet reached the Mariana Islands, those who survived were weak from hunger and sickness. The Spaniards seized food and water from the Micronesians who lived on the islands. Magellan called these islands *Islas de los Ladrones*, or *Islands of Thieves*, because he believed the inhabitants were robbers.

His Death. Again Magellan sailed west, and, in a few days, he reached the island of Cebu in the southern Philippines. He estimated that he had passed the longitude of the East Indies. The great navigator knew that the way was open to return to Spain through the Indian Ocean.

Magellan converted the chief of the island of Cebu to Christianity. But he made the mistake of assisting him in a war against his enemy, Chief Cilapulapu of nearby Mactan. Magellan was cut down by spears and cutlasses on April 27, 1521, while fighting Cilapulapu's tribesmen on the island of Mactan. The chief of Cebu then turned against the Spaniards, murdering some of them and driving the rest from the island.

The End of the Voyage. The Spanish ships wandered around the East Indies for many months. The *Concepción* became unseaworthy and was burned. The *Trinidad* and the *Victoria* finally reached the Spice Islands and each took on a load of cloves. The commander of the *Trinidad* tried to sail to the Isthmus of Panama, but the ship was wrecked by unfavorable winds. The remaining ship, the *Victoria*, returned to Spain, traveling through the Indian Ocean and around the Cape of Good Hope.

The *Victoria* reached Sanlúcar de Barrameda, Spain, on Sept. 6, 1522. It was commanded by Juan Sebastián del Cano who receives credit for being the first man to sail around the earth. Only Del Cano and 17 men returned with the ship.　　　Charles Edward Nowell

See also World, History of (picture: Magellan's Ship).

MAGELLAN, STRAIT OF, is a narrow, rough waterway that separates the islands of Tierra del Fuego from the mainland of South America. The Strait of Magellan

is almost at the southern end of the continent. In 1520, Ferdinand Magellan, the Portuguese explorer, discovered the strait during the first voyage around the world.

The Strait of Magellan is 350 miles long and varies from 2 to 20 miles in width. Before the Panama Canal opened, the strait and Cape Horn were the shortest water routes that sailors could use in order to sail from the Atlantic Ocean to the Pacific Ocean.　Robert N. Burr

See also Cape Horn; Magellan, Ferdinand.

MAGELLANIC CLOUDS. See Galaxy; Nebula.

MAGERØY. See North Cape.

MAGGIORE, LAKE. See Lake Maggiore.

MAGGOT, *MAG ut*, is the larva, or young, of many kinds of flies. The maggot has a soft body which usually tapers toward the front. It looks somewhat like a worm or caterpillar. It has no legs and no distinct head. Maggots move by wriggling or flipping their bodies. They are usually white, but may be colored.

Most maggots live buried in their food. Some are scavengers and live in dead or decaying matter. Others are parasites in animal and plant tissue. Still others prey on insects.　　　　　　　　　　E. G. Linsley

See also Fly (The Life of a Fly); Larva.

MAGI, *MAY jie*, were the priests of the ancient Medes and Persians. After the rise of Zoroaster, the Magi became the priests of the Zoroastrian religion (see Zoroastrianism). The ancient Greeks and Hebrews knew them as astrologers, interpreters of dreams, and givers of omens. The Greek word "magic" originally meant the work of the Magi. Later, the Magi became corrupt. The "wise men from the East" who brought gifts to the baby Jesus are supposed to have been Magi (see Stained Glass [color picture]; Botticelli, Sandro [picture: *Adoration of the Magi*]). According to one tradition, the three wise men who visited Jesus were Melchior, Balthasar, and Gaspar.　　　　　Bruce M. Metzger

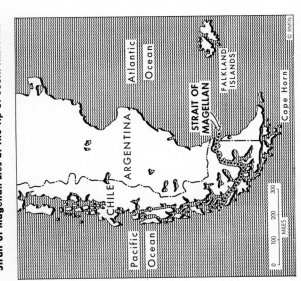

Strait of Magellan Lies at the Tip of South America.

Pacific Ocean

Atlantic Ocean

CHILE

ARGENTINA

STRAIT OF MAGELLAN

FALKLAND ISLANDS

Cape Horn

0　100　200　300

MILES

© RMRN

MAGIC

MAGIC is the practice of trying to control events by supernatural means, or of appearing to do so by the use of trickery. It includes the mystic learning and practices which are used to support the magician's claim of supernatural powers. Most primitive peoples believe in magic. Their view of the world and of the workings of nature makes it easy for them to accept the idea of a magician with strange powers over the laws of nature. Tricks of so-called magic performed on stage are called *conjuring* or *sleight of hand*. See CONJURING.

In simple cultures, magic is often closely related to religion. Many primitive peoples think that magic brings man closer to the powers above him. For them, it protects against evil and prevents disease, solves the problems of life, and lifts the dark curtain of the future.

Magic links itself with the mysteries of human life in this world and the next. In the happenings of nature, it sees a prediction of future events. It sees spirit forces moving the sun, moon, and stars, and causing wind, rain, and lightning. Magic links itself with the ancient belief in the survival of ancestral ghosts. It creates an unseen world peopled with spirits that control human fate. It surrounds life with constant duties and dangers.

The task of the magician in a primitive society is to ward off the dangerous forces of nature. He is expected to secure good fortune for his people and to show them how to avoid misfortune. Science and magic are similar in that they both deal with cause and effect. But science rejects the supernatural. Magic depends on it. Magic is sometimes used as an aid to science. A farmer in a primitive society may use all his knowledge of cultivation, planting, and climate. But he may also plant a magic charm to try to ensure a good crop.

When people believe in magic, it shapes their beliefs generally. It tells what must be done to avoid evil and secure good fortune. The teachings of magic develop special regulations for the cure of disease. There are rites for the punishment of enemies, for farming, for hunting, for making war, and for the common affairs of life.

Kinds of Magic

Communicating with Spirits is one of the most common kinds of magic. The magician's most dreaded power lay in his claim that he could communicate with the spirit world. In the Middle Ages, the magician proved his powers by calling spirits. He could do nothing without their aid. This idea appears in the story of Faust, who sold his soul to the devil. Primitive peoples believe that magic comes from spirit forces. They think that sick persons are under a spell, and that evil spirits live within them. One important duty for magicians is to perform ceremonies over the sick. They try to *exorse* (drive out) evil spirits to cure the patient.

People once thought that evil spirits made them yawn. The spirits then jumped down their throats while their mouths were open. Today, people cover their mouths when they yawn, out of politeness. But they did this originally to keep out evil spirits.

Since the 1840's, many people have believed in friendly communication with the dead. Persons who claim to be able to contact spirits of the dead are called *mediums*. Many mediums have been exposed as frauds, and have been arrested and convicted for making false

claims. But many persons still believe in their powers. A medium may claim to be able to call the spirits by means of an *incantation* (spell). This is a formula or group of words recited or sung for its supernatural effect. Primitive peoples also use such spells to bring rain or to heal the sick. The phrases repeated in some children's games may have come down to us from incantations used in earlier times.

Foretelling the Future, or fortunetelling, is another common practice of magic. It is as old as history. But it is not as popular as it once was. Some people still believe in methods of *divination* (foretelling events by means of signs or omens). But such methods as astrology, palmistry, and numerology arouse interest mainly as novelties. See FORTUNETELLING.

Black Magic. Primitive peoples believe that an enemy can spoil crops and cause sickness and death if he uses the proper ceremonies. This belief is deeply rooted in the human race, and survives in many parts of the world today. Such black magic, or *sorcery*, was forbidden by Jewish laws (Leviticus 20:27) and by Roman law. It was also forbidden by English laws until about a hundred years ago.

Witchcraft in some form is the most widespread magical belief. Many persons in all parts of the world have been punished or killed by their neighbors because they were suspected of witchcraft. People for many years have used *amulets*, or objects that are supposed to have certain magical powers (see AMULET). A primitive hunter may wear a tiny carved figure on a string around his neck. He believes that the amulet will protect him from all dangers because of its shape or some other characteristics. Some people today carry amulets in the form of a rabbit's foot or a good-luck charm. People also believe in *fetishes*. A *fetish* is an object which people think has power because a spirit supposedly resides in it (see FETISH).

Other Practices. An idea common to all magic is the belief that man can affect an object by doing something to another object that represents it. Islanders in the West Indies and the South Pacific practice this type

Witch Doctors claim that they can cure aches and pains, such as this earache, with magic spells, charms, and gestures.

Gendreau

of magic. For example, if a friend is wounded by an arrow, they put the arrow among cool leaves, believing that this action will heal the wound. But if the arrow wounds an enemy, they put it into the fire, believing that the enemy will then die. Another common practice consists of making a small image of an enemy, then cutting it, driving pins into it, or burning it. Some persons think that these actions will cause the enemy pain.

History

In Early Civilizations, many magical beliefs became established as customs. The people believed that they could do certain things, but could not do others, for fear of offending the spirits. Magical beliefs were extremely important in ancient Babylonia, Assyria, and Egypt. The ancient Egyptians believed that some days were "good" and some "evil," and determined them by studying the stars. They would start a new project, plant crops, or "bleed" the sick only on "good" days.

Early magical beliefs entered Greece and Rome, and some of them survived there for hundreds of years. A famous story about Cato the Censor suggests that the educated classes may have scorned magic. Cato supposedly asked whether one pagan priest, or fortuneteller, could meet another on the street without laughing. The ragged fortunetellers would advise a man on how to become wealthy, and then take a small coin as payment for their worthless advice.

In the Middle Ages, magic had a widespread revival. Magical practices entered Western Europe through the Greeks and Romans, and became part of the people's beliefs. The so-called science of *alchemy* was closely related to magic. It aimed at discoveries like the *philosophers' stone*, which could change base metals such as iron into precious metals such as gold and silver (see ALCHEMY). In medieval times, someone might give a *love potion* to a person whose love he desired, believing that the person would then fall in love.

Magic Today. Magic began to lose ground as man gained a better understanding of the operations of nature around him. In the age of discoveries and inventions after the Middle Ages, magic was usually limited to strange cults and some folk customs. But it was never erased from the minds of uneducated persons.

Many persons study magic beliefs today because of the light they shed on various present-day beliefs and on the beginnings of customs that have lost their original meanings.

There are many traces of magic in the history of thought. They appear in the old view that learning was a secret pursuit, in which students were introduced to mysteries, rather than acquiring knowledge. Recent organizations have made use of the belief in magic. They claim to reveal the secrets and mysteries of the ages. Such organizations claim years of devoted study in far-off places of learning. These groups often appear in the Western world with stories of their Oriental background. Often the stories are false, but the prestige of the Orient helps the groups to spread. See OCCULT.

The cult of theosophy was founded in New York in 1875. It moved to Madras, India, in 1879, where it revived the notion of *mahatmas* (persons who were supposed to possess strange powers). They could work miracles, such as moving objects through space without visible means. The leader of the cult claimed that its members were reborn spirits of people long dead. He was convicted of fraud, but his organization continued to prosper. Such cults are numerous.   JOHN MULHOLLAND

Related Articles in WORLD BOOK include:

Astrology	Mesmer, Franz	Suggestion
Clairvoyance	Mind Reading	Superstition
Divination	Necromancy	Telepathy
Evil Eye	Psychical Research	Trance
Exorcism	Shaman	Voodoo
Hypnotism	Spiritualists	Witchcraft

MAGIC FLUTE. See MOZART, WOLFGANG A.

MAGINOT LINE, *MAZH uh noh,* is a fortified line of defense along the eastern border of France. It was constructed after World War I. Forts stand above ground, flanked by pillboxes and barbed-wire entanglements. Underground chambers provide space for communications systems, hospitals, storerooms, garages, and living quarters for the officers and men, as shown in the picture *below.* In June, 1940, the Germans invaded France through Belgium, passing north of the Maginot Line. In three weeks, they swept past and then behind the line, and captured it from the rear. The line was overhauled in the 1950's for possible use in case of atomic war.   THEODORE ROPP

See also SIEGFRIED LINE.

MAGLOIRE, PAUL E. See HAITI (Recent Developments).

MAGMA. See ROCK (Igneous Rock); VOLCANO.

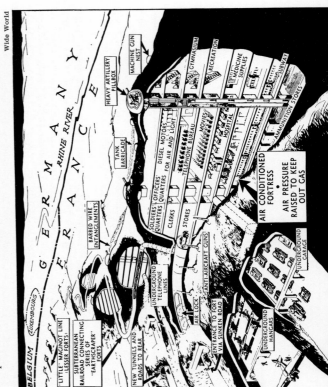

Wide World

The Maginot Line was designed to protect France from a German attack. It included huge underground fortresses, complete with garages and hangars. This drawing was made shortly before World War II.

Derek Gilby

The Magna Carta Memorial at Runnymede stands in a meadow southwest of London, England. King John approved historic Magna Carta on this site in 1215. The granite shaft inside the circular stone structure bears the inscription, "To Commemorate Magna Carta—Symbol of Freedom Under Law." Members of the American Bar Association contributed the funds to build the monument. The organization dedicated the memorial in 1957.

MAGNA CARTA, *MAG nuh KAHR tuh,* is a document that marked a decisive step forward in the development of constitutional government in England. In later centuries, much of the rest of the world also benefited from it, because many other democratic countries followed English law in creating their own governments. These countries include the United States and Canada.

The Latin words *Magna Carta* mean *Great Charter.* In the charter, King John was forced to grant many rights to the English aristocracy. The ordinary Englishman gained little. English barons forced the king to approve the charter in June, 1215. The historic action took place at Runnymede, a meadow alongside the River Thames southwest of London. A monument now stands there.

It is an error to say that Magna Carta guaranteed individual liberties to all men. In later centuries, it became a model for those who demanded democratic government and individual rights for all. In its own time, however, the greatest value of Magna Carta was that it placed the king under the law, and decisively checked royal power.

Bryce Lyon, the contributor of this article, is Professor of Medieval History at Brown University and the author of several books on medieval history, including A Constitutional and Legal History of Medieval England.

Reasons for the Charter. Normans from northern France conquered England in A.D. 1066. Able kings then ruled the country for more than a hundred years. They respected feudal law and tried to govern justly. But there was no real control over the kings' power. When John became king in 1199, he abused his power. He demanded more military service from the feudal class than did the kings before him. He sold royal positions to the highest bidders. He increased taxes without obtaining the consent of the barons, which was contrary to feudal custom. John's courts decided cases according to his wishes, not according to the law. Persons who lost cases had to pay crushing penalties.

In 1213, a group of barons and church leaders met at St. Albans, near London. They called for a halt to the king's injustices, and drew up a list of rights they wanted John to grant them. The king twice refused. After the second time, the barons raised an army to force the king to meet their demands. John saw that he could not defeat the army, and so he agreed to the articles on June 15, 1215. Four days later, the articles were *engrossed* (written out in legal form) as a royal charter. Copies of the charter were made for distribution throughout the kingdom.

Promises in the Charter. Magna Carta contained 63 articles, most of which pledged the king to uphold feudal law. These articles chiefly benefited the barons and other members of the feudal class. Some granted the church freedom from royal interference. A few articles guaranteed the rights of the rising middle class in the towns. Ordinary freemen and peasants were hardly mentioned in the charter, even though they made up by far the biggest part of England's population.

Some articles that in 1215 applied only to the feudal class later became important to all the people. For example, the charter stated that the king must seek the advice and consent of the barons in all matters important to the kingdom. It also said that no special taxes could be raised without the consent of the barons. Later, such articles were used to support the argument that no law should be made or tax raised without the consent of England's *Parliament* (the lawmaking body that represents all the people).

Still other articles became foundations for modern justice. One article says that no freeman shall be imprisoned, deprived of property, sent out of the country, or destroyed, except by the lawful judgment of his *peers* (equals) or by the law of the land. The idea of due process of law, including trial by jury, developed from this article. In John's time, however, there was no such thing as trial by jury in criminal cases.

The charter contained several articles designed to make the king keep his promises. A council of barons was formed to make certain that John did so. If John violated the charter and ignored the warnings of the council, it had the right to raise an army and force him to live by the charter's provisions.

The Charter After 1215. Magna Carta did not end the struggle between John and the barons. Neither side intended to abide by the charter completely. War broke out immediately, and John died in the midst of it in 1216. But in the years that followed, other English kings agreed to the terms of the charter. It came to be

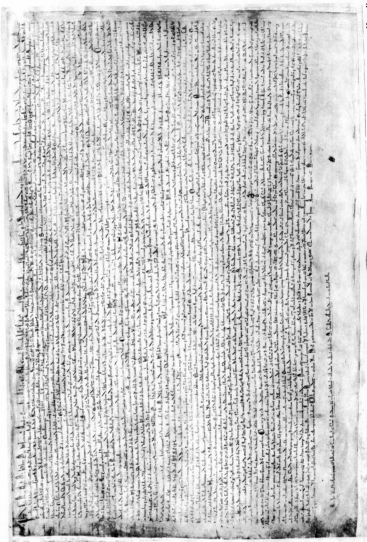

Mansell

An Original Copy of Magna Carta, *above,* is preserved in the British Museum in London. It is one of several copies of the charter that were sent to various cathedrals and castles throughout England in 1215. Altogether, four copies still survive—two in the British Museum, one in the cathedral at Salisbury, and one in the Lincoln Cathedral. No one knows which of the four, if any, was the "original" document. Like other medieval charters, Magna Carta was written in Latin on parchment. An enlargement of a portion of the charter is shown at *right.* Royal charters were sealed rather than signed. The Seal of King John, *above,* authenticated Magna Carta.

recognized as part of the fundamental law of England. Magna Carta was largely forgotten during the 1500's. But members of Parliament brought it to life again during the 1600's. They used it to rally support in their struggle against the despotic rule of the Stuart kings. Members of Parliament came to view the charter as a constitutional check on royal power. They cited it as a legal support for the argument that there could be no laws or taxation without the consent of Parliament. These men used the charter to demand guarantees of trial by jury, safeguards against unfair imprisonment, and other rights.

In the 1700's, Sir William Blackstone, a famous lawyer, set down these ideals as legal rights of the people in his famous *Commentaries on the Laws of England* (see BLACKSTONE, SIR WILLIAM). Also in the 1700's, colonists carried these English ideals on legal and political rights to America. The ideals eventually became part of the framework of the Constitution of the United States.

Four originals of the 1215 charter remain. Two are in the British Museum in London, one in Salisbury Cathedral, and one in Lincoln Cathedral. The one in Lincoln Cathedral is considered to be in the best condition. For many years, the document was commonly known as *Magna Charta*. But in 1946, the British government officially adopted the Latin spelling, *Magna Carta*.

BRYCE LYON

See also FEUDALISM; JOHN (king).

MAGNA CARTA OF LABOR. See LEO (XIII).

MAGNA CUM LAUDE. See DEGREE, COLLEGE (The Bachelor's Degree).

MAGNALIUM. See ALLOY (Alloys for Strength and Lightness).

MAGNEL, *MAN TELL,* **GUSTAVE PAUL ROBERT** (1889-1955), a Belgian professor and civil engineer, pioneered in the development of prestressed concrete. Prestressed concrete structures are stronger than structures made of reinforced concrete. He developed principles for the design and analysis of reinforced concrete structures. He was also noted as a consulting engineer on many engineering projects. Magnel wrote *Design and Analysis of Reinforced Concrete, Strength of Materials, Prestressed Concrete,* and *Analysis of the Vierendeel Trusses.* He also wrote more than a hundred technical papers.

He was born in Esschen, Belgium, and was graduated from the University of Ghent. He became a professor there in 1927.

ROBERT W. ABBETT

MAGNESIA, *mag NEE shuh,* or **MAGNESIUM OXIDE** (chemical formula, MgO), is a white, tasteless, earthy substance. It is used as an antacid and a mild cathartic. It is an alkali that does not release carbon dioxide. This property makes it a good antidote against poisoning by acids where an accumulation of gas might rupture the stomach. Manufacturers use magnesia in refining metals from their ores, in making crucibles and insulating material, and in making special cements. Milk of magnesia is a mixture of water and magnesia. Doctors prescribe it as an antacid and a laxative. They also use magnesia medically as a dusting powder. Manufacturers make large quantities of magnesia from magnesium chloride.

AUSTIN EDWARD SMITH

MAGNESIUM, *mag NEE shih um* (chemical symbol Mg), is the lightest metal that man uses to build things. This grayish-white element has a specific gravity of 1.74. This means that it weighs only 1.74 times as much as an equal volume of water. Steel is $4\frac{1}{2}$ times heavier than magnesium. Even aluminum weighs $1\frac{1}{2}$ times as much as magnesium.

Magnesium also ranks as the third most abundant *structural* (building) metal in the earth's crust. Only aluminum and iron are more plentiful. But the earth is not the most important source of magnesium. Most of the metal comes from sea water. The oceans contain 0.13 per cent of magnesium chloride, a compound of magnesium. A cubic mile of sea water contains 6 million tons of magnesium.

Magnesium has an atomic number of 12, and an atomic weight of 24.312. Its melting point is 651°C. See ELEMENT, CHEMICAL (tables).

Uses of Magnesium. Pure magnesium does not have enough strength for general structural uses. However, *alloys* (mixtures) of magnesium and other metals have been developed to meet specific needs (see ALLOY [Alloys for Strength and Lightness]). Magnesium alloys are made by adding small amounts of aluminum, lithium, manganese, silver, thorium, zinc, zirconium, and the rare earths (see RARE EARTH). Manufacturers use magnesium alloys in building airplanes, guided missiles, electronic equipment, trucks, portable tools, furniture, ladders, and other equipment where light weight is important. Magnesium is also used widely in baseball catchers' masks, snowshoes, skis, boats, horseshoes, and in the wheels and bodies of racing cars. Other uses of magnesium alloys include automobile parts, cameras, hospital equipment, and motion-picture and television equipment. Magnesium's *damping capacity* (the ability to absorb vibration) has opened many new uses for it.

Magnesium has a great many non-structural uses. For example, magnesium is alloyed with aluminum to produce most of the usable forms of aluminum. Magnesium plays an important part in the chemical reactions used to produce such important metals as titanium, beryllium, uranium, and zirconium. Magnesium is also used to protect pipelines, underground storage tanks, and the hulls of ships from corrosion. In the home, the ability of magnesium to protect other metals keeps rust and corrosion from water heaters and oil tanks. Magnesium also finds a place in home medicine chests in such compounds as milk of magnesia and Epsom salts.

Producing Magnesium. Because magnesium is so plentiful in sea water, it is available to most of the countries of the world. Even nations that do not border on the oceans can produce magnesium because the metal is so common in the earth's crust. It usually occurs in combination with other elements in such mineral rocks as dolomite, magnesite, brucite, and olivine. These rocks are available in many places. The only limit to the production of magnesium is the availability of a low-cost source of power to produce the metal from sea water or rocks.

The United States produces about 75,000 tons of magnesium a year. Russia produces about 35,000 tons a year. Most of the magnesium produced in the United States comes from plants in Texas using the water of the Gulf of Mexico. Two other plants in the United States, one in Alabama and the other in Connecticut, produce magnesium by another process. Other magnesium-producing nations include Canada, France, Great Britain, Italy, Japan, Norway, and Poland.

Manufacturers use two chief processes to produce magnesium. These processes use either electrolytic cells or thermal reduction. The electrolytic process uses sea water, and the thermal-reduction process uses dolomite, magnesite, and other rocks.

Electrolytic Cells produce most of the magnesium in the United States. In this process, sea water is mixed with lime (calcium hydroxide). From this mixture, the magnesium in the sea water *precipitates* (separates) as magnesium *hydrate* (hydroxide). This is filtered out of the mixture. Hydrochloric acid is added to the magnesium hydrate to form magnesium chloride. Workmen feed the magnesium chloride into an electrolytic cell. In this cell, an electric current breaks the magnesium chloride into magnesium metal and chlorine gas. See ELECTROLYSIS.

Thermal Reduction produces magnesium by the direct reduction of one of the mineral rock sources of the metal (see REDUCTION). Reducing agents, such as ferrosilicon, are used to break down the rock. The reducing agents cause vapors of magnesium to form at temperatures above the boiling point of the metal. The workmen distill these vapors to form solid magnesium crystals (see DISTILLATION). They melt the crystals and pour the molten metal into forms as *ingots* (blocks) of pure magnesium metal.

History of Magnesium. The British chemist Sir Humphry Davy first produced magnesium metal in 1808. In 1833, the British physicist and chemist Michael

Faraday produced magnesium by the electrolysis of magnesium chloride. The German scientist Robert Bunsen developed an electrolytic cell for the production of magnesium in 1852. Bunsen's cell was the basis for the cell used by German manufacturers in the late 1800's and early 1900's. By 1909, the Germans were producing magnesium on a commercial scale. American production of magnesium began in 1915 when World War I cut off imports from Germany.

Until the 1930's, manufacturers found few uses for magnesium and few changes were made in production processes. New uses were found during World War I, but these were largely military uses in incendiary bombs and *pyrotechnics* (fireworks). Magnesium burns with a brilliant white light which makes it useful for flares and tracer bullets.

Interest in magnesium grew during the 1930's. By the start of World War II in 1939, the need for a lightweight metal for airplane construction and other uses resulted in a number of applications. The Germans pioneered in using magnesium in aircraft parts as well as other military uses. American magnesium production reached its peak in 1943, when almost 184,000 tons were produced.

Since World War II, scientists and engineers have developed new applications of magnesium as a result of a need for a lightweight metal that can be handled easily. Magnesium can now be made in a variety of shapes for specific uses.

See also EPSOM SALT; MAGNESIA.

JERRY SINGLETON

Magnesium Hydrate settles to the bottom of huge tanks which contain sea water mixed with lime. The hydrate is pumped off and used to complete the magnesium extraction process.
Dow Chemical Co.

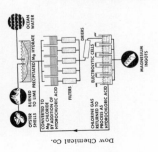

Dow Chemical Co.

OYSTER SHELLS → BURNED TO LIME → CONVERTED TO Mg CHLORIDE BY ADDITION OF HYDROCHLORIC ACID

OCEAN WATER → PRECIPITATED Mg HYDRATE

FILTERS → DRIERS

CHLORINE GAS RETURNED TO PROCESS AS HYDROCHLORIC ACID

ELECTROLYTIC CELLS → MAGNESIUM INGOTS

Electrolysis of sea water produces magnesium, above. The pure metal weighs less than ¼ as much as steel, below.

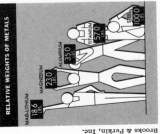

Brooks & Perkins, Inc.

RELATIVE WEIGHTS OF METALS

MAG-LITHIUM 18.6 LBS.
MAGNESIUM 23.0 LBS.
ALUMINUM 35.0 LBS.
TITANIUM 57.0 LBS.
STEEL 100.0 LBS.

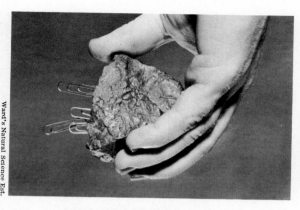

Ward's Natural Science Est.

Man First Discovered Magnetism in a loadstone, above, which can pick up a few paper clips or other small iron or steel objects. Today a powerful electromagnet, right, can lift many large, heavy bars of iron or steel.

Interlake Steel Corp.

MAGNET AND MAGNETISM

MAGNET AND MAGNETISM. Magnetism is a force that acts between certain objects called magnets. We often think of magnets as toys that pick up nails or other bits of iron and steel. But magnetism is an important force in nature. The earth itself acts as if its center contained a large magnet. Surrounding the earth is a *magnetic field* where magnetism can be found. Magnetic fields lie around every magnet. Fields a million times stronger than the earth's field are inside tiny pieces of matter called atoms. A field a million times weaker than the earth's field surrounds our Galaxy.

Every day, we use magnets and magnetism in many ways. Magnets in telephones, television sets, and radios help change electrical impulses into sounds. Compasses made with magnets help navigators guide ships safely. Without magnetism, we could not produce large amounts of electricity. Nor could we use electricity to do all the jobs that it does.

Anyone who has played with a bar magnet knows that it will pick up and hold more objects on its ends than on its middle. The areas at the ends where the magnetism is strongest are called the *poles* of the magnet. Every magnet has at least two poles. If a bar magnet is broken in the middle, new poles will appear at the broken ends.

If we hold a bar magnet by a string tied around its center, one end will point toward the north. The other end will point toward the south. If we turn the magnet

around, it will swing back to the north. The poles are named by the direction they point. The north and south poles of the magnet point as they do because the earth's magnetic poles attract them. The magnetic poles of the earth are near the North and South geographic poles.

The poles on opposite ends of a magnet act differently toward each other. We can see how the poles of a magnet act by experimenting with two bar magnets on a table. If the north pole of one magnet comes close to the north pole of another magnet, the two poles *repel* (push away from) each other. Two south poles also repel each other. But a north and a south pole attract each other and stick together. Two like magnetic poles always repel each other, and two unlike poles always attract each other.

Making and Using Magnets

How Magnets Are Made. The best-known magnets
are pieces of metal that attract some other kinds of metal. These magnets keep their magnetism permanently and are called *permanent magnets*. Most permanent magnets are made of steel or mixtures of iron, nickel, cobalt, and other substances. These materials are called *magnetically hard* because they can be magnetized only in strong fields.

A permanent magnet can be made from hard magnetic substances in several ways. Moving another permanent magnet in one direction across the steel or other material will magnetize it. An electric current flowing through a coil of wire will also magnetize the steel.

Hammering or tapping a substance while it is in a magnetic field will help magnetize it. In fact, magnetic substances can be magnetized slightly by hammering them in the weak magnetic field of the earth.

Henry H. Kolm, the contributor of this article, is one of the founders of the Francis Bitter National Magnet Laboratory at the Massachusetts Institute of Technology.

MAGNETS OF DIFFERENT SHAPES

WORLD BOOK photo

Zenith Radio Corp.
WORLD BOOK photo

Bar Magnets placed near doors are used as magnetic latches to keep the doors closed.

Horseshoe Magnets create magnetic fields for small motors like those used in slot cars.

Circular Magnets in electronic computers "remember" numbers and instructions.

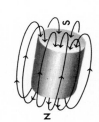

Disk Magnets in radio speakers help create sounds from electric impulses.

Cylindrical Magnets in some machines hold in place the object being worked on.

When a permanent magnet picks up an object, such as an iron nail, the nail becomes a *temporary magnet*. The nail can pick up other bits of metal and will be attracted or repelled by the poles of another magnet. But the nail will keep its magnetism only so long as it is near a permanent magnet. If the permanent magnet is taken away, the nail no longer acts like a magnet. Materials such as the iron in the nail are called *magnetically soft* because they can be magnetized in weak fields.

Some magnets are made from certain metals after the metals have combined with the element oxygen. These magnets, known as *ceramic magnets* or *ferrites*, can be either hard or soft.

Many common magnetic materials are mixtures of hard and soft substances. They can be magnetized easily, and they keep some permanent magnetization.

A coil of wire acts just like a permanent magnet when an electric current flows through it. One end of the coil becomes the north pole and the other end becomes the south pole of the *electromagnet*. But if the flow of current changes direction, the poles will also switch places. An electromagnet will remain magnetized only so long as electricity flows through it.

Sometimes, a magnetically soft material, such as iron, is put in the center of the coil. The iron makes the field of the electromagnet stronger.

How Magnets of Different Shapes Are Used. Magnets are made in many shapes and have their poles in different places. Each of these magnets has special uses. For example, permanent bar magnets are used in magnetic compasses. The compass needle is a bar magnet that points toward the earth's north magnetic pole. Some doors have bar magnets fastened near them to hold them shut.

A permanent bar magnet can be bent into a horseshoe, bringing the poles closer together and making a stronger magnetic field between them. Horseshoe magnets are used when a strong magnetic field is needed in a small space. The electronic tubes in radar sets need powerful horseshoe magnets to work properly. Horseshoe magnets also are used in some small electric motors.

Circular magnets look like small doughnuts. They do not have poles. Instead, the magnetism moves around the inside of the magnet in one direction or the other. Many electronic computers use large quantities of circular magnets to store numbers or other information. These magnets, sometimes called *cores*, are made of hard magnetic materials. They are connected to the computer by wires that run through their centers.

Magnets shaped like disks have one pole around the edge and the other pole in the center. They are used in radio and television loudspeakers.

Magnets shaped into long, round cylinders look like round bar magnets. Cylindrical magnets have some special uses, such as holding magnetic substances in place on a machine.

Electromagnets are used if magnetism is not needed all the time. For example, an electromagnet on the hook of a crane will pick up scrap iron to be loaded on a railroad car when electricity flows through the magnet. When the iron is hanging over the car, the electricity is turned off and the iron falls into the car.

Electromagnets have many uses in the home, indus-

MAGNET AND MAGNETISM

try, and scientific research. They not only can be turned on and off, but they also make stronger magnetic fields than permanent magnets can. Electric door bells and electric motors used in home appliances contain electromagnets. Larger electric motors used in industry also have electromagnets. Magnetic vibrators use electromagnets to make vibrations so rapid that they cannot be heard. Such vibrators can wash dirt out of watches and other delicate mechanisms, and cut hard substances such as silicon and germanium. They can even drive pipes into the ground. Scientists have built especially powerful electromagnets to help them study the effects of strong fields on various substances.

How Magnets Work

What Causes Magnetism? Although the most common magnets are made from magnetic materials,

EXPERIMENTING WITH MAGNETISM
A WORLD BOOK SCIENCE PROJECT

The purpose of this project is to demonstrate magnetic fields from permanent magnets and the magnetic effects of an electric current. The materials needed for the project are shown below. They can be purchased at most hardware or hobby stores.

MATERIALS NEEDED

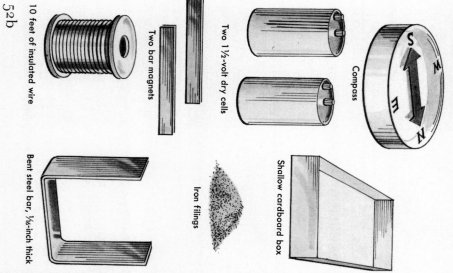

Two bar magnets

Two 1½-volt dry cells

Compass

Iron filings

Shallow cardboard box

10 feet of insulated wire

Bent steel bar, ⅛-inch thick

magnetism can be produced without any magnetic substances at all. A coil of wire can make a magnetic field exactly like the field around a permanent magnet. But the coil will be a magnet only so long as electric current flows through it. This fact gave scientists the first clue to the discovery that magnetism is caused by moving electric charges. They found that a bar magnet contains moving electric current just as a coil electromagnet does. But the current is a permanent part of the bar magnet.

To understand how electricity can be present in a bar magnet, we must know about the tiny particles, called *atoms*, that make up all things. Every atom has a central core called a *nucleus*. Moving around the nucleus, like planets around the sun, are even smaller particles called *electrons*. The electrons carry an electric charge, and their motion makes an electric current. As happens with a coil of wire, electric current produces a magnetic field. In most atoms, the electrons spin in

MAPPING MAGNETIC FIELDS

To Map the Field of a Bar Magnet, place the magnet under a sheet of white paper. Sprinkle iron filings on the paper, and tap the paper gently. The filings will line up as shown.

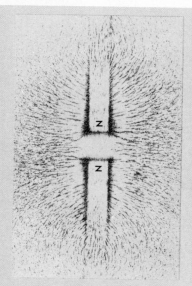

The Field Between Two Magnetic Poles curves outward from the gap between the poles if they are alike, above. If opposite poles are used, the field extends across the gap from one pole to the other, below.

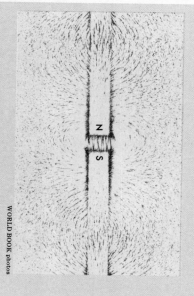

WORLD BOOK photos

Other Experiments include mapping the field when one of the magnets is turned to a different position, or when several magnets are placed under the paper. You can also study the effect of placing a steel coat hanger, coins, or other metal objects in contact with one or more magnets.

MAGNET AND MAGNETISM

different directions and their magnetic fields cancel each other. But in atoms of magnetic elements, such as iron and nickel, the fields do not cancel each other. These magnetic atoms are sometimes called atomic *dipoles*. Materials which contain many atomic dipoles can be magnetized. These materials are called *ferromagnetic* because atomic magnets were first discovered in iron, and *ferrum* is the Latin word for iron.

To understand how ferromagnetic materials become magnetized, we can look at what happens to a piece of steel that moves into a magnetic field. The steel contains small bunches of atomic dipoles, called *magnetic domains*, that are already magnetized. But the magnetic domains cancel each other because they point in different directions and the steel is not a magnet. As the magnetic field around the steel becomes stronger, the domains in line with the magnetic field grow larger. As the domains in line with the field grow larger, the steel becomes magnetized more strongly until it is com-

pletely magnetized. If the direction of the magnetic field is reversed, the domains will turn around and line up in the opposite direction. The north and south poles of the magnet will also turn around.

The steel becomes demagnetized if the domains move out of line. The domains will shift, for example, if the steel is heated or hit. If the magnet is not in a magnetic field, the domains may shift out of line. This explains why heating or hitting a substance can help magnetize or demagnetize it.

Ferromagnetic materials are magnetically hard or soft, depending on how their atomic dipoles behave. The dipoles in hard materials behave as though they were sticky. It takes a strong magnetic field to line them up, but they will remain lined up when the field is gone. The dipoles in soft materials act slippery and even a weak field will line them up temporarily.

MAGNETISM AND ELECTRICITY

To See the Magnetic Effects of Electricity, wrap about 10 turns of wire around a small box, below. Then strip the insulation from the ends of the wire.

To Observe the Magnetism, place a compass inside the box, below, and turn the box so that the compass needle lines up with the wire. Connect the wire to the terminals of a dry cell, and see how the compass needle moves.

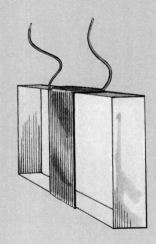

To Experiment Further, try switching the wires from one terminal to the other to see how the compass needle changes direction. By switching the wires at the proper rate, you may be able to make the needle spin completely around. You can also try changing the number of turns of wire to see the effect this has on the compass.

EXPERIMENTING WITH AN ELECTROMAGNET

To Make an Electromagnet, wind two layers of wire around a flat iron bar that is bent into the shape shown below. Strip the insulation from the ends of the wire.

To Use the Electromagnet, connect the wire to two dry cells, below. When you hold the compass between the poles of the electromagnet, the needle will point to the poles. The electromagnet will pick up iron objects when the current is on.

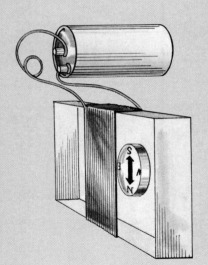

Electromagnet Experiments. Try mapping the field of your magnet. You can also change the number of turns of wire and the number of dry cells to increase the lifting power of the magnet. The more turns of wire you add, or the more dry cells you connect, the stronger your magnet will be.

MAGNET AND MAGNETISM

Most materials cannot be picked up by an ordinary magnet and are not ferromagnetic. Their action in even a strong magnetic field cannot be discovered except with sensitive instruments. Some elements, such as sodium and oxygen, have magnetic atoms that do not form magnetic domains. Scientists call these elements *paramagnetic* substances. They are only slightly attracted to strong magnets. Other materials, such as glass and water, move away from a magnetic field. These materials are called *diamagnetic* substances.

The Nature of Magnetic Fields. We can examine the magnetic field surrounding a magnet by using another magnet, such as a compass needle. As we move the compass around the magnet, the needle will stay in line with the direction of the field. The field can be thought of as a bunch of imaginary lines pointing in the direction shown by the compass. These imaginary lines, called *flux lines*, curve from the north pole to the south pole of the magnet. We can think of flux lines as closed loops, with part of the loop inside the magnet, and part forming the field outside.

The magnetic field is strongest at the poles, where the flux lines are close together. There are fewer lines farther away from the poles, showing that the field becomes weaker in those areas. If we measured the strength of the field, we would find that it is one-fourth as strong 2 inches away from a pole as it is 1 inch away from the pole.

In addition to applying force on magnetic poles, a magnetic field also applies force on electric charges. But to apply the force, either the field or the charge must be moving. Magnetic fields change the direction of moving charges. Such charges may be beams of electrons in television picture tubes. Moving magnetic fields, for example, cause electricity to flow in transformers. See ELECTROMAGNETISM.

Measuring Magnetic Fields. The strength of a magnetic field is usually measured in units of *gauss*. The earth's magnetic field at the surface is about ½ gauss. The field near the poles of a toy horseshoe magnet is likely to be several hundred gauss. The most powerful permanent magnet can produce a field of about 1,000 gauss.

An electromagnet using a soft iron center can make a maximum field of about 30,000 gauss. Fields above 250,000 gauss have been made with electromagnets that are *pulsed* (turned on for only an instant).

The Study of Magnetism

Early Discoveries. Man has known about magnets at least since the beginning of written history. But he did not learn much about how they work or how to use them until several hundred years ago. The first magnets known to man were hard black stones called *loadstones*. No one knows when or by whom these stones were discovered, but the ancient Greeks knew of the loadstone's power to attract iron.

Throughout the Middle Ages, many people believed that loadstones had a variety of medical powers. During this period, it was discovered that a loadstone would point to the north. In 1269, Petrus Peregrinus de Maricourt of France traced the lines of force on a loadstone and discovered the loadstone's two poles. In 1600,

William Gilbert, an English physician, discovered the earth's magnetism and explained the action of a loadstone compass.

Real progress in understanding magnetism came after the relationship between electricity and magnetism was discovered. Hans Christian Oersted of Denmark found in 1819 that electric current moves a compass needle. He established the first connection between electricity and magnetism. Michael Faraday, a British scientist, then discovered that a moving magnet produces an electric current. Another British scientist, James Clerk Maxwell, expressed the relationship between electricity and magnetism in a mathematical theory.

Current Research. Magnetism is a valuable research tool because it can penetrate matter and interact with the nuclei and electrons that make up atoms. Scientists generate strong magnetic fields to make electrons in *semiconductors* (partial conductors of electricity) produce infrared rays. In other experiments, nuclear physicists use magnetic fields to change the direction of high energy particles.

Magnetism itself is the object of much current research, and its mysteries are far from solved. For example, scientists do not know what produces the enormous electric currents deep within the earth that appear to be responsible for the earth's magnetic field. The deepest mystery of all is the question of why no one has ever found a single magnetic pole. Some of the world's leading physicists have searched for such a pole without success.

HENRY H. KOLM

Related Articles in WORLD BOOK include:

Compass	Electricity	Gauss
Dipping	(Electricity	Loadstone
Needle	and	Magnetic Equator
Electric	Magnetism)	Magnetohydro-
Generator	Electromagnet	dynamics
Electric Motor	Electromagnetism	Permalloy

Outline

I. **Making and Using Magnets**
   A. How Magnets Are Made
   B. How Magnets of Different Shapes Are Used
II. **How Magnets Work**
   A. What Causes Magnetism?
   B. The Nature of Magnetic Fields
III. **The Study of Magnetism**

Questions

How are permanent magnets used?
Who discovered the connection between electricity and magnetism? When?
What are magnetic poles?
What is a temporary magnet?
What are some things that scientists still do not know about magnetism?
What is a *gauss*?
What happens to the poles of an electromagnet when the electric current is reversed?
What are *flux lines*?
What is a *magnetically hard material*?
When are electromagnets used in place of permanent magnets?

MAGNET COVE. See ARKANSAS (Places to Visit).

MAGNETIC AMPLIFIER, also called a *saturable reactor,* is a device used to control large amounts of electric power. It is used where currents are too large, or other conditions are too severe, for transistor or vacuum tube amplifiers. For example, magnetic amplifiers are often used to control the speed of large motors or the brightness of airport runway lights.

A magnetic amplifier consists of two coils of wire—a *main coil* and a *control coil*—wound around an iron core. An alternating current flows through the main coil and creates a changing magnetic field around the core. This changing field limits the amount of current that can flow. But if another current is passed through the control coil, the core becomes *saturated* (completely magnetized). The saturation cancels the limiting effect of the changing field, and enables much more current to flow through the main coil.   HENRY H. KOLM

MAGNETIC COMPASS. See COMPASS; MAGNET AND MAGNETISM (Science Project).

MAGNETIC DECLINATION. See COMPASS.

MAGNETIC EQUATOR is an imaginary line that circles the earth close to the geographic equator. Scientists believe that the earth is like a huge magnet with magnetic North and South poles. The magnetic equator marks the place on the earth's surface where the magnetic attraction of the North and South magnetic poles is equal. The magnetic poles lie close to the geographic North and South poles. The North Magnetic Pole is near Prince of Wales Island, in northern Canada. The South Magnetic Pole is in Wilkes Land, in the Antarctic. Scientists often call the magnetic equator the *aclinic line.* At all points along the line, a magnetic needle will remain horizontal with no dip to either side.

See also DIPPING NEEDLE.

MAGNETIC FIELD. See MAGNET AND MAGNETISM.

MAGNETIC POLE. See EARTH (The Earth's Magnetism); NORTH POLE; SOUTH POLE.

MAGNETIC STORM is a violent and widespread disturbance in the earth's magnetic field. The earth is like a huge magnet. For example, the earth's poles can attract and move the needle of a compass. Like any other magnet, the earth is surrounded by a *magnetic field.* Scientists believe that magnetic storms are caused by great clouds of electrified particles that come from the sun and penetrate into the earth's magnetic field. During magnetic storms, compass needles may act strangely, radio communications may be interrupted, and lights called *auroras* may appear in the sky (see AURORA BOREALIS).   WALTER J. SAUCER

See also SUN (Sunspots).

MAGNETIC TAPE. See TAPE RECORDER; COMPUTER (Input Equipment); TELEVISION (Videotape Recording).

MAGNETITE. See IRON AND STEEL (Kinds of Iron Ore); LOADSTONE; MINERAL (color picture).

MAGNETO, *mag NEE toh,* is a device that generates electric current. It operates on the principle that an electric current is generated in a conductor moving through a magnetic field. One essential part of the machine is a powerful horseshoe magnet. Another is a coil of fine wire which revolves between the two poles in front of the magnet. An alternating current is set up in the coil as it moves through the magnetic field.

A reciprocating gasoline engine used in an airplane has two magnetos which supply electric current to the spark plugs. The current ignites the mixture of fuel and air in the cylinders.   H. S. STILLWELL

See also ELECTRIC GENERATOR; ELECTROMAGNETISM; IGNITION.

MAGNETOHYDRODYNAMICS, *mag NEE toh HY droh dy NAM iks,* is the study of electric and magnetic effects in fluids that conduct electricity. These fluids include liquid metals and *ionized* (electrically charged) gases. Magnetohydrodynamics is abbreviated *MHD.*

One branch of magnetohydrodynamics is the study of electric and magnetic effects around the earth and on the sun. These effects include sunspots, magnetic storms in the earth's magnetic field, and *auroras* (northern and southern lights) in the upper atmosphere. Scientific theories about these effects are based on a physical law that describes the motion of an electrically charged particle in a magnetic field. This law says that the particle's path is governed by the strength of the magnetic field and by the particle's speed, direction, and charge.

A second branch of magnetohydrodynamics is the study of a method for generating electricity. This branch is based on a physical law that describes the voltage generated along an electrical conductor as it moves through a magnetic field. The law says that the voltage depends on the strength of the magnetic field and on the length, speed, and direction of motion of the conductor through the field. In magnetohydrodynamics, this law is used in designing generators that produce electricity from a high-speed stream of ionized gas called a *plasma.* The gas is shot through a strong magnetic field where it produces a voltage between two electrodes. In theory, this kind of generator is more efficient than an ordinary electric generator. But many technical difficulties must be overcome before MHD generators can be widely used.   WILLIAM W. SEIFERT

See also AURORA BOREALIS; MAGNETIC STORM; PLASMA (in physics); SUNSPOT.

MAGNETOMETER, *mag nuh TOM uh tur,* is a device for measuring the strength of magnets and magnetic fields. Geologists often use magnetometers to search for underground deposits of oil. The earth's magnetic field varies slightly, depending on the kind of rock structures below the earth's surface. The magnetometer records these variations in the earth's magnetic field and shows where the earth has structures that might contain oil. A plane trailing a magnetometer at the end of a long cable can quickly search a wide area for deposits of petroleum. In a magnetometer, a small magnet is suspended from a fiber or pivoted so that it can be moved by a magnetic field. A compass needle may record the amount the magnet moves. This shows the strength of the magnetic field.

See also COAST AND GEODETIC SURVEY (picture: Measuring Magnetic Fields); PETROLEUM (Analyzing Earth Conditions; picture: Hunting for Petroleum).

MAGNETOSPHERE. See EARTH (The Earth's Magnetism).

MAGNETRON. See ELECTRONICS (Microwave Tubes).

MAGNIFYING GLASS is a lens which makes close objects appear larger. Both sides of the lens are usually curved to form a double convex lens. The magnifying glass can give two kinds of images. A page in a book forms a *virtual image*. The light rays which produce this image *diverge* (spread out) as they pass through the lens and appear to originate on the same side of the lens as the page. The virtual image appears upright and larger than the object.

A *real image* is formed when light rays from an object pass through the lens and are focused on the other side. The real image appears inverted, or upside down. Its size depends on the distance of the object from the lens. The distance from the center of the lens to the point where parallel light rays are focused is called the *focal length*. If the object is more than twice the focal length away from the lens, the image will be smaller. If it is less than twice the focal length away, the image will be larger.

The magnifying power of a lens depends on its focal length. The greater the curve of a lens, the shorter its focal length. It bends the rays more, and they meet at a smaller distance from the lens. The focal length of most magnifying glasses is about 10 inches.

A magnifying glass held between a piece of paper and the sun can be used to start a fire. Heat from the many rays focusing at a common point (focus) on the paper will make the paper burn.

S. W. HARDING

See also LENS; MICROSCOPE.

MAGNITOGORSK, *mag .NEE toh gawrsk* (pop. 357,-000; alt. 1,880 ft.), is the principal steel center of Russia. The city also makes mining machinery. It lies in the Ural Mountains, about 800 miles east of Moscow. For location, see RUSSIA (political map). The city received its name from its rich deposits of magnetite, a type of iron ore. When the city was founded in 1931, coal had to be transported from the Kuznetsk Basin in Siberia. Coal was later discovered in Karaganda, closer to Magnitogorsk.

THEODORE SHABAD

MAGNITUDE, in astronomy, refers to the relative brightness of a star. Astronomers classify stars according to *magnitude*. They call the brightest ones stars of the first magnitude.

Modern astronomers use 23 degrees of brightness. Each degree is 2⅔ times as bright as the next. A star of the first magnitude is 630 million times as bright as a star of the twenty-third magnitude. *Aldebaran* and *Altair* are first-magnitude stars. The naked eye cannot see stars fainter than the sixth magnitude.

The *apparent magnitude* of a star is its brightness as seen from the earth. It is determined by the star's *intrinsic* (actual) brightness and its distance. *Absolute magnitude* is a measure of a star's intrinsic brightness. It is an important physical property.

Astronomers actually use a system of classification that was started about 2,000 years ago. The first star catalogue was issued by Claudius Ptolemy, a Greek philosopher who lived in Alexandria.   R. WILLIAM SHAW

See also SIRIUS; STAR (How Bright Are the Stars?).

MAGNOLIA, *mag NOH lih uh,* is the name of a group of trees and shrubs that grow in North America and Asia. Eight of the 35 kinds of magnolia grow wild in the eastern United States. They have large, snowy-white or colored flowers, conelike fruits, and large leaves. *Southern magnolia* is especially popular because of the beauty and fragrance of its large whitish flowers. This evergreen is native from North Carolina to Texas.

It is the state tree and flower of Mississippi and the state flower of Louisiana. *Sweet bay,* also called *swamp magnolia,* has smaller flowers. It has leaves that are green on top and whitish underneath.

The leaves of the *umbrella tree* and the *big-leaf magnolia* tend to stretch out from the ends of the branches like the ribs of an open umbrella. Big-leaf magnolia has the largest flowers of any native tree in the United States. They measure about 10 inches across the six creamy-white petals. It also has the biggest undivided leaves, with blades 15 to 30 inches long and up to 10 inches wide.

Magnolia lumber is used mainly for furniture. The *cucumber tree,* which gets its name from the shape of its fruits, has wood similar to that of the yellow poplar, or the tulip tree.

Scientific Classification. Magnolias belong to the magnolia family, *Magnoliaceae.* The southern magnolia is genus *Magnolia,* species *M. grandiflora.* The sweet bay magnolia is *M. virginiana;* the umbrella tree is *M. tripetala;* the big-leaf is *M. macrophylla;* and the cucumber tree is *M. acuminata.*

ELBERT L. LITTLE, JR.

See also BAY TREE; TREE (picture; Types of Tree Flowers); TULIP TREE.

MAGNOLIA GARDENS. See CHARLESTON (S.C.).

MAGNOLIA STATE. See MISSISSIPPI.

MAGOG. See GOG AND MAGOG.

MAGPIE is a bird that belongs to the same family as the crows and the jays. The black-billed magpie lives in western North America from Mexico to Alaska. The yellow-billed magpie lives only in California. Other kinds of magpies live in Europe and Asia.

The black-billed magpie is black, with white feathers on the underparts and wing tops. Its long tail narrows at the tip. Its bill is heavy and black.

Magpies eat almost all kinds of food, including the eggs and young of other birds. Their bulky nests are domed over and have an opening in the side. A magpie usually places its nest in thorny bushes for added protection. The female lays 5 to 10 grayish-white eggs spotted with brown and tan. The maximum life span of the magpie is about 12 years.

Gottfried Hampfler, The Flower Grower

Sweet-Smelling Magnolia Blossoms often grace gardens in the southern United States. This beautiful blossom extends its large, snowy petals over rich, dark-green leaves.

These birds usually travel in groups, and are noisy and quarrelsome. They delight in imitating other birds' notes. Magpies can be tamed and taught to speak simple syllables. Superstitious people consider it a bad omen if a magpie comes to live near the home.

Scientific Classification. Magpies are in the crow family, *Corvidae.* The black-billed magpie is genus *Pica,* species *P. pica.* The yellow-billed is *P. nuttalli.*
GEORGE J. WALLACE

MAGSAYSAY, *mahg sy sy,* **RAMÓN R.** (1907-1957), became the third president of the Philippines on Dec. 30, 1953. He served as president until his death in a plane crash. During World War II, he commanded guerrillas in their fight against the Japanese in western Luzon. He helped prepare the way for the U.S. invasion of the Philippines in 1944.

He became secretary of national defense in 1951, and reformed the army. He ended the revolt by Hukbalahaps (Communist guerrillas) with a combination of armed attacks and land awards to the Huks (see PHILIPPINES [The 1950's]). His success led to his election as president. Magsaysay was born in Zambales province, the son of a farmer.
GEORGE E. TAYLOR

MAGUEY, *MAG way,* is the name given to several kinds of agave plants which grow in Mexico. The name is usually used for the *pulque agave.* Mexicans often drink the juice of this plant. They use it to make *pulque* (a fermented drink) and *tequila* (a distilled liquor). The plant's leaves are green with gray spines, and may grow 9 feet long and a foot wide. The greenish flowers grow on stalks 20 feet high. People often eat parts of the stems and flowers.

Scientific Classification. The maguey is in the agave family, *Agavaceae.* The pulque agave is genus *Agave,* species *A. atrovirens.*
HAROLD NORMAN MOLDENKE

See also CENTURY PLANT.

The Magpie is a noisy, aggressive cousin of the crow, and has the crow's thievish habits. It can imitate various birdcalls.

Schünemann, Bavaria

H. Armstrong Roberts

The Maguey, or Pulque Agave, grows in dry places in southern Mexico. People make beverages from the juice of its leaves.

MAGYAR, *MAG yahr,* is a descendant of the people who first settled what is now Hungary. Most of these descendants prefer to be called Magyars, rather than Hungarians.

The Magyars are a mixed race. They have dark skin, hair, and eyes, and are of medium height. They have round heads and broad faces. The basic stock of the Magyars is Neo-Danubian, with strong Alpine and Dinaric strains. Magyars also have some Turkish (non-Mongoloid) mixture, and traces of a Mongoloid type (see RACES OF MAN). They are members of the Finno-Ugric language group.

Ancestors of today's Magyars entered Hungary a little more than a thousand years ago as wild, barbarian horsemen. They terrorized southeastern Europe.

By 1914, Hungary's Magyar population had grown to 10 million. Hungary was among the Central Powers defeated in World War I. It lost about two-thirds of its territory to Yugoslavia, Czechoslovakia, and Romania under terms of the Treaty of Trianon. About one-third of Hungary's Magyar population then lived in the area that went over to these countries.

Hungary became a military ally of Nazi Germany and Italy in the 1930's. It regained many Magyars when Germany gave it large areas of Czechoslovakia in 1938 and of Romania in 1940. Allied forces defeated Hungary during World War II, and forced it to give up the territory it had received since 1938.
R. JOHN RATH

See also HUNGARY (The People; History).

57

MAH JONGG

MAH JONGG, *MAH ZHONG,* is a game that has been played in China since about 500 B.C. It is now played in many parts of the world.

Mah jongg is similar to many card games. But small, rectangular tiles engraved with Chinese drawings and symbols are used instead of playing cards. The "deck" consists of 136 standard tiles and several additional tiles. In the Orient, players use eight additional tiles, for a total of 144. In the United States, the number of additional tiles varies from year to year, as determined by the National Mah Jongg League in New York City.

Four persons usually play mah jongg, but two, three, five, or six can also play. Each person plays for himself. The object of the game is to form winning combinations of tiles by drawing from a pile of tiles, exchanging tiles with other players, and by discarding tiles. The rules of play are easy to learn, but scoring is more difficult. Players use a rule book while playing mah jongg. The book lists point values for the various winning combinations. Usually, each player begins the game with chips equaling 5,000 points. Losers give chips to the winner equal to the value of the winning hand. Play may con-

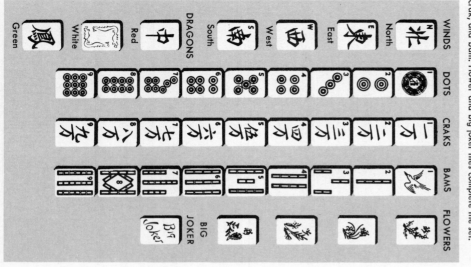

WINDS North N, East E, South S, West W

DRAGONS Red, White, Green

DOTS 1 2 3 4 5 6 7 8 9

CRAKS 1 2 3 4 5 6 7 8 9

BAMS 1 2 3 4 5 6 7 8 9

FLOWERS

JOKER BIG JOKER

A Mah Jongg Set has four tiles of each wind, dragon, dot, crak, and bam. Flower and big joker tiles complete the set.

tinue for a set number of rounds or until one player wins a certain number of points.

LILLIAN FRANKEL

MAHABHARATA, *muh HAH BAH ruh tuh,* is one of the two main epic poems of India. It describes events which took place chiefly in northern India about 1200 B.C. Some of the heroes in the poem are taken from history, and some are personifications of human ideals or divine beings.

The Mahabharata is an adventure tale. But it is also a religious drama, and has been used more than 2,000 years to educate Hindu youth. Poet-storytellers have sung the Mahabharata, and Brahman priests have explained it.

The dialogue between Krishna and Prince Arjuna, called the *Bhagavad-Gita* (*Song of the Blessed One*), was inserted into this epic, perhaps in the first hundred years A.D. Sir Edwin Arnold's *The Song Celestial* is a translation of this portion. Extracts from the two chief epics of India appear in many collections of world poetry under the title *The Ramayana and the Maha-bharata.* Many present-day poets admire the *Bhagavad-Gita.*

FRANZ ROSENTHAL

See also RAMAYANA; SANSKRIT LANGUAGE AND LITERATURE.

MAHAN, *mah HAN,* **ALFRED THAYER** (1840-1914), an American admiral, wrote many books on naval strategy and the influence of sea power on a nation's affairs. He became one of the world's great authorities on sea power. His books influenced the naval policies of many nations. His great work, *The Influence of Sea Power upon History, 1660-1783,* which he wrote in 1890, influenced President Theodore Roosevelt in his naval building program. It is also believed to have caused Kaiser Wilhelm II of Germany to build a powerful German navy.

Brown Bros.
Alfred Thayer Mahan

Mahan was born at West Point, N.Y. His father was a professor at the United States Military Academy and had written notable books on military engineering. Mahan studied at Columbia University and at the United States Naval Academy. He was graduated in 1859, and served in the South Atlantic and Gulf of Mexico squadrons during the Civil War.

He spent interesting years in travel and historical study before he wrote his first book, *Gulf and Inland Waters.* It was published in 1883. Mahan served as president of the Naval War College in Newport, R.I., in 1886 and in 1892. While there, he wrote *The Influence of Sea Power upon History.* He retired from the Navy in 1896 after 37 years of active service. But he returned to serve on the Naval Board during the Spanish-American War.

Admiral Mahan's importance in history is due to his thorough study of sea power. Mahan's studies convinced him that a country's strength and its position in the world is of great importance to its prosperity and its position in the world. He tried through his books to convince Americans of this fact and to obtain a powerful U.S. naval force.

His works include *The Influence of Sea Power upon the French Revolution and Empire, 1793-1812*, published in 1892; *Lessons of the War with Spain* (1899); *Types of Naval Officers* (1901); and *Armaments and Arbitration* (1912). He also wrote his autobiography, *From Sail to Steam* (1907), and biographies of Farragut (1894) and Nelson (1897).
DONALD W. MITCHELL.

MAHARAJAH. See RAJAH.
MAHATMA. See GANDHI, MOHANDAS KARAMCHAND.
MAHATMAS. See MAGIC (Magic Today).
MAHAVIRA. See JAINISM.
MAHAYANA. See BUDDHISM.
MAHICAN INDIANS. See MOHICAN INDIANS.

MAHLER, GUSTAV (1860-1911), was a Bohemian composer and one of the greatest conductors of his time. He is best known as the composer of nine symphonies. He failed to finish his 10th. Mahler tried to write music so varied and grandiose that the whole world was reflected in it. He used a larger orchestra than any composer before him, and added choruses and vocal soloists in several of the symphonies. His largest work, the *Symphony No. 8* (1907), is known as the "Symphony of a Thousand" because of the number of performers it requires. He also wrote *The Song of the Earth* (1908), an orchestral song cycle based on old Chinese poems.

Gustav Mahler

Mahler was born in Kalischt, and began to study piano at the age of 6. He was already an accomplished pianist when he entered the Vienna Conservatory at 15. He became an opera conductor in 1880, and later became director of the Vienna Court Opera. His energy and competence soon made the Vienna Opera the finest company in Europe. He came to the United States in 1907, and became the conductor of the New York Philharmonic Orchestra. He also conducted the Metropolitan Opera Company for three years. He was especially noted for the excellence of his Mozart and Wagner productions.
HOMER ULRICH.

MAHOGANY is often called the finest cabinet wood of the world, because it has most of the qualities desired for furniture making. It is strong and hard enough to stand ordinary use as furniture, yet soft enough to be easily sawed, planed, and carved. Mahogany does not shrink, swell, or warp as much as many other equally hard woods. The wood has an attractive color and grain, and a high luster.

The color of mahogany varies from light tan to dark reddish-brown. The wood darkens when exposed to daylight. It usually has an interlocking pattern or grain. Sometimes mahogany has curly, wavy, raindrop, or speckled figures. When woodmen cut lengthwise through forks in the tree trunk, the wood shows a beautiful ostrich-plume effect. Workers often quartersaw or quarterslice mahogany into *veneer*, or thin sheets. They saw through the center of the log lengthwise so as to divide it into four sections. Then they cut planks alternately from each face of the quarter. The wood usually shows a ribbon or stripe figure when quartersawed. Fur-

MAHOGANY

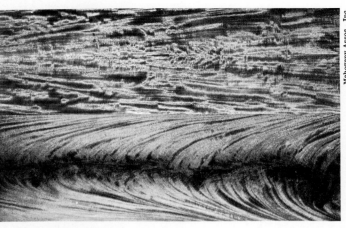
African Mahogany, *left*, has a crotch figure. Honduras mahogany, *right*, has a mottled effect.

A Huge Log of Philippine Mahogany is sawed into usable sizes in a lumber mill. Philippine Mahogany is the trade name for several types of hardwoods that are not true mahogany trees.

Philippine Mahogany Has an Even Ribbon Grain.

niture manufacturers glue the mahogany veneer to plain wood to make a beautiful surface finish.

Experts consider mahogany one of the heavier woods. Mahogany trees grow scattered throughout forests. The long, clean tree trunk may reach a height of 60 to 80 feet before the first branch appears. The heaviest and finest mahogany comes from the West Indies, where the tree *Swietenia mahagoni* grows to a height of more than 100 feet. This kind of mahogany is very scarce. Most mahogany comes from southern Mexico, northern South America, and Africa. In Mexico and South America, the wood comes from the *Swietenia macrophylla* tree. In Africa, it is found in trees of the genus *Khaya*. Wood from trees of the genus *Cedrela* looks like mahogany, but is softer, lighter, and more brittle than true mahogany.

The Cathedral of Santo Domingo in the Dominican Republic was the first building to use mahogany woodwork. The church was completed in 1540. People believe Sir Walter Raleigh used mahogany in 1595 to repair his ships in the West Indies. In the 1700's, Chippendale, Hepplewhite, and other furniture makers made mahogany furniture popular.

HARRY E. TROXELL.

MAHOMET. See MOHAMMED.

MAHOUT, *muh* RAT *uh,* or MARATHA, is the name of a vigorous people of India. More than 18 million Mahrattas live in the western part of the Deccan, south of the Ganges River. They are a mixed Indic subgroup of the Mediterranean race. The Mahrattas have great physical endurance. They are related to the Maharashtra, Kannada, Guzrat, Andhra, and Tamilnadu peoples of India. Mahrattas follow the Hindu religion. Their language is called *Marathi.*

The Mahrattas carried on endless wars against the Moslem rulers of the Mogul Empire. Their greatest leader was Sivaji. He freed them from the religious persecutions of the Moslems and established a strong kingdom in the Deccan region in the 1600's. These wars broke the power of the Mogul Empire and made possible the British conquest of India. In the early 1800's, the British destroyed the power of the Mahrattas in a series of wars. See also HINDUISM. WILTON MARION KROGMAN

MAIA. See PLEIADES.

MAID MARIAN. See ROBIN HOOD.

MAID OF ORLÉANS. See JOAN OF ARC, SAINT.

MAIDENHAIR FERN is the name of a group of delicate, graceful ferns that grow on damp rocks and in woods of North America and southern Europe. It has beautiful *fronds* (leaves), which are divided into two parts. The maidenhair fern gets its name from its leaf-stalks, which are slender, shiny, and brown or black in color. The maidenhair has been used to make a cough medicine called *syrup of capillaire.*

Scientific Classification. The maidenhair fern is a member of the common fern family, *Polypodiaceae.* The common maidenhair fern is genus *Adiantum,* species *A. pedatum.*

ROLLA M. TRYON

MAIDENHAIR TREE. See GINKGO.

MAIDU INDIANS, *MY'doo,* once lived in the Feather and American river valleys of what is now north-central California. These Indians formed one of the seed-gathering tribes (see INDIAN, AMERICAN [California-Intermountain Indians]).

The Maidu lived in small settlements that banded together to form village communities. Each village of 100 or more persons claimed the right to the territory surrounding it. No other tribe could gather food in that area. Acorns provided an important food for the Maidu. These bitter nuts contain poisonous tannic acid. The Maidu removed the poison by grinding the kernels into meal and pouring hot water over it to dissolve the acid. The Maidu also caught salmon and hunted rabbits, birds, and deer. Like the Pomo and other Indians of the area, the Maidu built sweat houses for steam baths (see POMO INDIANS). The men used them as ceremonial centers and meeting places.

Most Maidu today still live in California, working as farmers and woodcutters.

CHARLES E. DIBBLE

MAIL. See POST OFFICE.

MAIL-ORDER BUSINESS includes companies that sell their products through catalogues or circulars or by letter. These companies are often called *mail-order houses.* Smaller mail-order houses usually offer their goods by mail only. Larger firms permit customers to order by mail, by telephone, and through sales offices where shoppers can make selections from catalogues and from samples of goods on display. Some mail-order companies also operate retail department stores.

The catalogues of larger mail-order houses offer everything from safety pins to diamond rings. Some of the largest catalogues list as many as 135,000 separate items.

Before the establishment of mail-order houses, some retail stores sold certain types of goods by mail. In 1872, Montgomery Ward and Company of Chicago started the first mail-order house to sell general merchandise (see WARD, AARON MONTGOMERY). Today, it ranks as the second largest mail-order firm in the world. The world's largest mail-order house, Sears, Roebuck and Company, was founded in North Redwood, Minn., in 1886. T. Eaton Co., Ltd. and Simpson-Sears are the largest mail-order houses in Canada.

When the leading present-day mail-order firms were established, most of their customers lived on farms and in small towns. After World War I, the mail-order business began to decline. Improved roads and the increased use of automobiles made it easier for country people to travel to larger towns and cities to shop. This development led the larger firms to open retail stores.

In spite of a decreasing farm population, the mail-order business began to grow again after World War II. New firms selling specialized types of goods entered the business. Older firms developed new sales techniques. The mail-order industry recognized the importance of the rapidly growing city and suburban markets, and developed new methods of reaching customers there. These methods included telephone-order services, separate catalogue-sales offices in towns and suburbs, and increased circulation of catalogues in city areas.

The modern mail-order catalogue reflects the fact that city people as well as country people buy from these books. Although some larger catalogues offer farm equipment, they also offer clothes and other products that keep pace with the latest fashions.

MAILER, NORMAN (1923-   ), is an American author. Critics have often attacked his work, but Mailer's readers usually find his essays and novels fascinating and disturbing. Mailer has tried to analyze the myths and unconscious impulses that underlie human behavior. He often stresses sex and violence. But he uses these elements for serious artistic purposes, not merely to shock.

Mailer first achieved success with his war novel *The Naked and the Dead* (1948). In *Barbary Shore* (1951), he wrote about politics. *The Deer Park* (1955) describes the corruption of artistic and social values in Hollywood. *An American Dream* (1965) concerns events surrounding a man's murder of his wife. But it is really a surrealistic journey through the power structures and obsessions of modern urban America. Some of Mailer's best essays were collected in *Advertisements for Myself* (1959). *The Armies of the Night* (1968), which describes his experiences and observations during a peace demonstration, shared the 1969 Pulitzer prize for general nonfiction. *Miami and the Siege of Chicago* (1968) presents his reactions to the 1968 national political conventions. Mailer was born in Long Branch, N.J. EUGENE K. GARBER

MAILLOL, ARISTIDE (1861-1944), was a French sculptor. Like many sculptors of his generation, Maillol reacted against the emotionalism and irregular forms of Auguste Rodin, who had dominated French sculpture to that time. Maillol turned instead to a serene balanced style of broadly proportioned figures. Solid and clear forms were his primary aims. Maillol tried to return to what he believed to be the calm, harmonious spirit of early classical Greek sculpture. His *The Mediterranean* is reproduced in color in the SCULPTURE article.

Maillol was born in Banyuls. He began his career as a painter and designer of tapestries before turning to sculpture in the late 1890's. He dealt almost exclusively with the female figure, and his style changed little during his career. Maillol gave his subjects stationary poses and restful expressions. MARCEL FRANCISCONO

MAIMONIDES, *my MAHN'ih deez* (1135-1204), was a Jewish philosopher. His principal philosophical work,

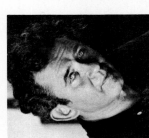

Norman Mailer

Pictorial Parade

The Guide of the Perplexed, completed in 1190, was an attempt to harmonize Judaism with the teachings of Aristotle. It influenced Christian theologians like Saint Thomas Aquinas because of its use of Aristotle's doctrines. Maimonides was a rabbi. His full name was Moses ben Maimon. Persecution forced him to leave his home in Córdoba, Spain, in 1148. After years of wandering, he settled in Egypt. He wrote many works on law, logic, astronomy, and medicine. W.T. JONES

MAIN, in sewerage systems, is the large pipe that is used to collect sewage from smaller pipes connected to buildings. In water or gas systems, a main is the pipe that delivers the water or gas to smaller pipes which are linked to buildings. RAY K. LINSLEY

See also SEWAGE; WATER.

MAIN RIVER, *mayn,* or *mine,* is the largest eastern branch of the Rhine River in Germany. The Main rises in the highlands of Bavaria and winds westward for 307 miles. It empties into the Rhine near the city of Mainz. The winding course of the river and its many sand bars make it difficult for large ships to sail up the Main. During dry seasons, only barges, small boats, and rafts can use this part of the waterway. A canal has been dug in the river bed between Mainz and Frankfurt for river traffic. The Ludwigs Canal connects the Main with the Danube River near Regensburg. JAMES K. POLLOCK

MAINE. The sinking of the United States battleship *Maine* helped cause the Spanish-American War. The *Maine* arrived in Havana, Cuba, on Jan. 25, 1898, to protect American lives and property in case of riots. On Feb. 15, 1898, it blew up, killing about 260 of the crew, and sank to the bottom of Havana Harbor. A naval court of inquiry concluded that a submarine mine had caused the explosion. The United States accused Spain in this matter because Havana was then a Spanish port. But Spanish authorities maintained that an explosion inside the ship caused the disaster. The slogan "Remember the Maine" spread throughout the United States. It aroused patriotic sentiment in favor of war against Spain. FRANK FREIDEL

See also SPANISH-AMERICAN WAR.

National Archives, Washington

The Sinking of the Maine in Havana Harbor on Feb. 15, 1898, angered the American people and helped spark the Spanish-American War. "Remember the Maine" became a popular patriotic slogan.

MAINE forms the northeastern corner of the United States. West Quoddy Head, a small peninsula of Maine, is the country's easternmost piece of land. Nearby Eastport lies farther east than any other U.S. city. On a map, northern Maine looks like a giant wedge between the Canadian provinces of New Brunswick and Quebec. Augusta is the capital of Maine, and Portland is the largest city.

Maine, the largest New England state, is probably best known for its beautiful shore on the Atlantic Ocean. Along this famous "rock-bound" coast are lighthouses, sandy beaches, quiet fishing villages, thousands of offshore islands, and Acadia National Park—New England's only national park. Jagged rocks and cliffs, and thousands of bays and inlets, add to the coast's rugged beauty. Inland Maine has sparkling lakes, rushing rivers, green forests, and towering mountains.

Many cities and towns lie in the lowlands of southeastern Maine. But forests cover nearly 90 per cent of the state. Trees from the forests are the raw materials of a giant wood-processing industry—the backbone of Maine's economy. Factories in Maine make paper, pulp, toothpicks, and a variety of other products from trees. The nation's largest producer of *newsprint* (paper used for newspapers) has factories in Maine. Maine leads the states in toothpick production, and ranks high

in other wood products. Maine's nickname, the *Pine Tree State*, came from the tall pines that once made up most of the state's forests.

Maine is also an important farming and fishing state. Only Idaho grows more potatoes than Maine. Maine is a leader in raising *broilers* (chickens 9 to 12 weeks old). Maine fishermen trap the nation's largest lobster catch. More sardines are packed every year in Maine than in any other state.

Pioneering Englishmen first settled in Maine in 1607, thirteen years before the Pilgrims landed at Plymouth Rock. Cold weather and lack of supplies forced the settlers back to England in 1608. Englishmen made permanent settlements in Maine in the 1620's. Maine was a part of Massachusetts for the better part of 200 years. Then, on March 15, 1820, it became the 23rd state of the United States.

The name *Maine* probably means *mainland*. Early English explorers used the term *The Main* to distinguish the mainland from the offshore islands. New Englanders often refer to Maine as *Down East*. They call Maine's people *Down Easters* or *Down Easterners*. These terms probably came from the early New England use of the word *down* to mean *north*. Maine lies farther north than the rest of New England. For the relationship of Maine to other states in its region, see NEW ENGLAND.

MAINE

THE PINE TREE STATE

Ralph Crowell, Sanford

Traditional New England Church in Wiscasset

Ralph Crowell

Fishing for Trout in a Maine Stream

The contributors of this article are Roger W. Remington, Editor of the Editorial Page of the Bangor Daily News; Joseph M. Trefethen, Professor of Geology at the University of Maine at Portland; and Robert M. York, Maine State Historian and Dean of Gorham State College.

Maine (blue) ranks 39th in size among all the states, and is the largest of the New England States (gray).

FACTS IN BRIEF

Capital: Augusta.

Government: *Congress*—U.S. senators, 2; U.S. representatives, 2. *Electoral Votes*—4. *State Legislature*—senators, 32; representatives, 151. *Counties*—16.

Area: 33,215 square miles (including 2,282 square miles of inland water), 39th in size among the states. *Greatest Distances*—(north-south) 332 miles; (east-west) 207 miles. *Coastline*—228 miles.

Elevation: *Highest*—Mount Katahdin, 5,268 feet above sea level; *Lowest*—sea level along the Atlantic Coast.

Population: *1970 Preliminary Census*—977,260; density, 29 persons to the square mile. *1960 Census*—969,265, 36th among the states; distribution, 51 per cent urban, 49 per cent rural.

Chief Products: *Agriculture*—beef cattle, broilers, eggs, milk, potatoes. *Fishing Industry*—clams, lobsters, ocean perch, sardines. *Manufacturing*—food and food products, leather and leather products, lumber and wood products, paper and related products, textiles, transportation equipment. *Mining*—clays, feldspar, peat, sand and gravel, stone.

Statehood: March 15, 1820, the 23rd state.

State Motto: *Dirigo* (*I direct or I guide*).

State Song: "State of Maine Song." Words and music by Roger Vinton Snow.

63

Constitution. Maine is governed under its original constitution. The constitution was adopted in December, 1819, about three months before Maine became a state. *Amendments* (changes) to the constitution may be proposed by a two-thirds vote in both houses of the state Legislature. To become law, these amendments need the approval of a majority of the voters in a regular election. Amendments also can be proposed by a constitutional convention. A two-thirds vote in both houses of the Legislature is needed to call a constitutional convention. Maine has never held such a convention.

Executive. The governor is the only Maine executive official elected by the people. He serves a four-year term and receives a $20,000 yearly salary plus a $15,000 annual expense account. The governor may serve any number of terms, but he may not serve more than two terms in succession. For a list of all the governors of Maine, see the *History* section of this article.

Maine has no lieutenant governor, but it does have a seven-member executive council. Members of this council are elected by the state Legislature to two-year terms. They serve as advisers to the governor, and must approve most of the top officials appointed by the governor. These officials include the commissioners of banking, finance, health and welfare, industry and commerce, and labor and industry. The Legislature elects the attorney general, secretary of state, and state treasurer to two-year terms. It elects the state auditor to a four-year term.

Legislature of Maine consists of a 32-member Senate and a 151-member House of Representatives. Voters in Maine's 16 counties elect from 1 to 4 senators, and from 3 to 28 representatives, depending on the population of the county. Legislators serve two-year terms. Legislative sessions begin on the first Wednesday of January in odd-numbered years and have no time limit. In 1966, Maine voters approved a constitutional

amendment requiring the Senate to be *reapportioned* (redivided) to give equal representation based on population. The Legislature drew up a reapportionment plan but the governor vetoed it. In 1967, the state Supreme Judicial Court ordered a plan which required a 32-member Senate. The plan became effective in 1968.

Courts. The Supreme Judicial Court is Maine's highest court of appeals for all civil and criminal cases. It has a chief justice and five associate justices. The governor, with the executive council's approval, appoints the justices to seven-year terms. Maine's superior court handles all cases requiring trial by jury, and all cases appealed from lower courts. The governor appoints the nine superior court justices to seven-year terms.

Each county has a probate court, whose judges are elected by the people to four-year terms. Maine's 13 district courts hear cases involving damages of less than $1,200. They also hear divorce cases and minor criminal cases. District court judges are appointed by the governor to seven-year terms.

Local Government. Maine's 21 cities operate under charters granted by the state Legislature. The Legislature must approve changes in city charters. Most cities have a mayor-council or city-manager government.

Maine has more than 450 towns and *plantations* (small incorporated areas). A town in Maine is similar to a township in many other states. It is a geographic division of the state rather than a single community. Several communities may exist in the same town. But the entire town is governed as a unit. The town meeting is the most common form of government in Maine towns. It allows citizens to take a direct part in government. Each year, town voters assemble to elect officials, approve budgets, and conduct other business. The chief town officials are called *selectmen*. Maine's plantations are governed in much the same way as towns. A board of assessors heads a plantation's government. Each of Maine's 16 counties has its own government.

Taxation provides about three-fourths of the state government's income. Almost all the rest comes from federal grants and other U.S. government programs. Sales taxes bring in the largest part of Maine's income. These taxes, ranked in order of importance, include a general sales tax, personal and corporation income taxes, and taxes on motor fuels, tobacco products, public utilities, alcoholic beverages, insurance, and horse racing. License fees are Maine's second most important kind of tax. The state also has a death and gift tax. A state property tax is the chief source of income for Maine's cities, towns, and plantations.

Politics. Maine was a Democratic state before the 1850's. But most Maine voters became Republicans in the period shortly before the Civil War. They favored the Republican Party's antislavery and pro-Northern policies. For about a hundred years, until the 1950's, Maine voters almost always elected Republicans in state, congressional, and presidential elections. The Republicans are still the state's strongest party. But the Democrats have gained support since the 1950's.

Maine has voted for more Republican presidential candidates than any other state except Vermont. Since 1856, only three Democrats—Woodrow Wilson in 1912,

Governor's Mansion stands across the street from the Capitol. The residence is usually called Blaine House, because James G. Blaine, a leading political figure of the late 1800's, once owned it.

Maine Dept. of Economic Development

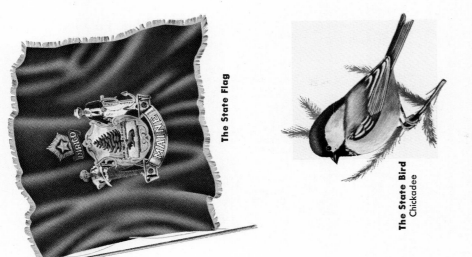

The State Flag

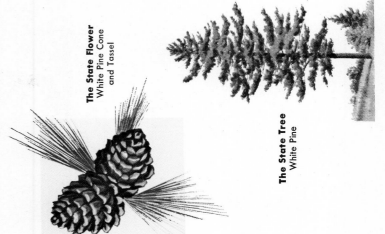

The State Bird
Chickadee

The State Flower
White Pine Cone and Tassel

The State Tree
White Pine

The State Seal

Symbols of Maine. On the seal, the farmer and the seaman represent two of Maine's chief occupations. The pine tree on the shield symbolizes Maine's many forests, and the moose represents its wildlife. The North Star above the shield stands for the state's northern location. The motto, *Dirigo*, means *I direct*. The seal was adopted in 1820. The state flag bears a reproduction of the seal on a field of blue. It was adopted in 1909.

Seal, flag, bird, and flower illustrations, courtesy of Eli Lilly and Company

Lyndon B. Johnson in 1964, and Hubert H. Humphrey in 1968—have won Maine's electoral votes. For years, Maine held its elections for Congress and governor in September. Its voters often chose candidates from the party that won November elections in other states. This led to the slogan, "As Maine goes, so goes the nation." In 1960, Maine began voting in November. For Maine's voting record in presidential elections, see ELECTORAL COLLEGE (table).

State Capitol is in Augusta. The original structure, designed by Charles Bulfinch, was completed in 1832. Portland was Maine's capital from 1820 until 1832, when Augusta became capital.

Maine Dept. of Economic Development

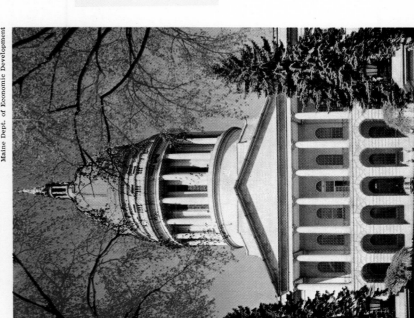

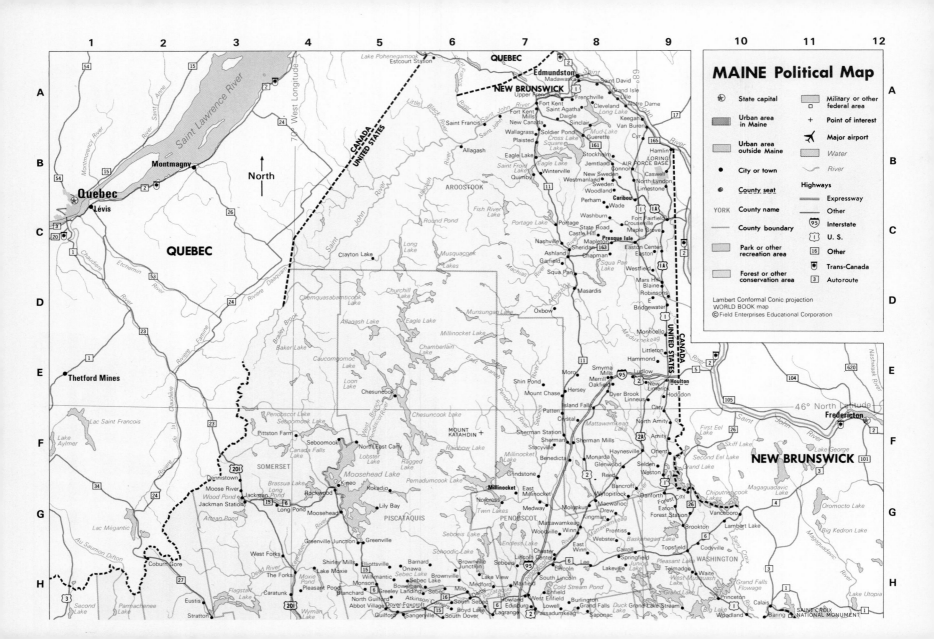

MAINE Political Map

Legend:

- State capital
- Urban area in Maine
- Urban area outside Maine
- City or town
- County seat
- YORK — County name
- County boundary
- Park or other recreation area
- Forest or other conservation area
- Military or other federal area
- Point of interest
- Major airport
- Water
- River

Highways
- Expressway
- Other
- 95 Interstate
- 1 U.S.
- 16 Other
- Trans-Canada
- 3 Autoroute

Lambert Conformal Conic projection
WORLD BOOK map
© Field Enterprises Educational Corporation

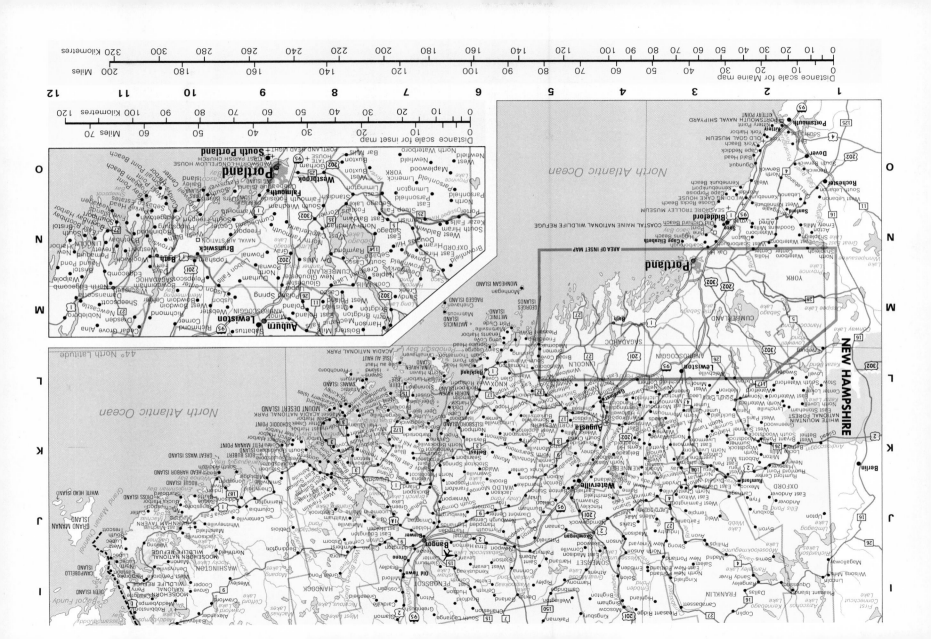

MAINE MAP INDEX

Population

977,260	..Census..1970
969,265	" ..1960
913,774	" ..1950
847,226	" ..1940
797,423	" ..1930
768,014	" ..1920
742,371	" ..1910
694,466	" ..1900
661,086	" ..1890
648,936	" ..1880
626,915	" ..1870
628,279	" ..1860
583,169	" ..1850
501,793	" ..1840
399,455	" ..1830
298,335	" ..1820
228,705	" ..1810
151,719	" ..1800
96,540	" ..1790

Metropolitan Areas

Lewiston-Auburn .71,624
Portland 139,959

Counties

Androscog-
gin ......90,127..L 3
Aroostook ..92,533..B 6
Cumber-
land ....190,007..M 2
Franklin ..21,882..I 3
Hancock ..33,443..I 8
Kennebec ..95,425..K 4
Knox ....27,983..L 6
Lincoln ..19,823..L 5
Oxford ..42,891..K 2
Penobscot 123,299..I 7
Piscataquis 16,331..G 5
Sagadahoc 23,037..M 4
Somerset ..39,670..F 4
Waldo ....22,874..K 6
Washington 29,106..I 10
York ....108,829..M 2

Cities and Towns

Abbot* ......442▲..H 5
Abbot Village ....H 5
Abbotts Mill ....K 2
Acton ......619▲..N 1
Addison ....743▲..J 9
Albion ....1,034▲..K 5
Alexander ..156▲..I 10
Alfred ..1,169▲○N 2
Allagash ....419..B 6
Allens Mills ....J 4
Alna ....311▲..M 11
Alton ......334▲..I 7
Amherst ....133▲..J 8
Amity ......143▲..F 9
Andover ....776▲..J 2
Anson ....2,178▲..J 4
Appleton ....619▲..L 6
Arrowsic ....202▲..N 11
Arundel ..1,315▲..O 2
Ash Point ......L 6
Ashland ..1,542▲..C 8
Ashville ....K 8
Athens ....642▲..I 5
Atkinson* ..204▲..H 6

Atkinson Corners ..H 6
Atlantic ......L 8
Auburn ..23,408.○M 9
Augusta ..22,104.○K 4
Aurora ......67▲..J 8
Avon ....465▲..I 3
Bailey Island ....O 10
Baileyville ..2,103▲..I 10
Bald Head ......O 2
Baldwin* ....862▲..N 7
Bancroft ......49▲..G 9
Bangor ..32,390.○J 7
Bar Harbor* 3,631▲..K 8
Bar Harbor ..2,444▲..K 8
Bar Mills ....O 8
Baring ....I 10
Barnard ....H 6
Bath ......9,473.○M 4
Bay Point ......O 11
Bayside ....J 7
Beals ......658▲..K 10
Beddington ..22▲..J 9
Belfast ..5,780.○K 6
Belgrade ..1,306▲..K 4
Belgrade Lakes ..K 4
Belmont ....340▲..K 6
Bemis ....J 2
Benedicta ..181▲..F 8
Benton ....1,760▲..K 5
Benton Station ..K 5
Bernard ....L 8
Berwick* ..3,071▲..O 2
Berwick ..1,557▲..O 2
Bethel* ..2,172▲..K 2
Bethel ....1,117▲..K 2
Biddeford 19,784▲..N 3
Bingham* ..1,069▲..I 4
Bingham ..1,180▲..I 4
Birch Harbor ....J 9
Blaine ......894▲..D 9
Blanchard ....48▲..H 5
Blue Hill ..1,292▲..K 7
Blue Hill Falls ..K 7
Bolsters Mills ..M 8
Boothbay ..1,742▲..N 11
Boothbay
Harbor ..2,198▲..N 11
Bowdoin* ....844▲..M 10
Bowdoin Center ..M 10
Bowdoinham 1,295▲..M 10
Bowerbank ..21▲..H 6
Boyd Lake ......H 7
Bradford ....557▲..I 6
Bradley ....989▲..I 7
Bremen ......450▲..L 5
Brewer ....9,186▲..J 7
Bridgewater ..891▲..D 9
Bridgton* ..2,866▲..M 7
Bridgton ..1,715▲..M 7
Brighton ......45▲..I 5
Bristol ..1,643▲..N 12
Broad Cove ......L 5
Brooklin ....586▲..L 7
Brooks ......740▲..K 6
Brooksville ..646▲..K 7
Brownfield ..482▲..N 6
Brownville ..1,479▲..H 6
Brownville
Junction ......H 6
Brunswick* 16,059▲..N 10
Brunswick ..9,444▲..N 10
Bryant Pond ......K 2
Buckfield ....908▲..L 3
Bucks Harbor ..J 10
Bucksport ..3,577▲..K 7

Bucksport ..2,327..K 7
Burkettville ....L 6
Burlington ..258▲..H 8
Burnham ....786▲..J 5
Buxton ....3,137▲..O 8
Byron ....21▲..J 2
Calais ....3,886..H 10
Cambridge ..317▲..I 5
Camden* ..3,916▲..L 6
Camden ..3,523..L 6
Canaan ....869▲..J 5
Canton ......750▲..K 3
Cape
Elizabeth .7,809▲..N 3
Cape Neddick ....O 2
Cape Porpoise ....O 3
Cape Rosier ......K 7
Caratunk ......83..H 4
Cardville ....K 7
Caribou ..10,247..C 9
Carmel ....1,283▲..I 6
Carrabassett ......I 3
Carroll ......122..H 8
Carthage ....376▲..J 3
Cary ....181..F 9
Casco ....1,179▲..M 8
Castine ..1,072▲..K 7
Castle Hill ..502▲..C 8
Caswell ......680..B 9
Cedar Grove ....M 11
Center Lovell ....L 2
Center Montville ..K 6
Centerville ..19▲..J 10
Chapman ....332▲..C 8
Charleston ..886▲..I 6
Charlotte ....191▲..I 11
Chebeague Island ..O 9
Chelsea ..2,154▲..L 5
Cherryfield ..771▲..J 9
Chester ....253▲..H 7
Chesterville ..618▲..K 4
Chesuncook ....E 5
China ....1,811▲..K 5
Chisholm ..1,193..K 3
Clayton Lake ....C 5
Cleveland ....A 8
Clifton ......225▲..J 7
Clifton Corners ..J 7
Clinton ..1,948▲..J 5
Coburn Gore ......H 2
Codyville ....50..H 10
Columbia ....145▲..J 9
Columbia
Falls ......370▲..J 9
Connor ....B 9
Convene ....H 7
Cooks Mills ......M 8
Cooper ......81▲..I 10
Coopers Mills ....L 5
Coplin ....43..I 3
Corea ....K 9
Corinna ..1,677▲..I 6
Corinth ..1,220▲..I 6
Cornish ......822▲..N 7
Cornville ....609▲..J 5
Costigan ....I 7
Cranberry
Isles ......162▲..L 8
Crawford ......74▲..I 10
Crescent Lake ..M 8
Criehaven ....M 7
Crouseville ......C 8
Crystal ......267▲..F 8
Cumberland* 4,139▲..N 9
Cumberland
Center ....N 9

Cundys Harbor ..N 10
Cushing ....524▲..L 6
Cutler ......583▲..J 11
Cyr ....149..B 9
Daigle ....A 8
Dallas ....84..I 2
Damariscotta 1,241▲..M 12
Danforth ....772▲..G 9
Dark Harbor ......L 6
Days Ferry ......N 11
Dayton ....541▲..N 2
Deblois ......23▲..J 9
Dedham ....490▲..J 7
Deer Isle ..1,118▲..L 7
Denmark ....482▲..N 7
Dennistown ..40..G 3
Dennysville ..268▲..I 11
Derby ....H 6
Detroit ....657▲..J 6
Dexter* ..3,723▲..I 6
Dexter ....2,720..I 6
Dixfield* ..2,155▲..K 3
Dixfield ..1,334▲..K 3
Dixmont ....522▲..J 6
Dixmont Center ..J 6
Douglas Hill ......M 7
Dover-
Foxcroft* .4,124▲..H 6
Dover-
Foxcroft ..2,481.○H 6
Dresden ....758▲..M 11
Drew ....40..G 8
Dry Mills ....N 9
Dryden ....K 3
Durham ..1,250▲..M 9
Dyer Brook ..153▲..E 8
E ....18..D 9
Eagle Lake ..873▲..B 7
East Andover ......J 2
East Baldwin ....N 7
East Blue Hill ....K 7
East Boothbay ..N 11
East Brownfield ..N 7
East Corinth ....I 6
East Dixfield ....K 3
East Eddington ..J 7
East Franklin ....K 8
East Hiram ......N 7
East Holden ......J 7
East Lebanon ....O 2
East Limington ..O 7
East Livermore ..K 3
East
Machias ..1,056▲..J 10
East Madison ....J 5
East Milli-
nocket ..2,589▲..G 7
East Milli-
nocket ..2,295..G 7
East Monmouth ..L 4
East New
Portland ....I 4
East Newport ....J 6
East Orland ......K 7
East
Parsonfield ....O 7
East Peru ....K 3
East Pittston ....L 5
East Poland ......M 9
East Sebago ......N 8
East Stoneham ..L 2
East Sullivan ....K 8
East Sumner ....K 3
East Union ......L 6
East
Vassalboro ....K 5

East Waterboro ....N 2
East Waterford ....L 2
East Wilton ......J 3
East Winn ....H 8
East Winthrop ....K 4
Eastbrook ..172▲..J 8
Easton ....1,296▲..C 9
Easton Center ....C 9
Eastport ..1,951..I 11
Eaton ....G 9
Eddington ..1,351▲..J 7
Edgecomb ..553▲..N 11
Edinburg ......67▲..H 7
Eliot ......3,273▲..O 2
Elliottsville ..12..H 5
Ellsworth ..4,555.○K 8
Embden ......283▲..I 4
Emery Mills ......N 2
Enfield ....1,133▲..H 7
Estcourt Station ..A 6
Etna ....498▲..J 6
Eustis ......571▲..H 3
Exeter ......647▲..I 6
Fairbanks ....J 3
Fairfield* ..5,670▲..K 5
Fairfield ..3,766..K 5
Falmouth ..6,468▲..O 9
Falmouth
Foreside ..1,062..O 9
Farmingdale 2,386▲..L 4
Farmington* 5,603▲..J 3
Farmington ..2,749.○J 3
Farmington
Falls ....J 4
Fayette ......455▲..K 4
Five Islands ......N 11
Forest City ....G 9
Forest Station ....G 9
Fort
Fairfield* 4,805▲..C 9
Fort
Fairfield ..3,082..C 9
Fort Kent* ..4,387▲..A 7
Fort Kent ..2,787..A 7
Fort Kent Mills ....A 7
Fosters Corner ....N 8
Frankfort ....606▲..J 7
Franklin ......666▲..J 8
Freedom ....515▲..L 3
Freeport* ..4,696▲..N 10
Freeport ..1,801..N 10
Frenchboro ..54..L 8
Frenchville 1,376▲..A 8
Friendship ..826▲..M 5
Frye ....L 1
Fryeburg ..2,133▲..L 1
Gardiner ..6,742..L 4
Garfield ....103..D 8
Garland ....581▲..I 6
Georgetown ..420▲..N 11
Gilead ......136▲..K 1
Glen Cove ....L 6
Glenburn* ..1,181▲..I 7
Glenburn Center ..I 7
Glenwood ......6..F 8
Goodwins Mills ..N 2
Goose Rocks
Beach ....O 3
Gorham* ..7,722▲..O 8
Gorham ..2,322..O 8
Gouldsboro 1,279▲..K 9
Grand Falls ......6..H 9
Grand Isle ....777▲..A 8
Grand Lake
Stream ....177..H 9
Gray ......3,040▲..N 9

Great Pond ....I 8
Greeley Landing ..H 6
Green Lake ......J 7
Greenbush ..973▲..I 7
Greene ....1,758▲..L 3
Greenfield ..113▲..I 8
Greenville ..1,800▲..G 5
Greenville ..1,893▲..G 5
Greenville
Junction ....G 4
Greenwood ..619▲..K 2
Grindstone ....G 7
Grove ....I 10
Guerette ....B 8
Guilford* ..1,676▲..I 5
Guilford ..1,372▲..I 5
Hall Quarry ......K 8
Hallowell ..2,784▲..L 4
Hamlin ......354▲..B 9
Hammond ....74▲..E 9
Hampden ..4,601▲..J 7
Hampden
Highlands ....J 7
Hancock ..1,011▲..K 8
Hanover ....265▲..K 2
Harborside ....K 7
Harmony ....636▲..I 5
Harpswell* ..2,456▲..O 10
Harpswell
Center ....N 10
Harrington ..582▲..J 9
Harrison ..1,018▲..M 7
Hartford ....314▲..K 3
Hartland* ..1,366▲..I 5
Hartland ..1,016▲..I 5
Haynesville ..150▲..F 9
Hebron ......515▲..L 3
Hermon ..2,345▲..I 7
Hersey ....80▲..E 8
Higgins Beach ....N 3
Highland ......22..I 4
Hinckley ....J 4
Hiram ......604▲..N 7
Hodgdon ....909▲..E 9
Holden ....1,789▲..J 7
Hollis* ....1,524▲..N 2
Hollis Center ....N 2
Hope ....429▲..L 6
Houlton* ..8,037▲..E 9
Houlton ..5,976.○E 9
Howland* ..1,461▲..H 7
Howland ..1,313▲..H 7
Hudson ....475▲..I 7
Hulls Cove ......K 8
Indian Point ......K 8
Indian River ......K 10
Industry ....344▲..J 4
Island Falls ..897▲..F 8
Isle au Haut ..32▲..L 7
Islesboro ....411▲..K 7
Islesford ....L 8
Jackman ....820▲..G 3
Jackman Station ..G 3
Jackson ......165▲..J 6
Jacksonville ......J 10
Jay ....3,895▲..K 3
Jefferson ..1,209▲..L 5
Jemtland ....A 9
Jonesboro ..435▲..J 10
Jonesport* 1,337▲..K 10
Jonesport-West
Jonesport ..1,339..K 10
Keegan ....A 9
Kenduskeag ..723▲..I 6
Kennebunk 5,527▲..O 2
Kennebunk ..2,804..O 2

Kennebunk
Beach ....O 2
Kennebunk-
port ......2,123▲..O 3
Kents Hill ....K 4
Kezar Falls ......N 7
Kineo ....G 5
Kingfield ....826▲..I 3
Kingman ....I 8
Kingsbury ....I 5
Kittery* ..10,337▲..O 2
Kittery ..8,051..O 2
Kittery
Point ......1,259..O 2
Knox* ......438▲..K 6
Knox Center ......K 6
Kokadjo ....G 5
Lagrange ....376▲..I 7
Lake Moxie ......H 4
Lake View ....H 6
Lakeville ....11..H 8
Lakewood ....J 4
Lambert Lake ....G 10
Lamoine ....586▲..K 8
Lamoine Beach ..K 8
Lebanon ..1,947▲..O 2
Lee ....555▲..H 8
Leeds ......999▲..L 3
Leeds Junction ..L 4
Levant ......789▲..J 6
Lewiston ..41,817..L 3
Liberty ......449▲..K 6
Lille ....A 8
Lily Bay ....G 5
Limerick ....925▲..O 7
Limestone* 10,627▲..B 9
Limestone ..1,772..B 9
Limington ..958▲..O 7
Lincoln* ..4,640▲..H 7
Lincoln ..3,616..H 7
Lincoln ......51..I 1
Lincoln Center ..H 7
Lincolnville ..934▲..L 6
Lincolnville Center ..L 6
Linneus ....605▲..E 9
Lisbon* ..6,399▲..M 8
Lisbon ..1,542..M 9
Lisbon Center ..M 10
Lisbon Falls 2,640..M 10
Litchfield ..1,185▲..L 4
Litchfield
Corners ....L 4
Little
Deer Isle ....L 7
Littleton ....941▲..E 9
Livermore ..1,586▲..K 3
Livermore
Falls* ..3,398▲..K 3
Livermore
Falls ..2,832..K 3
Locke Mills ......K 2
Long Island* ..60..K 7
Long Pond ....G 4
Longcove ....M 6
Lovell ......593▲..L 2
Lowell ......156▲..H 8
Lubec* ..1,876▲..J 11
Lubec ..1,289..J 11
Lucerne in
Maine ....J 7
Ludlow ......254▲..E 9
Lyman ......853▲..N 2
Lynchville ....L 2
Machias* ..2,415▲..J 10
Machias ..1,523.○J 10
Machiasport ..871▲..J 10

Macwahoc ...127..G 8
Madawaska* 5,527▲.A 8
Madawaska .4,035...A 8
Madison* .4,197▲.J 4
Madison ..2,761...J 4
Madrid ....102▲.J 3
Magalloway ...49..I 1
Manchester .1,342▲.K 4
Manset ....L 8
Maple Grove ......C 9
Mapleton .1,579▲.C 8
Maplewood ......O 6
Mariaville ...104▲.J 8
Marion ....K 8
Marlboro ....K 8
Mars Hill* .1,845▲.D 9
Mars Hill .1,458...D 9
Marshfield .248▲.J 10
Martinsville .....M 6
Masardis ..301▲.D 8
Matinicus ....M 7
Matinicus
  Isle* .....86..M 7
Mattawam-
  keag ....974▲.G 8
Maxfield ...31▲.H 7
McKinley ....L 8
Mechanic
  Falls* ..2,160▲.M 8
Mechanic
  Falls .1,992..M 8
Meddybemps .79▲.I 10
Medford ...130▲.H 7
Medomak ......M 5
Medway .1,502▲.G 7
Mercer ....302▲.J 4
Merrill ...261▲.E 8
Mexico* .4,373▲.K 2
Mexico .3,951...K 2
Milbridge .1,134▲.K 9
Milford ..1,822▲.I 7
Millinocket* 7,672▲.G 7
Millinocket .7,318...G 7
Milo* ...2,537▲.H 6
Milo ...1,802..H 6
Milton ....M 9
Minot .....903▲.M 9
Minturn ....L 8
Molunkus ....G 8
Monarda ....F 8
Monhegan ...42..M 6
Monmouth .2,041▲.L 4
Monroe ....652▲.H 5
Monson ....652▲.H 5
Monticello .1,040▲.E 9
Montville ..427▲.K 5
Moose River .243▲.G 3
Moosehead ....G 5
Moro ....24..E 8
Morrill ....401▲.K 6
Moscow ....585▲.I 4
Mount Chase .176..E 8
Mount
  Desert ..1,641▲.K 8
Mount
  Vernon ..670▲.K 4
Naples ....966▲.N 8
Nashville ...49..C 8
New Canada .304..B 7
New
  Gloucester 2,771▲.N 9

New Harbor ......N 12
New Limerick 414▲.E 9
New Portland 561▲.J 4
New Sharon .709▲.J 4
New Sweden .630▲.B 8
New Vineyard 433▲.J 3
Newagen ....N 11
Newburgh ..811▲.J 6
Newburgh Center .J 6
Newcastle ..961▲.M 12
Newfield ...414▲.O 7
Newport* .2,234▲.J 6
Newport .1,589...J 6
Newry .....189▲.K 2
Nobleboro ..824▲.M 12
Norcross ....G 7
Norridge-
  wock ...1,919▲.J 4
North Amity ....I 5
North Anson ....J 4
North Belgrade ..K 4
North Ber-
  wick* ...2,151▲.O 2
North Ber-
  wick .....1,295..O 2
North Bridgton ..M 7
North Brooksville .K 7
North Chesterville .J 4
North East Carry ..F 5
North Edgecomb .M 11
North Guilford ...H 5
North Haven ..350▲.L 7
North Jay ....K 3
North Leeds .....K 3
North Livermore ..K 3
North Lovell .....L 2
North Lubec ....I 11
North Lyndon ...B 9
North Monmouth ..L 4
North New
  Portland ......I 4
North
  Parsonfield ...O 6
North Penobscot ..K 7
North Pownal ....N 9
North Searsmont ..K 6
North Shapleigh ..N 1
North Sullivan ...K 8
North Turner ....K 3
North Vassalboro .K 4
North Waldoboro .L 5
North Waterford ..O 7
North Waterford ..L 2
North Wayne ....K 4
North Whitefield ..L 5
North Windham ..N 8
North Woodstock .K 2
North Yar-
  mouth ...1,156▲.N 9
Northeast Harbor .K 8
Northfield ...48▲.J 10
Northport ..727▲.K 6
Norway* .3,584▲.L 2
Norway ..2,654...L 2
Notre Dame .....A 9
Oak Hill ....N 3
Oakfield ...792▲.E 8
Oakland* .3,499▲.K 5
Oakland .1,880...K 5
Ogunquit ....O 2
Olamon ....I 7

Old Orchard
  Beach* ...5,313▲.N 3
Old Orchard
  Beach ....4,431...N 3
Old Town .9,001...I 7
Onawa ....H 5
Oquossoc ....I 2
Orient .....76▲.F 9
Orland ...1,248▲.K 7
Orono* ..9,796▲.J 7
Orono ...3,234...J 7
Orrington .2,598▲.J 7
Orrs Island .....O 10
Osborn .....26..J 8
Otis ......119▲.J 8
Otisfield ...573▲.M 8
Otter Creek .....K 8
Owls Head .1,236▲.L 6
Oxbow .....83..D 7
Oxford ...2,271▲.L 3
Palermo ...629▲.K 5
Palmyra .1,084▲.J 5
Paris ....3,738▲.L 3
Parker Head ....N 11
Parkman ...436▲.I 5
Parsonfield .918▲.O 6
Passadumkeag 337▲.H 7
Patten* ..1,255▲.F 8
Patten ...1,099...F 8
Pejepscot ......N 10
Pemaquid ......N 12
Pembroke ..683▲.I 11
Penobscot .773▲.K 7
Perham ....423▲.C 8
Perry .....842▲.I 11
Peru .....1,268▲.K 3
Phillips ...946▲.J 3
Phippsburg .1,180▲.N 11
Pine Point ......N 3
Pittsfield* .4,140▲.J 5
Pittsfield .3,232...J 5
Pittston .1,613▲.L 4
Pittston Farm ....F 4
Plaisted ....B 7
Plantation
  Number 14* .27..I 10
Plantation
  Number 21* .83..I 10
Plantation
  Number 33* .44..I 8
Pleasant Island ..I 2
Pleasant Point ..M 6
Pleasant Pond ...H 4
Pleasant
  Ridge ....113..I 4
Plymouth ..527▲.J 6
Poland ...1,995▲.M 8
Poland Spring ...M 9
Popham Beach ...O 11
Port Clyde ......C 8
Portage ....C 8
Portage
  Lake* ....442▲.C 8
Porter ....652▲.N 6
Portland .64,304▲.N 9
Pownal ....806▲.N 9
Prentiss ...158▲.G 9
Presque Isle 11,110..C 9
Princeton .937▲.H 10
Pripet ....K 7
Prospect ...370▲.K 7

Prospect Harbor ...K 8
Pulpit Harbor ....L 7
Quimby ....B 7
Randolph* .1,766▲.L 4
Randolph .1,585...L 4
Rangeley* ..887▲.J 2
Rangeley ...35..J 2
Raymond .1,300▲.N 8
Readfield .1,276▲.K 4
Readfield Depot ..K 4
Reed ......259..G 8
Richmond* .2,153▲.M 11
Richmond .1,412...M 11
Richmond Corner .M 10
Ripley ....299▲.I 5
Riverside ....K 4
Robbinston .377▲.I 11
Robinhood ......N 11
Robinsons ....K 9
Rockland .8,197.▲L 6
Rockport .2,011▲.L 6
Rockwood ....G 4
Rome ......369▲.K 4
Roque Bluffs .147▲.J 10
Round Pond .....N 12
Roxbury ...275▲.J 2
Rumford* .9,289▲.K 2
Rumford .7,233...K 2
Rumford Center ..K 2
Rumford Point ...K 2
Sabattus ......M 10
Saco ....11,625...N 3
St. Agatha .856▲.A 8
St. Albans .995▲.I 5
St. David ....A 8
St. Francis .807..B 7
St. George .1,579▲.L 6
St. John ...360..A 7
Salem ....I 3
Salsbury Cove ...K 8
Sandy Creek ....M 7
Sandy Point ....J 6
Sandy River .49..I 2
Sanford* .15,646▲.N 2
Sanford .10,936...N 2
Sangerville .1,085▲.I 5
Saponac ....L 7
Sargentville .....L 7
Scarborough 7,689▲.N 3
Seal Cove ....L 8
Seal Harbor .....L 8
Searsmont .885▲.K 6
Searsport .1,869▲.K 6
Seawall ....L 8
Sebago ....686▲.N 7
Sebago Lake ....N 8
Sebasco Estates ..O 10
Sebec .....330▲.H 6
Sebec Lake .....H 6
Seboeis ....64..H 7
Seboomook ......F 4
Sedgwick ..560▲.K 7
Selden ....M 11
Shapleigh .462▲.N 2
Shawmut ....J 5
Sheepscot ......M 11
Sheridan ....C 8
Sherman ...945▲.F 8
Sherman Mills ...F 8
Sherman Station ..F 8
Shin Pond ......E 7

Shirley* ....169▲.H 5
Shirley Mills .....H 5
Sidney ...1,337▲.K 4
Sinclair ....B 8
Skowhegan* .7,639▲.J 5
Skowhegan .6,667.▲J 5
Small Point
  Beach ....O 11
Smithfield ..521▲.J 4
Smithville ....K 9
Smyrna ....311▲.E 8
Smyrna Mills .....E 8
Soldier Pond ....B 7
Solon .....674▲.I 4
Somerville ..215▲.K 5
Sorrento ...196▲.K 8
South Addison ...K 9
South
  Berwick* .3,498▲.O 2
South
  Berwick ..1,773...O 2
South
  Bristol ....655▲.N 12
South Casco .....N 8
South China .....K 5
South Dover .....I 6
South Eliot .1,730...O 2
South Freeport ..N 10
South Gouldsboro .K 8
South Harpswell ..O 10
South Hiram .....M 10
South Hope .....L 6
South Lagrange ..I 7
South Lebanon ...O 1
South Lincoln ...H 7
South Orrington ..J 7
South
  Paris ...2,063.▲L 2
South Penobscot ..K 7
South Port-
  land ...22,586...O 9
South Sebec .....B 6
South
  Thomaston .799▲.L 6
South Trescott ...J 11
South Warren ...L 6
South
  Waterford .....L 2
South Wind-
  ham ....1,142...O 8
South Windsor ...L 5
South
  Woodstock .....K 2
Southport ..456▲.N 11
Southwest
  Harbor ..1,589▲.L 8
Springfield ..324▲.H 8
Springvale .2,379...N 2
Spruce Head ....M 6
Squa Pan ....D 8
Stacyville ..528▲.F 7
Standish .3,088▲.O 8
Starboard ....J 10
Starks ....324▲.J 4
State Road ......J 5
Steep Falls .....N 7
Stetson ...385▲.I 6
Steuben ...657▲.K 9
Stickney
  Corner ....L 5
Stockholm ..376▲.B 8

Stockton
  Springs .1,108▲.K 7
Stoneham* ..163▲.L 2
Stonington .1,264▲.L 7
Stow ......103▲.L 1
Stratton ....J 3
Strong ...1,097▲.J 3
Sullivan ...797▲.K 8
Sumner ....490▲.K 3
Sunset ....L 7
Sunshine ....L 7
Surry .....600▲.K 7
Swans
  Island ....305▲.L 8
Swanville ..475▲.K 6
Sweden ....103▲.L 2
Sweden ....B 8
Talmadge ...23▲.H 9
Temple ....354▲.J 3
Tenants Harbor ..M 6
The Forks ...33..H 4
Thomaston .2,583▲.L 6
Thomaston .2,342...L 6
Thorndike ..423▲.K 6
Topsfield ....H 9
Topsham* .4,959▲.N 10
Topsham ..2,240...N 10
Tremont ...970▲.K 8
Trenton ...373▲.K 8
Trevett ....N 11
Troy ......499▲.J 6
Turner ...2,194▲.L 3
Turner Center ...L 3
Union ....1,153▲.L 6
Unity .....1,208▲.J 5
Unity* ......42..J 5
Upper French-
  ville ....A 8
Upper Gloucester .M 9
Upton ......46▲.J 1
Van Buren* .3,960▲.B 9
Van Buren .3,589...B 9
Vanceboro .239▲.G 10
Vassalboro .2,640▲.K 4
Veazie ...1,530▲.J 7
Verona ....421▲.K 7
Vienna ....208▲.K 4
Vinalhaven .1,181▲.L 7
Wade .....248▲.B 8
Waite ......69▲.H 9
Waldo .....418▲.K 6
Waldoboro .3,054▲.L 5
Wales .....602▲.L 4
Wallagrass .622..B 7
Walpole ....N 12
Waltham ...167▲.L 8
Warren ...1,851▲.L 6
Washburn* .1,916▲.C 8
Washburn .1,055...C 8
Washington .688▲.L 5
Waterboro .1,158▲.N 2
Waterboro Center .N 2
Waterford ..751▲.L 2
Waterville .18,143...K 5
Wayne .....548▲.K 4
Webster ....65..G 8
Webster* .4,747...J 7
Webster .1,658▲.M 10
Weeks Mills .....K 5
Welchville ......L 3
Weld .....332▲.J 3

Wellington .222▲.I 5
Wells ....4,158▲.O 2
Wesley ....110▲.I 10
West Appleton ...K 6
West Baldwin ....N 7
West Bath ..828▲.N 10
West Bethel .....K 2
West Bowdoin ...M 10
West Buxton .....O 8
West Cumberland .N 9
West Enfield ....H 7
West Farmington ..J 3
West Forks ...66..H 4
West Franklin ...K 8
West
  Gardiner .1,431▲.L 4
West Gouldsboro .K 8
West Kennebunk ..O 2
West Lebanon ...O 1
West Levant .....I 6
West Lubec .....I 11
West Minot ......L 3
West Mount
  Vernon ....K 4
West Newfield ...O 6
West Paris .1,146▲.K 2
West Peru ....K 3
West Point ......M 8
West Poland .....M 8
West Rockport ...L 6
West Scarboro ...N 3
West Sullivan ...K 8
West Sumner ....K 3
West Tremont ...K 8
West Trenton ....L 8
Westbrook .14,428...O 9
Westfield ...516▲.D 9
Westmanland .38..B 8
Weston ....156▲.G 9
Westport ...209▲.N 11
Whitefield .1,119▲.L 5
Whiting ....266▲.J 11
Whitneyville .165▲.J 10
Willimantic ..566▲.H 5
Wilsons Mills ....I 1
Wilton* ..3,756▲.K 3
Wilton ..1,761...K 3
Windham* .6,526▲.N 8
Windsor .1,125▲.K 5
Winn ......540▲.G 8
Winslow* .7,459▲.K 5
Winslow .3,640...K 5
Winslows Mills ...L 5
Winter
  Harbor .1,017▲.K 9
Winterport .1,954▲.J 7
Winterville ..150..B 7
Winthrop .4,247▲.K 4
Winthrop .2,260...K 4
Wiscasset .2,183.▲M 11
Woodland .1,208▲.B 8
Woodland .1,393...I 10
Woodstock .1,003▲.K 2
Woodville ..56▲.G 8
Woolwich .1,681▲.N 11
Wytopitlock ......G 9
Yarmouth* .4,814▲.N 9
Yarmouth .2,913...N 9
York .....5,561▲.O 2
York Beach ......O 2
York Harbor .....O 2

▲Population of entire town (township), including rural area
*Does not appear on map; key shows general location.
○County seat

Sources: Latest census figures (1970 preliminary census where available or 1960 census). Cities and towns without population information are unincorporated places under 1,000 in population and are not listed in census reports.

MAINE/People

The 1970 preliminary United States census reported that Maine had 977,260 persons. The population had increased about 1 per cent over the 1960 census figure of 969,265.

About 51 per cent of Maine's people live in urban areas. That is, they live in or near municipalities with 2,500 or more persons. Maine's largest cities, in order of size, are Portland, Lewiston, Bangor, Auburn, South Portland, and Augusta. Most of the large cities are in the southern part of the state, near the coast. See the separate articles on Maine cities listed in the *Related Articles* at the end of this article.

Maine has two Standard Metropolitan Statistical Areas (see METROPOLITAN AREA). These areas are (1) Lewiston-Auburn and (2) Portland. More than a fifth of the state's people live in these two areas. For the populations of these areas, see the *Index* to the political map of Maine.

Most of Maine's people were born in the United States. Their ancestors include settlers from Canada and most of the European countries. Roman Catholics make up Maine's largest single religious group. But there are more Protestants than Catholics in the state. The Protestant groups with the largest memberships include Baptists, Episcopalians, Methodists, and members of the United Church of Christ.

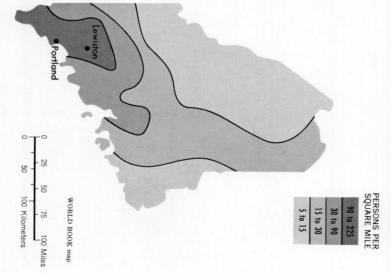

John C. Olson, Portland Press-Herald

Crowds of Shoppers stroll along Congress Street in downtown Portland. Portland is Maine's largest city.

Eric M. Sanford

Veteran Lobstermen mend their traps in Friendship. Almost every community on Maine's coast has at least a small fishing fleet.

POPULATION

This map shows the *population density* of Maine, and how it varies in different parts of the state. Population density means the average number of persons who live on each square mile.

PERSONS PER SQUARE MILE
90 to 225
30 to 90
15 to 30
5 to 15

Portland

Lewiston

0 25 50 75 100 Miles
0 25 50 100 Kilometers

WORLD BOOK map

MAINE / Education

Schools. Colonial Maine offered little opportunity for formal education. Parents and local ministers often served as teachers. The first school in Maine may have been an Indian mission founded in 1696 by Sebastian Rasle, a Roman Catholic priest. Maine's first known school for white children opened in York in 1701. The state's first schoolhouse was built in Berwick in 1719. A school fund was provided by the legislature in 1828. Schools began to receive tax support in 1868.

A commissioner of education and a 10-member board of education head Maine's public-school system. The governor appoints the board members, and they choose the commissioner. Children must attend school between the ages of 7 and 17. For the number of students and teachers in Maine, see EDUCATION (table).

Libraries. One of Maine's earliest libraries was formed in 1751. This collection of books alternated between parish houses in Kittery and York. Maine now has about 250 public libraries. Bookmobiles serve many areas that do not have a library.

Maine's biggest library is the State Library in Augusta. This library and the Maine Historical Library in Portland own large collections of books about Maine and its history. Maine's largest public libraries are the Bangor Public Library and the Portland Public Library. The libraries of Bowdoin College, Colby College, and the University of Maine rank among the state's largest school libraries.

Museums. The Maine State Museum, in the State House in Augusta, features exhibits on natural history. The Bowdoin College Museum of Art has paintings and drawings by American, European, and Oriental artists. The Portland Museum of Art owns large collections of paintings and sculptures. The Robert Abbe Museum of Stone Age Antiquities features Indian items. Other museums include the Treat Gallery in Lewiston, the Brick Store Museum in Kennebunk, the William A. Farnsworth Library and Art Museum in Rockland, and the L.D.M. Sweat Memorial in Portland. See also the *Places to Visit* section of this article.

UNIVERSITIES AND COLLEGES

Maine has nine universities and colleges accredited by the New England Association of Colleges and Secondary Schools. For enrollments and further information, see UNIVERSITIES AND COLLEGES (table).

Name	Location	Founded
Bangor Theological Seminary	Bangor	1905
Bates College	Lewiston	1855
Bowdoin College	Brunswick	1794
Colby College	Waterville	1813
Maine, University of	*	1864
Nasson College	Springvale	1912
Ricker College	Houlton	1949
St. Francis College	Biddeford	1953
St. Joseph's College	North Windham	1915

*For the campuses of the University of Maine, see UNIVERSITIES AND COLLEGES (table).

The University of Maine is in Orono. The Memorial Union, *background*, and the Raymond H. Fogler Library, *right*, stand at the center of the campus. The university also has campuses in Aroostook, Farmington, Gorham, and Portland.

University of Maine

Maine's beautiful coastal area attracts thousands of vacationers yearly. Visitors enjoy the rugged beauty of Atlantic waters pounding against rocky shores, and the many lighthouses along the coast. Hundreds of sandy beaches, bays, coves, and inlets provide recreation for swimmers, fishermen, and sailing enthusiasts. Inland, hunters stalk bears, deer, and many other game animals in the vast wilderness of the north. Fishermen can try their luck in 2,500 lakes and ponds and 5,000 rivers and streams. Skiers and climbers enjoy Maine's mountains. Maine's skiing season lasts from about mid-December to mid-April. The state also has many historic sites, and picturesque landmarks such as small white churches.

Boothbay Harbor, a Resort Village on Maine's Atlantic Coast

Kabel Art Photo, Publix

Lobster Bake on the Maine Coast

Maine Dept. of Economic Development

PLACES TO VISIT

Following are brief descriptions of some of Maine's many interesting places to visit.

Black Mansion, in Ellsworth, is often called *Maine's Mount Vernon*. It resembles George Washington's Virginia home, *Mount Vernon*. Built about 1820, the Black Mansion has a low porch supported by five tall columns. Other features include fine china, silverware, furniture, and a winding staircase.

Burnham Tavern, in Machias, is the place where colonists met in 1775 to plot the capture of the British ship *Margaretta*. The capture was made during the first naval battle of the Revolutionary War. Burnham Tavern, built about 1770, still displays its original sign: "Drink for the thirsty, food for the hungry, lodging for the weary, and good keeping for horses."

First Parish Church is a Unitarian church in Portland. It was the site of Maine's only constitutional convention, in 1819. Many of Portland's wealthiest families worshiped in the church during the 1700's and 1800's. **Fort Western**, in Augusta, dates from 1754. It was at

this fort that Benedict Arnold and his men met before marching up Maine to attack Quebec in 1775.

Old Gaol Museum, in York, is the oldest public building in Maine. It was built in 1653, and served as a *gaol* (jail) until 1860. Old Gaol Museum now houses local history relics.

Penobscot Marine Museum, in Searsport, displays valuable paintings, ship models, old sailing charts, navigation instruments, fishing and whaling equipment, ships' logs, books, and other historical items.

Portland Head Light, near Portland, towers 101 feet amid surf-beaten rocks. Built in 1791, it ranks among the oldest and most famous American lighthouses.

Seashore Trolley Museum, near Kennebunkport, is the largest U.S. museum that exhibits only electric railroad equipment.

Tate House is the oldest house in Portland. This three-story wooden structure was built in 1775. It includes quarters once used by slaves.

Wadsworth-Longfellow House, in Portland, ranks

72

Wedding Cake House in Kennebunk

Dearborn's Studio

Portland Head Light in Portland Harbor

Maine Dept. of Economic Development

Ox-Pulling Contest at the Fryeburg Fair

Dick Smith

Thunder Hole in Acadia National Park

David Corson, Shostal

Wadsworth-Longfellow House in Portland

Greater Portland Chamber of Commerce

as Maine's most popular historic site. This three-story brick building was the boyhood home of Henry Wadsworth Longfellow, the famous poet.

Wedding Cake House, in Kennebunk, is a two-story, square house with elaborate outside decorations. According to legend, a sea captain was ordered to sea in an emergency, and his bride had no wedding cake. So he added the decorations to make the house look like a wedding cake.

National Park and Forest. Acadia National Park, in southeastern Maine, is the only national park in New England. See ACADIA NATIONAL PARK.

White Mountain National Forest lies chiefly in New Hampshire, but part of it extends into southwestern Maine. See NATIONAL FOREST (table).

State Parks and Memorials. Maine has 22 state parks and 15 state memorials. It has no state forest system. For information on the state parks and memorials, write to Director, Maine State Park and Recreation Commission, State House, Augusta, Me. 04330.

Many of Maine's most popular annual events are sports contests. The summer months feature boat races and other water-sports contests. Among the state's outstanding annual events is the Maine Seafoods Festival. This celebration is held in Rockland during the first weekend in August.

Other annual events include the following.

January-June: Winter activities in Auburn, Bethel, Camden, Farmington, Jackman, Kingfield, Locke Mills, and other places (January and February); Corpus Christi processions in Fort Kent, Frenchville, St. Agatha, and Van Buren (first Sunday in June).

July-December: Windjammer Days at Boothbay Harbor (July); Maine Broiler Festival in Belfast (July); Blueberry Festival in Union (August); Retired Skippers Race in Castine (August); Fairs in Bangor, Cumberland Center, Farmington, Fryeburg, Presque Isle, Skowhegan, Topsham, Union, and Windsor (various times during the summer and in early autumn); Maine State Fair in Lewiston (first week in September).

ANNUAL EVENTS

73

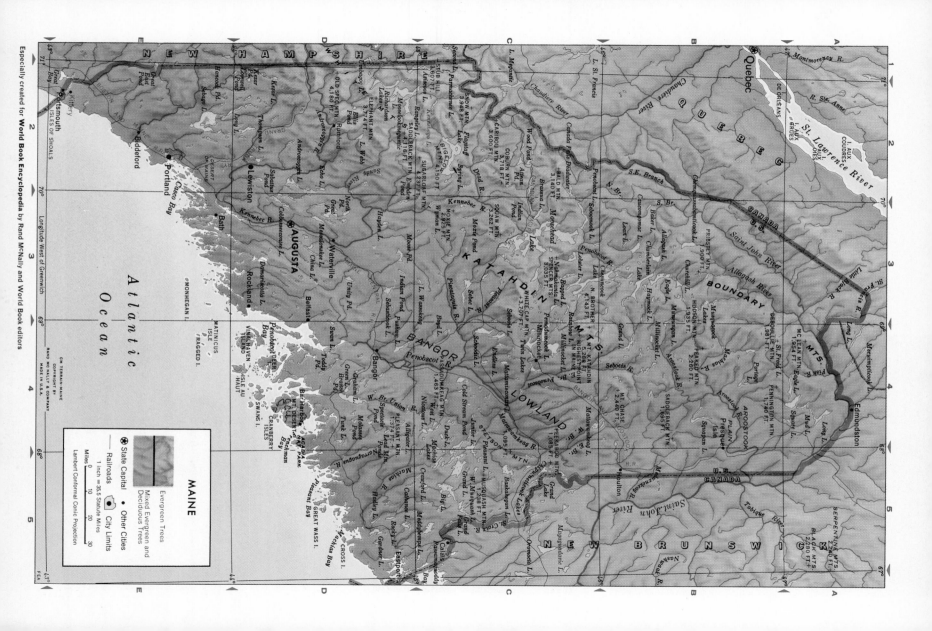

Longitude West of Greenwich

QUEBEC

CANADA
U.S.

BOUNDARY

NEW BRUNSWICK

KATAHDIN

LOWLAND

BANGOR

Atlantic
Ocean

NEW HAMPSHIRE

MAINE

Evergreen Trees

Mixed Evergreen and
Deciduous Trees

⊛ State Capital
● Other Cities
━━ Railroads
City Limits
Miles 0   10   20   30
1 inch = 35.5 Statute Miles
Lambert Conformal Conic Projection

Portsmouth
Kittery
ISLES OF SHOALS
Biddeford
Portland
Casco Bay
Bath
Lewiston
AUGUSTA
Waterville
Rockland
Belfast
Bangor
Houlton
Presque Isle
Calais
Eastport
Edmundston

MAINE / The Land

Land Regions. Maine has three natural land regions. They are, from southeast to northwest: (1) the Coastal Lowlands, (2) the Eastern New England Upland, and (3) the White Mountains Region.

The Coastal Lowlands cover southeastern Maine. They are part of a large region of the same name that stretches along the entire New England coast. In Maine, the region extends from 10 to 40 miles inland from the Atlantic Ocean. Sandy beaches line the coast in the south. Old Orchard Beach, with 11 miles of hard-packed sand, is one of the longest and smoothest beaches on the Atlantic Coast. Salt marshes, crossed by tidal creeks, lie west of the beaches. In the northeast, the beaches shrink to small bays or strips of sand between high cliffs.

Most of the Coastal Lowlands lie near sea level. The land was once much higher. It was pushed down thousands of years ago, during the Ice Age, by the great weight of ice and snow. The tops of sunken hills form more than 400 offshore islands between about 2 and 25 square miles in area, and thousands of smaller islands. Mount Desert, Maine's largest island, covers about 100 square miles.

The Eastern New England Upland lies northwest of the Coastal Lowlands. The entire upland extends from the Canadian border to Connecticut. In Maine, the region is from 20 to 50 miles wide. The land rises from elevations near sea level in the east to several thousand feet in the west. The Aroostook Plateau lies in the northeasternmost part of the region. The plateau's deep fertile soil is good for agriculture. Farmers there grow the country's second largest potato crop. Many lakes dot the Eastern New England Upland south of the Aroostook Plateau. Swift streams also flow through this area. Most of them are fed by springs and by melted snow. Mountains cut through the center of the region.

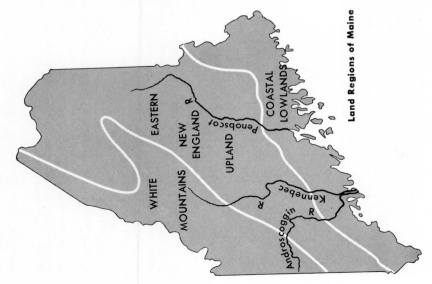

Land Regions of Maine

WHITE MOUNTAINS
EASTERN NEW ENGLAND UPLAND
COASTAL LOWLANDS
Penobscot R.
Kennebec R.
Androscoggin R.

Erle M. Sanford

Fields of Potatoes thrive in the deep fertile soil of Aroostook County. This area is part of Maine's Eastern New England Upland region, which extends from the Canadian border to Connecticut.

The White Mountains Region covers northwestern Maine and part of New Hampshire and Vermont. In Maine, the region is about 5 miles wide in the north and 30 miles wide in the south. The White Mountains Region includes hundreds of lakes and most of Maine's highest mountains. The mountains are an extension of New Hampshire's White Mountains. A series of *eskers* (also called *kames, horsebacks,* or *hogbacks*) covers part of the White Mountains Region. These long, low gravel ridges vary from 1 to about 150 miles long. The eskers were formed during the Ice Age by streams that flowed beneath the glaciers.

Coastline of Maine has thousands of bays, coves, and inlets. Measured in a straight line, the coastline totals 228 miles. But if all the coastal area washed by water is measured, the coastline totals 3,478 miles. The Maine coastline includes many deep harbors.

Mountains. Mount Katahdin is the highest peak in Maine. It rises 5,268 feet in the central part of the state. Nine other Maine mountains are more than 4,000 feet high, and 97 others are over 3,000 feet high. Most mountains in Maine are heavily forested and look green all year long. Cadillac Mountain towers 1,530 feet on Mount Desert Island. It is the highest point on the Atlantic coast between Labrador, Canada, and Rio de Janeiro, Brazil.

Rivers and Lakes. Maine has more than 5,000 rivers and streams. Two of the chief rivers, the Androscoggin and the Saco, begin in New Hampshire. They flow across southern Maine and empty into the Atlantic Ocean. Two other important rivers, the Kennebec and the Penobscot, rise in lakes of north-central Maine. They wind down the center of the state, and empty into coastal bays. The St. Croix River forms the southern part of the border between Maine and New Brunswick. In northern Maine, the Saint John River also is part of the border with New Brunswick. The Saint John is the longest river in the northern part of the state.

Many of Maine's more than 2,500 lakes and ponds gleam like blue gems among dark forests. Moosehead, the largest lake, covers about 120 square miles in the west-central part of the state. Other large lakes in Maine include the Belgrades, the Grands, the Rangeley, and the Sebago.

Ralph Crowell

Mount Katahdin, below, is the highest point in Maine. It rises 5,268 feet near the center of the state. Mount Katahdin is one of many tall rugged peaks that add beauty to Maine and help make it a favorite recreation center.

Maine Dept. of Economic Development

Fort Knox State Park, above, is near Bucksport in the Coastal Lowlands. The land in this region varies. Sandy beaches and high cliffs line the shore, and salt marshes lie inland.

MAINE / Climate

Maine has cooler weather than most of the rest of the United States. Arctic air and coastal winds keep the state from being warmed by Gulf Stream air. This makes Maine winters colder than winters in many places that are as far north. Maine has few hot summer days.

January temperatures in Maine average 24° F. July temperatures average 67° F. Maine's record low temperature, −48° F., was recorded in Van Buren on Jan. 19, 1925. The state's highest temperature, 105° F., was recorded in North Bridgton on July 10, 1911.

Maine's yearly *precipitation* (rain, melted snow, and other forms of moisture) averages about 43 inches. The annual snowfall varies from about 70 inches near the coast to about 100 inches in the interior.

Maine Dept. of Economic Development

Heavy Winter Snow blankets Sugarloaf Mountain near King-field. Low temperatures keep the snow in ideal condition for skiing.

SEASONAL TEMPERATURES

JANUARY

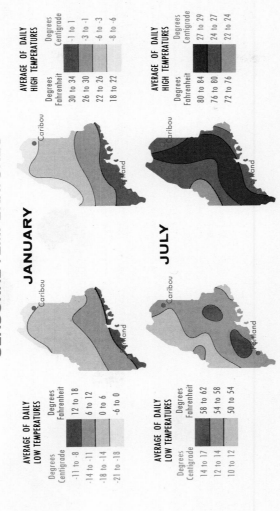

AVERAGE OF DAILY HIGH TEMPERATURES

Degrees Fahrenheit	Degrees Centigrade
30 to 34	−1 to 1
26 to 30	−3 to −1
22 to 26	−6 to −3
18 to 22	−8 to −6

AVERAGE OF DAILY LOW TEMPERATURES

Degrees Centigrade	Degrees Fahrenheit
−11 to −8	12 to 18
−14 to −11	6 to 12
−18 to −14	0 to 6
−21 to −18	−6 to 0

JULY

AVERAGE OF DAILY HIGH TEMPERATURES

Degrees Fahrenheit	Degrees Centigrade
80 to 84	27 to 29
76 to 80	24 to 27
72 to 76	22 to 24

AVERAGE OF DAILY LOW TEMPERATURES

Degrees Fahrenheit	Degrees Centigrade
58 to 62	14 to 17
54 to 58	12 to 14
50 to 54	10 to 12

AVERAGE YEARLY PRECIPITATION
(Rain, Melted Snow, and Other Moisture)

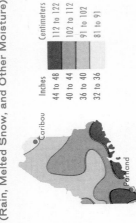

Inches	Centimeters
44 to 48	112 to 122
40 to 44	102 to 112
36 to 40	91 to 102
32 to 36	81 to 91

0	100	200 Miles
0	100	200	300 Kilometers

MONTHLY WEATHER IN CARIBOU AND PORTLAND													
		JAN	FEB	MAR	APR	MAY	JUNE	JULY	AUG	SEPT	OCT	NOV	DEC
CARIBOU	Average of: High Temperatures	18	20	31	43	59	69	75	72	63	51	36	22
	Low Temperatures	−1	0	13	26	38	48	54	51	43	33	22	7
	Days of Rain or Snow	14	13	13	13	14	14	12	11	11	11	13	14
PORTLAND	Days of Rain or Snow	12	11	12	13	12	9	9	8	8	8	11	11
	High Temperatures	31	32	41	52	63	73	79	77	70	60	47	35
	Low Temperatures	11	11	22	32	42	51	57	55	47	37	28	16

Temperatures are given in degrees Fahrenheit.

Source: U.S. Weather Bureau

Manufacturing is Maine's most important economic activity. The tourist industry ranks second, followed by agriculture. The southeast is Maine's chief manufacturing center. The more than 3½ million tourists who visit Maine annually contribute about $400 million to the state's economy. The coastal area attracts the most tourists. Farms thrive in southern and northeastern Maine.

Natural Resources of Maine include forests, swift rivers and streams, fertile soils, and mineral deposits.

Soil in Maine ranges from sand in the coastal area to rich loams in the potato-growing districts of Aroostook County and other regions. Clay soils cover much of Maine's lowlands. These soils once supported many small farms. But most of the farms have been abandoned or made into tree farms. Gravelly soils are common at Maine's higher elevations. These soils once supported farms. But they are not well suited to crops, and have been largely abandoned since 1930.

Minerals. Central Maine has many granite and limestone deposits, but few of them are mined. Slate deposits lie near Brownville and Monson. The one at Monson is mined. Large feldspar mines operate in Oxford County. Mica, and gemstones including beryl and tourmaline, are found in small quantities with the feldspar. Aroostook County has one of the country's largest reserves of low-grade manganese and iron ore. Other Maine minerals include brick clay, copper, peat, sand and gravel, and zinc.

Forests cover more than 17,425,000 acres in Maine, or 87 per cent of the total land area. The forests supply the raw material for many manufactured products of Maine. Private companies and individuals control almost 99 of every 100 acres of Maine's forest land. Until the late 1700's, the white pine tree was Maine's greatest resource. It was used mainly to make masts for ships. By the mid-1800's, the pines had been cut down throughout the state. Today, Maine's many pines are second-growth trees. Other valuable trees include the balsam fir, basswood, beech, hemlock, maple, oak, spruce, and white and yellow birch.

Plant Life. The speckled alder, a common shrub, thrives in Maine's swamps and pastures. Witch hazel borders much of the state's forest land. Chokeberries, shadbush, sumac, and thorn apples grow along country roads and farm fences, and in old cellar holes. Blueberry bushes carpet the ground in much of Hancock and Washington counties and in a few other areas.

Maine's most common wild flowers are the anemone, aster, bittersweet, black-eyed Susan, buttercup, goldenrod, harebell, hepatica, Indian pipe, orange and red hawkweed, white oxeye daisy, and wild bergamot. The delicate mayflower and the lady's-slipper are found scattered through many of Maine's wooded areas. Jack-in-the-pulpit, knotgrass, lavender, and wild lily of the valley grow along the coast and border the shores of many lakes in the state.

FARM, MINERAL, AND FOREST PRODUCTS

This map shows where the state's leading farm, mineral, and forest products are produced. The major urban areas (shown on the map in red) are the state's important manufacturing centers.

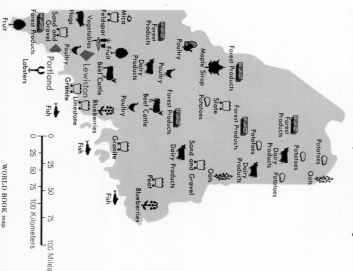

WORLD BOOK map

74d

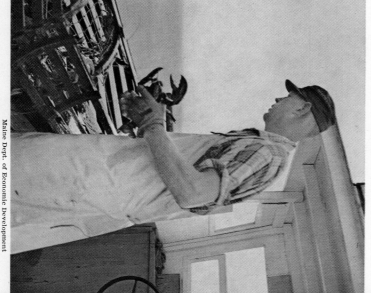

Lobsterman carefully removes a day's catch from his traps near Deer Isle. Maine leads all the states in the amount of lobsters caught—about 20 million pounds annually.

Maine Dept. of Economic Development

Mounds of Logs fill the yard of a paper mill in Bucksport. Wood processing is Maine's leading manufacturing activity. The most important manufactured products are paper and pulp. Factories get their raw materials from the state's vast forests.

Devaney

MAINE'S PRODUCTION IN 1967

Total value of goods produced—$1,340,755,000

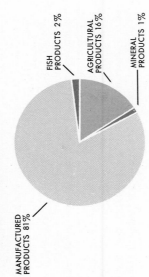

MANUFACTURED PRODUCTS 81%

FISH PRODUCTS 2%

AGRICULTURAL PRODUCTS 16%

MINERAL PRODUCTS 1%

Note: Manufacturing percentage based on value added by manufacture. Other percentages based on value of production.

Source: U.S. Government statistics

MAINE'S EMPLOYMENT IN 1967

Total number of persons employed—343,600

	Number of Employees
Manufacturing	119,800
Wholesale & Retail Trade	62,400
Government	57,200
Services & Mining	41,700
Transportation & Public Utilities	17,800
Construction	17,600
Agriculture	16,200
Finance, Insurance & Real Estate	10,900

Source: U.S. Department of Labor

Animal Life. Black bears roam the wooded areas of northern Maine. Bobcats and lynxes live in all parts of the state, but especially in Aroostook and Penobscot counties. Other fur-bearing animals of the forests include beavers, foxes, martens, minks, raccoons, and skunks.

Game animals are found in almost every part of Maine. They include chipmunks, rabbits, squirrels, and white-tailed deer. Deer are Maine's leading attraction for hunters. Moose live in isolated areas and are protected from hunters by law. A herd of caribou was brought to Mount Katahdin from Canada in 1963. Caribou were once common in Maine, but none had lived in the state for many years.

More than 320 kinds of birds live in Maine. The most common ones are buntings, chickadees, grackles, owls, sparrows, swallows, thrushes, and wrens. Ducks, gulls, loons, and other sea birds live on the coastal islands. In early spring and late fall, thousands of migratory ducks and geese congregate at Merrymeeting Bay, where the Androscoggin and Kennebec rivers meet.

Maine's most common game fishes in lakes and streams are brook trout and landlocked salmon. Other fishes include bass, white and yellow perch, and pickerel. Every spring, thousands of alewives swim up the coastal rivers to lay their eggs. Then they return to the ocean. Atlantic salmon are found in the Dennys, Machias, and other rivers. Fishes in Maine's coastal waters include flounders, mackerel, pollack, striped bass, and tuna.

Manufacturing, including processing, accounts for about 81 per cent of the value of goods produced in Maine. Goods manufactured there have a *value added by manufacture* of about $1 billion a year. This figure represents the value created in products by Maine in-

74e

74f

dustries, not counting such manufacturing costs as materials, supplies, and fuel.

Paper and Related Products are Maine's leading manufactured products. These products have a value added of about $283,200,000 yearly. The manufacture of paper ranks as Maine's most important industry. There are large paper and pulp mills in Augusta, Brewer, Bucksport, East Millinocket, Jay, Lincoln, Madawaska, Millinocket, Rumford, Topsham, Waterville, Winslow, and Woodland. The Great Northern Paper Company, with factories in Millinocket and East Millinocket, is the nation's largest producer of newsprint. Spruce and fir trees provide most of the wood used in Maine's paper and pulp industries.

Leather and Leather Products in Maine have a value added of about $200 million a year. The manufacture of shoes, Maine's chief leather product, employs more workers than any other single industry. Shoes and other footwear are made in Bangor, Belfast, Farmington, Gardiner, Livermore Falls, Norridgewock, North Jay, Old Town, Skowhegan, Wilton, and many other cities and towns.

Food and Food Products. Maine is an important food canning and food freezing state. Blueberries, French fried potatoes, and peas are the chief frozen foods processed in the state. Maine leads the states in the number of sardines packed each year. Maine factories also pack large quantities of clams, lobsters, scallops, and shrimps. Other processed foods include apple juice, beans, cucumbers, pickles, and sweet corn. The Aroostook County, Eastport-Lubec, and Portland areas are centers of Maine's food processing industry.

Lumber and Wood Products. Sawmills in Maine turn out about 450 million board feet of lumber and about 3 million cords of pulpwood a year. Maine's toothpick production, about 100 million a day, is the largest in the United States. Other products made from wood include boxes, canoes, clothespins, fencing, furniture, ice cream sticks, lobster traps, matches, skis, splints, toys, and wood flour. Millions of Maine fir trees are cut each year to be used as Christmas trees.

Textiles. Maine's textile industry has gradually declined since the 1920's. But the industry still plays an important part in the state's economy. Cotton mills are located in Augusta, Biddeford, and Lewiston. Woolen mills operate in the communities of Guilford, Kezar Falls, Lisbon, Oakland, and Waterville.

Other Industries. Maine has many small, thriving boatyards that build fishing and sailing craft. Blue Hill, Camden, East Boothbay, Mount Desert, Southwest Harbor, and Thomaston are the leading boat-building areas. The Bath Iron Works in Bath is one of the nation's largest shipbuilders. Machine tools, metal products, snowplows, and textile machinery are also manufactured in Maine.

Agriculture. Farm products account for about 16 per cent of the value of goods produced in Maine. Maine has a yearly farm income of about $221,600,000. The state's 12,900 farms average about 200 acres in size. About 8,000 Maine farms are full-time commercial farms, and about 3,200 are worked only part time. *Livestock and Livestock Products* account for about

65 per cent of the income earned by Maine farmers. Broiler raising earns more than any other livestock activity. Maine farmers raise almost 74 million broiler chickens worth more than $48 million each year. Eggs bring in about $38 million yearly. Dairy products, chiefly milk, earn about $36 million a year. Maine farmers also raise beef cattle, hogs, and turkeys.

Potatoes, Maine's leading field crop, earn about $50 million a year. Among the states, only Idaho grows more potatoes than Maine. Most of Maine's $3\frac{1}{2}$ billion pound annual potato crop comes from Aroostook County. Large amounts of potatoes also come from farms in Cumberland, Penobscot, Piscataquis, and Waldo counties.

Other Field Crops. Oats are an important field crop in Maine. Many farmers rotate oats and potatoes to keep soil fertile. Hay, once an important commercial product, is now raised chiefly as cattle feed. Many farmers also grow corn to feed cattle. Other crops raised in Maine include barley, buckwheat, dry beans, peas, sugar beets, and sweet corn.

Fruits. Apples, Maine's most valuable fruit, are grown chiefly in Androscoggin, Franklin, and Oxford counties. The chief varieties of apples include Cortland, Delicious, and McIntosh. Other Maine fruits include blueberries, raspberries, and strawberries.

Fishing Industry. Maine's annual fish catch is valued at about $23 million. Maine is a leading state in the value of fish caught. Its yearly lobster catch, which totals about 20 million pounds, is the largest of any state. Maine fishermen also bring in valuable amounts of bloodworms, clams, ocean perch, sardines,

Making Skis, this worker in a Paris factory smoothes the wood with a sander. Skis are one of Maine's many wood products.

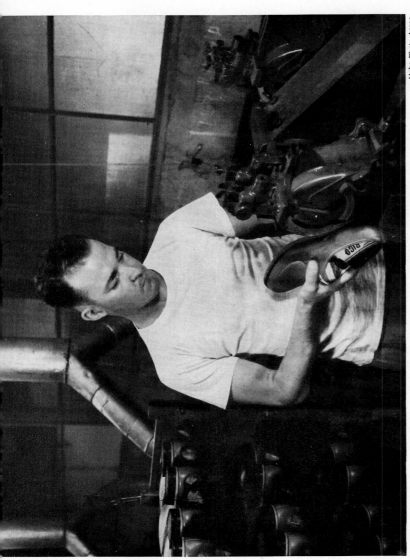

A Maine Shoemaker grinds the edge of a shoe sole to a smooth finish in an Auburn factory. Shoe manufacturers employ more

workers than any other industry in Maine. Shoes and other kinds of footwear are made in many communities throughout the state.

shrimps, and whiting. Portland and Rockland are the most important fishing ports in Maine. Almost every community along the coast has at least a small fleet of fishing boats.

Mining brings in about $15 million a year. Feldspar, used to make pottery and scouring powder, is an important mining product. Beryl and other gemstones are by-products of Maine's feldspar mining industry.

Maine has over a hundred granite quarries, but only a few of them are worked today. The most important ones are in southern and coastal Maine.

Limestone is also mined in Maine. Limestone is used in making cement. The only cement factory in New England is in Thomaston. Other products mined in Maine include clay and peat. The clay is chiefly used to make bricks. Peat is used to cover growing plants as protection against cold weather.

Electric Power. About two-thirds of Maine's electricity is produced by steam generating plants. Water power provides almost all of the rest. Most of Maine's hydroelectric plants are on the Androscoggin, Kennebec, Penobscot, and Saco rivers. For Maine's kilowatt-hour production, see ELECTRIC POWER (table).

Transportation. Maine began developing good roads during the early 1800's. Today, the state has about 21,200 miles of roads and highways, most of which are surfaced. The Maine Turnpike runs 106 miles between Kittery and Augusta. U.S. Interstate Highway 95 extends the turnpike from Augusta to Houlton, near the Canadian border. U.S. Highway 1 follows the coast of Maine.

Maine's first railroad was built in 1836 to carry lum-

ber between Bangor and Old Town. Railroads in the state now operate on about 1,800 miles of track. The Maine Central Railroad operates on about 800 miles of track, and the Bangor and Aroostook Railroad has about 550 miles of track. Neither of these freight railroads provides passenger service. The chief passenger line in the state is the Canadian Pacific Railroad.

Northeast Airlines provides Maine's only air passenger and airmail link with other parts of the United States. Maine has about 135 airports. In remote areas, pontoon planes often land vacationers on lakes.

Large ocean-going vessels can dock at some Maine ports. Portland and Searsport have the state's busiest docks. Portland is 116 miles nearer to Europe than any other large U.S. port. The 1,000-foot-long State Pier at Portland has $1\frac{1}{2}$ miles of track, and can hold as many as 110 freight cars.

Communication. Maine publishers issue 9 daily newspapers and about 35 weekly ones. The *Bangor Daily News* has the largest circulation of any newspaper in Maine. The Gannett newspaper chain publishes the *Daily Kennebec Journal*, the *Morning Sentinel* in Waterville, the *Portland Press Herald*, the *Portland Express*, and Maine's only Sunday newspaper, the *Maine Sunday Telegram* in Portland. The *Falmouth Gazette*, Maine's first newspaper, began in Falmouth (now Portland) in 1785.

Maine's first radio station, WABI, began operating in Bangor in 1924. The state's first television station, WABI-TV, started broadcasting in 1953, also from Bangor. Today, about 45 radio stations and 7 television stations operate in the state.

74g

HISTORIC MAINE

Northern Boundary with Canada was fixed by treaty in 1842. Earlier border disputes, called the Aroostook War, centered around Fort Kent.

● Fort Kent

In 1775, Benedict Arnold led an American army through the Kennebec Valley into Canada to attack Quebec.

Maine Entered the Union in 1820 as a free state (without slaves). Its admission was part of the Missouri Compromise.

Massachusetts Bought Maine for about $6,000 in 1677 from the heirs of Ferdinando Gorges, who had received the land as a gift in 1622.

An Early Sawmill was established near York in 1634. York (then called Gorgeana) became the nation's first incorporated English city in 1641.

● Portland

Invention of the Doughnut Hole in 1847 by Captain Hanson Gregory is still commemorated at Camden.

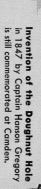

★ AUGUSTA

Shipbuilding became Maine's first industry. The first ship built by English colonists in America was launched on the Kennebec River in 1607.

Camden ●

● Kittery

● York

The Ranger, built at Kittery in 1777 and commanded by John Paul Jones, received the first salute given a man-of-war flying the Stars and Stripes.

The Popham Colony, the state's first settlement, was established in 1607 by English colonists near the mouth of the Kennebec River.

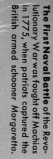

Machias ●

The First Naval Battle of the Revolutionary War was fought off Machias in 1775, when patriots captured the British armed schooner *Margaretta.*

MAINE / History

Indian Days. Thousands of Indians lived in what is now Maine before the white man came. The Indians belonged to the Abnaki and Etchemin tribes of the Algonkian Indian family. The Abnaki lived west of the Penobscot River, and the Etchemin lived east of the river. The Indians had villages, but often moved in search of food. Their enemy, the Iroquois, frequently raided their villages. Maine Indians lived in peace with the earliest white settlers.

Exploration and Settlements. Vikings, led by Leif Ericson, probably visited Maine about A.D. 1000. Many historians believe that John Cabot, an Italian sea captain in the service of England, reached Maine in 1498. France sent many explorers to Maine. These explorers and the dates they reached Maine included Giovanni da Verrazano (1524), Pierre du Guast, Sieur de Monts (1604), and Samuel de Champlain (1604). Champlain discovered and named Mount Desert, the largest island along Maine's coast.

In 1605, Sir Ferdinando Gorges and Sir John Popham, two wealthy Englishmen, sent George Waymouth to explore the Maine coast. Waymouth's favorable reports about the area led Gorges and Popham to attempt a settlement in Maine. In 1607, they financed a group of colonists who established Popham Plantation, near the mouth of the Kennebec River. Cold weather and other hardships forced the settlers to return to England in 1608. While in Maine, the settlers built a boat called the *Virginia*. It was the first boat built by English colonists in America. The English made many permanent settlements in Maine during the early 1620's. Perhaps the first one was the settlement made near present-day Saco in 1623.

Ownership Disputes developed over Maine during the 1600's. In 1622, the Council for New England, an agency of the English government, gave Ferdinando Gorges and John Mason a large tract of land in present-

day Maine and New Hampshire. The land was divided between the two men in 1629, and Gorges received the Maine section. Gorges established Maine's first government in 1636. In 1641, he made the community of Gorgeana (now York) a city. It was the first chartered English city in what is now the United States.

After Gorges died in 1647, the people of Kittery, Wells, and York united under a new government. Between 1652 and 1658, they and the people of Casco Bay,

Fort Popham Memorial is a brick and granite fortification begun in 1861 but never completed. Troops were stationed there as late as World War I. The fort stands near Popham Beach, where the first English settlement in Maine was established in 1607.

Maine Dept. of Economic Development

74i

Maine Dept. of Economic Development

A Fine Colonial Home, Montpelier, is a faithful reproduction of the mansion built by General Henry Knox in 1793. Knox was one of George Washington's most trusted advisers and the first U.S. Secretary of War. The 18-room home in Thomaston contains some of the original furnishings.

Kennebunk, Saco, and Scarborough agreed to make Maine a part of the Massachusetts Bay Colony. In 1660, the heirs of Gorges disputed Massachusetts' ownership of Maine, and claimed Maine for themselves. In 1664, an English board of commissioners ordered Maine restored to the Gorges family. Massachusetts finally gained clear title to Maine in 1677, when it bought the area from the Gorges family for about $6,000.

French and Indian Wars were fought in Maine and the rest of New England off and on from 1689 to 1763. The French and their Indian allies battled to gain control of the area from the English colonists. William Pepperell of Maine led the capture of a French fort at Louisbourg, Nova Scotia, in 1745. The capture was one of the major events of the war. The wars ended with the Treaty of Paris in 1763. The treaty ended all French claims to Maine and most of the rest of North America.

The Revolutionary War. During the 1760's, Great Britain passed a series of laws that caused unrest in Maine and the rest of colonial America. Most of these laws either imposed severe taxes or restricted colonial trade. In 1774, a group of Maine men burned a supply of British tea stored at York. This event, called the *York Tea Party*, resembled the more famous Boston Tea Party of 1773. Like the Boston Tea Party, the action symbolized colonial opposition to British taxation and trade policies.

The Revolutionary War (1775-1783) started at Lexington and Concord, Mass. Hundreds of Maine men joined the colonists' fight for independence. The war brought great hardships to Maine towns. The British blocked trade, causing a shortage in food and other vital goods. In 1775, British troops burned the town of Falmouth (now Portland) to punish the townspeople for opposing the king's policies.

The first naval battle of the Revolutionary War was fought off Machias in June, 1775. In the battle, a group of Maine patriots captured the British ship *Margaretta*. Also in 1775, Benedict Arnold and his troops made a long march from Augusta to Quebec. They tried to capture Quebec from the British, but were pushed back. British troops occupied Castine in 1779. Colonial troops tried to recapture the town, but were badly defeated.

Maine's population increased greatly after the war. Massachusetts rewarded its soldiers with gifts of land in Maine, and sold Maine land to other persons.

In the early 1800's, Maine's economy depended on its pine forests. Wood from the forests was used to build ships and many other products. It was also traded for a variety of goods. The Embargo Act of 1807, which limited U.S. trade with other countries, hurt Maine's thriving shipping industry. But the slowdown in shipping forced Maine to seek new income by developing its manufacturing industries.

Statehood. In 1785, a movement began for the separation of Maine from Massachusetts and for Maine's admission to the Union. Many people in Maine protested heavy taxation, poor roads, the long distance to the capital city of Boston, and other conditions. But before the War of 1812, most voters wanted Maine to remain a part of Massachusetts. The separation movement grew much stronger after the war. Many men who favored separation won election to the legislature. They swayed many voters to their side. The people voted for separation in 1819, and Maine entered the Union as the 23rd state on March 15, 1820. William King became the first state governor, and Portland was the first capital of Maine. Augusta became the capital in 1832.

Maine's admission to the Union became involved in the Missouri Compromise. The compromise called for Maine to enter the Union as a *free state* (a state without slaves) and Missouri to enter the Union as a slave state. This arrangement kept the number of slave and free states equal. See MISSOURI COMPROMISE.

Ever since 1783, the boundary between Maine and New Brunswick had been disputed. The argument led to the so-called Aroostook War of 1839. The U.S. government sent General Winfield Scott to Maine, and he reached a temporary agreement with Canadian officials. No fighting took place. The boundary was finally set by the Webster-Ashburton Treaty of 1842. See WEBSTER-ASHBURTON TREATY.

In 1851, Maine became the first state to pass a law prohibiting the manufacture and sale of alcoholic beverages. This law remained in force until 1934. Antislavery feelings grew strong in Maine during the

Published by Nathaniel Currier, 1855, The Mariners Museum,
Eldredge Collection, Newport News, Va.

early 1830's. The state's Baptists and Congregationalists opposed slavery especially strongly. About 72,000 Maine men served with the Union forces during the Civil War (1861-1865). Hannibal Hamlin, a former U.S. Senator and governor of Maine, served as Vice-President of the United States during the war under President Abraham Lincoln.

Industrial Development increased greatly after the Civil War. The textile and leather industries were among those that grew at record rates. Farming activity and rural populations decreased as industry grew. During the 1890's, Maine began developing hydroelectric power on its swift-running rivers. Businessmen competed for the best power sites, and the state legislature acted to protect the state's power interests. In 1909, the Maine legislature outlawed the sale of hydroelectric power outside the state. The legislature wanted to keep the power in Maine to attract new industries. The law remained in force until 1955.

The Early 1900's. In 1907, Maine adopted an initiative and referendum law (see INITIATIVE AND REFERENDUM). The state adopted a direct primary voting law in 1911. This law gives Maine voters a voice in choosing candidates for state elections.

THE GOVERNORS OF MAINE

		Party	Term
1.	William King	Democratic	1820-1821
2.	William D. Williamson	Democratic	1821
3.	Benjamin Ames	Democratic	1821-1822
4.	Albion K. Parris	Democratic	1822-1827
5.	Enoch Lincoln	Democratic	1827-1829
6.	Nathan Cutler	Democratic	1829-1830
7.	Joshua Hall	Democratic	1830
8.	Jonathan Hunton	National Republican	1830-1831
9.	Samuel E. Smith	Democratic	1831-1834
10.	Robert Dunlap	Democratic	1834-1838
11.	Edward Kent	Whig	1838-1839
12.	John Fairfield	Democratic	1839-1841
13.	Edward Kent	Whig	1841-1842
14.	John Fairfield	Democratic	1842-1843
15.	Edward Kavanagh	Democratic	1843-1844
16.	Hugh J. Anderson	Democratic	1844-1847
17.	John W. Dana	Democratic	1847-1850
18.	John Hubbard	Democratic	1850-1853
19.	William G. Crosby	Whig	1853-1855
20.	Anson P. Morrill	Republican	1855-1856
21.	Samuel Wells	Democratic	1856-1857
22.	Hannibal Hamlin	Republican	1857
23.	Joseph H. Williams	Republican	1857-1858
24.	Lot M. Morrill	Republican	1858-1861
25.	Israel Washburn, Jr.	Republican	1861-1863
26.	Abner Coburn	Republican	1863-1864
27.	Samuel Cony	Republican	1864-1867
28.	Joshua L. Chamberlain	Republican	1867-1871
29.	Sidney Perham	Republican	1871-1874
30.	Nelson Dingley, Jr.	Republican	1874-1876
31.	Seldon Connor	Republican	1876-1879
32.	Alonzo Garcelon	Democratic	1879-1880
33.	Daniel F. Davis	Republican	1880-1881
34.	Harris M. Plaisted	Democratic	1881-1883
35.	Frederick Robie	Republican	1883-1887
36.	Joseph R. Bodwell	Republican	1887
37.	S. S. Marble	Republican	1887-1889
38.	Edwin C. Burleigh	Republican	1889-1893
39.	Henry B. Cleaves	Republican	1893-1897
40.	Llewellyn Powers	Republican	1897-1901
41.	John Fremont Hill	Republican	1901-1905
42.	William T. Cobb	Republican	1905-1909
43.	Bert M. Fernald	Republican	1909-1911
44.	Frederick W. Plaisted	Democratic	1911-1913
45.	William T. Haines	Republican	1913-1915
46.	Oakley C. Curtis	Democratic	1915-1917
47.	Carl E. Milliken	Republican	1917-1921
48.	Frederic H. Parkhurst	Republican	1921
49.	Percival R. Baxter	Republican	1921-1925
50.	Ralph O. Brewster	Republican	1925-1929
51.	William Tudon Gardiner	Republican	1929-1933
52.	Louis J. Brann	Democratic	1933-1937
53.	Lewis O. Barrows	Republican	1937-1941
54.	Sumner Sewall	Republican	1941-1945
55.	Horace A. Hildreth	Republican	1945-1949
56.	Frederick G. Payne	Republican	1949-1952
57.	Burton M. Cross	Republican	1952-1955
58.	Edmund S. Muskie	Democratic	1955-1959
59.	Robert Haskell	Republican	1959
60.	Clinton Clauson	Democratic	1959
61.	John Reed	Republican	1959-1967
62.	Kenneth M. Curtis	Democratic	1967-

75

The number of small farms in Maine continued to decrease during the 1920's. Many large farms were started, especially in Aroostook County. These farms specialized in potato growing and in dairy and poultry products. Industrial growth also continued during the 1920's. However, some Maine textile mills moved to the South because of lower labor costs there. The state made up its loss with a greatly expanded paper and pulp industry. The Great Depression of the 1930's slowed Maine's economy. But conditions improved as the depression eased in the late 1930's.

The Mid-1900's. Margaret Chase Smith, a Maine Republican, won fame during the 1940's. She became the first woman to win election to both houses of the United States Congress. Mrs. Smith served in the House of Representatives from 1940 to 1949 and has served in the Senate ever since.

During World War II (1939-1945), Maine mills and factories produced military shoes and uniforms. Shipyards in Bath and South Portland built cargo and combat vessels. After the war, the state legislature passed laws to encourage industry to come to Maine. These laws included reduced tax rates for new businesses. The state also expanded its highway system, and businessmen built many motels for the growing tourist trade.

During the 1950's, Maine's economy was helped by the construction of Air Force bases in the state. Small-scale farming all but ended in Maine, and some of the state's oldest textile mills closed. Many small electronics companies were established in the state during this period.

The state Department of Economic Development, established in 1955, and various community development groups helped bring new industries to Maine during the 1960's. Paper and pulp companies expanded, and Maine's food-processing industry also grew. Improved skiing facilities attracted thousands of winter tourists. Politically, most Maine voters remained Republicans. But the Democratic Party gained strength during the 1950's and 1960's. In 1955, Edmund S. Muskie became Maine's first Democratic governor since 1937. In 1958, he became the first Democrat ever elected to the U.S. Senate from Maine. Muskie won re-election in 1964, and the Democrats won control of the state legislature. President Lyndon B. Johnson won Maine's electoral votes in 1964—the first time Maine voted for a Democratic presidential candidate in more than 50 years.

In 1966, the Republicans regained control of the state legislature. Muskie was the Democratic vice-presidential candidate in 1968. Maine supported him and presidential candidate Hubert H. Humphrey. In 1969, the Maine legislature approved state personal and corporate income taxes for the first time.

Maine Today is working to attract more people to live in the state and to bring in additional industries. Several developments indicate improvement for Maine's economy during the 1970's. Small farms in the state continue to decrease in number, but agriculture in general remains vital to Maine's economy. More plants are being built to process Maine potatoes, and the future of the state's broiler-chicken industry continues bright.

Paper and pulp manufacturing, the foundation of Maine's economy, is still expanding. Shoe and textile production contributes greatly to the economy, but both industries have been hurt by imported shoes and fabrics. An increase in the number of shrimp caught off the coast has boosted Maine's fishing industry, and tourism has become a year-round operation in the state.

Maine and other New England coastal states have claimed the rights to oil and other offshore resources beyond the traditional three-mile limit. But the federal government has disputed the claim. An oil refinery has been proposed for Machiasport, regardless of whether Maine wins its claim. Such a refinery could be expected to create jobs, lower fuel costs, and promote industrial growth.

ROGER W. REMINGTON, JOSEPH M. TREFETHEN, and ROBERT M. YORK

American Telephone and Telegraph Co.

Satellite Station near Andover is part of a worldwide communications system. This system includes the Telstar and Early Bird satellites. The station sends and receives signals, and tracks satellites as they orbit the earth. An inflated dome 161 feet high, background, covers an antenna. The control building, foreground, houses the station's computing and tracking equipment.

MAINE / Study Aids

Related Articles in WORLD BOOK include:

BIOGRAPHIES

Blaine, James G.
Coffin, Robert P. T.
Fessenden, William Pitt
Gilbreth, Frank B.
Hamlin, Hannibal
King (William)
Muskie, Edmund S.
Reed, Thomas B.
Sewall, Arthur
Smith, Margaret Chase

CITIES

Augusta
Bangor
Bar Harbor
Bath
Lewiston
Portland
Presque Isle

HISTORY

Acadia
Colonial Life in America
French and Indian Wars
Missouri Compromise
Webster-Ashburton Treaty

PHYSICAL FEATURES

Acadia National Park
Aroostook River
Kennebec River
Mount Desert
Passamaquoddy Bay
Penobscot River
Saint John River

PRODUCTS

For Maine's rank among the states in production, see the following articles:

Leather   Potato   Slate   Vegetable

OTHER RELATED ARTICLES

New England
Patriot's Day
Portsmouth Naval Shipyard

Outline

I. Government
  A. Constitution
  B. Executive
  C. Legislature
  D. Courts
  E. Local Government
  F. Taxation
  G. Politics

II. People

III. Education
  A. Schools
  B. Libraries
  C. Museums

IV. A Visitor's Guide
  A. Places to Visit
  B. Annual Events

V. The Land
  A. Land Regions
  B. Coastline
  C. Mountains
  D. Rivers and Lakes

VI. Climate

VII. Economy
  A. Natural Resources
  B. Manufacturing
  C. Agriculture
  D. Fishing Industry
  E. Mining
  F. Electric Power
  G. Transportation
  H. Communication

VIII. History

Questions

What caused the Aroostook War?
What is Maine's most popular historic site?
What are the most important duties of Maine's executive council?
What is the legend of Wedding Cake House?
When did the English first try to settle in Maine?
What is Maine's most important economic activity?
What is Maine's largest island?
In what way was Maine involved in the Missouri Compromise?
To what state did Maine belong before it joined the Union?
What man from Maine served as Vice-President?

Books for Young Readers

BRAGDON, ELSPETH. *That Jud!* Viking, 1957. The story of a boy on a Maine island.
COATSWORTH, ELIZABETH J. *Five Bushel Farm.* Macmillan, 1939. *Fair American.* 1940. *White Horse.* 1942. *Away Goes Sally.* 1934. Reissue, 1951. Early American life.
FIELD, RACHEL. *Hitty, Her First Hundred Years.* Macmillan, 1929. In this Newbery medal winner, a wooden doll tells of her 100-year life, starting in Portland. *Calico Bush.* 1931. The story of a "bound-out" girl in Maine.
McCLOSKEY, ROBERT. *One Morning in Maine.* Viking, 1952. *Time of Wonder.* 1957. Caldecott medal winner.
SAWYER, RUTH. *Maggie Rose.* Harper, 1952. The story of a little girl who sells berries in Maine.
WILSON, HAZEL H. *His Indian Brother.* Abingdon, 1955. An Indian boy trains a white youth in the ways of the wilderness.

Books for Older Readers

BECK, HORACE P. *The Folklore of Maine.* Lippincott, 1957.
CARROLL, GLADYS H. *As the Earth Turns.* Macmillan, 1933. The life of a Maine farming family during one year.
CHASE, MARY E. *Mary Peters.* Macmillan, 1934. A family story set in a seacoast village of Maine.
CLIFFORD, HAROLD B. *Maine and Her People.* 2nd ed. Bond Wheelwright, 1963.
COFFIN, ROBERT P. T. *Kennebec: Cradle of Americans.* Rinehart, 1937. History and legend.
DIETZ, LEW. *Pines for the King's Navy.* Little, Brown, 1955.
FULLER, NATHAN C., ed. *The Down East Reader; Selections From the Magazine of Maine.* Lippincott, 1962.
MOORE, RUTH. *Jeb Ellis of Candlemas Bay.* Morrow, 1952. A boy of 16 in a Maine fishing background.
OGILVIE, ELISABETH. *Whistle for a Wind.* Scribner, 1954. A story of Maine in the 1820's.
RICH, LOUISE D. *Start of the Trail: The Story of a Young Maine Guide.* Lippincott, 1949. *My Neck of the Woods.* 1950. *Trail to the North.* 1952.
ROBERTS, KENNETH. *Arundel.* Rev. ed. Doubleday, 1933. Benedict Arnold's march to Quebec.

MAINE, UNIVERSITY OF, is a coeducational, state-supported school in Orono, Me. It has a branch in Portland, and teacher-training colleges in Aroostook, Farmington, and Gorham. The Orono campus has colleges of arts and sciences, business administration, education, life sciences and agriculture, and technology. The faculty of Graduate Studies offers programs leading to M.A., M.S., M.Ed., and Ph.D. degrees. Founded in 1865 as the State College of Agriculture and Mechanic Arts, the school changed to its present name in 1897. For enrollment of the University of Maine, see UNIVERSITIES AND COLLEGES (table).   EDWIN YOUNG

MAINLAND is the name of two islands. See ORKNEY ISLANDS; SHETLAND ISLANDS.

MAINSPRING. See CLOCK (Spring Clocks).

MAINTENON, *man t'NAWN,* **MARQUISE DE** (1635-1719), FRANÇOISE D'AUBIGNÉ, became the second wife of Louis XIV of France in 1683. She had great influence over the king and in France until Louis' death in 1715. Madame de Maintenon was born in Niort, France. Her parents died when she was a child, and relatives cared for her. She married Paul Scarron, a crippled poet who was much older than she, in 1652. After he died in 1660, she became the governess of Louis XIV's children by his mistress, Madame de Montespan.

Louis grew to love and respect the governess more than the mistress. Six months after the death of the queen in 1683, he secretly married her. She was never officially recognized as the king's wife.

After her marriage to the king, Madame de Maintenon founded a school for girls at St. Cyr, where she retired after the king's death.

RICHARD M. BRACE

See also LOUIS (XIV).

MAINZ, *mynts* (pop. 143,093; alt. 269 ft.), is the capital of Rhineland-Palatinate, a West German state. Mainz lies on the rising ground along the left bank of the Rhine River. It was founded on the site of a Roman camp and is one of the oldest German cities. Mainz has chemical and cement factories, flour mills, and motor and locomotive plants. The city has been the seat of Johannes Gutenberg University since 1946. JAMES K. POLLOCK

MAIPU, or MAIPO. See MOUNTAIN (table).

MAIR, CHARLES (1838-1927), was a Canadian journalist and poet. He was a reporter for the Montreal *Gazette,* and helped found the "Canada First" movement which tried to stir up national feeling after the Dominion of Canada was formed. Rebels held him prisoner during the first Riel Rebellion (see CANADA, HISTORY OF [The Struggle for Unity]). He wrote *Dreamland and Other Poems* (1868), *Tecumseh, a Drama* (1886), and *Through the Mackenzie Basin* (1908). He was born in Lanark, Ont., and attended Queen's University, Kingston, Ont. He died in British Columbia.

DESMOND PACEY

MAISONNEUVE, SIEUR DE. See MONTREAL (History).

MAITLAND, FREDERICK WILLIAM (1850-1906), an English historian, pioneered in the study of early English legal history. His scholarship produced much of what is known today about the history of Anglo-Saxon law. Maitland was able to sift through masses of contradictory and confusing evidence and find the truth. His important works include *History of the English Law* (1895), which he wrote with Frederick Pollack, and *Domesday Book and Beyond* (1897).

Maitland was born in London, and attended Eton school and Cambridge University. He studied law at Lincoln's Inn, one of the four famous "Inns of Court" in London, where lawyers lived and studied. He practiced law for several years, then became a professor of English law at Cambridge in 1888. ROLAND N. STROMBERG

MAÎTRE D'HOTEL. See RESTAURANT (Careers).

MAIZE, *mayz,* is common corn. It is sometimes called *Indian corn.* Field corn, or dent corn, is one kind of maize that is more widely grown than any of the other types. It is used for silage or for grain. The grain contains much starch and little sugar. Maize is widely used to feed livestock, and is of great importance in industry. Other types of maize, such as sweet corn and popcorn, are used primarily as food for man. In Great Britain and most other parts of the English-speaking world, *maize* is used to mean all forms of corn. See also CORN.

Scientific Classification. Maize is in the grass family, *Gramineae.* It is genus *Zea,* species *Z. mays.* GUY W. MCKEE

MAJESTY. It was once believed that emperors, kings, and queens were too far above ordinary people to be spoken of or addressed simply by name. Instead of addressing a ruler simply as "King Charles," a person said "Your Most Gracious Majesty." In this way, he could feel that he was speaking, not to the king as a person, but to the king's *majesty,* which meant his royal power or dignity.

The word *majesty* comes from the Latin *majestas,* meaning *greatness* or *grandeur.* In the Middle Ages, this title was given to the rulers who followed the Roman emperors. Later, it was applied to kings, and a distinction was made between *imperial* majesty and *royal,* or *kingly,* majesty.

Henry VIII was the first English ruler to claim the title of majesty. But the word *majesty* was not generally used until the time of the Stuart kings. Before that time, English kings were spoken of as "His Grace" or "His Highness." The king of Spain had the title "His Catholic Majesty." The king of France was called "His Most Christian Majesty."

MARION F. LANSING

MAJLIS. See IRAN (Government).

MAJOLICA, *muh JAHL ih kuh,* or MAIOLICA, *muh YAHL ih kuh,* is a type of white-glazed pottery. The name probably comes from the Spanish island of Majorca in the Mediterranean Sea, a shipping point for Moorish lusterware that was exported to Italy. The word *majolica* was first used in the middle 1500's, and referred to a variety of white earthenware pottery decorated with bright colors. It now refers to wares more properly called *faïence,* and technique (see FAÏENCE).

Examples of majolica include vases, jars, pitchers, plates, bowls, bottles, and flasks. The best majolica came from northeastern Italy. The earliest signed piece was dated 1489, but the art of majolica was lost by 1570. Since that time, craftsmen have been unable to reproduce the beauty of the old ware. EUGENE F. BUNKER, JR.

See also POTTERY.

MAJOR. See RANK IN ARMED SERVICES.

MAJOR AXIS. See ELLIPSE.

MAJOR GENERAL. See RANK IN ARMED SERVICES.

MAJOR LEAGUE. See BASEBALL (The Major Leagues).

MAJORCA, *muh JAWR kuh,* or MALLORCA (pop. 363,199), is the largest island of the Balearic group. It lies a little more than 100 miles off the eastern coast of Spain, and is a Spanish possession. The island has an area of about 1,400 square miles. Palma de Mallorca is the only large city. It has a cathedral that overlooks the harbor. For location, see SPAIN (color map).

Farming is the chief occupation on Majorca. Products include almonds, figs, olives, oranges, and wine. The island also has limestone and marble quarries and some manufacturing.

See also BALEARIC ISLANDS; MAJORICA.

MAJORITY RULE is a principle of democratic government. It means that the laws of a country are decided according to the will of the greatest number of people, and that they will be binding on all the people. The candidate who receives the greatest number of votes wins an election. Here the term *majority* differs from the term *plurality.* A candidate with a majority receives more than half the votes cast. A candidate with a plurality receives more votes than any other candidate, but does not necessarily have a majority of the votes.

R. C. MARTIN

MAKALU, MOUNT. See MOUNT MAKALU.

MAKARIOS, ARCHBISHOP (1913-   ), is the religious and political leader of Cyprus. He is head of the Greek Orthodox Church of Cyprus, and *ethnarch* (national leader) of the *Greek Cypriots* (Cyprus citizens of

Wide World

Archbishop Makarios

Greek descent). He was elected the first president of Cyprus in 1959.

Archbishop Makarios led the Greek Cypriot movement for independence from Great Britain and *enosis* (union with Greece) in the 1950's. Britain exiled him to the Seychelles Islands in 1956, but freed him in 1957. Archbishop Makarios was elected president after Britain agreed to independence for Cyprus.

Archbishop Makarios was born in Pano Panayia, Cyprus. His real name is MICHAEL MOUSKOS. He entered a monastery when he was 13 years old. He later studied theology in the United States. He was elected bishop of Kitium in 1948, and archbishop and ethnarch of Cyprus in 1950.

FRANCIS NOEL-BAKER

MAKASAR, *muh KAS ur* (pop. 384,159; alt. 5 ft.), is the capital of the province of South Sulawesi, on the island of Celebes in Indonesia. Makasar is one of the 10 largest cities in Indonesia. It exports coffee, copra, teak, spices, vegetable oils, and corn. In 1512, the Portuguese built a fort on the site. The Dutch gained control of the area in 1668. Japanese forces occupied Makasar during World War II.

MAKASSAR STRAIT separates Borneo and Celebes, two islands of Indonesia. The strait joins the Celebes Sea in the north with the Java and Flores seas in the south. It is about 450 miles long, and 80 to 240 miles wide. Its waters are dotted with small volcanic islets. The largest of these islets are Laut and Sebuku. The port of Makasar, on Celebes, lies at its southeast end. Balikpapan, Borneo's oil port, lies on the west. The Allies repulsed the Japanese in a World War II naval battle near there early in 1942.

J. E. SPENCER

MAKEMIE, *muh KEM ih,* or *muh KAYM ih,* **FRANCIS** (1658?-1708), a minister and a businessman, founded the first Presbyterian presbytery in America in Philadelphia in 1706. He was born near Rathmelton, County Donegal, Ireland. Makemie chose to be a minister, although Presbyterians were being persecuted in his homeland at the time. He became an ordained minister to the American Colonies. He traveled widely in America and also went to the West Indies. But he did his most important ministerial work on the eastern shore of Maryland and Virginia, where he founded a number of churches. He was prosecuted in New York colony in 1707 for preaching without a license, but won acquittal. This was an important victory for religious toleration in America.

LEFFERTS A. LOETSCHER

MAKEUP. See THEATER (Makeup Techniques); COSMETICS.

MALACCA, *muh LACK uh* (pop. 69,848; alt. 15 ft.), is the capital of the state of Malacca in Malaya. Malacca lies on the southwest coast of the Malay Peninsula, 125 miles northwest of Singapore. For location, see MALAYSIA (map). Malacca lies in an area that produces pepper, rice, and sage. It exports copra, nuts, rattan, rubber, and tin. During the 1400's, the city of Malacca became the most important commercial port in South-

east Asia. The Portuguese captured the city in 1511. The Dutch seized Malacca in 1641, and the British gained control of the city in 1824.

MALACCA, STRAIT OF, is a channel between the Malay Peninsula and the island of Sumatra. The strait connects the China Sea and the Indian Ocean. It is about 500 miles long, and from 25 to 100 miles wide. The city of Singapore lies on Singapore Island at the southeastern end of the strait. See INDONESIA (map).

MALACHI, *MAL uh ky,* is the name given to the author and to the title of the last book of the Old Testament. The name means *my messenger.* Malachi is probably not the real name of the writer, but a title taken from chapter 3, verse 1, of the book itself. The book was probably written about 470 or 460 B.C. The people of Jerusalem were discouraged and were losing their religious faith. Malachi, a prophet, took up their questions and criticisms one by one, and answered that the fault lay with the people. They and their priests had grown careless in religion. If they would correct this, God was ready to bless them. Malachi spoke, too, about the return of Elijah, and the coming Day of the Lord, a day of triumph of good over evil.

WALTER G. WILLIAMS

MALACHITE, *MAL uh kite,* is a beautiful, green copper ore formed of copper, carbon, oxygen, and hydrogen. It is used for ornaments and mosaics. Malachite is formed in layers that vary in color from apple green to dark gray-green. Fine pieces of malachite are mined in the Ural Mountains; in Cornwall, England; and in Australia and Arizona.

See MINERAL (color picture).

A. PABST

MALADJUSTMENT sometimes results when a person is unable to adapt himself to conditions in which he must live. The term means *bad adjustment.* In maladjustment, this failure may have damaged the person's own ability to act effectively, so it may not help merely to move somewhere else. The symptoms of the damage may be constant gloom, worry, and irritability. Sometimes these become very serious, and the person may need a psychiatrist to help him make a readjustment.

Many psychiatrists believe the real causes of maladjustment go back to training in early childhood. In later life, an especially important time for making adjustments is puberty.

WILLIAM C. BEAVER

MÁLAGA, *MAL uh guh* (pop. 307,162; alt. 32 ft.), is an important seaport and a manufacturing and resort center in Spain. It lies 65 miles northeast of Gibraltar, and is the capital of Málaga province. For location, see SPAIN (color map).

Málaga wine is made in the city from Málaga grapes grown nearby. Exports include olives, olive oil, wine, raisins, lead, almonds, lemons, grapes, and esparto grass, used to make baskets and shoes. Factories produce cotton and linen goods, pottery, soap, chemicals, iron products, and sugar.

Málaga Cathedral was begun in the 1500's. The Phoenicians founded Málaga.

WALTER C. LANGSAM

MALAGASY REPUBLIC

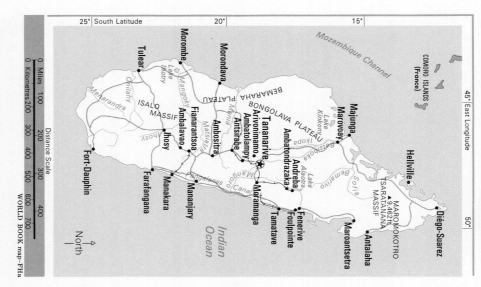

- ⊛ Capital
- • Other City or Town
- ‖ Road
- ┿ Rail Line
- ▲ MOUNTAIN
- ∿ River
- ⎯ Canal

Distance Scale

0 Miles 100 200 300 400 500 600 700

0 Kilometers 200 300 400 500 600 700

WORLD BOOK map–FHa

North

MALAGASY REPUBLIC is an independent country which includes Madagascar—the world's fourth largest island—and small nearby islands. It lies in the Indian Ocean about 240 miles off the southeast coast of Africa. It covers an area about four times that of Illinois, and it has about as many people as there are in the Chicago metropolitan area. Most of the people are farmers and herders of either Indonesian or African Negro descent.

The island was a favorite base for sea pirates in the 1600's and 1700's, including the famous Captain William Kidd. The pirates founded a republic called *Libertalia* there, but it lasted only a short time.

France governed Madagascar from 1896 until it became self-governing in 1958. The Malagasy Republic became fully independent in 1960. Tananarive, a city of about 300,000, is the capital and largest city. The country's official name is REPOBLIKA MALAGASY in Malagasy and RÉPUBLIQUE MALGACHE in French.

Government. The president, who also serves as prime minister, is head of state and head of the government. The people elect the president for a seven-year term. Parliament consists of a 107-member National Assembly and a 54-member Senate. The people elect the National Assembly members for five-year terms. Two-thirds of the senators are elected, and the rest are appointed by the government. Senators serve six-year terms. All persons 21 years of age or older may vote.

The central government closely controls all local governments. The country is divided into six provinces, which are divided into prefectures and subprefectures.

People. The people belong to two major groups—those of African Negro descent and those of Indonesian descent. The Negroes live in the coastal regions, and make up the larger group. The people of Indonesian descent live in the central and south-central highlands.

Political rivalries have developed between the two groups. The coastal people of African descent control the government. Their leaders favor close ties with France and other Western countries. The Merina, who are of Indonesian descent, are better educated than the coastal people and resent being governed by them. They want their country to have closer relations with non-Western countries. But they are in the minority, and have little chance of coming to power through elections.

Malagasy is the language spoken throughout the country. It resembles Malay and Indonesian. French and Malagasy are the official languages. Almost one-third of the people are Christians. The rest—especially those living along the coasts—practice tribal religions. They worship their ancestors and spirits, and perform cattle sacrifices and other ceremonies at family tombs.

Many Malagasys wear European-style clothing. However, people of isolated southern tribes often wear little clothing. Most houses are built of brick and many are several stories high. They have tile or thatched

Richard Adloff, the contributor of this article, is Research Associate at The Hoover Institution, Stanford University, and coauthor of The Malagasy Republic—Madagascar Today.

FACTS IN BRIEF

Capital: Tananarive.

Official Languages: Malagasy and French.

Form of Government: Republic. *Head of State*—President.

Area: 226,658 square miles. *Greatest Distances*—(north-south) 980 mi.; (east-west) 360 mi. *Coastline*—2,600 mi.

Population: No complete census. *Estimated 1971 Population*—6,979,000; distribution, 87 per cent rural, 13 per cent urban; density, 31 persons to the square mile. *Estimated 1976 Population*—7,858,000.

Chief Products: *Agriculture*—cattle, coffee, rice, vanilla. *Mining*—graphite, mica, semi-precious stones. *Manufacturing*—chemicals, cigarettes, sisal, sugar, textiles.

Flag: A white vertical stripe appears at the left, with a red horizontal stripe over a green one at the right. White is for purity, red for sovereignty, and green for hope. See FLAG (color picture; Flags of Africa).

Money: *Basic Unit*—franc. See MONEY (table: Values).

roofs. The people eat rice, vegetables, fruit, and sometimes meat and fish.

About half the people can read and write. Almost 50 per cent of the school age children attend primary schools and about 4 per cent attend secondary schools. The University of Madagascar, founded in 1961, has about 3,000 students. About 6,000 students attend teachers colleges and technical schools.

Land. Northern Madagascar has fertile soil. Mountains separate it from the rest of the island. Western Madagascar has wide plains, some fertile river valleys, and a fairly sheltered coast. A narrow plain lies along the east coast, but reefs and storms make the east coast dangerous for ships. Some coastal shipping uses the Pangalanes Canal, which runs along the east coast between Foulpointe and Farafangana. The climate is warm and humid on the coast. The southern end of the island is mainly desert, and has a hot, dry climate.

Central Madagascar consists of highlands ranging in altitude from 2,000 feet to 4,000 feet, with some higher mountains. The soil there is *eroded* (worn away) and the region is *deforested* (cleared of trees), but it has the densest population. The highlands are cool and temperatures at Tananarive range between 55° F. and 67° F.

Economy. Four-fifths of the people are farmers and herders. Rice is their chief food crop, but cassava, corn, and potatoes are also grown. Coffee is the most valuable export, and the Malagasy Republic is the world's greatest vanilla producer. Other exports include sisal, which is used to make binding twine, and sugar.

The country has more cattle (about 8½ million) than people. There are also about 450,000 pigs and 600,000 sheep and goats. Many of these animals are of poor quality, because they receive little care.

Most of Madagascar's few industries process hides, meat, ores, sisal, and sugar for export. Beverages, cigarettes, sacks, shoes, soap, and textiles are manufactured for the local market. Big French import-export companies and Chinese and Indian retailers control local

trade. Most of the foreign trade is with France. But the United States buys coffee, cloves, and vanilla from the Malagasy Republic.

Madagascar has about 1,300 miles of paved roads, 3,900 miles of unpaved roads, and 535 miles of railroads. Tamatave and Majunga are the leading seaports.

History. Immigrants from Indonesia came to the island in successive waves starting long before the time of Christ and lasting until the A.D. 1400's. They settled in the central highlands. Immigrants from Africa and the Arabian peninsula settled on the coasts. A number of kingdoms developed on the island, but by about 1800 the Merina kingdom ruled most of the island.

Radama I welcomed English and French traders and missionaries to the island after he became king in 1810. The missionaries opened churches and schools and persuaded the king to end the slave trade. In the 1840's, Queen Ranavalona I tried to end European influence and expelled Europeans from the island. European returned after she died in 1861. French influence increased after 1869. Merina resentment against the French led to the Franco-Malagasy wars of the 1880's and 1890's. Madagascar became a French colony in 1896.

During World War I, Merina leaders began to demand independence. France gave the Malagasys some control of financial matters and the right to elect an assembly in 1945. It also allowed them to elect representatives to the French parliament. But this did not satisfy the Malagasys. An armed revolt that lasted almost two years broke out in 1947.

Madagascar moved toward self-government in peaceful stages in the late 1950's. A government council with some power to administer laws was elected in 1956. In 1958, Madagascar became the Malagasy Republic, a self-governing republic in the French Community. It became fully independent on June 26, 1960. Philibert Tsiranana became the country's first president in 1959. He was re-elected in 1965.   RICHARD ADLOFF

See also TANANARIVE; LEMUR; ROSEWOOD; VANILLA.

The Narrow Streets of Tananarive, capital of the Malagasy Republic, are crowded on market day.

Sammer, Three Lions

Irrigation In Dry Southern Malagasy has helped the people develop plantations. Most Malagasy farmers also raise cattle.

Frederick Ayer, Photo Researchers

MALAMUD, BERNARD

MALAMUD, BERNARD (1914-   ), an American author, has written chiefly about Jews in the United States. His works often mix realism with supernaturalism, and humor with morality and sympathy for those who suffer. Malamud's novel *The Assistant* (1957) tells of a young man who robs a poor Jewish grocer. The young man returns to work for the grocer, and eventually saves the grocer from suicide and becomes a Jew himself. *The Fixer* (1966) is the story of an insignificant Jew in Czarist Russia who becomes, through persecution, a sort of hero. Malamud's other novels include *The Natural* (1952) and *A New Life* (1961). His short stories have been published in *The Magic Barrel* (1954) and *Idiots First* (1963). *Pictures of Fidelman* (1969) is a collection of related short stories about an American artist in Europe. Malamud was born in Brooklyn.   PHILIP YOUNG

MALAR. See FACE.

MALAMUTE. See ALASKAN MALAMUTE.

MALARIA, *muh LAIR ee uh,* is a serious infectious disease of man. It occurs most often in tropical and subtropical countries. But it also occurs in temperate regions during summer months. The word *malaria* comes from two Italian words that mean *bad air.* People gave the disease this name because of its association with the musty, bad-smelling air of swamps.

Malaria ranks as a leading cause of death in many tropical regions of the world. About 1 million persons die of it every year. Malaria was common in the southern states before World War II. It has been wiped out in the United States, although many persons catch it while traveling in other parts of the world.

Cause. Malaria is caused by one-celled animals, called *protozoans,* of the genus *Plasmodium.* These animals are parasites. They spend part of their lives in the red blood cells of human beings, and part in female *Anopheles* mosquitoes. These mosquitoes carry and spread the malaria parasites. When an *Anopheles* mosquito bites a person who has malaria, it sucks up the blood cells that contain the parasites. The parasites de-

FemaleAnophelesMosquito has a long proboscis with which it pierces the skin, spreading malaria.

American Museum of Natural History

Malaria Parasites are microscopic animals that multiply in human red blood cells, above, causing a fever.

WHO

velop and multiply in the mosquito's stomach, then move into its salivary glands or mouth parts. When the mosquito bites another person, it injects saliva containing the malaria parasites into the victim. The parasites enter the person's red blood cells. There they grow and burst the blood cells, causing anemia (see ANEMIA).

Symptoms. A person who has malaria suffers intense attacks of chills, fever, sweats, and great weakness. There are three kinds of malaria. The *falciparum,* or *estivo-autumnal,* type ranks as the most dangerous. In this type, fever and chills occur at irregular intervals. In the second type, *quartan* malaria, fever occurs about every 72 hours. In the most common type, *vivax,* or *tertian,* malaria, the fever often occurs every other day. Although vivax malaria is relatively mild, it causes much chronic illness. Persons with this type of malaria often have *relapses* (recurrent periods of fever).

Treatment. Doctors treat malaria with drugs that destroy the parasites. For centuries doctors used quinine to prevent and treat this disease. But during World War II, the supply of quinine from the East Indies was cut off. Scientists then developed many new compounds that were even more effective than quinine. Among these were atabrine, chloroquine, and primaquine. Some malaria parasites found recently cannot be checked with these drugs, and doctors are again using quinine.

Control and Prevention. Malaria may be controlled and prevented by destroying the *Anopheles* mosquitoes and their breeding places. This can be done by draining swamps and by spraying breeding places with oil or chemicals that destroy the larvae. But extensive drainage projects are impractical in many parts of the world. Therefore, scientists developed a highly effective control method based on killing infected mosquitoes. This method, now used throughout the world, depends on the use of insecticides and makes use of the habits of the mosquitoes as well. Many of these mosquitoes bite only when they are indoors at night. Immediately after biting, they usually seek rest on a nearby surface. People spray the walls and ceilings of rooms with insecticides such as DDT and dieldrin, which remain active a long time. When a mosquito rests on these surfaces, the insecticide destroys it. In some areas, mosquitoes have become resistant to commonly used insecticides.

History. Many years ago, the Indians of Peru used the bark of the cinchona tree to treat malaria. But the study of the cause of malaria involved the work of many scientists. In 1880, the French scientist Charles Laveran discovered the protozoa that caused malaria. In 1898, Sir Ronald Ross, an English scientist, showed that certain mosquitoes infect birds with malaria. Soon afterward, Giovanni Grassi of Italy worked out the lifecycle of the human malaria parasite.   THOMAS H. WELLER

Malaria in Animals. Malaria parasites also infect birds, lizards, and monkeys. The *Culex* mosquito carries the parasites that infect birds. Scientists have used these animals to learn about malaria in humans.

MALASPINA GLACIER. See ALASKA (Glaciers); GLACIER (Kinds of Glaciers; Famous Glaciers).

MALAWI

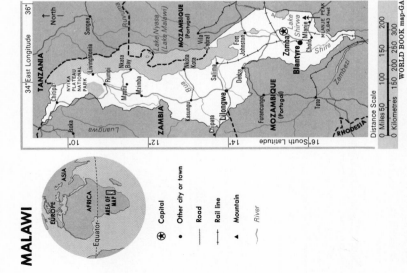

Capital
• **Other city or town**
—— **Road**
+++ **Rail line**
▲ **Mountain**
~ **River**

Distance Scale
0 Miles 50   100   150   200
0 Kilometres 50 100 150 200 250 300
WORLD BOOK map·GA

MALAWI, *muh LAH wee,* is a small scenic country in the eastern part of southern Africa. It is a country about 520 miles long and from 50 to 100 miles wide, an area slightly larger than the state of Pennsylvania. Malawi lies on the western shore of Lake Nyasa, called Lake Malawi in that country.

Malawi is a farming country, but only about one-third of the land is suitable for agriculture. Mountains, forests, and rough pastures cover most of the country. Most of the people grow only enough food to feed their own families. The country has little industry, and thousands of the men go to neighboring countries to work. Most of them work in mines in Rhodesia, South Africa, and Zambia. They send the money they earn back to their families.

The country takes its name from the Malawi group of people who settled there in the 1500's. Once the British protectorate of Nyasaland, it became independent in 1964. Zomba, a city of about 20,000, is the capital. The government plans to build a new capital near Lilongwe in central Malawi.

Government. Malawi is a republic, with a president as its head of state and chief executive. The people elect the president to a five-year term. The president appoints a council of ministers to assist him. The people elect the 53 members of parliament to five-year terms.

Only one political party, the Malawi Congress party, is allowed. The party includes Europeans and Asians, and they may run for parliament.

People. Most of Malawi's 4,642,000 persons are Negro Africans who live in small villages. In these rural areas, the people live in round or oblong houses that have mud walls and thatched roofs. Most of the people belong to Bantu tribes. The leading tribes are the Chewa (Cewa), Ngura, Nyanja, Yao, and Ngoni (Angoni). About 9,000 Europeans and about 14,000 Asians and persons of mixed origin also live in Malawi.

In most western cultures, the father is the head of the family and descent is determined through him. But most Malawi tribes determine descent through the mother. Today, thousands of men go to neighboring countries to work for periods ranging from nine months to two years. While they are gone, the women farm to raise food for their families. *Maize* (corn) is their main food crop. The people grow sorghum and millet where the climate is unsuitable for maize.

By custom, the land belongs to the family. Each member of the family can cultivate a part of the land, but he cannot sell it or pass it down to his children. The land always remains the property of the entire family.

English is Malawi's official language, but the people speak African languages. Nyanja and Yao are the most popular languages in central and southern Malawi. Most of the people in northern Malawi speak Tumbuka. Many of the Malawi tribes practice tribal religions. About 700,000 of the people are Christians, and about 500,000 are Moslems.

About 400,000 children attend primary schools, and about 4,500 attend the country's 17 secondary schools. Malawi relies heavily on Great Britain and the United States for the money and teachers to operate its schools. The government opened Malawi's first university at Zomba in 1965.

Land. Malawi is a land of great scenic beauty. Grassland and *savanna* (areas of coarse grass and trees) cover much of the land. The African Rift Valley runs the length of Malawi from north to south. Lake Nyasa fills most of the valley. It is 1,550 feet above sea level. The Shire River flows out of the southern end of the lake to join the Zambezi River. West of the lake, the land rises steeply to a plateau about 4,000 feet

—— **FACTS IN BRIEF** ——

Capital: Zomba.

Official Language: English.

Form of Government: Republic. *Head of State:* President (5-year term).

Area: 45,483 square miles.

Population: *1966 Census*—4,042,412; distribution, 95 per cent rural, 5 per cent urban. *Estimated 1971 Population*—4,642,000; density, 102 persons to the square mile. *Estimated 1976 Population*—5,303,000.

Chief Products: *Agriculture*—coffee, cotton, hides and skins, peanuts, tea, tobacco, tung oil. *Manufacturing and Processing*—bricks, cement, cotton goods, furniture, soap.

Flag: The flag has black, red and green horizontal stripes, with a red rising sun on the black stripe. See FLAG (color picture: Flags of Africa).

Money: *Basic Unit*—pound. See MONEY (table: Values).

W. E. F. Ward, the contributor of this article, is the author of several books on Africa, and is former deputy educational adviser in the British Colonial Office.

above sea level. Malawi's highest mountain peak, Mlanje Peak (9,843 feet), rises on another plateau southeast of the Shire River.

The lowlands in the Shire Valley and along the lake have a hot, humid, tropical climate. The temperature in this area averages between 74° F. and 78° F. The plateaus are much cooler, averaging about 65° F. in higher areas and about 58° F. in lower areas. The northern parts of the country average about 70 inches of rainfall a year. The southwestern parts get an average of only 30 inches a year.

Economy. Malawi is a poor country. It has no important mineral deposits. Its economy is based on agriculture, but only about a third of the land is suitable for farming. The most important export crop is tea, which is grown on estates in the highlands that are owned by Europeans. Important crops grown by Africans include tobacco, cotton, and peanuts. Many farmers raise livestock. Fishing on Lake Nyasa has also become an important industry. Malawi's few manufacturing industries produce such goods as soap, cotton goods, fishing nets, furniture, and bricks. Valuable hardwood forests cover the northwest part of the country, but they are too difficult for workmen to reach.

Malawi has nearly 6,000 miles of roads, but only about 500 miles are paved. A main road runs the length of the country, and Malawi has roads linking it with Rhodesia, Tanzania, and Zambia. A railroad running down the Shire Valley connects Malawi with the Mozambique port of Beira on the Indian Ocean. An international airport near Blantyre provides air service to eastern and southern Africa.

History. The Malawi group of Bantu people entered what is now Malawi from the north in the 1500's. In the 1830's, two other Bantu tribes, the Ngoni and Yao, invaded the area. The Yao were slave-traders who sold their slaves to the Arabs along the eastern coast of Africa.

The British missionary David Livingstone reached the area in 1859. He found it torn by tribal wars, and saw the suffering the slave-traders caused. Livingstone called for "commerce and Christianity" to bring peace to the area. In 1875, the Free Church of Scotland set up a mission that later became an important religious center. Scottish businessmen, in support of the missionaries, formed the African Lakes Corporation three years later to introduce lawful business instead of the slave trade. In 1889, the British made treaties with the tribal chiefs on the western shore of Lake Nyasa. Two years later, Britain proclaimed the territory as the Protectorate of Nyasaland.

In 1953, the British made the protectorate part of a federation with Northern and Southern Rhodesia, the Federation of Rhodesia and Nyasaland. The Africans living there opposed the creation of the federation, and protested strongly against it. After a British government study, the federation was dissolved in 1963. Hastings Kamuzu Banda, a physician educated in the United States, then became prime minister of a self-governing protectorate. In July, 1964, the protectorate became the independent nation of Malawi, a constitutional monarchy that recognized Queen Elizabeth II as queen of Malawi. In 1966, Malawi adopted a new constitution and became a republic, with Banda serving as president of the country.

See also ZOMBA.

W. E. F. WARD

Mealtime in Malawi. Children dry fish before cooking them at a village near Nkota Kota. Malawi fishermen use mosquito netting to catch thousands of these fish in Lake Nyasa.

S. T. Darke, Three Lions

MALAY is the general name for the short, brown-skinned peoples of Malaysia. About 100 million Malays make their homes on the Malay Peninsula and on the islands in Southeast Asia that include Indonesia and the Philippines.

Anthropologists classify the Malays racially as southern Mongoloids. Scientists believe that they spread out over the area several thousand years ago, and displaced such earlier populations as the Negritos, who still live in isolated places in the region. Rice and fish are the main staples of the Malays. The Malays have formed such new nations as the Philippines, the Republic of Indonesia, and Malaysia. The term *Malay* also may be applied to the languages spoken by many of the Malay peoples.

FELIX M. KEESING

See also RACES OF MAN (Mongoloids; table; pictures).

MALAY ARCHIPELAGO, also called the EAST INDIAN ARCHIPELAGO or MALAYSIA, is in a part of the Pacific Ocean which contains the largest group of islands in the world. The equator runs squarely through the middle of the group. The archipelago lies between southeastern Asia and Australia, and includes the Philippine Islands, Indonesia (including the Moluccas and the Lesser Sunda Islands), New Guinea, and several smaller groups. The archipelago covers about 943,250 square miles. See the maps with INDONESIA; PACIFIC ISLANDS.

The islands have much fine, fertile soil. Oranges, mangoes, guavas, rice, corn, sugar, coffee, cacao, coconuts, sago, breadfruit, and yams flourish. Exports include *gutta-percha* (a substance similar to rubber), camphor, and other forest products. Several of the Malayan islands also contain deposits of gold, manganese, chromium, iron, sulfur, oil, tin, and phosphate rock.

Naturalists and other scientists have discovered much valuable scientific material in the islands. Their most famous find was the fossil bones of the Java Man. Scientists believe he lived about 1½ million years ago (see JAVA MAN). About 163 million people live in the islands of the Malay Archipelago. Most of them belong to the Malaysian or Papuan racial groups.

JOHN F. CADY

See also EAST INDIES.

MALAYA, *muh LAY uh,* is a region in Southeast Asia on the southern end of the Malay Peninsula. The region is occupied by West Malaysia, a geographic section of the Federation of Malaysia. Kuala Lumpur, Malaysia's capital, is the largest city in Malaya.

Formerly a British colony, Malaya became one of Great Britain's most valuable possessions. It is the world's leading source of tin and one of the leading sources of natural rubber. Its location between the Bay of Bengal and the South China Sea makes the area a leading trade and shipping center (see MALAYSIA [map]).

Malaya was an independent country from 1957 to 1963. In 1963, it united with Singapore, Sarawak, and Sabah (formerly North Borneo) to form Malaysia. Singapore later withdrew from the federation.

The Land. Malaya covers 50,700 square miles, almost three-fourths of the Malay Peninsula. Thailand borders Malaya on the north. Sumatra lies across the Strait of Malacca to the west and Singapore lies off Malaya's southern coast. Borneo is east, across the China Sea.

Thick rain forests cover four of every five acres in Malaya. Several mountain ranges cross Malaya from north to south. Malaya's highest mountain, Tahan (7,186 ft.), rises in the northern section of the state.

The People and Their Work. Malaya has a population of about 9,660,000. About half the people are Malays (see MALAY). There are also many people from India and southern China. Most Malays are Moslems and speak a language called Malay.

Rubber ranks as the most important forest product. The forests also furnish vast supplies of timber, coconuts, oil palms, and other products. Tin mines are found throughout western Malaya. Other natural resources include bauxite, coal, iron ore, and tungsten.

Malaya's tin and rubber factories provide employment for thousands of workers. Other Malayans work as farmers, fishermen, and shopkeepers. Malayan farmers raise more rice than any other product. They also raise coffee, bananas, and yams. Malayan fishermen catch dorab, herring, mackerel, and other kinds of fish.

History. Until the late 1800's, Malaya's ports were important stops on the trade route between Europe and Asia. Few people lived in the interior of the Malay Peninsula. The only settled areas included the Kra Isthmus and the coast along the Strait of Malacca. During the late 1300's, Arab and Indian Moslems brought their religion, Islam, to the Malays. They also established small states ruled by sultans. In the 1400's, the city of Malacca was the most important port in southeast Asia. In 1511, the Portuguese captured the city. They lost control of the area to the Dutch in 1641.

British Possession. In the late 1700's, Great Britain became interested in Malayan ports. In 1786, the British bought Penang, an island off Malaya's western coast. By the early 1800's, Singapore, Malacca, and Penang-Wellesley formed a British colony called the Straits Settlements. During the late 1800's, the opening of the Suez Canal stimulated European trade with all southeastern Asia. At the same time, the tin industry became important. Great Britain needed control over local politics in order to control Malaya's tin mines. In 1895, treaties enabled the British to form the Federated Malay States from four Moslem states on the western third of the Peninsula. In 1909, the Malay States acquired several northern sultanates from Siam (now Thailand). The other states on the Peninsula became known as the Unfederated Malay States.

The Federation of Malaya. During World War II, Japanese forces occupied Malaya. After the war, the British proposed the formation of a Malayan Union, including all Malaya except Singapore. But this plan failed. In 1948, the Federation of Malaya was established. But the Malayans demanded full independence. At the same time, Communists in Malaya began creating trouble. During the 1950's, Great Britain defeated the Communists in a war. The Federation of Malaya held its first election in 1955. The British gave the Malayans control over their own affairs in 1956.

On Aug. 31, 1957, the federation joined the British Commonwealth of Nations as an independent constitutional monarchy. Plans to form Malaysia began in 1961. Tunku Abdul Rahman, Malaya's prime minister, was a leading force behind the formation of the federation, which began in 1963. For further information on the Federation of Malaysia, see MALAYSIA.

JOHN F. CADY

See also JOHORE; KUALA LUMPUR; MALACCA; SINGAPORE; STRAITS SETTLEMENTS.

MALAYSIA

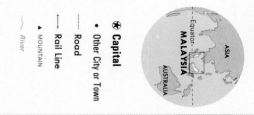

Equator—
MALAYSIA

ASIA
AUSTRALIA

✷ **Capital**
● **Other City or Town**
— **Road**
→ **Rail Line**
▲ MOUNTAIN
~ River

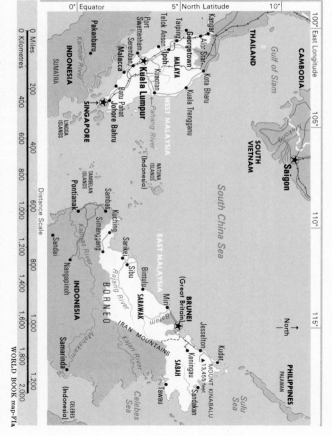

WORLD BOOK map–Fla

MALAYSIA, *muh LAY zhuh*, is a country in Southeast Asia. Its official name is the FEDERATION OF MALAYSIA. The federation was formed on Sept. 16, 1963, when Malaya, Singapore, and the British protectorates of Sarawak and Sabah (formerly North Borneo) united. Singapore was excluded in 1965. Malaysia is an independent member of the Commonwealth of Nations. Kuala Lumpur, in Malaya, is the capital.

Malaysia is made up of 13 states. Eleven once formed the independent country of Malaya. They are Johore, Kedah, Kelantan, Malacca, Negri Sembilan, Pahang, Penang, Perak, Perlis, Selangor, and Trengganu. Malaysia's other states are Sarawak and Sabah.

The Land. Malaysia lies in extreme southeastern Asia. It covers the southern half of the Malay Peninsula and most of the northern part of the island of Borneo. The part of the country on the Malay Peninsula is the geographic region of West Malaysia. The part on Borneo is East Malaysia. The Malay Peninsula

---
FACTS IN BRIEF

Capital: Kuala Lumpur.

Official Language: Malay.

Form of Government: Federation; 13 states. *Head of Government*—Prime minister.

Area: 128,430 square miles.

Population: No complete census. *Estimated 1971 Population* —11,370,000; density, 89 persons to the square mile. *Estimated 1976 Population*—13,225,000.

Chief Products: *Agriculture*—rice, pineapples, tobacco. *Mining*—tin, petroleum, iron, bauxite. *Forestry*—rubber.

Flag: A yellow crescent and star lie on a blue canton. The star's 14 points and the 14 alternating red and white stripes represent Malaysia's 14 original states. The crescent symbolizes Islamic faith. The flag was adopted in 1963. See FLAG (color picture: Flags of Asia).

Money: *Basic Unit*—Malaysian dollar. See MONEY (table).

and Borneo are separated by 400 miles of the South China Sea. Malaysia is about as big as New Mexico.

Malaysia is a tropical country with many dense rain forests. Forest-covered mountains run down the center of the Malay Peninsula. The western half of the peninsula has some unforested plains, and includes most of Malaysia's chief cities. Dense rain forests make it impossible to live in much of Sarawak and Sabah. Most cities in these states are along the coast. Malaysia's highest peak, Mount Kinabalu, rises 13,455 feet in Sabah.

The People. Malaysia has a population of 11,370,000. Over 9½ million persons live in Malaya, about 1,019,000 in Sarawak, and about 691,000 in Sabah.

Malays and Chinese form the largest groups of people (see MALAY). Dyaks form the largest group in Sarawak (see DYAK). Dusuns, tribesmen related to the Dyaks, make up the largest part of Sabah's population. Malays and Chinese also live in Sarawak and Sabah.

Most Malaysians speak Malay. Many speak English, Chinese, Tamil, and tribal dialects. Islam is the state religion, and most Malaysians are *Moslems* (followers of Islam). Confucianists, Christians, and members of other religions also live in Malaysia. Many people in Sarawak and Sabah practice tribal religions.

The Economy. Rubber and tin are Malaysia's chief natural resources. Rubber trees are the main source of income. Malaysia and Indonesia rank as the world's leading producers of natural rubber. Valuable tin deposits on the Malay Peninsula make Malaysia the world's leading tin producer. Other natural resources include petroleum, lumber, iron, bauxite, and coal.

The country's rubber plantations, tin mines, and oil fields provide employment for thousands of workers. Many Malaysians are farmers. Most of them grow rice, Malaysia's chief food product. The farmers also raise crops of coconuts, peppers, pineapples, and tobacco. Industry has begun to develop in the states that form

Malaysia. Many raw materials are still exported and refined in factories in other countries. But Malaysia hopes to attract more industry by offering tax exemptions to companies that build factories there.

Government. The prime minister heads the government. The Malaysian parliament is made up of a Senate and a House of Representatives. The people elect all the representatives. The Senate has 58 members. Each of Malaysia's 13 state legislatures elects 2 members. The Supreme *Head of State* appoints the others. The Supreme Head of State is a ruler in title only. Sultans of nine Malaysian states take turns filling the office.

History. Plans to create the Federation of Malaysia began in 1961. Several factors made the federation desirable. Singapore faced economic and political problems after its independence from Great Britain in 1959. It had trouble competing economically with larger nations. Singapore's government believed union with Malaya would improve its trade and add to its resources.

Communists took advantage of Singapore's economic problems to gain political influence in the country. Singapore proposed a merger with Malaya in 1959. Malaya rejected the proposal at first, but reconsidered when Communist influence continued to grow in Singapore. Malaya did not want a Communist nation as its neighbor to the south. Malaya finally agreed to unite with Singapore if Sarawak, Sabah (North Borneo), and Brunei were included. Malaya believed the Borneo states and their resources would strengthen the federation. Britain favored including the Borneo states so it could end its colonial rule on the island. Many people in northern Borneo wanted to end British rule, but not in exchange for rule by China or Indonesia. In July, 1963, Brunei announced that it would not join the federation.

The Federation of Malaysia was formed Sept. 16, 1963. Tunku Abdul Rahman of Malaya became the prime minister. Soon after federation, Malaysia ended diplomatic relations with the Philippines and Indonesia. The Philippines claimed that part of Sabah belonged to it. Malaysia and the Philippines resumed relations in 1965. President Sukarno of Indonesia charged that Sabah had been forced into the federation, and he threatened to "crush Malaysia." Border fighting began between Malaysia and Indonesia in 1964. When Indonesia tried to land troops in Malaysia, British forces were sent to support Malaysia. Malaysian and Indonesian leaders agreed to end the fighting in 1966, after Sukarno had lost power. Malaysia and Indonesia restored relations in 1967.

Malaysia excluded Singapore from the federation on Aug. 9, 1965. Singapore and the rest of Malaysia had developed many differences (see SINGAPORE).

After early returns in the 1969 national election, political rivalry led to rioting between Maylays and Chinese in Kuala Lumpur. During the riots, Malaysia's parliamentary government was suspended. It was replaced by the National Operations Council led by Deputy Prime Minister Tun Abdul Razak.   JOHN F. CADY

Related Articles in WORLD BOOK include:

Borneo	Kuala Lumpur	Rubber (table)
Colombo Plan	Malacca	Sarawak
Johore	Malaya	Tin (table)

MALCOLM X (1925-1965) was a leader of a movement to unite black people throughout the world. He was assassinated in New York City on Feb. 21, 1965. His followers interpreted his death as a sacrifice for the "black revolution," and he quickly became a hero of that movement.

In 1946, Malcolm X was sentenced to prison in Massachusetts for burglary. While in prison, he adopted the beliefs of the Black Muslims, members of a religious movement which believes in separation of the races. After his release from prison in 1952, Malcolm X became a leading spokesman for the Black Muslims. In 1964, following a disagreement with the leader of the Black Muslims, Malcolm X formed a rival group, the Organization of Afro-American Unity (OAAU). Malcolm was killed before the OAAU was firmly established. Three men, including two Black Muslims, were sentenced to life in prison for Malcolm's murder. Malcolm X was born Malcolm Little in Omaha, Nebr. *The Autobiography of Malcolm X* was published in 1965.   C. ERIC LINCOLN

See also BLACK MUSLIMS.

MALDEN, Mass. (pop. 57,676; alt. 35 ft.), is a residential and manufacturing city about five miles north of Boston (see MASSACHUSETTS [political map]). Factories produce aircraft engine parts, canned foods, cans, clothing, dolls and doll clothing, electronics equipment, paints, and rubber footwear. The first permanent settlers were Puritans who came between 1630 and 1640. In 1649, the settlement was incorporated as *Maulden*, also spelled *Mauldon*. It received a charter as *Malden* in 1881. It has a mayor-council government.   WILLIAM J. REID

Frank Castoral, Photo Researchers
Malcolm X

Kuala Lumpur, the capital of Malaysia, has colorful mosques and modern buildings. It is the largest city in Malaysia.

Launois, Black Star

MALDIVES

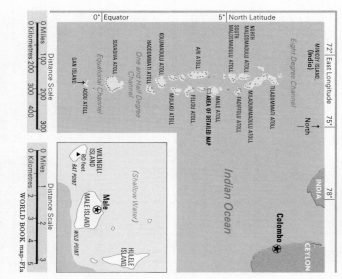

★ Capital

▲ Highest Known Elevation

Shallow Water

WORLD BOOK map–Fla

MALDIVES, *mal DEEVZ,* is the smallest independent country in Asia and one of the smallest in the world. It consists of about 2,000 small coral islands that form a chain 475 miles long and 80 miles wide in the Indian Ocean. The northern tip of the Maldives is about 370 miles south of India and 420 miles southwest of Ceylon. These green tropical islands cover a total land area of only 115 square miles, slightly greater than the area of Milwaukee, Wis. Milwaukee has about seven times as many people.

The Maldivian people live a simple life that has changed very little for hundreds of years. Most of the men are fishermen who go out to sea daily to catch bonito and tuna.

Great Britain governed the Maldives as a protectorate for 78 years. The islands became independent in 1965. The country's official name in Divehi, the official language, is DIVEHI RAAJJE (REPUBLIC OF MALDIVES). Male, a town of about 11,000, is the capital.

Government. A national convention elects the sultan to serve for life as head of state. The sultan appoints a prime minister to run the government for five years. The prime minister appoints Cabinet ministers to assist him. The Cabinet members also serve five-year terms. An elected committee handles local government on each *atoll* (cluster of islands). The government appoints a *kateeb* (headman) for each island. The sultan also appoints a chief justice to administer the laws. Law in the Maldives is based on the Sunni Moslems' code of law.

People. Most Maldivians are descendants of Sinhalese people who came from Ceylon. Some Maldivians are descendants of people from southern India and Arab traders and sailors. Almost all Maldivians belong to the Sunni Moslem sect.

Maldivians are small, slight, quiet people. They live on only about 210 of the country's islands. Most of them have just enough food for their families. They *barter* (trade) for other things they need.

Maldivian men go to sea every day in thousands of boats to catch fish. They build their boats of coconut or other timber that grows there. Most of the boats are 36 feet long and 8 or 9 feet wide at the widest point. Each boat can hold about a dozen fishermen. The fishermen sail 15 or 20 miles out from the islands, throw live bait fish into the water, and use rods and reels to haul in big fish.

When the boats return home, the women take over the job of preparing the fish. They cook and smoke them over a fire. Most of the fish are exported to Ceylon. The people eat some of the fish. Their diet also includes coconuts, papayas, pineapples, pomegranates, and yams.

Land. The 2,000 small islands are grouped together in about 12 clusters called *atolls.* Barrier reefs around

FACTS IN BRIEF

Capital: Male.

Official Language: Divehi.

Form of Government: Constitutional monarchy.

Head of State: Sultan.

Legislature: The *Majlis* has 54 members who serve five-year terms. Sultan appoints eight members; voters elect 46.

Local Government: An elected committee governs each atoll. Each inhabited island has a government-appointed *kateeb* (headman).

Political Divisions: 19 districts.

Total Land Area: 115 square miles. *Greatest Distances*—(north-south) 550 miles; (east-west) 100 miles.

Elevation: *Highest*—80 feet above sea level, on Wilingili Island. *Lowest*—sea level.

Population: *1967 Census*—103,801; distribution, 90 per cent rural, 10 per cent urban. *Estimated 1971 Population*—113,000; density, 983 persons to the square mile. *Estimated 1976 Population*—126,000.

Chief Products: *Agriculture*—breadfruit, coconuts, papaya, pineapples, pomegranates, yams. *Fishing*—bonito, tuna. *Handicrafts*—coir yarn, cowrie shells, lacquer ware, woven mats.

Flag: The flag has a white crescent on a dark green rectangle with a red border. The colors and the crescent on the flag stand for Islam. Adopted 1965. See FLAG (color picture: Flags of Asia and the Pacific).

Money: *Basic Unit*—rupee.

Robert I. Crane, the contributor of this article, is Ford-Maxwell Professor of South Asian History at Syracuse University.

History. Little is known about the islands before they came under Portuguese rule in the 1500's. From 1656 to 1796, the Dutch ruled the islands from Ceylon.

In 1887, the Maldives officially became a British protectorate. As a protectorate, the Maldives had internal self-government, and Britain handled the islands' foreign affairs. A dispute developed in the 1950's between the Maldivians and the British over an air base on Gan Island. The dispute led to the *secession* (withdrawal) of three southern atolls. The Maldivian government accused Britain of backing the rebellion. It crushed the rebellion in 1960.

In 1960, Britain and the Maldives signed an agreement that gave Britain free use of the Gan Island base until 1986. The Maldivians received the right to conduct most of their foreign affairs. Britain promised the islands about $2 million for economic development.

On July 26, 1965, Britain and the Maldives signed a new agreement that gave the islands complete independence. The Maldives joined the United Nations on Sept. 21, 1965.

See also COLOMBO PLAN; MALE.   ROBERT I. CRANE

MALE (pop. 11,202) is the capital and leading town of the Maldives. It is located on Male Island, which is part of Male Atoll (see MALDIVES [map]). Male Island is about a mile long and half a mile wide. The town has a radio station. An airfield on nearby Hulele Island serves Male.   ROBERT I. CRANE

MALEMUTE. See ALASKAN MALAMUTE.

MALENKOV, *mal un KAWF,* or *muh lyun KAWF,* **GEORGI MAXIMILIANOVICH** (1902-   ), became premier of Russia after the death of Joseph Stalin in March, 1953. Nikita S. Khrushchev forced him to resign as premier in February, 1955, and Malenkov became deputy premier under Premier Nikolai Bulganin. In June, 1957, Malenkov tried to unseat Khrushchev as first secretary of the Soviet Communist Party. He failed, and lost his high political posts. He was sent to Kazakhstan to manage a power plant. He was expelled from the Communist Party in 1964.

Malenkov was born in Orenburg. He became Stalin's private secretary in 1925. He became a member of the Politburo in 1946, and second secretary of the Presidium in 1952.   ALBERT PARRY

MALETSUNYANE FALLS, *MAH lay tsoon YAH nay,* is a waterfall in south-central Lesotho, about 20 miles from the mouth of the Maletsunyane River. Its 630-foot drop makes it one of the highest in Africa.

MALHERBE, *mal EHRB,* **FRANÇOIS DE** (1555-1628), was a French poet who became a haughty critic of French poetic language and style. He ridiculed the French poets of the 1500's, mercilessly attacking their flowery vocabularies and elaborate sentence structures. Some scholars believe he smothered French lyric poetry by setting rigid rules that dominated poets until the romantic period of the early 1800's. But he gave the language simplicity, clarity, force, and dignity.

Malherbe insisted that poetry be understandable, even to the poorest people of Paris. But he sternly avoided expressing personal feelings. Instead, he wrote about love and death, the great moral truths, and patriotic subjects of his day. His poetry consists of *Odes* and *Stanzas* (1600-1628). He was born in Caen. JOEL A. HUNT

Wide World

A Maldivian Fisherman Heads for Home with his share of the day's catch. Fish is a leading food and also the chief export.

the atolls help to protect the islands from the sea.

None of the islands covers more than 5 square miles, and most of the islands are smaller than that. Most are like little platforms about 6 feet above sea level. An 80-foot elevation on Wilingili Island is the highest point. The islands have clear lagoons and white sand beaches. The land is covered with grass and low-growing tropical plants. Clusters of coconut palms and fruit trees grow on the islands.

The climate is hot and humid. Daytime temperatures average about 80° F. The northern islands receive at least 100 inches of rain a year, and those in the south receive almost 150 inches a year. The two *monsoons* (seasonal winds) that blow over the islands each year bring most of the rain.

Economy is based on the government-controlled fishing industry. The sale of dried fish in Ceylon is one of the chief sources of the government's income.

The people raise breadfruit, coconuts, papaya, pineapples, pomegranates, and yams. Women use the coconut husk fibers, called *coir,* to make yarn and ropes. The women also collect cowrie shells from the shores and weave reed mats. The men make lacquer ware. Dried fish is the Maldives' chief export. Other exports include coir yarn, *copra* (dried coconut meat), cowrie shells, and fish meal. Rice, sugar, and wheat flour are the major imports. Ceylon is the country's chief trading partner.

Sailboats are the most common form of transportation in the Maldives. Steamships sail regularly between Male and Ceylon.

MALI

Clement Henry Moore, the contributor of this article, is Assistant Professor of Political Science at the University of California, Berkeley.

MALI is a big, underdeveloped country in western Africa. Most of it is flat or rolling grassland, but the northern part is desert. Mali covers a larger area than Arkansas, Louisiana, Oklahoma, and Texas combined. But it has only about half as many people as Texas.

Mali is an agricultural country. It lacks the mineral wealth and other resources needed for economic development. About 90 per cent of Mali's people live in rural areas. They include wandering Arab and Moorish herdsmen and Negro farmers.

From 1895 to 1959, France ruled Mali as the French Sudan. Mali merged with Senegal in 1959 to form the Federation of Mali, but the federation broke up in 1960. Mali then became a republic on Sept. 22, 1960. Its name in French, the official language, is RÉ-PUBLIQUE DU MALI (REPUBLIC OF MALI). Bamako, a city of about 130,000, is the capital and largest city.

Government. Mali is a republic. On Nov. 19, 1968, military officers overthrew the government, dissolved all political organizations, and jailed important government officials including President Modibo Keita. The military leaders set up a 14-man Committee of National

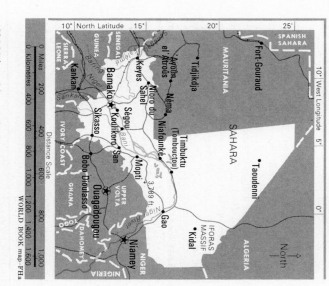

Capital

• **Other City or Town**

| **Road**

→ **Rail Line**

+ **Highest Known Elevation**

~ **River**

Liberation to supervise a provisional government. They promised a new constitution and elections in 1969.

Before the revolt, Mali had a strong central government. It was headed by an elected president and it was supported by Mali's one political party, the Sudanese Union.

Mali is divided into 6 regions, 42 *cercles* (districts), and 224 *arrondissements* (wards). The central government appoints local officials.

People. Mali's population is made up of three major groups—the white tribes, the Peuls, and the Negroes. There are about 500,000 members of the white tribes, which include the Tuareg, Moors, and Arabs. Most whites are wandering Moslem herders who live in the desert. They have a simple diet of millet, dates, and camel milk and live in camel-hair tents. Their loosely organized tribes are coordinated by *marabouts* (holy men) and are divided into *castes* (social classes).

The 700,000 Peuls live in the Niger Valley between the northern whites and the southern Negroes. Some Peuls are wandering Moslem cattle-raisers. They wear long white or brown robes and large cone-shaped straw hats. The herdsmen live in low huts made of straw mats or tree branches. Some of them wear only an animal skin tied around the waist. Some Peuls have mixed with the Negroes. They are settled farmers, and many are *animists* (people who believe that all objects have souls). They live in mud brick houses.

More than half the people are settled Negro farmers who live in southern Mali. Most Negroes belong to the Mandingo group of tribes which includes the Bambara, the Malinke, and the Sarakole. Most Bambara, the largest group, are animists. Some are woodworkers and others make cotton clothes. The Malinke include both animists and Moslems. The Sarakole are mainly farmers, cattle-raisers, and merchants. The Negroes live in neat villages of circular, sun-dried mud brick huts. Their diet consists of corn, yams, manioc, peanuts, and rice. Other important Negro groups in Mali include the Songhai, the Bozo, and the Dogons.

About 95 per cent of Mali's adults cannot read and write. Only about 10 per cent of the school age children in Mali attend primary, secondary, and technical schools.

FACTS IN BRIEF

Capital: Bamako.

Official Language: French.

Form of Government: Republic. *Head of State*—President.

Area: 478,767 square miles. *Greatest Distances*—(north-south) 1,000 mi.; (east-west) 1,150 mi. *Coastline*—none.

Population: No complete census. *Estimated 1971 Population*—5,065,000; distribution, 89 per cent rural, 11 per cent urban; density, 11 persons to the square mile. *Estimated 1976 Population*—5,565,000.

Chief Products: *Agriculture*—cotton, livestock, millet, peanuts, rice, shea nuts, sorghum. *Fishing*—fresh and dried fish. *Mining*—gold, iron, salt.

Flag: The flag has three vertical stripes of green, gold, and red which symbolize devotion to republicanism and the Declaration of the Rights of Man. See FLAG (color picture: Flags of Africa).

Money: *Basic Unit*—franc. See MONEY (table: Values).

Land. The southern half of Mali is a flat or rolling plateau covered with grass and trees. Highlands rise in the south and in the east. The highest point, in the southeast, is 3,789 feet above sea level. The northern half of Mali lies in the Sahara.

Most people live in the valleys of the Sénegal and Niger rivers and their tributaries. The Sénegal and its tributaries flow through southwestern Mali toward the northwest. The Niger River system flows northeast and then makes a great loop to the southeast. Mali's most fertile area is the lowland region that lies along the Niger between Bamako and Timbuktu.

Mali's climate is generally hot and dry. The annual temperature averages about 86° F. along the Sénegal and Niger rivers. Northern Mali is hotter. The average annual rainfall varies from 40 to 60 inches in the south to less than 10 inches in the north. Mali has three seasons. It is cool and dry from November to February; hot and dry from March to May; and cool and rainy from June to October.

Economy. Mali's economy is based chiefly on farming and livestock-raising. Mali produces more than enough food for its people and exports some agricultural products. But its natural resources are limited and the country has few industries. Mali receives economic aid from France, the United States, Communist China, and other countries.

The main crops include cotton, millet, peanuts, rice, shea nuts, and sorghum. Shea nuts provide an oil that is used for making butter, cooking oil, and soap. *Nomadic* (wandering) herdsmen raise millions of cattle, goats, and sheep, and also raise camels, donkeys, and horses.

Exports include peanuts, hides and skins, live animals, meat, and wool. About 8,000 tons of fish caught in the rivers are exported annually. Imports include automobiles and machinery. Most of Mali's foreign trade is with France and neighboring African countries. Mali's chief industries process agricultural products such as cotton, rice, and peanuts. Mali also produces some gold, salt, and iron.

The country has about 8,000 miles of roads, but many are impassable during the rainy season. A railroad runs 800 miles from Koulikoro to Dakar, Senegal. Air-Mali, the country's airline, operates within Mali and also has flights to other African countries and to Europe.

History. Areas in what is now Mali were part of powerful Negro empires from about the A.D. 300's to the 1500's. These empires—Ghana, Mali, and Songhai—were important trading centers.

The Ghana Empire lasted from about the 300's to the 1200's. It lay in what are now western Mali and southeastern Mauritania. See GHANA EMPIRE.

The Mali Empire flourished from about 1240 to 1500. It covered a large part of West Africa, including most of what is now Mali. The former city of Mali, northeast of Ségou, Mali, was its capital. See MALI EMPIRE.

The Songhai Empire probably began in the mid-800's. It reached its peak in the mid-1400's and included parts of what are now Mali, Niger, and Upper Volta. The city of Gao, Mali, was its capital. Moroccan invaders overran Songhai in 1591. But the Moroccan army was too small to control the huge empire, and many small kingdoms later ruled the area. See SONGHAI EMPIRE.

France entered what is now Mali in the mid-1800's. In Mali, it met one of the strongest movements that resisted colonial rule in Africa. From the 1850's to the 1890's, El Hadj Omar, a Tukulor conqueror, and Samory, a Malinke marabout, fought the French. But France crushed the resistance in 1895 and made the area a French colony which they called the Sudan. The colony became a territory in the French Commu-

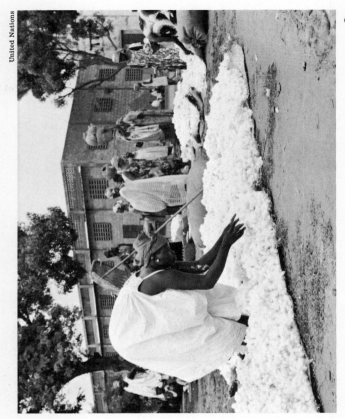

United Nations

Ségou, in Southern Mali, has a central market place where cotton and other important crops are sold.

85

nity in 1946. In 1958, it became the Sudan Republic, a self-governing republic within the French Community. In 1959, it joined Senegal to form the Federation of Mali. The federation became an independent political unit within the French Community in June, 1960, but it broke up in August, 1960. On Sept. 22, 1960, the Sudan Republic became the Republic of Mali. Modibo Keita became the country's first president.

Keita tried to develop the country's economy. But Mali seems to lack the resources for agricultural and industrial development. In 1962, Mali tried to achieve economic independence from France by setting up its own currency. This led Mali into debt. In 1968, military leaders overthrew Keita. Moussa Traore, a military officer, took control of the country as head of a military committee.

See also BAMAKO; FRENCH WEST AFRICA; NIGER RIVER; SENEGAL; TIMBUKTU.

MALI EMPIRE was a Negro empire that flourished in West Africa from about 1240 to 1500. At its height, the Mali Empire controlled most of what is now Gambia, Guinea, Mali, and Senegal, and parts of Mauritania, Niger, and Upper Volta.

Between 1235 and 1240, Sundiata, the king of Kangaba, conquered the nearby lands of the Sosso. He built a new city, Mali, to be the capital of his expanding empire. Later, under Mansa Musa, who ruled from 1312 to 1337, the empire spread eastward as far as Gao. Mansa Musa brought the empire to the peak of its political power and cultural achievement. Timbuktu

became a famous center of learning, especially in law and the study of Islam, the Moslem religion.

The cities of the Mali Empire were centers for the caravan trade from beyond the Sahara. The people were successful farmers and herders. Members of the governing classes were Moslems, but most of the people continued to worship tribal gods.

Control of the vast empire required skill and power that Mansa Musa's successors lacked. After about 1400, Songhai and other states conquered Mali's outlying areas. Tuareg raiders captured southern Sahara market towns. By 1500, the Songhai Empire controlled most of the Mali Empire.

See also TIMBUKTU.

LEO SPITZER

THE MALI EMPIRE IN 1337

This map shows the Mali Empire, in dark gray, at the height of its power in 1337. Mali controlled an area in West Africa including most of what are now the countries of Gambia, Guinea, Senegal, and Mali. The present boundaries are shown as white lines. The Tuareg and Songhai tribes conquered most of Mali by 1500.

North Atlantic Ocean

Gulf of Guinea

TEKRUR
WANGARA
KANGABA
KINGDOM OF KANGABA
MALI
Mali
Jenne
SOSSO
To Gold Coast
Walata
Timbuktu
Taghaza
BERBERS
To Europe
To Europe
SAHARA
Gao
SONGHAI
To Slave Coast
To Tunisia
TUAREG

Distance Scale
0 Miles 300 600 900
0 Kilometres 600

WORLD BOOK map
CLEMENT HENRY MOORE

MALIBRAN, *MAH lee BRAHN,* **MARIA FELICITA** (1808-1836), was a French-Spanish mezzo-contralto. She became noted for the peculiar tone and unusual range of her voice, and for her fiery temperament. At the age of 5, she played in Paer's opera *Agnese* in Naples, Italy. She created a sensation at her debut in Paris in 1824. She repeated her success in London in 1825, and appeared in New York in 1826 and 1827. She was born in Paris.

SCOTT GOLDTHWAITE

MALICE is ill will toward another person. In law, a crime is said to be malicious if it is committed for the sole purpose of injuring someone. Malice usually involves damage to property or damaging property. *Malicious mischief* is damage to property without cause.

MALIGNANCY is the tendency of a disease to be severe and possibly cause death. It most frequently refers to a *malignant tumor,* or cancer, in contrast to a *benign* (mild) tumor (see CANCER; TUMOR). Benign tumors remain in one part of the body and grow slowly. Malignant tumors spread to many parts of the body and grow rapidly. They are made up of actively dividing cells that vary in size and shape. The cells have little resemblance to the cells from which they originate. These features make the tumor malignant. Many people say *malignancy* when they mean *cancer.* J. F. A. McMANUS

MALINOWSKI, *MAH lee NAWF ski,* **BRONISLAW** (1884-1942), was a British anthropologist. He became known for his intensive study of the culture of the peoples of the Trobriand Islands in the southwest Pacific, and for his contributions to theories on human culture. Malinowski was born in Poland, and studied at Jagiellonian University and the University of London. He taught at the University of London for many years, and at Yale University from 1939 until his death. He wrote *Crime and Custom in Savage Society, Sexual Life of Savages in North West Melanesia,* and *Coral Gardens and Their Magic.*

DAVID B. STOUT

MALL is a broad, parklike thoroughfare. In Washington, D.C., the Mall stretches between the Capitol and the Lincoln Memorial (see WASHINGTON, D.C. [Washington from the Air; map]). In London, the Mall leads from Buckingham Palace to Trafalgar Square (see LONDON [Trafalgar Square and Whitehall]).

MALLARD, *MAL erd,* is a wild duck which lives in Europe, northern Asia, and throughout North America. It is about 2 feet long, and has curly upper tail feathers. The male mallard is beautifully colored during the breeding season and in the winter. It is grayish-brown on the back, and purplish-chestnut colored underneath. Its head and neck are glossy green, shaded with Prussian blue and purple. Glossy black feathers cover the lower back, rump, and tail. Two white and two black bars mark each of the side wings. A white band circles the neck. The bill is greenish-yellow and the feet are orange-red.

The female mallard is a tawny and dusky-brown color. She lays from 6 to 15 olive-colored eggs. The nest is made of grass or weeds and lined with down.

Scientific Classification. The mallard belongs to the surface duck family, *Anatidae*. It is a member of genus *Anas*, and is species *A. platyrhynchos*.   JOSEPH J. HICKEY

See also BIRD (color picture: Wild Ducks and Wild Geese); DUCK (Domestic Ducks).

MALLARMÉ, *mah lahr MAY,* **STÉPHANE** (1842-1898), was a French poet and critic born in Paris. He is best known for his dream poem *L'Après-midi d'un faune* (*The Afternoon of a Faun,* 1865). Except for weekly meetings with a group of European poets and artists in Paris, Mallarmé lived detached from society. He considered society hostile to the values of the poet.

Recognized by the younger generation as a master of poetic theory, Mallarmé became the mentor of a literary movement known as *symbolism* (see SYMBOLISM). According to him, the poet must suggest, not describe, the natural object. He must deliberately make his poetic image ambiguous, so that reality is presented in an atmosphere of mystery. Mallarmé's other works include esoteric sonnets; a metaphysical prose poem, *Igitur*; and *L'Hérodiade*, a long poem about Salome. His last poem, "Un Coup de dés jamais n'abolira le hasard" (1897) expresses the confrontation between the chaos of the universe (*le hasard*) and man's desire to shape his own destiny (*le coup de dés*).   ANNA BALAKIAN

See FRENCH LITERATURE (Poetry Reborn).

MALLEABILITY, *MAL ee ah BIL ih tih.* When metals can be hammered or rolled into thin sheets, they are said to be *malleable*. Gold, for example, is one of the most malleable of metals. It can be hammered into gold leaves so thin that they are almost transparent. The other common metals in the order of their malleability are silver, copper, aluminum, tin, zinc, and lead. Cast iron is stiff and brittle and has practically no malleability. Its stiffness is caused by the carbon atoms which are united with the iron. Cast iron can be made slightly malleable by heating it for a long time with some substance which will remove some of the carbon atoms. Cast iron which has been treated in this way is called *malleable iron* and has many uses in industry. Any metal becomes more malleable when it is heated and usually when it is purified. Another property similar to malleability is *ductility*. This means that metal can be drawn out into wire.   LOUIS MARICK

See also DUCTILITY.

MALLEIN TEST. See GLANDERS.

MALLEUS. See EAR (The Middle Ear).

MALLOPHAGA. See INSECT (table).

MALLORCA. See MAJORCA.

MALLORY, STEPHEN RUSSELL (1813?-1873), was an American lawyer and political leader who served as secretary of the Confederate Navy. He was born in the West Indies. His father was a Connecticut shipbuilder, but was living in Trinidad when Stephen was born. The family settled in Key West, Fla., in 1820.

Mallory was appointed inspector of customs in Key West in 1833, and studied law while holding that position. After he was admitted to the bar, President Polk appointed him collector of customs in Key West. In 1850, Mallory was elected to the United States Senate from Florida.

Florida seceded from the Union in 1861, and Mallory resigned from the Senate. President Jefferson Davis appointed him secretary of the Confederate Navy, which was then almost nonexistent. Mallory had to organize the Navy and direct it. He also had to build the ships and equip them from what little material he found available.

Mallory attacked his task with great ability. He succeeded in building a small but efficient Navy, and showed much foresight in ordering ironclads built instead of the older type of wooden warships. His naval experts developed deadly torpedoes and underwater devices which kept the Union Navy out of the great rivers of Virginia until late in the war.

After the fall of Richmond, Mallory fled south with President Davis and was captured in Georgia. He was held prisoner for nearly a year, but was pardoned by President Andrew Johnson in 1867.   RICHARD N. CURRENT

MALLOW, *MAL oh,* is the popular name of a large family of plants. The mallow family includes about 1,000 kinds of herbs, shrubs, and trees that grow in tropical and temperate regions of the world. The plants of this family have fibrous stems and sticky sap. Many well-known flowers, such as the hibiscus, hollyhock, and marsh mallow, belong to the mallow family. The cotton plant and okra are also members.

Scientific Classification. The mallows make up the mallow family, *Malvaceae*.   ROBERT W. HOSHAW

Related Articles in WORLD BOOK include:

Cotton	Indian Mallow
Flower (color picture: Flowers	Marsh Mallow
That Grow in Wet Places)	Okra
Hibiscus	Rose of Sharon
Hollyhock	

MALMAISON. See JOSEPHINE.

MALMÖ, *MAHL muh* (pop. 245,803; met. area 259,-707; alt. 18 ft.), is the third largest city in Sweden. It lies at the southern tip of Sweden, 16 miles from Copenhagen, Denmark (see SWEDEN [political map]). The city exports food and other products to European ports. Eight railroad lines connect it with other cities of Sweden. Malmö has a modern airport. Its beautiful town hall dates from 1546.   JAMES J. ROBBINS

MALNUTRITION, *mal noo TRISH uhn,* is an unhealthy condition caused by poor intake, absorption, or use of nutrients by the body. Symptoms of malnutrition include cramps, diarrhea, weakness, and weight loss. *Primary malnutrition* results when the body does not get enough food or the right kinds of food. *Secondary malnutrition* occurs when, because of disease, the body cannot use nutrients even though they are present in the food.

There are a number of types of malnutrition, depending on the nutrient or nutrients missing. *Protein-calorie malnutrition* occurs when the diet is low in both proteins and calories. This condition is called *marasmus* if the diet is particularly low in calories. It is called *kwashiorkor* if the diet is especially low in proteins.

Malnutrition caused by a low intake of vitamins may lead to *vitamin deficiencies.* Various diseases result from deficiencies of different vitamins (see VITAMIN). Malnutrition may also be due to *mineral deficiencies*. For example, lack of iron or copper can cause an abnormal condition of the blood called *anemia*.

Social and economic conditions as well as natural conditions such as flooding and drought may produce malnutrition. Poverty, war, disease, and ignorance concerning a balanced diet also cause countless cases of malnutrition.

JEAN MAYER

Related Articles in WORLD BOOK include:

Anemia	Food
Beriberi	Goiter
Diet	Nutrition
	Pellagra
	Rickets
	Scurvy

MALOCCLUSION. See DENTISTRY (Orthodontics); TEETH (Malocclusion).

MALONE COLLEGE. See UNIVERSITIES AND COLLEGES (table).

MALORY, *MAL oh rih*, SIR THOMAS (? -1471), was an English writer who collected and rewrote stories for his romance of knighthood *Le Morte Darthur* (The Death of Arthur). This was the first important English prose romance. It tells of King Arthur and his knights of the Round Table, their search for the Holy Grail, and their downfall (see ARTHUR, KING; HOLY GRAIL).

William Caxton, the first English printer, edited and published his version of the original Malory *Le Morte Darthur* in 1485 (see CAXTON, WILLIAM). Until 1934, Caxton's was the only version of the work known. Great poets like Edmund Spenser and Alfred, Lord Tennyson used it as a basis for their poems, and readers took it as Malory's own work. Tennyson titled his poem *Morte d'Arthur*, and this became the popular spelling. In 1934, an old manuscript of *Le Morte Darthur* was discovered in the library of Winchester College, a boy's school in England. Scholars recognized it as an example of Malory's original work.

In 1947, Professor Eugène Vinaver published an edition of *Le Morte Darthur* based on this manuscript. There are now two versions of the work, Malory's original, and Caxton's rewriting of it. Malory wrote eight separate stories. Caxton united them into one work. Versions published before 1947 are Caxton's.

Malory was probably a knight of Warwickshire, but he apparently did not live up to the high ideals of knighthood. He served in Parliament in 1445. Later, he was arrested and convicted several times for armed robbery, assault, and other crimes. He wrote much or all of his work in prison. In one place he calls himself "knyht prisoner," and in another he prays for "good delyveraunce sone hastely."

ARNOLD WILLIAMS

MALPEQUE BAY. See PRINCE EDWARD ISLAND (Places to Visit; picture).

MALPIGHI, *mahl PEE gee*, MARCELLO (1628-1694), an Italian anatomist, has been called the first histologist (see HISTOLOGY). He discovered the capillary blood vessels that carry the blood between the arteries and veins. He was the first to describe the red blood corpuscles, and one of the first to use the microscope in medicine. Malpighi's book, *Anatomical Treatise on the Structures of the Viscera*, appeared in 1666. His descriptions of the minute structure of the lungs, spleen, and kidneys are considered to be among the classics of medicine.

Malpighi was born near Bologna, Italy. He studied at the University of Bologna. At 28, he became a professor of medicine at the University of Pisa. He returned to Bologna in 1659, and stayed there more than 30 years teaching, writing, and doing research. He served as personal physician to Pope Innocent XII from 1691 until his death.

CAROLINE A. CHANDLER

MALPIGHIAN TUBE. These tube-shaped glands in insects and related animals secrete urine into the alimentary canal. They are named after the Italian anatomist Marcello Malpighi.

MALRAUX, *mal ROH*, ANDRÉ (1901-), is a French author who has combined intellectual achievement with political activity. Malraux was born in Paris. From 1923 to 1927, he traveled in the Far East as a student of archaeology, Oriental languages, and art. While there, he became involved in local revolutionary struggles for freedom. In the 1930's, Malraux participated in the struggles against Nazism in Germany, and Fascism in Spain. During World War II, he fought with the French resistance forces against the Germans. In 1959, he became France's first secretary of cultural affairs.

United Press Int.

André Malraux

Malraux's novels reflect his involvement in battles for freedom. However, his books are not autobiographical. Even in his autobiography, *Anti-Memoirs* (1967), he does not write about himself so much as about some of the great political figures of his day. Malraux's fiction explores man's devotion to ideals. He wants art "to give men a consciousness of their own hidden greatness." His style is simple, concise, and fact-filled. But it may burst into poetic imagery and suggests man's solitude and ever-present sense of death. Malraux's best novels include *The Royal Way* (1930), *Man's Fate* (1933), *Days of Wrath* (1935), and *Man's Hope* (1937).

Malraux has also written several important works on art that compare works of different periods and civilizations.

EDITH KERN

MALT is a food product which results when barley and certain other grains are specially treated. Beermakers use most of the malt made. It is also used in distilling, baking, and making other foods and drugs.

In the malting process, manufacturers steep grain in water for 24 to 96 hours. They then spread it on large, ventilated floors and allow it to sprout and grow for 5 to 10 days. Temperature and moisture are carefully controlled during this time. Next, large *kilns* (ovens) dry the grain for 2 or 3 days. The drying is started at low temperatures and gradually increased to 180°F. Finally, the malt is aged for 4 to 8 weeks before manufacturers use it.

During the malting process, certain chemical changes take place in the grain. The insoluble starch changes into a sugar called *maltose*. Malting also releases certain *enzymes*. The enzymes are *diastase*, which has the power to convert starch into sugar, and *peptase*, which can change certain proteins.

See also BREWING; MALTOSE.

H. F. PEROT

MALTA

MALTA is an independent island country in the Mediterranean Sea, about 60 miles south of Sicily. It is one of the most densely populated countries in the world, with 2,500 persons to a square mile.

Malta is important because of its strategic location and its natural harbors. British Mediterranean fleet headquarters are there. The North Atlantic Treaty Organization (NATO) also has its Mediterranean area headquarters in Malta.

Terrace-farming over much of Malta makes the countryside look much like giant steps. The balmy climate attracts many visitors. Tourists also come to Malta to view some of the world's finest examples of Baroque and Renaissance art and architecture.

Malta was once a British crown colony. In 1962, it became the State of Malta within the British Commonwealth, with powers of internal self-government. In September, 1964, Malta became an independent country. Valletta, on the island of Malta, is the capital and chief port of the country. See VALLETTA.

Government. Malta is a constitutional monarchy. The British queen is recognized as Malta's queen and is represented in Malta by a governor general. The prime minister is head of government and leader of the majority party in parliament. He is elected to a five-year term. The prime minister, assisted by a Cabinet of not more than seven ministers, directs the government. The 50 members of the House of Representatives are elected by the people to five-year terms.

People. Malta has a population of about 305,000. The Maltese have the medium height, regular features, black hair, and dark eyes of most Mediterranean peoples. Most of them speak Maltese, a West Arabic dialect with some Italian words. Both English and Maltese are official languages. Maltese is used in the courts. The country has both Maltese and English newspapers. Roman Catholicism is the state religion of Malta.

Land. Malta covers a total area of 122 square miles. It consists of the islands of Malta, Comino, Cominotto, Filfla, and Gozo. Malta and Gozo are the largest and most important. Malta island covers 95 square miles and has a 62-mile coastline. Gozo covers 26 square miles. Cominotto and Filfla are tiny and uninhabited. Malta has a mild climate. Frost in the winter is unusual, and sea breezes moderate the summer heat. Winters are moist and mild, and summers are hot and dry. Temperatures average 66° F. Malta gets about 21 inches of rainfall annually. Strong northwest winds sometimes reach hurricane force in autumn and winter.

Economy. Most of the people work at the dockyards and in the building industry. The economy of Malta is becoming more dependent upon tourists. The onetime British naval dockyards are now used for commercial shipbuilding and repair work. A few light industries have been set up in the country.

Maltese farmers raise citrus fruits, barley, grapes, onions, potatoes, and wheat. However, crops are small because of the rocky soil. Malta must import most of its food. The country has no minerals or natural resources, except salt and limestone.

Malta imports more goods than it exports. It carries on nearly half of its trade with Great Britain. Italy is its second most important trade partner.

The country has over 600 miles of road. There is a ferry service between Malta and Gozo. British airlines maintain local and international service for Malta.

Malta has compulsory elementary education for all children from 6 to 14 years old. There are about 120 Roman Catholic primary and secondary schools operated by the government. The country also has about 80 private primary and secondary schools. Parents may choose whether their children are taught in English or Maltese. Until World War II, the schools taught Italian. But English has replaced Italian in the schools. The Royal University of Malta is in Valletta.

History. Malta is a region of great historical interest. Remains of late Stone Age and Bronze Age men have been found in limestone caverns on the islands. Rough stone buildings from early ages have also been discovered in Malta. The Phoenicians colonized Malta

FACTS IN BRIEF

Capital: Valletta.

Official Languages: Maltese and English.

Form of Government: Constitutional monarchy.

Area: 122 square miles.

Population: *1967 Census*—315,765; distribution, 64 per cent urban, 36 per cent rural. *Estimated 1971 Population*—305,000; density, 2,500 persons to the square mile. *Estimated 1976 Population*—293,000.

Chief Products: *Agriculture*—barley, grapes, onions, potatoes, wheat. *Manufacturing and Processing*—beverages, processed food, shipbuilding and repair.

Flag: A silver replica of the George Cross, a British medal awarded to Malta for bravery in World War II, appears on a red and white field. See FLAG (picture: Flags of Europe).

Money: *Basic Unit*—Maltese pound. See MONEY (table).

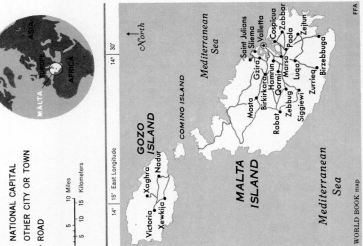

NATIONAL CAPITAL
OTHER CITY OR TOWN
ROAD

0   5   10 Miles
0 5 10 15 Kilometers

GOZO ISLAND

Victoria Xaghra Nadur
Xewkija

COMINO ISLAND

MALTA ISLAND

Mediterranean Sea

Mediterranean Sea

North

14° 15' East Longitude 14° 30'

36°

35° 50' North Latitude

Saint Julians Sliema
Gzira Valletta
Birkirkara Cospicua Zabbar
Mosta Hamrun Paola
Rabat Qormi Marsa Zejtun
Zebbug Luqa
Siggiewi Zurrieq Birzebbuga

Mediterranean Sea

WORLD BOOK map

FFA

ASIA
EUROPE
MALTA
AFRICA

MALTA

in about 1000 B.C. Temples, tombs, and other relics of the Phoenicians still stand. Greek, Carthaginian, Roman, and Arab conquerors followed the Phoenicians into Malta. According to tradition, Saint Paul the Apostle was shipwrecked near Malta about A.D. 60 and converted the inhabitants to Christianity.

Malta passed to the Norman kings of Sicily around 1090. Around 1520, the Holy Roman Emperor Charles V inherited the area when he received the crown of Spain. In 1530, Charles V gave Malta to the Knights of the Order of Saint John of Jerusalem. The Knights are sometimes called the Hospitallers. The Knights of Saint John wore the Maltese cross as their badge (see Cross). They had fought against the Moslems since the time of the First Crusade in the 1090's. In 1565, the Turks laid siege to Malta with great naval and military forces. Though heavily outnumbered, the Knights held out against the Turks for months, and finally defeated them. The town of Valletta was named after Jean de la Vallette, the Grand Master who led the Knights' defense against the Turks.

The French under Napoleon Bonaparte took Malta from the Knights of Saint John in 1798. British forces drove out the French in 1800. The people of Malta offered control of the colony to Great Britain. Britain's control was not completely recognized, however, until peace was made with France in 1815, after the Napoleonic Wars. Great Britain developed its Mediterranean headquarters on Malta.

During World War I, Malta served as a strategic naval base for Allied forces. Great Britain granted Malta a measure of self-government in 1921. However, political crises in Malta caused Britain to revoke the Maltese political power. Malta's constitution was suspended in 1930 because of a dispute between the state and Roman Catholic authorities. They disagreed about the role of the church in state affairs. The constitution

was re-established in 1932, then withdrawn a year later. This time the pro-Italian sympathies of the Maltese ministry led Britain to suspend the constitution. Full authority was reinvested in the governor in 1936.

During World War II, Malta controlled the vital sea lanes between Italy and Africa. The natural rocks and deep inlets of the colony concealed anchorages and submarine bases. Many underground passages provided bomb shelters. Fighter planes based on Malta defended convoys of ships. The colony suffered heavy bomb damage. In 1942, King George VI of England awarded the George Cross to Malta in recognition of the courage and endurance of its people during the war.

The constitution of 1947 gave the colony increased partial self-government. The Maltese Labour party gained control of the assembly and proposed political integration with Great Britain. In a 1956 referendum, the people voted for integration. A bill was prepared in the British Parliament, providing for local government in Malta and giving it three members in Britain's House of Commons. No further progress was made, because the Maltese wanted guarantees of employment in the dockyards. An independence movement began to grow in Malta in 1958. A constitution approved in 1962 provided that the colony become a state with internal self-government. The new legislative assembly favored full independence. Great Britain agreed to grant full independence, effective in May, 1964. But disagreement among Malta's political factions delayed the action until September, 1964.

Malta's political parties could not agree on whether to become a republic or a constitutional monarchy after independence. Some factions did not even want independence from Great Britain. But the Nationalist party defeated the Labour party on these measures and Malta became an independent constitutional monarchy on Sept. 21, 1964. Dr. Borg Oliver, leader of the Nationalists, became prime minister. Later that year, Malta joined the United Nations.

FRANCIS H. HERRICK

Three Lions

Valletta, The Capital of Malta, is also the country's most important port. The city has been Malta's capital since 1571.

New York Zoological Society

The Mamba of Africa Is a Graceful But Deadly Snake.

MALTA, KNIGHTS OF. See KNIGHTS OF SAINT JOHN.

MALTA FEVER is the name once given to undulant fever, an infectious disease first known in Malta. See UNDULANT FEVER.

MALTED MILK POWDER. See MILK (Other Processes).

MALTESE was probably the world's first lap dog. It developed on the Mediterranean island of Malta more than 2,000 years ago. Ladies in Greek and Roman noble families were fond of these little dogs. They carried them in the long sleeves of their robes, and waited on them like babies. The Maltese grew to be one of the gentlest of all toy dogs. It usually weighs from 4 to 6 pounds. Its black eyes have dark rims that make the eyes look large. Its white coat falls from a part down its back, and sometimes grows so long it trails on the ground. See also Dog (picture: Toy Dogs).
JOSEPHINE Z. RINE

MALTESE. See CAT (Breed Colors).

MALTESE CROSS. See CROSS (picture); KNIGHTS OF SAINT JOHN.

MALTHUS, *MAL thus,* **THOMAS ROBERT** (1766-1834), was an English economist. He is best known for his *Essay on the Principle of Population,* published in 1798. Malthus' main idea in this book is that population tends to increase more rapidly than food supplies. He believed that wars and disease would have to kill off the extra population, unless people decided to limit the number of their children.

Malthus' *Essay* suggested to Charles Darwin the relationship between progress and the survival of the fittest. This was a basic idea in Darwin's theory of evolution (see DARWIN [Charles R.]). Few people today believe in Malthus' theory. Improved methods of agriculture usually provide enough food for all, though some have starved because of faulty economic organization or distribution. Some conservationists have warned, however, that food production cannot keep pace with population increases indefinitely. The *neo-Malthusians* of the 1900's urge planned parenthood. Malthus himself had rejected this belief in his *Essay.*

Malthus was born on Feb. 17, 1766, in Surrey. He decided to be a clergyman, and was graduated from Cambridge University. About 1796, he took a parish in Surrey. He became a professor of history and political economy in the college of the East India Company in 1805, and held this post until his death.
H. W. SPIEGEL

See also POPULATION (Overpopulation).

MALTOSE, *MAWL tohs,* is the chemical term for malt sugar. The formation of maltose in the body is the first step in the digestion of starchy foods. The enzyme *ptyalin* in saliva changes starch into maltose. Other enzymes in the body split the maltose into glucose (see GLUCOSE). Commercially, the enzyme *diastase* in malt changes starch into maltose. Fermentation changes maltose into alcohol. This is recovered by distillation. Maltose is used for sweetening some foods. See also BREWING; DIGESTION; MALT.
W. NORTON JONES, JR.

MAMBA, *MAHM bah,* is the name of three of the most dreaded snakes of Central and South Africa. They are closely related to the cobras, but do not have a hood.

The mambas are slender and look somewhat like whips. They are usually about 6 to 8 feet long, but may be as long as 14 feet. Mambas glide very rapidly in trees as well as on the ground. They produce a poison as powerful as that of the African cobras and vipers. The black mamba is green when young and dark brown

when adult. The green mamba is green throughout life.

Scientific Classification. The mambas belong to the terrestrial poisonous snake family, *Elapidae.* They make up the genus *Dendroaspis.* The black mamba is genus *Dendroaspis,* species *D. polylepis.* The green mamba is *D. angusticeps.*
CLIFFORD H. POPE

MAMELUKE, *MAM uh lyook.* The Mamelukes were Turkish and Circassian prisoners of Genghis Khan. They were sold as slaves to the Sultan of Egypt. The Egyptians trained them as soldiers, and eventually promoted them to high government posts. In A.D. 1250, the Mamelukes seized control of Egypt, and ruled it for more than 250 years. See EGYPT (History; picture).

The Mameluke sultans overran Asia Minor, Syria, and the island of Cyprus. Selim I of Turkey finally defeated them in 1517 and conquered Egypt. But even under Turkish rule, the Mamelukes remained powerful. They organized cavalry squadrons and attacked Napoleon I when he invaded Egypt in 1798. After the French defeated the Mamelukes in the Battle of the Pyramids, some of them joined the French Army.

Egypt's Viceroy Mehemet Ali ordered the massacre of all Mamelukes in 1811. The few who escaped fled to Nubia and tried to organize an army of Negroes. When they failed, the Mamelukes disappeared.
A. E. R. BOAK

Mameluke Warriors serving under Napoleon I during the French invasion of Spain massacred many Spaniards on May 2, 1808.
The Charge of the Mamelukes (The Second of May, 1808) by Francisco Goya, 1814, The Prado, Madrid

MAMMAL

MAMMAL, *MAM ul*, is an animal with hair and *mammary glands* on its body. The name *mammal* comes from the Latin word *mamma* (breast). The mammary glands of female mammals produce milk the females feed to their young. This feeding is called *nursing*. No other animals —fishes, insects, birds, or snakes—nurse their young.

There are about 3,500 different *species* (kinds) of mammals, and they live in all parts of the world. Human beings are mammals. So are dogs and cats, dolphins and bats, and big game animals, such as lions and tigers. The blue whale, the largest animal that has ever lived, is a mammal. The smallest mammal is a shrew that weighs less than a dime. To learn where mammals fit into the whole animal kingdom, see ANIMAL (chart: A Classification of the Animal Kingdom).

Scientists believe the first mammals developed from a group of reptiles about 180 million years ago. This was during what geologists call the Mesozoic Era, when reptiles were the *dominant* (ruling) animals on the earth. Over the last 65 million years, mammals have slowly become the dominant land *vertebrates* (animals with backbones). See PREHISTORIC ANIMAL.

Features of Mammals. During these millions of years, mammals have developed different ways to protect themselves against the weather and other forces in their *environment* (surroundings). Some mammals migrate to warmer areas when winter comes. Others hibernate to survive when the weather is cold and there is little food.

Most mammals, such as bears, are covered with hair from head to tail. The hair helps to protect them from harsh weather. Most animals shed some of the hair in warm weather, and their coats grow thick again when cold weather returns. A coat of thick, sharp hair called *spines* or *quills* helps to protect the porcupine from other animals. Porcupines strike attackers with their quilled tails. Some mammals, such as the whale and hippopotamus, have only a few bristles. But they both have thick, tough skin. Generally, the thicker the mammal's skin is, the less hair it has.

Mammals usually have brown, black, or reddish hair that blends with their surroundings. The hair of some, such as the fox and weasel, turns white during the winter. Their hair color helps them hide from other animals that might eat them.

All mammals are warm-blooded. When the surrounding temperature gets hot, they can cool themselves off. Some do this by panting or sweating. They can also warm themselves up when the weather is cold, sometimes by shivering or exercising. Mammals keep their body temperature constant, regardless of the air temperature. For example, a human being's normal body temperature is 98.6° F. However, the body temperature may vary when a mammal is sick, and it drops when a mammal hibernates.

Mammals have a keen sense of smell and communicate with others by making sounds. Mammals can reason better and learn more easily than other animals. This is because a mammal thinks and remembers with a larger and more complex brain than any other animal. Human beings have the most complex brain and nervous system of all the mammals.

Kinds of Mammals. Mammals are classified in three different groups according to the way young mammals develop. Most young mammals develop inside the mother's body before birth. In the *placental mammals*, the young receive nourishment through a special organ in the female body called the *placenta*. This group includes human beings, horses, goats, and most other mammals.

The second group of mammals are called the *pouched mammals* or *marsupials*. This group includes kangaroos and opossums. Most marsupials give birth to their young earlier than other mammals. Because of this, marsupial young are smaller and less developed. Consequently, after birth they crawl into the mother's protective pouch where they get nourishment from the mammary glands. There they feed and develop until they are better able to care for themselves.

In the third group of mammals, the young develop outside of the mother's body. They are called *monotremes* or *egg-laying mammals*. This group includes the platypus and spiny anteaters. The female lays eggs and nurses the young after they hatch. Monotremes are the only living mammals that lay eggs. They are only found in Australia and parts of Asia.

The *gestation time* (period of development before birth) of mammals varies from 12½ days in opossums to 20 to 22 months in elephants. The larger mammals usually have the longer gestation periods. The placental mammals have the longest gestation period and are born more developed and more nearly able to take care of themselves. See GESTATION.

Scientific Classification. Mammals make up the class *Mammalia* in the phylum *Chordata*.

Related Articles. See the separate articles in WORLD BOOK on the mammals mentioned in this article. See also the following articles with their lists of Related Articles:

Animal	Insectivore	Rodent
Carnivore	Man	Sirenia
Cetacean	Marsupial	Ungulate
Edentate	Primate	

WILLIAM V. MAYER

MAMMARY GLANDS are glands in the breasts of all mammals, both male and female. They produce milk. They are one of the major features that distinguish mammals from other kinds of animals (see MAMMAL).

In males, the mammary glands remain undeveloped. In females, they enlarge and develop. The gland itself consists of many *lobules* (sacks) which secrete milk. Many *ducts* (tubes) are connected to these lobules. The ducts combine to form several main ducts which empty the milk into the nipple. Milk is released through the nipple.

T. B. SCHWARTZ

MAMMOTH, *MAM uth*, was a prehistoric animal closely related to present-day elephants. Mammoths were huge, lumbering beasts. Some measured more than 14 feet high at the shoulders. Like the elephants of today, mammoths had trunks and tusks. Many had tusks 13 feet long. The tusks curved down from the animal's upper jaw, then curved up and crossed in front of the trunk. Certain kinds of mammoths, called *woolly* or *hairy* mammoths, had long hair on their bodies to help protect them from the severe cold of the Ice Age.

Mammoths rank among the most common fossils. The bodies of mammoths have been found perfectly preserved in ice in Siberia. Alaskan miners often wash petrified mammoth bones and teeth out of gravel when they pan for gold. Fossils of these enormous beasts have also been found in New York and Texas.

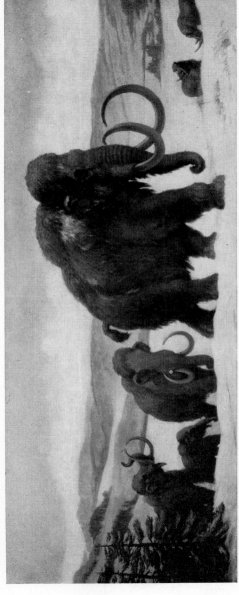

The Hairy Mammoth was a relative of the modern elephant. Mammoths lived in the frozen regions of North America, Europe,

and Asia, but died out many thousand years ago. On the right are woolly rhinoceroses, which lived in Europe.

The oldest known mammoth bones date from 4 million years ago in India. Mammoths spread to other continents and reached North America about 500,000 years later, at the beginning of the Ice Age. Prehistoric men hunted these animals for food. Pictures of mammoths drawn by cave dwellers can still be seen on the walls of caves in southern France. Mammoths died out about 10,000 years ago.

Scientific Classification. Mammoths belong to the elephant family, *Elephantidae*. They make up the genus *Mammuthus*.

SAMUEL PAUL WELLES

See also ELEPHANT (Kinds); FOSSIL (Whole Animals); MASTODON; PREHISTORIC ANIMAL (color picture).

MAMMOTH CAVE NATIONAL PARK surrounds Mammoth Cave, the largest single cave in the world. The park lies in central Kentucky, about 100 miles south of Louisville. It includes 51,354.40 acres of wooded hill country. Two rivers, the Green and the Nolin, wind through the park. Mammoth Cave National Park was established in 1941. Each year, the park attracts about 500,000 visitors.

Mammoth Cave is often called one of the wonders of the Western Hemisphere. Visitors can explore about 150 miles of corridors on five different levels within the cave. The lowest level lies 360 feet below the surface. Beautiful rock formations, called *stalactites* and *stalagmites*, fill the cave (see STALACTITE; STALAGMITE). Many of the rocks in the cave have interesting and unusual shapes and colors. They resemble flowers, fruits, trees, and waterfalls.

The cave contains two lakes, three rivers, and eight waterfalls. The largest river, Echo River, varies in width from 20 to 60 feet and in depth from 5 to 25 feet. Visitors may take a half-mile trip over the river in flat-bottomed boats. Strange eyeless fish live in Echo River (see BLINDFISH). These colorless creatures are about 4 inches long and have no scales. Other blind creatures living in Mammoth Cave include beetles, crayfish, and crickets. Many small brown bats live in parts of the cave that are not visited frequently by people.

According to popular legend, a hunter named Robert

Houchins found Mammoth Cave in 1799 while chasing a wounded bear. But moccasins, simple tools, torches, and the remains of mummies found in the cave indicate that it was known to prehistoric Indians. Saltpeter, used to make gunpowder, was mined in the cave during the War of 1812. The cave contained the only large supply of saltpeter known in the United States at that time. After the war ended, miners stopped working in the cave. Mammoth Cave then became a public showplace.

Another famous cave, Floyd Collins Crystal Cave, lies in a privately-owned area within the national park. Collins, a cave explorer, discovered Crystal Cave in 1917. About 30 miles of it have been surveyed. At least 15 other caves lie under the same ridge as Crystal Cave. Many cave authorities believe that Crystal Cave is the central unit tying all of these caves together into one vast cave system.

HERBERT E. KAHLER

MAMMOTH HOT SPRINGS. See YELLOWSTONE NATIONAL PARK.

MAMMOTH SPRING. See ARKANSAS (Springs).

Mammoth Cave National Park, Kentucky, is a noted sight-seeing attraction. Stalactites hang from the roof of the "Onyx Chamber," below, in the Frozen Niagara section of the cave. The stalagmite on the floor is 67 feet in circumference at its base.

HOW MAN DIFFERS FROM ANIMALS

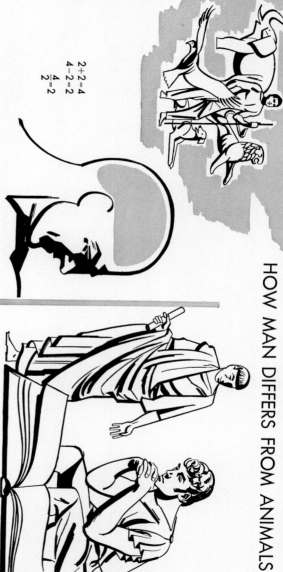

Man has greater brain capacity, and can reason.

$$2+2=4$$
$$4-2=2$$
$$\frac{4}{2}=2$$

He can create new ideas.

He can live in the cold Arctic—

or in the hot tropics.

Man adapts himself to his climate and surroundings.

He uses and changes plants,

tames and uses animals,

and uses the power of rivers.

Man changes his surroundings to meet his needs.

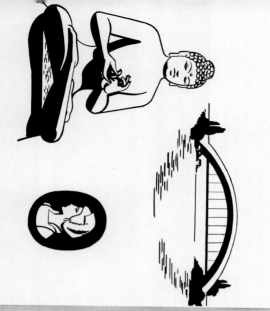

Man creates things of lasting use and beauty.

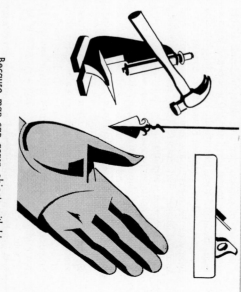

Because man can grasp objects with his hands, he can use the tools he makes to create or change his surroundings.

MAN is the most remarkable of all the creatures that live in the world. He is the only creature that lives in all climates, makes and uses tools, creates fire, prays, talks, and destroys his own kind in wars. Through science, man has unlocked many secrets of the universe, such as knowledge of the shape of the earth, the structure of atoms, and the composition of plants and animals.

Several branches of science help man learn about himself and understand how he fits into the world he lives in. *Anatomy* studies the structure of the human body. *Physiology* investigates how the body works. Through *psychology*, man explores the human mind. He studies *sociology* to see how people behave in groups. *Anthropology* helps him learn about the differences between the various races and cultures of mankind. All these branches of science have separate articles in WORLD BOOK. These studies, and many more, help man to understand himself, to conquer diseases, and to plan for the future in the hope of achieving a more perfect way of life for his descendants.

Man's Unique Characteristics

The main difference between man and other creatures is that only man has intellectual faculties and spiritual qualities along with physical ones. The spiritual side of man's nature is often called his *soul*. Members of most religious faiths believe that this soul is *immortal*, or that it never dies. The belief in a home for the soul, usually called *heaven*, comes from this version of the nature of man.

Reason. Man differs greatly from animals because of his brain, which is probably the most complex living structure yet known (see BRAIN). Human behavior reflects man's superior brain. The function of the brain and other parts of the central nervous system is to receive signals from the sense organs, to coordinate them, and to respond to them. Insofar as these receptions and responses are largely automatic, man's brain shares its function with the brains of the lower animals. Both men and animals learn by experience, and learning influences the planning and carrying out of simple actions. But man can go a step farther because his brain gives him the ability to reason. Without any direct stimulus, such as hunger, a man can retire into the world of his mind and think up a scheme, then decide whether or not to carry it out. He may reason: "I have a new bow to shoot animals with. I have a stone-tipped drill that I bore holes with by twirling the shaft between my hands. Why wouldn't it be easier to combine them and make a bow drill?" Scientists have not discovered any other creature that can create things in its mind by reasoning, and then put ideas into action.

Man can reason because his brain is able to establish and recognize symbols. A symbol is something that stands for something else. A picture of a mountain is a symbol of a mountain, which we can see when the mountain is out of sight. The word *mountain* when spoken also gives a person the idea of the object through his sense of hearing. A blind person can read the word *mountain* by feeling letters printed in Braille. So the idea of *mountain* can be understood through at least three senses.

Language. Almost everyone can recognize a realistic picture. But only a person who knows the language of which a word forms a part can recognize a verbal sym-

bol. For example, *mountain* is *jebel* in Arabic, *kuh* in Persian, and *yama* in Japanese. Some animals also communicate with each other. Porpoises and gibbons, for example, may have 20 or more sounds with separate meanings. But animals use sounds only to express emotions, and they cannot express ideas. Animal languages have to be learned, but the process is simple, rapid, and more closely controlled by heredity than with man. All porpoises or gibbons of a given species understand each other. But man alone inherits the ability to learn specialized, complete, and elaborate languages.

Scientists do not know whether man's ability to create language has anything to do with his physical equipment for making sounds. Man's tongue, teeth, lips, and vocal cords and other throat organs resemble those of most of the other primates. Some scientists believe that man can produce a variety of sounds because his remote ancestors may once have lived in trees. These scientists believe that tree-living animals, such as birds, tree toads, and monkeys, can be noisier than ground-living animals, because they are safer. All primates have long been able to communicate in a simple and direct way by making faces. The facial muscles also serve to modify sounds. Man and other primates can actually change the sounds with their mouths by "making faces."

Culture. Speech forms the basis of culture, the sum total of all distinctly human activities. Some scientists believe that certain animals, particularly the apes, show the beginnings of culture. For instance, chimpanzees can invent clumsy tools in order to reach food beyond their grasp. But they have no way of passing on their knowledge. Human parents tell their children what to do during their long period of growing up, which is unique in man. In the same way, man can pass on to future generations the knowledge he has gained through thousands of years. Language unites men for common purposes. Apes, which cannot talk, have no organization larger than the family. Human beings, through their power of communication, can organize themselves into bands of hunters, villages of farmers, cities of craftsmen and traders, and great nations and empires. For a more complete discussion of the meaning and scope of human culture, see CULTURE.

Man's Place Among Living Things

Scientific Classification. Scientists who study living things *classify* them, or divide them into groups. For a discussion of the reasons for and methods of scientific classification, see CLASSIFICATION. Classification shows that man's physical characteristics resemble those of many members of the animal kingdom. His bones are made of the same material as those of horses and sheep, and he has the same number of eyes as a bird or a fish. Scientific investigators in many fields have pointed out how closely man's bodily structure is related to that of animals. Studies of the way man and animals grow have also indicated that man is governed by the same biological laws that govern animals. Where does man fit in?

Within the animal kingdom, scientists place man in the subkingdom *Metazoa*, which includes all living things made up of many cells instead of just one. He belongs to the phylum *Chordata*, which includes all creatures with a nerve cord and a *notochord* (other stiffening structure) along the back. Man's backbone places him in the subphylum *Vertebrata*. Vertebrates form several classes, among them *Mammalia*, to which man belongs. Almost all mammals give birth to live young and nurse them with milk.

The 3,500 or so species of mammals make up 16 orders. Scientists place men, apes, monkeys, lemurs, and tarsiers in the order *Primates*, because all have nails instead of claws or hoofs. Primates possess opposable thumbs or big toes, with which they can grasp objects easily. They also have semierect posture and *stereoscopic* (overlapping) vision, which helps them see objects in three dimensions at a short distance. Men, apes, and monkeys make up the superfamily *Anthropoidea*. Men and apes alone form the superfamily *Hominoidea* (manlike creatures). Man's own family, the *Hominidae*, includes fossil men of prehistoric times as well as all races of modern men. Some scientists divide this family into only two groups, genus *Australopithecus* and genus *Homo*. Others identify several genera. Both groups further divide man into several species. Man eats many kinds of food and lives in all life-supporting regions. When he began expanding over the earth, he probably competed for food with other, less intelligent species, and killed them off. Scientists agree that all living humans today are genus *Homo*, species *sapiens*, Latin words which mean *wise man*. For the story of other members of the family *Hominidae*, see PREHISTORIC MAN. For a discussion of the racial differences among men, see RACES OF MAN.

Physical Differences Between Man and Animals. Man differs physically from the apes in five main ways. (1) Man walks erect on two legs, with his hands free for carrying and working. Apes sometimes walk erect, but more often use both their hands and feet. (2) Man's legs are longer than his arms, but the apes' arms are longer than their legs. (3) Man's body has little hair, but apes are hairy. (4) Man has small teeth and short *canines* (eye teeth). Apes have large teeth for eating coarse, uncooked food, and long canine teeth for fighting. Man cooks much of his food, and fights with his hands. (5) Man's highly developed brain makes it possible for him to speak, to think, and to reason. It also makes it possible for him to create ideas and inventions. All of these things help him build a culture. The development of man's brain puts him on a level of life far above all the animals. See BRAIN.

Several other physical characteristics also set man apart from the apes. Many of these differences concern the head and face. Man's profile is more or less straight up and down. An ape's profile is *prognathous*, with the jaws projecting outward. An ape has a massive lower jaw with strong muscles, but no chin like man's. Man's nose is much more prominent than that of the apes, and his nostrils smaller and less flaring. Apes have thinner, more mobile lips than man.

Additional differences relate to man's upright walk. To support his weight, his spine has a double curve, rather than a single one. Man has a shorter torso than the apes. His foot is arched both across and lengthwise, but cannot grasp objects. Most of these characteristics differ in degree, rather than in kind.

In spite of the distinctions that set man apart from animals, scientists refer to him as a *generalized* being. That is, man has not developed special features that would seriously limit his activities. For example, a seal has a body streamlined for swimming, but it has difficulty moving about on land. The specialized front teeth of squirrels and other rodents help them chew through the strongest wood. But a rodent must gnaw almost continuously or these teeth will grow through his head. Man cannot swim so well as a seal, but he can walk, run, climb, and crawl. Man has four different kinds of teeth, so he can eat both animal and vegetable food. Because man is generalized, he is very adaptable, and can live almost anywhere in the world.

Man in the World

Because man has working hands, a creative brain, and the power of speech, he has come to dominate most other living things. Over three billion strong and still increasing, he occupies all ice-free continents and most islands. He has adapted himself to his surroundings, and has also adapted nature to himself. The changing seasons, the surrounding areas of land and water, and other factors important to many animals may be relatively unimportant to man. Man has even created an indoor climate for himself, either warm or cool. Man has domesticated such animals as cattle, horses, and dogs, has used them and selected them, and has made them provide him with food and clothing.

Man has gradually perfected his ability to cut and shape materials, fire furnaces to high temperatures, and smelt and fabricate metals. He has learned how to convert heat into energy, and how to span and dam rivers. He has built machines that carry him around the world by land, air, and sea. He has constructed cities that hold millions of people. He has split atoms, shot rockets into space, and spun satellites around the earth.

Man has made great progress in technology; but he also continues the age-old search for values that give meaning to his life. His sense of beauty finds expression in works of art that create an international language. Philosophy mirrors man's need for truth. Religion has taken on new strength in an increasingly disturbed world.

Many problems remain unsolved. Nations still fight among themselves. The increased powers of destruction released by atomic energy haunt men's minds. In spite of man's successes in adapting himself to his environment, he must always work to make that environment a suitable one in which to live. He must wage constant warfare against insects and bacteria. Insects destroy the foods that man raises for his use. Bacteria not only attack man and cause disease, but also attack animals and plants upon which man depends for food. Man can never stop fighting the forces that endanger his existence. He may harness nature, but he is not free from the laws which govern all living things. Man has more and more come to realize that he must conserve the earth's resources so that future generations will be able to carry on the great heritage that he has created. CARLETON S. COON

Related Articles. See the Trans-Vision three-dimensional color pictures with HUMAN BODY. See also:

Anthropology	Culture	Races of Man
Archaeology	Human Relations	World
Civilization	Prehistoric Man	

MANAGEMENT

The need for management has increased as modern society becomes more complex. This is particularly true of business, whose great growth has been a characteristic of the modern world. In earlier days, an individual might operate his own small business or farm without too much planning regarding the exact way he did it. But today, some businesses employ tens of thousands of workers, use millions of dollars worth of equipment, and sell products throughout a nation and even in all parts of the world. It has become important to make all decisions in the light of carefully chosen objectives.

Management in Business became a separate function with the development of joint-stock companies in the 1500's (see JOINT-STOCK COMPANY). Before that time, the proprietors or partners who owned a business also managed it. The discovery of ocean-trade routes to all parts of the world created new opportunities for trade. They also created a need for large amounts of money to finance this trade. But the amounts needed were more than single individuals could supply or were willing to risk. The joint-stock company could bring together individuals with money to assist in the financing of trade even if they knew little or nothing about the business. The stock owners could hire managers with skill and experience. The managers often had little or no ownership in the businesses they managed.

The need for large *capital* (amounts of money) to operate a business brought about the separation of management from ownership. This need for capital has continued ever since. Managements today usually have relatively little share in the ownership of the companies they operate. The term *management* has become a general term used in business in contrast to stockholders, on the one hand, and labor, on the other.

Industrial Management is the aspect of business management which has been most important in the United States in the 1900's. The invention and improvement of machines has made it especially important to plan the entire process of production carefully. Modern machines are efficient, but they are also expensive. A company must decide exactly what is to be made and how the work is to be done. Materials must be available in a smooth flow as they are needed. The work must be planned through every step, from the raw material to the finished product. In present-day industry every step depends on the previous steps, and an interruption at any point can halt the entire production process.

Personnel Management. One or more persons who become ill, angry, or emotionally upset can interrupt production just as quickly and completely as a serious fire or accident that puts machines out of operation. As industries and businesses have become larger, managements of companies have had to pay more attention to *personnel* (employee) problems. A friendly spirit between workers in various departments and between workers and management helps as much as mechanical efficiency to make a business a success. In fact, wise management strives to link the human and the technical aspects of its activities. Good morale among employees is a vital goal. See PERSONNEL RELATIONS.

Market Management becomes necessary when a firm grows so large that it has only a few competitors of similar size. It would not be possible for a single businessman

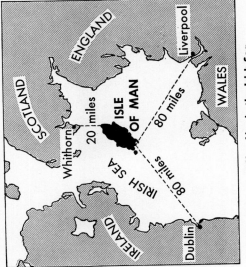

The Isle of Man Lies in the Irish Sea.

MAN, ISLE OF. The Isle of Man lies in the Irish Sea, halfway between England and Ireland, and 20 miles south of Scotland. The island is a favorite summer resort for the people of the British Isles. Scholars believe that its name comes from a Celtic word which means *hilly land*. A breed of cats, usually without tails, called *Manx*, originated on the Isle of Man (see CAT).

The island has an area of 227 square miles. Farms, rolling moorlands, and low mountains cover the island. It has a coastline of 50 miles. The coast in many places is rocky and beautiful. A low mountain chain runs the length of the island. It rises to its highest point in Snaefell, 2,034 feet above sea level.

The Isle of Man has a population of about 50,000. The people are Celtic and are called *Manx* or *Manxmen*. In some parts of the island, the people speak English and Manx, their own Celtic language. The chief industries include the tourist trade, farming, cattle raising, and fishing. Douglas, the capital of the Isle of Man, lies beside a beautiful bay on the east coast. The Court of Tynwald, the island's 1,000-year-old parliament, is the oldest parliament in the British Commonwealth. The ruins of Rushen Castle, built in A.D. 947, stand near Castletown, the ancient capital. The Isle has full harbor radar control.

The Isle of Man has been ruled by Ireland, Wales, Norway, Scotland, and England. In 1765, Great Britain bought the island. The Isle of Man still has its own representative assembly and courts. The British Crown appoints the governor.   FREDERICK G. MARCHAM.

MAN FRIDAY. See ROBINSON CRUSOE.

MAN IN THE IRON MASK. See IRON MASK, MAN IN THE.

MAN-OF-WAR BIRD. See FRIGATE BIRD.

MAN O' WAR. See HORSE RACING (Famous Horses).

MAN WITHOUT A COUNTRY, THE. See HALE, EDWARD EVERETT.

MANAGEMENT means directing businesses, government agencies, foundations, and many other organizations and activities. The central idea of management is to make every action or decision help achieve a carefully chosen goal. The word *management* is also used to mean the group of persons called *executives*, who perform management activities.

or small firm to think of *managing* the market in which it sells its products. The market controls the company, not the other way around. But large businesses produce and sell a great portion of the total of their type of product. They must plan the marketing of their products as carefully as they plan production. Because they are large, they can do this. Such companies can set carefully planned prices, confident that no competitor is likely to undercut them. They can plan a system to distribute the product that will keep the goods moving steadily from the factory to the consumer. They make sure that no interruption occurs anywhere in their production and distribution systems.

Financial Management depends on and measures the success of other management processes. Financial management must obtain the capital required to support the production and distribution of a company's goods. If the firm produces and distributes its products successfully, it should yield a profit. In turn, if it has a record of profitable operation, it becomes an attractive place for investors to put their capital. In this way, a company finds it easier to obtain capital for the business. The objective of privately owned businesses is to make a profit. Financial management provides the capital with which a business can begin. It also tests its operation continuously to ensure that all uses of capital in the business help make a profit.

The Importance of Management. In addition to the branches of business management already mentioned, the terms *land management, water management, natural resource management* and the like are frequently used. In fact, wherever complex problems appear that can be controlled by human beings, the skills of management are called into play. The growth of management in business has been greater than in other fields, however. Business executives with skill and experience in management are in great demand by companies of all kinds. Such individuals can often shift from firm to firm, wherever their skills are needed, even between different kinds of businesses. This kind of mobility between firms has served to make business managers a professional management class that has become one of the most influential in our present-day society. The management class makes decisions that can determine the prosperity of entire nations.

ROBERT D. PATTON

Related Articles in WORLD BOOK include:

Centralization	Industrial Revolution	Labor
Corporation	Industry	Manufacturing
Industrial Relations	Joint-Stock Company	Partnership
		Stock, Capital

MANAGEMENT AND BUDGET, OFFICE OF. See PRESIDENT OF THE UNITED STATES (Executive Office of the President).

MANAGUA, *muh NAH gwah* (pop. 262,047; alt. 195 ft.), is the capital and largest city of Nicaragua. It lies on the south shore of Lake Managua, 25 miles east of the Pacific. For location, see NICARAGUA (color map).

The National Palace, city hall, and cathedral face Central Park. Between Central Park and Lake Managua is Rubén Darío Park, dedicated to the great Nicaraguan poet (see DARÍO, RUBÉN). Avenida Roosevelt, the main street, leads south from Central Park to the Presidential Palace on Tiscapa Hill.

Managua's industries manufacture cement, textiles, soap, candles, perfume, drugs, and food products.

When the Spaniards arrived in the 1500's, they found a large Indian community on the present site of Managua. Managua became the capital of Nicaragua in 1855. An earthquake in 1931 almost completely destroyed the city. It has been rebuilt in checkerboard pattern, and is one of the most up-to-date small cities in Latin America.

See also NICARAGUA (picture).

ROLLIN S. ATWOOD

MANAMA, *muh MAN muh* (pop. 79,098; alt. 10 ft.), is the capital and chief port of the Arab sheikdom of Bahrain (see BAHRAIN). It is on the northeast corner of the island of Bahrain. It is a commercial center and the headquarters for pearling and fishing fleets in the area.

MANASSAS, BATTLES OF. See CIVIL WAR (First Bull Run; Second Bull Run; table: Major Battles).

MANASSEH. See JOSEPH (son of Jacob).

MANATE. See JOSEPH (son of Jacob).

MANATEE, *MAN uh TEE,* sometimes called SEA COW, is a large water mammal. It belongs to the same group of mammals—the order *Sirenia*—as the dugong. The manatee is found in the West Indies and along the coasts of eastern Central America, northeastern South America, and western Africa. In the United States, manatees are found in bays and rivers along the Florida coast. However, manatees have been much hunted for their flesh, hide, and oil, and they are becoming increasingly rare.

The manatee feeds on water plants in either fresh or salt water. Its upper lip is divided into halves, which close on the plants like pliers. On quiet nights, a manatee can be heard feeding 200 yards away.

A manatee may grow about 14 feet long and weigh about 1,500 pounds. It has light to dark gray skin, with short, bristlelike hairs scattered over its body. The manatee's front legs are paddle shaped, and its tail is rounded. It has no hind legs.

Scientific Classification. The manatee belongs to the family *Trichechidae*. It is genus *Trichechus*. There are three species of manatees. *T. manatus* lives in the coastal waters of the Southeastern United States, in the Caribbean Sea, and along the northeast coast of South America. *T. inunguis* lives in the Amazon and Orinoco rivers. *T. senegalensis* lives along the coast and in rivers of western Africa.

KARL W. KENYON

See also DUGONG; SEA COW; SIRENIA.

Jim Mitchell, Black Star

Managua's F. D. Roosevelt monument, foreground, stands at one end of Avenida Roosevelt. Lake Managua is at the other end.

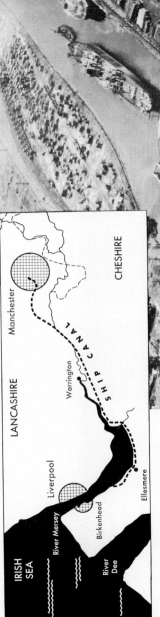

IRISH SEA

LANCASHIRE

Manchester

Warrington

Liverpool

SHIP CANAL

River Mersey

Birkenhead

River Dee

Ellesmere

CHESHIRE

The Manchester Ship Canal has made Manchester a great British port. The smaller Bridgewater Canal, center, crosses over it by an aqueduct. The aqueduct rests on an island in the main canal and swings open to allow ships to pass. The map, above, shows how the canal links Manchester with the Irish Sea.

MANOEL CARDOZO

MANAUS, *muh NOWS* (pop. 242,000; alt. 141 ft.), is a major inland city of Brazil, and the capital of the state of Amazonas. Manaus lies on the Negro River, 10 miles from the meeting place of the Negro and Amazon rivers. It is 1,000 miles from the mouth of the Amazon, but can be reached by ocean liners. The city is the trading center for the area around the Amazon Basin. It trades in products of the Amazon forests, including hardwoods, Brazil nuts, and rubber. For location, see BRAZIL (political map).

MANCHESTER (pop. 602,790; met. area 2,440,520; alt. 275 ft.) is the fourth largest city in England. It is the center of one of the greatest manufacturing districts in the world. The only larger English cities are London, Birmingham, and Liverpool.

Manchester is situated in Lancashire, on the Irwell River. It lies 32 miles northeast of Liverpool. The city of Salford, on the west bank of the Irwell, is connected with Manchester by 16 bridges. The two cities are almost like one municipality. For location, see GREAT BRITAIN (political map).

Industry and Trade. Manchester has long been known as a world center of cotton manufacture, but it has more than 700 other industries. Great engineering works have been established, as well as factories which produce automobiles and rubber goods.

Many mills and workshops stand outside the city itself. As a result, an ever-widening circle of dense population has grown up around the center of the city. This outer area distributes the numerous and varied products that the city sends to every part of the world. Manchester exports chemicals, dyes, oil, and cotton goods.

Manchester lies more than 30 miles from the Irish Sea. But the construction of the Manchester Ship Canal made the city a great ocean port. Other canals lead out from the city in all directions. Manchester has 6 miles of wharves and 120 acres of water for dock accommodations. It also serves as a leading railroad center. In 1830, the first passenger railroad in England was built between Manchester and Liverpool.

Buildings and Public Works. A fine town hall of Gothic design stands in Manchester. The clock tower, 286 feet high, contains a chime of 21 bells. Manchester

The Manatee, commonly called a *sea cow*, can stand partly out of the water, balanced on its broad tail. The animal is helpless on land.

Field Museum of Natural History

has a number of excellent libraries, including the John Rylands Library. The Victoria University of Manchester is well known among scholars. The *Guardian* (formerly *Manchester Guardian*), a world-famous newspaper, was founded in 1821. During World War II, German planes bombed Manchester heavily. But the city has rebuilt most of its industries and buildings.

Manchester Ship Canal. This remarkable canal made the inland town of Manchester a great seaport. It was completed in January, 1894. In the following May, officials opened it in the presence of Queen Victoria. The canal is 35½ miles long, about 120 feet wide, and 28 to 30 feet deep. It connects directly with all the barge canals of the kingdom. Seagoing vessels can pass through it and into the heart of Manchester. The canal was built at a cost of $75,000,000.

FREDERICK G. MARCHAM

MANCHESTER, Conn. (pop. 42,102; alt. 180 ft.), lies in north-central Connecticut. For location, see CONNECTICUT (political map). Factories in the city make furniture, wood products, paper, machinery, textiles, fabricated metals, and aircraft and electrical equipment. The Cheney Silk Mills, begun in 1838, gave Manchester the title the *Silk City*. Manchester was settled in 1672. It has a council-manager form of government.

ALBERT E. VAN DUSEN

MANCHESTER, N.H. (pop. 88,282; met. area 102,861; alt. 175 ft.), is the largest city and chief manufacturing center of New Hampshire. Manchester lies in the south-central part of the state, about 17 miles south of Concord, the capital. The city covers nearly 34 square miles along both banks of the Merrimack River. The Uncanoonuc Mountains curve around the western part of the city. For location, see NEW HAMPSHIRE (political map).

Most of the people of Manchester are foreign-born or the descendants of foreign-born. Nearly half of the population are French-Americans from Canada.

The city is the home of the Manchester Institute of Arts and Sciences, the Currier Gallery of Art, the Association Canado-Americaine, and the Carpenter Memorial Library. The residence of General John Stark, a famous figure of the Revolutionary War, is in Manchester. His body is buried in a park named for him.

Manchester was once known as the home of the largest cotton mills in the world. The mills failed in the 1930's and today Manchester's industries are more varied. Chief products of the city include boots and shoes and cotton and woolen goods. Manchester is an insurance center and a distributing point. The city is served by railways and several bus lines. Manchester receives its water power from Amoskeag Falls of the Merrimack River. The city receives its water supply from Lake Massabesic, about 5 miles to the east.

The first white settlement there was started in 1722. Manchester was first called Harrytown, and then Derryfield. It received its present name in 1810. Manchester became a city in 1846. It has a mayor-council form of government.

J. DUANE SQUIRES

MANCHESTER COLLEGE. See UNIVERSITIES AND COLLEGES (table).

MANCHESTER TERRIER is a slender, lively dog that was first bred in the 1800's in Manchester, England. It has a small head and a short, shiny coat. It is jet black,

---

marked with reddish tan. The Manchester stands about 16 inches high and weighs from 12 to 22 pounds. Breeders produced the first Manchesters by mating a whippet with a rat-catching terrier. The Manchester became an excellent rat-catching breed of dog. Manchesters were also known for their ability at fighting badgers and otters. See also Dog (color picture: Terriers); TOY MANCHESTER TERRIER.

JOSEPHINE Z. RINE

MANCHINEEL, *man chih NEEL*, is a tree that grows on sandy beaches in Florida and in many parts of tropical America. It stands from 10 to 50 feet high. The manchineel has smooth, pale brown bark, and long, drooping branches. The egg-shaped leaves are about 3 inches long. They have jagged edges. The manchineel has small purple flowers. Its fruit resembles a crab apple.

The milky sap and yellowish-green fruits of the manchineel are extremely poisonous to man and to many animals. Even dew or rainwater that drips from the leaves can cause blisters on the skin. Sap or smoke from burning wood that comes into contact with the eye can cause temporary blindness.

Scientific Classification. Manchineel is in the spurge family, *Euphorbiaceae*. It is genus *Hippomane*, species *H. mancinella*.

H. E. CHEN

MANCHU, *MAN choo*. The Manchus were a people who conquered China in the 1600's. Most Manchus lived in Manchuria, in northeast China. They were related to a Tungusic people whom the Chinese called *Nüchên* or *Juchên*. The Tungus lived in Manchuria as early as the 200's B.C. In A.D. 1644, the Manchus set up a dynasty in China that became known as the *Ch'ing* (*Pure*) dynasty. The dynasty prospered in the 1700's, but declined rapidly in the 1800's. It ended in 1912, when the Chinese overthrew their Manchu rulers.

The Manchu rulers forbade marriage between their people and the Chinese people until the early 1900's. Since that time, many have intermarried, and most of the Manchus have adopted Chinese names. See also MANCHURIA (History).

MANCHUKUO. See CHINA (War with Japan); MANCHURIA (History and Government).

MANCHURIA, *man CHOOR ih uh*, lies in the northeast corner of China. It covers the provinces of Heilungkiang, Kirin, and Liaoning, and part of the autonomous region of Inner Mongolia. It has an area of 309,499 square miles. For location of the provinces, see CHINA (political map).

Description. Manchuria is a great plain, bordered by three separate ranges of mountains. The Greater Khingan Mountains on the west separate Manchuria from Mongolia. The Lesser Khingan Mountains lie in the northeastern part of Manchuria. The third mountain region, a series of broken hills and mountains, makes up the Kwantung Peninsula. The Yalu River, in the southeast, divides Manchuria from Korea. Other principal rivers are the Liao and Hun in the southwest and the Nonni and Sungari in the north. Most of Manchuria's cities, and its best farming land, lie in the south.

Climate. Manchuria has cold winters, with temperatures dropping as low as −49° F. in the north. Summers are mild, with an average temperature of 75° F. Rainfall averages 20 to 40 inches annually in most of Manchuria.

Natural Resources. Manchuria has vast deposits of coal and iron. One of the largest coal seams in the world is at Fushun, near Mukden. Other minerals include

Eastfoto

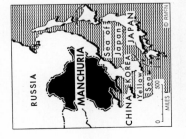

Manchuria, shown in black above, lies in northeastern China. Public housing in a Manchurian city, *right*, follows traditional styles of architecture.

aluminum, asbestos, copper, gold, magnesite, and molybdenum. Salt is taken from the sea water.

Manchuria has fertile soil, excellent grazing lands, and rich forests. Fur-bearing animals and many kinds of fish are found in the region.

The People. Manchuria has about 51,500,000 people. About 90 out of 100 of the Manchurians are descendants of Chinese who poured into Manchuria after 1900. The Chinese have developed Manchuria into an important agricultural and industrial region.

Manchuria has about a million Mongols, who live in the northern plains and in the Khingan Mountains. About a million Koreans have moved into Manchuria.

Cities. The major cities are Mukden, Harbin, Dairen, Changchun, and Port Arthur. WORLD BOOK has articles on these cities.

Agriculture. Manchuria produces more food than it needs. Principal crops include soybeans and *kaoliang*, a grain sorghum. Barley, corn, cotton, fruit, millet, rice, tobacco, and wheat are also grown. Manchurian farmers raise cattle, hogs, horses, mules, and sheep.

Manufacturing and Trade. Manchuria is China's chief heavy-industry region. Manchuria has a great steel works and a large plant for refining oil from shale. It also has factories that produce aircraft, cement, and munitions.

Most of the trade is carried on with Russia. Manchuria exports soybeans, soybean oil, and coal. Manchuria's imported products include flour, machinery, paper, and sugar.

Transportation. Manchuria has about 2,100 miles of railroads operated by the Changchun Railway. The rivers and roads provide poor transportation.

Education. Manchuria has a well-developed system of elementary schools, secondary schools, and colleges. It also has teacher-training and vocational schools.

History and Government. Mongols and Tungus (later Manchus) lived in Manchuria as early as the 200's B.C. From 1644 to 1912, the Manchu tribes of Manchuria ruled the vast Chinese empire. The Man-

chus gave their name to Manchuria. During the last years of Manchu rule, Russia and Japan contended for control of Manchurian trade. Russia controlled trade during the late 1800's. But after the Russo-Japanese War in 1905, Russia ceded the railroad in southern Manchuria to Japan. Japan also gained control of important territory on the Liaotung Peninsula.

Chinese revolutionaries ousted the Manchu Dynasty in 1912. The government of China then began to strengthen and develop Manchuria. The Japanese opposed China's interests in the area. Japanese troops seized the area in 1931, and established a puppet state called *Manchukuo*. In 1937, Japan invaded China. This invasion, based chiefly in Manchuria, became an early part of World War II. After the war, Russia gained Manchuria's chief ports. But in 1946, Russia turned over control of Manchuria to Communist China. In 1949, Manchuria became part of China, with a Communist government.   THEODORE H. E. CHEN

Related Articles in WORLD BOOK include:

Changchun	Japan (The Rise	Port Arthur
China (History)	of Militarism)	Russo-Japanese War
Dairen	Manchu	Trans-Siberian
Harbin	Mongol Empire	Railroad
	Mukden	Yalu River

MANDALAY, *MAN duh LAY* (pop. 195,348; alt. 252 ft.), is Burma's second largest city and chief inland river port. It lies 350 miles north of Rangoon on the Irrawaddy River. For location, see BURMA (map).

Mandalay is best known for its old pagodas, temples, and monasteries. The chief industry is silk weaving. Silk is sold in the city's *bazaars* (market places).

The Burmese founded Mandalay in 1857. It was the capital of Burma from 1860 to 1885, when the British captured the city. The British moved the capital to Rangoon. About 85 per cent of Mandalay was destroyed during World War II. The Burmese rebuilt parts of it after the war.   JOHN F. CADY

MANDAMUS, *man DAY mus,* is a court order which requires a person, lower court, government official, or an officer of a corporation to do his legal duty. On many occasions, a public official may be required to perform an act, such as to make a commission or sign a paper. If the official refuses to do the act, a *writ of mandamus* may be sought against him, and a court may order him to perform his duty.

Mandamus can be obtained only where the law says the official must do the act, but not where the law says he may decide whether or not he will do it. In such a case, a court will not compel the official to decide in favor of the person seeking the writ of mandamus. But the court may compel him to decide one way or the other. A court may not issue a writ of mandamus if it believes that some other remedy is available to handle the situation, such as a suit for money damages against the official.

ERWIN N. GRISWOLD

See also INJUNCTION; WRIT.

MANDAN INDIANS were the most famous traders of the western plains. They built large villages of earth-covered lodges along the Missouri River in what is now North Dakota. Here the Mandan cultivated fields of corn, beans, squash, and tobacco. They exchanged these products for buffalo meat and hides which nearby wandering tribes brought to them. In later years, they traded their corn and tobacco for guns, tools, and cloth which northern tribes got from white traders, and for horses brought by southern tribes from New Mexico. They also welcomed white traders and explorers.

The Mandan performed elaborate ceremonies to ensure growth of their crops. Men's warrior societies held dances in which members wore colorful costumes and carried symbolic staffs. In the 1830's, the white artists George Catlin and Karl Bodmer drew and painted many portraits of Mandan Indians and scenes of tribal life. These are some of the finest pictures of American Indians. At that time the Mandan ranked as the most advanced tribe of the upper Missouri. They were a happy, healthy people. Yet, in 1837, a smallpox epidemic nearly wiped out the tribe. The remnant of the once proud and prosperous Mandan found refuge among the nearby Hidatsa and Arikara. Members of these tribes intermarried. Their descendants live on Fort Berthold reservation in North Dakota.

JOHN C. EWERS

See also CATLIN, GEORGE; INDIAN, AMERICAN; MIGRATION (picture: Migration or Starvation).

MANDARIN, *MAN´ duh rin,* English-speaking people used the name *mandarin* for any high military or civil official of the Chinese Empire. The Chinese term is *kwan,* which means *a public official.* The dialect of North China, which is the language these officials spoke, is also called *Mandarin.* Today it is the national language of China.

A Chinese became a mandarin by taking promotional examinations. He showed his rank by the color of the buttons on his cap. Governors and generals had red coral buttons. Lieutenant governors and judges wore blue ones. Lower officers had other colors.

Each mandarin had an official robe. The military man's robe had beasts embroidered on it. The civil official had decorative birds on his robe. Judges wore plainer robes.

To ensure the honesty of a mandarin, he was never assigned to the province from which he came. He could neither marry nor acquire property in the province to which he was sent. And he could not serve over three years in one province.

THEODORE H. E. CHEN

MANDARIN. See TANGERINE.

MANDARIN DIALECT. See CHINESE LANGUAGE.

MANDATED TERRITORY. After World War I, certain colonies and territories were taken from the defeated nations and placed under the administration of one or more of the victorious nations. These regions were called *mandated territories.* The League of Nations supervised the administration of these territories. The League expected the governing countries to improve conditions for the people in the mandated territories, and to prepare the people in the territories for self-government.

The mandated territories included areas once controlled by Germany and Turkey. Great Britain received mandates for Iraq, Palestine (including Jordan), and Togoland. Belgium received Ruanda-Urundi. Japan was given former German islands in the North Pacific Ocean. Australia received German islands in the South Pacific, including the northeastern section of New Guinea and Nauru. New Zealand received Western Samoa, and the Union of South Africa (now South Africa) obtained German South West Africa.

The League appointed a commission to supervise the mandate system. The commission had no power to govern, but usually persuaded the nations with mandates to improve education, public health, and the economy in the mandated regions. However, the governing nations

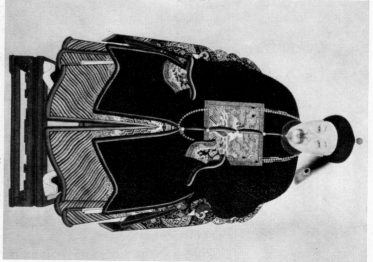

Chinese Mandarins served as important government officials. This mandarin was an imperial high commissioner during the Ch'ing dynasty. The bird on the gown indicates he was a civil official.

Museum of Fine Arts, Boston

often failed to train the people to govern themselves.

The mandate system came to an end in 1947. By that time, several of the mandated territories, including Iraq, Syria, Lebanon, and Jordan, had become independent countries. The remaining mandated territories, with the exception of South West Africa, were placed under the stronger United Nations trusteeship system. The same countries continued to administer the territories, but they were under the control of the UN Trusteeship Council and General Assembly (see TRUST TERRITORY). South Africa resisted UN attempts to bring South West Africa into the trusteeship system.

MANDIBLE, *MAN duh b'l,* or lower jawbone, is shaped like a horseshoe. A person can feel the entire bone from chin to temple. The *corpus* (body) of the mandible runs backwards from the chin to the *angle,* at which point it turns upward to form the *ramus.* The ramus makes a joint at the temple. This joint allows the mouth to open and close. In adults, the body of the mandible contains eight teeth on each side. The chewing muscles attach to the ramus, and the tongue muscles attach to the body. See also HEAD (picture). IRVIN STEIN

MANDINGO. See GAMBIA (People); SENEGAL (People).

MANDOLIN, *MAN doh lin,* is a musical instrument with strings. It was probably copied from the lute, a much older instrument (see LUTE). The mandolin is

shaped like a pear cut in half lengthwise. It has four or five double strings of wire, a fretted neck, and a flat headpiece with tuning screws. The player produces a tone with a rather stiff *plectrum* (pick), which he holds between his right thumb and forefinger. Musical sounds can be sustained by *trilling* (shaking the strings rapidly). The four-stringed mandolin in common use is tuned in fifths, like the violin. It is often used to accompany informal singing.

MANDRAKE is the name of two similar plants that belong to the nightshade family. Mandrakes grow wild in southern Europe and Asia. The stem of the man-

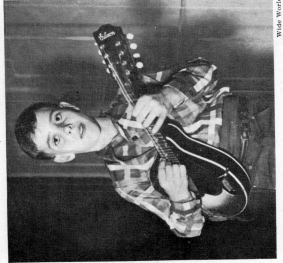

Wide World

The Mandolin has been popular for hundreds of years, particularly among southern Europeans and Latin Americans.

drake cannot be seen, and the leaves seem to grow directly from the roots. The roots are large and shaped like a carrot. The white, bluish, or purple flowers of the mandrake grow on stalks among the leaves.

People have long had superstitious beliefs about the mandrake. According to one superstition, the mandrake shrieks when it is pulled out of the soil. Many persons also believe that it brings good luck to a household when it is properly consulted. The root of the mandrake was once used as a narcotic and anesthetic, and in so-called *love potions.* The mandrake was also described as growing best under a gallows.

People in the United States and Canada often use the name *mandrake* for the *May apple,* which belongs to the barberry family (see MAY APPLE).

Scientific Classification. Mandrakes belong to the nightshade family, *Solanaceae.* They make up the genus *Mandragora.* The species of mandrakes include *M. autumnalis,* and *M. officinarum.* JULIAN A. STEYERMARK

MANDRILL is a large, colorful baboon that lives in the forests of Cameroon and other parts of western Africa. This odd-looking monkey has long arms, small piglike eyes, large canine teeth, and a muzzle similar to that of a dog. The male mandrill is strikingly colored. Its cheeks are blue, its long flat nose is red, and its rump is red and blue.

Like other baboons, mandrills live in groups. They usually move about on the ground, roaming through the forests eating fruits and other vegetation, and perhaps insects.

Scientific Classification. The mandrill belongs to the Old World monkey family, *Cercopithecidae.* It is genus *Papio,* species *P. sphinx.* GEORGE B. SCHALLER

MANED WOLF. See ANIMAL (Bodies [picture]); SOUTH AMERICA (Animals [picture]).

MANES. See MANICHAEISM.

MANET, *MAH NEH,* **EDOUARD** (1832-1883), a French artist, is sometimes called the first modern painter because of his interest in analyzing vision and the process of painting. He is important in the history of painting because he emphasized structure, color, and form in his works, instead of telling pretty stories in paint. He went back to the traditional ideas of painting that Diego Velázquez and Francisco Goya, two Spanish masters, had shared with the Venetians and Dutch. As a result, he helped clear the way for the development of impressionism and all subsequent contemporary movements in painting which emphasize formal elements more than the story or scene being painted.

Manet studied for six years with the painter Thomas Couture. He was always at odds with Couture, who was not particularly interested in formal structure. But Manet learned a subtle handling of color from him. He added to this by studying Velázquez, Goya, Rembrandt van Rijn, Frans Hals, and the Venetian masters.

The Salon, at which official exhibitions of painting were held, refused to exhibit Manet's *The Absinthe Drinkers* in 1859. When it was shown privately, it met with criticism from people who were not accustomed to Manet's new style. His stiff, self-conscious poses, his sober, flatly silhouetted forms, and his lack of story-telling content also ran against the painting style of the day. In 1863, Manet exhibited *Luncheon on the Grass* and in 1865, *Olympia*. These paintings provoked such scandal, because they included a nude in a contemporary setting, that Manet left for Spain. Upon his return, he became a rallying point for a group of younger artists who had met at the Café Guerbois. The impressionist movement grew out of this group of young artists, who had been inspired by Manet.

In 1873, Manet's picture *Le Bon Bock* scored a triumph. He continued to show at the Salon and not with the impressionists. Although he produced pictures such as *Boating* (1874) and *Argenteuil* (1875), which used impressionist colors, Manet did not dissolve forms in the impressionist manner. *Boating* appears in color in the PAINTING article. Manet's last great pictures were of scenes in restaurants and cabarets, climaxed by the *Bar at the Folies Bergère*, a masterpiece of his career. Manet was born in Paris. He received the Legion of Honor in 1881.

ROBERT GOLDWATER

See also the picture with the ALABAMA (ship) article.

MANGANESE, *MANG guh nees* (chemical symbol, Mn), is one of the most important metals used in industry. Its chief use is to strengthen steel and to remove impurities from it. Steelmakers have found few substitutes for it. But U.S. mines do not produce enough manganese for the country's steel industry. The United States imports about 98 per cent of the manganese it uses. Johann Gahn discovered the element in 1774.

Uses. Pure manganese metal is seldom used commercially. It is usually used in ores, compounds, or alloys. About 95 per cent of the manganese used in the United States goes into the production of steel.

To produce a ton of steel, steelmakers need about 13 pounds of manganese. They may add the manganese to the steel in scrap steel; in *ferromanganese*, an alloy of iron containing a high percentage of manganese; or in *spiegeleisen*, an alloy of iron containing a lower percentage of manganese. Manganese removes harmful oxygen and sulfur from the molten steel. It takes up the oxygen or sulfur and forms *manganous oxide* or *manganous*

sulfide. These compounds do not dissolve easily in molten iron. They separate from the iron and become part of the slag, which is poured off. Manganese that remains in the steel increases its strength. *Manganese steel* is an especially hard alloy used in making mining machinery and such heavy-duty machinery as rock crushers.

Manganese oxide is used in dry-cell batteries to prevent *polarization* (the formation of hydrogen, which does not conduct electricity) on the carbon electrode. In the past, manufacturers used manganese oxide in making glass. Iron impurities in the sand that was used to make glass gave it a yellowish color. Manganese oxide eliminated this color. But, after a few years of exposure to the sun, glass containing manganese turned purple. For this reason, glass manufacturers now use selenium in place of manganese.

Manganese sulfate is an important ingredient in the fertilizers used in parts of the United States. It is hard to grow citrus fruits in Texas and Florida unless manganese is added to the soil. If such crops as tomatoes, beans, potatoes, and corn are grown in soils containing large amounts of lime, they will not mature fully unless treated with fertilizers containing manganese.

Potassium permanganate is an important chemical. It is used as an oxidizing agent in various industrial processes (see OXIDATION). It also has value in quantitative analysis, because it changes color when the concentration of hydroxide ions in a solution changes (see CHEMISTRY [Branches of Chemistry]).

Manganese dioxide is used in manufacturing *hydroquinone*, a chemical used as a photographic developer. It is also used to *bond* (hold) enamels to steel. Manganese dioxide and certain manganese salts are used to make paint and varnish dry faster. Manganese salts produce attractive colors in bricks, pottery, and tiles. Other uses for manganese compounds include welding-rod coatings, pigments, and insecticides.

Chemistry. Pure manganese is a silver-gray metal with a pinkish tinge. It is relatively soft, compared with

Courtauld Institute Gallery, London

Edouard Manet completed *Bar at the Folies Bergère*, left, in 1882. The painting shows the firm modeling and bright, vivid colors that are typical of much of his work. The portrait of Manet, above, was painted by his friend Henri Fantin-Latour in 1867.

Art Institute of Chicago

iron. Manganese is unstable, and reacts easily with other chemicals to form many compounds. If placed in cold water, manganese will react with the water and release hydrogen gas from it. The atomic weight of manganese is 54.9380, and its atomic number is 25. See ELEMENT, CHEMICAL (tables).

Manganese can be prepared from its oxides by reduction with carbon or aluminum. It can also be reduced by electrolysis or by an electric furnace. See ELECTRIC FURNACE; ELECTROLYSIS; REDUCTION.

Sources. Geologists estimate that manganese ranks as the 11th most abundant element in the earth's crust. But it is rare compared with other elements such as iron, oxygen, magnesium, and silicon, which total 93 per cent of the earth. Meteorites probably have about twice as large a percentage of manganese as does the earth. Manganese does not exist naturally in its pure state, because it reacts so easily with other elements. More than a hundred different manganese minerals are known. Of these, the three most abundant in ores are the black oxides, *pyrolusite* and *psilomelane*, and the pink carbonate, *rhodochrosite*.

The most important known manganese ores lie in rocks in Russia. The *residual* deposits in India, Africa, and China rank next in importance. Residual deposits have been enriched by the *leaching* (washing and dissolving away) of impurities near the surface.

Mining and Metallurgy. The black oxides are usually mined from shallow pits or open cuts, and from shallow underground mines. Most of the pink carbonate is mined from veins, usually along with other minerals.

Manganese ore may be improved in grade by several methods, including hand sorting and simple "gravity" methods using water for washing. The pink carbonate ore is usually concentrated by the flotation process, using soap reagents (see FLOTATION PROCESS). This process is followed by *sintering* (heating fine particles of ore at high temperatures) so that they form lumps.

LEADING MANGANESE-MINING COUNTRIES
Tons of manganese mined in 1967

Country	Tons
Russia	*7,940,000 tons
South Africa	*1,930,000 tons
India	1,763,000 tons
Gabon	1,264,000 tons
Brazil	1,248,000 tons
China (Communist)	*770,000 tons
Australia	*600,000 tons

*Estimate

Source: *Minerals Yearbook, 1967*, U.S. Bureau of Mines

Production. The chief manganese-producing countries include Russia, South Africa, India, and Gabon. Brazil, China (Communist), Australia, and Ghana also produce manganese. Brazil became the leader in manganese production in the Western Hemisphere with the opening of its Amapá deposit in 1957.

The small amount of manganese produced in the United States comes mainly from Montana and New Mexico. At times, the government has encouraged production by giving subsidies and by setting up protective tariffs (see TARIFF [Revenue and Protective Tariffs]). Known high-grade ore reserves in the United States are limited. But Minnesota, Maine, South Dakota, and Arizona have large reserves of low-grade material that

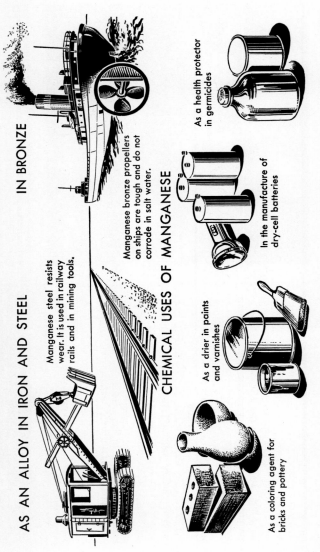

SOME USES OF MANGANESE

AS AN ALLOY IN IRON AND STEEL
Manganese steel resists wear. It is used in railway rails and in mining tools.

IN BRONZE
Manganese bronze propellers on ships are tough and do not corrode in salt water.

CHEMICAL USES OF MANGANESE
As a drier in paints and varnishes

In the manufacture of dry-cell batteries

As a health protector in germicides

As a coloring agent for bricks and pottery

could be made available in times of extreme need. Manganese found at the bottom of the sea may be important in the future. Blast-furnace slag is a potential source of manganese. A ton of slag has about 23 pounds of manganese. Because of the limited reserves in the United States and the importance of manganese in wartime, the United States has stockpiled manganese ores since the 1940's.

See also ALLOY (Alloys of Iron); IRON AND STEEL (Methods of Making Steel).

HARRISON ASHLEY SCHMITT

MANGE, *maynj*, is a skin disease that affects dogs, horses, sheep, and cattle. It is much like the itch in human beings. Mange usually attacks dirty, neglected animals which live in groups or herds, or in crowded shelters. The disease is caused by tiny mites that burrow into the skin and live there. Different kinds, or species, of mites attack different kinds of animals. They produce soreness, swelling, and itching. Tiny pimples and sores form on the skin, and the hair or wool falls out in patches. The sores and breaks in the skin become worse as a result of the animal's continuous scratching.

Mange can be treated by dipping or hand rubbing the skin with sulfur, lime, and arsenic mixtures. In most cases, a veterinarian should be consulted. Mange can be prevented by general cleanliness and by washing and brushing the animal.

See also MITE.

D. W. BRUNER

MANGEL-WURZEL. See BEET.

MANGO, *MANG goh.* The mango is the fruit of an evergreen tree which grows in tropical regions throughout the world. It originally grew wild in southeastern Asia. Settlers brought it to America in the 1700's.

The mango tree is attractive. It is thick and dark green, and may grow 40 to 50 feet tall. The slender, pointed leaves are about a foot long. Tiny pink flowers grow in clusters at the ends of small branches.

The fruit of the mango tree is usually about the size of an apple, but it may weigh as much as 3 pounds. It

Clusters of Mangoes hang from an evergreen mango tree. Residents of the tropics like to roast mango seeds and eat them.

J. Horace McFarland

consists of a soft, juicy, yellow or orange pulp covered by a skin that may be yellow, red, or green. A thick husk surrounds the large flat seed of the mango. Many tough fibers grow into the pulp. The fruits, or mangoes, are usually shaped like a kidney, but they may be round or egg-shaped. There are about 500 varieties. Finer, grafted varieties of the mango have no fibers, and the fruit can be eaten with a spoon. The mango has a delicious, spicy flavor.

The fiberless Indonesian and Philippine varieties of mango have become popular in southern Florida. In 1900, the U.S. Department of Agriculture brought these varieties to the United States. Small amounts of the fruit have been sent to northern markets. Frost easily destroys the mango tree. Grafted mangoes bear fruit after 2 or 3 years. Seedlings require a year or two longer.

Scientific Classification. The mango belongs to the cashew family, *Anacardiaceae.* It is in the genus *Mangifera,* and is species *M. indica.*

See also PLANT (color picture: Fruits Unknown to Our Forefathers).

JULIAN C. CRANE

MANGOSTEEN, *MANG goh steen,* is a tree which grows in Indonesia. It is about 30 feet tall. The shining green leaves are leathery, thick, and about 8 inches long. The pinkish flowers of the mangosteen measure almost 2 inches across. The reddish-purple edible fruit is shaped like a tangerine, with thick, juicy, white flesh. They are about 2½ inches across. Cold weather kills the mangosteen. A few of these plants grow in gardens in the southernmost parts of the United States.

The Fruit of the Mangosteen tastes much like an orange. The fruit has a reddish-purple rind.

Ewing Galloway

Scientific Classification. Mangosteens belong to the garcinia family, *Guttiferae.* They are classified as genus *Garcinia,* species *G. mangostana.*

MANGROVE, *MANG grohv,* is a tropical tree that grows in salty ocean water. As the mangrove develops, it sends down roots from its branches. At last, hundreds of roots support its leafy crown above the water. The roots look like stilts. In hot regions, large thickets or forests on stilts, grow in shallow water. Mangroves flourish along bays, lagoons, and river mouths.

Mangrove thickets form the chief plant growth along thousands of miles of coast in the tropics. The thickets grow only in places by quiet ocean water. The thousands of stiltlike roots catch silt, which piles up in the quiet water. At the mouths of streams, the roots slow down the current and help settle the silt. In this way, the mangroves aid in building up dry land. At last, the

Mangroves Grow in Shallow Salt Water near seacoasts of tropical countries. Their spreading roots catch and hold particles of dirt and sand. This action helps build up shorelines.

Nature Magazine

plant remains standing in the mud above the reach of the tide. But it kills itself in forming the land, for its roots need to be washed in ocean water, at least during high tide.

The seed often germinates while the mangrove fruit is attached to the tree. It sends down a root sometimes several feet long. When the fruit falls, the heavy root holds it upright as it floats on the water. Sometimes when the root tip strikes mud, it begins to grow and form a new tree.

The red mangrove grows along the coasts from Florida to northern South America. It grows about 25 feet high and has a round top, with thick, oval leaves. People use the wood for wharf piles and fuel. They use the bark for tanning hides and making dyes.

Scientific Classification. The mangrove belongs to the mangrove family, *Rhizophoraceae*. The red mangrove is genus *Rhizophora*, species *R. mangle*. K. A. ARMSON

MANHATTAN COLLEGE. See UNIVERSITIES AND COLLEGES (table).

MANHATTAN ISLAND (pop. 1,698,281) is one of the commercial, financial, and cultural centers of the world. It has an area of 31 square miles and forms the borough of Manhattan, New York City's smallest borough. The East River is its eastern border, with Upper New York Bay on the south, the Hudson River on the west, and the Harlem River and Spuyten Duyvil Creek on the north. A series of bridges and tunnels connects the island with the other boroughs and with New Jersey (see NEW YORK CITY [map]).

Manhattan Island has many famous landmarks and tourist attractions. They include Broadway, Chinatown, the Empire State Building, Greenwich Village, Rockefeller Center, Times Square, the United Nations headquarters, Wall Street, and many churches, colleges, museums, skyscrapers, and theaters. Most of New York City's municipal buildings stand on Manhattan Island.

Peter Minuit, governor of the Dutch West India Company, bought the island in 1626 from the Manhattan Indians. He paid for it with beads, cloth, and trinkets worth $24. About 200 people lived in the settlement, then called New Amsterdam. WILLIAM E. YOUNG

See also MINUIT, PETER; NEW YORK CITY.

MANHATTAN PROJECT was created by the United States government in 1942 to produce the first atomic bomb. The official agency that produced the bomb was the Corps of Engineers' Manhattan Engineer District, commanded by Major (later Lieutenant) General Leslie R. Groves. He directed industrial and research activities at such sites as Oak Ridge, Tenn., and Los Alamos, N.Mex. See also ATOMIC BOMB. RALPH E. LAPP

MANHATTAN SCHOOL OF MUSIC. See UNIVERSITIES AND COLLEGES (table).

MANHATTANVILLE COLLEGE. See UNIVERSITIES AND COLLEGES (table).

MANIA. See MENTAL ILLNESS (Manic-Depressive Psychosis).

MANIC-DEPRESSIVE. See MENTAL ILLNESS.

MANICHAEISM, *MAN uh key izm,* is a religious system based on the doctrines of Manes, a Persian born about A.D. 215. Manes combined the Christian theory of salvation and the Zoroastrian concept of *dualism,* or the belief that two opposing principles govern the universe (see ZOROASTRIANISM). According to this system, the world originated as a mixture of light and darkness, which represent good and evil. Manichaeans believe that man's soul, which arose from the Kingdom of Light, wants to escape from the body, which represents the Kingdom of Darkness. They believe that the soul can attain release only through wisdom, not through the renunciation of material or sensual things. They also believe that a savior will provide the wisdom necessary for release. Manichaeism was suppressed in Persia, but was important in other countries through the 900's.

MANICURE. See GROOMING, PERSONAL; NAIL (picture: Care of the Nails).

MANIFEST is a detailed list of the goods a vessel is carrying. It also tells who owns the goods. The ship's captain certifies that the manifest is correct. The port collector uses it in figuring the *duty* (tax) on goods.

MANIFEST DESTINY was a term used to describe the belief in the 1840's in the inevitable territorial expansion of the United States. Persons who believed in manifest destiny maintained that the United States, because of its economic and political superiority, and its rapidly growing population, should rule all North America. The phrase was first used in 1845 by John L. O'Sullivan in an article on the annexation of Texas. The spirit of manifest destiny was revived at the end of the 1800's, during and after the Spanish-American War (see SPANISH-AMERICAN WAR). See also UNITED STATES, HISTORY OF (The Compromise of 1850). RAY ALLEN BILLINGTON

MANIFOLD, INTAKE. See CARBURETOR; GASOLINE ENGINE (Fuel System; picture).

MANILA

MANILA, *muh NIL uh* (pop. 1,356,000; alt. 30 ft.), is the leading port and chief cultural, social, and commercial city of the Philippines. Spanish invaders of the Philippines founded the city nearly 400 years ago. Manila now serves as the world's greatest market for abacá, a kind of hemp. Manila is also a center for the cigar, coconut oil, and sugar industries. The city's beautiful setting and architectural landmarks earned it the name of the *Pearl of the Orient.*

Location and Size. Manila stretches along the east shore of Manila Bay on the island of Luzon. A crescent of mountains surrounds the city on the north, east, and south. The Pasig River flows down from the mountains and divides the city into two sections. Manila covers a total area of about 14 square miles. For location, see PHILIPPINES (color map).

Description. Intramuros, or the Walled City, stands on the south bank of the Pasig River. Spaniards began construction of Intramuros in 1571, and completed it in 1739. They built high city walls and surrounded them with a wide moat to protect themselves from attacks by unfriendly Filipinos. The walls and some of the churches, convents, monasteries, and public buildings still stand in this old Spanish colonial town, despite heavy bombing during World War II. Outstanding among the old buildings is St. Augustine Church, built in 1599 by Spaniards and Filipinos.

The Luneta, one of Manila's favorite parks, looks across Manila Bay from just outside Intramuros. The Philippine Armed Forces Band gives concerts every Sunday in the park. A statue of Dr. José Rizal stands on the spot in the park where this national hero was executed by the Spanish on Dec. 30, 1896. Roxas Boulevard (formerly Dewey Boulevard) runs south along Manila Bay from the Luneta. This picturesque drive passes the mansions of wealthy Manilans and lovely hotels, apartment buildings, restaurants, and night clubs. The United States Embassy and the headquarters of the Philippine Navy also lie along the boulevard.

The modern business district of Manila lies on the north bank of the Pasig River. Six bridges connect the two parts of the city. The Escolta and the Avenida

Rizal, Manila's fashionable shopping streets, run through this newer section. A large Chinatown lies next to the Escolta. Many tourists travel to Quiapo, just north of the river, to visit its colorful market and lively restaurants, shopping centers, and movie houses. Thousands of people go to the Quiapo Church every Friday to worship before the shrine of the miraculous image of the Black Nazarene. Tondo, in the northwestern corner of the city, presents a sharp contrast to the modern buildings elsewhere in the newer business district. Many of the people in Tondo live in primitive huts thatched with nipa palm.

Important buildings in Manila include the Malacañang Palace, home of the Philippine president, and the José Rizal Memorial Stadium. Outstanding government buildings are the Legislative Building, the City Hall, the Post Office, and the Agricultural and Finance department buildings. Japanese bombings during World War II destroyed the Manila Cathedral, originally built in 1654, but it was rebuilt in 1958.

Industry and Trade. Industries in Manila turn out a variety of textiles, and clothing and accessory manufacturers produce hats, leather goods, pearl buttons, and shoes. Handmade items include embroidered goods and rattan furniture. Processing plants produce beer, coconut oil, soap, sugar, and tobacco products. The city also has an automobile assembly plant. Other manufactured products include building materials, cosmetics, drugs, glassware, ink, machinery, matches, nails, paints, pencils, radio equipment, and rope and twine.

Manila ranks as one of the leading trade centers of East Asia. Nearly half of the abacá sold in the city goes to the United States to make rope and twine. The United States also purchases about half of Manila's copra exports. Other leading exports include copal, dried fish, fruits, kapok, lumber, ramie fiber, and sugar, and chromite, iron, and manganese ores.

Transportation and Communication. Manila's superb harbor and location make it an important port on most of the Pacific and Far East trade routes. Four large piers in the harbor can handle up to 12 large ships at one time. Manila also has an international airport. Two north banks of the Pasig River. Six bridges connect the railways, the Manila Railroad Company and the

The Manila Post Office, center, stands on the south bank of the Pasig River, just across from the main business district. The muddy river cuts through the heart of the city and forms an essential part of the harbor on Manila Bay.

Chas. W. Miller

Philippine Association

Manila's City Hall, *left*, Is Near the Legislative Building. *right*, Where the Philippine Congress Meets.

Philippine Railway Company, also serve the city.

Manila has six radio stations, including one in suburban Quezon City and the government-owned station, DZFM. The city also has one television station. Publishers print several periodicals in English, including 7 daily newspapers, 7 weekly magazines, and a quarterly magazine. The city also has 7 newspapers printed in Spanish, 2 dailies and 10 weeklies in Tagalog, and 7 Chinese dailies.

Education. Manila has 12 universities. The University of Santo Tomás, founded in 1611, is older than Harvard. The University of the Philippines stands in Quezon City. Dozens of colleges also operate in Manila. The National Museum and Santo Tomás Museum have an interesting variety of collections. The city also has 14 public libraries. The Manila Symphony Orchestra, the Filipino Youth Symphony, the Army Band, and college orchestras play concert music. Ballet and opera groups are active.

Government. Manila is divided into 14 municipal districts for administrative purposes. A mayor heads the executive department of the city government. The people elect him to office for a four-year term. The municipal board makes up the legislative branch of the government. It consists of three elected members. The municipal court of Manila has eight branches.

History. Before the coming of Europeans, the Manila area belonged to the monarchies ruled by Rajah Soliman and Rajah Lakandula. Miguel López de Legazpi, a Spanish conquistador, founded Manila in 1571. The Ayuntamiento in Intramuros was built in 1735 to house the city council and the mayor's office. This building became the seat of the national government when the United States took possession of the Philippines. An earthquake destroyed a large part of the city in 1863. Spain surrendered Manila to the United States in 1898, during the Spanish-American War. The American administration of the city installed a modern water supply system, electric lighting, and made several other improvements.

Japanese forces seized Manila on Jan. 2, 1942, just

four weeks after the beginning of World War II in the Pacific. American forces began the liberation of the city on Feb. 3, 1945, and a bitter three-week battle followed. Among the first places liberated were the Santo Tomás internment camp and the Bilibid Prison, where the Japanese had kept American prisoners. Few buildings remained standing in Manila when the Japanese finally surrendered the city on February 24. But the Filipinos began rebuilding the city almost immediately.

Manila became the national capital of the Philippines when independence was proclaimed on July 4, 1946. But in 1948, Philippine President Elpidio Quirino signed an act that recognized Quezon City as the official capital of the country. Manila continued to act as the seat of the Philippine government in the 1960's, pending the completion of new government buildings in Quezon City.

RUSSELL H. FIFIELD

See also WORLD WAR II (The War in Asia and the Pacific).

MANILA BAY is the entrance to the city of Manila on Luzon in the Philippines. The bay faces southwesterly towards the South China Sea. For location, see PHILIPPINES (color map). Manila Bay is about 40 miles long and 35 miles wide. Its waters are deep enough to accommodate large ships. There are two excellent harbors at Cavite and Manila.

The rocky, fortified island of Corregidor is at the mouth of Manila Bay. Some of the most bitter fighting of World War II took place on Corregidor. It was attacked by the Japanese during the first days of the war. During the Spanish-American War, an American fleet under Commodore George Dewey destroyed a Spanish fleet in a battle at Manila Bay.

F. G. WALTON SMITH

See also BATAAN PENINSULA; CORREGIDOR; SPANISH-AMERICAN WAR.

MANILA BAY, BATTLE OF. See SPANISH-AMERICAN WAR.

MANILA HEMP. See ABACÁ.

MANIOC. See TAPIOCA.

MANITO. See INDIAN, AMERICAN (Beliefs).

Manitoba Dept. of Industry and Commerce

Ice Fishing on a Frozen Lake in Manitoba
Manitoba Dept. of Industry and Commerce

Atikameg Lake in Clearwater Provincial Park

MANITOBA

— FACTS IN BRIEF —

Capital: Winnipeg.

Government: *Parliament*—senators, 6; members of the House of Commons, 14. *Provincial Legislature*—members of the Legislative Assembly, 57. *Voting Age*—18.

Area: 251,000 square miles (including 39,225 square miles of inland water), sixth in size among the provinces. *Greatest Distances*—(north-south) 761 miles; (east-west) 493 miles. *Coastline* (Hudson Bay)—410 miles.

Elevation: *Highest*—Baldy Mountain, 2,727 feet above sea level. *Lowest*—sea level, along Hudson Bay.

Population: *1966 Census*—963,066, fifth among the provinces; density, 4 persons to the square mile; distribution, 67 per cent urban, 33 per cent rural. *Estimated 1971 Population*—1,007,000.

Chief Products: *Manufacturing*—cement, clothing, food products, lumber and wood products, petroleum products, transportation equipment. *Agriculture*—barley, beef cattle, flaxseed, milk, oats, rye, sugar beets, wheat. *Mining*—copper, nickel, petroleum, zinc. *Fishing Industry*—pickerel, pike, sauger, whitefish.

Entered the Dominion: July 15, 1870, the fifth province.

The contributors of this article are Peter McLintock, Executive Editor of the Winnipeg Free Press; W. L. Morton, Vanier Professor of History at Trent University and author of Manitoba: A History; and Thomas R. Weir, Professor and Head of the Department of Geography of the University of Manitoba.

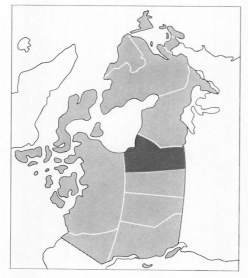

Manitoba (Blue) Is the 6th Largest Province of Canada.

Sawmill Near Cedar Lake in Western Manitoba

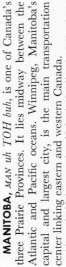

MANITOBA, *MAN uh TOH buh,* is one of Canada's three Prairie Provinces. It lies midway between the Atlantic and Pacific oceans. Winnipeg, Manitoba's capital and largest city, is the main transportation center linking eastern and western Canada.

About half the people of Manitoba live in Winnipeg and its suburbs. This area is the province's major industrial center. Busy food-processing plants and other factories there help make manufacturing the chief source of income in Manitoba. St. Boniface, a suburb of Winnipeg, has the largest stockyard in Canada. The area also has clothing factories, petroleum refineries, and railway equipment plants.

Winnipeg lies in rolling plains that cover the southern section of Manitoba. This fertile region has the province's richest farmlands. In summer, hundreds of square miles of wheat and other grains wave in the sun. Large numbers of beef cattle graze in fenced pastures. Other important farm products include flaxseed, milk, sugar beets, and vegetables.

A vast, rocky region lies across the northern two-thirds of Manitoba. This thinly populated region has great deposits of copper, gold, nickel, and zinc. Thompson has the only facilities in the western world for all stages of nickel production, from mining to processing. The thriving town was carved out of the wilderness after prospectors discovered vast deposits of nickel. Manitoba ranks among the leading North American producers of nickel and zinc. Thick forests stretch across the southern half of the region. Balsam firs, spruces, and other trees provide wood for Manitoba's furniture factories and paper mills. Much of the northern half of the region is too cold for trees to grow.

Manitoba's many rivers and lakes cover almost a sixth of the province and help make it a popular vaca-

tionland. Tourists enjoy boating and swimming in the clear, sparkling waters. Fishermen come from many parts of North America to cast for bass, pike, and trout. In the rugged forests, hunters track caribou, elk, moose, and smaller game. In the marshes and prairies, they shoot ducks, geese, and partridges.

Beavers and other fur-bearing animals made the Manitoba region important during the late 1600's. English fur traders entered the rich fur country from Hudson Bay in the northeast. French-Canadian traders came westward from Quebec during the early 1700's. The adventurous fur traders paddled their birchbark canoes up Manitoba's rivers and traveled through unexplored forests and plains. They traded with the Indians of the region and built forts and trading posts in the wilderness. Irish and Scottish farmers began breaking up the plains in the early 1800's. Vast wheat fields were created in the fertile Red River Valley. Manitoba began exporting wheat, and the grain became famous for its high quality.

The word *Manitoba* probably came from the Algonkian language of the Indians. The tribes thought the *Manito* (great spirit) made the echoing sounds that came from a strait of Lake Manitoba. These sounds were actually made by waves dashing against limestone ledges on the shore. The Indians called this narrow part of the lake *Manito waba* (great spirit's strait). Manitoba has the nickname of the *Keystone Province.* The nickname came from Manitoba's location in the center, or keystone, of the "arch" formed by the 10 Canadian provinces.

For the relationship of Manitoba to the other Canadian provinces, see the articles on CANADA; CANADA, GOVERNMENT OF; CANADA, HISTORY OF; PRAIRIE PROVINCES.

111

Manitoba Dept. of Industry and Commerce

The Legislative Building's Grand Staircase is flanked by buffaloes. Manitoba has a single-house legislature called the general assembly.

Manitoba Dept. of Industry and Commerce

Government House stands east of the Legislative Building in Winnipeg. The mansion is the home of the lieutenant-governor of Manitoba. He serves as Queen Elizabeth's official representative in the province.

Lieutenant-Governor of Manitoba represents Queen Elizabeth in the province. He is appointed by the governor-general-in-council of Canada. The lieutenant-governor's position is largely honorary, like that of the governor-general.

Premier of Manitoba is the actual head of the provincial government. The province, like the other provinces and Canada itself, has a *parliamentary* form of government. The premier is a member of the legislative assembly, where he is the leader of the majority party. The voters elect him as they do the other members of the assembly. The premier receives a salary of $18,000 a year, in addition to allowances he gets as a member of the assembly. For a list of all the premiers of Manitoba, see the *History* section of this article.

The premier presides over the executive council, or cabinet. The council also includes ministers chosen by the premier from among his party's members in the legislative assembly. Each minister directs one or more branches of the provincial government. The executive council, like the premier, resigns if it loses the support of a majority of the assembly.

Legislative Assembly is a one-house legislature that makes the provincial laws. It has 57 members elected from 57 electoral districts. Their terms may last up to five years. However, the lieutenant-governor, on the advice of the premier, may call for an election before the end of the five-year period. If he does so, all members of the assembly must run again for office.

Courts. The highest court in Manitoba is the court of appeal. It is made up of the chief justice of Manitoba and five *puisne* (associate) judges. The court of queen's bench hears all major civil and criminal cases. Although Manitoba has no counties, it has county courts in the six judicial districts. Each district has one county judge, except that which includes Winnipeg and St. Boniface. This district, because of its large population, has five judges.

The governor-general-in-council appoints all Manitoba's higher-court judges. They serve until the age of 75. Minor court officials, such as police magistrates and judges of family and juvenile courts, are appointed by provincial authorities.

Local Government. Manitoba has about 200 incorporated cities, towns, and rural municipalities. Each is governed by a council headed by a mayor or a reeve. Most of these officials are elected to two-year terms. The number of council members ranges from 4 to 18, depending on the area's population. The province also has about 20 local government districts in thinly settled areas. These districts are governed by resident administrators appointed by the provincial government.

The nine cities of Manitoba received their charters under special acts of the legislative assembly. The towns, villages, and rural municipalities were incorporated under the province's municipal act. They are supervised by the provincial department of municipal affairs.

The Metropolitan Corporation of Greater Winnipeg includes Winnipeg and 15 suburbs, among them St. Boniface and St. James. The area is governed by a 10-man council elected from 10 districts. This council has no connection with the various governments of Winnipeg and the suburbs. It was created in 1960 to deal

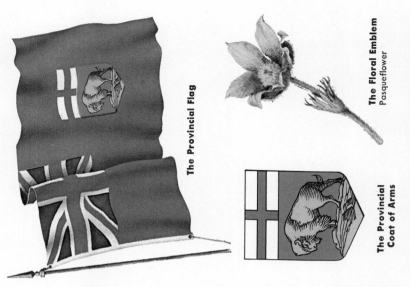

The Provincial Flag

The Floral Emblem
Pasqueflower

**The Provincial
Coat of Arms**

Manitoba Dept. of Industry and Commerce

Legislative Building in Winnipeg rises 255 feet. A statue of *Golden Boy*, symbolizing enterprise, tops the dome. Winnipeg became the capital in 1870. Manitoba has had no other capitals.

Symbols of Manitoba. On the coat of arms, the buffalo symbolizes the importance of the Red River buffalo in Manitoba's history, and the position of Manitoba as a Prairie Province. The cross of St. George represents Manitoba's bond with Great Britain. The coat of arms was adopted in 1870. The provincial flag, adopted in 1965, bears Manitoba's coat of arms and the British Union flag.

with such metropolitan problems as flood control, highway construction, sewage disposal, and urban growth.

Taxation provides almost a third of the provincial government's income. A gasoline tax provides much of the tax money. Manitoba also has corporate and personal income taxes and a 5 per cent general sales tax. About 40 per cent of its income is from federal-provincial tax-sharing arrangements, and about 15 per cent from license and permit fees. Other income is chiefly from the sale of liquor, which is government controlled.

Politics. In 1969, the New Democratic Party, a socialist party, won control of Manitoba's Legislative Assembly and formed its first government. The major political parties of Manitoba have been the Progressive Conservative and the Liberal parties, or earlier forms of these groups. The Progressive Conservative Party was formerly named the Conservative Party, and today the members are usually simply called Conservatives. In 1932, the Liberals joined the provincial government headed by a farmers' organization called the Progressives. They called themselves Liberal Progressives until 1961.

Smaller political parties of Manitoba are the Communist Party and the Social Credit Party. A Manitoba citizen must be at least 18 years old to vote.

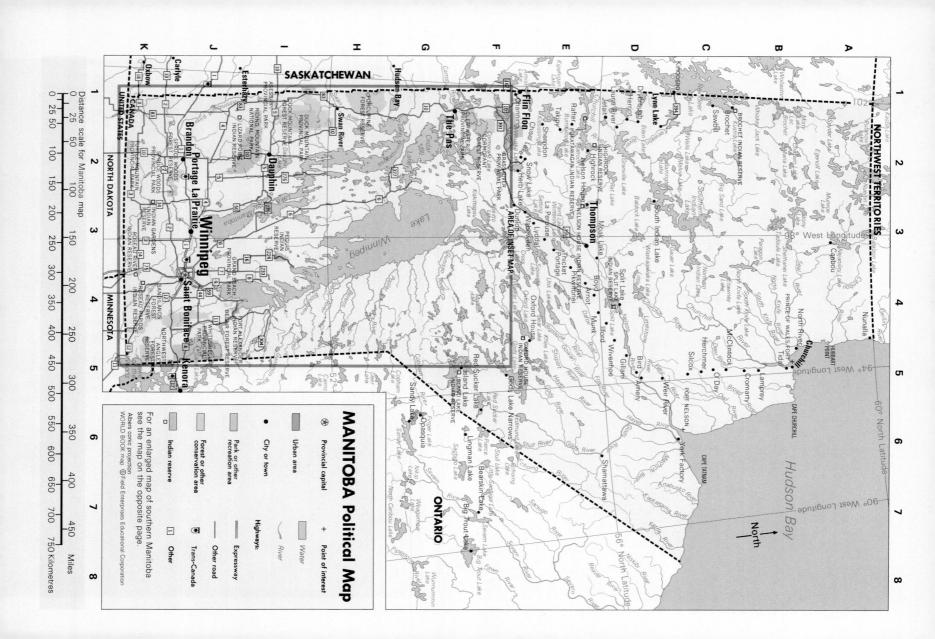

MANITOBA Political Map

Legend:
- ⊛ Provincial capital
- + Point of interest
- ● City or town

Highways:
- Expressway
- Other road
- Trans-Canada
- Other

Water
River
Urban area
Park or other recreation area
Forest or other conservation area
Indian reserve

For an enlarged map of southern Manitoba see the map on the opposite page.

WORLD BOOK map © Field Enterprises Educational Corporation
Albers conic projection

Distance scale for Manitoba map

Miles
Kilometres

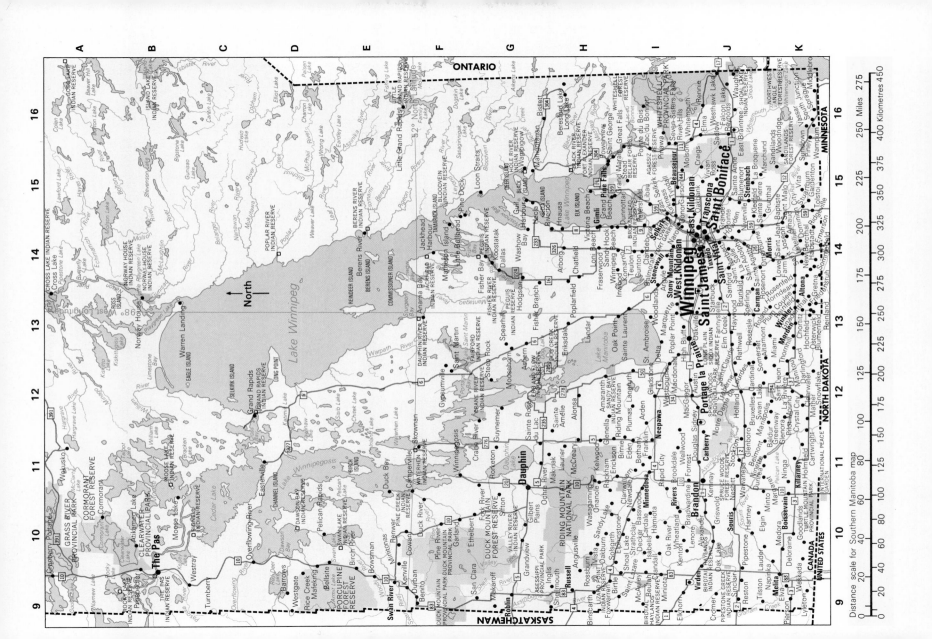

116

*Does not appear on map; key shows general location.
†Town on Manitoba-Saskatchewan border; total population 10,201.

Source: Latest census (1966). Places without population figures are unincorporated and have less than 50 persons.

MANITOBA/People

The 1966 Canadian census reported that Manitoba had 963,066 persons. The population had increased 5 per cent over the 1961 figure of 921,686. By 1971, Manitoba had an estimated population of 1,007,000 persons.

About two-thirds of the people of Manitoba live in cities and towns. About half—508,759 persons—live in the metropolitan area of Winnipeg. Winnipeg has the province's only Census Metropolitan Area as defined by the Dominion Bureau of Statistics.

Besides Winnipeg, Manitoba has nine cities and towns with populations of more than 10,000. They are, in order of size, St. Boniface, St. James, Brandon, St. Vital, East Kildonan, West Kildonan, Transcona, Portage la Prairie, and Flin Flon. See the separate articles listed in the *Related Articles* at the end of this article. More than 80 of every 100 Manitobans were born in Canada. The province also has large numbers of persons

born in Germany, Great Britain, Poland, and Russia. About 40 per cent of the people have English, Irish, or Scottish ancestors. Some descendants of French settlers live in towns where French is still the chief language. Manitoba has about 30,000 *métis* (persons of mixed white and Indian ancestry). About 32,000 Indians and 200 Eskimos live in the province. Southwestern Manitoba has more than a hundred Indian reservations. Most of the Eskimos live near Churchill.

The United Church of Canada has the largest church membership in Manitoba. Other large religious groups are Roman Catholics, members of the Anglican Church of Canada, and Lutherans.

POPULATION

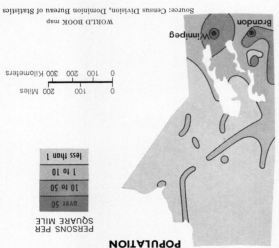

This map shows the *population density* of Manitoba, and how it varies in different parts of the province. Population density means the average number of persons who live on each square mile.

PERSONS PER SQUARE MILE

over 50	
10 to 50	
1 to 10	
less than 1	

WORLD BOOK map
Source: Census Division, Dominion Bureau of Statistics

0   100   200 Miles
0   100   200   300 Kilometers

Winnipeg
Brandon

MANITOBA/Education

Schools. The first school in the Manitoba region was a log cabin built in 1818 at St. Boniface. Roman Catholic priests established the school for the children of French-Canadian settlers. Other missionaries opened Roman Catholic or Protestant schools after new settlements developed.

In 1871, the church-supported educational system was ended. The province created a board of education to direct the schools and provide them with public funds. Roman Catholic board members managed the Roman Catholic schools, and Protestant board members supervised theirs. In 1890, the province abolished the board of education and its double school system. The provincial Department of Education was created to head a single education system. In 1908, the cabinet office of minister of education was established in Manitoba.

A Manitoba law of 1965 requires children between the ages of 7 and 16 to attend school. The province has

about 1,800 public schools. For information on the number of students and teachers in Manitoba, see EDUCATION (table). Brandon University is in Brandon, and the University of Manitoba and the University of Winnipeg are in Winnipeg. Each of these universities has a separate article in WORLD BOOK.

Libraries and Museums. Two of the most important libraries in the province are the University of Manitoba Library and the Legislative Library, both in Winnipeg. Students of early Manitoban history use a special library operated by the Hudson's Bay Company in its Winnipeg offices. The Winnipeg Museum and Art Gallery and the St. Boniface Historical Museum attract thousands of visitors yearly.

National Film Board of Canada

Traders Bid in Winnipeg's Grain Exchange. About half of Manitoba's people live in or near Winnipeg, the province's chief city.

MANITOBA / A Visitor's Guide

Visitors to Manitoba can see many reminders of the province's colorful history. Forts and trading posts of the early fur-trading days are popular attractions. The site of the first Roman Catholic church in western Canada. It is perhaps the most beautiful cathedral in the region. Many men who helped make Manitoba history are buried in the churchyard. They include Louis Riel, who led two uprisings of the métis.

PLACES TO VISIT

Following are brief descriptions of some of Manitoba's many interesting places to visit.

International Peace Garden lies partly in Manitoba and partly in North Dakota. It honors the long friendship between Canada and the United States. A *cairn* (memorial made of stones) consisting of rocks from both countries marks the international boundary. The cairn was built in 1932.

Lower Fort Garry, 20 miles north of Winnipeg, is the only stone fur-trading fort in Canada still standing complete. It was built during the 1830's by the Hudson's Bay Company on the west bank of the Red River. The area became a national historic park in 1951.

Norway House, built in 1826, stands at the northern end of Lake Winnipeg. This old Hudson's Bay Company post has many articles from fur-trading days.

Prince of Wales Fort, near Churchill, overlooks Hudson Bay. It has the massive remains of the northernmost fortress in North America. The stone structure was

116b

Lake Winnipeg and many other beautiful lakes of Manitoba have popular summer resorts that offer boating and swimming. The province also has fine golf courses. Sportsmen come from most parts of North America to fish for bass, pike, and trout in the province's lakes and rivers. Hunters seek ducks, geese, and moose in the forests and swamps. Many visitors attend performances by the Royal Winnipeg Ballet or Winnipeg Symphony Orchestra, or other cultural events.

built by the Hudson's Bay Company between 1733 and 1771. The area became a national historic park in 1941.

Red River Valley, near Winnipeg, was the region where the first Manitoba colony was founded. Historic sites, old houses, and early stone churches dot the prairies and grain fields.

The Pas is a historic northern crossroads town about 45 miles north of Lake Winnipegosis. Its name came from the Cree Indian word *opas* (narrows). Much north and south traffic passes through it.

National and Provincial Parks. Riding Mountain National Park, Manitoba's only national park, lies in the western part of the province, west of Lake Winnipeg. For its area and chief features, see CANADA (National Parks).

Manitoba has nine provincial parks. For information on these parks, write to Provincial Forester, Department of Mines and Natural Resources, 808 Norquay Building, York Ave. and Kennedy St., Winnipeg, Man.

Fishermen Cast for Trout in a Rushing Manitoba Stream

Lower Fort Garry on the Red River North of Winnipeg

Photos, Malak, Miller Services

ANNUAL EVENTS

Manitoba's outstanding annual event is probably the World Championship Dog Derby, a dog sled race over snow. The event is part of the famous Trappers' Festival, held in The Pas each February. Other annual events in Manitoba include the following.

February-April: Winnipeg Bonspiel (February); Manitoba Musical Festival in Winnipeg (March); Manitoba Winter Fair in Brandon (April).

June-July: Red River Exhibition in Winnipeg (June); Trout Festival in Flin Flon (June); Selkirk Interlake Fair and Regatta (July); Manitoba Stampede (July); Northwest Roundup and Fair in Swan River (July); Provincial Exhibition in Brandon (July); Scottish Highland Games in Winnipeg (July).

August: Icelandic Celebration in Gimli.

The Royal Winnipeg Ballet Performs Throughout Canada

Manitoba Dept. of Industry and Commerce

MANITOBA/The Land

Land Regions. Manitoba has four main land regions. They are, from northeast to southwest: (1) the Hudson Bay Lowland, (2) the Canadian Shield, (3) the Manitoba Lowland, and (4) the Saskatchewan Plain.

The Hudson Bay Lowland is a wet plain that curves around the southern part of Hudson Bay. In Manitoba, this almost treeless flatland extends into the interior for about a hundred miles. Very few persons live in this region.

The Canadian Shield is a vast, horseshoe-shaped region that covers almost half of Canada and dips into the northern United States. The rough shield, made up of ancient granites and other rocks, covers nearly two-thirds of Manitoba. It has countless lakes and streams, great forests, and deposits of copper, nickel, and other minerals. See CANADIAN SHIELD.

The Manitoba Lowland forms part of the Western Interior Plains, the Canadian section of the North American Great Plains. It is a flat area of forests, lakes, limestone rock, and swamps. The forests have great stands of timber, and the lakes are rich in fish.

The Saskatchewan Plain also forms part of the Western Interior Plains. This region is a rolling plain broken by low hills. Its rich, well-drained soils make it the main farming region of Manitoba.

Mountains. The Duck, Porcupine, and Riding mountain ranges form the Manitoba Escarpment. It rises between the two plains regions. The highest point in Manitoba is 2,727-foot Baldy Mountain, in the Duck Mountain range near the Saskatchewan border. The

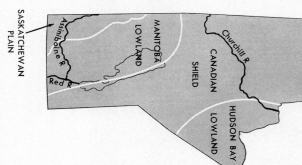

Land Regions of Manitoba

SASKATCHEWAN PLAIN

CANADIAN SHIELD

HUDSON BAY LOWLAND

MANITOBA LOWLAND

Churchill R.

Assiniboine R.

Red R.

Cattle Graze along the banks of the Red River. A large part of Manitoba's dairy production comes from the Red River Valley.

Rowed, Miller Services

MANITOBA

Hudson Bay
All islands within Hudson Bay
lie within Northwest Territories.

Longitude West of Greenwich

Legend:
- Evergreen Trees
- Deciduous Trees
- Grass
- Tundra
- Provincial Capital
- Cities and Towns
- City Limits
- Rail Lines

1 inch = 95 Statute Miles

Miles 0 10 20 40 60 80 Statute Miles

Lambert Conformal Conic Projection

ONTARIO

N. W. T.

SASKATCHEWAN

MINN.

N. DAK.

CANADA
U. S.

WINNIPEG

St. Boniface

Churchill

CAPE CHURCHILL

CAPE TATNAM

York Factory

Hudson Bay

Nelson River

Churchill River

Reindeer Lake

Southern Indian Lake

Lake Winnipeg

Lake Winnipegosis

Lake Manitoba

Cedar Lake

Moose Lake

Cross Lake

Split Lake

Island Lake

Oxford Lake

Gods Lake

God's Lake

Red Lake

Kenora

Fort Frances

Emerson

Brandon

Dauphin

Yorkton

Portage la Prairie

The Pas

Flin Flon

Brochet

Lynn Lake

Grand Rapids

Red Deer Lake

Wollaston Lake

Kasba Lake

Nueltin Lake

Big Trout Lake

North Caribou Lake

Sachigo Lake

Severn River

Echoing River

Winisk River

Pipestone River

Attawapiskat River

Big Sand Lake

Caribou Lake

Reindeer River

Saskatchewan River

Assiniboine River

Red River

Pembina River

Souris River

Winnipeg River

Lake of the Woods

Rainy Lake

Lac des Mille Lacs

QUETICO PROV. PARK

RIDING MOUNTAIN NAT'L. PARK

DUCK MTN. PROV. PARK

TURTLE MTS.

PORCUPINE MTN.

PEMBINA MTS.

BALDY MTN. 2,727 FT. + HIGHEST POINT IN MANITOBA

HART MTN. 2,700 FT.

1,642 FT.

2,500 FT.

1,228 FT. +

Grand Rapids Dam

CANADIAN NATIONAL RYS.

CANADIAN PACIFIC RY.

TM TERRAIN MANITOBA
COPYRIGHT BY
RAND McNALLY & COMPANY
MADE IN U.S.A.

Specially created for **World Book Encyclopedia** by Rand McNally and World Book editors

MANITOBA

Turtle and Pembina hills of North Dakota extend into the southern part of Manitoba.

Rivers and Lakes cover almost a sixth of Manitoba, or 39,225 square miles. The rivers form a great waterway system that drains western Canada from as far west as the Rocky Mountains. The Red, Saskatchewan, and Winnipeg rivers flow into Lake Winnipeg. Important branches of the Red River are the Assiniboine and Pembina rivers. The Nelson River flows northeast out of Lake Winnipeg across the Canadian Shield, and empties into Hudson Bay. The Churchill and Hayes rivers also drain the northern part of the province.

Three lakes are so large that they are often called the *Great Lakes of Manitoba*. Lake Winnipeg, which covers 9,398 square miles, is the largest body of water entirely within any province or state. Lake Winnipegosis covers 2,103 square miles, and Lake Manitoba spreads over 1,817 square miles. Other principal lakes include Dauphin, Gods, Island, Reindeer, Southern Indian, and Tadoule. Cedar, Cross, and Moose lakes were enlarged and joined together during construction of the Grand Rapids hydroelectric project on the Saskatchewan River. The resulting reservoir, completed in 1965, covers 2,000 square miles. The three sections of the reservoir kept their original names.

Rich Farmland Surrounds a Village near Portage la Prairie in southern Manitoba. This area lies in the Manitoba Lowland, an important agricultural region.

Photographic Survey Corp., from Photo Researchers

George Hunter, Publix

Mines at Flin Flon, *right,* produce most of Manitoba's zinc and copper. The area lies in the Canadian Shield. This rocky region has many lakes and streams, forests, and mineral deposits.

Churchill is one of the few towns in the Hudson Bay Lowland of Manitoba. This region's heavy clay soil is not good for farming.

George Leavens, Photo Researchers

MANITOBA/Climate

Manitoba has long, bitterly cold winters and warm summers. In general, the temperature decreases from the southwestern part of the province to the northeastern section. The average January temperature is 0° F. in the south and −17° F. in the north. The lowest recorded temperature in Manitoba, −61° F., occurred in Waskada on Feb. 15, 1936. Southern Manitoba has an average July temperature of 68° F., and the north's July average is 55° F. The province's highest temperature was 112° F., recorded in Treesbank, near Wawanesa, on July 11, 1936, and in Emerson on July 12, 1936. Manitoba's *precipitation* (rain, melted snow, and other forms of moisture) averages 17 inches a year. About 50 inches of snow falls annually. The snow lies deep on the ground from December to March.

Warm Summer Sunshine brightens the southern Manitoba countryside. Winter will bring bitter cold and deep snow to the area.

Manitoba Dept. of Industry and Commerce

SEASONAL TEMPERATURES

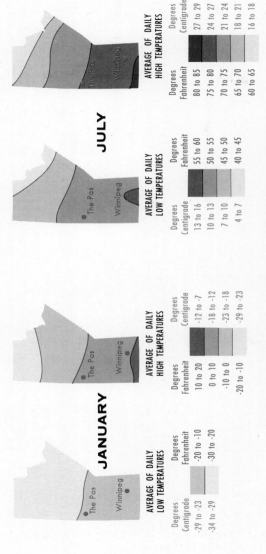

JANUARY

AVERAGE OF DAILY LOW TEMPERATURES

Degrees Centigrade	Degrees Fahrenheit
-29 to -23	-20 to -10
-34 to -29	-30 to -20

AVERAGE OF DAILY HIGH TEMPERATURES

Degrees Fahrenheit	Degrees Centigrade
10 to 20	-12 to -7
0 to 10	-18 to -12
-10 to 0	-23 to -18
-20 to -10	-29 to -23

JULY

AVERAGE OF DAILY LOW TEMPERATURES

Degrees Centigrade	Degrees Fahrenheit
13 to 16	55 to 60
10 to 13	50 to 55
7 to 10	45 to 50
4 to 7	40 to 45

AVERAGE OF DAILY HIGH TEMPERATURES

Degrees Fahrenheit	Degrees Centigrade
80 to 85	27 to 29
75 to 80	24 to 27
70 to 75	21 to 24
65 to 70	18 to 21
60 to 65	16 to 18

AVERAGE YEARLY PRECIPITATION
(Rain, Melted Snow, and Other Moisture)

Inches	Centimeters
20 to 25	51 to 64
15 to 20	38 to 51
10 to 15	25 to 38

0 100 200 300 400 Miles
0 200 400 600 Kilometers

WORLD BOOK maps

MONTHLY WEATHER IN THE PAS AND WINNIPEG

		JAN	FEB	MAR	APR	MAY	JUNE	JULY	AUG	SEPT	OCT	NOV	DEC
THE PAS	Average of: High Temperature	3	10	25	44	60	69	76	73	61	47	25	9
	Low Temperature	-16	-12	1	21	36	46	53	50	40	29	9	-8
	Days of Rain or Snow	7	7	7	7	9	11	11	10	10	10	9	8
WINNIPEG	Days of Rain or Snow	12	10	9	9	10	12	10	11	8	8	11	11
	High Temperatures	9	14	28	48	64	73	80	78	66	52	30	15
	Low Temperatures	-8	-5	9	28	41	51	57	54	45	34	16	1

Temperatures are given in degrees Fahrenheit.

Source: Meteorological Branch, Canadian Department of Transport

For many years, the economy of Manitoba was based chiefly on agriculture. Many new industries developed during the 1940's, and industrial production increased rapidly. Since the 1950's, manufacturing has been Manitoba's chief source of income.

All values given here are in Canadian dollars. For their value in U.S. money, see MONEY (table).

Natural Resources of Manitoba include fertile soils, rich minerals, valuable forests, and much wildlife.

Soil. The deep, fertile soils of the southern plains are perhaps the province's chief natural resource. Some were deposited by ancient glacial lakes or by glaciers that covered the region. The soils of the Manitoba Lowland vary from fertile clays to bog and peat. Fertile clay covers thousands of acres of the Canadian Shield north of Lake Winnipeg. The soils of the Hudson Bay Lowland contain much clay.

Minerals. The Canadian Shield has large deposits of copper, gold, nickel, silver, zinc, and other minerals. Great deposits of gypsum lie in the Manitoba Lowland, and the uplands have salt deposits. Bentonite, petroleum, and potash are found in the southwest.

Plant Life. Manitoba has about 58,000 square miles of forests that produce some lumber, but chiefly pulp for paper. The province has 65,000 square miles of less valuable forests. The most common trees are spruces.

Others include balsam firs, birches, cedars, jack pines, poplars, and tamaracks.

Animal Life. Caribou, elk, and moose live in the northern forests. Deer thrive there and in most parts of southern Manitoba. Fur-bearing animals of the forests include bears, beavers, foxes, lynxes, martens, minks, and wolves. Coyotes, foxes, muskrats, rabbits, and skunks also live in Manitoba.

Thousands of ducks and geese fly north in spring to breed in Manitoba's lakes and ponds. Grouse, partridges, prairie chickens, ptarmigans, and other game birds live in the province. Fish there include bass, pickerel, pike, saugers, trout, and whitefish.

Manufacturing. Goods manufactured in Manitoba have a *value added by manufacture* of about $315,235,000 yearly. This figure represents the value created in producing Manitoba's industries, not counting such costs as materials, supplies, and fuels.

Food-processing is the major industry. It accounts for about two-fifths of all manufacturing in Manitoba. Large flour mills operate in Winnipeg, the chief manufacturing center, and in St. Boniface and Virden. Butter production is important in Brandon, Portage la Prairie, St. Boniface, Winnipeg, and many small towns. Vegetables are canned in Carberry, Morden, Portage la Prairie, and Winkler. St. Boniface has the largest stockyard in Canada.

Winnipeg has one of North America's largest railway yards. Repairing locomotives and other railroad equipment is an important industry. Winnipeg also produces boilers, bus and truck bodies, cement, clothing, steel, and tractors, and is a printing and publishing center.

The manufacture of furniture, paper, and other wood products thrives in Kleefield, Pine Falls, Piney, Steinbach, The Pas, and other towns. In 1961, the second largest nickel-processing plant in North America opened in Thompson. Only the one in Port Colborne, Ont., is bigger. Copper and zinc are processed in Flin Flon. Several cities have oil refineries.

Agriculture. Manitoba's farm products have a value of about $116,040,000 a year. The province has about 40,000 farms. They cover a total of about 19,084,000 acres and average about 480 acres in size.

Wheat ranks as the most important crop. Manitoba No. 1 Hard is the grade name for the finest wheat in many of the world's grain markets. Canada's major grain market is in Winnipeg. Manitoba ranks among the leading provinces and states in the production of barley and rye. Farmers grow flaxseed, mustard seed, rapeseed, and sunflowers—all for their oil. Other important crops include buckwheat, corn, field peas, oats, potatoes, sugar beets, and vegetables.

Beef cattle are raised and fattened in many parts of Manitoba. Dairying is important in the Red River Valley and other parts of the Manitoba Lowland. Farmers also raise excellent hogs and sheep.

Fur farming is another important agricultural industry. More than 200 fur farms in southern Manitoba produce most of the province's furs. Almost all the fur farmers raise minks. About a third of the fur production, chiefly muskrat fur, comes from trapping. The provincial government leases the trapping areas, mostly to

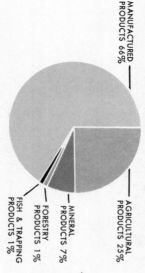

PRODUCTION IN MANITOBA

Total yearly value of goods produced—$474,371,000

- MANUFACTURED PRODUCTS 66%
- AGRICULTURAL PRODUCTS 25%
- MINERAL PRODUCTS 7%
- FORESTRY PRODUCTS 1%
- FISH & TRAPPING PRODUCTS 1%

Source: Dominion Bureau of Statistics

Note: Percentages based on net value of production (total value of shipments less such costs as materials, fuel, electricity, and supplies).

EMPLOYMENT IN MANITOBA

Average yearly number of persons employed—263,962

	Number of Employees
Services	55,031
Wholesale & Retail Trade	48,218
Manufacturing	44,853
Transportation, Communications & Utilities	38,143
Government & Defense	26,523
Construction	17,211
Finance, Insurance & Real Estate	11,381
Agriculture	8,477
Mining	5,566
Forestry	1,233
Fishing & Other	7,326

Source: 1961 Census of Canada

Indians and métis. In Canada, the Winnipeg fur market ranks second only to that of Montreal.

Mining production in Manitoba has an annual value of about $34,060,000. Nickel is the most valuable mineral, followed by zinc, petroleum, and copper, in that order. A huge nickel deposit was found in the Mystery Lake-Moak Lake area of north-central Manitoba in 1956. The discovery led to the development of the important mining center of Thompson. Manitoba ranks among the leading provinces and states in zinc production. The Flin Flon mine, started in 1930, produces most of the province's zinc and copper. Mines at Lynn Lake produce copper, nickel, and zinc.

In 1950, prospectors discovered oil near Virden. Today, Manitoba's oil wells produce about 4,000,000 barrels of oil annually. Gold is mined east of Lake Winnipeg and near Flin Flon and Lynn Lake. Other important minerals include bentonite, chromite, gypsum, potash, and salt. Quarries of granite, limestone, and marble provide building materials.

Forestry. Logs and pulpwood cut in Manitoba have an annual value of about $4,261,000. Lumberjacks cut about 35,000,000 board feet of lumber yearly. Pulpwood, used in making paper, is cut throughout the province.

Fishing Industry. Manitoba fishermen annually catch about 30,000,000 pounds of fish, valued at about $3,174,000. More than 90 per cent of the catch is shipped to the United States. Pickerel are the most valuable fish, followed in order by saugers, whitefish, and pike. Lake Winnipeg, the center of the provincial fishing industry, provides about a third of the catch. Lakes Manitoba and Winnipegosis provide much of the rest. Some belugas, often called *white whales*, are caught in Hudson Bay.

Electric Power. The production of hydroelectric energy has been important in Manitoba since the 1920's. Hydroelectric power serves nearly all manufacturing industries in the province. Most of it is developed at sites on the Winnipeg River northeast of Winnipeg, and on the Saskatchewan River near Grand Rapids. The $140,000,000 Grand Rapids project began operating in 1964. Some power plants in the province operate on steam. For Manitoba's kilowatt-hour production, see ELECTRIC POWER (table).

Transportation. Four major airlines serve Manitoba. One of them connects Winnipeg and London, England, by an arctic route. A number of smaller airlines connect Winnipeg and The Pas with distant northern mining and fishing operations.

The province has about 5,000 miles of railroad tracks. Canada's two main railways enter Winnipeg and branch out to many points in Manitoba. One branch line connects Churchill, The Pas, and Thompson. Two U.S. railroads have terminals in Winnipeg.

About 40,000 miles of roads and highways, most of them in southern Manitoba, serve the province. The most important one is the cross-country Trans-Canada Highway, which crosses Manitoba through Winnipeg and Brandon. Other major roads link Flin Flon and Winnipeg with North Dakota, and Winnipeg with Grand Rapids. In winter, tractors make snow trails on frozen lakes in the north. They draw trains of *cat-swings* (loaded sleighs) that carry supplies and other materials to and from mines and logging camps.

Rivers and lakes provide many waterways throughout the province. A steamboat operates between Winnipeg and Selkirk on the Red River, and to all ports on Lake Winnipeg. Churchill, on Hudson Bay, is the chief seaport. About 20,000,000 bushels of wheat yearly are carried to Churchill by railway, and loaded on ships for export to Great Britain and other European countries. Trappers and prospectors use dog sleds in winter, and canoes and outboard motorboats after the ice melts.

Communication. The first newspaper published in Manitoba, *The Nor' Wester*, was issued in 1859 in Fort Garry (now Winnipeg). Today, the province has six daily newspapers, the largest of which are the *Free Press* and *Tribune*, both of Winnipeg. Weekly newspapers are published in more than 50 cities and towns. The *Free Press Prairie Farmer*, printed in Winnipeg, has the largest circulation of these papers. The largest French-language weekly, *La Liberté et le Patriote*, is published in St. Boniface. The first radio station in Manitoba, CKY, began broadcasting from Winnipeg in 1922. The first television station, CBWT, began operating there in 1954. French-language radio and television stations broadcast from St. Boniface. Manitoba has 13 radio stations and 5 major television stations.

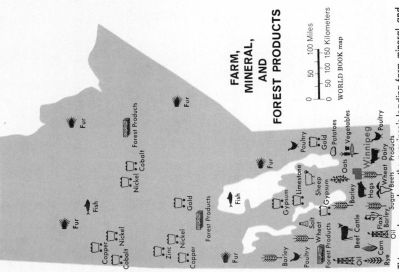

FARM, MINERAL, AND FOREST PRODUCTS

0   50   100 Miles
0   50   100 150 Kilometers
WORLD BOOK map

This map shows where the province's leading farm, mineral, and forest products are produced. The major urban area (shown in red) is the province's most important manufacturing center.

HISTORIC MANITOBA

First Railway to Hudson Bay. The Hudson Bay Railway to Churchill, completed in 1931, gave Manitoba a sea route to world grain markets.

Churchill

Henry Hudson and his men discovered a great bay in 1610 and explored its shores. This vast body of water was later named Hudson Bay.

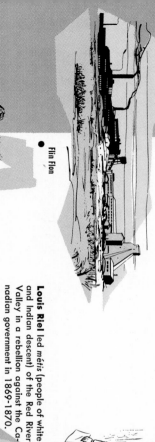

Flin Flon

Mining Operations at Flin Flon were begun in 1930 by the Hudson Bay Mining and Smelting Company. Flin Flon has deposits of copper, gold, silver, and zinc.

The Hudson's Bay Company received its charter from King Charles II of England in the late 1600's. His cousin, Prince Rupert, was the first governor of the company.

Louis Riel led *métis* (people of white and Indian descent) of the Red River Valley in a rebellion against the Canadian government in 1869-1870.

WINNIPEG ★

Winnipeg, the capital of Manitoba, grew around Fort Garry, one of the chief centers of the Hudson's Bay Company in the 1800's.

The First Permanent Settlement in Manitoba, called the Red River Colony, was established in 1812 by settlers sent by Thomas Douglas, the Earl of Selkirk.

Canada's First Transcontinental train arrived in Winnipeg in 1886.

Indian Days. Five Indian tribes lived in the Manitoba region when the first explorers and fur traders arrived. The Chipewyan Indians hunted caribou across the northern section. The Woods Cree, who were wandering hunters of beavers and moose, lived in the central forests. The Plains Cree fished and trapped animals in the prairies and wooded lowlands. The Assiniboin lived on the southwestern plains. These allies of the Cree were buffalo hunters. The Chippewa, who also hunted buffalo, lived in the southeastern section of the plains.

Exploration. Sir Thomas Button, an English explorer, was the first white man in the Manitoba region. He sailed down the west coast of Hudson Bay in 1612. Button spent the winter at the mouth of the Nelson River, and claimed the land for England. Two English seamen, Luke Foxe and Thomas James, explored Hudson Bay and its west coast in 1631.

In 1670, King Charles II of England granted trading rights in the region to the Hudson's Bay Company of London. The region was called Rupert's Land. By 1690, English fur traders had fought many battles with their French-Canadian rivals, who were pushing westward into the Hudson Bay region. The company sent Henry Kelsey on an expedition to find new sources of fur. Kelsey left the company's outpost in York Factory and traveled among the Indians of central and southern Manitoba from 1690 to 1692. He persuaded many of them to bring furs north to the company trading posts. See HUDSON'S BAY COMPANY; RUPERT'S LAND.

In 1731, Pierre Gaultier de Varennes, Sieur de la Vérendrye, left Montreal in search of an overland route to the Pacific Ocean. He and his men were French-Canadian fur traders. They built a series of forts between the Lake Superior area and the lower Saskatchewan River. These outposts included Fort Rouge, which La Vérendrye built on the site of present-day Winnipeg in 1738. The fur trade that he established cut heavily into that of the Hudson's Bay Company.

In 1763, the British defeated the French in the French and Indian War. France gave up its Canadian lands to Great Britain, and French exploration and trade in the Manitoba region stopped. In 1783, the North West Company was established in Montreal to compete with the Hudson's Bay Company. This competition forced the Hudson's Bay Company to build posts to defend its trade. See NORTH WEST COMPANY.

The Red River Colony. While the two fur companies competed for trade, plans were being made for the Manitoba region's first farming settlement. In 1811, Thomas Douglas, fifth Earl of Selkirk, obtained a land grant from the Hudson's Bay Company. It involved more than 100,000 square miles along the Red River. Selkirk sent several groups of Scottish Highlanders and Irishmen there. The first settlers arrived in 1812. See SELKIRK, EARL OF.

The early colonists suffered great hardships. Frosts, floods, and grasshoppers ruined many of their crops. At first, the settlers depended almost entirely on buffaloes and other game animals for food. Farm equipment, livestock, and supplies were brought from the United States, and production gradually increased.

The Red River colony lay in the heart of the North West Company's area of operations. As the colony expanded, it interfered with the fur trade. The company became increasingly hostile. Company trappers in the region were *métis* (people of mixed white and Indian ancestry). The North West Company turned them against the settlers. The métis tried to force the farmers to leave by burning their homes and destroying their crops. The violence reached a climax in 1816. The métis massacred Robert Semple, the colonial governor, and about 20 men in the Battle of Seven Oaks, near present-day Winnipeg. Peace was restored after the North West Company combined with the Hudson's Bay Company in 1821.

The Red River Rebellion. The Dominion of Canada was created in 1867. Almost immediately, it sought to acquire Rupert's Land, including the Manitoba region, from the Hudson's Bay Company. Under pressure from the British government, the company agreed in 1869 to give up its rights in almost all of Rupert's Land for $1,500,000. Great Britain began making plans to unite this vast region with Canada. However, the métis of the Red River Valley opposed the union and rebelled later in 1869. The métis held no legal title to their lands. They feared they would lose the lands to British-Canadian settlers who would pour in after union with Canada.

Louis Riel, the leader of the métis, used buffalo hunters as soldiers. They turned back federal surveyors and William McDougall, whom Canada had sent to govern the territory. The métis captured Fort Garry, in present-day Winnipeg, and set up their own government. In 1870, the Canadian government granted the métis a bill of rights in the Manitoba Act. This act made Manitoba Canada's fifth province on July 15, 1870. The province covered the southeastern section of what is now Manitoba. Winnipeg became the capital, and Alfred Boyd was the first premier. See RED RIVER REBELLION.

Growth as a Province. The expected land rush of settlers into Manitoba began after 1870. Between 1871 and 1881, the population more than doubled—from 25,228 to 62,260. In 1876, Manitoba began to export wheat. Farmers in the Red River Valley collected 857 bushels of wheat in homemade wooden carts from farms around Winnipeg. They loaded the carts onto steamboats, and shipped them up the Red River. The wheat was taken to a railroad center in Minnesota and then to Toronto, Ont. Wheat soon replaced fur as Manitoba's most valuable product.

In 1878, the first railroad in the province connected Winnipeg and St. Paul, Minn. Another line linked Winnipeg with cities in eastern Canada in 1881, and the wheat-producing region with Lake Superior in 1882. Huge quantities of Manitoba grain were shipped to Canadian and European markets through ports on the Great Lakes.

During the 1890's, thousands of settlers came to Manitoba from European countries. Winnipeg grew rapidly. By 1901, the population of the province had increased to more than 10 times that of 1871. The Canadian government extended the provincial boundary west to what is now Saskatchewan in 1881, and east to Ontario in 1884. In 1912, the northern boundary was extended to Hudson Bay. This extension gave Manitoba its present size and shape.

Industrial Developments. Great agricultural expansion took place in Manitoba from 1900 to 1913. Manitoba remained almost entirely a farming province until the 1920's. But even before 1913, when the great land boom ended, Manitoba was beginning to build industrial plants. Most of these early factories were in Winnipeg. After 1912, St. Boniface began to develop stockyards and meat-packing plants.

Manitoba's boundary extension to Hudson Bay in 1912 opened up lands for mineral development. In 1915, prospectors discovered huge deposits of copper and zinc on the site of Flin Flon. The town developed rapidly after mining operations became fully developed in 1930. Extensive mining of gold, nickel, and silver also began during the 1930's, particularly in areas around northern Lake Winnipeg.

During the early 1900's, Winnipeg became the manufacturing and transportation center of western Canada. In Winnipeg, railroads exchanged the products of eastern and western Canada. Livestock, lumber, minerals, and wheat were shipped east for export to European markets.

Cheap power and plentiful water encouraged the growth of many industries during the 1920's and 1930's. A pulp and paper plant opened in Pine Falls in 1927. Fur-processing and clothing trades developed rapidly in Winnipeg during the 1930's.

Political Developments. The Conservative Party, led by Sir Rodmond P. Roblin, controlled the provincial government from 1900 until 1915. This government did much to develop Manitoba's economy, and got its boundaries extended in 1912. A Liberal government,

headed by T. C. Norris, replaced it. The Liberal administration passed many progressive and social-reform laws. These laws included giving women the right to vote, setting minimum wages, enforcing school attendance until the age of 14, and providing money for needy mothers.

In 1922, a group of organized farmers called the United Farmers of Manitoba, or Progressives, defeated the Liberal government. This group was actually a citizens' movement, and not really a political party. The members opposed political parties, and elected independent candidates. They formed a government under John Bracken, principal of the Manitoba Agricultural College. The Liberals and the Progressives combined in 1932 to form the Liberal Progressive Party.

During the 1930's, two new political parties appeared in Manitoba. The Co-operative Commonwealth Federation, later called the New Democratic Party, was made up of farmers and factory workers. The other was the Social Credit Party. Its members believed that governments should pay all citizens a dividend based on economic production.

The Mid-1900's. World War II (1939-1945) created a great demand for Manitoba cattle, metals, wheat, and wood. Many industries built new plants in the province during the war, and manufacturing continued to grow rapidly in the late 1940's. By 1950, for the first time in Manitoba's history, manufacturing outranked agriculture as the province's main source of income.

After World War II, Manitoba needed fewer farmworkers because of the increased use of machines and new farming methods. Thousands of Manitobans moved from rural areas to cities and found jobs in factories.

Geologists discovered important mineral deposits in Manitoba during the 1940's and 1950's. Copper, nickel, and zinc ores were found in a northwestern area in 1945. Oil companies developed rich oil fields near Virden in the early 1950's. In 1956, prospectors found huge nickel deposits in the Moak Lake-Mystery Lake area. The International Nickel Company built a giant nickel complex at Thompson, and nickel mining began there in 1960. Thompson became one of the largest centers of nickel production in the Western world. In the late 1960's, International Nickel began a $100-million expansion of its facilities in Manitoba.

THE PREMIERS OF MANITOBA

		Party	Term
1.	Alfred Boyd	None	1870-1871
2.	Marc A. Girard	Conservative	1871-1872
3.	Henry J. H. Clarke	None	1872-1874
4.	Marc A. Girard	Conservative	1874
5.	Robert A. Davis	None	1874-1878
6.	John Norquay	Conservative	1878-1887
7.	David H. Harrison	Conservative	1887-1888
8.	Thomas Greenway	Liberal	1888-1900
9.	Hugh J. MacDonald	Conservative	1900
10.	Rodmond P. Roblin	Conservative	1900-1915
11.	Tobias C. Norris	Liberal	1915-1922
12.	John Bracken	Liberal Progressive	1922-1943
13.	Stuart S. Garson	Liberal Progressive	1943-1948
14.	Douglas L. Campbell	Liberal Progressive	1948-1958
15.	Duff Roblin	Progressive Conservative	1958-1967
16.	Walter Weir	Progressive Conservative	1967-1969
17.	Edward R. Schreyer	New Democratic	1969-

The province continued to develop its rich sources of electric power in the 1950's and 1960's. By 1954, all rural areas had electricity. The first laboratories began operating at the Whiteshell Nuclear Research Establishment near Winnipeg. A nuclear reactor went into operation there in 1965.

During the 1960's, several chemical companies built large facilities in Brandon. Many companies in various fields expanded, particularly those in the aerospace, electronics, farm machinery, and wood processing industries. Huge shipments of Manitoba wheat were exported to many countries, including Communist China and Russia. Also during the 1960's, the provincial and federal governments built a $63-million flood control system on the Red River.

Premiers of the Liberal Progressive Party governed Manitoba during the 1940's and most of the 1950's. The Progressive Conservatives won power in 1958 and held it until 1969. That year, Manitoba voters elected the first socialist government ever to hold office in Canada outside Saskatchewan. The government was headed by Edward R. Schreyer of the New Democratic Party.

Manitoba Today. The industrial expansion that began in Manitoba during the 1940's continued into the 1970's. But it has presented challenges to the province. Rapidly growing urban areas face the need for more schools, increased public services, and expanded highways. Differences in income between urban and rural Manitobans continue to widen. Living standards in northern Manitoba are far below those of more developed areas in the province.

Since the late 1960's, increasing competition in the world wheat market has greatly reduced the income of many Manitoba farmers. The government is encouraging these farmers to decrease their dependence on wheat by growing other crops and by raising livestock.

PETER McLINTOCK, W. L. MORTON, and THOMAS R. WEIR

MANITOBA / Study Aids

Questions

What is Manitoba's largest city?
Why is Manitoba called the *Keystone Province*?
How much of Manitoba do rivers and lakes cover?
Who were the *métis*? Why did they rebel in 1869?
What is the province's most important crop?
Why did the English and French Canadians fight each other during the region's early days?
Where do Manitoba's Indians and Eskimos live?
Where is Manitoba's nickel-producing center?
Which land region covers two-thirds of the province?
What is the largest body of water entirely within any province or state?

Books for Young Readers

CAMERON, ALEXANDER A., and THORDARSON, LEO. *Prairie Progress.* Dent (Toronto), 1954.
CHALMERS, J. W. *Red River Adventure: The Story of the Selkirk Settlers.* Macmillan (Toronto), 1957. This book describes the hardships and massacre of Manitoba's first immigrants.
HAYES, JOHN F. *Buckskin Colonist.* Copp (Toronto), 1947.
SCOTT, JOSEPH M. *Story of Our Prairie Provinces.* Dent (Toronto), 1943. A history of the provinces.
SHIPLEY, NANCY. *Whistle on the Wind.* Ryerson (Toronto), 1961.
THARP, LOUIS H. *Company of Adventurers: The Story of the Hudson's Bay Company.* McClelland (Toronto), 1946.

Books for Older Readers

CARD, BRIGHAM Y. *The Canadian Prairie Provinces from 1870 to 1950: A Sociological Introduction.* Dent (Toronto), 1960.
DONNELLY, MURRAY S. *The Government of Manitoba.* Univ. of Toronto Press (Toronto), 1963.
GRAY, JOHN M. *Lord Selkirk of Red River.* Macmillan (Toronto), 1964.
MORTON, WILLIAM L. *Manitoba: A History.* Univ. of Toronto Press, 1957.
ROSS, ALEXANDER. *Red River Settlement.* Ross & Haines, 1957. A valuable reprint of an early detailed history first published in 1846.
SHIPLEY, NANCY. *Return to the River.* Fell, 1964.
STANLEY, GEORGE F. G. *The Birth of Western Canada: A History of the Riel Rebellions.* 2nd ed. Univ. of Toronto Press, 1963. *Louis Riel.* Ryerson (Toronto), 1963.
WEIR, THOMAS R., ed. *Economic Atlas of Manitoba.* Dept. of Industry, Province of Manitoba, 1960.

Related Articles in WORLD BOOK include:

BIOGRAPHIES

Riel, Louis
Roy, Gabrielle
Selkirk, Earl of
Stefansson, Vilhjalmur
Strathcona and Mount Royal, Baron of

CITIES AND TOWNS

Brandon
Churchill
Flin Flon
Portage la Prairie
Saint Boniface
Winnipeg

PHYSICAL FEATURES

Assiniboine River
Canadian Shield
Churchill River
Hudson Bay
Lake Agassiz
Lake Manitoba
Lake Winnipeg
Lake Winnipegosis
Nelson River
Red River of the North
Saskatchewan River
Winnipeg River

OTHER RELATED ARTICLES

Athabaska
Barley (table)
Flax (table)
Fur
Hudson's Bay Company
Manitoba, University of
North West Company
Red River Rebellion
Rye (table)
Wheat

Outline

I. Government
A. Lieutenant-Governor
B. Premier
C. Legislative Assembly
D. Courts
E. Local Government
F. Taxation
G. Politics

II. People

III. Education
A. Schools
B. Libraries and Museums

IV. A Visitor's Guide
A. Places to Visit
B. Annual Events

V. The Land
A. Land Regions
B. Mountains
C. Rivers and Lakes

VI. Climate

VII. Economy
A. Natural Resources
B. Manufacturing
C. Agriculture
D. Mining
E. Forestry
F. Fishing Industry
G. Electric Power
H. Transportation
I. Communication

VIII. History

MANITOBA, UNIVERSITY OF, is a coeducational, government-supported school in Winnipeg, Canada. It is the only institution in the province of Manitoba that offers courses in almost all fields. It grants degrees in agriculture, architecture, arts, commerce, dentistry, education, engineering, environmental studies, fine arts, home economics, interior design, law, medicine, music, nursing, occupational therapy, pharmacy, physical education, physiotherapy, science, and social work. It also gives diplomas in agriculture, anesthesiology, art, dairying, dental hygiene, occupational therapy, physiotherapy, psychiatry, radiology, and surgery. The university has a graduate school and a summer school. It was founded in 1877. For enrollment, see CANADA (table: Universities).

HUGH H. SAUNDERSON

MANITOU. See FOLKLORE (Indian Folklore).

MANITOULIN ISLANDS, *MAN uh TOO lin* (pop. 11,045), in Lake Huron, are famed for their resorts. The islands lie northwest of Georgian Bay and are separated from the northern shore of Lake Huron by the North Channel. They are formed by cliffs of the northern section of the Niagara Escarpment, a long series of cliffs. There are three large islands and many smaller ones with a total area of 1,389 square miles. Most of the islands are in Ontario. They include Manitoulin Island, which has an area of 1,068 square miles and is the world's largest inland island; and Cockburn Island (68 square miles). Drummond Island, in Michigan, covers about 176 square miles. Manitoulin is an Indian name for *sacred isles.*

JOHN BRIAN BIRD

MANKATO STATE COLLEGE. See UNIVERSITIES AND COLLEGES (table).

MANLIUS. See GOOSE (History and Literature).

MANN, *mahn,* is the family name of three German authors. All three left Germany in 1933 when the Nazis took power, and eventually moved to the United States.

Thomas Mann (1875-1955) won the 1929 Nobel prize for literature. His writings combine wisdom, humor, and philosophical thought. His intellectual scope, keen psychological insight, and critical awareness of cultural and political conditions made him one of the foremost humanistic writers of his time. His writing has a tone of gentle irony, which creates an atmosphere of artistic detachment and tolerance. He often wrote in a highly stylized, stilted manner as a *parody* (mock imitation) of earlier writers, especially Goethe.

A superb literary craftsman, Mann maintained a balance between the traditional realism of the 1800's and experimentation with style and structure. He was a critical, yet sympathetic, analyst of the European middle class. The central theme in his writings is a dualism between spirit and life. Mann expressed *spirit* as intellectual refinement and creativity, and *life* as naïve and unquestioning vitality. He often presented this dualism through the conflict between the attitudes of the artist and the middle class.

Mann's first novel, *Buddenbrooks* (1901), made him famous. It describes the physical decline and accompanying intellectual refinement of a merchant family similar to Mann's. Variations on this theme appear in two shorter works, *Tristan* (1903) and *Tonio Kröger* (1903). The short novel *Death in Venice* (1912) portrays

a writer's moral collapse through an uncontrollable and humiliating passion for a young boy.

Mann published the novel *The Magic Mountain* in 1924, after working on it for 12 years. In the book, patients of a tuberculosis sanitarium represent the conflicting attitudes and political beliefs of European society before World War I. Mann's longest work is *Joseph and His Brothers* (1933-1943). This four-novel series expands on the Biblical story of Joseph by analyzing it from the standpoint of both psychology and mythology.

Doctor Faustus (1947) is Mann's most despairing novel. In it, a German composer rejects love and moral responsibility in favor of artistic creativity. His story symbolically parallels the rise of Nazism. *Confessions of Felix Krull, Confidence Man* (1954) is a delightful novel about a rogue's adventures in middle class society.

Mann's brilliant essays deal with politics, literature, music, and philosophy. Collections include *Order of the Day* (1942) and *Essays of Three Decades* (1947). *Last Essays* was published in 1959, after his death.

Mann was born into a wealthy family in Lübeck. He lived in Switzerland from 1933 to 1938, when he moved to the United States. He became a U.S. citizen in 1944. He returned to Switzerland in 1952 and died there.

Heinrich Mann (1871-1950) was Thomas Mann's brother. Most of his novels are passionate criticisms of the middle class and political and social conditions in Germany. They express a violent opposition to nationalism, militarism, and capitalism, and they call for a democratic and humanistic socialism. The Nazis banned Mann's books. Mann's masterpieces are *Professor Unrat* (1905, translated in English as *The Blue Angel*), *The Little Town* (1909), and *The Patrioteer* (1918). Mann was born in Lübeck and died in California.

Klaus Mann (1906-1949) was Thomas Mann's son. He moved to the United States in 1936 and became a citizen in 1943. Out of despair over the political and cultural decline of Europe, he committed suicide. His writings include *Symphonie Pathétique* (1935), a novel about the composer Peter Tchaikovsky; and *The Turning Point* (1942), an autobiography. With his sister Erika Mann, he wrote *Escape to Life* (1939) and *The Other Germany* (1940).

WERNER HOFFMEISTER

MANN, HORACE (1796-1859), played a leading part in establishing the elementary school system of the United States. He aroused public interest in educational problems. He summed up his great desire to serve mankind in his last public statement: "Be ashamed to die until you have won some victory for humanity."

Mann gave up his law practice in 1837 to become the secretary of the newly established Massachusetts State Board of Education. He fought so well for educational reforms that nearly every one of the states profited. He has been called the *Father of the Common Schools.*

Mann strengthened education in his own state through a series of laws that improved the financial support and public control of schools. He founded the first state normal school in the United States in 1839 in Lexington, Mass. This improved the quality of public-school teachers. His study of European educational methods in 1843 was the subject of one of his famous 12 annual reports. These influential reports covered almost every phase of the problems facing the U.S. educational system.

Mann resigned from the State Board of Education in 1848 to take a seat in the U.S. House of Representatives as an antislavery Whig. Mann was defeated as a Free Soil Party candidate for governor of Massachusetts. He became president of Antioch College at Yellow Springs, Ohio, in 1853 and held this office until his death.

Mann was born on May 4, 1796, at Franklin, Mass., and was graduated from Brown University. He began his public career as a member of the Massachusetts state legislature in 1827. He was elected to New York University's Hall of Fame when it was established in 1900 to honor great Americans.　CLAUDE A. EGGERTSEN

MANNA, *MAN uh,* was the food given to the Israelites during their 40 years of wandering in the wilderness (Exod. 16 and Num. 11). It looked like small, round flakes of a yellowish-white color, and tasted like wafers made with honey. Manna rained from heaven each morning. It was gathered early, because it melted in the sun. The daily portion of each person was an *omer* (about six pints). The people gathered up just enough food for each day. The manna spoiled and was unfit to eat if more was gathered. But twice the usual amount was said to fall on the sixth day. Each person then took two omers, because the Sabbath was a day of worship and rest. This manna stayed fresh two days. The fall stopped when the Israelites crossed into Canaan, the Promised Land. Some historians say manna was a gluey sugar from the tamarisk shrub.　CYRUS H. GORDON

MANNED SPACECRAFT CENTER is headquarters for all U.S. manned spacecraft projects conducted by the National Aeronautics and Space Administration (NASA). The center covers about 1,600 acres of land near Clear Lake City, Tex., about 20 miles southeast of Houston. See CLEAR LAKE CITY.

The center serves as the training site for United States astronauts and their flight crews. It contains equipment that simulates actual space and ground conditions that might occur during space flights, and it works out recovery techniques. The center serves as command post for such space projects as the Apollo program (three-man moon flights). It maintains central control during orbital rendezvous and lunar missions. Scientists and engineers also work at the center to develop spacecraft for future manned flights.

Facilities include space environment simulation chambers and other training devices that imitate actual space conditions, laboratories for spacecraft research and systems evaluations, an auditorium, and office buildings. The center employs about 4,300 workers.

The Manned Spacecraft Center resulted from a longrange project of the Space Task Group. This group was created by NASA in 1958. The center's first headquarters were at Langley Field, Virginia. Operations shifted to temporary quarters near Houston in 1962. In 1964, the permanent spacecraft center was opened near Clear Lake City.　PAUL P. HANEY

See also ASTRONAUT (Training); SPACE TRAVEL (Manned Spacecraft); TEXAS (picture).

MANNERHEIM, CARL GUSTAV EMIL VON (1867-1951), a Finnish military and political leader, helped found the Republic of Finland in 1919. He had a fortified line built across the Karelian Isthmus called the *Mannerheim Line.* He directed the Finnish defense against Russian invaders in the famous "Winter War" of 1939-1940, and in fighting that lasted from 1941 to 1944. He was president of Finland from 1944 to 1946.

Mannerheim was born in Villnäs, Finland, which was then under Russian control. He served in the Russian Army in the Russo-Japanese War (1904-1905) and in World War I. An anti-Communist, he left Russia after the Communist revolution of 1917.

Mannerheim took command of the Finnish Army in January, 1918, after Finland declared its independence from Russia. In December, 1918, he became *regent* (temporary ruler) of Finland, and toured Europe seeking recognition for his country and food for his people. In 1919, Mannerheim ran unsuccessfully for president. He then retired from public life until the 1930's, when he took over command of Finnish defenses.　ALFRED ERICH SENN

MANNERHEIM LINE. See MANNERHEIM, CARL VON.

MANNERISM is a term that refers to certain stylistic features of European art from about 1520 to 1600. These features appear most fully and typically in central Italian art. But some Mannerist traits can be found in all European art of the time, including architecture and the late works of the Renaissance artists Raphael and Michelangelo.

Mannerist artists tended to consider artistic invention and imagination more important than faithful reproduction of nature. Space in many Mannerist paintings appears illogical or unmeasurable, with abrupt and disturbing contrasts between figures close to the viewer and those far in the distance. Most Mannerist paintings stress surface patterns. Strongly three-dimensional forms compressed within these patterns create an effect of confinement or of a struggle between a figure and its setting. Many figures are distorted in proportion and have contorted poses. The most striking Mannerist was the Spanish painter El Greco (see GRECO, EL). MARCEL FRANCISCONO

See also SCULPTURE (Michelangelo); CELLINI, BENVENUTO; TINTORETTO.

MANNERS. See ETIQUETTE.

MANNERS AND CUSTOMS. See CUSTOM.

MANNHEIM, *MAN hïme* (pop. 326,949; alt. 318 ft.), is an important river port in West Germany. It lies near the point where the Rhine and Neckar rivers meet (see GERMANY [political map]). Mannheim's large docks make up one of Europe's largest inland harbors. Its factories produce precision instruments, motors, and farm machinery. Much coal and iron is traded there.

Mannheim began as a small fishing village. It was fortified and chartered in 1606-1607. The great German poet and playwright Friedrich von Schiller wrote plays for the city's National Theater.　JAMES K. POLLOCK

MANNING, WILLIAM THOMAS (1866-1949), served as bishop of the Protestant Episcopal diocese of New York from 1921 to 1946. His outspoken statements against divorce and pacifism, and on many other topics, made him one of the best-known churchmen in the United States. As bishop, he raised more than $15 million to help finance building the Cathedral of Saint John the Divine in New York City (see SAINT JOHN THE DIVINE, CATHEDRAL OF).

Bishop Manning was born in Northampton, England. He came to the United States with his parents at the age of 16. He was graduated from the University of the South at Sewanee, Tenn.　L. J. TRINTERUD

MANOLETE, *MAH noh LEH tay* (1917-1947), won fame as a Spanish *matador* (bullfighter). He was a national hero, and hundreds of paintings, statues, and monuments honor him. He was awarded *La Cruz de la Beneficencia*, Spain's highest civilian decoration. Manolete was born Manuel Laureano Rodríguez y Sánchez in Córdoba, Spain, the son of a matador. He began his career in 1938 and by 1946 received the highest fees ever paid a matador to that time. On the eve of his retirement, he was gored to death by a bull in Linares, Spain.

MANOMETER, *muh NAHM ee ter,* is an instrument used to measure the pressure of a gas or vapor. There are several types of manometers. The simplest kind consists of a U-shaped tube with both ends open. The tube contains a liquid, often mercury, which fills the bottom of the U and rises a short distance in each of the arms. The person using this type connects one of the arms to the gas whose pressure is to be measured. The other arm remains open to the atmosphere. In this way, the liquid in the manometer is exposed to the pressure of the gas in one arm and atmospheric pressure in the other.

If the pressure of the gas is greater than that of the atmosphere, the liquid rises in the arm of the tube exposed to the air. The user measures the difference between the heights of the liquid in the two arms to determine the pressure of this amount of liquid. The sum of this pressure and of the atmospheric pressure is the pressure of the gas. Gas pressure is often measured in units of the height of the liquid in the manometer. For example, gas pressure is often expressed as centimeters of mercury, where normal atmospheric pressure is 76 centimeters.

In some manometers, the air is removed from one arm of the tube and that end is sealed. This eliminates difficulties caused by changes in atmospheric pressure. The difference between the levels of the liquid in the arms shows the pressure of the gas. This manometer is often called a *vacuum gauge* or *pressure gauge*. Some manometers work on the principle of a spring attached to an indicator. The indicator moves in front of a graduated scale that gives direct pressure readings. Doctors use a type of manometer, called the *sphygmomanometer,* to measure blood pressure.

CLARENCE E. BENNETT

See also BAROMETER; GAUGE.

MANON. See OPERA (Some of the Famous Operas).

MANORIALISM was the economic system of Europe from the end of the Roman Empire to the 1200's. The name comes from *manorium,* the Latin word for *manor,* meaning a large estate controlled by a lord and worked by *peasants.* Manors covered most of Europe. They supplied food, clothing, shelter, and nearly everything else needed by the lords and peasants.

Most manors were made up of the lord's land and small plots of land held by the peasants. The lord lived in a manor house, which was usually surrounded by a garden, an orchard, and farm buildings. The peasants' huts were clustered nearby. Most manors also included a church, a mill for grinding grain into flour, and a press for making wine.

The peasants depended on the lord for protection from enemies, for justice, and for what little government there was. The peasants farmed both the lord's land and their own. They were *bound to the soil.* This means that they were part of the property, and they

A. J. Jaffe, the contributor of this article, is Director of the Manpower and Population Program in the Bureau of Applied Social Research at Columbia University.

and their families remained on the land if a new lord acquired it. Unlike slaves, they could not be sold apart from the land. Peasants rarely traveled more than a few miles from the manor.

The manorial system began to decline when trade and industry revived. This revival brought back an economic system based on payment with money for goods and services. Manorialism ended first in western Europe. It remained as late as the 1800's in some parts of central and eastern Europe. Large family estates in Great Britain and other parts of Europe still exist as reminders of manorialism.

BRYCE LYON

See also FEUDALISM; MIDDLE AGES; SERF; VIL-LEIN.

MANPOWER is that part of the total population of a country which produces—or could produce—its goods and services. A nation's manpower includes all persons who work or seek work, or who could be encouraged to take jobs if the nation so desired. The manpower supply includes farmers, factory workers, dentists, government officials, and all other employed workers. It also includes all unemployed persons, as well as housewives, students, and even some retired persons.

A nation's economic growth and standard of living are influenced by the size and quality of its manpower. If the people are healthy, well fed, and reasonably well educated, a nation can produce more goods and services more efficiently. This, in turn, means that each person is better-off. A few nations have too few people to do all the work that might be done, and are not as well off economically as they might be if they had more manpower. Some *underdeveloped* (poor) countries have plenty of people. But because they are poorly fed and poorly educated and have little machinery, they are unable to produce much and have a very low standard of living.

Manpower and the Labor Force. *Labor force,* in the United States, includes all persons 16 years of age and over who have jobs or are looking for jobs. Persons who receive no money for their work or who are not looking for work are not included in the labor force. Other countries refer to the labor force as the *economically active population,* the *work force,* or the *gainfully employed.* The manpower of the United States and other economically developed countries is always larger than the labor force. See LABOR FORCE; LABOR (chart: Men and Women in the United States Labor Force).

How Manpower Requirements Change. During short periods of time, the number of workers that employers wish to hire depends largely on current business conditions. The types of workers employers want also remain about the same within short periods. Over long periods of time—perhaps 10 years or longer—manpower requirements may change considerably. In the long run, the total number of workers needed depends on the growth of the population and the level of *technological development. Technology* means applying scientific methods to change the world around us. Through technology, man has developed tools and machinery to produce goods and services, instead of doing the work by hand.

In business and industry, for example, computers now perform many tasks with little or no human help. See TECHNOLOGY; COMPUTER; AUTOMATION.

Several factors can cause changes in the kinds of workers needed. One of the most important factors is the development of technology. Technological changes in the United States have always been rapid. Such changes have reduced job opportunities in certain industries or occupations. But inventions and other technological changes have increased job opportunities in other industries and occupations, so total unemployment has not increased.

Technological changes that are accompanied by changes in consumer tastes and preferences can significantly affect the manpower requirements of certain industries. In the U.S. coal-mining industry, for example, the use of machinery has greatly increased the amount of coal that can be mined per unit of labor. At the same time, many who once used coal now prefer to heat with oil and natural gas. These conditions have greatly reduced the number of jobs for coal miners, while job opportunities in the oil and gas industries have expanded rapidly. How much unemployment results from such changes depends on how able and willing workers are to move from one job to another.

Also, the kinds of work people do have changed. Over the years in the United States, for example, the number of jobs requiring mainly manual labor has dropped. The number of jobs requiring special skills and education has risen.

A nation's position in international affairs also affects its manpower needs. For example, U.S. defense commitments in the 1960's required a much larger military force than during the 1930's. Many of these servicemen would otherwise have been in the civilian labor force. The production of military equipment also requires many workers with special skills, and the U.S. space program requires technicians and other workers with special skills.

Developing a Nation's Manpower is a responsibility of private business as well as of local, state, and federal governments. Elementary and secondary school education provides the most important manpower training program. This schooling provides young people with the basic skills needed to learn most jobs. A person who has satisfactorily completed high school can be trained for many different kinds of work. However, certain professional and administrative jobs require additional education, training, and work experience.

On-the-job training provided by employers is the second most important training program. Sometimes that training can be given by the foreman in as little as an hour or two. Or it may be provided in apprenticeship programs. Such programs often are sponsored jointly by an industry and a labor union or government organization. There also are technical schools that train workers to become such specialists as barbers, television repairmen, and automobile mechanics.

As a result of technological change, there are always some jobs passing out of use and new jobs being created. Generally, workers can be retrained within a short time. The number of completely new jobs that come into being at any one time and that require extensive training is very small. But over a period of many years, enough changes will occur so that a worker can expect to be retrained at least once during his lifetime. Some workers will be unable to adjust to a new job or will be rejected by employers, and become permanently unemployed.

The U.S. Congress, recognizing the importance of the efficient use of the nation's manpower, passed the Manpower Development and Training Act of 1962. One of the act's chief provisions is to train those workers having the most difficulty finding jobs. Such persons tend to be the poorly educated, older workers, young persons with no job experience, and persons from minority groups.

A. J. JAFFE

MANPOWER DEVELOPMENT AND TRAINING ACT. See LABOR, DEPARTMENT OF (Functions).

MANSARD ROOF. See ROOF.

MANSFIELD, Ohio (pop. 51,418; met. area pop. 117,761; alt. 1,155 ft.), one of the state's leading industrial centers, lies about 64 miles northeast of Columbus. For location, see OHIO (political map).

Rich farmlands surround Mansfield, and coal and natural gas deposits lie nearby. The city produces aircraft parts, bedding, electrical equipment, plumbing fixtures, and brass, rubber, and steel products.

The city was named for U.S. Surveyor General Jared Mansfield (1759-1830), who laid it out in 1808. It was incorporated as a village in 1828, and as a city in 1857. It is the county seat of Richland County and has a mayor-council government.

JAMES H. RODABAUGH

MANSFIELD, KATHERINE (1888-1923), a British author, wrote symbolic short stories about everyday human experiences and inner feelings. Many of her stories are studies of childhood, based on her early years in Wellington, New Zealand. Miss Mansfield often used herself and her brother as models for the main characters. Her stories were published in *In a German Pension* (1911), *Prelude* (1918), *Bliss* (1920), and *The Garden Party* (1927). *Her Journal* (1927) gives a fascinating picture of her mind and the development of her writing.

Miss Mansfield was born Kathleen Mansfield Beauchamp in Wellington. She began her literary career after moving to England in 1908. She suffered from tuberculosis, and spent much of her life in hospitals and sanitariums.

JOHN ESPEY

MANSFIELD, MIKE (1903-), entered the United States Senate in 1953, and became the Senate majority leader in 1961. A Montana Democrat, Mansfield served five terms in the U.S. House of Representatives between 1943 and 1953. Born Michael Joseph Mansfield in New York City, he moved with his family to Montana when he was 3 years old. He was graduated from Montana State University and taught history there before entering politics.

THOMAS A. CLINCH

MANSFIELD, RICHARD (1854?-1907), was one of the best-known actors in the United States during the 1890's. He excelled in both romantic and tragic character roles. He was especially good in portrayals of evil old men. His great stage successes included *Beau Brummell, Cyrano de Bergerac, The Scarlet Letter,* and *Dr. Jekyll and Mr. Hyde.*

Mansfield also was a skilled dancer and singing comedian. His career began in England, where he sang in Gilbert and Sullivan comic operettas. He was probably born in Berlin, Germany.

CLIFFORD EUGENE HAMAR

MANSFIELD STATE COLLEGE. See UNIVERSITIES AND COLLEGES (table).

MANSHIP, PAUL (1885-1966), was an American sculptor. His works appear in public buildings throughout the United States. He worked in stone and metals. Many of his sculptures recall the traditions of European art. One of his best-known works, *Prometheus*, is in Rockefeller Center in New York City. Manship was born in St. Paul, Minn. He studied under Solon Borglum in New York City and at the Pennsylvania Academy of Fine Arts.

WILLIAM L. MacDONALD

MANSLAUGHTER is the legal term for the wrongful unplanned killing of another person. It is different from *murder* in that it is not done with malice.

The law recognizes two kinds of manslaughter, *voluntary* and *involuntary*. Voluntary manslaughter is a killing done in the heat of the moment, without previous plan. If one man kills another in a violent quarrel without first planning to do so, he is guilty of voluntary manslaughter. Involuntary manslaughter is done as the result of criminal carelessness, or while the offender is engaged in some wrongful act. If a reckless driver kills someone, he is guilty of involuntary manslaughter.

Punishment for manslaughter varies in different states and countries. The usual penalty in the United States is imprisonment of from 1 to 14 years. This is less severe than are the penalties for murder.

See also HOMICIDE; MURDER; MALICE.

FRED E. INBAU

MANSON, SIR PATRICK (1844-1922), a Scottish physician, was called the *father of tropical medicine*. He demonstrated in 1877 that the parasite *Filaria* caused the tropical disease, elephantiasis. Later he showed that mosquitoes carried the parasite (see FILARIA). In 1900, he confirmed that malaria was transmitted to man in this way. He allowed his own son and another volunteer to be bitten by a mosquito infected with the parasite. He made many valuable contributions to our knowledge of other tropical diseases, including leprosy and beriberi. He wrote a manual entitled *Tropical Diseases*.

Manson was born in Aberdeenshire, Scotland, and was graduated from the University of Aberdeen. He began his career in medicine in China. Manson started a school of medicine in Hong Kong. He worked in China for 24 years, and returned to London in 1890. He was a leader in founding the London School of Tropical Medicine. Manson was knighted in 1904.

HENRY J. L. MARRIOTT

MANTA. See PARAGUAY (Way of Life).

MANTEGNA, *mahn TEN'yah,* **ANDREA** (1431-1506), an Italian painter, is considered by many to be the father of engraving. His works are powerful and moving, and show sculptural form, deep emotion, and great perspective. Both Raphael and Albrecht Dürer made copies from his drawings, and were deeply influenced by them. His paintings include *St. Sebastian, Parnassus,* and *The Infancy of Jesus.* He was born near Padua, and worked mainly in Mantua.

S. W. HAYTER

MANTID is an insect that is sometimes called *praying mantis* because it often lifts its front legs as if it were praying. Mantids usually live in warm countries, but the common European mantid can live in the northern United States.

The mantid takes the praying position when it rests. This position does not reveal the insect's real character. The many kinds of mantids are among the greediest of all insects. They feed not only on other kinds of insects, but on other mantids as well. A female mantid does not hesitate to devour her own mate if she is hungry. These insects prefer to eat their prey alive.

A full-grown, large mantid varies from 2 to 5 inches in length, depending on the kind. It easily escapes notice. In form and color it closely resembles the plants on which it stays. The first segment of the body behind the head, the prothorax, is long and thin, and held almost erect. The rest of the body is thicker, but its shape is long and slender.

The wings are short and broad. The armlike forelegs have sharp hooks that hold the victim as if in a vise.

Female mantids lay their eggs in masses. They glue the eggs to trees and shrubs with a sticky substance from their bodies. The eggs remain there throughout the winter, and the young hatch in spring. The mantid helps man by eating harmful insects.

Scientific Classification. The mantid belongs to the order Orthoptera. It makes up the praying mantis family, *Mantidae.* Some scientists consider the mantid to be a separate order, *Mantodea.*

URL LANHAM

Ralph Buchsbaum

The Praying Mantis

MANTILLA. See SPAIN (Way of Life).

MANTISSA. See LOGARITHMS (Common Logarithms).

MANTLE is a membrane or a tissue. See SHELL; CLAM; OYSTER; SCALLOP; MOLLUSK.

MANTLE. See EARTH (Inside the Earth); MOHOLE.

MANTLE, MICKEY CHARLES (1931-   ), ranks among the leading home run hitters in baseball history. During his career, he hit 536 home runs in regular season play. He also hit 18 home runs in World Series competition, an all-time record. Mantle was a *switch-hitter* (batted both right- and left-handed). He spent his entire major league career (1951 through 1968) with the New York Yankees. He won the American League Most Valuable Player award in 1956, 1957, and 1962. In 1956, Mantle led the league in batting (.353), home runs (52), and runs batted in (130). He had a .298 lifetime batting average. Mantle was born in Spavinaw, Okla.

JOSEPH P. SPOHN

MANU, *MAN oo,* is believed by the Hindus of India to be the ancestor of the human race. *Manu* is a Sanskrit word meaning *man.* A Hindu book of sacred poems, the *Rig-Veda,* describes him as the first man. According to the *Mahabharata,* an epic poem, he is the only man on earth who survived the Deluge (see DELUGE). Manu is believed to be the author of *The Code of Manu,* the holy book of the law.

See also HINDUISM (The Scriptures of Hinduism).

PADRAIG COLUM

MANUA ISLANDS. See AMERICAN SAMOA.

MANUAL TRAINING. See INDUSTRIAL ARTS with its list of Related Articles.

MANUEL, DON JUAN. See SPANISH LITERATURE (The Middle Ages).

MANUEL II. See PORTUGAL (The 1800's).

MANUFACTURERS, NATIONAL ASSOCIATION OF. See NATIONAL ASSOCIATION OF MANUFACTURERS.

Chrysler Corporation

Manufacturing Provides Jobs for Millions of People in the United States and Canada, two of the leading manufacturing countries. U.S. automobile plants produce about half the world's cars.

MANUFACTURING is the industry that makes automobiles, books, clothing, furniture, paper, pencils, and thousands of other products. The word *manufacture* comes from the Latin words *manus* (hand) and *facere* (to make). But, today, manufacturing means the making of articles by machinery as well as by hand.

Manufacturing plants have great importance to the welfare of their communities. When a factory hires 100 workers, for example, it also creates about 175 jobs outside the factory. These include jobs for waitresses, store clerks, and other persons who provide the factory employees with the goods and services they need.

Until the early 1900's, the world's greatest manufacturing centers were in western Europe. The United States became the leading manufacturing nation during World War I, when its industries expanded to make war materials. Since then, the United States has ranked as the world's greatest producer of manufactured goods.

Manufacturing is the chief industry in the United States and Canada. It earns about a third of each nation's income and employs about a fourth of their workers.

Kinds of Manufacturing

Manufactured items may be divided into heavy or light, and durable or nondurable goods. A *durable* product lasts for a long time. A *nondurable* product is used up quickly. For example, a locomotive is a heavy durable product. A sweater is a light durable product. A loaf of bread is a light nondurable item.

All manufactured products are either consumer goods or producer goods. Retail stores, such as groceries or drugstores, sell *consumer goods* to millions of buyers. These products include radios, rugs, food, and thousands of other items. *Producer goods* are products that are used to make other products. They include springs, bearings, printing presses, and many other items.

Manufacturing Around the World

Manufacturing industries are usually located in regions that have abundant natural resources, good transportation, mild climates, and large populations. North America, Europe, and Asia rank as leaders in all these categories and the three regions produce more than 90 per cent of the world's manufactured goods.

In the United States, nearly 300,000 companies make about half the world's manufactured goods, ranging from airplanes to zippers. More than $164 billion has been invested in these firms. U.S. manufacturing firms employ more than 19 million persons, and pay over $100 billion annually in wages, salaries, and stock dividends (see STOCK, CAPITAL). Manufacturing accounts for about $31 of every $100 earned in the United States.

Most big U.S. manufacturers are near large cities, chiefly in the northeastern quarter of the country. The 15 major manufacturing regions, in order of importance, are New York City, Chicago, Los Angeles, Detroit, Philadelphia, Cleveland, Boston, Newark, St. Louis, Pittsburgh, San Francisco-Oakland, Baltimore, Milwaukee, Buffalo, and Cincinnati. See UNITED STATES (Manufacturing).

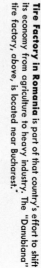

Cotton Mill in Brazil helps make textiles one of the most important manufactured products on the South American continent.

Brazilian Embassy, London

Shipyards in Gydnia, Poland, and those in neighboring Danzig form one of the busiest shipbuilding centers in the world.

Embassy of the Polish People's Republic

Adding Machine Factory in Italy is part of one of the country's major industries, the manufacture of business machines.

Olivetti Underwood Corp.

Tire Factory in Romania is part of that country's effort to shift its economy from agriculture to heavy industry. The "Danubiana" tire factory, *above,* is located near Bucharest.

Embassy of the Romanian People's Republic

MANUFACTURING

In Canada. Canada ranks among the leading manufacturing countries. Its major manufacturing industry produces wood pulp and paper. Other important industries smelt and refine metals, and produce petroleum products, food products, and transportation equipment. About half of Canada's manufactured goods comes from Ontario and nearly a third from Quebec. The nation has about 33,500 factories that employ about 1,400,000 persons. They produce goods with a value added by manufacture of more than $16½ billion a year. See CANADA (Manufacturing).

In Europe. Western Europe and Russia rank after the United States as the world's main manufacturing regions. The major manufacturing nations of western Europe are France, Great Britain, Italy, The Netherlands, Sweden, and West Germany. The governments of some European countries own many or all the factories. The Swedish government controls about half of Sweden's manufacturing. In Russia and other Communist nations, the government owns all the factories. See EUROPE (Manufacturing); EUROPEAN COMMUNITY.

In Asia, large-scale manufacturing is mostly centered in China, India, Japan, and Russia. Most countries produce only a few goods which workers make by hand. But Asia leads the world in the production of silk. See ASIA (Mining and Manufacturing).

In Africa, there is almost no manufacturing. Most of the land is dry or tropical. The continent has poor transportation and includes vast areas with sparse populations. Africa has about a third of the world's potential water power. But most of the sites for power plants are in regions where it would be difficult to develop water power is used. See AFRICA (Manufacturing).

In Latin America, manufacturing is still largely in the handicraft stage. Latin Americans make furniture,

pottery, silverware, textiles, and tinware by hand for tourists. Argentina, Brazil, and Chile produce textiles, shoes, and wine. Argentina and Uruguay have important meat-packing industries. Argentina and Brazil manufacture automobiles. See the Manufacturing sections of CENTRAL AMERICA; SOUTH AMERICA.

The Main Steps in Manufacturing

Design. Manufacturers of consumer goods often change the styles of their products. The new designs attract the public's interest and frequently include improvements on the old styles. Manufacturers also spend much time and money designing attractive packages for their products.

Manufacturers must design products that will be easy to use, and that will not be too expensive to produce or to ship from place to place. Sometimes, after a company designs a new product, it builds and tests a *prototype* (sample of the product) before selling the item to customers.

Raw Materials used in manufacturing come from farms, forests, fisheries, mines, and quarries. Some manufacturers, such as those that make food products, buy most of their raw materials from nearby areas. Others may require raw materials that must be shipped from the other side of the world. For example, Ohio manufacturers make the most tires in the world. But most of the natural rubber the factories use comes from Asia.

Making Products involves one or more of three processes: (1) synthetic, (2) analytic, and (3) conditioning. Manufacturers who use the *synthetic* process mix ingredients or assemble ready-made parts. A paint manufacturer mixes chemicals to produce paint, and an

The Steps in Manufacturing are the same for nearly all types of products. First, the manufacturer designs the product, *above left.* Then, he buys the raw materials needed to make it. Workmen at the factory use the raw materials to produce the finished product, *above right and below left.* After the product is completed, a salesman sells it to customers.

100 LEADING U.S. MANUFACTURERS

#	Manufacturer	*Net Sales	*Assets	Employees
1	General Motors	22,755.4	14,010.2	757,231
2	Standard Oil (N.J.)	14,091.3	16,786.4	151,000
3	Ford Motor	14,075.1	8,953.2	415,039
4	General Electric	8,381.6	5,743.8	400,000
5	Chrysler	7,445.3	4,398.1	231,089
6	International Business Machines	6,888.5	6,743.4	241,974
7	Mobil Oil	6,221.0	6,871.8	78,300
8	Texaco	5,459.8	8,687.0	78,475
9	Gulf Oil	4,558.5	7,498.3	60,300
10	United States Steel	4,536.7	6,391.3	201,017
11	International Tel. & Tel.	4,066.5	4,022.4	293,000
12	Western Electric	4,031.9	2,722.0	177,970
13	Standard Oil of California	3,634.8	5,769.6	47,885
14	McDonnell Douglas	3,609.3	1,335.1	124,740
15	E. I. du Pont de Nemours	3,481.2	3,289.3	114,100
16	Shell Oil	3,317.0	4,230.0	39,080
17	Westinghouse Electric	3,294.6	2,271.4	138,000
18	Boeing	3,213.7	2,186.1	142,400
19	Standard Oil (Ind.)	3,176.4	4,737.5	47,809
20	RCA Corporation	3,106.2	2,365.5	125,000
21	Gen. Telephone & Electronics	3,037.6	6,157.5	161,000
22	Goodyear Tire & Rubber	2,925.7	2,377.1	119,744
23	Bethlehem Steel	2,857.1	3,060.4	131,000
24	Swift	2,827.1	734.9	46,200
25	Ling-Temco-Vought	2,769.7	2,648.2	114,579
26	Union Carbide	2,662.2	3,208.6	100,448
27	General Dynamics	2,652.2	865.9	101,400
28	Eastman Kodak	2,644.1	2,565.2	108,400
29	North American Rockwell	2,639.8	1,361.6	114,430
30	Procter & Gamble	2,542.6	1,611.8	42,125
31	International Harvester	2,540.0	1,902.2	106,190
32	Kraftco	2,450.8	948.1	47,007
33	United Aircraft	2,428.1	1,357.8	76,377
34	Continental Oil	2,401.6	2,537.4	34,384
35	Lockheed Aircraft	2,251.6	936.8	95,404
36	Firestone Tire & Rubber	2,217.4	1,882.6	102,400
37	Phillips Petroleum	2,131.4	2,888.8	35,359
38	Armour	2,106.9	560.5	32,800
39	Tenneco	2,096.4	3,888.3	62,000
40	Litton Industries	2,063.5	1,207.9	106,600
41	Monsanto	1,855.0	1,895.3	59,849
42	Sun Oil	1,792.9	2,362.6	29,446
43	Singer	1,778.2	1,044.7	135,000
44	General Foods	1,754.6	1,677.9	37,000
45	W. R. Grace	1,739.7	1,604.8	69,000
46	Caterpillar Tractor	1,738.4	891.7	61,553
47	Textron	1,704.1	788.2	72,000
48	Occidental Petroleum	1,699.0	1,788.2	22,000
49	Borden	1,669.4	1,023.1	39,819
50	Dow Chemical	1,652.5	2,312.2	47,400
51	American Can	1,633.0	1,337.1	54,400
52	Burlington Industries	1,619.3	1,192.7	83,000
53	Sperry Rand	1,562.8	1,095.2	101,016
54	International Paper	1,561.8	1,713.6	53,657
55	Union Oil of California	1,536.0	2,297.9	17,250
56	Continental Can	1,487.5	881.8	48,408
57	TRW	1,465.1	851.3	80,314
58	Sinclair Oil	1,439.7	1,851.3	19,802
59	Cities Service	1,421.4	1,872.5	23,100
60	Uniroyal	1,413.7	1,121.4	67,595
61	Atlantic Richfield	1,405.0	2,450.9	19,756
62	Minnesota Mining & Mfg.	1,399.5	1,162.9	58,193
63	Republic Steel	1,388.7	1,607.8	50,076
64	Bendix	1,376.2	905.2	82,226
65	FMC	1,375.2	822.6	53,754
66	Armco Steel	1,352.8	974.3	45,427
67	Aluminum Co. of America	1,318.0	2,192.3	46,532
68	Signal Companies	1,313.9	1,352.8	37,000
69	Gulf & Western Industries	1,283.4	1,227.5	75,000
70	U.S. Plywood-Champion Papers	1,281.5	2,055.3	38,686
71	Ralston Purina	1,281.3	626.9	23,800
72	Honeywell	1,278.1	987.4	74,483
73	Allied Chemical	1,264.7	1,494.6	35,700
74	R. J. Reynolds Tobacco	1,255.8	1,197.1	21,332
75	Celanese	1,216.8	1,659.2	38,706
76	Consolidated Foods	1,185.8	802.1	45,000
77	Coca-Cola	1,183.4	1,185.8	26,422
78	Avco	1,158.0	1,824.6	50,000
79	Raytheon	1,152.6	465.7	51,588
80	Grumman Aircraft Eng.	1,152.2	354.3	36,400
81	Owens-Illinois	1,139.7	1,161.8	61,384
82	B. F. Goodrich	1,139.1	1,035.0	45,800
83	National Steel	1,137.9	869.2	17,000
84	CPC International	1,117.4	1,512.1	41,600
85	American Brands	1,102.2	1,117.6	40,540
86	National Cash Register	1,098.1	531.3	91,000
87	Colgate-Palmolive	1,085.8	784.9	24,500
88	Getty Oil	1,085.6	680.5	12,974
89	American Home Products	1,075.2	948.6	38,405
90	American Standard	1,073.7	680.5	82,300
91	Inland Steel	1,068.4	1,175.1	30,552
92	Ashland Oil & Refining	1,052.4	736.8	17,000
93	Beatrice Foods	1,051.4	343.4	63,000
94	Ogden	1,051.0	574.3	43,000
95	Anaconda	1,044.0	1,685.4	43,765
96	PPG Industries	1,039.1	1,094.8	39,300
97	General Tire & Rubber	1,032.8	812.7	45,800
98	Weyerhaeuser	1,030.5	1,376.8	37,620
99	Deere	1,026.5	2,055.3	42,195
100	Boise Cascade	1,027.8	1,027.8	29,930

*Sales and assets in millions of dollars

Source: "The Fortune Directory," Fortune, May 15, 1969. © 1969 Time Inc.

25 LEADING MANUFACTURERS OUTSIDE THE U.S.

#	Manufacturer	*Net Sales	*Assets	Employees
1	Royal Dutch/Shell Group	9,215.8	14,303.3	171,000
2	Unilever	5,533.7	3,431.8	312,000
3	British Petroleum	3,260.2	5,056.3	68,000
4	ICI (Imperial Chemical Industries)	2,969.5	4,387.1	187,000
5	Volkswagenwerk	2,925.0	1,604.8	145,401
6	Philips' Gloeilampenfabrieken	2,685.3	3,406.8	265,000
7	British Steel	2,624.9	3,336.9	254,000
8	Montecatini Edison	2,315.7	4,561.3	142,326
9	Hitachi	2,281.7	2,618.3	154,195
10	British Leyland Motor	2,222.2	1,506.5	188,247
11	General Electric & English Electric	2,155.2	2,519.1	233,000
12	Fiat	2,135.5	1,628.3	158,445
13	Siemens	2,097.3	1,611.1	256,400
14	Nestlé	1,938.7	1,568.0	90,075
15	Farbwerke Hoechst	1,906.8	1,817.8	91,052
16	Mitsubishi Heavy Industries	1,806.8	2,801.5	95,344
17	August Thyssen-Hütte	1,777.0	1,408.4	88,387
18	Renault	1,733.1	844.0	122,000
19	Farbenfabriken Bayer	1,731.3	1,912.5	82,300
20	Daimler-Benz	1,699.3	830.6	108,127
21	Matsushita Electric Industrial	1,688.4	1,320.6	73,058
22	Toyota Motor	1,677.6	1,297.9	90,075
23	Nissan Motor	1,662.3	1,817.8	44,576
24	Tokyo Shibaura Electric	1,597.8	2,031.0	67,938
25	Cie Française des Pétroles	1,560.8	894.7	24,000

*Sales and assets in millions of dollars

Source: "The Fortune Directory," Fortune, August 15, 1969. © 1969 Time Inc.

automobile company assembles parts to make a car.

In the *analytic* process, the manufacturer breaks down a raw material. Oil refineries break crude oil down into gasoline, oil, and other parts. A hog goes through an analytic process at a packing house and comes out as ham, bacon, and other pork products.

The *conditioning* process changes the form of raw materials. Carloads of ore from mines become ingots (bricks) or sheets of metal. Rocks from quarries are made into various grades of gravel.

Besides making the product, a manufacturer must have a system of *quality control*. Specially trained workers check the raw materials and examine the finished products. They make sure that the products meet the standards of the company. Careful *production control* is also essential. Experts make sure that the right materials in the right amounts go to the proper place in the factory at the proper time.

Distribution and Sales account for a large part of the prices that we pay for all products. For example, a gallon of paint costs much more than the chemicals and labor needed to make it. The final price includes the costs of advertising, packaging, shipping, storage, commissions to salesmen, office work, and taxes. In addition to all these costs, the price must give a fair profit to the manufacturer, the wholesalers, and the retailers.

How Science Helps Manufacturing

Engineers and scientists continually experiment and search for new materials that will improve manufactured items. As a result of research since the early 1800's, manufacturers use hundreds of kinds of plastics. Plastics products have replaced less sturdy, less attractive, and more expensive materials. See PLASTICS.

Research not only develops new products, but also finds new uses for old ones. In addition, it leads to lower

prices as manufacturers discover more efficient ways to make products. For example, until automobile companies developed the assembly-line method of manufacturing in the early 1900's, only the wealthiest families could afford cars (see ASSEMBLY LINE).

Widespread industrial research began after World War I, when research became more and more important as a part of manufacturing. Today, companies in the United States pay about $8 billion a year for research. About 225,000 scientists and technicians do this work in some 9,000 company laboratories and 500 gov-

LEADING MANUFACTURED PRODUCTS IN THE U.S.

Value added by manufacture in 1967

Transportation Equipment	$28,901,000,000
Machinery	$27,697,000,000
Food Products	$26,352,000,000
Electrical Machinery	$24,855,000,000
Chemicals	$23,440,000,000
Primary Metals	$20,148,000,000
Metal Products	$17,054,000,000
Printing & Publishing	$14,155,000,000
Clothing	$9,693,000,000
Paper & Allied Products	$9,676,000,000

Source: U.S. Bureau of the Census

LEADING MANUFACTURING STATES AND PROVINCES

Value added by manufacture in 1967

State/Province	Value
New York	$25,331,000,000
California	$23,416,000,000
Ohio	$20,457,000,000
Illinois	$20,005,000,000
Pennsylvania	$19,484,000,000
Michigan	$17,244,000,000
New Jersey	$12,798,000,000
Texas	$10,969,000,000
Indiana	$10,309,000,000
Ontario	$9,012,000,000

Sources: Dominion Bureau of Statistics; U.S. Bureau of the Census

LEADING MANUFACTURING COUNTRIES

Value added by manufacture in 1967

United States	$259,301,000,000
Russia	$132,886,000,000
Japan	$43,121,000,000
Germany (West)	$37,015,000,000
Great Britain	$32,021,000,000
France	$22,348,000,000
Canada	$16,699,000,000
Italy	$16,638,000,000
Brazil	$14,438,000,000
Germany (East)	$13,723,000,000

Sources: Dominion Bureau of Statistics; Statistical Office of the UN; U.S. Bureau of the Census ernment, university, and independent laboratories. See RESEARCH.

How Governments Help Manufacturing

Thousands of government laws and regulations protect a manufacturer's property in noncommunist nations. The government also provides legal, orderly ways to buy and sell property and to establish companies. Government helps keep money stable so that the value of a dollar does not change greatly from day to day and from one area to another. The government permits manufacturers the right to patent an invention. Patents and from business exclusive rights to new products or methods that the manufacturers develop (see PATENT).

Governments furnish businesses with statistics that help them plan their sales and purchases. They give manufacturers loans at low rates of interest, and sometimes give them *subsidies*, or outright grants (see SUBSIDY). Governments protect home industries by levying tariffs on goods imported from other countries (see TARIFF). Many nations encourage manufacturers to build factories by not levying taxes on their profits for a certain number of years.

FRANK F. GROSECLOSE

Related Articles. See the sections on Manufacturing in each state, province, and country article. See also articles on specific products such as AUTOMOBILE. Other related articles in WORLD BOOK include:

Appliances	Industrial	Publishing
Chemical Industry	Revolution	Technology
Clothing	Industry	Textile
Factory	Machine	Transportation
Food (The Food	Mass	Value Added
Industry)	Production	by Manufacture
Forest and Forest	Metal	Vocations
Products	Printing	

MANURE, *muh NOOR* or *muh NYOOR,* is any substance applied to the soil to make it more fertile. In the United States, the word *manure* usually applies to animal *excrement* (waste). In Europe, the word is used for almost any type of fertilizer, including both animal manure and green crops that are plowed under and decay in the soil.

Most animal manure in the United States is from the wastes of cattle and chickens. Horses, pigs, and sheep also provide manure. Animal manure is a valuable source of the *organic* (carbon-containing) matter that plants need for growth. However, it contains only a small amount of other necessary plant foods such as nitrogen, phosphoric acid, and potash. Animal manure should be used in combination with commercial fertilizer and green manure to provide a well-balanced supply of plant food.

Green manure crops provide a large amount of organic matter. They also provide other necessary plant foods as they decay in the soil. These crops are usually grown between the growing seasons of *cash crops* (the crops the farmer sells), or during the winter and early spring. Most farmers use grasses and *legumes* (plants with pods, such as beans and peas) for green manure.

All forms of manure and organic matter improve the soil because they absorb plant food and improve the soil's texture and condition. They also may increase the size and quality of the crop. WILLIAM RAYMOND KAYS

See also FERTILIZER; GARDENING (Plant Foods).

MANUS ISLAND. See ADMIRALTY ISLANDS.

MANUSCRIPT, *MAN, yoo skript.* This word comes from the Latin *manuscriptum,* which means something *written by hand.* But today we also speak of typewritten manuscripts, which we also call *typescripts.*

Handwritten manuscripts were the chief records of human history for about 5,000 years, until the time when printing became general throughout the Western World. These manuscripts make up some of the most valuable collections of the world. Many are kept in glass display cases or are stored in underground vaults of the great museums and libraries of the world. There are many valuable old manuscripts in such libraries as the Bibliothèque Nationale of Paris and the Vatican Library.

The typewritten manuscripts of modern authors are also valuable to collectors, because they show the authors' original work, before editing and publication.

Manuscripts of the Western World

Manuscripts of the Western World can usually be traced to certain periods in history by the materials on which they are written. In ancient times, papyrus, wood and wax tablets, and parchment or vellum (made from animal skins) were used for manuscripts. During the Middle Ages, parchment and paper were used. And, in modern times, we use paper for manuscripts.

Papyrus Manuscripts were first written in Egypt about 4,500 years ago. The ancient Egyptians prepared the writing material from a reedlike plant, called the *papyrus.* The manuscript sheets were pasted together into rolls or "volumes" which were usually twenty to thirty feet long. Many were even longer. The British Museum has copies of the Egyptian *Book of the Dead* which are well over 100 feet long.

The long papyrus rolls of the ancient Egyptians and Greeks were filed in an unusual way. The filers attached documents on the same subject to the end of the same roll, and then indexed the various rolls.

There are papyrus manuscripts dating from about 2500 B.C., and others written as late as A.D. 1000. Papyrus was used in all the lands around the Mediterranean Sea. Scholars believe that all the great works of Greek and Roman literature were written on papyrus.

The University of Michigan has nearly 7,000 papyrus manuscripts, making up the largest collection of its kind in the United States. There are 40 or 50 smaller collections of papyrus manuscripts in the United States.

Wax Tablets, with a wooden frame and back, look very much like the slates which were used in American schools in the 1800's. In ancient times these tablets were used for school exercises, letters, contracts, and other documents. Sometimes two or three tablets were tied together, much as the pages of a book are put together.

Parchment Manuscripts. The use of skins as writing material is probably as old as the invention of writing. But the parchment *codex* (book) did not become more popular than the papyrus roll in Europe until about A.D. 300. Parchment, also called *vellum,* was first used as a manuscript material because it was more durable than papyrus. It was also easier to write on with a pen, and more widely available. The monks and other scribes of the Middle Ages copied many ancient classics onto parchment from decaying papyrus rolls.

The word *palimpsest* is generally used to mean a type

est manuscripts on narrow wood or bamboo strips, or on silk rolls. After they learned to make paper, they sought methods of making it easier to handle. By the 600's, they had begun to fold their paper rolls into "accordion-pleated" books. The Library of Congress has the largest collection of valuable Chinese paper manuscripts in the United States.

Palm Leaves have been used for manuscripts by the people of India from ancient times to the present day. There are 107 collections of Indian manuscripts in the United States and Canada. About 10,000 of these documents were written before 1800.

Pens and Inks

Various instruments and fluids have been used for writing manuscripts through the ages. The ancient Egyptians used a brush made from reeds, and dipped it into an ink made from a mixture of lampblack and water. They used the brush much as we do a pen. The Chinese also used a brush, lampblack, and water.

Later the Egyptians began to use pens made of reeds. The Romans also used reeds, but had some metal pens. For writing on materials like wax or palm leaves, they used a sharp-pointed *stylus* made of wood, metal, or bone. Pens made of feather quills came into use in the early Middle Ages.

The people of ancient times also knew how to make colored inks. Many ornamental letters and illustrations of this period are written in red, yellow, blue, and green. Some are written in purple, gold, and silver.

Illuminated Manuscripts

Manuscripts, like any other handiwork, can be works of art. The handwriting in many early manuscripts

Aztec Manuscript of the mid-1500's shows property records of a Mexican village. It is made of fiber from the maguey plant.

Newberry Library, Ayer Collection

Trinity College, Dublin, Ireland, The Green Studio Ltd.

The Book of Kells is an illuminated manuscript of the four Gospels created in Kells, Ireland, in the 700's or 800's.

of parchment which was washed or scraped and written on again. Hundreds of palimpsests remain, but they are mostly in small pieces. On many, the first writing was not completely removed, and still can be read. In some cases, a palimpsest may be the only manuscript of early writings which historians have been able to find. Cicero's *Republic* was handed down from a palimpsest.

Paper Manuscripts. The Chinese knew how to make paper as early as A.D. 100. But the Western World did not learn the secret until the time of the Crusades. During the 1400's, especially after printing was invented, paper took the place of parchment as manuscript material. Men still used parchment, usually for legal documents, for some time. Most valuable paper manuscripts of the West belong to modern times. The most valuable paper manuscripts in the United States deal with early American history. The largest collection of these is in the United States National Archives at Washington, D.C. The Clements Library at the University of Michigan; the Henry E. Huntington Library in San Marino, Calif.; the New York Historical Society; and the Historical Society of Pennsylvania have large collections dealing with early American history.

Manuscripts of the Orient

The great manuscripts of the Eastern World are written on paper, bamboo, silk, and palm leaves.

Paper Manuscripts. Paper was an invention of the Chinese, even though the word *paper* comes from the Egyptian *papyrus*. The ancient Chinese wrote their earli-

shows great beauty of line, form, and design. The letters and documents written by professional handwriters, or *scribes*, often were done with remarkable design.

The ornamentation and illustration of manuscripts are called *illumination*. In papyrus manuscripts, ornamentation was limited to the first letters. These were usually colored red or blue. In later years, the first letters were sometimes colored gold.

The first illustration of manuscripts on record is in the Egyptian *Book of the Dead* (see EGYPT, ANCIENT [Religion]). The same type of illumination is shown in other works dating from about A.D. 300.

From the 600's to the 900's, Irish monastic schools developed beautiful and extraordinary ornamentation. Lines, geometric figures, and miniature plant and animal forms filled in vacant spaces in the text. Vine tendrils sprouted out into the margins from elaborate initial letters. These decorations sometimes framed the page.

Ornaments and pictures were combined in French and other continental European manuscripts of the 800's. The pictures, sometimes very tiny, were placed within or close to the first letter of the page.

In the last 100 years of the handwritten manuscript period, pictures became larger and more elaborate. They were no longer united with the ornamental lines and letters of the page. The heavy use of color and gold leaves gave them a great splendor. This type of ornamentation inspired the gradual change to the decoration of the printed book with "printer's ornaments," head and tail pieces, and inset and full-page illustrations.

In the United States, some beautiful and valuable illuminated manuscripts may be seen at the Pierpont Morgan Library and the Public Library in New York City, and at the Walters Art Gallery in Baltimore. An example appears in color in the PAINTING article.

Related Articles in WORLD BOOK include:

Bible	Library	Paper	Scribe
Book	(History)	Papyrus	Scroll
Book of Kells	Middle Ages	Parchment	Stylus
Gouache	(pictures)	Pen	Writing
Ink	Paleography		

MANX. See CAT (Breeds of Cats); CELT; MAN, ISLE OF.

MANZANITA, *MAN zuh NEE tuh,* is a shrub of the heath family. It grows from British Columbia to Cali-

"Dick" Whittington

Bright Red Berries and Brilliant Green Leaves make the manzanita a popular evergreen shrub for ornamental use.

fornia. The manzanita is about 20 feet tall, and has attractive evergreen leaves. The leaves have smooth edges. White fuzz covers their under surface. The small, bell-shaped flowers of the manzanita are pink or white. The fruit is red and fleshy. The kind known as bearberry (*Arctostaphylos uva-ursi*) is a hardy creeping evergreen common in sandy soils. The leaves are often used in medicine for their action on the kidneys and bladder.

Scientific Classification. The manzanita belongs to the heath family, *Ericaceae*. It is genus *Arctostaphylos*, species *A. tomentosa*.

GEORGE B. CUMMINS

See also HEATH.

MANZONI, ALESSANDRO (1785-1873), ranks as one of Italy's greatest novelists because of his only novel, *The Betrothed*. This work, published in 1827 and revised in 1840, set the standard for modern Italian prose style. *The Betrothed* is a long historical story set in Lombardy during the 1600's, when the province was ruled by Spain. It describes the adventures of two simple, young silk weavers, Renzo and Lucia, whose marriage is prevented by a local tyrant, Don Rodrigo.

Manzoni was born in Milan. At the age of 16, he began writing poetry, classical in style and patriotic in inspiration and content. Manzoni was born a Roman Catholic, but paid little attention to his faith until 1810. He then underwent a crisis that led him back to Catholicism. That crisis deeply influenced all his works. In addition to *The Betrothed*, he wrote five religious *Sacred Hymns* (1812-1822), an ode to Napoleon, and two historical plays.

SERGIO PACIFICI

See also ITALIAN LITERATURE (In the 1800's).

MANZÙ, GIACOMO. See SCULPTURE (Modern International; color picture: Modeling in Clay).

MAO TSE-TUNG, *MAH oh DZUH DOONG* (1893-   ), the leader of Com-

Mao Tse-tung

Eastfoto

munist China, became one of the most powerful men in the world. He led the long struggle that made China Communist in 1949. As ruler of China, he controlled all artistic, intellectual, military, industrial, and agricultural planning and policy.

Mao's round face with the mole on the chin became familiar throughout the world. Pictures of him appeared everywhere in

China. Young and old learned his slogans and studied his writings. His writings, particularly on guerrilla warfare and the role of peasants in Communist revolutions, were influential outside of China. Mao also wrote poetry.

His Life. Mao was born to a peasant family in Shaoshan, a village in Hunan province. He was still a student when the revolution of 1911-1912 overthrew the Manchu government and made China a republic. While attending the National University at Peking in 1918, Mao became attracted to Communism. In 1921, Mao and 11 others founded the Chinese Communist Party in Shanghai.

The Communists joined forces with Sun Yat-sen's *Kuomintang* (Nationalist Party) in the effort to unite

An Old Maori Chief in native costume stands before the skillful and intricate carvings on the front of his home.

New Zealand Government

133

China. But distrust between the Communists and Chiang Kai-shek, who became Nationalist leader after Sun's death in 1925, soon led to open warfare between the two groups. Mao and other Communist leaders led small bands to Kiangsi province in 1928. By 1931, Kiangsi province had become Chiang's chief target. He launched a series of "extermination campaigns" that nearly wiped the Communists out. In 1934, Mao led the Communists to Shensi province, in what is called *The Long March*. The 6,000-mile march lasted more than a year, and welded the survivors into a tightly-knit group under Mao's leadership.

Japan had invaded Manchuria in 1931, and launched full-scale war against China in 1937. The Communists and Nationalists joined in an uneasy alliance until World War II ended in 1945. As the Nationalist armies were driven inland during the war, Mao organized guerrilla warfare to spread Communism. By 1945, the Communists controlled areas populated by nearly 100 million Chinese.

In 1946, fighting between Communists and Nationalists began in Manchuria. The Communists gained control of China by October, 1949, and the Nationalists withdrew to Formosa (Taiwan).

His Leadership. Mao formed the Chinese into a tightly-controlled society more quickly than most observers thought possible. After taking power, he made an alliance with the Russians, who helped strengthen the Chinese army when Chinese forces aided North Korea during the Korean War (1950-1953).

After the Korean War, Mao began a series of programs to expand China's agricultural and industrial production. In 1958, a crash program called the *Great Leap Forward* failed. Russia refused to give China atomic help in the mid-1950's and Mao began independent atomic research which led to Chinese nuclear explosions in the 1960's.

In 1959, Mao gave up his title of chairman of the People's Republic. But he kept control of the country and of the Communist Party. By the 1960's, disputes between China and Russia had expanded into a struggle for leadership of the Communist world. Mao considered himself the true interpreter of Marx, Lenin, and Stalin. Mao believed that poor nations would inevitably revolt against richer nations. Mao also accused the Russian Communist Party of being too soft toward the United States.

In the mid-1960's, China suffered a series of diplomatic defeats, and Mao launched a campaign against so-called *revisionists* (those favoring changes), to maintain revolutionary enthusiasm. Young *Red Guards* publicly disgraced many officials. In the late 1960's, a power struggle seemed to be taking place among followers of the aging Mao. In 1969, Lin Piao was named as Mao's eventual successor (see LIN PIAO).   MARIUS B. JANSEN

See also CHINA (History).

MAORI, *MAH oh rih*, is the name of the native inhabitants of New Zealand. In their language the word means *native*. They belong to the Polynesian race of the Pacific. They have a strong brunet white element, with Negroid or Negritoid and Mongoloid elements.

The Maoris are above the average in height, and range from light brunet to medium brown in skin color. Their hair and their eyes are brown to very dark brown or black. Their hair is straight to wavy and is thick and crisp. The face tends to be broad, with fairly prominent cheekbones. The nose is prominent and usually straight.

In physical development, the Maoris are among the strongest races known. Until recently, they tattooed their faces with fantastic figures which gave them a wild appearance. They were one of the fiercest peoples of the South Pacific and waged bloody wars with the white invaders. But since the English conquered New Zealand, the Maoris have been greatly changed by their contact with civilization. The Maoris wear European clothing like that of the white residents of the islands, and they have taken up the ways of white civilization with ease.

The Maoris are highly respected by the New Zealanders, and were not brushed aside by the settlers as the aborigines of Australia were. Maori forces fought in Europe in World Wars I and II. Maoris have full political rights in New Zealand. They have been converted to Christianity. Many Maoris have intermarried with New Zealand whites. But there are still about 200,000 pure Maoris in New Zealand.

See also NEW ZEALAND (The People; History); PACIFIC ISLANDS; DANCING (picture).

WILTON MARION KROGMAN

MAP

MAP is a graphic picture of a part or all of the earth. Maps have lines, words, symbols, and colors that show the distribution and arrangement of features upon the earth's surface. Maps may also show objects in space, such as stars and planets. Each feature is drawn in a reduced size so it can be shown on paper or on a globe. In some ways, a map is like an architect's drawing of a building. But there is a much greater reduction in size of the area shown on a map. One inch on a map, for example, may show a distance of 100 miles on the earth's surface.

Almost everyone uses a map at one time or another. Maps help us travel from place to place, and to understand the world around us. They help us plan vacation trips and follow news events in all parts of the world. Businessmen use maps to find good places to sell and ship their products. Armed forces use maps to plan attack and defense strategy. Special kinds of maps serve different uses. One kind of map may show the number of people in every country in the world. Another map may compare the amount of rain that falls in different lands. Still another may show the different types of trees that grow in various parts of the world.

Types of Maps

There are many different kinds of maps, but every map may be classed as one of two types: a *general reference map*, or a *special* or *thematic map*.

General Reference Maps show general information such as continents, countries, rivers, cities, and other features. A *transportation map* is a type of general reference map. It usually shows features of the earth's surface that the traveler will easily recognize, such as roads

and towns, as he goes from one place to another. The most familiar transportation map is the automobile *road map*. Transportation maps are also especially designed for soldiers, hunters, prospectors, and hikers. Maps used by airplane pilots and ship captains are usually called *charts* (see CHART).

The traveler uses his map to find out where he is and to show him where he wants to go. The map helps him decide what direction he should take, which route to follow, how far he must travel, and how long it will take him to reach his destination.

Students and other persons use general reference maps of a slightly different kind in school, at home, in business, or in government when they want information about a specific region, or about the world as a whole. These are the general reference maps found in textbooks, in encyclopedias, and in books of maps called *atlases* (see ATLAS). These maps may be used to show many things besides the location of a place. For example, a map can answer such questions about a city as: Does it lie inland or on the coast? Is it on a river that appears large enough to be navigable? How does the city compare in size and population with nearby cities?

Although most maps are flat, a general reference map can be mounted on a ball called a *globe*. There are two kinds of globes. A *terrestrial* globe shows continents,

Ayer Collection, Newberry Library: H. Armstrong Roberts

Maps Depict Man's Knowledge of the Earth in a way that everyone can understand. Early explorers had only crude maps to follow compared with the accurate charts and globes of today.

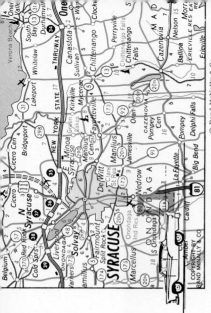

Road Maps help drivers find their way across country. They show the roads in a region, and the distances between cities and towns.

General Reference Maps show elevations and political features. The map above shows high areas in orange, and low areas in green.

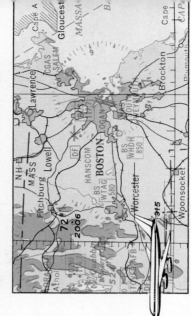

Aeronautical Charts provide information for fliers. They show airports, compass directions, and radio station frequencies.

U.S. Geological Survey Maps show the exact locations of features on the earth. Surveyors rely on these maps for facts.

oceans, and other surface features of the earth. It presents a more nearly perfect map picture of the earth than any other kind of map. A *celestial* globe shows the stars and planets. See GLOBE.

Although globes are good maps of the world for many purposes, they have several disadvantages. One is that only about half of the earth's surface can be seen at a time. Another is that most globes are too small to give much information about any one country or region. Some globes are so big and heavy that they are awkward to move.

Special Maps, or thematic maps, show or emphasize some particular feature, such as rainfall, the distribution of people, or particular kinds of crops. There are as many kinds of special maps as there are features whose location is to be shown. People use special maps to learn how different parts of the earth vary in many ways. THE WORLD BOOK has many useful special maps.

Maps on which different colors indicate various countries are called *political maps.* The relative size and arrangement of countries are easier to remember when shown by colors.

Maps that emphasize in some way the roughness of the earth's surface are called *physical maps.* Sometimes color indicates elevation above sea level. Shading is often used to suggest mountains and hills as they would appear from an airplane. Colors may also be used to show differences in rainfall or temperature. Frequently, the darker color indicates a heavier concentration of the subject. The lines between the colors are called *isolines.* They pass through points that have equal value. For example, a 30-inch rainfall line is drawn through places that have 30 inches of rainfall annually. Land on one side of the line has more rainfall than this amount, and land on the other side has less. On other special maps, colors or other symbols may show the distribution of vegetation or where various languages are spoken.

Map Language

The amount of information a person learns from a map depends on his ability to read it. For example, if a motorist goes on a long trip, he must know how to read a road map in order to know what highways to follow.

Scale. A map must be *drawn to scale* in order to be accurate. The scale of a map shows how much of the actual earth's surface is represented by a given measurement on a map. The scale must be shown so that the map reader can use the distances and areas shown on the map in measuring or figuring out the real distances and areas on the earth's surface. A *large-scale* map covers only a small region and shows most of the details of an area, such as roads and small rivers. A *small-scale* map leaves out many details and covers a much larger area, such as the world.

Scale can be expressed in three different ways. But all three ways do not always appear on every map.

Graphic Scale. On many maps, scale is shown graphically by means of a straight line on which distances have been marked off. Each mark usually represents a certain number of miles on the earth's surface.

Words and Figures. The scale of a map is often expressed as so many units on the map equaling so many units on the ground. This scale might appear as 1 inch = 15 statute miles. In other words, 1 inch on the map

MAP

136

equals 15 miles when measured on the earth's surface. *Representative Fraction (R.F.)*. The most common method of expressing scale is to write a representative fraction. For example, a scale might be written as 1:62,500 or $\frac{1}{62,500}$. This means that one unit of measurement on the map represents 62,500 of the same units on the surface of the earth. The advantage of this method is that the scale is expressed by the fraction regardless of what measurement system is used. An inch is the unit of measurement used in the United States and most other English-speaking countries. Most other nations use the metric system of measurement, in which the unit of measurement is the centimeter.

Symbols. Using many symbols on a map makes it possible to put a large amount of information on a single map. A map usually has a *legend* that explains what each symbol means. Some of these symbols represent *man-made*, or *cultural*, features of the landscape, such as highways, railroads, farms, dams, and cities. Others represent *natural* features, such as mountains, lakes, and plains. The symbols may be lines, dots, circles, squares, triangles, words, letters, colors, or combinations of these. The symbol often looks like or suggests the feature it represents. For example, some maps use a tree symbol for a forest or an orchard. Sometimes, however, there is little resemblance between the symbol and the feature represented by it. For example, a circle or a dot usually indicates a town or a city.

Color. Most maps are printed in color, and the different colors used on a map are part of the map language. On political maps, color can be used to indicate different cities or countries or other types of political information. On physical maps, color can tell the map reader the elevation of various places. The map maker can use a standard series of colors called *layer tints* to show altitude. White may show land below sea level, and green shows land less than 1,000 feet above sea level. Yellow can represent the land between 1,000 and 2,000 feet. Tan can mark the land between 2,000 and 5,000 feet above sea level. Orange may be used for land between 5,000 and 10,000 feet, and dark brown for land more than 10,000 feet above sea level.

Map makers can use color to tell the map reader what the surface of the land is like, to illustrate the nature of the landscape, to show differences in temperature or rainfall among areas, and to indicate where different crops are grown. Color can also be adapted for many other uses.

On most general reference maps, map makers use blue for rivers and bodies of water. Contours, or lines that link points of equal elevation, are usually shown in brown, and man-made features in black or red.

Geographic Grids. A network of accurately spaced north-south and east-west lines is necessary on every map for finding and describing locations. The entire system of these *grid lines* (called *meridians* and *parallels*) is worked out from the North and South poles. All grid lines are circles or parts of circles. Grid lines are labeled in degrees because circles are measured in degrees.

Meridians. By drawing a line from pole to pole through any place on the equator, we have a meridian, or north-south line. Each meridian is a half circle, be-cause it runs halfway around the globe from pole to pole. By agreement among all countries, the meridian passing through the original site of the observatory at Greenwich, England, is called the *prime meridian* (see GREENWICH MERIDIAN). The prime meridian is labeled 0°. All other meridians are numbered in degrees east and west of this meridian up to 180°. See INTERNATIONAL DATE LINE; MERIDIAN.

Parallels are lines drawn around a globe, with all points along each line an equal distance from a pole. The *equator* is the parallel drawn with all points along the line an equal distance from either pole. All the lines parallel the equator and are true east-west lines. Using the equator as 0°, parallels are numbered north and south to the poles. The distance from the equator to a pole is one-fourth of a circle, or 90°.

Longitude and Latitude. The distance in degrees of any place east or west of the prime meridian is known as its longitude. Longitude is marked by meridians, and is usually labeled along the top and bottom margins of a map. On the color map of MARYLAND in this volume, the meridians run from $75\frac{1}{2}°$ to $79\frac{1}{2}°$ west longitude. See LONGITUDE.

Distance in degrees north and south of the equator is called latitude. Latitude is marked by parallels, and is usually labeled along the side margins of a map. Parallels on the MARYLAND color map run from 38° to $39\frac{1}{2}°$ north latitude. See LATITUDE.

How to Read a Map

What Maps Tell Us. There are several ways by which the surface features of the earth, such as mountains, plains, valleys, and deserts, are shown on physical maps.

A pictorial way of showing the earth's surface is the *terrain map.* THE WORLD BOOK uses this method on the physical maps with state, province, country, and continent articles. Shades of various colors suggest the color of the ground and vegetation as the map reader would see them from high in the air. For example, if the ground is barren or exposed rock or sand, the color is light gray or yellow. A lush growth of tall evergreens is shown by a deep blue-green. These maps also give elevations of principal terrain features so the map user may make comparisons.

Each of the state and province articles is also accompanied by a general reference political map. These maps give place-name references and locations. They indicate the network of principal highways, and show rivers, lakes, and reservoirs. The legend with each map explains special features. Wide red lines outline the states, and gray lines separate the counties. The size of type used in printing the name of a city gives the map reader an idea of the city's population. The larger the type, the more important the city.

Special maps with each state and province article provide information on the average yearly rainfall, average daily low and high temperatures for January and July, population density, and farm, mineral, and forest products.

How to Find Places on Maps. The location of a place can be given by longitude and latitude. A place at 77° west longitude could be anywhere along the meridian that extends from pole to pole, about one-fifth of the way around the world west from the prime meridian. But, if this place is also known to be at 39° north

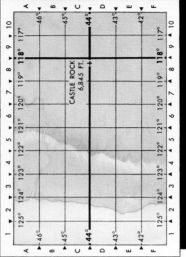

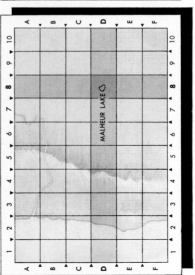

1 Inch=240 Statute Miles

Miles 0 50 100 150 200 250

How far is it from Chicago, Illinois, to Montreal, Canada?

1. The scale on the map indicates that 1 inch = 240 miles.

2. Using a ruler, the distance between the two cities is about 3 inches.

240 (miles to an inch.)
× 3 (inches.)
about 720 miles.

left, the lake lies in the area where the number and letter meet. You can also find places by longitude and latitude. Castle Rock, Ore., lies near 118° W. Longitude and 44° N. Latitude. You can find this feature by tracing inward on the map, as *below right.*

Marginal Symbols help you use maps. You can find distances as shown above. The map index and the letters and numbers in the margins help you locate places. If you want to find Malheur Lake, Ore., the map index will show the symbol D8. On the map, below

latitude, it can easily be located, because there is only one place along the meridian where it could be. A look at the MARYLAND map will show this location to be just north of Washington, D.C.

North, south, east, and west are usually indicated on maps by the initials N., S., E., and W. Thus, 77° west longitude is usually written 77°W., and 39° north latitude is written 39°N.

The *index* of a map provides an even easier way to find places. The index is an alphabetical list of cities

and physical features represented on the map. After each place name, the index has two symbols—a letter and a number—which can be used to locate the place on the map.

Large cities can be located easily by just looking at a map. But smaller towns, such as Frederick on the MARY-LAND map, are harder to find. The index to the MARY-LAND map shows the letter "B" and a number "5," after the name Frederick. Map makers letter and number the squares that are formed on maps by the lines

137

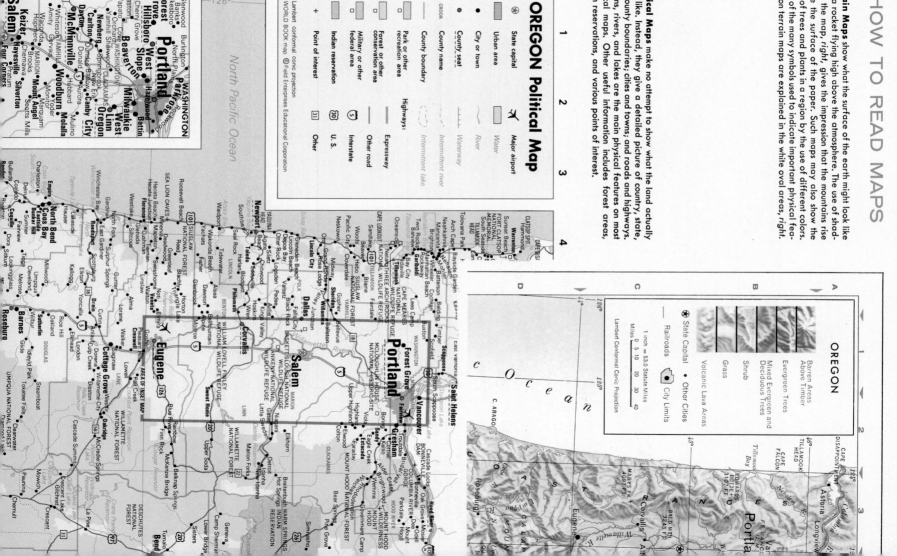

HOW TO READ MAPS

Terrain Maps show what the surface of the earth might look like from a rocket flying high above the atmosphere. The use of shading in the map, *right*, gives the impression that the mountains rise above the surface of the paper. Such maps may also show the kinds of trees and plants in a region by the use of different colors. Some of the many symbols used to indicate important physical features on terrain maps are explained in the white oval areas, *right*.

Political Maps make no attempt to show what the land actually looks like. Instead, they give a detailed picture of country, state, and county boundaries; cities and towns; and roads and highways. Oceans, rivers, and lakes are the main physical features on most political maps. Other useful information includes forest areas, Indian reservations, and various points of interest.

OREGON Political Map

- ⊛ State capital
- ■ Urban area
- ● City or town
- ○ County seat
- County name
- County boundary
- ▭ Park or other recreation area
- ▭ Forest or other conservation area
- ▭ Military or other federal area
- ▭ Indian reservation
- + Point of interest
- ✈ Major airport

Highways:
- Expressway
- Other road
- Ⓢ Interstate
- ⨀ U.S.
- ▣ Other

Water
River
Waterway
Intermittent river
Intermittent lake

Lambert conformal conic projection
WORLD BOOK map © Field Enterprises Educational Corporation

OREGON (terrain map legend)

- ⊛ State Capital
- ● Other Cities
- ▣ City Limits
- — Railroads
- Volcanic Lava Areas

- Barren Areas Above Timber
- Evergreen Trees
- Mixed Evergreen and Deciduous Trees
- Shrub
- Grass

1 inch = 53.0 Statute Miles

Miles 0 5 10   20   30   40

Lambert Conformal Conic Projection

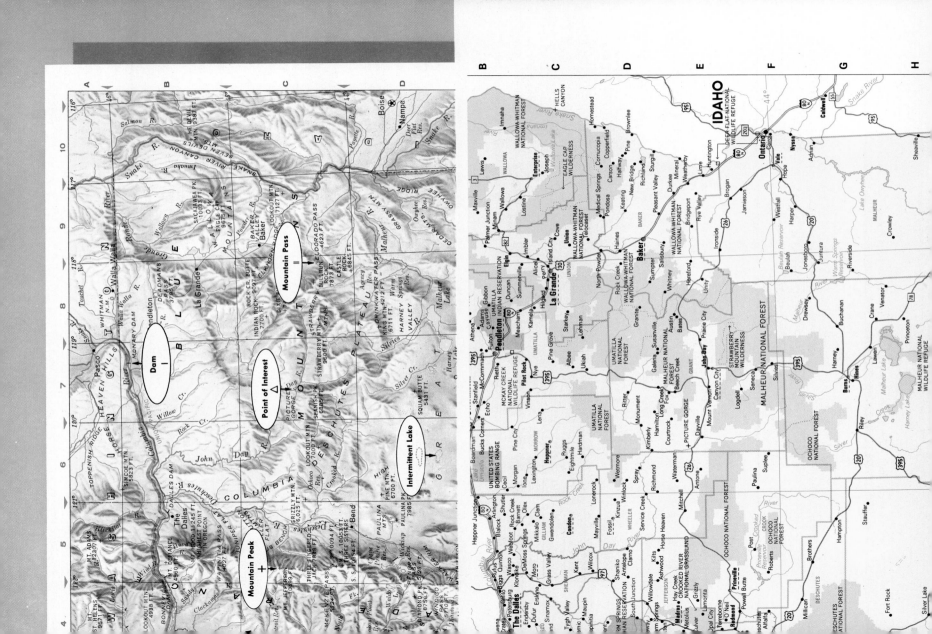

Map Projections

of longitude and latitude. Letters run along the side margins of a map, and numbers along the top and bottom margins. The "B$_5$" after Frederick indicates that the town lies in the square "B$_5$." To find the square, the map reader looks along the side of the map to find the letter "B," then along the top or bottom to find the number "5." He then finds the square where "B" and "5" meet on the map, and looks for Frederick in that square. This method can be used for finding places easily on most maps.

Any drawing on a flat surface that shows a globe's network of meridians and parallels is called a *projection*. This term comes from the fact that one way to transfer lines and points from a globe to a flat map is to use a transparent globe with a light inside it. The light projects the lines on the globe onto a large sheet of paper, where they can be copied.

In actual practice, a map maker works out a flat pattern of meridians and parallels mathematically. It is not possible to make a flat map of the round earth that shows all distances, directions, shapes, and areas as accurately as a globe does. Every flat map has some distortion, or error.

Many different map projections have been developed throughout the years, but only a few are in common usage. A map should be drawn on a projection that comes closest to showing accurately the features that are required for some specific purpose. For example, a map that compares the sizes of two countries should show areas accurately. A square inch on one part of the map should equal the same number of square miles as

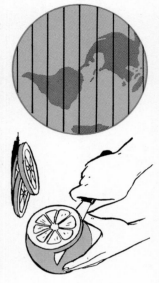

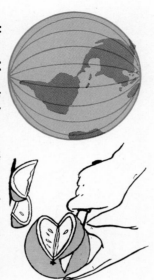

Lines of Latitude, or *parallels,* run around a globe from east to west so that all points along their path are an equal distance from the poles. You would be cutting along parallels of latitude on an orange if you sliced the fruit at right angles to its pith.

Lines of Longitude, or *meridians,* run from north to south on a globe from pole to pole. They cross the parallels of latitude at right angles. You could cut along the meridians of an orange by slicing wedges from the fruit that were parallel to its pith.

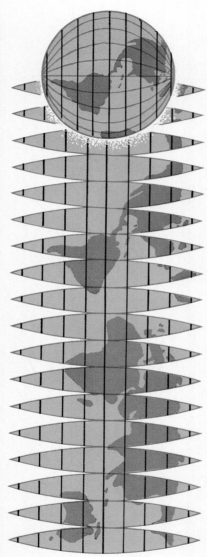

Maps on Flat Surfaces attempt to show the world as it appears on a globe, with as little distortion as possible. An accurate map can be made by cutting a globe apart along the meridians and flattening it. But its many parts make such a map hard to read.

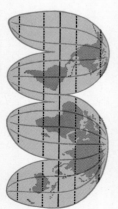

Accurate Maps can be made in ways that are less difficult to read. A nearly flat map results from cutting a globe as shown at left, and opening it as far as possible. The map can then be flattened by stretching the parts that are still curved, *right.*

KINDS OF MAP DISTORTION

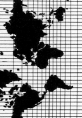

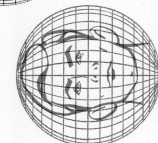

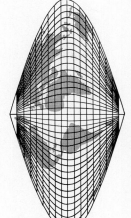

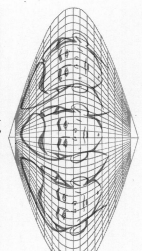

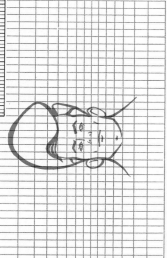

A Globe presents a picture of the earth with practically no distortions. If you imagined a man's face printed on the surface of the globe, the face would look completely natural.

A Sinusoidal Projection does not have lines of longitude of equal length. It squeezes shapes near the top and bottom, and bends them at the left and right, as the faces below indicate.

A Mercator Projection does not show lines of longitude converging at the poles. As a result, areas near the poles appear larger than they are, as the face below indicates.

a square inch on another part. A map used by a ship captain should show compass directions accurately by straight lines.

How to Find Distortions on Maps. Since all flat maps have some distortion, a way to find the inaccuracies is useful. This can be done by comparing the latitude and longitude lines and the rectangles made by them on a map with those on a globe. The following grid (pattern of latitude and longitude lines) facts can be seen on a globe:

(1) All longitude lines are equal in length and meet at the poles.

(2) All latitude lines are parallel.

(3) The length of latitude lines around the globe decreases from the equator to the poles.

(4) Distances along lines of longitude between any two latitude lines are equal.

(5) All latitude and longitude lines meet at right angles, or 90°.

If the grid of a map projection disagrees with one or more of these five facts, the distortion on the map can be found. For example, the longitude lines on the Mercator projection (see diagram on this page) do not converge to meet at the poles, and the latitude lines do not decrease in length toward the poles. Therefore, the scale increases and areas are exaggerated away from the equator.

Although most projections are systematic arrangements of the latitude and longitude lines according to a mathematical formula, it is easier to visualize their general form and characteristics if the earth's surface is considered to be projected upon a plane, a cylinder, or a cone. The projections described below are grouped in this order.

Azimuthal Projections. The azimuthal group of projections is developed by projecting the surface of a globe on a flat surface that touches the globe at a single point. The point of the projection is called an *eye point*, and may be on the globe itself, inside it, or some distance from it.

Gnomonic Projection is perhaps the best-known azimuthal projection. The grid is set up by projecting the surface of the globe from an eye point that is at the center of the globe. Distortion of shape, areas, and scale are very great in this projection. The gnomonic projection has only one true quality, but it is important for long-distance airplane flights. A straight line between two places on a gnomonic projection represents the *great circle route* or the shortest distance between these two points (see GREAT CIRCLE ROUTE). From this, a navigator can determine the latitude and longitude of places that lie along his course. Then he can transfer these positions to a Mercator chart of the same area. Straight lines drawn between these positions on the Mercator chart give him the directions for each part of his flight, so that the route will follow a great circle as closely as possible.

Cylindrical Projections. The cylindrical group of projections is worked out as if a cylinder, or tube, were rolled around a globe along the equator. The parallels and meridians are usually straight lines at right angles to each other.

Mercator Projection, a type of cylindrical projection, is drawn so that the distances between parallels, which are the same on a globe, become greater and greater as

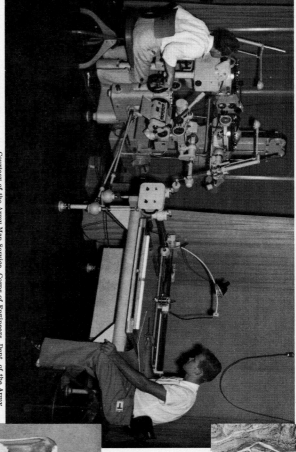

The Stereoplanigraph, *above,* draws contour maps from aerial photographs. The operator at left follows the contours on the photograph through eyepieces. The machine traces the contours on paper on the table at right.

The Aerial Photograph, *above,* shows hills and a river;

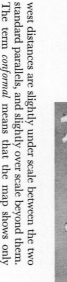

Even a Cow can be shown by means of a contour map.

the parallels approach the poles. This distortion makes up for the fact that the distances between meridians remain the same from the equator to the poles on this type of map. The Mercator projection makes areas in high latitudes seem much larger than they are. But it is ideal for navigation charts. Shapes of features, such as islands and harbors, are accurate, and any compass course between two points on the map can be shown as a straight line.

Miller Cylindrical Projection is a modification of the Mercator projection. East-west distances are fairly accurate between 45°N. and 45°S. latitudes. The exaggeration of areas in high latitudes is not nearly so great as in the Mercator projection. For this reason, the Miller projection is useful for a map of the world, because it does not greatly distort the parts of the world where most of the people live.

Conic Projections. The conic group of projections is made as if a cone were laid over the globe, and touched it along some line of latitude. The parallels, which are arcs of concentric circles, are spaced evenly along the meridians, which are straight lines. As on the globe, the meridians come closer and closer together as they approach the pole. The simple conic projection, although neither equal-area nor conformal, is fairly accurate when used for small areas. It is often used for maps in atlases. See the physical map with OHIO.

Lambert Conformal Conic Projection is an accurate conic projection for large areas with greater east-west than north-south dimensions. The cone is thought of as cutting through the surface of the globe so that east-west distances are true along two parallels. These are known as the *standard parallels.* North-south and east-west distances are slightly under scale between the two standard parallels, and slightly over scale beyond them. The term *conformal* means that the map shows only true shapes. Distances, directions, and areas are shown fairly accurately. The small errors of azimuth or direction, and the closeness with which a straight line follows a great circle, make this type of projection useful in air navigation. The International Civil Aviation Organization has adopted it for its series of aeronautical charts covering the world. For an example of this type of map, see the political map with MASSACHUSETTS.

Polyconic Projection may be thought of as a projection of strips of the earth's surface upon a series of touching cones. In practice, however, this principle is modified. A vertical straight line marks a central meridian that is divided to space the parallels truly. Each parallel is divided truly, and the curved lines that connect the division points form the meridians. Distortion is small near the central meridian. For this reason, the projection is excellent for showing areas of small east-west direction. For an example of this type of map, see the physical map with ALASKA.

Other Types of Projections. There are other projections, purely conventional in design, which cannot be related to these three general groups. They include the sinusoidal projection, the oval-shaped homolographic projection, and the interrupted homolosine projection, a combination of the sinusoidal and homolographic projections. For an example of a sinusoidal projection map, see the terrain map with SOUTH AMERICA.

How Maps Are Made

Many skilled scientists and technicians must work together to make a map. The information shown by a

The Contour Map, above, shows the results produced by the stereoplanigraph.

The Lines on the map, below, indicate the outline and the contours of a cow.

The Pantograph Router, above, makes a three-dimensional model of the features shown on a contour map. The operator traces the lines on the map, and a cutting blade forms the model.

Plastic Relief Maps can be made from the model produced by the router. A die is made from the model and placed on a forming machine. The machine uses pressure and heat to form maps.

map is the result of scientific observation and the study of some part of the earth's surface. Many maps, however, are made from other maps by carefully selecting facts to be shown and by simplifying and reducing the scale. In general, a map goes through the following steps as it is made.

Observation. Various experts observe, plot, survey, photograph, and describe facts about the earth. The surveyor works out the exact location of places by measuring distances, directions, and elevations. In this way, places on the earth's surface are related to other parts of the earth to provide the correct space relations between places on maps. Surveyors use precision instruments to make these measurements. Aerial photography helps them with much of their work. Other specialists, including the explorer, the geographer, the geologist, the geodesist, the photogrammetrist, and the meteorologist, may carry on additional observations.

Organization. Any new information is added to the facts that are already known about the area to be mapped. The results are organized, simplified, and generalized so they can be translated into the language of maps. This is the work of another group of scientists, chosen according to the kind of facts to be presented and the purpose of the map. These men might be geographers, geologists, climatologists, sociologists, historians, or military strategists.

Planning. All the facts to be shown on the map are gathered together and analyzed. A *cartographer*, or map maker, plans the map. Sometimes a cartographic editor and a cartographic designer share the job.

Drafting. The map is put on paper as an original drawing or as a series of drawings by a cartographic artist or draftsman. Usually, this drawing is larger than

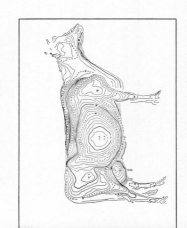

the final map. It is the draftsman's job to bring together the facts and ideas of the scientists and cartographers to make the map easy to read, accurate, and pleasing to the eye.

Reproduction. If a large number of persons are to use a map, many copies must be made. The map drawing must be put on a material from which it can be printed directly, or from which printing plates can be made.

The Map Industry. Each year, several thousand new maps are made and hundreds of millions of maps are used. Government agencies make many of the maps. Governments need maps of various scales and types to help them carry out their duties. Many special maps are needed for military purposes. In the United States, they are made by the Army Map Service, the largest governmental mapping agency. The United States Geological Survey prepares large-scale topographic maps of areas within the United States. The U.S. Hydrographic Office makes charts of the ocean. Commercial map companies make maps chiefly on smaller scales and for special needs, such as road maps. These firms include Rand McNally & Company, C. S. Hammond & Company, and the General Drafting Company, Inc. Private organizations such as the American Geographical Society and the National Geographic Society also publish maps.

History

Old maps can tell us a great deal about where people traveled in ancient times. Men have made and used maps ever since people first moved about the earth exploring other territories, trading, or conquering other peoples. By comparing old maps, we can learn the extent of knowledge that various peoples had of the world

143

early 300's B.C. They became one of the first peoples to realize that the earth is round. They designed the first projection and developed a longitude and latitude system. No ancient Greek maps exist today. The Romans used maps for taxing land and to assist in military campaigns. They were excellent surveyors, and were among the first to make road maps. But few of their maps have been preserved.

The most famous ancient maps were made by Claudius Ptolemy, a scholar who lived in Alexandria, Egypt, around A.D. 150. A map of the world as known at that time, and 26 regional maps of Europe, Africa, and Asia, formed part of his eight-book *Geographia*. Only a few scholars knew about Ptolemy's maps until the late 1400's, when they were printed in an atlas. Maps showing North and South America, and the route around Africa to the East Indies, were added to the later editions of Ptolemy's atlas during the 1500's.

Map Making in Europe. The *portolano*, or sailor's chart, came into common use during the 1300's and 1400's. It was developed as an aid to navigation along the coasts of the Mediterranean Sea. Maps of this type were drawn on sheepskin. They showed the outline of coasts and harbors, and located shipping ports. The oldest examples of portolano charts date from about 1300. But their fine workmanship indicates they were probably patterned after even earlier maps.

Christopher Columbus was a map maker. As a navigator, he used portolano charts. But, as a student of geography, he was also familiar with the maps of scholars. No map made by Columbus himself is known to exist today. But the Naval Museum in Madrid, Spain, has a large, hand-drawn map showing the first discoveries of Columbus. It was made by one of his pilots, Juan de la Cosa, and is dated 1500. The discovery of America and the voyages of the Portuguese around Africa led to great progress in map making during the 1500's. See COLUMBUS, CHRISTOPHER (map).

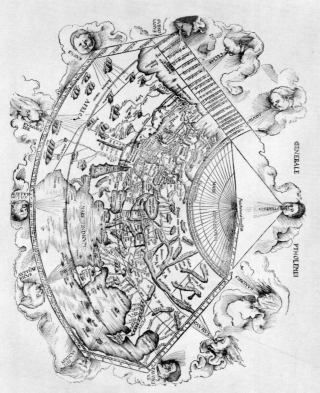

The Oldest Map Known is a clay tablet found in Iraq. Made about 2300 B.C., it probably shows a man's estate in a valley.

throughout the ages. We usually think of maps in connection with reading and writing. But peoples who do not have written languages have often used maplike aids when traveling from place to place. The Eskimos scratched such maps on scraps of wood or ivory. Polynesians of the Pacific Islands made charts of rattan to indicate prevailing winds and ocean currents.

Ancient Maps. The oldest known map was made about 2300 B.C. It is a small clay tablet from Babylonia that probably shows a man's estate in a mountain-lined valley. The Egyptians made maps as early as 1300 B.C. One of the few remaining ancient Egyptian maps shows the route from the Nile Valley to the gold mines of Nubia, part of ancient Ethiopia.

The Greeks made maps of the inhabited world in the

Until the 1500's, maps were based on the writings of Ptolemy, a Greek geographer and astronomer who lived about A.D. 150. The map, *left*, was made in 1520. Although it is not accurate, the map shows the earth as being round.

MAP

145

The growth of knowledge about the world can be traced in maps that were drawn to record discoveries. Almost every voyage of exploration had a chart maker who drew sketch maps of coast lines, harbors, and islands. He also drew a general map of each expedition from the sketch maps and the ship's log. Then scholars and cartographers added these latest discoveries to their atlas and globes.

Famous Map Makers. Martin Behaim (1459?-1507), a German merchant-navigator, made the oldest existing globe in 1492. The first map to use the name *America* was made in 1507 by a German map maker, Martin Waldseemüller (1470?-1518). This was a large world map printed in 12 sheets and measuring about 4½ by 8 feet. Each sheet was separate, printed from a woodcut, and measured about 18 inches by 24 inches.

One of the greatest map makers of the 1500's was Gerhard Kremer, who used the Latinized name of Mercator (1512-1594). This Flemish geographer not only produced some of the best maps and globes of his time, but also developed a new map projection of great value to sailors (see MERCATOR, GERHARDUS). Another Flemish map maker, Abraham Ortelius (1527-1598), produced the first modern atlas in 1570. The German mathematician Johann Lambert (1728-1777) made contributions to the mathematical projection of maps.

Early Map Making in America. The first map made after English settlers came to Jamestown was a map of Virginia by the famous adventurer, John Smith (1580-1631). It was published in England in 1612. Smith also made the first English map of New England.

There were no professional map makers in the American Colonies, but skilled amateurs drew many maps of the area. Lewis Evans (c. 1700-1756) of Philadelphia produced *A General Map of the Middle British Colonies in America* in 1755. It measured about 26 by 20 inches, and is considered the best map produced by a colonist before the Revolutionary War. *A Map of the British and French Dominions in America* was produced in England in 1755 by John Mitchell (? -1768). It measured about 76 by 53 inches. A copy of this map was used at the peace conference of 1783 to mark the boundary of the newly established United States of America.

As the pioneers moved westward, travelers and scholars made newer and better maps. Meriwether Lewis and William Clark used an English map of North America made by Aaron Arrowsmith (1750-1823) to guide them across the continent. Upon their return, they drew their own map. Other explorers, including Zebulon Pike, Jedediah Smith, and John C. Frémont, provided additional information about the West. Their information was put on maps used in the immigration to Oregon during the 1800's and the Gold Rush to California in 1849. Later, the government sent army engineers into the West to make railroad and geographical surveys. The maps that illustrated the reports of these surveys became the foundation of the first accurate and fairly complete maps of the United States, dating from about 1875. Four years later, the United States Geological Survey was organized and began making large-scale, detailed topographical maps.

Map Making in the 1900's. Road maps for automobile travel came into wide use about 1910 (see ROAD MAP [History]). Oil companies give away road maps at most gasoline service stations. These maps are up-to-date, because new editions are printed every year. The airplane made necessary many new kinds of maps and charts for pilots and passengers. The use of vertical and oblique air photographs increased the speed with which maps can be made. The entire United States has been photographed, and air photos are used in making nearly all large-scale, detailed maps. The science of making maps from air photos is called *photogrammetry*. The United States Air Force has special target maps for bombing, with concentric circles around the targets. For night flying, charts are printed on fluorescent paper which makes the map glow under ultraviolet light. Since the end of World War II, people have used more maps and atlases than they ever did before.

E. B. ESPENSHADE, JR.

Related Articles. See the color and black-and-white maps with the state, province, country, and continent articles. See also the following articles:

Airplane (color diagram:	Longitude
Navigation Aids)	Mercator, Gerhardus
Atlas	Meridian
Aviation (maps)	Navigation
Azimuth	Photogrammetry
Boundary	Radar (Recent
Chart	Developments)
Coast and Geodetic Survey	Relief Map
Colonial Life in	Road Map
America (color map:	Surveying
Long Island)	Topography
Earth	Weather (Weather Fore-
Geodesy	casting; color pictures:
Geography	How to Read a
Globe	Weather Map)
Greenwich	World, History
Meridian	of (picture: An
Latitude	Exploration Map)

Outline

I. **Types of Maps**
   A. General Reference Maps   B. Special Maps

II. **Map Language**
   A. Scale   C. Color
   B. Symbols   D. Geographic Grids

III. **How To Read a Map**
   A. What Maps Tell Us
   B. How to Find Places on Maps

IV. **Map Projections**
   A. How to Find Distortions on Maps
   B. Azimuthal Projections
   C. Cylindrical Projections
   D. Conic Projections
   E. Other Types of Projections

V. **How Maps Are Made**

VI. **History**

Questions

What two general kinds of features do symbols represent on a map?

What is a geographic grid? Why is it useful in map reading?

What is the prime meridian? How are other meridians numbered from the prime meridian?

Why is the globe the best kind of map for many purposes?

For what main purposes did the Romans use maps?

What does the scale on a map show? What are the three most common ways of showing scale?

What is meant by latitude? Longitude?

What is a map projection? What are the main types of map projections?

What are some kinds of general maps? Special maps?

Why is it valuable to know about distortion on a map?

MAPLE

The Stately Norway Maple grows straight and tall, sometimes reaching a height of 90 feet. These handsome trees line the parkways of many cities. Their wide, even shape provides excellent shade during the summer months. In autumn, the Norway maple's shiny, dark-green leaves turn to a pale yellow.

MAPLE. The maple is a handsome tree from which we get maple sugar and a valuable wood. More than a hundred species of the maple family are known. They grow throughout the north temperate regions of the world. Thirteen species are native to the United States.

All maples which grow in the open have full, rounded tops. They furnish much of the welcome shade along our streets. Most people also find pleasure in their beautiful leaves and strange winged fruits. All maple leaves grow opposite each other, in pairs. They are broad and flat, with veins and lobes like fingers. There are from three to seven lobes. One species, the *box elder*, has a true compound leaf, made up of separate leaflets. See BOX ELDER.

The fruits of these trees are called *key fruits*, or *keys*. Each has a thin flat wing. Usually two seeds grow together with the wings on each side of the seeds. Often a pair of seeds looks like the propeller of an airplane. Maple-tree seeds supply food for squirrels, birds, and chipmunks.

The Sugar Maple. The *sugar*, *rock*, or *hard maple* is the most important of the maples. It grows from Newfoundland to the Great Lakes, south to Georgia, and west to Manitoba and Texas. The sugar maple may reach a height of 135 feet. Its trunk may be 5 feet across. The sugar maple has gray bark and dark-green leaves. In autumn the leaves turn to beautiful yellow, orange, and red. The maple leaf is the national emblem of Canada, and appears on the Canadian flag.

The delicious golden-brown maple syrup comes from the sugary sap of the hard maple. Manufacturing syrup and sugar from maple sap is an important business, especially in Ontario, Quebec, New York, and Vermont. See MAPLE SUGAR.

The hard maple also outranks all other maples as a lumber tree. Its wood is heavy, hard, and strong and takes a fine polish. The color is a light reddish-brown. From colonial times, it has had so many uses that it is hard to count them all. Furniture makers have used maple since furniture was first made in America. Hard maple is widely used for floors. Other maple products are saddles, shoe lasts, wooden kitchenware and novelties, boxes, crates, and parts of many musical instruments. Hard maple is much used as a fuel. Veneer, railroad ties, and pulpwood are also cut from this tree. The pioneers used its ashes to make soap.

Bird's-Eye Maple. The wood in a small percentage of hard maple trees shows a beautiful spotted design. Each spot is about ¾ inch across, and looks a little like a bird's eye. These spots are caused by numerous indented places, more or less close together, in the annual

rings of growth. Special methods of sawing are necessary to bring out the design. A method called *plain sawing*, or *tangent sawing*, gives bird's-eye lumber. Veneer is cut by slicing round and round the tree, cutting in the same direction as the growth rings. The saw pares off a thin layer from the surface as the log turns. Smoothing the surface by planing and careful polishing brings out the full richness of the design.

The bird's-eye design is seldom found in any other kind of wood. It is not known exactly what causes the indented places in the rings. They are not due to buds growing underneath the bark, as many people think. Most bird's-eye veneer comes from the northern peninsula of Michigan.

Curly and Wavy Grained Maple are other woods with special patterns. The fibers take either an irregular, curly course, or are arranged in regular waves. These growths produce beautiful effects of light and shade. The cause of curly and wavy grain also is unknown. Unlike bird's-eye grain, they appear in many other kinds of wood besides maple. They are found in both hardwoods and softwoods.

Figured maple with twisted wood fibers is highly prized both as lumber and veneer. It is used for bedroom furniture, desks, wall paneling, fancy gunstocks, and violin backs. The design preferred for violins is a fine wavy grain that has been given the name "fiddleback" figure. The figure has the same name when it appears in other woods that are not used for violins, such as mahogany.

Other American Maples include the *silver maple*, which is grown in many places. This is a hardy tree that grows quickly. It has beautiful shimmering silver and green leaves, but light, brittle wood. The *big-leaf*, or

William M. Harlow

SUGAR MAPLE   SYCAMORE MAPLE   SILVER MAPLE

Maple Leaves are easy to identify because of their handlike shape. In Canada, the maple leaf is the national symbol. Maple leaves are usually green, but those of the silver maple are green on top and silver below. A pair of U-shaped wings holds the seeds. When the wind blows, the wings spin like a propeller, carrying the seeds downward and away from the tree so they can take root.

Oregon maple is one of the few valuable hardwoods of the Pacific coast. The *red, scarlet,* or *swamp maple* is a valuable ornamental and lumber tree. Its red or scarlet flowers appear in the spring before the leaves. The leaves turn to a beautiful scarlet in early fall. The *striped maple* and the *mountain maple* are two smaller trees usually found together in the northern woods.

In Canada, the government has furnished many trees for planting as protection against wind and snow. Of all the trees furnished, 30 per cent are maples.

Foreign Maples. The *sycamore maple* is an important hardwood tree in Europe. The branches of this tree spread wide, and its thick leaves look like those of the sycamore. It is planted in America to some extent. The *Norway maple* is a large tree with thick leaves and a milky sap. It resembles the sugar maple tree, and produces a vast amount of fruit, which covers the ground around the tree like a carpet. The tree's green leaves turn to pale yellow in autumn. The Norway maple is popular in England and the United States. A variety of Norway maple, the *Schwedler maple*, has bright red leaves

when young. The leaves turn dark green in summer. The Schwedler maple is a popular ornamental tree. *Japanese maples* also find wide use as ornamental trees. They seldom grow above 20 feet high. Their feathery leaves have delicate shades of red and green in the spring. These leaves have beautiful tints in autumn.

Insect Enemies. Several harmful insects attack the maple. Some bore into the bark while others eat the leaves. Maples are often damaged by tent caterpillars, sugar-maple borers, plant lice, scales, and galls. Various washes are good cures for scales.

Scientific Classification. The maple family is *Aceraceae.* The sugar, or rock, maple is genus *Acer,* species *A. saccharum.* The silver maple is *A. saccharinum.* The big-leaf, or Oregon, is *A. macrophyllum.* The striped maple is *A. pensylvanicum.* The mountain maple is *A. spicatum.* The red maple is *A. rubrum.* The sycamore maple is *A. pseudoplatanus.* The Norway maple is *A. platanoides.* The Japanese maple is *A. palmatum.*

THEODORE W. BRETZ

See also Box Elder; Leaf (picture, Kinds of Leaves); Maple Sugar; Tree (picture, Tree Shapes; color pictures, Ornamental Trees, Autumn Colors).

Devereux Butcher

Flower Cluster of the Norway maple sprouts yellowish-green flowers in early spring.

The Huge Silver Maple makes an excellent shade tree because of its thick foliage.

Tom Burns, Jr.

Japanese Maples have delicate, shrublike leaves, *left inset.* Their colors include purple, crimson, scarlet, and yellow.

Maple Sap Runs When Spring Returns. Workmen bore tapholes in the trunks of the trees, above. They insert the spouts so that a watertight seal is made with the sapwood and the bark. They hang either plastic bags or galvanized buckets on the spouts to collect the sap, *right*. The buckets are covered to keep out rain and falling debris.

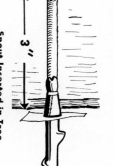

M. C. Audsley, USDA;
Vermont Extension Service

Spout Inserted in Tree

3″

State of New Hampshire

Sap Gathered in the Maple-Sugar Grove, *left*, is transferred to storage tanks, foreground above. In the sap house, background above, water is boiled from the sap to make maple syrup.

LEADING MAPLE SYRUP PRODUCING STATES AND PROVINCES

Gallons of maple syrup produced in 1967

Quebec	2,723,000 gals.	🍁🍁🍁🍁🍁🍁🍁🍁🍁🍁🍁🍁🍁🍁🍁🍁🍁🍁🍁🍁🍁
Vermont	310,000 gals.	🍁🍁
New York	275,000 gals.	🍁🍁
Ontario	271,000 gals.	🍁🍁
Wisconsin	100,000 gals.	🍁
Ohio	69,000 gals.	🍁

Includes maple syrup later made into maple sugar and maple taffy.

Sources: U.S. Department of Agriculture; Dominion Bureau of Statistics

MAPLE, FLOWERING. See FLOWERING MAPLE.

MAPLE LEAF FOREVER is a song which has been popularly used as the Canadian unofficial hymn. The words and music were written in 1867 by Alexander Muir, a public schoolteacher in Toronto. He was born in Scotland, and was brought to Canada when he was 3 years old. The maple leaf was made the official emblem of Canada in 1860.　　　　RAYMOND KENDALL.

MAPLE SUGAR is made chiefly from the sap of the sugar-maple tree. Late in the winter and in early spring, farmers in eastern Canada and in the midwestern and northeastern states begin the yearly job of tapping these trees. They bore a hole about 3 inches deep into the tree trunk, at a height of $3\frac{1}{2}$ to 4 feet from the ground. Then they drive a small metal spout or wooden trough into the hole. A bucket hangs from the spout to collect the sap that flows out of the hole. The bucket is usually covered to keep the sap clean.

Each day, the farmers collect the sap in large tanks and take it by sled or cart to the sap house. Here, the farmers boil it until most of the water in the sap has boiled away as steam. They once did this out-of-doors in large iron kettles. Now they use a modern machine called an evaporator. When some of the water has boiled off, maple syrup remains. If the sap is boiled longer, it forms maple cream, soft sugar, and then hard sugar. Farmers make more syrup than sugar because there is more demand for it. The syrup is passed through a woolen strainer after it is boiled. It is then so pure that no further refining is needed.

The black, silver, and red maples are all sources of maple sugar, but the largest amounts come from the sugar-maple tree. New York is the leading sugar-maple state. In Canada, Quebec leads the provinces in maple sugar production.　　　　PERRY H. MERRILL.

MAQUIS, *MAH kees*, were French patriots who formed a secret army to fight German occupation forces in France during World War II. *Maquis* is a French word for the tough, scrubby vegetation of the Mediterranean Coast. People from all classes joined the Maquis to support the Free French, and to escape from being forced into German labor camps. The Maquis conducted intelligence and small-scale operations, blowing up trains, killing sentries, and sabotaging military production. Members lived in hiding in the mountains of southern and eastern France in units of up to 60 men. The Allies parachuted supplies to them. When the war ended, the French government publicly thanked the Maquis for their services.　　　　STEFAN T. POSSONY

MARA. See CAVY.

MARABOU, *MAR uh boo*, is a stork that has beautiful white feathers. Manufacturers once used marabou feathers to make scarves, and to trim hats and gowns. Marabous live in Africa and Asia. The best-known marabou lives in Africa. It is a large, white bird with greenish-gray wings and a large pouch beneath its bill. It eats birds, small mammals, and lizards, and is also useful as a scavenger. The marabou is also called the *adjutant* (see ADJUTANT).

Scientific Classification. Marabous belong to the stork family, *Ciconidae*. The African marabou is genus *Leptoptilus*, species *L. crumeniferus*.　　　　GEORGE E. HUDSON

MARACAIBO, *mar uh KY boh* (pop. 621,109; alt. 30 ft.), is Venezuela's chief coffee-exporting port and second largest city. The discovery of petroleum in

1912 made Maracaibo one of the world's great oil cities, and a thriving metropolis. Maracaibo lies on the west shore of the narrows that connect the Gulf of Venezuela with Lake Maracaibo. For location, see VENEZUELA (color map). The city has a good harbor. A $5\frac{1}{2}$-mile-long bridge across the lake connects Maracaibo with the mainland. The University of Zulia is located there. Maracaibo was founded in 1529 by Ambrosio Alfinger, an officer who led 150 soldiers there from Coro, Venezuela.

MARACAIBO, LAKE. See LAKE MARACAIBO.

MARACAS. See VENEZUELA (The Arts).

MARAJÓ, *MAH ruh ZHO*, is a large island that covers an area of 22,859 square miles between the estuaries of the Amazon and Pará rivers in northeastern South America. The island belongs to Brazil.

Marajó is a plain just above sea level. Most of it is flooded during the six-month rainy season. In the six-month dry season, the extensive grasslands make good pasture. Most of the island is grassland with forests fringing the shores and banks of waterways. Some rubber trees are scattered through these forests.

About 164,450 people make their homes on Marajó. Wandering herders and rubber hunters visit the island during the dry season.　　　　H. F. RAUP

See also BRAZIL (physical map).

MARAÑÓN RIVER. See AMAZON RIVER.

MARASCHINO CHERRIES, *MAR uh SKEE noh*, are preserved cherries used to decorate and add flavor to desserts and beverages. The cherries received their name because they were originally preserved in *maraschino*, a liqueur distilled from the fermented juice of the marasca cherry. Today, the cherries are artificially colored, flavored, and preserved. Several varieties of cherries are used. They are picked before they have fully ripened, and are pitted by a machine.　　　　RICHARD A. HAVENS

The Marabou Stork Has a Long Bill and Spindly Legs.
F. E. Westlake from National Audubon Society

MARAT, JEAN PAUL

MARAT, *mah RAH,* **JEAN PAUL** (1743-1793), was one of the most radical leaders of the French Revolution. With Georges Danton and Maximilien Robespierre, Marat was responsible for the Reign of Terror. When the revolution broke out in 1789, Marat was a physician. He became a violent revolution-

Portrait by Joseph Boze,
Carnavalet, Paris (Bulloz)

Jean Paul Marat

ist. He began publishing a newspaper which he called *L'Ami du Peuple* (The Friend of the People). It grew to be the mouthpiece of the murderous mobs of Paris. Marat was the idol and leader of the worst element in France. He demanded the death of all Frenchmen who spoke against him. At one time he demanded that 270,000 men be guillotined.

Marat became a member of the Commune of Paris, the city's governing body, in 1792. Mobs stirred up by his writings joined eagerly in the September Massacre of 1792, in which more than 1,000 persons were killed. Marat's writings were so violent that he was tried for *sedition* (causing rebellion) by the Revolutionary Tribunal in April, 1793. But he was freed and was welcomed back by his followers.

His wickedness had angered Charlotte Corday, a young girl from the northern province of Normandy. She blamed Marat for the fall of the Girondists, a party that supported neither nobility nor peasantry. The girl believed he incited the people to violence. Obsessed with the idea that Marat's death would mean the relief of France, she stabbed him to death while he was sitting in his bathtub on July 13, 1793. She was arrested and beheaded on the guillotine. See CORDAY, CHARLOTTE.

Marat was born at Boudry, near Neuchâtel, Switzerland, where his father was a doctor. Marat studied medicine in Paris and later practiced there and in London.

See also DANTON, GEORGES J.; FRENCH REVOLUTION; REIGN OF TERROR.

MARATHI is the name of a language spoken mainly by the Mahratta people of India. See MAHRATTA.

MARATHON, *MAHR uh thahn,* is a plain in Greece on which one of the decisive battles of history was fought. The plain of Marathon is about 25 miles from Athens. There the Athenians and their allies, the Plataeans, defeated the army of King Darius of Persia in 490 B.C.

Darius controlled Asia Minor, which included Greek cities in Ionia (western Asia Minor). The Ionians revolted against Persia in 499 B.C., and the other Greeks came to their aid. Darius decided to punish the Greeks for aiding the Ionians. He gathered a powerful army and a great fleet and sent them to Greece under two generals, Datis and Artaphernes. The Persians captured the island of Euboea and set up a base there. From this point the Persian army landed on the mainland of Greece and the fleet anchored near the Persian camp. The Greeks watched the Persians from the surrounding hills. After a few days, part of the Persian force, includ-

ing the cavalry, boarded its ships and set sail for the Bay of Phalerum. This force planned to attack Athens from the southwest. The main Persian force of about 20,000 men remained facing the Greeks on the plain of Marathon.

The Greeks had a force of 10,000 Athenians and 1,000 Plataeans. They sent Pheidippides, their swiftest runner, to bring help from Sparta—about 150 miles away. But the Spartan army was delayed because of religious observances and did not arrive until after the battle. The Athenian general Miltiades attacked the Persians with a running charge. The Persian bowmen fired a great shower of arrows, but the speed and heavy armor of the Greeks enabled them to reach the Persians with small losses. When the two armies came to grips, the superior weapons and bodily strength of the Greeks were decisive. The Greeks drove the Persians to their ships. The Persians lost 6,400 men, but the Athenians lost only 192. The Greek dead were buried under a mound of earth which may still be seen on the battlefield at Marathon.

As the fleet sailed away, Miltiades feared that the ships would attack Athens by sea. He was afraid that the city might surrender without knowing of the victory at Marathon. According to legend, he sent Pheidippides to carry news of the victory to Athens. Pheidippides, weary from his record journey to Sparta and back, raced the 25 miles to Athens. He reached the city and gasped out, "Rejoice, we conquer," then fell to the ground, dead.

The word *marathon* is now often used to refer to a long-distance foot race of slightly more than 26 miles. This foot race is one of the sporting events at Olympic Games today (see OLYMPIC GAMES). *Marathon* also refers to any other long-distance race.

RICHARD N. FRYE

MARBLE, *MAHR b'l,* is any limestone that is hard enough to take polish. It is used for buildings, interiors, and statues. The finest marble is white, and is called statuary marble. All marble is composed of crystals of the minerals *calcite* or *dolomite,* which when pure are perfectly white. Colored marbles result from the presence of other minerals or small amounts of staining matter mixed with the calcite or dolomite. Black, gray, pink, reddish, greenish, and many kinds of mottled and banded marbles are used in the designs of buildings and in monuments. The color of red marble is due to tiny particles of hematite from the presence of crystals. *Serpentine* marbles are principally green and yellowish-green silicates. *Fossiliferous* marbles are limestones which are full of fossil shells. On polished surfaces of such marbles, the cross sections of the shells can be seen through the rock.

Its Qualities. Marble, in the geological sense, is limestone that has been *metamorphosed* (changed) through the action of heat far below the earth's surface. Ordinary limestone is made up of fragments of shells or irregular grains of calcium carbonate. But in marble it has been changed to a mass of crystals grown firmly together. Metamorphism has made marble more uniform in hardness and grain throughout, so that it can be carved better than ordinary limestone. Metamorphism has also made marble harder, and has freed it from small cavities and pores. As a result, marble takes a higher polish, and sculptors and architects prefer to work with it. Ancient peoples made their finest buildings of either

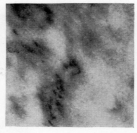

Florentine Gray Marble

Marble Walls give a striking, elegant look to the interior of buildings. Marble is also often used for table tops, left.

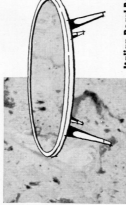

Italian Pearl Beige Marble

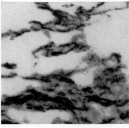

Pavanazzo Marble

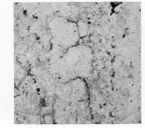

Travertine Marble

granite or marble. The Egyptians worked chiefly with granite. The Greeks were skillful in carving and design, and found marble more suited to their needs. Their temples and arcades at Athens and Corinth stand as monuments to their skill and the materials used. The ancient Greeks used Pentelic marble from Mount Pentelicus, north of Athens, for their finest work. The Parthenon, which stands on the Acropolis at Athens, is built of Pentelic marble. The Romans copied the forms of Greek sculpture and architecture, and also used marble with great skill.

The most famous quarries for any stone are the marble quarries at Carrara, Italy. Stone from them was used in Rome at the time of the Emperor Augustus. The finest varieties were discovered much later and were made famous by the great sculptors Leonardo da Vinci and Michelangelo.

In the United States, marble has been used for memorials since colonial days. Marble headstones for men who fell in the Revolutionary War have lasted longer than most other kinds. This stone has been a favorite in architecture from the time of the Erie Customhouse, erected in 1836, to the impressive building of the Supreme Court of the United States in Washington, D.C., completed in 1935.

Today, marble and granite are used less as building stone. Steel, aluminum, concrete, and artificial stone replace marble and granite in many large present-day buildings. White marble has lost much of its popularity, but colored or textured varieties are still in considerable demand.

The largest American marble quarry is in Vermont. In past years, this state often led others in the production of marble. Other important marble producing states are Tennessee, Missouri, Georgia, and Alabama. One of the largest blocks of marble ever quarried came from Vermont. This block weighed 93 tons. It was used for *The Covered Wagon*, a carving on the Oregon Capitol in Salem, Ore. (see OREGON [picture]). ERNEST E. WAHLSTROM

Related Articles in WORLD BOOK include:

Building Stone	Onyx
Carbonate	Quarrying
Dolomite	Rosso Antico
Limestone	Sculpture
Metamorphism	Vermont (color picture)

MARBLE, ALICE. See TENNIS (Famous Players).

MARBLE BONES. See OSTEOSCLEROSIS.

MARBLE CANYON NATIONAL MONUMENT is a scenic canyon area in northern Arizona. It extends for about 50 miles along the Colorado River. The Grand Canyon lies to the south. Marble Canyon's red sandstone and white limestone walls rise almost straight up from the river. They are about 3,000 feet high. The monument covers about 26,000 acres. The government established it in 1969. For location, see ARIZONA (political map).

GEORGE B. HARTZOG, JR.

MARBLES is a children's game played with little balls of many colors. It is a very old game. Egyptian and Roman children played with marbles before Christ was born. In the United States, the neighborhood marbles game is one of the signs of spring. The game is so popular that many cities and states have marble tournaments, with special referees and scorekeepers.

How to Play Marbles

Most American children play a game called *ringer*. Two to six children can play. A circle 10 feet across is marked on the ground. When two or more are playing, 13 marbles are placed on a cross marked at the center of the ring. Two lines, each about 9 inches long, form the cross. One marble is placed at the center and three each on the four parts of the cross. Each marble lies about 3 inches from the next one. Each

IMMY

GENUINE CARNELIAN

MOONSTONE

FIRST AMERICAN

RAINBOW

JAPANESE CAT'S EYE

SCRAP GLASS

MARINE

PEPPERMINT STRIPE

CAT'S EYE

Harold M. Lambert; Berry Pink Industries, Inc.

Marble Players gather around marble rings at the first sign of spring, left, and shouts of "Knuckle down!" and "No hunchin'!" fill the air. Ringer, one of the most popular marble games, is played on a circle 10 feet in diameter, above. Boys today favor Rainbows and Japanese Cat's Eyes among the many kinds of marbles on the market, below.

Lag line

Pitch line

10-Foot
Diameter

player uses a larger marble, the shooter, to knock, or "shoot," the small marbles out of the ring. Some boys and girls call their shooters *taws, glassies,* or *moonies*. The marbles in the ring, or object marbles, are called *mibs, miggs, ducks, commies,* or *hoodles*. The player who shoots the most marbles out of the ring wins the game.

Players start the first game by *lagging* for turns. They toss or shoot their shooters from a *pitch line* drawn outside the circle, with its center touching the circle. On the opposite side of the circle, also with its center touching the circle, is a *lag line*. The player whose shooter comes closest to the lag line plays first, and others follow in order of the nearness of their shooters to the line. In the games that follow, the winner of the game before plays first, and all others lag for their shooting turn.

All shots except the lag are made in a position called *knuckling down*. One knuckle of the hand must touch

---

TERMS USED WHEN TALKING ABOUT MARBLES

Knuckling Down is a position in which one knuckle must touch the ground until the shooter has left the hand.

Lofting, a difficult shot, occurs when a player shoots in an arc through the air to hit a marble.

Marbles are the object marbles only. They can also be called *mibs, miggs, ducks, commies,* or *hoodles*.

Miss occurs when a player fails to knock a marble from the ring on a shot.

Roundsters, or *circling,* is the act of selecting the best location outside the ring for knuckling down.

Shooter is the attacking marble. It also can be called a *taw,* a *glassy,* or a *moony*.

Shot is the act of snapping the shooter at a marble by a quick extension of the thumb.

TERMS USED WHEN TALKING ABOUT MARBLES

Bowling occurs when a player rolls a shot on the ground.

Edgers are marbles near the edge of the ring.

For Fair means playing for the fun of the game. After each game, the marbles are returned to their owners.

For Keeps occurs when each player keeps the marbles that he shoots out of the ring.

Histing occurs when a player raises his hand from the ground when shooting.

Hit occurs when a player knocks a marble out of the ring on a shot.

Hunching occurs when a player moves his hand forward across the ring line when shooting from the ring line, or when his hand advances from the spot where the shooter stopped, when shooting inside the ring.

the ground until the shooter marble has left the hand. *Histing* (raising the hand from the ground) and *hunching* (moving the hand forward) are forbidden. The player holds the shooter between his forefinger and thumb, and shoots it out with his thumb.

A player starts his turn from any spot outside of the ring. If he knocks an object marble out of the ring, he may shoot again from the spot where the shooter has come to rest. If the shooter also leaves the ring, the player takes *roundsters*. That is, he may shoot from any position on, or outside of, the ring line. In case the shooter slips from the player's hand and does not move more than 10 inches, the player calls "slips." He may then shoot again. Each player's turn continues until he misses the marbles with his shooter. He then picks up his shooter and waits for his next turn. He starts every new turn by taking roundsters.

The player who first shoots seven marbles out of the ring wins. When the seventh marble is shot from the ring, the shooter marble must also leave the ring. If it does not, the object marble is put back on the cross lines for the next player. Histing, hunching, smoothing the ground, or removing pebbles and other obstacles are penalized by loss of one shot.

Any player who changes shooters during the game must leave the game. Any player who walks across the ring must give up one of the marbles he has won. A player who talks with a coach during play gives up all the marbles he has won up to that point. Marbles given up are put back on the cross lines. In case of a tie score, the winners play another game. Sometimes, boys like to play marbles *for keeps*. Each keeps the marbles he shoots from the ring. But often the game is played *for fair*, and the marbles are returned to their owners.

Composition of Marbles. The ordinary marble is made of glass. A pigment is often inserted to color the marbles. Most of these marbles come from West Virginia, where plants in Clarksburg and St. Marys manufacture millions every year. *Aggies*, marbles made of agate, a fine-grained variety of quartz, are made in Idar-Oberstein, Germany. Germany also supplies marbles made from limestone. At one time, many marbles in the United States were composed of painted and glazed clay. Many people collect marbles as a hobby.

Marble Tournaments. The National Youth Activities Department of the Veterans of Foreign Wars holds an annual national marble tournament. Over 200,000 boys and girls take part. The youths advance through elimination contests on state and regional levels to the national meet. An organization such as the Young Men's Christian Association may sponsor a local meet, and then send the champion through the later stages of the tournament.

CARL A. TROESTER, JR.

MARBURY V. MADISON marked the first time the U.S. Supreme Court declared a federal law unconstitutional. This 1803 case is one of the most important decisions in history. It established the supremacy of the Constitution over laws passed by Congress and the right of the court to review the constitutionality of legislation.

In 1801, President John Adams appointed William Marbury justice of the peace in the District of Columbia. But Adams' term ended before Marbury took office, and James Madison, the new secretary of state, withheld the appointment. Marbury asked the Supreme Court, under Section 13 of the Judiciary Act of 1789, to force Madison to grant the appointment. But the court refused to rule on the appointment because Section 13 gave the Supreme Court powers not provided by the Constitution and, therefore, the court declared Section 13 unconstitutional.

STANLEY I. KUTLER

See also JEFFERSON, THOMAS (The Courts).

MARCEL. See HAIRDRESSING.

MARCEL, GABRIEL (1889-   ), is a French philosopher. He is an unsystematic thinker who has presented his philosophy for the most part in three philosophical diaries: *Metaphysical Journals* (1927), *Being and Having* (1935), and *Presence and Immortality* (1959). His philosophy consists of reflections on concrete human experiences such as love and fidelity. He believes that human experience can be understood only by directly participating in it. Therefore, he attempts not merely to observe, but to relive these experiences in the course of his reflections. Marcel's other works include *Homo Viator* (1944), an analysis of hope; and *Man Against Society* (1951), an examination of the effects of a technological society on the human personality.

Marcel was born in Paris. He became a Roman Catholic at 39, and is often classified as a Christian existentialist (see EXISTENTIALISM).

IVAN SOLL

MARCELLUS is the name of two popes of the Roman Catholic Church whose reigns were brief.

Saint Marcellus I governed the church in 308 and 309. Little is known about his life, except that he divided the parishes of Rome into seven regions, each with its own burial places.

Marcellus II (1501-1555) governed the church until he died, 22 days after his election. As a cardinal, he served as one of the reform leaders in the court of Pope Paul III, who ruled from 1534 to 1549. He was one of Paul's three legates to the first session of the Council of Trent in 1545. Marcellus pledged himself to reconvene the Council of Trent to finish its work of reform and definition of doctrine, but he died before this could be done.

THOMAS P. NEILL AND FULTON J. SHEEN

MARCH is a highly rhythmic piece of music first used by military bands to accompany marching. The march usually has one dominant tune repeated over and over with other tunes coming in between. The tempo of military marches varies with the occasion. In the U.S. Army, soldiers march about 120 steps a minute. This march is called *quick time*. A *double-time* march is about 180 steps a minute. In the British Army, soldiers march about 75 steps a minute to a slow march, and about 108 steps a minute to a quick march. People often call a quick march *quickstep*.

One of the most famous composers of march music was John Philip Sousa. His works include "The Stars and Stripes Forever," "The Washington Post," and "Semper Fidelis." Sir Edward Elgar wrote the well-known *Pomp and Circumstance*, a set of six military marches, in honor of the coronation of Edward VII.

Composers have used the march as an art form in operas and oratorios. Famous marches occur in Verdi's opera *Aida* and Mozart's *Marriage of Figaro*. The march from Handel's *Scipio* became the parade march of the British Grenadier Guards.

See also BAND; ELGAR, SIR EDWARD; SOUSA, JOHN P.

MARCH

MARCH is the third month of the year. It was the first month on the ancient Roman calendar, and was called *Martius*. When Julius Caesar revised the calendar, he moved the beginning of the year from March to January. March then became the third month. March has always had 31 days. Its name honors Mars, the Roman god of war.

March brings in spring and ends the winter. Spring in the northern half of the world begins with the *vernal equinox*, which almost always occurs on March 21. On this day, the sun rises directly in the east and sets directly in the west, so that the length of the day is exactly equal to the length of the night. March can be both wintry and springlike. Blustery, windy days occur as frequently as mild, sunny days.

In the Northern Hemisphere, many animals and plants awaken, or come to life again, during March. Sap flows in the trees, and green buds begin to appear. The first pussy willows and wild flowers can be found in the woods. Most frogs lay their eggs. Hibernating animals, such as bears, chipmunks, and woodchucks, leave their winter sleeping places. Wild geese and ducks begin their northward flights. In March, people begin to look for the first robin as a sign that spring has really come. Early songbirds appear.

Special Days. March has no national holidays, but there are several important state and religious holidays. Nebraskans celebrate the admission of their state to the Union on March 1. Texas celebrates March 2 as the anniversary of its independence from Mexico. On March 4, the people of Pennsylvania commemorate the anniversary of Penn's Charter. The Irish celebrate March 17 as the feast day of St. Patrick. In Maryland, March 25 is set apart for a celebration of the arrival of the first Maryland colonists in 1634. The Jewish festival of Purim usually occurs in March. It is held on the day corresponding to the 14th day of Adar on the Hebrew calendar.

IMPORTANT MARCH EVENTS

1 Ohio became the 17th state, 1803.
— William Dean Howells, American novelist, born 1837.
— Augustus Saint-Gaudens, American sculptor, born 1848.

2 Nebraska became the 37th state, 1867.
— De Witt Clinton, American statesman, born 1769.
— Sam Houston, American political leader, born 1793.
— Bedřich Smetana, Bohemian composer, born 1824.
— Carl Schurz, American political leader, born 1829.
— Texas declared its independence from Mexico, 1836.
— Pope Pius XII born 1876.

3 Missouri Compromise passed, 1820.
— Kurt Weill, German composer, born 1900.
— George Pullman, American inventor and business-man, born 1831.
— Florida became the 27th state, 1845.
— Inventor Alexander Graham Bell born 1847.

4 William Penn received grant of Pennsylvania, 1681.
— Russia signed the Treaty of Brest-Litovsk, 1918.
— The new U.S. Constitution went into effect, 1789. This date was used as Inauguration Day until 1937.
— Vermont became the 14th state, 1791.
— Heitor Villa-Lobos, Brazilian composer, born 1887.
— The Hall of Fame was founded, 1900.
— Joseph Stalin, Russian dictator, died 1953.

5 Gerhardus Mercator, Flemish geographer, born 1512.
— Knute Rockne, American football coach, born 1888.

6 Michelangelo, the most famous artist of the Italian Renaissance, born 1475.
— British soldiers fired on a mob in the Boston Massacre, 1770.
— Elizabeth Barrett Browning, English poet, born 1806.
— Philip H. Sheridan, Union cavalry general, born 1831.
— James Ives, American painter and lithographer, born 1824.
— Santa Anna captured the Alamo, 1836.

7 Sir John Herschel, English astronomer, born 1792.
— Luther Burbank, American horticulturist, born 1849.
— Ring Lardner, American humorist, born 1885.
— Heitor Villa-Lobos ...

7 Sir John Herschel, English astronomer, born 1792.
— Luther Burbank, American horticulturist, born 1849.

8 Alexander Graham Bell patented the telephone, 1876.
— Oliver Wendell Holmes, Jr., born 1841.

9 Amerigo Vespucci, Italian explorer, born 1451.
— Leland Stanford, American business leader, born 1824.

9 The *Merrimack* fought the *Monitor*, 1862.
— Ulysses S. Grant commissioned as commander-in-chief of the Union armies, 1864.

10 Barry Fitzgerald, Irish-born actor; born 1888.

11 Arthur Honegger, French composer, born 1892.

12 Canadian politician William Mackenzie born 1795.
— Manufacturer Clement Studebaker born 1831.
— Adolph S. Ochs, American newspaper publisher, born 1858.
— Gabriele d'Annunzio, Italian poet, born 1863.
— Juliette Low founded the Girl Scout movement in America, 1912.

13 Joseph Priestley, English chemist and clergyman, born 1733.
— First transatlantic radio broadcast, 1925.
— President Harry S. Truman announced the Truman Doctrine, 1947.

14 Johann Wyss, Swiss author, born 1781.
— Eli Whitney patented the cotton gin, 1794.
— Johann Strauss, Austrian composer, born 1804.
— Paul Ehrlich, German biochemist, born 1854.
— Albert Einstein, German-born scientist, born 1879.

15 Julius Caesar assassinated, 44 B.C.
— Andrew Jackson, seventh President of the United States, born in Waxhaw settlement, Lancaster County, S.C., 1767.
— Maine became the 23rd state, 1820.
— American Legion founded, 1919.

16 James Madison, fourth President of the United States, born at Port Conway, King George County, Va., 1751.
— Georg S. Ohm, German physicist who studied electric currents, born 1787.
— United States Military Academy founded at West Point, N.Y., 1802.

16-17 Ferdinand Magellan discovered the Philippines, 1521.

JACKSON

MADISON

CLEVELAND

Popular Beliefs. There are many superstitions about March. We often hear that "March comes in like a lion and goes out like a lamb." This means that the first day of March is often stormy, and the last day is mild and warm. Another saying is, "April borrowed from March three days, and they were ill." This refers to the first three days of April, which are generally rough and blustery like March. A third saying calls the first three days of March "blind days" because they are "unlucky." If rain falls on these days, farmers supposedly will have poor harvests. Some farmers are so superstitious about the three "unlucky" days that they will not plant seed until March 4.

March Symbols. The flower for March is the violet. The birthstones are the bloodstone (a variety of chalcedony) and the aquamarine.

GRACE HUMPHREY

Related Articles in WORLD BOOK include:

Aquamarine	Chalcedony	Mars	St. Patrick's	Spring
Calendar	Equinox	Purim	Day	Violet

Quotations

The stormy March has come at last,
With wind, and cloud, and changing skies;
I hear the rushing of the blast
That through the snowy valley flies.

William Cullen Bryant

I wonder if the sap is stirring yet,
If wintry birds are dreaming of a mate,
If frozen snowdrops feel as yet the sun,
And crocus fires are kindling one by one.

Christina Rossetti

And the Spring arose on the garden fair,
Like the Spirit of Love felt everywhere;
And each flower and herb on Earth's dark breast
Rose from the dreams of its wintry rest.

Percy B. Shelley

The year's at the spring
And day's at the morn,
God's in His Heaven—
All's right with the world.

Robert Browning

TYLER

IMPORTANT MARCH EVENTS

17 St. Patrick's Day.
—British evacuated Boston, 1776.
—Chief Justice Roger B. Taney born 1777.
—Jim Bridger, American frontier scout, born 1804.
—Kate Greenaway, English illustrator, born 1846.
—Bobby Jones, American golf champion, born 1902.

18 John C. Calhoun, American statesman, born 1782.
—Grover Cleveland, 22nd and 24th President of the United States, born in Caldwell, N.J., 1837.
—Nicholas Rimsky-Korsakov, Russian composer, born 1844.
—Rudolf Diesel, German inventor, born 1858.
—British statesman Neville Chamberlain born 1869.

19 Missionary and explorer David Livingstone born 1813.
—Political leader William Jennings Bryan born 1860.
—Ballet producer Sergei Diaghilev born 1872.
—Joseph Stilwell, American general, born 1883.

20 Henrik Ibsen, Norwegian poet and dramatist, born 1828.
—Charles W. Eliot, American educator, born 1834.
—Lauritz Melchior, Danish-American tenor, born 1890.

21 Johann Sebastian Bach, German composer, born 1685.
—Benito Juárez, Mexican political leader, born 1806.
—Modest Mussorgsky, Russian composer, born 1839.

22 Anthony Vandyke, Flemish painter, born 1599.
—Randolph Caldecott, English illustrator, born 1846.
—Robert Millikan, American physicist, born 1868.
—Arthur Vandenberg, U.S. political leader, born 1884.

23 Patrick Henry declared "Give me liberty, or give me death!" 1775.
—Roger Martin du Gard, French novelist and Nobel prize-winner for literature, born 1881.

24 William Morris, English poet and artist, born 1834.
—Andrew Mellon, American financier, born 1855.
—George Sisler, American baseball player, born 1893.

25 Lord Baltimore's colonists landed in Maryland, 1634.
—British Parliament abolished slave trade, 1807.
—Arturo Toscanini, Italian conductor, born 1867.
—Gutzon Borglum, American sculptor, born 1871.

25 Béla Bartók, Hungarian composer, born 1881.

26 A. E. Housman, English poet, born 1859.
—Robert Frost, American poet, born 1874.
—James Conant, American chemist and educator, born 1893.

27 Louis XVII of France born 1785.
—George Washington signed the act that created the United States Navy, 1794.
—Lithographer Nathaniel Currier born 1813.
—Wilhelm Roentgen, German physicist who discovered X rays, born 1845.

28 Pierre Laplace, French astronomer and mathematician, born 1749.
—Aristide Briand, French statesman, born 1862.

29 John Tyler, 10th President of the United States, born at Greenways Estate, Charles City County, Va., 1790.
—Parliament passed the British North America Act, 1867.
—Cy Young, American baseball player, born 1867.

30 Francisco Goya, Spanish painter, born 1746.
—Treaty of Paris ended the Crimean War, 1856.
—United States purchased Alaska from Russia, 1867.
—Amendment 15 to the U.S. Constitution, stating that a person cannot be denied the ballot because of race or color, proclaimed, 1870.
—Jo Davidson, American sculptor, born 1883.
—Albert Einstein announced revised Unified Field Theory, 1953.

31 René Descartes, French philosopher-scientist, born 1596.
—Joseph Haydn, Austrian composer, born 1732.
—Edward FitzGerald, English translator of the *Rubáiyát* of Omar Khayyám, born 1809.
—Commodore Matthew C. Perry made the first treaty between the United States and Japan, 1854.
—Jack Johnson, American boxer, born 1878.
—United States took possession of the Virgin Islands by purchase from Denmark, 1917.
—Daylight Saving Time went into effect in the United States, 1918.
—Civilian Conservation Corps created, 1933.
—Newfoundland became the 10th province of Canada, 1949.

MARCH, PEYTON CONWAY

MARCH, PEYTON CONWAY (1864-1955), was chief of staff of the United States Army during World War I. He directed the operations that landed about 2 million American troops in France. March has been called the father of the modern U.S. Army. He combined the Regular Army, the National Guard, and the National Army divisions into a single force. He also reorganized the War Department, and built a small, well-organized army around a core of professional soldiers. March believed that a small corps of trained officers could build a large, powerful army in time of emergency.

March was born in Easton, Pa. He graduated from the United States Military Academy (West Point) in 1888, and fought in the Spanish-American War. March retired from active service in the Army in 1921. He wrote an account of his World War I experiences, *The Nation at War* (1932).

MAURICE MATLOFF

MARCH HARE. See HARE.

MARCH OF DIMES. See NATIONAL FOUNDATION.

MARCIANO, ROCKY (1923-1969), was the world heavyweight boxing champion from 1952 to 1956. He retired in 1956 after winning all of his 49 professional fights. Marciano won the title on Sept. 23, 1952, by knocking out Jersey Joe Walcott in the 13th round in Philadelphia. Eight months later, in his first title defense, Marciano knocked out Walcott in the first round. Marciano then successfully defended his title five more times. Marciano is generally considered one of the hardest punchers in boxing history. His victories include 43 knockouts, with 11 coming in the first round. In 1951, Marciano ended the comeback of former world champion Joe Louis by knocking him out in the 8th round.

Marciano was born Rocco Marchegiano in Brockton, Mass. He turned professional in 1948. HERMAN WEISKOPF

MARCO POLO. See POLO, Marco.

MARCONI, *mahr KOH nee,* **GUGLIELMO** (1874-1937), an Italian inventor and electrical engineer, won recognition for his work in developing *wireless telegraphy,* or radio. This led to present-day radio broadcasting. He produced a practical wireless telegraph system in 1895 from basic discoveries that had previously been made in wireless telegraphy (see Radio [History]). He produced the first transatlantic wireless signal in history on Dec. 12, 1901, and patented the horizontal directional aerial in 1905. He shared the 1909 Nobel prize in physics with Ferdinand Braun for their development of wireless telegraphy. Braun, working independently of Marconi, developed a cathode-ray tube. Marconi invented the beam system of wireless for long-distance communication.

Early Life. Marconi was born on April 25, 1874, in Bologna, Italy. His father was a wealthy Italian, his mother Irish. He grew up as a delicate and studious child. He read widely as a boy, in the excellent scientific library in the Marconi home, and became interested in the study of electromagnetic waves. He was educated by tutors, and later studied at the University of Bologna.

First Experiments. In 1894, Marconi set up apparatus at his father's estate. With this apparatus, he sent and received signals by electrical waves over a longer distance than had ever been done before. But the Italian government took no interest in the early stages of his work. Marconi went to England in 1896 to seek capital for a wireless telegraph company. He applied for and received from the British government the first wireless patent, the famous No. 7777. The patent was based in

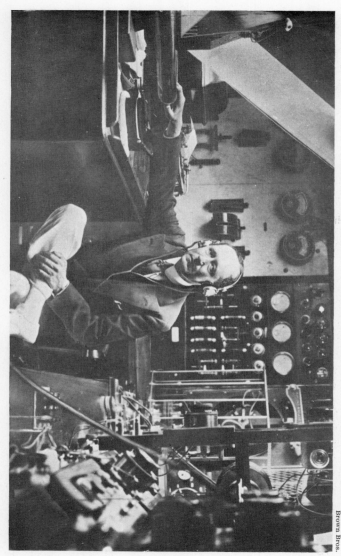

Guglielmo Marconi centered his life around wireless telegraphy. He outfitted his yacht, the *Elettra,* with a complete wireless laboratory. He experimented in this "floating laboratory," sending and receiving messages while crossing the Atlantic.

Brown Bros.

part on the theory that the distance of communication increases rapidly as the height of aerials is increased.

Marconi formed the first wireless company in 1897. The company installed wireless sets in lighthouses along the English coast. In March, 1899, Marconi sent the first wireless telegraph message across the English Channel, a distance of 85 miles.

The value of the wireless for emergencies at sea was shown on April 28, 1899. Heavy seas had pounded the Goodwin Sands lightship off the English coast, and parts of the deckhouses had been swept away. The vessel communicated with a nearby station by wireless, and help arrived at the ship in time to prevent loss of life.

The First Transatlantic Signal. Marconi decided to try to send signals across the Atlantic in 1901. He built a sending station at Poldhu, Cornwall, England. He sailed to Newfoundland and set up receiving equipment at St. John's. The first signal sent, the letter "S," came through as scheduled, though exceedingly faint, on Dec. 12, 1901. See KITE (Other Uses).

Marconi showed the next year that wireless signals can be received over greater distances at night than in the day. While aboard the steamship *Philadelphia* bound for the United States, Marconi received signals sent from a distance of 2,099 miles.

Marconi lost his right eye in an automobile accident in 1912. But he continued to work. He volunteered for active service when Italy entered World War I, and became commander of the Italian wireless service. He began experimenting with very short waves while he was in the wireless service.

Marconi's work brought him honors from governments throughout the world. The Italian government made him a senator of the kingdom of Italy for life in 1909. He received the hereditary title of *marchese* (marquis) in 1929.   W. RUPERT MACLAURIN

MARCOS, FERDINAND (1917-), became president of the Philippines in 1965. In 1969, he became the first president to win election to a second term. Marcos served in the Philippine House of Representatives from 1949 to 1959. He was elected to the Senate in 1959, and later became president of the Senate.

Marcos was born in Sarrat. While a law student at the University of the Philippines, Marcos was accused, tried, and convicted of murdering a man who had defeated his father in a local election. But Marcos argued his own case in an appeal to the Supreme Court and won an acquittal. During World War II, he fought with the Filipino-American forces on Bataan Peninsula, and later he fought as a guerrilla officer. The United States awarded Marcos the Distinguished Service Cross and the Silver Star.   JEAN GROSSHOLTZ

See also ASIA (picture: Leaders of Asia).

MARCUS, SIEGFRIED. See GASOLINE ENGINE (Development of the Gasoline Engine).

MARCUS AURELIUS, *aw REE lih us* (A.D. 121-180), was a Roman emperor devoted to Stoic philosophy. He defended the empire against the first heavy barbarian attacks from outside. He is perhaps the best known of all the Roman emperors because of his *Meditations*, a diary of philosophical reflections. The *Meditations* contain Marcus' own rules for living and for accepting the difficulties of life. They are considered among the most readable of all Stoic writings.

Marcus was born in Rome to a noble family. He was adopted by Antoninus Pius, who later became emperor. Marcus succeeded Antoninus in 161. Marcus' soldiers won victories in Parthia, but they brought a plague back to Rome that spread across the empire. At the height of the plague, barbarian tribes overran the northern frontiers. Marcus spent most of his later years fighting barbarians along the Danube and Rhine rivers. He died in Vienna. Carvings on a column in Rome illustrate some of his campaigns.   RAMSAY MACMULLEN

MARCUS ISLAND is a low, isolated island in the northwest Pacific. It belongs to Japan. Marcus Island lies 1,160 miles southeast of Tokyo, and 816 miles northeast of Saipan Island. It covers 740 acres. It was administered by the United States from after World War II until 1968, when it was returned to Japan. The island is uninhabited.

MARCY, WILLIAM L. See JACKSON, ANDREW (The Spoils System); PIERCE, FRANKLIN (table: Pierce's Cabinet); POLK, JAMES KNOX (table: Polk's Cabinet).

MARDAL FALLS is a waterfall in western Norway, about 100 miles southwest of Trondheim. It lies on the Akers River, near the head of the Sogne Fiord. Its waters drop 650 feet, making it one of the highest waterfalls in Europe.

MARDI GRAS, *MAHR dee GRAH,* is a gay, colorful celebration held on Shrove Tuesday, the day before Lent begins. The date of Mardi Gras depends on the date of Easter. The celebration takes place at the end of a long carnival season which begins on January 6, or Twelfth Night (see TWELFTH NIGHT). It is celebrated in many Roman Catholic countries and other communities. *Mardi Gras* is a French term meaning *fat Tuesday.* The term arose from the custom of parading a fat ox through the streets of Paris on Shrove Tuesday.

French colonists introduced Mardi Gras into America in 1766. The custom became popular in New Orleans, La., and spread throughout the Southern States. Mardi Gras is a legal holiday in Alabama, Florida, and in eight *parishes* (counties) of Louisiana. The New Orleans celebration is the most famous. But Biloxi, Miss., and Mobile, Ala., also celebrate Mardi Gras.

Mardi Gras in New Orleans attracts tourists from everywhere. Street parades begin about two weeks before Mardi Gras Day. Societies called *Krewes* organize and pay for the parades and other festivities. The best-known Krewes are Comus, the oldest, founded in 1857, and Rex, founded in 1872. During the carnival season, the Krewes give balls and private parties. Their members parade in the streets in masks and fancy dress. A parade of beautiful floats and marching bands climaxes the carnival on Tuesday, Mardi Gras Day. Each year, the festivities carry out a specific theme.

Rex, King of Carnival, reigns for the day. He is the only one who parades unmasked. When his parade passes the reviewing stand, the King and Queen of Carnival exchange toasts in front of it. After the parade, the Krewes hold fancy-dress balls. Rex and Comus, god of mirth, preside over the two grandest balls.

The Mardi Gras celebration goes back to an ancient Roman custom of merrymaking before a period of fast. In Germany it is called *Fasnacht,* and in England it is called *Pancake Day.*   ELIZABETH HOUGH SECHRIST

See also LOUISIANA (picture); SHROVE TUESDAY.

MARDONIUS

MARDONIUS. See XERXES (I).

MARDUK, *MAHR dook,* was the chief god of the ancient Babylonians. He was originally a god of only the city of Babylon. But when the Dynasty of Babylon came to power in Mesopotamia in about 2000 B.C., Marduk became the most important god of the area. The largest Babylonian temple honored him. Marduk's temple and its buildings covered more than 60 acres. His worshipers called him the "great lord, the lord of heaven and earth." His great power was said to lie in his wisdom, which he used in governing the good people of the earth, in supporting the good people, and in punishing the wicked.

I. J. GELB

MARE. See HORSE (Life History).

MARE ISLAND lies at the east end of San Pablo Bay, 25 miles northeast of San Francisco, Calif. It is located at Vallejo, Calif., about 25 miles northeast of San Francisco. The 1,400-acre shipyard is part of the 12th Naval District. The shipyard repairs, overhauls, and converts ships of all types, and builds nuclear-powered submarines. During World War II, Mare Island Naval Shipyard built or repaired 1,598 ships and boats.

The shipyard was established in 1854 as the home port of the 12 ships which at that time made up the entire Pacific Fleet of the U.S. Navy.

JOHN A. OUDINE

MARE ISLAND NAVAL SHIPYARD is the largest and oldest U.S. naval yard on the West Coast. It is located at Vallejo, Calif., about 25 miles northeast of San Francisco. The 1,400-acre shipyard is part of the 12th Naval District. The shipyard repairs, overhauls, and converts ships of all types, and builds nuclear-powered submarines. During World War II, Mare Island Naval Shipyard built or repaired 1,598 ships and boats. connects Mare Island with the city of Vallejo, across a half-mile-wide strait. The Mare Island Naval Shipyard covers most of the island.

MARENGO, BATTLE OF, was the most important battle of Napoleon's second Italian campaign. Although outnumbered, his forces decisively defeated the Austrians at Marengo, near Alessandria, on the Lombardy Plains, on June 14, 1800.

At first, the battle went against the French. Baron Michael von Melas, the Austrian general, felt so sure of victory that he sent a courier to Vienna with news of the triumph. But Napoleon fought stubbornly.

Two generals helped Napoleon save the day for France. Louis Desaix, who was killed during the fighting, brought 5,000 reinforcements. François Étienne Kellermann led a brilliant cavalry charge that proved to be a decisive point in the battle.

Napoleon's troops suffered heavy losses, about 3,500 dead and the same number wounded. Austrian losses totaled about 3,000 prisoners and 7,000 dead or wounded. The victory gave France undisputed control of Milan, Genoa, and Piedmont. It also made Napoleon a popular hero in France.

ROBERT B. HOLTMAN

See also NAPOLEON I (Wars Against Austria).

MARGARET, QUEEN. See DENMARK (A Great Power).

MARGARINE, *MAHR juh reen,* is a manufactured mixture of vegetable fats and oils. It can be produced more cheaply than butter, and is often used as a substitute. When vitamin A is added, margarine has about the same food value as butter (see BUTTER).

Margarine is made by mixing water and salt with vegetable fats and oils such as those obtained from cotton seed, coconuts, soybeans, peanuts, and corn. The mixture is then churned with pasteurized skimmed milk. Most margarine is a creamy yellow color. But a few states prohibit the sale of colored margarine. In such states, it is bleached and a capsule of yellow coloring is included in each package. Butter manufacturers, too, usually add color to obtain a bright yellow product.

The first margarine was called "oleomargarine." It developed from a contest which Napoleon III conducted to get a satisfactory butter substitute during the Franco-Prussian War of 1870. A French chemist, Hippolyte Mege-Mouries, made this oleomargarine by churning beef oleo oil, milk, water, and *annatto* (a vegetable dye) together.

Margarine was introduced to the United States in 1874. Farmers and dairymen throughout the nation protested that margarine would ruin the butter market. In 1886, Congress began taxing margarine to restrict the use of this butter substitute. Manufacturers were required to pay a tax of 10 cents a pound on margarine sold in its natural color; if bleached, one fourth of a cent a pound. Manufacturers also had to pay a license fee of $600. Wholesalers of colored margarine had to pay $480; wholesalers of uncolored margarine, $200. A license fee of $48 for colored, and $6 for uncolored margarine was required of retail dealers. These federal taxes on margarine were repealed in 1950. But another federal law was passed requiring retailers to sell margarine in packages not exceeding one pound. The packages must be labeled "oleomargarine" or "margarine." The ingredients must also be listed. The federal government can impose fines up to $5,000 a day on persons who sell margarine as butter. Restaurants and boarding houses using colored margarine must clearly identify it or serve it in triangular cuts. Several states still tax the manufacture and sale of margarine. Such states as Connecticut, Delaware, and Illinois lifted the ban on the sale of colored margarine in 1951. The rivalry between margarine and butter producers has helped to set high standards for both products.

LEONE RUTLEDGE CARROLL

MARGARITA. See VENEZUELA (Location, Size, and Surface Features; color map).

MARGAY, *MAHR gay,* is a wildcat that lives in Central and South America from northern Mexico to Bolivia and Brazil. Its reddish or grayish fur is thickly marked with black spots and streaks. Its tail is longer than the head and body. The margay is 2½ to 4 feet long and weighs 10 to 20 pounds. It closely resembles

The Margay of South America looks much like a domestic cat. This playful-looking margay is still a kitten, but it will soon reach an adult weight of 10 to 20 pounds.

Hollister

the *ocelot* (tiger cat) but is smaller, more slender, and has a longer tail. The name of the margay may have come from an Indian term for "little ocelot" or "small cat." Zoologists know little about its habits. It probably lives much like the ocelot (see OCELOT).

Scientific Classification. The margay belongs to the cat family, *Felidae.* It is classified as genus *Felis,* species *F. wiedii.*

ERNEST S. BOOTH

MARGE. See CARTOON (Leading Cartoonists).

MARGIN in a stock exchange refers to funds that a speculator deposits with his broker to protect the broker against loss. The deposit safeguards the broker, in case the speculator loses money after he has bought stocks. It must cover the difference between the selling price of the stocks and the amount the broker can borrow from a bank, plus an amount to cover possible losses that might result from stocks quickly changing prices. In the United States, the Federal Reserve System sets the amount of margin required. See also BUCKET SHOP.

MARGINAL LAND. See RENT.

MARGRAVE, *MAHR grayv,* is the English form of the German word *Markgraf* (count of the border). In the Carolingian Empire, the title of margrave was given the ruler of a frontier province called a *mark* or *march.*

MARIA. See MARS (Surface).

MARIA THERESA, *muh REE uh tuh REE suh* (1717-1780), was Holy Roman empress, queen of Hungary and Bohemia, and archduchess of Austria. She was an important figure in the affairs of Europe for 40 troubled years in the 1700's. She ranked as a wise and able ruler. With the aid of her brilliant foreign minister, Prince Kaunitz, she managed foreign affairs skillfully. Her economic reforms promoted the prosperity of her empire. She was the mother of 16 children. One of her daughters, the beautiful and tragic Marie Antoinette, became queen of France (see MARIE ANTOINETTE).

Maria Theresa of Austria, portrait by Martin Van Mytens, Brooks Memorial Art Gallery, Memphis, Tenn.

Maria Theresa of Austria

Maria Theresa was born in Vienna. Her father, Emperor Charles VI, was the last male Hapsburg heir. He issued a decree called a Pragmatic Sanction in 1713. By its terms, he made his daughter heir to his territories. The rulers of the principal states of Europe agreed to it, and promised not to attack Maria Theresa's lands (see PRAGMATIC SANCTION).

Charles VI died in 1740. Prussia, Spain, Bavaria, and France immediately attacked in the War of the Austrian Succession. They all claimed parts of Maria Theresa's territories in spite of their earlier promises. Maria Theresa fled to Pressburg, where she made a dramatic appeal to her Hungarian subjects. They rallied loyally to her defense. The war ended in 1748 with the Peace of Aix-la-Chapelle. By this treaty, Maria Theresa lost the rich province of Silesia to Frederick II of Prussia (see FREDERICK [II] of Prussia). The powers of Europe recognized her rights to her other possessions. Her husband, Francis Stephen, Duke of Lorraine, became Emperor as Francis I (see FRANCIS

[I], Holy Roman Emperor). But Maria Theresa kept control over most state affairs (see SUCCESSION WARS).

In 1756, while the queen was planning to avenge the loss of Silesia, Frederick II suddenly attacked again. The Seven Years' War followed. After much bloodshed, Maria Theresa was forced to give up all claims to Silesia (see SEVEN YEARS' WAR). Her husband died in 1765, and her eldest son succeeded him as Joseph II. Maria Theresa, however, allowed her son only limited powers at first. In 1772 she joined with Russia and Prussia in the first partition of Poland, taking Galicia and Ludomeria. Then she took Bucovina from Turkey in 1775. She died in Vienna.

ROBERT G.L. WAITE

MARIAN COLLEGE. See UNIVERSITIES AND COLLEGES (table).

MARIAN COLLEGE OF FOND DU LAC. See UNIVERSITIES AND COLLEGES (table).

MARIANA ISLANDS, *MAIR ih AN uh,* are formed by the summits of 15 volcanic mountains in the Pacific Ocean. They are the southern part of a submerged mountain range which extends 1,565 miles from Guam almost to Japan. The Marianas have an area of 396 square miles and a population of 136,986. Most of the people live on Guam, which has a population of 126,-000. The islands' total coastline is 220 miles long. For location, see PACIFIC ISLANDS (color map).

The 10 northern Marianas are rugged islands. Some of them have volcanoes that erupt periodically. Pagan, Agrihan, and Anatahan are the largest islands in this group. The limestone or reef rock terraces on volcanic slopes in the five southern Marianas show that they are older than the northern group. Guam is the largest of the southern islands. Other important islands are Rota, Saipan, and Tinian. Farmers raise food crops and make *copra* (the dried meat of coconuts). Natural resources include phosphate and manganese ore.

Ferdinand Magellan, the Portuguese navigator, discovered Guam and Rota in 1521. His sailors called them the *Islas de los Ladrones,* or *Islands of Thieves,* because the islanders helped themselves to articles on the ships after furnishing supplies of food and water. The islands received their present name from Spanish Jesuits who arrived in 1668. Spain governed the islands from 1668 to 1898. After the Spanish-American War, the United States kept Guam as a naval base. Spain sold the rest of the islands to Germany. Japan occupied Guam in 1941, but American armed forces recaptured the island in July, 1944, and built naval air bases on several of the islands. The Mariana Islands, except for Guam, are governed by the United States as part of the United Nations Trust Territory of the Pacific Islands.

EDWIN H. BRYAN, JR.

Related Articles in WORLD BOOK **include:**

Anatahan	Pacific Islands, Trust	World War II
Chamorro	Territory of the	(Island
Guam	Pagan	Rota	Saipan	Hopping)
		Tinian

MARIANA TRENCH. See PACIFIC OCEAN; DEEP.

MARIE ADÉLAÏDE. See LUXEMBOURG (History).

MARIE ANTOINETTE, *AN twah NET* (1755-1793), was the beautiful queen of France who died on the guillotine during the French Revolution. Her frivolity and plotting helped undermine the monarchy and start the revolution.

MARIE ANTOINETTE

The young queen was lively, witty, and extravagant. The stiff formalities of court life bored her, so she amused herself with such pleasures as fancy balls, theatricals, attending the horse races, and gambling. Marie lacked a good education and cared very little for serious affairs. She gave no heed to the nation's financial crisis. Marie did not hesitate to urge the dismissal of the able ministers of France whose efforts to reduce royal spending threatened her pleasures. Louis XVI gave her the château called the Petit Trianon, where the queen and her friends amused themselves (see VERSAILLES).

Marie became very unpopular, and was blamed for the corruption of the French court. She lavished money on court favorites, and paid no attention to France's financial crisis. False and vicious stories were told about her. It was even rumored that she was a spy for Austria. The haughty attitude people associated with her name is illustrated by a story. She once asked an official why the Parisians were angry. "Because they have no bread," was the reply. "Then let them eat cake," said the queen. The suffering people of Paris readily believed such stories, true or false.

Her Early Life.

Marie was born in Vienna. She was the youngest and favorite daughter of Emperor Francis I and Maria Theresa, rulers of the Holy Roman Empire. From childhood, Marie was brought up in the hope that she might one day be queen of France.

She married the French *dauphin* (crown prince) in 1770 at the age of 15. Four years later, the prince became King Louis XVI, and Marie became queen of France.

Marie Antoinette was a beautiful teenager when she became queen of France in 1774. She was executed less than 20 years later.

Marie Antoinette and Her Children in the Petit Trianon Park (detail) by Ulrich Wertmuller, Nationalmuseum, Stockholm

The Revolution.

Tragedy struck Marie twice in 1789. Her eldest son died, and the French Revolution started. Her weak-willed husband gradually lost control of the nation, but Marie faced danger courageously. She tried to stiffen King Louis' will, but only made people angrier by her stubborn opposition to the revolutionary changes.

The king, partly on her advice, assembled troops around Versailles twice in 1789. Both times violence followed, and royal authority became weaker. The second time, early in October, 1789, a hungry and desperate Parisian mob that included many women marched to Versailles, and forced the royal family to move to the Tuileries palace in Paris. From then on, Louis and Marie were virtual prisoners in Paris.

The rulers might have been able to rally the nation in support of a constitutional monarchy like that of England, had they followed the advice of moderate statesmen like the Comte de Mirabeau (see MIRABEAU, COMTE DE). Instead, Marie Antoinette plotted for military aid from the rulers of Europe, especially from her brother, Joseph II of Austria. She refused to make any concessions at all to the revolutionists.

Downfall of the Monarchy.

Finally, Marie influenced Louis to flee from Paris on the night of June 20, 1791. The royal family set out in disguise by carriage for the eastern frontier of France. But an alert patriot recognized the king from his picture on French paper money. The king and queen were halted at Varennes, and returned under guard to Paris. The flight made Frenchmen distrust their rulers even more. But Louis promised to accept a new constitution that limited his powers.

Marie now worked to get aid from abroad, and, when war with Austria and Prussia came in 1792, she passed military secrets on to the enemy. The people suspected

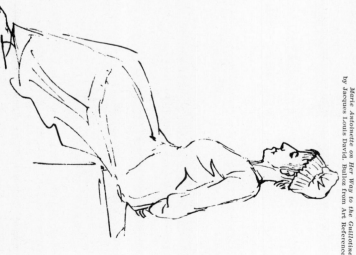

later, following the French Revolution. The strain of the revolution had aged her so that she resembled an old woman at her death.

Marie Antoinette on Her Way to the Guillotine by Jacques Louis David, Bulloz from Art Reference

such treason. On Aug. 10, 1792, they threw their rulers into prison. The king was suspended from office, and the monarchy was ended. Louis XVI died on the guillotine on Jan. 21, 1793. After bravely enduring terrible sufferings, Marie Antoinette, called Widow Capet by the revolutionists, was brought to trial on a charge of treason. She was executed on the guillotine on Oct. 16, 1793.

RAYMOND O. ROCKWOOD

Related Articles in WORLD BOOK include:

French Revolution   Louis (XVI)   Swiss Guards
Furniture (Louis XVI)   Maria Theresa

MARIE DE L'INCARNATION. See CANADIAN LITERATURE (Before 1760).

MARIE LOUISE (1791-1847) was the second wife of Napoleon Bonaparte and the daughter of Emperor Francis II of the Holy Roman Empire. She married Napoleon in 1810 after his divorce from Josephine. Napoleon and Marie Louise had a son in 1811 who became known as Napoleon II (see NAPOLEON II).

Marie Louise was not permitted to go with Napoleon when he was exiled. She and her son lived at Schönbrunn, near Vienna. She received the Italian duchies of Parma, Piacenza, and Guastalla in 1816, and governed them until her death. She was married twice after Napoleon died.

See also JOSEPHINE; NAPOLEON I.

MARIETTA, Ohio (pop. 16,847; alt. 600 ft.), the oldest town in Ohio, is an important manufacturing and trading center. The city lies on the north bank of the Ohio River at the mouth of the Muskingum River. For location, see OHIO (political map).

Marietta serves as a market for farm products of the Muskingum Valley. The chief manufactures include furniture, paints, safes, gasoline, lubricating oils, concrete products, alloys, phenol, and polystyrene.

Pioneers led by General Rufus Putnam founded Marietta in 1788. The city was named for Queen Marie Antoinette of France. Four Ohio governors and Vice-President Charles G. Dawes came from Marietta. The town has a mayor-council form of government, and is the seat of Washington County.

JAMES H. RODABAUGH

See also PUTNAM, RUFUS.

MARIETTA COLLEGE. See UNIVERSITIES AND COLLEGES (table).

Marie Louise was Napoleon's second wife. This painting by Franque shows her with her son, who became Napoleon II.

MARIGOLD is a hardy annual flower grown in Europe and America. Most marigolds stand 1 to 2 feet high and have deeply cut leaves on long stalks.

The attractive flowers are usually yellow or orange, sometimes reddish or brown. They have an odor which some people do not like. But scientists have developed some odorless marigolds. The *Aztec* and *French marigolds* originally grew wild in Mexico, but the French transplanted them. Marigolds can be raised from seed in ordinary soil. They should be planted about a foot apart. They usually bloom late in summer. The marsh marigold belongs to the crowfoot family.

Scientific Classification. Marigolds belong to the composite family, *Compositae*. The pot marigold is genus *Calendula*, species *C. officinalis*. The Aztec marigold is *Tagetes erecta*; the French, *T. patula*.   ALFRED G. HOTTES

See also FLOWER (color pictures; Flowers that Grow in Wet Places, Fall Garden Flowers).

The Aztec Marigold is an attractive marigold variety. It is a common garden flower of North America.

Marigolds are popular fall flowers. Some varieties, such as the one below, have yellow flowers that look like chrysanthemums.

MARIJUANA

MARIJUANA, MAR uh WAH nuh, is a drug made from the flower tops of hemp plants. The drug has no medical value. Marijuana, usually used in the form of cigarettes, generally produces a mild intoxication. Marijuana is also called hashish. The word assassin originated in South Africa as an adaptation of the xylophone.

Marijuana is classified as a narcotic drug under U.S. federal law. But it does not cause addiction (a physical and mental need) in the same way as such narcotic drugs as heroin and morphine. Marijuana users do not become physically dependent on it and crave it. However, its use carries other major dangers. A person with psychological problems may have intense emotional disturbances after taking marijuana. Or, a person may become reckless and begin taking heroin or morphine when he sees that he can do without marijuana for long periods without ill effects.

Some persons mistakenly believe that marijuana can improve the ability of musicians. Actually, the use of marijuana only makes a musician think he is playing better.

See also Drug Addiction; Hemp; Narcotic.

SOLOMON GARB

MARILLAC COLLEGE. See Universities and Colleges (table).

MARIMBA, muh RIM buh, is a percussion instrument similar to the xylophone. It is larger, and has a deeper and richer tone. It consists of wooden bars of different lengths with tuned resonators underneath, mounted on a large, tablelike frame. Each resonator (sound box) has a piece of bladder covering a hole in one end. The bladder vibrates, intensifying the sound and producing

The Mellow Tones of the Marimba come from the tubes below the wooden bars that the musician strikes with mallets.

J. C. Deagan, Inc.

a peculiar buzzing sound characteristic of the marimba. The marimba has a five-octave range. A player hits the wooden bars with drumsticks. Four performers can play the marimba at one time, each using a pair of drumsticks of varying lengths and sizes. The marimba is popular in Mexico, and in Central and South America. It originated in Mexico, and in Central and South America. It phone.

See also Xylophone; Guatemala (Recreation).

CHARLES B. RIGHTER

MARIN, DON FRANCISCO DE PAULA. See Hawaii (The Kingdom of Hawaii).

MARIN, MAH rin, JOHN (1870-1953), a leading American painter, became famous for his water-color landscapes. The Maine seacoast became his favorite subject. He painted in bold, brilliant splashes of color. His water colors range from fairly faithful nature studies to almost abstract color compositions. Late in life, he turned to painting in oils, and did colorful circus scenes. Marin was born in Rutherford, N.J. He studied engineering and worked as a draftsman. He began to study art at the Pennsylvania Academy of Design in 1899. His painting Sun and Grey Sea appears in color in the Painting article.

MILTON W. BROWN

MARINA is a dock or basin for small boats. Some marinas have repair, service, and supply shops; fueling stations; and restaurants and clubhouses, as well as slips and moorings for craft.

MARINA FALL, or PRINCESS MARINA FALL, is a horseshoe-shaped waterfall in west-central Guyana. It lies on the Kuribrong River, about 20 miles northwest of the famous Kaieteur Fall. Marina Fall has a sheer drop of 300 feet and a total fall of 500 feet. For location, see Guyana (map).

MARINE is a sea-soldier. Marines serve as assault landing forces. They keep units as national forces in readiness, prepared for instant expeditionary service. Marines are specially recruited, trained, and organized for service at sea and in land and air operations. Nearly all the world's major maritime nations, including the United States, maintain marine forces or some type of naval infantry. For the marines of the United States, see Marine Corps, United States.

Marines of Other Lands. The British Royal Marines force operates under the Admiralty in London, England. Its commandant-general is a lieutenant general. Its motto is Per Mare, Per Terram, or "By Sea and By Land." The 12,000-man Royal Marines fire ships' guns, provide bands for the navy, conduct amphibious raids, and operate landing craft. Their three main commands are the Portsmouth and Plymouth groups and the commando brigade.

The 5,000-man Royal Netherlands Korps Mariniers serves at sea and as expeditionary forces in the Dutch colonies. Its motto is Qua Patet Orbis, or "Throughout the Wide World."

Other countries that also have marines or naval infantry include Argentina, Brazil, Cambodia, Chile, Nationalist China, Colombia, Dominican Republic, France, Indonesia, Iran, South Korea, Mexico, the Philippines, Poland, Romania, Russia, Spain, Thailand, Venezuela, and Yugoslavia.

History. The first marines were the epibatae, or "heavily armed sea-soldiers," of the Greek navies in the 500's B.C. Later, Roman warships carried milites classiarii, or "soldiers of the fleet." Both the Greeks and Romans

Metropolitan Museum of Art, New York. Alfred Stieglitz Collection

Peter A. Juley & Son

John Marin, *above,* became famous for his brilliant water colors. *Movement No. 2, right,* often called *The Black Sun,* shows Marin's use of simplified, relaxed forms in place of realistic sharp lines.

used their marines to fight at sea, while sailors maneuvered the ships.

During the Middle Ages, nations did not maintain organized navies and marine forces. But it was common practice to put ordinary soldiers aboard ship whenever fighting was expected. In the 1600's, both Great Britain and The Netherlands realized the need for regular troops aboard men-of-war. The British formed a corps of marines in 1664, and the Dutch did so in 1665. When the American colonies revolted in 1775, the Continental Congress authorized the first marines.

The oldest role of marines is service aboard warships. In some countries, marines only perform guard duty at naval bases, or man sea coast defenses. France's *Infanterie coloniale,* or "colonial infantry," wears an anchor for its badge as a symbol that the regiment originated as a marine service.

ROBERT D. HEINL, JR.

See also NAVY.

MARINE ANIMAL. See MARINE BIOLOGY with its list of Related Articles.

MARINE BAND, UNITED STATES. See BAND (Concert Bands).

A Swedish Marine, *right,* serves with the Royal Navy of Sweden. Royal marines of Great Britain, *lower right,* leap ashore in an amphibious training operation.

Royal Swedish Navy;
Royal Marines Photo

Royal Netherlands Navy; Sovfoto

Dutch Marines of the Royal Netherlands Navy, *above,* act as the honor guard for their ruler, Queen Juliana. A Russian marine of the Soviet navy, *right,* stands guard with his machine gun.

Marine Biologists Study Marine Life In Its Environment. These scientists may travel thousands of miles to a lonely beach or stream, where they can study a particular fish community. They collect data on the fish and how they use light, water, and food.

MARINE BIOLOGY

MARINE BIOLOGY is the study of plants and animals that live in the sea. It deals with all forms of marine life, from huge whales to tiny creatures only a fraction of an inch long. Marine organisms live in all parts of the ocean, from shallow shore areas to the deepest points on the ocean floor. The scientists who study life in the sea try to classify all marine plants and animals, and try to discover how they develop and grow, how their bodies function, how they get food, and how they live in relation to other marine plants and animals. Marine biology has become increasingly important in recent years because it has helped human beings better understand their own basic life processes.

Many biologists who specialize in studying marine plants and animals never see them in their natural surroundings. They do most of their work in specially equipped laboratories. They are often called marine biologists. Some marine biologists study the environment of marine life, as well as the marine plants and animals. They are often called biological oceanographers.

John H. Ryther, the contributor of this article, is the Director of the Department of Biology at Woods Hole Oceanographic Institution, Woods Hole, Mass.

Marine Biologists use marine organisms in laboratory experiments that are designed to increase man's knowledge of human life processes. For example, much of man's knowledge of human reproduction and development has been developed through experiments with marine animals. Chemical substances that influence different animal *embryos* (developing young) were first discovered in experiments with marine organisms. The sea urchin is one of the animals most often used by biologists in these experiments. It produces many large eggs that make experiments and observations easier (see SEA URCHIN).

Marine biologists have used the squid's giant nerve fibers to do valuable research in discovering how nerves work. The squid's nerve fibers are larger and easier to handle and observe than those of most animals. The fibers are so large that scientists can place instruments inside different parts of the nerve. The instruments are then used to record the mechanical, chemical, and electrical responses of the nerves. These experiments may lead to greater understanding of how messages are sent from the brain to various points of action in the human body.

Marine biologists also use organisms from the sea to produce substances that are valuable to human beings.

Laboratory scientists have found substances in sponges, sea cucumbers, corals, and seaweed that can be used in treating such things as viral and bacterial infections, and cancer. Substances from certain subtropical sponges can be used to treat skin infections, food and blood poisoning, and pneumonia caused by *staphylococcal* bacteria (see STAPHYLOCOCCUS).

Some marine biologists have found that the poisons from certain kinds of shellfish and puffers are 200,000 times more powerful as anesthetics than drugs that are now being used for this purpose. They have found that the saliva of the octopus contains a substance that can be used as a powerful heart stimulant. The octopus also uses its saliva to paralyze crabs and then eat them. Scientists specializing in the study of marine life believe that many of these substances will eventually be refined for use as commercial drugs.

Most of the experiments with marine organisms are carried out at marine laboratories. Among the oldest and most famous of these are the Stazione Zoologica in Naples, Italy; the Laboratory of the Marine Biological Association of the United Kingdom in Plymouth, England; and the Marine Biological Laboratory at Woods Hole, Mass.

Biological Oceanographers try to find out how marine organisms live in relationship to one another and to their environment. They watch how organisms live in the sea, and try to trace how they *evolved* (gradually developed), adapted, and spread. They try to find out how the body organs of marine creatures can work deep in the sea at pressures as low as 15,000 pounds per square inch. They want to learn how organisms living on the sea floor can locate their mates and find their food, despite the fact that they live in constant darkness, where there are no seasons or temperature changes.

Some marine oceanographers go down into the sea to observe and conduct experiments in the natural environment of marine organisms. Ocean-going vessels with deep-sea nets and dredges are used to capture organisms for study. Scientists often record environmental conditions, such as water temperature and the salt and oxygen content in given ocean areas, on special mechanical equipment that can be fastened to a *buoy* (floating marker). Deep-sea cameras are used to map the sea floor and to locate certain types of organisms. Scientists also now use special types of underwater cameras to make detailed photographic records of various types of marine life at great depths. Special sound devices are used to record the vertical movements of fish. Among the leading U.S. organizations equipped for such studies are the Woods Hole (Mass.) Oceanographic Institution, the Scripps Institution of Oceanography in La Jolla, Calif., the Lamont Geological Observatory in New York City, and the Institute of Marine Science, in Miami, Fla.

Many marine oceanographers use scuba diving equipment to make underwater studies, especially in clear tropical waters along coral reefs. To observe life in the deep sea, they use special equipment, such as deep-sea research submarines. Some of them, such as the bathyscaph called the *Trieste*, can withstand the great pressures found at the deepest parts of the ocean. The *Trieste*, built by the Swiss scientists Auguste and

Jacques Piccard, made a record dive of 35,800 feet in the deepest known spot in the ocean, Challenger Deep in the Mariana Trench of the Pacific Ocean off Guam, in 1960. Scientists can stay submerged for longer periods of time in vessels such as this. See BATHYSCAPH (picture); OCEAN (Discovering the Secrets of the Deep).

The French undersea explorer Jacques-Yves Cousteau pioneered in using undersea stations where observers can live for relatively long periods to study sea life (see COUSTEAU, JACQUES-YVES). The U.S. Navy, in its Man-in-the-Sea program conducted off the California coast, and scientists at the Oceanic Institute in Hawaii have also used this method.   JOHN H. RYTHER

Related Articles. See OCEAN (Life in the Ocean; color pictures). See also the following articles:

ANIMAL LIFE

Animal (Animals of the Ocean)	Echinoderm	Sea Horse
Coelenterate	Fish	Seal
Crustacean	Mollusk	Sponge
Dolphin	Porpoise	Turtle
Dugong	Puffer	Walrus
	Sea Cow	Whale

PLANT LIFE

Algae	Diatom	Irish Moss	Kelp	Seaweed

OTHER RELATED ARTICLES

Diving, Underwater	Plankton	Sargasso Sea

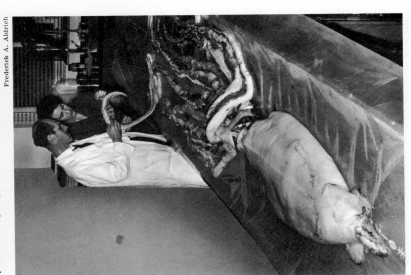

Marine Biologists Also Use Laboratories to study marine life. Scientists examine the sucking disks on the arm of a dead squid. Later they may cut the body apart for further study.

Frederick A. Aldrich

163

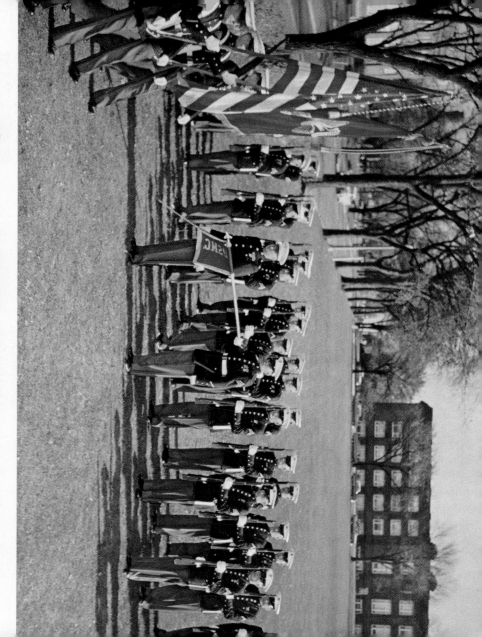

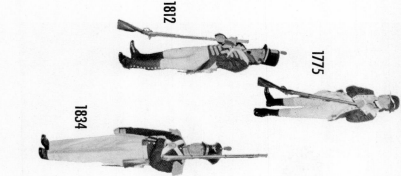

1812

1775

1834

1861

1898

1917

DEVELOPMENT OF THE MARINE CORPS UNIFORM

MARINE CORPS, UNITED STATES, is the branch of the armed services that is especially trained and organized for landing operations. Marine assault troops, supported by air units, attack and seize enemy beachheads and bases. As the nation's amphibious force, marines in many strategic parts of the world stand alert to speed to any trouble spot. A well-known military saying is "The marines have landed, and the situation is well in hand." Marines have been the first to fight in almost every major war of the United States. Since 1775, these "soldiers of the sea" have grown from two battalions

MARINE CORPS, UNITED STATES

of sharpshooters into a combat organization of highly mobile ground divisions and air wings. Marines have made more than 300 landings on foreign shores, and have served from the polar regions to the tropics.

In the mid-1960's, the Marine Corps had a strength of about 277,500 men and 2,100 women. It is a separate branch of the armed forces within the Department of the Navy in the Department of Defense. Marines are often called *leathernecks*, because in the early days they wore leather bands around their throats. The *WM's*, or women marines, have the same ranks as male marines.

The motto of the corps, adopted in 1868, is *Semper Fidelis* (Always Faithful). The Marine emblem was also adopted that same year. "The Marines' Hymn," written in the 1800's, begins with the stirring words "From the halls of Montezuma to the shores of Tripoli." John Philip Sousa wrote the corps' march, "Semper Fidelis," while serving as leader of the Marine band. The band is called "The President's Own," because it plays for state affairs in the White House. The official colors of the corps are scarlet and gold.

Why We Have a Marine Corps

Every great maritime nation such as the United States must be able to defend its interests on land and sea, and protect the lives and property of its citizens in other regions. During war and other emergencies, the United States must be ready to send well-trained, disciplined forces to accomplish these goals.

The Marine Corps maintains fleet marine forces of

Marine Corps Emblem

Marine Corps Color Guard, left, escorts the national colors while a platoon stands at attention and presents arms. A marine, center, dips the guidon, or unit flag, in salute.

Photos taken especially for THE WORLD BOOK ENCYCLOPEDIA through the courtesy of the U.S. Marine Corps.

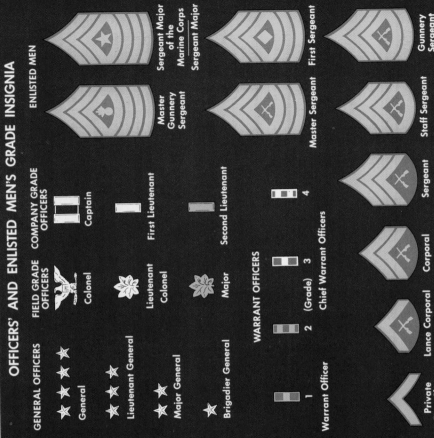

OFFICERS' AND ENLISTED MEN'S GRADE INSIGNIA

GENERAL OFFICERS
General
Lieutenant General
Major General
Brigadier General

WARRANT OFFICERS
Warrant Officer
1   2   3   4
(Grade)
Chief Warrant Officers

FIELD GRADE OFFICERS
Colonel
Lieutenant Colonel
Major

COMPANY GRADE OFFICERS
Captain
First Lieutenant
Second Lieutenant

ENLISTED MEN
Sergeant Major of the Marine Corps
Sergeant Major
Master Gunnery Sergeant
First Sergeant
Gunnery Sergeant
Master Sergeant
Staff Sergeant
Sergeant
Corporal
Lance Corporal
Private First Class

Today

MARINE CORPS, UNITED STATES

166

combined air and ground units to seize and defend advance bases, and for land operations that are carried out as part of a naval campaign. It develops the tactics, techniques, and equipment for the amphibious landing operations. The corps provides detachments for service aboard warships and for the protection of naval bases and stations. It guards U.S. embassies, legations, and consulates in other countries, and performs such other duties as the President may direct.

Life in the Marine Corps

Training a Marine. Every man receives 9 weeks of basic training in "boot camp." Recruits are called "boots," because in early days they wore leather leggings that look like boots. Recruits undergo physical conditioning and learn how to shoot, drill, obey orders, and to know the traditions of the corps. Enlisted women marines undergo basic training at the recruit depot in Parris Island, S.C. Enlisted men are also trained there, or at the recruit depot in San Diego, Calif. After "boot camp," a marine goes to four weeks of infantry training at Camp Lejeune, N.C., or Camp Pendleton, Calif. There he masters more advanced infantry weapons and marine combat tactics.

Training an Officer. Marine Corps officers come from five main sources: (1) the U.S. Naval Academy, (2) the U.S. Military Academy, (3) civilian universities, (4) the enlisted ranks of the corps, and (5) the U.S. Marine Corps aviation cadet program. Each officer receives five or more months of rigorous initial training at the U.S. Marine Corps Basic School in Quantico, Va. Much basic school training consists of field tactics, about a third of which is night training. Women officer candidates also receive training at the U.S. Marine Corps Schools. After being commissioned, they attend an officers' indoctrination course there.

A Typical Day. Because of the wide variety of marine duties, there is no completely typical day. Neverthe-

less, the following routine would be familiar to any marine in peacetime. At 6 A.M. the "field music" (bugler) sounds reveille. The marine rises, washes, makes his bunk, and has setting-up drill. A hearty breakfast is followed by police call, when quarters and outside areas are carefully *policed* (cleaned and ticked). At 8 A.M. comes morning colors, when the flag is hoisted while the band plays the National Anthem. After colors, troop inspection and guard mounting take place. All men are inspected and drilled, and the guard is relieved. Throughout the forenoon, drills and instructions go on until recall at 11 A.M. Dinner is served at 11:30 A.M. At 1 P.M. drill call sounds again, and afternoon training continues until the day's work is finished. Liberty call then announces that eligible marines may "go ashore," or leave the post if they wish. Supper is served at 5 P.M., and evenings are free unless night training is planned. Taps sounds at 10 P.M.

Careers in the Marine Corps. Young men between the ages of 17 and 28 may enlist in the corps for three, four, or six years. Women between the ages of 18 and 30 may enlist in the corps. Male marines may serve in combatant-type, administrative, or communications jobs. Women marines can perform more than 200 military jobs, ranging from clerical tasks to operating aviation control towers.

Marines who remain in the corps after their first enlistment may expect, if qualified, to rise to responsible jobs as senior noncommissioned officers. The most capable marines can win appointments to the U.S. Naval Academy, receive direct commissions as officers, or be chosen as warrant officers. Marines may retire with pay after 20 years' service. For ranks and pay in the Marine Corps, see RANK IN ARMED SERVICES.

Weapons of the Marine Corps

Marine Ground Weapons. The M14 rifle is the basic infantry weapon of the corps. Marines also use grenades, pistols, submachine guns, machine guns, and flame throwers.

Artillery provides support for Marine infantry. Marine artillery includes mortars, rocket launchers, guns, and howitzers. Armored units have tanks with heavy guns and flame throwers. Antiaircraft units have *Hawk* guided missiles. Special marine teams ashore use radio to direct gunfire and missile support from warships.

Marine Aviation provides close air support for fleet marine and other troops. It reinforces naval aviation. It attacks enemy forces so close to marine land operations that detailed coordination between air and ground units is required. The Marines have aviators with ground units at the front lines to control and direct air support. They fly the same kinds of aircraft as the Navy (see Navy, UNITED STATES [Ships and Weapons of the Navy]). The Marines also operate assault helicopters to land men from naval helicopter carriers.

Organization of the Marine Corps

Headquarters of the Marine Corps is in Washington, D.C. The corps is one of the two naval services. It is a partner, but not literally a part, of the Navy. A commandant commands the corps. The President appoints him with the approval of the Senate. The commandant usually serves four years, and has the rank of general. He is responsible directly to the secretary of the navy.

MAJOR MARINE CORPS POSTS

Name	Location
Albany Marine Corps Supply Center	Albany, Ga.
Barstow Marine Corps Supply Center	Barstow, Calif.
Beaufort Marine Corps Air Station	Beaufort, S.C.
*Camp H. M. Smith	Oahu, Hawaii
*Camp Lejeune	Jacksonville, N.C.
*Camp Pendleton	Oceanside, Calif.
*Camp Smedley D. Butler	Okinawa
*Cherry Point Marine Corps Air Station	Cherry Point, N.C.
*El Toro Marine Corps Air Station	Santa Ana, Calif.
Iwakuni Marine Corps Air Station	Iwakuni, Japan
Kaneohe Bay Marine Corps Air Station	Oahu, Hawaii
*Parris Island Marine Corps Recruit Depot	Parris Island, S.C.
Pearl Harbor Marine Barracks	Oahu, Hawaii
Philadelphia Marine Corps Supply Activity	Philadelphia, Pa.
*Quantico Marine Corps Development and Education Command	Quantico, Va.
*San Diego Marine Corps Recruit Depot	San Diego, Calif.
Twentynine Palms Marine Corps Base	Twentynine Palms, Calif.
Washington Marine Barracks	Washington, D.C.

*Has a separate article in THE WORLD BOOK ENCYCLOPEDIA.

MARINE CORPS, UNITED STATES

His principal assistants include the assistant commandant, the chief of staff, deputy and assistant chiefs of staff, and directors of headquarters divisions. In matters of direct concern to the corps, the commandant serves as a member of the Joint Chiefs of Staff (see JOINT CHIEFS OF STAFF).

Operating Forces include (1) the fleet marine forces, (2) marines aboard ships, and (3) security forces. The fleet marine forces form parts of the Atlantic and Pacific fleets. They include three Marine divisions, three Marine aircraft wings, and supporting units. One division and wing are usually stationed on each coast of the United States, and the rest in the Far East.

Marine air reserve training command has headquarters at the naval air station in Glenview, Ill. A director at Marine headquarters supervises all reserve matters.

History

The Revolutionary War. The Continental Congress established a marine corps on Nov. 10, 1775, to fight in the Revolutionary War. Marines also served with the continental army in the battles of Trenton, Assunpunk, Morristown, and Brandywine. After the Revolutionary War, no marine corps as such existed. Congress re-created the corps as a military service in 1798.

The Shores of Tripoli. Marines took part in the hard-fought naval battles that United States ships fought against France in 1797. In 1805, marines led the

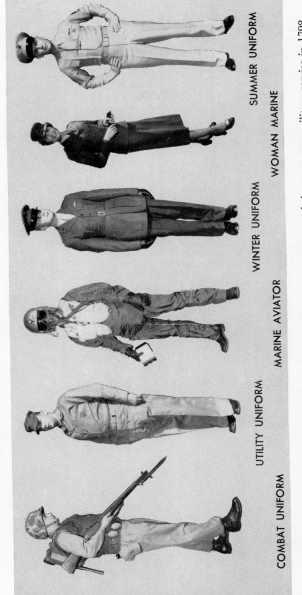

COMBAT UNIFORM

UTILITY UNIFORM

MARINE AVIATOR

WINTER UNIFORM

WOMAN MARINE

SUMMER UNIFORM

The fleet marine forces account for more than half the strength of the Marine Corps.

Marines serve aboard many warships. They operate guns, serve as guards and orderlies, and provide a trained backbone for the ships' landing forces. Marine airplane and helicopter squadrons may fly from carriers. Security forces include marines who guard American embassies and other important government installations and Marine barracks at naval bases.

Support Organization provides, trains, maintains, and supports the operating forces. The Marine schools combine all officer education and military development activities of the corps. The corps' two recruit depots handle basic training. The Marine supply centers provide logistic support for the corps. Marine bases, barracks, and air stations also support Marine Corps activities.

Regulars and Reserves. The regular Marine Corps includes men and women who enter it as a professional career. The reserves consist of (1) the *fleet marine reserve* of former enlisted marines with more than 20 years' service, (2) the *organized reserve* consisting of a Marine division and a Marine aircraft wing with supporting units that can be mobilized into the fleet marine forces, and (3) the *volunteer reserve* of all reservists not assigned to the fleet or the organized reserves.

The Marine Corps administers its reserve program through seven reserve and recruiting districts. The

— **IMPORTANT DATES IN MARINE CORPS HISTORY** —

1775 The Continental Congress authorized the formation of two battalions of marines.

1776 Marines made their first landing, on the Bahama Islands during the Revolutionary War.

1798 Congress re-created the Marine Corps as a separate military service.

1805 Marines stormed the Barbary pirates' stronghold at Derna on the shores of Tripoli.

1834 Congress placed the Marine Corps directly under the Secretary of the Navy.

1847 Marines occupied "the halls of Montezuma" in Mexico City during the Mexican War.

1913 The Marine Corps established its aviation section.

1918 Marines fought one of their greatest battles at Belleau Wood in France during World War I.

1942 Marines invaded Guadalcanal Island in the first United States offensive of World War II.

1945 Marines seized Iwo Jima Island in the western Pacific in the largest all-marine battle.

1950 Marines stormed ashore at Inchon, Korea, in the first major landing of the Korean War.

1952 The marine commandant became a member of the Joint Chiefs of Staff.

1965 Marines landed at Da Nang and Chu Lai, Vietnam, in the first amphibious assaults of the Vietnam War.

THE MARINES IN ACTION

The Marine Corps has been the first to fight in every major war of the United States. It has carried out more than 300 landings on foreign shores. Marines have served everywhere, from the poles to the tropics.

storming of the Barbary pirates' stronghold at Derna, Tripoli. Their action helped end the pirate menace in the Mediterranean Sea.

The War of 1812 saw marines in all major American naval victories. Captain John Gamble showed such ability that he was given command of a captured British warship. He became the only marine officer ever to command a naval ship. Marines helped Andrew Jackson's army administer the worst defeat of the war to the British in the defense of New Orleans in 1815.

The Creek and Seminole Wars. In 1836, the army was assigned to move the Creek and Seminole Indians of Georgia and Florida to new reservations. When the tribes refused to move, marine commandant Archibald Henderson personally led marines to reinforce the army. He was promoted to brigadier general for gallantry at the Battle of Hatchee-Lustee in Florida in 1837. Henderson became the corps' first general officer.

The Halls of Montezuma. During the Mexican War, from 1846 to 1848, marines made many landings on

Marines' Astronaut Medal

was first awarded to Marine Lt. Col. John H. Glenn, Jr., in 1962 for orbiting the earth.

The Halls of Montezuma, the royal palace in Mexico City, fell to invading marines during the Mexican War. Marines were the first United States troops to enter the capital. Marines also helped take California.

THE MARINES' HYMN

From the Halls of Montezuma
To the shores of Tripoli,
We fight our country's battles
In the air, on land, and sea,
First to fight for right and freedom,
And to keep our honor clean,
We are proud to claim the title of
UNITED STATES MARINE.

both coasts of Mexico. Marines were the first to enter the city gates of Mexico City. They raised the American flag over the National Palace, which later became known as "the halls of Montezuma."

The Civil War. When John Brown and his followers captured the army arsenal at Harpers Ferry, Va., in 1859, marines from Washington were the only troops available. They captured Brown and occupied the arsenal. In the Civil War itself, marines fought in many land and naval battles.

In the Far East. During the late 1800's and early 1900's, marines landed 17 times in China to protect American interests. They defended the besieged legations in Peking during the Boxer Rebellion in 1900, and fought at Tientsin in the Peking relief force.

The Spanish-American War. Marines were the first American troops to land in Cuba. A battalion seized Guantánamo Bay in 1898. Marines were also the first American forces to land in the Philippines. They occupied Guam, and took part in the seizure of Puerto

First Marine Landing took place during the Revolutionary War. Marines invaded New Providence Island in the Bahamas and seized supplies.

The Shores of Tripoli came under marine attack in 1805 during the campaign against the Barbary pirates. Marines raised the U.S. Flag for the first time in the Eastern Hemisphere.

The Marines' Hymn has been traced back to the 1850's. The music may have been composed by Jacques Offenbach, or by an unknown marine who based the tune on an ancient Spanish melody.

Belleau Wood in France was the scene of the greatest marine battle in World War I. Marines helped crush a German offensive that threatened Paris. The French named the battle area "the Wood of the Brigade of Marines."

MARINE CORPS, UNITED STATES

the Central Pacific. The conquest of Iwo Jima during February and March of 1945, was the largest all-marine battle in history (see Iwo Jima; Washington, D.C. [color picture]). Strength of the corps reached nearly 500,000 during World War II.

The Korean War. In August, 1950, marines arrived in Korea to help rescue the crumbling Pusan perimeter. They later made the amphibious landing at Inchon. After Chinese Communist troops entered the war, Marines smashed seven enemy divisions in their winter march south from the Chosin Reservoir.

Recent Developments. During the Suez crisis in 1956, a Marine battalion covered the evacuation of American citizens from the trouble zone. In 1958, a reinforced marine regiment landed in Lebanon and helped prevent the Lebanese government from being overthrown. The corps also completed reorganizing the combat structure of its fleet marine forces. In 1965, Marine units landed in the Dominican Republic to end the fighting there. Also in 1965, Marines landed in Da Nang, South Vietnam. From 1965 through mid-1969, over 376,000 marines served in the Vietnam War.

T. P. Gogin

Related Articles. See the table *Major Marine Corps Posts* with this article. See also Navy, Department of the; Navy, United States. Additional related articles in World Book include:

BIOGRAPHIES

Smith, Holland M.   Vandegrift, Alexander A.

HISTORY

Civil War	Revolutionary War in America	War of 1812
Korean War	Spanish-American War	World War I
Mexican War	Vietnam War	World War II

OTHER RELATED ARTICLES

Air Force,	Military	Rank in Armed
United States	Discharge	Services
Decorations	Military	Recruiting
and Medals	School	Regiment
Flag (color picture:	Military	Uniform
Flags of the	Training	War Aces
Armed Forces)		
Marine		

Outline

I. Why We Have a Marine Corps

II. Life in the Marine Corps
 A. Training a Marine
 B. Training an Officer
 C. A Typical Day
 D. Careers in the Marine Corps

III. Weapons of the Marine Corps
 A. Marine Ground Weapons
 B. Marine Aviation

IV. Organization of the Marine Corps
 A. Headquarters
 B. Operating Forces
 C. Support Organization
 D. Regulars and Reserves

V. History

Questions

What is the Marine Corps motto? What does it mean?
Why are marines often called *leathernecks?*
What are some operating forces? Support forces?
What are the duties of marines aboard warships?
What are some marine ground weapons?
What is the chief purpose of the Marine Corps?
What is "boot camp"? The fleet marine force?
Why is marine aviation important to marine ground units?
When did the corps establish its aviation section?
Where did the marines make their first landing?

Rico. A Marine brigade served with the army during the Philippine insurrection from 1899 to 1903.

In Central America. Marines landed in Panama six times between 1885 and 1903 to protect American lives and property, and to keep the Isthmus of Panama open. They also fought in two campaigns to stabilize Nicaragua, in 1912 and again from 1926 to 1933. Marine brigades exercised American protectorates over Haiti and Santo Domingo in the early 1900's.

World War I. The Marines arrived in France in June, 1917, with the first troops of the American Expeditionary Force. They dismayed the Germans with their accurate, long-range rifle fire, and their fierce assaults at Soissons, Saint Mihiel, Blanc Mont Ridge, and the Meuse-Argonne.

World War II. In August, 1942, the Marines invaded Guadalcanal in the Solomon Islands and launched the first American offensive of the war. Marines under Lieutenant General Holland M. Smith led the amphibious landings of the island-hopping drive westward through

---

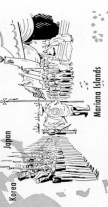

Pacific Island campaigns brought the Allies victory in World War II. Marines launched the first U.S. offensive, and led the westward sweep through the Solomon, Gilbert, Marshall, Mariana, Palau, Volcano, and Ryukyu islands.

Marshall Islands

Mariana Islands

Solomon Islands

Japan

Korea

Japan opened its ports to international trade after a visit by Commodore Matthew C. Perry in 1853 and 1854. Perry's marine troops were the first to land on Japanese soil.

Korea tested the combat readiness of the marine corps. During the Korean War, marine aviators flew helicopters for the first time in battle.

MARINE ENGINEERING

United States Capitol Building, Library of Congress

Francis Marion was a daring military leader in the Revolutionary War. Because of his shrewd, daring raids, Marion became known as the Swamp Fox. According to legend, he once invited a British officer to dinner at his swamp encampment. Artist John Blake White portrayed the legend, *left*, in *General Marion Inviting a British Officer to Share His Meal.*

MARINE ENGINEERING. See ENGINEERING (table).

MARINE INSURANCE. See INSURANCE (Marine).

MARINE PLANT. See MARINE BIOLOGY with its list of Related Articles.

MARINER SPACE PROBE. See SPACE TRAVEL (Space Probes); VENUS (planet); MARS.

MARINER'S CHART. See CHART.

MARINER'S COMPASS. See COMPASS.

MARINERS' MEASURE. See WEIGHTS AND MEASURES (Linear Measure—Nautical).

MARINETTI, FILIPPO. See FUTURISM.

MARINUS is the name of two popes of the Roman Catholic Church. Some historians later listed them as Martin II and Martin III.

Marinus I (Martin II) was pope from 882 to 884. He was the first bishop elected to the papacy. He thought highly of the English and freed the Anglo-Saxon center in Rome from taxes. He was born in Tuscany.

Marinus II (Martin III) was pope from 942 to 946. He was not a brilliant pope, but he worked gently for church reforms.

MARION, FRANCIS (1732?-1795), was an American general whose shrewd, daring raids won him the nickname the *Swamp Fox* in the Revolutionary War. He and his men darted out of the marshes to attack the British, then vanished before they could strike back.

Marion became a member of the South Carolina Provincial Congress in 1775, and voted for war. Soon after, he became captain of a volunteer group and fought in many engagements. He sprained his ankle in 1780, and was forced to leave Charleston before the town surrendered. This fortunate accident saved Marion from capture, and he later commanded the forces in the northern part of the state.

He had the only American troops left in South Carolina after the British defeated General Horatio Gates and General Thomas Sumter. His forces were too small to fight the British in open battle. So Marion organized them into a guerrilla band. The soldiers provided their own food and horses. Blacksmiths made their swords from saw blades. Their bullets were melted pewter plates, and ammunition was so scarce in many battles that each man had only three rounds.

Marion had a secret hideout on Snow Island in the Pee Dee River, and the British had great difficulty finding it. From there he and his men made quick raids on British communications and supply depots and rescued captured Americans. The British cavalry officer, Banastre Tarleton, spent much time and energy pursuing Marion, but he could never catch him. After the war, Marion served in the South Carolina senate several times. He died on his plantation at Pond Bluff.

Marion was born in Berkeley County, South Carolina. He spent his youth on his parents' farm near Georgetown, S.C. He had his first taste of war as a lieutenant of colonial militia, when he fought against the Cherokee Indians in 1761.

WILLIAM O. STEELE

MARION COLLEGE. See UNIVERSITIES AND COLLEGES (table).

MARION PRISON is a maximum-security federal penitentiary located near Marion, Ill. The modern prison is designed to hold dangerous and long-term prisoners. The penitentiary houses about 700 inmates on a 921-acre reservation. A staff of about 220 operates the prison. When Marion was opened in 1963, it was the first new penitentiary built in the United States since 1940.

JAMES V. BENNETT

MARIONETTE. See PUPPET (Types).

MARIOTTE'S LAW. See GAS (Gas Laws).

MARIPOSA GROVE. See YOSEMITE NATIONAL PARK.

MARIPOSA LILY is a group of hardy, spring-blooming flowers of the lily family. The beautiful flowers are sometimes called *fairy lantern, globe tulip,* or *butterfly lily.* Native to the western United States, mariposa lilies have narrow leaves shaped like large blades of grass. The cup-shaped flowers grow singly or in small clusters, and resemble tulips. Colors range from white to purple to deep yellow or orange. Mariposa lilies grow well in sandy, porous soil, but need a lot of water. They grow from underground bulbs. Bulbs should be

J. Horace McFarland

The Mariposa Lily has three beautiful petals. Six pollen stalks surround its *pistil* (center part). The flowers vary in color.

dried out in summer for fall planting. Mariposa lilies make excellent flowers for woodland or rock gardens.

Scientific Classification. Mariposa lilies belong to the lily family, *Liliaceae*. The white mariposa is genus *Calochortus*, species *C. albus*.

ROBERT W. SCHERY

See also PLANT (color picture: Some Members of the Lily Family); SEGO LILY.

MARIS, ROGER. See BASEBALL (Recent Developments; picture).

MARIST COLLEGE. See UNIVERSITIES AND COLLEGES (table).

MARITAIN, *MA rih TAN,* **JACQUES** (1882-   ), a French educator and philosopher, helped lead the revival of *Thomistic* (scholastic) philosophy in the 1900's (see SCHOLASTICISM). He lectured on scholasticism in Europe and America, and taught at such universities as Toronto, Chicago, Columbia, and Notre Dame. His books include *An Introduction to Philosophy* (1937), *Degrees of Knowledge* (1938), *Man and the State* (1951), and *Creative Intuition* (1955). Maritain was awarded the French Grand Prize for Letters in 1963. He was born in Paris.

THOMAS P. NEILL and FULTON J. SHEEN

MARITIME ADMINISTRATION (MA) is an agency under the United States Department of Commerce that promotes U.S. shipping. The goal of the agency is to assure U.S. shippers of sufficient available, up-to-date ships to carry the nation's domestic water-borne commerce and a substantial portion of its foreign commerce. Merchant ships are available to the defense effort in time of war or national emergency. See MERCHANT MARINE.

The MA insures mortgages and loans made by private lending institutions for building or reconstructing ships. It determines ocean routes essential for maintaining U.S. foreign commerce and requirements of ships to provide adequate service on these routes. It also designs new ships and does research to improve the efficiency of merchant shipping operations.

The Maritime Subsidy Board, established within the MA in 1961, awards subsidies to United States firms for building and operating ships. These payments help make up the difference between U.S. and foreign costs.

Critically reviewed by the MARITIME ADMINISTRATION

See also FEDERAL MARITIME COMMISSION.

MARITIME COLLEGE is a professional school for men at Fort Schuyler, N.Y. It is a member college of the

State University of New York. The oldest maritime school in the United States, it was originally established in 1847 as the New York Nautical School. Courses lead to bachelor's degrees, and prepare students for the maritime industry. For the enrollment of Maritime College, see UNIVERSITIES AND COLLEGES (table [New York, State University of]).

MARITIME COMMISSION, UNITED STATES. See FEDERAL MARITIME COMMISSION.

MARITIME LAW regulates commerce and navigation on the high seas or other navigable waters, including inland lakes and rivers. It involves all vessels, from huge passenger liners to small pleasure boats, and covers such matters as contracts, insurance, property damage, and personal injuries. Maritime law is sometimes referred to as *admiralty law*, because at one time it was administered under the jurisdiction of admirals.

Although a general maritime law has developed internationally, it operates in any nation according to the laws and usages of that country. Each nation bases its own maritime law on the general law, with whatever modifications and qualifications it thinks are necessary and proper. Maritime law, in general, does not have any legal force of its own. There is no international court to enforce maritime decisions. But all nations that have vessels on the sea set up national maritime courts. These courts consider maritime cases in much the same way that civil courts hear other kinds of complaints. Federal district courts administer maritime law in the United States. Admiralty courts handle maritime law cases in Great Britain.

WARREN A. JACKMAN

See also FLOTSAM, JETSAM, AND LAGAN; SALVAGE; BARRATRY.

MARITIME PROVINCES, or ATLANTIC PROVINCES, are the four eastern provinces of Canada: Nova Scotia, New Brunswick, Prince Edward Island, and Newfoundland. Maritime means *sea*.

See also ATLANTIC PROVINCES.

MARITSA RIVER. See BULGARIA (The Land).

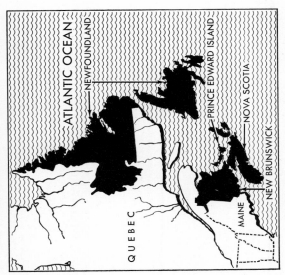

The Maritime Provinces Are Shown in Black.

171

MARIUS, GAIUS

MARIUS, GAIUS (157-86 B.C.), was a Roman general and statesman. He was not of noble ancestry, but he worked his way into political leadership. He served seven times as one of the two *consuls* (chief government officials) of Rome, between 107 and 86 B.C. He opposed Rome's aristocratic *oligarchy* (rule by few).

As a general, Marius reorganized Rome's infantry legions, improved training methods, and opened military service to men of the lowest social classes. A strong professional army developed. The troops, if treated well, often became more loyal to their generals than to the state, so successful military command became a means to political power.

Marius was born near Arpinum, in central Italy. He won his greatest military victories against the Numidians in North Africa, and the Cimbri and Teutone tribes in northern Italy.

HENRY C. BOREN

J. Horace McFarland

Marjoram

MARIVAUX, *mar ii` voh,* **PIERRE** (1688-1763), was a French playwright and novelist. His works deal chiefly with the rising middle class, which was slowly replacing the nobility as the ruling social force in France.

Marivaux is best known for his comedies. His originality lies in his basing his comedies on the problem of love as seen by women. His heroines are elegant, intellectual, and cunning, and their speech is delicate and refined. His comedies include *The Double Inconstancy* (1723), *The Game of Love and Chance* (1730), and *The False Confessions* (1737). Marivaux also wrote two unfinished novels, *The Life of Marianne* (1731-1741) and *The Successful Peasant* (1735-1736). These books were among the first French novels to give a realistic picture of the middle class. Marivaux was born PIERRE CARLET DE CHAMBLAIN DE MARIVAUX in Paris.

JULES BRODY

MARJORAM, *MAHR joh rum,* is the popular name of a group of herbaceous plants which belong to the mint family. These plants grow wild in the Mediterranean region and in Asia. Several kinds are cultivated in North America. Marjoram is also called *organo.*

The marjoram plant stands 1 to 2 feet tall and bears small whitish or purplish flowers. *Sweet marjoram* is grown in American gardens. Its leaves, stems, and flowers can be used to flavor stews, soups, and dressings. Manufacturers use oil of sweet marjoram in making toilet soaps. *Common marjoram* also grows in the United States. It is used to season foods. It has purple flowers which grow in clusters. Marjoram is often used in commercial oils such as salad oils.

Scientific Classification. Marjoram belongs to the mint family, *Labiatae.* Sweet marjoram is classified as genus *Majorana,* species *M. hortensis.* Common marjoram is *Origanum vulgare.*

HAROLD NORMAN MOLDENKE

MARK is the monetary unit of Germany. After World War I, it became almost valueless, but in 1924 it was stabilized and called the *reichsmark.* It is now called the *Deutsche mark.* See also MONEY (table).

MARK, GOSPEL OF. See GOSPELS; MARK, SAINT.

MARK, SAINT, according to tradition, was the author of the second Gospel in the New Testament. This book is supposed to report Peter's teachings as Mark remembered them (see GOSPELS). Mark was brought up in Jerusalem. His mother, Mary, lived there, and her home was a gathering place for Christians.

Mark went with Saint Paul and Barnabas, Paul's friend, on their first missionary journey. But there was a quarrel, and Mark returned to Jerusalem. Later he sailed for Cyprus with Barnabas. For 10 years no one heard from him. Then he suddenly joined Paul at Rome.

He probably worked with both Paul and Peter for the rest of his life. Another tradition tells that he founded the church at Alexandria.

FREDERICK C. GRANT

MARK ANTONY. See ANTONY, MARK.

MARK TWAIN. See TWAIN, MARK.

MARKET is a term in economics that has several meanings related to buying and selling. The term comes from the Latin word *mercatus* (*trade,* or *market place*).

One meaning of a market is a place where goods are brought to be sold. The earliest markets were of this type. Buyers and sellers met at certain times and places to exchange cotton, cloth, grains, wool, and many other basic goods. The sellers were usually the producers of the goods, and the buyers were the *consumers* (users). As large cities developed and production became more specialized, personal contact between producers and consumers became impractical. Most goods now are handled by many *middlemen,* including wholesale and retail sellers, before being distributed to consumers.

Today's markets are highly organized places where goods are bought and sold with speed. Such markets include grain and stock exchanges. The commodities traded are not present at most markets. Instead, a title of ownership is transferred from seller to buyer.

A second meaning of *market* is the total demand of potential buyers. For example, economists may refer to "the overseas market" or "the teen-age market." In each case, the total demand of a particular geographical area or group of individuals is involved.

The term *market* is used in still another way. In the United States, Canada, and a few other countries, individuals and companies are free to make most economic decisions for themselves. Consumers express their wants by the prices they are willing to pay for goods and services. Economists use the term *market* to refer to the field in which economic forces operate to determine those prices. For information on how supply, demand, and other market forces determine price, see PRICE.

An economic system that permits individual economic decisions is often called a *free enterprise system* or a *market economy.* For detailed explanations of how such systems operate, see the articles on ECONOMICS and FREE ENTERPRISE SYSTEM.

See also DISTRIBUTION; BOARD OF TRADE; STOCK EXCHANGE; BLACK MARKET.

ROBERT F. LANZILLOTTI

MARKET RESEARCH. See ADVERTISING (Research).

MARKETING. See DISTRIBUTION; AGRICULTURE (introduction); The Agricultural Revolution); COOPERATIVE; FOOD (Marketing); MANAGEMENT (Market Management); RETAILING.

MARKHAM, *MAHR kum,* **EDWIN** (1852-1940), an American poet and lecturer, won recognition with his poem "The Man with the Hoe" (1899). He also wrote the books of poems *Lincoln and Other Poems* (1901) and

New Poems (1932); and a sermon entitled "The Social Conscience" (1897). Markham was born in Oregon City, Ore., but his mother took him to California when he was 5. He graduated from Christian College in Santa Rosa, Calif. For several years, he worked as a schoolteacher and superintendent of schools in California communities. He lived near New York City after 1899.
                                          PETER VIERECK

MARKKA, *MAHRK kah,* is the gold monetary unit of Finland. It also has been made of an alloy of nickel and bronze. The markka is equal to 100 pennia. For its value in dollars, see MONEY (table: Values).

MARKLE FOUNDATION, JOHN AND MARY R. See FOUNDATIONS.

MARKOVA, DAME ALICIA (1910-   ), is considered the first great English ballerina. At 14, she joined the Sergei Diaghilev ballet company and became a soloist. After that company disbanded in 1929, she spent almost a decade with Sadler's Wells (now the Royal) Ballet and then with the Markova-Dolin Ballet. Her greatest role was the title character in *Giselle.*

In 1938, Alicia Markova joined the Ballet Russe de Monte Carlo, the leading international company. By this time, her movements were perfect and her pure, soaring style was flawless at any speed. During World War II, she danced with the Ballet Theatre. She retired in 1963 and became director of the Metropolitan Opera Ballet. She received the title *Dame Commander of the British Empire* in 1963.
                                          P. W. MANCHESTER

MARKS AND MARKING. See GRADING.

MARL is the name for different kinds of clay mixtures. Usually, marl contains clay, sand, and calcium carbonate. The fresh-water marls of Michigan and Indiana are examples of such a mixture. *Shell marl* contains many shells. *Greensand marl* is found in some of the Atlantic Coast states. It does not have much calcium carbonate, but it is rich in potash and phosphorus. Farmers used marl for fertilizer before the commercial fertilizers became popular. They still use it where it is plentiful. Marl acts against soil acidity.
                                          A. PABST

MARLBORO COLLEGE. See UNIVERSITIES AND COLLEGES (table).

MARLBOROUGH, *MAWL buh ruh,* **DUKE OF** (1650-1722), JOHN CHURCHILL, was one of England's greatest generals. He won a series of brilliant victories at Blenheim, Ramillies, Oudenarde, and Malplaquet in his campaigns in the War of the Spanish Succession (see BLENHEIM, BATTLE OF; SUCCESSION WARS [The War of the Spanish Succession]).

His character and motives have been criticized, but his military genius has never been questioned. He had a winning personality, and was a successful diplomat. He was an ancestor of Sir Winston Churchill, who wrote a biography of him.

Marlborough deserted King James II to support William of Orange when the English Parliament invited William to accept the English throne in 1688

The Duke of Marlborough
Detail from portrait by Sir Godfrey Kneller, reproduced by kind permission of His Grace, The Duke of Marlborough

(see JAMES [II]; WILLIAM [III] of England). William made him earl of Marlborough, and gave him commands in the army. Marlborough's position became stronger when William died and Princess Anne came to the throne as Queen Anne (see ANNE). Marlborough's wife, Sarah Jennings (1660-1744), was the queen's closest friend. Anne made him commander of all the armed forces at home and in Europe. In the War of the Spanish Succession, Marlborough, who was then a duke, won a series of victories.

At the peak of his success, Marlborough lost his influence at home. His political enemies had turned the queen against him and his wife. He was removed from his command, and retired from public life. His final downfall was not due to lack of ability. It was the fault of his wife, who was domineering and ill tempered. England generously rewarded him for his services. He received an estate in Oxfordshire, and Blenheim Castle was built for him there in 1705.

Marlborough was born in Devonshire. He served in the war against The Netherlands, under the French Marshal Turenne, the greatest military leader of that day. He won rapid promotion.
                                          W. M. SOUTHGATE

MARLIN, *MAHR lin,* or SPEARFISH, is the name of a group of large game fishes that live in the ocean. They are related to the swordfishes and sailfishes. Most marlins weigh from 50 to 400 pounds, but some weigh much more. The marlin has a pointed spear about as long as that of the swordfish. The marlin's *dorsal* (back) fin looks like a sickle, and its tail is crescent shaped. *Blue* and *white marlins* live in the Atlantic Ocean, and *striped marlins* live in the Pacific. Marlins usually swim singly, and often leap high in the air.

Scientific Classification. The marlin belongs to the family *Istiophoridae.* The blue marlin is genus *Makaira,* species *M. ampla.* The white marlin is *M. albida,* and the striped marlin is *M. holei.*
                                          LEONARD P. SCHULTZ

See also FISHING (table: Game-Fishing World Records); SAILFISH; SWORDFISH.

The Marlin Is a Strong, Exciting Game Fish.
California Dept. of Fish and Game

MARLOWE, CHRISTOPHER (1564-1593), was the first great Elizabethan writer of tragedy. His most famous work, *The Tragical History of Doctor Faustus* (1588?), is an imaginative view of a legendary scholar's fall to damnation through lust for forbidden knowledge, power, and sensual pleasure. Never before in English literature had a writer so powerfully shown the individual soul's conflict with the laws defining man's place in a universal order. See FAUST.

Marlowe was born in Canterbury and studied at Cambridge. Evidently at some time during his university years, he did secret service work for the government. The few years before his death in a tavern fight have left evidence of his duels and reports of his unconventional, skeptical political and religious thought.

Marlowe established his theatrical reputation with *Tamburlaine* (Parts I and II, c. 1587). These plays concern an awe-inspiring conqueror, Tamburlaine. In "high astounding" poetry and spectacle, they express Renaissance man's fascination with the reach and limits of the human will's desire for dominion. In *Tamburlaine*, Marlowe influenced later drama with his concentration on a heroic figure and his development of *blank verse* (unrhymed poetry) into a flexible poetic form for tragedy. But artificial and crude elements make *Tamburlaine* less attractive today than Marlowe's more mature plays—*The Jew of Malta* (c. 1589), *Edward II* (c. 1592), and *Doctor Faustus*. Marlowe's nondramatic poetry includes the unfinished *Hero and Leander*—regarded by some readers as his finest poetic achievement—and the pastoral lyric "The Passionate Shepherd to His Love."

LAWRENCE J. ROSS

MARMARA, *MAHR muh ruh, MAHR moh ruh,* **SEA OF,** is part of the trade waterway which connects the Black Sea with the Mediterranean Sea. The Strait of Bosporus connects Marmara with the Black Sea on the east. The Dardanelles connects it with the Aegean Sea on the west. The Sea of Marmara is about 140 miles long and about 40 miles across at its widest point. It covers about 4,300 square miles.

JOHN D. ISAACS

See also BOSPORUS; DARDANELLES.

MARMION. See LOCHINVAR.

MARMOLADA. See DOLOMITES.

MARMOSET, *MAHR moh set.* Marmosets are the world's smallest monkeys. Some marmosets are only about as big as a rat. Marmosets live in warm regions of South and Central America and Mexico. In South America, the *oustiti* marmoset is a common pet.

The common marmoset is covered with soft fur. Large, beady eyes stare out from its furry, round head. The biggest thing about the marmoset is its tail, which is usually longer than its body. Some marmosets have tufts of hair on the top of their ears. Some marmosets have a large pompadour of long fur. The *silver marmoset* has a bald head and its face is a bright pink. Marmosets live in trees. But they do not use their tails to hold on to branches as some other South American monkeys do. They eat mostly fruits and insects.

Scientific Classification. Marmosets make up the marmoset family, *Callithricidae*. The common marmoset belongs to the genus *Callithrix*. The silky marmoset is in the genus *Leontideus*.

GEORGE B. SCHALLER

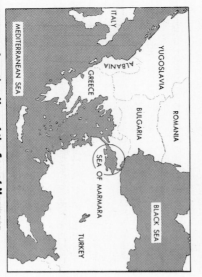

Location Map of the Sea of Marmara

Cy La Tour

Oustiti Marmosets Are Popular Pets in South America.

MARMOT, *MAR mut,* is the largest member of the squirrel family. Marmots live in the ground, and are common in Europe, western North America, and in much of Asia. They are rodents, as are beavers, chipmunks, and mice. The woodchuck is a kind of marmot that lives in open areas (see WOODCHUCK). North American marmots are between 1 and 2 feet long. They have short legs, small ears, and furry tails up to 9 inches long. Most marmots have gray fur on their backs and yellowish-orange fur on their bellies. Marmots eat plants. They grow fat in autumn and sleep through winter. Female marmots give birth to four or five young in May. Marmots live in *colonies* (groups) in loose rock on mountain slopes. They make their homes in burrows.

Scientific Classification. Marmots belong to the squirrel family, *Sciuridae*. The common marmot is genus *Marmota*, species *M. flaviventris*.

DANIEL H. BRANT

MARNE, BATTLES OF THE. See WORLD WAR I (table: Highlights of World War I; The March Through Belgium; The Last Campaigns).

MARNE RIVER, *mahrn,* is the largest branch of the Seine River in France. The Marne rises in the hills of eastern France and follows a winding course north and west for 310 miles. It empties into the Seine River 4 miles above Paris. The rapid current of the Marne provides water power for flour mills on its banks. Its fertile valley offers good soil for wheat growing. Large barges can navigate the Marne. The Marne is connected to the east by a canal that runs through Nancy to Strasbourg on the Rhine River.

MAROT, *mar OH,* **CLEMENT** (1496-1544), was a French poet who served in the households of King Francis I and Marguerite de Navarre. Marot composed light, elegant, witty verse that pleased the gay, wealthy members of court society. But his poetry also reveals,

ROBERT E. DICKINSON

with great artistry and devotion to truth, the social and intellectual realities of the time. Shortly before his death, he published a significant translation of the Psalms. Some critics consider Marot an unimportant court poet. Others, especially present-day critics, call him a genuine moralist who wrote with delicacy and discretion.

Marot was born in Cahors. He died in Italy, exiled from Roman Catholic France because of his Protestant beliefs.

JOEL A. HUNT

MARQUAND, *mahr QUAHND,* **JOHN PHILLIPS** (1893-1960), an American novelist, pictured the decayed aristocratic society in Boston with gentle but effective satire. He won a Pulitzer prize in 1938 for *The Late George Apley.* This, and *Wickford Point* (1939), *H. M. Pulham, Esq.* (1941), and *Point of No Return* (1949) are usually considered his best works. They show how the inheritors of wealth conform to old customs without understanding the duties of a new age.

Marie S. Newberry

John P. Marquand

He also wrote *Repent in Haste* (1945); *Melville Goodwin, USA* (1951); *Sincerely, Willis Wayde* (1955); and *Stopover: Tokyo* (1957). *Thirty Years* (1954) contains essays and reports on his own observations. Marquand won his first success with romantic novels and with serialized detective stories about Mr. Moto, a secret agent.

Marquand was born in Wilmington, Del. He was graduated from Harvard University, and became a reporter on the Boston *Transcript.*

HARRY R. WARFEL

MARQUE AND REPRISAL, *mahrk, re PRĪZ ul.* Governments at once granted written *commissions* (licenses) to private owners of ships, giving them the authority to wage war against enemy shipping. These commissions were called *letters of marque and reprisal.* Vessels sailing under such commissions were known as *privateers.* See also PRIVATEER.

MARQUESAS ISLANDS, *mahr KAY sus,* are a group of 11 volcanic islands which lie about 740 miles northwest of Tahiti, in the south Pacific Ocean. They belong to France. The islands cover an area of 492 square miles, and have a population of about 5,000. The capital of the islands is Atuona, on Hiva Oa. The people are governed from Papeete in Tahiti. For location, see PACIFIC ISLANDS (color map).

The Land. The Marquesas, in order of size, are Nuku Hiva (the largest), Hiva Oa, Ua Pu, Fatu Hiva, Ua Huka, Tahuata, Eiao, Hatutu, Motane, Fatu Huku, and Motu Iti. All are fertile and mountainous. The highest point, on Hiva Oa, is 4,130 feet above sea level. There are sheltered harbors in deep bays. The Marquesas have a healthful climate with variable rainfall. The chief crops include breadfruit, taro, bananas, sweet potatoes, and coconuts. The chief export is *copra,* the dried meat of coconuts.

The People. The Marquesans were once populated by at least 100,000 Polynesians, a brown-skinned people famous for their daring voyages over thousands of miles in the Pacific Ocean. They are related to the Tahitians, but have a civilization of their own. The first explorers found the Polynesians handsome, generous, and hospitable. They built houses on platforms made of stone blocks, and were clever at carving wood, shell, and bone. After contact with white men, diseases killed most of the Polynesians.

History. The islands were discovered by Álvaro de Mendaña, a Spaniard, in 1595. Captain James Cook, Joseph Ingraham, and others explored the islands. The Marquesas are famous in art and literature. Paul Gauguin, the French painter, lived, painted, died, and was buried on Hiva Oa. Herman Melville, the American novelist, described the islands in his novel *Typee.* It is a fictional tale of the actual adventures of Melville as a young man.

EDWIN H. BRYAN, JR.

See also PACIFIC ISLANDS (Polynesia).

MARQUETRY. See FURNITURE (William and Mary); INLAY.

Polynesians on the Marquesas Islands at one time decorated their bodies with elaborate tattoos, left. A drawing made in the late 1700's, below, shows the outrigger canoes they used.

American Museum of Natural History, New York

175

MARQUETTE, *mahr KET,* **JACQUES,** *zhahk* (1637-1675), was a French missionary and explorer in America. With the fur trader Louis Joliet and others, he discovered that the Mississippi River flowed into the Gulf of Mexico (see JOLIET, LOUIS). They are also believed to have been the first white men to enter what is now Illinois.

In 1673, Father Marquette, Joliet, and their party began a great expedition. They were sent by Governor Frontenac of Canada to look for a route to the Pacific Ocean. Marquette, Joliet, and five other Frenchmen left Lake Michigan and paddled their canoes up the Fox River to what is now Portage, Wis. They carried their canoes across land to the Wisconsin River. Here the two Indian guides deserted them for fear of what lay ahead. Marquette and his companions pushed on alone. They went down the Wisconsin River until suddenly they came to a broad, majestic stream. It was the Mississippi. They went south on this river, stopping for a peaceful meeting with the Illinois Indians. The chief of the Illinois gave them a *calumet* (peace pipe), which later saved their lives.

Marquette and Joliet led their party down the Mississippi to the mouth of the Arkansas River. Strange Indians with guns suddenly surrounded them there. Only the sight of the Illinois peace pipe kept these In-

Father Marquette and His Symbol of Peace, engraving by A. Bobbet, Newberry Library, Ayer Collection, Chicago

Father Jacques Marquette worked as a missionary among the American Indians. They loved him so much that he could travel freely among them merely by carrying a peace pipe.

dians from attacking. Some of them became friendly enough to tell Marquette that the guns came from other white men who were some 10 days' journey farther south. These could only be Spaniards, and it would have been dangerous to go on. So the French explorers ended their trip down the Mississippi. They returned to Canada by way of the Illinois River. They passed the present site of Chicago on this part of the trip.

Marquette was born in Laon, France, and became a Jesuit priest (see JESUIT [Missionary Work]). He was sent to Canada as a missionary in 1666. He had great influence with the Indians around Sault Sainte Marie and the Straits of Mackinac, because he learned their language and customs. He went into the Illinois country again in 1674, but his health was poor. He died on the return trip. In 1677, his remains were brought to St. Ignace, Mich., and buried there.   FRANKLIN L. FORD

See also CHICAGO (The First Settlers); ILLINOIS (French and English Control).

MARQUETTE UNIVERSITY is a coeducational school conducted by the Society of Jesus in Milwaukee, Wis. The university admits students of all faiths. The courses offered lead to degrees in liberal arts, business administration, journalism, engineering, nursing, speech, dentistry, law, and other fields. The university has a graduate school and a summer school. Marquette was chartered in 1864, opened in 1881, and became a university in 1907. The school colors are blue and old gold. The athletic teams are called the *Warriors.* For the enrollment of Marquette University, see UNIVERSITIES AND COLLEGES (table).   E. S. CARPENTER

MARQUIS. See WHEAT (Breeding Disease-Resistant Wheats).

MARQUIS, *MAHR kwis,* is a degree of nobility in the British peerage. A marquis ranks higher than an earl or a baron, and second only to a duke. The name *marquis* once meant the ruler of an outlying province.

MARQUIS, "DON," DONALD PERRY (1878-1937), was a noted American writer and newspaper columnist. His daily columns, "The Sun Dial" in the New York *Sun* and "The Lantern" in the New York *Herald Tribune,* became highly popular. He introduced *archy,* the cockroach, and *mehitabel,* the cat. Marquis published *archy and mehitabel* in 1927.

Marquis wrote humorous books, including *Love Sonnets of a Cave Man* (1928). His *The Old Soak* (1921) was made into a successful play in 1922. His serious books include *The Dark Hours* (1924) and *Out of the Sea* (1927). He was born in Walnut, Ill.   EDWIN H. CADY

MARQUIS OF QUEENSBERRY RULES. See QUEENSBERRY RULES.

MARRAKECH, *muh RAH kesh* (pop. 255,000; alt. 1,535 ft.), is the third largest city in Morocco and one of its traditional capitals. It lies in the southwestern part of the country (see Morocco [color map]). It is noted for its *mosques* (Moslem houses of worship), parks, gardens, and pink clay buildings. The chief industries in Marrakech include food processing, flour milling, and leather and textile manufacturing.

Marrakech was once the capital of a vast Berber empire. The city was founded by the Berber ruler Yusuf ibn-Tashfin in 1062, and reached the height of its prosperity in the 1400's. Its importance declined when a succession of Arab rulers replaced the Berbers in Morocco.   KEITH G. MATHER

Ewing Galloway

Marriage Begins with a wedding. Many girls dream of elaborate gowns and services, but others prefer a simple wedding.

MARRIAGE is a relationship uniting a man and a woman. It is a contract, requiring an agreement between the two persons. But it is much more than the usual contract. The relationship arising from the agreement to live together as husband and wife is imposed by law. It is known as a *status* (legal relationship).

Marriage is a social institution that is set up to provide for family life. It gives responsibility and permanence to the relationships between a man and a woman. People everywhere feel that the regulations of marriage are necessary to protect women and children and to maintain the stability of the community. Every known society has prescribed marriage as the normal and accepted way of expressing adult love and of establishing a family. From the earliest times, marriage has been an important part of man's legal and religious systems.

Marriage is the basis for the family. The rights, duties, and obligations of marriage are expected to continue during the lives of husband and wife, unless the marriage is ended by a legal action. The husband and wife are legally responsible for their children. They must protect and care for them, and not leave them to be supported by the community.

After two people have been dating, or courting, for some time, they may agree to marry. Their agreement is known as an *engagement*, or a *betrothal*. The promises they make are binding, but neither party can be forced to perform them by entering into the marriage. Some states allow one party to bring suit for breach of promise if the other party refuses to carry out the promise. But breach of promise suits are not as common today as they once were.

A person may marry for one or for many reasons. Among these are the desire for such things as economic or emotional security, a home and children, companionship, protection, and social position. In addition, contemporary society is organized in such a way that people are expected to marry.

Marriage Laws

The legal basis of marriage is the government. Each state or nation sets up its own requirements for a valid

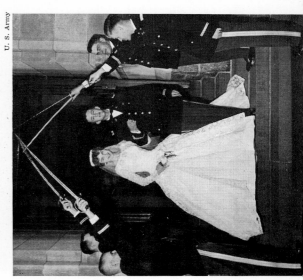

U. S. Army

A Military Wedding, such as this one at the Cadet Chapel of West Point, adds military customs to the traditional ceremonies.

marriage. In general, the United States and Canada have the same basic laws. Neither country has federal marriage laws that apply to all the people. Instead, marriage laws differ from state to state and from province to province. Most of these laws apply to (1) minimum ages for the parties involved, (2) provision for a license, (3) necessity of a ceremony, and (4) other restrictions.

Age. The two persons who intend to marry must be above a certain age that is set by law. Most states require the boy to be at least 18 and the girl at least 16. However, a few states allow the girl to be as young as 14, and two states allow the boy to be 15. The laws of most states also provide that their parents must consent to the marriage if the boy is under 21, or the girl is under 18.

License. The couple must have a marriage license. Many states require that both persons have medical

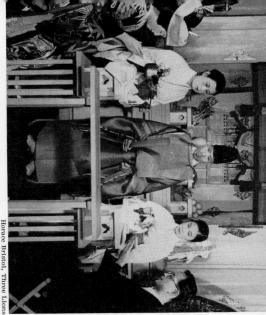

During a Japanese Shinto Wedding, the bride and groom drink rice wine in front of a priest to seal their marriage vows.

examinations and blood tests before they can obtain a marriage license. Some states require a waiting period of three to five days between the time the couple applies for a license and the time of the marriage.

Ceremony. The marriage ceremony itself may be a religious ceremony, performed in a church by a minister or a priest, or in a synagogue by a rabbi. Or it may be a civil ceremony, performed anywhere by a civil official such as a judge. By tradition, the captain of a ship is regarded as authorized to conduct a ceremony while a ship is at sea.

Some states require couples to announce their intention of marrying a certain length of time before the ceremony. Many couples follow this practice, started by the Roman Catholic Church, by having their engagement announced in church for several Sundays. These announcements are called *banns*.

Other Restrictions are imposed by most states, such as laws that first cousins may not marry each other. *Miscegenation*, or marriage between persons of different races, was once illegal in a number of states. But in 1967, the Supreme Court of the United States ruled that states cannot outlaw miscegenation. Persons of unsound mind, persons with epilepsy or some other specified disease, or persons with physical incapacity are often prohibited by state laws from marrying.

A common requirement is that both parties freely consent to the marriage. If it can be shown that either the bride or the groom was threatened or forced, the marriage may be declared void.

State laws do not permit a person who has been married once to marry again while the first marriage is still in effect. Marrying a second time in such a case constitutes the crime of *bigamy*, and the second marriage is considered void.

In some states, so-called *common-law marriages* are recognized as valid. These are informal marriages in which the parties have not complied with the legal requirements for a license or a ceremony. They simply carry out an agreement to live as husband and wife. The community recognizes them as a married couple.

In some states where an agreement to live together is all that is necessary, marriages by mail or telephone may be possible. A *marriage by proxy* is common in

some countries and may be recognized in some states. In this ceremony, one of the parties is not present. Someone else substitutes for him as his *proxy*.

A marriage is usually considered valid according to the laws of the state where the ceremony was performed. But two persons who are not qualified to marry under the laws of one state may go to another state where the laws are different, have the ceremony performed, and then return. The couple's home state may, and often does, refuse to recognize the validity of the marriage.

Certain religions or organizations restrict *intermarriage* of their members with persons of different faiths or social groups.

Religious Ceremonies

All churches recognize the religious element in marriage, and have a special marriage ceremony.

Protestant ceremonies usually take place before the altar, with the minister facing the bridal couple and the congregation. The minister sometimes begins with a short sermon on the sacredness of married life. His text is partly for the benefit of the congregation, but also includes some instruction for the couple getting married. The bride and groom then exchange promises to "love, honor, and cherish" each other as long as they both shall live. They join hands, and the groom gives the bride a ring. As he places it on her finger, he says, "With this ring I thee wed." In a *double-ring ceremony*, the bride also gives the groom a ring. Finally, the minister declares that they "are husband and wife," and concludes by saying "Those whom God hath joined together, let not man put asunder." But there are variations in these procedures and in the exact words used.

Roman Catholic weddings are part of the ceremony of the Nuptial Mass. At one time, the Mass followed the wedding ceremony. But since 1964, the ceremony takes place during the Mass—after the Gospel. The couple kneels at the altar, where the priest begins Mass. During the wedding ceremony, the priest instructs the couple and asks each to express willingness to marry the other. Bride and groom join right hands, and repeat the marriage vows after the priest. The priest then confirms the marriage vows with the words, "I join you together in matrimony . . ." He sprinkles the couple with holy water and blesses the ring or rings. He assists the couple in the ring ceremony and ends by repeating a series of prayers and blessings. Mass then continues. Usually, the husband and wife receive Holy Communion. They are given a special blessing for their marriage.

Jewish wedding ceremonies usually take place under a special canopy. As the bride and groom enter, the rabbi greets them and says, "Blessed be you who come here in the name of the Lord." Later, the rabbi offers a series of seven special prayers, praising God and His creations. Near the middle of the ceremony, he blesses some wine, and both bride and groom drink from the same cup. Each of the partners makes appropriate vows, and takes part in the ring ceremony. Near the end, the rabbi pronounces the couple husband and wife. After the ceremony, an empty wine glass is placed on the floor, and the new husband smashes it with his foot. This act commemorates the destruction of the Jewish Temple, and reminds the couple that marriage, too, might be broken unless protected. Other people interpret this act as a reminder to the couple that sadness can enter into life.

Other Religious Groups have marriage ceremonies that differ from these. For example, Quakers have little ceremony at all. The bride and groom simply stand before the congregation and announce that they intend to live together as husband and wife. They then sign a marriage document. Most Mormon weddings take place in Temples, and have lengthy ceremonies. Mormons believe these marriages will be good, not only "until death do you part," but for the next life as well.

Marriage Customs

When two persons agree to marry, the man usually gives the girl a ring as a token of his promise to marry

Courtesy of Dr. Leonard C. Mishkin

A Traditional Jewish Wedding takes place under a special canopy. This marriage custom is hundreds of years old.

her. This is the *engagement ring*. Legally, this ring belongs to the man until the marriage takes place. If the engagement is broken, the woman is supposed to return the ring. After the wedding, the ring is hers. The use of a ring as an engagement token comes from the ancient custom of using a ring to seal any sacred or important agreement. Many types of gems have been used in engagement rings, but the diamond has come to be the most popular. An old superstition tells that the diamond's sparkle originated in the alchemists' fires of love.

When a couple marries, the groom presents his bride with another ring, known as the *wedding ring*. Many weddings today involve double-ring ceremonies, in which both bride and groom exchange rings. Wedding rings are worn as long as husband and wife live together, as reminders of their marriage vows. A single unadorned band has always been the most popular style of wedding ring. Many people believe that its roundness represents eternity, and that it is a symbol that the couple is united forever. The wedding ring is usually worn on the third finger of the left hand. Many people once thought that a vein or nerve in this finger ran directly to the heart.

There are many other customs surrounding marriage, but they have nothing to do with civil or church laws. Many of these customs have developed from the wedding rites of earlier times. Many persons believe that the best man today fills the same function as the groom's strong-armed friend of earlier times. He helped the groom escape from the bride's father. The wedding veil may have developed from the Roman custom of having the bride wear a full-length veil that was later used as her burial shroud. The bride often tosses her bouquet to the unmarried girls as she leaves. This custom is said to have started in France in the 1300's. At that time, the bride threw a garter or a stocking. The lucky girl who caught it was supposed to be the next in the group to be married. The custom of having the groom carry the bride over the threshold probably comes from the ancient practice of capturing a wife. The honeymoon tradition may also have started in the days of marriage by capture. During the honeymoon, the groom waited, hoping his wife's parents would stop being angry.

MARITAL STATUS OF THE U.S. POPULATION

Persons 14 years old and over

Year	Single	Married	Widowed	Divorced
1890	16,307,000	22,331,000	2,970,000	121,000
1900	19,427,000	27,770,000	3,896,000	199,000
1910	23,327,000	35,781,000	4,647,000	341,000
1920	24,622,000	43,176,000	5,676,000	508,000
1930	28,637,000	52,503,000	6,759,000	1,062,000
1940	31,529,000	60,282,000	7,844,000	1,447,000
1950	25,461,000	74,860,000	9,263,000	2,148,000
1960	27,651,000	84,406,000	10,551,000	2,850,000
1965	31,947,000	89,441,000	10,944,000	3,508,000
1968	34,642,000	92,122,000	11,447,000	3,970,000

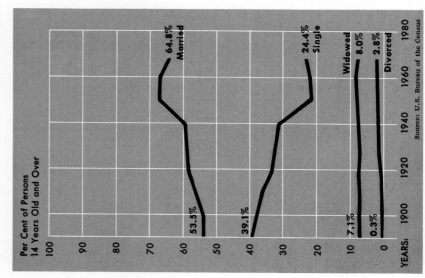

Per Cent of Persons 14 Years Old and Over

Married 53.5% → 64.8%
Single 39.1% → 24.4%
Widowed 7.1% → 8.0%
Divorced 0.3% → 2.8%

YEARS: 1900 1920 1940 1960 1980

Source: U.S. Bureau of the Census

179

MARRIAGE

Other customs are old superstitions that are supposed to bring luck to the marriage. Some persons believe that the bride will insure her luck if she wears "something old, something new, something borrowed, something blue, and a lucky sixpence in her shoe." It is supposed to be bad luck for a bride and bridegroom to see each other before the ceremony on their wedding day. At the end of the ceremony, guests often toss rice and old shoes as a wish for prosperity and children. Both of these customs are of ancient origin. The ancient Assyrians, Hebrews, and Egyptians gave or traded sandals as a symbol of good faith in making a bargain. Rice was an emblem of fruitfulness among many early peoples, and it was thrown after weddings to symbolize the wish for children. Or it may have been an offering to the evil spirits, asking them to stay away from the couple.

Marriage customs in other English-speaking countries and in Europe are much like those of the United States, except that there are many local additions and changes to fit each particular culture. Laws regulate only a few customs, but even those vary from country to country. When custom and law require different things, people generally try to comply with both. For instance, in some countries, it is quite common for couples to have two marriage ceremonies. One is a civil ceremony, to comply with the law, and the other is a religious ceremony, to satisfy the requirements of their faith.

Various peoples have followed the custom of making engagements for children while they are young, or even of having children marry. This custom is common in parts of India and Indonesia. In many countries that have the system of civil law developed from Roman law, a bride's parents pick her husband while she is still a child. The girl has no choice in the matter. The prospective husband and his family present gifts to the father and other relatives of the bride. This payment is called the *bride price*. In return, the bride's family may give the groom or his family a *dowry* (a gift of money, goods, or land). The custom of giving a dowry is followed in many countries. In some countries, members of the ruling house or higher nobility make *morganatic marriages* when they marry women of lower social ranks. Children of such marriages may inherit neither the father's rank nor estate.

Some peoples have practiced *polygamy* (*poh LIG ah mee*), in which one man has more than one wife, or one woman has more than one husband. *Polyandry* (*PAHL-*

In Yugoslavia, the couple's oldest relative is the first to enter the new household with traditional gifts, bread and salt.

Dever, Black Star

ih AN dree), in which a woman may have more than one husband, is practiced in parts of India, Ceylon, and Tibet, and among some Eskimo tribes.

The marriage of one man to two or more women, called *polygyny* (*poh LIJ ih nee*), is more common than polyandry, particularly in Oriental countries and in primitive societies. In most communities that practice polygyny, wives are considered to be property. The women do most of the work in the household, and a great deal of agricultural work. But polygyny is usually limited to wealthy men, because most men cannot afford to pay for more than one wife.

In primitive times, the marriage relationship did not last long. Often the woman was simply a captured slave. When there was no war to supply wives, men could purchase women. Among many savage tribes, the custom of wife-capture was practiced for hundreds of years. It was sometimes accepted even among civilized nations. The early history of Greece, Rome, and Northern Europe shows that these practices existed until Christian times. Most primitive marriages are *endogamous*, which means a man may not marry a woman from another tribe. The reverse of this custom is *exogamy*. In exogamous marriages a man can marry only a woman from some other tribe.

HAROLD T. CHRISTENSEN

Related Articles in WORLD BOOK include:

Annulment	Dower
Banns of Marriage	Eugenics
Bigamy	Family
Breach of Promise	Gretna Green
Divorce	Hymen
Polygamy	
Proxy	
Roman Catholic Church (picture)	
Wedding Anniversary	

MARRIAGE OF FIGARO, THE. See OPERA (Some of the Famous Operas).

MARROW. See BONE (Structure of the Bones).

MARRYAT, FREDERICK (1792-1848), was an English author whose novels about life at sea were widely read during the 1800's. The novels have declined in popularity, but they remain fine examples of adventure stories.

Marryat was born in London. As a boy he tried to run away to sea several times. When Marryat was 14 years old, his father allowed him to join the navy. Marryat's 23 years of sea adventures in the British navy provided material for his writing. *The Naval Officer, or Scenes and Adventures in the Life of Frank Mildmay* (1829), for example, is largely an autobiographical novel. Marryat's other sea novels include *The King's Own* (1830), *The Pirate and the Three Cutters* (1836), and *Mr. Midshipman Easy* (1836). He also wrote children's stories, including *Masterman Ready* (1841-1842). JAMES D. MERRITT

MARS, son of Jupiter and Juno, was the god of war in Roman mythology. He is generally ranked second in importance only to his father. He was originally a god of agriculture and fruitfulness, but later became a god of war. At this time he became identified with the Greek *Ares*, and most of the stories about him are taken from the legend of Ares. Mars and Venus became lovers and had a daughter, Harmonia.

Mars supposedly was the father of Romulus and Remus, the legendary founders of Rome (see ROMULUS AND REMUS). His temple and festivals were important at Rome. The month of March, named for him, began the Roman year (see MARCH). Wolves and chickens were especially sacred to him, and many soldiers going into battle carried chickens with them. Under the emperor Augustus, Mars became known as *Ultor*. H. LLOYD STOW

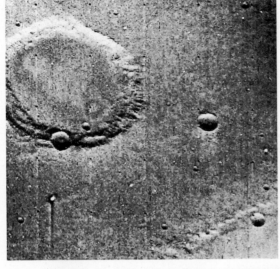

Jet Propulsion Laboratory, California Institute of Technology

Craters on Mars were photographed by the U.S. *Mariner VI* space probe in 1969. This picture was taken 2,300 miles from the planet. The large crater is about 24 miles across.

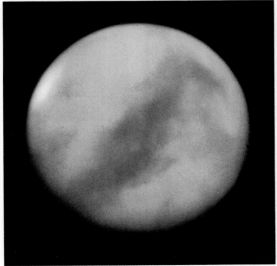

Mount Wilson and Mount Palomar Observatories

Mars' Surface Features, including light areas, dark areas, and polar cap, are visible in this photograph taken from the earth. The atmosphere of the earth makes the picture blurred.

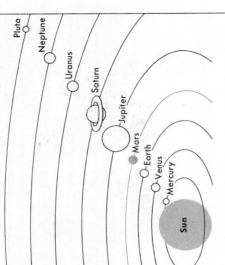

MARS is the only planet whose surface can be seen in detail from the earth. It appears red from the earth, and was named Mars after the bloody red god of war of the ancient Romans.

Mars is the fourth closest planet to the sun, and the next planet beyond the earth. Its mean distance from the sun is about 141,500,000 miles, compared with about 93,000,000 miles for the earth. At its closest approach to the earth, Mars is 35,000,000 miles away. Venus is the only planet that comes closer to the earth.

The diameter of Mars is about 4,200 miles, a little more than half that of the earth. Pluto and Mercury are the only planets that are smaller than Mars.

Orbit. Mars travels around the sun in an *elliptical* (oval-shaped) orbit. Its distance from the sun varies from about 155 million miles at its farthest point, to about 128 million miles at its closest point. Mars takes about 687 earth-days to go around the sun, compared with about 365 days, or 1 year, for the earth.

Rotation. As Mars orbits the sun, it spins on its *axis,* an imaginary line drawn through its center. Mars' axis is not *perpendicular* (at an angle of 90°) to the planet's path around the sun. The axis tilts at an angle of about 25° from the perpendicular position. For an illustration of the tilt of an axis, see PLANET (The Axes of the Planets). Mars rotates once every 24 hours and 37 minutes. The earth rotates once every 24 hours.

Surface. The surface conditions on Mars are more like the earth's than are those of any other planet. But the plants and animals of the earth could not live on Mars. The temperature on Mars averages about

The contributor of this article is Hyron Spinrad, Associate Professor of Astronomy at the University of California in Berkeley.

—80° F. (−62° C.). There is not enough water on the planet to fill even a small lake on the earth. The atmosphere surrounding Mars contains almost no oxygen. In spite of these conditions, some astronomers believe that some form of plant life exists on Mars.

As seen from the earth through a telescope, the surface of Mars has three outstanding features—bright areas, dark areas, and polar caps. At least part of the planet's surface is covered by craters, caused by meteors crashing into it.

Bright Areas of Mars are yellow-orange in color, and cover about two-thirds of the planet's surface. They are dry, desertlike regions and are believed to be covered with dust. These regions give Mars its red appearance when the planet is viewed from the earth.

Dark Areas of Mars cover about one-third of the planet's surface. They form irregular patterns, and generally appear greenish or bluish gray in color. These dark regions are called *maria* (seas), even though they do not have any measurable amounts of water.

Astronomers once thought the bright areas of Mars were higher than the maria. But after bouncing radar beams off the surface of the planet, some astronomers think the dark areas are higher. The difference in height between the two regions probably averages about five miles. The slopes from high ground to low ground are probably gradual rather than steep.

The color and size of Mars' dark areas vary throughout the planet's year. Parts of the maria become lighter in color or disappear during the Martian fall and winter. They become darker and larger during the Martian spring and summer. This variation has caused some astronomers to believe that the dark areas consist of some form of plant life. The growth and death of this plant life during the various Martian seasons would cause the changes in color and size. Other astronomers think the changes are caused by blowing sand and dust that covers and uncovers parts of Mars' surface.

A series of lines running between Mars' dark areas was discovered in 1877 by Giovanni V. Schiaparelli, an Italian astronomer. Schiaparelli called these lines "channels," but when the word was translated from Italian into English, it became "canals." As a result, some scientists thought the lines might be man-made waterways. Astronomers now know the canals on Mars are not man-made, and do not carry water. The canals change color during the Martian seasons, and some astronomers think they are cracks lined with the same type of plant life as that on the maria.

Polar Caps of Mars cover small areas at the planet's north and south poles. The polar caps appear white from the earth, and consist of either frozen water or frozen carbon dioxide. Like the maria, each cap grows and shrinks with the Martian seasons. A cap appears to evaporate and become smaller when it is tilted toward the sun, and then freeze and get larger when it is tilted away from the sun. The evaporating polar caps may provide some of the water on Mars' surface.

Atmosphere of Mars is thinner and contains fewer gases than that surrounding the earth. For many years, astronomers thought Mars' atmosphere consisted chiefly of nitrogen, with small amounts of carbon dioxide. More recent observations indicate that it consists mainly

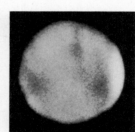
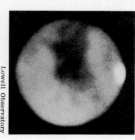

Seasons on Mars cause changes in the planet's surface features. During a Martian winter, the polar cap is large and the dark areas are small, *left*. During a Martian summer, the polar cap shrinks and the dark areas become larger, *right*.

Lowell Observatory

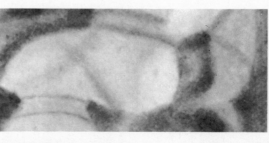
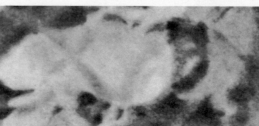

The Canals on Mars' Surface appear as solid straight lines in a drawing, *left*, made under average viewing conditions. A drawing made under excellent viewing conditions, *right*, shows the canals as uneven, broken markings.

Dr. Audouin Dollfus, Paris Observatory

The Two Satellites of Mars appear in a photograph of the planet taken through a telescope. Phobos, *left*, is a bright spot near Mars. Deimos, *right*, is fainter and farther from the planet.

Lowell Observatory

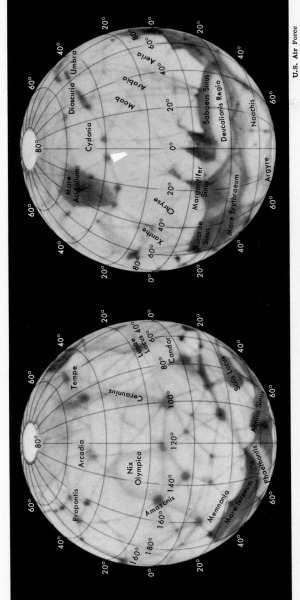

Maps of Mars' Surface Show the Names Astronomers Have Given to General Areas of the Planet.

U.S. Air Force

of carbon dioxide, with small amounts of water vapor, and possibly nitrogen and argon. The *atmospheric pressure* (force exerted by the weight of the gases) on Mars is only about 0.15 pounds per square inch, compared with about 14.7 pounds per square inch for the earth.

Three general types of clouds can be seen in the Martian atmosphere. Yellow clouds, which astronomers believe are dust clouds, sometimes cover large areas of the planet. Thin blue clouds appear to be made up of ice crystals. Thicker white clouds, thought to consist of water vapor, occasionally move across the planet at a speed of about 10 miles per hour.

By using a colored lens, astronomers photograph Mars with red or yellow light so that details on its surface can be seen more clearly. But if Mars is photographed with blue light, it becomes a gray disk with no features at all. A blue haze in its atmosphere hides its surface details. At various times, the blue haze has cleared for short periods. Astronomers do not know what causes the blue haze, or what causes it to clear.

Temperature. The tilt of Mars' axis causes the sun to heat the planet's northern and southern halves unequally, resulting in seasons and temperature changes. The seasons on Mars last about twice as long as those on the earth, because Mars takes almost twice as long to go around the sun as the earth does.

Temperatures on Mars are generally lower than those on the earth, because Mars is farther from the sun than the earth is. The average temperature for the entire planet is about −80° F. (−62° C.). There is a wide variation between daytime and nighttime temperatures. The average daytime temperature is about −10° F. (−23° C.). But in areas near Mars' equator, daytime temperatures may rise as high as 70° F. (21° C.). The average nighttime temperature on Mars has never been accurately measured, but astronomers estimate it to be about −150° F. (−101° C.).

Density and Mass. Mars is about four-fifths as *dense* as the earth (see DENSITY). The *mass* of Mars is only about a tenth that of the earth (see MASS). Because of the planet's smaller mass, its force of gravity is about three-eighths as strong as the earth's. A 100-pound object on the earth would weigh about 38 pounds on Mars.

Satellites. Two small *satellites* (moons) travel around Mars. The closest and largest one, named Phobos, is about 5,800 miles from the center of Mars. It travels around Mars once about every 7½ hours. Deimos, the smaller of the two satellites, is about 14,600 miles from the center of the planet, and circles Mars once about every 30 hours. Each satellite has a diameter of less than 10 miles. Both were discovered in 1877 by an American astronomer, Asaph Hall, at the U.S. Naval Observatory in Washington, D.C.

Flights to Mars. Mars and Venus are the only two planets that have been observed by a passing spacecraft. The U.S. spacecraft *Mariner IV* flew within 8,000 miles of Mars in 1965. *Mariner VI* and *Mariner VII* flew within about 2,000 miles of Mars in 1969.

Photographs sent back to the earth from *Mariner IV* revealed the meteor craters on the surface of Mars. Astronomers had never seen craters in observations from the earth. The photographs did not show any canals or any sign of life on Mars, but the area photographed was only about 1 per cent of the surface.

Measurements made by *Mariner IV* showed that Mars has no measurable *magnetic field*. That is, a compass on Mars would not point to either of the planet's poles. Other measurements showed that Mars' atmosphere is similar to that predicted by astronomers.

More spacecraft will explore Mars in the future. Some of them will land on Mars, and someday there will be manned space flights to the planet.   HYRON SPINRAD

See also ASTRONOMY; PLANET; SOLAR SYSTEM; SPACE TRAVEL (Reaching the Planets and Stars).

MARS HILL, or HILL, OF ARES. See AREOPAGUS.

MARS HILL COLLEGE. See UNIVERSITIES AND COLLEGES (table).

MARSEILLAISE, *MAHR seh LAYZ*, is the national hymn of France. A young captain of the engineers named Claude Joseph Rouget de Lisle (1760-1836) wrote it during the French Revolution. It is believed that he composed both the words and the music in one night. Some historians believe he took the music from an old Protestant hymn and the words from war slogans. Others say he wrote the song in 1792 at a banquet the mayor of Strasbourg gave for 600 army volunteers. It aroused such enthusiasm that 400 more men joined the company. Some of the best known lines are the following:

Allons enfants de la patrie,
Le jour de gloire est arrivé.
Aux armes citoyens! Formez vos bataillons.
Marchons, marchons, qu'un sang impur
Abreuve nos sillons.

The song was first heard in Paris when the Marseille battalion sang it as they marched to storm the Tuileries. After that, it was called "Song of the Marseillais," and finally "The Marseillaise." The composer died in 1836 in Choisy-le-Roi. A monument to his memory has been built there. In 1875, France adopted the song as its national hymn.

RAYMOND KENDALL

MARSEILLE, *mahr SAY* (pop. 889,029; met. area 964,412; alt. 150 ft.), is the greatest seaport of France, and the greatest on the Mediterranean. Only Paris is larger among French cities. Marseille is the chief city of the department of Bouches-du-Rhône, and is 27 miles east of the Rhône River's mouth. For location, see FRANCE (political map).

The city is built in the shape of a half-circle around a natural harbor of fair size, known as the Old Harbor. A newer harbor was built about 1850. It has a water area of 414 acres and a depth great enough to float the largest ocean-going vessels. About 4,500 ships enter and clear the port of Marseille each year. The city is often called the *port of all men* because ships from most countries anchor in its harbor.

Marseille is also a great manufacturing center. Raw materials brought in by sea from all parts of the world are processed in the Marseille area. The chief manufactures include soap, steam engines and automobiles, oil, candles, macaroni, tiles, and brick. There are also sugar and petroleum refineries, lead, tin, and copper plants, tanneries, and flour mills. Harbor improvements and the construction of the Marseille-Rhône Canal have improved the city's position in world trade.

Famous buildings include a large cathedral built in the style of a Byzantine basilica, and the well-known church of Notre-Dame-de-la-Garde. The church stands on a high hill and has a great image of the Virgin on its lofty steeple. The image can be seen far out at sea.

Marseille is one of the oldest seaports in Europe. The Greeks founded the seaport about 600 B.C. They set up a colony on the site of the Old Harbor and called it *Massilia*. It became a great trading center in ancient times, and joined with Rome in the wars against Carthage. Bloody struggles took place there during the French Revolution, and the name of the city was given to the great hymn of the Revolutionary period—"The Marseillaise" (see MARSEILLAISE).

Marseille had no connection with the canal system of France until 1928 when engineers dug a great tunnel through the mountains back of the city. They linked the tunnel with a canal to the Rhône River. It is about 4½ miles long, the largest of its kind in Europe. The canal is 72 feet wide and 51 feet deep, with a 6-foot towpath along each wall. The cost, 135 million francs ($5,292,000), was shared by France and the city.

ROBERT E. DICKINSON

MARSH is an area of soft, wet land. It is periodically covered with water. It is treeless, but usually has many grasses, cattails, and other plants. It is often called a swamp or morass. See also SWAMP.

MARSH, REGINALD (1898-1954), was an American artist famous for his vigorous and realistic pictures of American city life. He excelled in portraying crowds on skid row and the waterfront, and in burlesque houses. Some of his scenes are grim in feeling, but filled with vitality. Marsh worked in various painting media, and also made drawings. Some of his best works are drawings.

Marsh was born in Paris of American parents. He grew up in New Jersey and graduated from Yale University. He worked as an illustrator of books and magazine articles, and as a graphic artist for the *New York Daily News*. He taught art at the Art Students League in New York from the early 1930's until his death.

GEORGE EHRLICH

MARSH GAS. See METHANE.

MARSH HAWK is the only harrier hawk that lives in North America. The marsh hawk is one of the best known birds of prey in North America. It visits almost every part of the continent at some time during the year. Marsh hawks are seldom seen over 24 inches long. The male is usually about 19 inches long with a wingspread of 40 to 45 inches. The female is 2 to 3 inches longer.

The Marsh Hawk is a friend to the North American farmer. This valuable bird kills rats, mice, snakes, and other harmful pests.

Allen Cruickshank

The male is light gray and white. The female is a rich brown and tan. Both have a white patch above the base of the tail. Marsh hawks eat mice, poultry, game birds, and snakes.

Scientific Classification. The marsh hawk belongs to the Old World vulture family, *Accipitridae*. It is genus *Circus*, species *C. cyaneus*.   OLIN SEWALL PETTINGILL, JR.

See also HARRIER; BIRD (Bird Courtship); HAWK.

MARSH MALLOW is a coarse plant which belongs to the mallow family. It grows wild in meadows and marshes of eastern Europe, and is now grown in the United States. The marsh mallow has woody stalks which grow 2 to 4 feet high. The leaves are large and wide. Soft, downy hair covers both stalks and leaves. The marsh mallow has pale pink flowers. Its root is white and shaped like a carrot. During periods of famine, people have eaten marsh mallow roots. The root once was used as a basis for the candy called marshmallow. It is sometimes used to make glue.

Scientific Classification. The marsh mallow belongs to the mallow family, *Malvaceae*. It is genus *Althaea*, species *A. officinalis*.   HAROLD NORMAN MOLDENKE

J. Horace McFarland

The Marsh Mallow Flower has rounded, pale pink petals. The leaves have notched edges and come to a sharp point.

MARSH MARIGOLD. See COWSLIP.

MARSHAL is the highest title in the armies of many countries. *Marshal* is also the title of a police officer in many small towns or villages.

In England, the word *marshal* was used to mean *commander of the army* as early as the 1100's. Under the early Frankish kings, the marshal was first a master of horse and later a commander of cavalry. The title grew in dignity and honor until *Maréchal de France* (Marshal of France) became one of the highest honors that could be conferred upon a man. The countries of Europe have given the title *marshal* to top-ranking military commanders. Joseph Stalin, former dictator of Russia, used the title *Marshal* during World War II. The British Army uses the title *field marshal*, and the head of the air forces is called an *air marshal*. The *provost marshal* is the highest military police officer.

A *United States marshal* is an officer of the federal court. He opens and closes sessions of district courts and courts of appeals, and may serve the processes of the courts in his district. *Deputy United States marshals* can make arrests for violation of federal laws. A United States marshal is assigned to each federal court district. Temporary police are sometimes called marshals, and in some towns the head of the fire department is called the *fire marshal*.   ERWIN N. GRISWOLD

MARSHALL, ALFRED (1842-1924), was a British educator and the most influential economist of his day. Marshall combined two different theories about what determines the value or price of a good. "Classical" theorists had said price was determined mainly by the cost of producing the good, and theorists of the late 1800's had stressed the *utility* (usefulness) of the good and the consumer demand for it. In *Principles of Economics* (1890), Marshall concluded that all of these factors helped to determine price.

Marshall also believed that a self-regulating economy, free of major government interference and based on free competition and private enterprise, would lead to better social conditions, a fair distribution of income, and full employment. Marshall's emphasis on consumer welfare led to the development of *welfare economics*. This branch of economics judges economic systems according to how well they contribute to consumer satisfaction and human well-being.

Marshall was born in London. In 1883, he began teaching economics at Oxford University. He taught at Cambridge University from 1885 to 1908. At Cambridge, Marshall helped train a generation of economists who made the "Cambridge school" the most important of its time.   DANIEL R. FUSFELD

MARSHALL, GEORGE CATLETT (1880-1959), an American soldier and statesman, served as chief of staff of the United States Army during World War II (1939-1945). He also served as secretary of state from 1947 to 1949 and as secretary of defense from 1950 to 1951. Marshall was the first professional soldier to become secretary of state. In 1947, while serving in that post, he proposed the European Recovery Program, also called the Marshall Plan. Under this plan, the United States spent billions of dollars to rebuild war-torn western Europe. The Marshall Plan is credited with helping check the spread of Communism in Europe. Marshall's role in European reconstruction earned him the 1953 Nobel peace prize.

His Early Life. Marshall was born on Dec. 31, 1880, in Uniontown, Pa. He was the youngest of four children. His father owned coal and coke properties. The senior Marshall was extremely proud of his distant cousin John Marshall, the former chief justice of the Supreme Court (see MARSHALL, JOHN).

George C. Marshall
U.S. Army

George Marshall graduated from the Virginia Military Institute in Lexington, Va., in 1901. He was not an outstanding student, but his grades ranked him in the upper half of his class. He received an army commission as a second lieutenant of infantry in 1902. Marshall married Elizabeth Carter Coles in 1902. She died in 1927, and Marshall was married to Katherine Tupper Brown in 1930. He had no children.

His Early Career. Marshall began his army career in 1903, and attended the Army Staff College at Fort Leavenworth, Kans. He was graduated first in his class from the School of the Line. Marshall said later of this achievement, "Ambition had set in." He also served at various military posts in the United States.

Assigned to the Philippines again in 1913, he showed great ability for planning and tactics in mock battles. In 1916, he returned to the United States and was promoted to captain. When the United States entered World War I in 1917, Marshall sailed for France with the first field units to go overseas. He served for a year as training officer and then as chief of operations of the First Division. He was transferred to the First Army in 1918, and served as chief of operations in the closing months of the war.

Marshall helped plan the First Army's attack on St. Mihiel. He directed the movement of more than 400,-000 men and 2,700 guns from St. Mihiel to the Meuse-Argonne front for the final American battle of the war. This transfer, made at night in less than two weeks, completely surprised the Germans. General John J. Pershing, commander of the U.S. forces, hailed it as one of the great accomplishments of the war.

Marshall served as senior aide to Pershing from 1919 to 1924. From 1924 to 1927, he served in China as executive officer of the 15th Infantry Regiment.

From 1927 until 1932, Marshall was assistant commandant in charge of training at the Infantry School, Fort Benning, Ga. He did much to raise the level of instruction there. He later helped organize and administer Civilian Conservation Corps (CCC) camps.

World War II. Marshall was made a brigadier general in 1936. In 1938, he became chief of the war plans division of the War Department and then deputy chief of staff of the army. On Sept. 1, 1939, the day World War II began in Europe, Marshall became chief of staff of the U.S. Army, which then totaled less than 200,000 men, including the Army Air Corps. He also became a four-star general.

Marshall introduced mass maneuvers in which soldiers gained experience under combatlike conditions. He organized the army into units especially trained to take part in desert, mountain, and jungle warfare.

Marshall helped make the U.S. Army the greatest fighting force in history by 1945. He remained in Washington, D.C., throughout the war. His work there was so important that he could not be spared to serve as a battle leader. He was responsible for building, arming, and supplying a military force of 8,250,000 soldiers and airmen. He was a leader in planning the overall strategy of the war, and the directing force behind the movements of the United States armies. Under his command, General Dwight D. Eisenhower and General Douglas MacArthur led American forces to victory in Europe and the Pacific.

On Dec. 16, 1944, Marshall became a General of the Army. In November, 1945, a few months after the war ended, he retired as chief of staff. After he retired, President Harry S. Truman appointed him special representative to China. He spent the next year in China trying to end the civil war between the Chinese Nationalists and the Communists.

Statesman. Marshall returned to the United States in January, 1947, to assume the post of secretary of state in President Truman's Cabinet. As secretary, he urged Congress to pass the European Recovery Program. Under the plan, the United States sent about $13 billion in aid to European countries. Marshall also worked to secure aid for Greece and Turkey and to supply food to West Berlin when the Communists blockaded that city. These programs and the Marshall Plan did much to check Communist influence in Europe (see MARSHALL PLAN; BERLIN AIRLIFT). Marshall also began negotiations that led to the North Atlantic Treaty Organization (NATO). In January, 1949, he resigned his Cabinet post because of poor health.

Marshall served as president of the American Red Cross in 1949 and 1950. When the Korean War began in 1950, Truman asked Marshall to head the Department of Defense. An act of Congress set aside the rule that the secretary of defense must be a civilian. Marshall helped strengthen NATO and build up the United Nations fighting forces in Korea. He resigned as secretary of defense in September, 1951.

Marshall died on Oct. 16, 1959, and was buried at Arlington National Cemetery. In 1964, the George C. Marshall Research Library, containing Marshall's papers and his souvenirs, was dedicated in Lexington, Va.

FORREST C. POGUE

MARSHALL, JAMES WILSON (1810-1885), discovered gold in California on Jan. 24, 1848. He found small pieces of gold while he was building a sawmill for John Sutter 48 miles north of Sutter's Fort. When the secret of Marshall and Sutter leaked out, it started the great gold rush of 1849. In spite of his important discovery, he died a poor and bitter man. The first persons who came to the gold site paid a small fee, but later arrivals refused to pay. The claims of Marshall and Sutter were swept aside. Marshall was born in Hunterdon County, New Jersey.

HOWARD R. LAMAR

MARSHALL, JOHN (1755-1835), is known as the *great chief justice.* When Marshall became chief justice of the United States in 1801, the Supreme Court of the United States was so poorly respected that it was difficult to get able men to serve as justices. Many felt that the court would never settle important questions. But 34 years later, when Marshall's term as chief justice ended with his death, the Supreme Court had become a vigorous and fully equal third branch of the government. The structure of the government had been made clear through his decisions. Later court interpretations have rested heavily upon the strong principles he created.

Marshall's service as chief justice featured a continuous argument between the Supreme Court and the Democratic-Republicans, led by Thomas Jefferson, James Madison, and, later, Andrew Jackson. Jefferson and his followers believed in a weak judiciary and "states' rights." Marshall opposed these beliefs. His decisions established a powerful Supreme Court and a strong national government, with the right to override the states whenever national and state interests clashed. The Democratic-Republicans often threatened to impeach Marshall and to make constitutional changes that would take away the Court's power. But the clarity and persuasiveness of Marshall's decisions always kept those who opposed him on the defensive, and so they were unable to carry out their plans.

Early Life. John Marshall was born on Sept. 24, 1755, in Germantown, Va. His father was a colonel in the Revolutionary War. Marshall grew up on his father's farm and had little formal schooling. He was a tall, awkward boy, but he had great strength and agility. When the Revolutionary War broke out, he joined the patriot army and fought in several battles. By 1777, he had risen to the rank of captain. He served in Virginia, New Jersey, New York, and Pennsylvania, and was at Valley Forge during the winter of 1777-1778. During the war years, he saw much of his country for the first time. Later, he said that he had gone into the army a Virginian and had come out an American.

Marshall became a lawyer in 1781, after studying law on his own and attending some lectures at William and Mary College. He joined the Federalist party, and served in the Virginia legislature. In 1788 he became a delegate to the state convention that adopted the new federal Constitution. He and James Madison wanted it adopted, and led the debate in favor of ratification. Marshall's reputation as a lawyer grew rapidly. President Washington offered him the position of attorney general. He declined, but in 1797 agreed to go to Paris with Charles Pinckney and Elbridge Gerry to try to

Portrait by Richard N. Brooke, U.S. Capitol, House Wing (Library of Congress)

John Marshall, the fourth chief justice of the United States, established the Supreme Court's power to review legislative acts.

settle various questions growing out of French interference with American trade (see XYZ AFFAIR). Marshall was elected to the U.S. House of Representatives as a Federalist on his return. In 1800, President John Adams appointed him secretary of state.

The Chief Justice. Marshall, appointed by President Adams, began his great career as the fourth chief justice on Feb. 4, 1801. At that time the present relationship among the executive, legislative, and judicial branches of the government had not been established. Nor was the relationship between the national government and the states well defined. It fell to Marshall, as chief justice, to solve these problems.

In the famous case of *Marbury v. Madison* (1803), Marshall established the power of the Supreme Court to declare laws unconstitutional. This doctrine, which we know today as the power of "judicial review," is now accepted without question. But, if it had not been established, over strong opposition, the Constitution might have become the same kind of weak charter as the Articles of Confederation.

His Decisions. Marshall believed in a strong federal government to enable the United States to act effectively as a nation. A series of his decisions made this principle vital. In *McCulloch v. Maryland* (1819), Marshall upheld the power of Congress to create the United States Bank. In doing so, he laid down the principle of broad interpretation of the federal powers. In this case, also, he firmly established the doctrine that federal power must prevail over state power in case of conflict. In cases defining the national power over interstate commerce, Marshall's broad interpretation set out principles which are as applicable in the most recent cases as they were in his time.

The force and persuasiveness of Marshall's constitutional interpretations became most apparent after 1811. From that time until Marshall's death in 1835, most of the justices of the Court were appointed by Presidents who strongly opposed him. The new justices also opposed Marshall, but they soon found themselves agreeing with his important opinions.   JERRE S. WILLIAMS

See also SUPREME COURT OF THE UNITED STATES.

MARSHALL, PETER (1902-1949), was a Presbyterian minister who served as chaplain of the United States Senate from January, 1947, until his death. His prayers as chaplain of the Senate were in striking language, and parts of them were widely quoted. His wife, Catherine Marshall, wrote a biography of him, *A Man Called Peter* (1951). This story was later made into a motion picture.

Marshall was born in Coatbridge, Scotland. His father died when he was 4, and he struggled against poverty through childhood. He came to the United States in 1927, and was graduated from the Columbia Seminary in Decatur, Ga., in 1931. He served three pastorates, the last being the New York Avenue Presbyterian Church in Washington, D.C. He preached there the last 12 years of his life.   LEFFERTS A. LOETSCHER

MARSHALL, THOMAS RILEY (1854-1925), served as Vice-President of the United States from 1913 to 1921, under President Woodrow Wilson. He made the famous remark: "What this country needs is a good five-cent cigar." He was the first Vice-President in nearly 100 years to serve two terms with the same President. He was also the first Vice-President to preside at a Cabinet meeting in the absence of the President. Marshall refused to listen to those who urged him to declare himself President after President Wilson became seriously ill in 1919.

Marshall was born in North Manchester, Ind., and was graduated from Wabash College. He practiced law, and served as governor of Indiana from 1909 to 1913. Marshall sought the Democratic presidential nomination in 1912. However, he was nominated for the vice-presidency instead.

See also VICE-PRESIDENT OF THE UNITED STATES (picture).

IRVING G. WILLIAMS

MARSHALL, THURGOOD

MARSHALL, THURGOOD (1908-   ), became the first Negro to serve as an associate justice of the Supreme Court of the United States. He was nominated by President Lyndon B. Johnson in 1967. Marshall served as chief counsel for the National Association for the Advancement of Colored People (NAACP) from 1938 to 1961. He presented the legal argument that resulted in the 1954 Supreme Court decision that racial segregation in public schools is unconstitutional. In 1961, Marshall became the first Negro appointed to the U.S. Court of Appeals. In 1965, he was appointed solicitor general of the United States.

Marshall was born in Baltimore. He graduated from Lincoln University, and studied law at Howard University. He began practicing law in 1933. Marshall won the Spingarn Medal in 1946.

See also SUPREME COURT OF THE U.S. (picture).

CARL T. ROWAN

MARSHALL FORD DAM is an irrigation, power, and flood-control structure on the Colorado River in Texas. Marshall Ford Dam stands northwest of Austin. It is 278 feet high and 5,093 feet long. Its reservoir is 9 miles long and can hold 2,200,200 acre-feet of water.

CARL T. ROWAN

MARSHALL ISLANDS are a group of 34 low-lying coral atolls and islands in the central Pacific Ocean. They lie east of the Caroline Islands and northwest of the Gilbert Islands in the part of the Pacific called Micronesia, meaning *small islands*.

Marshall Islands Villagers are noted for their expert handicraft work. Women on the tiny island of Rong Rong gather near their thatched-roof huts for a "weaving bee."

Wide World

The Land and Its Resources.
The Marshall Islands have an area of about 70 square miles and a coastline of 75 miles. They lie in two parallel chains about 130 miles apart. Each chain extends about 650 miles in a curve from northwest to southeast. The eastern group is called the *Radak* or *Sunrise Chain;* the western group, the *Ralik* or *Sunset Chain.* About 1,150 islets are scattered along the reefs that form the atolls.

The climate is tropical, but ocean breezes cool the air. Rainfall is light on the northern islands, but heavier on those to the south. Only a few kinds of plants, such as coconut palms and breadfruit trees, can grow in the coral sand. *Copra* (dried coconut meat) is the chief product. Fish are plentiful among the reefs.

The People are called Micronesians. They are noted for their handicraft, and their sailing and fishing skills. Many Micronesians died of diseases brought to the islands by Europeans in the early 1900's. The islands' population is 18,925.

History. The first white man to visit the Marshall Islands was probably Alvaro de Saavedra, a Spanish navigator who sailed the Pacific in 1529. The islands were named for John Marshall, a British sea captain who explored them in 1788. Germany gained possession of the islands in 1886 and bought them from Spain along with the Mariana and Caroline islands in 1899. Japanese forces occupied the Marshalls during World War I. After the war, Japan was allowed to rule the islands under a mandate of the League of Nations. But in 1933 Japan left the League. The Japanese declared themselves the owners of the Marshalls. They closed the islands to Europeans and built war bases on them.

Early in 1944, American forces landed on Kwajalein and Eniwetok, in the eastern Marshalls, and, later, took possession of all the islands. The Marshall Islands are governed by the United States as part of the United Nations Trust Territory of the Pacific Islands. Kwajalein is an aircraft base, and Eniwetok is an atomic proving ground.

See also ENIWETOK; KWAJALEIN; WORLD WAR II (Island Hopping).

EDWIN H. BRYAN, JR.

MARSHALL PLAN encouraged European nations to work together for economic recovery after World

War II. The United States agreed to send aid to Europe if the countries would meet to decide what they needed. The official name of the plan was the European Recovery Program. It is called the Marshall Plan because U.S. Secretary of State George C. Marshall first suggested it.

The Marshall Plan began in April, 1948, when Congress established the Economic Cooperation Administration (ECA) to administer foreign aid. Seventeen nations formed the Organization for European Economic Cooperation (OEEC) to assist the ECA and develop cooperation among its members. The United States sent about $13 billion in food, machinery, and other products to Europe. Aid ended in 1951.

In 1961, the Organization for Economic Cooperation and Development (OECD) succeeded the OEEC. Twenty nations, including the United States and Canada, formed the OECD to promote the economic growth of member nations and to aid underdeveloped areas.

EDWARD McNALL BURNS

See also EUROPE (History); FOREIGN AID; MARSHALL, GEORGE C.; TRUMAN, HARRY S. (The Marshall Plan).

MARSHALL UNIVERSITY. See UNIVERSITIES AND COLLEGES (table).

MARSILIUS OF PADUA (1275?-1343?), an Italian political theorist, defended the claims of the Holy Roman Empire against those of the papacy. He held that the clergy should be concerned only with the soul's salvation and not with the affairs of this world. Unlike most medieval thinkers, Marsilius emphasized will rather than reason in his definition of law. "A law is useless," he said, "unless it is obeyed." Marsilius was born in Padua, Italy.

W. T. JONES

MARSTON, JOHN (1576-1634), was an English playwright. Two of his plays reflect the pessimism of their time, when the glories of the Elizabethan Age were becoming clouded by the uncertainties of life in the 1600's. *Antonio's Revenge* (1600) is a sensational drama of revenge about the assassination of a tyrant. With *Hamlet*, it is among the first examples of the great flowering of tragedy in English drama. *The Malcontent* (1604) is a far-from-joyous comedy of intrigue, bitter in its satire but intended to correct, not to condemn.

Marston was educated at Oxford. His talent for satire led to a running quarrel with Ben Jonson. He was briefly imprisoned in 1608 for critical comments about King James I. Later, Marston studied theology and in 1616 became rector of a country parish. ALAN S. DOWNER

MARSTON MOOR, BATTLE OF. See CHARLES (I) of England.

MARSUPIAL, *mahr SOO pee uhl*, is an animal whose young are raised in a pouch in the mother's body. The pouch is called the *marsupium*. There are over 250 *species* (kinds) of marsupials. Almost all marsupials live in Australia, New Guinea, or the islands of Australasia. Marsupials of these regions include the bandicoot, cuscus, dasyure, kangaroo, koala, Tasmanian devil, Tasmanian wolf, and wombat. The opossum of North, South, and Central America is the only marsupial that lives outside these regions.

Kangaroos are the biggest marsupials. Some grow to be more than 7 feet tall. The smallest marsupials are the so-called marsupial "mice." Marsupial "mice" is a general name for several tiny marsupials that are about as big as house mice.

Some marsupials eat only insects, some eat only meats, and some eat only plants. Other marsupials eat any kind of food they can find.

Marsupials are very small at birth. About 20 newborn opossums could easily fit into a teaspoon. Marsupials are not developed enough at birth to live outside the mother's pouch. After birth, they crawl from the birth canal along the mother's fur and into the pouch. Once inside the pouch, they attach themselves to the nipples of the *mammary* (milk) glands. To get enough food to stay alive, the young remain attached to the nipples continuously until they are developed enough to leave the pouch. Therefore, when there are more offspring than there are nipples, the extra offspring die. The young marsupials may stay in the pouch for several months. For some time after they leave the pouch, they stay near the mother. They sometimes return to the pouch when frightened.

The number of marsupials in the world has decreased during the 1900's. Man has brought dogs, foxes, and other animals to areas where marsupials live. These animals prey upon marsupials and compete with them for food. Farmers kill many marsupials because marsupials eat crops. Hunters kill kangaroos for food and hides. The opossum is an exception to the trend. The opossum population has increased because the animal will eat almost any kind of food, and it has a high reproduction rate.

Scientific Classification. Marsupials make up the order *Marsupialia* in the class *Mammalia* and the phylum *Chordata.* To learn where the order fits into the whole animal kingdom, see ANIMAL (table: A Classification of the Animal Kingdom).

For pictures and more detailed information on specific marsupials, see KANGAROO; KOALA; OPOSSUM; TASMANIAN DEVIL; TASMANIAN WOLF; WOMBAT; AUSTRALIA (animal map). See also BANDICOOT; CUSCUS; DASYURE.

WILLIAM V. MAYER

MARTEL, CHARLES. See CHARLES MARTEL.

MARTEN, *MAHR ten,* is a slim, fur-covered mammal that looks somewhat like a weasel. It lives in northern forests around the world.

One of the best-known American martens is the *pine marten* or *American sable.* It is fairly common only in the northern Rockies and in the Far North from Quebec to Alaska. The pine marten has thick, soft, rich brown hair and grayish-brown fur. It is about 2 feet long, including its bushy tail. Martens weigh 2 to 3 pounds. The pine marten eats mice, rabbits, squirrels, and small partridges and other birds. It lives in hollow trees and in rock formations. The female usually gives birth to two or three young in April, about nine months after mating.

From November to March, the pine marten's coat is thick and soft. During this season, marten trappers in Canada and the United States kill about 30,000 animals for use of the fur in coats, hats, and muffs.

The *fisher,* or *pekan,* is a large *species* (kind) related to the pine marten. A male fisher weighs about 15 pounds. It has dark brown or grayish-brown fur. Now rare, the fisher lives in nearly the same areas as the marten. The fisher lives on the ground or in trees. It eats rodents, including porcupines.

Well-known European martens include the *stone mar-*

ten, which has a white throat and chest, and the *baum marten*, which has yellowish fur on its throat and chest.

Scientific Classification. Martens are in the fur bearers family, *Mustelidae*. The pine marten is genus *Martes*, species *M. americana*. The fisher is *M. pennanti*; the stone, *M. foina*; and the baum, *M. martes*.
E. LENDELL COCKRUM

See also FUR; SABLE.

MARTHA. See OPERA (Some of the Famous Operas).

MARTHA was a friend of Jesus and the sister of Mary and Lazarus of Bethany. Jesus often stayed at their home. Martha busied herself about the house to provide comfort for Jesus. But Mary preferred to sit and listen to His teachings. For this reason, in later times, Martha became the symbol of the active life and Mary became the symbol of the thoughtful life. The Gospels of Luke and John mention Martha.
FREDERICK C. GRANT

MARTHA'S VINEYARD, an island four miles off the southeastern coast of Massachusetts, is a popular summer resort. Vineyard Sound separates it from the mainland. The island covers about 100 square miles. For location, see MASSACHUSETTS (physical map). Its attractions include a mild climate, beaches, fishing, and yachting. About 6,000 people live on the island. However, over 40,000 tourists visit the island in the summer. Explorer Bartholomew Gosnold named the island for his daughter and for the grapevines he found when he visited there in 1602.

See also MASSACHUSETTS (color picture).
WILLIAM J. REID

MARTÍ, *mahr TEE*, **JOSÉ JULIÁN** (1853-1895), was a Cuban patriot, author, and journalist. He dedicated his life to Cuba's struggle for independence from Spain, and became known to his people as the *Apostle*. Martí was jailed and exiled many times for his revolutionary writings and activities. He emerged from each setback with greater strength and appeal. He was finally ambushed and killed during a battle with the Spaniards.

Martí's books of verse, including *Ismaelillo* (1882) and *Simple Verses* (1891), show him to be a sensitive, sincere poet. His journalism set new standards of brilliance in Latin America.

Martí was born in Havana. He lived in exile in the United States from 1881 to 1895 and wrote many articles about life in the United States. He founded the Cuban Revolutionary party in 1892.
MARSHALL R. NASON

MARTIAL, *MAHR shul* (A.D. 40?-104?), was a Roman writer of epigrammatic verses. His main work is in 14 books. His first, *A Book of Spectacles*, contains poems on the shows given to celebrate the opening of the Colosseum by Emperor Titus in A.D. 80. Books 13 and 14 consist of mottoes to accompany holiday gifts and greetings. Martial's best work is in the first 12 books. They contain witty epigrams on the silly or affected people who made up Roman society. Born in Bilbilis, Spain, Martial moved to Rome in A.D. 64.
MOSES HADAS

MARTIAL LAW, in the strict sense, exists in wartime when an area is occupied by a hostile or lawless force that prevents the civil courts from functioning. Military authorities who have the job of keeping order administer martial law. Martial law differs from *military law*, since it applies to all persons in the area. Military law is limited only to military personnel in most cases.

Martial law in a qualified sense may exist in peacetime. When civilian authorities cannot keep public order, armed forces may take over and act for the government of a community. A strike or a riot, for example, may be regarded as serious enough to endanger public safety. If the police forces of the city or state prove unable to control the situation, the governors of many states may send a military force into the city to place it under martial law.

Under peacetime martial law, the civil government still remains in control of the community. But even in peacetime, the military commander holds absolute power over all the citizens until order is restored. He may order the destruction of property, or even of human life, if he feels it is necessary. Military control ends when normal conditions return.
JOHN W. WADE

MARTIN is the name for several birds in the swallow family. The *purple martin* is the best-known martin in North America. This bird is about 8 inches long. The male is a beautiful dark purplish-blue color. The birds migrate to Central and South America in the winter. They have been seen in summer as far north as the Saskatchewan Valley in Canada.

Purple martins usually build their nests in large bird-

Walt Disney Productions

The Agile Marten usually builds its moss-lined den in a hollow tree, some distance above the ground. It chases squirrels through the treetops, leaping easily from one branch to another.

MARTIN, JOSEPH WILLIAM, JR.

MARTIN was the name of five popes of the Roman Catholic Church. Martin II and Martin III are also called Marinus I and Marinus II (see MARINUS). The popes Martin served as follows:

Martin I, Saint	(649-655)
Martin II (Marinus I)	(882-884)
Martin III (Marinus II)	(942-946)
Martin IV	(1281-1285)
Martin V	(1417-1431)

Saint Martin I convoked a council of more than 100 bishops to condemn heresies about Christ.

Martin IV, a Frenchman, excommunicated Pedro III of Aragon whom the Sicilians had elected king after he drove out the French. He also excommunicated the Byzantine emperor.

Martin V reorganized the Papal States and introduced a just government into Rome. He also called the Council of Basel in 1431.

THOMAS P. NEILL and FULTON J. SHEEN

MARTIN, ABRAHAM. See PLAINS OF ABRAHAM.

MARTIN, ARCHER JOHN PORTER (1910-   ), is a noted English biochemist. With Richard L. M. Synge, he was awarded the 1952 Nobel prize in chemistry (see SYNGE, RICHARD L. M.). They did important work in *partition chromatography*, a method of chemical analysis. It led to the use of this technique in separating carbohydrates, amino acids, and other compounds important in biochemistry. Martin was born in London, and studied at Cambridge and Leeds universities. Later, he became head of the physical chemistry division at the National Institute for Medical Research located in London.

HENRY M. LEICESTER

MARTIN, GLENN LUTHER (1886-1955), was an American aircraft designer and manufacturer. One Martin bomber, designed during World War I, was standard in the Army Air Force for many years. The Martin B-10 bomber was flown for the first time in 1932. The B-10 set a new standard for bomber aircraft, because it could fly faster than most of the pursuit planes of its day.

During World War II, Martin directed production of bombers and flying boats, including the B-26 bomber. He pioneered in building large transoceanic flying boats.

Martin was born in Macksburg, Iowa. After several years of working and learning to glide, he flew for the first time in 1909 in an airplane he had designed and built himself. By 1911 he had become one of the best-known flyers in the United States. He flew at fairs and exhibitions to publicize aviation. Martin was involved in several manufacturing firms, including a partnership with the Wright brothers (see WRIGHT BROTHERS).

ROBERT B. HOTZ

MARTIN, JOSEPH WIL-LIAM, JR. (1884-1968), a Republican from Massachusetts, served in the United States House of Representatives from 1925 to 1967. He was Speaker of the House from 1947 to 1949 and from 1953 to 1955. Martin served as the

Joseph W. Martin, Jr.
Wide World

Field Museum of Natural History

The Purple Martin has unusually long, pointed wings and a short, forked tail. This makes its flight easy and graceful.

houses which people make especially for them. They nest in *colonies* (large groups). They may build their nests in trees in regions where few people live. Martins will return to the same birdhouse year after year. The martin lays from 3 to 8 white eggs.

Martins help man by eating ants, flies, beetles, and other winged insect pests. In New England, English sparrows and starlings have driven most of the martins from their homes.

Scientific Classification. Martins belong to the swallow family, *Hirundinidae*. The purple martin is genus *Progne*, species *P. subis*.

See also BIRD (picture: Other Kinds of Birdhouses; color picture: Birds' Eggs).

HERBERT FRIEDMANN

Martins require very little room in which to build a nest. This bird house is divided into 18 separate martin "apartments."
Allan Cruickshank

Republican leader in the House for 20 years—from 1939 until Charles A. Halleck of Indiana replaced him in 1959.

A skillful party leader in Congress, Martin became noted for keeping in touch with the voters in his district. He was permanent chairman of the Republican national conventions of 1940, 1944, 1948, 1952, and 1956.

Martin was born in North Attleboro, Mass. He started work as a newspaper reporter. He became a newspaper publisher in 1908 when he bought the North Attleboro *Evening Chronicle*. He went into politics in 1912.　RICHARD L. WATSON, JR.

MARTIN, SAINT. See MARTINMAS.

MARTINDUGARD, *mahr TAN dyoo GAHR,* **ROGER** (1881-1958), ranked among the most skillful French novelists. He received the 1937 Nobel prize for literature. His novel *Jean Barois* (1913) is perhaps the best literary presentation of the intellectual agonies that the unjust treatment of Captain Alfred Dreyfus caused in thoughtful Frenchmen (see DREYFUS, ALFRED). He published the 10-volume saga-novel *The World of the Thibauls* between 1922 and 1940. He was born in Neuilly-sur-Seine, and was graduated from the École des Chartes. HENRI PEYRE

MARTINELLI, *MAHR tih NEL ee,* **GIOVANNI** (1885-1969), sang as a leading tenor with the New York Metropolitan Opera Company in more than 50 operas. He was a dynamic actor. Much of his success resulted from his belief that an opera singer must also have dramatic ability. Martinelli made his debut at the Metropolitan in 1913 in *La Bohème.* A special testimonial concert at the Metropolitan Opera House in 1938 celebrated his 25th year with that institution.

Martinique Market Places overflow with bananas and other tropical fruits. Women do most of the buying and selling.

Alcoa Steamship Co., Inc.

Giovanni Martinelli

United Press Int.

Martinelli was born in Montagnana, Italy, and played the clarinet in an Italian regimental band. He studied voice in Rome, and made his concert debut in Rome's *Stabat Mater* in Milan in 1910. He sang at Covent Garden in London in 1912.　DANIEL A. HARRIS

MARTINGALE. See HARNESS.

MARTINIQUE, *MAHR t'n EEK,* is a French island in the West Indies. It is roughly oval in shape and covers an area of 425 square miles. The island is about 40 miles long and 16 miles wide. Its capital is Fort-de-France. For location, see WEST INDIES (map).

Martinique has many volcanic mountains. The highest and most famous of these is Mont Pelée (4,800 feet). This volcano suddenly erupted in 1902, and destroyed the entire city of Saint-Pierre. About 38,000 people died, and only one man in Saint-Pierre escaped.

Martinique has a population of 357,000. Many of the people are Negroes. Others have a mixture of both Latin and Negro blood. The island's chief crop is sugar cane. Pineapples, bananas, tobacco, and cotton also grow there. Rum distilling is the only important industry.

Christopher Columbus discovered Martinique in 1502, on his fourth voyage. The French began to colonize it in 1635. They made Fort-de-France the capital. The Empress Josephine, first wife of Napoleon I, was born at Trois-Îlets in Martinique. The French government made Martinique an overseas *department* (state) in 1946. The island sends three deputies to the French National Assembly. In 1958, Martinique chose to remain in the French Community as an overseas department. It has its own local government.   W. L. BURN

See also FORT-DE-FRANCE; MONT PELÉE.

MARTINMAS is a feast day celebrated in the Roman Catholic Church on November 11. It honors Saint Martin (316?-397?), a bishop of Tours, France (then called Gaul), and a patron saint of the French. Martinmas falls at the end of the harvest season, and people throughout Europe celebrate it with feasts and new wine. In Belgium and other countries, children receive apples and nuts on this day. They also parade through the streets carrying lanterns and singing special songs. People in the British Isles usually eat goose dinners on Martinmas. In parts of Great Britain, Martinmas also marks the ending of one of the legal quarters into which the year is divided.

MARTINSBURG, W.Va. (pop. 14,625; alt. 430 ft.), is the gateway city to the Shenandoah Valley. It was named for Colonel Thomas B. Martin, nephew of Lord Fairfax. The Potomac River curves east and north about 10 miles from the city (see WEST VIRGINIA [political map]). Martinsburg factories make cement, cooking ware, explosives, metal containers, stockings, textiles, and wood veneer. The city markets apples and peaches. The Newton D. Baker Veterans Administration Hospital and the Internal Revenue Service National Computer Center are near Martinsburg. The city has a mayor-council government.   FESTUS PAUL SUMMERS

MARTYR is a person who defends a principle, even though it means he must sacrifice many things, perhaps even his life. Almost every religious movement has had such dedicated persons. Stephen was the first Christian martyr. He was stoned to death because he protested against the wickedness of his fellow citizens (Acts 7:59-60). Many early Christians became martyrs because the Romans persecuted them for not worshiping official Roman gods. Many social and political movements have created martyrs. The word *martyr* comes from the Greek, and means *witness*.   FLOYD H. ROSS

MARVEL-OF-PERU. See FOUR-O'CLOCK.
MARVELL, ANDREW (1621-1678), was perhaps the finest of the English nonreligious poets who were influenced by John Donne and Ben Jonson in the mid-1600's. Marvell's best poems are a series of lyrics written about 1650, including such classics as "The Garden" and "To His Coy Mistress," with its witty opening:

Had we but world enough, and time,
This coyness, lady, were no crime,

and its grand ending:

Let us roll all our strength, and all
Our sweetness, up into one ball;
And tear our pleasures with rough strife,
Through the iron gates of life.
Thus, though we cannot make our sun
Stand still, yet we will make him run.

Marvell was born in Winestead. During the Puritan revolution, he supported Oliver Cromwell. He assisted John Milton when Milton was a high government official. Marvell served in Parliament from 1659 to his death. During his later years, he wrote political satire against the king and court.   RICHARD S. SYLVESTER

See also METAPHYSICAL POETS.

Karl Marx

Brown Bros.

MARX, KARL

Marx was sometimes ignored or misunderstood, even by his followers. Yet many of the social sciences—especially sociology—have been influenced by his theories. Many important social scientists of the late 1800's and the 1900's can be fully understood only by realizing how much they were reacting to Marx's beliefs.

MARX, KARL (1818-1883), was a German philosopher, social scientist, and professional revolutionary. Few writers have had such a great and lasting influence on mankind. Marx was the chief founder of two of the most powerful mass movements in history—democratic socialism and revolutionary communism.
See COMMUNISM; SOCIALISM.

The Life of Marx

Karl Heinrich Marx was born and raised in Trier, in what was then Prussia. His father was a lawyer. Marx showed intellectual promise in school and went to the University of Bonn in 1835 to study law. The next year, he transferred to the University of Berlin. There he became much more interested in philosophy, a highly political subject in Prussia, where citizens were not permitted to participate directly in public affairs. Marx joined a group of radical leftist students and professors whose philosophic views implied strong criticism of the severe way in which Prussia was governed.

In 1841, Marx obtained his doctorate in philosophy from the university in Jena. He tried to get a teaching position but failed because of his opposition to the Prussian government. He became a free-lance journalist and helped create and manage several radical journals. After his marriage in 1843, he and his wife moved to Paris. There they met Friedrich Engels, a young German radical, who became Marx's best friend and worked with him on several articles and books. Marx lived in Brussels, Belgium, from 1845 to 1848, when he returned to Germany. He edited the *Neue Rheinische Zeitung*, which was published in Cologne during the German revolution of 1848. This journal made Marx known throughout Germany as a spokesman for radical democratic reform. See GERMANY (History [The Revolution of 1848]).

After the collapse of the 1848 revolution, Marx fled from Prussia. He spent the rest of his life as a political exile in London.

Marx led a hand-to-mouth existence because he was too proud—or too much a professional revolutionary—to work for a living. He did write occasional articles for newspapers. His most regular job of this kind was that of political reporter for the *New York Tribune*. But generally, Marx, his wife, and their six children survived only

Alfred G. Meyer, the contributor of this article, is Professor of Political Science and Director of the Center for Russian and East European Studies at the University of Michigan.

because Engels sent them money regularly. In 1864, Marx founded *The International Workingmen's Association*, an organization dedicated to improving the life of the working classes and preparing for a socialist revolution (see INTERNATIONAL, THE).

Marx suffered from frequent illnesses, many of which may have been psychological. Even when physically healthy, he suffered from long periods of apathy and depression and could not work. Marx was learned and sophisticated, but he was often opinionated and arrogant. He had many admirers but few friends. Except for Engels, he lost most of his friends—and many of them became his enemies. He broke all contact with his mother and was cool to his sisters. But with his wife and children, Marx was relaxed, witty, and playful.

Marx's Writings

Most of Marx's writings have been preserved. They include not only his books, but also most of his correspondence and the notes of his speeches.

Philosophic Essays. Some of Marx's philosophic essays were published during his lifetime, but others were not discovered until the 1900's. Marx wrote some of them alone and some with Engels. The essays range from over 15 sentences to a 700-page book, *The German Ideology* (1845-1846), written with Engels.

Marx wrote his essays between 1842 and 1847. They spell out the philosophic foundations of his radicalism. The chief themes in the essays include Marx's bitter view that economic forces were increasingly oppressing mankind and his belief that political action is a necessary part of philosophy. The essays also show the influence of the philosophy of history developed by the German philosopher Georg Wilhelm Friedrich Hegel (see HEGEL, GEORG WILHELM FRIEDRICH).

The Communist Manifesto was a pamphlet written jointly with Engels on the eve of the German revolution of 1848. Its full title is the *Manifesto of the Communist Party*. The manifesto is a brief but forceful presentation of the authors' political and historical theories. It is the only work they produced that can be considered a systematic statement of the theories that became known as *Marxism*. The *Communist Manifesto* considers history to be a series of conflicts between classes. It predicts that the ruling middle class will be overthrown by the working class. The result of this revolution, according to Marx and Engels, will be a classless society in which the chief means of production are publicly owned.

Das Kapital (Capital) was Marx's major work. He spent about 30 years writing it. The first volume appeared in 1867. Engels edited the second and third volumes from Marx's manuscripts. Both of these volumes were published after Marx's death. The fourth volume exists only as a mass of scattered notes.

In *Das Kapital*, Marx described the free enterprise system as he saw it. He considered it the most efficient, dynamic economic system ever devised. But he also regarded it as afflicted with flaws that would destroy it through increasingly severe periods of inflation and depression. The most serious flaw in the free enterprise system, according to Marx, is that it accumulates more and more wealth but becomes less and less capable of using this wealth wisely. As a result, Marx saw the accu-

mulation of riches being accompanied by the rapid spread of human misery. See FREE ENTERPRISE SYSTEM.

Other Writings. Marx and Engels also wrote what today might be called political columns. They discussed all sorts of events in and influences on national and international affairs—personalities, overthrowing of governments, cabinet changes, parliamentary debates, wars, and workers' uprisings.

Marx also wrote about the practical problems of leading an international revolutionary movement. The major source of these comments is his correspondence with Engels and other friends.

Marx's Theories

Marx's doctrine is sometimes called *dialectical materialism*, and part of it is referred to as *historical materialism*. These terms were taken from Hegel's philosophy of history. Marx never used them, but Engels did and so have most later Marxists. The concepts of dialectical and historical materialism are difficult and obscure and may be unnecessary for an understanding of Marx's theories. See MATERIALISM.

Marx's writings cover more than 40 years. His interests shifted and he often changed his mind. But his philosophy remained surprisingly consistent—and very complex. Aside from the brief *Communist Manifesto*, he never presented his ideas systematically.

Production and Society. The basis of Marxism is the conviction that socialism is inevitable. Marx believed that the free enterprise system, or capitalism, was doomed and that socialism was the only alternative.

Marx discussed capitalism within a broad historical perspective that covered the history of mankind. He believed that man, not God, is the highest being. Man has made himself what he is by his own labor. He uses his intelligence and creative talent to dominate the world by a process called *production*. Through production, man makes the goods he needs to live. The means of production include natural resources, factories, machinery, and manpower.

The process of production, according to Marx, is a collective effort, not an individual one. Organized societies are the chief creative agents in human history, and historical progress requires increasingly developed societies for production. Such societies are achieved by continual refinement of production methods and of the *division of labor*. By the division of labor, Marx meant that each person specializes in one job, resulting in the development of two classes of men—the rulers and the workers. The ruling class owns the means of production. The working class consists of the nonowners, who are *exploited* (treated unfairly) by the owners.

The Class Struggle. Marx believed there was a strain in all societies because the social organization never kept pace with the development of the means of production. An even greater strain developed from the division of mankind into two classes.

According to Marx, all history is a struggle between the ruling and working classes, and all societies have been torn by this conflict. Past societies tried to keep the exploited class under control by using elaborate political organizations, laws, customs, traditions, ideologies, religions, and rituals. Marx argued that man's personality, beliefs, and activities are shaped by these institutions. By recognizing these forces, he reasoned, man will be able to overcome them through revolutionary action.

Marx believed that private ownership of the chief means of production was the heart of the class system. For man to be truly free, he declared, the means of production must be publicly owned—by the community as a whole. With the resulting general economic and social equality, every person would have an opportunity to follow his own desires and to use his leisure time creatively. Unfair institutions and customs would disappear. All these events, said Marx, will take place when the *proletariat* (working class) revolts against the *bourgeoisie* (owners of the means of production).

Political Strategy. It is not clear what strategy Marx might have proposed to achieve the revolution he favored. An idea of this strategy can come only from his speeches, articles, letters, and political activities. As a guideline for practical politics, Marxism is vague. Marx's followers have quarreled bitterly among themselves over different interpretations and policies.

Marx Today

Today, Marx is studied as both a revolutionary and an economist. His importance as a pioneer in the social sciences is being recognized increasingly. Marx has often been attacked because he rebelled against all established societies, because he was an arrogant writer who scorned his critics, and because of his radical views.

As the founding father of the Communist movement, Marx is regarded in most Communist countries as one of the greatest thinkers of all time. In those countries, many people believe that Marx's writings are the source of all important truths in social science as well as philosophy. They believe that a person cannot be an intelligent student of society, history, economics, philosophy, and numerous other fields without first studying Marx or his principal disciples.

Scholars in the Western world were slow to recognize the importance of Marx. For many years, few Americans bothered to study his writings. But today, in a variety of fields, it has become essential to have some knowledge of Marx. One of these fields is economics. Although his methods of analyzing capitalism are considered old-fashioned, many scholars recognize the brilliance of this analysis. Many people consider his criticism of capitalism and his gloomy view of what man has made of his world as timely today as they were 100 years ago. Even Marx's analysis of the business cycle is still studied as one of the many explanations of inflation and depression.

In sociology, Marx's work is also regarded with increasing respect. Without his contributions, sociology would not have developed into what it is today. Marx did pioneering work in many of the areas of inquiry with which sociology deals. For example, he wrote on social classes, on the relationship between the economy and the state, and on the principles that underlie a political or economic system.

Many people still turn to Marx for an explanation of current social, economic, and political evils. But most of them are unlikely to agree with his view of the ease and speed with which the working class will overthrow the class system and establish a Communist classless society.

See also ENGELS, FRIEDRICH; LENIN, V. I.; CIVILIZATION (Theories About Civilization).

ALFRED G. MEYER

MARX BROTHERS are a family of comedians who became famous for a series of crazy, unpredictable motion pictures. The Marx Brothers began their career on the stage, but gained their greatest success in the movies. Their most successful films include *Animal Crackers* (1930), *Duck Soup* (1933), *A Night at the Opera* (1935), and *A Day at the Races* (1937).

The family includes Chico (Leonard, 1891-1961), Harpo (Arthur, 1893-1964), Groucho (Julius, 1895-), and Zeppo (Herbert, 1901-). Groucho became known for his insults, cigar, and bushy mustache. Chico used an exaggerated Italian accent and played the piano. Harpo, who never spoke, played the harp. Zeppo played the straight man and romantic lead until he left the team in the mid-1930's. The brothers were born in New York City.

RICHARD GRIFFITH

The Marx Brothers starred in *Horse Feathers*, a zany 1932 motion picture comedy. They are Chico, left, holding an apple; Groucho, smoking the cigar; and Harpo, far right.

United Press Int.

MARY was the name of three queens of England.

Mary I (1516-1558) was the daughter of Henry VIII and Catherine of Aragon. She became queen in 1553, after Edward VI, her brother, died. An attempt to set her aside in favor of Lady Jane Grey, "the nine-day queen," failed. See CATHERINE OF ARAGON; EDWARD (VI) of England; HENRY (VIII) of England.

Mary was a devout Roman Catholic and tried to bring England back to the Roman Catholic Church. She repealed all the religious laws of Edward VI. She revived certain severe laws against heresy or disbelief in church doctrine. She became known as "Bloody Mary" because of the persecutions she caused. More than 300 persons were burned at the stake during her brief reign. Among

Mary I of England by Master John, National Portrait Gallery, London

Queen Mary I of England became known as "Bloody Mary" because of the bitter persecutions she caused the Protestants in her attempt to bring England back to the Roman Catholic faith.

them were Thomas Cranmer, Nicholas Ridley, and Hugh Latimer, all high-ranking Protestant clergymen. See CRANMER, THOMAS; LATIMER, HUGH; RIDLEY, NICHOLAS.

Mary married Philip II of Spain. Their marriage was unpopular, because many Englishmen looked upon Spain as their greatest enemy. Philip persuaded Mary to join Spain in a war against France. The war ended disastrously in 1558. Mary died soon after, deserted by her husband and saddened at the thought that she would be succeeded by her Protestant sister, Elizabeth (see ELIZABETH I). See PHILIP (II) of Spain.

Mary II (1662-1694) was the older of the two Protestant daughters of James II. She married William of Orange, the chief executive of the Dutch Republic. During the Glorious Revolution of 1688, Parliament offered the throne to William and Mary as joint rulers. William accepted on the understanding that he would be responsible for the administration of affairs. Mary died from smallpox in 1694. William served as king until his death in 1702. See JAMES (II) of England; FURNITURE (William and Mary); STUART, HOUSE OF; WILLIAM (III) of England.

Mary of Teck (1867-1953) was the queen *consort* (wife) of King George V. Mary endeared herself to the British by her homely virtues. In place of the gay court of Edward VII, she and her husband lived conservatively. Through their efforts, the monarchy regained the prestige it had enjoyed under Queen Victoria. After the death of George V in 1936, Mary retired to Marlborough House in London. Her eldest son became king as Edward VIII. After his abdication, her second son became

George VI. Upon his death her granddaughter became Queen Elizabeth II (see ELIZABETH II). During these years Queen Mary took an active part in public affairs. Her plain dress and old-fashioned hats were famous throughout the British Empire. See also GEORGE (V, VI) of England; EDWARD (VII, VIII). W. M. SOUTHGATE

MARY, QUEEN OF SCOTS (1542-1587), was the last Roman Catholic ruler of Scotland. The life story of this beautiful woman who was beheaded by her cousin Elizabeth I is one of the great tragedies of history.

Mary was the only child of James V of Scotland and Mary of Guise. The princess was only a week old when her father died, but she was immediately proclaimed queen of Scotland. She was sent to France at the age of 6 to be educated. She married the French *dauphin* (crown prince) at the age of 16. He became king soon after their marriage, but died in 1560 (see FRANCIS [II] of France).

Her Reign. Mary returned to Scotland in 1561. She found Scotland becoming a Protestant country, and she was a Roman Catholic. She did not oppose the spread of the Protestant faith at first. But, in 1565, she married her cousin, Henry Stuart, who was known as Lord Darnley. This young Catholic nobleman's rise to power caused the powerful Protestant lords to revolt. The rebellion was quickly put down. But the queen soon discovered that she had married a weak and worthless husband, and she came to hate him.

An Italian musician, David Rizzio (1533?-1566), was Mary's private secretary, and became one of her favorites. Scottish tongues began to wag about the relationship between Rizzio and the queen. A band of men led by two Scottish earls burst into Mary's private supper room in March, 1566. They dragged Rizzio from the table, and stabbed him to death. Darnley, Mary's husband, was one of the leaders in the murder, but Mary fled with him to Dunbar. Mary gave birth to a son two months later. He later became King James I of England (see JAMES [II]).

Mary still hated her husband. Before long she began to show marked attention to James Hepburn, Earl of Bothwell (see BOTHWELL, EARL OF). Early in 1567, the house in which Darnley was living was blown up by a charge of gunpowder, and he was found dead. All Scotland believed that Bothwell had planned the crime. Three months later, Mary married Bothwell.

Her Death. This marriage was Mary's fatal mistake. She was forced to abdicate in favor of her son in 1567, and she became a prisoner on the island of Loch Leven. She escaped in 1568, and raised a small army. But almost all Scotland was against her. Her forces were defeated, and she fled to England for protection. Mary was the center of plots against her cousin, Queen Elizabeth I, because she had a claim to the English throne and wanted to bring England back to the Roman Catholic faith (see ELIZABETH I). Mary lived almost as a prisoner in the house of the Earl of Shrewsbury. When plots against her became increasingly serious, Elizabeth moved Mary to a prison. Mary became involved in a plot to kill Elizabeth in 1586. She maintained her innocence. The court found her guilty, and she was beheaded on Feb. 8, 1587. W. M. SOUTHGATE

MARY, VIRGIN. See VIRGIN MARY.

MARY BALDWIN COLLEGE, at Staunton, Va., is the second oldest college for women in the United States.

Mary, Queen of Scots, Married Francis II, the Future King of France, When She Was 16 Years Old.

A Principal Marriage (1600) by Georges Boba, Musée de Dijon, Dijon, France

It is affiliated with the Presbyterian Church. It offers liberal arts courses. The college was founded in 1842. The Rev. Joseph Wilson, father of Woodrow Wilson, headed the school at one time. William McGuffey, of *McGuffey's Readers* fame, was a counselor. For the enrollment of Mary Baldwin College, see UNIVERSITIES AND COLLEGES (table).

MARY COLLEGE. See UNIVERSITIES AND COLLEGES (table).

MARY HARDIN-BAYLOR COLLEGE, at Belton, Tex., became the first college for women west of the Mississippi River. It was chartered in 1845. The Baptist Church controls the school. The college offers courses in music, art, dramatics, speech, journalism, elementary education, and home economics. Men are now admitted on a limited basis. Mrs. Miriam W. Ferguson, the only woman governor of Texas, attended the college. For enrollment, see UNIVERSITIES AND COLLEGES (table).

MARY IMMACULATE SEMINARY AND COLLEGE. See UNIVERSITIES AND COLLEGES (table).

MARY MAGDALENE, *MAG duh leen*, was a faithful follower of Jesus. She was called Magdalene because she was born in the village of Magdala. Luke gives her name at the head of a list of women of Galilee (Luke 8: 2). Mary Magdalene was known as the one out of whom Jesus "had cast seven demons." She followed Jesus the rest of His life, and stood at the cross when He was crucified. She was the first person to see Him after He arose from the tomb (John 20). FREDERICK C. GRANT

MARY MANSE COLLEGE. See UNIVERSITIES AND COLLEGES (table).

MARY OF BETHANY was the sister of Martha and Lazarus. Jesus often visited their home. Mary sat at His feet and listened to His teaching (Luke 10: 39). When Martha complained that she was not helping with a meal, Jesus said, "Only one thing is needful; Mary has chosen the better part, which shall not be taken from her." FREDERICK C. GRANT

See also LAZARUS; MARTHA.

MARY ROGERS COLLEGE is a Roman Catholic school at Maryknoll, N.Y. The student body is restricted to members of the Maryknoll Sisters of St. Dominic. Courses prepare students to teach in foreign missions. For the enrollment of Mary Rogers College, see UNIVERSITIES AND COLLEGES (table).

MARY WASHINGTON COLLEGE OF THE UNIVERSITY OF VIRGINIA. See VIRGINIA, UNIVERSITY OF.

MARYCREST COLLEGE is a liberal arts college for women at Davenport, Iowa. The Roman Catholic Sisters of Humility of Mary conduct it. Marycrest College was chartered as a division of St. Ambrose College. In 1954, Marycrest became an independent school. For enrollment, see UNIVERSITIES AND COLLEGES (table).

MARYGROVE COLLEGE. See UNIVERSITIES AND COLLEGES (table).

MARYHILL CASTLE. See WASHINGTON (Places to Visit).

MARYKNOLL COLLEGE. See UNIVERSITIES AND COLLEGES (table).

MARYKNOLL SEMINARY. See UNIVERSITIES AND COLLEGES (table).

193

MARYLAND

The Old Line State

MARYLAND is an important industrial and shipping state. It lies in the northeastern corner of the Southern States. Chesapeake Bay, which cuts deep into Maryland, gives the state several excellent harbors. Baltimore, the state's largest city, is one of the greatest port cities in the world. Annapolis, the home of the United States Naval Academy, is the capital of Maryland.

Chesapeake Bay divides Maryland into two parts. The part of Maryland east of the bay is called the Eastern Shore. The part west of the bay is the Western Shore. The two parts join north of the bay in the northeastern corner of the state. The Eastern Shore shares the Delmarva Peninsula with parts of Delaware and Virginia. The Eastern Shore and part of the Western Shore are low and flat. But western Maryland has rolling plains, hills and valleys, mountains, and plateaus. Most parts of Maryland have good farmland. Forests cover nearly half the state.

The leading products of Maryland's industries include basic metals, food products, and transportation equipment. Most of the state's manufacturing is centered in the Baltimore area. The Bethlehem Steel Corporation plant outside Baltimore is one of the world's largest steel mills.

Tobacco farms cover much of southern Maryland. Vegetable farming thrives on the Eastern Shore. Most mining and fruit growing takes place in the west. Dairy farming prospers throughout the state. Maryland is a leading producer of soft-shell clams and oysters.

Maryland was named for Queen Henrietta Maria, the wife of King Charles I of England. In 1632, Charles chartered the Maryland region to Cecil Calvert, the second Lord Baltimore. Calvert, a Roman Catholic, believed in religious freedom, and welcomed settlers of all faiths to Maryland.

The Lords Baltimore ruled Maryland during most of the period it was an English colony. During the Revolutionary War, the Second Continental Congress met for about three months in the city of Baltimore. After the war, the Congress of the Confederation met for several months in the Maryland State House in Annapolis. In 1791, Maryland gave part of its land to the federal government for the District of Columbia.

Francis Scott Key wrote "The Star-Spangled Banner" while watching the British bombard Baltimore's Fort McHenry during the War of 1812. Maryland, although a southern state, remained loyal to the Union during the Civil War. Several Civil War battles were fought in Maryland, including the Battle of Antietam—one of the bloodiest of the war.

Maryland is nicknamed the *Old Line State* because its heroic "troops of the line" won praise from George Washington during the Revolutionary War. For Maryland's relationship to the other states in its region, see SOUTHERN STATES.

Maryland (blue) ranks 42nd in size among all the states, and 13th in size among the Southern States (gray).

The contributors of this article are George Beishlag, Professor of Geography at Towson State College; Aubrey C. Land, Research Professor at the University of Georgia, and former Professor of History at the University of Maryland; and Fred Theroux, Editorial Writer of The News American in Baltimore.

The Star-Spangled Banner Flies Day and Night Over Historic Fort McHenry in Baltimore Harbor.

FACTS IN BRIEF

Capital: Annapolis.

Government: *Congress*—U.S. senators, 2; U.S. representatives, 8. *Electoral Votes*—10. *State Legislature*—senators, 43; delegates, 142. *Counties*—23, and the independent city of Baltimore.

Area: 10,577 square miles, including 686 square miles of inland water (not including Chesapeake Bay), 42nd in size among the states. *Greatest Distances*—(east-west) 198.6 miles; (north-south) 125.5 miles. *Coastline*—31 miles; including Chesapeake Bay, 3,190 miles.

Elevation: *Highest*—Backbone Mountain in Garrett County, 3,360 feet above sea level. *Lowest*—sea level, along the Atlantic Ocean.

Population: *1970 Preliminary Census*—3,874,642; density, 366 persons to the square mile. *1960 Census*—3,100,689, 21st among the states; distribution, 73 per cent urban, 27 per cent rural.

Chief Products: *Agriculture*—beef cattle, broilers, corn, greenhouse and nursery products, milk, soybeans, tobacco. *Fishing Industry*—clams, crabs, flounder, menhaden, oysters, shad, striped bass, swellfish, white perch. *Manufacturing and Processing*—chemicals, clothing, food and food products, machinery, metal products, primary metals, printing and publishing, transportation equipment. *Mining*—clays, coal, natural gas, sand and gravel, stone.

Statehood: April 28, 1788, the 7th state.

State Motto: *Fatti Maschii Parole Femine* (Deeds are manly, words are womanly), Italian motto of the Calvert family.

State Song: "Maryland, My Maryland," sung to the music of the German tune "O, Tannenbaum." Words by James Ryder Randall.

Constitution. Maryland has had the same constitution since 1867, shortly after the Civil War. Earlier constitutions were adopted in 1776, 1851, and 1864.

An *amendment* (change) in the constitution may be proposed by the state legislature or by a constitutional convention. Legislative amendments must be approved by three-fifths of the members of both houses of the legislature. All amendments must be approved by a majority of the voters who cast ballots on the amendment.

Executive. Maryland's governor serves a four-year term. He may be elected to two terms in a row. But he must be out of office for at least a year before running for a third term. The governor receives a yearly salary of $25,000. Maryland has no lieutenant governor. If the governor dies or leaves office, the president of the Senate takes his place until the state legislature elects a new governor. For a list of Maryland's governors, see the *History* section of this article.

The governor appoints the secretary of state, the adjutant general, and members of state boards. The people elect the attorney general and the comptroller to four-year terms. The state treasurer is elected by the legislature. He also serves a four-year term.

Legislature, called the *general assembly*, consists of a 43-member Senate and a 142-member House of Delegates. Each of Maryland's 16 senatorial districts elects from one to seven senators, depending on population. Each of the state's 23 counties and each of Baltimore city's six legislative districts elects from 1 to 22 delegates, depending on population. All Maryland legislators serve four-year terms. The legislature meets each year. Sessions begin on the third Wednesday in January and last 70 calendar days. The governor may call special sessions lasting no longer than 30 calendar days.

Courts. Maryland's highest court is the state Court of Appeals. It has seven judges. The governor selects one of the judges to serve as chief judge. Maryland has eight judicial circuits, including the city of Baltimore. Each circuit has a circuit court. Baltimore's circuit court is called the Supreme Bench of Baltimore City. It

has a chief judge and 21 associate judges. The other circuit courts have a chief judge and up to 11 associates.

Judges of courts of appeals and of circuit courts are first appointed by the governor to serve for at least one year. These judges may then be elected by the voters to serve 15-year terms. Seven counties have people's courts. The number of judges and the length of their terms vary in these courts.

Judges of the Municipal Court of Baltimore City are elected to 10-year terms by the voters of Baltimore. Judges of the People's Court of Baltimore City are first appointed by the governor for eight years. Then they may be elected by the voters to additional eight-year terms. Judges of the people's court of Montgomery County are appointed by the county council for 10-year terms. Probate court judges serve four-year terms. Trial magistrates serve in Maryland counties that do not have people's courts. The magistrates are appointed to two-year terms.

Local Government in Maryland is centered in the state's 23 counties. Incorporated cities function as independent units of government. But all other areas in a county come under the jurisdiction of the county government. Baltimore, which is not part of any county, is governed by a mayor, an 18-member city council, and a council president. Most of the other incorporated cities use the mayor-council or commissioner form of government.

Anne Arundel, Baltimore, Howard, Montgomery, and Wicomico counties are governed by county councils, whose members are elected to four-year terms. Voters in each of the other counties elect the members of a board of county commissioners to four-year terms. Elected county administrative officers include clerk of the circuit court, state's attorney, sheriff, register of wills, surveyor, and treasurer or financial director.

Cities and counties in Maryland may adopt *home rule* (self-government) to the extent that they may govern their own affairs without control by the state legislature. All the cities and five of the counties in Maryland have adopted home rule.

Governor's Mansion stands west of the Capitol and faces it. The residence was completed in 1869. The end chimneys, gables, and two wings were added in 1935.

The State Flag

The State Bird
Baltimore Oriole

The State Flower
Black-Eyed Susan

The State Tree
White Oak

The State Seal

Symbols of Maryland. The front of the seal shows Lord Baltimore, founder of Maryland, as a knight. A shield on the back of the seal bears the coats of arms of the Calvert and Crossland families. Lord Baltimore was related to both families and used the combined arms. The farmer beside the shield symbolizes Maryland. The fisherman represents Lord Baltimore's Avalon colony in Newfoundland. The seal was adopted in 1876. The flag, with an adaptation of Baltimore's arms, was adopted in 1904.

Seal, Maryland Department of Economic Development;
flag illustration, courtesy Eli Lilly and Company

Taxation. Sales and gross receipts taxes account for about 35 per cent of the state government's income. Individual state income taxes account for another 25 per cent. Other income includes a corporate income tax, estate and gift taxes, licenses, and property taxes. About 15 per cent of the state income comes from federal grants and other U.S. government programs.

Politics. In most state elections, the Republican Party's strength is limited to a few counties in southern and western Maryland. The rest of the state is strongly Democratic, with the greatest Democratic strength in the city of Baltimore. Only five Republicans have ever served as governor of Maryland. But in presidential elections since 1900, a nearly equal number of Democratic and Republican candidates have won the state's electoral votes. For Maryland's electoral votes and for the state's voting record in presidential elections, see ELECTORAL COLLEGE (table).

State Capitol is in Annapolis. The building, begun in 1772, is the nation's oldest statehouse in daily use. St. Mary's City was the capital from 1634 until 1694, when Annapolis became the capital.
M. E. Warren

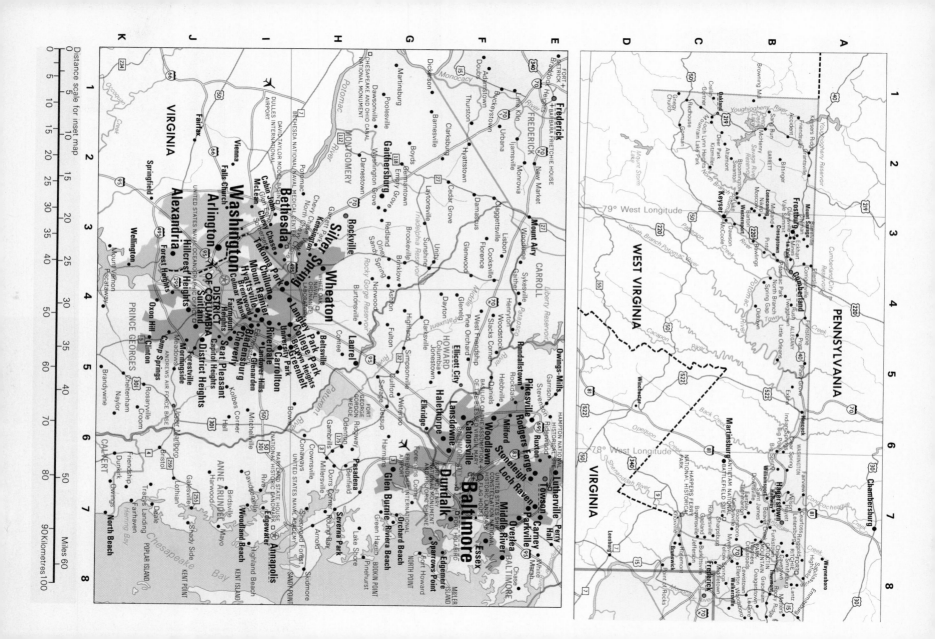

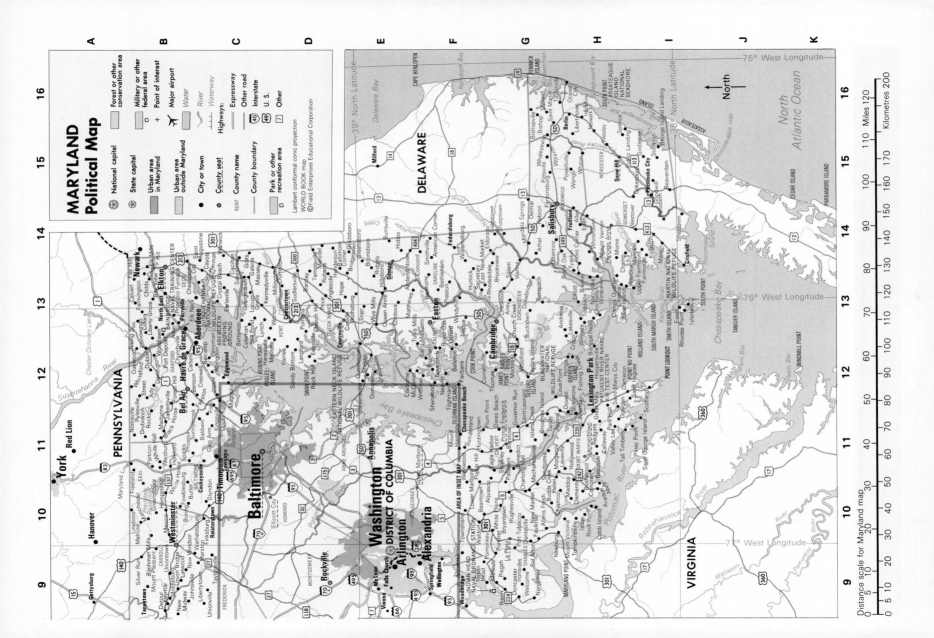

Place	Pop.	Ref.
Overlea	10,795	F 7
Owings		K 7
Owings-Mills	3,810	E 5
Oxford	852	K 4
Oxon Hill		H 1
Parkton		C 11
Parkville	27,236	G 15
Parsonsburg		G 11
Pasadena		G 7
Patuxent		E 8
Perry Hall		G 11
Perryman	2,040	C 12
Phoenix		B 11
Pikesville	18,737	E 6
Pinehurst		H 8
Pine Orchard		H 5
Piney Grove		B 5
Piney Point		I 11
Pinto		B 3
Piscataway		K 4
Pisgah		G 9
Pittsville	488	G 15
Plum Point		F 11
Pocomoke City	3,496	I 15
Point of Rocks	326	C 8
Pomfret		D 7
Pomona		G 1
Pomonkey	298	G 7
Poolesville		K 5
Poplar Hill	953	B 13
Port Deposit		B 11
Port Herman		G 10
Port Tobacco		G 3
Potomac		B 3
Potomac Park	1,016	B 3
Powellville		H 15
Pratt		E 6
Preston	469	F 13
Price		D 13
Prince Frederick		°G 11
Princess Anne	1,351	°H 14
Principio Furnace		B 13
Public Landing		H 16
Pylesville		B 12
Quantico		G 14
Queen Anne	283	E 13
Queenstown	355	F 12
Randallstown		B 3
Rawlings		H 1
Redgate		C 11
Redhouse		B 1
Redland		G 3
Rehobeth		G 15
Reisterstown	4,216	C 10
Relay*		B 11
Rhodes Point		I 13
Rhodesdale		G 14
Riderwood		E 6
Ridgely	886	E 13
Ridgway		H 6
Ringgold		B 8
Rising Sun	824	B 3
Rison		G 9
Riva		G 4
Riverdale	5,758	I 4
Riviera Beach	4,902	G 7
Roberts		D 12
Rock Hall	1,084	D 11
Rock Point		H 6
Rockville	41,164	°H 3
Rocky Ridge		B 2
Rodgers Forge		E 7
Rohrersville		C 7
Rosaryville		K 5
Rosemont	212	B 11
Round Bay		G 7
Royal Oak		F 12
Royal Oak		F 12
Rush		B 4
Ruthsburg		E 13
Ruxton		E 6
Sabillasville		B 8
St. Augustine		C 14
St. George Island		I 11
St. Inigoes		I 12
St. James		B 7
St. Leonard		G 11

Place	Pop.	Ref.
St. Martin		G 16
St. Marys City		I 12
St. Michaels	1,429	F 12
Salem		G 13
Salisbury	15,166	°G 14
Sandgates		D 12
Sandy Bottom		B 3
Sandy Spring		G 4
Sang Run		B 1
Sassafras		C 14
Savage		G 3
Scotland		I 12
Seat Pleasant	7,147	J 5
Secretary	351	F 13
Severna Park	3,728	H 7
Shady Side		H 7
Sharpsburg	861	C 7
Sharptown	620	G 14
Shelltown		H 15
Sherwood		F 12
Sherwood Forest		G 16
Showell		G 16
Silver Hill		E 10
Silver Run		B 9
Silver Spring	66,348	I 4
Simpsonville		H 5
Skidmore		H 8
Slacks Corner		F 4
Smithsburg	586	B 7
Smithville		E 13
Snow Hill	2,189	°H 15
Solomons		H 12
Somerset	1,329	I 4
Sparks		B 11
Sparrows Point		G 7
Spence		H 15
Spring Gap		B 4
Starr		E 13
Stevenson		E 6
Stevensville		E 12
Still Pond		C 13
Stoakley		G 11
Stockton		I 15
Stoneleigh	15,645	E 7
Street		B 12
Sudlersville	394	D 14
Suitland	10,300	J 4
Sunderland		F 11
Sunnybrook		B 10
Sunshine		G 4
Swanton		C 2
Sykesville	1,373	F 4
Takoma Park	18,323	I 4
Tall Timbers		I 11
Taneytown	1,714	B 9
Taylors Island		G 12
Taylorsville		C 9
Templeville	98	D 14
Thomas		H 6
Thurmont	2,313	B 8
Thurston		F 2
Tilghman		B 7
Tilghmanton		C 11
Timonium		C 11
Toddville		H 13
Tompkinsville		H 10
Townshend		F 10
Towson	19,090	°E 7
Tracys Landing		F 13
Trappe	358	F 13
Tunis Mills		F 12
Twiggtown		B 4
Twin Rivers*		C 12
Tyaskin		H 14
Tylerton		I 13
Union Bridge	833	B 9
Uniontown		B 9
Unionville		C 9
Unity		G 4
University Park	2,921	I 4
Upper Fairmount		H 14
Upper Falls		C 12
Upper Marlboro	673	°J 6
Urbana		F 3
Vale Summit		C 3
Valley Lee		I 11
Vienna	420	G 14
Wagners Crossroads		B 7

Place	Pop.	Ref.
Waldorf	1,048	F 10
Walkersville	1,265	C 8
Wango		H 15
Warfieldsburg		B 10
Warwick		C 14
Washington Grove	576	H 3
Waterloo		G 5
Weisburg		B 10
Welcome		G 9
Wenona		I 15
Wesley		H 15
West Friendship		F 4
Westernport	3,044	C 3
Westminster	7,143	°B 10
Westover		I 14
Westwood		F 11
Whaleyville		G 15
Wheaton	54,635	H 4
White Hall		B 11
White House		B 10
White Marsh		E 8
White Plains		G 10
Whiteford		B 12
Whitehaven		H 14
Whiton		H 15
Willards	531	G 15
Williamsburg		F 14
Williamsport	2,281	B 7
Wilson		B 9
Windyhill		F 13
Wingate		H 12
Wittman		F 12
Woodbine		F 4
Woodland Beach	1,855	F 7
Woodlawn	19,234	F 6
Woodlawn		B 13
Woodsboro	430	B 9
Woodstock		F 5
Woolford		G 12
Worton		D 13
Wye Mills		E 13
Yellow Springs		C 8
Zihlman		B 3

*Does not appear on the map; key shows general location.
°County seat

Sources: Latest census figures (1970 preliminary census where available or 1960 census). Cities and towns without population are unincorporated places under 1,000 in population and are not listed in census reports.

MARYLAND/People

The 1970 preliminary United States census reported that Maryland had a population of 3,874,642. The population had increased 25 per cent over the 1960 figure of 3,100,689.

Nearly three-fourths of Maryland's people live in urban areas. That is, they live in or near cities and towns of 2,500 or more persons. Slightly more than a fourth of the people live in rural areas. About 53 of every 100 persons live in the Baltimore metropolitan area. This is the state's only Standard Metropolitan Statistical Area (see METROPOLITAN AREA). For the population of the politi-cal map of Maryland. Almost a third of the people live in the Maryland portion of the Washington, D.C., metropolitan area.

Baltimore is the state's largest city. Other large population centers, in order of population, are Dundalk, Silver Spring, Bethesda, and Wheaton. See the separate articles listed under Cities in the Related Articles at the end of this article.

About 97 of every 100 persons living in Maryland were born in the United States. Roman Catholics make up Maryland's largest single religious group, followed by Methodists. Other large religious groups in the state include Baptists, Episcopalians, Jews, Lutherans, and Presbyterians.

POPULATION

This map shows the population density of Maryland, and how it varies in different parts of the state. Population density means the average number of persons who live on each square mile.

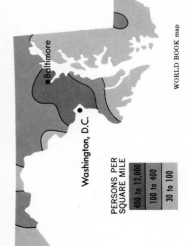

Washington, D.C.

Baltimore

WORLD BOOK map

PERSONS PER SQUARE MILE
- 400 to 12,000
- 100 to 400
- 30 to 100

Miles 0 25 50 75 100

Kilometers 0 25 50 75 100

Schools. Church leaders and private tutors taught children in the early days of the Maryland colony. Only the children of wealthy families received schooling. The colony first provided funds for public education in 1694. King William's School (now St. John's College) in Annapolis was the colony's first free school. It was founded as an academy in 1696. In 1826, Maryland provided for the establishment of public schools throughout the state. The state board of education and the office of superintendent of public instruction were created in 1865.

Today, the Board of Education administers Maryland's public school system. The governor appoints the seven members of the board to five-year terms. The board appoints the superintendent of public instruction to carry out its policies. A state law requires children between the ages of 6 and 16 to attend school. For the number of students and teachers in Maryland, see EDUCATION (table).

Libraries. In 1699, the Reverend Thomas Bray, an Episcopal minister, set up 30 *parish* (church district) libraries in the colony, with a central library in Annapolis. These were Maryland's first libraries. In 1882, Enoch Pratt, a Baltimore iron merchant, established the Enoch Pratt Free Library of Baltimore. Today, this library ranks as one of the outstanding libraries in the nation. The Enoch Pratt's main library, together with its branches and bookmobiles, has the largest collection of books in Maryland.

The Johns Hopkins University library in Baltimore has a large collection of medical books. The Maryland Historical Society, founded in 1844, has an outstanding collection of books and manuscripts dealing with the history of Maryland. The Peabody Institute Library in Baltimore has rare books, pamphlets, and reference works. The University of Maryland has a large collection of current East Asian materials.

Museums. The Peale Museum, also called the Municipal Museum of the City of Baltimore, is one of the oldest museums in the United States. It opened in 1814 as the Baltimore Museum and Gallery of the Fine Arts. Rembrandt Peale, the founder, was the son of the famous painter, Charles Willson Peale. The museum displays many works including those of both Peales.

M. E. Warren

Thousands of miles of shoreline along the Atlantic Ocean and Chesapeake Bay attract swimmers, boaters, and fishermen to Maryland. Sportsmen hunt game birds and animals in the fields and forests, and along rivers. Old mansions and historic sites throughout the state appeal to sightseers. Visitors can still watch old English sports such as jousting tournaments, in which galloping riders try to catch small rings on a spear.

PLACES TO VISIT

Barbara Frietchie House, in Frederick, is a reproduction of the home from which Barbara Frietchie supposedly defied Confederate forces. The 1½-story brick building contains her clothing, spinning wheel, china, and Bible. See FRIETCHIE, BARBARA.

Basilica of the Assumption of the Blessed Virgin Mary, in Baltimore, was the first Roman Catholic cathedral in the United States. Benjamin Henry Latrobe designed the cathedral, which was completed in 1821.

Flag House, in Baltimore, was the home of Mary Pickersgill. In this brick building, built in 1793, she made the huge flag that inspired Francis Scott Key to write "The Star-Spangled Banner."

St. Mary's City, a village near Leonardtown, became Maryland's first colonial settlement in 1634. A copy of the first Maryland state house stands in the village.

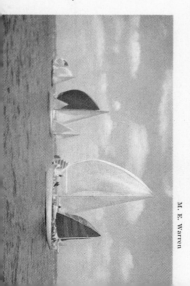

Annual Jousting
Championships
in St. Margarets

▲

Sailing in
Chesapeake Bay ▶

M. E. Warren

National Monuments and Historic Sites. Antietam National Battlefield Site, near Sharpsburg, was the site of one of the bloodiest Civil War battles. On Sept. 17, 1862, Union forces at Antietam turned back the first Confederate invasion of the North. The State House of Maryland in Annapolis was made a national historic landmark in 1960. It served as the U.S. Capitol in 1783 and 1784, and is the oldest state Capitol still in daily use. Fort McHenry National Monument and Historic Shrine in Baltimore honors the defense of Baltimore against the British during the War of 1812. During that defense, on Sept. 13 and 14, 1814, Francis Scott Key was inspired to write "The Star-Spangled Banner." Other sites include Antietam National Cemetery in Sharpsburg, Chesapeake and Ohio Canal National Monument between Seneca and Cumberland, Hampton National Historic Site in Towson near Baltimore, and *U.S.S. Constellation* National Historic Landmark in Baltimore. Maryland shares Harpers Ferry National Historical Park with West Virginia.

State Parks and Forests. Maryland has 19 state parks, 11 state forests, 5 state recreational areas, and a state forest nursery. For information on the state parks of Maryland, write to Director, Department of Forests and Parks, Forests and Parks Commission, State Office Building, Annapolis, Md. 21404.

The Baltimore Museum of Art has exhibits of paintings, prints, sculpture, and colonial interiors. Its collection of paintings by Henri Matisse is the largest in any public gallery.

The Maryland Historical Society in Baltimore owns the original manuscript of "The Star-Spangled Banner." It also displays portraits of many prominent Americans. The society's Noel Wyatt and Elizabeth Patterson Bonaparte collections include Empire furniture, miniatures, glass, jewelry, and lace. The society also has a collection dealing with ships and the sea.

Other important museums in Maryland include the Walters Art Gallery in Baltimore and the U.S. Naval Academy Museum in Annapolis.

UNIVERSITIES AND COLLEGES

Maryland has 24 universities and colleges accredited by the Middle States Association of Colleges and Secondary Schools. For enrollments and further information, see UNIVERSITIES AND COLLEGES (table).

Name	Location	Founded	Name	Location	Founded
Bowie State College	Bowie	1867	Notre Dame of Maryland, College of	Baltimore	1895
Columbia Union College	Takoma Park	1904	Peabody Conservatory of Music	Baltimore	1857
Coppin State College	Baltimore	1900	St. John's College	Annapolis	1696
Frostburg State College	Frostburg	1902	St. Joseph College	Emmitsburg	1809
Goucher College	Towson	1885	St. Mary's Seminary and University	Baltimore	1791
Hood College	Frederick	1893	Salisbury State College	Salisbury	1925
Johns Hopkins University	Baltimore	1876	Towson State College	Baltimore	1865
Loyola College	Baltimore	1852	United States Naval Academy	Annapolis	1845
Maryland, University of	*	1807	Washington College	Chestertown	1782
Morgan State College	Baltimore	1867	Western Maryland College	Westminster	1867
Mount Saint Agnes College	Baltimore	1890	Woodstock College	Woodstock	1869
Mount Saint Mary's College	Emmitsburg	1808			

*For the campuses of the University of Maryland, see UNIVERSITIES AND COLLEGES (table).

ANNUAL EVENTS

One of Maryland's most famous annual events is the Preakness Stakes, a horse race run each May at the Pimlico race track in Baltimore. The Preakness, with the Kentucky Derby and the Belmont Stakes, makes up the famous *Triple Crown* of horse racing. Other annual events in Maryland include the following.

January-March: Governor's Open House in Annapolis (January 1); Ratification Day in Annapolis (January 14); Maryland Day, statewide (March 25).

April-June: Steeplechase Races in Baltimore County (April); Governor's Cup Sports Car Races in Upper Marlboro (April); Tobacco Auctions in Upper Marlboro (April-July); House and Garden Pilgrimages in the Eastern Counties (April-May); National Sports Car Races in Cumberland (May); June Week at the U.S. Naval Academy in Annapolis (first week in June); Flag Day Ceremonies at Flag House in Baltimore (June 14).

July-September: Miles River Yacht Club Regatta in St. Michaels (July); National Hard Crab Derby in Crisfield (Labor Day weekend); Old Defender's Day, statewide (September 12); State Jousting Championships near Baltimore (September).

October-December: Autumn Glory Time in Garrett County (October); Heritage Month in Annapolis (October); Old Princess Anne Days in Princess Anne (October); International Horse Race at Laurel Race Track in Laurel (November 11); Eastern Livestock Show in Timonium (middle of November).

Graduation at U.S. Naval Academy in Annapolis

M. E. Warren

Antietam National Battlefield Site near Sharpsburg

Zehrt, FPG

Barbara Frietchie House in Frederick

Roche, FPG

PENNSYLVANIA

MT. DAVIS
3,213 FT.

NEGRO MTN.

MT. NEBO
2,762 FT.

Cumberland

Youghiogheny R.

MEADOW MTN.

Deep Creek
Lake

Savage
River Res.

Savage R.

DANS MTN.

Patterson Cr.

KNOBLY MTN.

N. Br. Potomac R.

Potomac R.

SIDELING HILL

TOWN HILL

TUSCARORA MTS.

WESTERN MD.

HEARTHSTONE
MTN. + 1,980 FT.

QUIRAUG MTN.
2,145 FT.

GETTYSBURG
NAT'L. MIL. PARK

Conococheague Cr.

Hagerstown

Conococheague Creek

Monocacy River

WESTERN MD.

Prettyboy
Res.

Susquehanna River

Octoraro Cr.

White Clay Cr.

Philadelphia

Wilmington

Newark

NEW
JERSEY

Salem Cr.

HIGH KNOB
1,980 FT.

SLEEPY CREEK MTN.

CACAPON MTN.

Antietam Cr.

ANTIETAM NAT'L.
BFLD. SITE
& CEM.

HIGH
KNOB
1,531 FT.

Frederick

SUGARLOAF
1,281 FT.

PARRS RIDGE

Westminster

S. Br. Patapsco R.

Patapsco
Res.

Loch
Raven
Res.

SPESUTIE I.

TURKEY
PT.

TAYLOR I.

ROBBINS PT.

POOLES I.

Gunpowder Falls

Gunpowder R.

Sassafras River

DELMARVA

OHIO R.R.

Chesapeake
& Del. Canal

Nottingham
Pond

BOMBAY
HOOK
PT.

EGG
ISLAND
PT.

Delaware River

BACKBONE MTN.

APPALACHIAN MOUNTAINS

ALLEGHENY MOUNTAINS

BACKBONE MTN.
3,360 FT.
HIGHEST POINT
IN MARYLAND

WEST
VIRGINIA

HIGH KNOB
2,844 FT.

HARPERS FERRY
NAT'L. HIST. PARK

NORTH MTN.

SOUTH MOUNTAIN

CATOCTIN MOUNTAIN

Potomac

River

Triadelphia
Res.

Rocky Gorge
Res.

Middle Patuxent R.

Patapsco R.

Baltimore

NORTH
PT.

BODKIN
PT.

LOVE
PT.

SANDY
PT.

EASTERN
NECK I.

Chester River

POOLES I.

PENN. CENTRAL R.R.

Dover

Delaware

Bay

DELAWARE

Monocacy Creek

SHENANDOAH

Shenandoah River

N. Fk. Shenandoah River

S. Fk. Shenandoah River

SHENANDOAH VALLEY

GREAT VALLEY

BLUE RIDGE MTNS.

Monocacy R.

CHESAPEAKE & OHIO
CANAL NAT'L. MON.

Occoquan Cr.

Arlington

WASHINGTON
D.C.

ANNAPOLIS

KENT
ISLAND

KENT
PT.

TILGHMAN I.

BLACKWALNUT
PT.

COOK
PT.

Eastern
Bay

South R.

Severn R.

Choptank River

Marshope Cr.

Rehoboth
Bay

CAPE
HENLOPEN

Miles River

SHENANDOAH

NATIONAL

PARK

PIEDMONT

Rappahannock
River

Piscataway Cr.

Zekiah Swamp

MARYLAND
PT.

SOUTHERN MD. R.R.

Wicomico R.

Patuxent River

JAMES I.

Cambridge

Savannah
Lake

Nanticoke River

Great Pocomoke
Swamp

Assawoman
Bay

Rapidan River

VIRGINIA

FREDERICKSBURG R.R.

B. AND O. POTOMAC R.R.

Fredericksburg

GEORGE WASHINGTON
BIRTHPLACE

Potomac

BLAKISTONE I.

River

CEDAR
PT.

HOOPER I.

Fishing
Bay

Hooper Strait

BLOODSWORTH I.

DEAL I.

HOLLAND
STRAITS

SOUTH
MARSH
I.

TANGIER I.

Manokin R.

Pocomoke River

Sinepuxent
Bay

COASTAL

PLAIN

Charlottesville

N. Anna River

Mattaponi River

PT.
NO
POINT

PONE I.

HOLLAND
I.

SOUTH
PT.

DEAL I.

Pocomoke Sound

ASSATEAGUE
ISLAND

Rivanna R.

S. Anna River

Rappahannock River

GREAT
PT.

PT.
LOOKOUT

SMITH I.

SOUTH
PT.

TANGIER I.

SMITH
PT.

Tangier Sound

VA.

Chincoteague Bay

ASSATEAGUE
ISLAND

Atlantic
Ocean

Chesapeake

Bay

FENWICK I.

Great Pocomoke
Swamp

Delaware
Bay

Sinepuxent
Bay

MARYLAND

	Mixed Evergreen and Deciduous Trees
	Deciduous Trees
	Grass

⊛ State Capitals   • Cities and Towns

— Rail Lines   ▨ City Limits

1 inch = 28 Statute Miles

Miles 0 5 10 15 20 25

Lambert Conformal Conic Projection

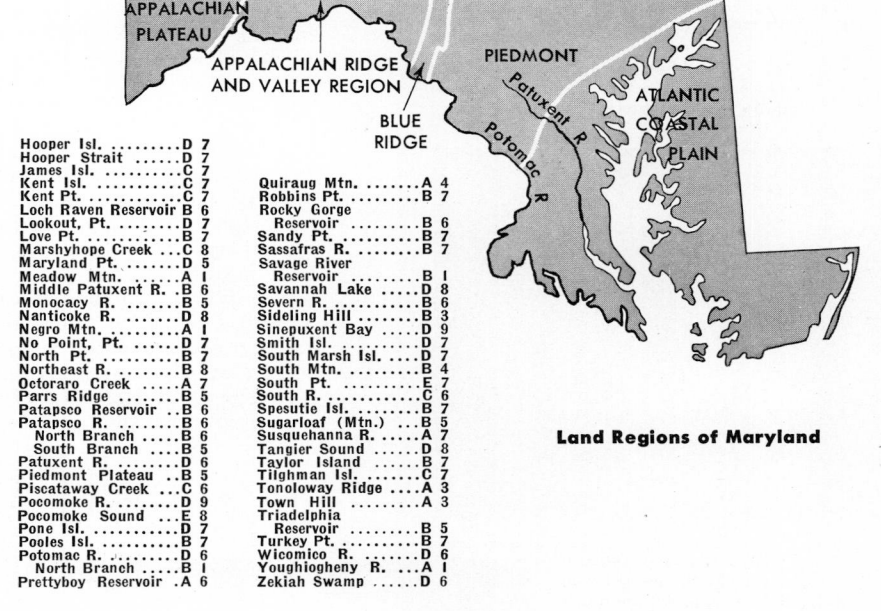

Land Regions of Maryland

MARYLAND / The Land

Land Regions. Chesapeake Bay divides most of Maryland into two parts. The area east of Chesapeake Bay is called the Eastern Shore. The area west of the bay is called the Western Shore. Maryland has five main land regions. They are, from east to west: (1) the Atlantic Coastal Plain, (2) the Piedmont, (3) the Blue Ridge, (4) the Appalachian Ridge and Valley, and (5) the Appalachian Plateau.

The Atlantic Coastal Plain stretches along the east coast of the United States from New Jersey to southern Florida. In Maryland, the coastal plain covers the entire Eastern Shore and part of the Western Shore. The plain touches a narrow tip of northeastern Maryland. It extends across a wide portion of southern Maryland, from the southeastern corner of the state almost to Washington, D.C. The coastal plain is flat on the East-ern Shore, but it rises to about 400 feet on the Western Shore.

The Eastern Shore has some marshy areas. The two-mile-wide Pocomoke Swamp extends from Pocomoke Sound to the Delaware border. The part of the Western Shore south of Baltimore is called Southern Maryland. Tobacco has been raised in Southern Maryland since colonial times.

The Piedmont extends from New Jersey to Alabama. In Maryland, the Piedmont is about 50 miles wide. It stretches from the northeastern to the central part of the state. Low, rolling hills and fertile valleys cover the region. The Piedmont rises to about 880 feet at Parrs Ridge, and to about 1,200 feet at Dug Hill Ridge on the Pennsylvania border. Both these ridges run in a southwesterly direction. They form the divide between streams flowing westward into the Potomac River and those flowing eastward into Chesapeake Bay. Fred-erick Valley, along the Monocacy River, is one of the richest dairy-farming areas in the United States.

The Blue Ridge region extends from southern Pennsyl-vania to northern Georgia. In Maryland, the region is a narrow, mountainous strip of land between the Pied-mont and the Appalachian Ridge and Valley region. South Mountain and Catoctin Mountain form most of the Blue Ridge. Nearly all the region is over 1,000 feet above sea level. It rises to a height of over 2,000 feet near the Pennsylvania border. The Blue Ridge region was named for the blue haze that sometimes hangs over its forest-covered ridges.

The Appalachian Ridge and Valley is a land region that stretches southwestward from New Jersey to Ala-bama. The Maryland portion of the region is a strip of land that separates Pennsylvania from West Vir-ginia. At Hancock, Maryland measures less than two miles from its northern to its southern borders.

The Great Valley, known in Maryland as Hagers-town Valley, covers the eastern portion of the state's ridge and valley region. Much of this fertile valley is filled with orchards and farms. West of the valley, a series of ridges crosses the state from northeast to south-west. Some of the ridges rise to almost 2,000 feet. Forests cover about two-thirds of the region.

The Appalachian Plateau extends from New York to Georgia. It covers a triangle-shaped area in the extreme western part of Maryland. The Allegheny Mountains cover most of the region. The Alleghenies make up part of the huge Appalachian range. Backbone Mountain, in the southwestern corner of the state, is the highest point in Maryland. It rises 3,360 feet. Streams have cut deep valleys into the Appalachian Plateau. These valleys served as early trails to the West. Forests cover nearly three-fourths of the plateau region.

Coastline of Maryland measures only 31 miles along the Atlantic Ocean. But the many arms and inlets of Chesapeake Bay give Maryland a total coastline of 3,190 miles. These arms and inlets provide excellent harbors. Important islands in Chesapeake Bay include Bloodsworth, Deal, Hooper, Kent, Smith, South Marsh, Taylors, and Tilghman.

Maryland State Roads Comm.

M. E. Warren

A. Aubrey Bodine

Blue Haze, *above,* hangs over the hills and valleys of the Blue Ridge region, a narrow strip of land in northern Maryland.

Fertile Farmland, *left,* makes Frederick County one of Maryland's finest agricultural areas. It is in the Piedmont region.

Rivers and Lakes. Most of Maryland is drained by rivers that flow into Chesapeake Bay. Seven large rivers cross the Eastern Shore area. They are the Chester, Choptank, Elk, Nanticoke, Pocomoke, Sassafras, and Wicomico. The Susquehanna River flows into the state from Pennsylvania and empties into Chesapeake Bay. The Gunpowder, Patapsco, and Patuxent rivers all drain the Western Shore and flow into the bay.

The Potomac River forms Maryland's southern and southwestern boundary. South of Washington, D.C., the Potomac widens into an arm of Chesapeake Bay. Tributaries of the Potomac River drain a large part of western Maryland.

All Maryland lakes are man-made. The largest, Deep Creek Lake in the Allegheny Mountains, covers about 4,000 acres. This lake was formed by a dam built across a small tributary of the Youghiogheny River. The dam provides hydroelectric power.

FPG

"The Narrows," *above,* lies near Cumberland. This area of Maryland is in the Appalachian Ridge and Valley region.

Hunters Watch for Ducks, *right,* on Chesapeake Bay in the Atlantic Coastal Plain.

MARYLAND/Climate

Maryland has a humid climate, with hot summers and generally mild winters. Temperatures in the mountainous regions of the northwest are lower than those along the Atlantic coast and in the Chesapeake Bay region. January temperatures average 29° F. in Garrett County in the northwest, and 39° F. along the coast. Average July temperatures range from 68° F. in Garrett County to the mid-70's in the Chesapeake Bay region. The state's record high temperature, 109° F., occurred at Boettcherville on July 3, 1898, and at Cumberland and Frederick on July 10, 1936. Oakland recorded the state's lowest temperature, —40° F., on Jan. 13, 1912.

Maryland's *precipitation* (rain, melted snow, and other forms of moisture) averages about 44 inches a year. Rain falls fairly evenly throughout the state. Snow ranges from about 9 inches a year in the southeast to about 78 inches in the Appalachian Plateau.

Deep Creek Lake, in the Allegheny Mountains, is Maryland's largest lake. It lies in the Appalachian Plateau region.

M. E. Warren, Alpha

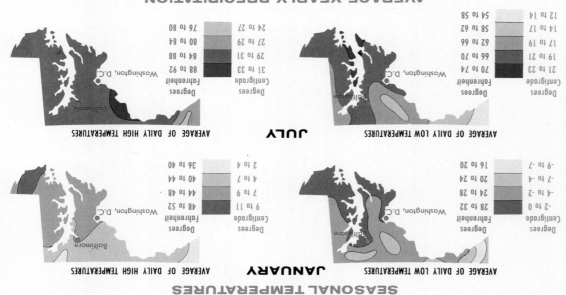

SEASONAL TEMPERATURES

JANUARY

AVERAGE OF DAILY HIGH TEMPERATURES

Degrees Fahrenheit	Degrees Centigrade
48 to 52	9 to 11
44 to 48	7 to 9
40 to 44	4 to 7
36 to 40	2 to 4

AVERAGE OF DAILY LOW TEMPERATURES

Degrees Fahrenheit	Degrees Centigrade
28 to 32	-2 to 0
24 to 28	-4 to -2
20 to 24	-7 to -4
16 to 20	-9 to -7

JULY

AVERAGE OF DAILY HIGH TEMPERATURES

Degrees Fahrenheit	Degrees Centigrade
88 to 92	31 to 33
84 to 88	29 to 31
80 to 84	27 to 29
76 to 80	24 to 27

AVERAGE OF DAILY LOW TEMPERATURES

Degrees Fahrenheit	Degrees Centigrade
70 to 74	21 to 23
66 to 70	19 to 21
62 to 66	17 to 19
58 to 62	14 to 17
54 to 58	12 to 14

AVERAGE YEARLY PRECIPITATION
(Rain, Melted Snow, and Other Moisture)

Inches	Centimeters
48 to 52	122 to 132
44 to 48	112 to 122
40 to 44	102 to 112
36 to 40	91 to 102

0   25   50   75   100 Miles
0   50   100 Kilometers

WORLD BOOK maps

MONTHLY WEATHER IN BALTIMORE AND WASHINGTON, D.C.

	Average of:	JAN	FEB	MAR	APR	MAY	JUNE	JULY	AUG	SEPT	OCT	NOV	DEC
BALTIMORE	High Temperatures	43	44	53	63	73	83	87	85	78	67	55	44
	Low Temperatures	27	26	33	42	53	62	66	64	58	46	36	27
	Days of Rain or Snow	11	10	11	11	11	10	9	10	7	6	9	6
WASHINGTON, D.C.	Days of Rain or Snow	11	10	12	11	11	11	12	11	9	6	8	10
	High Temperatures	44	46	55	65	76	84	87	85	79	68	57	46
	Low Temperatures	29	29	36	45	55	64	68	67	61	49	39	31

Temperatures are given in degrees Fahrenheit.

Source: U.S. Weather Bureau

Baltimore is Maryland's major manufacturing center. Other manufacturing cities in the state include Cambridge, Cumberland, Frederick, Hagerstown, Salisbury, and Westminster. Most of the state has good farmland. Most mining takes place on the Western Shore. The state's tourist industries thrive along Chesapeake Bay; in the areas near Washington, D.C., and Baltimore; and at Maryland's many historic sites.

Natural Resources of Maryland include fertile soils, trees, waters filled with sea life, and many minerals.

Soil. Light, sandy loams and stiff, clay soils cover much of the Eastern Shore, although the northern part has heavier soils. The Western Shore south of Baltimore also has loam and clay soils. North-central Maryland has fertile, limestone soils. The valleys of western Maryland have a thin covering of soil. Orchards thrive there.

Forests cover about 2,900,000 acres, or nearly half the state's land area. A belt of hardwood forest stretches across much of central Maryland. Over 150 kinds of trees grow in the state. Oaks are the most common. Others include the ash, beech, black locust, hickory, maple, tulip tree, tupelo, and walnut.

Plant Life. The black-eyed Susan, Maryland's state flower, grows on the Western Shore. The Western Shore also has many kinds of berries, including blackberries, dewberries, raspberries, and wild strawberries. Grasses and grasslike plants called *sedges* grow on the Eastern Shore. Azaleas, laurel, and rhododendrons grow along the edges of the woods.

Animal Life includes eastern cottontail rabbits, minks, opossums, raccoons, red and gray foxes, and white-tailed deer. The north-central part of the state has chipmunks, otters, squirrels, and woodchucks. Hunters find grouse, partridge, wild turkeys, and woodcocks in western Maryland, and wild ducks and geese along the coastal plain. Songbirds are plentiful. The Baltimore oriole is not common but was chosen as the state bird because it is orange and black, the colors of the Lords Baltimore, Maryland's first rulers.

Maryland's coastal waters have great quantities of bluefish, crabs, diamondback terrapins, menhaden, oysters, sea trout, shad, shrimps, and striped bass (called *rockfish* or *rock* in Maryland). Each spring, shad, croakers, alewives, and other fishes swim up Chesapeake Bay to lay their eggs in the larger rivers. Trout live in the cold rivers and streams of northern and western Maryland. Bullheads, carp, catfish, and suckers are found in the waters of the Piedmont and the coastal plain.

Minerals. Sand and gravel deposits are found in many counties on Maryland's Western Shore. Baltimore County has valuable deposits of stone. Other minerals in the state include clays, granite, lime, limestone, natural gas, soapstone, and talc.

Manufacturing, including processing, accounts for 89 per cent of the value of goods produced in Maryland. Manufactured goods have a *value added by manufacture* of about $3,800,000,000 a year. This figure represents the value created in products by Maryland's industries, not counting such costs as materials, supplies, and fuels. Maryland's chief manufactured products, in order of importance, are (1) food and food products, (2) primary metals, and (3) transportation equipment.

Food and Food Products have a value added of about $530,700,000 yearly. Factories in Baltimore process meats and manufacture spices, food concentrates, and other food products. Baltimore is the center of the state's sugar refining. Frederick has vegetable canning plants. Factories in Cambridge process, can, and freeze foods. Salisbury is Maryland's leading poultry processor.

Primary Metals industries manufacture products that have a value added of about $524,400,000 a year. These industries smelt, refine, and roll metals, and manufacture nails, bolts, and basic metal products such as castings. Most primary metals plants are in the Baltimore area. The Bethlehem Steel Corporation plant in Sparrows Point is one of the largest steel mills in the world. Most metals are imported from outside the state.

Transportation Equipment has a value added of about $463,400,000 a year. Much of Maryland's transportation industry is centered around Baltimore. The Baltimore area has shipbuilding and repair facilities, and factories that make railroad and automobile equipment. Hagerstown factories build trucks. Cumberland has railroad shops. Cambridge has boat-building plants.

Other Leading Industries. Chemicals and allied products rank fourth in Maryland as sources of manufacturing income. Electrical machinery is fifth. Baltimore leads the state in both these industries. Maryland industries also manufacture clothing and related products,

MARYLAND'S PRODUCTION IN 1967

Total value of goods produced—$4,258,575,000

MANUFACTURED PRODUCTS 89%

AGRICULTURAL PRODUCTS 9%

FISH AND MINERAL PRODUCTS 2%

Note: Manufacturing percentage based on value added by manufacture. Other percentages based on value of production. Fish Products are less than 1 per cent.

Source: U.S. Government statistics

MARYLAND'S EMPLOYMENT IN 1967

Total number of persons employed—1,220,000

	Number of Employees
Manufacturing	283,200
Wholesale & Retail Trade	264,000
Government	212,600
Services	205,300
Construction	87,200
Transportation & Public Utilities	77,700
Finance, Insurance & Real Estate	61,600
Agriculture & Mining	28,400

Source: U.S. Department of Labor

FARM, MINERAL, AND FOREST PRODUCTS

This map shows where the leading farm, mineral, and forest products are produced. The major urban areas (shown in red) are the important manufacturing centers.

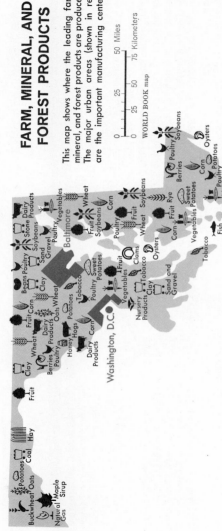

WORLD BOOK map

fabricated metal products, and nonelectrical machinery. Printing and publishing are also important.

Agriculture. Farm products in Maryland earn an annual income of about $377,800,000, or 9 per cent of the value of goods produced in the state. Farmland covers about half the state. Maryland's 20,800 farms average about 153 acres in size.

Livestock and Livestock Products have an annual value of about $218,106,000. Milk is Maryland's leading farm product, earning about $88 million a year. Frederick County leads the state in milk production, followed by Carroll, Washington, Harford, and Montgomery counties. *Broilers* (chickens between 9 and 12 weeks old) are the second leading farm product. They earn about $83 million a year. Most of the state's broilers are raised in the central and southern parts of the Eastern Shore. Other important livestock products include cattle and calves, eggs, and hogs.

Crops in Maryland have an annual value of about $112 million. Corn is Maryland's leading cash crop, bringing in about $27 million a year. Corn is grown throughout the state. Maryland is a leading tobacco state, and tobacco is the state's second leading cash crop. Soybeans rank third. Other important crops include apples, barley, hay, snap beans, sweet corn, sweet potatoes, tomatoes, and wheat.

Mining in Maryland has an annual value of about $72,820,000. Stone ranks as Maryland's most valuable mineral. Quarries in the northern and western regions produce most of the stone. Allegany and Garrett counties, in western Maryland, mine *bituminous* (soft) coal. Fire clay is produced in western Maryland and in Cecil County in the northeast. Large quantities of sand and gravel come from pits on the Western Shore. Baltimore, Frederick, and Washington counties, all on the Western Shore, produce limestone. Natural gas comes from Garrett County. Other important minerals include crushed stone, soapstone, and talc.

Fishing Industry. The annual fish catch in Maryland is valued at about $17,356,000. Maryland leads all states in the production of soft-shell clams, and is a leading source of oysters. Valuable catches in Chesapeake Bay include alewives, catfish, crabs, eels, men-

haden, oysters, shad, soft-shell clams, striped bass, swellfish, and white perch. The Atlantic coastal waters provide flounders, hard clams, oysters, porgy, sea bass, striped bass, and tuna.

Electric Power. Steam plants, operated on coal, supply most of Maryland's electric power. Most of the plants are privately owned. Some hydroelectric power comes into the state from Pennsylvania. For Maryland's kilowatt-hour production, see ELECTRIC POWER (table).

Transportation. Early transportation in the Maryland region was provided by steamboats traveling over Chesapeake Bay and its tributaries. In 1828, construction began on the Baltimore and Ohio Railroad. This railroad was the first in the Western Hemisphere to carry both passengers and freight. The Chesapeake and Delaware Canal was completed in 1829, connecting Chesapeake Bay with the Delaware River. In the 1920's, motor trucks and buses replaced steamboat transportation in the Chesapeake Bay country.

Today, nearly all Maryland's 25,600 miles of roads are surfaced. In 1963, the John F. Kennedy Expressway became the state's first modern tollway. It is part of a major nonstop highway that extends from Washington, D.C., to Boston. Maryland has about 80 airports. Friendship International Airport near Baltimore is a major national and international terminal. It serves both Baltimore and Washington, D.C. Railroads operate on about 1,300 miles of track in Maryland. Baltimore ranks as a leading U.S. seaport.

Communication. The *Maryland Gazette,* published in Annapolis from 1727 to 1734, was the first colonial newspaper south of Philadelphia, and one of the first in the colonies. In 1844, the first telegraph line in the United States opened between Baltimore and Washington, D.C. Maryland's oldest radio stations, WCAO and WFBR of Baltimore, began broadcasting in 1922. The state's first television station, WMAR-TV, was established in Baltimore in 1947.

Today, Maryland has about 90 newspapers, 12 of which are dailies, and about 115 periodicals. *The News American* and *The Sun,* both in Baltimore, are the largest dailies. The state has about 80 radio stations and 6 television stations.

Indian Days. Indians probably lived in the Maryland region hundreds of years before white men came. Early white explorers found Algonkian Indians and a few Susquehannock in the region. The Algonkian tribes included the Choptank, Nanticoke, Patuxent, Portobago, Wicomico, and others. Most of the Indians left the region during the early years of white settlement. But they gave their names to many of Maryland's rivers, towns, and counties.

Exploration and Settlement. The Spaniards became the first white men to visit the Maryland region when they explored Chesapeake Bay in the 1500's. In 1608, Captain John Smith of Virginia sailed northward up Chesapeake Bay into the Maryland region. Smith wrote a description of what he saw. In 1631, William Claiborne, also of Virginia, opened a trading post on Kent Island in the bay. Claiborne's was the first white settlement in the Maryland region.

In 1632, King Charles I of England granted the Maryland region to George Calvert, the first Lord Balti-

---

IMPORTANT DATES IN MARYLAND

1608 Captain John Smith explored Chesapeake Bay.

1631 William Claiborne established a trading post on Kent Island.

1632 King Charles I of England granted the Maryland charter to Cecil Calvert, second Lord Baltimore.

1634 The first settlers arrived in Maryland.

1649 Maryland passed a religious toleration act.

1654 William Claiborne seized control of the colony.

1658 Lord Baltimore regained control.

1691 England assumed direct rule of the colony.

1715 The Lords Baltimore regained proprietorship of the colony.

1767 Mason and Dixon completed their survey of the Maryland-Pennsylvania boundary, begun in 1763.

1774 Marylanders burned the *Peggy Stewart* and its cargo of tea in protest against the Boston Port Bill.

1776 Maryland declared its independence.

1776-1777 The Second Continental Congress met in Baltimore.

1783 George Washington resigned his commission as commander in chief at Annapolis.

1788 Maryland became the seventh state on April 28.

1791 Maryland gave land for the District of Columbia.

1814 Francis Scott Key wrote "The Star-Spangled Banner" during the British bombardment of Fort McHenry.

1828 Construction of the Baltimore & Ohio Railroad began.

1850 The National (Cumberland) Road, west from Cumberland, was completed.

1862 Federal forces drove back the Confederates from Antietam Creek near Sharpsburg.

1864 A constitution abolishing slavery was adopted.

1919-1933 Maryland resisted the nation's prohibition laws and became known as the *Free State*.

1950 Baltimore's Friendship International Airport began operating.

1952 The Chesapeake Bay Bridge was opened to traffic.

1954 The Baltimore-Washington, D.C., Expressway was completed.

1957 The Baltimore Harbor Tunnel opened.

1962-1966 Maryland reapportioned its legislative and congressional districts.

HISTORIC MARYLAND

The Battle of Antietam, near Sharpsburg, in September, 1862, halted General Lee's first invasion of the North.

Religious Toleration Law was passed in 1649. Called the *Act Concerning Religion,* it gave equal rights to all faiths.

Washington, D.C., occupies land Maryland gave the U.S. in 1791, after George Washington chose that site for the capital.

---

more. But George Calvert died before the king signed the charter. King Charles then chartered the region to Calvert's son, Cecil, the second Lord Baltimore. The region was named *Maryland* in honor of Queen Henrietta Maria, the wife of Charles. Cecil Calvert sent colonists to Maryland on two ships, the *Ark* and the *Dove*. In 1634, the ships anchored off St. Clements Island (now Blakiston Island) in the Potomac River. The colonists established St. Mary's City near the southern tip of the Western Shore.

Colonial Days. Lord Baltimore appointed his brother, Leonard Calvert, as governor of the Maryland Colony. Lord Baltimore encouraged the colonists to suggest laws and to assist his brother in the colony's administration. Lord Baltimore was a Roman Catholic, and he wanted freedom of worship for those of his faith. But he also wanted persons of other faiths to settle in Maryland. He believed that religious restrictions would interfere with the colony's growth and development. In 1649, the colonial assembly approved Lord Baltimore's

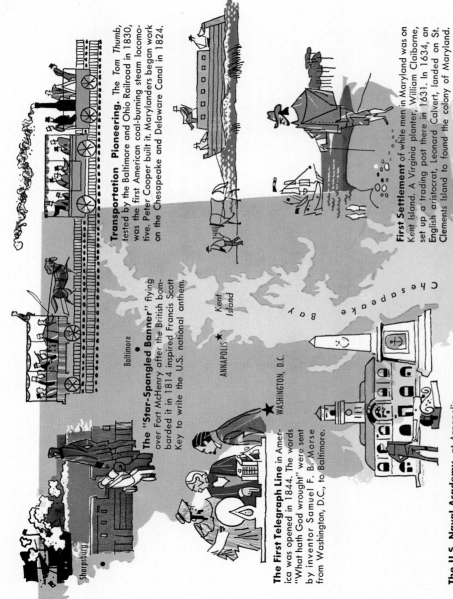

Transportation Pioneering. The *Tom Thumb*, tested by the Baltimore and Ohio Railroad in 1830, was the first American coal-burning steam locomotive. Peter Cooper built it. Marylanders began work on the Chesapeake and Delaware Canal in 1824.

First Settlement of white men in Maryland was on Kent Island. A Virginia planter, William Claiborne, set up a trading post there in 1631. In 1634, an English aristocrat, Leonard Calvert, landed on St. Clements Island to found the colony of Maryland.

The Chesapeake Bay Bridge, opened in 1952, crosses the bay. The 7.7-mile bridge provides fast transportation between Maryland's two "shores."

Chesapeake Bay

Baltimore

Kent Island

ANNAPOLIS ★

★ WASHINGTON, D.C.

Sharpsburg

The First Telegraph Line in America was opened in 1844. The words "What hath God wrought" were sent by inventor Samuel F. B. Morse from Washington, D.C., to Baltimore.

The "Star-Spangled Banner," flying over Fort McHenry after the British bombarded it in 1814 inspired Francis Scott Key to write the U.S. national anthem.

The U.S. Naval Academy, at Annapolis, has trained midshipmen since 1845. The Academy moved to Newport, R.I., during the Civil War, but returned to Annapolis in 1865.

draft of a religious toleration law, granting religious freedom to people of all faiths. After the law was passed, a band of Puritans fled from Virginia and came to Maryland. Maryland became famous for its religious freedom.

William Claiborne's trading settlement on Kent Island was part of the Maryland Colony. But Claiborne refused to recognize Lord Baltimore's authority. In 1654, Claiborne led a group of Protestant settlers who overthrew Lord Baltimore's government. Claiborne controlled Maryland for four years.

On orders from the English government, Claiborne returned Maryland to Lord Baltimore in 1658. Lord Baltimore promised to uphold the religious freedoms established in 1649. But many Protestants in Maryland resented a Roman Catholic as owner of the colony. In 1689, the Protestant Association, a group led by John Coode, seized control of the colony. Coode demanded that England take over the government of Maryland. As a result, royal governors appointed by the English crown began to rule the colony in 1691.

The Calvert family regained control of Maryland in 1715 under the fourth Lord Baltimore, a Protestant. Maryland remained in the hands of the Lords Baltimore until the Revolutionary War. Maryland prospered during the years before the Revolution. Tobacco farming in the colony became profitable. Many colonists grew wealthy and built beautiful mansions. Maryland's population grew rapidly. In the 1700's Maryland and Pennsylvania quarreled over the boundary line between them. In 1763, both colonies agreed to have Charles Mason and Jeremiah Dixon of England survey the land. The survey was completed in 1767, and the Maryland-Pennsylvania boundary became known as *Mason and Dixon's Line.*

The Revolutionary War. In the mid-1700's, Great Britain found itself deeply in debt. To help raise money, Britain placed severe taxes and trade restrictions on the American colonies. The people of Maryland, like those of the other colonies, opposed these measures.

Marylanders resisted the Stamp Act of 1765 (see STAMP ACT). In 1774, colonists in Maryland protested the Boston Port Bill. This bill was a British attempt to punish the people of Boston for the Boston Tea Party (see BOSTON PORT BILL.) Marylanders burned the British ship *Peggy Stewart* and its cargo of tea in Annapolis.

In 1774, delegates from Maryland attended the First Continental Congress in Philadelphia. They supported a policy forbidding the colonists to trade with Great Britain. The Revolutionary War began in Massachusetts in April, 1775. That May, the Second Continental Congress met in Philadelphia, and on July 2, 1776, Maryland delegates voted for independence. Maryland adopted its first constitution on Nov. 8, 1776. In December, 1776, the Continental Congress moved to Baltimore because the British threatened Philadelphia. The congress remained there until the following March. Thomas Johnson, Maryland's first governor under its constitution, took office on March 21, 1777.

Maryland troops fought throughout the Revolutionary War. Baltimore industries built ships and cannons for the colonial forces. But little fighting took place on Maryland soil. The British admiral Richard Howe sailed up Chesapeake Bay in 1777 and landed troops at the mouth of the Elk River. The troops moved into Pennsylvania that same year, and they defeated General George Washington in the Battle of Brandywine.

Statehood. During the war, the Continental Congress formed a government of the United States under the Articles of Confederation. Some of the states claimed western land that extended beyond their colonial boundaries. Maryland refused to sign the Articles of Confederation until the states promised to turn these western lands over to the United States government. Maryland signed the Articles on March 1, 1781. See ARTICLES OF CONFEDERATION; CONGRESS OF THE CONFEDERATION.

After the war, the Congress of the Confederation accepted Maryland's invitation and met in Annapolis from November, 1783, to June, 1784. George Washington resigned his commission as Commander in Chief of the Continental Army in the Maryland State House.

During the 1780's, Maryland and Virginia disagreed over navigation rights in Chesapeake Bay and on the Potomac River. The dispute led to a series of interstate conferences. These and other problems were finally taken up in 1787 by the state delegates to a constitutional convention in Philadelphia. The delegates drew up the United States Constitution. Maryland *ratified* (approved) the Constitution on April 28, 1788, and became the seventh state of the Union. In 1791, Maryland gave land to Congress for the District of Columbia, the new national capital.

The War of 1812 and Industrial Development. Several battles of the War of 1812 were fought in Maryland. In 1813, the British raided a number of Maryland towns and farmhouses along Chesapeake Bay. During the summer of 1814, a large British force under General Robert Ross sailed up the Patuxent River. Ross's troops defeated American forces in the Battle of Bladensburg on Aug. 24, 1814. The British moved on to Washington,

D.C., that same day. They burned the Capitol and other government buildings.

On Sept. 12, the British attacked Baltimore. British troops landed at North Point, southeast of Baltimore at the mouth of the Patapsco River. British ships sailed up the river and fired on Fort McHenry. But American forces defended the city and drove the British out of Maryland. The Battle of Baltimore inspired Francis Scott Key to write "The Star-Spangled Banner," which later became the national anthem of the United States. See STAR-SPANGLED BANNER.

During the early and middle 1800's, Baltimore grew into an important industrial city. It became a leading seaport, and one of the nation's shipbuilding centers. Goods were shipped between Baltimore and the West on the Baltimore and Ohio Railroad, on the Chesapeake and Ohio Canal, and on the Chesapeake and Delaware Canal. In 1830, Peter Cooper built the *Tom Thumb*, the first coal-burning American steam locomotive. The Baltimore and Ohio Railroad used the *Tom Thumb* between Baltimore and Ellicotts' Mills (now Ellicott City). The *De Rosset*, the first ocean-going iron steamship built in the United States, was completed in Baltimore in 1839. Maryland adopted a new constitution in 1851, its first since 1776.

The Civil War. Maryland was a slave state, but it also was one of the original 13 states of the Union. When the Civil War began in 1861, Marylanders were divided in their loyalties between the Union and the Confederacy. After Virginia joined the Confederacy, the fate of Washington, D.C., depended on whether Maryland remained in the Union. If Maryland joined the Confederacy, Washington, D.C., would be surrounded by Confederate territory. Union forces rushed across Maryland to defend the nation's capital. Maryland finally decided to stay in the Union, but many Marylanders joined the Confederate armies.

Several Civil War battles were fought on Maryland soil. In 1862, General Robert E. Lee's Confederate troops invaded Maryland. Union forces fought them in the Battle of Antietam, near Sharpsburg, on September 17. That day, more than 12,000 Union soldiers and 10,000 Confederates were killed or wounded. Lee withdrew to Virginia the next day. In June, 1863, Lee led his troops across Maryland into Pennsylvania, where he was defeated in the Battle of Gettysburg. In 1864, Confederate General Jubal A. Early crossed the Potomac River into Maryland. He defeated a Union division in the Battle of Monocacy, near Frederick, on July 9. Early's forces advanced to within sight of Washington, D.C., before Union forces drove them back.

In 1864, Maryland adopted a constitution that abolished slavery. The new constitution also placed harsh penalties on Marylanders who had supported the Confederate cause. A less severe constitution was adopted in 1867, and is still in effect.

Maryland maintained its industrial and commercial development after the Civil War. Baltimore, already a great industrial city, became a well-known cultural center in the middle and late 1800's.

The Early 1900's. Maryland's industrial expansion continued into the 1900's. The state's factories and shipyards expanded greatly after the United States entered World War I in 1917. The U.S. Army established the Aberdeen Proving Ground, its first testing center, along the northwest shore of Chesapeake Bay in 1917.

Between 1916 and 1935, Maryland adopted many reforms. They included improvements in state government and in the care of prisoners and mental patients.

In 1919, the U.S. Congress passed a law making it illegal to manufacture, sell, and transport alcoholic beverages. Marylanders were among the leading opponents of prohibition law, because they considered it a violation of their state's rights. As a result, Maryland became known as the *Free State*. This nickname is still sometimes used to honor Maryland's traditions of political and religious freedoms.

The Great Depression of the 1930's struck the industrial city of Baltimore particularly hard. Maryland passed social and welfare laws in cooperation with the federal government to ease hardships. In 1938, the state legislature approved the first state income tax law and a $15-million federal housing project.

The Mid-1900's. During World War II (1939-1945), manufacturing activity increased greatly in Maryland. Thousands of workers came to the state from the Appalachian mountain region and other parts of the South.

After the war, Maryland's industry and population continued to grow, and the state improved its transportation systems. Baltimore's Friendship International Airport opened in 1950. Between 1952 and 1963, the state completed the Baltimore Harbor Tunnel, the Chesapeake Bay Bridge (now the William Preston Lane, Jr., Memorial Bridge), the John F. Kennedy Expressway, and an expressway connecting Baltimore and Washington.

The growth of Maryland's urban population created political problems. Until the 1960's, voters in thinly populated rural areas were electing most of the state's legislators. Between 1962 and 1966, Maryland *reapportioned* (redivided) its state legislative and U.S. congressional districts. These changes provided more equal representation based on population.

Maryland expanded its school system during the 1960's. The University of Maryland, which has its main campus in College Park, opened branches in Baltimore and Catonsville. Five state teachers' colleges became general state colleges, and seven two-year community colleges opened.

In 1967, Spiro T. Agnew became the fifth Republican governor in Maryland's history. In 1969, Agnew took office as Vice-President of the United States under President Richard M. Nixon.

Maryland Today. Maryland's industrial growth and its location on Chesapeake Bay have tied the state economically to the northeastern industrial states. Many new cities, suburbs, and industrial communities have grown up between Baltimore and Washington. In the 1970's, the state faces the challenge of providing these expanding areas with schools, water and power supplies, and other services. Maryland is also seeking solutions to the problems of air and water pollution.

The population increase during and after World War II brought changes in housing and education that are still going on in Maryland. Thousands of the people who moved to Maryland from the South were Negroes. As more and more Negroes settled in Baltimore, increasing numbers of white families moved to the city's suburbs. At this time, Negro children in Maryland attended segregated schools, as required by state law. But in 1954,

the Supreme Court of the United States ruled that compulsory segregation of public schools was unconstitutional. Baltimore desegregated its public schools almost

THE GOVERNORS OF MARYLAND

	Party	Term
Under the Articles of Confederation		
1. Thomas Sim Lee	None	1779-1782
2. William Paca	None	1782-1785
3. William Smallwood	Unknown	1785-1788
Under the United States Constitution		
1. William Smallwood	Unknown	1785-1788
2. John Eager Howard	Federalist	1788-1791
3. George Plater	Federalist	1791-1792
4. James Brice	Unknown	1792
5. Thomas Sim Lee	Federalist	1792-1794
6. John H. Stone	Federalist	1794-1797
7. John Henry	Federalist	1797-1798
8. Benjamin Ogle	Federalist	1798-1801
9. John Francis Mercer	*Dem.-Rep.	1801-1803
10. Robert Bowie	Dem.-Rep.	1803-1806
11. Robert Wright	Dem.-Rep.	1806-1809
12. James Butcher	Unknown	1809
13. Edward Lloyd	Dem.-Rep.	1809-1811
14. Robert Bowie	Dem.-Rep.	1811-1812
15. Levin Winder	Federalist	1812-1816
16. Charles Ridgely	Federalist	1816-1819
17. Charles Goldsborough	Federalist	1819
18. Samuel Sprigg	Dem.-Rep.	1819-1822
19. Samuel Stevens, Jr.	Dem.-Rep.	1822-1826
20. Joseph Kent	Dem.-Rep.	1826-1829
21. Daniel Martin	Democratic	1829-1830
22. Thomas King Carroll	Democratic	1830-1831
23. Daniel Martin	Democratic	1831
24. George Howard	Democratic	1831-1833
25. James Thomas	Whig	1833-1836
26. Thomas W. Veazey	Whig	1836-1839
27. William Grason	Democratic	1839-1842
28. Francis Thomas	Democratic	1842-1845
29. Thomas G. Pratt	Democratic	1845-1848
30. Philip Francis Thomas	Democratic	1848-1851
31. Enoch Louis Lowe	Democratic	1851-1854
32. Thomas Watkins Ligon	Democratic	1854-1858
33. Thomas Holliday Hicks	Democratic	1858-1862
34. Augustus W. Bradford	Union	1862-1866
35. Thomas Swann	Democratic	1866-1869
36. Oden Bowie	Democratic	1869-1872
37. William Pinkney Whyte	Democratic	1872-1874
38. James Black Groome	Democratic	1874-1876
39. John Lee Carroll	Democratic	1876-1880
40. William T. Hamilton	Democratic	1880-1884
41. Robert M. McLane	Democratic	1884-1885
42. Henry Lloyd	Democratic	1885-1888
43. Elihu E. Jackson	Democratic	1888-1892
44. Frank Brown	Democratic	1892-1896
45. Lloyd Lowndes	Republican	1896-1900
46. John Walter Smith	Democratic	1900-1904
47. Edwin Warfield	Democratic	1904-1908
48. Austin L. Crothers	Democratic	1908-1912
49. Phillips Lee Goldsborough	Republican	1912-1916
50. Emerson C. Harrington	Democratic	1916-1920
51. Albert C. Ritchie	Democratic	1920-1935
52. Harry W. Nice	Republican	1935-1939
53. Herbert R. O'Conor	Democratic	1939-1947
54. Wm. Preston Lane, Jr.	Democratic	1947-1951
55. Theodore R. McKeldin	Republican	1951-1959
56. J. Millard Tawes	Democratic	1959-1967
57. Spiro T. Agnew	Republican	1967-1969
58. Marvin Mandel	Democratic	1969-

*Democratic-Republican

MARYLAND

immediately. School desegregation in the rest of the state has proceeded slowly but steadily. Baltimore, like many cities, had racial violence after the assassination of civil rights leader Martin Luther King, Jr., in 1968. Since then, federal, state, and local agencies have increased their efforts to end discrimination in education, employment, and housing.

Today, Maryland is a national center for space research, development, and production. Basic planning for space projects is carried out at the National Aeronautics and Space Administration's Goddard Space Study Center in Greenbelt.

GEORGE BEISLAG, AUBREY C. LAND, and FRED THEROUX

MARYLAND/Study Aids

Related Articles in WORLD BOOK include:

BIOGRAPHIES

Agnew, Spiro T.
Baltimore, Lord
Carroll (family)
Chase, Samuel
Davis, David
Decatur, Stephen
Few, William
Hanson, John
Hopkins, Johns
Jenifer, Daniel of St. Thomas

Johnson, Thomas
Key, Francis Scott
McHenry, James
Paca, William
Shehan, Lawrence J. Cardinal
Shriver, Sargent
Stoddert, Benjamin
Stone, Thomas
Taney, Roger B.

CITIES

Annapolis
Baltimore
Bethesda

Cambridge
Cumberland
Frederick

Hagerstown
Salisbury

HISTORY

Civil War
Claiborne's Rebellion
Colonial Life in America
Mason and Dixon's Line

Revolutionary War in America
Star-Spangled Banner
War of 1812

NATIONAL MONUMENTS

Chesapeake and Ohio Canal National Monument
Fort McHenry National Monument and Historic Shrine

PHYSICAL FEATURES

Allegheny Mountains
Appalachian Mountains
Chesapeake Bay

Delmarva Peninsula
Potomac River
Susquehanna River

PRODUCTS

Chicken   Oyster   Tobacco

OTHER RELATED ARTICLES

Aberdeen Proving Ground
Andrews Air Force Base
Bethesda National Naval Medical Center
Edgewood Arsenal

Fort George G. Meade
Maryland Day
Oceanographic Office, United States Naval
Southern States

For Maryland's rank among the states in production, see the following articles:

Outline

I. Government
  A. Constitution
  B. Executive
  C. Legislature
  D. Courts
  E. Local Government
  F. Taxation
  G. Politics

II. People

III. Education
  A. Schools
  B. Libraries

IV. A Visitor's Guide
  A. Places to Visit
  B. Annual Events
  C. Museums

V. The Land
  A. Land Regions
  B. Coastline
  C. Rivers and Lakes

VI. Climate

VII. Economy
  A. Natural Resources
  B. Manufacturing
  C. Agriculture
  D. Mining
  E. Fishing Industry
  F. Electric Power
  G. Transportation
  H. Communication

VIII. History

Questions

For whom was Maryland named?

Why did Maryland delay signing the Articles of Confederation?

What important developments in transportation occurred in Maryland during the 1800's?

What two agricultural products earn the greatest income for Maryland farmers?

What Confederate general made the farthest advance toward Washington, D.C., during the Civil War?

What are Maryland's two leading manufacturing industries? What is the leading manufacturing city of Maryland?

By what name has the Maryland-Pennsylvania boundary become known? Why?

What famous Marylander wrote "The Star-Spangled Banner"? Under what circumstances?

When and why did Maryland give land to the U.S. government?

Why is Maryland called the *Old Line State?* The *Free State?*

Books for Young Readers

AGLE, NAN H. and BACON, FRANCES A. *The Lords Baltimore.* Holt, Rinehart & Winston, 1962. A story of the family of English lords who founded Maryland.

DILLARD, MAUD E. *Ahoy, Peggy Stewart!* Dutton, 1956. A story about the burning of the brig *Peggy Stewart* at Annapolis.

KAESSMANN, BETA E. and others. *My Maryland: Her Story for Boys and Girls.* Rev. and enl. ed. Maryland Historical Society, 1955.

MANAKEE, HAROLD R. *Indians of Early Maryland.* Maryland Historical Society, 1959.

SCHAUN, GEORGE and VIRGINIA. *Everyday Life in Colonial Maryland.* 3rd ed. Greenberry Pubs., Annapolis, 1960.

SWANSON, NEIL H. and ANNE S. *The Star-Spangled Banner.* Winston, 1958.

Books for Older Readers

BARD, HARRY. *Maryland Today: The State, the People, the Government.* Oxford Book Co., 1961.

BODINE, A. AUBREY. *Chesapeake Bay and Tidewater.* 2nd ed. Viking, 1961. *The Face of Maryland.* 1961. Photographs of typical scenes in Maryland.

BURGESS, ROBERT H. *This Was Chesapeake Bay.* Cornell Maritime Press, 1963.

KANE, HARNETT T. *The Amazing Mrs. Bonaparte; A Novel Based on the Life of Betsy Patterson.* Doubleday, 1963. *Maryland; A Guide to the Old Line State.* Oxford, 1946.

TUFTS, ANNE. *Rails Along the Chesapeake.* Holt, 1957. An adventurous young New Englander comes to Baltimore in 1830 to work on the *Tom Thumb,* the first steam locomotive built to burn coal.

University of Maryland campus in College Park, Md., lies in a wooded area, about eight miles northeast of Washington, D.C. Buildings on the campus include the Memorial Chapel, *center,* and dormitories, *upper right.*

University of Maryland

MARYLAND, UNIVERSITY OF, is a state-assisted, coeducational university with campuses in College Park, Baltimore, and Catonsville, Md. The university also includes Maryland State College in Princess Anne, Md., and overseas centers in Germany, Japan, and 22 other countries.

The main campus is in College Park. It has colleges of agriculture, arts and sciences, business and public administration, education, engineering, home economics, and physical education, recreation, and health; schools of architecture and of library and information services; and an evening division, a summer school, and a graduate school. It grants bachelor's, master's, and doctor's degrees.

The university's schools of dentistry, law, medicine, nursing, pharmacy, and social work, and the university hospital and psychiatric institute are in Baltimore. The Baltimore County campus in Catonsville offers bachelor's degrees in liberal arts. Maryland State College offers bachelor's degrees in liberal arts and sciences. The overseas centers provide programs for military and government personnel.

The university was founded in 1807. For the enrollment, see Universities (table). **Wilson H. Elkins**

MARYLAND DAY is a holiday observed on March 25 in the state of Maryland. It commemorates the first Roman Catholic Mass which colonists celebrated when they landed in 1634. Their first act after landing on St. Clements (now Blakiston) Island in the Potomac River was to celebrate the Feast of the Annunciation.

MARYLAND INSTITUTE. See Universities and Colleges (table).

MARYLAND STATE COLLEGE. See Maryland, University of.

MARYLHURST COLLEGE. See Universities and Colleges (table).

MARYMOUNT COLLEGE. See Universities and Colleges (table).

MARYMOUNT MANHATTAN COLLEGE. See Universities and Colleges (table).

MARYVILLE COLLEGE. See Universities and Colleges (table).

MARYVILLE COLLEGE OF THE SACRED HEART. See Universities and Colleges (table).

MARYWOOD COLLEGE. See Universities and Colleges (table).

MASACCIO, *mah ZAHT choh* (1401-1428), was the greatest painter in Florence during the early Renaissance. Both Michelangelo and Raphael studied his art. Masaccio's wall paintings in the Brancacci Chapel of the Carmine Church in Florence rank among his major works of art. His works also include frescoes in Rome and several altarpieces in art galleries in Florence and London. Masaccio was the first painter who used perspective and foreshortening according to scientific rules. His powerful figures stand firmly on the ground. They appear three-dimensional, and look like statues.

Masaccio was born Tommaso Gudi in San Giovanni di Valdarno. A detail of his painting *The Tribute Money* appears in color in the Painting article. **Wolfgang Lorz**

MASAI. See Kenya (The People).

MASARYK, *MASS uh rick,* was the family name of two Czechoslovak statesmen, father and son.

Tomáš Garrigue Masaryk (1850-1937) was a scholar and a statesman who, with his student Eduard Beneš, founded Czechoslovakia in 1918 (see Beneš, Eduard). Masaryk became the first president of Czechoslovakia in 1918, and served until 1935.

He began his career in 1891 in the Austro-Hungarian parliament, where he fought for the rights of Slavic minority groups. When World War I broke out, he fled to Switzerland and then to England. In his absence, the Austro-Hungarian government in 1916 sentenced him to death for high treason.

Masaryk came to the United States in 1917 to seek support for his dream of an independent Czechoslovakia. He met with Pres-

Tomáš Masaryk
Czechoslovak Embassy

ident Woodrow Wilson, and with Czechs, Slovaks, and Ruthenes who lived in America. He gained his objective when the Allied armies defeated Austria-Hungary in 1918. The Republic of Czechoslovakia was created from a part of Austria-Hungary.

Masaryk's 17-year term as president of the Czechoslovakian republic was generally a time of peace and prosperity. But the Slovaks gradually became restless, because they thought he had not fulfilled a promise to grant them the right of self-government. Also, the German minority group turned increasingly to Nazi Germany for sympathy and help. Masaryk resigned in 1935 because of poor health. Beneš succeeded him.

Masaryk was born on an estate in Moravia, where his father served as a coachman to the Austrian emperor, Francis Joseph. He was educated at the universities of Vienna and Leipzig. He taught philosophy and sociology at Charles University in Prague.

Jan Garrigue Masaryk (1886-1948), the son of Tomáš, entered the Czechoslovak foreign service in 1919, and served as minister to London from 1925 to 1938. In 1940 he became foreign minister of the Czechoslovak government-in-exile. When the government returned to Czechoslovakia after World War II, Masaryk kept the post of foreign minister. He fought a losing battle from 1945 to 1948 against the increasing Communist domination of his country.

Masaryk died mysteriously in 1948. His body was found in a courtyard, three stories under his apartment window in Prague. It has never been determined whether he was murdered or killed himself in protest against the Communist seizure of the government in February, 1948. He was born in Prague.   R. V. BURKS

See also CZECHOSLOVAKIA (History).

MASBATE. See PHILIPPINES (The Islands).

MASCAGNI, *mah SCAH nyee,* **PIETRO** (1863-1945), was an Italian opera composer. He studied music in Leghorn, his birthplace, and at the Milan Conservatory. In 1888, Mascagni entered a one-act opera in a competition and won first prize. The opera, *Cavalleria Rusticana,* was a drama of raw passion in a Sicilian village. It was presented in Rome in 1890 and made Mascagni world famous as the leader of a realistic, boisterous operatic style called *verismo.* Another verismo success was Ruggiero Leoncavallo's two-act *Pagliacci* (1892). The two operas are usually performed together.

Mascagni never came close to repeating his first success. His only other opera that is still performed is *L'Amico Fritz* (1891). *Cavalleria Rusticana* remains popular because of its emotional melodies and the theatrical force of its *libretto* (words).

HERBERT WEINSTOCK

MASCONS. See Moon (Gravity).

MASCULINE GENDER. See GENDER.

MASEFIELD, JOHN (1878-1967), an English writer, in 1930 became the 16th poet laureate of England (see POET LAUREATE). His vigorous and sympathetic pictures of the poor and unfortunate made him "the poet of the people." His best-known long poems are "The Everlasting Mercy," "Dauber," "Reynard the Fox," and "The Widow in the Bye Street." They tell tales of love and tragedy among the people of Shropshire, and among the men of the sea. Masefield wrote over a hundred works. He wrote an

autobiography, *So Long to Learn* (1952) at 74. His best-known novels are *Captain Margaret* (1908), *Multitude and Solitude* (1909), *Sard Harker* (1924), and *Odtaa* (1926). His plays include *The Tragedy of Pompey the Great* (1909) and *End and Beginning* (1933). He also wrote the books of poetry *Salt-Water Ballads* (1902), *Ballads* (1903), *A Mainsail Haul* (1905), and *The Bluebells and Other Verse* (1961).

His individual poems include "A Consecration," "On Growing Old," and "Sea Fever."

Masefield was born in or near Ledbury, in Herefordshire, England. He received the Companions of Literature award in 1961 for his distinctive contribution to English letters.   JOHN HOLMES

MASER is an electronic device that generates and amplifies radio and light waves. Masers are used as atomic clocks (see ATOMIC CLOCK). They are also used to amplify weak radio signals, such as those from distant stars. Lasers (optical masers) produce an extremely narrow beam of light (see LASER). Scientists hope that laser beams may be used to transmit radio and television signals. The word *maser* stands for *Microwave Amplification by Stimulated Emission of Radiation.*

The essential part of a maser is a substance that has been put into an *excited* (high energy) state, the atoms of the substance are able to radiate energy of a particular frequency when *stimulated* (triggered) by a radio or light wave of the same frequency. The energy released by the atoms is added to the stimulating wave, amplifying it.

In the *ammonia maser,* heat is used to excite ammonia gas. In the *ruby maser,* radio waves are used to excite the chromium in a synthetic ruby placed in a magnetic field. Ruby masers are operated at temperatures of only a few degrees above absolute zero.

Some lasers also use a ruby. The chromium in the ruby is excited by an intense light. When the chromium atoms release energy, they produce a light wave of a precise frequency. The light is called *coherent* light because all the atoms that add to it act in step with one another. As a result, the beam acts as though it comes from one tiny source. Some lasers produce a beam that spreads only one foot at a distance of a mile.

The first ammonia maser was built in the United States in 1953. Several years later, American and Russian scientists developed the ruby maser. The first continuously operating laser was produced in the United States in 1961.

JOHN ROBINSON PIERCE

MASERU, *MAZ uh roo* (pop. 14,000; alt. 5,125 ft.), is the capital of Lesotho, a country in southern Africa. Maseru lies near the northwestern border of the country. A railroad links it with cities in South Africa. The city is the seat of government for the country, and has a hospital and technical training school where manual and local arts are taught. Most of the people are Africans, but there are a few Europeans who live and work there. See also LESOTHO.

HERBERT V. B. KLINE, JR.

MASH. See WHISKEY; BREWING.

John Masefield

British Combine

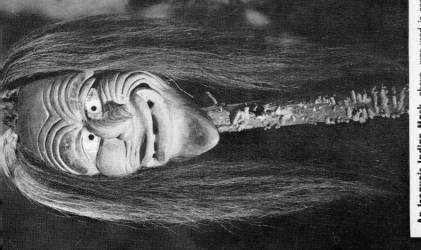

MASK is a disguise or covering for the face or head. Children wear masks at Halloween or other times for fun. Peoples in different parts of the world use masks in religious ceremonies. They believe the masks have magical powers. Such masks may represent animals or identify gods. Prehistoric cave paintings in Spain and other places show masked human figures.

In ancient Greece, people used masks in dramas that grew out of older religious ceremonies. Masked singers and dancers represented gods and mythological heroes. The masks also expressed such emotions as anger, joy, and love. In ancient China, actors wore masks to indicate their character. Japan borrowed this custom from China about A.D. 500. Italian clowns in the 1500's first used the *domino*, or half mask. People still wear masks like this at costume balls and masquerades. A type of play known as a *masque* developed from the use of such masks (see MASQUE).

The tribal peoples of West Africa, New Guinea, and the Amazon region of South America make some of the most dramatic masks. They carve their masks out of

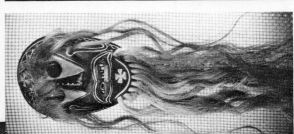

An Iroquois Indian Mask, above, was used in ceremonial dances around flickering campfires. The Indians believed such masks frightened away disease-bearing spirits.

Mexican Yaqui Indians wear the long, bewhiskered mask, below left, on the back of the head. Similar masks are used to entertain the gay crowds at festivals.

Ceylonese Devil Dancers sometimes wear tall, beautifully decorated masks, below right. The finely detailed figures are set off by many bright colors.

Brazilian Indians wore the elaborate costume, above, in their Jaguar dance. Both the mask and the robe are made of bark cloth.

MASK-MAKING

Heyman for School Arts Magazine

The Weird-Looking Masks, *right,* were made from light cardboard covered with papier-mâché and colored with tempera paint.

Millick for School Arts Magazine

Aluminum Foil makes an excellent sculpture like mask, *below.* It can easily be shaped to show different facial features and skin textures.

Scrap-Paper Excelsior mixed with plaster of Paris and water makes unusual hairy, white masks, *right.* These masks must be shaped quickly because the plaster mixture hardens rapidly.

McCaughey for School Arts Magazine

Humorous Paper-Bag Masks that slip over the head are inexpensive and fun to make. First, cut out a nose, mouth, eyes, and eyebrows from colored paper, *upper left,* and glue them on a flat paper bag, *upper right.* Glue the whites of the eyes in position, and cut a small hole in each at eye level. Then cut a jagged strip of paper, *bottom left,* and glue it on the top of the bag for hair, *bottom right.* Water colors and crayons can be used to draw in different facial expressions.

Al Barry, Three Lions, Inc.

The Bird-Shaped Body Mask, *below,* has a wire frame, and is covered with papier-mâché.

Baranski for School Arts Magazine

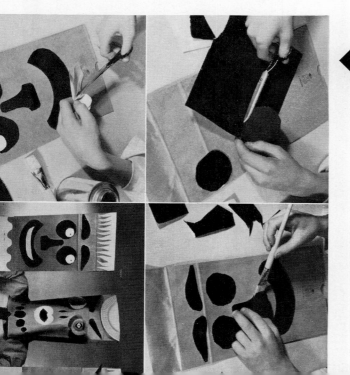

The Metal Mask, *right,* makes a weird-looking false face with fantastic eyes and mouth. Such masks may be made of copper, brass, or aluminum foil. A thin stick was used to produce the deep lines in the face.

Baranski for School Arts Magazine

Colored Construction Paper, paste, and scotch tape can also be used to create an interesting mask, *above.*

Baranski for School Arts Magazine

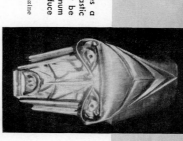

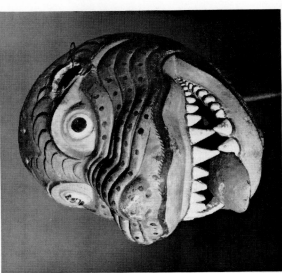

Monks of Tibet use this dark mask of a snarling face to imitate an evil spirit during religious dances in sacred enclosures near their temples. The mask is made of papier-mâché.

Devil Dancers in Ceylon often use ugly masks such as this one in their ancient ceremonies. The Devil Dance is intended to frighten away disease demons and other evil spirits.

George Mason

wood in elaborate and sometimes fantastic shapes. They usually represent animals or birds. Sometimes they represent ghosts of the dead. The men often use masks to frighten women and children.

Many North American Indians wore masks in their ceremonies. In the ceremonial dances of the Hopi Indians, masked figures representing gods visit the villages and bring rain for the corn and presents for the children. These figures, called *kachinas*, are also carved into wooden dolls for the Hopi girls. Sometimes masked clowns dressed in funny costumes come to play games and make people laugh. Some fierce-looking kachinas punish Hopi children who have misbehaved.

Masks may be carved from wood or stone. They may also be made from leather, grass, or cloth, and be painted in different designs and colors. The *false face* is a type of mask made of papier-mâché or cloth. Clay is used to model the features of the false face. A plaster cast is made of this model. Papier-mâché may then be pressed over the cast (see Papier-Mâché). After the mask dries, it can be painted and decorated. Hair and whiskers can be glued on.

Death masks are sometimes used to preserve the features of dead people. A plaster cast is made of the face. Plaster likenesses can then be made from this mold. Famous death masks include those of George Washington, Abraham Lincoln, and the French emperor, Napoleon Bonaparte.

Fred Eggan

See also Bolivia (picture, The Devil Mask); Clothing (Interesting Facts); Tin (picture).

MASOCHISM. See Mental Illness (table, Terms).

MASON (bricklayer). See Building Trade.

MASON (Freemason). See Masonry.

MASON, CHARLES. See Mason and Dixon's Line.

MASON, GEORGE (1725-1792), was a Virginia statesman during and after the Revolutionary War. He played an important part in the Constitutional Convention, although he refused to sign the final draft of

the Constitution. He disliked the way public affairs were conducted, and refused many public offices that were offered to him. But his writings and his leadership made him an influential figure in the colonies.

Mason also helped extend the western borders of the United States. He was a sponsor of the George Rogers Clark expedition to the Northwest Territories. His paper, *Extracts from the Virginia Charters* (1773), formed a basis for American claims to all land south of the Great Lakes.

The Declaration of Rights. Perhaps Mason's most important work was his part in writing the Declaration of Rights as a member of the Virginia Convention of May, 1776. Thomas Jefferson drew on this document when he wrote the Declaration of Independence. It formed the basis for the Bill of Rights, which was added in the form of amendments to the original federal Constitution. It was popular in France during the French Revolution.

His Constitutional Views. He favored the proposed federal Constitution, but objected to the compromise arrangement made between the New England states and those of the extreme South on the tariff and slavery questions. He refused to sign the federal Constitution as it was finally adopted, because the Constitutional Convention refused to change or include certain clauses he favored. He worked hard during the last weeks of the convention, but was unsuccessful. Later years proved, however, that he was right on several points. Mason insisted that the

Constitution should include a Bill of Rights. It became obvious a few years later that Mason was correct. The first 10 amendments passed constitute the Bill of Rights. Mason also maintained that the judiciary section of the Constitution was weak. The Eleventh Amendment repaired this weakness.

Mason was one of the first Southerners to favor freeing the slaves. His greatest objection to the Constitution was that it compromised on the slavery question. He believed that slaves should be educated first and then set free, and that the process should be gradual.

Early Life. Mason was born in Fairfax County, Virginia, where his family had extensive landholdings. He later built Gunston Hall there. His father died when he was 10, and he was educated by tutors. He studied law under the guidance of his guardian, John Mercer. He managed his plantation and took an active part in community affairs. Mason repeatedly refused public office. Finally, at the insistence of his neighbors, he agreed to become a member of the third Virginia Convention that met in Richmond in 1775. Mason wrote a large part of the Virginia Constitution.

ROBERT J. TAYLOR

MASON, JOHN. See NEW HAMPSHIRE (Settlement).
MASON, JOHN L. See CANNING (History).
MASON, JOHN YOUNG. See OSTEND MANIFESTO.
MASON, LOWELL (1792-1872), an American hymnwriter and music educator, wrote more than 1,650 religious compositions. He published many popular works, including hymn collections and books on music and music education. His best-known compositions include "Nearer My God to Thee" and "From Greenland's Icy Mountains." Mason was the first music teacher in American public schools, and became superintendent of music for Boston public schools in 1838. Mason founded the Boston Academy of Music in 1833. Mason was born in Medfield, Mass.

ARTHUR L. RICH

MASON AND DIXON'S LINE is usually thought of as the line that divides the North and the South. Actually it is the line that separates Pennsylvania from Maryland and part of West Virginia, and the north-south boundary between Maryland and Delaware. Before the Civil War, the southern boundary of Pennsylvania was considered the dividing line between the slave and nonslave states.

In the 1700's, a boundary quarel arose between Pennsylvania and Maryland. The two agreed to settle the dispute by having the land surveyed. In 1763, they called in two English astronomers, Charles Mason and Jeremiah Dixon. They completed their survey in 1767. The line was named after them.

The surveyors set up milestones to mark the boundary. Through the years souvenir hunters removed many stones and used them as doorsteps and curbstones. Authorities finally recovered many of them, however, and replaced nearly all of the stolen markers. Occasionally a dispute arose as to the exact location of the line. But surveys made in 1849 and in 1900 showed that there was no important error in the line. Mason and Dixon decided upon. The line has remained at 39° 43' 26.3" north latitude.

MASON AND SLIDELL, *SLY' d'l*, Confederate statesmen, are famous because of a Civil War event that nearly caused war between the United States and Great Britain (see TRENT AFFAIR).

James Murray Mason (1798-1871) drafted the Fugitive Slave Law that became part of the Compromise of 1850 (see COMPROMISE OF 1850). He served as a Democrat from Virginia in both houses of Congress, and was one of the leaders of the states' rights group. After the Trent Affair, he served as Confederate Commissioner to England, but failed to win England's recognition of the Confederacy. He lived in Canada until 1868. He was born in Fairfax County, Virginia.

John Slidell (1793-1871), a Louisiana Democrat, served in both houses of Congress. President James K. Polk sent him on a secret mission to Mexico in 1845. Mexico's refusal to confer with him was one cause of the Mexican War (see MEXICAN WAR). After the Trent Affair, he served as Confederate Commissioner to France. He was born in New York City.

FRANK E. VANDIVER

MASON CITY, Iowa (pop. 30,711; alt. 1,125 ft.), is an industrial and transportation center in a fertile agricultural region in north-central Iowa. Besides its farm crops and dairy and meat industries, the city is known especially for its Portland cement, brick, and clay tile products. Six railroads serve Mason City. The town was settled as Shibboleth in 1854, and became Mason City in 1855. It is the seat of Cerro Gordo County. Mason City has a mayor-council government. For location, see Iowa (political map).

WILLIAM J. PETERSEN

MASONRY, or FREEMASONRY, is the name of one of the largest and oldest fraternal organizations in the world. Its full title is ANCIENT FREE AND ACCEPTED MASONS. It aims to promote brotherhood and to foster morality among its members. The Masons spend millions of dollars annually for hospitals; homes for widows, orphans, and the aged; relief for people in distress; and scholarships for students.

Masons try to promote "religion in which all men agree, that is, to be good men and true." Throughout its history, Masonry has brought together men of varied beliefs and opinions. It does not sponsor any particular denomination of faith. Men of any religion that professes belief in one God may join. But some faiths forbid their members to become Masons.

Masons call God the "Great Architect of the Universe." They base most of their symbols and rituals on the tools and practices of the building professions. At times, some Masons dress in elaborate, colorful costumes, and take part in dramatic rituals, many of which are secret to all except members.

The Lodges and Degrees of Masonry. When a man enters the Masons, he joins a *Blue Lodge*, the basic organization of Masonry. Members of Blue Lodges may hold three degrees. When they join, they automatically

Mason and Dixon's Line

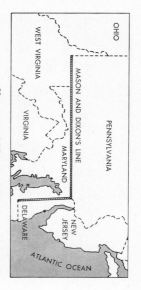

George Washington, wearing his regalia as a member of the Masons, laid the cornerstone of the United States Capitol in Washington, D.C., in 1793. The historic ceremony was under the auspices of the Grand Lodge of Maryland.

Master Mason

MASONIC EMBLEMS

Knights Templars

33rd Degree Mason

32nd Degree Mason

receive the *Entered Apprentice* degree. Later, they may earn the second degree, called *Fellowcraft*, and the third degree, called *Master Mason*. Each degree in Masonry teaches moral lessons. To earn the degree, a Mason must learn the lessons and participate in a ceremony that illustrates them. After a Mason acquires the third degree in a Blue Lodge, he may receive further degrees in either or both of the two branches of advanced Masonry, the *Scottish Rite* and the *York Rite*.

If a Mason enters the Scottish Rite, he may advance through 29 degrees, designated both by names and numbers. The first degree in the Scottish Rite is the fourth degree in Masonry. The highest is the 33rd, an honorary degree that members receive in recognition of outstanding service to Masonry, the community, or the nation. Names of the 33 degrees vary from one area to another. Some of the names commonly used include *Knight of the Sun* for the 28th degree, *Grand Inspector Inquisitor Commander* for the 31st degree, and *Sovereign Grand Inspector General* for the 33rd degree.

If a Mason chooses to advance in the York Rite, the first four degrees he receives are called *Degrees of the Chapter*. They include *Mark Master*, *Past Master*, *Most Excellent Master*, and *Royal Arch*. The next three degrees make up the *Degrees of the Council*. They are *Royal Master*, *Select Master*, and *Super-Excellent Master*. Members of the York Rite do not have to receive the Degrees of the Council in order to go on to higher degrees in the rite. The three highest degrees make up the *Orders of the Commandery* called *Knight of the Red Cross*, *Knight of Malta*, and *Knight Templar*, which is the highest degree in the York Rite.

The names *Scottish Rite* and *York Rite* are symbols of early times in Masonry. The earliest Masonic traditions are associated with Scotland and with the city of York, England.

Organization. In most countries, all the Blue Lodges come under the jurisdiction of one *National Grand Lodge*, at the head of which is a *Grand Master*. But in the United States and Canada, each state and province has a Grand Lodge and a Grand Master at the head of all the local Blue Lodges in the area. The Masons in the United States and Canada do not have a National Grand Lodge, but they do hold an annual conference for Grand Masters in North America each February in Washington, D.C. The conference has no administrative authority, but it gives the delegates an opportunity to discuss plans, problems, and other matters of interest to their state or province and local lodges.

The chapters, councils, and commanderies in the York Rite each come under the jurisdiction of a state *Grand Body*. Most state grand bodies adhere to the leadership of the general grand bodies, which have nationwide jurisdiction.

The Scottish Rite in the United States has two groups, called *jurisdictions*. Separate supreme councils govern each group. The Southern Jurisdiction includes the 35 states south of the Ohio or west of the Mississippi rivers (including Alaska and Hawaii) and all the territories of the United States. The Northern Jurisdiction covers the remaining 15 states. All other countries have only one Supreme Council to head the Scottish Rite.

More than a hundred fraternal organizations have a relationship with Masonry, but they do not form part of its basic structure. One of the best known is the *Order of the Eastern Star*, an organization for women relatives of Masons who have achieved at least the degree of Master Mason. Girls and boys who have Masons in their immediate families have their own organizations. The girls may join *Job's Daughters* and the boys may become members of the *Order of De Molay.* *The Rainbow for Girls* accepts only girls who are recommended for membership by members of the Order of the Eastern Star or by Masons.

The Ancient, Arabic Order of Nobles of the Mystic Shrine admits members who are at least 32nd-degree Masons in the Scottish Rite or Knights Templar in the York Rite. Wives of Shrine members may belong to an organization called the *Daughters of the Nile.*

History. Many of the ideas and rituals of Masonry stem from the period of cathedral building from the 900's to the 1600's. At that time, *masons* (stoneworkers) formed associations called *guilds* in various European cities and towns. Freemasons were stoneworkers who traveled from community to community. They had organizations, sometimes referred to as *lodges.* With the decline of cathedral building in the 1600's, many of the masons' organizations became purely social societies. The groups began accepting members who had never been stoneworkers, and called these men *speculative masons.*

In 1717, four fraternal lodges, which may have been originally founded as masons' organizations, united under the Grand Lodge of England. The Masons of today consider the formation of the Grand Lodge of England to be the beginning of their society. The order spread quickly to other lands, and included such famous persons as Benjamin Franklin, Frederick the Great of Prussia, Wolfgang Amadeus Mozart, George Washington, and Voltaire.

British colonists brought the organization to North America. Some historians believe that it may have been a group of Masons who staged the Boston Tea Party in 1773 (see Boston Tea Party). After 1832, the Masons abandoned their political activities, and the organization assumed the social and fraternal character that it has today.

The Masons now emphasize the fact that they do not foster any specific religious, political, or economic creeds. As a result, the organization has constantly attracted more and more members. During the past 10 years, their membership has increased by almost a million. The number of Masons in the United States is twice that of the rest of the world. About 1 of every 12 adult American males is a Mason. James D. Carter

See also Cedar Rapids; De Molay, Order of; Fraternal Society; Job's Daughters, International Order of; Rainbow for Girls.

MASQAT. See Muscat and Oman.

MASQUE, *mask,* is a form of dramatic entertainment named after the masks worn by the performers. It originated in England, where it was first called *mummery.* It developed into a folk play. Italy adopted it later as a court spectacle including songs, dances, and scenery. From Italy it went to France, then back to England during the early 1500's. The performances were usually given at court, with nobles and ladies taking parts. Ben Jonson developed the literary form of the masque in the 1600's. He also introduced the antimasque, using two sets of performers. Inigo Jones, architect and scene designer, used elaborate designs and staging methods for masques. The masques generally lacked story, action, crisis, or ending. The performers recited long, poetic speeches. John Milton's *Comus* is considered a masque. Charles W. Cooper

See also Jonson, Ben; Milton, John (His Early Life and Works).

MASQUERADE, *mas ker AID,* is the name of a party or dance at which fancy masks and costumes are worn. The word as a verb also means *to disguise* or *falsely pretend.*

MASS is often defined as the amount of matter in an object. However, scientists usually prefer to define mass as a measure of *inertia,* the property of all matter that represents its resistance to being *accelerated* (speeded up) or *decelerated* (slowed down). See Inertia.

The greater an object's mass, the more difficult it is to speed it up or slow it down. For example, a railroad locomotive has a greater mass than an automobile. For this reason, it takes more force to stop a moving locomotive than it does an automobile. It also takes more force to start a locomotive moving.

Force, mass, and acceleration are related by Newton's *second law of motion* (see Motion [Newton's Laws of Motion]). This law is represented by the equation $F=ma$, where F is force, m is mass, and a is acceleration. See Acceleration.

The unit of mass depends on the system of *mechanical units* used (see Mechanical Unit). Scientists prefer the Meter-Kilogram-Second (MKS) absolute system in which the unit of mass is the kilogram (1,000 grams). Engineers prefer the Foot-Pound-Second (FPS) gravitational system in which the unit of mass is the slug. A slug equals 14.594 kilograms.

Mass and Weight are not the same thing. Weight is the force on an object due to the pull of earth's gravity. A body weighs less, the farther it gets from the surface of the earth. But its mass remains constant, no matter where it is. For example, crewmen in a spaceship would be "weightless" beyond the earth's gravitational field (see Space Travel [Flying a Spacecraft]).

Conservation of Mass. Scientists once thought that matter could not be created or destroyed. This was based on the *law of the conservation of mass* (or *matter*), which states that the mass of materials that take part in a chemical reaction is the same as the mass of the products. For example, burning a piece of coal produces carbon-dioxide gas, water vapor, and ash. The mass of these products is the same as the mass of the piece of coal. But atomic reactions, such as those that take place in an atomic bomb or nuclear reactor, result in a loss of mass accompanied by a release of energy. Scientists now say that the *total* mass and energy in the universe does not change. However, the quantity of each does vary.

Mass and energy are related by Albert Einstein's famous equation $E=mc^2$. In this formula, E represents energy, m represents mass, and c is the velocity of light. See Atomic Energy (Mass Into Energy; The Energy of Fission). Robert Lindsay

Related Articles in World Book include:

Density	Gravitation	Matter
Energy	Lavoisier,	Weight
Force	Antoine L.	

MASS is the celebration of the Eucharist in the Roman Catholic Church. According to Catholic teaching each Mass is a true sacrifice, in which the risen Christ becomes bodily present on the altar as a Victim who is offered anew by the Church to God the Father as expiation for the sins of men. The Mass is understood by Catholics to be a renewal, in an unbloody manner, by the mandate of Christ, of the one universally effective sacrifice freely offered by Christ Himself in His crucifixion, for the redemption of the world. The principal parts of the Mass are the Offertory, the Consecration, and the Communion.

The priest who performs the Mass is called the *celebrant*. He speaks or sings the Mass prayers, usually in the *vernacular* (language of the area). The people attending the Mass and the *altar boys* (celebrant's helpers) speak or sing the responses to the celebrant's prayers. Before the 1960's, Latin was used in most Masses. The altar boys, and sometimes a choir, responded to the prayers.

Masses have different names, but are the same in essentials. Mass in which most of the prayers and responses are spoken is *Low Mass*. At *High Mass*, most of the prayers and responses are sung. A Mass for repose of souls of the dead is a *Requiem Mass.*   FULTON J. SHEEN

The Episcopal Church also celebrates Mass. It is sometimes called the Service of Holy Eucharist. Celebration of the Eucharist in the Eastern Orthodox Church is generally called *Liturgy.* The Lutheran Church has the Order of Service or Order of Worship. It is called Mass in some European countries.

See also CHRISTMAS; COMMUNION; LITURGY; PALESTRINA, GIOVANNI.

MASS MEDIA. See COMMUNICATION.

MASS NUMBER. See ATOM (Atomic Weight).

MASS PRODUCTION is the production of machinery and other articles in standard sizes in large numbers. The United States leads the world in mass production. Nearly every article made in the United States—from freezers to automobiles—is manufactured by mass-production methods. Mass production makes it possible to manufacture more things faster. It also means that whenever any part of a machine breaks down, a replacement part that fits perfectly can be obtained.

Mass production began in 1800, when the United States was building up its army for protection from the Indians and from warring European nations. Until that time, gunsmiths used only a ruler for measuring. They changed tools as they made each part. They started a second gun only after they had completed the first one. This meant that each gun was a little different.

In 1798, the federal government contracted with Eli Whitney, the inventor, for the manufacture of 10,000 muskets for delivery in two years. By 1800, Whitney had delivered only 500. He was called to Washington to explain what he was doing to fulfill his contract.

Whitney opened a box in front of a board of experts. He placed 10 musket barrels, 10 stocks, 10 triggers, and so on, in separate piles. Then he suggested that one of the board members take a piece from each pile and lay the pieces together. Then Whitney assembled the pieces from each pile into a complete musket. He continued until he had assembled 10 muskets. Any man could do this once the parts were properly made.

During the years when Whitney had seemed to be doing nothing toward producing muskets, he had been making *machine tools.* One machine tool shaped and bored barrels. Another shaped the stocks. Others made separate intricate parts. By 1800, Whitney had completed making his series of machine tools, which made perfectly fitting parts. He could then produce 10,000 muskets while the artisan gunsmith was making one.

Whitney's system of mechanical measurement was exact. He used metal patterns called *jigs* to guide some of his machines, so that all parts were made to measure the same. Other machines were *repetitive* (made exactly the same motions over and over again).

After Whitney had designed the machine tools, his next job was to make mass production as automatic as possible. But compared with the mass production practices of today, he did not accomplish much. Many of the parts of his muskets had to be finished and polished by hand, and they had to be assembled entirely by hand.

This hand method of assembly and polishing seems almost primitive in comparison to modern methods of manufacture and assembly. In 1918, five engineering societies established the American Engineering Standards Committee (now the American Standards Association). The association studies and sets up standards of quality and methods of mass production in most of the industries of the country. Its work has greatly increased the speed of production.

In the early 1900's, American automobile manufacturers originated the moving assembly line. After the automobile parts are made, the automobile frame is placed on a moving belt. Workers are stationed all along the belt in what is called an assembly line. Each worker has a particular job to do in assembling the automobile. As the car moves slowly along the assembly line, the worker does his special task, perhaps with the aid of a machine. He must do it in a certain length of time, and with exactness, for the work of the entire line is stopped if it is necessary to stop the moving belt (see ASSEMBLY LINE; CONVEYOR BELT).

Mass production has made possible the *division-of-labor* system in which each worker becomes skilled in a single operation. Mass production enables industry to produce goods in far greater quantity and at less cost than by hand methods.   ROBERT D. PATTON

See also AUTOMOBILE (How the Auto Industry Grew); LABOR; MACHINE TOOL; PAPER BAG; WHITNEY, ELI.

MASS SPECTROSCOPY, *spek TRAHS koh pih,* is a method of separating a mixture of molecules or atoms into its component parts. In the simplest *mass spectroscope,* electrons bombard a gas at low pressure. The beam of ions formed goes through electric and magnetic fields. The fields deflect the lighter ions more than the heavier ions. Thus, if the original beam contains ions of various masses (weights), it spreads into a number of beams called a *mass spectrum.* This is similar to what happens when a beam of white light passes through a prism and forms an *optical spectrum.* If the beams are detected with a photographic plate, the apparatus is called a *mass spectrograph;* if with electrical instruments, a *mass spectrometer.*   ALFRED O. NIER

See also ASTON, FRANCIS WILLIAM; ION AND IONIZATION; MASS (matter); SPECTROSCOPE.

MASSACHUSETTS

THE BAY STATE

Massachusetts (blue) ranks 45th in size among all the states and 4th in size among the New England States (gray).

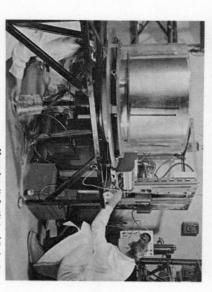

Laboratory at the Massachusetts Institute of Technology

Massachusetts Institute of Technology

Lexington Common, Where the Revolutionary War Began

Fred Bond, Publix

MASSACHUSETTS is the sixth smallest state, but it stands among the leaders in many fields. Only New Jersey, Hawaii, Connecticut, Delaware, and Rhode Island have smaller areas. Yet Massachusetts ranks among the nation's top manufacturing states. Boston, the capital and largest city of Massachusetts, is a major U.S. seaport and air terminal. The many great universities in and around Boston make the area one of the world's great educational, research, and cultural centers. A wealth of historic landmarks makes Massachusetts one of America's main tourist spots.

The land in Massachusetts is a series of hills and valleys. From sea level near the Atlantic Ocean, the state reaches a height of about 3,500 feet near its western border. The best farmland lies in the river valleys and near the coastline. Massachusetts produces more cranberries than any other state. Boston and

Fishing Boats in Gloucester

Sunny Day—Gloucester by Emile A. Gruppe for the Field Enterprises Educational Corporation Collection. Courtesy Findlay Galleries, Inc.

Gloucester are important fishing ports and centers of fish canning and fish processing industries. New Bedford is another important fishing port.

The Norse explorer Leif Ericson may have visited the Massachusetts region about the year 1000. Ericson was one of the first Europeans to sail to North America. In 1620, the Pilgrims landed in what is now Provincetown harbor. The Puritans arrived in 1630. Both these groups left England in search of religious freedom. The first newspaper, printing press, and library in the British colonies were established in Massachusetts. The first college in the colonies, Harvard, was founded at Cambridge in 1636. Boston Latin School, the first secondary school in the colonies, opened in 1635. The first public high school in the United States, Boston English High School, opened in 1821.

Many of the events that led up to the Revolutionary War took place in Massachusetts. These included the Boston Massacre in 1770 and the Boston Tea Party in 1773. On the night of April 18, 1775, Paul Revere made his famous ride to warn his fellow patriots that British troops were coming. On April 19, 1775, minutemen at Lexington and then at Concord fought the first battles of the Revolutionary War. On Feb. 6, 1788, Mas-

sachusetts became the sixth state to join the Union.

Three U.S. Presidents came from Massachusetts. John Adams, the second President, and his son, John Quincy Adams, the sixth President, were both born in Braintree (now Quincy). John F. Kennedy, the 35th President, was born in Brookline. Calvin Coolidge, the 30th President grew up in Massachusetts.

Massachusetts gets its name from the Massachuset Indian tribe, which lived in the region when the Pilgrims arrived. The name probably means *near the great hill*, or *the place of the great hill*. Historians believe it refers to the Great Blue Hill south of Boston. Massachusetts is often called the *Bay State* because the Puritans founded their colony on Massachusetts Bay. Massachusetts is one of four states officially called *commonwealths*. The others are Kentucky, Pennsylvania, and Virginia.

For the relationship of Massachusetts to other states in its region, see NEW ENGLAND.

The contributors of this article are C. Edward Holland, Managing Editor of the Boston Record American; Benjamin W. Labaree, Professor of History at Williams College; and Michael G. Mensoian, Professor of Geography at Boston State College.

The Sacred Cod hangs over the rear of the chamber of the Massachusetts House of Representatives in Boston. The fish, carved from a solid block of pine, is about 5 feet long. It symbolizes the importance of the fishing industry in the state's growth and development.

Devaney from Publix

Constitution. Massachusetts adopted its constitution in 1780, during the Revolutionary War. It is the oldest state constitution still in use.

The constitution provides for two kinds of *amendments* (changes). *Initiative amendments* are introduced to the legislature on petitions signed by a specified number of qualified voters. *Legislative amendments* are introduced by members of the legislature. Both types of amendments must be approved during joint sessions of the legislature. Initiative amendments must be approved by one-fourth of the legislators. If the legislature votes against an initiative amendment, the petitioners can still bring it to the voters by collecting a certain number of additional signatures. Legislative amendments require approval by a majority of the legislature. All amendments must then be approved in a similar manner by the next legislative body. Finally, an amendment must be approved by a majority of the persons voting on the amendment in a general election. An initiative amendment must also receive approving votes equal to 30 per cent of the total ballots cast in the election.

A state law permits amendments to be proposed by a constitutional convention. Before a constitutional convention can meet, it must be approved by a majority of the legislators and by a majority of the voters.

Executive. In 1964, Massachusetts voters approved a constitutional amendment that increased the terms of office of the governor and lieutenant governor from two years to four years. Also increased from two to four years were the terms of the other elected state officials. These include the secretary of the commonwealth, the treasurer and receiver general, the attorney general, and the state auditor. The amendment provided for the four-year terms to begin in 1967.

The governor is assisted by an executive group called the governor's council. The council consists of the lieutenant governor and one member elected from each of eight state districts. The governor has the power to appoint the heads of state departments and the members of state agencies. The governor receives a yearly salary of $40,000. For a list of Massachusetts' governors, see the *History* section of this article.

Legislature, called the *general court*, consists of a 40-member senate and a 240-member house of representatives. Each of the state's 40 senatorial districts elects one senator. Each of the 175 representative districts elects

from one to three representatives. All members of the general court serve two-year terms. Both houses meet every year beginning on the first Wednesday in January. They stay in session until all business is completed.

In 1960, Massachusetts redrew its senatorial and representative districts to all its people. Representative districts were redrawn in 1967. In 1970, the state supreme judicial court ordered the legislature to redraw the senatorial districts again.

Courts. The governor appoints all Massachusetts judges to serve for life. The governor also has the power to remove judges from office. The governor's council must approve these appointments and removals.

The state's highest court is the supreme judicial court. It has a chief justice and six associate justices. The superior court is the main trial court in the state. It consists of a chief justice and 41 associate justices. Other state courts include land, probate, district, and municipal courts. Massachusetts' 73 district and municipal courts are the lowest courts in the state. Juvenile cases are handled in the Boston juvenile court, and in special closed sessions of district courts.

Local Government in Massachusetts is centered in 39 chartered cities and in 312 incorporated towns. Most cities have a mayor-council form of government. Some cities use the council-manager system. A *town* in Massachusetts is similar to a *township* in other states. It is a geographic division of a county rather than a single community. Several communities and rural areas may exist in the same town. But the entire town is governed as a unit. Towns are governed by annual town meetings. Voters gather once each year to discuss the town's business. They express their opinions, and make plans for the coming year. The voters choose *selectmen* to carry out the town's business until the next annual meeting. Massachusetts cities and towns have *home rule* (self government) to the extent that they may pass local laws without interference from the state government.

Counties serve mainly as judicial boundaries. The state's 14 counties are divided into districts. Each county has one or more district courts. Each county elects a register of deeds, a register of probate and insolvency, a district attorney, a sheriff, and clerks of court. Most counties elect commissioners and treasurers.

Taxation. During the late 1960's, gross receipts and excise taxes accounted for about 28 per cent of

The State Flag

The State Bird
Chickadee

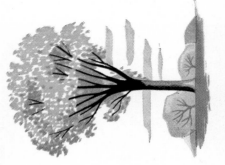

The State Flower
Mayflower

The State Tree
American Elm

The State Seal

Symbols of Massachusetts. The state seal bears the coat of arms of the Commonwealth of Massachusetts. The Indian points an arrow downward, symbolizing peace. The star over his right shoulder represents Massachusetts as a state. The arm and sword above the shield stand for the state motto. The seal was adopted in 1898. The flag, adopted in 1908, has the coat of arms on one side, and a green pine tree on a blue shield on the other side.

Flag, bird, flower, and tree illustrations, courtesy of Eli Lilly and Company

the state government's income. A state income tax provided another 18 per cent. Other sources of income include license fees, estate and gift taxes, and taxes on corporate income, property, and document and stock transfers. U.S. government grants and programs provide about 22 per cent of Massachusetts' income. In 1967, the legislature passed a limited 3 per cent sales tax.

Politics. In Massachusetts, most cities vote Democratic and most towns support Republican candidates. Massachusetts has elected about an equal number of Democrats and Republicans to the United States Senate. In 1967, Massachusetts Republican Edward Brooke became the first Negro U.S. senator since the post-Civil War period. More Republicans than Democrats have served as governor. In presidential elections, about the same number of Democrats and Republicans have won the state's electoral votes since 1900. For Massachusetts' electoral votes and voting record in presidential elections, see ELECTORAL COLLEGE (table).

The State House in Boston, with its golden dome and impressive columns, overlooks Boston Common. The building was constructed in 1798. Boston has been the capital of Massachusetts since 1630.
Arthur Griffin

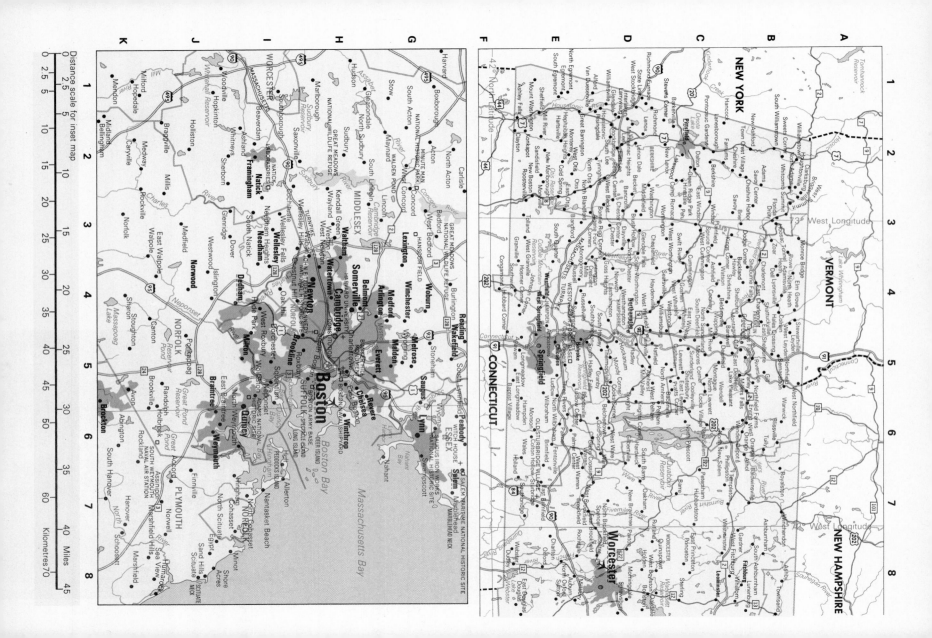

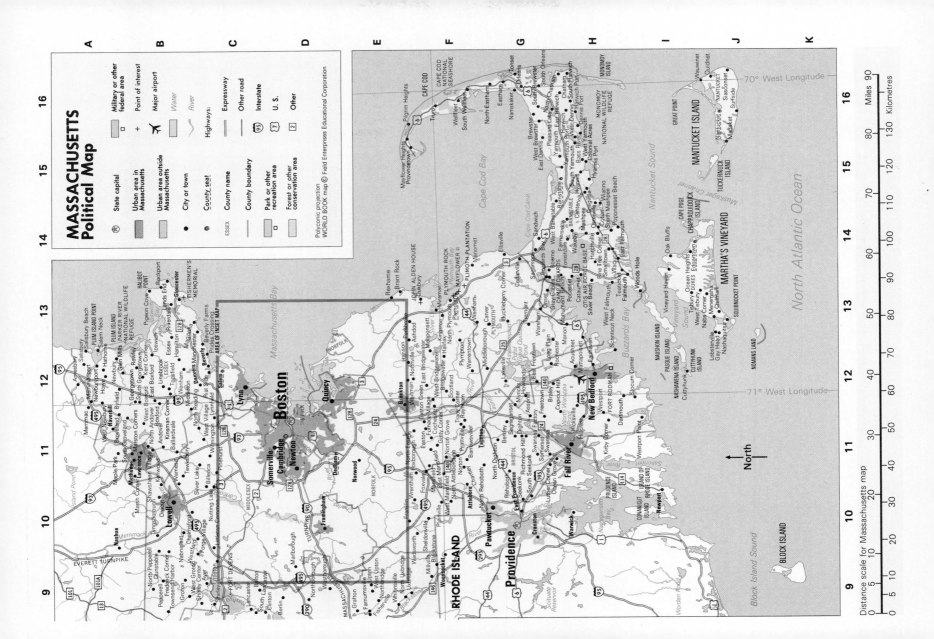

MASSACHUSETTS
Political Map

⊛	State capital
▢	Military or other federal area
	Urban area in Massachusetts
+	Point of interest
	Urban area outside Massachusetts
✈	Major airport
	Water
•	City or town
	River
	County seat
	Highways:
ESSEX	County name
	Expressway
	County boundary
	Other road
▢	Park or other recreation area
(95)	Interstate
	Forest or other conservation area
(17)	U.S.
		(2)	Other

Polyconic projection
WORLD BOOK map © Field Enterprises Educational Corporation

Distance scale for Massachusetts map

Miles
Kilometres

70° West Longitude
71° West Longitude

North Atlantic Ocean

North

Population

	Census
5,630,224	1970
5,148,578	1960
4,690,514	1950
4,316,721	1940
4,249,614	1930
3,852,356	1920
3,366,416	1910
2,805,346	1900
2,238,947	1890
1,783,085	1880
1,457,351	1870
1,231,066	1860
994,514	1850
737,699	1840
610,408	1830
523,287	1820
472,040	1810
422,845	1800
378,787	1790

Metropolitan Areas

Boston	2,730,228
Brockton	186,839
Fall River	148,430
Fitchburg-Leominster	96,289
Lawrence-Haverhill	229,325
Lowell	210,597
New Bedford	151,934
Pittsfield	79,154
Springfield-Chicopee-Holyoke	523,502
Worcester	342,529

Counties

Barnstable	88,639 H 14
Berkshire	147,841 A 12
Bristol	441,130 I G 11
Dukes	6,501 I 13
Essex	633,632 C 12
Franklin	58,680 B 4
Hampden	453,485 E 4
Hampshire	122,557 D 4
Middle- sex	1,388,129 C 10
Nantucket	3,824 I 16
Norfolk	605,413 E 10
Plymouth	328,929 G 13
Suffolk	721,152 D 11
Worcester	633,785 C 7

Cities and Towns

Sources: Latest census figures (1970 preliminary census where available or 1960 census). Cities and towns without population information are unincorporated places under 1,000 in population and are not listed in census reports.

Springfield is a transportation center for western New England. Downtown improvements planned for completion in the early 1970's include an office-hotel-store complex and Interstate 91. This photograph shows models of the complex, center, and the expressway.

Greater Springfield Chamber of Commerce

MASSACHUSETTS/People

The 1970 preliminary United States census reported that Massachusetts had a population of 5,630,224. The population had increased about 9 per cent over the 1960 figure of 5,148,578.

About five-sixths of the people of Massachusetts live in urban areas. That is, they live in or near municipalities of 2,500 or more persons. About one-sixth of the people live in rural areas of the state. About 85 of every 100 persons in Massachusetts live in one of the state's 10 Standard Metropolitan Statistical Areas (see METROPOLITAN AREA). These areas are Boston, Brockton, Fall River, Fitchburg-Leominster, Lawrence-Haverhill, Lowell, New Bedford, Pittsfield, Springfield-Chicopee-Holyoke, and Worcester. For the populations of these metropolitan areas, see the *Index* to the political map of Massachusetts.

Boston is the state's largest city and the state capital. Other large cities in the state, in order of population, are Worcester, Springfield, New Bedford, and Cambridge. See the separate articles on the cities of Massachusetts listed in the *Related Articles* at the end of this article.

Almost 90 of every 100 persons living in Massachusetts were born in the United States. The largest groups of persons born in other countries came from Canada, Italy, and Ireland.

More than half the people of Massachusetts belong to the Roman Catholic Church. The United Church of Christ has the second largest membership of all religious denominations in the state, and the Episcopal Church ranks third.

A Tired Young Marcher rests after Boston's St. Patrick's Day parade. The ancestors of many Bostonians came from Ireland.

Boston Herald

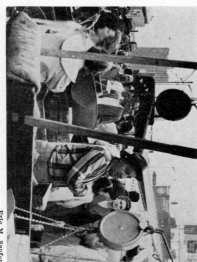

Eric M. Sanford

Customers Crowd a Boston Market to look for unusual foods. This market features foods common in Italy and eastern Europe.

POPULATION

This map shows the population density of Massachusetts, and how it varies in different parts of the state. Population density is the average number of persons who live on each square mile.

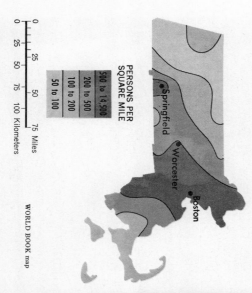

WORLD BOOK map

PERSONS PER SQUARE MILE

- 500 to 14,500
- 200 to 500
- 100 to 200
- 50 to 100

Springfield

Worcester

Boston

0   25   50   75   100 Kilometers

0   25   50   75 Miles

Ewing Galloway

Harvard University in Cambridge is the oldest institution of higher learning in the United States. A statue on the campus honors John Harvard, who gave the school its first large gift.

MASSACHUSETTS / *Education*

Schools. The Puritans of Boston built Massachusetts' first school in 1635, just five years after Boston was settled. In 1642, the Massachusetts Bay Colony government gave each town the responsibility of educating all boys whose parents could not teach them. In 1647, the colony ordered elementary schools set up in all towns of 50 or more families. This was the first time that any government in the world provided free public education at public expense. In 1852, Massachusetts became the first state to require its children to attend school.

Today, public education up through secondary schools is controlled by local school committees. The state department of education has only general control. The department has a commissioner, a deputy commissioner, and an 11-member board of education. All are appointed by the governor. Massachusetts children between the ages of 7 and 16 must attend school. For the number of students and teachers in Massachusetts, see EDUCATION (table).

Massachusetts has some of the nation's most highly regarded *prep schools* (private schools that prepare students for college). Universities and colleges in Massachusetts rank among the world's outstanding educational institutions.

Libraries. The first library in the American colonies was established in Massachusetts in 1638, when John Harvard gave his collection of books to Harvard College. Massachusetts, with its interest in education, had many of the earliest colonial libraries. Today, nearly all the state's cities and towns have public libraries.

Several Boston libraries own outstanding collections. These include the Athenaeum, which has George Washington's collection of books; the Massachusetts Historical Society; and the state library, in the State House.

Other libraries with important or unusual collections include the Boston Public Library, the Essex Institute in Salem, and the American Antiquarian Society in Worcester. The Harvard library owns important collections of rare books, maps, and old Indian manuscripts.

Museums. The Museum of Fine Arts in Boston ranks as one of the world's great museums. It has the finest collection of Oriental art in the world. The Isabella Stewart Gardner Museum in Boston has many outstanding Renaissance paintings. Boston's famous Children's Museum is one of the oldest and largest museums for young people in the nation. The George Walter Vincent Smith Art Museum in Springfield and the Worcester Art Museum are among the nation's best-known smaller museums. The Addison Gallery of American Art of Phillips Academy in Andover owns one of the nation's most valuable collections of American paintings. The Sterling and Francine Clark Art Institute in Williamstown has a collection of paintings by French artists of the 1800's. Several of the state's colleges and universities maintain art galleries and exhibits. These include Harvard's William Hayes Fogg Art Museum, and museums at Amherst, Massachusetts Institute of Technology, Smith, and Wellesley.

Other museums in Massachusetts include the Museum of Science in Boston, the Whaling Museum in New Bedford, the Peabody Museum of Salem, and the John Woodman Higgins Armory in Worcester.

UNIVERSITIES AND COLLEGES

Massachusetts has 58 universities and colleges accredited by the New England Association of Colleges and Secondary Schools. For enrollments and further information, see UNIVERSITIES AND COLLEGES (table).

Name	Location	Founded
American International College	Springfield	1885
Amherst College	Amherst	1821
Anna Maria College	Paxton	1946
Assumption College	Worcester	1904
Atlantic Union College	South Lancaster	1882
Babson College	Wellesley	1919
Bentley College	Waltham	1961
Boston College	Newton	1863
Boston Conservatory of Music	Boston	1867
Boston State College	Boston	1852
Boston University	Boston	1839
Brandeis University	Waltham	1948
Bridgewater State College	Bridgewater	1840
Cardinal Cushing College	Brookline	1958
Clark University	Worcester	1887
Eastern Nazarene College	Quincy	1900
Emerson College	Boston	1880
Emmanuel College	Boston	1919
Fitchburg State College	Fitchburg	1894
Framingham State College	Framingham	1839
Gordon College	Wenham	1889
Harvard University	Cambridge	1636
Hebrew College	Brookline	1921
Holy Cross, College of the	Worcester	1843
Lesley College	Cambridge	1909
Lowell State College	Lowell	1894
Lowell Technological Institute	Lowell	1895
Massachusetts, University of	Amherst	1863
Massachusetts College of Art	Boston	1873
Massachusetts Institute of Technology	Cambridge	1861
Merrimack College	North Andover	1947
Mount Holyoke College	South Hadley	1836
New England Conservatory of Music	Boston	1867
Newton College of the Sacred Heart	Newton	1946
Nichols College	Dudley	1958
North Adams State College	North Adams	1894
Northeastern University	Boston	1898
Our Lady of the Elms, College of	Chicopee	1928
Radcliffe College	Cambridge	1879
Regis College	Weston	1927
St. Hyacinth College and Seminary	Granby	1957
St. Stephen's College	Dover	1955
Salem State College	Salem	1854
Simmons College	Boston	1899
Smith College	Northampton	1871
Southeastern Massachusetts University	North Dartmouth	1949
Springfield College	Springfield	1885
Stonehill College	North Easton	1948
Suffolk University	Boston	1906
Tufts University	Medford	1852
Wellesley College	Wellesley	1870
Western New England College	Springfield	1919
Westfield State College	Westfield	1839
Wheaton College	Norton	1834
Wheelock College	Boston	1888
Williams College	Williamstown	1793
Worcester Polytechnic Institute	Worcester	1865
Worcester State College	Worcester	1871

Skiing brings many visitors to the Berkshire Hills and to other parts of Massachusetts. The Atlantic Ocean and the state's many lakes and rivers attract swimmers, fishermen, and boaters. But Massachusetts offers perhaps its greatest rewards to the student of American history. Historic sites date back to the Pilgrims, to colonial witchcraft trials, and to the Revolutionary War.

Concert at Tanglewood Music Shed near Lenox

Eric M. Sanford

Saugus Iron Works National Historic Site in Saugus

Jack Zehrt, Publix

PLACES TO VISIT

Boston is a major cultural center and one of the nation's great historic cities. The city became known as the *Cradle of Liberty* when it led the American colonies in their struggle for independence. Visitors can see many of Boston's historic shrines by strolling along the *Freedom Trail.* See Boston (The City; table: The Freedom Trail).

Bunker Hill Monument, on Breed's Hill in the Charlestown section of Boston, honors one of the early battles of the Revolutionary War. The 220-foot granite shaft was built between 1825 and 1842. A small museum has portraits, statues, and engravings of soldiers who fought in the Battle of Bunker Hill.

Cape Cod, a peninsula in southeastern Massachusetts, is a famous summer resort and vacation area. The peninsula faces Cape Cod Bay on the north, Nantucket Sound on the south, and the Atlantic Ocean on the east. Long sandy beaches stretch along the cape.

Constitution, or *Old Ironsides,* lies at anchor at the Boston Naval Base in the Charlestown section of Boston. This early U.S. Navy frigate became famous during the War of 1812. Oliver Wendell Holmes honored the ship with his famous poem "Old Ironsides."

Fishermen's Memorial, in Gloucester, is a statue that overlooks the city's harbor. The statue honors the many Gloucestermen who lost their lives while fishing. Gloucester has been an important fishing port since colonial days.

Harvard University, in Cambridge, is one of the world's most famous universities. Harvard was founded in 1636. It is the oldest institute of higher learning in the United States. Harvard Yard, the center of the original college, still retains much of its early charm. The school has several libraries and museums.

John and Priscilla Alden House, in Duxbury, is probably the only house still standing that was occupied by Pilgrims who sailed on the *Mayflower.* It was built about 1653.

Old Sturbridge Village, in Sturbridge, is a replica of a typical New England town of about 1800.

Plimoth Plantation, in Plymouth, is a reconstruction of the first Pilgrim village. *Mayflower II,* built the way the original *Mayflower* is thought to have looked, is maintained by the plantation.

Walden Pond, near Concord, is the small lake near which Henry David Thoreau lived with nature for two years. He told of his beliefs, and described his experiences at the pond, in his famous book *Walden.*

Witch House, in Salem, was the home of Jonathan Corwin, a judge at the Salem witchcraft trials in the 1690's.

National Historical Parks, Seashores, and Historic Sites. Minute Man National Historical Park is located between Lexington and Concord. Cape Cod National Seashore covers about 45,000 acres on outer Cape Cod. Saugus Iron Works National Historic Site in Saugus is a reconstruction of the first successful ironworks in North America. Other national historic sites in Massachusetts are the Adams National Historic Site in Quincy, Dorchester Heights National Historic Site in Boston, John Fitzgerald Kennedy National Historic Site in Brookline, and Salem Maritime National Historic Site in Salem.

State Parks and Forests. Massachusetts has 44 state parks, 97 state forests, and 8 state recreational reservations. For information on the state parks of Massachusetts, write to Director, Division of Forests and Parks, 15 Ashburton Place, Boston, Mass. 02108.

ANNUAL EVENTS

One of the outstanding yearly events in Massachusetts is the Berkshire Festival of the Boston Symphony Orchestra. Each July and August, musicians from many parts of the world perform in the Tanglewood Music Shed near Lenox.

Other annual events in Massachusetts include the following.

January-March: Winter Carnival in Greenfield (January); Evacuation Day, when the British left Boston in 1776, in South Boston (March 17); Spring Flower Show in Revere (March).

April-June: Patriots' Day in Boston, Concord, and Lexington (April 19); Boston Symphony Pops Concerts in Boston (May-June); Militia Day, Old Sturbridge Village (June 10); Bunker Hill Day in Charlestown (June 17); Brandeis Creative Arts Festival in Waltham (June).

July-September: Salt-Water Fishing Derbies in coastal towns (July-August); Sailing Regatta, all yacht clubs (weekends and special days); Esplanade Concerts in Boston (July); Jacob's Pillow Dance Festival in Becket (July-September); United States Lawn Tennis Association National Doubles Championship in Chestnut Hill (August); Fishermen's Memorial Service in Gloucester (August); Pilgrim Progress Procession in Plymouth (every Friday, August-November); Eastern States Exposition in West Springfield (September).

October-December: Fall Foliage Tours in the Berkshire Hills, along the Mohawk Trail (scenic drive), and in Worcester County (October); Pilgrim Thanksgiving Day in Plymouth (Thanksgiving Day); Forefathers' Day, observance of the landing of the Pilgrims, in Plymouth (December 21).

A Pilgrim House and the *Mayflower II* in Plymouth

Jack Zehrt, Publix

223

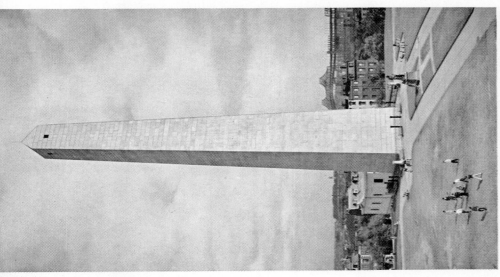

Bunker Hill Monument on Breed's Hill in Charlestown

Jack Zehrt. Publix

Minuteman Statue in Lexington

Ewing Galloway

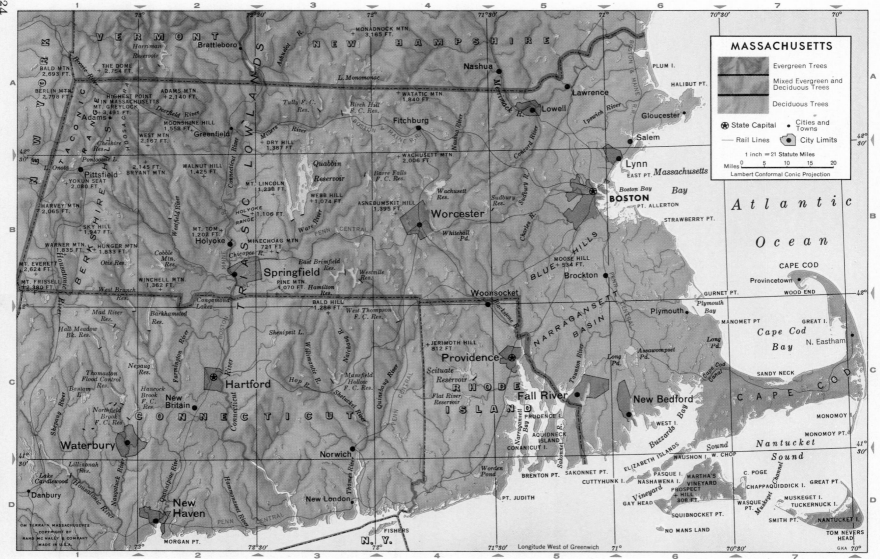

224

MASSACHUSETTS

Evergreen Trees

Mixed Evergreen and Deciduous Trees

Deciduous Trees

⊛ State Capital   • Cities and Towns

— Rail Lines   City Limits

1 inch = 21 Statute Miles

Miles 0   5   10   15   20

Lambert Conformal Conic Projection

VERMONT

NEW HAMPSHIRE

MONADNOCK MTN. 3,165 FT.

Brattleboro

Harriman Reservoir

BALD MTN. 2,693 FT.

THE DOME 2,754 FT.

BERLIN MTN. 2,798 FT.

Nashua

WATATIC MTN. 1,840 FT.

HIGHEST POINT IN MASSACHUSETTS MT. GREYLOCK 3,491 FT.

ADAMS MTN. 2,140 FT.

Adams

MOONSHINE HILL 1,558 FT.

WEST MTN. 2,167 FT.

Greenfield

Lawrence

Lowell

Fitchburg

DRY HILL 1,387 FT.

Tully F.C. Res.

Birch Hill F.C. Res.

WACHUSETT MTN. 2,006 FT.

Gloucester

HALIBUT PT.

PLUM I.

Salem

Lynn

EAST PT. *Massachusetts Bay*

Pittsfield

2,145 FT. BRYANT MTN.

WALNUT HILL 1,425 FT.

Quabbin Reservoir

Barre Falls F.C. Res.

WACHUSETT RES.

BOSTON

YOKUN SEAT 2,080 FT.

MT. LINCOLN 1,238 FT.

WEBB HILL 1,074 FT.

ASNEBUMSKIT HILL 1,395 FT.

Worcester

PT. ALLERTON

STRAWBERRY PT.

Atlantic Ocean

HARVEY MTN. 2,065 FT.

SKY HILL 1,947 FT.

MT. TOM 1,202 FT.

HOLYOKE RANGE 1,106 FT.

Whitehall Pd.

CAPE COD

WARNER MTN. 1,835 FT.

HUNGER MTN. 1,833 FT.

Holyoke

MINECHOAG MTN 721 FT.

MOOSE HILL 534 FT.

Provincetown

WOOD END

Cobble Mtn. Res.

East Brimfield Res.

Springfield

Brockton

GURNET PT.

Cape Cod Bay

GREAT I.

MT. EVERETT 2,624 FT.

WINCHELL MTN. 1,362 FT.

PINE MTN. 1,070 FT.

Hamilton Res.

Westville Res.

Woonsocket

Plymouth

Plymouth Bay

MANOMET PT

MT. FRISSELL 2,380 FT.

West Branch Res.

BALD HILL 1,286 FT.

West Thompson F.C. Res.

JERIMOTH HILL 812 FT.

Long Pd.

Assawompset Pd.

N. Eastham

Mad River Res.

Barkhamsted Res.

NARRAGANSETT BASIN

Hall Meadow Bk. Res.

Nepaug Res.

Shenipsit L.

Providence

New Bedford

SANDY NECK

Thomaston Flood Control Res.

Hancock Brook F.C. Res.

Northfield Brook F.C. Res.

Mansfield Hollow F.C. Res.

Hartford

New Britain

CONNECTICUT

Scituate Reservoir

RHODE ISLAND

Fall River

PRUDENCE I.

WEST I.

Buzzards Bay

C. POGE

MONOMOY

MONOMOY PT.

Nantucket Sound

Waterbury

Bantam L.

Flat River Reservoir

AQUIDNECK ISLAND

CONANICUT I.

NAUSHON I. W. CHOP

CHAPPAQUIDDICK I.

GREAT PT.

Lillinonah Res.

Lake Candlewood

Norwich

Worden Pond

BRENTON PT.

SAKONNET PT.

ELIZABETH ISLANDS

PASQUE I.

NASHAWENA I.

MARTHA'S VINEYARD

PROSPECT HILL 308 FT.

MUSKEGET I.

TUCKERNUCK I.

Danbury

New London

PT. JUDITH

CUTTYHUNK I.

GAY HEAD

WASQUE PT.

NANTUCKET I.

New Haven

MORGAN PT.

FISHERS

N. Y.

SQUIBNOCKET PT.

NO MANS LAND

SMITH PT.

TOM NEVERS HEAD

Longitude West of Greenwich

GM TERRAIN MASSACHUSETTS COPYRIGHT BY RAND McNALLY & COMPANY MADE IN U.S.A.

GKA

Specially created for **World Book Encyclopedia** by Rand McNally and World Book editors

**Land Regions
of Massachusetts**

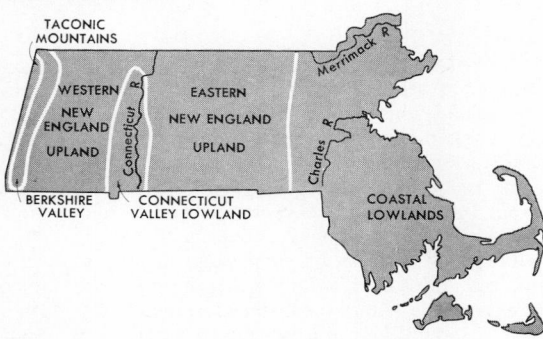

MASSACHUSETTS / The Land

Land Regions. Massachusetts has six main land regions. They are, from east to west: (1) the Coastal Lowlands, (2) the Eastern New England Upland, (3) the Connecticut Valley Lowland, (4) the Western New England Upland, (5) the Berkshire Valley, and (6) the Taconic Mountains.

The Coastal Lowlands are part of a large land region that extends over the entire New England coastline. The lowlands make up the eastern third of Massachusetts. They also include Nantucket Island, Martha's Vineyard, the Elizabeth Islands, and other smaller offshore islands. The region has many rounded hills, swamps, small lakes and ponds, and short shallow rivers. The lowlands are dotted with glacial deposits. These were left by glaciers thousands of years ago during the Ice Age. The Great Blue Hill, south of Boston, rises to a height of about 635 feet. Several excellent harbors lie along the coast. They include Boston, Gloucester, and New Bedford.

The Eastern New England Upland makes up part of a land region that stretches from Maine to New Jersey. The upland is an extension of the White Mountains of New Hampshire. In Massachusetts it extends westward from the Coastal Lowlands for 40 to 60 miles. The upland region rises to a height of about 1,000 feet, then gradually slopes downward toward the Connecticut Valley Lowland. Many streams cut through this region.

The Connecticut Valley Lowland is a long, sausage-shaped region. It extends from northern Massachusetts to southern Connecticut. In Massachusetts, the 20-mile-wide valley is hemmed in by hills to the north, east, and west. The Connecticut River flows through the flat land of the valley region. Rich soil and a mild climate provide good farming.

The Western New England Upland extends through Vermont, Massachusetts, and Connecticut. In Massachusetts, the region stretches 20 to 30 miles westward from the Connecticut Valley Lowland to the Berkshire Valley. The Berkshire Hills, a range that covers this region, is an extension of the Green Mountains of Vermont. In Massachusetts, the Western New England Upland region itself is often called the *Berkshire Hills*. The land rises from the lowlands of the Connecticut Valley to rugged, beautiful heights of more than 2,000 feet. Majestic 3,491-foot-high Mount Greylock is the highest point in the state (see BERKSHIRE HILLS [picture]). Farms and towns lie on the region's slopes.

The Berkshire Valley is a narrow path of lower land that extends into northern Connecticut. In Massachusetts, it winds between the Berkshire Hills and the Taconic Mountains. This valley region is less than 10 miles wide. Its many green meadows are good for dairy farming.

The Taconic Mountains extend into Vermont. This region skirts the extreme western edge of Massachusetts. At its widest point, the region measures no more than 5 or 6 miles across. The Taconic Range slopes from northwestern Massachusetts to the southwestern corner of the state, where Mount Everett rises 2,624 feet.

Coastline of Massachusetts measures 192 miles. If the coastline of each bay and inlet were added to the total, the state's coastline would measure more than 1,500 miles. Boston is the state's most important harbor. Other important harbors include Gloucester in the north, Quincy and Weymouth in Boston Bay, and New Bedford and Fall River in the south.

On a Tobacco Farm, *left,* near Hadley, workers harvest the leaves. Cigar tobacco is an important crop in the Connecticut Valley Lowlands region.

Quabbin Reservoir, *right,* near Ware, is a huge manmade lake in the Eastern New England Upland region of central Massachusetts.

Massachusetts Metropolitan Dist. Comm.

Eric M. Sanford

Martha's Vineyard, a famous resort area, has many beaches. The island is part of the Coastal Lowlands region of New England.

FPG

Islands. The Elizabeth Islands, Martha's Vineyard, and Nantucket Island are the state's largest and most important islands. Together with Cape Cod, these islands form the boundaries of Nantucket Sound. Martha's Vineyard and Nantucket Island are important resort centers. A number of smaller islands also lie along the state's coast.

Rivers and Lakes. Massachusetts has 4,230 miles of rivers. The Connecticut River is the state's most important waterway. It flows southward and provides water for the most fertile Massachusetts farmlands. The Connecticut's chief tributaries include the Deerfield and Westfield rivers to the west, and the Chicopee and Millers rivers to the east. The far western part of the state has two important rivers—the Hoosic and the Housatonic. The Hoosic flows northward and westward into Vermont, and finally drains into the Hudson River. The scenic Housatonic River flows southward into Connecticut. The Blackstone River drains Massachusetts' eastern upland region and flows southeastward into

Rhode Island. The Merrimack River is the most important river in the Coastal Lowlands. It enters the state from New Hampshire. Then the Merrimack turns abruptly northeastward and flows almost parallel to the Massachusetts border until it empties into the Atlantic Ocean at Newburyport. The Nashua and Concord rivers are the Merrimack's main tributaries. The Charles, Mystic, and Neponset rivers all empty into Boston harbor. The Taunton River flows southward into Rhode Island's Mount Hope Bay.

Massachusetts has more than 1,300 lakes and ponds. More than a fourth of these lakes supply drinking water to nearby cities and towns. The state's two largest lakes—Quabbin and Wachusett—are man-made reservoirs. Quabbin Reservoir, near Ware in the center of the state, is one of the nation's largest reservoirs of drinking water. It covers more than 39 square miles. Wachusett Reservoir, north of Worcester, covers $6\frac{1}{2}$ square miles. These reservoirs supply water to Boston and to many cities and towns in its metropolitan area.

MASSACHUSETTS/Climate

Eric M. Sanford

Winter snow covers the Berkshire Valley near North Adams. The mountains may get as much as 75 inches of snowfall a year.

The hills and mountains in western Massachusetts have colder temperatures than the eastern part of the state. Boston, on the coast, has an average July temperature of 72° F. and an average January temperature of 29° F. In the west, Pittsfield averages 68° F. in July and 21° F. in January. Worcester, in the central portion of the state, has a July average of 70° F. and a January average of 24° F. The highest temperature ever recorded in the state was 106° F. at Lawrence on July 4, 1911. The lowest recorded temperature, —34° F., occurred at Birch Hill Dam on Jan. 18, 1957.

The state's *precipitation* (rain, melted snow, and other forms of moisture) averages about 44 inches a year in the west. A yearly average of about 42 inches of precipitation occurs in the central part of the state, and about 40 inches near the coast. Between 55 and 75 inches of snow falls in the western mountains each year. The central part of the state averages about 42 inches a year. The coastal area about 42 inches annually. Damaging hurricanes occasionally lash the Massachusetts coastline. Two of the most destructive hurricanes hit the state in 1938 and 1944.

SEASONAL TEMPERATURES

JANUARY

AVERAGE OF DAILY HIGH TEMPERATURES

Degrees Fahrenheit	Degrees Centigrade
40 to 44	4 to 7
36 to 40	2 to 4
32 to 36	0 to 2
28 to 32	-2 to 0

AVERAGE OF DAILY LOW TEMPERATURES

Degrees Fahrenheit	Degrees Centigrade
24 to 28	-4 to -2
20 to 24	-7 to -4
16 to 20	-9 to -7
12 to 16	-11 to -9
8 to 12	-13 to -11

JULY

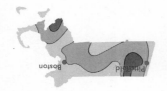

AVERAGE OF DAILY HIGH TEMPERATURES

Degrees Fahrenheit	Degrees Centigrade
76 to 80	24 to 27
80 to 84	27 to 29
84 to 88	29 to 31

AVERAGE OF DAILY LOW TEMPERATURES

Degrees Fahrenheit	Degrees Centigrade
60 to 64	16 to 18
56 to 60	13 to 16
52 to 56	11 to 13

AVERAGE YEARLY PRECIPITATION
(Rain, Melted Snow, and Other Moisture)

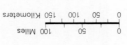

Inches	Centimeters
48 to 52	122 to 132
44 to 48	112 to 122
40 to 44	102 to 112

0   50   100 Miles

0   50   100   150 Kilometers

WORLD BOOK maps

MONTHLY WEATHER IN BOSTON AND PITTSFIELD

	Average of:	JAN	FEB	MAR	APR	MAY	JUNE	JULY	AUG	SEPT	OCT	NOV	DEC
BOSTON	High Temperatures	37	37	45	55	66	76	80	79	73	63	52	40
	Low Temperatures	22	22	30	39	49	58	64	64	56	47	37	26
	Days of Rain or Snow	12	10	12	11	11	10	10	10	9	9	10	11
PITTSFIELD	Days of Rain or Snow	14	13	13	14	14	11	12	9	10	8	12	13
	High Temperatures	30	31	40	53	66	74	79	78	70	59	46	33
	Low Temperatures	13	13	22	31	43	52	56	54	47	36	28	16

Temperatures are given in degrees Fahrenheit.

Source: U.S. Weather Bureau

Much of the state's manufacturing is centered in the industrial cities of the Coastal Lowlands. Springfield and Worcester in the central portion of the state are also important manufacturing centers. Massachusetts' huge tourist industry thrives around the Boston area, on Cape Cod, and in the Berkshires. The tourist industry has an annual value of about $500 million. The most profitable farms lie along the river valleys, especially in the Connecticut Valley Lowland.

Natural Resources of Massachusetts include thick forests, hundreds of miles of rivers and streams and coastal waters filled with sea life.

Soil. Most of the river valleys have deep soils that are rich in peat. The Connecticut River Valley has the most fertile soil in the state. The marshy soils of the Coastal Lowlands, with underground peat deposits, are also quite rich. But much of the state's soil contains sand and gravel. Stones and boulders, deposited long ago by melting glaciers, are also common. These gravel and sandy acid soils are not very fertile. Farmers must treat them with large amounts of fertilizer.

Minerals. Most of the minerals found in Massachusetts are valuable building stones. Sand and gravel deposits lie throughout much of the state. The richest granite deposits are near West Chelmsford. Deposits of dolomitic marbles are found in Ashley Falls, Lee, and West Stockbridge.

Forests cover more than 3 million acres, or about three-fifths of the land area of Massachusetts. The most common softwood trees include the hemlock, pitch pine, and white pine. Common hardwoods include ash, beech, birch, maple, and oak trees. The 120 state forests and parks have about 220,000 acres of woodland in Massachusetts.

Plant Life. Every spring, blue and white violets blossom along the river valleys and in the lower portions of the upland regions. Marsh marigolds, skunk cabbages, and white hellebores also cover these regions in the springtime. Common shrubs and plants in the western hilly regions include azaleas, dogwoods, ferns, mountain laurels, rhododendrons, and viburnums. Mayflowers, Solomon's-seals, and trilliums are also common in the western regions of Massachusetts. Rushes and sedges thrive along the seacoast and in the Coastal Lowlands.

Animal Life. Massachusetts' forests and woodlands are filled with foxes, muskrats, porcupines, rabbits, raccoons, and skunks. The tiny meadow mouse is the state's most common animal. Deer live throughout the state. Great numbers of beavers live in the streams of the Berkshire Hills, and the state permits limited trapping. Partridge, pheasant, and other game birds are found in the fields and forests. Many kinds of water, marsh, and shore birds, especially gulls and terns, nest along the seacoast. Bass, pickerel, sunfish, trout, and white and yellow perch swim in the lakes and ponds. Clams, fishes, lobsters, and oysters are found in the coastal waters. Massachusetts has many kinds of snakes. Poisonous copperheads and timber rattlesnakes live in the Berkshire and Blue hills.

Manufacturing accounts for 97 per cent of the value of goods produced in Massachusetts. Manufactured goods have a *value added by manufacturing* of about $8,748,000,000 a year. This figure represents the value created in products by Massachusetts' industries, not counting such costs as materials, supplies, and fuels. Massachusetts ranks among the leading manufacturing states. Its chief manufacturing industries, in order of importance, are (1) electrical machinery, (2) nonelectrical machinery, and (3) fabricated metal products.

Electrical Machinery has a value added of about $1,-340,000,000 yearly. Massachusetts factories produce appliances, electronic instruments, lamps, measuring instruments, radios, television sets and components, and turbines. Much of this industry is centered near Boston in Lynn, Quincy, Salem, and Waltham. Waltham leads the state in the manufacture of electrical machinery. Other cities that make these products include Haverhill and Lawrence in the northeast, and Chicopee, Holyoke, Pittsfield, and Springfield in the west. The Boston area is an important center for electronics research and development. Many electronics research laboratories stand along Route 128, which swings in an arc around Boston. This highway has been nicknamed the *Electronic Superhighway.*

Nonelectrical Machinery has a value added of about $1,231,000,000 a year. Plants in Worcester make machine tools, textile machinery, valves, looms for weaving cloth, and other products. Plants in Boston, Cambridge, and Springfield make metal products. Beverly manufac-

MASSACHUSETTS' PRODUCTION IN 1967

Total value of goods produced—$8,999,080,000

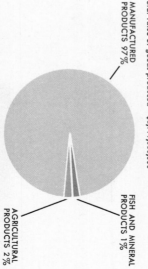

MANUFACTURED PRODUCTS 97%

FISH AND MINERAL PRODUCTS 1%

AGRICULTURAL PRODUCTS 2%

Note: Manufacturing percentage based on value added by manufacture. Other percentages based on value of production.

Sources: U.S. Government statistics

MASSACHUSETTS' EMPLOYMENT IN 1967

Total number of persons employed—2,200,500

	Number of Employees
Manufacturing	690,900
Wholesale & Retail Trade	451,700
Services & Mining	423,400
Government	290,700
Finance, Insurance & Real Estate	117,900
Transportation & Public Utilities	110,900
Construction	100,300
Agriculture	14,700

Source: U.S. Department of Labor

FARM, MINERAL, AND FOREST PRODUCTS

This map shows where the state's leading farm, mineral, and forest products are produced. The major urban areas (shown on the map in red) are the state's important manufacturing centers.

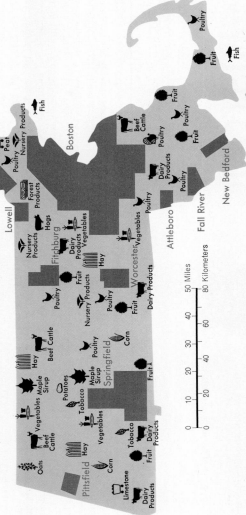

WORLD BOOK map

turers produce machinery for shoe factories. Peabody plants manufacture tanning machines for the leather industry. Other factories throughout the state produce many types of metal products, and foundry and machine-shop products.

Fabricated Metal Products have a value added of about $620,400,000 annually. Factories in Boston and Worcester make aluminum windows. Ducts and pipe are produced in Boston and Cambridge. Plants in Boston also make fans and metal tanks. Jewelry is produced in Attleboro. Factories in Fitchburg and Springfield make saws and hardware.

Other Leading Industries. Instruments and printed materials rank fourth and fifth as sources of manufacturing income in Massachusetts. The Boston area is a leading producer of measuring devices and scientific instruments. Boston is also a major printing and publishing center.

Other important industries in the state include chemicals, clothing, food and food products, leather products, paper and paper products, rubber and plastic products, and textiles.

Massachusetts ranks as one of the nation's leading textile producers. Most of the state's textile mills and clothing factories are in the Coastal Lowlands. Boston, Cambridge, and Clinton are leaders in the state's candy industry, which supplies a nationwide market.

Agriculture in Massachusetts has a yearly gross income of about $171 million. Farms in the state cover an average of only 113 acres in size. But Massachusetts farms earn one of the highest per-acre incomes in the nation.

Milk is the leading source of farm income, earning about $50 million a year. Greenhouse and nursery products, such as flowers and ornamental shrubs, rank second among the state's farm products with a value of about $25 million each year. Dairying activities and nursery and greenhouse products supply about two-fifths of Massachusetts farm income. Eggs rank third, with an income of about $19 million yearly. Beef cattle,

broilers (chickens between 9 and 12 weeks old), and hogs are the leading livestock products of the state.

Massachusetts farmers plant more acreage in hay than in any other crop. They use the hay to feed their dairy cattle. Truck gardeners near the towns and cities raise strawberries, tomatoes, and fresh vegetables such as asparagus and sweet corn. Cigar tobacco is an important product of the Connecticut Valley Lowland. Farmers in this region also raise cucumbers, sweet corn, and other vegetables. Farmers grow fine apples in the Connecticut and Nashua river valleys. The Cape Cod area supplies about two-fifths of the nation's cranberries.

Fishing Industry. Massachusetts ranks among the leading commercial fishing states. The state's annual fish catch is valued at about $40 million. New Bedford fishermen bring in the most fish. They account for about two-thirds of the sea scallops produced in the United States. Gloucester's fish catch is the second largest in the state. Its chief products include haddock, ocean perch, and whiting. Boston fishermen specialize in haddock. Other valuable products of the fishing industry include clams, cod, flounder, mackerel, pollack, and swordfish. Massachusetts is one of the nation's chief lobster producers.

Mining in Massachusetts has a value of about $41 million a year. The state's most valuable mining products include building stones such as crushed stone, granite, gravel, and sand. Quarries near Hingham, West Chelmsford, and Weymouth produce building granite. However, many granite quarries in the state lie idle because the increased use of concrete in buildings has caused a great decline in the need for granite. Other products mined in Massachusetts include basalt, clay, limestone, and peat.

Electric Power. Most of the state's electric power is steam-generated. Coal, oil, and other fuels produce over 95 per cent of this power. Hydroelectric projects produce most of the rest of the state's power. In 1960, New England's first atomic energy plant went into operation in Rowe. For Massachusetts' kilowatt-hour production, see ELECTRIC POWER (table).

Transportation. Massachusetts has about 110 airports and airfields. Logan International Airport in Boston is the state's busiest airport. Boston is served by about 20 airlines.

Railroads operate on about 1,600 miles of track in Massachusetts. Three main railroad systems provide freight and passenger service in the state. Massachusetts has about 28,000 miles of roads and highways. All but about 1,600 miles are paved or surfaced. The Massachusetts Turnpike, a toll road, stretches westward from Boston to the New York state line. The Circumferential Highway swings in an arc around Boston and its suburbs, from Gloucester to Weymouth.

Boston is the main seaport for Massachusetts and for much of New England. It handles more than 20 million tons of cargo a year. Fall River, the second most important port in the state, handles mostly building cement, coal, and petroleum products.

HISTORIC MASSACHUSETTS

John Adams
both born in Braintree (now Quincy)

John Quincy Adams
born in Quincy

John F. Kennedy
born in Brookline

The Telephone was invented by Alexander Graham Bell in Boston in 1876.

The Sewing Machine was invented by Elias Howe at Cambridge in 1845.

The Slavery Abolition Movement was started in New England by William Lloyd Garrison in the 1830's.

MASSACHUSETTS/History

Indian Days. Indians probably lived in the Massachusetts region more than 3,000 years ago. Early white explorers saw Algonkian Indians in the region about 1500. The Algonkian tribes included the Massachuset, Mohican, Nauset, Nipmuc, Pennacook, Pocomtuc, and Wampanoag. Disease killed many of these Indians in 1616 and 1617. By the time the Pilgrims arrived in 1620, the Indian population had dropped from about 30,000 to about 7,000.

Early Exploration. The first Europeans to reach Massachusetts were probably vikings led by Leif Ericson in about the year 1000. Some French and Spanish fishermen may have visited the region during the 1400's. Historians believe that John Cabot sighted the Massachusetts coast in 1498, six years after Christopher Columbus discovered America. In 1602, Bartholomew Gosnold of England landed on Cuttyhunk Island in the Elizabeth Islands. He gave Cape Cod its name. In 1605

and 1606, Samuel de Champlain of France drew maps of the New England shoreline. John Smith, an English sea captain, sailed along the Massachusetts coast in 1614. Smith's book, *A Description of New England*, guided the Pilgrims to Massachusetts.

The Pilgrims. In the early 1600's, a group of English Protestants separated from the Church of England. They wanted to worship God in their own way, but they were not permitted to do so. In 1620, more than a hundred of these people decided to make a *pilgrimage* (religious journey) to America. They hoped to find religious freedom there. On Sept. 16, 1620, these Pilgrims sailed from Plymouth, England, in the *Mayflower*. That November, the *Mayflower* anchored in what is now Provincetown harbor. Before leaving the ship, the Pilgrims drew up a plan of self-government, which they called the Mayflower Compact (see MAYFLOWER COMPACT). In December, the Pilgrims sailed across Cape

224f

MASSACHUSETTS

Communication. In 1639, Stephen Daye set up the first printing press in the English colonies in Cambridge. This was only 19 years after the Pilgrims landed in Massachusetts. In 1640, Daye printed *The Bay Psalm Book*, the first English-language book published in America.

The first two newspapers in the colonies were published in Boston. *Publick Occurrences Both Forreign and Domestick* was established in 1690. The *Boston News-Letter*, which was established in 1704, was the first successful newspaper in America.

Today, Massachusetts publishers issue over 250 newspapers. About 55 of them are dailies. The chief newspapers include the *Boston Globe*, *Boston Herald-Traveler*, and *Christian Science Monitor* and *Record American–Sunday Advertiser* (published in Boston), *Evening Gazette* in Worcester, *New Bedford Standard Times*, *Patriot Ledger* in Quincy; *Springfield Daily News*, *Springfield Union*, and *Worcester Telegram*. About 250 periodicals are published in the state.

The state's oldest radio station, WGI, began broadcasting in Medford in 1920. The first television stations, WBZ-TV and WNAC-TV, started in Boston in 1948. Today, Massachusetts has about 100 radio stations and 11 television stations.

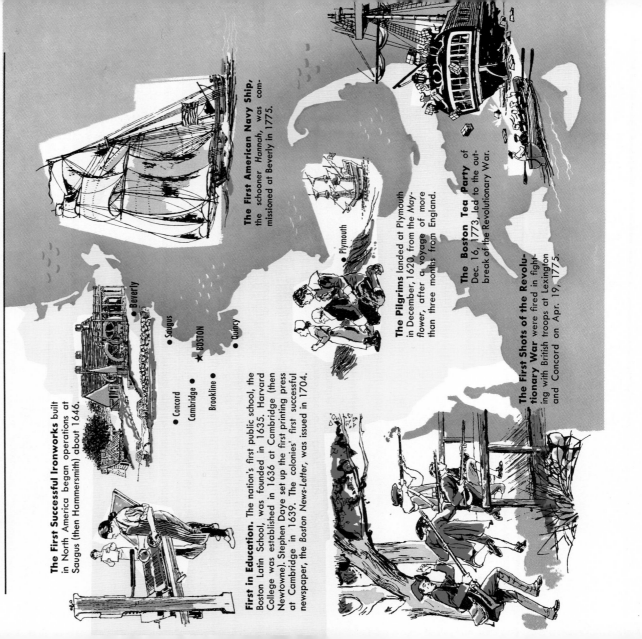

The First Successful Ironworks built in North America began operations at Saugus (then Hammersmith) about 1646.

First in Education. The nation's first public school, the Boston Latin School, was founded in 1635. Harvard College was established in 1636 at Cambridge (then Newtowne). Stephen Daye set up the first printing press at Cambridge in 1639. The colonies' first successful newspaper, the *Boston News-Letter*, was issued in 1704.

• Beverly

• Saugus

• Concord

• Cambridge

★ BOSTON

• Brookline

• Quincy

The First American Navy Ship, the schooner *Hannah*, was commissioned at Beverly in 1775.

• Plymouth

The Pilgrims landed at Plymouth in December, 1620, from the Mayflower, after a voyage of more than three months from England.

The Boston Tea Party of Dec. 16, 1773, led to the outbreak of the Revolutionary War.

The First Shots of the Revolutionary War were fired in fighting with British troops at Lexington and Concord on Apr. 19, 1775.

Cod Bay and settled in Plymouth. See PILGRIM; MAY-FLOWER.

The Pilgrims suffered great hardships during their first winter in America. They had little food other than the game they could hunt. Their houses were crude bark shelters. About half the settlers died during the winter of 1620-1621.

Early in 1621, the Pilgrims became friendly with some Indians. The Indians taught them how to plant corn and beans. By the time cold weather came again, the settlers were living more comfortably. They had enough food to last through the winter. The Pilgrims celebrated the first Thanksgiving in 1621. They gave thanks to God for delivering them from hunger and hardship (see THANKSGIVING DAY).

More settlers came to the Plymouth Colony during the years that followed. Within 20 years after the Pilgrims landed, Plymouth Colony had eight towns and about 2,500 persons.

The Puritans. In 1629, King Charles I of England granted a charter to a group called the Puritans. The charter gave the Puritans the right to settle and govern an English colony in the Massachusetts Bay area. John Winthrop, a London lawyer, led about 1,000 Puritans to Massachusetts in 1630. They joined a settlement that had been established in Salem about three years earlier. In 1630, the Puritans left Salem and founded a new settlement in the area of present-day Boston. The Puritan colony prospered and grew. By 1640, the Massachusetts Bay Colony had about 10,000 settlers. See PURITAN.

Colonial Days. The Massachusetts Bay Colony established political freedom and a representative form of government. In 1641, the first code of laws of the colony was set down in a document known as the Body of Liberties. But the Puritans permitted no religion except their own in the colony. Some religious groups were put out of the colony, and others left on their own. These Massachusetts settlers helped colonize other parts of New England in their search for religious freedom. They established settlements in Connecticut in 1635, Rhode Island in 1636, New Hampshire in 1638, and Maine in 1652. Connecticut and Rhode Island soon became independent colonies. New Hampshire did not separate from Massachusetts until 1680. Maine remained a part of Massachusetts until 1820.

King Philip's War. Massasoit, chief of the Wampanoag tribe, had been a close friend of the Plymouth colonists. But his son, King Philip, who became chief in 1662, feared the white settlers. He believed that they would wipe out the Indians and seize their lands.

In 1675, King Philip rose up against the colonists in an attempt to protect his people and their homelands. He planned to massacre all white settlers in New England. The struggle became known as King Philip's War. White and Indian settlements were burned and hundreds of men, women, and children died on both sides. An Indian serving with colonial troops killed King Philip in 1676, but the struggle dragged on until 1678. The Indian danger in eastern, central, and southern Massachusetts ended. But a tenth of Massachusetts' white male population had been wiped out.

Troubles with England. Although Massachusetts belonged to England, the colonists often resisted controls from across the sea. England believed that its colonists should trade only with the mother country. But many Massachusetts colonists disagreed, and traded with other countries. Attempts at stricter control had little effect on some of the colonists. In 1684, King Charles II canceled the Massachusetts charter. James II became king of England in 1685.

In 1686, King James established a government in Massachusetts and other northern colonies called the Dominion of New England. The king made Sir Edmund Andros governor of the dominion. King James was overthrown in 1688. His daughter, Mary, and her husband, Prince William of Orange, became joint rulers of England. When the Massachusetts colonists received the news, they put Andros out of office and set up a temporary government of their own. William and Mary granted a new charter to Massachusetts in 1691. This charter combined the Plymouth Colony with the Massachusetts Bay Colony and added the island of Martha's Vineyard.

In 1692, Sir William Phips became Massachusetts' first royal governor. One of his most important acts was to end the persecution of persons believed to be witches (see WITCHCRAFT).

The French and Indian Wars. In 1689, the first of the four French and Indian Wars broke out. The English colonists fought the French colonists and France's Indian allies. Between 1689 and 1713, settlers along Massachusetts' northern and western borders fought off continuous French and Indian attacks. In 1713, Great Britain, France, and other European nations signed a peace treaty at Utrecht, Holland. An era of prosperity began in Massachusetts. Dozens of towns sprang up in the central and western areas of the colony.

The French and Indian Wars broke out again in the 1740's. They finally ended in 1763 with victory for the British.

Pre-Revolutionary Days. The colonial wars left Britain in debt. To help pay for defense of the colonies, the British placed severe taxes on the American colonies. The Massachusetts colonists ignored most of these taxes. But the Stamp Act of 1765 led to bitter protests (see STAMP ACT). The cry of "no taxation without representation" spread through the colony. An angry mob destroyed the lieutenant governor's home. The presence of British soldiers in Boston added to the bitterness between the colonists and the Crown. In 1770, British soldiers killed several colonists while fighting a Boston mob. This incident became known as the Boston Massacre. In 1773, angry colonists staged the Boston Tea Party to protest a British tea tax. The colonists dumped 340 chests of British tea into Boston Harbor.

The British passed a series of measures to punish the colonists. But these measures merely angered the colonists more and helped bring all the American colonies together. On April 18, 1775, British troops marched from Boston to seize supplies of gunpowder hidden by the colonists at Concord. Paul Revere and others rode across the Massachusetts countryside to warn their fellow patriots that the British were coming. The next morning, American minutemen at Lexington fought the opening battle of the Revolutionary War (see MINUTEMAN).

Halliday Historic Photo

Boston Harbor in 1768 is shown in an engraving by Paul Revere. British warships fill the harbor, and soldiers pour into the city.

The Revolutionary War began in Massachusetts. Much of the early fighting took place on Massachusetts soil. Massachusetts soldiers fought bravely at Lexington, Concord, and at Bunker Hill. On July 3, 1775, General George Washington took command of the Continental Army in Cambridge. In the spring of 1776, Washington drove the British out of Boston in the first major American victory of the war. Much of the fighting moved out of Massachusetts and into New York, New Jersey, and Pennsylvania in 1776. But Massachusetts continued to send men and supplies to the American forces. At sea, Massachusetts ships inflicted heavy damage on British merchant ships.

The effects of the Revolutionary War in Massachusetts were felt most by the farmers. Prices of farm products dropped after the war ended in 1783. Money became so scarce that many farmers could not pay their taxes or debts. The farmers, facing the danger of losing their farms and going to prison, grew restless. In September, 1786, Daniel Shays led a group of angry farmers to protest in front of the courthouse in Springfield. Fighting broke out between the farmers and government troops. The fighting, which became known as Shays' Rebellion, ended when the farmers surrendered in February, 1787.

Massachusetts farmers also opposed *ratification* (approval) of the United States Constitution. They felt that the Constitution was more favorable to trade and finance than to agriculture. On Feb. 6, 1788, Massachusetts ratified the Constitution and became the sixth state in the Union. Massachusetts ratified the Constitution only on the condition that a bill of rights be added. The Bill of Rights to the United States Constitution went into effect on Dec. 15, 1791.

Progress as a State. Massachusetts prospered during its early years as a state. In the early 1800's, France and Britain were at war. American shipowners who were willing to send their vessels into European waters could make huge profits. But both the British and the French tried to attack ships bound for their enemy's ports. President Thomas Jefferson feared that such an attack on an American ship might force the United States into the war. In 1807, he persuaded Congress to pass an embargo act, which stopped all American trade with other countries.

Hardships resulting from the embargo and the War of 1812 forced a new way of life upon the people of Massachusetts. Goods had to be manufactured at home rather than imported. In 1814, Francis Cabot Lowell built a textile factory in Waltham. It was one of the first factories in the United States. A number of other textile mills were soon operating in eastern Massachusetts. With the opening of New York's Erie Canal in 1825, crops could be brought to New England from the west. Farming in Massachusetts suffered. Many farmers left the state or went to work in factories.

The whaling industry flourished in New Bedford, Nantucket, and Boston until the early 1860's. It declined after kerosene replaced whale oil.

The *abolitionist* (antislavery) movement received wide support in Massachusetts. In 1831, William Lloyd

---

IMPORTANT DATES IN MASSACHUSETTS

1602 Bartholomew Gosnold, an English explorer, visited the Massachusetts region.

1620 The Pilgrims landed at Plymouth.

1630 The Puritans founded Boston.

1636 Harvard became the first college in the colonies.

1641 Massachusetts adopted its first code of law, the Body of Liberties.

1675-1678 Massachusetts colonists won King Philip's War against the Indians.

1689-1763 Massachusetts colonists helped the British win the French and Indian Wars.

1691 Plymouth and the Massachusetts Bay colonies were combined into one colony.

1764 The colonists began to resist enforcement of British tax laws.

1770 British soldiers killed several colonists in the Boston Massacre.

1773 Patriots dumped British tea into Boston Harbor during the Boston Tea Party.

1775 The American Revolutionary War began at Lexington and Concord.

1780 Massachusetts adopted its constitution.

1788 Massachusetts became the sixth state in the Union on February 6.

1797 John Adams of Massachusetts became President of the United States.

1807 The Embargo Act ruined Massachusetts shipping, and led to the rise of manufacturing.

1825 John Quincy Adams of Massachusetts became President of the United States.

1831 William Lloyd Garrison began publishing his antislavery newspaper *The Liberator* in Boston.

1912 A strike of textile workers at Lawrence led to improved conditions in the textile industry.

1919 Settlement of the Boston police strike brought national prominence to Governor Calvin Coolidge.

1938 A hurricane killed several hundred persons and caused millions of dollars in damages in Massachusetts.

1959 The U.S. Navy launched its first nuclear-powered surface ship, the cruiser *Long Beach*, at Quincy.

1961 John F. Kennedy of Massachusetts became President of the United States.

1969 The Massachusetts legislature approved a plan for a major reorganization of the state government. The plan was to go into effect in 1971.

MASSACHUSETTS

Garrison of Boston began publishing his antislavery newspaper *The Liberator*. In 1832, abolitionists formed the New England Anti-Slavery Society in Boston. The society helped slaves escape to Canada. Some people in Massachusetts opposed the abolitionist movement. They objected to what they considered extremist tactics. They also feared that Southern planters might cut off the cotton supply for the Massachusetts textile industry.

In 1850, Congress passed a series of acts which it hoped would settle the conflict between slave owners and those who opposed slavery. These acts were called the Compromise of 1850 (see COMPROMISE OF 1850). Senator Daniel Webster of Massachusetts defended the compromise as necessary to preserve the Union. But many persons in Massachusetts disagreed. Abraham Lincoln and the Republican Party carried the state in the 1860 presidential election.

Massachusetts gave strong support to the Union during the Civil War (1861-1865). The state furnished more than 125,000 men to the Union army and about 20,000 men to the navy. Massachusetts shipbuilders built and equipped many Union ships.

Industry in the state expanded after the war. The textile industry prospered, and the leather and metal products industries also grew rapidly. Thousands of immigrants poured into the state to meet the great demand for industrial labor.

In 1876, Alexander Graham Bell invented the telephone in Boston. A 45-mile, long-distance line between Boston and Providence, R.I., opened in 1881.

The Early 1900's. Massachusetts' population swelled to about $2\frac{1}{2}$ million by 1900. About 30 per cent of the state's people came to the United States from other countries. This huge number of people, with their variety of backgrounds, brought new problems into the state. Communities had to provide such services as water supply, sewage, housing, and police protection.

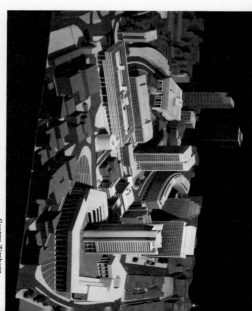

Boston's New Government Center, shown in this model, was built in Scollay Square in the 1960's and 1970's.

George Zimberg

THE GOVERNORS OF MASSACHUSETTS

Under Articles of Confederation

		Party	Term
1.	John Hancock	None	1780-1785
2.	James Bowdoin	None	1785-1787
3.	John Hancock	None	1787-1793

Under United States Constitution

		Party	Term
1.	John Hancock	None	1787-1793
2.	Samuel Adams	None	1793-1797
3.	Increase Sumner	Federalist	1797-1800
4.	Caleb Strong	Federalist	1800-1807
5.	James Sullivan	*Dem.-Rep.	1807-1809
6.	Levi Lincoln	Dem.-Rep.	1809
7.	Christopher Gore	Federalist	1809-1810
8.	Elbridge Gerry	Dem.-Rep.	1810-1812
9.	Caleb Strong	Federalist	1812-1816
10.	John Brooks	Federalist	1816-1823
11.	William Eustis	Dem.-Rep.	1823-1825
12.	Marcus Morton	Dem.-Rep.	1825
13.	Levi Lincoln	Dem.-Rep.	1825-1834
14.	John Davis	Whig	1834-1835
15.	Samuel Armstrong	Whig	1835-1836
16.	Edward Everett	Whig	1836-1840
17.	Marcus Morton	Democratic	1840-1841
18.	John Davis	Whig	1841-1843
19.	Marcus Morton	Democratic	1843-1844
20.	George N. Briggs	Whig	1844-1851
21.	George S. Boutwell	Democratic	1851-1853
22.	John H. Clifford	Whig	1853-1854
23.	Emory Washburn	Whig	1854-1855
24.	Henry J. Gardner	†American	1855-1858
25.	Nathaniel P. Banks	Republican	1858-1861
26.	John A. Andrew	Republican	1861-1866
27.	Alexander H. Bullock	Republican	1866-1869
28.	William Claflin	Republican	1869-1872
29.	William B. Washburn	Republican	1872-1874
30.	Thomas Talbot	Republican	1874-1875
31.	William Gaston	Democratic	1875-1876
32.	Alexander H. Rice	Republican	1876-1879
33.	Thomas Talbot	Republican	1879-1880
34.	John D. Long	Republican	1880-1883
35.	Benjamin F. Butler	Democratic	1883-1884
36.	George D. Robinson	Republican	1884-1887
37.	Oliver Ames	Republican	1887-1890
38.	John Q. A. Brackett	Republican	1890-1891
39.	William E. Russell	Democratic	1891-1894
40.	Frederic T. Greenhalge	Republican	1894-1896
41.	Roger Wolcott	Republican	1896-1900
42.	Winthrop M. Crane	Republican	1900-1903
43.	John L. Bates	Republican	1903-1905
44.	William L. Douglas	Democratic	1905-1906
45.	Curtis Guild, Jr.	Republican	1906-1909
46.	Eben S. Draper	Republican	1909-1911
47.	Eugene N. Foss	Democratic	1911-1914
48.	David I. Walsh	Democratic	1914-1916
49.	Samuel W. McCall	Republican	1916-1919
50.	Calvin Coolidge	Republican	1919-1921
51.	Channing H. Cox	Republican	1921-1925
52.	Alvin T. Fuller	Republican	1925-1929
53.	Frank G. Allen	Republican	1929-1931
54.	Joseph B. Ely	Democratic	1931-1935
55.	James M. Curley	Democratic	1935-1937
56.	Charles F. Hurley	Democratic	1937-1939
57.	Leverett Saltonstall	Republican	1939-1945
58.	Maurice J. Tobin	Democratic	1945-1947
59.	Robert F. Bradford	Republican	1947-1949
60.	Paul A. Dever	Democratic	1949-1953
61.	Christian A. Herter	Republican	1953-1957
62.	Foster Furcolo	Democratic	1957-1961
63.	John A. Volpe	Republican	1961-1963
64.	Endicott Peabody	Democratic	1963-1965
65.	John A. Volpe	Republican	1965-1969
66.	Francis Sargent	Republican	1969-

Industrial workers became unhappy with wages and working conditions. A textile strike in Lawrence in 1912 brought nationwide attention to poor working conditions in the textile industry. Improvements followed the strike.

The United States entered World War I in 1917. The Yankee (26th) Division of Massachusetts was the first national guard division to reach the battlefields of France. Prices climbed in Massachusetts during the war, and workers demanded higher wages to meet the increased cost of living. But often such demands were not met. In 1919, the mayor of Boston refused to let the city's policemen form a union. About three-fourths of the Boston police force went on strike. Governor Calvin Coolidge helped end the strike by sending the national guard into Boston. Coolidge gained nationwide fame because of his action and was elected Vice-President of the United States in 1920. Three years later, Coolidge became President after President Warren G. Harding died.

Massachusetts' economy suffered during the 1920's because of competition from the textile and shoe industries in southern and western states. But other industries in Massachusetts continued to prosper. In 1929, the Great Depression hit the United States. Massachusetts carried on its own unemployment-relief program until the federal government organized nationwide programs. In 1938, a hurricane killed hundreds of persons in Massachusetts and caused great property damage.

The Mid-1900's. The state's economy soared during World War II (1939-1945). Massachusetts factories and shipyards produced huge quantities of war materials. The economy continued to prosper after the war.

Many traditional Massachusetts industries, including the manufacture of shoes and textiles, declined greatly during the 1950's and 1960's. Between 1959 and 1963, the state's employment rate fell below the national average. Many industries in the state began to switch to space and rocket research or the production of electronics equipment. Hundreds of research laboratories developed in and around Boston, using the facilities and personnel of the area's many colleges and universities. The U.S. Navy launched its first nuclear surface ship, the cruiser *Long Beach*, at Quincy in 1959. In 1960, an atomic energy plant began operating in Rowe.

Like many other states, Massachusetts faced serious racial problems during the mid-1900's. In 1957, the state legislature prohibited segregation in public hous-

ing. New legislation in 1963 made it illegal in most private dwellings as well.

During the 1950's and 1960's, the Kennedy family of Brookline became powerful in state and national politics. John F. Kennedy served as President of the United States from 1961 until his assassination in 1963. When elected President, Kennedy was representing Massachusetts in the United States Senate. His brother, Robert F. Kennedy, served as U.S. attorney general from 1961 to 1964. Robert Kennedy was elected to the U.S. Senate from New York in 1964. He was assassinated in 1968 while campaigning for the Democratic presidential nomination. The youngest Kennedy brother, Edward M. Kennedy, was elected a U.S. senator from Massachusetts in 1962.

Massachusetts Today faces several problems common to many states in the 1970's. These problems include air and water pollution, overcrowded cities, racial tension, and rising taxes. Many Massachusetts industries are moving from cities to suburban areas. These areas offer lower real estate taxes, more space, and better transportation facilities.

The high cost of Massachusetts' government and government services, especially its welfare program, contributes to the state's high tax rate. In 1969, the Massachusetts legislature approved a reorganization plan for the state government. This plan, designed to help reduce costs, was to go into effect in 1971. It called for the creation of nine departments that will absorb hundreds of smaller departments and agencies.

Massachusetts' shoe and textile industries continue to decline. In addition, a decrease in defense spending by the federal government has cut into atomic energy and research in the state. But expansion in other areas promises to help steady the Massachusetts economy during the 1970's. The growth rate has increased in the computer industry and in such businesses as banking and insurance. It has also increased in the fields of education and medicine.

In 1970, Massachusetts became the first state to challenge the federal government on the role of the United States in the Vietnam War. The state legislature passed a law that allows Massachusetts servicemen to refuse combat duty if Congress has not declared war.

C. EDWARD HOLLAND,
BENJAMIN W. LABAREE, and MICHAEL G. MENSOIAN

MASSACHUSETTS/Study Aids

People

Knox, Henry
Lodge (family)
Lowell, Amy
Lowell, James Russell
Mann, Horace
Martin, Joseph W., Jr.
Massasoit
Mather (family)
McCormack, John W.
Otis, James
Paine, Robert T.
Phillips, Wendell
Pickering, Timothy
Prescott, William
Randolph, Edward
Revere, Paul
Saltonstall, Leverett

Samoset
Sewall, Samuel
Shirley, William
Squanto
Standish, Miles
Sumner, Charles
Thoreau, Henry David
Volpe, John A.
Ward, Artemas
Warren, Joseph
Weeks, Sinclair
White, Peregrine
Whittier, John G.
Williams, Roger
Wilson, Henry
Winslow, Edward
Winthrop (family)

Cities and Towns

Arlington
Boston
Brockton
Brookline
Cambridge
Chelsea
Chicopee
Concord
Everett

Fall River
Fitchburg
Gardner
Gloucester
Haverhill
Holyoke
Lawrence
Lowell
Lynn

Malden
Medford
Nantucket
New Bedford
Newton
Northampton
Pittsfield
Plymouth
Quincy

Revere
Salem
Somerville
Springfield
Taunton
Waltham
Watertown
Weymouth
Worcester

History

Boston Massacre
Boston Tea Party
Brook Farm
Civil War
Colonial Life in America
Massachusetts Bay Colony
Mayflower
Mayflower Compact
Pilgrim

Pine-Tree Shilling
Plymouth Colony
Plymouth Rock
Puritan
Revolutionary War in America
Shays' Rebellion
War of 1812
Witchcraft

Physical Features

Berkshire Hills
Cape Cod
Cape Cod Canal
Connecticut River

Housatonic River
Martha's Vineyard
Merrimack River

Products and Industry

Clothing
Leather

Publishing
Textile

For Massachusetts' rank among the states in production, see the following articles:

Other Related Articles

Boston Naval Base
Hoosac Tunnel
New England

Patriots' Day
Westover Air Force Base
Winsor Dam

Outline

I. Government
A. Constitution
B. Executive
C. Legislature
D. Courts
E. Local Government
F. Taxation
G. Politics
II. People
III. Education
A. Schools
B. Libraries
C. Museums
IV. A Visitor's Guide
A. Places to Visit
B. Annual Events

V. The Land
A. Land Regions
B. Coastline
C. Islands
D. Rivers and Lakes
VI. Climate
VII. Economy
A. Natural Resources
B. Manufacturing
C. Agriculture
D. Fishing Industry
E. Mining
F. Electric Power
G. Transportation
H. Communication
VIII. History

Questions

What nationwide holiday was first observed in Massachusetts? What was the occasion?

What distinction does the Massachusetts constitution have among all state constitutions?

What section of the state has the most fertile soil?

When and where was the first printing press in the British colonies set up?

What was Shays' Rebellion?

What great stride in education took place in the Massachusetts Bay Colony in 1647?

Why did Britain tax the American colonies after the French and Indian Wars? How did these taxes start a chain of events that led to the Revolutionary War?

Which three Presidents of the United States were born in Massachusetts?

How does local government operate in Massachusetts towns?

Books for Young Readers

ALBRECHT, LILLIE V. *Deborah Remembers*. Hastings, 1959. A museum doll tells what she has seen during 250 years of Massachusetts history.

CHASE, MARY ELLEN. *Donald McKay and the Clipper Ships*. Houghton, 1959.

DAUGHERTY, JAMES H. *The Landing of the Pilgrims*. Random House, 1950.

DEWEY, ANNE P. *Robert Goddard, Space Pioneer*. Little, Brown, 1962.

FORBES, ESTHER. *Johnny Tremain*. Houghton, 1943. This Newbery medal winner tells of Revolutionary War days.

HALL, ELVAJEAN. *Pilgrim Stories*. Rand, 1962. A revision of the Margaret Pumphrey book.

JACKSON, SHIRLEY. *The Witchcraft of Salem Village*. Random House, 1956. The trials of 1692 and 1693.

KINGMAN, LEE. *The Best Christmas*. Doubleday, 1949. A story of Finnish Americans living on Cape Ann.

LATHAM, JEAN L. *Carry On, Mr. Bowditch*. Houghton, 1955. This Newbery medal winner is a biography of the famous Massachusetts navigator.

LENSKI, LOIS. *Berries in the Scoop*. Lippincott, 1956. Cape Cod and its cranberry bogs.

MORISON, SAMUEL E. *The Story of the Old Colony of New Plymouth (1620-1692)*. Knopf, 1956.

SMITH, ERIC BROOKS, and MEREDITH, R. K., eds. *Pilgrim Courage*. Little, Brown, 1962.

SPYKMAN, ELIZABETH C. *A Lemon and a Star*. Harcourt, 1955. A story about a Massachusetts family in the early 1900's.

Books for Older Readers

AMERICAN HERITAGE. *The Pilgrims and Plymouth Colony*. Meredith, 1961.

FAST, HOWARD. *April Morning*. Crown, 1961.

FORBES, ESTHER. *Paul Revere and the World He Lived In*. Houghton, 1962.

HOWE, HENRY F. *Salt Rivers of the Massachusetts Shore*. Rinehart, 1951.

Massachusetts: A Guide to Its Places and People. Houghton, 1937.

MORISON, SAMUEL E. *The Maritime History of Massachusetts, 1783-1860*. New ed. Houghton, 1961.

REID, WILLIAM J. *Massachusetts: A Students' Guide to Localized History*. Teachers College Press, 1965.

MASSACHUSETTS, UNIVERSITY OF, is a state-supported coeducational university with campuses in Amherst and Boston, Mass. The Amherst campus has a college of agriculture and a college of arts and sciences; schools of business administration, education, engineering, home economics, nursing, and physical education; a department of public health; and a graduate school. It grants bachelor's, master's, and doctor's degrees. The Boston campus offers liberal arts programs leading to bachelor's degrees.

The University of Massachusetts and Amherst, Smith, and Mount Holyoke colleges have set up several cooperative programs. One program allows a student to take courses at any of the other three schools if they are not offered at his own school. The four schools also offer doctor's degrees jointly in several fields.

The University of Massachusetts was chartered in 1863 as Massachusetts Agricultural College. It took its present name in 1947. The Boston campus opened in 1965. For enrollment, see UNIVERSITIES AND COLLEGES (table).

JOHN W. LEDERLE

MASSACHUSETTS BAY COLONY was one of the first settlements in New England. It was established in 1628 in Salem, Mass., by a group of English Puritans. These Puritans wished to keep their religion pure, and free from what they felt were evils of the Church of England. John Endecott led the first group of 100 settlers. In 1630, John Winthrop, who had become governor of the colony, led 1,000 more settlers to Boston.

The Puritans firmly believed that their simple way of carrying on a religious meeting and of organizing a congregation was the only correct one. They were unfriendly to newcomers to their settlements who proposed any form of worship that differed from their own. They also refused to obey trade laws passed by the English. As a result, in 1684, the Puritans lost the royal charter they had been given in 1629. In 1691, after they agreed to observe the king's rules, a new charter was issued. This charter included the Plymouth Colony as part of the Massachusetts Bay Colony. The colonists were governed under this charter until 1775, when the Revolutionary War began.

The colony's government expelled some settlers who disagreed with the religious beliefs of the founders. Many of those who left found new homes in Rhode Island or New Hampshire.

The colonists of the Massachusetts Bay Colony made many important contributions to American life. Among the most important of these were a practical, local self-government and a love for learning.

MARSHALL SMELSER

See also ENDECOTT, JOHN; MASSACHUSETTS (History); PURITAN; WILLIAMS, ROGER; WINTHROP (family).

MASSACHUSETTS COLLEGE OF ART. See UNIVERSITIES AND COLLEGES (table).

MASSACHUSETTS INSTITUTE OF TECHNOLOGY (M.I.T.) is a coeducational university engaged in research and teaching in many areas centering upon science and its applications. It was founded in Boston in 1861, and moved to its present location on the Charles River in Cambridge, Mass., in 1916.

The institute includes schools of architecture and planning, science, engineering, humanities and social science, and management. All of the schools offer graduate programs. Students may wait until the end of their second year to choose a professional field for

M.I.T.

The M.I.T. Chapel is capped by a modern steeple. The Kresge Auditorium, *left, partly hides campus domes, background.*

specialization. M.I.T. also offers a wide sports program as well as activities in music, drama, publications, and other cultural areas.

M.I.T. has over 70 special laboratories with a wide range of scientific and technical facilities. The laboratories conduct research programs in all the fields represented at the institute. There are major research centers in several broad areas including communications sciences, earth and life sciences, international and urban studies, and nuclear and space science. For the enrollment of M.I.T., see UNIVERSITIES AND COLLEGES (table).

HOWARD W. JOHNSON

MASSACRE OF SAINT BARTHOLOMEW'S DAY. See SAINT BARTHOLOMEW'S DAY, MASSACRE OF.

MASSAGE, *muh SAHZH,* is a type of medical treatment given by stroking, kneading, and striking certain muscular parts of the body. It is used to improve circulation, soothe the nerves, and stimulate the digestive organs. Massage also helps to increase the tone of muscles after a long illness. The person who gives the massage should be well trained, and should have a knowledge of human anatomy. He must be able to use his hands skillfully in stroking motions on muscles. A man who gives a massage is called a *masseur,* and a woman, a *masseuse.*

Massage was a luxury to the ancient Greeks and Romans. The Chinese, Egyptians, Japanese, and Turks have used it for hundreds of years.

W. W. BAUER

MASSALIA. See MARSEILLE.

MASSANUTTEN. See VIRGINIA (Land Regions).

MASSASOIT, *MAS uh SOIT* (1580?-1661), was a chief of the Wampanoag tribe of Indians that lived in what is now southern Massachusetts and Rhode Island. He made a treaty with Governor John Carver of Plymouth Colony in the spring of 1621, shortly after the Pilgrims landed in America.

He agreed that his people would not harm the Pilgrims as long as he lived. In turn, the Pilgrims guaranteed to protect the Indians and their rights. Massasoit kept the peace all his life.

As a reward for the Indians' friendship, Massasoit and a number of his braves are said to have been invited to join the feast in Plymouth Colony on the first Thanksgiving Day. Afterward, the chief solemnly told the English: "The Great Spirit surely must love his white children best."

When Massasoit died, he was succeeded by his elder son, Wamsutta, known as Alexander. Massasoit's younger son, Metacomet, known as King Philip, succeeded Alexander.

See also PHILIP, KING; PLYMOUTH COLONY (The First Year in the New Land).

MASSECUITE. See MOLASSES.

MASSENET, *mas NAY,* **JULES** (1842-1912), was a French composer best known for his operas. Massenet's operas are noted for their dramatic sense and graceful melodies. Perhaps the best known of his 25 operas is *Manon* (1884). The leading roles of Manon and her lover, Des Grieux, are still popular with singers. Massenet's other operas include *Werther* (1892), *Thaïs* (1894), and *Don Quichotte* (1910). He also wrote more than 200 orchestral works, works for orchestra and voice, and more than 200 songs that rank among his best compositions.

Jules Émile Frédéric Massenet was born in Montaud, near St.-Étienne. While a student at the Paris Conserva-

tory, he studied composition with the composer Ambroise Thomas. From 1878 to 1896, Massenet was a professor of composition at the conservatory. MILOŠ VELIMIROVIĆ

MASSEUR and **MASSEUSE.** See MASSAGE.

MASSEY, VINCENT (1887-1967), became the first Canadian-born governor-general of Canada in 1952. He served in the post until 1959.

Massey had a long career in public service. During World War I, he served on the staff of the Military District No. 2 (Canada). He became secretary of the Government Repatriation Committee of Canada in 1918.

In 1926, Massey was appointed to the Canadian delegation that attended the Imperial Conference in London. At this conference, Canada won the right to name its own diplomatic representatives to the United States. Massey was minister to the United States from 1926 to 1930. From 1935 to 1946, he served as high commissioner for Canada in Great Britain.

Massey became noted for his great interest in education. In 1949, the Canadian government made him chairman of a royal commission to obtain information on the needs and desires of the people in relation to science, literature, and the arts. The commission made recommendations to strengthen the arts and sciences.

Vincent Massey

United Press Int.

Massey was born in Toronto of a prominent industrial family. He studied at St. Andrew's College, and was graduated from the University of Toronto. After receiving a postgraduate degree at Oxford University, he lectured at the University of Toronto from 1913 to 1915. He later served there as chancellor from 1947 to 1953. He was president of the Massey-Harris Company, manufacturers of farm implements, from 1921 to 1925.

LUCIEN BRAULT

MASSINE, *mah SEEN,* **LEONIDE** (1896-), is a great Russian dancer and *choreographer* (dance composer). Massine invented a dance form called *symphonic ballet,* in which dances with no story were choreographed to well-known symphonies. His successful *Les Présages* to Tchaikovsky's *Fifth Symphony* in 1933 was the first of these ballets. It led to what has become a standard ballet form. Massine also choreographed and danced key roles in the ballets *The Three-Cornered Hat, Le Beau Danube,* and *Gaîté Parisienne.*

Massine was born in Moscow. He joined Sergei Diaghilev's Ballets Russes in 1913. Massine was director, dancer, and choreographer of Col. W. de Basil's Ballets Russes from 1932 to 1938. He served in the same capacity with the Ballet Russe de Monte Carlo from 1938 to 1941.

MASSINGER, PHILIP (1583-1640), an English playwright, is best known for his comedy *A New Way to Pay Old Debts* (1621 or 1622). The play's chief character, the monstrous villain Sir Giles Overreach, so appealed to actors and audiences that the play was performed longer than any other non-Shakespearean play of the 1600's. The character of Sir Giles Overreach is based on the

P. W. MANCHESTER

A Statue of Massasoit by the American sculptor Cyrus Dallin stands on a Pilgrim burial ground in Plymouth, Mass.

Dallin

E. ADAMSON HOEBEL

scandalous activities of a real nobleman, and the action is taken from Thomas Middleton's play *A Trick to Catch the Old One* (1608).

Massinger was born in Salisbury of a prominent family, and he was educated at Oxford. He wrote nearly 40 plays, some of them in collaboration with other playwrights. About 20 of his plays survive. From 1625 to his death, Massinger wrote one or two plays a year for The King's Men, the leading acting company of the day.
ALAN S. DOWNER

MASSYS, *MAHS ice,* **QUENTIN** (1465?-1530), was the leading painter in Antwerp, Belgium, in the early 1500's. He painted traditional religious themes and satirical subjects, mocking folly, greed, and hypocrisy. He also painted portraits in which he caught his models in lifelike poses. His altar paintings include *The Holy Kinship* and *The Lamentation of Christ.* His works reveal the influence in Belgium and The Netherlands of the art of the Italian Renaissance, especially of Leonardo da Vinci. He was born in Louvain.
JULIUS S. HELD

MAST. See SAILING (Spars); SHIP AND SHIPPING (History).

MASTERS, EDGAR LEE (1869-1950), was an American author. He wrote novels, poetry, plays, biography, and history, but he became famous chiefly for one volume of poems, *Spoon River Anthology* (1915).

Masters modeled the *Anthology* on a collection of ancient Greek short poems and sayings called *The Greek Anthology.* Spoon River is an imaginary Midwestern village. Masters' work consists of more than 200 short poems in free verse. Each poem is spoken by a former resident of the village, now dead and buried in the Spoon River cemetery. Each of the dead persons seeks to interpret, from the grave, the meaning of life on earth.

Through the words of the dead, the village of Spoon River comes to life again, sometimes relating the histories of whole families. The community is seen as a place where life was hard but where it could be good and satisfying. Among the best-known poems in the *Anthology* is one spoken by Petit, the Spoon River poet. Another poem is spoken by Ann Rutledge, a real-life girl whom young Abraham Lincoln supposedly loved.

Masters was born in Garnett, Kans., and grew up in Illinois. He studied law in his father's office in Lewiston, and was an attorney in Chicago from 1895 to 1920 when he devoted himself full-time to writing. Masters published his autobiography, *Across Spoon River,* in 1936.
CLARK GRIFFITH

MASTERSINGER was one of a group of German poet-musicians who treated literary art as a sort of craft or trade. The name is a translation of the German word *meistersinger.*

The tradition of the mastersingers began in the late Middle Ages when middle-class poets tried to revive the declining art of the *minnesingers.* The minnesingers were wandering poet-musicians, chiefly aristocrats (see

MINNESINGER). Between the late 1200's and the late 1400's, the mastersingers developed rules for song composition and organized song schools modeled after medieval guilds. Members passed examinations for admission and promotion. Singing competitions were held and prizes were awarded.

Most mastersingers were businessmen and craftsmen. The most famous mastersinger was Hans Sachs, a Nuremberg shoemaker. The mastersingers reached their peak in the early 1500's, although the tradition continued into the 1800's.

In the early period, the *Tabulatur* (rule book) permitted composition only to prescribed melodies. But by the 1500's, original compositions were required to gain the title of *master.* Poetic themes were usually instructive stories. Mastersingers did not produce great literature, but achieved lasting fame through Richard Wagner's opera *Die Meistersinger.*
JAMES F. POAG

MASTHEAD. See NEWSPAPER (table: Newspaper Terms).

MASTIC is a resin extracted from *Pistacia lentiscus,* a tree or small shrub that grows chiefly in southern Europe. Pharmacists use mastic as an ingredient in a mild cathartic. Mastic was once widely used as a protective dressing for wounds, and as a temporary protection for tooth cavities. It has also been used as a coating for tablets. Industry uses mastic for lacquers, varnishes, plasters, and tile cements, and also for calking.

Mastic resin has a pale yellowish color. It smells somewhat like balsam.
K. L. KAUFMAN

See also CALKING; RESIN.

MASTICATION, *mas tuh KAY shun,* is the first process in the digestion of food. The term is taken from a Latin word which means *to chew.* Mastication involves chewing or breaking the food into small pieces by grinding with the teeth. Mastication mixes the food with saliva, which reacts chemically with the food and also gives it a pasty texture. Saliva contains the enzyme *ptyalin,* which digests cooked starches into sugars. It also contains a slimy *mucus* that lubricates the food so it can be swallowed. Poor mastication causes overworking of digestive organs, and indigestion. ARTHUR C. GUYTON

See also DIGESTION; INDIGESTION.

Library of Congress

Edgar Lee Masters

MASTIFF, or OLD ENGLISH MASTIFF, is a breed of dog that was developed in England, perhaps about 55 B.C. It has a coat of short hair and an undercoat of dense hair. The coat is usually apricot, silver fawn (yellow brown), or dark fawn. Most mastiffs have a dark brown or black mouth, nose, and ears. They stand about 30 inches high at the shoulder, and weigh about 165 to 185 pounds.
OLGA DAKAN

See also Dog (color picture: Working Dogs); GREAT DANE; BULLMASTIFF.

MASTODON, *MASS toh dahn,* was an animal much like the elephant. It is now extinct. Mastodons first lived in Egypt about 35 million years ago. They spread to Asia, Europe, and Africa. Mastodons reached America about 12 million years ago, and lived there until at least 8,000 years ago, long after the Indians arrived.

There were about 100 different kinds of mastodons. They were stockier than and not as tall as elephants. Early mastodons had tusks in both jaws. Some of the later species lost the lower tusks. Others developed great, flat, lower tusks. These species are called *shovel-tuskers*. The teeth of the mastodon were 2 inches wide and 4 inches long. Each tooth consisted of four to six cross-rows of heavy enamel cones which the mastodon used to grind the plants it ate.

See also MAMMOTH; PREHISTORIC ANIMAL.

Scientific Classification. Mastodons belong to the mastodon family, *Mammutidae*. The American mastodon is genus *Mammut*, species *M. americanum*. The European mastodon is *M. angustidens*.

SAMUEL PAUL WELLES

MASTOID, *MASS toid*, is one of the five parts of the temporal bone of the skull. It is located at the side of the skull, just behind the ear. The name *mastoid* means *nipple-shaped*. This describes the bottom of the mastoid, which extends downward, forming the *mastoid process*. The mastoid process may be felt as the hard area just behind and below the ear. Some people call it the *mastoid bone*.

The mastoid process is porous, like a sponge. The *pores*, or hollow spaces, are called the *mastoid cells*. They vary greatly in size and number in different individuals. The mastoid cells connect with a larger, irregularly shaped cavity called the *tympanic antrum*, or *cavity*. The tympanic antrum opens into the middle ear. The mucous membrane of the middle ear extends into the tympanic antrum and the mastoid cells. Infections of the middle ear spread through these connections and may infect the mastoid cells. Doctors call infection of the mastoid cells *mastoiditis*.

Mastoiditis may be serious, because the mastoid cells are close to the organs of hearing, to important nerves, to the covering of the brain, and to the jugular vein. A mastoid infection may spread to any of these.

Mastoiditis may result from blowing the nose the wrong way. If a person closes both nostrils when he blows his nose, he may force germs from the throat into the *Eustachian tubes*. These tubes connect the throat with the middle ear. Antibiotics have been effective in curing mastoiditis, but severe cases may require surgery (see ANTIBIOTIC).

See also EAR (The Middle Ear); HUMAN BODY (Trans-Vision three-dimensional color picture).

WILLIAM V. MAYER

MASURIAN LAKES, *muh ZOOR ih un*, lie in a low, marshy, hilly region of central Europe. The many small lakes have belonged to both Poland and Germany. Poland has had them since 1945. A major battle in World War I was fought on their shores. See WORLD WAR I (The Eastern Front).

MASURIUM. See TECHNETIUM.

MAT. See PAPIER-MÂCHÉ; STEREOTYPING.

MATA HARI (1876-1917), a Dutch dancer, was executed by the French on charges of being a German spy during World War I. She began her stage career after an unhappy marriage to a Dutch colonial officer. She soon became popular throughout Europe, pretending to be a Javanese temple dancer. She apparently became associated with the German spy network when her strange dances lost their popularity. She was born Margaretha Gertrud Zelle at Leeuwarden, in The Netherlands. See also SPY.

JOHN R. ELTING

MATADOR. See BULLFIGHTING.

MATANUSKA VALLEY is the site of a large-scale farming experiment carried on by the federal government in Alaska. The valley lies in south-central Alaska about 48 miles northeast of the city of Anchorage. High mountains to the north help to protect Matanuska from extreme climate. The soil is fertile. The government organized the new farming community in 1935. It established on farms about 200 families who had suffered from the economic depression in Michigan, Minnesota, and Wisconsin. Long, warm, summer days account for the high quality of vegetables grown in the area. Dairying and poultry raising also are important occupations. The Alaska Railroad and a modern highway carry produce out.

LYMAN E. ALLEN

Mastodon Americanus, painting by Charles R. Knight, The American Museum of Natural History, New York

The Prehistoric Mastodon of America once roamed over all of North America. The animal was an ancient relative of present-day elephants. It resembled the elephant, but was smaller, had a furry coat, and its teeth were different.

MATCH

MATCH. The average person in the United States lights about nine matches every day. Every time he does so, he produces fire in a fraction of a second. This way of making fire is very different from that of primitive man. He had to rub dry sticks together very fast until the friction of the rubbing sent off sparks which set fire to a pile of dry moss. The flint, steel, and tinder with which man later learned to make fire was not much better than the cave man's dry sticks. In the 1800's Charles Dickens complained that it took a man about half an hour to light a fire with flint and steel.

Kinds of Matches

The matches we use today are of two chief types, the strike-anywhere match and the safety match.

Strike-anywhere Matches will light when drawn across any rough surface. They are wooden matches with heads of two colors, usually red and white, or black and white. The white tip, called the *eye*, contains the firing substance. It is made chiefly of the chemical preparation, sesquisulfide of phosphorus. The rest of the bulblike head will not fire if struck, but will burn after the flaming eye sets it afire. It is larger around than the eye. This protects the matches from setting fire to each other by friction when they are packed into a box. When the match is lighted, the paraffin in which the matchstick had been dipped carries the flame from the head to the wood part.

Safety Matches can be lighted only by striking them across a special surface, usually on the side of the box in which they are contained. The head of the match is made of a substance containing chlorate of potash, and has a kindling temperature of 360° Fahrenheit. The striking surface is formed of a compound of red phosphorus and sand. *Book* matches are a type of safety match made of paper and bound into a folding paper cover. The striking surface is on the outside. The book should be closed before striking a match.

Matches Can Be Dangerous

Many disastrous fires and hundreds of deaths have been caused by the careless use of matches. All kinds of matches should be stored where children cannot reach them. Strike-anywhere matches should be placed out of the reach of mice. Rats or mice can set off matches by gnawing at the striking heads. You should never strike a match unnecessarily.

Matches burn best when held in a slanting position with the flame downward. The size of the flame and the

rate of the burning can be reduced, if desired, by turning the flame upward. After the match is out, it should not be thrown away until the user is certain that the flame is out. Even then, it should be placed in a metal or other fireproof container.

The Match Industry

More than 510,000,000,000 matches are produced every year in the United States. About half of this number are book matches. The paper covers of book matches provide excellent surfaces for advertising for all sorts of products. Therefore, thousands of companies use book matches for advertising purposes, spending some $27,000,000 a year. About 90 per cent of all the book matches produced are given away with the sale of cigars, cigarettes, and tobacco.

Ranking next to the United States in the production of matches are Great Britain, Russia, Sweden, Norway, and Japan. The match industry is owned by the government in many foreign countries.

How Matches Are Made

Wooden Matches are made in one continuous operation by a series of automatic machines. These machines slice thin veneer of pine, aspen, or other wood into matchsticks. The matchsticks are treated with chemicals, dried, and packed into boxes at a rate of more than a million matches an hour. Match-making machines are from 60 to 90 feet long, and as tall as a two-story house. They have an endless belt of steel or aluminum plates that each have 800 small holes.

The veneer is cut into sticks called *splints* and then a machine places a stick in each hole of the plates. Matches made in this way can be identified by the tiny indented collar at their end. This collar marks the place where the stick was shoved into the plate hole.

As the chain of plates fills up with matches, it moves the matchsticks through a series of five chemical dips and sprays. First there is a bath in an antiafterglow solution, which prevents the formation of embers after a burned match is blown out. The tips are then dipped in paraffin, which forms a base to carry the flame from

Match Books, printed with colorful advertising, are made in many shapes and sizes. Hobbyists make interesting collections of unusual match books.
Universal Match Corp.

HOW WOODEN MATCHES ARE MADE

Wooden Matches are produced on three assembly lines. Wood veneer enters machines on one line to make box covers and on another to make box trays. A third machine cuts veneer into sticks and drops them into a tank of fireproofing solution that prevents afterglow. The solution also keeps the sticks from turning to ashes when they burn.

match head to wood. The base bulbs and the eyes of the matches are applied as the plates pass through grooves formed by rollers turning in composition baths. A final bath gives the heads a hard coating which protects them from moisture in the air. The completed matches are then punched from their plates and poured into a machine which counts them and packs them.

There are several modifications of this method. One of these is shown in the diagram with this article. In this method, the sticks are dropped into tanks containing the antiafterglow solution. From the tanks, the matches move on a conveyor belt that carries them through a drier to a tumbler that polishes the sticks and removes the splinters. A sorter then removes any matches that are too small, and then the sticks are stacked into wooden trays.

The trays go to a machine that coats the sticks with wax, and then to another machine that automatically coats the tips. Finally, the sticks reach a box-filling machine that puts them in boxes that have been made on another assembly line.

Modern match factories conduct all the operations necessary to manufacture and package the finished matches. Plants usually operate printing plants which prepare covers, labels, and wrappings. Most plants also have a box and carton department where the finished matches are packed and shipped.

Book Matches are made by two machines from rolls of specially treated *paperboard*, or heavy paper. The first machine slices the paperboard into *combs*, or strips, of 60 or 100 matches. The machine then separates every other match so that one match is just ahead of or behind the one next to it. This prevents the heads from touching each other when they are put on. In the last step, the machine dips the combs into paraffin and the match-head solution.

The combs next go to a *booking machine*. This device

cuts the combs to match-book size and fits them into the books. Finally, the combs are stapled to the books, and then the matches are packaged in various sized boxes.

Collecting Match-Book Covers

Collecting match-book covers is an interesting and enjoyable hobby shared by thousands of persons. Match hobbyists collect covers from places they visit, trade covers with other collectors, and even buy rare or unusual covers from hobby shops or through advertisements in hobby magazines. Some match covers have become valuable because of their rarity. A single cover has sold as high as $50, and a set of eight covers has

Matches Are Tested to be sure they strike and burn properly. A worker samples matches from combs taken off the machines.

Diamond Gardner Corp.

HOW PAPER

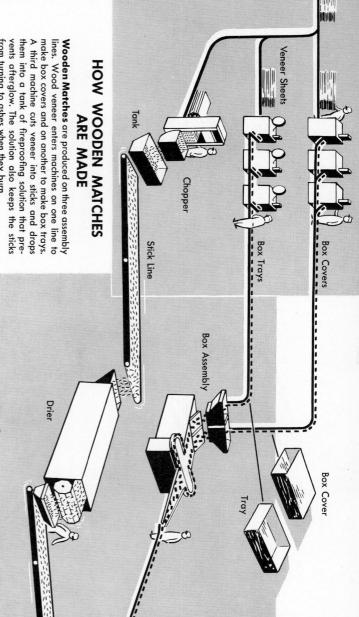

Veneer Sheets

Tank

Chopper

Stick Line

Box Trays

Box Covers

Box Assembly

Drier

Tray

Box Cover

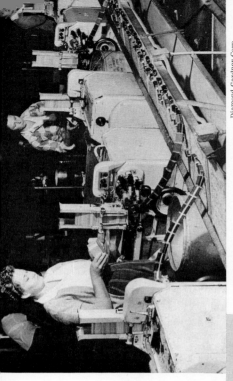

Machines Make Match-Box Covers from strips of veneer that workers feed into the hoppers. A conveyor then takes the covers to a machine that assembles complete match boxes.

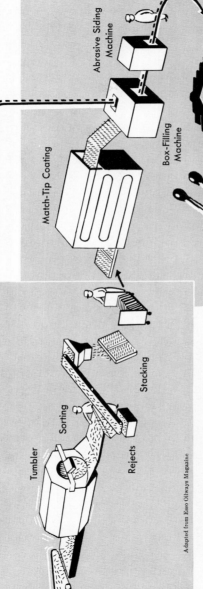

Abrasive Siding Machine

Match-Tip Coating

Box-Filling Machine

MATCHES

Assembled-Box Overhead Conveyor

Tumbler

Sorting

Rejects

Stacking

Assembly Lines move boxes and trays to a machine that puts them together. The match sticks go to a tumbler that polishes them and removes splinters. Then they pass over a screen that sorts out any that are too small. The rest go to stacking machines, are stacked on wooden trays, and taken to a coating machine. This machine coats each tip with inflammable chemicals as the sticks move on an endless belt. Finally, a machine puts the sticks in the boxes, and another applies the abrasive striking area to the boxes.

MATCHES ARE MADE

1. **Rolls of Thick Paper** called paperboard provide the raw material to make book matches.

2. **The Paperboard Is Cut** into strips called combs, usually about 1/8 of an inch wide.

3. **The Heads Are Added** by dipping the comb tips in an inflammable chemical solution.

4. **The Combs Are Stacked** two or more deep after the solution on the tips has dried.

5. **The Combs Are Cut** to the proper size, then stapled into the match-book covers.

been valued at as much as $75.

Match-book collectors often form clubs to help them trade covers and meet fellow hobbyists. The clubs hold meetings and conduct contests that award prizes to the best collections. Several clubs are organized on a nationwide basis. The largest of these is the Rathkamp Matchcover Society with headquarters at 20966 Greenview, Southfield, Mich. 48076.

Because of the great variety of match-book covers, collectors classify them in order to store or display them more easily. Collectors often specialize in certain kinds of covers, such as those from hotels, railroads, government organizations, and so on. Match-book covers can also be classified by size. Most collectors prefer covers that have not been used. However, they often keep a used cover until they can find an unused one to replace it in their collections.

Collectors usually store covers in albums which they buy from hobby shops or make themselves. A match-book album should have slots to hold the covers. A cover that is pasted in an album loses its value.

History

Early Developments. It is surprising that it took so long from the time man first learned to make fire until he produced the match.

Chemical fire-making devices came before the first real matches. These were not very convenient. The Phosphoric Candle, or Ethereal Match, was invented in France in 1781. This was a twist of paper tipped with phosphorus and sealed in a glass tube. When the tube was broken, fire was fanned into life by the oxygen which rushed in. In 1786 the Pocket Luminary was invented in Italy. This was a bottle lined with oxide of phosphorus. Chemically treated splints were rubbed on the oxide and withdrawn into the air, where they burst into flame. The Instantaneous Light Box was developed in France in 1805. It was a bottle which contained a fabric soaked with sulfuric acid. The Instantaneous Light Box, with fifty chemically treated splints, sold for $2 in the United States, where it was popular for about forty years.

The First Match that was at all like those of today appeared in 1827. John Walker (1781?-1859), an English pharmacist, made and sold three-inch splinters of wood tipped with antimony sulfide, chlorate of potash, and gum arabic. Walker's matches, which came to be known as *Congreves*, were sold with a sheet of *glass paper*, somewhat like sandpaper.

When the Congreve was drawn through a fold of this paper, it burst into flame with a series of small explosions which showered the user with sparks. The burning was accompanied by a sharp and unpleasant smell. Samuel Johnes, another early match maker, called his matches *Lucifers*, and printed on their boxes this warning: "If possible, avoid inhaling gas that escapes from the combustions of the black composition. Persons whose lungs are delicate should by no means use Lucifers."

The first strike-anywhere match was produced by Dr. Charles Sauria of France in 1830. The striking tip of this match was composed of white or yellow phosphorus. Dr. Sauria did not suspect it at the time, but phosphorus fumes from matches of this type were to cripple and kill thousands of persons with a disease called *necrosis*. In addition to the deaths caused by the fumes from white and yellow phosphorus matches, the deadly poison at their tips was used in murders and suicides.

Alonzo Dwight Phillips patented the first phosphorus matches in the United States in 1836. He made his matches and boxes by hand at Springfield, Mass., and when he had filled a wagon he set out on a sales trip, selling his matches from door to door. As the match industry grew from a home industry to a factory industry, more and more workers were exposed to phosphorus fumes, and the death rate from necrosis became alarming. In 1900 the Diamond Match Company purchased a French patent for making matches with a nonpoisonous compound. It was found, however, that the French formula would not work in the United States because of the difference in climate.

In 1910, because of the spread of necrosis, the United States placed such a high tax on white and yellow phosphorus matches that the match industry was threatened with extinction. In 1911 William Armstrong Fairburn, a young naval architect, solved the problem by adapting the French formula for sesquisulfide of phosphorus to the climate of the United States. The patent was made public and the threat of necrosis was ended.

The First Safety Matches were invented by Gustave E. Pasch, a Swedish chemist, in 1844. John Lundstrom, a Swedish manufacturer, began to produce them in large quantities in 1852.

For many years the match industry was centered in Sweden. In 1913 Ivar Kreuger, a Swedish promoter, formed the Swedish Match Company. This was a giant international match empire which owned forests, mines, and factories. This company had match factories in forty-three countries of the world and manufactured most of the world's matches. Kreuger himself was often called the *Match King*, and is said to have invented the superstition that *three on a match* is unlucky, in order to sell more matches. Kreuger's match empire lasted until 1932, when it was discovered that he had used company funds for private speculation. Kreuger later committed suicide. See KREUGER, IVAR.

The Invention of Book Matches. Book matches were invented by Joshua Pusey, a Philadelphia patent lawyer, in 1892. Pusey made his matches in packages of 50. The striking surface was on the inside cover, dangerously near the heads of the matches. Because of this, book matches did not become popular until World War I (1914-1918). By that time, the Diamond Match Company had purchased Pusey's patent and made book matches safe and usable.

During World War II, when the United States Army found it was to fight the Japanese in areas where long rainy seasons prevailed, the match industry was called upon to produce a waterproof match. In 1943 Raymond Davis Cady of Oswego, N.Y., produced a formula which so protected wooden matches that they would light even after eight hours under water. This waterproof match is coated with a water- and heat-resistant substance which does not interfere with the creation of enough friction to light it.

See also FAIRBURN, WILLIAM A.; FIRE (table, Antidotes for Some Common Poisons); FIRST AID (table, Methods of Starting Fires); SAFETY (Burns and Scalds).

BROR L. GRONDAL

MATCHLOCK. See HARQUEBUS.

MATE is the title of a merchant marine officer or naval petty officer. The word comes from the Old English *gemaca*, meaning *comrade* or *companion*. On merchant ships, the first mate is second in command. In the U.S. Navy, mates serve under warrant officers.

MATÉ, *MAH tay*, or **PARAGUAY TEA,** is a drink made from the dried leaves and shoots of a holly tree which grows in South America. People make the tea by pouring boiling water over the leaves and stems. Maté has a large amount of caffeine and produces a stimulating effect. The plant has three-cornered leaves 3 to 6 inches long. Its small flowers grow at the base of the leaf stems. Maté growing is a large industry in Paraguay, Argentina, and southern Brazil. Exporters ship large amounts of the leaves to other countries in South America. Maté is sometimes called *yerba maté*.

Scientific Classification. The maté plant is a member of the family *Aquifoliaceae*. It is genus *Ilex*, species *I. paraguariensis*.

JULIAN C. CRANE

A Maté Drinker of Uruguay draws the aromatic tea from a gourd container through a special straw called a *bombilla*.

Julien Bryan

MATERIALISM is a philosophy based on the ideas that matter is the only thing in the universe that has reality, and that matter is the basis of all that exists. The word comes from the Latin *materia*, which means *matter*. Materialists think that physical changes in the body and nervous system cause all mental processes. They justify this belief by pointing out that men can really know only what they see, hear, smell, taste, or touch. They deny the existence of mind or soul as distinct from matter, and insist that feelings, thoughts, and will have no independent existence.

This form of materialism was first expressed by two Greek philosophers, Democritus and Leucippus, in the 400's B.C. They stated that invisible material particles make up the physical world, and that similar particles make up the mind. Some later philosophers, including Epicurus and Lucretius, accepted this idea.

Materialism has always been a popular philosophy among scientists, because, if everything in the world is

made of matter, then we can analyze and understand the world according to the laws which govern the way matter behaves. This idea is called *scientific materialism*. According to it, everything that exists now is the result of factors and conditions that existed before, and everything that will exist in the future must develop from some combination or change in the factors and conditions that exist now. This idea is often called *mechanism*. It was first fully stated by Baruch Spinoza.

A German philosopher, G. W. F. Hegel, explained this idea of the development of the universe, and gave it the name *dialectic*. Hegel was not a materialist, but his ideas influenced the development of a new philosophy, *dialectical materialism*. Karl Marx, Friedrich Engels, and V. I. Lenin developed it. In this system, the world develops along a dialectical path, with mechanical changes in what exists today producing what will exist tomorrow. The doctrine is materialist in its emphasis on the physical world and its denial of values based on man's mind or soul. Dialectical materialism is the philosophic basis for Communism, a political and economic movement. But the Communists have used dialectical materialism to suit their own purposes, and have not necessarily kept it logically coherent. See PHILOSOPHY (Philosophy and Government).

Except in its scientific or dialectical forms, materialism has not attracted as widespread popularity among philosophers as it has among scientists and laymen. Materialist philosophers of the past include Ludwig Büchner, Denis Diderot, Ernst Haeckel, Thomas Hobbes, and Julien de la Mettrie.

H. M. KALLEN

Related Articles in WORLD BOOK include:

Communism	Epicurus	Marx, Karl H.
Democritus	Haeckel, Ernst H.	Mechanist
Diderot, Denis	Hobbes, Thomas	Philosophy

MATERIALIZATION. See ECTOPLASM.
MATERIALS SCIENCE. See METALLURGY (Careers).
MATHEMATICAL ASSOCIATION OF AMERICA is a national organization of persons interested in mathematics. Its purpose is to assist in promoting the interests of mathematics in America. The association has about 19,000 members in 28 sections throughout the United States. It holds annual meetings and sponsors college and university programs. Its publications include *The American Mathematical Monthly, Mathematics Magazine,* books, and monographs. The association was founded in Columbus, Ohio, in 1915. Its headquarters are at 1225 Connecticut Avenue NW, Washington, D.C. 20036.

Critically reviewed by the MATHEMATICAL
ASSOCIATION OF AMERICA

MATHEMATICAL SOCIETY, AMERICAN, is an association of mathematicians in the United States. Its purpose is to promote research and scholarship in pure and applied mathematics. The society has about 13,000 members. It publishes books and journals on mathematics, provides cataloging and indexing services, sponsors technical meetings, and cooperates with similar organizations in joint projects. The society was founded in New York City in 1888. Its headquarters are at 321 S. Main Street, Providence, R.I. 02904.

Critically reviewed by the AMERICAN MATHEMATICAL SOCIETY
MATHEMATICAL SYMBOL. See SYMBOL; ALGEBRA (Symbols in Algebra); SET THEORY.

MATHEMATICS is one of the most useful and fascinating divisions of human knowledge. It helps us in many important areas of study, and has the power to solve some of the deepest puzzles man must face.

Mathematics includes many different subjects. So the term *mathematics* is usually hard to define. But here is a definition that fits most of the mathematics we learn in school or college. *Mathematics is the study of quantities and relations through the use of numbers and symbols. Arithmetic*, for example, deals with quantities expressed by numbers. *Algebra* uses quantities and relations expressed by symbols. *Geometry* involves quantities associated with figures in space, such as length and area, and the relationships between figures in space. *Trigonometry* is concerned with the measurement of angles and with the relationships of angles. *Analytic geometry* applies algebra to geometric studies. And *calculus* works with pairs of associated quantities and the way one quantity changes in relation to the other.

The Importance of Mathematics

In Everyday Life. We use mathematics daily, even in such simple ways as telling time from a clock or counting the change returned by the grocer. A customer in a store uses mathematics whenever he buys something. A man and his wife use mathematics to make up a household budget or to figure out their income tax. The wife uses mathematics to make the proper measurements from a recipe in her cookbook. The husband uses mathematics to estimate how much paint he needs to refinish the kitchen. And the children use mathematics in many games and hobbies.

In Science. "Mathematics," wrote the English scientist Roger Bacon in 1267, "is the gate and key of the

sciences." Most scientists depend on mathematics for exact descriptions and formulas of observations and experiments. Many scientific problems have become so complicated that only highly trained mathematicians working with giant electronic computers can supply the answers. The physical sciences, such as astronomy, chemistry, and physics, lean heavily on mathematics. And there is increasing use of mathematics in such social sciences as economics, psychology, and sociology.

In Industry. Almost all companies realize the tremendous value of mathematics in research and planning. Many major industrial firms employ trained mathematicians. Mathematics has great importance in all engineering projects. For example, the design of a superhighway requires extensive use of mathematics. The construction of a giant dam would be impossible without first filling reams of paper with mathematical formulas and calculations. The large number of courses an engineering student must take in mathematics shows the importance of mathematics in this field.

In Business, all transactions that involve buying and selling call for mathematics. Any business establishment, large or small, needs mathematics to keep its records. Bankers use mathematics to handle and invest money. Many companies employ *accountants* to keep their records and *statisticians* to analyze large groups of figures, such as the records of sales in a certain area. Insurance companies employ *actuaries* who specialize in computing the rates charged for insurance.

Kinds of Mathematics

Arithmetic is the first branch of mathematics learned in school, and almost everyone uses it daily. It includes the study of numbers and methods for *computing*, or

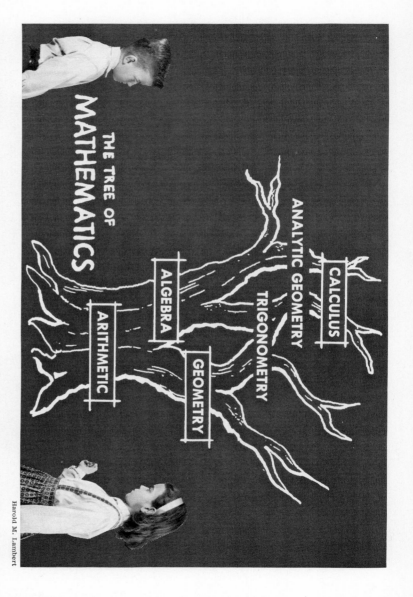

THE TREE OF
MATHEMATICS

CALCULUS

ANALYTIC GEOMETRY

TRIGONOMETRY

ALGEBRA

GEOMETRY

ARITHMETIC

Harold M. Lambert

solving problems, with numbers. Arithmetic furnishes the basis for many other branches of mathematics. It includes four basic operations: addition, subtraction, multiplication, and division. See ADDITION; ARITHMETIC; DIVISION; MULTIPLICATION; SUBTRACTION.

Algebra, as learned in high school, forms one of the branches of mathematics used widely in business, industry, and science. It deals with numbers, but it differs from arithmetic because it is much more general than arithmetic. Arithmetic uses specific numbers. Algebra uses letters, such as x or y, to solve problems in which certain numbers are unknown. See ALGEBRA.

Algebra has produced a number of useful inventions in mathematics, such as *logarithms*. Logarithms are numbers developed by algebra that can be used to solve extremely long multiplications and divisions in arithmetic problems. Logarithms form the basis of the *slide rule*, a computing device frequently used by engineers. See LOGARITHMS; SLIDE RULE.

Geometry, as learned in high school, makes up one of the branches of mathematics most useful in building or measuring things. Architects, astronomers, construction engineers, navigators, physicists, and surveyors depend on geometry in their work. *Plane geometry* deals with figures, such as squares and circles, that lie on a *plane*, or flat surface. *Solid geometry* deals with figures that have three dimensions, such as cubes, spheres, and pyramids. See GEOMETRY.

Trigonometry forms a branch of mathematics widely used by astronomers, navigators, and surveyors. The basic idea in trigonometry is computing the relations between the sides of a right triangle. These relations are called *trigonometric ratios*. *Plane trigonometry* deals with triangles on a plane. *Spherical trigonometry* deals with triangles on the surface of a sphere. See TRIGONOMETRY.

Analytic Geometry comes from the application of algebra to geometry. Using analytic geometry, a person can draw a curved line that represents an equation from algebra, such as $y=x^2$. Similarly, he can write an equation that is a mathematical description of a certain curved line. Engineers and physicists use analytic geometry in many ways. For example, designing an airplane calls for many equations that describe curves. See GEOMETRY (Analytic Geometry).

Calculus deals with changing quantities. It forms one of the most useful branches of advanced mathematics. Calculus has hundreds of practical applications in engineering, physics, and other branches of science. Suppose a gun fires a projectile into the air. The projectile's speed changes during the course of its flight. *Differential calculus* finds the rate at which the speed of the projectile changes. *Integral calculus* finds the speed of the projectile when the rate of change is known. These problems of changing quantities also relate to geometry. See CALCULUS.

Probability is the mathematical study of the likelihood of events. It has many important practical uses. Almost all scientific predictions use probability. Insurance companies use it to compute the rates they charge for insurance. The armed forces use probability to plan artillery fire and bombing. See PROBABILITY.

Statistics forms a branch of mathematics that analyzes large bodies of numbers. Scientists and other investigators often begin work on a problem by gathering facts. These facts usually come from measurements and count-

ings of various kinds, and appear as collections of numbers. Statisticians analyze collections of numbers and show important trends. Using the study of probability, they can make predictions. See STATISTICS.

Non-Euclidean Geometry contributed much to the development of the theory of relativity, one of the outstanding advances in scientific thought (see RELATIVITY). It also helped explore the fundamental nature of mathematics itself. About 1830, János Bolyai of Hungary and Nikolai Lobachevsky of Russia, two mathematicians working independently of each other, produced new and sometimes strange systems of geometry. For example, in Lobachevsky's geometry, the angles of a triangle do not add up to 180°. But, as logical systems, these geometries are just as consistent and regular as the Euclidean geometry we learn in high school. See GEOMETRY (Non-Euclidean Geometry).

Pure and Applied Mathematics

Mathematics arose from attempts to solve practical problems, such as counting farm animals or measuring pieces of land. The ancient Greeks developed two kinds of mathematics, pure and applied.

Pure Mathematics includes systems of mathematics that need not have any practical applications. A storyteller can describe a mythical kingdom that never existed. In the same way, a mathematician can make up a system of mathematics, such as a system of geometry.

Applied Mathematics results from the use of pure mathematics in concrete situations. A pure mathematical system often has a number of separate practical applications. For example, we use geometry to build machines, design houses and furniture, and measure land. Behind almost every operation of applied mathematics lies a piece of pure mathematics.

Mathematics for Fun

Mathematics has a lighter side. It includes hundreds of entertaining puzzles, tricks, and problems. Perhaps this is one of the reasons why so many persons have followed careers in mathematics and so many others have made mathematics their hobby.

Which Salary Would You Choose? The president of a company interviews Jones and Smith, two young applicants for a job. The job requires a person with a sharp mind. "Which would you prefer," the president asks the men, "a starting salary of $4,000 a year with a $200 increase every year, or a starting salary of $2,000 every half year with a $50 increase every half year?" Jones says he prefers the first arrangement and Smith says he prefers the second. The president hires Smith. Why did he choose him?

Make a chart to show the salary arrangements by the year.

	JONES' CHOICE	SMITH'S CHOICE
First year	$4,000	$2,000+$2,050 = $4,050
Second year	4,200	2,100+ 2,150 = 4,250
Third year	4,400	2,200+ 2,250 = 4,450
Fourth year	4,600	2,300+ 2,350 = 4,650

Contrary to Jones' impression, the second arrangement gives the higher salary.

A Little Pile of Paper. Suppose you take a huge sheet of extremely thin paper. The paper is only $\frac{1}{1,000}$ of an inch thick. Then you cut the sheet in half and put one piece on top of the other. Cut these two pieces in half and put the resulting four pieces together in a pile. Cut the pile of four pieces in half and put the resulting eight pieces in a pile. Suppose you cut the pile in half 50 times and each time pile up the resulting pieces.

Ask your friends how high they think the final pile of paper will be. Some persons suggest a foot, others suggest several feet, and occasionally someone guesses a mile. Usually, they show surprise when you tell them the pile is more than 17,000,000 miles high!

But you can easily prove this. After the first cut, you have 2 pieces. After the second cut, you have 2×2, or 2^2 pieces. After the third cut, you have $2 \times 2 \times 2$, or 2^3 pieces. Clearly, after the fiftieth cut, the number of pieces is the product of fifty 2's, or 2^{50}. The number 2 multiplied by itself 50 times is about 1,126,000,000,000,000. Because there are 1,000 sheets of paper to the inch, the pile is about 1,126,000,000,000 inches high. Divide this number by 12 to find the number of feet. Divide the number of feet by 5,280 to find the number of miles. You will find that the pile is over 17,000,000 miles high.

A Mind-Reading Trick. Many amusing "mind-reading" tricks have simple mathematical explanations. Suppose you ask a friend to think of a number and keep it secret. Then ask him—still keeping the number to himself—to multiply his number by 5, add 6, multiply by 4, add 9, and multiply by 5. Now ask him to tell you the result. When he does, you need only a moment's thought to tell him his original number.

Suppose your friend chooses 13. He multiplies $13 \times 5 = 65$. He adds 6: $65 + 6 = 71$. He multiplies by 4: $71 \times 4 = 284$. He adds 9: $284 + 9 = 293$. And he multiplies by 5: $293 \times 5 = 1,465$. He tells you the number 1,465. *Without telling him, you subtract 165 from the number he tells you, divide by 100 (drop two zeros), and tell him his original number.* In the case of 1,465, subtract 165: $1,465 - 165 = 1,300$. Divide by 100: $1,300 \div 100 = 13$.

You can explain the trick by using n to represent the unknown number. Here are the steps. (1) n. (2) $5n$. (3) $5n + 6$. (4) $4(5n + 6) = 20n + 24$. (5) $20n + 24 + 9 = 20n + 33$. (6) $5(20n + 33) = 100n + 165$. So $100n + 165$ equals x, or the number your friend tells you. You solve $100n + 165 = x$ by subtracting 165 from x and dividing it by 100. No matter what number your friend chooses, you can find it by following the rule given above.

Where Is My Missing Horse? After Mr. Klopstock's death, his estate consisted of 17 horses. His will provided that his friend Mr. Thom should be his executor. The terms of the will were these: one half of the horses should go to the widow, one third to the older son, and one ninth of the horses to the younger son. Mr. Thom found himself in great trouble. It seemed evident that Mr. Klopstock had miscalculated in drawing up his will. It would be impossible for any of the persons to receive a fraction

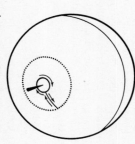

of a horse. Yet Mr. Thom solved the problem. How did he do it?

Mr. Thom found that the fractions $\frac{1}{2}$, $\frac{1}{3}$, and $\frac{1}{9}$ added together make $\frac{17}{18}$. In order to start with $\frac{18}{18}$, which equals one, he put his own horse into the corral with the other 17. Then he gave the widow $\frac{1}{2}$ of the horses, or 9. The elder son received $\frac{1}{3}$ of the horses, or 6. The younger son got $\frac{1}{9}$ of the horses, or 2. Then Mr. Thom rode away on his own horse and everybody was happy.

One Equals Two. A tricky problem in algebra seems to establish the fact that one equals two. Of course, such a conclusion seems impossible. The trick starts simply enough. Suppose that $a = b$. Here is what you can do:

(1) Multiply by a, then $ab = a^2$.
(2) Subtract b^2, then $ab - b^2 = a^2 - b^2$.
(3) Factor, then $b(a - b) = (a + b)(a - b)$.
(4) Divide by $(a - b)$, then $b = a + b$.
(5) Substitute a for b, then $b = a + a$.
(6) $a = 2a$.
(7) Divide by a, then $1 = 2$.

At first glance, all seems well. These processes appear to agree with principles in algebra. But there is an oversight in the application of these principles. It lies in the fact that $(a - b)$ in the third and fourth steps is equal to zero, because b equals a. For this reason, the conclusion reached is wrong. Division by zero is not permitted.

A Matter of Direction. From what point on the earth's surface can a man walk 12 miles due south, then walk 12 miles due east, then walk 12 miles due north, and find himself back at his starting point? The usual answer to this old riddle is the North Pole. But the earth actually has an infinite number of points from which such a walk could be taken.

In theory, the equator forms a circle around the middle of the earth. Going north or south from the equator, progressively smaller circles of latitude ring the earth until they reach the points of the North and South poles. Somewhere near the South Pole, there must be a circle of latitude whose circumference is exactly 12 miles long. And there must be a second circle of latitude exactly 12 miles north of the first circle. Suppose a man starts his walk at any point on this second circle. He walks 12 miles due south and finds himself on the first circle whose circumference is 12 miles. He walks 12 miles due east. That is, he walks around the 12-mile circle. Then he walks 12 miles due north to his starting point on the first circle!

But other points can solve the problem. There must be circles of latitude north of the South Pole with circumferences of 6 miles, 4 miles, 3 miles, and so on. By starting at any point on a circle of latitude 12 miles north of any one of these circles, the man can take the required walk. For example, when he walks 12 miles due east on the 4-mile circle, he will walk around the circle three times before he starts his 12-mile journey north to his first circle.

An Extra Square. Suppose you mark off a square piece of cardboard into 64 little squares. The area of the cardboard is 8×8 little squares, or 64 little squares. Cut the cardboard into two triangles and two trapezoids, as shown in the accompanying picture.

Now rearrange the two triangles and two trapezoids to form the rectangle shown in the picture.

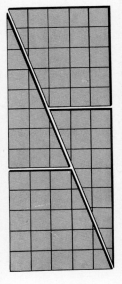

But this new rectangle has sides of 5 little squares and 13 little squares. It must have an area of 5×13 little squares, or 65 little squares. Where did the extra square come from?

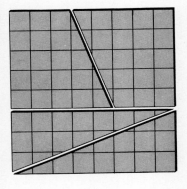

The answer to this problem is that the edges of the two triangles and two trapezoids do not really form a diagonal in the new rectangle. Instead, they form the flat parallelogram that is shown in exaggerated form in the bottom picture. The area of this parallelogram is exactly one little square.

A Strange Twist. You may find it difficult to predict the outcome of some experiments in geometry. Suppose you have a strip of paper about 1 inch wide and about 10 inches long, with a dotted line down the middle of its length. Mentally, paste the ends of the strip together to form a ring like a section of a cylinder. If, with a pair of scissors, you cut this ring along the dotted line, you will obtain two rings just like the first

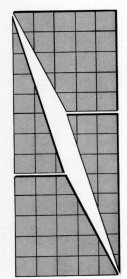

ring, but only half as wide. Now imagine the unpasted strip of paper again. This time give the strip a half-twist (a twist of 180°) before mentally pasting the ends together. With the ends pasted and the strip in a half-twist, what will happen when you cut this new ring along the dotted line?

You should actually do this experiment at home with a strip of paper, paste, and a pair of scissors. When you discover what happens when you cut the ring with one half-twist, imagine what will happen with two, three, four, and five half-twists, or—in general—m half-twists on the strip.

In terms of geometry, if m, the number of half-twists, is even, the ring will be a surface with two sides and two edges. If you cut it along the line, it will become two rings, each with m half-twists, linked together $\frac{m}{2}$ times. If m, the number of half-twists, is odd, the ring will be a surface with only one side and one edge. If you cut it along the line, it will remain one ring with $2m+2$ half-twists. If m is greater than 1, the ring will be knotted. You may want to try cutting the twisted rings along two ruled lines, instead of one.

The ring with one half-twist takes its name—Möbius strip—from August Ferdinand Möbius (1790-1868), a German astronomer and mathematician. Möbius helped establish a study in geometry called *topology*. Topology deals with geometrical figures that are *deformed*, or pulled and twisted out of shape in various ways. See TOPOLOGY.

The Earth with a Pipeline Around It. Suppose that someone wants to lay a pipeline around the earth. Also suppose that the circumference of the earth is exactly 25,000 miles. The manufacturer made the pipeline exactly 20 feet too long. Still, it was proposed to put it in by position, supported above the surface of the earth by posts of equal length. How high above the surface of the earth would the pipeline be?

In a diagram, let R represent the radius of the earth, h the height of one of the posts, and C the circumference of the earth.

Now $2\pi R = C$.
The radius of the circle of pipeline is $R+h$.
Then $2\pi (R+h) = C+20$.
Substitute $2\pi R$ for C.
$2\pi R + 2\pi h = 2\pi R + 20$.
Subtract $2\pi R$ from each side, and $2\pi h = 20$.
Then $2 \times 3.1416 h = 20$.
And $h = \dfrac{20}{2 \times 3.1416}$
Finally, $h = 3.18$ feet.

It may be hard to believe that adding only 20 feet to 25,000 miles would result in raising the pipeline more than 3 feet above the earth. But try adding the same number of feet to a much smaller circumference, such as 10 feet. The answer is the same, though you have used a different figure for the original circumference. In fact, the length of the original circumference makes no difference. The answer will always be found by dividing the added length by 2×3.1416.

History

Ancient Times. Prehistoric men took the first great steps toward mathematics. Before the time of recorded history, they learned to count such things as the animals in their herds and flocks. They probably first used their fingers or pebbles to help keep track of small numbers. They learned to use the length of their hands and arms and other standards of measure. And they learned to use regular shapes when they molded pottery and chipped stone arrowheads.

By 3000 B.C., the peoples of ancient Babylonia, China, and Egypt had developed a practical system of mathematics. They used written symbols to stand for numbers, and knew the simple arithmetic operations. They used this knowledge in business and government. They also developed a practical geometry helpful in agriculture and engineering. For example, the ancient Egyptians knew how to survey their fields and to make the intricate measurements necessary to build huge pyramids. The Babylonians and Egyptians had even explored some of the fundamental ideas of algebra. But this early mathematics solved only practical problems. It was applied, rather than pure, mathematics.

The Greeks and the Romans. Between 600 and 300 B.C., the Greeks took the next great step in mathematics. They inherited a large part of their mathematical knowledge from the Babylonians and Egyptians. But they became the first people to separate mathematics from practical problems. For example, they separated geometry from practical applications and made it into an abstract exploration of space. They based this study of points, lines, and figures, such as triangles and circles, on logical reasoning rather than on facts found in nature. Thales of Miletus (c. 640-546 B.C.), a philosopher, helped begin this new viewpoint

of geometry. The philosopher Pythagoras (c. 580-c. 500 B.C.) and his followers explored the nature of numbers. In geometry, the Pythagoreans developed the famous theorem that bears their name (see PYTHAGOREAN THEOREM). Thales, Pythagoras, and many other Greek mathematicians built up a large body of geometrical knowledge. Euclid (c. 300 B.C.), one of the foremost Greek mathematicians, organized geometry as a single logical system. His book, *The Elements*, remains one of the basic works in studying mathematics.

The Greeks also advanced other branches of mathematics. As early as 450 B.C., Greek mathematicians recognized *irrational numbers* such as the square root of 2. About 370 B.C., Eudoxus of Cnidus (c. 400-355 B.C.), a Greek astronomer and mathematician, formulated a surprisingly masterful definition of proportions. Archimedes (287?-212 B.C.), the leading mathematician of ancient times, devised processes that foreshadowed those of integral calculus. Archimedes made many other contributions to mathematics and physics. The Greek astronomer Ptolemy (c. A.D. 150) helped develop trigonometry. Diophantus (c. A.D. 275), a Greek mathematician, worked on numbers in equations. He earned the title of the father of algebra.

Although the Romans constructed many impressive buildings, they showed little interest in pure mathematics. Roman mathematics dealt largely with practical matters such as business and military science.

The Middle Ages. After the fall of Rome in A.D. 476, Europe saw no new developments in mathematics for

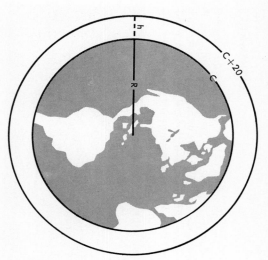

--- RED-LETTER DATES IN MATHEMATICS ---

c. 300 B.C. Euclid organized geometry as a single system of mathematics.

c. 225 B.C. Archimedes invented processes that foreshadowed those used in integral calculus.

c. A.D. 275 Diophantus helped found algebra.

c. 820 Al-Khowarizmi helped organize algebra as a branch of mathematics.

1614 John Napier published his invention of logarithms, an important mathematical aid.

1637 René Descartes published the first work on analytic geometry.

1640 Pierre Fermat founded the modern theory of numbers.

1654 Pierre Fermat and Blaise Pascal established the mathematical theory of probability.

c. 1675 Sir Isaac Newton and Baron von Leibniz, working independently, invented calculus.

1733 Leonhard Euler began a series of publications on calculus that started modern mathematical analysis.

c. 1830 János Bolyai and Nikolai Lobachevsky, working independently, invented non-Euclidean geometry systems.

1843 Sir William Hamilton invented a system of algebra that differed in many ways from traditional algebra.

1854 Georg Riemann invented a non-Euclidean geometry later used in the relativity theory.

1910-1913 Alfred North Whitehead and Bertrand Russell published *Principia Mathematica*, a work that tries to develop mathematics entirely from logic.

1915 Albert Einstein announced his general theory of relativity.

1929 Einstein published his unified-field theory.

1950 Einstein announced a major revision of his unified-field theory.

hundreds of years. But the Arabs preserved the mathematical tradition of the Greeks and Romans. One of the greatest discoveries in the history of mathematics appeared in Europe during the Middle Ages. Mathematicians in India developed zero and the decimal number system. After A.D. 700, the Arabs adopted these inventions from the Indians and used the new numbers in their mathematics. The Arabs also preserved and translated many of the great works of Greek mathematicians. They made important contributions of their own. For example, the mathematician Al-Khowarizmi (c. 820) organized and expanded algebra. The word *algebra* comes from an Arabic word in the title of one of his books on the subject. See ALGEBRA (History).

After 1100, Europeans began to borrow the mathematics of the Arab world. For example, European merchants started to use the decimal number system. At the same time, European scholars began to study Arab works on algebra and geometry. Leonardo Fibonacci (c. 1200), one of the leading European mathematicians of the Middle Ages, contributed to algebra, arithmetic, and geometry.

The Renaissance, from the 1400's to the 1600's, produced many great advances in mathematics. The exploration of new lands and continents called for better mathematics for navigation. The growth of business demanded better mathematics for banking and finance. The invention of printing brought the appearance of hundreds of popular arithmetic textbooks. Many of the computation methods used today date from this period, such as the procedure used for doing a long multiplication.

Interest also grew in pure mathematics. Michael Stifel (1487-1567), Nicolò Tartaglia (c. 1500-1557), Girolamo Cardano (1501-1576), and François Viète (1540-1603) pioneered in algebra. Viète introduced the use of letters to stand for unknown numbers. These men also helped develop trigonometry. Nicolaus Copernicus (1473-1543), the astronomer who defended the theory that the universe had the sun as its center, contributed to mathematics through his work in astronomy.

The 1600's brought many brilliant contributions to mathematics. John Napier (1550-1617), a Scottish mathematician, invented logarithms. Two Englishmen, Thomas Harriot (1560-1621) and William Oughtred (1574-1660), worked out new methods for algebra. The astronomers Galileo (1564-1642) and Johannes Kepler (1571-1630) expanded mathematical knowledge through their studies of the stars and planets. Gérard Desargues (1593-1662) helped expand geometry through his study of sections of cones. René Descartes (1596-1650) invented analytic geometry and aided many other branches of mathematics. Pierre de Fermat (1601-1665) founded the modern numbers theory. Blaise Pascal (1623-1662) and Fermat invented the mathematical theory of probability. Then, toward the end of this period, Sir Isaac Newton (1642-1727) and Baron von Leibniz (1646-1716) invented calculus. The invention of calculus marked the beginning of modern mathematics.

The 1700's saw wide applications of the new calculus. Abraham de Moivre (1667-1754) used calculus to contribute to the study of probability. Brook Taylor (1685-1731) helped develop differential calculus. Colin Maclaurin (1698-1746) also helped with calculus. But one of the greatest contributors to calculus was Leonhard

Euler (1707-1783), a Swiss mathematician. Euler worked in almost every branch of mathematics. His contributions to calculus reached into so many fields that many mathematicians call him the founder of modern mathematical analysis. Count Lagrange (1736-1813) used calculus for the study of forces in physics. Gaspard Monge (1746-1818) applied calculus to geometry.

The 1800's brought further application of calculus throughout mathematics. The Marquis de Laplace (1749-1827) used calculus in physics, particularly in astronomy. Jean Baptiste Fourier (1768-1830) used it for the study of heat in physics. Adrien Marie Legendre (1752-1833) also worked with calculus and contributed to the theory of numbers. But the early work in calculus often rested on shaky theoretical foundations. As a result, many disturbing paradoxes appeared. The great achievements in mathematics in the 1800's included rebuilding the theoretical foundations of calculus and mathematical analysis. Four mathematicians—Baron Cauchy (1789-1857), Karl Friedrich Gauss (1777-1855), Georg Friedrich Riemann (1826-1866), and Karl Theodor Weierstrass (1815-1897)—helped carry out this important work.

Another outstanding advance of the 1800's was the invention of non-Euclidean geometry by János Bolyai (1802-1860) and Nikolai Lobachevsky (1793-1856). During the same period, Arthur Cayley (1821-1895) and Sir William Rowan Hamilton (1805-1865) invented new systems of algebra. These discoveries liberated geometry and algebra from their traditional molds and did much to shape present-day mathematics.

Recent Developments. The invention of new systems of algebra and geometry and the revision of the theoretical foundations of calculus had far-reaching effects on mathematics. In the 1900's, mathematicians began to explore the foundations of mathematics itself. Many philosophies of mathematics appeared, as well as attempts to give mathematics a basis in logic. Luitzen Brouwer (1881-1966), Georg Cantor (1845-1918), David Hilbert (1862-1943), Bertrand Russell (1872-1970), and Alfred North Whitehead (1861-1947) made important studies of the foundations of mathematics. The work of Albert Einstein (1879-1955) opened a whole new area for mathematical research.

At the same time, new developments in science required a tremendous expansion of applied mathematics. Fields such as electronics, nuclear physics, and the exploration of space have used new inventions from pure mathematics to solve problems. For example, the giant electronic computers used in modern science had their own systems of mathematics designed for their use by mathematicians.

Careers in Mathematics

Mathematics offers many career opportunities. A young person can work as a mathematician in business, government, or industry. Or, he can teach mathematics in a school or college. Many other careers, such as professional work in architecture, banking, and engineering, demand extensive mathematical training.

Training. The amount of training needed for a career in mathematics depends on the career itself. A man or woman who wants to become a high-school mathe-

MATHEMATICS

matics teacher must earn at least a bachelor's degree in college. This degree must include the required courses in mathematics. At the same time, a student with this career in mind should take as much work as possible in both the physical and social sciences. For a teaching career in a college or university, a person must do graduate work. A doctor's degree in mathematics is an almost universal requirement.

A person who wants to become a statistician must have a strong college or university background in mathematics with emphasis on subjects allied to statistics, such as calculus. In addition, a would-be statistician should prepare himself in the field in which he will use statistics.

Industry needs mathematicians at all levels of preparation, from the bachelor's to the doctor's degree. Persons with a bachelor's degree or limited training usually work at computing. Persons with a doctor's degree or more extensive training often serve industry as consultants. These consultants in industry are mathematicians with a flair for applied mathematics and the solution of industrial problems. Mathematics careers in government resemble those in industry. A mathematician's civil-service rating depends on his training and ability. The federal government employs mathematicians in the research laboratories and offices of such agencies as the Atomic Energy Commission, the Bureau of the Census, the Coast and Geodetic Survey, and the Department of Defense.

Actuaries usually work for insurance companies. An actuary must know statistics and general mathematics. In addition, he must have a good background in economics and finance.

Professional Associations. Mathematicians have a number of professional associations. These associations publish regular journals for their members. Many elementary and high-school teachers belong to the National Council of Teachers of Mathematics. Many college and university teachers are members of the Mathematical Association of America. Mathematicians engaged in research may join the American Mathematical Society. Many statisticians belong to the American Statistical Association. Mathematicians in industry may join the Society for Industrial and Applied Mathematics. Actuaries may join the Society of Actuaries or the Casualty Actuarial Society. Many mathematicians belong to specialized groups and societies devoted to their particular interests.

Related Articles in WORLD BOOK include:

AMERICAN MATHEMATICIANS

Banneker, Benjamin
Bowditch, Nathaniel
Fisher, Irving
Gibbs, Josiah W.
Peirce, Charles S.
Rittenhouse, David
Steinmetz, Charles P.
Von Neumann, John
Wiener, Norbert

BRITISH MATHEMATICIANS

Napier, John
Newton, Sir Isaac
Russell, Bertrand A. W.
Whitehead, Alfred North

FRENCH MATHEMATICIANS

Cauchy, Augustin L.
Descartes, René
Fermat, Pierre de
Lagrange, Joseph L.
Laplace, Marquis de
Legendre, Adrien M.
Pascal, Blaise
Poincaré, Jules H.

GERMAN MATHEMATICIANS

Bessel, Friedrich W.
Clausius, Rudolf J. E.
Gauss, Karl F.
Hilbert, David
Kepler, Johannes
Leibniz, Gottfried W.

OTHER MATHEMATICIANS

Archimedes
Bernoulli
Euclid
Euler, Leonhard
Huygens, Christian
Omar Khayyám
Ptolemy
Pythagoras
Torricelli, Evangelista

APPLIED MATHEMATICS

Accounting
Actuary
Biomathematics
Bookkeeping
Budget
Discount
Engineering
Insurance
Interest
Map
Measurement
Mechanical Drawing
Navigation
Surveying
Weights and Measures

BRANCHES OF MATHEMATICS

Algebra
Arithmetic
Calculus
Geometry
Probability
Statistics
Topology
Trigonometry

MATHEMATICAL MACHINES AND DEVICES

Abacus
Adding Machine
Business Machines
Calculating Machine
Computer
Differential Analyzer
Slide Rule
Vernier

ORGANIZATIONS

Mathematical Association of America
Mathematical Society, American

OTHER RELATED ARTICLES

Determinant
Number
Numeration Systems
Permutations and Combinations
Progression
Series
Set Theory
Square Root

HOWARD W. EVES

Outline

I. The Importance of Mathematics
  A. In Everyday Life
  B. In Science
  C. In Industry
  D. In Business

II. Kinds of Mathematics
  A. Arithmetic
  B. Algebra
  C. Geometry
  D. Trigonometry
  E. Analytic Geometry
  F. Calculus
  G. Probability
  H. Statistics
  I. Non-Euclidean Geometry

III. Pure and Applied Mathematics

IV. Mathematics for Fun

V. History

VI. Careers in Mathematics

Questions

How does mathematics help solve various problems in everyday life?

What invention has algebra produced to help solve long arithmetic problems?

How does analytic geometry combine two different kinds of mathematics?

What kinds of problems does calculus solve?

What are some contributions of non-Euclidean geometry to mathematics and science?

How does pure mathematics differ from applied mathematics?

In what ways did the Arabs help to contribute to mathematics?

How did the Renaissance stimulate mathematics?

What have been some main trends in mathematics in the 1900's?

Why is mathematics important in science?

Portrait c. 1727 by Peter Pelham,
American Antiquarian Society,
Worcester, Mass.

Cotton Mather

MATHER, *MATH* er, was the name of a famous family of clergymen in early America. The Mather family of Massachusetts stood out in an age when ministers were the leaders in public and intellectual life.

Richard Mather (1596-1669), the founder of "the Mather dynasty," was born in Lancashire, England. He studied at Oxford, and was ordained a minister in 1620. His Puritan beliefs led him into difficulties with the authorities of the Church of England. In 1633 he was suspended from the ministry.

Mather left England in 1635 to begin a new life in Massachusetts. From 1636 until his death he was pastor of the Congregational Church in Dorchester. His influence spread beyond his own congregation, and he was a leading figure in all the disagreements that shook the churches of early Massachusetts. He was a principal author of the *Bay Psalm Book.*

Increase Mather (1639-1723) was the son of Richard Mather. He was pastor of the Second (or North) Church of Boston from 1664 to his death.

Mather's intense conservatism made him an enemy of every kind of new change in the old New England order of church and state. He opposed those clergymen who were trying to liberalize Puritan doctrine and church organization. He also opposed attempts by the British government to reduce the historic independence of the Massachusetts colony. Mather spent four years in London between 1688 and 1692 pleading the cause of his colony before William III. He got a new charter in 1691 that united Plymouth and Massachusetts.

From 1685 to 1701, Mather served as head of Harvard University. He was an early friend of scientific investigation, despite his political and religious conservatism, and supported the campaign to introduce inoculation for smallpox. He was troubled by the witch trials in Salem, and protested against the extreme methods of the prosecution. His *Cases of Conscience Concerning Evil Spirits,* published in 1693, helped end executions for witchcraft. He wrote *A Brief History of the War with the Indians* and many religious and political articles. He was born in Dorchester and studied at Harvard, and at Trinity College in Dublin. After several years of preaching in the British Isles, he returned to Massachusetts in 1661.

Cotton Mather (1663-1728) was the son of Increase Mather. He was ordained in 1685, and became his father's associate in Boston's North Church. He served as pastor during his father's trip to England, and carried on after his father's death in 1723.

Mather is remembered mainly as the leading scholar of early American Puritanism. He wrote more than 450 books. His *Magnalia Christi Americana* (1702) is a treasure house of materials and opinions on the church history of New England. *Essays to Do Good* (1710), a book of Puritan morality, influenced Benjamin Franklin.

Like his father, Cotton Mather was a friend of education and science. He helped found Yale College, and was the first American to be elected a fellow of the Royal Society in London. He was born in Boston, and studied at Harvard.

CLINTON ROSSITER

MATHEWSON, "CHRISTY," CHRISTOPHER (1880-1925), was one of baseball's greatest right-handed pitchers. He won 372 games in the National League, 371 for the New York Giants and one for the Cincinnati Reds. He became the first pitcher in the 1900's to win 30 games a season for three consecutive years. He won 37 games in 1908, and pitched three shutouts in the 1905 World Series against Philadelphia. Mathewson was born in Factoryville, Pa. See also BASEBALL (National Baseball Hall of Fame; picture).

ED FITZGERALD

MATHIAS, "BOB," ROBERT BRUCE. See TRACK AND FIELD (Famous Track and Field Champions).

MATINS, *MAT inz,* are the first part of the Divine Offices (prayers, psalms, and commentary on the scriptures) read each day by the clergy of the Roman Catholic Church. The Anglican Church sometimes uses the word *Matins* to refer to Morning Prayers.

MATISSE, *mah TEESE,* **HENRI** (1869-1954), was a noted French painter. His colorful, rhythmic, and posterlike paintings and drawings rank him as the foremost decorative painter of his time. He and Pablo Picasso are probably the most influential painters of the 1900's (see PICASSO, PABLO). Matisse became the leader of a group of radical painters in Paris whom critics called *fauves,* or *wild beasts,* because they thought the art of these painters was outrageous and savage.

His paintings include *Odalisque, Desserte, The Red Studio,* and *Piano Lesson.* His painting, *The Purple Robe,* appears in color in the PAINTING article. His paintings are deceptively simple in appearance. They are not supposed to be true to life. He said they are intended for relaxation, "something like an armchair." Matisse's favorite subjects included women, interior scenes, and still lifes. But the important part of his art is what present-day painters call "form," or "plastic design." This is found in the colors, lines, rhythms, textures, and patterns that make up the pictures. The subject matter is little more than a framework on which to hang the harmonies and contrasts.

In 1892, he studied in the Paris studio of William Bouguereau, an academic master of the nude. Such artificial art did not suit Matisse. He soon changed to the studio of Gustave Moreau. This imaginative artist encouraged him to paint in his own way.

The Impressionists strongly influenced him in 1896 and 1897 (see IMPRESSIONISM). But he was also influenced by the simplicity, strength, and colorfulness of Oriental art, particularly that of Persia (now Iran) and the Middle East. He also studied European painting and the stained glass of the Middle Ages. Meanwhile, he was developing his own manner. He settled on a boldly

Matisse (Self-Portrait)
Collection of S. Max Becker, Jr.,
Glencoe, Ill.

simple style. He held his first independent exhibition in 1906. Soon he became internationally famous.

He was born in Le Cateau, France. He studied law for a time, but gave it up to become an artist. He moved from Paris to Nice in 1917.

MATO GROSSO, *MAT oo GROHS oo,* or *MATTO GROSSO,* is a state which covers an area of 475,502 square miles in western Brazil. The region lies in the center of a forest area. Its name means *great forest.* The land has never been fully explored. Archaeologists think it may contain relics of ancient civilizations.

MATRIARCHAL FAMILY. See FAMILY (Home Life).

MATRIX, in anatomy. See NAIL.

MATRIX. See LINOTYPE.

MATSU. See FORMOSA (Location; map).

MATTE is a mixture of sulfides formed in the smelting of metal ores such as copper, lead, and nickel.

MATTER is one of the two ways in which nature shows itself to man. Energy is the second way in which nature shows itself. All objects consist of matter. The objects may differ widely from one another. But they have one thing in common—they all occupy space. Therefore, scientists usually define matter as anything that occupies space. All matter has *inertia.* This means that it resists any change in its condition of rest or of motion. Scientists call the quantity of matter in an object *mass.* The earth's gravitational attraction for a given mass gives matter its *weight.* Gravity's pull on an object decreases as it moves away from the center of the earth. For this reason, objects that move from the earth's atmosphere into outer space "lose weight" even though the mass, or quantity of matter, remains the same.

When we see people, animals, or machines working, feel heat from a fire, or see light from an electric bulb,

The Royal Museum of Fine Arts, Rump Collection, Copenhagen.

Portrait of Madame Matisse, painted in 1905, shows Matisse's emphasis on color, which is typical of the fauve movement.

JOSEPH C. SLOANE

we become aware of *energy.* All these processes involve energy. Scientists often define energy as the ability to do work, or to move matter. Heat is the variety of energy most familiar to us. All other kinds of energy may be changed into heat. Therefore, scientists also define energy as heat, or anything that can be changed into heat. See ENERGY.

Matter can be changed into energy and energy into matter. However, such changes occur only under unusual circumstances. For example, matter changes into energy when radium and other radioactive elements disintegrate and when atomic bombs explode.

The Properties of Matter

All of us easily recognize many varieties of matter. Each variety possesses certain characteristics common to all samples of its special kind. We base our recognition of each variety on knowledge of these special characteristics, or *properties.* These properties distinguish one kind of matter from other kinds. Matter has two main types of properties—physical and chemical.

Physical Properties. People recognize certain kinds of matter by sight, smell, touch, taste, or hearing. We can recognize gold and copper by color, sugar by taste, and gasoline by odor. These are examples of some of the physical properties of matter. Another physical property of matter is *density,* or the amount of mass for each unit of volume. Because of the difference in density, a block of cork weighs less than a block of all common woods the same size. *Solubility* (the ability of one kind of matter to dissolve in another) and *conductivity* (the ability of matter to conduct heat or electricity) are also physical properties.

Chemical Properties of matter describe how a substance acts when it undergoes chemical change. For example, a chemical property of iron is its ability to combine with oxygen in moist air to form iron oxide, or rust. Scientists call such changes in the composition of matter *chemical changes.* Some changes alter the value of physical properties, such as weight or density, but produce no change in the composition of the matter. Scientists call these *physical changes.* When water changes to steam it undergoes physical, but not chemical, change (see PHYSICAL CHANGE).

Materials and Substances. Any variety of matter recognized as a certain type or kind, such as wood or coal, is a *material.* If all samples of a given material have identical or similar properties, the material is a *substance.* For example, pure sand is a substance, but glass is a material. Many materials are mixtures of several varieties of matter. This means that substances in a mixture retain their individual chemical and physical properties. For example, salt and sand mixed together remain salt and sand. You can separate one from the other without changing its individual properties. Scientists usually separate the components of mixtures without changing their chemical properties. When they can obtain no further separation by physical means, pure, *homogeneous* (uniform) substances remain.

By using chemical processes, scientists may be able to separate a substance into two or more simpler kinds of matter with new properties. If so, they call the substance a *compound substance,* or a *chemical compound.* Substances that do not break down into simpler varieties of matter by chemical means are called *elementary*

KINDS AND PROPERTIES OF MATTER

3 STATES OF MATTER

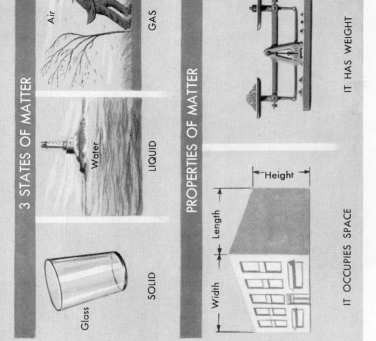

GAS
Air

LIQUID
Water

SOLID
Glass

KINDS OF MATTER

ORGANIC
Plants
Animals

INORGANIC
Earth
Rock

PROPERTIES OF MATTER

Height
Length
Width

IT OCCUPIES SPACE

IT HAS WEIGHT

---

substances, or *chemical elements* (see ELEMENT, CHEMICAL).

Structure of Matter

An atom is the smallest particle of an element that can enter into chemical reaction to form a compound (see ATOM). When atoms combine with other atoms they form larger particles called *molecules* (see MOLECULE). But they may also unite by acquiring charges to form electrically charged atoms, or groups of atoms, called *ions*. Water consists of molecules, each of which contains two atoms of hydrogen and one of oxygen. Atoms and most ions and molecules are extremely small. If the molecules in a single drop of water were counted at the rate of ten million each second, a person would need about five million years to complete the job.

When two or more chemical elements unite, they form a compound. Compounds may be organic or inorganic. Organic compounds contain the element carbon. They are called *organic* because most of the compounds found in living organisms (plants and animals) contain carbon. All other compounds are classed as *inorganic*. However, these classifications are not rigid.

States of Matter

Matter can exist in three physical states—solid, liquid, and gas. For example, ice is solid water. When heated, it melts at a definite temperature to form liquid water. When heat causes the temperature of the water to rise to a certain point, the water boils, producing steam, which is a gas. Removal of heat reverses these processes. Experiments show that in spite of these changes, the chemical composition of water remains the same. Therefore, the changes that take place are physical.

Solids. All solids have *form*. They also have *hardness* and *rigidity*, or the ability to oppose a change of shape. For example, stone does not change shape easily. Some solids, like salt or sulfur, are *brittle* and will shatter when

struck. Others have considerable *tensile strength* and resist being pulled apart. Still others, particularly metals, have *malleability* (the ability to be beaten into thin sheets) and *ductility* (the ability to be drawn into wires). These properties depend on the kinds of particles that make up the substance and on the forces acting among them. See SOLID.

Liquids have no shape of their own. But they have the ability to flow. They take the shape of any container in which they are placed. They fill the container only when their volume equals that of the container itself. Iron and steel are rigid in their solid state. But manufacturers often melt these metals and pour them into molds. See LIQUID.

Gases. All gases, regardless of the composition of their molecules, have almost identical physical behavior. Compared with liquids or solids, they have low densities. They exert pressure equally in all directions. All are compressible. When heated, gases expand greatly or exert a greater pressure when confined in a vessel of fixed volume. See GAS.

Conservation of Matter

At one time people thought that atoms were the smallest particles of nature. But scientists found that atoms are complex structures made up of still smaller particles. Each atom has a small, heavy nucleus that contains tiny particles called protons and neutrons. Outside the nucleus, but within the atom, are a number of very light particles called electrons. The size of the atom is about 50,000 times that of its nucleus. Thus the atom is mostly empty space, allowing room for the electrons to move freely about the nucleus. Atoms of different elements differ only in the number and arrangement of their neutrons, protons, and electrons.

The small particles that atoms contain often behave like small bundles of energy. Scientists sometimes give matter the name of *organized energy*, because these

MATTER

bundles of energy arranged in definite patterns make up the atoms of all the earth's matter. Scientists call energy used to do work *disorganized energy* because it is not organized into matter and becomes even more disorganized with use. In all ordinary chemical processes that take place in homes, laboratories, and factories, the mass of end products obtained is equal to the mass of starting materials used. For all ordinary processes,

The Matterhorn Towers Majestically above the old mountain village of Zermatt in southern Switzerland. The spectacular peak rises from a field of snow-packed glaciers.

Conzett & Huber

we say that matter cannot be created or destroyed. In the same manner, energy is neither created nor destroyed. Scientists found that when an atomic bomb explodes, a tiny quantity of matter is converted into a relatively large quantity of energy. Thus, we seem to be destroying matter. But the matter has not been destroyed. It has been converted into energy. Therefore, physicists evolved a modern statement of the conservation law. This law states that mass-energy may not be created or destroyed, but each may be converted into the other.

W. NORTON JONES, JR.

Related Articles in WORLD BOOK include:

Adhesion	Expansion	Liquid
Atom	Gas	Malleability
Cohesion	Gravitation	Molecule
Density	Inertia	Plasma
Elasticity	Lavoisier,	(in physics)
Element, Chemical	Antoine L.	Solid
Energy		

MATTERHORN, *MAT er hawrn,* is a famous mountain peak in the Pennine Alps. It stands 14,685 feet high on the boundary between Valais, Switzerland, and the Piedmont region of Italy. It is about 40 miles east of Mont Blanc. For location, see SWITZERLAND (color map). The Matterhorn rises like a pyramid from the mountains around it. Snow always covers the upper slopes of this peak. Many experienced climbers have scaled its steep sides. The first man to make the dangerous climb to the top of the Matterhorn was Edward Whymper in 1865.

FRANKLIN C. ERICKSON

See also ALPS; MOUNTAIN (picture chart; table).

MATTHEW, SAINT, was one of the apostles of Christ. In the Gospel of Mark, he is called *Levi,* the son of Alphaeus. If this Alphaeus is the same as the one mentioned in Matthew 10:3, he and James the Less may have been brothers (see JAMES [Saint James the Less]). He was a *publican* (professional tax collector). After becoming a disciple, Matthew gave a dinner in Jesus' honor, which was attended by many of his friends. It was there that Jesus rebuked the Pharisees.

Matthew is usually regarded as the author of the first Gospel. After Pentecost and the church's early years in Jerusalem, he preached in Syria, and perhaps in Ethiopia and Persia. Early writers said that he died a natural death, but, according to later stories, he was a martyr. His feast day is celebrated on September 21 except in the Eastern Orthodox Church, where it is November 16.

FULTON J. SHEEN and MERRILL C. TENNEY

MATTHIAS, *muh THIE us,* **SAINT,** was elected to take the place of Judas Iscariot as an apostle of Jesus Christ. He was chosen by lot from the 120 disciples who had gathered in the upper room before the day of Pentecost. According to Acts 1:15-26, he was one of Jesus' original disciples and had been with Him since the baptism of John. He is not mentioned again in the New Testament, and nothing is known about the later career of Matthias.

FULTON J. SHEEN and MERRILL C. TENNEY

MATTHIAS CORVINUS. See HUNGARY (Early Days).

MATO GROSSO. See MATO GROSSO.

MATTRESS. See BED.

MATURATION is the process by which living things grow and develop. It includes the processes involved in changing a green, immature fruit into the ripened form. It also includes advanced stages of cell division in man, animals, and plants in which cells specialize in activity and structure. Another type of maturation is the ripening of the reproductive cells of man and higher animals. In medical practice, maturation is the ripening of an abscess and the formation of pus.   NEAL D. BUFFALOE

See also INSTINCT (The Modern View).

MATZAH, *MAHT suh,* is the Hebrew name for an unleavened bread. Jews eat matzahs during the Passover festival in memory of the flight of the ancient Hebrews from Egypt. The Bible says that the Hebrews baked matzahs because they had no time to bake leavened breads. People often use matzahs as tea biscuits or crackers.   LEONARD C. MISHKIN

MAU MAU, *mou mou,* was a secret movement that included Africans who wanted to end European colonial rule in Kenya. Most who took the oath of unity were Kikuyu people who lived in overcrowded areas. The movement began in the late 1940's. British forces started a drive to wipe out the movement after a series of murders and other terrorist attacks by the Mau Mau started in 1952. Jomo Kenyatta, who later became president of Kenya, was convicted of leading the movement and was held in a remote area until 1961. When the fighting ended in 1956, about 11,500 Kikuyu had been killed. About 2,000 other Africans, 95 Europeans, and 29 Asians lost their lives supporting the government. See also KENYA (History).   CARL GUSTAF ROSBERG

MAUGHAM, *mawm,* **W. SOMERSET** (1874-1965), a fiction and drama writer, became one of the most popular British authors of the 1900's. His reputation stood far higher with the public than with critics.

Maugham usually wrote in a detached, ironic style, yet he often showed sympathy for his characters. His semiautobiographical novel *Of Human Bondage* (1915) established his position as a serious writer. Considered his finest work, it is a realistic story of a medical student's bondage to his lameness and his love for an unappreciative woman. *Cakes and Ale* (1930) is generally ranked next among Maugham's novels. It is a comic satire about an English author (possibly Thomas Hardy, although Maugham denied it). Maugham based his novel *The Moon and Sixpence* (1919) on the life of the painter Paul Gauguin. Maugham's experiences in the British secret service during World War I provided the background for a group of related stories published as *Ashenden* (1928).

Maugham's short story collections include *The Trembling of a Leaf* (1921), *On a Chinese Screen* (1922), and *First Person Singular* (1931). *The Summing Up* (1938) and *A Writer's Notebook* (1949) are the direct, personal observations of a professional writer.

Maugham wrote many sophisticated plays, beginning with *Lady Frederick* (1907). His most popular comedies include *The Circle* (1921) and *The Constant Wife* (1927).

Maugham was born in Paris, the son of a British embassy official. His full name was WILLIAM SOMERSET MAUGHAM. At his family's request, Maugham studied medicine, but never practiced after his internship.   HARRY T. MOORE

W. Somerset Maugham
Balkin, Pix

Courtesy of Mr. and Mrs. Sidney Simon, New York, New York

"Beautiful view! Is there one for the enlisted men?"

Cartoonist Bill Mauldin accurately pictured the favorite gripes and the plight of the common soldier in World War II. This drawing lampooning officers became one of his most famous.

MAUI. See HAWAII (The Islands).

MAULDIN, BILL (1921-   ), became a noted soldier cartoonist during World War II, and won 1945 and 1959 Pulitzer prizes for his cartoons. Mauldin portrayed war and the combat infantrymen as they really were. His best-known book, *Up Front* (1945), is a collection of war cartoons and their stories. His other cartoon collections include *Sicily Sketchbook* (1943), *Mud, Mules, and Mountains* (1944), *Back Home* (1947), *Bill Mauldin in Korea* (1952), and *What's Got Your Back Up?* (1961). Born in Mountain Park, N.Mex., WILLIAM HENRY MAULDIN was an editorial cartoonist for the *St. Louis Post-Dispatch* from 1958 to 1962 when he became editorial cartoonist for the *Chicago Sun-Times*. DICK SPENCER III

See also KENNEDY, JOHN F. (picture: The Nation's Sorrow).

MAUNA KEA, *MOU nah KAY ah,* is a volcano on the island of Hawaii. It is the highest island peak (13,796 feet) in the world. Measured from its underwater base, Mauna Kea is 33,476 feet tall, 4,448 feet higher than Mount Everest. Its name means *white mountain.*

MAUNA LOA, *MOU nah LOH ah,* a volcanic mountain on the island of Hawaii, rises 13,680 feet above sea level in Hawaii Volcanoes National Park (see HAWAII [physical map]). At the top is Mokuaweoweo, a crater. Kilauea volcano lies on the southeastern slope. Mauna Loa averages one eruption about every three years. The longest eruption lasted for 18 months in 1855-1856. Eruptions in 1859 and 1950 each produced more than 600 million cubic yards of lava. Most of the lava flows come from the sides of the mountain, and not from the peak crater. In 1926, lava destroyed a fishing village. Parts of other villages were buried in 1950. Lava flows sometimes threaten the nearby city of Hilo. In 1935 and 1940, bombs were dropped from airplanes in an effort to divert the lava flows. Mauna Loa also erupted in 1959 and again in 1960. GORDON A. MACDONALD

See also KILAUEA; VOLCANO.

MAUNDY THURSDAY, or HOLY THURSDAY, comes three days before Easter. It commemorates two events of Christ's last week on earth: washing the feet of His disciples, and sharing the Last Supper with them. The name *Maundy* probably comes from the Latin *mandatum,* or *commandment.* It refers to Christ's words to the disciples (John 13: 34): "A new commandment I give unto you: that ye love one another."

Traditionally, the priest girded himself with a linen towel, took a vessel of water, and washed the feet of the faithful. In Austria, Portugal, Russia, and Spain, the emperor or king used to wash the feet of 12 poor persons on Maundy Thursday. In England, servants known as *yeomen of the laundry* washed the feet of the poor while the king or queen watched. James II was the last to perform the rite in full in the 1680's.

Roman Catholic bishops consecrate the oil used in the sacraments on Maundy Thursday. The altar is stripped for the rite of *Tenebrae* (darkness). In some cathedrals, the bishop washes the feet of 12 or 13 men or boys. Pope John XXIII revived the foot-bathing custom by a pope on Maundy Thursday in 1961. Popes had not observed the rite since the reign of Pope Pius IX, who died in 1878.

Martin Luther and his followers condemned the practice of washing feet. A few Protestant groups still practice it. The ceremony is intended as a visible token of Christian brotherly love.

FLOYD H. ROSS

MAURI, or MAURE. See MOOR.

MAURIAC, *maw REE ahk,* **FRANÇOIS** (1885-1970), a French author, won the 1952 Nobel prize for literature. Mauriac's novels are set among middle-class people in his native Bordeaux. The attitudes toward sin and love expressed in his fiction reflect his Roman Catholic faith. Mauriac's novels explore the mysteries of human existence, the nature of man's destiny, and man's guilt before a judging though forgiving God. His stories are also noted for their psychology and the beauty of their language. Mauriac's major novels include *Flesh and Blood* (1920), *A Kiss to the Leper* (1922), *Genitrix* (1923), *Thérèse Desqueyroux* (1927), and *The Knot of Vipers* (1932).

In 1934, Mauriac began to write essays on his view of life and literature for the newspaper *Le Figaro.* These essays have been republished periodically in collections called *Journals.* Mauriac also wrote several plays, including *Asmodée* (1938) and *Le Feu sur la terre* (1951). His poetry was collected in *Le Sang d' Atys* (1940). His biographies include two studies of Christ, *The Life of Jesus* (1936) and *The Son of Man* (1958).

Mauriac was elected to the French Academy in 1933. Claude Mauriac (1914-   ), his son, is also a well-known novelist. EDITH KERN

MAUPASSANT, GUY DE. See DE MAUPASSANT, GUY.

MAURETANIA. See MOROCCO (History); MOOR; ROMAN EMPIRE (map).

MAURITANIA

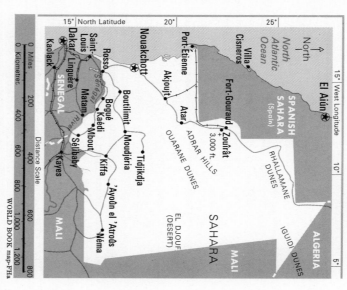

15° North Latitude

• Capital
• Other City or Town
↔ Road
↔ Rail Line
+ Highest Known Elevation
～ River

WORLD BOOK map-FHa

MAURITANIA is a big country in western Africa. It covers a larger area than the states of California, Oregon, and Washington combined, but it has only about half as many people as the San Francisco metropolitan area. Mauritania stretches eastward from the Atlantic coast into the dry, hot Sahara. The people are Negro farmers and wandering Moorish tribesmen.

Mauritania was once a colony in French West Africa. It became independent in 1960. Its name in French is RÉPUBLIQUE ISLAMIQUE DE MAURITANIE (ISLAMIC REPUBLIC OF MAURITANIA). The name comes from the fact that almost all the people are Moslems. Nouakchott, a town of about 15,000, is the capital and largest city.

Government. Mauritania is a republic headed by a president. Mokhtar Ould Daddah, the president, is head of state and head of the government. He is also leader of the Mauritanian People's Party, the only political party. As president and party leader, he has great power. But he is not a dictator. Ould Daddah must cooperate with other government leaders.

Clement Henry Moore, the contributor of this article, is Assistant Professor of Political Science at the University of California, Berkeley.

Marc & Evelyne Bernheim, Rapho Guillumette

A Holy Man in Mauritania belongs to one of the highest castes (social classes) in this Islamic republic. The tablet he holds contains verses from the Koran, sacred book of the Islamic faith.

MAURITANIA

Capital: Nouakchott.

Official Language: French. *National Language*—Arabic.

Form of Government: Republic. *Head of State*—President.

Area: 397,956 square miles. *Greatest Distances*—(north-south) 800 mi.; (east-west) 780 mi. *Coastline*—414 mi.

Population: No complete census. *Estimated 1971 Population*—1,189,000; distribution, 90 per cent rural, 10 per cent urban; density, 3 persons to the square mile. *Estimated 1976 Population*—1,312,000.

Chief Products: *Agriculture*—dates, gum arabic, millet (cattle, sheep, goats), millet. *Mining*—iron ore. *Fishing*—ocean and fresh-water fish.

Flag: The flag is green and has a yellow star and crescent in the center. The green color and the star and crescent stand for Mauritania's ties to Islam and north Africa. The yellow stands for the country's ties to nations south of the Sahara desert. See FLAG (color picture: Flags of Africa).

Money: *Basic Unit*—franc.

The People's Party selects a candidate for the presidency and then submits his name to the voters for approval. It nominates the 40 members of the National Assembly (legislature) for five-year terms. Voters then approve the nominees. All persons 21 years of age or older may vote.

Mauritania is divided into seven regions and one district. The capital makes up the district.

People. About 99 per cent of the people are Moslems, but the way of life differs among the various groups.

About one-fifth of the people are settled Negro farmers who live in neat villages along the Sénégal River. Their circular huts, which have walls made of sun-dried mudbrick, stand along narrow, twisting village pathways. Most of them speak the Tukulor language. The Negroes were the first to gain a modern education, and many hold jobs in government and as teachers.

The majority of people are Moors, descendants of Arabs and Berbers. Most Moors speak Arabic. They lead a *nomadic* (wandering) life, living in camel-hair tents and moving over the desert and other regions with their cattle in search of waterholes and sparse pastureland. The Moors are divided into two groups, the nomadic warrior tribes and the *marabout* (saintly) tribes.

Until the French came, the warriors were a nobility who kept Negro slaves. Other tribes served the warriors, whose chief occupation was fighting.

The peaceful marabout tribes have always raised livestock, such as cattle and sheep. Before French rule, leading marabout families were a learned class who studied religion and law and advised the warriors.

Mauritania has two chief languages. French is the official language, but most of the people speak Arabic. Arabic is called the national language. The Moors want to make Arabic the official language, but the Negroes want to keep the two-language system. This dispute over language is the most dangerous threat to the country's unity.

There are few educated persons in Mauritania. Only 10 per cent of the children attend primary school. About 20 students complete high school each year. Those who want higher education study in France or Senegal.

Land. An imaginary line drawn between Nouakchott on the coast and Néma in the southeast divides Mauri-

tania into two major land regions. The Sahara covers most of the country that lies north of the Nouakchott-Néma line. It is broken only by rocky plateaus and a few oases.

The small part of the country south of the line receives enough rainfall to support farming and livestock-raising. It contains two fertile areas—a narrow plain along the Sénégal River and a *savanna* (grassland) area in the southeast. Farmers raise millet, rice, and other crops on the muddy soil of the plain. Herders raise livestock in the savanna area. Eighty per cent of the people live in the south.

Mauritania's climate is hot, but temperatures vary greatly. Desert temperatures may fall from over 100° F. during the day to 45° F. at night. Port-Étienne's average monthly temperatures vary from a 91° F. high in September to a 54° F. low in January. There is little rain in the north. The south receives over 20 inches of rain a year, usually in late summer and fall.

Economy. Mauritania's economy is based on agriculture and 90 per cent of the people are farmers and livestock herders. The chief food crops include millet, dates, corn, red beans, and rice. Gum arabic, which is used to make mucilage, and livestock on the hoof are important exports. One of the world's richest fishing grounds lies off the Mauritanian coast, and Mauritania exports dried fish to other African countries.

Large high-grade iron ore deposits near Fort-Gouraud are Mauritania's most important mineral resource. A French-operated company mines the deposits. The iron ore is exported chiefly to Great Britain, Germany, and Italy. Taxes on these exports make up almost one-third of the government's revenue.

Incomes in Mauritania are low and most workers make only enough to feed and clothe themselves and their families. The government depends upon aid from other countries—chiefly France—to balance its budget. The government is trying to develop a meat-processing industry and to expand the fishing industry. But poor communications and transportation block economic development.

Mauritania's 420-mile-long railroad links Fort-Gouraud and Akjoujt with Port-Étienne, the chief port. Mauritania has about 3,100 miles of dirt roads.

History. From the A.D. 300's to the 1500's, areas of what is now Mauritania were part of two great West African empires—Ghana and Mali. In the early 1900's, archaeologists identified a ruins in southeastern Mauritania as part of Kumbi, the capital of the Ghana Empire. See GHANA EMPIRE; MALI EMPIRE.

The Portuguese landed in Mauritania in the 1400's, but continuous European contact did not begin until the 1600's. Between the 1600's and the 1800's, France, Great Britain, and The Netherlands competed for the Mauritanian gum arabic trade.

France began to occupy Mauritania in 1902 and set up a protectorate there in 1903. Xavier Coppolani became the first governor. Modern Mauritania is largely the result of Coppolani's work in extending French rule over the country. Mauritania became a French colony in 1920.

After World War II, Mauritanian political leaders began to gain power. In 1946, Mauritania became a territory in the French Union. It became a self-governing republic in the French Community in 1958. Mokhtar Ould Daddah was elected prime minister in 1959. Supported by many Moorish leaders and the small group of educated Negro leaders, he favored independence and close ties with west African countries. But Morocco claimed that Mauritania was historically Moroccan and did not recognize its independence. Some of Ould Daddah's opponents fled to Morocco and worked to unite the two countries until 1962.

On Nov. 28, 1960, Mauritania became fully independent. In 1961, it adopted a new constitution which set up a presidential system of government. Ould Daddah, elected the first president, merged Mauritania's four political parties into a single party, the Mauritanian People's Party. A 1965 constitutional amendment officially made Mauritania a one-party state.

Mauritania maintains close ties with France and has diplomatic relations with both Russia and Communist China. During the Middle East crisis in 1967, it joined with six Arab countries in breaking diplomatic relations with the United States. It resumed diplomatic relations with the United States in 1969.

CLEMENT HENRY MOORE

See also FRENCH WEST AFRICA; NOUAKCHOTT.

MAURITIUS

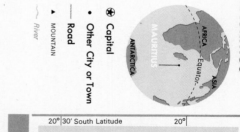

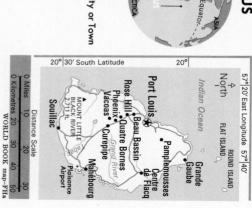

MAURITIUS, *maw RISH us,* is an island nation in the Indian Ocean. It lies about 500 miles east of Madagascar and about 2,450 miles southwest of India. Population is one of the island's problems. Mauritius is about half as big as Rhode Island, but it has almost as many people as that state.

Sugar cane fields cover about half of the island. Bare, black volcanic peaks tower over the sugar cane fields.

Sugar is the island's leading export, and two-thirds of all workers are employed in the sugar industry.

The Dutch claimed Mauritius in 1598. Later, France and then Great Britain ruled the island. Mauritius became independent in 1968. Port Louis, a city of about 134,900 persons, is the capital and leading port.

Government. Mauritius is a constitutional monarchy. A governor general, appointed by Great Britain, represents the Crown. But a premier, who is chosen by the majority party in the assembly, runs the government.

Burton Benedict, the contributor of this article, is Professor of Anthropology at the University of California at Berkeley and the author of Mauritius: Problems of a Plural Society.

———— FACTS IN BRIEF ————

Capital: Port Louis.

Official Language: English.

Form of Government: Constitutional monarchy.

Area: 720 square miles. *Greatest Length*—38 miles. *Greatest Width*—29 miles. *Coastline*—100 miles.

Elevations: *Highest*—2,711 feet. *Lowest*—sea level.

Population: *1962 Census*—681,619; distribution, 54 per cent rural, 46 per cent urban. *Estimated 1971 Population*—843,000; density, 1,171 persons to the square mile. *Estimated 1976 Population*—944,000.

Chief Product: *Agriculture*—sugar.

Flag: The flag's four horizontal stripes are red, blue, yellow, and green (top to bottom). Red stands for the struggle for freedom, blue for the Indian Ocean, yellow for the light of independence shining over the island, and green for agriculture. Adopted 1968. See FLAG (color picture: Flags of Africa).

Money: *Basic Unit*—rupee.

Mauritius controls several other islands. The chief one is Rodrigues, about 350 miles east of Mauritius. Others are Agalega, two small islands about 580 miles north of Mauritius, and the Cargados Carajos Archipelago, about 250 miles north of Mauritius.

The 70-member Legislative Assembly passes laws for the country. Elections for the assembly are held at least once every five years. Adults cast three votes, and elect three assemblymen from each of the island's 20 districts. To guarantee fair representation for minority groups, an electoral supervisory commission chooses eight more assemblymen from among unsuccessful candidates. They choose four assemblymen from minorities that do not have enough representatives in the assembly in proportion to their numbers in the population. They choose the other four on the basis of minority groups and political party. The people of Rodrigues elect two members to the Legislative Assembly.

Throughout Mauritius, councils govern villages and towns. Their members are elected by adult voters.

People. The people of Mauritius are descendants of European settlers, African slaves, Chinese traders, and Indian laborers and traders. About 2 out of 3 persons are Indians, and about 3 out of 10 are persons of European and African or European and Indian ancestry called *Creoles*. The rest are Chinese or Europeans. Most Europeans are of French descent.

About two-thirds of the people live in villages throughout the island. But most Europeans live in the towns. In the past, most villagers lived in houses that had mud walls and thatched roofs. But now many villagers are building houses with concrete and wood walls and corrugated iron roofs. Most men wear Western-style clothes. Indian women wear the colorful *sari* (a straight piece of cloth draped around the body).

English is the official language, but French may also be used in the Legislative Assembly. Most of the people speak *Creole*, a French dialect. Some Indians speak one or more of six Indian dialects, and the Chinese speak two Chinese dialects. Most Europeans speak French.

About half the people are Hindus, and about a third are Christians. Hindu temples, Moslem mosques, Buddhist pagodas, and Christian churches dot the island. Primary education is free, but not compulsory. About 60 per cent of the people can read and write. Mauritius has an agricultural college, a teachers' training college, and a university college.

Land. The island was formed by volcanoes that left the land covered with rocks and with a layer of lava from 2 to 20 inches thick. Farmers have to clear the rocks from their fields before they can plant crops.

A misty plateau in the center of the island rises 2,200 feet above sea level. This area may receive as much as 200 inches of rain a year. In the north, the plateau slopes gradually to the sea. But it drops sharply to the southern and western coasts. Dry regions that receive only about 35 inches of rain a year lie in the southwest. Coral reefs surround all but the southern part of the island.

Summer lasts from November to April, and the temperatures then average about 79° F. Southeast winds bring heavy rains to the plateau, and sometimes destructive cyclones strike the island. Winter lasts from June to October. Temperatures then average about 72° F.

Economy. More than a third of the nation's income comes from the sugar industry, and almost all its exports are sugar or sugar products. About two-thirds of all workers grow, harvest, or process sugar cane. About 90 per cent of the farmland is planted with sugar cane. Twenty-five large sugar estates own over half of the cane fields. The rest are cultivated by individual planters whose holdings range from less than an acre to over 500 acres. The cane is crushed and the sugar is processed in factories on the island.

Farmers also raise tea in the wet uplands. About two-thirds of the tea crop is exported. Some tobacco is raised and made into cigarettes. People grow vegetables in small gardens or between the rows of sugar cane. A few keep cattle, goats, or chickens. But almost all of the island's food, including rice, cattle, grain, meat, oils and fats, and wheat flour, must be imported. Mauritius has about 550 miles of paved roads. An airline owned partly by the government began operating between Mauritius and nearby Réunion in 1967.

History. Portuguese sailors were the first Europeans to visit Mauritius. In the 1500's, they stopped there for food and water. Mauritius was uninhabited until the Dutch claimed the island in 1598, and named it after Prince Maurice of Nassau. The Dutch brought slaves from the island of Madagascar to cut down the ebony forests, but they abandoned Mauritius in 1710.

In 1715, France took possession of the island, and renamed it Île de France. French colonists from the neighboring island of Bourbon (now Réunion) moved to Mauritius in 1722. They imported slaves, built a port, and planted coffee, fruit, spices, sugar, and vegetables. During the Anglo-French wars of the 1700's, the French launched attacks from the island against British shipping in the Indian Ocean and against British settlements in India. The British captured the island in 1810, made it a colony, and renamed it Mauritius.

In 1833, the British abolished slavery throughout their empire. More than 75,000 slaves were freed in Mauritius. Most of the freed slaves refused to continue working on the sugar plantations. As a result, planters brought nearly 450,000 Indian laborers to Mauritius from 1835 to 1907.

In the 1950's, Mauritius began to achieve self-government. By 1962, the leader of the majority party in the assembly served as chief minister. Later, the chief minister (now called premier) and his cabinet were given partial control of the government. Mauritius became independent on March 12, 1968. BURTON BENEDICT

See also PORT LOUIS; DODO.

MAUROIS, *moh RWAH,* **ANDRÉ** (1885-1967), was the pen name of Emile Herzog, a French novelist and biographer. Maurois tried to attain in his life and writings the spirit of the French writer Michel de Montaigne —a skeptical detachment from life, mixed with humor. These qualities appear in his best works.

Maurois's place in literature probably rests with his biographies of English and French authors. His most notable works include the lives of Percy Shelley (*Ariel,* 1923), Benjamin Disraeli (*The Life of Disraeli,* 1927), Lord Byron (*Don Juan,* 1930), George Sand (*Lélia,* 1952), Victor Hugo (*Olympio,* 1954), and three generations of the Alexandre Dumas family (*The Titans*, 1957).

His first works were two humorous novels based on his war experiences, *The Silence of Colonel Bramble* (1918) and *Les Discours du Docteur O'Grady* (1922), established Maurois as a skillful novelist with an elegant style. He also wrote popular histories of France, England, and the United States. Maurois was elected to the French Academy in 1938.

EDITH KERN

MAURY, *MAW rih,* **MATTHEW FONTAINE** (1806-1873), was a United States naval officer and scientist who did much to improve ocean travel. He has been called the *Pathfinder of the Seas.* Maury spent years collecting information on winds and currents from ships' records and from his own travels. His *Wind and Current Charts* formed the basis for all pilot charts that were issued by the U.S. government. He published works on navigation, naval reform, meteorology, and astronomy, including the *Physical Geography of the Sea and Its Meteorology.* In the 1850's, he aided in laying the Atlantic Cable (see CABLE [Atlantic Telegraph Cable]).

Maury entered the navy as a midshipman in 1825. He took charge of the Navy Department's Depot of Charts and Instruments in 1842. The Naval Observatory and the Hydrographic Office grew out of this office, and were developed according to his plans. He became a commander, effective in 1855.

During the Civil War, Maury joined the Confederate forces. He was in charge of all coast, harbor, and river defenses. The Confederacy sent him to England as a special envoy. While there, he invented an electric mine for harbor defense. He went to Mexico after the war and tried unsuccessfully to set up a colony of Virginians there. Later, he went to England, where he received honors and financial aid. When President Andrew Johnson pardoned Confederate leaders in 1868, Maury returned home. He became a professor of meteorology at the Virginia Military Institute in Lexington, Va.

Maury was born near Fredericksburg, Va. In 1930, he was elected to the Hall of Fame. RICHARD S. WEST, Jr.

MAURYA EMPIRE, *MOW ree uh,* was the first empire of India to provide a uniform government for almost the entire country. The Maurya emperors ruled from about 321 to 185 B.C. During its early period, the empire provided efficient, stern government, resulting in prosperity but little freedom.

Chandragupta Maurya, who ruled from about 321 to 298 B.C., conquered much of North India and West Pakistan and part of Afghanistan. His son Bindusara held the throne from about 298 to 272 B.C., and Bindusara's son Asoka governed from about 272 to 232 B.C. Both expanded the empire far into South India. Asoka eventually gave up further conquest. The empire broke up into smaller units after Asoka's death.

During the Maurya Empire, public irrigation works helped farms produce good harvests. Craftsmen made cloth, gold, jewelry, and wood products. Many persons worked in farms, forests, mines, and workshops owned by the state. Many peasants and war prisoners worked as slaves to develop new agricultural lands. A system of royal inspectors, spies, and informers made sure

that officials and citizens alike obeyed the emperor's will. The Maurya Empire traded with Ceylon, Greece, Malaya, Mesopotamia, and Persia. Broach, near the mouth of the Narbada River, was a seaport for commerce with the Persian Gulf states.

Pataliputra, the Maurya capital, stood at what is now Patna. It was surrounded by a wall with 570 watchtowers and 64 gates. The wooden palace of Chandragupta was in a park filled with flowering trees, fountains, and fish ponds. Asoka built a new palace of stone and also erected many stone monuments. J. F. RICHARDS

See also ASOKA; CHANDRAGUPTA MAURYA.

MAUSOLEUM. See TOMB.

MAUSOLEUM AT HALICARNASSUS. See SEVEN WONDERS OF THE WORLD.

MAUVE is a delicate pale purple or violet dye. In 1856, W. H. Perkin, an English chemist, discovered that the oxidation of *aniline* and *potassium dichromate* produces mauve dye (see OXIDATION). It is a mixture of derivatives of phenazine. It was the first synthetic coloring obtained from coal tar chemicals. FRED FORTESS

MAVERICK, SAMUEL AUGUSTUS (1803-1870), was a prominent Texas pioneer and statesman. He helped establish the Republic of Texas. His name has become part of the American language. In 1845, Maverick took a herd of 400 cattle in payment of a debt. He did not mark his cattle with a brand. They strayed, and neighboring ranchers called them *mavericks.* This came to be the term given to all unmarked cattle.

Maverick was born in South Carolina. He was graduated from Yale University and practiced law in Virginia and Alabama before going to Texas. THOMAS D. CLARK

MAVIS. See THRUSH (bird).

MAWSON, SIR DOUGLAS. See EXPLORATION AND DISCOVERY (table: Famous Explorers).

MAXILLAE. See FACE; LABIUM.

MAXIM, *MACK sim,* was the family name of three famous American-born inventors.

Sir Hiram Stevens Maxim (1840-1916) invented the automatic gun that bears his name. The Maxim gun uses the force of recoil caused by the explosion of a cartridge to throw out the empty shell and ram home a new one. The invention changed many warfare methods.

Maxim was born near Sangerville, Me. He worked for a time in a machine shop and in a shipbuilding yard. He did early inventive work on gas-generating plants and electric lighting. He lost his rights to an important patent in a lawsuit with Thomas Edison. Maxim then moved to England, where he set up the Maxim Gun Company. The company later merged with the Vickers munitions company. Maxim experimented with internal-combustion engines for automobiles and airplanes. In 1894, he tested a steam-powered airplane that actually lifted itself off the ground. Maxim became a British citizen in 1900, and was knighted in 1901. See AIRPLANE (Early Experiments; picture: Sir Hiram Maxim's Airplane); MACHINE GUN.

Hudson Maxim (1853-1927), Sir Hiram Maxim's brother, invented *maximite,* an explosive one and a half times as powerful as dynamite. Maxim also invented a smokeless powder, a self-propelled torpedo, and a torpedo ram. He was born in Orneville, Me., and worked first as a book publisher. He later became interested in explosives, and worked briefly for his brother. He set up a company, but sold out to E. I. du Pont de Nemours

& Company and acted as an adviser to Du Pont. **Hiram Percy Maxim** (1869-1936), son of Sir Hiram S. Maxim, invented a silencer for guns. Maxim also worked on mufflers to eliminate noises in gasoline engines, and developed several electrical appliances. His silencer was later used to quiet the roar of jet engines. He wrote the books *Life's Place in the Cosmos* (1933), and *Horseless Carriage Days* (1937). He was born in Brooklyn, N.Y., and was graduated from the Massachusetts Institute of Technology. CHARLES EDWARD CHAPEL

MAXIMILIAN, *MACK suh MIL ih un* (1832-1867), ruled as Emperor of Mexico from 1864 to 1867. He was a victim of a European nation's attempts to gain possessions and influence in North America.

Emperor Napoleon III of France used Maximilian to further his attempt to control Mexico. The French had landed in Mexico in 1862 to collect debts. They advanced inland and captured Mexico City. At this time, Napoleon III decided that he wanted to control Mexico. He offered the crown to Maximilian, then Archduke of Austria. Maximilian accepted on the basis of "proof" given by Napoleon and by Mexican exiles in France that the Mexican people wanted him. The United States was involved in the Civil War. It could not enforce the Monroe Doctrine, which forbade European intervention in the Americas.

Benito Juárez, president of Mexico, resisted the French (see JUÁREZ, BENITO PABLO). In 1865, Maximilian ordered that Juárez supporters be shot on sight. His advisers assured him that resistance had ended, and that this order would prevent further trouble.

Maximilian's empire was doomed when the Civil War in the United States ended. The United States could now enforce the Monroe Doctrine. Napoleon III was forced to withdraw his troops from Mexico, leaving Maximilian without support. Maximilian's wife Carlota (1840-1927) went to Europe to seek aid, but failed.

Maximilian left Mexico City in 1867 to fight Juárez. He and his soldiers marched to Querétaro, where General Gómez, a trusted aide, betrayed him. He was captured by troops of the Mexican Republic, and was executed by a firing squad on June 19, 1867.

Maximilian was born in Vienna. He was a brother of Austrian Emperor Francis Joseph. He trained with the Austrian navy and served briefly as its commander in chief. He married Carlota, daughter of King Leopold I of Belgium, in 1857. DONALD E. WORCESTER

See also MEXICO (The French Invasion).

MAXIMILIAN I (1459-1519), reigned as Holy Roman Emperor from 1493 to 1519 (see HOLY ROMAN EMPIRE). He is noted for extending the power of the House of Hapsburg through wars and marriages (see HAPSBURG).

Maximilian, son of Emperor Frederick III, married Mary, daughter of Charles the Bold of Burgundy, in 1477. He fought Mary's war with Louis XI of France for possession of Burgundy and The Netherlands. He won the war, but the Netherland states, hostile to him, signed a treaty with Louis XI in 1482. The treaty forced Maximilian to give Burgundy back to Louis XI. Mary died the same year.

Maximilian became emperor in 1493. He married Bianca, daughter of the Duke of Milan, in 1494. He fought another long war with France for control of possessions in Italy, and lost. He was forced to grant Switzerland its independence after a war in 1499.

Maximilian arranged the marriage of his son, Philip, to Joanna, daughter of Ferdinand and Isabella of Spain, in 1496. The marriage gave Spain to the Hapsburgs when Philip and Joanna's son became king of Spain and, later, emperor as Charles V. Maximilian established claims on Hungary and Bohemia when his grandchildren married heirs of these countries. He was born in Wiener Neustadt, Austria. FRANKLIN D. SCOTT

MAXIMITE. See MAXIM (Hudson).

MAXIXE DANCE. See DANCING (The 1900's).

MAXWELL is a unit of magnetic flux. It represents a single line of force. Flux density of 1 maxwell to a square centimeter is a *gauss* (see GAUSS).

MAXWELL, JAMES CLERK (1831-1879), a British scientist, was one of the greatest mathematicians and physicists of the 1800's. He is most famous for his studies of electricity in motion and the kinetic theory of gases (see GAS). He was an excellent experimental, as well as theoretical, physicist.

Maxwell used the experimental discoveries of Michael Faraday to arrive at exact mathematical descriptions of electric and magnetic fields (see FARADAY, MICHAEL). He assumed that these fields acted together to produce a new kind of energy called *radiant energy*. This led him to predict in 1864 the existence of electromagnetic waves that move through space with the speed of light. The discovery of these waves by Heinrich Hertz in 1887 led to the development of radio, television, and radar (see ELECTRONICS; HERTZ, HEINRICH R.).

Maxwell's conclusion that light waves were electromagnetic and not mechanical in nature made the field of physical optics a subdivision of electricity. His findings provided the framework for later studies of the nature of X rays and ultraviolet rays. His work on the theory of gases in motion paved the way for great advances in thermodynamics. Using statistical methods, Maxwell could predict how many molecules of a gas had a particular speed at any given moment (see THERMODYNAMICS).

Maxwell was born in Edinburgh, Scotland, the son of wealthy parents. His mother died when he was nine. He was educated at the University of Edinburgh, which he entered at the age of 16, and at Trinity College, Cambridge. He was the pupil at Cambridge of William Hopkins, who was considered one of the ablest mathematics teachers of the time. Maxwell taught natural philosophy in 1856 at Marischal College which is located in Aberdeen, Scotland.

From 1860 to 1865, Maxwell served as professor of natural philosophy at King's College, London. He left retirement in 1871 to install the Cavendish Laboratory and to become the first teacher of experimental physics at Cambridge University. He was interested in theories of color and vision, and investigated the eye disorder known as color blindness.

Maxwell published many of the discoveries which Henry Cavendish, the physicist, had made about 60 years before (see CAVENDISH, HENRY). Maxwell's best-known work, *Treatise on Electricity and Magnetism*, was published in 1873. It is now recognized as the foundation of present-day electromagnetic theory (see ELECTROMAGNETISM). SIDNEY ROSEN

MAXWELL AIR FORCE BASE. See AIR UNIVERSITY.

MAY is one of the most beautiful months of the year in the North Temperate Zone. The snow and ice have melted, and summer's intense heat has not yet begun. The first garden crops begin to sprout in May. The trees and grass are green, and wild plants are in bloom. Wild flowers that blossom in different parts of the United States include the jack-in-the-pulpit, anemone, hepatica, forsythia, dogwood, and blue, yellow, and white violets. Many birds have already built their nests, and mother birds are sitting on the eggs which will soon hatch.

May was the third month on the early Roman calendar, and March was the first. January and February were the 11th and 12th months. Julius Caesar changed the calendar to begin with January, making May the fifth month. May has always had 31 days.

There are several stories about how this month was named. The most widely accepted one is that it was named for Maia, the Roman goddess of spring and growth. But some scholars say that May is short for *majores*, the Latin word for *older men*. They believe that May was the month sacred to the *majores*, just as June

was considered sacred to the *juniors* (young men).

May Customs. Even in ancient times, May 1 was a day for outdoor festivals. In Rome, May 1 fell at a time that was sacred to Flora, the goddess of flowers. The Romans celebrated the day with flower-decked parades. The English also observed many beautiful May-day customs. Maypoles were erected in village parks. On the morning of May 1, the village youths went to the woods and gathered "Mayflowers," or hawthorn blossoms, to trim the Maypole. The girls wore their prettiest dresses, each hoping that the people would elect her as May queen. The queen danced around the Maypole with her "subjects."

Special Days. In most states of the United States, the last Monday in May is observed as Memorial Day, or Decoration Day. It is a legal holiday in memory of those who died in the Civil War, Spanish-American War, World Wars I and II, the Korean War, and the Vietnam War. The graves of war heroes are decorated with flowers. Memorial Day was first observed in 1868.

Two special days in May have been designated by Presidential proclamations. Mother's Day, first observed in 1907, was recognized officially by Congress and the

---

IMPORTANT MAY EVENTS

1 —Joseph Addison, English essayist, born 1672.
—The Act of Union joined England and Wales with Scotland to form Great Britain, 1707.
—George Inness, American painter, born 1840.
—Admiral Dewey won the Battle of Manila Bay, 1898.

2 —Leonardo da Vinci, Italian Renaissance artist and scientist, died 1519.
—Hudson's Bay Company chartered 1670.
—Catherine the Great of Russia born 1729.

3 —Niccolò Machiavelli, author of *The Prince*, born 1469.
—First American medical school opened in Philadelphia, 1765.

4 —Jacob A. Riis, American newspaperman and social reformer, born 1849.
—Rhode Island declared its independence, 1776.
—Horace Mann, American educator, born 1796.
—Thomas Huxley, English biologist, born 1825.
—Haymarket Riot took place in Chicago, 1886.

5 —Christopher Columbus discovered Jamaica, 1494.
—Karl Marx, author of *Das Kapital*, born 1818.
—Napoleon died on St. Helena, 1821.
—Mexicans defeated French at Puebla, 1862.

6 —Christopher Morley, American author, born 1890.
—Robespierre, French statesman, born 1758.
—First postage stamp issued in England, 1840.
—Robert E. Peary, American explorer who reached the North Pole, born 1856.
—Psychoanalyst Sigmund Freud born 1856.

7 —Rabindranath Tagore, Hindu poet, born 1861.
—Works Progress Administration (WPA) set up, 1935.
—Airship *Hindenburg* blew up and burned, 1937.
—United States forces on Corregidor surrendered to Japanese, 1942.

8 —Robert Browning, English poet, born 1812.
—Composer Johannes Brahms born 1833.
—Peter Ilich Tchaikovsky, Russian composer, born 1840.
—A German submarine sank the *Lusitania*, 1915.
—Harry S. Truman, 33rd President of the United States, born in Lamar, Mo., 1884.
—First V-E Day celebrated, 1945.

9 —John Brown, American abolitionist, born 1800.
—Sir James Barrie, Scottish author, born 1860.
—Mother's Day became a public holiday, 1914.
—Admiral Richard E. Byrd flew to North Pole, 1926.

10 —Ethan Allen captured Ticonderoga, 1775.
—Second Continental Congress met, 1775.
—Confederate General Stonewall Jackson died, 1863.
—First transcontinental railway completed in Promontory, Utah, 1869.

11 —Franco-Prussian War ended, 1871.
—Robert Gray discovered mouth of Columbia River, 1792.
—Ottmar Mergenthaler, Linotype inventor, born 1854.
—Minnesota admitted to the Union, 1858.
—Irving Berlin, American songwriter, born 1888.

12 —King Gustavus I of Sweden born 1496.
—Edward Lear, English author of nonsense verse, born 1812.
—Florence Nightingale, English nurse, born 1820.
—Henry Cabot Lodge, U.S. political leader, born 1850.

13 —Lincoln Ellsworth, American polar explorer, born 1880.
—Roald Amundsen flew over the North Pole, 1926.
—Austrian Empress Maria Theresa born 1717.
—Sir Arthur Sullivan, English composer, born 1842.
—United States declared war on Mexico, 1846.
—President Dwight D. Eisenhower signed a bill authorizing construction of the St. Lawrence Seaway, 1954.

14 —First permanent English settlement in America established in Jamestown, Va., 1607.

—Gabriel Fahrenheit, German physicist, born 1686.
—Robert Owen, social reformer, born 1771.
—Edward Jenner, a British physician, performed the first vaccination against smallpox, 1796.
—William Hickling Prescott, American historian, born 1796.
—Lewis and Clark began trip up Missouri River from what is now St. Louis, 1804.
—Israel became an independent country as the last British troops left Palestine, 1948.

Harry S. Truman

President in 1914. It is celebrated in honor of the nation's mothers on the second Sunday in May. The third Saturday of the month is Armed Forces Day, when the United States honors the men and women of the military services. In 1950, the Armed Forces Day celebration combined for the first time the army, navy, and air force tributes, which had been held at separate times.

The Kentucky Derby, the most famous horse race in the United States, takes place on the first Saturday in May at Churchill Downs, Louisville, Ky.

May Symbols. The hawthorn and the lily of the valley are considered the flowers for May. The birthstone is the emerald.

GRACE HUMPHREY

Quotations

Then came fair May, the fairest maid on ground,
Deck'd all with dainties of the season's pride,
And throwing flowers out of her lap around.

Edmund Spenser

The voice of one who goes before to make
The paths of June more beautiful is thine,
Sweet May!

Helen Hunt Jackson

Hail, bounteous May, that doth inspire
Mirth, and youth, and warm desire;
Woods and groves are of thy dressing,
Hill and dale doth boast thy blessing.

John Milton

When May, with cowslip-braided locks,
Walks through the land in green attire.

Bayard Taylor

Here's to the day when it is May
And care as light as a feather,
When your little shoes and my big boots
Go tramping over the heather.   *Bliss Carman*

'Twas as welcome to me as flowers in May.

James Howell

The maple puts her corals on in May.

James Russell Lowell

Related Articles in WORLD BOOK include:

Armed Forces Day
Calendar
Emerald
Hawthorn
Kentucky Derby
Lily of the Valley
May Day
Memorial Day
Mother's Day

IMPORTANT MAY EVENTS

15 —Élie Metchnikoff, Russian biologist, born 1845.
—Pierre Curie, codiscoverer of radium, born 1859.
—U.S. began first regular air-mail service, 1918.
16 —William Seward, American statesman who arranged the purchase of Alaska, born 1801.
17 —Edward Jenner, English physician, born 1749.
—King Alfonso XIII of Spain born 1886.
—King George VI became the first reigning British monarch to visit Canada, 1939.
18 —Abraham Lincoln nominated for the Presidency for the first time, 1860.
—Czar Nicholas II of Russia born 1868.
—Selective Service Act passed, 1917.
19 —Johns Hopkins, American philanthropist, born 1795.
20 —Honoré de Balzac, French novelist, born 1799.
—John Stuart Mill, English philosopher, born 1806.
—Emile Berliner, American inventor, born 1851.
—Homestead Act signed by President Lincoln, 1862.
—Sigrid Undset, Norwegian novelist, born 1882.
—Amelia Earhart began the first solo flight by a woman across the Atlantic Ocean, 1932.
21 —Albrecht Dürer, German engraver, born 1471.
—Alexander Pope, English poet, born 1688.
—First Democratic National Convention held, 1832.
—Glenn Curtiss, American aviator and inventor, born 1878.
—Clara Barton founded what became the American Red Cross, 1881.
—Charles Lindbergh finished first transatlantic solo flight, 1927.
22 —Richard Wagner, German composer, born 1813.
—Sir Arthur Conan Doyle, British author and creator of Sherlock Holmes, born 1859.
—Sir Laurence Olivier, British actor, born 1907.
23 —Carolus Linnaeus, Swedish botanist, born 1707.
—South Carolina became the eighth state, 1788.
—James Eads, American engineer, born 1820.
24 —Ambrose E. Burnside, Union general, born 1824.
—Queen Victoria of England born 1819. Her birthday is celebrated as Commonwealth Day.
—Jan Christiaan Smuts, South African statesman, born 1870.
—Brooklyn Bridge opened to traffic, 1883.
25 —Constitutional Convention opened in Philadelphia with George Washington as president, 1787.

26 —Ralph Waldo Emerson, American essayist and poet, born 1803.
—Edward Bulwer-Lytton, English writer, born 1803.
—Lord Beaverbrook, British publisher, born 1879.
—Igor I. Sikorsky, aviation pioneer, born 1889.
27 —Julia Ward Howe, American poet who wrote "The Battle Hymn of the Republic," born 1819.
—Jay Gould, American financier, born 1836.
—Arnold Bennett, English novelist, born 1867.
—Isadora Duncan, American dancer, born 1878.
—Golden Gate Bridge opened at San Francisco, 1937.
28 —William Pitt, English statesman, born 1759.
—Thomas Moore, Irish poet and composer, born 1779.
—Jean Louis Agassiz, American naturalist, born 1807.
—P. G. T. Beauregard, Confederate general, born 1818.
—Dionne quintuplets born 1934.
29 —The Turks captured Constantinople, 1453.
—King Charles II of England born 1630.
—Monarchy restored to England, 1660.
—Patrick Henry, American statesman and orator, born 1736.
—Rhode Island ratified the Constitution, becoming the 13th state, 1790.
—Wisconsin became the 30th state, 1848.
—G. K. Chesterton, English author, born 1874.
—Bob Hope, American comedian, born 1903.
—John F. Kennedy, 35th President of the United States, born in Brookline, Mass., 1917.
30 —Joan of Arc burned at the stake, 1431.
—Christopher Columbus began his third voyage, 1498.
—Kansas-Nebraska Bill became a law, 1854.
—Memorial Day first observed, 1868.
—Hall of Fame opened in New York, 1901.
31 —U.S. copyright law enacted, 1790.
—Walt Whitman, American poet, born 1819.
—Johnstown (Pa.) flood, 1889.
—Amendment 17 to the Constitution, providing direct election of senators, proclaimed, 1913.
—Battle of Jutland fought in the North Sea, 1916.

John F. Kennedy

MAY APPLE is an American plant which belongs to the barberry family. It grows wild in wooded areas of the eastern half of the United States. People often call the May apple *mandrake*.

The May apple grows in large groups or colonies. Its large leaves have 5 to 7 lobes. The leaves look somewhat like small umbrellas. They usually grow in pairs, on a stem about a foot high. A white flower grows on a short stalk in a fork of the stem. It is about 2 inches wide.

The yellow fruit looks much like a small lemon. It can be eaten and has a sweet taste. People sometimes use the fruit to make preserves.

The root of the May apple contains *podophyllin*, a poisonous substance. When dried, the roots can be used for making a cathartic drug.

Scientific Classification. The May apple belongs to the barberry family, *Berberidaceae*. It is genus *Podophyllum*, species *P. peltatum*.

GEORGE H. M. LAWRENCE

See also FLOWER (color picture, Flowers of the Woodland).

J. L. Kenner

The May Apple's large leaves and tall stem, *above*, make it resemble an umbrella. Its white blossom, *right*, is shaped like a cup. Its fruit, *far right*, is edible and has a sweet flavor.

MAY BEETLE. See JUNE BUG.

MAY DAY (May 1) is celebrated as a spring festival in many countries. It marks the revival of life in early spring after winter. Some people believe that the celebrations on May Day began with the tree worship of the Druids (see DRUID). Others believe they go back to the spring festivals of ancient Egypt and India.

The English and other peoples whom the Romans conquered developed their May Day festivals from the *Floralia*. In their April festival of Floralia, the Romans gathered spring flowers to honor the goddess of springtime, *Flora* (see FLORA).

In medieval times, May Day became the favorite holiday of many English villages. People gathered spring flowers to decorate their homes and churches. They sang spring carols and received gifts in return. They chose a King and Queen of May. Villagers danced around a Maypole, holding the ends of ribbons that streamed from its top. They wove the ribbons back and forth until the Maypole was covered with bright colors.

Children Salute May Day and Spring throughout the world by dancing around gaily decorated maypoles. Here children in many national costumes dance in New York. The maypole probably originated in England as branches decorated with flowers.

Rockefeller Center, Inc.

Other European countries had their own May Day customs. In some, the day became a time for courting. In Italy, boys serenaded their sweethearts. In Switzerland, a May pine tree was placed under a girl's window. German boys secretly planted May trees in front of the windows of their sweethearts. In Czechoslovakia, boys at night placed Maypoles before their sweethearts' windows. But in France, May Day had religious importance. The French considered the month of May sacred to the Virgin Mary. They enshrined young girls as May queens in their churches. The May queens led processions in honor of the Virgin Mary.

The Puritans frowned on May Day. For this reason, the day has never been celebrated with the same enthusiasm in the United States as in Great Britain. But, in many American towns and cities, children celebrate the return of spring with dancing and singing. Children often gather spring flowers, place them in handmade paper May baskets, and hang them on the doorknobs of the homes of friends and neighbors on May Day morning. At May Day parties, children select May queens, dance around the Maypole, and sing May Day songs. These festivals are often held in parks or in schools.

In 1889, a congress of world Socialist parties held in Paris voted to support the United States labor movement's demands for an eight-hour day. It chose May 1, 1890, as a day of demonstrations in favor of the eight-hour day. Afterwards, May 1 became a day for Socialist labor demonstrations in Europe. In many parts of the world today, members of Communist-dominated political parties and others celebrate May Day with demonstrations. In Russia, May Day is a national holiday.

Communist leaders celebrate it by making speeches and holding military parades. ELIZABETH HOUGH SECHRIST

See also MAY (May Customs).

MAY FLY is a dainty insect with lacy wings and a slender tail which trails behind it in flight. May flies are often called *dayflies* because of their short lives. Adult May flies live only a few hours or a few days. They do not eat, and usually have no mouth or stomach. May flies are not true flies. A true fly has two wings, and a May fly has four wings. May flies are also called *shad flies* or *duns*. Fishermen often use imitation May flies as lures for fish.

A *nymph*, or young May fly, hatches from eggs laid in streams and ponds. It breathes through gills and feeds on water plants. A nymph lives for a few months to two years in the water. It then leaves the water, sheds its skin, and becomes a winged *subimago*, or subadult. May flies are the only insects that go through this stage. After a few hours, the subimago sheds its skin and becomes a full-grown adult.

May flies are most common in early spring, but may occur until late fall. The nymphs serve as a source of food for fish.

Scientific Classification. May flies make up the order *Ephemeroptera*. E. G. LINSLEY

The May Fly

Gayle Pickwell

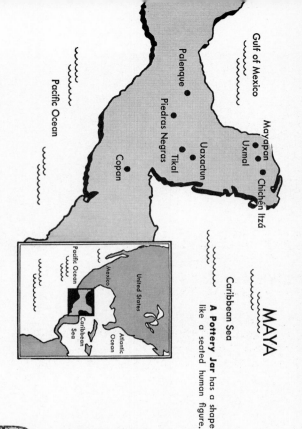

A Pottery Jar has a shape
like a seated human figure.

From *The Rise and Fall of Maya
Civilization* by J. Eric S. Thompson.
© 1954 by Univ. of Oklahoma Press

MAYA

(map labels:) Gulf of Mexico · Pacific Ocean · Mayapán · Uxmal · Chichén Itzá · Palenque · Piedras Negras · Uaxactun · Tikal · Copan · Caribbean Sea

(inset map labels:) Pacific Ocean · Mexico · United States · Caribbean Sea · Atlantic Ocean

MAYA, *MAH yuh.* The Maya Indians built a remarkable civilization in Central America. At its height, from the A.D. 300's to the 800's, this society may have included about 2,000,000 persons. The Maya achieved outstanding success in astronomy and in arithmetic. They were the only Indians in America to develop an advanced form of writing. Maya architecture and art have won the admiration of the world.

The Maya lived in most of present-day Guatemala, British Honduras, and parts of Mexico, including the territory of Quintana Roo and the states of Yucatán, Campeche, Tabasco, and eastern Chiapas. They also lived in western El Salvador and Honduras. Much of the Maya homeland was covered with a dense tropical forest and lay only 200 to 600 feet above sea level.

Today, the ruins of Maya cities that once hummed with activity lie abandoned, deep in the jungles. Tree roots force the stones of great buildings apart, and, season by season, rains wear away the stone. But much yet remains to show us how the people once lived.

Life of the Maya

The Maya Indians were short, stocky people. They had dark skins, black hair, and remarkably round heads. The people admired sloping foreheads, and flattened their babies' heads with boards. Mothers dangled

258

El Castillo, a temple-topped pyramid with four staircases, rises 75 feet above the jungle floor at Chichén Itzá.

Ewing Galloway

*Courtesy of the American
Museum of Natural History*

Hieroglyphics, as well as dots and dashes representing numbers, give important dates in the Mayan calendar in this page from the Dresden Codex.

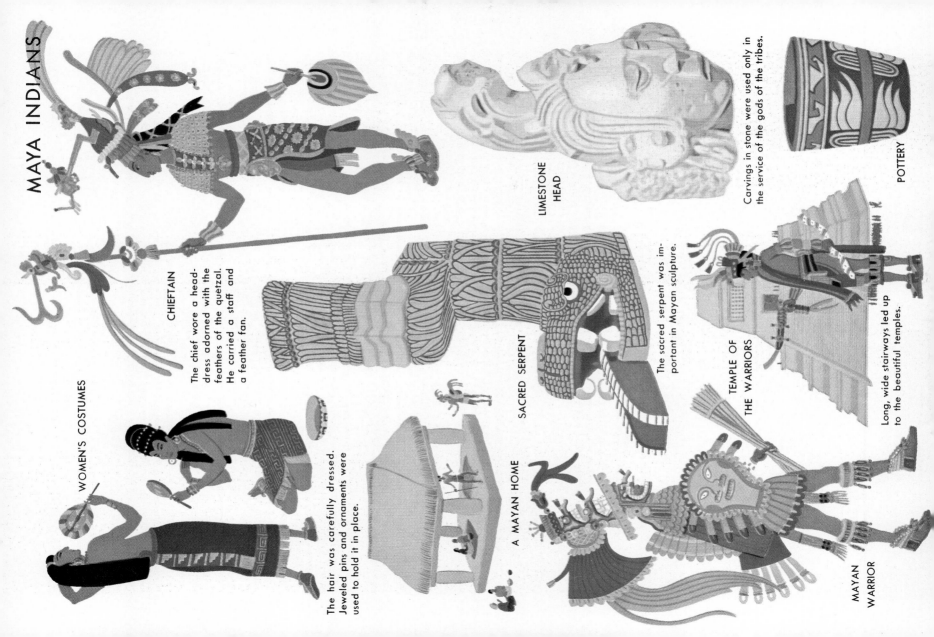

MAYA INDIANS

CHIEFTAIN

The chief wore a headdress adorned with the feathers of the quetzal. He carried a staff and a feather fan.

WOMEN'S COSTUMES

The hair was carefully dressed. Jeweled pins and ornaments were used to hold it in place.

A MAYAN HOME

SACRED SERPENT

The sacred serpent was important in Mayan sculpture.

LIMESTONE HEAD

Carvings in stone were used only in the service of the gods of the tribes.

POTTERY

TEMPLE OF THE WARRIORS

Long, wide stairways led up to the beautiful temples.

MAYAN WARRIOR

beads in front of their babies' eyes so they would develop a squint. They may have done this to honor the sun god, who was represented as cross-eyed. The Maya spoke several dialects of the same language.

Daily Life. Maya cities were centers for religious festivals, markets, and courts of justice, but they had no permanent inhabitants. Priests lived in the cities only for periods before great religious ceremonies. The people lived in single huts or small settlements of a few houses scattered throughout the countryside.

Shelter. The Maya built rectangular or oval huts with walls of poles, sometimes covered with mud. They thatched the roofs with palm leaves or grass. Most huts had a single room with wooden beds at one end and a hearth at the other. There were no windows, and smoke escaped through the roof. Until marriage, boys and young men lived in separate men's houses, somewhat like college dormitories.

Food. Corn, beans, squash, and chili peppers formed the main Maya dishes. The people enjoyed stews and flat corncakes similar to Mexican *tortillas* of today. They rarely ate meat, because their only domestic animals were turkeys and dogs.

Clothing. Men wore loincloths with long ends hanging down in front and back. In cold weather, they wrapped themselves in blankets. Women wore tight skirts or long smocklike garments. Most clothes were made of cotton, often embroidered or painted with many-colored designs, and decorated with feather fringes. Some people wore clothes made of pounded tree bark, like the tapa cloth of the Polynesians. Priests and many Maya wore necklaces of seeds or beetle wings. They pierced their ear lobes for large ornaments of jade, shell, obsidian, or wood.

Recreation. The Maya liked to dance, and did so on almost every religious or social occasion. Usually, only men danced and women were not allowed to watch. Almost every city had at least one ball court for the favorite Mayan game, which somewhat resembled basketball. Two teams tried to hit a rubber ball through a high vertical stone ring with their knees or hips. Getting the ball through the ring was so difficult that the game ended as soon as one team scored.

Religion. The Maya worshiped rain gods, gods of the soil, a sun god, a corn god, and the rulers of the underworld and of death. Several gods had more than one form. For instance, there were four main rain gods, called *Chacs.* Each was identified with a direction and a color. The moon goddess looked out for women's activities, particularly weaving and childbirth. She was the wife of the sun. The Maya believed that the gods and all human beings descended from the moon and the sun. Their descendants still call the moon and the sun "our mother" and "our father." Beginning in the 900's, the people worshiped Kukulcan, a feathered-serpent god who was the Mexican god Quetzalcoatl under another name. The Maya practiced human sacrifice, but never on such a large scale as the Aztec.

Science and Learning were in the hands of the Maya priesthood. The priests were mainly interested in problems of time. They believed that every division of time was lucky or unlucky, and was ruled by a separate god. The priests made accurate tables of dates on which to

Carving on a Stone Pillar shows a priest wearing a huge headdress of quetzal feathers. He carries a scepter in the form of a serpent. Hieroglyphics give a date equivalent to A.D. 849.

R. E. Leslie, from *Natural History*

expect eclipses of the sun, and prepared tables to determine when the orbit of the planet Venus would cross that of the sun. The priests also worked out 360- and 365-day civil years, and a 260-day sacred year. Each day in each of the three kinds of years had its own number and symbol. The relation of the various years to each other was very important in Mayan life. Priests consulted the calendars to decide which days were lucky for every undertaking, from sowing crops or building a hut to starting a war.

The Mayan system of numbering was based on the number 20 instead of 10, as in our number system. Numbers were written with dots and dashes. The Maya developed a symbol roughly equivalent to our zero, although it really stood for completion. Their use of this sign resembled our use of 0 to change 1 to 10.

The Maya recorded time on large stone shafts called *stelae*, and on altars, monumental stairways, doorways, and wall panels. The priests also recorded dates and astronomical and religious information in folding books made of bark-cloth paper. The Maya had a more advanced type of writing than any other Indian group. Their symbols stood partly for sounds and partly for ideas, and formed a kind of hieroglyphic writing (see HIEROGLYPHIC).

The Arts had a close relationship to religion. Low-relief carvings of gods and religious ceremonies decorated the stelae, altars, and temples. The designs may seem somewhat crowded today. But, according to Mayan tradition, sculpture had to show all the characteristics of the gods in formal religious symbols. Painters had more freedom to picture everyday life. They painted scenes on pottery vases and on temple walls. The bright colors and complete absence of shadow or perspective create an extremely decorative effect. A Maya wall painting appears in color in the PAINTING article.

Maya architecture consisted mainly of high stone pyramids with small temples on top. Priests climbed steep stairways to the temples, while the people stood in a court below. The Maya also built low, many-roomed "palaces" that probably served as sleeping quarters for the priests during their fasting periods before great ceremonies, and for storage, reception, and administration. The Maya never learned the principle of the true arch (see ARCH). They used *corbeled* vaulting, building the sides of two walls closer and closer together until they could bridge the gap between them with a row of flat stones. With this architecture, the Maya could build only tall, narrow, windowless rooms.

Education. Most children learned at home from their parents. Sons of chiefs and priests went to schools where they studied history, hieroglyphic writing, astronomy, and medicine, and learned how to foretell the future. Children had to know by heart the chants that told the history and legends of their people.

Work of the Maya

Farming. Almost all the Maya were farmers. They worked hard to clear land for their fields, cutting down trees with stone axes. They burned the felled trees and brush, and used digging sticks to plant seeds in the ashes. The Maya had no beasts of burden, but the thin soil would have made plows useless anyway. Their main crops included corn, beans, squash, sweet potatoes, cassava, cotton, tobacco, and cacao. The people let forests cover the cleared land after one or two seasons, because of the weeds and the poor soil. Many families kept hives of stingless bees for their honey.

Transportation and Trade. In some areas, stone-surfaced roads, usually about 30 feet wide, connected cities or parts of cities. The Maya had no wheeled vehicles, and probably used the roads chiefly for religious and civic processions. Chiefs traveled in litters carried by slaves. Traders also used the roads, but wherever possible they preferred water travel by canoes. People of the lowlands traded jaguar pelts, feathers, copal incense, lime, flint knives, and edible hearts of palm trees. In return, they received the highly prized quetzal feathers and jade of the highlands, and sharp *obsidian* (volcanic glass), which was used for knives. Yucatán exported salt and finely brocaded cottons to Honduras for cacao beans, which the people used as money.

Government. Little is known about the Maya system of government, especially in the early days. Each large city probably controlled the region around it, forming a kind of city-state, somewhat like those of ancient Greece (see CITY-STATE). A group of priests ruled each city-state. The city-states may have united in loose federations. In late Maya times, such cities as Chichén Itzá (pronounced *chee CHAYN eet SAH*), and Mayapán ruled larger areas, and controlled several city-states.

History

The ancestors of the Maya came from Asia thousands of years ago. Scholars disagree about how to relate the dates of Maya history to the present-day calendar. However, most historians accept the dates used here. Others follow a system that places these dates about 260 years earlier.

The Classic Period began about A.D. 350. During this period, the Maya produced the arts and intellectual achievements that made them famous. Cities such as Palenque (pronounced *pah LAYNG kay*), Piedras Negras (pronounced *PYAY thrahs NAY grahs*), Tikal, and Uaxactun (pronounced *WAH shakk TOON*) grew up in the lowlands of northern Guatemala and nearby Mexico. The city of Copán in Honduras also belongs to this period, which reached its peak in the 700's. During the 800's, the Maya abandoned these great cities one by one. We do not know why this happened. Many experts believe that the peasants revolted, and massacred or drove out the priest-ruler group. This revolt may have occurred when the priests tried to introduce new religious ideas and practices. Peasants probably continued to farm in the region, but they allowed the cities to fall into ruin.

The Mexican Period. In the 900's, the Maya of Yucatán and the Guatemalan highlands developed a culture with Mexican influences. Warriors called the *Itzas* enlarged Chichén Itzá and ruled much of Yucatán. This group introduced many new ideas, such as militarism and the worship of Kukulcan. We do not know whether the Itzas came from Mexico, or were Mexican-influenced Maya from an outlying area. But archaeologists have traced many of their innovations to Tula, a Toltec settlement north of Mexico City (see TOLTEC INDIANS).

About 1200, a warrior named Hunac Ceel led a revolt against Chichén Itzá, and established a new capital at Mayapán. This city ruled a large area until 1450, when its rulers were defeated by leaders of dissatisfied city-states under their control. Yucatán then split into several groups, and Maya art and learning declined.

Coming of the White Man. Spanish conquerors invaded Maya territory in the early 1500's, and subdued most of the people with little difficulty. Pedro de Alvarado led troops into Guatemala in 1523. Francisco de Montejo and his son conquered Yucatán in the 1540's. Bishop Diego de Landa ordered the Spanish to burn as many of the Mayan bark-cloth books as they could find, because he thought they "contained nothing but superstitions and falsehoods of the Devil." Only three of the books, each called a *codex*, survived.

In the late 1700's, explorers rediscovered the ruins of Maya civilization. The Spaniard Antonio del Rio excavated at Palenque in 1785. In the years that followed, several travelers and archaeologists braved the dense jungles to add to our knowledge of the Maya. John L. Stephens, an American, published two books on the Maya in the 1840's, after extensive travels. Later in the 1800's, Alfred Maudslay of Great Britain copied most of the known inscriptions and made many casts of monuments. Edward H. Thompson, the U.S. consul in Yucatán, gained world-wide fame when he dredged the well of sacrifice at Chichén Itzá in the early 1900's.

Present-Day Maya. More than 1½ million descendants of the Maya still live in the area where Maya civilization flourished. They belong to various tribes, such as the Chol and Lacandon of Chiapas, and the Yucatec of Yucatán. They speak the Maya language and observe some of the old religious practices, but know little about their ancestors' great achievements. The governments of several countries have made national monuments of the most important Maya ruins.   J. ERIC S. THOMPSON

Related Articles in WORLD BOOK include:

Guatemala
Indian, American
Mexico (History)

Races of Man (picture: The Americas)

Rubber (picture: The Original Rubber Shoes)

MAYAGÜEZ, *MAH yah GWATS* (pop. 50,147; met. area pop. 83,850; alt. 7 ft.), is the third largest city in Puerto Rico. It lies on the west coast. Many of Puerto Rico's needlework factories are in or near Mayagüez. Exporters ship large amounts of sugar from the city. Much of Mayagüez was rebuilt after an earthquake in 1918.

JAIME BENITEZ

MAYBACH, *MY bahk,* **WILHELM** (1846-1929), a German engineer, pioneered in building automobiles. He worked with his friend, Gottlieb Daimler, from the late 1860's until Daimler died in early 1900 (see DAIMLER, GOTTLIEB). They developed the first Mercedes automobile. Maybach left the Mercedes company in 1907. He invented the honeycomb radiator. Maybach was born in Heilbronn, Germany.

SMITH HEMPSTONE OLIVER

MAYER, *MY er,* **JULIUS ROBERT VON** (1814-1878), was a German physician and physicist. He and James Joule shared credit for discovering the universal law of conservation of energy (see JOULE, JAMES). This principle, known as the first law of thermodynamics, states that the total energy of the universe remains the same, and cannot be increased or lessened.

Mayer published his article on heat and energy in 1842. Joule, an English physicist, reached the same conclusions while working independently. It has never been determined which scientist made the first discovery. Mayer was born at Heilbronn.

R. T. ELLICKSON

MAYER, MARIA GOEPPERT- (1906-), a German-born physicist, shared the 1963 Nobel prize in physics with J. Hans Jensen of Germany. Working independently, they prepared almost identical papers on the shell structure of atomic nuclei. They discovered that atomic nuclei possess shells similar to the electron shells of atoms. These shells contain varying numbers of protons and neutrons, which permits systematic arrangement of nuclei according to their properties. Mrs. Mayer was born in Kattowitz, Germany (now Katowice, Poland), and studied at the University of Göttingen. She married the American chemist, Joseph E. Mayer, in 1930, and moved to the United States. In 1960, she and her husband joined the faculty of the University of California at La Jolla.

G. GAMOW

MAYFLOWER. See ARBUTUS; LILY OF THE VALLEY.

MAYFLOWER was the ship that carried the first Pilgrims to America, in 1620. It was built around 1610 and probably looked like other ships of its time, which had three masts, two decks, and resembled a cod's head and a mackerel's tail in shape. It probably measured about 90 feet long and weighed about 180 tons. Its quarter-owner, Christopher Jones, served as master.

The *Mayflower* sailed from Plymouth, England, on Sept. 16, 1620, with 102 passengers. The ship reached the Cape Cod coast 65 days after it left England, and dropped anchor off what is now Provincetown Harbor on Nov. 21, 1620. It reached the present site of Plymouth, Mass., on December 26, five days after a small party had explored the site and decided to make Plymouth their new home.

The *Mayflower* left America on April 5, 1621. Historians are not certain what happened to the ship after it returned to England. Some believe it was dismantled after Jones died in 1622, although a ship called *Mayflower* made frequent trips to America after that. Others believe that William Russell bought the *Mayflower* for salvage, and used its hull as a roof for his barn. The barn stands in the village of Jordans, outside London.

The *Mayflower II*, built the way the original *Mayflower* is thought to have looked, is kept in Plymouth, Mass. In 1957, it crossed the Atlantic in 54 days. The Britons who built the replica gave it to the American people as a symbol of friendship.

MARSHALL SMELSER

See PLYMOUTH ROCK; PLYMOUTH COLONY; PILGRIM.

MAYFLOWER COMPACT was the first agreement for self-government ever put in force in America. On Nov. 21 (then Nov. 11), 1620, the ship *Mayflower* anchored off Cape Cod, Mass. The Pilgrim leaders persuaded 41 male adults aboard to sign the *Mayflower*

The First Written Agreement for Self-Government in America was signed on the ship *Mayflower*, before the new colonists built their settlement at Plymouth. The agreement, called the Mayflower Compact, promised "just and equal" laws.

The Signing of the Compact by Percy Moran, Pilgrim Hall, Plymouth, Mass. (Pilgrim Society)

Mayflower II, built the way the original *Mayflower* is thought to have looked, made a 54-day voyage across the Atlantic Ocean in 1957. This was 11 days less than the Pilgrims' trip in 1620.

Compact, and set up a government in Plymouth Colony. The original compact has since disappeared. The version below follows the spelling and punctuation given in the manuscript history *Of Plimoth Plantation,* written by William Bradford, second governor of Plymouth colony.

"In ye name of God Amen. We whose names are underwriten, the loyall subjects of our dread soveraigne Lord King James, by ye grace of God, of Great Britaine, Franc, & Ireland king, defender of ye faith, &c.

Haveing undertaken, for ye glorie of God, and advancemente of ye Christian faith and honour of our king & countrie, a voyage to plant ye first colonie in ye Northerne parts of Virginia, doe by these presents solemnly & mutualy in ye presence of God, and one of another, covenant, & combine ourselves togeather into a Civill body politick; for our better ordering, & preservation & furtherance of ye ends aforesaid; and by vertue hereof to enacte, constitute, and frame such just & equall Lawes, ordinances, Acts, constitutions, & offices, from time to time, as shall be thought most meete & convenient for ye generall good of ye colonie: unto which we promise all due submission and obedience. In witnes whereof we have hereunder subscribed our names at Cap-Codd ye -11- of November, in ye year of ye raigne of our soveraigne Lord King James of England, France, & Ireland ye eighteenth, and of Scotland ye fiftie fourth. Ano Dom. 1620." MARSHALL SMELSER

See also PLYMOUTH COLONY.

MAYFLOWER DESCENDANTS, GENERAL SOCIETY OF, is an organization of persons descended from the Pilgrims. The general society has more than 13,000 adult members in 51 state societies. Members have proved their descent from 50 of the passengers who sailed to New England aboard the *Mayflower.* The organization was founded in 1897 to perpetuate the memory and promote the ideals of the Pilgrims. It publishes *The Mayflower Quarterly* and material about the Pilgrims and the Mayflower Compact. Headquarters are in Plymouth, Mass. *Critically reviewed by the* GENERAL SOCIETY OF MAYFLOWER DESCENDANTS

MAYHEM, *MAY hem,* in law, is the offense of making a person less able to defend himself by maiming his body or by destroying or injuring one of its members. Such injuries call for legal distinctions, because not all injuries which result from assault are mayhem. Biting off a man's ear or nose was not mayhem under the old common law. But cutting off a finger or destroying an eye came under that law, because such an injury would make a man less able to defend himself.

Modern statutes now regard as mayhem any crime of violence which causes a permanent bodily injury. The person who inflicts the injury is subject to a civil suit as well as to criminal prosecution. The word is an old form of the word *maim.* FRED E. INBAU

MAYNOR, DOROTHY (1910-   ), is an American Negro soprano with an international reputation. Sergei Koussevitzky heard her at the Berkshire Music Festival in 1939, and immediately hired her as soloist with the Boston Symphony Orchestra. He called her singing "a musical revelation." Within three months, she had appeared with four of the country's leading orchestras. Her vocal performances include selections from works by the composers George Handel and Wolfgang Mozart, and from German *lieder* (songs) and Negro folk songs.

Dorothy Maynor was born in Norfolk, Va., the daughter of a Methodist clergyman, and first sang in the choir of her father's church. MARTIAL SINGHER

MAYO, *MAY oh,* is the family name of four American surgeons who made the Mayo Clinic in Rochester, Minn., internationally famous (see MAYO CLINIC).

William Worrall Mayo (1819-1911) and his two sons started the Mayo Clinic in 1889 at St. Mary's Hospital in Rochester.

Mayo started practicing medicine in Minnesota in 1855. He became the leading physician and surgeon in the area. He was one of the first doctors in the West to use a microscope in diagnosis. In 1883, when a cyclone struck Rochester, Mayo was placed in charge of an emergency hospital for the injured. Sisters of the Order of St. Francis assisted him during the emergency, and two years later the order started to build St. Mary's Hospital, with Mayo as its head. The hospital is still affiliated with Mayo Clinic.

Mayo took an active part in organizing the Minnesota Territory. He served in 1862 as an Army surgeon during a Sioux Indian outbreak. He became provost surgeon for southern Minnesota in 1863.

Mayo was born in Manchester, England, and studied at Owens College there. He came to the United States in 1845. He was graduated in medicine in 1854 from the University of Missouri.

William James Mayo (1861-1939), the older son of William Worrall Mayo, won fame for his surgical skill in gallstone, cancer, and stomach operations. He and his brother, Charles, founded the Mayo Foundation for Medical Education and Research at the graduate school of the University of Minnesota. The Mayo brothers donated $1½ million in 1915 to establish the foundation, and later contributed more. The foundation became one of the most important graduate medical centers in the world.

Mayo was graduated in medicine from the University of Michigan in 1883. He served during World War I in the Army Medical Corps and became a brigadier general in the medical reserve in 1921. He was born in Le Sueur, Minn.

Charles Horace Mayo (1865-1939), the younger son of William Worrall Mayo, was famous for reducing the death rate in goiter surgery. He was professor of surgery at the Mayo Clinic from 1915 to 1936 and at the University of Minnesota Medical School from 1919 to 1937. He was health officer of Rochester from 1912 to 1937. He also served in the armed forces during World War I and became a brigadier general in the medical reserve in 1921.

Mayo was graduated in medicine from Northwestern University in 1888. He was born in Rochester, Minn.

Charles William Mayo (1898-1968), the son of Charles Horace Mayo, became a member of the board of governors of the Mayo Clinic in 1933. He became a professor of surgery in the Mayo Foundation Graduate School of the University of Minnesota in 1947. He was an alternate delegate to the UN General Assembly in 1953. He also served as editor of *Postgraduate Medicine*. He retired from the Mayo Clinic in 1963. Mayo was born in Rochester, Minn., and was graduated from the University of Pennsylvania in 1926.

NOAH D. FABRICANT

MAYO CLINIC, in Rochester, Minn., is one of the world's largest medical centers. Staff physicians care for clinic patients through an integrated group practice of medicine. An 11-man board of governors, which functions through several committees, administers the clinic. Board members and committee members are chosen from the clinic staff of over 400. About 650 younger physicians work with the staff, doing graduate work in medical and surgical specialties under fellowships from the Mayo Foundation.

William Worrall Mayo and his sons, William James and Charles Horace Mayo, started the clinic in 1889 in Rochester (see Mayo [family]). They developed it to care for surgical patients, and gradually added physicians and surgeons to the staff. The name Mayo Clinic dates from about 1903. Just before World War I,

the brothers turned the clinic into a general medical center. The clinic now registers more than 200,000 patients a year. It has cared for about 2½ million patients since its founding.

Critically reviewed by MAYO CLINIC

MAYO FOUNDATION, in Rochester, Minn., provides training for young physicians at the graduate level in the special fields of medicine and surgery, and in sciences related to medicine. The Mayo Foundation includes the Mayo Graduate School of Medicine, a part of the University of Minnesota. The Mayo Foundation is separate from the Mayo Clinic, but the two cooperate closely. Foundation members use the teaching facilities at the Mayo Clinic. Physicians and surgeons of the clinic hold academic appointments on the staff of the Mayo Graduate School of Medicine.

The Mayo Foundation was established in 1919 by William James Mayo and Charles Horace Mayo in collaboration with the University of Minnesota. It is governed by a board of trustees. Alumni of the foundation teach and practice medicine in all parts of the world.

Critically reviewed by MAYO CLINIC

MAYOR is the head of a city government in the United States and many other countries. The people of England have used the title for hundreds of years. Colonists in America brought the name and office with them from England. In the United States, two kinds of mayors, called strong and weak, developed.

In cities that have a *strong mayor* government, the mayor takes a leading part in city administration. He enforces laws passed by the council, and can veto council rulings. He appoints lesser officials. He may name a managing director or chief administrative officer to supervise operations of the city government. San Francisco was the first city to set up this kind of office.

In cities that have a *weak mayor* government, the mayor has little executive authority. He is the head of the government, but he does not actually direct the administration of the city. The council has the final say in governing the city.

More than half of the United States cities with a population of 5,000 or more operate under a mayor form of government. This includes 14 of the 15 largest cities. The average salary for mayors of cities with populations over 50,000 is about $15,000 a year.

In Austria, Belgium, Germany, and The Netherlands, the mayor is often called the *burgomaster*. The duties of a burgomaster are substantially those of a mayor in the United States. The position of mayor in Great Britain is largely honorary. In Canada, the mayor enforces ordinances, supervises lower officials, and presents proposals to the city council.

H. F. ALDERFER

See also BURGOMASTER; CITY GOVERNMENT; ADDRESS; FORM OF (Mayors).

MAYPOLE. See May Day; May (May Customs).

MAYPOP. See PASSIONFLOWER.

MAYS, BENJAMIN ELIJAH (1895-   ), is an American Baptist minister, educator, and public speaker. He was president of Morehouse College in Atlanta, Ga., from 1940 to 1967. Civil rights leader Martin Luther King, Jr., attended Morehouse. King's admiration for Mays influenced his decision to become a minister. Mays delivered a nationally televised speech at a memorial service for King, who was killed in 1968.

Mays was born in Epworth, near Greenwood, S.C. He earned a B.A. degree at Bates College in Maine and a Ph.D. degree at the University of Chicago. He became a minister in 1922. Mays was dean of the School of Religion at Howard University in Washington, D.C., from 1934 to 1940. He wrote *The Negro's Church* (1933). EDGAR ALLAN TOPPIN

MAYS, WILLIE HOWARD (1931-　), became one of the most exciting players in baseball history. He electrified crowds with his timely hits, "breadbasket" catches, accurate throws, and daring base running. A center fielder, Mays joined the New York (now San Francisco) Giants in 1951. He spent most of the next two years in the United States Army. He returned to the Giants in 1954, and won the National League batting title and Most Valuable Player award.

Mays hit more home runs during his career than anyone in baseball history except Babe Ruth. In 1961, Mays hit four home runs in a single game. He also led the National League four times in stolen bases. Mays was born in Fairfield, Ala. JOSEPH P. SPOHN

See also BASEBALL (picture: "The Catch").

MAYTAG, FREDERICK LOUIS (1857-1937), was an American businessman. He founded the Maytag Company, and built it into one of the world's largest washing machine manufacturers. Maytag had only 22 months of formal schooling, but his reputation for honesty and hard work won the confidence of inventors and investors, who helped build the company. Maytag became the first budget director for the state of Iowa. He also served in the Iowa Senate for 10 years, and as mayor of Newton, Iowa. He was born in Elgin, Ill.

MAYVILLE STATE COLLEGE. See UNIVERSITIES AND COLLEGES (table).

MAZARIN, *MAH zah RAN,* **JULES CARDINAL** (1602-1661), was a French statesman, and a cardinal of the Roman Catholic Church. When Cardinal Richelieu died in 1642, Mazarin became chief minister of France. Anne of Austria, mother of the 4-year-old king, Louis XIV, ruled as her son's regent after Louis XIII died in 1643. She relied heavily on Mazarin's advice.

Mazarin sought to strengthen the French rulers at the expense of the power-loving aristocracy. Abroad, he employed diplomacy and the army to break out of the encirclement imposed upon France by the Spanish and Austrian Hapsburgs. This program helped the French rulers, but placed a heavy tax burden upon the common people. Mazarin managed to keep his office except during the Fronde Rebellion, when he fled Paris twice for short periods. In 1653, he returned to Paris and ruled France for the monarchy until he died.

In serving his king, Mazarin never lost an opportunity to enrich himself. When he died a wealthy man, he was mourned by both the monarchy and the browbeaten aristocrats. The people disliked him because he taxed them heavily and thought little about their needs.

Mazarin was born in the south-central Italian district of Abruzzi. He served as a captain of infantry in the pope's army in the early campaigns of the Thirty Years' War. His skill in diplomacy resulted in a mission to France, where he attracted the notice of Cardinal Richelieu, Louis XIII's chief minister. Mazarin entered the service of France and became a French citizen. In 1641, he became a cardinal. RICHARD M. BRACE

See also LOUIS (XIV); LIBRARY (The 1600's and 1700's).

MAZARIN BIBLE. See GUTENBERG, JOHANNES.

MAZATLÁN, *MAH sah TLAHN* (pop. 75,751; alt. 10 ft.), is western Mexico's trade and industry center, and the country's largest Pacific Ocean port. It stands at the foot of the Sierra Madre Mountains, near the mouth of the Gulf of California. For location, see MEXICO (political map). Beaches, water sports, and deep-sea fishing make Mazatlán a popular winter resort. The city has a sugar refinery, cotton gins, textile mills, and frozen seafood packing houses. It was founded by Spaniards in the 1500's. JOHN A. CROW

MAZE. See LABYRINTH.

MAZEPA, or MAZEPPA, *muh ZEP uh,* **IVAN STEPANOVICH** (1632?-1709), was a famous Cossack *hetman,* or chieftain (see COSSACK). Mazepa was born in western Russia and became a page at the court of King John Casimir of Poland. According to a story, Mazepa offended a nobleman there. He was strapped to a wild horse, and sent into the wilderness. The horse eventually reached a camp of Cossacks in the Ukraine. Mazepa grew up among them, and became their leader. Later, he fought without success for the independence of the Ukraine by aiding Charles XII of Sweden against Peter the Great of Russia. Byron's poem *Mazeppa* (1819) and Tchaikovsky's opera *Mazeppa* (1883) are based on his life story. ARTHUR M. SELVI

MAZURKA. See FOLK MUSIC (The Three Types).

MAZUROV, *muh ZOO rawf,* **KIRILL TROFIMOVICH** (1914-　), became a member of the Politburo, the policy-making body of the Russian Communist Party, in 1965. He also serves as first deputy chairman of the Soviet Council of Ministers. The council is the Russian government's highest executive body.

Mazurov was born in what is now the village of Rudnya-Pribytovskaya, near Gomel', in Byelorussia. He worked with the Young Communist League from 1939 to 1947. He headed the Byelorussian Communist Party from 1956 to 1965, and served in the Presidium of the Supreme Soviet from 1958 to 1965. WALTER C. CLEMENS, JR.

MAZZINI, *maht TSEE nee,* **GIUSEPPE** (1805-1872), was a gifted Italian patriot and republican leader who played an important part in uniting Italy. He spent many years in exile because he wanted to free the country from Austrian rule and unite it as a republic.

Mazzini began his political career in 1830 by joining the *Carbonari*, a group that wanted to unify Italy. He was a bold and active leader, and was exiled from Italy in 1830. He lived in exile for 18 years, first in Marseille, France, and later in Switzerland. During this time, he kept in contact with the liberal republicans in Italy.

In 1832, Mazzini organized a new society, called *Young Italy*, to work for Italian unity. One of his followers was Giuseppe Garibaldi, who later played an important role in unifying Italy.

Mazzini returned to Italy in 1848, when revolutions broke out in many European countries. He helped organize a republic at Rome, and became one of its leaders. But French troops attacked the new government and captured Rome. Mazzini again fled to Switzerland, and later to London.

Italy finally was united in 1861 under King Victor Emmanuel II of Sardinia, but only half of Mazzini's dream was realized. He wanted a republic, not a monarchy. He tried to organize a republican revolt in

Palermo, Sicily, in 1870, but it failed. Mazzini was born in Genoa.

See also ITALY (History).

MBABANE, 'm bah BAHN (pop. 13,800; alt. 3,200 ft.), is the capital of Swaziland, a country in southern Africa. Mbabane lies in a mountainous region of Swaziland 200 miles east of Johannesburg, South Africa. For location, see SWAZILAND (map). Mbabane was founded as a mining camp. Tin mining and farming are major occupations for the town's residents. Most of the people living there are members of the Swazi group of Bantu tribesmen.

HIBBERD V. B. KLINE, JR.

Mc. See MAC.

McADAM, JOHN LOUDON (1756-1836), a British engineer, originated the *macadam* type of road surface. He was the first man to recognize that dry soil supports the weight of traffic, and that pavement is useful only for forming a smooth surface and keeping the soil dry. His macadam pavements consist of crushed rock packed into thin layers. McAdam's methods of road building spread to all nations. He was born in Ayr, Scotland. See also ROADS AND HIGHWAYS (Surfacing). ROBERT W. ABBETT

McADOO, WILLIAM GIBBS (1863-1941), served as secretary of the treasury in President Woodrow Wilson's Cabinet from 1913 to 1918. The Federal Reserve System was created during his term (see FEDERAL RESERVE SYSTEM). He also served as director general of United States railroads from 1917 to 1919, while the government operated them as a wartime measure.

McAdoo became president of the New York and New Jersey Railroad in 1902, and built the first traffic tunnels under the Hudson River. He served as acting chairman of the Democratic National Committee in 1912, when Wilson was first elected President. He was a Democratic U.S. senator from California from 1933 to 1939. McAdoo was born near Marietta, Ga., and attended the University of Tennessee. R. E. WESTMEYER

McAFEE, MILDRED HELEN (1900-), an American educator, commanded the WAVES during World War II. She received the Distinguished Service Medal in 1945 for her work as the first director of the WAVES, the women's reserve of the U.S. Navy. She was president of Wellesley College from 1936 to 1949.

Mildred McAfee was born in Parkville, Mo. She was graduated from Vassar College, and received her master's degree from the University of Chicago. In 1945, she married Douglas Horton, a clergyman. She retired in 1949. She was the first woman to become a member of the board of directors of Radio Corporation of America (RCA). JOHN S. BRUBACHER

McBRIDE, RICHARD. See BRITISH COLUMBIA (History).

McCARRAN, PATRICK ANTHONY (1876-1954), served as United States senator from Nevada from 1933 to 1954. McCarran sponsored the *Internal Security Act* (1950) and the *Immigration and Nationality Act* (1952), also known as the McCarran-Walter Act. The Internal Security Act established close controls over Communists. The Immigration and Nationality Act tightened controls over aliens and immigrants. Although a Democrat, McCarran often opposed the policies of Presidents Franklin D. Roosevelt and Harry S. Truman. McCarran was born in Reno, Nev. A statue of McCarran represents Nevada in Statuary Hall in the U.S. Capitol in Washington, D.C. F. JAY TAYLOR

McCARRAN-WALTER ACT. See IMMIGRATION AND EMIGRATION (U.S. Immigration and Emigration Laws);

McCARTHY, EUGENE JOSEPH (1916-), a United States senator from Minnesota, was an unsuccessful candidate for the 1968 Democratic presidential nomination. As a candidate, he consolidated the widespread opposition among Americans to the Vietnam War. McCarthy attracted much student support, and won important primary elections in New Hampshire, Wisconsin, and Oregon.

McCarthy's success in the New Hampshire primary influenced Senator Robert F. Kennedy of New York to enter the Democratic race. It also helped persuade President Lyndon B. Johnson not to run for re-election. McCarthy lost in three states to Kennedy, and Vice-President Hubert H. Humphrey won the presidential nomination.

Eugene J. McCarthy

McCarthy was born in Watkins, Minn. He earned degrees from St. John's University and the University of Minnesota, and taught high school and college for 10 years. He was acting head of the sociology department at St. Thomas College in St. Paul, Minn., when he ran for the U.S. House of Representatives in 1948. He served in the House from 1949 to 1959, when he became a senator. In October, 1968, he announced that he would not run for re-election in 1970. CHARLES BARTLETT

McCARTHY, JOSEPH RAYMOND (1908-1957), a Republican United States senator from Wisconsin, was one of the most controversial figures in American politics. He gained worldwide attention in the early 1950's by charging that Communists had infiltrated the government. McCarthy conducted several public investigations of Communist influence on U.S. foreign policy. Some persons praised him as a patriot, but others condemned him for publicly accusing people of disloyalty without sufficient evidence. His widely scattered charges gave rise to a new word, *McCarthyism.*

McCarthy was elected to the Senate in 1946. He attracted national attention in 1950 by accusing the Department of State of harboring Communists. President Harry S. Truman, a Democrat, and Secretary of State Dean Acheson denied McCarthy's charges. But most of McCarthy's fellow senators of both parties were aware of his widespread support and were anxious to avoid challenging him. So was General Dwight D. Eisenhower, both as Republican presidential candidate and soon after becoming President in 1953. McCarthy also accused the Eisenhower administration of treason.

A number of circumstances caused many Americans to believe McCarthy's charges. These included the frustrations of the Korean War, the Chinese Communist conquest of mainland China, and the arrest and conviction of several Americans as Russian spies.

During nationally televised hearings in 1954, McCarthy accused the U.S. Army of "coddling Communists." The Army made countercharges of improper

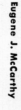

conduct by members of McCarthy's staff. As a result of the hearings, McCarthy lost the support of millions of people. The Senate censured McCarthy in 1954 for "contemptuous" conduct toward a subcommittee that had investigated his finances in 1952, and for his abuse of the committee that recommended his censure.

Joseph R. McCarthy
United Press Int.

graduated from Marquette University. He wrote two books, *America's Retreat from Victory: The Story of George Catlett Marshall* (1951) and *McCarthyism: The Fight for America* (1952).

CHARLES BARTLETT

McCARTHY, MARY (1912-   ), is an American author. She has written novels, short stories, criticism, essays, travel books, and autobiography. In each form she has shown originality, especially in her combination of intellectual analysis and satirical wit.

Mary McCarthy was born in Seattle. She described her early years in *Memories of a Catholic Girlhood* (1957). Her novel *The Oasis* (1949) deals with an experiment in group living. Another novel, *The Groves of Academe* (1952), is a study of life at an experimental college. *The Stones of Florence* (1959) received high praise for its successful blend of history and art criticism.

Mary McCarthy's first novel to reach a wide audience was *The Group* (1963).

Mary McCarthy
Pix from Publix

Partly autobiographical, it relates the stories of several girls who graduate from Vassar College and enter the world of the 1930's. In the novel, the author examines politics, suicide, psychiatry, and economics. *On the Contrary* (1961) is a collection of articles.

JOHN CROSSETT

McCARTNEY, PAUL. See BEATLES.
McCARTY, HENRY. See BILLY THE KID.
McCAULEY, MARY. See PITCHER, MOLLY.
McCLELLAN, *muh KLEL un,* **GEORGE BRINTON** (1826-1885), a Union Army commander, served for a time as the general in chief of all armies during the Civil War. He was a brilliant organizer of troops. Some authorities rank him as the greatest Northern general, while others contend that he was too cautious to lead an army. He was the Democratic candidate for President in 1864, but lost to Abraham Lincoln.

George B. McClellan
Brown Bros.

Military Career. At the outbreak of the Civil War, McClellan became a major general in command of Ohio volunteers. After clearing western Virginia of Confederate forces, he became a major general in the regular Army. In the summer of 1861, he took command of the Union Army in the East, which became known as the Army of the Potomac. He organized it into an efficient force. Later, he became general in chief of all armies. President Lincoln grew impatient because McClellan did not move against the Confederates. He relieved him as supreme general early in 1862. McClellan stayed on as Army commander.

McClellan finally advanced in the spring of 1862, moving against Richmond from the east in the Peninsula campaign. After fighting at Yorktown, Williamsburg, and Fair Oaks, he drew within a few miles of Richmond. The Confederates under General Robert E. Lee then attacked him in the Battle of the Seven Days, and drove him back to Harrison's Landing on the James River. Washington authorities then transferred McClellan's army to northern Virginia, placing most of his troops temporarily under General John Pope's command. After Pope's defeat at the second Battle of Bull Run, or Manassas, McClellan became commander of all troops in the Washington area. He led his army into Maryland to meet a Confederate invasion. He forced the Confederates to withdraw to Virginia in the Battle of Antietam, the bloodiest one-day battle of the war, in September, 1862. Lincoln, displeased with McClellan's delay in following up his victory, replaced him with General Ambrose Burnside, and his military career ended.

Other Activities. McClellan was born in Philadelphia, Pa., and was graduated from the U.S. Military Academy in 1846, second in his class. He served as an engineer in the Mexican War. He went to Europe in 1855 as a member of a commission to study European military systems, and saw a part of the Crimean War. He also devised a cavalry saddle that was adopted by the Army. In 1857, McClellan resigned from the Army to become chief engineer of the Illinois Central Railroad. Later, he served as vice-president of that railroad, then served as president of the eastern division of the Ohio and Mississippi Railroad. He was governor of New Jersey from 1878 to 1881.

T. HARRY WILLIAMS

See also CIVIL WAR (The War in the East).

McCLOSKEY, JOHN CARDINAL (1810-1885), was the Roman Catholic archbishop of New York from 1864 until his death. He became the first American cardinal in 1875. He was well known as a preacher, and knew many European Catholic leaders. Persuasive rather than forceful, he was extremely influential during a period of tremendous growth in the numbers of Roman Catholics in the United States. Cardinal McCloskey was responsible for building the cathedral in Albany, N.Y., where he was bishop before he went to New York City, and the famous St. Patrick's Cathedral on Fifth Avenue in New York City. He was born in Brooklyn, N.Y.

JOHN T. FARRELL and FULTON J. SHEEN

McCLOSKEY, ROBERT (1914-   ), is an American artist, and writer and illustrator of children's books. He won the Caldecott medal in 1942 for *Make Way for Ducklings,* and again in 1958 for *Time of Wonder.* He is the first person to win this award twice. McCloskey wrote about his boyhood experiences in his first book, *Lentil* (1940) and in *Homer Price* (1943). His summer home on a Maine island was the background for *Blueberries for Sal* (1948) and *One Morning in Maine* (1952). He was born in Hamilton, Ohio.

RUTH HILL VIGUERS

McCLURE, SIR ROBERT. See NORTHWEST PASSAGE.

McCLURE, SAMUEL SIDNEY (1857-1949), was an American editor and publisher. He founded the McClure Syndicate in New York City in 1884. This was one of the first newspaper syndicates.

In 1893, McClure founded *McClure's Magazine*, one of the first successful magazines in the 15-cent (and, later, 10-cent) field. For a short time, he was connected with the S. S. McClure Newspaper Corporation, which was formed in 1915 when McClure bought and became editor of the *New York Mail*.

McClure was born in Forcess, Ireland. His parents brought him to America when he was a child. His works include *My Autobiography*, *Obstacles to Peace*, and *The Achievements of Liberty*.

JOHN ELDRIDGE DREWRY

McCOLLUM, ELMER VERNER (1879-1967), an American biochemist and educator, originated the letter system of naming vitamins. He and his associates presented evidence in 1915 that more than one vitamin existed. McCollum classified these substances as "fat-soluble A" and "water-soluble B" vitamins (see VITAMIN). He is also known for his work on the role of calcium and magnesium in the diet, and the effect of vitamin D on bone formation. He was coauthor of the book *The Newer Knowledge of Nutrition*. McCollum was born in Fort Scott, Kan. He was a professor of biochemistry at Johns Hopkins University.

PAUL R. FREY

McCORMACK, JOHN (1884-1945), was perhaps the most famous of Irish tenors. His popularity as a concert artist was almost unrivaled. It enabled him to amass a fortune estimated at more than $1 million. He had a light clear voice and perfect diction. He sang airs of the 1700's and Irish ballads equally well.

McCormack began his career at the age of 18 by winning a gold medal at the National Irish Festival in Dublin. After study in Italy, he won immediate success in Naples, London, New York, Boston, and Chicago. McCormack abandoned opera after 1913 in favor of concerts. He was born in Athlone, Ireland, but became a U.S. citizen in 1917.

SCOTT GOLDTHWAITE

McCORMACK, JOHN WILLIAM (1891-), a Democrat from Massachusetts, became speaker of the United States House of Representatives in 1962. Before his election as speaker, McCormack had been deputy to Sam Rayburn, the top House Democrat from 1940 until his death in 1961.

McCormack was born in Boston and attended public schools there. He served in the Massachusetts legislature from 1920 to 1926, and has represented his South

John McCormack
Brown Bros.

Boston district in the U.S. House of Representatives since 1928. McCormack gained a reputation in Congress as a strong supporter of his party's legislative programs. In 1969, a group of liberal House Democrats tried to replace McCormack as speaker, but he was re-elected by a wide margin. In 1970, McCormack announced that he would retire from the House when his term expired in January, 1971.

CHARLES BARTLETT

McCORMICK, CYRUS HALL (1809-1884), invented a reaping machine that stands as the symbol of the mechanical revolution in agriculture. It was not a brilliant or even a particularly original device. Other men had developed all its main features. But McCormick's reaper came at a time when the rich prairie wheatlands of the United States were ready for development if means could be found to harvest huge crops.

The problem had two parts. (1) There were too few farmhands to do the harvesting, so a substitute for manpower had to be found. (2) The great stretches of flat, stoneless prairie presented an ideal terrain for a mechanical reaper. McCormick saw the need for this machine and made the most of it. His drive and ability made him a millionaire before the age of 40.

He was born on a farm in Walnut Grove, Va. His father had tinkered unsuccessfully for years with a reaper. But Cyrus was determined to succeed. He built a reaper and first demonstrated it in 1831. At the age of 38, with $60 in his pocket, McCormick went to Chicago. There, he set up his own factory to manufacture reapers. Through years of court action and by purchasing others' patent rights, he established the superiority of his machines, and made his company the leader. In 1902, the McCormick holdings were merged into the present International Harvester Company.

See also INTERNATIONAL HARVESTER COMPANY; REAPING MACHINE.

RICHARD D. HUMPHREY

Cyrus Hall McCormick, *inset upper right*, gave a public demonstration of his first successful grain reaper in 1831, *above*.
Chicago Historical Society

McCORMICK, ROBERT RUTHERFORD (1880-1955), an American editor and publisher, made the *Chicago Tribune* one of the nation's most important newspapers. His grandfather, Joseph Medill, gave the *Tribune* its first fame (see MEDILL, JOSEPH). With his cousin, Joseph Medill Patterson, McCormick built an enterprise that included the *Tribune*, the *New York Daily News*, and the *Washington* (D.C.) *Times-Herald*. He took over sole control of the *Tribune* in 1925. A conservative Republican, McCormick fought the New Deal (see NEW DEAL). He was born in Chicago. KENNETH N. STEWART

McCORMICK THEOLOGICAL SEMINARY is a coeducational graduate school of religion in Chicago. It grants bachelor's degrees in divinity and master's degrees in theology, Christian education, and church and community. The seminary was founded in 1830. It is controlled by the United Presbyterian Church in the U.S.A. The seminary has about 200 students.

McCRAE, *muh KRAY,* **JOHN** (1872-1918), was a Canadian physician, soldier, and poet. He contributed verses to Canadian periodicals before World War I. But he did not become famous until 1915 when he published "In Flanders Fields" in *Punch,* an English magazine. His poems were published after his death under the title *In Flanders Fields, and Other Poems* (1919). The second stanza of his famous poem is:

"We are the Dead. Short days ago
We lived, felt dawn, saw sunset glow,
Loved and were loved, and now we lie
In Flanders fields." Reprinted by permission of Punch

McCrae was born in Guelph, Ont., and was graduated from the University of Toronto. In 1900, he became a pathologist at McGill University and at Montreal General Hospital. As the chief medical officer at a general hospital in Boulogne, France, in World War I, he witnessed the suffering and death he wrote about. He died of pneumonia 10 months before the end of World War I. DESMOND PACEY

McCULLERS, CARSON (1917-1967), was a prominent American writer. She is known particularly for her sensitive account of a lonely, thwarted adolescent girl in *The Member of the Wedding* (1946). *The Heart Is a Lonely Hunter* (1940) is an account of two deaf-mutes. She also wrote *The Ballad of the Sad Café* (1951) and *Clock Without Hands* (1961). Her work is often full of fantasy. She was born in Columbus, Ga. RICHARD ELLMANN

McCULLOCH V. MARYLAND resulted in one of the most important decisions in the history of the U.S. Supreme Court. The court ruled in 1819 that Congress has implied powers in addition to those specified in the Constitution. The court also ruled that when federal and state powers conflict, federal powers prevail.

James McCulloch, cashier of the Baltimore branch of the Bank of the United States, refused to pay a Maryland state tax on the bank. The court first upheld the implied power of Congress to create a bank, because Congress needed a bank to exercise its specified powers. It then declared the tax unconstitutional because it interfered with an instrument of the federal government. In a famous opinion, Chief Justice John Marshall said that the American people "did not design to make their government dependent on the states." STANLEY I. KUTLER

McCUTCHEON is the family name of two American brothers, an author and a cartoonist. Both were born near Lafayette, Ind.

George Barr McCutcheon (1866-1928) wrote *Graustark* (1901) and five sequels. These were popular romances about adventures in an imaginary Balkan kingdom. *Castle Craneycrow* (1902) and *Brewster's Millions* (1903) also were popular. EDWARD WAGENKNECHT

John Tinney McCutcheon (1870-1949) won the Pulitzer prize in 1932 for his cartoons. The *Chicago Tribune* has reprinted his "Injun Summer" (1907) cartoon annually since 1912. Books of his cartoons include *Bird Center Cartoons* (1904), *Entertaining Prince Henry Cartoons* (1904), and *An Heir at Large* (1922). DICK SPENCER III

McDIVITT, JAMES. See ASTRONAUT (table; picture).

McDONALD, DAVID JOHN (1902-), was president of the United Steelworkers of America from 1952 to 1965. He played a leading part in the merger of the American Federation of Labor and the Congress of Industrial Organizations (AFL-CIO) in 1955. He became a vice-president and member of the executive committee of the AFL-CIO. McDonald stressed the need to help steelworkers whose jobs are threatened by automation. He was born in Pittsburgh. JACK BARBASH

McDONNELL DOUGLAS AIRCRAFT COMPANY. See AIRPLANE (Leading Airplane Companies).

McDOUGALL, WILLIAM. See RED RIVER REBELLION.

McDOWELL, EPHRAIM (1771-1830), a skilled American frontier surgeon, performed the first *ovariotomy* (removal of a tumor of the ovary). He performed the operation without anesthesia in Danville, Ky., in 1809. He published an account of three similar cases in 1817, and performed eight of these operations in 17 years.

McDowell studied medicine in Virginia and at the University of Edinburgh. He was born in Rockbridge County, Virginia. Kentucky honors him with a statue in the U.S. Capitol in Washington, D.C. HENRY H. FERTIG

McDOWELL, IRVIN. See CIVIL WAR (The War in the East, 1861-1864).

McELROY, MARY ARTHUR. See ARTHUR, CHESTER ALAN (Life in the White House; picture).

McGILL, JAMES (1744-1813), a wealthy Canadian merchant, founded McGill University in Montreal, Quebec. He willed money and property to the institution, which was chartered in 1821 and opened in 1829. Born in Glasgow, Scotland, McGill settled in Montreal in 1770, and became a fur trader. He served in the first parliament of Lower Canada. GALEN SAYLOR

McGILL UNIVERSITY is a privately endowed coeducational university in Montreal, Canada. It is controlled by a board of governors and a senate. McGill has faculties of agriculture, arts and science, dentistry, education, engineering, graduate studies, law, medicine, music, and research. It has schools of architecture, commerce, graduate nursing, household science, library science, physical and occupational therapy, and social work. Macdonald College, in Ste. Anne de Bellevue near Montreal, houses the faculties of agriculture and education, and the school of household science. McGill was chartered in 1821.

For the enrollment of McGill University, see CANADA (table: Universities and Colleges). COLIN M. McDOUGALL

McGILLICUDDY, CORNELIUS. See MACK, CONNIE.

McGILLIVRAY, ALEXANDER (1759-1793), became a powerful Creek Indian chief. His father was a wealthy Scot, and his mother was half Creek and half French. He served as a British agent during the Revolutionary War, and kept the southern Indian tribes loyal to England. After the war, McGillivray tried to unite these tribes. He tried unsuccessfully to force the United States to return lands to the Indians. He worked at times for the governments of Great Britain, Spain, and the United States. He was born near what is now Montgomery, Ala. REMBERT W. PATRICK

McGINLEY, PHYLLIS

McGINLEY, PHYLLIS (1905–), is an American poet who writes light verse. Her collection *Times Three: Selected Verse from Three Decades* won the 1961 Pulitzer prize for poetry. With affection and humor, Phyllis McGinley praises the virtues of the ordinary life. She satirizes the absurdities in life and defends femininity, morality, and domestic and suburban living in

Phyllis McGinley

Times Three and in two books of witty essays, *The Province of the Heart* (1959) and *Sixpence in Her Shoe* (1964). She sums up her point of view by quoting a man who said he had failed as a philosopher because "cheerfulness was always breaking in." She has written more than a dozen books for young people, including *The Horse Who Lived Upstairs* (1944) and *Sugar and Spice* (1960). *Saint-Watching* (1969) is an analysis of the lives of several Christian saints.

Phyllis McGinley was born in Ontario, Ore. She lives in a suburb of New York City, which provides the setting for much of her writing.

MONA VAN DUYN

McGOVERN, GEORGE STANLEY (1922–), a South Dakota Democrat, was elected to the United States Senate in 1962 and won re-election in 1968. He was the first Democratic senator from South Dakota in 26 years. McGovern made an unsuccessful bid for the Democratic presidential nomination in 1968. In his campaign, he criticized the Vietnam War and military spending and received support from some backers of the late Robert F. Kennedy.

In 1969, McGovern became chairman of a commission to recommend ways to reform the Democratic Party and its method of choosing delegates to its national conventions.

George S. McGovern

McGovern was born in Avon, S. Dak. He graduated from Dakota Wesleyan University and later taught history there. He earned master's and doctor's degrees from Northwestern University. During World War II, McGovern served as a bomber pilot and won the Distinguished Flying Cross.

In 1956, McGovern was elected to the U.S. House of Representatives. He was re-elected in 1958 and ran unsuccessfully for the Senate in 1960. In 1961, President John F. Kennedy named him director of the Food for Peace program.

McGUFFEY, WILLIAM HOLMES (1800-1873), was an American educator and clergyman. From 1836 to 1857, he published illustrated reading books for the first six grades of elementary schools. More than 120 million copies of his *Eclectic Reader* were sold, and for many years

nearly all American school children learned to read from it.

The simple readers told stories designed to win the students' interest. They taught children to respect the United States governmental and economic system. They played an important part in forming the moral ideas and the literary tastes of the United States in the 1800's.

McGuffey was born on Sept. 23, 1800, in Washington County, Pennsylvania. He was graduated from Washington College, and became a Presbyterian minister in 1829.

William H. McGuffey, above, was an American educator. His *Eclectic Reader* was used in all parts of the United States. Millions of copies were sold during the 1800's.

McGuffey taught at Miami University in Ohio from 1826 to 1836, and he was president of Ohio University from 1839 to 1845. After 1845, he taught at the University of Virginia.

CLAUDE A. EGGERTSEN

14   NEW SECOND READER.

LESSON II.

THE SCHOOL-BOY.

flew	trees	catch	ver'y	lit'tle
once	birds	think	po'ny	tall'er
been	knew	found	ta'ble	a-way'
come	grass	would	wi'ser	sum'mer
much	shone	school	stud'y	morn'ing

1. I once knew a boy. He was not a big boy.

2. If he had been a big boy, he would have been wi-ser.

3. But he was a lit-tle boy. He was not much tall-er than the ta-ble.

DAVID S. BRODER

McGUIGAN, *muh GWIG ahn,* **JAMES CHARLES CARDINAL** (1894-   ), is a Canadian cardinal of the Roman Catholic Church. He was ordained a priest in 1918. He was elevated to archbishop of Regina in 1930, and became archbishop of Toronto in 1934. He was made a cardinal in 1946.

Cardinal McGuigan was born in Hunter River, Prince Edward Island. He studied in Charlottetown at Prince of Wales College and St. Dunstan's University (now joined as the University of Prince Edward Island). He attended the Grand Seminary of Laval University, Quebec, and the Catholic University of America in Washington, D.C.   WILLIAM R. WILLOUGHBY

McGUIRE AIR FORCE BASE, N.J., is the site of headquarters of the Twenty-first Air Force of the Military Airlift Command (MAC). The base is a departure point for MAC flights over the Atlantic Ocean and the Caribbean Sea. Fighter-interceptor aircraft, air-defense missiles, and a Strategic Air Command air-refueling unit are also based there. The 3,547-acre base lies beside Fort Dix, about 18 miles southeast of Trenton. It was established in 1942. In 1949, the Air Force named the base for Major Thomas B. McGuire, Jr., a U.S. fighter pilot killed in World War II. McGuire was the second ranking Air Force ace of the war.   RICHARD M. SKINNER

McHENRY, FORT. See FORT McHENRY NATIONAL MONUMENT AND HISTORIC SHRINE.

McHENRY, JAMES (1753-1816), was an American soldier and statesman. As a Maryland delegate to the Constitutional Convention of 1787, he signed the United States Constitution and was Secretary of War from 1796 to 1800. During the Revolutionary War, he served as secretary to General George Washington, on Marquis de Lafayette's staff, and as a surgeon. Born in Ballymena, Ireland, he served in the Congress of the Confederation from 1783 to 1786.   KENNETH R. ROSSMAN

McINTYRE, JAMES FRANCIS CARDINAL (1886-   ), served as the Roman Catholic Archbishop of Los Angeles from 1948 until he resigned in 1970. He was named a cardinal by Pope Pius XII in 1953. He left a promising business career in New York City in 1915, and was ordained six years later. He was an auxiliary bishop and coadjutor archbishop in New York City. In Los Angeles, he worked to make more educational facilities available to the growing numbers of Roman Catholics in the area. Cardinal McIntyre was born in New York City.   JOHN T. FARRELL and FULTON J. SHEEN

McIVER, HELENE MADISON. See SWIMMING (Famous Swimmers).

McKAY, ALEXANDER (?-1811), a Canadian fur trader and explorer, spent most of his life as a member of the North West Company. He accompanied Alexander Mackenzie on the first overland trip made by white men across North America (see MACKENZIE, SIR ALEXANDER). They reached the Pacific Coast in 1793.

McKay and others from the North West Company joined John Jacob Astor's Pacific Fur Company in 1810. They sailed to Oregon to build Astoria, their western headquarters. Shortly after their arrival, hostile Indians boarded their ship, *Tonquin.* The Indians killed McKay and all others on board.   HOWARD R. LAMAR

McKAY, CLAUDE (1890-1948), was a Negro poet and novelist. His poetry is noted for its lyricism and its powerful statements of Negro feelings. His four novels include *Home to Harlem* (1928), the story of a

black soldier's return from France to the United States after World War I. McKay also wrote an autobiography, *A Long Way from Home* (1937), and *Harlem* (1940), a study of Negro life in New York City.

McKay was born in Jamaica. His first two works were collections of poetry published there—*Songs of Jamaica* (1911) and *Constab Ballads* (1912). McKay moved to the United States in 1912 and studied briefly at Tuskegee Institute and Kansas State University. He then lived in New York City, London, and Paris. McKay was associate editor of the socialist newspaper *The Liberator* for several years.   DEAN DONER

McKAY, DONALD (1810-1880), was a Canadian master craftsman who designed and built over 90 clipper ships. They were the fastest sailing vessels ever built, famed for grace and seaworthiness. McKay's beautiful *Flying Cloud,* 1,783 tons, was launched in 1851. It sailed around Cape Horn from New York to San Francisco in 89 days, and covered 374 nautical miles in one day. Both the speed of the cruise and the speed of the day's run set world records for sailing ships. McKay launched the *Great Republic,* the largest sailing ship ever built, in 1853. McKay was born in Shelbourne County, Nova Scotia. V. E. CANGELOSI and R. E. WESTMEYER

McKEAN, THOMAS (1734-1817), was a Delaware signer of the Declaration of Independence. He served as a delegate to the Continental Congress and the Congress of the Confederation from 1774 to 1783, and was governor of Pennsylvania from 1799 to 1808. During his career as governor, he restrained radical politicians whose plans might have reduced the state to a condition of anarchy. McKean was born in New London, Pa. He studied law, and wrote most of the Delaware state constitution.   CLARENCE L. VER STEEG

McKEE JUNGLE GARDENS. See FLOWER (Famous Flower Gardens).

McKEESPORT, *muh KEES pohrt,* Pa. (pop. 45,489; alt. 750 ft.), lies in the heart of the natural-gas and coal fields of southwestern Pennsylvania. It is located about 14 miles southeast of Pittsburgh. For location, see PENNSYLVANIA (political map). McKeesport was named after its first settler, David McKee, who operated a ferryboat service there in the early 1700's. McKeesport is often called the *Tube City* because it is the home of one of the greatest steel-tube works in the world. A great iron and steel center, it also produces tin plate, automobile wheels and bodies, tools and dies, cans, glass, and candy.

McKeesport was founded in 1795 by John McKee, son of the first settler. In 1830, miners opened the first coal fields nearby. McKeesport became a borough in 1842 and a city in 1890. The commission form of government was adopted in 1913.   S. K. STEVENS

McKIM, CHARLES FOLLEN (1847-1909), was an American architect. He helped make popular the building styles of the Renaissance and of classic Greece and Rome. These styles dominated American architecture for the 40 years from 1880 to 1920. McKim and his associates designed the Boston Public Library and the Pennsylvania Railway Station in New York City. He worked with Stanford White (see WHITE, STANFORD). He was born in Isabella Furnace, Pa.   HUGH MORRISON

McKINLEY, MOUNT. See MOUNT McKINLEY.

WILLIAM McKINLEY

25TH PRESIDENT OF THE UNITED STATES 1897-1901

B. HARRISON
23rd President
1889 — 1893

CLEVELAND
24th President
1893 — 1897

T. ROOSEVELT
26th President
1901 — 1909

TAFT
27th President
1909 — 1913

The United States Flag had 45 stars when McKinley took office.

McKINLEY, WILLIAM (1843-1901), guided the United States into the path toward world leadership. During his term, American business flourished at home and abroad, and American soldiers and sailors won the nation a world power. This victory made the Spanish-American War. Guam, Hawaii, the Philippines, Puerto Rico, and American Samoa all came under the Stars and Stripes.

McKinley, a Republican, succeeded Grover Cleveland, and twice defeated William Jennings Bryan for the presidency. An assassin shot McKinley six months after the start of his second term, and Vice-President Theodore Roosevelt took office. McKinley was the third President to be assassinated, and the fifth to die in office.

His friends considered McKinley tactful and charming. Others sometimes regarded him as cold and pompous, perhaps because of his rigid bearing, piercing eyes, and his tight, thin lips. He went to church regularly and lavished great care and affection upon his invalid wife. He combined a stubborn dedication to the major goals of his administration with a politician's shrewd sense for compromise. This political flexibility was demonstrated by McKinley's changing attitudes toward tariffs and silver coinage in his later years.

The number of business trusts reached a new high under McKinley, and his administration did little to enforce the antitrust laws. Cries for change from farmers, labor leaders, and other reformers received scant notice from a people enjoying newly found economic prosperity and international prestige.

Electric lights and telephones added to the excitement of McKinley's day, along with snorting "horseless carriages." The people sang such hit tunes of the Gay 90's as "My Wild Irish Rose" and "Because." Lillian Russell reigned as the leading star of Broadway. The farm workers and immigrants who crowded into the sprawling tenement districts of big cities worked hard and long, often 85 hours a week.

Early Life

Childhood. William McKinley was born on Jan. 29, 1843, in Niles, Ohio, a rural town with a population of about 300. A country store occupied part of the first floor of the long, two-story family home. McKinley's father, also named William, and his mother, Nancy Allison McKinley, were of Scotch-Irish ancestry. His great-great-grandfather had sailed to America from Ireland in 1743 and settled in Pennsylvania. His grandfather, James McKinley, moved to Ohio about 1830 and set up an iron foundry.

Education. William, the seventh of nine children,

— IMPORTANT DATES IN McKINLEY'S LIFE —

1843	(Jan. 29) Born in Niles, Ohio.
1871	(Jan. 25) Married Ida Saxton.
1876	Elected to U.S. House of Representatives.
1891	Elected governor of Ohio.
1896	Elected President of the United States.
1900	Re-elected President of the United States.
1901	(Sept. 6) Shot by assassin in Buffalo, N.Y.
1901	(Sept. 14) Died in Buffalo from bullet wounds.

McKINLEY, WILLIAM

first attended school in Niles. When he was 9 years old, his parents decided that the school was not adequate. The family, except his father, moved to the town of Poland, near Youngstown. His father had to remain in Niles for a time because of his iron-manufacturing business.

William entered the Poland Seminary, a private school. He studied hard and recited his lessons easily. At the age of 10, he joined the Methodist Episcopal Church. He attended Sunday school regularly, and his mother hoped that he might become a bishop.

At 17, McKinley entered the junior class of Allegheny College in Meadville, Pa. Severe illness soon forced him to return home. He later taught briefly in a country school.

Bravery Under Fire. When the Civil War broke out in 1861, McKinley was the first man in his home town to volunteer. He became a commissary sergeant in a regiment commanded by another future President,

Rutherford B. Hayes. McKinley carried food and coffee to the regiment during the Battle of Antietam. His bravery under fire earned him a commission as second lieutenant. By the end of the war he had been promoted to brevet major.

After the war, McKinley decided to become a lawyer. He studied for about 18 months in the office of County Judge Charles E. Glidden in Youngstown. In 1866, he entered law school in Albany, N.Y. He was admitted to the bar in 1867, and began practicing law in Canton, Ohio.

Political and Public Activities

Entry into Politics. Early in life McKinley developed a strong interest in politics, and an ambition for high office. Many years later, he said: "I have never been in doubt since I was old enough to think intelligently

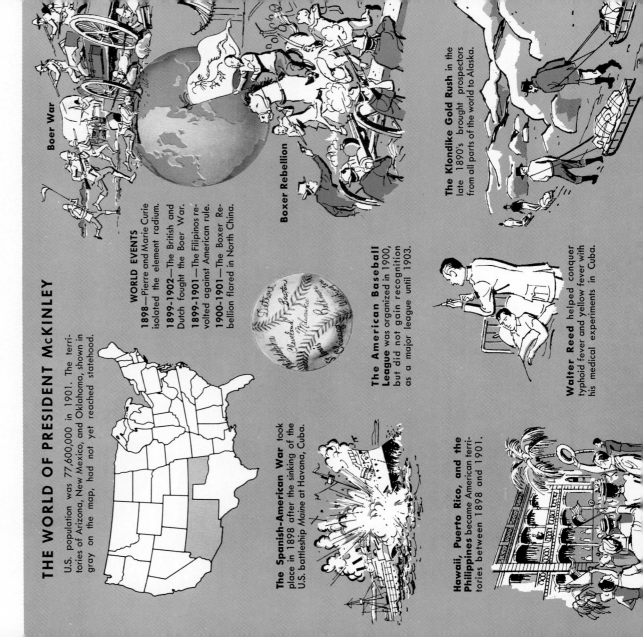

THE WORLD OF PRESIDENT McKINLEY

U.S. population was 77,600,000 in 1901. The territories of Arizona, New Mexico, and Oklahoma, shown in gray on the map, had not yet reached statehood.

The Spanish-American War took place in 1898 after the sinking of the U.S. battleship Maine at Havana, Cuba.

Hawaii, Puerto Rico, and the Philippines became American territories between 1898 and 1901.

The American Baseball League was organized in 1900, but did not gain recognition as a major league until 1903.

Walter Reed helped conquer typhoid fever and yellow fever with his medical experiments in Cuba.

WORLD EVENTS

1898—Pierre and Marie Curie isolated the element radium.

1899-1902—The British and Dutch fought the Boer War.

1899-1901—The Filipinos revolted against American rule.

1900-1901—The Boxer Rebellion flared in North China.

Boer War

Boxer Rebellion

The Klondike Gold Rush in the late 1890's brought prospectors from all parts of the world to Alaska.

that I would sometime be made President." In 1869, he won his first public office as prosecuting attorney of Stark County. This victory came as a personal tribute, because McKinley was a Republican and the county usually voted Democratic.

McKinley's Family. On Jan. 25, 1871, McKinley married Ida Saxton (June 8, 1847-May 26, 1907), whose grandfather had founded the first newspaper in Canton. At the time of her marriage, she was working as a cashier in her father's bank. The McKinleys had two daughters. The other daughter, Ida, died in 1873 when she was only 4 months old. Mrs. McKinley's mother also died that year. The younger one, Katherine, died at the age of 4 in 1876. Overwhelmed by shock and grief, Mrs. McKinley remained an invalid the rest of her life. She later developed epilepsy. McKinley was devoted to his wife and constantly cared for all her needs. When he was governor of Ohio, he would turn his back before entering the state house in Columbus, then remove his hat and bow to his wife in their hotel room window across the street. He waved to her from a window at 3 o'clock every afternoon.

Congressman. McKinley was elected to the United States House of Representatives in 1876. He served until 1891, except for one break of 10 months. In May, 1884, the House voted to unseat McKinley, upholding the claim of Jonathan H. Wallace, a lawyer, that he had defeated McKinley in the election of 1882.

McKinley gained his greatest fame as a Congressman by vigorously supporting high tariffs to protect American industries from foreign competition. "Let England take care of herself," he cried, "let France look after her own interests, let Germany take care of her own people, but in God's name let Americans look after America." In 1890, he sponsored a tariff bill that raised duties to new highs.

In Congress, McKinley allied himself with men who favored an expansion of silver currency. He voted for bills providing for unlimited and, later, limited purchase and coinage of silver.

Governor. In 1890, McKinley lost his bid for an

eighth term in Congress. His tariff measure had proved unpopular, and he ran for office in a district that the Democratic-controlled state legislature had gerrymandered (see GERRYMANDER). The next year, McKinley rose from his defeat to win the governorship of Ohio. He improved the state's canals, roads, and public institutions. He established a state board of arbitration to settle labor disputes. His widening political fame brought him into contact with many men of national influence, including the Cleveland millionaire Marcus A. Hanna. In 1892, Hanna opened an unofficial McKinley-for-President headquarters at the Republican national convention in Minneapolis. McKinley received 182 votes, second only to the nominee, Benjamin Harrison. In 1893, McKinley won re-election as governor.

Crisis and Triumph. A personal financial crisis almost sidetracked McKinley's political career in 1893. He had cosigned notes totaling $100,000 to help a friend enter the manufacture of tin plate. The enterprise failed, and the banks came to McKinley for payment. Threatened with bankruptcy, McKinley appealed to Hanna for help. His wealthy political sponsor and a few other men raised enough money to pay off the entire debt, thus saving McKinley's future.

Hanna now set out to have McKinley nominated as the Republican candidate for President in 1896. He did his work so well that two thirds of the delegates arrived at the national convention with instructions to vote for McKinley. The convention also nominated a friend of Hanna, state Senator Garret A. Hobart of New Jersey, for Vice-President (see HOBART, GARRET A.).

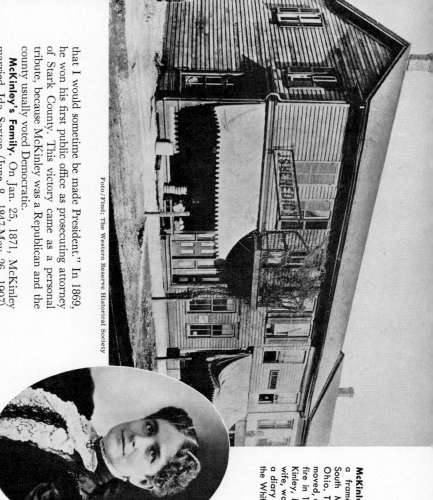

Foto/Findt: The Western Reserve Historical Society

McKinley's Birthplace, left, a frame building, stood on South Main Street in Niles, Ohio. The house was later moved, and then destroyed by fire in 1937. Ida Saxton McKinley, below, the President's wife, was an invalid. She kept a diary during his last year in the White House.

McKINLEY'S FIRST ELECTION

Place of Nominating Convention..St. Louis

Ballot on Which Nominated.....1st

Democratic Opponent..........William Jennings Bryan

Electoral Vote................271 (McKinley) to
176 (Bryan)

Popular Vote.................7,102,246 (McKinley) to
6,492,559 (Bryan)

Age at First Inauguration......54

The Democrats nominated the great orator William Jennings Bryan for President, and chose Arthur Sewall, a wealthy Maine shipbuilder, as his running mate. They campaigned against McKinley and Hobart as symbols of the plutocracy, or "rule of the rich."

The "Front Porch" Campaign. Hanna collected more than $3,500,000 in campaign funds, an astounding sum then. McKinley refused to leave his invalid wife for long campaign tours, so Hanna arranged to have thousands of visitors travel to Canton. McKinley stood on his front porch and gave brief, well-rehearsed talks keyed to the interests of the delegations.

McKinley expected to make high protective tariffs the chief issue of the campaign. But, at the Democratic national convention, Bryan delivered his famous "cross of gold" speech and raised the currency issue to first place in the campaign (see BRYAN [William Jennings]). As a Congressman, McKinley had favored the limited coinage of silver. He now took the opposite view. Business conditions favored a Republican sweep, and McKinley won by over 600,000 votes.

McKinley's Administration (1897-1901)

True to his campaign promise, McKinley persuaded Congress to pass a protective tariff in 1897 that sent rates higher than ever before. Congress also enacted another important bill, the Gold Standard Act of 1900 (see MONEY [U.S. Monetary Standards]).

The Spanish-American War. A Cuban revolt against Spanish rule had been under way for two years when McKinley took office in 1897. Despite pressure for American support of the revolutionists, McKinley sought to maintain neutrality. Then, on Feb. 15, 1898, the battleship U.S.S. Maine blew up in Havana harbor. The exact cause of the explosion has never been discovered, but many Americans thought the ship had been sunk by the Spaniards. Public clamor for war with Spain increased and soon reached fever pitch. Many Congressmen, the newspapers of William Randolph Hearst and some other publishers, and such expansion-minded men as Assistant Secretary of the Navy Theodore Roosevelt urged McKinley to declare war. For weeks McKinley pondered an answer. Roosevelt called him a "white-livered cur" who had "prepared two messages, one for war and one for peace, and doesn't know which one to send in." McKinley finally yielded to the demands for war. In his war message to Congress on April 11, McKinley declared: "In the name of humanity, in the name of civilization, in behalf of endangered American interests which give us the right and duty to speak and act, the war in Cuba must stop." See SPANISH-AMERICAN WAR.

America Enters World Affairs. The war with Spain lasted only 113 days. But it brought the nation into world politics, in both Europe and the Far East. In the peace treaty with Spain, the United States acquired Guam, the Philippines, and Puerto Rico. American expansion and influence soon extended to other areas. Pressured by American business interests, Congress annexed Hawaii in 1898. As the United States consolidated its Pacific possessions, the Filipinos revolted against American rule. McKinley finally concluded that "there was nothing left for us to do but to take them all, and educate the Filipinos, and uplift and civilize and Christianize them . . ."

In 1899, the United States issued the "Open-Door" notes asking for equality of trade in the vast and promising China market (see OPEN-DOOR POLICY). That same year, Tutuila and several smaller islands in the

Front Porch Campaign. McKinley remained at home in Canton, Ohio, during his presidential campaigns and gave rehearsed speeches. He refused to leave his wife for tours about the country.

Culver

VICE-PRESIDENTS AND CABINET

Vice-President...........*Garret A. Hobart
*Theodore Roosevelt(1901)

Secretary of State......*John Sherman
William R. Day (1898)
*John M. Hay (1898)

Secretary of the Treasury.....Lyman J. Gage

Secretary of War..............Russell A. Alger
*Elihu Root (1899)

Attorney General.............Joseph McKenna
John W. Griggs (1898)
*Philander C. Knox (1901)

Postmaster General...........James A. Gary
Charles E. Smith (1898)

Secretary of the Navy........John D. Long

Secretary of the Interior....Cornelius N. Bliss
Ethan A. Hitchcock (1898)

Secretary of Agriculture.....James Wilson

*Has a separate biography in WORLD BOOK.

McKINLEY, WILLIAM

Samoan group came under United States control.

Life in the White House remained simple during McKinley's administration. Because of her illness, Mrs. McKinley did not take part in managing the White House. Her relatives and the President's nieces often served as official hostesses. McKinley reserved a private room on the second floor of the White House to greet his many visitors. Mrs. McKinley usually sat in a chair beside the President as he stood in the receiving line at receptions. The devoted couple often enjoyed long drives in their horse-drawn carriage.

At official dinners, McKinley seated his wife at his right so he could help her if necessary. In doing this, he ignored protocol which directed that the President's wife sit across the table from him.

"The Full Dinner Pail." The Republicans renominated McKinley by acclamation in 1900. For Vice-President, the delegates selected Theodore Roosevelt, who had returned as a hero from the Spanish-American War to be elected governor of New York.

The Democrats again nominated Bryan, and named Adlai E. Stevenson, Vice-President from 1893 to 1897, as his running mate. They campaigned for free silver and against imperialism.

But prosperity became the real issue of the campaign. The Republicans claimed that McKinley's re-election would give the people "four years more of the full dinner pail." The President won a sweeping victory.

Second Term. McKinley's second term also saw several events of international significance. The Supreme Court affirmed in the "Insular Cases" that the residents of the newly acquired dependencies did not have the rights of citizens and that Congress could impose tariffs on their trade. The United States had established civil government in Puerto Rico, and set up free trade with it. In June, 1901, Cuba added to its constitution an amendment that recognized the right of the United States to intervene in Cuban affairs under certain circumstances. In the Philippines, the appointment of William Howard Taft as civil governor paved the way for peace in the islands in 1902.

Assassination. McKinley delivered one of the most important speeches of his career at the Pan-American Exposition in Buffalo, N.Y., on Sept. 5, 1901. He expressed the hope that "by sensible trade relations which will not interrupt our home production, we shall extend the outlets for our increasing surplus . . . The period of exclusiveness is past." Such a position meant that McKinley had modified his high-tariff policy.

The next day, McKinley held a public reception in the exposition's Temple of Music. Hundreds of persons waited to shake his hand. Standing in the crowd was

---

McKINLEY'S SECOND ELECTION

Place of Nominating Convention.	Philadelphia
Ballot on Which Nominated.	1st
Democratic Opponent.	William Jennings Bryan
Electoral Vote.	292 (McKinley) to 155 (Bryan)
Popular Vote.	7,218,491 (McKinley) to 6,356,734 (Bryan)
Age at Second Inauguration.	58

---

an anarchist named Leon F. Czolgosz. As McKinley drew near, Czolgosz extended his left hand to grasp McKinley's outstretched hand. Czolgosz fired two bullets into the President's body with a revolver concealed by a handkerchief in his right hand. McKinley slumped forward, gasping, "Am I shot?" The crowd pounced on the assassin and began beating him. McKinley pointed to Czolgosz, imploring, "Let no one hurt him." He whispered to his secretary: "My wife—be careful, Cortelyou, how you tell her—oh, be careful." An ambulance rushed the wounded President to a hospital for emergency surgery. For a time, McKinley appeared to be recovering, but he died on September 14. Czolgosz, who had confessed a great urge to kill a "great ruler," was later electrocuted.

Roosevelt, who had been vacationing in the Adirondack Mountains, did not arrive in Buffalo until after McKinley had died. He then took the oath of office as President.

Mrs. McKinley, at the home of the president of the exposition, did not learn of the shooting until several hours later. She was so shocked that she never returned to the White House. Nor did she attend the burial rites. During her final years she lived in Canton. She died in 1907, and was buried there beside her husband at the McKinley Memorial.

An authoritative biography of McKinley is *In the Days of McKinley* by Margaret Leech.   OSCAR HANDLIN

Related Articles in WORLD BOOK include:

Bryan (William Jennings)	Ohio (Places to Visit)
Buffalo (Interesting	Philippines (History)
Places to Visit)	President of the United States
Cuba (History)	Puerto Rico (History)
Hanna, "Mark,"	Spanish-American War
Marcus A.	Tariff
Hobart, Garret	Trust
Augustus	

Outline

I. Early Life
  A. Childhood
  B. Education
  C. Bravery Under Fire

II. Political and Public Activities
  A. Entry into Politics
  B. McKinley's Family
  C. Congressman
  D. Governor
  E. Crisis and Triumph
  F. The "Front Porch" Campaign

III. McKinley's Administration (1897-1901)
  A. The Spanish-American War
  B. America Enters World Affairs
  C. Life in the White House
  D. "The Full Dinner Pail"
  E. Second Term
  F. Assassination

Questions

Why was McKinley's election to his first public office a personal tribute?

What conditions favored his election in 1896?

Why did he seat Mrs. McKinley at his right at official dinners in defiance of diplomatic custom?

What were two of McKinley's achievements while he served as governor of Ohio?

What was McKinley's relationship to: (1) Marcus A. Hanna? (2) William Jennings Bryan? (3) Theodore Roosevelt?

When did he reverse his position on silver coinage?

Who assassinated McKinley? Where and when did the assassination occur?

In what ways did his administration encourage the expansion of American industry?

How did the world position of the United States change during McKinley's administration?

McKINLY, JOHN. See Delaware (The Revolutionary War).

McKISSICK, FLOYD BIXLER (1922-   ), a black American leader, became a spokesman for the doctrine of *Black Power*. This doctrine urges black Americans to gain political and economic control of their own communities. It also urges blacks to adopt their own standards rather than the values of white America. It rejects the idea of complete nonviolence, and calls for black Americans to meet violence with violence. See Negro (Black Power).

McKissick was born in Asheville, N.C. He earned a B.A. degree in 1951 and a law degree in 1952 at North Carolina College. He became a legal adviser to CORE (Congress of Racial Equality) in 1960, and served as its national chairman from 1963 to 1966. He was national director of CORE from 1966 to 1968.   C. Eric Lincoln

McLOUGHLIN, *muk LOF lin,* **JOHN** (1784-1857), is sometimes called the *father of Oregon*. He played a leading part in settling Oregon Territory. He was a partner in the North West Company, and had charge of Fort William. After the North West and Hudson's Bay companies merged, he directed their business in the Oregon country from 1824 to 1846. He developed trading posts and friendly relations with the Indians. He had to resign for helping new settlers at his company's expense. McLoughlin was born at La Rivière du Loup, Quebec. Oregon placed his statue in the Statuary Hall collection in the U.S. Capitol in 1953.   Kenneth R. Rossman

McLUHAN, MARSHALL (1911-   ), is a Canadian professor and writer whose theories on mass communication have caused widespread debate. According to McLuhan, electronic communication—especially television—dominates the life of all Western peoples. It affects their ways of thinking as well as their institutions. McLuhan analyzed the effects of communications media on man and society in such works as *The Mechanical Bride* (1951), *The Gutenberg Galaxy* (1962), *Understanding Media* (1964), *The Medium Is the Massage* (1967), and *War and Peace in the Global Village* (1968).

McLuhan argued that each major period in human history takes its character from the medium of communication used most widely at the time. For example, he called the period from 1700 to the mid-1900's the *age of print.* During that time, printing was the principal means by which men acquired knowledge and shared it with others. McLuhan claimed that printing encouraged individualism, nationalism, democracy, the desire for privacy, specialization in work, and the separation of work and leisure.

According to McLuhan, the electronic age has replaced the age of print. Electronics speeds communication so greatly that people in all parts of the world become deeply involved in the lives of everyone else. As a result, said McLuhan, electronics leads to the end of individualism and nationalism and to the growth of new international communities. Electronics creates public participation and involvement and the need for general, rather than specialized, knowledge.

Herbert Marshall McLuhan was born in Edmonton, Alta. He received a Ph.D. from Cambridge University in England in 1942 and has taught at the University of Toronto since 1946.   James W. Carey

McMANUS, GEORGE. See Comics (Bringing Up Father).

McMASTER UNIVERSITY is a privately controlled co-educational university at Hamilton, Ont. Courses in the humanities and social sciences and in science and engineering lead to bachelor's, master's, and doctor's degrees. The university operates a nuclear reactor as part of an extensive research program. The Baptist Church controls McMaster Divinity College, which is affiliated with the university. McMaster University was founded in 1887. For enrollment, see Canada (table: Universities and Colleges).   Henry George Thode

McMATH TELESCOPE. See Kitt Peak National Observatory.

McMILLAN, EDWIN MATTISON. See Nobel Prizes (table [1951]); Synchrotron.

McMURRY COLLEGE. See Universities and Colleges (table).

McNAIR, ALEXANDER. See Missouri (Statehood).

McNAIR, LESLEY JAMES. See World War II (Invasion of Europe).

McNAMARA, ROBERT STRANGE (1916-   ), was secretary of defense from 1961 to 1968. He served under Presidents John F. Kennedy and Lyndon B. Johnson. As secretary, McNamara became an important adviser to the Presidents in economic and foreign affairs as well

United Press Int.

Robert S. McNamara

as in military matters. He introduced systems of estimating military needs and costs 10 to 15 years into the future. In 1968, McNamara became president of the International Bank for Reconstruction and Development, often called the World Bank.

McNamara was born in San Francisco. He graduated from the University of California and the Harvard Business School, and taught at Harvard from 1940 to 1943. He was in the Army Air Forces in World War II, and then joined the Ford Motor Company. He became president of Ford shortly before he was named secretary of defense.   F. Jay Taylor

McNARY, CHARLES LINZA (1874-1944), served as a United States senator from Oregon from 1917 until his death. He was the Republican candidate for Vice-President of the United States in 1940. He and presidential candidate Wendell L. Willkie were defeated by President Franklin D. Roosevelt and Henry A. Wallace. McNary served as Senate minority leader from 1932 until his death. His chief interests were farm and conservation legislation. McNary was born near Salem, Ore. He attended Stanford University.   Jesse L. Gilmore

McNAUGHTON, *muk NAW t'n,* **ANDREW GEORGE LATTA** (1887-1966), was a noted Canadian soldier of World Wars I and II. He took command of the First Canadian Army at the outbreak of World War II in 1939. He helped plan the Canadian raid on Dieppe, France, in 1942. Ill health forced him to retire in 1944. He served as defense minister under Prime Minister Mackenzie King in 1944. He was chairman of the Canadian section of the Canada-United States Permanent Joint Board on Defense from 1945 to 1962.

McNaughton served as a gunnery officer in World War I, and became a brigadier general in 1918. He was credited with inventing the *rolling barrage*, an artillery attack made against the enemy to protect advancing infantry.

McNaughton was the co-inventor of a cathode-ray direction finder used in airplanes (see CATHODE; CATHODE RAYS). He served as chairman of the Canadian National Research Council from 1935 to 1939. McNaughton was born in Moosomin, Sask.

McNEESE STATE COLLEGE. See UNIVERSITIES AND COLLEGES (table).

McPHERSON, AIMEE SEMPLE (1890-1944), an American evangelist, founded the International Church of the Foursquare Gospel. For membership, see RELIGION (table). She also founded the Lighthouse of International Foursquare Evangelism Bible College. She stressed salvation, divine healing, baptism by the Holy Spirit, and the Second Coming of Christ. She worked briefly as a missionary in Hong Kong until 1908. She built Angelus Temple in Los Angeles in 1922. She was born in Salford, Ont., Canada.

EARLE E. CAIRNS

McPHERSON COLLEGE. See UNIVERSITIES AND COLLEGES (table).

McREYNOLDS, JAMES CLARK (1862-1946), was one of the "nine old men" of the Supreme Court of the United States during the 1930's. McReynolds served as an associate justice from 1914 to 1941. He consistently opposed President Franklin D. Roosevelt's New Deal measures. To offset this opposition, Roosevelt proposed in 1937 that when a justice reached 70 years of age, a younger justice be appointed to sit with him on the court. The proposal was never approved (see ROOSEVELT, FRANKLIN D. [The Supreme Court]).

McReynolds was born in Elkton, Ky. He practiced law in Nashville, Tenn., and served from 1903 to 1907 as assistant attorney general under President Theodore Roosevelt. President Woodrow Wilson named him U.S. attorney general in 1913, and appointed him to the Supreme Court in 1914.

DAVID A. SHANNON

MEAD, LAKE. See LAKE MEAD.

MEAD, MARGARET (1901-   ), is an American anthropologist. She became famous for her studies of the cultures of the Pacific Islands, Russia, and the United States. She also served in several important advisory posts for the United States government during and after World War II. From 1926 to 1969, she was a curator of anthropology at the American Museum of Natural History in New York City. She has written many books, including *Coming of Age in Samoa* (1928), *Growing Up in New Guinea* (1930), *Sex and Temperament in Three Primitive Societies* (1935), *Male and Female* (1948), and *Culture and Commitment: A Study of the Generation Gap* (1970).

Margaret Mead was born in Philadelphia. She was graduated from Barnard College, and received her Ph.D. degree from Columbia University.

DAVID B. STOUT

MEADE, GEORGE GORDON (1815-1872), was a Union general in the Civil War. He commanded the victorious Union Army at the Battle of Gettysburg, from July 1 to 3, in 1863. This has been called the greatest engagement ever fought on American soil.

When the Civil War began, Meade became a brigadier general of Pennsylvania volunteers. He fought

in most of the important battles in the East, including the battles of the Peninsula, the Seven Days, second Bull Run, Antietam, Fredericksburg, and Chancellorsville. He became a major general of volunteers after Antietam, and a corps commander after Fredericksburg. Late in June, 1863, he replaced General Joseph Hooker as commander of the Army of the Potomac. At Gettysburg,

George Meade

Meade defeated the Confederates in a defensive battle. When General Ulysses S. Grant became supreme Union commander in 1864, he kept Meade as commander of the Army of the Potomac.

Meade was born in Cadiz, Spain, the son of an American naval agent. He was educated in the United States, and was graduated from the U.S. Military Academy. After serving in the Seminole War in Florida, he resigned from the Army to become a civil engineer. He returned to the Army in 1842 as a topographical engineer. He also served in the Mexican War. After the Civil War, Meade commanded various military departments.

T. HARRY WILLIAMS

MEADOW LARK is a common North American bird that usually lives in grassy fields, meadows, and marshes. Meadow larks are found in many areas, particularly in the United States. They spend the summer as far north as southern Canada. In the winter, they live as far south as northern South America. There are two kinds of meadow larks, the *eastern* and the *western*.

Meadow larks are not true larks. Meadow larks belong to the same family as blackbirds and orioles. They are about the size of a robin, but have heavier bodies, shorter tails, and longer bills. The feathers of the back and wings are brownish, marked with black. The throat and under parts are bright yellow with a large black crescent on the breast. The white outer tail feathers can easily be seen when the farmer by eating many harmful insects.

The meadow lark's song is a clear, tuneful whistle. It is one of the first songs to be heard in the spring. The song of the western meadow lark is considered especially beautiful.

The meadow lark builds its nest on the ground, usually with a roof of grass so that the eggs cannot be seen and stolen. It lays three to seven white eggs, speckled with cinnamon and reddish brown.

Meadow larks eat some waste grain, and they help the farmer by eating many harmful insects.

See also BIRD (table: State Birds; color pictures: Other Bird Favorites, Birds' Eggs).

Scientific Classification. Meadow larks belong to the icterid family, *Icteridae*. The eastern meadow lark is genus *Sturnella*, species *S. magna*. The western meadow lark is *S. neglecta*.

GEORGE E. HUDSON

MEADOW SAFFRON is another name for the colchicum plant. See COLCHICUM.

MEADOWSWEET. See SPIRAEA.

MEAL. See DIET; FOOD; HOMEMAKING (Food); NUTRITION.

MEALY BUG. See SCALE INSECT (picture).

MEAN, in mathematics, is the sum of a series of numbers divided by the number of cases. Suppose five boys weigh 67, 62, 68, 69, and 64 pounds. The sum of their weights is 330 pounds. Divide this sum by 5, the number of boys, or cases: 330 ÷ 5 = 66. The *mean* of this series of numbers is 66 and the *mean weight* of the boys is 66 pounds. This single weight of 66 pounds can be used to represent the differing weights of all five boys, even though none weighs exactly 66 pounds. The mean is often called the *arithmetic average* or *arithmetic mean.*

By using averages or means, we can often compare groups that could not easily be compared directly. Suppose we wanted to compare two long series of numbers. We can find the sum of each series, compute the two averages, and compare the averages.   ALBERT E. WAUGH

See also AVERAGE; MEDIAN; MODE; STATISTICS (picture).

MEAN SOLAR DAY. See TIME (Measuring Time).

MEANY, GEORGE (1894-   ), has been president of the American Federation of Labor and Congress of Industrial Organizations since its founding in 1955. He had served as president of the A.F. of L. since the death of William Green in 1952 (see GREEN, WILLIAM). Before that, he had served as secretary-treasurer of the A.F. of L. since 1940.

One of Meany's most important tasks in the A.F. of L.-C.I.O. was the enforcement of the ethical-practice codes against corrupt union leaders. He has also taken part in the international activities of the A.F. of L.-C.I.O., and has aimed to strengthen the anti-communist forces in labor throughout the world.

As A.F. of L. president, Meany was influential in expelling the International Longshoremen's Association on grounds of corruption. He played an important part in merging the A.F. of L. and the C.I.O.

Before the merger he helped negotiate a "no-raiding" agreement between the two labor groups.

Meany was born in New York City, where his father was president of a plumbers' union local. He became an apprentice at the age of 16. He rose from business agent of the local to the presidency of the New York Federation of Labor in 1934. In 1963, Meany received the Presidential Medal of Freedom.   JACK BARBASH

MEASLES, *MEE z'lz,* is a highly contagious disease. The first symptoms of measles are almost like those of a bad cold. The patient suffers from a headache. "Sniffles," another symptom, results from a discharge from the eyes and nose. The temperature rises toward evening and the person feels extremely exhausted. A cough is common. Usually, on the fourth day a rash appears on the face, and spreads to the neck, chest, and other parts of the body. The rash first appears as small red spots on the forehead and behind the ears, but soon changes to blotches or patches that may cover most of the body. The spots are darker in *black measles,* a more serious form of the disease. Usually before the rash appears, marks, called *Koplik spots,* form on the mucous

Miller of Washington
George Meany

membranes on the inside of the cheeks. Three or four days later the rash begins to disappear, and the skin scales and peels. The eyes often become sensitive to light. Complications which may develop include pneumonia, middle-ear disease, and occasionally encephalitis. Measles should never be considered as simply a mild disease.

Measles has an *incubation* period of eight to twelve days, usually ten. This is the length of time between exposure and the first appearance of symptoms.

Cause and Spread. A virus which is present in the secretions of the nose and throat causes measles. The virus is spread by the secretions on handkerchiefs and other objects, and by coughing and sneezing.

People usually consider measles a disease of children. But the disease may attack human beings of any age over six months. The highest death rate from measles is in children under five years old.

Treatment. Patients who suffer from measles usually recover, but should be given very careful treatment because of the danger of complications. Black measles is very often fatal, but fortunately is rare.

In the treatment of measles the patient should be kept warm at all times, the cough relieved, and the eyes protected from bright light for comfort. The diet should be light, or even chiefly liquid, and the bowels kept well regulated. The patient must be kept warm and quiet for several weeks after the symptoms have disappeared, because the lungs and mucous lining of the intestine may easily become inflamed.

The patient should be isolated after the first symptoms appear. All cases of measles should be under the care of a competent physician.

Physicians often use antibiotics to treat cases of measles which have been complicated by pneumonia or bronchial infections.

Prevention. At one time, measles was often prevented by giving *convalescent serum* to the patient during the incubation period of the disease. This serum came from the blood of people recovering from measles. In place of this serum, doctors sometimes gave serum or whole blood from someone who had the disease, or placental extract that contained antibodies against the measles virus. A part of the blood plasma called *gamma globulin* was found to be effective in preventing the disease or making it milder.

In the early 1960's, two vaccines were developed that give immunity against measles. A "live" virus vaccine made from the weakened viruses gives permanent protection against the disease. A "killed" virus vaccine produces immunity for about one year. Booster doses repeated every year maintain the immunity.

Parents should not expose their children to measles to "get it over with." If a child passes his tenth year without getting the disease, he may not get it at all, or may have only a mild case.   AUSTIN EDWARD SMITH

See also DISEASE (tables: Main Contagious Diseases in the U.S., Some Common Communicable Diseases); GAMMA GLOBULIN; GERMAN MEASLES; VACCINATION.

MEASURE. See WEIGHTS AND MEASURES.

MEASURE. In music, a measure is a division of equal portions of time. Each measure is made up of a certain number of beats. See also MUSIC (Rhythm; Notation).

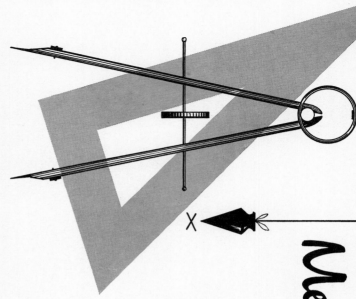

Measurement

MEASUREMENT. What is the temperature outdoors today? How long should we cut a board to make a new shelf? How far is it to London, Paris, or Moscow? How much paint do we need to paint the kitchen? How much flour do we use to bake a cake? How fast does a jet airplane travel? The answers to all these questions can be found by measurement. Measurement, or the way to find the size of things, is one of our most important tools. We use it daily at home, in school, on the farm, and in industry and science. One of the first things that happens to a newborn baby is the measurement of his weight and length.

For tables of various weights and measures, see WEIGHTS AND MEASURES.

How Measurements Are Made

When we drive into a service station, an attendant pumps gasoline into the tank of our automobile. The pump measures the gasoline in *gallons* as it feeds the fuel into the tank. The amount of *money* we pay for the gasoline depends on the number of gallons measured by the pump. We can find the total cost by multiplying the price of one gallon by the number of gallons we received.

Buying gasoline shows us some things that are true of all measurements. *Measurements are numbers*. We use *units*, such as *gallons*, *inches*, and *hours*, to measure things. To measure, we must find *how many* units there are in what we are measuring.

We can make some measurements *directly*. For example, we can measure a kite string with a foot ruler by holding it against the string. But suppose we want to

Measuring Length and Width. Ancient workmen measured rough lengths in cubits, the distance from the elbow to a fingertip. Workmen today find precise widths with the micrometer.

measure the distance a ship has traveled. We cannot apply a unit, such as a mile, directly. So we must find the answer *indirectly* with arithmetic, using the speed of the ship and the length of time it has been traveling.

Most measurements involve reading some kind of scale. No matter how many subdivisions the scale has, the object being measured is likely to fall between two of them. This means that *every measurement is an approximation*. A measurement may come very close, but it never matches the scale perfectly. For example, with the unaided eye, we cannot read an ordinary ruler that is *graduated*, or marked, much more closely than within sixty-fourths of an inch. But a machinist makes simple shop measurements with *micrometer calipers* that can be read to a thousandth of an inch (see MICROMETER). So a workman or a scientist must choose the kind and quality of measuring instrument that will give him the precision he needs.

Measuring Space

People in the United States and Canada use the *English system of measurement*. This system includes such units as *feet*, *rods*, and *pints*. Scientists and most other countries use the *metric system*. This system includes such units as *meters* and *liters*. It uses divisions of 10 or multiples of 10, and fits in with the decimal number system. See DECIMAL NUMERAL SYSTEM; METRIC SYSTEM.

Length and Distance. Man's first measurements probably consisted of finding lengths. He needed to measure materials for a house or a temple. Or he told his friends the length of the journey to another place.

For long distances, early men often used *a day's journey* as a unit. But the length of a day's journey varies, because it depends on the distance each person can travel and whether he walks, runs, rides a horse, drives a car, or flies in an airplane. A more precise unit for long distances is the *mile*. Our word *mile* comes from the Latin words *milia passuum*, which mean *a thousand paces*. The ancient Roman pace consisted of two steps (about 5 feet), and 1,000 paces nearly equals our *land mile* or *statute mile* of 5,280 feet. See MILE.

For shorter distances or lengths, early men used the *cubit*. The cubit was the length of a man's forearm from his elbow to the tip of his middle finger. Archaeologists have found the cubit cut on wooden rods and stone slabs in Egypt dating back to 3000 B.C. The Egyptians had several cubits, averaging about 21 inches in length. They divided the cubit into seven *palms*, and subdivided each palm into four *digits*. The word *digit* also means *finger*. So every person carried his own "ruler" with him in his fingers, palm, and forearm. But, of course, everyone had a slightly different ruler, because arm lengths vary. See CUBIT; DIGIT.

The Romans introduced a cubit of about 26.6 inches into the lands they conquered north of Italy. This cubit consisted of two *feet*, and each foot had 12 *unciae*. The basic Roman piece of money, the *as*, also consisted of 12 unciae. So the uncia measured the weight of metal in coins, as well as measuring length. Our words *inch* and *ounce* came from *uncia*. The units *inch*, *foot*, *yard*, and *rod* in the English system can be traced all the way back to the Roman and the Egyptian cubit. See FOOT; INCH; ROD; YARD.

In the United States and many other countries, units of length are defined by law in terms of the meter. For example, in the United States, 1 yard is defined as 0.9144 of a meter. The meter was defined by international agreement in 1960 as 1,650,763.73 wavelengths of the orange-red light produced by artificially excited atoms of *krypton-86* (an isotope of the element krypton). This standard for the meter replaced the platinum-iridium bar that had previously served as the international standard of length.

The distance to the stars is so great that astronomers need a large distance unit, something far larger than a mile. So they define a *light-year* as the distance traveled by a ray of light in one year. Light travels at a speed of about 186,000 miles a second, so a light-year measures about 6,000,000,000,000 miles! Except for the sun, the star nearest to us, Proxima Centauri, is about 4.3 light-years away. See ASTRONOMY.

Area is measured in *square units*, such as square inches and square feet. You can picture the measurement of the area of a wall by imagining it covered with rows of

square feet. To find the area, you could count the square feet in each row and multiply this number by the number of rows. Suppose the wall has 8 rows, each containing 12 square feet. The area of the wall is 12 × 8, or 96 square feet. See AREA; SQUARE MEASURE.

Land is sold in area units called *acres* and *sections*. An acre consists of 160 square rods, and a section is a square mile. Early area measurements varied from person to person, just as distance measurements did. For example, an acre originally consisted of the area of land that a man could plow in one day with a *yoke*, or pair, of oxen. See ACRE.

Volume or Capacity. Every time we buy such things as gasoline, milk, or grain, we use measurements of *volume* or *capacity*. These are measures of liquid or of materials that fill containers. These are measures of *volume* or *capacity*. In the measurement of volume, the simplest container is a box whose top, bottom, and sides are squares. This kind of box is a *cube* (see CUBE). Units for measuring volume include the *cubic inch*, *cubic foot*, and *cubic yard*.

Suppose you want to measure the volume of a box whose bottom and sides are rectangles. You can imagine that its bottom is covered with a layer of cubic inches. There are as many cubic inches in this layer as there are square inches in the bottom area. Next, imagine that you pile new layers of cubic inches on the bottom layer until the box is full. The total number of cubic inches would be the number of layers multiplied by the number of cubic inches in each layer.

We often use units that do not include the word *cubic* in their names. To measure liquids, for example, we use *gallons*, *quarts*, and *pints*. But we define the gallon as 231 cubic inches, and we define the pint and quart in terms of the gallon. That is, two pints equal a quart, and four quarts make a gallon. So the cubic units are really the basic ones. The *Imperial gallon*, used in Canada and Great Britain, measures 277.420 cubic inches. The Imperial gallon is about ⅕ larger than the United States gallon. See GALLON; PINT; QUART.

We also use the words *pint* and *quart* to measure dry substances, such as grains and fruits. But the dry pint is larger than the liquid pint. The dry pint contains 33.6 cubic inches, and the liquid pint contains 28.875 cubic inches. A dry quart consists of two dry pints. Eight dry quarts equal a *peck*, and four pecks make a *bushel*. See BUSHEL; PECK.

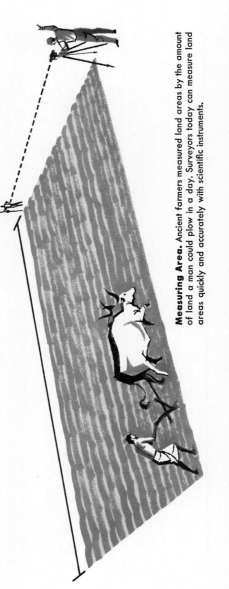

Measuring Area. Ancient farmers measured land areas by the amount of land a man could plow in a day. Surveyors today can measure land areas quickly and accurately with scientific instruments.

The measurement of grains and berries by the capacities of their containers is less accurate than measuring liquids in this way. Shippers may pack grains and fruits tightly or loosely, and can heap up or level off the filled containers. For these reasons, many state laws define bushels of special products by weight rather than by volume or capacity. For example, Michigan law defines a bushel of wheat as 64 pounds, a bushel of rye as 56 pounds, and a bushel of hard coal as 80 pounds.

Measuring Weight

We use scales and machines to weigh quantities of things we buy and sell, and amounts of materials used in chemical and manufacturing processes. The earliest trading probably did not require weights or standard units, because people exchanged goods in direct barter. For example, a man traded an ax blade for a clay pot.

The oldest known weights appear in prehistoric graves in Egypt, dating from about 4000 B.C. The oldest records of weighing show stone weights being used on balances to weigh gold in Egyptian temple treasuries (see BALANCE). These records date from about 2500 B.C. The Babylonians used seeds of grain as weights, and we still use a unit called a *grain* to measure drugs and precious metals (see GRAIN).

Our *pounds* and *ounces*, like the units of length, came from Roman units. The pound belongs to the *avoirdupois* system of weights. The word *avoirdupois* comes from French and means *to have weight*. We define the pound as 0.43359237 kilograms. The National Bureau of Standards keeps the *United States Prototype Kilogram* in Washington, D.C. This kilogram is a copy of the *International Prototype Kilogram* at Sèvres. See AVOIRDUPOIS; OUNCE; POUND.

We define *ounces* and *tons* in terms of pounds. That is, 16 ounces equal one pound and 2,000 pounds make one ton (see TON). The ordinary ton of 2,000 pounds is sometimes called a *short ton*. Miners often use a *long ton* of 2,240 pounds to weigh coal and iron ore. The *metric ton*, used in many European countries, measures 2,204.6 pounds. Other systems of weight include *troy weight* for precious metals and *apothecaries' weight* for drugs and medicines. The troy pound and the apothecaries' pound measure about $\frac{10}{12}$ of an avoirdupois pound. See APOTHECARIES' WEIGHT; TROY WEIGHT.

Measuring Time

The calendars of the ancient Babylonians and Egyptians were probably the earliest methods of measuring time. Later, peoples of ancient times used sundials and water clocks to measure short time intervals. See CALENDAR; CLOCK; TIME.

The Babylonians used a number system based on 60. They also thought that a year consisted of 360 days. These two practices led them to use fractions based on sixtieths, in astronomy. When the ancient Greeks began to study astronomy, they used the ideas of the Babylonians. Later, when scholars in the Middle Ages translated Greek astronomy into Latin, they called a sixtieth *pars minuta prima*, or *first small part*. They called a sixtieth of a sixtieth *pars minuta secunda*, or *second small part*. Our words *minute* and *second* come from these Latin names for Babylonian fractions. See MINUTE.

We define all units of time in terms of the movement of the earth with reference to the stars. But the earth's

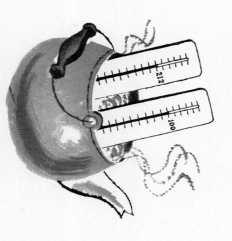

Liquid Measurements Differ Throughout the World. The Imperial gallon, used for measurement in Canada, contains more liquid than the gallon used for measurement in the United States.

Paul Granger, © 1957 by Street & Smith Publications, Inc., reprinted from *Science World*

Weight Measurements Differ with Materials. In the United States, most heavy measurements appear in short tons. But mining companies use the long ton to weigh coal and iron ore. People in Canada use the long ton to measure all heavy weights.

Temperature Measurements Differ with the Job. On a scientist's thermometer, water boils at 100° celsius. On a kitchen thermometer, water boils at 212° Fahrenheit.

A Radar Telescope measures the distance from the earth to the moon. Astronomers of the U.S. Navy use this device to bounce radar signals off the moon. The signals help astronomers to measure the distance to the moon and the relative sizes of the moon and the earth. This radar telescope has a 600-inch antenna.

speed changes during the year. We want time intervals to have the same length, so our clocks will tell time accurately. Astronomers must make daily observations of the sun and stars to compute the time. The United States Naval Observatory at Washington, D.C., broadcasts official time signals continuously. Canada's Dominion Observatory in Ottawa broadcasts similar time signals. These signals help us to set clocks accurately. See NAVAL OBSERVATORY, UNITED STATES.

Measuring Speed

Units that measure speed combine measurements of distance and time. For example, a speed of 30 *miles an hour* means that if we travel at this speed for one hour we will travel 30 miles. Other combinations of distance and time units include *feet a second* and *miles a minute.* See SPEEDOMETER.

We measure the speed of a ship in *knots* (nautical miles an hour). The name *knot* grew out of the way seamen once measured a ship's speed. See KNOT.

Measuring Temperature

Temperature is one of the quantities that we can measure only indirectly. Heat makes liquids and metals expand. We "measure" temperature in degrees by measuring the change in a length of liquid in a narrow tube, or of a piece of metal. We have two systems of units for measuring temperature, *celsius* and *Fahrenheit.* On the celsius scale, water freezes at 0 degrees and boils at 100 degrees. Most scientists use celsius temperatures, because they tie in with the metric system. But some countries, including the United States, use the Fahrenheit scale invented by Gabriel Daniel Fahrenheit, a German physicist. On the Fahrenheit scale, water freezes at 32 degrees and boils at 212 degrees. See CENTIGRADE SCALE; THERMOMETER.

Measurement of temperature has great importance in manufacturing, science, and even in cooking. We use several other thermometer scales and instruments for special purposes. For example, *pyrometers* record extremely high temperatures, such as the temperature of molten steel (see PYROMETRY). Doctors use special kinds of thermometers to measure body temperatures.

Other Measurements

The basic quantities measured by scientists and engineers are distance, time, and weight. But various instruments help make many other measurements. The *barometer* measures the pressure of air and helps predict the weather (see BAROMETER). Some *altimeters* use the barometer principle to tell airplane pilots their distance above the earth (see ALTIMETER). *Voltmeters* and *ammeters* measure properties of electricity (see AMMETER; VOLTMETER). Photographers use *light meters* to measure the intensity of light (see LIGHT METER).

Another field of measurement includes the tests and measurements used in education and psychology. See TESTING.

Standardizing Measurement

Merchants find trade easier if they use the same units of measure. Scientists can exchange information more easily if they all use the same units. Different systems of measurement tend to hamper trade and communication. So *standardized units of measure,* or units that are

the same for all persons in all places, have become important. The metric system has been one of the most useful international systems since its adoption by France in 1799. The United States began to base its standard measures on the metric system after 1866.

Manufacturers in many parts of the world produce goods with interchangeable parts. For this reason, we need standard precision measurements in addition to standard units. As measuring methods improve, the definitions of standard units must be improved.

A recent step in improving standard units was the adoption in 1960 of a new definition for the international standard meter. The wavelength of orange-red light emitted by krypton-86, an isotope of the gas krypton, was selected as the new standard for the meter (see ISOTOPE). It measures a meter about 100 times more accurately than before.

PHILIP S. JONES

Related Articles in WORLD BOOK include:

MEASUREMENT

Outline

I. How Measurements Are Made
II. Measuring Space
  A. Length and Distance
  B. Area
  C. Volume or Capacity
III. Measuring Weight
IV. Measuring Time
V. Measuring Speed
VI. Measuring Temperature
VII. Other Measurements
VIII. Standardizing Measurement

Questions

Why must many measurements be indirect?

Why are measurements really approximations, regardless of their accuracy?

What unit of measurement did the early Egyptians and Romans use to measure short distances?

What Roman measure is found in both the inch and the ounce?

How do you measure the area of a wall?

How do you measure the volume of a box?

How do capacity units differ for dry and liquid materials?

How is the measurement of time corrected daily?

How is speed used as a measure of distance in astronomy?

How can standardized measures help science and trade?

MEASUREMENT, EDUCATIONAL. See TESTING.

MEASURING WORM is a green or brown caterpillar that crawls by looping its body. It brings its hind feet up to the forefeet, and then stretches the forefeet out again, as if it were measuring the ground. An old superstition says that if a measuring worm measures a person's length, the person will die.

The measuring worm is also called the *looper* or *inch worm*. The *omnivorous looper* is one of the best-known measuring worms in the United States. It can hold itself straight out from a branch so that it looks like a small twig. Some members of the measuring-worm family, such as the cankerworm, are serious pests (see CANKERWORM). If the worms become numerous, they may completely strip the leaves from the trees. Farmers use poison sprays to help control them. Similar kinds of measuring worms live in Europe and Asia.

The measuring worm becomes a delicate, butterfly-like moth. It develops in a cocoon or in a cell in the ground.

Scientific Classification. The measuring worm is the caterpillar of a moth in the measuring-worm moth and cankerworm moth family, *Geometridae*. The omnivorous looper is genus *Sabulodes*, species *S. caberata*. E. G. LINSLEY

The Measuring Worm

Gayle Pickwell

MEAT is animal flesh that is used as food. Meat consists mainly of the muscle, fat, and certain other tissues of animals. The most commonly eaten meats come from cattle (beef and veal), hogs (pork), sheep (lamb and mutton), fish, and such poultry as chickens, ducks, and turkeys. The white and dark meat of fish and poultry are considered separately from the red meat of cattle, hogs, and sheep. See FISH; POULTRY.

Americans eat about 32 billion pounds of red meat each year. People in the United States eat an average of about 170 pounds of red meats per person each year. About 100 pounds of this is beef; 58 pounds, pork; 4 pounds, veal; and 4 pounds, lamb and mutton.

But in several other countries, the people eat more red meat than Americans. Uruguayans average about 235 pounds per person a year. New Zealanders average 234 pounds a year; Australians, 210 pounds; and Argentines, 198 pounds.

Meat is necessary for a well-balanced diet. It is an energy food, and contains the five basic food elements that human beings need—proteins, minerals, vitamins, fats, and carbohydrates.

Food Value of Meat

Meat protein is well balanced and contains all the essential tissue-building elements called *amino acids* (see AMINO ACID). Nearly all meats contain the minerals iron and copper, which are needed for the blood. Liver is especially rich in iron and copper. Most meats also contain phosphorus, which aids in building strong bones and teeth.

Meat is an excellent source of vitamins. Nearly all of the vitamin B complex group are found in lean beef, lamb, pork, and veal. Thiamine (B_1) is important for the growth and working of the heart and nerves. Riboflavin (B_2) is needed for healthy skin and normal vision. Nicotinic acid (niacin) helps prevent a disease called *pellagra*, which leaves victims tired and nervous (see PELLAGRA). Pyridoxine (B_6) and vitamin B_{12} are also found in meat. Liver also is very rich in vitamin A, which is needed for normal vision and healthy skin. It also contains vitamin D, which builds bones and teeth, and vitamin C, which prevents a skin disease called *scurvy*.

The fat in meat is one of the best sources of body heat and energy. Some meats contain small amounts of carbohydrates in the form of glycogen (see GLYCOGEN). Carbohydrates supply energy and are necessary for normal body functioning.

Kinds of Meat

The meat of cattle, hogs, and sheep is known by several different names. Cattle meat, for example, is divided into two general classes—beef and veal.

Veal is the flesh of calves from 2 to 14 weeks old. Calves which are older are usually sold as calves or yearling beef. Veal is more tender than beef. It contains a higher percentage of water and less fat.

Beef is the flesh of full-grown cattle. In the United States, it is generally considered a tastier meat than yearling beef. Good beef has white fat and bright, cherry-red colored lean meat.

Lamb is the flesh of young sheep. The meat of a sheep becomes mutton when the animal is about a year old. Lamb has a light-pink color. The fat is white. Lamb has a much milder flavor than mutton.

Mutton has a darker color and a stronger flavor than lamb. The people of Great Britain and many other European countries like this high flavor, and prefer mutton to lamb.

Pork is the flesh of hogs. It is sold as pork no matter how old the hog is. All hogs have a high percentage of fat (from 20 per cent to 40 per cent). The eating quality of pork does not change much with the animal's age. Bacon, ham, pork chops, and spareribs are favorite pork meats.

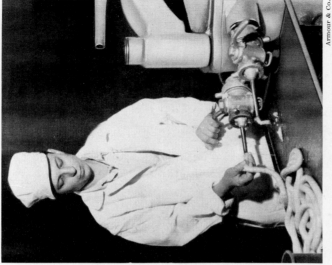

Armour & Co.

A Sausage Maker Works in a Large Packing House.

Variety Meats. Various organs of animals are called variety meats. These meats may be sold as extra parts, fancy meats, or meat sundries. Variety meats are usually rich and full of flavor.

The variety meats from beef cattle include the heart, liver, kidney, *tripe* (first and second stomachs), brains, tongue, and *sweetbreads* (thymus glands). Sweetbreads may be taken from animals of all ages, but most sweetbreads are sold as "calf sweetbreads."

More variety meats come from hogs than from any other farm animal. They include liver, heart, kidneys, brain, and tongue. In addition, feet, ears, lips, and snouts are sold as pork variety meats. These meats may be sold fresh, pickled, or canned. The intestines of hogs are sold as *chitterlings*, which are regarded as special delicacies in the southern United States.

Lamb and mutton variety meats are the heart, liver, tongue, kidney, and brain.

How to Buy Meat

The housewife who knows how to buy meat properly can save money and provide her family with tastier

MEAT CARVING

Diagrams prepared through the cooperation of the National Live Stock and Meat Board

PORK LOIN ROAST

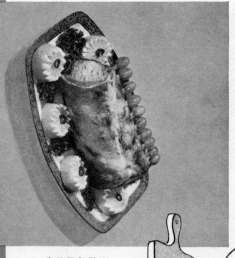

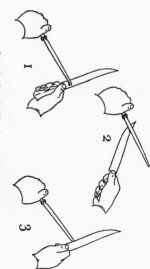

Steel the Knife by passing the blade lightly over the steel. Work from heel to tip on one side of the blade, then from tip to heel on the other side.

Remove the Backbone before you bring the roast to the table. To cut between the backbone and the rib ends, place the roast so the ribs face you, and use them as a guide.

Slice the Roast with the fork inserted firmly in the top. Cut close to each rib. The size of the loin determines the number of boneless slices you can cut between the ribs.

Turn the Shank Bone to your right. Insert the fork firmly and carve two or three lengthwise slices from the thin side opposite the thick meaty cushion section of the roast.

ROAST LEG OF LAMB

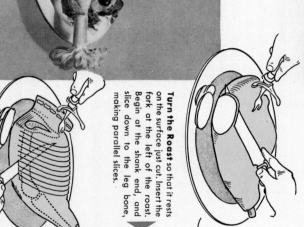

Turn the Roast so that it rests on the surface just cut. Insert the fork at the left of the roast. Begin at the shank end, and slice down to the leg bone, making parallel slices.

Release All the Slices at the same time by running the knife along the leg bone.

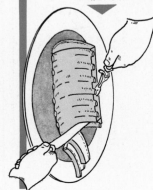

TIPS TO THE CARVER

Carving will be easier if you remember a few helpful hints. A good knife needs sharpening only occasionally. But always steel it before using it. Always cut across the grain to avoid stringy-textured slices, except when carving steaks. To get neat slices, keep the blade at the same angle while cutting each slice.

TIPS TO THE HOSTESS

A few thoughtful precautions help the carver. Allow a large roast to stand for about 30 minutes after you take it from the oven. This makes it easier to cut. Give the carver enough room on the table and on the platter. If one platter is not big enough to hold the roast and the slices, use an additional one. Place glasses and dishes where they will not interfere with the carver.

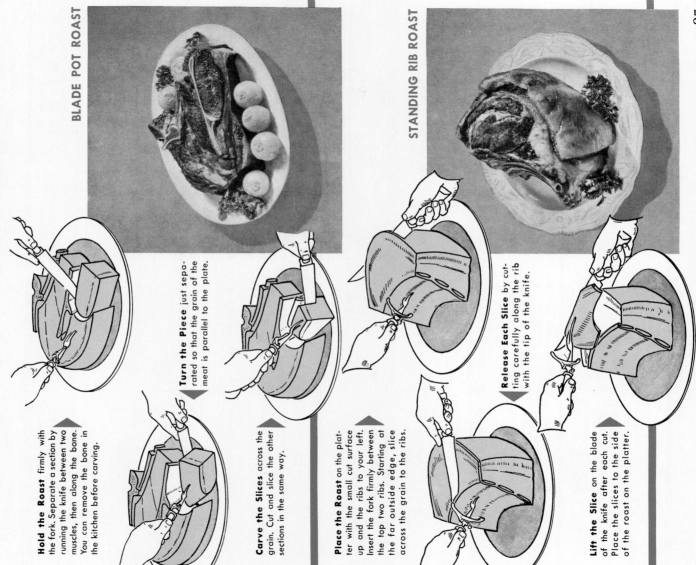

BLADE POT ROAST

Hold the Roast firmly with the fork. Separate a section by running the knife between two muscles, then along the bone. You can remove the bone in the kitchen before carving.

Turn the Piece just separated so that the grain of the meat is parallel to the plate.

Carve the Slices across the grain. Cut and slice the other sections in the same way.

STANDING RIB ROAST

Place the Roast on the platter with the small cut surface up and the ribs to your left. Insert the fork firmly between the top two ribs. Starting at the far outside edge, slice across the grain to the ribs.

Release Each Slice by cutting carefully along the rib with the tip of the knife.

Lift the Slice on the blade of the knife after each cut. Place the slices to the side of the roast on the platter.

ROAST TURKEY

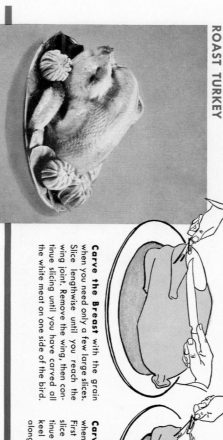

Courtesy Better Homes & Gardens Magazine

Remove the Drumstick by turning the turkey on its side with its breastbone away from you. Hold the end of the drumstick, and pull it forward, as the knife cuts through the joint.

Carve the Drumstick into lengthwise slices by standing it on its thick end and holding the thin end in your hand.

Carve the Thigh after the drumstick. Expose the thigh bone by slicing down to it. Remove the thigh bone by prying it loose with the tip of the knife. Then finish slicing the thigh meat.

Carve the Breast with the grain when you need only a few large slices. Slice lengthwise until you reach the wing joint. Remove the wing, then continue slicing until you have carved all the white meat on one side of the bird.

Carve the Breast across the grain when you need several small slices. First remove the wing, then carve a slice at an angle of about 45°. Continue carving slices until you reach the keel bone. Loosen the slices by cutting along the bone under them.

OTHER CUTS

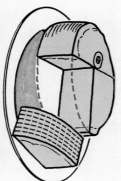

Beef Tongue should be cut in thin, even, parallel slices. Start carving from the large end and continue to the tip.

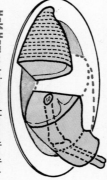

Half Ham contains a cushion section that you can easily remove and slice. Separate the other section from the shank and remove the bone. Then slice the meat.

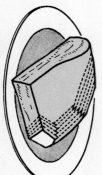

Center-Cut Ham Slice should be cut into three sections before you slice it. Carve across the grain. Make the slices any thickness you desire. Remove the bone before you slice the end section.

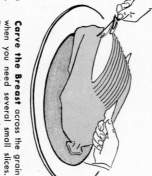

Beef Brisket often contains excess fat that you should trim off before you begin to carve. Place the round side of the brisket away from you. Take the slices from three sides in rotation.

Beef Cuts	Veal Cuts	Lamb and Mutton Cuts	Pork Cuts
Rump Roast	Rump Roast	Leg Roast	Butt Roast
Round Steak	Cutlets		Pork Steak
Hind Shank	Hind Shank		Fresh Ham Hocks
Porterhouse Steak	Loin End Chops	Loin Chops	Shoulder End Chops
Sirloin Steak	Loin Chops	Kidney Chops	Center Cut Chops
Club Steak			Rib Chops
T-Bone Steak			Ham End Chops
			Shoulder End Loin Roast
			Ham End Loin Roast
Flank Steak	Flank Steak	Rolled Breast	Sausage
Plate Boil	Rolled Veal Breast	Riblets	
Beef Short Ribs	Stew		
Brisket			
Rib Steak	Rib Chops	Rib Chops	Loin
Rolled Rib Roast	Rolled Rib Roast		
First Cut Rib Roast			
Center Cut Rib Roast			
Blade Rib Roast			
Chuck Arm Roast	Shoulder Arm Chops	Shoulder Roast	Boston Butt
Chuck Arm Steak	Shoulder Arm Roast	Shoulder Arm Chops	Sliced Shoulder
Chuck Blade Steak	Shoulder Blade Chops	Shoulder Blade Chops	Picnic Shoulder
Chuck Blade Roast	Shoulder Blade Roast		Skinned Shoulder
	Stew		Pork Fore Shank
Boiling Beef		Shank in Stew or Rolled Breast	

meals. The smart buyer of meat knows the different cuts of meat which are sold. The wide variety of cuts which can be bought at retail shops are listed on the chart with this article.

Not all meat markets or butchers have all of these cuts. But all markets—both city and rural—have cuts which fall within certain price ranges. Supply and demand, as well as the quality of the meat, determine how much meat cuts cost. In general, chops and steaks are costly. The prime rib cut of beef is also expensive. Chuck, shoulder cuts, and shanks are less expensive, and a section of backbone called the *chine* is an excellent low-cost cut for boiling and roasting.

Steaks and chops are most popular because they are flavorful and easy to prepare. Less popular cuts are just as high in food value, however, and they cost much less. Lower grades of meat have less calorie value, but many yield more protein, minerals, and vitamins.

How to Cook Meat

There are two chief methods for cooking meat, dry heat and moist heat. *Dry-heat* methods, such as roasting, broiling, pan broiling, frying, and deep fat frying, are best for cooking tender cuts. These methods use as little water as possible, which helps meat keep its natural flavor. Cooks usually roast meat by placing it in an uncovered pan in an oven. Broiling means to cook by applying heat directly to the meat. Cooks place the meat under the gas flame or electric heating unit of an oven, or over hot coals. *Moist-heat* methods include braising, baking, simmering, and cooking in water. These methods are best for meats that are not very tender. Dry heat tends to harden the connective tissues of less tender meats, making them harder. Moist heat softens the tissues and makes the meat more tender.

How to Carve Meat

Meat must be carved, or cut in pieces, before it can be served. Except for steaks, all meats are cut across the grain to avoid giving a stringy texture to the slices. To cut neat and uniform slices of meat, the carver should hold the knife blade at the same angle for each slice. A meat platter or a carving board allows more room for cutting and makes carving easier. See the pictures with this article for a detailed discussion on how to carve various kinds of meat, including beef, pork, and poultry.

JOHN C. AYRES

Related Articles in WORLD BOOK include:

KINDS OF MEAT

Beef	Ham	Mutton	Poultry
Fish	Lamb	Pork	Veal

OTHER RELATED ARTICLES

Amino Acid	Diet	Nutrition
Calorie	Food	Protein
Cooking	Meat Packing	Vitamin

MEAT EXTRACT is a concentrated paste made by boiling fresh, lean meat in vacuum kettles. The meat is boiled until the water takes on a brown color and the meat loses nearly all its color. Then the meat is removed, and the juice is boiled again until most of the liquid has evaporated, leaving the paste. Meat extract has a yellowish-brown color, and a pleasing, meaty odor and flavor.

Meat extract has little food value. It usually contains only about 7 per cent protein, and some minerals. The meat which is left over after boiling, even though flavorless, generally contains more food value than the extract. To add to the food value of extract, the boiled meat is sometimes ground or powdered and placed in the broth.

Meat extract has an appetizing flavor, stimulating to the appetite. It is often fed to sick persons or convalescents. It can be added to milk for persons who cannot digest milk alone. Meat extract is used to flavor soups and sauces.

JOHN C. AYRES

MEAT INSPECTION ACT OF 1906. See UNITED STATES, HISTORY OF (The Square Deal).

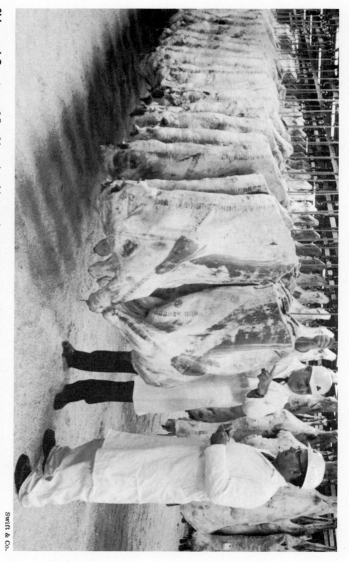

Swift & Co.

Sides and Quarters of Beef hang in refrigerated rooms at meat-packing plants until they are cut into smaller pieces. About 60 per cent of a steer's original weight can be used as meat.

MEAT PACKING

MEAT PACKING is the business of slaughtering cattle, hogs, and sheep, and preparing the meat for transportation and sale. Meat packing is an important industry in many countries. The United States produces the most *red meat* (meat of cattle, hogs, and sheep). Russia, France, West Germany, and Argentina rank next in order of production.

In the United States alone, the meat-packing industry produces more than 35 billion pounds of meat each year. More than 140 million farm animals must be slaughtered each year to produce this amount of meat. Raising and slaughtering these animals and processing the meat provide jobs for thousands of farmers, ranchers, butchers, and meat packers. The 4,000 meat-packing and processing plants in the United States employ about 230,000 workers. The industry pays out about $14 billion a year to the farmers and ranchers who raise livestock. It produces about $18 billion worth of meat and meat by-products.

Marketing of Livestock

Market Centers. Stockyards provide a central point where large numbers of animals can be collected. Each weekday, farmers and ranchers in the United States ship almost 500,000 meat animals to market. A farmer may ship several hundred head by train or truck to a *terminal* (central) market. Or, he may load a few cattle or hogs in his own truck and deliver them to one of the thousands of smaller markets called *auction markets* or *sale barns* that are scattered throughout farming areas in the United States. About 50 terminal markets operate in the United States.

Many meat packers operate slaughterhouses in ter-

minal-market cities. But not all animals shipped to terminal markets are sold and processed in that area. Some are shipped on to other markets and then sold. Others are bought and shipped on to meat-packing plants in other cities.

The Omaha, Nebr., stockyards receives the largest number of cattle of any stockyards in the United States. Other large yards are in Chicago; Sioux City, Iowa; Kansas City, Mo.; and South St. Paul, Minn. The South St. Paul and Milwaukee stockyards handle the most calves. Other leading calf markets are Sioux City; Oklahoma City, Okla.; and Fort Worth, Tex.

The market center in Omaha receives the greatest number of hogs. Sioux City; East St. Louis, Ill.; and St. Paul, and St. Joseph, Mo. are also large hog-marketing centers.

The San Angelo, Tex., stockyards receives the most sheep. Other sheep markets are in Sioux Falls, S. Dak.; South St. Paul; Omaha; and West Fargo, N. Dak.

Selling the Stock.

Most farmers and ranchers have a commission firm at the stockyards sell their animals to local slaughterers or ship the stock to packers at another location. The commission firm receives a *commission* (payment) for this service.

The stockyards charges the stock owner for the feed and water the livestock use, and for the pens the stock occupy in the stockyards. It also charges for handling the animals. These *yardage charges* and the commission fees charged by the agents who sell the stock are deducted from the check the owner receives from the commission firm. Animals sent directly to packers are paid for by the packers. Livestock commission firms and meat packers usually pay by check for all livestock they

290

Swift & Co.

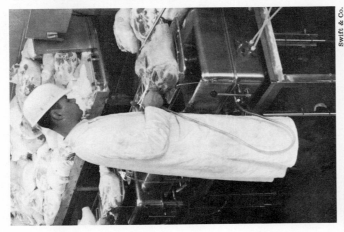

Swift & Co.

A Special Flavor is given to hams and other meats by pumping in a solution including salt and water.

A Frankfurter Assembly Line includes fast machinery that stuffs the meat into long tubes and shapes them into links.

buy within an hour after the animals are weighed in. Livestock buyers pay so much money per hundred pounds, on the basis of live weight. Factors such as age, sex, weight, grade of the animal, and degree of fatness help buyers determine the price they will pay for livestock. Expert livestock buyers can accurately estimate the meat yield of a live animal. Their judgment is seldom more than 1 per cent away from the actual meat yield after slaughtering and *dressing* (preparing meat for sale).

Packing Processes

Meat goes through more than 25 operations before it hangs dressed in packing-house coolers. Skilled workmen perform these operations with great speed. Many packing plants slaughter and dress as many as 150 head of cattle or 600 to 1,200 hogs in an hour.

Slaughtering and Dressing. Workmen use mechanical stunners to make the cattle unconscious, after which the animals are killed and dressed. The carcasses are suspended from an overhead rail for the dressing operation, in which the hide and *viscera* (internal organs) are removed. Workers cut the dressed carcasses into halves, wash them, and move them along the rail to refrigerated rooms. There the carcasses chill to about 35° F. for 12 hours. Then workers may cut the halves into forequarters and hindquarters.

At wholesale or retail establishments, butchers divide the hindquarter cuts into *round* (hind shank and rump), loin end, short loin, and flank. These cuts make up about half of a dressed beef carcass. The forequarter cuts, the other half, are divided into rib, plate, chuck, and shank. A choice grade steer that weighs 1,000

pounds when alive will yield a carcass of about 600 pounds of meat.

Calves and lambs are made unconscious by an electric shock. Then workmen slaughter and dress them in much the same way as cattle. Packers ship most calves to wholesalers and retailers as whole carcasses. Workers skin out lamb carcasses by hand.

Hogs are made unconscious by electricity or gas before they are killed. The carcasses are scalded, dehaired, and washed before being cooled overnight in a hog-chill cooler at a temperature of about 35° F. The next day, butchers in the hog-cutting room cut the carcasses into wholesale cuts—hams, shoulders, loins, backs, bellies, spareribs, and other cuts. These cuts are then sent to the shipping room to be graded by weight, boxed, and marked for shipment to markets.

Lard makes up about 20 per cent of the weight of a dressed hog. Grinding and heating operations *render* (separate) the lard from the protein in the raw fat. The fat around the kidneys may be made into leaf lard, the best grade.

Curing and Smoking processes were once used to preserve meat. Now they are used to produce the special flavor that is associated with bacon, ham, and other cuts.

Packers cure most meat by pumping a curing solution into the arteries of the meat, or by injecting the solution directly into the meat. The curing solution is made up largely of salt and water, but sugar may be included. Other ingredients are usually added to help develop the cherry-red color of cured meat.

Smoking produces the distinctive smoked-meat flavor which consumers demand in certain meats. Modern

Processing Meat to produce corned beef or other special meat products may involve adding various seasonings and cutting it into the desired size and shape. Tenderizers also may be added.

smokehouses consist of air-conditioned, stainless-steel rooms. Controlled amounts of smoke from special hardwood sawdust are drawn into the rooms. The warm, fragrant smoke gives the meat a unique flavor and color.

Tenderizing. Consumers want tenderness, as well as flavor, in the meat they buy. Less-tender cuts of meat may be ground to tenderize them. For example, ground beef makes up about 30 per cent of all fresh beef consumed in the United States.

In recent years, chemical tenderizers that are enzymes taken from fruits such as pineapple, papaya, and figs, have been used by both packers and consumers to make beef tender. When meat is cooked, the heat activates these tenderizers. Consumers may buy these tenderizers in liquid or powder form.

Sausage Making. Packers make more than 200 varieties of sausage, but they use the same basic process to make most varieties. Meat is chopped and mixed with seasonings and curing ingredients in high speed chopping machines. Generally, this mixture is forced out into *casings* (long tubes made from cellulose). The casings are then tied or twisted at regular intervals to form sausage links. Then the sausage may be smoked, cooked, or dried, depending upon the type of sausage being made.

Some sausages are ready to eat. Others require cook-

Meat Processing Magazine

ANIMAL BY-PRODUCTS

BLOOD

Adhesives
Leather Preparations
Pharmaceuticals
Plaster Retardants
Plastics
Textile Sizing

BONES, HORNS, AND HOOFS

Bone China
Gelatin
Inedible Bone Meal
Ornaments and Novelties (such as combs, buttons, and umbrella handles)

HAIR

Air Filters
Brushes
Felt Padding
Plastering Materials
Rug Pads
Upholstery

HIDE

Athletic Equipment
Belting
Chamois
Drumheads
Fertilizer
Furniture
Glue
Harnesses
Jewelry
Luggage
Shoes and Soles
Wallets and Pocketbooks
Wearing Apparel

FATS AND OILS

Antifreeze
Candles
Candles
Cellophane
Chewing Gum
Cosmetics
Detergents
Food Preservatives
Frozen Desserts
Illuminating and Industrial Oils
Insecticides
Lard
Leather Dressing
Medicinal Capsules
Nitroglycerin
Ointments
Paints
Plastics
Shortenings
Soap
Solvents
Synthetic Rubber
Tar
Weedkillers

ORGANS, GLANDS, AND VISCERA (for medical use)

ACTH
Adrenalin
Bile Salts
Cortisone
Epinephrine
Insulin
Liver Extract
Pepsin
Progesterone
Rennet
Surgical Sutures
Thyroid Extract

ing. The most popular sausage is the frankfurter, or hot dog.

By-Products

Modern production methods make it possible for meat packers to use much material that was once considered waste. In fact, packers are sometimes credited with using "every part of the pig but the squeal." Livestock producers would get less money for the animals they sell if meat packers depended only upon the sale of the carcass to make a profit. The sale of by-products is almost as profitable as the sale of carcasses.

The manufacturer divides his by-products into two classes: (1) variety meats and their by-products, and (2) by-products such as hides that are not used as food.

The variety meats of cattle include the heart, liver, kidney, tongue, brains, *sweetbreads* (thymus glands), and *tripe* (first and second stomachs). In addition to variety meats, hogs yield edible by-products such as ears, feet, *chitterlings* (small intestines), and lard.

More than a hundred different articles are made as by-products of meat packing. Some of these by-products, and what they are derived from, are listed in a table that appears in this article.

U.S. Government Inspection

The Wholesome Meat Act of 1967 requires each state to provide inspection equal to federal standards for packers who sell in and have plants in that state. The U.S. Department of Agriculture must impose federal inspection standards on all plants in a state if that state's inspection standards do not equal federal standards. The law also requires that all meat produced in one state and sold in another must be inspected by the U.S. Department of Agriculture.

The inspection process extends through each stage of preparation of meat for sale. Labels used on federally inspected meat products must be approved, and they must give complete and accurate information.

The U.S. Department of Agriculture inspects about 85 per cent of all meat produced in the United States. It administers federal laws that control the slaughtering and dressing of animals, and the preparation of meat for sale. It also inspects meat and meat products brought into the United States, and inspects the wholesomeness of meat exported to other countries.

Government inspectors, many of them veterinarians, examine each animal to be certain it is produced under sanitary conditions. They make sure that meat products are wholesome and *unadulterated* (have no improper substances added). They check the construction, equipment, and sanitation in slaughtering and processing plants. They also inspect plants that make prepared meat products such as luncheon meats; frozen meat pies and dinners; and canned and dehydrated soups.

History

William Pynchon (1590?-1662) founded the first meat-packing plant in Springfield, Mass., in 1641. The plant packed pork in salt for shipment to West Indies plantations. The number of packing houses grew as communities developed that did not produce their own meat animals. In most cases, a packing house then

served only one small community. When that community's farms failed to produce enough livestock, animals were herded in from other communities.

Before 1850, packing plants operated only during the winter. Many meat-packing plants were connected with icehouses. Men cut ice from rivers and lakes in winter, and stored it in icehouses for use in warm weather. Meat packing became a year-round business when artificial refrigeration was developed.

However, until the industry developed refrigerated railway cars, packing plants had trouble keeping meat fresh during the time needed to ship it to big Eastern cities. By the 1880's, meat packers had perfected refrigerated railway cars. In the early 1900's, inventor Frederick McKinley Jones developed a refrigeration process that could be used in trucks.

Modern meat packing also began during this period when packers perfected assembly line production methods. In 1890, Congress passed a meat inspection law for meats to be exported. In 1906, a law was passed providing for federal inspection of meats shipped in interstate commerce.

Recent Developments. Since 1945, several hundred meat-packing plants have been built in towns and cities close to the farms and ranches where livestock are raised. Companies have lowered their transportation costs by building packing plants where livestock are raised. Chicago, Omaha, and other large cities are no longer the largest meat-packing centers. Many plants which make prepared foods have been built in and near big cities. These plants supply the processed meats that are sold in neighborhood supermarkets, butcher shops, and grocery stores.

The increased use of machinery in the 1950's and 1960's has helped speed up meat-packing operations. Mechanical developments include continuous-process, frankfurter-making machines; semiautomatic slicing and weighing systems for packaged bacon; and mechanical knives and saws. Mechanically refrigerated railway cars have eliminated the need for ice and salt to preserve meat that is shipped long distances. Some packers now use computers in their production operations.

Trends in new product development include more prepackaging of retail meat items containing recipes and detailed cooking instructions, and more precooked meat products. Many meat packers offer the consumer canned meats—hams, luncheon meats, sandwich spreads, and combination dishes which consumers can store easily and serve quickly. Nearly all meat is sold in prepackaged form. Much of it is boned, shaped, and ready for cooking. New methods of breeding and feeding have produced younger animals of desired market weight and quality. As a result, meat is leaner and more tender.

Critically reviewed by the AMERICAN MEAT INSTITUTE

Related Articles in WORLD BOOK include:

Armour, Philip D.	Ham	Sausage
Bacon	Lamb	Suet
Beef	Meat	Sweetbread
Cudahy, Michael	Meat Extract	Swift
Fat	Mutton	(family)
Food (The Food	Pork	Tripe
Industry)	Pure Food and	Veal
Food Preservation	Drug Laws	

MEATBIRD. See JAY.

MECCA, *MECK uh* (pop. 185,000; alt. 919 ft.), in Saudi Arabia, is the chief holy city of the Moslems. Mohammed, the founder of the Moslem religion, was born in Mecca. The city stands in a narrow, sandy valley about 40 miles east of its Red Sea port, Juddah. Mecca is also the capital of Saudi Arabia's Hejaz Province. For location, see SAUDI ARABIA (color map).

The Great Mosque, in Mecca, is the center of worship for Moslems all over the world. It consists of an *arcade* (series of arches supported by pillars). The arcade encloses an area about 600 by 800 feet. Tall *minarets* (towers) stand at the corners of the arcade. A small, flat-roofed stone building called the *Kaaba* is in the center of an open area. Moslems throughout the world face the Kaaba when they pray. The Kaaba contains the Black Stone, which Moslems consider sacred. Moslems believe this stone was sent down from heaven by God. It is on the Kaaba's south wall.

Mohammed taught his followers that one of the five duties of a Moslem is to make a *hajj* (pilgrimage) to Mecca if he can afford it. Moslems who complete the hajj earn the title of *hajji* (pilgrim). Moslems make the pilgrimage to Mecca during the tenth and eleventh months and the first 10 days of the twelfth month of the Moslem year. The ceremonies required of a pilgrim include marching seven times around the Kaaba and kissing the Black Stone.

Moslem pilgrims from all parts of the world come to Mecca during the pilgrimage. Each Moslem tries to visit Mecca at least once during his life. Caring for these pilgrims is the city's chief industry. Many citizens serve as mosque officials, scribes, or guides. As many as 250,000 pilgrims often visit the area at one time. Moslem law forbids non-Moslems to enter Mecca.

History. Mecca was a commercial and religious center many years before Mohammed was born about

A.D. 570. *Emirs* (local rulers) governed the city. The Egyptians controlled Mecca from 1258 to 1517, when the Turks conquered the city. The Turks made it the capital of the province of Hejaz. Hejaz became an independent kingdom during World War I, and Mecca was its capital. Ibn Saud, the king of Nejd, the area to the east of Hejaz, united Hejaz and Nejd in 1926. Mecca became the religious capital of this kingdom (Riyadh is the political capital). Ibn Saud named the kingdom Saudi Arabia in 1932.

DOUGLAS D. CRARY

Related Articles in WORLD BOOK include:

Hegira	Islam	Mohammed
Hejaz	Kaaba	Moslems

MECHANIC. See REPAIRMEN AND MECHANICS.

MECHANICAL ADVANTAGE. See MACHINE.

MECHANICAL DRAWING is a drawing made with the aid of instruments. Such drawings show exactly how to construct or use machines, buildings, or other objects. No ship, airplane, dam, engine, or any of the tools of industry could be made without mechanical drawings.

Mechanical drawings do not show objects as they appear in photographs, because photographs do not indicate true dimensions. Instead, a mechanical drawing shows as many views of an object as may be necessary to define its exact shape and size. The most common method of doing this is called *orthographic*, or *right-angle*, projection. This presents views of an object as seen from the front, side, and above. After the *draftsman* (one who draws the plans) completes the necessary number of views, and has indicated all dimensions, he gives each part a number or letter. The parts are then listed in a bill that shows the kinds and sizes of materials needed to build the object.

Materials Needed. A set of instruments is necessary to make mechanical drawings. A simple set consists of at least a drawing board, a scale, a T square, triangles,

Pan-Asia, Black Star

Mecca, the Moslem Holy City, attracts thousands of Moslems on pilgrimages. Each Moslem tries to visit Mecca at least once during his life. The symbolic meeting place for all Moslems is the square, dark building, far left, known as the Kaaba.

shop practices as patternmaking, molding, blacksmithing, and welding. HARRY MUIR KURTZWORTH

See also BLUEPRINT; COMPUTER (picture: Computerized Drawing Board); PANTOGRAPH; PROTRACTOR; WORKING DRAWING.

MECHANICAL EFFICIENCY. See MACHINE (Efficiency).

MECHANICAL ENGINEERING. See ENGINEERING (Main Branches of Engineering).

MECHANICAL UNIT is a standard for measuring different mechanical quantities. Canada and the United States use the *English system*. The countries in Europe use the *Metric system*. The following examples compare the two systems.

Force. In the metric system, one dyne will give a mass of one gram an acceleration of one centimeter per second per second. In the English system, one poundal will give a mass of one pound an acceleration of one foot per second per second.

Velocity is measured in centimeters per second in the metric system, and feet per second in the English system.

Work. One dyne acting through one centimeter equals one erg. One pound raised one foot equals one foot-pound.

Pressure. A pressure of 1 million dynes per square centimeter equals one bar. One pound per square foot equals 479 dynes per square centimeter. PHILIP FRANKLIN

See also METRIC SYSTEM; WEIGHTS AND MEASURES.

MECHANICS is the science that studies the effects of forces on bodies or fluids at rest or in motion. Civil

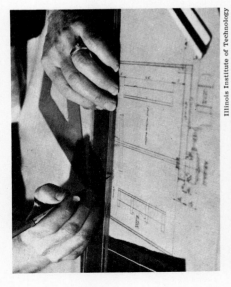

Illinois Institute of Technology

Mechanical Drawing demands attention to detail. The finished drawing must show exact views of all parts of the object.

a compass, thumbtacks, masking tape, hard pencils, an eraser, and drafting paper. Draftsmen also use curves, inking pens, dividers, protractors, a ruler, and blueprinting or other copying machines.

Career Opportunities. Mechanical drawing is exacting work, and expert draftsmen are in great demand. Courses are taught in high schools and colleges. Engineers who wish to concentrate on design must have a good background in drafting. They also must be thoroughly acquainted with mathematics, physics, chemistry, mechanics, thermodynamics, and projection. In addition, they should have a detailed knowledge of such

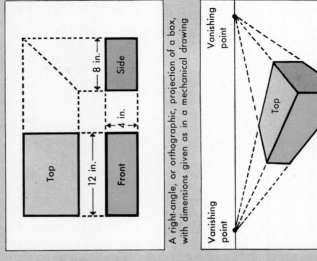

Top

8 in.

Side

12 in.

4 in.

Front

A right-angle, or orthographic, projection of a box, with dimensions given as in a mechanical drawing

Vanishing point

Top

Front

Side

Vanishing point

The box in perspective, as it would appear to the eye

MECHANICAL DRAWING

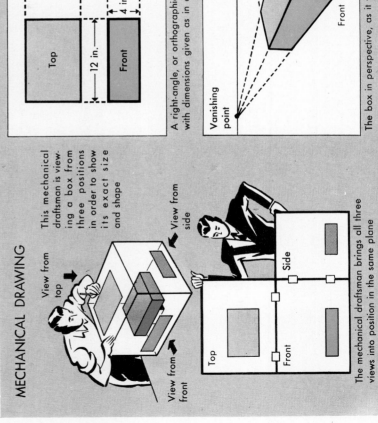

View from top

This mechanical draftsman is viewing a box from three positions in order to show its exact size and shape

View from side

View from front

Top

Side

Front

The mechanical draftsman brings all three views into position in the same plane

engineers use mechanics to determine stresses on bridges, dams, and other structures. Mechanics is also used to design rockets and airplanes. An important use of mechanics in physics is the study of the motion of atomic particles. Astronomers use the principles of mechanics to determine the motions of stars, planets, and other celestial bodies. Sir Isaac Newton first used the term to describe the science of building and using machines.

Solid mechanics includes *statics*, the study of bodies at rest or in equilibrium, and *dynamics* or *kinetics*, the study of motion or change of motion of moving bodies. *Kinematics* deals with pure motion, or motion apart from any cause. Scientists sometimes use the term *dynamics* to cover the whole field of mechanics.

Fluid mechanics includes *hydrostatics*, the study of the mechanics of still liquids, and *hydraulics*, which treats of the mechanics of liquids in motion. *Aerodynamics* is the study of air as it moves around objects.

Related Articles in WORLD BOOK **include:**

Aerodynamics	Hydraulics	Kinematics	Statics
Dynamics	Hydrostatics	Machine	

MECHANIC'S LIEN is a claim for materials or labor furnished by a contractor in the construction of a building. When filed with the proper public official, the lien must be paid before there is a clear title to the property involved. A mechanic's lien is usually paid even before a mortgage. See also LIEN.

MECHANIST PHILOSOPHY, *MECK* **uh** *nist,* states that the universe behaves like a giant machine. Everything happens according to physical laws of cause and effect. The mechanist believes that no living thing has a choice in the way it behaves. He says that events of yesterday determine what happens today. Only the past and the present can control the future.

The mechanist admits that no one can predict exactly what will happen in the future. He thinks this is true because no one knows the present state of all the matter in the universe. If anyone did, the mechanist believes, he could predict the future accurately.

Mechanism is one of the two great philosophical theories of cause and effect in the universe. Opposed to the theory of mechanism is the theory of *teleology.* Anything that grows and develops can be explained in two ways. Mechanism explains it from behind, in terms of its origins. Teleology explains it from the front, in terms of the goal it is seeking. The word *teleology* comes from a Greek word meaning *end* or *purpose.* Teleologists believe that events may be determined not only by the past, but also by the future. They believe man can choose his goals. Greek philosophy is dominated by this idea that effort and growth are inspired by goals to be achieved. An ideal, purpose, or goal at work in the universe may direct the way in which events follow one another. The mechanist would say, "I passed the examination because I studied." The teleologist would say, "I studied because I knew there would be an examination and I intended to pass it."

The first great philosopher who made clear the full meanings of the teleological and mechanistic views was Baruch Spinoza (see SPINOZA, BARUCH).

MECKLENBURG is a farming region in northern East Germany. Before World War II, it consisted of huge estates held by powerful land owners called *Junkers.*

Junkers played a major role in German history between the mid-1700's and mid-1900's (see JUNKER). In Mecklenburg, peasants lived and worked on the estates, but owned no property. The land owners controlled Mecklenburg's economy and ruled their estates with absolute authority. Peasants had few rights and often found themselves at the mercy of cruel land owners.

In 1945, Mecklenburg became part of East Germany. The East German government destroyed the power of the land owners. The government also tried, with little success, to develop industry there.

THEODORE S. HAMEROW

MECKLENBURG DECLARATION OF INDEPENDENCE refers to a resolution supposedly passed on May 20, 1775, by a group of citizens living in Mecklenburg County, North Carolina. There are no written records of such a resolution, or of the meeting at which it was supposed to have been passed. The only evidence for the story is the statement of several men who claimed, in 1819, that they had attended the meeting, where they declared their independence from Great Britain.

There is no good reason to believe that such a meeting took place. There is proof, however, that Mecklenburg citizens did meet on May 31, 1775, to protest against unjust treatment of the colonies by Great Britain. Most historians believe the May 20 meeting was imagined by some who attended the May 31 meeting. But the state of North Carolina recognizes the Mecklenburg Declaration of Independence.

JOHN R. ALDEN

MECOPTERA is an order of slender insects with long legs. In some of these insects, the end of the abdomen curves upward much like a scorpion's tail. For this reason, they are commonly called scorpion flies. See also INSECT (table); SCORPION FLY.

MEDAILLE COLLEGE. See UNIVERSITIES AND COLLEGES (table).

MEDAL. See DECORATIONS AND MEDALS.

MEDAL OF HONOR. See DECORATIONS AND MEDALS.

MEDAN, *may DAHN* (pop. 479,098; alt. 82 ft.), is a city on the island of Sumatra, Indonesia. It lies 400 miles northwest of Singapore. Medan is a commercial center for a forested and agricultural area. Its chief products include rubber, tobacco, palm oil, tea, and fibers. Medan's factories make machinery, bricks, and tile.

MEDAWAR, *MEHD* **uh** *wuh,* **SIR PETER BRIAN** (1915-   ), an English zoologist, shared the 1960 Nobel prize in physiology and medicine with Sir Macfarlane Burnet. In 1953, Medawar and his colleagues proved Burnet's idea on *acquired immunological tolerance* to be correct. This idea suggested that under certain conditions, tissues and organs can be transplanted from one animal to another and function properly even though the animals are not related.

Medawar was born in Brazil and educated in England. He became professor of zoology at University College, London, in 1951.

See also BURNET, SIR MACFARLANE.

IRWIN H. HERSKOWITZ

MEDE. See MEDIA.

MEDEA, *me DEE uh,* was an evil sorceress in Greek mythology. Her magic spells helped Jason obtain the Golden Fleece, which was kept in Colchis. A dragon guarded the treasure, but Medea put him to sleep and escaped with Jason and the Golden Fleece. Her father Aeëtes, King of Colchis, pursued them. But Medea delayed him by cutting up her younger brother Absyrtus and dropping pieces of his body along the way.

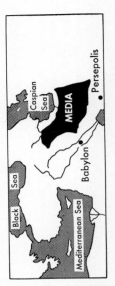

Location Map of Media, About 600 B.C.

Culver

The Story of Medea is the subject of a modern verse play by Robinson Jeffers. Dame Judith Anderson played the role of Medea.

Medea and Jason fled to Corinth and lived happily for 10 years. Jason deserted Medea and married Creusa, also called Glauce. Medea poisoned a golden robe and sent it to Creusa. Creusa died in agony. Medea cut the throats of her own children. Then she got into her dragon chariot and disappeared.

Medea was the subject of plays by Euripides and Robinson Jeffers and Cherubini's opera. PADRAIC COLUM

See also GOLDEN FLEECE; JASON.

MEDELLÍN, *MAY thay YEEN,* or *MAY duh LEEN* (pop. 1,096,790; alt. 4,880 ft.), is the second largest city in Colombia, and the country's chief commercial center. Medellín is high in the inland mountains. Nearby mines furnish coal for Medellín's factories. The city's markets sell coffee brought in from neighboring farms. The University of Antioquia and the National School of Mines are located in Medellín. For the location of Medellín, see COLOMBIA (color map). E. TAYLOR PARKS

MEDFORD, Mass. (pop. 64,971; alt. 15 ft.), is the home of the famous Medford-built ships that sailed the seas in the 1800's. Today, Medford is chiefly a residential area. It is located about five miles northwest of Boston on the Mystic River, and about five miles inland from the Atlantic Ocean (see MASSACHUSETTS [political map]).

Medford factories make paper, furniture, mattresses, toys, paper boxes, and storage batteries. Tufts University in Medford includes Jackson College for women. The Barnum Museum at Tufts houses the zoological collection of showman P. T. Barnum.

Puritans settled Medford in 1630. It ranks as one of the oldest cities in the state, and a number of colonial buildings still stand there. In colonial days, shipbuilding and rum distilling became leading industries in the settlement. Both industries declined after the Civil War. The Medford-built ships of the 1800's, with their 200- to 300-ton capacity, could navigate the shallow bays of the Pacific Northwest. Medford was incorporated as a town in 1864 and chartered as a city in 1892. It has a council-manager government. WILLIAM J. REID

MEDIA, *ME dih uh,* was an ancient country in what is now Northern Iran. It became the center of a large empire in the 500's B.C. Media was the homeland of the Medes, a nomadic people. The Medes settled in Media in the 900's B.C., and moved slowly southward.

Scholars have traced the recorded history of the Medes back to 836 B.C., when the Assyrians under King Shalmaneser III invaded Media. This was the first of many Assyrian invasions of Media. The Medes reached the peak of their power under Cyaxares, who reigned from 625 to 585 B.C. Cyaxares defeated Assyria and built an empire that included parts of what are now Turkey, Iran, Afghanistan, and Pakistan. Astyages, the son of Cyaxares and the last Median king, was defeated by Cyrus the Great of Persia about 550 B.C. Cyrus incorporated Median lands into the Persian Empire and made Media a Persian province. JACOB J. FINKELSTEIN

See also CYRUS THE GREAT; NABOPOLASSAR; SCYTHIAN.

MEDIA. See ADVERTISING (Ways of Advertising).

MEDIAN, *ME dih un,* is the middle value in a group of numbers arranged in order of size. Suppose five boys weigh 67, 62, 68, 69, and 64 pounds. To find the median, arrange the values in order of size: 62, 64, 67, 68, and 69. The number in the middle is now 67. The *median* of this group is 67, and the *median weight* is 67 pounds. The *arithmetic average* or *mean weight* of the boys is 66 pounds. If the number of cases is even, there will be no number in the middle. Under these circumstances, the median is the arithmetic average of the two middlemost values.

If we learn that the median mark on a test is 84, we know that just as many students received marks above 84 as marks below 84. The median is always settled so that there are as many values larger than the median as there are values smaller. ALBERT E. WAUGH

See also AVERAGE; MEAN; MODE; STATISTICS (illustration).

MEDIATION BOARD, NATIONAL. See NATIONAL MEDIATION BOARD.

MEDIC ALERT FOUNDATION is a nonprofit organization that issues identification emblems to persons with certain medical problems. The emblems are available to anyone who has diabetes, epilepsy, or any other problem that a doctor should know about before he begins medical treatment. For example, a person with a severe allergy may become seriously ill or die if he takes certain drugs. He might someday require emergency medical care while unconscious. If he wears a Medic Alert emblem that identifies his problem, the doctor will know not to give him the harmful drugs.

The metal emblems are available in the form of bracelets or necklaces. The symbol of the medical pro-

Medic Alert Emblem

Medic Alert Foundation

fession and the words *Medic Alert* appear on the front. The person's medical problem, his serial number, and the foundation's telephone number are engraved on the back. The doctor can call the foundation collect for further information about the patient. Medic Alert Foundation headquarters are in Turlock, Calif.

Critically reviewed by the MEDIC ALERT FOUNDATION

MEDICAID. See MEDICARE.

MEDICAL ASSOCIATION, AMERICAN. See AMERICAN MEDICAL ASSOCIATION.

MEDICAL CORPS is the name of the branch that handles health and medical matters in each of the United States armed services.

MEDICAL SCHOOL. See MEDICINE (Careers in Medicine; table: Accredited Medical Schools).

MEDICARE is a popular name for the U.S. government system of financing medical care for persons who are 65 years of age and over. The law establishing Medicare was passed in 1965. Medicare consists of two parts—hospital insurance and supplementary medical insurance.

Hospital Insurance helps pay the cost of hospital care, certain skilled nursing-home care after leaving the hospital, and post-hospital home health services. Hospital insurance is available to nearly all persons 65 and over. See BLUE CROSS.

A person pays the first $52 of his hospital bill in each period or "spell of illness." Medicare then pays the cost of the rest of the patient's covered hospital expenses for 60 days, and all but $13 a day for an additional 30 days. If extended care nursing-home facilities are also needed, Medicare pays all covered expenses for the first 20 days and all but $6.50 a day for the next 80 days. Within each "spell of illness," a person may use the full 90 days of hospital and 100 days of nursing-home benefits. He is eligible again for these benefits anytime he has not been in a hospital or extended care facility for 60 days in a row. In addition, he has a "lifetime reserve" of 60 hospital days. These can be used at any time, and cover all costs over $26 a day.

Hospital insurance is financed by a special tax paid by workers, their employers, and self-employed persons. This tax is collected along with the regular Social Security contributions. The federal government pays the cost for uninsured persons.

Medical Insurance helps pay the cost of physicians' services and certain other medical costs not covered by hospital insurance. Except for certain aliens, all persons 65 and over may sign up for this insurance. The insured member pays the first $50 of covered medical expenses in a calendar year. Medical insurance then pays 80 per cent of the cost of covered services for the rest of the year. The program is financed by payments of $5.30 a month from each insured member and by matching payments from the federal government.

Medicaid is a popular name for a section of the same law that established Medicare. It provides federal assistance to states to set up new medical care programs for the needy. Under these programs, the federal government pays between 50 and 83 per cent of the medical care costs for eligible persons of all ages. Each state determines who is eligible for benefits.

Critically reviewed by the SOCIAL SECURITY ADMINISTRATION

Portrait by Giorgio Vasari, Uffizi, Florence (Alinari)

Lorenzo de' Medici

MEDICI, *MEH dee chee*, was the name of a ruling family of Florence, Italy. Members of the family played important parts in the history of Italy and France from the 1400's to the 1700's. Their great wealth and influence as bankers first gave them control of the government of Florence.

Except for brief periods, the Medici ruled Florence until 1737. The cultural interests of the family led them to become patrons of the arts, and Florence became a center of artistic life under their rule. Michelangelo and Raphael were among the great artists the Medici helped.

The Medici influence extended to Rome when three members of the family became popes. Leo X reigned from 1513 to 1521 and Clement VII from 1523 to 1534 (see LEO [X]; CLEMENT [VII]). Leo XI was pope for only 27 days in 1605.

Two women of the Medici family became queens of France. They adopted the French spelling of the name, de Médicis.

Catherine de Médicis, the wife of Henry II and mother of three French kings, virtually ruled France from 1559 until her death in 1589 (see CATHERINE DE MÉDICIS). Marie de Médicis married Henry IV. After his death in 1610, Marie reigned until her son, Louis XIII, came of age and took over the throne.

Sculpture by Benvenuto Cellini,
M. H. De Young Memorial Museum,
Roscoe and Margaret Oakes
Collection, San Francisco

Cosimo de' Medici

Giovanni de' Medici (1360-1429) made a fortune in banking and commerce. Giovanni de' Medici is considered the first of the great Medici.

Cosimo de' Medici (1389-1464), the son of Giovanni, became the first Medici to win wide fame. He gave large sums of money to promote the arts. Cosimo wielded great influence in the city of Florence, and was called the *Father of his Country*.

Lorenzo the Magnificent (1449-1492), the grandson of Cosimo, became the most famous Medici. Lorenzo made Florence the most powerful state in Italy, and worked to make it one of the beautiful cities in the world. He built beautiful buildings and promoted the establishment of large libraries.

While the people of Florence devoted themselves to luxury, Lorenzo took over the government. The Medici first lost power under Pietro de' Medici (1471-1503), the weak son of Lorenzo, FRANKLIN D. SCOTT

See also FLORENCE (History); MICHELANGELO; PAWNBROKER (picture).

MEDICINAL FLOWERS AND PLANTS. See DRUG; FLOWER (In Industry).

MEDICINE

MEDICINE is the art and science of healing. It seeks to save lives and relieve suffering. Doctors of medicine devote their lives to fighting illness and disease.

At any time of day or night, the physician must be ready to help persons in trouble. He answers an emergency call from a mother with a sick child. His skillful hands set a broken bone or remove a tumor that might cause death. When disasters such as earthquakes, floods, or epidemics strike, he helps the sick and injured. The doctor takes much responsibility for the health of his community as well as for that of his patients. He is also a pioneer, because he constantly seeks new and better ways to heal people.

The practice of medicine is often called a *science*. Without scientific knowledge of the human body and how it works, medicine could not have progressed. But every person differs from every other person. No two illnesses are ever exactly alike. Physicians have many scientific tools to help them. But they must depend on their own wisdom, judgment, and skill to identify and treat illnesses. For these reasons, the practice of medicine is also an *art*.

Every doctor has to have certain basic knowledge and skills. Most important, he must understand how the human body works. He must know how it works when it is healthy and when it is sick. Every doctor chooses how to use his medical knowledge. Most physicians throughout the world conduct a *general practice* of medicine. These doctors, called *general practitioners*, treat all kinds of illness. Other doctors become *specialists*. They usually limit their practices to one field of medicine. Still other doctors are *researchers*. They work in laboratories and hospitals to learn more about disease and how to treat it. Some doctors spend all or part of their time as teachers in medical schools.

One of the doctor's closest co-workers is the nurse who helps him care for his patients. The druggist, who prepares the medicines prescribed by the doctor, is another ally. So is the company that makes the medicines. Health officials help doctors and dentists by enforcing laws that protect the public health. Educators aid in the fight against disease by teaching both children and adults how to keep their bodies healthy. This article deals chiefly with doctors of medicine. For information on others in the medical field, see DENTISTRY; NURSING; PHARMACY; PUBLIC HEALTH.

The Practice of Medicine

The practice of medicine involves three main activities. These are (1) *diagnosis*, the identification of illness; (2) *therapy*, the treatment of disease and injuries; and (3) *prevention*, the search for ways to avoid illness. All these activities require detailed knowledge of the human body.

Diagnosis of Disease. A patient might complain of pain in the abdomen, along with fever and vomiting. These are *symptoms* of disease. Symptoms are changes in the body that occur when disease is present. The doctor first examines the patient. He listens to the patient's heart and lungs through an instrument called a *stethoscope*. He gently prods the patient's abdomen with

The Hippocratic Oath states the ideals that are every doctor's goal. Hippocrates (460?-377? B.C.) required his students to take this oath. Today, graduating doctors still repeat the vow.

his hands. In this way, he can feel such organs as the kidneys, the liver, and the intestines. The doctor knows where each organ is because he studied *anatomy* to learn the structure of the human body. His knowledge of *physiology* helps him know how various body parts work. He learned from his study of *biochemistry* that chemical reactions take place constantly in the cells that make up the body.

The doctor knows what is normal in the body, so he can recognize any changes that have occurred. Every disease causes certain symptoms. As he examines the patient, the doctor thinks of all the diseases that could cause the patient's symptoms. He rules them out, one by one, until he can decide what is wrong with the patient. Disease may result from some change in the form of a body part. It could also be caused by an upset in the function of an organ. Or it might come from a breakdown in the reactions in the body. On the other hand, disease itself may cause such changes.

To help identify the disease and learn what caused it, the physician may send his patient to a hospital or a medical laboratory for tests. These tests usually include examinations of the patient's blood, urine, and other body fluids. An X-ray examination may be made. The doctor studies the results of these tests. His knowledge of what various diseases do to the body helps him make a diagnosis. See DIAGNOSIS.

Treatment of Disease. The doctor knows that the human body has a great ability to heal itself. One of his most important jobs is to find ways to help the body do so.

In some cases, the best treatment is simply to protect the body against further damage until healing takes place. The doctor may give his patient drugs that help the body heal itself. Perhaps an operation must be performed to remove or repair a damaged organ. Some diseases cannot be cured. The doctor tries to slow down the progress of such diseases, and makes the patient as comfortable as possible.

In any illness, the doctor seeks to relieve pain and lessen suffering while healing takes place. To do so, he must understand drugs and how they affect the body. This study is called *pharmacology*. Closely connected with it is *therapeutics*, the study of the many kinds of treatments.

Prevention of Disease. The doctor can prevent many diseases, even serious ones. He urges his patients to have a complete physical examination at least once a year. During this examination, the physician looks for signs of disease. He advises the patient about health problems. The doctor may give the patient a drug that builds up the body's resistance to disease. He gives "shots" for protection against diphtheria, whooping cough, and other diseases. He recommends diets to prevent such diseases as rickets and scurvy.

All doctors are concerned with public health. They help protect the health of their communities by supporting public health programs. Some doctors serve as public health officers. They help enforce health laws that regulate housing conditions, garbage disposal, and water supply. They also aid victims of such disasters as floods and earthquakes. See PUBLIC HEALTH.

The Medical Profession

There are so many kinds of illness, and so many forms of treatment, that we need many kinds of doctors. Most doctors belong to one of three groups: (1) general practitioners, (2) specialists, or (3) researchers.

General Practitioners. When illness or injury strikes, most people first consult a general practitioner. He is the "family doctor." He cares for patients with all kinds of illnesses, from a common cold to appendicitis. The *G.P.*, as he is often called, may not have special training in any one field of medicine. But he develops a wide knowledge of all kinds of illness. He delivers babies, diagnoses diseases, performs surgery, and sets broken bones. The general practitioner often becomes extremely skillful in the art of medical practice. He develops an understanding of people and diseases that cannot be taught in medical textbooks. In the United States, about 40 per cent of the physicians in private practice are general practitioners. In Canada, the figure is about 50 per cent.

Some general practitioners live and work in isolated communities. They must treat all types of illnesses and injuries. But where specialists are available, the G.P. consults them when a patient has a difficult or unusual illness.

Specialists. Certain fields of medicine require special advanced training and skill. One specialist is the *surgeon*, who treats diseases by means of surgical operations. Most doctors perform certain kinds of surgery in their everyday practices. They may make an *incision* (cut) to allow an infection to drain. Or they may take out a patient's tonsils. Difficult operations are usually performed by highly skilled surgeons. Surgeons, like other specialists, often work only with certain parts of the body. *Orthopedic surgeons* specialize in bone and joint diseases. *Cardiac surgeons* operate on the heart and large blood vessels.

Some physicians prefer to treat only certain kinds of illnesses. They become specialists in their chosen fields. Other doctors often consult them when a patient needs their special skill and knowledge. A general practitioner might refer a pregnant woman to an *obstetrician*. The obstetrician cares for her and delivers her baby. A *pediatrician*, who specializes in childhood diseases, then takes over the care of the infant.

Doctors do not need special licenses to become specialists. But most specialists take advanced training in their fields. Doctors in each specialty have set up

WHAT DOCTORS DO

Vortes Fischer

Doctors Interview patients as a normal part of a medical examination, left. This helps the doctor diagnose his patients' medical problems.

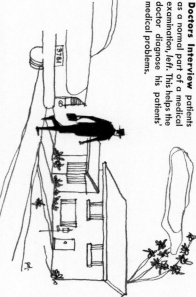

Making House Calls. The doctor must be prepared to hurry to the home of a sick person at any time of day or night.

Operating. Every doctor is trained in surgery. He may have to perform an operation to cure a disease or to save a patient's life. A team of doctors and nurses, *left*, helps the surgeon.

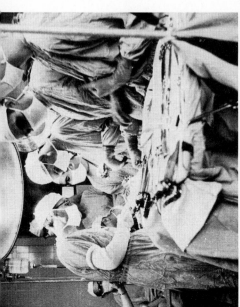

Rus Arnold

Examining Patients, *below*, often enables a doctor to find early signs of disease. He then can correct disorders that could cause trouble later.

Gus Pasquarella, courtesy *The Saturday Evening Post*, © 1959, Curtis Publishing Co.

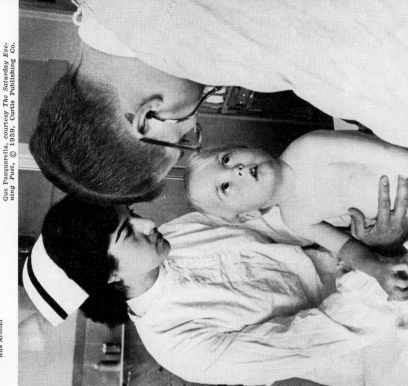

Keeping Informed about advances in medicine is important to every physician. Doctors share information at professional meetings and seminars, *above*.

Du Pont Magazine

Diagnosing Diseases. Doctors use X rays, *below*, to identify diseases and to find their location and cause.

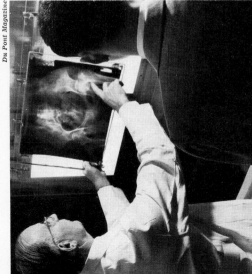

Research projects are conducted by many doctors. Some physicians are full-time researchers. Others also have regular practices.

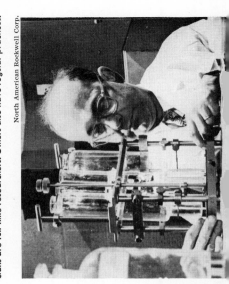

North American Rockwell Corp.

examination boards. These boards make sure that a specialist's knowledge and experience stay at a high level. The American Board of Medical Specialists establishes standards of professional knowledge in various specialties. It recognizes 18 specialty fields, which are described in the accompanying table. Canada and other countries have similar specialty boards.

Researchers. Some physicians do not practice medicine. They prefer to devote their time to medical research. These doctors often help teach future physicians in medical schools. At the same time, they use the laboratories and hospital facilities of the medical schools to conduct research programs. Some earn special degrees in chemistry, biochemistry, physiology, or pharmacology.

Many medical researchers work in large hospital research centers. Their projects are supported by private foundations or by government grants of money. Other researchers work for manufacturing companies, seeking new kinds of medicines and treatments. Medical research is not limited to doctors who work full time in research laboratories. Many physicians conduct research programs in addition to their private practices. Medical journals publish the results of medical research. In this way, doctors pass on new knowledge to other physicians.

What a Doctor Does

A doctor's day is long and busy. It usually begins early in the morning and often ends late at night. A family doctor may begin his day by going to the hospital to check the progress of his patients there. After lunch, he might see patients in his office. Then perhaps he makes house calls, treating patients in their homes.

He may have office hours again in the evening. He spends some time reading medical journals to keep up with the latest developments. If he is lucky, the doctor gets to bed about midnight and can sleep until morning. But frequently his telephone rings during the night. The caller may be a woman who is about to have a baby. Or it could be a man who has just had a heart attack. No matter what emergencies interrupt his sleep, the doctor must be alert to care for his patients again the next day.

In the Office. Most patients go to the doctor's office if they are not too ill. There the physician can see a wide variety of cases conveniently. He also can deal at once with his patients' problems. A doctor's office usually has several rooms. In a consulting room, the doctor and his patient can discuss the patient's problems. An examining room, where the doctor gives physical examinations, is nearby.

The doctor has a supply of drugs in his office for emergency use. He also has sterilized bandages and instruments for such treatments as sewing a deep wound or opening a boil. An *X-ray machine* helps him locate broken bones. Another machine, the *electrocardiograph*, aids in the diagnosis of heart ailments. Most offices include a small laboratory for examinations of blood and urine. A treatment room may have heat lamps and other physical therapy equipment.

Many doctors employ nurses to help them in their offices. The nurse assists the doctor in the examining room, and may administer drugs or treatments. Some doctors have large offices and see many patients every day. They may require the help of more than one office nurse. Such a doctor might have a receptionist to greet his patients and to arrange appointments. He may employ an X-ray technician or a laboratory technician to help with special examinations.

KINDS OF MEDICAL SPECIALTY FIELDS

Anesthesiology is the study of anesthesia and anesthetics. Physicians who have advanced training in this field are anesthesiologists. They give anesthetics during operations or direct the services of anesthetists.

Dermatology is the diagnosis and treatment of diseases of the skin. Specialists in this field are dermatologists.

Internal Medicine deals with diseases that cannot be treated by surgery. Specialists in this field are called *internists*. Some limit their work to *allergies* (diseases caused by sensitivities to certain substances), *cardiovascular diseases* (diseases of the heart and blood vessels), or *gastroenterology* (diseases of the stomach and intestines).

Neurological Surgery, or neurosurgery, concerns the surgical treatment of diseases and disorders of the nervous system. Doctors who specialize in this field are neurosurgeons.

Obstetrics and Gynecology are specialties dealing with women's health. Obstetricians limit their practice to treating women during pregnancy and labor. Gynecologists limit their practice to the treatment of women's diseases.

Ophthalmology is the study of the eye and its diseases. Specialists are ophthalmologists.

Orthopedic Surgery, or *orthopedics*, treats all parts of the skeletal system, including bones, joints, and ligaments. Specialists are orthopedic surgeons or orthopedists.

Otolaryngology is the study of the ear and throat and their diseases. Doctors who specialize in this field are otolaryngologists. Those who treat only the ear are otologists. Those who treat only the throat are laryngologists.

Pathology deals with the nature of disease. Pathologists study changes in the body that cause disease or are caused by disease. Clinical pathologists use laboratory tests to diagnose diseases.

Pediatrics concerns treatment of children's diseases. Specialists are pediatricians.

Physical Medicine and Rehabilitation, or *physiatrics*, treats diseases by such physical means as exercise or light, heat, or water therapy. Doctors who limit their practice to this field are physiatrists. They direct the work of such experts as *physical therapists* and *occupational therapists*.

Plastic Surgery restores or rebuilds certain parts of the body that are imperfect or have been damaged. Specialists in this field are *plastic surgeons*.

Preventive Medicine deals with the prevention of disease. Physicians and surgeons in this field may limit their practice to such fields as *public health, aviation medicine,* or *industrial medicine*.

Proctology is concerned with diseases of the rectum. Specialists are proctologists.

Psychiatry and Neurology deal with the mind and nervous system. Psychiatrists treat mental illnesses. Neurologists treat disturbances and diseases of the nervous system.

Radiology uses X rays and radium to diagnose and treat disease. Doctors in this field are radiologists.

Surgery is the treatment of disease by operations. Doctors who limit their practice to this field are surgeons. Thoracic surgery deals with the surgical treatment of diseases of the thorax (chest). Specialists are thoracic surgeons.

Urology concerns the treatment of diseases of the organs that produce and excrete urine. It also includes treatment of diseases of the reproductive organs. Specialists are urologists.

Most doctors specify their daily office hours. In emergencies, they see patients at any hour. Some doctors see patients on a first-come, first-serve basis. Others see patients only by appointment.

At the Hospital. A patient may need an operation or special tests that can be done only in a hospital. The doctor also hospitalizes patients with severe illnesses that require nursing care, close observation, or special drugs.

The physician arranges for his patient's admission to the hospital. At the hospital, he writes orders for each patient. These directions guide the nurses who care for the patient. The doctor makes daily "rounds" at the hospital, visiting all his patients. He studies each patient's chart, which gives him details of the person's progress. The chart also shows the care given, and the patient's reactions to drugs and other treatments.

While the doctor is at the hospital, he may schedule operations that he will perform there. In the operating room, he is assisted by specially trained nurses and doctors-in-training. Most babies are delivered by a doctor in a hospital. The hospital's well-equipped obstetrical department helps care for mothers and their babies. The doctor also may use the hospital emergency room when he treats accident victims.

House Calls may take much of a doctor's time. But in recent years, doctors have reduced the number of house calls they make. They believe that office calls take less time and provide better care than calls at the patient's home. In emergencies, of course, doctors respond as quickly as possible. Each doctor carries the familiar black bag, which contains a stethoscope, thermometer, hypodermic syringe, gauze bandages, and instruments and drugs.

To Keep Informed. The physician must keep up with medical advances. He subscribes to medical journals, which tell him about new medical discoveries. Drug manufacturers send doctors information about new drugs and treatments. Representatives of these firms visit the doctor and explain the uses of new products. From time to time, the doctor also attends meetings, seminars, and postgraduate medical courses.

The Doctor in the Community

Government and Medicine. Most countries have laws that regulate how doctors practice. Laws also establish standards that doctors must meet before they can treat patients.

Licensing. A doctor cannot practice medicine just because he has been graduated from a medical school and has finished training in a hospital. He must pass special examinations to obtain a license to practice. This license also permits him to prescribe drugs.

In most countries, a physician's license permits him to practice anywhere in that country. In the United States and Canada, each state and province gives its own examination and grants its own license. Most states and provinces have "reciprocal agreements." That is, doctors licensed in one state or province can practice in another without taking a second examination. However, there is no reciprocity between the United States and Canada or any other nation. Many doctors in the United States take National Board Examinations given by a federal board. They take these examinations in addition to, or instead of, the state examinations. Licenses obtained in this way are accepted by all but a few states.

Regulation of Narcotics. The United States government controls the importation, purification, and sale of narcotic drugs. A physician must obtain a permit from the federal government before he can give narcotics to patients. His permit has a number that is recorded by the United States Bureau of Narcotics and Dangerous Drugs. The doctor must put this number on every prescription for a narcotic drug. Narcotics such as morphine and codeine are used as pain killers. But overdoses of these drugs can cause death, and prolonged use can be habit-forming. For these reasons, the government controls the manufacture of narcotics and allows only responsible physicians to prescribe them. See NARCOTIC; NARCOTICS AND DANGEROUS DRUGS, BUREAU OF.

Government Aid and Support. Governments contribute to the medical profession in many ways. Most states help support medical schools. These schools train doctors and provide laboratories for medical research. County and city governments offer care and hospitalization for persons who cannot pay.

The federal government supports military and Veterans Administration hospitals throughout the United States. Other government agencies deal with nationwide health care. They include the U.S. Public Health Service; the Department of Health, Education, and Welfare; and the National Research Council.

Socialized Medicine is a general name for government health programs paid for in whole or in part by tax money. In some countries, the government pays doctors and supplies free medical and hospital facilities. In 1965, the U.S. Congress passed *Medicare*, a program designed to help aged persons pay hospital and nursing home expenses. The cost of this program, which started in 1966, is paid through higher Social Security taxes. See SOCIALIZED MEDICINE; MEDICARE.

Ethics and Legal Responsibilities. The relationship between a doctor and his patient is more than a mere business contract. Each has confidence and trust in the other. Ethical and moral rules govern doctors in their practices. These rules require that the doctor guard the confidence of his patient and accept responsibility for the patient's care. Hippocrates, an ancient Greek physician, was the father of modern medicine. He established the guiding principles of medical ethics. Graduating medical students vow to follow his principles when they take the Hippocratic oath. See HIPPOCRATES.

Physicians cannot guarantee to cure illness or to save lives. But they promise to do the best that their training and experience permits. A doctor who fails to uphold his responsibility to his patients is guilty of *malpractice*, a legal offense. If a patient suffers because of a doctor's negligence, the doctor can be held legally responsible. A surgeon who makes a mistake in the operating room because of negligence may be charged with malpractice.

Some physicians make a special study of the legal aspects of medicine. They become specialists in *forensic* medicine. Many legal cases and civil law suits involve medical questions. Lawyers often ask physicians to testify in court on medical matters.

Doctors do not advertise, even though no law forbids their doing so. Physicians believe that advertising their services hurts the dignity of their relationship with patients.

Fees and Salaries. In most countries, a doctor may charge his patients whatever he thinks proper for his services. Fees vary widely among doctors and from community to community. Specialists often charge higher fees than do general practitioners. In countries with socialized medicine, the fee for a service is likely to be the same throughout the nation.

Some doctors receive fixed salaries every year. They include physicians who work only on hospital staffs or in large industrial plants, and those who do only research work. Doctors with large practices often employ other doctors as salaried assistants. The *median* (middle) net income of self-employed physicians, the largest group, is $25,000 a year in the United States and $15,800 in Canada.

Medical Organizations. The largest medical organization in the United States is the *American Medical Association (AMA)*, a nationwide federation of doctors who are members of their respective state medical societies. County medical societies also form part of the association. The *Canadian Medical Association*, with provincial and local units, is the largest medical group in Canada. These organizations help standardize medical practice and discipline the profession. They help enforce medical ethics, hear public complaints against doctors, and provide medical libraries. Sometimes they act as spokesman for the medical profession on problems that affect the nation or the profession itself. An organization of national medical associations from over 60 countries forms the *World Medical Association*. This organization provides an international code of ethics.

In most hospitals, the doctors on the staff make up a hospital staff organization. This group helps direct the work of the hospital. It also tries to maintain high standards of practice in the hospital. Doctors in some communities have formed another kind of organization,

the *medical service bureau*. They sponsor a type of medical insurance that provides medical service at moderate cost to families with low incomes.

Most medical specialties have their own organizations. These groups hold conferences and sponsor educational programs that help maintain their high standards of training.

Careers in Medicine

Young men and women who choose careers in medicine face a long, difficult, and expensive training period. First, the future doctor spends at least three, but usually four, years in a liberal arts college. He studies for more years in a medical school. Then he takes at least a year's training in a hospital. If he wants to specialize, he needs even more time before he begins to practice.

Expenses vary greatly. They depend on the college and the medical school, on whether the student is married or single, and on the student's personal needs. The cost of a single year in a U.S. medical school ranges from $2,700 to $5,350. This includes money for food, clothing, and housing. Most medical students are too busy with their studies to hold part-time jobs. About two of every five medical students must borrow money to complete their studies. They borrow an average of about $1,500 per student per year.

The most important personal qualification for a medical career is a deep and unwavering desire to be a doctor. The person who chooses medicine as a career must like people and want to help them. He has to make good-to-excellent grades in college and in medical school. He also should have a natural aptitude for these skills for success in medicine.

Premedical Education has two major goals. First, it gives the future doctor a broad general college edu-

Basic Education. High school courses provide a test for a person's interest and ability in science. General courses in the physical and biological sciences offer an excellent background for more detailed courses in college. Students also learn fundamental study habits and develop their ability to concentrate. They need these skills for success in medicine.

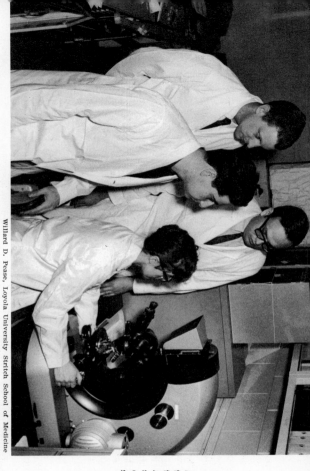

Willard D. Pease, Loyola University Stritch School of Medicine

Medical Education combines the study of real patients with textbook and laboratory work. A group of medical students studies the activities of a human cell through a powerful microscope, left.

cation. The student takes such liberal arts courses as English composition, literature, sociology, and foreign languages. Second, premedical training provides a scientific background for medical studies. The student must take such courses as zoology, physics, and organic and inorganic chemistry. Some medical schools admit students with only three years of premedical education. But most medical schools require a candidate to study for four years and earn a bachelor's degree.

Admission to medical schools is highly competitive. In the United States, only about 56 of every 100 candidates are accepted. Medical schools choose candidates largely on the basis of their grades in premedical courses. If a student is not in the upper half of his class, he is urged not to study medicine. Medical schools also discourage students who have had trouble with science courses. The student should apply to the medical school of his choice about a year before he finishes premedical training. He should also apply to several other schools to increase his chances of acceptance by one of them. Many medical schools use standard tests to screen applicants. Such tests may be taken during the student's junior or senior year in college.

Medical Education. Every doctor spends four years in medical school. During the first two years, called *preclinical years*, the future physician studies the basic

ACCREDITED MEDICAL SCHOOLS

U.S. Schools

ALABAMA	Medical Coll. of Alabama	Birmingham
ARKANSAS	Univ. of Arkansas	Little Rock
CALIFORNIA	Univ. of California	Irvine, Los Angeles, San Francisco
	Loma Linda Univ.	Loma Linda
	Univ. of Southern California	Los Angeles
	Stanford Univ.	Stanford
COLORADO	Univ. of Colorado	Denver
CONNECTICUT	Yale Univ.	New Haven
DISTRICT OF COLUMBIA	George Washington Univ.	Washington
	Georgetown Univ.	Washington
	Howard Univ.	Washington
FLORIDA	Univ. of Miami	Miami
	Univ. of Florida	Gainesville
GEORGIA	Emory Univ.	Atlanta
	Medical Coll. of Georgia	Augusta
ILLINOIS	Chicago Medical School	Chicago
	Loyola Univ.	Chicago
	Northwestern Univ.	Chicago
	Univ. of Chicago	Chicago
	Univ. of Illinois	Chicago
INDIANA	Indiana Univ.	Indianapolis
IOWA	Univ. of Iowa	Iowa City
KANSAS	Univ. of Kansas	Kansas City
KENTUCKY	Univ. of Kentucky	Lexington
	Univ. of Louisville	Louisville
LOUISIANA	Louisiana State Univ.	New Orleans
	Tulane Univ.	New Orleans
MARYLAND	Johns Hopkins Univ.	Baltimore
	Univ. of Maryland	Baltimore
MASSACHUSETTS	Boston Univ.	Boston
	Harvard Univ.	Boston
	Tufts Univ.	Boston
MICHIGAN	Univ. of Michigan	Ann Arbor
	Wayne State Univ.	Detroit
MINNESOTA	Univ. of Minnesota	Minneapolis-St. Paul
MISSISSIPPI	Univ. of Mississippi	Jackson
MISSOURI	Univ. of Missouri	Columbia
	St. Louis Univ.	St. Louis
	Washington Univ.	St. Louis
NEBRASKA	Creighton Univ.	Omaha
	Univ. of Nebraska	Omaha
NEW JERSEY	New Jersey College of Medicine and Dentistry	Jersey City
NEW MEXICO	Univ. of New Mexico	Albuquerque
NEW YORK	Union Univ.	Albany
	Yeshiva Univ.	New York
	Columbia Univ.	New York
	Cornell Univ.	New York
	New York Medical Coll.	New York
	New York Univ.	New York
	State Univ. of N.Y. at:	Buffalo
	Downstate Medical Center	New York
	Upstate Medical Center	Syracuse
	Univ. of Rochester	Rochester
NORTH CAROLINA	Univ. of North Carolina	Chapel Hill
	Duke Univ.	Durham
	Wake Forest Univ.	Winston-Salem
OHIO	Univ. of Cincinnati	Cincinnati
	Case Western Reserve Univ.	Cleveland
	Ohio State Univ.	Columbus
OKLAHOMA	Univ. of Oklahoma	Oklahoma City
OREGON	Univ. of Oregon	Portland
PENNSYLVANIA	Hahnemann Medical Coll.	Philadelphia
	Jefferson Medical Coll.	Philadelphia
	Temple Univ.	Philadelphia
	Univ. of Pennsylvania	Philadelphia
	Woman's Medical Coll.	Philadelphia
	Univ. of Pittsburgh	Pittsburgh
PUERTO RICO	Univ. of Puerto Rico	San Juan
SOUTH CAROLINA	Medical Coll. of South Carolina	Charleston
TENNESSEE	Univ. of Tennessee	Memphis
	Meharry Medical Coll.	Nashville
	Vanderbilt Univ.	Nashville
TEXAS	Univ. of Texas	Dallas, Galveston
	Baylor Univ.	Houston
UTAH	Univ. of Utah	Salt Lake City
VERMONT	Univ. of Vermont	Burlington
VIRGINIA	Univ. of Virginia	Charlottesville
	Virginia Commonwealth Univ.	Richmond
WASHINGTON	Univ. of Washington	Seattle
WEST VIRGINIA	West Virginia Univ.	Morgantown
WISCONSIN	Univ. of Wisconsin	Madison
	Marquette School of Medicine	Milwaukee

Canadian Schools

ALBERTA	Univ. of Alberta	Edmonton
BRITISH COLUMBIA	Univ. of British Columbia	Vancouver
MANITOBA	Univ. of Manitoba	Winnipeg
NOVA SCOTIA	Dalhousie Univ.	Halifax
ONTARIO	Queen's Univ.	Kingston
	Univ. of Western Ontario	London
	Univ. of Ottawa	Ottawa
	Univ. of Toronto	Toronto
QUEBEC	McGill Univ.	Montreal
	Univ. of Montreal	Montreal
	Laval Univ.	Ste. Foy
SASKATCHEWAN	Univ. of Saskatchewan	Saskatoon

medical sciences. His courses include anatomy, physiology, biochemistry, and pharmacology. The student's first contact with patients comes near the end of this period. He learns to *take case histories*—that is, to ask patients about their symptoms and previous illnesses. He also learns to give physical examinations.

The second two years of medical school are the *clinical years*. Medical schools and hospitals work together to train the student. The medical student spends most of his time in the hospital. There, he studies the illnesses of patients. He helps with their care while he learns about diagnosis and treatment. The student works in the medical wards, in the labor and delivery rooms, and in the operating rooms. He also attends lectures and has regular reading assignments in his textbooks. Upon graduation from medical school, he receives a Doctor of Medicine (M.D.) degree.

Internship. Every graduate doctor serves a year as a hospital intern. He tries to choose a hospital that will give him the additional training he wants. Most hospitals offer *rotating internships*. Under this system, the intern spends some time in each of the hospital's *services* (medical departments). He might start in pediatrics, then move to internal medicine, and then to surgery. Some hospitals have *straight internships*. The intern spends all his time in one of the four major services—internal medicine, surgery, pediatrics, or obstetrics and gynecology. Other hospitals offer *mixed internships*. The intern's assignments include only two or three major services.

The intern works under the close supervision of doctors on the staff. He "makes rounds" with them, visiting hospital patients. He may help give special treatments. He answers emergency calls in the hospital at any time of day or night. Some hospitals provide living quarters for interns. Hospitals in the United States pay interns an average of about $360 a month.

Residency. Most young physicians spend another year or more in a hospital as residents. This additional training gives them even more experience. If the doctor wants to become a specialist, he may spend two to five years as a resident. He concentrates all his work on his chosen specialty. The resident who wants to be a surgeon, for example, watches as many operations as possible. Like the intern, he learns by observing the work of others. But the resident has much more responsibility than the intern. He often assists experienced surgeons during operations. In an emergency, he may take over the work of the staff surgeon.

The resident chooses a hospital that offers the best training in his specialty. U.S. hospitals pay residents an average of about $360 a month. Some hospitals provide living quarters for their residents.

History

Primitive Medicine. In the earliest days of medicine, people believed that evil spirits and angry gods caused diseases. Tribal witch doctors acted as "physicians." The people thought the witch doctors had special powers to get rid of evil spirits. Primitive physicians discovered many drugs and treatments that are still used today. They found that chewing the leaves of the foxglove plant (digitalis) could slow a rapidly beating heart. They used the bark of certain trees (quinine) to

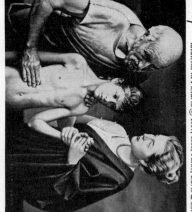

Paintings by Robert A. Thom, from *A History of Medicine in Pictures* © 1957, 1958, Parke, Davis & Co.

Hippocrates, a Greek physician of the 400's B.C., is called the father of medicine. He established principles that are still used by physicians.

Galen, a physician in Rome during the A.D. 150's, studied how the body works. Doctors used his methods of treatment, *right*, for hundreds of years.

HIGHLIGHTS IN MEDICINE

An Egyptian Physician of the 1400's B.C. treats a patient with symptoms of lockjaw. Ancient Egyptian doctors diagnosed and treated many kinds of diseases.

300 B.C. 200 B.C. 100 B.C. A.D. 1 A.D. 100 A.D. 200

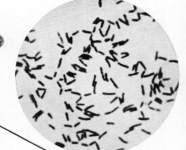
Brown Bros.

Human Anatomy was first described completely in the 1500's by Andreas Vesalius, *left,* a physician who was born in what is now Belgium.

The Microscope enabled scientists to see germs. Anton van Leeuwenhoek, a Dutch amateur scientist of the 1600's, studied them under his microscope, *right.* He was the first to record his observations of germs.

The Germ Theory of disease was proved in the 1800's by Louis Pasteur of France and Robert Koch of Germany.

Tuberculosis Germs, *above,* were discovered and described by Koch in 1882. He also developed a test for the disease.

NASA

Space Medicine. Machines such as the centrifuge, below, are used to create space conditions. Doctors test the body's reactions in them.

1500 1600 1700 1800 1900 2000

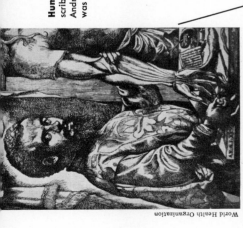
World Health Organization

X Rays were discovered in 1895 by Wilhelm Roentgen, a German physicist. Doctors often use X-ray pictures, below, to diagnose diseases.

Penicillin Mold, *left,* produced the first "wonder drug." The drug was purified in the early 1940's by Alexander Fleming, a British bacteriologist, and his co-workers.

Chas. Pfizer & Co., Inc.

Open Heart Surgery, *below,* was perfected in the 1950's. A machine pumps the patient's blood during the operation. It keeps the patient alive and the heart dry.

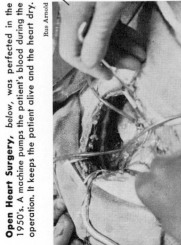
Rus Arnold

help control fever. They squeezed the juice from the belladonna plant (atropine) and used it to relieve suffering caused by abdominal cramps. See ATROPINE; DIGITALIS; QUININE.

Egyptian, Greek, and Roman Medicine. As early as 2500 B.C., Egyptian physicians were famous for their diagnosis and treatment of hundreds of diseases. They performed many kinds of operations, including surgery to relieve pressure in the skull.

The physicians of ancient Greece made outstanding contributions. They realized the importance of reasoning, observation, and research in medical practice. Hippocrates, who lived in the 400's B.C., developed great skill in diagnosis. Doctors still use his descriptions of certain diseases, such as pneumonia and pleurisy, and many of his methods of diagnosis.

Greek civilization declined about 200 to 100 B.C. The city of Alexandria in Egypt then became the medical center of the ancient world. A great medical school flourished there for several hundred years. This school was particularly famous for its experiments in anatomy. Its library preserved and recorded the medical knowledge of the time.

The Romans got their knowledge of medicine from the Greeks, and developed it. Greek physicians began to practice in Rome about 300 B.C. In 46 B.C., Julius Caesar gave Roman citizenship to all free-born Greek physicians in Rome. The Greeks established the importance of personal hygiene, and the Romans developed public health. The Romans recognized the need for sanitary engineering. They drained swamps and built great aqueducts to carry fresh water from the mountains to their cities. The ancient Romans also built a system of sewers to carry off wastes. Many medical historians rank Galen as the most

famous physician of Rome. He studied anatomy at the school in Alexandria, and was the physician of the gladiators in Pergamum before he went to Rome. Galen's greatest interest was the human body and how it works. He recorded his principles of medicine in books that were used by physicians for hundreds of years. Doctors now know that Galen had many wrong ideas.

The Middle Ages. Medicine made little progress during the Middle Ages, from about the 400's to the 1400's. Great plagues such as the *black death* (bubonic plague) killed millions of persons (see BUBONIC PLAGUE). Other diseases, including syphilis and smallpox, made hundreds of thousands of persons ill. Doctors had no defenses against these diseases.

During this period, medicine was practiced largely in the great monasteries. The monks grew herbs for use as medicines. They also collected and studied manuscripts that described the work of Greek and Roman doctors.

Several famous medical schools were established. But they served as libraries of past medical knowledge, rather than as centers of progress. One of them, the medical school at Salerno in Italy, reached its peak in the 1100's. All the great discoveries of Greek, Alexandrian, Hebrew, and Arabian medicine were taught there. The medical schools at Montpellier in France, and Oxford in England also became famous.

The 1400's to 1700's. Two men gave doctors a better understanding of anatomy and physiology. The great Italian artist Leonardo da Vinci studied the human body in detail during the late 1400's. He pioneered in dissection. Da Vinci drew accurate pictures of bones, muscles, tendons, the heart, the lungs, and other parts of the body. In the 1500's, Andreas Vesalius, a professor at the University of Padua, made extensive studies of

Rhazes, an Arab physician who lived from A.D. 865 to 925, studied children's diseases. He was the first physician to describe measles and smallpox. Arab doctors contributed much to medicine during a time when European doctors were making little progress.

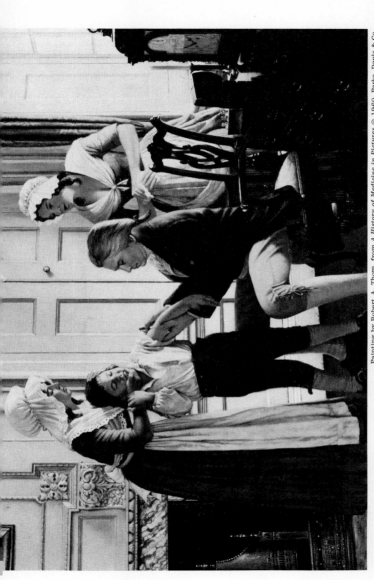

The First Smallpox Vaccination was performed in 1796. Edward Jenner, an English physician, scratched fluid from cowpox blisters into a boy's arm.

Painting by Robert A. Thom, from *A History of Medicine in Pictures* © 1960, Parke, Davis & Co.

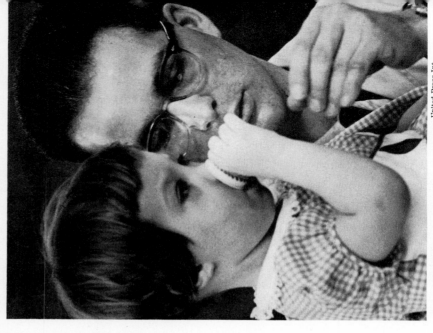

Today's Oral Polio Vaccination is painless. Children and adults swallow the vaccine, and avoid the discomfort of injections.

United Press Int.

anatomy and physiology. He published his findings in a book—the first complete descriptions of human anatomy. Doctors now know that some of his observations were wrong. But Vesalius helped destroy many false beliefs about the structure of the human body.

Philippus Paracelsus, a Swiss physician, contributed to the treatment of diseases with drugs. Doctors of his time used drugs to treat all diseases. Often their medicines consisted of 20 or more ingredients. Paracelsus pointed out that in many of these remedies, one ingredient made another useless. He introduced the idea of finding the drug that was most effective against the disease being treated. Doctors today use this method for prescribing drugs.

The English physician William Harvey proved in the early 1600's that the blood circulates through the body. For hundreds of years, men had believed that the blood flowed back and forth in the body, much like the ebb and flow of ocean tides. Harvey showed that the heart pumps blood into the arteries, and that the veins return blood to the heart. He experimented with animals, actually seeing and feeling the heart beat. Harvey used mathematics to estimate how many ounces of blood the heart pumps every hour. This was probably the first use of mathematics in medical research. Harvey's work showed that the study of how the body works cannot be separated from knowledge of the structure of the body.

Harvey did not know how the arteries and veins were linked so that blood could flow from one to the other. In 1661, four years after Harvey's death, an Italian anatomist named Marcello Malpighi showed that capillaries join the arteries to the veins.

The microscope gave doctors a way to study germs. In the late 1600's, Anton van Leeuwenhoek, a Dutch amateur scientist, saw many kinds of germs through his simple microscope. But the role of germs as a cause of disease was not established until about 150 years later.

During the late 1700's, the English physician Edward Jenner discovered a method of vaccination against smallpox. Jenner did not know why vaccination worked. But he proved that people could be saved from smallpox even after being exposed to the disease. Jenner's discovery led to the science of *immunology*, the prevention of disease by building up resistance to it. See VACCINATION.

The 1800's. Medicine moved ahead rapidly during the 1800's. The brilliant research of Louis Pasteur and Robert Koch firmly established the germ theory of disease. Since the 1500's, various scientists had suggested that "invisible seeds" could cause disease. Many believed that these "seeds" came into being in the body of a sick person. Pasteur, a French bacteriologist, and Koch, a German physician, proved that the "seeds" were germs. They showed that germs exist everywhere, and do not come into being in a patient's body. Both men proved that sterilization kills germs.

Two doctors, Ignaz Semmelweis of Hungary and Joseph Lister of England, used the new knowledge of germs to make surgery safe. They introduced the basic idea of *antisepsis*, the killing of germs that cause infection. They also showed the need for *asepsis* (the complete cleanliness that keeps germs out of wounds).

In the United States, Crawford Long and William T. G. Morton made anesthesia safe for surgery. Until the early 1840's, the pain and shock of operations had limited the usefulness of surgery. Long, a physician, and Morton, a dentist, developed ether as an anesthetic. Surgeons could now control pain in operations.

As medicine advanced, the need grew for trained physicians. Many medical schools were established in Europe and the U.S. Teachers such as Sir William Osler of Canada helped set high training standards.

The 1900's. Research in physics, chemistry, biochemistry, and bacteriology helped medicine advance. The French physicists Marie and Pierre Curie discovered radium, a weapon against cancer. X rays, discovered by the German physicist Wilhelm Roentgen, provided a way to diagnose many diseases, and also to treat cancer. The German chemist and physician Gerhard Domagk found that a group of chemicals, the *sulfonamides*, fought germs. This discovery started the age of "miracle drugs." Doctors could now treat such diseases as meningitis, blood poisoning, and venereal diseases. Sir Alexander Fleming, a British biochemist, discovered *penicillin*, the first *antibiotic* drug. Another antibiotic, *streptomycin*, was discovered by the American biochemist Selman A. Waksman. It helped the fight against tuberculosis. Numerous other antibiotics have since been developed.

Medical researchers have developed machines that do the work of a diseased or missing part of the body. The iron lung, for example, can keep a polio victim alive for years. It takes over the work of paralyzed breathing muscles. Other machines such as the artificial kidney and mechanical heart pump body fluids while surgeons repair the vital organs.

The development of strong, lightweight materials gave doctors a way to replace damaged body parts. Orthopedic surgeons can insert a plastic plate for a shattered part of the skull. They substitute plastic or metal shafts for destroyed arm or leg bones. Mechanical hands made of metal can take the place of amputated hands. The mechanical parts are covered with a plastic hand so lifelike that it even has fingerprints and hairs.

Challenges for the Future. Experts consider the four major challenges to medical research as cancer, hypertension (high blood pressure), arteriosclerosis (hardening of the arteries), and geriatrics (old age). But man still cannot control many of the most common diseases. Scientists seek ways to kill viruses in the body without destroying the body cells. If they succeed, doctors could conquer such troublesome diseases as the common cold and influenza. In addition, physicians need to know more about the exact causes of mental illness and heart diseases. Such knowledge would help them find ways to prevent these ailments.

ALAN E. NOURSE

Related Articles in WORLD BOOK include:

CONTRIBUTORS TO MEDICAL PROGRESS

AMERICAN

Beadle, George W.
Beaumont, William
Billings, John S.
Blackwell, Elizabeth
Bloch, Konrad Emil
Cournand, André F.
Crile, George W.
Cushing, Harvey
De Lee, Joseph B.
Dooley, Thomas A., III
Drew, Charles R.
Enders, John F.
Goldberger, Joseph
Gorgas (William C.)
Gorrie, John
Hench, Philip S.
Holmes, Oliver W.
Howe (Samuel G.)
Kendall, Edward C.
Kornberg, Arthur
Lawless, Theodore K.
Lazear, Jesse W.
Lipmann, Fritz A.
Loeb, Jacques
Long, Crawford W.
Mayo (family)
McCollum, Elmer V.
McDowell, Ephraim
Menninger (family)

Minot, George
Morgan, Thomas H.
Morton, William T. G.
Mudd, Samuel A.
Murphy, John B.
Northrop, John H.
Reed, Walter
Robbins, Frederick C.
Rush, Benjamin
Sabin, Albert B.
Salk, Jonas E.
Shaw, Anna H.
Smith, Theobald
Spock, Benjamin M.
Stanley, Wendell
Sumner, James B.
Szent-Györgyi, Albert
Tatum, Edward L.
Theiler, Max
Thornton, Matthew
Trudeau, Edward L.
Waksman, Selman A.
Walker, Mary E.
Warren, John C.
Weller, Thomas H.
White, Paul D.
Williams, Daniel H.
Wright, Sewall

BRITISH

Addison, Thomas
Bright, Richard
Brown, Robert
Bruce, Sir David
Chain, Ernst B.
Colles, Abraham
Fleming, Sir Alexander
Florey, Lord
Graves, Robert J.
Grenfell, Sir Wilfred
Harvey, William
Huxley (Julian S.)
Jenner, Edward
Jenner, Sir William

Lister, Sir Joseph
MacLeod, John J.
Manson, Sir Patrick
Martin, Archer J. P.
Medawar, Sir Peter

Brian

Pearson, Karl
Roget, Peter M.
Ross, Sir Ronald
Sherrington, Sir C. S.
Simpson, Sir James Y.
Sloane, Sir Hans
Sydenham, Thomas
Synge, Richard L. M.

CANADIAN

Banting, Sir Frederick G.
Best, Charles H.

Black, Davidson
McCrae, John

Osler, Sir William

Selye, Hans

FRENCH

Bernard, Claude
Bichat, Marie François
Carrel, Alexis
Halpern, Bernard N.
Jacob, François
Laënnec, René T. H.

Laveran, Charles L. A.
Lwoff, André
Monod, Jacques
Paré, Ambroise
Pasteur, Louis

GERMAN

Baer, Karl E. von
Behring, Emil von
Billroth, Albert C. T.
Cohn, Ferdinand J.
Domagk, Gerhard
Ehrlich, Paul
Fischer, Hans
Forssmann, Werner
Gall, Franz J.
Hahnemann, Samuel F.

Koch, Robert
Krebs, Hans A.
Löffler, Friedrich
Lynen, Feodor
Mayer, Julius R. von
Schweitzer, Albert
Spemann, Hans
Virchow, Rudolf
Wassermann, August von
Weismann, August

ITALIAN

Galvani, Luigi
Golgi, Camillo
Malpighi, Marcello

Morgagni, Giovanni B.
Spallanzani, Lazzaro

OTHERS

Avicenna
Barnard, Christiaan N.
Bovet, Daniel
Burnet, Sir Macfarlane
Cori
Einthoven, Willem
Fibiger, Johannes A. G.
Finlay, Carlos J.
Finsen, Niels R.
Freud, Sigmund
Galen
Gullstrand, Allvar
Hippocrates
Houssay, Bernardo A.

Imhotep
Kitasato, Shibasaburo
Kocher, Emil T.
Landsteiner, Karl
Mesmer, Franz
Metchnikoff, Élie
Moniz, Antônio C.
Ochoa, Severo
Paracelsus, Philippus A.
Pavlov, Ivan P.
Schick, Béla
Semmelweis, Ignaz P.
Theorell, Hugo
Vesalius, Andreas

DIAGNOSIS

Biopsy
Blood Count
Bronchoscope
Diagnosis
Electro-
  cardiograph
Electro-
  encephalograph
Fehling's Solution
Fluoroscope
Gastroscope
Liquid Crystal
Manometer

Metabolimeter
Ophthalmoscope
Schick Test
Spirometer
Stethoscope
Wassermann Test
X Rays

See DISEASE and MENTAL ILLNESS with their lists of Related Articles.

MEDICAL ORGANIZATIONS

American Medical
  Association
Armed Forces Institute
  of Pathology
Cancer Society, American
Heart Association,
  American
Medic Alert
  Foundation

Menninger Foundation
National Medical
  Association
National Society for
  Medical Research
Public Health Service
Rockefeller University
World Health Organization
World Medical Association

PREVENTIVE MEDICINE

Health
Immunity

Inoculation
Mental Health

Sanitation
Vaccination

SPECIAL FIELDS OF MEDICINE

Antibody
Antitoxin

Allopathy
Anatomy
Aviation
  Medicine
Bacteriology

Biochemistry
Chiropractic
Dentistry
Dermatology
Embryology

Genetics
Geriatrics
Histology
Homeopathy
Nursing

Pediatrics
Pharmacology
Physiology
Podiatry
Prosthetics

Psychiatry
Psychoanalysis
Veterinary
  Medicine

Nutrition
Ophthalmology
Osteology
Osteopathy
Pathology

SURGERY

Amputation
Anesthesia
Artificial Limbs
Bloodletting
Chloroform

Ether
Hysterectomy
Leech
Lobotomy
Nitrous Oxide

Novocain
Plastic Surgery
Skin Grafting
Surgery
Trephining

TREATMENT

Chemotherapy
Diathermy
Diet
Drug
First Aid
Gamma Ray
Hydrotherapy
Hypodermic
  Injection
Infrared Rays

Intravenous
  Injection
Iron Lung
Irradiation
Isotope
Massage
Naprapathy
Occupational
  Therapy

Oxygen Tent
Physical Therapy
Plasma
Psychotherapy
Serum
Sun Bath
Sun Lamp
Ultraviolet Rays

OTHER RELATED ARTICLES

Aesculapius
Blood Bank
Bone Bank
Electricity
  (In Science)
Eye Bank
Hospital
Hygeia

Invention
  (In Medicine)
Nobel Prizes
Optometry
Pharmacy
Plastics
  (In Medicine)
Prescription
Psychosomatic
  Medicine

Pure Food and
  Drug Laws
Rx
Sanitarium
Socialized
  Medicine
Tissue
  Transplant
Transfusion,
  Blood

Outline

I. **The Practice of Medicine**
   A. Diagnosis of Disease
   B. Treatment of Disease
   C. Prevention of Disease

II. **The Medical Profession**
   A. General Practitioners
   B. Specialists
   C. Researchers

III. **What a Doctor Does**
   A. In the Office
   B. At the Hospital
   C. On House Calls
   D. To Keep Informed

IV. **The Doctor in the Community**
   A. Government and Medicine
   B. Ethics and Legal Responsibilities
   C. Fees and Salaries
   D. Medical Organizations

V. **Careers in Medicine**
   A. Basic Education
   B. Premedical Education
   C. Medical Education
   D. Internship
   E. Residency

VI. **History**

Questions

Why is medical practice both a science and an art?
What is the most important personal qualification for a man or woman who wants to be a doctor?
What three main areas of activity does the practice of medicine include?
What are the goals of premedical education?
How do doctors learn about medical advances?
Why do physicians not advertise?
What are four challenges to medical research?
How does a doctor obtain a license to practice?
What Greek physician developed methods of diagnosis that are still used by doctors?
How does a specialist's practice differ from that of a general practitioner?

MEDICINE, PATENT. See PATENT MEDICINE.

Medicine Hat Chamber of Commerce

Medicine Hat, a trade center in southeastern Alberta, has large grain elevators along the rail lines.

MEDICINE HAT, Alberta (pop. 25,574; alt. 2,181 ft.), is situated on the South Saskatchewan River. It lies about 195 miles southeast of Calgary (see ALBERTA [political map]). The Chinook belt of warm winds usually keeps Medicine Hat warmer (average annual temperature 42° F.) than other cities in the same latitude.

One of the largest known natural-gas fields in the world surrounds Medicine Hat and provides the basis for its industries. The city owns the gas field.

The town's name is the translation of the Blackfoot Indian word *saamis* (the headdress of a medicine man). A Blackfoot legend says a saamis was found there.

The city serves as a trading center for a large farming and ranching area. Its factories use gas for power, and this keeps Medicine Hat free from smoke. The chief products include flour, glass, linseed oil, cement, brick and tile, pottery, and machinery. Workers process slate, lignite coal, and clay found nearby. The city has a fertilizer plant, tire plant, and 16 greenhouses. One of these greenhouses, with 10 acres under glass, ranks as the second largest in Canada.

Medicine Hat was founded in 1883 and chartered as a city in 1906. It has a mayor-council form of government.　　　　　　　　　　　W. D. McDOUGALL

MEDICINE MAN. See INDIAN, AMERICAN (Shamans and Priests); SHAMAN; ESKIMO (Religion).

MEDICINE ROCKS. See MONTANA (Places to Visit).

MÉDICIS, CATHERINE DE. See CATHERINE DE MÉDICIS.

MEDICO. See DOOLEY, THOMAS ANTHONY, III.

MEDIEVAL PERIOD. See MIDDLE AGES.

MEDILL, *muh DILL,* **JOSEPH** (1823-1899), a crusading American editor and publisher, made the *Chicago Tribune* one of the world's most successful newspapers. He served as managing editor from 1855 to 1863, as editor in chief from 1863 to 1866, and as publisher from 1874 until his death. Many of his editorials concerned government reforms. Medill worked hard to build the Republican party.

Some authorities believe he named the party. He helped sponsor Abraham Lincoln as a candidate for the presidency. Medill served at the Illinois Constitutional Convention of 1869, on the Civil Service Commission under President Ulysses S. Grant, and as mayor of Chicago from 1872 to 1874. He was born near St. John, New Brunswick, Canada.　　　　　　　　　　　JOHN TEBBEL

MEDINA, *muh DEE nuh* (pop. 72,291; alt. 2,024 ft.), is a Moslem holy city in Saudi Arabia. The tomb of Mohammed, founder of the Islamic religion, lies there. The tomb is in a mosque that Mohammed built after he made his hegira from Mecca to Medina in A.D. 622 (see HEGIRA). Thousands of Moslem pilgrims visit the city each year. Non-Moslems are forbidden to enter Medina. A wall surrounds the old section of the city. For location, see SAUDI ARABIA (color map).

Medina lies in a fertile plain. It has a plentiful supply of water, and is noted for the vegetables and the dates and other fruit grown nearby.

Jewish settlers founded Medina more than 2,000 years ago. In 1924, Ibn Saud conquered Medina and added it to his kingdom, which today is called Saudi Arabia.　　　　　　　　　　　DOUGLAS C. CRARY

See also HEJAZ; IBN SAUD; MOHAMMED.

MEDINA, *muh DEE nuh,* **HAROLD RAYMOND** (1888-), an American judge, won international fame for his fair conduct of the trial of 11 American Communist party leaders in 1949. The Communist leaders were convicted of conspiring to teach and advocate the overthrow of the U.S. government by force. Medina urged the jury to be calm and patient, and cautioned that "justice does not flourish amidst emotional excitement and stress."

Judge Medina was born in Brooklyn, N.Y., and was graduated from Princeton University. He received his law degree from Columbia University in 1912, and taught there from 1915 to 1947. He practiced law in New York City until he was appointed a federal judge in 1947. He retired from that post in 1958.　　　H. G. REUSCHLEIN

MEDINA ANGARITA, ISAÍAS. See VENEZUELA (Struggle for Power).

MEDITERRANEAN FRUIT FLY is an insect that destroys fruits and vegetables. It is an even greater enemy of man than the corn borer, because it attacks more than 70 kinds of crops. The watermelon and pineapple are about the only fruits that this fruit fly does not destroy.

Scientists believe that the Mediterranean fruit fly first came from the Azores. Long ago it made its way to Africa, southern Europe, and Asia. Early in the 1900's, it appeared in Brazil and Hawaii. In 1929, it was discovered in Florida. Congress immediately provided $4¼ million to destroy the harmful insect. A strict quarantine was immediately ordered in the infested area. By July 25, 1930, all of these flies in the United States apparently had been destroyed. The fly invaded Florida again in 1956 and in 1962. It was destroyed both times by spraying infested areas.

This dangerous insect is about the size of a common

Mediterranean Fruit Fly
USDA

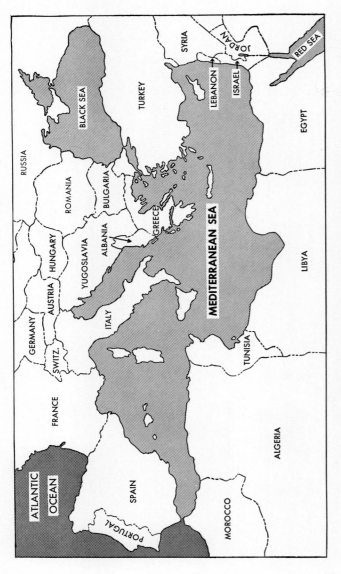

The Mediterranean Sea Lies Between Africa and Europe.

house fly. A person can tell it from a house fly by its spotted wings, and the way it holds its wings at an angle with its body. The female fruit fly selects a ripe fruit while it is still on the tree and drills tiny holes into the skin or rind. Here the fly lays many tiny eggs. These eggs soon hatch into larvae. Then the larvae eat their way through the fruit, which soon drops to the ground. Larvae finish this stage of growth in three or four months. Then they burrow into the ground. When they come out, they are adult insects with wings.

The Mediterranean fruit fly thrives best in a warm climate, but sunlight kills the larvae. There are several insect parasites that destroy the eggs and larvae without doing other damage. These parasites alone cannot check the fruit fly. The only way to destroy the larvae completely is to boil the fruit for several hours, or burn it completely. If a person suspects that fruit is infested, he should have it examined by an expert.

Scientific Classification. The Mediterranean fruit fly belongs to the family *Tephritidae*, or *Trypetidae*. It is genus *Ceratitis*, species *C. capitata*.   Robert L. Usinger

MEDITERRANEAN RACE. See Races of Man (Caucasoids; table; pictures).

MEDITERRANEAN SEA, *MED uh tuh RAY nee un.* The Romans first named this body of water *Mare Internum,* or *Inland Sea.* They later gave it its present name, which means *middle of the earth.* The Mediterranean formed the center of life in the ancient world. Many of the great cultures of the period grew up along its shores. Today, the Mediterranean still serves as one of the chief trade routes of the world.

Location and Description. The Mediterranean Sea lies between Europe, Asia, and Africa. The Strait of Gibraltar connects its western end with the Atlantic Ocean. In the southeast, the Suez Canal allows ships to sail into the Red and Arabian seas and the Indian Ocean. The Dardanelles and Bosporus connect the northeastern part of the Mediterranean with the Black Sea.

Many arms stretch northward from the Mediterranean. Some are large enough to be called seas by themselves. The Tyrrhenian, Ionian, and Adriatic seas surround Italy. The Aegean Sea lies east of Greece. Another of these arms, the Black Sea, is south of Russia. The Mediterranean, with all its arms, covers about 1,145,100 square miles.

The Mediterranean reaches its deepest point, 15,000 feet, in the Ionian section. At the Strait of Gibraltar it is about 1,000 feet deep. Atlantic Ocean water flows into the Mediterranean at the surface, and Mediterranean water flows out at the bottom. More than 400 kinds of fish live in the sea, but commercial fisheries are not of great importance. The Mediterranean contains rich growths of sponges. Several important islands lie in the Mediterranean, including Corsica, Crete, Cyprus, Sardinia, Sicily, and the Balearic Islands.

History. The Phoenicians were the boldest sailors of the Mediterranean in the ancient world. They traveled to all parts of the sea from their homes in Syria as early as 1500 B.C. Much later, according to legend, they found a message carved on rocks at Gibraltar that said *Ne Plus Ultra* meaning *no more beyond.* Despite this, the daring Phoenicians sailed on into the Atlantic.

The Greeks and Romans followed trade routes established by the Phoenicians, and the Mediterranean became the greatest water route of the world. The Romans controlled the Mediterranean from about 133 B.C. to A.D. 337. They sometimes referred to it as *Mare Nostrum,* or *Our Sea.* The Italians used this same expression in the 1930's. The Mediterranean lost some of its importance when explorers from Europe found new routes around Africa and across the Atlantic Ocean. But it became the chief water route between Europe and the Far East after 1869, when the Suez Canal opened. European

309

powers built outposts in northern Africa and the Middle East to gain a foothold for trade along the Mediterranean Sea.

During World War I, France and Great Britain tried to open a supply route from the Mediterranean to the Black Sea and Russia. They landed troops on the Gallipoli Peninsula, but Turkish troops decisively defeated them. In World War II, both the Allies and the Axis Powers considered it necessary to control the Mediterranean. The Allied Powers sent armies into North Africa and Italy, even though their main enemy was Nazi Germany.

Since World War II, Middle Eastern and North African countries have driven out most European powers and attained independence. Egypt nationalized the Suez Canal in 1957, taking it away from France and Great Britain. But the Suez remains open for world commerce.

ROBERT O. REID

Related Articles in WORLD BOOK include:

Adriatic Sea	Cyprus	Phoenicia
Aegean Sea	Dardanelles	Sardinia
Balearic Islands	Gallipoli Peninsula	Sicily
Black Sea	Gibraltar	Sirocco
Bosporus	Gibraltar, Strait of	Suez Canal
Corsica	Ionian Sea	Tyrrhenian
Crete	Ligurian Sea	Sea

MEDIUM. See ECTOPLASM; SPIRITUALISTS; MAGIC (Communicating with Spirits).

MEDIUM, in biology: See CULTURE (laboratory).

MEDLAR, MED ler, or MESPIL, is a pome, the same kind of fruit as the apple. It grows on a bush or small tree. Medlars are more popular in Europe than in America. They grow well in the southern United States and as far north as New York state. The Dutch variety is two and one-half inches across. The Nottingham is smaller. The fruit stays hard until the first mellows it. Growers usually pick it after the first frost and lay it aside to ripen. The ripening is called bletting. The medlar has a slightly sour taste. It can be eaten fresh but people use it chiefly for preserves.

Scientific Classification. The medlar belongs to the rose family, Rosaceae. The medlar is genus Mespilus, species M. germanica.

ROY E. MARSHALL

MEDULLA OBLONGATA. See BRAIN (The Medulla Oblongata; color picture, The Parts of the Brain).

MEDULLARY CAVITY. See BONE (Structure of the Bones).

MEDUSA, muh DOO suh, is a jellyfish which is shaped like an umbrella or bell. This name comes from the animal's feelers, which look like the serpents in the hair of Medusa, a monster in Greek mythology. The tentacles (feelers) of the medusa encircle its umbrellalike body. Its mouth is an opening at one end of a tube which hangs from its body. The medusa has stinging organs on its tentacles. It uses these to paralyze small sea animals which it feeds on. The tentacles also grasp and carry

Eric J. Hosking, NAS

The Medlar, shaped like an apple, has a tart, sour taste.

the food to the mouth. The medusa reproduces in two different ways—from eggs and by budding.

Scientific Classification. The medusae belong to the phylum Coelenterata. They belong to the classes Hydrozoa and Scyphozoa.

See also JELLYFISH; CAMEO (picture).

The Medusa appears more like a flower than a marine animal, as it floats on the water to feed. When hungry, the medusa rises to the surface and rolls over. It then extends its tentacles and floats slowly downward. It catches worms, shrimp, and small fish.

Roy M. Allen

MEDUSA, muh DOO suh, was one of the three Gorgons, the daughters of the sea god Phorcus in Greek mythology (see GORGON). She was the only mortal Gorgon. Medusa had been beautiful in her youth, and was still proud of her hair. She boasted of her beauty to Athena, who became jealous and changed her into a hideous person. Medusa and her sisters had staring eyes, protruding fangs for teeth, and withing snakes for hair. They were so ugly that anyone who saw them turned to stone.

Perseus killed Medusa by looking in his mirrorlike shield as he cut off her head (see PERSEUS). The winged horse Pegasus sprang from her beheaded body; and poisonous snakes arose from the blood that dripped from her head. Athena saved blood from Medusa's body and gave it to Aesculapius, the physician (see AESCULAPIUS). The blood from her left side was a fatal poison, but that from her right side had the power to revive the dead.

O. M. Pearl

MEEKER, EZRA (1830-1928), was an American pioneer and author. In 1852, he took a five-month journey by ox-cart along the Oregon Trail from Iowa to Portland, Ore., with his wife and infant son. He returned to Iowa by the same route in 1906, painting inscriptions on landmarks along the way as part of a memorial observance. He made a similar trip by automobile in 1915. He spent much of his time after the age of 75 promoting the memory of the Oregon Trail. Meeker founded the Oregon Trail Association. His books include Ox-Team Days on the Oregon Trail (1922) and Kate Mulhall (1926). Meeker was born in Huntsville, Ohio. See also OREGON TRAIL (picture).

JESSE L. GILMORE

MEGARON. See ARCHITECTURE (Greek).

MEGATON. See ATOMIC ENERGY (The Hydrogen Bomb).

MEHMET ALI, *meh MET ah LIH,* or MOHAMMED ALI (1769-1849), an Albanian soldier of fortune, made himself the master of the Turkish province of Egypt in 1805. He fought under the sultan of Turkey, leading a group of Balkan soldiers. His forces successfully put down the Greek rebellion of 1821. He was to acquire the Peloponnesus as a reward, but the navies of Great Britain, France, and Russia destroyed his fleet at the Battle of Navarino in 1827. In Egypt, Mehmet Ali introduced cotton and hemp farming, and developed irrigation. He was born in Kavalla, Greece, then in the Turkish empire. See also EGYPT (The 1800's). R. V. BURKS

MEI LAN-FANG, *moy lan fawng* (1894-1961), was a famous Chinese actor. At 19 he won an acting contest and was crowned "King of Actors." He toured the United States, England, and Russia during the 1920's. Mei acted only in the Chinese classical dance-dramas, and always played female parts. Mei was born in Peking. RICHARD MOODY

MEIGHEN, *MEE un,* **ARTHUR** (1874-1960), became the youngest prime minister in the history of Canada. He took office on July 10, 1920, at the age of 46, when Prime Minister Sir Robert Borden retired (see BORDEN, SIR ROBERT LAIRD). He also became secretary of state for external affairs on the same date. But his strong support of military conscription during World War I angered many Canadians, and he was defeated in 1921. He became prime minister again in 1926. The Conservatives lacked an overall majority, however, and a few months later he was defeated in Parliament and in the general election that followed. The Conservatives returned to power in 1930 under Prime Minister Richard Bedford Bennett, and Meighen became minister without portfolio in 1932 (see BENNETT, RICHARD BEDFORD).

A Cheerleader Shouts Through a Megaphone.

Meerschaum Miners use heavy iron picks to dig in clay for the whitish mineral used to make meerschaum pipe bowls.

MEERSCHAUM, *MEER shum,* is a soft, whitish fibrous or flaky clay. Manufacturers use it to make tobacco pipes. Meerschaum is also called *sepiolite*. It is so light that it will float in water. In German, the word *meerschaum* means *sea foam*. The mineral gets its name because it floats and has the look of foam. Large quantities of meerschaum are found in Asia Minor. Lumps of meerschaum are found in masses of other clays. Meerschaum is a compound of magnesium, silicon, oxygen, and water. It is a water-bearing magnesium silicate.

Many smokers prefer meerschaum tobacco pipes. The bowls of meerschaum pipes are white when new. With careful handling and use, the bowl slowly colors a rich brown. Meerschaum pipes break easily. CECIL J. SCHNEER

MEETING. See PARLIAMENTARY PROCEDURE (Holding Meetings); CONVENTION.

MEGACYCLE. See MEGAHERTZ.

MEGADYNE. See DYNE.

MEGAERA. See FURIES.

MEGAHERTZ, formerly called MEGACYCLE, is a unit used to measure the frequency of waves such as light and television waves. It is 1 million *hertz* (cycles a second). See also KILOHERTZ.

MEGALITHIC MONUMENTS, *meg uh LITH ic,* are structures made of large stones and used as tombs or places of ritual. The best known are those built by people of the New Stone and Bronze ages in western Europe. Some, called *dolmens,* served as tombs. Stone circles called *cromlechs* appear at Stonehenge, England (see STONEHENGE). *Menhirs* are single erect stones, and *alignments* are parallel rows of stones. CARLETON S. COON

MEGALOMANIA. See MENTAL ILLNESS (Paranoia).

MEGALOSAURUS. See DINOSAUR (Lizard-Hipped).

MEGANTIC, LAKE. See CHAUDIÈRE RIVER.

MEGAPHONE is a hollow, cone-shaped device used to make a person's voice sound louder. A person using a megaphone speaks or shouts into the small opening at one end. His voice comes out at the much wider opposite end. The megaphone makes the voice sound louder because it points sound waves in one direction and keeps them from spreading out in all directions. Megaphones may be from several inches to 2 or more feet long. Cheerleaders often use megaphones. A portable, battery-powered loudspeaker called a *bullhorn* is now often used in place of a megaphone. PAUL J. SCHEIPS

MEGARA. See HERCULES.

He also became government leader in the Senate in the same year. He retired from the Senate to run for a seat in the Canadian House of Commons in 1942. But he was defeated in the election.

Arthur Meighen

Meighen was born in Anderson, Ont., Canada. He moved to Manitoba in 1898, where he entered business and studied law. He entered politics in 1908 when he was elected a Conservative member of the Canadian House of Commons from Portage la Prairie, Manitoba. Later he served as secretary of state, minister of mines, and minister of the interior. He accompanied Prime Minister Robert Laird Bor-den to the conference of prime ministers of the British Dominions in London in 1918.
G. F. G. STANLEY

MEIGS, *meigz,* **CORNELIA LYNDE** (1884-   ), an American author, has written more than two dozen books for children. Most of them are based on incidents in American history. In 1934, she won the Newbery medal for *Invincible Louisa,* the life of Louisa May Alcott. Her other works include *Kingdom of the Winding Road* (1915), *Rain on the Roof* (1925), *The Trade Wind* (1927), and *As the Crow Flies* (1927). She was editor in chief and coauthor of *A Critical History of Children's Literature* (1953). She also wrote a play, *The Steadfast Princess,* that won a Drama League prize in 1916.

Cornelia Meigs was born in Rock Island, Ill. She spent her summers in New England. Some of her books relate the New England stories her parents and grandparents told her. She was graduated from Bryn Mawr College, and taught there 18 years.
EVELYN RAY SICKELS

MEIJI. See MUTSUHITO.

MEIN KAMPF is a book by Adolf Hitler. The title is German for *My Struggle.* In the book, Hitler gave a fanciful account of his life and set down his political ideas. He described the alleged superiority of the German people, and said that the good of Germany ranked above all other values. The book stated Hitler's ideas on "race purity." These beliefs led to World War II and the slaughter of millions of Europeans. *Mein Kampf* was the "bible" for German Nazis and a guide for Nazi sympathizers in other countries.
STEFAN T. POSSONY

See also HITLER, ADOLF (Mein Kampf).

MEIOSIS. See CELL (Cell Division; illustration).

MEIR, *meh ihr,* **GOLDA** (1898-   ), became Israel's prime minister in 1969 after the death of Levi Eshkol. She served as Israel's first minister to Moscow in 1948, as minister of labor from 1949 to 1956, and was minister for foreign affairs from 1956 to 1966. She was secretary-general of the Mapai (Labor) Party in Israel from 1966 to 1969.

Mrs. Meir was born GOLDA MABOVITZ in Kiev, Russia. In 1906, her family moved to Milwaukee, Wis., and she later taught school there. In 1921, she went to Palestine and joined a collective farm village. ELLIS RIVKIN

MEISTERSINGER. See MASTERSINGER.

MEITNER, *MITE ner,* **LISE** (1878-1968), was an Austrian physicist. Her discoveries in nuclear physics played a large part in developing atomic energy. Otto Hahn and Fritz Strassmann, German physical chemists, split the uranium atom in 1938 when they bombarded uranium with neutrons and produced *barium* (see BARIUM). This discovery was not recognized officially until January, 1939, when Miss Meitner and Otto Frisch announced their interpretation of the work of Hahn and Strassmann.

She developed a mathematical theory to explain the splitting of the uranium atom into two fragments. She calculated the energy released in nuclear fission. The Hahn-Strassmann experiment and the Meitner-Frisch explanation of it were important events in the development of the atomic bomb and other uses of atomic energy.

Miss Meitner was born on Nov. 7, 1878, in Vienna, and started her studies in atomic physics there. From 1908 to 1911, she served at the University of Berlin as assistant to Max Planck, originator of the quantum theory (see QUANTUM THEORY). She was a leading professor at the Kaiser Wilhelm Institute for Chemistry during World War I. She won fame for her studies there on radioactive radium, thorium, and actinium. In 1917, she and Hahn discovered radioactive *protactinium,* element 91 (see PROTACTINIUM). She became a professor of physics at the Catholic University of America in 1946. Later the same year, Miss Meitner returned to Europe to become a member of the University of Stockholm staff.

See also ATOMIC ENERGY (Splitting Uranium).
RALPH E. LAPP

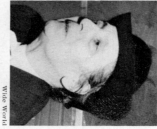

Lise Meitner

Wide World

MEKKA. See MECCA.

MEKNÈS, *mek NES* (pop. 185,000; alt. 1,890 ft.), one of Morocco's four capitals, is a main trading center in northern Morocco. The city lies about 35 miles southwest of Fez. For location, see Morocco (color map). Meknès was founded in the 1100's, and became Morocco's capital when Sultan Ismail built a large palace there in the 1670's.

MEKONG RIVER, *ma KAWNG,* is the largest stream on the Indochinese peninsula. The Mekong is about 2,600 miles long. It flows southeastward from eastern Tibet, and forms part of the boundary between Thailand (Siam) and Laos. The river crosses Laos, Cambodia, and Vietnam, and branches into several streams before it empties into the China Sea near Saigon. One branch rises in Cambodia and drains the Tonle Sap (Great Lake). In the region of the lower delta, the Mekong is known as the Saigon River. See THAILAND (color map).

Ships can sail only about 350 miles up from the mouth of the Mekong. Farther inland, the river is interrupted by rapids and sand bars.
J. E. SPENCER

See also RIVER (chart: Longest Rivers).

MELAMINE. See PLASTICS (table: Kinds of Plastics).
MELANCHOLIA. See MENTAL ILLNESS (Manic-Depressive Psychosis).

MELANCHTHON, mel LANK thon, PHILIPP (1497-1560), a German humanist and scholar, was Martin Luther's chief associate in starting and leading the Protestant Reformation. Melanchthon wrote the *Loci Communes* (*Commonplaces*, 1521), a widely-read handbook that set down Lutheran doctrines in a systematic way for easy reference. He was also the chief author of the Augsburg Confession, which became the basic statement of faith of the Lutheran Church.

Melanchthon had a calmer personality than did Luther. He continually tried to find compromise solutions to issues that divided Protestants and Catholics, and Protestants from each other. Melanchthon declared that many such issues were unimportant and should not block Christian unity. But he also believed that the Roman Catholic Church had forsaken the true Christian tradition several hundred years after Christ. He especially opposed the power of the popes.

Melanchthon was born near Karlsruhe. Like Luther, he was a professor at the University of Wittenberg. He was a brilliant student of classical literature and of the works of the early church fathers. Melanchthon has been called the founder of the German educational system because he established public schools where boys learned to read and write Greek, Latin, and German. RICHARD MARIUS

See also LUTHER, MARTIN; AUGSBURG CONFESSION; REFORMATION.

MELANESIA. See PACIFIC ISLANDS.

MELANIN. See SKIN; HAIR (The Color of Hair).

MELBA, NELLIE (1861-1931), was a famous coloratura soprano. Her real name was Helen Porter Mitchell.

Nellie Melba

U&U

She adopted her stage name from Melbourne, Australia. She was born in Richmond, a suburb of Melbourne. She first sang in public at the age of 6 in Melbourne. She made her operatic debut in 1887 in Brussels, Belgium, as Gilda in *Rigoletto*. She sang in Italy, Russia, Denmark, and England, and made her American debut in 1893. SCOTT GOLDTHWAITE

MELBOURNE (pop. 75,709; met. area 2,108,499; alt. 30 ft.) is the capital of the state of Victoria, Australia. The city, with its widespread suburbs, ranks with Sydney as one of the two largest metropolitan areas in Australia. Melbourne lies at the mouth of the Yarra River on Port Phillip Bay (see AUSTRALIA [political map]).

Melbourne is one of the leading commercial centers of Australia. Its factories manufacture automobiles, aircraft, textiles, clothing, shoes, paper, and processed foods. Melbourne's port has been developed to provide 62,000 feet of wharfage. It is one of the chief Australian ports that handles overseas and interstate shipping.

Governor Philip King of New South Wales commissioned David Collins to settle the area around Port Phillip Bay in 1803. But Collins had opposed the settlement, and was soon transferred to the nearby island of Tasmania, then called Van Diemen's Land. He served as governor of Tasmania from 1804 until 1810. Settlers from Tasmania came to the Melbourne region in 1835. They formed the Port Phillip Association to seek grazing lands across Bass Strait from Tasmania. Their representative, John Batman, sailed to the mainland in 1835, and bought 600,000 acres of land from the people of the Melbourne region. Batman paid for the land with blankets, tomahawks, flour, and other goods. Another group of settlers, led by John Fawkner, arrived soon after Batman had claimed the land. The settlement eventually developed into the city of Melbourne. A gold rush in Victoria during the 1850's

Melbourne, Australia, on the Yarra River, Has One-Sixth of Australia's People in Its Metropolitan Area.

Australian News & Information Bureau

MELCHER, FREDERIC GERSHOM

brought many more settlers to Melbourne. New South Wales governed the city until 1851, when a separate government was set up in Melbourne. The city served as the seat of government from 1901 until 1927, when the capital was established in Canberra.

Robert Hoddle planned the city in 1837. He designed a city of rectangular blocks, with each main street 99 feet wide and the streets crossing at 220-yard intervals. The streets were named for prominent figures in early Australian history. Today, they are broad and pleasant thoroughfares. Narrow streets, lined with shops and offices, run between the thoroughfares in the center of the city. Two of the most famous of the wide, tree-lined streets are Collins Street and St. Kilda Road. The Melbourne metropolitan area has about 7,000 acres of parks, including the 100-acre Botanic Gardens.

The University of Melbourne was founded in 1853. Other landmarks in the city include the Anglican and Roman Catholic cathedrals and the Exhibition Building. A new art gallery, the first part of a planned cultural center, opened in 1968.

C. M. H. CLARK

MELCHER, FREDERIC GERSHOM (1879-1963), won the Regina medal in 1962 for his contributions to children's literature. In 1919, he helped found Children's Book Week. He established the Newbery medal in 1921 for the outstanding children's book of the year, and the Caldecott medal in 1937 for the best-illustrated children's book of the year. Born in Malden, Mass., Melcher was co-editor of *Publishers' Weekly* for 40 years, and also served as board chairman of the R. R. Bowker Publishing Company. See also CALDECOTT MEDAL; LITERATURE FOR CHILDREN (Children's Book Week); NEWBERY MEDAL; REGINA MEDAL.

MELCHIOR. See MAGI.

MELCHIOR, *MEL kih aur,* **LAURITZ LEBRECHT HOMMEL** (1890-   ), is a Danish operatic tenor. He won fame for his performances of roles in Richard Wagner's operas. He sang the role of Siegfried more than 100 times. Melchior was a member of the Metropolitan Opera Company from 1926 to 1950.

Melchior began his career as a boy soprano in Copenhagen, where he was born. He studied at the Royal Opera School there, and made his adult debut in 1913 as a baritone in *La Traviata.* He first appeared as a tenor in 1918. Melchior sang in the famed Wagner festival at Bayreuth, Germany, in 1924, and won acclaim for his performance in *Parsifal.*

DANIEL A. HARRIS

Lauritz Melchior
William Morris

Andrew Mellon
U&U

MELILOT is a type of sweet clover. See CLOVER.

MELLETTE, ARTHUR CALVIN. See SOUTH DAKOTA (History).

MELLON, ANDREW WILLIAM (1855-1937), was an American financier. President Warren G. Harding appointed him secretary of the treasury in 1921. He served until 1932 under Presidents Harding, Calvin Coolidge, and Herbert Hoover. Mellon was often called the greatest secretary of the treasury after Alexander Hamilton. While he was in office, the government reduced its World War I debt by $9 billion, and Congress cut income-tax rates substantially.

Mellon was born in Pittsburgh of wealthy parents. In 1886, he joined his father's bank, Thomas Mellon and Sons, and became a shrewd judge of which new businesses and young businessmen deserved loans. Mellon served as an officer or director of many financial and industrial corporations. He became especially active in the development of the coal, coke, oil, and aluminum industries. By 1921, he had become one of the wealthiest men in the United States.

Mellon served as ambassador to Great Britain in 1932 and 1933. In 1937, he gave his $25 million art collection to the United States government. He also donated $15 million for a museum to house it. This museum, the National Gallery of Art in Washington, D.C., is part of the Smithsonian Institution. It was opened in 1941.

See also NATIONAL GALLERY OF ART.

DONALD L. KEMMERER

MELLON INSTITUTE. See CARNEGIE-MELLON UNIVERSITY.

MELLOPHONE is a wind instrument made of brass. It has three valves and is shaped like the French horn. The mellophone is less expensive and easier to play than the French horn. It is sometimes used as a substitute for the French horn in school and marching bands. Its curved tube is half the length of the French horn's tube. The two instruments play in the same pitch. But the mellophone cannot produce the rich tones of the French horn.

See also FRENCH HORN.

MELODEON. See ORGAN (The Reed Organ).

MELODRAMA, *MEL oh DRAH muh,* is a kind of drama that depends for interest on romance, thrills, and narrow escapes. The term comes from the Greek words *melos,* meaning *song,* and *drama,* meaning *play* or *action.* Originally, a melodrama was a dramatic performance with intervals of song and instrumental music.

MELODY is a series of single sounds that follow each other in the form of a musical pattern. *Melody* may also refer to the main part of a musical composition. See also MUSIC (Melody).

MELON is the name of the fruit of several plants that belong to the *cucurbit* family. Melon plants have trailing or climbing stems that fasten themselves with tendrils to the objects they climb over. *Tendrils* are modified leaves that look like small coils of wire. The fruits, or melons, are round or somewhat egg-shaped. They range from only a few inches to a foot or more across. The fruits vary from tan and yellow to light or dark green. The flesh may be green, white, yellow, pink, or red.

Scientific Classification. Melons belong to the gourd family, *Cucurbitaceae.*

See also CASABA; MUSKMELON; WATERMELON; ARTHUR J. PRATT GOURD (picture).

MELOS, *ME lahs*, or *Mîlos* is a Greek island in the Aegean Sea. It lies about midway between Athens and Crete. For location, see GREECE (map). Melos is famous as the place where a remarkable statue of Venus was found in 1820. This statue is called the Aphrodite of Melos, or, more commonly, the Venus de Milo (see VENUS DE MILO).

Melos is about 13 miles long and up to 8 miles wide. It has an area of about 60 square miles and a population of about 4,900. In the Stone Age, Melos was famous for its *obsidian* (volcanic glass) which people used for cutting tools. The Athenians seized this island in 416 B.C., and brutally massacred the men who lived there. Thucydides, the Greek historian, wrote about this in his *History*. During World War I, the British used the harbor of Melos for their naval expedition against the Turks at Gallipoli.

JOHN H. KENT

MELPOMENE. See MUSE.

MELTING POINT is a term in physics which means the temperature at which a solid melts or becomes a liquid. It is also called *fusing point*. Different solids may have widely different melting points. Helium, for example, melts at a temperature below −271° Celsius under a pressure of 26 times atmospheric pressure. But tungsten melts at a temperature of 3410° C.(±20° C.).

The very high melting point of tungsten is the reason why it is used for the filaments of incandescent lamps. The higher the temperature a filament can withstand, the greater is the amount of light which can be produced by a given amount of electrical current. Tungsten has the highest melting point of all of the metallic elements.

The more nearly pure a metal is, the higher its melting point. Zinc, tin, lead, and some other metals have comparatively low melting points. Alloys of these metals are used for fuses in electric circuits because they melt before the fuse or the copper wire in the circuit gets hot enough to cause a fire.

RALPH G. OWENS

See also BOILING POINT; FREEZING.

MELTING POT. See UNITED STATES (Population and Ancestry).

MELTON, JAMES (1904-1961), an American tenor, gained a wide following in radio, television, motion pictures, concerts, and operas. He made his radio debut in 1927, and made his operatic debut in Cincinnati in 1932 as Lieutenant Pinkerton in Puccini's *Madame Butterfly*. Melton also sang with the Metropolitan Opera. He was born in Moultrie, Ga.   MARTIAL SINGHER

MELTING POINTS OF IMPORTANT ELEMENTS AND ALLOYS

Element or Alloy	Degrees Celsius	Element or Alloy	Degrees Celsius
Aluminum	660.2	Neodymium	1024
Antimony	630.5	Nickel	1453
*Arsenic (gray)	817(28 atm.)	Niobium	2468(±10)
Babbitt Metals	181-248	Osmium	3000(±10)
Barium	725	Palladium	1552
Beryllium	1278(±5)	Pewter	295
Bismuth	271.3	Platinum	1769
Boron	2300	Plutonium	639.5(±2)
Brass	900-1000	Potassium	63.65
Bronze	800-1000	Radium	700
Cadmium	320.9	Rhenium	3180
Calcium	848	Rhodium	1966(±3)
Carbon (graphite)	>3550	Rubidium	38.89
Cerium	795	Selenium (gray)	217
Cesium	28.5	Silicon	1410
Chromium	1890	Silver	960.8
Cobalt	1495	Sodium	97.81(±0.03)
Copper	1083(±0.1)	Solder	183-250
Gallium	29.78	Stainless Steel	1350-1550
Germanium	937.4	Steel	1400-1550
Gold	1063.0	Strontium	769
Hafnium	2150	Tantalum	2996
Indium	156.61	Tellurium	449.5(±0.3)
Iridium	2410	Thallium	303.5
Iron	1535	Thorium	about 1700
Lanthanum	920	Tin	231.89
Lead	327.5	Titanium	1675
Lithium	179	Tungsten	3410(±20)
Magnesium	651	Uranium	1132.3(±0.8)
Manganese	1244(±3)	Vanadium	1890(±10)
Mercury	−38.87	Zinc	419.4
Molybdenum	2610	Zirconium	1852(±2)
Monel Metals	1300-1350		

*28 atm. means 28 atmospheres of pressure or 28(14.7 lbs./in.). ± means plus or minus. > means more than.

HOW MELTING POINTS DIFFER

Mercury is liquid, *left*, at normal room temperatures.

Tungsten, in lights, *right*, has a high melting point.

Iron melts, *right*, when heated to 1535°C.

Copper, with high melting point, makes good wire, *left*.

MELVILLE, HERMAN

MELVILLE, HERMAN (1819-1891), ranks among America's major authors. He wrote *Moby-Dick*, one of the great novels in literature, and his reputation rests largely on this book. But many of his other works are literary creations of a high order—blending fact, fiction, adventure, and subtle symbolism. Melville's wealth of personal experience in faraway places was remarkable even in the footloose and exploring world of the 1800's.

His Early Life. Melville was born in New York City. The family name was Melvill, and he added the "e" to the name. Melville's father was a well-to-do merchant from New England, and his mother came from an old and socially prominent New York Dutch family. Melville lived his first 11 years in New York City. Then his father died after a financial and mental breakdown in 1831 and the family moved to Albany, N.Y.

Young, inexperienced, and now poor, Melville tried a variety of jobs between 1832 and 1841. He was a clerk in his brother's hat store in Albany, worked in his uncle's bank, taught in a school near Pittsfield, Mass., and, in 1837, sailed to Liverpool, England, as a cabin boy on a merchant ship. He described this voyage in his novel *Redburn*. Melville returned to America and signed on the newly-built whaling ship *Acushnet* for a trip in the Pacific Ocean. From this trip came the basic experiences recorded in several of his books, and above all, the whaling knowledge he put into *Moby-Dick*.

Melville sailed from New Bedford, Mass., on Jan. 3, 1841. He stayed on the *Acushnet* for 18 months, helping to catch and cut up whales. But when the *Acushnet* put in at Nukahiva in the Marquesas Islands, he and a shipmate *jumped* (deserted) ship. The two men headed inland until they accidentally came to the lovely valley of the Types, a Polynesian tribe with a reputation as fierce cannibals. However, the natives turned out to be gentle and charming hosts. Melville described his experiences with these people in *Typee*.

Melville lived in the valley for about a month. He then joined another whaling ship, but he soon deserted it with other sailors in a semimutiny at Tahiti. After a few days in a local jail, Melville and a new friend began roaming the beautiful and unspoiled islands of Tahiti and Moorea. Melville described his life during these wanderings in the novel *Omoo*.

After short service on a third whaling ship, Melville landed at the Sandwich Islands, where he lived by doing odd jobs. On Aug. 17, 1844, he enlisted as a seaman on the frigate *United States*, flagship of the Navy's Pacific Squadron. He recounted his long voyage around Cape Horn to the United States in the novel *White-Jacket*. Melville arrived in Boston Harbor in October, 1844. He was released from the Navy and headed home to Al-

bany, his imagination overflowing with his adventures.

His Literary Career. Melville wrote about his experiences so attractively that he soon became one of the most popular writers of his time. The books that made his reputation were *Typee* (1846); *Omoo* (1847); *Mardi* (1849), a complex allegorical romance set in the South Seas; *Redburn* (1849); and *White-Jacket* (1850).

Melville then began *Moby-Dick*, another "whaling voyage," as he called it, similar to his successful travel books. He had almost completed the book when he met Nathaniel Hawthorne. Hawthorne inspired him to radically revise the whaling documentary into a novel of both universal significance and literary complexity.

Moby-Dick, or The Whale (1851), on one level, is the story of the hunt for Moby Dick, a fierce white whale actually known to sailors of Melville's time. Captain Ahab is the captain of the whaling ship *Pequod*. He has lost a leg in an earlier battle with Moby Dick, and is determined to catch the whale. The novel brilliantly describes the dangerous and often violent life on a whaling ship, and contains information on the nature of the whaling industry and a discussion of the nature of whales. On another level *Moby-Dick* is a deeply symbolic story. The whale represents the mysterious and complex force of the universe, and Captain Ahab represents the heroic struggle against the limiting and crippling constrictions which confront an intelligent and non-passive man.

Curiously, Melville's popularity began to decline with the publication of his masterpiece. The novel, either ignored or misunderstood by critics and readers, damaged Melville's reputation as a writer. When Melville followed *Moby-Dick* with the pessimistic and tragic novel *Pierre* (1853), his readers began to desert him, calling him either eccentric or mad. The public was ready to accept unusual and exciting adventures, but they did not want ironic, frightening exposures of the terrible double meanings in life.

His Later Life. Melville turned to writing short stories. Two of them, "Benito Cereno" and "Bartleby the Scrivener," rank as classics. Several of the stories were collected in *The Piazza Tales* (1856). But the haunting and disturbing question of the meaning of life that hovered over the stories also displeased the public. In 1855, Melville published *Israel Potter*, a novel set in the American Revolution. After *The Confidence-Man* (1856), a bitter satire on mankind, he gave up writing.

Melville began writing prose again after his retirement. At his death, he left the manuscript of *Billy Budd*. This short novel, published in 1924, is considered Melville's finest book after *Moby-Dick*. It is a symbolic story about the clash between innocence and evil, and between social forms and individual liberty.

The 1920's marked the start of a Melville revival among critics and readers. By the 1940's, Americans at last recognized Melville's genius. His reputation has since spread throughout the world.

To make a living, Melville worked as deputy inspector of customs in the Port of New York from 1866 to 1885. For private pleasure he wrote poetry, which he published at his own expense. He toured the Holy Land in 1856 and 1857. The trip resulted in a 10,000-line narrative poem *Clarel* (1876), one of Melville's least read works. The poem gives a powerful picture of a man's struggle to find his faith in a skeptical, materialistic world.

HOWARD P. VINCENT

MELVILLE ISLAND is one of a group of islands in the Arctic Ocean, north of Canada. It lies between Prince Patrick and Bathurst islands, and is one of the Parry Islands. Melville Island covers an area of about 16,400 square miles. It stretches nearly 200 miles from east to west, and measures about 130 miles at its widest north to south point. Ice floes and frozen seas surround the island for at least nine months of each year.

Sir William Parry discovered Melville Island in 1819, when he was searching for a northwest passage to Asia. The island is governed as part of the Northwest Territories of Canada.

See also CANADA (physical map).

D. F. PUTNAM

MELVILLE PENINSULA is a wilderness region north of Hudson Bay in the Northwest Territories of Canada. It is about 250 miles long and about 140 miles wide at its widest point. Rae Isthmus connects it with the mainland. The straits of Fury and Hecla on the north separate it from Baffin Island. West of Melville is Committee Bay. East is Foxe Channel.

D. F. PUTNAM

MEMBRANE, *MEM brain,* is a thin sheet of tissues that covers surfaces or separates spaces in the body. There are three types of membranes—fibrous, serous, and mucous. These vary greatly in thickness and in the types of cells composing them.

Fibrous Membranes are tough and add strength to the parts they cover. They are made up entirely of fibrous connective tissue (see TISSUE [Connective Tissue]). The fibrous membrane that lines the inside of the skull is called *dura mater.* The *periosteum* is a fibrous membrane that covers the bones. The periosteum also serves as an attachment for muscles, and contains the blood vessels and nerves of the bones.

Serous Membranes line body cavities which do not open to the outside, such as the thorax and abdomen. They also cover the outside of the digestive organs and support them. The serous membranes secrete a watery fluid. This fluid keeps them moist and prevents their sticking to each other or to the organs they touch. A serous membrane lines the *pericardium,* the sac around the heart (see HEART [Its Parts and Development]). Other serous membranes include the *pleura,* which lines the lung cavities, and the *peritoneum,* which lines the cavity of the abdomen (see PLEURA; PERITONEUM). Inflammation of the peritoneum is known as *peritonitis.* A serous membrane called the *synovial membrane* lines the cavities of the joints. It secretes a watery fluid that lubricates the joints and helps them move easily and smoothly. The largest of the synovial cavities is in the knee.

Mucous Membranes line organs and passages of the body that open to the outside. A clear, sticky fluid called *mucus* covers mucous membranes (see MUCUS). Glands just under the membranes produce the mucus. Mucous membranes form the lining of the mouth, throat, alimentary canal, reproductive system, nose, windpipe and lungs, the inner surfaces of the eyelids, and the Eustachian tube.

WILLIAM V. MAYER

MEMEL, *MAY mul,* or KLAIPĔDA, *KLY peh dah* (pop. 115,000; alt. 20 ft.), is the chief seaport of Lithuania. It lies at the north end of the Kurisches Haff (Courland Lagoon) on the Baltic Sea. Memel has shipyards, and textile, paper, and lumber industries. Founded in 1252, it has been ruled by Sweden, Prussia, Germany, and the League of Nations. Now Russia controls the city. See also MEMEL, TERRITORY OF.

FRANCIS J. BOWMAN

MEMEL, TERRITORY OF, was made up of the town of Memel (Klaipėda) and a small strip of land on the coast of the Baltic Sea near Lithuania. Germany controlled the territory until the end of World War I. The Treaty of Versailles forced Germany to turn the territory over to the Allies. For the next three years, Memel remained under their control. In January, 1923, citizens of Lithuania seized Memel to get an outlet to the Baltic Sea. The Council of the League of Nations accepted the seizure, and Memel became part of Lithuania.

The president of Lithuania appointed a governor to rule the territory. The governor, in turn, appointed a council of five Memel citizens to assist him. A legislature of Memel citizens passed on the decisions of the council, but the governor could veto any acts of the legislature. The legislature objected to the governor's power. However, the Permanent Court of International Justice of the League of Nations ruled that the governor was within his rights.

Germany gained control of the territory in 1939. During World War II, Russian forces drove German troops out of Memel, and it became part of the Lithuanian Soviet Socialist Republic.

FRANCIS J. BOWMAN

MEMEL RIVER. See NEMAN RIVER.

MEMLING, HANS (1430?-1494), was a Flemish painter. His works are noted for their poetic beauty and technical perfection. He painted religious subjects, but is better known for the excellence of his portraits. Particularly famous are the small panels with which he decorated the Reliquary Shrine of St. Ursula in Bruges, Belgium. Memling was born in Seligenstadt, Germany, but spent most of his life in Bruges. Groups of his paintings hang in museums in Bruges.

JULIUS S. HELD

MEMMINGER, CHRISTOPHER GUSTAVUS (1803-1888), an American statesman, served as secretary of the treasury for the Confederacy from 1861 to 1864. He tried unsuccessfully to reduce the amount of Confederate currency. When the credit of the Confederate government collapsed, many southerners blamed him and he resigned. Memminger was born in Würtemberg, Germany. He came to Charleston, S.C., as a child.

MEMNON was an Ethiopian king in Greek mythology. He entered the Trojan War to help his uncle, Priam, fight the Greeks after the death of Hector. Memnon fought bravely and killed Antilochus, a Greek leader. But Achilles gained revenge for the Greeks by killing Memnon after a long struggle. Memnon's mother, the goddess Aurora, mourned his death. She was the goddess of dawn, and the Greeks believed that dewdrops were her tears of sorrow for Memnon (see AURORA). Zeus, the king of the gods, took pity on Aurora, and made Memnon immortal.

The Vocal Memnon is one of two huge stone statues near Thebes in Egypt built by Pharaoh Amenhotep III about 1400 B.C. It was damaged in an earthquake in 27 B.C. The damaged statue gave a musical sound at dawn when the sun struck it. The sudden change of temperature at sunrise probably caused vibrations in the statue that made the sound. The Egyptians believed that the sound was Memnon's greeting to Aurora. The sounds stopped after the Roman emperor Septimius Severus had the statue repaired.

I. J. GELB

MEMORABILIA OF SOCRATES. See XENOPHON.

The Memorial Madonna in Portage Des Sioux, Mo., was erected by residents after they were miraculously spared from a flood.

George Harris, *Life* © 1958 Time, Inc.

MEMORIAL may take the form of a statue, monument, building, or park. Frequently, highways and streets, schools, churches, mountain peaks, and books are dedicated to the memory of heroes, public servants, or loved ones. Since ancient times, men have built memorials to preserve the memory of great persons, or to commemorate events and achievements.

Sometimes, men who wish to make sure they will not be forgotten build monuments to themselves. The rulers of ancient Egypt built pyramids as memorials to their own glory. These pyramids, which also served as tombs, were among the wonders of the ancient world. In more recent times, memorials have been erected, sometimes through public donations, to honor great soldiers and statesmen.

The Arc de Triomphe in Paris is a memorial to the victories of Napoleon from 1805 to 1809. The Lincoln and Jefferson memorials and the Washington Monument in Washington, D.C., stand as tributes to three men who helped shape American history. The Tomb of the Unknowns in Arlington National Cemetery is a national shrine. On each Memorial Day, the President of the United States places a wreath on this tomb in memory of those who died in American wars. Monuments have been erected on battlefields, on the sites of historically important events, in public squares, and in cemeteries. They express the wish that the memory of both public and private persons may be cherished.

Many memorials are dedicated to peace. The famous Christ of the Andes stands in Uspallata Pass on the border between Argentina and Chile. It is a memorial to the peaceful settlement of a boundary dispute between these two countries. The memorial helps to remind everyone who sees it of the promise that all future disputes will be settled in a peaceful manner. The Statue of Liberty, in New York Harbor, is a memorial commemorating the friendship between France and the U.S.

The most common memorials are the grave markers seen in cemeteries. These monuments often represent beautiful craftsmanship.

Wealthy persons frequently create "living memorials" to honor their loved ones. These memorials may be in the form of bequests that serve useful public needs. Some persons have given grants to universities for buildings, libraries, professorships, lectureships, and scholarships. Others have endowed memorial hospitals, public auditoriums, and public parks.

CHARLES L. WALLIS

Related Articles in WORLD BOOK include:

Arc de Triomphe de L'Étoile
Christ of the Andes
Jefferson Memorial
John F. Kennedy Center for the Performing Arts
Liberty, Statue of
Lincoln Memorial
Monument
National Park System
Sarcophagus
Unknown Soldier
Washington Monument

MEMORIAL DAY, or DECORATION DAY, is a patriotic holiday in the United States. It is a day to honor American servicemen who gave their lives for their country. Originally, Memorial Day honored men who had died in the Civil War. It now also honors those who died in the Spanish-American War, World Wars I and II, the Korean War, and the Vietnam War.

Memorial Day is a legal holiday in most states. Most Northern States and some Southern States observe Memorial Day the last Monday in May. This date was made a federal holiday by a law that became effective in 1971. Most of the Southern States also have their own days for honoring the Confederate dead. Mississippi sets aside April 25, and Alabama and Georgia celebrate April 26 as Confederate Memorial Day. North Carolina and South Carolina observe this holiday on May 10. Kentucky and Louisiana celebrate June 3, Jefferson Davis' birthday, in honor of the President of the Confederacy.

Observance. On Memorial Day, people place flowers and flags on the graves of servicemen. Many organizations, including Boy Scouts, Girl Scouts, and fraternal groups march in military parades and take part in special programs. These programs often include the reading of Abraham Lincoln's "Gettysburg Address." Memorials are often dedicated on this day. Military exercises and special programs are held at Gettysburg National Military Park and at the National Cemetery in Arlington, Va.

To honor members of the armed forces who died at sea, some ports of the United States also organize ceremonies where tiny ships filled with flowers are set afloat on the water. Easton, Pa., holds such a ceremony each year. A boat filled with flowers made by Easton High School students is set afloat on the Delaware River.

Since the end of World War I, Memorial Day has also been Poppy Day. Ex-servicemen sell small, red artificial poppies to help disabled veterans (see POPPY WEEK.) In recent years, the custom has grown in most families to decorate the graves of loved ones on Memorial Day.

History. No one knows exactly when or where Memorial Day was first observed. According to tradition, Memorial Day originated during the Civil War when some Southern women chose May 30 to decorate soldiers' graves. The women honored the dead of both the Union Army and the Confederate Army.

Major General John A. Logan in 1868 named May 30 as a special day for honoring the graves of Union

Memorial Day Services are held each year to honor the memory of the dead. Military services honor the war dead. People often decorate the graves of loved ones with flowers on Memorial Day.

soldiers. Logan served as commander in chief of the Grand Army of the Republic, an organization of Union veterans of the Civil War. They had charge of Memorial Day celebrations in the Northern States for many years. The American Legion took over this duty after World War I.   ELIZABETH HOUGH SECHRIST

See also CONFEDERATE MEMORIAL DAY; GRAND ARMY OF THE REPUBLIC.

MEMORIAL UNIVERSITY OF NEWFOUNDLAND at St. John's is a coeducational university supported by the province. It offers courses in arts, commerce, education, nursing, physical education, and science, and grants bachelor's, master's, and doctor's degrees. The university also offers diplomas in architecture, engineering, and forestry. Affiliated with the university are Queen's College, an Anglican divinity college; St. Bride's Academy, a Roman Catholic college for women; and the Christian Brothers' Training College, a Roman Catholic college located at Mono Mills, Ont.

Memorial University was founded in 1925 as the Memorial University College. It became a degree-granting university in 1949. For its enrollment, see CANADA (table: Universities and Colleges).   M. O. MORGAN

MEMORY. See COMPUTER (Memory).

MEMORY is the ability to keep a mental record of earlier experiences. Basically, memory is learning. Every person learns a great many things. For example, a person may learn to ride a bicycle. This is a *skill*. Or he

may learn the names of all the Presidents of the United States. This is a *verbal response.* He also may learn to be afraid of snakes. This is an *emotional response.* A person may remember some skills, verbal responses, and emotional responses all his life. He may forget others. Verbal responses are usually forgotten more easily than are skills or emotional responses.

Why We Forget

Psychologists are interested in the problems of memory. They want to find out why we forget things, and what we can do to remember better.

Look at the following list of grocery items: milk, butter, eggs, bread, steak, LETTUCE, peas, potatoes, apples, and pudding. With practice, a person could learn this list of 10 items. An hour after first learning it, he might be able to remember about five of the items. A day or two later he might remember only one or two items. A week later he might not remember any of them.

The above example shows that time is one of the important factors in forgetting. Usually, a person forgets more and more as time goes on. The greatest memory loss occurs shortly after the original learning. After that, memory loss is more gradual. There are some kinds of material that a person remembers better a little while after learning, rather than immediately after learning. For example, a person who spends five minutes memorizing a poem may find he can recite it better the next day than immediately after the five minutes of study. This improvement of memory after a period of time is called *reminiscence*.

Some psychologists believe that time by itself does not produce loss of memory. They believe that the events that occur in time produce the failure to remember. A person will remember more items on a list eight hours later if he learns them just before going to bed, than if he learns them in the morning. Less forgetting occurs during sleep than during the day, probably because fewer events interfere with the recently learned material. The events during the day, rather than the passage of time, interfere with the ability to remember learned material.

Some forms of activity interfere with remembering more than others do. Learning to ride a bicycle should have no effect on the number of items remembered on the grocery list. But learning another grocery list, with different items, would almost certainly interfere with remembering the first list accurately. This type of interference is called *retroactive inhibition*. In general, the more similar the second activity is to the first, the more it interferes with remembering the first activity.

The Process of Remembering

What Do We Remember? In a list of items, such as the grocery list, some of the items will be remembered better than others. One of the important things that determines whether an item is easily remembered or not is its position in the list. If the item is near the beginning of the list or near the end, it will be remembered fairly easily. If it is near the middle, it will not be easily remembered. For example, in the grocery list, milk and pudding should be fairly easy to remember. Psychologists call this the *serial position effect*.

The same difficulty in remembering material near the middle also occurs in material that is not in list form. For example, if a person hears a great many arguments during a debate, he will best remember those arguments near the beginning and end. Good public speakers know that in order to convince people of a point of view, they should place their best arguments at the beginning and at the end of their speeches.

In a list, any item that stands out in any way will be better remembered than the other items. On the grocery list, the word *LETTUCE* will be easier to remember because it is the only word written in capital letters. Anything that can be done to give emphasis to a word will help that word to be remembered.

A person can remember words that mean something to him more easily than words that do not. Familiar words are easier to remember than unfamiliar words. A grocery list is much easier to remember than a list of *nonsense syllables*. Nonsense syllables are a series of letters that do not make up a word, and do not immediately suggest any word. Many nonsense syllables are made up of three letters: a consonant, a vowel, and another consonant. For example, *kuf* would be a nonsense syllable. Psychologists use nonsense syllables to study memory.

How Much Do We Remember? Psychologists use three methods to determine how much a person remembers. These methods are: (1) recall, (2) recognition, and (3) relearning.

The most natural way to find out how much a person remembers of a grocery list is to ask him what he remembers. This is called the method of *recall*. Another method, called *recognition*, is to ask the person to separate items on the original list from items that were not on the list. Usually a person will be able to recognize much material that he cannot recall. However, he will not be able to recall material that he cannot remember. Police sometimes use the method of recognition to identify a man in a lineup. If a person selects the correct man from a number of other men, he has recognized and remembered that man.

A third method of determining how much a person remembers is called the method of *relearning*. Here the individual is asked to relearn the original list. He will probably learn the list the second time faster than he did the first time. The difference in the time it takes him to relearn the list is considered a measure of how much he has remembered. Sometimes a person will not be able to recall the grocery list, and he may not even be able to recognize it. Yet, he will be able to relearn the material more quickly than he learned it the first time. This shows that something was remembered, even though the person was not aware of remembering.

How to Remember. If a person really learns material well, he will remember well. Suppose a person wanted to remember the grocery list of 10 items for a week or two. This might require *overlearning*. If he practices the list only until he is able to recall each item once, he may not remember the entire list for long. But if he continues to memorize the list long after he thinks he knows it perfectly, he will remember the list much longer.

Recitation during the original learning process also helps the memory. While learning the list, a person should repeat the items over and over to himself.

A person should try to remember the entire list as one *single unit*, rather than learn the first half one day and the second half another day. This may be discouraging at first when he tries to remember a very long list. But, in the long run, he will learn it faster and remember it longer.

The longer the list is, the more items a person will remember. He will remember more if he has learned more. But, he will remember most of the things that he has learned only if he has not learned too much.

Memorizing. Teachers and psychologists have differed widely in their opinions about the value of memorizing. But they generally agree there is little use memorizing things that have no particular meaning for the person who memorizes them. A child should not be encouraged to learn facts in the language of a textbook and repeat them word for word. It is much more important for him to understand the meaning of what he is learning, and to use facts to connect new knowledge with things he has learned previously. If he does this, he is more likely to remember what he learns.

Improving the Memory. A reliable memory is so important to success in life that people have spent much time inventing ways of improving the memory. The art of strengthening the memory by using certain formal or mechanical methods of remembering is called *mnemonics*. Mnemonics tries to make remembering easy by using various kinds of tricks or associations. For example, almost everyone remembers how many days there are in each month by repeating to himself a jingle that begins:

"Thirty days hath September,
April, June, and November,
All the rest have thirty-one
Excepting February alone . . ."

But in order to remember a great many facts by using such devices, a person also has to remember a great many devices. It may then become harder to remember the device than the thing he wants to remember.

Loss of Memory. Sometimes a person cannot remember the name of a person that he knows well. Or, perhaps he cannot remember something that was "on the tip of his tongue." Such failures to remember things that are well known may be *motivated*. This means that the person may have wanted to forget the person's name because he did not like him. He may be unable to remember what he was about to say for some equally good reason.

Sometimes things that are forgotten remain in the unconscious mind, and reveal themselves in dreams or in some other way. A person may shrink from high places, or be afraid in the dark, without knowing why. The reason may be that as a child he had unpleasant experiences which he forgot later.

Some people suffer from the condition known as *amnesia*. A person suffering from amnesia has lost his memories, not his memory. He has forgotten, at least in his conscious mind, everything that happened before the emotional shock or accident that caused the amnesia. But he may be able to remember perfectly what happened just afterward, and his ability to memorize a set of historical dates or some other group of facts is usually as good as ever. See AMNESIA.

Individual Differences

Unusual Memories. One often hears of people who have miraculous memories. They never forget a face or a name. They can repeat whole books word for word, or they can play whole symphonies after having heard them once. Some persons who have excellent memories for detail may actually "see" the material when they remember it. This is known as *eidetic imagery*. Many persons with eidetic imagery can tell the exact position of a statement on a textbook page. They can glance at an object for only a second or two, and then give a complete description of it, based on their image.

A person with eidetic imagery is often said to have a *photographic memory*. Actually, his memory is not photographic. If a person had a true photographic memory, he would be able to glance at a page and then recite the words on the page from left to right or from bottom to top. A person with eidetic imagery cannot do this. Eidetic imagery is rare in adults. But many children under 14 years of age can visualize objects with amazing clarity, and correctly answer detailed questions about them.

Normal Memories. Ordinary persons are likely to feel discouraged when they read about persons with extraordinary memories. Many people have trouble remembering the motion picture they saw last week or the errand they promised to do today. They may say to themselves, "I have no memory." But this is not true. Every person has a memory. A person who had no memory would not be able to recognize his own parents, or even his own face in the mirror.

Some persons have excellent memories, and others have poor memories. However, certain general statements can be made about the memories of most persons. Memory tends to improve up to the time of maturity. After that, there may be a very gradual decline in the ability to remember things. Furthermore, the higher the person's intelligence, the better the person will be able to remember.

RUSSELL M. CHURCH

MEMPHIS, *MEM fis*, was the first capital of ancient Egypt. According to tradition, Menes, who lived about 3100 B.C. and was the first king of Egypt, founded the city and made it his capital. Memphis stood near the site of present-day Cairo. During the Old Kingdom (2700-2200 B.C.), kings built pyramids at Giza and Sakkara near Memphis. The city was Egypt's capital until about 2200 B.C., and was an important religious and political center until about 330 B.C. Nothing remains of the ancient city itself. But cemeteries and the pyramids at Giza and Sakkara stand as reminders of the city's past glory.

BARBARA MERTZ

See also EGYPT, ANCIENT (map; History).

MEMPHIS, Tenn. (pop. 536,585; alt. 275 ft.), is the largest city in the state. It lies on the Mississippi River in the southwest corner of Tennessee. A Cotton Carnival held every May dramatizes the city's position as the largest U.S. spot cotton market. During five days of city-wide celebration, the carnival tells in pageantry the story of the city and of cotton.

The city ships cotton and hardwood lumber to all parts of the world. Its metropolitan area includes Crittenden County, Arkansas, and has a population of 674,583 persons. Memphis was named for Egypt's ancient capital of Memphis.

Location, Size, and General Description. Memphis stands on high bluffs on the east bank of the Mississippi River. Its location has made it the trade and cultural center of western Tennessee and parts of neighboring states. It is the largest city on the Mississippi River between New Orleans (about 408 miles to the south) and St. Louis (about 306 miles to the north). For location, see TENNESSEE (political map).

The city blends old southern traditions with the vigor of a modern industrial center. Wealthy planters built many of its fine homes. Memphis is often called the *City of Churches* because of its many beautiful churches. With 26 hospitals, Memphis serves as one of the great medical centers of the South. Military installations include a U.S. naval air station, a U.S. naval hospital, Memphis General Depot, and Memphis Municipal Airport, which has an air force reserve training center.

The People. Memphis originally was settled by the Scottish, Scotch-Irish, and Germans. The people today have varied backgrounds. About one-third are Negroes.

Cultural Life. Schools in Memphis include University of Tennessee medical units, Christian Brothers College, LeMoyne-Owen College, Memphis State University, and Southwestern at Memphis. It also has a natural-history museum, an art gallery, an art academy, a symphony orchestra, a little theater, the Front Street Theater, the Goodwin Institute, a cultural cen-

ter. W. C. Handy, the jazz composer, made busy Beale Street famous in his song "Beale Street Blues."

Industry and Trade. Memphis has about 800 manufacturing plants, including sprawling foundries and machine shops, and paper and rice mills. It is the world's largest inland hardwood lumber market and one of the largest producers of cottonseed products in the United States. Memphis is a major distributor of rolled steel products, drugs, and chemicals. It is one of the leading wholesale, livestock, and meat-packing centers in the South. A Piggly Wiggly store, opened there in 1916, was the first grocery in the country where people served themselves. A $50 million harbor project has helped Memphis make rapid industrial strides.

Transportation. Rail, truck, bus, and air lines connect Memphis with all parts of the nation. Four barge lines serve its port. Three bridges enable cars and trains to cross the Mississippi River at Memphis.

History. Hernando de Soto, Spanish explorer, first discovered the Mississippi River near here in 1541 and raised a Spanish flag on the bank. The French explorers, Father Jacques Marquette, Louis Joliet, and Sieur de la Salle, visited the region in the 1600's. About 1682, La Salle built Fort Prudhomme near Memphis. France and Spain claimed the land, but it was given to England by treaty. In 1783, the area became a part of the United States. In 1798 and 1799 the U.S. government built Fort Adams. Soon afterwards, the Indians were forced to leave the region. General Andrew Jackson, Judge John Overton, and General James Winchester became owners of the land. They organized a small settlement in 1819. It was incorporated as a city in 1826.

During its early days, Memphis was a stopping point for showboats. In 1878, the last of five yellow fever epidemics left the city nearly deserted. As a result, the state legislature took away Memphis' name and charter and did not restore them until 1891. Memphis has a commission government.

JEWELL A. PHELPS

MEMPHIS ACADEMY OF ARTS. See UNIVERSITIES AND COLLEGES (table).

MEMPHIS STATE UNIVERSITY is a state-supported school at Memphis, Tenn. It has colleges of arts and sciences, law, business and education, and a graduate school. Founded in 1909 as a normal school, it became a four-year college in 1925 and a university in 1957. It awards bachelor's and master's degrees. For enrollment, see UNIVERSITIES AND COLLEGES (table).

MEMPHREMAGOG. See LAKE MEMPHREMAGOG.

MENAGERIE. See CIRCUS (The Side Shows); Zoo (History).

MENAM, river. See THAILAND (Location).

MENANDER (342 B.C.-291 B.C.) was a Greek playwright who wrote over 100 comedies. However, we know his work only through fragments of his plays, adaptations of his plots by the Roman comic dramatists Terence and Plautus, and one complete play *Dyscolos* (The Grouch), which was discovered in 1959.

Menander was born and lived in Athens during a troubled political period when powerful figures like Alexander the Great controlled political and military affairs. Writers then turned their attention to the individual and his experience in society. Menander's semiserious comedies dramatize humorous situations in middle class society, especially the complications of love affairs. He is noted for his clarity of style, expert plot construction, delicate characterization, and a sympathetic view of humanity.

NORMAN T. PRATT

MENCKEN, *MENG kun,* **HENRY LOUIS** (1880-1956), was an editor and critic who greatly influenced American writing in the 1920's. He made the American public, which he called the "booboisie," the special target of his criticism. He disliked what he considered low standards of taste and culture in the United States. Mencken admired literary works that satirized American life. He encouraged such realistic writers as Sinclair Lewis, Sherwood Anderson, and Theodore Dreiser.

Mencken did not approve of many American customs, but he loved the American language. In 1918, he published *The American Language,* a long study and commentary on the growth and history of American speech. The book was widely read, and later revised three times. Mencken published *Supplement One* to the work in 1945, and he published *Supplement Two* in 1948.

He wrote books and essays nearly all his life. Some of his other writings include *The Philosophy of Friedrich Nietzsche* (1908), *In Defense of Women* (1917), *Prejudices*

Henry Louis Mencken

A. Aubrey Bodine

(in six series [1919-1927]), *Treatise on the Gods* (1930), *Treatise on Right and Wrong* (1934), *Christmas Story* (1946), and *A Mencken Chrestomathy* (1949). He also edited *A New Dictionary of Quotations*, and wrote memoirs.

Mencken was born in Baltimore, Md., on Sept. 12, 1880, and studied engineering at the Baltimore Polytechnic Institute. He began his literary career as a reporter on the Baltimore *Morning Herald* in 1899. He spent most of his life, from 1906 to 1936, as a reporter, editor, and columnist for the Baltimore *Sun*. He joined the staff of *Smart Set* magazine as a literary critic in 1908, and later became coeditor. In 1924, Mencken and the literary critic George Jean Nathan founded *The American Mercury*, a magazine of satire and comment on American life, politics, and customs. Mencken edited the magazine until 1933.   I. W. COLE

MENDAÑA DE NEYRA, ÁLVARO. See SOLOMON ISLANDS; MARQUESAS ISLANDS.

MENDEL, GREGOR JOHANN (1822-1884), an Austrian botanist and monk, discovered the principles of heredity. Observing the contrasting characteristics of different members of a species, he grew successive generations of such plants, and studied how these characteristics were inherited.

Mendel's experiments in growing garden peas proved that there is a definite pattern in the way contrasting characteristics are inherited. He discovered that one of each pair of characteristics is dominant, while the other is recessive. He found that it was possible to raise a line of plants that showed only the recessive character, as well as a line that showed only the dominant character. See HEREDITY.

In 1866, Mendel reported his experiments and findings in a paper printed by the Natural History Society of Brünn (now Brno). His discoveries laid the foundation for the scientific study of heredity. The importance of his work was not realized, however, until 1900.

Mendel was born on July 22, 1822, in Heinzendorf, Austria. He became interested in plants while a youth on his father's farm. In 1843 he entered the Augustinian monastery in Brünn. Except for his education at the University of Vienna and short periods of teaching natural history at nearby schools, Mendel spent his life in the monastery.   ROGERS MCVAUGH

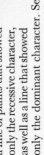

Gregor Mendel

Brown Bros.

MENDELEEV, *MEN duh LAY yef,* **DMITRI IVANOVICH** (1834-1907), a Russian chemist, introduced order into inorganic chemistry. He devised the Periodic Table that systematized the properties of the elements and permitted prediction of the existence of such new ones as gallium and germanium. The later synthesis of new elements has been based on his work.

Mendeleev was born in Tobolsk, Siberia, and was educated in St. Petersburg (now Leningrad). He taught there until 1890. Later, he worked out the standards for the Russian units of weights and measures. He wrote *Elements of Chemistry* (1868).   HENRY M. LEICESTER

See also ELEMENT, CHEMICAL; MENDELEVIUM; CHEMISTRY (picture: Famous Men).

MENDELEVIUM, *MEN duh LEE vih um* (chemical symbol, Md) is a man-made radioactive element. Its atomic number is 101 and its most stable isotope has a mass number of 258. Mendelevium is chemically similar to thulium. It was discovered in 1955 by Albert Ghiorso, Bernard G. Harvey, Gregory R. Choppin, Stanley G. Thompson, and Glenn T. Seaborg. They named it in honor of the famous Russian chemist Dmitri Mendeleev. Mendelevium was first produced by bombarding einsteinium, element number 99, with helium ions. It has not been isolated in weighable amounts. Mendelevium 256 has such a short life that half of any sample will decay in about one hour (see RADIOACTIVITY [Half-Life]). The decayed sample becomes an isotope of fermium, element 100, which also decays. See also ELEMENT, CHEMICAL; SEABORG, GLENN THEODORE; TRANSURANIUM ELEMENTS.   GLENN T. SEABORG

MENDEL'S LAWS. See HEREDITY; MENDEL, GREGOR.

MENDELSSOHN, *MEN d'l sun,* **ERIC** (1887-1953), a German architect, was famed for his free and imaginative approach to architectural problems. His work in Germany includes the Einstein tower in Potsdam (1920), a factory in Luckenwalde, and department stores in Breslau and Chemnitz. Fleeing persecution in Germany, he worked in England from 1933 to 1937. Then he lived in Palestine until 1941, and designed the government hospital in Haifa. He moved to the United States in 1941 and became an American citizen in 1947. His work in the United States includes the Maimonides Hospital in San Francisco and synagogues in St. Louis and Cleveland.   WILLIAM T. ARNETT

MENDELSSOHN, FELIX (1809-1847), was a German composer, pianist, and conductor. He made his first public appearance as a pianist when he was 9. He wrote his first music when he was 10, and by the time he was a teen-ager he was a respected composer. He became probably the most famous composer of his time.

One of Mendelssohn's most significant achievements was his role in reviving interest in the music of Johann Sebastian Bach. In 1829, Mendelssohn organized and conducted a performance of Bach's "Passion According to St. Matthew." It was the first performance of that work since Bach's death, and it greatly contributed to renewed interest in Bach.

Perhaps more than any other conductor, Mendelssohn contributed to shaping audiences' taste for music. He had excellent musical taste and demanded excellence in performance. He deserves much of the credit for increasing the performances of works by Beethoven and Mozart. Mendelssohn also was the first conductor to organize concerts aimed at presenting composers representing particular periods in music history.

His Life. Mendelssohn was born in Hamburg on Feb. 3, 1809. His full name was JAKOB LUDWIG FELIX MENDELSSOHN. He was the son of a wealthy banker

Felix Mendelssohn

Portrait by Wilhelm Von Schadow, Dr. Felix Wach, Dresden, Germany (Historical Pictures Service, Chicago)

MENDELSSOHN, FELIX

and grandson of the German-Jewish philosopher Moses Mendelssohn. In 1812, the Mendelssohn family moved to Berlin. There Felix received private music lessons from the best teachers available, including Carl Zelter. Zelter was so impressed with his young pupil that he took Mendelssohn, then only 11 years old, to visit the famous German poet Goethe. The young Mendelssohn and the 72-year-old writer became close friends.

During Mendelssohn's teen-age years, his home became the gathering place for the most respected intellectuals in Berlin. His family made an orchestra available so that Mendelssohn could try out the compositions flowing from his pen. At the age of 17, he wrote an orchestral overture, *A Midsummer Night's Dream* (1826), based on Shakespeare's play. Its lively and brilliant orchestration and catchy melodies established him as one of the leading composers of his day. Another 17 years passed before Mendelssohn wrote the incidental music, including the familiar "Wedding March," for that play. But the two works are so similar in style that they sound as though they had both been composed at the same time.

In 1829, Mendelssohn made the first of 10 trips to England. There he achieved immediate fame as a composer, soloist, and conductor. Even today, Mendelssohn's works are admired and performed more in England than in any other country. In England, he wrote perhaps his greatest work, the oratorio *Elijah*, first performed in Birmingham in 1846. England also inspired his third symphony, *Scotch* (1842), and his famous overture *The Hebrides* (1830–1832), also known as *Fingal's Cave*.

In 1835, Mendelssohn became conductor of the orchestra of the *Gewandhaus* (Cloth Hall) in Leipzig. Except for a few interruptions, he held the post until he died.

His Music has the basic elements of the "classical" period. His works contain smooth *progressions* (changes) in the harmony accompanying melodies that are easy to sing. Several of his works also show his skill in using *counterpoint* (the combination of several melodies at the same time). Mendelssohn was gifted in creating melody and in organizing the forms of his compositions so they would be clear and easily understood. This clarity can be found particularly in *Songs Without Words*, an eight-book collection of well-organized song forms.

Mendelssohn's compositions tend to be "classical" in form, but they are also filled with the emotion typical of the romantic spirit. During his lifetime, Mendelssohn was considered an experimenter and a champion of modern music. But later critics considered him as basically a conservative composer. Music historians do not agree on where to place Mendelssohn in the history of musical styles. He has been called both a "classical" and a "romantic" composer.

Many of Mendelssohn's works contain elements of descriptive music, as in *A Midsummer Night's Dream*. This quality is not surprising, because Mendelssohn was also a talented painter. When he traveled, he always tried to find time for sketching and drawing.

Of Mendelssohn's large output of 200 musical compositions, audiences today most frequently hear only fragments of some of his best work. Among the Men-

delssohn compositions still performed as complete works, the most popular are the fourth of his five symphonies (the *Italian*, 1833), and his concerto for violin in E minor (1844).

MILOŠ VELIMIROVIĆ

MENDICANT AND MENDICANT ORDERS. See FRIAR.

MENELAUS, *MEN uh LAY us*, a King of Sparta, was the husband of Helen of Troy. Paris, a Trojan prince, persuaded Helen to elope with him to Troy. Menelaus and his brother, Agamemnon, gathered a huge army and attacked Troy. This started the Trojan War. After 10 years they took the city, and Menelaus recovered Helen. They wandered for eight years, but finally reached Sparta. Menelaus and Helen lived there peacefully for many years.

See also AGAMEMNON; HELEN OF TROY; PARIS; TROJAN HORSE; TROY.

JOSEPH FONTENROSE

MENELIK. See ETHIOPIA (History).

MENÉNDEZ DE AVILÉS, PEDRO. See FLORIDA (Exploration and Spanish Settlement); GEORGIA (Exploration).

MENES. See EGYPT, ANCIENT (Early Days).

MENHADEN, *men HAY d'n*, or MOSSBUNKER, is a fish that lives in the Atlantic Ocean off the Americas from Nova Scotia to Brazil. Its name comes from an Indian word meaning *that which enriches the earth*. Early Indians often used these fish for fertilizing their crops. The fish has many local names, such as *pogy*, *bony fish*, *bunker*, *bugfish*, and *fatback*. The menhaden grows to be from 12 to 18 inches long and weighs from three quarters of a pound to a pound.

Countless numbers of young menhaden appear along the east coast of the United States in the summer. They swim near the surface in compact schools. These fish make easy prey for fishermen as well as for the shark, tuna, and other flesh-eating fish. Menhaden themselves feed chiefly on tiny plants and animals in the sea, called *plankton* (see PLANKTON).

Menhaden can be eaten by humans, but only small quantities are sold for food. Menhaden yield a valuable oil, used in the manufacture of soap, linoleum, oilskin garments, paint and varnish, and in the tempering of steel. Ground menhaden meal serves as livestock feed and menhaden scrap is used for fertilizer. Menhaden meal is high in protein content. There are many menhaden-processing plants along the coasts of the Atlantic Ocean and Gulf of Mexico in the United States. Menhaden are also used for bait in fishing for mackerel, cod, and tuna.

Scientific Classification. Menhaden belong to the herring family, *Clupeidae*. They are members of the genus *Brevoortia*, and are species *B. tyrannus*. LEONARD P. SCHULTZ

The Menhaden swims along the eastern coast of America. It has silvery sides, and its fins are usually yellowish.

MENINGES. See BRAIN (Brain Membranes); MENINGITIS.

MENINGITIS, *MEN in JYE tis,* is a disease of the *meninges* (coverings of the brain and spinal cord). It may be caused by a variety of microorganisms, or germs, that invade the human body. The bacteria that most commonly cause meningitis are meningococcus, tubercle bacillus, influenza bacillus, pneumococcus, streptococcus, and staphylococcus. Many kinds of viruses may also cause meningitis.

The disease is usually associated with infections that develop elsewhere in the body, as in the lungs. Germs travel from these infections to the meninges through the blood stream. If enough bacteria reach the meninges, and if the body's defense forces are weak enough, meningitis will occur.

Meningitis may also result when disease-producing germs invade any tissue in contact with the covering of the brain. Infections may spread from the nose, throat, sinuses, and ears. The microorganisms usually travel through the short, wide veins that meet the veins of the meninges. The microorganisms also may spread by traveling along the outer coverings of the nerves from the nose. They sometimes spread directly from infected bones, such as the sinuses and mastoid bones.

Symptoms. Meningitis frequently occurs in the course of some other illness. Meningitis usually starts with severe headaches, nausea, vomiting, and a rise in temperature. A spasm of the neck and back muscles pulls the head back. This spasm may be so severe that the patient cannot bend his head forward. The back may also be bowed backward. The patient may become delirious, and then fall into a coma.

Diagnosis. Doctors diagnose meningitis by examining the spinal fluid. They insert a needle between the vertebrae in the lower part of the back, and draw the fluid from the canal that contains the spinal cord. If they find pus, or an excess of white blood corpuscles, the diagnosis of meningitis is confirmed. The germ that causes the meningitis sometimes may be identified by staining the sediment of the spinal fluid, or by making cultures of the fluid or the patient's blood.

Treatment and Recovery. The development of sulfa drugs and a variety of antibiotics has increased the chances for recovery from meningitis. Most cases of influenzal meningitis can be cured. The length of time necessary for recovery depends on the severity of the infection. Many cases of pneumococcus meningitis, tuberculous meningitis, and influenzal meningitis in infants are still fatal. Persons who come in close contact with meningitis patients often receive sulfa drugs or antibiotics to protect them from the disease.

Epidemic Cerebrospinal Meningitis is the term often applied to meningitis caused by meningococcus bacteria. This microorganism causes more cases of meningitis than any other germ, but the cases seldom reach epidemic form. However, epidemics do occur, especially when many young people live together under conditions that favor the rapid spread of bacteria from person to person. An example of such conditions is when hundreds of new recruits live together in barracks during wartime.

This type of meningitis, commonly called *spinal meningitis,* usually is *primary.* This means that it reaches the brain directly from the nose and throat, without any infection developing there first. Sometimes the blood is heavily infected with meningococci. This most frequently happens in infants. In such instances, spots appear all over the body. Because of these spots, the disease was once called *spotted fever.*

Nonpurulent Meningitis is caused by microorganisms that do not form pus in the spinal fluid. The viruses of lymphocytic meningitis, mumps, infectious mononucleosis, or poliomyelitis are probably the chief causes of this type.

PAUL S. RHOADS

MENLO COLLEGE. See UNIVERSITIES AND COLLEGES (table).

MENNINGER, *MEN ing ur,* is the family name of two noted American psychiatrists. With their father, Charles Frederick Menninger (1862-1953), they founded the Menninger Clinic and the Menninger Foundation in Topeka, Kan. They pioneered in treating mental and physical disorders in a community clinic setting. The Menninger Clinic owes much of its renown to the zeal with which the family attacked problems in the treatment of mental disorders.

Karl Augustus Menninger (1893-   ) serves as chairman of the board of trustees of the Menninger Foundation. He has crusaded for the improvement of hospital facilities for psychiatric care and for greater individual and personal attention toward mental patients. His many writings, especially *The Human Mind* (1930), widely influenced public attitudes toward mental illness. His other works include *Man Against Himself* (1938), *Love Against Hate* (1942), and *The Vital Balance* (1963, with others).

Menninger was born in Topeka, Kan., and was graduated from the University of Wisconsin. He received his M.D. from Harvard University. He built an active medical practice, but devoted most of his time to the teaching and research program and the administration of the Menninger Foundation. The writings of Sigmund Freud interested Menninger, and his writings reflect many of Freud's concepts.

William Claire Menninger (1899-1966) became general secretary of the Menninger Foundation. He was chief consultant on psychiatry to the Surgeon General of the United States Army during World War II, and won the Distinguished Service Medal for this work. He also became a leader in the Boy Scout movement.

He was born in Topeka, and was graduated from Washburn College (now Washburn University of Topeka). He received his M.D. from Cornell University.

William C. Menninger

Menninger Foundation

Karl A. Menninger

Menninger Foundation

Like his brother, he built an active private medical practice, but spent most of his time working with the Menninger Foundation. His writings include *Psychiatry in a Troubled World* (1948) and *Psychiatry: Its Evolution and Present Status* (1948).

KENNETH E. CLARK

MENNINGER FOUNDATION

MENNINGER FOUNDATION is a nonprofit organization for psychiatric treatment, training, and research, and for the prevention of mental illness. It is the outgrowth of the Menninger Clinic, founded in 1919 by Dr. C. F. Menninger and his sons, Dr. Karl A. and Dr. William C. Menninger. The clinic operated a private psychiatric hospital, a school for problem children, and a small research and training program. In 1946, the Menningers turned their assets over to the Menninger Foundation. The foundation conducts research and runs a department for children, an industrial mental-health program, and a marriage-counseling training program. The foundation is at 3617 W. 6th Street, Topeka, Kans. 66606. See also MENNINGER (family); KANSAS (picture: The Menninger Foundation).

WILLIAM C. MENNINGER

MENNONITES, *MEN un ites,* belong to a Protestant group known for its emphasis on plain ways of dressing, living, and worshiping. There are many branches of Mennonites. Those who live in rural areas dress and live much more simply than urban groups.

Mennonites base their beliefs on the Bible, especially the New Testament. Their *creed* (statement of beliefs) is the Sermon on the Mount (Matt. 5-7). Mennonites believe it forbids going to war, swearing oaths, or holding offices that require the use of force.

The first Mennonites belonged to a church organized in Zurich, Switzerland, in 1525. The members called themselves *Swiss Brethren.* They believed that church and state should be separate, and that Reformation leaders had not reformed the church enough. They also believed that baptism and church membership should be given only to those who voluntarily gave up sin. They baptized only persons who proved their goodness in their daily lives. They were nicknamed *Anabaptists,* meaning *rebaptizers* (see ANABAPTISTS). The name *Mennonite* came from Menno Simons, a Roman Catholic priest who led the Anabaptists in The Netherlands and northern Germany in the 1530's. The Mennonites later split into groups, including the Amish (see AMISH).

The Mennonites were persecuted in many countries. Dutch Mennonites moved to northern Germany and Prussia in the 1600's, and to the Russian Ukraine in the 1700's. In 1874, many moved from Russia to Canada and to Kansas, Nebraska, and nearby states. Swiss Mennonites settled in southern Germany and France, and moved to Pennsylvania in 1683 after William Penn offered them religious liberty. They are part of the group called *Pennsylvania Dutch* (see PENNSYLVANIA DUTCH).

There are about 400,000 Mennonites in the world, including about 320,000 in North America. For U.S. membership, see RELIGION (table).

MENOMINEE INDIANS, *mee NAHM uh nee,* were swift runners and brave warriors. According to tradition, no other tribe could capture one of them alive. The Menominee belonged to the eastern woodland group of North American tribes. They lived at the mouth of the Menominee River in Green Bay, and on the headwaters of the Rock River, farther south in Wisconsin.

JOHN A. HOSTETLER

Some lived in northern Illinois. Their Algonkian language resembled that of the Sauk, Fox, and Kickapoo.

The word *Menominee* means *wild rice people.* The Indians received this name because their main food was the wild rice that grew along the lake shores in the areas where they lived. They harvested this grain from the water by canoe. The Menominee knew how to plant seed and raise grain, but refused to do so because they did not want to "wound their mother, the earth." They lived in long lodges made of poles covered with bark.

The Menominee usually had peaceful relations with white men, but remained bitter enemies of nearby Algonkian Indian tribes. By the late 1600's, wars had killed off most of the Menominee, but they continued to live along the Menominee River and in northern Illinois until about 1852. At that time, they were assigned a reservation along the Wolf River in northeastern Wisconsin.

See also INDIAN, AMERICAN.

WAYNE C. TEMPLE

MENOPAUSE. See MENSTRUATION.

MENORAH. See B'NAI B'RITH.

MENOTTI, *meh NAW tih,* **GIAN CARLO** (1911-), an American composer, wrote some of the most popular operas of the mid-1900's. Unlike most composers, he also writes the *librettos* (words) for his operas and stages most of their premières. Menotti won the 1950 Pulitzer prize for music for *The Consul* (1950) and the 1955 prize for *The Saint of Bleecker Street* (1954). His best operas are noted for their vivid theatrical quality.

Menotti's first performed opera, *Amelia Goes to the Ball,* was staged in 1938 at the Metropolitan Opera.

Gian Carlo Menotti

NBC Television

In 1947, his tragedy *The Medium* and comedy *The Telephone* had a long run on Broadway. Menotti's next stage successes were *The Consul,* a tragedy about political refugees in Europe, and *The Saint of Bleecker Street,* which tells of life in New York City's Italian section. He wrote *Amahl and the Night Visitors,* perhaps his best-known opera, for television in 1951. Based on the story of the three wise men, it has been rerun many times on TV at Christmas. *Help! Help! The Globolinks!* (1969) is a comic opera about an invasion from outer space.

Menotti was born in Cadegliano, near Milan, Italy, and moved to the United States in 1928. In 1958, he founded the Festival of Two Worlds, an international festival of the arts that is held each summer in Spoleto, Italy.

GILBERT CHASE

MENSHEVIK, *MEN shuh vik,* was the name given to a group in the Russian Social Democratic Labor Party. In 1903, the party split over a disagreement about membership. V. I. Lenin, a Russian revolutionary, became the leader of the *bolshinstvo* (majority), or Bolsheviks. His opponents became known as the *menshinstvo* (minority), or Mensheviks. The Bolsheviks favored party membership restricted to a small number of professional revolutionaries. The Mensheviks wanted fewer limitations on membership. See also BOLSHEVIK; LENIN, V. I.

MENSTRUATION

MENSTRUATION, *men stroo AY shun,* is the normal bleeding that occurs about every four weeks in women. This bleeding, the *menstrual period,* usually lasts from three to seven days. During this period, part of the lining of the *uterus,* a pear-shaped sex organ, comes off and is discharged with blood. The beginning and end of menstruation, and the duration of the periods, may vary widely among individual women. The first menstrual period is called the *menarche.* It usually occurs at about 12 years of age. Menstruation then occurs rhythmically until about age 50. The ending of the menstrual cycles is called the *menopause.*

Menstruation results from the way certain glands and organs prepare a woman's body for having children. These glands produce powerful chemicals called *hormones.* One kind of hormone causes the *ovary* (female sex gland) to give off an *ovum* (egg or female sex cell) about

once a month. If the ovum unites with a *sperm* (male sex cell), a new human being develops in the uterus.

Menstruation occurs in a rhythmical cycle that can be divided into four phases. These are (1) the postmenstrual phase, (2) intermenstrual phase, (3) premenstrual phase, and (4) menstrual phase.

ALLAN C. BARNES

PARTS OF THE FEMALE REPRODUCTIVE SYSTEM

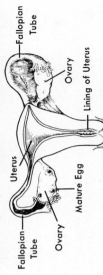

Fallopian Tube

Ovary

Lining of Uterus

Uterus

Fallopian Tube

Ovary

Mature Egg

THE FOUR PHASES OF MENSTRUATION

Postmenstrual Phase. When menstrual bleeding stops, preparations for a new cycle begin at once. The pituitary gland gives off FSH (folliclestimulating hormone). This hormone causes an egg to begin ripening within a follicle (tiny sac) in an ovary. Each ovary contains as many as 400,000 potential egg cells, but usually only one egg matures during any one menstrual cycle.

Intermenstrual Phase. The ovaries produce their own hormones. One of these, called *estrogen,* makes the cells lining the uterus divide rapidly to form a new lining, *right.* In this way, the uterus prepares to receive a *fertilized egg* (an egg united with a sperm). The ovary releases the egg about eight or nine days after the bleeding stops, *right.* After the egg is released, the ovaries produce a hormone called *progesterone* that also helps build the uterine lining.

Premenstrual Phase. The egg released by the ovary makes its way slowly down the Fallopian tube to the uterus. The journey takes about five days. If sperm are present, fertilization takes place in the Fallopian tube. This egg-sperm combination then settles into the lining of the uterus, which has become thick and spongy with many blood vessels and watery fluids, *right.* When this happens, the menstrual cycle usually stops until after the baby is born.

Menstrual Phase. If the egg does not become fertilized in the Fallopian tube, it dies in a day or two. It cannot attach itself to the uterine lining. Then the ovary stops making estrogen and progesterone. Without these hormones, the uterine lining breaks down and begins to shed, *right.* This shedding causes some bleeding. During this bleeding, or menstrual period, most of the lining and about 1½ ounces of blood are discharged from the body. After the bleeding ends, the menstrual cycle begins again.

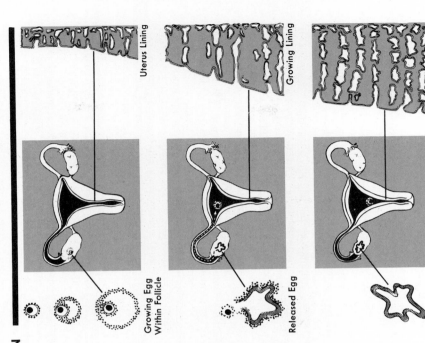

Uterus Lining

Growing Egg Within Follicle

Growing Lining

Released Egg

Mature Lining

Empty Follicle

Degenerating Lining

Degenerating Follicle

WORLD BOOK diagrams by Johns Hopkins University Art Department

MENSURATION

MENSURATION, *MEN shoo RAY' shun,* is the measurements of lines, surfaces, and solids. A line has one dimension—length. Length is measured in linear units, such as inches, feet, miles, or kilometers. A surface has two dimensions, length and width. The area of a surface is measured in square units, such as square inches.

A solid has three dimensions, length, width, and thickness. The volume of a solid is measured in cubic units, such as cubic feet or cubic meters.

For a more complete discussion of mensuration, see Measurement; Weights and Measures; Denominate Number.

MENTAL HEALTH includes the prevention of mental and emotional disorders, and the detection, treatment, and rehabilitation of the mentally ill. It also involves the promotion of mental well-being.

Prevention. In general, doctors can prevent mental illness in only a relatively few types of cases. These include mental illnesses resulting directly from brain injury, food deficiencies, and certain poisons. The basic causes of mental illness remain the object of scientific research involving both physical and psychological factors. Doctors believe that stress may bring on mental illness. Such stress may be pressures from relationships with other persons or from social conditions, or they may result from physical or chemical processes within the body. Some mental illnesses may be prevented by avoiding pressures that become too great to handle.

Detection, Treatment, and Rehabilitation of persons suffering from mental illnesses require many services. These include the establishment and maintenance of child-guidance clinics in schools, community mental-health clinics to treat children and adults suffering from mental disorders, and full-treatment programs for the mentally ill in general hospitals and mental hospitals. Research into the causes, nature, and treatment of mental illness is also important.

Promotion of Mental Health deals with helping people to feel comfortable about themselves and others, and to meet the demands of life. These attitudes have their roots in a stable family life that provides children with good physical care and emotional satisfaction. Other elements contributing to mental health include communities as free as possible of social, moral, and physical dangers; schools that offer both knowledge and the opportunities for children to develop their full potentials and to learn to get along with others; warm friends; and steady, rewarding work.

The National Association for Mental Health was formed in 1950 through the merger of the National Committee for Mental Hygiene, the National Mental Health Foundation, and the Psychiatric Foundation. The association has more than 800 state and local affiliates. They work for improved treatment and care for mental hospital patients, expanded community mental health services, special treatment services for mentally ill children, and rehabilitation services for discharged patients. The association also conducts a research program. It has headquarters at 10 Columbus Circle, New York, N.Y. 10019. PHILIP E. RYAN

See also BEERS, CLIFFORD; HEALTH (Keeping Your Mind Healthy); MENTAL ILLNESS; PSYCHIATRY; PSYCHOLOGY.

PHILIP S. JONES

For a more complete discussion of mensuration, see Measurement; Weights and Measures; Denominate Number.

MENTAL ILLNESS

MENTAL ILLNESS means sickness of the mind. It may involve a mental breakdown so serious that the patient must have special care or enter a mental hospital. Or it may mean personality traits or quirks that lead to personal unhappiness. Mental illness can result in difficulty in getting along with others, and lack of ability to live a useful life.

Mentally ill persons are sick people, just as persons suffering from sore throats or heart disease are sick people. Like other sick persons, the mentally ill need specialized treatment by a physician.

Mental illness occurs in every country and among all peoples. No social or economic class of persons is free of it. About 10,000,000 persons in the United States suffer some form of mental illness, and more than 250,000 new patients enter mental hospitals every year. Mental patients occupy about half the hospital beds in the United States.

At present we know little about preventing mental illness. Medical science knows neither specific causes of all kinds of mental illnesses nor specific ways of preventing them. Experts believe that early family life influences the development of some mental illnesses. A happy home life during the first years may do more than anything else to prevent many mental illnesses.

What Is Mental Illness?

Mental illness covers a wide range of conditions of the mind. Almost everyone has some minor disturbances of personality, character, and behavior. These include periods of depression, worry, and outbursts of unjustifiable anger. But these disturbances usually do not keep a person from living a satisfactory life. Doctors

---

MENTAL ILLNESS TERMS

Adaptation is the ability to adjust to the problems of life.

Amnesia is the inability to remember past experiences, produced by some impending danger whose cause is largely unknown. This contrasts to fear of the known.

Anxiety is a condition of worry, tension, or uneasiness

Complex is a group of related repressed ideas or feelings.

Conscious means to be freely aware, or knowing, as contrasted with *unconscious*, or not being aware.

Defense is a conscious or unconscious process of hiding one's feelings.

Delusion is a false belief that a person keeps, in spite of its being proved false.

Hallucination means seeing, hearing, or otherwise sensing something that does not really exist.

Inhibition is a blocking of thoughts or behavior.

Masochism means receiving pleasure from one's own pain and suffering.

Neurosis is a mild emotional disorder.

Phobia is a strong, unreasonable fear, such as fear of water or of height.

Psychosis is a severe mental disorder.

Rationalization is a person's attempt to make reasonable and logical any unreasonable thinking, feeling, or behavior.

Regression means a return to childish behavior, because of the inability to meet difficulties in life.

Repression means to keep an idea or feeling out of the conscious mind.

Sadism means receiving pleasure from causing pain and suffering to others.

Sublimation means to replace childish tendencies with socially accepted behavior.

MENTAL ILLNESS

do not consider such disturbances as illnesses unless they are severe or occur frequently. Sometimes, however, the disturbances cause personal unhappiness, difficulties in personal relations, or behavior that breaks the rules of society. Then the condition may be considered a mental illness.

People in some countries accept as perfectly healthy persons whom we would call mentally ill. Mental illness appears in many forms, varying from culture to culture. Behavior can be judged *abnormal* (sick) only when it is considered in relation to the background in which the person lives. For example, our culture considers as abnormal a person who has an attitude of constant suspicion. But among the people of Dobu Island in Melanesia, the typical personality trait is a suspicious nature. Anthropological studies show that the social organization and religion of the Dobu Islanders are such that constant suspicion is the normal and expected attitude. According to the standards of our culture, such a mental state would probably be considered unhealthy. See CULTURE; BEHAVIOR.

Unhealthy Behavior. Mentally ill persons may be confused, unhappy, depressed, and uncertain about themselves. On the other hand, they may not know about their illness, because they explain their behavior by blaming other persons. Sometimes they withdraw into their own make-believe world, and become only dimly aware of what goes on around them. In the most serious stages of mental illness, people may cause physical harm to themselves or to others.

A break with reality is commonly called a *nervous breakdown.* This term has no meaning in medicine, and doctors do not use it. However, laymen often use the term to describe any unusual behavioral disturbance that takes place in a previously healthy person and that requires hospitalization or absence from the ordinary activities of life. The legal term *insanity* refers to any mental illness that requires a court to confine a person in a mental institution, or to appoint a legal guardian for him.

Even mentally healthy persons sometimes have moods of anxiety, depression, and discouragement, and are not always happy. At times, all normal people become worried, depressed, or angry. A doctor would probably suspect that a person who never showed any of these emotions was not entirely normal.

Causes of Mental Illness. Mental illnesses are sometimes related to defects in the brain that may result from various causes. Some defects may be *congenital.* That is, they occur before birth. For example, a child may be born with an incompletely developed brain. Or, the defects may be *accidental,* as when brain injury occurs during birth. Such brain defects usually result in *mentally retarded* children. See MENTAL RETARDATION; HANDICAPPED (The Mentally Disabled).

Accidental brain damage from injury to the head may also occur after birth, and cause mental disorder. Hardening of the arteries, a disease of old age, may harm the nerve cells of the brain, because the blood does not flow properly to the brain. Sometimes the brain cells simply wear out, as in senility, and the mind does not function properly (see SENILITY). Poisons from body infections may harm the brain, or infection may occur in the brain itself. Disorders in body metabolism, such as too little sugar in the blood, may affect the way the mind functions (see METABOLISM). Some experts believe that defects in the adrenal glands may also affect the mind. Other researchers believe that chemical and metabolic disturbances may occur in the brain and cause certain mental disorders.

Most mental illness occurs without any apparent brain damage. Some psychiatrists believe that heredity may cause such conditions (see HEREDITY [Mental Traits]). The influence of heredity in mental illness is difficult to prove, however. Other psychiatrists believe that childhood experiences help cause mental illness. They believe that overprotection or frustration during the first year or two of life can make a person

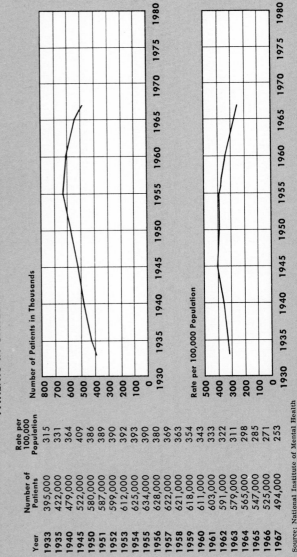

PATIENTS IN UNITED STATES MENTAL HOSPITALS

Year	Number of Patients	Rate per 100,000 Population
1933	395,000	315
1935	422,000	331
1940	479,000	364
1945	522,000	409
1950	580,000	386
1951	587,000	389
1952	599,000	390
1953	612,000	392
1954	625,000	393
1955	634,000	390
1956	628,000	380
1957	622,000	369
1958	621,000	363
1959	618,000	354
1960	611,000	343
1961	603,000	333
1962	591,000	322
1963	579,000	311
1964	565,000	298
1965	547,000	285
1966	525,000	271
1967	494,000	253

Number of Patients in Thousands

Rate per 100,000 Population

Source: National Institute of Mental Health

MENTAL ILLNESS

maladjusted, or unable to face later difficulties (see MALADJUSTMENT).

Anything that interferes with the normal development of the ability to face life can cause later trouble. Such trouble may not occur unless the person meets a particular crisis in later life. Depending on our past experiences and current problems, we all have weak spots. Anyone can reach a "breaking point" and become mentally ill.

The term *psychosomatic* is often used to describe illnesses in which emotional disturbances affect a person's physical health. Such conditions as asthma, ulcers, migraine headaches, and hay fever are often called psychosomatic illnesses, because of their close relationship to emotional health. This term also refers to the relationship between mind and body. Doctors do not consider psychosomatic illness as a special kind of mental illness. See PSYCHOSOMATIC MEDICINE.

Kinds of Mental Illnesses

Doctors classify mental illnesses into two general types: (1) organic and (2) functional. *Organic* mental illnesses result from defects that occur in the brain before birth, or when injury or illness cause damage to the brain. *Functional* mental illnesses involve no apparent change in the brain, yet the mind does not work properly. Most mental illness is functional.

Conditions such as drug addiction, alcoholism, delinquency, and criminality are symptoms of severe emotional illness. They may appear in any type of neurosis or psychosis.

Neurosis is a mild emotional disorder in which a person's thinking or behavior harms his relationships with other people or his own happiness. Neurotic persons frequently have *repressed* (hidden) ideas or memories called *complexes*. A neurosis reduces a person's ability to live happily, but he does not seriously lose his sense of reality.

Psychiatrists believe that neuroses usually result when childhood experiences lead to poor adjustment to the difficulties of later life. A child may develop a neurosis during the critical years of adolescence (see ADOLESCENCE). On the other hand, some persons may not suffer neurotic disturbances until they meet a particular crisis in life. Still others, who suffer neuroses from early childhood, have severe changes in personality.

There are several common types of neuroses. Certain symptoms of all neuroses may appear in one person, or various mixtures of symptoms may occur.

An *anxiety neurosis* involves mental and physical symptoms caused by the abnormal fear or dread of death, insanity, or other conditions that could destroy the individual. *Conversion hysteria* causes physical symptoms such as paralysis, numbness, or even convulsions (see HYSTERIA). *Depressive reactions* include "blue" and sad feelings, lack of decision, loss of appetite, and feelings of being inadequate to face life. *Hypochondria* is an overconcern for symptoms or diseases that do not exist (see HYPOCHONDRIA). Persons with *obsessive* and *compulsive neuroses* have repeated urges to perform certain acts. The patient spends much of his time thinking in the same manner, or performing the same acts over and over again. He may needlessly want to wash his hands dozens

of times a day. Or, he may be excessively concerned about keeping things in order or scheduling his time. *Phobias* involve unreasonable fears about objects and situations, such as a fear of high places. The patient avoids the object of his phobia in order to lessen his worry (see PHOBIA). *Character neuroses* include passiveness, aggressiveness, moodiness, and elation. See NEUROSIS.

Personality Disorders occur in persons who have character traits such as extreme selfishness, that make it difficult for them to get along with others. Such disorders do not keep the person from enjoying the usual activities of life, as do the neuroses.

The *psychopathic personality* is the worst of these disorders. Doctors find it in persons who repeatedly perform unsocial acts, and apparently do not learn from their experience. The psychopathic personality may be a sexual pervert, a narcotics addict, or a criminal. This kind of disorder can rarely be treated successfully, because it is associated with conscience. Psychiatrists and psychologists believe that if conscience is not instilled in early childhood, it cannot be created later.

Manic-Depressive Psychosis is a major emotional illness. It involves periods of *mania* (elation) and *depression* (blueness). Several members of a family often suffer this condition.

In *melancholia* (depression appearing with or without manic attacks), a person may have difficulty sleeping and eating. He may lose weight, and even try to commit suicide. He usually feels worst in the early morning, but somewhat better at night, after the day's activities have been finished. Many depressed persons cry frequently.

In contrast, some people are only manic, and never become depressed. They talk excessively and move about a great deal. They seem to be happy, but many are sad inside. They act impulsively and are easily distracted.

Between attacks, manic-depressive persons return to their normal state without treatment. They may go through long periods with no attacks of mania or depression. But doctors find it difficult, if not impossible, to prevent such attacks. See PSYCHOSIS.

Schizophrenia means a "splitting" of the personality. The patient's intelligence may remain normal, but his emotions do not fit real-life situations. Schizophrenia does not mean that the patient has more than one personality.

Schizophrenic patients may be emotionally disturbed, aggressive, and destructive. They may return to childish behavior and be unable to care for themselves. Some withdraw into fantasy and hallucination. Most have serious difficulties in adjusting to reality. In general, doctors can rarely prevent or cure this disorder; but they can often help the patient. Schizophrenia occurs in several forms, and is the most frequent psychosis found among patients in mental hospitals.

In *catatonic schizophrenia*, a person may become completely inactive and immobile, and not seem to respond to reality. His muscles may become rigid and he may stay in one position for hours. Often he must be fed and his toilet needs cared for. On the other hand, he may become wildly excited and behave in violent and strange ways. When catatonic, such persons do not seem to know what is going on around them. However, they remember

Play Therapy is often used in work with disturbed children. The child plays with dolls or toys and often acts out the emotional problems. The doctor interprets the child's play.

their experiences during the course of their illnesses.

In *hebephrenic schizophrenia*, a person talks and acts in an irrational manner. He may behave childishly. These patients suffer rapid mental deterioration. In many cases, they must remain in mental hospitals throughout their lives.

The *paranoid schizophrenic* believes that other persons persecute him, and he behaves accordingly. He thinks that people talk about him and wish to harm him. He may even accuse members of his own family. He may accuse others of poisoning him or of following him on the street.

A person who suffers *simple schizophrenia* is emotionally dull, withdrawn, and isolated. He shows no strange symptoms, and often goes along for some time before his illness is detected. His emotions slowly disappear. This slow change led to the original term for schizophrenia, *dementia praecox*. This term was based on the belief that the disease began early in adolescence (*praecox*) and ended in loss of mental ability (*dementia*). Doctors now know that schizophrenia may begin at any age and that it may never be associated with dementia.

Medical science has discovered that schizophrenic persons suffer from a disturbed function of the adrenal glands. Brain-wave tests show that these patients also have changes in the function of the brain. If the reason for these physical disorders can be found, doctors may be able to find a way to correct them and to help schizophrenic patients.

Paranoia, a disorder that doctors often consider a type of schizophrenia, may also be present separately. Such persons show *megalomania*, or an exaggerated degree of selflove. They believe that other people act

hostile and persecute them. However, unlike the paranoid schizophrenics, persons suffering from paranoia seem to be able to behave properly.

How Mental Illnesses Are Treated

Mental illness, like all illnesses, should be treated by physicians. Specialists in the diagnosis and treatment of mental disorders are called *psychiatrists*. A psychiatrist is trained as a medical doctor and has an M.D. degree. He must serve a three-year residency in a mental hospital as part of his training. See PSYCHIATRY.

Diagnosis. Psychiatrists use a number of methods to diagnose mental illnesses. The first step is a thorough medical examination to find any physical causes for the mental disturbance. Then the psychiatrist interviews the patient. The psychiatrist asks questions and encourages the patient to talk freely. The doctor also usually talks with members of the patient's family, his friends, and other associates. These talks help show how the person behaves in many situations. Sometimes the psychiatrist suggests a brain-wave test to detect any organic changes in the brain.

A *psychologist* often helps the psychiatrist diagnose cases. Psychologists test and measure a wide variety of behavior and mental reactions. For example, the psychiatrist may ask a psychologist to give the patient a Rorschach Ink-Blot Test. In this test, the patient tells the psychologist what he sees in a series of 10 standardized ink blots. The psychologist and psychiatrist are trained to interpret the patient's replies as expressions of his inner feelings. The psychologist, who usually holds a Ph.D. degree, is particularly concerned with conscious acts and learning processes. *Clinical psychologists* help people who have problems of adjustment. See

MENTAL ILLNESS

PSYCHOLOGY (Clinical Psychology).

Psychotherapy, the major type of treatment given by a psychiatrist, involves talks between the doctor and the patient. It gives the patient a chance to *ventilate*, or talk out, his deepest feelings toward persons who have played important parts in his life. Psychotherapy may enable a person to realize that relationships with people do not always cause discomfort.

The various forms of psychotherapy differ in goals, according to how the patient needs to be helped, and how much change the patient can make in his own personality. Psychotherapy may seek to give the patient confidence, or to help him understand the nature of his problems. Sometimes the psychiatrist tries to uncover unconscious reasons for the patient's feelings, in order to help him understand his actions.

Physicians and psychologists often use a form of psychotherapy called *counseling*. They do not try to diagnose a person's problems or tell him what to do. The doctor listens while the patient talks about his problems. He may offer advice, but often serves only as a sympathetic listener. The patient, simply by talking about his problems, may arrive at a decision or reach a conclusion by himself. Many experts feel that counseling bolsters the person's self-confidence and helps him meet his problems. See PSYCHOTHERAPY.

Psychoanalysis is a technique developed by Sigmund Freud to uncover a patient's unconscious feelings. The patient lies down on a couch and tells the *psychoanalyst* whatever comes into his mind. A psychoanalyst is a psychiatrist who has had additional training in psychoanalysis. Psychoanalysis requires three or four 50-minute sessions a week, and may last for several years. Psychiatrists find it useful in treating neuroses. See FREUD, SIGMUND; PSYCHOANALYSIS.

Drug Therapy calms patients and enables them to sleep at night. Sometimes persons who are extremely

upset may be given sleep-producing drugs to put them into prolonged *narcosis*, a deep sleep that lasts for several days. They are awakened for food and to attend to their toilet needs. In *narco-analysis*, the physician puts the patient into a state of grogginess, or "twilight sleep," and encourages him to describe or act out painful experiences that he represses when awake.

Doctors may use *tranquilizing drugs* to quiet disturbed patients so they can receive therapy. These tranquilizers do not cure, but simply lessen the patient's anxiety and activity. See TRANQUILIZER.

Shock Treatment consists of induced coma or convulsions. It frequently helps victims of severe psychoses. Doctors use *insulin shock* to treat schizophrenic patients (see INSULIN). Large doses of insulin produce daily periods of coma by reducing the sugar content of the blood. The coma may last for an hour or more. Often, after several months of such treatment, the patient becomes free of his psychosis for a period of time. This *remission*, or period of freedom, may last for a few months, or even years. Remissions occur faster when the doctor uses insulin than if they occur naturally. However, they usually last no longer and produce no better results.

In *electric shock*, the physician applies an electric current to the patient's head. This causes a convulsion that lasts about 50 seconds, followed by a stupor that lasts about an hour. Psychiatrists use this treatment for depressions, melancholia, and sometimes mania. It occasionally produces amnesia for several weeks. Electric-shock treatment shortens the period of depression, but does not prevent further attacks. See SHOCK TREATMENT.

Lobotomy is the removal by surgery of small areas of the frontal lobes of the brain. These parts of the brain are concerned with worry and future consequences of behavior (see BRAIN). Physicians have used this operation for patients suffering severe anxiety. But most psychiatrists no longer recommend it, because lobotomy

Larry Fried, Pix

In Group Therapy, several mental patients, led by a psychiatrist, discuss their problems and ways to solve them. The patients gain insight and assurance from the group.

often severely damages the patient's initiative and concern for the future.

Physiotherapy includes *hydrotherapy* (water baths), *diathermy* (application of heat), and *massage*. Mental institutions use these methods to relax and quiet disturbed patients. The use of physiotherapy has declined, however, because doctors have discovered that tranquilizing drugs offer a simpler way to produce similar results.

Special Techniques of treatment for mental illness include psychodrama, play therapy, group therapy, and hypnosis.

Psychodrama. Under the direction of a psychiatrist, a group of patients act out their problems. They may play the roles of themselves and of other persons in their lives. This acting-out frequently helps a person understand his disturbance.

Play Therapy is often used in work with children. The doctor gives the child dolls and toys to play with, and the youngster generally uses them to act out his family life. As the child directs the actions and speech of the mother-doll and father-doll in relation to the child-doll, he reveals details of his own troubles. The doctor then interprets the child's play to the young patient. The child is often able to understand the importance of his play in terms of his illness.

Group Therapy involves groups of 8 to 10 persons, led by a psychiatrist. Mental patients seem to be helped by knowing that other people have similar problems. They often talk out their own problems better within a group than when alone with a doctor.

Hypnosis is often used to help the patient bring hidden memories to the surface. It usually does not work when used to command the patient to forget his symptoms. Injections of pentothal sodium, a hypnotic drug, also help the patient remember what he consciously has forgotten. See HYPNOTISM.

Institutional Care may be recommended for patients who need long-term care that their families cannot afford in private hospitals. About 98 of every 100 mentally ill hospital patients in the United States are in state and county hospitals and veterans' hospitals. After a patient spends several years in an institution, his family may become unwilling to take him back, even if he is well enough to leave. This is one of the most serious difficulties in rehabilitating patients who have been in mental institutions.

Care at Home. Many types of mental illness can be treated while the patient lives at home. He may receive treatment from a psychiatrist, either at the doctor's office or at a psychiatric clinic. A patient living at home during treatment remains a part of his family, and does not feel forgotten as often happens when he is placed in an institution for a long period of time.

History

Superstition and Folklore. Mental illness is as old as the history of man. Prehistoric man sometimes treated disturbances of the mind by drilling holes in the skull to let the "evil spirits" escape. Later, pagan priests and witch doctors performed rituals to drive out the "devils." People treated mental illness with magic, prayers, advice, and various home remedies. The people of ancient Greece believed that mental illness was caused by breathing diseased air.

During the Middle Ages, people still believed that mentally ill persons were possessed by devils. Beating, starvation, and other tortures were used in an attempt to drive the devils out of a sick person's body.

As late as the 1600's, the mentally ill were still tortured or put to death as witches, or chained in dungeons. The hospital of Saint Mary of Bethlehem in London became famous as *Bedlam*, where "mad" persons were publicly beaten and tortured for the entertainment of visitors. Today, the word *bedlam* has come to mean uproar and confusion. See BEDLAM.

Humane Treatment. During the late 1700's, Philippe Pinel, a French physician, and William Tuke, an English merchant, pioneered in improving the treatment of the mentally ill in France and England. Under their leadership, mental hospitals stopped chaining patients and began more humane treatment. By the early 1800's, physicians everywhere recognized mental illness as a form of illness, and it became the subject of medical research and treatment. During the late 1800's, Sigmund Freud developed his concepts of how unconscious forces can disrupt mental health. His theories became the basis for psychoanalytic treatment of the mentally ill. Alfred Adler and Carl Jung, students of Freud, developed their own modifications of his method. See ADLER, ALFRED; JUNG, CARL GUSTAV.

Clifford W. Beers, once a mental patient, wrote a book in 1908 describing his experiences in two mental hospitals in Connecticut. This book, *A Mind That Found Itself*, spurred the growth of the mental-health movement in the United States. Beers helped establish the National Committee for Mental Hygiene, now the National Association for Mental Health, in 1909. This committee, composed of psychiatrists, psychologists, and public-spirited citizens, aimed to promote public understanding of the problems of mental illness. Ten years later, the movement had spread to become an international organization sponsoring work in the diagnosis, treatment, prevention, and cure of mental illness. See MENTAL HEALTH.

Research Programs. World War II brought additional emphasis on the treatment of mental illness. Physicians recognized that "battle fatigue," which afflicted thousands of fighting men, was the same thing as the "shellshock" of World War I. The symptoms included sleeplessness, battle dreams, anxiety, tremors, and loss of appetite. The doctors began investigating ways to combat and treat this form of mental illness. Today, medical units of the army, navy, and air force, along with the National Mental Health Institute of the United States Public Health Service, and various private foundations, support many programs of research in mental illness. The Veterans Administration also conducts a wide research program in its hospitals.

The 1950's brought intensive research into the relationship of body chemistry and mental disorders. The discovery of the benefits of tranquilizing drugs aided psychiatrists in treating many "hopeless" patients, and opened new channels for research and investigation.

Physicians no longer put special emphasis on any one aspect of human life as leading to mental illness. They recognize many factors that contribute to mental illness, and consider them all in treating patients. They realize that there are other factors which, when known, may lead to further improvements and progress in the treatment of mental illness.

Critically reviewed by WILLIAM C. MENNINGER

Related Articles in WORLD BOOK include:

KINDS OF MENTAL ILLNESS

Alcoholism	Drug Addiction	Neurosis
Alexia	Hallucination	Phobia
Amnesia	Hypochondria	Psychosis
Anxiety	Hysteria	Pyromania
Catalepsy	Kleptomania	Regression
Delusion	Maladjustment	

TREATMENT

Adler, Alfred	Hypnotism	Psychosomatic
Beers, Clifford	Jung, Carl Gustav	Medicine
Freud, Sigmund	Psychiatry	Psychotherapy
Hallucinatory	Psychoanalysis	Shock Treatment
Drug	Psychology	

OTHER RELATED ARTICLES

Cataplexy	Intelligence	Nervous Breakdown
Extrovert	Quotient	Personality
Heredity	Introvert	Subconscious
Imagination	Mental Health	Testing
Insanity	Mind	

Outline

I. **What Is Mental Illness?**
  A. Unhealthy Behavior
  B. Causes of Mental Illness
II. **Kinds of Mental Illnesses**
  A. Neurosis
  B. Personality Disorders
  C. Manic-Depressive Psychosis
  D. Schizophrenia
  E. Paranoia
III. **How Mental Illnesses Are Treated**
  A. Diagnosis
  B. Psychotherapy
  C. Psychoanalysis
  D. Drug Therapy
  E. Shock Treatment
  F. Lobotomy
  G. Physiotherapy
  H. Special Techniques
  I. Institutional Care
  J. Care at Home
IV. **History**

Questions

What does mental illness mean?
How do organic and functional mental illness differ?
What is the origin of the word *bedlam*?
What is a psychosomatic illness? Give an example.
Is it normal for people to be depressed, anxious, frustrated, and angry? When do such conditions indicate mental illness?
What is a nervous breakdown?
What is a psychopathic personality?
What is psychotherapy?
How did early man sometimes treat mental illness?
Who is considered to be the father of psychoanalysis?

MENTAL RETARDATION is a condition in which intelligence does not develop normally. A mentally retarded child develops mentally at a below-average rate. He is not able to learn or to use what he learns as well as the average person of his age, and he does not reach the ability level of normal adults when he reaches adult age. There were more than $5\frac{1}{2}$ million retarded persons in the United States in the mid-1960's.

There are many degrees of mental retardation. Some retarded persons lead normal lives. Most retarded persons can learn to read and write and to hold supervised jobs. A smaller number can take care of their personal needs and can learn to perform useful, simple, routine tasks. A still smaller number are so mentally handi-capped that they cannot care for themselves or even protect themselves against common dangers.

Scientists are studying mental retardation and are constantly learning new things about causes and treatment. Research in mental retardation involves many fields of study, including medicine, genetics, neurology, physiology, education, psychology, and social work. With a rapidly increasing body of knowledge, authorities use many different terms and definitions and have different theories. This article presents facts and interpretations accepted by most authorities today.

Causes. More than 200 causes of mental retardation have been identified, but many of these occur only rarely. The reason for retardation can be determined in only about 15 to 25 per cent of the cases.

Some causes of mental retardation occur before birth. Certain combinations of blood types in the parents can produce mental retardation (see RH FACTOR). Syphilis occurring during pregnancy can cause damage to the entire nervous system of the unborn child. An unborn child can suffer brain damage if his mother has German measles during the first three months of her pregnancy. *Phenylketonuria* (PKU) is an inherited condition in which the body cannot use protein properly. This failure of metabolism produces progressive brain damage. *Galactosemia* is another specific condition produced by metabolic disorder. *Mongolism* is a type of mental retardation produced by abnormalities in the *genes* (units that determine inherited traits).

Other causes of mental retardation occur during or after birth. Brain damage can occur during the birth process when the baby's brain does not receive enough oxygen. This can happen during a long or difficult birth, or when the mother receives too much anesthesia. Brain damage can occur in childhood from illness or disease which produces a high fever that lasts a long time. Head injuries can also cause brain damage.

Specific causes of mental retardation among mildly retarded children cannot be determined as often. Some authorities believe that the learning ability of these children has been damaged by their environment, which has not provided enough stimulation for learning.

Diagnosis and Treatment. Intelligence quotient (I.Q.) tests help determine the degree of retardation. Persons of average intelligence have I.Q. scores between 90 and 109. Persons with I.Q. scores of 70 to 89 are called *slow learners* and are not considered mentally retarded. Persons with I.Q. scores of 50 to 69 are considered mildly retarded; 35 to 49 are moderately retarded; 20 to 34 are severely retarded; and below 20 are profoundly retarded. See INTELLIGENCE QUOTIENT.

Mildly retarded children are considered *educable*. They can attend special *educable mentally handicapped* (EMH) classes in public schools. These children may reach fifth or sixth grade levels of achievement. Most of them will become partially or completely self-supporting adults. Since about 1950, some schools have developed special classes for *trainable* (moderately retarded) children. These children will make little or no progress with reading, writing, and arithmetic, but they can learn to care for themselves and to take part in many family and community activities. As adults, some of them can do routine jobs under supervision, in order to contribute to their own support. Severely and profoundly retarded persons are totally dependent on others and are generally cared for in special institutions. Additional information about mental retardation can be obtained from the National Association for Retarded Children, 420 Lexington Avenue, New York, N.Y. 10017.

HARRIET E. BLODGETT

MENTAL TELEPATHY. See TELEPATHY.

MENTAL TEST. See INTELLIGENCE QUOTIENT; TESTING.

MENTHOL, *MEN thohl,* is an ingredient used widely in salves and cold or cough medicines. It has a pleasing odor, and gives the sensation of coolness because it is a *differential anesthetic.* Differential anesthetics anesthetize only certain sensations. Menthol partially anesthetizes most sensations except cold. It has little, if any, other medical effect. Some cigarettes use it to produce a cooling effect on the throat. But menthol does not reduce the dangers of smoking. It is a soft white solid found in oil of peppermint. It is also made synthetically. The chemical formula of menthol is $C_{10}H_{20}O$.

SOLOMON GARB

MENTOR was the companion and friend of Ulysses (Odysseus) in Greek mythology. When Ulysses went to the Trojan War, he made Mentor the guardian of his house. In Mentor's shape, the goddess Athena helped Ulysses' son, Telemachus. The word *mentor* today refers to any friendly adviser. See also ULYSSES.

MENU. See RESTAURANT.

MENUHIN, *MEN yoo in,* **YEHUDI,** *yeh HOO dih* (1916-   ), is an American violinist who had spectacular success as a child prodigy. He promoted the works of contemporary composers and revived neglected, but valuable, music of the past. He took his first violin lessons at the age of 4. Three years later, he appeared as a soloist with the San Francisco Orchestra. At the age of 10, he played with the New York Symphony Orchestra. Menuhin won popular acclaim, and also the admiration of the greatest musicians. He retired temporarily from the concert stage in 1935. But he resumed giving concerts two years later. Menuhin was born in New York City.

Yehudi Menuhin, master violinist, gave his first recital at the age of seven. At eleven, he gave a concert in Berlin. Albert Einstein, the great physicist, came backstage after the concert, greeted Yehudi, and said, "You have once again proved to me that there is a God in heaven."

RCA

MENZIES, *MEN zeez,* **SIR ROBERT GORDON** (1894-   ), was prime minister of Australia from 1939 to 1941, and from 1949 to 1966. He entered the Australian House of Representatives in 1934 as a member of the United Australia (now the Liberal) Party, and served as attorney general of the nation from 1934 to 1939. He was leader of the opposition to the Labour Party government from 1943 to 1948. Menzies was born in Jeparit, Victoria. He attended Grenville College, and graduated from Melbourne University.

CHARLES LOCH MOWAT

MEPACRINE. See ATABRINE.

MEPHISTOPHELES, *MEF uh STAHF uh leez,* is the devil in the medieval legend about a magician named Faust. Faust sold his soul to Mephistopheles in return for the devil's services for 24 years. The name *Mephistopheles* may come from three Greek words meaning *not loving the light* or, possibly, from the Hebrew *mephiz* (destroyer) and *tophel* (liar).

In Johann Wolfgang von Goethe's great drama, *Faust,* Mephistopheles is a clever evil spirit who forever tempts man. But the devil loses in the end, because the troubles he causes only help man to find wisdom and true faith. Mephistopheles also appears in Charles François Gounod's opera *Faust* (1859), in Arrigo Boïto's opera *Mefistofele* (1868), and in Christopher Marlowe's best-known play, *The Tragical History of Doctor Faustus* (1604).

ARTHUR M. SELVI

See also DEVIL; FAUST; OPERA (Faust).

MER DE GLACE. See GLACIER (Famous Glaciers).

MERAK. See NORTH STAR (picture).

MERCANTILISM, *MUR kun til ism,* or MERCANTILE SYSTEM, is a system by which a government regulates its agriculture, industry, and commerce to create a favorable balance of trade. Under the system, the country exports more goods than it imports. It brings into the government's treasury more money because more goods are sold than are bought.

Mercantilists believe that gold and money are the same as wealth. More exports than imports means increased wealth. Mercantilists favor government protection of industry against competition from industries of other countries. They also favor government subsidies to industries, and high tariffs on goods imported from other lands. The system was in use during the 1500's and 1600's. After a period of free trade, it again came into use in the late 1800's. See also FREE TRADE.

MERCATOR, *mer KAY ter,* **GERHARDUS** (1512-1594), a Flemish geographer, became famous for his invention of the Mercator map projection. He was the most notable geographer of his time. He published an accurate map of Europe, and built globes that showed the earth and heavens. Mercator won lasting fame with his world map of 1569. He originated the term *atlas* for a collection of maps.

On his Mercator map, the *meridians* (lines of longitude) and the *parallels* (lines of latitude) appear as straight lines drawn at right angles to each other (see Map [Cylindrical Projections]). Many navigators favor this projection, because a straight line drawn anywhere on the map shows a constant compass direction, and the shapes of very small areas are nearly perfect. But the Mercator map magnifies areas near the poles, and does not show areas in their true proportions.

Mercator was born Gerhard Kremer on March 5, 1512, in Rupelmonde, Flanders. He studied mathematics and surveying at the University of Louvain, and became a surveyor, map maker, and lecturer in geography. Mercator surveyed and prepared a map of Flanders with such accuracy that he became the official geographer to Emperor Charles V. Later he became the official map maker for the Duke of Jülich and Cleves in Germany.

MERCATOR PROJECTION. See MAP (Cylindrical Projections).

J. RUSSELL WHITAKER

MERCED RIVER. See YOSEMITE NATIONAL PARK.

MERCENARY, *MUR suh NEHR ih,* is a soldier who offers his services for hire. Persia, Greece, and Rome all employed mercenaries. But mercenaries became most prominent from the 1200's to the 1500's, when Swiss and German soldiers were in great demand. National armies eventually replaced mercenaries. But they existed until recently in a unique kind of military unit, the Foreign Legion (see FOREIGN LEGION). For more detailed information on mercenaries, see ARMY (Mercenaries).

THEODORE ROPP

MERCER UNIVERSITY is a coeducational liberal arts school in Macon, Ga. It is affiliated with the Baptist Church. Mercer was founded in 1833 in Penfield, Ga. In 1871, the school moved to Macon. For enrollment, see UNIVERSITIES AND COLLEGES (table).

MERCERIZING, *MUR sur iz ing,* is a process of treating cotton fabric or yarns with a strong solution of sodium hydroxide. The treatment causes the fiber to become round, so that it resembles a rod, rather than the flattened, twisted ribbon of the cotton fiber that has not been treated.

Mercerization increases luster and strength, and enables dye to penetrate the cloth more easily. John Mercer of Lancashire, England, invented the mercerizing process in 1850.

HAZEL B. STRAHAN

MERCHANDISE MART, in Chicago, is the world's largest commercial building and wholesale buying center. It is also one of the largest buildings in the world. The Merchandise Mart stands on the north bank of the Chicago River. It is the home of THE WORLD BOOK ENCYCLOPEDIA.

Every year more than 500,000 visitors come to the Merchandise Mart from all parts of the world to purchase new goods to sell in retail stores. Over 3,200 manufacturers have permanent displays in the Mart. These displays include about 1,200,000 separate items of merchandise. Special "markets" or shows for buyers are held throughout the year. About 20,000 people work in the Mart and every day another 20,000 visit it on business.

The main structure of the Mart was originally 18 stories high, but another story has been added. The Mart's tower is 25 stories high. The building covers two city blocks. The Mart's total floor space equals almost 95 acres.

Marshall Field and Company built the Mart in 1930 at a cost of $32 million. In 1945, the Mart was purchased by Joseph P. Kennedy, former United States Ambassador to Great Britain and father of the late President John F. Kennedy.

The Merchandise Mart Hall of Fame honors great American merchants. Giant bronze busts of its members are located on the plaza in front of the Merchandise Mart. The men honored thus far are Marshall Field I, Edward A. Filene, George H. Hartford, Julius Rosenwald, John R. Wanamaker, Robert E. Wood, and Frank W. Wool-

The Merchandise Mart houses the home office of WORLD BOOK and other Field Enterprises Educational Corporation publications.

The Merchandise Mart

The Mercator Map of America, 1538, by Gerhardus Mercator, The New York Public Library; Astor, Lenox, and Tilden Foundations; Newberry Library, Chicago.

Gerhardus Mercator, above, worked out a basic system for map-making. His world map of 1538, left, shows many of the new lands discovered by explorers, including America.

worth. The Merchandise Mart Hall of Fame was founded in 1953.

SARGENT SHRIVER

MERCHANDISING. See RETAILING.

MERCHANT. See RETAILING (Careers); TRADE (History).

MERCHANT MARINE is a fleet made up of a nation's commercial ships and the men who operate them. It includes both cargo and passenger ships.

The importance of a country's merchant marine is measured by its *gross tonnage*, rather than by the number of ships. Gross tonnage is the total space within the hull and enclosed deck space on a ship. Each 100 cubic feet of space in a ship equals one gross ton.

Technically, the tiny African country Liberia has the world's largest merchant marine. About 1,700 ships with more than 29 million gross tons fly the Liberian flag. But few of these ships are actually Liberian vessels. Many ship owners from other countries register their vessels in Liberia because taxes are lower there. The United States has the fifth largest merchant marine, after Japan, Great Britain, and Norway. The United States has about 3,100 ships with about $19\frac{1}{2}$ million gross tons.

For a list of the leading merchant fleets of the world, see SHIP AND SHIPPING (table).

The United States Merchant Marine. The American colonies had a large merchant fleet before the Revolutionary War. By 1800, America's merchant fleet ranked second in the world only to the British fleet. But much United States shipping was destroyed during the Civil War. Most of the remaining ships became *obsolete* (out-of-date) when steel hulls and steam power were developed.

The United States Shipping Board was created in 1916. It improved the merchant marine by building and purchasing ships and regulating shipping. Since 1950, the Maritime Administration has assisted the merchant marine through programs designed to help U.S. shippers build and operate modern ships (see MARITIME ADMINISTRATION).

Careers in the Merchant Marine. One way to become an officer in the U.S. merchant marine is to gain admission to the U.S. Merchant Marine Academy in Kings Point, N.Y. Young men can get information about the academy by writing to the Division of Maritime Academies, Maritime Administration, U.S. Department of Commerce, Washington, D.C. 20235. See UNITED STATES MERCHANT MARINE ACADEMY.

A young man can also earn an officer's license by studying at a state nautical school. But only a few states have these schools. The courses generally require three or four years of study. A seaman can also earn an officer's license by spending three years at sea, working either on the deck or in the engine room to advance in unlicensed ratings. Then he can pass the licensed officer's examination. Young men may obtain unlicensed positions aboard ship if they can get seamen's certificates from the Coast Guard. Wages are set by contracts between shipping companies and maritime unions.

Young men may train to become officers or seamen in the British merchant fleet by studying aboard training ships or enrolling in special nautical schools for two or three years of study.

See also MATE.

MERCHANT MARINE ACADEMY. See UNITED STATES MERCHANT MARINE ACADEMY.

MERCHANT OF VENICE. See SHAKESPEARE, WILLIAM (Synopses of Plays).

MERCHANTS' GUILDS. See GUILD.

MERCIA. See EGBERT; ANGLO-SAXON.

MERCIER, *mair STAY,* **DÉSIRÉ CARDINAL** (1851-1926), was a Belgian archbishop and a cardinal of the Roman Catholic Church. He was a renowned educator, and established an institute of philosophy at the University of Louvain in Belgium. In August, 1914, the great library there was destroyed by invading German troops. The library's precious collection of books and manuscripts represented much of his life's work. When he returned to Belgium, he found the country almost completely occupied by the Germans. For the next four years, Cardinal Mercier was the soul of Belgian resistance. The Germans were unable to stop his preaching or suppress his pastoral letters.

Cardinal Mercier was born in Braine-l'Alleud in Brabant.

JOHN T. FARRELL and FULTON J. SHEEN

MERCURIC CHLORIDE. See BICHLORIDE OF MERCURY.

MERCURIC OXIDE (chemical formula, HgO) is a compound of mercury and oxygen. It is a yellow or orange-red powder which dissolves in acids, but not in water. Its molecular weight is 216.6. When heated, mercuric oxide decomposes, or breaks down, giving off 7.4 per cent oxygen. It is considered a good oxidizing agent for this reason.

Mercuric oxide is used in the manufacture of mercury salts, pigments, paints, and pottery. It also is used in ointments for the treatment of parasitic skin diseases and eye diseases.

GEORGE L. BUSH

MERCUROCHROME is the trade name for a weak antiseptic that is used in a water solution. The official name is *merbromin.* Mercurochrome is one of a group of antiseptics called *organic mercurials* that contain mercury. Mercurochrome is a coarse, green powder, but in a water solution it is a deep red. Mercurochrome's chemical formula is $C_{20}H_8O_6Na_2Br_5Hg$. Mercurochrome solutions normally do not burn or irritate the tissues when applied to wounds.

SOLOMON GARB

See also ANTISEPTIC.

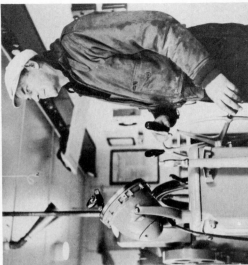

Merchant Marine Crewmen are civilians. However, the United States government has authority to lease privately owned merchant ships to carry troops and supplies during war.

Maritime Administration

Critically reviewed by the MARITIME ADMINISTRATION

338

MERCURY (chemical symbol, Hg). This silver-white metallic element is a liquid which flows so freely that it was named for the fleet-footed messenger of the gods in Roman mythology. Because of its fluid quality, it is sometimes called *quicksilver*. The discoverer is unknown but mercury was known to ancient Chinese and Hindus and was found in Egyptian tombs of 1500 B.C.

Mercury has many qualities which distinguish it from other metals. It is the only metal which stays liquid at ordinary temperatures. It is 13.55 times as heavy as water. Under ordinary atmospheric conditions mercury melts at −38.87° C. (about −37.9° F.). Mercury boils at 356.58° C. (about 673° F.). Its atomic weight is 200.59 and its atomic number is 80.

One of the most interesting and valuable qualities of mercury is that it expands and contracts in regular degrees when subjected to changes of temperatures. This quality makes mercury an excellent metal for filling tubes of thermometers and barometers, instruments that measure temperature and atmospheric pressure.

Mercury has a wide variety of other uses. It may be combined with oxygen to form a red oxide which is used in laboratory experiments to prove the presence of oxygen. Mercury combines with chlorine to make *mercurous chloride*, which is used as a medicine under the name of *calomel*. *Mercuric chloride*, another compound, is often used as a disinfectant. *Vermilion*, a compound of mercury and sulfur, is used in some red paints. All mercury compounds are poisonous and should not be used as medicine except under a doctor's careful direction.

A glass tube containing an isotope of mercury, called a *mercury lamp*, serves as a precise measuring device. Scientists use the light waves given off from the mercury for measuring by passing them through an optical instrument called an *interferometer* (see INTERFEROMETER).

BAROMETERS AND THERMOMETERS

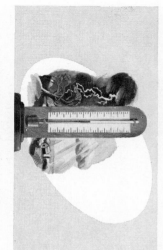

Revere Electric Mfg. Co.; Ewing Galloway

MEDICAL LABORATORY RESEARCH

HARRISON ASHLEY SCHMITT

TOOTH FILLINGS

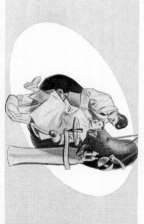

By using this method, an object can be measured to within one billionth of an inch.

A large part of the mercury which is produced is used in the form of *mercury fulminate*. This is a chemical mixture of alcohol, nitric acid, and mercury. It is highly explosive, and is used chiefly for the percussion caps on shells and cartridges. At one time, the most important use of mercury was to extract gold and silver from their ores. The powdered ore was mixed with water and run over copper plates coated with a thin layer of mercury. The mercury combined with the gold or silver to form an *amalgam*, which remained on the plates while the water washed away the rocks and earth. Then the amalgam was heated until the mercury boiled and became gas, leaving the gold or silver free.

The chief ore mineral of mercury is *cinnabar*, or mercuric sulfide, although pure mercury can be mined. Usually cinnabar is mined from deposits less than 500 feet below the surface of the earth. But some cinnabar is found in deposits at the outlets of active hot springs. Miners consider the ore practical for mining when it has as little as 10 pounds of mercury to the ton.

Mercury is removed from its ore by roasting the cinnabar in a current of air. Heating drives off the sulfur, which combines with the oxygen in the air to form a gas.

Spain is the leading producer of mercury. Other producers include China, Italy, and Russia, and California and Nevada in the United States.

Related Articles in WORLD BOOK include:

Amalgam	Metallurgy (Amalgamation)
Barometer	Pump (Mercury Vacuum
Bichloride of	Pumps)
Mercury	Thermometer
Cinnabar	Vermilion
Gold (The Milling	
Process)	

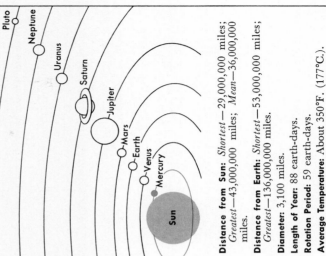

Russ Kinne, Photo Researchers

Mercury Appears as a Tiny Dot against the sun when it is directly between the sun and the earth. Mercury is so small and so near the sun that a telescope is needed to see it at this point.

MERCURY AT A GLANCE

Mercury, shown in blue in the diagram, is the closest planet to the sun. The ancient symbol for Mercury, *right*, is still used by astronomers.

Pluto
Neptune
Uranus
Saturn
Jupiter
Mars
Earth
Venus
Mercury
Sun

Distance from Sun: *Shortest*—29,000,000 miles; *Greatest*—43,000,000 miles; *Mean*—36,000,000 miles.

Distance from Earth: *Shortest*—53,000,000 miles; *Greatest*—136,000,000 miles.

Diameter: 3,100 miles.

Length of Year: 88 earth-days.

Rotation Period: 59 earth-days.

Average Temperature: About 350°F. (177°C.).

Atmosphere: Carbon dioxide (?).

Number of Satellites: None.

MERCURY is the smallest planet and the planet nearest the sun. It has a diameter of about 3,100 miles, about two-fifths the earth's diameter. Mercury's mean distance from the sun is about 36,000,000 miles, compared to 67,250,000 miles for Venus, the second closest planet to the sun.

Because of Mercury's size and nearness to the brightly shining sun, the planet is often hard to see from the earth without a telescope. At certain times of the year, Mercury can be seen low in the western sky just after sunset. At other times, it can be seen low in the eastern sky just before sunrise.

Orbit. Mercury travels around the sun in an *elliptical* (oval-shaped) orbit. It is about 29 million miles from the sun at its closest point, and more than 43 million miles from the sun at its farthest point. At its closest approach to the earth, Mercury is about 53 million miles away.

Mercury moves around the sun faster than any other planet because it is the closest planet to the sun. The ancient Romans named it Mercury in honor of the swift messenger of their gods. Mercury travels about 30 miles per second, and goes around the sun once every 88 earth-days. The earth goes around the sun once every 365 days, or one year.

Rotation. As Mercury moves around the sun, it rotates on its *axis*, an imaginary line through its center. The planet rotates once about every 59 earth-days, slower than any other planet except Venus. A day on Mercury lasts about 180 earth-days because Mercury rotates so slowly. The earth rotates once a day.

Until 1965, astronomers believed that Mercury rotated once every 88 earth-days, the same time the planet takes to go around the sun. If Mercury did this, the sun would seem to stand still in Mercury's sky. One side of the planet would always face the sun, and the other side would always be dark. In 1965, astronomers bounced radar beams off Mercury. The scientists found that the signals returning from one side of the planet differed from those from the other side. Using these beams, the astronomers measured the movement of the opposite sides and found that Mercury rotates once in about 59 days.

Phases. When viewed through a telescope, Mercury can be seen going through "changes" in shape and size. These apparent changes are called *phases*, and resemble those of the moon. They result from different parts of Mercury's sunlit side being visible from the earth at different times.

As Mercury and the earth travel around the sun, Mercury can be seen near the other side of the sun about every 116 days. At this point, almost all its sunlit area is visible from the earth. It looks like a bright, round spot with almost no visible marks. As Mercury moves around the sun toward the earth, less and less of its sunlit area can be seen. After about 36 days, only half its surface is visible. After another 22 days, it nears the same side of the sun as the earth, and only a thin sunlit

The contributor of this article is Hyron Spinrad, Associate Professor of Astronomy at the University of California in Berkeley.

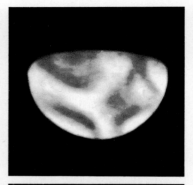

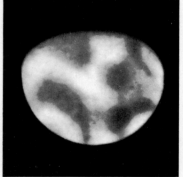

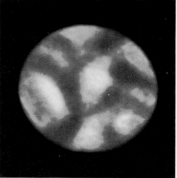

The Phases and Surface Markings of Mercury can be seen in drawings made by the French astronomer Audouin Dollfus on July 16, July 22, and Aug. 8, 1942. Detailed photographs of Mercury have not been made, because the planet is so close to the sun.

Dr. Audouin Dollfus, Paris Observatory

area is visible. The amount of sunlit area that can be seen increases gradually after Mercury passes in front of the sun and begins moving away from the earth.

When Mercury is on the same side of the sun as the earth is, its dark side faces the earth. The planet is usually not visible at this point, because Mercury and the earth orbit the sun at different angles. As a result, Mercury does not always pass directly between the earth and the sun. Sometimes Mercury is directly between the earth and the sun. When this occurs, every 3 to 13 years, the planet is in *transit* and can be seen as a black spot against the sun. Most transits occur in May and November, with twice as many in November as in May. Astronomers can get valuable information about Mercury by observing it during transits.

Surface and Atmosphere. Mercury's surface appears to be much like that of the moon. It reflects about 6 per cent of the sunlight it receives, about the same as the moon's surface reflects. Many astronomers believe Mercury is covered by craters, like those found on the moon. They think these craters were formed by meteors crashing into the planet. Mercury does not have enough atmosphere to slow down approaching meteors and burn them up by friction.

Mercury is dry, extremely hot, and almost airless. The sun's rays are about seven times as strong on Mercury as they are on the earth. The sun also appears about $2\frac{1}{2}$ times as large in Mercury's sky as in the earth's. Mercury does not have enough gases in its atmosphere to reduce the amount of heat and light it receives from the sun. The temperature on the planet is about 625° F. (329° C.) during the day, and lower than 80° F. (27° C.) at night. Because of the lack of atmosphere, Mercury's sky is black, and stars probably can be seen during the day.

Mercury is surrounded by either a very small amount of gas or by no gas at all. For many years, astronomers studying Mercury were unable to find any of the gases found on other planets. Then, in 1965, the Russian astronomer Vasili I. Moroz reported evidence of carbon dioxide gas on Mercury. If Moroz's findings are correct, the greatest possible *atmospheric pressure* (force exerted by the weight of gases) on Mercury would be less than 0.04 pounds per square inch. The atmospheric pressure

on the earth is about 14.7 pounds per square inch. The plant and animal life of the earth could not live on Mercury, because of the lack of oxygen and the intense heat. Astronomers do not know whether the planet has any form of life.

Density and Mass. Mercury's *density* is slightly less than the earth's (see DENSITY). That is, a portion of Mercury would weigh about the same as an equal portion of the earth. Mercury is smaller than the earth, and has much less *mass* (see MASS).

If Mercury's mass were the same as the earth's, and its size were unchanged, its force of gravity would be about six times that of the earth. But Mercury's smaller mass makes its force of gravity only about a third as strong. An object that weighs 100 pounds on the earth would weigh only about 37 pounds on Mercury.

Flights to Mercury. Unmanned spacecraft will probably be sent to observe Mercury during the 1970's. Manned flights to the planet will not be attempted for many more years.

The first spacecraft to Mercury will simply fly past the planet. Instruments will make measurements and take pictures, and the results will be sent to the earth by radio. Later, unmanned spacecraft may go into orbit around Mercury, crash into it, or even land on it.

Spacecraft will take about six months to reach Mercury. As the spacecraft approach the planet, the increasing heat from the sun will present the most serious problem. Scientists may be able to use the sun's rays as a valuable source of energy for the spacecraft.

Photographs from spacecraft flying past Mercury will be used to prove the existence of craters on the planet's surface. They also may provide clues to the presence of any form of life on the planet.

Spacecraft flying past Mercury will make measurements that will determine whether the planet has any atmosphere. They also will take more accurate measurements of the planet's temperature, especially on areas that have not had any sunlight for several weeks.

Spacecraft will also be used to obtain a more accurate measurement of Mercury's mass. The effect of the planet's gravity on the spacecraft will determine the mass of Mercury.

See also EVENING STAR; PLANET; SOLAR SYSTEM.

HYRON SPINRAD

MERCURY was the swift messenger of the gods in Roman mythology. He was the god of commerce and travel, and the patron of thieves, gamblers, and ambassadors. The Greeks called him Hermes or Cyllenius, because he was born on Mount Cyllene, in Arcadia. He was the son of Jupiter (Zeus) and Maia, a daughter of Atlas. Pan, the god of shepherds, was the son of Mercury (see PAN).

Mercury showed great talents on the very day that he was born. He invented a musical instrument, the lyre, before noon of that day. Before evening he stole the cattle of Apollo. Apollo intended to punish him for this, but Mercury gave him the lyre. This pleased Apollo so much that he gave Mercury a magic wand called the *caduceus*. Mercury used this to guide the souls of the dead to the Lower World. He also could control the living and the dead with it, or turn anything to gold. The caduceus had wings

Mercury is a bronze statue by Giovanni Bologna of Italy.

The Louvre, Cossé Brissac collection, Paris (Alinari)

at its top and snakes twined around it. It is an emblem of the medical profession and military medical corps.

Mercury had more duties than any other god. He was a favorite of Jupiter, for whom he killed the monster Argus (see ARGUS). The other gods also favored him. Mercury led Priam, king of Troy, to the tent of the Greek warrior Achilles. He carried Bacchus (Dionysus), god of wine, to the nymphs, and led Proserpina, the Greek goddess, back from the Lower World.

Mercury wore a winged cap and sandals, and carried a short sword and the caduceus. He used these to perform many wonders as the messenger of Jupiter. He is often shown carrying a purse. The festival of Mercury was held in Rome on May 15.

VAN JOHNSON

See also HERMES OF PRAXITELES; IO (picture).

MERCURY, PROJECT. See ASTRONAUT.

MERCURY ARC. See ARC LIGHT; ELECTRIC LIGHT.

MERCURY GLASS. See GLASSWARE.

MERCURY-VAPOR LAMP. See ELECTRIC LIGHT.

MERCY, SISTER OF. See SISTER OF MERCY.

MERCY COLLEGE. See UNIVERSITIES AND COLLEGES (table).

MERCY COLLEGE OF DETROIT. See UNIVERSITIES AND COLLEGES (table).

MERCY KILLING. See EUTHANASIA.

MERCY SEAT. See TABERNACLE.

MERCYHURST COLLEGE. See UNIVERSITIES AND COLLEGES (table).

MEREDITH, GEORGE (1828-1909), was an English novelist and poet. He wrote his novels in a subtle poetic

prose, rich in metaphor. His best-known novel, *The Ordeal of Richard Feverel* (1859), is the story of the harm done a young man who is sheltered by his father and educated at home. It is one of several Meredith novels in which a duel is fought over a woman. *The Egoist* (1879) and *Diana of the Crossways* (1885) show Meredith's support of the emancipation of women. The heroine exercises freedom of choice in love and marriage.

Meredith thought his poetry had more merit than his novels, and many scholars agree. His *Modern Love* (1862) is one of the finest poetic works of the Victorian Age. It is a long beautifully written sequence of 16-line sonnets inspired by his unhappy marriage to his first wife, who deserted him. Meredith was born in Portsmouth. He worked for many years as a journalist and literary critic.

HARRY T. MOORE

MEREDITH, JAMES HOWARD (1933-), was the first Negro to attend the University of Mississippi. He tried to register at the school in the fall of 1962. He was accompanied by federal marshals, but police and other state officials repeatedly barred his entrance. A large protest group that gathered on the campus rioted against Meredith and the marshals. Two persons were killed. However, Meredith succeeded in registering, and federal troops were stationed on the campus to protect him until he graduated in 1963.

In 1966, Meredith led a march in the South to encourage Negroes to vote. A sniper shot him in Mississippi, but he recovered, and later completed the march.

Meredith was born in Kosciusko, Miss. He wrote the book *Three Years in Mississippi* (1966).

C. ERIC LINCOLN

MEREDITH COLLEGE. See UNIVERSITIES AND COLLEGES (table).

James Meredith

United Press Int.

MERGANSER, *mer GAN ser,* is the name of a group of ducks that eat fish. Mergansers grasp fish in their straight narrow bills which are hooked at the tips and notched at the edges. For this reason, people sometimes call them *sawbills* or *sheldrakes*. Mergansers live in many

The Merganser Is One of the Most Handsome Ducks, but has little commercial value because its meat has a fishy flavor.

Allan D. Cruickshank

parts of the world. The *American*, *red-breasted*, and *hooded mergansers* live in North America. They range from Mexico to Alaska and Greenland.

Mergansers have tufts of feathers on their heads. The male's feathers are black and white, and the female's are grayish-brown. The American merganser has a glossy greenish-black head and upper neck. The red-breasted merganser has a cinnamon-red breast. The hooded merganser has a large black-and-white head crest with two curving bands of black on the sides.

Scientific Classification. Mergansers belong to the water fowl family, *Anatidae*. The American merganser is genus *Mergus*, species *M. merganser*. The red-breasted merganser is species *M. serrator*. The hooded merganser is genus *Lophodytes*, species *L. cucullatus*.

LEÓN A. HAUSMAN

MERGENTHALER, *MER gun TAH ler,* **OTTMAR** (1854-1899), invented the Linotype typesetting machine. Linotype machines set most of the newspapers and other material printed in the United States. Mergenthaler made a device with a keyboard that composed *matrices* (molds) for letters, and then cast an entire line of type at once. He demonstrated the Linotype in 1883. It was patented in 1884 and first used in 1886. Mergenthaler was born in Württemberg, Germany, and came to the United States in 1872.

See also LINOTYPE.

RICHARD D. HUMPHREY

MERGER is a combination of two or more business companies under one management. Usually one corporation buys all the capital stock of another corporation and dissolves the firm it has purchased. Some persons object to mergers on the grounds that they lead to monopolies. Those who favor mergers say they develop competition by making companies stronger, more efficient, and better able to supply things at reasonable prices. See also MONOPOLY AND COMPETITION.

MERICI, SAINT ANGELA. See URSULINE.

MÉRIDA, *MAY' ree thah* (pop. 190,390; alt. 65 ft.), is the largest city on Mexico's Yucatán Peninsula. It stands in a region of henequen farms and cattle lands. It is connected by railroad with the nearby port of Progreso, and by roads with the ancient Mayan centers of Chichén Itzá and Uxmal. For location, see MEXICO (political map). Mérida has a beautiful cathedral and other buildings built by early Spanish settlers. Its museum contains handicraft of the Mayan Indians. The Spaniards founded Mérida in 1542.

JOHN A. CROW

MERIDEN, Conn. (pop. 51,850; alt. 150 ft.), is known as the *Silver City* because it leads the nation in the production of sterling and plated silverware. The city lies in the south-central part of the state (see CONNECTICUT [political map]). Peaks of the volcanic Hanging Hills rise as high as 1,000 feet west of the city. Factories of Meriden make electrical apparatus, tools, machinery, and plastics. The Meriden area was first settled in 1661. Meriden became a city in 1867. It has a mayor-council form of government.

ALBERT E. VAN DUSEN

MERIDIAN, *muh RID ee un.* If you look at a globe of the earth you will see a number of lines drawn from the north to south poles. Each line goes halfway around the globe and meets another line at both poles. These lines are called *meridians*. Two *meridians* that meet at the poles make a *meridian circle*. Meridian lines are used to measure longitude, which is the distance east or west of a line passing through Greenwich, England. See MAP (illustration: Lines of Longitude).

Geographers think of the whole world as being covered by meridians. Wherever you are, an imaginary line called a meridian passes through the place where you are standing. When the sun shines directly down on that line, it is noon *all along the meridian*.

In order to measure distance, everyone had to start counting meridians from the same place. Geographers who met at Washington, D.C., in 1884 decided that a line passing through the observatory at Greenwich, England, would be called the *prime meridian*. Distances on the map are measured east or west of this line. The *longitude* of a place is its distance east or west of the prime meridian. Pilots and sailors can tell where they are in the sky or on the sea if they know the degrees of longitude and latitude. Changes in time can be measured by degrees of longitude. Longitude is measured in degrees, minutes, and seconds. At the equator, a degree is about 69.20 miles wide. Distances to the north and south of the equator are measured in *latitude*.

See also GREENWICH MERIDIAN; INTERNATIONAL DATE LINE; LATITUDE; LONGITUDE; STANDARD TIME.

MERIDIAN, Miss. (pop. 49,374; alt. 345 ft.), the second and largest city in the state, is an industrial and trading center. Meridian lies in the eastern part of Mississippi. For location, see MISSISSIPPI (political map). For monthly weather, see MISSISSIPPI (Climate).

Leading industries include cotton, feed, grain, hosiery, and lumber mills; garment and mattress factories; railroad shops; and woodworking and box plants. It also is headquarters for the Mississippi Air National Guard.

Meridian was settled about 1854 where the tracks of the Mobile and Ohio, and Vicksburg and Montgomery railroads cross. It is the seat of Lauderdale County, and has a council-manager form of government.

CHARLOTTE CAPERS

MÉRIMÉE, *MAY ree MAY,* **PROSPER** (1803-1870), a French author, is best known for his *novelettes* (long short stories). One of them, "Carmen" (1845), was the source for Georges Bizet's famous opera of the same name. Set in Spain, Mérimée's "Carmen" tells of the love of Don José for Carmen, a gypsy girl. Don José's love leads him to army desertion, smuggling, and finally the murder of the unfaithful heroine. Mérimée's other novelettes include "Mateo Falcone" (1829) and "Colomba" (1840), tales of violence set in Corsica. "The Venus of Ille" (1837) is a fantastic tale in which the hero is apparently killed by a statue.

Mérimée was born in Paris. His first works were *Theatre of Clara Gazul* (1825), a group of plays; and *La Guzla* (1827), a book of ballads. He fooled the public by saying these works were translations. He wrote during the romantic age, and his work has elements of both romantic and classical literature. It is romantic in the violent passions it portrays, and in the strong personalities of its characters. It is classical in its unemotional presentation, formal style, and its attention to detail.

IRVING PUTTER

MERINO. See SHEEP (Fine-Wooled; picture); OHIO (Agriculture); AUSTRALIA (Agriculture).

MERIT BADGE. See BOY SCOUTS (Boy Scouting).

MERIT SYSTEM. See CIVIL SERVICE.

MERLIN. See ROUND TABLE.

MERMAID was a mythical creature that lived in the sea. According to popular belief, mermaids had bodies

The Mermaids by Arnold Böcklin. Kunstmuseum, Basel, Switzerland

Beautiful Mermaids appear in many myths. They are usually pictured with human upper bodies and fish tails instead of legs.

MERRIAM, CLINTON HART (1855-1942), was an American physician and zoologist. He led several expeditions to study wildlife in western United States and later studied the Pacific Coast Indians.

Merriam was director of the United States Biological Survey (now Fish and Wildlife Service) from 1885 to 1910. He helped found the National Geographic Society in 1888. Merriam's book, *Studies of California Indians*, was published in 1955, after his death. Merriam was born in New York City. He graduated from Yale University and Columbia University College of Physicians and Surgeons. LORUS J. MILNE and MARGERY MILNE

MERRILL-PALMER INSTITUTE is a specialized institution of higher education in Detroit, Mich. Its chief functions are instruction and research in the fields of human development and family life. College seniors and graduate students attend the institute through a cooperative arrangement with over a hundred colleges and universities throughout the United States. Credits earned at the institute may be applied toward degrees at the participating schools.

The institute also sponsors an interdisciplinary research program. This program centers on the intellectual, physical, and social aspects of human growth and development. The Merrill-Palmer Institute was founded in 1920. D. KEITH OSBORN

MERRILL'S MARAUDERS, sometimes called MERRILL'S RAIDERS, were about 3,000 United States infantrymen who fought under Brigadier General Frank Merrill during World War II. The Marauders were tough jungle fighters who won fame in the China-Burma-India theater. They went to India in October, 1943, after President Franklin D. Roosevelt called for volunteers for a "dangerous and hazardous" mission.

In March, 1944, after a 100-mile march, the Marauders surprised the enemy by blocking the only Japanese supply line in the Hukawng Valley. CHARLES B. MACDONALD

MERRIMACK. See MONITOR AND MERRIMACK.

MERRIMACK COLLEGE. See UNIVERSITIES AND COLLEGES (table).

MERRIMACK RIVER is noted for its six waterfalls which furnish electric power for manufacturing centers in Massachusetts and New Hampshire. The river is formed where the Winnepesaukee and Pemigewasset streams meet at Franklin, N.H. It empties into the Atlantic Ocean at Newburyport, Mass. *Merrimack* is an Indian name meaning *swift water.* For location, see NEW HAMPSHIRE (physical map).

MERRY-GO-ROUND is an amusement ride that has been standard equipment of amusement parks and carnivals for many years. The merry-go-round consists of a revolving, circular platform. Brightly painted wooden horses and other animals are mounted to the platform on vertical metal poles. The animals go up and down as the merry-go-round whirls around. Merry-go-rounds are powered by a piston engine or electricity. The first merry-go-round was made in Europe, perhaps in France, in the late 1700's or early 1800's. It was called a *carrousel,* after an elaborate tournament-type entertainment first given at the court of France in the reign of Henry IV. See also AMUSEMENTS (picture).

MERRY WIVES OF WINDSOR. See SHAKESPEARE, WILLIAM (table: The Second Period).

that were half human and half fish. They attracted mortal men by their beauty and their singing. They would sit and comb their golden hair. A magic cap lay beside them. They would slip the cap on the head of the man they wanted, and take him away with them. A human being could live in the sea by wearing the cap. There were also mermen, who captured mortal maidens.

Mermen and mermaids are often found in art and poetry. Certain sea animals such as the seal look a little like human beings from a distance. This similarity in appearance may explain the stories. H. LLOYD STOW

See also SIRENIA.

MERMAID TAVERN was one of the most famous of Elizabethan inns. It was located on Bread Street, Cheapside, in the heart of old London. The name of the tavern came from the painted sign of a mermaid hanging outside its door. Brilliant English literary men often met there, including William Shakespeare, Ben Jonson, Francis Beaumont, John Fletcher, John Selden, John Donne, and Robert Herrick. KNOX WILSON

MERODACHBALADAN. See CHALDEA.

MEROPE. See PLEIADES.

MEROVINGIAN, *MER oh VIN jih un,* was the name given to the line of the first Frankish kings who governed Gaul. These kings were the founders of the French state. The name Merovingian came from *Merovech,* the name of an early leader of the Franks.

Clovis I was the first powerful Merovingian king. At his death, in A.D. 511, the Merovingian kingdom included northern Gaul, Aquitaine, and some territory east of the Rhine River. His four sons divided up the kingdom. During their reign, the Merovingian kingdom grew to include Burgundy, Provence, Thuringia, and Bavaria. But the kingdom was held together very loosely.

The Merovingian rulers finally became so weak that they were called the "do-nothing" kings. After the battle of Testry in A.D. 687, they were gradually pushed aside by the forerunners of the new royal line, the Carolingians. FRANKLIN D. SCOTT

See also CAROLINGIAN; CHARLES MARTEL; CLOVIS; FRANK; PEPIN THE SHORT.

New Mexico State Tourist Bureau

MERSEY, RIVER, in northwest England, is one of the most important trade waterways in the world. The Mersey rises in the Pennine Hills, flows southwest to Runcorn, and enters the Irish Sea at Liverpool. The Mersey is about 70 miles long, and has a wide *estuary* (mouth).

A system of docks and basins extends along both banks of the estuary, and serves Liverpool and Birkenhead. A railway tunnel under the river connects the two manufacturing centers. An underwater tunnel for highway traffic was completed in 1934. Birkenhead has become the greatest cattle market in Great Britain. The Manchester Ship Canal connects Manchester with the river (see MANCHESTER [map]).

JOHN W. WEBB

MERTHYR TYDFIL, *MUR ther TID vil* (pop. 57,200; alt. 670 ft.), is the center of the iron trade of south Wales. The city lies on the River Taff, on the northern rim of the coal district. The city became an early center for iron and steel manufacture, because of nearby iron and limestone deposits.

JOHN W. WEBB

MERTON, THOMAS (1915-1968), was an American poet and religious writer. He became a Roman Catholic and entered the Trappist monastery of Our Lady of Gethsemani in Kentucky in 1941. He later became a priest, and was known as Father M. Louis. Merton described his life in *The Seven Storey Mountain* (1948) and life in a Roman Catholic religious order in *The Sign of Jonas* (1953). He was born in France.

DAVID WILLIAMS

MERV is an oasis in central Asia. It has been a center of life and industry for hundreds of years, although it lies in the midst of a great wasteland. The ancient Persians called the Merv "the cradle of the human race." The Merv covers about 2,000 square miles in the vast plateau desert in the southeastern part of the Russian state, Turkmenistan. For the location of the Merv, see RUSSIA (physical map). Farming is the chief occupation. Some cotton and wool are produced. The ancient town of Merv is in ruins. The modern city, Mary, stands 25 miles west of the old site. It was founded by Russians in 1881.

HARRY R. WARFEL

MERWIN DAM, formerly called Ariel Dam, stands on the Lewis River in the state of Washington. It is a combination gravity- and arch-type dam, 303 feet high and 1,250 feet long. It creates a reservoir 12 miles long that will hold 650,200 acre-feet of water. The power installation is 100,000 kilowatts. The dam was completed in 1931.

See also DAM.

T. W. MERMEL

MESA, *MAY suh*. In the western and southwestern United States there are many flat-topped land forms that the early Spanish settlers called *mesas*. Mesa is Spanish for *table*. These mesas were once part of larger plateaus that were worn away by erosion over a long period of time. Mesas usually have steep sides. Grasses, desert bushes, or other plants cover the mesa tops. Two of the best-known mesas are the *Mesa Encantada*, or the Enchanted Mesa, of New Mexico and the *Mesa Verde*, or the Green Mesa, in Colorado. See also MESA VERDE NATIONAL PARK.

ELDRED D. WILSON

MESA VERDE NATIONAL PARK, *MAY suh VUR dee*. Hundreds of years ago Indians built high cliff dwellings of stone along the canyon walls of a huge plateau in southwestern Colorado. Some of the cliff dwellings are still standing. In 1906, the federal government set aside this region as a national park. The park was named Mesa Verde (Spanish for *green table*), because it is covered with forests of juniper and piñon pines. The park covers about 52,000 acres of high tablelands cut by deep canyons.

The Cliff Dwellers built their homes along overhanging walls of these canyons for protection against other tribes. Cliff Palace, the largest cliff house, contains more than 200 living rooms. About 400 people lived in Cliff Palace at one time. The structure is built much like a modern apartment building. It has sections which are two, three, and four stories high. Cliff Palace also has many underground rooms, known as *kivas*, where the Indians held religious ceremonies. Spruce Tree House, the second largest ruin in the park, has 100 living rooms. Scientists believe most of these homes were built in the late 1100's. Cliff Palace was probably begun in 1066. Historians believe that the Cliff Dwellers left this region in the late 1200's because of a great drought.

Desert and mountain plants grow in the park, and there is a wide variety of animal life.

See also COLORADO (color picture).

HERBERT E. KAHLER

MESABI RANGE, *muh SAH bih*, is a chain of hills in northeastern Minnesota. The range was once one of the great iron-ore mining regions of the world. *Mesabi* is the Indian word for *hidden giant*. Most of the Mesabi range is located in St. Louis County, which is bordered on the southeast by Lake Superior. The range itself is from 60 to 75 miles northwest of the lake.

The Mesabi range was first leased for mining in 1890 by Leonidas Merritt and his six brothers. By 1896, 20 mines were producing nearly 3 million tons of ore a year. The ore was so near the surface that *open-pit mining* was used. Usually, steam or electric shovels scooped out the ore and transferred it to waiting railway cars for shipment to Lake Superior ports.

See also MINNESOTA (Natural Resources).

WALLACE E. AKIN

MESCAL. See CENTURY PLANT.

MESCALINE, or PEYOTE, is a drug obtained from a small cactus plant that grows in the Rio Grande region of the United States and Mexico. Indian tribes of the region use it for medical and religious purposes.

Mescaline produces visions, often with flashes of brilliant color. It also produces psychological disturbances and trances. Psychological investigation indicates that mescaline causes confusion of personality and a sense of unreality. This is similar to some kinds of mental illness. Psychiatrists and biochemists have experimented with mescaline for many years. However, no use for it has been found in modern medicine, and it is considered a dangerous drug.   WALTER MODELL.

MESETA (plateau). See SPAIN (Land Regions).

MESHA. See MOABITE STONE.

MESHED, *muh SHED* (pop. 409,616; alt. 3,197 ft.), is Iran's third largest city and a leading religious center. It lies on a fertile plain in northeastern Iran, near Russia. Thousands of persons travel to Meshed each year to visit the huge, gold-domed tomb of Imam Reza, a Moslem leader.

MESMER, *MEHS mer,* **FRANZ,** or **FRIEDRICH ANTON** (1734-1815), an Austrian physician, pioneered in the practice of hypnotism. He developed a theory called "animal magnetism," later named *mesmerism.* Mesmer believed that a mysterious fluid penetrates all bodies, and allows one person to have a powerful, "magnetic" influence over another.

Mesmer was born at Iznang in Austria. He studied medicine in Vienna. He went to Paris to lecture and practice in 1778. Mesmer's sessions, or *séances,* in which he supposedly "magnetized" patients, created a sensation. But the medical profession considered him a fraud. His theories have been discarded, but hypnotism has been accepted as a subject for scientific study and as a possible means of treatment.   GEORGE ROSEN

See also HYPNOTISM (History).

MESODERM. See EMBRYO (Human Development).

MESOLITHIC PERIOD. See STONE AGE; PREHISTORIC MAN (color diagram).

MESON, *MESS ahn,* is an elementary nuclear particle. Mesons, pi-mesons particularly, are responsible for most forces acting between the protons and neutrons in the nuclei of atoms. Mesons are unstable, and spontaneously *decay,* or break down, into other particles (see RADIOACTIVITY [Half-Life]). Mesons exist in several forms, classed by their weights.

K-mesons, the heaviest mesons, have a weight about 967 times that of an electron. They may have a positive or a negative electrical charge, or they may be neutral. K-mesons decay in a variety of ways, producing lighter-weight kinds of mesons and sometimes electrons and neutrinos. K-mesons belong to the class of particles called *strange particles.* They were discovered in 1947.

Pi-mesons, also called *pions,* exist in positive, negative, and neutral forms. Charged pi-mesons have a weight 273 times that of an electron. Neutral pi-mesons have a weight 264 times that of an electron. A charged pi-meson decays into a neutrino and a mu-meson, the lightest variety of meson. The neutral pi-meson decays into quanta of light or radiation. Pi-mesons were discovered in 1947.

Mu-mesons, also called *muons,* exist in positive and negative forms. They have a weight about 207 times that of an electron. They decay into electrons and neutrinos. Mu-mesons do not contribute to nuclear forces like other mesons. They resemble electrons and neutrinos and should logically be grouped with these particles. Mu-mesons were discovered in 1936. See LEPTON.

Physicists originally found mesons only among the particles produced by cosmic rays as they passed through matter. But various types of high-energy atom smashers can produce mesons artificially. Physicists have recently found new types of mesons (or mesonlike states of matter), heavier than K-mesons and with extremely short lifetimes.   C. D. ANDERSON and HIDEKI YUKAWA

See also ANDERSON, CARL D.; YUKAWA, HIDEKI; ATOM (Inside the Atom; table: Known Atomic Particles).

MESOPHYTE. See PLANT (Where Plants Live).

MESOPOTAMIA. See ARGENTINA (Land Regions).

MESOPOTAMIA, *MES oh poh TAY mi uh,* was an area between the Tigris and Euphrates rivers now known as Iraq and southeastern Turkey. Several ancient civilizations grew there. In Greek, *Mesopotamia* means *between the rivers.* The mountains of Iran and Turkey rise east and north of the Mesopotamian region. The great Syrian desert lies to the west, and the Persian Gulf lies directly south of it. North of the city of Baghdad, the region is a fertile plateau that has cool temperatures and receives some rain. But the southern part, a plain of silt left behind by the rivers, is now being covered with sand and saturated with salt.

Settlers from the north came into Mesopotamia before 4000 B.C. These settlers may have been related to early settlers of Turkey and Syria. But scholars have found no clear records to identify their language or their race.

Sometime after 4000 B.C., the Sumerians invaded Mesopotamia. They probably came from the mountainous regions of present-day Iran and Turkey. They moved south to the Persian Gulf, building towns and draining much of the marshland around the gulf. By

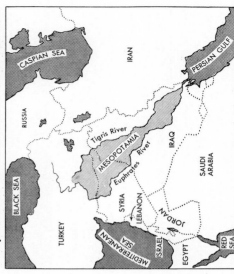

Mesopotamia Stretched North from the Persian Gulf.

345

The Mesquite Tree casts a small patch of shade in hot, dry areas. Its roots may burrow 60 feet into the ground to obtain water.

John Dominis, *Life*, © 1957 Time, Inc.

2700 B.C., the Sumerians had developed a flourishing civilization in Mesopotamia. They developed a form of writing with wedge-shaped symbols called *cuneiform writing*, and used it to record their way of life (see CUNEIFORM).

While this great civilization was growing, Semitic peoples moved in from the west. The Semites adopted much of the Sumerian culture, but they spoke Akkadian, a language similar to Arabic and Hebrew. Semites made up nearly all the empires that controlled Mesopotamia between 2300 and 539 B.C. These included the Akkadian, Babylonian, Assyrian, and Neo-Babylonian (Chaldean) empires.

In 539 B.C., the Persians made Mesopotamia part of their empire. Alexander the Great conquered the Persians between 334 and 330 B.C. Later the Romans, Sassanians, Arabs, Mongols, and then Turks ruled Mesopotamia. Iraq was created at the end of World War I, when the Ottoman Empire broke up. JOHN W. SNYDER

Related Articles in WORLD BOOK include:

Assyria	Euphrates River	Persia, Ancient
Babylonia	Iraq	Sumer
Chaldea	Mitanni	Tigris River

MESOZOIC ERA. See EARTH (The Mesozoic Era; table: Outline of Earth History).

MESQUITE, *mehs KEET*, is a thorny, low shrub which grows in dry climates. The shrub is common in the southwestern United States, Mexico, the West Indies, and parts of western South America. The mesquite also grows in the Hawaiian Islands, where it was brought by missionaries. The mesquite needs little water, and it will grow in deserts too hot and dry for other plants.

Stories of desert life often mention the mesquite. When the mesquite has plenty of water, it grows into a large tree. It may become 50 to 60 feet high with a trunk 3 feet across. People use the wood of the mesquite for fuel, to make fence posts, and to erect buildings. The seeds or beans serve as food for cattle and horses and were once an important food for the Indians of the Southwest. Two kinds of gum taken from the mesquite are used to make candies and Mexican dyes. J. J. LEVISON

Scientific Classification. The mesquite belongs to the pea family, *Leguminosae*. The mesquite is genus *Prosopis*, species *P. juliflora*.

MESS CALL. See BUGLE (illustration).

MESSAGE TO GARCÍA. See GARCÍA Y IÑIGUEZ, CALIXTO; HUBBARD, ELBERT; ROWAN, ANDREW SUMMERS.

MESSENGER. See MERCURY; POST OFFICE (History).

MESSENIA, *meh SEE nee ah*, is a *department* (political division) of present-day Greece. It was also an important region in ancient times. Messenia is located in the southwestern *Peloponnesus* (Greece's southern peninsula). It has an area of 1,155 square miles and a population of about 212,000. Kalámai is the capital of the department. Messenia's farmland is the richest in Greece.

During the Late Bronze Age in Greece (1580-1100 B.C.), eastern Messenia was controlled by King Menelaus of Sparta, and western Messenia by King Nestor of Pylos (now Pílos). According to legend, both Nestor and Menelaus took part in the Greek invasions that destroyed the city of Troy about 1200 B.C. In the 1100's B.C., Dorian invaders from the north overran Messenia. Many Dorians settled in the region. Nestor's palace at Pylos was uncovered in 1939 by American archaeologist Carl Blegen. It is considered one of the great monuments of Bronze Age Greece.

In the late 700's B.C., Sparta conquered Messenia and enslaved the people. Messenians revolted unsuccessfully twice, and they stayed under Spartan rule. But in 371 B.C., Thebes defeated Sparta in the Battle of Leuctra and freed the Messenians. The Theban leader Epaminondas helped the Messenians build a new capital and fortress at Messene (now Messíni). The walls of that fortress are still standing. Messenia remained independent under the protection of Macedonia and the Achaean League until the Romans conquered all of Greece in 146 B.C.

During the Middle Ages (A.D. 476 to about 1500), Slavs, Franks, Venetians, and Turks occupied Messenia. Frankish and Turkish castles still stand at Kalámai, Koróni, Methóni, and Pílos. NORMAN A. DOENGES

MESSERSCHMITT, a German airplane. See AIR FORCE (color picture); JET PROPULSION (Development).

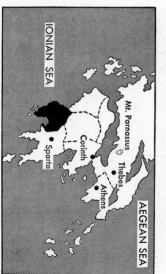

Messenia Lies in Southwestern Greece.

IONIAN SEA

AEGEAN SEA

Mt. Parnassus

Corinth

Sparta

Thebes

Athens

Koróni

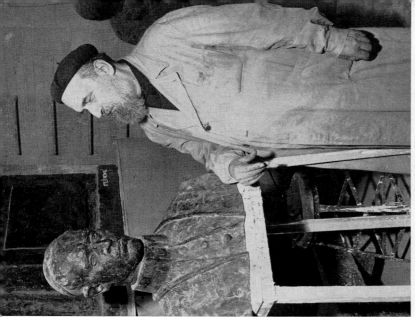

Art Gallery, University of Notre Dame

Ivan Mestrovic stressed mass in such sculptures as his bust of Pope Pius XII. He worked in bronze, wood, and stone.

MESSIAH, *muh SYE uh,* is a Hebrew word meaning *the anointed one.* It has the same meaning as the Greek *Christos,* or *Christ.* The ancient Hebrews often called their high priests and kings *Messiahs* because they had been anointed with holy oil. Later, the prophets spoke of a king who would redeem Israel and bring about a period of peace and justice on earth. They believed that he would be a direct descendant of King David. The term *Messiah* came to refer to this ideal king.

Paul and the early Christians taught that Jesus was "Ho-Christos," the Messiah. In Christian literature, the term *Messianic prophecy* means all prophecy about the person, work, and kingdom of Jesus. The term *Messianic times* refers to the period when Jesus lived on earth and to the new era that He introduced. See JESUS CHRIST.

But the Jews did not accept Jesus as the Messiah the prophets had spoken of. They continued to look forward to the future coming of a Messiah. During the 1600's, Shabbetai Zebi, a Turkish Jew, claimed that he was the Messiah, and had come to revenge the suffering of the Jews. His revolutionary preachings gained him many followers throughout the world. He was finally forced to accept conversion to Islam in order to avoid being put to death. His messianic movement gradually died out. Jews refer to him as a *false Messiah.*

Today, most Orthodox Jews still speak of the coming of a personal Messiah. But many Conservative and Reform Jews look forward to a *Messianic Age* when peace and freedom will reign on earth. See JUDAISM.

MESSIAH, oratorio. See HANDEL, GEORGE F.

MESSIAH COLLEGE. See UNIVERSITIES AND COLLEGES (table).

MESSINA, *muh SEE nuh* (pop. 258,118; alt. 10 ft.), is the third largest city in Sicily. It lies on the northeastern coast of the island, on the Strait of Messina. Messina is noted for its exports of fruit, wine, fine silk, and damask. For location, see ITALY (political map).

Historians believe that pirates founded the city in the 700's B.C. About 500 B.C., it was a well-known Greek colony. The Greeks gave Messina its name. The First Punic War was fought for control of Messina. At the end of this war, the colony fell into Roman hands. The city suffered in many wars and earthquakes. In 1908, an earthquake destroyed Messina, but it was soon rebuilt into a modern city.   BENJAMIN WEBB WHEELER

MESSINA, STRAIT OF, is a stretch of water separating the island of Sicily from Italy. The strait is about 24 miles long. At one time, sailors would not attempt to cross its narrow northern end because of the jagged rocks and strong current. The strait serves as a travel route, but ships find it a dangerous crossing. Reggio di Calabria in Italy and Messina, Sicily, are ports on the strait. See also SCYLLA.   JOHN D. ISAACS

MESTIZO, *mes TEE zoh,* is a Spanish word that comes from the Latin *mixtus,* meaning *mixed.* The word refers to a person whose parents belong to different races. A mestizo may be someone of mixed white and Negro or Malay ancestry. More commonly, the term is applied to a person of mixed white and American Indian parentage, especially in Latin America. Scholars estimate that there are about 39 million mestizos in the Western Hemisphere. Countries with a high proportion of mestizos include Chile, Colombia, El Salvador, Honduras, Mexico, Nicaragua, Paraguay, and Venezuela.   WILTON MARION KROGMAN

MESTROVIC, *MESH troh vich,* **IVAN** (1883-1962), a Yugoslav-born sculptor, often used strong religious and patriotic themes in his work. These characteristics can be seen in his marble *Maiden of Kossovo* (1907), in a series of low reliefs in wood executed during World War I, and in his marble *Pietà* (1942-1946). Mestrovic executed the sculptural decoration of churches in Cavtat and Split.

Mestrovic was born at Vrpolje. He learned carving from a master mason in Split. During the World War I period, he gained a reputation as a Yugoslav patriot. He worked and taught in Yugoslavia until 1946, when he moved to the United States.   WILLIAM MACDONALD

METABOLIMETER, *muh TAB oh LIHM uh tur.* When a person is quiet, his body cells function at "cruising speed" rather than at top speed. The cells then take less food and oxygen from the blood stream, and do not discharge as much waste into the blood. Physicians call this cruising speed *basal metabolism.* The *metabolimeter* is a device used to determine a person's basal metabolism. It does this by measuring the amount of oxygen a patient takes into his body while he is resting. Oxygen is a major fuel of the body, so doctors can tell how quickly body tissues burn food if they know how much oxygen the patient uses. A mask with two tubes is put over the patient's mouth. The tubes connect to a reservoir of oxygen. Dials on the oxygen reservoir register the amount of oxygen that the patient is using. The patient's basal metabolism can be calculated from the number of cubic centimeters of oxygen that he absorbs each minute.   A. C. GUYTON

See also METABOLISM.

347

METABOLISM

The Vital Process of Metabolism breaks down food to produce energy. The body uses this energy for growth, to repair tissues, and to produce heat. Metabolism also provides the energy people need for such physical processes as walking, talking, and the pumping of the heart.

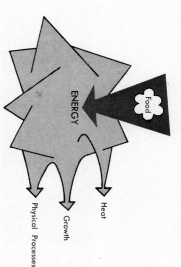

METABOLISM, *meh TAB oh lizm,* is the process by which all living things—men, animals, and plants—transform food into energy and living tissue. It can be thought of as the sum of two related chemical processes that take place inside the body. *Catabolism,* or destructive metabolism, is the breaking down of food substances to release energy. *Anabolism,* or constructive metabolism, involves the *synthesis,* or building up, of new cells and tissues, and the repair of worn-out tissues.

Energy released during catabolism is used in three ways: (1) to make the reactions of anabolism work, (2) to heat the body, and (3) to enable the body's muscles and nerves to do their work. Materials used in the processes of metabolism are formed during digestion and put to work through respiration in the cells.

Digestion. Food consists of three main kinds of organic compounds: proteins, fats, and carbohydrates (starches and sugars). After food enters the body, it is broken down in the digestive tract. Chemicals in the digestive tract split the complex molecules of proteins, fats, and carbohydrates into smaller chemical units. For example, proteins are broken into amino acids and starches are split into sugars. These smaller units, or "food fuels," pass through the walls of the intestine into the blood stream. The blood carries them to all the tissues of the body. In the tissues, the cells may use these products of digestion as building blocks for new and growing tissue. Or they may burn the food fuels during the process of respiration. See Digestion.

Respiration is commonly understood to mean breathing. But breathing makes up only the first part of the whole process of respiration. During breathing, the lungs take in air. Oxygen in the air passes from the lungs into the blood stream, which carries it to the tissues. The second part of respiration is called *tissue respiration.* In this process, the cells use the oxygen to burn the food fuels. In addition to supplying energy for tissue building, tissue respiration also supplies the heat that man

and warm-blooded animals need to maintain body temperature. See Respiration.

In addition to proteins, carbohydrates, and fats, the body needs certain inorganic compounds, or minerals. These include calcium, iron, and salts. Water is also necessary. Certain complex compounds, called vitamins, are essential for metabolism. They are needed only in very small amounts. Man and animals depend mainly on plants as a source of vitamins. See Vitamin.

Basal Metabolism. The rate of metabolism depends on various factors, including amount of food eaten, activity, and temperature. However, at rest, at room temperature, and several hours after a meal, metabolism settles down to a minimum constant rate. Doctors call this rate the *basal metabolic rate.* Normal persons of the same body size, age, and sex, have much the same *basal metabolic rate,* or rate at which the tissues burn food. The rate may be expressed as a plus or minus percentage of the normal rate. The basal metabolism provides a standard to compare metabolism under the varying conditions of health and disease.

The thyroid hormone, which is secreted into the blood by the thyroid gland, performs most of the regulation of the rate of metabolism. By measuring the basal metabolic rate, doctors can determine whether or not the thyroid is operating properly. A low rate indicates *hypothyroidism,* or too little thyroid hormone. A high rate indicates *hyperthyroidism,* or too much thyroid hormone. Physicians use a device called a *metabolimeter* to measure basal metabolism. It has a metal drum that measures the amount of oxygen the patient uses within a certain time. The physician can calculate the metabolic rate from the amount of oxygen used. FRITZ LIPMANN

See also Food (How Our Bodies Use Food); KREBS CYCLE; METABOLIMETER; SPIROMETER; THYROID GLAND.

METACARPAL BONE. See HAND.
METACOMET. See PHILIP, KING.

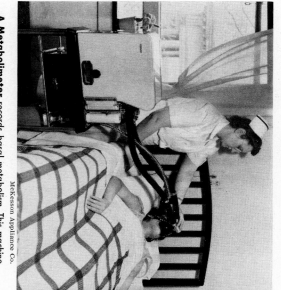

A Metabolimeter records basal metabolism. This machine measures how much oxygen a patient uses while resting. The amount of oxygen indicates how rapidly the body is using up food and producing heat and other forms of energy.

METAL forms a large part of the earth on which we live. The earth's crust is said to be made up of about 8 per cent aluminum, 5 per cent iron, and 4 per cent calcium. Potassium, sodium, and magnesium also occur in large amounts. The core of the earth is much heavier than the crust, and scientists believe that it is made up mainly of nickel and iron. They also believe that more of the heavy metals, such as gold, lead, and mercury, lie in the core than near the surface.

What Metal Is. When chemists wish to learn whether an element is metallic or nonmetallic, they conduct what they call an *electrolysis* test. This test consists of dissolving the element in acid and running an electric current through the solution. If the element is metallic, the tiny atoms which make it up will show a positive charge. This means that when electricity is run through the solution, they will seek the point where the electricity enters the solution, or the *negative* pole.

Thus, chemists define metals as "those elements which, when in solution in a pure state, carry a positive charge and seek the negative pole in an electric cell." Only one nonmetallic element, hydrogen, is an exception to this definition.

Most metals have a silvery color. They are shiny, and usually heavier than water. Most of them conduct heat and electricity very well. Many of the most important metals can be hammered into thin sheets, and are described as *malleable*. They also can be drawn out into wires, and are called *ductile*.

A few metals, such as gold, copper, and strontium, are colored. Several others are not as heavy as water. Potassium, sodium, and lithium, for example, will float on water. Some metals are not malleable and ductile, but are so brittle that they break quickly when worked. Calcium is an example of such a metallic element.

Some substances such as boron and selenium are called *nonmetals*. Chemically, they are not metals, but they have one or more of the physical properties of metals.

Certain combinations, or *alloys*, of metals with other metals also are called metals. Among these are bronze, bell metal, gun metal, and type metal. Alloys and metals that do not contain iron are referred to as *nonferrous*.

Metals Through the Ages. Ancient man knew and used many native metals. Gold was used for ornaments, plates, and utensils as early as 3500 B.C. Gold objects showing a high degree of culture have been excavated at the ruins of the ancient city of Ur in Mesopotamia. Silver was used as early as 2400 B.C., and many ancients considered it to be more valuable than gold, because it was rarer in the native state. Native copper also was used at an early date in tools and utensils, because it was found near the surface of the ground in the native state and could be easily worked and shaped.

Since about 1000 B.C., iron and steel have been the chief metals for construction. Today, supplies of the best iron ore for steelmaking are being exhausted. The same is true for copper, lead, and zinc deposits. Metallurgists now substitute aluminum for steel in many cases. The supply of aluminum is almost unlimited.

Magnesium, another light, strong metal, has also become important. It is extracted from sea water and the common rock called *dolomite*. The atomic bomb is made from uranium, one of the important radioactive metals.

HARRISON ASHLEY SCHMITT

Related Articles in WORLD BOOK include:

METALS

Actinium	Gold	Promethium
Aluminum	Hafnium	Protactinium
Americium	Holmium	Radium
Antimony	Indium	Rhenium
Arsenic	Iridium	Rhodium
Barium	Iron	Rubidium
Berkelium	Lanthanum	Ruthenium
Beryllium	Lead	Samarium
Bismuth	Lithium	Scandium
Cadmium	Lutetium	Silver
Calcium	Magnesium	Sodium
Californium	Manganese	Strontium
Cerium	Mendelevium	Tantalum
Cesium	Mercury	Technetium
Chromium	Molybdenum	Terbium
Cobalt	Neodymium	Thallium
Copper	Neptunium	Thorium
Curium	Nickel	Thulium
Dysprosium	Niobium	Tin
Einsteinium	Nobelium	Titanium
Erbium	Osmium	Tungsten
Europium	Palladium	Uranium
Fermium	Platinum	Vanadium
Francium	Plutonium	Ytterbium
Gadolinium	Polonium	Yttrium
Gallium	Potassium	Zinc
Germanium	Praseodymium	Zirconium

OTHER RELATED ARTICLES

Alloy	Malleability
Assaying	Metallurgy
Corrosion	Mineral
Ductility	Mining
Element, Chemical	Rare Earth

Jet Engines depend on parts made of titanium, a light, strong, heat-resistant metal.

Calcium Carbide, produced in electric furnaces, is used in acetylene and other compounds.

Damascus Swords of the Middle Ages contained tungsten. It is still used to harden steel.

Niobium is mined in western Africa. It must be separated from tin and tantalum ores.

Union Carbide Corp.

The purpose of this project is to learn how to recognize the chemical composition of different kinds of steel by observing the kinds of sparks given off when a piece of the metal is pressed against a high-speed grinding wheel.

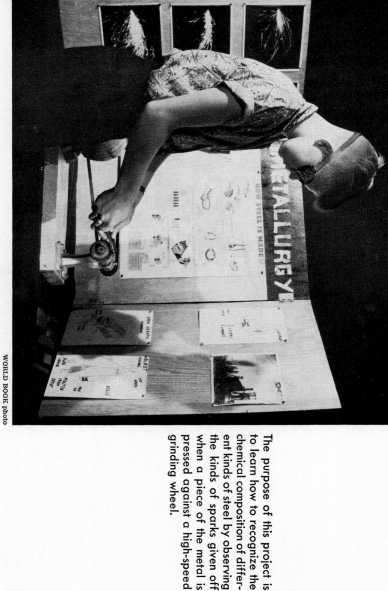

WORLD BOOK photo

MATERIALS

You can get the materials you need for this project from a store that sells machine-shop supplies. The grinding wheel, made of coarse, hard abrasive, should be about 2 inches in diameter.

It should run at a speed of about 9,000 revolutions per minute. The goggles are essential. Use them whenever you use the grinder. They protect your eyes from flying bits of steel and abrasives.

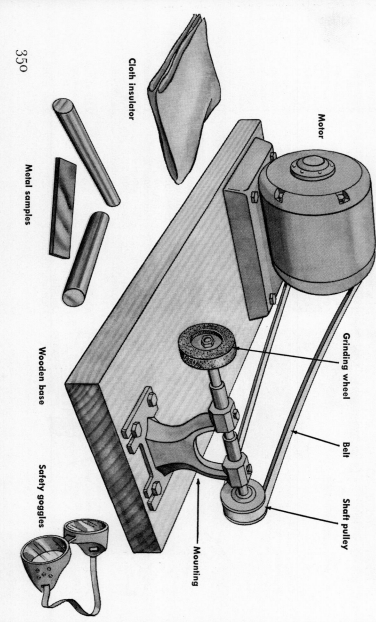

Cloth insulator

Motor

Metal samples

Grinding wheel

Belt

Shaft pulley

Wooden base

Mounting

Safety goggles

350

PROCEDURE

To conduct a spark test, get several samples of steel at least 3 inches long. Set up the grinder in a draft-free area. Wrap an insulating cloth around one end of a steel piece. Turn the lights off and start the grinder. Hold the tip of the steel against the wheel and note the shape of the sparks. Compare the shapes with those shown in the diagrams, below.

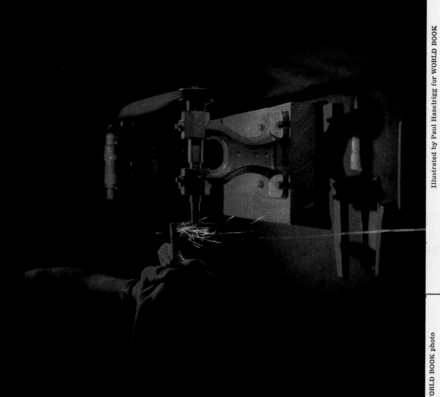

WORLD BOOK photo

Illustrated by Paul Hazelrigg for WORLD BOOK

SAMPLE SPARKS

Sparks are caused when the abrasive wheel tears tiny particles off the steel sample so fast that the particles glow with heat. As these glowing particles hurl through the air, they explode, forming patterns that are typical for the chemicals in the metal. Spark patterns for some common kinds of steel are shown, *right* and *below*. To make your own spark patterns, get samples of other kinds of steel and test them. Make a drawing of the pattern made by each sample.

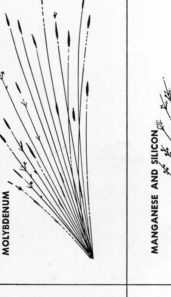

MOLYBDENUM

MANGANESE AND SILICON

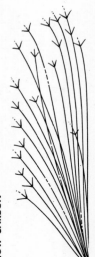

NICKEL

HIGH CARBON

LOW CARBON

METAL FATIGUE. See FATIGUE, METAL.

METALLOGRAPHY, *MET 'l AHG ruh fih,* is the study of the internal structure of metals and alloys. It is a branch of physical metallurgy. Metallographers use microscopes and X rays to explore the effects of heat on metal, and to find out what happens to its internal structure when molten metal is cooled. The success of new missiles and rockets often depends on the reaction of metals to high temperatures.

METALLURGICAL ENGINEERING. See METAL-LURGY (Careers); ENGINEERING (table: Specialized Engineering Fields).

METALLURGY, *MET uh gee,* is the science of separating metals from their ores and preparing them for use. All metal objects which we use are made possible by the work of metallurgy. Metals carry electricity to our homes and factories, and make up the framework of skyscrapers. Automobiles, trains, airplanes, and rockets are made of metal. So are many of the tools we use. Modern industry and manufacturing would be impossible without the use of metals.

The important science of metallurgy falls into two major divisions. One division is called *extractive,* or *recovery,* *metallurgy;* the other is *physical,* or *alloy, metallurgy.*

Extractive Metallurgy

Extractive metallurgy deals with taking metals from their ores and refining them to a pure state. It includes a wide variety of specialized commercial processes, such as mineral dressing, roasting, sintering, smelting, leaching, electrolysis, and amalgamation.

Mineral Dressing is a step in extractive metallurgy which occurs between the mining of the ore and extracting the metals from it. Mineral dressing removes as much of the waste materials as possible from the ore. This is usually done by grinding the ore so that the metals in it, along with certain nonmetallic materials, separate from the waste. Then the dirt and some of the other waste materials may be floated or washed away. In this *flotation process,* crushed ore is *agitated* (set in motion) in water with air or gas bubbles. Various chemicals or oils cause the mineral particles to stick to the bubbles. The minerals are then removed in a froth. The waste materials that occur along with mineral ore are called *gangue.* By the removal of the gangue, the amount of ore that must be handled during the actual process of metal extraction is reduced.

Roasting is a type of extractive metallurgy which removes sulfur and other impurities from the ore. When the ore is heated in air, the sulfur and certain other impurities combine with the oxygen of the air, and pass off as gases. The remaining solid material contains a *metallic oxide* (combination of metal and oxygen). This material must be further purified or reduced to yield the pure metal.

Sintering may occur when the temperature at which ores are roasted becomes very high. In this process, fine particles in contact with one another join together to form coarse lumps. The joining is caused by surface tension. It is the same force that causes small water drops to combine into larger drops. The sintering is sometimes accompanied by partial melting of the fine particles, but the particles often remain entirely solid throughout the process. The coarse lumps produced by sintering can be used more easily in later processes.

Smelting. After the ores have been subjected to such preliminary processes as dressing, roasting, or sintering, processors begin the actual work of extracting the metal. The usual method of metal extraction is by *smelting* (melting the ore in such a way as to remove impurities). In the case of iron, for example, the ore is placed in a huge, brick-lined furnace called a *blast furnace,* and subjected to high heat. Quantities of coke and limestone also are placed in the furnace. As the heat of the furnace is raised, the coke begins to burn and give off carbon monoxide. This gas takes oxygen from the iron, helping to purify the metal. Many of the other impurities of the ore melt and combine with the limestone to form a liquid collection of *refuse* (waste materials) which is lighter than the iron. This refuse rises to the top of the molten metal, and is taken from the furnace as slag. The slag is drawn off from holes in the side of the furnace at a height above the level of the molten iron. The molten iron is still not completely free of impurities. But all the iron has been taken from the ore. The metal must now be refined further to purify it.

Leaching. Some metals can be effectively separated from their ores by *hydrometallurgy* (leaching). This is a method of dissolving the metal out of the ore with a chemical solvent. The metal may then be recovered from the chemical solution by a process called *precipitation.* For example, gold is usually separated from its ore by treating the ore with a dilute alkaline solution of sodium cyanide. After the gold is dissolved in the sodium cyanide, it is placed in contact with metallic zinc. This causes all the gold to *precipitate* (separate) from the solution and gather on the metallic zinc.

Electrolysis. After the metal has been taken from its ore by leaching, it is sometimes recovered from the leaching solution by electrolysis. For example, copper is leached from some ores with sulfuric acid. Then it is placed in an electrolytic cell. There, electric current flows from a lead *anode* (positive pole) through the solution to a copper *cathode* (negative pole). The copper particles in the solution have a positive charge. These particles then seek their opposites, or the negatively charged copper cathode. Aluminum and magnesium also are recovered by electrolysis. This is done at a high temperature and from a solution of their molten salts.

Electrolysis is also used to purify the metal. Copper is one of the metals that can be refined by electrolysis. The impure metal is used as the anode. When electric current is passed through the solution, the atoms of pure copper on the anode give up electrons and pass into solution as positively charged particles. These particles pass through the solution toward the cathode. There, they acquire the necessary electrons to become neutral copper atoms on the cathode. Most impurities are left behind, and a plating of purified copper forms on the cathode.

Amalgamation is a method that is sometimes used to recover gold and silver from their ores. The finely

William W. Mullins, the contributor of this article, is Dean of Carnegie Institute of Technology at Carnegie-Mellon University.

ground particles of ore are carried by a solution over plates covered with mercury. The mercury attracts the metal and combines with it. The mercury forms an alloy, called an *amalgam*, with the gold or silver. Then the amalgam is heated. The heat causes the mercury to come to a boil and pass off as gas, leaving a metallic sponge of pure gold or silver.

Physical Metallurgy

Physical metallurgy is the branch of metallurgy which adapts metals to human use. It includes any operation used to convert a refined commercial metal into a useful finished product. This involves combining metals into alloys to get a metal with special properties. For example, physical metallurgy includes combining steel with nickel to make a chemically resistant, strong steel. It also includes the improvement of these properties by heat treatments, such as the tempering of steel and certain other metals to add strength. The forming of the metal into its final shape, and the surface treatment of the finished product also are classified as physical metallurgy. When a blacksmith heats and hammers a horseshoe, he is practicing metallurgy. The metal may be formed into its final shape by casting, rolling, forging, welding, pressing, extrusion, drawing, stamping, and other methods. Surface treatment may include heat treatment at the surface, and *carburizing* (combining with carbon). The application of a surface coating, such as in galvanizing, and the final surface cleaning are also considered parts of physical metallurgy.

History

Although we usually think of metallurgy as a modern science, it is one of the oldest. The people of prehistoric times knew something of physical metallurgy. The ancient Chinese and Egyptians found gold and silver in their pure state as grains and nuggets, and molded the metal into many different kinds of ornaments. The American Indians found large amounts of pure copper in the area near Lake Superior and molded the metal into weapons and implements.

Sometime before written history began, some of the ancient peoples discovered the simplest principles of smelting metals from their ores. Lead was probably the first metal ever to be separated from its ore by smelting, because it is very easy to reduce. But as long as 4,000 years ago, the Egyptians knew how to separate iron from its ore—and this metal is considered one of the hardest to reduce. By the time of the Assyrian civilization, smelting iron was a highly developed art. The ancient Assyrians even knew how to change iron into steel.

During the Middle Ages, when the alchemists were studying ways to make gold from other substances, great advances were made in metallurgy. The alchemists learned much about the behavior of metals and about various methods of using metals. They are credited with laying the foundations of the modern science of metallurgy. See METAL (Metals Through the Ages).

Careers in Metallurgy

The growing use of metals in industry has increased the importance of metallurgy as a career. *Metallurgists*, also called *metallurgical engineers*, can find jobs chiefly in the metal industry, especially in the manufacture of iron and steel. The mining industry also employs large numbers of metallurgists. Other openings can be found in other industries, in government, and in research. Metallurgists are usually classified into two groups. *Extractive* metallurgists are those who work on the extraction of metals from ores. *Physical* metallurgists are those concerned with the content and structure of metals and their alloys.

Since the mid-1940's, metallurgists have greatly increased their efforts to explain complex metallurgical behavior in terms of the basic laws of physics and chemistry. They also have extended the use of metallurgical research methods and skills to such nonmetallic materials as ceramics, semiconductors, plastics, organic solids, and glass. The name *materials science* has been given to this broadened field that deals with both metals and nonmetals.

A person interested in metallurgy or materials science as a career should have an interest in science and the ability to do mechanical jobs. He should take as many high-school science and mathematics courses as possible. Most jobs require a bachelor of science degree in metallurgical engineering. Research positions usually require advanced degrees.

WILLIAM W. MULLINS

Related Articles in WORLD BOOK include:

Alchemy	Iron and Steel
Alloy	Machine Tool
Amalgam	Metallography
Electrolysis	Powder Metallurgy
Flotation Process	Sintering
Flux	Slag
Forging	Solder
Ion Microscope	

METAMORPHIC ROCK is rock that has been changed in appearance, and sometimes in composition. These rocks are changed by heat, pressure, and chemical solutions at great depths below the earth's surface. The action of the weather also changes rocks, but most geologists do not classify these rocks as metamorphic rocks.

Most metamorphic rocks are very old. They are seen only because they have been heaved up to the surface during changes in the earth's crust.

Many metamorphic rocks contain layers and streaks of different mineral composition and texture. Geologists call these *gneiss*. Some metamorphic rocks are uniform in composition and contain minerals that appear in parallel plates. Geologists call these *schist*. Schist generally splits into thin plates. Metamorphosed sandstone is called *quartzite*. Metamorphism changes limestone into marble.

ERNEST E. WAHLSTROM

See also METAMORPHISM; ROCK (Metamorphic Rock; table).

METAMORPHISM, *MET uh MAWR fiz'm*, is a general name for the changes in the form and composition of rocks. During metamorphism, rocks change because of the growth of new mineral crystals from the original minerals in the rocks. They also change because the solutions that move through the rocks add or take away chemical substances. The number of kinds of changes that geologists can call *metamorphic* is almost unlimited.

The causes of metamorphism include heat, pressure, and hot fluids that are active deep below the surface of

COMPLETE METAMORPHOSIS OF A BUTTERFLY

EGGS

LARVA

PUPA (CHRYSALIS)

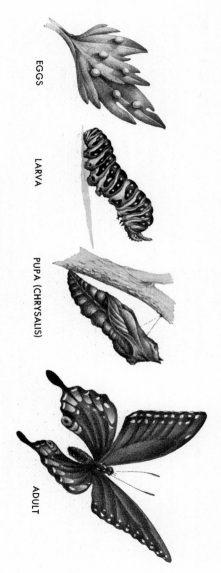

ADULT

the earth. Some rocks are metamorphosed by the heat of hot igneous rocks, such as those formed from lava. This kind of change is called *contact*, or *local*, *metamorphism*. The earth's heat and mountain-forming movements in the earth's crust often metamorphose very large bodies of rocks. This process is called *regional metamorphism*.

See also METAMORPHIC ROCK (Metamorphic Rock; table).

ERNEST E. WAHLSTROM

METAMORPHOSIS, *MET uh MAWR foh sis*, is a Greek word that means *to transform*. Biologists use the word to describe the rather abrupt changes, or transformations, which occur in the form and structure of many lower animals from the time of their birth until they reach the stage of maturity, or adulthood.

Many young animals, such as cats, dogs, and horses, look like their parents in form and structure. They differ chiefly in size from mature animals. But when such insects as the butterfly, other invertebrates such as the sea urchin, and the frog come from the egg, they appear to be different from the mature animal. In many of these young animals, striking changes in appearance and structure—that is, *metamorphosis*—must take place before they reach their adult condition.

The changes that occur in the life cycle of a butterfly or moth are among the most striking examples of metamorphosis. Because the butterfly passes through

four separate stages of growth, scientists consider it an example of *complete metamorphosis*. The first stage of the butterfly is as an *embryo* that forms inside the egg (see EMBRYO).

The Larva. When the future butterfly is newly hatched, it is known as a *larva*. Scientists call the first stage of development after the creature comes out of the egg the *larval stage*. The larva of a butterfly or moth is a crawling, often fuzzy caterpillar. It may be smooth, or hairy, or green. It may be smooth, or hairy, or may have many long spines. In any case, the larva does not look at all like a beautiful, winged adult butterfly. The larva has a greater number of legs, and biting jaws instead of the long, slender, sucking tube of the butterfly. The larva has no wings. It eats a great deal and grows rapidly, *molting* (shedding its skin) several times. After about a month in the larval stage, it enters its third period of existence, called the *pupal stage*.

The Pupa. The third stage in a butterfly's life history is a very quiet one. The larva changes into an almost motionless, stiff object called a *chrysalis*. A chrysalis usually hangs from a twig or from the underside of a leaf. Most moth larvae spin a silk covering called a *cocoon*. Within this cocoon, the larva changes into a pupa. During the period when the moth or butterfly lies quietly in its covering, the wings, legs, and body of the mature insect develop. At the same time,

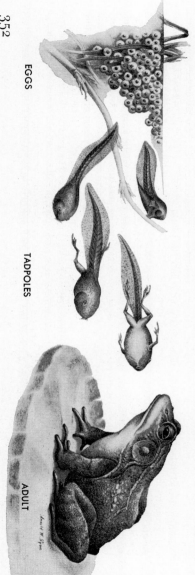

EGGS

TADPOLES

METAMORPHOSIS OF A FROG

ADULT

other changes take place in the body of the insect.

The Adult, or Imago. The pupal period may last from two weeks to many months. When the end of the pupal period arrives, the case splits open, and the fully developed insect, or *imago*, emerges and expands its wings.

Other Examples. The grasshopper is an insect which passes through three stages of development, omitting the pupal period entirely. The frog undergoes a wholly different type of metamorphosis. It comes out of the egg as a small, wriggling tadpole. The tadpole lives under water and breathes by means of gills. But as it grows larger, it develops lungs and pairs of forelegs and hind legs. Gradually, the tadpole loses its gills and tail by absorbing them into its body. Chemical substances which the tadpole secretes from ductless glands bring about all these *metamorphoses* (changes). When the tadpole is ready to leave its home in the water and live mostly on the land, the metamorphosis is finished. ALEXANDER B. KLOTS

Related Articles in WORLD BOOK include:

Butterfly	Fly (The Life of a Fly)	Molting	Nymph
Chrysalis	Larva	Moth	Pupa
Cocoon			

METAPHOR, *MET uh for,* a figure of speech, is an expression taken from one field of experience and used to say something in another field. For example, when we say, "He's a sly fox," we are using metaphor. That is, we are using the name of an animal to describe a man.

A metaphor suggests a comparison without using the word *like* or *as.* The statement "He is *like* a sly fox," or "He is sly *as* a fox," is a simile (see SIMILE).

Everyday speech is rich in metaphors. If we ask someone, "Did you *land* a job today?" the reply may be, "No, not a *bite.*" These words from the special language of *fishing* are used to express thoughts about job-hunting. Common words, like *hunting,* actually develop new senses when they are repeatedly used as metaphors. For instance, we hardly realize that in the phrase "table leg," the word *leg* was originally a metaphor. And we may understand the meaning of "rocket fins," without imagining the shape of a fish. But when we are told not to "make pigs of yourselves," we are probably aware of the unpleasant comparison that the metaphor suggests.

Metaphors are important in the speech of statesmen, scientists, and journalists. In 1946, Sir Winston Churchill used the now-famous phrase "iron curtain" to describe an international problem. Scientists speak of the "wave theory of light." And the phrase "priming the pump" is sometimes used to refer to government spending to stimulate a nation's business and industry. In each of these cases, the metaphor has been an important tool of thought.

Great works of literature are enriched by metaphor. Psalm 23 of the Bible is based on a metaphor. It begins with the words, "The Lord is my shepherd," and suggests the relationship of God to man by considering the relation of shepherd to his sheep. The plays of Shakespeare contain brilliant metaphors, such as the passage in *As You Like It* beginning, "All the world's a stage." Poets often use surprising and beautiful metaphors, as in the line from Alfred Noyes' poem "The Highwayman," "The road was a ribbon of moonlight . . ." Mixed metaphors, using two or more unrelated metaphors in the same expression, are often unintentionally amusing. An example: "I smell a rat, but we shall nip it in the bud." CHARLES W. COOPER

METAPHYSICAL POETS is the name commonly given to a group of English poets of the 1600's. John Donne, the most important poet in the group, influenced the other members. Donne wrote on both religious and nonreligious topics. The group also included Richard Crashaw, George Herbert, and Henry Vaughan, who wrote mainly on religious subjects; and Lord Herbert of Cherbury, John Cleveland, Abraham Cowley, and Andrew Marvell, who wrote chiefly on nonreligious topics.

At its best, metaphysical poetry was truly *metaphysical.* That is, it explored the philosophical problems of the one and the many, unity and division, and the spirit and the flesh. The metaphysical poets often ignored traditional stanza forms. They used vividly colloquial language, irregular rhythms, clever but obscure or outlandish imagery, and, occasionally, extravagant diction.

Their diction and rhythms made the metaphysical poets unfashionable in the late 1600's and 1700's. Critic Samuel Johnson first used the term "metaphysical" in his *The Lives of the English Poets* (1779-1781). Johnson criticized the group for what he felt was an excessive use of learning. In the 1900's, the essays of T. S. Eliot helped stimulate interest in the metaphysical poets. Modern poets influenced by the group include Eliot, Wallace Stevens, Hart Crane, Elinor Wylie, and Richard Eberhart.

RICHARD S. SYLVESTER

See also COWLEY, ABRAHAM; DONNE, JOHN; HERBERT, GEORGE; MARVELL, ANDREW; VAUGHAN, HENRY.

METAPHYSICS, *MET uh FIZZ iks,* is the name given to research about the eternal, universal nature of things. The natural scientist deals with the kinds of fundamental and basic properties that make up matter. The *metaphysician* (philosopher who deals with metaphysics) studies the basic kinds of things and properties that make up the entire *cosmos* (universe).

Branches of Metaphysics. Traditionally, metaphysics is subdivided into two branches. These are *ontology* and *cosmology.* Ontology deals with questions about the ultimate nature of things; whether a thing is one or many, or of what kind. Cosmology considers the type of organization of the world. If all things are determined, cosmology seeks to find out how, or by what method. If they are not, cosmology then tries to find out what causes the breakdown of determinism. Cosmology also seeks to discover whether things are arranged in some *hierarchy* (ascending order). If they are, it then tries to discover the *apex* (top) of that hierarchy, and how things ascend to various levels.

A person may realize that very often things are not what they appear to be. He then begins to ask whether the things that he knows are what they appear to be or whether they are *manifestations* (appearances) of something quite different. A person may ask such questions as these: "Are all things matter, or is there something else which appears to us as matter?" "Would the world appear different if we had other types of experience than taste, touch, smell, hearing, and seeing?" Answers to these questions may be classified as *qualitative* and *quantitative.* Qualitative ontology tries to answer the question, "What is the nature of reality?"

METAPHYSICS

Quantitative ontology seeks replies to "How many kinds of ultimate substances are there?"

Doctrines of Metaphysics. *Idealism* asserts that mind or spirit is in some sense basic to everything that exists. Most religions are based on idealistic ontologies. *Absolute idealism* asserts that there is only one universal spirit, of which all things are manifestations. *Supernaturalism*, a form of idealism, believes in the existence of something (God) beyond nature. *Naturalism*, opposed to supernaturalism, insists that there is only nature and that all things are to be explained in materialistic or scientific terms. *Materialism* affirms that matter is fundamental. Marxism is rooted in a materialistic ontology. *Dialectical materialism* says that the universe is composed of matter which develops through a series of conflicts to form the great variety of things found throughout the world.

Monism holds that there is only one ultimate substance, out of which all things are constructed. Materialism and some forms of idealism are examples of monistic systems. *Dualism* maintains that there are two ultimate substances, usually mind and matter. *Pluralism* insists that there are many kinds of ultimate substances.

Many of these doctrines differ on the nature of change. Some cosmologies have maintained that change is unreal. Others have tried to describe the way in which things have changed and do change. *Dialectics* explains change as the result of conflict between opposites which then, so to speak, fuse into a new kind of thing that embraces both opposites. The greatest advocate of this type of explanation was the German philosopher Georg W. F. Hegel (see HEGEL, GEORG W. F.). *Evolution* explains change as the result of a development out of a given stage into something new. The cause may be either an internal drive or external compulsion. Henri Bergson, a French philosopher, advocated this doctrine (see BERGSON, HENRI). *Creation* explains change as the result of a creative act. This act may be either of God or of some principle of creativity inherent in the universe, such as love. Alfred North Whitehead, an English philosopher, advocated a similar view (see WHITEHEAD, ALFRED NORTH).

These questions metaphysicians raise cannot be answered by experimental observation in a laboratory. The laboratory method of solving questions assumes that nature is such that it can be observed in a laboratory. Metaphysics tries to justify its conclusions either by generalizing from the natural sciences or by *inferring*, or drawing conclusions, from the process of knowing to the nature of things known. Some metaphysicians have insisted that there is a process of knowing that reveals to us the structure of things in general (knowledge by acquaintance or intuition).

Opinions About Metaphysics. The progress of natural science and the diversity of answers to metaphysical questions have caused some philosophers to insist that these questions are meaningless because they cannot be answered. For example, we know of no way to answer the question, "Is reality mind or matter?" once and for all. Therefore, these philosophers consider it a meaningless question.

Other philosophers try to discover means of replying

to metaphysical questions. They say that such questions are not really about the universe as it is, but about our methods of talking about the universe. Philosophers who take this position are called *linguistic analysts*. They do not affirm that there *are* particular things but that their words *assume* there are. These analysts claim that the function of metaphysics is to analyze the ways in which language is used. If a person says that there are only particular things like *this* stone and *this* book, and that there are no general things like beauty and book, he intends to say that the words in his language are never general terms but singular terms.   LOUIS O. KATTSOFF

See also IDEALISM; MATERIALISM; SUPERNATURALISM.

METATARSAL. See TRANSVERSE ARCH.

METAURUS, BATTLE OF. See Army (Famous Land Battles of History).

METAXAS, *meh tah KSAHS*, **JOANNES** (1871-1941), was dictator of Greece from 1936 until his death. He became an army officer in 1890. He studied in a German military academy from 1899 to 1903, and became an admirer of German militarism. In 1934 he formed a Greek fascist-monarchist party. This group helped him become the Italian dictator of Greece in 1936. Metaxas admired the Italian dictator, Benito Mussolini, but led Greece against the Italian invaders in 1940. Metaxas was born in Cephalonia.   ALBERT PARRY

METAZOAN is an animal made up of many different kinds of cells. Scientists classify these animals in the subkingdom *Metazoa*. This subkingdom includes all animals except the protozoans, which have only one cell (see PROTOZOAN). Sponges have many cells, but they differ so much from other many-celled animals that many scientists do not classify them as metazoans.

See also CELL; CLASSIFICATION.

METCALFE, CHARLES THEOPHILUS (1785-1846), BARON METCALFE, a British statesman, served as Governor-General of Canada from 1843 to 1845. His dispute with the Canadian Cabinet over official appointments started a bitter struggle between the Reform and Conservative parties. The election of 1844 showed that a small majority favored his policy. But health soon forced him to resign. Metcalfe was born in Calcutta, India. He served in India from 1801 to 1836, and as Governor of Jamaica from 1839 to 1842. He attended Eton College in England.   JAMES L. GODFREY

METCHNIKOFF, *MECH nih kawf*, **ÉLIE** (1845-1916), was a great Russian biologist. He made important studies of the functions of *phagocytes*. These are white blood cells that attack disease germs. Doctors at first opposed his theory that inflammation at a wound is caused by a struggle between phagocytes and germs. But the theory was generally accepted before his death. Metchnikoff shared the 1908 Nobel prize for medicine. The biologist spent his $20,000 share of the Nobel prize on his studies.

His writings include *The Nature of Man, Lectures on the Comparative Pathology of Inflammation,* and *Immunity in Infective Diseases.* In *The Prolongation of Life*, he suggested that people should eat cultures of sour-milk bacteria to slow down the process of growing old.

Metchnikoff was born at Ivanovka in Kharkov province. He studied in Russia and Germany, and taught zoology at Odessa University. He joined the staff of the Pasteur Institute in Paris in 1892, and became its sub-director in 1895.   MORDECAI L. GABRIEL

All meteors belong to the solar system of which the earth is a part. They travel in a variety of orbits and velocities about the sun. The faster ones move at about 26 miles a second. The earth travels at about 18 miles a second. When meteors meet the earth's atmosphere head-on, the combined velocity reaches about 44 miles a second. Those traveling in the same direction as the earth hit the atmosphere at much slower speeds. Meteors rarely blaze for more than a few seconds. But occasionally one leaves a shining trail that lasts as long as several minutes. Most of the meteors we see are originally no larger than a pinhead or a grain of sand.

Meteor Showers. The earth meets a number of swarms of meteors every year. When this happens, the sky seems filled with a shower of flying sparks. Some meteor swarms have orbits similar to the orbits of comets. This shows that these swarms are fragments of comets.

IMPORTANT METEOR SHOWERS

Shower	Date
Quadrantid	January 3
Lyrid	April 21
Eta Aquarid	May 4
Delta Aquarid	July 29
Perseid	August 12
Orionid	October 22
Taurid, North	November 1
Taurid, South	November 16
Leonid	November 17
Geminid	December 12

The most brilliant meteoric shower took place on Nov. 13, 1833. The earth encounters this swarm, called the *Leonid* meteor shower, every November. It consists of a great ring of particles that revolves continually around the sun. In the 1800's, the earth passed through the thickest part of the swarm every 33 years, and several brilliant displays of meteors occurred. The earth now misses the thickest part of the swarm.

Astronomers name meteor showers after the constellations from which they appear to come. The table above lists some of the important annual showers and the dates of their greatest activity.

Meteorites sometimes explode into fragments with a noise that can be heard for miles when they strike the

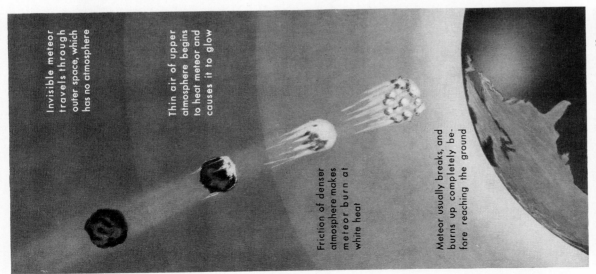

The Atmosphere Screens the Earth from Meteors, and prevents all but a few of them from reaching the ground.

Invisible meteor travels through outer space, which has no atmosphere

Thin air of upper atmosphere begins to heat meteor and causes it to glow

Friction of denser atmosphere makes meteor burn at white heat

Meteor usually breaks, and burns up completely before reaching the ground

METEOR, *ME tee or,* is a piece of metallic or stony matter that hurtles into the earth's atmosphere from space. Meteors cannot be seen until they enter the atmosphere. Then friction with the air makes them so hot they glow with brilliant light, and we can see them shine. People often call meteors *shooting stars* or *falling stars,* because they look like stars falling from the sky.

Scientists estimate that as many as 200,000,000 visible meteors enter the earth's atmosphere every day. These and other meteorites are estimated to add more than 1,000 tons daily to the earth's weight. We first see most of these meteors when they are about 65 miles above the earth. Air friction heats them to about 4000° F., and they burn out at altitudes of 30 to 50 miles. Meteors that reach earth before burning up are *meteorites.*

The Great Meteor Crater of Arizona lies between the towns of Flagstaff and Winslow. Scientists believe that a giant meteorite struck the earth about 50,000 years ago and dug this huge hole. It measures about 4,150 feet across and 570 feet deep.

Ernest Chilson, Flagstaff Chamber of Commerce

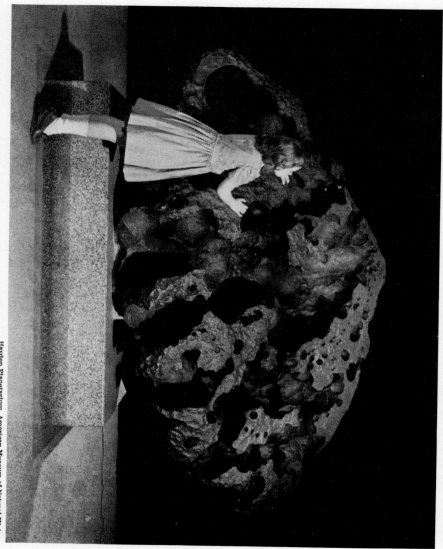

Willamette Meteorite is the largest meteorite ever found in the United States. It weighs about 15½ tons. Rust and atmospheric friction pitted one side. The meteorite was named after the Willamette Valley in Oregon, where it was unearthed in 1902.

earth or its atmosphere. In 1908, the famous Tunguska meteorite crashed into the earth in Siberia. People hundreds of miles away saw this meteorite in full daylight, and felt its blast at a distance of 50 miles. The Tunguska meteorite had a weight estimated at a few hundred tons. It scorched the earth, and flattened forests like matchsticks. In 1947, a meteorite exploded into fragments over the Sikhote-Alin Mountains in eastern Siberia. It left more than 200 holes and craters.

There are two kinds of meteorites, stony and iron. *Stony meteorites* are made up of many different stony minerals mixed with particles of iron. Some resemble minerals that come from volcanoes. *Iron meteorites* consist chiefly of iron combined with nickel. They also may have small amounts of cobalt, copper, phosphorus, carbon, and sulfur.

Scientists collect meteorites for study, because they are the only actual objects that come from outside the earth. The largest meteorite, at Hoba West in South West Africa, weighs about 60 metric tons (66 U.S. tons). The Hayden Planetarium in New York City owns the Ahnighito, a 34-ton nickel-iron meteorite that Arctic explorer Robert E. Peary brought to the United States from western Greenland in 1897.

In the 1950's, scientists discovered a 400-mile wide depression on the eastern shore of Hudson Bay in Canada

which may be the earth's largest meteorite crater. It is larger in size than the moon's largest crater, Bailly, which is about 180 miles wide. Canada also has four other craters found in the 1950's. These are a crater 7 to 8 miles wide at Deep Bay, Saskatchewan; the 2-mile-wide Chubb crater on the Ungava Peninsula; and a 2-mile-wide crater at Brent and a 1½-mile-wide crater at Holleford, both in Ontario. Southern Algeria has a crater 1¼ miles wide. The Meteor Crater in Arizona is about 4,150 feet wide and 570 feet deep. The rim of the Meteor Crater towers over 150 feet above the surrounding ground level.

See also Comet; Fireball; Leonids; Tektite.

Fletcher G. Watson

METEOROLOGICAL SATELLITE. See Space Travel (Artificial Satellites).

METEOROLOGICAL SOCIETY, AMERICAN, is an international organization that encourages the study of the atmospheric sciences. Its members include scientists and other persons interested in weather.

The society prepares educational films, and publishes books and papers on meteorological subjects. It provides career information and makes awards to college students. The society certifies consulting meteorologists. The American Meteorological Society was founded in 1919. It has headquarters at 45 Beacon Street, Boston, Mass. 02108.

METEOROLOGY, ME tee ur AHL oh jih, is the study of the atmosphere and the weather. It includes both what we can observe about the weather and the attempt to explain what we see. Meteorology borrows much from other sciences, including chemistry, physics, and mathematics.

Meteorology at Work. Meteorology tries to get a complete picture of what the atmosphere is like. Weather observations are taken regularly from land stations in all parts of the world, from ships at sea, and from airplanes and balloons in the sky.

Meteorologists are interested in many things about the atmosphere. They want to know its temperature, which they measure with *thermometers*; its pressure, which they determine with *barometers*; and its moisture, which they measure with *hygrometers*. Meteorologists measure *wind* (the motion of the atmosphere) with *anemometers* and *wind vanes*. *Rain gauges* tell about rainfall, *ceilometers* give information about cloud heights, and *nephoscopes* report cloud motion.

The meteorologist uses chemistry to study the nitrogen, oxygen, and other gases that make up the air we breathe. Chemistry also helps in the study of *smog* and other impurities that pollute air (see SMOG). Meteorologists use physics to explain the motion of the atmosphere, lightning and other electrical effects, and the formation of rain, snow, and hail. Mathematics helps meteorologists to improve weather forecasts, to understand what makes the wind blow, and to calculate accurately the speed of storms.

Careers in Meteorology. The meteorologist performs different tasks on different jobs. If he works for the United States Weather Bureau or the meteorological services of Canada and Great Britain he may do one of several jobs. Some meteorologists observe the weather. Others analyze and forecast the weather, study climate, or work on weather instruments.

A good weather observer takes great care in his work. He may work in an unusual and interesting place such as the South Pole. Or he may work in your home town. A weather observer does not need a great deal of formal training. But he should have a careful and inquiring mind, and the desire to do the best possible job. The weather observer must be especially reliable. His work often goes unchecked, and he may be responsible for the lives of many persons. For example, careless weather observations have caused airplane accidents.

Weather analysts and forecasters have more training than observers. They usually work in larger cities where they prepare weather forecasts for the public. Some forecasts are made especially for airplane pilots, farmers, and highway-maintenance departments. Meteorologists also make forecasts that help people plan fishing trips, picnics, or a day at the beach.

Weather forecasters and observers are on the job around the clock, every day in the week. The weather goes on day and night, throughout the year. This does not mean that observers or forecasters work longer than other persons. The meteorologist who studies climate or works on weather instruments usually has fairly regular hours.

The U.S. Army, Navy, and Air Force have all kinds of meteorologists, most of them in uniform. These men do about the same jobs as civilian meteorologists who work for the Weather Bureau. Private industry has a few

jobs for meteorologists. Airlines employ some of their own weathermen, but they use the government weather services as much as possible. Large electric and gas companies employ some weather forecasters to help them determine their needs in advance. But most utilities also rely on government forecasts. Small private companies that sell weather information are increasing in importance. They service a variety of businesses including ice cream companies, department stores, and oil firms.

Most universities and colleges offer courses in meteorology. Because of this, teaching is an important field for the meteorologist. Some college meteorology courses give only a broad idea of the subject. Others are more detailed and intensive for the student who wants to be a meteorologist. High-school students interested in meteorology should have a good background in physics, chemistry, and mathematics. An interest in geography also may prove helpful, because the weather is world-wide.

GEORGE F. TAYLOR

See also WEATHER with its list of Related Articles.

METER, in poetry, is the number of feet in a line of verse. The word *meter* means *measure*. It can also refer to the *metrical pattern*—the foot, meter, and rhyme scheme—of a poem. See POETRY (Verse and Melody).

When poetry like this is read aloud, the flow of word sounds is rhythmical. A definite pattern of rising and falling sounds becomes apparent. *Scanning* (marking accented syllables) may help to discover this pattern:

Lives of great men all remind us
We can make our lives sublime,
And, departing, leave behind us
Footprints on the sands of time.

The metrical pattern of a traditional poem is described in terms of the basic *foot* (rhythmic unit), the *meter* (verse length), and the line scheme. There are four or five different kinds of feet used in metrical patterns: the iamb (*de-DUMM*), anapest (*de-de-DUMM*), trochee (*DUMM-de*), dactyl (*DUMM-de-de*), and occasionally amphibrach (*de-DUMM-de*). The *meter* (verse length) is the number of feet to the line: monometer (a line of only one foot), dimeter (a line of two feet), trimeter (three), tetrameter (four), pentameter (five), hexameter (six), heptameter (seven), and octameter (eight). The meter of the above example is trochaic tetrameter (four *DUMM de* feet per line). The second and fourth lines lack a final syllable.

Lives' of/great' men/all' re/mind' us
We' can/make' our/lives' sub/lime'

The *rhyme scheme* of a metrical pattern is the sequence or grouping of lines, often in stanzas that use rhyme. The above stanza is a *quatrain* (four-line stanza) with *crossed rhymes* (alternate lines rhyme, *abab*).

But meter is not necessary to poetry. There are some non-metrical types of verse. For example, free verse has no meter (see FREE VERSE). In such poetry, there is no regular beat. The rhythm will follow the meaning of the phrases and arrangement of the verses on the page.

CHARLES W. COOPER

See also POETRY (Metrical Patterns); BLANK VERSE; COUPLET.

357

METER is the basic unit of length in the metric system. A meter is equal to 39.37 inches. Scientists define the length of the meter as 1,650,763.73 wavelengths of the orange-red light from the isotope krypton-86, measured in a vacuum. The International Bureau of Weights and Measures adopted this standard in 1960 in place of the platinum-iridium meter bar. See also CENTIMETER; METRIC SYSTEM; YARD.

E. G. STRAUS

METER, ELECTRIC. See ELECTRIC METER.

METHANE, *METH ayn,* is an important industrial compound that makes up a large part of natural gas. It is formed when plants decay in places where there is very little air. Methane is often called *marsh gas* because it is found around stagnant water and swamps. It is also the chief substance in *firedamp,* a gas that causes serious explosions in mines.

The chemical industry uses methane as a starting material for many other chemicals. Methane reacts with a limited amount of air at high temperatures to form acetylene. Under similar conditions, it reacts with ammonia to produce hydrogen cyanide. It also undergoes *partial combustion* (incomplete burning), producing hydrogen and carbon monoxide gases. This mixture serves as a source for commercial hydrogen, and for carbon monoxide used in making methyl alcohol (methanol).

Methane is a colorless, odorless, flammable gas, soluble in alcohol but only slightly soluble in water. Its chemical formula is CH_4, and it is the first member of the *paraffin* series of hydrocarbons. It burns with a colorless flame. Mixtures of methane with air, oxygen, or chlorine are explosive.

See also ACETYLENE; DAMP; GAS (The Composition of Natural Gas); HYDROCARBON; WOOD ALCOHOL.

LEWIS F. HATCH

METHANOL. See WOOD ALCOHOL.

METHODIST COLLEGE. See UNIVERSITIES AND COLLEGES (table).

METHODIST YOUTH FELLOWSHIP. See UNITED METHODIST YOUTH FELLOWSHIP.

METHODISTS belong to Protestant religious denominations that trace their beginnings back to John Wesley, a Church of England clergyman in the 1700's. In the United States, more than 15 denominations share the name *Methodist* and a common heritage in Wesley's teaching. The largest Methodist body is the United Methodist Church, formed in 1968 through a union of The Methodist Church and the Evangelical United Brethren Church. Other major denominations include the African Methodist Episcopal Church, the African Methodist Episcopal Zion Church, the Christian Methodist Episcopal Church, the Free Methodist Church of North America, and the Wesleyan Church. For membership of major U.S. bodies, see RELIGION (table).

There is no central organization of Methodist denominations in the United States, but many denominations are part of a World Methodist Council. However, this council has no legislative power and serves primarily as a *fraternal* (brotherly) association.

Doctrine. Methodist churches are *evangelical.* That is, they try to convince non-Methodists of the soundness of the Methodist approach to religion. All Methodists stress salvation through faith, and emphasize an orderly, active Christian life and God's forgiveness of personal sins. But Methodists emphasize that salvation comes through work as well as faith. They believe in a personal religious experience in which each individual gives proof of his belief in Jesus Christ as his personal savior. This experience may be sudden and highly emotional for some. For others, it may involve periods of study and prayer. But all Methodist denominations expect their members to declare their faith in Jesus Christ publicly. Each denomination strongly emphasizes the necessity of being a church member. Methodists accept the Bible as the supreme rule of faith and religious practice.

History. In the early 1700's, John Wesley began trying to find ways to reform the Church of England. He did not set out to found a new church.

The name *Methodist* first appeared in 1729 when Wesley was a tutor at Oxford University. While there, he and his brother Charles became leaders of a small group called the Holy Club. Other students noticed the strict, methodical way in which this group approached their religious life and began calling them *methodists.*

John Wesley tried unsuccessfully to find religious satisfaction by closely following the rules of the Church of England. A turning point in his life came in London in 1738, when he said his heart was "strangely warmed." Wesley said he discovered that inner peace comes by faith in God's mercy and grace, not through personal efforts alone.

Wesley became unwelcome in Anglican churches because of his evangelistic vigor in preaching and the strict discipline he urged on his followers. He and his followers then began to preach wherever people would gather to listen—on streets, in public squares, and in fields. Wesley believed that salvation was free to all men, not just to a select few, and that God's grace is equal to every need. Such a doctrine appealed to many persons in England at that time, especially to the poor and oppressed.

As the movement spread, Wesley established what he called the United Societies, in which he used many *lay* (unordained) preachers. Wesley trained, appointed, and supervised the preachers, and his doctrine spread mainly because of their devotion and enthusiasm. He organized the preachers into a Methodist conference in 1744.

Painting about 1817 by Joseph B. Smith, Museum of the City of New York; Horizon

The First Methodist Church in New York City Was the John Street Methodist Church, center, Built in 1768.

Wesley realized that this growing movement could not continue to work within the framework of the Church of England. Under his guidance, the United Societies developed as an independent church, although Wesley continued as an ordained Anglican clergyman. Wesley sent preachers to America. Philip Embury preached in New York City about 1766. Robert Strawbridge went to Maryland about the same time. Wesley later sent Francis Asbury and Thomas Coke, who became the first American Methodist bishops.

In 1784, about 60 ministers organized the Methodist Episcopal Church in Baltimore. The denomination grew quickly, as traveling preachers called *circuit riders* carried the Methodist religion to the frontier (see CIRCUIT RIDER). In 1828, a group insisting on more lay representation in church affairs separated and formed the Methodist Protestant Church. Like Methodism in England, this new church did not have bishops. In 1844, a group left the Methodist Episcopal Church to form the Methodist Episcopal Church, South. This division occurred over the issues of slavery and constitutional powers within the denomination. The Methodist Episcopal Church, the Methodist Protestant Church, and the Methodist Episcopal Church, South reunited in 1939 as The Methodist Church.

Methodists in Canada organized into the United Church of Canada in 1925. British Methodists, after periods of division, reunited in 1925. EARL KENNETH WOOD

Related Articles in WORLD BOOK include:

African Methodist Episcopal Church	Free Methodist Church
African Methodist Episcopal Zion Church	Oxnam, Garfield Bromley
	United Church of Canada
Asbury, Francis	United Methodist Church
Camp Meeting	United Methodist Youth Fellowship
Cartwright, Peter	Wesley
Delaware (Places to Visit [Houses of Worship])	Wesleyan Methodist Church
	Whitefield, George

METHUEN TREATY. See PORTUGAL (Years of Decline).

METHUSELAH, *mee THOO zuh luh,* was the son of Enoch and the grandfather of Noah in the Old Testament. According to the Bible, he lived 969 years (Gen.

5: 25-27). The expression "as old as Methuselah" describes a very old person. Babylonians believed that some of their heroes lived 36,000 years. JOHN BRIGHT

METHYL, *METH ul,* is the simplest hydrocarbon *radical* (group of atoms that acts as a unit in chemical reactions). It makes up part of many organic compounds. The methyl radical, CH_3-, contains one carbon atom and three hydrogen atoms.

The word *methyl* is used in naming many compounds that contain the radical. For example, CH_3OH is called methyl alcohol (methanol); CH_3COOCH_3 is methyl acetate, a solvent, and CH_3Cl is methyl chloride, a refrigerant. E. CAMPAIGNE

See also HYDROCARBON; METHANE; RADICAL; WOOD ALCOHOL.

METHYL BENZENE. See TOLUENE.

METHYLATED SPIRIT is denatured alcohol. See ALCOHOL.

METIC. See ATHENS (Industry and Trade).

MÉTIS. See MANITOBA (People; The Red River Colony); RED RIVER REBELLION; RIEL, LOUIS; SASKATCHEWAN REBELLION.

METIS, the goddess. See MINERVA.

METONYMY, *mee TAHN uh mih.* We often use words figuratively, rather than literally. Some of these forms of expressions are called *metonymy.* When we "turn on the light," we actually flip a switch, closing an electric circuit and causing the light. But we give the name of the effect to the cause. When we "listen to records," we really hear music, but we name the cause to mean the effect. When we pledge allegiance to the flag, we mean "the Republic for which it stands." The symbol replaces the thing symbolized. When we ask for "another cup," we really mean more coffee. The container symbolizes what it contains. These are common forms of metonymy.

In *synecdoche,* which is related to metonymy, we name the part for the whole. For instance, we use the name of an athletic team, but actually mean the school the team represents. CHARLES W. COOPER

See also FIGURE OF SPEECH.

METRE. See METER; METRIC SYSTEM.

359

METRIC SYSTEM

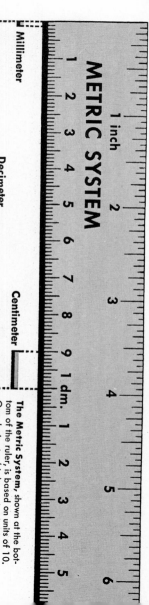

1 inch
2
3
4
5
6

METRIC SYSTEM

Millimeter Decimeter Centimeter

The Metric System, shown at the bottom of the ruler, is based on units of 10. One decimeter (dm) equals 3.937 inches, top, or one-tenth of a meter.

METRIC SYSTEM, *MET rick.* Scientists throughout the world measure lengths, distances, weights, and other values by a standard method, called the *metric system.* The word comes from *meter,* the principal unit of length in this system.

A commission of French scientists developed the metric system. France adopted it as the legal system of weights and measures in 1799. Its use was made compulsory in 1837. Most countries now use the metric system. After World War II, China, Egypt, and India adopted it. During the 1960's, Great Britain and most of the Commonwealth of Nations began to convert to the system. But the United States and Canada still use the English system. The metric system is generally considered easy to learn and to use.

How It Is Organized. In the metric system all units have a uniform scale of relation, based on the decimal. The principal unit is the *meter* which corresponds to the *yard* as a unit of length. The meter is 39.37 inches, or 1.093 yards. The scale of multiples and subdivisions of the meter is ten. All units of surface, volume, capacity, and weight are directly derived from the meter.

The relation between them is very simple because a definite volume of water is taken as the unit of capacity and mass. The *liter* corresponds to the *quart* as a unit of capacity. The liter also has multiples and subdivisions of ten. One liter contains one cubic *decimeter* of water and weighs one *kilogram.*

The following table shows the use of the decimal scale:

Ten millimeters = one centimeter
Ten centimeters = one decimeter
Ten decimeters = one meter
Ten meters = one decameter
Ten decameters = one hectometer
Ten hectometers = one kilometer
Ten kilometers = one myriameter

The same system applies to the other units, the *liter* and the *gram.* Ten *liters* are equal to one *decaliter,* or *dekaliter,* and ten *decigrams* are equal to one *gram.*

This uniform system of names is one of the advantages of the metric system. The various units of measure get their names by adding other prefixes to the chief units. Divisions of the chief units are tenths, hundredths, thousandths, and so on. They are formed by adding Latin prefixes. For example, *deci* means *one-tenth* (.1), *centi* means *one-hundredth* (.01), and *milli* means *one-thousandth* (.001). Higher denominations are formed by multiplying the basic unit by ten, a hundred, a thousand, and so on. Greek prefixes are added to the chief unit. For example, *myria* means 10,000; *kilo* means 1,000; *hecto* means 100, and *deca* means 10. The units to which these prefixes are added are the *meter, liter,* and *gram.*

Metric numbers are written decimally. The decimal point is placed immediately after the unit. For example, 156.735 m. reads 156 meters and 735 millimeters. Or, 156.735 g. reads 156 grams and 735 milligrams. Calculations with the metric system are easy because they

---

Wide World

International Track Events are usually measured in meters. Here, two runners battle to win a race of 1,500 meters, or slightly less than a mile.

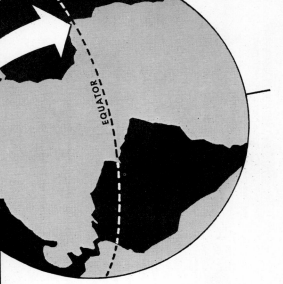

The Basis of the Metric System is the distance between the North Pole and the equator, which is about 6,200 miles. A line running from the North Pole to the equator has 10,000,000 equal parts. Each part is a meter, or 39.37 inches.

are made according to the decimal system. Any denomination may be changed to the next higher by moving the decimal point to the left. Any denomination may be reduced to the next lower by moving the decimal point to the right.

The Unit of Length. The unit of length is described in the article METER. The kilometer (1,000 meters) is used, like the English mile, to measure long distances. For example, Versailles is nineteen and one-half kilometers from Paris.

The Unit of Surface. Surface is measured with the square meter which is the area of a square whose sides each measure one meter. The multiples and subdivisions go by the square of ten, which is 100. One square decameter is equal to 100 square meters. One square decimeter is one-hundredth part of a square meter. The *are* and the *hectare* are used in most land measurements. The *are* has 100 square meters. The hectare has 100

METRIC SYSTEM

Meter	= 1.093 yards
	= 3.281 feet
	= 39.370 inches
Kilometer	= 0.621 mile
Square meter	= 1.196 square yards
	=10.764 square feet
Square centimeter	= 0.155 square inch
Square kilometer	= 0.386 square mile
Hectare	= 2.471 acres
Cubic meter	= 1.308 cubic yards
	=35.314 cubic feet
Cubic centimeter	= 0.061 cubic inch
Stere	= 0.275 cord (wood)
Liter	= 1.056 U.S. liquid quarts or
	0.880 English liquid quart
	= 0.908 dry quart
	= 0.264 U.S. gallon or
	0.220 English gallon
Hectoliter	= 2.837 U.S. bushels or
	2.75 English bushels
Gram	=15.432 grains
	= 0.032 troy ounce
	= 0.0352 avoirdupois ounce
Kilogram	= 2.2046 pounds avoirdupois
Metric ton	=2204.62 pounds avoirdupois
Carat	= 3.08 grains avoirdupois

ENGLISH MEASUREMENTS

Length	Yard	= 0.9144 meter
	Foot	= 0.3048 meter
	Inch	= 0.0254 meter
	Mile	= 1.609 kilometers
Surface	Square yard	= 0.836 square meter
	Square foot	= 0.092 square meter
	Square inch	= 6.45 square centimeters
	Square mile	= 2.590 square kilometers
	Acre	= 0.405 hectare
Volume	Cubic yard	= 0.764 cubic meter
	Cubic foot	= 0.028 cubic meter
	Cubic inch	=16.387 cubic centimeters
	Cord	= 3.624 steres
Capacity	U.S. liquid quart	= 0.946 liter
	Dry quart	= 1.111 liters
	U.S. gallon	= 3.785 liters
	English gallon	= 4.543 liters
	U.S. bushel	= 0.352 hectoliter
	English bushel	= 0.363 hectoliter
Weight	Grain	= 0.0648 gram
	Troy ounce	=31.103 grams
	Avoirdupois ounce	=28.35 grams
	Pound	= 0.4536 kilogram
	Short ton	= 0.907 metric ton

10 DECILITERS

equals

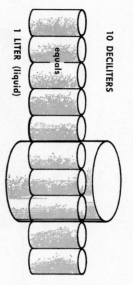

1 LITER (liquid)

The Liter Is the Basic Unit of Capacity in the metric system. It holds slightly more than the U.S. liquid quart.

ares or 10,000 square meters. Large areas, such as countries, are measured by square kilometers.

The Unit of Volume. A cubic meter is the unit used to measure volume. A cubic meter is a cube of which each edge is one meter. The multiples and subdivisions go by the cube of ten, which is 1,000. One cubic decameter is equal to 1,000 cubic meters. One cubic decimeter is equal to one-thousandth part of a cubic meter. When the cubic meter is used to measure wood it is called a *stere.*

The Unit of Capacity. A *liter* is the unit of capacity. A liter contains the quantity of one cubic decimeter of distilled water at its greatest density, or, at the temperature of 39.2 degrees Fahrenheit and at sea level. The liter is used to measure liquids such as milk and wine, and also for small fruit. Grain, vegetables, and liquids in casks are usually measured with the *hectoliter.*

The Unit of Weight. A *gram* is the unit of weight. A gram is the weight of one cubic centimeter of distilled water at its greatest density, or at a temperature of 39.2° F. at sea level. One thousand cubic centimeters, which equal one cubic decimeter, have the capacity of one liter and weigh 1,000 grams, or a kilogram. The kilogram is used to compute most weights. The metric ton (1,000 kilograms) is used for heavy articles. All the units in the metric system are related. A thousand kilograms, or a metric ton, is the weight of 1,000 cubic decimeters, or a cubic meter of water with a capacity of 1,000 liters, or a kiloliter.

The American five-cent piece weighs five grams and has a diameter of two centimeters. A silver half dollar of United States money weighs twelve and one-half grams. Eighty half dollars weigh one kilogram. In fine scientific weights, the unit is the *microgram,* which is a thousandth part of a milligram, or a millionth part of a gram. The *carat,* the weight for measuring diamonds and other precious stones, also has been standardized since 1913. The new international carat weighs 200 milligrams, or one fifth of a gram. Before it was standardized, the carat weighed 205.3 milligrams.

The Metric System in Modern Science. Scientists use the metric system in defining physical and chemical constants, or the "laws of nature." A spectrum is used to measure such microscopic distances as the diameter of an atom or electron. The unit of measure for radio waves and other infrared radiations is the meter. In dealing with visual light (all the colors from deep red to violet), the ultra-violet, X rays, and cosmic rays, the unit is the *micron.* A micron is one thousandth of a millimeter. A millimicron is one millionth of a millimeter. The Angstrom unit is one tenth of a millimicron, or 0.00000003937 inches. Scientists working with spectra can measure distances as small as one thousand-billionths of an inch. Many scientists now use a wave length of orange light to determine the length of a meter.

In defining scientific constants involving lengths, masses, and time, the centimeter-gram-second or C.G.S., units are used. For example, a mass of one gram is sus-

—— TABLES OF THE METRIC SYSTEM ——

MEASURES OF LENGTH

A myriameter (mym) is equal to 10,000 meters
A kilometer (km) is equal to 1,000 meters
A hectometer (hm) is equal to 100 meters
A decameter (dkm) is equal to 10 meters

A Meter

A decimeter (dm) is equal to 0.1 of a meter
A centimeter (cm) is equal to 0.01 of a meter
A millimeter (mm) is equal to 0.001 of a meter

SURFACE MEASURES

A square kilometer (km^2) is equal to 1,000,000 square meters
A square hectometer or hectare (ha) = 10,000 square meters
A square decameter or are (a) = 100 square meters

A Square Meter

A square decimeter (dm^2) = 0.01 of a square meter
A square centimeter (cm^2) = 0.0001 of a square meter
A square millimeter (mm^2) = 0.000,001 of a square meter

CUBIC MEASURES

A cubic hectometer = 1,000,000 cubic meters
A cubic decameter = 1,000 cubic meters

Cubic Meter

A cubic decimeter (dm^3) = 0.001 of a cubic meter
A cubic centimeter (cm^3) = 0.000,001 of a cubic meter
A cubic millimeter (mm^3) = 0.000,000,001 of a cubic meter

MEASURES OF CAPACITY

A hectoliter (hl) = 100 liters
A decaliter (dkl) = 10 liters

Liter

A deciliter (dl) = 0.1 liter
A centiliter (cl) = 0.01 liter
A milliliter (ml) = 0.001 liter

MEASURES OF WEIGHT

A metric ton (t) = 1,000 kilograms
A kilogram (kg) = 1,000 grams
A hectogram (hg) = 100 grams
A decagram (dkg) = 10 grams

Gram

A decigram (dg) = 0.1 gram
A centigram (cg) = 0.01 gram
A milligram (mg) = 0.001 gram

The abbreviations in the tables above were officially adopted by the International Congress of Weights and Measures.

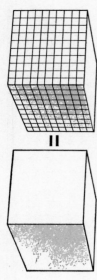

1 CU. METER equals 35.3 CU. FT.

pended by a long silk thread in a room free of air currents. A constant force, strong enough to give the gram mass a horizontal velocity of one centimeter a second in one second of time, is applied. The resulting unit of force is one *dyne*.

Scientists use the kilogram as the standard of mass in the meter-kilogram-second, or M.K.S., system, which also is based on the metric system. The system uses the kilogram, or 1,000 grams, as the unit of mass, the meter as the unit of length, and the second as the unit of time. The unit of force measured by this system is the *newton*, which is equal to 100,000 dynes.

The metric system is also used in electricity. For example, the *ampere*, a unit used to measure electric current, is defined in terms of newtons.

Use in the United States. In 1866 Congress passed a law making the metric system legal in the United States for those who wish to use it. The Bureau of Standards in Washington adopted the metric system in 1893 as the standard to be used in legally defining the yard and the pound. It is now used in the Coast and Geodetic Survey, in all government departments dealing in tariff operations, in coining money, and in weighing foreign mail. Government departments dealing in tariff operations use it, and it is the legal unit for electrical measure. Eyeglass lenses are prescribed and ground by metric tables. Radio stations use it in defining the wave lengths which are assigned to them.

Several attempts have been made to bring the metric system into general use in the United States. As far back as 1790, Thomas Jefferson, who was then Secretary of State, recommended that Congress introduce a decimal system in this country. Later, in 1821, John Quincy Adams advocated the adoption of the metric system in a report to Congress on weights and measures. With engineers and the business world using both the metric and older units of measure, there is some confusion. Probably in a few generations the metric system will be used generally. Anyone who plans a career in business, foreign trade, civil service, engineering or any branch of pure or applied science should understand the metric system.

International Use. The International Bureau of Weights and Measures is located at Sèvres, France, just outside Paris. It was established by representatives of all the civilized countries in the world. International standards for the meter and the kilogram are set up there. The standard for the kilogram is made of a special alloy of platinum and iridium. Exact duplicates of this standard are kept by every country represented at the International Bureau. The one in the United States is kept at the Bureau of Standards in Washington, D.C. It was received on Jan. 2, 1890, by President Benjamin Harrison. Before 1960, the standard for the meter was a platinum-iridium meter bar. Now, the meter is more accurately defined as 1,650,763.73 wavelengths of the orange-red light from the isotope krypton-86, measured in a vacuum. OLIVER J. LEE

Related Articles in WORLD BOOK include:

Ampere	International Bureau of Weights and Measures	Liter
Angstrom Unit	Kilogram	Meter
Carat	Kilogram-meter	Micron
Centimeter	Kilometer	Ton
Dyne		Weights and Measures
Gram		

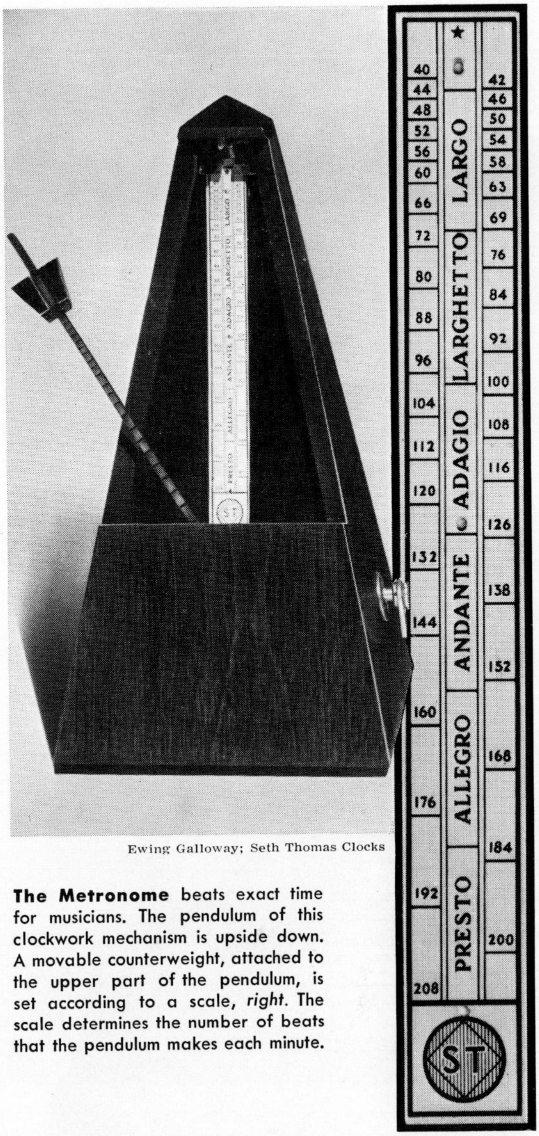
LARGO
LARGHETTO
ADAGIO
ANDANTE
ALLEGRO
PRESTO
40 44 48 52 56 60 66 72 80 88 96 104 112 120 132 144 160 176 192 208
42 46 50 54 58 63 69 76 84 92 100 108 116 126 138 152 168 184 200
ST

Ewing Galloway; Seth Thomas Clocks

The Metronome beats exact time for musicians. The pendulum of this clockwork mechanism is upside down. A movable counterweight, attached to the upper part of the pendulum, is set according to a scale, *right*. The scale determines the number of beats that the pendulum makes each minute.

METRONOME, *MET roh nohm*, is an instrument that beats time for musicians. Dietrich Winkel of Amsterdam, a Dutch inventor, probably invented it. But the German Johann Maelzel patented it in 1816. The common type consists of a hollow wooden box with a weighted pendulum. A movable counterweight is attached to the pendulum. The mechanism ticks as the pendulum moves. The lower the counterweight is set, the faster the machine ticks. Most metronomes are wound by hand. But some metronomes operate by electricity. CHARLES B. RIGHTER

METROPOLITAN is the title of an archbishop of the Eastern Orthodox Church. Occasionally, Roman Catholic archbishops are called *metropolitans*. In A.D. 341, the Council of Antioch decreed that the bishop of the *metropolis* (capital city) of an ecclesiastical province should rank above the other bishops of the province. The bishops were to consult the metropolitan about all matters other than regular diocesan affairs. See also ARCHBISHOP. R. PIERCE BEAVER

George Woodruff

METROPOLITAN AREA

METROPOLITAN AREA includes a central city and the area that surrounds it. The cities, boroughs, villages, towns, or townships in the metropolitan area outside the central city are called *suburbs*. In the United States, metropolitan areas are officially called *standard metropolitan statistical areas*. Two adjacent metropolitan areas may form a *standard consolidated area*. The United States government defines a metropolitan area as a region with at least one city with a population of 50,000 or more. The area also includes the entire county in which the city is located. At least 75 per cent of the county's labor force must be nonagricultural. The term *greater* as applied to a city, such as Greater Paris, means a metropolitan area.

Metropolitan areas have developed in every country in the world. As cities grow, people move outside the city boundaries and form suburbs. Since the early 1900's, the most important population shift has been an almost steady flow of families from large cities to the surrounding suburbs. The development of modern transportation and paved roads and streets has been chiefly responsible for this mass movement.

Suburbanites, the people who live in the suburbs, view the city as the hub of their work and business activities. They also use its recreational, professional, commercial, and cultural facilities and services. As the workday begins, thousands of commuters speed toward the city by automobile or train on paths that resemble spokes on a wheel. People live miles away, but travel the distance twice daily between work and home. Commuters like to live in suburbs because they may enjoy uncongested outdoor living, open spaces, and the countryside. A few commuters may travel from the city to work in the suburbs.

Industries and businesses often follow households into the suburbs. They seek locations where parking is plentiful, where land is cheaper and available in larger plots, and where building restrictions may be less confining than in the cities. As this process continues,

Greater Chicago, a standard metropolitan area, includes towns and villages far beyond the city limits. It covers eight Illinois and Indiana counties. Railroads and highways link Chicago with the many suburbs that spring up as people move out from the city.

Commuters may spend several hours a day traveling to and from work. Trains, buses, and cars speed them to their jobs.

WISCONSIN
ILLINOIS

50 MILES

McHENRY COUNTY

Woodstock

LAKE COUNTY

KANE COUNTY

Elgin

DU PAGE COUNTY

COOK COUNTY

Aurora

Joliet

WILL COUNTY

COOK COUNTY

25 MILES

Kenosha

CHICAGO

ILLINOIS
INDIANA

Hammond

Gary

LAKE COUNTY

PORTER COUNTY

Valparaiso

SCALE IN MILES
0 5 10 15 20 25

SYMBOLS

City of Chicago

Incorporated Places of 2,500 or More

Urban Places

County Lines

State Lines

Railroads

Tollroads and Expressways

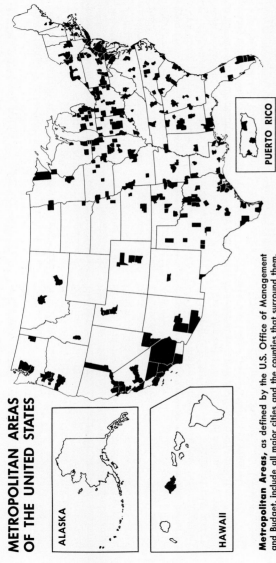

METROPOLITAN AREAS OF THE UNITED STATES

ALASKA

HAWAII

PUERTO RICO

Metropolitan Areas, as defined by the U.S. Office of Management and Budget, include all major cities and the counties that surround them.

another great metropolitan area may be established.

In the United States, over 119 million persons, or nearly two-thirds of the population, live in the 233 standard metropolitan areas (including 3 in Puerto Rico). In Canada, about half of the people live in 19 metropolitan areas. More than one-third of the people in England live in the country's six large conurbations. In France, one out of every six persons lives in metropolitan Paris.

Most of the people of a metropolitan area live in the city, but an increasing number drift toward the suburbs. For example, about 40 of every 100 persons in metropolitan Chicago live outside the city limits. About 60 of every 100 persons in Greater Buenos Aires live in the adjacent suburbs. Almost 60 of every 100 residents in Greater Los Angeles live in surrounding suburbs.

Problems of Metropolitan Areas

Conflict in Authority. Most metropolitan areas have no centralized, metropolitan government to handle problems that affect the entire area. Government is almost completely decentralized. Each city, town, village, or other municipality usually has its own government. Little or no relationship exists between these governments and that of the central city. Some rural areas have no local government except that of the county in which they are located. The 233 standard metropolitan areas of the United States have more than 18,400 local government units. These include over 300 counties, 2,500 townships, 4,100 municipalities, 5,400 special districts, and 6,000 school districts.

The process of government becomes scrambled with overlapping authority, and the results can only be unsatisfactory. Local government within the area remains fragmented. Many metropolitan areas straddle county and even state lines. Economic and social organizations, such as telephone companies, usually deal with the metropolitan area as a single unit. Some special districts and municipal authorities have been set up to provide centralized, but limited, administration and services to a metropolitan area.

People who live in a metropolitan area often have

little feeling of political unity among themselves. Many able, civic-minded citizens who work in the city live in the suburbs. They have nothing to say about the government of the city. Yet this government may have a profound effect on their businesses, because it influences the entire metropolitan area. In this way, many cities lose the civic interests and moral resources that city workers contribute to their suburban communities.

Finances. The widespread movement from the city to the suburbs affects the financial position of both areas. A city finds its land values declining, its tax resources dropping, and blighted areas appearing. Industries may contribute to the development of the suburbs in which they are located. But they do not contribute to the maintenance of the central city.

A city often finds that it must provide services, such as health inspections, for the suburbs as well as for people within its own borders. It may impose taxes, because of the decline in the value of city land. Suburbanites usually resist such taxes.

Many suburbs have been built up almost overnight because of a growing need for housing. Some suburbs have only homes, and no taxable businesses and industries. They cannot raise enough money to provide the services needed by all new urban communities, especially with young families and small children. Such services include schools, police and fire protection, water and sewage systems, paved streets, building inspection, public-health services, recreational facilities, street and traffic lights, and zoning.

A large industry may be located in a region and be taxed by the government there. But its workers may live in the surrounding areas that do not receive any tax revenue from the industry. As a result, slums and blighted areas may appear quickly in suburbs that lack tax resources and means of financing their services.

Metropolitan Area Plans

Various plans have been devised in attempts to provide urban areas with the kinds of governments they need and deserve. But no agreement has been reached as to what the solution should be. The objectives of a metropolitan plan could include: (1) unity of government in the area, (2) supplying all the people with the services of government that an urban area needs, and (3) allowing these services to be provided locally rather than by state and national governments. Many authorities believe that long-range regional planning that considers the needs of both city and suburbs is essential to any solution. See City Planning.

Intergovernmental Cooperation. In the United States, many neighboring local units have agreed to work together. For example, they may agree to cooperate in such services as police and fire protection, public utilities, centralized purchasing, and regional planning. Authorities believe that these useful arrangements may answer the needs of the moment. But they do not permanently solve the problem of providing efficient and economical metropolitan government.

Annexation has long been used as one solution. Under this plan, the city *annexes* (absorbs) its outlying areas. In the past, cities usually grew to their present size by annexation. But people who live on the outskirts now generally oppose this method. They do not want to lose their governmental independence. They do not want to be merely small parts of a large city.

Extramural Jurisdiction. In some states, central cities have the power to exercise government control in areas outside municipal boundaries. For example, Alabama grants municipalities the right to exercise broad powers three miles outside their city limits. These powers include police and sanitary regulation. Municipalities also may levy business taxes and control subdivisions across city lines.

County Government in some states provides urban services for areas outside city limits. California has county governments that supply police and fire protection, health and welfare services, and other aid to such areas. But, in most states, counties lack the personnel or organization to handle these functions efficiently.

A metropolitan county government provides urban services for the entire county. For example, Dade County, which includes Greater Miami, Fla., operates under this plan. Its 13-man county commission hires a county manager. The commission carries out plans for serving and developing the entire county. Municipalities within the county handle only local affairs. Voters from Miami and from counties and districts in the metropolitan area elect members of the commission. Cities that reach 60,000 population elect other members.

City-county consolidation has been achieved in a number of cities, including Philadelphia, San Francisco, and New York City. It merges city and county functions under one government.

Special Districts or municipal authorities may consist of two or more local units in a metropolitan area. They have been set up to provide specific services of government, such as water supply and sewage disposal. Many districts or authorities must use the revenue from their services to pay for the construction, maintenance, and operation of the necessary facilities.

Districts and authorities have paved the way for more governmental unity. But they have also added to, rather than reduced, the complexity of local government. One of the largest and most successful municipal authorities

is the Port of New York Authority. It handles port development and transportation matters within a 20-mile radius of New York City, in both New York and New Jersey (see Port of New York Authority). Another authority, the Metropolitan Water District of Southern California, serves about $3\frac{1}{2}$ million persons in 13 cities, including Los Angeles. Pennsylvania has more than 1,000 municipal authorities to build and operate schools, waterworks, sewage disposal systems, parking facilities, and other utilities. Many authorities serve more than one local unit.

Metropolitan Federation merges all local governments in a metropolitan area into a new unit called *the federated city*. The local units retain their own identities and carry on the functions of local government that they are best fitted to handle. The federated city accepts specific functions for the entire region. It is then given the necessary taxing authority to finance them. London operates under a metropolitan federation.

The Municipality of Metropolitan Toronto merges the city with 12 suburban units of government. The federation controls water supply and distribution, sewage disposal, trunk sewers, metropolitan road systems, land-use planning, police protection, welfare services, and public transportation. Member municipalities are responsible for such functions as fire protection and health services. The federation covers about 240 square miles and serves about 1,900,000 persons.   H. F. Alderfer

Related Articles in World Book include:

City (table: 50 Largest Community
  Metropolitan Areas)   State
City Government   Government
City Planning   Urban Renewal
Local   Suburb
Government

METROPOLITAN LIFE INSURANCE COMPANY is one of the largest private business organizations in the world. It has more life insurance in force than any other company. It insures about one of every five persons in the United States and Canada. Metropolitan Life is a *mutual company* (operated exclusively for the benefit of its policyholders). The company's home office is in New York City. For assets and the amount of life insurance in force, see Insurance (table: 30 Largest U.S. and Canadian Life Insurance Companies).

Metropolitan Life sells both personal and group insurance. Its main business is in life insurance, but it also sells health insurance and annuities. It is one of the world's largest private owners and developers of real estate. It also ranks among the world's leading mortgage holders. The company carries on an extensive program of health and safety education. As part of this program, the company has distributed almost 2 billion booklets on various health subjects.

Metropolitan Life was formed in 1868. It was one of the successors of the National Union Life and Limb Insurance Company. This earlier company had insured servicemen during the Civil War. Metropolitan Life gained much of its early success by selling small amounts of insurance to immigrants, laborers, and other persons with low incomes. Few U.S. insurance companies in the late 1800's made any attempt to insure such people. From 1909 to 1953, the company provided a visiting nurse service for its policyholders. This visiting nurse service pioneered in setting up public health nursing services.

The Metropolitan Life Insurance Company

METROPOLITAN MUSEUM OF ART

public restaurant features a pool that has eight life-size fountain sculptures in it.

The Collections of Ancient Art include Egyptian prehistoric pottery, wall paintings, sculpture, and jewelry. An original Egyptian tomb dated about 2460 B.C. also belongs to these collections. Articles from Greece and Rome include vases and stone sculptures, bronzes, gems, jewelry, glass, and wall paintings. Etruscan art includes terra-cotta work. Ceramics, ivories, metalwork, and sculpture represent art from Mesopotamia and ancient Persia.

The Collections of Eastern Art include oriental paintings, sculpture, pottery, lacquerware, and jade from India, Japan, and China. These collections also contain examples of Islamic art such as rugs and textiles, pottery, wood carvings, and glass.

The Collections of European Art include 43 galleries of paintings from the 1200's to the present day. The museum also has examples of European sculpture, furniture, tapestries, textiles, pottery, glassware, metalwork, and other decorative arts from the Middle Ages and later periods. The museum also has collections of arms and armor, musical instruments, prints, and drawings.

American Art is represented by paintings from the Colonial period to the present time, and by sculptures. The museum also has American rooms with furniture and decorations dating from 1640 to the early 1800's.

The Junior Museum in the south wing of the museum is the center for children's activities. It has its own special exhibitions, library, auditorium, and studio. The Costume Institute collection has more than 15,000 articles of dress that cover 400 years of world history and five continents.

The Cloisters, located in Fort Tryon Park, is a branch of the museum devoted to medieval art. Its collections include tapestries, ivories, metalwork, sculpture, and

Spanish Renaissance Patio is the entrance to the Thomas J. Watson Library at the Metropolitan Museum of Art. The patio was once part of a private New York City home. It was dismantled and reassembled at the museum. The library was opened in 1965.

D. Jordan Wilson, Pix from Publix

METROPOLITAN MUSEUM OF ART in New York City is the largest art museum in the United States. It has a collection of over 365,000 works of art. The city of New York owns the building, but the collections belong to a corporation which runs the museum under a charter granted in 1870. The museum contains an auditorium which seats about 700 persons. Its store sells art books, color reproductions of art, silver, and jewelry. The

C. A. Peterson, Publix

Metropolitan Museum of Art in New York City attracts millions of visitors each year. The museum was opened at its present site on Fifth Avenue and 82nd Street in 1880. It now contains about 20 acres of floor space in a building 1,000 feet long.

METROPOLITAN OPERA ASSOCIATION

Culver

stained glass. The Cloisters features parts of original monasteries and churches that were brought from France and Spain, and lovely outdoor gardens.

Critically reviewed by METROPOLITAN MUSEUM OF ART

METROPOLITAN OPERA ASSOCIATION is one of the most important opera companies in the world. The company performs at the Metropolitan Opera House in the Lincoln Center for the Performing Arts in New York City. The 14-story opera house, which opened in 1966, cost over $42½ million and seats over 3,700 persons. It replaced the original Metropolitan Opera House, which opened in 1883. The first production in the old Metropolitan Opera House was Charles Gounod's *Faust*. During the 1932-1933 season, the company changed its name to the Metropolitan Opera Association. The "Met" broadcast its first performance in 1931, and televised its first complete opera, Giuseppe Verdi's *Otello*, in 1948. See also BING, RUDOLF.

Critically reviewed by the METROPOLITAN OPERA ASSOCIATION

METTERNICH, *MET er nick,* **PRINCE VON** (1773-1859), an Austrian statesman and diplomat, dominated Europe from 1814 to 1848. That period is often called "The Age of Metternich." Metternich believed that democracy and nationalism would lead to disaster. He became the guiding force behind the efforts of Austria, Prussia, and Russia to crush nationalist revolts throughout Europe.

Metternich began his long diplomatic career in 1797. He became Austrian ambassador to Prussia in 1803 and to France in 1806. As Austrian minister of foreign af-

Prince Von Metternich

Brown Bros.

Prince Von Metternich, *left,* met with Napoleon at Dresden on June 26, 1813, and assured him of Austrian neutrality in Europe. But in August, Austria joined Prussia and Russia against Napoleon.

fairs (1809-1848), he helped establish the *Vienna System*, which controlled Europe after Napoleon's defeat in 1815. He lost office in the 1848 Revolution, and fled to England. He returned to Vienna in 1851, but never held office again.

His full name was KLEMENS WENZEL NEPOMUK LOTHAR VON METTERNICH. He was born in Koblenz. He married the granddaughter of Prince Wenzel Kaunitz, chancellor of Austria.

ROBERT G. L. WAITE

See also AUSTRIA (Metternich and Revolution); VIENNA, CONGRESS OF.

METZ, *mets* (pop. 102,771; met. area 147,154; alt. 565 ft.), is a manufacturing center about 175 miles northeast of Paris. The city serves as the capital of the department of Moselle. The factories of Metz produce munitions, muslin, hats, and hosiery.

The history of the city goes back to the Roman conquest, after which it was known as *Divodurum,* then *Mediomatrica,* and finally, *Metz.* The Huns plundered Metz in A.D. 451. It was part of the Holy Roman Empire from 962 until the French captured the city in 1552. But France did not get formal possession of Metz until 1648. The Germans captured Metz in 1870, and held it until the Treaty of Versailles returned the city to France after World War I. German troops captured Metz early in World War II. Allied forces freed the city in 1944.

MEUSE RIVER, *muz,* rises in the Langre Plateau of eastern France, and flows north past Verdun through the Ardennes highlands. The river then flows northeast through Belgium past Namur and Liège. North of Liège, the river enters The Netherlands. Here, it makes

EDWARD W. FOX

a sweeping curve northwest and empties into the North Sea south of Rotterdam. The Meuse River is 575 miles long. In Belgium and The Netherlands, it is called the MAAS.

Several navigable canals join the Meuse along its course. Near Toul, France, it connects with the Marne-Rhine Canal. At Liège, the Meuse is linked with the Albert Canal, which goes to Antwerp. At Maastricht, the river meets the Juliana Canal.   ROBERT E. DICKINSON

MEXICAN HAIRLESS is a dog that has no coat of hair. Its skin is bare, except for a little tuft of hair on its forehead and a slight fuzz along its tail. The rest of the skin is a spotted, pinkish color. A Mexican hairless dog weighs about 12 pounds. It has a narrow head and a pointed nose. Its body is lightly built, with a rounded back and a long tail. The dog's skin feels hot to the touch. People at one time believed that the warmth of the dog would cure ailments if it was held against their bodies. The Mexican hairless probably originated in China in the 1300's. The dogs were first imported into Mexico by sailors.

JOSEPHINE Z. RINE

MEXICAN WAR (1846-1848) was fought between the United States and Mexico over disagreements that had been accumulating for two decades. In the course of the war, United States forces invaded Mexico and occupied the Mexican capital, Mexico City. By the Treaty of Guadalupe Hidalgo, the United States acquired from Mexico the regions of California, Nevada, and Utah, most of Arizona and New Mexico, and parts of Colorado and Wyoming. But many historians believe the war was an unnecessary attack on a weaker nation.

Causes of the War

Background of the War. When Texas revolted against the Mexican government in 1836, Mexico refused to recognize its independence. The Mexican government warned the United States that if Texas were admitted to the Union, Mexico would declare war. James K. Polk was elected President of the United States in 1844. He had declared himself in favor of annexing Texas. In

1845, Texas was made a state. Mexico broke off relations with the United States, but did not declare war. The question of annexing Texas could thus have been settled by peaceful means. However, other quarrels began to develop.

One of these disputes was the question of the boundary between Texas and Mexico. Texas claimed the Rio Grande as its southwestern border. Mexico said that Texas had never extended farther than the Nueces River. In the second place, Mexico owed citizens of the United States about $3 million in compensation for lives and property lost in Mexico through revolution, theft, and confiscation since the 1820's. By the 1840's, many Americans demanded that the United States collect these debts by force.

Most important of all, feeling was growing in the United States that the country had a "manifest destiny" to expand westward into new lands (see MANIFEST DESTINY). The frontier movement had brought Americans into Mexican territory, especially California. Mexico was too weak either to control or to populate its northern territories. Both American and Mexican inhabitants were discontented with the government of Mexico City. California seemed almost ready to declare itself independent.

Events Leading Up to the War. In the fall of 1845, President Polk sent John Slidell to Mexico as American minister. Slidell was to offer to pay Mexico $25 million and cancel all claims for damages, if Mexico would accept the Rio Grande boundary and sell New Mexico and California to the United States. If Mexico refused to sell New Mexico and California, Slidell was to offer to cancel the claims on condition that Mexico agreed to the Rio Grande boundary.

A revolution was going on in Mexico when Slidell arrived. Both the old and new presidents were afraid

Americans at Home followed the course of the war in newspaper reports. Many felt the war could have been averted.

War News from Mexico by Richard Caton Woodville,
National Academy of Design, New York City.

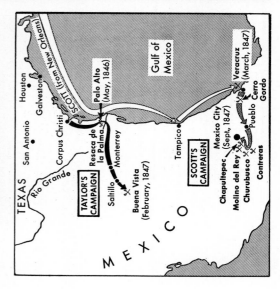

Campaigns of the Mexican War

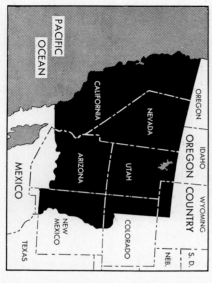

Mexico Lost This Land to the United States.

their enemies would denounce them as cowards if they made concessions to the United States. They refused to see Slidell, who came home and told Polk that Mexico needed to be "chastised." Meanwhile, Polk had ordered Major General Zachary Taylor, who was stationed with 3,000 men on the Nueces River, to advance to the Rio Grande. Taylor reached the river in April, 1846. A Mexican force crossed the river to meet him. On April 25, a small body of American cavalry was defeated by a larger body of Mexicans.

Polk had already decided to ask Congress to declare war on Mexico. The news of the battle gave him the chance to say that Mexico had "invaded our territory and shed American blood on American soil." In reality, Mexico had as good a claim as the United States to the soil where the blood was shed. But on May 13, 1846, Congress declared war on Mexico.

The War

The Campaigns. The United States had two aims. The Americans wanted to occupy the territory that Mexico had been asked to sell. They also wished to invade Mexico in order to force the Mexicans to agree to peace.

The Occupation of New Mexico and California. Brigadier General Stephen W. Kearny set out from Fort Leavenworth in June, 1846, with about 1,700 troops. He occupied Santa Fe, N.Mex., in August. Part of his force marched south, crossed the Rio Grande, and occupied the Mexican city of Chihuahua in March, 1847. Meanwhile, Kearny himself pushed across the desert to California, where Captain Robert F. Stockton of the Navy and Captain John C. Frémont of the Army were leading American forces in a second campaign. By January, 1847, the Stars and Stripes flew over all the territory the United States had demanded. But Mexico was still not ready to yield.

Taylor's Campaign. Before war officially began, General Zachary Taylor had driven the Mexicans across the lower Rio Grande to Matamoros in the two battles of Palo Alto and Resaca de la Palma. On May 18, 1846, he crossed the river and occupied Matamoros. After waiting for new troops, he moved his army up the river

and marched against the important city of Monterrey. Monterrey fell on September 24, after a hard-fought battle. Before the end of the year, Taylor had occupied Saltillo and Victoria, important towns of northeastern Mexico. But Mexico still refused to negotiate.

Polk and his advisers decided to land an army at Veracruz, on the east coast, and strike a blow at Mexico City. Many of Taylor's best troops were ordered to join Major General Winfield Scott, who was placed in charge of the new campaign. President Antonio Santa Anna of Mexico was in command of the Mexican Army. He learned of the American plans and immediately led a large army against Taylor at Buena Vista, in the mountains beyond Saltillo. The Mexicans were badly defeated. Taylor became a hero because of his victories, and was elected President of the United States in 1848.

Scott's Campaign. General Scott was at this time the officer of highest rank in the United States Army. With a force of about 10,000 men, he landed near Veracruz on March 9, 1847. Twenty days later he captured the city, and on April 8 he began his advance toward the Mexican capital. The American Army stormed a mountain pass at Cerro Gordo on April 17 and 18 and pushed on. A few miles away from Mexico City, American troops fought and won the battles of Contreras and Churubusco on August 19 and 20. The Mexican Army was superior in numbers but, again, was poorly equipped and poorly led.

After a two weeks' armistice, the Americans won a battle at Molino del Rey and stormed and captured the hilltop fortress of Chapultepec. On the following day the Americans marched into Mexico City.

The Peace Treaty. Despite the succession of American victories, Polk could not induce the Mexican government to negotiate a peace treaty. In April, 1847, he sent Nicholas P. Trist, Chief Clerk of the Department of State, to join Scott's army in Mexico and attempt to open diplomatic negotiations with Santa Anna. When the armistice of August failed, the President recalled Trist. But Santa Anna resigned shortly after Scott entered the Mexican capital. Mexico established a new government, and it was willing to accept the American demands. At the request of the Mexican leaders and General Scott, Trist agreed to remain in Mexico and negotiate a settlement.

The treaty was signed on Feb. 2, 1848, at the little village of Guadalupe Hidalgo, near Mexico City. By this time, many people in the United States wanted to annex all Mexico. But the treaty required Mexico to give up only the territory Polk had originally asked for—the Rio Grande region, New Mexico, and California. The United States paid Mexico $15 million for this territory. Later, in 1853, the Gadsden Purchase gave the United States an additional 29,640 square miles (see GADSDEN PURCHASE).

Results of the War. The United States gained more than 525,000 square miles of territory as a result of the Mexican War. But the war also revived the quarrels over slavery. Here was new territory. Was it to be slave or free? The Compromise of 1850 made California a free state and set up the principle of "popular sovereignty." That meant letting the people of a territory decide whether it would be slave or free. But popular sovereignty later led to bitter disagreement and became one of the underlying causes of war. So the Mexican

The Battle of San Pasqual was a short, bloody fight between United States and Mexican troops near San Diego, Calif., on Dec. 6, 1846. Col. Stephen Watts Kearny led the United States forces.

Oil painting by Walter Francis, The Bancroft Library, University of California, Berkeley

War was an indirect cause of the Civil War. See COMPROMISE OF 1850; SQUATTER SOVEREIGNTY.

The Mexican War gave training to many officers who later fought in the Civil War. Those who fought in the Mexican campaigns included Ulysses S. Grant, William T. Sherman, George B. McClellan, George Gordon Meade, Robert E. Lee, Thomas "Stonewall" Jackson, and Jefferson Davis.

Principal Battles

The chief battles of the Mexican War included:

Palo Alto, *PAL oh AL toh,* was one of the earliest battles of the war. Gen. Taylor's troops defeated Mexican forces under Gen. Mariano Arista on May 8, 1846, on a plain 8 miles northeast of Brownsville, Tex.

Resaca de la Palma, *rreh SAH kah thay lah PAHL mah.* A 2,300-man army under Taylor crushed Arista's 5,000 Mexican soldiers in Cameron County, near Brownsville, Tex., on May 9, 1846. Taylor's two victories allowed him to cross the Rio Grande and invade Mexico.

Buena Vista, *BWAY nah VEES tah.* Near the ranch of Buena Vista, Mexico, Taylor's 5,000-man force successfully defended a narrow mountain pass against Santa Anna's army of from 16,000 to 20,000 men. Through this battle, fought on Feb. 22 and 23, 1847, the Americans established their hold on northeastern Mexico.

Cerro Gordo, *SEHR oh GAWR doh,* ranks among the most important battles the United States forces fought on the march from Veracruz to Mexico City. A mountain pass near Jalapa, Cerro Gordo lies 60 miles north-

west of Veracruz. General Scott's 9,000-man force attacked 13,000 Mexicans under Santa Anna, and forced them to flee. The battle, fought on April 17 and 18, 1847, cleared the way to Mexico City.

Churubusco, *CHOO roo VOOS koh.* In the small village of Churubusco, six miles south of Mexico City, Scott's invading army won another major victory on Aug. 20, 1847. Scott's soldiers stormed the fortified camp of Contreras, then attacked the Mexican force at Churubusco. The Mexicans finally fled, and sought refuge within the walls of the capital city. The Americans had about 9,000 men in the battle; the Mexicans, about 30,000.

Chapultepec, *chah POOL tay PEK,* was the last battle of the war before the capture of Mexico City. On Sept. 12, 1847, Scott's men attacked Chapultepec, a fortified hill guarding the city gates. The attacks continued the following day until the Mexicans retreated to Mexico City. On September 14, Scott's troops entered the Mexican capital.

NORMAN A. GRAEBNER

Related Articles in WORLD BOOK include:

Arista, Mariano
Davis, Jefferson
Frémont, John C.
Grant, Ulysses S.
  (Early Army Career)
Guadalupe Hidalgo,
  Treaty of
Jackson, "Stonewall,"
  Thomas J.
Lee, Robert E.
  (The Mexican War)

McClellan, George B.
Mexico (War with Texas
  and the U.S.)
Polk, James K.
Santa Anna,
  Antonio L. de
Scott, Winfield
Sherman (William T.)
Taylor, Zachary
Texas (History)
Wilmot Proviso

MEXICO

MEXICO is the northernmost country of Latin America. It lies just south of the United States. The Rio Grande forms about two-thirds of the boundary between Mexico and the United States. Among all the countries of the Western Hemisphere, only the United States and Brazil have more people than Mexico. Mexico City is the capital and largest city of Mexico. New York City and Chicago are the only cities in North America that are larger than Mexico City.

To understand Mexico, it is necessary to view the nation's long early history. Hundreds of years ago, the Indians of Mexico built large cities, developed a calendar, invented a counting system, and used a form of writing. The last Indian empire in Mexico—that of the Aztec—fell to Spanish invaders in 1521. For the next 300 years, Mexico was a Spanish colony. The Spaniards took Mexico's riches and kept the Indians poor and uneducated. But they also introduced many changes in farming, government, industry, and religion.

During the Spanish colonial period, a third group of people developed in Mexico. These people, who had both Indian and white ancestors, became known as *mestizos*. Today, the great majority of Mexicans are *mestizos*. Some of them think of the Spaniards as intruders and take great pride in their Indian ancestry. A number of government programs stress the Indian role in Mexican culture. In 1949, the government made an Indian the symbol of Mexican nationality. He was

Cuauhtémoc, the last Aztec emperor. Cuauhtémoc's bravery under Spanish torture made him Mexico's greatest hero.

Few other countries have so wide a variety of landscapes and climates within such short distances of one another. Towering mountains and high, rolling plateaus cover more than two-thirds of Mexico. The climate, land formation, and plant life in these rugged highlands may vary greatly within a short distance. Mexico also has tropical forests, dry deserts, and fertile valleys.

Manufacturing is Mexico's fastest-growing industry, but agriculture has great importance. Leading manufactured products include cement, chemicals, clothing, and processed foods. About a million tourists visit Mexico each year and account for a large part of the nation's income. Crops are grown on only about an eighth of Mexico's total land area. The rest of the land is too dry, mountainous, or otherwise unsuitable for crops. But Mexico is one of the world's leading pro-

The contributors of this article are Homer Aschmann, of the University of California, author of The Central Desert of Baja California: Demography and Ecology; Frank Brandenburg, of The American University, author of The Making of Modern Mexico; Dwight S. Brothers of Harvard University, co-author of Mexican Financial Development; and Robert E. Quirk of Indiana University, author of The Mexican Revolution, 1914-1915.

WORLD BOOK photo by Henry Gill

Snow-Capped Mountains tower over over what has been the heart of Mexico since the days of the Aztec Indians. The three peaks of Ixtacíhuatl, an inactive volcano, rise southeast of Mexico City and can be seen from the capital.

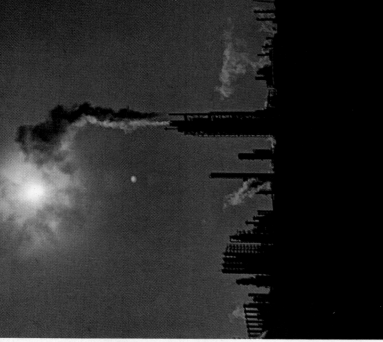

Guadalupe Day honors the Virgin of Guadalupe, Mexico's patron saint. On December 12, thousands go to the Basilica of Our Lady of Guadalupe near Mexico City.

Marilu Pease, Monkmeyer

Mexico's Industrial Production is among the largest in the Western Hemisphere. Refineries of the government-owned petroleum industry have rapidly expanded their production of chemicals since 1960.

WORLD BOOK photo by Henry Gill

ducers of coffee, corn, cotton, oranges, and sugar cane. Large herds of beef cattle graze on the northern plains. Mexico is rich in minerals, and is one of the leading producers of silver. The country also has important deposits of copper, gold, petroleum, and sulfur.

The Mexicans overthrew Spanish rule in 1821. But they believe their real revolution started in 1910, when they began a long struggle for social justice and economic progress. During this struggle, the government took over huge, privately owned farmlands and divided them among millions of landless farmers. It established a national school system to promote education, and has built many hospitals, housing projects, and roads. Since the 1940's, the government has especially encouraged the development of manufacturing. But all these changes have not kept up with Mexico's rapid population growth. More than a third of the people still live in poverty, and the government keeps expanding its programs to help them. As a result, many Mexicans believe their revolution is still going on.

FACTS IN BRIEF

Capital: Mexico City.

Official Language: Spanish.

Official Name: *Estados Unidos Mexicanos* (United Mexican States).

Form of Government: Republic—29 states, 2 territories, 1 federal district. *Head of State*—President (6-year term). *Congress*—Senate (60 members, 6-year terms); Chamber of Deputies (about 200 members, 3-year terms).

Area: 761,602 square miles. *Greatest Distances*—(north-south) 1,250 miles; (east-west) 1,900 miles. *Coastline*—6,320 miles.

Elevation: *Highest*—Orizaba (Citlaltépetl), 18,701 feet above sea level. *Lowest*—near Mexicali, 33 feet below sea level.

Population: *1960 Census*—35,970,823; distribution, 51 per cent urban, 49 per cent rural. *Estimated 1971*

Population—52,406,000; density, 69 persons to the square mile. *Estimated 1976 Population*—62,242,000.

Chief Products: *Agriculture*—alfalfa, beans, coffee, corn, cotton, fruits, henequen, livestock, rice, sugar cane, tobacco, vegetables, wheat. *Fishing*—abalones, oysters, sardines, shrimp, tuna. *Forestry*—chicle, ebony, mahogany, pine, rosewood. *Manufacturing*—cement, chemicals, clothing, fertilizers, iron and steel, handicraft articles, household appliances, processed foods, wood pulp and paper. *Mining*—coal, copper, fluorspar, iron ore, lead, manganese, natural gas, petroleum, silver, sulfur, tin, zinc.

National Anthem: *Himno Nacional de México* (National Hymn of Mexico).

National Holiday: Independence Day, September 16.

Money: *Basic Unit*—peso. One hundred centavos equal one peso. For the value of the peso in dollars, see MONEY (table: Values). See also PESO.

373

MEXICO/Government

Mexico is a democratic republic with a president, a national legislature called the Congress, and a Supreme Court. There is no vice-president. If the president does not finish his term, the Congress chooses a temporary president to serve until a special or regular presidential election is held.

Constitution. The Mexican government is based on the constitution of 1917. The constitution, like that of the United States, provides for three branches of federal government—executive, legislative, and judicial. The constitution also establishes state governments with elected governors and legislatures.

The constitution of Mexico gives the federal government powers much greater than those of the U.S. government. These powers apply to economic matters, education, and state affairs. They provide for the goals of economic progress and social justice that were fought for in the Mexican Revolution of 1910 and afterward. The government has used its powers to break up privately owned farmlands and divide them among the poor, and to set up a national school system. The government has also taken over a number of industries, including railroads, telegraph operations, and the petroleum industry. It can suspend a state's constitutional powers, remove the governor from office, and appoint a temporary governor. This has happened many times to settle struggles for leadership, especially during the 1920's and 1930's.

Politics. Mexico has an "official" political party, the *Partido Revolucionario Institucional* (Institutional Revolutionary Party). It was established in 1929 as the *Partido Nacional Revolucionario* (National Revolutionary Party). The party is generally considered the official promoter of the economic and social goals of the Mexican Revolution. Its candidates have won all state and national elections by huge majorities.

Other Mexican political parties include the *Partido Revolucionario Democrático* (Democratic Revolutionary Party). It is established in 1929 as the *Partido Nacional Revolucionario* (National Revolutionary Party). The party is generally considered the official promoter of the economic and social goals of the Mexican Revolution. Its candidates have won all state and national elections by huge majorities.

Other Mexican political parties include the *Partido*

The National Palace, *right,* in Mexico City houses the office of the president of Mexico. It faces Constitution Plaza, called the Zócalo. The National Cathedral, *left,* also faces this public square.

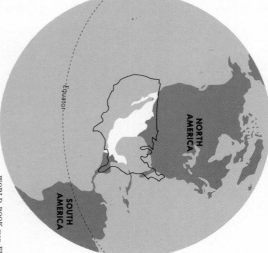

Mexico is about a fourth as large as the United States, not counting Alaska and Hawaii. It lies just south of the United States.

Mexico's Flag was adopted in 1821. The green stands for independence, white for religion, and red for union. The coat of arms is in the center.

Coat of Arms. A legend says the Aztec Indians built their capital Tenochtitlán (now Mexico City) where they saw the eagle shown in this symbol.

H. E. Harris & Co.

WORLD BOOK photo by Henry Gill

The Palace of Justice, which houses Mexico's Supreme Court, has paintings by José Orozco telling of true and false justice.

Dick Davis, Photo Researchers

The Chamber of Deputies, lower house of Mexico's Congress, has about 200 members.

Auténtico de la Revolución Mexicana (Authentic Party of the Mexican Revolution), the *Partido de Acción Nacional* (National Action party), the *Partido Nacionalista de México* (Nationalist Party of Mexico), and the *Partido Popular Socialista* (Socialist Popular party).

Married Mexican men and women who are at least 18 years old can vote in national, state, and local elections. Single persons must be at least 21 to vote.

Armed Forces. Mexican men are required to serve a year in the army or the national guard after reaching the age of 18. The regular army, navy, and air force have a total of about 60,000 men.

MEXICAN GOVERNMENT IN BRIEF

Form: Republic.

Divisions: 29 States, 2 Territories, 1 Federal District.

Head of State: President (can be elected to only one 6-year term).

Congress: Senate (60 members; 2 elected from each state and the Federal District; 6-year terms); Chamber of Deputies (about 200 members; 178 elected from districts; minority-party candidates elected according to percentage of total national vote; 3-year terms). Members of Congress cannot serve two terms in a row.

Courts: Highest court, Supreme Court of Justice (21 members appointed for life by the president). The Su-

preme Court appoints the judges of the 6 Federal Appeals Courts and the 44 District Courts to life terms. A Superior Court of Justice is the highest court in each state and territory.

State Government: Governor (can be elected to only one 6-year term). Chamber of Deputies (7 to 15 members; cannot serve two terms in a row).

Territorial Government: Governor (appointed by the president to an indefinite term). No legislature.

Local Government: Divisions, about 2,300 *municipios* (cities or townships). Governed by elected municipal presidents and councils (3-year terms).

STATES, TERRITORIES, AND FEDERAL DISTRICT OF MEXICO

STATES

Map Key	Name	Area (sq. mi.)	Population	Capital
E 5	Aguascalientes	2,158	299,549	Aguascalientes
B 1	Baja California	27,071	1,014,984	Mexicali
F 10	Campeche	21,666	217,795	Campeche
G 9	Chiapas	28,528	1,528,401	Tuxtla
B 4	Chihuahua	95,400	1,654,604	Chihuahua
C 6	Coahuila	58,522	1,093,366	Saltillo
F 5	Colima	2,106	223,610	Colima
D 6	Durango	46,196	885,963	Durango
E 6	Guanajuato	11,810	2,152,358	Guanajuato
G 7	Guerrero	24,631	1,457,774	Chilpancingo
F 7	Hidalgo	8,103	1,128,443	Pachuca
F 5	Jalisco	30,941	3,202,097	Guadalajara
F 7	México	8,286	2,435,653	Toluca
F 6	Michoacán	23,113	2,294,579	Morelia
F 7	Morelos	1,908	511,179	Cuernavaca
E 5	Nayarit	10,664	494,858	Tepic
D 7	Nuevo León	24,925	1,461,638	Monterrey
G 8	Oaxaca	36,820	2,021,182	Oaxaca
F 7	Puebla	13,096	2,307,852	Puebla
F 7	Querétaro	4,544	422,369	Querétaro
E 6	San Luis Potosí	24,266	1,234,231	San Luis Potosí
B 3	Sinaloa	22,429	1,047,972	Culiacán
D 4	Sonora	71,403	1,106,114	Hermosillo
G 9	Tabasco	9,522	639,103	Villahermosa
D 7	Tamaulipas	30,822	1,363,415	Ciudad Victoria
F 7	Tlaxcala	1,511	406,540	Tlaxcala
F 8	Veracruz	28,114	3,447,544	Jalapa
F 10	Yucatán	16,749	705,492	Mérida
E 6	Zacatecas	28,973	965,613	Zacatecas

TERRITORIES AND FEDERAL DISTRICT

Map Key	Name	Area (sq. mi.)	Population	Capital
D 2	Baja California Sur	28,447	103,339	La Paz
F 11	Quintana Roo	16,228	82,715	Chetumal
F 7	Federal District	579	7,101,774	Mexico City

Source: Official population estimates (1968). Each state and territory has a separate article in WORLD BOOK.

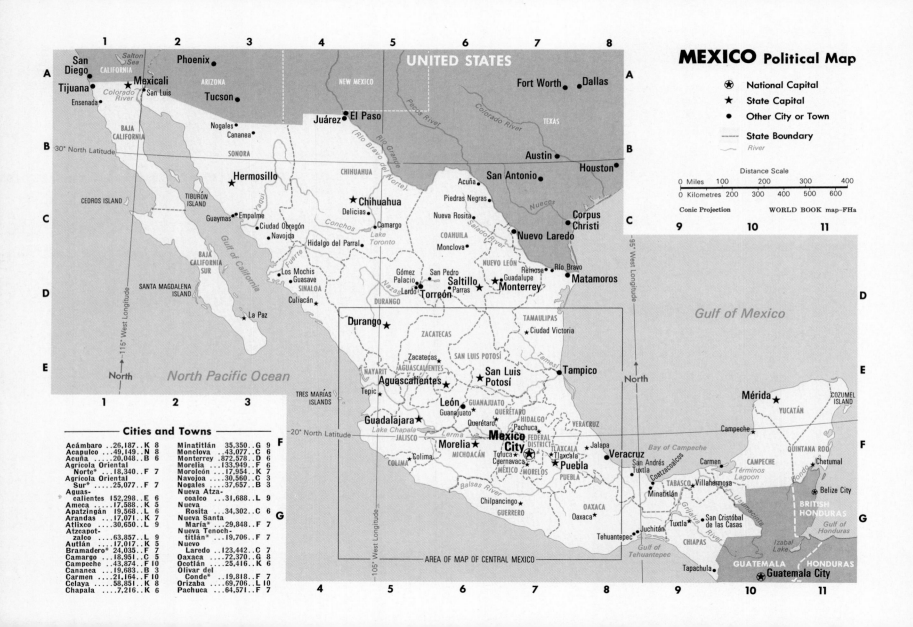

MEXICO Political Map

- ✪ National Capital
- ★ State Capital
- ● Other City or Town
- - - - State Boundary
- ～ River

Distance Scale

| 0 Miles | 100 | 200 | 300 | 400 |

| 0 Kilometres | 200 | 300 | 400 | 500 | 600 |

Conic Projection   WORLD BOOK map—FHa

UNITED STATES

San Diego
Tijuana
Ensenada
Mexicali
San Luis
Phoenix
Tucson
Nogales
Cananea
Juárez
El Paso
Fort Worth
Dallas
Austin
Houston
San Antonio
Acuña
Piedras Negras
Nueva Rosita
Corpus Christi
Nuevo Laredo
Monclova
Reinosa
Río Bravo
Matamoros
Guadalupe
Monterrey
Saltillo
San Pedro
Parras
Gómez Palacio
Lerdo
Torreón
Ciudad Victoria
Durango
Tampico
Ciudad Obregón
Navojoa
Hidalgo del Parral
Delicias
Camargo
Chihuahua
Hermosillo
Guaymas
Empalme
Los Mochis
Guasave
Culiacán
La Paz
Zacatecas
San Luis Potosí
Aguascalientes
Tepic
León
Guanajuato
Querétaro
Pachuca
Guadalajara
Morelia
Mexico City
Toluca
Cuernavaca
Puebla
Tlaxcala
Jalapa
Veracruz
Colima
Chilpancingo
Oaxaca
Tehuantepec
Juchitán
Tapachula
Mérida
Campeche
Carmen
Villahermosa
Minatitlán
Coatzacoalcos
San Andrés Tuxtla
Tuxtla
San Cristóbal de las Casas
Chetumal
Belize City
Guatemala City

North Pacific Ocean

Gulf of Mexico

Gulf of California

Gulf of Tehuantepec

Bay of Campeche

Gulf of Honduras

CALIFORNIA
ARIZONA
NEW MEXICO
TEXAS
Salton Sea
Colorado River
Pecos River
Rio Grande
Colorado River
Nueces
Salado River
Conchos
Lake Toronto
Yaqui
Fuerte
Nazas
Tamesí
Lerma
Lake Chapala
Balsas River
Grijalva River
Usumacinta
Hondo
Izabal Lake
Términos Lagoon

BAJA CALIFORNIA
BAJA CALIFORNIA SUR
SONORA
CHIHUAHUA
COAHUILA
NUEVO LEÓN
SINALOA
DURANGO
TAMAULIPAS
ZACATECAS
NAYARIT
AGUASCALIENTES
SAN LUIS POTOSÍ
JALISCO
GUANAJUATO
QUERÉTARO
HIDALGO
VERACRUZ
COLIMA
MICHOACÁN
MÉXICO
MORELOS
PUEBLA
TLAXCALA
FEDERAL DISTRICT
GUERRERO
OAXACA
CHIAPAS
TABASCO
CAMPECHE
YUCATÁN
QUINTANA ROO
BRITISH HONDURAS
GUATEMALA
HONDURAS

CEDROS ISLAND
TIBURÓN ISLAND
SANTA MAGDALENA ISLAND
TRES MARÍAS ISLANDS
COZUMEL ISLAND

30° North Latitude
20° North Latitude
115° West Longitude
105° West Longitude
95° West Longitude
North

AREA OF MAP OF CENTRAL MEXICO

Cities and Towns

Acámbaro ...26,187...K 8	Minatitlán ..35,350...G 9
Acapulco ...49,149...N 8	Monclova ..43,077...C 6
Acuña ...20,048...B 6	Monterrey 872,578...D 6
Agrícola Oriental	Morelia ..133,949...F 6
Norte* ..18,340...F 7	Moroleón ..17,954...K 7
Agrícola Oriental	Navojoa ..30,560...C 3
Sur* ...25,077...F 7	Nogales ..37,657...B 3
Aguas-	Nueva Atza-
calientes 152,298...E 6	coalco* ..31,688...L 9
Ameca ...17,588...K 5	Nueva
Apatzingán 19,568...L 6	Rosita ..34,302...C 6
Arandas ..17,071...K 7	Nueva Santa
Atlixco ...30,650...L 9	María* ..29,848...F 7
Atzcapot-	Nueva Tenoch-
zalco ...63,857...L 9	titlán* ..19,706...F 7
Autlán ...17,017...K 5	Nuevo
Bramadero* 24,035...F 7	Laredo 123,442...C 7
Camargo ..18,951...C 5	Oaxaca ..72,370...G 8
Campeche ..43,874...F10	Ocotlán ..25,416...K 6
Cananea ..19,683...B 3	Olivar del
Carmen ...21,164...F10	Conde* ..19,818...F 7
Celaya ...58,851...K 8	Orizaba ..69,706...L10
Chapala ...7,216...K 6	Pachuca ..64,571...F 7

CENTRAL MEXICO

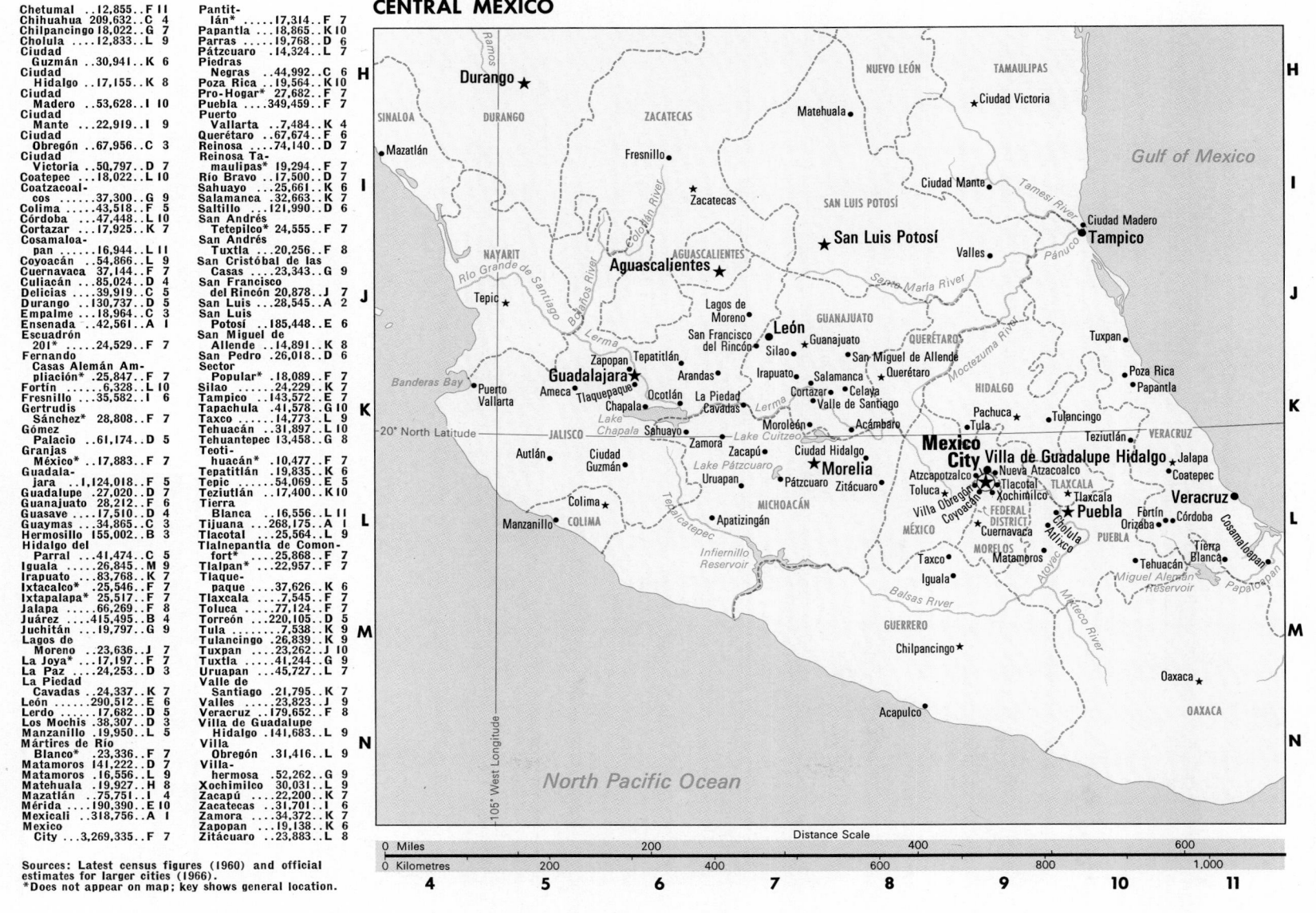

Sources: Latest census figures (1960) and official estimates for larger cities (1966).
*Does not appear on map; key shows general location.

374c

Mexico has over 52 million persons. This population is increasing almost $3\frac{1}{2}$ per cent a year, one of the greatest annual "population explosions" in the world. The growth rate is the result of Mexico's traditionally high birth rate and its sharply reduced death rate. Since the 1930's, improved living conditions and expanded health services have cut the death rate by more than half. Perhaps the government's chief problem is trying to provide housing, jobs, and schools for the rapidly increasing population.

The great majority of the Mexican people are *mestizos* (persons of mixed white and Indian ancestry). Their white ancestors were Spaniards who came to what is now Mexico during and after the Spanish conquest of 1519-1521. Their Indian ancestors were living in the region when the Spaniards arrived. Negroes and some Asians are also part of the racial mixture. The nation has some Indians and whites of unmixed ancestry. But most Mexicans think of themselves as mestizos. Being a mestizo is generally a matter of national pride.

Being an Indian in Mexico does not depend chiefly on ancestry. It is mostly a matter of way of life and point of view. For example, a Mexican is considered an Indian if he speaks an Indian language, wears Indian clothes, and lives in a village where the people call themselves Indians. This is true even if the person is actually a mestizo.

Language. Almost all Mexicans speak Spanish, the official language of Mexico and nearly all other Latin-American countries. Many words that are used in the United States came from Mexico. They include *canyon, corral, desperado, lariat, lasso, patio, rodeo,* and *stampede.*

Most Mexican Indians speak Spanish in addition to their own ancient language. But more than a million speak only an Indian language. The major Indian languages include Maya, Mixtec, Nahuatl, Otomí, Tarascan, and Zapotec. See SPANISH LANGUAGE.

Religion. Nearly all of Mexico's people belong to the Roman Catholic Church. Mexico also has some Protestants, Jews, and other religious groups.

Roman Catholic missionaries and priests first arrived from Spain in the early 1500's. They baptized millions of Indians. But the rain, sun, and other forces of nature remained an important part of religion to the Indians. Today, millions of Indian villagers still combine ancient religious practices with Catholicism.

During the Spanish colonial period, the Roman Catholic Church was closely linked with the government as the official state church. The church became wealthy and powerful, and prohibited other religions. Beginning in the mid-1800's, the Mexican government greatly reduced the political and economic power of the church. Today, Mexican law provides freedom of worship, but it forbids any church to own land or to take part in political affairs.

The Virgin of Guadalupe is the patron saint of Mexico. According to Roman Catholic legend, she was seen twice by Juan Diego, a poor Indian, in December, 1531. She appeared as an Indian maiden on Tepeyac Hill near Mexico City. She asked Diego to tell Bishop Juan de Zumárraga to build a shrine in her honor on the hill. To prove her identity, she caused a picture of herself to appear on Diego's cloak. The bishop built the shrine and placed the cloak in it.

WORLD BOOK photo by Henry Gill

Distance Scale

0 Miles	200 400 600
0 Kilometres	400

WORLD BOOK map-FHa

POPULATION

This map shows the population distribution of Mexico. Each dot represents 25,000 persons. The cities shown on the map have the largest populations.

Tijuana · Mexicali
Juárez
Chihuahua
Guadalajara · León · Torreón · Monterrey
Mexico City · Puebla
Mérida

Crowded Mexico City is the third largest city in North America, after New York City and Chicago. Most Mexicans are mestizos (people of mixed Indian and white ancestry).

HISTORICAL POPULATION

1976 Estimate	62,242,000
1971 Estimate	52,406,000
1960	35,970,823
1950	25,791,017
1940	19,653,552
1930	16,552,722
1921	14,334,780
1900	13,607,259
1856	7,661,520
1823 Estimate	6,800,000
1521 Estimate	9,120,000

The way of life in Mexico includes many features from the nation's long Indian past and the Spanish colonial period. But Mexico has changed rapidly during the 1900's. In many ways, life in its larger cities is similar to that in the United States and Canada. Mexican villagers follow the older way of life more than the city people do. Even in the villages, however, government economic and educational programs are doing much to modernize the people's lives. These programs are bringing the Indian villagers into the general life of Mexico, and making them think of themselves as Mexicans rather than Indians. These Indians will probably be blended into the national life by about the year 2000.

City Life. Only a little more than half the people of Mexico live in cities and towns with populations of at least 2,500. Twenty-two Mexican cities have more than 100,000 persons. Mexico City, the capital and largest city, has over 3 million persons. Five other cities have populations of over 300,000. They are, in order of size, Guadalajara, Monterrey, Juárez, Puebla, and Mexicali. See the separate articles on the cities of Mexico listed in the *Related Articles* at the end of this article.

Many Mexican cities and towns began as Indian communities. After the Spaniards arrived, they rebuilt the communities and made them more like Spanish towns. The main church and the chief public and government buildings were built around a *plaza* (public square). The plaza is still the center of city life. In the evenings and on Sunday afternoons, the people gather in the plaza to talk with friends or to listen to music.

Modern houses and apartment buildings in the new suburbs look like those in the United States and Canada. The older parts of the cities have rows of homes built in the Spanish colonial style. Most of these houses are made of stone or *adobe* (sun-dried clay) brick. Small balconies extend from some windows. A Spanish-style house also has a *patio* (courtyard), which is the center of family life. This gardenlike area may have a fountain,

flowers, vines, and pots of blooming plants. The poorest Mexicans live in slum shacks or rooms with almost no furniture. *Petates* (straw mats) serve as beds, and clay bowls may be the only dishes.

Village Life. Many Mexican farmers live in small villages near their fields. The village homes stand along dusty streets that are simple dirt roads or are paved with cobblestones. In most villages, a Roman Catholic church stands on one side of the plaza, the center of the community. On the other sides of most plazas are a few stores and government buildings.

Almost every village, and every city and town, has a market place. Going to market is one of the chief activities of the people in farm areas. Men, women, and children take along clothes, food, lace, pictures, toys, baskets, or whatever else they have to sell or trade. They either rent stalls in which to display their goods, or spread the merchandise on the ground. The people spend the day chatting with friends and doing a little business. Farmers often trade their goods instead of selling them, and much bargaining takes place.

The shape and style of village houses vary according to the climate. People on the dry central plateau build homes of adobe, brick, cement blocks, or stone, with flat roofs of red tile, sheet metal, or straw. Some of these houses have only one room, a hard-packed dirt floor, a door, and few or no windows. The kitchen may be simply a lean-to built of poles and cornstalks placed against an outside wall. If a house does not have a lean-to kitchen, the family may build a cooking fire on the floor. The smoke from the fire curls out through the door and windows.

In areas of heavy rainfall, many houses have walls built of poles coated with lime and clay. This mixture lasts longer in the rain than adobe does. The houses have sloping roofs to allow the water to run off easily. Some Indians in southern Mexico build round houses. In Yucatán, most village houses are rectangular with

Village Markets are social centers for Mexican families, as well as places to buy or trade food and other products.

WORLD BOOK photo by Henry Gill

Blindfolded Mexican Children take turns trying to break a *piñata*, a decorated container filled with candy and toys. The piñata, often shaped like an animal, is hung from a tree or ceiling at parties and before Christmas and Easter.

Ardean Miller, Alpha

Housewives in Mexico's Big Cities look for bargain prices in large discount stores like those in the United States and Canada. The cities also have fashionable shops and traditional open-air markets.

WORLD BOOK photo by Henry Gill

Housing Projects are common in Mexico's rapidly growing big cities. Some projects in Mexico City include medical centers, nurseries, schools, shops, and theaters.

WORLD BOOK photo by Henry Gill

Mexican Craftsmen, such as these leather workers, are famous for their skill in creating beautiful objects of Indian, Spanish, or modern design. They sell many of their products to tourists.

WORLD BOOK photo by Henry Gill

Leisure Time in Mexico has greatly increased since the 1940's, when the nation's rapid industrial growth began. Large crowds attend art shows and other attractions in city parks.

WORLD BOOK photo by Henry Gill

rounded ends. The roofs are made of neatly trimmed palm leaves.

Many Indian villages are in the wilds of Yucatán and in rugged areas of central and southern Mexico. There, the Indians still follow their ancient customs and live much as their ancestors did before the white man arrived. For example, some Maya Indians sacrifice turkeys to their gods in hope of getting rain.

Family Life. Mexican households consist of an average of five or six persons. In many homes, several generations of the same family live together. Most women, like those of other Latin-American countries, have few activities outside the home besides marketing. But many women in the cities have jobs, and the women in farm areas often help cultivate the fields. Mexican girls do not have so much individual freedom as girls in the United States. Farm boys work in the fields, and many city youths have part-time or full-time jobs.

Food. Thousands of years ago, the Indians of what is now Mexico discovered how to grow corn. It became their most important food. Today, corn is still the chief food of most Mexicans, especially in rural areas. Mexican housewives generally soften the corn in hot limewater, boil it, and then grind it into meal.

The main corn-meal food is the *tortilla,* a thin pancake shaped by hand or machine and cooked on an ungreased griddle. The tortilla is the bread of the poorer people. It can be eaten plain or as part of (1) the *taco,* a folded tortilla filled with chopped meat, chicken, or cheese, and then fried; (2) the *enchilada,* a rolled-up tortilla with a similar filling and covered with a hot sauce; or (3) the *tostada,* a tortilla fried in deep fat until it becomes crisp, and served flat with beans, cheese, lettuce, meat, and onions on top.

Many Mexicans eat *frijoles* (beans) that are boiled, mashed, and then fried and refried in lard. Poorer Mexicans may eat frijoles every day, often using a folded tortilla to spoon up the beans. Rice is also boiled and then fried. Other popular foods include *atole* (a thick, soupy corn-meal dish) and *tamales* (corn meal steamed in corn husks or banana leaves, and usually mixed with

John Stage, Photo Researchers

W. R. Wilson

Ancient Ways of Life are still followed in many of Mexico's Indian villages, but are slowly being replaced by modern customs. The Tarascan Indians, like their ancestors, use dugouts and butterfly nets to catch fish in Lake Pátzcuaro.

Mexican Farmers in many areas cultivate their fields with old-fashioned equipment, including wooden hoes and ox-drawn plows.

pork or chicken). Most Mexicans like their foods highly seasoned with hot, red chili pepper or other strong peppers. Turkey is a popular holiday dish. It is often served with *mole*, a sauce made of chocolate, chili, sesame seed, and spices.

The poorer families eat little meat because they cannot afford it. They may vary their basic diet of corn and beans with fruit, honey, onions, tomatoes, squash, or sweet potatoes. Favorite fruits include avocados, bananas, mangoes, oranges, and papayas. The fruit and leaves of the prickly pear, a type of cactus, are boiled, fried, or stewed. Richer Mexicans have a more balanced diet, and also eat tortillas and beans.

Popular beverages include water flavored with a variety of fruit juices, and cinnamon-flavored hot chocolate cooked with water and beaten into foam. Mexicans also drink coffee and milk. Alcoholic beverages include *mescal, pulque,* and *tequila,* which are made from the juice of the maguey plant, and beer and wine.

Clothing. Mexicans in the cities and larger towns wear clothing similar to that worn in the United States and Canada. The village people wear simple types of clothing that date back hundreds of years. Men generally wear plain cotton shirts and trousers, and leather sandals called *huaraches.* Wide-brimmed felt or straw hats called *sombreros* protect them from the hot sun. During cold or rainy weather, they may wear *ponchos* (blankets that have a slit in the center for the head and are draped over the shoulders). At night the men may wrap themselves in colorful *serapes,* which are blankets carried over one shoulder during the day. The village women wear blouses and long, full skirts, and usually go barefoot. They cover their heads with fringed shawls called *rebozos.* A mother may wrap her baby to her back with a rebozo.

Some of the villagers' clothing is homemade. Hand weaving was an ancient Indian art, and today the Indians are famous for their beautiful home-woven fabrics. Styles of weaving vary throughout Mexico, and an Indian's region can be identified by the colors and designs of his poncho or serape. For example, blankets with

a striped rainbow pattern come from the Saltillo area.

Some Indians wear unusual clothing. Large capes made of straw are worn in Oaxaca state. On holidays, Indian women on the Isthmus of Tehuantepec wear a wide, lacy white headdress called a *huipil grande.* According to legend, this garment was copied from baby clothes that were washed ashore from a Spanish shipwreck. The Indian women thought the clothes were head shawls. In Yucatán, Maya women wear long, loose white dresses that are embroidered around the neck and bottom hem.

Mexicans sometimes wear national costumes on holidays and other special occasions. The men's national costumes include the dark-blue *charro* suit, made of doeskin or velvet. It has a *bolero* (short jacket) and tight riding pants with gold or silver buttons down the sides. A flowing red bow tie, spurred boots, and a fancy white sombrero complete the costume.

Probably the best-known women's costume is the *china poblana.* It is usually worn in the *jarabe tapatío* ("Mexican Hat Dance"), the national dance of Mexico. A legend says the china poblana was named for a Chinese princess of the 1600's who was kidnaped by pirates and sold in the slave market. She was brought to Acapulco, where a kindly merchant of Puebla bought her. In Puebla, she dedicated her life to helping the poor. The princess adopted a costume that the local women later imitated. Today, it consists of a full red and green skirt decorated with beads and other ornaments, a gaily embroidered short-sleeved blouse, and a bright sash. See CLOTHING (color picture: Mexico).

Holidays. Mexicans celebrate their Independence Day, September 16, and other holidays with colorful *fiestas* (festivals). Every Mexican city, town, and village also holds a yearly fiesta to honor its local patron saint. Most fiestas begin before daylight with a shower of rockets, loud explosions of fireworks, and ringing of bells. During the fiestas, the people pray and burn candles to their saints in churches decorated with flowers and colored tissue paper. They dance, gamble, hold parades, and buy refreshments in the crowded

John Stage, Photo Researchers

Bullfighting is the most popular spectator sport in Mexico. Many small towns have bull rings where amateur bullfighters perform against young bulls. The major rings are in the big cities.

John Stage, Photo Researchers

Corn Is Mexico's Chief Food. Many Mexican women soak, boil, and grind the corn themselves, as the ancient Indians did. The corn meal is often flattened like a pancake to make *tortillas*.

Farm Women and Girls of Teotihuacán do their laundry in a creek. Many Mexican families in dry regions use water from wells.

WORLD BOOK photo by Henry Gill

market places and public square. Fireworks are again set off at night.

In the smaller towns and villages, amateur bullfights are also held during fiestas. In the larger towns and the cities, fiestas resemble carnivals or county fairs in the United States. Most of them include less religious worship than do the village fiestas. The people watch plays and professional bullfights, ride merry-go-rounds and Ferris wheels, and buy goods at merchants' booths.

Guadalupe Day is Mexico's most important religious holiday. It is celebrated on December 12, when the Virgin is believed to have made a sign of her appearance on Tepeyac Hill near Mexico City.

On the nine nights before Christmas, friends and neighbors gather and act out the journey of Mary and Joseph to Bethlehem. These nine ceremonies are called *posadas*. Each night after the posada, the children play the *piñata* game. Piñatas are containers made of earthenware or papier-mâché. Many are shaped like animals, and are filled with candy, fruit, and toys. A piñata is hung above the heads of the children. Then the youngsters are blindfolded and take turns trying to break the piñata with a stick. After it breaks, they scramble for the presents. On Twelfth Night, 12 days after Christmas, parents fill their children's shoes with presents. See CHRISTMAS (color picture: Christmas Is Children's Time). See also EASTER (In Mexico).

Sports popular in Mexico include baseball, soccer, swimming, and volleyball. Many amateur and professional baseball teams play throughout the country. Most Mexicans also enjoy watching bullfights. Mexico City has the largest bullfighting arena in the world. It seats about 50,000 persons. There are about 35 other major bullfighting arenas in Mexico.

Another popular sport is jai alai, which resembles handball. The players hit the ball against a wall with a basketlike racket. Jai alai is sometimes called the fastest game in the world because the ball travels so rapidly. Richer Mexicans also enjoy such sports as golf, horseback riding, polo, tennis, and yachting.

MEXICO / Education

Throughout the Spanish colonial period, the Roman Catholic Church controlled education in what is now Mexico. During the 1800's, the newly independent government and the church struggled for power, and the government won control of the schools. Mexico's present constitution, adopted in 1917, prohibits religious groups and ministers from establishing schools or teaching in them. The government does permit churches to operate private schools. However, less than 15 per cent of the nation's elementary schools are private.

During the early 1900's, fewer than 25 per cent of Mexico's people could read or write. Since the Revolution of 1910, and especially since the early 1940's, the government has done much to promote free public education. It has built thousands of new schools and established teachers' colleges. The government spends increasing sums on education each year—more than a fifth of its national budget. Today, about 65 per cent of the people can read and write.

Mexican law requires all children from the age of 6 through 14 to go to school. But there are not enough schools or trained teachers. About 30 per cent of the youngsters do not attend school, especially in farm areas. There, less than 10 per cent of the schools go beyond the fourth grade. The population of Mexico increases about 3½ per cent a year, and the school-expansion program simply cannot keep up.

Mexico's school system is managed by the national Ministry of Public Education. After kindergarten, a child has six years of elementary school. The relatively few students who plan to go to college study in high schools for five years. Others may attend three-year high schools, most of which stress job training. Courses of higher education at Mexico's many universities, specialized colleges, and technical institutes last from three to seven years. The oldest and largest Mexican university is the National Autonomous University of Mexico near Mexico City. It was founded in 1551 and has about 80,000 students. See MEXICO, NATIONAL AUTONOMOUS UNIVERSITY OF.

Marc & Evelyne Bernheim, Rapho Guillumette

The Boldly Modern Campus of the National Autonomous University of Mexico, near Mexico City, was built during the 1950's.

Hilda Bijour, Monkmeyer

Mexico's Village Schools generally have at least two grades, but some have only one. Less than a tenth go above fourth grade.

Carl Frank

Research Institutes of Mexico have fine libraries for specialized study in various sciences and other fields. Most of these institutes are in Mexico City, the education center of Mexico.

Maya Murals were painted on temple walls in Bonampak, a religious center in what is now the state of Chiapas. These murals date from the 700's.

Stone Mosaics by Juan O'Gorman decorate the Central Library of the National Autonomous University of Mexico. About 7½ million stones were used to make the mural for the building.

Otto Done, Shostal

Reconstruction of *Presentation of a Prince* (Euramex Photographie)

Religious Art of the Spanish colonial period is represented by this highly decorated altar in the Church of Santa Prisca, built in Taxco during the 1750's.

WORLD BOOK photo by Henry Gill

MEXICO/Arts

The arts have been an important part of Mexican life since the days of the ancient Indian civilizations. The Maya and Toltec Indians built beautiful temples and painted *murals* (wall paintings) in them. The Aztec composed music and poetry. The Spaniards brought a love for beautiful buildings and for literature. They also built thousands of impressive churches. During the 1900's, Mexico has given the world many important architects, artists, composers, and writers.

Architecture of the ancient Indians was related chiefly to religion. The Indians built stone temples on flat-topped pyramids, and decorated them with murals and sculptured symbols. These symbols represented the feathered-serpent god Quetzalcoatl and the Indians' other gods. Many ancient structures still stand near Mexico City and at Chichén Itzá in Yucatán. See the Arts sections of the AZTEC and MAYA articles.

After the Spanish conquest, the earliest mission churches were designed in a simple style. The huge National Cathedral in Mexico City, begun in 1573, was designed in a more ornamental style. Churches built during the 1700's were even more highly decorated. During the 1900's, Félix Candela and other Mexican architects have combined ancient Indian designs with modern construction methods. Their work includes the beautiful buildings of the National Autonomous University of Mexico. Another example is the 44-story Latin-American Tower, one of the tallest buildings in Latin America, in Mexico City.

Painting. During the Spanish colonial period, many artists painted murals in churches or portraits of government officials. But Mexican painting is best known for the artists who did their work after the Mexican Revolution of 1910. Beginning in the 1920's, José

374j

Gianni Tortoli, Photo Researchers

Ancient Pyramids and Temples attract visitors to Teotihuacán (House of the Gods) northeast of Mexico City. The Pyramid of the Sun, rear, covers more than 10 acres and is over 200 feet high.

Olle Stackman, Pix from Publix

The Story of the Mexican Revolution is told in murals by David Siqueiros and other well-known Mexican artists. Siqueiros is shown with part of his 175-foot mural, *The March of Humanity.*

Euramex Photographic

The Mexican Hat Dance is the national dance of Mexico. It is often performed by the Ballet Folklórico, a dance company that appears regularly in the Palace of Fine Arts in Mexico City.

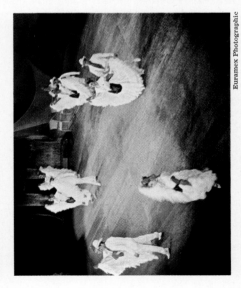

WORLD BOOK photo by Henry Gill

Beautiful Silver Objects including candlesticks, jewelry, and tableware are produced by skilled silversmiths of Taxco. Silver shops line the city's streets and attract many tourists.

Orozco, Diego Rivera, and David Siqueiros painted the story of the revolution on the walls of public buildings. Important Mexican painters of later years include Rufino Tamayo and José Luis Cuevas. During the 1960's, many younger Mexican painters have turned from revolutionary themes and have followed the latest art influences from other countries.

Literature. Outstanding colonial writers included the dramatist Juan Ruiz de Alarcón and the poet Sor Juana Inés de la Cruz. In 1816, José Joaquín Fernández de Lizardi published one of the first Latin-American novels, *The Itching Parrot.* After 1910, revolutionary themes became important in novels by such writers as Mariano Azuela and Martín Luis Guzmán, and later by Carlos Fuentes and Agustín Yáñez. Leading Mexican poets of the 1900's include Amado Nervo, Octavio Paz, Carlos Pellicer, and Alfonso Reyes.

Music. The early Indians used drums, flutes, gourd rattles, and seashells as well as the human voice for music and dances. This ancient music is still played in some parts of Mexico. Much church music was written during the colonial period. In addition, popular Spanish music was combined with Indian or Negro styles of music. The *jarabe* style was prohibited by the Spaniards as "indecent and disgraceful." The *jarabe tapatío,* or Mexican hat dance, later became the national dance of Mexico.

Folk songs called *corridos* have long been popular in Mexico. They may tell of the Mexican Revolution, of a bandit or a sheriff, or of the struggle between church and state. During the 1900's, Mexican composers including Carlos Chávez and Silvestre Revueltas have used themes from these folk songs or from ancient Indian music.

Mexico has six main land regions: (1) the Pacific Northwest, (2) the Plateau of Mexico, (3) the Gulf Coastal Plain, (4) the Southern Uplands, (5) the Chiapas Highlands, and (6) the Yucatán Peninsula. Within these regions are many smaller ones that differ greatly in altitude, climate, land formation, and plant and animal life.

The Pacific Northwest region of Mexico is generally dry. The Peninsula of Lower California, the region's westernmost section, consists largely of rolling or mountainous desert. During some years, the desert receives no rain at all. It has a few oases, where farmers in small settlements grow dates and grapes. The northwestern corner and southern end of the peninsula get enough rain for a little farming. The lowest point in Mexico is in the far northern area, near Mexicali. This area, 33 feet below sea level, is the southern end of the huge Imperial Valley of California.

The most valuable land of Mexico's Pacific Northwest lies along the mainland coastal strip. There, in fertile river valleys, is some of Mexico's richest farmland. The valleys are irrigated with the waters of the Colorado, Fuerte, Yaqui, and other rivers. Steep, narrow mountain ranges extend in a north-south direction in the state of Sonora, east of the coastal plain. The ranges lie parallel to each other and separate the upper river valleys. In these basins are cattle ranches, irrigated farmland, and copper and silver mines.

The Plateau of Mexico is the largest of Mexico's land regions. It has most of the Mexican people and the largest cities. The plateau is the most varied land region, and consists of five sections.

The Volcanic Axis, a series of volcanoes, extends across Mexico at the plateau's southern edge. Many of the volcanoes are active. The volcanic soils of this rugged zone are fertile and receive enough rain for agriculture. Corn, beans, and other crops have been grown on the steep slopes since the days of the ancient Indian civilizations. The highest point in Mexico is 18,701-foot Orizaba (Citlaltépetl), the third tallest mountain in North America. Southeast of Mexico City

are the snow-capped volcanoes Ixtacihuatl and Popocatépetl, both more than 17,000 feet high. To the west is 417-square-mile Lake Chapala, the largest lake in Mexico. See IXTACIHUATL; ORIZABA; POPOCATÉPETL.

The Bajío (Flat), which lies north of the Volcanic Axis on the plateau, is the heart of Mexico. It averages about 7,000 feet above sea level. The rainfall of this section is hardly enough to raise corn or beans, but wheat and barley grow well there. The Aztec capital of Tenochtitlán stood at the Bajío's southern edge, in the beautiful Valley of Mexico. Mexico City was built on the same site after the Spanish conquest, and became the capital during the colonial period. Today, it is also the country's leading center of culture, industry, and transportation. Several small lakes, including famous Lake Xochimilco, are in the Mexico City area (see LAKE XOCHIMILCO).

The Mesa del Norte (Northern Plateau) makes up more than half the Plateau of Mexico. It extends from the Bajío north to the United States. The mesa is highest in the south and west, with altitudes between 6,000 and 9,000 feet. In the north and east, it is less than 4,000 feet high. Low mountains rise from 2,000 to 3,000 feet above the mesa's rolling plains. This section receives little rainfall except in the higher mountains, where frost is a constant threat to farming. Only in such irrigated places as the Saltillo and Torreón areas is farming really successful.

The low mountains of the mesa have the richest silver mines in the world. The Spaniards began developing these mines during the 1500's. They also established huge ranches in the nearby dry hills and plains to supply the miners with beef, horses, and mules. In the Durango and Chihuahua areas, *vaqueros* (cowboys) developed skills at riding, roping cattle, and fighting Indians. American cowboys later copied these skills from the vaqueros.

The Sierra Madre Occidental is a long mountain range that forms the western rim of the Plateau of Mexico. For hundreds of years, this range was a natural barrier to transportation between the plateau and the west

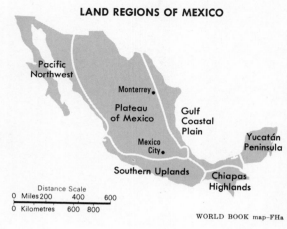

LAND REGIONS OF MEXICO

Pacific Northwest

Monterrey

Plateau of Mexico

Gulf Coastal Plain

Mexico City

Southern Uplands

Yucatán Peninsula

Chiapas Highlands

Distance Scale
0 Miles 200   400   600
0 Kilometres   600   800

WORLD BOOK map-FHa

coast. Paved roads and a railroad were not built across it until the 1900's. The range includes some of Mexico's most rugged land. Short, steep streams flowing to the Pacific Ocean have cut canyons more than a mile deep through the mountains. The largest canyon is the spectacular Barranca del Cobre, cut by the Urique River. This deep, wide gorge is so wild that parts of it have not been explored on foot.

The Sierra Madre Oriental, the plateau's eastern rim, is actually a series of mountain ranges. In many places between the ranges, highways and railroads climb up to the plateau from the east coast. Monterrey, located near large deposits of coal and iron ore, is second only to Mexico City among the nation's industrial centers. It is the major center of the expanding Mexican steel industry. See SIERRA MADRE.

The Gulf Coastal Plain. North of Tampico, the plain is largely covered by tangled forests of low, thorny bushes and trees. This section of the plain is generally dry, and farming is possible only along rivers and with the aid of irrigation. South of Tampico, the rainfall increases. The plant life gradually changes

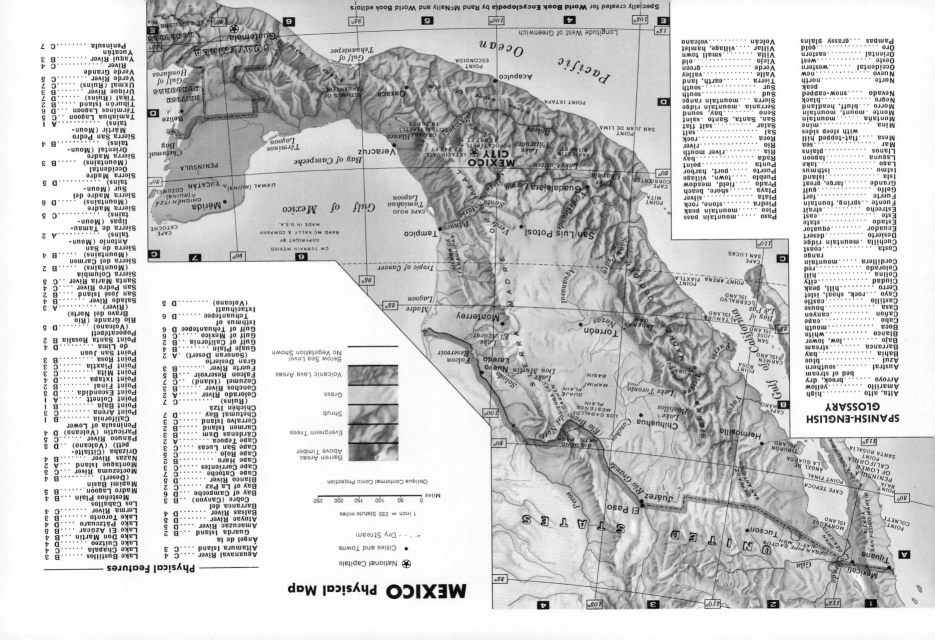

MEXICO Physical Map

Specially created for World Book Encyclopedia by Rand McNally and World Book editors

Legend
- ⊛ National Capitals
- • Cities and Towns
- ---- Dry Stream

Oblique Conformal Conic Projection

Miles 0 50 100 150 200 250

1 inch = 232 statute miles

Vegetation:
- Barren Areas Above Timber
- Evergreen Trees
- Shrub
- Grass
- Volcanic Lava Areas
- Below Sea Level
- No Vegetation Shown

SPANISH-ENGLISH GLOSSARY

Spanish	English
Alta, Alto	high
Amarillo	yellow
Arroyo	brook, dry bed of stream
Austral	southern
Azul	blue
Bahía	bay
Bajo	low, lower
Barranca	stream
Blanco	white
Boca	mouth
Cabo	cape
Cañon	canyon
Casa	house
Castillo	castle
Cayo	rock, shoal, islet
Cerro	hill, peak
Ciudad	city
Colina	hill
Colorado	red
Cordillera	mountain range
Costa	coast
Cuchilla	mountain ridge
Desierto	desert
Ecuador	equator
Estado	state
Este	east
Estrecho	strait
Fuerte	fort
Fuente	spring, fountain
Golfo	gulf
Grande	large, great
Isla	island
Istmo	isthmus
Lago	lake
Laguna	lagoon
Llanos	plains
Mar	sea
Mesa	flat-topped hill with steep sides
Mina	mine
Montaña	mountain
Monte	mount, mountain
Morro	bluff, headland
Negro	black
Nevado	snow-capped
Norte	north
Nuevo	new
Occidental	western
Oeste	west
Oriental	eastern
Oro	gold
Pampas	grassy plains
Paso	mountain pass
Pico	mountain peak
Piedra	stone, rock
Plata	silver
Playa	shore, beach
Prado	field, meadow
Pueblo	town, village
Puerto	port, harbor
Punta	point
Rada	bay
Ría	river mouth
Río	river
Roca	rock
Sal	salt
Salar	salt flat
San, Santa, Santo	saint
Seno	bay, sound
Serranía	mountain ridge
Sierra	mountain range
Sud	south
Sur	south
Tierra	earth, land
Valle	valley
Verde	green
Viejo	old
Villa	village
Villar	village, hamlet
Volcán	volcano

Physical Features

Feature	Grid
Aguanaval River	C 4
Altamura Island	C 4
Angel de la Guarda Island	D 5
Amanzac River	D 5
Balsas River	D 4
Barranca del Cobre (Canyon)	B 3
Bay of Campeche	B 6
Bay of La Paz	C 3
Blanco River	C 5
Cape Catoche	C 7
Cape Corrientes	C 3
Cape Haro	B 3
Cape Rojo	C 5
Cape San Lucas	C 3
Cape Tepoca	A 2
Cardenas Dam	D 3
Cerralvo Island	C 3
Chetumal Bay	D 7
Chichen Itzá (Ruins)	C 7
Colorado River	A 1
Conchos River	C 2
Cozumel (Island)	C 7
Falcon Reservoir	B 5
Fuerte River	B 3
Gran Desierto (Sonoran Desert)	A 2
Guaje Plain	A 2
Gulf of California	B 2
Gulf of Mexico	C 6
Gulf of Tehuantepec	D 6
Isthmus of Tehuantepec	D 6
Ixtacíhuatl (Volcano)	D 5
Lake Bustillos	B 3
Lake Chapala	D 4
Lake Cuitzeo	D 4
Lake Don Martin	B 3
Lake Pátzcuaro	D 4
Lake El Azúcar	B 5
Lake Toronto	B 3
Lerma River	D 4
Los Caballos	B 5
Mapimí Basin	B 4
Madre Lagoon	C 5
Mestenos Plain	B 5
Montague Island	A 1
Moctezuma River	C 5
Orizaba (Citlaltépetl) (Volcano)	D 5
Nazas River	C 3
Cape Rojo	C 5
Cape San Lucas	C 3
Cape Tepoca	A 2
Cardenas Dam	D 3
Peninsula of Lower California (Volcano)	B 1
Paricutín (Volcano)	D 4
Pánuco River	D 5
Point Arena	B 1
Point Colnett	B 1
Point Baja	B 1
Point Escondida	C 2
Point Final	B 2
Point Ixtapa	D 5
Point Mita	C 3
Point Rosa	C 3
Point San Juan	B 4
de Lima (River)	D 5
Point Santa Rosalía	B 2
Popocatépetl (Volcano)	D 5
Rio Grande (Río Bravo del Norte)	D 5
Salado River	B 4
San José Island	C 3
San Pedro River	C 5
Santa María River	C 3
Sierra Columbia	B 2
Sierra del Carmen (Mountains)	B 4
Sierra de San Antonio (Mountains)	A 2
Sierra de Tamaulipas (Mountains)	C 5
Sierra Madre Occidental (Mountains)	C 3
Sierra Madre del Sur (Mountains)	D 5
Sierra Madre Oriental (Mountains)	B 4
Sierra San Pedro Martir (Mountains)	A 1
Tamiahua Lagoon	C 5
Términos Lagoon	C 6
Tiburón Island	B 2
Trail (Ruins)	C 7
Uxmal (Ruins)	C 7
Urúapan River	B 3
Verde River	C 5
Verde Grande River	C 3
Yaqui River	B 3
Yucatán Peninsula	C 7

CM TERRAIN MEXICO
COPYRIGHT BY
RAND McNALLY & COMPANY
MADE IN U.S.A.

Longitude West of Greenwich

MEXICO

southward, and becomes a tropical rain forest in Tabasco. The southern section has some rich farmland.

Many of Mexico's longest rivers flow into the Gulf of Mexico from the coastal plain. They include the Rio Grande, which forms about 1,300 miles of Mexico's border with the United States. Large petroleum deposits lie beneath the plain and offshore. Huge sulfur deposits occur near the Gulf of Mexico in the 130-mile-wide Isthmus of Tehuantepec, the narrowest part of Mexico. See GULF OF MEXICO; RIO GRANDE.

The Southern Uplands consist largely of steep ridges and deep gorges cut by mountain streams. The region includes a large, hot, dry valley just south of the Volcanic Axis. This valley is drained by the Balsas River. The Sierra Madre del Sur, a rugged mountain range, rises southwest of the valley along the Pacific Ocean. The famous beach resort of Acapulco is on this coast. A little farming takes place on the steep mountainsides. The Oaxaca Plateau makes up the eastern part of the Southern Uplands. Monte Albán, an ancient Indian religious center, was built there on a flattened mountaintop. Much of the gold of the Aztec empire probably came from the Oaxaca Plateau.

The Chiapas Highlands have great blocklike mountains that rise more than 9,000 feet above sea level. There are also many relatively flat surfaces at high altitudes. These tablelands are farmed by Indians who speak Maya and other ancient languages. Most of the region's modern farming development is taking place in deep, broad river valleys. With irrigation, farmers grow coffee, fruits, and other crops.

The Yucatán Peninsula is a low limestone plateau with no rivers. Limestone dissolves in water, and rainfall reaches the sea through underground channels dissolved out of the rock. Great pits have formed where the roofs of these channels have fallen in. The pits were the sacred wells of the ancient Maya Indians. The northwestern part of the region is dry bushland. There, leaves of agave plants provide a yellow fiber called henequen, which is used in making twine. To the south, the rainfall increases, and tropical rain forests cover the land. See YUCATÁN PENINSULA.

The Pacific Northwest region of Mexico includes the Peninsula of Lower California. Much of the peninsula is a desert which receives no rain in some years.

Phil Stern, Globe Photos

The Plateau of Mexico is the largest and most varied of the country's six main land regions. It has fertile uplands, snow-topped mountains, and dry plains.

WORLD BOOK photo by Henry Gill

WORLD BOOK photo by Henry Gill

The Southern Uplands include the Oaxaca Plateau in the eastern part of the region. There, on a flattened mountaintop, are ruins of Monte Albán, an ancient religious center of the Zapotec Indians.

The Yucatán Peninsula is a low plateau of limestone with many large pits. These pits were sacred wells of the Maya Indians. Ruins of Chichén Itzá, a Maya city, stand near one of the pits.

Carver, Photo Researchers

Ian Graham, Photo Researchers

Bullaty-Lomeo from Nancy Palmer

The Gulf Coastal Plain is covered by tropical rain forests and some rich farmland in the south. Forests of low, thorny bushes and trees grow in the dry northern section.

The Chiapas Highlands rise more than 9,000 feet above sea level. They include many flatlands with Indian farm villages. Broad, deep valleys cut through the mountains.

MEXICO/Climate

The climate of Mexico varies sharply from region to region. These differences are especially great in tropical Mexico, south of the Tropic of Cancer. In the south, the wide variety in altitude results in three main temperature zones. The *tierra caliente* (hot land) includes regions up to 3,000 feet above sea level. It has long, hot summers, and mild winters with no frost. The *tierra templada* (temperate land), from 3,000 to 6,000 feet, has temperatures that generally stay between 80° F. and 50° F. the year around. Most crops can be grown there. The *tierra fría* (cold land) lies above 6,000 feet. Frost is rare in this zone up to 8,000 feet, but may occur at almost any time. The highest peaks are always covered with snow.

In tropical Mexico, most rain falls during the summer, usually as short, heavy, afternoon showers. Toward the south, the rainy season generally begins earlier and lasts longer.

The northern half of Mexico is usually dry, and consists largely of deserts and semideserts. Only the mountainous sections receive enough rainfall for growing good crops without irrigation. Most of northern Mexico's rainfall also occurs during the summer. But northwestern Lower California receives most of its rainfall in winter. Above 2,000 feet, summer days are hot and nights are cool. During the winter, days are warm and nights are cold. The coastal lowlands are hot, except on the cool Pacific coast of Lower California.

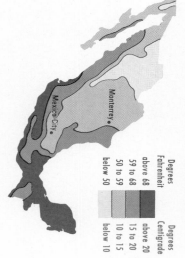

AVERAGE JANUARY TEMPERATURES

Degrees Fahrenheit	Degrees Centigrade
above 68	above 20
59 to 68	15 to 20
50 to 59	10 to 15
below 50	below 10

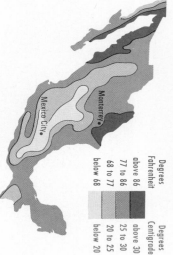

AVERAGE JULY TEMPERATURES

Degrees Fahrenheit	Degrees Centigrade
above 86	above 30
77 to 86	25 to 30
68 to 77	20 to 25
below 68	below 20

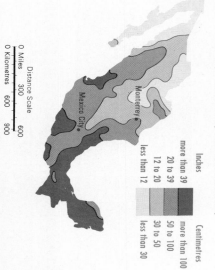

AVERAGE YEARLY PRECIPITATION
(Rain, Melted Snow, and Other Moisture)

Inches	Centimetres
more than 39	more than 100
20 to 39	50 to 100
12 to 20	30 to 50
less than 12	less than 30

Distance Scale

0 Miles   300   600

0 Kilometres   300   600   900

Sunny Acapulco, a popular winter resort on Mexico's Pacific coast, has an average January temperature of 78° F.

WORLD BOOK photo by Henry Gill

MONTHLY WEATHER IN MEXICO CITY AND MONTERREY

		JAN	FEB	MAR	APR	MAY	JUNE	JULY	AUG	SEPT	OCT	NOV	DEC	Average of:
Mexico City		66	69	75	77	78	76	73	73	74	70	68	66	High Temperatures
		42	43	47	51	54	55	53	54	53	50	46	43	Low Temperatures
		4	5	9	17	21	27	27	23	13	6	4		Days of Rain or Snow
Monterrey		68	72	76	84	87	91	92	86	80	71	65		High Temperatures
		48	52	57	62	68	71	72	70	64	55	50		Low Temperatures
		6	5	7	9	8	7	10	9	13	6			Days of Rain or Snow

Temperatures are given in degrees Fahrenheit.

Sources: Meteorological Office, London; *Atlas Geográfico General de México*, by Jorge L. Tamayo, published by Instituto Mexicano de Investigaciones Económicas.

WORLD BOOK maps-FHa

The economy of Mexico is growing much faster than those of most other Latin-American countries. Mexico's economic expansion is based on government policies and programs that developed after the Mexican Revolution of 1910. At that time, Mexico was mainly a land of huge estates owned by wealthy landlords. The government has broken up most of these holdings and distributed them among millions of landless Mexicans. Since the 1940's, the government has especially promoted industrialization. Today, manufacturing is Mexico's fastest-growing industry.

Mexico's economic expansion has made the nation a leader in the production of many products. For Mexico's rank in production, see the separate articles listed under *Products* in the *Related Articles* at the end of this article.

Natural Resources. Mexico has a wide variety of natural resources that support its rapidly expanding economy. They include rich farmland, rich mineral deposits, thick forests, and much plant and animal life. There are also many rivers for irrigating farmland and producing hydroelectric power. The warm climate, sandy beaches, and clear waters of the Pacific coast provide popular vacationlands for tourists.

Farmland. The various farming regions of Mexico vary greatly in altitude, rainfall, and temperature. As a result, many kinds of crops can be grown. However, most of the country is mountainous or receives little rainfall, and is naturally unsuited for growing crops. Crops are grown on only 12 per cent of the total land area.

The best farmlands are in the southern part of Mexico's central plateau. There, rich soils, enough rainfall, and a mild climate permit heavy cultivation. The northern part of the central plateau has little rainfall, and is used mainly for cattle grazing. Large irrigation projects there have developed some rich croplands. Fertile soils are found in the rainy, hot regions of the south and east, and in the eastern coastal plains. However, much work must be done to turn them into productive farmlands. This work includes clearing and draining the land, and controlling floods, insects, and plant diseases. The western coast has fertile soils, but much of it is mountainous and dry.

Minerals. During the 1500's, Mexico's gold and silver attracted European explorers to the region. There are rich mineral deposits throughout Mexico. Northwestern Mexico has the country's largest deposits of copper. Gold, lead, silver, and zinc are found in the central regions. The northeast has much coal, and petroleum is found along the east coast. The chief deposits of iron ore are in the southwest and the state of Durango. The Isthmus of Tehuantepec has enormous sulfur deposits.

Forests and Plant Life. Forests cover about a fifth of Mexico, providing millions of board feet of lumber yearly. The largest forests are in the northwestern and central mountains, and in the rainy south and southeast. The forests include ebony, mahogany, rosewood, walnut, and other valuable hardwoods used in making furniture. Large pine forests also grow in the mountains, and supply timber for Mexico's pulp and paper industry. Sapodilla trees in the south provide chicle, a gumlike, milky juice used in making chewing gum. Mexico also has a great variety of flowers and cactus

plants. The country's thousands of kinds of flowers include azaleas, chrysanthemums, geraniums, orchids, and poinsettias. The northern deserts have hundreds of kinds of cactus plants.

Animal Life. Bears, deer, and mountain lions live in Mexico's mountains. The northern deserts have coyotes, lizards, prairie dogs, and rattlesnakes. Mexico also has some alligators, jaguars, and opossums. Chihuahuas, the world's smallest dogs, originally came from Mexico.

Mexico has hundreds of kinds of birds, including the beautifully colored quetzals of the southern forests. Other birds include flamingoes, hummingbirds, herons, parrots, and pelicans.

Fish and shellfish are plentiful in the coastal waters, lakes, and rivers. Abalones, oysters, sardines, shrimp, and tuna are the most important commercial catches. Sportsmen catch marlin, swordfish, and tarpon in the seas off Mexico.

Manufacturing has expanded rapidly in Mexico since

MEXICO'S GROSS NATIONAL PRODUCT IN 1965

Total gross national product—$19,400,000,000

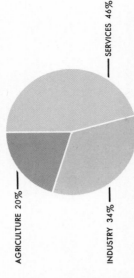

AGRICULTURE 20%

INDUSTRY 34%

SERVICES 46%

The Gross National Product (GNP) is the total value of goods and services produced by a country in a year. The GNP measures a nation's total economic performance for the year. It can also be used to compare the economic output and growth of countries.

PRODUCTION AND WORKERS BY ECONOMIC ACTIVITIES

Economic Activities	Per Cent of GNP Produced	Labor Force* Number of Persons	Labor Force* Per Cent of Total
Trade	26	1,288,000	10
Manufacturing	25	1,923,000	15
Agriculture, Forestry, & Fishing	20	6,909,000	52
Other Services	13	1,812,000	14
Transportation & Communication	4	437,000	3
Construction	3	499,000	4
Government	3	†	†
Petroleum & Coke	3	**	**
Mining	2	174,000	1
Utilities & Other	1	174,000	1
Total	100	13,216,000	100

*1964, latest information available.
†Included in Other Services.
**Included in Manufacturing.
Sources: ILO; National Bank of Foreign Commerce, Mexico; UN.

MEXICO

the 1940's. This expansion has led to related developments throughout the entire economy. For example, the production of raw materials for new factories has increased. Banking, marketing, and other services have expanded. Heavy government spending on construction has provided additional housing for the growing industrial centers. Power plants have been built for the new industries, as well as highways and railroads for carrying goods. Mexico's industrialization has been financed chiefly by the nation's businessmen, but the government and foreign investors have also contributed much.

Mexico City is the leading industrial center, followed by Monterrey and Guadalajara. Other expanding manufacturing centers include Puebla, Querétaro, Saltillo, San Luis Potosí, Toluca, and Veracruz. A government program of the 1960's is spreading industry still farther from the main centers, especially to northern cities.

Mexico's leading products include chemicals, clothing, and processed foods. The production of iron and steel is expanding rapidly. Until the 1960's, Mexican automobile factories merely assembled parts, most of which were imported. Today, Mexican plants are producing the parts in increasing quantities. Other important products include cement, fertilizers, household appliances, rubber, and wood pulp and paper.

Mexico has long been famous for the skill of its craftsmen who make various handicraft articles. These crafts-

FARM, MINERAL, AND FOREST PRODUCTS

This map shows where the leading farm, mineral, and forest products of Mexico are produced. The map also shows the crop, livestock, forest, and nonagricultural areas, and the major manufacturing centers. Most of Mexico's farming and manufacturing activities are within 300 miles of Mexico City.

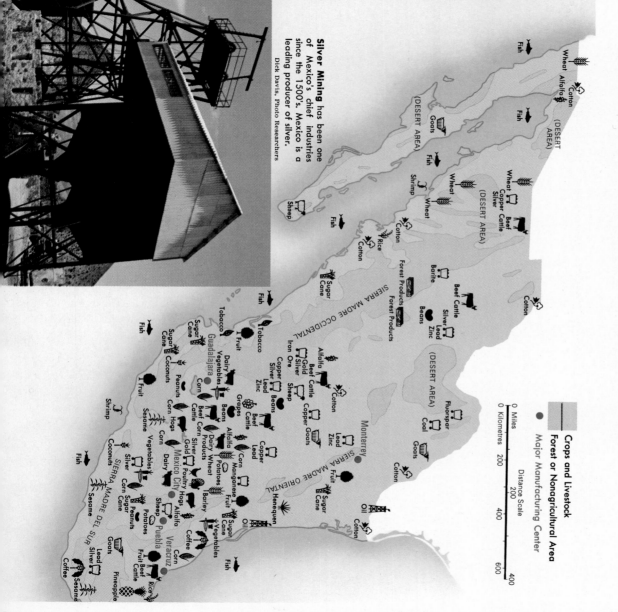

Silver Mining has been one of Mexico's chief industries since the 1500's. Mexico is a leading producer of silver.

Dick Davis, Photo Researchers

Crops and Livestock

Forest or Nonagricultural Area

● **Major Manufacturing Center**

Distance Scale

Miles
0   200   400   600

Kilometres
0   200   400

men follow beautiful old Indian or Spanish-colonial designs. Their products generally vary by area. The articles include silver jewelry from Taxco, glassware and pottery from Guadalajara and Puebla, and hand-woven baskets and blankets from Oaxaca and Toluca. Many of the products are sold to tourists, about a million of whom visit Mexico every year.

Agriculture. For hundreds of years, most Mexicans worked on huge haciendas. These estates were owned by wealthy Spaniards or by *creoles* (persons of Spanish ancestry born in the New World). A majority of the peasants were bound to the land for life in payment of debts. This system, called *peonage*, was declared illegal in 1917. Since then, the government has broken up most of the haciendas and distributed more than 130 million acres of the land to the peasants. See PEONAGE.

The Mexican constitution of 1917 recognized the old system of *ejidos* (farmlands held in common by communities). On the ejidos, farmers either work on individual sections by themselves, or they work the land as a group and share in the crops. Mexico has about 18,000 ejidos, most of which are worked in individual sections. A farmer can pass his land on to his children, but he cannot sell or rent it.

The standard of living on most ejidos is extremely low. The plots are small, and more than half of them cover fewer than five acres. The ejidos consist mostly of poor cropland, forests, dry grazing land, or even land that is completely unproductive. They include about 45 per cent of Mexico's total cropland. The rest of the cropland consists of cooperatives, small family farms, or haciendas that the government has not broken up.

Since 1937, the government has promoted modern farming methods by means of educational programs, financial aid, and expansion of irrigation and transportation systems. As a result, production has greatly increased in many areas. But ancient methods are still used in many other sections, especially on the ejidos and smaller family farms.

More farmland is used for corn, the people's basic food, than for any other crop. Other leading crops, in order of acreage, include beans, wheat, cotton, sugar cane, and coffee. Also important are alfalfa, fruits, henequen, rice, tobacco, and vegetables.

Livestock is raised throughout Mexico. Beef cattle graze in the dry northern pasturelands. Dairy cattle are raised chiefly in central Mexico. Farmers also raise chickens, goats, hogs, horses, sheep, and turkeys.

Mining. The mining industry of Mexico has long been based on copper, gold, lead, silver, tin, and zinc. Today, antimony, bismuth, fluorspar, manganese, and mercury are also mined in large quantities. Mexico is a leading silver producer, mining about 38 million ounces a year. Large iron ore and coal deposits support the nation's growing steel industry.

Mexico was once the world's leading producer of petroleum. Today, Mexico pumps more than 133 million barrels of oil annually. The petroleum industry is operated by a government agency. Mexico also produces much natural gas. Since the 1950's, sulfur has become one of the country's chief exports.

Electric Power. Mexico generates about 15 billion kilowatt-hours of electricity a year. The government handles almost all power production and distribution. Almost half the power is produced by hydroelectric plants, and steam or diesel stations produce most of the rest. About 70 per cent of the power is used by industries. During the late 1960's, several huge projects were being built to provide electricity in millions of Mexican homes.

Foreign Trade of Mexico consists chiefly of exporting raw materials and partly processed goods, and importing manufactured products. Cotton is the leading export. Other major agricultural exports include coffee, henequen, shrimp, sugar, and tomatoes. The chief mineral exports are copper, fluorspar, lead, sulfur, and zinc. The principal imports include automobiles, machines and machinery, and industrial equipment.

In most years, the value of Mexico's imports is greater than that of its exports. The nation's industries are expanding steadily. But the new factories need much equipment and materials, and simply cannot supply the country's needs for industrial goods. To help pay for imports, Mexico depends on its large tourist income and on foreign loans and investments.

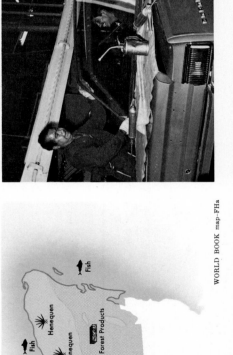

Automobile Production in Mexico has expanded rapidly during the 1960's. Mexico City is the center of the automobile industry.

Chrysler Corporation

WORLD BOOK map—FHa

381

MEXICO

More than two-thirds of Mexico's trade is with the United States, but trade with Western European countries and Japan is increasing. Trade with other Latin-American countries is relatively unimportant. But Mexico is trying to increase it through the Latin American Free Trade Association, an economic union of Mexico and eight other Latin-American nations.

Transportation in Mexico ranges from modern methods to ancient ones. Airlines, highways, and railroads connect all the major cities and towns. But some farmers still carry goods to market on their heads and backs, or by burros and oxcarts.

Mexico has more than 20,000 miles of paved highways, including several that extend from the United States. There are also about 15,000 miles of unpaved, all-weather roads. The government is continually improving and extending the highway system. Mexicans own more than a million motor vehicles, including almost 700,000 automobiles. Many buses connect the cities and towns.

There are about 30 major airports in Mexico. Mexican and foreign airlines provide air service within Mexico and to all parts of the world. Mexico City is an important center of international air travel.

The government-owned national railway system includes almost all of the country's more than 15,000 miles of track. The system consists of almost 15 railroads.

Mexico has more than 30 seaports, but only a few are important. They include Coatzacoalcos, Tampico, and Veracruz on the Gulf of Mexico, and Ensenada and Mazatlán on the Pacific Ocean. The nation has a small merchant fleet.

Communication. The first book known to be published in the Western Hemisphere was a catechism printed in Mexico City in 1539. Today, books and magazines published in Mexico City are read widely throughout Mexico and all of Latin America. Mexico has about 200 newspapers with a total circulation of nearly 4½ million copies. About 20 daily newspapers in Mexico City account for almost half the total circulation. The largest newspapers include *Excélsior*, *La Prensa*, *Novedades*, and *Ovaciones* of Mexico City; *El Occidental* of Guadalajara; and *El Norte* of Monterrey.

Mexico has nearly 450 radio stations and about 25 television stations. Telephone and telegraph lines connect all parts of the country. Mexico's motion-picture industry produces about 65 films a year, more than any other Latin-American nation.

TRANSPORTATION

This map shows the major roads, rail lines, airports, and seaports of Mexico. Mexico's few inland waterways are also shown. Several branches of the Pan American Highway extend from the Mexican-U.S. border. They meet near Mexico City, and the highway continues south to Central America.

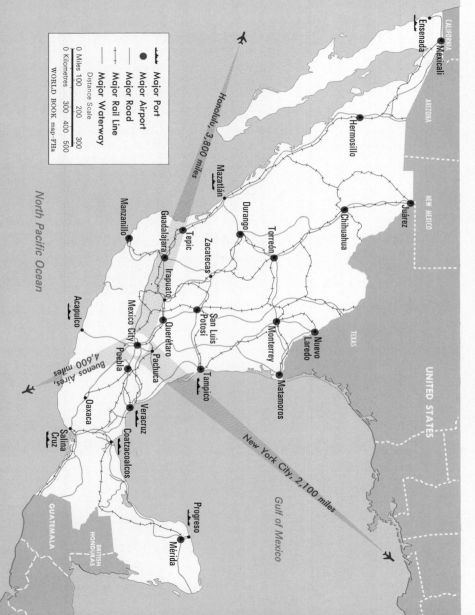

Legend:
- Major Port
- Major Airport
- Major Road
- Major Rail Line
- Major Waterway

Distance Scale
0 Miles 100   200   300
0 Kilometers 100 200 300 400 500

WORLD BOOK map–FHa

Honolulu, 3,800 miles

Buenos Aires, 4,600 miles

New York City, 2,100 miles

North Pacific Ocean

Gulf of Mexico

CALIFORNIA
ARIZONA
NEW MEXICO
TEXAS
UNITED STATES
GUATEMALA
BRITISH HONDURAS

Ensenada
Mexicali
Hermosillo
Mazatlán
Durango
Chihuahua
Juárez
Manzanillo
Guadalajara
Tepic
Zacatecas
Torreón
Irapuato
Acapulco
Mexico City
Querétaro
San Luis Potosí
Monterrey
Nuevo Laredo
Pachuca
Puebla
Tampico
Matamoros
Oaxaca
Veracruz
Coatzacoalcos
Salina Cruz
Progreso
Mérida

Ancient Times. The first people who lived in what is now Mexico probably arrived as early as 10,000 B.C. They were Indians of unknown tribes who migrated from the north. These Indians were hunters who lived in small, temporary communities. They followed the herds of buffalo, mammoths, mastodons, and other large animals that roamed the land. About 7500 B.C., the climate changed and became drier. The herds could not find enough grass to eat, and they died off. The Indians then lived on small wild animals or the berries and seeds of wild plants.

Beginning about 5000 B.C., Indians in what is now the Puebla region discovered how to grow plants for food. They grew corn, which became their most important food, and avocados, beans, peppers, squashes, and tomatoes. These Indians were among the first people to cultivate these vegetables. They also raised dogs and turkeys for food. The wandering bands of hunters became groups of farmers in permanent settlements.

The Growth of Villages. By 1500 B.C., large farm villages stood along Lake Texcoco in the fertile southcentral Valley of Mexico, and in the southern highlands and forests. The farmers used irrigation to improve their crops. The villages grew and new classes of people developed, including pottery makers, priests, and weavers. Trade in polished stones, pottery, and seashells was carried on with distant communities.

By 500 B.C., the villagers began to build flat-topped pyramids with temples on them. Some villages, including Cuicuilco near what is now Mexico City, became religious centers. Indians came from other communities to worship in the temples. Because these people were farmers, they worshiped gods that represented such natural forces as the rain and the sun. The villages grew into towns, from the Valley of Mexico to the Gulf and Pacific coasts, and south to what is now Guatemala.

The Olmec Indians of the southern Gulf Coast made the first great advance toward civilization in the Mexico region. Between 1200 B.C. and about 100 B.C., the Olmec developed a counting system and calendar. They also carved beautiful stone statues. See OLMEC INDIANS.

The Classic Period. Great Indian civilizations thrived between A.D. 300 and 900, the Classic Period of Mexico. Huge pyramids dedicated to the sun and the moon were built at Teotihuacán, near what is now Mexico City. In the religious centers of southern Mexico and northern Central America, the Maya Indians built beautiful homes, pyramids, and temples of limestone. They recorded important dates on tall, carved blocks of stone, and wrote in a kind of picture writing. In what is now the state of Oaxaca, the Zapotec Indians flattened a mountaintop and built their religious center of Monte Albán. See MAYA; ZAPOTEC INDIANS.

The reasons for the fall of these classic civilizations are not clear. The climate probably became even drier about A.D. 900, and not enough crops could be produced to feed the large population. Perhaps the city people attacked their neighbors to get more land. Or the farmers may have revolted against the priests who had been their rulers. In the north, wild Chichimec tribes attacked and destroyed many cities.

The Toltec and the Aztec. Many wars took place after the Classic Period. The fierce Toltec Indians established an empire during the 900's, with a capital at Tula, north of present-day Mexico City. The Toltec invaded the Yucatán Peninsula and rebuilt Chichén Itzá, an old Maya religious center. Toltec influence spread throughout the central and southern regions. This influence included the use of stone pillars to support roofs, the worship of the feathered-serpent god Quetzalcoatl, and human sacrifice in religion. See TOLTEC INDIANS.

The Aztec built the last and greatest Indian empire during the early 1400's, after invading tribes ended the Toltec power. The Aztec empire extended between the Pacific and Gulf coasts, and from the Isthmus of Tehuantepec north to the Pánuco River. The Aztec were skilled in medicine, and composed music and poetry. They were rich with gold, silver, and other treasure paid

IMPORTANT DATES IN MEXICO

c. 1500 B.C. Village life developed in the Valley of Mexico.

c. A.D. 300-900 Great Indian civilizations thrived during the Classic Period.

c. 900-1200 The Toltec empire controlled the Valley of Mexico.

1325 The Aztec Indians founded Tenochtitlán (now Mexico City).

1519-1521 Hernando Cortes conquered the Aztec empire for Spain.

1535 Antonio de Mendoza, the first Spanish viceroy, arrived in Mexico City to rule New Spain (now Mexico).

1810 Miguel Hidalgo y Costilla began the Mexican struggle for independence.

1821 Mexico won independence.

1823 Mexico became a republic.

1836 Texas won independence from Mexico.

1846-1848 The United States defeated Mexico in the Mexican War, and won much Mexican territory.

1855 A liberal government began a period of reform.

1863 French troops occupied Mexico City.

1864 Maximilian became emperor of Mexico.

1867 Liberal forces led by Benito Juárez regained power.

1876-1880 and 1884-1911 Porfirio Diaz ruled Mexico as dictator.

1910-1911 Francisco I. Madero led a revolution that overthrew Díaz.

1914 United States forces occupied Veracruz.

1917 A revolutionary constitution was adopted.

1920 The government began making revolutionary reforms.

1929 The National Revolutionary party was formed.

1934 The government began extensive land distribution to farmers.

1938 Mexico took over foreign oil-company properties.

1942-1945 Mexico's industries expanded rapidly during World War II to supply the Allies with war goods.

1953 Women received the right to vote in all elections.

1963 Mexico and the United States settled the 99-year-old Chamizal border dispute.

1966 Work began on the Chamizal project to shift the course of the Rio Grande.

1968 The Summer Olympic Games were held in Mexico City.

yearly by tribes they had conquered. Every year, thousands of prisoners of war were sacrificed to the Aztec gods. The Aztec capital, Tenochtitlán, founded in 1325, stood on an island in Lake Texcoco at the site of Mexico City. When the Spaniards arrived there in 1519, Tenochtitlán had a population of about 100,000. No Spanish city of that time had so many people. See AZTEC.

The Spanish Conquest. The Spaniards began to occupy the West Indies during the 1490's, and discovered Mexico in 1517. That year, Diego de Velásquez, the governor of Cuba, sent ships under Francisco de Córdoba to explore to the west and search for treasure. Córdoba found the coast of the Yucatán Peninsula and brought back reports of large cities. Velásquez sent Juan de Grijalva in 1518. Grijalva explored the Mexican coast from Yucatán to what is now Veracruz.

Reports of the strangers on the coast were carried to the Aztec emperor Montezuma II, or Moctezuma II, in Tenochtitlán. The tales of Spanish guns and horses—which the Indians had never seen before—and of men in armor made him fear that the Spaniards were gods.

A third expedition of about 550 soldiers sailed from Cuba under Hernando Cortes, or Hernán Cortés, in February, 1519. Cortes' 11 ships followed Grijalva's route along the coast. At various points, Cortes defeated large Indian armies with his horses and cannons. He founded Veracruz, the first Spanish settlement in what is now Mexico.

Montezuma sent messengers with rich gifts for Cortes, but also ordered the Spaniards to leave the land. Instead, Cortes marched toward Tenochtitlán. He was joined by thousands of the Aztec's Indian enemies, who looked on him as the godlike destroyer of the cruel Aztec. Montezuma decided not to oppose the Spaniards because he feared Cortes was the god Quetzalcoatl. The invaders arrived in Tenochtitlán in November, 1519. They were far too few to control the great Aztec capital by themselves. Cortes soon seized Montezuma and held him as hostage for the safety of the Spaniards.

In June, 1520, the Aztec revolted. After a week of bitter fighting, they drove the Spaniards from Tenochtitlán. Cortes built a fleet of boats to cross Lake Texcoco,

and attacked the city in May, 1521. The Spaniards killed thousands of Aztec and destroyed Tenochtitlán almost completely. The city surrendered in August. Cortes then sent soldiers to take over the rest of the Aztec empire. See HERNANDO.

Spanish Rule. King Charles I of Spain granted huge estates to Cortes and the other *conquistadores* (conquerors). In 1522, Charles named Cortes governor and captain-general of New Spain, which the colony was called. But Charles distrusted Cortes, and soon limited his power. In 1524, the king appointed a Council of the Indies to make laws for the Spanish-American colonies. In 1527, he established the first *audiencia* (court of judges) to govern New Spain. Antonio de Mendoza, a Spanish nobleman, arrived in 1535 to head the government as the first *viceroy* (king's representative).

The people had no elected legislature. Power was held by the *peninsulares* (persons born in Spain). Only they received high posts in the government of New Spain or in the Roman Catholic Church there. *Creoles* (persons of Spanish ancestry born in the New World) held only unimportant government or church posts. *Mestizos* (persons of mixed white and Indian ancestry) were free craftsmen, farmers, and laborers. Most Indians were forced to live and work on estates almost like serfs, or remained in their own villages. Negro slaves from Africa worked in mines or on estates.

AZTEC EMPIRE—1521

■ Aztec Empire
▭ Present Boundary

Tenochtitlán

Distance Scale
0 Miles ___ 500 ___ 1,000
0 Kilometres ___ 1,000 ___ 1,500

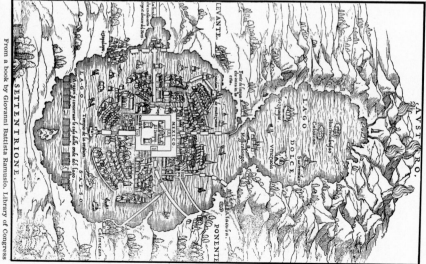

The Aztec Capital, Tenochtitlán (now Mexico City), stood on an island in Lake Texcoco. Raised roads connected it with the mainland. This map, published in 1556, is based on one believed to have been drawn by Hernando Cortes, conqueror of the Aztec.

From a book by Giovanni Battista Ramusio, Library of Congress

Spanish priests tried to turn the Indians to Roman Catholicism as early as the 1520's. The priests established missions in farm areas and built churches in the cities. Millions of Indians were baptized. But the forces of nature remained an important part of religion to them. Many Indians worshiped their old gods in private, and most continued ancient religious practices.

The Spaniards brought new kinds of animals and crops from Europe. Burros, for example, became a basic part of Indian life. But generally, the Indians still lived as they had for hundreds of years. They ate the same foods, lived in the same huts, and worked their fields in the same ancient ways.

Revolt Against the Spaniards. Most groups in New Spain opposed Spanish rule. The creoles were not allowed to hold power, and the mestizos and Indians were kept in ignorance and poverty. But for almost 300 years, until 1810, the people did not revolt.

By 1800, the creoles were ready for independence. The American Revolutionary War and the French Revolution provided examples of successful revolts against hated kings. New books from France preached freedom from harsh rule. The royal government became unbearable to the creoles. In addition, political confusion developed after the French invaded Spain in 1808.

Late on the night of Sept. 15, 1810, a creole priest named Miguel Hidalgo y Costilla launched the Mexican War of Independence. In the town of Dolores (now Dolores Hidalgo), he called Indians and mestizos to church. Hidalgo raised the *Grito de Dolores* (Cry of Dolores), in which he demanded independence from Spanish rule. Today, late on September 15, Mexico's president rings a bell and repeats the Grito de Dolores. Mexicans celebrate September 16 as Independence Day.

Hidalgo's untrained followers armed themselves with axes, clubs, and knives. They gained followers as they marched across estates and through such cities as Guanajuato and Guadalajara. The revolution spread into other regions, and Hidalgo soon controlled much of New Spain. Spanish troops captured Hidalgo in 1811 and executed him.

Hidalgo's struggle was continued by José María Morelos y Pavón, another priest. Morelos organized a trained army that was equipped with guns taken from the Spaniards. Morelos won many victories, and captured Acapulco in 1813. He then declared Mexico independent and organized a government.

Morelos' government outlined a liberal program of reform. It had three main goals: (1) establishing a republic in which all races had equal rights, (2) ending the special rights of the army and of the Roman Catholic Church, and (3) breaking up the large estates into small farms for the people.

Most creoles did not want Morelos' social and economic reforms, however. They turned against him and supported the viceroy. The Spanish forces began winning important victories in 1814, and Morelos was captured and shot the next year. The fight for independence was carried on by only a few small bands in the mountains. Most creoles and peninsulares united behind Ferdinand VII, the king of Spain.

Independence. In 1820, a liberal revolt swept Spain. Ferdinand was forced to accept a constitution that greatly limited his power. The liberal victory alarmed the conservatives in New Spain. They feared that social

reforms in the colony would soon follow. To prevent such reforms, conservative leaders who had supported the viceroy decided secretly to bring about independence in their own way.

The conservatives persuaded the viceroy to send their military leader, Agustín de Iturbide, to crush the revolutionaries, now led by Vicente Guerrero. Instead, Iturbide and Guerrero agreed in February, 1821, to make Mexico independent. The new government was planned to grant equal rights to creoles and Spaniards. Liberals and conservatives both supported Iturbide, and his army increased by the thousands. Only a few Spanish forces remained loyal to Spain, and little fighting took place. Mexico became independent by the end of 1821.

The various Mexican groups had stayed united only because they opposed the Spanish government. The revolution broke apart soon after Spanish power had been driven from the country. Conservatives wanted a member of Spain's royal family to be king. Liberals called for a republic. A third group wanted Iturbide to take over. Iturbide seized power and was declared Emperor Agustín I in 1822. But he was a poor ruler, and most groups turned against him. A revolt led by General Antonio López de Santa Anna, a former officer in Iturbide's army, drove Iturbide from power in 1823. Mexico became a republic.

A convention met in 1823 and began to write a constitution. The conservative delegates called for *centralism*, under which a strong central government would control the republic. But a majority of the delegates were liberals and favored *federalism*, which granted the states more power. A federalist constitution was completed in 1824, and a two-house Congress was established. The newly created state legislatures elected Guadalupe Victoria, a former follower of Hidalgo and Morelos, to be Mexico's first president.

War with Texas and the United States. During the mid-1800's, struggles for power shook Mexico. Santa Anna switched his loyalty from one group to another, and became the leading political figure. He joined the liberals in 1832, and was elected president. After the Congress approved many liberal measures, the conserva-

Miguel Hidalgo y Costilla set off Mexico's War of Independence in 1810. Freedom from Spain was won in 1821.

From a mural by José Orozco. Guadalajara, Mexico (Ralph Mandol, DPI)

tives rebelled. Santa Anna then switched over to the conservatives and seized the powers of a dictator. He threw out the constitution, forced the liberals out of office, and established a centralist government.

Texas was then a part of Mexico, even though many persons from the United States lived there. In 1835, the Americans in Texas revolted against Santa Anna's government. In 1836, Santa Anna defeated a Texas force in the famous Battle of the Alamo at San Antonio. But later that year, the Texans crushed Santa Anna's troops at San Jacinto and captured him. To regain his freedom, Santa Anna signed a treaty recognizing Texan independence. The new republic of Texas included parts of present-day Colorado, Kansas, New Mexico, Oklahoma, and Wyoming. The Mexican government did not recognize Santa Anna's treaty, and removed him from office.

Texas wanted to be part of the United States, and joined the Union in 1845. But Mexico still claimed Texas, and border disputes developed. In April, 1846, American forces crossed the disputed region and were attacked by Mexican troops. The United States declared war on Mexico the next month.

American armies drove deep into Mexico and occupied much of the country. General Zachary Taylor fought Santa Anna in the Battle of Buena Vista in February, 1847, and both sides claimed victory. Taylor became a national hero in the United States, and was elected President the next year. In September, 1847, General Winfield Scott captured Mexico City after the bitter Battle of Chapultepec. In this battle, a number of young military students threw themselves

WORLD BOOK map—FHa

REPUBLIC OF MEXICO—1823

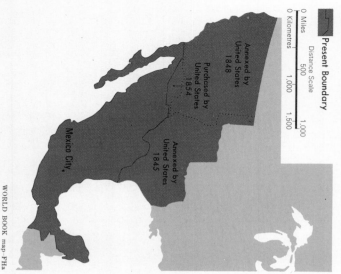

Present Boundary

Distance Scale

| 0 Miles | 500 | 1,000 |
| 0 Kilometres | 1,000 | 1,500 |

Annexed by United States 1848

Purchased by United States 1854

Annexed by United States 1845

Mexico City.

over a cliff to their deaths, rather than surrender. Today, the Monument to the Boy Heroes stands at the foot of Chapultepec Hill in their honor.

The Treaty of Guadalupe Hidalgo, signed in February, 1848, ended the Mexican War. Under the treaty, Mexico gave the United States the land that is now California, Nevada, and Utah; most of Arizona; and parts of Colorado, New Mexico, and Wyoming. Mexico also recognized Texas, down to the Rio Grande, as part of the United States. In return, Mexico received $15 million from the United States. In the Gadsden Purchase of 1854, the United States paid Mexico $10 million for territory in what is now southern Arizona and New Mexico.

For fuller accounts of this period, see the separate articles on ALAMO; GADSDEN PURCHASE; GUADALUPE HIDALGO, TREATY OF; MEXICAN WAR; SAN JACINTO, BATTLE OF; SANTA ANNA, ANTONIO; TEXAS (The Texas Revolution).

Reform. The Mexican War exhausted the country's economy, and great political confusion developed. Santa Anna again seized power in 1853 and ruled as a dictator. But the liberals had been gaining strength since the war. In 1855, they revolted and drove Santa Anna from power.

Benito Juárez, a Zapotec Indian, and other men gave the liberal movement effective leadership. The liberals promoted the private ownership of land. After they took over in 1855, they passed laws to break up the large estates of the Roman Catholic Church and the lands of Indian villages. In 1857, a new constitution brought back the federal system of government.

The new reforms resulted in a conservative revolt in 1858. Juárez fled from Mexico City. The liberals declared him president, and he set up a government in Veracruz. During the civil war that followed—the War of the Reform—a conservative government operated in Mexico City. The Catholic bishops supported the con-

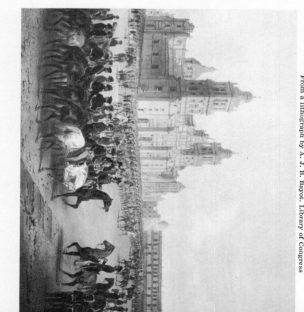

U.S. Forces Captured Mexico City in September, 1847, during the Mexican War. They were led by General Winfield Scott.

From a lithograph by A. J. B. Bayot. Library of Congress

servatives because of the liberals' opposition to the church. In 1859, Juárez issued his Reform Laws in an attempt to end the church's political power in Mexico. The laws ordered the separation of church and state, and the takeover of all church property. The liberal armies defeated the conservatives late in 1860, and Juárez returned to Mexico City in 1861.

The French Invasion. The Mexican government had little money after the War of the Reform. Juárez stopped payments on the country's debts to France, Great Britain, and Spain. Troops of the three nations occupied Veracruz in 1862. The British and Spaniards soon left after they saw that the French were more interested in political power than in collecting debts. The French emperor, Napoleon III, took this opportunity to invade and conquer Mexico. French troops occupied Mexico City in 1863. Juárez escaped from the capital.

In 1864, Napoleon named Maximilian, brother of the Austrian emperor, to be emperor of Mexico. Maximilian was supported by Mexican conservatives. The United States opposed the French occupation of Mexico, but could do nothing because of its own Civil War. After the war ended in 1865, the United States put heavy pressure on France to remove its troops. In addition to this pressure, Napoleon needed his soldiers in Europe because he feared war would break out between France and Prussia. The French troops sailed from Veracruz in 1867. Juárez' forces then captured Maximilian and shot him. The conservative movement broke up. Juárez returned to Mexico City, and the country was united behind the liberals. After Juárez died in 1872, his Reform Laws were made part of the constitution.

The Dictatorship of Porfirio Díaz. After the election of 1876, a revolt overthrew the new government. The revolt was led by Porfirio Díaz, a mestizo general. He ignored the federal constitution and controlled all Mexico with his troops. His enemies were killed, jailed, or sent out of the country. Díaz had called for a policy of no re-election during his revolt, but served eight terms. Except from 1880 to 1884, Díaz held office until 1911. He allowed no effective opposition in his "elections."

Under Díaz, mines, oil wells, and railroads were built, and Mexico's economy improved. But industrial wages were kept low, and attempts to form labor unions were crushed. Indian communities lost their land to big landowners. Peasants were kept in debt and were prevented from leaving the estates. The great majority of Mexicans remained in poverty and ignorance. The benefits of Mexico's improved economy went chiefly to the big landowners, businessmen, and foreign investors.

The Revolution of 1910. Opposition to Díaz' rule began to grow after 1900. Francisco I. Madero, a liberal landowner, decided to run against him in 1910. During the campaign, Madero became widely popular. Díaz had him jailed until after the election, which Díaz won. Madero then fled to the United States.

In November, 1910, Madero issued a call for revolution. He had opposed violence, but he saw no other way to overthrow Díaz. Revolutionary bands developed throughout Mexico. They defeated federal troops, destroyed railroads, and attacked towns and estates. In May, 1911, members of Díaz' government agreed to force him from office, in hope of preventing further bloodshed. Díaz resigned and left Mexico, and Madero became president later that year.

Madero meant well, but he was a weak president. He could not handle the many groups that opposed him. Some of these groups wanted a dictatorship again. Others called for greater reforms than Madero put through. In 1913, General Victoriano Huerta seized power, and Madero was shot.

Many Mexicans supported Huerta's dictatorship, hoping for peace. But Madero's followers united behind Venustiano Carranza, a landowner, and the bitter fighting continued. President Woodrow Wilson of the United States refused to recognize Huerta's government, and openly sided with Carranza's revolutionaries. After some American sailors were arrested in Tampico in 1914, U.S. forces seized Veracruz. Wilson hoped to prevent the shipment of arms from the seaport to Huerta's army. Later in 1914, Carranza's forces occupied Mexico City, and Huerta was forced to leave the country. See WILSON, WOODROW (Crisis in Mexico).

The Constitution of 1917. The victorious revolutionary leaders soon began to struggle among themselves for power. Carranza's armies fought those of Francisco "Pancho" Villa and Emiliano Zapata. Villa and Zapata demanded more extreme reforms than Carranza planned. In 1915, the United States supported Carranza and halted the export of guns to his enemies. In revenge, Villa crossed the border in 1916 and raided Columbus, N.Mex. His men killed 16 Americans. President Wilson sent General John J. Pershing into Mexico, but Pershing's troops failed to capture Villa.

In 1916, Carranza's power was recognized throughout most of Mexico. He called a convention to prepare a new constitution. The constitution, adopted in 1917, combined Carranza's liberal policies with more extreme reforms. It gave the government control over education, farm and oil properties, and the Roman Catholic

"Pancho" Villa, a bandit chief, became a general in the Mexican Revolution of 1910. He controlled much of northern Mexico.

Bettmann Archive

Church. The constitution limited Mexico's president to one term, and it recognized labor unions.

Also in 1917, during World War I, Germany invited Mexico to join in declaring war on the United States. In return, Germany promised that Mexico would get back all the territory lost in the Mexican War. Carranza refused Germany's offer.

Carranza, like Madero, was a weak president and did little to carry out the new constitutional program. In 1920, he was killed during a revolt led by General Álvaro Obregón, who later became president.

Economic and Social Changes. Obregón distributed some land among the peasants, built many schools throughout the countryside, and supported a strong labor-union movement. Plutarco Elías Calles, who had fought Huerta and Villa, became president in 1924. Calles carried on the revolutionary program. He encouraged land reform and enforced constitutional controls over the Roman Catholic Church. The bishops protested by closing the churches from 1926 to 1929.

For several years after Calles' term ended in 1928, he remained the real power behind the presidency. In 1929, Calles formed the National Revolutionary Party. Until then, Mexican political parties had been temporary combinations of various groups organized by presidential candidates. The National Revolutionary Party stood for the goals of the Mexican Revolution. It included all important political groups and became a permanent party. It was reorganized as the Party of the Mexican Revolution in 1938, and as the Institutional Revolutionary Party in 1946. The party has won all state and national elections by large majorities.

By the early 1930's, the push for reform had slowed down. Calles and many other old revolutionary leaders were now wealthy landowners and opposed extreme changes. Younger politicians called for speeding up the revolutionary program. As a result, the National Revolutionary Party adopted a six-year plan of social and economic reform. General Lázaro Cárdenas was named to carry it out.

After Cárdenas became president in 1934, he ended Calles' power and gave Mexico strong leadership. He divided among the peasants more than twice as much land as all previous presidents combined had done. Cárdenas also promoted government controls over foreign-owned companies and strongly supported labor unions. In 1938, during a strike of oil workers, the government took over the properties of American and British oil companies. The companies and the British government protested angrily. But the United States government recognized Mexico's right to the properties as long as the companies received fair payment. During the 1940's, Mexico and the American and British companies agreed on payments that Mexico later made.

Industrial Growth was a major goal after General Manuel Ávila Camacho became president in 1940. Cárdenas had thought of Mexico as a land of farms and small local industries. Ávila Camacho recognized the need for heavy industries and production of all kinds of goods. The growth of modern industrial Mexico began.

In 1942, during World War II, German submarines sank Mexican oil tankers. Mexico then declared war

on Germany and its allies, Italy and Japan. Mexico sent an air force group to fight the Japanese in the Philippines. But Mexico's contribution to the war effort was almost entirely economic. Mexico supplied many laborers and raw materials to the United States. It also exported war goods manufactured in factories that the United States helped set up. Mexico's total exports nearly doubled in value during the war. Mexico became a charter member of the United Nations in 1945, the year World War II ended.

Mexico kept up its industrial growth after the war. New factories were built to produce automobiles, cement, chemicals, steel, and such consumer goods as clothing and processed foods. The government expanded Mexico's highway, irrigation, and railway systems. Many apartment buildings went up, especially in Mexico City. In 1953, Mexican women received the right to vote in all elections. During the 1950's, increasing numbers of tourists from the United States brought new wealth to Mexico.

Mexico Today is continuing the industrial expansion that began during the 1940's. Industrial growth has been especially rapid in the production of automobiles, chemicals, electrical appliances, and steel. In spite of this expansion, more than a third of the people still do not have proper food or housing. Living conditions are especially bad in the farm areas, where about half the people live, and in the city slums. Few farms have modern equipment, and farm wages are very low.

Mexico's population increase of almost $3\frac{1}{2}$ per cent a year is a major reason for the low standard of living. The increase also makes the nation's education program difficult. The government spends increasing sums of money each year for education. But the construction of new schools cannot keep up with the rapidly growing population. Also, the many new government housing projects in the cities cannot meet the increasing needs.

In 1961, the United States proposed the Alliance for Progress. Under this program, Mexico and other Latin-American countries began receiving United States loans for economic and social development (see ALLIANCE FOR PROGRESS).

In 1963, Mexico and the United States settled a 99-year-old border dispute. The Rio Grande had changed its course in 1864, putting part of Juárez on the north side of the river, in El Paso, Tex. Under the 1963 treaty, the United States agreed to shift part of the river about a mile north to downtown El Paso, and transfer 437 acres of land to Mexico. The treaty provided that the two nations would share the cost of shifting the river. The first steps were taken in 1966 to provide a new channel for the Rio Grande at Juárez and El Paso. The United States began moving a number of industries in the Chamizal district of El Paso northward beyond the planned new channel. All the factories were moved by the end of 1967.

Gustavo Díaz Ordaz, a former Cabinet minister, became president of Mexico in 1964. In 1966, he met in Mexico City with President Lyndon B. Johnson of the United States. Both presidents hailed the "firm friendship" of their countries, based on "freedom, human dignity, and a mutual respect." In 1970, Luis Echeverría Álvarez, a former Cabinet member, was elected president of Mexico.

HOMER ASCHMANN, FRANK BRANDENBURG, DWIGHT S. BROTHERS, and ROBERT E. QUIRK

MEXICO, NATIONAL AUTONOMOUS UNIV.

MEXICO/Study Aids

Related Articles in WORLD BOOK include:

BIOGRAPHIES

Alemán Valdés, Miguel
Ávila Camacho, Manuel
Calles, Plutarco E.
Cárdenas, Lázaro
Carranza, Venustiano
Chávez, Carlos
Cortés, Hernando
Díaz, Porfirio
Díaz Ordaz, Gustavo
Hidalgo y Costilla, Miguel
Iturbide, Agustín de

Juárez, Benito P.
López Mateos, Adolfo
Montezuma
Obregón, Álvaro
Orozco, José C.
Rivera, Diego
Ruiz Cortines, Adolfo
Santa Anna, Antonio
Tamayo, Rufino
Villa, "Pancho"
Zapata, Emiliano

CITIES

Acapulco
Aguascalientes
Chihuahua
Cuernavaca
Guadalajara
Juárez
León
Mazatlán

Mérida
Mexico City
Monterrey
Morelia
Oaxaca
Orizaba
Puebla
San Luis Potosí

Tampico
Taxco
Tijuana
Torreón
Veracruz
Villa de Guadalupe
Hidalgo

HISTORY

Alamo
Aztec
Guadalupe Hidalgo, Treaty of
Indian, American
Maya

Mexican War
Olmec Indians
San Jacinto, Battle of
Toltec Indians
Zapotec Indians

PHYSICAL FEATURES

Cárdenas Dam
El Boquerón
Gulf of California
Gulf of Mexico
Ixtacíhuatl

Lake Xochimilco
Orizaba
Parícutin
Popocatépetl
Río Grande

Sierra Madre
Tehuantepec,
Isthmus of
Vizcaíno Desert
Yucatán Peninsula

PRODUCTS

For Mexico's rank in production, see:

Cattle
Chicle
Coconut Palm
Coffee

Corn
Cotton
Gas
Guayule

Horse
Lead
Mahogany
Orange

Silver
Sugar
Sugar Cane

STATES AND TERRITORIES

See the separate article on each state and territory listed in the *Government* section of this article.

OTHER RELATED ARTICLES

Adobe
Bullfighting
Cactus

Enchilada
Guadalupe Day
Henequen

Latin America
Tin (pictures)

Outline

I. **Government**
II. **People**
   A. Language
III. **Way of Life**
   A. City Life
   B. Village Life
   C. Family Life
   D. Food
   E. Clothing
   B. Religion
   F. Holidays
   G. Sports
IV. **Education**
V. **Arts**
   A. Architecture
   B. Painting
   C. Literature
   D. Music
VI. **The Land**
   A. The Pacific Northwest
   B. The Plateau of Mexico
   C. The Gulf Coastal Plain
   D. The Southern Uplands
   E. The Chiapas Highlands
   F. The Yucatán Peninsula
VII. **Climate**
VIII. **Economy**
   A. Natural Resources
   B. Manufacturing
   C. Agriculture
   D. Mining
   E. Electric Power
   F. Foreign Trade
   G. Transportation
   H. Communication
IX. **History**

Questions

To which racial group do most Mexicans belong?
About how much of Mexico can support crops?
Why do Mexicans celebrate their Independence Day on September 16?
What are some words that came from Mexico and are used in the United States?
What is Mexico's "official" political party?
Who were the *peninsulares*? The *creoles*?
Why did United States forces seize Veracruz in 1914?
How does the voting age differ between married and single persons in Mexico?
What is Mexico's most important religious holiday?

Books for Young Readers

ETS, MARIE HALL, and LABASTIDA, AURORA. *Nine Days to Christmas.* Viking, 1959. Caldecott Medal Winner.
GARTLER, MARIAN, and HALL, G. L. *Understanding Mexico.* Laidlaw, 1963.
RITCHIE, BARBARA. *Ramón Makes a Trade (Los Cambios de Ramón).* Parnassus, 1959.
ROSS, PATRICIA F. *Mexico.* Fideler, 1965.
WOOD, FRANCES E. *Mexico.* Childrens Press, 1964.

Books for Older Readers

BLACKER, IRWIN R. *Cortes and the Aztec Conquest.* American Heritage, 1965.
BRANDENBURG, FRANK R. *The Making of Modern Mexico.* Prentice-Hall, 1964.
BROTHERS, DWIGHT S., and SOLÍS M, LEOPOLDO. *Mexican Financial Development.* Univ. of Texas Press, 1966.
COE, MICHAEL D. *Mexico.* Praeger, 1962.
QUIRK, ROBERT E. *The Mexican Revolution, 1914-1915.* Indiana Univ. Press, 1960.
ROSS, BETTY. *Mexico: Land of Eagle and Serpent.* Roy, 1965.
SIMPSON, LESLEY BYRD. *Many Mexicos.* Rev. ed. Univ. of California Press, 1966.
VERNON, RAYMOND. *The Dilemma of Mexico's Development.* Harvard Univ. Press, 1963.

MÉXICO, a state of Mexico, lies mainly within the beautiful Valley of Mexico. It borders the Federal District, which includes Mexico City (see MEXICO [political map]). México covers 8,286 square miles and has a population of 2,435,653. Farmers grow barley, corn, wheat, alfalfa, and vegetables. Toluca is the capital of México.
CHARLES G. CUMBERLAND

MEXICO, GULF OF. See GULF OF MEXICO.

MEXICO, NATIONAL AUTONOMOUS UNIVERSITY OF, is the largest university in Mexico. It was founded in 1551, in Mexico City, as the Royal and Pontifical University. The Roman Catholic Church operated it until the government closed it in 1867. It was reopened in 1910 as the National University of Mexico. The university became *autonomous* (free of government control) in 1929. A new campus was built near Mexico City in the early 1950's. Today, about 80,000 students go there. Courses are offered in law, philosophy, medicine, science, music, political and social science, commerce, engineering, architecture, and nursing. The university also has research and teaching institutes in Mexico.
EMILE DELAVENAY

See also MEXICO (pictures).

Marc & Evelyne Bernheim, Rapho Guillumette

Colorful Mexico City has one of the most beautiful boulevards in the world, the Paseo de la Reforma, *left*. Skyscrapers rise over a statue of Christopher Columbus in one of the avenue's landscaped circles. The Plaza México, the world's largest bullfight ring, *right*, is also in the city.

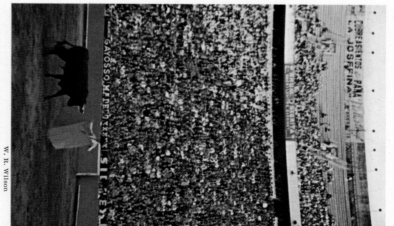

W. R. Wilson

390

MEXICO CITY is the capital and largest city of Mexico. Among all the cities of North America, only New York City and Chicago are larger. Mexico City has almost as many people as Mexico's six next largest cities combined. The Mexico City metropolitan area is the country's commercial and industrial center, and more than half of Mexico's labor force lives there. The capital is also the center of Mexican culture, education, tourism, and transportation.

The Aztec Indians controlled a mighty empire from Tenochtitlán, which they built in 1325 where Mexico City now stands. During the early 1500's, Spanish invaders conquered the Aztec. The Spaniards built Mexico City on the ruins of Tenochtitlán, and made it the capital of their colony. Today, most of Mexico City's people have both Indian and Spanish ancestors.

Mexico City has many beautiful palaces that were built during the Spanish colonial period. They now house government offices, museums, or shops. The city also has new homes, industries, and skyscrapers of extremely modern styles. Many of the new buildings are constructed of concrete strengthened with steel, and are decorated with bright colors, stones, and tiles.

A large number of Spanish colonial homes still stand. Each has a gardenlike patio, which is the center of family life. The modern houses and apartment buildings in the new districts and suburbs look much like those in

the United States and Canada. The poorest people live in slum shacks or rooms with almost no furniture. Their beds are *petates* (straw mats), and clay bowls may be their only dishes.

Mexico City and its suburbs have more than 350 neighborhood districts called *colonias*. Like Mexico's cities and towns, many colonias have their own *plazas* (public squares). The parklike plazas are centers of neighborhood life, and band concerts and local *fiestas* (festivals) are held there. Facing the plazas are churches, markets, restaurants, and theaters.

The soil under Mexico City is spongy, and about 85 per cent of it is water. Much of the city's water is pumped from the soil, which causes the ground to sink unevenly. Since the 1930's, parts of Mexico City have been sinking as much as a foot a year. New buildings and monuments have special foundations that prevent them from sinking. These supports also prevent damage from earthquakes that sometimes shake Mexico City.

Mexico City lies in the high, bowl-shaped Valley of Mexico. Mountains surround the valley, and there is no natural drainage through them. Canals carry rain water out of the valley, but especially heavy rains may cause

Robert E. Quirk, the contributor of this article, is Professor of History at Indiana University and the author of The Mexican Revolution, 1914-1915.

floods. Rain falls briefly nearly every day in Mexico City from late May or early June until October. The nearby bed of Lake Texcoco, which has been drained, becomes swampy during the rainy season. During the dry months, Mexico City is troubled by smog from automobiles and factories. Much dust also blows in from the dry lake bed. Although Mexico City is in the tropics, its high altitude gives it a mild climate. Nights are cool throughout the year.

Famous Landmarks. Constitution Plaza, called the Zócalo, is Mexico City's chief plaza. It covers the site of the old Aztec capital's main square, where the emperor's palace and the Great Temple once stood. Today, the City Hall, National Cathedral, National Palace, National Pawnshop, and Supreme Court of Justice all surround the Zócalo. The National Pawnshop, founded in 1775, offers loans on personal property at low rates of interest. Some Aztec ruins also are near the Zócalo.

The block-long National Palace was built during the 1600's as the Spanish governor's home. It now houses the offices of Mexico's president and other officials. Paintings by the famous Mexican artist Diego Rivera are on the walls, and Mexico's Liberty Bell hangs over the main entrance. Late each September 15, on the eve of Mexico's Independence Day, the president rings the bell in a public celebration.

The heart of Mexico City extends westward from the Zócalo along busy *avenidas* (avenues). It ends near the Paseo de la Reforma, one of the most beautiful boulevards in the world. Facing the Avenida Juárez stands the majestic Palace of Fine Arts. The palace has the National Theater, in which concerts, dance programs, operas, and plays are presented. It also includes art galleries and auditoriums. The palace is built almost entirely of marble. Its great weight has caused it to sink about 15 feet into the spongy soil underneath. Nearby rises the 44-story Latin-American Tower, one of the tallest buildings in Latin America. It "floats" on special supports topped by steel and concrete mats, which prevent sinking or earthquake damage.

The wide, tree-lined Paseo de la Reforma includes seven *glorietas* (landscaped circles in street intersections). A monument honoring a national hero or important event stands in each circle. At the Avenida de los Insurgentes, the main north-south road, the glorieta monument honors Cuauhtémoc, the last Aztec emperor. His bravery under Spanish torture made him Mexico's greatest hero.

North of the downtown area is the Plaza of the Three Cultures. It has ruins of ancient Aztec temples and of a Spanish church built in 1524. Nearby, representing the third culture—that of today—is a huge government housing project of boldly modern architecture.

The Basilica of Our Lady of Guadalupe is Mexico's most famous religious shrine. It stands in Villa de Guadalupe Hidalgo, north of Mexico City, at the foot of Tepeyac Hill. This church, built in the 1700's, honors the Virgin of Guadalupe, Mexico's patron saint. According to Roman Catholic legend, she appeared on the

——————— **FACTS IN BRIEF** ———————

Population: 3,269,335.

Area: 53 square miles.

Altitude: 7,575 feet above sea level.

Climate: *Average temperature*—December, 54° F.; May, 66° F. *Average annual precipitation* (rainfall, melted snow, and other forms of moisture)—29 inches.

Government: *Chief executive*—head of the Department of the Federal District (appointed by the president).

Founded: 1325 (as Tenochtitlán).

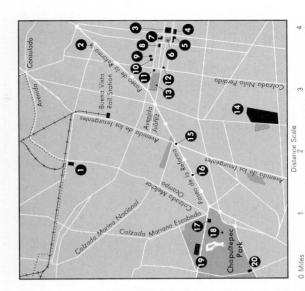

WORLD BOOK maps-FHa

INNER MEXICO CITY

+ Rail Line

Major Street

Park

MEXICO CITY

Alameda Park	13
Chamber of Deputies	9
Chapultepec Hill	18
City Hall	5
Cuauhtémoc Monument	15
Independence Monument	16
Latin-American Tower	12
Los Pinos	20
Medical Center	14
Museum of Modern Art	17
National Cathedral	7
National Museum of Anthropology	19
National Palace	6
National Pawnshop	8
National Polytechnic Institute	1
Palace of Fine Arts	11
Plaza of the Three Cultures	2
Senate House	10
Supreme Court of Justice	4
Zócalo (Constitution Plaza)	6

MEXICO CITY

.... City Limits

Federal District

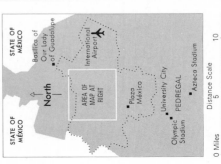

STATE OF MÉXICO

Basilica of Our Lady of Guadalupe

STATE OF MÉXICO

International Airport

North

AREA OF MAP AT RIGHT

Plaza México

University City

PEDREGAL

Olympic Stadium

Azteca Stadium

Distance Scale

hill to Juan Diego, a poor Indian, in December, 1531. Pilgrims from all parts of Mexico and from other countries come to worship at the shrine throughout the year. On Guadalupe Day, December 12, thousands of pilgrims pass through the church.

Other attractions north of Mexico City include handsome Spanish colonial churches in Acolman and Tepozotlán. Also to the north are ancient Indian pyramids and temples at San Juan Teotihuacán, Tenayuca, and Tula. Lake Xochimilco, southeast of the capital, is famous for its "floating gardens."

Parks. The downtown area of Mexico City includes the Alameda, a park developed by a Spanish governor during the late 1500's. He planted it with *álamos* (poplar trees), which gave the Alameda its name. During the colonial period, victims of the Spanish Inquisition were burned at the stake there (see INQUISITION). The Alameda is now the scene of holiday celebrations and of band concerts twice a week.

Chapultepec Park, the largest park in Mexico City, was first used by Aztec emperors. It is a popular family picnic area, with several lakes for boating. The park also includes large flower gardens, lovely fountains, a zoo, and an amusement area with rides and games. On Sundays, horsemen ride in the park. They often wear colorful national costumes.

In 1847, during Mexico's war with the United States, American troops captured Mexico City after the bitter Battle of Chapultepec. A number of young military students, who had defended Chapultepec Hill, threw themselves over a cliff rather than surrender. Today, the Monument to the Boy Heroes stands at the foot of the hill in their honor. Chapultepec Castle, on the hill, houses the National Museum of History. Also in the park are the National Museum of Anthropology, with many ancient and present-day Indian exhibits, and *Los Pinos* (The Pines), the home of Mexico's president.

Education. In Mexico City, as in other parts of Mexico, the law requires children between the ages of 6 and 14 to go to school. Much of Mexico offers no education beyond fourth grade, but Mexico City provides full educational opportunities. The city and its suburbs have more than 2,000 elementary and high schools, as well as schools of higher learning.

Mexico's oldest and largest university is the National Autonomous University of Mexico. It was founded in 1551, and has more than 70,000 students. In 1954, its new campus was completed in University City on the *Pedregal*, a plain of ancient lava south of the capital. Many of Mexico's leading architects and artists designed and decorated the colorful campus in a mixture of Indian, Spanish colonial, and modern styles (see MEXICO, NATIONAL AUTONOMOUS UNIVERSITY OF). Other schools of higher learning in Mexico City include the National Polytechnic Institute. There are also several schools devoted to such special subjects as engineering and the fine arts.

Sports. Bullfighting is the national sport of Mexico, and Mexico City has two bullfighting rings. One of them, the Plaza Mexico, seats about 50,000 persons and is the largest in the world. Baseball, football, and soccer are also popular. Soccer teams of Mexico and other countries play in the Azteca Stadium, which holds 105,000 persons. An Olympic Stadium stands south of Mexico City in a sports area built for the 1968 Summer Olympic Games.

Jai alai, a game similar to handball, attracts many Mexicans and tourists. The players hit the ball against a wall with a basketlike racket. The ball travels so fast that jai alai is sometimes called the fastest game in the world. Other popular sports in Mexico City include basketball, golf, horse racing, swimming, and tennis.

Manufacturing. Mexico City and its suburbs have about 25,000 factories. They account for about half the total value of all goods manufactured in Mexico. Important products include automobiles, chemicals, clothing, drugs, iron and steel, machinery, and textiles. Many foreign-owned factories assemble or finish products for sale in the Latin-American countries. About 3,000 Americans, most of them in commercial or industrial activities, live in the capital.

More than half the nation's labor force lives in Mexico City. Every year, great numbers of workers from other parts of Mexico come to the city in search of jobs. Most of the newcomers are unskilled laborers, and many cannot find work. Their families live in extreme poverty. The increasing population places great strain on Mexico City's food supplies. As a result, food prices

The Plaza of the Three Cultures combines ruins of Indian and Spanish buildings near a modern housing project. The plaza honors the mixture of Indian and Spanish ancestry of Mexico's people.

WORLD BOOK photo by Henry Gill

rise and cause the cost of living to go far higher than in the rest of Mexico.

Transportation. Almost all roads in Mexico lead to Mexico City. Highways connect the capital with other large Mexican cities and with the United States and Central America. Mexico City is also the center of Mexico's railroad network.

Mexico City is one of the main centers of international air travel in the Western Hemisphere. The huge Mexico City International Airport opened in 1952. It provides direct flights to almost 25 countries, including the United States, Canada, and nations in Central and South America, Europe, and the Far East. Flights also connect the capital with other large Mexican cities.

Communication. Mexico City has about 20 daily newspapers, and they account for almost half the total newspaper circulation in Mexico. The largest dailies include *El Universal, Excélsior, La Prensa, Novedades,* and *Ovaciones.* Several newspapers have a page printed in English. There are also English-language newspapers. Leading weekly magazines are *Tiempo* and *Siempre.*

The capital is Mexico's broadcasting center. Mexico City has about 30 radio stations, 5 commercial television stations, and an educational TV channel.

Government. Mexico City forms part of the 579 square-mile Federal District, which is politically similar to the District of Columbia in the United States. Like Washington, D.C., Mexico City has no local legislature. It is governed by the head of the Department of the Federal District, who is appointed by the president of Mexico. Its laws are passed by the federal Congress. The people of Mexico City, unlike those of Washington, elect members of the Congress.

History. People have lived in what is now Mexico City for thousands of years. By 1500 B.C., several farm villages stood along Lake Texcoco. In 1325, the Aztec Indians founded their capital, Tenochtitlán, on an island in the lake. During the 1400's, the Aztec built an empire that controlled much of what is now Mexico.

Spanish invaders came to Tenochtitlán in 1519. Their leader, Hernando Cortes, or Hernán Cortés, destroyed the city almost completely in 1521. He built Mexico City on the ruins, and took over the rest of the Aztec empire for Spain. Mexico City became the capital of New Spain, which the Spaniards called their colony.

Thousands of people died in floods because Mexico City had no natural drainage. After 30,000 died in 1629, the Spaniards built a large canal to drain Lake Texcoco and to carry off rain water. But especially heavy rains still caused floods.

Mexico City remained under Spanish rule for 300 years, and was the largest city in the Western Hemisphere. In 1821, Mexico became independent after an army led by General Agustín de Iturbide took over Mexico City. A series of civil wars, fought for control of Mexico, began soon afterward and lasted until the 1920's. Mexico City was attacked many times. For the story of these struggles, see MEXICO (History).

Mexico City was captured by American troops in 1847, during Mexico's war with the United States. The Americans occupied the capital until the war ended in 1848. Mexico City fell again in 1863, to invading French troops. France named Maximilian, an Austrian archduke, emperor of Mexico in 1864. He ruled until 1867, when Mexican forces overthrew him.

General Porfirio Díaz led a revolt and seized power in Mexico City in 1876. Díaz ruled as a dictator, and the capital became the center of tight, harsh control over all Mexico. The Mexican Revolution began in 1910, and Díaz resigned the next year.

Many factories were built in Mexico City during the 1940's, and the city expanded rapidly. The Lerma Waterworks were built during the 1950's to increase the capital's water supply.

President Lyndon B. Johnson of the United States visited Mexico City in 1966. He and President Gustavo Díaz Ordaz hailed the "firm friendship" of their countries. In 1968, the Summer Olympic Games were held in the Mexico City area.

ROBERT E. QUIRK

Related Articles in WORLD BOOK include:

Aztec	Ixtacihuatl
Cortes, Hernando	Juárez, Benito
Díaz, Porfirio	Lake Xochimilco
Guadalupe Day	Maximilian
Iturbide, Agustín de	Mexican War

Mexico (country)
Montezuma
Orozco, José C.
Popocatépetl
Rivera, Diego

MEYER, ALBERT GREGORY CARDINAL (1903-1965), a cardinal of the Roman Catholic Church, became archbishop of Chicago in 1958. Pope John XXIII named him a cardinal in December, 1959. Cardinal Meyer was born in Milwaukee. He studied at St. Francis Seminary in Milwaukee and at the North American College in Rome. He was ordained a priest in 1926, and was elevated to bishop of Superior, Wis., in 1946. In 1953, he became archbishop of the Milwaukee archdiocese.

THOMAS P. NEILL

MEYER, JULIUS LOTHAR (1830-1895), a German chemist, showed the relation between the atomic weights and properties of the elements. His work and that of the Russian chemist Dmitri Mendeleev led to the development of a periodic chart of the elements, which groups the elements according to their atomic weights and properties (see ELEMENT, CHEMICAL [Periodic Table of the Elements]). Meyer also concluded that elements were composed of several kinds of smaller particles. This idea led other persons to study the structure of atoms. Meyer was born in Tübingen. K. L. KAUFMAN

See also CHEMISTRY (Development of Inorganic Chemistry).

MEYERBEER, GIACOMO (1791-1864), was one of the most popular opera composers of his day. He was born in Berlin, but achieved his greatest success while composing in Paris. The trend in French opera during the early 1800's was toward grand opera, which emphasized many performers on stage and impressive stage effects. These features replaced dramatic quality in many productions. Meyerbeer used this stress on the spectacular in his first Paris opera, *Robert le Diable* (1831), which gained him immediate fame. This work was followed by *Les Huguenots* (1836) and *Le Prophète* (1849). *L'Africaine,* perhaps his most interesting opera, was first performed in 1865, after his death.

Meyerbeer had an acute sense for building climaxes and for creating spectacular effects. Richard Wagner's early operas owe much to the influence of Meyerbeer's music.

MELOŠ VELIMIROVĆ

MEZZO and **MEZZO FORTE.** See MUSIC (table: Terms Used in Music).

MEZZO-RILIEVO. See RELIEF (in art).

MEZZOTINT. See ENGRAVING (Mezzotint).

MIAMI

Miami's Glistening Skyscrapers tower above the palm trees that line Biscayne Boulevard, *right,* and beautifully landscaped Bayfront Park, which borders on Biscayne Bay. The Miami River, *foreground,* flows through Miami into Biscayne Bay.

Miami-Metro News Bureau

MIAMI, Fla. (pop. 291,688; met. area 935,047; alt. 10 ft.), is often called the *Magic City* because of its rapid growth since its incorporation in 1896. Miami is one of the fastest-growing cities in the United States. It ranks as Florida's second largest city in both area and population. Jacksonville ranks first. Millions of tourists visit Miami each year.

Location. Miami lies at the mouth of the Miami River, 2½ miles west of Miami Beach. It covers about 41 square miles. Five causeways cross Biscayne Bay, the eastern border of Miami. Satellite communities border Miami on the north, west, and south. These include North Miami, Miami Shores, Hialeah, Miami Springs, West Miami, Coral Gables, and South Miami. The Greater Miami metropolitan area consists of Miami, its mainland satellites, Miami Beach, and other ocean localities. For the location of Miami, see FLORIDA (political map).

Interesting Places to Visit. Besides the beaches and tourist centers, Miami has many other points of interest. Among the attractions are the Fairchild Tropical Gardens, the Serpentarium, the Aquarium, the Kendall Rare Bird Farm, the Vizcaya Art Museum, and the Miami Public Library. Bayfront Park, landscaped with tropical foliage, consists of land reclaimed from the bottom of Biscayne Bay. An unsuccessful attempt to assassinate President Franklin D. Roosevelt in 1933 took the life of Mayor Anton J. Cermak of Chicago in the

amphitheater at Bayfront Park. Many visitors to Miami attend the annual Orange Bowl football game each New Year's Day. The city is the home of the National Football League's Miami Dolphins. Other attractions include golf, fishing, and tennis tournaments; regattas; horse and greyhound races; and fashion and air shows. Miami is the home of the Miami Symphony Orchestra, and Biscayne and Florida Memorial colleges. The University of Miami and Barry College are nearby.

The People. Only about one-fourth of Miami's residents are native-born Floridians. Many of the people have moved there from northern and midwestern states. Miami also has a large Latin-American population.

Tourism. Greater Miami, with its elaborate beach resorts and luxurious hotels, has developed a thriving tourist trade. Visitors come to Miami to enjoy the tropical marine climate and the abundant recreational areas. Miami's temperature varies little, averaging 78° F. in the summer and 69° F. in the winter. For rainfall and temperature information on Miami, see FLORIDA (Climate). Most tourist accommodations operate throughout the year. Rates are lowered in the summer. The area has many parks, swimming pools, and beaches. Fishing in the waters off Miami is popular.

Trade and Industry. Miami is not merely a tourist city. About 1,800 factories manufacture a variety of products, including furniture, food products, iron and steel fabrications, plastics, chemical products, and lumber products and millwork. The city has become a fashion capital, and produces garments, jewelry, hand-

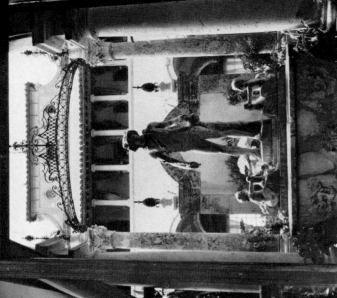

The Torch of Friendship stands in Miami's Bayfront Park as a symbol of friendship to Latin America. Built in 1960 by the city, it contains U.S. and Latin American flags and official seals.

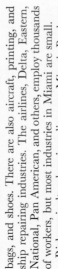

Miami-Metro News Bureau

Italy in Miami is featured at Vizcaya Art Museum. The Italian marble statue and fountain stand in a formal Italian garden. Once an elegant mansion, the museum has many priceless antiques.

bags, and shoes. There are also aircraft, printing, and ship repairing industries. The airlines, Delta, Eastern, National, Pan American, and others, employ thousands of workers, but most industries in Miami are small.

Rich agricultural regions lie near Miami. Products include winter vegetables, dairy products, citrus fruits, pineapples, avocados, mangoes, and guavas. Miami ships its manufactured and agricultural products to all parts of the country.

Transportation. Miami's two railroads, the Florida East Coast and the Seaboard, connect Miami with all the principal cities of the East Coast and the Middle West. Airlines link Miami with many parts of the world, and the city is a major air terminal. The International Airport is one of the busiest passenger and freight terminals in the United States. This airfield serves as the main gateway for air traffic to and from Latin America. Two of Florida's most colorful highways pass through Miami. They are the Tamiami Trail, which runs between Miami on the east coast and Tampa on the west coast; and the Sunshine State Parkway, a turnpike that stretches north from Miami. Steamship lines also link the city to northern ports in the United States, and to the Bahamas and other points in the West Indies.

Government. Miami is the county seat of Dade County. The city adopted a commission-manager form of government in 1921. In 1957, residents of the Miami metropolitan area voted to form the first metropolitan government in the United States. The community hired a metropolitan manager, and increased its commission from 5 to 13 members, or 1 member for every 50,000 people. The new administration, designed to end conflicting and overlapping local governments, served as a model for other metropolitan areas in the nation (see METROPOLITAN AREA).

History. During the first half of the 1900's, Miami grew from a small village on Biscayne Bay to the largest metropolis in the state. The city was founded after severe frosts in the winter of 1894-1895 destroyed the citrus fruit crop in central Florida. Mrs. Julia Tuttle, a Florida pioneer, urged railroad builder Henry Morrison Flagler to bring his railroad into the Biscayne Bay area. She sent him flowers to convince him that Miami had escaped the frost. Flagler extended the Florida East Coast Railroad to the area in exchange for land. At that time, Miami consisted chiefly of sand trails through palmetto growths. Early business places were often tents and pine shacks.

Miami received its charter in 1896. Until that time the settlement had been called Fort Dallas, after a military outpost established in the area in 1835. The name *Miami* comes from the Miami River.

The area first received national attention when real estate promoters began to turn the mangrove swamps of the island across Biscayne Bay into the resort city of Miami Beach. During the 1920's, a great real estate boom centered in Miami. More than $100,000,000 was spent in one year to build homes, hotels, and resorts in the city. Land prices rose sharply, and real estate changed hands rapidly. Just as the boom began to decline in 1926, a devastating hurricane struck Miami. Another severe storm hit Miami in 1928. Before the city could recover, a national depression began in 1929. In spite of these setbacks, Miami recovered and prospered.

During World War II, Miami became an important training center for the armed services. Most of the hotels housed servicemen. After the war, Miami shared another Florida population boom. Luxurious resorts sprang up, and the tourist trade flourished. Many people moved there to live permanently, and new industries were established.

KATHRYN ABBEY HANNA

395

MIAMI, UNIVERSITY OF

MIAMI, UNIVERSITY OF, is a private, nondenominational, coeducational university in Coral Gables, Fla. It has a college of arts and sciences; schools of business administration, education, engineering, law, and music; and a full graduate program. The School of Medicine is in Miami. In addition, the School of Environmental and Planetary Sciences conducts research and offers graduate programs in atmospheric science, marine sciences, and molecular evolution. The Center for Advanced International Studies offers graduate programs in international and inter-American studies. The university was founded in 1925. For the enrollment of the University of Miami, see UNIVERSITIES AND COLLEGES (table).

HENRY KING STANFORD

MIAMI BEACH, Fla. (pop. 63,145; alt. 10 ft.), is one of North America's most famous resort centers. It lies on an island 2½ miles across Biscayne Bay from the city of Miami. The island measures 10 miles from north to south and is one to three miles wide. Four causeways connect it with the mainland. For location, see FLORIDA (political map).

The city's major industry is the tourist trade. It can accommodate more than 200,000 visitors at one time. Miami Beach has more than 400 hotels and 2,100 apartment buildings. About 85 per cent of these hotels and apartment buildings remain open all year. The tropical climate, white sandy beaches, and recreational areas attract more than 2 million tourists to the city annually. A number of the city's resort hotels are among the most luxurious in the world. The city has many parks, fishing piers, playgrounds, beaches, recreation centers, and swimming pools. Tropical trees and shrubs line its modern boulevards, and gardens of brilliantly colored flowers border its green lawns.

Tequesta Indians lived in the Miami Beach area in the 1400's, and a Spanish mission was built in 1567. An attempt by a group of businessmen to start a coconut plantation failed in the 1880's. But John S. Collins, a member of the group, pioneered in developing the resort city. Other city founders include Carl G. Fisher, Thomas J. Pancoast, and John N. Lummus. In 1912, rock and sand were pumped from the bottom of Biscayne Bay and spread over mangrove roots and soft sand to create the modern city. Miami Beach was incorporated as a town in 1915. It was incorporated as a city in 1917. Miami Beach has a council-manager form of government.

KATHRYN ABBEY HANNA

See also FLORIDA (pictures).

MIAMI INDIANS, *my AM' ee,* formed an important tribe in North America's eastern woodlands. They were closely related to the Illinois Indians, even though these two tribes frequently fought each other. Two groups of the Miami, the Piankashaw and the Wea, ranked as separate tribes.

The customs and Algonkian language of the Miami closely resembled the customs and language of the Illinois (see ILLINOIS INDIANS). According to early French explorers, the Miami were mild-mannered and polite. Miami chiefs had greater authority than other Algonkian leaders. The Miami raised corn and hunted buffalo.

When white men first discovered the Miami, they lived in the Green Bay area of Wisconsin. Gradually they split into various groups and moved southeast into Illinois and Michigan. Some groups also settled along the Wabash River in Indiana and on the Miami and Maumee rivers in the western part of Ohio.

The Miami played a prominent part in the Indian wars of the Ohio Valley in the 1790's. Under their most important leader, Little Turtle, they fought fiercely against United States forces led by Generals Josiah Harmar and Arthur St. Clair. General "Mad Anthony" Wayne defeated the Miami at the Battle of Fallen Timbers in 1794 (see INDIAN WARS [Other Midwestern Conflicts]).

Soon after the War of 1812, the remaining Miami moved westward. They then settled in Oklahoma with groups of the Illinois Indians.

WAYNE C. TEMPLE

See also INDIAN, AMERICAN (Indians of the Eastern Woodlands); LITTLE TURTLE.

MIAMI RIVER, or GREAT MIAMI RIVER, flows through western Ohio (see OHIO [physical map]). It rises in Logan County and flows southwestward for about 160 miles. It empties into the Ohio River at the southwestern corner of Ohio. Towns along the river include Dayton, Hamilton, Sidney, and Troy. The river is an important source of power for industries along its course.

GEORGE MACINKO

MIAMI UNIVERSITY is a coeducational state university at Oxford, Ohio. It has a college of arts and science; schools of education, business administration, fine arts, and applied science; and a graduate school. It also has a summer school. Miami University has academic centers that provide extension courses in many Ohio cities. The university library has collections of the Scripps Foundation for Research in Population Problems, the McGuffey Library, and the Covington Library of Ohio Valley History. Miami is called the *mother of fraternities.* The university was established in 1809. For enrollment, see UNIVERSITIES AND COLLEGES (table).

JOHN D. MILLETT

"Hotel Row" in Miami Beach cuts through the center of the resort city. Miami Beach has over 30,000 hotel rooms and almost as many apartments to accommodate thousands of vacationers.

City of Miami Beach

MICA, *MI kah,* is a mineral that contains silica. It can be split into sheets so. thin that 1,000 sheets make a pile only an inch high. Mica has *perfect cleavage,* because when it is struck, it splits cleanly along parallel planes into flat sheets or layers. Mica may be colorless, black, brown, green, red, or yellow.

There are several kinds of mica, including *muscovite* and *biotite.* Muscovite, which contains aluminum, oxygen, potassium, silicon, and water, is a light-colored mica. Most muscovite is very clear. It is so named because the Russians, or "Muscovites," used it instead of window glass. Biotite, one of the dark-colored micas, consists of aluminum, hydrogen, iron, magnesium, oxygen, potassium, and silicon. Mica is often confused with isinglass, a form of gelatin (see ISINGLASS).

Mica is an essential material in the manufacture of electronic and electrical devices, including guided missiles, ion counters, proximity fuses, and radar equipment. It is also used in delicate measuring and sighting instruments. Mica serves as insulation in electric irons and toasters and is used in armature-winding tape, capacitors, spark plugs, and transformers. Finely ground mica is used as a preservative and a lubricant, like talcum powder, in the manufacture of automobile tires and other items. Ceramics and various kinds of glass are replacing mica for many purposes.

Crystals of mica are found in such igneous rocks as granite, and in gneiss and other metamorphic rocks (see ROCK [Igneous Rock; Metamorphic Rock]). Mica is mined in Brazil, Canada, India, the Malagasy Republic, South Africa, Tanzania, and the United States. The largest amount comes from India, where the abundant supply and inexpensive labor make mica low in cost. In the United States, major deposits of mica are found in Alabama, Georgia, New Mexico, New Hampshire, North Carolina, South Carolina, and South Dakota.

During World War II (1939-1945), when mica imports were cut off, the United States and several other nations tried to make synthetic mica. However, natural high-quality mica is still cheaper to produce than synthetic mica. A process has been developed that molds small flakes of mica into large sheets suitable for most purposes. This process uses mica from factory scrap and mine scrap.   CECIL J. SCHNEER

See also VERMICULITE.

MICA SCHIST, *MY' kuh shist,* is a type of rock formed mostly of quartz and mica. Schists will crack into many *laminations* (thin layers). The property of splitting in this way is called *foliation.* It is due to the internal structure of the schist.

MICAH was a Judean prophet in the late 700's B.C. The name *Micah* means *Who is like the Lord?* Micah criticized people because they concerned themselves more with beautiful ceremonials than with true religious conduct. He found fault with the rich for oppressing and cheating poor people. He also distinguished between "true" and "false" prophets, and said that sincerity was the distinguishing mark of a true prophet.

The book of Micah is the sixth of the minor prophets in the Old Testament. The first three chapters contain Micah's own words. The last four have been enlarged, and contain writings from much later periods. The most famous passages in the book are the summary of true religion (6:6-8), and the expectation of the Messiah from Bethlehem (5:2):

But thou, Bethlehem . . . .
Which art little to be among the thousands of Judah,
Out of thee shall one come forth unto Me that is to
be ruler in Israel;
Whose goings forth are from of old . . . .

The name *Micah* is given to another Old Testament hero in chapters 17 and 18 of the Book of Judges. In the *Douay* (Roman Catholic) version, Micah is spelled as *Micheas.*   WALTER G. WILLIAMS

See also PROPHET (picture).

MICE. See MOUSE.

MICHAEL. See ROMANOV.

MICHAEL, *MY' kuhl* (1921-   ), served as king of Romania from 1927 to 1930 and from 1940 to 1947. His Romanian name was *Mihai.* He succeeded his grandfather, Ferdinand I. His father Carol II gave up his right to be king in 1925. But Carol took over the throne in 1930, and made Michael crown prince.

Michael regained the throne in 1940 when disorders forced Carol to abdicate and flee. But Michael was only a puppet, first, of the Romanian fascists and their German allies, later, of the invading Russians. He abdicated in December, 1947, and left Romania. He moved with his wife and children to Switzerland. He took a job with an aircraft company, teaching European fliers how to use American instruments.   ALBERT PARRY

See also CAROL (II); ROMANIA (History).

MICHAEL, SAINT, is one of the seven archangels, or chief angels, named in the Old Testament. He appears with Gabriel as one of the four great angels. In Revelation 12:7, he is pictured as a military leader in the war between God and Satan. The feast of Saint Michael is on September 29 in the Roman Catholic and Anglican churches and on November 8 in the Greek Church. Milton makes the archangel Michael a prominent character in his epic *Paradise Lost.* See also ARCHANGEL; MICHAELMAS.

FREDERICK C. GRANT and FULTON J. SHEEN

MICHAEL PALAEOLOGUS. See BYZANTINE EMPIRE (Final Decline).

MICHAELMAS, *MIK uhl muhs,* is a festival held on September 29 in the Roman Catholic and Anglican churches and several other countries, Michaelmas is one of the four quarter days of the year when rents and bills come due. It is also the beginning of a quarterly court term and an academic term at Oxford and Cambridge. The people celebrate the day with meals of roast goose, a custom that started hundreds of years ago when people included a goose in their rent payments to landlords. An English proverb says, "If you eat goose on Michaelmas Day you will never want money all the year round."   ELIZABETH HOUGH SECHRIST

MICHAELMAS DAISY. See ASTER.

MICHELANGELO (1475-1564) was one of the most famous artists in history and a great leader of the Italian Renaissance. Michelangelo was mainly interested in creating large marble statues, but his consistent creative energy also led him to become a great painter and architect, and an active poet. In addition, he was one of the most famous persons of his time.

Michelangelo is best known for his treatment of the human body in painting and sculpture. His figures convey a sense of grandeur and power, and arouse strong emotions in many spectators. Both in physical size and strength and in emotional intensity, these figures seem to go beyond real people. The figures have an emotional

yet unsentimental quality and their physical strength gives more than the effect of mere bulk. Physical and spiritual strengths build on each other, producing a powerful product that seems to widen human experience. Michelangelo's work pressed toward the extremes of heroism and tragedy, but never seems false or artificial. See the picture of the statue with the DAVID article.

Early Life. Michelangelo was born on March 6, 1475. His full name was MICHELANGELO BUONARROTI. He came from a respectable Florence family, and was born in the village of Caprese, where his father was a government agent. After a brief classical education, he became an apprentice at the age of 12 to the most popular painter in Florence, Domenico Ghirlandajo.

But it was the work of the sculptor Donatello that had the strongest influence on Michelangelo. Before his apprenticeship was completed, Michelangelo stopped

Michelangelo *Pietà* (1498-1499), St. Peters, Vatican City, Camera Clix

Michelangelo's *Pietà* was the most important work of his youth, and established his reputation as a sculptor. The marble statue shows the Virgin Mary cradling the dead Jesus after the Crucifixion. The simple and solemn quality of the statue makes it one of Michelangelo's most enduring works.

Creighton Gilbert, the contributor of this article, is Professor of the History of Art at Brandeis University.

painting and began working as a sculptor under the guidance of a pupil of Donatello. Michelangelo attracted the support of the ruler of Florence, Lorenzo de' Medici, who invited the young artist to stay at his house. Michelangelo's earliest surviving sculpture is a small relief of a battle, completed when he was about 16. This work shows the obvious influence of a collection of fragments of ancient Roman marble sculpture belonging to Lorenzo. But the relief shows the force and movement that became typical of Michelangelo's style.

After the Medici family lost power in 1494, Michelangelo began traveling. He lived in Rome from 1496 to 1501. There he had his first marked success when he carved in marble a life-sized statue of the Roman wine god Bacchus. At 23, Michelangelo carved a version of the traditional Pietà subject, the dead Christ on the knees of the mourning Mary. Both figures are larger than life size. This statue, now in St. Peter's Church in Rome, established him as a leading sculptor. The work was plainer and less decorative than most statues of the time, and thus looked stronger and more solemn.

Michelangelo lived in Florence from 1501 to 1505. There he met Leonardo da Vinci. The new democratic government of Florence wanted to display the talents of the city's two outstanding artists. So it asked both Leonardo and Michelangelo to create large battle scenes for the walls of the city hall. Michelangelo's work, now lost, is known to us through his sketches and through copies by other artists. It displayed his expert ability to render human anatomy. On this project, Michelangelo learned from Leonardo how to show flowing and vibrant movement. Leonardo carried this manner of showing life and action farther than any previous artist. Amazingly, Michelangelo's ability to project solid forms did not decrease. The result was his fundamental style, showing figures that are both massive and full of intense vitality.

From about 1505 on, Michelangelo devoted nearly all his time to large projects. In his enthusiasm for creating grand and powerful works of art, he accepted projects that were far too large for him to complete. The first one was a tomb ordered by Pope Julius II that was to include 40 marble statues. The artist accepted the commission in 1505, but 40 years later, after changes and interruptions, he had completed only a few statues.

The Sistine Chapel. Julius II was a patron of the arts with a sweeping imagination equal to Michelangelo's. He gave the artist a more practical commission, painting the ceiling of the Sistine Chapel in the Vatican. This became Michelangelo's most famous work. The 1,000 square yards of frescoes show nine scenes from the Old Testament—three scenes each of God creating the world, the story of Adam and Eve, and Noah and the flood. These are surrounded by 12 larger than life size Old Testament prophets and classical prophetic women called *sibyls*. See pictures with JEREMIAH; DAVID.

Michelangelo began the ceiling in 1508 and finished the first half in September, 1510. At first, he approached this task in a style resembling his earlier works. But soon he gained confidence, and developed new ways of showing tension and violence. After a pause, Michelangelo began the second half with scenes that are relaxed though powerful, such as *The Creation of Adam*,

reproduced in color in the PAINTING article. Again he progressed to richer and more active compositions. But in the second half the mood is more restrained.

The Tomb of Julius II. Michelangelo finished the ceiling in 1512 and resumed work on the pope's tomb. He carved three famous figures that resemble the painted prophets and decorative figures on the Sistine ceiling. These figures are Moses and two prisoners, sometimes called the *Heroic Captive* and the *Dying Captive*. The figure of Moses in deep thought was later used as the centerpiece of the tomb. The statue is now located in the Church of St. Peter in Chains in Rome and is reproduced in the ART AND THE ARTS article. The *Captives* did not fit into the final reduced design of the tomb. Its figures are interpreted as symbolizing either lands conquered by Julius II or elements of civilization hurt by his death. They fight their bonds with anxiety and muscular pressure, but the tension has declined in a way that suggests their coming defeat.

The Medici Chapel. Michelangelo spent the years from 1515 to 1534 working mainly for the Medici family, which had regained control of Florence. He designed and carved tombs for two Medici princes, and also designed the Medici Chapel, in which the tombs are placed. This project is more complete than any of his other large sculptural or architectural works.

Along with the statues of the two young princes, the tombs include the famous figures of Day and Night on one tomb and Dawn and Evening on the other. The figures recline on curving lids, conveying a sense of fate or individual tragedy. They make a great impact on spectators as an intensely significant observation about human destiny. Some read the parts of the monument from floor to ceiling as a symbol of the rising of the soul after its release from the body. Others see the four statues on the curved lids as a sign of the endless movement of time, in which life is only an incident. The tomb

The Crucifixion of Saint Peter was completed by Michelangelo when he was 75. This fresco and a companion work, *The Conversion of Saint Paul*, were commissioned by Pope Paul III.

Detail from The Vatican Museum

Duomo, Florence (Shostal)

The Vatican Museum

Florentine Pietà, above, was intended for Michelangelo's own tomb. The bearded figure at the top of the group is an idealized self portrait of the sculptor when he was about 80 years old.

The Heroic Captive, right, shows the physical strength and emotional tension found in Michelangelo's sculpture. The 7-foot statue was completed in 1516 for the tomb of Pope Julius II.

Sistine Ceiling, below, was probably Michelangelo's greatest achievement as a painter. He completed this scene in 1511. The fresco shows God creating the sun, the moon, and the planets.

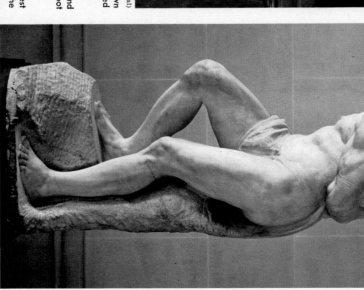

The Louvre, Paris

containing Dawn and Evening is reproduced in color in the SCULPTURE article.

Michelangelo also designed the architecture of the Medici Chapel. He planned the walls like a carved relief, with projections and hollows and long, narrow shapes to give an elongated effect. This approach, resembling carved architecture, is carried farther in the entrance hall and staircase to the Laurentian library in Florence, which he designed at the same time. It was his first architecture to come close to completion.

The Last Judgment. In 1534, the Medici officially became the ruling dukes of Florence. Michelangelo, who favored the republic, left the city and settled in Rome. He spent the next 10 years working for Pope Paul III. Most notable among his painting projects is the fresco *The Last Judgment* (1534-1541). The pope commissioned this work for the altar wall of the Sistine Chapel. In a single scene almost as large as his ceiling, Michelangelo showed the souls of mankind rising on one side and falling on the other. These figures move with a slow heaviness that suggests the fateful importance of their action. At the top, Christ controls them with a powerful gesture, like a puppet master. At the bottom, in a smaller scale, tombs open and the dead are rowed across a river in a scene based on Dante's *Divine Comedy*.

Later Years. The small amount of sculpture in Michelangelo's later years includes works to complete old commissions and two unfinished Pietà groups. He created both Pietàs for his own satisfaction and not for a patron. The Pietà now in the Cathedral of Florence was meant for his own tomb. It is designed as a massive pyramid, with Christ's body slumping down to the ground. In the Rondanini *Pietà*, now in Milan, the marble limbs are reduced to a ghostlike thinness. The bodies seem to lack substance, while the material of the stone is emphasized by the hacking chisel marks left on the unfinished surface. Because of this technique, many modern sculptors, including Henry Moore, admire this work above all others Michelangelo produced.

Michelangelo devoted much time after 1546 to architecture and poetry. In 1546, Pope Paul III appointed him supervising architect of St. Peter's Church, one of Julius II's unfinished projects. Michelangelo started the construction of its dome, still the largest of any church (see SAINT PETER'S CHURCH; ARCHITECTURE [Renaissance]). He also planned a square for the civic center of Rome and the buildings around it. The square, built after his death, avoids ordinary rectangles and focuses on key points leading to the Senate House.

In the works Michelangelo created after he was 70, he showed an ever wider range of interests and capacities, but less stress and violence. He still created works in complex patterns. But beginning with *The Last Judgment*, the Florentine *Pietà*, and the late buildings, he no longer emphasized complicated design. This applies also to his buildings, the interlocking of bodies in his paintings and sculpture, and the sentence structure of his poems. However, his earlier work is more popular with many people because it has a more immediate and exciting impact.

The Life of Michelangelo, by John Addington Symonds, is a good biography of the artist. CREIGHTON GILBERT

MICHELET, *MEESH LEH,* **JULES** (1798-1874), a French historian, is best known for his 19-volume *History of France*. He was chief of the historical department of the archives of France, and professor of history and moral sciences at the College of France. He was liberal in his beliefs, and lost those posts when he refused to take an oath of loyalty to Napoleon III in 1851. Michelet was born in Paris. FRANCIS J. BOWMAN

MICHELSON, *MI kul sun,* **ALBERT ABRAHAM** (1852-1931), an American physicist, spent over 50 years studying the problems of light. He received the 1907 Nobel prize in physics, the first American scientist to win that award. He worked for many years to determine the exact speed of light (see LIGHT [Speed of Light]).

In 1880, Michelson invented the interferometer (see INTERFEROMETER). He used this instrument in 1920 to make the first accurate measurement of a star's diameter. The star measured was Betelgeuse (Alpha Orionis).

He worked with Edward Williams Morley (1838-1923), a chemist and physicist, to determine the relative motion of the earth and ether. Their findings furnished a basis for Einstein's work on the theory of relativity (see RELATIVITY [Special Theory of Relativity]).

Another of Michelson's outstanding achievements was his work on a standard unit of length. In analyzing the spectrum lines of various elements, he recognized that the red line of cadmium could be precisely measured. He suggested using the measurement as a standard unit of length. In 1925, the International Committee on Weights and Measures adopted his standard. He was born at Strelno, Germany, and came to the United States at the age of 2. R. T. ELLICKSON

MICHENER, DANIEL ROLAND (1900-   ), became governor-general of Canada in 1967. He was Canada's *high commissioner* (ambassador) to India from 1964 until his appointment. He served as a Progressive Conservative in the Canadian House of Commons from 1953 to 1962, and was speaker from 1957 to 1962. He became a member of the Queen's Privy Council for Canada in 1962.

Michener was born in Lacombe, Alberta, the son of a provincial legislator. He graduated from the University of Alberta, and studied at Oxford University as a Rhodes Scholar. Michener served in the Ontario legislature from 1945 to 1948. The last two years of that term he was provincial secretary and registrar for Ontario. He practiced law in Toronto from 1923 to 1957.

MICHENER, *MICH uh ner,* **JAMES ALBERT** (1907-   ), an American novelist, won the 1948 Pulitzer prize for fiction with *Tales of the South Pacific* (1947). This book describes the life of United States servicemen among the people of the Solomon Islands during World War II. Richard Rodgers and Oscar Hammerstein II based their successful musical play *South Pacific* (1949) on Michener's book.

Michener's other novels include *The Fires of Spring* (1949), *The Bridges at Toko-ri* (1953), *Sayonara* (1954), *Hawaii* (1960), and *The Source* (1965). He reported events in *The Voice of Asia* (1951), *Rascals in Paradise* (1957), and *The Bridge at Andau* (1957), and wrote on art. Michener was born in New York, and was graduated from Swarthmore College. HARRY R. WARFEL

Ford Motor Company Plant Near Detroit

MICHIGAN
THE WOLVERINE STATE

The contributors of this article are Willard M. J. Baird, Capitol Bureau Chief of the State Journal of Lansing, and State Bureau Chief of Federated Publications, Inc.; William Rogers Bruckheimer, Head, Department of Geography at Florida State University; and former Head, Department of Geography and Geology at Western Michigan University; and Sidney Glazer, Professor of History at Wayne State University.

MICHIGAN is an important industrial, mining, farming, and tourist state in the Great Lakes region of the Midwest. It is one of the nation's leading manufacturing states. Michigan leads in the manufacture of automobiles. Detroit, Michigan's largest city, is called the *Automobile Capital of the World* and the *Motor City*. It produces more cars and trucks than any other city. Flint, Pontiac, and Lansing, the state capital, also are important automaking cities. Michigan is a leading state in food processing and steel production.

Michigan touches four of the five Great Lakes—Erie, Huron, Michigan, and Superior. The state's 3,288-mile shoreline is longer than that of any other inland state.

Michigan consists of two separate land areas, called the Upper Peninsula and the Lower Peninsula. The two peninsulas are connected by the 5-mile-long Mackinac Bridge across the Straits of Mackinac.

Michigan ranks second only to Minnesota in the production of iron ore. It is also a leading copper-mining state. Michigan is one of the leading states in salt production. Salt and other minerals are mined in the Lower Peninsula.

Most farming in Michigan takes place in the Lower Peninsula. The best farmland lies in the southern part of the state. The Lake Michigan shores of the Lower Peninsula are an excellent fruit-growing region. Michigan leads the nation in the production of cherries, and is a top producer of many other fruits. It is also the leading producer of dry beans.

Michigan is one of the leading tourist states. More than 10,000,000 persons visit the state each year. Both the Upper and Lower peninsulas offer resort and recreation facilities, and scenic beauty. In addition to the Great Lakes, Michigan has more than 11,000 smaller

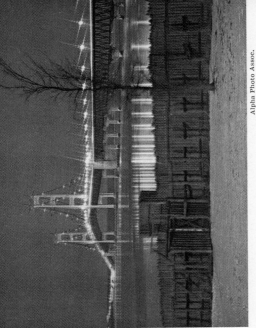

Alpha Photo Assoc.

Mackinac Bridge

K. Snyder, Alpha

Sparkling Lake Michigan, for Which the State Is Named

Michigan (blue) ranks 23rd in size among all the states and 7th in size among the Midwestern States (gray).

FACTS IN BRIEF

Capital: Lansing.

Government: *Congress*—U.S. senators, 2; U.S. representatives, 19. *Electoral Votes*—21. *State Legislature*—senators, 38; representatives, 110. *Counties*—83.

Area: 58,216 square miles (including 1,399 square miles of inland water), 23rd in size among the states. *Greatest Distances in Upper Peninsula:* (east-west) 334 miles; (north-south) 215 miles. *Greatest Distances in Lower Peninsula:* (north-south) 286 miles; (east-west) 200 miles. *Shoreline*—3,288 miles (including 1,056 miles of island shoreline).

Elevation: *Highest*—1,980 feet above sea level in Baraga County. *Lowest*—572 feet above sea level along Lake Erie.

Population: *1970 Preliminary Census*—8,778,187; density, 151 persons to the square mile. *1960 Census*—7,823,194, 7th among the states; distribution, 73 per cent urban, 27 per cent rural.

Chief Products: *Agriculture*—beef cattle, cherries, corn, dry beans, eggs, greenhouse and nursery products, hogs, milk, soybeans, wheat. *Fishing Industry*—alewives, chubs, lake herring, whitefish, yellow perch, yellow pike. *Manufacturing and Processing*—automobiles, buses, trucks; chemicals; electrical equipment; fabricated metal products; food and food products; furniture and fixtures; nonelectrical machinery; paper and paper products; primary metals; printing and publishing; rubber and plastic products; stone, clay, and glass products. *Mining*—bromine, copper, iron ore, petroleum, salt, sand and gravel, stone.

Statehood: Jan. 26, 1837, the 26th state.

State Motto: *Si quaeris peninsulam amoenam, circumspice* (If you seek a pleasant peninsula, look about you).

State Song (unofficial): "Michigan, My Michigan." Words of 1863 version by Winifred Lee Brent. Words of more widely used version of 1902 by Douglas M. Malloch.

---

lakes. Forests cover more than half the state. Michigan offers sportsmen excellent hunting and fishing.

French explorers of the early 1600's were the first white men to visit the Michigan region. France controlled the region for nearly 150 years, but did little to develop it. Great Britain gained control of the Michigan region after defeating France in the French and Indian Wars (1689-1763). In 1787, after the Revolutionary War, Michigan became part of the Northwest Territory of the United States. In 1805, Congress established the Territory of Michigan. In 1837, Michigan became the 26th state of the Union.

Michigan is named for Lake Michigan. The Chippewa Indians called the lake *Michigama*, which means *great*, or *large, lake*. Michigan is nicknamed the *Wolverine State* because the early fur traders brought valuable wolverine pelts to trading posts in the region. The state is also known as the *Water Wonderland*, because of its beautiful lakes and streams. Including its share of the Great Lakes, Michigan has more water than any other state. The Upper Peninsula is sometimes called the

Land of Hiawatha because it is described in Henry Wadsworth Longfellow's poem, *The Song of Hiawatha*. For the relationship of Michigan to other states in its region, see MIDWESTERN STATES.

Constitution. Michigan's present Constitution went into effect in 1964. Earlier constitutions were adopted in 1835, 1850, and 1908.

Constitutional *amendments* (changes) may be proposed in three ways. *Initiative amendments* are introduced by petitions signed by a specified number of voters. *Legislative amendments* are introduced by members of the state Legislature. Legislative amendments must be approved by two-thirds of the members of both houses of the Legislature. Amendments can also be proposed by *constitutional conventions*. Beginning in 1978, and every 16 years thereafter, the voters will decide whether to call a constitutional convention. All proposed amendments must be approved by a majority of the voters who cast ballots on the amendment.

Executive. The Constitution of 1964 increased the governor's term of office from two years to four years. Michigan's governor may be re-elected any number of times. Also increased from two to four years were the terms of the lieutenant governor, secretary of state, and attorney general. The Constitution provided that the four-year terms begin with officials elected in 1966. Also, beginning in 1966, each party's candidates for governor and lieutenant governor began running for office as a team. Thus, voters cast a single vote for the governor and lieutenant governor together. The governor receives a yearly salary of $40,000. For a list of the state's governors, see the *History* section of this article.

The governor, with the consent of the state Senate, appoints various state officials who are not elected. These officials include the treasurer, members of boards and commissions, and department heads. Officials elected to eight-year terms include regents of the University of Michigan, trustees of Michigan State University, governors of Wayne State University, and members of the state board of education.

To run for governor, candidates of major political parties must be nominated by the people in a primary election. Candidates for other elective offices are nominated at party conventions. A *recall* law gives the people

the right to vote to remove from office any elected officials other than judges. A specified number of qualified voters must sign a petition to hold such a recall vote.

Legislature of Michigan consists of a 38-member Senate and a 110-member House of Representatives. The 1964 Constitution increased the terms of office of state senators from two to four years, beginning with the 1966 election. Representatives serve two-year terms. In 1964, both legislative houses were redrawn according to population. This action was designed to give fairer representation to all persons in the state. Legislative sessions begin on the second Wednesday of every January, and last until all business has been completed. The governor may call special sessions of the Legislature.

Courts. Michigan's highest court is the state Supreme Court. This court has seven justices, elected to eight-year terms. The justices elect one of their members to serve as chief justice. The 1964 Constitution provided for a new nine-judge court of appeals, elected from three districts drawn according to population. Michigan has circuit courts in each of 42 districts. Circuit courts are the highest trial courts in the state. Each county has a probate court with from one to six judges, appeals, circuit, and probate court judges are elected to six-year terms. Other courts include common pleas and district courts.

Local Government. The county is Michigan's chief unit of local government. The state's 83 counties are divided into townships. Each county has a county board of commissioners as its legislative body. The board consists of representatives from each township and city in the county. Other county officers include the county clerk, county treasurer, prosecuting attorney, register of deeds, and sheriff.

The Constitution permits counties and cities to have *home rule* (self-government) to the extent that they may frame, adopt, and amend their own charters. However, these powers can be restricted by the Constitution and the Legislature. More than a hundred Michigan cities

Penrod Studios

Statue of Austin Blair, by Edward Clark Potter, stands in front of the entrance to the Capitol. Blair was governor of Michigan during the Civil War.

Penrod Studios

Office of the Governor is in the Capitol in Lansing. The office is on the second floor, on the east side of the building.

The State Flag

The State Seal

The State Bird
Robin

The State Flower
Apple Blossom

The State Tree
White Pine

Symbols of Michigan. On the seal, the sun rising over water and the man in a field appear on a shield supported by an elk and a moose. They represent Michigan's wealth, resources, and people. An eagle above the shield symbolizes the superior authority and jurisdiction of the U.S. government over state governments. The Latin word *Tuebor* means *I will defend.* The seal was adopted in 1835 and appears on the state flag. The flag was adopted in 1911.

Flag, bird, and flower illustrations, courtesy of Eli Lilly and Company

have the city-manager form of government. Most of the other cities have the mayor-council form.

Taxation. Sales and excise taxes account for more than 40 per cent of the state government's income. Other sources of income include personal and corporate income taxes, estate and gift taxes, licenses, and property taxes. About 20 per cent of the state government's income comes from federal grants and programs.

Politics. The Republican party is strongest in rural areas of Michigan. Democratic strength lies in Detroit and other urban areas. Voting in state-wide elections has been fairly evenly divided since 1930. In the 1962 election, George W. Romney, a Republican, was elected governor. It was the first time in 14 years that a governor of Michigan had a state legislature controlled by his own political party. From 1964 to 1966, the Democrats controlled both houses of the state legislature for the first time in over 30 years. For Michigan's electoral votes and voting record in presidential elections, see ELECTORAL COLLEGE (table).

The State Capitol is in Lansing, Michigan's capital since 1847. Detroit was the state capital from 1837 to 1847.

John Penrod

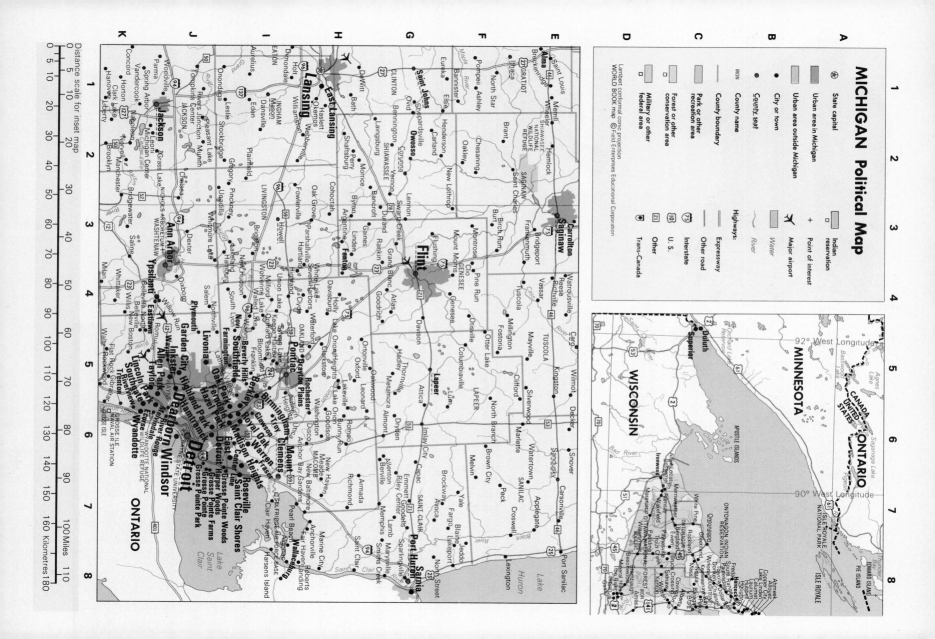

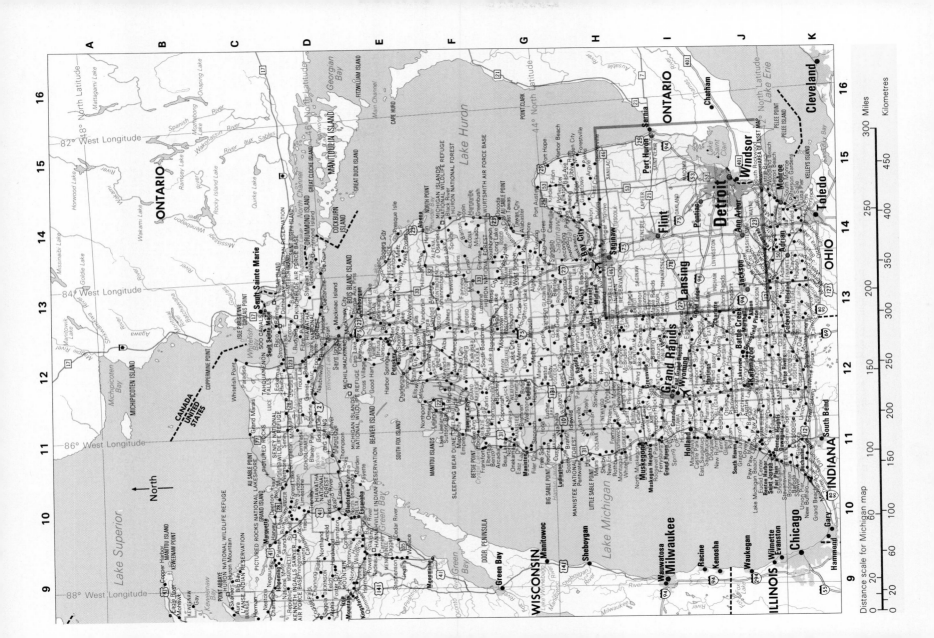

Holt 4,818 I 1
Homer 1,595 J 13
Honor 278 F 11
Hope H 13
Hopkins 556 J 12
Horton K 1
Houghton 6,052 °C 8
Houghton Lake G 13
Houghton Lake Heights 1,195 G 13
Howard City 1,047 H 12
Howell 5,202 °I 3
Hoxeyville G 12
Hubbard Lake F 14
Hubbardston 381 I 13
Hubbell 1,429 B 9
Hudson 2,600 K 13
Hudsonville 3,502 I 12
Hulbert D 12
Huntington Woods* 8,313 I 6
Huron Mountain C 9
Ida K 14
Idlewild H 12
Imlay City 2,000 G 6
Indian River E 13
Ingalls E 9
Inkster 38,264 J 5
Ionia 6,284 °I 12
Iron Mountain 8,622 °E 9
Iron River 2,667 D 8
Irons G 11
Ironton E 12
Ironwood 8,476 D 7
Ishpeming 8,137 D 9
Ithaca 2,728 °I 13
Jackson 45,733 °J 13
Jasper K 14
Jeddo F 8
Johannesburg F 13
Jones K 12
Jonesville 2,041 K 13
Kalamazoo 84,444 °J 12
Kaleva 348 G 11
Kalkaska 1,554 °F 12
Karlin G 12
Kawkawlin H 14
Keego Harbor 3,081 I 5
Keeler J 11
Keweenaw Bay C 8
Kent City 617 I 12
Kenton D 8
Kentwood* 20,176 I 12
Kewadin F 12
Kinde 624 G 15
Kingsford 5,210 E 9
Kingsley 586 G 12
Kingston 456 E 5
Kinross D 13
Kiva D 10
Lachine F 14
Laingsburg 1,156 H 2
Lake H 12
Lake Angelus* 231 I 14
Lake Ann 106 F 11
Lake City 718 °G 12
Lake George G 12
Lake Leelanau F 12
Lake Linden 1,206 B 9
Lake Michigan Beach 1,092 J 11
Lake Odessa 1,918 I 12
Lake Orion 2,893 H 5
Lake Orion Heights 1,918 H 5
Lakeland J 3
Lakeport F 8
Lakeside* 1,569 I 14
Lakeview 1,106 H 12
Lakeview 10,384 J 12
Lakeville H 6
Lakewood* 1,815 K 14
Lamb G 7
Lambertville 1,168 K 14
L'Anse 2,506 °C 9
Lansing 129,021 I 13
Lapeer 6,372 °G 5
La Salle K 14
Lathrup Village 4,613 J 5
Laurium 2,799 B 8
Lawrence* 773 J 11
Lawton 1,366 J 12
LeRoy 267 G 12
Leland °F 12
Lennon G 3
Leonard 359 H 6
Leoni K 2
Leslie 1,880 J 1
Level Park-Oak Park* 3,017 J 12
Levering E 13
Lewiston F 13
Lexington 722 F 8
Liberty K 1
Limestone D 10
Lincoln 441 F 14
Lincoln Park 52,988 K 6
Linden 1,540 H 3
Linwood H 14
Litchfield 1,162 J 13
Livonia 109,746 J 5
Long Lake G 14

Lowell* 3,051 I 12
Lucas G 12
Ludington 8,889 °H 11
Lum G 6
Luna Pier 1,403 K 14
Lupton G 14
Luther 325 G 12
Luzerne F 13
Lyons* 687 I 13
Macatawa I 11
Mackinac Island 942 D 13
Mackinaw City 934 E 13
Madison Heights 38,560 I 6
Mancelona 1,208 F 12
Manchester 1,644 K 3
Manistee 7,762 °G 11
Manistique 4,274 °D 11
Manitou Beach-Devil's Lake 1,544 K 13
Manton 1,095 G 12
Maple City F 11
Maple Rapids 683 I 13
Marcellus 1,145 K 12
Marenisco D 7
Marine City 4,562 H 8
Marion 898 G 12
Marlette 1,682 E 6
Marne I 12
Marquette 21,501 °C 10
Marshall 7,183 °J 13
Martin 483 J 12
Marysville 5,600 G 8
Mason 5,483 °I 1
Mass C 8
Mattawan* 1,492 J 12
Maybee 459 K 14
Mayfield F 12
Mayville 896 E 5
McBain 551 G 12
McBrides 265 H 12
McMillan D 12
Meade H 7
Mears H 11
Mecosta 303 H 12
Melvin 196 F 7
Melvindale 13,998 J 6
Memphis 1,112 G 7
Mendon* 867 K 12
Menominee 10,637 °F 9
Merrill 963 E 2
Merritt G 12
Merriweather C 7
Mesick 304 G 12
Metamora 452 G 5
Metz E 14
Michiana 135 K 11
Michigan Center 4,611 K 2
Middleton I 13
Middleville 1,846 I 12
Midland 34,691 °H 13
Mikado F 14
Milan 3,978 K 4
Milford 4,725 I 4
Millbrook H 12
Millersburg 280 E 13
Millington 1,089 F 4
Minden City 369 H 15
Mineral Hills 311 D 8
Mio °F 13
Mohawk B 9
Moline I 12
Monroe 23,623 °K 14
Montague 2,397 H 11
Montgomery 362 K 13
Montrose 1,757 F 3
Moorestown G 12
Moran D 13
Morenci 1,872 K 13
Morley 445 H 12
Morrice 530 H 2
Mount Clemens 20,129 °I 7
Mount Morris 3,783 F 4
Mount Pleasant 19,961 °H 13
Muir 610 I 13
Mullett Lake E 13
Mulliken 484 I 13
Munger H 14
Munising 3,664 °D 10
Munith J 2
Munson K 13
Muskegon 44,377 °I 11
Muskegon Heights 17,041 I 11
Nadeau E 10
Nahma E 10
Napoleon K 2
Nashville 1,528 J 12
National City G 14
National Mine D 9
Naubinway D 12
Negaunee 5,207 D 9
Nestoria C 9
New Baltimore 4,054 I 7
New Boston K 5
New Buffalo 2,465 K 11
New Era 403 H 11
New Haven 1,826 H 7
New Hudson I 4
New Lothrop 510 F 3
New Richmond J 11

Newaygo 1,373 H 12
Newberry 2,330 °D 12
Newport J 15
Niles 12,942 K 11
Nisula C 8
North Adams 494 K 13
North Bradley H 13
North Branch 901 F 6
North Escanaba E 10
North Muskegon 4,219 I 11
North Star F 1
North Street G 8
Northland D 9
Northport 530 F 12
Northville 5,387 J 5
Norton Shores* 22,160 I 11
Norvell K 2
Norwalk G 11
Norway 3,030 E 9
Novi 9,526 I 5
Nunica I 11
Oak Grove H 3
Oak Park 36,700 J 6
Oakley 417 F 2
Oakwood H 5
Ocqueoc E 13
Oden E 13
Okemos H 1
Old Mission F 12
Olivet 1,640 J 13
Omena F 12
Omer 322 G 14
Onaway 1,247 E 13
Onekama 469 G 11
Onondaga J 1
Onsted* 526 K 13
Ontonagon 2,402 °C 8
Orchard Lake 1,490 I 5
Ontonville 771 H 5
Oscoda G 14
Ossineke F 14
Otisville 701 F 4
Otsego 3,900 J 12
Ottawa Lake K 14
Otter Lake 562 F 5
Ovid 1,651 G 1
Owendale 298 H 14
Owosso 17,282 G 2
Oxford 2,501 H 5
Ozark D 12
Painesdale C 8
Palmer D 9
Palms H 15
Paradise C 12
Parchment 2,015 J 12
Paris H 12
Parma 770 K 1
Parshallville I 4
Patterson Gardens 1,747 K 14
Paulding D 8
Paw Paw 3,148 °J 12
Paw Paw Lake 3,518 J 11
Paynesville C 8
Pearl Beach 1,224 I 8
Peck 548 F 7
Pelkie C 8
Pellston 429 E 13
Pentwater 1,030 H 11
Perkins D 10
Perrinton 424 I 13
Perronville E 10
Perry 1,553 H 2
Petersburg* 1,242 K 14
Petoskey 6,159 °E 12
Pewamo* 415 I 13
Pickford D 13
Pierson 219 H 12
Pigeon 1,174 H 14
Pinckney 732 J 3
Pinconning 1,310 H 14
Pine Run F 4
Plainfield I 2
Plainwell 3,230 J 12
Pleasant Lake J 2
Pleasant Ridge* 3,990 J 15
Plymouth 11,394 J 5
Pompeii F 1
Pontiac 84,951 °J 13
Port Austin 706 G 15
Port Hope 349 G 15
Port Huron 35,530 °I 15
Port Sanilac 361 E 8
Portage* 33,151 J 12
Portland 3,809 I 13
Posen 341 E 14
Potterville 1,258 J 13
Powers 415 E 10
Prattville K 13
Prescott 308 G 14
Presque Isle E 14
Princeton D 10
Prudenville G 13
Pullman J 11
Quakertown* 482 J 14
Quincy 1,593 K 13
Quinnesec E 9
Raco D 13
Ralph D 9
Ramsay 1,158 D 7
Rankin G 4
Rapid City F 12
Rapid River D 10

Ravenna 1,050 I 11
Reading 1,114 K 13
Reed City 2,364 °H 12
Reeman H 11
Reese 1,053 E 4
Remus H 12
Republic D 9
Rexton D 12
Rhodes H 13
Richland* 511 J 12
Richmond 3,183 H 7
Richville E 4
Ridgeway K 14
Riley Center G 7
River Rouge 15,574 J 6
Riverdale H 13
Riverview 11,368 K 6
Rives Junction J 1
Roberts Landing I 8
Rochester 6,966 I 6
Rockford 2,434 I 12
Rockland C 8
Rockwood 3,203 K 6
Rodney H 12
Rogers City 4,032 °E 14
Romeo 3,967 H 6
Romulus 1,798 K 5
Roosevelt Park 4,101 I 11
Roscommon 867 °G 13
Rose City 435 G 13
Rosebush H 13
Roseville 60,505 I 6
Rothbury H 11
Royal Oak 84,081 I 6
Rudyard D 13
Ruth H 15
Saginaw 90,603 °H 14
Sagola D 9
St. Charles 2,040 F 2
St. Clair 4,724 H 8
St. Clair Shores 87,378 J 7
St. Helen G 13
St. Ignace 2,889 °D 13
St. Johns 6,682 °G 1
St. Joseph 10,978 °J 11
St. Louis 4,029 E 1
Salem J 4
Saline 4,770 K 4
Sand Lake 394 I 12
Sandusky 2,059 °E 7
Sanford H 13
Saranac* 1,208 I 12
Saugatuck 1,004 J 11
Sault Ste. Marie 14,812 °C 13
Sawyer K 11
Schaffer E 10
Schoolcraft 1,262 J 12
Scottville 1,199 H 11
Sears H 12
Sebewaing 2,040 H 14
Seney D 11
Shaftsburg H 2
Shelby 1,706 H 11
Shepardsville G 1
Shepherd 1,401 H 13
Sheridan 606 I 12
Sherwood 356 K 12
Shingleton D 11
Shoreham 443 K 11
Sidnaw C 8
Sidney I 12
Silverwood E 5
Six Lakes H 12
Skandia D 10
Skanee C 9
Smiths Creek G 8
Snover E 6
Somerset Center J 13
South Boardman F 12
South Haven 6,419 J 11
South Lyon 2,654 J 4
South Monroe 2,919 K 14
South Range 760 C 8
South Rockwood 1,481 J 15
Southbranch G 14
Southfield 68,844 J 5
Southgate 33,723 K 6
Spalding E 10
Sparlingville 1,877 G 8
Sparta 3,086 I 12
Spring Arbor K 1
Spring Lake 3,008 I 11
Springfield 3,914 J 12
Springfield Place 5,136 J 12
Springport 693 J 13
Spruce F 14
Stalwart D 13
Stambaugh 1,444 D 8
Standish 1,161 °G 14
Stanton 1,085 °I 12
Stanwood 205 H 12
Stephenson 820 E 9
Sterling 470 G 14
Sterling Heights* 58,843 J 15
Stevensville 1,070 K 11
Stockbridge 1,192 J 2
Stronach G 11
Strongs D 12
Sturgis 9,179 K 12
Sundell D 10

Sunfield 626 I 13
Sunrise Heights* 1,569 J 12
Suttons Bay 421 F 12
Swartz Creek 4,893 G 3
Sylvan Lake 2,223 I 5
Tawas City 1,625 °G 14
Taylor 69,673 K 5
Tecumseh 7,048 K 14
Tekonsha 744 J 13
Temperance 2,215 K 14
Temple G 12
Thompson D 11
Thompsonville 243 G 11
Thornville G 5
Three Oaks 1,738 K 11
Three Rivers 7,441 K 12
Tipton K 14
Toivola C 8
Tompkins Center J 1
Topinabee E 13
Tower E 13
Traunik D 10
Traverse City 17,687 °F 12
Trenary D 10
Trenton 25,196 K 6
Trout Creek D 8
Trout Lake D 12
Troy 39,143 I 6
Turner 206 G 14
Tustin 248 G 12
Twin Lake H 11
Twining 199 G 14
Ubly 819 H 15
Unadilla J 3
Union K 12
Union City 1,716 J 12
Union Lake I 4
Union Pier K 11
Unionville 629 H 14
Utica 3,463 I 6
Vandalia 357 K 11
Vanderbilt 509 F 13
Vandercook K 1
Vassar 2,790 E 4
Vermontville 768 J 13
Vernon 754 G 3
Vestaburg H 13
Vicksburg 2,131 J 12
Vulcan E 9
Wakefield 2,550 D 7
Waldron 454 K 13
Walhalla H 11
Walker* 11,443 I 12
Walkerville 261 H 11
Wallace E 9
Walled Lake 3,743 I 5
Walloon Lake E 12
Waltz K 5
Warren 179,217 I 6
Washington H 6
Waterford H 5
Waters F 13
Watersmeet D 8
Watervliet 2,045 J 11
Watrousville E 4
Watton C 8
Wayland 2,056 J 12
Wayne 21,223 J 5
Webberville 1,240 I 2
Weidman H 12
Wells E 10
Wellston G 11
West Branch 1,869 °G 13
Westland* 86,291 J 14
Weston K 14
Westphalia* 560 I 13
Wetmore D 11
Wheeler E 1
White Cloud 1,032 °H 12
White Lake-Seven Harbors 2,748 H 4
White Pigeon 1,453 K 12
White Pine C 7
Whitefish Point C 12
Whitehall 2,999 H 11
Whitmore Lake J 4
Whittaker K 4
Whittemore 460 G 14
Williamsburg F 12
Williamston 2,572 I 2
Willis K 4
Willow Run K 4
Wilmot E 5
Wilson E 10
Winn H 13
Winona C 8
Wixom 2,003 I 4
Wolf Lake 2,525 I 11
Wolverine 292 E 13
Wolverine Lake 4,282 I 4
Wood Creek Farms* 684 J 14
Woodhaven* 2,025 J 15
Woodland 374 I 12
Woodland Beach 1,944 K 15
Woodville K 1
Wyandotte 40,832 K 6
Wyoming 56,196 I 12
Yale 1,491 F 7
Ypsilanti 29,260 K 4
Zeeland 4,714 I 11
Zilwaukee* 2,062 H 14

*Does not appear on the map; key shows general location.
°County seat

Sources: Latest census figures (1970 preliminary census where available or 1960 census). Cities and towns without population information are unincorporated places under 1,000 in population and are not listed in census reports.

MICHIGAN/People

The 1970 preliminary United States census reported that Michigan had a population of 8,778,187. This was an increase of about 12 per cent over the 1960 figure of 7,823,194.

Nearly three-fourths of Michigan's people live in

Factory Workers stream out of a factory in Dearborn, near Detroit, at the end of a day. Many Detroit area factories have thousands of employees and operate in two or even three shifts. Most of Michigan's people live in or near large industrial cities.

The Detroit News

urban areas. That is, they live in or near cities and towns of 2,500 or more persons. Slightly more than a fourth of the people live in rural areas. More than 75 per cent of the people make their homes in one of the state's 10 Standard Metropolitan Statistical Areas (see METROPOLITAN AREA). These are Ann Arbor, Bay City, Detroit, Flint, Grand Rapids, Jackson, Kalamazoo, Lansing, Muskegon-Muskegon Heights, and Saginaw. For the populations of these metropolitan areas, see the *Index* to the political map of Michigan. Most of the people of Michigan live in the Lower Peninsula. Only about 300,000 persons, or about 3 of every 100, live in the Upper Peninsula.

Detroit is Michigan's largest city, and the fifth largest city in the United States. Other large cities in Michigan, in order of population, are Grand Rapids, Flint, Warren, Lansing, Livonia, Dearborn, Ann Arbor, Saginaw, and St. Clair Shores. All have populations of more than 80,000, and all are in the Lower Peninsula. The largest city in the Upper Peninsula of Michigan is Marquette. It has a population of more than 21,000 persons. See the separate articles on the cities of Michigan which are listed in the *Related Articles* at the end of this article.

About 93 of every 100 persons in Michigan were born in the United States. Of the more than 500,000 persons from other countries who live in the state, the largest group came from Canada. Other groups born outside the United States include, in order of size, those from Poland, Italy, England, Germany, Russia, Scotland, and The Netherlands.

Roman Catholics make up the largest religious group in Michigan. Other large church groups in the state include Baptists, Episcopalians, Lutherans, Methodists, and Presbyterians. The House of David, a small but well-known religious organization, has its headquarters in Benton Harbor (see HOUSE OF DAVID).

POPULATION

This map shows the *population density* of Michigan, and how it varies in different parts of the state. Population density means the average number of persons who live on each square mile.

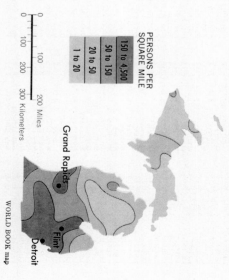

PERSONS PER SQUARE MILE
150 to 4,500
50 to 150
20 to 50
1 to 20

Grand Rapids
Flint
Detroit

0 100 200 300 Kilometers
0 100 200 Miles

WORLD BOOK map

MICHIGAN / Education

Wayne State University's McGregor Memorial Community Conference Center was designed by Minoru Yamasaki.

Schools. Roman Catholic missionaries who came to the Michigan region in the 1600's established schools for the Indians. In 1798, Father Gabriel Richard came to Detroit as pastor of Ste. Anne's Roman Catholic Church. He set up schools to provide regular classes and vocational training for Indian and white children.

In 1809, the territorial legislature passed Michigan's first school law. The law provided for school districts, school taxes, and the building of public schools. It also required children between the ages of 4 and 18 to attend school. In 1827, the legislature provided for community schools maintained by townships. German settlers in Washtenaw and other nearby counties built many schools during the 1830's. After Michigan entered the Union in 1837, the state Legislature approved a state-wide system of public education, including a university. The Legislature also provided for the appointment of a superintendent of public instruction to administer the public school system. The Michigan superintendent was the first such administrator in the United States.

Eastern Michigan University, established in 1849, was the first state teachers college west of New York. Michigan State University, founded in 1855, was the first state school to offer agriculture courses for credit. In 1879, the University of Michigan became one of the first state universities to establish a *chair* (special teaching position) in education.

Today, Michigan has about 2,700 public elementary schools and about 1,100 public junior and senior high schools. The state board of education directs Michigan's public school system. It consists of eight members elected to the board by the voters. The board appoints the superintendent of public instruction. A state law requires children between the ages of 6 and 16 to attend school. For the number of students and teachers in Michigan, see EDUCATION (table).

Libraries. Michigan's state library was founded in Detroit in 1828. At that time, large numbers of settlers were beginning to move into the Michigan territory. The state library was later moved to Lansing. It now has over 1 million volumes. Michigan has 24 library systems and 344 public libraries with 165 branches. Bookmobiles serve many rural communities. The state provides aid to local library systems. Small libraries receive funds to improve their reference collections from the McGregor Fund of Detroit.

The William L. Clements Library at the University of Michigan is famous for its collection on early America. The University of Michigan's library has about 4 million volumes. The Detroit Public Library has the Burton Historical Collection, containing fine reference works on Michigan and the Great Lakes area. Other large libraries are located at Wayne State University and at Michigan State University.

Museums. The Detroit Institute of Arts was established in 1885. Its collection of paintings and sculptures includes murals by the Mexican artist Diego Rivera. The Detroit Historical Museum has exhibits on the history of Detroit and Michigan. The Children's Museum of the Detroit Public Schools has displays for young people about U.S. and Michigan history. Greenfield Village, in Dearborn, is a museum made

up of a group of historical buildings. Its exhibits deal with American industrial history, and life in the 1700's and 1800's. The Grand Rapids Public Museum features natural history exhibits. The Baker Museum and Craft Shop, also in Grand Rapids, has displays of furniture and furnishings. The Michigan Historical Commission Museum in Lansing displays pioneer items. The Kingman Museum of Natural History in Battle Creek has exhibits of wildlife, prehistoric mammals, and ancient relics. Mackinac Island has seven museums. One of them features writings of William Beaumont, a surgeon of the early 1800's, who made important discoveries about human digestion.

UNIVERSITIES AND COLLEGES

Michigan has 34 universities and colleges accredited by the North Central Association of Colleges and Secondary Schools. For enrollments and further information, see UNIVERSITIES AND COLLEGES (table).

Name	Location	Founded
Adrian College	Adrian	1845
Albion College	Albion	1835
Alma College	Alma	1886
Andrews University	Berrien Springs	1874
Aquinas College	Grand Rapids	1922
Calvin College	Grand Rapids	1876
Central Michigan University	Mount Pleasant	1892
Cranbrook Academy of Art	Bloomfield Hills	1942
Detroit, University of	Detroit	1877
Detroit Institute of Technology	Detroit	1891
Duns Scotus College	Southfield	1930
Eastern Michigan University	Ypsilanti	1849
Ferris State College	Big Rapids	1884
General Motors Institute	Flint	1919
Grand Valley State College	Allendale	1960
Hillsdale College	Hillsdale	1844
Hope College	Holland	1851
Kalamazoo College	Kalamazoo	1833
Lawrence Institute of Technology	Southfield	1932
Madonna College	Livonia	1947
Marygrove College	Detroit	1905
Mercy College of Detroit	Detroit	1941
Michigan, University of	Ann Arbor	1817
Michigan State University	East Lansing	1855
Michigan Technological University	*	1885
Nazareth College	Kalamazoo	1897
Northern Michigan University	Marquette	1899
Oakland University	Rochester	1959
Olivet College	Olivet	1844
Sacred Heart Seminary	Detroit	1919
Siena Heights College	Adrian	1919
Spring Arbor College	Spring Arbor	1873
Wayne State University	Detroit	1868
Western Michigan University	Kalamazoo	1903

*For the campuses of Michigan Technological University, see UNIVERSITIES AND COLLEGES (table).

Michigan is a year-round playground for sportsmen and lovers of the outdoors. Thousands of lakes, rivers, and streams attract swimmers, water skiers, fishermen, and boaters. Thick forests and scenic woodlands attract hunters and campers. Winter sportsmen travel to Michigan for skiing, skating, tobogganing, iceboat racing, and ice fishing. Sightseers are drawn to the many beautiful waterfalls and dunes, and to the rugged "Copper Country" of the western Upper Peninsula.

Pictured Rocks near Munising

John Calkins, Shostal

Following are brief descriptions of some of Michigan's many interesting places to visit.

PLACES TO VISIT

American Ski Hall of Fame, in Ishpeming, honors famous American skiers, skiing events, and persons who have made outstanding contributions to the sport.

Arboretums of Michigan have some of the country's finest collections of plants, shrubs, and trees. *Leila Arboretum,* in Battle Creek, is a beautifully landscaped park with rare plants and a wildlife museum. *Nichols Arboretum,* in Ann Arbor, has a famous garden and a collection of about 140 kinds of hybrid lilacs.

Automobile Plants in Dearborn, Detroit, Flint, Lansing, and Pontiac provide guided tours for visitors.

Big Spring, or *Kitch-iti-ki-pi,* near Manistique, is a 40-foot-deep pool fed by more than 200 bubbling springs. The water is so clear that visitors can watch coins drift all the way to the bottom of the pool.

Detroit, the *Motor City,* produces more cars and trucks than any other city in the world. Detroit is the fifth largest city in the United States, and a leading port. Its famous Cultural Center includes libraries, museums, and Wayne State University. See DETROIT.

Fort Michilimackinac, in Mackinaw City, is a reconstruction of the fort built in the 1700's. Buildings include the home of British commander Robert Rogers, and Ste. Anne's Jesuit church.

Greenfield Village, in Dearborn, is a collection of historic buildings restored by Henry Ford. The village includes the Edison Institute School, and buildings made famous by such persons as Abraham Lincoln, Thomas Edison, William H. McGuffey, and Stephen Foster. The Henry Ford Museum is next to the village. See GREENFIELD VILLAGE.

House of David is a well-known religious community in Benton Harbor. Members operate a summer resort. See HOUSE OF DAVID.

Kellogg Bird Sanctuary, on Gull Lake near Battle Creek, is a 100-acre refuge for ducks, geese, pheasants, swans, and other wild birds.

Mackinac Island is a famous resort island in the Straits of Mackinac, between the Upper and Lower peninsulas. No automobiles are permitted on the island. See MACKINAC ISLAND.

Pictured Rocks, near Munising on Lake Superior, are beautifully colored cliffs carved into spectacular shapes by the action of waves.

Sleeping Bear Dune, near Glen Arbor, is a 600-foot-high mound of sand shaped like a sleeping bear. The sand is so fine that the dune is used as a ski slide in summer. Favorable wind conditions allow sportsmen to fly gliders from the Sleeping Bear Dune. See DUNE (picture).

Soo Canals, at Sault Ste. Marie, permit ships to travel between Lake Huron and Lake Superior through huge locks. See SOO CANALS.

Tahquamenon Falls, near Newberry, are among the most beautiful sights of the Upper Peninsula. Henry Wadsworth Longfellow wrote about both the upper and lower falls of the Tahquamenon River in his poem *The Song of Hiawatha.*

National Forests and Parks. Michigan has four national forests. The largest, Ottawa National Forest, lies in the western part of the Upper Peninsula. Hiawatha National Forest is in the central and eastern parts of the Upper Peninsula. Huron National Forest occupies much of the Au Sable River basin of the eastern Lower Peninsula. Manistee National Forest covers most of the Manistee River basin in the western Lower Peninsula. For the areas and other features of these forests, see NATIONAL FOREST (table).

Michigan's only national park, Isle Royale, is in northwestern Lake Superior, about 45 miles from the mainland. It includes Isle Royale and about 200 nearby small islands. The park has one of the largest remaining herds of great-antlered moose in the United States. See ISLE ROYALE NATIONAL PARK.

State Parks and Forests. Michigan has over 70 state parks, 29 state forests, and over 150 roadside parks and rest areas. Michigan's park system has over 13,000 prepared campsites, more than any other state. The state also has about 85 organized winter-sport areas. The 500-foot artificial ski jump at Iron Mountain is one of the highest in the world.

For information on the state parks of Michigan, write to Director, Parks Division, Department of Conservation, Stevens T. Mason Building, Lansing, Mich. 48926.

ANNUAL EVENTS

One of Michigan's most popular annual events is the week-long Tulip Festival, held each May in Holland. The people of the city dress in traditional Dutch costumes and sell souvenirs made by craftsmen in the area. The festival includes parades, dancing in wooden shoes, group singing, and a marionette show. Other annual events in Michigan include the following.

January-March: Semiannual Furniture Show in Grand Rapids (first week in January); Ski tournaments at Iron Mountain and Ishpeming (February).

April-June: Smelt Jamboree in Escanaba (first weekend in April); Maple Syrup Festival in Vermontville (April); Blossom Festival in Benton Harbor-St. Joseph (May); Music Festival in Ann Arbor (May); Semiannual Furniture Show in Grand Rapids (last week in June); Music Festival in Interlochen (June-August).

July-September: Cherry Festival in Traverse City (mid-July); International Freedom Festival in Detroit (July); Yacht Races at Mackinac Island (July); Mexican Fiesta in Hart (July); National Junior and Boys Tennis Tournament in Kalamazoo (July); Re-enactment of the landing of Father Marquette at St. Ignace (second Sunday in August); Upper Peninsula State Fair in Escanaba (mid-August); State Fair in Detroit (late August).

October-December: Fall color tours, state-wide (October); Hunting season, parts of Upper and Lower peninsulas (October-November); state-wide (November); Red Flannel Days in Cedar Springs (November); Automobile Show in Detroit (November).

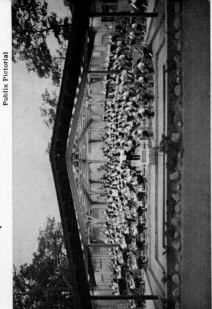

Publix Pictorial

National Music Camp in Interlochen

International Bridge Authority

International Bridge at Sault Ste. Marie

Ellis-Sawyer, FPG

Washing the Street for the Tulip Festival in Holland

Alpha Photo Assoc.

Greenfield Village Store in Dearborn

John Freeman, Publix

Tahquamenon Falls near Newberry

Land Regions. Michigan has two main land regions: (1) the Superior Upland and (2) the Great Lakes Plains.

The Superior Upland extends along Lake Superior in Michigan, Wisconsin, and Minnesota. In Michigan, the Superior Upland covers the western half of the Upper Peninsula. Much of the region is a rugged plateau, rising from about 600 feet to nearly 2,000 feet above sea level. Michigan's mountains are in this region. The Porcupine Mountains in extreme northwestern Michigan rise from the shores of Lake Superior. Baraga County has the highest point in the state, 1,980 feet above sea level. Forests cover many of the hills and mountains. The Superior Upland region has some of the nation's richest iron and copper deposits.

The Great Lakes Plains stretch along the Great Lakes from Wisconsin to Ohio. In Michigan, the region covers the eastern Upper Peninsula and the entire Lower Peninsula. In the Upper Peninsula, parts of the Great Lakes Plains are lowlands covered by swamps. A short growing season and thin soils make many parts of the area unsuitable for farming. The Great Lakes Plains are part of a large midwestern land region called the *Interior Lowland.*

Much of the Lower Peninsula is fairly level, but some parts are rolling and hilly. The north-central Lower Peninsula rises to between 1,200 and 1,400 feet above sea level. Many high bluffs and sand dunes border Lake Michigan. The state's lowest point, 572 feet above sea level, is along the shore of Lake Erie. Parts of the northern Lower Peninsula have sandy wastes, covered with jack pine trees, scrub, and stumps. The southern half of the Lower Peninsula has good farmland.

Shoreline of Michigan is 3,288 miles long, including 1,056 miles of island shoreline. Michigan's shoreline is longer than that of any other inland state. Four Great Lakes touch the state—Erie, Huron, Michigan,

A. M. Wettach

Sleek Dairy Cattle graze in a rich pasture near East Lansing. Michigan's best farmland lies in the southern Lower Peninsula. This area is part of the Great Lakes Plains region.

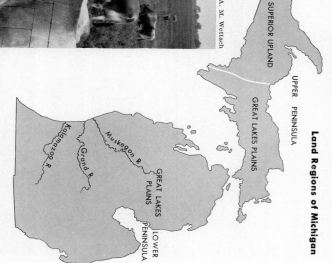

Land Regions of Michigan

SUPERIOR UPLAND

GREAT LAKES PLAINS

UPPER PENINSULA

Kalamazoo R.

Grand R.

Muskegon R.

GREAT LAKES PLAINS

LOWER PENINSULA

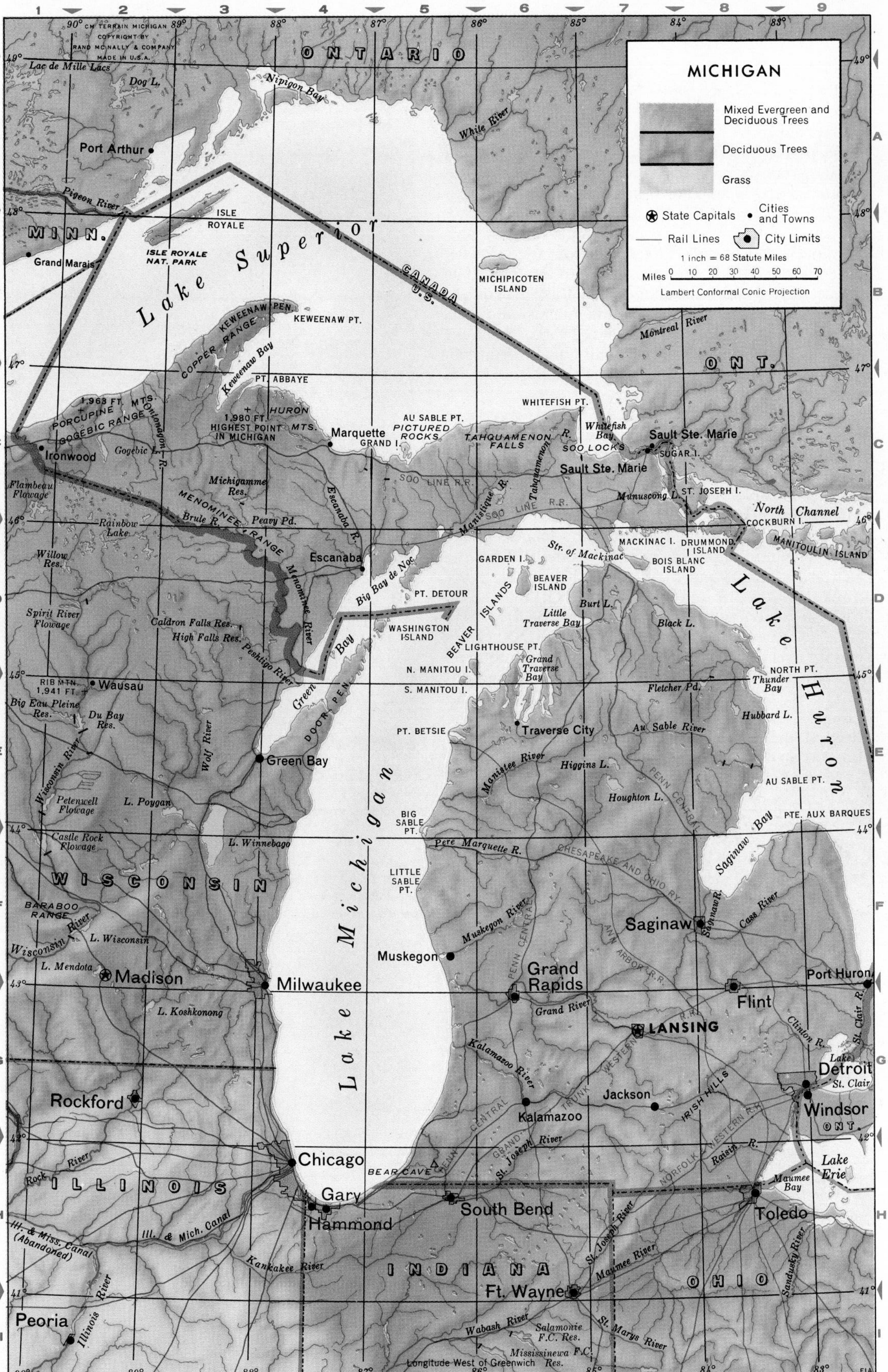

MICHIGAN
Mixed Evergreen and Deciduous Trees
Deciduous Trees
Grass
State Capitals
Cities and Towns
Rail Lines
City Limits
1 inch = 68 Statute Miles
Miles 0 10 20 30 40 50 60 70
Lambert Conformal Conic Projection
CM TERRAIN MICHIGAN COPYRIGHT BY RAND McNALLY & COMPANY MADE IN U.S.A.
ONTARIO
ONT.
MINN.
WISCONSIN
ILLINOIS
INDIANA
OHIO
CANADA
U.S.
Lake Superior
Lake Michigan
Lake Huron
Lake Erie
North Channel
Lac de Mille Lacs
Dog L.
Nipigon Bay
White River
Port Arthur
Pigeon River
ISLE ROYALE
ISLE ROYALE NAT. PARK
Grand Marais
MICHIPICOTEN ISLAND
Montreal River
KEWEENAW PEN.
KEWEENAW PT.
COPPER RANGE
Keweenaw Bay
PT. ABBAYE
1,963 FT.
PORCUPINE MTS.
GOGEBIC RANGE
1,980 FT.
HIGHEST POINT IN MICHIGAN
HURON MTS.
Marquette
GRAND I.
AU SABLE PT.
PICTURED ROCKS
WHITEFISH PT.
Whitefish Bay
TAHQUAMENON FALLS
Tahquamenon R.
SOO LOCKS
Sault Ste. Marie
SUGAR I.
ST. JOSEPH I.
Munuscong L.
COCKBURN I.
MANITOULIN ISLAND
Ironwood
Gogebic L.
Ontonagon R.
Flambeau Flowage
Michigamme Res.
SOO LINE R.R.
MENOMINEE RANGE
Brule R.
Peavy Pd.
Escanaba R.
Manistique R.
Rainbow Lake
Willow Res.
Escanaba
Big Bay de Noc
Str. of Mackinac
MACKINAC I.
DRUMMOND ISLAND
BOIS BLANC ISLAND
GARDEN I.
BEAVER ISLAND
PT. DETOUR
BEAVER ISLANDS
Little Traverse Bay
Burt L.
Black L.
Spirit River Flowage
Caldron Falls Res.
High Falls Res.
Menominee River
Peshtigo River
WASHINGTON ISLAND
LIGHTHOUSE PT.
Grand Traverse Bay
RIB MTN. 1,941 FT.
Wausau
Green Bay
DOOR PEN.
N. MANITOU I.
S. MANITOU I.
NORTH PT.
Thunder Bay
Fletcher Pd.
Big Eau Pleine Res.
Du Bay Res.
Wolf River
PT. BETSIE
Traverse City
Hubbard L.
Au Sable River
Wisconsin River
Green Bay
Manistee River
Higgins L.
Petenwell Flowage
L. Poygan
PENN CENTRAL
Houghton L.
AU SABLE PT.
BIG SABLE PT.
Saginaw Bay
PTE. AUX BARQUES
Castle Rock Flowage
L. Winnebago
Pere Marquette R.
CHESAPEAKE AND OHIO RY.
LITTLE SABLE PT.
BARABOO RANGE
L. Wisconsin
Muskegon River
Saginaw
Saginaw R.
Cass River
Wisconsin River
L. Mendota
Madison
Milwaukee
Muskegon
ANN ARBOR R.R.
Grand Rapids
Port Huron
Flint
L. Koshkonong
Grand River
LANSING
St. Clair R.
Clinton R.
Kalamazoo River
GRAND TRUNK WESTERN
Lake St. Clair
Detroit
Rockford
Jackson
IRISH HILLS
Kalamazoo
Windsor
CENTRAL
St. Joseph River
NORFOLK WESTERN R.R.
Raisin R.
Rock River
Chicago
BEAR CAVE
Maumee Bay
Gary
Hammond
South Bend
Toledo
Ill. & Mich. Canal
Ill. & Miss. Canal (Abandoned)
St. Joseph River
Kankakee River
Maumee River
Sandusky River
Illinois River
Ft. Wayne
Peoria
Wabash River
Salamonie F.C. Res.
St. Marys River
Mississinewa F.C. Res.
Longitude West of Greenwich
FIA

Specially created for **World Book Encyclopedia** by Rand McNally and World Book editors

and Superior. No part of Michigan is more than 85 miles from one of these four lakes.

Bays along the Lower Peninsula include Grand Traverse and Little Traverse on Lake Michigan, and Saginaw on Lake Huron. The Upper Peninsula has Whitefish and Keweenaw bays on Lake Superior, and Big Bay de Noc on Lake Michigan. Green Bay touches the southern tip of the Upper Peninsula.

Islands. Michigan's largest island, Isle Royale, covers about 210 square miles in Lake Superior. The Beaver and Manitou islands are in Lake Michigan. Bois Blanc, Mackinac, and Round islands are in the Straits of Mackinac. Drummond Island, in Lake Huron, lies off the eastern tip of the Upper Peninsula. The Detroit River has a number of small islands, including Belle Isle and Grosse Ile.

Rivers, Waterfalls, and Lakes. The chief rivers of the Upper Peninsula include the Escanaba, Manistique, Menominee, Ontonagon, Sturgeon, Tahquamenon, and Whitefish. Principal rivers in the Lower Peninsula are the Au Sable, Clinton, Grand, Huron, Kalamazoo, Manistee, Muskegon, Raisin, Saginaw, and St. Joseph. The 260-mile-long Grand River is the longest in the state. The most important rivers for commerce are the Detroit, St. Clair, and St. Marys. The Detroit River connects Lakes Erie and St. Clair. Lakes Huron and St. Clair are joined by the St. Clair River. The St. Marys River connects Lakes Huron and Superior. Other important rivers include the Cass and the Pere Marquette.

Michigan's Upper Peninsula has about 150 beautiful waterfalls. The best known falls are the Upper and Lower Tahquamenon Falls on the Tahquamenon River. Other important waterfalls include the Agate, Bond, Laughing Whitefish, Miners, and Munising—all in the Upper Peninsula.

Michigan has more than 11,000 inland lakes. They range in size from small bodies of water to 30-square-mile Houghton Lake in the north-central Lower Peninsula. Most of the larger lakes are in the Lower Peninsula. They include Black, Burt, Charlevoix, Crystal, Higgins, Mullet, and Torch lakes. Lake Gogebic is the largest lake in the Upper Peninsula.

Mackinac Island, a famous resort area, lies in the Straits of Mackinac between Michigan's Upper and Lower peninsulas.

John Freeman, Publix

Shostal

Lake of the Clouds is cradled in a valley in Porcupine Mountains State Park. This region has some of the highest elevations in the Middle West. It is part of Michigan's Superior Uplands region.

High Sand Dunes in Warren Dunes State Park near Bridgman spread over more than two miles of Lake Michigan's shore. The sand, kept moving by air currents, may cover plants and even trees.

Tad Stamm, Alpha

MICHIGAN / Climate

Michigan has a moist climate with cold winters and warm summers in the south and cool summers in the north. Winds blowing across the Great Lakes tend to prevent extremely hot or cold temperatures in the Lower Peninsula. But they do bring much cloudiness. The state has partly cloudy days about 6 of every 10 days in summer and about 7 of every 10 days in winter. Fall and winter are especially cloudy in the western Lower Peninsula and the eastern Upper Peninsula.

Temperatures in the Lower Peninsula are generally higher than those in the Upper Peninsula. Average January temperatures range from 15° F. in the western Upper Peninsula to 26° F. in the southern Lower Peninsula. July temperatures average 65° F. in the eastern Upper Peninsula and 73° F. in the southern Lower Peninsula. Michigan's record low temperature, −51° F., occurred in Vanderbilt on Feb. 9, 1934. Mio recorded the highest temperature, 112° F., on July 13, 1936. Air cooled by Lake Michigan in the spring usually prevents the budding of fruit trees until the danger of frosts has passed.

Michigan's yearly *precipitation* (rain, melted snow, and other forms of moisture) ranges from about 25 to 35 inches. Annual snowfall varies from less than 30 inches in the southwestern Lower Peninsula to about 160 inches in the western Upper Peninsula. In some areas of the Upper Peninsula, the snowfall occasionally measures 50 feet or more in a single winter.

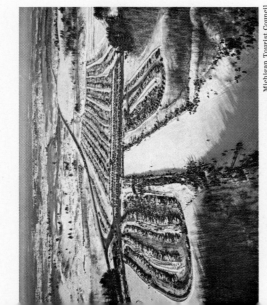

Heavy Winter Snow blankets Michigan's Upper Peninsula, a winter sports center. Many ski tournaments are held at Iron Mountain, which has one of the highest artificial ski jumps in the world.

Michigan Tourist Council

AVERAGE YEARLY PRECIPITATION
(Rain, Melted Snow, and Other Moisture)

Inches	Centimeters
36 to 44	91 to 112
28 to 36	71 to 91
20 to 28	51 to 71

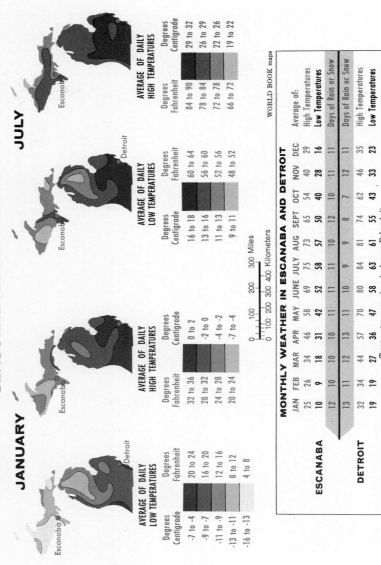

SEASONAL TEMPERATURES

JANUARY

AVERAGE OF DAILY LOW TEMPERATURES

Degrees Centigrade	Degrees Fahrenheit
-7 to -4	20 to 24
-9 to -7	16 to 20
-11 to -9	12 to 16
-13 to -11	8 to 12
-16 to -13	4 to 8

AVERAGE OF DAILY HIGH TEMPERATURES

Degrees Centigrade	Degrees Fahrenheit
0 to 2	32 to 36
-2 to 0	28 to 32
-4 to -2	24 to 28
-7 to -4	20 to 24

JULY

AVERAGE OF DAILY LOW TEMPERATURES

Degrees Centigrade	Degrees Fahrenheit
16 to 18	60 to 64
13 to 16	56 to 60
11 to 13	52 to 56
9 to 11	48 to 52

AVERAGE OF DAILY HIGH TEMPERATURES

Degrees Centigrade	Degrees Fahrenheit
29 to 32	84 to 90
26 to 29	78 to 84
22 to 26	72 to 78
19 to 22	66 to 72

WORLD BOOK maps

0 100 200 300 400 Kilometers
0 100 200 300 Miles

MONTHLY WEATHER IN ESCANABA AND DETROIT

		JAN	FEB	MAR	APR	MAY	JUNE	JULY	AUG	SEPT	OCT	NOV	DEC
ESCANABA	Average of: High Temperatures	25	26	34	46	58	69	75	73	65	54	40	29
	Low Temperatures	10	9	18	31	42	52	58	57	50	40	28	16
	Days of Rain or Snow	12	11	12	13	11	11	10	9	12	11	12	11
DETROIT	Days of Rain or Snow	13	11	13	12	11	9	8	7	8	7	12	11
	High Temperatures	32	34	44	57	70	80	84	81	74	62	46	35
	Low Temperatures	19	19	27	36	47	58	63	61	55	43	33	23

Temperatures are given in degrees Fahrenheit.

Source: U.S. Weather Bureau

The production of transportation equipment ranks as Michigan's most important industry. Detroit is the state's leading manufacturing center. Other important manufacturing cities include Battle Creek, Flint, Grand Rapids, Kalamazoo, Lansing, Muskegon, Pontiac, and Saginaw. The southern Lower Peninsula has the state's best farmland. Most livestock and crops are raised there. Fruit growing thrives along the Lake Michigan shoreline of the Lower Peninsula. Michigan's valuable iron-ore and copper mines are in the western Upper Peninsula. Salt is mined around Detroit and in other parts of the Lower Peninsula.

Michigan is a leading tourist state. It ranks second only to Pennsylvania in the amount of money collected from the sale of hunting licenses. Each year, nearly 10 million persons visit the state. Natural attractions, and resort and recreation areas, can be found in many parts of both the Upper and Lower peninsulas.

Natural Resources of Michigan include fertile soils, rich mineral deposits, widespread forests, and plentiful plant and animal life.

Soil. The Upper Peninsula has soils that vary from fertile loams to areas of poor soils and infertile sands. The northern section of the Lower Peninsula has sandy and loamy soils similar to those of the Upper Peninsula. A variety of soils covers former glacial lake beds around Saginaw Bay and along the shoreline of eastern Michigan. These glacial soils range from rich, dark-brown or black loams and gray sands, to infertile soils that are shallow and poorly drained. The state's richest soils are in the southern half of the Lower Peninsula. These are mostly gray-brown forest soils.

Minerals. Michigan's Upper Peninsula has vast iron-ore and copper deposits. Great stores of iron ore lie in the Marquette Range of the central Upper Peninsula. The Menominee Range in the southern Upper Peninsula, and the Gogebic range in the western corner, also have enormous iron-ore deposits. These iron deposits extend into Wisconsin and Minnesota, and are part of the greatest known iron-ore region in the world. The Keweenaw Peninsula, which forms the northernmost tip of Michigan, has been called the state's *treasure chest.* It is one of the few sources of *native* (pure) copper in the United States.

The Lower Peninsula has great deposits of salt. These deposits are so vast that they could probably supply the whole world with salt for a million years. The central and southern parts of the Lower Peninsula have rich petroleum deposits. Small reserves of coal are also found in the central Lower Peninsula. Limestone and shale occur throughout the state. Gypsum deposits lie under much of the Lower Peninsula. Almost every county in Michigan has deposits of sand and gravel. Natural gas is found in central Michigan.

Forests cover about 20 million acres, or more than half of Michigan. About 12 million acres are privately owned. The rest are in state and national forests in the Upper Peninsula, and in the northern portion of the Lower Peninsula.

About three-fourths of Michigan's forest land is covered by such hardwood trees as aspens, beeches, birches, elms, maples, and oaks. Softwoods cover most of the remaining forest land. These include cedars, firs, hemlocks, pines, spruces, and other softwood trees. Michigan's state tree is the white pine. In order to keep a good supply of lumber in the state, Michigan foresters plant more trees each year than they cut down.

Plant Life. Bittersweet, clematis, grapes, moonseed, and several kinds of smilax grow wild in Michigan's thickest forests. Shrubs such as blackberry, currant, elder, gooseberry, raspberry, rose, and viburnum thrive in the more open forest areas. Ferns and mosses grow in the swamps, as do cranberries and lady's-slippers. Such flowers as the arbutus, mandrake, trillium, and violet bloom in early spring. Flowers that bloom later in the year include the daisy, iris, orange milkweed, rose, shooting star, and tiger lily. Other common flowers in the state include the aster, chicory, goldenrod, and sunflower.

Animal Life. Great numbers of fur and game animals make Michigan a paradise for hunters. Michigan probably has more deer than any other state. Other common fur and game animals in Michigan include badgers, black bears, bobcats, minks, muskrats, opossums, otters, rabbits, raccoons, red foxes, skunks, and weasels. Hundreds of kinds of birds live in the state. The game birds most prized by hunters include ducks, partridges, and pheasants.

Many kinds of fish are found in Michigan's lakes, rivers, and streams. They include bass, crappie, perch,

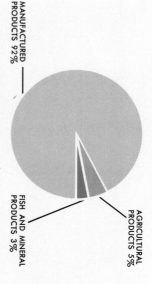

MICHIGAN'S PRODUCTION IN 1967
Total value of goods produced—$18,789,719,000

Note: Manufacturing percentage based on value added by manufacture. Other percentages based on value of production. Fish Products are less than 1 per cent.

MANUFACTURED PRODUCTS 92%
AGRICULTURAL PRODUCTS 5%
FISH AND MINERAL PRODUCTS 3%

Sources: U.S. Government statistics

MICHIGAN'S EMPLOYMENT IN 1967
Total number of persons employed—2,855,200

	Number of Employees
Manufacturing	1,037,600
Wholesale & Retail Trade	547,000
Government	438,800
Services	374,600
Transportation & Public Utilities	143,300
Construction	129,600
Finance, Insurance & Real Estate	102,900
Agriculture & Mining	81,400

Source: U.S. Department of Labor

pike, and trout. Smelt runs occur each spring in streams that empty into parts of Lake Huron and Lake Michigan. Other fishes common in Michigan's waters include alewives, catfish, and chubs. Carp, lake herring, and whitefish are common in the Great Lakes.

Manufacturing, including processing, accounts for about 92 per cent of the value of goods produced in Michigan. Goods manufactured in the state have a *value added by manufacture* of about $17 billion a year. This figure represents the value created in products by Michigan's industries, not counting such manufacturing costs as materials, supplies, and fuels. Michigan ranks among the leading manufacturing states. Its chief manufactured products are, in order of importance: (1) transportation equipment, (2) nonelectrical machinery, (3) fabricated metal products, (4) primary metals, (5) chemicals and related products, and (6) food and food products.

Transportation Equipment has a value added of about $5,825,000,000 a year, or about one-third of the state's manufacturing income. Automobiles, buses, trucks, and other vehicles manufactured in Michigan may be seen in all parts of the world. The transportation equipment industries employ nearly one-third of all the industrial workers in the state. Michigan's transportation industries use about two-thirds of the nation's total rubber supply. These industries account for about two-fifths of the plate glass used in the United States. They also use more than three-fifths of the nation's upholstery leather.

Michigan is the leading manufacturer of automobiles among the states. Detroit factories account for more than half the yearly income earned by the state's transportation industries. Detroit is called the *Automobile Capital of the World* and the *Motor City.* Other important automobile-manufacturing cities in Michigan include Dearborn, Flint, Kalamazoo, Lansing, and Pontiac. Factories in Jackson and Muskegon produce airplane engines and parts.

Nonelectrical Machinery has a value added of about $2,100,000,000 annually. Detroit factories account for nearly 60 per cent of this income. Michigan produces large quantities of agricultural machinery, machine-shop products, office machines, and pumps. Stoves and furnaces are manufactured in Albion, Detroit, Dowagiac, and Holland.

Fabricated Metal Products have an annual value added of about $1,969,000,000. Products manufactured in Detroit account for more than half this total. Flint and Grand Rapids are also important producers of fabricated metal products. These goods include cutlery, hand tools, hardware, and other products made from metals.

Primary Metals industries in Michigan turn out products that have a value added of about $1½ billion

FARM, MINERAL, AND FOREST PRODUCTS

This map shows where the leading farm, mineral, and forest products are produced. The major urban areas (shown in red) are the important manufacturing centers.

Copper Mine near Mohawk taps some of Michigan's richest ore deposits. This area has supplied man with copper for thousands of years.

David W. Corson, Devaney

100 Miles

150 Kilometers

WORLD BOOK map

yearly. Detroit accounts for about two-thirds of this total. The primary metals industries smelt, refine, and roll metals. They also manufacture such items as nails, bolts, and basic metal products such as castings. Michigan produces large quantities of foundry products. It stands among the leading producers of steel. The largest gray-iron foundry in the United States is in Muskegon. Detroit has the nation's largest forge.

Chemicals and Related Products have a value added of about $1,040,000,000 yearly. The state's chief chemical plants are in Ludington, Marquette, Midland, Muskegon, and Wyandotte. Drug manufacturers have plants in Ann Arbor, Detroit, and Kalamazoo.

Food and Food Products rank high in the state, with a value added of about $917,300,000 yearly. Michigan is among the leading food processing states. Detroit is the state's largest processor of foods. Grand Rapids is also an important food processing center. Battle Creek, the *Cereal Center of the World*, produces more breakfast cereal than any other city in the world. Fremont has the largest baby foods plant in the United States. The state has important fruit and vegetable canneries and sugar refineries.

Other Leading Industries. Industries that produce electrical machinery, and paper and paper products, also rank among the leaders, as does printing and publishing. The products of each of these industries have a value added of more than $400 million yearly. Kalamazoo is the center of the state's paper manufacturing industry.

Michigan is among the leading states in the manufacture of sporting goods and athletic equipment. Muskegon has the nation's largest plant for making billiard and bowling alley equipment. Alpena has the largest cement plant in the United States. Grand Rapids is sometimes called the *Furniture Capital of America* because of its many furniture factories. Other important industries in the state manufacture clothing; scientific instruments; furniture and fixtures; petroleum and coal products; rubber and plastics products; and stone, clay, and glass products.

418b

Mining in Michigan has an annual value of about $521,373,000. Iron ore is Michigan's most valuable mineral. In 1844, the earliest discoveries of iron-ore deposits in the state were made near Ishpeming and Negaunee in the Upper Peninsula. During the next 40 years, millions of tons of iron ore were mined in Michigan. The opening of the Soo Canal in 1855 brought a great increase in the state's iron-ore production. The canal provided an important transportation route from the mines near Lake Superior to steel-making centers along the Great Lakes. Michigan was the leading producer of iron ore from about 1890 to 1900. Today, Minnesota mines more iron ore. But Michigan still supplies about 15 per cent of the nation's output. Most of Michigan's iron mining takes place in the western Upper Peninsula—in Dickinson, Iron, and Marquette counties. Mining companies in the Upper Peninsula ship ore across the Great Lakes to steel mills in the eastern and midwestern United States.

Indians were the first to mine copper in the Michigan region. They made tools and utensils from the copper of the Upper Peninsula. White settlers mined copper near Copper Harbor on Lake Superior, and later throughout the copper range of the Keweenaw Peninsula. Michigan led the United States in copper production from 1850 until 1887, when Montana became the leading U.S. producer. Production in Michigan gradually decreased during the early 1900's, when other states began to produce copper more cheaply than Michigan. A revival of copper mining in Michigan began in 1955 with the completion of the White Pines project near Ontonagon. Today, Michigan ranks among the leading copper-mining states. Copper is mined in Houghton, Keweenaw, and Ontonagon counties in the western Upper Peninsula.

Michigan is among the leaders in salt production. One of the world's largest salt mines is beneath the city of Detroit. Salt is also produced from natural brines in Gratiot County, and from artificial brines in Gratiot, Manistee, Midland, Muskegon, St. Clair, and Wayne counties. Most salts mined in Michigan are for in-

General Motors

Automobile Workers Check Car Frames that move along an assembly line in a Detroit factory. Detroit produces more cars and trucks than any other city in the world.

Michigan Conservation Dept.

Workers Plant Seedling Trees as part of a conservation project in Higgins Lake State Park. Each year, to preserve Michigan's forests, the state plants more trees than are cut.

dustrial purposes, not as table salt. Bromine is taken from the natural brines of Michigan's salt mines. The state's drug and chemical industries also use some of the salt from Michigan mines.

Oil is one of the state's most valuable mineral products. Natural gas fields in St. Clair County supply nearly half of the state's total production. Some gas fields are used to store gas piped in from southwestern states. Rogers City has one of the world's largest limestone quarries. Michigan is the leading producer of gypsum and peat. Gypsum is mined in Iosco and Kent counties. Michigan is a leading producer of clay, marl, and sand and gravel.

Agriculture. Farm products in Michigan have a yearly gross income of about $1 billion. Farmland covers about 40 per cent of the state's land area. Michigan's 93,500 farms average about 145 acres in size.

Livestock and Livestock Products have an annual value of about $456 million. Milk, Michigan's leading farm product, earns about $238 million a year. Michigan ranks among the leading producers of milk. Cattle and calves rank second in importance among livestock and livestock products. Other such products include hogs and eggs. Most cattle, calves, and hogs are raised in the Lower Peninsula. Dairying is also important throughout the Lower Peninsula. Zeeland is a center of baby chick hatcheries. Ottawa County has large turkey farms, and chicken, duck, geese, and turkey hatcheries.

Crops in Michigan have an annual value of about $395 million. Michigan stands among the leaders in the production of many crops of the northern United States. Corn is the state's leading cash crop. It earns about $46½ million a year. Wheat ranks second, followed by dry beans, greenhouse and nursery products, soybeans, apples, and cherries.

The land along Lake Michigan in the Lower Peninsula is one of the most productive fruit-growing belts in North America. Michigan leads the nation in the production of cherries. It also ranks among the leaders in raising apples, cantaloupes, grapes, peaches, pears, plums, and strawberries. Fruit tree blossoms attract many bees in spring, and honey is an important by-product of the fruit industry. Most of the grapes are grown in Berrien and Van Buren counties. Berrien County is the leading producer of fruit in the state. Traverse City is famous for its cherries.

The state has more than a thousand vegetable farms. Much vegetable farming takes place around Grand Rapids, Muskegon, and other industrial cities. Michigan is the leading producer of dry beans. Other important vegetables include asparagus, cabbages, carrots, cucumbers, lettuce, onions, potatoes, snap beans, sugar beets, and tomatoes. Most farmers in the state raise alfalfa, corn, hay, and oats—usually as feed for livestock rather than as cash crops. Large quantities of celery are grown in Michigan's western counties.

Fishing Industry. Michigan has an annual fish catch valued at about $2,846,000. The most valuable fishes taken from the Great Lakes include alewives, chubs, lake herring, whitefish, yellow perch, and yellow pike. Every spring, commercial fishermen take smelts from the state's rivers and streams.

Electric Power. Michigan has over 200 generating plants. About 80 are powered by coal and natural gas. The state has about 60 hydroelectric power plants.

Nuclear-power generating plants are near Charlevoix, Monroe, and South Haven. For Michigan's kilowatt-hour production, see ELECTRIC POWER (table).

Transportation. Indians and early pioneers in Michigan traveled in canoes along the waterways. The first roads followed Indian trails. The first highway in Michigan was built in the 1820's. It ran from Detroit across the Maumee River in what is now Ohio. The Erie and Kalamazoo Railroad was completed in 1836. Horses pulled the railroad's first trains. In 1837, the Erie and Kalamazoo started to operate what was probably the first steam locomotive west of the Allegheny Mountains. By the mid-1800's, stagecoach routes connected Detroit with Chicago. The state highway department was established in 1905. In 1908, Michigan became the first state to build a concrete highway—a mile-long stretch in Detroit. In 1957, the Mackinac Bridge was completed across the Straits of Mackinac. This was the first bridge to connect the Upper and Lower peninsulas. The International Bridge, across the St. Marys River at Sault Ste. Marie, was completed in 1962. It links Michigan with Ontario. This two-mile bridge replaced ferry boats that once carried people across the river. Other links between Michigan and Ontario include a Detroit to Windsor bridge, a Detroit to Windsor tunnel, and a Port Huron to Sarnia bridge.

Today, Michigan has more than 114,000 miles of roads, about 80 per cent of which are surfaced. Railroads operate on about 6,900 miles of track. Michigan is served by about 280 airfields, of which 127 are public. Commercial airlines serve the state's major cities. Detroit is served by three airports.

Ships from Michigan ports carry huge cargoes of minerals and manufactured goods across the Great Lakes and through the Great Lakes-St. Lawrence Seaway system to other countries. The Soo Canals rank among the busiest ship canals in the Western Hemisphere, even though ice closes the canals from December to April. The canals handle about 90 million tons of cargo each year. Detroit, the state's largest port, handles over 33 million tons yearly. Other major ports are Calcite (near Rogers City), Escanaba, Grand Haven, Presque Isle, Saginaw, and Stoneport. Ferries from Frankfurt, Ludington, and Muskegon carry railroad and auto passengers across Lake Michigan to ports in the Upper Peninsula and Wisconsin.

Communication. Michigan's first regularly published newspaper, the *Detroit Gazette*, was established in 1817. Radio station WWJ in Detroit began broadcasting in 1920. WWJ and Pittsburgh's KDKA were the nation's first regular commercial radio stations. Michigan's first television station, WWJ-TV, began operating in Detroit in 1947.

Michigan has about 55 daily newspapers. The *Detroit Free Press* is the only English-language morning paper published in the state. Afternoon newspapers with the largest circulations include the *Detroit News*, the *Flint Journal*, and the *Grand Rapids Press*. Michigan publishers produce more than 360 weekly newspapers, several foreign-language papers, and about 185 periodicals. The state has 18 television stations and about 190 radio stations.

Indian Days. About 15,000 Indians lived in the Michigan region when white men first arrived. Most of the tribes belonged to the Algonkian language group. They included the Chippewa and Menominee tribes in the Upper Peninsula, and the Miami, Ottawa, and Potawatomi tribes in the Lower Peninsula. The Wyandot, who settled around what is now Detroit, belonged to the Iroquois language group. Only about 3,000 Indians lived in the forests of the Upper Peninsula.

French Exploration and Settlement. Étienne Brulé of France explored the Upper Peninsula around 1620. He was probably the first white man to visit the Michigan region. Brulé was sent to Michigan from Quebec by Governor Samuel de Champlain of New France (Canada). In 1634, Champlain sent another explorer, Jean Nicolet, to the region to search for a route to the Pacific Ocean. Nicolet sailed through the Straits of Mackinac and explored parts of the Upper Peninsula. In 1660, Father René Ménard, a Jesuit missionary, established a mission at Keweenaw Bay. In 1668, Father Jacques Marquette founded Michigan's first permanent settlement, at Sault Ste. Marie.

During the late 1600's, Father Marquette; Louis Joliet; Robert Cavelier, Sieur de la Salle; and other Frenchmen explored much of the region. They mapped many of the lakes and rivers. By 1700, the French had built forts, missions, and trading posts at several places in both the Upper and Lower peninsulas. In 1701, Antoine de la Mothe Cadillac founded Fort Pontchartrain, which grew into the city of Detroit.

The Michigan region made little progress under the French. Only a few settlers established farms in the region, mostly along the Detroit River. The main French interests were to convert the Indians to Christianity and to develop a profitable fur trade. They also hoped to use the region as a passage to the west.

British Control. During the late 1600's and the 1700's, France and Great Britain struggled to gain control of North America. British and French settlers fought a series of wars called the French and Indian Wars. The French were defeated in 1763. Britain won most of the French holdings in North America, including the Michigan region. See FRENCH AND INDIAN WARS.

In 1763, Indians massacred the British at Fort Michilimackinac in Mackinaw City. Indians also attacked a number of other forts, killing many of the settlers. Detroit stood under Indian attack for more than five months, but the warriors were finally turned away. In 1774, the British made Michigan a part of the province of Quebec. The British were more interested in fur trading than in settling the region.

During the Revolutionary War (1775-1783), the British sent raiding parties of Indians and whites from Detroit to attack American settlements. Spain and Britain were also at war during the American Revolution. In 1781, Spanish forces captured Fort St. Joseph in Niles, and held it for one day. The Revolutionary War ended in 1783, and the Michigan region came under the control of the United States. The British wanted to hold on to the valuable fur trade as long as possible. They did not surrender Detroit or Fort Mackinac to the United States until 1796.

Territorial Period. In 1787, the Michigan region became part of the Northwest Territory—the first territory established by the United States government. In 1800, Congress created the Indiana Territory, which included part of Michigan. The Indiana Territory obtained the entire Michigan region in 1803. In 1805, Congress

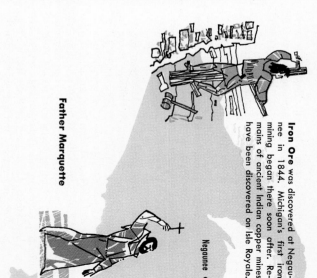

Iron Ore was discovered at Negaunee in 1844. Michigan's first iron mining began there soon after. Remains of ancient Indian copper mines have been discovered on Isle Royale.

Father Marquette

Negaunee ●

IMPORTANT DATES IN MICHIGAN

1620? Étienne Brulé, a French explorer, visited what is now Michigan.

1668 Father Jacques Marquette founded Michigan's first permanent settlement at Sault Ste. Marie.

1701 Antoine Cadillac founded what is now Detroit.

1763 The British took possession of Michigan.

1783 The United States gained Michigan from the British after the Revolutionary War.

1787 Congress made Michigan part of the Northwest Territory.

1800 Michigan became part of the Indiana Territory.

1805 Congress created the Territory of Michigan, including the entire Lower Peninsula and the eastern Upper Peninsula.

1837 Michigan became the 26th state on January 26. Congress gave Michigan the entire Upper Peninsula.

1845 The state's iron mining industry began at Negaunee.

1854 The Republican Party was formally named at Jackson.

1855 The Soo Canal was completed.

1899 Ransom E. Olds established Michigan's first automobile factory in Detroit.

1914 The Ford Motor Company established a minimum daily wage of $5.

1935 Michigan workers formed the United Automobile Workers union.

1942-1945 Michigan's entire automobile industry converted to war production during World War II.

1957 The Straits of Mackinac Bridge was opened to traffic between Mackinaw City and St. Ignace.

1964 Michigan's new Constitution went into effect.

1967 Michigan's legislature adopted a state income tax.

1968 Michigan voters approved $435 million in bond issues to expand recreational areas and to fight water pollution.

HISTORIC MICHIGAN

The Soo Canals at Sault Sainte Marie rank among the busiest ship canals in the Western Hemisphere. The first canal on the Michigan side was completed in 1855. Father Marquette founded Michigan's first permanent settlement there in 1668.

Sault Ste. Marie

Mackinac Island

The American Fur Company, founded by John Jacob Astor, made the Mackinac Island trading post its Michigan headquarters in 1817.

Thomas Alva Edison, the famous inventor, built his first electric battery at Fort Gratiot (Port Huron) in 1861.

The Lumberman's Memorial, in Iosco County, honors Michigan's early lumbermen, who helped develop the Middle West. From 1870 to 1890, Michigan led the states in lumbering.

The Republican Party was founded, and the name formally adopted, at Jackson in 1854 after an earlier meeting at Ripon, Wis.

Detroit, the fifth largest city in the nation, was founded as Fort Pontchartrain in 1701 by the French explorer Cadillac.

Port Huron

Detroit

The First Railroad in Michigan was the Erie and Kalamazoo, completed in 1836. The 35-mile line linked Adrian, Mich., with Toledo, Ohio.

LANSING

Jackson

Adrian

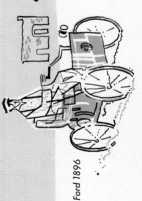

Oldsmobile 1899

Henry Ford built his first workable automobile at Detroit in 1896. Three years later, Ransom E. Olds established Michigan's first automobile factory at Detroit.

Ford 1896

MICHIGAN

established the Territory of Michigan. It included the Lower Peninsula and eastern Upper Peninsula.

During the War of 1812, the British captured Detroit and Fort Mackinac. American forces regained Detroit in 1813. The British returned Fort Mackinac after the United States won the war in 1814.

The Erie Canal was completed in 1825. It linked the Great Lakes with the Atlantic Ocean, and provided a transportation route between the eastern states and the western territories. Many settlers came to Michigan, especially from New York and New England.

In 1835, a convention drew up a state constitution. The people *ratified* (approved) the Constitution on Oct. 5, 1835, and elected 23-year-old Stevens T. Mason as their first state governor. But Congress delayed admitting Michigan to the Union because of a dispute between Michigan and Ohio. The dispute involved a strip of land near Toledo. Congress settled the question in 1836 by giving the 520-square-mile "Toledo Strip" to Ohio, and the entire Upper Peninsula to Michigan.

Progress as a State. Michigan became the 26th state of the Union on Jan. 26, 1837. The western Upper Peninsula soon proved to be a source of many valuable minerals. In 1842, the state obtained Isle Royale and the Keweenaw Peninsula in a treaty with the Indians. Iron-ore mining began near Negaunee in 1845. Large numbers of miners and prospectors soon came to the Upper Peninsula. By the late 1840's, mining was prospering in the state. But the miners needed some way to ship the ore from western Michigan to the iron and steel centers along the Great Lakes. This need was one of the chief reasons for the construction of the Soo Canal, which was completed in 1855 (see Soo Canals).

The Republican Party was named in 1854 in Jackson. Delegates to a Michigan state convention met there on July 6, 1854. They were the first to formally adopt the name *Republican* (see Republican Party).

Michigan soldiers fought in the Union army during the Civil War (1861-1865). General George A. Custer, a famous Union officer, led the Michigan cavalry. On May 10, 1865, the Fourth Michigan Cavalry captured Jefferson Davis, President of the Confederacy, near Irwinville, Ga.

After the Civil War, lumbering became an important industry in Michigan. The construction of sawmills aided the rapid development of manufacturing in the state. Michigan lumber was used in building many cities, towns, and farms of the Midwest. Michigan hardwood lumber helped develop the furniture industry, which started in Grand Rapids in the 1830's. By 1870, Michigan led the nation in lumber production.

Between 1870 and 1900, Michigan's population more than doubled. Agriculture developed as settlers poured into Michigan and cleared the land. Michigan took the lead among the states in the support of public education. Railroads and steamship lines promoted Michigan resorts, and the state's tourist industry began to develop.

The Early 1900's brought further industrial expansion to Michigan. In 1899, Ransom E. Olds founded the Olds Motor Works in Detroit. By 1901, the factory was mass-producing Oldsmobiles. Henry Ford organized the Ford Motor Company in 1903. Detroit soon became the center of the nation's automobile industry. This new industry increased Michigan's population and also its prosperity.

In 1914, Henry Ford announced that the Ford Motor Company would share its profits with its workers. Ford also established a minimum wage of $5 a day. At that time, most unskilled workers earned only $1 a day, and skilled workers earned $2.50.

After the United States entered World War I in 1917, Michigan factories built trucks, armored vehicles, airplane engines, and other military products. The improvement of Michigan's highways during the 1920's contributed to the growth of the automobile industry and related businesses. By the late 1920's, Michigan's tourist industry had become a leading source of income in the state.

Depression and Recovery. Michigan was hit hard by the Great Depression of the 1930's. Hundreds of thousands of workers lost their jobs. Federal measures to end the depression had important effects in Michigan. The state had more than a hundred Civilian Con-

Mass Production of Automobiles was begun by Oldsmobile in 1901. These workers pose with the parts for assembling the engines. The company made 425 cars in 1901. Today, the Oldsmobile factory in Lansing produces about 400,000 cars annually.

Oldsmobile Div., General Motors

servation Corps (CCC) camps. In these camps, the government employed young men to work on conservation projects. The Works Progress Administration (WPA) employed about 500,000 persons in Michigan to work on public works projects. Before and during the depression, copper mining in other states became less costly than in Michigan. It cost more to mine copper in Michigan because the ore lies so deep in the earth. Michigan's copper mining decreased, and more unemployment resulted in the Upper Peninsula.

In 1935, workers in the automobile industry organized the United Automobile Workers union. In December, 1936, the union went on strike at the Fisher Body and Chevrolet plants in Flint. The strikers demanded a *closed shop* (an industry in which only union members can be hired). The union also called for *collective bargaining* (discussion of differences between company and union representatives). The Fisher and Chevrolet plant officials rejected the union's demands. The strikers then locked themselves inside the plants, and fought off police attempts to remove them. The union received collective bargaining rights on Feb. 11, 1937, and the strike ended. By 1941, the United Automobile Workers represented the workers of all the large automobile companies, and had won its chief demands. These included higher pay and recognition of the union as representative of the workers.

The Mid-1900's. During World War II (1939-1945), Michigan's entire automobile industry switched to manufacturing war materials. The production of airplanes, ships, tanks, and other military equipment brought prosperity back to the state.

Michigan's prosperity continued after the war. Millions of Americans bought new cars and other Michigan products. The state's mining industry began to recover. In 1955, a new copper mine opened near Ontonagon. Iron-mining companies in the Upper Peninsula developed new methods of recovering iron from nonmagnetic ore and new ways of processing ore for shipment to steel plants. In 1957, the 5-mile-long Mackinac Bridge was completed, linking the Upper and Lower peninsulas.

The state faced financial problems during the late 1950's and early 1960's. A nationwide recession caused a slump in Michigan automobile sales and production. As a result, other business activities in the state also slowed down. Michigan's financial picture brightened as the nation began to prosper again during the 1960's, and purchases of automobiles and other Michigan products increased.

In 1961, Michigan voters authorized a constitutional convention to revise the outdated state constitution, adopted in 1908. The convention submitted a new constitution to the voters in 1962. They approved the constitution in 1963, and it went into effect in 1964. Also in 1964, both houses of the state legislature were *reapportioned* (redivided) to provide more equal representation based on population.

George W. Romney, a Michigan businessman, served as the state's governor from 1963 to 1969. Romney, a Republican, had played a leading role in the constitutional convention. As governor, he fought for passage of the new constitution. Romney's administration modernized the state tax structure. New taxes, including a state income tax adopted in 1967, enabled Michigan to increase spending for education, mental health facilities, welfare programs, and other government services. In 1969, Romney became secretary of housing and urban development under President Richard M. Nixon.

In July, 1967, an eight-day riot broke out in a predominantly Negro section of Detroit. Rioters burned buildings and looted stores. Forty-three persons were killed, and about $45 million worth of property was damaged or destroyed.

In 1968, Michigan voters approved a $100-million bond issue to pay for more parks and other recreational facilities. Much of the money was to be used to improve living conditions in inner core areas of Detroit and other cities. Also in 1968, voters approved a $335-million bond issue to fight water pollution.

Michigan Today. In the 1970's, Michigan faces increasing costs of education, mental health services, welfare programs, pollution control, and other government services. The state is continuing to work to change conditions that lead to racial tensions. Some govern-

THE GOVERNORS OF MICHIGAN

		Party	Term
1.	Stevens T. Mason	Democratic	1837-1840
2.	William Woodbridge	Whig	1840-1841
3.	James W. Gordon	Whig	1841-1842
4.	John S. Barry	Democratic	1842-1845
5.	Alpheus Felch	Democratic	1846-1847
6.	William L. Greenly	Democratic	1847
7.	Epaphroditus Ransom	Democratic	1848-1849
8.	John S. Barry	Democratic	1850
9.	Robert McClelland	Democratic	1851-1853
10.	Andrew Parsons	Democratic	1853-1854
11.	Kinsley S. Bingham	Republican	1855-1858
12.	Moses Wisner	Republican	1859-1860
13.	Austin Blair	Republican	1861-1864
14.	Henry H. Crapo	Republican	1865-1868
15.	Henry P. Baldwin	Republican	1869-1872
16.	John J. Bagley	Republican	1873-1876
17.	Charles M. Croswell	Republican	1877-1880
18.	David H. Jerome	Republican	1881-1882
19.	Josiah W. Begole	Democratic and Greenback	1883-1884
20.	Russell A. Alger	Republican	1885-1886
21.	Cyrus G. Luce	Republican	1887-1890
22.	Edwin B. Winans	Democratic	1891-1892
23.	John T. Rich	Republican	1893-1896
24.	Hazen S. Pingree	Republican	1897-1900
25.	Aaron T. Bliss	Republican	1901-1904
26.	Fred M. Warner	Republican	1905-1910
27.	Chase S. Osborn	Republican	1911-1912
28.	Woodbridge N. Ferris	Democratic	1913-1916
29.	Albert E. Sleeper	Republican	1917-1920
30.	Alexander J. Groesbeck	Republican	1921-1926
31.	Fred W. Green	Republican	1927-1930
32.	Wilber M. Brucker	Republican	1931-1932
33.	William A. Comstock	Democratic	1933-1934
34.	Frank D. Fitzgerald	Republican	1935-1936
35.	Frank Murphy	Democratic	1937-1938
36.	Frank D. Fitzgerald	Republican	1939
37.	Luren D. Dickinson	Republican	1939-1940
38.	Murray D. Van Wagoner	Democratic	1941-1942
39.	Harry F. Kelly	Republican	1943-1946
40.	Kim Sigler	Republican	1947-1948
41.	G. Mennen Williams	Democratic	1949-1960
42.	John B. Swainson	Democratic	1961-1962
43.	George W. Romney	Republican	1963-1969
44.	William G. Milliken	Republican	1969-

ment officials feel that Michigan's tax structure must again be changed to pay for all these programs.

Michigan remains strong industrially. The manufacture of transportation equipment still provides the greatest income to the state, and Michigan continues to lead the nation in automobile production. But in the 1970's, state leaders want to attract new industries and to stimulate economic growth in the Upper Peninsula. They also hope to find new markets for Michigan products, both in the United States and in other countries.

WILLIAM ROGERS BRUECKHEIMER, and SIDNEY GLAZER

MICHIGAN/Study Aids

Related Articles in WORLD BOOK include:

Biographies

Cadillac, Antoine de la M.
Cass, Lewis
Chandler, Zachariah
Chrysler, Walter P.
Coughlin, Charles E.
Couzens, James
Dodge (family)
Ford (family)
Ford, Gerald R.
Griffin, Robert P.
Guest, Edgar A.

Humphrey, George M.
Kellogg, W. K.
Lindbergh, Charles A.
Marquette, Jacques
Murphy, Frank
Olds, Ransom E.
Pontiac
Romney, George W.
Vandenberg, Arthur H.
Williams, G. Mennen

Cities

Ann Arbor
Battle Creek
Bay City
Dearborn
Detroit
Flint
Grand Rapids
Hamtramck

Highland Park
Holland
Jackson
Kalamazoo
Lansing
Lincoln Park
Muskegon

Pontiac
Roseville
Royal Oak
Saginaw
Saint Clair
Shores
Warren

Physical Features

Detroit River
Great Lakes
Isle Royale National Park
Lake Erie
Lake Huron
Lake Michigan

Lake Saint Clair
Lake Superior
Mackinac, Straits of
Mackinac Island
Manitoulin Islands
Saint Marys River

Products and Industry

Apple
Automobile
Bean
Cherry
Copper

Gypsum
Iron and Steel
Manufacturing
Onion

Paper
Salt
Sugar Beet
Wine

Other Related Articles

Dune (picture)
Midwestern States
National Music Camp

Northwest Ordinance
Soo Canals
War of 1812

For Michigan's rank among the states in production, see the following articles:

Outline

I. Government
  A. Constitution
  B. Executive
  C. Legislature
  D. Courts
  E. Local Government
  F. Taxation
  G. Politics

II. People

III. Education
  A. Schools
  B. Libraries
  C. Museums

IV. A Visitor's Guide
  A. Places to Visit
  B. Annual Events

V. The Land
  A. Land Regions
  B. Shoreline
  C. Islands
  D. Rivers, Waterfalls, and Lakes

VI. Climate

VII. Economy
  A. Natural Resources
  B. Manufacturing
  C. Mining
  D. Agriculture
  E. Fishing Industry
  F. Electric Power
  G. Transportation
  H. Communication

VIII. History

Questions

Why does Michigan have so many cloudy days?

Why did the Michigan region not prosper under French control?

Why did copper production in Michigan belong to before becoming a state?

What important event brought many settlers to Michigan in the 1820's?

How did Michigan's lumber industry aid the growth of the state?

What Michigan canals rank among the busiest ship canals in the Western Hemisphere?

What territories of the United States did Michigan obtain the early 1900's?

How did Michigan obtain the Upper Peninsula?

What are two of the chief provisions of the Michigan Constitution adopted in 1963?

What city produces more breakfast cereal than any other city in the world?

Books for Young Readers

ABBOTT, ETHELYN M. Abbott's Michigan History Stories for Boys and Girls. Hillsdale School Supply Co., 1960.

BAIRD, WILLARD. This Is Our Michigan. Federated Publications, Inc., 1959.

CARR, HARRIETT H. Where the Turnpike Starts. Macmillan, 1955.

DERLETH, AUGUST W. Land of Sky-Blue Waters. Dutton, 1955.

HOLLING, HOLLING C. Paddle-to-the-Sea. Houghton, 1941.

HOWARD, ELIZABETH. Candle in the Night. Morrow, 1952.

JUDSON, CLARA I. The Mighty Soo: Five Hundred Years at Sault Ste. Marie. Follett, 1955.

LEWIS, FERRIS E. My State and Its Story. Rev. Hillsdale School Supply Co., Hillsdale, Mich., 1955.

NEWCOMB, DELPHINE. Exploring Michigan. Follett, 1954.

Books for Older Readers

BALD, FREDERICK C. Michigan in Four Centuries. Harper, 1961.

DUNBAR, WILLIS F. Michigan Through the Centuries. 4 vols. Lewis Historical Publishing Co., New York City, 1955.

Michigan: A History of the Wolverine State. Eerdmans, 1965.

HODGINS, BERT. Michigan: Geographic Backgrounds in the Development of the Commonwealth. 4th ed. J. W. Edwards, Ann Arbor, Mich., 1961.

MAYBEE, ROLLAND H. Michigan's White Pine Era, 1840-1900. John M. Munson Michigan History Fund Pamphlet Number 1. Michigan Historical Commission, 1960.

Michigan: A Guide to the Wolverine State. Rev. printing. Oxford, 1946.

QUAIFE, MILO M., and GLAZER, SIDNEY. Michigan, from Primitive Wilderness to Industrial Commonwealth. Prentice-Hall, 1948.

RUBIN, LAWRENCE A. Mighty Mac: The Official Picture History of the Mackinac Bridge. Wayne State Univ. Press, 1958.

MICHIGAN, LAKE. See LAKE MICHIGAN.

University of Michigan

The University of Michigan has a Diagonal Walk, or "Diag," that cuts through the center of the main campus. Students hurry along this famous landmark on the way to their classes.

MICHIGAN, UNIVERSITY OF, was founded in Detroit, Mich., in 1817, and has been in Ann Arbor, Mich., since 1837. It is called the "mother" of state universities because, in 1837, it became the first university to be controlled by regents elected by the voters.

The coeducational university has colleges of liberal arts, engineering, pharmacy, architecture and design, medicine, law, dentistry, education, business administration, forestry, nursing, music, public health, social work, and graduate studies. In 1959, the Institute of Science and Technology was founded. It offers undergraduate, graduate, and extension courses.

The university libraries contain over 2,800,000 books and documents. The William L. Clements Library of American History is noted for its collection of original documents relating to the Revolutionary War.

The Phoenix Project, the university's World War II memorial, has provided a fund of $9½ million to finance research on peacetime uses of atomic energy. For the enrollment of the university, see UNIVERSITIES AND COLLEGES (table).

See also LAW (picture: Famous University Law Schools).

ERICH A. WALTER

MICHIGAN STATE UNIVERSITY is a state-supported coeducational school in East Lansing, Mich. It offers undergraduate degrees in 130 fields, and graduate degrees in 70. It has colleges of agriculture, arts and letters, business and public service, communication arts, education, engineering, home economics, natural science, social science, science and arts, and veterinary medicine. It also has a School of Advanced Graduate Studies.

Michigan State was founded in 1855, and served as a model for the land-grant colleges and universities founded later in the United States. It was the first state school to offer courses in agriculture for credit. Until 1955, it was called Michigan State College. Michigan State ranks as one of the 10 largest institutions of higher learning in the United States.

Oakland University, near Rochester, Mich., has the same Board of Trustees as Michigan State. Oakland was founded in 1957. It is coeducational, and grants bachelor's and master's degrees in business and economics, engineering, liberal arts and science, and teacher education. For the enrollments of Michigan State University and Oakland University, see UNIVERSITIES AND COLLEGES (table).

JOHN A. HANNAH

MICHIGAN TECHNOLOGICAL UNIVERSITY is a state-supported coeducational school in Houghton, Mich. It grants bachelor's degrees in nine branches of engineering and in business administration, chemistry, forestry, geology, geophysics, mathematics, medical technology, and physics. It offers graduate degrees in civil, chemical, electrical, geological, mechanical, metallurgical, mining, and nuclear engineering, and in chemistry, engineering mechanics, geology, geophysics, and physics. The university participates in the Argonne National Laboratory atomic energy program. The school was chartered in 1885. For enrollment, see UNIVERSITIES AND COLLEGES (table).

THEODORE PEARCE

MICHOACÁN, *MEE choh ah KAHN,* is one of the most beautiful states in Mexico. The 23,113-square-mile state borders the Pacific Ocean in the southwest part of the country. For location, see MEXICO (political map). Mountainous Michoacán has won fame for its

picturesque lakes such as Pátzcuaro, and for Parícutin and other volcanoes. Morelia is the capital. The state has a population of 2,294,579. See also PARÍCUTIN; TARASCAN INDIANS; MORELIA.

CHARLES C. CUMBERLAND

MICMAC INDIANS. See NEW BRUNSWICK (Indian Days); PRINCE EDWARD ISLAND (introduction; Places to Visit); NOVA SCOTIA (Indian Days).

MICROBE. See MICROBIOLOGY; AIR (Particles).

MICROBIOLOGY is the study of microscopic organisms. These organisms include algae, bacteria, molds, protozoans, viruses, and yeasts. They are sometimes called *microbes*. Most cannot be seen without a microscope.

Many biologists specialize in the study of certain kinds of microorganisms. For example, *bacteriologists* work with bacteria, *mycologists* are concerned with fungi, and *virologists* study viruses.

Microorganisms. Nearly all microorganisms measure less than $\frac{4}{1000}$ of an inch across. Most microorganisms must be studied with microscopes that magnify objects at least 1,500 times. The smallest microorganisms, the viruses, can be seen only with electron microscopes that magnify as much as 100,000 times.

Viruses are called *acellular* microorganisms because they do not have true cell structures. All other microorganisms are *cellular*. They have cell membranes, cytoplasm, and a nuclear body. Bacteria are the smallest single-celled organisms. The smallest bacteria may be as small as $\frac{4}{10}$ of a *micron* (a micron is $\frac{1}{25,400}$ of an inch). About 10,000 small viruses could be packed into a cell the size of one of these bacteria. More than a billion

421

such cells could be packed into one of the largest *mi-crobial* cells—the cells of a certain kind of algae.

Fields of Microbiology. Many microbiologists study the relationships between microbes and man, animals, and plants. Medical microbiologists investigate the role of microorganisms in human and animal diseases and seek ways to prevent and cure these diseases. Dental microbiologists are concerned with the microorganisms found in the mouth, especially their role in tooth decay and other oral diseases. Agricultural microbiologists study plant diseases, the role of microorganisms in soil fertility, and spoilage of farm products by microorganisms. Industrial microbiologists use microorganisms to produce such products as alcoholic beverages, amino acids, antibiotics, citric acid, and vitamin C. General microbiologists study the basic features of microorganisms, including ecology, genetics, metabolism, physiology, and structure.

Related Articles in World Book include:

Algae	Mold	Virus
Bacteria	Mycology	Yeast
Bacteriology	Protozoan	

SELMAN A. WAKSMAN

MICROBIOLOGY, INSTITUTE OF, is a part of Rutgers, The State University in New Brunswick, N.J. Scientists at the institute study the structure and function of bacteria, fungi, yeasts, protozoa, viruses, and other microorganisms. They also study the antibiotics, vitamins, and enzymes produced by microorganisms. The institute was founded in 1954 with royalties received from manufacturers of streptomycin. This antibiotic was first isolated by Selman A. Waksman and his associates at the New Jersey Agricultural Experiment Station in 1944. See also Microbiology.

MICROCHEMISTRY is the branch of chemistry that deals with extremely small quantities of chemical substances. Chemists make both qualitative and quantitative analyses on the minute samples. These substances usually weigh about 1 milligram. *Ultramicrochemistry* deals with microgram quantities, and *semimicrochemistry* with centigram quantities. See Metric System.

Chemists use microchemistry to identify and isolate microscopic amounts of substances located in large volumes of other substances. For example, chemists first isolated one of the sex hormones from a large amount of urine. Only 18 milligrams of the hormone were isolated from a total of 13,000 liters of urine.

Some of the instruments used in microchemistry are smaller versions of standard laboratory equipment. For example, a standard *burette* (scaled tube) can usually be read only to .02 milliliters. But microchemists use burettes that read as low as .0002 milliliters. Sensitive balances and high-powered microscopes, with or without special attachments, are also important microchemical tools (see Balance; Ultramicroscope). Other equipment used by microchemists includes special filter paper, spectroscopes, and *photometers*, or light meters (see Spectroscope). *Coulometry* is another method used to determine microscopic quantities of materials in solution. This method measures the amount of electric current required to deposit the sample electrochemically, or to produce a chemical change. Sometimes the radioactive rate at which a substance breaks down helps scientists determine the size of a sample (see Radioactivity).

Friedrich Emich (1860-1940), an Austrian chemist, pioneered in the development of microanalytic techniques in the 1890's. Since then, many chemists have made important advances in the field. American chemists working on the atomic bomb project first developed ultramicrochemical methods in 1943.   K. L. KAUFMAN

MICROCLINE. See FELDSPAR.

MICROCRYSTALLINE WAX is widely used in making special types of paper for packaging. Paper treated with microcrystalline wax is strong enough to replace tin and steel in many types of containers. These waxes are extracted from the residual oils driven off during the process of refining petroleum (see PETROLEUM [Chemical Treatment]). Microcrystalline waxes were first used during the 1920's.

A popular wrapping material is made from a paper sheet coated with microcrystalline wax. This sheet is highly resistant to grease. It is pliable and self-sealing. Laminated paper—made of several sheets pressed together—and greaseproof paper, both made with microcrystalline waxes, have many uses in industry.

Microcrystalline waxes are used in rust compounds, in condenser coils for electrical systems, and for lining tank cars and concrete tanks used in shipping and storing wine and vinegar. They are also used in waterproofing rope, twine, and textiles. These waxes are flexible and adhesive, and resist moisture and chemical change. They come from a heavier part of petroleum than do the paraffin waxes.   WILLIAM B. HARPER

MICROENCAPSULATION is the process of enclosing a substance in a capsule so that the substance can be easily released. Such capsules are made of gelatin, plastic, starch, or other materials. Solids, liquids, and gases can be encapsulated.

Microencapsulation is used in making carbonless duplicator paper. This paper has a top sheet—coated on the underside with millions of capsules—and a bottom sheet. The capsules release a colorless dye when broken by the pressure of writing or typing. The dye reacts with a thin layer of white clay on the surface of the lower sheet, forming ink.

Microencapsulation is also used in making *timed-release* medicines. Such medicines are slowly released in the body so that their effect is extended for as long as 12 hours.   KENNETH SCHUG

MICROFARAD. See FARAD.

MICROFILM is a small photographic film on which reduced images of printed and other material are photographed. Because the images are reduced, microfilm can store a large amount of material in a small space. For example, the contents of an entire book can be photographed, page-by-page, on a strip of microfilm less than 2 inches wide and a few feet long. The strip can then be wound into a small roll and stored in a fraction of the space occupied by the book.

The microfilm copy of the book can be read easily by putting it through a projection machine to enlarge the image. Some projection machines will make an enlarged paper copy of the image on the film. This copy may be made the same size as the original page of the book. Most microfilm is black and white because color is more expensive and usually not necessary.

A microfilm strip which has been cut into short pieces and placed in a plastic card is called a *microfiche*. The microfiche measures about 4 inches by 6 inches. Two or three of these cards can hold a book's contents.

Individual frames cut from a strip of microfilm can be inserted in punched cards used by high-speed business machines. This makes it possible to locate information on the microfilm quickly by running the cards through a sorting machine. See BUSINESS MACHINES (Punched-Card Machines).

Microfilm has many industrial, scientific, and educational uses. Two or three rolls can store four drawers of business records. A few small boxes of microfiche cards can store enough books to make a small library. Newspapers, libraries, and government offices make extensive use of microfilm. Copies of rare books and manuscripts are made for schools and libraries for much less than it would cost to print them. Architects and engineers can store their large, detailed drawings on microfilm.

The process of making microfilm copies is called *microphotography*. This process has been known since the

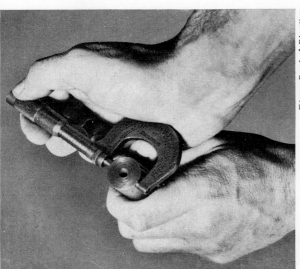

Chicago Board of Education

The Micrometer Caliper is used by mechanics to measure exceedingly small distances in doing precise work.

earliest days of photography. It became a large industry after the Library of Congress began to microfilm books about 1928.

See also FILMSTRIP. BEAUMONT NEWHALL

MICROGRAM. See METRIC SYSTEM.

MICROMETEOROID. See SPACE TRAVEL (Dangers in Space).

MICROMETER, *my KRAHM uh tur*, is an instrument for measuring small dimensions. The simplest micrometer is a glass disk marked with squares in hundredths of an inch. The size of the object is determined by the number of squares it covers. Surveyor's instruments have micrometers which measure distances by a screw with a very fine thread. The head of the screw rests against the scale. The surveyor takes his measurements by turning the screw to raise it up and down along the scale.

Several kinds of micrometers measure the V threads on bolts and screws. Scientists use one kind of micrometer to measure the distances of stars on photographic plates. Measuring microscopes often have micrometers attached. One type of *caliper*, an instrument similar to a geometry compass, has a micrometer screw attached. Scientists call this instrument a *micrometer caliper*. It can be closed on the object by turning a screw scaled to show the measurements of how far it is turned. It can measure one ten-thousandth of an inch.

People sometimes use the term micrometer for the *micron*, one-millionth of a meter. HERMAN J. SHEA

See also CALIPER.

MICRON is a unit of measure in the metric system. It is a small measure, and comes from the Greek word *mikros*, meaning *small*. A micron is equal to $\frac{1}{1000}$ of a millimeter, and is therefore $\frac{1}{1000000}$ of a meter, or .000039 inch. In chemistry, a micron is a particle that measures between .01 and .0001 millimeter in diameter. See also METRIC SYSTEM. OLIVER J. LEE

MICRONESIA. See PACIFIC ISLANDS.

MICROORGANISM. See MICROBIOLOGY.

Eastman Kodak

A Microfiche, above, can store many pages of information as tiny images on a plastic card. The cards are made by a photographic process, as are microfilms. A reading projector, below, enlarges the images on a viewing screen or copies them on paper.

Eastman Kodak

423

A Miniature Microphone, developed for television and motion-picture sound pickup, weighs only 3 ounces.

RCA

MICROPHONE

MICROPHONE is a device for changing sound into electrical signals. These signals can then be broadcast through the air or sent over wires to distant points where they are changed back into sound again. All radio and television stations use microphones to pick up the sounds they want to broadcast. Microphones serve a similar purpose in public-address systems, and in making phonograph recordings and the sound portion of motion pictures. A telephone transmitter is a simple type of microphone.

Kinds of Microphones. Various kinds of microphones have been developed for different uses. Small, neat *pencil,* or *studio,* microphones and *interview* microphones are used when they will be seen by an audience. Speakers and entertainers often wear personal microphones called *lavalier* or *lapel* microphones. These types permit the wearer to move through an audience or to walk about a stage while talking.

Microphones can be built so that they will pick up sounds from any direction or only certain directions. *Nondirectional* microphones detect sounds from any direction. A *bidirectional* microphone picks up sounds from in front of and behind the microphone, but not from the sides. *Unidirectional* microphones are sensitive to sounds from only one direction. A metal arm called a *boom* may often be used to hold one or more unidirectional microphones over the heads of actors appearing before cameras. The boom can be raised, lowered, and tilted to follow the actors and yet keep the microphones outside the range of the cameras.

How a Microphone Works. Microphones can be divided into two groups, according to the method by which they respond to sound waves. These are (1) the pressure type and (2) the velocity type.

The Pressure Type of microphone contains a thin metal diaphragm stretched somewhat like a drumhead inside a rigid frame. This diaphragm is part of an electrical circuit. When sound waves strike the diaphragm, they make it vibrate. These vibrations produce corresponding electrical signals by changing the electric current that flows through the circuit.

Types of pressure microphones include the *condenser* or *capacity* microphone, the *moving coil* or *dynamic* microphone, the *crystal* microphone, and the *carbon* microphone. In the condenser microphone, the vibrating diaphragm changes the capacitance of a condenser (see CAPACITOR.) A moving coil microphone works opposite to the way a loudspeaker does (see LOUDSPEAKER). In a crystal microphone, the vibrating diaphragm twists a piezoelectric crystal producing an electric current. A carbon microphone works like a telephone transmitter (see TELEPHONE [The Transmitter]).

The Velocity Type of microphone has a light ribbon of aluminum foil loosely suspended in a strong magnetic field. Sound waves make the ribbon vibrate. The movement of the ribbon in the magnetic field generates varying amounts of current in the ribbon.

History. Efforts to improve the telephone transmitter invented by Alexander Bell in 1876 led to the development of the microphone. David Edward Hughes, of the United States, invented the first real microphone in 1878. Other microphone inventors included Emile Berliner, Thomas Edison, Philip Reis, Francis Blake, and Henry Hunnings.

Related Articles in WORLD BOOK include:
Berliner, Emile
Edison, Thomas A.
Motion Picture (Sound)
Phonograph
Public Address System
Radio
Telephone
Television

SAMUEL SEELY

MICROPHOTOGRAPHY. See MICROFILM.
MICROPYLE, *MI'kroh pile,* is a tiny opening in several kinds of plant and animal structures. One kind is the opening in the ovule of a plant through which the sperm reaches the egg. Other kinds of micropyles are found in the membrane around animal eggs.

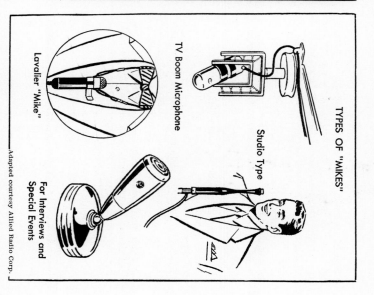

TYPES OF "MIKES"

Adapted courtesy Allied Radio Corp.

Lavalier "Mike"

For Interviews and Special Events

TV Boom Microphone

Studio Type

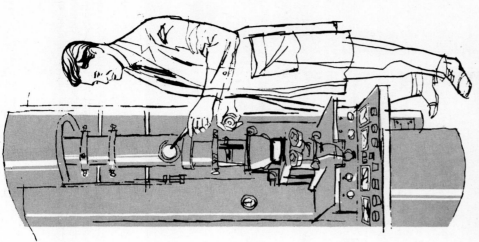

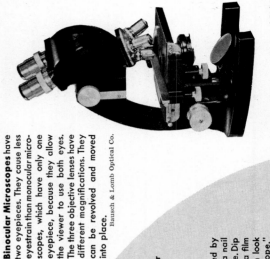

MICROSCOPE, *MY′ kroh skohp,* is an instrument that sees little things. It *magnifies* objects by producing images larger than the original. The microscope serves as one of the most important tools of science. Doctors, bacteriologists, botanists, and other researchers use it to examine bacteria, blood cells, and other objects whose details cannot be seen with the naked eye.

Optical microscopes magnify because light rays reflected from the object bend as they pass through one or more lenses. The bent rays form an image larger than the original. *Electron microscopes* replace light rays with a beam of electrons and use special electronic lenses to bend the beam.

The simplest optical microscope is the magnifying glass (see MAGNIFYING GLASS). Magnifying glasses can give satisfactory results up to a magnification of about 10X, or 10 times the diameter of the object (see DIAM-ETER). After that, the image becomes fuzzy. Scientists obtain greater magnifications by using *compound* microscopes that have two systems of lenses: (1) the *objective lens* that magnifies the object, and (2) the *ocular lens* that magnifies the image from the objective.

Parts of a Microscope. The kind of microscope used in most schools and colleges for teaching has three parts: (1) the foot, (2) the tube, and (3) the body. The *foot* is the base on which the instrument stands. The *tube* contains the lenses, and the *body* is the upright support that holds the tube.

The body, which is hinged to the foot so that it may be tilted, has a mirror at the lower end. The object lies on the *stage,* a platform attached above the mirror. The mirror reflects light through an opening in the stage to illuminate the object. The upper part of the body is a slide that holds the tube and permits the operator to move it up and down with a *coarse-adjustment* gear. This focuses the microscope. Most microscopes also have a *fine adjustment* gear which moves the tube a few thousandths of an inch for final focusing of a high-power lens.

The lower part of the tube carries the objective lens. Many microscopes have several objectives with varying powers of magnification. The objectives are mounted on a revolving *nosepiece* that the operator can rotate to bring the desired lens into place. The upper end of the tube holds the ocular lens, often called the *eyepiece.* Usually, microscopes have a standard ocular of 10X and standard objectives of 3.5X, 10X, and 40X. These,

Electron Microscope uses streams of electrons to magnify objects too small to be seen by a regular microscope. It can magnify up to 1,000,000 times.

Binocular Microscopes have two eyepieces. They cause less eyestrain than monocular microscopes, which have only one eyepiece, because they allow the viewer to use both eyes. The three objective lenses have different magnifications. They can be revolved and moved into place.

Bausch & Lomb Optical Co.

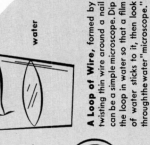

MAKE YOUR OWN MICROSCOPE

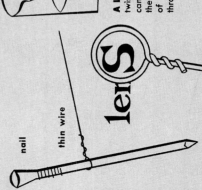

nail

thin wire

water

lens

A Loop of Wire, formed by twisting thin wire around a nail can be a simple microscope. Dip the loop in water so that a film of water sticks to it, then look through the water "microscope."

The purpose of this project is to use a microscope to study the tiny animals that live in ponds and streams. By using a camera that takes time exposures, you can take pictures through the microscope.

SMALL ANIMALS IN PONDS AND STREAMS

Protozoa

Water samples · Microscope · Light · Specimens · Glass slides · Formalin

Life in the Pond

Sporozoa · Mastigophora · Ciliophora · Sarcodina

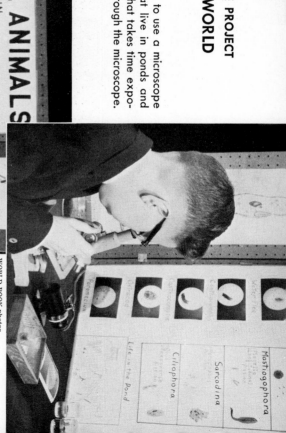

WORLD BOOK photos

MATERIALS

Materials for this project include a microscope, glass slides with covers, and samples of water dipped from a pond or stream. The microscope should be able to obtain at least 400X magnification. If you want to take pictures of the specimens, you will also need a camera that can be set to take time exposures.

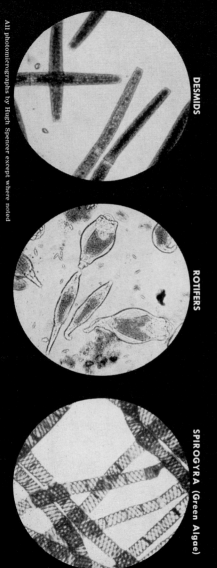

DESMIDS

ROTIFERS

SPIROGYRA (Green Algae)

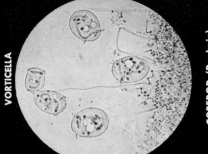

VORTICELLA

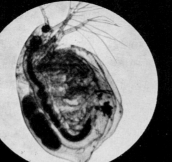

COPEPOD (Daphnia)

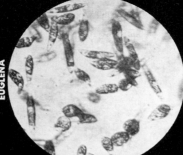

EUGLENA

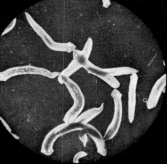

PLANARIA

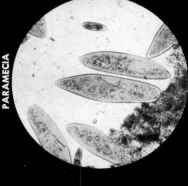

PARAMECIA

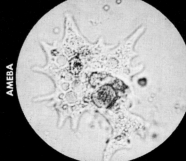

AMEBA

STUDYING THE ANIMALS

Use a medicine dropper to draw up a few drops of pond water from the container. Put one or two drops of the water near one end of a clean, dry glass slide. Place the end of another slide on the water, which will spread between the slides. Then gently push the top slide along until it covers the bottom slide. Put the slides under the microscope. Vary the magnification and move the covered slide around to see all of it.

MAKING PHOTOMICROGRAPHS

Mounting the Camera. To make photographs, put formalin on the slide to kill the specimens. Focus the microscope and mount the camera over the microscope eyepiece. To focus the camera, remove the back. Place a piece of waxed paper in the camera and adjust the camera and the lens to get a sharp picture on the waxed paper.

Taking the Pictures. After you have focused the camera, put in the film, replace the camera back, and take the pictures. Increase the exposure time as you increase magnification. For example, use 5 seconds for 100X magnification, and 10 seconds for 200X. You can use the pictures on these pages to help you identify your specimens.

425

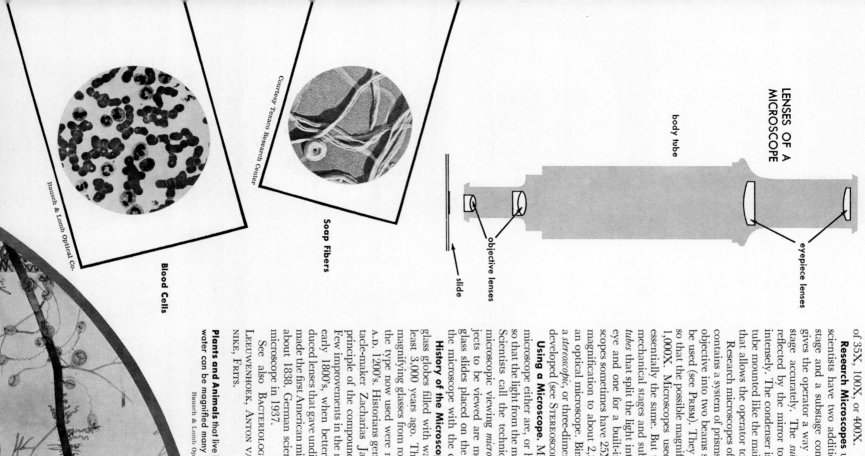

LENSES OF A MICROSCOPE

body tube

eyepiece lenses

objective lenses

slide

Courtesy Texaco Research Center

Soap Fibers

Bausch & Lomb Optical Co.

Blood Cells

Plants and Animals that live in pond water can be magnified many times.

Bausch & Lomb Optical Co.

---

combined with the ocular, give a total magnification of 35X, 100X, or 400X.

Research Microscopes used by physicians and other scientists have two additional features—a mechanical stage and a substage condenser. The *mechanical stage* gives the operator a way to position an object on the stage accurately. The *substage condenser* focuses light reflected by the mirror to illuminate the object more intensely. The condenser is held by the *substage*, a short tube mounted like the main tube on an adjustable gear that allows the operator to focus the light.

Research microscopes often have a *binocular tube* that contains a system of prisms that splits the light from the objective into two beams so that a pair of oculars may be used (see Prism). They usually have 97X objectives so that the possible magnification is increased to almost 1,000X. Microscopes used in advanced research are essentially the same. But they have more complicated mechanical stages and substages. Some have *trinocular tubes* that split the light into three beams—one for each eye and one for a built-in camera. Advanced microscopes sometimes have 25X oculars that bring the total magnification to about 2,500X, the practical limit for an optical microscope. Binocular microscopes that give a *stereoscopic*, or three-dimensional, effect have also been developed (see Stereoscope).

Using a Microscope. Most objects viewed through a microscope either are, or have been made, transparent so that the light from the mirror will shine through them. Scientists call the technique of preparing objects for microscopic viewing *microtomy* (see Microtomy). Objects to be viewed are mounted on 3-inch by 1-inch glass slides placed on the stage. The operator focuses the microscope with the coarse and fine adjustments.

History of the Microscope. Engravers probably used glass globes filled with water as magnifying glasses at least 3,000 years ago. The Romans may have made magnifying glasses from rock crystal, but glass lenses of the type now used were not introduced until the late A.D. 1200's. Historians generally credit the Dutch spectacle-maker Zacharias Janssen with discovering the principle of the compound microscope in about 1590. Few improvements in the microscope occurred until the early 1800's, when better glass-making methods produced lenses that gave undistorted images. C. A. Spencer made the first American microscopes in Canastota, N.Y., about 1838. German scientists developed the electron microscope in 1937.

Peter Gray

See also Bacteriology; Electron Microscope; Leeuwenhoek, Anton van; Ultramicroscope; Zernike, Frits.

MICROTOME is a device used to cut materials very thin so that they can be seen in cross section under a microscope. It has a holder in which the specimen is clamped, a razor-sharp knife, a guide for the knife, and a turnscrew which regulates the thickness of the slice. See also MICROSCOPE; MICROTOMY.

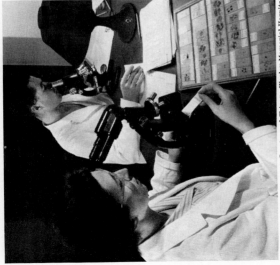

Courtesy of Chicago Wesley Memorial Hospital

Doctors Use the Techniques of Microtomy to make slides of diseased tissues taken from a patient's body.

MICROTOMY originally meant *microscopic cutting.* But it now means the art of preparing objects for examination with a microscope. Without preparation, few objects can be properly examined with a microscope (see MICROSCOPE). A piece of metal, for example, must be highly polished and etched before its structure can be seen. Rocks are sawed into slices thin enough to see through by the techniques of microtomy.

Scientists prepare biological materials either as smears, squashes, wholemounts, or sections. *Smears* are made by applying a thin layer of blood or other organic fluid to a microscopic slide. Technicians dry and stain the layer so the cells can be seen. Geneticists make *squashes* by crushing cells in order to see the number and shape of the chromosomes (see CHROMOSOME). *Whole-mounts* are prepared from whole microscopic animals and plants that are killed in a *fixative* to keep their shape. They are then stained. Alcohol removes the water, and clove or cedar oil makes the objects transparent. Technicians next mount the objects in a drop of resin on a glass slide, which they cover with a glass *coverslip* about $\frac{1}{5,000}$ of an inch thick.

Scientists study plant and animal tissues in *sections* about $\frac{1}{2,500}$ of an inch thick. After being hardened and dried out, the tissues are soaked in wax and shaped into rectangular blocks. The wax supports the tissues so they can be sliced into sections on a *microtome* (see MICROTOME). The sections are then cemented to slides with egg white and the wax is dissolved. They are then stained and preserved under a coverslip. PETER GRAY

MICROWAVE is a short radio wave. It varies from .03937 of an inch to 1 foot in length. Microwaves travel in straight lines. Like light waves, they may be reflected and concentrated. But they pass easily through rain, smoke, and fog that block light waves. Thus they are well suited for long-distance communication and for control of navigation.

Microwaves first came to public notice through the applications of radar in World War II. In television, microwave transmission sends programs from pickup cameras in the field to the television transmitter. It is also used for linking stations in different cities. Microwaves transmit pictures and printed matter at great speed in a process called *Ultrafax.* V. K. ZWORYKIN

See also RADAR; RADIO (Transmitter); TELEVISION (How TV Travels); ULTRAHIGH FREQUENCY WAVE.

MICROZOAN. See PROTOZOAN.

MICRURGY is the study of microorganisms and cells under the microscope. Tiny instruments are used to separate, inject, and isolate the organisms and cells for detailed study.

MIDAS, *MY'dus,* was a character in Greek mythology. He was king of Phrygia, an ancient country in central Asia Minor. The god Dionysus (Bacchus) gave Midas the power to turn everything he touched into gold, because he had helped Silenus, who was Dionysus' old teacher (see BACCHUS).

At first, Midas' miraculous power pleased him. But soon it became a curse, because even his food turned to gold the moment he touched it. He prayed to Dionysus to help him, and the god told him to bathe in the river Pactolus. Midas washed himself, and the magic touch left him. But the sands of the river turned to gold.

Midas acted as judge at a musical contest between Apollo and Pan (see APOLLO; PAN). He awarded the prize to Pan, and Apollo angrily turned Midas' ears into those of an ass. Midas was ashamed and kept his ears covered. But he could not hide his ears from the slave who was his barber. The slave did not dare tell anyone, because he feared punishment. He dug a hole in the ground and whispered the truth into it. Reeds grew out of the soil, and spread the secret, whispering it when the wind blew.

The expression *to have the Midas touch* is used to describe a person who makes money in everything he does. A *Midas* is a wealthy person. O. M. PEARL

Midas Bathed in a River to Lose His Golden Touch.
Midas at the Source of the Pactolus by Nicolas Poussin. Musée Fesch, Ajaccio, Corsica. Giraudon

MIDDLE AGES

MIDDLE AGES were the period between ancient and modern times in western Europe. Before the Middle Ages, western Europe was part of the Roman Empire. After the Middle Ages, western Europe included the Holy Roman Empire, the kingdoms of England and France, and a number of smaller states. The Middle Ages are also known as the *medieval* period, from the Latin words *medium* (middle) and *aevum* (age). Sometimes the Middle Ages are incorrectly called the *Dark Ages*.

The history of the Middle Ages extends from the end of the Roman Empire to the 1500's. Historians today do not give exact dates for the end of the Roman Empire, because it ended over a period of several hundred years. This article uses the A.D. 400's as the starting date of the Middle Ages. By that time, the Roman Empire was so weak that Germanic tribes were able to conquer it. The Germanic way of life gradually combined with the Roman way of life to form the civilization which we call *medieval*. Medieval civilization was greatly influenced by the Moslems in Spain and the Middle East, and by the Byzantine Empire in southeastern Europe.

This article tells about life in western Europe between the A.D. 400's and the 1500's. To understand how other civilizations influenced medieval civilization, see the WORLD BOOK articles on BYZANTINE EMPIRE; MOSLEMS; and ROMAN EMPIRE. For the relationship of the Middle Ages to other periods in history, see WORLD, HISTORY OF.

THE BEGINNINGS

The Germanic Invasions. The Germanic peoples came from Scandinavia in northern Europe. They began moving into central Europe about 1000 B.C. By the A.D. 200's, they occupied regions in the Rhine and Danube river basins along the northern and north-

Bryce Lyon, the contributor of this article, is Professor of Medieval History at Brown University and author of The High Middle Ages and The Middle Ages in Western Europe.

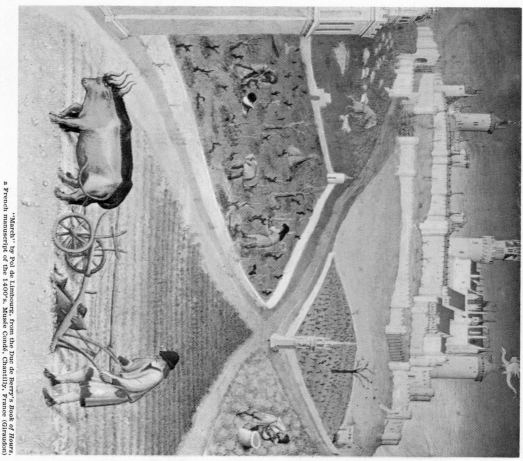

"March," by Pol de Limbourg, from the Duc de Berry's Book of Hours, a French manuscript of the 1400's. Musée Condé, Chantilly, France (Giraudon)

Spain about A.D. 416. The Angles, Jutes, and Saxons began to settle in Britain about 450. The Franks established a kingdom in Gaul (now France) in the 480's. The Ostrogoths invaded Italy in 489. See ANGLE; FRANK; GOTH; JUTE; SAXON.

Barbarian Europe. The barbarian invasions divided the huge Roman Empire into many kingdoms. The barbarians were loyal only to their tribal chiefs or to their own families. Each group of tribesmen kept its own laws and customs. As a result, the strong central and local governments of the Romans disappeared.

In the Roman Empire, a strong system of laws protected the citizens and gave them the safety and security that comes from law and order. Barbarian superstitions replaced many Roman laws. For example, *trial by ordeal* became a common way of determining whether a person was guilty of a crime. The accused person plunged his arm into a pot of boiling water or picked up a red-hot iron bar with his bare hand. If his burns healed within three days, he was judged innocent. Otherwise, he was hanged. See also TRIAL BY COMBAT.

The barbarian invasions also destroyed most of the European trade that the Romans had established. Few persons used the great system of stone roads that had encouraged trade and communication among the prosperous cities of the Roman Empire. Without trade, money went out of use almost completely. The people were forced to make their living from the soil.

By the 800's, most of western Europe was divided into large estates of land called *manors*. A few wealthy landowners, called *landlords* or *lords*, ruled the manors, but most of the people were poor peasants who worked the land. Each village on a manor produced nearly everything needed by its people. This system of obtaining a living from the land was called *manorialism*. See MANORIALISM.

Towns lost their importance under manorial conditions. Most people who had lived in the towns went to the countryside and became peasants on the manors. Some towns were completely abandoned and gradually disappeared. The middle class, which had engaged in trade and industry, also disappeared.

Education and cultural activities were almost forgotten. Almost all state and city schools disappeared. Few persons could read or write Latin, the language of the well-educated. Even fewer were educated enough to preserve the little that remained of ancient Greek and Roman knowledge. The great skills of ancient literature, architecture, painting, and sculpture were forgotten.

The Christian Church was the only civilizing force of the early Middle Ages. It provided leadership for the people and saved western Europe from complete ignorance.

Little by little, the church made Christians of the barbarians. Although the people of Europe no longer honored one ruler, they gradually began to worship the same God. Men called *missionaries* traveled great distances to spread the Christian faith. They also helped civilize the barbarians by introducing Roman ideas of government and justice into their lives.

The popes, bishops, and other leaders of the church took over many functions of government after the Ro-

Illumination from *Roman Customs,* a French manuscript of the 1400's. Bibliothèque Nationale, Paris

Life in the Middle Ages centered around the control of land. Land was ruled by a powerful lord, defended by his knights, and farmed by his peasants. The peasants plowed the lord's fields, trimmed his grapevines, and did many other tasks. The lord's home, left, a mighty stone castle built for defense against his enemies, provided protection for the peasants. Lords, ladies, and knights feasted in the castle's huge banquet hall, entertained by wandering poets and singers, above.

eastern boundaries of the Roman Empire. Some Germans adopted the civilization of their Roman neighbors. They traded with Roman merchants, learned to farm the land, and accepted Christianity as their religion.

But most Germans were rough, ignorant people. The Romans called them *barbarians* (uncivilized people). The Germans lived in tribes, each governed by a chief. The few laws that these people had were based on tribal customs and superstition. The tribesmen were fierce in appearance—big, bearded, and clothed in animal skins or coarse linen. They fought with spears and shields, and were brave warriors. The Germans lived mainly by hunting and by a crude type of farming. They worshiped such Scandinavian gods as Odin and Thor. Few Germans could read or write.

During the A.D. 400's, the Germanic tribes began invading Roman territory. By then, the Roman Empire had lost much of its great power, and its armies could not defend the long frontier. The Visigoths invaded

man emperors lost power. The church collected taxes and maintained law courts to punish criminals. Church buildings also served as hospitals for the sick, and as inns for travelers.

Two church institutions—the *cathedral* and the *monastery*—became centers of learning in the early Middle Ages. Cathedrals were the churches of bishops. Monasteries were communities of men called *monks*, who gave up worldly life to serve God through prayer and work. The monks of some monasteries and the clergy of the cathedrals helped continue the reading and writing of Latin, and preserved many valuable ancient manuscripts. They also established most of the schools in Europe.

The Carolingian Empire united most of western Europe under one ruler in the late 700's. The *Carolingians* were a family of Frankish kings who ruled from the mid-700's to 987. The most important Frankish rulers were Charles Martel, his son Pepin the Short, and Pepin's son Charlemagne.

Charles Martel united the Frankish kingdom in the early 700's, when he captured lands held by powerful Frankish lords. Pepin the Short strengthened the Carolingians' control over the Frankish kingdom. In 768, Charlemagne became ruler of the kingdom. He then conquered much of western Europe, and united Europe for the first time since the end of the Roman Empire.

In creating their empire, the Frankish rulers depended on the assistance of loyal noblemen called *vassals*. A nobleman became a vassal when he pledged his loyalty to the king and promised to serve him. The king then became a *lord* to his vassal. Most vassals held important positions in the king's army, where they served as *knights*. Many vassals had their own knights, whose services they also pledged to the king.

The Carolingian kings rewarded their vassals by granting them estates called *fiefs*. A fief included the manors on the land, the buildings and villages of each manor, and the peasants who farmed the manors.

The early Middle Ages reached their highest point of achievement during the long rule of Charlemagne. He worked to protect the church from its enemies and to keep the people of Europe united under the church. Although Charlemagne never learned to write, he did improve education. He established a school in his palace at Aachen, and teachers from throughout Europe gathered there. They organized schools and libraries, and copied ancient manuscripts. These activities caused a new interest in learning called the *Carolingian Renaissance.* See CHARLEMAGNE.

Charlemagne's empire and the revival of learning did not last long after his death. His three grandsons fought each other for the title of emperor. In 843, the Treaty of Verdun divided the empire into three parts, one for each grandson. Soon after, the divided empire was attacked from outside by Magyars, Moslems, and Vikings. By the late 800's, the Carolingian Empire no longer existed.

FEUDAL EUROPE

Feudalism. After the end of Charlemagne's empire, Europe was again divided into many kingdoms. Most of the kings were weak and had little control over their kingdoms. As a result, hundreds of vassals—with such titles as *prince, baron, duke,* or *count*—became independent rulers of their own fiefs. These noblemen ruled their fiefs through a form of government called feudalism.

Under feudalism, the noblemen who controlled the land also had political, economic, judicial, and military power. Each nobleman collected taxes and fines, acted as judge in legal disputes, and maintained an army of knights within his own territory. He also supervised the farming of the manors on his fief. The fiefholders were the ruling class in Europe for more than 400 years.

A typical member of the ruling class under feudalism was a nobleman, a knight, a vassal, and a lord—all at the same time. He was a nobleman because he had been born into the noble class. He became a knight when he decided to spend his life as a professional warrior. He became a vassal when he promised to serve a king or other important person in return for a fief. Finally, he became a lord when he gave part of his own land to persons who promised to serve him.

Suppose that Sir John, a nobleman, was a vassal of William the Conqueror, king of England and duke of Normandy. When John pledged his loyalty to William, he also promised to supply the king with 10 knights. In return, William gave 20 manors to John as a fief. If the king called his army to battle, John had to go—and take nine other knights with him. If John did not have nine knights living in his household, he hired wandering knights. As payment, John gave each knight one manor as a fief. The knights then pledged their loyalty and service to John. In this way, they became John's vassals, and he became their lord.

A lord and a vassal had rights and duties toward each other. A lord promised his vassal protection and justice, and the vassal gave the lord various services, most of which were military. Feudal warfare was common in Europe. If a lord and his vassal performed their duties, there was peace and good government. But if either disregarded his duties, war broke out between them. The lords fought among themselves as well, because they often tried to seize each other's land. The church, which had its own princes and fiefs, was part of the feudal system, so it also suffered in the warfare. See FEUDALISM.

Feudal Government. During the 900's and 1000's, most of western Europe was divided into feudal states. A powerful lord ruled each state as if he were king. The kings themselves ruled only their own royal lands.

In France, the king ruled only the area called the *Île-de-France,* a narrow strip of land centered near Paris. The rest of France was divided into such feudal states as Aquitaine, Anjou, Brittany, Flanders, and Normandy. In some feudal states, no lord was powerful enough to establish a strong government. But in Anjou, Flanders, and Normandy, capable lords provided strong governments. The dukes of Normandy maintained tight control over the noblemen living there. No one could build a castle, collect taxes, regulate trade, or hold important court trials without the duke's permission. Only he could order an army into battle.

Under William the Conqueror, England became the strongest feudal state in Europe. William, who was duke of Normandy, invaded England in 1066. After defeating the Anglo-Saxon army, he became king of England. He then established the feudal system in England by making all landholders his vassals. See NORMAN CONQUEST; NORMANDY; WILLIAM (I, the Conqueror).

MIDDLE AGES

The strong governments in the feudal states of France and England provided some peace and security for the people. Strong feudal government allowed rulers in the 1100's and 1200's to establish strong central governments in France and England.

Feudalism did not provide strong government in Germany or Italy. For hundreds of years, powerful dukes fought the kings. Otto I, one of the most powerful German kings, won control over the dukes in the mid-900's. He then tried to create an empire similar to Charlemagne's. After conquering lands east of Germany, Otto invaded Italy. In 962, the pope crowned Otto *Holy Roman Emperor*. The Holy Roman Empire was small and weak, and included only Germany and northern Italy. In time, the German dukes tried to regain control of

their kingdoms, and the empire was continually divided by warfare. Neither Germany nor Italy became united countries until the 1800's.

The Power of the Church became the single great force that bound Europe together during the feudal period. The church touched almost everyone's life in many important ways. The church baptized a person at his birth, performed the wedding ceremony at his marriage, and conducted the burial services at his death.

The church also became the largest landholder in western Europe during the Middle Ages. Many feudal lords gave fiefs to the church in return for services performed by the clergy. At first, feudal lords controlled the

FEUDAL STATES OF EUROPE: 1096

| Kingdom of France |
| Holy Roman Empire |

Distance Scale

0 Miles 100 200 300

0 Kilometres 300 400

This map shows the political divisions of Europe in 1096. France and the Holy Roman Empire were made up of many feudal states, each ruled by a lord. The kings ruled only their own royal lands. In France, the king ruled the Île-de-France, shown in yellow. England was a unified kingdom ruled by William II.

Data for map from *Mediaeval History*, by Bryce Lyon; Harper & Row, 1962.

WORLD BOOK map—FHa

church, but it gradually won a large degree of freedom. Although clergymen did not take a direct part in feudal warfare, they controlled the lords with their own types of weapons. One great power of the church was its threat of *excommunication*. To excommunicate a person meant to cut him off completely from the church and take away his hope of going to heaven. If a lord continued to rebel after being excommunicated, the church disciplined him with an *interdict*. This action closed all the churches on the lord's land. No one on the land could be married or buried with the church's blessing, and the church bells never rang. The people usually became so discontented that they rebelled, and the lord finally yielded to the church.

Life of the People. Europe during the 900's was poor, underdeveloped, and thinly populated. At least half the land could not be farmed because it was covered with thick forests or swamps. War, disease, famine, and a low birth rate kept Europe's population small. People lived an average of only 30 years. There was little travel or communication, and fewer than 10 miles from their birthplace.

The people of western Europe consisted of three groups. The *lords* governed the large fiefs and did all the fighting. The *clergy* served the church. The *peasants* worked on the land to support themselves, the clergy, and the lords.

The Lords. A lord's life centered around fighting. He believed that the only honorable way to live was as a professional warrior. The lords and their knights, wearing heavy armor and riding huge war horses, fought with lances or heavy swords.

The behavior of all fighting men gradually came to be governed by a system called *chivalry*. Chivalry required that a man earn knighthood through a long and difficult training period. A knight was supposed to be courageous in battle, fight according to certain rules, keep his promises, and defend the church. Chivalry also included rules for gentlemanly conduct toward women. In times of peace, a lord and his knights entertained themselves by practicing for war. They took part in *jousts* (combat between two armed knights) and in *tournaments* (combat between two groups of knights). See KNIGHTS AND KNIGHTHOOD.

The lord lived in a manor house or a castle. Early castles were simple forts surrounded by fences of tree trunks. Later castles were mighty fortresses of stone. In the great hall of the castle, the lord and his knights ate, drank, and gambled at the firesides. They played dice, checkers, and chess.

The lord's wife, called a *lady*, was trained to sew, spin, and weave, and to rule the household servants. She had few rights. If she did not bear at least one son, the lord could end their marriage. Neither the lords nor their ladies thought education was necessary, and few could read or write.

The Clergy. Most bishops and other high-ranking clergymen were noblemen who devoted their lives to the church. They ruled large fiefs and lived much like other noblemen. Some of these clergymen were as wealthy and powerful as the greatest military lords. Monks who lived in a monastery were required to live according to its rules. They had to spend a certain num-

ber of hours each day studying, praying, and taking part in religious services. Some monks who were outstanding scholars left the monastery and became advisers to kings or other rulers.

Many peasants who became clergymen served as priests in the peasant villages. Each village priest lived in a small cottage near his church. He gave advice and help to the peasants, settled disputes, and performed church ceremonies. The priests collected fees for baptisms, marriages, and burials. But most priests were as poor as the peasants they served.

The Peasants had few rights, and were almost completely at the mercy of their lords. With the help of his wife and children, a peasant farmed both the lord's fields and his own. He also performed whatever other tasks the lord demanded, such as cutting wood, storing grain, or repairing roads and bridges.

The peasant had to pay many kinds of rents and taxes. He had to bring his grain to the lord's mill to be ground, bake his bread in the lord's oven, and take his grapes to the lord's wine press. Each of these services meant another payment to the lord. Money was scarce, so the peasant usually paid in wheat, oats, eggs, or poultry from his own land.

The peasant lived in a crude hut and slept on a bag filled with straw. He ate black bread, eggs, poultry, and such vegetables as cabbage and turnips. Rarely could he afford meat. He could not hunt or fish because game on the manor belonged to the lord.

THE HIGH MIDDLE AGES

Medieval civilization reached its highest point of achievement between the 1000's and the late 1200's. This period is called the *High Middle Ages*.

During the 1000's, many capable lords provided strong governments and periods of peace and security under the feudal system. As a result, the people were able to devote themselves to new ideas and activities.

Economic Recovery. As government improved, so did economic conditions. Merchants again traveled the old land routes and waterways of Europe. Towns sprang up along the main trade routes. Most early towns developed near a fortified castle, church, or monastery where merchants could stop for protection. The merchants, and the craftsmen who made the goods sold by the merchants, gradually settled in the towns.

Europe's population began to increase during the 1000's, and many persons moved to the towns in search of jobs. At the same time, peasants began to leave the manors to seek a new life. Some became merchants and craftsmen. Others farmed the land outside the towns and supplied the townspeople with food. Medieval towns, which arose mainly because of the growth of trade, encouraged trade. The townspeople bought goods, and also produced goods for merchants to sell.

The peasants learned better ways of farming and produced more and more food for the growing population. Peasants began to use water power to run the grain mills and sawmills. They gained land for farming by clearing forests and draining swamps.

For the first time since the days of the Roman Empire, Europeans took notice of the world beyond their borders. Merchants traveled afar to trade with the peoples of the Byzantine Empire in southeastern Europe. The *crusades*, a series of holy wars against the Moslems, encouraged European trade with the Middle East (see CRUSADES). Italians in Genoa, Pisa, Venice, and other towns built great fleets of ships to carry the merchants' goods across the Mediterranean Sea to trade centers in Spain and northern Africa. The Italians brought back goods from these seaports. Many of the goods were exports from cities in India and China. Leaders in the towns of northern Germany created the Hanseatic League to organize trade in northern Europe.

Merchants exchanged their goods at great international trade fairs held in towns along the main European trade routes. Each fair was held at a different time of the year, and merchants traveled from one fair to another. The county of Champagne in northeastern France became the site of the first great European fairs. Its towns lay on the trade routes that linked Italy with northern Europe. Flemish merchants brought woolen cloth to the fairs. Italian merchants brought silks, spices, and perfumes from the Middle East, India, and China. Merchants from northern and eastern Europe brought furs, lumber, and stone. The merchants not only traded their goods, but also exchanged ideas about new methods of farming, new industries, and events in Europe and the rest of the world. See FAIRS AND EXPOSITIONS (Fairs of the Middle Ages).

Medieval Towns. Early towns were only small settlements outside the walls of a castle or a church. As the towns grew larger, walls were built around them. Soldiers on the walls kept a lookout for attacking armies.

The towns were crowded because the walls limited the amount of land available. Houses stood crowded together. The people had to build upward because land was expensive, and many buildings were five or six stories high.

Streets were narrow, crooked, dark, and filthy. Until about 1200, they were not paved. The people threw all their garbage and rubbish into the streets, and disease spread quickly. During the 1200's, the people in some towns began to pave their streets with rough cobblestones. They also took some steps toward sanitation.

A citizen who went out at night took his servants along for protection against robbers. The servants carried lanterns and torches because no town had any street lighting. The wide use of lamps, torches, and candles made fire one of the great dangers for a medieval town. Wealthy citizens had stone and brick houses, but most houses were made of wood. A large fire was likely to wipe out a whole town. The city of Rouen, in France, burned to the ground six times between 1200 and 1225.

After the merchants and craftsmen settled in the towns, they set up organizations called *guilds*. A guild protected its members against unfair business practices, established prices and wages, and settled disputes between workers and employers.

Guilds played an important part in town government. When the first guilds were organized, the towns had few laws to protect merchants or craftsmen. Most laws were made and enforced by the lord who owned the land on which a town stood. As the townspeople gained power, they demanded the right to govern themselves. Often, a guild forced a lord to grant the people a charter giving them certain rights of self-government. The guilds led the fight for self-government, and so their members often ran the new town governments. See GUILD.

The Decline of Feudalism. Economic recovery brought many changes to the social and political organi-

A Medieval City Scene shows many small shops crowded together along a narrow cobblestone street. Shopkeepers and their families lived in the upper part of the wooden buildings. This scene includes a druggist, *right;* a tailor cutting cloth, *left;* and a barber shaving a customer, *background.*

Illumination from the French manuscript *Book of Government of Kings and of Princes* written by Gilles Romain in the 1500's. Bibliothèque de l'Arsenal, Paris (Bulloz)

Building a Medieval Stone Wall required great engineering skill. In this illustration, workers cut stone into squares and carry it to a crane. A man provides power for the crane by walking on the steps of a large moving wheel. Another worker carries mortar up a ladder to the man who cements the pieces of stone together.

Illumination from a French manuscript of the 1200's. The Pierpont Morgan Library, New York

zation of Europe. Money came back into use with the growth of trade and industry, the rise of towns, and the crusades. The manorial system began to break down as people grew less dependent on the land. Many peasants ran away from the manors to the towns. Others bought their freedom with money they made by selling food to the townspeople. The lords of some towns encouraged new settlers to come. Many lords granted freedom to peasants who settled in their towns.

The feudal system, which was based on manorialism, began to break down, too. Ruling lords could pay for military and political service with money instead of fiefs. Their wealth provided better pay for the soldiers and officials they hired. In return, the lords received better service. They and their governments grew increasingly powerful.

During the 1100's and 1200's, great nation-states arose in England and France. Such powerful kings as Henry II of England and Louis IX of France forced feudal lords to accept their authority. These kings developed new and better forms of government. They also organized national armies to protect the people, and established royal laws and courts to provide justice throughout the land. See HENRY (II) of England; LOUIS (IX).

At the same time, small but well-organized governments took form in Flanders, and in Italian city-states

including Florence, Genoa, Siena, and Venice.

Learning and the Arts during the high Middle Ages were devoted to glorifying God and strengthening the power of the church. From 1100 to 1300, almost all the great ideas and artistic achievements reflected the influence of the church.

Princes and laborers alike contributed money to build the magnificent stone cathedrals that rose above medieval towns. The stained glass windows and sculptured figures that decorated the cathedrals portrayed events in the life of Christ and other stories from the Bible. The cathedrals still standing in the French cities of Chartres, Reims, Amiens, and Paris are reminders of the faith of medieval people. See GOTHIC ART (picture); REIMS (picture).

Increasing contact with Arab and Byzantine civilizations brought back much learning that had been lost to Europe since the end of the Roman Empire. Scholars translated Greek and Arabic writings from these civilizations into Latin, and studied their meanings. More and more scholars became familiar with the writings of the Greek philosopher Aristotle. The scholars argued whether Aristotle's teachings opposed those of the church. A field of thought called *scholasticism* grew out of their discussions and writings (see SCHOLASTICISM). Among the great teachers and writers of this period were Peter Abelard, Albertus Magnus, and Thomas Aquinas (see ABELARD, PETER; ALBERTUS MAGNUS, SAINT; AQUINAS, SAINT THOMAS).

Students gathered at the cathedrals where the scholars lectured. Students and scholars formed organizations called *universities*, which were similar to the craftsmen's guilds. From the universities came men to serve the church and the new states, to practice law and medicine, to write literature, and to educate others.

THE LATE MIDDLE AGES

Between 1300 and 1500, medieval Europe gradually gave way to modern Europe. During this period, the Middle Ages overlapped the period in European history called the *Renaissance*. For a discussion of the great developments in art and learning during this period, see the WORLD BOOK article on RENAISSANCE.

A Halt in Progress. Although art and learning advanced, other areas of medieval civilization stood still or fell back. Europe had moved forward economically and socially almost without interruption during the high Middle Ages. The population had grown steadily, social conditions had improved, and industry and trade had expanded greatly. These developments ended in the 1300's. The population decreased, the people became discontented, and industry and trade shrank.

Wars and natural disasters played a large part in the halt of European progress. From 1337 to 1453, England and France fought the Hundred Years' War, which interrupted trade and exhausted the economies of both nations (see HUNDRED YEARS' WAR). In addition, the breakdown of feudalism and manorialism caused civil war throughout most of Europe. Peasants rose in bloody revolts to win freedom from lords. In the towns, workmen fought the rich merchants who kept them poor and powerless. To add to the miseries of the people, the *Black Death* killed about a fourth of Europe's population between 1347 and 1350. The Black Death, a form of bubonic plague, was one of the worst epidemic diseases (see BUBONIC PLAGUE). Severe droughts and floods also brought death, disease, and famine.

The Growth of Royal Power. By the 1300's, the breakdown of feudalism had seriously weakened the feudal lords. At the same time, economic recovery had enriched the kings. With the help of hired armies, they enforced their authority over the lords. Royal infantry—newly armed with longbows, spears called *pikes*, and guns—defeated armies of feudal knights. Meanwhile, the kings greatly increased their power by gaining the support of the middle classes in the towns. The towns-people agreed to support the kings by paying taxes in return for peace and good government. These developments gave birth to the nations of modern Europe.

Troubles in the Church. The power of the popes grew with that of the kings, and bitter disputes arose between the rulers of church and state. Churchmen took an increasing part in political affairs, and kings interfered in church affairs more and more. The popes sometimes surrendered their independence and gave in to the kings. This happened especially from 1309 to 1377, when the popes ruled the church from Avignon, France. After the popes returned to Rome, disputes over the election of popes divided the church. Two, and sometimes three, men claimed the title of pope. Such disputes hurt the influence of the church. They also caused criticism of church affairs and of church teaching. The religious unity of western Europe was weakened, leading to the Protestant Reformation of the 1500's. See CHRISTIANITY (Heresies and Schisms); POPE (Troubles of the Papacy); REFORMATION.

The Growth of Humanism. During the late Middle Ages, scholars and artists were less concerned with religious thinking, and concentrated more on understanding man and the world about him. This new outlook was called *humanism*. The scholars and artists of ancient Greece and Rome had emphasized the study of man. Scholars and artists of the late Middle Ages rediscovered the ancient works and were inspired by them. Architects began to design nonreligious buildings, rather than cathedrals. Painters and sculptors began to glorify man and nature in their works. Scholars delighted in the study of pre-Christian authors of ancient times. More and more writers composed prose and poetry not in Latin but in the *vernacular* (native) languages, including French and Italian. This increasing use of the vernacular opened a new literary age, and gradually brought learning and literature to the common people.

The political, economic, and cultural changes of the late Middle Ages gradually changed Europe, and by the early 1500's it was no longer medieval. But the culture and institutions of the Middle Ages continued to influence modern European history.   BRYCE LYON

Related Articles. For a discussion of political developments in western Europe during the Middle Ages, see the History sections of the articles on AUSTRIA; BELGIUM; ENGLAND; FRANCE; GERMANY; ITALY; the NETHERLANDS; SPAIN; and SWITZERLAND. See also WORLD, HISTORY OF with a table of Major Events of the Middle Ages. Other related articles in WORLD BOOK include:

Architecture (Romanesque; Gothic)	Curia Regis	Literature (The Middle Ages)
Armor	Dancing (The Middle Ages)	Magna Carta
Barbarian	Dark Ages	Manorialism
Byzantine Empire	Domesday Book	Manuscript
Carolingian	Drama (Medieval Drama)	Moslems
Carolingian Art	Education, History of	Music (The Middle Ages)
Castle	Exploration and Discovery	Norman
Charlemagne	Feudalism	Parliament
Christianity	Furniture	Reformation
Clothing (The Middle Ages)	Gaul	Renaissance
Crusades	Glass (The Middle Ages)	Roman Empire
	Gothic Art	Serf
	Guild	Shelter (Shelter in the Middle Ages)
	Hanseatic League	Tournament
	Holy Roman Empire	Verdun, Treaty of
	Homage	Viking
	Humanism	Villein
	Hundred Years' War	Wait
	Knights and Knighthood	Wat Tyler's Rebellion
	Labor (pictures)	Yeoman
	Library (The Middle Ages)	

Outline

I. The Beginnings
   A. The Germanic Invasions
   B. Barbarian Europe
   C. The Christian Church
   D. The Carolingian Empire
II. Feudal Europe
   A. Feudalism
   B. Feudal Government
   C. The Power of the Church
   D. Life of the People
III. The High Middle Ages
   A. Economic Recovery
   B. Medieval Towns
   C. The Decline of Feudalism
   D. Learning and the Arts
IV. The Late Middle Ages
   A. A Halt in Progress
   B. The Growth of Royal Power
   C. Troubles in the Church
   D. The Growth of Humanism

Questions

How did the Germanic invasions of the A.D. 400's change European life?

What two church institutions preserved learning during the early Middle Ages?

What were Charlemagne's accomplishments?

What was *feudalism?* What did it accomplish for medieval Europe?

What were the three classes of medieval society during feudal times?

Why did towns develop during the high Middle Ages?

What was a *fief?* a *manor?* a *vassal?* a *guild?* the *Black Death?*

Why did economic and social progress come to a halt in the late medieval period?

What forces weakened the church in the late Middle Ages?

What was *humanism?* How did it affect medieval society?

MIDDLE AMERICA is a term geographers use for the area between the United States and South America. Middle America includes Mexico, Central America, and the West Indies. All the countries, except El Salvador, have coasts on the Caribbean Sea.

Related Articles in WORLD BOOK include:

Caribbean Sea	Dominican Republic	Mexico
Central America	Haiti	Puerto Rico
Cuba	Jamaica	West Indies

MIDDLE ATLANTIC STATES

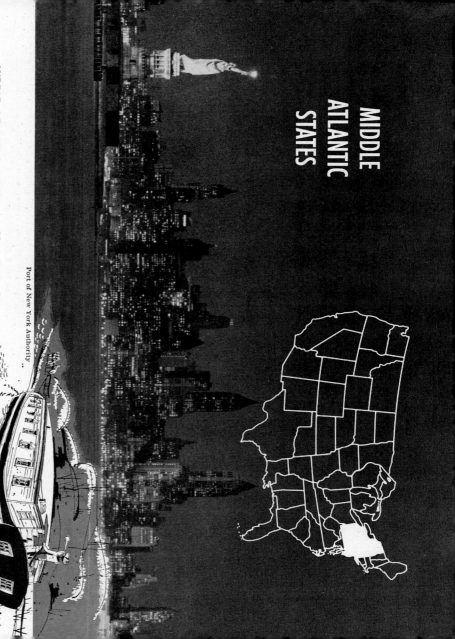

The Statue of Liberty in New York's Harbor faces Lower Manhattan's impressive skyline. In the early days horses on shore pulled boats along canals in the Middle Atlantic States.

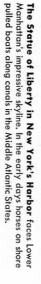

Port of New York Authority

MIDDLE ATLANTIC STATES are New York, New Jersey, and Pennsylvania. They give the United States one of its most important gateways to other parts of the world. Through their deep harbors come nearly half the goods shipped into the country. Their great cities rank among the most important trade centers of the world. Behind this threshold, the Middle Atlantic States are a heavily populated region of great industry. Nearly one of every five persons in the U.S. lives within its 102,745 square miles. About three-fourths of the more than 33 million people of the region live in cities and suburbs.

The people of the Middle Atlantic States come from as many parts of the world as do the ships that dock at their busy ports. This has been true since colonial days, when such leaders as William Penn welcomed all newcomers to the region and encouraged them to live together in harmony. Successive waves of immigrants from various countries moved into the region. The population of these states today includes individuals from more than 60 different countries.

Of every 100 employed persons in the Middle Atlantic States, about 32 work in manufacturing. Clothing factories in New York make about a third of the clothes worn by Americans. Great steel mills in and near Pittsburgh manufacture a fifth of the nation's steel.

Only about 2 of every 100 persons in the Middle Atlantic States earn their living from agriculture. Many of these cultivate the rich truck farms of the New Jersey coastal plain that supply food for city markets.

The area is a center for publishing, higher education, and the cultural arts. Since the days of Benjamin Franklin, it has been the home of leading newspapers, magazines, and book publishing firms. Some of the na-

tion's greatest universities are located here. New York City is a world leader in drama, opera, and music.

The Middle Atlantic region played a key role in the Revolutionary War. Philadelphia was the seat of the Continental Congress and the birthplace of the Declaration of Independence. Military campaigns swirled through the Middle Atlantic region. The battles at Brandywine, Germantown, Princeton, and Trenton were turning points of the war. General George Washington's troops spent their most rugged winters at Valley Forge and Morristown. General John Burgoyne surrendered his troops to the colonists at Saratoga. And when independence had been won, leaders from the Middle Atlantic region helped greatly in framing the Constitution of the United States at Philadelphia.

The Land and Its Resources

The Middle Atlantic States stretch westward between New England and the Southern States. New York and New Jersey face the Atlantic Ocean. Ocean-going ships steam up the Delaware River to reach the Pennsylvania ports of Chester and Philadelphia.

Land Regions. The landscape of the Middle Atlantic region has great variety. It includes a broad coastal

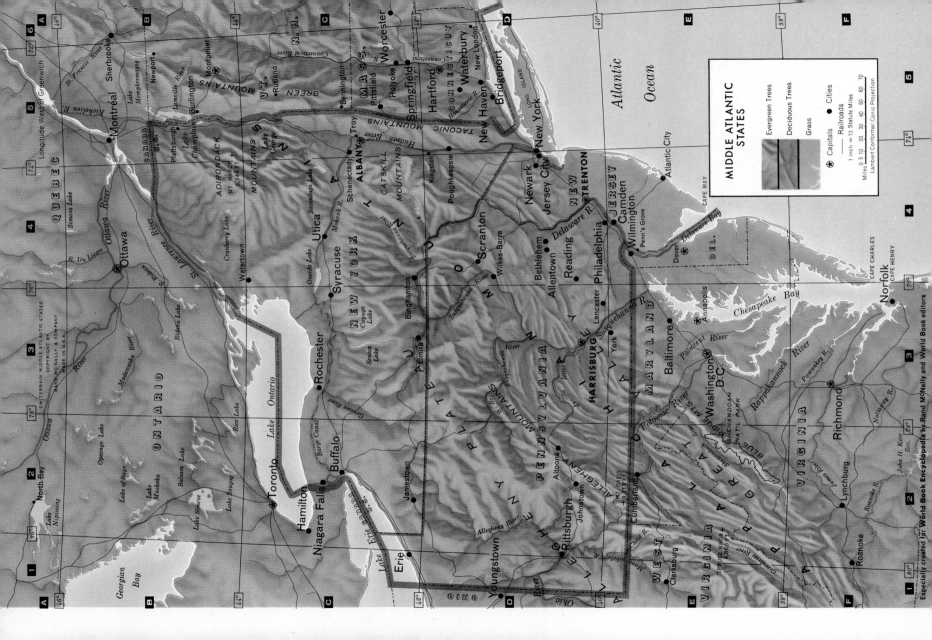

MIDDLE ATLANTIC STATES

Evergreen Trees
Deciduous Trees
Grass

⊛ Capitals   Railroads
• Cities

Miles 0 5 10 20 30 40 50 60 70
1 inch = 73 Statute Miles
Lambert Conformal Conic Projection

plain, mountainous ridges, deep valleys, and flat, fertile lowlands bordering the Great Lakes.

The Appalachian Plateau, made up of round-topped hills and ridges, extends southward from east-central New York, and covers most of northern and western Pennsylvania. Herds of dairy cattle graze on its hills. Miners take coal and stone from southwestern Pennsylvania.

The Appalachian Ridge and Valley Region is a land of wide, scenic valleys. It runs from east-central New York, through northwestern New Jersey, and into central Pennsylvania. Here, also, dairy cattle graze on the slopes, many of which are too steep for other farming.

The New England Upland Region is a narrow strip that rises in southeastern New York and extends through northern New Jersey to eastern Pennsylvania. Hard rock covers the region's flat-topped ridges. Its scenic landscape, cool air, and sparkling lakes make it a favorite summer resort.

The Piedmont begins in the southern tip of New York. It covers a wide area running diagonally through Pennsylvania. Rolling plains, rough uplands, and fertile valleys mark the region. Almost three-fourths of New Jersey's people live in the Piedmont. It includes the principal cities, factories, and highways of the state.

The Coastal Plain consists of gently rolling lowlands that front on the Atlantic Ocean. Most of southern New Jersey lies on this plain. White, sandy beaches stretch along the coast. Fisheries also operate there. Truck farms cover much of the plain's open land. The region also has large deposits of sand, clay, and gravel.

The Adirondack Mountains make up a circular region in northern New York. The wild beauty of its forests, rivers, and waterfalls makes it a popular recreation area. Many of the people who live in the region work at lumbering and mining.

Natural Resources of the Middle Atlantic States include rich farm land, abundant woodlands, large mineral reserves, and plentiful water. All three states use water from the Delaware River.

Forests cover more than two-fifths of the region. During the late 1800's, lumbermen cut most of the virgin timber. Second-growth pine, hemlock, hickory, elm, oak, and maple trees now cover the mountain slopes.

Anthracite coal is found in north-central Pennsylvania. Oil fields in southwestern New York and northern Pennsylvania supply petroleum and natural gas. The nation's first commercially successful oil well was drilled near Titusville in northern Pennsylvania in 1859. The Middle Atlantic States have deposits of clay, granite, limestone, sand, slate, and talc. The portland cement industry is centered in Pennsylvania. The three-state region also provides garnet, gypsum, iron ore, kaolin, titanium, and zinc.

Climate of the Middle Atlantic region varies with the altitude and land surface. Brief extremes of temperature occur, but only for short periods at a time. The highest mountain area, the Adirondacks, has the coldest climate. January temperatures there have dropped as low as −50°F. Sometimes during January the mercury hits −10°F. in northern Pennsylvania. January temperatures in the three states average about 27°F. Ocean breezes usually hold the region's July temperatures to an average of about 74°F. But coastal temperatures sometimes

reach 100°F. in July. The region has an average annual rainfall of 42 inches, which is generally well distributed. However, some sections of the mountains have more than 50 inches of rain a year, while the Great Lakes region averages barely 30 inches.

Snowfall averages only about 14 inches annually at Cape May in New Jersey, but more than 50 inches in the Adirondacks. Occasional heavy snowstorms strike the great cities, creating a serious problem of snow removal. Spring thaws sometimes cause severe floods.

Activities of the People

The Middle Atlantic region played a vital role in America's development because of its location and natural resources. In colonial days, it served as a bridge between Puritan New England and the more easy-going life of the South. As the nation grew, it became the natural center of commerce. As a result of the Industrial Revolution, many farmers became factory workers, and the coal and iron of the Middle Atlantic States provided raw materials for the new industries.

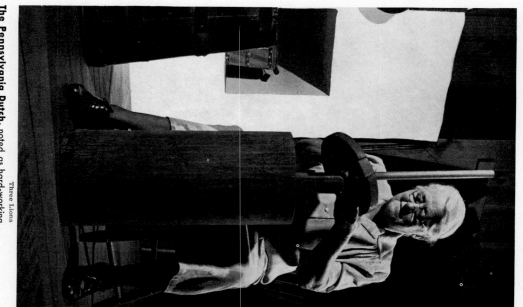

Three Lions

The Pennsylvania Dutch, noted as hard-working farmers, still maintain many traditional customs.

Rich Rolling Farmland covers about half of the Middle Atlantic States. Southeastern Pennsylvania and New Jersey have the richest soil.

Grant Heilman

Richard A. Peer

Fine Inland Waterways, such as the Saint Lawrence Seaway, open the area to world shipping.

WORLD BOOK photo by Three Lions

Giant Industrial Centers in the Middle Atlantic States make the region a manufacturing center.

The People. The character of the people helped to build the Middle Atlantic States into national leadership. During the early 1600's, the trade-and-commerce-minded Dutch settled in New Netherland. This area included parts of present-day New Jersey, Delaware, New York, and Pennsylvania. To cultivate their land, the Dutch brought farmers from Denmark, France, Germany, Ireland, and Norway. In 1664, the Dutch surrendered New Netherland to the English.

In Pennsylvania, William Penn created a new society based upon tolerance and concern for the welfare of others. He pioneered in the care of the poor, the sick, and the insane. His promise of religious freedom to everyone brought the first Mennonites from Holland and Germany to settle at Germantown in 1682. By the time of the Revolutionary War, the region had become established as a place where all people could find equal opportunity. Philadelphia was the largest city of the colonies and the leading center of government and culture.

As the young industries of the Middle Atlantic States began to grow, they attracted thousands of new im-

migrants. Families of Italian and Slavic descent settled in the fast-expanding steel centers. Irish immigrants moved into the cities during the mid-1800's. Welshmen came to Pennsylvania in the 1840's. Many had had mining experience in the coal mines of Great Britain.

The industry and thrift of the Pennsylvania Dutch are apparent in their neat, prosperous farms. Their imaginative folk art and their delicious German cooking bring thousands of visitors each year to festivals at Hershey. These devout people live simply. Many Mennonites still drive to market in old-fashioned buggies. See MENNONITES; PENNSYLVANIA DUTCH.

Manufacturing and Processing industries grew upon a solid foundation of natural resources, strategic location, and a large and varied supply of labor. All three Middle Atlantic States stand among the 10 leading industrial states. The region earns about 12 times as much income in value of production from manufacturing and processing as it does from farming and mining.

Pennsylvania's factories and mills make durable goods, such as iron and steel, machinery, transportation

435

436

equipment, and aluminum and other metal products. New York and New Jersey manufacture mostly nondurable products, such as food and clothing. The region also ranks high in printing and publishing, chemical production, feed manufacturing, electrical equipment, and paper and paper products. Philadelphia is a shipbuilding center. Rochester leads the world in manufacturing photographic film, cameras, and optical goods.

Mining. The most important mineral deposits of the Middle Atlantic States are found in Pennsylvania. This state is the nation's only source of *anthracite* (hard) coal, and ranks among the country's leading producers of *bituminous* (soft) coal. Great quantities of coal are needed to make iron and steel, and these rich fields keep Pennsylvania in front in its production. Pennsylvania's coal production has declined as other fuels have replaced coal for many purposes. This cutback in production has created hardships in mining areas, where people had come to depend upon the mines for their living.

The Middle Atlantic region also provides petroleum, as well as stone and clay products. In the 1850's, coal oil was widely used in lamps and lanterns. For more than 50 years, Pennsylvania led the states in the production of petroleum. Several other states now produce more petroleum, but Pennsylvania oil is still considered one of the best bases for lubricating oils.

Agriculture. Farms cover about half of the Middle Atlantic region. Farmers plant crops on nearly two-fifths of the land. The rest is grass, upon which livestock graze. The average farm covers about 107 acres.

The area's best soils are in the limestone region of southeastern Pennsylvania and the clay-marl belt extending from southwest to northeast through central New Jersey. Because of its fertile soil, New Jersey is called *The Garden State*. Much of the soil in the region must be fertilized to produce profitably.

Dairying and poultry production are the most important farm activities. New York and Pennsylvania rank among the 10 leading producers of dairy cattle. Farmers in New York raise much hay for feed. The state ranks among the leading states in milk and cheese production. New York has many poultry farms, especially turkey farms. Pennsylvania ranks among the 10 leading egg-producing states.

Truck farming ranks next in importance after dairying and poultry raising. The flat coastal plain around Camden is one of the most intensive truck-gardening areas in the country. Farmers raise beans, celery, lettuce, onions, potatoes, sweet potatoes, and tomatoes.

Vineyards and orchards add color to the famous Finger Lakes region in New York and the Lake Erie area in northwestern Pennsylvania. New York wines are famous throughout the nation. Central Pennsylvania is noted for its apples and peaches.

Other Industries. New Jersey fishermen take crabs, lobsters, and oysters from the Atlantic waters and Delaware Bay. The development of fast transportation and the frozen-food industry enabled many of these sea delicacies to be shipped to such far-inland cities as St. Louis, Denver, and Salt Lake City.

United States Steel Corporation

Great Steel Mills in the Middle Atlantic States supply much of the steel in the United States. Steel comes out of a hot strip mill, foreground, at speeds up to 2,300 feet a minute at U.S. Steel's Fairless Works, near Morrisville, Pa.

The tourist industry provides the largest source of income for New Jersey. The broad beaches and resorts of this state attract throngs of vacationers and conventioners every year. Atlantic City is known throughout the world as a popular seaside resort.

Transportation. The great harbors of New York and the Delaware River are lined with ships from every part of the world. Sleek passenger liners dock at the Manhattan piers on the Hudson River. On the New Jersey side of the Hudson and in the Delaware River, freighters unload cargo from a number of countries.

Nature not only gave the Middle Atlantic region fine harbors, but also endowed it with a first-class system of inland waterways. Early settlers used the routes of the Hudson, Delaware, Mohawk, and lesser rivers to explore the interior. Pioneers in Pennsylvania built the first Conestoga wagons in the early 1700's. These wagon bodies were shaped somewhat like a boat, so they could cross the rivers without being unloaded. The region developed as roads pushed through the mountains. The opening of the Pennsylvania Turnpike in 1940 marked the beginning of a new transportation era in America.

More than 23,000 miles of railroad track provide the Middle Atlantic States with their most important freight transportation system. Hundreds of airports, seaplane bases, and heliports meet the needs of the air age.

Regional Cooperation. Some of the industrial centers of the Middle Atlantic States overlap state boundaries. The Port of New York, for example, lies partly in New Jersey. The Delaware River harbor is in both Pennsylvania and New Jersey. About one of every six New Jerseyites works in either New York or Pennsylvania, and commutes to his job.

As early as 1783, the Middle Atlantic States began to realize the need of working together to solve interstate problems. New Jersey and Pennsylvania ratified the Delaware River Compact that year. This agreement regulated the use of the river and the construction of dams across it. The compact has been changed from time to time to meet new needs.

In 1936, the Middle Atlantic States and Delaware created the Interstate Commission on the Delaware River Basin. This commission works to develop the natural resources of the basin, upon which all the states depend. The four states share the water supply of the basin according to careful agreement.

By means of interstate agencies, the Middle Atlantic States deal with common matters of sanitation, recreation, forestation, transportation, and commerce. The Port of New York Authority was established in 1921 to plan and develop the port facilities of the New York-New Jersey area. This authority built shipping piers, bridges, tunnels, truck and bus terminals, and airports (see PORT OF NEW YORK AUTHORITY). Pennsylvania and New Jersey created the Delaware River Port Authority in 1952. This authority also builds bridges and it operates a transit line between the cities of Philadelphia and Camden.

S. K. STEVENS

Related Articles. For additional information on the Middle Atlantic states, see the separate article on each state in this region with its list of Related Articles. Other related articles in WORLD BOOK include:

HISTORY AND GOVERNMENT

City Government	State Government
Civil War	United States,
Colonial Life in America	Government of
Local Government	United States,
Metropolitan Area	History of
Revolutionary War in America	

PHYSICAL FEATURES

Adirondack Mountains	Delaware Bay
Allegheny Mountains	Delaware River
Allegheny River	Delaware Water Gap
Appalachian Mountains	Hudson River
Catskill Mountains	Piedmont Region

Outline

I. The Land and Its Resources
   A. Land Regions
   B. Natural Resources
   C. Climate
II. Activities of the People
   A. The People
   B. Manufacturing and Processing
   C. Mining
   D. Agriculture
   E. Other Industries
   F. Transportation
   G. Regional Cooperation

Questions

What percentage of the people of the Middle Atlantic States work in factories?

How did the location of the Middle Atlantic states influence the region's growth?

In what way did freedom of religion under William Penn help the region develop?

What are the most important mineral deposits of the region and where are they found?

What is the greatest source of income for New Jersey?

What are three reasons for the Middle Atlantic States' rise as a great manufacturing area?

What are three problems that have required cooperation among the states?

What reminders of early times might a visitor to the region see today?

MIDDLE CLASS refers to people who belong to the class in a society between the upper class and the working and lower classes. In the United States, members of the middle class usually enjoy a better-than-average education and standard of living. The traditional occupations of the middle class include business managers and owners, such professional workers as physicians, lawyers, and teachers, and many "white collar" workers.

Middle class people usually do not own large amounts of inherited wealth, and generally do not live in the manner of the upper class. The incomes of the middle class, however, vary considerably. The poorest paid may receive less money than the better-paid people of the working class.

Members of the middle class usually live in comfortable, but not the most expensive or exclusive, sections of a community. They usually send their children to college, and are generally prominent in the civic and governmental affairs of the area.   JOHN F. CUBER

See also SOCIAL CLASS.

437

438

MIDDLE EAST is a large region that covers parts of northeastern Africa, southwestern Asia, and southeastern Europe. Scholars disagree on which countries make up the Middle East. But many say the region consists of Bahrain, Cyprus, Egypt, Iran, Iraq, Israel, Jordan, Kuwait, Lebanon, Muscat and Oman, Qatar, Saudi Arabia, Southern Yemen, Sudan, Syria, the Trucial States, Turkey, and Yemen. Altogether, these countries cover about 3,730,000 square miles and have a population of more than 155 million.

Most of the people of the Middle East are Arabs. Other peoples include African Negroes, Armenians, Copts, Greeks, Iranians, Jews, Kurds, and Turks. Almost all these peoples have the same culture, except for differences in language and religion. A visitor to the Middle East finds little difference, for example, between life in Iran and life in Egypt. Israel is the chief exception.

Much of the Middle East is desert. The people live crowded along the seacoasts, in river valleys, and in mountain valleys that have enough water for growing crops. Most of the people are poor farmers.

Oil has been discovered in Iran, Iraq, Kuwait, Saudi Arabia, and most of the Middle Eastern countries. Income from it is being used to develop these countries and is improving the lives of the people.

Two of the world's first great civilizations—those of ancient Egypt and of Babylonia—developed in the Middle East about 4000 B.C. The region also gave birth to three religions—Christianity, Islam, and Judaism.

Sydney N. Fisher, the contributor of this article, is Professor of History at Ohio State University and the author of The Middle East: A History *and the author of* The Military in the Middle East: Problems in Society and Government.

Bo Dahlin, Carl Östman

A Pipeline on Das Island, part of Abu Dhabi, carries petroleum pumped from the bottom of the Persian Gulf to oil tankers. Oil is the Middle East's most important natural resource.

Throughout its long history, the Middle East has been torn by conflicts among its own peoples and between its people and invaders. Today, three important power struggles are being waged in the Middle East. One struggle is between Arabs and Israelis. A second is between Greeks and Turks in Cyprus. The third struggle is between Arab monarchies, such as Jordan and Saudi Arabia, and Arab republics, such as Egypt and Iraq. Many Middle Eastern nations are also torn by conflict within their borders between people who want to keep the old ways of life and those who want change to keep pace with the modern world.

People

Most people of the Middle East belong to the Mediterranean branch of the *Caucasoid* (white) race. But some mixing with Nordic and Alpine Caucasoids has produced variations in appearance, especially among the peoples of Iran and Turkey. In southern Sudan, most of the people are *Negroid* (black).

Way of Life. Most Middle Eastern people live in villages and farm the nearby land. Many use the same kinds of tools that their ancestors did hundreds of years ago. Some of the people are nomadic tribesmen. They live in the desert and herd cattle, sheep, and goats. Many of the people who live in cities and towns are poor, unskilled workers. Others are business or professional people who lead comfortable lives.

Most people of the Middle East have strong ties with their families and with their villages or tribes. They also consider themselves part of both a language group and a religious group. But many of the people do not feel strongly patriotic toward their countries, most of which were created between the 1920's and the 1960's. As a result, most Middle Eastern countries are weak. The

MIDDLE EAST

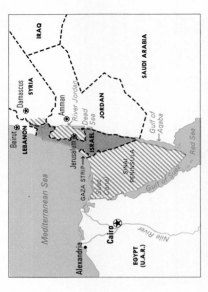

The map below shows the Middle East countries in white.
Asia, Africa, and Europe come together in this region.
The smaller map, *right*, shows the territory occupied by
Israel in the Arab-Israeli war of 1967.

⊛ Capital
● Other city or town
···· Oil Pipeline
▲ MOUNTAIN
~ River
▨ Israeli–occupied territory

ASIA
MIDDLE EAST
AFRICA
Equator

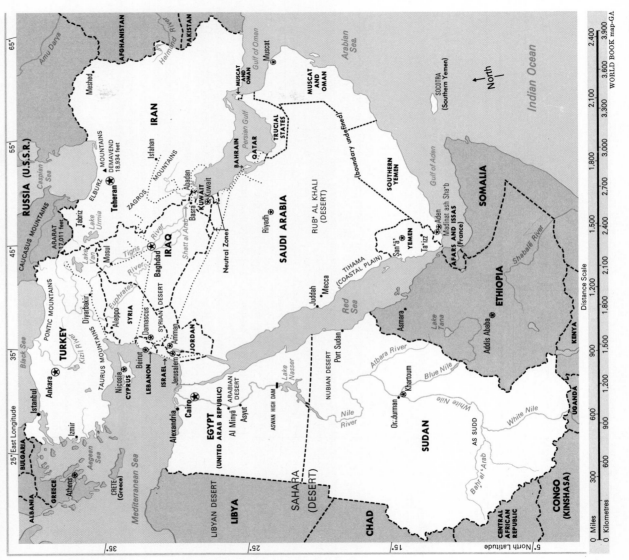

IRAQ
SYRIA
Damascus ⊛
Amman ●
JORDAN
SAUDI ARABIA
LEBANON
Beirut ⊛
Jerusalem →
(ISRAEL)
GAZA STRIP
Mediterranean Sea
River Jordan
Dead Sea
Gulf of Aqaba
SINAI PENINSULA
Gulf of Suez
Red Sea
Cairo ⊛
EGYPT (U.A.R.)
Alexandria ●
Nile River

65°
AFGHANISTAN
PAKISTAN
Amu Darya
Helmand River
Meshed ●
IRAN
Teheran ⊛
ELBURZ MOUNTAINS
▲ DEMAVEND 18,934 feet
Caspian Sea
Isfahan ●
MOUNTAINS
Tabriz ●
Lake Urmia
Lake Van
Mosul ●
ZAGROS MOUNTAINS
Abadan ●
Basra ●
Baghdad ●
IRAQ
Tigris River
Euphrates River
Shatt al Arab
KUWAIT
Kuwait ⊛
BAHRAIN
QATAR
Muscat ●
MUSCAT AND OMAN
Gulf of Oman
Persian Gulf
TRUCIAL STATES
Arabian Sea
MUSCAT AND OMAN
(boundary undefined)
Riyadh ⊛
SAUDI ARABIA
RUB' AL KHALI (DESERT)
Neutral Zone
SOUTHERN YEMEN
Gulf of Aden
SOCOTRA (Southern Yemen)
North
Indian Ocean

RUSSIA (U.S.S.R.)
55°
45°
CAUCASUS MOUNTAINS
ARARAT 17,011 feet
Black Sea
PONTIC MOUNTAINS
Diyarbakir ●
TURKEY
Ankara ⊛
Kizil River
TAURUS MOUNTAINS
Aleppo ●
SYRIA
Damascus ●
SYRIAN DESERT
Mecca ●
Juddah ●
Red Sea
TIHAMA (COASTAL PLAIN)
Ṣan'a' ⊛
YEMEN
Ta'izz ●
Aden ●
Madinat ash Sha'b
AFARS AND ISSAS (France)
SOMALIA
ETHIOPIA
Asmara ●
Lake Tana
Addis Ababa ⊛
Shabalē River
KENYA

35°
Istanbul ●
Izmir ●
Aegean Sea
BULGARIA
GREECE
Athens ⊛
ALBANIA
CRETE (Greece)
Mediterranean Sea
Nicosia ⊛
CYPRUS
LEBANON
Beirut ⊛
ISRAEL
Jerusalem ●
Damascus ●
Amman ●
JORDAN
EGYPT (UNITED ARAB REPUBLIC)
ARABIAN DESERT
Cairo ⊛
Alexandria ●
Al Minyā ●
Asyūṭ ●
ASWAN HIGH DAM
Lake Nasser
NUBIAN DESERT
Port Sudan ●
Nile River
LIBYAN DESERT
LIBYA
SAHARA (DESERT)
CHAD
SUDAN
Khartoum ⊛
Omdurman ●
Blue Nile
White Nile
AS SUDD
Baḥr el 'Arab
Baḥr el Jebel
NUBIAN DESERT
Atbara River
CENTRAL AFRICAN REPUBLIC
CONGO (KINSHASA)
UGANDA

25° East Longitude
35°
25°
15°
5° North Latitude

Distance Scale
Miles 0   300   600   900   1,200   1,500   1,800   2,100   2,400
Kilometres 0   600   900   1,200 1,500 1,800 2,400 2,700 3,000 3,300 3,600 3,900

WORLD BOOK map-GA

439

The Nile Valley in Egypt has rich soil and plentiful water for farming. Most of the people of the Middle East are farmers.

United Nations

majority of Israel's people, however, came from other countries to create and build a Jewish state. They are loyal to Israel, and it is strong.

Religion and Language. Most Middle Eastern people are Moslems. Their religion, Islam, has many *sects* (branches), including Shi'a and Sunni. Christians make up the second largest religious group. The churches include the Coptic, Greek Orthodox, and Maronite. Most Israelis practice Judaism.

Arabic is spoken in most Middle Eastern countries. Other languages include Armenian, Greek, Hebrew, Kurdish, Persian, and Turkish.

The Land

The Arabian Peninsula covers much of the central part of the Middle East. The peninsula is a desert plateau that begins at sea level along the Persian Gulf and gradually slopes upward to highlands along the Red Sea. In Yemen, these highlands reach about 12,000 feet. The Syrian Desert covers much of Syria, Iraq, and Jordan. Another desert, the Sahara, covers large parts of Egypt and Sudan.

Mountains. In northeastern Turkey, the land rises more than 17,000 feet. From this high point, four large mountain ranges spread out into Iran and Turkey. These ranges are the Elburz and Zagros mountains of Iran and the Pontic and Taurus mountains of Turkey. A smaller chain of mountains extends into Lebanon.

Rivers. The Middle East has two great river systems —the Nile River system and the Tigris-Euphrates-Karun river system. The Nile River flows northward through Sudan and Egypt to the Mediterranean Sea. Almost all of Egypt's farmland lies along the Nile, and almost all the Egyptian people live in the Nile Valley or on the Nile Delta.

The Tigris and Euphrates rivers rise in Turkey. They meet in Iraq and form the Shatt al Arab. The Karun River rises in Iran and flows into the Shatt al Arab. The Shatt al Arab empties into the Persian Gulf.

Climate

The Middle East has a long, intensely hot summer and a mild winter. Temperatures vary with location. Summer temperatures may climb to 115° F. or more in Egypt, Iran, Saudi Arabia, Sudan, and Turkey. Winter temperatures range from 40° F. in the north to 50° F. in the south. Temperatures in the northern mountains

in Iran and Turkey often drop below zero in winter.

The only parts of the Middle East that receive more than 10 inches of rain a year are some coastal regions and the mountain regions of Iran, Lebanon, Turkey, and Yemen. Most areas have rain only in winter. The heaviest rain, about 30 inches a year, falls along the Black, Caspian, and Mediterranean seas.

Economy

The Middle East is largely an underdeveloped region. Most of the people make a bare living from farming or herding. Industry has been expanding, but many more new industries are needed—and capital is scarce. Oil and gas are the most important natural resources.

Agriculture. Wheat is the most important crop of the Middle East. Other cereal crops include barley, corn, millet, oats, and rice. Fruits, nuts, and vegetables are grown in many areas. These crops include apricots, beans, dates, figs, filberts, grapes, melons, olives, oranges and other citrus fruits, peaches, and pistachios. Other important crops are cotton and tobacco. The people raise cattle for meat, leather, and dairy products. Sheep are raised for meat and wool.

Since the 1950's, agricultural production has grown because of improved equipment, scientific farming methods, better seeds, and increased irrigation. Many all-weather roads have been built, and trucks have been imported to carry farm products to markets.

Manufacturing has also increased since the 1950's, especially in Egypt, Iran, Israel, Kuwait, Saudi Arabia, and Turkey. The chief manufactured products include cement, chemicals, light industrial goods, processed foods, and textiles. Many factories have been built in large cities, and more are needed. But the increasing industrialization has worsened such problems as pollution and overcrowding.

Mining. The Middle East has more than 60 per cent of the world's proved oil reserves. Iran, Kuwait, and Saudi Arabia each produce more than 2 million barrels of oil a day. Other important oil-producing countries are Abu Dhabi, in the Trucial States; Bahrain; Egypt; Iraq; Muscat and Oman; and Qatar.

Most Middle Eastern oil is sold to European countries and Japan. Altogether, the oil-producing countries receive from $3 billion to $4 billion a year for their oil. They spend much of this income on economic development, such as construction of airports, canals, dams, factories, harbors, highways, pipelines, power plants, and railroads. The money is also used to build hospitals and schools and to carry out programs to cure and prevent disease. In addition, a large part of the oil income is spent on arms and military training.

Other minerals produced in the Middle East include chrome, coal, cobalt, copper, gold, iron, manganese, phosphates, and silver.

Trade. The Middle East does not export enough products to pay for its imports. The difference is made up by loans, investments in the region by foreign countries, gifts from friends, and tourist spending. Only Abu Dhabi, Kuwait, Lebanon, Qatar, and Saudi Arabia support themselves.

History

Men lived in many parts of the Middle East as early as 25,000 B.C. About 4000 B.C., two of the world's earliest great civilizations—those of ancient Egypt and of Babylonia—developed in the region. The Egyptian civilization arose in the Nile Valley of Egypt (see EGYPT, ANCIENT). Babylonia developed on the fertile plain between the Tigris and Euphrates rivers of Iraq (see BABYLONIA). About 1900 B.C., a people called the Hittites came to power in Turkey. The three great civilizations balanced one another for 500 years. In the land between the three empires, many other peoples organized societies. These peoples included the Arameans, Hebrews, and Phoenicians. The Arameans developed a language that spread throughout the Middle East. The Hebrews firmly established a belief in one God. The Phoenicians may have developed an alphabet.

Beginning in the 800's B.C., all these civilizations were destroyed by a series of invaders. The invaders included the Assyrians, Chaldeans, Medes, Persians, and finally Alexander the Great.

The Hellenistic Age. Alexander conquered the Middle East in 331 B.C. He introduced the Greek language and Greek customs and united the region into one empire. The next 300 years, called *the Hellenistic Age*, brought great achievements in scholarship, science, and the arts. Since the Hellenistic Age, the Middle East has had basically a single culture.

The Romans conquered most of the Middle East by 31 B.C. Roman armies, governors, and tax collectors controlled the people, and Latin became the language of the government. During the Roman rule, Jesus

Christ was born in Bethlehem and died in Jerusalem.

Arab Rule. In the A.D. 600's, the followers of the Prophet Mohammed, called Moslems, swept out of the Arabian Peninsula and conquered what are now Egypt, Iran, Iraq, Israel, Jordan, Lebanon, and Syria. Many of the conquered people adopted the Arabic language and the Moslem religion. Many non-Arab Moslems in the conquered lands joined the army or entered government service. In time, a united society was formed. The Seljuk Turks from central Asia conquered much of the Arab empire in the 1000's. The Seljuk Turks, in turn, were followed by the Ottoman Turks in the 1300's.

Under Ottoman rule, the Middle East declined in power. Meanwhile, strong states were developing in Europe. In 1869, French engineers completed the Suez Canal, which shortened the water route between Europe and the East. During the late 1800's, Great Britain gained influence in Egypt and in *sheikdoms* (kingdoms) on the Arabian Peninsula to protect its trade routes.

World War I. During World War I (1914-1918), the Arabs fought with the Europeans against the Turks to gain their independence. Turkey was defeated and, in 1923, it became a republic. But most Arab lands were divided into mandated territories by the League of Nations and placed under British and French rule (see MANDATED TERRITORY). The Arabs continued to demand independence. One by one, the territories were made independent states during the 1930's and 1940's. In the 1960's, Britain withdrew from many sheikdoms on the Arabian Peninsula.

Palestine was one of the Arab territories mandated to Great Britain. In 1917, Britain issued the Balfour Declaration, which supported the creation of a Jewish homeland in Palestine—but without violating the civil or religious rights of the Arabs there. Many Jews moved to Palestine during the 1920's and 1930's. The Palestinian Arabs resented the growing Jewish immigration. They believed that Palestine was their homeland, and they wanted it to become an independent Arab state. The Arabs and the Jews fought each other, and both fought the British for control of Palestine.

In 1947, Britain asked the United Nations (UN) to help solve the conflict. The UN proposed that Palestine be divided into two states, one Arab and one Jewish.

The Suez Canal has separated Egyptian and Israeli forces since the six-day war of 1967. Continual fighting along the canal has caused many deaths and great destruction.

Pix from Publix

44I

The Arabs, who made up the majority of the population, rejected the plan. They said the UN did not have the right to divide their land. The Jews accepted the plan. In May, 1948, they established the state of Israel on land assigned to them by the UN. See PALESTINE.

The 1948 and 1956 Wars. After the creation of Israel, several Arab states joined the Palestinians in their fight against the Jewish state. The UN arranged a cease-fire late in 1948. When the war ended, Israel controlled 75 per cent of Palestine, about 2,000 square miles more than the UN had assigned to it. Egypt and Jordan held the rest of Palestine.

About 700,000 Arabs who had been living in what became Israel fled or were driven from their homes. They became refugees in the Arab countries around Israel. During the early 1950's, they sent raiding parties into Israel. Israel struck back at the Arab countries.

In 1956, President Gamal Abdel Nasser of Egypt asked the Western nations for aid to defend his country. The West refused, and Nasser turned to Russia for aid. The United States then withdrew its offer to help Egypt build a dam across the Nile River near Aswan. Nasser reacted by seizing the Suez Canal from its British and French owners in July, 1956. Egypt then built the Aswan High Dam with Russian help.

In October, 1956, Great Britain, France, and Israel responded to the seizing of the canal by invading Egypt. Pressure from the United States, Russia, and other nations forced the invaders to withdraw. A UN peace-keeping force was stationed in Egypt along the Israeli border. Israel refused to permit the UN troops on its land.

The Six-Day War. In 1967, the Arabs believed that Israel planned a major attack on Syria. At Nasser's demand, the UN troops were withdrawn from Egypt's border with Israel. Nasser then sent military forces into the Sinai Peninsula and closed the Straits of Tiran, the entrance to the Israeli port of Elat. Israel considered the closing of the straits to be an act of war. On June 5, 1967, Israeli planes wiped out the air forces of Egypt, Jordan, and Syria. Israeli forces then seized Egypt's Sinai Peninsula, including the east bank of the Suez Canal, all of Jordan west of the River Jordan, and the Golan Heights in Syria. The UN arranged a cease-fire on June 10, ending the six-day war. See UNITED NATIONS (The Arab-Israeli Wars).

The Middle East Today. Since the six-day war, no armistice has been signed, and no solution has been found to the Arab-Israeli conflict. The Arab countries want Israel to withdraw from the land it conquered in 1967. Israel, in turn, wants the Arab governments to recognize its right to exist. Russia has rearmed Egypt and Syria. It has also sent military advisers and pilots to Egypt. The United States has supplied arms to Israel. The cease-fire has been ignored by both the Arabs and the Israelis, and frequent fighting continues.

The UN troops prevented raids across the Israeli-Egyptian border after the 1956 war. But raids continued back and forth along Israel's borders with Jordan and Syria. In 1966, Israel attacked the Jordanian village of As Samū'. The attack was so severe that King Hussein of Jordan was almost overthrown because his people felt he had not defended them.

Meanwhile, many Palestinian Arabs in Israel and the refugees outside the country have abandoned hope that Arab or other states will help them regain their home-land. As a result, they have formed guerrilla groups to fight Israel.

Because the United States has supported Israel, Russia has been able to gain wide influence in some Arab countries. Russia has also increased its naval power in the Mediterranean Sea. In August, 1970, the United States arranged a cease-fire and tried to settle the Middle East conflict.

SYDNEY N. FISHER

Related Articles in WORLD BOOK include:

COUNTRIES

Bahrain	Israel	Qatar	Syria
Cyprus	Jordan	Saudi Arabia	Trucial
Egypt	Kuwait	Southern	States
Iran	Lebanon	Yemen	Turkey
Iraq	Muscat and Oman	Sudan	Yemen

OTHER RELATED ARTICLES

Ancient Civilization	Desert	Mediterranean Sea
	Islam	Petroleum

MIDDLE ENGLISH. See ENGLISH LANGUAGE (Development of English).

MIDDLE TENNESSEE STATE UNIVERSITY. See UNIVERSITIES AND COLLEGES (table).

MIDDLE WEST. See MIDWESTERN STATES.

MIDDLEBURY COLLEGE. See UNIVERSITIES AND COLLEGES (table).

MIDDLEMAN. See DISTRIBUTION (Distribution of Goods).

MIDDLETON, ARTHUR (1742-1787), was one of the South Carolina signers of the Declaration of Independence. He was also an American Revolutionary War leader. He served in the Colonial Legislature and in the First Provincial Congress of South Carolina. He became an opponent of the Tories, and served as a member of the first South Carolina Council of Safety (see TORY). Middleton was a delegate to the Continental Congress in 1776, 1777, and in 1781. He was also elected in 1778, 1779, and 1780, but he refused the election. The British captured him in 1780 at the siege of Charleston.

Middleton was born near Charleston, S.C. He was educated in the colony and in England. ROBERT J. TAYLOR

MIDDLETON GARDENS. See FLOWER (Famous Flower Gardens; picture).

MIDDLEWEIGHT. See BOXING (The Classes).

MIDDLINGS. See FLOUR (How Flour Is Milled).

MIDGET. See DWARF.

MIDIANITE was the name of a northern Arabian tribe, said to be descended from Midian, a son of Abraham. The Midianites lived east of the northern tip of the Red Sea. Moses lived with them after fleeing from Egypt, and married a daughter of Jethro, a Midianite priest. In a later age, the Israelite hero, Gideon, defeated the Midianites at Jezreel.

GLEASON L. ARCHER, JR.

MIDLAND, Tex. (pop. 62,625; met. area 67,717; alt. 2,770 ft.), a financial center of the oil industry, lies midway between Fort Worth and El Paso. For location, see TEXAS (political map). Many oil companies and legal and professional agencies have home offices in Midland. Midland has long been a cattle center and holds a world's championship rodeo each year.

THE LAND OF THE MIDNIGHT SUN

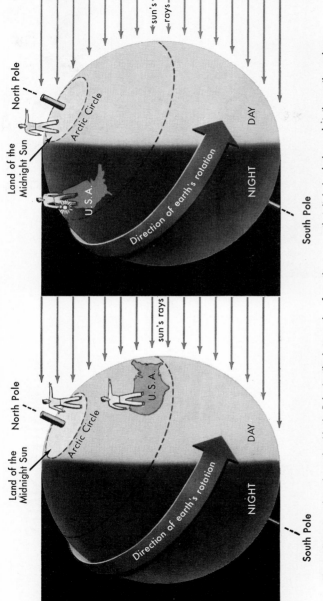

North Pole

Land of the Midnight Sun

U.S.A.

Arctic Circle

sun's rays

Direction of earth's rotation

DAY

NIGHT

South Pole

These diagrams show how the North Pole is tilted toward the sun at midsummer. In the diagram on the left, both the United States and the arctic regions are in daylight. In the diagram on the right, the earth's rotation has turned the United States away from the sun so that it is in darkness, but the arctic regions are still in daylight. All areas north of the Arctic Circle have the midnight sun at least one night in the year. At the North Pole the sun does not set for six months of the year.

Midland was settled in 1885. It has a mayor-council form of government. Midland is the seat of Midland County. H. BAILEY CARROLL

MIDLAND EMPIRE. See BILLINGS.

MIDLAND LUTHERAN COLLEGE. See UNIVERSITIES AND COLLEGES (table).

MIDNIGHT SUN. The sun shines at midnight at certain times of the year in the polar regions. At the Arctic Circle, this occurs about June 22. Farther north, the periods of midnight sun last longer. For example, in northern Norway, the *Land of the Midnight Sun,* there is continuous daylight from May through July. At the North Pole, the sun does not set for six months, from about March 20 to about September 23. At the Antarctic Circle, 24 hours of sunlight occurs about December 21, and the South Pole has midnight sun from about September 23 to about March 20.

The midnight sun is caused by the tilting of the earth toward the sun. As the earth travels around the sun, first the South Pole, and then the North Pole, faces the sun. While one polar region faces the sun, it has continuous daylight. At the same time, the other polar region faces away from the sun and has continuous darkness.

See also ANTARCTIC CIRCLE; ARCTIC CIRCLE; DAY.

MIDSHIPMAN is a student at the United States Naval Academy at Annapolis, Md. Upon graduation, midshipmen receive commissions as ensigns in the Navy or as second lieutenants in the Marine Corps. Canadian naval cadets are also called midshipmen.

The term *midshipman* goes back to the 1600's, when the British Navy placed junior officers amidships to relay orders. In 1954, Great Britain substituted the rank of acting sublieutenant for that of midshipman. These men serve in a training program on shore. THEODORE ROPP

See also UNITED STATES NAVAL ACADEMY.

MIDSUMMER NIGHT'S DREAM, A. See SHAKESPEARE, WILLIAM (Synopses of Plays).

MIDWAY, BATTLE OF. See WORLD WAR II (The Battle of Midway); MIDWAY ISLAND.

MIDWAY CHURCH. See GEORGIA (Places to Visit).

MIDWAY ISLAND lies 1,300 miles northwest of Honolulu in the Pacific Ocean. It is made up of two islands in an atoll 6 miles in diameter, and has an area of 2 square miles and a total coastline of about 20 miles. Midway has a population of 2,356. The United States discovered Midway in 1859, and annexed it in 1867. United States companies built a cable relay station there in 1903, and an airport in 1935. The U.S. Navy Department controls the island.

The Battle of Midway was one of the most important naval battles in World War II. From June 4 to June 6, 1942, United States land- and carrier-based planes attacked a Japanese fleet approaching the islands. They sank four aircraft carriers and one heavy cruiser. The United States lost the destroyer *Hammann* and the aircraft carrier *Yorktown.*

The Battle of Midway was the first decisive naval victory United States forces won against the Japanese in World War II. It crippled Japan's naval air power and ended Japan's attempt to seize Midway as a base from which to strike Hawaii. Many military experts believe this battle was the turning point in the Pacific campaign. The Japanese aircraft carriers were never replaced. EDWIN H. BRYAN, JR.

See also WORLD WAR II (The Battle of Midway).

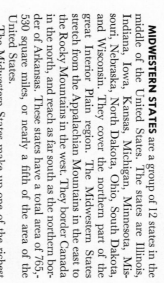

MIDWESTERN STATES

MIDWESTERN STATES are a group of 12 states in the middle of the United States. The states are Illinois, Indiana, Iowa, Kansas, Michigan, Minnesota, Missouri, Nebraska, North Dakota, Ohio, South Dakota, and Wisconsin. They cover the northern part of the great Interior Plain region. The Midwestern States stretch from the Appalachian Mountains in the east to the Rocky Mountains in the west. They border Canada in the north, and reach as far south as the northern border of Arkansas. These states have a total area of 765,530 square miles, or nearly a fifth of the area of the United States.

The Midwestern States make up one of the richest and most important regions of the world. Midwestern farmers have taken advantage of the fertile soils and favorable climate of this area to make it the country's main food supplier. The farmers can use nearly all the land for raising crops or grazing cattle. The region has few areas too rugged, dry, or rocky for agriculture.

The Midwestern States have rich mineral deposits. Minnesota mines more iron ore than any other state. Indiana leads in limestone production, and South Dakota in gold. Michigan and Ohio are leading producers of salt.

Since the early days of exploration and settlement, the people in the Midwest have benefited from the region's excellent waterway system. This system is made up of the Great Lakes and of the Mississippi River and its main tributaries, the Ohio and Missouri rivers. Completion of the Lakes-to-Gulf Waterway in 1933 connected the Great Lakes and the Mississippi by way of the Illinois and Des Plaines rivers. Construction of the St. Lawrence Seaway in the late 1950's made it possible for large ships to sail between the Atlantic Ocean and Great Lakes ports. See SAINT LAWRENCE SEAWAY.

Midwestern manufacturers have prospered because of the availability of raw materials. Factories and mills in

Early Settlers Traveled to the Midwestern States over the National Road. Fertile farm lands in the Midwest have made it the leading agricultural area of the United States.

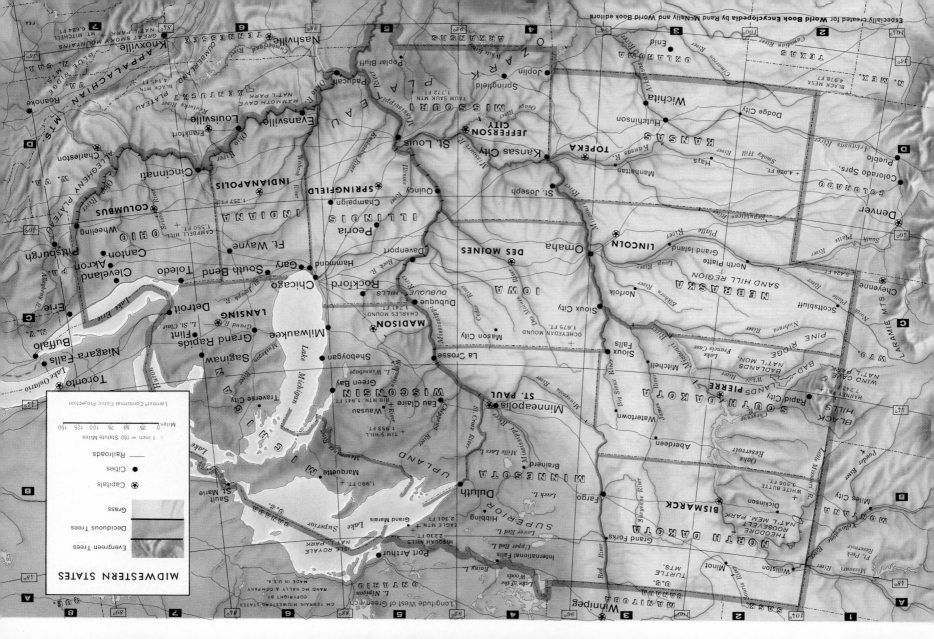

The Rich, Rolling Farmland of the Midwest produces much of the nation's food. Midwestern States are leaders in producing corn, wheat, vegetables, and dairy products.

the Midwest produce more food, iron and steel, fabricated metal products, machinery, transportation equipment, paper, and rubber products than those in any other region of the United States.

The combination of favorable geographic factors—good soil, comparatively mild climate, generally level land surface, and accessibility to the ocean—makes the Midwest different from the interior of any other continent. More people live in the Midwest than in any other area so far from the sea. The 55,000,000 Midwesterners make up about one-third of the population of the United States.

The Land and Its Resources

The area covered by the 12 Midwestern States is basically a lowland whose eastern and western edges rise above the rest of the terrain. The elevation ranges from 230 feet above sea level near Cardwell, Mo., to 7,242 feet on Harney Peak, in the Black Hills of South Dakota. To the northeast, the Great Lakes form the world's largest group of fresh-water lakes.

Land Regions. The Midwest has five general land regions. The glaciers that moved over most of the Midwest during the Ice Age leveled the land and left few rugged areas. The flatness and vast expanse of the landscape awe visitors. They can look over the Midwestern farmlands stretching flat to the horizon, as far as the eye can see.

The Great Plains have a higher elevation than any other section of the Midwest. They form the western part of the region and extend through the western areas of North Dakota, South Dakota, Nebraska, and Kansas. The plains rise toward the west, and reach average elevations of 3,000 to 4,000 feet in all four states. The Great Plains are generally flat, broken occasionally by river valleys, canyons, and buttes. The region receives less rain and snow than other parts of the Midwest. As a result, farmers are limited to crops requiring little moisture, such as wheat, or crops dependent on irrigation. Cattle graze on grasses that cover much of the land. See GREAT PLAINS.

The Ozark Plateau, an upland of lakes, hill farms, and scenic forests, rises in southern Missouri. Its elevation ranges from 500 to about 2,000 feet. Vacationers enjoy the good fishing and hunting, cool summers, and natural beauty. See OZARK MOUNTAINS.

Midwestern Farm Life still includes such traditional community events as the farm auction sale, presided over by an auctioneer.

Dawson L. Jones, Palmer

Ohio Dept. of Development

Scenic Recreation Areas can be found throughout the Midwest. The region has many lakes and rivers that attract campers, fishermen, and tourists.

Ewing Galloway

Great Industrial Centers have developed in Detroit, Chicago, and other Midwestern cities.

Van Bucher, Photo Researchers

Beef Cattle and Other Livestock raised in the Midwest supply much of the nation's meat.

The Superior Upland surrounds the southern and western parts of Lake Superior. This rugged area reaches its highest point (2,301 ft.) at Eagle Mountain in Minnesota. Miners have tapped iron deposits there to supply the nation's iron and steel industry.

Great pine forests originally covered the land. During the 1800's, this area had many logging and lumbering camps. The lumbermen used the Great Lakes and south-flowing streams to ship the lumber to settlers in the prairies who needed wood. By the early 1900's, little remained of the great forests. Since then, foresters have controlled cutting and planted new trees, so that second-growth timber now covers much of the area. The upland has more than 6,000 square miles of lakes that were gouged out by glaciers long ago. Campers, fishermen, and boating enthusiasts enjoy summer holidays there.

The Appalachian Plateau, an extension of the Appalachian Mountains, covers eastern Ohio. This hilly, eroded region has deposits of coal, oil, and other minerals. Farms lie chiefly in the valleys, and sheep and cattle graze on the hills. See APPALACHIAN MOUNTAINS.

The Interior Lowland makes up the remainder of the 12-state region. The rich soils of this prairie area are the food-producing heart of the nation, and one of the richest agricultural areas in the world. The lowland may be divided into three main parts: (1) the green fields of tall corn stretching from western Ohio to eastern Nebraska; (2) golden, waving wheat fields that cover much of the western two-thirds of Kansas, western Minnesota, western Nebraska, and the eastern Dakotas; and (3) America's dairyland which extends through Wisconsin, northern Illinois, eastern Minnesota, northeastern Iowa, and southern Michigan.

Climate. The extreme western part of the Midwest is very dry. Farmers depend on irrigation to raise many crops. In the north, the winters are long and cold, and the summers short. North Dakota has an average January temperature of 9° F., but only receives about 30 inches of snow a year. In northern Minnesota, Wisconsin, and Michigan, heavy snows often blanket the countryside.

Summers are long and hot in the southern part of the Midwest. Winter temperatures generally average below freezing. The eastern section receives much more precipitation than the western part. Southern Illinois and

MIDWESTERN STATES

Missouri are noted for long, hot summers. Temperatures in these regions in July average about 80° F.

Water Conservation.

The lack of water on the Great Plains affected settlers even before they began farming. Because of the dryness of the region, few trees grew and the pioneers lacked firewood and lumber for building. As early as 1855, a Nebraska settler, J. Sterling Morton, began a tree-planting program. Today, the Nebraska National Forest is the largest man-planted forest in the country. The tree-planting program gained new vigor after the dust storms of the 1930's. Farmers had plowed up so much land to produce crops that no trees or deeproot grasses were left to hold the soil down.

The Mississippi River system is the chief water source of the agricultural Middle West. In the west and north, tributaries such as the Platte in Nebraska carry little water. But widespread irrigation projects, begun on the Platte in the 1930's, have increased the productivity of large areas. In 1914, Ohio passed the first Conservancy Act in the United States. The act provided for the construction of dams and reservoirs to prevent flooding. In general, the Missouri River carries too little water in the north, but causes floods in its lower course. The federal Missouri River Basin Project, begun in 1944, was designed to correct this condition (see Missouri River Basin Project).

Certain areas in the Midwest have a shortage of ground water, or water stored in natural underground reservoirs. Cities and farms depend on ground water for farming and for home and industrial uses. Some sections, such as Kansas, southern Illinois, and the Dakotas, suffered from a shortage of ground water during the 1950's, because of a severe drought. The U.S. Department of Agriculture established a program to build small dams and channels that prevent water from small streams from pouring into rivers and being lost.

The heavily industrial Midwestern States surrounding the Great Lakes have no water shortage. Their problem comes from pollution, created by the intensive industrial use of water.

Work of the People

About two-thirds of all Midwesterners live in towns and cities, and the rest live on farms. The farm population outnumbers town and city dwellers in Nebraska, Iowa, Kansas, and especially in North and South Dakota. Most large Midwestern cities grew up along the shores of the Great Lakes or on the main river routes. Chicago, the region's largest city, sprawls on a plain along the shores of Lake Michigan. Detroit, the second largest Midwestern city, is on the banks of the Detroit River close to Lake Erie. St. Louis and Minneapolis lie along the Mississippi River, Cincinnati by the Ohio River, and Kansas City, Mo., at the junction of the Kansas and Missouri rivers. Water transportation plays a major part in the importance of these cities, but they all also bustle with air, rail, and highway traffic.

Manufacturing accounts for the greatest share of the value of goods produced in the Midwest. It accounts for about 75 per cent of the value of production. Agriculture contributes over 20 per cent, and mining earns the rest.

Agriculture. There are about 1,277,000 farms in the

Midwest. Their average size ranges from 915 acres in South Dakota to 145 acres in Michigan. The four westernmost states have the largest and fewest farms, mainly because the people use much of the land for grazing cattle on large ranches, or for farming large wheat crops.

No agricultural region in the world is more mechanized than the Midwest. Farmers use power equipment to plow the land, to apply specially prepared liquid fertilizers, and to plant crops. Mechanized pickers harvest corn, and combines gather grains and beans. Special machinery cuts, bales, and chops hay and other forage. Power equipment unloads grain from trucks to elevators. Dairy farmers use machinery to milk their cows.

Soon after World War I, prices dropped and farmers could not pay for the equipment and land they had bought on credit. The National Grange and especially the American Farm Bureau Federation accomplished much toward obtaining federal legislation that would ease the farmers' problems.

Federal help came in 1933 with the establishment of the Agricultural Adjustment Administration. Congress passed the Agricultural Act in 1948, and the Agricultural Act in 1954. These and other measures limit the amount of cropland and thus the amount of farm products on the market. The federal government pays farmers to let part of the land lie idle.

Since the 1920's, the Midwest has had the problem of farm surpluses, resulting from mechanization, generally abundant rainfall, and the increased size of farms. Except during World War II and the Korean War, farmers have produced more of some crops, such as wheat, than the market has demanded. The government buys the excess crops and puts them in sealed storage. This prevents the excess crops from flooding the market, and forcing prices down. Row upon row of cylindrical metal storage bins containing surplus food products stand in small towns throughout the Midwest.

Corn is worth more than $3 billion a year for Midwestern farmers, and leads in value among agricultural products. Cattle and hogs follow, and dairy products rank fourth. Nine leading corn states lie in the Midwest. Farmers of Iowa, Illinois, and Indiana lead the nation in hog raising. Wisconsin and Minnesota, two states in the dairy belt, lead in dairy products. Wisconsin ranks first in wheat production, followed by North Dakota. In other agricultural products, North Dakota leads the states in barley, rye, and flaxseed. Iowa leads in corn production. Iowa and Indiana rank among the top 10 states in egg production. Five of the top 10 beef-cattle states are in the Midwest.

The states bordering the Great Lakes produce large quantities of vegetables and fruits. Ohio, Indiana, Illinois, and Michigan rank among the leaders in tomatoes, and Minnesota and Wisconsin in green peas. Michigan and Wisconsin rank high in total vegetable production. Michigan orchards yield more cherries than those in any other state.

Manufacturing and Processing

industries have developed chiefly in the five Midwestern States east of the Mississippi River—Illinois, Indiana, Michigan, Ohio, and Wisconsin. All these states, except Wisconsin, rank among the nation's top 10 industrial leaders in value added by manufacture. Only New York and California have a greater industrial output than Ohio.

In the Midwest, transportation equipment leads all other manufactured products in value. It is followed by machinery, processed foods, primary metals, metal products, and electrical machinery. Detroit is the automobile capital of the world. The leadership of Benjamin Goodrich and Harvey Firestone, who founded their companies in Akron, established Ohio as the nation's leader in manufacturing tires and other rubber products.

The Midwest also pioneered in farm-machinery production. The first combine (harvester-thresher combination) was used in Michigan in 1837. Factories in Illinois, Indiana, and Minnesota now produce most of the nation's combines. John Deere made America's first steel plow in Grand Detour, Ill., in 1837. Cyrus McCormick built the nation's first reaper factory in Chicago in 1847. Chicago's International Harvester Company, one of the largest farm-implement makers in the world, resulted from a merger in 1902 of a number of companies in Chicago, Milwaukee, and Springfield, Ill.

The Midwest's food industry processes, prepares, and packs countless products. Wheat comes to Minneapolis, Chicago, Kansas City, Mo., Duluth, and Superior for milling. Plants in these and other cities turn corn, soybeans, and other grains into foods, beverages, and industrial products.

The Armour and Swift families helped establish Chicago as the world's largest livestock and meat-packing center. Other Midwestern cities also rank among the country's leading meat processors. These industries have grown out of the Midwest's abundant supply of cattle and hogs.

Furnaces and mills in Illinois, Indiana, Ohio, and Michigan have almost half the ironmaking and steelmaking capacity of the United States. Limestone for steelmaking comes chiefly from Indiana, which leads the nation in the production of this mineral. Coal abounds in states bordering the Midwest, such as West Virginia, and can be imported cheaply.

Missouri is the nation's leading lead producer. The electrical machinery and automobile industries use large quantities of metal.

Pipelines bring oil from the Gulf Coast to great refineries that line the southern end of Lake Michigan. One of the world's largest oil refineries operates in Whiting, Ind.

Transportation. Farm products from the sprawling agricultural Midwest must travel great distances to reach far-off markets. For this reason, farmers throughout the years have sought ways to keep transportation rates low. They accomplished this mainly through legislation and cooperative movements.

The growth of railroads during the 1800's did much to speed settlement. But, as agriculture prospered, farmers found that they depended greatly on the railroads to bring in supplies, and especially to carry farm products to markets. The railroads took advantage of this dependence by charging rates that the farmers could not afford. In the 1870's, the National Grange fought the railroads by winning the passage of state laws regulating railroad rates. Cooperatives helped cut farmers' costs chiefly in two ways. By banding together, the farmers could afford to build storage facilities, such as grain elevators, previously supplied by railroads at high costs. By pooling their shipments, the farmers could obtain bulk rates for transporting their products.

In the early 1900's, many Midwestern States launched great highway-improvement programs. Trucking began to develop rapidly after World War I. Cooperatives took advantage of the expanded highways by forming their own trucking firms. In this way, they avoided paying railroad rates, especially on short hauls.

The population of Midwestern cities has been growing since the industrial expansion that followed the Civil War. Many persons moved to the cities in search of work. Others moved out of the crowded business and factory districts to the suburbs that now surround most metropolitan areas. To bring these people to work every day, and to take them home, cities have had to improve their transportation systems.   JOHN H. GARLAND

Related Articles. For additional information on the Midwestern States, see the separate article on each state in this region with its list of Related Articles. Other Related Articles in WORLD BOOK include:

HISTORY AND GOVERNMENT

City Government	State Government
Colonial Life	United States,
in America	Government of
Indian, American	United States,
Indian Wars	History of
Local Government	Western Frontier Life
Northwest Territory	Westward Movement
Pioneer Life in America	

PHYSICAL FEATURES

Appalachian	Mississippi River
Mountains	Missouri River
Detroit River	Ohio River
Great Lakes	Ozark Mountains
Great Plains	

Outline

I. The Land and Its Resources
  A. Land Regions
  B. Climate
  C. Water Conservation
II. Work of the People
  A. Agriculture
  B. Manufacturing and Processing
  C. Transportation

Questions

Why is the Midwest one of the world's best areas for farming?

What are the three main agricultural regions of the Midwest?

How is the terrain of the Midwest unusual in appearance?

What products manufactured in the Midwest have the greatest value?

Why is it sometimes said that Midwestern farmers produce too much?

Where do most of the Midwest's largest cities lie?

Why do the westernmost states of the area have the largest farms?

In what kind of machinery did Midwestern manufacturers pioneer?

Why do the Midwestern States surrounding the Great Lakes have water-pollution problems?

What are the four geographic factors that make the Midwest different from the interior of any other continent in the world?

What percentage of Midwesterners live in towns and cities?

How many Midwestern States are there? Name them.

MIDWESTERN UNIVERSITY is a state-controlled co-educational school of arts and sciences in Wichita Falls, Tex. It grants bachelor's and master's degrees. The university was founded in 1922 as a junior college and became a four-year school in 1946. For enrollment, see UNIVERSITIES AND COLLEGES (table).

MIDWIFE is a woman who assists women who are in childbirth. The need for services of midwives is strongest in overcrowded and rural communities where a physician is not available.

MIDWIFE TOAD. Two small toads of Central and Southwestern Europe are called *midwife*, or *obstetrical*, toads because the male helps care for the eggs. Midwife toads are about 2 inches long. The female lays from 20 to 60 eggs in two strings. The male fastens them to his legs and carries them until they hatch. The male toad usually hides under a stone or in some other place while he carries the eggs. He comes out only after dark and bathes the eggs in a nearby pond or stream. After three weeks he takes them into the water, where tadpoles hatch from the eggs.

Scientific Classification. The midwife toad belongs to the toad family, *Discoglossidae*. One of the toads is genus *Alytes*, species *A. obstetricans*. The classification of the other midwife toad is *A. cisternasi*.

W. FRANK BLAIR

American Museum of Natural History

The Male Midwife Toad carries the fertilized eggs like a bunch of grapes attached to its hind legs until the tadpoles hatch.

MIES VAN DER ROHE, *ME us vahn der ROH uh,* **LUDWIG** (1886-1969), a German architect, won fame for the clean, uncluttered design of his buildings of brick, steel, and glass. He built his first steel-framed building, an apartment house, in 1927 at an exposition he directed in Stuttgart, Germany. Two years later he directed the German exhibition at the international exposition in Barcelona, Spain. Here, Mies built his famed Barcelona pavilion, with its marble walls reaching out beyond the building, its hovering roof slab, and its great expanse of glass. The sparse appearance of his buildings illustrates his motto, "Less is more."

Mies was born in Aachen, Germany. In 1930, he became director of the Bauhaus school in Dessau. That same year, he built his widely-known Tugendhat house in Brno, Czechoslovakia. Two years later, he moved the Bauhaus to Berlin, where it remained until it was closed in 1933 (see BAUHAUS).

Mies came to the United States in 1938. He became architect for the Illinois Institute of Technology (then Armour Institute), and headed its school of architecture, planning, and design until his retirement in 1958. He planned the I.I.T. campus on an eight-block site in Chicago. He left the steel skeletons of the buildings exposed, and combined them with great expanses of glass and carefully arranged panels of brick. In his apartment buildings at I.I.T., he exposed the reinforced concrete to view. He was elected to the National Institute of Arts and Sciences in 1961.

WILLIAM T. ARNETT

See also SHELTER (picture).

Ezra Stoller

Illinois Institute of Technology

Ludwig Mies van der Rohe, *right*, pioneered in glass-and-steel architecture. Mies and Philip Johnson designed the 38-story, bronze-covered Seagram skyscraper in New York City, *above*. Associate architects were Kahn and Jacobs.

MIFFLIN, THOMAS (1744-1800), was an American soldier and politician. He became a member of the First Continental Congress in 1774. He served as an aide to General George Washington during the Revolutionary War, and later as quartermaster general of the Continental Army. Mifflin also served in the Congress of the Confederation from 1782 to 1784. He represented Pennsylvania at the Constitutional Convention of 1787, and signed the United States Constitution. He served from 1788 to 1799 as the chief executive of Pennsylvania. He was born in Philadelphia of Quaker parents.

KENNETH R. ROSSMAN

MIGNON. See OPERA (Some of the Famous Operas).

MIGNONETTE, *MIN yun ET,* is an attractive garden plant of North America and Europe. Its name comes from a French word which means *little darling*. The mignonette has a low, bushy mass of smooth, soft-green leaves. The tiny flowers grow on tall spikes. They are yellowish white with reddish pollen stalks inside, and have a delightful fragrance. Gardeners have produced larger-flowered mignonettes, but they are not so fragrant. Some of the cultivated varieties make excellent border plants. The mignonette grows best in a cool temperature and a light soil. It is hardy and may be grown from seed plantings in May and July.

Scientific Classification. Mignonettes belong to the mignonette family, *Resedaceae*. They are genus *Reseda,* species *R. odorata.*

ALFRED C. HOTTES

MIGRAINE. See HEADACHE.

MIGRANT LABOR is a farm labor force that moves into a region temporarily to help harvest and process crops. Migrants usually harvest crops like fruits and vegetables that must be picked as soon as they ripen. The United States has about 500,000 migrant workers. They usually work in several areas during a year without becoming permanent members of any community. Migrant labor is paid by the day or by the number of units produced. Migrant workers generally receive very low wages, and live under substandard conditions. The

J. HORACE MCFARLAND

The Fragrant Mignonette Blooms Almost All Summer.

use of migrant labor may lead to serious housing, health, and education problems. Workers often live in camps that have poor sanitary facilities. Communicable diseases are an ever-present problem. Children in migrant families may not get adequate schooling.

U.S. farmers employed up to 500,000 Mexican migrant laborers a year between 1951 and 1963, under a special seasonal labor importation law. The U.S. House of Representatives refused to renew the law in 1964.

During the depression of the 1930's, many farm families in the United States left their farms in the dustbowl region of the Great Plains because they could not make a living (see DUST BOWL). Many moved west and became migrant laborers, but some of these families settled in California.

GERALD G. SOMERS

Van Bucher, Photo Researchers

Migrant Workers harvest broccoli in a field near Salinas, Calif. Many of these workers live in nearby camps. During the harvesting seasons, migrant laborers and their families travel from one area to another looking for work.

MIGRATION is the movement of people or animals from one place to another. Throughout history, entire groups of people and animals have at times left their homes and moved to new ones. People may migrate because they are forced to move, or merely because they want to move. Wars, famines, floods, and volcanic eruptions have all caused migrations.

The causes of animal migrations have remained basically the same for thousands of years. Animals cannot control their surroundings in the way that men can. Wild animals must move from area to area to find the physical conditions in which they can survive.

In prehistoric times, men often moved from one area to another much as the animals did. They seldom stayed anywhere for a long time, because the food supply usually ran out. As men learned to cultivate crops and domesticate animals, they could stay in one place longer than before. But when the soil no longer produced good crops, or when drought, floods, or fire ruined the crops, men had to migrate in search of food.

Human migration today is much different from migrations of animals and prehistoric man. People usually move to improve their economic or social conditions, or because of political changes. Some migrations cause long-range changes in populations, because they bring together peoples with different backgrounds.

Migration includes both *emigration* (the movement of people *out* of an area) and *immigration* (the movement of people *into* an area.) *International migration* occurs between two countries, and *intercontinental migration* between two continents. When people move within one country, from one region, state, or province to another, the movement is called *internal migration.*

For an explanation of immigration and emigration, see the article on IMMIGRATION AND EMIGRATION.

Why People Migrate

Since earliest times, man has migrated for three chief reasons: (1) because he has used up or destroyed his natural resources, (2) because he seeks to improve or change some aspects of his way of life, or (3) because of wars, conquests, and invasions. These reasons are usually taken together and called *population pressure.*

Shortage of Resources. Early man often had to migrate because of the shortage of natural resources where he lived. The population grew so large that the land could not produce enough food to support everyone. People also had to migrate because they outgrew their water supply. This might happen because more and more persons used the water, or because of a drought. The Indians of Mesa Verde, in Colorado, left their cliff dwellings and migrated to new lands around A.D. 1300, partly because of a 20-year drought. The potato crop in Ireland failed in the 1840's. The famine that followed caused more than 1½ million persons to migrate from Ireland and settle in other countries, principally the United States.

Improvement of Life. In the late 1700's and early 1800's, individuals and families began moving from one country or region to another in search of better economic opportunities. Others moved for political or religious reasons. The western expansion across the United States was an internal migration. It resulted from people wanting free land and a chance to improve their way of life. Floods, volcanic eruptions, and other natural disasters have wiped out homes and crops, causing people to migrate. Epidemics and plagues, particularly those of the Middle Ages, caused thousands to flee from their homes.

Wars and Conquests have caused people to migrate ever since tribes or nations first began attacking each other to gain power and riches. The victors have often forced the defeated peoples either to flee elsewhere or to become slaves. The resulting movement often stimulated other migrations. The peoples driven out by invading tribes had to force out their neighbors, or perish. Some invaders wandered into settled agricultural regions. Often they conquered these regions, adopted new ways of life, and became the rulers. When the region became overcrowded, new rulers would conquer or drive out the old ones. This type of migration occurred continuously for thousands of years, extending well into the era of written history.

Some peoples first began raiding their neighbors because of population pressure, but quickly found the attacks a profitable occupation. Drawn by the hope of wealth, they adopted raiding as a way of life.

History

Prehistoric Migrations were often caused by changes in climate. Men and animals moved southward through the ages to escape the great glaciers, or ice sheets, that gradually spread down over thousands of years from the North Pole. The people returned north after the glaciers melted. As many areas in northern Africa slowly dried up, hunters of the Stone Age followed the animals on which they lived into the fertile Nile Valley.

We do not know definitely how prehistoric man migrated over the earth's surface. One of the earliest known migrations took place when prehistoric men moved

Forced Migrations were common among tribes living in Gaul during the 100's B.C. The Helvetians set fire to their homes and fled as conquering Roman soldiers approached their village.

Drawing by Rodney Thompson, from Mankind Throughout the Ages by Rugg and Krueger, published by Ginn & Co.

from North Africa to Europe. These migrants were of a type superior to the Neanderthal men of Europe, and seem to have replaced them. Most anthropologists and archaeologists believe that the Alpine people of eastern Europe migrated to central Europe in prehistoric times. But they disagree as to the size and importance of that migration. Nomads from the steppes (plains) of Russia seem to have migrated to central Europe at an early date.

Language similarities in the countries of Asia and Europe provide evidence that a people speaking an Indo-European tongue migrated widely over the world in early times. These people may have originated in the Caspian Sea region, but there is little evidence to confirm this theory.

Another great migration took place across the Bering Strait when people from Asia moved into the Americas. Anthropologists once thought this was a single migration that occurred about 20,000 years ago. Now they generally believe that the total migration took place over a long period, and that men came to America in several migrations (see ESKIMO [History]; INDIAN, AMERICAN). The most recent migration from Asia to America may have occurred not more than 1,000 years ago.

Invasions and Conquests. During the 200's B.C., a group of tribes pushed out of Mongolia. They drove some people westward toward the Ural Mountains, and others southeast into China. The Chinese called these people the *Hsiung-Nu*, and Europeans later gave them the name *Huns*. By the early A.D. 300's, the Huns had overrun most of northern China. After the Huns were driven west by fierce Mongolian tribes, they pushed into eastern Europe.

Other tribes fled from the Huns, and swept into Europe in what historians call *the barbarian invasion*. The Huns drove the Ostrogoths and Visigoths from southwestern Russia, and forced them to press into the Roman Empire. Other peoples, driven into what is now Germany, forced the Germanic nomads to fight their

way south. One group, the Vandals and Suevians, made their way through Gaul and down into Spain. The Huns finally moved into what is now Hungary. Their migration ended after their chief, Attila, died in 453 (see ATTILA).

For hundreds of years, the military might of the Roman Empire prevented large migrations in northern Africa and the Middle East. But the slow decay of the empire gave the nomads of Arabia a chance to push forward in one of the greatest migrations in history. During the 600's and 700's, they occupied Arabia, Armenia, Egypt, Persia (now Iran), and Syria. The nomads swept along the entire length of North Africa, carrying the Berbers and other peoples with them. They moved north into Spain and Gaul. Their migrations into Asia forced other nomadic people northeast toward China. This set off another chain of Asiatic migrations that later reached into Europe.

Genghis Khan, a Mongol chief, led a great migration in the 1200's. He conquered Afghanistan, Persia, most of eastern Europe, Asia Minor, Mesopotamia, Syria, and southern China. The Mongols drove the Ottoman Turks from central Asia. The Turks slowly made their way across Asia Minor to the Balkan countries. They captured Constantinople (now Istanbul) in 1453, ending the Byzantine, or East Roman, Empire. See GENGHIS KHAN.

Seaborne Migrations. Important sea migrations include the movement of the Angles, Saxons, and Jutes into England beginning in the 450's. The most daring sea migrations were probably those of the Polynesians. They traveled thousands of miles by canoe from their homes in southeast Asia to islands in the Pacific Ocean.

Large seaborne migrations from Europe began about 1500. The Portuguese, Spanish, French, Italians, and English ventured across the oceans in search of new

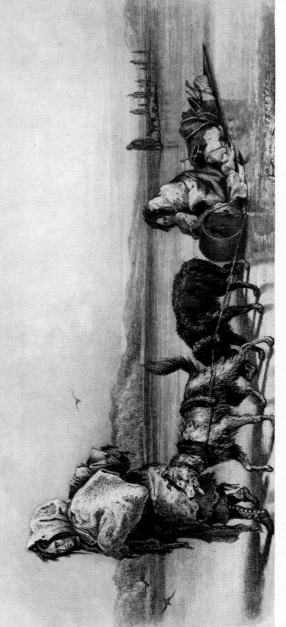

Migration or Starvation, the choices that faced many peoples, usually led to migration. The Mandan Indians of North Dakota, shown in this lithograph from a painting by Karl Bodmer, set out for places where they could find more food during the winter.

Made to accompany *Travels in the Interior of North America* by Maximilian, Prinz von Wied-Neuwied, London, 1843. Newberry Library, Ayer Collection, Chicago

land. They gradually settled the coast of America, which Christopher Columbus had discovered in 1492. This set off a new migration that lasted almost 400 years. Adventurous explorers sailed the seven seas to find new trade routes and establish colonies (see Exploration and Discovery). The major European colonial powers—France, Great Britain, Portugal, Spain, and The Netherlands—began to compete for new lands to conquer, develop, and colonize. The English set up the Virginia colony in 1607 and Plymouth Colony in 1620. Each of these colonies had about 100 settlers at the beginning. By 1700, migration and a high birth rate had increased the population of the English colonies in New England to about 275,000.

A Wave of Immigration. About 250,000 Europeans migrated to America between 1700 and 1820, and 750,000 persons arrived during the next 20 years. Most of them came from Europe. From 1840 to 1900, the United States admitted about 18,000,000 newcomers. During this period of migration, thousands of Europeans also migrated to Australia, Africa, Canada, New Zealand, and South America.

As Europeans settled in America, they forced the Indians to migrate westward. The Spaniards brought horses to the Americas. With horses, the Indians could hunt buffalo on the great Western plains. Indian tribes began to find the plains a desirable place in which to hunt, fish, and live. From all directions, they poured into the plains area in a vast migration that changed the population pattern of the United States. By horseback, the Blackfoot migrated from the north, the Sioux and Cheyenne from the east, the Comanche from the west, and the Pawnee from the south.

Migration in the 1900's. Heavy immigration continued from Europe to the United States and other countries until the early 1920's. Then many nations began to limit sharply the number of people who could immigrate. By 1930, almost all governments had placed restrictions on the number or types of people who could enter or leave their countries. These laws ended the relatively free movement of people as it had taken place in the past. During the 1930's, German Jews and other persons fleeing political and religious persecution sought refuge in other countries. Some escaped, but the great majority of oppressed people found no place in which to hide from the tyranny of dictatorships.

World War II drove millions of persons from their homes in Europe and Asia. About 50,000,000 people migrated from one country to another during the 10 years after the war, to seek political and economic security. About 20,000,000 of them were displaced persons, refugees, expellees, and escapees. Five countries that came under Communist rule—Czechoslovakia, Hungary, Poland, Romania, and Yugoslavia—expelled more than 12,000,000 Germans and sent them to Germany. Of this number, more than 8,000,000 migrants poured into West Germany. Millions of Czechs and Poles moved into lands formerly occupied by the expelled Germans. During the 1950's, thousands of anti-Communists fled to West Germany from Russian-dominated East Germany. Mass transfers of populations also took place between Bulgaria and Turkey, and between Yugoslavia and Italy. After the Hungarian revolt of 1956, nearly 200,000 refugees fled to Austria, Yugoslavia, the United States, and Great Britain.

Large shifts of populations also took place in Asia after World War II. After the partition of India in 1947, about 17,000,000 persons moved to new homes in a two-way movement of refugees between India and Pakistan. Israel became an independent country in 1948. By the end of 1955, more than 770,000 Jews had migrated to Israel, chiefly from eastern Europe, Asia, and Africa. The war between Israel and the Arab states forced more than 800,000 Arabs living in Palestine to leave their homes. Many of these Arab refugees lived in camps along the Israeli border.

Huge migrations followed the defeat of the Chinese Nationalists in 1949. More than 1,000,000 Chinese fled

United Nations

Fleeing the Weather, nomadic tribes of Kurds migrate twice a year between Iraq and Iran, crossing at a frontier bridge. They move to avoid the intense Iraqi heat in summer, and the cold winters on the plateaus of Iran.

MIGRATORY BIRD LAWS

to Formosa, and about the same number sought refuge in Hong Kong. Migrations also came after the Indochina and Korean wars in Asia. More than 800,000 refugees poured into South Vietnam from North Vietnam in the 1950's. Over 700,000 persons migrated from North Korea to South Korea by 1952 as a result of the Korean War.

During the 1900's, millions of persons in the United States have moved from one state to another. The chief currents of this migration include movements (1) from northern and southern states to western states, mainly California, (2) from the South to the North, (3) from rural areas to cities, and (4) from cities to suburbs.

The volume of internal migration fell during the depression years of the 1930's. But, during this period, many families moved out of the dust bowl region of the middle west to seek jobs in California (see MIGRANT LABOR). During World War II, job opportunities drew thousands to Western and Eastern states.

People in the United States may move to any part of the country whenever they wish to do so. Every state has received migrants from other states. Freedom of internal migration has been a factor in making the United States "the great melting-pot," because it allows immigrants and their children from other countries to mix freely with people of many nationalities.

Migration of Animals

Birds, fishes, insects, and other animals migrate regularly. Birds fly south for the winter and return north in the spring. Salmon swim from fresh water to salt water, and later return to their birthplaces to spawn and die. Caribou migrate from woodlands to tundra regions (see TUNDRA). Animals move about to find places with the most food. They seek regions with the best climate in which to breed and care for their young.

Most migrations take place between breeding grounds and regions where animals feed. For some animals, such as the lemming, the move is a one-way trip. Some scientists call this movement *emigration*, because these animals never return to their homes. For other animals, such as birds, the migration includes a return trip home. Birds move in *periodic* migrations, or at regular times during their lives. Lemmings move in *sporadic* migrations, once every 5 to 20 years. The painted lady

butterflies breed north of the Sahara Desert in Africa during the winter, then fly northward across the Mediterranean Sea to Europe, where they lay their eggs. The insects that hatch from these eggs fly southward in the fall, but the parents never return.

Scientists do not agree on the reasons that cause animals to migrate. Some believe that the increase in the number of animals causes overpopulation in one region. This threatens to wipe out the food supply, and the animals must move to other regions in search of food. We do not know how some birds and fishes find their way to the same spot to breed year after year. Many believe that sunlight and the length of day have effects on the migrations of animals from their homes.

Animals have also migrated with men traveling across the oceans. Ships brought the first rabbits to Australia in 1859, and the first English sparrows to the United States in the middle 1800's.   ROBERT C. COOK

Related Articles in WORLD BOOK include:

Animal (Animal Travelers)
Bird (Bird Migration)
Eskimo (History)
Exploration and Discovery
Goth
Hun
Immigration and Emigration
Indian, American (History)
Migrant Labor
Population
Refugee
Roman Empire (History)
Seal
War (Causes of War)

MIGRATION OF ANIMALS. See ANIMAL (Animal Travelers).

MIGRATION OF BIRDS. See BIRD (Bird Migration).

MIGRATORY BIRD CONSERVATION COMMISSION considers and approves acquisitions of land for migratory bird refuges. The land is acquired by the Bureau of Sport Fisheries and Wildlife of the Department of the Interior. The commission makes an annual report to Congress. The commission consists of the secretary of the interior, who serves as chairman; the secretary of agriculture; the secretary of commerce; two U.S. senators; and two U.S. representatives. Congress created the agency in 1929.

Critically reviewed by MIGRATORY BIRD CONSERVATION COMMISSION

MIGRATORY BIRD LAWS AND TREATIES. See BIRD (Protective Laws).

Fleeing Persecution, Hungarian patriots crossed makeshift bridges to Austria after the rebellion in Hungary in 1956. Russian troops blasted bridges across a canal at the border, but could not stop the steady flow of refugees.

MIHAILOVICH, *mee HY' loh vich,* **DRAŽA** (1893-1946), was a Yugoslav resistance leader during World War II. When the Germans invaded Yugoslavia in 1941, Mihailovich refused to surrender. He retreated to the mountains with a fighting patriot group called the *Chetniks* (see CHETNIK). The Yugoslav government-in-exile of King Peter II named Mihailovich its minister of war and the chief of staff of the Yugoslav Army in January, 1942.

But the Chetniks were not the only resistance fighters in Yugoslavia. The Communist Partisans, led by Tito, formed a second group (see TITO). Russia insisted that the Allies aid Tito more than Mihailovich. Tito accused Mihailovich of collaborating with the Germans, and the Chetniks and Communist Partisans fought each other. Mihailovich's troops dwindled to almost nothing, and Tito's men captured him in March, 1946. He was charged with treason. He denied collaborating with the Germans, but admitted receiving supplies from Italy. He was found guilty as charged and shot. Mihailovich was born near Belgrade.

ALBERT PARRY

MIKADO, *mih KAH doh,* was the ancient title of the Emperor of Japan. The term was also used by foreigners. The term *Mikado* comes from the Japanese words that mean *exalted gate.* This shows the reverence the Japanese people held for their ruler. After Chinese civilization came to Japan in the A.D. 500's, the Japanese came to call their emperor *Tenno,* which means *Heavenly Emperor.* The emperor is never referred to by his personal name. Recent emperors and their reigns are called by a name selected for them. The Emperor Hirohito is known as the *Showa Tenno* or *Showa Emperor.*

Many historians consider Japan's ruling dynasty the oldest in the world. Japanese legend assigns the date 660 B.C. to the reign of Jimmu, the first Mikado. According to tradition, he descended from the Sun Goddess. Japanese historians consider this date too early, but they trace the same family of emperors back through 124 reigns. See JAPAN (Early History).

William S. Gilbert and Arthur S. Sullivan wrote a popular operetta, *The Mikado. See GILBERT AND SULLIVAN.

MARIUS B. JANSEN

MIKAN, GEORGE. See BASKETBALL (Great Basketball Players and Coaches).

MIKIMOTO, KOKICHI. See PEARL (Cultured Pearls).

MIKLOSICH, FRANZ. See LINGUISTICS (The Comparativists).

MIKOYAN, *mee koh YAHN,* **ANASTAS** (1895-   ), was president of Russia in 1964 and 1965. He previously had served as the first vice-premier of Russia. He also served for many years as commissar of food supply and minister of trade. He first visited the U.S. in 1936 and introduced a few U.S. foods in Russia. He became supply chief of the Russian army during World War II.

Mikoyan was born in Russian Armenia, the son of a carpenter. Although he completed a theological course, he did not become a priest. He became a Communist in 1915, and took part in the Russian civil war of 1918-1920. He has been a member of the party's Central Committee since 1922, and of its Politburo since 1926.

ALBERT PARRY

MILAM, BENJAMIN. See TEXAS (History).

MILAN, *mih LAN* (pop. 1,666,300; alt. 397 ft.), is the second largest city in Italy. It is the capital of the province of Milan, and also the capital of Lombardy, one of Italy's political regions. Milan is the chief financial and banking city of northern Italy. In Italian, its name is MILANO (pronounced *mee LAH noh*) Milan lies about 165 miles west of Venice in the Lombardy plain (see ITALY [political map]). The Italian lake country can be reached easily from Milan.

Famous Landmarks. The modern appearance of Milan sets it apart from such cities as Rome, Naples, and Venice. It lacks the ancient ruins that give other Italian cities so much of their interest, but it has many famous buildings.

The Piazza del Duomo, or Cathedral Square, is the center of the city. The Duomo of Milan, the famous Gothic cathedral, towers over the square (see MILAN CATHEDRAL). Modern streets, streetcar lines, and a subway lead outward from the square in all directions, and connect with an excellent transportation system outside the city. The Archiepiscopal and Royal palaces can be seen to the south of the cathedral. In 1918, King Victor Emmanuel gave the Royal Palace of Milan, with its art collection, to the city. The Church of San Carlo Borromeo, modeled after the Pantheon at Rome, lies to the southeast of the cathedral. San Carlo Borromeo is the patron saint of Milan.

To the southeast of the cathedral stands the Ambrosian Library, a treasure house of rare books and ancient manuscripts. An elaborate system of arcades takes up the section just north of the cathedral. In this group of buildings is the Gallery of Victor Emmanuel, which contains some of Milan's finest shops. Built in the form of a cross, it is sheltered by a glass roof. Still farther north lies the Piazza della Scala. La Scala Theater, the largest opera house in Italy, faces this square. Many of the operas of Giuseppe Verdi and Giacomo Puccini were first performed there.

On a wall in the monastery dining room next to the Church of Santa Maria delle Grazie, Leonardo da Vinci painted *The Last Supper.* This treasure is the pride of Milan. The Brera Palace, however, contains the city's finest picture gallery. It has a collection of 600 paintings and works by Raphael, Titian, Bernardino Luini, the Bellinis, and other masters. The treasures of this gallery include Raphael's *Marriage of the Virgin* and Gentile Bellini's *Saint Mark.*

Education. Milan has been a leading center of culture for many hundreds of years. The Milan Conservatory of Music is world-famous. The city has a number of technical and academic schools. The Bocconi University is one of the great educational institutions of Italy.

History. Milan's written history began about 222 B.C., when the Romans took the city from the Gauls. In the time of Constantine the Great it was considered the second city of the Roman Empire. It was attacked and again partly destroyed by the Huns under Attila and again by the Goths, who killed most of the people and then burned the city. It was rebuilt, but was again burned to the ground by the Emperor Frederick I. Milan was rebuilt again and became the strongest of the great Italian cities that defeated Frederick in 1176. Milan became a duchy of the powerful Visconti family 100 years later.

Milan's La Scala, background, is a world-famous opera house. Its full name is *Teatro alla Scala* (*Theater at the Stairs*). The

The Viscontis were followed by the Sforza family, whose rule ended in 1535. Charles V then united Milan with Spain. In 1713, Milan passed into the hands of Austria, and later became the capital of the Napoleonic kingdom of Italy. Milan was restored to Austria in 1815, and continued to be the capital of the Austro-Italian kingdom until 1859. In that year it became a part of united Italy under the House of Savoy.

Milan was a thriving city at the outbreak of World War II. It had a prosperous trade in food products, and manufactured artificial silk, cars, and other commodities. It was the center of the Italian book trade.

During World War II, Allied bombs destroyed much of the city. The defeat of Italy left Milan poverty-stricken. The Italians dragged the body of Premier Mussolini through the streets of Milan. He was buried in a pauper's cemetery there until August, 1957. After World War II, the city began an extensive rebuilding program. New homes, offices, and factories rose on the damaged sites. The first skyscrapers in Italy were in Milan.

SHEPARD B. CLOUGH

See also FAIRS AND EXPOSITIONS (picture).

MILAN CATHEDRAL. The great Gothic cathedral of Milan, Italy, is the third largest church in Europe. It ranks next to Saint Peter's at Rome and the cathedral at Seville, Spain. Its foundation was laid by Gian Visconti in 1385. From 1805 to 1813, it was completed by order of Napoleon I. Marble was carried by boat on the Ticino River and the *Naviglia Grande* (Grand Canal) from the quarries of Candoglia for its construction.

The cathedral is built of white Carrara marble, in the form of a Latin cross. It is 490 feet long and 180 feet wide. The tower rises 354 feet high. It affords a beautiful view of the distant Alps and the country surrounding Milan. Over 2,000 statues set in niches in

historic structure was built in 1778 on the site of a church. A monument honors Leonardo da Vinci, who worked in Milan.

the walls cover the outside of the cathedral. A maze of marble spires, each bearing a life-size statue of a saint, Biblical character, or historical figure, rises from the roof of the cathedral. The windows tell Biblical stories in stained glass. Many great figures of Milan's history are buried in the cathedral.

BENJAMIN WEBB WHEELER

Milan Cathedral in Italy is Europe's third largest church. Its roof is covered with 135 marble spires, each bearing a statue.

455

MILAN DECREE

MILAN DECREE was a fundamental step in Napoleon's Continental System, a blockade against Great Britain. Napoleon issued it on Dec. 17, 1807, in retaliation against Britain. The British cabinet had ordered that neutral ships stop at British ports to have their cargoes examined, and to obtain licenses before going to ports under French control.

The Milan Decree provided that any ship that obeyed these instructions would be subject to capture. In 1806, Napoleon had issued the Berlin Decree, barring British ships from ports under French control. His aim now was to keep the British from using neutral ships to carry goods to these ports. Napoleon hoped that, by setting up an economic blockade of Europe, he could bring about Great Britain's downfall.

Although the Milan Decree increased the effectiveness of Napoleon's blockade, he could not adequately enforce it because the British had the most powerful navy afloat. But Napoleon did cause great distress to neutral powers. The decree led the United States to adopt severe acts to protect its commerce. Napoleon used these acts to his own advantage, and convinced the United States that he would withdraw his decree. In this way, he turned American anger against the British, and furnished a cause for the War of 1812 between the United States and Great Britain.   ROBERT B. HOLTMAN

See also CONTINENTAL SYSTEM; NAPOLEON I (Dominates Europe); WAR OF 1812 (Causes).

MILDEW is a fungus which attacks plants and some products made from plants and animals. It comes as suddenly as the dew of night. Its name comes from a Middle English word, *meoldeu*, which means *spoiled meal*. There are two main classes of mildew which damage useful plants: *powdery mildew* and *downy mildew*.

Powdery mildews attack green plants. There are about 50 different kinds of powdery mildews, and some of them can attack several different plants. About 1,500 different kinds of flowering plants may be infected by powdery mildew. These include such common plants as the gooseberry, pea, peach, rose, apple, cherry, and grape. The mildew fungus usually grows on the outside of the leaves. Sometimes it also forms flowerlike blotches on the stems and fruits. These blotches consist of a great many fungus threads that send out short branches with sucking organs into the stem or fruit. Copper sprays and sulfur dusts protect plants from powdery mildew.

Downy mildews produce yellow spots on the upper surfaces of the leaves or young fruits. The fungus grows from a single fertilized cell called a *spore*. When the mildew attacks the top of a leaf, small spores come out of the breathing pores on the bottom of the leaf. These spores produce even tinier spores which swim in the dewdrops on the surface of the leaf. The spores start new infections by sending out minute threads into the leaf.

Downy mildews attack many plants, including the grape, cucumber, cabbage, onion, and lettuce. One way to protect plants from downy mildew is to spray them with a Bordeaux mixture (see BORDEAUX MIXTURE). In 1845 and 1846, one of the downy mildews almost destroyed the Irish potato crop. A terrible famine followed in which hundreds of thousands of people died.

Mildew is a serious problem in damp tropical countries because it attacks clothes unless they are kept dry. Even in temperate regions, clothing should not be allowed to remain wet long.

Mildew often attacks bookbindings in damp climates. Books kept in damp or poorly ventilated places also are subject to mildew. To protect books from mildew, keep the volumes in an enclosed bookcase along with a form of paraformaldehyde powder. The powder evaporates to form a protective atmosphere. If books must be stored in an open place, good air circulation will help prevent the formation of mildew. Once mildew has formed, dusting or wiping may remove it from the outside of the book. However, this will not stop mildew from continuing to grow.

Several chemical solutions will prevent mildew when applied to the bookbindings. Most of the solutions contain mercurials, such as mercuric chloride. They are highly poisonous and should be used with care. One solution, which is less poisonous and is sold commercially, contains 0.2 per cent of 8-hydroxy quinoline in carbon tetrachloride.   WILLIAM F. HANNA

Scientific Classification. Mildews belong to the fungi phylum, *Eumycophyta*. The powdery mildews are in the class *Ascomycetes* and the family *Erysiphaceae*. The downy mildews are in the class *Phycomycetes* and the family *Peronosporaceae*.

See also FUNGI; FUNGICIDE; MOLD.

MILE is a unit of length. In the English system of measurement, the unit of length used to measure distances on land is called the *statute*, or *land*, *mile*. It is equal to 5,280 feet or 320 rods. The mile was first used by the Romans. It was about 5,000 feet long and contained 1,000 paces, each 5 feet in length. The term *mile* comes from *milia passuum*, the Latin words for *a thousand paces*. Around the year 1500, the 5,000 feet of the Roman mile was changed to the 5,280 feet of today, although many countries still kept their own length for the mile. Most continental European countries have officially adopted the kilometer as their standard. A kilometer equals 3,280.8 feet, or about $\frac{5}{8}$ of a mile.

Distances on the sea are measured in *nautical*, *geographical*, or *sea miles*. The nautical mile is obtained by dividing the circumference of the earth into 360 degrees and then dividing each degree into 60 minutes. One nautical mile equals one minute, or is $\frac{21}{1,600}$ of the circumference of the earth. The *international nautical mile* used in the United States and other countries equals 6,076.11549 feet. This makes the international nautical mile equal to 1.15079 statute or land miles.

A "knot" is a unit of speed, not of length. A ship traveling one nautical mile per hour is said to have a speed of *one knot*.

See also FURLONG; KILOMETER; KNOT; LEAGUE; WEIGHTS AND MEASURES.

MILES, NELSON APPLETON (1839-1925), a noted American soldier, fought in the Civil War, the Indian wars, and the Spanish-American War. He is an outstanding example of a citizen soldier, one who rose to the rank of lieutenant general in the United States Army without a formal military education.

Miles entered the army as a volunteer captain when the Civil War started. He fought in nearly every battle in the East. He was wounded several times, and won rapid promotion. At the age of 26, he became a major   PHILIP S. JONES

one mile

Chicago Aerial Industries, Inc.

How Long Is a Mile? Different miles measure distances on land, on the sea, and in the air. The ancient Roman mile was 5,000 feet. The metric system uses kilometers to measure distances. An air or sea mile equals $\frac{1}{60}$ of one degree of the distance around the earth. In the 1500's, Englishmen measured distances in 660-foot furlongs, so Queen Elizabeth I made the land or statute mile 8 furlongs, or 5,280 feet.

Roman Mile 5,000 Feet

Kilometer 3,280.8 Feet

Air or Sea (Nautical) Mile 6,076.1 Feet

Land or Statute Mile 5,280 Feet

general of volunteers and commanded an Army corps. He entered the regular Army in 1865. For the next 15 years, he directed campaigns against Indians in the West. In 1894, Miles commanded the troops that President Grover Cleveland sent to Chicago following the Pullman Strike disorders. In 1895, he became commanding general of the Army. Miles headed the expedition to Puerto Rico in 1898, during the Spanish-American War, and retired in 1903. He was born near Westminster, Mass.   T. HARRY WILLIAMS

MILETUS, *my LEE tus,* was one of the largest cities of ancient Greece. It stood on the western coast of Asia Minor in the district of Ionia (see GREECE, ANCIENT [color map]). Miletus' excellent harbor made the city an important trading center. In the 700's and 600's B.C., colonists from Miletus settled along the coast of the Hellespont (a channel now called the Dardanelles) and Black Sea. About 600 B.C., Thales founded the famous Milesian school of philosophy.

The city had a privileged position when the Persians took over the area in the mid-500's B.C. But in 499 B.C., the Milesian ruler Aristagoras led the Ionian Greeks in an unsuccessful revolt, and the Persians looted Miletus in 494 B.C. Miletus lost importance when its harbor silted up in the A.D. 400's.   DONALD W. BRADEEN

MILHAUD, DARIUS *(mee YOH, dah RYOOS)* (1892-   ), is a French-born composer noted for his works for the stage. Milhaud has written 15 operas, 13 ballets, and music for other ballets and for motion pictures. The French poet Paul Claudel wrote the *librettos* (words) for several of Milhaud's stage works, including his most famous opera, *Christophe Colomb* (1928). Milhaud's best-known ballet, *The Creation of the World* (1923), reflects his interest in jazz.

Milhaud was born in Aix-en-Provence in southern France, and this region inspired his *Suite Provençale* for orchestra (1936). Milhaud received his music training at

the Paris Conservatory from 1910 to 1915. In 1917 and 1918, he served with the French Embassy in Rio de Janeiro, Brazil, and became acquainted with Brazilian popular music. Milhaud used this music in *Saudads do Brasil* (*Memories of Brazil,* 1920-1921), which he composed both for orchestra and for piano.

During the 1920's, Milhaud belonged to a group of young French composers called *Les Six.* He left France in 1940 during World War II. That year, he joined the faculty of the music department at Mills College in Oakland, Calif.   GILBERT CHASE

MILHOUS, KATHERINE (1894-   ), an American author and illustrator of children's books, received the Caldecott medal in 1951 for *The Egg Tree.* She was born in Philadelphia. Her books include *Lovina, Herodia, Appolonia's Valentine,* and *With Bells On.*   RUTH HILL VIGUERS

MILITARY ACADEMY, UNITED STATES. See UNITED STATES MILITARY ACADEMY.

MILITARY AIRCRAFT. See AIR FORCE; AIR FORCE, UNITED STATES; BOMBER; GUIDED MISSILE; HELICOPTER.

MILITARY AIRLIFT COMMAND (MAC) provides air transportation of more than 350,000 tons of cargo and about $1\frac{1}{2}$ million U.S. armed forces military personnel each year. It also provides air weather services, rescue and recovery, and charting and photographic services. It is a major command of the U.S. Air Force.

MAC is the world's largest air transport service. It has routes stretching more than 100,000 miles throughout the world. The 21st Air Force handles routes across the Atlantic and Caribbean. The 22nd Air Force flies routes in the United States and across the Pacific. In 1948, the Air Force and Navy air transport operations were merged to form the Military Air Transport Service (MATS). In 1966, MATS became MAC, and an Air Force responsibility. Headquarters are at Scott Air Force Base, near Belleville, Ill.   RICHARD M. SKINNER

MILITARY ATTACHÉ. See ATTACHÉ.

457

MILITARY DISCHARGE

MILITARY DISCHARGE ends a person's period of service in the armed forces. Members of the Armed Forces of the United States receive one of five types of discharges: (1) honorable, (2) general, (3) undesirable, (4) bad conduct, and (5) dishonorable.

Honorable discharges are issued to all those whose military behavior has been proper and whose performance of duty has been "proficient and industrious." A person holding such a discharge is entitled to all benefits available to veterans.

General discharges are given to those whose military records do not entitle them to an honorable discharge. A general discharge may be issued if a person has been found guilty by a general court-martial in any service. Veterans with general discharges are eligible for the same benefits as those holding honorable discharges.

Undesirable discharges are given to persons considered unfit for military service. They cancel many veteran benefits, and prohibit re-enlistment in any service.

Bad conduct discharges are given for reasons such as absence without leave, insubordination, and destruction of private property. They deprive the holder of all veteran benefits and certain citizenship rights.

Dishonorable discharges may be given for such reasons as theft, desertion, and destruction of government property. They cancel all veteran benefits and some citizenship rights.

CHARLES B. MACDONALD

MILITARY INSIGNIA. See INSIGNIA; also the color pictures in AIR FORCE, UNITED STATES; ARMY, UNITED STATES; MARINE CORPS, UNITED STATES; NAVY, UNITED STATES.

MILITARY JUSTICE, UNIFORM CODE OF. See UNIFORM CODE OF MILITARY JUSTICE.

MILITARY LAW. See MARTIAL LAW.

MILITARY POLICE. The armed forces of the United States have their own trained policemen. On military posts, these men have powers similar to those of civil police, including authority to arrest where necessary. Military policemen keep order among the soldiers on

leave in cities near military posts. They check soldiers' papers and tickets at railway stations. Under combat conditions, they help move civilians, direct traffic, and guard enemy prisoners. Military policemen learn various methods of fighting with weapons such as the knife and hand grenade, and a form of wrestling called judo.

Police duties are carried out by Military Police (MP) for the Army and Marine Corps, by the Shore Patrol (SP) for the Navy and Coast Guard, and by the Air Police (AP) for the Air Force.

JOHN W. WADE

See also AIR POLICE; PROVOST MARSHAL GENERAL; SHORE PATROL.

MILITARY PREPAREDNESS. See NATIONAL DEFENSE.

MILITARY SCHOOL is an institution that educates and trains persons in military arts and sciences. All major countries operate military schools. Many U.S. military schools are privately operated.

Government Military Schools. In the United States, each branch of the armed forces has its own military schools. Courses in these schools for enlisted men and women range from the repair of guided missiles to food service. The armed forces maintain service academies, officer-candidate schools, and reserve officers training corps for persons learning to become officers. Service academies are the U.S. Air Force Academy at Colorado Springs, Colo.; the U.S. Coast Guard Academy at New London, Conn.; the U.S. Military Academy at West Point, N.Y.; and the U.S. Naval Academy at Annapolis, Md.

Military schools prepare officers for duties they may have to perform in peace or war. Courses at the first level cover specialized subjects. Schools at the next level stress command and staff work. They include the Air Command and Staff College and Air War College of Air University, Army War College, Command and General Staff College, Marine Corps Senior School, Naval Postgraduate School, and the Naval War College. Joint-service colleges operate at the highest level. They are the Armed Forces Staff College in Norfolk, Va., and the Industrial College of the Armed Forces and the National War College, both in Washington, D.C.

Pennsylvania Military College Cadets Snap to "Eyes Right" as They Pass in Review.

H. Armstrong Roberts

Private Military Schools and Colleges train boys of junior high school, high school, and college age. Students wear distinctive uniforms, and learn the fundamentals of military training, strategy, and tactics. Leading private military schools include Culver Military Academy in Culver, Ind.; Staunton Military Academy in Staunton, Va.; The Citadel in Charleston, S.C.; and Virginia Military Institute in Lexington, Va.

In Other Countries. Great Britain trains its officers at the Royal Military Academy in Sandhurst, the Army Staff College in Camberley, the Joint Services Staff College in Latimer, and the Imperial Defense College in London. Canada has the Royal Military College of Canada in Kingston, Ont., Royal Roads Military College near Victoria, B.C., and Collège militaire royal de Saint-Jean in St. Jean, Que. The chief French military school is Saint-Cyr, in Coëtquidan, Brittany. Russia has the Frunze Academy in Moscow.   CHARLES B. MACDONALD

Related Articles in WORLD BOOK include:

Air University	Quantico Marine Corps Schools
Armed Forces Staff	Royal Military College of Canada
College	United States Air Force Academy
Army War College	United States Coast Guard
Citadel, The	Academy
Industrial College of	United States Military Academy
the Armed Forces	United States Naval Academy
National War College	Virginia Military Institute
Naval War College	

MILITARY SCIENCE is the study of scientific principles which control the conduct of war. It is also the application of those principles to battle conditions. Military science covers five areas. They are tactics, strategy, logistics, engineering, and communications.

Related Articles in WORLD BOOK include:

Air Force	Logistics
Air Force, U.S.	Marine Corps, U.S.	Navy
Army	Military Training	Navy, U.S.
Army, U.S.		War

MILITARY SERVICE, COMPULSORY. See DRAFT, MILITARY.

MILITARY TANK. See TANK, MILITARY.

MILITARY TRAINING is training in the art and science of war. Modern military training is a great deal more complex than in ancient times. Battles then involved relatively simple formations, weapons, and equipment. Today, fighting troops must understand and be prepared to use mechanized equipment and intricate scientific instruments. They must be backed up by many more service troops than there are actual fighters. During World War II, nations trained both men and women in a variety of jobs. In some countries, such as Russia, women also engaged in combat.

All soldiers first learn to obey orders. Combat soldiers learn to handle various types of weapons: machine guns, bayonets, rifles, pistols, and grenades. They learn how to handle explosives. A soldier assigned to some specialized branch of the army receives additional training for his particular job. He may learn to drive an automobile, to jump from an airplane, or build a bridge.

Training Schools. The army, navy, and air force maintain a system of schools or training stations for officers and enlisted personnel. In addition, each of these branches of the service has specialized schools for higher officer training. These include the Army War College, the Naval War College, and the Air University. Schools operated jointly by the services include the Armed Forces Staff College, the Industrial College

of the Armed Forces, and the National War College. The National War College teaches strategy and related subjects in politics, economics, and social problems. The Industrial College of the Armed Forces prepares officers for duties connected with *procurement* (purchase), storage, and maintenance of supplies and equipment.

Military Training for Civilians. Many colleges and universities have Reserve Officers Training Corps units of the army, navy, and air force, which offer instruction for prospective officers. Students who successfully complete such training may be eligible for commissions in the regular army, navy, or air force. The army also conducts a junior branch of its ROTC in high schools and preparatory schools. The National Guard and Air National Guard are other volunteer organizations offering training to civilians. The individual states and territories conduct these groups.

Compulsory Military Training. From the days of the ancient Romans, many European countries have tried some form of enforced military service. France introduced a conscription law in 1792. Germany made the greatest progress in developing a military machine under nationwide conscription. It began its program after the Franco-Prussian War.

In the United States, the federal government first tried compulsory military training during the Civil War. Conscription laws providing for military training for male citizens were also in effect in the United States during World Wars I and II. The first U.S. peacetime draft law was enacted in 1940.   CHARLES B. MACDONALD

Related Articles in WORLD BOOK include:

Air Force, United States	National Guard
Army, United States	Navy, United States
Draft, Military	Reserve Officers
Military School	Training Corps
Militia	Selective Service
National Defense	System

MILITARY UNIFORM. See UNIFORM.

MILITIA, *muh LISH uh,* includes all able-bodied men liable to be called into the armed forces in time of national emergency. The U.S. militia includes the Air Force Reserve, Air National Guard, Army National Guard, Marine Corps Reserve, and Naval Reserve.

Each of the 13 colonies in America required its citizens to enroll and train in the militia. Militiamen formed almost half of the Continental Army that fought in the American Revolutionary War. The United States Constitution gave Congress the right to call up the militia to "execute the laws of the Union."

The Militia Act of 1792 placed every "free able-bodied white male citizen" at the age of 18 in the militia. But it left the control and training of these units to each state. The act of 1903 made all male citizens subject to military service, and set up the National Guard as the organized militia (see NATIONAL GUARD).

The governments of ancient Egypt, Greece, and Rome all formed militias. The Spartans, for example, used the militia to organize their professional armies. Switzerland's militia system was set up in 1291. Militiamen in feudal England had to keep armor and weapons that were inspected twice a year.   CHARLES B. MACDONALD

See also DRAFT, MILITARY (History); PURITAN (picture); SWITZERLAND (Defense).

MILK is often called "the most nearly perfect food." We drink milk as a liquid, and eat it in butter, cheese, ice cream, and other foods. Milk contains all the *nutrients* (food elements) that we need for growth and good health. Other foods contain these same nutrients. But only milk has these elements in such amounts that they can work as a "team." That is why milk does more for our bodies than any other single food.

Cows provide most of the milk used in the United States and Canada. But other animals produce the main supply of milk in many parts of the world. Goats rank second to cows as suppliers of milk. Their milk is popular in the Mediterranean region, Norway, Switzerland, Latin America, parts of Asia and Africa, and in the mountain areas of the southwestern United States. Camels furnish milk in the deserts of Arabia and Central Asia. Some South Americans drink llama milk. In Arctic regions, people get milk from reindeer. Sheep serve as milk animals in Spain, Italy, the Balkans, and The Netherlands. The water buffalo and the Brahman supply milk in the hot, wet jungles of India, in the Philippines, and in many parts of Asia.

Many products besides food are made with certain parts of milk. For example, manufacturers use a part of milk called *casein* to make waterproof glues, cold-water paints, plastics, and certain cements. Another part of milk, called *lactose*, is used in medicines.

Food Values of Milk

Milk is one of the easiest foods for the body to digest. It contains proteins, carbohydrates, fats, minerals, and vitamins, all the nutrients needed for healthy bodies and sturdy bones and teeth. An 8-ounce glass of milk supplies about 170 calories of energy (see CALORIE).

All kinds of milk, human or animal, contain the same nutrients. But the amounts differ. For example, cows' milk averages about 3.5 per cent proteins, 3.8 per cent fats, 4.8 per cent carbohydrates, 0.7 per cent minerals, and 87.2 per cent water. Reindeer milk has almost 4½ times as much fat, 3 times as much protein, and 2 times as much minerals. But it contains only about half as much sugar as cows' milk. Human milk has fewer proteins and minerals than cows' milk, and about 1½ times as much sugar.

Milk is the first food of newborn babies, whether they are breast-fed or bottle-fed. Children who drink milk grow faster than those on the same diets, but who do not drink milk. Milk is a "protective" food that makes up deficiencies in the diet. Doctors urge children and teen-agers to drink from 1½ pints to 1 quart of milk daily. They recommend 1 pint of milk daily for adults, and from 1 quart to 1½ quarts for mothers-to-be and mothers who are nursing their babies.

Proteins in milk furnish energy and serve as important body-building blocks. Nutrition experts call them *complete* proteins, because they contain every amino acid essential for building blood and tissue (see AMINO ACID). They not only have more amino acids than plant proteins, but also provide them in greater amounts than the proteins of eggs and most meats. One quart of cows' milk supplies between 30 and 35 grams of protein, or about half the daily requirement for an adult. About four fifths of this protein is *casein*, and the rest consists mostly of *lactalbumin* and *lactglobulin*. Casein occurs only in milk, and gives milk its white color (see CASEIN). Lactalbumin is similar to, but not exactly like, the albumin found in our blood. Scientists believe lactoglobulin is the same as serum globulin in the blood. Some chemical analyses have shown traces of other proteins, such as *fibrin*, in milk. See PROTEIN.

Fats. Milk fat, sometimes called *butterfat*, provides energy and essential fatty acids that our bodies cannot make. Fat also gives milk its flavor. Milk fat contains the vitamins A, D, E, and K; traces of lecithin and cholesterol; and carotene, a pigment that supplies vitamin A and gives milk a golden tint. A quart of cows' milk contains from 34 to 44 grams of fat in the form of beadlike *globules* that the unaided eye cannot see. A drop of milk contains about 100,000,000 fat globules. When milk stands for awhile, the lightweight globules rise to the top, forming a layer of cream. See FAT.

Carbohydrates. *Lactose* (milk sugar) makes up most of the carbohydrate content of milk, along with traces

U.S. Dept. of Agriculture

The Morning Milk Delivery is a familiar sight in most communities. The milkman is the last link in the chain of workers who bring this health-giving food from farm to table.

Glenn H. Beck, the contributor of this article, is Dean of Agriculture at Kansas State University.

of *glucose* (another sugar). Bodies burn milk sugar for energy. Doctors believe that lactose, combining with calcium and phosphorus in milk, helps build strong bones and teeth. A quart of cows' milk contains from 45 to 50 grams of lactose. See CARBOHYDRATE.

Minerals. Milk contains calcium, phosphorus, potassium, sodium, sulfur, magnesium, and chlorine. It has smaller amounts of iodine, iron, copper, manganese, zinc, and aluminum. Calcium and phosphorus are the most important milk minerals. Both are needed for building bones and teeth. Milk is our most important food source of calcium. One quart contains about 1.2 grams of calcium and 0.8 grams of phosphorus.

Vitamins. Few natural foods besides milk contain as many vitamins in amounts so close to what our bodies need. Cows' milk is an excellent source of vitamin A and vitamin B_2 (riboflavin), and a good source of vitamin B_1 (thiamine). It has some vitamin D, but not enough to supply the needs of children. Other vitamins in milk include vitamin B_6 (pyridoxine), vitamin B_{12}, vitamin C (ascorbic acid), vitamin E (alphatocopherol), vitamin K, niacin (nicotinic acid), pantothenic acid, folic acid, biotin, inositol, choline, p-amino-benzoic acid, and citrin. See VITAMIN.

From Farm to Table

Every state of the United States and every province of Canada produces milk. The chief dairy belt in the United States extends from Minnesota to Maine. It includes the three leading milk-producing states: Minnesota, New York, and Wisconsin. Ontario and Quebec lead in Canadian milk production.

Production. Milk as it comes from the cow is called *raw milk.* Some farmers still milk cows by hand. But most farmers use milking machines (see MILKING MACHINE). Farmers store fresh milk in stainless steel cans, each holding 8 or 10 gallons. The cans of milk are kept in a *cooler* that may be a refrigerated compartment or a tank of cold water. Many dairy farmers pipe milk directly from the milking machines into a refrigerated storage tank instead of using cans.

The composition of milk depends mainly on the breed of the cows. The flavor and quality of milk vary according to how the cows are cared for, what they are fed, and how the milk is handled. Milk must be kept cool and clean from the moment it comes from the cows. Bacteria multiply rapidly unless milk is kept at temperatures below 60°F. Wise dairy farmers keep their cows and barns clean, and sterilize all milking utensils.

In spite of these measures, disease-producing bacteria sometimes get into raw milk. Because of this, raw milk is generally not considered safe to drink unless it has been certified. All *certified milk* is produced under conditions and regulations set by the American Association of Medical Milk Commissions. Local medical milk commissions supervise the quality of certified milk. They do this by laboratory examination of milk, sanitary inspection of farms and dairies, veterinary inspection of cows, and medical examination of all persons who handle the milk on the farm or in the dairy.

Most cities and towns have special laws dealing with the production of *Grade A* milk. They deal generally with the health of cows and workers, and with sanitary conditions at farms and processing plants. Most Grade A laws require milk to be pasteurized.

Transportation. Insulated trucks usually pick up milk from dairy farms every day. They bring the milk directly to processing plants, or to receiving stations that ship it to processing plants. Milk must be protected against exposure to bacteria, and must be kept cool until it reaches the processing plants. Here, technicians immediately check its flavor and temperature. They reject any milk that does not meet the required high standards for quality and for the prevention of contamination and spoilage.

Testing. Milk processors make many tests to ensure the quality and purity of milk. Trained laboratory technicians test milk upon arrival, and during and after processing. Odor, taste, and appearance are tested by smelling, tasting, and observing the milk.

The Babcock Test, invented in 1890 by Stephen M. Babcock of the University of Wisconsin, shows the butterfat content of milk. Milk is mixed with sulfuric acid, which melts the fat. A bottle of this mixture is whirled in a machine called a *centrifuge.* The percentage of fat can be read on a scale on the bottle. See BABCOCK, STEPHEN M.

The Methylene Blue Test is a simple method of indicating the approximate number of bacteria in milk. This blue dye is added to a small quantity of milk which is heated and examined every hour. The longer it takes the blue color to disappear, the fewer bacteria are present.

The Lactometer determines the weight of milk compared to an equal amount of water. It shows whether the milk has been watered, or whether any cream has been removed. It also shows the amount of solids in milk.

The Acidity Test shows the amount of acid in milk. Milk that contains too much acid tastes sour and cannot be properly processed. An alkaline solution is added to a sample of milk, and a color indicator, such as phenolphthalein, shows the acid content (see ALKALI; PHENOLPHTHALEIN).

The Breed Test, a method of counting bacteria in milk, was developed by R. S. Breed of Geneva, N.Y., in 1925. A tiny drop of milk is spread on a glass slide. After it is dried and stained, the bacteria can be counted under a microscope.

The Standard Plate Count is another way of counting bacteria in milk. Milk diluted with sterile distilled water is placed in a germ-free dish and mixed with a solution called sterile agar medium (see AGAR-AGAR).

--- **INTERESTING FACTS ABOUT MILK** ---

California Cows average the highest milk production in the United States, about 5,000 quarts each a year.
Daily Food for a dairy cow includes 10 to 20 gallons of water, up to 45 pounds of *roughage* (hay and silage), and as much as 12 pounds of grain and other concentrates.
Dairy Cows are descended from wild cattle that once roamed the forests of northeastern Europe.
Dairy Industry began in America in 1611 when dairy cows were brought to the Jamestown colony in Virginia.
Marco Polo reported in the 1300's that every Tartar Mongol warrior carried 10 pounds of dried milk as part of his food rations.
Mosaics from Mesopotamia about 5,000 years old show cows being milked.
One-Fourth the total weight of the food used in the United States consists of milk and other dairy products.

MILK

—FROM THE FARM TO YOUR HOME

The cow turns grass and grain into milk.

F.S.A.

She is milked at least twice a day.

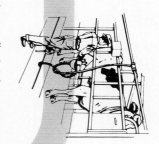

Each cow's milk production record is kept.

A veterinarian tests her health regularly.

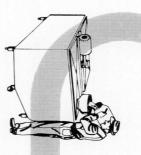

In the milkhouse, the warm milk is strained and cooled immediately.

462

Each day a milk truck takes milk to a city plant or . . . .

All equipment is washed, sterilized, and stored in the milkhouse.

. . . . to a country receiving station. Here the milk is weighed, tested, cooled, and shipped to a city plant by tank truck or tank car.

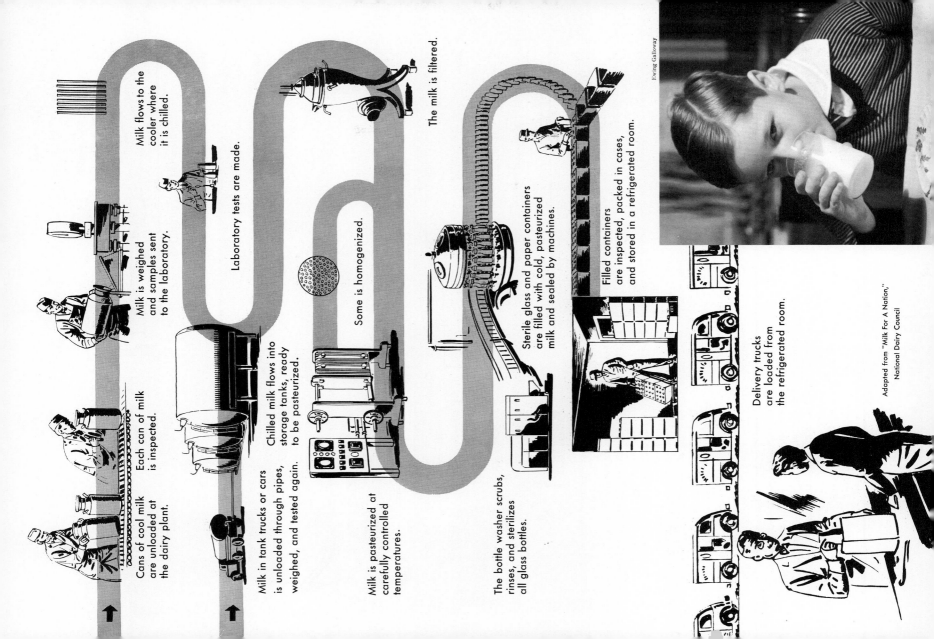

Cans of cool milk are unloaded at the dairy plant.

Each can of milk is inspected.

Milk in tank trucks or cars is unloaded through pipes, weighed, and tested again.

Milk is weighed and samples sent to the laboratory.

Laboratory tests are made.

Milk flows to the cooler where it is chilled.

Chilled milk flows into storage tanks, ready to be pasteurized.

Milk is pasteurized at carefully controlled temperatures.

Some is homogenized.

The milk is filtered.

The bottle washer scrubs, rinses, and sterilizes all glass bottles.

Sterile glass and paper containers are filled with cold, pasteurized milk and sealed by machines.

Filled containers are inspected, packed in cases, and stored in a refrigerated room.

Delivery trucks are loaded from the refrigerated room.

Adapted from "Milk For A Nation," National Dairy Council

Ewing Galloway

USES OF MILK

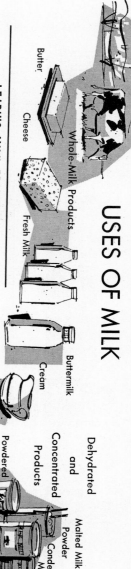

Butter

Cheese

Fresh Milk

Whole-Milk Products

Buttermilk

Cream

Dehydrated and Concentrated Products

Malted Milk Powder

Powdered Milk

Condensed Milk

Evaporated Milk

Lactose

Special Diets

Drugs

Baby Foods

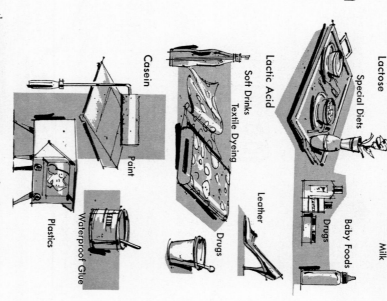

Casein

Lactic Acid

Soft Drinks

Textile Dyeing

Leather

Drugs

Paint

Plastics

Waterproof Glue

LEADING MILK PRODUCING STATES AND PROVINCES

U.S. gallons of milk produced in 1967

State/Province	Gallons
Wisconsin	2,157,791,000 gal.
New York	1,209,419,000 gal.
Minnesota	1,199,535,000 gal.
California	1,014,419,000 gal.
Pennsylvania	797,209,000 gal.
Ontario	774,320,000 gal.
Quebec	770,807,000 gal.
Iowa	654,302,000 gal.
Ohio	550,116,000 gal.
Michigan	545,698,000 gal.

Sources: U.S. Department of Agriculture; Dominion Bureau of Statistics

Bacteria grow in this medium and form colonies which appear as small, scattered spots that can be counted.

Pasteurization. After the milk has been tested it is often put through a *clarifier*. This machine gets rid of any foreign object such as hair or dust. Then milk is *pasteurized*, or heated to kill disease-causing bacteria. In the United States, almost all milk sold for drinking is pasteurized, including Certified Milk and Grade A milk.

There are two common methods of pasteurization: (1) high-temperature, and (2) low-temperature. In the *high-temperature* process, also called the *flash* or *hot-short-time* method, the milk is quickly heated to at least 161° F., kept at that temperature for at least 15 seconds, and immediately cooled. In the *low-temperature* or *holding* method, milk is heated to at least 145° F. for at least 30 minutes. Most large dairy plants use the high-temperature method. See PASTEURIZATION.

Homogenization. Before pasteurization, milk may be homogenized. This process breaks up the fat globules and distributes the fat equally throughout the milk so that it does not rise to the top. It forces the milk through tiny openings at a pressure of about 2,000 pounds per square inch. This gives every drop of homogenized milk

the same cream content as every other drop. More than three-fourths of the milk sold in the United States is homogenized. See HOMOGENIZATION.

Adding Vitamins and Minerals. Milk normally contains some vitamin D, but many farmers and dairies increase its vitamin D content. This is done in one of three ways: (1) by *irradiation* (exposing the milk to ultraviolet light); (2) by feeding the cows irradiated yeast that is rich in vitamin D; or (3) by adding concentrated vitamin D directly to the milk. Some dairies increase the amounts of all vitamins and some of the minerals in milk. Such milk is often sold as *fortified milk*.

Bottling. After the milk is processed, pipes carry it from large tanks to automatic bottling and capping machines. These machines fill sterilized glass bottles or coated paper containers, and cap or seal them in one operation. Some machines fill 175 quarts of milk a minute. The filled containers are put in cases and stored in a refrigerated room until they are loaded onto refrigerated delivery trucks.

Other Processes. Only about half the milk produced in the United States is processed into the milk we drink. The rest is made into such dairy products as butter, cheese, and ice cream (see BUTTER; CHEESE; ICE CREAM).

Mechanical separation removes the fat from whole milk and provides cream for bottling and buttermaking. Cream separation leaves behind skim milk which is bottled as a low-calorie drink. Skim milk also may be further processed to make cottage cheese and buttermilk (see BUTTERMILK).

Concentration and canning processes provide condensed milk and evaporated milk (see CONDENSED MILK; EVAPORATED MILK). Special *dehydration* (drying) processes produce nonfat dry milk solids from skim milk; dry whole milk powder; and malted-milk powder from a mixture of barley malt, whole milk, and wheat flour. Fermented milk foods include yogurt and acidophilus milk (see ACIDOPHILUS MILK; YOGURT). Treating milk with mechanical action and enzymes produces *soft-curd* milks (see ENZYME). Softening the curd makes milk easier to digest. These milks are used for infant foods and special diets.

The Milk Industry

The milk industry is one of the largest in the United States. More than 1½ million farmers earn all, or a large part, of their income from dairying. Over 30,000 dealers process and deliver milk and milk products. They employ more than 200,000 workers to bring milk from farms to plants, process it in the plants, and deliver it to consumers. Thousands of other plants make evaporated, condensed, and powdered milks; cheeses; and other milk products. These plants employ more than 100,000 persons. About 125 billion pounds, or 58 billion quarts, of milk are produced in the United States each year. This amounts to an average of about four-fifths of a quart a day for every person. Consumption is about evenly divided between fresh milk and manufactured milk foods. Canada produces about 8½ billion quarts of milk yearly.

History

No one really knows how long man has used milk and milk products. Records from ancient Babylon, Egypt, and India show that men raised dairy cattle at least 6,000 years ago.

For hundreds of years, the family cow served as the chief source of milk. A family used as much milk as it needed, and sold or traded the rest to neighbors. This was especially common in colonial days in the United States, and continued until about the 1850's. Gradually, farmers began owning several cows, and supplied milk to nearby homes.

With the growth of cities, laws prohibited keeping cows within city limits. Dairy farmers outside the cities then began to increase the size of their herds and to establish dairy businesses. Cheese and butter factories began operating about 1850. Eventually, plants developed for processing fresh milk. Glass jars and bottles began to be used around 1885. The invention of a bottle filler in 1886 made filling easier and faster than by hand.

In the 1850's, cities began to control the sale of milk by law. Some early laws made it illegal to add water to milk or to remove cream from it. The first such law was passed in Boston in 1856. That same year, Gail Borden (1801-1874), a surveyor and inventor, received a patent for the first successful milk-condensing process. Early laws did not cover the cleanliness of milk, and it became a common practice to add chemical preservatives. When some of these were found to be harmful, laws prohibited their use. City and state supervision of the milk industry developed gradually.

In the late 1800's, French scientist Louis Pasteur discovered pasteurization, the process of killing bacteria in fluids by heat. About 20 years later, a German scientist named Franz Von Soxhlet (1848-1926) proposed boiling milk before feeding it to babies. By 1897, commercial pasteurization had been introduced in some American cities. Later, practically all cities and towns required pasteurization. With the development of pasteurizing equipment, separators, coolers, and other processing machinery, more and more milk came to be processed in plants. These developed into the large modern dairy plants of today.

GLENN H. BECK

Related Articles in WORLD BOOK include:

MILK PRODUCTS

Acidophilus Milk	Evaporated Milk
Butter	Ice Cream
Buttermilk	Yogurt
Casein	
Cheese	
Condensed Milk	

PRODUCING MILK

Dairying	Milking Machine
Dehydration	Pasteurization
Farm and Farming	Pure Food and
Homogenization	Drug Laws

SOURCES OF MILK

Camel	Reindeer
Cattle (Dairy Cattle)	Sheep
Goat (Domestic Goats)	Water Buffalo
Llama	Yak

Outline

I. Food Values of Milk
 A. Proteins C. Carbohydrates E. Vitamins
 B. Fats D. Minerals

II. From Farm to Table
 A. Production F. Adding Vitamins
 B. Transportation and Minerals
 C. Testing G. Bottling
 D. Pasteurization H. Other Processes
 E. Homogenization

III. The Milk Industry

IV. History

Questions

How much milk should children and teen agers drink each day? Adults?

How is milk used other than as a food?

What are some common milk food products?

What diseases may be carried by infected milk? How do germs get into milk?

What happens to milk during pasteurization? Homogenization?

Why is milk considered the "most nearly perfect food"?

What animals besides cows furnish milk for human use?

What are the three leading milk-producing states?

What is Certified milk? Grade A milk? Fortified milk? Raw milk?

What are the two most common methods of pasteurization?

MILK GLASS. See GLASSWARE (Milk Glass).
MILK RIVER. See MONTANA (Rivers).

MILK SNAKE

MILK SNAKE. One type of king snake is called *milk snake* because farmers once believed that it took milk from cows. Today, scientists know that no snake is physically able to take milk from a cow. But any snake might drink milk it finds in a pail, mistaking it for water. Like other king snakes, the milk snake helps man by killing harmful rodents, such as rats and mice. It often helps farmers by coming into barnyards to hunt for rodents that nest there.

The milk snake may be 4 feet long, whereas other king snakes grow to be 6 feet in length. Milk snakes are gray with dark-bordered chestnut blotches on the back and sides. However, milk snakes found in the Western and Southern United States vary in size and color pattern. Some persons also call these snakes *house snakes*.

Scientific Classification. The milk snake is a member of the common snake family, *Colubridae*. It is genus *Lampropeltis*, species *L. doliata*.

See also KING SNAKE.

The Milk Snake Is Valuable to Farmers because it eats the rats and mice that live in and around farm buildings.

New York Zoological Society

CLIFFORD H. POPE

MILK SUGAR. See SUGAR (Milk Sugar); MILK (Carbohydrates).

MILKING MACHINE is a device that milks cows. A motor-driven vacuum pump sucks the milk through rubber-lined cups that fit over the cow's teats. Hoses link the cups to the pump. The milk flows into a closed pail or through a pipeline to a tank. The action of the cups resembles the sucking of a calf. The pump creates alternately a vacuum and pressure in the cups. Part of the time the cups milk the cow, and part of the time they are idle or massage the teats. This permits blood to circulate in the teats to keep them healthy.

Most modern dairy farms use milking machines. The machines provide a closed system from the cow to the milk container. This keeps the milk cleaner than the milk from hand-milked cows. The machines lower the cost of producing milk by reducing the labor needed to milk a herd of cows.

Anna Baldwin, an American woman, patented the first suction milking machine in 1878. However, a Swedish engineer, Carl Gustaf de Laval (1845-1913), developed the first commercially successful machine. It grew out of a series of models he built, starting in 1894, and it went on the market in 1918.

A. D. LONGHOUSE

See also CATTLE (color picture: Guernseys in a Dairy Barn); DAIRYING (The Milking Parlor of a Dairy).

MILKING SHORTHORN. See CATTLE (Dual-Purpose Cattle; color picture: Milking Shorthorn); DAIRYING (Dairy Cattle).

MILKWEED is the name of several plants which have tufts of silky hairs on the seeds, and stout stems filled with a milky juice. The *common milkweed* is one of the best-known milkweeds in North America. It grows along roadsides and in fields and waste places as far south as Georgia and Kansas.

The stems of the common milkweed stand about 4 feet high, and bear large, hairy, pale-green leaves on short stalks. The purplish flowers grow in clusters at the tip of the stem. The flowers bloom from June to August, and have a sweet odor which attracts insects. Each flower is shaped so that an insect has to walk through masses of pollen before it reaches the nectar. The insect then flies away with two bundles of pollen strapped together like saddlebags on its legs, and thus brings about *cross-pollination* (see POLLEN AND POLLINATION).

In the autumn, large, rough seed pods take the place of the flower clusters of the milkweed. When the pods ripen and burst open, clouds of seeds are scattered by the wind. The milkweed can also reproduce itself from its creeping roots. In 1942, milkweed floss was collected as a wartime substitute for the kapok fiber used in life belts. The juice of the milkweed contains small amounts of a rubberlike substance. One of the most attractive milkweeds is the brilliant *butterfly weed*.

Scientific Classification. The milkweed is a member of the milkweed family, *Asclepiadaceae*. The common milkweed is classified as genus *Asclepias*, species *A. syriaca*. The butterfly weed is *A. tuberosa*.

EARL L. CORE

See also FLOWER (color picture: Flowers that Grow in Wet Places [Swamp Milkweed]).

MILKY WAY is a glowing band of starlight coming from the billions of stars within our own *galaxy* (star system). The galaxy is shaped like a pancake. But at night, we see it as a milky-looking strip of stars because we are inside it. Actually, the stars fan out from the center in many wide, curving arms that would give the galaxy a *spiral* (coil) shape if we could see it from above. Astronomers call the Milky Way a *spiral galaxy*.

Size of the Galaxy. The diameter of the galaxy is about 10 times greater than its thickness. It is so big that light, which travels 186,282 miles per second, takes about 100,000 years to travel from one end to the other. Our solar system is a tiny speck located about 30,000 light-years from the center of the galaxy. It is about midway between the upper and lower edges of the galaxy. See ASTRONOMY (illustration: The Milky Way).

On a dark, clear summer night, the Milky Way can

Flowers of the Milkweed bloom along roadsides and in fields in the summer. They may be purple, red, orange, or yellow.

J. Horace McFarland

The Rough-Coated Milkweed Pod is about to burst and scatter its seeds.

The Pod Splits, showing the brown, overlapping seeds and their silky tufts.

The Silky Floss carries the seeds away on the breeze as they pop out.

Lynwood M. Chace

be seen extending from the southern constellation Sagittarius, where it is brightest, to Cygnus, the great northern cross. During winter, it is dimmer and crosses the sky near Orion and Cassiopeia (see Astronomy [illustration: Skies of the Seasons]). The Milky Way has dark gaps in many places. These are formed by clouds of dust that blot out the stars behind them.

Composition of the Galaxy. The Milky Way contains clouds of dust and gas; planets; star clusters; and stars, each with its own distinctive pattern. For example, young stars and the open star clusters lie near the middle *plane* (imaginary flat surface) of the galaxy. The oldest stars and dense clusters, containing millions of stars, make a ball-shaped halo near the center of the galaxy.

Gravity holds the Milky Way together, and all of its stars rotate around the center. However, not all stars rotate with the same speed. Their speed depends on their position in relation to the *mass* (matter) in the galaxy. Stars such as our sun, which are far from the center, rotate around the center much as the planets

rotate around the sun. They move this way because, for them, most of the mass lies toward the center. Our sun moves in a circular path at a speed of 130 miles per second. Yet even at that speed, a complete trip around the center of the Milky Way takes the sun 200 billion years. The stars slightly closer to the center move faster, because they are attracted with greater force. However, the stars very close to the center move slower. For them, most of the mass lies toward the edges of the Milky Way. A study of this motion reveals that the mass of the Milky Way is equal to 200 billion suns.

The Center of the Galaxy. Light from the center cannot reach us through the dust, but scientists know from studying radio waves and infrared rays that there is intense activity there. Astronomers have found that gas streams out from the center at 1,000 miles per second, but they do not know why this occurs. Charles A. Whitney

See also Galaxy; Nebula; Solar System; Star.

MILL is a *money of account*, or coin term used in keeping accounts in the United States. A mill, which is not a coin, has the value of one-tenth of a cent.

Mount Wilson & Palomar Observatories

The Milky Way is made up of many billions of stars. It can be easily seen as a bright haze on a clear summer night.

MILL was the family name of two famous British writers, father and son. They won distinction in the fields of philosophy, history, psychology, and economics.

James Mill (1773-1836) established his reputation as a writer with the publication of *A History of British India* (1817). This work was partly responsible for changes in the Indian government. It also won him a job with the East India Company in 1819. He headed the company from 1830 until his death.

In 1808, Mill met Jeremy Bentham, a political economist called the *father of utilitarianism*. The utilitarians believed that the greatest happiness of the greatest number should be the sole purpose of all public action (see BENTHAM, JEREMY; UTILITARIANISM). Mill adopted the utilitarian philosophy, and became Bentham's ardent disciple and the editor of *St. James's Chronicle*.

His writings helped clarify the philosophical and psychological basis of utilitarianism. *Analysis of the Phenomena of the Human Mind* (1829) is a study of psychology. He wrote *Elements of Political Economy* (1821) as a textbook for his son, and it became the first textbook of English economics. *Fragment on Mackintosh* (1835) states his views of utility as the basis of morals.

Mill was born in Scotland and was graduated from Edinburgh University where he studied for the ministry. He became a Presbyterian minister in 1798, but left the ministry in 1802 to become a journalist.

John Stuart Mill (1806-1873), a distinguished philosopher and economist, became the leader of the utilitarian movement. Mill was one of the most advanced thinkers of his time. He tried to help the English working people by promoting measures leading to a more equal division of profits. He favored a cooperative system of agriculture and increased rights for women. He served as editor of the *Westminster Review* from 1835 to 1840, and wrote many articles on economics.

His greatest contribution to philosophy and his chief work, *System of Logic* (1843), ranks with Aristotle's work in that field. Mill applied economic principles to social conditions in *Principles of Political Economy* (1848). His other works include *Utilitarianism* (1863), *On Liberty* (1859), *The Subjection of Women* (1869), and *Autobiography* (1873).

Mill was born in London and was educated completely by his father. He began to study Greek at the age of 3, and, at 14, had mastered Latin, classical literature, logic, political economy, history, and mathematics. He entered the East India Company as a clerk at 17. Like his father, he became director of the company. He retired after 33 years of service, and was elected to parliament in 1865.

H. W. SPIEGEL

MILLAIS, *mih LAY*, SIR JOHN EVERETT (1829-1896), an English painter, was a founder of the Pre-Raphaelite Brotherhood in 1848. The others were Holman Hunt and Dante Gabriel Rossetti. This group believed that art should be simple and sincere as they considered it to be in the days before Raphael. Millais' Pre-Raphaelite paintings resembled colored photographs. He chose subjects from the Bible, history, legends, and poems. Millais painted *Christ in the House of His Parents* in this style. His other paintings include *Ophelia* and *The Eve of Saint Agnes*. He left the Pre-Raphaelite movement in

1859, and became a typical Victorian academic painter. He was born in Southampton.

LESTER D. LONGMAN

MILLAY, EDNA ST. VINCENT (1892-1950), was an American poet. Many of her poems have romantic themes. She wrote about love and death, about the self and the universe, and about the feelings of rebellious youth. In her treatment of these subjects, she combined sentimentality with wit and sophistication.

Miss Millay was born in Rockland, Me., and graduated from Vassar College in 1917. She did some of her best work while very young. "Renascence," a poem about a personal religious experience, was written when she was only 19 years old. *A Few Figs from Thistles* (1920) was one

Culver

Edna St. Vincent Millay

of three works for which she won a Pulitzer prize in 1923. The other two works were *The Ballad of the Harp-Weaver* and eight sonnets.

Miss Millay's later poetry became increasingly concerned with modern history. *Conversation at Midnight* (1937) deals with events that were leading to World War II. *The Murder of Lidice* (1942) tells about the destruction of a Czechoslovak town by German troops during the war. Miss Millay was fond of the sonnet form, and her many sonnets were published in 1941. A definitive collection of her poems appeared in 1956. She also wrote several plays, including the one-act poetic fantasy *Aria da Capo* (1919).

CLARK GRIFFITH

MILLEDGEVILLE, Ga. (pop. 11,117; alt. 275 ft.), a distributing center for surrounding farms, lies 30 miles northeast of Macon (see GEORGIA [political map]).

Milledgeville was established in 1803, and was named for Governor John Milledge. It was the state capital from 1807 to 1868. Georgia's first state Capitol still stands there. Milledgeville is the home of the Georgia College at Milledgeville and of Georgia Military College. The city's factories make textiles, brick, tile, medical supplies, and mobile homes. Milledgeville has a mayor-council form of government.

ALBERT B. SAYE

MILLEFIORI GLASS. See GLASSWARE (Early Glassware).

MILLENNIUM, *muh LEHN ee um*, means any period of 1,000 years. But it is usually used to refer to the period mentioned in the New Testament book of Revelation (20: 1-6) as the time when holiness will prevail throughout the world (see REVELATION).

Some people have interpreted the passage in Revelation as meaning that Christ will reign on earth either before or after the 1,000-year period. These views are known as *premillennialism* and *postmillennialism*.

Because the book of Revelation frequently uses numbers symbolically, other people have interpreted this passage spiritually. They regard the millennium as the long period of time between Christ's first coming and His second coming. St. Augustine was the first to set forth this view, known as *amillennialism*. It is expressed in *The City of God*.

See also ADVENTISTS.

MILLEPEDE. See MILLIPEDE.

BRUCE M. METZGER

MILLER, ARTHUR (1915-   ), is a leading American playwright. His works record the conflict between the individual and the society which establishes the individual's moral code. Miller showed society's morality as valid in *All My Sons* (1947) and *A View from the Bridge* (1955). But in *Death of a Salesman* (1949), *The Crucible* (1953), and *Incident at Vichy* (1964), he showed its morality as false. *Death of a Salesman*, which received a Pulitzer prize, is generally considered Miller's masterpiece. It tells of Willy Loman, a traveling salesman who chooses popularity and material success as his goals in life. Destroyed by his choice, Loman commits suicide in the end. The play typifies Miller's belief that the "common man" is the modern tragic hero.

Miller's work generally follows the Ibsen school of realistic drama. But much of the action in *Death of a Salesman* is seen through Loman's mind, thus establishing Miller's debt to expressionistic drama.

Miller was born in New York City. He was married to actress Marilyn Monroe from 1956 to 1961. His play *After the Fall* (1964) contains elements of this and other autobiographical episodes.   MARDI VALGEMAE

MILLER, CINCINNATUS H. See MILLER, JOAQUIN.

MILLER, GLENN. See POPULAR MUSIC.

MILLER, HENRY (1891-   ), became one of the most controversial American authors of his time. His emphasis on sex and his obscene language have led to censorship trials and literary quarrels.

Miller's first important book, *Tropic of Cancer* (1934), was banned from publication in the United States until 1961. It was written in Paris where Miller had exiled himself from an America he despised. As in all of Miller's work, the plot is not as important as the message. He believes that modern civilization is diseased. Man, to be healthy again, must win freedom from society and glorify the self and the senses.

Tropic of Capricorn (1939) is even more poetic and has a stronger sense of prophecy. It mixes moments of mystic joy with descriptions of what Miller sees as the American cultural wasteland. Miller's basic position has never changed, though his later subjects became more literary. He has greatly influenced the "Beat" writers, including Jack Kerouac, Allen Ginsberg, and Lawrence Ferlinghetti. Miller was born and grew up in New York City.   EUGENE K. GARBER

MILLER, JOAQUIN, *wah* KEEN (1839?-1913), was the pen name of the American poet CINCINNATUS HINER MILLER. He once wrote an article in defense of the Mexican bandit Joaquin Murietta. When he published his first book, he took Joaquin as a pen name. Miller is perhaps best remembered today for the poem "Columbus."

He was born in Liberty, Ind., but spent much of his early life in the West. His family settled in Oregon in 1852. At the age of 15, Miller ran away from his Oregon home. He lived in various mining camps and with the Indians in California. An Indian tribe adopted him, and he was married to a chief's daughter. After she was

Wide World
Arthur Miller

killed in an accident, Miller returned to Oregon in about 1860 and became a lawyer. But he spent his time writing.

In 1871, he visited England, where he published his first notable collection, *Songs of the Sierras* (1871). He also wrote *Songs of the Sunlands* (1873), the autobiographical *Life Amongst the Modocs* (1873), and the play *The Danites of the Sierras* (1877).   PETER VIERECK

MILLER, "JOE," JOSEPH (1684-1738), was a famous English comedian. He was a member of the Drury Lane Company from 1709 until his death. His acting in William Congreve's plays was largely responsible for their success. After Miller's death, John Mottley published a collection of coarse jokes and called it *Joe Miller's Jest Book* or *The Wit's Vade Mecum*. But only three of the jokes had ever been told by Joe Miller.

MILLER, JOHN. See NORTH DAKOTA (History).

MILLER, LEWIS. See CHAUTAUQUA.

MILLER, WILLIAM. See ADVENTISTS.

MILLER, WILLIAM EDWARD (1914-   ), was the Republican nominee for Vice-President of the United States in the 1964 election. Senator Barry M. Goldwater and Miller were defeated by a Democratic ticket headed by President Lyndon B. Johnson and Hubert H. Humphrey.

Miller, a New Yorker, served in the U.S. House of Representatives from 1951 to 1965, and was Republican national chairman from 1961 to 1964. He gained a reputation as a tough debater and campaigner, and a good organizer. Miller headed his party's congressional campaign committee in 1960. The Republicans gained 22 seats in the House, even though their presidential candidate, Richard M. Nixon, was defeated. Republican leaders gave Miller much credit for the victories. Miller also became known for his barbed comments about Democrats. Goldwater indicated this was one reason he chose Miller as his running mate.

Miller was born in Lockport, N.Y. He attended the University of Notre Dame and Albany Law School. He served in the army during World War II, and later helped prosecute German war criminals at the Nuremberg trials. Miller entered politics when Governor Thomas E. Dewey of New York appointed him district attorney of Niagara County in 1948.   ERIC SEVAREID

MILLER'S-THUMB. See SCULPIN.

MILLERSVILLE STATE COLLEGE. See UNIVERSITIES AND COLLEGES (table).

MILLES, *MIL lus,* **CARL WILHELM EMIL** (1875-1955), was a Swedish-American sculptor. He became famous for creating fountains that combine graceful figures with splashing water. Examples are *Fountain of Faith,* in Falls Church, Va., and *Meeting of the Waters,* in St. Louis, Mo. (see SAINT LOUIS [picture]).

Milles was born near Uppsala, Sweden, and studied in Stockholm, Paris, Munich, and Rome. He came to the United States in 1929, and became a citizen in 1945. He taught for many years at the Cranbrook Academy of Art in Bloomfield Hills, Mich. The academy has a fine collection of his works. Many of his statues and fountains are beautifully displayed in a famous park, the Millesgarden, in Stockholm.   WILLIAM MACDONALD

See also SWEDEN (color picture: Statues).

MILLET, *MILL et.* Almost one-third of the people of the world depend on millet for grain feeds and flours.

MILLET

Many kinds of grain and hay grasses are called millet. These grasses have different uses in different parts of the world. In Canada and the United States, farmers grow various kinds of millet for hay, for enriching the soil, and for producing seed. But in large areas of Europe and Asia, millet is grown for human food. In India, farmers plant about 40 million acres with millet annually to provide grain and flour. In Japan, 35 million bushels of millet seed are ground into flour each year.

Farmers in the United States usually grow *foxtail millet*. There are several varieties of foxtail millet, but all have thick, rounded flower heads at the top of slender stems. In *Hungarian millet*, a variety of foxtail millet, these spikes are purple. Foxtail millet grows chiefly in Kansas, Missouri, Texas, and neighboring states. Foxtail millet makes the best hay when the grass is cut just after the flowers are in full bloom.

Broomcorn millet, which grows in Europe, is also raised in North and South Dakota, Montana, Wyoming, and Colorado. Broomcorn millet has loose and bushy flower heads. They look somewhat like small brush brooms. Farmers use the different varieties of broomcorn millet for seed rather than for hay.

Barnyard millet is a cultivated form of the weed called barnyard grass. Farmers grow it chiefly as hay.

Planting. The planting season for millet varies with the location. Millet may be planted as early as May and as late as August. Most varieties of millet are

Millet Is Grown to Feed Cattle in the United States, but in many parts of the world, people use it as food.

J. Horace McFarland

sensitive to cold. They should not be planted until the sun has thoroughly warmed the ground. Rich, loamy soils are best for all kinds of millet. The soil is prepared for planting millet in the same way that it is for other grasses. Insects and plant diseases do not usually attack millet. Hay crops as large as 2 or 3 tons to the acre are sometimes obtained from Hungarian millet within 50 to 80 days after seeding.

Feeding Value. A little millet hay makes satisfactory feed for farm animals, if it is not used continuously. Ripe millet seeds are a good food for poultry and birds. Crushed and ground millet seeds can be fed to livestock. But no millet hay or seed is fed to horses.

Scientific Classification. Millet belongs to the grass family, *Gramineae*. Foxtail millet is genus *Setaria*, species *S. italica*. Broomcorn millet is genus *Panicum miliaceum*, species *P. miliaceum*. Barnyard millet, *Echinochloa frumentacea*.

WILLIAM R. VAN DERSAL

MILLET, *MEE LEH*, JEAN FRANÇOIS (1814-1875), a French painter, is famous today for a few paintings, such as *The Gleaners*, *The Man with the Hoe*, and *The Angelus* (see ANGELUS). He worked largely in dark, muddy colors. He painted figures of farmers and workers in the fields as symbols rather than as individuals. Millet is seen today by many as a traditionalist whose handling of his themes seems sentimental.

Millet was born near Cherbourg, in Normandy, of rural stock. He showed early talent. In 1836, the town council of Cherbourg gave Millet a small pension, and he went to Paris. He studied with Paul Delaroche, but Millet left Delaroche because he was temperamentally unable to learn by art school methods. Millet began to teach himself. He supported himself by painting signs and portraits and doing other work. After many exhibits, he was admitted to the French Academy in 1847.

Millet moved to the village of Barbizon in 1848, where he became a leading figure in the group of landscape and nature painters living there. He painted at Barbizon the scenes from rural life for which he is famous. His paintings were then considered revolutionary. Millet was poor, but after his death, his paintings became valuable. By 1890, a collector had bought *The Angelus* for $150,000.

ROBERT GOLDWATER

See also TABLEAU (picture).

MILLIGAN, EX PARTE, *eks PAHR tih*, was a legal case in which the U.S. Supreme Court ruled that civilians cannot be tried by military courts if civil courts are available. This 1866 ruling, one of the most important in the history of American civil liberties, defined the limits of military power over civilians in wartime.

During the Civil War, a military court in Indiana convicted Lambdin Milligan of cooperating with Confederate forces. Milligan appealed to the Supreme Court to determine if he was being justly imprisoned. The Supreme Court ruled unanimously that the military court, authorized by the President, was illegal because civil courts were open nearby. Milligan was freed. The Supreme Court also ruled, by a five-to-four majority, that if civil courts are open, not even Congress can create military courts to try civilians.

STANLEY I. KUTLER

MILLIGAN COLLEGE. See UNIVERSITIES AND COLLEGES (table).

MILLIGRAM. See METRIC SYSTEM.

MILLIKAN, ROBERT ANDREWS (1868-1953), an American physicist, was one of the most illustrious U.S. scientists. He is noted for his measurement of the elec-

The Louvre, Paris

Jean Millet's Painting *The Gleaners* Shows His Interest in Portraying Farmers and Scenes from Nature.

trical charge carried by the electron, and for his contributions to cosmic-ray research.

Born at Morrison, Ill., Millikan studied at Oberlin College and received a Master's degree in 1893. He entered Columbia University, where he became the only graduate student in physics, and obtained his Ph.D. degree. Millikan then went to the University of Chicago and its newly-opened Ryerson Laboratory. He remained until 1921. In 1909, he began a series of experiments to study the electrical charge carried by an electron. He found the charge by spraying tiny drops of oil into a specially-built chamber. For this work he won the 1923 Nobel prize for physics. Millikan became director of the Norman Bridge

Robert A. Millikan
Kourken

Laboratory of Physics at the California Institute of Technology in 1921. He held this post until 1945. Under his guidance, the institute became famous for its brilliant contributions to science. Millikan conducted research in cosmic-ray phenomena and pioneered in measuring the intensity of cosmic rays by means of instrument-carrying balloons. He also developed techniques for

investigating the nature of cosmic rays in deep lakes. His interest in cosmic-ray research led to the establishment of a powerful research team that made many fundamental discoveries at the California Institute of Technology. Their most important discovery was that of the *meson*, a fundamental atomic particle.

The challenge of education stimulated Millikan to write or collaborate in writing textbooks. They include *Electricity, Sound and Light* (1908), *Elementary Physics* (1936), and *Mechanics, Molecular Physics, Heat and Sound* (1937). Millikan was aware of the importance of science in the modern world, and for the general reader he wrote *Science and Life* (1923).

RALPH E. LAPP

See also COSMIC RAYS; ELECTRON; ELECTROSCOPE; MESON.

MILLIKIN UNIVERSITY. See UNIVERSITIES AND COLLEGES (table).

MILLILITER. See METRIC SYSTEM.

MILLIMETER. See METRIC SYSTEM.

MILLINERY. See HAT.

MILLING. See CORN (Processing); FLOUR; GOLD.

MILLING MACHINE. See MACHINE TOOL.

MILLION is a thousand 1,000's. One million is written 1,000,000. An idea of the size of a million is given in these facts: 1 million minutes is 16,667 hours, or 694 days, or 1.9 years; 1 million hours is 41,667 days, or 114 years; and 1 million days is 2,740 years. As a power of 10, one million is written 10^6 (see POWER). See also DECIMAL NUMERAL SYSTEM (Larger Numbers).

471

MILLIPEDE, or **MILLIPEDE,** is a wormlike, many-legged animal. Millipedes have segmented bodies. Two pairs of legs attach to each of their body segments, except to the first three or four segments and the last one or two segments. The word *millipede* means thousand-footed, but none of the millipedes has as many as 1,000 feet. Some *species* (kinds) have up to 115 pairs of legs. The animals range from less than one-eighth inch to 8 or 9 inches long. They have round heads which bear a pair of short antennae. Millipedes usually feed on decaying plant life, but some species also attack crops growing in damp soil. They live in dark, damp places, under stones and rotting logs. More than a

thousand species of millipedes are found in all parts of the world except in the polar regions.

Scientific Classification. Millipedes are classified in the phylum *Arthropoda.* They make up the class *Diplopoda.*

EDWARD A. CHAPIN

Cornelia Clarke

Most Millipedes Resemble Worms with Many Legs.

MILLS, ROBERT (1781-1855), was one of the first Americans trained as an architect and engineer. He studied with Thomas Jefferson. He designed the Washington Monument in Washington, D.C., which for many years was the tallest structure in the world (see WASHINGTON MONUMENT). He designed more than 50 important buildings, including the United States Post Office, Treasury, and Patent Office buildings in Washington, D.C. He also designed canals, churches, homes, and many courthouses. Mills was born in Charleston, S.C.

HUGH MORRISON

MILLS, WILBUR DAIGH (1909-   ), a Democratic congressman from Arkansas, has been chairman of the powerful House Ways and Means Committee since 1958. Mills plays a central role in determining the taxes paid by Americans because this committee handles all federal tax legislation.

During the 1960's, Mills's control over tax bills brought him into frequent dispute with Presidents John F. Kennedy and Lyndon B. Johnson. Mills refused to support many of their proposals until he was certain of enough votes to pass them. But he helped win passage of the 1964 tax cut, the 1965 bill establishing Medicare, and the 1968 income tax surcharge bill.

Mills was born in Kensett, Ark. He graduated from Hendrix College and attended the Harvard University law school. He served as county and probate judge of White County, Arkansas, from 1934 to 1938, and has been a member of the House since 1939.

CHARLES BARTLETT

MILLS COLLEGE. See UNIVERSITIES AND COLLEGES (table).

MILLS COLLEGE OF EDUCATION. See UNIVERSITIES AND COLLEGES (table).

MILLSAPS COLLEGE. See UNIVERSITIES AND COLLEGES (table).

MILNE, *mihln,* **ALAN ALEXANDER** (1882-1956), an English writer, became widely known for his children's verses and stories. His Winnie-the-Pooh stories became particularly popular. He also wrote several successful plays, including *Mr. Pim Passes By* (1919) and *The Dover Road* (1922). He published a series of poems, *The Norman Church* (1948); a collection of short stories, *A Table Near the Band* (1950); and a novel, *Chloe Marr* (1946).

Milne wrote his first children's book of verse, *When We Were Very Young* (1924), about his 3-year-old son,

Culver

A. A. Milne

Christopher Robin. It was followed by another book of verse, *Now We Are Six,* in 1927. *Winnie-the-Pooh* (1926) and *The House at Pooh Corner* (1928) are delightful stories that Milne wrote about his son's stuffed animals.

Milne's books for children proved immensely popular with young and old alike. Christopher Robin, Winnie-the-Pooh, Piglet, and James James Morrison Morrison are only a few of the characters which Milne made famous. Milne was born in London, and was graduated from Cambridge University. In 1906 he became assistant editor of the humor magazine, *Punch.* He began to write plays while serving in World War I.

JOSEPH E. BAKER

MILO is a grain. See SORGHUM.

MILSTEIN, *MILL stine,* **NATHAN** (1904-   ), is one of the world's greatest violinists. He became known particularly for his interpretations of Bach violin sonatas. Milstein came to the United States in 1929 to make his American debut with the Philadelphia Orchestra. After that, his stature as an artist grew steadily. Milstein was born in Odessa, Russia. He studied in Russia under Peter Stoliarski who also developed the great Russian violinist David Oistrakh. He also studied with Leopold Auer in Russia, and Eugène Ysaÿe in Brussels, Belgium.

DOROTHY DELAY

MILTIADES, *mil TY uh deez* (540?-488? B.C.), was a famous general of ancient Athens. He defeated the Persians at the Battle of Marathon in 490 B.C., during the wars between Greece and Persia (see MARATHON).

Miltiades was a member of an aristocratic Athenian family. About 516 B.C., while securing trade routes for Athens, he made himself ruler of what is now the Gallipoli Peninsula in Turkey. He probably fought against Persian forces led by Darius. He lost his throne about 492 B.C., and was forced to flee to Athens.

Persians invaded Greece in 490 B.C., and the Athenians made Miltiades a general. Because of his experience in fighting the Persians, he convinced the other generals to attack the enemy at Marathon. After defeating the Persians and driving them from Greece, he commanded a fleet in the Aegean Sea. He died in Athens after being wounded in an accident at sea.

RICHARD NELSON FRYE

MILTON, JOHN (1608-1674), an English poet and political writer, wrote one of the world's greatest epics, *Paradise Lost* (1667). He composed this famous epic and two other works, *Paradise Regained* (1671) and *Samson Agonistes* (1671), when he was totally blind.

Paradise Lost is a 12-book epic in blank verse based on the Bible story of the creation and of the fall of Satan and of Adam and Eve. *Paradise Regained*, a blank verse poem in four books, shows Christ overcoming Satan's temptations. *Samson Agonistes*, modeled after Greek tragedies, tells how Samson, betrayed by Dalila (Delilah) and blinded by the Philistines, finally defeats his captors. These three works established Milton as one of England's greatest poets.

Milton was a Puritan and a deeply religious man. He studied the Bible intensely and based many of his firmest beliefs directly on its words. He was a man of high moral character who expressed his literary creed by saying that the writer "ought himself to be a true poem." In a lofty and powerful style, Milton wrote about love, politics, and religion. His works fulfill his own definition of a good book. They pulse with "the precious lifeblood of a master spirit."

His Early Life and Works. Milton was born in London. He showed promise of unusual literary abilities while at Christ's College, Cambridge. There he wrote several poems in Latin, and an ode celebrating the birth of Christ, "On The Morning of Christ's Nativity" (1629). His early training pointed to a religious career. But Milton came to believe that "tyranny had invaded the church." He decided that he could not honestly become a clergyman under the doctrines of the Church of England. He chose to become a poet. While he was still a student, he wrote "L'Allegro" and "Il Penseroso" (1631?), two companion-poems noted for their charm and human interest. "L'Allegro" describes the pleasures of a mirthful man; "Il Penseroso" depicts the joys of a thoughtful, serious man. Milton graduated from Cambridge in 1632 and went to his father's country home, Horton, to study and write.

Milton wrote two major pieces at Horton, *Comus* (1634), and "Lycidas" (1637). *Comus*, a masque (dramatic presentation with music), concerns the nature of virtue. Milton wrote the words for the masque, and a friend, Henry Lawes, wrote the music. "Lycidas," a pastoral elegy, commemorates the death of a school friend, Edward King.

Milton left Horton in 1638 for a 15-month European tour. He heard while in Italy that a conflict was growing between the bishops of the Church of England and the Puritans. Milton returned to England to support the Puritan cause through a series of political writings.

Middle Years. Civil discord divided England from 1640 to 1660. King Charles I and the bishops clashed with Parliament over policies of church and state. Civil war broke out in 1642. The Puritans won. Charles was beheaded in 1649, and a Commonwealth government was established (see ENGLAND [The Civil War]).

During this period, Milton wrote a series of pamphlets supporting the Puritans. He believed that the Church of England was corrupt, and argued in *Of Reformation in England* (1641) that the bishops should be deprived of power. In 1649, he published *The Tenure of Kings and Magistrates*, which declared that the people had the right to choose and depose their rulers. Leaders of the

Yale University Art Gallery, George Heard Hamilton Collection, New Haven
Blindness Failed to Halt Milton's Work. He composed *Paradise Lost* and other poems while blind. According to legend, he dictated *Paradise Lost* to his daughters. This painting, *Milton Dictating Paradise Lost To His Daughters*, is by Eugène Delacroix.

Commonwealth government noticed the pamphlet and appointed Milton secretary for foreign tongues to the Council of State to translate dispatches to other countries into Latin. He also wrote tracts defending the Commonwealth as part of this job. He wrote, among other essays, "Defensio Pro Populo Anglicano" (1651), and "Eikonoklastes" (1649).

Milton had married Mary Powell, a 16-year-old girl, in 1643. Their marriage was unhappy. She left Milton after a month or two, and did not return for two years. Milton wrote a series of pamphlets advocating divorce in certain cases. *The Doctrine and Discipline of Divorce* (1643) was the most notable. In 1644, Milton published his most famous prose work, *Areopagitica*, a defense of freedom of the press.

Milton's work and constant study strained his weak eyes, and he became blind in 1652. He wrote a sonnet on his blindness, "When I Consider How My Light Is Spent" (1655). His wife died in 1652, and he married Catharine Woodcock in 1656. She died 16 months later. He probably wrote the sonnet "Me-Thought I Saw My Late Espoused Saint" (1658) about her.

Retirement. After the restoration of Charles II in 1660, the government executed several Puritans held responsible for the death of Charles I. Milton was arrested, but was not punished. He went into retirement, and married Elizabeth Minshull in 1663. He devoted the rest of his life to writing poetry. The three poems of his retirement were *Paradise Lost*, *Paradise Regained*, and *Samson Agonistes*. They present his mature views on man and his destiny, and stand as great monuments to England's most dedicated poet.   GEORGE F. SENSABAUGH

MILTON COLLEGE. See UNIVERSITIES AND COLLEGES (table).

MILWAUKEE is the largest city in Wisconsin and the 11th largest in the United States. It is one of the world's leading producers of heavy machinery, such as electric generators and mining equipment. The city is known for its honest and progressive government, its traffic safety record, its low crime rate, and its beautiful harbor on Lake Michigan. Tree-shaded parkways run along Milwaukee's rivers and the lake shore.

Location and Description. Milwaukee lies on a bluff overlooking a bay on the southwestern shore of Lake Michigan. The Milwaukee, Menomonee, and Kinnickinnic rivers flow through the city to the bay. The city's name comes from the Milwaukee River. The river's Algonkian Indian name *Millioke* means *good land.* Milwaukee is about 40 miles *north of Wisconsin's* southern boundary, and 85 miles north of Chicago. For location, see WISCONSIN (political map).

The streets of Milwaukee run north, south, east, and west in a regular pattern. This gives the city a checkerboard appearance from the air. West Canal Street divides Milwaukee into north and south sides. Most of the city's office buildings and the municipal headquarters stand near the lake front. Many manufacturing plants have been built along the rivers. Lincoln Memorial Drive runs north from the center of the city along Lake Michigan. Other beautiful streets include Prospect Avenue, Lake Drive, and Capitol Drive.

FACTS IN BRIEF

Population: 741,324; metropolitan area, 1,278,850.
Area: 96 sq. mi.; metropolitan area, 1,489 sq. mi.
Altitude: 635 feet above sea level.
Climate: For information on the monthly weather in Milwaukee, see WISCONSIN (Climate).
Government: Mayor-council (four-year terms).
Founded: 1818. Incorporated as a city, 1846.
Seal: Four scenes representing rail transportation, government, water transportation, and industry surround a lake front.
Flag: An industrial gear, symbolic of Milwaukee's industry, is in the center. Other symbols around or on the gear include a stalk of barley, the County Stadium, the Arena, the City Hall, a factory, and a ship. The flag has a blue background; red, gold, and white lettering; and a gold fringe. See FLAG (color picture: Flags of Cities of the United States).

City of Milwaukee

Milwaukee lies on the western shore of Lake Michigan. Its port is a major gateway to the Midwest for ships traveling from the Atlantic Ocean through the St. Lawrence Seaway and the Great Lakes.

The metropolitan area of Milwaukee includes Milwaukee and Waukesha counties. Suburbs border the city on three sides. They include Shorewood, Whitefish Bay, and Brown Deer on the north; Wauwatosa, Brookfield, and West Deer on the west; and Greenfield, Cudahy, South Milwaukee, and Oak Creek on the south.

The People. Descendants of German and Polish immigrants make up a large part of Milwaukee's population. These two nationality groups once lived almost entirely apart from each other. Today, in spite of intermarriage and relocation, the north side of Milwaukee remains more German, and the south side more Polish. Roman Catholics and Lutherans form the city's two largest religious groups.

Manufacturing industries employ nearly half a million persons in metropolitan Milwaukee. The city's 2,000 manufacturing companies produce more than $3 billion worth of goods each year. The chief manufactured products are equipment and machinery for the generation, transmission, and distribution of electric power. The largest single firm, Allis-Chalmers Manufacturing Company, produces industrial equipment and farm machinery. The city's construction and mining-machinery plants make the nation's largest cranes. Other important manufactured products include automobiles and automobile parts, castings and forgings, leather and leather goods, and motorcycles. Milwaukee's large breweries have given it the name of the *Beer Capital* of the United States.

Transportation and Communication. Milwaukee's busy harbor has helped in the city's development as an industrial center. Many docks stand along the rivers and the lake front. Ships connect Milwaukee with the world's leading cities, particularly by way of the St. Lawrence Seaway. Six railroad systems serve Milwaukee, two of them by ferry across Lake Michigan from Ludington and Muskegon, Mich. Airlines use General Mitchell Field, on the city's southern edge. Milwaukee has two daily newspapers, the *Journal* and the *Sentinel.* Six television stations and 11 radio stations broadcast from the city.

Education. More than 100,000 students attend Milwaukee's 140 public schools. The Milwaukee Voca-

Huge Glass Domes in Mitchell Park feature desert and tropical plants from many parts of the world. The domes are part of the park's Horticultural Conservatory, one of the most interesting places to visit in Milwaukee.

tional School is one of the largest trade schools in the United States, with an enrollment of about 30,000. Milwaukee has over 120 private and parochial schools, with more than 50,000 students. Universities and colleges include Marquette University; the University of Wisconsin at Milwaukee; St. Francis Seminary; and Alverno, Cardinal Stritch, and Mount Mary colleges.

The Milwaukee Public Library has a notable collection of periodicals of the 1800's. The Milwaukee Public Museum emphasizes natural history. The Milwaukee County Historical Society maintains historic buildings and local history exhibits. The War Memorial building at the lake front houses the Milwaukee Art Center.

Recreation. The county maintains more than 10,000 acres of parks, which offer a variety of summer and winter activities. Whitnall Park has an arboretum and botanical gardens. Mitchell Park includes a conservatory and sunken gardens. The Milwaukee County Zoo is at the western limits of the city. The Milwaukee Symphony Orchestra performs at the Milwaukee Center for the Performing Arts and in the Municipal Auditorium.

The downtown Civic Center includes the Municipal Auditorium and Arena. Their halls can seat a total of 24,500 persons, and they have 140,000 square feet of floor area for exhibits. The Milwaukee Brewers of the American League play baseball in County Stadium. The Green Bay Packers of the National Football League also play some of their games there.

History. French explorers, missionaries, and fur traders began stopping at the site of Milwaukee in the late 1600's. Robert Cavelier, Sieur de la Salle, found an Indian village on the lake shore in 1679. Jacques Vieau operated a fur-trading post there in the late 1700's. His son-in-law, Solomon Laurent Juneau, was the first permanent settler. He settled in the area in 1818 and established a town in 1833.

Settlers from New England and New York started arriving in the 1830's. In 1846, a charter merged several towns into the city of Milwaukee. The people elected Juneau their first mayor. Beginning in the 1840's, many immigrants came to Milwaukee from Germany. The German language became common in homes, business, newspapers, and schools.

Harbor improvements, and the construction of canals, plank roads, and railroads, encouraged growth during the 1840's and 1850's. By the time of the Civil War, Milwaukee had become a leading market for the wheat and flour of western farmers. Industries, including meat packing, tanning, brewing, and steelmaking, developed from 1880 to 1900.

In 1910, Milwaukee elected its first socialist mayor, Emil Seidel. He served until 1912. Since then, the city has had two other socialist mayors, Daniel W. Hoan from 1916 to 1940, and Frank P. Zeidler from 1948 to 1960. Their programs demanded reform rather than socialism. Only under Seidel did the city council have a socialist majority. Milwaukee is the largest American city to elect socialist mayors.

After World War II, Milwaukee began redeveloping its downtown and lake front areas, and building expressways to the suburbs. During the 1950's, it improved the harbor to handle ocean shipping coming to the city through the St. Lawrence Seaway and the Great Lakes.

FREDERICK I. OLSON

MIMEOGRAPH is a stencil duplicating machine. See DUPLICATOR.

MIMICRY, *MIM ik rih,* is the condition in which one living organism closely resembles, or mimics, its surroundings or another animal or plant. It is usually the result of similar color or construction. Mimicry may enable the organism to protect itself in its struggle for existence. For example, the monarch butterfly and the viceroy butterfly resemble each other in size, shape, and colors. The monarch is believed to be distasteful to birds, while the viceroy is not. But the viceroy often escapes being eaten because it resembles the monarch.

Another example of mimicry is the *Kallima,* or "dead leaf," butterfly of India, which brings its wings together over its back and places the "tails" of its wings against a twig when it rests. The *Kallima* escapes notice because the undersides of its wings resemble a dead leaf in color and texture.

C. BROOKE WORTH

See also ANIMAL (Animal Defenses; pictures: Animal Camouflage); BIRD (How Birds Protect Themselves; color picture: Color Protects Them); BUTTERFLY (color pictures: Kallima, The Monarch); PROTECTIVE COLORATION.

Leaves and Blossoms of the Mimosa have a featherlike appearance. The handsome tree is native to the tropics.

Gendreau

MIMOSA, *mih MO suh,* is the name of a group of trees, shrubs, and herbs which have featherlike leaves. The mimosa grows chiefly in warm and tropical lands. The tree is similar to the acacia. The seed, or fruit, grows in flat pods. The small flowers may be white, pink, lavender, or purple. Mimosa grows throughout Asia, Africa, Mexico, and Australia. In the United States, it grows along the valley of the Rio Grande and in many states, including West Virginia, Virginia, Alabama, Kentucky, Louisiana, and Indiana.

Scientific Classification. The mimosas are members of the pea family, *Leguminosae*. They make up a genus called *Mimosa*.

J. J. LEVISON

MINARET, *MIN uh RET,* is a tower of the Moslem house of worship called a *mosque.* The minaret is one of the most typical features of Islamic architecture and one of the most beautiful. From the top of the minaret, a crier, or *muezzin,* calls the people to prayer. Minarets are built of brick and stone. Most of them are tall and

Four Minarets covered with intricate mosaics, and a low rounded dome with the same decoration, top the great mosque in Teheran. All mosques have at least one minaret.

Joseph Covello, Black Star

slender, but some are short and heavy. The minaret may be round, square, or many-sided. Some mosques possess only one minaret, but others have several.

The minaret may stand by itself, but it is usually a part of the mosque. An inside stairway leads to the top. In a few early minarets, this stairway wound around the outside. One or more balconies surround the minaret.

Minarets are found in Iraq, Iran, Syria, North Africa, Spain, Turkey, and India. Those built between the 1200's and 1500's are the finest. The oldest-known minaret belongs to the mosque in Buṣrá ash Shām, Syria. It was built in the 600's.

KENNETH J. CONANT

See also MOSQUE.

MINAS BASIN. See BAY OF FUNDY.

MINCH, THE, is a broad strait which separates the island of Lewis, of the Hebrides group, from the west coast of Scotland. Its average width is about 30 miles. It is sometimes called North Minch to distinguish it from Little Minch, a narrow channel to the southwest.

MIND. Psychologists have held many different views on the nature of the mind, and even today they have by no means reached agreement.

Early theories of mind held that man was made up of two different substances, *mind* and *matter.* Matter was something that could be seen and felt. Matter occupied space and had weight. Mind was a substance present in a person, but it took up no space and could not be weighed, seen, or touched. The mind was divided into several *faculties,* such as will, reason, and memory. Some people thought that the mind, like the muscles, developed through exercise, so that the way to strengthen the mind was to give the faculties work to do.

Some psychologists and philosophers who questioned the mind-substance idea offered the view that mind was the sum total of all a person's conscious states. This meant that the mind was simply a mass of thoughts, memories, feelings, and emotions. At any given moment, there would be only a few things in a person's consciousness, the things to which a person was giving attention; and there would be some other things of which he was aware without thinking about them, somewhat as we see things "out of the corner of our eye." Below this level of consciousness would be a whole vast mass made up of all the conscious states an individual had experienced since his birth. Whenever a new idea or impression made its way into a person's consciousness, all the earlier impressions that were like it or in some way related to it were supposed to rise up into consciousness and welcome the newcomer. In this way, the mind kept growing and rearranging itself.

The Nature of Mind. During the 1800's, psychologists began to try out some of these ideas on the nature of mind. For example, one man set himself the task of memorizing nonsense syllables over a period of time, and checking how long it took him each time he tried. He reached the conclusion that a person could memorize and memorize without in any way improving his memory. Other psychologists began to ask why it was, if mind and matter were separate substances, that drugs or illness or a blow on the head could so greatly disturb a person's mind. They wondered also why the mind seemed to fail as people grew very old.

Some of these psychologists went so far as to suggest that perhaps everything a person did could be explained in terms of the body, without using such ideas as mind or consciousness at all. These psychologists held that actual physical movements of the brain and central nervous system could account for all the events we speak of as "mental," if only we knew enough about them. The person who spoke of "mind" or "consciousness," according to this view, was simply an animal impelled through experiences and habits. This animal had built up certain associations in his nervous system, to make specific sounds on specific occasions.

This theory, sometimes called *extreme behaviorism*, made rapid headway among psychologists. However, its limitations soon became apparent. The modern psychologist, while still a behaviorist, has accepted many modifications of the original viewpoint.

Another view began to develop that perhaps mind, like matter, is just something that happens, and is not a separate, identifiable thing. For example, everyone knows that water is wet. But atoms of hydrogen and oxygen are not wet, and neither are the energy charges that make them up. We can say that wetness is a quality that comes into being when energy charges, organized in the form of hydrogen and oxygen atoms, are brought together to form water. If we break water down into its parts, the wetness is gone, and so is the water itself.

In the same way, mind is a quality that comes into being as people interact with the world around them. According to this theory, mind, like wetness, is something that emerges or comes into being when organisms reach a certain level of complexity in development.

Another theory states that mind is the foundation and the source of feeling, thinking, and willing. This foundation is distinct from the acts which it produces. The mind is the ultimate source of sensations, images, feelings, and thoughts. The thoughts are the mental activities. The *soul* is an even broader concept. It is the source of both mental and other life activities, such as breathing and walking.

Physical and Mental Relationship. Most people believe that a practical separation between mind and body is impossible. The mind can move the body, as when a man decides to flex his muscles. Almost any human reaction has both physical and mental sides, so that men smile with pleasure, frown in anger, or quiver with fear. Physicians tell us that mental states can actually produce heart disease, ulcer of the stomach, kidney trouble, and other diseases.

The body also affects the mind. Everyone can note for himself the difference in his mental state when he is hungry or well-fed, cold or warm, sick or well. It is known also that certain glands have a profound effect upon emotions, attitudes, and behavior. See Behavior.

The influence of the mind and the body on each other is difficult to explain. Some people explain it by discarding the mind. Others discard matter in order to explain it. A more common-sense view insists that they both exist and interact. According to the interaction theory, each human being is composed of both body and mind. However, the body and mind are incomplete until they form a unity called a *person*, or *ego*. Man is a single composite substance made up of two distinct principles. It is the *person* who thinks and remembers, not the mind, and not the body.

The discussion above deals with some of the many questions and problems involved in the nature of mind. The discussion shows that serious work is being done on the subject. No one statement of the nature of mind is acceptable to all authorities.

Related Articles in World Book include:

Emotion	Intuition	Reason	Thought and
Feeling	Memory	Subconscious	Judgment
Intelligence	Psychology	Suggestion	Will

FRANK J. KOBLER

MIND READING is a term loosely applied to various forms of *extrasensory perception (ESP)*, especially *telepathy* and *clairvoyance*. Telepathy is an awareness of another person's thoughts, knowledge, or feelings without the aid of the senses of hearing, sight, smell, taste, or touch. Clairvoyance is an awareness of events, objects, or persons without the use of the known senses. The term *mind reading* may be considered a synonym for *telepathy*. But the term has little more than historical interest today because of changing ideas about the concept of the mind.

In the past, each person was considered to have a mind more or less independent of his body and behavior. It was also thought that one mind could "read" another mind without using the known senses. Today, scientists do not believe that the mind is independent of the rest of the body.

Magicians and other performers have popularized the term *mind reading*. However, they use a variety of clever tricks and codes to imitate telepathy and do not have telepathic powers.   WILLIAM M. SMITH

See also Extrasensory Perception; Telepathy; Clairvoyance; Parapsychology.

MINDANAO. See Pacific Ocean (The Islands).
MINDANAO DEEP. See Pacific Ocean (Location and Size); Philippines (Coast Line, Bays, and Harbors).
MINDORO. See Philippines (The Islands); Sulu Sea.
MINDSZENTY, *MIND sent ee*, JOSEPH CARDINAL (1892-   ), a Hungarian cardinal of the Roman Catholic Church, became a national religious leader in Hungary. He was a strong enemy of Communism, and soon found himself the main target of the Communist-dominated secret police. When Hungary was taken over by the Communists in 1948, Cardinal Mindszenty was arrested and condemned to life imprisonment for treason. But Hungarian rebels dramatically released him during their revolt in November, 1956, and he took refuge in the United States Legation in Budapest.

Mindszenty was born Joseph Pehm in Csehimindszenty. His father was of German ancestry. He was ordained a priest in 1915. During the Nazi occupation of Hungary, he changed his name to indicate his completely Hungarian nationality, using the name of his birthplace. He was named bishop of Veszprém in 1944, and then archbishop of Esztergom and Hungarian Prince Primate in 1945. Pope Pius XII made him a cardinal in February, 1946.   JOHN T. FARRELL and FULTON J. SHEEN

See also Hungary (Communist Hungary).

Cardinal Mindszenty

United Press Int.

MINE, MILITARY

MINE, MILITARY, is an explosive device that is used to destroy enemy forces and equipment. Mines can be fired in many different ways. Some explode when they are stepped on. Some go off when a ship or vehicle passes over or near the mine. Others fire after a certain number of targets pass by. Mines can also be exploded by remote control, or they can be set to go off at a certain time.

Mines are important weapons, and they have been used extensively in recent wars. They are highly destructive because they explode close to their target, and they are very inexpensive and easy to make.

The term *mine* comes from the early practice of mining tunnels under enemy trenches and forts, packing them with tons of gunpowder, then exploding the charge. During the Civil War, the Union Army mined a section of the Confederate trenches at Petersburg, Va., and blew a hole in the lines in what is called the Battle of the Crater. TNT mines of this type were used in World War I. But they became outdated in later wars, because armies used fast-moving armored equipment and no longer fought in trenches.

Land Mines

Hundreds or thousands of land mines may be laid in planned patterns called *mine fields*. Mine fields stop or slow down an enemy or make it impossible for him to use the land. Sometimes harmless *dummy* mines are planted to slow down the enemy, who must stop to remove them before he can be sure they are not explosive.

U.S. Army

Antitank Mines are one of the most destructive types of land mines. Filled with high explosives, they are buried in the ground. They explode with great force when heavy vehicles such as tanks roll over them and push down the triggerlike detonators.

Sometimes mines called *booby traps* are hidden under harmless looking objects such as a dead soldier or a floorboard in an abandoned building. When someone moves the dead soldier or steps on the floorboard, the booby trap explodes.

Specially trained soldiers usually lay mines. They dig a shallow trench, set the mine's fuse, plant the mine, and cover it with dirt. Sometimes, mechanical mine layers are used to lay mines. Mines that are set to go off several days or weeks after they are laid can also be dropped by airplanes. During World War II, Allied planes dropped thousands of such mines along the roads that retreating German forces were expected to use.

Types of Land Mines include antipersonnel mines, antitank mines, and chemical mines.

Antipersonnel Mines are designed to kill or injure enemy soldiers. They have sensitive fuses and can be set off by the weight of a small man. They vary in size, shape, and weight. Some will kill persons within a few yards of the blast. Others can kill soldiers more than 200 yards away. Fragmentation mines hurl jagged metal fragments that will kill or injure anyone they strike. The "Bouncing Betty," developed by Germany during World War II, is a deadly mine. It shoots a cylinder three or four feet into the air. Then the cylinder explodes and sprays fragments in all directions. The Claymore mine can be aimed to shoot fragments in one direction.

Antitank Mines destroy tanks and other vehicles. Some stop a tank by blowing off one of the *tracks* (metal belts) on which the tank moves. Others are designed to

U.S. Army

Mine Detector aids a soldier in finding booby traps that might be hidden by the enemy. Extremely sensitive electronic detectors have also been perfected that can usually locate even the most skillfully concealed booby traps and mines.

explode only when the tank is directly over the mine. A common type of antitank mine weighs about 20 pounds, including 12 pounds of explosives. It takes from 200 to 300 pounds of pressure to set it off.

Chemical Mines are used against enemy soldiers or tanks to spread chemicals and gases.

Land Mine Detection is a slow and dangerous job. The best method of detection calls for men to creep slowly across the mine fields on their hands and knees, carefully sticking bayonets into the ground probing for mines. When a soldier finds a mine, he cautiously digs it out and removes it.

Electrical mine detectors are used to find certain types of metal mines or mines with timing devices. An automatic mine detector has been perfected for use on jeeps. It stops the jeep when it locates a mine. The detector can cover a 6-foot path directly in front of the jeep, and can be moved to cover the area on either side of the jeep.

The safest way to remove mines is by *countermining*. In countermining, large explosive charges are set off to blow up all the mines in the field. The *snake* is a device that is often used to cross mine fields. It is a long pipe filled with explosives that can be pushed across a mine field by a tank to explode the mines along its path.

Naval Mines

Mines have been used in naval warfare to block harbors and shipping routes for at least 200 years. Naval mines are laid by ships called *mine layers*. They can also be laid by airplanes and submarines.

Soldiers Remove a Mine planted by the Viet Cong along a highway in Vietnam. A detonator made of bamboo lies beside the sergeant's left hand. The Army has specially trained men who carry out this delicate and dangerous work.

Kinds of Naval Mines. Some mines, called *buoyant mines*, float on or just below the surface of the water. Others, called *ground mines*, rest on the ocean's floor. The following kinds of mines may be either buoyant or ground mines:

Pressure Mines are designed to explode when a passing ship causes a change in the water pressure. They can be set to explode at almost any change in pressure. Sometimes, they are fitted with timers that explode them at a certain time.

Anchored Floating Mines are held just below the surface by a cable connected to an anchor resting on the ocean floor. They are set off when a ship hits the mine or an *antenna* (rodlike extension on top of the mine). These mines were used more than any other naval mines during World War II.

Unanchored Floating Mines are usually connected by cables. They are usually floated in pairs. Both unanchored floating mines go off when a ship hits either one of them.

Influence Mines are set off by the magnetic field created by a passing ship. Some ships carry a belt of electrical cables called a *degaussing belt* around the hull, to reduce the ship's magnetic field. *Acoustic mines* are exploded by the sound of a passing ship. These mines have small microphones connected to their triggers.

Naval Mine Detection. Ships called *mine sweepers* find and remove naval mines. Two mine sweepers can work together by dragging a long cable between them. The cable cuts loose the anchored mines so that the mines come to the surface where they can be exploded by rifle fire. The cable may also pull a noisemaker and a magnetic device that explodes acoustic and influence mines.
JOHN D. BILLINGSLEY

See also MINE LAYER; MINE SWEEPER; PARAVANE.

MINE LAYER is a warship that is used to lay mines in the water. A surface ship drops mines from a slide or track on its stern. A mine-laying submarine usually drops mines through special tubes, or from its torpedo tubes. See also MINE, MILITARY (Naval Mine Detection).
RAYMOND V. B. BLACKMAN

See also MINE, MILITARY.

MINE SWEEPER is a warship that clears enemy explosives from coastal waters. It tows a *paravane* that has a cutter which severs the cable anchoring a mine (see PARAVANE). After the mine floats to the surface, it can be exploded harmlessly. See also MINE, MILITARY (Naval Mine Detection).
RAYMOND V. B. BLACKMAN

MINE WORKERS OF AMERICA, UNITED. See UNITED MINE WORKERS OF AMERICA.

MINER. See MINING.

MINER, JACK (1865-1944), was a Canadian bird conservationist. He established a bird sanctuary on his farm near Kingsville, Ont., in 1908. Miner freed many birds after putting numbered metal anklets on them. He urged hunters to return the numbered bands from birds they shot. In this way, he learned where the migrating birds went. Friends established the Jack Miner Migratory Bird Foundation in 1931 to help him continue his work on the migrating habits of birds. Miner was born in Dover Centre, Ohio. His full name was JOHN THOMAS MINER.
LORUS J. MILNE and MARGERY MILNE

See also ONTARIO (Places to Visit).

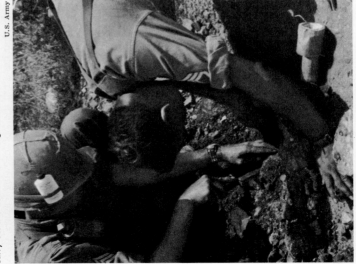

U.S. Army

479

MINERAL

MINERAL is the most common solid material found on the earth. The earth's land and oceans all rest on a layer of rock made of minerals. All rocks found on the earth's surface also contain minerals. Even soil contains tiny pieces of minerals broken from rocks.

Minerals include such common substances as salt and pencil "lead," and such rare ones as gold, silver, and gems. There are about 2,000 kinds of minerals, but only about 100 of them are common. Most of the others are harder to find than gold.

Man digs minerals from the earth and uses them to make many products. He uses minerals to make cement and steel for building, fertilizers for farming, chemicals for manufacturing, and many other materials.

Scientists have given many minerals names that end in *ite*. Salt is the mineral halite, and pencil lead is graphite. Hematite is the world's most important source of iron. Other common minerals include gypsum, used in making wallboard, and talc, used in talcum powder and crayons.

Many persons use the term *mineral* for any substance taken from the earth. Such substances include coal, petroleum, natural gas, and sand—none of which is a mineral. Certain substances in food and water, such as calcium, iron, and phosphorus, also are called minerals. But mineralogists, the scientists who study minerals, do not consider any of them minerals. Mineralogists use the term *mineral* to mean a sub-

stance that has all of the four following features. (1) A mineral is found in nature. A natural diamond is a mineral, but a man-made diamond is not. (2) A mineral is made up of substances that were never alive. Coal, petroleum, and natural gas are not minerals because they were formed from the remains of animals and plants. (3) A mineral has the same chemical makeup wherever it is found. Sand is not a mineral because samples from different places usually have different chemical makeups. (4) The atoms of a mineral are arranged in a regular pattern, and form solid units called *crystals*. The calcium and phosphorus found in milk are not minerals because they are dissolved in a liquid and are not crystals.

This article discusses only substances that mineralogists consider minerals. For information on coal, petroleum, and other mined products, see the articles listed in the *Related Articles* section of the MINING article. For information on other materials that are often called minerals, see the articles on FOOD (How Our Bodies Use Food) and OCEAN (The Ocean—A Liquid Mine).

William H. Dennen, the contributor of this article, is the Chairman of the Department of Geology at the University of Kentucky and author of Principles of Mineralogy.

Rocks Are Made of Minerals. A chunk of granite, *left*, contains bits of hornblende, feldspar, quartz, and mica. Alone, these minerals appear as shown, *right*.

Mica

Quartz

Feldspar

Hornblende

photos by E. F. Hoppe, courtesy the Field Museum of Natural History, Chicago.

MINERAL/Identifying Minerals

Minerals vary greatly in appearance and feel. Some have glasslike surfaces that sparkle with color. Others look dull and feel greasy. The hardest minerals can scratch glass. The softest ones can be scratched by a fingernail. Four of the main characteristics of minerals are (1) luster, (2) cleavage, (3) hardness, and (4) color.

Luster of a mineral may be metallic or nonmetallic. Minerals with metallic luster shine like metal. Such minerals include galena, gold, and ilmenite. Minerals with nonmetallic luster vary in appearance. Quartz looks glassy, talc has a pearly surface, and varieties of cinnabar appear dull and claylike. The luster of a mineral also may differ from sample to sample. Some kinds of cinnabar, for example, have a metallic luster rather than a dull luster.

Cleavage is the splitting of a mineral into pieces that have flat surfaces. Minerals differ in the number of directions they split, and in the angles at which the flat surfaces meet. Mica splits in one direction and forms thin sheets. Halite has three cleavage directions, and it breaks into tiny cubes. A diamond may split in four directions, forming a pyramid. Other minerals, such as quartz, do not split cleanly, but break into pieces with irregular surfaces.

Hardness of minerals may be tested by scratching one mineral with another. The harder mineral scratches the softer one, and mineralogists use a scale of hardness based on this principle. Friedrich Mohs, a German mineralogist, invented the scale in 1822. The Mohs hardness scale lists 10 minerals from the softest to the hardest. These minerals are numbered from 1 to 10. The hardness of other minerals is found by determining whether they scratch, or are scratched by, the minerals in the Mohs scale. For example, galena scratches gypsum (number 2), but is scratched by calcite (number 3). Therefore, galena's hardness is $2\frac{1}{2}$—about halfway between that of gypsum and calcite. A person's fingernail has a hardness of about 2.

Color of some minerals depends on the substances that make up the crystals. The black of ilmenite, the red of cinnabar, and the green of serpentine all result from the chemical composition of these minerals. Other minerals get their color from chemical impurities. Pure quartz, for example, has colorless crystals. But tiny amounts of other substances in quartz crystals can give quartz a pink or green tint, or even make it black.

Other Identification Tests. Some minerals may be recognized by their *habit* (general appearance). Gold is found in the form of nuggets, and diamonds are found as crystals. Halite may have the form of grains, clumps of crystals, or large chunks. Mineralogists can also identify minerals by feeling, tasting, or smelling them. Talc and serpentine feel greasy. Epsomite and halite taste salty, and borax and melanterite taste sweet. Kaolinite has an earthy smell.

A *streak test* uses color to identify a mineral. The mineral is rubbed across a slightly rough, white porcelain plate. The rubbing grinds some of the mineral to powder and leaves a colored streak on the plate. But the streak is not always the same color as the sample. Hematite varies from reddish brown to black, but always leaves a red streak. Chalcopyrite, a yellow mineral, produces a green-black streak.

Many chemical tests can identify minerals. One of the simplest consists of pouring a warm, weak acid on the sample. If the acid fizzes, the sample belongs to a group of minerals called *carbonates*. Calcite, aragonite, and dolomite are examples of carbonates. These minerals contain carbon and oxygen, together with other chemicals. When attacked by acid, the minerals release carbon dioxide gas which forms bubbles in the acid. This test may be made at home, using vinegar for the acid. In the *flame test*, a bit of a mineral is ground into powder near the air holes at the base of a lighted Bunsen burner. Air carries the powder up into the flame. The powder gives the flame a color that identifies the mineral.

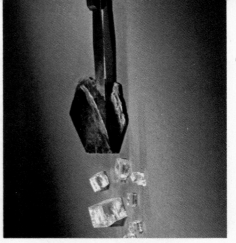

Common Identification Tests. A mineral's hardness is tested by scratching it against minerals listed in the Mohs scale, *left.* A streak test of hematite, *center,* leaves a red streak. The tester rubs the mineral against rough porcelain and wipes the streak with his finger. *Right,* calcite cleaves into blocks, and mica into sheets.

MOHS HARDNESS SCALE

MINERAL	HARDNESS	COMMON TESTS
Talc	1	Scratched by a fingernail
Gypsum	2	
Calcite	3	Scratched by a copper coin
Fluorite	4	Scratched by a knife blade or window glass
Apatite	5	
Feldspar	6	
Quartz	7	Scratches a knife blade or window glass
Topaz	8	
Corundum	9	
Diamond	10	Scratches all common materials

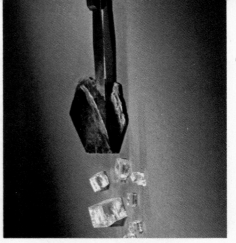

482

Rutile TiO$_2$. Red to black with gem-like luster. May be transparent. Hardness 6-6½. Cleaves.

Magnetite Fe$_3$O$_4$. Black. Attracted by magnet and may act as magnet. Hardness 5½-6½. Does not cleave.

Galena PbS. Bright metallic lead-gray cubes. Hardness 2½. Cleaves to form cubes.

Bornite Cu$_5$FeS$_4$. Copper-red with purple-blue tarnish. Hardness 3. Cleaves.

Silver Ag. Silver-white (above, as flecks in barite), tarnishing to black. Hardness 2½-3. Does not cleave.

Pyrite FeS$_2$. Pale yellow. Leaves green- to brown-black streak. Hardness 6-6½. Does not cleave.

Gold Au. Yellow nuggets, grains, and flakes. Does not tarnish. Hardness 2½-3. Does not cleave.

Chalcopyrite CuFeS$_2$. Yellow. Leaves a green-black streak. Hardness 3½-4. Does not cleave.

Stibnite Sb$_2$S$_3$. Gray columns with black tarnish. Hardness 2. Cleaves in one direction.

Pyrrhotite FeS. Bronze-yellow. Weakly attracted to magnet. Hardness 3½-4½. Does not cleave.

Graphite C. Steel-gray. Feels greasy. Hardness 1-2. Cleaves into tablets and sheets.

Copper Cu. Copper-red with brown tarnish. Hardness 2½-3. Does not cleave.

COMMON MINERALS WITH NONMETALLIC LUSTER

Fluorite CaF₂. Green or violet cubes. Hardness 4. Cleaves in four directions.

Muscovite KAl₂(AlSi₃O₁₀)(OH)₂. Colorless. Hardness 2½-3. Cleaves to form tablets and sheets.

Rhodochrosite Mn(CO₃). Pink. Leaves white streak. Hardness 3½-4. Polyhedral cleavage.

Wulfenite Pb(MoO₄). Orange-yellow square tablets. Hardness 3. Cleaves into tablets.

Cinnabar HgS. Dark red, earthy to metallic luster. Hardness 2-2½. Earthy form does not cleave.

Malachite Cu₂(CO₃)(OH)₂. Bright green. Hardness 3½-4. Cleaves irregularly.

Quartz SiO₂. Clear or tinted glassy crystals. Hardness 7. Does not cleave.

Talc Mg₃(Si₄O₁₀)(OH)₂. Pale green. Feels greasy. Hardness 1-1½. Cleaves into tablets and sheets.

Azurite Cu₃(CO₃)₂(OH)₂. Blue. Hardness 3½-4. Cleaves irregularly.

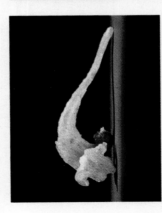

Gypsum Ca(SO₄)·2H₂O. Colorless, white, gray, or yellow to brown. Hardness 2. Cleaves into plates.

Orthoclase K(AlSi₃O₈). White to pink. Leaves white streak. Hardness 6. Cleaves.

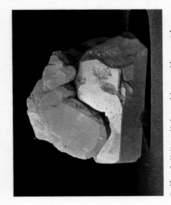

Sulfur S. Yellow. Melts and burns with a match. Hardness 1½-2½. Cleaves irregularly.

Mineral Crystals occur in many sizes. A giant crystal of beryl or feldspar may weigh several tons. Tiny crystals of kaolin may be too small to be studied even with a microscope. Regardless of their size, all crystals are basically the same. They are groups of atoms arranged in a regular pattern.

To imagine what it is like inside a crystal, you can think of "rooms" formed by the crystal's atoms. A room in a copper crystal is formed by 14 copper atoms. The room has an atom at each corner of the floor and ceiling and an atom at the centers of the floor, the ceiling, and each of the four walls. A copper crystal consists of many of these rooms side by side and one on top of the other. The rooms share copper atoms where they meet. Mineralogists call such rooms *unit cells*.

Most minerals are composed of more than one kind of atom. Halite, for example, consists of sodium atoms and chlorine atoms. Other minerals may have as many as five kinds of atoms in complicated arrangements. Some unit cells have six walls instead of four, and others have slanted walls. Such differences in the shape of unit cells produce differences in the shape of mineral crystals.

Chemical Bonds are forces that hold atoms together in a crystal. These forces are electrical. They result when atoms exchange or share some of their electrons. Chemical bonds can hold two or more atoms together only in definite positions. The positions depend on the size of the atoms and on the number of bonding electrons. In turn, the shape of a unit cell depends on the positions the atoms take when they are bonded together.

Bonds between atoms are not all equally strong. Atoms may be held in some positions by powerful bonds, and in other positions by weak bonds. This variation in bonding explains why some crystals can be cleaved. Cleavage can take place when the weak bonds lie along a flat surface called a *cleavage plane*. When the crystal is cut along this plane, the weak bonds break and the crystal splits, exposing the flat surface.

How Minerals Grow. Almost all minerals grow in liquids. For example, some crystals grow in a liquid called *magma* deep inside the earth. This extremely hot substance contains all the kinds of atoms that make up the earth's minerals. When magma cools, some atoms become bonded together and form tiny crystals. The

HOW ATOMS ARE ARRANGED IN MINERALS

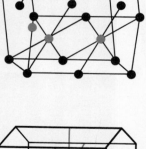

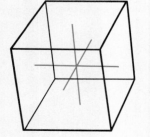

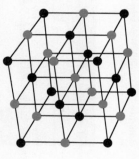

A Corundum Crystal, *above left,* has six sides. Its unit cell, *center,* is a six-sided "room" containing 21 oxygen atoms (black) and 6 aluminum atoms (blue). Corundum belongs to the hexagonal system, *right,* which has four axes.

A Halite Crystal, *above left,* has four sides and is made up of billions of four-sided unit cells. Each cell, *center,* contains 14 sodium atoms (shown in black) and 13 chlorine atoms (blue). Halite belongs to the isometric crystal system—one of six systems into which all mineral crystals are grouped. A general diagram for the isometric system, *right,* includes three axes (imaginary lines) that show the directions followed by the edges of the crystal.

crystals grow by adding layers of atoms to their flat outer surfaces. The new atoms must be the right size, and they must have the right number of bonding electrons to fit into the growing crystals.

The atoms of many chemicals are almost alike in size and electrical characteristics. Such atoms can take one another's place in a growing crystal. Some minerals have the same kind of crystal but differ in one of the atoms that make it up. For example, olivine has a basic crystal made of oxygen and silicon atoms. Either iron or magnesium atoms can fit into this crystal. As a result, there are two kinds of olivine—forsterite, which contains magnesium, and fayalite, which contains iron. Mineralogists use the term *isomorphic* for minerals that have the same form but different compositions.

Some mineral crystals are made of the same kinds of atoms but differ in the way the atoms are arranged. For example, quartz, coesite, and tridymite contain the same relative number of oxygen and silicon atoms, but their crystals have different forms. Mineralogists use the term *polymorphic* for minerals that have different forms but the same composition.

Minerals were among the first substances to be used and described by man. Egyptian paintings of 5,000 years ago show that minerals were used in weapons and jewelry, and in religious ceremonies. Theophrastus, a Greek philosopher, wrote a short work on minerals about 300 B.C. Pliny the Elder of Rome wrote about metals, ores, stones, and gems about A.D. 77. Other early writings about minerals were done by German scientists. These writings include *De Mineralibus* (1262) by Albertus Magnus and *De Re Metallica* (1556) by Georgius Agricola.

Early Studies of crystals began in the 1600's. In 1665, Robert Hooke, an English scientist, showed that metal balls piled in different ways duplicated the shapes of alum crystals. In 1669, Nicolaus Steno, a Danish physician, found that the angles between the faces of quartz crystals were the same even though the crystals had different shapes. A French scientist, Romé de l'Isle, suggested in 1772 that Steno's discovery could be explained only if the crystals were composed of identical units stacked together in a regular way.

By the late 1700's, scientists had studied and described many minerals. But they had only guessed about the makeup of crystals and the reasons for their shape. About 1780, chemists began to develop correct ideas about the nature of chemical elements and other substances. These ideas helped scientists understand the chemical makeup of minerals, but did not remove the mystery about crystal shape and internal structure.

The 1900's. During the 1900's, X-ray studies provided the key to the internal structure of minerals. The first X-ray experiment on minerals was performed in 1912 by the German scientist Max von Laue. At that time, scientists did not fully understand either X rays or crystals. Laue set up an experiment to investigate each at the same time. He believed that if X rays act like light rays, and if the atoms in a crystal have a regular arrangement, a beam of X rays sent through a crystal would be divided into several narrow beams. When Laue sent an X ray beam through a crystal of sphalerite, he found that the beam was divided. With the help of similar experiments, scientists finally learned how atoms are arranged to form crystals.

Mineralogists are still trying to answer many questions. They would like to know how billions of atoms can move relatively long distances to join a growing crystal in exactly the right places. For example, how do ice crystals form such perfect shapes as those shown in the Snow article? Mineralogists also would like to know more about the "wrong" things that happen in a growing crystal. What controls the kind and the number of atoms that form impurities in a crystal? Why do such impurities affect a crystal's mechanical and electrical properties? The operation of electronic devices called *semiconductors* depends on the presence of impurities in crystals (see SEMICONDUCTOR).

New uses are constantly being found for such chemical elements as beryllium, indium, titanium, tantalum, and the rare earths. Mineralogists are trying to find minerals containing these elements. They are also developing methods for removing these elements from the minerals.

WILLIAM H. DENNEN

WHY SOME MINERALS CLEAVE

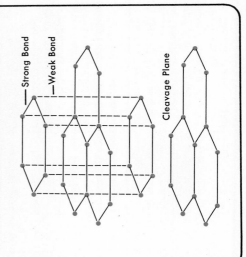

Graphite, *above*, consists of layers of carbon atoms. Weak bonds hold the layers together and form cleavage planes, *below*. The crystal splits into tablets along these planes.

Strong Bond

Weak Bond

Cleavage Plane

MINERAL / Study Aids

Related Articles. For information on the minerals found in specific parts of the world, see the Natural Resources section of the articles on each country, state, and province. See also the following articles:

MINERALS

Alabaster	Dolomite	Malachite
Amphibole	Emery	Meerschaum
Argentite	Feldspar	Mica
Asbestos	Flint	Molybdenite
Azurite	Fluorite	Pyrite
Bauxite	Galena	Pyroxene
Beryl	Glauconite	Quartz
Calcite	Graphite	Rutile
Carnotite	Gypsum	Salt
Chalcocite	Hematite	Serpentine
Cinnabar	Hornblende	Sillimanite
Columbite	Ilmenite	Talc
Corundum	Kyanite	Vermiculite
Cryolite	Limonite	Wolframite
Diopside	Loadstone	Zeolite

OTHER RELATED ARTICLES

See GEM; METAL; MINING; and ROCK with their lists of Related Articles. See also the following articles:

Alumina	Conservation (Mineral
Ceramics	Conservation)
Clay	Crystal and Crystallization
	Hardness
	Mica
	Mineral Wool

Outline

I. Identifying Minerals
  A. Luster
  B. Cleavage
  C. Hardness
  D. Color
  E. Other Identification
    Tests

II. Inside Minerals
  A. Mineral Crystals
  B. Chemical Bonds
  C. How Minerals Grow

III. History of Mineralogy

Questions

Why does quartz have a variety of colors?
What is a unit cell?
What mineral has a salty taste? A sweet taste?
Why can some minerals be split into pieces with flat surfaces?
Why is a man-made diamond not a mineral?
What did Max von Laue discover about minerals?
What holds together the atoms in a crystal?
How many kinds of minerals are there?
What kind of mineral is a carbonate? Why does acid fizz when poured on a carbonate?
How do minerals grow?

Books to Read

DANA, EDWARD S. *Minerals and How to Study Them.* Rev. by Cornelius S. Hurlbut, Jr. 3rd ed. Wiley, 1949. A general and brief introduction to mineralogy. *Dana's Manual of Mineralogy.* 17th ed. 1959. A more detailed and advanced book.

DENNEN, WILLIAM H. *Principles of Mineralogy.* Revised printing with determinative tables. Ronald, 1960. An introductory college text.

DIETRICH, R. V. *Mineral Tables: Hand Specimen Properties of 1500 Minerals.* Virginia Polytechnic Institute, Bulletin 160, Engineering Experiment Station Series. Blacksburg, Va., 1966.

LOOMIS, FREDERIC B. *Field Book of Common Rocks and Minerals.* Rev. ed. Putnam, 1948. A book useful for both children and adults.

ZIM, HERBERT S., and SHAFFER, PAUL R. *Rocks and Minerals.* A pocket handbook with many illustrations that is useful for both children and adults.

MINERAL OIL is a clear, colorless, oily liquid with almost no taste or odor. It is also called *liquid petrolatum, white mineral oil,* and *white paraffin oil.* Mineral oil is used in medicinal and cosmetic preparations such as laxatives and hair tonics. It is also used as a *diluent* (dissolver) in the manufacture of plastics, and as a lubricant in industrial operations. Mineral oil is obtained when petroleum *fractions* (separated parts) are boiled at 600° to 750° F. (316° to 399° C.). The fractions are refined to make pure mineral oil. See also PETROLATUM.

CLARENCE KARR, JR.

MINERAL WATER, or AERATED WATER, is spring water with a high content of mineral matter or of gas. (The term *aerated* means *charged with gas.*) The mineral matter includes salt, Epsom salt, lime, magnesia, iron, silica, boron, fluorine, and many others, including radioactive substances. The most common gases are carbonic acid and hydrogen sulfide.

In most cases, the water is rain water that has seeped underground through rocks, dissolving mineral matter on the way. Other springs may contain *magmatic* or *juvenile* water, which rises from deep in the earth after forming through a chemical process in rocks. Some of these springs are hot springs. Others have cooled to ordinary temperatures.

People have used mineral water since ancient times to cure such ailments as rheumatism, skin infections, and poor digestion. The temperature of the water, the location, the altitude, and the climate at the springs are all considered in the treatment.

There are many thousands of mineral springs in North America. About 800 of these have at one time or another had *spas* (resorts) where people used to come for the waters. Most of these resorts are in the Eastern and Midwestern states. Their popularity has greatly declined since the turn of the century and many have gone out of business. The best-known mineral springs today are at Saratoga Springs, N.Y.; Hot Springs, Ark., and French Lick, Ind. Hot Springs has been made a national park.

The waters from some foreign springs are imported to the United States. Among these waters are the Apollinaris from Germany, Hunyadi-Janos from Hungary, and Vichy from France.

Water taken from mineral springs is sold in sterilized glass bottles. Bottling companies usually make every effort to keep the bottled water as pure as when it comes from the ground.

RAY K. LINSLEY

See also BLACK FOREST; HOT SPRINGS NATIONAL PARK; SARATOGA SPRINGS.

MINERAL WOOL is an insulating material made from the minerals which are taken from iron-making blast furnaces as refuse, or *slag.* To make mineral wool, the molten slag is forced by steam pressure through a crescent-shaped opening. It cools in long fibers which are pressed into mats.

Mineral wool does not conduct heat and cannot be set on fire. It is used for packing around heated objects, such as steam pipes and boilers, to prevent the escape of heat. It also is used to protect water pipes from frost, and as matting under floors to deaden sound. Mineral wool is sometimes called *mineral cotton* or *slag wool* in the industry.

GEORGE W. WASHA

See also ASBESTOS; INSULATION.

MINERALOGY. See MINERAL.

Vatican Museum, Rome. (Alinari)

Minerva, a Greek sculpture, was made in the 400's B.C.

The Art Institute of Chicago

Ming Dynasty Pottery is highly valued by museums.

MINERALS IN DIET. See NUTRITION.

MINERVA was the goddess of wisdom and war in Roman mythology. She was also a goddess of arts and of such crafts as spinning and weaving. The Greeks called her ATHENA. Minerva and Neptune (Poseidon) had a contest for the protection of Athens. Minerva produced the olive, and Neptune the horse. The gods decided that the olive was of greater benefit to mankind, and named the city Athens after her.

She was the daughter of Jupiter (Zeus) and Metis (Wisdom). Jupiter swallowed Metis before Minerva was born, and Minerva sprang fully grown and dressed in armor from the forehead of Jupiter (see JUPITER).

Minerva carried the magic shield called the *aegis*. This had the head of Medusa in the center of it, and it could turn enemies to stone (see AEGIS; MEDUSA). Minerva is usually shown in art wearing a helmet.   VAN JOHNSON

See also ATHENAEUM.

MINES, BUREAU OF, an agency of the United States government, works to ensure efficient mining, processing, and use of mineral and fuel resources. The bureau conducts research on new mining methods to help assure adequate supplies of essential raw materials. It also estimates the commercial potential of the country's mineral deposits and provides information on mineral resources throughout the world. It produces most of the helium used in non-Communist nations.

Safety is one of the bureau's chief concerns. The bureau conducts safety inspections of mines and helps train workers in accident prevention and rescue procedure. The Bureau of Mines was created in 1910. It is part of the Department of the Interior.

Critically reviewed by the DEPARTMENT OF THE INTERIOR

MING DYNASTY ruled China from A.D. 1368 to 1644, a period of Chinese rule between two foreign conquests. It was preceded by the Mongol empire and followed by the Manchu dynasty. Ming rulers restored traditional institutions, such as the civil service, which the Mongols had temporarily suspended. Chinese authority extended into Mongolia, Korea, Southeast Asia, and the Ryukyu Islands.

Ming means *bright* in Chinese, and the period was important especially in the arts. Ming architects built the imperial palace, which is called the *Forbidden City*,

in Peking. Many other buildings from this period are still standing. Artists produced beautiful porcelain, bronze, and lacquer ware. Western traders came to China for the first time. The Chinese also welcomed Jesuit missionaries from Europe.   THEODORE H. E. CHEN

MING TREE is an imitation of the dwarf trees grown in Asia. Ming trees are made by gluing several gnarled branches or twigs together into the form of a windswept tree. Covering the branches with moss or lichens makes them look old and weathered. Ming trees can be placed in a low bowl along with a figurine and used as an ornament or table decoration.   GEORGE B. CUMMINS

See also DWARF (picture: Dwarf Trees).

MINHOW. See FOOCHOW.

MINIATURE PINSCHER is a toy dog of the terrier family. It comes from the Rhine Valley of Germany. The Germans sometimes call the dog a *reh pinscher* because it looks like the small deer found in forests. It has a wedge-shaped head and bright black eyes. The dog may be red, or it may be black with a tan spot over each eye and stripes on its toes. The dog resembles the Doberman pinscher, but weighs only 6 to 10 pounds. JOSEPHINE Z. RINE

See also DOG (color picture: Toy Dogs).

MINIATURE SCHNAUZER. See SCHNAUZER.

MINIM is the smallest measure druggists and apothecaries use for liquids. It is a unit in the *apothecaries' measure* of the United States and Great Britain. The word *minim* comes from the Latin word *minimus*, meaning the *smallest*. The minim is equal to one drop, or $\frac{1}{60}$ of a liquid dram, in the apothecaries' measure. One minim equals $\frac{1}{480}$ ounce, because eight drams equal one ounce.   E. G. STRAUS

MINIMUM WAGE is the smallest amount of money per hour that an employer may legally pay a worker. It may be established by law to cover all workers, or only those in a particular industry or industries. It is usually set so a person working a normal number of hours can support a family at acceptable minimum standards. See WAGES AND HOURS.

A minimum wage is usually well below the average wage paid to factory workers. Self-employed persons usually are not covered by minimum wage laws. Employees of small businesses often are not covered.

Several U.S. states have minimum wage laws or boards that set minimum wages. Boards also set minimum wages for certain kinds of work done for the U.S. government. The U.S. Fair Labor Standards Act covers most workers in businesses engaged in interstate commerce. The original act, passed in 1938, set a minimum wage of 25 cents an hour, and provided that the wage be raised to 40 cents by 1945. The minimum wage has since been increased by amendments to the Fair Labor Standards Act in 1949, 1955, 1961, and 1966.

The 1966 amendment provided that the 30 million workers already covered would receive minimum rates of $1.40 an hour in 1967 and $1.60 in 1968. The amendment also extended coverage to 8 million other workers. Their minimum wage started at $1 an hour in 1967 and would reach $1.60 in 1971.

In Great Britain, wage boards set minimum wages for particular industries. In Great Britain and some other European countries, labor unions and employers set unofficial minimum wages by mutual agreement.

MINING

MINING is the process of taking mineral substances from the earth. A mineral substance is almost any non-living thing that is found in the earth. These substances include metal compounds, coal, sand, oil, natural gas, and many other useful things.

Almost every substance that man gets from the earth is obtained by mining. Mining provides iron and copper for making airplanes, automobiles, and refrigerators. Mines also supply salt for food; gold, silver, and diamonds for jewelry; and coal for fuel. Men mine uranium for atomic energy, stone for buildings, phosphate to make plants grow, and gravel for highways.

Some minerals can be mined more cheaply than others because they are found at the surface of the earth. Others lie buried thousands of feet beneath the surface. They can be removed by digging deep underground. Still other mineral elements are found in oceans, lakes, and rivers.

Man has mined the earth for thousands of years. About 6,000 B.C., men dug pits and tunnels to obtain flint, a hard stone used to make tools and weapons. By 3,000 B.C., men were mining tin and copper. These metals were combined to make bronze, a hard alloy (mixture of metals) that made better tools and weapons.

The ancient Romans probably were the first people to realize that mining could make a nation rich and powerful. Merchants traded valuable stones and metals and brought riches to the Roman Empire. The Romans took over the mines of every country they conquered.

The Roman Empire ended in the A.D. 400's. For about a thousand years, few advancements were made in mining. During the 1400's, coal, iron, and other minerals were mined in Europe, especially in Germany and France. Mining also began to develop in South America. The Inca Indians and other tribes of South America used metals to make tools, jewelry, and weapons.

Mining began in what is now the United States during the early 1700's. French explorers mined lead and zinc in the valley of the Mississippi River. In the mid-1800's, men began to dig up large amounts of coal in Pennsylvania. At about the same time, thousands of persons rushed to California hoping to find gold. In the West, the gold rush led to the discovery of copper, lead, silver, and other useful mineral substances.

J. Donald Forrester, the contributor of this article, is Dean of the College of Mines of the University of Arizona, and Director of the Arizona Bureau of Mines.

Rotkin, PPI

In an Open-Pit Copper Mine in Utah, electric power shovels dig the pit and railroad cars carry out the ore. The equipment moves to and from the pit over a continuous road formed by a series of connected, steplike ledges called benches.

MINING/*Kinds of Mining*

There are many methods of mining, but each is based on where and how a mineral deposit is found in the earth. Some mineral deposits lie at or near the earth's surface, and others are far underground. Some minerals are found as a compact mass, but others are widely scattered. Minerals also vary in hardness and in the ease with which the ore can be separated from the surrounding rocks. Certain mineral substances are liquids, or can be changed into liquids, and are obtained by various methods of pumping. For a discussion of the methods of mining a particular mineral, see the WORLD BOOK article on that mineral, such as GOLD.

Surface Mining Methods

Surface mining methods are used when deposits occur at or near the surface of the earth. These methods include placer mining, dredging, open-pit mining, strip mining, and quarrying.

Placer Mining is a way of obtaining gold, platinum, tin, and other so-called *heavy minerals* from gravel and sand deposits where nearby water supplies are plentiful. The mineral-bearing gravel and sand are shoveled into the upper end of a slanting wooden trough called a *riffle box*. In the box, they are washed by water. The valuable minerals are heavier than the sand and gravel, and settle in grooves on the bottom of the box. The noneconomic gravel and sand are washed away. The mineral-bearing gravel and sand may also be moved directly from a deposit into the riffle box by the force of water shooting out through a large nozzle called a *hydraugiant*. Placer mining done in this way is called *panning*. Sometimes a form of placer mining called *panlicking* is used to get gold and other minerals from streams.

Dredging is used especially where mineral-bearing sand and gravel layers are exceptionally thick. In dredging, a pond or lake must be formed so that a large, bargelike machine called a *dredge* can be floated. An endless chain of buckets is attached to a *boom* (long beam) at the front end of the dredge. The buckets dip into the water when one end of the boom is lowered. They dig up the mineral-bearing sand and gravel and move the material to a bin on the deck of the dredge. The material is taken from the bin and washed in much the same way as in placer mining. After the valuable minerals are collected, the sand and gravel are put on a conveyor belt and dumped back into the pond behind the dredge. By digging forward while at the same time disposing of the waste sand and gravel to the rear, the pond and the dredge move ahead as the deposit is mined.

When mining some kinds of loose gravel deposits, machines called *draglines* or *slacklines* are used. These machines have a scoop attached to a high boom. The scoop is pulled back and forth along the deposit to gather material, which is put into a separating bin.

Open-Pit Mining is used to dig valuable minerals from large deposits in hard rock. Often whole mountains are removed or large pits are dug by this method. When digging the mine, the miners make a series of connected, steplike ledges called *benches*. Each bench is lower than the one above. The benches form a road around the sides of the mine, so that the ore can be brought up from the pit by truck or railroad train.

Maurice Broomfield, Diamond Corp. West Africa Ltd.

Panning for Diamonds, African miners swirl water and diamond-bearing gravel around in pans. The water washes away lightweight gravel, leaving the diamonds and heavy gravel.

W. W. Bacon, III, Rapho Guillumette

A Mining Dredge digs for gold in Alaska. A revolving chain of buckets scoops up a mixture of gold and sand. The dredge separates the gold and sand, and dumps the sand into the pond.

MINING

Miners use explosives to break up great masses of ore-bearing hard rock. The men load the broken rock into large trucks or trains. By using electric power shovels, large amounts of a mineral can be collected cheaply by the open-pit method. Many important copper, iron, diamond, phosphate, and gypsum mines are operated as open pits.

Strip Mining involves removing the material that covers the deposit so the deposit can be dug up. Power shovels remove this material, called the *overburden*. Smaller shovels are then used to load the deposit into huge trucks. Coal which lies near the surface of the earth can often be mined cheaply by this method.

Quarrying is a method in which large blocks of rock are wedged loose or sawed out of a deposit that lies near the surface. Chains and pulleys are used to lift the blocks from the pit. Miners quarry such rock materials as marble, granite, sandstone, limestone, and slate.

Gravel and sand also are quarried. Power shovels dig into the gravel or sand deposit and load the material into trucks or trains. It is then taken to be washed or cleaned, or is hauled directly to a construction site.

Underground Mining Methods

Underground methods are used when the mineral deposit lies deep beneath the earth's surface. First the miners *drive* (dig) an opening to the mine. A vertical opening is called a *shaft*. A passage that is nearly horizontal, dug into the side of a hill or mountain, is called an *adit*. The miners usually make the opening by blasting with explosives. Timber may be needed to support the roof and walls of the passage. If the deposit is extremely hard, the miners must also use explosives to loosen the mineral-bearing mass.

The miners load the ore on trucks or small trains and remove it from the mine. Much of the machinery used to remove ore from underground mines is operated by electric power or compressed air. Engines that burn gasoline or diesel fuel are not generally used. These fuels may give off poisonous gases that could injure the men.

If the mine has a vertical opening to the surface, the mineral is hauled to the shaft. An elevator is installed in the shaft to carry the miners to and from the mine, and to remove the ore. An elevator car used to haul miners is called a *cage*. A bucketlike car that removes ore is called a *skip*.

There are two main types of underground mining: (1) level and shaft mining and (2) room and pillar mining.

Level and Shaft Mining is used especially when the mass of ore slants so that it extends downward into the earth. The miners dig a shaft that may reach a depth of a mile or more. They then remove the ore through a system of horizontal passages called *levels*. These passages are dug at different depths, usually 100 to 200 feet from each other. The levels are connected by a shaft, steeply sloping passages called *raises*, and openings called *stopes*, which have been formed by the removal of ore. The miners often remove the ore by working upward from one level to the next. The ore falls through the raises to be hoisted in small train cars and carried to the shaft to be hoisted to the surface.

This method of mining is much more selective than surface mining. Miners make an effort to remove only the ore, and leave the useless rock surrounding it. Level and shaft mining is expensive because it takes more time to follow the mass of ore. It also requires a richer

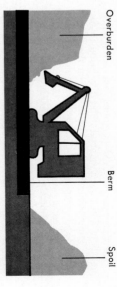

Overburden   Berm   Spoil

In Strip Mining, huge power shovels strip away the shallow layer of soil and rock which covers the mineral deposit. Miners use this method to remove coal lying near the surface of the earth.

A **"Continuous Miner"** is used to mine underground potash deposits. The rotating cutters of this 132-ton machine can rip out 7½ tons of potash a minute.

Westinghouse Air Brake Co.

MINING TERMS

Adit is a nearly horizontal passage from the earth's surface into a mine.

Crosscut is a horizontal mine passage whose direction is at a right or sharp angle to the directions of the veins or other geologic structures in a mine.

Drift is a horizontal mine passage that has been driven along or parallel to the course of a vein.

Footwall is the wall or zone of rock under an inclined vein. It is beneath the miner's feet as he excavates the ore.

Gangue is the worthless material mixed with the ore in a mineral deposit.

Hanging Wall is the wall or zone of rock above an inclined vein. It hangs above the miner as he excavates the ore.

Level is the group of drifts and crosscuts made at one depth in an underground mine. Miners usually develop several levels, each at a different depth.

Ore is a natural mass of minerals that can be mined at a profit. Most ores contain metal, but they also may be such nonmetallic substances as sulfur or fluorite.

Outcrop is the exposed surface of a mineral deposit.

Overburden is the soil or rock that covers a mineral deposit.

Quarry is an open or surface excavation from which building stone is usually obtained.

Raise is a passage driven upward from a lower level toward an upper level in an underground mine.

Shaft is a vertical passage from the earth's surface into a mine. It is shaped like an elevator shaft.

Stope is an underground excavation formed by the removal of ore between one level and the next in a mine.

Stripping is the process of removing the overburden from a mineral deposit.

Sump is an excavation made at the bottom of a shaft to collect water in order to remove it from a mine.

Tunnel is a horizontal underground passage that opens to the surface at both ends.

Vein is a mineral deposit with definite boundaries that separate it from the surrounding rock.

Winze is a passage that has been driven downward from a level in an underground mine.

AN UNDERGROUND MINE

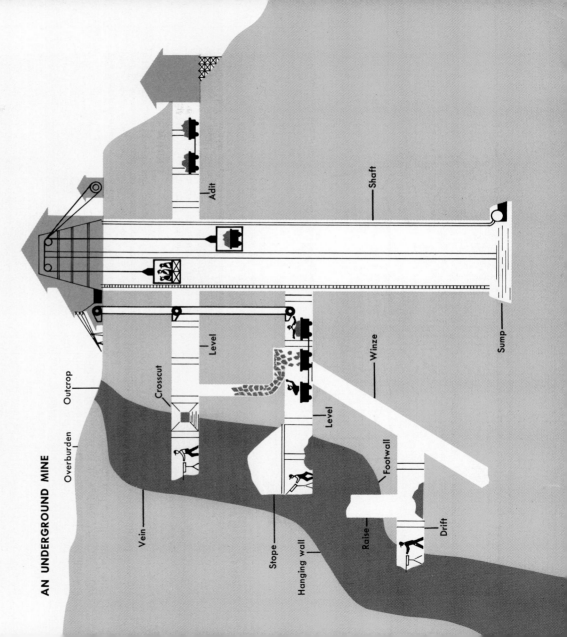

Overburden

Outcrop

Crosscut

Level

Winze

Level

Adit

Shaft

Sump

Vein

Stope

Hanging wall

Footwall

Raise

Drift

MINING

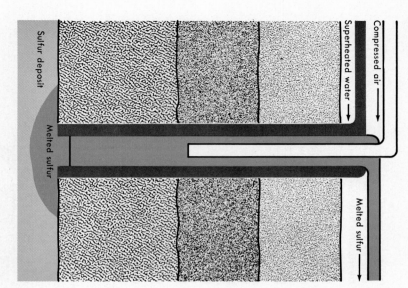

Compressed air →

Superheated water →

→ Melted sulfur

Sulfur deposit

Melted sulfur

deposit than mining that is not selective. Copper, lead, zinc, gold, and silver are frequently mined by this method.

Room and Pillar Mining is often used for mineral deposits that lie flat. The mine may be developed at a single depth. The miners dig a large horizontal chamber and divide it into rooms. Pillars of some of the mineral-bearing rock are left to support the roof of the chamber so that the mine does not collapse. This method of mining is selective and is used for some types of lead, zinc, salt, potash, coal, and other mineral deposits.

Pumping Methods

The waters of the ocean and of some lakes, including Great Salt Lake in Utah, contain huge amounts of mineral elements. They often are obtained by pumping the water into plants where it is treated. Pumps move large amounts of seawater through *precipitators* (separators) so that the minerals can be removed. Most of the magnesium used today is obtained by this method.

Pumping is sometimes used to get salt from beds beneath the earth's surface. Workers drill holes and circulate water underground to dissolve the salt and form a salt-water solution called *brine*. The brine is pumped to the surface and taken to a factory. There, the water is evaporated, and the salt forms a solid again. A somewhat similar method called *leaching* is used for some ores that contain copper (see COPPER [Leaching]).

The Frasch process, another pumping method, is often used in mining sulfur, a mineral that melts easily. Miners bore holes in a buried sulfur bed and then inject superheated water. The sulfur melts and forms a liquid which is pumped to the surface. After the sulfur cools, it becomes a solid again, and can be stored until needed.

Petroleum and natural gas also are pumped from the ground (see PETROLEUM; GAS [fuel]).

The Frasch Method of mining sulfur uses hot water that flows into a deposit through the outer of three pipes. The sulfur melts and begins to rise through the middle pipe. Compressed air from the inner pipe forces the sulfur through the middle pipe.

UNDERWATER MINING

This diagram shows mining equipment that pumps sulfur from beneath the ocean floor off the coast of Louisiana. The Frasch process is used to mine sulfur deposits that lie as much as 2,500 feet below sea level. The main units of the mine stand on platforms which rest on steel supports more than 60 feet above the water. A series of 200-foot-long bridges connects the platforms and provides a road for transporting equipment and workers. Workers live on this steel island in modern, air-conditioned living quarters. They travel to and from the shore by helicopter.

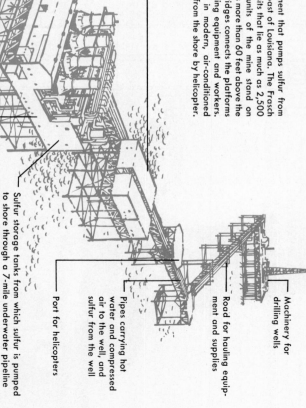

Warehouses and machine shops

Living quarters and offices

Power plant has three chief functions. It (1) heats the water used to melt the sulfur, (2) supplies the compressed air which lifts the melted sulfur to the surface, and (3) provides electric power to run drilling machinery and other equipment.

Sulfur storage tanks from which sulfur is pumped to shore through a 7-mile underwater pipeline

Port for helicopters

Road for hauling equipment and supplies

Pipes carrying hot water and compressed air to the well, and sulfur from the well

Machinery for drilling wells

MINING / The Mining Industry

In the late 1960's, the annual value of mining production in the United States was about $23 billion. In Canada, the value of mineral production was about $4½ billion a year. For the value of mining in the states and provinces, see the *Economy* section of the WORLD BOOK articles on each state and province.

The value of the world's mining production outside the United States is probably about equal to that of the United States. However, worldwide production figures are not known. Reliable figures for many countries, including Communist nations, are not available.

About 640,000 persons earn their living in the U.S. mining industry. The industry offers a wide variety of careers for professional, skilled, and semiskilled workers.

Management in the industry consists mainly of businessmen and engineers. These men manage mines, smelters, and refineries, and direct the search for new deposits. They try to improve mining methods, and to develop new operating and engineering practices.

Many universities and colleges offer training for various specialized careers in mining industry engineering. The *geological engineer* or *exploration engineer* guides the search for mineral deposits and estimates their value. The *production engineer* or *mining engineer* decides on the best and cheapest method of removing minerals from the earth. The *beneficiation engineer* or *metallurgical engineer* directs the *beneficiation* (milling, smelting, and refining) of minerals so they can be sold or used by his company. Some business firms own and operate their own mines to obtain minerals needed to manufacture their products. For example, many steel companies operate coal mines to get coke for making steel. Such mines are called *captive mines*. The minerals they produce are used only by the company that owns the mine.

Jon Brenneis

Mining Exploration Teams of geologists, geophysicists, and other experts search for minerals. Mining companies use their reports on the probable size, shape, and value of deposits.

LEADING MINING STATES AND PROVINCES
Value of minerals produced in 1967

Texas $5,315,000,000	
Louisiana $3,962,000,000	
California $1,573,000,000	
Ontario $1,067,000,000	
Oklahoma $1,032,000,000	
West Virginia $938,000,000	
Alberta $887,000,000	
New Mexico $874,000,000	
Pennsylvania $789,000,000	
Quebec $651,000,000	

Sources: Dominion Bureau of Statistics; U.S. Bureau of Mines

LEADING MINING COUNTRIES
Value of minerals produced in 1967

United States $22,658,000,000	
Canada $4,271,000,000	
Germany (West) $2,874,000,000	
Venezuela $2,568,000,000	
South Africa $1,802,000,000	
France $1,750,000,000	
Great Britain $1,680,000,000	
Iran $1,600,000,000*	
Saudi Arabia $1,400,000,000*	
Kuwait $1,300,000,000*	

*Estimates
Data from Russia, China, and other Communist countries are unavailable. Includes cement for all cement-producing countries except the United States and Canada.

Sources: Dominion Bureau of Statistics; U.S. Bureau of Mines

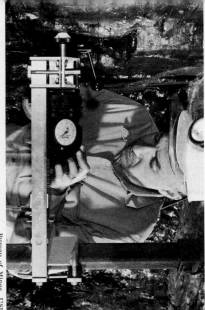

Bureau of Mines, USDI

Mining Engineers use scientific instruments to find the easiest and cheapest way of removing minerals from the earth.

Some mining engineers specialize in mine safety. Their programs have been so effective that working as a miner today is no more dangerous than working in many other industries.

The mining industry also employs salesmen, surveyors, and scientists, including chemists and physicists.

Among the workers in mines are men skilled in operating and maintaining various kinds of cranes, shovels, and machines. Other mineworkers include mechanics, electricians, truck drivers, hoistmen, and laborers.

Further information on mining careers may be obtained by writing the American Institute of Mining, Metallurgical and Petroleum Engineers, 345 E. 47th St., New York, N.Y. 10017.

J. Donald Forrester

MINING/Study Aids

Related Articles. See also Mineral and the Economy section of the various country, state, and province articles. Other related articles in World Book include:

Alchemy	Iron and Steel	Salt
Assaying	Lead	Silver
Coal	Magnesium	Tin
Coke	Metal	United Mine Workers
Copper	Metallurgy	of America
Damp	Mines, Bureau of	Uranium
Diamond	Ore	Well
Engineering	Petroleum	Western Frontier Life
Gas (fuel)	Prospecting	(The Search for
Gem	Quarrying	Gold and Silver)
Gold	Safety Lamp	Zinc

Outline

I. Kinds of Mining
 A. Surface Mining Methods
 B. Underground Mining Methods
 C. Pumping Methods
II. The Mining Industry

Questions

What are captive mines?
What are the two chief types of underground mining?
What minerals are often obtained by open-pit mining?

What are some specialized positions for mining engineers?
When are draglines used in dredging?
How do miners obtain sulfur by the Frasch process?
What determines the method used to mine a mineral?
What is the difference between a shaft and an adit?
What is the overburden?
Why are selective methods of mining more expensive than other methods?

MINING ENGINEERING. See Mining (The Mining Industry); Engineering (Main Branches; table).

MINISTER, in international relations, is a diplomatic agent who represents his country in a foreign land. He is appointed by the head of his country, and ranks below an ambassador. The President of the United States appoints ministers. Like all diplomatic agents in the United States, ministers get their credentials from the Secretary of State. Most countries tend to exchange ambassadors, rather than ministers.

In some countries, the name *minister* is also given to high administrative officers who make up the cabinet or executive body (see Cabinet).

Payson S. Wild, Jr.

See also Ambassador; Diplomacy (table); Ministry.

MINISTER is the general term for an ordained, professional officer of a Christian church. Specifically, it is the usual title of the pastor of a congregation in most Protestant churches. He conducts worship, administers the sacraments, preaches, and assumes responsibility for the pastoral care of the people. Orthodox, Roman Catholic, and Anglican churches have three "orders" of ministers: bishops, priests, and deacons. Protestant churches that stress the priesthood of all believers do not regard the minister as of a different "order" from the laity. He is considered to be the leader of a congregation of ministering disciples.

The word *minister* comes from Christ's description of Himself as one who "came not to be ministered unto, but to minister" (Matt. 20:28), and from His charge to the Apostles, "Whosoever will be great among you shall be your minister" (Mark 10:43).

R. Pierce Beaver

MINISTER PLENIPOTENTIARY. See Ambassador.

MINISTER RESIDENT. See Ambassador.

MINISTRY, in government, is a body of executive officers who advise the head of a country or directly control a nation's affairs. Often, the members are members of parliament and heads of executive departments.

Ministries are part of the governmental setup of countries which have a parliamentary form of government. The ministry of Great Britain has furnished the model for all nations using the parliamentary system.

The British ministry consists of the prime minister and a number of other officers known as the *ministers.*

The monarch appoints the prime minister. He usually selects the leader of the party in control of the House of Commons. He bases his selections of the other ministers on the recommendations of the prime minister. British ministers are members of Parliament and are divided into *cabinet ministers* and *ministers not in the cabinet.* Cabinet ministers vary from cabinet to cabinet.

Major bills are introduced by ministers.

The British ministry represents the political party or parties that control the House of Commons. When it can no longer get parliamentary support, the ministry resigns.

Robert G. Neumann

See also Cabinet (The Cabinet System of Government); Prime Minister.

MINK

The **Mink** is a small, swift, agile mammal. It is a member of the weasel family. Its beautiful fur is prized for making expensive coats.

Valleywood Mink Farm, Swanton, Ohio

The **White Mink** has one of the most sought-after mink furs. Its color, extremely rare among minks, is known as a *mutation*.

Large Mink Ranches provide many of the mink pelts used to make coats. Mink ranchers try to improve the pelts by using selective breeding methods.

MINK is a small member of the weasel family. Its furs are made into costly coats for women. Minks live on wooded streams, lakes, and marshes of North America, from the Gulf of Mexico to the Arctic Circle, and in the northern parts of Europe and Asia. The mink is a swift and agile animal, at home on land or in the water. The male American mink is between 14 and 25 inches long, with a bushy tail extending another 8 or 9 inches. It is 4 or 5 inches high at the shoulders and sometimes weighs 2 pounds. The female is much smaller, sometimes weighing only half as much as the male. The European mink is a little smaller. Wild mink fur varies from light brown or tan to a dark chocolate color, with a white patch on the chin and several spots of white on the throat and chest.

Minks have many of the land habits of the weasel, and the water habits of the otter. They like watercourses where food such as frogs, crayfish, and fish are plentiful. They also feed on many small mammals such as mice, as well as on any birds that they can catch on the ground. A litter of 4 to 10 young minks, called *kits*, is born in the spring in a den among the rocks, under the roots of a tree, or in a hollow log. The family stays together until late summer or fall, when the young scatter to find hunting ranges of their own.

The mink has a strong, acrid, unpleasant odor. Unlike the skunk, the mink cannot spray its scent at a distance, but the odor is stronger and, to many persons, more nauseating. As a rule it is not noticeable except when the mink is in a rage. Like the other members of the weasel family, it can fight ferociously when it is cornered. Its chief enemies include the lynx, the bobcat, the fox, the great horned and snowy owls, and man. Trappers kill more minks than all the animals do.

The beautiful and costly mink furs never go out of fashion for coats, capes, jackets, neckpieces, stoles, and trimmings. The color of the fur often determines its value, and single pelts have sold for as much as $750 apiece. The value of a good dark-colored wild mink pelt is about $20. About 75 per cent of all the furs marketed come from mink ranches. These pelts bring $15 to $250 apiece. Minks in captivity have been bred to produce fur from white and pale silver to darkest brown. Such specially-developed fur is called *mutation mink*.

Scientific Classification. Minks belong to the family *Mustelidae*. The North American mink is genus *Mustela*, species *M. vison*. The European mink is genus *Mustela*, species *M. lutreola*.

E. Lendell Cockrum

See also Fur.

MINKOWSKI, HERMANN. See Fourth Dimension.

Minneapolis lies on both sides of the mighty Mississippi River. The downtown business district stretches out behind the city's river-front industrial development.

Minneapolis Chamber of Commerce

MINNEAPOLIS, *MIN ee AP oh lis,* Minn. (pop. 482,872; alt. 815 ft.), is the state's largest city and the younger of its *Twin Cities* (Minneapolis and Saint Paul). The Minneapolis-Saint Paul metropolitan area has a population of 1,482,030. The name *Minneapolis* combines the Indian word *minne* (water) and the Greek word *polis* (city). The city got this name because of the 22 natural lakes within the city limits. People often call Minneapolis the *Vacation Capital* because it is the gateway to the lake country of northern Minnesota.

Minneapolis is a city of trade and industry. Ships can sail from the Gulf of Mexico up the Mississippi River beyond the city. The city is an important producer of flour. More farm equipment is bought and sold in Minneapolis than in any other U.S. city.

Location, Size, and Description. Minneapolis lies in southeastern Minnesota, about 350 miles northwest of Chicago. The city covers more than 58 square miles. The Mississippi River divides Minneapolis into two areas, the larger part west of the river, and the smaller to the east. See MINNESOTA (political map).

In the downtown district, the main streets run from northwest to southeast, parallel to the Mississippi. Parks and wide boulevards separate many of the city's skyscrapers and large commercial buildings. Residential streets in the rest of the city run in a straight north-south direction. A system of connected boulevards called the *Grand Rounds* carries traffic rapidly through the city.

Cultural Life. Minneapolis is the home of the University of Minnesota, one of the leading educational institutions in the United States. Other colleges in the city include Augsburg College, MacPhail College of Music, Minneapolis College of Music, Minneapolis School of Art, and Minnesota Bible College. It also has North Central Bible College, Northwestern College, and Northwestern Lutheran Theological Seminary.

Many people rate the Minneapolis Symphony Orchestra as one of the best in the United States. The Tyrone Guthrie repertory theater, opened in 1963, produces plays during a 20-week season each summer. The Minneapolis Institute of Art holds annual exhibits of paintings by Twin-Cities artists. The Walker Art Center displays paintings and jade and ceramic objects.

Recreation. Minneapolis has over 150 public parks. Most of them line the shores of the Mississippi or surround the many small lakes within the city. Lake Minnetonka, about 12 miles southwest of the city, is a popular swimming, fishing, and boating area. The Minnesota Twins of the American Baseball League and the Minnesota Vikings of the National Football League play at Bloomington, a Twin-City suburb.

Visitors to Minneapolis often visit Fort Snelling, which was established in 1819. This military post formed the center of the first permanent settlement in Minneapolis. A $2 million veterans hospital now occupies part of the grounds at Fort Snelling. Many people visit the Stevens House. In 1849, John H. Stevens received a permit to settle on the west shore of the Mississippi in return for providing ferry service.

Industry and Commerce. Flour mills in Minneapolis can produce nearly 17,700,000 pounds of flour a day. The city's grain elevators have a capacity of about 100

boards, such as the school board. The city adopted a nonpartisan system of nominating city officers in 1912. A city planning board was established in 1919.

History. In 1680, a Belgian explorer and missionary named Louis Hennepin traveled up the Mississippi River and discovered a waterfall which he called the Falls of Saint Anthony (see HENNEPIN, LOUIS [picture]). He became the first white man to visit the present site of Minneapolis. Fort Snelling was established in 1819 at the point where the Minnesota and Mississippi rivers meet. Early settlers in Minneapolis included many lumbermen who moved from Maine in the 1840's. The federal government opened the lands west of the river for settlement in 1854. The town that developed west of the river was called Minneapolis. It remained separate from the settlement at St. Anthony until 1872, when the two towns were joined. The lumber industry flourished in Minneapolis until the nearby forests were exhausted.

CEDRIC M. ADAMS

For information on the monthly weather in Minneapolis and St. Paul, see MINNESOTA (Climate). See also MINNESOTA (picture: Tyrone Guthrie Theatre).

MINNEAPOLIS SCHOOL OF ART. See UNIVERSITIES AND COLLEGES (table).

MINNEHAHA was an Indian maiden in Henry Wadsworth Longfellow's poem *The Song of Hiawatha.* She married Hiawatha. See also HIAWATHA.

MINNEHAHA FALLS is a beautiful waterfall in Minneapolis, Minn. A bronze statue of Hiawatha and his Indian bride stands at the top of the falls. Water is sometimes pumped over the top to keep the 54-foot-high falls going. Henry Wadsworth Longfellow made the falls famous in his poem *The Song of Hiawatha.*

See also MINNESOTA (color picture).

MINNESINGER, *MIN uh sing er,* was one of a group of German love poets who flourished from the 1100's to the 1300's. The minnesingers sang their poetry to music at court festivals.

Minne was an old German word meaning *love.* The minnesingers' expressions of love were regulated by the courtly society that placed much value on form. Courtly love, as many minnesingers portrayed it, was the hopeless love of a knight for a lady of high station. The knight's plea that the lady answer his love was often expressed in feudal terms such as a vassal might use in begging a favor from his lord. The lady usually remained unapproachable.

The doctrines and forms of courtly love developed in southern France and spread to Germany. In addition to ideas of the feudal system, several literary traditions influenced the minnesingers. These included Arabic poetry transmitted from Spain, classical literature such as Ovid's *The Art of Love,* and medieval Latin poetry. The homage paid to the Virgin Mary in the 1100's also contributed to the idealization of women so basic to much of courtly love poetry.

The leading minnesingers included Dietmar von Aist, Kürenberger, Heinrich von Veldeke, Friedrich von Hausen, Heinrich von Morungen, Reinmar von Hagenau, Walther von der Vogelweide, Neidhart von Reuental, Tannhäuser, and Ulrich von Lichtenstein. JAMES F. POAG

See also TANNHÄUSER; WALTHER VON DER VOGELWEIDE.

Minneapolis Chamber of Commerce

Scenic Minneapolis has about 150 parks. Minnehaha Falls, above, in Minnehaha Park, is one of the city's most beautiful spots.

Visual Education Service

Fort Snelling stands south of Minneapolis near the junction of the Minnesota and Mississippi rivers. It was established in 1819.

million bushels. Large plants in Minneapolis include foundries, machine and railroad shops, and factories that make wood products. Manufacturers also produce farm and electrical machinery, food and dairy products, furniture, heat controls, knitted materials, and linseed oil. The city is one of the nation's leading electronics manufacturing centers.

Nine railroads serve Minneapolis. Buses and trucks enter from all parts of the nation. Eleven bridges cross the Mississippi River at Minneapolis. Airlines use the Minneapolis-St. Paul International Airport.

Government. Minneapolis was incorporated as a city in 1867. Administrative power for the city lies in the hands of a mayor, a city council, and several special

St. Paul's Skyline Rises Beyond a Bend of the Mississippi River

Lloyd Schnell

MINNESOTA

The Gopher State

Camping on the Shores of Snowbank Lake

Minnesota Dept. of Economic Development

Minnesota (blue) ranks 12th in size among all the states, and is the largest of the Midwestern States (gray).

Minnesota Farmland

Minnesota Winter by Adolf Dehn for the Field Enterprises Educational Corporation Collection

MINNESOTA is one of the chief food-producing states in the United States. The state's wheat crops, flour mills, and dairy products give Minnesota one of its nicknames—the *Bread and Butter State*. But Minnesota is usually called the *Gopher State*, because many gophers live on its southern prairies.

More than a million milk cows graze on the rich pastures of Minnesota's dairy farms. The farmers of this midwestern state also raise great numbers of beef cattle, calves, and hogs. Minnesota is a leading producer of corn, flaxseed, hay, potatoes, soybeans, and sugar beets. All these farm products bring in an enormous income. But manufacturing is even more important to Minnesota's economy than agriculture.

One of Minnesota's most important industries is processing the products of its farms. Minnesota makes more butter than any other state, and is a leading producer of milk and cheese. It is one of the top meat-packing, flour-producing, and vegetable-canning states.

About three-fifths of all the iron ore mined in the United States comes from Minnesota. The known deposits of the state's richest iron ore have been exhausted. But the Minnesota earth still contains billions of tons of valuable low-grade ore. Minnesota also has millions of acres of trees, although lumber companies have logged its forests heavily. These woodlands furnish raw materials for making pulp, paper, and other products.

Minnesota's scenic beauty, thousands of sparkling lakes, and deep pine woods make the state a vacation wonderland. It is a favorite state of hunters and fishermen because of its plentiful game animals and fish. In northern Minnesota, campers, canoeists, and hikers can explore thousands of square miles of wilderness.

The state's history is much the story of the development of its great natural resources. The fur-bearing animals of Minnesota's forests first attracted fur traders. Next, the fertile soil brought farmers, who poured into the region from the eastern states and from Europe. The thick forests of tall pines attracted lumberjacks from Maine, Michigan, and Wisconsin. Finally, miners came to dig the vast deposits of rich iron ore.

The name *Minnesota* comes from two Sioux Indian words meaning *sky-tinted waters*. St. Paul is the capital of Minnesota, and Minneapolis is the largest city. For the relationship of Minnesota to other states in its region, see the article on the MIDWESTERN STATES.

The contributors of this article are John R. Finnegan, Assistant Executive Editor of the St. Paul Dispatch-Pioneer Press; Harold T. Hagg, Professor of History and Chairman, Division of Social Sciences, at Bemidji State College; and Philip L. Tideman, Associate Professor of Geography at the University of Wyoming and former Assistant Professor of Geography at St. Cloud State College.

FACTS IN BRIEF

Capital: St. Paul.

Government: *Congress*—U.S. senators, 2; U.S. representatives, 8. *Electoral Votes*—10. *State Legislature*—senators, 67; representatives, 135. *Counties*—87.

Area: 84,068 square miles (including 4,779 square miles of inland water; excluding 2,212 square miles of Lake Superior), 12th in size among the states. *Greatest Distances*—(north-south) 411 miles; (east-west) 357 miles. *Shoreline*—180 miles.

Elevation: *Highest*—Eagle Mountain, 2,301 feet above sea level in Cook County. *Lowest*—602 feet above sea level, along Lake Superior.

Population: *1970 Preliminary Census*—3,767,975; density, 45 persons to the square mile. *1960 Census*—3,413,864, 18th among the states; distribution, 62 per cent urban, 38 per cent rural.

Chief Products: *Agriculture*—barley, beef cattle, corn, dairy products, eggs, hogs, oats, soybeans, turkeys, wheat. *Fishing Industry*—buffalo fish, carp, catfish, chubs, lake herring, tullibee, yellow pike. *Manufacturing and Processing*—chemicals; clothing; electrical machinery; food and food products; lumber and wood products; metal products; nonelectrical machinery; paper and related products; primary metals; printing and publishing; stone, clay, and glass products. *Mining*—clays, iron ore, sand and gravel, stone.

Statehood: May 11, 1858, the 32nd state.

State Motto: *L'Étoile du Nord* (The Star of the North).

State Song: "Hail! Minnesota." Words by Truman E. Rickard and Arthur E. Upson; music by Truman E. Rickard.

Constitution.
Minnesota is still governed under its original constitution, adopted in 1858. The constitution may be *amended* (changed) in two ways. An amendment may be proposed in the legislature, where it must be approved by a majority of the lawmakers. Next, it must be approved by a majority of the voters in an election. The constitution may also be amended by a constitutional convention. A proposal to call such a convention must be approved by two-thirds of the legislature and by a majority of the voters in an election. Proposals made by a convention become law after they have been approved by three-fifths of the voters casting ballots on the proposals.

Executive.
The governor of Minnesota holds office for a four-year term. He can be re-elected any number of times. The governor receives a yearly salary of $27,500. For a list of all the governors of Minnesota, see the *History* section of this article.

The lieutenant governor, secretary of state, attorney general, treasurer, and auditor are also elected to four-year terms. The governor appoints the heads of most state departments, boards, and commissions. Their terms range from two to six years.

Legislature
consists of a 67-member senate and a 135-member house of representatives. Minnesota has 67 legislative districts. Voters in 66 districts elect one senator and two representatives. Voters in one district elect one senator and three representatives. Senators serve four-year terms, and representatives serve two-year terms. State legislators are elected on a *nonpartisan* ballot—the ballot has no political party labels. Nebraska is the only other state in which the legislators are chosen in nonpartisan elections.

The legislature meets in regular session on the Tuesday after the first Monday in January in odd-numbered years. The constitution limits regular sessions to 120 legislative days. The governor may call special sessions.

Courts.
The state supreme court heads Minnesota's court system. The supreme court has a chief justice and six associate justices. All are elected to six-year terms. Minnesota has one district court. It is divided into 10 judicial districts. Each judicial district has three or more judges, who are elected to six-year terms. Each county has a probate court, presided over by at least one judge. Probate judges are elected to six-year terms. Some cities and villages have municipal courts. Municipal judges serve six years. Justices of the peace, elected to two-year terms, serve in townships, and in cities and villages that do not have municipal courts. All Minnesota judges are elected on nonpartisan ballots.

Local Government.
Minnesota has 87 counties. Each is governed by a board of commissioners, usually consisting of five members. The board's powers include borrowing money, collecting taxes, and determining how funds are to be spent. The board members are elected to four-year terms. Other county officials include the attorney, auditor, coroner, sheriff, and treasurer. These officials also serve four-year terms.

Minnesota has more than 800 cities and villages. The state constitution allows cities to adopt *home rule* charters. This means that a city may choose the form of government best suited to its needs. About 90 cities operate under home rule charters. Most cities use the mayor-council form of government. The rest use the commission or council-manager form. Minnesota villages operate under a village code adopted by the legislature.

Taxation.
Taxes bring in about 70 per cent of the state government's income. Almost all the rest comes from federal grants and other U.S. government programs. Taxes on personal income provide more than a third of the state's income. The state adopted a 3 per cent selective sales tax in 1967 to provide additional funds for municipalities and local school districts. Iron mining companies must pay a tax on all minerals they take from the ground.

Politics.
Throughout most of its history, Minnesota has strongly favored Republicans for state offices and for President. About two-thirds of Minnesota's gover-

The Golden Quadriga, a sculptured group of gilded figures, stands above the south entrance to Minnesota's Capitol. The figures symbolize prosperity.

Statue of Floyd B. Olson stands on the Capitol grounds in St. Paul. Olson, the first Farmer-Laborite governor of Minnesota, served from 1931 until 1936.

Photos, Minnesota Dept. of Economic Development

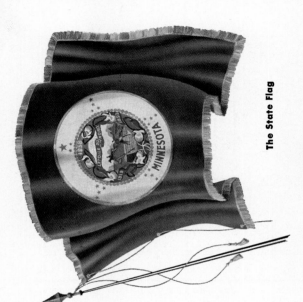

The State Flag

The State Flower
Pink and White Lady's-Slipper

The State Bird
Common Loon

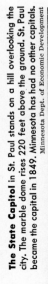

The State Tree
Norway Pine

The State Seal

Symbols of Minnesota. On the seal, the Indian riding into the sunset and the farmer symbolize the white man's rise and the Indian's decline in pioneer Minnesota. The waterfall and the forest represent the state's natural features. The seal was adopted in 1858. The state flag, adopted in 1957, has the seal and 19 stars. The stars symbolize Minnesota's entry into the Union as the 19th state after the original 13 states.

nors have been Republicans. Between 1860 and 1931, Minnesota had only three Democratic governors. For Minnesota's electoral votes and voting record in presidential elections, see ELECTORAL COLLEGE (table).

In 1920, a third party, the Farmer-Labor party, was founded in Minnesota. The party sought to improve economic conditions of farmers and workers. The party soon became a powerful force in the state. From 1931 to 1939, Minnesota's governors belonged to the Farmer-Labor party. In 1944, the party joined with the Minnesota Democratic party to form the Democratic-Farmer-Labor party. Two leaders of the Democratic-Farmer-Labor party were Orville L. Freeman and Hubert H. Humphrey. Freeman served as governor from 1955 to 1961. He was U.S. secretary of agriculture from 1961 to 1969. Humphrey served in the U.S. Senate from 1949 to 1964, and was Vice-President of the United States from 1965 to 1969. He was the Democratic nominee for President in 1968, but lost.

The State Capitol in St. Paul stands on a hill overlooking the city. The marble dome rises 220 feet above the ground. St. Paul became the capital in 1849. Minnesota has had no other capitals.
Minnesota Dept. of Economic Development

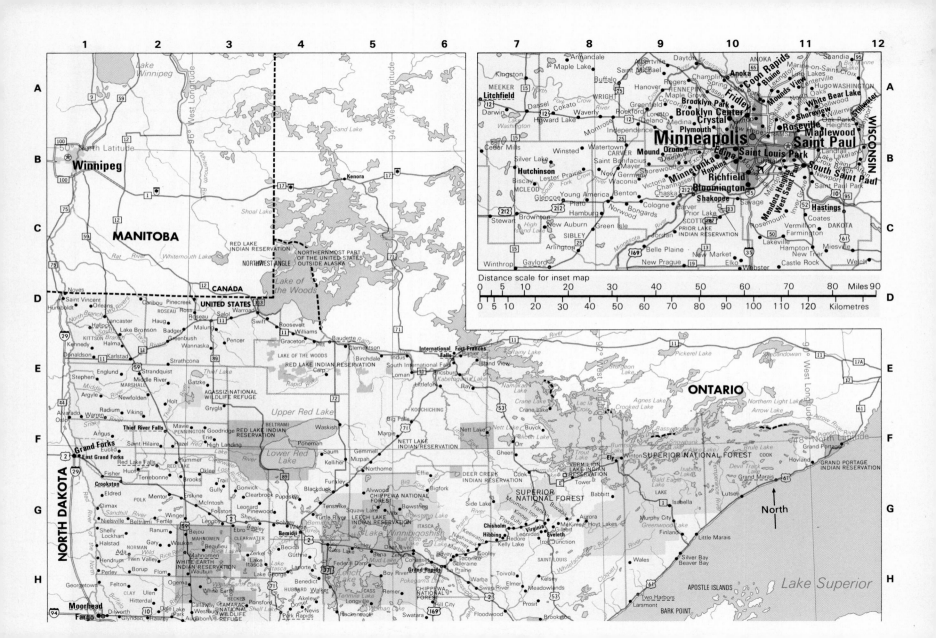

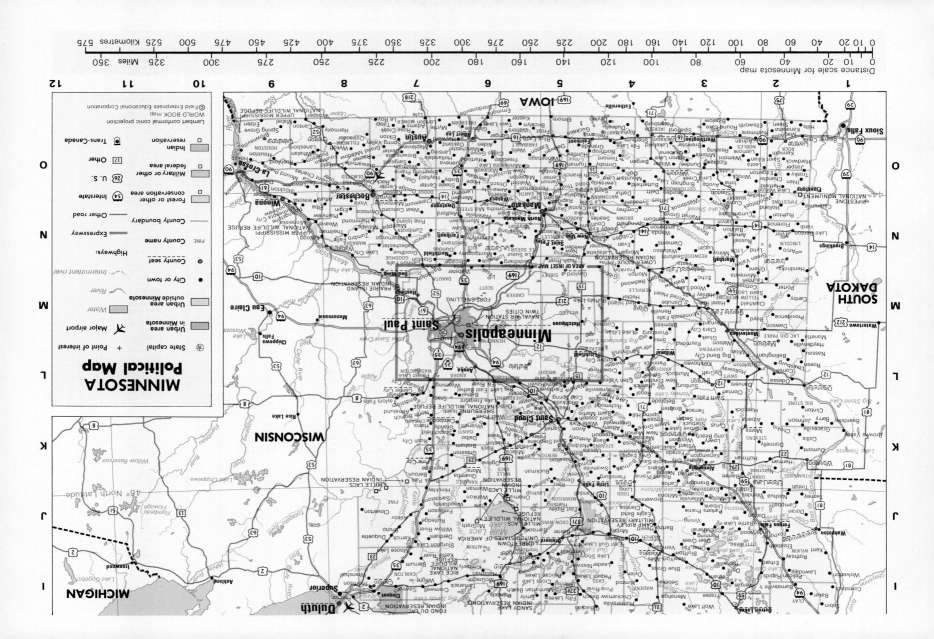

Population

3,767,975	..Census..	1970
3,413,864	.." " ..	1960
2,982,483	.." " ..	1950
2,792,300	.." " ..	1940
2,563,953	.." " ..	1930
2,387,125	.." " ..	1920
2,075,708	.." " ..	1910
1,751,394	.." " ..	1900
1,310,283	.." " ..	1890
780,773	.." " ..	1880
439,706	.." " ..	1870
172,023	.." " ..	1860
6,077	.." " ..	1850

Metropolitan Areas

Duluth-Superior (Wis.) 261,963
(218,533 in Minn., the rest in Wis.)
Minneapolis-St. Paul 1,805,081
Moorhead-Fargo (N. Dak.) 118,555
(45,845 in Minn., the rest in N.Dak.)

Counties

Aitkin ....11,031..J 6
Anoka ....153,557..L 6
Becker ....23,687..H 3
Beltrami ....25,886..F 4
Benton ....20,728..K 5
Big Stone ....8,020..L 2
Blue Earth ....52,453..O 5
Brown ....28,621..N 4
Carlton ....27,677..I 7
Carver ....28,102..M 6
Cass ....16,614..H 5
Chippewa ....14,649..L 3
Chisago ....17,340..K 7
Clay ....45,845..H 2
Clearwater ....7,877..G 3
Cook ....3,346..F 10
Cottonwood ....14,825..O 3
Crow Wing ....33,815..J 5
Dakota ....138,613..M 7
Dodge ....12,946..O 7
Douglas ....22,612..J 3
Faribault ....20,833..O 5
Fillmore ....21,550..O 8
Freeborn ....37,625..O 6
Goodhue ....34,241..N 7
Grant ....7,269..K 2
Hennepin ....955,617..M 6
Houston ....17,396..O 9
Hubbard ....10,268..H 4
Isanti ....16,283..K 6
Itasca ....35,060..G 6
Jackson ....14,172..O 4
Kanabec ....9,656..K 6
Kandiyohi ....29,991..L 4
Kittson ....6,788..E 1
Koochiching ....16,819..F 6
Lac Qui Parle ....11,031..M 2
Lake ....12,860..G 9
Lake of the Woods ....3,819..E 4
Le Sueur ....21,259..N 6

Lincoln ....8,202..N 2
Lyon ....24,092..N 2
Mahnomen ....5,563..G 3
Marshall ....12,871..E 2
Martin ....24,098..O 4
McLeod ....27,404..M 5
Meeker ....18,367..L 4
Mille Lacs ....15,180..J 6
Morrison ....26,848..J 5
Mower ....43,065..O 7
Murray ....12,369..O 3
Nicollet ....24,378..N 5
Nobles ....22,959..O 2
Norman ....9,888..H 2
Olmsted ....81,268..O 8
Otter Tail ....45,934..J 2
Pennington ....13,261..F 2
Pine ....16,620..J 7
Pipestone ....12,665..O 2
Polk ....33,830..G 2
Pope ....11,023..K 3
Ramsey ....474,823..M 7
Red Lake ....5,264..F 2
Redwood ....19,730..N 3
Renville ....20,709..M 4
Rice ....40,856..N 6
Rock ....11,212..O 2
Roseau ....11,352..D 2
St. Louis ..218,533..H 7
Scott ....32,148..M 6
Sherburne ....17,765..L 6
Sibley ....15,732..M 5
Stearns ....93,588..K 4
Steele ....26,600..N 6
Stevens ....11,014..K 2
Swift ....12,996..L 3
Todd ....21,634..J 4
Traverse ....6,205..K 2
Wabasha ....17,134..N 8
Wadena ....12,241..I 4
Waseca ....16,492..O 6
Washington ....82,471..L 7
Watonwan ....13,258..O 4
Wilkin ....9,255..J 2
Winona ....43,462..O 9
Wright ....38,251..L 5
Yellow Medicine ....14,184..M 2

Cities and Towns

Ada ....2,013..°H 2
Adams ....806..O 7
Adrian ....1,338..O 2
Afton ....158..B 12
Aitkin ....1,538..°I 6
Akeley ....434..H 4
Albany ....1,590..K 4
Albert Lea 19,212..°O 6
Alberta ....149..K 2
Albertville ....279..A 9
Alden ....694..O 6
Aldrich ....65..J 4
Alexandria ....6,905..°K 3
Alpha ....207..O 4
Altura ....420..O 8
Alvarado ....282..F 1
Amboy ....629..O 5
Angus ....F 1
Annandale ....1,210..A 8
Anoka ....13,545..°L 6
Appleton ....1,783..L 2
Arco ....140..N 2
Arden Hills ....5,662..A 11
Argyle ....789..E 1
Arlington ....1,797..C 8
Ashby ....426..J 2

Askov ....331..J 7
Atwater ....899..L 4
Audubon ....245..I 2
Aurora ....2,506..G 8
Austin ....24,831..°O 7
Avoca ....226..O 3
Avon ....443..K 5
Babbitt ....3,031..G 8
Backus ....317..I 5
Badger ....338..D 2
Bagley ....1,299..°G 3
Balaton ....723..N 2
Barnesville ....1,766..I 2
Barnum ....417..I 7
Barrett ....345..K 2
Barry ....60..K 1
Battle Lake ....733..J 3
Baudette ....1,499..°E 4
Baxter ....1,538..J 5
Bayport ....2,985..B 12
Beardsley ....410..K 1
Beaver Bay ....287..H 9
Beaver Creek ....250..O 2
Becker ....279..L 5
Bejou ....164..G 2
Belgrade ....666..L 4
Belle Plaine 2,305..C 9
Bellechester ....184..N 7
Bellingham ....327..L 2
Beltrami ....186..G 2
Belview ....400..M 3
Bemidji ....11,398..°G 4
Bena ....286..H 5
Benson ....3,468..°L 3
Benton ....63..C 9
Bertha ....562..J 4
Bethel ....302..L 6
Big Falls ....526..F 6
Big Lake ....610..L 6
Bigelow ....256..O 3
Bigfork ....464..G 6
Bingham Lake ....254..O 4
Birchwood* ....598..L 7
Bird Island ....1,320..M 4
Biscay ....70..B 7
Biwabik ....1,494..G 8
Bixby ....O 7
Blackduck ....765..G 4
Blaine ....19,935..A 10
Blomkest ....171..M 4
Blooming Prairie* ....1,776..O 7
Bloomington ....81,761..B 10
Blue Earth ....3,927..°O 5
Bluffton ....211..I 3
Bock ....91..K 6
Borup ....145..H 2
Bovey ....1,086..H 6
Bowlus ....263..K 5
Boy River ....51..H 5
Boyd ....419..M 2
Braham ....728..K 6
Brainerd ....11,421..°J 5
Brandon ....353..K 3
Breckenridge 4,163..°J 1
Brewster ....500..O 3
Bricelyn ....542..O 6
Brook Park ....108..K 7
Brooklyn Center ....34,717..A 10
Brooklyn Park ....25,979..A 10
Brooks ....148..G 2
Brookston ....144..I 7
Brooten ....661..L 4
Browerville ....744..J 4

Browns Valley ....1,033..K 1
Brownsdale ....622..O 7
Brownsville ....382..O 9
Brownton ....698..C 7
Bruno ....116..J 7
Buckman ....166..K 5
Buffalo ....3,220..°L 5
Buffalo Lake ....707..M 4
Buhl ....1,285..G 7
Burnsville ....19,813..B 10
Burtrum ....160..K 4
Butterfield ....601..O 4
Byron ....1,404..O 7
Caledonia ....2,633..°O 9
Callaway ....235..H 2
Calumet ....799..H 6
Cambridge ....2,691..°K 6
Campbell ....365..J 2
Canby ....2,060..M 2
Cannon Falls ....2,050..N 7
Canton ....467..O 8
Carlos ....262..K 3
Carlton ....862..°I 8
Carver ....467..C 9
Cass Lake ....1,283..H 4
Castle Rock ....D 11
Cedar Mills ....96..B 7
Center City ....293..°L 7
Centerville ....338..A 11
Ceylon ....554..O 4
Champlin ....2,263..A 10
Chandler ....388..O 2
Chanhassen ....4,347..B 9
Chaska ....4,312..°B 9
Chatfield ....1,875..O 8
Chickamaw Beach ....76..I 5
Chisago City 1,062..L 7
Chisholm ....5,836..G 7
Chokio ....464..L 2
Circle Pines* 3,906..L 6
Clara City ....1,489..M 3
Claremont ....466..O 7
Clarissa ....569..J 4
Clarkfield ....1,071..M 3
Clarks Grove ....353..O 6
Clear Lake ....316..L 5
Clearbrook ....650..G 3
Clearwater ....274..L 5
Clements ....269..N 4
Cleveland ....389..N 5
Climax ....310..G 1
Clinton ....565..L 2
Clitherall ....138..J 3
Clontarf ....139..L 3
Cloquet ....8,640..I 8
Coates ....202..C 11
Cobden ....114..N 4
Cohasset ....605..H 6
Cokato ....1,733..A 8
Cold Spring 2,031..L 5
Coleraine ....1,088..H 6
Cologne ....454..C 9
Columbia Heights* ..23,789..M 6
Comfrey ....616..N 4
Comstock ....138..I 1
Conger ....215..O 6
Cook ....527..F 7
Cooley ....87..H 6
Coon Rapids ....30,225..A 10
Corcoran ....1,648..A 9
Correll ....101..L 2

Cosmos ....487..M 4
Cottage Grove* ..13,338..M 7
Cottonwood ....717..M 3
Courtland ....239..N 5
Crane Lake ....F 7
Cromwell ....187..I 7
Crookston ....8,221..°G 1
Crosby ....2,199..I 5
Cross Lake ....522..I 5
Crystal ....30,564..A 10
Currie ....438..O 3
Cuyuna ....86..I 5
Cyrus ....362..K 3
Dakota ....339..O 9
Dalton ....239..J 2
Danube ....494..M 4
Danvers ....132..L 3
Darfur ....191..O 4
Darwin ....273..A 7
Dassel ....1,049..A 7
Dawson ....1,677..M 2
Dayton ....456..A 10
Deephaven ....3,833..B 10
Deer Creek ....312..J 3
Deer River ....992..H 6
Deerwood ....527..I 5
De Graff ....196..L 3
Delano ....1,872..A 9
Delavan ....322..O 5
Delhi ....124..M 3
Dellwood ....310..A 11
Denham ....71..J 7
Dennison* ....179..N 7
Dent ....176..I 3
Detroit Lakes ....5,676..°I 3
Dexter ....313..O 7
Dilworth ....2,298..I 1
Dodge Center ....1,604..O 7
Donaldson ....64..E 1
Donnelly ....358..K 2
Doran ....136..J 2
Dover ....312..O 8
Dovray ....148..N 3
Duluth ....99,761..°I 8
Dumont ....226..K 2
Dundas ....488..N 6
Dundee ....148..O 3
Dunnell ....260..O 4
Eagle Bend ....611..J 4
Eagle Lake ....506..N 5
East Bethel* ..2,561..L 6
East Grand Forks ....7,555..F 1
East Gull Lake 311..J 5
Easton ....411..O 5
Echo ....459..M 3
Eden Prairie* ....6,881..B 10
Eden Valley ....793..L 4
Edgerton ....1,119..O 2
Edina ....44,039..B 10
Effie ....195..G 6
Eitzen ....181..O 9
Elba ....152..O 8
Elbow Lake ....1,444..°J 2
Elgin ....521..N 8
Elizabeth ....168..J 2
Elk River ....2,036..°L 6
Elko ....116..C 10
Elkton ....147..O 7
Ellendale ....501..O 6
Ellsworth ....634..O 2
Elmdale ....88..K 5

Elmore ....1,078..O 5
Elrosa ....205..K 4
Ely ....4,848..F 8
Elysian ....382..N 6
Emily ....351..I 5
Emmons ....408..O 6
Erdahl ....150..J 2
Ericsburg ....E 6
Erskine ....614..G 2
Euclid ....F 1
Evan ....153..N 4
Evansville ....411..J 3
Eveleth ....4,668..G 7
Excelsior ....2,538..B 9
Eyota ....558..O 8
Fairfax ....1,420..N 4
Fairhaven ....L 5
Fairmont ....10,679..°O 5
Falcon Heights* ....5,659..M 6
Faribault ..16,459..°N 6
Farmington ....3,075..C 11
Farwell ....106..K 3
Federal Dam ....151..H 5
Felton ....201..H 2
Fergus Falls ..12,731..°J 2
Fertile ....968..G 2
Fifty Lakes ....143..I 5
Finland ....G 9
Finlayson ....213..J 7
Fisher ....326..G 1
Flensburg ....280..K 4
Floodwood ....677..H 7
Florence ....87..N 2
Foley ....1,257..°K 5
Forada ....98..K 3
Forest Lake 3,198..L 7
Foreston ....266..K 6
Fort Ripley ....55..J 5
Fosston ....1,674..G 3
Fountain ....297..O 8
Foxhome ....181..J 2
Franklin ....45..G 7
Franklin ....548..N 4
Fraser ....95..G 7
Frazee ....1,007..I 3
Freeborn ....314..O 6
Freeport ....615..K 4
Fridley ....28,993..A 10
Frost ....381..O 5
Fulda ....1,232..O 3
Funkley ....28..G 5
Garfield ....240..K 3
Garrison ....118..J 6
Garvin ....205..N 3
Gary ....262..G 2
Gaylord ....1,710..°N 5
Gem Lake* ....305..L 7
Geneva ....439..O 6
Genola ....108..K 5
Georgetown ....178..H 1
Ghent ....326..N 2
Gibbon ....896..N 4
Gilbert ....2,253..G 8
Gilman ....212..K 5
Glencoe ....4,231..°C 8
Glenville ....643..O 6
Glenwood ....2,569..°K 3
Glyndon ....489..I 1
Golden Hill ..2,190..O 8
Golden Valley* ..24,189..M 6
Gonvick ....363..G 3
Good Thunder 468..O 5

Goodhue ....566..N 7
Goodridge ....134..F 3
Goodview ....1,810..O 9
Graceville ....823..K 2
Granada ....418..O 5
Grand Marais ....1,200..°G 11
Grand Meadow 837..O 7
Grand Portage ....F 12
Grand Rapids ....7,122..°H 6
Grandy ....K 6
Granite Falls ....3,189..M 3
Grasston ....146..K 7
Green Isle ....331..C 8
Greenbush ....706..E 2
Greenfield ....639..A 9
Greenwald ....266..K 4
Greenwood* ....520..L 5
Grey Eagle ....372..K 4
Grove City ....466..L 4
Grygla ....192..F 3
Gully ....168..G 3
Hackensack ....204..H 5
Hadley ....151..O 2
Hallock ....1,454..°D 1
Halma ....115..E 2
Halstad ....639..G 1
Hamburg ....288..C 8
Hammond ....205..N 8
Hampton ....305..C 11
Hancock ....942..L 3
Hanley Falls ....334..M 3
Hanover ....263..A 9
Hanska ....491..N 5
Harding ....111..J 5
Hardwick ....328..O 2
Harmony ....1,128..O 8
Harris ....552..K 7
Hartland ....330..O 6
Hastings ..12,026..°C 12
Hatfield ....95..O 2
Hawley ....1,362..I 2
Hayfield ....889..O 7
Hayward ....258..O 6
Hazel Run ....115..M 3
Hector ....1,165..M 4
Heidelberg ....44..N 6
Henderson ....728..N 5
Hendricks ....797..N 2
Hendrum ....305..H 1
Henning ....980..J 3
Henriette ....65..K 7
Herman ....764..K 2
Heron Lake ....852..O 3
Hewitt ....267..J 4
Hibbing ..16,069..G 7
Hill City ....429..H 6
Hillman ....80..J 5
Hills ....516..O 2
Hilltop ....1,008..A 10
Hinckley ....851..J 7
Hitterdal ....235..H 2
Hoffman ....605..K 3
Hokah ....685..O 9
Holdingford ....526..K 5
Holland ....264..N 2
Hollandale ....363..O 6
Holloway ....242..L 2
Holt ....114..E 2
Homer ....O 9
Hopkins ..13,395..B 10
Houston ....1,070..O 9
Hovland ....F 11

Howard Lake 1,164..A 8
Hoyt Lakes .3,595..G 8
Hugo ......538..A 11
Humboldt ...169..D 1
Huntley .....O 5
Hutchinson .7,790..M 5
Ihlen ......111..O 2
Independ-
ence ...1,955..B 9
International
Falls ...6,332.°E 6
Inver Grove (In-
ver Grove
Heights) .12,022..B 11
Iona ......328..O 3
Iron Junction .187..G 7
Ironton .....724..J 5
Isanti ......521..L 6
Island View ..13..E 6
Isle ....529..J 6
Ivanhoe ....°O 2
Jackson ...3,505.°O 4
Janesville ..1,545..O 6
Jasper .....850..O 2
Jeffers .....489..O 3
Jenkins .....144..I 5
Johnson ......64..K 2
Jordan ...1,818..C 9
Kandiyohi ...312..L 4
Karlstad ....720..E 2
Kasota .....649..N 5
Kasson ...1,942..O 7
Keewatin ..1,370..G 7
Kelliher ....297..F 5
Kellogg ....446..N 8
Kelly Lake ....G 7
Kennedy ....458..E 2
Kenneth ....111..O 2
Kensington ..324..K 3
Kent ....134..J 1
Kenyon ...1,565..N 7
Kerkhoven ..645..L 3
Kerrick .....110..I 7
Kettle River ..234..I 7
Kiester .....741..O 6
Kilkenny ....221..N 6
Kimball
Prairie ....535..L 5
Kinbrae ......55..O 3
Kingston ......A 7
Kinney .....240..G 7
La Crescent .3,106..O 9
Lafayette ...516..N 5
Lake Benton ..905..N 2
Lake Bronson ..421..D 2
Lake City ..3,591..N 8
Lake Crystal 1,799..O 5
Lake Elmo* ..550..M 7
Lake Fremont .302..L 6
Lake George ....H 4
Lake Henry ...91..L 4
Lake Lillian ..335..M 4
Lake Park ...730..I 2
Lake St. Croix
Beach ...1,107..B 12
Lake Shore ..264..I 5
Lake Wilson ..436..O 2
Lakefield ..1,810..O 3
Lakeland ....598..B 12
Lakeland
Shores* ....52..M 7
Lakeville ..7,516..C 10
Lamberton ..1,141..N 3
Lancaster ...462..D 1
Landfall ....731..B 11
Lanesboro ..1,063..O 8
Lansing ....O 7

Laporte ......155..H 4
La Prairie ...243..H 6
La Salle .....147..O 4
Lastrup .....138..J 5
Lauderdale .2,493..B 11
Le Center .1,836.°N 6
Lengby .....181..G 3
Le Roy .....971..O 8
Lester
Prairie ...1,159..B 8
Le Sueur ..3,723..N 5
Lewiston ....890..O 9
Lewisville ...375..O 5
Lexington .1,942..A 11
Lilydale .....116..B 11
Lindstrom ..1,237..L 7
Lino Lakes .3,661..A 11
Lismore .....306..O 2
Litchfield ..5,306.°L 5
Little
Canada* ..3,523..M 7
Little Chicago ....N 6
Little Falls .7,556.°K 5
Littlefork ...805..E 6
Long Beach ..236..K 3
Long Lake* .1,511..M 5
Long Prairie 2,253.°K 4
Longville ....159..H 5
Lonsdale ....541..N 6
Loretto .....271..A 9
Louisburg ....91..L 2
Lowry ......294..K 3
Lucan ......216..N 3
Luverne ...4,650.°O 2
Lyle ....607..O 7
Lynd ....259..N 2
Mabel ......815..O 9
Madelia ...2,295..O 5
Madison ...2,257.°M 2
Madison
Lake* ......477..N 5
Magnolia ....280..O 2
Mahnomen .1,286.°H 2
Mahtomedi* .2,634..M 7
Manchester ..131..O 6
Manhattan
Beach ......62..I 5
Mankato .30,943.°N 5
Mantorville ..498.°O 7
Maple Grove 6,231..A 9
Maple Lake .1,109..A 8
Maple Plain* 1,154..M 5
Mapleton ..1,312..O 5
Mapleview ...183..G 7
Maplewood .25,279..A 11
Marble ....1,153..H 6
Marietta ....327..M 2
Marine-on-St.
Croix ......454..A 12
Marshall ..9,850.°N 3
Max ....G 5
Mayer ......179..B 8
Maynard ....429..M 3
Mazeppa ....444..N 7
McGrath .....96..J 6
McGregor ....283..I 6
McIntosh ....785..G 3
McKinley ....408..G 8
Meadowlands .176..G 7
Medford .....567..N 6
Medicine
Lake* ......323..M 6
Medina ...2,390..A 9
Meire Grove ..167..K 4

Melrose ...2,260..K 4
Menahga ....799..I 4
Mendota .....259..B 11
Mendota
Heights ..6,115..B 11
Mentor ......281..G 2
Merrifield ......J 5
Middle River .414..E 2
Miesville .....126..C 12
Milaca ....1,922.°K 6
Milan ......482..L 2
Millerville ...119..J 3
Millville ....171..N 8
Milroy ......268..N 3
Miltona .....163..J 3
Minneapo-
lis .....431,977.°M 6
Minneiska ....110..N 9
Minneota ..1,321..N 2
Minnesota City 190..O 9
Minnesota
Lake ....697..O 5
Minnetonka 35,480..B 10
Minnetonka
Beach* .....544..M 7
Minnetrista* 2,839..L 6
Mizpah .....140..F 5
Montevideo .5,435.°M 3
Montgomery .2,282..N 6
Monticello .1,354..L 6
Montrose ....360..A 8
Moorhead .29,026.°I 1
Moose Lake .1,409..I 7
Mora .....2,554.°K 6
Morgan .....975..N 4
Morningside .1,981..B 10
Morris ....5,120.°K 2
Morristown ...616..N 6
Morton .....624..N 4
Motley ......430..J 4
Mound ....7,462..B 9
Mounds View 9,946..A 11
Mountain
Iron .....1,684..G 7
Mountain
Lake .....1,965..O 4
Murdock .....381..L 3
Myrtle ....89..O 7
Nashua ......146..J 2
Nashwauk .1,333..G 6
Nassau ......182..L 2
Nelson ......150..K 3
Nerstrand ....584..N 7
Nett Lake ......F 7
Nevis ....344..H 4
New Auburn ..299..C 7
New
Brighton* 19,384..M 7
New Germany .274..B 8
New Hope .23,087..B 10
New London ..721..L 4
New Market ...211..C 10
New Munich ..296..K 4
New Prague .2,677..D 9
New
Richland .1,109..O 6
New Trier ....106..C 11
New Ulm ..12,908.°N 5
New York
Mills ......828..I 3
Newfolden ...370..E 2
Newport ...2,970..B 11
Nicollet .....493..N 5
Nielsville ....183..G 1
Nimrod ......60..I 4
Nisswa .....742..I 5
Norcross ....153..K 2

North
Branch ...1,110..L 7
North
Mankato ..7,372..N 5
North Oaks .2,106..A 11
North
Redwood ...179..N 4
North St.
Paul* ...12,001..M 7
Northfield .10,123..N 7
Northome ....291..F 5
Northrop .....189..O 5
Norwood ...1,053..C 8
Oak Park ......K 6
Oak Park
Heights ..1,237..A 12
Oakland ......O 7
Odessa ......234..L 2
Odin ....184..O 4
Ogema ......224..H 2
Ogilvie .....376..K 6
Okabena ....244..O 3
Oklee ......529..F 3
Olivia ....2,503.°M 4
Onamia .....145..I 6
Ormsby ......221..O 4
Orono ....6,741..B 9
Oronoco .....361..F 7
Orr ....361..F 7
Ortonville .2,816.°L 2
Osakis ....1,329..K 4
Oslo ....372..F 1
Osseo ....2,892..A 10
Ostrander ....216..O 8
Otter Tail ....164..J 3
Owatonna .15,213.°O 6
Palisade .....180..I 6
Park Rapids 2,734.°H 4
Parkers
Prairie .....884..J 3
Paynesville .1,897..L 5
Pease ....191..K 6
Pelican Lakes 134..I 5
Pelican
Rapids ...1,823..I 2
Pemberton ...177..O 6
Pennock .....257..L 4
Pequot Lakes .461..I 5
Perham ....1,979..I 3
Perley ......165..H 1
Peterson .....283..O 9
Pierz ....816..K 5
Pillager .....261..J 5
Pine City ..2,121.°K 7
Pine Island 1,645..N 7
Pine River ...775..I 5
Pine Springs* 142..M 7
Pipestone ..5,274.°O 2
Plainview ..2,082..N 8
Plato ....280..C 8
Pleasant Lake .58..L 5
Plummer .....283..F 2
Plymouth .17,985..B 10
Porter ......261..M 2
Preston ...1,416.°O 8
Princeton ..2,526..K 6
Prinsburg ....462..M 3
Prior Lake .1,104..C 10
Proctor ...2,999..I 7
Quamba ......95..K 6
Racine .....180..O 8
Randall .....516..J 5
Randolph ....315..N 7
Ranier ......262..E 6
Raymond ....608..M 3
Red Lake
Falls ....1,603.°F 2

Red Wing ..10,191.°N 7
Redwood
Falls .....4,731.°N 4
Regal ....53..L 4
Remer ......492..H 5
Renville ...1,227..M 3
Revere ......201..N 3
Rice ....387..K 5
Richfield ..47,215..B 10
Richmond ....751..L 5
Richville .....91..I 3
Riverton .....121..J 5
Robbins-
dale* ...16,948..L 6
Rochester .51,568.°O 8
Rockford ....533..A 9
Rockville ....357..L 5
Rogers .....378..A 9
Rollingstone .392..O 9
Ronneby ......84..K 5
Roosevelt ....145..D 4
Roscoe ......168..L 5
Rose Creek ...351..O 7
Roseau ...2,530.°D 3
Rosemount .1,354..C 11
Roseville .34,472..B 11
Rothsay .....457..I 2
Round Lake ...449..O 3
Royalton .....580..K 5
Rush City ..1,122..K 7
Rushford ..1,313..O 9
Rushford* ....581..O 9
Rushmore ....382..O 2
Russell .....449..N 2
Ruthton .....476..N 2
Rutledge .....146..J 7
Sabin ....251..I 1
Sacred Heart .696..M 3
St. Anthony ...72..K 4
St. Anthony* 9,708..M 6
St. Bonifacius 576..B 9
St. Charles .1,922..O 8
St. Clair .....373..O 5
St. Cloud .39,286.°K 5
St. Hilaire ...370..F 2
St. James ..4,032.°O 4
St. Joseph .1,758..K 5
St. Leo ......129..M 2
St. Louis
Park ....48,812..B 10
St. Martin ...215..L 4
St. Marys
Point* .....271..M 7
St. Michael .1,025..A 9
St. Paul .308,686.°M 7
St. Paul
Park .....5,567..B 11
St. Peter ..8,271.°N 5
St. Rosa ......62..K 4
St. Stephens ..276..K 5
St. Vincent ...217..D 1
Sanborn .....521..N 4
Sandstone .1,613..J 7
Sargent ......113..O 7
Sartell ....1,307..K 5
Sauk Centre .3,689..K 4
Sauk Rapids .5,027..K 5
Savage ....1,568..C 10
Scandia ......A 12
Scanlon ...1,142..I 8
Seaforth .....131..N 3
Sebeka .....823..I 4
Sedan ....91..K 3
Shafer ......310..G 1
Shakopee ..6,815.°C 10
Shelly ......310..G 1
Sherburn ..1,161..O 4

Shevlin .....203..G 3
Shoreview .10,842..A 11
Shorewood .4,181..B 9
Silver Bay .3,272..H 9
Silver Lake ..646..B 7
Skyline .....354..N 5
Slayton ...2,336.°O 3
Sleepy Eye .3,446..N 4
Sobieski .....190..K 5
Solway ......100..G 4
South Haven ..328..L 5
South Inter-
national
Falls ....2,126..E 6
South
St. Paul .24,895..B 11
Spicer ......589..L 4
Spring Grove 1,297..O 9
Spring Hill ...105..K 4
Spring Lake
Park .....6,398..A 10
Spring Park* 1,063..M 6
Spring
Valley ...2,468..O 8
Springfield .2,508..N 4
Squaw Lake ..129..G 5
Stacy ....211..L 7
Staples ...2,662..J 4
Starbuck ..1,124..K 3
Steen ....198..O 2
Stephen .....858..E 1
Stewart .....676..C 7
Stewartville .2,805..O 8
Stillwater .10,110.°A 12
Stockton ....242..O 9
Storden .....390..O 3
Strandquist ..160..E 2
Strathcona ...64..E 2
Sturgeon Lake 151..J 7
Sunburg .....589..L 4
Sunfish Lake* 181..B 11
Swanville ....342..K 4
Swatara ....I 6
Taconite .....376..H 6
Tamarack ....112..I 7
Taopi ....92..O 7
Taylors Falls .546..L 7
Tenney ......35..J 2
Tenstrike ....147..G 4
Thief River
Falls .....8,648.°F 2
Thomson .....179..I 8
Tintah ......228..J 2
Tonka Bay* .1,386..M 6
Tower ......878..G 8
Tracy .....2,570..N 3
Trail ....100..G 3
Trimont ...1,042..O 4
Trommald .....101..I 5
Trosky ......122..O 2
Truman ....1,131..O 5
Turtle River ...58..G 4
Twin Lakes ...153..O 6
Twin Valley ..841..H 2
Two Harbors 4,325.°H 9
Tyler .....1,058..N 2
Ulen ....481..H 2
Underwood ...314..J 2
Upsala ......356..K 4
Urbank ......177..J 3
Utica ....218..O 8
Vadnais
Heights* .3,551..M 7
Vergas ......292..I 3
Vermillion ...284..C 11
Verndale ....606..J 4

Vernon Center 333..O 5
Veseli ....N 6
Vesta ....318..N 3
Victoria ....425..B 9
Viking ......128..F 2
Villard .....235..K 3
Vining ......136..J 3
Virginia .12,291..G 7
Wabasha ..2,357.°N 8
Wabasso .....789..N 3
Waconia ...2,425..B 9
Wadena ...4,576.°J 4
Wahkon .....172..J 6
Waite Park .2,825..K 5
Waldorf .....270..O 6
Walker ....1,065.°H 4
Walnut Grove .886..N 3
Walters .....133..O 6
Waltham .....207..O 7
Wanamingo ...540..N 7
Wanda ......160..N 3
Warba ......162..H 6
Warren ...2,027.°F 1
Warroad ...1,064..D 3
Warsaw ......N 6
Waseca ...6,686.°O 6
Watertown .1,387..B 9
Waterville .1,585..N 6
Watkins .....744..L 5
Watson ......267..M 3
Waubun .....350..H 2
Waverly .....574..A 8
Wayzata* ..3,660..M 6
Webster ......N 6
Welcome .....733..O 4
Wells .....2,791..O 6
Wendell .....253..J 2
West Concord .810..N 7
West St.
Paul ....18,554..B 11
West Union ...83..K 4
Westbrook .1,012..O 3
Westport .....92..K 4
Whalan ......146..O 8
Wheaton ...2,011.°K 2
White Bear
Lake ....22,795..A 11
White Earth ...H 3
Wilder ......107..O 3
Willernie ....664..A 11
Williams ....317..D 4
Willmar ..12,833.°L 4
Willow River .343..J 7
Wilmont .....473..O 2
Wilton ......112..G 4
Windom ...3,922.°O 4
Winger ......292..G 2
Winnebago .1,765..O 5
Winona ..26,036.°O 9
Winsted ...1,292..B 8
Winthrop ..1,385..D 7
Winton ......182..F 8
Wolf Lake ....I 3
Wolverton ...204..I 1
Wood Lake ...506..M 3
Woodland* ...449..M 6
Woodstock ...213..O 2
Worthington 9,733.°O 3
Wrenshall ....189..I 7
Wright ......169..I 7
Wykoff ......391..O 8
Wyoming ....435..L 7
Young
America ...536..C 8
Zemple ......82..H 6
Zumbro Falls .164..N 8
Zumbrota ..1,867..N 7

*Does not appear on the map; key shows general location.
°County seat

Sources: Latest census figures (1970 preliminary census where available, 1960 census, or special census). Cities and towns without population information are unincorporated places under 1,000 in population and are not listed in census reports.

MINNESOTA

MINNESOTA/People

The 1970 preliminary United States census reported that Minnesota had 3,767,975 persons. The population had increased 10 per cent over the 1960 figure, 3,413,864.

Almost two-thirds of the people of Minnesota live in cities. Almost half live in the Minneapolis-St. Paul metropolitan area. Minnesota has three Standard Metropolitan Statistical Areas (see METROPOLITAN AREA). For the populations of these metropolitan areas, see the *Index* to the political map of Minnesota.

Minneapolis is the largest city in Minnesota. It adjoins St. Paul, Minnesota's capital and second largest city. The *Twin Cities*, as they are called, serve as the state's leading cultural, financial, and commercial cen-

ter, Duluth, Minnesota's third largest city, is the westernmost port on the Great Lakes and an important industrial center. See the separate articles on the cities of Minnesota listed in the *Related Articles* at the end of this article.

About 96 of every 100 Minnesotans were born in the United States. Most Minnesotans who were born in other countries came from Denmark, Finland, Norway, and Sweden. Many also came from Canada, Czechoslovakia, Germany, Great Britain, Poland, and Russia.

Lutherans and Roman Catholics are the largest religious groups in Minnesota. Other large religious groups include Baptists, Congregationalists, Episcopalians, Methodists, and Presbyterians.

Minnesota Dept. of Economic Development

Minnesota Indians, father and son, harvest wild rice. They gather the grain the same way their ancestors did. Minnesota has one of the largest Indian populations in the Midwest.

Merle Morris

Baseball Fans cheer the Minnesota Twins in a game in Bloomington, a suburb of Minneapolis and St. Paul. About one of every two Minnesotans lives in the Twin Cities area.

POPULATION

This map shows the *population density* of Minnesota, and how it varies in different parts of the state. Population density means the average number of persons who live on each square mile.

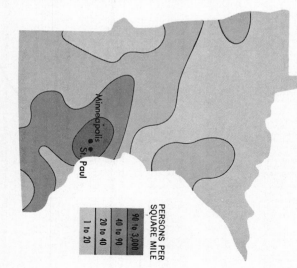

WORLD BOOK map

PERSONS PER SQUARE MILE
90 to 3,000
40 to 90
20 to 40
1 to 20

0   50   100   150 Miles
0   50   100   150   200 Kilometers

University of Minnesota in Minneapolis is the state's oldest and largest university. Students attend lectures and concerts in the Cyrus Northrop Memorial Auditorium.

Minnesota Dept. of Economic Development

MINNESOTA / Education

Schools. The first teachers in Minnesota were missionaries who worked among the Indians. About 1820, the first school for white children was opened at Fort St. Anthony (later renamed Fort Snelling). Missionaries set up many Indian schools during the 1830's. In 1849, the territorial legislature passed a law providing for the establishment of public schools in Minnesota.

The state board of education directs the state department of education. The board has seven members. They are appointed to seven-year terms by the governor with the approval of the state senate. The board appoints its chief administrative officer, the commissioner of education. The commissioner serves a six-year term. Minnesota children must attend school between their 7th and 16th birthdays. For the number of students and teachers in Minnesota, see EDUCATION (table).

Libraries. Minnesota has about 175 public libraries. The largest public libraries in the state are those serving Minneapolis, St. Paul, and Hennepin County. The library at the University of Minnesota in Minneapolis is the largest library in the state. It has more than 2 million books. The Minnesota Historical Society library in St. Paul dates from 1849. It has one of the nation's largest collections of historical books about Minnesota and the Midwest. The University of Minnesota library owns the largest collection of books in the United States about Scandinavian countries. Other special collections include the State Law Library in St. Paul, the medical library of the Mayo Foundation in Rochester, and the James J. Hill Reference Library in St. Paul.

Museums. The Minneapolis Institute of Arts and the Walker Art Center, also in Minneapolis, have many outstanding paintings and other works of art. The Minnesota Historical Society Museum in St. Paul features exhibits dealing with the state's history. The American Swedish Institute in Minneapolis has textiles, glassware,

antique furniture, and other items. The Science Museum in St. Paul has exhibits on biology, anthropology, and other sciences. The University of Minnesota operates the James Ford Bell Museum of Natural History. The Minnesota Museum of Mining in Chisholm features mining equipment. The Mayo Foundation sponsors the Mayo Medical Museum in Rochester.

UNIVERSITIES AND COLLEGES

Minnesota has 24 universities and colleges accredited by the North Central Association of Colleges and Secondary Schools. For enrollments and further information, see UNIVERSITIES AND COLLEGES (table).

Name	Location	Founded
Augsburg College	Minneapolis	1869
Bemidji State College	Bemidji	1919
Bethel College and Seminary	St. Paul	1871
Carleton College	Northfield	1866
Concordia College	Moorhead	1891
Concordia College	St. Paul	1893
Gustavus Adolphus College	St. Peter	1862
Hamline University	St. Paul	1854
Macalester College	St. Paul	1885
Mankato State College	Mankato	1867
Minneapolis School of Art	Minneapolis	1886
Minnesota, University of	*	1851
Moorhead State College	Moorhead	1887
St. Benedict, College of	St. Joseph	1913
St. Catherine, College of	St. Paul	1905
St. Cloud State College	St. Cloud	1869
St. John's University	Collegeville	1857
St. Mary's College	Winona	1912
St. Olaf College	Northfield	1874
St. Paul Seminary	St. Paul	1896
St. Scholastica, College of	Duluth	1912
St. Teresa, College of	Winona	1907
St. Thomas, College of	St. Paul	1885
Winona State College	Winona	1858

*For campuses, see UNIVERSITIES AND COLLEGES (table).

Minnesota is one of the nation's most popular playgrounds. Every year, about 3,500,000 residents and out-of-state visitors spend their vacations in Minnesota. Thousands of sparkling blue lakes attract swimmers, water skiers, and boaters. Fishermen find the cool northern waters filled with a great variety of fighting game fish. The many animals of the fields and forests challenge the hunter's skill. Only California sells more fishing licenses and duck stamps every year than Minnesota. Wooded parks and deep forests are scattered throughout the state. Many campers pitch their tents under the tall pines, and sleep and cook outdoors.

PLACES TO VISIT

Following are brief descriptions of some of Minnesota's most interesting places to visit.

High Falls, on the Pigeon River in northeastern Minnesota, plunges over cliffs 120 feet high. Nearby are the remains of Fort Charlotte, an important trading post of the late 1700's.

Lumbertown, U.S.A., in Brainerd, is a reconstruction of a typical early logging town.

Mayo Clinic and Foundation, in Rochester, offers tours of the world-famous medical center.

Northwest Angle is the most northern part of the United States outside Alaska. A scenic boat trip runs from Warroad across Lake of the Woods to the angle.

Red Lake Indian Reservation, in northwestern Minnesota, is the home of the Red Lake Chippewa tribe. The tribe operates the largest sawmill in Minnesota.

Sibley House, in Mendota, is the oldest stone house in Minnesota. Henry H. Sibley, the state's first governor, built it in 1835. The house has displays of pioneer furniture.

Statues of Paul Bunyan and Babe, in Bemidji, honor the legendary lumberman and his giant blue ox. Brainerd also has huge statues of Paul and his ox.

Tyrone Guthrie Theatre, in Minneapolis, is a strikingly designed playhouse that opened in 1963. Its permanent company of actors presents a series of plays every year.

National Forests and Monuments. Minnesota has two national forests. Superior National Forest lies in the northeast. Chippewa National Forest covers much of Itasca County and parts of Beltrami and Cass counties. In 1964, Congress set aside part of the Superior National Forest as a national wilderness area. The area will be kept in its natural state, with no roads or other developments. For the area and chief features of each national forest, see NATIONAL FOREST (table). Grand Portage National Monument, on the northwestern shore of Lake Superior, marks the site of a historic canoe route and trading post. Indians once made peace pipes from the red pipestone found at Pipestone National Monument. See the separate articles on these national monuments.

State Parks and Forests. Minnesota has about 65 state parks and about 35 state forests. It began developing its state park system in the 1890's. For information on the state parks of Minnesota, write to Commissioner, Division of State Parks, Department of Conservation, State Office Building, St. Paul, Minn. 55101.

506

High Falls on the Pigeon River
Minnesota Dept. of Economic Development

Lumbertown, U.S.A., in Brainerd
Minnesota Dept. of Economic Development

Statues of Paul Bunyan and Babe in Bemidji

Robert J. Kohl

Minnesota Theatre Company Foundation

Tyrone Guthrie Theatre in Minneapolis

Snow Sculpture at Winter Carnival in St. Paul

St. Paul Winter Carnival Assn.

Minnesota Dept. of Economic Development

Grand Portage National Monument

Minnesota's long, cold winters are ideal for winter carnivals and sports festivals. The St. Paul Winter Carnival begins the last week in January. It features ice-skating races, ski-jumping contests, and a snowmobile race from Canada into Minnesota. Minnesota's birthday (May 11) is celebrated in a statewide festival which centers near Minneapolis. The Minneapolis Aquatennial, held in July, features more than 230 events, including parades, sky diving, water sports, and an art fair. Minnesota holds its State Fair in St. Paul from late August through Labor Day. Other annual events in Minnesota include the following.

January-March: Snowmobile derbies in Alexandria, Crane Lake, Fergus Falls, Lake City, Roseau, and Walker (February); Snow Frolics in North St. Paul (February); Red River Valley Winter Show in Crookston (February); Pancake Days in Redwood Falls (February); Spring Bonspiel in Eveleth (March).

ANNUAL EVENTS

April-June: Syttende Mai (Swedish Festival) in Minneapolis (May); Inventors Congress in Redwood Falls (June); Fiesta Days in Montevideo honoring sister city in Uruguay (June); Soybean Days in Clara City (June); Kaffe Fest in Willmar (June).

July-September: Logging Days in Park Rapids (July); "Boulevard of Roses" Camera Day in Kenyon (July); Raspberry Festival in Hopkins (July); Sauerkraut Festival in Henderson (July); Kolacky Day in Montgomery (August); Robin Hood Days in St. Louis Park (August); Lake of the Woods Regatta in Baudette (August); Berne Swissfest in West Concord (August); Corn-on-the-Curb Days in Le Sueur (August).

October-December: Greater Moorhead Days in Moorhead (September); Giant Hallowe'en Parade in Anoka (October); St. Olaf College Christmas Festival in Northfield (December); Christmas Choral Pageant in St. Paul (December).

507

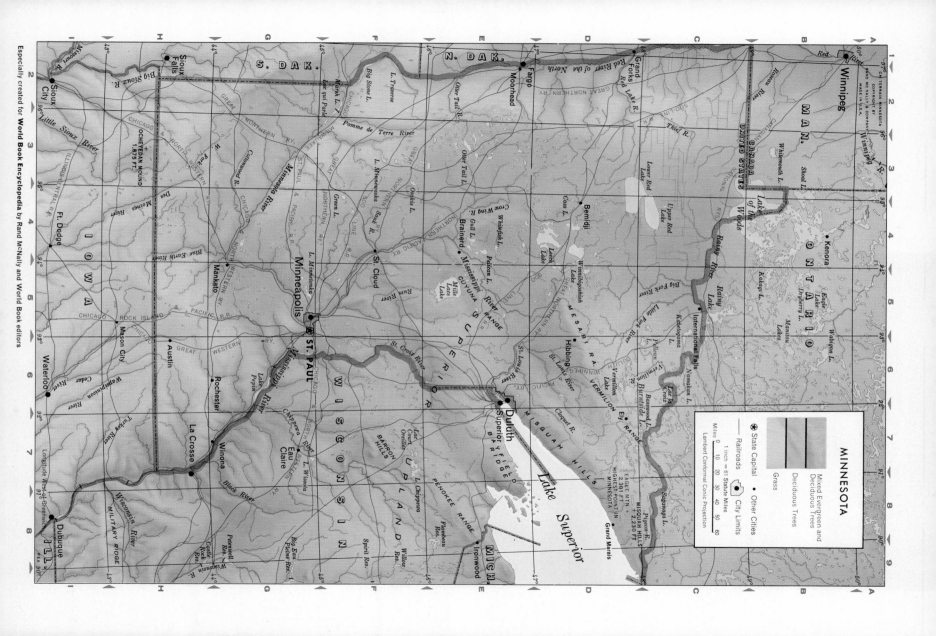

MINNESOTA

⚹ State Capital
● Other Cities
⬟ City Limits

Railroads

1 inch = 61 Statute Miles

Miles 0 10 20 30 40 50 60

Lambert Conformal Conic Projection

Mixed Evergreen and Deciduous Trees

Deciduous Trees

Grass

EAGLE MTN.
2,301 FT.
HIGHEST POINT IN
MINNESOTA

MISQUAH HILLS
2,230 FT.

Winnipeg

Red River

MAN.

ONTARIO

CANADA
UNITED STATES

Kenora

Lake of the Woods

Rainy River Lake

Rainy River

International Falls

Grand Marais

N. DAK.

S. DAK.

Fargo
Moorhead

Grand Forks

Red River of the North

Bemidji

Leech Lake

Mille Lacs Lake

MESABI RANGE

Hibbing

Duluth

Lake Superior

Brainerd

St. Cloud

Minneapolis

ST. PAUL

Mankato

Rochester

Austin

Winona

La Crosse

Eau Claire

WISCONSIN

IOWA

Sioux City

Sioux Falls

Ft. Dodge

Mason City

Waterloo

Dubuque

MICH.

Ironwood

MISSISSIPPI RIVER

OCHEYEDAN MOUND
1,675 FT.

MINNESOTA / *The Land*

During the Ice Age, which began about a million years ago, a series of glaciers moved across Minnesota. Scientists believe the last glacier retreated from the region about 12,000 years ago. As the glaciers advanced southward across Minnesota, they leveled most of the land. Only a small area in the southeast was untouched. The glaciers created gently rolling plains over most of the state. Thousands of low places formed by the glaciers filled with water. These places became lakes, swamps, or marshes.

Land Regions. Minnesota has four major land regions: (1) the Superior Upland, (2) the Young Drift Plains, (3) the Dissected Till Plains, and (4) the Driftless Area.

The Superior Upland is part of the southern tip of the Canadian Shield. The Canadian Shield is a vast area lying over old, hard rock. It covers about half of Canada (see CANADIAN SHIELD). The glaciers had less effect on the hard rock of the Superior Upland than on most other regions of the state. That is why this region includes the most rugged part of Minnesota. The area just north of Lake Superior is the roughest, most isolated part of the state. The highest point in Minnesota is 2,301-foot-high Eagle Mountain in Cook County. The northeastern tip of the Superior Upland has an arrowhead shape, and is called the *Arrowhead Country*. Most of Minnesota's iron ore deposits are in the Superior Upland region.

The Young Drift Plains consist mainly of gently rolling farmlands. Glaciers smoothed the surface of this region, and deposited great amounts of fertile topsoil called *drift* as they melted. The region has some of the

Land Regions of Minnesota

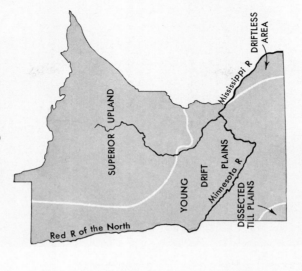

Map Index

Basswood Lake	C 7
Big Fork R.	C 5
Big Stone Lake	F 2
Blue Earth R.	H 4
Burntside Lake	D 6
Cass Lake	D 4
Cedar R.	I 6
Chippewa R.	G 7
Cloquet R.	D 7
Cottonwood R.	G 3
Crow Wing R.	E 4
Cuyuna Range	E 5
Des Moines R.	H 3
Eagle Mtn. (Highest Point in Minnesota)	D 8
Green Lake	F 4
Gull Lake	E 4
Kabetogama Lake	C 6
Lac la Croix (Lake)	C 6
Lac qui Parle (Lake)	F 2
Lake Minnetonka	G 5
Lake Minnewaska	F 3
Lake of the Woods	C 4
Lake Pepin	G 6
Lake Superior	D 8
Lake Traverse	F 2
Leech Lake	D 4
Little Fork R.	C 5
Lower Red Lake	C 3
Marsh Lake	F 2
Mesabi Range	D 5
Mille Lacs Lake	E 5
Minnesota R.	G 3
Misquah Hills	D 7
Misquah Hills	D 8
Mississippi R.	D 6
Namakan Lake	C 6
Osakis Lake	F 3
Otter Tail Lake	E 2
Otter Tail R.	E 2
Pelican Lake	E 4
Pelican Lake	E 4
Pigeon R.	C 9
Pomme de Terre R.	F 2
Rainy Lake	C 5
Rainy R.	C 5
Red Lake R.	D 2
Red River of the North	D 2
Roseau R.	B 2
Rum R.	F 5
Saganaga Lake	C 8
St. Croix R.	F 6
St. Louis R.	D 6
St. Louis R.	E 6
Sauk R.	F 4
Superior Upland	E 5
Thief R.	C 2
Upper Red Lake	C 4
Vermilion Lake	D 6
Vermilion Range	C 6
Vermilion R.	C 6
Whitefish Lake	E 4
Winnibigoshish Lake	D 4

Duluth Harbor on Lake Superior is a St. Lawrence Seaway terminal. It joins the Superior, Wis., harbor to form one of the largest ports in the United States.

Minnesota Dept. of Economic Development

MINNESOTA

Minnehaha Falls in Minneapolis is in Minnesota's Young Drift Plains region.

An Indian Entertains Visitors at Pipestone National Monument. The red rock, called pipestone, is in the Dissected Till Plains.

You Can Walk Across the Mississippi River, above, where the river begins in the Superior Upland. This region includes the loneliest, most rugged parts of Minnesota. Apple orchards, below, thrive near La Crescent in the Driftless Area.

nation's richest farmland, and it is the most important farming area in Minnesota. Parts of the Drift Plains are sandy or stony, and not so well suited for crop farming. *Moraines* can be found in some places, especially in central Minnesota. These are deposits of stones and other earth materials pushed before or along the sides of the glaciers. The moraine areas are hilly and have many lakes. The northernmost tip of the Drift Plains was once part of the bed of Lake Agassiz, a huge lake that drained away at the end of the Ice Age (see LAKE AGASSIZ). Marshlands and wooded areas lie in parts of this northern section. But most of it is a level and almost treeless plain.

The Dissected Till Plains cover the southwestern corner of Minnesota. There, the glaciers left a thick deposit of *till*—a soil-forming material of sand, gravel, and clay. Streams have *dissected* (cut up) the region. The region's few level areas make excellent farmland.

The Driftless Area lies along the Mississippi River in the southeastern corner. Although glaciers never touched this region, the western part is almost flat. Swift-flowing streams have cut deep valleys into the eastern part, giving it a broken surface.

Lakes, Rivers, and Waterfalls. Minnesota has one of the greatest water areas of any state. Its thousands of inland lakes cover more than 4,000 square miles—almost a twentieth of the state's area. The number of lakes in Minnesota has been estimated as high as 22,-000. There are over 15,000 known lake basins in the state that cover 10 acres or more. But opinions differ on how large a body of water must be to be properly called a lake.

The largest lake within the state, Red Lake, covers 430 square miles. Other big northern lakes include Cass Lake, Lake of the Woods, Leech Lake, Vermilion Lake, and Winnibigoshish Lake. Large lakes in other parts of Minnesota include Big Stone Lake and Lake Traverse, in the west; and Mille Lacs Lake and Lake Minnetonka, near the center of the state.

The mighty Mississippi River has its source in Lake Itasca, in north-central Minnesota. The Mississippi flows out of the lake as a small, clear stream about 10 feet wide and less than 2 feet deep.

The Mississippi and its branches drain about 57 per cent of Minnesota. The Mississippi's chief branches include the Crow Wing, Minnesota, Rum, St. Croix, and Sauk rivers. The Rainy River and the Red River of the North drain the northern and northwestern areas of the state. The St. Louis and other rivers that empty into Lake Superior drain the land north of Lake Superior.

One of Minnesota's most beautiful waterfalls is Minnehaha Falls, on Minnehaha Creek in Minneapolis. Henry Wadsworth Longfellow made this 50-foot falls famous in his poem *The Song of Hiawatha*. The 49-foot Falls of St. Anthony, on the Mississippi River in Minneapolis, was an important source of power in the early development of Minneapolis. The state's highest waterfall is 124-foot Cascade Falls, on the Cascade River in Lake County. Another famous waterfall is High Falls, along the Minnesota-Ontario border in Cook County. High Falls drops 120 feet.

MINNESOTA / Climate

July temperatures in Minnesota average about 68° F. in the north, and 74° F. in the south. The state's record high temperature, 114° F., was set at Beardsley on July 29, 1917, and at Moorhead on July 6, 1936. January temperatures average 2° F. in the north, and 15° F. in the south. The record low, −59° F., was set at Leech Lake Dam on Feb. 9, 1899, and at Poke-gama Falls (now Pokegama Dam) on Feb. 16, 1903.

The entire state receives enough *precipitation* (rain, melted snow, and other forms of moisture) for farming. Northwestern Minnesota has about 19 inches of pre-cipitation yearly, and southeastern Minnesota receives about 32 inches. Snowfall ranges from about 20 inches annually in the extreme southwest to more than 70 inches in the northeastern corner.

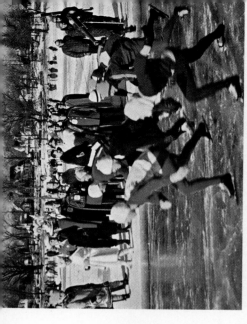

Ice Skaters race in St. Paul. Many Minnesota cities hold exciting sports carnivals during the long, severe winters.

St. Paul Winter Carnival Assn.

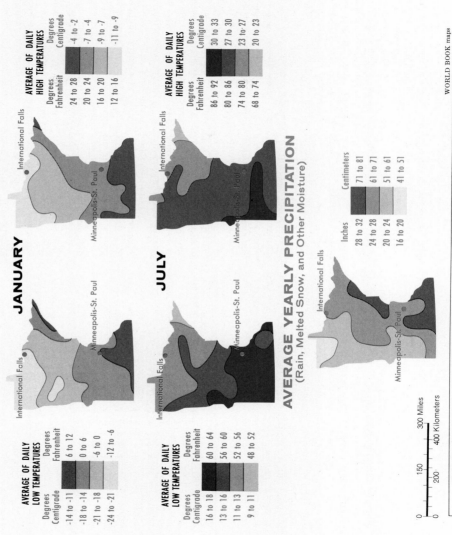

SEASONAL TEMPERATURES

JANUARY

AVERAGE OF DAILY LOW TEMPERATURES

Degrees Centigrade	Degrees Fahrenheit
-14 to -11	6 to 12
-18 to -14	0 to 6
-21 to -18	-6 to 0
-24 to -21	-12 to -6

AVERAGE OF DAILY HIGH TEMPERATURES

Degrees Fahrenheit	Degrees Centigrade
24 to 28	-4 to -2
20 to 24	-7 to -4
16 to 20	-9 to -7
12 to 16	-11 to -9

JULY

AVERAGE OF DAILY LOW TEMPERATURES

Degrees Centigrade	Degrees Fahrenheit
16 to 18	60 to 64
13 to 16	56 to 60
11 to 13	52 to 56
9 to 11	48 to 52

AVERAGE OF DAILY HIGH TEMPERATURES

Degrees Fahrenheit	Degrees Centigrade
86 to 92	30 to 33
80 to 86	27 to 30
74 to 80	23 to 27
68 to 74	20 to 23

AVERAGE YEARLY PRECIPITATION
(Rain, Melted Snow, and Other Moisture)

Inches	Centimeters
28 to 32	71 to 81
24 to 28	61 to 71
20 to 24	51 to 61
16 to 20	41 to 51

0 — 150 — 300 Miles
0 — 200 — 400 Kilometers

MONTHLY WEATHER IN INTERNATIONAL FALLS AND MINNEAPOLIS-ST. PAUL		Average of:	JAN	FEB	MAR	APR	MAY	JUNE	JULY	AUG	SEPT	OCT	NOV	DEC
INTERNATIONAL FALLS		High Temperatures	14	19	32	48	63	73	79	75	65	52	32	18
		Low Temperatures	-8	-5	8	26	38	48	53	51	42	32	16	0
		Days of Rain or Snow	12	11	11	10	12	13	11	10	12	9	9	12
MINNEAPOLIS-ST. PAUL		Days of Rain or Snow	8	7	11	9	11	13	11	10	7	8	8	9
		High Temperatures	23	27	39	56	69	79	85	82	73	60	41	27
		Low Temperatures	6	9	23	36	48	58	63	61	52	41	25	12

Temperatures are given in degrees Fahrenheit.

WORLD BOOK maps

Source: U.S. Weather Bureau

Natural Resources of Minnesota include fertile soil, important mineral deposits, thick evergreen forests, and a wealth of plant and animal life.

Soil is Minnesota's most important natural resource, because it is the basis of the state's great farm economy. Minnesota has several types of soil. Most of them were formed from the drift deposited by the glaciers. The color and fertility of the soil indicate the direction from which the ice sheets came. Drift brought from the north was generally gray and more fertile. Drift from the northeast was reddish and less fertile. In some places, different kinds of drift were deposited in layers or mixed. In parts of southern Minnesota, the wind deposited a fine, silty material called *loess* on top of the drift. The loess formed a fertile, rock-free topsoil.

Minerals. Minnesota has four iron ore ranges. The first ore mined in the state came from the Vermilion Range, in Lake and St. Louis counties. The Mesabi Range, in Itasca and St. Louis counties, yields more than nine-tenths of Minnesota's ore. Ore from the Cuyuna Range, just north of Mille Lacs Lake, contains manganese, an important element in steelmaking. Deposits of *taconite*, a low-grade ore, are found in the Mesabi Range (see TACONITE). Iron ore also comes from the Spring Valley Range, in Fillmore County.

Large deposits of granite are found near St. Cloud and along the upper Minnesota River. Quarries in southern Minnesota produce limestone and sandstone. Sand and gravel are found throughout the state.

Forests cover almost 40 per cent of Minnesota. Forests of jack, Norway, and white pine grow in various sections of the north. Other northern trees include the aspen, balsam fir, spruce, and white birch. Scattered groves of ash, black walnut, elm, maple, and oak trees grow in the south.

Other Plant Life in northern Minnesota includes blackberries, lilies of the valley, raspberries, rue anemones, wild geraniums, and wild roses. Blueberries, honeysuckles, sweet ferns, trailing arbutus, and wintergreen cover natural openings in the pine forests. Wild flowers in southern, western, and northwestern Minnesota include asters, bird's-foot violets, blazing stars, goldenrod, and prairie phlox.

Animal Life. White-tailed deer can be found over most of the state. Black bears and moose roam the woods and swamps of the north. Smaller animals found in various parts of Minnesota include beavers, bobcats, foxes, gophers, minks, muskrats, raccoons, and skunks. Quail and ring-necked pheasants feed in the grainfields. Ducks nest in the lakes and swamps during the summer. Fishermen catch bass, muskellunge, pike, trout, and other fishes.

Manufacturing, including processing, accounts for more than three-fifths of the value of all goods produced in Minnesota. Goods manufactured in the state have a *value added by manufacture* of about $4 billion yearly. This figure represents the value created in products by Minnesota's industries, not counting such costs as materials, supplies, and fuel. Minnesota's chief manufacturing industries, in order of importance, are (1) production of nonelectrical machinery, (2) food processing, and (3) production of electrical machinery.

Nonelectrical Machinery manufactured in Minnesota has a value added of about $911,700,000 yearly. The most important part of this industry is the production of service industry machinery. Most farm machinery is manufactured in Minneapolis. Several factories in the Twin Cities turn out machinery for construction, mining, printing, and paper manufacturing.

Food Processing. Food and related products processed in Minnesota have a value added of about $759,100,000 yearly. Meat packing is the most important food-processing activity, and Minnesota is one of the nation's leading meat-packing states. The largest plants are in Albert Lea, Austin, Duluth, South St. Paul, and Winona. Large poultry-processing plants operate in southwestern Minnesota.

Minnesota leads the nation in butter production, and ranks high in milk and cheese production. Its creameries make about 160,000 tons of butter a year. About a tenth of the nation's flour comes from Minnesota. In addition to wheat flour, the state's mills produce breakfast cereals, cake mixes, and other products.

Minnesota is a top producer of canned vegetables. Most of the canning plants are in southern Minnesota. Sugar-beet refineries operate in the Red River Valley and along the Minnesota River. Minnesota is one of the

Sources: U.S. Government statistics

MINNESOTA'S PRODUCTION IN 1967
Total value of goods produced—$6,687,157,000

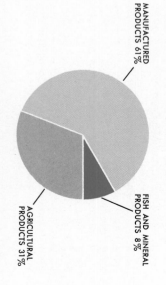

MANUFACTURED PRODUCTS 61%

FISH AND MINERAL PRODUCTS 8%

AGRICULTURAL PRODUCTS 31%

Note: Manufacturing percentage based on value added by manufacture. Other percentages based on value of production. Fish Products are less than 1 per cent.

MINNESOTA'S EMPLOYMENT IN 1967
Total number of persons employed—1,430,000

	Number of Employees
Manufacturing	311,800
Wholesale & Retail Trade	287,400
Government	213,200
Agriculture	199,900
Services	183,400
Transportation & Public Utilities	87,100
Construction	73,300
Finance, Insurance & Real Estate	58,300
Mining	15,600

Source: U.S. Department of Labor

leading processors of soybean oil in the United States. Large soybean-oil plants are located in Blooming Prairie, Columbia Heights, Dawson, Mankato, Minneapolis, and Savage. Minnesota also ranks high in the production of malt beverages.

Electrical Machinery manufactured in the state has a value added of over $320 million yearly. The manufacture of electric industrial equipment is the most important part of the industry. Plants in the Twin Cities make most of the electrical machinery.

Other Manufacturing Industries. Printing and publishing is an important industry in the state. The nation's largest law book publisher is in St. Paul. Mills in Cloquet, St. Paul, and several other cities manufacture paper and paperboard products. The Twin Cities produce chemicals and related products. Automobiles are assembled in St. Paul, and railroad equipment is manufactured in Brainerd, Fairmont, and St. Cloud.

St. Paul has a large sandpaper factory. Other St. Paul plants produce *abrasives* (grinding and polishing materials), and a variety of adhesive tapes and industrial adhesives. Plants in several cities manufacture linseed oil and meal. Other Minnesota products include carpets, cement, cosmetics, fur and knitted goods, furniture, glass, leather, and stone products.

Agriculture. Farm products account for almost a third of the value of all goods produced in Minnesota. The state's yearly farm income totals about $2 billion,

making Minnesota one of the leading farming states. Minnesota has about 131,000 farms. They average about 235 acres in size. Minnesota farms cover a total of about 30,805,000 acres.

Thousands of Minnesota farmers sell their produce through cooperatives. Minnesota has more farm cooperatives than any other state. Most of them are dairy cooperatives, but many handle grain and livestock. See COOPERATIVE.

Meat Animals are the chief source of farm income. They account for about $687,280,000 yearly. Minnesota farmers raise great numbers of beef cattle, calves, hogs, lambs, and sheep. The state is a leader in raising turkeys. Minnesota also ranks high in raising chickens and producing eggs.

Dairy Products provide about $404,469,000 a year. Minnesota has about $1\frac{3}{4}$ million dairy cattle. The cows produce about $10\frac{1}{2}$ billion pounds of milk annually, making Minnesota one of the leading milk-producing states. Most of Minnesota's milk is made into butter and cheese.

Field Crops. Minnesota leads the states in the production of oats. It also ranks high in corn production. The state's farmers feed much of their corn and oats to their cattle and hogs. Minnesota's annual hay crop ranks among the largest in the country. The state is also a leading producer of flaxseed, potatoes, soybeans, and sugar beets. Farmers in the Red River Valley grow

Gallagher's Studio

Hull-Rust Mine, near Hibbing, is one of the world's largest open-pit iron mines. Minnesota's iron ore ranges produce about three-fifths of the total mined in the United States. The state also produces large amounts of granite and limestone.

FARM, MINERAL, AND FOREST PRODUCTS

This map shows where the state's leading farm, mineral, and forest products are produced. The major urban areas (shown on the map in red) are the state's important manufacturing centers.

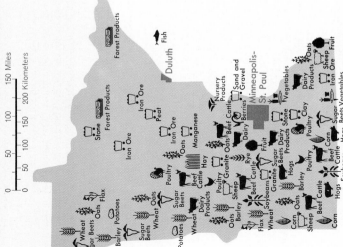

WORLD BOOK map

potatoes, spring wheat, sugar beets, and sunflowers. Minnesota ranks high in potato and sugar-beet production. Other crops include barley and rye.

Fruits and Vegetables. Apples are Minnesota's chief fruit. Most of the apple orchards are in southern Minnesota. Other fruits include cherries, grapes, plums, and strawberries. Minnesota raises a variety of vegetables for canning and freezing. It leads the other states in the production of sweet corn for processing, and ranks among the leaders in producing green peas and potatoes for processing. Other vegetables include cabbages, carrots, dry beans, and onions.

Mining. The value of Minnesota's mineral output totals about $523 million a year. About three-fifths of the iron ore mined in the United States comes from Minnesota. The state produces about 55 million tons of ore yearly, including taconite. Most ore is mined by the *open-pit* method. The ore lies close to the surface and often can be uncovered by stripping away a thin layer of dirt. One of the world's largest open-pit mines is near Hibbing. This huge hole is over 3 miles long, about 1 mile wide, and over 500 feet deep.

Minnesota began large-scale taconite mining in the 1950's. Taconite plants, which concentrate the low-grade ore, produce about 27 million tons of taconite pellets yearly.

Quarries in central Minnesota yield granite of unusually fine quality. Limestone is taken from extensive deposits in southern Minnesota. Clay comes from many areas, and is used in making bricks and tile. Sand and gravel are also produced throughout the state.

Fishing Industry. Minnesota's annual fish catch is valued at about $930,000. The most valuable fishes taken from the Mississippi River include buffalo fish, carp, catfish, and yellow pike. Chubs and lake herring are the chief products of the Lake Superior catch. Minnesota's commercial fishermen also catch large amounts of tullibee and yellow pike in inland lakes.

Electric Power. Steam plants produce almost 90 per cent of Minnesota's electric power. The fuel used by the steam plants must be imported from other states. Although few of Minnesota's rivers are swift and large enough for hydroelectric development, the state has

MINNESOTA/History

Indian Days. White men first entered the Minnesota region in the last half of the 1600's. They found Sioux Indians in the northern forests. The Sioux lived in dome-shaped wigwams. They raised crops, and were skilled hunters. By 1750, large numbers of Chippewa Indians were moving westward into Minnesota. They took over the northern forests, and forced the Sioux to move to the southwest. The Sioux became wanderers, and the two tribes remained enemies for many years. See INDIAN, AMERICAN (table: Indian Tribes).

Exploration. Two famous French fur traders, Pierre Esprit Radisson and Médart Chouart, Sieur de Groseilliers, were perhaps the first white men to set foot in Minnesota. They arrived in the area north of Lake Superior between 1659 and 1661. Another Frenchman,

several large hydroelectric plants. They are on the Minnesota, Mississippi, Rainy, and St. Louis rivers. In 1964, a nuclear power plant at Elk River began producing electricity. For Minnesota's kilowatt-hour production, see ELECTRIC POWER (table).

Transportation. Minnesota's great network of rivers and lakes provided transportation for the explorers, fur traders, missionaries, and settlers who first entered the region. In the 1820's, the first steamboats sailed on the upper Mississippi. Railroad construction in the state progressed rapidly after 1865. In time, railroads replaced steamboats in importance.

Today, railroads operate on about 8,700 miles of track in the state. Eight major rail lines operate in Minnesota. The Twin Cities are the chief rail center of the upper Mississippi Valley. Seven airlines serve Minneapolis and St. Paul. Local airlines link the state's principal cities. Minnesota has over 260 airports.

More than 125,000 miles of roads and highways cross the state. Nine-tenths of the roads and highways are surfaced. The nation's largest bus system, Greyhound Bus Lines, had its start in Hibbing in 1914.

Barges bring coal, oil, and other products to Minnesota ports on the Minnesota, Mississippi, and St. Croix rivers. The barges return downriver with grain and other products. Most of Minnesota's water traffic is on Lake Superior. The harbor at Duluth and Superior, Wis., is one of the busiest ports in the world. It handles about 38 million tons of cargo yearly. Iron ore makes up most of the outgoing cargo.

Communication. In 1849, James Madison Goodhue began publishing Minnesota's first newspaper, the *Minnesota Pioneer*, in St. Paul. Today, Minnesota has about 30 daily newspapers and about 390 weeklies. Dailies with the largest circulations include the *Duluth News-Tribune*, the *Minneapolis Star*, the *Minneapolis Tribune*, the *St. Paul Dispatch*, and the *St. Paul Pioneer Press*. Minnesota also publishes over 200 magazines.

Minnesota's first licensed radio station was WLB (now KUOM), an educational station owned by the University of Minnesota. The station was licensed in Minneapolis in 1922. The first commercial station, WDGY, began broadcasting from Minneapolis in 1923. KSTP-TV, Minnesota's first television station, started broadcasting in Minneapolis in 1948. Minnesota now has over 100 radio stations and 12 television stations.

Daniel Greysolon, Sieur Duluth (or Du Lhut), entered Minnesota about 1679. Duluth was an adventurer who hoped to blaze a trail to the Pacific Ocean. Duluth landed on the western shore of Lake Superior, and then pushed on into the interior of Minnesota. He claimed the entire region for King Louis XIV of France.

In 1680, Father Louis Hennepin, a Belgian missionary, set out from the Illinois region to explore the upper Mississippi. But Sioux Indians captured Hennepin and his two companions. The Indians took them into Minnesota. Although a captive, Hennepin saw much of the region. He became the first white man to visit the site of present-day Minneapolis, where he discovered and named the Falls of St. Anthony. Meanwhile, Duluth heard that Indians had captured three white men. He

HISTORIC MINNESOTA

Rich Iron Deposits were discovered in Minnesota in 1865 by geologist H. H. Eames. The first ore was mined from the Vermilion Range in 1884, and from the great Mesabi Range in 1892.

Source of the Mississippi. Henry Schoolcraft discovered the source of the Mississippi River in 1832 at Lake Itasca.

Record Balloon Flight. Major David G. Simons set a new altitude record when he rose 102,000 feet in 1957 from a mining pit near Crosby, Minn. He remained aloft in his 400-foot-high balloon for 32 hours.

Lumberjacks began cutting timber on a commercial basis in the late 1830's in the Saint Croix Valley. Railroads created a lumbering boom that lasted from 1870 to 1910.

Lake Superior

Duluth •

Falls of Saint Anthony were discovered by Father Hennepin when he visited the region around Mille Lacs in 1680.

• Crosby

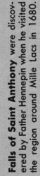

Minneapolis •

ST. PAUL ★

Rochester •

The Mayo Clinic was established at Rochester, Minn., in 1889 by William W. Mayo and his two sons, William and Charles. It is one of the greatest medical research centers in the world.

Fort Snelling was built in 1819 as Fort Saint Anthony. It was later named for Colonel Josiah Snelling. Count Zeppelin, a German military observer, made tests in balloon flying there in 1864.

The First Flour Mill in Minnesota was built at the Falls of St. Anthony in 1823. Minneapolis was the state's leading flour center by the late 1800's.

Early Minnesota Farmers. Five Swiss families settled on the military reservation at Fort Snelling in 1821. They may have been the first settlers in the state to devote themselves to farming.

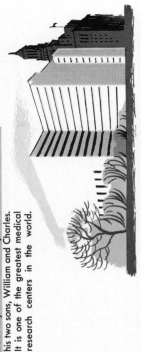

MINNESOTA

found the Indians and successfully demanded that they release the captives.

Struggle for Control. In 1762, France gave Spain all its land west of the Mississippi River, including western Minnesota. But the Spaniards did not try to explore or settle the region, and French trappers continued to collect furs there. In 1763, the French and Indian War ended. France lost this war with Great Britain over rival claims in North America. France gave Britain almost all its land east of the Mississippi, including eastern Minnesota. During the next 50 years, the North West Company and other British fur trading firms established posts in the region.

In 1783, the Revolutionary War ended. Great Britain gave its land south of the Great Lakes and east of the Mississippi to the United States. This vast area became part of the Northwest Territory, which Congress created in 1787. But British fur companies continued to trade in the region, and the United States did not gain full control until after the War of 1812.

The Louisiana Purchase. In 1800, Napoleon Bonaparte forced Spain to return the region west of the Mississippi River to France. France sold this region, called Louisiana, to the United States in 1803 (see LOUISIANA PURCHASE). Two years later, Zebulon M. Pike was sent to explore the upper Mississippi and the Minnesota wilderness.

In 1819, American soldiers under Colonel Josiah Snelling built Fort St. Anthony (renamed Fort Snelling in 1825). The fort stood at the point where the Minnesota and Mississippi rivers meet. It became a center of industry and culture, as well as of military duty. Explorers used the fort as a base from which to set out for undiscovered parts of Minnesota. These explorers in-

——— IMPORTANT DATES IN MINNESOTA ———

1659-1661 Pierre Esprit Radisson and Médart Chouart, Sieur de Groseilliers, possibly visited the Minnesota region.

1679? Daniel Greysolon, Sieur Duluth, explored the western shore of Lake Superior.

1680 Louis Hennepin discovered and named the Falls of St. Anthony.

1783 Great Britain granted the land east of the Mississippi River to the United States.

1803 The United States obtained the western Minnesota area through the Louisiana Purchase.

1819 The U.S. Army established Fort St. Anthony.

1832 Henry R. Schoolcraft discovered Lake Itasca, the source of the Mississippi River.

1837 The Sioux and Chippewa Indians sold their claim to the St. Croix Valley.

1849 Congress created the Minnesota Territory.

1851 The Indians gave up their rights to millions of acres of land west of the Mississippi River.

1858 Minnesota became the 32nd state on May 11.

1862 Minnesota militiamen and U.S. troops put down a Sioux uprising.

1884 The first shipment of iron ore from the Vermilion Range left Minnesota.

1889 William W. Mayo and his two sons founded the Mayo Clinic in Rochester.

1892 The first ore was shipped from the Mesabi Range.

1944 The Farmer-Labor party joined the Minnesota Democratic party to form the Democratic-Farmer-Labor party.

1955 A large taconite-processing plant was opened at Silver Bay.

1964 Minnesota voters approved a constitutional amendment assuring taconite producers that taxes on taconite will not be raised at a higher rate than taxes on other businesses for 25 years.

Fort Snelling in southeastern Minnesota protected settlers and traders in the early 1800's. Canadian artist Paul Kane painted a view of the fort in *Fort Snelling, Sioux Scalp Dance,* above.

Royal Ontario Museum of Archaeology, University of Toronto

cluded Lewis Cass, Stephen H. Long, and Henry R. Schoolcraft. In 1832, Schoolcraft discovered and named Lake Itasca, the source of the Mississippi River.

Lumbering began in the St. Croix Valley during the 1830's. In 1837, the Sioux and Chippewa Indians sold their claim to the logging area around the St. Croix River. A land boom followed. Towns sprang up as lumbermen and settlers from New England flocked to the new land to cut timber and to build homes.

Territorial Days. Through the years, parts of Minnesota had belonged to the territories of Illinois, Indiana, Iowa, Michigan, Missouri, and Wisconsin, and to the territory and district of Louisiana. On March 3, 1849, Congress created the Minnesota Territory. Its southern, northern, and eastern boundaries were the same as those of the state today. The western boundary extended to the Missouri and White Earth rivers. Alexander Ramsey was appointed as the first territorial governor. About 4,000 white persons lived in Minnesota when it became a territory.

In 1851, the Sioux Indians, under pressure from the U.S. government, signed two treaties giving up their rights to millions of acres of land west of the Mississippi River. Most of the land was in southern Minnesota. This new rich territory was opened to white settlement, and newcomers poured in.

Statehood. On May 11, 1858, Congress admitted Minnesota into the Union as the 32nd state. The people elected Henry H. Sibley as the first governor of their state. Sibley had been an agent of the American Fur Company, and had worked for the creation of the Minnesota Territory. Minnesota had a population of about 150,000 when it became a state.

The Civil War began in 1861. Minnesota became the first state to offer troops for the Union armies. In August, 1862, the Sioux went on the warpath in Minnesota. They were making a last effort to drive the white men from their old hunting grounds. By that time, many

Minnesota men were away fighting for the Union. The Indians swooped down on the frontier towns, killing hundreds of settlers and destroying much property. Federal troops in the state helped Minnesota militiamen put down the uprising.

Industrial Development occurred rapidly in Minnesota during the late 1800's. Railroads expanded across the state, and the old Sioux hunting grounds became wheat lands. Flour mills sprang up throughout the wheat region, but most were in the Minneapolis area. Minneapolis mills produced such huge quantities of flour that Minneapolis became known as the *Mill City*.

Minnesota waged a vigorous drive to attract newcomers. The railroads sent pamphlets to Europe, describing the opportunities in Minnesota. During the 1880's and 1890's, thousands of immigrants, especially Germans, Norwegians, and Swedes, settled in the state.

The outstanding event of the late 1800's was the development of rich iron ore resources. In 1884, the first ore was shipped from the Vermilion Range. In 1890, Leonidas Merritt and one of his six brothers discovered ore near Mountain Iron in the Mesabi Range. Two years later, the seven Merritt brothers shipped the first load of ore from the Mesabi Range. The Merritts became known as the *Seven Iron Men*.

In 1889, William W. Mayo and his two sons, William and Charles, established the Mayo Clinic in Rochester. The clinic's fame spread rapidly, and the Mayos turned it into a general medical center. The clinic became one of the world's leading medical research centers.

In 1894, a great forest fire swept across about 400 square miles of eastern Minnesota. It wiped out the villages of Hinckley and Sandstone. More than 400 persons were killed, and property valued at over $1,000,-000 was destroyed.

Treaty of Traverse des Sioux was signed by the Sioux Indians and the U.S. government in 1851. The Indians gave up rights to millions of acres of land in Minnesota. Frank B. Mayer, who painted this picture, was present when the treaty was signed.
The Minnesota Historical Society

The Early 1900's. In 1911, the first shipment of iron ore left the Cuyuna Range. Five years later, in 1916, a huge steel mill began operating in Duluth. After the United States entered World War I in 1917, there were heavy demands for Minnesota's products. Great crops of wheat and other grains were raised to feed the armed forces. Iron ore production totaled almost 90 million tons during the war years of 1917 and 1918.

In 1918, Minnesota was struck by another disastrous forest fire. Strong winds fanned a number of small fires into one huge fire that roared across large areas of Carlton and St. Louis counties in the northeast. The fire killed more than 400 persons and destroyed property valued at about $25 million.

During the 1890's and early 1900's, many Minnesota farmers joined cooperatives. They joined together to provide their own financial and storage services, and transportation for their products. The farmers felt that the railroads, banks, and grain companies charged too much for these services. During the 1920's, the new Farmer-Labor party supported the farmers. In 1931, Floyd B. Olson became the first Farmer-Labor governor.

The Great Depression of the 1930's hit Minnesota hard. Unemployment was widespread in the cities. About 70 per cent of the iron-range workers lost their jobs. Farm income fell sharply. The state government took many steps to fight the depression, and federal agencies were set up to provide employment and relief.

The Mid-1900's. Minnesota's economy recovered during World War II (1939-1945). The state's lumber and mining industries turned out huge amounts of raw materials for the armed forces. Until the early 1950's, Minnesota provided almost 60 per cent of the nation's iron ore. But the supply of high-grade ore suddenly dropped, as did the demand for the ore. The industry declined and several mines closed.

As a result of the mining slump, the state's iron industry began to develop low-grade taconite ore. Taconite contains about 30 per cent iron in the form of specks of iron oxide. Many Minnesota communities also formed industrial development corporations to attract new industries to the state.

The Farmer-Labor party joined the state Democratic party in 1944 to form the Democratic-Farmer-Labor party. The D.F.L. grew in strength in the 1950's. But it began to weaken in 1960 when Orville Freeman was defeated for governor by Elmer L. Andersen, a Republican. But in 1962, a recount of the vote resulted in Andersen being replaced by Karl Rolvaag of the D.F.L. A serious split in the D.F.L. occurred in 1966 when younger party members challenged Rolvaag. The split widened in 1968 when U.S. Senator Eugene J. McCarthy and Vice-President Hubert H. Humphrey, both members of the party, sought the Democratic presidential nomination.

Minnesota Today faces the continuing problems caused by the growth of its cities and the decline of rural areas. Several agencies have been set up to handle these problems. The Minnesota Municipal Commission reviews requests for the incorporation and expansion of communities. A metropolitan council is responsible for the Twin Cities area of Minneapolis-St. Paul, which covers seven counties.

Other Minnesota areas are establishing planning agencies. The problems of such groups in the 1970's include consolidation of public services and school districts, expansion of city schools, pollution, preservation of parks and open spaces, and transportation.

A large taconite-processing plant opened at Silver Bay in 1955, and another started operations at Hoyt Lakes in 1957. In 1964, Minnesota voters approved an amendment to the state constitution that boosted investment in the iron industry. The so-called taconite amendment guaranteed that taxes on taconite would not be raised at a higher rate than taxes on other products for 25 years. Previously, iron mining companies had been taxed at a higher rate, and producers had delayed plans to build taconite plants. After passage of the taconite amendment, producers invested more than $1 billion in taconite plants by 1970.

Many new industries began to operate in Minnesota during the 1950's and 1960's. The products of these industries include aerospace equipment, chemicals, computers, electronic equipment, heavy machinery, and processed foods.

In Minnesota, as in other states, the number of farms and farm workers decreased. Large numbers of families moved from rural areas to cities. By 1950, the state's total city population had grown larger than the rural population for the first time. In 1964, a federal court ordered Minnesota to *reapportion* (redivide) its legislative districts to give the city population equal representation in the state legislature. The reapportionment went into effect in the 1966 state elections.

THE GOVERNORS OF MINNESOTA

		Party	Term
1.	Henry H. Sibley	Democratic	1858-1860
2.	Alexander Ramsey	Republican	1860-1863
3.	Henry A. Swift	Republican	1863-1864
4.	Stephen Miller	Republican	1864-1866
5.	William R. Marshall	Republican	1866-1870
6.	Horace Austin	Republican	1870-1874
7.	Cushman K. Davis	Republican	1874-1876
8.	John S. Pillsbury	Republican	1876-1882
9.	Lucius F. Hubbard	Republican	1882-1887
10.	Andrew R. McGill	Republican	1887-1889
11.	William R. Merriam	Republican	1889-1893
12.	Knute Nelson	Republican	1893-1895
13.	David M. Clough	Republican	1895-1899
14.	John Lind	Democratic	1899-1901
15.	Samuel R. Van Sant	Republican	1901-1905
16.	John A. Johnson	Democratic	1905-1909
17.	Adolph O. Eberhart	Republican	1909-1915
18.	Winfield S. Hammond	Democratic	1915
19.	Joseph A. A. Burnquist	Republican	1915-1921
20.	Jacob A. O. Preus	Republican	1921-1925
21.	Theodore Christianson	Republican	1925-1931
22.	Floyd B. Olson	Farmer-Labor	1931-1936
23.	Hjalmar Petersen	Farmer-Labor	1936-1937
24.	Elmer A. Benson	Farmer-Labor	1937-1939
25.	Harold E. Stassen	Republican	1939-1943
26.	Edward J. Thye	Republican	1943-1947
27.	Luther W. Youngdahl	Republican	1947-1951
28.	C. Elmer Anderson	Republican	1951-1955
29.	Orville L. Freeman	*D.F.L.	1955-1961
30.	Elmer L. Andersen	Republican	1961-1963
31.	Karl F. Rolvaag	*D.F.L.	1963-1967
32.	Harold E. LeVander	Republican	1967-

*Democratic-Farmer-Labor

JOHN R. FINNEGAN, HAROLD T. HAGG, and PHILIP L. TIDEMAN

MINNESOTA/Study Aids

Related Articles in WORLD BOOK include:

BIOGRAPHIES

Donnelly, Ignatius
Duluth, Sieur
Freeman, Orville L.
Hench, Philip S.
Hennepin, Louis
Hill, James J.
Humphrey, Hubert H.
Kellogg, Frank B.
Kendall, Edward C.
Lewis, Sinclair

Mayo (family)
McCarthy, Eugene J.
Nier, Alfred O. C.
Pike, Zebulon M.
Pillsbury, John S.
Radisson, Pierre E.
Rice, Henry M.
Schoolcraft, Henry R.
Stassen, Harold E.
Volstead, Andrew

CITIES

Bloomington
Duluth
Hibbing
Minneapolis

Northfield
Rochester
Saint Cloud

Saint Paul
Stillwater
Winona

HISTORY

Indian, American (Indians
of the Plains)

Louisiana Purchase
Northwest Territory

PHYSICAL FEATURES

Lake Agassiz
Lake of the Woods
Lake Superior
Mesabi Range

Minnehaha Falls
Minnesota River
Mississippi River

Rainy Lake
Red River of
the North

PRODUCTS

For Minnesota's rank among the states in production,
see the following articles:

Agriculture
Alfalfa
Barley
Cattle
Cheese
Corn
Flax

Hog
Honey
Iron and Steel
Milk
Oats
Pea

Potato
Rye
Soybean
Sugar Beet
Taconite
Turkey

OTHER RELATED ARTICLES

Bunyan, Paul
Farmer-Labor Party
Grand Portage National Monument

Midwestern States
Pipestone National
Monument

Outline

I. Government
   A. Constitution
   B. Executive
   C. Legislature
   D. Courts
   E. Local Government
   F. Taxation
   G. Politics
II. People
III. Education
   A. Schools
   B. Libraries
   C. Museums
IV. A Visitor's Guide
   A. Places to Visit
   B. Annual Events
V. The Land
   A. Land Regions
   B. Lakes, Rivers, and Waterfalls
VI. Climate
VII. Economy
   A. Natural Resources
   B. Manufacturing

   C. Agriculture
   D. Mining

E. Fishing Industry
F. Electric Power
VIII. History

G. Transportation
H. Communication

Questions

What two cities in Minnesota and Wisconsin make up
one of the world's leading ports?
Why was Minnesota nicknamed the *Gopher State?* The
Bread and Butter State?
The flags of which four nations have flown over Minnesota?
What is the chief manufacturing industry of Minnesota?
What are some of Minnesota's products?
Near what city is one of the largest open-pit iron mines
in the world?
What political party was founded in Minnesota?
How much of the iron ore mined in the United States
comes from Minnesota?
Why did Minnesota redivide its legislative districts
in the 1960's?
How many state constitutions has Minnesota had?
Why is taconite so important to Minnesota?

Books for Young Readers

BORCHERT, JOHN R. *Minnesota's Changing Geography.* Univ.
of Minn. Press, 1959.
BROCK, EMMA L. *Drusilla.* Macmillan, 1937. The story of
a cornhusk doll who goes to Minnesota in a covered
wagon.
DERLETH, AUGUST W. *Land of Sky-Blue Waters.* Dutton,
1955. Schoolcraft's search for the Mississippi headwaters.
LIERS, EMIL E. *A Black Bear's Story.* Viking, 1962. Set in
the wild north country of Minnesota.
POATGIETER, ALICE H., and DUNN, JAMES T., eds. *The
Gopher Reader: Minnesota's Story in Words and Pictures.*
Minnesota Historical Society, 1958.
WILDER, LAURA I. *On the Banks of Plum Creek.* New uniform ed. Harper, 1953. A story of pioneer life in
Minnesota.

Books for Older Readers

BLEGEN, THEODORE C. *Minnesota: A History of the State.*
Univ. of Minn. Press, 1963.
BRINGS, LAWRENCE M., ed. *Minnesota Heritage: A Panoramic Narrative of the Development of the North Star State.*
Denison, 1960.
FOLWELL, WILLIAM W. *A History of Minnesota.* 4 vols.
Minnesota Historical Society, 1956.
FRIDLEY, RUSSELL W. *Minnesota: A Students' Guide to Localized History.* Teachers College Press, 1966.
HOLMQUIST, JUNE D., and BROOKINS, J. A. *Minnesota's
Major Historic Sites: A Guide.* Minnesota Historical Society, 1963.
JAQUES, FLORENCE P. *Canoe Country.* Univ. of Minn.
Press, 1938. *Snowshoe Country.* 1944. Travels in northern Minnesota.
LOVELACE, MAUD H. *Early Candlelight.* Univ. of Minn.
Press, 1949. A novel about frontier life.
MITAU, GUNTHER T. *Politics in Minnesota.* Univ. of Minn.
Press, 1960. A historical review.
O'CONNOR, WILLIAM VAN, ed. *A History of the Arts in
Minnesota.* Univ. of Minn. Press, 1958.
OLSON, SIGURD F. *Singing Wilderness.* Knopf, 1956. Essays
about the Quetico-Superior country.
POTTER, MERLE. *101 Best Stories of Minnesota.* 3rd ed.
Schmitt Publications, Inc., Minneapolis, 1956.
SCHWARTZ, GEORGE M., and THIEL, G. A. *Minnesota's
Rocks and Waters: A Geological Story.* Rev. ed. Univ. of
Minn. Press, 1963.
WILDER, LUCY. *The Mayo Clinic.* 2nd ed. Thomas, Springfield, Ill., 1955.

MINNESOTA, UNIVERSITY OF, is a state-supported coeducational institution. Its main campus is in Minneapolis-St. Paul, but it also has campuses in Crookston, Duluth, and Morris.

The Minneapolis-St. Paul campus awards bachelor's, master's, and doctor's degrees. A special program allows some juniors and seniors to follow individual courses of study. The university has colleges of biological sciences, education, liberal arts, medical sciences, pharmacy, and veterinary medicine; a general college; an institute of technology; an institute of agriculture that includes a college of agriculture, forestry, and home economics; schools of business administration, dentistry, and law; a general extension division; a summer session; and a graduate school. The Mayo Graduate School of Medicine in Rochester is part of the graduate school.

The Duluth campus offers liberal arts courses leading to bachelor's and master's degrees. The Morris campus offers bachelor's degrees in arts and science. The Technical Institute in Crookston offers two-year programs in agriculture, business, and food management. The university also operates the Southern School of Agriculture in Waseca, the Hormel Institute in Austin, the Lake Itasca Forestry and Biological Station in Itasca State Park, the Forest Research Center in Cloquet, the Cedar Creek Natural History Area near Bethel, the Landscape Arboretum and the Fruit Breeding Farm in Excelsior, and the Rosemount Research Center. The university operates an agricultural extension service and six agricultural experiment stations.

The University of Minnesota was chartered in 1851, and first operated as a preparatory school. It closed during the Civil War, and was reorganized as a four-year college in 1868. For enrollment, see UNIVERSITIES AND COLLEGES (table).

MALCOLM C. MOOS

MINNESOTA RIVER. This large branch of the Mississippi River flows through a wide valley that was cut by the outlet of an ancient glacial lake (Lake Agassiz). The Minnesota rises in the Coteau des Prairies (*little hills of the prairie*), a group of hills in northeastern South Dakota. The river flows southeastward to Big Stone Lake on the boundary between South Dakota and Minnesota. It follows the lake southward to Ortonville. There it leaves the lake and flows southeastward to Mankato, Minn. The river then turns sharply to the northeast and enters the Mississippi a few miles south of St. Paul, Minn. The river is 332 miles long. It drains an area of about 16,600 square miles. For location, see MINNESOTA (physical map).

Early explorers and fur traders sailed up the Minnesota River in their westward journeys. Today, the river is an important trade route.

WALLACE E. AKIN

See also LAKE AGASSIZ.

MINNOW is a common name for fish in the carp family. This is the largest family of fresh-water fishes, with more than 1,000 species in North America, Europe, Asia, and Africa. Most of the American minnows are small, less than 6 inches long. But a few grow quite large. The *squawfish*, one of the largest minnows, reaches a length of from 2 to 4 feet. Minnows usually have only a few teeth, arranged in rows. The main row has about 4 or 5 teeth, and the other rows, if present, usually have fewer teeth. Minnows are one of the most difficult groups to classify because of their uniform size, form, and color.

Greater Minneapolis Chamber of Commerce

University of Minnesota campus in Minneapolis has a wide mall at its center. Cyrus Northrup Memorial Auditorium, top, stands at the end of the mall. The Minneapolis Symphony Orchestra performs there.

Field Museum of Natural History

The Common Shiner is used as live bait by many fishermen. It can be found in streams, rivers, and lakes from the East Coast west to the Rocky Mountains and as far south as Louisiana.

Minnows are used as live bait to catch larger fish, and also as forage fish. Forage fish furnish the food which allows game fish to reach a large size. In many places, so many minnows have been caught for bait that there are few left, and some states have outlawed or limited the taking of minnows. Minnows are usually caught with nets. They are often raised in ponds and fish hatcheries. Some of the most common minnows in North America include the *common shiner*, the *golden shiner*, and the *creek chub*.

Scientific Classification. The minnow belongs to the family *Cyprinidae*. The golden shiner is genus *Notemigonus*, species *N. crysoleucas*. The common shiner is genus *Notropis*, species *N. cornutus*, and the creek chub, genus *Semotilus*, species *S. atromaculatus*. CARL L. HUBBS

See also CHUB.

MINOAN CIVILIZATION. See AEGEAN CIVILIZATION; ARCHITECTURE (Greek); CRETE; PAINTING (Ancient Civilizations).

MINOR is a person who is under legal age. In most states the legal age is 21. In some, the legal age for women is 18. According to law, a minor reaches legal age on the day before his twenty-first or her eighteenth birthday.

In the eyes of the law, a minor has many privileges which are not given to adults. For example, he is not held responsible for a contract with an adult and can refuse to carry out his part of the bargain. The minor may even demand the return of money or property which he has given to the adult under a contract. But he is liable for the reasonable value of *necessaries*, such as food, clothing, lodging, medical care, and education. The law gives these privileges to the minor because he is considered too inexperienced to be fully responsible for his actions. In some states, these privileges can be removed by a court action.

Minors may be held responsible for wrongdoing, such as damages they do to others, though age and inexperience may be taken into consideration.

At common law, infants under 7 years old were presumed to be incapable of committing a crime. Between the ages of 7 and 14, this presumption could be rebutted. If the child was over 14, the presumption was that he had criminal capacity. Punishment today varies with the minor's age and usually differs from that for adults. In most cities in the United States, there are special courts for minors. JOHN W. WADE

See also JUVENILE COURT.

MINOR AXIS. See ELLIPSE.

MINOR LEAGUE. See BASEBALL (The Minor Leagues).

MINORCA. See CHICKEN (Mediterranean Class; color picture: Black Minorcas).

MINORCA, or MENORCA, is the second largest island of the Balearic Islands, which lie off the eastern coast of Spain (see BALEARIC ISLANDS). Minorca has an area of 266 square miles, and a population of 42,955. Some iron is mined there. Farm crops include cereals and hemp, and grapes, olives, and other fruits. Metalware, textiles, soap, wine, and sandals are manufactured on the island. Mahón, the chief city and port, is an important naval and air base. For the location of the island, see SPAIN (color map).

Spain owns the island. England and France captured it several times. England ceded Minorca to Spain by the Treaty of Amiens in 1802. WALTER C. LANGSAM

MINORITY GROUP is composed of people in a society who differ in some ways from the dominant group, which exercises greater control in the society. For example, members of the minority group may look or speak differently or have a different cultural background than members of the dominant group. The dominant group generally discriminates against minorities. Thus, members of minority groups often do not have an equal chance in the economic, political, and social life of the society.

Social scientists often refer to minorities as racial or ethnic minorities. A *racial minority* is identified chiefly by distinctive physical characteristics that are shared by members of the group. These may include skin color, type of hair, body structure, and shape of the head or nose. Negroes are a racial minority in the United States. An *ethnic minority* is identified chiefly by distinctive cultural practices. For example, its language or speaking accent, religion, or manner of living is different from that of the dominant group. The Amish people of the United States and Canada are an ethnic minority. Many Amish dress in plain styles that are different from the clothing worn by most Americans.

Some minority groups combine the characteristics of both racial and ethnic minorities. For example, most Chinese in California in the 1850's were distinguished from other Americans by their yellow-brown skin color and "inner" eyefolds as well as by their language, style of dress, food preferences, and other cultural characteristics.

The term *minority* literally means "less than half of the whole." Yet when used in relation to people, it does not refer to numerical size. A minority group is not always smaller in number than the dominant group. For example, Negroes form a majority of the population in some parts of the South in the United States. But they are still a minority group, because most members of the dominant white group treat them as inferiors.

How a Group Becomes a Minority

A minority group usually develops when people leave their homeland and settle in another society. Members of the minority may move into or be brought within the territory of the dominant group either voluntarily or against their will. Or the dominant group may move in and take over the minority's territory. When these groups meet, the dominant group controls the minority because it has greater economic or military power, or some other superior strength.

When the minority group becomes enclosed in the territory of the dominant group, the process is generally called *incorporation*. Bringing Negro slaves to America from Africa from the early 1600's to the mid-1800's is an example of one type of incorporation. Immigration is another type. The United States has admitted many immigrants from Europe since the late 1700's, and many of these peoples become minority groups. Incorporation also occurs through *annexation* of adjoining

James W. Vander Zanden, the contributor of this article, is Associate Professor of Sociology at Ohio State University and author of American Minority Relations.

territory. After the Mexican War (1846-1848), for example, the United States gained many Spanish-speaking persons in areas that formerly belonged to Mexico.

The dominant group may move into the territory of the minority group. When one group sends some of its people to gain control over another territory and to use it as a source of wealth for the settlers' homeland, the process is called *colonialism*. The settlers retain close political, economic, and cultural ties with their homeland. Usually, the dominant group wants to use the colony for its natural resources, as a source of laborers, or as a trading partner. For example, countries such as Belgium, France, Great Britain, Portugal, and Spain set up colonies in Africa. In some cases, the dominant group breaks away from the mother country's political control. This happened when English settlers in North America revolted against Great Britain's political control.

After establishing control over the minority, the dominant group may try to remove them from its territory. The dominant group may expel them from its territory, as white Americans did in the 1830's when they forced the Cherokee Indians to move from the Southeastern United States to reservations in what is now Oklahoma. Or the dominant group may attempt *annihilation* (complete destruction) of the minority. For example, American settlers gained control of North America by killing many of the native Indians. *Genocide* is a form of annihilation in which one organized group—usually a government—systematically kills members of another group. Between 1933 and 1945, the Nazis in Germany persecuted Jews on a regular basis. In the early 1940's, they murdered about 6 million European Jews.

Relationships Between Groups

The dominant and minority groups usually develop a manner of living together when incorporation or colonialism occur. The dominant group regulates these relationships, which usually lead to segregation, assimilation, or pluralism.

Segregation is the separation of groups of people by custom or by law. Segregation is often a territorial separation. For example, Indian reservations and Negro slums physically set minorities apart in the United States. But a minority can be physically intermixed in a society and still be separated from the dominant group because of discrimination. See Segregation.

Assimilation occurs when a dominant group absorbs members of a minority, and the minority no longer exists as a group. In assimilation, both groups want the minority to join the dominant group. The minority group generally alters its way of life to fit the culture of the dominant group. But the minority does not necessarily adopt the new way of life completely. It may keep some of its old customs, and modify some of the new customs while adopting them. Most Irish and Italian immigrants in the United States have assimilated in this way.

But assimilation has not been possible for all minorities. Usually, physical differences make it difficult for a minority group to assimilate. Thus far, most Negroes in the United States have not been able

to assimilate completely because of their black skin. Some minorities, such as the Amish people, deliberately avoid assimilation. See Assimilation.

Pluralism is a compromise between the extremes of segregation and assimilation. Pluralism permits a minority group to retain some of its own cultural practices, if it also conforms to dominant group practices that are considered essential to the well-being of society. For example, the United States has followed a pluralistic policy in permitting religious freedom for many different groups.

Results of Minority Status

Minority group members generally recognize that they belong to a less-favored group, and this affects their behavior. A sense of isolation and common suffering is a strong social glue that binds group members together. Common cultural and physical traits also help to draw the group together. Identification with the minority may continue even after a minority group member is assimilated into the dominant group. For instance, a person of Jewish descent may no longer practice the traditional Jewish religion, and may become a member of dominant group society in the United States. Yet he may continue to think of himself primarily as a Jew.

In responding to domination, minority group members must decide whether to attempt assimilation or to try to avoid contact with the dominant group. Assimilation is often the most common adjustment that members of minority groups make. But if they find assimilation impossible or if they do not want to assimilate, minorities may try to achieve territorial separation from the dominant group. They may try to live together in one section of a country or in one city neighborhood. But avoidance can involve more extreme separatism. An example of this approach is *Zionism*, a movement that began in the 1800's among Jews. It resulted in the establishment of the Jewish nation of Israel.

Minorities in the United States

The United States has become the home of many minority groups. These minorities include Negroes, Jews, European immigrants, Spanish-speaking Americans, Orientals, and American Indians.

Negroes form the largest minority group in the United States. They make up about 11 per cent of the population. Negroes were brought to America as slaves beginning in the early 1600's, and most blacks remained slaves until after the Civil War (1861-1865). But even as they gradually gained legal freedom, most Negroes could not assimilate into American life because of widespread discrimination. In the 1960's, some Negroes reacted to their exclusion from society by starting *black nationalist* or *black power* movements. These movements called for separation and strengthening of Negro group identity. See Negro.

Jews have often fled to the United States to avoid persecution, only to meet continued discrimination. Today, there are about 5½ million Jews in the United States. Most Jews have retained their religious beliefs and many traditional cultural practices. See Jews.

European Immigrants who came to the United States often became minority groups. Most of these minorities were eventually assimilated into American society. Before the 1880's, most Europeans who came to America were from northern and western Europe. Beginning in the 1880's, most immigrants came from southern and eastern Europe. Most European immigrants have come from Germany, Italy, Ireland, Great Britain, and Austria-Hungary. See IMMIGRATION AND EMIGRATION.

Spanish-Speaking Americans in the United States include Puerto Ricans, Hispanos, and Mexican Americans. They live primarily in the Southwest and in a few large cities, such as New York.

Puerto Ricans have migrated to the United States mainland in large numbers since World War II (1939-1945). Most of them have settled in New York City. Many Puerto Ricans have retained Spanish as their principal language.

Hispanos are former Mexicans who became United States citizens when the U.S. annexed large parts of Mexico in 1848. They have retained many customs that were common in Mexico hundreds of years ago. *Mexican Americans* have come to the United States seeking employment since the 1890's. They are usually farmworkers who come to work at harvesting crops. There are about 3 million Mexican Americans in the United States.

Orientals in the United States include Chinese and Japanese. There are about 700,000 Orientals in the United States today. See ORIENTAL EXCLUSION ACT.

Chinese have often been discriminated against. They often live in city neighborhoods called *Chinatowns*. *Japanese* immigrants have often suffered the same injustices as the Chinese. During World War II, many Japanese were segregated in special camps.

American Indians were driven from their homes by European settlers and then were denied their rights for hundreds of years. Indians have been forced to live on reservations, and they were not granted United States citizenship until 1924. There are more than 500,000 Indians in the United States. See INDIAN, AMERICAN (Indians Today).

Minority Groups in Other Countries

Many nations have minority groups. European countries have often had minority nationality groups living within their boundaries. For example, before World War II, Germans lived in a part of Czechoslovakia called the Sudetenland. Religious minorities have also lived in Europe. Today, the Roman Catholics living in Northern Ireland are a minority, and Jews form a minority in many parts of Europe.

In South Africa, the dominant whites discriminate against Negroes and other nonwhites, though nonwhites make up about four-fifths of the population. Whites follow a governmental policy of *apartheid* (apartness). Nonwhites are segregated from whites and face official discrimination in education, employment, politics, and many other ways. See SOUTH AFRICA (Life of the People).

There are 14 major and many smaller national minority groups living in Russia. During World War II, the Volga Germans, Chechen-Ingush, Crimean Tartars, and Kalmuks were expelled from their homelands, supposedly for disloyalty. Antisemitism has been practiced in Russia since the czars came to power.   JAMES W. VANDER ZANDEN

Related Articles in WORLD BOOK include:

Acculturation	Genocide	Prejudice
Alienation	Gentlemen's Agreement	Races of Man
Culture	Ghetto	

MINOS, *MY nahs,* a king of Crete in Greek legend, was the son of Zeus (Jupiter) and Europa. He was famed as a lawmaker and ruler of a great empire. The great age of Crete is called Minoan, because of Minos' fame. Stories told about Minos by the Athenians show him as a cruel conqueror. They tell that Minos overcame Athens, and required the Athenians to send seven boys and seven girls each year as a sacrifice to the Minotaur.

Other stories picture Minos as a wise ruler. He defeated the pirates who were attacking ships, and enacted just laws on the advice of his father, Zeus. Minos and his brother, Rhadamanthus, became judges in the Lower World after their death (see RHADAMANTHUS).   O. M. PEARL

See also MINOTAUR.

MINOT, *MY nut,* N.Dak. (pop. 33,477; alt. 1,590 ft.), is the trade center of northwest North Dakota. The city lies on the Souris River, 59 miles west of the geographic center of North America. Two railroads, one airline, and three U.S. highways serve Minot. It has flour and alfalfa mills. Lignite coal mines and a major oil field lie nearby. Minot has a U.S. Air Force base and a $5 million Veterans Hospital. Minot State College is there. Minot was settled in 1885 and incorporated in 1887. It became the seat of Ward County in 1891, and has a council-manager government.   RUSSELL REID

MINOT, *MY nut,* **GEORGE** (1885-1950), an American physician, was one of the world's greatest authorities on blood diseases. In 1926, he announced the liver treatment for pernicious anemia patients. His research showed that when the patients were treated with a diet containing a large amount of liver, the anemia disappeared and the red blood count returned to normal. His discovery opened a new era for patients with anemia, a disease that had always been fatal.

Minot and his co-workers, G. H. Whipple and W. P. Murphy, received the 1934 Nobel prize in medicine for this research. He also received the 1929 Kuber Medal of the Association of American Physicians, the 1930 Cameron Prize of the University of Edinburgh, and the 1933 Medal of the Royal College of Physicians in London. Minot wrote many articles on the blood and its disorders, and on dietary deficiency. One of his works, written with William B. Castle, is *Pathological Physiology and Clinical Description of the Anemias* (1936).

Minot was born in Boston, Mass. He received his medical degree from Harvard University in 1912. He taught and did research work at Johns Hopkins University in 1914 and 1915. During World War I, he served as a contract surgeon for the United States Army. From 1928 to 1948, Minot was professor of medicine at Harvard Medical School, and director of Boston's Thorndike Memorial Laboratory.   NOAH D. FABRICANT

MINOT STATE COLLEGE. See UNIVERSITIES AND COLLEGES (table).

MINOTAUR, *MIN oh tawr,* was a mythical monster with the head of a bull and the body of a man. King Minos of Crete kept it in the Labyrinth, a mazelike building from which no one could escape (see LABYRINTH; MINOS). Minos sacrificed seven Athenian youths and seven Athenian maidens to it each year. Theseus of Athens finally killed the Minotaur, and escaped from

Sovfoto

Opera and Ballet Are Performed in This Large, Modern Theater in Minsk.

The Minotaur in Greek mythology had a bull's head and a man's body. Theseus, a Greek hero, killed it on the island of Crete.

the Labyrinth by following a thread given to him by Minos' daughter, Ariadne (see ARIADNE; THESEUS). He took Ariadne with him, but later deserted her.

The palace excavated at Knossos in Crete has so many passageways that it resembles the legendary Labyrinth (see Knossos). Paintings and mosaics found there show bulls and bull-baiting games. O. M. PEARL

MINSK (pop. 772,000; alt. 640 ft.), is the capital of the Byelorussian Soviet Socialist Republic. It lies on the Svisloch River, about 470 miles southwest of Mos-

Minstrels and Jugglers Entertain at a Royal Dinner during the Middle Ages. Many were highly skilled performers.

Newberry Library, Chicago

Theseus and the Minotaur (1848) by Antoine Louis Barye. The Walters Art Gallery, Baltimore, Md.

cow on the railway route to Warsaw, Poland. For location, see Russia (political map).

Factories in Minsk produce ball bearings, machine tools, peat-digging machines, radios, trucks, and tractors. Woodworkers in the city produce prefabricated houses and furniture.

Minsk is the home of the Byelorussian state university, medical and polytechnic schools, an academy of sciences, a state museum, and an opera and ballet theater. The city suffered heavy damage during the fighting in World War II.

THEODORE SHABAD

MINSTREL. The wandering poet musicians who flourished during the Middle Ages were known by various names in the different countries of Europe. They were called *troubadours* and *jongleurs* in France, and *minnesingers* in Germany. Other names were *skald* in Scandinavia and *bard* in Ireland. The early English minstrel was called a *scop*. But the name *minstrel* was used for the later poet musicians of England.

Some minstrels belonged to the households of kings and noblemen. Some traveled about and gave entertainments at the castles along their way. Sometimes they entertained the village folk. The minstrels often

Treasury Department

A Mint Is a Coin Factory. A worker feeds coin blanks into the hopper of a stamping press, *right*. The finished coins drop into a bin, *lower left*. An inspector examines them for possible defects.

made up their own songs and stories as they entertained. But they also repeated ballads and folk tales of the time, thus helping to preserve them. The minstrels began to die out by the late 1400's. The printing press eventually replaced the storytellers.

Many songs and literary works tell about the deeds of the minstrels. Sir Walter Scott's novel *The Talisman*, tells of Blondel, the favorite minstrel of Richard the Lionhearted, king of England.   REGINALD FRENCH

Related Articles in WORLD BOOK include:

Bard	Trouvère
Harp (pictures)	Mastersinger Skald
	Minnesinger Troubadour

MINSTREL SHOW is one of the few purely American forms of entertainment. It was a kind of vaudeville show in which the performers blackened their faces with burnt cork to appear on the stage as Negroes. They sat in a semicircle, with a band behind them. An *interlocutor* ("straight man") served as master of ceremonies. The star performers were the *end men*, who sat at each end of the row. Their stage names, Mr. Bones and Mr. Tambo, came from the ivory bones and the tambourine that they played. Minstrel shows featured comedy routines, sentimental songs, variety acts, and dancing. Performers often toured on floating theaters, or *showboats* (see SHOWBOAT).

Minstrel shows began in the 1840's, and enjoyed great popularity until about 1900. They probably originated in the dancing and singing of Negro slaves, but almost all the performers were white men. Famous troupes included the Virginia Minstrels and Christy's Minstrels. Stars such as Primrose and West, McIntyre and Heath, and Lew Dockstader delighted audiences from coast to coast. The entertainer Al Jolson began in show business as a member of Dockstader's troupe. Stephen C. Foster wrote many songs for minstrel shows, among them "My Old Kentucky Home" and "Old Black Joe."   GLENN HUGHES

MINT is a place where coins are made. In the United States and *most* other countries, only the federal government may *mint* (manufacture) coins. U.S. mints are supervised by the Bureau of the Mint, a division of the Department of the Treasury. Mints now operate in Denver and Philadelphia, and on a temporary basis in San Francisco. They make only coins. The Bureau of Engraving and Printing in Washington, D.C., makes paper money (see ENGRAVING AND PRINTING, BUREAU OF).

U.S. mints make half dollars, quarters, dimes, nickels, and cents. The government stopped minting gold dollars in 1933, and silver dollars in 1935. For a description of how U.S. coins are minted and what they are made of, see MONEY (Minting Coins).

Historians believe the world's first mint was founded during the 600's B.C. in Lydia, now a part of Turkey. Coins were used in commerce by ancient Mediterranean civilizations, including Greece and Rome. The use of coins gradually spread throughout Europe and Asia.

The first mint in the United States was established in Boston in 1652. It produced coins under the authority of the General Court of the Massachusetts Bay Colony. The Articles of Confederation of 1781 gave both the U.S. Congress and the individual states authority to mint money and regulate its value. The first federal mint opened in Philadelphia in 1792, and is still in operation. Other federal mints have operated at Carson City, Nev.; Charlotte, N.C.; Dahlonega, Ga.; Denver; New Orleans; and San Francisco.

Coins were minted in England before the coming of the Romans in A.D. 43. The present British Royal Mint has operated in London since 1810. The Canadian mint was established in Ottawa in 1870 as a branch of the British Royal Mint. It became a part of the Canadian Department of Finance in 1931.   ARTHUR A. WICHMANN

See also BULLION.

In the Mint Oil Extraction Process, *left,* a mixture of water and oil collects in a receiver, where it separates into layers.

A workman then draws the oil off through a discharge spout. Mint flowers grow on spikes above the leaves, *right.*

USDA

MINT. Most people think of the pleasant flavor of peppermint when they hear the word *mint.* But, actually, mint is the name of a whole family of plants. Mint plants have square stems. Some plants have stems called *rootstocks* which take root along the ground. The leaves grow on the stems in twos, one on each side of the stem. Most mint plants have small, white, bluish, or pinkish two-lipped flowers. The flowers sometimes grow on spikes at the end of the stem, rather far above the pleasantly scented leaves.

Mint grows in all parts of the world. Both the leaf and the oil are used for flavoring in cooking and in making perfume. Mint is also used in medicine. There are about 3,200 different kinds of mint. The best known members of the mint family are balm, horehound, catnip, hyssop, lavender, marjoram, peppermint, rosemary, sage, spearmint, and thyme.

Scientific Classification. Mint makes up the mint family, *Labiatae.*

Related Articles in WORLD BOOK include:

Balm	Hyssop	Peppermint
Basil	Lavender	Rosemary
Bergamot	Marjoram	Sage
Catnip	Patchouli	Spearmint
Horehound	Pennyroyal	Thyme

HAROLD NORMAN MOLDENKE.

MINTO, EARL OF (1845-1914), GILBERT JOHN EL-LIOT-MURRAY-KYNYNMOND, served as Governor-General of Canada from 1893 to 1904 and as Viceroy of India from 1905 to 1910. As Canada's governor-general, he won permission from the British prime minister to send Canadian forces to fight in the Boer War of 1899 (see BOER WAR).

The Earl of Minto served as an attaché to the Turkish Army during the Russo-Turkish war in 1877. He became chief of staff during the Second Riel Rebellion of 1885 (see CANADA, History of [Growth of the Dominion]).

He was born in London, the grandson of the first Earl of Minto. In 1891, he became head of the Minto estate at Hawick, Scotland.

LUCIEN BRAULT

MINUET, *MIN yoo EHT,* is a popular dance which originated in France about 200 years ago. The name *minuet* comes from the French word *menu,* meaning small, because of the dance's short, mincing, dainty

steps. People danced the minuet in $\frac{3}{4}$ time, with a slow tempo. The minuet was introduced at the French court of Louis XIV about 1650, and reached its greatest popularity in the 1700's. In the 1800's, dancers walked the minuet as a *quadrille.* The minuet has come to represent dignity and gracefulness. It made a strong impact on the music of its time.

WALTER SORELL.

MINUIT, *MIN yoo it,* **PETER** (1580-1638), was a Dutch colonial governor. He bought Manhattan Island from the Indians in 1626 for trinkets costing 60 Dutch *guilders,* or about \$24 (see MANHATTAN ISLAND). This legalized the occupation of the island by the Dutch West India Company. Minuit made New Amsterdam, a settlement on the lower half of the island, the center of the company's activities. The community already was protected by water on three sides, but Minuit built Fort Amsterdam for further protection against the hostile Indians. New Amsterdam was the beginning of New York City.

The Dutch West India Company recalled Minuit in 1631 for granting too many privileges to the *patroons* (wealthy landowners). Later, the Swedish government asked him to lead its first expedition to America, and he returned to America in 1638. He built Fort Christina, named after the queen of Sweden, near the present city of Wilmington, Del. Shortly after the establishment of the fort, Minuit was drowned at sea during a hurricane.

Minuit was born at Wezel, Germany, but moved to The Netherlands when he was a young man. In 1626, he became the governor and director-general of New Netherland, the Dutch colony in North America.

IAN C. C. GRAHAM

See also TREATY (picture).

Peter Minuit bought Manhattan Island from the Indians.

Brown Bros.

"The Rude Bridge That Arched the Flood" in Concord, Mass., was built of wood and has long since disappeared. But it has been duplicated as a memorial to the minutemen of the American Revolutionary War. The statue of an alert minuteman, *left,* stands at one end of the bridge. The figure is the work of the American sculptor Daniel Chester French.

MINUTE, *MIN it,* is a unit used to measure both time and angles. In time, 60 minutes make up one hour. Each minute is divided into 60 seconds. Because an hour is $\frac{1}{24}$ of a day, a minute is $\frac{1}{1440}$ of a day. In measuring angles, 60 minutes make up one degree. A circle is divided into 360 degrees, so one minute is $\frac{1}{21,600}$ of a complete circle. Each minute of an angle is divided into 60 seconds.

The minute in time is an exact measurement, which means exactly so much time. The minute of an angle is an exact portion of a circle, and is independent of the size of the circle. But if the angle is denoted by a linear measurement along the circumference of the circle, the distance of a minute depends on the diameter of the circle. For example, a minute on a baseball measures only a small fraction of an inch. On the earth's surface it is one nautical mile, about 6,076 feet (see MILE).

The circle was first divided into 360 degrees by ancient civilizations, either the Babylonians, the Egyptians, or the Chaldeans. The Babylonians figured everything in units, 10's, and 60's instead of 10's and 100's, as we do. The degree was divided into 60 parts and each of these parts was divided into 60 parts.

The Romans called the first divisions of the degree the *partes minutae primae,* or "first small parts." The second division they called the *partes minutae secundae,* or "second small parts." These terms were finally shortened to *minute* and *second.*   DONALD H. MENZEL

See also DEGREE; HOUR; MOMENT (time).

MINUTE MAN NATIONAL HISTORICAL PARK. See NATIONAL PARK (National Historical Parks).

MINUTEMAN, a missile. See GUIDED MISSILE (Recent Developments).

MINUTEMEN. In the years just before the Revolutionary War, volunteers were organized into military companies and trained to bear arms. These men were called *minutemen* because they were prepared to fight "at a minute's notice."

When the Massachusetts militia was reorganized in 1774, the Provincial Congress provided that one-third of all the new regiments were to be made up of minutemen. In 1775, several colonies trained military companies at the suggestion of the Continental Congress.

The most famous minutemen came from Massachusetts. Minutemen fought side by side with the militia at Lexington and Concord. The minutemen groups disappeared when regular armies were formed.   JOHN R. ALDEN

MINUTES OF MEETING. See PARLIAMENTARY PROCEDURE (Minutes).

MIOCENE EPOCH. See EARTH (table: Outline of Earth History).

MIQUELON. See SAINT PIERRE AND MIQUELON.

MIRA, a giant red star, was the first star of variable brightness to be discovered. The German astronomer David Fabricius observed the changing brightness of the star in 1596. Its variation in brightness was the first indication that objects outside the solar system undergo any change. Because of this discovery, astronomers named the star *mira* (Latin for *wonderful*). Changes in Mira's size and temperature cause it to change from dim to bright and back to dim about every 11 months. At its brightest, Mira is about 300 times brighter than it is at its dimmest.

Mira is so big that if its center were where the center of the sun is, its surface would lie beyond the orbit of Mars. Mira is about 270 light-years from Earth.   CHARLES A. WHITNEY

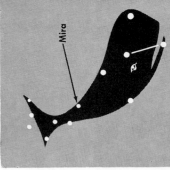

Mira appears in the whale-shaped constellation Cetus.

MIRABEAU, COMTE DE

MIRABEAU, *MIR uh boh* or *MEE RAH BOH,* **COMTE DE** (1749-1791), Honoré Gabriel Victor Riqueti, was a French statesman, orator, and revolutionary leader. He was called "the tribune of the people."

Mirabeau was always in debt, and lived an unsavory private life. But his wonderful powers of oratory made him one of the leaders of France. He became the most powerful enemy of the royal court.

But, after the first weeks of the French Revolution, he tried to place his abilities at the king's service and to work with the government. He believed that France needed both the king and the assembly. He wanted a constitutional monarchy similar to that in England. But the king and the revolutionists both were suspicious of him.

Mirabeau was born in Bignon. In 1767, he entered a military school in Paris. In the same year he became an officer in a cavalry regiment, but was imprisoned for misconduct. He was released on condition that he would join the Corsican expedition of 1769. He agreed and soon became a captain, but left the army in 1771. In 1774, Mirabeau was again in jail, this time for debt. From 1777 to 1780 he was imprisoned again, and left France on his release. He lived in The Netherlands and England, but returned to France in 1788. In 1789, he was elected to represent Aix in the States-General, the Third Estate, the term used for the common people (see STATES-GENERAL).

Shortly afterward, the king's chamberlain ordered the deputies of the Third Estate to leave their place of assembly at Versailles. Mirabeau rose in his seat and thundered, "Go and tell your master that we are here by the will of the people and that we shall not budge save at

the point of a bayonet." The deputies stayed.

In 1790, Mirabeau was elected president of the Jacobin Club, a powerful organization of French political leaders (see JACOBIN). In 1791, he became president of the National Assembly, a position where his influence might have done much good. But years of bad living habits had ruined his health. In three months he died, with the prophetic words, "I carry with me the ruin of the monarchy."

ANDRÉ MAUROIS

Comte de Mirabeau

Bust of Mirabeau by Jean Antoine Houdon, Chateau de Versailles (Alinari from Art Reference Bureau)

MIRACLE is an event of such supernatural or unusual character that the beholders believe that God or some agent unknown to man caused it. Miracles in the Bible were performed by God, sometimes through His spokesmen, such as the prophets in the Old Testament, the apostles in the New Testament. Miracles in the Old Testament include the parting of the Red Sea and the fall of manna in the desert. The greatest miracle in the New Testament is the resurrection of Jesus Christ. Other important miracles include Christ's healing of the sick and His feeding 5,000 persons with only a few loaves and fishes.

The Roman Catholic Church accepts as miraculous certain events which have occurred since biblical times. These miraculous events include cures at Lourdes, France, and other shrines.

See also CANONIZATION.

MIRACLE DRUG. See ANTIBIOTIC.

BERNARD RAMM

Victoria and Albert Museum, London

The *Miraculous Draught of Fishes* was painted by the Italian artist Raphael in 1516. This pictures one of Christ's early miracles which took place on Lake Gennesaret (now the Sea of Galilee). Jesus told Simon to cast out his net and the catch almost sank the boat.

MIRACLE PLAY is a form of religious drama which was popular in the Middle Ages. It was based on the lives of the saints. At first, the plays were presented as a part of Roman Catholic Church services. But, like the mystery plays out of which they developed, they lost the approval of the church. The plays were driven from the church to the streets or public squares.

In England, trade guild members performed these plays on feast days. Miracle plays have been revived from time to time, but interest in this type of drama has become chiefly literary. CHARLES W. COOPER

See DRAMA (Medieval Drama).

MIRAFLORES LOCKS. See PANAMA CANAL (The Pedro Miguel and Miraflores Locks).

MIRAGE, *mih RAHZH.* Sometimes when we drive in summer on a paved road, we see something ahead of us on the highway that looks like a distant pool of water. Men in deserts often think they see a cool lake or pool of water, only to discover nothing but wastes of sand when they draw near. Mirages are also seen at sea. The term *mirage* comes from a Latin word, *mirare,* meaning *to look at.*

All of these mirages are caused by hot air near the surface of the earth. The warm air *refracts* (bends) light rays from the sky toward our eyes. For example, sometimes when we are on a highway, we seem to see part of the sky on the road in front of us. Light rays from the sky strike the layers of hot air just above the pavement and are refracted along our line of vision. Sometimes, the resulting image of the sky includes part of a cloud, and what we see looks like a distant lake. Because mirages are actual light rays, they can be photographed, just as the reflection in a mirror can be photographed.

Some mirages are very striking. Because the layers of hot air vary in position, the mirage lake we see may apparently have ripples, just like a real lake disturbed by the wind. Trees are sometimes seen upside down, just as they look when reflected in a pool of water. Light rays from the treetop coming at an angle downward are bent upward again along our line of vision. We actually "see" the top of the tree which lies beneath the horizon.

At sea, the dense layers of air next to the surface of the water often focus rays from a distant object into an upside-down image in the sky. Sometimes men at sea cannot see a distant ship because of hot air layers, but they do "see" the ship in the sky, upside down.

Mirages were known to the ancients, but they were not scientifically explained until Tobias Gruber in 1781 and 1786 showed they were caused by the bending of light waves in the atmosphere. Gaspard Monge, who traveled with Napoleon's expedition to Egypt, saw the mirage and also gave the right explanation. Some scientists believe that *flying saucers* are mirages (see FLYING SAUCER). The Fata Morgana is a well-known mirage of a city that sometimes appears in the Strait of Messina off the coast of Sicily. SAMUEL W. HARDING

MIRAMICHI RIVER, *MIHR uh mih SHEE,* is one of the greatest salmon streams in the world. It is the second largest waterway in New Brunswick, Canada, ranking next to the Saint John River. The Miramichi forms where the Northwest Miramichi and the Southwest Miramichi meet and join in northeastern New Brunswick. The river flows northeastward for 135 miles and empties into the Gulf of Saint Lawrence through Miramichi Bay. Large ships can sail up to Newcastle, about 30 miles from the mouth of the river. D. F. PUTNAM

MIRANDA, *mee RAHN dah,* **FRANCISCO DE** (1750-1816), a Venezuelan patriot, fought in the American, French, and Spanish-American revolutions. He took the lead in declaring Venezuela's independence from Spain in 1811 (see VENEZUELA [Struggle for Independence]). Unsuccessful as a dictator, he surrendered his forces to the Royalists. His former subordinates, including Simón Bolívar, handed him over to the Spanish (see BOLÍVAR, SIMÓN). Miranda died in a Spanish dungeon. He was born in Caracas. HARVEY L. JOHNSON

MIRANDA V. ARIZONA. See SUPREME COURT OF THE UNITED STATES (Landmark Decisions).

MIRÓ, *mee ROH,* **JOAN,** *hwahn* (1893-   ), became a leader of the Surrealist art movement in 1924 (see SURREALISM). In contrast to the Cubists, who had made art formal and severe, Miró made paintings that were imaginative and gay. His playful subjects are freely drawn, and sometimes grow out of accidental splashes of color. He sprinkled childlike symbols of men, women, and dogs on gaily colored landscapes. The titles of these works are often humorous, such as *Still Life with Old Shoe.* One of his paintings, *Dutch Interior I,* appears in color in the PAINTING article. Miró was born near Barcelona, Spain. GEORGE D. CULLER

MIRAGE

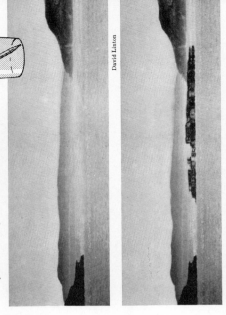

Bending Light Rays Cause Mirages. Light rays bend when they pass through substances of different densities, such as air and water. This bending makes a pencil in a glass of water look broken.

David Linton

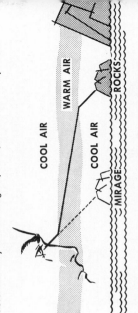

Layers of Cool and Warm Air Produce a Mirage. Light rays from an object, such as the distant rocks, *top,* bend as they pass from the cool, heavy air near the surface to the warm, light air above. This produces a mirage, *center,* that makes the rocks appear closer than they are. The diagram, *below,* shows how the rays bend.

COOL AIR

WARM AIR

COOL AIR

MIRAGE — ROCKS

A Mirror, or other highly polished surface, reflects, or sends back, light rays that fall on it. The direction the light is reflected depends on the angle at which it falls on the mirror.

The Uses of Mirrors vary greatly. They may reflect the image of an object, or reflect and direct the rays of a source of light.

Telescope

Microscope

Motion-Picture Projector

Periscope

MIRROR

MIRROR. People use mirrors, or looking glasses, every day. Any smooth surface which reflects light rays rather than absorbs them is a mirror. Most mirrors are made of a pane of glass which is coated on the back so that the light cannot pass through, but is reflected. The amount of light reflected depends on the kind of material, the angle at which light strikes it, and how polished the surface is. The more mirrors are polished, the more light they will be able to reflect. But even the best mirrors never reflect all the light which falls upon them.

The angle at which light strikes the mirror from the object is called the *angle of incidence*. The angle at which light is reflected is called the *angle of reflection*. The angle of incidence is always equal to the angle of reflection. A perpendicular to the mirror which strikes the mirror at the point of reflection is called the *normal*.

When you stand close in front of a *plane* (flat) mirror, your image is the same size as yourself, and seems to be as far behind the mirror as you are in front of it. If you are 3 feet from the mirror, your image seems 6 feet away. In a sense it is, because the light rays travel 6 feet before you see them—3 feet to the mirror, and 3 feet back to your eyes.

The image is always reversed. If you lift your right hand, your image seems to be raising its left hand.

If you want to see yourself full length in a mirror, the mirror must be at least half as tall as you are. This is because the angle of incidence must equal the angle of reflection. Suppose the top of the mirror is about on a line with the top of your head. Then the light rays

Popular Science Monthly

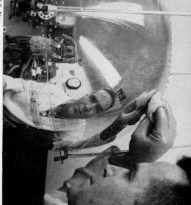

U.S. Navy

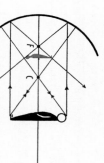

Object Beyond C produces a real, inverted, smaller image.

Object Between C and F produces a real, inverted image that is farther from the surface of the mirror than the original reflected object.

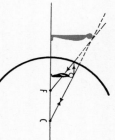

Object at C produces a real, inverted, equal-sized image.

Object Between F and the Mirror produces an erect image, larger than the object. The image appears to be behind the mirror.

In a Concave Mirror, such as those used for shaving, the position and size of the image (in gray) depend on the position of the object (in black) in relation to the mirror's center of focus (F)

and center of curvature (C). The object's position also determines whether the image is *real* (formed in front of the mirror), or *virtual* (appears formed behind the mirror).

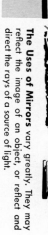

way between the mirror and its center of curvature. This point is called the *principal focus*. When the object is between the center of curvature and the principal focus, the image formed is larger than the object, and inverted. It appears beyond the center of curvature. The reflectors in automobile lights, bicycle lights, and in special surgical mouth mirrors used by dentists are concave mirrors.

Convex mirrors are just the opposite of concave mirrors. They curve toward the object instead of inward, away from it. They are parts of the outsides of imaginary spheres. The center of curvature and the principal focus are behind the mirror now. The reflected rays have to be extended behind the mirror in order to meet these points and form the image. The image is always behind the mirror, smaller than the object, and right side up. A polished ball will reflect such an image. Convex mirrors are often used to reflect a large field of vision smaller than it appears normally. Some automobile rear-view mirrors are convex for this reason.

County fairs, carnivals, and circus side shows use convex and concave mirrors for amusement. People stand before a convex mirror and see themselves stretched out grotesquely. Then they look in a concave mirror and see themselves short and round. S. W. HARDING

See also ABERRATION; PARABOLA; REFLECTION; SEARCHLIGHT; TELESCOPE.

MISDEMEANOR is any violation of the law which is less serious than a felony. Assault and battery, the theft of a small sum of money, and other such acts against the public safety and welfare, are misdemeanors. So are most traffic offenses.

Not all courts of law draw the line between misdemeanors and felonies at the same point. A felony in one court may be a misdemeanor in another. Persons guilty of misdemeanors are usually fined or given a short jail sentence. FRED E. INBAU

See also FELONY.

MISÉRABLES, LES. See Les MISÉRABLES.

MISHNAH. See TALMUD.

MISSAL, *MIS ul*, is the book containing the prayers and ceremonial directions of the complete yearly service, or *liturgy*, for the celebration of Mass in the Roman Catholic Church. The word comes from the Latin *missa*, meaning *mass*. All the separate books formerly used in the service were united into one volume to form the missal. In order to correct variations, the Council of Trent ordered its revision. Pope Pius V accomplished this in 1570.

The revised book was ordered to be used in every church which failed to show that its form of service had been in unbroken use for 200 years. Pope Clement VIII made further revisions in 1604, and Pope Urban VIII made others 30 years later. In 1884 and in 1898 Pope Leo XIII also revised the rules slightly. FULTON J. SHEEN

See also BREVIARY.

MISSILE, GUIDED. See GUIDED MISSILE.

MISSING LINK. See EVOLUTION (Missing Evolutionary Links).

MISSION FURNITURE. See FURNITURE (American Furniture).

MISSIONARY RIDGE, BATTLE OF. See CIVIL WAR (Chattanooga).

In a Plane Mirror, the image is at the mirror, but appears to be as far beyond the mirror as the object is in front of it. In a mirror, *top*, the angle of incidence (A) equals the angle of reflection (B). Because of this, a mirror must be at least half the height of a person to reflect a full-length image, *below*.

which come from your feet and which are reflected back to your eyes by the mirror must strike the mirror at least half the distance between your feet and head. If you are 5 feet tall, the mirror must be at least 2½ feet high. No matter how far away you stand from a smaller mirror, you will never be able to see yourself in it at full length.

A concave spherical mirror is shaped like the inside of an imaginary sphere. No matter how much or how little the mirror curves, it will fit the surface of some sphere. The center of this imaginary sphere is called the *center of curvature*. A line from the center of the mirror to this center of curvature is called the *principal axis* of the mirror. When parallel light rays strike the mirror, they are reflected so that they meet at a spot half-

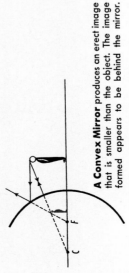

▶ **A Solar Cooker** uses a concave mirror to focus the sun's rays on a single spot that can cook foods by the sun's heat.

A Convex Mirror produces an erect image that is smaller than the object. The image formed appears to be behind the mirror.

The Reflector of a Searchlight is made in the shape of a parabola in order to produce a beam of light that does not spread out.

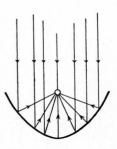

▶ **The Shiny Surface of an Artificial Satellite** acts as a convex mirror and reflects the face of a scientist.

MISSIONS AND MISSIONARIES

MISSIONS AND MISSIONARIES

MISSIONS AND MISSIONARIES spread religious doctrine and try to win converts to the faith they represent. Missionaries establish churches and set up schools, hospitals, and other services. Several religious have carried on missionary work. But Christianity probably depends more strongly than other faiths on missions and missionaries for its growth and expansion.

Early Missionaries. The apostles were the first Christian missionaries. St. Peter preached among the Jews. According to early tradition, he died a martyr at Rome. St. Paul preached among the Gentiles. The work of the apostles and of many others made Christianity the main faith of the Roman Empire by the middle of the 300's.

During the next thousand years, Christianity spread through many parts of the world, although it lost some ground to the militant religion of Islam. Missionaries went to the barbarians of northern and eastern Europe, who worshiped pagan gods. Ulfilas, an Arian bishop, brought Christianity to the Goths. St. Patrick went from Britain to Ireland. Later, Saints Columba and Columban, Irish missionaries, preached in Scotland and Europe. St. Augustine established Christianity in southern England in the 500's, and became the first Archbishop of Canterbury. An English monk, St. Boniface, became known as the *Apostle of Germany*. He cut down a huge ancient oak sacred to Thor, and built a Christian church with the wood. This action won many converts among the German tribes.

During the 800's, St. Anskar of France carried the Christian faith to Scandinavia. Missionaries traveled from Constantinople (now Istanbul) to convert Russia and the Balkans to the Eastern Church. King Vladimir became a Christian leader among the Russian tribes. However, the people of Lapland and the far north did not learn of Christianity until the Reformation.

The Nestorian Church spread through Central Asia and entered China as early as the 600's. But Christianity did not take root in southern and eastern Asia until about the late 1600's.

When a missionary went into a strange region, he first tried to convert the ruler. Then he would teach and baptize the people. It usually took several hundred years to make Christianity the faith of all the people.

Roman Catholic Missionaries. Beginning in the 1200's, the Roman Catholic church sent Franciscan and Dominican missionaries to preach Christian doctrine in many parts of the world. Missions and missionaries increased with the exploration and discovery that began in the late 1400's. Christopher Columbus and others took missionaries on their voyages, and introduced Christianity in new lands. In the 1500's, St. Francis Xavier traveled widely in India, Ceylon, Malacca, Japan, and other parts of Asia. Jesuit and Dominican missions spread steadily from that time.

Protestant Missions did not develop until about the 1700's. The spread of *evangelicalism* (revival movements) in Europe, and the Methodist revival in England, contributed to the first Protestant missionary work. At first, people did charity work in their own countries. Later, churches began sending people to other areas.

Members of various denominations traveled to many regions. In 1793, William Carey, a Baptist missionary, sailed from England to India. In 1807, Robert Morrison went to China to carry on similar work. Other mission-

MISSIONS AND MISSIONARIES

aries included Adoniram Judson in Burma, and the explorer David Livingstone in Africa. After Commodore Matthew Perry of the United States negotiated a treaty with Japan in 1854, missionaries moved there.

Later Missions. During the late 1800's and early 1900's, churches began to coordinate missionary work. Many Protestant groups set up foreign missions boards that were responsible to individual churches.

The Roman Catholic Society for the Propagation of the Faith was organized in France in 1822. It guides most of the Catholic missionary program. The Roman Catholic Church has added other missionary societies. One of the best known is Maryknoll, the Catholic Foreign Missionary Society of America, founded in 1911.

Many churches have emphasized medical missions. Albert Schweitzer is noted for his work in Africa. Some denominations have also attempted to set up native Christian churches and clergy.

During the 1900's, many workers left missions because of wars and the rise of totalitarianism. In China, the Communists halted missionary work. They imprisoned some missionaries and killed others.

Home Missions help spread Christianity in the United States and Canada. The first missions in North America were those of the Jesuits of Canada. Roger Williams and other preachers in the English colonies carried on early missionary work. Other missionaries included Jean de Brébeuf, John Eliot, and David Brainerd. Many of these early missionaries also served as explorers. For example, Jacques Marquette traveled through much of the upper Mississippi River Valley. Franciscan friars established missions throughout California. One of the early missionaries to the Indians was Junipero Serra.

Many mission buildings still stand (see CALIFORNIA [color picture: Visitors at Mission Juan Capistrano; table: California's Franciscan Missions]).

During the westward expansion of the 1800's, missionaries helped promote settlement and education. Marcus Whitman did much to open up the Pacific Northwest region. After the Civil War, churches established missions in the South to help in the rehabilitation and education of Negroes.

Many Christian groups have expanded to include activities in the field of social work. Thousands of immigrants came to the United States during the 1800's, and missions grew up where they settled, especially in large cities. One of the most famous groups working in this area is the Salvation Army. Its members do both missionary and charitable work in large cities.

Home missions also work with racial minorities, and with industrial and migrant groups. They establish camps for underprivileged children, and work among Indians and Eskimos.

FRANK WILSON PRICE

Related Articles in WORLD BOOK include:

Asbury, Francis	Jones, Eli S.
Bingham (Hiram (1789-1869))	Judson, Adoniram
	Las Casas, Bartolomé de
Boniface, Saint	Lee, Jason
Brainerd, David	Marquette, Jacques
Brébeuf, Saint Jean de	Schweitzer, Albert
De Smet, Pierre J.	Serra, Junipero
Eliot, John	Whitman, Marcus
Grenfell, Sir Wilfred T.	Whitman, Narcissa
Hennepin, Louis	Xavier, Saint Francis
Jogues, Saint Isaac	

Mission San Xavier del Bac, *left,* completed by Catholic missionaries in 1797, stands in the desert near Tucson, Ariz. A Protestant missionary among the Auca Indians of Ecuador, *below,* strives to learn the difficult language from an Auca woman.

Western Ways; Cornell Capa, Magnum

Stanton Hall, a Mansion near Natchez

Ragsdale, FPG

MISSISSIPPI

THE MAGNOLIA STATE

MISSISSIPPI is a state of the Deep South that is going through a period of great change. It was once a land of farmers and quiet towns, but is becoming a state of factory workers and busy cities. Since the 1930's, the people of Mississippi have worked to build a modern economy based on industry as well as agriculture.

But tradition still plays an important part in Mississippi life. The people have great pride in their state's history, and Mississippi retains many reminders of the Old South. Stately *ante-bellum* (pre-Civil War) mansions bring back memories of Mississippi plantation life before the Civil War. Monuments throughout the state recall the heroic deeds of the Confederate soldiers who fought on the state's many battlefields.

Rich natural resources form the basis for Mississippi's industrial growth. The state is a leading producer of cotton, petroleum, and natural gas. These products

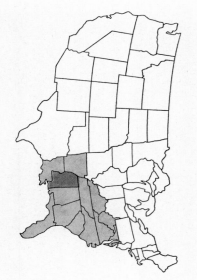

Mississippi (blue) ranks 32nd in size among all the states, and 7th in size among the Southern States (gray).

supply many of the raw materials and fuels used by the rapidly growing manufacturing industries. Mississippi manufactures a wide variety of goods. They include, in order of importance, clothing, lumber and wood products, food and related products, and chemicals and related products. Shipbuilding is also an important Mississippi industry.

Farmland and forest-covered hills spread over most of the state. The farmland of northwestern Mississippi is one of the nation's major cotton-producing areas. Many Mississippi farmlands are used to raise beef or dairy cattle. Other farmlands are used to grow crops. Mississippi ranks as a leading producer of soybeans and sweet potatoes.

Mississippi takes its name from the mighty river that forms most of its western border. *Mississippi* means the *Great Water,* or the *Father of Waters,* in the language of the Indians who lived in the region in early times. Mississippi's nickname, the *Magnolia State,* comes from the beautiful magnolia trees that grow in most parts of the state. Mississippi gardens also have many colorful azaleas and camellias. They bloom for months each year because the climate is generally warm and moist.

The mild climate attracts many tourists to Mississippi, especially in winter. The Mississippi Gulf Coast is a popular winter vacationland. It has large, sunny beaches lined with fine hotels.

Jackson is the capital and largest city of Mississippi. For the relationship of Mississippi to other states in its region, see the article on SOUTHERN STATES.

The contributors of this article are Charlotte Capers, Special Projects Assistant at the Mississippi Department of Archives and History; T. M. Hederman, Jr., Editor in Chief of the Mississippi Publishers Corporation; and M. W. Myers, Professor of Geography at Mississippi State University. The photographs were taken for WORLD BOOK by W. R. Wilson unless otherwise indicated.

—— FACTS IN BRIEF ——

Capital: Jackson.

Government: *Congress*—U.S. senators, 2; U.S. representatives, 5. *Electoral Votes*—7. *State Legislature*—senators, 52; representatives, 122. *Counties*—82.

Area: 47,716 square miles (including 358 square miles of inland water), 32nd in size among the states. *Greatest Distances*—(north-south) 352 miles; (east-west) 188 miles. *Coastline*—44 miles.

Elevation: *Highest*—Woodall Mountain (806 feet), in Tishomingo County; *Lowest*—sea level along the coast.

Population: *1970 Preliminary Census*—2,158,872; density, 45 persons to the square mile. *1960 Census*—2,178,141, 29th among the states; distribution, 62 per cent rural, 38 per cent urban.

Chief Products: *Agriculture*—beef cattle, broilers, chickens, corn, cotton, dairy products, eggs, forest products, hogs, pecans, rice, soybeans, sweet potatoes, wheat. *Fishing Industry*—menhaden, oysters, red snapper, shrimps. *Manufacturing*—chemicals, clothing, food and related products, furniture and fixtures, lumber and wood products, machinery, metal products, paper and paper products. *Mining*—clays, natural gas, petroleum, sand and gravel.

Statehood: Dec. 10, 1817, the 20th state.

State Motto: *Virtute et armis* (By valor and arms).

State Song: "Go Mis-sis-sip-pi." Words and music by Houston Davis.

Building Merchant Ships in Pascagoula Shipyards

Constitution. Mississippi adopted its present constitution in 1890. The state had four earlier constitutions, adopted in 1817, 1832, 1865, and 1869. The constitution of 1869 was written so that Mississippi could qualify to re-enter the Union after the Civil War. An *amendment* (change) to the constitution must be approved by two-thirds of the members of each house of the state Legislature. Then the amendment must be approved by a majority of the people voting on the amendment in an election. The constitution may also be amended by a constitutional convention called by a majority of each house.

Executive. The governor of Mississippi is elected to a four-year term. He receives a yearly salary of $25,000. Other executive officers elected to four-year terms include the lieutenant governor, secretary of state, treasurer, auditor, superintendent of public education, attorney general, and commissioners of agriculture and commerce, insurance, and land. The governor and treasurer may not serve two terms in a row. For a list of all the governors of Mississippi, see the *History* section of this article.

Legislature of Mississippi consists of a Senate of 52 members and a House of Representatives of 122 members. Mississippi state legislators are elected to four-year terms. Regular legislative sessions begin on the Tuesday after the first Monday in January each year, unless the governor calls the sessions to order earlier. Most of the sessions last 90 days. The legislature may extend the sessions 30 days. Every fourth year, the regular sessions last 125 days. The governor may call special sessions of the legislature.

In the 1960's, Mississippi's legislative districts were *reapportioned* (redivided) to provide equal representation based on population.

Courts in Mississippi are headed by a State Supreme court. The people elect the nine justices of the Supreme Court to eight-year terms. Three are elected from each of three districts that were set up for electing Supreme Court justices. The justice who has served the longest acts as chief justice. All other judges in the state are elected to four-year terms. Mississippi's chief trial courts are 19 chancery courts and 18 circuit courts. Chancery court judges handle civil cases. Circuit court judges handle both civil and criminal cases. Other courts include county, justice, and juvenile courts.

Local Government. The county is the chief unit of local government in Mississippi. The state has 82 counties, each with five districts. The people of each district elect one of the five members of a county board of supervisors which administers the county. Most cities have the mayor-council form of government. The Legislature controls the county and city governments.

Taxation provides about 65 per cent of the state government's income. Almost all the rest comes from federal grants and other U.S. government programs. The state receives about half of its revenue from a sales tax. Individual and corporation income taxes provide another large source of income. Profit and taxes on alcoholic beverages rank as the third leading source of revenue. Additional income comes from property, inheritance and gift taxes, and license fees.

Politics. The Democratic party has controlled Mississippi politics throughout most of the state's history.

Mississippi Agricultural & Industrial Board

The Governor's Mansion in Jackson was completed in 1842. The building and the landscaped grounds around it occupy an entire block along the city's main business street. The stately old house served as General William Sherman's Union headquarters for a time during the Civil War.

Inside the Governor's Mansion, graceful furniture and elaborate decorations reflect the dignity of the Old South. State guests are often entertained in this parlor.

The State Flag

The State Bird
Mockingbird

The State Flower
Magnolia

The State Tree
Magnolia

The State Seal

Symbols of Mississippi. On the seal, the American eagle holds an olive branch, representing peace, and three arrows, symbolizing war. The seal was adopted in 1817. The flag, adopted in 1894, reflects Mississippi's ties to the United States and to the Confederacy. The red, white, and blue bars stand for the colors of the national flag. A replica of the Confederate Army's battle flag occupies the upper left portion.

Seal, flag, bird, and flower illustrations, courtesy of Eli Lilly and Company

Since 1876, all Mississippi governors, and most state and local officials, have been Democrats. Before the 1963 election, Republicans rarely nominated candidates for many state and local offices. As a result, nomination by the Democratic party in primary elections almost always meant election to office.

In presidential elections since 1876, Mississippi has cast its electoral votes for the Democratic candidate in every election except four. In 1948, Mississippi voted for the Dixiecrat party (see Dixiecrat Party). In 1960, the state chose electors who voted for Senator Harry F. Byrd of Virginia rather than for the Democratic nominee, Senator John F. Kennedy of Massachusetts. In 1964, Mississippi gave a huge majority to the Republican candidate, Senator Barry M. Goldwater of Arizona. Goldwater was the first Republican presidential candidate to win in Mississippi since 1872. In 1968, the state's electors voted for former Alabama governor George C. Wallace, leader of the American Independent Party. For Mississippi's electoral votes and voting record in presidential elections since 1820, see Electoral College (table).

The State Capitol is in Jackson, which became the capital in 1822. Earlier capitals were Natchez (1798-1802), Washington (1802-1817), Natchez (1817-1821), and Columbia (1821-1822).

Mississippi Agricultural & Industrial Board

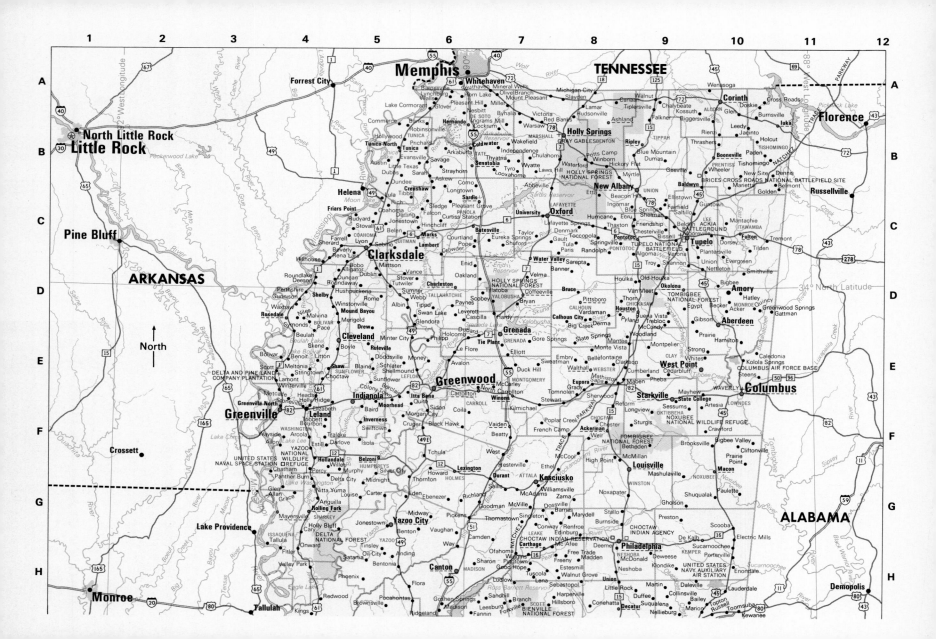

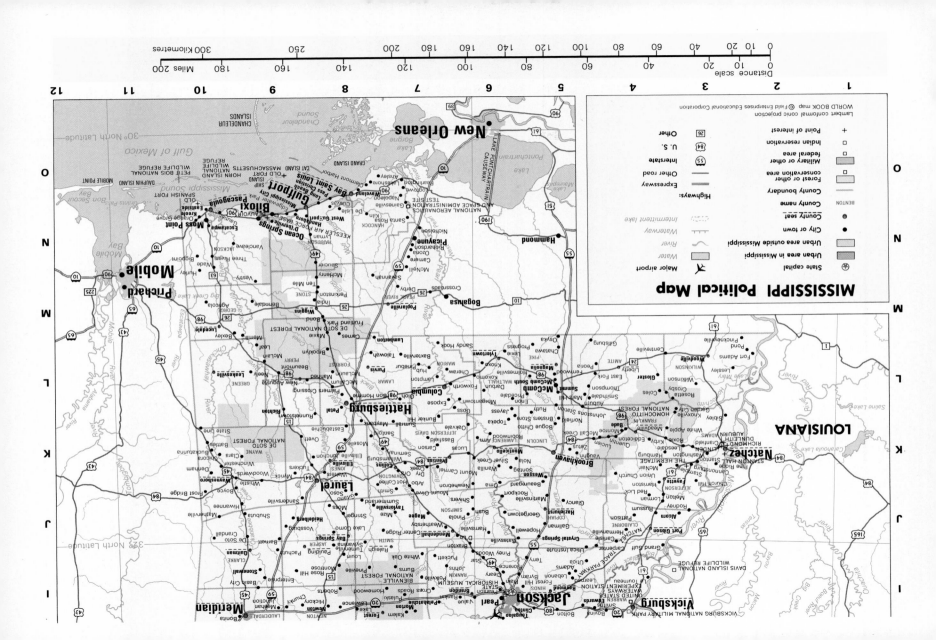

Population

2,158,872	Census	1970
2,178,141	"	1960
2,178,914	"	1950
2,183,796	"	1940
2,009,821	"	1930
1,790,618	"	1920
1,797,114	"	1910
1,551,270	"	1900
1,289,600	"	1890
1,131,597	"	1880
827,922	"	1870
791,305	"	1860
606,526	"	1850
375,651	"	1840
136,621	"	1830
75,448	"	1820
31,306	"	1810
7,600	"	1800

Metropolitan Area

Biloxi-
Gulfport 131,268
Jackson 252,713

Counties

Adams ...36,925..K 3
Alcorn ...26,362..A 10
Amite ...12,965..L 4
Attala ...19,115..G 7
Benton ...6,976..B 8
Bolivar ...48,202..D 4
Calhoun ...14,264..D 8
Carroll ...8,966..F 6
Chickasaw ..16,583..D 9
Choctaw ...8,063..F 8
Claiborne ...9,850..J 4
Clarke ...14,703..J 9
Clay ...18,449..E 9
Coahoma ..39,302..C 5
Copiah ...23,918..J 5
Covington ..13,629..K 7
De Soto ..35,247..A 6
Forrest ...56,699..L 8
Franklin ...7,932..K 4
George ...12,547..M 10
Greene ...8,372..L 9
Grenada ..19,224..E 7
Hancock ..16,566..N 7
Harrison ..131,268..N 9
Hinds ...209,513..I 5
Holmes ...22,605..G 6
Humphreys ..13,973..F 5
Issaquena ..2,663..G 4
Itawamba ..16,615..C 10
Jackson ...85,471..N 10
Jasper ...15,267..J 8
Jefferson ...8,676..J 3
Jefferson
Davis ...12,460..K 7
Jones ...55,043..K 8
Kemper ...9,988..H 9
Lafayette ..24,055..C 8
Lamar ...16,174..L 7
Lauderdale ..65,451..I 9
Lawrence ..10,868..K 6
Leake ...16,883..G 7
Lee ...45,332..C 9
Leflore ...40,033..E 5
Lincoln ...24,909..K 5
Lowndes ...48,399..F 10
Madison ...28,644..H 6
Marion ...22,372..L 7
Marshall ...23,322..B 7
Monroe ...32,751..D 10

Cities and Towns

Abbeville ....B 7
Aberdeen ..6,117.°D 10
Acker ....D 10
Ackerman ...1,418.°F 8
Adams ....I 5
Agricola ....M 10
Albin ....D 5
Alcorn ....J 3
Algoma ....C 9
Alligator ...227..D 5
Amory ...7,010..D 10
Anding ....G 4
Anguilla ...580..G 4
Ansley ....Q 8
Arbo ....K 7
Arcola ...366..F 4
Arkabutla ....B 6
Arm ....K 6
Artesia ...469..F 10
Ashland ...309.°B 8
Askew ....B 6
Auburn ....L 5
Austin ....B 5
Avalon ....F 5
Avon ....F 4
Bailey ....H 9
Baird ....F 5
Baldwyn ...2,378..B 10
Banks ....B 6
Banner ....B 8
Barnes ....G 8
Barnesville .....A 6
Barnett ....I 9
Basic City ......I 9
Bassfield ...295..K 7
Batesville ..3,747.°C 6
Battles ....K 10
Baxterville .....L 7
Bay
  St. Louis .6,478.°O 9
Bay Springs .1,786.°J 8
Beacon Hill .....C 9
Beatty ....F 7

Beaumont ...1,064..L 9
Beauregard ...193..K 5
Becker ....D 10
Belden ....C 9
Belen ....C 5
Bellefontaine ...E 8
Belmont ...901..B 11
Belzoni ...3,073.°F 5
Benndale ....M 9
Benoit ...453..E 4
Benton ....G 6
Bentonia ...511..H 5
Berclair ....E 5
Bethelen ....F 9
Beulah ...421..E 4
Beverly ....C 5
Bexley ....M 10
Big Creek ...100..D 8
Bigbee ....D 10
Bigbee Valley ...F 10
Biggersville ....B 10
Bigpoint ....N 10
Biloxi ...47,814..N 9
Bissell ....C 9
Black Hawk ......F 6
Blaine ....E 5
Blue Mountain 741..B 9
Blue Springs ..99..C 9
Bobo ....D 5
Bogue Chitto ....K 5
Bolivar ....E 4
Bolton ...797..I 5
Bon Homme ....L 8
Bonita ....I 9
Booneville ..5,509.°B 10
Bourbon ....F 4
Bovina ....I 4
Boyce ....K 10
Boyle ...848..E 5
Branch ....H 7
Brandon ...2,677.°I 6
Braxton ...191..J 6
Bristers Store ..L 7
Brooklyn 10,564.°K 5
Brooklyn ....M 8
Brooksville ..857..F 10
Brownsville .....H 5
Bruce ...2,009..D 8
Bryan ....D 7
Buckatunna .....J 9
Bude ...1,206..K 4
Buena Vista .....B 9
Bunker Hill .....L 7
Burns ....I 7
Burnside ....A 8
Burnsville ...416..A 10
Bush ....J 6
Byhalia ...674..A 7
Byram ....I 5
Caledonia ...289..E 10
Calhoun City 1,812..D 8
Camden ....H 7
Canaan ....A 8
Cannonsburg .....K 3
Canton ..10,138.°H 6
Carlisle ....J 4
Carnes ....M 8
Carpenter ....J 5
Carriere ....N 7
Carrollton ...343.°F 6
Carson ....K 7
Carter ....G 4
Carthage ...2,971.°H 7
Cary ...428..G 4
Cascilla ....D 6
Cedarbluff ......E 9
Center Ridge ....J 7
Centreville ..1,778..L 4
Chalybeate ......A 9
Charleston ..2,811.°D 6

Chatawa ....M 5
Chatham ....G 4
Cheraw ....L 7
Chester ....F 8
Chesterville ....C 9
Chicora ....K 10
Choctaw ....E 4
Chulahoma ....B 7
Chunky ...224..I 9
Church Hill .....K 3
Clara ....K 9
Clarksdale .21,158.°C 5
Clarkson ....E 8
Cleary ....I 6
Clermont Harbor .O 8
Cleveland .13,079.°E 5
Cliftonville ....F 10
Clinton ...7,525..I 5
Coahoma ....C 5
Cockrum ....B 7
Coffeeville ..1,007.°D 7
Coila ....F 6
Coldwater ...1,425..B 6
Coles ....L 4
Collins ...1,894.°K 7
Collinsville ....H 9
Colony Town .....F 4
Columbia ...7,248.°L 7
Columbus .25,176.°E 10
Commerce ....B 5
Como ...789..B 6
Conehatta ....H 8
Conway ....G 7
Corinth ..11,349.°A 10
Courtland ...242..C 6
Crandall ....J 10
Cranfield ....K 3
Crawford ...317..F 10
Crenshaw ...1,246..B 6
Crosby ...705..L 4
Cross Roads .....A 10
Cross Roads .....I 7
Crossroads ......M 7
Crowder ...528..C 6
Cruger ...362..F 6
Crystal
  Springs ..4,281..J 5
Cuevas ....O 8
Curtiss Station ..C 6
Daleville ....H 9
Darbun ....L 6
Darling ....C 6
Darlove ....F 4
Decatur ...1,275.°H 8
Deemer ....H 8
Deeson ....D 4
De Kalb ...1,045.°G 9
De Lisle ....O 8
Delta City ......G 4
Denham ....K 10
Denmark ....C 8
Dennis ....B 11
Derby ....M 7
Derma ...578..D 8
De Soto ....H 9
Deweese ....H 9
D'Iberville ..3,005..N 9
D'Lo ...428..J 6
Doddsville ...190..E 5
Dorsey ....C 10
Doskie ....C 10
Dossville ....G 7
Drew ...2,572..E 5
Dry Creek ....K 6
Dubard ....J 7
Dubbs ....D 5
Dublin ....D 5
Duck Hill ...674..E 7
Duffee ....I 9
Dumas ....B 9

Duncan ...465..D 4
Dundee ....B 5
Durant ...2,697..G 7
East Fork ....K 5
Eastabuchie .....K 8
Eastside ...4,318..O 10
Ebenezer ....G 6
Ecru ...442..C 9
Eddiceton ....K 4
Eden ...218..G 5
Edgewater Park ..N 9
Edinburg ....G 8
Edwards ...1,229..I 5
Egypt ....D 9
Electric Mills ..G 10
Elizabeth ....F 4
Elliott ....E 7
Ellistown ....C 9
Ellisville ..4,139.°K 8
Ellisville Junction K 8
Embry ....K 4
Enid ...128..D 6
Enon ....G 6
Enondale ....H 10
Enterprise ...532..I 9
Escatawpa ..1,464..N 10
Estesmill ....H 7
Estill ....F 4
Ethel ...566..F 8
Etta ....C 8
Europa ...1,654..E 8
Eureka Springs ..C 7
Evansville ......B 5
Evergreen ....C 10
Expose ....L 7
Fairfield ....C 9
Falcon ....C 6
Falkner ....A 9
Fannin ....I 6
Farrell ....F 5
Fayette ...1,677.°K 4
Fernwood ....L 5
Fitler ....H 4
Flora ...743..H 6
Florence ...360..I 6
Flowood* ...486..I 6
Forest ...3,997.°I 8
Forest Hill .....I 6
Forkville ....I 7
Fort Adams ......L 2
Foxworth ....L 7
Free Trade ......H 8
Freeny ....H 8
French Camp .123..F 8
Friars Point 1,177..C 5
Friendship ......C 9
Frost Bridge ....K 10
Fruitland Park ..M 8
Fulton ...2,689.°C 10
Gainesville .....O 7
Gallman ...100..J 5
Garden City .....L 3
Gatesville ......J 6
Gattman ...145..D 11
Gault ....H 9
Gautier ....N 10
Geeville ....H 9
Georgetown ...285..J 6
Gholson ....G 9
Gibson ....B 10
Gillsburg ....M 5
Gitano ....H 8
Glancy ....J 5
Glen ....J 10
Glen Allan ......G 4
Glendora ...147..D 6
Gloster ...1,278..L 4
Glover ....A 6
Golden ...121..B 11
Good Hope ....H 7

Goodman ...1,151..G 6
Gore Springs ....E 7
Goshen Springs ..H 7
Goss ....G 7
Grace ....G 4
Grady ....E 8
Grand Gulf ......J 4
Greenville .38,834.°F 4
Greenville
  North ...2,516..F 4
Greenwood .20,640.°E 6
Greenwood
  Springs ....D 10
Grenada ..9,710.°E 7
Gulfport ..39,415.°O 9
Gunnison ...448..D 4
Guntown ...269..C 9
Hamburg ....K 4
Hamilton ....D 10
Handsboro ..1,577..N 9
Hardy ....D 7
Harperville .....H 8
Harriston ....K 4
Harrisville .....J 6
Hatley ....D 10
Hattiesburg 37,461.°L 8
Hazlehurst ..4,238.°J 5
Heads ....I 5
Heidelberg ..1,071..J 9
Hermanville .....J 4
Hernando ..2,463.°B 6
Hesterville .....F 7
Hickory ...539..I 9
Hickory Flat ...344..B 8
High Point ......F 8
Hillhouse ....D 4
Hillsboro ....H 7
Hinchcliff ......C 6
Hiwannee ....J 9
Holcomb ...97..E 6
Holcut ....B 10
Hollandale ..2,417..F 4
Holly Bluff .....G 5
Holly Ridge .....F 4
Holly
  Springs ..5,497.°B 8
Hollywood ....B 5
Holmesville .....L 5
Homewood ....I 7
Hopewell ....I 4
Horn Lake ....A 6
Hot Coffee ......K 7
Houlka ...547..D 9
Houston ...2,687.°D 9
Howard ....G 8
Hub ....L 7
Hudsonville .....A 7
Hurley ....N 10
Hurricane ....C 8
Hushpuckena .....D 4
Independence ....B 7
India ....M 8
Indianola ..8,859.°F 5
Ingomar ....C 9
Ingrams Mill ....J 7
Inverness ..1,088..F 5
Isola ...481..G 5
Itta Bena ..2,478..E 5
Iuka ...2,354.°B 11
Jackson 150,332.°I 6
Jayess ....L 6
Johns ....I 7
Johnstons
  Station ....L 5
Jonestown ..1,123..C 5
Jonestown ....J 8
Kalem ....I 7
Kewanee ....I 10
Kilmichael ...532..F 7

Kiln ....N 8
Kings ....I 4
Kirby ....K 4
Klondike ....H 9
Knoxo ....L 6
Knoxville ....L 3
Kokomo ....L 6
Kolola Springs ..E 10
Kosciusko ..7,170.°G 7
Kossuth ...178..A 9
Kreole ...1,870..N 10
Lafayette
  Springs ....C 8
Lake ...297..I 8
Lake Como ....J 8
Lake
  Cormorant ....A 6
Lakeshore ....O 8
Lamar ....L 3
Lambert ...1,490..C 6
Lamont ....D 4
Lampton ....L 7
Lauderdale ......H 9
Laurel ..23,521.°K 8
Lawrence ....H 8
Laws Hill ....B 7
Leaf ....L 9
Leakesville ..1,065.°L 10
Learned ...96..I 5
Lebanon ....I 7
Leedy ....B 10
Leesburg ....E 8
Leesdale ....K 3
Le Flore ....E 6
Leland ...6,080..F 4
Lena ...307..H 7
Lessley ....H 3
Le Tourneau .....D 6
Leverett ....D 4
Lexie ....L 6
Lexington ..2,753.°G 6
Liberty ...642.°L 4
Little Rock .....H 9
Little Texas ....A 8
Litton ....E 4
Logtown ....O 7
Long Beach ..5,990.°O 8
Longtown ....B 6
Longview ....F 8
Looxahoma ....B 7
Lorman ....J 4
Louin ...389..J 8
Louise ...481..G 5
Louisville ..6,453.°F 9
Lucas ....K 5
Lucedale ..2,309.°M 10
Lucien ....K 5
Ludlow ....H 7
Lula ...484..C 5
Lumberton ..2,111..M 8
Lyman ....N 8
Lynchburg ....A 6
Lyon ...393..C 5
Maben ...696..E 8
Macon ...2,573.°G 10
Madden ....H 8
Madison ...703..H 6
Magee ...2,897..J 7
Magnolia ..1,738.°L 5
Mahned ....K 8
Malvina ....D 4
Mantachie ...246..C 10
Mantee ...166..E 8
Marietta ....B 10
Marion ....I 10
Marks ...2,588.°C 6
Mars Hill ....H 3
Martin ....K 4
Martinsville ....J 5
Marydell ....G 8

Mashulaville ....G 9	Nicholson ....N 7	Prairie Point .....F 10	Shellmound ....E 6
Matherville ....J 10	Niles ....D 4	Prentiss ...1,661.°K 7	Sherard ....C 5
Mathiston ....597..E 8	Nitta Yuma ....G 4	Preston ....G 9	Sherman ....403...C 9
Mattson ....D 5	Nola ....K 6	Pricedale ....L 6	Sherwood ....E 8
Maxie ....M 8	Norfield ....K 5	Prichard ....B 6	Shivers ....J 6
Maybank ....K 8	North Carroll-	Progress ....M 5	Shubuta ....718...J 9
Mayersville ......°G 4	ton ....521...F 6	Puckett ....302...I 7	Shuford ....C 7
Mayhew ....E 10	Noxapater ..549...G 9	Pulaski ....I 7	Shuqualak ...550..G 10
McAdams ....G 7	Oakland ....488..D 6	Purvis ...1,880.°L 8	Sibley ....L 4
McAfee ....H 8	Oakvale .....99..K 6	Pyland ....D 8	Sidon .....410...F 6
McCall Creek .....K 5	Ocean	Quentin ....K 4	Silver City ..431..G 5
McCallum ....L 8	Springs ..5,775..N 9	Quincy ....D 10	Silver Creek ..229..K 6
McCarley ....E 7	Otahoma ....H 7	Quitman ...2,605.°J 9	Singleton ....G 7
McComb ...11,640..L 5	Oil City ....H 5	Quito ....J 5	Skene ....C 5
McComb	Okolona ...2,984.°D 9	Raleigh ...1,000.°J 7	Slate Springs .123..E 8
South ...1,865..L 5	Old Houlka ....D 9	Randolph ...131...C 8	Slayden ....A 8
McCondy ....D 9	Olive	Rankin ....I 6	Sledge .....440...C 6
McCool ....211...F 8	Branch ...1,497..A 7	Raymond ...1,471.°I 5	Smith ....K 7
McDonald ....H 8	Oloh ....J 7	Red Banks ....B 7	Smithdale ....L 5
McHenry ....N 8	Oma ....K 6	Red Lick ....J 4	Smiths ....C 7
McLain ....L 9	Onward ....H 4	Redwood ....H 4	Smithville ...489..D 10
McLaurin ....L 8	Ora ....J 7	Reform ....D 4	Sontag ....K 6
McMillan ....F 8	Orange Grove .....N 10	Rena Lara ....D 4	Soso ....J 8
McNair ....K 4	Osyka .....712...M 5	Renfroe ....G 8	Southaven ....A 6
McNeill ....N 7	Ovett .....290...K 9	Rich ....C 5	Springville ....D 8
McVille ....G 7	Oxford ...9,147.°C 7	Richardson ....N 7	Stallo ....G 8
Meadville ....611.°K 4	Ozona ....N 7	Richland ....G 6	Stampley ....K 3
Meehan ....I 9	Pace ......420...E 4	Richton ...1,065..L 9	Stanton ....K 3
Melton ....J 4	Pachuta ...271...J 9	Ridgeland .1,605..I 6	Starr ....J 4
Meltonia ....E 4	Paden .....134..B 10	Rienzi .....375..B 10	Starkville .10,631.°E 9
Mendenhall .2,329.°J 7	Palmers Crossing ..L 8	Ripley ...3,484.°B 9	State College .....E 9
Meridian ..44,405.°I 9	Panther Burn .....G 4	Roberts ....I 8	State Line ...653..K 10
Merigold ...602...D 5	Paris ....J 8	Robinsonville .....B 5	Steens ....E 10
Merrill ....M 9	Pascagoula 26,512.°O 10	Robinwood ....K 6	Stewart ....162..F 8
Metcalfe ....F 4	Pass	Rockport ....J 6	Stoneville ....F 4
Michigan City .....A 8	Christian .2,792..O 8	Rodney ....J 3	Stonewall .1,186..I 9
Midnight ....G 5	Pattison ....J 4	Rolling Fork 2,017.°G 4	Stovall ....C 5
Midway ....G 6	Paulding ....°J 9	Rome ......279...D 5	Stover ....D 6
Miller ....G 6	Paulette ....G 10	Rose Hill ....J 8	Strayhorn ....B 6
Mineral Wells .....A 7	Paynes ....D 6	Rosedale ..2,423.°D 4	Stringer ....J 8
Minter City ....E 6	Pearl ...5,081...I 6	Rosetta ....L 3	Stringtown ....E 4
Mississippi	Pearlington ....O 7	Roundaway ....D 5	Strong ....E 10
City ....4,169..O 9	Pearson ....I 6	Roundlake ....D 4	Sturgis ....358...F 9
Mize ......371...J 7	Pelahatchie .1,259..I 7	Roxie .....585...K 4	Sucarnoochee ......H 10
Money ....E 6	Peoria ....L 5	Rudyard ....C 5	Summerland ....J 8
Monroe ....K 4	Percy ....G 4	Ruleville .2,292..E 5	Summit ...1,602...L 5
Monte Vista ....E 8	Perkinston ....M 8	Runnelstown ....L 8	Sumner .....551.°D 5
Monticello .1,795.°K 6	Perthshire ....D 4	Russell ....I 10	Sumrall ....797...K 7
Montpelier ....E 9	Petal ...4,007...L 8	Russum ....J 4	Sunflower ...662...E 5
Montrose ...169...I 8	Pheba ....E 9	Ruth ....L 5	Suqualena ....H 9
Mooreville ....C 10	Philadelphia 6,186.°H 8	Sabino ....C 5	Swan Lake ....D 5
Moorhead ..2,243..F 5	Philipp ....E 6	Sallis ....223...G 7	Sweatman ....E 7
Morgan City ....F 5	Phoenix ....H 6	Saltillo ...536...C 9	Swiftown ....F 5
Morgantown ....L 4	Picayune .10,388..N 7	Sandersville .1,517..J 9	Sylvarena ....69...J 8
Morton ...2,588..I 7	Pickens ...727...G 6	Sandhill ....H 7	Symonds ....D 4
Moselle ....K 8	Piggtown ....J 7	Sandy Hook ....M 7	Tallula ....H 4
Moss ....J 8	Pinckneyville .....M 3	Sanford ....K 8	Talowah ....L 8
Moss Point 18,746..N 9	Pine Ridge ....K 3	Santa Rosa ....N 7	Taylor .....122...C 7
Mound	Pinebur ....L 7	Sapa ....E 8	Taylorsville .1,319..J 8
Bayou ....2,133..D 4	Pineville ....B 6	Sarah ....B 6	Tchula ...1,721..F 6
Mount Carmel .....K 7	Piney Woods ....J 6	Sardis ...1,829.°C 6	Ten Mile ....M 8
Mount Olive ..841..J 7	Pinola ....116...J 6	Sarepta ....D 8	Terry .....585...J 6
Mount Pleasant ....A 7	Pittsboro ..205.°D 8	Satartia ...126...H 5	Thaxton ....C 8
Murphy ....G 5	Plain ....I 6	Saucier ....N 8	Thomastown ....G 7
Myrick ....K 9	Plantersville ..572..C 9	Savage ....B 6	Thompson ....L 5
Myrtle ....313...B 8	Pleasant Grove ....C 6	Savannah ....N 8	Thorn ....D 8
Napoleon ....L 9	Pleasant Hill .....H 6	Schlater ....D 5	Thornton ....G 6
Natchez ..19,777.°K 3	Pocahontas ....H 6	Scobey ....D 7	Thrashers ....B 10
Neely ....L 9	Polkville ....I 7	Scooba ....513...G 10	Three Rivers .....N 10
Nellieburg ....I 9	Pond ....L 2	Scott ....E 4	Thyatira ....B 7
Nesbitt ....H 8	Pontotoc ..3,466.°C 9	Sebastopol ..343...H 8	Tibbs ....B 7
Neshoba ....H 8	Pope ......246...C 6	Seminary ...288...K 8	Tie Plant ...1,491..E 7
Nettleton .1,534..D 10	Poplar Creek .....F 7	Senatobia .4,170.°B 6	Tilden ....C 10
New Albany .6,355.°B 9	Poplarville .2,255.°M 7	Sessums ....D 9	Tillatoba ..102...D 7
New Augusta ..275.°L 9	Port Gibson .2,287.°J 4	Shannon ...554...D 9	Tinsley ....H 5
New Site ....B 10	Porterville ....H 10	Sharon ....H 6	Tiplersville ......A 9
Newhebron ...271...K 6	Potts Camp ..429...B 8	Shaw .....2,515..E 4	Tippo ....D 6
Newton ...3,442..I 8	Prairie ....112...E 9	Shelby ...2,614..D 4	Tishomingo ..415..B 10

*Does not appear on the map; key shows general location.
°County seat

Shoppers Stroll along one of the main streets in Jackson, the largest city in Mississippi. Jackson, the state capital, is a business and financial center.

Toccopola ...198...C 8	Vance ....D 5	Weir ......522...F 8
Tomnolen ....E 8	Vancleave ....N 10	Wenasoga ....A 10
Toomsuba ....I 10	Van Vleet ....D 9	Wesson ...1,238...K 5
Topeka ....K 6	Vardaman ...637...D 8	West ......282...F 7
Topton ....I 6	Vaughan ....K 5	West Gulf-
Tougaloo ....I 6	Vaughn ....K 5	port .....3,323..N 9
Tralake ....F 4	Velma ....D 7	West Point .8,513.°E 10
Trebloc ....D 9	Verona ...1,846..C 9	Wheeler ....B 10
Tremont ....C 10	Vestry ....N 9	Whistle ....K 9
Tribbett ....F 4	Vicksburg .24,679.°I 4	White Apple ....K 4
Troy ....K 9	Victoria ....A 7	White Oak ....J 7
Tuckers ....K 9	Vossburg ....J 9	Whites ....E 10
Tula ....K 9	Wade ....N 10	Wiggins ....H 7
Tunica ...1,661.°B 5	Wakefield ....B 7	Wiggins ...2,969.°M 8
Tunica	Walls ....A 6	Wilkinson ....M 3
North .....1,025..B 5	Walnut ....390...A 9	Willet ....L 3
Tupelo ...20,046.°C 9	Walnut Grove .433..H 8	Williamsburg ......K 7
Turnerville ....H 7	Walters ....K 8	Williamsville .....G 7
Tuscola ....H 7	Walthall ....153.°E 8	Winborn ....B 8
Tutwiler .1,102...D 5	Wanilla ....K 6	Winchester ....K 9
Tylertown .1,711.°L 6	Warsaw ....B 7	Winona ...5,509.°E 7
Tyro ....B 7	Washington ....K 3	Winstonville ......D 4
Union ....C 9	Water Valley 3,185.°C 7	Winterville ....F 4
Union ....1,794..H 8	Waterford ....B 8	Woodland ....E 8
Union Church ......K 4	Waveland ..2,903..O 8	Woodville ..1,597.°L 3
University .3,597..C 7	Waxhaw ....D 4	Woodwards ....K 10
Utica .....764...I 5	Way ....H 6	Wyatte ....B 7
Utica Institute ...I 5	Waynesboro .4,287.°K 10	Yazoo
Vaiden ....475.°F 7	Wayside ....F 4	City ....10,712.°G 5
Valley Park ....I 4	Weathersby ....80...J 7	Zama ....K 5
Value ....I 6	Webb ......686...D 5	Zetus ....K 5

Sources: Latest census figures (1970 preliminary census where available, 1960 census, or special census). Cities and towns without population information are unincorporated places under 1,000 in population and are not listed in census reports.

MISSISSIPPI

MISSISSIPPI/People

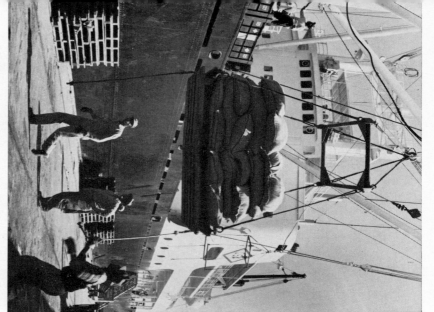

The 1970 preliminary United States census reported that Mississippi had 2,158,872 persons. This figure was a decrease of about 1 per cent from the 1960 figure, 2,178,141.

More than 60 per cent of Mississippi's people live in farming areas. Fewer than 40 per cent live in cities and towns. But Mississippi's urban population is growing as people move from country areas to the cities where manufacturing industries are being developed. Mississippi's urban population more than doubled between 1930 and 1960.

The largest city is Jackson, the state capital and center of Mississippi's business and financial activities. Jackson is the state's largest Standard Metropolitan Statistical Area (see METROPOLITAN AREA). The metropolitan area of Biloxi-Gulfport ranks second in population to Jackson. Expanding activity in shipbuilding and oil refining made the port city of Pascagoula one of the fastest growing cities of Mississippi during the 1960's. Mississippi has several large cities on the Mississippi River. These cities include Greenville, Natchez, and Vicksburg. See the separate articles on the cities of Mississippi in the *Related Articles* at the end of this article.

Almost all Mississippians were born in the United States. The 1960 census showed that 42 of every 100 persons in Mississippi are Negroes. This is a larger proportion of Negroes than in any other state.

More than half of all Mississippians who are church members are Baptists, and more than a fourth are Methodists. Other religious groups with large membership in Mississippi include Roman Catholics, Presbyterians, and Episcopalians.

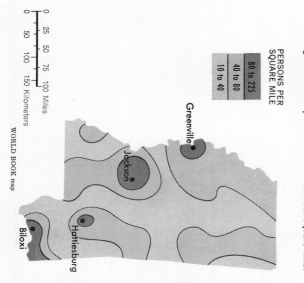

POPULATION

This map shows the *population density* of Mississippi, and how it varies in different parts of the state. Population density means the average number of persons who live on each square mile.

PERSONS PER
SQUARE MILE

80 to 225
40 to 80
10 to 40

Greenville

Jackson

Hattiesburg

Biloxi

WORLD BOOK map

0 25 50 75 100 Miles

0 50 100 150 Kilometers

Dockworkers at Gulfport unload fish meal from a merchant ship. Industries in the busy port cities of Gulfport and Pascagoula hire many workers. Pascagoula has large shipyards and oil refineries.

Livestock Buyers gather in a sale barn near Macon to bid for farm animals. Mississippi stockmen tend large herds of beef cattle and dairy cows. They also raise chickens, hogs, and sheep.

Mississippi Agricultural & Industrial Board

MISSISSIPPI / Education

Schools. The Mississippi public-school system was established by the constitution of 1869. The state set up a board of education and provided that every child should receive free schooling for four months each year. At first, most Mississippians opposed public schools. The Civil War had caused hard times and the people had little money for school taxes. The opposition decreased as conditions improved, and by the 1890's the public-school system had won general approval. In 1904, the state established a textbook purchasing board. The board supplies books to all schoolchildren, whether they attend public or private schools. In 1910, Mississippi set up agricultural high schools.

The state's entire school system was re-organized during the 1950's and early 1960's. The aim was to improve the schools by a program of consolidation of small districts (see CONSOLIDATED SCHOOL). To meet the manpower needs of new industry and business, Mississippi has also established a statewide network of vocational-technical training centers at both the high school and junior college levels.

A state law of 1920 required children to attend school between their 7th and 16th birthdays. Like other southern states, Mississippi had separate schools for Negroes and whites. In 1954, the Supreme Court of the United States ruled that school segregation on the basis of race was unconstitutional. In 1956, Mississippi repealed its law that required children to go to school.

The state superintendent of public education directs Mississippi's elementary and secondary schools. The people elect him to a four-year term. Mississippi spends about 65 per cent of its tax revenue for public education. For the number of students and teachers in Mississippi, see EDUCATION (table).

Libraries. The Mississippi Library Commission, established in 1926, directs the state's public libraries. It also lends books to public and school libraries. County and regional libraries serve thousands of Mississippians, and bookmobiles bring library services to farming areas.

In 1946, Mississippi's state department of education began a school-library program. Under this program, consultants help develop libraries in many schools.

A library established in 1818 in Port Gibson is probably the first Mississippi library that served the public. The state library in Jackson was established in 1838.

Museums. Mississippi has one of the nation's finest historical museums, in the restored Old Capitol in Jackson. It is a division of the Department of Archives and History. Other historical museums include the Old Courthouse Museum in Vicksburg, and the Jefferson Davis Shrine at Beauvoir House near Biloxi. Art museums include the Jackson Municipal Art Gallery, the Mary Buie Museum in Oxford, and the Lauren Rogers Library and Museum of Art in Laurel. The State Wildlife Museum of the Mississippi Game and Fish Commission in Jackson has many exhibits of natural history.

UNIVERSITIES AND COLLEGES

Mississippi has 14 universities and colleges accredited by the Southern Association of Colleges and Schools. For enrollments and further information, see UNIVERSITIES AND COLLEGES (table).

Name	Location	Founded
Alcorn Agricultural and Mechanical College	Lorman	1871
Belhaven College	Jackson	1894
Blue Mountain College	Blue Mountain	1873
Delta State College	Cleveland	1924
Jackson State College	Jackson	1877
Millsaps College	Jackson	1892
Mississippi, University of	University	1844
Mississippi College	Clinton	1826
Mississippi State College for Women	Columbus	1884
Mississippi State University	State College	1878
Mississippi Valley State College	Itta Bena	1950
Southern Mississippi, University of	Hattiesburg	1910
Tougaloo College	Tougaloo	1869
William Carey College	Hattiesburg	1906

The Gulf Coast of Mississippi is one of the nation's most popular winter resort regions. This vacationland has won fame for its large, sunny beaches and fine hotels. In other parts of the state, historic monuments and pleasant wooded areas are the chief attractions. Thousands of visitors also take tours of Mississippi's many old mansions and plantations. There, they can get some idea of what life was like in Mississippi before the Civil War. Pretty hostesses dressed in billowing hoop skirts serve as guides.

Excellent hunting and fishing in about 25 Wildlife Management areas attract many sportsmen to Mississippi. Hunters may shoot wild doves, ducks, geese, quail, turkeys, deer, rabbits, raccoons, and squirrels. Thousands of ponds and lakes have been stocked with fish. Freshwater fishermen can cast for bass, bream, crappies, and other fishes. Or they may sit lazily on a Mississippi river-bank and wait for catfish to take their bait. Salt-water fishermen fight big game fish in the waters off the Gulf Coast.

Beauvoir, Last Home of Jefferson Davis

Captured Cannon at Pascagoula's Old Spanish Fort

PLACES TO VISIT

Following are brief descriptions of some of Mississippi's most interesting places to visit.

Ackia Battleground, in northeastern Mississippi, marks the site of the Chickasaw fort that was attacked by the French in 1736. The Chickasaw defeated the French and kept them from gaining control of the entire Mississippi Valley. Ackia Battleground was a national monument from 1938 until 1961, when it became part of the Natchez Trace Parkway.

Capitols, in Jackson, offer many reminders of the state's rich history. The *Old Capitol,* now the State Historical Museum, was built chiefly by slave labor between 1833 and 1842. Here, Mississippi voted in January, 1861, to secede from the Union. Jefferson Davis, president of the Confederacy, made his last speech here in 1884. The *New Capitol,* built in 1903, houses the state legislature, the state library, Hall of Governors, and the state supreme court.

Churches. The Church of the Redeemer in Biloxi is one of the most interesting churches in the South. This ivy-covered Episcopal church, erected in 1890, is built in Gothic style. A Confederate flag drapes the pew of Jefferson Davis. The pew was moved from an older church in which the Confederate president had worshiped. The Presbyterian church in Port Gibson dates from 1829.

Delta and Pine Land Company Plantation covers 38,000 acres near Scott. It is one of the largest cotton plantations in the world. The Fine Spinners and Doublers, Ltd., of Manchester, England, has owned it since 1911.

Fort Massachusetts, on Ship Island, was a Union stronghold during the Civil War. Confederate troops captured the fort early in the war. They partly destroyed it when they evacuated the island in 1861. Union forces then rebuilt the fort and used it as a prison until the end of the war. Another interesting fort is the Old Spanish Fort in Pascagoula.

Kansas Monument in Vicksburg

Priest Blesses Fleet at the Biloxi Shrimp Festival

Azaleas Brighten a Spring Festival Along the Gulf

Stately Old Homes in or near Natchez are reminders of the way of life of wealthy Mississippians before the Civil War. These mansions include *Auburn* (built in 1812), *D'Evereux* (1840), *Dunleith* (1847), *Edgewood* (1860), *Gloucester* (1804), *Linden* (1789), *Melrose* (1840), *Monteigne* (1853), *Richmond* (1786), *Rosalie* (1800's), and *Stanton Hall* (1857). The *Hermitage* stands near Port Gibson. *Anchuca* (1830) and *McRaven* (1797) are in Vicksburg. Other homes include *Waverly* (1856) near Columbus, *Gray Gables* (1830) in Holly Springs, and *Hampton Hall* (1832) near Woodville.

Jefferson Davis spent his boyhood at *Rosemont* near Woodville. At Biloxi stands *Beauvoir*, Davis' last home. The building later became a home for Confederate veterans and their wives or widows. Beauvoir is now a shrine and a museum.

United States Waterways Experiment Station. The station has two branches—one near Vicksburg and one near Clinton. They display concrete models of many U.S. dams, harbors, and waterways. The U.S. Army Corps of Engineers operates the station as part of its programs of flood control and improvement of inland waterways.

Vicksburg National Military Park honors the siege of Vicksburg, which lasted from May 18 to July 4, 1863. The siege, which ended in a Union victory, was a major turning point of the Civil War. Museum exhibits show the history of the region from Indian days to the present.

National Forests. Mississippi has six national forests. The largest is De Soto in southeastern Mississippi. The others are Homochitto in the southwest; Bienville, Delta, and Tombigbee in central Mississippi; and Holly Springs in the north. For the area and chief features of each national forest, see NATIONAL FOREST (table).

State Parks. Mississippi has 14 state parks. For information on the state parks of Mississippi, write to Comptroller, State Park System, 502 Milner Building, Jackson, Miss. 39201.

ANNUAL EVENTS

The highlight of Mississippi's many annual events is the Shrimp Festival in Biloxi during the first week of June. It marks the opening of the shrimp-fishing season. The celebration includes colorful balls and parades, the crowning of a shrimp queen, and the blessing of the shrimp fleet.

Other annual events in Mississippi include the following.

January-March: United States Field Trials for Hunting Dogs in Holly Springs (February); Biloxi Mardi Gras (second week before Lent); Azalea Trail and Spring Festival along the Gulf Coast (March); Vicksburg Historical Tours (March).

April-June: Garden Pilgrimages in Aberdeen, Columbus, Greenwood, Holly Springs, Jackson, Meridian, Natchez, and Port Gibson (April— some start in March); Confederate Memorial Day (April 26); Mississippi Arts Festival in Jackson (April); Southern Mississippi Singing Convention in Hattiesburg (first week of June).

July-September: Summer Sports Carnival in Biloxi (the 10 days before July 4); Regatta in Biloxi (July 4); Yacht Club Regatta in Gulfport (July); Mississippi Deep Sea Fishing Rodeo in Gulfport (July); Tarpon Rodeo in Pass Christian (July); Delta Staple Cotton Festival in Clarksdale (late August or early September); Choctaw Indian Fair in Philadelphia (late August or early September).

October-December: Mississippi Fair and Dairy Show in Meridian (first week of October); State Fair in Jackson (second week of October); Hospitality Regatta in Jackson (October); Chrysanthemum Society Meeting in Jackson (early in November); Annual Band Festival in Greenwood (early in December).

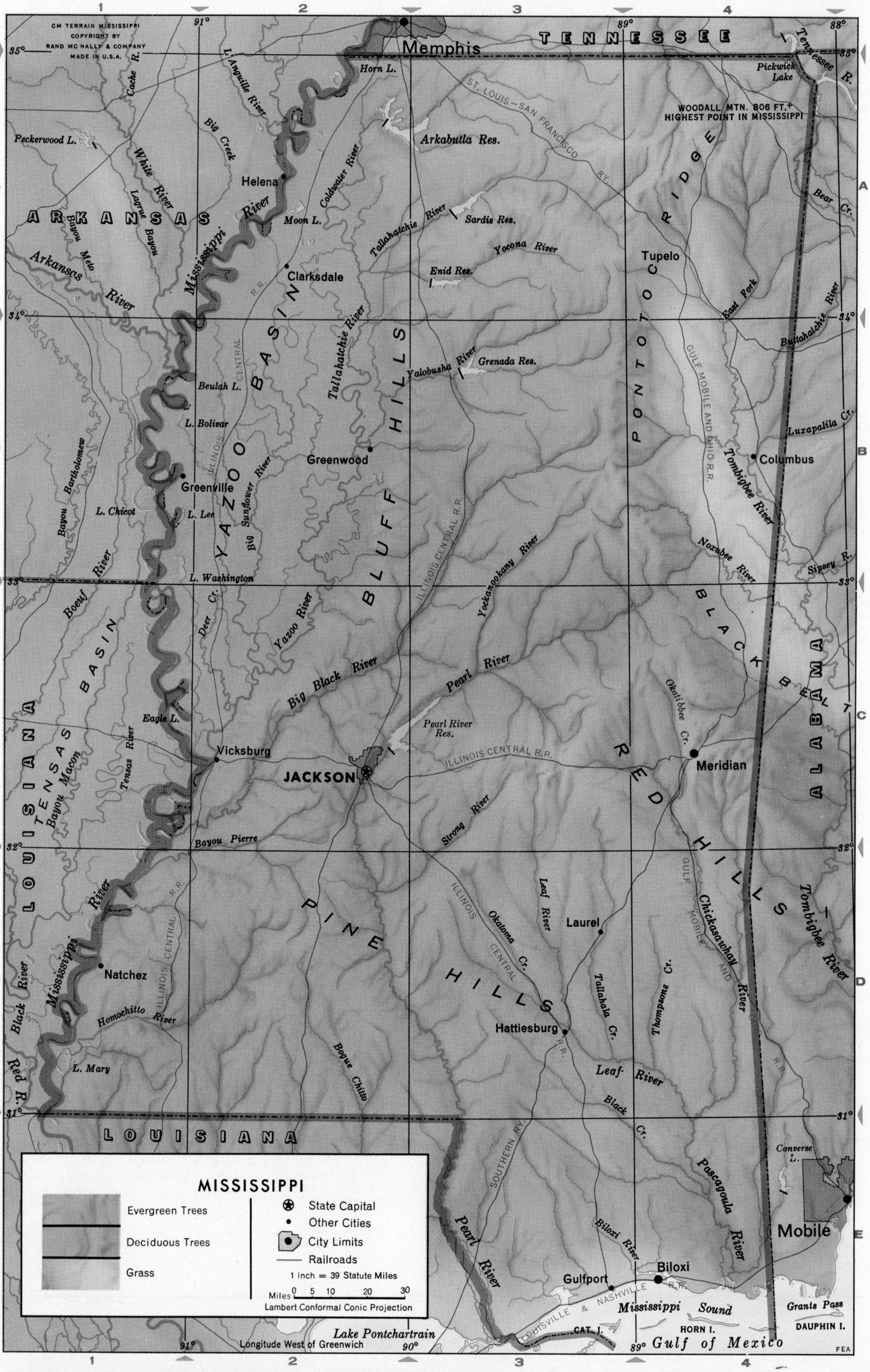

MISSISSIPPI

⊛ State Capital
• Other Cities
City Limits
Railroads

Evergreen Trees
Deciduous Trees
Grass

Miles
0 5 10 20 30
1 inch = 39 Statute Miles

Longitude West of Greenwich
Lambert Conformal Conic Projection

LOUISIANA

LOUISIANA

ARKANSAS

TENNESSEE

ALABAMA

TENSAS BASIN

YAZOO BASIN

BLUFF HILLS

PINE HILLS

PONTOTOC RIDGE

BLACK PRAIRIE

Red R.
Black River
Mississippi River
L. Mary
Homochitto River
ILLINOIS CENTRAL R.R.
Bayou Macon
Tensas River
Eagle L.
Deer Cr.
L. Washington
Big Sunflower River
Yazoo River
Boeuf River
Bayou Bartholomew
Bayou
L. Chicot
L. Lee
Greenville
L. Bolivar
Beulah L.
ILLINOIS CENTRAL R.R.
Greenwood
Tallahatchie River
Moon L.
Coldwater River
Clarksdale
Helena
Mississippi River
White River
Lagrange Bayou
Big Creek
L. Lagrange River
Cache R.
Peckerwood L.
Arkansas River
Arkabutla Res.
Sardis Res.
Yocona River
Enid Res.
Tallahatchie River
Yalobusha River
Grenada Res.
Horn L.
Memphis
ST. LOUIS-SAN FRANCISCO RY.
Pickwick Lake
WOODALL MTN. 806 FT.
HIGHEST POINT IN MISSISSIPPI
Tupelo
GULF MOBILE AND OHIO R.R.
East Fork
Bay Springs Lake
Buttahatchie River
Columbus
Tombigbee River
Luxapalila Cr.
Sipsey R.
Noxubee River
Meridian
Chickasawhay River
Okatibbee Cr.
Pearl River
Yockanookany River
Yalobusha River
ILLINOIS CENTRAL R.R.
Big Black River
Pearl River Res.
Strong River
Bogue Chitto
Pearl River
Bayou Pierre
Natchez
Vicksburg
JACKSON
SOUTHERN RY.
Oktoma Cr.
Leaf River
Okatoma Cr.
Hattiesburg
Laurel
Tallahala Cr.
Leaf River
Thompsons Cr.
Chunky River
Black Cr.
GULF MOBILE AND OHIO R.R.
Pascagoula River
Biloxi
Gulfport
LOUISVILLE & NASHVILLE R.R.
Mississippi Sound
Gulf of Mexico
HORN I.
Converse L.
Tchoutacabouffa River
DAUPHIN I.
Grants Pass
Mobile
ILLINOIS CENTRAL R.R.

FEA

MISSISSIPPI/The Land

Land Regions. Mississippi has two main land regions: (1) the Mississippi Alluvial Plain, and (2) the East Gulf Coastal Plain.

The Mississippi Alluvial Plain covers the entire western edge of the state. It consists of fertile lowlands and forms part of the 35,000-square-mile *Alluvial Plain* of the Mississippi River. The region is quite narrow south of Vicksburg. North of the city, the plain spreads out and covers the area between the Mississippi River and the Yazoo, Tallahatchie, and Coldwater rivers. Floodwaters of the rivers have enriched the soil of the region with deposits of silt. The fertile soil of the Mississippi Alluvial Plain is famous for its large cotton and soybean crops. Most Mississippians call this region the *Delta.*

The East Gulf Coastal Plain extends over all the state east of the Alluvial Plain. Most of the region is made up of low, rolling, forested hills. The coastal plain also has prairies and lowlands. Yellowish-brown *loess* (soil blown by winds) covers the region in the west. Most Mississippians call these deposits the Cane, Bluff, or Loess Hills. The Tennessee River Hills rise in northeastern Mississippi. They include the highest point in the state, 806-foot Woodall Mountain. The Pine Hills, often called the Piney Woods, rise in the southeastern part of the region. They are covered largely with longleaf and slash-pine forests.

The main prairie is called the *Black Belt* or *Black Prairie* because its soil is largely black in color. This long, narrow prairie lies in the northeast. It stretches through 10 counties. Livestock graze there, and corn and hay grow well on the farmlands of the Black Belt. Small prairies also lie in central Mississippi, east of Jackson. Along the Mississippi Sound, lowlands stretch inland over the southern part of the region.

Coastline. Mississippi has a 44-mile-long coastline along the Gulf of Mexico. With bays and coves, it has a total shoreline of 359 miles. The largest bays include Biloxi, St. Louis, and Pascagoula. The nation's longest sea wall protects more than 25 miles of coastline between Biloxi and Point Henderson at Bay St. Louis. Other coastal towns include Gulfport, Pass Christian, and Ocean Springs. Deer Island is near the mouth of Biloxi Bay, and a chain of small islands lies off the

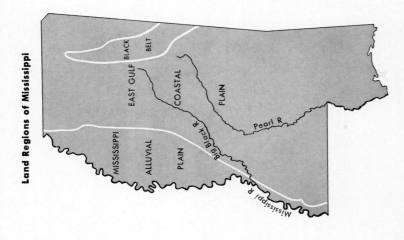

Land Regions of Mississippi

The Broad Mississippi River forms almost all of Mississippi's western border. Huge cotton crops grow in the Mississippi Alluvial Plain region that lies along the river. Powerful towboats push heavy barges past the cotton fields.

U.S. Army Corps of Engineers

Mississippi's Famous Piney Woods Country forms part of the East Gulf Coastal Plain region. Pine trees in this area provide pine oil, rosin, and turpentine as well as lumber.

Vicksburg Harbor, foreground, provides a navigation channel of quiet water away from the Mississippi River, background. Construction of the harbor created 245 acres of industrial land.

coast. They include Cat, Horn, Ship, and Petit Bois islands. Mississippi Sound separates these islands from the mainland.

Rivers and Lakes. Mississippi has many rivers and lakes. The nation's most important river, the Mississippi, forms most of the state's western border. Its floodwaters, in earlier times, often deposited silt on the land, and helped make the land fertile. In some years, heavy floods damaged crops and homes. Today, wide *levees* (man-made walls) help protect many areas against damaging floods (see LEVEE; MISSISSIPPI RIVER).

The state has several main river basins. The rivers of the western and north-central basin drain into the Mississippi River. These rivers include the Big Black River and the Yazoo River with its large tributaries, the Coldwater, Sunflower, and Tallahatchie rivers. Rivers of the eastern basin drain into the Gulf of Mexico. They include the Pearl, Pascagoula, and Tombigbee. Many of Mississippi's lakes are man-made reservoirs. The Tennessee River, for example, flows through Pickwick Lake in the northeastern section of Mississippi. Other man-made lakes in the state include Arkabutla, Enid, Grenada, and Sardis reservoirs, all of which are in north-central Mississippi. All these lakes lie behind flood-control dams. In the early 1960's, the large Ross Barnett Reservoir was built on the Pearl River near Jackson. The Mississippi River has formed many *oxbow lakes,* mostly north of Vicksburg. These lakes form when a river changes its course to take short cuts (see OXBOW LAKE). Mississippi's oxbow lakes include Beulah, Lee, Moon, and Washington. Mississippi also has many slow-moving streams called *bayous.* Some bayous connect the lakes with the rivers in the Delta. Others link the inland waterways with the Gulf of Mexico.

MISSISSIPPI / Climate

Mississippi has a warm, moist climate, with long summers and short winters. In July, Mississippi temperatures average about 82° F. Winds from the Gulf of Mexico, and frequent thundershowers, have a cooling effect on much of the state during the summers. Even in the interior part of the state, the temperature seldom goes above 100° F. However, temperatures of 90° F. or higher occur about 55 days a year on the Gulf Coast and more often in the interior. The highest temperature recorded in Mississippi was 115° F. at Holly Springs on July 29, 1930.

January temperatures average 48° F. in Mississippi. The lowest temperature was −16° F., recorded at French Camp on Feb. 13, 1899, and at Batesville on Feb. 2, 1951. Northern and central Mississippi occasionally have ice and snow. The Gulf Coast ordinarily has a frost-free season of 250 to 300 days. *Precipitation* (rain, melted snow, and other forms of moisture) ranges from

Warm, Sunny Weather all year around attracts many vacationers to the sandy beaches along Mississippi's Gulf Coast.

about 50 inches a year in the northwest to about 65 inches in the southeast. Hurricanes sometimes sweep over parts of Mississippi as they travel northward from the Gulf in late summer and fall.

Mississippi Agricultural & Industrial Board

SEASONAL TEMPERATURES

JANUARY

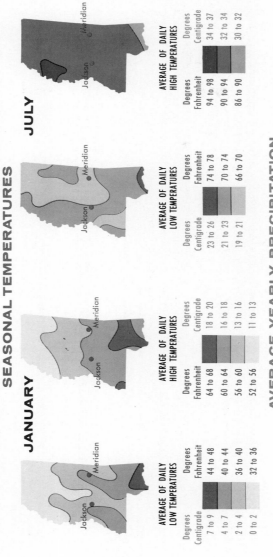

AVERAGE OF DAILY LOW TEMPERATURES

Degrees Centigrade	Degrees Fahrenheit
7 to 9	44 to 48
4 to 7	40 to 44
2 to 4	36 to 40
0 to 2	32 to 36

AVERAGE OF DAILY HIGH TEMPERATURES

Degrees Fahrenheit	Degrees Centigrade
64 to 68	18 to 20
60 to 64	16 to 18
56 to 60	13 to 16
52 to 56	11 to 13

JULY

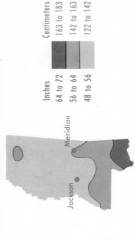

AVERAGE OF DAILY LOW TEMPERATURES

Degrees Centigrade	Degrees Fahrenheit
23 to 26	74 to 78
21 to 23	70 to 74
19 to 21	66 to 70

AVERAGE OF DAILY HIGH TEMPERATURES

Degrees Fahrenheit	Degrees Centigrade
94 to 98	34 to 37
90 to 94	32 to 34
86 to 90	30 to 32

AVERAGE YEARLY PRECIPITATION
(Rain, Melted Snow, and Other Moisture)

Inches	Centimeters
64 to 72	163 to 183
56 to 64	142 to 163
48 to 56	122 to 142

0   50   100   200 Miles
0   100   200   300 Kilometers

WORLD BOOK maps

MONTHLY WEATHER IN JACKSON AND MERIDIAN

		JAN	FEB	MAR	APR	MAY	JUNE	JULY	AUG	SEPT	OCT	NOV	DEC
JACKSON	Average of: High Temperatures	59	62	68	76	84	91	94	93	89	80	67	59
	Low Temperatures	38	40	46	54	61	68	71	70	65	53	43	39
	Days of Rain or Snow	11	11	10	9	9	9	11	7	7	5	8	10
MERIDIAN	Days of Rain or Snow	10	10	10	8	10	10	12	10	7	5	7	10
	High Temperatures	59	62	68	77	84	91	92	92	87	78	67	60
	Low Temperatures	37	39	45	52	59	67	70	69	64	51	41	37

Temperatures are given in degrees Fahrenheit.

Source: U.S. Weather Bureau

The annual value of Mississippi's manufactured products is greater than that of its farm products. However, agriculture remains an important industry in the state. Many manufacturing industries, such as food processing and the clothing and textile industries, depend on the farms for their raw materials.

Natural Resources of Mississippi include rich soils, abundant water supplies, valuable mineral deposits, large forests, and a wide variety of wildlife.

Soil and Water are the state's most important natural resources. The Mississippi Alluvial Plain has some of the richest soil in the United States. Much of this fertile earth is largely silt deposited by floodwaters of the Mississippi River. Another fertile area of clay loam soils is in the Black Belt. These soils are gray or black in color. Sandy loam soil covers most of the East Gulf Coastal Plain. Mississippi has great supplies of surface water, and also many wells. Together, they furnish abundant fresh water for home and industrial use.

Minerals. Petroleum is the most valuable mineral resource of Mississippi. The state has reserves of about 350 million barrels of oil. The chief oil deposits are in southern Mississippi. The state probably has over 1½ trillion cubic feet of natural gas, chiefly in the south-central and southwestern counties.

Mississippi has many kinds of clays that are used by important industries. Such clays include bentonite, used to lubricate oil well drills, and fuller's earth, used in refining certain fats and oils. Other valuable Mississippi clays are ball clays, kaolin, and certain clays suitable for making brick and tile. Low-grade bauxite is found in an area that extends from Tippah County to Kemper County. Large deposits of sand and gravel are found in various places, and Tishomingo County has large deposits of sandstone. Other important minerals produced in Mississippi include iron ore, lignite, limestone, and salt.

Forests cover more than half of Mississippi. They provide the raw materials for a huge output of products that make Mississippi a leading forest industry state. About 120 kinds of trees grow in Mississippi. The most important are the loblolly, longleaf, and slash pines of the Piney Woods area, and the shortleaf pine of northern and central Mississippi. Other trees include the ash, bald cypress, cottonwood, elm, hickory, oak, pecan, sweet gum, and tupelo. Mississippi conducts a widespread program of planting young trees to replace those that are cut down. Mississippi has over 4,000 tree farms —more than any other state.

Plant Life. The magnolia, an evergreen tree with fragrant white flowers, grows throughout the state. The magnolia is Mississippi's state flower. Many parts of the state also have azaleas, black-eyed Susans, camellias, crepe myrtle, dogwood, redbud, violets, Virginia creepers, and pink and white Cherokee roses.

Animal Life includes beavers, deer, foxes, opossums, rabbits, and squirrels. Among the state's game birds are wild doves, ducks, quail, and turkeys. The mockingbird is Mississippi's state bird. Fresh-water fish include bass, bream, catfish, and crappies. In the Gulf waters are crabs, oysters, shrimps, menhaden, mackerel, and speckled trout.

Manufacturing accounts for about 57 per cent of the value of all goods produced in Mississippi. Goods manufactured in the state have an annual *value added by manufacture* of about $1,635,000,000. This figure represents the value created in products by Mississippi's industries, not counting such costs as materials, supplies, and fuels. Clothing has the highest annual value added of Mississippi's manufactured products, about $175 million. Lumber and wood products rank second, with an annual value added of about $167 million. The other chief manufactured products, in order of importance, are food and food products, chemicals, and nonelectrical machinery.

The Mississippi clothing industry produces dresses, gloves, hosiery, shirts, and slacks. Clothing centers include Aberdeen, Booneville, and Tupelo. Textiles are manufactured chiefly in Grenada, Meridian, Rolling Fork, and Stonewall.

Mississippi foresters cut about a billion board feet of lumber yearly. The state's most important lumber region is the Piney Woods, where common trees include loblolly, longleaf, and slash pines. Products of the pine forests include pine oil, rosin, and turpentine. Other trees, such as black tupelo, cottonwood, hickory, sweet gum, tulip tree, and willow, are cut chiefly in the Delta

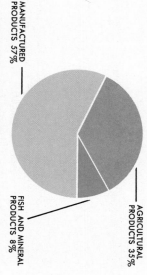

MISSISSIPPI'S PRODUCTION IN 1967
Total value of goods produced—$2,860,547,000

MANUFACTURED PRODUCTS 57%

FISH AND MINERAL PRODUCTS 8%

AGRICULTURAL PRODUCTS 35%

Note: Manufacturing percentage based on value added by manufacture. Other percentages based on value of production. Fish Products are less than 1 per cent.
Sources: U.S. Government statistics

MISSISSIPPI'S EMPLOYMENT IN 1967
Total number of persons employed—643,500

	Number of Employees
Manufacturing	167,000
Government	115,500
Agriculture	109,200
Wholesale & Retail Trade	100,100
Services	65,100
Construction	34,100
Transportation & Public Utilities	27,900
Finance, Insurance & Real Estate	18,700
Mining	5,900

Source: U.S. Department of Labor

FARM, MINERAL, AND FOREST PRODUCTS

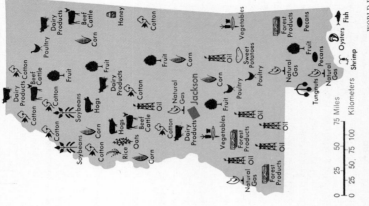

This map shows where the state's leading farm, mineral, and forest products are produced. The major urban area (shown on the map in red) is the state's important manufacturing center.

WORLD BOOK map

Ewing Galloway

Harvesting Cotton. Many Mississippi farmers use machines to pick cotton. As the machines move through the rows of plants, barbed spindles pull the raw cotton fibers from the bolls.

and in the Loess Hills. The wood of these trees is used largely in the manufacture of boxes, crates, furniture, pallets, and veneer. Wood-product centers include Greenville, Hattiesburg, Jackson, Laurel, McComb, Meridian, Moss Point, and Natchez.

Food-processing plants operate throughout the state. Most of the plants that process cheese and other dairy products are in or near the Black Belt. Meat packers have large plants in Jackson, Tupelo, and West Point. Poultry is processed largely in Forest, Morton, and Pelahatchie. Large canneries and freezing plants operate in Biloxi and Pascagoula. These plants process crab meat, oysters, and shrimps.

Industrial chemicals are made by large plants in Columbus, Yazoo City, and Vicksburg, and on the Gulf Coast. Chemical plants in the Delta process oil from cottonseeds and soybeans to make cooking oil and margarine. The hulls are made into feed meal and fertilizer.

Mississippi has many paper mills and factories that manufacture paper products. They make up one of the state's most important industries. The paper and paper products industry uses about 2 million cords of the state's pulpwood yearly. The nation's largest fiberboard factory is in Laurel.

Large shipyards in Pascagoula build freighters, passenger liners, tankers, and nuclear submarines. One of America's most highly automated oil refineries is also in Pascagoula. Factories throughout the state produce metal and machine products, and many products made of clay, glass, leather, rubber, and stone.

Agriculture. Mississippi's farm products provide an annual income of about $1 billion. Farms cover about three-fifths of the state, and average about 165 acres in size.

Cotton is Mississippi's most important farm crop. The cotton crop earns about $165 million a year, or about one-fifth of the farm income in the state. Most of the cotton is raised on the Mississippi Alluvial Plain. The fertile lowlands of the alluvial plain make it one of the leading cotton-growing regions in the United States.

Mississippi ranks among the leading states in the production of soybeans and sweet potatoes. Field crops, such as corn and hay, are raised chiefly as livestock feed.

Other grains that are grown in the state include oats, rice, wheat, and grain sorghums. Some Mississippi farmers grow sweet sorghum and sugar cane for making syrup.

Mississippi is an important livestock-raising state, largely because of its fine pastures and a long growing season for hay and other feed. Angus, Hereford, and *polled* (hornless) Hereford beef cattle graze in many parts of the state. Large herds of dairy cattle also are raised in many parts of Mississippi. The largest herds are found near heavily populated areas. They supply milk for Mississippi's dairies and cheese and ice cream plants. Livestock farmers also raise hogs and sheep. Mississippi ranks as a leading broiler-raising state. Most of the chickens raised in Mississippi are sold as *broilers* (chickens that are 9 to 12 weeks old). Other important Mississippi poultry products include eggs and turkeys.

Mississippi truck farms and fruit farms produce a wide variety of products. Truck farmers grow beans, cabbage, cowpeas, cucumbers, okra, peas, potatoes, sweet corn, tomatoes, and turnips. Mississippi fruits include apples, cantaloupes, figs, peaches, pears, plums, strawberries, and watermelons. Pecans are Mississippi's leading edible-nut crop. Tung trees are grown chiefly in southeastern Mississippi. Their nuts supply the state's tung-oil processing industry. This oil is used in making ink, paint, and varnish. Mississippi was the nation's leading producer of tung nuts for many years. But in 1969, a hurricane destroyed or damaged two-thirds of the state's tung trees.

Mining. Mississippi ranks as a leading producer of petroleum and natural gas. These products account for about $180 million, or about four-fifths of the value of the state's mined products. Mississippi produces about 57 million barrels of petroleum each year from about 2,500 wells. The annual natural gas production is about 140 billion cubic feet.

Mississippi quarries produce more than 14 million tons of sand and gravel a year. Clay production is over 1½ million tons annually. The most important clays include bentonite and fuller's earth, both used in refining certain oils. Fire clay, used for lining furnaces and stoves, is also an important product.

Mississippi Agricultural & Industrial Board

Workers Package Shirts in a clothing plant in Decatur. The manufacture of clothing and textiles is one of the state's chief activities. Mississippi, traditionally an agricultural state, has been developing a strong industrial economy since the early 1930's.

Fishing Industry. Mississippi has an annual fish catch valued at over $9 million. Mississippi is a leading shrimp-fishing state, with a shrimp catch valued at over $3 million a year. Biloxi is the chief shrimp-packing port and the center of Mississippi's commercial fishing industry. The salt-water catch includes crabs, menhaden, red snapper, and oysters. The fresh-water catch includes buffalo fish, carp, and catfish.

Electric Power. Steam plants produce all the electricity generated in Mississippi. The chief plants are in Cleveland, Gulfport, Hattiesburg, Jackson, Meridian, Natchez, and Vicksburg, Mississippi also buys some of its power from the Tennessee Valley Authority (TVA). For Mississippi's kilowatt-hour production, see ELECTRIC POWER (table).

Transportation. The state has one of the finest highway systems in the South. There are more than 60,000 miles of surfaced highways and about 3,000 miles of nonsurfaced roads. Mississippi has about 150 airports. The chief ones serve the Biloxi and Gulfport area, Columbus, Greenville, Jackson, and Meridian. Three major airlines link Mississippi with cities in other states. Eight major railroads operate on about 3,600 miles of track in Mississippi. These railroads serve every county in the state.

Mississippi has two deep-water seaports, Gulfport and Pascagoula. Together, the dock facilities of these ports handle over 12,700,000 tons of cargo every year. The Mississippi River connects Mississippi with many inland states. The chief river ports are Greenville, Natchez, and Vicksburg.

Communication. More than 130 newspapers, 20 of them dailies, are published in Mississippi. About 40 periodicals also are published. The state has over 100 radio stations and 9 television stations.

Mississippi's earliest newspapers, all published in Natchez, were the *Mississippi Gazette* (established in 1799), the *Intelligencer* (1801), and the *Mississippi Herald* (1802). The oldest newspaper still published in Mississippi, the *Woodville Republican*, was founded in 1823. Dailies with the largest circulations include the *Biloxi-Gulfport Daily Herald,* the *Meridian Star,* the *Clarion-Ledger* of Jackson, and the *Jackson Daily News.*

"View of Vicksburg," State of Mississippi Department of Archives and History, Jackson, Miss. Hiatt-Ford Photography

The Port of Vicksburg in the 1800's was an important stop for Mississippi riverboats. The city is still a major river port.

Indian Days. Three powerful Indian tribes once ruled the Mississippi region. The Chickasaw lived in the north and east, the Choctaw in the central area, and the Natchez in the southwest. They held power over the Chakchiuma, Tunica, and Yazoo tribes that lived along the Yazoo River, and the Biloxi and Pascagoula tribes of the Gulf Coast. Between 25,000 and 30,000 Indians lived in the Mississippi region when the first white explorers arrived. See INDIAN, AMERICAN (table: Indian Tribes).

Exploration and Early Settlement. In 1540, the Spanish explorer Hernando de Soto became the first European to enter the Mississippi region. De Soto discovered the Mississippi River in 1541 while searching for gold. The Spanish explorers found no treasure in the region and made no settlements there. In 1682, the French explorer Robert Cavelier, Sieur de la Salle, traveled down the Mississippi River from the Great Lakes to the Gulf of Mexico. Cavelier claimed the entire Mississippi Valley for France, and named it *Louisiana* for King Louis XIV. The region included present-day Mississippi.

In 1699, Pierre le Moyne, Sieur d'Iberville, established the first French settlement of the region at Old Biloxi (now Ocean Springs). In 1716, a second settlement was established by Jean Baptiste le Moyne, Sieur de Bienville, at Fort Rosalie (now Natchez). Three years later, in 1719, the first Negro slaves were brought to the region from West Africa. They worked in the rice and tobacco fields of the French colonists.

During the early 1700's, a scheme to develop the region was launched by John Law, a Scottish economist. Law's scheme failed and many Frenchmen lost the money they had invested in his company. However, Law's venture brought much attention to Louisiana. As a result, thousands of settlers were attracted to the region (see MISSISSIPPI SCHEME). Old Biloxi, New Biloxi (now Biloxi), and Fort Louis de la Mobile (now Mobile, Ala.) served as capital of the region at various times during the early 1700's. In 1722, the French made New Orleans, in present-day Louisiana, the capital of the region. At that time, Louisiana made up a vast territory that extended from the Allegheny Mountains to the Rocky Mountains.

Many difficulties delayed development of the region. At first, the Indians fought the settlers. Later, the British battled the French for possession of the newly settled land. In 1730, the French put down an uprising of the Natchez Indians. But in 1736, British troops helped the Chickasaw Indians defeat the French colonists in the northeastern part of present-day Mississippi. That defeat stopped the French from gaining control of the Mississippi Valley. During the French and Indian War (1754-1763), the British and the Chickasaw blocked the French in the lower Mississippi Valley from joining the French forces in the Ohio Valley. The Treaty of Paris, signed after the war, gave the British all the land east of the Mississippi River. Thus, the Mississippi region came under British rule. The southern portion became part of the British province called West Florida. Nearly all of the remaining area became part of the Georgia colony.

Territorial Days. During the Revolutionary War (1775-1783), most of the settlers of West Florida remained loyal to Great Britain. But the Indians, trappers, and scouts of the rest of the Mississippi region supported the American colonies. In 1781, because the British were so busy with their war with the colonies, Spain was able to take over West Florida. Two years later, Great Britain granted West Florida to Spain. After the British lost the war, the Mississippi region north of about the 32nd parallel was made part of the United States. In 1795, the Spanish government accepted the 31st parallel as the U.S. border in a treaty signed in Madrid.

Congress organized the Mississippi Territory in 1798, with Natchez as the capital. Winthrop Sargent became the first governor of the new territory. It was bounded on the south by the 31st parallel, on the west by the Mississippi River, on the north by a line east from the mouth of the Yazoo River, and on the east by the Chattahoochee River. In 1803, the Louisiana Purchase made the Mississippi River part of the United States. Development of the territory was aided because the river allowed Mississippi trading ships to sail to the Gulf of Mexico.

In 1804, Congress extended the Mississippi Territory north to the border of Tennessee. More land was added in 1812. That year, the part of the West Florida Republic lying east of the Pearl River was incorporated into the Mississippi Territory. The republic had been formed in 1810 after American settlers took control of the region from Spain. The republic consisted of the land south of the 31st parallel between the Mississippi River and the Perdido River.

During the War of 1812, the Choctaw Indians under Chief Pushmataha remained friendly to the Americans. The Choctaw joined the Mississippi militia in helping General Andrew Jackson put down uprisings of the Creek Indians and in defeating a British army in the Battle of New Orleans.

Statehood. In 1817, Congress divided the Mississippi Territory into the state of Mississippi and the Alabama Territory. On Dec. 10, 1817, Mississippi was admitted to the Union as the 20th state. The first Mississippi state governor, David Holmes, had been territorial governor since 1809. Columbia, Natchez, and Washington served as the state capital at various times until Jackson became the capital in 1822.

In territorial days, Indian tribes had controlled almost two-thirds of Mississippi. The tribes gradually gave up their lands to the U.S. government. By 1832, most of the Indians had moved to the Indian Territory (now Oklahoma). The lands they left were opened for settlement. Many settlers came from the East to farm the fertile soil. Much of the soil was excellent for growing cotton. Cotton production had increased throughout the South after Eli Whitney invented the cotton gin in 1793.

After 1806, an improved type of cottonseed helped increase Mississippi's cotton production. The improved variety was developed from some seeds brought to Mississippi from Mexico. It was called Petit Gulf, the name of the Claiborne County area in which it was developed. The cotton producers used slave labor to operate large cotton plantations. Mississippi became one of the wealthiest states of the period.

During the 1850's, Mississippi farmers built many levees in the Delta region to control the floodwaters of the Mississippi and Yazoo rivers. In 1858, the legislature set up a board of levee commissioners. Many acres of swampland in the state were drained and made suitable for farming.

The Civil War and Reconstruction. Most Mississippians did not favor secession (withdrawal) from the Union when South Carolina threatened to do so in 1832 (see NULLIFICATION). But their feelings changed during the next 29 years. The reasons for the change included violations of the Fugitive Slave Law, the struggle over slavery in Kansas, the founding of the Republican Party, and the economic differences between the North and the South. Mississippi became a strong defender of states' rights. See CIVIL WAR (Causes of the War).

On Jan. 9, 1861, a convention met in the Old Capitol in Jackson and adopted the Ordinance of Secession. Mississippi became the second state, after South Carolina, to secede from the Union. About five weeks later, Jefferson Davis of Mississippi became president of the Confederacy. He had been a soldier, planter, and a U.S. Senator. Davis also had served as Secretary of War under President Franklin Pierce.

More than 80,000 Mississippi troops served in the Confederate armies. Union and Confederate forces clashed in Mississippi, or on its borders, in many places. Important battles were fought at Corinth, Harrisburg (now Tupelo), Holly Springs, Iuka, Jackson, Meridian, and Port Gibson. In June, 1864, at Brice's Cross Roads, General Nathan Bedford Forrest of Mississippi defeated

a larger Union cavalry force. Forrest supposedly explained his military successes by saying that he tried "to git thar fustest with the mostest men."

The Battle of Vicksburg ranks as the most important military action in Mississippi. The Confederate stronghold in Vicksburg fell to General Ulysses S. Grant's Union forces on July 4, 1863, after a 47-day defense. General Grant's capture of Vicksburg gave the Union control of the Mississippi River. The Union victories at Vicksburg and Gettysburg marked the turning point of the Civil War.

After the war, in 1867, the United States placed Mississippi under military rule during the Reconstruction period (see RECONSTRUCTION). Mississippi was readmitted to the Union in 1870, after adopting a new state constitution and ratifying amendments 14 and 15 to the United States Constitution. It took many years for Mississippi to recover from its war losses.

The Early 1900's were years of progress in agriculture, education, and industry. The lumber industry reached a high peak just before World War I began in 1914. New drainage projects in Mississippi opened large swampy areas to agriculture. County agricultural high schools were established in 1908. The state established an illiteracy commission in 1916 to start a special educational program for adults who could not read or write. In 1912, the Mississippi legislature passed laws regulating child labor.

After the United States entered World War I in 1917, Payne Field was established at West Point, Miss., as a training base for army pilots. Camp Shelby, near Hattiesburg, became one of the army's chief centers for preparing troops for overseas duty.

Legislative measures during the 1920's included the establishment of a state commission of education in 1924, and of a state library commission in 1926. The first milk condensery in the South opened at Starkville in 1926. Mississippi suffered greatly in the Mississippi River flood of 1927. About 100,000 persons fled from their flooded homes in the Delta. The damage to crops and property in Mississippi totaled over $204 million. The next year, Congress made the U.S. Army Corps of Engineers responsible for controlling floods on the Mississippi River.

Economic Development. During the Great Depression of the 1930's, Mississippi launched an important program of economic development. The program, called Balancing Agriculture With Industry (BAWI), was helped by special laws passed by the legislature in 1936. These laws freed new industries from paying certain taxes. The laws also allowed cities and counties to issue

---

IMPORTANT DATES IN MISSISSIPPI

1540 Hernando de Soto entered the Mississippi region.

1699 Pierre le Moyne, Sieur d'Iberville, established the first French colony at Old Biloxi.

1763 Mississippi became English territory after the French and Indian War.

1781 Spain occupied the Gulf Coast.

1798 The Mississippi Territory was organized.

1817 Mississippi became the 20th state on December 10.

1858 Mississippi started a swamp drainage program in the Delta.

1861 Mississippi seceded from the Union.

1863 Union forces captured Vicksburg in the Civil War.

1870 Mississippi was readmitted to the Union.

1936 Mississippi adopted special laws to encourage manufacturing.

1939 Petroleum was discovered at Tinsley.

1954 The Mississippi legislature passed a law banning required union membership.

1960 Mississippi passed laws that broadened the tax-free privilege of industrial properties.

1964 Atomic scientists set off the first nuclear test explosion east of the Mississippi River at Baxterville, Miss.

1969 Charles Evers became the first black mayor in Mississippi since Reconstruction. He was elected in Fayette.

HISTORIC MISSISSIPPI

Hernando de Soto, the Spanish explorer, discovered the Mississippi River in 1541 near the northern border of Mississippi. He died one year later and was buried in the river near Natchez.

Vicksburg is often called the Gibraltar of the Confederacy. Here, Confederate soldiers controlled the Mississippi River during the Civil War until 1863.

Cotton Became King in Mississippi after 1806 when an improved variety of the plant was developed from seeds brought from Mexico. The cottonseed-oil industry was established in Natchez during the 1870's.

The Petroleum Industry developed in Mississippi after oil was discovered at Tinsley in 1939 and at Vaughan in the next year.

King's Tavern, probably the oldest building in Natchez, stood at the end of Natchez Trace, an important early road. River-boatmen used it to return northward after floating down the Mississippi.

Mississippi's First Colony, Old Biloxi, was established by French settlers in 1699 on the present site of Ocean Springs.

Casquette Girls were sent to Mississippi about 1721 as wives for the colonists. France gave each girl a small amount of money and a chest of wedding clothes.

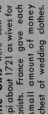

Aaron Burr's preliminary treason trial was held in Washington (Miss.) in 1807. He was accused of trying to set up a republic in the West.

• Ocean Springs

Vaughan•

Tinsley•

★ JACKSON

• Vicksburg

Natchez•

bonds and use the bond money to build factories for new industries. The BAWI program is administered by the state's Agricultural and Industrial Board. In developing the BAWI program, Mississippi became one of the first states to use national advertising to promote new industries. Mississippi's industrial development was strongly aided by the discovery of petroleum at Tinsley in 1939 and at Vaughan in 1940.

The Mid-1900's. During World War II (1939-1945), many war plants operated in Mississippi. The port of Pascagoula became an assembly center for ships sailing in convoys. After the war, the state's industrial development continued. In 1954, the legislature passed a right-to-work law. This law provided that no worker has to join a union if he or she does not want to do so. The law became part of the state's constitution in 1960.

During the 1960's, Mississippi worked to attract new industries. The legislature passed laws in 1960 broadening the tax-free position of industry. In 1964, a huge oil refinery was built in Pascagoula. The state set up the Mississippi Research and Development Center. The center encourages new industries to move into the state and helps established companies expand. By 1966, more Mississippians worked in manufacturing than in agriculture. In 1968, the Ingalls shipyards began a $130-million expansion program in Pascagoula. In other coastal areas, the tourist industry boomed. During the 1960's, tourists spent about $200 million annually.

Mississippi became active in the work of the Atomic Energy Commission (AEC) and the National Aeronautics and Space Administration (NASA). In 1964, AEC scientists set off a nuclear device near Baxterville. It was the first nuclear test explosion east of the Mississippi River. In 1965, NASA engineers began to test-fire engines of the Saturn V rocket near Gulfport. Saturn V rockets are used to launch U.S. spacecraft to the moon.

Like many other states, Mississippi has had racial problems. The state's constitution had provided for segregated schools. But in 1954, the Supreme Court of the United States ruled that compulsory segregation of public schools was unconstitutional. Efforts by civil rights groups to bring about integration were sometimes met with violence. In 1962, two persons were killed in riots that broke out when James Meredith enrolled as the first black student at the University of Mississippi. In 1963, Medgar Evers, Mississippi field secretary of the National Association for the Advancement of Colored People (NAACP), was shot and killed. In 1964, three civil rights workers were murdered near Philadelphia, Miss. Both white and Negro leaders in Mississippi spoke out against the violence. They called for all citizens to obey the laws.

The Mississippi Test Facility, a testing ground for rockets, was built near Gulfport in the mid-1960's. Saturn rockets tested here launched the Apollo 11 astronauts to the moon.

NASA

THE GOVERNORS OF MISSISSIPPI

	Party	Term
1. David Holmes	*Dem.-Rep.	1817-1820
2. George Poindexter	Dem.-Rep.	1820-1822
3. Walter Leake	Dem.-Rep.	1822-1825
4. Gerard C. Brandon	Dem.-Rep.	1825-1826
5. David Holmes	Dem.-Rep.	1826
6. Gerard C. Brandon	Dem.-Rep.	1826-1832
7. Abram M. Scott	Dem.-Rep.	1832-1833
8. Charles Lynch	Democratic	1833
9. Hiram G. Runnels	Democratic	1833-1835
10. John A. Quitman	Whig	1835-1836
11. Charles Lynch	Democratic	1836-1838
12. Alexander G. McNutt	Democratic	1838-1842
13. Tilghman M. Tucker	Democratic	1842-1844
14. Albert G. Brown	Democratic	1844-1848
15. Joseph W. Matthews	Democratic	1848-1850
16. John A. Quitman	Democratic	1850-1851
17. John I. Guion	Democratic	1851
18. James Whitfield	Democratic	1851-1852
19. Henry S. Foote	Union Democratic	1852-1854
20. John J. Pettus	Democratic	1854
21. John J. McRae	Democratic	1854-1857
22. William McWillie	Democratic	1857-1859
23. John J. Pettus	Democratic	1859-1863
24. Charles Clark	Democratic	1863-1865
25. William L. Sharkey	Whig-Democratic	1865
26. Benjamin G. Humphreys	Whig	1865-1868

	Party	Term
27. Adelbert Ames	†U.S. Mil. Gov.	1868-1870
28. James L. Alcorn	Republican	1870-1871
29. Ridgley C. Powers	Republican	1871-1874
30. Adelbert Ames	Republican	1874-1876
31. John M. Stone	Democratic	1876-1882
32. Robert Lowry	Democratic	1882-1890
33. John M. Stone	Democratic	1890-1896
34. Anselm J. McLaurin	Democratic	1896-1900
35. Andrew H. Longino	Democratic	1900-1904
36. James K. Vardaman	Democratic	1904-1908
37. Edmond F. Noel	Democratic	1908-1912
38. Earl L. Brewer	Democratic	1912-1916
39. Theodore G. Bilbo	Democratic	1916-1920
40. Lee M. Russell	Democratic	1920-1924
41. Henry L. Whitfield	Democratic	1924-1927
42. Dennis Murphree	Democratic	1927-1928
43. Theodore G. Bilbo	Democratic	1928-1932
44. Martin Sennett Conner	Democratic	1932-1936
45. Hugh L. White	Democratic	1936-1940
46. Paul B. Johnson	Democratic	1940-1943
47. Dennis Murphree	Democratic	1943-1944
48. Thomas L. Bailey	Democratic	1944-1946
49. Fielding L. Wright	Democratic	1946-1952
50. Hugh L. White	Democratic	1952-1956
51. James P. Coleman	Democratic	1956-1960
52. Ross R. Barnett	Democratic	1960-1964
53. Paul B. Johnson	Democratic	1964-1968
54. John Bell Williams	Democratic	1968-

*Democratic-Republican; †United States Military Governor

In the fall of 1964, the first public schools in Mississippi began to desegregate. In 1969, the United States Supreme Court ordered an immediate end to all segregated public schools. As a result, a federal court in New Orleans ordered 33 Mississippi school districts to desegregate by December, 1969. Many white people then established segregated private schools and enrolled their children. Also in 1969, Charles Evers, brother of Medgar, was elected mayor of Fayette. He became the first black mayor in Mississippi since Reconstruction.

Mississippi Today has the lowest *per capita* (per person) income in the nation. Thousands of farmworkers in the Delta region are jobless because of increased use of machinery and the inability of many farm operators to pay minimum wages. Many high school and college graduates leave Mississippi to find jobs.

During the 1970's, Mississippi faces the challenge of fully developing its economic program. Mississippi hopes to keep young people from leaving the state by attracting industries that require higher skills and pay higher wages. To attract such industries, many cities are working to improve transportation and other services and to increase cultural and educational opportunities.

CHARLOTTE CAPERS, T. M. HEDERMAN, JR., and M. W. MYERS

MISSISSIPPI/Study Aids

Related Articles in WORLD BOOK include:

BIOGRAPHIES

Bilbo, Theodore G.
Davis, Jefferson
De Soto, Hernando
Eastland, James O.
Evers (family)
Faulkner, William
George, James Z.

Lamar, Lucius Q. C.
Turner, Roscoe
Vardaman, James K.
Welty, Eudora
Williams, Tennessee
Wright, Richard
Young, Stark

CITIES

Biloxi
Greenville
Hattiesburg

Jackson
Laurel
Meridian

Natchez
Vicksburg

HISTORY

Civil War
Confederate States of America
Louisiana Purchase
Mississippi Scheme
Natchez Trace

Paris, Treaties of (1763, 1783)
Reconstruction (Southern Resistance)

PHYSICAL FEATURES

Gulf of Mexico
Mississippi River

Tombigbee River
Yazoo River

PRODUCTS

For Mississippi's rank among the states in production, see the following articles:

Chicken
Cotton
Horse
Soybean
Sweet Potato

OTHER RELATED ARTICLES

Education, History of (Recent Developments)
Negro
Sardis Dam
Southern States

Outline

I. **Government**
  A. Constitution
  B. Executive
  C. Legislature
  D. Courts
  E. Local Government
  F. Taxation
  G. Politics
II. **People**
III. **Education**
  A. Schools
  B. Libraries
  C. Museums
IV. **A Visitor's Guide**
  A. Places to Visit
  B. Annual Events
V. **The Land**
  A. Land Regions
  B. Coastline
  C. Rivers and Lakes
VI. **Climate**
VII. **Economy**
  A. Natural Resources
  B. Manufacturing
  C. Agriculture
  D. Mining
  E. Fishing Industry
  F. Electric Power
  G. Transportation
  H. Communication
VIII. **History**

Questions

Where is Mississippi's chief cotton-producing area?
Why is its soil so fertile?
What important social change was brought about by the growth of factories in Mississippi?
Why is Mississippi a leading winter vacationland?
Where are the state's chief winter resorts?
What special event marks the opening of Mississippi's shrimp-fishing season?
How does Mississippi protect its great resources of valuable trees?
Why did the early Spanish explorers make no settlements in the Mississippi region?
Why does the Battle of Vicksburg rank as one of the most important battles of the Civil War?
How does Mississippi try to attract new industries?
How is Mississippi playing an important part in the U.S. space travel program?
Why did public opinion in Mississippi about secession change during the 29 years before the Civil War?

Books for Young Readers

BAILEY, BERNADINE F. Picture Book of Mississippi. Rev. ed. Whitman, 1966.
BETTERSWORTH, JOHN K. Mississippi Yesterday and Today. Steck, 1964.
GUYTON, PEARL V. Our Mississippi. 3rd ed. Steck, 1964.
McLEMORE, R. A. The Mississippi Story. Rev. ed. Laidlaw, 1964.
RAND, CLAYTON. Men of Spine in Mississippi. Dixie Press, 1940.

Books for Older Readers

BEARS, EDWIN C. Decision in Mississippi. Mississippi Commission on the War Between the States, 1962.
BETTERSWORTH, JOHN K. Mississippi: A History. Steck, 1959. Edited with J. W. SILVER, Mississippi in the Confederacy. 2 vols. Louisiana State Univ. Press, 1961.
COOPER, J. WESLEY. Natchez: A Treasure of Ante-Bellum Homes. Southern Historical Publications, 1957. Color photographs with text on history and architecture.
KANE, HARNETT T. Natchez on the Mississippi. Morrow, 1947. Stories of the people who built and lived in the great houses of Natchez.
Mississippi: A Guide to the Magnolia State. Hastings, 1949.
PERCY, WILLIAM A. Lanterns on the Levee: Recollections of a Planter's Son. Knopf, 1941.
SMITH, FRANK E. The Yazoo River. Rinehart, 1954.

The Lyceum Building at the University of Mississippi houses the School of Commerce and Business Administration.

University of Mississippi

MISSISSIPPI, UNIVERSITY OF, is a state-supported coeducational school at University, near Oxford, Miss. It has a college of liberal arts, a graduate school, and schools of pharmacy, law, engineering, education, and commerce and business administration. The school of medicine is located on the Jackson, Miss., campus. Courses lead to B.A., M.A., and Ph.D. degrees.

The library has the Deavours collection of Mississippiana, and also the James Wilford Garner Library, which contains books on political science and international law. Two summer sessions in foreign languages are held each year, one in France and one in Mexico. The university cooperates in an education program with the Oak Ridge Institute of Nuclear Studies and the Gulf Coast Research Laboratory. The university also has an extension division.

The university has army, navy, and air force ROTC units. Notable buildings include the chapel, the Kennon Observatory, and the Lyceum, built in 1848. The university was founded in 1844. For enrollment, see UNIVERSITIES AND COLLEGES (table).

JOHN B. MORRIS

MISSISSIPPI BUBBLE. See MISSISSIPPI SCHEME.

MISSISSIPPI COLLEGE is a coeducational liberal arts school at Clinton, Miss. It is controlled by the Mississippi Baptist Convention. The school was founded in 1826 as Hampstead Academy and received its present name in 1830. Courses at Mississippi College lead to A.B., B.S., and M.A. degrees. For enrollment, see UNIVERSITIES AND COLLEGES (table).

MISSISSIPPI RIVER. A pageant of American history has passed up and down the Mississippi; the largest river in the United States and one of the greatest trade waterways in the world. The waters of this mighty river bore the canoes of the Indians, who compared the size of the river with other streams they knew, and named it "great river."

Hernando de Soto, the Spanish explorer, was probably the first white man to find this river road into the North American wilderness. De Soto discovered the river near the present Memphis, Tenn., in 1541. He led a company of adventurers across it and wandered through its valley for a year. When the great explorer died of fever, his body was buried in the river to protect it from mistreatment by hostile Indians.

The Mississippi carried the rafts and boats of the early settlers who established homesteads in its valley. Later, paddle-wheeled steamboats traveled up and down the Mississippi, exchanging the products of the towns and cities that sprang up along the riverbanks from north to south. The Mississippi was the stage for the colorful showboat, a peculiarly American contribution to the history of the theater (see SHOWBOAT). Poets, novelists, and song writers have gathered material from the rich history of the Mississippi. Mark Twain's *Life on the Mississippi* is a famous description of the river.

To the millions of persons who live along its banks in thriving cities, on great plantations, and in humble shanties, the Mississippi is affectionately and respectfully known as "Old Man River." They have come to regard the river almost as a living thing, which can bring both good and evil to its valley. The area that the river drains is one of the richest farming regions in the world. For thousands of years the floodwaters have brought fertile silt to the lower part of the Mississippi Valley. But the raging floods of the Mississippi have often caused death and severe property damage to the downstream portion of the region.

The Mississippi and its chief tributary, the Missouri River, together make up one of the longest river systems in the world (about 3,710 miles) Army engineers estimate the Mississippi winds about 2,350 miles from its source near the northern boundary of the United States to its mouth in the Gulf of Mexico. The entire river system affords about 14,000 miles of navigable waterways and drains about 1,250,000 square miles, or about one-third of the total area of the United States.

The Mississippi River makes up part of the boundaries of 10 mid-American states. East of the river lie Wisconsin, Illinois, Kentucky, Tennessee, and Mississippi. On the west are Iowa, Missouri, Arkansas, Louisiana, and part of Minnesota.

Its Course and Tributaries. A clear little stream about 18 feet wide and less than a foot deep rushes out of the northern end of Lake Itasca in north-central Minnesota. This is the source of the river that later in its course stretches about a mile from shore to shore, and digs a bed deeper than 100 feet in many places. The stream twists and bends through a region of small lakes and swamps. Finally it settles into its generally southeastward flow at the rate of about 2 mph. Steep limestone bluffs line the banks of the Mississippi's course in many parts of Minnesota, Wisconsin, Iowa, and Illinois.

Before the Mississippi pours its waters into the Gulf of Mexico below New Orleans, La., it is joined by more

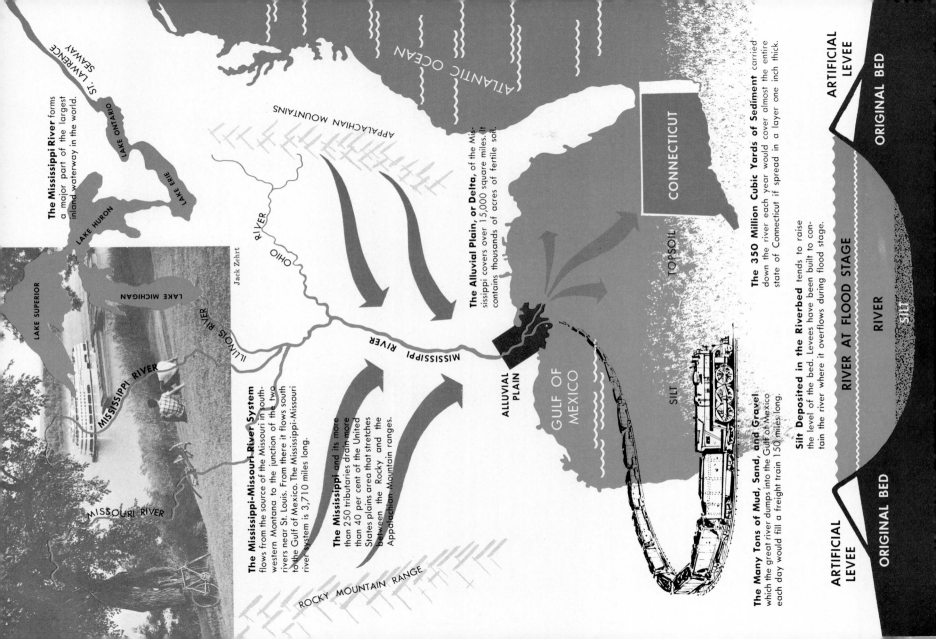

The Mississippi River forms a major part of the largest inland waterway in the world.

ST. LAWRENCE SEAWAY

LAKE ONTARIO
LAKE ERIE
LAKE HURON
LAKE MICHIGAN
LAKE SUPERIOR

Jack Zehrt

MISSISSIPPI RIVER

MISSOURI RIVER

ILLINOIS RIVER

OHIO RIVER

MISSISSIPPI RIVER

APPALACHIAN MOUNTAINS

ATLANTIC OCEAN

CONNECTICUT

TOPSOIL

ALLUVIAL PLAIN

GULF OF MEXICO

SILT

ROCKY MOUNTAIN RANGE

The Mississippi-Missouri River System flows from the source of the Missouri in southwestern Montana to the junction of the two rivers near St. Louis. From there it flows south to the Gulf of Mexico. The Mississippi-Missouri river system is 3,710 miles long.

The Mississippi and its more than 250 tributaries drain more than 40 per cent of the United States plains area that stretches between the Rocky and the Appalachian Mountain ranges.

The Alluvial Plain, or Delta, of the Mississippi covers over 15,000 square miles. It contains thousands of acres of fertile soil.

The 350 Million Cubic Yards of Sediment carried down the river each year would cover almost the entire state of Connecticut if spread in a layer one inch thick.

The Many Tons of Mud, Sand, and Gravel, which the great river dumps into the Gulf of Mexico each day would fill a freight train 150 miles long.

Silt Deposited in the Riverbed tends to raise the level of the bed. Levees have been built to contain the river where it overflows during flood stage.

ARTIFICIAL LEVEE

RIVER AT FLOOD STAGE

RIVER

SILT

ORIGINAL BED

ARTIFICIAL LEVEE

ORIGINAL BED

than 250 tributaries. Some of these branches are as large as, or larger than, the Mississippi when they meet it. Others are small streams. These tributaries spring from as far west as Montana and Wyoming, and from as far east as western New York and western North Carolina. They gather the excess rainfall and the overflow of springs and lakes throughout this vast region and pour them into the Mississippi. From the East come the Ohio River, the Illinois River, the Wisconsin, and the Yazoo. From the West flow the Arkansas, the Red, and the Missouri. The Ohio River system passes through an area that has an annual rainfall of 40 to 50 inches. The Ohio pours the greatest amount of water into the Mississippi. The Mississippi is connected to the Great Lakes by the Illinois Waterway, which includes the Illinois River and the Chicago Sanitary and Ship Canal.

The Mississippi reaches its greatest width after the Missouri joins it north of St. Louis, Mo. For miles, the two big rivers flow side by side in one bed while their waters scarcely mingle. The red waters of the Missouri are in sharp contrast to the clear current of the Mississippi. Later, the waters mix, and the Mississippi shows the muddy color for which it is famous in the South.

The lower course of the Mississippi is between wide, flat shores formed of mud carried by the river current. This has formed a valley as fertile as that of the Nile River in Egypt. In this section, the Mississippi *meanders* (winds) through bayous, lakes, and swamps. The river often cuts off the loops of its long bends, changing its course and varying its length as much as 50 miles a year. The loops then often become oxbow lakes.

Finally, the Mississippi reaches its present delta below New Orleans. Here it divides into several arms (known as *distributaries*) which empty into the Gulf of

Mexico. During the high-water season, the Mississippi pours about 2,300,000 cubic feet of water into the Gulf every second. The average amount of water carried to the Gulf during a year is 611,000 cubic feet per second. The Mississippi also carries to its mouth about 350,000,000 cubic yards of mud, sand, and gravel every year. A part of this deposit is added to the muddy delta, and part is carried out to sea.

Floods. Heavy rains over a long period of time and melting snow swell the Mississippi. Normal floodwaters rise as much as 50 to 55 feet above the river's lowest stage. Heavy floods from the Ohio and Missouri have also caused floods along the Mississippi that have covered large areas of the river valley. One of the worst of these floods took place in the spring of 1927. Over 300 people were drowned or otherwise killed as a result of the flood. About $250 million worth of property was destroyed. Homes and barns were swept from their foundations and carried down the river. Crops were ruined. Another damaging flood occurred during April and May of 1965. Severe floods on the upper Mississippi caused an estimated $140 million damage to cities, towns, and farmland along the river in Minnesota, Wisconsin, Illinois, Iowa, and Missouri.

Attempts to prevent these floods have included the dredging of the riverbed to make it deeper, and the building of levees and dams along the lower course of the Mississippi.

Levees made of earth and strengthened with metal cables and mesh, sometimes held together with asphalt, protect the banks of the Mississippi south of Cairo, Ill. Some levees are built only of earth and brush. These are meant to be weak, so that the waters may break through them and flood regions where there are no

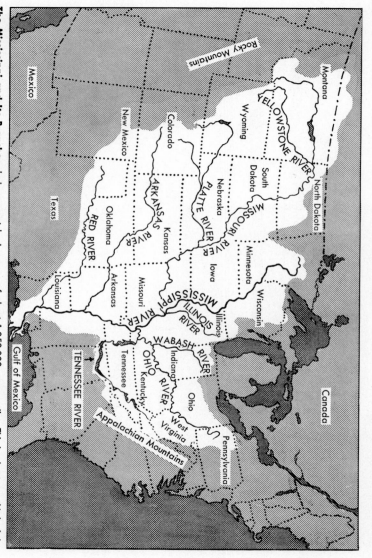

The Mississippi and its Branches drain a great basin extending from the Appalachian to the Rocky Mountains, an area of about 1,250,000 square miles. This is about one-third of the total land area of the United States.

farms or villages. The Morganza and West Atchafalaya floodways along the Atchafalaya River in Louisiana provide floodwater outlets. The Bonnet Carré Spillway, which was built near New Orleans by the federal government in 1932, drains floodwaters into Lake Pontchartrain.

Water Power. Dams and turbines harness the current of the Mississippi to provide electric power for industries of the various cities along its course. The most northern of these dams is at Bemidji, Minn., northeast of Lake Itasca. Other dams are at Grand Rapids and Brainerd, Minn. One of the largest sources of power from the Mississippi is provided by the Falls of Saint Anthony near Minneapolis. Iowa's Keokuk Dam, completed in 1913, was built with private funds under a permit issued by the federal government. The Des Moines Rapids have been replaced by an artificial lake that is about 1 mile wide and more than 50 miles long.

Bridges. The Mississippi River is crossed by hundreds of bridges along its course. Probably the oldest bridge across the Mississippi is the Stone Arch Bridge that crosses the river between Minneapolis and St. Paul, Minn. One of the most famous is the Eads Bridge that connects St. Louis, Mo., and East St. Louis, Ill. One of the largest railway bridges is the Atchison, Topeka, and Santa Fe Bridge at Fort Madison, Iowa. There are also large bridges at Memphis, Tenn.; at Natchez and Vicksburg, Miss.; and at Baton Rouge and New Orleans, La.

Transportation Today. The great era of the Mississippi River commerce was from 1840 to about 1880. This river commerce was responsible for the growth of such Mississippi ports as Minneapolis and Saint Paul, Minn.; La Crosse, Wis.; Keokuk, Dubuque, and Davenport, Iowa; Rock Island, Quincy, and Cairo, Ill.; St. Louis, Mo.; Memphis, Tenn.; Vicksburg, Miss.; and Baton Rouge and New Orleans, La. River traffic declined with the coming of the railroads to the Mississippi Valley.

But the Mississippi River again became an important transportation route in the 1920's, when tugboats were developed that were powerful enough to push strings of barges more than a thousand feet long. One of these small tugs can push a line of barges carrying as much weight as 16 loaded railroad freight cars.

In 1963, a 76-mile canal between New Orleans and the Gulf of Mexico opened. The canal provided a short cut for ocean-going ships. During the late 1960's, the Mississippi River system carried about 335 million tons of freight annually. This freight included inland and coastal traffic, as well as imports and exports.

WALLACE E. AKIN

Related Articles in WORLD BOOK include:

Arkansas River	Minnesota
Dam	(color pictures)
Delta	Missouri
De Soto, Hernando	(color picture)
Eads Bridge	Missouri River
Floods and	Ohio River
Flood Control	Red River
Illinois River	River (color chart;
Jetty	Longest Rivers)
Keokuk Dam	Wisconsin River
Le Sueur, Pierre	Yazoo River
Levee	
Louisiana (pictures)	

MISSISSIPPI SCHEME was a wild financial project formulated in France in 1717. John Law, a Scottish economist, originated the scheme, which resulted in the organization of a concern known as The Mississippi Company. The French regent, Philip, Duke of Orléans, gave the company a *monopoly* (exclusive rights) to carry on far-reaching business operations in French-held Louisiana and Canada. At first, the scheme won widespread approval. Thousands of Frenchmen bought shares in Law's company without really knowing how their money was to be used. But when the stockholders discovered that the company actually did little to develop business enterprises in America, they became frightened, and began to sell their shares at greatly reduced prices. The result was a financial panic in 1720, known as the bursting of "The Mississippi Bubble." A few investors who sold their shares early at high prices made huge profits. But others suffered heavy losses, or were ruined financially. The scheme was a failure, but it helped advertise Louisiana and attracted thousands of settlers and slaves to the colony.   OSCAR O. WINTHER

MISSISSIPPI STATE COLLEGE FOR WOMEN, in Columbus, Miss., is a school of arts and sciences. It is the oldest state supported college for women in the United States. Courses include the humanities, commerce, and medical technology. The school was founded in 1884. For enrollment, see UNIVERSITIES AND COLLEGES (table).

MISSISSIPPI STATE UNIVERSITY is a coeducational school in State College, Miss. It receives state and federal support. It has colleges of agriculture, arts and sciences, business and industry, education, and engineering; a school of forest resources; and a graduate school. There is also an agricultural experiment station and an agricultural extension service. The university is noted for its seed technology and aerophysics laboratories. Its full name is MISSISSIPPI STATE UNIVERSITY OF AGRICULTURE AND APPLIED SCIENCE.

The university was founded in 1878, and took its present name in 1958. For enrollment, see UNIVERSITIES AND COLLEGES (table).

WILLIAM LINCOLN GILES

MISSISSIPPI VALLEY STATE COLLEGE. See UNIVERSITIES AND COLLEGES (table).

MISSISSIPPIAN PERIOD was the early part of the Carboniferous Period in the Paleozoic Era of geologic history. See EARTH (table: Outline of Earth History).

MISSOULA, *muh ZOO luh,* Mont. (pop. 29,232; alt. 3,210 ft.), is the agricultural trading center of five fertile valleys. It lies on the Pacific slope of the Rocky Mountains, 115 miles west of Helena. For location, see MONTANA (political map).

Missoula is the site of Montana State University and the Montana Forest Tree Nursery. It also serves as the headquarters of Region One of the United States Forest Service. Industries include sugar refining, flour milling, and a pulp and paper mill for making wood products.

The name *Missoula* comes from a Flathead Indian word, *Im-i-su-la* or *Im-i-sul-a-tiko,* meaning *by or near the cold, chilling waters.* Some think the word refers to Hell Gate Canyon, just east of Missoula, where Blackfoot Indians ambushed Flathead Indians.

Missoula was founded in 1860. It has a mayor-council form of government.

DONALD H. WELSH

MISSOURI

The Show Me State

Cave Spring by Thomas Hart Benton for the
Field Enterprises Educational Corporation Collection

Ozark Scene in Southern Missouri

MISSOURI, *muh* ZOOR *ee,* or *muh* ZOOR *uh,* is an important industrial and farming state of the Midwest. Its location and its two great rivers have made Missouri a center of water, land, and air transportation.

The mighty Mississippi River forms Missouri's eastern border. The wide Missouri River winds across the state from west to east. A tremendous wealth of food, manufactured products, and raw materials is shipped on these waterways—the nation's longest rivers. Twenty major railroads and many national and interstate highways crisscross Missouri. Five transcontinental airlines serve the state, and St. Louis and Kansas City are among the nation's chief air terminals.

Vast fields of golden grain and green grasses cover the state's rolling plains in the north and west. Swift streams tumble through the rugged, wooded plateau of southern Missouri. This scenic region, called the Ozarks, is a major playground of the Midwest.

Missouri's factories turn out airplanes, automobiles, railroad cars, and other vehicles. The state ranks high in shoe manufacturing and flour milling. Missouri plants also pack meat and process dairy products and other foods. Missouri stands high among the states in corn and soybean production, and it is a leading livestock center. Missouri produces more lead than any other state. It also has valuable deposits of clay, coal, iron, marble, and other minerals.

Missouri is sometimes called the *Mother of the West*

because it once lay at the frontier of the United States. The state supplied many of the pioneers who settled the vast region between Missouri and the Pacific Ocean. St. Louis, St. Charles, Independence, St. Joseph, and Westport Landing (now Kansas City) served as jumping-off places for the westbound pioneers. The historic Santa Fe Trail led from Independence to the rich, faraway Southwest. Thousands of settlers also followed the Oregon Trail from Independence to the Pacific Northwest. Furs brought from the Northwest made St. Louis the fur capital of the world.

During the Civil War, Missourians were torn between their loyalties to the South and to the Union. After the war, manufacturing developed rapidly, and St. Louis and Kansas City grew into industrial giants. Agriculture also expanded, and Missouri became a great farming state.

Many outstanding Americans have lived in Missouri. They include Harry S. Truman, the nation's 33rd President; Mark Twain, the creator of Tom Sawyer and Huckleberry Finn; Eugene Field, the beloved children's poet; General John J. Pershing, commander of U.S. forces in Europe during World War I; George Washington Carver, the great Negro scientist; Joseph Pulitzer, the famous journalist; General Omar N. Bradley, a brilliant commander in World War II; and Thomas Hart Benton and George Caleb Bingham, noted painters.

The state's name comes from the Missouri River. The word *Missouri* probably came from an Indian word meaning the *town of the large canoes*. Missouri's nickname is the *Show Me State*. This nickname is usually traced to a speech by Congressman Willard Duncan Vandiver of Missouri in 1899. Speaking in Philadelphia, Vandiver said: ". . . frothy eloquence neither convinces nor satisfies me. I am from Missouri. You have got to show me."

Jefferson City is the capital of Missouri, and St. Louis is the largest city. For Missouri's relationship to the other states in its region, see MIDWESTERN STATES.

FACTS IN BRIEF

Capital: Jefferson City.

Government: *Congress*—U.S. senators, 2; U.S. representatives, 10. *Electoral Votes*—12. *State Legislature*—senators, 34; representatives, 163. *Counties*—114, and the city of St. Louis.

Area: 69,686 square miles (including 640 square miles of inland water), 19th in size among the states. *Greatest Distances*—(north-south) 284 miles; (east-west) 308 miles.

Elevation: *Highest*—Taum Sauk Mountain, 1,772 feet above sea level. *Lowest*—230 feet above sea level, along the St. Francis River near Cardwell.

Population: *1970 Preliminary Census*—4,636,247; density, 67 persons to the square mile. *1960 Census*—4,319,813, 13th among the states; distribution, 67 per cent urban, 33 per cent rural.

Chief Products: *Agriculture*—beef cattle, corn, hogs, milk, soybeans, wheat. *Manufacturing and Processing*—chemicals, clothing, fabricated metal products, machinery, printing and publishing, processed foods, transportation equipment. *Mining*—coal, iron ore, lead, sand and gravel, stone.

Statehood: Aug. 10, 1821, the 24th state.

State Motto: *Salus populi suprema lex esto* (The welfare of the people shall be the supreme law).

State Song: "Missouri Waltz." Words by J. R. Shannon; music from an original melody obtained from John Valentine Eppel.

Winter on the Missouri River near Jefferson City

Gerald R. Massie

Missouri (blue) ranks 19th in size among all the states, and 6th in size among the Midwestern States (gray).

The contributors of this article are James E. Collier, Professor of Geography at Southern Illinois University (formerly of the University of Missouri); Lew Larkin, Reporter and Columnist for the Kansas City Star; and William E. Parrish, Professor of History at Westminster College.

Constitution of Missouri was adopted in 1945. The state had three earlier constitutions, adopted in 1820, 1865, and 1875. An amendment to the constitution may be proposed by a majority of the members of the state legislature. Or it may be proposed by a petition signed by 8 per cent of the voters in two-thirds of the state's congressional districts. To become part of the constitution, an amendment must be approved by a majority of the voters voting on the amendment. The constitution requires that the people vote every 20 years, starting in 1962, on whether to call a convention to amend the constitution. In 1962, the voters rejected a proposal for a constitutional convention.

Executive. The governor of Missouri is elected to a four-year term. He is limited to two terms. The governor receives a yearly salary of $37,500. He appoints the members of all boards and commissions, and the heads of all departments of the state government. For a list of all the governors of Missouri, see the *History* section of this article.

The other top state officials—the lieutenant governor, secretary of state, state treasurer, attorney general, and state auditor—are elected to four-year terms. The treasurer may not serve two terms in a row. The other officials may be re-elected to consecutive terms.

Legislature of Missouri is known as the General Assembly. It consists of a Senate of 34 members and a House of Representatives of 163 members. Missouri has 34 senatorial districts and 163 representative districts. Voters in each senatorial district elect one senator. Voters in each representative district elect one representative. Senators serve four-year terms, and representatives serve two-year terms.

In 1966, a commission composed of 10 Democrats and 10 Republicans reapportioned the House of Representatives. The *reapportionment* (redivision) provided equal representation on the basis of population.

The General Assembly meets on the first Wednesday after January 1 in odd-numbered years. A regular ses-

sion may last until July 15. But after June 30, the lawmakers cannot consider new bills. The governor may call special sessions, limited to 60 calendar days.

Courts in Missouri are headed by the state Supreme Court, composed of seven judges. The state has three courts of appeals—in Kansas City, St. Louis, and Springfield. The governor appoints the judges of the Supreme Court and the appeals courts for 12-year terms. He selects them from candidates proposed by nonpartisan commissions. After a judge has been in office for a year, he must be approved by the voters in the next general election. When his term expires, each judge must again be approved by the voters if he wishes to serve another term. No political party designation is allowed on the ballot. Every two years, the Supreme Court selects one of its members to serve as chief justice.

The state constitution also provides for circuit courts, courts of common pleas, probate courts, magistrate courts, the St. Louis courts of criminal correction, and municipal courts. Circuit-court judges serve six-year terms, and the rest serve four-year terms. Judges of circuit and probate courts in St. Louis and Jackson County, and of the St. Louis criminal courts, are selected like the judges of the Supreme Court. The people elect all the other judges.

Local Government. Voters in Missouri's 114 counties elect local officials. These officials generally include three judges of the county court, a sheriff, recorder of deeds, prosecuting attorney, collector of revenue, assessor, treasurer, coroner, public administrator, surveyor, and superintendent of public schools. The county court judges serve as the chief administrators of the county. They are responsible for health, welfare, and public works in the county, and set the county tax rate. The constitution provides that any county with more than 85,000 residents, or any city with over 10,000 persons, may organize its government in the way that best suits its people. Most Missouri cities have the mayor-council form of government.

Walker, Missouri Division of Commerce

The Governor's Mansion stands south of the Missouri Capitol. The three-story residence was completed in 1871.

The State Flag

The State Bird
Bluebird

The State Flower
Hawthorn

The State Tree
Flowering Dogwood

The State Seal

Flower illustration, courtesy of Eli Lilly and Company

Symbols of Missouri. On the state seal, adopted in 1822, two grizzly bears represent the state. They hold shields of the United States and Missouri to show that the state supports itself and the Union. The helmet symbolizes enterprise and hardiness. The stars show that Missouri was the 24th state in the Union. The Roman numerals give the date that Missouri's first constitution was adopted. The seal appears on the flag, adopted in 1913.

Taxation. Taxes and licenses bring in about two-thirds of Missouri's income. The federal government provides about one-third of the income. Missouri receives about half its income from a sales tax, individual and corporation income taxes, a gasoline tax, and vehicle licenses. Taxes are also collected on cigarettes, liquor, property, and other items.

Politics. Missouri voters tend to favor Democratic candidates, but the balloting between parties is usually close. In presidential elections since 1900, Missouri has voted for the winner every time except once—in 1956. For the state's voting record in presidential elections since 1820, see ELECTORAL COLLEGE (table).

St. Louis and Kansas City vote strongly Democratic, but the region around St. Louis is Republican. Northeastern Missouri, most of the counties along the Missouri River, and southeastern Missouri are Democratic. North-central and southwestern Missouri are Republican. About 30 counties switch back and forth between the two major parties. The party that wins these counties generally controls the state legislature. Missouri has had only five Republican governors since 1900.

The State Capitol, in Jefferson City, was completed in 1917. Jefferson City has been Missouri's capital since 1826. Former capitals were St. Louis (1820) and St. Charles (1821-1826).

Walker, Missouri Division of Commerce

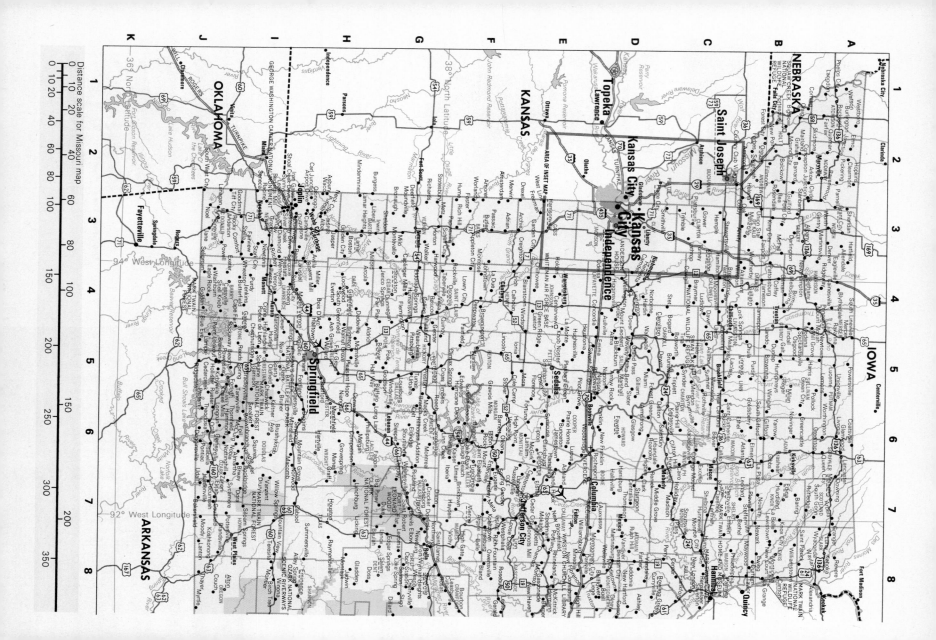

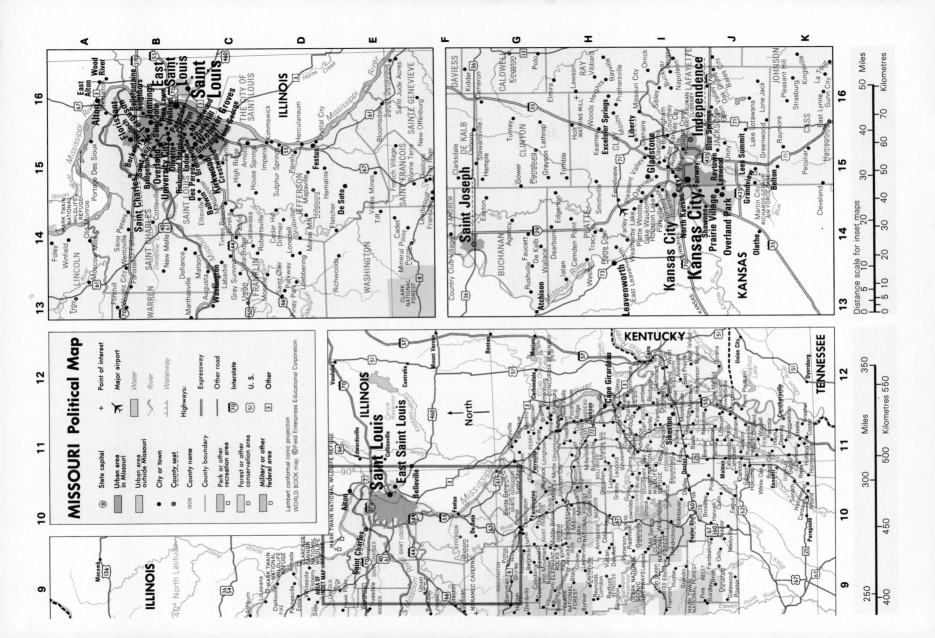

Population

Metropolitan Areas

Counties

Cities and Towns

Index of cities and towns with 1970 preliminary census figures (or 1960 census where available), map grid coordinates.

Holliday ...181 .C 7
Hollister ...600 .K10
Hollywood ...104 .K16
Holt ...281 .H 6
Hopkins ...710 .A 4
Hornersville ...742 .H17
Houston 2,420 .H 1
Houston Lake 261 .E 5
Howardville 190 .H15
Howardsville 134 .G 6
Humansville 745 .G 3
Hume 369 .F 3
Humphreys 163 .B 5
Hunnewell 284 .C 7
Hunter ...105 .H 0
Huntsville 1,374 .E10
Hurdland 205 .B 7
Hurley ...117 .I 5
Deck ...117 .F 6
Iberia 694 .F 7
Illmo 1,224 .H12
Independence 110,790 .D 3
Ionia ...114 .F 3
Iron Gates 312 .I 5
Irondale 335 .G10
Ironton 1,436 .G10
Isabella ... .I 6
Jackson 5,841 .H11
Jacksonville 153 .C 6
Jamesport 622 .B 4
Jamestown 216 .E 6
Jasper 746 .H 3
Jefferson City 31,921 .E 7
Jennings 19,455 .B16
Jerico Springs 27 .G 4
Johnstown ... .F 4
Jonesburg 415 .E 7
Joplin 38,424 .I 2
Junction City 260 .H10
Kahoka 2,167 .A 8
Kansas City 495,405 .D 3
Kearney 678 .D 3
Kelso 258 .H12
Kennett 9,671 .K11
Keytesville 644 .C 6
Kidder 224 .C 4
Kimmswick 303 .D 8
King City 1,005 .B 3
Kingston 311 .C 4
Kingsville 225 .E 4
Kinloch 5,444 .B16
Kirksville 15,413 .B 6
Kirkwood 31,451 .C16
Knob Noster 2,235 .E 5
Knox City 330 .B 7
Koshkonong 216 .I 8
La Belle 786 .B 7
La Plata 1,364 .B 6
Laredo 370 .B 5
Larussell 129 .I 3
Latham 131 .E 6
Lathrop 1,231 .C 4
La Tour 68 .K16
Lawson 1,008 .H11
Leadington 365 .G10
Leadwood 1,422 .F15
Leasburg 176 .F 8
Leawood 152 .G 6
Lebanon 8,492 .G 2

Lees Summit 16,188 .I16
Leeton 371 .E 5
Leonard 142 .B 6
Leslie 224 .H11
Lewistown 454 .B 7
Lexington 5,375 .D 4
Liberal 835 .H 1
Liberty 13,604 .D 7
Licking ... .H 7
Liege 78 .I 4
Lilbourn 1,149 .J16
Lincoln 446 .F 5
Linn 1,297 .C 8
Linn Creek 174 .G 1
Linneus 471 .B 5
Lithium 54 .G11
Livonia 154 .A 6
Lock Springs 117 .B 4
Lohman 128 .E 7
Longtown 113 .G11
Louisiana 4,437 .D 8
Lowry City 437 .F 4

Luerne ...157 .A 5
Ludlow 235 .C 6
Lupus 154 .E 7
Luray ...158 .A 7
Lutesville 658 .H11
Mackenzie 1,803 .B16
Mackerel Creek 123 .G 5
Macon 5,528 .C 7
Madison 427 .D 7
Malden 5,278 .J11
Malta Bend 338 .D 5
Manchester 12,737 .B16
Mansfield 1,039 .G 1
Maplewood 12,737 .B16
Marble Hill 497 .H16
Marceline 2,616 .C 5
Margona E10
Marionville 1,260 .E10
Marlborough 631 .A 2
Marquand ...392 .H16
Marshall 12,052 .D 5
Marshfield 2,964 .H 1
Marston 631 .J11
Martinsville 339 .B13
Martinsburg 330 .D 7
Marsville ...79 .A 3
Marvin Terrace E10
Mary Ridge 631 .A 2
Matthews 450 .G 3
Maysville 1,033 .B 3
Maywood 270 .B 7
McFall 206 .B 3
McKittrick 97 .E 8
Meadowbrook E10
Downs 639 .E10
Meadville 447 .C 6
Melbourne 27 .C 4
Memphis 2,094 .A 7
Mendon 287 .C 6
Menfro H16
Merwin 368 .A 5
Mercer 422 .F 7
Merwin 76 .D 3
Meta 137 .F 7
Mexico 11,760 .D 7
Miami 156 .D 5
Middle Grove 59 .D 7
Middletown 199 .D 7
Midway* 67 .E 7
Milan 1,752 .B 5
Mill Spring 226 .H 9
Milo 108 .G 3
Mindenmines 356 .H 1
Miner 548 .H15
Mineral Point 332 .G 9
Missouri City 404 .I16
Modena 66 .A 4
Mokane 419 .E 7
Moline Acres 3,689 .E10
Monett 5,854 .I 4
Monroe City 2,446 .C 7
Montevallo 50 .G 3
Montgomery City 2,168 .D 8
Montier ... .I 7
Montrose 526 .F 4
Morehouse 1,326 .J10
Morgan 492 .H 1
Morley 801 .J 6
Morrisville 357 .J 5
Morrison 232 .E 8
Mosby 293 .H11
Moscow Mills 304 .D13
Mound City 1,129 .B 3
Moundville 21 .G 3
Mount Leonard 147 .D 5
Mount Moriah 225 .A 4
Mount Vernon 2,993 .I 4
Mountain Grove 3,367 .I 7
Mountain View 1,313 .I 8
Napoleon 371 .I16
Naylor 499 .J10
Neck City 110 .H 3
Neelyville 385 .J10
Nelson 126 .D 5
Neosho 7,570 .I 3
Nevada 9,516 .G 3
New Bloomfield 359 .E 7
New Cambria 270 .C 6
New Court 64 .O 8
New Florence 616 .E 8
New Franklin 1,080 .D 6
New Hamburg 197 .I16
New Hampton 289 .B 7
New Haven 1,752 .E 8
Newburg 287 .H 2
Newtonia 153 .A 3
Newtown 265 .A 5
Nianqua 1,236 .G 7
Nixa 1,852 .J 5
Noel 965 .I 2
Normandy 6,360 .A 1
North Kansas City 5,290 .I15
Norborne 965 .D 4
Norwood 263 .J 1
Norwood Court 186 .E10
Osgood 135 .B 5
Otterville 416 .E 6
Overland 24,825 .B16
Owensville 2,394 .E 8
Ozark 2,360 .J 5
Pacific 3,207 .C14
Pagedale 5,218 .C16
Palmyra 3,158 .O 6
Paris 1,429 .O 7
Parkdale 696 .F14
Parkville 4,577 .D 3
Parkway D13
Parma 263 .J11
Pasadena 260 .A 3
Pasadena Hills* 1,011 .E10
Park* 680 .E10
Pasola 228 .J 1
Passaic 84 .F 3
Pattonsburg 753 .B 3
Peach Orchard 57 .J11
Peculiar 1,245 .E 4
Perkins 153 .H11
Perry 802 .C 8
Perryville 4,932 .G11
Pevely 416 .D15
Phelps City 81 .A 1
Phillipsburg 142 .H 4
Piedmont 1,899 .H10
Pierce City 1,102 .I 4
Pilot Knob 524 .G10
Pine Lawn 5,732 .B16
Piney Park 97 .J 2
Platte City 2,015 .I16
Platte Woods 393 .I16
Plattsburg 1,794 .C 3
Pleasant Green 14 .E 5
Pleasant Hill 3,334 .I16
Pleasant Hope 216 .H 5
Pleasant Valley 1,537 .I16
Pocahontas 128 .H11
Point Pleasant J11
Polk 115 .J16
Polo 469 .G16
Poplar Bluff 16,471 .I10
Portage Des Sioux 371 .A15
Portageville 3,016 .J11
Potosi 2,690 .G 9
Powe 97 .J 3
Powersville 189 .A 5
Prairie Hill 84 .C 6
Prairie Home 213 .E 7
Prathersville 148 .H16
Preston 117 .G 2
Princeton 1,314 .A 5
Purcell 265 .H 3
Purdin 207 .B 5
Purdy 467 .I 4
Puxico 743 .J 9
Queen City 599 .A 6
Quitman 113 .A 2
Qulin 587 .J 9
Ravanna 127 .A 5
Ravenswood 282 .H 4
Raymondville 202 .H 1
Raymore 32,965 .I16
Raytown 32,965 .I16
Rayville 200 .H11
Rea 16 .B 3
Red Oak 175 .H11
Oak Ridge 175 .H11
Redings Mill 1,583 .I 2

Reeds Spring 327 .I 5
Reger 190 .D 6
Renick 63 .C 6
Rensselaer 178 .J 1
Republic 2,415 .I 4
Revere 190 .A 8
Rhineland 190 .E 8
Rich Hill 1,639 .F 3
Richards 133 .G 3
Richland 1,767 .G 6
Richmond 4,856 .D 4
Richmond Heights 13,690 .B15
Ridgeway 502 .J 1
Risco 449 .G10
Ritchey 128 .I 3
Rivermines 97 .J 5
Riverside 2,097 .I15
Riverview* 3,692 .J12
Rives 34 .D 6
Roanoke ... .J 5
Rocheport 375 .D 6
Rock Hill 6,623 .C16
Rockaway Beach 884 .K10
Rockport 1,553 .A 1
Rockville 255 .F 3
Rocky Comfort 151 .I 4
Rogersville 447 .J 6
Rolla 13,257 .G 8
Roscoe 288 .F 2
Rosebud 234 .E 8
Rosendale 138 .C 6
Rothville 132 .D 6
Rush Hill 253 .D 7
Russellville 442 .E 7
Rutledge 158 .A 7
Saginaw 188 .I 2
St. Ann 18,391 .B16
St. Charles 31,668 .O 6
St. Clair 2,957 .D 7
St. Elizabeth 272 .F 7
St. George 524 .C16
St. James 2,588 .G 8
St. John 8,978 .B16
St. Joseph 71,996 .C 3
St. Jude Acres 144 .E16
St. Louis 607,718 .E16
St. Marys 620 .G11
St. Peters 404 .B14
St. Robert 1,274 .G 7
Ste. Genevieve 4,476 .G11
view 50 .G 4
Salisbury 1,963 .C 6
Sandy Hook 50 .E 7
Saroxie 1,153 .I 4
Savannah 3,283 .B 3
Schell City 343 .G 3
Schuermann Heights* 288 .E10
Scott City 2,456 .H12
Sedalia 22,549 .E 5
Sedgewickville 91 .H11
Seligman 387 .J 4
Senath 1,534 .K10
Seneca 1,598 .I 2
Seymour 1,116 .J 1
Shelbina 2,031 .C 7
Sheldon 657 .G 3
Sheridan 134 .A 4
Shoal Creek Drive 415 .I 3
Shrewsbury* 5,900 .C16
Sibley 97 .I16
Sikeston 14,488 .H15
Silex 176 .D13
Silver Creek 425 .I 2
Skidmore 503 .A 3
Slater 2,503 .D 5
Sleeper 111 .G 6
Smithton 395 .E 5
Smithville 1,381 .I16
South Gifford 64 .C 6
South Gorin 279 .A 7
South Green- field 179 .H 4
South Lineville 76 .A 5
South West City 504 .I 2
Sparta 272 .J 6
Spickardsville 450 .B 5
Spring Garden 37 .F 6
Springfield 118,950 .H 5
Stanberry 1,450 .B 3
Stark City 37 .I 3
Steele 2,066 .K11
Steelville 1,381 .G 9
Stella 166 .I 3
Stewartsville 466 .C 3
Stockton 1,037 .F 3
Stotesbury 64 .G 3
Stotts City 221 .I 4
Stoutland 225 .G 6
Stoutsville 109 .C 7
Stover 757 .F 6
Strasburg 213 .K16
Sturgeon 619 .D 6
Sugar Creek 4,746 .I15
Sullivan 5,104 .F 8
Summersville 336 .H 8
Sumner 111 .C 6
Sunrise Beach 78 .F 6

Sunset Hills* 4,617 .E10
Sweet Springs 1,676 .D 5
Sycamore Hills* 942 .E10
Syracuse 180 .E 6
Taneyville 134 .K 5
Tarkio 2,490 .A 1
Tarsney Lakes* 294 .D 3
Taylor 1,522 .B 8
Thayer 1,238 .J 8
Times Beach 1,238 .C15
Tina 199 .D 6
Tindall 94 .B 4
Tipton 1,957 .E 6
Town and Country 2,669 .E10
Tracy 6,032 .H14
Trenton 231 .B 5
Trimble 2,523 .D 3
Triplett 217 .O 5
Truesdale 144 .C 7
Tuscumbia 231 .F 7
Twin Oaks 206 .O15
Union 5,067 .F 9
Union Star 392 .B 3
Unionville 2,066 .A 5
Unity Village 153 .J15
University City 45,902 .B15
Uplands Park* 549 .C16
Urbana 348 .G 5
Urbandale 56 .O 6
Urich 408 .F 4
Valley Park* 3,614 .C16
Van Buren 575 .H 9
Vandalia 3,069 .D 7
Vanduser 45 .J10
Vanduser 272 .J 1
Velda Village 524 .E10
Velda Village Hills* 2,181 .E10
Verona 401 .I 4
Versailles 2,185 .F 6
Vibbard 535 .H16
Vienna 620 .F 7
Vinita Park* 3,412 .E10
Vista 50 .G 4
Waco 143 .H 3
Wakenda 146 .D 5
Walker 235 .G 3
Walnut Grove 373 .H 4
Wardell 331 .J11
Warrensburg 13,242 .E 4
Warrenton 1,994 .E 8
Warsaw 1,407 .F 5
Warson Woods* 2,620 .E10
Washington 8,475 .C13
Watson 181 .A 1
Waverly 837 .D 5
Wayland 384 .A 8
Waynesville 3,304 .G 7
Weatherby 450 .B 3
Weatherby Lake 376 .I14
Weaubleau 349 .G 4
Webb City 6,754 .I 3
Webster Groves 27,250 .C16
Wellington 169 .D 4
Wellston 6,958 .B16
Wellsville 1,564 .D 7
Wentworth 174 .I 3
Wentzville 3,196 .B14
West Line 88 .E 4
West Plains 6,272 .J 7
Westboro 262 .A 1
Weston 1,243 .H14
Westphalia 316 .F 7
Westwood 291 .E10
Wheatland 305 .G 4
Wheaton 341 .I 4
White Oak 302 .C 6
Whiteoak 349 .H 3
Whitewater 122 .H11
Wilbur Park* 684 .C16
Willard 357 .H 4
Williamsville 412 .I10
Wilson City 274 .H15
Winchester* 1,381 .C16
Windsor 2,301 .E 4
Winfield 564 .D13
Winigan 64 .C 6
Winona 827 .H 8
Winston 236 .B 3
Woods Heights 107 .H16
Woodson Terrace* 5,964 .E10
Woolridge 100 .E 6
Worth 135 .A 3
Wright City 738 .B14
Wyaconda 356 .A 7
Wyatt 402 .J11
Zalma 141 .H11

Oakview 543 .I15
Oakwood 159 .I15
Oakwood Manor 178 .I15
Odessa 2,824 .D 4
O'Fallon 7,184 .B14
Old Monroe 290 .B14
Olean 135 .F 7
Olivette 9,329 .B15
Oran 1,212 .H15
Oregon 887 .O 8
Orrick 513 .H16
Osage Beach 1,101 .F 6
Osborn 274 .C 3
Osceola 1,066 .F 4
New Haven 875 .E 8
New London 116 .O 8
New Madrid 2,682 .J12
Newark 153 .B 7
North Lilbourn 301 .J11
Northmoor 696 .I15
Northwoods 4,577 .A16
Norwood 263 .J 1

Sources: Latest census figures (1970 preliminary census where available, 1960 census, or special census). Cities and towns without population information are unincorporated places under 1,000 in population and are not listed in census reports.

*Does not appear on the map; key shows general location.
○County seat

The 1970 preliminary United States census reported that Missouri had 4,636,247 persons. The population had increased 7 per cent over the 1960 figure, 4,319,813.

Two-thirds of the people of Missouri live in cities and towns. Most of these persons live in metropolitan areas. Missouri has four Standard Metropolitan Statistical Areas (see METROPOLITAN AREA). They are Kansas City, St. Joseph, St. Louis, and Springfield. For the populations of these metropolitan areas, see the *Index* to the political map of Missouri.

St. Louis and Kansas City, the state's largest cities, rank among the leading transportation, grain, and livestock centers of the United States. See the separate articles on Missouri cities listed in the *Related Articles* at the end of this article.

Fewer than 2 of every 100 Missourians were born outside the United States. Most of the American-born whites have Czech, English, French, German, Irish, Italian, Polish, or Swiss ancestors. About 9 of every 100 Missourians are Negroes.

More than half of Missouri's church members are Protestants. The largest groups include the Baptists, Disciples of Christ, Episcopalians, Lutherans, Methodists, Presbyterians, and members of the United Church of Christ. About one of every six Missourians is a Roman Catholic.

Competition Among Farmers is popular at local fairs. These Missouri farmers near St. Louis are watching a contest to determine which team of horses can pull the heaviest load.

Jack Zehrt, Publix

Handicraft Skills are often passed down from generation to generation. A quilting bee provides a friendly social gathering for this group of Missouri women.

Tom Hollyman, Photo Researchers

POPULATION

This map shows the *population density* of Missouri, and how it varies in different parts of the state. Population density means the average number of persons who live on each square mile.

PERSONS PER SQUARE MILE

| 5 to 20 | 20 to 40 | 40 to 120 | 120 to 12,500 |

St. Joseph

Kansas City

Springfield

St. Louis

0 50 100 150 200 Miles
0 50 100 200 300 Kilometers

WORLD BOOK map

552

Missouri Division of Commerce

The William Rockhill Nelson Gallery of Art and Mary Atkins Museum of Fine Arts in Kansas City

MISSOURI / *Education*

Schools. Missouri's first school was a private elementary school established in St. Louis in 1774. In 1820, Missouri's first constitution included a provision for establishing a system of public education. The system was not founded until 1839, however.

The state board of education supervises Missouri's public school system. The board has eight members appointed by the governor to eight-year terms. One term expires each year. The board appoints a commissioner of education, who serves as the chief administrative officer of the public school system. His term of office is indefinite. All children between the ages of 7 and 16 must attend school. For the number of students and teachers in Missouri, see EDUCATION (table).

Libraries. Many of Missouri's public libraries grew out of public school libraries. Some started as *subscription libraries*, in which members contributed money and used the books free of charge. In 1865, the St. Louis public library was established. It was supported by money from the school board and by fees and donations. In 1893, the library became tax-supported. Today, Missouri has about 170 public libraries and 70 college and university libraries. The library of the University of Missouri at Columbia is the largest in the state.

Museums. Missouri's largest art museums are the City Art Museum in St. Louis and the William Rockhill Nelson Gallery of Art and Mary Atkins Museum of Fine Arts in Kansas City. The City Art Museum has a collection from many countries and periods. The Nelson Gallery-Atkins Museum owns noted collections of Oriental and American art. The Capitol in Jefferson City houses a museum with collections of Missouri materials of historical, geological, scientific, and cultural interest. The Missouri Historical Society building in Forest Park in St. Louis displays trophies and gifts received by Charles A. Lindbergh, the aviator. The Harry S. Truman Library in Independence exhibits the souvenirs of the nation's 33rd President.

UNIVERSITIES AND COLLEGES

Missouri has 38 universities and colleges accredited by the North Central Association of Colleges and Secondary Schools. For enrollments and further information, see UNIVERSITIES AND COLLEGES (table).

Name	Location	Founded
Avila College	Kansas City	1867
Cardinal Glennon College	St. Louis	1818
Central Methodist College	Fayette	1854
Central Missouri State College	Warrensburg	1870
Culver-Stockton College	Canton	1853
Drury College	Springfield	1873
Evangel College	Springfield	1955
Fontbonne College	St. Louis	1917
Harris Teachers College	St. Louis	1875
Immaculate Conception Seminary	Conception	1883
Kansas City Art Institute	Kansas City	1962
Lincoln University	Jefferson City	1866
Lindenwood College	St. Charles	1827
Marillac College	St. Louis	1954
Maryville College	St. Louis	1846
Missouri, University of	*	1839
Missouri Southern College	Joplin	1967
Missouri Valley College	Marshall	1889
Missouri Western College	St. Joseph	1915
Northeast Missouri State College	Kirksville	1867
Northwest Missouri State College	Maryville	1905
Notre Dame College	St. Louis	1954
Ozarks, School of the	Point Lookout	1964
Park College	Parkville	1875
Rockhurst College	Kansas City	1910
St. Louis College of Pharmacy	St. Louis	1932
St. Louis University	St. Louis	1818
St. Mary's Seminary	Perryville	1834
Southeast Missouri State College	Cape Girardeau	1873
Southwest Baptist College	Bolivar	1966
Southwest Missouri State College	Springfield	1906
Stephens College	Columbia	1833
Tarkio College	Tarkio	1883
Washington University	St. Louis	1853
Webster College	St. Louis	1915
Westminster College	Fulton	1851
William Jewell College	Liberty	1849
William Woods College	Fulton	1870

*For the campuses of the University of Missouri, see UNIVERSITIES AND COLLEGES (table).

Missouri's mild climate and many varied attractions make the state a popular vacationland. Missouri has abundant wildlife, rugged hills, rushing streams, and peaceful woodlands to delight sportsmen, hikers, and photographers. Fishermen can try their luck for bass, trout, and other game fish in clear, spring-fed streams. Hunting for foxes and raccoons in the hills has long been a favorite sport. Visitors can take guided boat trips down rapid streams. The state's most unusual sights include great bubbling springs and deep caverns.

Harry S. Truman Library in Independence

Jack Zehrt, Publix

Elephant Rocks near Pilot Knob

John H. Gerard

Following are brief descriptions of some of Missouri's many interesting places to visit.

Altenburg, in Perry County, is a historic German community established in 1839. Its buildings include the log Concordia Seminary, erected in 1839.

Anderson House, built near Lexington in 1853, was used as a hospital during the Civil War Battle of Lexington. The house is now a museum with furniture, firearms, and other items of the 1860's.

Climatron is a revolutionary greenhouse in the Missouri Botanical Garden in St. Louis. The great domed structure is completely air-conditioned and moisture-controlled. It displays a variety of plants.

Elephant Rocks, near Pilot Knob, are huge granite boulders worn into weird shapes by the forces of nature.

Harry S. Truman Library, in Independence, opened in 1957. The 700-foot-long building houses about 3,500,000 documents dealing with the history of U.S. foreign relations.

Mark Twain Cave, near Hannibal, is a cave that the famous author Mark Twain learned about as a boy. In the novel *The Adventures of Tom Sawyer,* Tom and his friend Becky Thatcher get lost in this cave.

Mark Twain Home and Museum, in Hannibal, is the restored boyhood home of the writer. The museum has many objects connected with Mark Twain's life.

McDonnell Planetarium, in St. Louis, offers exciting exhibits and lectures on the mysteries of the universe. The striking building rests on 12 pillars.

PLACES TO VISIT

Meramec Caverns, near Stanton, is a legendary hideout of the outlaw Jesse James. The first room of this huge cave is large enough to hold 300 automobiles.

Winston Churchill Memorial and Library, in Fulton, was formerly the Church of St. Mary Aldermanbury. It was dismantled and moved from London after World War II, and rebuilt on the campus of Westminster College in Fulton. Winston Churchill delivered his famous "iron curtain" speech on the campus in 1946.

National Forests and Monument. Missouri's two national forests are Clark and Mark Twain. For their areas and chief features, see NATIONAL FOREST (table). George Washington Carver National Monument, near Diamond Grove, honors the famous Missouri-born Negro scientist. See GEORGE WASHINGTON CARVER NATIONAL MONUMENT.

State Forests and Parks. Missouri has six state forests. They are Canay Mountain (5,527 acres) in Ozark County; Daniel Boone (2,250 acres) in Warren County; Deer Run (115,105 acres) in Carter, Reynolds, Ripley, Shannon, and Texas counties; Dupont (1,242 acres) in Pike County; Indian Trail (13,255 acres) in Dent County; and Rockwoods (3,406 acres) in St. Louis County. Missouri has 36 state parks. Many of them have features of historical interest, such as the home in which Mark Twain was born, as well as recreational facilities. For information about Missouri's state parks, write to Director, Missouri State Park Board, Box 176, Missouri City, Mo. 65102.

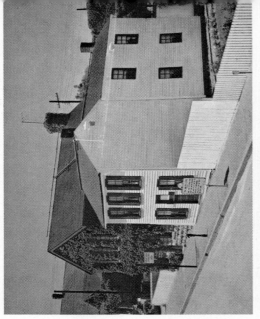

Mark Twain's Home in Hannibal

Winston Churchill Memorial and Library in Fulton

Climatron at Missouri Botanical Garden in St. Louis
Jack Zehrt, Publix

McDonnell Planetarium in St. Louis

ANNUAL EVENTS

Missouri's best-known annual event is perhaps its State Fair, held the third week in August in Sedalia. The fair attracts about 250,000 persons from Missouri and neighboring states. Other annual events in Missouri include the following.

January-March: Orchid Show at Missouri Botanical Garden in St. Louis (February); National Intercollegiate Basketball Tournament in Kansas City (March).

April-June: Journalism Week at the University of Missouri in Columbia (May); Apple Blossom Festival in St. Joseph (May); Maifest in Hermann (May); Current River Canoe Race, which begins near Van Buren and ends near Doniphan (May); Singing Event in Ava (May); Governor's Fish Fry in Branson (June); J Bar H Rodeo in Camdenton (June).

July-September: Mark Twain Fence Painting Contest in Hannibal (July); Ozark Empire Fair in Springfield (August); Jaycee Boot Heel Rodeo in Sikeston (September).

October-December: Flaming Fall Revue in Ava (October); Veiled Prophet's Parade in St. Louis (Wednesday after first Tuesday in October); Future Farmers of America National Convention in Kansas City (October); American Royal Livestock and Horse Show in Kansas City (October); Thanksgiving Day Turkey Shoots in many communities (November); Silver Skates Tournament in St. Louis (December); La Guignolée Festival (traditional French New Year's celebration) in Ste. Genevieve and Old Mines (December 31).

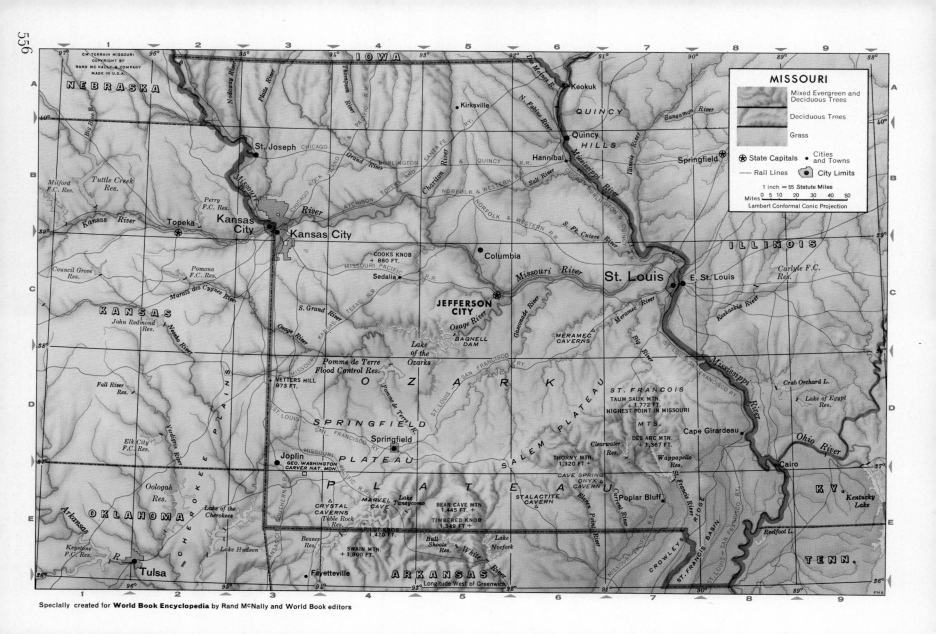

556

MISSOURI

Legend
Mixed Evergreen and Deciduous Trees
Deciduous Trees
Grass
✪ State Capitals
• Cities and Towns
— Rail Lines
◉ City Limits

1 inch = 55 Statute Miles

Miles 0 5 10 20   30   40   50

Lambert Conformal Conic Projection

CM TERRAIN MISSOURI
COPYRIGHT BY
RAND McNALLY & COMPANY
MADE IN U.S.A.

NEBRASKA

IOWA

ILLINOIS

KANSAS

OKLAHOMA

ARKANSAS

KY.

TENN.

Nodaway River
Platte River
Thompson River
Grand River
Chariton River
Des Moines R.
N. Fabius River
Salt River
Illinois River
Sangamon River
Mississippi River

Keokuk
Kirksville
Quincy
QUINCY HILLS
Hannibal
Springfield ✪

St. Joseph
CHICAGO
Missouri River
BURLINGTON
ATCHISON TOPEKA
SANTA FE
QUINCY
NORFOLK & WESTERN
NORFOLK & WESTERN R.R.
CHICAGO BURLINGTON & QUINCY

Big Blue R.
Milford F.C. Res.
Tuttle Creek Res.
Kansas River
Topeka ✪
Kansas City ✪
Kansas City
Perry F.C. Res.
Pomona F.C. Res.
CHICAGO ROCK ISLAND
PACIFIC
MISSOURI PACIFIC

Council Grove Res.
Marais des Cygnes River
Pomona F.C. Res.
COOKS KNOB + 880 FT.
Sedalia
Columbia
Missouri River
St. Louis
E. St. Louis
Carlyle F.C. Res.

John Redmond Res.
Neosho River
S. Grand River
JEFFERSON CITY ✪
Osage River
Gasconade River
Meramec River
Kaskaskia River

KANSAS TEXAS R.R.
S. PK. Cuivre River
MISSOURI

Fall River Res.
Osage River
Pomme de Terre Flood Control Res.
VETTERS HILL 973 FT.
Lake of the Ozarks
BAGNELL DAM
MERAMEC CAVERNS
Big River
ST. LOUIS SAN FRANCISCO RY.
Crab Orchard L.
Lake of Egypt Res.

OZARK

SALEM PLATEAU
ST. FRANCOIS MTS.
TAUM SAUK MTN. + 1,772 FT. HIGHEST POINT IN MISSOURI
DES ARC MTN. + 1,367 FT.

ST. LOUIS SAN FRANCISCO RY.
Pomme de Terre R.
Cape Girardeau

Elk City F.C. Res.
Verdigris River
SPRINGFIELD PLATEAU
Springfield
Clearwater Res.
THORNY MTN. 1,320 FT. +
Wappapello Res.
Ohio River

Joplin
GEO. WASHINGTON CARVER NAT. MON.
PLATEAU
CAVE SPRING ONYX CAVERN
Current River
Poplar Bluff
Cairo

Oologah Res.
Lake of the Cherokees
MARVEL CAVE
Lake Taneycomo
BEAR CAVE MTN. 1,445 FT. +
STALACTITE CAVERN
Eleven Point River
ST. FRANCIS RIDGE

CHEROKEE

CRYSTAL CAVERNS
Table Rock Res.
PILOT KNOB 1,420 FT.
TIMBERED KNOB 1,349 FT. +
Black River
Reelfoot L.
Kentucky Lake

Keystone F.C. Res.
Lake Hudson
Beaver Res.
SWAIN MTN. + 1,800 FT.
Bull Shoals Res.
Lake Norfork
White River
CROWLEYS RIDGE
ST. FRANCIS BASIN

Arkansas R.
Tulsa
Fayetteville
ARKANSAS
ST. LOUIS SAN FRANCISCO RY.
MISSOURI PACIFIC RY.

Longitude West of Greenwich

Land Regions of Missouri

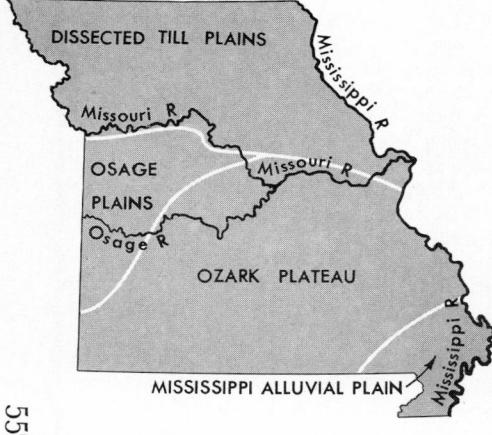

Land Regions. Missouri has four main land regions. These are, from north to south: (1) the Dissected Till Plains, (2) the Osage Plains, (3) the Ozark Plateau (or Ozarks), and (4) the Mississippi Alluvial Plain.

The Dissected Till Plains lie north of the Missouri River. Glaciers once covered this region. The great ice sheets left a rich, deep deposit of soil-forming materials especially suited to the growing of corn. Many slow-moving streams drain the rolling surface of the Dissected Till Plains.

The Osage Plains lie in western Missouri. This is a region of flat prairie land, broken in places by low hills. Glacial ice never covered the region, and the soil is not so rich as that of the Dissected Till Plains. The chief crops are corn and other grains.

The Ozark Plateau is the state's largest land region. Forested hills and low mountains give it scenic beauty. The plateau rises from 500 feet to more than 1,700 feet above sea level. In the extreme southwestern corner of the state, a high, wooded tableland has soil especially good for gardening and raising strawberries. The river valleys are about the only level land in the Ozark region. The plateau is one of the nation's major tourist areas because of its many caves, large springs and lakes, and clear, fast-flowing streams.

The St. Francois Mountains rise in the southeast. This series of granite peaks, knobs, and domes covers about 70 square miles. The St. Francois Mountains do not form a continuous range. They rise more or less in groups, usually of two or three peaks. The mountains make up the highest and most rugged part of the state. One of the peaks, Taum Sauk (1,772 feet), is the highest point in Missouri.

The Mississippi Alluvial Plain covers the southeastern corner of Missouri. This region was once a swampy wilderness. Much of the area has been cleared and drained, and the soil is unusually rich for farming. The southern part of the plain is known as the *Boot Heel* because of its shape.

Rivers and Lakes. Missouri owes much of its commercial and industrial importance to the two largest rivers in the United States—the Mississippi and the Missouri. These rivers and their branches provide water highways for transportation, water supplies for cities and industries, and hydroelectric power for homes and factories.

The Current River is one of Missouri's most beautiful rivers. It starts from Montauk Spring in the Ozarks, which has a daily flow of about 40 million gallons. The river's name comes from the swift flow of its cold, sparkling waters. Like the Black, James, St. Francis, and other rivers of the Ozark Plateau, the Current is noted for its game fish. Other rivers favored by fishermen include the Gasconade, Little Piney, Meramec, and White.

Lake of the Ozarks, Missouri's largest lake, is man-made. It provides a popular recreation area in the heart of the scenic Ozarks.

Missouri Division of Commerce

MISSOURI

Lake of the Ozarks, a man-made lake, is the largest lake in the state. It stretches snakelike through the heart of the scenic Ozarks. Lake of the Ozarks has a shoreline of more than 1,300 miles, and covers about 60,000 acres. It is a popular recreation area. Other important man-made lakes include Bull Shoals, Pomme de Terre, Table Rock, and Taneycomo.

Springs and Caves. About 10,000 springs bubble from the ground in the Ozark Plateau. More than a hundred springs have a daily water flow of over a million gallons each. The largest is Big Spring, near Van Buren. It has an average flow of about 278 million gallons of water a day. In addition to its fresh-water springs, Missouri has about 30 mineral springs.

More than 1,450 caves have been found in Missouri. Underground streams formed these caves beneath the Ozarks. One of the largest caves, Marvel Cave, is near Branson. An underground railroad winds through its 10 miles of passageways. Every year, about 20 marriages are performed in Bridal Cave, near Camdenton.

Jack Zehrt, Publix

The Mighty Mississippi River forms the eastern border of the state. Old-time stern-wheel boats still carry crowds on sightseeing trips.

Big Spring, largest in the state, is near Van Buren. Many springs feed the clear lakes and swift rivers of Missouri's Ozark Plateau.

Jack Zehrt, Publix

Rich Farmland covers the Mississippi Alluvial Plain. This region was once useless swampland.

Jack Zehrt, Publix

Missouri Division of Commerce

Fields of Wheat, such as these near Clinton, spread across the Osage Plains region in western Missouri.

MISSOURI/*Climate*

Both winters and summers are milder in the mountain areas of Missouri than in the lower-lying plains farther north. In July, average temperatures range from about 81° F. in the Boot Heel section to about 79° F. in the north and in areas of highest elevation. The state's record high temperature is 118° F. It was set at Clinton on July 15, 1936; at Lamar on July 18, 1936; and at Union and Warsaw on July 14, 1954.

Average January temperatures vary from 29° F. in the north to about 38° F. in the Boot Heel. Missouri's record low temperature of −40° F. was set at Warsaw on Feb. 13, 1905. The state's average yearly *precipitation* (rain, melted snow, and other forms of moisture) ranges from about 50 inches in the southeast to about 30 inches in the northwest. Snowfall averages from about 8 to 12 inches a year in the southernmost counties to 18 to 22 inches north of the Missouri River. The growing season ranges from 225 days in the southeast to about 170 days in the north.

Country Scene near Gray Summit shows the natural beauty made possible by Missouri's mild temperatures and ample rainfall.

John H. Gerard

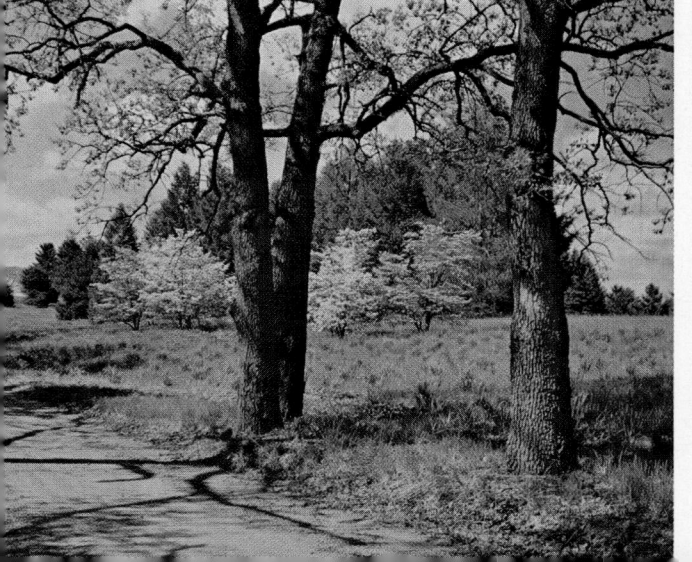

SEASONAL TEMPERATURES

JANUARY

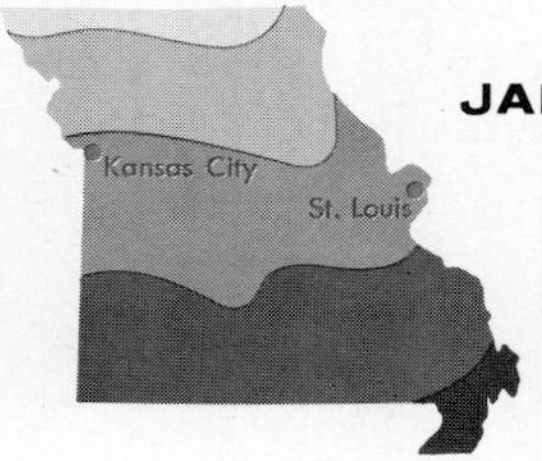
AVERAGE OF DAILY LOW TEMPERATURES
Degrees Centigrade
Degrees Fahrenheit
-2 to 0
28 to 32
-4 to -2
24 to 28
-7 to -4
20 to 24
-9 to -7
16 to 20
-11 to -9
12 to 16
Kansas City
St. Louis

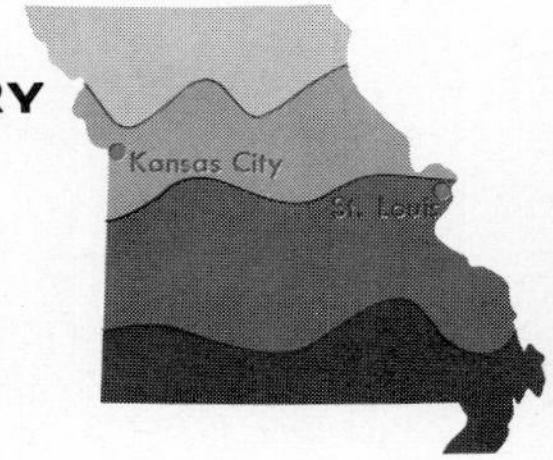
AVERAGE OF DAILY HIGH TEMPERATURES
Degrees Fahrenheit
Degrees Centigrade
46 to 50
8 to 10
42 to 46
6 to 8
38 to 42
3 to 6
34 to 38
1 to 3
Kansas City
St. Louis

JULY

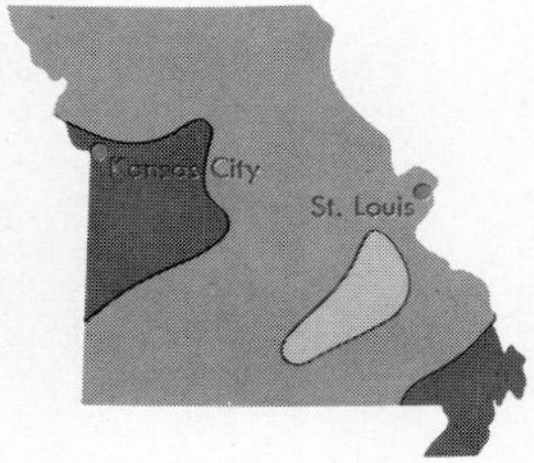
AVERAGE OF DAILY LOW TEMPERATURES
Degrees Centigrade
Degrees Fahrenheit
20 to 22
68 to 72
18 to 20
64 to 68
16 to 18
60 to 64
Kansas City
St. Louis

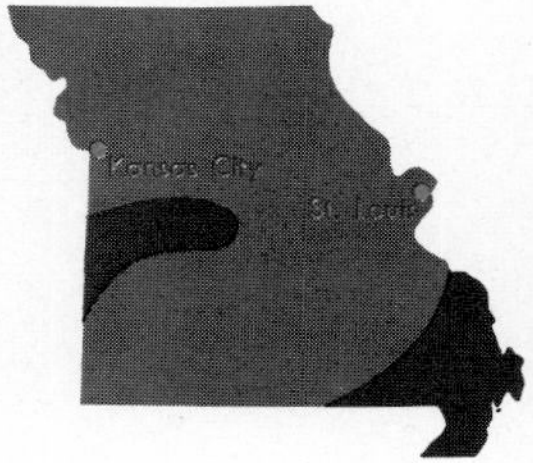
AVERAGE OF DAILY HIGH TEMPERATURES
Degrees Fahrenheit
Degrees Centigrade
92 to 94
33 to 34
90 to 92
32 to 33
Kansas City
St. Louis

AVERAGE YEARLY PRECIPITATION

(Rain, Melted Snow, and Other Moisture)

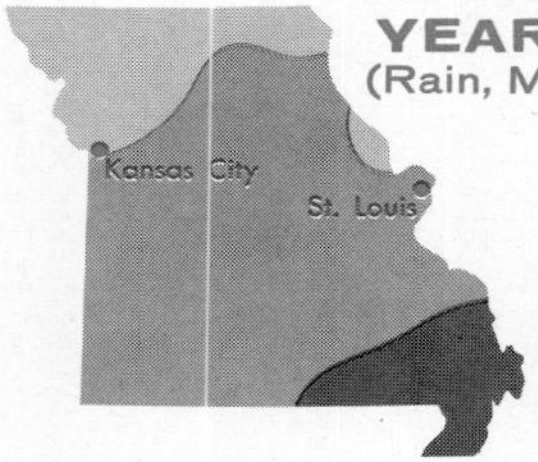
Inches
Centimeters
44 to 52
112 to 132
36 to 44
91 to 112
28 to 36
71 to 91
Kansas City
St. Louis
0 50 100 200 Miles
0 100 200 300 Kilometers

WORLD BOOK maps

MONTHLY WEATHER IN KANSAS CITY AND ST. LOUIS

	JAN	FEB	MAR	APR	MAY	JUNE	JULY	AUG	SEPT	OCT	NOV	DEC	Average of:
KANSAS CITY	39	44	54	66	75	85	91	89	81	70	54	42	High Temperatures
	21	25	34	46	56	66	71	69	60	49	35	25	Low Temperatures
	7	7	9	11	12	11	8	9	7	7	6	7	Days of Rain or Snow
ST. LOUIS	9	9	11	12	12	11	8	8	7	7	8	9	Days of Rain or Snow
	41	45	54	66	75	85	90	88	80	70	54	44	High Temperatures
	26	29	37	47	57	67	72	70	62	52	38	29	Low Temperatures

Temperatures are given in degrees Fahrenheit.

Source: U.S. Weather Bureau

Natural Resources

Natural Resources of Missouri include fertile soils, large mineral deposits, dense forests, and abundant plant and animal life.

Soil. The soils of the Dissected Till Plains are mainly glacial soils (clay mixed with sand and gravel) and *loess* (a brownish wind-blown dust). A band of rich loess, usually more than 50 feet deep, lies along the Missouri River. The Osage Plains have soils of medium fertility, ranging from dark-brown loam to lighter-colored sandy or silt loams.

Brown limestone soils cover most of the southwestern part of the Ozarks. Elsewhere in the Ozarks, the soils are shallow and stony. The Mississippi River has deposited highly productive soils on the Mississippi Alluvial Plain. There are also about 714,000 acres of rich alluvial soil along the Missouri River.

Minerals. The state's most important metal is lead. It is produced chiefly in Crawford, Iron, Reynolds, St. Francois, and Washington counties. Large clay deposits occur across central Missouri. One of the nation's most important barite reserves lies south of St. Louis. Limestone, Missouri's leading quarry product, is found throughout most of the state. Miners take most of Missouri's dolomite limestone from the eastern Ozarks. Marble is quarried in southwestern Missouri. Other important quarry products include granite and sandstone.

Coal is found in more than 50 counties stretching across the state from the southwest to the northeast. Missouri's coal reserves total about 45 billion tons. The state has iron deposits, chiefly in the Ozark Plateau. Production of iron ore from newly discovered high-grade reserves began in 1964 in Washington County. In the 1960's, mining companies discovered several other extensive deposits of iron ore in the eastern Ozarks. Missouri also has small amounts of oil and natural gas along its western border. Other minerals include asphalt, cobalt, copper, silver, and zinc.

Forests. Commercially important forests cover about a third of the state, chiefly in the Ozarks. Missouri's forests are largely hardwoods. About two-thirds of the forests are of various types of oak or hickory. The state also has large growths of ash, bald cypress, cottonwood, elm, maple, shortleaf pine, and sweet gum.

Other Plant Life. Plants that grow throughout Missouri include asters, dogwood, goldenrod, milkweed, roses, sweet Williams, verbenas, violets, and many kinds of mint and hawthorn. Mistletoe grows on many trees on the Mississippi Alluvial Plain. The Ozarks probably have more flowers than any region in the state.

Animal Life. White-tailed deer are the most numerous of Missouri's big-game animals. Other animals include beavers, cottontail rabbits, foxes, muskrats, opossums, raccoons, skunks, and squirrels. Bobwhite quail are Missouri's most plentiful game bird. Fish include bass, bluegills, catfish, crappies, jack salmon, and trout.

Manufacturing accounts for over three-fourths of the value of all goods produced in Missouri. Goods manufactured in the state have a *value added by manufacture* of about $5,891,000,000 a year. This figure represents the value created in products by Missouri's industries, not counting such costs as materials, sup-

plies, and fuel. About two-thirds of the state's more than 6,000 factories are in Kansas City and St. Louis.

Transportation Equipment from Missouri has a value added of about $1,234,000,000 a year. Factories in St. Louis and Kansas City produce airplanes, railroad cars, truck and bus bodies, and truck trailers. Missouri ranks high in automobile production. There are large automobile assembly plants in St. Louis and Kansas City. Missouri is also a leading state in the aerospace industry. The Mercury capsules in which U.S. astronauts orbited the earth were made in St. Louis. St. Louis also manufactures the two-man Gemini spaceship and the Phantom II supersonic fighter plane. Engines for missiles and rockets are built in Neosho.

Processed Food has a yearly value added of $804,400,-000. Slaughtering and meat-packing plants are centered in Kansas City, St. Louis, and St. Joseph. The nation's largest dairy-processing plant is in Springfield. It handles about a million pounds of milk a day. Missouri ranks high among the states in the production of butter and cheddar cheese. St. Louis is a leading beer-brewing center. Kansas City, in the heart of the U.S. winter-wheat belt, has large flour mills. The nation's largest pancake-flour factory is in St. Joseph.

Chemicals and Related Products. Most of Missouri's chemical plants are in St. Louis and Kansas City. They

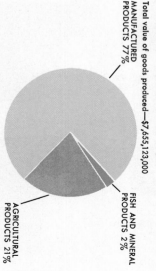

turn out agricultural chemicals, drugs, insecticides, lubricants, medicines, paints, and many other products. The state produces chemicals and related products with a value added of about $545,600,000 a year.

Other Important Industries in Missouri include clothing, electrical machinery, metal products, nonelectrical machinery, primary metals, and printing and publishing.

St. Louis and Kansas City have iron smelters, and lead smelters operate in Joplin and Herculaneum. Workers in Joplin process zinc. The city of Mexico has the nation's largest refractory brick factory. Festus-Crystal City is the site of one of the country's largest plate-glass factories.

Agriculture. Missouri is one of the nation's leading agricultural states. Its yearly farm income is $1,574,000,000. This amount is about a fifth of the value of all goods produced in the state. Missouri has about 147,000 farms. The average farm covers about 222 acres. Missouri has about 32,692,000 acres in farmland. Most Missouri farms support only the owner and his family. Farms in the northern part of the state usually have a greater gross income than other farms in Missouri.

Field Crops. Soybeans rank as Missouri's leading crop. Corn ranks second. Soybeans are raised throughout the northern third of Missouri and in the southeastern corner. Farmers plant about a third of their cropland in corn. Corn is grown mainly in northwestern Missouri. Wheat and cotton are the state's third and fourth most important crops. Barley, grain sorghum, greenhouse nursery products, hay, oats, popcorn, rice, rye, seed crops, and tobacco are also important crops of Missouri farms.

Fruits and Vegetables. Farmers throughout the state grow apples. The biggest orchards are along the bluffs

of the Mississippi and Missouri rivers and in the Ozark Plateau. Missouri stands high among the states in the production of watermelons, which are raised chiefly in the southeast. The state also ranks high in the production of dewberries and blackberries. Other fruits include cherries, grapes, peaches, pears, and plums. Farmers in southeastern Missouri produce most of the state's commercial vegetables.

Livestock. Missouri ranks high among the states in the number of beef cattle and dairy cows. The raising of beef cattle and hogs is profitable because of the abundance of corn, small grains, and hay. Sheep graze in the northern and western parts of the state. Missouri is an important state in poultry production, with over 40½ million chicks hatched every year. The state's farmers also raise about 20 million chickens, ducks, geese, and turkeys annually.

Farmers throughout the state raise horses. Missouri was once famous for its mules, and the state was the nation's leading mule producer. Missouri mules—strong, smart, and tireless—did much of the work on farms before World War II. Since then, machinery has largely replaced them.

Mining accounts for about 2 per cent, or about $189,200,000, of the value of goods produced in Missouri each year. Missouri ranks first in the nation in lead production. Miners take about 153,000 tons of lead annually from mines in the state. More than 2 million tons of clay and over 330,000 tons of barite come from Missouri mines each year.

Missouri's main quarrying region is in the Ozarks. Quarries there produce about 35½ million tons of limestone annually. Sand and gravel production totals about 10 million tons a year.

About 98 per cent of Missouri's coal comes from open-

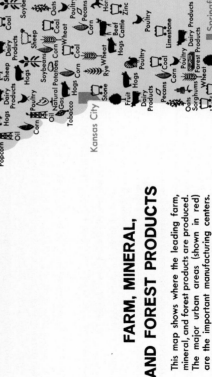

St. Louis

Springfield

Kansas City

100 Miles
50 100 150 Kilometers
0 50

FARM, MINERAL, AND FOREST PRODUCTS

This map shows where the leading farm, mineral, and forest products are produced. The major urban areas (shown in red) are the important manufacturing centers.

WORLD BOOK map

556e

pit mines. The leading coal-producing counties are Boone, Henry, Macon, Putnam, and Vernon. Iron ore also ranks high in Missouri's mineral production. The state produces small amounts of asphalt, copper, natural gas, oil, and zinc.

Electric Power. Steam plants generate about 90 per cent of Missouri's electric power. The Ozark Plateau has several large hydroelectric installations. The power plant at Bagnell Dam generates electricity mainly for the St. Louis area.

The Taum Sauk Project near Lesterville is the largest pumped-storage hydroelectric plant in the United States. The plant stores and uses the same supply of water over and over again. The water is pumped from a lower reservoir to a higher one. When the water is released from the upper reservoir and flows to the lower one, its flow is used to generate electricity. The Taum Sauk Project, completed in 1963, has a capacity of 350,-000 kilowatts. For the state's kilowatt-hour production, see ELECTRIC POWER (table).

Transportation. Missouri's central location, its nearness to raw materials, and the great Mississippi and Missouri waterways have made Kansas City and St. Louis leading transportation centers.

Missouri has more than 270 airports. Lambert-St. Louis Municipal Airport in St. Louis and the Kansas City Municipal Airport are among the busiest in the country. The Kansas City International Airport is another important airport in the state.

Railroads operate on about 7,500 miles of track in

MISSOURI/History

Indian Days. Indians known as Mound Builders lived in the Missouri region long before white men came there. The Indians built large earthwork mounds that still may be seen in various sections of the state (see MOUND BUILDERS). Many tribes of Indians lived in Missouri when the white man first arrived. The Missouri Indians dwelt in what is now east-central Missouri. The Osage, a tribe of unusually tall Indians, lived and hunted in the areas to the south and west. Other tribes included the Fox and the Sauk Indians, who lived in

Missouri, Kansas City and St. Louis are among the most important U.S. railroad centers.

Missouri has about 115,000 miles of roads and highways. Over 90 per cent of them are surfaced. The first land traffic in Missouri followed old Indian trails. In 1860 and 1861, St. Joseph was the eastern terminal of the pony express mail system. The famous Oregon and Santa Fe trails ran from Independence.

Boats and barges can use the Mississippi River for 490 miles along the state's eastern border. The Missouri River has a navigable channel throughout its course in Missouri. River barges on the Missouri and Mississippi rivers carry much heavy freight.

Communication. Two famous Missouri journalists made newspaper history. They founded the state's leading papers and influenced journalism across the country. William Rockhill Nelson, founder of the *Kansas City Star*, was a crusading editor who fought for government reform. Joseph Pulitzer, who founded the *St. Louis Post-Dispatch*, established the Pulitzer prizes (see PULITZER PRIZES).

The first Missouri newspaper, the *Missouri Gazette*, began publication in St. Louis in 1808. Today, Missouri has more than 50 daily newspapers and about 330 weeklies. Newspapers with the largest daily circulations include the *Kansas City Star*, the *Kansas City Times*, the *St. Louis Globe-Democrat*, and the *St. Louis Post-Dispatch*. Missouri publishers also issue more than 200 periodicals. Firms in St. Louis and Kansas City publish textbooks.

The first radio station in Missouri, WEW of St. Louis University, began broadcasting in 1921. The state's first TV station, KSD-TV, started in 1947 in St. Louis. There are now 129 radio stations and 17 TV stations.

the north. See INDIAN, AMERICAN (table: Indian Tribes).

Exploration and Settlement. The daring French explorers Father Jacques Marquette and Louis Joliet were probably the first white men to see the mouth of the Missouri River. In 1673, they marked the spot where the Missouri joins the Mississippi. In 1682, another French explorer, Robert Cavelier, Sieur de la Salle, traveled down the Mississippi River and claimed the Mississippi Valley for France. La Salle named the region *Louisiana* in honor of King Louis XIV.

IMPORTANT DATES IN MISSOURI

1673 Father Jacques Marquette and Louis Joliet discovered the mouth of the Missouri River.

1682 Robert Cavelier, Sieur de la Salle, claimed the Mississippi Valley, including Missouri, for France. He named the region *Louisiana*.

c. 1735 Settlers from what is now Illinois established Missouri's first permanent white settlement, at Ste. Genevieve.

1762 France gave the Louisiana region to Spain.

1764 Pierre Laclède Liguest and René Auguste Chouteau established St. Louis.

1800 Spain returned the Louisiana region to France.

1803 France sold the Louisiana region to the U.S.

1812 Congress made Missouri a territory.

1815 Indian attacks on Missouri settlements ended when the Indians and United States government officials signed a peace treaty at Portage des Sioux.

1821 Missouri became the 24th state on August 10.

1837 Missouri gained its six northwestern counties as a result of the Platte Purchase.

1854 Border warfare began between antislavery Kansans and proslavery Missourians.

1861-1865 Missouri became a battleground during the Civil War.

1904 The Louisiana Purchase Centennial Exposition was held in St. Louis.

1931 Bagnell Dam on the Osage River was completed, forming the 60,000-acre Lake of the Ozarks.

1945 Harry S. Truman of Independence became the 33rd President of the United States.

1965 The last section of the 630-foot-high stainless steel Gateway Arch, the nation's tallest monument, was put in place in St. Louis.

HISTORIC MISSOURI

Harry S. Truman born in Lamar

The Missouri Compromise, passed by Congress in 1820, brought Missouri into the Union the next year as a slave state.

The Dred Scott Decision was made by the Supreme Court of the United States in 1857. It prevented the Missouri slave, Dred Scott, from gaining his freedom, and was one of the events that led to the Civil War.

Mark Twain grew up in Hannibal

• Hannibal

The Pony Express linked St. Joseph, Mo., and Sacramento, Calif., in 1860. Riders covered the 1,966 miles in 8 to 9 days. The Pony Express operated for 18 months.

• St. Joseph

Lewis and Clark started their famous journey from near St. Louis to the Pacific Northwest in 1804. They gave the United States a strong claim to the great Oregon region.

• St. Louis

St. Louis was founded in 1764 by Pierre Laclède Liguest, a French fur trader. The city's location near where the Mississippi and Missouri rivers meet has made it a great transportation center.

• Ste. Genevieve

The Lead Mines near Ste. Genevieve have been worked since about 1720. Ste. Genevieve was the first permanent settlement in the Missouri region.

★ JEFFERSON CITY

• Independence

Independence, where the Oregon and Santa Fe trails began, became the "Gateway to the West" for pioneers in the mid-1800's.

• Lamar

Jesse James, one of the nation's most dangerous bandits, terrorized Missouri for about 16 years following the Civil War. He was born near Centerville (now Kearney).

The Great Mississippi Steamboat Race, in 1870, ended with the victory of the *Robert E. Lee* over the *Natchez.* The historic three-day race between New Orleans and St. Louis was close until the *Natchez* got lost in fog near Cairo, Ill.

MISSOURI

During the years that followed, French trappers and fur traders established trading posts along the river. French missionaries, eager to convert the Indians, founded a number of missions. Indian tales of gold and silver attracted other Frenchmen. These adventurers found lead and salt in what is now St. Francois County and remained to mine these minerals. About 1700, Jesuit missionaries established the first white settlement in Missouri, the Mission of St. Francis Xavier. They built it near the present site of St. Louis. The mission was abandoned in 1703 because of unhealthful swamps nearby. About 1735, settlers from what is now Illinois established Missouri's first permanent white settlement, at Ste. Genevieve. In 1764, Pierre Laclède Liguest and René Auguste Chouteau founded St. Louis.

By a secret treaty, signed in 1762, France gave up all its territory west of the Mississippi River to Spain. France and Spain had been allies in the Seven Years' War (see SEVEN YEARS' WAR). The Spaniards encouraged pioneers from the East to come to the region, and settlers poured into the Spanish land. One of the pioneers was Daniel Boone, the famous frontiersman. He moved to what is now St. Charles County in 1799, after the Spanish had granted him about 800 acres of land. In 1800, the Spanish appointed Boone a *syndic*, or judge (see BOONE, DANIEL).

Napoleon Bonaparte, the ruler of France, forced Spain to return the territory west of the Mississippi to France in 1800. By that time, much of present-day Missouri had been explored and many communities had been established. Napoleon, badly in need of money to finance his wars in Europe, sold the Louisiana Territory to the United States in 1803 (see LOUISIANA PURCHASE). The northern part of the territory was called Upper Louisiana, and included the present state of Missouri. Upper Louisiana extended northward from the 33rd parallel to Canada, and westward to the Rocky Mountains. In 1812, Congress organized the Missouri Territory.

Territorial Days. The Missouri Territory began with a population of more than 20,000. The farming and mining industries were well established, and schools and

churches had been built. So many settlers poured into the territory that the Indians became aroused by the loss of their ancient hunting grounds. For several years, the Indians led frequent, bloody raids on the frontier settlements.

In 1812, war broke out between the United States and Great Britain (see WAR OF 1812). The British gave weapons to the Indians and encouraged them to attack the Missouri pioneers. The settlers built forts and blockhouses for protection. Even after the war between the United States and Britain ended, the Indians continued to raid many settlements. The attacks ended in 1815, when the Indians and U.S. government officials signed a peace treaty at Portage des Sioux.

Statehood and Expansion. In 1818, Missouri asked Congress to be admitted into the Union. The territory had been settled mainly by Southerners who had brought Negro slaves with them. Missouri's application for admission as a slave state caused a nationwide dispute between slavery and antislavery sympathizers. This dispute was not settled until 1820, when Congress passed the Missouri Compromise. Under this legislation, Missouri entered the Union as a slave state on Aug. 10, 1821 (see MISSOURI COMPROMISE). A census taken in 1820 showed that the territory had 66,586 persons, including 10,222 slaves. Missourians elected Alexander McNair as the first governor of the state.

When Missouri entered the Union, it was the western frontier of the nation. The fur trade was the state's most important industry. In 1822, John Jacob Astor organized a St. Louis branch of the American Fur Company. Within the next 12 years, Astor ruined or bought out most other fur companies. He had a near monopoly on the fur trade west of the Mississippi River.

In 1836, Congress approved the purchase from the Indians of an area known as the Platte Country. By presidential proclamation, it became part of Missouri in 1837. This region extended the northern part of Missouri's western border to the Missouri River.

Since the 1820's, Missourians had been carrying on a regular trade with Mexicans over the Santa Fe Trail. This famous trail linked Independence, Mo., with Santa Fe in the Southwest. Tremendous wealth from the Southwest poured into Missouri, and Independence became a busy, thriving village. The great Oregon

The Santa Fe Trail and the Oregon Trail played important roles in the history of Missouri during the early 1800's. Both trails ran from Independence. This mural shows Independence as a village during the years when it was the starting point of the

Trail, which thousands of settlers followed to the Northwest, also began in Independence. See SANTA FE TRAIL; OREGON TRAIL.

The Civil War. In 1857, the Supreme Court of the United States issued the historic Dred Scott Decision. The court ruled that Scott, a Missouri slave, was merely property and did not have citizenship rights. The ruling greatly increased ill feeling between the North and the South (see DRED SCOTT DECISION). Meanwhile, many Missourians who lived near the western border of the state feared that the newly organized Kansas Territory would become a free state. As more and more antislavery families settled in Kansas, scattered warfare broke out between Missourians and Kansans (see BROWN, JOHN; KANSAS ["Bleeding Kansas"]). Kansas became a free state in 1861. Fighting between Kansans and Missourians continued into the Civil War.

Missouri became the center of national interest in 1861. The nation wondered whether Missouri would *secede* (withdraw) from the Union and join the Confederacy. Early in 1861, Governor Claiborne F. Jackson recommended that a state convention be called to determine the will of the people. The convention was held in February and March. Jackson and some members of the convention were strongly pro-South, but the convention voted to remain in the Union. Most Missourians wanted to stay neutral if war should come.

After the Civil War began in April, 1861, President Abraham Lincoln called for troops from Missouri. Governor Jackson refused Lincoln's call. Union soldiers and the Missouri state militia, which Jackson commanded as governor, clashed at Boonville on June 17, 1861. This battle was the first real fighting of the Civil War in Missouri. The Union troops, under General Nathaniel Lyon, routed the militiamen and gained control of northern Missouri. Jackson and his militiamen retreated to southwestern Missouri, where they reorganized their forces. They then advanced to Wilson's Creek, near Springfield. There, in August, the militiamen defeated the Union forces in a bloody battle.

On July 22, the state convention had met again. It voted to remove pro-Confederate state leaders from office. The convention replaced them with pro-Union men. Hamilton R. Gamble became governor. In September, 1861, Jackson called for the legislature to meet

in Neosho in October. Not enough members attended to hold a legal session. But those present voted to secede from the Union and join the Confederacy.

The Confederate forces controlled a foothold in southwestern Missouri until March, 1862, when Union forces defeated them at Pea Ridge, Ark. In 1864, General Sterling Price tried to recapture Missouri for the South in a daring raid. He was defeated at Westport, which is a part of present-day Kansas City. Price's defeat marked the end of full-scale fighting in the state. Throughout the war, however, bands of both Union and Confederate guerrillas terrorized the countryside. They burned and looted towns and murdered innocent people.

After the war ended in 1865, Missouri adopted a new constitution. It included a clause that denied the right to vote to anyone who refused to swear that he had not sympathized with the South. This unpopular clause was repealed in 1870.

Progress as a State. Between 1850 and 1870, big changes took place in Missouri. St. Louis and Kansas City became important transportation centers. The frontier disappeared. Trade with Mexico over the Santa Fe Trail ended. The fur trade grew less important, although St. Louis remained one of the world's great fur markets. Tenant farmers replaced the relatively few slaves who worked the fields.

In 1875, Missouri adopted a new constitution. It reestablished the governor's term from two to four years. It also established a state railroad commission to regulate rates and shipping conditions.

For almost 20 years after the Civil War, many former Confederate guerrillas turned to crime. They held up banks, stagecoaches, and trains. In 1881, Governor Thomas T. Crittenden began a campaign to stop the outlaws. He offered a $5,000 reward for the arrest of Jesse James, one of the most notorious bandits. James was killed by one of his own gang in 1882.

The Louisiana Purchase Centennial Exposition was held in St. Louis in 1904. This world's fair attracted almost 20 million visitors from the United States and other countries. A popular exhibit featured automobiles. One of the automobiles had been driven all the way

Oregon Trail to the Northwest. The mural, painted by Thomas Hart Benton, is in the Harry S. Truman Library in Independence.
Independence And The Opening of The West mural by Thomas Hart Benton, Harry S. Truman Library, Independence, Mo.

trails. The Santa Fe Trail brought Missouri great wealth from Mexico and the Southwest. Thousands of settlers followed the

Jefferson National Expansion Memorial in St. Louis is a vast project that includes the 630-foot-high Gateway Arch. The stainless steel arch was completed in 1965.

Missouri Division of Commerce

THE GOVERNORS OF MISSOURI

	Party	Term			Party	Term
1. Alexander McNair	*Dem.-Rep.	1820-1824		24. Thomas T. Crittenden	Democratic	1881-1885
2. Frederick Bates	*Dem.-Rep.	1824-1825		25. John S. Marmaduke	Democratic	1885-1887
3. Abraham J. Williams	*Dem.-Rep.	1825-1826		26. Albert P. Morehouse	Democratic	1887-1889
4. John Miller	*Dem.-Rep.	1826-1832		27. David R. Francis	Democratic	1889-1893
5. Daniel Dunklin	Democratic	1832-1836		28. William Joel Stone	Democratic	1893-1897
6. Lilburn W. Boggs	Democratic	1836-1840		29. Lon V. Stephens	Democratic	1897-1901
7. Thomas Reynolds	Democratic	1840-1844		30. Alexander M. Dockery	Democratic	1901-1905
8. Meredith M. Marmaduke	Democratic	1844		31. Joseph W. Folk	Democratic	1905-1909
9. John C. Edwards	Democratic	1844-1848		32. Herbert S. Hadley	Republican	1909-1913
10. Austin A. King	Democratic	1848-1853		33. Elliott W. Major	Democratic	1913-1917
11. Sterling Price	Democratic	1853-1857		34. Frederick D. Gardner	Democratic	1917-1921
12. Trusten Polk	Democratic	1857		35. Arthur M. Hyde	Republican	1921-1925
13. Hancock Lee Jackson	Democratic	1857		36. Sam A. Baker	Republican	1925-1929
14. Robert M. Stewart	Democratic	1857-1861		37. Henry S. Caulfield	Republican	1929-1933
15. Claiborne F. Jackson	Democratic	1861		38. Guy B. Park	Democratic	1933-1937
16. Hamilton R. Gamble	Union	1861-1864		39. Lloyd C. Stark	Democratic	1937-1941
17. Willard P. Hall	Union	1864-1865		40. Forrest C. Donnell	Republican	1941-1945
18. Thomas C. Fletcher	Republican	1865-1869		41. Phil M. Donnelly	Democratic	1945-1949
19. Joseph W. McClurg	Republican	1869-1871		42. Forrest Smith	Democratic	1949-1953
20. B. Gratz Brown	†Lib. Rep.	1871-1873		43. Phil M. Donnelly	Democratic	1953-1957
21. Silas Woodson	Democratic	1873-1875		44. James T. Blair, Jr.	Democratic	1957-1961
22. Charles H. Hardin	Democratic	1875-1877		45. John M. Dalton	Democratic	1961-1965
23. John S. Phelps	Democratic	1877-1881		46. Warren E. Hearnes	Democratic	1965-

*Democratic-Republican

†Liberal Republican

from New York City to St. Louis under its own power.

In 1905, Governor Joseph W. Folk began one of the state's most progressive administrations. Under his leadership, Missouri adopted state-wide primary elections and began political, social, and industrial reforms. Laws were passed calling for the inspection of factory working conditions. Other new laws regulated child labor and public utilities.

After the United States entered World War I in 1917, Missouri's mining, manufacturing, and agriculture expanded to supply the demands of the armed forces. General John J. Pershing, who was born in Linn County, became commander in chief of the U.S. forces in France. General Enoch H. Crowder, who was born in Grundy County, was named the first director of the Selective Service System.

Bagnell Dam, an important source of electric power for the St. Louis area, was completed in 1931. The waters held back by the dam formed Missouri's great man-made lake, Lake of the Ozarks. Many Missourians lost their jobs during the Great Depression of the 1930's, and farmers suffered because of low prices. Under Gov-

ernor Guy B. Park, the number of state government employees was cut and operating costs of government were reduced. The federal government set up several agencies in Missouri to provide employment and relief.

The Mid-1900's. During World War II (1939-1945), many new industries were developed in Missouri to provide supplies for the armed forces. In 1944, U.S. Senator Harry S. Truman of Independence was elected Vice-President. He became President after President Franklin D. Roosevelt died in 1945. Truman was elected to a full term as President in 1948.

New industrial plants boosted Missouri's economy during the 1950's. An electronics plant opened in Joplin, and factories in St. Louis and Neosho began producing parts for spacecraft. A uranium-processing plant went into operation in Weldon Spring.

During the 1960's, Missouri conducted a vigorous drive to attract more new industries. The state also encouraged tourism, which became a $500-million business annually. The mining industry expanded during the 1960's with the discovery of new iron ore deposits in Crawford, Dent, Franklin, Iron, and Washington counties.

By the early 1960's, most public schools in Missouri were desegregated. The state constitution had provided for segregated schools. But in 1954, the Supreme Court of the United States ruled that compulsory segregation of public schools was unconstitutional.

Missouri Today. Missouri faces serious problems in the 1970's. The state needs more money for education, health and welfare programs, and new highways. In 1969, the General Assembly increased personal and corporate income taxes. But in a special election in 1970, Missouri voters defeated the increases.

Urban problems have become increasingly serious in Missouri. In St. Louis, for example, about half the population is Negro, partly because many middle-class white families have moved to the suburbs. This population shift has drained the city of much financial support. To a lesser extent, this has also been happening in Kansas City. Inadequate transportation and an increase in crime have added to the problems of Missouri's cities.

In spite of its many problems, Missouri entered the 1970's relatively strong economically. The state's farms are continuing to produce large quantities of corn, cotton, livestock, soybeans, and wheat. Each year, Missouri spends increasingly more money for agricultural research. St. Louis, Kansas City, and many smaller cities annually report many new and expanded factories. The aerospace industry continues to thrive. Many

firms, especially smaller companies, are relocating in smaller towns, where they can recruit workers from nearby farms. Iron ore reserves remain plentiful in Missouri. Tourism continues to grow and is expected to become a billion-dollar industry during the 1970's.

JAMES E. COLLIER, LEW LARKIN, and WILLIAM E. PARRISH

MISSOURI/Study Aids

Related Articles in WORLD BOOK include:

BIOGRAPHIES

Ashley, William H.
Atchison, David R.
Benton, Thomas Hart (senator)
Benton, Thomas Hart (painter)
Blair (Francis P., Jr.)
Bland, Richard P.
Brown, Benjamin Gratz
Carver, George Washington
Chouteau (family)
Field, Eugene
James, Jesse W.
Nelson, William R.
Pulitzer, Joseph
Robidoux (brothers)
Symington, Stuart
Truman, Harry S.
Twain, Mark

CITIES

Cape Girardeau
Columbia
Hannibal
Independence
Jefferson City
Joplin
Kansas City
Saint Joseph
Saint Louis
Sedalia
Springfield
University City

HISTORY

Civil War
Dred Scott Decision
Latter Day Saints, Reorganized Church of Jesus Christ of
Lewis and Clark Expedition
Louisiana Purchase
Missouri Compromise
Pony Express
Sante Fe Trail
Western Frontier Life

PHYSICAL FEATURES

Lake of the Ozarks
Mississippi River
Missouri River
Ozark Mountains
White River

PRODUCTS

For Missouri's rank among the states in production, see the following articles:

Agriculture
Automobile
Cattle
Cheese
Corn
Hog
Horse
Lead
Leather
Publishing
Soybean
Turkey

OTHER RELATED ARTICLES

Bagnell Dam
Clearwater Dam
Eads Bridge
Fort Leonard Wood
George Washington Carver National Monument
Memorial (picture: The Memorial Madonna)
Midwestern States
Osage Indians

Outline

I. Government
A. Constitution
B. Executive
C. Legislature
D. Courts
E. Local Government
F. Taxation
G. Politics

II. People

III. Education
A. Schools
B. Libraries
C. Museums

IV. A Visitor's Guide
A. Places to Visit
B. Annual Events

V. The Land
A. Land Regions
B. Rivers and Lakes
C. Springs and Caves

VI. Climate

VII. Economy
A. Natural Resources
B. Manufacturing
C. Agriculture
D. Mining
E. Electric Power
F. Transportation
G. Communication

VIII. History

Questions

From which Missouri city did the famous Santa Fe and Oregon trails run?

What is Missouri's leading crop?

Which political party has been the stronger in Missouri's history?

To what two rivers does Missouri owe much of its commercial and industrial importance?

Why is Missouri sometimes called the *Mother of the West?* Why was it nicknamed the *Show Me State?*

What are Missouri's three most important manufactured products?

Missouri leads all states in producing what metal?

Why did Missouri become a transportation center?

What was the Missouri Compromise? The Dred Scott Decision?

Why did Missouri become the center of national interest in 1861?

Books for Young Readers

BAKER, NINA B. *Boy for a Man's Job: The Story of the Founding of St. Louis.* Winston, 1952.

BURRESS, JOHN. *Punkin Summer.* Vanguard, 1957. Three generations of a family share happy days in a small Missouri town.

KARSCH, ROBERT. *Missouri Under the Constitution.* Rev. ed. Lucas, 1968.

KEITH, HAROLD. *Rifles for Watie.* Crowell, 1957. This Newbery medal winner tells the story of a teen-age recruit during the Civil War.

MEYER, FRANKLYN E. *Me and Caleb.* Follett, 1962. The escapades of two Missouri brothers.

PEARE, CATHERINE O. *Mark Twain, His Life.* Holt, 1954.

SAVELAND, ROBERT N. *Geography of Missouri: A Story of the People and the Regions of the Show Me State.* State Publishing Co., St. Louis, 1954.

Books for Older Readers

AMERICAN HERITAGE. *Steamboats on the Mississippi.* Meredith, 1962.

BATTAGLIA, ELIO L. *The Face of Missouri.* Univ. of Missouri Press, 1960.

ERDMAN, LOULA G. *Life Was Simpler Then.* Dodd, 1963. Life on a Missouri farm 50 years ago.

HECKMAN, WILLIAM L. *Steamboating: Sixty-Five Years on Missouri's Rivers.* Burton, 1950.

McREYNOLDS, EDWIN C. *Missouri: A History of the Crossroads State.* Univ. of Oklahoma Press, 1962.

MEYER, DUANE. *The Heritage of Missouri.* State Publ. Co., St. Louis, 1963.

MIERS, EARL S. *Mark Twain on the Mississippi.* World, 1957. This account is based on fact and describes the early life of Twain.

Missouri: A Guide to the Show Me State. Rev. ed. Hastings, 1954.

MISSOURI, UNIVERSITY OF,

MISSOURI, UNIVERSITY OF, is a coeducational state university with campuses in Columbia, Kansas City, Rolla, and St. Louis, Mo. Founded in 1839 in Columbia, it is the oldest state university west of the Mississippi River. For enrollment, see UNIVERSITIES AND COLLEGES (table).

The University of Missouri at Columbia campus grants degrees in agriculture, arts and science, business and public administration, education, engineering, forestry, home economics, journalism, law, library science, medicine, nursing, social and community services, and veterinary medicine. It has a graduate program and an extension division. Its school of journalism, founded in 1908, is the oldest in the world.

The University of Missouri at Rolla campus offers degrees in engineering and science. It has a graduate school. The Rolla campus was founded in 1870.

The University of Missouri at St. Louis campus grants degrees in arts and science. It was established in 1960 as a junior college and became a four-year college in 1965.

The University of Missouri at Kansas City campus grants degrees in arts and science, business and public administration, dentistry, education, law, music, and pharmacy. It was founded as the privately controlled University of Kansas City in 1933. It became part of the University of Missouri in 1963.

MISSOURI COMPROMISE.

MISSOURI COMPROMISE. In 1818, the Territory of Missouri, which had been carved out of the middle of the Louisiana Purchase, applied for admission to the Union. Slavery was legal in the territory, and about 8,000 to 10,000 slaves already lived there. Most people expected Missouri to become a slave state.

When the question arose of admitting Missouri to the Union, there were exactly as many slave states as free states. Six of the original 13 states and five new states still permitted slavery, while seven of the original states and four new states had abolished it. This meant that the free states and the slave states each had 22 senators in the United States Senate. The admission of Missouri seemed certain to break this balance.

This balance had been temporarily upset a number of times, but it had always been easy to decide whether states east of the Mississippi River should be slave or free. Mason and Dixon's Line and the Ohio River formed a natural and well-understood boundary between the two sections. No such line had been drawn west of the Mississippi River. In addition, some parts of

IRVIN F. COYLE

Missouri Territory lay to the north of the Ohio River, while other parts of it lay to the south.

A heated debate broke out in Congress when Representative James Tallmadge of New York introduced an amendment to the bill enabling Missouri to become a state. Tallmadge, although a Democrat, proposed to prohibit the bringing of any more slaves into Missouri, and to grant freedom to the children of slaves born within the state after its admission. This proposal disturbed the South, which found cotton growing by means of slave labor increasingly profitable, and feared national legislation against slavery. Because the free states dominated the House of Representatives, the South felt it must keep the even balance in the Senate.

The Tallmadge amendment passed the House, but the Senate defeated it. During the next session of Congress, Maine applied for admission to the Union. Missouri and Maine could then be accepted without upsetting the Senate's balance between free and slave states, and the Missouri Compromise became possible.

The compromise, introduced into the Senate by Jesse B. Thomas of Illinois and adopted by Congress in March, 1820, admitted Maine as a free state and authorized Missouri to form a state constitution. A territory had to have an established constitution before it could become a state. The compromise also banned slavery from the Louisiana Purchase north of the southern boundary of Missouri, the line of 36° 30' north latitude, except in the state of Missouri.

The people of Missouri felt that it was their business to decide about slavery. So they wrote into their new constitution a clause which forbade any free Negroes or mulattoes to enter the state.

Before Congress would admit Missouri, a second Missouri Compromise was necessary. This agreement, worked out in part by Henry Clay, required the Missouri legislature not to deny Negro citizens of the United States their constitutional rights. With this understanding, Missouri was admitted to the Union in 1821. Most newcomers to the state did not own slaves.

In 1848, Congress passed the Oregon Territory bill, which prohibited slavery in the area. President James K. Polk signed the bill on the grounds that the territory lay north of the Missouri Compromise line. Later proposals tried to extend the line by law across the continent to the Pacific Ocean. These efforts failed. The Missouri Compromise was repealed by the Kansas-Nebraska Act of 1854 (see KANSAS-NEBRASKA ACT).

RAY ALLEN BILLINGTON

University of Missouri

Missouri University's famous columns are its most widely-known landmark. They stand in the center of the Red Campus in Columbia, and are all that remains of the old administration building, destroyed by fire in 1892.

MISSOURI RIVER

MISSOURI RIVER is the second longest river in the United States, running 2,315 miles from its farthest headwaters to its mouth, where it joins the Mississippi River. Pioneers nicknamed the river the *Big Muddy* because of the vast amounts of silt carried in its waters. Geographers say that the Missouri, once held to be a branch of the Mississippi, is really its headstream.

The muddy waters of the Missouri have served as one of the main highways to the American West ever since pioneer days. The river allowed explorers and pioneers to travel quickly and easily from the swamps along the Mississippi to the snow-covered peaks of the Rocky Mountains. Hardy frontiersmen passed Indian villages, fur-trading posts, and forts on their trips west. Today, the river flows past prosperous farms and ranches. Several busy cities depend on the Missouri for water supply and transportation facilities.

The Course of the River. The Missouri River begins at the point where three rushing mountain streams unite in southwestern Montana to form a single tumbling river. The Gallatin and Madison rivers merge with the Jefferson River about halfway between the towns of Three Forks and Logan. At this point, the Missouri lies 4,032 feet above sea level.

The river flows first north and then east as it makes its way across Montana. The Yellowstone River, the largest branch of the Missouri, joins the river just after it crosses into North Dakota. The Missouri sweeps across North Dakota in a great curve toward the south. It turns eastward again in South Dakota, and forms part of the boundary between the eastern parts of South Dakota

and Nebraska. Turning southeastward again, the river separates Nebraska from Iowa and Missouri. The Missouri River also forms a small part of the northeastern boundary of Kansas. It winds across Missouri and finally joins the Mississippi a few miles north of St. Louis.

The Missouri River empties into the Gulf of Mexico through the Mississippi River. The more important branches of the Missouri include the Big Sioux, Cheyenne, James, Kansas, Milk, Osage, Platte, and White rivers. With its branches, the river drains an area of nearly 600,000 square miles, or about half the entire Mississippi drainage system. Important trade centers along the Missouri include Sioux City, Iowa; Omaha, Neb.; and St. Joseph and Kansas City, Mo.

The Character of the River. Near its source, the Missouri is a small rushing mountain stream. But it soon spreads out and becomes a wide waterway, measuring more than a mile across. As the Missouri cuts through the mountains, it gathers sand and gravel in its waters. Many rivers, like the Mississippi, build up a large flood plain with the solid deposits they carry. But the Missouri drops the sand and gravel it carries on the bed of its channel. As a result, the river runs over a thick bed of gravel and silt, 125 feet deep in some places.

The Missouri River pours an average of 69,300 cubic feet of water per second into the Mississippi. It also carries a huge amount of silt along with it. Every year, it pours about 250,000,000 cubic yards of silt into

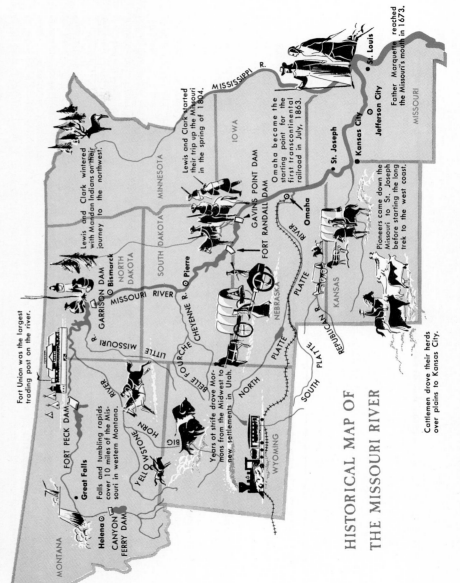

HISTORICAL MAP OF
THE MISSOURI RIVER

Fort Union was the largest trading post on the river.

Falls and tumbling rapids cover 10 miles of the Missouri in western Montana.

Years of strife drove Mormons from the Midwest to new settlements in Utah.

Lewis and Clark wintered with Mandan Indians on their journey to the northwest.

Lewis and Clark started their trip up the Missouri in the spring of 1804.

Omaha became the starting point for the first transcontinental railroad in July, 1863.

Pioneers came down the Missouri to St. Joseph before starting the long trek to the west coast.

Father Marquette reached the Missouri's mouth in 1673.

Cattlemen drove their herds over plains to Kansas City.

the Mississippi. Farmers along the shores of the river jokingly say that its waters are "too thick to drink, too thin to plow." But people have always considered the water from the Missouri especially pure once the silt has been removed. Many cities depend on the river for their drinking water.

History. The French explorers Louis Joliet and Father Jacques Marquette were probably the first white men to see the lower Missouri. They explored the eastern end of the river in 1673, and marked the spot where the Missouri joins the clearer waters of the Mississippi. In 1738, Pierre Gaultier, Sieur de la Vérendrye, led a party to the upper Missouri from one of the French fur-trading posts in Manitoba. They were the first white men to reach the upper part of the river. They returned with reports of vast herds of buffalo and of large Mandan Indian villages in what is now North Dakota.

Between 1804 and 1806, Meriwether Lewis and William Clark thoroughly explored the area crossed by the Missouri River (see LEWIS AND CLARK EXPEDITION). John Colter, a member of the group, remained in the Rocky Mountain area. He reported on the painted canyons, waterfalls, and geysers in what is now Yellowstone National Park (see COLTER, JOHN). Colter and his fellow frontiersmen became known as *mountain men*. They lived and trapped in the remote regions near the headwaters of the Missouri.

At first, oar-powered keelboats hauled supplies up the Missouri. In 1819, a steamboat made the first trip up the river. Fur companies soon used large numbers of steamboats to carry passengers and supplies up the river, and cargoes of precious furs back down. More than 300 steamboats were destroyed by explosions and other accidents during the period of steamboat transportation from the 1820's until the 1860's.

Pioneers traveling west to Oregon and California during the 1840's and 1850's went part of the way on the Missouri River. They continued their journeys by wagon or on horseback across the mountains, along the valley of the Platte River. In 1846 and 1847, the Mormons followed the Missouri River on their way to Utah. River traffic declined after 1860 because of the competition of the railroads. But today the Missouri is again an important trade waterway. Levees have been

built and sand bars removed to make water traffic easier. Congress passed several laws in the 1900's to make the Missouri a more useful waterway. The most important of these measures was the Flood Control Act of 1944. This act provided for irrigation, flood control, and hydroelectric power in much of the Missouri River Basin. The act launched the basin-wide Pick-Sloan plan (see MISSOURI RIVER BASIN PROJECT). A stabilization and navigation project was undertaken from the mouth of the Missouri River to Sioux City, Iowa. The project provides for 9-foot navigation for 760 miles from Sioux City to the river's mouth. It also provides for reinforcement of the river banks for this stretch of the river. A number of dams were built between this stretch of the river and Sioux City. Huge reservoirs stand at intervals north of Sioux City.

Great destructive floods along the Missouri have caused serious damage to homes, farm lands, and factories. The Missouri has tremendous power at flood stage. In 1937, the river's floodwaters formed a 30-foot-wide channel with a depth of 104 feet. In 1947, two destructive floods resulted in the loss of 26 lives and the flooding of about 3,000,000 acres of land. ORRO G. HOBERG

See also RIVER (color chart: Longest Rivers).

MISSOURI RIVER BASIN PROJECT is a large-scale federal flood control, electric power, and irrigation program for the parts of the United States drained by the Missouri River. Government planners believe the project will increase trade, market, and business opportunities along the river. Congress authorized the program with the Flood Control Act of 1944. The Missouri Basin Survey Commission submitted a detailed report early in 1953 on the best way to develop land and water resources in the Missouri Valley. The Federal Bureau of Reclamation and the United States Army Corps of Engineers are building the project.

The Missouri River Basin covers about one-sixth of the United States. The river and its tributaries drain all, or parts of, Colorado, Iowa, Kansas, Minnesota, Missouri, Montana, Nebraska, North and South Dakota, and Wyoming. For years, the great river system has overflowed its banks in the spring, causing millions of dollars of damage. Disastrous droughts frequently plague farmers during the summer. The western parts

Wide World

KANSAS CITY

The Missouri River is an important avenue for American shipping. Powerful tugboats move up and down the river daily, carrying huge loads of such industrial materials as coal, gravel, and limestone to cities along the river's shores.

of the valley usually have too little water, while the eastern parts have too much. In general, the Bureau of Reclamation works in the west to develop water resources for irrigation. The Corps of Engineers works in the east to promote flood control and navigation projects. See MISSOURI RIVER.

Plans call for the construction of 137 dams and reservoirs. They will store millions of acre-feet of water. The project will provide flood control and irrigation for more than 10 million acres of land. Planners believe that the overall project will reduce soil erosion and help develop mineral resources in the Missouri Valley. The project will also help to control floods on the lower Mississippi River. Hydroelectric plants in the project should generate about 3,200,000 kilowatts of electric power.

Many dams have been built. They include Fort Peck and Yellowtail dams in Montana, Fort Randall and Big Bend dams in South Dakota, Garrison Dam in North Dakota, and Gavins Point Dam which spans the river between South Dakota and Nebraska. It may take over 50 years to complete the project. WALLACE E. AKIN

See also FORT PECK DAM; FORT RANDALL DAM; GARRISON DAM.

MISSOURI SOUTHERN COLLEGE. See UNIVERSITIES AND COLLEGES (table).

MISSOURI VALLEY COLLEGE. See UNIVERSITIES AND COLLEGES (table).

MIST. See FOG.

MISTLETOE, *MIS'l toh*, is a plant which grows as a parasite on the trunks and branches of various trees. It grows most often on apple trees, but may grow on other trees such as the lime, hawthorn, sycamore, poplar, locust, fir, and occasionally on oak.

Mistletoe is an evergreen with thickly clustered leaves. It has tiny yellow flowers which bloom in February and March. Birds eat the white, shiny fruits called berries. The seeds of the berries cling to the bills of birds and are scattered when the birds sharpen their bills against the bark of trees. The berries are poisonous to man.

Mistletoe is associated with many traditions and holidays, especially Christmas. Historians say the Druids, or ancient priests of the Celts, cut the mistletoe which grew on the sacred oak, and gave it to the people for charms. In Northern mythology, an arrow made of mistletoe killed Balder, son of the goddess Frigg. Early European peoples used mistletoe as a ceremonial plant. The custom of using mistletoe at Christmastime probably comes from this practice. In many countries, a person caught standing beneath mistletoe must forfeit a kiss.

Scientific Classification. Mistletoe belongs to the mistletoe family, *Loranthaceae*. American mistletoe is genus *Phoradendron*, species *P. flavescens*. European mistletoe is *Viscum album*. J. J. LEVISON

See also CHRISTMAS (Mistletoe); OKLAHOMA (color picture: The State Flower); PARASITE.

MISTRAL, *MIS truhl*, is a swift, dry, cold northerly wind that blows down from the western Alps and the plateau of southern France and out over the Mediterranean. The cold heavy air from the high lands moves faster and faster as it approaches the warmer, lighter air over the sea in winter. This causes gusty, strong winds, as the cold air sinks to the level of the sea and the warm air rises above it. The mistral may cause extensive frost damage to plants. It is especially bad for the vineyards of southern France. It often blows 100 days a year.

MISTRAL, FRÉDÉRIC (1830-1914), was a famous French poet who won the 1904 Nobel prize for literature. He wrote in modern Provençal, the language of southern France. Mistral led a movement of the 1800's called the *Félibrige*. This movement tried to revive the literary tradition and enrich the language of the medieval troubadours (see TROUBADOUR).

In 1859, Mistral published his masterpiece, *Mireille*, an epic describing the tragic love of a farmer's daughter in the valley of the Rhône River. The poem's success did much to gain sympathy for the Provençal revival in literature. In addition to *Song of the Rhône* (1897) and other poems, Mistral compiled *Lou Tresor dòu Felibrige* (1878-1886), a dictionary of *langue d'oc*, the general term used for the dialects of southern France. He was born near Arles. LEROY C. BREUNIG

MISTRAL, *mees TRAHL,* **GABRIELA** (1889-1957), was the pen name of LUCILA GODOY ALCAYAGA, a Chilean poet and educator. In 1945, she became the first Latin-American writer to win the Nobel prize for literature. A tragic love affair frustrated her hopes for love and motherhood, so she devoted herself to love of God and good causes. Her poems show compassion for the humble and the needy. Her best-known books of poetry include *Desolation* (1922), *Tenderness* (1924), *Felling of Trees* (1934), and *Winepress* (1954).

Miss Mistral was born in Vicuña, Chile. She was a rural schoolteacher and later became a prominent educator in Chile. She served in the foreign service of Chile and at the League of Nations. She later taught at Barnard College and Middlebury College in the United States. MARSHALL R. NASON

American Mistletoe bears small, white berries and thick clusters of leaves. It is used to decorate homes at Christmastime

J. Horace McFarland

MITANNI, *mih TAWN ee,* was an ancient kingdom in northern Mesopotamia. The kingdom was located in what is now southwestern Turkey. The Mitannians used horses, and were skilled in the use of chariots in war. The neighboring Hittites learned how to use chariots in warfare from the Mitannians.

In the 1400's B.C., the Mitannians fought the Egyptians for control of Syria. But both kingdoms feared the rise of Hittite power. A Mitannian princess married into the Egyptian royal family as a sign of unity between the kingdoms. About 1370 B.C., however, the Hittites defeated the Mitannians. Civil war further weakened the Mitannians, and the kingdom was finally absorbed into the Assyrian empire by about 1350 B.C.

THOMAS W. AFRICA

MITCHEL, JOHN PURROY (1879-1918), was elected reform mayor of New York City in 1913. His election ended, for a time, control by Tammany Hall, a notorious political group. Mitchel reduced the city debt, fought against dishonesty in the city's police department, and set up a relief fund and workshops for the unemployed. However, many of Mitchel's actions angered powerful interests, and he lost his bid for re-election in 1917.

Mitchel was born in Fordham, N.Y., and graduated from New York Law School. In 1906, as commissioner of accounts for the city, he exposed dishonest practices of two borough presidents, the fire department, and the licenses bureau.

CHARLES FORCEY and LINDA FORCEY

MITCHEL AIR FORCE BASE, N.Y., served as a United States military post in all major wars from the Revolutionary War until 1961. The base lies about 25 miles east of New York City and covers 1,117 acres. It was named *Mitchel Field* in 1918 after Major John P. Mitchel, a World War I flier and former mayor of New York City. The first transcontinental air-mail flight took off from Mitchel Field in 1924. In 1929, famed American flier James H. Doolittle gave the first public demonstration of "blind flying" there. Long Island University founded Mitchel College, the only college on a military post, on the base in 1957.

MITCHELL, "BILLY," WILLIAM (1879-1936), an army general, became one of the most controversial figures in American military history. An early and vigorous advocate of air power, he was court-martialed for defiance of his superiors in 1925. He resigned from the army rather than accept a five-year suspension. He was branded at first as an extremist and insurgent. But early in World War II, events confirmed many of Mitchell's predictions. In 1946, the United States Congress authorized the Medal of Honor for Mitchell.

Mitchell enlisted in the army as a private at the start of the Spanish-American War in 1898. He remained in the army and rose rapidly in the signal corps, which first controlled the development of aviation in the U.S. Army. Mitchell learned to fly in 1916, and became air adviser to General John Pershing in World War I. He was in Europe when the United States entered the war, and quickly got in touch with Allied air leaders. Major General Hugh M. Trenchard, head of the British Royal Flying Corps, heavily influenced Mitchell's thinking. Mitchell commanded several large air units in combat, including the largest concentration of Allied air power

of World War I, during the Battle of the Argonne. He became a brigadier general by the end of the war.

After the war, Mitchell became assistant chief of the Air Service, and the leading advocate of an air force independent of the army and the navy. He found a natural resistance among leaders of the older services, and appealed to the public through books, magazine articles, newspaper interviews, and speeches. Because airplanes were then limited in size and range, many people thought his claims for air power were exaggerated. But he persuaded many others, especially after a 1921 experiment when he sunk by air attack three German ships—a destroyer, a cruiser, and a battleship. He repeated this success in later tests against obsolete U.S. battleships—one in September, 1921, and two in September, 1923. But Mitchell failed to achieve his goal, perhaps partly because he was frequently violent in argument and bitter in his condemnation of superiors who did not agree with him.

Mitchell wrote *Our Air Force* (1921), *Winged Defense* (1925), and *Skyways* (1930). He was born in Nice, France, of American parents.

ALFRED GOLDBERG

MITCHELL, JAMES PAUL (1900-1964), an American personnel expert, served as secretary of labor under President Dwight D. Eisenhower from 1953 until 1961. Earlier in 1953, he served briefly as assistant secretary of the Army in charge of manpower and forces.

Mitchell spent more than 20 years in personnel and management-employee relations work with such firms as R. H. Macy and Company. Before World War II, he served with the New York City division of the Works Progress Administration (WPA). From 1942 to 1945, he directed the civilian personnel division of the War Department's Services of Supply. Mitchell was born in Elizabeth, N.J.

CAROL L. THOMPSON

MITCHELL, JOHN (1870-1919), was president of the United Mine Workers of America from 1898 to 1908. At this time, many considered it the best-organized union in the United States. Mitchell became famous in the Pennsylvania hard coal strike of 1902. He united 150,000 immigrant miners, and won better wages and shorter hours for them. He was second in prestige to Samuel Gompers in the labor movement. Mitchell was born in Braidwood, Ill., and went to work in the mines at the age of 12. He wrote *Organized Labor* (1903).

JACK BARBASH

General "Billy" Mitchell stands, left, during his court-martial. Later events proved that his air-power theories were correct.

MITCHELL, JOHN NEWTON (1913-   ), became attorney general of the United States under President Richard M. Nixon in January, 1969. He came to be regarded as one of Nixon's most influential advisers on both domestic and international problems.

Mitchell was born in Detroit. He grew up in New York City, and graduated from Fordham University and Fordham Law School. He was a Navy commander in World War II and served in the same PT boat squadron as President John F. Kennedy. As a lawyer, Mitchell specialized in handling state and municipal bond issues, and was considered a leading expert in public finance. His New York City law firm merged with Nixon's in 1967. Mitchell served as Nixon's presidential campaign manager in 1968.

DAVID S. BRODER

MITCHELL, MARGARET (1900-1949), won the 1937 Pulitzer prize for *Gone with the Wind*, a world-famous novel she wrote about the Civil War. The American Booksellers Association selected it as the outstanding novel of 1936. The book, which reflects the Confederate view of the Civil War, became one of the best-selling books of all time. *Gone with the Wind* was published in Braille, and was translated into 20 languages. The motion-picture version of the novel appeared in 1939, and broke all attendance records.

Margaret Mitchell was born in Atlanta, Ga., the scene of much of the action of *Gone with the Wind*. She attended Smith College for one year. She worked for the *Atlanta Journal* from 1922 until 1926, when she began working on *Gone with the Wind*. She took the title of the book from a poem by the English poet Ernest Dowson. Miss Mitchell was married to John R. Marsh in 1925.

BERNARD DUFFEY

MITCHELL, MARIA (1818-1889), an American astronomer, became known for her studies of sunspots and of satellites of planets. She discovered a new comet in 1847. The king of Denmark gave her a gold medal for this discovery. Although she was largely self-educated, she served as professor of astronomy at Vassar College from 1865 to 1888. She was elected to membership in several learned societies. In 1848, she became the first woman admitted to membership in the American Academy of Arts and Sciences. She later became a fellow of the society. She was elected to the Hall of Fame in 1905. Miss Mitchell was born in Nantucket, Mass. As a child, she spent many hours in her father's poorly equipped laboratory.

HELEN E. MARSHALL

MITCHELL, WESLEY CLAIR (1874-1948), an American economist, devoted his life to a study of business cycles. He pioneered a new approach to the study of economics, insisting that economic theories should be based on detailed statistics rather than on general ideas or a few observations. He measured changes in prices, production, and other factors during periods of prosperity, crisis, depression, and revival. Mitchell believed that ups and downs in business activity are bound to occur in regular cycles in a modern, free enterprise economy.

Mitchell was born in Rushville, Ill., and graduated from the University of Chicago. He taught economics at the University of California from 1902 to 1912 and at Columbia University from 1913 to 1944. Mitchell was a founder of the National Bureau of Economic Research and served as its director from 1920 to 1945. Mitchell's books include *Business Cycles: The Problem and*

Its Setting (1927), and *The Backward Art of Spending Money* (1937).

DANIEL R. FUSFELD

MITE is the common name for small ticks. Scientists do not separate mites and ticks on the basis of structure, but most people call the smallest species mites and the larger ones ticks. These creatures are not insects, but are related to spiders and scorpions.

Some mites live on land, while others live in water. Some are too small to be seen easily with the naked eye and must be studied under a microscope. The male usually has a saclike body with a slight dividing line between its abdomen and thorax, and has four pairs of legs. The mouth has piercing and grasping organs. The digestive system begins in the sucking beak. The young larvae of most species hatch from eggs and have six legs. They shed their skins and change into nymphs with eight legs. After one or more other moltings, the nymphs change into adults.

More than half the different kinds of mites live at least part of their lives as parasites. They suck the blood of animals or the juice from plants, and eat cell tissues as well. Other mites eat feathers, cheese, flour, cereal, drugs, and other stored products. Several kinds of mites burrow into the skin of man and other mammals, especially horses, cattle, and sheep. They cause the skin to break out and itch, forming scabs and mange. The troublesome *chiggers*, or *red bugs*, which torment people in the woods are mites. Another kind which attacks man is a long wormlike mite which burrows into the hair follicles and the oil glands. It is said to cause blackheads, but many scientists disagree. All these mites except the last can be killed by sulfur preparations.

Several kinds of mites attack poultry. The best-known is the common *chicken mite*, which, like the bedbug, sucks the blood of its victims at night and hides in cracks during the day. Kerosene will kill it.

Sometimes a mite called the *red spider* destroys greenhouse plants. Sulfur fumes will kill this mite. The *pear-tree blister mite* damages fruit trees. *Gall mites* form small lumps on leaves and twigs. Unlike other mites, they have only two pairs of legs. *Clover mites* attack plants and fruit trees. In the South, they spend the winter on clover plants.

Other mites attack bulbs and roots of plants. A few species prey on plant lice, or aphids, and others on in-

Mites Annoy Man, Most Animals, and Some Plants.

P. S. Tice

sects and grasshopper eggs, but the majority of mites do not help man.

Scientific Classification. Mites belong to the order *Acarina*. The itch mite of man is genus *Sarcoptes*, species *S. scabiei*. The skin mite of horses and cattle is *Psoroptes communis*. The chicken mite is *Dermanyssus gallinae*. The red spider is *Tetranychus bimaculatus*, or some closely related species. EDWARD A. CHAPIN

See also CHIGGER; MANGE; PARASITE; TICK.

MITHRAS, *MITH ras,* was a god of the ancient Persians and the Aryans of India. The Aryans made him one of their 12 high gods. In the Zoroastrian religion of ancient Persia, he was an angel of light who fought on the side of the god Ahura Mazda against the forces of evil (see ZOROASTRIANISM). The Zoroastrian scriptures called Mithras "the Heavenly Light."

The Persians carried their belief in Mithras to Assyria and Asia Minor, where many people identified him with the sun. Mithraism took on the form of a mystery religion, with elaborate rites and ceremonies. It came into the ancient Roman world about 75 B.C., and ranked as a principal competitor of Christianity for 200 years. CLIFTON E. OLMSTEAD

MITHRIDATES VI, *MITH rih DAY teez* (120?-63 B.C.), was king of Pontus, an area in what is now Turkey. One of Rome's most dangerous enemies, Mithridates opposed Roman expansion into Asia Minor.

He fought three wars against Rome. When Rome's Italian allies in central and southern Italy revolted in 90 B.C., Mithridates drove the Romans from Asia. He ordered every Roman citizen in Asia Minor killed—an estimated 80,000 were put to death.

Culver

Tom Mix and His Horse, Tony, made many motion pictures. Mix's adventures later became a popular radio program.

When Rome attacked Mithridates' allies in Greece, he sent two armies there. But Sulla, a Roman general, defeated them, and Mithridates had to make peace in 84 B.C. The greatest war broke out in 75 B.C. when Rome took over Bithynia, a region adjoining Pontus. The Roman general Pompey drove Mithridates out of Asia Minor. Mithridates planned to continue the war from the Crimea in what is now southern Russia. But his son, Pharnaces, rebelled against him, and Mithridates killed himself by taking poison.

HENRY C. BOREN

MITOSIS. See PONTUS; SULLA, LUCIUS CORNELIUS.

MITRAL VALVE. See CELL (Cell Division; illustration).

MITRE, BARTOLOMÉ. See HEART (Parts of the Heart).

MITROPOULOS, *mih TRAHP uh lus,* DIMITRI, *dee MEE tree* (1896-1960), was a Greek-born American operatic and orchestral conductor. He directed the Minneapolis Symphony Orchestra from 1937 to 1949, and the New York Philharmonic-Symphony Orchestra from 1949 to 1958. He conducted at the Metropolitan Opera Company from 1954 until his death. He also conducted at London, Milan, Moscow, and Paris. Mitropoulos was born in Athens, and studied music in Athens, Berlin, and Brussels. He made his American debut in 1936, and became a United States citizen in 1946.

DAVID EWEN

MITSCHER, *MICH er,* MARC ANDREW (1887-1947), an American naval officer, commanded two famous Task Force 58 in the South Pacific during World War II. From January to October, 1944, his force of aircraft carriers, battleships, cruisers, and destroyers sank or damaged 795 Japanese ships and destroyed 4,425 enemy planes.

Mitscher took command of the aircraft carrier *Hornet* in October, 1941. James Doolittle's bombers made the first air raid of the war on Japan from the decks of the *Hornet* on April 18, 1942. Several weeks later, Mitscher played an important role in the U.S. victory at the Battle of Midway. For several months in 1943, he commanded all air forces in the Solomon Islands.

Mitscher was born in Hillsboro, Wis. He graduated from the U.S. Naval Academy in 1910, and was one of the first U.S. Navy officers to adopt aviation as a career. He became a vice-admiral in 1944. After World War II, he became deputy chief of naval operations for air. He became an admiral in 1946 and took command of the Eighth Fleet. DONALD W. MITCHELL

MIX, TOM (1880-1940), became one of America's most famous motion-picture cowboys. He entered the movies in 1910. His expert horsemanship and easygoing manner made him a star. He appeared in such western motion pictures as *Riders of the Purple Sage*. Mix and his horse, Tony, were given a reception by the Lord Mayor of London in 1925.

Mix was born in Driftwood, Pa. He fought in the Spanish-American War at the age of 18, and in China during the Boxer Rebellion. NARD REEDER CAMPION

MIXED NUMBERS are numbers made up of a whole number and a fraction. Thus, $6\frac{1}{2}$ years and $2\frac{1}{4}$ feet are mixed numbers. They must be reduced to their simplest forms for any calculation. See also FRACTION.

MIXTURE, in chemistry. See COMPOUND.

MIZAR. See DOUBLE STAR.

MNEMONICS. See MEMORY (Improving the Memory).

MNEMOSYNE. See MUSE.

Sea. The Moabites were Semites, related to the Hebrews. The Moabites often fought against the Israelites, who lived to the west and to the north, and against the Edomites, who lived to the south.

MOABITE STONE. This ancient stone bears some of the earliest writing in Hebrew-Phoenician characters. The stone is of black basalt. It is about 3 feet 8 inches high and 2 feet 3 inches wide. F. A. Klein, a missionary, found it in 1868 at Diban, in ancient Moab. The writing on it was probably carved by a Moabite scribe sometime in the 800's B.C. It is a good example of the Hebrew-Phoenician characters used at the time.

When the French tried to buy the stone at Constantinople, the Arabs in the district became greedy. The Arabs broke the priceless, irreplaceable stone into many parts, hoping to get more money by selling the pieces. The French collected the larger pieces. An official of the French embassy at Constantinople had also made a paper impression of the stone before it was broken.

The 34-line inscription tells of the deeds of Mesha, King of the Moabites, in his wars against the kings of Israel and against the Edomites. For a description of part of this conflict from the point of view of the people of Israel, see II Kings 3:4-27. The restored stone is in the Louvre, in Paris.

JOSEPH WARD SWAIN

MOAT. See CASTLE; ZOO.

The Oriental Institute, The University of Chicago

The Moabite Stone bears an historical inscription which was carved with Hebrew-Phoenician writing in the 800's B.C.

Amer. Mus. of Natural History

The Moa was a large bird that looked somewhat like an ostrich. It lived in New Zealand, and was killed for food.

MOA, *MOH uh,* is any one of about 20 *species* (kinds) of extinct birds that once lived in New Zealand. Moas ranged in size from those as big as a large turkey to some that were 10 feet tall. Moas could not fly. They had small heads, long necks, stout legs, and no wings. They ate green plants and roots.

Moas existed until the 1600's, and one small kind may have survived until the mid-1800's. Maoris, the Polynesians who settled in New Zealand about 600 years ago, hunted moas for food. They may have been responsible for wiping out the bird.

Scientific Classification. Moas belong to the moa order, *Dinornithiformes,* and to the families *Dinornithidae* and *Anomalopteryginae.*

RAYMOND A. PAYNTER, JR.

MOAB, Utah (pop. 4,682; alt. 4,000 ft.), lies 240 miles southeast of Salt Lake City. For location, see UTAH (political map).

Uranium processing has been one of Moab's most important industries since 1952. At that time, increased developments of uranium ores began in the Colorado Plateau region of southeastern Utah. The people also work in milling, and trade in livestock and in fruit and other truck crops that are raised in the area around Moab.

The city has an airport, a library, and a museum. Arches National Monument, north of Moab, and Dead Horse Point, in the plateau country to the west, attract tourists to the city. Moab was founded in 1855, and was permanently settled between 1877-1879. It has a mayor-council form of government, and is the seat of Grand County.

A. R. MORTENSEN

MOABITE, *MO ub ite.* The Moabites lived in the land of Moab from the 1200's to the 500's B.C. The region of Moab lay east of the lower Jordan River and the Dead

recall the erosion effects of wind or water, or imaginative flight forms in space. Sculptors use many colors, textures, and materials for mobiles.

Most mobiles are suspended from above, so they can move freely overhead. Some are pivoted on a base. They are planned to present artistic interest not only in their actual shape, but also in the moving shadows they cast on walls and floor. Mobiles usually move as the result of natural currents of air, or the vibration of the earth. A few are designed for mechanical power.

A mobile's movement is of greater aesthetic value than its actual shape. The constantly swinging projections form arcs that cut shapes or volumes out of space. These volumes have no weight or substance, but they do remain fixed in our memory. The real design of a mobile is in this variety of space shapes, and in their abstract relationships with one another. Artists of many times and many places have created things that depend on movement for some part of their expression. But an American sculptor, Alexander Calder, was the first to create the true mobile, in which movement is the basic aesthetic purpose. Calder is regarded as the foremost creator of mobiles.

Wide acceptance of this new art form is obviously based on two significant facts. First, our art concepts have quite naturally grown to include the beauty of the machine in motion. Second, our minds have been freed to think and feel in terms of volumes of space that our eyes cannot see.

See also CALDER, ALEXANDER; SCULPTURE (Form and Treatment; picture: Red Petals).

BERNARD FRAZIER

MOBILE, *moh BEEL,* Ala. (pop. 202,779; met. area 363,389; alt. 15 ft.) is the only seaport of Alabama, and one of the largest ports in the United States. Several streets of the city and its suburbs form the 35-mile Azalea Trail, featuring thousands of flowering azalea plants every spring.

Location, Size, and Description. Mobile is the second largest city in Alabama. It lies on the Mobile River at its entrance to Mobile Bay, 31 miles north of the Gulf of

MAKING MOBILES

MOBILE, *MOH beel,* is a contemporary type of sculpture. It is distinctive from other types of sculpture in that it achieves expression or meaning through movement. Traditional sculpture achieves its expression through the arrangement of solid forms. Mobiles are usually frail constructions of many rod-like projections loosely joined together. They are delicately balanced so they can swing freely in an infinite variety of moving arcs. The rods may end in *finials* (ending shapes) that

Mobiles sway gracefully in the wind, casting shadows on the walls or the floor.

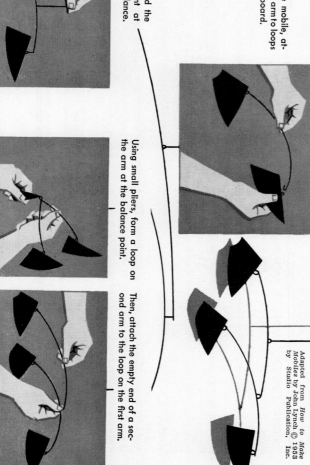

To make a simple mobile, attach a curved wire arm to loops on pieces of cardboard.

Next, tie a string around the arm and find the point at which the two pieces balance.

Using small pliers, form a loop on the arm at the balance point.

Then, attach the empty end of a second arm to the loop on the first arm.

Adapted from *How to Make Mobiles* by John Lynch © 1953 by Studio Publication, Inc.

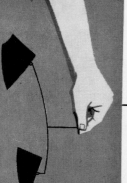
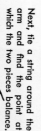

Thigpen, Mobile Chamber of Commerce

Fort Gaines, on Dauphin Island at the entrance to Mobile Bay, protected Mobile from the Union Navy during the Civil War.

Mexico. For location, see ALABAMA (political map). Huge moss-draped oak trees towering over historic Government Street form the entrance to the city from the west. Large trees and handsome homes line the residential streets. In the downtown district, small parks with giant shade trees provide relief from the office buildings. Beautiful suburbs such as Chateauguay, Delwood, and Spring Hill surround the city. Mobile is the home of Spring Hill College.

Industry and Commerce. Mobile is an important industrial and transportation center. Brookley Air Force Base, with more than 13,000 civilian employees, is Mobile's largest single employer. Paper and wood pulp used for paper is Mobile's largest single industry. Wood pulp is also the basic raw material for a large rayon fiber plant. Other important products include aluminum, lumber, rayon, roofing, cement, naval stores, chemicals, clothing, fertilizer, paint, and petroleum products. Shipbuilding and repair, and shipping itself, are other important industries. The Alabama State Docks can accommodate 30 ocean-going vessels at one time. The Port of Mobile handles over 17 million tons of cargo a year. Commercial fishermen in the area do a lively business in fish and oysters.

The city is served by four railroads and four bus lines. Four major airlines use Mobile's busy Bates Field. Bankhead Tunnel, the first underwater tunnel in the South, handles traffic under the Mobile River.

History. Founded originally in 1702 as Fort Louis de la Mobile, Mobile is one of the oldest cities in the United States. The settlers moved to the present site in 1711 because of flood waters. Mobile is often called *The City of Six Flags.* It has been ruled by the French, British, and Spanish, and has also flown the flags of the Republic of Alabama, the Confederate States, and the United States. The United States captured Mobile from the Spanish in 1813. Mobile was the last Southern stronghold to surrender to the Union forces at the end of the Civil War. Mobile received a city charter in 1819, and adopted commission government in 1910. It is the seat of Mobile County.

For the monthly weather in Mobile, see ALABAMA (Climate). See also ALABAMA (pictures); IBERVILLE, SIEUR D'.

MOBILE BAY, BATTLE OF. See CIVIL WAR (Mobile Bay).

MOBILE COLLEGE. See UNIVERSITIES AND COLLEGES (table).

MOBILE HOME. See TRAILER.

MOBILE RIVER is a short stream in southwestern Alabama. It offers transportation for cotton and other farm products of its valley. The Mobile was named for the Mobile, or Maubila, Indians who once lived along its banks. The Mobile River is formed where the Alabama and Tombigbee rivers meet in Clarke County. The Mobile flows southward for 38 miles before it empties into the Gulf of Mexico through Mobile Bay. For location, see ALABAMA (physical map). The port of Mobile lies at the mouth of the river.   WALLACE E. AKIN

MÖBIUS, AUGUST FERDINAND. See MATHEMATICS (A Strange Twist).

MOBUTU, *mo BOO too,* **JOSEPH DÉSIRÉ** (1930-   ), seized control of the government in Congo (Kinshasa) in 1960 and again in 1965. In 1965, he declared himself president for five years.

Mobutu was born in a small village in what was then the colony called the Belgian Congo. He studied in Belgium and served in the colonial army. Trouble broke out among Congolese groups when the colony gained independence in 1960, and it threatened to destroy the nation. Mobutu headed a military government that restored order. He ruled for five months. Mobutu seized power again when new trouble broke out in 1965.

MOBY DICK. See MELVILLE, HERMAN.

MOCCASIN, *MAHK uh sin.* The American Indians called their slipperlike footwear *moccasins.* They made moccasins of animal skin and often decorated them with beads, and sometimes porcupine quills. Moccasins are soft, closely fitted, and have no heels. They may be ankle-length or extend to the hip. Hair is left on the skin of winter moccasins to serve as a lining. See also INDIAN, AMERICAN (color picture).   LYNN FARNOL

MOCCASIN FLOWER. See LADY'S-SLIPPER.

MOCCASIN SNAKE. See WATER MOCCASIN.

MOCHA. See COFFEE (Kinds).

MOCK ORANGE, sometimes called *syringa,* is a bush covered with clusters of small, single or double, white or creamy flowers. The flowers of some kinds of mock orange have purple spots at the base of their petals. In most plants, the flowers are fragrant, but some are odorless. Some types of mock orange have leaves with toothed edges. The bush generally does not grow very high, although some species do reach 20 feet.

Gardeners in the United States and Mexico grow many different kinds of mock orange. A few kinds also grow in Asia and Europe. Almost all types of this hardy plant bloom in June. Breeders have produced many beautiful hybrids of mock orange. One of these hybrids, *Philadelphus virginalis,* is among the best and most fragrant of the mock oranges. Many mock orange plants escape from gardens and grow wild. The syringa is the state flower of Idaho (see IDAHO [color picture]).

Scientific Classification. Mock oranges belong to the saxifrage family, *Saxifragaceae.* They make up the genus *Philadelphus.*   J. J. LEVISON

MOCK-UP. See AIRPLANE MODEL.

MOCKINGBIRD is an American bird famous for its ability to imitate the sounds of other birds. One naturalist reported a mockingbird in South Carolina that imitated the songs of 32 different kinds of birds in 10 minutes. The mockingbird's own song is one of the most versatile of all bird songs.

Mockingbirds live only in North, Central, and South America. In the United States, most mockingbirds live in the Southern States. However, some mockingbirds range as far north as Massachusetts and Michigan.

The bird has an ashy-white breast and an ash-gray coat. Its wings and tail are darker gray with white markings. Males and females have almost the same coloring, but the female has a little less white in its feathers. The mockingbird grows from 9 to 11 inches long. It has a long slender body and a long slender tail.

The birds build their nests in thickets, low trees, and bushes. They lay from four to six pale greenish-blue or bluish-white eggs spotted with brown. Mockingbirds help man by eating insects and weed seeds. They often pick insects off the radiators of parked cars. This represents a recent change in food habits. Mockingbirds also eat wild fruits, and sometimes damage fruit crops.

Scientific Classification. The mockingbird belongs to the mockingbird family, *Mimidae*. It is classified as genus *Mimus*, species *M. polyglottos*.

See also Bird (color pictures: Birds' Eggs; Favorite Songbirds).

GEORGE J. WALLACE

MODE, in grammar. See Mood.

MODE, in mathematics, is that value in any group that occurs most frequently. Suppose a boy counts the eggs in 77 birds' nests. He finds that four nests have one egg each, 65 have two eggs each, five have three eggs, and three have four eggs. The nests that contain two eggs are by far the most common. Therefore, two is the *mode,* or *modal value,* in this group of numbers. The mode is a type of *average* that is often useful in the study of statistics. See also Average; Mean; Median; Statistics (picture).

ALBERT E. WAUGH

MODEL CITIES is a federally aided program to help make cities in the United States more livable. It is administered by the Department of Housing and Urban Development. The program provides federal grants and technical assistance to selected cities to help them solve physical, social, and economic problems of slum and blighted neighborhoods. It is designed to encourage new approaches to the solution of these problems.

The Model Cities program was established by the Demonstration Cities and Metropolitan Development Act of 1966. The act requires widespread citizen participation in the program. A participating city establishes a city demonstration agency, which drafts broad plans for rebuilding or restoring blighted areas. The agency coordinates the many separate urban improvement projects in the target area. Federal funds help pay the cost of planning and carrying out approved Model Cities programs. These funds supplement the federal grants many cities already receive for such projects as slum clearance, on-the-job training, low-rent housing, and preschool education. Specific programs vary from city to city.

MODEL MAKING is one of the oldest crafts. In museums, we can see small models of boats, household articles, and tools made by ancient peoples more than 6,000 years ago. Today, many people make models as a hobby or a profession.

There are two kinds of models: copies and original forms. Making small-scale *copies* of such things as boats or airplanes is a fascinating and sometimes profitable hobby. These models require skill if they are carried out in great detail. But simple models can be made by almost anyone. Even small children can make models of houses and furniture from heavy paper, cardboard, or balsa wood. They can also use clay or *Plasticine,* an artificial modeling material.

Professional model makers are usually employed to make *original forms,* which show how something will work or look before it is actually made. Models of large objects, like buildings or bridges, are made to a small scale. Models of smaller articles, such as electric toasters, are usually made full size. Models of very small things, like coins, are made much larger than actual size. The model maker often uses materials different from those used in the final structure or product. He may, for instance, paint wood to make it look like metal or use clear plastic instead of glass.

Architects use small-scale models of buildings to demonstrate their plans. Engineers construct models of dams, bridges, and other structures to exact scale, out of the materials they intend to use for the actual projects. Then they test the models and correct faults that may appear in their designs. Aviation engineers test small airplane models in wind tunnels, and shipbuilders try out miniature ships in specially constructed basins. Inventors use models to demonstrate ideas they wish to patent. Industrial designers and manufacturers make models of products ranging from fountain pens to steam shovels, before ordering the expensive tools necessary to produce them.

See also Airplane Model; Railroad, Model; Ship Model.

RALPH R. KNOBLAUGH

MODEL PARLIAMENT was the parliament that met at Westminster in 1295. It is considered representative of early assemblies from which today's parliament gradually emerged. When Edward I of England ordered parliament to meet, he summoned not only churchmen

An Architect's Scale Model shows how this honeycomb-designed building will actually look when it is constructed.

Fred Stone

Chicago Sun-Times

A Fashion Model takes an unusual stance to give the most striking and effective display possible to her clothing and accessories.

and nobles, but also two knights elected from each county and two townsmen from each of many towns. Knights and townsmen later made up the House of Commons. Historians of the 1800's believed that the parliament of 1295 served as a model. But research indicates that knights and townsmen had been summoned before 1295, and that some later parliaments included only nobles and churchmen. BASIL D. HENNING

See also PARLIAMENT.

MODEL T. See FORD (Henry Ford; picture).
MODELING. See SCULPTURE; SOAP SCULPTURE; WOOD CARVING.

MODELING is the art of posing before a photographer or a painter as the subject of a picture, or before an audience in order to display new fashions. Photographic modeling is the most important aspect of modeling, because of the extensive use of photographs in advertising. The influence of advertising in everyday life has made modeling an increasingly important job.

Kinds of Modeling. There are three basic kinds of photographic modeling: (1) fashion; (2) illustration; and (3) commercial. *Fashion* models have always been important to the garment industry. But they now form a "sales force" for household products advertised in women's magazines. *Illustration* models are photographed to illustrate stories and articles. Their pictures often appear on magazine covers. Photographs of *commercial* models appear in magazine and newspaper advertisements, in brochures and catalogues, and on billboards. The photograph of an attractive person, when associated with a product, not only attracts attention, but often makes a product more appealing.

Not all modeling is done in front of a camera. An important part of the fashion industry is the fashion show, where designers and manufacturers introduce their new styles. Many charity organizations also use fashion shows as a way to raise money.

Most department stores in large cities employ models in departments where expensive clothes are sold. Manufacturers and designers also hire models for fitting garments and for showing them to prospective buyers.

Tradeshows, such as an automobile show, use models. Many companies hire models to display their products, because an attractive girl will call attention to the product or to the booth where the product is displayed. Models are also in demand for television commercials where no extensive dramatic ability is required.

But most young women find work as a photographer's model most desirable. They enjoy the glamour attached to having their pictures widely circulated, and they find that the fees for this type of work are generally higher than those for other types of modeling.

The Model's Work. Modeling is difficult and tiring work. Sometimes a model must work for hours under hot, bright lights. Because advertising is planned long in advance, many bathing suits are photographed in winter, and fur coats are photographed in summer.

A photographic model usually works on an hourly basis, and charges a set fee for her time. For fashion shows, the model usually works for a specific fee rather than an hourly one. This fee covers her time for fittings, rehearsals, and the show itself. Most models charge lower fees for artists, because artists require more time than photographers, and usually work on a smaller budget. The screen and television actors' unions regu-

late payment for performing in television commercials.

In an assignment to be photographed, models usually work at the photographer's studio. But pictures may be taken "on location." This may mean working indoors in another building, outdoors in the same city, or in some other place, sometimes many miles away. Most models have an hourly, daily, and weekly rate. However, a model usually charges a set fee if much of her work time is spent traveling to a location.

Model Agencies act as "clearinghouses" for the convenience of models and their employers. A client arranges with the agency to hire a model for a definite amount of time on a specified day. This is called a *booking.* The booking may be for a fashion show, television commercial, or time spent posing for a photographer or artist. Once the client has made a definite booking, he must pay the model, whether or not he goes through with the assignment. In the case of outdoor work, a client may make arrangements on a "weather-permitting" basis. In this case, he can have first demand on the model's time the following day if the weather makes his booking impossible. The model's agent must make all decisions concerning changes in bookings.

Most successful models are registered with a licensed model agency. The agency acts as the model's representative. It accepts bookings and assigns them to her, sends bills to the clients, and collects money owed to the model. In return, the model pays the agency a *commission* (specified percentage) on all her earnings.

Requirements for a Model. A model's basic requirement is physical appearance. She does not need classical beauty, but she must be attractive, according to the ideal of the time.

For fashion work, size is important. A "standard" dress is usually regarded as size 10 or 12. A girl should be at least 5 feet 6 inches tall for fashion work, because she can then show the clothes to best advantage. In the illustration field, height is not as important.

The other requirements of a good model, in any field, are good grooming and gracefulness. A model must also be able to understand and carry out directions, and have a certain amount of flexibility and acting ability in order to portray the mood that the client requires.

Careers in Modeling. The greatest demand is for young women models from 18 to 25 years old. Male models have limited opportunity. They often appear in illustrations and advertisements and as background in fashion photographs. There is sometimes one male model in a fashion show. The widest use of male models is in television commercials.

A career in modeling is usually short. Youth is an important asset for the successful model. A model sometimes becomes so successful that people recognize her face too easily, or associate it with one product.

Modeling can be a steppingstone to other interesting professions. For example, famous actresses and actors started their careers as models. Many successful women in the fashion field were once models. Making television commercials gives models experience that is helpful for acting and executive careers in television.

There are modeling opportunities throughout the world. In the United States, most modeling activity centers in New York, Chicago, and Los Angeles. But because New York City is the center of most national advertising, it usually provides the best opportunity for the career model.

See also FASHION.

JOHN ROBERT POWERS

MODELMAKING. See MODEL MAKING.

MODERATO. See MUSIC (Terms).

MODERATOR. See ATOMIC ENERGY (Chain Reactions); ATOMIC REACTOR (Operation).

MODERN MATHEMATICS. See NUMERATION SYSTEMS; SET THEORY.

MODERN WOODMEN OF AMERICA. See WOODMEN OF AMERICA, MODERN.

MODERNISM. See SPANISH LITERATURE (The 1900's [Poetry]); LATIN-AMERICAN LITERATURE (Modernism).

MODIFIER. See ADJECTIVE; ADVERB.

MODIGLIANI, *moh dee LYAH nee,* **AMEDEO** (1884-1920), an Italian artist, painted portraits of artists, poets, musicians, and models. He usually painted single figures with long bodies and oval heads, using lines to catch the

personality of a subject. One of his portraits, *Young Girl in Pink,* appears in color in the PAINTING article. He also did some sculpture. Modigliani was born in Leghorn (Livorno), Italy, but lived in Paris after 1906. He was poor, and supported himself for a time by sketching café portraits.

GEORGE D. CULLER

MODOC INDIANS, *MO dahk,* is the name of a small tribe of Indians which once lived in northern California and southern Oregon. The Modoc fought the early white settlers. They were subdued by U.S. troops and removed to reservations in Oregon and Oklahoma.

MODULATION. See MUSIC (Harmony).

MODULE. See SPACE TRAVEL (Space Travel Terms).

MOE, JØRGEN. See ASBJØRNSEN, PETER CHRISTEN.

MOFFAT, DAVID HALLIDAY. See MOFFAT TUNNEL.

MOFFAT TUNNEL is one of the longest railroad tunnels in the United States. It ranks among the longest in the world. The tunnel cuts through James Peak in Colorado for a distance of 6.23 miles.

Moffat Tunnel has two separate *bores* (tubes). The largest, 24 by 16 feet, is used for trains. The other bore, 8 by 8 feet, carries water from the Fraser River to Denver. Engineers bored through rock from each side of the Continental Divide, at an elevation of 9,200 feet. The tunnel shortened the distance between Salt Lake City and Denver by 176 miles. By using the tunnel, trains avoid snowstorms, snowslides, and steep grades. The tunnel was named for David H. Moffat, American banker and railroad builder. It was leased to the Denver & Salt Lake Railroad.

See also COLORADO (color map: Historic Colorado).

ARCHIBALD BLACK

MOFFATT, JAMES. See BIBLE (The Accepted Protestant Versions in English; Other Modern Versions).

MOGADISCIO, *MAHG uh DISH ee oh* (pop. 141,770; alt. 27 ft.), is the capital and chief port of Somalia, which became independent in 1960. For location, see AFRICA (political map). The city once served as the capital of the Italian trusteeship of Somaliland. Most of the people are Africans, but some are Italians.

MOGOLLON is the name of prehistoric Indians who lived in southeastern Arizona and southwestern New Mexico from about 500 B.C. to A.D. 1200. Scientists believe they disappeared about A.D. 1250. They may have resembled present-day Zuñi and Hopi Indians. The early Mogollon lived in villages of pit-houses. Later, they built crude one-story pueblo villages. The Indians gathered wild berries and seeds and later hunted and farmed corn. They used crude stone tools. The Mogollon made tobacco pipes of stone or baked clay. They decorated their pottery with figures and geometric designs in red and brown or black and white.

MOGUL EMPIRE, or MUGHAL EMPIRE, ruled most of India in the 1500's and 1600's. Life in Mogul India set a standard of magnificence for its region of Asia, and the empire had peace, order, and stability. The centralized government of the empire provided a model for later rulers of India. A distinctive culture developed that blended Middle Eastern and Indian elements, and the Persian language became widely used.

Babar, a prince from what is now Afghanistan, founded the Mogul Empire in 1526. His grandson Akbar established its governmental structure. Akbar, who ruled from 1556 to 1605, controlled north and central India and Afghanistan. Jahangir, Akbar's son, ruled from 1605 to 1627 and was a patron of painting.

His son Shah Jahan reigned from 1627 to 1658, during the height of the Mogul period. He encouraged architecture and built the famous Taj Mahal as a tomb for his wife. Shah Jahan's son Aurangzeb took the throne from his father in 1658 and imprisoned Shah Jahan.

The Mogul emperors were Moslems who ruled a largely Hindu nation. Under Akbar, Hindu warriors served as Mogul generals and governors, and other Hindus were administrators and clerks. Aurangzeb was not so tolerant of other religions. He imposed a tax on the Hindus and destroyed many of their temples. The Marathas, a Hindu warrior people of central India, revolted and seriously weakened the empire.

The Mogul Empire began to break up shortly after Aurangzeb's death in 1707. Moguls continued to rule a small kingdom at Delhi until Great Britain took control of India in the 1800's.

J. F. RICHARDS

See also AKBAR; AURANGZEB; BABAR; INDIA (The Mogul Empire); SHAH JAHAN.

MOHÁCS, BATTLE OF. See HUNGARY (Early Days); TURKEY (The Ottoman Empire).

MOHAIR is the name given to the hair of the angora goat. This animal is native to Asia Minor and also is raised in South Africa, California, and Texas. The name *mohair* is also applied to the lustrous, long-wearing fabrics which are made from the hair of the angora goat.

Mohair is smooth and resilient. It can be dyed to give brilliant permanent colors to decorative fabrics used to make draperies and clothing such as men's summer suits and women's coats. Mohair is also used to make fabrics that must withstand rough wear, such as furniture upholstery and the coverings of railroad-car seats. Mohair is sometimes incorrectly called alpaca, a fleece made from the alpaca (see ALPACA).   ERNEST R. KASWELL

See also GOAT (picture: The Angora Goat).

MOHAMMED, *moh HAM uhd* (A.D. 570?-632?), was the founder of the Islamic religion. He is called the *Prophet of Islam.* His followers are called *Moslems.*

Moslems believe Mohammed was the last messenger of God. They believe he completed the sacred teachings of such earlier prophets as Abraham, Moses, and Jesus. Moslems respect Mohammed, but they do not worship him.

Mohammed was one of the most influential men of all time. He felt himself called to be God's prophet. This belief gave him the strength to bring about many changes in Arabia. When Mohammed began to preach in the 600's, Arabia was a wild, lawless land. The fierce tribes of the deserts fought continual bloody wars.

In Mecca, a city in southwestern Arabia, there was poverty and suffering among the poor. Most of Mohammed's countrymen worshiped many gods, and prayed to idols and spirits.

Mohammed brought a new message to his people from God. He taught that there is only one God, and that this God requires men to make *Islam* (submission) to Him. Mohammed replaced the old loyalty to tribes with a new tie of equality and brotherhood among all Moslems. He also preached against the injustice of the wealthy classes in Mecca, and tried to help the poor.

During his lifetime, Mohammed led his countrymen to unite in a great religious movement. Within a hundred years after his death, Moslems carried his teachings into other parts of the Middle East, into North Africa, Europe, and Asia. Today, there are about 465 million Moslems throughout the world.

The name *Mohammed* means *Praised One.* There are several common spellings of the name, including *Mohammad (moh HAM uhd), Muhammad (moo HAHM uhd),* and *Mahomet (muh HAHM uht).*

Early Life. Mohammed was born in Mecca, in southwestern Arabia. His father died before his birth, and his mother died when he was a child. Then his grandfather and later his uncle, Abu Talib, became his guardians. For a time, Mohammed lived with a desert tribe. He learned to tend sheep and camels. Later, he may have traveled with his uncle on caravan journeys through Arabia to Syria. Mohammed also probably attended assemblies and fairs in Mecca, where he may have heard men of different faiths express their ideas.

At the age of 25, Mohammed entered the service of Khadija, a wealthy widow. She was 15 years older than Mohammed, but he later married her. They had two sons and four daughters. The sons died young. One of the daughters, Fatima, married Ali, son of Abu Talib. Many Moslems trace their descent from Mohammed through this couple (see FATIMITE DYNASTY).

His Religious Life. The most sacred shrine in Mecca was the Kaaba. It had a black stone, believed to be especially sacred, in one corner. When Mohammed was 35, a flood damaged the Kaaba. Because of his moral excellence, Mohammed was chosen to set the sacred stone back into place. See KAABA.

Later, when Mohammed was meditating alone in a cave on Mount Hira, a vision appeared to him. Moslems believe that the vision was of the angel Gabriel, who called Mohammed to be a prophet and proclaim God's message to his countrymen.

At first, Mohammed doubted that his vision had come from God. But his wife Khadija reassured him. She became his first disciple. For a time, no more revelations came, and Mohammed grew discouraged. Then Gabriel came once more, and told him, "Arise and warn, magnify thy Lord, . . . wait patiently for Him."

At first, Mohammed may have told only relatives and friends of the revelations. But soon he began to preach publicly. Most of the people who heard Mohammed ridiculed him, but some believed. Abu Bakr, a rich merchant, became a disciple. Omar, one of the leaders of Mecca, persecuted Mohammed at first, but later accepted him as a prophet.

The Hegira. Mohammed continued to preach in Mecca until several calamities took place. First, both Khadija and Abu Talib died. Also the people of Mecca began to hate Mohammed for his claims and his attacks on their way of life.

Finally, in A.D. 622, Mohammed fled north to the nearby city of Medina, then called Yathrib. His emigration to Medina is called the *Hegira.* It is considered so important that the Moslem calendar begins with the year of the Hegira (see HEGIRA). The people of Medina welcomed Mohammed. His preaching and statesmanship soon won most of them as followers.

His Teachings. Mohammed was now the head of both a religion and a community, and he was able to make his religious message into law. He abolished the customs of worshiping idols and killing unwanted baby girls. He limited the practice of *polygyny* (marriage to more than one wife), and restricted divorce. He reformed inheritance laws, regulated slavery, and helped the poor. He also banned war and violence except for self-defense and for the cause of Islam.

Mohammed seems to have expected Jews and Christians to accept him as a prophet. At first he was friendly toward them. He chose Jerusalem as the direction to be faced in prayer, similar to the Jewish practice. He also set aside Friday as a Moslem day of congregational prayer, perhaps because the Jews began their Sabbath preparations then. But the Jews of Medina broke their alliance with Mohammed and conspired against him with his enemies in Mecca. Mohammed angrily drove them from the city and organized a purely Moslem society. To symbolize the independence of the new religion, he ordered Moslems to face Mecca, instead of Jerusalem, when praying.

The Meccans went to war against Mohammed and his followers. They attacked Medina several times, but they were always driven back. In 630, Mohammed entered Mecca in triumph. He offered forgiveness to the people there, most of whom accepted him as the Prophet of God. He destroyed the pagan idols in the Kaaba, prayed there, and proclaimed it a *mosque* (house of worship). Mohammed died two years later in Medina. His tomb is located in the Prophet's Mosque in Medina (see MEDNA).

See also ISLAM; MOSLEMS; KORAN; MECCA; FLAG (color picture: Historical Flags of the World).

Critically reviewed by ALI HASSAN ABDEL-KADER

MOHAMMED II (1430?-1481), called THE CONQUEROR or THE GREAT, was the seventh ruler of the Ottoman Empire. He conquered Constantinople (now Istanbul) in 1453. This brought the Byzantine Empire to an end (see BYZANTINE EMPIRE). His armies also won Serbia, Bosnia, Albania, and other areas of southeast Europe, and the Crimea, Trebizond, and other Black Sea regions. Mohammed became sultan in 1451 after the death of his father, Murad II. He reorganized the Ottoman government and established the Palace School for training government officials. He also built the Seraglio Palace in Constantinople (now Istanbul), a *mosque* (Moslem house of worship), several colleges, and many charitable institutions (see SERAGLIO).

See also TURKEY (The Ottoman Empire).

SYDNEY N. FISHER

MOHAMMED V (1844-1918) was the 35th sultan of the Ottoman Empire (Turkey). He had been kept a prisoner of the state until 1909 by his brother, the sultan Abdul-Hamid II. The revolutionary Young Turks deposed Abdul-Hamid in 1909 and placed Mohammed on the Ottoman throne. Throughout his nine-year reign, the Young Turks dominated Mohammed. They led the Ottoman Empire into the Balkan Wars and World War I. The empire lost much territory in these wars, and was greatly weakened (see TURKEY [The Young Turks]).

See also TURKEY (The Ottoman Empire).

SYDNEY N. FISHER

MOHAMMED V (1911-1961), SIDI MOHAMMED BEN YOUSSEF, became king of Morocco in 1957. He had ruled as sultan since 1927, and maintained a staunch friendship with Western nations despite harsh treatment from the French government. The French seized him in 1953 and banished him to Corsica because of anti-

French riots in Morocco. Affairs became so serious in 1955 that the French allowed him to return. Morocco gained its independence in 1956. In 1958, Mohammed V proposed that the countries of Morocco, Algeria, and Tunisia join together in a federated Arab State of North Africa. His son Hassan II succeeded him as king. See also Morocco (Independence).

SYDNEY N. FISHER

MOHAMMED AHMED. See SUDAN (History).

MOHAMMED ALI. See MEHMET ALI.

MOHAMMED REZA PAHLAVI, *rih ZAH PAH luh vee* (1919-   ), became *shah* (king) of Iran in 1941. He is best known for the help he gave the Allies during World War II (1939-1945) and for his social and economic reforms in Iran.

Mohammed was born in Teheran. His father was Reza Khan Pahlavi. Reza refused to let Great Britain and Russia use the Trans-Iranian Railway during World War II. British and Russian troops occupied Iran, and forced Reza to give up his throne in 1941. Mohammed then became

Mohammed Reza Pahlavi

Wide World

shah. He allowed Britain and Russia to use the railway, and he let the Allies station troops in Iran.

Mohammed began a series of reforms in the 1960's. For hundreds of years, landlords owned and kept most of the profits from most Iranian farmland. Mohammed started a land reform program which forced landlords to sell or lease land to the poor farmers who worked it. Mohammed started a Literacy Corps in 1963. Its workers have taught thousands of Iranians to read and write. In 1963, through Mohammed's efforts, Iranian women were given the right to vote.

SYDNEY N. FISHER

MOHAMMED ZAHIR (1914-   ) became *shah* (king) of Afghanistan in 1933. During his reign, Afghanistan has built roads, schools, and irrigation projects and has developed new industry.

Zahir Shah was born in Kabul, the capital of Afghanistan. He became shah after the death of his father, Nadir Shah, but other members of the royal family actually ran the country until the 1960's. In an effort to make Afghanistan more democratic, Zahir Shah forced his cousin to retire from the key post of prime minister in 1963. He then appointed a prime minister who was not a member of the royal family. In 1964, Zahir Shah gave Afghanistan a new constitution that guaranteed individual rights, limited the power of the royal family, and gave the people a greater voice in the government.

See also AFGHANISTAN (Recent Developments).

MOHAMMEDAN ART. See ISLAMIC ART.

MOHAMMEDANISM. See ISLAM; MOSLEMS.

MOHAWK INDIANS. See IROQUOIS INDIANS.

MOHAWK RIVER is the largest branch of the Hudson River. The east and west branches of the Mohawk meet in central New York. The river then flows southeastward for 148 miles and enters the Hudson at Cohoes, about ten miles north of Albany.

The Mohawk River was named for the Mohawk Indians who lived in the region. A confederacy of

Iroquois tribes also made its headquarters in the area. The Mohawk River valley has served as a highway from the Hudson Valley to the Great Lakes region since colonial days. The New York State Barge Canal and two railroads run parallel with the river. GEORGE MACINKO

MOHAWK TRAIL was a route westward along the Mohawk River from the Hudson River to the Great Lakes. The Iroquois Indian confederacy occupied the land it crossed. In pioneer days, thousands of settlers traveled westward along this route. Its importance declined after the building of the Erie Canal in 1825. The Penn Central Railroad and a modern highway now follow the course of the trail. W. TURRENTINE JACKSON

See also TRAILS OF EARLY DAYS (map).

MOHENJO-DARO. See INDUS VALLEY CIVILIZATION.

MOHICAN INDIANS, *moh HEE kun,* is the name often given to two separate but related tribes of the eastern United States. One group, properly called the *Mahican,* lived along the Hudson River in New York state. The other, the *Mohegan,* settled in Connecticut. They broke off from the Pequot tribe, and formed one of the most powerful Indian groups in New England. Their chief Uncas remained friendly to the colonists, but the other Indians hated him and accused him of treachery (see UNCAS). Both groups lived like other tribes of the area (see INDIAN, AMERICAN [Eastern Woodlands]). After the coming of the white men, most Mahican moved westward to Wisconsin and lost their tribal identity. A few Mohegan, who have mixed with whites, still live in Mohegan, Conn.

James Fenimore Cooper's famous novel *The Last of the Mohicans* has given the Mohicans a prominent place in American literature. WILLIAM H. GILBERT

See also INDIAN WARS (The Pequot War).

MOHL, HUGO VON (1805-1872), a German botanist, was the first to propose calling the living contents of plant cells *protoplasm.* Mohl helped develop the *Cell Theory.* According to this theory, all plants and animals are made up of cells. New cells are formed by the division of older cells, and the protoplasm carries on the work of the cells. Mohl was born in Stuttgart, Germany. ROGERS MCVAUGH

MOHOLE was a government-financed project to drill into the earth and bring up the first samples of the earth's *mantle.* The mantle is one of four *layers* (zones) in the earth. It lies below the *crust* (outer layer). The boundary between the crust and the mantle is called the *Mohorovičić discontinuity.* This name is shortened to *Moho.* The hole that was to be drilled was called *mohole.* Scientists hoped the mohole project would provide information about the mantle. They wanted to study its composition, radioactivity, and temperature.

Scientists planned to drill from a floating platform in the ocean, because the crust is only about 5 miles thick under the ocean. It is about 20 miles thick under land, deeper than man can drill. They made test drillings, but the project ended in 1966 when Congress refused to provide more money, chiefly because of the rising costs of the project and of the space program and the Vietnam War. ROBERT S. DIETZ

See also EARTH (The Earth's Crust).

MOHOROVIČIĆ DISCONTINUITY. See MOHOLE.

MOHS, FRIEDRICH. See MINERAL (Hardness).

MOIRÉ, *mwah RAY,* is any cloth which has wavy designs on it, such as corded silk or rayon. The pattern

is put on cloth with engraved rollers and heat. Moiré is a French word which means *watered.* The word moiré may also describe paper, rock, or metal which has a watered appearance. See also MOIRÉ PATTERN.

MOIRÉ PATTERN, *mwah RAY,* is a pattern of lines that results when two regular patterns overlap. For example, if an ordinary piece of window screen is folded over, wavy lines appear where the screen overlaps. These lines form a moiré pattern.

The two patterns used to create a moiré pattern can consist of straight lines, curved lines, wavy lines, or even rows of dots. Interesting artistic designs have been created with moirés. Moiré cloth is an early example of the use of these patterns. Modern artists have used moirés in op art paintings.

In the 1960's, scientists discovered uses for moiré patterns. For example, when some crystals overlap, they produce moirés that can be seen with an electron microscope. From these patterns, scientists can discover how the atoms in the crystal are arranged. GERALD OSTER

MOISTURE. See WEATHER (Moisture); HUMIDITY.

MOJAVE, *moh HAH vih,* in southeastern California, is a vast desert wasteland covering about 25,000 square miles. It lies between the Sierra Nevada and the Colorado River. The Pacific Ocean covered this region thousands of years ago. Over a long period, high mountains rose and blocked the entry of water from the sea.

Volcanic mountains erupted and covered the region with lava, mud, and ashes. Today, many small isolated mountain ranges and extinct volcanoes break up the great stretches of sandy soil. Dry lake beds include Searles and Owens lakes. These lake beds and the region south of them form the world's chief source of boron, a mineral that is used for jet-engine and rocket fuels. GEORGE SHAFTEL

See also CALIFORNIA (physical map); DESERT (picture).

MOLAR. See TEETH (Permanent Teeth).

A Moiré Pattern of Wide Curving Lines results where two groups of narrow-lined circles overlap.

Edmund Scientific Co.

MOLASSES, *moh LASS ez,* is a thick, sweet, sticky syrup. It is yellowish or dark-brown. Molasses is used for cooking, candymaking, and as a livestock feed.

Most molasses is obtained as a by-product in the manufacture of sugar from sugar cane. Therefore, countries that grow sugar cane produce most of the world's molasses (see SUGAR CANE). In the United States, Louisiana is the center of molasses production.

How Molasses Is Made. Molasses is a liquid that is obtained from sugar crystals by changing cane juice to sugar. Molasses may be made by the open kettle method or by the vacuum pan method.

In the *open kettle method,* the cane juice is boiled in a large open pan. After it has been boiled several times, most of the water evaporates as steam. The syrup that remains receives additional boiling until it becomes a stiff mass of syrup and crystals called *massecuite.* The massecuite is placed in barrels that have tiny holes in the bottom. The molasses seeps through these holes, leaving sugar crystals inside the barrels.

Large sugar factories generally use the *vacuum pan method,* in which they boil the massecuite in large, covered vacuum pans. After the massecuite has been boiled several times, it is thoroughly stirred in a mixer. The mixture is then spun in rotating containers called *centrifugals.* The centrifugals have walls of fine copper mesh that permit the molasses to pass through but hold the sugar crystals.

Further boiling of the molasses produces varying grades. The molasses left after several boilings is called *blackstrap.* It is used chiefly to feed farm animals, for fertilizer, and to distill rum or alcohol.

Food Value. Molasses contains about 69.3 per cent carbohydrates, 25 per cent water, 2.4 per cent protein, and 3.2 per cent ash or mineral. A pound has a high energy value of 1,290 calories.

RICHARD A. HAVENS

MOLASSES ACT was passed by the British Parliament in 1733. It taxed molasses and sugar coming into the North American colonies from parts of the West Indies not under British control. The purpose of the act was to limit this trade to British colonies. But most Americans ignored the act, and it was repealed in 1764.

MOLAY, JACQUES DE. See DE MOLAY, ORDER OF; KNIGHTS TEMPLARS.

MOLD is a hollow form. See CAST AND CASTING.

MOLD is a tiny, simple plant which belongs to the fungi group. It is closely related to the mildews, rusts, and mushrooms. Molds have no *chlorophyll,* or green coloring matter, and therefore cannot manufacture their own food. They must live on food made by other plants or animals, or on decaying matter. Some molds live as parasites on insects and certain fungi.

Common bread mold belongs to a group called the *black molds.* The group gets its name because all of these molds produce dark-colored spores. Common bread mold forms a cottony, soft, white growth on damp bread. A group of molds known as the *blue molds* also grow on bread. A green mold often grows on various kinds of cheeses. Other molds, called *water molds,* are often found in water and soil.

Molds develop from a tiny particle called the *spore.* When the spore settles on a damp food substance such as bread, it swells and begins to grow by producing

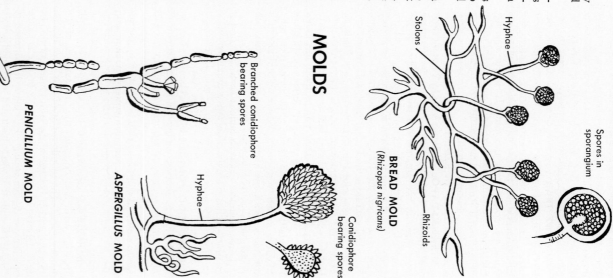

MOLDS

BREAD MOLD
(*Rhizopus nigricans*)

Spores in
sporangium

Hyphae

Stolons

Rhizoids

PENICILLIUM MOLD

Branched conidiophore
bearing spores

Conidiophore
bearing spores

ASPERGILLUS MOLD

Hyphae

tiny *hyphae* (threads). Some hyphae, called *rhizoids,* are like tiny roots. Others, called *stolons,* spread out on the surface.

As the plant body of the mold matures, many upright hyphae produce spore cases containing thousands of spores. Each spore case, called *sporangium,* is about the size of a pinhead. When the spore cases mature and break open, the spores are set free and are carried away by air currents. These spores in the air settle on damp foods and develop into new molds. In some molds, chains of spores are produced at the tips of certain hyphae, called *conidiophores.*

Moldy foods generally should be thrown away. But certain cheeses, such as Roquefort, owe their flavor to a mold which grows in them and ripens them.

Molds also are useful because they help to break up dead organisms and waste matter, and fertilize the soil. One mold produces the widely used drug penicillin (see PENICILLIN).

Scientific Classification. Molds belong to the phylum *Eumycophyta*. They are in the classes *Phycomycetes* and *Ascomycetes*.

WILLIAM F. HANNA

See also FUNGI; MILDEW; SLIME MOLD.

MOLDAVIA, *mŏl DAY´ vih uh,* is a region in south-central Europe. Part of it makes up the Moldavian Soviet Socialist Republic in the southwest corner of Russia. The western part (Moldavia proper) is a district in northeastern Romania. The Prut River divides the two. See RUSSIA (political map).

The Moldavian Soviet Socialist Republic (MSSR) (pop. 3,425,000) covers 13,012 square miles. Farmers raise cereals and tobacco in its fertile soil. Kishinev is its capital. This part of Moldavia belonged to Romania from the end of World War I until 1940. In 1940, Russia took it over and made it part of the MSSR.

Romanian Moldavia raises sheep and cattle, and grows wheat, corn, barley, sugar beets, grapes, and sunflowers. Coal and manganese are mined. Iaşi and Galaţi are the chief cities.

GEORGE KISH

See also BESSARABIA; ROMANIA; RUSSIA.

MOLE is a small, thick-bodied mammal that lives underground. The mole is a fast, tireless digger, and the shape of its body is well suited for burrowing through the earth. The mole has a narrow, pointed nose, a wedge-shaped head, and large forelegs. Its front paws, which turn outward, have long, broad nails. The forelegs work like shovels, scooping out the earth. The mole's hind legs are short and powerful. The animal is almost blind, with tiny eyes that are shaded by overhanging fur or skin. A mole does not have external ears, but it hears well.

A mole's home can be recognized by a mound of earth above it. This mound is considerably larger than the mound that the animal makes when digging for food. Moles eat mainly worms and insects and seldom eat plants. Their diggings often spoil gardens and fields, and farmers set traps in the animals' tunnels.

Mole fur has been used in making coats and jackets. Furriers prefer bluish-gray mole fur, but they also use black, brownish-black, and paler shades. Moleskin is lightweight, warm, soft, and thick. But it does not wear well and has lost popularity through the years.

The Common Mole of North America lives in the Eastern, Midwestern, and Southwestern regions of the United States. Its body is 8 to 9 inches long, including a short, almost hairless tail about an inch long. The common mole weighs from 1½ to 5 ounces and eats nearly its own weight in food every day. This mole lives almost its entire life underground. It tunnels near the surface when searching for food. Its nest may be several feet underground and is often lined with leaves.

One kind of common mole, the *star-nosed mole,* has a fringe of fleshy feelers around its nose. It has dark, brownish-gray fur on its upper parts, shading to a paler color underneath. The animal's long, hairy tail thickens at the base. The star-nosed mole lives in eastern Canada and in the Eastern United States as far south as Georgia. It likes to live near water and usually builds its home in the damp, muddy soil of a swamp or along the shore of a brook or pond. It is an expert swimmer. During the

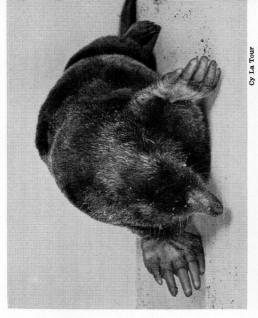

Cy La Tour

The Mole searches for earthworms and other food by digging tunnels with its sharp claws and powerful legs. The mole is nearly blind, but it does not need keen vision in its underground tunnels.

winter, the star-nosed mole burrows deep into the soil to avoid the frost.

The European Mole builds a home with many underground chambers. There is one central chamber that is connected to other smaller, round rooms. Passageways extend from these rooms in all directions. One passage, called the *bolt run,* serves as an exit in case of danger. The others lead to feeding grounds. In the central chamber is a nest in which three or four baby moles are born in early spring. The European mole is about the same size as the common mole of North America.

Moles also live in parts of Asia. The largest species of all moles is the Russian Desman, which is about 14 inches long, including the tail. It lives in southeastern Europe and central western Asia. The smallest species are the shrew moles and longtailed moles of Asia and the Pacific Coast of North America. They are about 5 inches long, including their tails.

Scientific Classification. Moles belong to the order *Insectivora.* They are in the mole family, *Talpidae.* The common mole of the Eastern United States is genus *Scalopus,* species *S. aquaticus.* The star-nosed mole is *Condylura cristata.* The European mole is *Talpa europaea.* The Russian Desman is *Desmana moschata.* FRANK B. GOLLEY

MOLE is a unit used in chemistry to measure amounts of chemicals that take part in chemical reactions. One mole of any substance equals 602,257,000,000,000,-000,000,000 (602.257 billion trillion) atoms, molecules, ions, or radicals. This number is usually written 6.02257×10^{23}. It is called *Avogadro's number* in honor of the Italian physicist Amedeo Avogadro.

The weight in grams of one mole of any substance is the same as the substance's *formula weight* (the sum of the atomic weights of all the atoms represented in its chemical formula). For example, one mole of carbon (chemical symbol C) weighs 12 grams, because carbon's atomic weight is 12 and only one atom is represented in its formula. One mole of oxygen (O_2) weighs 32 grams, because oxygen's atomic weight is 16 and two atoms are represented in its formula. One mole of carbon can be combined with one mole of oxygen to form one mole (44 grams) of carbon dioxide (CO_2).

MOLE is a spot on the skin. A mole is a birthmark, even though it may appear long after a person is born. There are two main kinds of moles, *vascular moles* and *non-vascular moles*. Most vascular moles are made up of swollen blood vessels. They are blue or deep red in color. Non-vascular moles are solid knots of skin tissue or connective tissue. They are seldom dangerous. A rare type of non-vascular mole, smooth and bluish-black in color, sometimes develops into a malignant tumor. The soft, hairy, brown mole is a common kind and is quite harmless. A fleshy mass or tumor that occasionally forms in the *uterus* (womb) is also called a mole.

See also TUMOR.

W. B. YOUMANS

MOLE CRICKET is a large cricket which burrows in the ground like a mole. The most common kind of mole cricket is about an inch and a half long, and is velvety brown. Its short front legs, like the mole's legs, are especially suited for burrowing. This insect has very short wings, but another kind of mole cricket has long wings and is able to fly. Mole crickets live throughout the tropical and temperate world.

Mole crickets live underground in the burrows which they dig. They eat insect larvae, earthworms, and root and tuber crops, including potatoes. The mole cricket, like other crickets, can make noise with its wings.

The *changa*, a mole cricket of Puerto Rico, is the worst insect pest of the sugar crop.

Scientific Classification. Mole crickets belong to the cricket family, *Gryllidae*. The American mole cricket is genus *Gryllotalpa*, species *G. borealis*. The changa is *Scapteriscus didactylus*.

URL LANHAM

MOLECULAR BIOLOGY is the study of the structure

and function of the large molecules essential to life. Among these molecules are proteins and nucleic acids. Proteins *catalyze* (speed up) chemical reactions that supply the energy for living cells. Nucleic acids carry the *genetic code* (information) necessary for the development of all living cells.

Molecular biologists try to find out how these molecules are built and how they work. They use X rays, electron microscopes, and chemical methods that purify and break down molecules for their studies. They also study microorganisms.

The discovery of the structure of *deoxyribonucleic acid* (DNA) was one of the most important advances in molecular biology. This discovery made it possible to explain the laws of heredity on a chemical basis. DNA also determines the structure of proteins. Scientists working in molecular biology have unraveled the structure of *myoglobin* and *hemoglobin*, two proteins that store and transport oxygen. They also have discovered how muscles contract and how certain viruses are built up. See NUCLEIC ACID; PROTEIN.

Molecular biologists as well as other scientists want to learn how proteins are made in a cell, and how they work. They hope to discover how single germ cells can grow into complex organisms such as humans, animals, and plants. They also hope to find out how the brain works.

M. F. PERUTZ

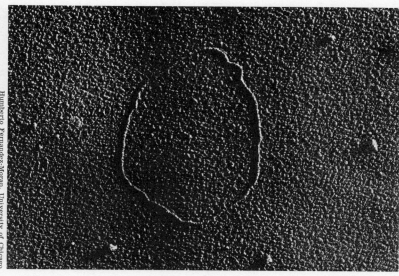

A Molecule of DNA looks like a thin thread when magnified 120,000 times by an electron microscope. DNA molecules are among the largest molecules known to scientists. They are thousands or millions of times larger than most other molecules. DNA is a chemical found in all living cells.

Humberto Fernandez-Moran, University of Chicago

MOLECULE, *MAHL uh kyool,* is one of the basic units of matter. It is the smallest particle into which a substance can be divided and still have the *properties* (characteristics) of the original substance. If the substance were divided further, only *atoms* (individual particles) of chemical elements would remain. For example, a drop of water contains billions of water molecules. If the drop could be divided until only a single water molecule remained, that final drop would still have all the properties of water. But if the water molecule were divided, only atoms of the elements hydrogen and oxygen would remain.

Molecules are made up of atoms held together in certain patterns. Every atom consists of a positively charged *nucleus* (central core) surrounded by negatively charged electrons. In a molecule, there are an equal number of positive and negative charges.

Scientists use chemical formulas to show the composition of molecules. For example, a water molecule consists of two hydrogen atoms and one oxygen atom, and has the formula H_2O. The size of a molecule depends on the size and number of its atoms. Molecules are made up of from two to thousands of atoms. A molecule that consists of only two atoms, such as nitric oxide (NO), is called a *diatomic* molecule. A molecule made up of three atoms, such as water, is called a *triatomic* molecule.

Almost all gases, most common liquids, and many solids consist of molecules. But some substances are made up of different units called *ions* (atoms with either a positive or a negative charge). These substances are called *ionic substances.*

Salts are examples of ionic substances. For example, sodium chloride, which is common table salt, consists of positive sodium ions and negative chloride ions. Electric forces among the ions hold the salt crystals together in a regular framework. Metals are also different from molecular substances. In addition to positive ions, metals consist of a large number of electrons that move about freely throughout the metal.

Molecules and Matter. Molecules are held together in a group by forces called *Van der Waals forces* (see VAN DER WAALS, JOHANNES DIDERIK). These forces are usually weaker than those that hold the molecule itself together. The force between molecules depends on how far apart they are. When two molecules are widely separated, they attract each other. When they come very close together, they *repel* (push apart) each other.

In a solid, the molecules are so arranged that the forces which attract and repel are balanced. The molecules vibrate about these positions of balance, but they do not move to different parts of the solid. As the temperature of a solid is raised, the molecules vibrate more strongly. When the Van der Waals forces can no longer hold the molecules in place, the solid melts and becomes a liquid.

In a liquid, the molecules move about easily, but they still have some force on one another. These forces are strong enough to form a filmlike surface on a liquid and prevent it from flying apart.

In a gas, the molecules move about so fast that the attractive forces have little effect on them. When two molecules in a gas collide with each other, the repelling force sends them apart again. Therefore, gas molecules fill a container completely, because they move freely through all the space available.

Most substances can be changed into solids, liquids, or gases by either raising or lowering their temperatures. But some substances remain solid until they are heated to very high temperatures. Other substances are gases except when cooled to very low temperatures. The temperature at which these changes occur—and also other characteristics of a substance—depends on the size, shape, and weight of the molecules and on the strength of the Van der Waals forces between them.

Individual Molecules. Certain atoms within a molecule have strong attractive forces between them. These forces produce *bonds* between the atoms. The forces within a molecule determine its shape. The molecule takes the shape that forms the strongest bonds and the least amount of strain among its atoms. For example, an ammonia molecule looks like a pyramid, with three hydrogen atoms forming the base and a nitrogen atom at the top. Normal butane molecules have four carbon atoms arranged in a zigzag chain with ten hydrogen atoms attached. A benzene molecule has six carbon atoms in a ring with six hydrogen atoms attached. Many protein molecules form long spiral chains.

The weight of a molecule is indicated by its *molecular weight.* Molecular weight can be found by adding the *atomic weights* of all the atoms in a molecule. The molecular weight of carbon dioxide (CO_2) can be found by adding the atomic weight of carbon, which is 12, and the weights of the two oxygen atoms, which are about 16 each. Carbon dioxide has a molecular weight of about

DIAGRAMS OF SOME COMMON MOLECULES

Scientists study chemical compounds to learn how many atoms of each element are in the molecules and how these atoms are joined to each other. With this information, diagrams of molecules can be drawn with balls representing the individual atoms.

WORLD BOOK diagram

A Carbon Dioxide Molecule has two oxygen atoms and a carbon atom.

An Ammonia Molecule has three hydrogen atoms and a nitrogen atom.

A Butane Molecule is a chain of carbon atoms with hydrogen atoms.

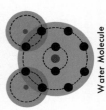

Hydrogen Atoms

Electron

Vacancies

Electrons

Electron

Vacancies

Oxygen Atom

A Molecule of Water forms when two atoms of hydrogen and one of oxygen, above, join together in sharing their electrons, below. The electrons fill the vacancies in all the atoms.

Water Molecule

44. A molecule's weight can also be measured with an instrument called a *mass spectrometer.*

The positive and negative charges in a molecule balance each other, but these charges are spread out unevenly in *polar* molecules. In a polar molecule, more positive charges collect at one end of the molecule and more negative charges collect at the other end. Some molecules are magnetic, because of the way the electrons move about within the molecule.

When two different kinds of molecules come near enough to each other, they may react and form one or more new molecules. Or two molecules of the same kind may combine and form one larger molecule. Molecules can also be broken down into smaller molecules. This can be done with ultraviolet light, fast-moving electrons, or nuclear radiation.

Studying Molecules. Scientists can study some molecules directly with an *electron microscope.* This method provides a picture of a molecule, but the picture is often too blurred to see fine details. Scientists also use several indirect methods to study molecules. For example, they study solids by *X-ray diffraction.* The way a solid deflects X rays tells them about the size, shape, and arrangement of the molecules in the solid. Scientists also use *neutron diffraction* to study solids. With this method, they pass a beam of *neutrons* (uncharged particles) through a solid, and observe how the beam is affected. Gases can be studied by *electron diffraction*—that is, by passing electrons through a gas.

Scientists also learn about molecules by studying the

way they absorb or give off light. Each kind of molecule has its own *spectrum* (band of colored light) when it absorbs or gives off light. By studying the spectrum of a substance, scientists can learn much about the molecules that make up the substance. For example, they can find the sizes and shapes of the molecules, the strength of the forces that hold the atoms together in the molecule, and the way the electrons move about in the molecules.

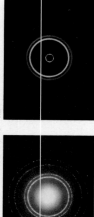

Diffraction Patterns are produced on photographic film when X rays or electrons pass through molecules of various substances. X rays produced the pattern at the left, and electrons made the one at the right.

Film Studio, Education Development Center

Related Articles in WORLD BOOK include:

Atom	Ion and	Liquid Crystal
Bond (chemical)	Ionization	Matter
Chemistry	Light	Solid
Gas (matter)	Liquid	

DAVID R. LIDE, JR.

MOLESKIN. See MOLE.

MOLIÈRE, *mo LYAIR* (1622-1673), was the stage name of Jean Baptiste Poquelin, the greatest French writer of comedy. Molière's plays emphasize one broad principle: the comic contrast between how people see

themselves and how others see them.

Molière experimented with many drama forms. During his short career, he wrote farce, high comedy, satire, and comedy-ballets. He wrote equally well in verse and prose. Molière was also a fine actor and director.

Molière was born in Paris, the son of a prosperous upholsterer. He earned a law degree, but he never practiced law. Instead, he

Molière in the Role of Caesar. Portrait by Nicolas Mignard, Comédie Française, Paris (National Photographic Service, Versailles)

Molière

and a group of friends founded the Illustre-Théâtre in 1643. From 1645 to 1647, the troupe toured France. In 1659, Molière staged *The Affected Young Ladies,* a one-act farce which he wrote. Its success attracted the attention of Louis XIV, who provided Molière with a permanent theater and asked him to write court entertainments.

Molière had no real philosophy, and his plays contain few ideas. But he had a knack for choosing controversial subjects that would attract public interest. *Tartuffe, or The Imposter* (1664) was a satire on religious hypocrisy. It aroused such great church opposition that the play could not be performed for several years. Church opposition also forced *Don Juan* (1665) to close after a short run. Molière then satirized universal human failings in *The Misanthrope* (1666), *The Miser* (1668), *The Learned Ladies* (1672), and other plays.

Late in his career, Molière wrote a series of comedy-ballets in which the dramatic script was accompanied by interludes of song and dance, somewhat like today's musical comedies. The most important of these works are *George Dandin* (1668), *The Would-Be Gentleman* (1670), and *The Imaginary Invalid* (1673).

See also FRENCH LITERATURE (Drama); DRAMA (French Neoclassical Drama).

MOLINA, TIRSO DE. See TIRSO DE MOLINA.

MOLINE, Ill. (pop. 42,705; alt. 585 ft.), a leading farm implement manufacturing center, is known as *the Plow City.* Located on the Mississippi River, it is adjacent to Rock Island and East Moline, Illinois, and opposite Davenport, Iowa. The four cities are linked by several bridges, and form a metropolitan area of 319,375 persons. Moline lies 150 miles west of Chicago (see ILLINOIS [political map]).

The name of the city comes from the Spanish word *molino,* meaning *mill,* and was probably suggested by the water power of the Mississippi. Moline was laid out in 1843, four years before John Deere decided to locate his plow factory there. Moline has a mayor-council government.

PAUL M. ANGLE

MOLINO DEL REY, BATTLE OF. See MEXICAN WAR (Scott's Campaign).

MOLLOY CATHOLIC COLLEGE FOR WOMEN. See UNIVERSITIES AND COLLEGES (table).

Walter Dawn

Bivalve (Common Edible Scallop)

Ralph Buchsbaum

Tooth Shell (Scaphopod)

Henning Lemche

Monoplacophoran (top and underside)

Russ Kinne, Photo Researchers

Chiton (Amphineura)

Douglas Faulkner, Publix

Gastropod (Pacific Islands Whelk)

N. J. Berrill

Squid (Cephalopod)

MOLLUSK is a soft-bodied animal without bones. Clams, octopuses, oysters, slugs, snails, and squids are mollusks. Most kinds of mollusks, including clams and oysters, have a hard armorlike shell that protects their soft bodies. Other kinds, such as cuttlefish and squids, have no outside shell. A special shell grows inside their bodies. This shell is called a *cuttlebone* in cuttlefish, or a *pen* in squids. A few kinds of mollusks, including octopuses and certain slugs, have no shell at all. For information about mollusk shells and how they are formed, see SHELL.

All mollusks have a skinlike organ called a *mantle*, which produces the substance that makes the shell. The edges of the mantle squeeze out liquid shell materials and add them to the shell as the mollusk grows. In mollusks with no outside shell, the mantle forms a tough wrapper around the body organs.

Mollusks live in most parts of the world. Some kinds live in the deepest parts of oceans. Others live on the wooded slopes of high mountains. Still others live in hot, dry deserts. Wherever mollusks live, they must keep their bodies moist to stay alive. Most land mollusks live in damp places such as under leaves or in soil.

The Importance of Mollusks

Mollusks are used mainly for food. People in many parts of the world eat mollusks every day. Most Americans do not eat them nearly so often. The most popular kinds used as food in the United States are clams, oysters, and scallops.

Mollusk shells are made into many useful products, including pearl buttons, jewelry, and various souvenir items. Perhaps the best known mollusk products are the pearls made by oysters.

Some mollusks are harmful to man. Certain small, fresh-water snails of the tropics carry worms that cause a fatal disease. Shipworm clams drill into rope, boats, and wooden wharves, and cause millions of dollars worth of damage a year.

Kinds of Mollusks

Mollusks make up the largest group of water animals. There are about 100,000 known kinds of living mollusks, and scientists find about 1,000 new species every year. The fossils of about 100,000 other species of mollusks have also been found.

The mollusks make up a *phylum* (major division) of the animal kingdom. The scientific name of the phylum

R. Tucker Abbott, the contributor of this article, holds the du Pont Chair of Malacology at the Delaware Museum of Natural History, and is the author of American Seashells *and* Sea Shells of the World.

MOLLUSK

is *Mollusca*, a Latin word meaning *soft-bodied*. A table with this article shows the six *classes* (large groups) of mollusks. To learn where the phylum fits into the whole animal kingdom, see ANIMAL (table: *A Classification of the Animal Kingdom*).

The six classes of mollusks are (1) univalves or *Gastropoda*, (2) bivalves or *Pelecypoda*, (3) octopuses and squids or *Cephalopoda*, (4) tooth shells or *Scaphopoda*, (5) chitons or *Amphineura*, and (6) *Monoplacophora*.

Univalves or Gastropods (*Gastropoda*) are the largest class of mollusks. They include limpets, slugs, snails, and whelks. Most kinds of univalves have a single, coiled shell. The name *univalve* comes from Latin words meaning *one shell*. Some kinds, including garden slugs and the sea slugs called *nudibranchs*, have no shells.

The name *Gastropoda* comes from Greek words meaning *belly* and *foot*. Gastropods seem to crawl on their bellies, but actually they move about by means of a large, muscular foot. The foot spreads beneath the body, and the foot muscles move in a rippling motion that makes the animal move forward. Most sea snails and a few land snails have a lidlike part called an *operculum* at the back of the foot. When danger threatens, the snail draws back into its shell and the operculum closes the shell opening.

Certain kinds of univalves have two pairs of *tentacles* (feelers) on their heads. One pair helps the animals feel their way about. Some species have an eye on each of the other two tentacles. Others have no eyes at all. A univalve also has a ribbon of teeth. This ribbon, called a *radula*, works like a rough file and tears apart the animal's food. Most univalves that eat plants have thousands of weak teeth. A few kinds eat other mollusks, and have several dozen strong teeth.

Bivalves (*Pelecypoda*) form the second largest class of mollusks. They include clams, oysters, mussels, and scallops. All bivalves have two shells that are held together by hinges that look like small teeth. The shells of bivalves are usually open. When the animals are frightened, strong muscles pull the shells shut and hold them closed until danger has passed.

The word *Pelecypoda* comes from Greek words that mean *hatchet* and *foot*. Bivalves have a strong, muscular foot shaped like a hatchet. Many kinds of these animals move about by pushing the foot out and hooking it in the mud or sand. Then they pull themselves up to the foot. Some bivalves, such as the geoduck and razor clam, use the foot to dig holes. They push the foot downward into mud or sand. First the foot swells to enlarge the hole, and then it contracts and pulls the animal is buried in mud or sand.

Most kinds of bivalves have no head or teeth. They get oxygen and food through a muscular *siphon* (tube). The siphon can be stretched to reach food and water if the animal is buried in mud or sand.

Octopuses and Squids (*Cephalopoda*) are the most active mollusks. The argonaut, cuttlefish, and nautilus also belong to this group. All live in the ocean, and most of them swim about freely.

The word *Cephalopoda* comes from Greek words meaning *head* and *foot*. A cephalopod seems to be made up of a large head and long tentacles that look like arms or feet. Octopuses and squids have dome-shaped "heads" surrounded by tentacles. Octopuses have 8 tentacles, and squids have 10. The tentacles grow around hard, strong, beaklike jaws on the underside of the head. These powerful jaws tear the animal's prey, and are far more dangerous than the tentacles. The animal uses its tentacles to capture prey and pull it into the jaws. Octopuses and squids eat fish, other mollusks, and shellfish.

Tooth Shells (*Scaphopoda*) have slender, curving shells that resemble tusks. These mollusks are often called *tusk shells*. The word *Scaphopoda* comes from Greek words that mean *boat* and *foot*. A tooth shell has a pointed foot that looks somewhat like a small boat. All tooth shells live in the ocean, where they burrow in the mud or sand. The top of the shell sticks up into the water. Tooth shells have no head or eyes. They feed on one-celled plants and animals that are swept into the mouth by tentacles.

Chitons (*Amphineura*) have flat, oval bodies covered by eight shell plates. The plates are held together by a tough girdle. The name *Amphineura* comes from Greek words that mean *around* and *nerve*. This name refers to two nerve cords that go around the chiton's body. Chitons have a large, flat foot. They can use the foot to move about, but they usually cling firmly to rocks. They roll up into a ball when forced to let go of the rocks. Chitons have a small head and mouth, but no eyes or tentacles. Their long radula is crisscrossed with teeth, which they use to scrape seaweed from rocks for food.

Monoplacophora are extremely rare. They live in the deepest parts of the ocean, and most kinds are found only as fossils. The name *Monoplacophora* comes from Greek words meaning *single*, *shell*, and *bearer*. Monoplacophorans have one shell that is almost flat, like a limpet shell. These mollusks are unusual because they have several pairs of gills, six or more pairs of kidneys, and many nerve centers. Like other mollusks, they have a mantle and radula. Scientists know little about their habits.

R. TUCKER ABBOTT

Related Articles in WORLD BOOK include:

Abalone	Geoduck	Scallop
Argonaut	Limpet	Shell
Chiton	Mother-of-Pearl	Shipworm
Clam	Mussel	Slug
Cockle	Nautilus	Snail
Conch	Octopus	Squid
Cowrie	Oyster	Whelk
Cuttlefish	Periwinkle	

CLASSES OF MOLLUSKS

Gastropoda (Univalves)	**Pelecypoda** (Bivalves)
Cephalopoda (Octopuses and Squids)	**Scaphopoda** (Tooth Shells)
Amphineura (Chitons)	**Monoplacophora**

MOLLY MAGUIRES was a secret society that used its power to aid its members in labor disputes. It was founded in Ireland and branches were started in Pennsylvania in 1867. Its members terrorized the hard-coal region of Pennsylvania. They were finally suppressed in 1877.

MOLNÁR, *MAHL nahr,* or *MAWL nahr,* **FERENC** (1878-1952), a Hungarian dramatist, wrote clever comedies. His best-known play, *Liliom* (1909), is more serious than many of his other works. It is an understanding and forgiving character-study of an amusement park barker who fails in everything he tries to do. It was made into the American musical comedy *Carousel* in 1945. Other Molnár plays that became popular are *The Devil* (1907), *The Guardsman* (1910), *The Swan* (1920), and *The Play's the Thing* (1925). His works also include the famous children's novel *The Paul Street Boys* (1907).

Molnár was born in Budapest, the son of a well-known physician. He studied law, but decided to become a journalist. He won fame as a witty conversationalist, as a man-about-town, and as the author of more than 40 plays. In 1940, he settled in the United States.   JOHN W. GASSNER

MOLOCH, *MOH lahk,* also spelled MOLECH, was an idol worshiped especially by the ancient Phoenicians and Amorites. From them, the idol-worshiping heretics of Israel borrowed the custom of sacrificing babies on the altar to Moloch, or else casting them on the lap of his image after it had been heated red-hot. The Bible forbids this worship (Lev. 18: 21; 20: 3-5). Kings Ahaz and Manasseh of Judah built altars to Moloch in the Valley of Hinnom, outside the walls of Jerusalem. King Josiah ended the practice.   GLEASON L. ARCHER, JR.

MOLOKAI. See HAWAII (The Islands).

MOLOTOV, *MAW loh tohv,* **VYACHESLAV MIKHAILOVICH** (1890-   ), became widely known during two terms as foreign minister of Russia. He was demoted in 1957 for his opposition to Nikita S. Khrushchev, first secretary of the Soviet Communist party. He was expelled from the Communist party's Presidium and sent into virtual exile as ambassador to Outer Mongolia. In 1960, he became Russia's delegate to the International Atomic Energy Agency. The Russian Communist party attacked him in 1961 and he returned to Moscow. In 1962, the Supreme Soviet (legislature) ordered his name removed from all Russian towns, buildings, and objects that had been named after him.

From 1939 to 1949 and from 1953 to June, 1956, Molotov served as commissar (later called minister)

Vyacheslav Molotov
Wide World

of foreign affairs. He helped create the Russian policy of hostility to the West, particularly to the United States. He attacked the North Atlantic Treaty Organization (NATO) as an agency that would lead to another war. Molotov proposed a collective security treaty for European countries that would exclude the United States.

Molotov joined the Bolshevik party at the age of 16 (see BOLSHEVIK). From 1906 to 1917, he helped plan the Bolshevik revolution. When the Bolshevik (now Communist) party seized power in Russia in 1917, Molotov received several important government positions. He served as premier of Russia from 1930 to 1941.

Molotov was born in the Kirov region of European Russia. His family name was Skriabin, but he changed it to Molotov, which means *of the hammer.*   ALBERT PARRY

MOLTING is the process an animal goes through in shedding worn-out hair, skin or feathers, and growing a new body covering. It often takes place at a definite time of year known as the animal's *molting season.*

The process of molting varies with different animals. In insects, the outer covering of the *larva* (the newly hatched insect) is too firm to expand with the growing creature, and so must be renewed periodically. The old covering becomes detached by a fluid that appears beneath it, and then dries, hardens, splits, and finally drops away. A new covering is secreted by a special layer of cells. The caterpillars of several kinds of butterflies shed their skins as many as five times before they reach the chrysalis stage in their development. See METAMORPHOSIS.

Birds shed their feathers at least once a year. Some kinds of birds even shed their feathers three times a year.

A Molting Snake rubs its nose against a hard, rough object, such as a rock or tree trunk, until its skin breaks away. Then it slides out of the old skin, leaving it turned inside out. The process takes only a few minutes.
John H. Gerard

Ferenc Molnár

Each complete molt takes from four to six weeks. Birds have a very systematic way of molting. The feathers fall out, one after another, in a regular order. As they fall out, they are replaced in a correspondingly regular order with new feathers. Because the molting is regularly spaced in some birds, they are able to fly during molting periods. When a bird has two molting seasons, the first is to replace bedraggled winter plumage, and the second is to deck the bird out for the mating season. See Bird (Feathers).

Many mammals (milk-giving animals) shed their hair once a year, usually in spring. Some animals replace body parts during molting. Deer shed their antlers and grow new ones. The lemming, an animal that looks like the guinea pig, and the ptarmigan, a grouselike bird, replace their claws. Scaly reptiles, such as snakes and lizards, and shellfish, such as lobsters and crabs, also undergo molts. They replace their outer coverings with new ones.

See also Crustacean (Life Story).

MOLTKE, *MAWLT kuh,* was the family name of two Prussian military leaders.

Count Helmuth Karl von Moltke (1800-1891) was a Prussian military genius. He ranked next to Prince Otto von Bismarck as a builder of the German Empire.

Von Moltke was appointed to the Prussian general staff in 1832. He became chief of staff in 1858. As the Prussian chief of staff, Von Moltke prepared the military plans for the wars with Denmark in 1864, with Austria in 1866, and with France in 1870. His campaigns always succeeded. A story has been told that while he was playing chess with another general, an excited officer told him that France had declared war on Prussia. Von Moltke calmly told the messenger which of his many war plans to put into effect. Then he turned to his chess opponent and said quietly, "Your move, I believe."

The great triumph of Von Moltke's career was the Prussian victory over France. His armies won decisively at Sedan on Sept. 2, 1870. Metz fell in October, and the Prussian armies entered Paris in triumph (see Franco-Prussian War). As a reward, the German government voted Von Moltke a fortune, and made him a count, a field marshal, and a life member of the upper house of parliament. He served as chief of staff until 1888. Von Moltke was born in the duchy of Mecklenburg-Schwerin and grew up in Lübeck. He was graduated from the Royal Military Academy in Copenhagen.

Count Helmuth Johannes von Moltke (1848-1916) was a nephew of Helmuth Karl von Moltke. He became chief of the German general staff in 1906. When World War I broke out in 1914, he followed General Alfred von Schlieffen's plan for a quick victory. This plan called for a sudden attack on France in a sweeping, fanlike movement through Belgium. But Von Moltke weakened his forces by sending troops to the Russian front, and the plan failed. The German government blamed Von Moltke for the failure, and removed him from command late in 1914. Von Moltke was born in Gersdorf, Germany.
Robert G. L. Waite

MOLTO. See Music (table: Terms Used in Music).

MOLUCCAS, *moh LUCK uz,* or Spice Islands, are a large group of islands in the eastern part of Indonesia. They are valued for their spice plants. The chief islands in the group are Ambon, Ceram, and Halmahera. For a discussion of these islands, see Indonesia.
L. B. Arey

MOLYBDENITE, *moh LIB duh nite,* is a bluish, lead-gray mineral. It is the chief source of molybdenum (see Molybdenum). Molybdenite is a compound of molybdenum and sulfur, and occurs in granite, limestone, and other rocks. A low-grade deposit is considered practical for mining purposes, even if it contains less than 20 pounds of molybdenite per short ton of the ore. It is found in several states in the United States, and in Australia, Canada, Germany, and Norway.

MOLYBDENUM, *moh LIB duh mum,* is a hard, silvery-white chemical element. Molybdenum is one of the strongest and most widely used *refractory metals* (heat resistant metals), because of its unusually high melting point of 2610° C. It also conducts heat and electricity easily. Molybdenum is mixed with steel and iron to produce strong *alloys*. Molybdenum steel is hard, strong, and resists *corrosion* (chemically wearing away).

Molybdenum is used in making parts for aircraft and missiles and for making wire filaments in electronic tubes. It is also used as a protective coating on other metals. Molybdenum compounds have many industrial uses. Molybdenum disulfide is used as a lubricant in greases and oils. Molybdenum trioxide increases *adhesion* (sticking qualities) of enamels for coating metals. Some molybdenum chemicals are used as dyes.

Molybdenum is found in the minerals molybdenite and wulfenite. Canada and the United States are the leading producers. Carl Wilhelm Scheele of Sweden discovered molybdenum in 1778. Molybdenum has the chemical symbol Mo, the atomic number 42, and the atomic weight 95.99. It boils at 5560° C.
Alan Davison

MOMBASA, *mahm BAH suh* (pop. 179,575; alt. 35 ft.), is an important seaport in Kenya, in eastern Africa. For the location of Mombasa, see Kenya (map). The products shipped from Mombasa include animal hides and skins, coffee, cotton, gold, sugar, tea, and tin.
Clarence E. Bennett

MOMENT, in physics, is the product of some quantity multiplied by a particular distance from a *fulcrum,* or axis. Moment of force is an example. A 100-pound boy sitting 10 feet from the center of a seesaw produces a moment of 1,000 pound-feet. Engineers use the knowledge of moments to determine stresses in bridges and other structures.

See also Lever (Law of Equilibrium); Gravity; Center of.

MOMENT is the smallest amount of time. It has no particular length. When most people speak of a moment, they mean a few seconds or a few minutes. But a moment is too small to be measured. Philosophers think of a moment as an instant or a point in time. The idea of a moment, or point in time, is important in philosophy, but has no practical scientific use.

In the Middle Ages, a moment was a definite period of time. People in the Middle Ages divided the hour into four *points*. Each point contained 10 *moments*. A moment was thus 1½ minutes long.

MOMENTUM, *moh MEN tum,* in physics, was called by Newton the quantity of motion of a moving body. When a baseball player swings his bat, the momentum of the bat depends on its mass and how fast it is swung.

The force exerted on the ball when the bat hits it depends on the rate of change in the bat's momentum.

To calculate the momentum of any moving object, multiply its *mass* (quantity of matter) by its *velocity* (speed and direction). An automobile that weighs 2,200 pounds has a mass of 1,000 kilograms. When driving north at 5 meters per second (about 11 miles per hour), it has a momentum of 5,000 (1,000 × 5) kilogram meters per second toward the north. An 11,000-pound truck has a mass of 5,000 kilograms. To have the same momentum as the car, the truck must drive north at only 1 meter per second (about 2 miles per hour).

An important law of physics states that momentum is conserved when two bodies act on each other without outside forces. If two objects collide, the total momentum of both objects after the collision equals their total momentum before collision. If the two objects have zero total initial momentum, their total final momentum also is zero. Thus, the momentum gained by one is equal and opposite to the momentum gained by the other. When a man dives off a still rowboat, the boat moves in a direction opposite to that of the man's dive. The boat's final momentum is equal and opposite to the man's final momentum, so that the total final momentum is zero, as it was before the dive.   LEON N. COOPER

See also FORCE; MASS; MOTION; VELOCITY.

MOMMSEN, *MAWM zun,* **THEODOR** (1817-1903), a German historian, won the 1902 Nobel prize for literature. His best-known work is his *History of Rome* (1854-1856). He was an expert on ancient Roman inscriptions. He taught law at the universities of Leipzig and Zurich, and history at Breslau. He was professor of history at the University of Berlin from 1858 until his death. He was born in Schleswig.   FRANCIS J. BOWMAN

MONA LISA. See PAINTING (color picture); DA VINCI, LEONARDO (Work in Florence).

MOMENTUM

When a man dives off a still boat, the boat moves in a direction opposite to the man's dive. The momentum gained by the boat is opposite and equal to the momentum gained by the man.

BEFORE DIVING
Boat's Momentum = 0   Diver's Momentum = 0

AFTER DIVING
Boat's Momentum + Diver's Momentum = 0

MONACO

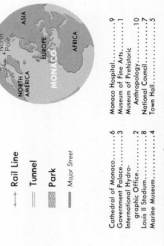

Rail Line
Tunnel
Park
Major Street

Cathedral of Monaco	6
Government Palace	3
International Hydrographic Office	2
Louis II Stadium	8
Marine Museum	4
Monaco Hospital	9
Museum of Fine Arts	1
Museum of Prehistoric Anthropology	10
National Council	7
Town Hall	5

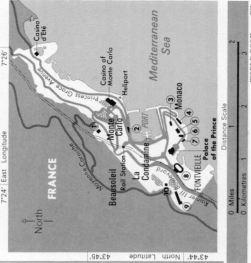

FRANCE

Mediterranean Sea

Casino d'Été
Casino of Monte Carlo
Monte Carlo
Heliport
Monaco
Beausoleil
Rail Station
La Condamine
Palace of the Prince
FONTVIEILLE

North

7°24′ East Longitude   7°26′
43°44′ North Latitude   43°45′

Distance Scale
0 Miles   1   2
0 Kilometres   1   2   3

WORLD BOOK map-FHa

MONACO, *MAHN uh koh,* is one of the smallest countries in the world, with an area of less than 1 square mile. It lies on the French Riviera coast of the Mediterranean Sea. France borders it on three sides. Monaco is a popular tourist resort, with many fine hotels, clubs, flower gardens, and places of entertainment. One of its chief attractions is the famous Monte Carlo gambling casino.

Monaco is also known for automobile sports events. Drivers from all over the world compete each year in the Monte Carlo Rally. They drive more than 2,000 miles from starting points in many parts of Europe for the competition at Monte Carlo. In the Monaco Grand Prix, top racing drivers guide their cars on a 200-mile automobile race through the twisting streets of Monaco.

The towns of Monaco and Monte Carlo perch on terraced cliffs overlooking the Mediterranean. The town of Monaco is the capital of the country. Prince Rainier III and Princess Grace, the former American actress Grace Kelly, rule from a stately castle, part of which was built in the 1200's.

The contributor of this article, Anthony Mann, is Chief of the Paris Bureau of the (London) Daily Telegraph.

MONACO

FACTS IN BRIEF

Capital: Monaco.

Official Language: French.

Form of Government: Principality.

Area: 0.58 square mile.

Population: *1961 Census*—22,297; distribution, 100 per cent urban. *Estimated 1971 Population*—24,000; density, 41,379 persons to the square mile. *Estimated 1976 Population*—28,000.

Chief Products: Beer, candy, chemicals, dairy products.

Flag: The flag has two horizontal stripes, red and white. See FLAG (color picture: Flags of Europe).

Money: *Basic Unit*—French franc. See MONEY (table).

Monaco's official language is French Its citizens are called *Monégasques*.

Government. Monaco is a *principality* (ruled by a prince). The prince represents Monaco in international affairs, such as the signing of treaties and agreements with other countries. Under the terms of a treaty with France in 1918, if Monaco's royal family has no male heirs, Monaco will come under French rule.

A minister of state, under the authority of the prince, heads the government. The minister is a Frenchman, and is nominated by the French government. Three councilors who are responsible for finance, police and internal affairs, and public works assist the minister of state. The 18-member National Council is the legislative body of the principality. Monégasques elect National Council members to five-year terms. The council must approve changes in Monaco's constitution.

People. Only about a seventh of Monaco's 24,000 people are Monégasque. Nearly half its residents are French, and most of the others are Italians, Germans, British, and Americans. Most people in Monaco speak French. Most Monégasque citizens converse in a local dialect called Monégasque, which is based on French and Italian. Many wealthy people from other countries

make Monaco their permanent home because the principality has no income tax. Since 1963, however, most Frenchmen living in Monaco have had to pay income tax at French rates.

The state religion is Roman Catholicism, but there is complete freedom of worship. Monaco's primary schools are run by the church. The principality also has a high school and a music academy.

The Monaco government awards the Rainier III prize for literature each year to a writer in the French language. Monaco's libraries include the Princess Caroline Library, which specializes in children's literature. Monaco also has a marine museum, a prehistoric museum, a zoo, and botanical gardens. The marine museum houses a collection of rare exhibits, and also has one of the world's leading aquariums and a laboratory for marine research. The Grand Theater of Monte Carlo presents performances by some of the world's greatest singers and ballet dancers. Some of the world's leading conductors and soloists perform with Monaco's national orchestra.

Land. Monaco lies at the foot of Mt. Agel (3,600 ft.). In some places, the principality stretches only 200 yards inland from the Mediterranean.

Monaco has four distinct parts—the three towns and a small industrial area. Monaco, the old town and former fortress, stands on a rocky point 200 feet high. It is dominated by the royal palace.

Monte Carlo has the famous gambling casino, the opera house, hotels, shops, beaches, and swimming pools. The port area, La Condamine, lies between the town of Monaco and Monte Carlo. The industrial zone, called Fontvieille, lies to the west of the town of Monaco.

The country has a mild winter climate, with an average January temperature of 50° F. Summer temperatures rarely exceed 90° F. On the average, rain falls only 62 days a year.

Economy. Monaco's income comes mainly from the tourist trade. Each year, more than 600,000 tourists from all parts of the world visit the principality. A

The Harbor in Monaco is nestled at the foot of terraced Alpine cliffs. Monaco's glittering buildings are clustered around the harbor's edge, at the foot of Mt. Agel.

Paul Popper, Ewing Galloway

company called the Société des Bains de Mer owns the casino and most of the hotels, clubs, beaches, and other places of entertainment. Monaco's colorful postage stamps are popular with collectors, and are an important source of income.

Many foreign companies have their headquarters in Monaco because of the low taxation there. Factories in Fontvieille produce beer, candy, and chemicals.

The principality has a local bus service. The main highway on the Riviera coast passes through Monaco, carrying motorists traveling between France and Italy. A railroad connecting France and Italy also runs through Monaco. The principality transmits its own radio and television programs. Its television transmitter stands on top of Mt. Agel, in French territory.

History. Monaco's museum contains much evidence, including remains and tools, of early man in the area. Phoenicians from the eastern Mediterranean probably settled in Monaco in about 700 B.C. In Greek and Roman times, Monaco was an important trading center, and its harbor provided shelter for ships from many lands.

The Genoese, from northern Italy, gained control of Monaco in the A.D. 1100's. They built the first fort there in 1215. In 1308, the Genoese granted governing rights over Monaco to the Grimaldi family of Genoa. The Grimaldi family became absolute rulers.

At various times from the 1400's to the 1600's, Monaco was occupied or controlled by France or Spain. France seized control of Monaco in 1793, during the French Revolution. But the Congress of Vienna restored control to the Grimaldi family in 1814. In 1866, Prince Charles III founded the town of Monte Carlo. In the early 1900's, Monte Carlo became a popular winter resort for the wealthy and famous of Europe.

The princes of Monaco ruled as absolute monarchs until 1911, when Prince Albert I approved a new constitution. Palace revolts and violence marked the early history of Monaco. Prince Jean II was murdered by his brother Lucien, who was later murdered by a relative. Prince Honoré I was drowned during a revolt.

Later rulers included Prince Albert, known as the *Scientist Prince.* He did much important marine research, and founded the famous Oceanographic Museum. Prince Louis II ruled from 1922 until 1949, except for the German occupation during World War II. His grandson Prince Rainier III succeeded him.

Rainier proclaimed a new constitution in 1962. The constitution provided votes for women, and abolished the death penalty. In 1963, under pressure from France, Monaco imposed a tax on business profits for the first time.

Rainier announced plans to build new hotels and reclaim land from the sea for new beaches and places of entertainment. After a long struggle with Aristotle Onassis, a wealthy Greek shipowner who controlled the Société des Bains de Mer company, Rainier enacted a law in 1966 giving the Monaco government greater control of the company. ANTHONY MANN

See also RAINIER III; KELLY, GRACE; MONTE CARLO.

MONAD. See LEIBNIZ, GOTTFRIED WILHELM.
MONADNOCK. See VERMONT (Land Regions); NEW HAMPSHIRE (Mountains).
MONARCH BUTTERFLY. See BUTTERFLY.

MONARCHY is a form of government in which one person who inherits, or is elected to, a throne holds executive power for life. These persons, or monarchs, have different titles, including *king, emperor,* or *sultan,* in various governments. The old idea of monarchy maintained that the power of the monarch was absolute. It sometimes held that the power of the monarch was responsible only to God. This doctrine became known as "the divine right of kings" (see DIVINE RIGHT OF KINGS).

Revolutions, particularly in England and France, destroyed much of the power of monarchs. In the 1640's, the English Parliament raised an army, defeated King Charles I, and condemned him to death. In 1688 the English people feared James II would restore the Catholic faith, and forced him to give up his throne. The French Revolution of 1789 limited the power of Louis XVI, and in 1793 the revolutionists put him to death. As a result, *limited,* or *constitutional,* monarchy developed, in which a legislature, a constitution, or both, limit the power of a monarch. Norway, Denmark, and Sweden have limited monarchies. The British monarch has little power. WILLIAM EBENSTEIN

Related Articles in WORLD BOOK **include:**

Coronation	Emperor	King	Queen
Czar	Kaiser	Majesty	Sultan

MONASH, SIR JOHN (1865-1931), commanded the Australian Army Corps during the last seven months of World War I. His strategy of combining the use of tanks and infantry helped bring the Allies victory in battles at Hamel, France, in July, 1918, and Amiens, France, in August, 1918. An excellent organizer, Monash once said, "Battles should be won before the barrage opens." Prime Minister David Lloyd George of Great Britain called Monash "the most resourceful general in the whole of the British Army."

Monash was born near Melbourne, Australia. He was trained as an engineer. He entered the army in 1887, and was given command of an infantry brigade in 1914. In May, 1918, he took command of the Australian Army and was promoted to lieutenant general. ROBIN W. WINKS

MONASTERY. See MONASTICISM; MONK; CLOISTER.

MONASTICISM, *moh NAS tuh sizˊm,* is the way of life of one who leaves the affairs of the world and devotes himself to religion. Such persons are called *monastics* or *monks* if they are men, and *nuns* or *sisters* if they are women. The word comes from the Greek word *monos,* meaning *alone.* Most followers of monasticism live in communities called *monasteries* (for men) or *convents* (for women). Those who live alone are *hermits.*

A Trappist Monk
The New World

Since ancient times, Buddhist and Hindu monastics have lived apart in order to devote their time to spiritual matters. Many scholars have regarded the Essenes, a Jewish sect, as the forerunners of Christian monasticism. Sometime during the A.D. 200's, individual Christians began to live as hermits. St. Anthony of Thebes became the first hermit to organize his followers into a group with fairly definite rules. He is known as the father of Christian monasticism. Later Christian monks formed orders that accepted a common mode of life, such as the orders of St. Benedict of Nursia, or St. Basil.

Related Articles in World Book include:

Convent	Fakir	Monk	Religious	Trappist
Essenes	Hermit	Nun	Life	

MONAZITE, MON uh zite, is a heavy, yellow-brown mineral. It is a compound of phosphates (phosphorus and oxygen) of the rare-earth metals and thorium. Its chemical formula is $(Th, Ce, La, Y)PO_4$. Monazite is one of the chief sources of thorium, a nuclear fuel used in nuclear power plants called *breeder reactors* (see Atomic Reactor ["Breeder" Reactors]). Monazite is also a chief source for the rare-earth elements and compounds. The rare earths are used widely in glass and metal manufacturing.

Monazite occurs naturally in granite and pegmatite rocks and veins. As these rocks weather and break up, the monazite settles in deposits in riverbeds and beach sand. Commercial supplies of monazite are taken from sand. The monazite is usually separated from other collected minerals by an electromagnetic process. The most important monazite deposits occur in India and Brazil. Other deposits are found in the United States, Australia, Ceylon, Malaysia, Indonesia, Canada, and South Africa.

CECIL J. SCHNEER

MONCK, mungk, **BARON STANLEY MONCK,** a British statesman, was the first governor general of the Dominion of Canada. He served as governor general of British North America from 1861 to 1867 and of the Dominion of Canada from 1867 to 1868. He was influential in uniting Upper and Lower Canada into one dominion. Monck was born in Tipperary County, Ireland, and was graduated from Trinity College, Dublin. He was elected to the English House of Commons in 1852, and also served as lord of the treasury.

MONCTON, New Brunswick (pop. 45,847; alt. 33 ft.), is the transportation and distributing center for the Atlantic Provinces of Canada. It lies on a bend of the Petitcodiac River near the Bay of Fundy. Railroads and highways connect Moncton to Nova Scotia. A railway and ferry provide service to Prince Edward Island (see New Brunswick [political map]). Daily air flights link Moncton with other parts of Canada and with the United States. The city has several industries. For the monthly weather, see New Brunswick (Climate).

The famous *bore* (tidal wave) of the Petitcodiac River rushes past Moncton twice a day. It comes up from the Bay of Fundy with a roar that can be heard for miles. The wall of water ranges from a few inches to 4 feet in height. This makes it necessary for even large boats to be tied firmly. See BORE; BAY OF FUNDY.

Baron Monck

oil portrait by an unknown artist, The Government House, Ottawa

LUCIEN BRAULT

1763. The town, then known as *The Bend,* became a shipbuilding center in its early days. The name was changed to Moncton in 1885, and a city charter was granted in 1890. During World War II, the Moncton airport was used as a training base for the British and Canadian air forces. Moncton has a mayor-council form of government.

W. S. MacNUTT

MONCTON, UNIVERSITY OF, is a coeducational school in Moncton, N.B. It is supported by the province. Courses at the university are taught in French. The university has a faculty of arts and a faculty of pure and applied sciences. It also has schools of commerce, education and psychology, home economics and social sciences, and nursing. The university was founded in 1963. For enrollment, see CANADA (table: Universities and Colleges).

CLEMENT CORMIER

MONDAY is the second day of the week. The word comes from the Anglo-Saxon *monandæg,* which means the *moon's day.* In ancient times, each of the 7 days was dedicated to a god or goddess. Monday was sacred to the goddess of the moon. Monday comes after Sunday.

Black Monday is the name given to Easter Monday, April 14, 1360. On this day, many of the troops of King Edward III of England, who were fighting the French, died on their horses outside Paris because of the cold.

Blue Monday is a term used in the United States to indicate that it is a dismal day. It is the day the workweek begins, and in many parts of the country it is the traditional family washday. In Bavaria, Blue Monday is the Monday before Lent. It is called that because of the color of the church decorations on that day. See also LABOR DAY; WEEK.

GRACE HUMPHREY

MONDRIAN, MAWN dree ahn, **PIET** (1872-1944), is known for pure geometric painting. His early works were brilliantly colored landscapes. In Paris in 1912, the cubist works of Georges Braque and Pablo Picasso impressed him. By 1919, Mondrian used only straight lines of black, white, and primary colors. His work affected later architecture and advertising. His painting *Composition in Red, Yellow, and Blue* appears in color in the PAINTING article. He was born in Amersfoort, The Netherlands, and lived in New York City. GEORGE D. CULLER

MONEL METAL, moh NEL, is an important alloy of nickel and copper. It contains about 67 per cent nickel and 28 per cent copper. The rest is made up of such elements as iron, manganese, or aluminum. Monel metal looks like nickel. It is about as hard as steel and can be forged and drawn into wire. It is easier to prepare than nickel, for some ores already contain nickel and copper in suitable proportions. The alloy is therefore cheaper than pure nickel. See ALLOY; COPPER; NICKEL.

Monel metal resists corrosion. It shows hardly any damage from steam, sea water, hot gas, air, or acids. This property makes it useful in sheet-metal work, in chemical plants, and on ships. It is used for pump fittings, propellers, and condenser tubes, and as a covering for sinks and soda fountains.

WILLIAM W. MULLINS

MONERA, MUH nih uh, is a group of tiny one-celled organisms. Members of the group are called *monerans.* Monerans have some characteristics of both animals and plants. Some scientists consider the monerans a separate *kingdom* (group) in the system of scientific classification. Monerans include bacteria and blue-green *algae* (seaweed), which are sometimes considered

Monet's *Water Lilies* was one of a series the artist painted near the end of his life, when he was almost blind. The emphasis on light and color gives the picture an almost abstract quality.

plants. Other scientists classify monerans and other one-celled organisms called *protozoa* in a single kingdom called *Protista*. Some protozoans have both animal and plant characteristics.

See also CLASSIFICATION; PROTISTA.

MONET, *maw NEH,* **CLAUDE** (1840-1926), was a founder and leader of the Impressionist group of French painters. The group took its name from one of Monet's pictures, *Impression, Rising Sun* (1874). For a color picture of this painting, see FRANCE (Arts). Monet and Pierre Renoir together developed the Impressionists' technique of *broken color* in the 1870's. This technique meant placing touches of pure color side by side and letting the eye blend them at a certain distance from the canvas (see PAINTING [In the 1800's]; RENOIR, PIERRE).

The public greeted the Impressionists with hostility and ridicule, and considered their art ugly and revolutionary. Monet continued to use and develop the Impressionist style throughout his life, becoming more and

more free as he grew older. From about 1890 on, he did many series of paintings showing the same subject at various hours of the day under different lighting. These paintings include *The Haystacks, Rouen Cathedral, The Thames,* and *Venice.* His famous painting *Old St. Lazare Station, Paris* appears in color in the PAINTING article. Monet devoted his last years to the famous series of lily-pond pictures, *The Water Lilies,* which carried his style to the edge of pure abstraction.

Monet was born in Paris but spent his early life in Le Havre. He studied in Paris. Monet disliked the classical type of painting then popular, and joined several artists whose ideas agreed with his own. This group became the Impressionists.   ROBERT GOLDWATER

See also IMPRESSIONISM (picture).

MONETARY CONFERENCE, INTERNATIONAL. See BRETTON WOODS.

MONETARY SYSTEM OF THE UNITED STATES. See MONEY (Money and the National Economy).

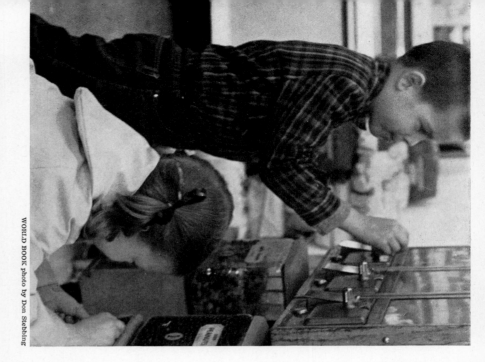

WORLD BOOK photo by Don Stebbing

MONEY

A Pocketful of Change can be spent for candy in a vending machine or dropped into a coin bank. But not all money is as handy as modern coins. Yap islanders still use primitive stone "coins" weighing hundreds of pounds, above. They place the money in front of their homes to represent their wealth.

MONEY is what people use to buy things. When you buy a pair of shoes, you may pay for them with paper bills and some coins. Or if you have money in a bank, you may give the merchant a check. The merchant accepts the bills, coins, or check for the shoes because he can use the money to buy things for himself.

People spend money for goods and services. They buy *goods* such as food, clothing, and books. They pay for *services* such as haircuts, hospital care, and television repairs. Many persons save some of their money by depositing it in a bank or a savings institution.

People earn money by performing services such as making refrigerators, selling shoes, or teaching school. They also earn money from *investments*, including government bonds and savings accounts.

Money can be anything that people agree to accept in exchange for the things they sell or the work they do. Ancient peoples used such varied things as beads, shells, and cattle for money. Today, most nations use metal coins, paper bills, and bank checks. The coins and bills of most countries differ from those of other countries. They look different and have different names. But if a nation wanted to do so, it might use beads, shells, sheep, or anything else for money.

The contributors of this article are G. L. Bach, Frank E. Buck Professor of Economics and Public Policy at Stanford University; and V. Clain-Stefanelli, Curator of the Division of Numismatics of the Smithsonian Institution.

588

MONEY TERMS

Bank Deposits consist of money in banks. Bank deposits in checking accounts can be spent by writing checks.

Bullion is uncoined gold and silver in such forms as bars, nuggets, or dust.

Credit Money is paper money with a face value greater than the reserves that *back it up* (guarantee its value).

Currency includes legal coins and paper bills.

Devaluation means lowering the value of a nation's currency in terms of its standard money or in terms of the currencies of other nations.

Fiat Money is money that has no gold or silver reserves to support it.

Fiduciary Money is money that is not full-bodied. It includes token coins and all paper money.

Fractional Money, such as a half dollar, is worth a certain portion of a standard monetary unit.

Full-Bodied Money refers to coins that have a face value equal to the value of the metal they contain.

Legal Tender is money which, by law, must be accepted in payment of debts.

Mint is a place where coins are made. *Minting* means manufacturing coins.

Representative Money is backed by reserves totaling the face value of the money.

Reserves consist of gold and silver bullion or coins that guarantee the value of fiduciary money.

Scrip is paper currency issued for temporary use, usually in an emergency.

Standard Money, such as gold or silver, serves as backing for a nation's circulating currency.

Token Coin is a coin with a face value greater than the value of the metal it contains.

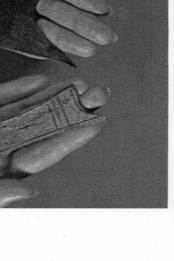

Babylonian "Due Bill," written in clay in the 3000's B.C., shows what a purchaser owed to a merchant in exchange for goods. Such bills are the earliest monetary documents.

Ancient Ring Money of gold, silver, and bronze served as convenient types of "coins."

Lumps of Salt were used as money to pay Roman soldiers. This practice led to the expression "not worth his salt" to describe a person who does not earn his wages.

Money of Ancient China was sometimes made in the form of bronze spades and knives. This kind of money developed from the custom of exchanging spades, knives, and other tools in barter.

Feathers of Jungle Birds were once used to make a rare kind of money. Tribesmen in the Santa Cruz Islands, northeast of Australia, trapped birds and glued their feathers to a rope coil.

Japanese Tree Money of the 1800's had coins that could be broken from "branches" to make change.

Money of Central African Tribes once included a copper cross about the size of an outspread hand, above, and an iron spearhead, below. A tribesman used a number of crosses to buy a wife. With several spearheads, he could buy a slave.

MONEY / *Money Around the World*

Every country has its own units of money. For example, the United States uses the *dollar*, England uses the *pound sterling*, and Japan uses the *yen*. These basic units are broken down into smaller units of money. The U.S. dollar has 100 *cents*, the English pound has 100 *new pence*, and the Japanese yen has 100 *sen*. A person can exchange his money for the money of

any country according to certain rates. For example, one pound sterling is worth about $2.40, and one dollar is worth about 356 yen. Usually, such rates are set by central banks (see BANKS AND BANKING [Central Banks]). The amount of goods or services one can buy with one unit of a currency changes as that country's economic and political conditions change.

1 DOLLAR (Canada)

1 POUND (England)

1 KRONA (Sweden)

2.50 PESETAS (Spain)

1,000 LIRE (Italy)

1 DEUTSCHE MARK
(West Germany)

1 DEUTSCHE MARK
(East Germany)

¼ BALBOA (Panama)

1 PESO (Mexico)

1 LIRA (Turkey)

1 RUPEE (India)

1 DRACHMA (Greece)

1,000 YEN (Japan)

1 FRANC (France)

1 RUBLE (Russia)

Russian Trade Delegation

1 PESO (Philippines)

WORLD BOOK photo

HALF DOLLAR
(Liberia)

All photos from Chase Manhattan Bank
Money Museum unless otherwise indicated.

590

VALUES OF MONETARY UNITS IN 1970

The table below lists the monetary units of many countries and shows their value in United States dollars. It also lists the number of these monetary units per U.S. dollar. The examples, *right*, show how some monetary units have changed in U.S. dollar value over the years.

Monetary Unit	1940	1950	1960	1970
British pound	$4.03	$2.80	$2.80	$2.40
Mexican peso	.18	.1157	.0800	.0801
Swedish krona	.2385	.1932	.1930	.1942
Swiss franc	.2315	.2331	.2322	.2325

Country	Monetary Unit	Value in U.S. Dollars	Units Per U.S. Dollar
Afghanistan	Afghani	$ .0133	75.00
Albania	Lek	.20	5.00
		*.08	*12.50
Algeria	Dinar	.2041	4.90
Argentina	Peso	.2857	3.50
Australia	Dollar	1.12	.8925
Austria	Schilling	.0385	26.00
Bahamas	Dollar	.9829	1.02
Barbados	Dollar	.5050	1.98
Belgium	Franc	.0200	50.00
Bolivia	Peso	.0843	11.86
Brazil	Cruzeiro	.2283	4.38
Bulgaria	Lev	.854	1.17
		*.5000	*2.00
Burma	Kyat	.2118	4.72
Burundi	Franc	.0115	86.86
Cambodia	Riel	.0180	55.54
Cameroon	Franc	.0036	277.61
Canada	Dollar	.9324	1.0725
Central African Rep.	Franc	.0036	277.71
Ceylon	Rupee	.1680	5.95
Chad	Franc	.0036	277.71
Chile	Escudo	.1010	9.90
China (Communist)	Yuan	.4000	2.50
Colombia	Peso	.0557	17.95
Congo (Brazzaville)	Franc	.0036	277.71
Congo (Kinshasa)	Zaire	1.99	.50
Costa Rica	Colon	.1505	6.62
Cuba	Peso	1.00	1.00
Czechoslovakia	Koruna	.138	7.20
		*.0619	*16.16
Dahomey	Franc	.0036	277.71
Denmark	Krone	.1332	7.51
Dominican Republic	Peso	1.00	1.00
Ecuador	Sucre	.0469	21.30
Egypt (U.A.R.)	Pound	2.30	.435
El Salvador	Colon	.40	2.50
Ethiopia	Dollar	.4030	2.48
Finland	Markka	.2392	4.18
Formosa (Taiwan)	Dollar	.0250	40.00
France	Franc	.1800	5.55
Gabon	Franc	.0036	277.71
Gambia	Pound	2.40	.41667
Germany (East)	Mark	.450	2.22
		*.2387	*4.19
Germany (West)	Mark	.2705	3.68
Ghana	Cedi	.9800	1.02
Great Britain	Pound	2.40	.41667
Greece	Drachma	.0335	29.85
Guatemala	Quetzal	1.00	1.00
Guinea	Franc	.0036	277.71
Haiti	Gourde	.20	5.00
Honduras	Lempira	.50	2.00
Hong Kong	Dollar	.1640	6.10
Hungary	Forint	.085	11.74
		*.0333	*29.97
Iceland	Krona	.0119	84.00
India	Rupee	.1334	7.50
Indonesia	Rupiah	.00307	326.00
Iran	Rial	.0133	75.00
Iraq	Dinar	2.83	.353
Ireland	Pound	2.40	.41667
Israel	Pound	.2857	3.50
Italy	Lira	.001589	629.00
Ivory Coast	Franc	.0036	277.71

Country	Monetary Units	Value in U.S. Dollars	Units Per U.S. Dollar
Jamaica	Dollar	$1.20	.833
Japan	Yen	.002803	356.00
Jordan	Dinar	2.80	.357
Kenya	Shilling	.1422	7.03
Korea (South)	Won	.00327	305.25
Kuwait	Dinar	2.80	.357
Laos	Kip	.0018	550.00
Lebanon	Pound	.3046	3.28
Liberia	Dollar	1.00	1.00
Libya	Pound	2.825	.35
Liechtenstein	Franc	.2325	4.30
Luxembourg	Franc	.0200	50.00
Malagasy Republic	Franc	.0036	277.71
Malawi	Pound	2.410	.41250
Malaysia	Dollar	.3247	3.08
Mali	Franc	.001800	555.00
Malta	Pound	2.42	.41250
Mauritania	Franc	.0036	277.71
Mexico	Peso	.0801	12.49
Monaco	Franc	.1800	5.55
Morocco	Dirham	.1904	5.25
Nepal	Rupee	.099	10.10
Netherlands	Guilder	.2752	3.69
New Zealand	Dollar	1.1270	.89
Nicaragua	Cordoba	.1429	7.00
Niger	Franc	.0036	277.71
Nigeria	Pound	2.78	.35833
Norway	Krone	.1404	7.12
Pakistan	Rupee	.2119	4.72
Panama	Balboa	1.00	1.00
Paraguay	Guarani	.0080	125.00
Peru	Sol	.02299	43.50
Philippines	Peso	.1640	6.10
Poland	Zloty	.25	4.00
		*.0418	*23.94
Portugal	Escudo	.0352	28.44
Puerto Rico	Dollar	1.00	1.00
Romania	Lev	.166	6.00
Russia	Ruble	1.10	.91
Rwanda	Franc	.01007	99.00
Saudi Arabia	Riyal	.2237	4.47
Senegal	Franc	.0036	277.71
Sierra Leone	Leone	1.204	.83
Somalia	Shilling	.1400	7.14
South Africa	Rand	1.4020	.71
Spain	Peseta	.01438	69.60
Sudan	Pound	2.89	.35
Sweden	Krona	.1942	5.14
Switzerland	Franc	.2325	4.30
Syria	Pound	.2380	4.20
Tanzania	Shilling	.1403	7.13
Thailand	Baht	.0484	20.67
Togo	Franc	.0036	277.71
Trinidad and Tobago	Dollar	.5000	2.00
Tunisia	Dinar	1.95	.512
Turkey	Lira	.1111	9.00
Uganda	Shilling	.1404	7.12
United States	Dollar	1.00	1.00
Upper Volta	Franc	.0036	277.71
Uruguay	Peso	.00400	250.00
Venezuela	Bolivar	.2232	4.48
Vietnam (South)	Dong	.00847	118.00
		*.0555	*18.00
Yugoslavia	Dinar	.0800	12.50
Zambia	Kwacha	1.418	.71

Sources: *Foreign Exchange Quotations*, March, 1970, The First National Bank of Chicago; *Monthly Bulletin of Statistics*, April, 1970, UN
*Preferential rate for tourists.

MONEY/How Money Developed

Long ago, no one needed money. People made their own food or hunted it. They made their own clothing and shelter. As time went on, some persons found that they could do a certain job better than their neighbors. They began to spend their time doing that one job. They then exchanged the things they produced for other things they needed but did not make themselves.

A man who liked to fish and was a good fisherman spent his time fishing. He traded some of the fish he caught for spears, clothing, and other items his neighbor made. This method of trading or exchanging goods is called *barter*. Barter works well when people do not need or use a wide variety of goods. Primitive tribes in various regions still use barter. See BARTER.

People often met problems in using the barter system. For example, a man who raised sheep might find that the only person who wanted a sheep was a fisherman. Suppose the sheepherder traded one sheep for a hundred fish. He would then have to exchange the fish he could not use before they spoiled. Frequently, he could not find people who would accept the fish in trade for other goods he needed. And so he lost the value of the unused fish.

The First Money. To avoid some of the problems of barter, people began to accept certain objects in exchange for any product. They agreed on objects that everyone valued. These objects served as the first money. They included animal skins, cattle, fish, grain, salt, shells, and metal objects such as fishhooks, hoes, pots, and rings.

Many ancient tribes measured the value of their money and the price of goods in terms of animals. Suppose, for example, that a man had 20 hoes, and the 20 hoes were worth 1 ox. The man could buy a canoe that was valued at 1 ox. In this way, oxen served as a

standard of value without actually being exchanged.

As time went on, people began to use metal money more than any other kind because it was more practical. Metal objects did not wear out easily. They also had a wide range of values depending on their weight, and they could be broken into smaller pieces. Historians believe that the Chinese may have used specially shaped metal money as early as the 1100's B.C. This money consisted of miniature bronze spades, knives, and other tools. The tool-shaped money represented the objects that commonly were exchanged in barter.

Gold and silver became especially valuable because they were scarce. People valued rings, bracelets, and other ornaments made from these metals, and used the ornaments as money. Sometimes gold and silver money was made in the form of bars. A bar of a certain weight might have the value of one ox. The major problem with such money was that it might not be pure. Articles made from gold and silver could contain varying amounts of less-valuable minerals.

The First Coins were made in order to assure the value of metal money. A government or some other authority made coins and stamped them with designs to guarantee their value. All coins with the same value contained the same amount of a valued metal.

Historians believe the first coins were made during the 600's B.C. in Lydia, a country in what is now Turkey. These coins were called staters. The word *stater* (meaning *standard*) was originally the name for a unit of weight. Staters were made of a natural mixture of gold and silver called *electrum*. Seagoing merchants brought these early coins to Greece. By the mid-500's B.C., similar coins were being used in every area where the Greeks had set up colonies.

The Romans began making coins during the 300's

Bargaining with Cattle was a common practice among ancient peoples who used animals as money. Cattle also were used as a standard for measuring the value of money and the price of goods.

United Nations

Barter Markets are the shopping centers of some countries where the people make their living mostly by farming. At these markets, persons exchange goods or use money to buy products.

Early Paper Money included giant Chinese bills almost as large as two outspread pages of this encyclopedia. The bills were printed during the 1300's on paper made from mulberry bark.

Chase Manhattan Bank Money Museum

Chase Manhattan Bank Money Museum

Greek Stater of the 600's B.C. was the first Greek coin made of silver. The shape of a turtle was stamped on the face, and a design resembling windmill vanes was punched into the reverse.

American Numismatic Association

Roman Denarius was issued in many designs from the 200's B.C. until the A.D. 200's. The face of this coin carries the portraits of the emperor Nero and his mother, Agrippina.

B.C. About 200 B.C., they issued the first denarius (see DENARIUS). The Romans brought their coins into all the countries they conquered. Roman coins greatly influenced the monetary systems of the Middle Ages, mainly those of England and the Holy Roman Empire.

The First Paper Money was probably made in China. The Italian adventurer Marco Polo saw it being used there in the late A.D. 1200's. Unlike gold and silver coins, this paper money had little value of its own. But it could be exchanged for valuable metals.

The paper money we use today developed from a custom that began in England during the 1600's. At that time, many persons stored their gold and other valuables in the vaults of goldsmiths. The goldsmiths gave written receipts for the valuables. The owners of the valuables then used the receipts as money. Businessmen accepted the receipts because they could use them to recover the valuables from the goldsmiths.

The use of paper money increased greatly after 1650 with the rise of national banks. For example, the Bank of Sweden, founded in 1656, printed paper *bank notes*. The notes were issued to persons who either deposited money in the bank or borrowed money from it. Each note stated the amount in coins that the person could get from the bank in exchange for the note.

Paper money appeared in North America for the first time in 1685. This money consisted of playing cards used in the Canadian colonies. Each card was marked with a certain value and signed by the French colonial governor. The French colonial authorities issued this unusual money because of a shortage of French currency in the Canadian colonies. They intended that the playing cards be used only until more money arrived from France. The people could then exchange the cards for regular French money. But even after the money arrived, the Canadian colonies continued to use the cards without cashing them. The cards were so widely accepted that they were issued for more than 70 years.

Playing Cards were used as money by early Canadian colonists. The back of each card was signed by the French colonial governor.

Criswell's Money Museum

The First Bank Notes in the Western world were printed in the 1600's. This bank note was issued in Denmark in 1819.

Spanish Dollar was a common coin of the early colonists. It could be cut into pieces to make change.

Pine-Tree Shillings and various other coins were made by colonists during the 1600's.

Colonial Paper Money of the 1700's included many bills printed by Benjamin Franklin.

Fugio Cent of 1787 was the first coin officially issued by the United States government.

"Continentals"—bills issued during the Revolutionary War—became worthless because there were not enough gold and silver coins in the colonies to back them up.

Money in the Colonies. Money did not play an important part in the economy of the early American colonies. Each family made most of the things it needed, and bartered with other families for goods it did not produce. Sometimes the colonists used Indian wampum as money. *Wampum* money consisted of strings or belts of beads made from the insides of shells (see WAMPUM).

The colonists made some coins, called *shillings* and *pence,* according to the money system used in Great Britain (see PINE-TREE SHILLING). But gold and silver for coinage were scarce. The colonists did not mine these metals and they could not afford to import them. Also, the English government opposed the making of coins in the colonies. The English said coinage was a privilege only of the mother country.

Most of the coins used in the colonies were Spanish. Colonial traders received these coins when dealing with Spanish settlements in the West Indies. The colonists also used some British, French, and Portuguese coins.

Paper money was first issued in the American colonies during the late 1600's. The colonial governments printed money to pay the cost of military attacks against Canadian colonists. In the 1700's, colonial governments continued to issue notes to pay their debts. Also, colonial banks sometimes issued paper notes as loans to persons and businesses.

By 1750, the colonies had much more paper money than they had gold or silver to exchange it for. As a result, many persons found that the notes were worth far less than the value printed on them. Merchants would not accept the notes at *face value* (the value printed on a

note). A purchaser might have to pay several times the price of an item if he bought it with paper money instead of coins. In 1751, the British Parliament took steps to keep the colonial notes from becoming worthless. It prohibited Connecticut, Massachusetts, New Hampshire, and Rhode Island from printing any more paper money. In 1764, Parliament ordered the rest of the colonies to stop issuing paper money.

New Nation, New Currency. During the Revolutionary War (1775 to 1781), the Continental Congress issued great amounts of notes called *continentals.* The value of these notes was stated in terms of Spanish silver coins called *dollars.* The continentals quickly lost value because they greatly outnumbered the supply of Spanish dollars. Americans began to describe any worthless thing as "not worth a continental."

During and after the Revolutionary War, the new states issued a variety of copper cents in small quantities. Private individuals also made and circulated some unofficial coins, including silver shillings and pence, and gold doubloons (see DOUBLOON).

The Coinage Act of 1792 established the first national *mint* (a place where coins are made). The act also set up the first system of money in the United States. Congress established an American dollar as the basic unit of this system. The American dollar had about the same value as the Spanish dollar. The new money system included both gold and silver coins. Congress chose the decimal system to count money units because it was easy to use (see DECIMAL NUMBER SYSTEM). Along with their new money, Americans continued

Bank Notes issued by the First and Second Banks of the United States in the 1800's were "as good as gold" because they could be exchanged for coins.

Gold Pieces, such as this $50 coin, or *slug,* were issued by the U.S. assay office in California in the 1850's.

All photos from Chase Manhattan Bank Money Museum unless otherwise indicated.

Greenbacks, first issued in 1861 to help pay the costs of the Civil War, soon decreased in value because they could not be exchanged for coins.

Confederate Currency was printed by the Confederate States of America during the Civil War. It was not backed by any gold or silver reserves.
WORLD BOOK photo by Don Stebbing

Gold Certificates were issued from 1865 to 1933. Persons could exchange them for gold coins.
Criswell's Money Museum

Silver Certificates, issued from 1878 to 1963, are gradually being withdrawn from circulation.

Gold Coins, such as this $10 gold "eagle," were last issued in 1933.

Federal Reserve Notes were first issued in 1914. The Jackson $10 bill, below, was issued until the late 1920's.
Criswell's Money Museum

to use many foreign coins. A law passed in 1793 made these coins a legal part of the U.S. coinage system. Under the law, the value of a foreign coin depended on the amount of gold or silver in it. In 1857, Congress passed a law removing foreign coins from circulation.

The Growth of Paper Money. During the early 1800's, American banks issued large amounts of paper notes to borrowers. The First and Second Banks of the United States supported their own notes with reserves of gold coins (see BANK OF THE UNITED STATES). People willingly used these notes because they could always exchange them for coins. Notes also were issued by state banks and by banks authorized by state governments. But these banks did not set aside enough coins to support their notes. Notes issued by one bank could not always be exchanged at another bank for coins. When the notes could be exchanged, their value in coins varied from bank to bank. The notes were often worth far less than the amount printed on them, and, in some cases, they were even worthless.

In 1861, the Department of the Treasury issued the first United States notes, called *greenbacks.* The government issued a large number of these notes to help pay the costs of the Civil War (1861 to 1865). Greenbacks could not be exchanged for gold or silver. As a result, they lost much of their value. See GREENBACK.

The National Bank Acts of 1863 and 1864 set up a system of national banks. The national banks had the power to issue bank notes backed by government bonds. To keep the notes from losing their value, the government limited the number that could be issued. But as a result, shortages of paper money occurred frequently. The government's efforts to overcome the money shortage led to the Federal Reserve Act of 1913. This law gave the United States a new type of paper money called *Federal Reserve notes.* It also provided a method of adjusting the money supply to fit the public's demand for money (see FEDERAL RESERVE SYSTEM).

At first, the government intended Federal Reserve notes to be just a small part of all the money in circulation. But by 1920, the value of the Federal Reserve notes in use was greater than the total value of all coins and other bills.

U.S. Money Today. In the mid-1960's, U.S. *currency* totaled about $4 billion in coins and about $38 billion in paper money. During the past hundred years, Americans have been paying their bills more and more by

MONEY/United States Money

bank check. In the mid-1960's, for example, between 75 and 80 per cent of all payments were made by check. More than $130 billion was deposited in bank checking accounts of individuals and business and other organizations. Because checks are used to make most payments, economists usually include checking deposits in banks as part of the money supply.

Just as the government controls the amount of coins and paper money created, so also it has the power to regulate the amount of checking deposits in banks. Congress gives this power to the Board of Governors of the Federal Reserve System (FRS). For a discussion of the ways in which the FRS regulates bank deposits, see FEDERAL RESERVE SYSTEM (What the System Does).

Two bureaus of the Department of the Treasury manufacture currency. The Bureau of the Mint makes

James Madison

George Washington/The Great Seal

Alexander Hamilton/U.S. Treasury

Thomas Jefferson/Monticello

Abraham Lincoln/Lincoln Memorial

Benjamin Franklin/Independence Hall

Andrew Jackson/The White House

William McKinley

Ulysses S. Grant/U.S. Capitol

Salmon P. Chase

Woodrow Wilson

Grover Cleveland

coins at mints in Philadelphia and Denver, and from time to time, at the assay office in San Francisco. The Bureau of Engraving and Printing in Washington, D.C., produces paper money. See MINT; ENGRAVING AND PRINTING, BUREAU OF.

Coins are minted in five *denominations* (values): (1) half dollar, (2) quarter, (3) dime, (4) nickel, and (5) cent. No silver dollars have been minted since 1935, but over 450 million are still in circulation.

A date appears on the front of a coin. This date is usually the year the coin was made. During the mid-1960's, mints attempted to discourage hoarding by making a large number of coins without changing the date from one year to the next. This practice was discontinued in 1966.

Many coins have a mint mark on the face or reverse. Coins made at the Denver mint are marked with the letter *D*, and those made at San Francisco with the letter *S*. To discourage hoarding, mint marks were left off coins dated 1965, 1966, and 1967. No mint marks appear on coins made at Philadelphia, except for Jefferson nickels of 1942 through 1945, which have the letter *P*.

The motto *In God We Trust* was placed on U.S. coins for the first time in 1864. Not all coins minted then have carried it. In 1955, Congress passed a law requiring that all U.S. coins and paper money carry the motto. The first bills to carry it were $1 bills issued in 1957. The law provided that the motto be added to all U.S. paper money when printing plates were made for new high-speed presses. The phrase *E Pluribus Unum* (*one out of many*) has appeared on the reverse side of many U.S. coins. The value of the coin and the inscription *United States of America* also appear on the backs of all coins.

From time to time, the government issues special coins to honor outstanding persons or events. For example, the Washington-Carver half dollar was issued from 1951 to 1954 in honor of Booker T. Washington and George Washington Carver. Such coins, called *commemoratives*, are issued for only a short time and in a limited quantity. Few commemoratives get into circulation because coin collectors buy and keep them.

Paper Money includes seven types of notes. But only two kinds of notes are now being issued—Federal Reserve notes and United States notes.

Federal Reserve notes are issued by Federal Reserve banks in denominations of $1, $5, $10, $20, $50, and $100. Their value is protected by gold reserves and by such securities as government bonds. These notes make up over 85 per cent of the money in circulation. Until 1969, Federal Reserve banks also issued notes in denominations of $500, $1,000, $5,000, and $10,000.

United States notes (also called legal tender notes or greenbacks) are issued by the Department of the Treasury in the $100 denomination. The Treasury also issued $2 notes until 1966 and $5 notes until 1969.

Five other types of notes are being withdrawn from circulation. (1) *Silver certificates* of $1, $5, and $10 are backed by reserves of silver. In 1963, the Department of the Treasury began withdrawing these notes so that the silver reserves could be used for coinage. (2) *Federal Reserve bank notes* have been gradually withdrawn since the 1930's. (3) *National Bank notes* were issued until 1935. Few of them remain in circulation. (4) *Gold certificates*, along with gold coins, were mostly withdrawn in 1933. But the Treasury still uses gold certificates in dealing with Federal Reserve banks. (5) *Treasury notes of 1890* have been almost entirely withdrawn.

Artists in the Bureau of Engraving and Printing design United States paper money. The secretary of the treasury must approve the final design. Every piece of paper money has a seal at the right or left side of the front portrait. The color and position of the seal vary with different types of money.

Penny

Abraham Lincoln/Lincoln Memorial

Nickel

Thomas Jefferson/Monticello

Dime

Franklin D. Roosevelt/Torch; Laurel and Oak Leaves

Quarter

George Washington/Eagle

Half Dollar

John F. Kennedy/Presidential Seal

Dollar

Liberty Head/Eagle

WORLD BOOK photos unless otherwise indicated

Chase Manhattan Bank Money Museum

Designing Paper Money. An artist draws the design into the steel plate. The Secretary of the Treasury must approve the finished design.

Making an Engraving. Engravers copy the artist's drawing, cutting the design into a steel plate.

Minting Coins. All U.S. coins are made of *alloys* (mixtures of metals). Pennies are an alloy of copper and zinc. Nickels are a mixture of copper and nickel. Dimes, quarters, and half dollars formerly contained 90 per cent silver and 10 per cent copper, but the Coinage Act of 1965 changed their composition. All silver was eliminated from dimes and quarters, and the percentage of silver in half dollars was greatly reduced. Dimes and quarters are made of three layers of metal *bonded* (sealed) together. The *core* (center) is pure copper, and the outer layers are an alloy of copper and nickel. Half dollars are made of three layers of a silver-copper alloy. The core contains a lower percentage of silver than the outer layers. No silver dollars have been minted since 1935, but those in circulation contain 90 parts of silver to 10 of copper.

The mint prepares the alloys for cents and nickels by melting the metals together in electric furnaces. The alloys are then molded into thin *ingots* (bars). A machine presses the ingots into strips about as thick as finished coins. The bonded strips used to make dimes, quarters, and half dollars are prepared by private companies and shipped to the mints.

Most of the remaining manufacturing steps are the same for all coins. A machine cuts the metal strips into *blanks* ("coins" without a design). Each blank then goes into a machine that produces a raised rim around its edge. These blanks are fed into a coining press that stamps a design on both sides. Besides stamping the coins, the press squeezes ridges called *reeding* on the rims of dimes, quarters, and half dollars.

The mint ships finished coins to Federal Reserve banks. These banks distribute the coins to banks that are members of the Federal Reserve System. Banks that do not belong to the system get coins from member banks. Federal Reserve banks remove worn and damaged coins from circulation. The mint remelts these coins and makes the metal into new coins.

Printing Paper Money begins with the preparation of engravings used to make printing plates. Skillful engravers cut the design of a bill into a steel plate. One engraver works on the portrait, another adds the lettering, and still others complete the rest of the design. The engraving then goes to a *transfer press*. This machine squeezes the engraving against a steel roller and presses the design into the roller's surface. In a similar way, the roller then presses the design into hundreds of printing plates used to print the bills.

The Bureau of Engraving and Printing uses two kinds of printing presses in making paper currency. High-speed rotary presses print sheets of 32 bills. Slower flatbed presses print 72 bills at a time. Plans call for all currency to be printed on high-speed presses.

The government uses special paper and ink made by secret processes. For example, the paper contains tiny red and blue threads that can easily be seen in new bills. The Bureau of Engraving and Printing guards its paper and ink carefully to prevent anyone from using them to make counterfeit money.

The design of the bills gets printed first. A second printing operation adds the serial number, seal, and signatures of the Secretary of the Treasury and the Treasurer of the United States. Next, the sheets are cut in half, inspected, and cut into separate bills. The approved bills are banded and wrapped for delivery to banks of the Federal Reserve System. Nonmember banks get their bills from Federal Reserve banks.

After paper money wears out, banks withdraw it from circulation and ship it to their Federal Reserve banks. The Federal Reserve banks burn unfit silver certificates and United States notes, and replace them with new bills. If the worn-out bills are Federal Reserve notes, the Federal Reserve banks ship them to the Department of the Treasury to be burned. A $1 bill wears out in about 18 months. Bills of higher denominations last longer because they are not handled as often in circulation.

Main Features of Federal Reserve Notes

[Illustration of a $1 Federal Reserve Note with labeled features]

Seal and letter
identifying Federal Reserve
district where issued

Printing plate
identification number

Serial number

Number of Federal Reserve
district where issued

Treasury seal

Serial number

Printing plate
identification number

Year in which bill
was designed

Printing. A high-speed rotary press prints sheets of 32 bills. The bill's design is printed first. Then the serial number, seal, and signatures are added.

Inspecting. The printed sheets are cut in half and examined. Inspectors mark any imperfect bills.

Cutting. Inspected sheets are cut into stacks of bills. Imperfect bills are removed and destroyed.

By special permission, U.S. Bureau of Engraving and Printing, U.S. Treasury

Making Printing Plates. In a transfer press, a roller squeezes the design into plates that will print the bills.

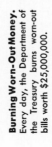

Burning Worn-Out Money. Every day, the Department of the Treasury burns worn-out bills worth $25,000,000.

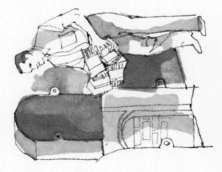

Shipping. A million dollars in $1 bills makes a wall of money. The wrapped bills are shipped to Federal Reserve Banks.

Money and Business.

The strength of a nation's economy depends, to a large degree, on how much money individuals and businesses have and how they spend it. If they do not spend enough money, depression and unemployment may result. If they spend too much, inflation will occur. See Economics (Booms and Depressions); Inflation and Deflation.

The government tries to promote a prosperous economy by controlling the amount of money individuals and businesses have to spend. If there is depression and unemployment, the Federal Reserve can provide more reserves to banks. This permits banks to lend more money. Persons and businesses then have more money to spend, and the increased spending helps provide new jobs and make the economy more prosperous. If there is inflation and too much spending, the Federal Reserve

Vaults at Fort Knox guard part of the U.S. gold supply. The Treasury also stores gold in mints in Denver and Philadelphia, and in assay offices in New York City and San Francisco.

U.S. Bureau of the Mint

can take away bank reserves. The banks then can lend less money.

Monetary Standards.

Throughout history, nations have used various *monetary standards* to regulate the amount of money it can issue. The standard must be something that the citizens consider valuable. During the past few hundred years, almost all nations have used a valuable metal, such as gold or silver, as partial backing for their money.

When nations use gold or silver as backing for money, the government's supply of these metals limits the amount of money it can issue. In the United States, for example, the Federal Reserve cannot issue paper money totaling more than four times the gold certificates it holds. These certificates represent the gold owned by the U.S. government. But there is no such limit on how many new reserves it can provide to banks to permit them to lend more. This reflects a gradual movement to put less stress on gold and silver as backing for money. Nations rely more and more on control of the money supply by governmental authorities to encourage a growing, prosperous economy.

Since the mid-1800's, many countries have used a *gold standard*. Such a standard is called a *monometallic* (one-metal) standard. Under the gold standard, a stated amount of gold can always be obtained from the government in exchange for coin or paper money. The government, therefore, must limit the amount of money in circulation so that it can meet demands for such exchanges. Thus, the amount of money a nation issues depends roughly on the size of the nation's supply of gold.

Some nations have used a *silver standard*. A nation that uses both gold and silver is said to be on a *bimetallic* (two-metal) standard. A nation whose money cannot be freely exchanged for gold or silver at a fixed rate is sometimes said to be on an *inconvertible paper standard*, or a *managed money standard*.

Most major nations had gold standards from 1870 until the outbreak of World War I in 1914. Then most nations abandoned the gold standard. Great Britain, then the world's monetary leader, stayed off the gold standard until 1925. During the Great Depression of the early 1930's, most nations again went off the gold standard. Since 1934, only a few nations have returned to the gold standard.

All nations, however, accept gold in payment for goods they sell to other countries, and use gold to make such payments. Nations must keep some gold reserves on hand to meet international payments. They also hold reserves in the form of other internationally acceptable money, especially U.S. dollars and British pounds. As a result of this, most major Western nations now are on an *international gold reserve standard*, no matter what their domestic monetary standards may be.

U.S. Monetary Standards

have changed several times since the nation was founded. The U.S. Constitution gives the federal government the power "to coin money and regulate the value thereof." Congress has used this power in different ways. Today's monetary arrangements reflect continuing adjustments to the changing needs of the economy.

The Bimetallic Standard, the first U.S. monetary standard, began with the Coinage Act of 1792. Under this standard, persons could get either gold or silver coins in exchange for bills. The bills were issued by the First and Second Banks of the United States and by state banks (see Bank of the United States). During the Civil War, the government stopped using the bimetallic standard and switched to an inconvertible paper standard. It issued greenbacks that could not be exchanged for gold or silver coins.

The Dispute Over Gold and Silver. In 1879, the government began exchanging metal coins for greenbacks. The secretary of the treasury could have chosen to give out either silver or gold coins. But in almost every case, the Treasury paid out only gold coins. This meant that the country was operating on an unofficial gold standard.

The government policy of redeeming paper money in gold brought strong protests from supporters of *free silver*. These persons believed that the standard should be based on both silver and gold. Many silver supporters came from the western regions that produced much silver. The United States did not return to a bimetallic standard. In 1878 and 1890, it agreed to buy large amounts of silver, but canceled these agreements in 1893.

The free-silver dispute came to a climax during the presidential election of 1896. The Republican candidate, William McKinley, favored the gold standard.

Gold Vault of New York City's Federal Reserve Bank has compartments for gold reserves of many nations. International debts are paid by transferring gold from one compartment to another.

Receiving a Gold Shipment. When a country ships gold to the gold vault, the bars are stacked in the country's own compartment.

Giant Scale can hold $300,000 in gold bars and weigh them accurately to within 35 cents.

Federal Reserve Bank of New York

McKinley defeated Democrat William Jennings Bryan, who led the free-silver supporters. In 1900, Congress passed the Gold Standard Act, which officially put the nation on a gold standard. See BRYAN (William Jennings Bryan).

Abandoning the Gold Standard. The United States went off the gold standard after entering World War I in 1917. But the government obtained large amounts of gold by selling wartime supplies to Great Britain, France, and other allies. At the end of the war in 1918, the United States owned the largest gold reserve in the world. In 1919, the United States returned to the gold standard.

The government abandoned the gold standard once more in March, 1933, during the Great Depression (see UNITED STATES, HISTORY OF [The Great Depression]). The government abandoned the gold standard to protect its gold reserve from being hoarded by individuals or exported to other countries.

The Gold Reserve Act, passed in 1934, established a modified form of gold standard. The government stopped minting gold coins, and individuals could no longer legally hold gold coins, except for rare or unusual coins. However, anyone could sell gold to the government at $35 an ounce, and gold was easily available to make international payments.

The Silver Purchase Act, approved in 1934, required the Department of the Treasury to issue silver certificates against silver which it bought from the public. The government issued $1, $5, and $10 silver certificates until 1963, when Congress did away with the Silver Purchase Act. That year, the Federal Reserve banks started to issue Federal Reserve notes to replace silver certificates and other forms of paper money.

The U.S. Monetary Standard Today is often called an *international gold reserve standard.* It is so called because the nation uses gold as payment in international trade, and allows other nations to exchange their U.S. dollars for gold at a fixed price. But people can not use gold as money in carrying on trade within the borders of the United States.

International Reserves. Gold and U.S. dollars serve today as the international monetary reserves of most major nations. Gold and dollars are the major forms of international money. However, British pounds and the money of some other nations are also widely accepted as international money.

When a nation buys more from other countries than

it sells to them, it usually must pay the difference in gold or some other widely acceptable money (see INTERNATIONAL TRADE [Financing International Trade]; BALANCE OF PAYMENTS). Gold owned by many countries is stored in the *gold vault* of the Federal Reserve Bank in New York City. The gold is stored in bars, each weighing about 27½ pounds and worth about $14,000. The New York bank keeps each country's gold in a separate compartment. Many adjustments in the Free World's gold supplies take place in the gold vault.

When persons speak of an outflow of gold from the United States, this does not always mean that gold is actually shipped out of the country. An outflow of gold may take place by having the Federal Reserve Bank in New York City transfer U.S. gold to another nation's compartment in the gold vault. The gold then belongs to that nation.

An outflow of gold takes place when other nations exchange some of their U.S. dollars for gold. Suppose, for example, that Sweden obtains a large supply of dol-

lars by selling steel to U.S. manufacturers. Swedish authorities could decide to convert some of these dollars into gold. They would work through the Federal Reserve Bank in New York City. The bank would buy the gold for Sweden from the U.S. government, and move the gold to Sweden's compartment in the gold vault. Sweden's dollars would be paid to the U.S. government.

As world trade has grown, nations have needed a growing volume of international reserves. In 1944, the International Monetary Fund (IMF) was established as a kind of international bank where nations could obtain temporary reserves. In the 1960's, the amount of gold mined each year was insufficient to satisfy the growing demand for international reserves. In 1969, the IMF voted to supplement gold as international currency by creating $9½ billion in "paper gold." These reserves were called Special Drawing Rights (SDR's). The first $3½ billion was made available in 1970, $3 billion more was scheduled for 1971, and the final $3 billion for 1972.

G. L. BACH and V. CLAIN-STEFANELLI

MONEY/Study Aids

Related Articles in WORLD BOOK include:

ASIATIC CURRENCIES

Baht	Piaster	Rupee	Yuan
Cash	Rial	Yen	

BRITISH CURRENCIES

Crown	Penny	Shilling
Farthing	Pound Sterling	Sixpence

CONTINENTAL CURRENCIES

Centime	Franc	Leu	Markka
Dinar	Guilder	Lev	Peseta
Drachma	Kopeck	Lira	Ruble
Escudo	Krona	Mark	Schilling
Florin	Krone		

LATIN-AMERICAN CURRENCIES

Balboa	Colon	Peso	Sol
Bolivar	Cordoba	Quetzal	Sucre
Centavo	Gourde		

CURRENCIES OF THE UNITED STATES AND CANADA

Cent	Dollar	Greenback	Nickel
Dime	Eagle (coin)	Mill	

HISTORIC CURRENCIES

Denarius	Guinea	Pine-Tree Shilling	Talent
Doubloon	Livre	Real	Thaler
Ducat	Napoleon	Shekel	Wampum
Groat	Piece of Eight	Sou	

MONETARY DOCUMENTS

Bill of Exchange	Money Order	Note
Check	Negotiable Instrument	Receipt
Draft		Traveler's Check
Letter of Credit		

MONETARY POLICIES AND STANDARDS

Convertibility	Gold Standard	Moratorium
Devaluation	Gresham's Law	Specie Payments,
Free Silver	Legal Tender	Resumption of

ORGANIZATIONS

Engraving and Printing, Bureau of
Federal Deposit Insurance Corporation
Federal Reserve System
International Monetary Fund
Secret Service, United States
Treasury, Department of the

OTHER RELATED ARTICLES

Banks and Banking	Counterfeiting	Inflation and
Barter	Depreciation	Deflation
Bretton Woods	Depression	Investment
Bullion	E Pluribus Unum	Mint
Coin Collecting	Economics	Silver
Colonial Life in	Gold	
America (Money)		

Outline

I. **Money Around the World**
II. **How Money Developed**
  A. The First Money
  B. The First Coins
  C. The First Paper Money
III. **United States Money**
  A. Money in the Colonies
  B. New Nation, New Currency
  C. The Growth of Paper Money
  D. U.S. Money Today
IV. **How Money Is Made**
  A. Minting Coins
  B. Printing Paper Money
V. **Money and the National Economy**
  A. Money and Business
  B. Monetary Standards
  C. U.S. Monetary Standards
  D. International Reserves

Questions

How did people obtain the things they needed before they used money?
What are some of the objects that ancient civilizations used as money?
What is a *gold standard?* An *international gold standard?*
When was the first U.S. mint established?
What metals are used to make U.S. cents?
In what country were the first coins made?
What bureau of the U.S. government makes coins?
Who controls the supply of money in the U.S.?
What are the main forms of money in the U.S.?
What are the chief forms of international money?
How do other nations convert U.S. dollars into gold?
What is "an outflow of gold from the United States"?

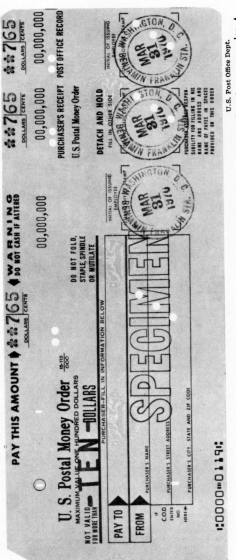

U.S. Post Office Dept.

United States Postal Money Orders are issued in amounts up to $100. The purchaser fills in his name and address and the name of the person to whom he is sending the money order. A post office employee fills in the rest of the form and dates it.

MONEY ORDER. The United States postal money order is a written document directing any post office to pay a sum of money to a certain person. The order is bought at a post office. Then the purchaser fills it out and mails it to the person he names on the money order. The person receiving it may cash the order at any bank or post office. He must identify himself so that the money will not be given to the wrong person. Since July 2, 1951, money orders have been issued on prepunched cards. These prepunched money orders are cleared through Federal Reserve Banks.

Postal money orders may be purchased at any post office in the United States. The highest amount of any single money order is $100. It is necessary to buy more than one order to get more than that amount. But there is no limit on the number of orders that a person may purchase at one time. Therefore, there is no limit to the amount of money that may be sent by money orders. The rates on money orders are graduated as follows:

Amount of Money Order	*Fee*
Not exceeding $10	25¢
Over $10 to $50	35¢
Over $50 to $100	40¢

A postal money order may be cashed at any time within 20 years from the date of issue. Postal orders may be endorsed once. International money orders may be sent to almost any part of the world. Fees for these money orders are twice the domestic fees.

Postal Notes were formerly used within the United States only. It was possible to obtain *postal notes* from all first-class U.S. post offices in amounts from 1¢ to $10. The notes were in denominations of dollars, from 1 to 10 inclusive. Eighteen different denominations of special *postal-note stamps* were used to get the exact amount wanted. They were issued in amounts from 1¢ to 10¢ inclusive, and in 20¢, 30¢, 40¢, 50¢, 60¢, 70¢, 80¢, and 90¢ denominations. Postal notes were abolished in 1951 when the new type of money order was put into use.

Canadian Postal Money Order. A Canadian money order cannot exceed $100, but an unlimited number can be purchased. Fees range from 5¢ to 25¢ for money orders issued in Canada for payment in Canada, Antigua, the Bahamas, Barbados, Bermuda, British Honduras, the Caicos Islands, Cayman Islands, Dominica, Grenada, Guyana, Jamaica, Montserrat, St. Christopher (St. Kitts)-Nevis-Anguilla, St. Lucia, St. Vincent, Trinidad and Tobago, Turks Islands, and the Virgin Islands. Money order fees for Great Britain, other British Commonwealth countries, and Ireland are from 10¢ to 53¢. For all other countries, fees are from 18¢ to $1.03. For the United States, U.S. dependencies, Mexico, and Poland, the fee can be higher or lower depending on the rate of exchange of U.S. dollars.

Critically reviewed by the POST OFFICE DEPARTMENT

MONEYLENDER. See PAWNBROKER.
MONEYWORT. See LOOSESTRIFE.

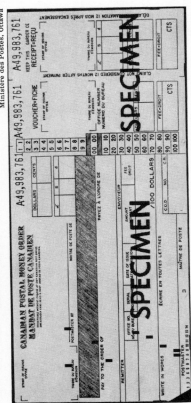

Ministère des Postes, Ottawa

A Canadian Postal Money Order is printed in both English and French. This type, the notched money order, may be used for payment at any post office in Canada or other countries.

MONGOL EMPIRE

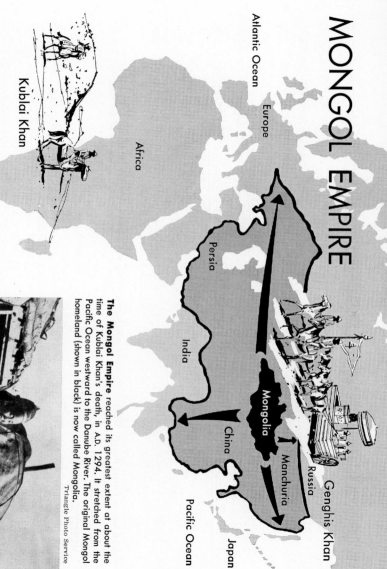

Kublai Khan

Atlantic Ocean

Europe

Africa

Persia

India

China

Mongolia

Manchuria

Russia

Genghis Khan

Japan

Pacific Ocean

The Mongol Empire reached its greatest extent at about the time of Kublai Khan's death, in A.D. 1294. It stretched from the Pacific Ocean westward to the Danube River. The original Mongol homeland (shown in black) is now called Mongolia.

Triangle Photo Service

MONGOL EMPIRE was the biggest land empire in history. Its territory extended from the Yellow Sea in eastern Asia to the borders of eastern Europe. At various times it included China, Korea, Mongolia, Persia (now Iran), Turkestan, and Armenia. It also included parts of Burma, Vietnam, Thailand, and Russia.

The Mongols were the most savage conquerors of history. But their vast empire contributed to increased contacts between peoples. Migrations fostered these contacts and promoted trade. Roads were built to connect Russia and Persia with eastern Asia. Many Europeans came to China, and Chinese found their way into Russia and other parts of Europe. Printing and other Chinese inventions such as paper, gunpowder, and the compass may have been introduced to the West during Mongol times.

The Mongols originally consisted of loosely organized nomadic tribes in Mongolia, Manchuria, and Siberia. They lived in felt tents called *yurts*, and raised ponies, sheep, camels, oxen, and goats. They ate mainly meat and milk. Every Mongol was a soldier, and learned to ride and use a bow and arrow skillfully.

Early Empire

Genghis Khan. In the 1100's, Temujin, a Mongol chieftain who later became known as Genghis Khan, rose to power as *khan* (see KHAN). He began to unify and organize the scattered Mongol tribes into a superior fighting force. Genghis Khan was shrewd, ruthless, ambitious, and a strict disciplinarian. After he became the undisputed master of Mongolia, and "lord of all the peoples dwelling in felt tents," he set out on a spectacular career of conquest.

Genghis Khan aimed to train the best disciplined and most effective army of his time. As part of his military

strategy, he formed an officer corps from picked Mongols who were trained in military tactics. These men were then stationed with various tribes as a training force. The Mongol tribes specialized in the art of siege. They learned to use storming ladders, and sandbags to fill in moats. Besiegers approached fortress walls under the protection of gigantic shields. Each tribe prepared a siege train, which consisted of special arms and equipment.

Invasions. Genghis Khan wanted to conquer China to the south. As a skillful strategist, he decided to attack first Hsi Hsia, a state in northwest China. Hsi Hsia represented the Chinese military pattern, with Chinese-trained armies and Chinese-built fortresses. In this campaign, Genghis Khan could evaluate his armies, and train them for war against China.

The Mongols subdued Hsi Hsia, and then turned to North China. There a nomadic tribe called the Juchen had established the Chin dynasty. The Mongols chose spring for his assault on China, so that his horses would have food when crossing the Gobi Desert. Warriors car-

avoided having too many Chinese in high offices. In Persia and other Islamic lands, many Mongols adopted Moslem customs and the Moslem faith.

European Contacts. Marco Polo was one of the most famous Europeans to travel to the Orient at this time. His travel records contain much interesting information about the Mongols. His reports of beautiful Chinese cities and the riches of the country he called *Cathay* did much to arouse the interest of Europeans in exploring the possibilities of trade with the Orient. Many Europeans, including Christopher Columbus, then sought to go to the Orient by the sea route.

The Khan expressed a desire to have more missionaries sent to China. Dominicans and Franciscans traveled to China and were welcomed by the Khan in Cambaluc. A Franciscan, John of Montecorvino, built a church in the capital and converted many people to Christianity.

Decline. The Mongol empire did not last long, because it was too big and had no unity of culture. Actually, it began to disintegrate shortly after it reached its peak of expansion in the late 1200's. The Mongols were dauntless fighters, but had little experience in administration. They relied upon other peoples to look after the affairs of their empire. They brought foreigners into China to avoid total reliance on the Chinese. The Mongols temporarily suspended the Chinese civil service system to allow these other peoples to assume positions.

Corrupt government and incompetent administration resulted in revolts in different parts of the empire. Even before the fall of the Yüan dynasty in China, the Mongols had lost control of many of their conquered lands. In some areas, they had never succeeded in firmly establishing their rule after their military conquests. Even at the peak of his power, Kublai Khan's authority did not extend to such distant places as Persia and Russia. The Mongols also lacked a firm hold in Southeast Asia.

Breakup. When Kublai Khan died, his empire broke up into several parts. These smaller empires were the Golden Horde on the steppes of southern Russia and the Balkans, the Mongolian-Chinese Chin Empire, and the realm of the Ilkhans in western Asia. A revolution in China in the 1300's resulted in the fall of the Yüan dynasty and restored Chinese rule in the form of the Ming dynasty.

The great Timur, or Tamerlane, a descendant of Genghis Khan, joined some of the Mongol empires together again and extended his rule over much of Asia in the late 1300's. A descendant of Tamerlane named Babar established a powerful Mongol state in India in 1526. Babar's realm was called the *Kingdom of the Great Moguls*. The term *Mogul* comes from the Persian word *mughul*, meaning *a Mongol*. A Mogul emperor, Shah Jahan, built the beautiful Taj Mahal in the early 1600's. The British destroyed the Mogul kingdom after it had begun to break up in the 1700's. THEODORE H. E. CHEN

Related Articles. See the History sections of the various countries where Mongols ruled, such as CHINA (History). See also the following:

Genghis Khan
Kublai Khan

Mongolia
Polo, Marco

Shah Jahan
Tamerlane

Medieval Tartar Huts and Waggons, drawing by Quinto Cenni. From *The Book of Sir Marco Polo* by Colonel Sir Henry Yule, London published by John Murrey, 1903 (Newberry Library)

Mongols of the Middle Ages, *above,* often carried their tents on large wooden wagons when moving. A team of many oxen drew the wagon, and the driver stood in the entrance of the tent.

▼ **Mongols of Today,** *left,* live in tents that closely resemble those of medieval times. A Mongol woman, dressed in warm clothing and heavy jewelry, stands in front of her felt-covered home.

ried everything they needed on the march, and each rider had a spare horse. The hordes drove herds of cattle for food in the desert. Genghis Khan conquered North China in 1215.

Before completing the conquest of China, Genghis Khan turned westward into central Asia and eastern Europe. His armies charged into the steppes of Russia and the Moslem lands, including Persia. They came within reach of Constantinople (now Istanbul), and destroyed much of Islamic-Arabic civilization.

All along their routes, the Mongol armies ruthlessly eliminated any resistance. They spread terror and destruction everywhere. When faced with resistance in conquered territories, the Mongols systematically slaughtered the population of entire cities. They laid waste to North China so completely that a horseman could ride for miles without stumbling over anything.

Genghis Khan died in 1227. The Mongols pushed into Europe under Ogotai, a son of Genghis Khan. In 1241, about 150,000 Mongol riders laid waste a large part of Hungary and Poland, and threatened the civilization of western Europe. Ogotai died in the midst of this campaign. His death forced the Mongol generals to break off their European campaign and return to Mongolia to elect a new khan.

Later Empire

Kublai Khan, a grandson of Genghis, completed the conquest of China after attacking the Sung dynasty in South China. Kublai Khan then founded the Yüan dynasty, which lasted from 1279 to 1368. He established the Mongol capital at Cambaluc, the site of present-day Peking. Successive attempts to extend the Mongol empire to Japan ended in failure. Mongol horsemen were not successful fighters on the seas or in the tropical climate of Southeast Asia.

The Mongols under Kublai Khan had a reputation for some tolerance. Kublai permitted the existence of various religions. He enlisted the services of Moslems, Christians, Buddhists, and Taoists. He accepted Confucianism and Chinese political ideas, although he

MONGOLIA

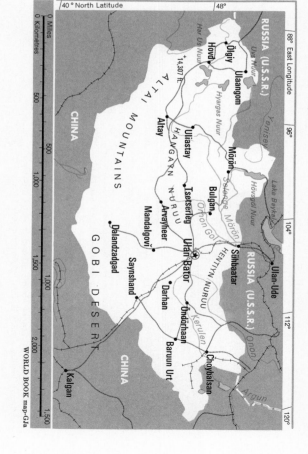

Geographical Terms

⊛ National Capital
● Other City or Town
━━ Road
┿┿ Rail Line
∿ River

Gol . . . . stream
Nuruu . . . . . mountain range
Nuur . . . . lake

40° North Latitude

WORLD BOOK map-G/a

MONGOLIA, *mahn GOH lee uh,* is a Communist country that lies between China and Russia in east-central Asia. Its official name is MONGOLIAN PEOPLE'S REPUBLIC. Mongolia is more than twice as large as Texas. However, a single Texas city—Houston—has about as many people as all of Mongolia.

Mongolia is a rugged land. Plateaus and towering mountain ranges cover much of the country. The bleak Gobi Desert blankets much of southeastern Mongolia. Temperatures are usually very cold or very hot. Mongolia's little rainfall occurs in a few summer storms.

Raising livestock has long been the country's chief economic activity. Mongolians once wandered over the grassy plateaus where their animals grazed. Today, more than half of them work on cooperative livestock farms that were set up by the government.

Mongolia is the original home of an Asian people called *Mongols.* The Mongols built the largest land empire in history during the 1200's. They conquered an area from eastern Asia to eastern Europe. China ruled Mongolia from the 1680's to 1911. Mongolia was then called *Outer Mongolia.* A Mongol region to the south, called *Inner Mongolia,* is still part of China.

Government. Mongolia is a Communist country. Its constitution calls the country "a socialist state in the form of a people's democracy." There is only one political party, however, the Mongol People's Revolutionary Party (MPRP). The party is called the "guiding and directing force of society and the state." Only MPRP candidates and some non-party candidates may be put up for election to national and local councils.

The people elect the members of the Great National Khural, Mongolia's legislature, to three-year terms. The Khural elects a seven-member Presidium, Mongolia's real governing body. The Presidium makes the important decisions in domestic and foreign affairs. Its chairman is the head of state. The Khural also elects a Council of Ministers, which runs the government.

For administrative and judicial purposes, the country is divided into 18 provinces called *aimaks,* and two

independent cities. These cities are Ulan Bator, Mongolia's capital, and Darhan, a new industrial area.

The People. Nearly all the people of Mongolia are Mongols. About 4 of every 100 persons belong to a group called *Kazakhs.* Some Chinese, Russians, and Tuvans also live in Mongolia. The official language of Mongolia is Mongolian. It is written in a special form of the Cyrillic alphabet, the alphabet Russians use. Many Mongolians believe in the form of Buddhism called *Lamaism.* The Communist government tries to discourage religious practices.

More than half the people live on livestock farms. The state has set up about 300 of these farms. The farms are like huge ranches with small towns in the center. The central buildings include houses, offices, shops, and medical posts for the people and animals. The state runs some farms for raising crops.

Few Mongolians still follow the traditional way of life of *nomadic* (wandering) herdsmen. Those who do, journey from place to place with their animals. They

---

FACTS IN BRIEF

Capital: Ulan Bator.

Official Language: Mongolian.

Form of Government: People's Democracy (Communist).

Area: 604,250 square miles. *Greatest Distances*—(north-south) 790 miles; (east-west) 1,500 miles.

Population: *1963 Census*—1,017,100; distribution, 59 per cent rural, 41 per cent urban. *Estimated 1971 Population*—1,332,000; density, 2 persons to the square mile. *Estimated 1976 Population*—1,559,000.

Chief Products: *Agriculture*—camels, cattle, goats, grain, horses, meat, milk, potatoes, sheep, vegetables, *Manu-facturing and Processing*—building materials, felt, processed foods, soap, textiles. *Mining*—coal, petroleum.

Flag: Vertical stripes of red, blue, and red, with gold symbols on the left stripe. Red stands for Communism and blue for the Mongols of the past. The flag was adopted in 1944. See FLAG (color picture: Flags of Asia and the Pacific).

Money: *Basic Unit*—tugrik, divided into 100 mungu.

live in collapsible felt tents called *ger* or *yurts*, which help protect them from the intense heat and cold. The government is gradually settling the nomads on farms.

The Mongolian State University was founded in Ulan Bator in 1942. The country has teacher training colleges and technical schools where students study such subjects as agriculture, economics, and medicine.

Land. No part of Mongolia lies less than 1,700 feet above sea level. The Altai Mountains in the west rise to more than 14,000 feet. A high plateau lies between the Altai Mountains and the mountains called Hangayn Nuruu in central Mongolia. This plateau has many lakes. Uvs Nuur, the largest, covers about 1,300 square miles. Dense forests cover the mountains called Hentiyn Nuruu, northeast of Ulan Bator. Eastern Mongolia is a lower plateau of grassland. It becomes less fertile as it nears the Gobi, a bleak desert area from southeastern Mongolia into Inner Mongolia.

Mongolia gets very hot and very cold. Temperatures ranging from −57° F. to 96° F. have been recorded in Ulan Bator. Snowfall and rainfall are generally light. Heavy rains may occur in July and August. Violent earthquakes sometimes shake Mongolia.

Economy. The state owns and operates most factories and the state farms in Mongolia. Livestock farms are co-operative property, owned by the members. Livestock-raising is the backbone of the economy. Herdsmen keep over 20 million animals, more than half of them sheep. Other animals include camels, cattle, goats, and horses. Cattle make up about 35 per cent of the country's exports, and wool about 40 per cent. Mongolia also exports dairy products, furs, hides, and meat.

The number of animals raised in the country has decreased during the 1950's and 1960's. During the same period, farmers have greatly increased their production of grains and other crops.

Mongolia has little industry. Building materials, processed foods, tent frames and felts, wool and woolen fabrics, furniture, glass and china, soap, and matches rank among the chief manufactured products. The government is trying to develop industry. Mongolia has deposits of coal, copper, gold, iron, and petroleum.

Mongolia's main railroad connects Ulan Bator with the Russian Trans-Siberian railroad in the north and with Chinese railroads in the south. The country has about 47,000 miles of roads. Most of these are dirt roads. Boats carry many goods traded between Mongolia and Russia on Hövsgöl Nuur, a lake; and Selenge Mörön, a river. Air service links Ulan Bator with other countries and with provincial capitals in Mongolia.

Mongolia's leading daily newspaper is *Unen* (*Truth*). It and 9 other newspapers and 13 periodicals circulate throughout the country. There are 18 provincial newspapers.

History. Various groups of Mongol peoples were united under Genghis Khan in the early 1200's. Genghis Khan and his grandson Kublai Khan extended the Mongol Empire from Korea and China westward into Europe. The empire broke up in the late 1300's. See MONGOL EMPIRE.

Mongol princes reunited Mongolia briefly in the late 1500's, and converted the people to Lamaism. In the early 1600's, the Manchu rulers of Manchuria gained control of Inner Mongolia. The Manchus conquered China in 1644 and seized Outer Mongolia in the 1680's. Mongolia, like China, had little contact with the rest of the world in the 1700's and the 1800's. See MANCHU.

The Mongolians drove Chinese forces out of Outer Mongolia in 1911. They appointed a priest, called the *Living Buddha*, as king, and appealed to Russia for support. In 1913, China and Russia agreed to give Outer Mongolia control over its own affairs. Legally, Outer Mongolia remained Chinese territory. But, in fact, it came largely under the control of Russia.

In 1920, during Russia's civil war, anti-Communist Russian troops occupied Outer Mongolia and ruled it through the Living Buddha. Mongolian and Russian Communists gained control of Outer Mongolia in 1921. They established the Mongolian People's Republic in 1924, after the Living Buddha died.

China did not recognize Mongolia's independence until 1946. Mongolia became a member of the United Nations in 1961. Mongolia supports Russia in the Russian-Chinese dispute for leadership of the Communist world. In 1966, Mongolia and Russia signed a new mutual-assistance pact. Many Soviet troops are in Mongolia for construction and defense.   CHARLES BAWDEN

Related Articles in WORLD BOOK include:

China (History)	Gobi	Lamaists
Genghis Khan	Kublai Khan	Ulan Bator

MONGOLIAN RACE. See RACES OF MAN (Mongoloids; tables; pictures).

Sovfoto

Ulan Bator, Mongolia's Capital, has many modern buildings and a central square that is larger than Moscow's Red Square. The theater, left, presents ballets, concerts, and operas.

Leavitt F. Morris

Home on the Mongolian Plains for centuries has been the ger or yurt, a portable hut made of layers of felt covered with canvas or hide. The huts are also used in many towns.

The Quick and Fierce Mongoose tackles a deadly cobra in a fight to the death. The little animal depends on its lightning-

Schaumburg, Pix

like speed to dodge the cobra's vicious thrusts. People in India often keep a mongoose around their homes to drive snakes away.

MONGOLISM is a form of mental deficiency characterized by certain bodily abnormalities. A flattened face and folded upper eyelids give the patient an Oriental appearance. Other abnormal body features include a small, round head; short arms and legs; a large abdomen; and thick, stubby hands, with the little finger often short and turned inward.

Mongoloids are quiet, good-natured, and affectionate. Their condition results from a *chromosome* abnormality. Chromosomes are the parts of a cell that contain the heredity-controlling *genes*. Normal cells have 46 chromosomes. But a Mongoloid's cells may have 47 chromosomes, or one of the 46 may be exceptionally large. Doctors believe excessive chromosome substance may cause overproduction of certain body materials. This increased production seems to interfere with the control of body and brain growth.

GEORGE A. ULETT

MONGOOSE, *MAHNG goos,* is the name of several closely related small animals that live in Africa, Madagascar, and southern Asia. All mongooses are related to the civet and the ichneumon. The common mongoose is about 16 inches long and has stiff, yellowish-gray hair that is grizzled with brownish-black. It has a fierce disposition, but can be easily tamed.

The mongoose is known for its ability to kill mice, rats, and snakes. It is not immune to poison, but its swiftness allows it to seize and kill poisonous snakes such as the cobra. The mongoose has been introduced into Jamaica, Cuba, Puerto Rico, Hawaii, and other parts of the world to destroy hordes of rats. The mongoose reproduces rapidly. After reducing the supply of snakes and rodents, the mongoose kills poultry, wild birds, and other beneficial small animals. It also eats birds' eggs and young birds. Laws forbid bringing the mongoose into the continental United States.

Scientific Classification. The mongoose belongs to the family *Viverridae.* There are about 16 genera. One, the Asiatic mongoose, is genus *Herpestes.*

See also CIVET; ICHNEUMON.

E. LENDELL COCKRUM

MONISM. See METAPHYSICS (Doctrines).

MONITOR, *MAHN uh ter,* is the name of a group of about 30 kinds of lizards that live in the Solomon Islands, New Guinea, Australia, the East Indies, southern Asia, and Africa. They have long heads and necks; short, powerful legs; and tails with whiplike ends. The different kinds are so much alike that scientists often find them hard to tell apart. The body is usually black or brown with yellow bands, spots, or mottling. The deeply forked tongue looks like a snake's tongue. These lizards have few rivals in size. They are usually at least 4 feet long. One of them, the *dragon of Komodo,* is often 10 feet long (see DRAGON OF KOMODO).

When a monitor is cornered, it pretends to be ferocious. It stands high on its legs, puffs up its body, and swings its tail like a whip. The teeth can make deep wounds and the tail can lash with some force.

A monitor will eat almost any animal it can kill, such as other reptiles, birds, small mammals, large insects, and crustaceans. Many monitors like to live near water, and they are all good swimmers and divers. When they swim, they hold their legs against their sides, driving themselves forward by weaving their bodies and tails. Monitors lay eggs, and climb well. The two best-known species are the *Nile monitor* of Africa and the *water monitor,* which lives from India to northern Australia.

Scientific Classification. Monitors are in the monitor family, *Varanidae.* Nile monitor is genus *Varanus,* species *V. niloticus.* Water monitor is *V. salvator.*

CLIFFORD H. POPE

MONITOR. See TELEVISION (The Control Room; picture: Monitors).

MONITOR AND MERRIMACK fought a famous naval battle in the American Civil War. These two ships were called *ironclads,* because they had been covered with iron. The *Monitor* was built of iron as well as being ironclad. The battle focused worldwide attention on the importance of armor-plated ships. It was also one of the first sea battles in which the opposing ships were maneuvered entirely under steam power.

The *Merrimack*, or *Merrimac*, originally was a wooden frigate. Federal troops scuttled the ship when they evacuated the Navy yard at Portsmouth, Va., in 1861. Confederate forces raised it, and covered it with iron plates. They renamed it the *Virginia* although it is usually known by its original name. On Mar. 8, 1862, the *Virginia* (*Merrimack*) sank two Northern ships at Hampton Roads, Va. When it returned the next day, it found a Union ironclad waiting, the *Monitor*. John Ericsson, a Swedish-American inventor, had designed this "cheese box on a raft" for the Northern Navy (see ERICSSON, JOHN). The two ships battled for about four hours. The *Monitor* moved about more easily than the *Virginia* (*Merrimack*), but its shells had little effect on the Confederate ship. When the *Monitor* withdrew temporarily, the *Virginia* (*Merrimack*) returned to the James River. Within the year, both ships were lost. The *Virginia* (*Merrimack*) was destroyed to keep it from being captured by the Union, and the *Monitor* foundered while being towed at sea in a storm. BERNARD BRODIE

See also CIVIL WAR (picture: The Battle of the Ironclads).

MONITORING STATION receives and measures signals from radio transmitters. These signals come from such sources as AM and FM radio stations, television stations, radios in airplanes and ships, and amateur radios. Some countries use monitoring stations as "listening posts" to obtain information from other countries.

In the United States, the Federal Communications Commission (FCC) operates monitoring stations. In Canada, the Department of Transport operates the stations. Both government agencies issue transmitter licenses and enforce operating regulations determined by national laws and international laws and treaties. These laws and treaties establish standards and procedures for equipping, installing, and operating radio stations. Monitoring stations measure radio transmissions often to make certain the stations are operating under these procedures and the terms of their licenses.

The FCC operates 19 monitoring stations in the United States. Canada has eight stations. Each country maintains many mobile monitoring vehicles. Long-range direction finders help locate sources of radio interference, unauthorized transmitters, and aircraft and ships in distress. See DIRECTION FINDER.

During World War II, the FCC operated as many as 102 monitoring stations, supported by automobiles with direction finders. This equipment was used to uncover radio transmitters operated by enemy agents.
Critically reviewed by the FEDERAL COMMUNICATIONS COMMISSION

MONIZ, *MOH neesh,* **ANTÔNIO CAETANO DE ABREU FREIRE EGAS** (1874-1955), shared the 1949 Nobel prize for physiology and medicine. Moniz introduced the *prefrontal leukotomy,* or *lobotomy,* operation as a therapeutic procedure in certain mental diseases. He and Almeida Lima operated on 29 patients with a hollow needle containing a steel-wire cutting loop. The tool cuts nerve fibers that connect parts of the brain.

Moniz was born in Avanca, Portugal. He became professor of neurology in Lisbon in 1911. He held a number of political posts from 1903 to 1919, including minister of foreign affairs. HENRY H. FERTIG

MONK, *mungk,* is a man who has taken religious vows and retired from worldly life to live with other monks. At first the term meant a person who lived entirely alone in order to devote himself to religion. Such persons were also called hermits, which is the name now reserved to them. The first group of Christian monks originated in northern Egypt early in the A.D. 300's. The members lived by themselves, but met at fixed times for worship. They studied the Scriptures, prayed, and thought of God.

Later, monks formed communities, with buildings known as *monasteries.* Many orders of monks now exist, especially in the Roman Catholic Church. All the monasteries of one order follow an identical rule of life. In any such order, the members take vows of poverty, chastity, and obedience. Monks differ from friars in that friars originally had no monasteries, and were committed to a life of preaching rather than one of retirement. FULTON J. SHEEN

See also FRIAR; HERMIT; MONASTICISM; RELIGIOUS LIFE; TONSURE.

MONK, or **MONCK,** *mungk,* **GEORGE** (1608-1670), DUKE OF ALBEMARLE, was an English general and naval commander. He arranged the restoration of the Stuarts to the English throne in 1660.

Monk joined the army at the age of 17. He commanded Irish troops for the king in the English civil war of 1642-1649, which ended with the triumph of Parliament and Oliver Cromwell (see CROMWELL, OLIVER). The parliamentary troops defeated Monk in 1644, and imprisoned him in the Tower of London for two years. Cromwell then offered to free him if he would serve in the army of the Commonwealth of England. Monk did so, and was made a lieutenant general.

He served the Commonwealth as commander-in-chief of Scotland from 1651 to 1652 and from 1654 to 1659. He helped command the English Navy in 1652 and 1653, and defeated the Dutch in several naval battles.

After the death of Cromwell in 1658, Monk made possible the peaceful return of Charles II. The Presbyterian members who had been driven out of Parliament in 1648 were brought back. Their presence in Parliament made certain a majority in favor of restoring the Stuart king. Monk quietly shifted the armed forces throughout England in such a way that there would be no chance of an uprising (see RESTORATION).

Monk brought back Charles II in 1660. Charles rewarded Monk by making him duke of Albemarle, privy councilor, and lord lieutenant of Devon and Middlesex. Monk was born in Devonshire. W. M. SOUTHGATE

MONK, THELONIOUS (1917-   ), is an American composer and pianist. He became closely identified with the *bebop* movement in jazz in the early 1940's. Many of Monk's compositions, including "Round Midnight," "Blue Monk," and "Straight No Chaser," have become jazz standards. Monk's unique and unpredictable piano style helped establish him as one of the most adventurous individualists in jazz.

Monk was born in Rocky Mount, N.C., and grew up in New York City. Beginning in 1939, he played in the small groups that helped develop bebop in such Harlem jazz clubs as Minton's Play House and Monroe's Uptown House. He gained an international reputation in the late 1950's, after years of comparative obscurity. He usually leads a quartet, but occasionally forms an orchestra for concerts and recordings. LEONARD FEATHER

The Capuchin Monkey is one of the most alert and intelligent members of the monkey family. It often appears in circuses.

Ylla, Rapho-Guillumette

MONKEY is a small, lively, intelligent mammal. There are nearly 200 kinds of monkeys, most of which live in the warm parts of the world. Monkeys vary greatly in size. The smallest kind, the *pygmy marmoset*, is no bigger than a rat. But some kinds of African baboons are more than 3½ feet long, excluding their long tails.

Zoologists place monkeys, together with apes, lemurs, and man, in the highest order of animals, the *primates.* Nearly all monkeys have tails. Apes, except for the gibbons, are larger than monkeys and have no tails. Unlike many other animals, monkeys can see both in depth and in color, as man does. Like most primates, monkeys can grasp things both with their hands and their feet.

Monkeys usually do well in intelligence tests designed for animals. Their ability to learn and their playfulness make them favorites in zoos and circuses. Tame monkeys make affectionate pets. But they are inquisitive and destructive animals, and have to be kept in cages most of the time. Monkeys live for 15 to 30 years in captivity. No one knows how long they live in the wild.

How Monkeys Live. Most monkeys live in tropical regions. But a few kinds, including the macaque of Japan, live in places that may be covered with snow in winter. Some monkeys, such as colobuses of Africa, live their entire lives in trees. Their long, slender bodies and long tails are well suited for moving among branches. Some other monkeys, including baboons, roam on the ground. Baboons may even live on grassy plains.

Monkeys usually eat leaves, buds, fruits, insects, and, occasionally, bird eggs. Baboons of the plains sometimes catch and eat young antelopes. Monkeys usually eat in the morning and afternoon, but some may

snack throughout the day. Most monkeys rest during the midday hours. At night, they sleep while crouched on a tree branch. Where there are no trees, they sleep on steep rock bluffs.

Almost all monkeys are sociable, and live together in groups. Some groups, such as groups of baboons, may have as many as 100 members. Males may protect the group and females care for the young. The mothers carry the children until they can travel safely on their own. Most kinds of female monkeys give birth to a single young once a year. Marmosets often have twins.

Monkeys are classified into two major groups: the *New World monkeys* of Central and South America, and the *Old World monkeys* of Africa and Asia.

New World Monkeys are smaller and lighter than most of their Old World relatives. New World monkeys have 36 teeth. Old World monkeys have 32 teeth, as man does. Many New World monkeys can grasp with their tails. They use the tail to swing through trees like talented acrobats. The beautifully colored marmosets of South America are the only monkeys that have claws on most of their toes. Only their big toes have toenails. Some marmosets weigh only 3 or 4 ounces. The spider monkey, an excellent acrobat, has long legs and a long tail. The intelligent capuchin monkey is often trained as a circus performer. The howler monkey gives a roaring cry that can be heard for a mile or two through the jungle. Woolly monkeys make gentle pets.

Old World Monkeys cannot grasp things with their tails. Their noses usually are narrower and more manlike in appearance than those of the New World monkeys. The baboons of Africa are known for their large size and doglike faces. The proboscis monkey of Borneo is probably the strangest looking Old World monkey. The male's fleshy nose is over 3 inches long and resembles a cucumber. Colobuses and langurs have stomachs that are divided into series of sacs. All other monkeys have single-sac stomachs, like man does. Guenon monkeys of Africa have brilliant colors. One guenon, the Diana monkey, has a black back, a white beard and belly, and a rusty-red-colored rump. The rhesus monkey of India has been used in many scientific experiments. A blood factor called the *Rh factor* was discovered in the rhesus monkey (see Rh Factor).

Scientific Classification. New World monkeys, except marmosets, belong to the New World monkey family, *Cebidae.* Marmosets belong to the marmoset family, *Callithricidae.* Old World monkeys belong to the Old World monkey family, *Cercopithecidae.* Each family contains many genera and species.

GEORGE B. SCHALLER

Related Articles in WORLD BOOK include:

Animal (Intelligence of Animals;
Baboon   color pictures)
Capuchin   Howler
Florida (Places to Visit [Monkey Jungle]) Lemur
                           Mandrill
MONKEY BREAD. See BAOBAB.   Marmoset
MONKEY FLOWER is the name given to a large group   Sapajou
of herbs and small shrubs which have flowers with *two lips*, or two large petals growing one over the other. The petals often have spots which make the flower look more like a monkey's face. There are many different species, growing from a few inches to 2 feet high. They grow in both South and North America, most of them along the Pacific Coast.

Monkey flowers can be grown in gardens, garden

A Moustache Guenon escapes danger by leaping through the treetops.

The Woolly Monkey lives mainly in the upper Amazon basin of South America.

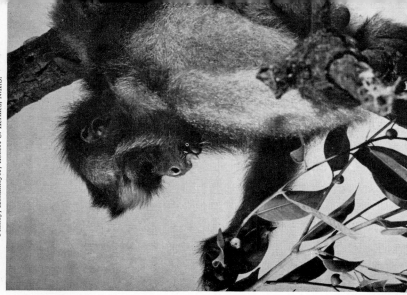

The Spider Monkey is a skilled acrobat. He can cover 30 feet in one flying leap.

Pinney, Monkmeyer; Robert C. Hermes, N.A.S.

Guenons are found only in Africa. They live mostly in trees, and can carry food in their cheek pouches.

Monkeys Are Devoted Parents. This rhesus mother will fight fiercely to protect her baby.

borders, and in greenhouses. They grow well in shady places and should be given plenty of water. Some of the shrubby kinds of monkey flower do not require much care.

Scientific Classification. The monkey flower belongs to the figwort family, *Scrophulariaceae*. It makes up the genus *Mimulus*. One kind of monkey flower is genus *Mimulus*, species *M. luteus*.

J. J. Levison

MONKEYPOD TREE, or RAIN-TREE, is a beautiful shade tree that grows in tropical regions from southern Florida to Brazil. Its short, stout trunk bears spreading branches. The top of the tree may measure 100 feet across. The monkeypod tree has delicate pink and white flowers. Its leaves fold up at night and on cloudy days.

Scientific Classification. The monkeypod tree belongs to the pea family, *Leguminosae*. It is genus *Samanea*, species *S. saman*.

Elbert L. Little, Jr.

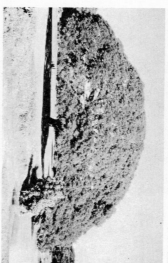

The Monkeypod Tree is grown in tropical countries as a shade tree. Its wood makes attractive trays and bowls.

J. L. Kenner

MONKSHOOD. See Aconite (picture).

MONMOUTH, BATTLE OF. See New Jersey (The Revolutionary War).

MONMOUTH, DUKE OF (1649-1685), James Scott, was an Englishman who led an unsuccessful rebellion against King James II (see James [II]). He was supposedly the son of Charles II and a Welsh woman named Lucy Walter, and was a pretender to the throne of England (see Charles [II] of England). There is some doubt about his real parentage, but Charles recognized him as his son.

Charles II became king in 1660 after Richard Cromwell fell from power. He called Monmouth back to England and made him Duke of Monmouth. In 1663, Monmouth married Anne, daughter of the Earl of Buccleuch. The Duke of York ascended the throne as James II in 1685. Monmouth gathered an army in The Netherlands to invade England and demand the crown. He landed at Lyme, and issued a proclamation which declared James to be a usurper, tyrant, and murderer. But Monmouth was defeated at the Battle of Sedgemoor and taken to his uncle the king. Before a court headed by Lord Jeffreys, he begged for his life. But he was imprisoned in the Tower of London and executed. He was born in Rotterdam, The Netherlands.

André Maurois

MONMOUTH COLLEGE. See Universities and Colleges (table).

MONNET, *muhn NAY*, **JEAN** (1888-), a French economist, led the movement to unify Western Europe in the 1950's and 1960's. He is called the *Architect of United Europe*. He proposed the European Coal and Steel Community in 1950 and became president of its executive branch in 1952. In 1955, he left the community and organized the Action Committee for a United States of Europe. He helped create the European Atomic Energy Community (Euratom), and the European Economic Community (Common Market) in 1957. See European Community.

His career as an international financial adviser began during World War I when he directed Allied supply operations. From 1919 to 1923, he served as deputy secretary-general of the League of Nations. He also helped to stabilize the economies of Algeria, Austria, China, Poland, and Romania after World War I. During World War II, Monnet served as a financial adviser to Great Britain and the United States. In 1947, he created the Monnet Plan, a five-year economic recovery plan for France.

In 1963, Monnet became one of the first Europeans to receive the Presidential Medal of Freedom, the highest civilian medal awarded by the United States. Monnet was born in Cognac.

Leonard B. Tennyson

MONOCLINIC SYSTEM. See Crystal and Crystallization (Classification of Crystals).

MONOCOQUE is a type of fuselage construction. See Airplane (The Airplane Comes of Age).

MONOCOTYLEDON, *MON oh KAHT uh LEE dun*, is a type of flowering plant that has one seed leaf, or *cotyledon*. The leaves of these plants have parallel veins. The flower parts usually grow in multiples of three. About 40,000 species of plants are monocotyledons, including bananas, pineapples, and corn. See also Cotyledon.

MONOCYTE. See Blood (White Blood Cells).

MONOD, JACQUES (1910-), a French biochemist, shared the 1965 Nobel prize for physiology and medicine with François Jacob and André Lwoff. The scientists, all members of the Pasteur Institute in Paris, studied the cells of bacteria. They discovered in these cells a class of genes that controls the activity of other genes. Radiation and some chemicals can cause these controlling genes to function improperly. If this happens, the other genes may get out of control and damage the cells. Some scientists believe the discovery will aid research on cancer, a disease in which uncontrolled cell division takes place.

Monod was born in Paris. He studied in the United States in the late 1930's, and received a doctoral degree in France in 1941. Monod joined the Pasteur Institute in 1946. He became head of its cellular biochemistry department in 1953. He is also a professor at the Faculté des Sciences in Paris.

Irwin H. Herskowitz

MONOECIOUS PLANT. See Botany (Terms); Flower (Variations in Form).

MONOFILAMENT. See Plastics (table: Terms).

MONOGAMY. See Family (Marriage); Culture.

MONOMER, *MAHN uh mer*. Monomers are small molecules that can combine with each other to form larger molecules called *polymers*. Polymers are used in the manufacture of paint, plastics, *synthetic* (man-made) rubber, and synthetic fibers. Heat, pressure, or chemical treatment may be used to cause monomers to combine. See also Polymer; Polymerization.

David R. Lide, Jr.

MONOMETALLIC STANDARD. See MONEY (Monetary Standards).

MONOMETER. See POETRY (table: Terms).

MONOMIAL. See ALGEBRA (Terms Used in Algebra).

MONONGAHELA RIVER, *moh NAHN guh HEE luh,* provides river transportation between the rich soft coal fields of southwestern Pennsylvania and the steel factories at Pittsburgh. The river is formed where the Tygart and West Fork rivers meet in Marion County, W.Va. The Monongahela winds northeastward across the boundary of Pennsylvania to the mouth of the Cheat River. Here it flows northward until it unites with the Allegheny at Pittsburgh to form the Ohio River. The Monongahela is 128 miles long. Boats can sail on all parts of the river that flow through Pennsylvania. The name *Monongahela* comes from an Indian word that means *river with sliding banks.*   GEORGE MACINKO

MONONUCLEOSIS. See INFECTIOUS MONONUCLEOSIS.

MONOPHONY, *moh NAHF oh nih,* is music written for a single, unsupported voice or part. It can also mean such music with a simple accompaniment. Monophony is the oldest type of music, and the only form used in ancient Greek music and European folk music.

MONOPLACOPHORA. See MOLLUSK.

MONOPLANE. See AIRPLANE (Kinds of Airplanes).

MONOPOLY AND COMPETITION are terms used to describe selling conditions in a market or industry. *Competition* exists when many persons or companies try to sell the same kinds of goods to the same buyers. *Monopoly* exists when a single producer or seller controls the supply of a product for which there is no close substitute. Monopoly conditions also exist when a group of sellers acts together to set prices or other terms of sale of a product. The word comes from the Greek *monos,* meaning *single,* and *polein,* which means *to sell.*

Maintaining competition has always been a major issue in the United States. It came to a head in the late 1800's and early 1900's. John D. Rockefeller, J. P. Morgan, Jay Gould, and other "captains of industry" created giant business complexes that controlled entire industries. With their monopoly power, they regulated the supply of goods and set high prices for their products. The public outcry that resulted led to the passage of the Sherman Antitrust Act in 1890 and to its first vigorous enforcement in the "trust-busting" days of President Theodore Roosevelt.

Kinds of Monopoly and Competition. Monopoly and competition exist in many different forms and degrees. Markets and industries in the United States, for example, range from almost *pure monopoly* to almost *pure competition.*

Pure, or *perfect, competition* occurs when the same kinds of goods or services are produced or sold by many firms. No producer or seller can control the price of the product, because no one controls a large part of the total production or supply. In the United States, the sale of some farm products comes closest to being pure competition.

A few large companies dominate in some U.S. industries. As few as three or four firms may make or sell three-fourths or more of an industry's products. This situation, where there are only a few competing producers, is called *oligopoly.* The term comes from the Greek *oligos* (few) and *polein* (to sell). Oligopolies develop most often in manufacturing industries that require such huge factories and expensive equipment that it is hard for new firms to enter the field.

Economists often divide oligopolies into two groups. The first includes industries whose products are made to a standardized size, shape, thickness, quality, or purity. Examples include certain grades of aluminum, steel, oil, and chemicals. A second type of oligopoly is called *differentiated oligopoly,* because producers differentiate their products from one another by emphasizing brand names. This type includes industries that produce cars, television sets, cigarettes, and soaps.

Monopolistic competition describes the case of many sellers—perhaps 20 or 30—selling differentiated products. Examples include clothing manufacturers, food packers, and retail merchants. Each seller has a limited form of monopoly, because his products differ in some ways from those of other sellers.

Effects of Limited Competition. Monopoly and oligopoly can adversely affect the quality and availability of what people buy. So long as customers feel they must have the product, a monopoly firm can sell a product of poor quality without fear of being undersold. In time, however, such practices may lead to the development of substitute products or even to the entry of new firms into the market.

Some economists believe a certain degree of monopoly may be desirable to encourage inventions and new ideas and practices in industry. They argue that monopoly and oligopoly firms can finance new projects better because they receive above normal profits and thus have money to put into new products. Other economists maintain that there is little evidence that this is the only, or even the best, way to bring about improvements and changes in products.

History. In the late 1800's and early 1900's, a few U.S. industrialists merged and combined many small firms into extremely large corporations. They tried to monopolize many industries, including the railroad, steel, and petroleum industries. In some industries, large corporations combined under unified control. These combinations were called *trusts.* Some firms engaged in price-cutting practices that forced smaller firms out of business. Then they restricted production and raised prices. See TRUST.

The abuses of monopolies and trusts led to a series of federal laws. The Sherman Antitrust Act of 1890 prohibited great combinations that restricted interstate trade. But it was almost 20 years before the power of the act was felt. On the basis of this act, President Theodore Roosevelt's Administration filed antitrust suits against many monopolies. In the best-known of these suits, the courts ordered the Standard Oil trust broken up in 1911 (see STANDARD OIL COMPANY).

Two other federal laws were passed in 1914 to give support and clarification to the Sherman act. The

MONORAIL RAILROAD

Federal Trade Commission Act prohibited unfair methods of competition and unfair or deceptive marketing practices. The act established the Federal Trade Commission to investigate certain suspect business practices and to prevent business firms from destroying competition. The Clayton Antitrust Act prohibited such monopolistic practices as price discrimination and mergers that substantially reduce competition.

The latest important federal antitrust legislation was the Celler-Kefauver Act of 1950. This act tightened control over business mergers that might lessen competition or lead to monopoly. Most states also have laws that forbid monopolistic practices.

Federal and state governments have relied on two different methods in dealing with monopoly. The main effort has been to prohibit monopoly and monopolistic practices. These are the chief provisions of the federal antimonopoly laws. But in the public utility field, federal and state governments permit and even encourage monopolies. Certain features of public utilities would make competition in this field costly and inefficient. However, government commissions regulate the prices and activities of public utilities.

See also MERGER; CARTEL; FREE ENTERPRISE SYSTEM.

Critically reviewed by JOHN R. COLEMAN

MONORAIL RAILROAD is a railroad that has only one rail. Monorail cars can run along a rail placed above or below them. Cars that run above the track have either a gyroscopic device to balance them, or guide wheels that grip the side of the rail to keep the cars from falling over (see GYROSCOPE). There are two types of suspended monorail systems. In the older type, the cars hang freely from wheels on a rail. The newer "split-rail" type suspends the cars from two rails spaced closely together and housed in one enclosure. The enclosure ensures quieter operation, and also keeps the track dry.

Monorail cars can be powered by electric motors, gas turbines, or gasoline engines. Rubber wheels cut noise considerably. Monorails are faster and cheaper to operate and maintain than two-rail elevated or subway lines. A two-way monorail system costs about $700,000 a mile, compared to around $6 million a mile for subway lines. The smaller amount of friction in monorails allows greater speeds with less operating cost.

The first monorail system, built in Wuppertal, Germany, in 1901, still carries passengers. Many cities in

the United States have studied the possibility of building monorail systems. Single-rail railroads can be built quickly and can operate above a busy street. Ground supports do not require much space, because they have only one rail.

The first monorail train in the U.S. began operating at Houston, Tex., in 1956. Other monorails in the United States are located at Seattle, Wash.; Disneyland, near Anaheim, Calif.; Dallas, Tex.; Lake Arrowhead, Calif.; Pomona, Calif.; and New York City. Tokyo, Japan, built an 8.2-mile monorail system for use during the 1964 Olympic Games there.   CARLTON J. CORLISS

See also MONOSODIUM GLUTAMATE. (Other Products).

MONOTHEISM. See RELIGION.

MONOTYPE is one of the two chief kinds of typesetting and type-casting devices. It casts and sets type one letter at a time in the proper sequence. It also spaces the letters in lines up to 10 inches wide, just as a compositor arranges letters into words by hand. The other machine is a *Linotype*. It casts and sets type in a *slug* (bar of metal) up to 7 inches wide (see LINOTYPE).

The Monotype sets type for fine books, catalogs, national magazines, dictionaries, technical books, and ordinary commercial printing. The Monotype machine is made up of two parts, the *keyboard* and the *casting machine*. They produce type in two separate operations.

The Keyboard resembles a large typewriter. Striking the keys *perforates* (punches holes) in a paper *controller ribbon* that controls the operation of the casting machine, which actually casts the type. The use of perforations in the controller paper is called *code control*, and is one of the earliest known applications of automation (see AUTOMATION). The keyboard provides 255 letters and characters used in printing. At the end of each word, the operator strikes a space bar. This space is important when the line is nearly completed, when a line is divided into equal parts. This leftover space is added to the spaces previously set between each word in the line. This operation is called *justifying the line*, and explains why the last character in a printed line falls exactly below the last character in the line above.

The Casting Machine casts type from molten metal (antimony, tin, and lead) and assembles each character and space in the proper sequence in the line. A frame that is called a *matrix case* holds 225 or 255 *matrices* (molds) that correspond to the characters on the key-

A Monorail Train at Disneyland in California takes riders on demonstration runs. A driver in the lead car pilots the train, but an automatic control system handles such operations as starting, slowing down on curves, and stopping. Monorail systems operate in various parts of the world. But they have been more successful in Europe than anywhere else.

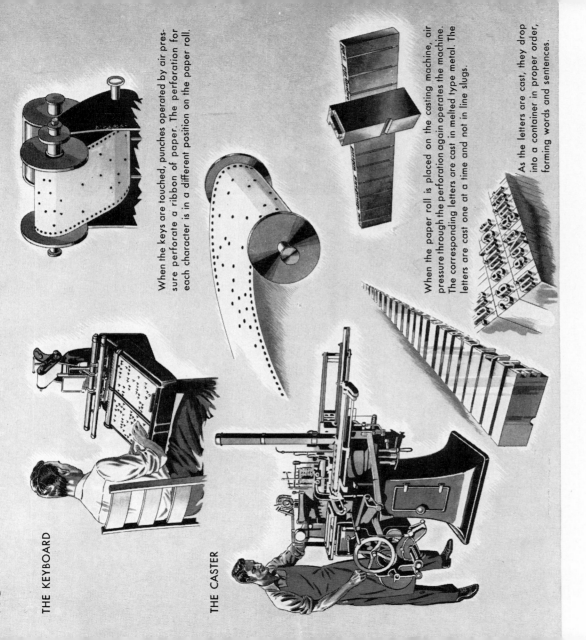

THE KEYBOARD

When the keys are touched, punches operated by air pressure perforate a ribbon of paper. The perforation for each character is in a different position on the paper roll.

THE CASTER

When the paper roll is placed on the casting machine, air pressure through the perforation again operates the machine. The corresponding letters are cast in melted type metal. The letters are cast one at a time and not in line slugs.

As the letters are cast, they drop into a container in proper order, forming words and sentences.

board. The perforated control paper "orders" a small device to pick up the proper matrix and carry it to the casting box. When the matrix is in place, molten metal pours over it to form the character. The type is then ejected from the casting machine.

One of the advantages of the Monotype is that errors can be corrected by changing single letters, since all letters and spaces are separate. An error in a Linotype slug can be corrected only by resetting and recasting the entire line.

DONALD H. NEALE

See also PRINTING (Setting the Type).

MONROE, La. (pop. 52,219; alt. 82 ft.), lies near one of the largest natural-gas fields in the world. It is a commercial and industrial center for northeastern Louisiana. The city stands on the banks of the Ouachita River, about 200 miles northwest of Baton Rouge, and 25 miles south of the Arkansas state line. For location, see ARKANSAS (color map).

Large industrial plants in Monroe produce carbon black, cotton products and cotton-seed oil, lumber, metal products, and paper. Three trunk-line railroads run into the city. Monroe is the home of Northeast Louisiana State College.

Don Juan Filhiol built Fort Miro in 1790. In 1807, it became the seat of government for Ouachita Parish. The town changed its name to Monroe in 1819, and was incorporated as a city in 1900. Gas, discovered in 1916, made power cheap, and attracted industries to Monroe. It has a commission government.

EDWIN A. DAVIS

MONROE, HARRIET (1860–1936), founded *Poetry: A Magazine of Verse* in Chicago in 1912. She served as its editor until 1936. Miss Monroe wrote poetry, but became famous chiefly as an editor. Her magazine helped initiate and develop modern American poetry. Miss Monroe was born in Chicago, and attended the Academy of the Visitation in Washington, D.C. She wrote an autobiography, *A Poet's Life,* published in 1938.

WILLIAM VAN O'CONNOR

JAMES MONROE

James Monroe

JEFFERSON
3rd President
1801—1809

MADISON
4th President
1809—1817

5TH PRESIDENT OF THE UNITED STATES 1817-1825

Sculpture by Attilio Piccirilli, Rotunda of the Virginia
State Capitol, Richmond, Va. (Elliott Erwitt, Magnum)

J. Q. ADAMS
6th President
1825—1829

JACKSON
7th President
1829—1837

The United States Flag had 15 stars
and 15 stripes when Monroe took office,
even though there were 19 states.

MONROE, JAMES (1758-1831), is best remembered for the Monroe Doctrine, which he proclaimed in 1823. This historic policy warned European countries not to interfere with the free nations of the Western Hemisphere.

Monroe became President after more than 40 years of public service. He had fought in the Revolutionary War. During the first years after independence, he had served in the Virginia Assembly and in the Congress of the Confederation. He later became a U.S. Senator; minister to France, Spain, and Great Britain; and governor of Virginia. During the War of 1812, he served as Secretary of State and Secretary of War at the same time.

In appearance and manner, Monroe resembled his fellow Virginian, George Washington. He was tall and rawboned, and had a military bearing. His gray-blue eyes invited confidence. Even John Quincy Adams, who criticized almost everyone, spoke well of Monroe. At his inauguration, Monroe still wore his hair in the old-fashioned way, powdered and tied in a queue at the back. He favored suits of black broadcloth with knee breeches and buckles on the shoes. To the people, he represented the almost legendary heroism of the generation which led the country to freedom.

As President, Monroe presided quietly during a period known as "the era of good feeling." He looked forward to America's glorious future, the outlines of which emerged rapidly during his presidency. The fron-

tier was moving rapidly westward, and small cities sprang up west of the Mississippi River. Monroe sent General Andrew Jackson on a military expedition into Florida which resulted in the purchase of Florida from Spain. Rapidly extending frontiers soon caused Americans to consider whether slavery should be permitted in the new territories. The Missouri Compromise "settled" this problem for nearly 30 years by setting definite limits to the extension of slavery in land lying within the Louisiana Purchase area.

Early Life

Boyhood. James Monroe was born in Westmoreland County, Virginia, on April 28, 1758. His father, Colonel Spence Monroe, came from a Scottish family that had settled in Virginia in the mid-1600's. The family

IMPORTANT DATES IN MONROE'S LIFE

1758 (April 28) Born in Westmoreland County, Virginia.
1783 Elected to the Congress of the Confederation.
1786 (Feb. 16) Married Elizabeth Kortright.
1790 Elected to the United States Senate.
1794 Named minister to France.
1799 Elected governor of Virginia.
1811 Appointed Secretary of State.
1814 Named Secretary of War.
1816 Elected President of the United States.
1820 Re-elected President.
1823 Proclaimed the Monroe Doctrine.
1831 (July 4) Died in New York City.

MONROE, JAMES

of his mother, Elizabeth Jones Monroe, came from Wales, and also had lived in Virginia for many years. James was the eldest of four boys and a girl.

James studied at home with a tutor until he was 12 years old. Then his father sent him to the school of Parson Archibald Campbell. The boy had to leave home early in the morning and tramp miles through the forest to reach Campbell's school. He often carried a rifle and shot game on the way. At the age of 16, James entered the College of William and Mary. But the stirring events of the Revolutionary War soon lured him into the army.

Soldier. Although only 18, Monroe was commissioned a lieutenant. He soon saw action, fighting at Harlem Heights and White Plains in the fall of 1776. His superior officers praised Monroe for gallantry in the Battle of Trenton, where he was wounded in the shoulder. During the next two years, he fought at Brandywine, Germantown, and Monmouth.

In 1778, Monroe was promoted to lieutenant colonel and sent to raise troops in Virginia. He failed in his mission, but it greatly influenced his future career. It

brought him into contact with Thomas Jefferson, then governor of the state. Monroe began to study law under Jefferson's guidance, and became a political disciple and lifelong friend of his teacher.

Political and Public Career

Monroe began his public career in 1782, when he won a seat in the Virginia Assembly. In 1783, he was elected to the Congress of the Confederation, where he served three years (see Congress of the Confederation). Monroe did not favor a highly centralized government. But he supported moderate measures intended to let Congress establish tariffs. Monroe worked to give pioneers the right to travel on the Mississippi River. He also aided Jefferson in drafting laws for the development of the West. Two hurried trips to the western region had left Monroe unimpressed with its beauty or fertility. But he still believed that the West would be important in the future growth of the country.

State Politics. In 1786, Monroe settled down to the

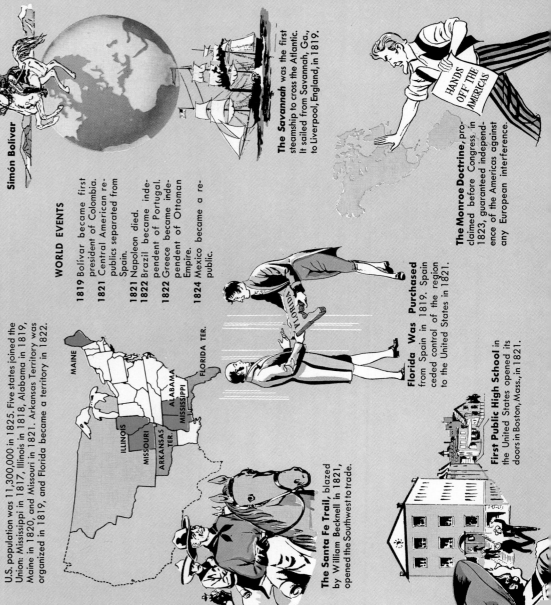

THE WORLD OF PRESIDENT MONROE

U.S. population was 11,300,000 in 1825. Five states joined the Union: Mississippi in 1817, Illinois in 1818, Alabama in 1819, Maine in 1820, and Missouri in 1821. Arkansas Territory was organized in 1819, and Florida became a territory in 1822.

Simón Bolivar

WORLD EVENTS

1819 Bolivar became first president of Colombia.
1821 Central American republics separated from Spain.
1821 Napoleon died.
1822 Brazil became independent of Portugal.
1822 Greece became independent of Ottoman Empire.
1824 Mexico became a republic.

The Savannah was the first steamship to cross the Atlantic. It sailed from Savannah, Ga., to Liverpool, England, in 1819.

The Monroe Doctrine, proclaimed before Congress in 1823, guaranteed independence of the Americas against any European interference.

HANDS OFF THE AMERICAS

MAINE

ILLINOIS

MISSOURI

ARKANSAS TER.

ALABAMA

MISSISSIPPI

FLORIDA TER.

Florida Was Purchased from Spain in 1819. Spain ceded control of the region to the United States in 1821.

The Santa Fe Trail, blazed by William Becknell in 1821, opened the Southwest to trade.

First Public High School in the United States opened its doors in Boston, Mass., in 1821.

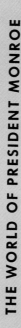

LIFE AND CAREER OF JAMES MONROE

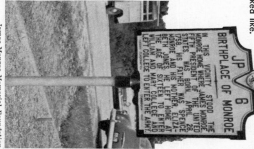

Monroe's Birthplace, near Colonial Beach, Va., fell into ruin, and no one knows exactly what the building looked like.

James Monroe Memorial Foundation

Monroe's Law Office in Fredericksburg, Va., has been preserved as a museum. It contains displays of many of Monroe's personal possessions.

Virginia Dept. of Conservation and Development

An Army Officer. Monroe served in many Revolutionary War battles. His superior officers especially praised him for bravery at Trenton, where he was wounded.

practice of law in Fredericksburg, Va. But politics drew him like a magnet. He ran for the Virginia Assembly, and won easily. Monroe remained in the assembly four years.

In 1788, Monroe served in the convention called by Virginia to ratify the United States Constitution. His distrust of a strong federal government aligned him with Patrick Henry and George Mason, who opposed the Constitution. But Monroe offered only moderate opposition, and he gracefully accepted ratification.

Monroe's Family. In 1786, Monroe married 17-year-old Elizabeth Kortright (June 30, 1768–Sept. 23, 1830), the daughter of a New York City merchant. The couple had two daughters, Eliza and Maria, and a son, but the boy died at the age of 2. Monroe's admiration for Jefferson became so strong that in 1789 he moved to Charlottesville, Va. There he built Ash Lawn, not far from Jefferson's estate, Monticello.

U.S. Senator. Monroe ran against James Madison for the first United States House of Representatives, but lost. In 1790, the Virginia legislature elected him to fill a vacancy in the United States Senate. As a Senator, Monroe aligned himself with Madison and with Jefferson, then Secretary of State, in vigorous opposition to the Federalist program of Alexander Hamilton. Assisted by such leaders as Albert Gallatin and Aaron Burr, the three Virginians founded the Democratic-Republican party. This party developed into one of the two great parties which have formed the basis of American politics ever since (see DEMOCRATIC-REPUBLICAN PARTY).

Opposition to Washington. In 1794, President George Washington appointed Monroe minister to France. The President knew that Monroe opposed many administration policies, but he needed a diplomat who could improve relations with the French. He also knew that Monroe strongly admired France.

During talks in France, Monroe criticized the Jay Treaty between the United States and Britain as "the most shameful transaction I have ever known." Furious,

Washington recalled Monroe in 1796. See JAY TREATY.

Upon his return, Monroe became involved in a bitter personal dispute with Hamilton which nearly led to a duel. The quarrel resulted from the publication of materials that slandered Hamilton. Monroe was blamed, but denied responsibility. Hamilton eventually dropped his charges. The quarrel, and the humiliation of being recalled from France, made these years among the unhappiest in Monroe's life.

Diplomat Under Jefferson. In 1799, Monroe was elected governor of Virginia. In this post, he played an important part in preserving democratic processes during the tense years following passage of the Alien and Sedition Acts (see ALIEN AND SEDITION ACTS). Early in 1803, President Thomas Jefferson sent Monroe to Paris to help Robert R. Livingston negotiate the purchase of New Orleans. By the time Monroe reached France, Napoleon had offered the astonished Livingston the entire Louisiana Territory. Monroe urged Livingston to accept the offer without waiting to consult Jefferson, and the two men made arrangements for the treaty. See LOUISIANA PURCHASE.

Jefferson was pleased with Monroe's initiative, and sent him to Madrid to help Charles Pinckney purchase the Floridas from Spain. They failed, but Jefferson still had confidence in Monroe. The President named him minister to Great Britain. In 1806, Monroe helped conclude a trade treaty that was so unsatisfactory that Jefferson refused to submit it to the Senate.

Monroe felt his usefulness in London had ended, and returned home in 1807. He became a reluctant candidate for the nomination to succeed Jefferson as President. But Madison won the nomination and the presidency. Monroe served in the Virginia Assembly until he was elected governor in 1811.

Secretary of State. Monroe resigned as governor after about three months to accept President Madison's appointment as Secretary of State. As his first task, he attempted to reach some understanding with the Brit-

Secretary of State. He headed Madison's Cabinet for six years.

Governor of Virginia. Monroe won the governorship in 1799 and 1811.

Virginia State Chamber of Commerce

Oak Hill, Monroe's retirement home, stands near Leesburg, Va. Thomas Jefferson helped draw the plans for this cream-colored brick mansion.

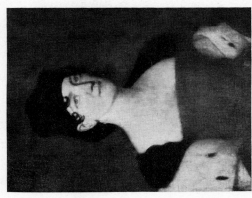

Painting by Benjamin West; Photo courtesy James Monroe Law Office Museum, Fredericksburg, Va.

Elizabeth Kortright Monroe closely observed European court life while her husband was a diplomat. As First Lady, she introduced more formal ways of White House entertaining.

ish over the impressment of American seamen. But he soon concluded that war could not be avoided.

At the beginning of the War of 1812, Monroe was eager to take command of the army. But Madison convinced him to stay in the Cabinet. Secretary of War John Armstrong was forced to resign in 1814 because of neglect of duty during the burning of Washington, D.C. Madison asked Monroe to become Secretary of War while continuing as Secretary of State. Monroe held both offices for the rest of the war. After he took over the War Department, American armies won several brilliant victories. These triumphs greatly increased Monroe's popularity. See WAR OF 1812.

In 1816, while still Secretary of State, Monroe was elected President of the United States. He received 183 electoral votes to 34 for Senator Rufus King of New York, the Federalist candidate. Monroe's running mate was Governor Daniel D. Tompkins of New York.

Monroe's Administration (1817-1825)

The years of Monroe's presidency are generally known as "the era of good feeling." The Federalist party had disappeared after the election of 1816, and nearly everyone belonged to the Democratic-Republican party. The country prospered because of fast-growing industries and settlement of the West. A depression in 1818-1819 caused only a temporary setback.

"The American System" provided the chief issue of Monroe's first term. House Speaker Henry Clay of Kentucky advanced this plan. The American System proposed to strengthen nationalism in two ways: (1) construction of new roads and canals to open the West, and (2) enactment of a protective tariff to encourage Northern manufacturers and develop home markets.

Monroe distrusted the American System, because he doubted that the federal government had the power for these activities. He studied the program during a 3½-month tour of the North and West. But this trip did not change his "settled conviction" that Congress did not have the power to build roads and canals.

Clay continued his fight, and finally won Congress over to his side. In 1822, Monroe vetoed a bill providing for federal administration of toll gates on the Cumberland Road. He urged a constitutional amendment to give Congress the power to promote internal improvements. In 1824, Monroe signed the Survey Act, which planned improvements in the future.

Clay had more success in pushing through the protective tariff, the second part of his American System. Congress had already raised tariff rates in 1816, and it further increased the duty on iron in 1818. In 1824, Congress raised tariff rates in general.

Life in the White House. The British had burned the White House during the War of 1812, and the mansion had not been rebuilt when Monroe took office. The new President maintained his residence on I Street, near 20th Street, for nine months. On New Year's Day, 1818, President and Mrs. Monroe held a public reception marking the reopening of the White House.

Monroe had observed court etiquette during his trips to Europe, and decided to adopt a strict social attitude for the White House. Partly because of ill health, Mrs. Monroe received only visitors to whom she had sent invitations. She refused to pay calls, sending her elder daughter, Mrs. Eliza Hay, in her place. Soon all Washington buzzed about the "snobbish" Mrs. Monroe. As time passed, the public realized that Mrs. Monroe

---

VICE-PRESIDENT AND CABINET

Vice-President	*Daniel D. Tompkins
Secretary of State	*John Quincy Adams
Secretary of the Treasury	*William H. Crawford
Secretary of War	*John C. Calhoun
Attorney General	Richard Rush
	William Wirt (1817)
Secretary of the Navy	Benjamin W. Crowninshield
	Smith Thompson (1819)
	Samuel L. Southard (1823)

*Has a separate biography in WORLD BOOK.

had followed the President's wishes in establishing protocol. During Monroe's second term, her Wednesday receptions became popular. The visit of the Marquis de Lafayette on New Year's Day, 1825, added a touch of splendor to the last months of Monroe's term.

Beginnings of Sectionalism. In 1819, Missouri applied for admission to the Union as a slave state. The House of Representatives aroused anger in the South by passing a bill to admit Missouri with the provision that no more slaves could be brought into the state. The Senate defeated this provision, and Congress eventually agreed on a bill known as the Missouri Compromise. This law permitted slavery in Missouri, but banned it from the rest of the Louisiana Purchase region north of the southern boundary of Missouri. Monroe avoided interfering with these debates. But he made it known that he would not sign a bill placing any special restraints on Missouri's admission to the Union. See MISSOURI COMPROMISE.

War with the Seminole. Since the War of 1812, Americans in Georgia had been harassed by bands of runaway Negroes and Indians in Spanish Florida. In 1817, fighting broke out between the Seminole Indians and settlers in southern Georgia. President Monroe ordered Major General Andrew Jackson to raise a force of militia and put down the uprising. Jackson chased the Indians into the Everglades of Florida. Then he captured Pensacola, the Spanish capital of Florida.

Jackson's easy conquest convinced the Spanish that they could not defend Florida. In 1819, the Spanish sold Florida to the United States in return for the cancellation of $5 million in American claims against Spain. See FLORIDA (History).

Diplomatic Achievements. Monroe's administration marked one of the most brilliant periods in American diplomacy. The Rush-Bagot Agreement, signed with Great Britain in 1817, prohibited fortifications on the Great Lakes. In 1818, Great Britain agreed to the 49th parallel as the boundary between the United States and Canada from Lake of the Woods on the Minnesota-Ontario border as far west as the Rocky Mountains. The British also consented to joint occupation of the Oregon region. American diplomats convinced Spain to give up its claims to Oregon in 1819, and the Russians agreed to a similar pact in 1824.

Re-election. In the election of 1820, Monroe was unopposed for the presidency. This was the second and last time in American history that there was only one presidential candidate. In 1792, George Washington had been unopposed for a second term. Monroe received every vote cast in the electoral college but one. William Plumer, an elector from New Hampshire, cast his vote for John Quincy Adams.

The Monroe Doctrine. During the Napoleonic Wars, the Spaniards had become deeply involved in European affairs, and took little interest in their American colonies. Most of the colonies took advantage of this situation and declared independence from Spain. The Latin-American revolutions aroused great sympathy in the United States. As early as 1817, Henry Clay had begun a campaign for recognition of these new countries. In March, 1822, Monroe finally recommended that their independence be recognized. In December, 1823, the President proclaimed the historic Monroe Doctrine in a message to Congress. This doctrine has remained a basic American policy ever since. See MONROE DOCTRINE.

The era of good feeling ended before Monroe finished his second term. Unlike the situation which followed the retirement of Jefferson and Madison, there was no single, outstanding figure who was the overwhelming choice to become the next President. Four candidates fought for the office. None won a majority of the votes, and the House of Representatives chose John Quincy Adams. See ADAMS, JOHN QUINCY (Election of 1824).

Later Years

Monroe retired to Oak Hill, his estate near Leesburg, Va. He served for five years as a regent of the University of Virginia. In 1829, he became presiding officer of the Virginia Constitutional Convention. His wife died on Sept. 23, 1830, and was buried at Oak Hill. Long public service had left Monroe a poor man, and he was too old to resume his law practice. Late in 1830, his financial distress forced him to move to New York City to live with his daughter and her husband. Monroe died there on July 4, 1831. In 1858, his remains were moved to Hollywood Cemetery in Richmond, Va. His law office in Fredericksburg has been preserved as a memorial. Authoritative books on the life of Monroe include James Monroe by William P. Cresson and The Autobiography of James Monroe, edited by Stuart Gerry Brown.

RALPH L. KETCHAM

Related Articles in WORLD BOOK include:

Adams, John Quincy	Jefferson, Thomas	President of
Clay, Henry	Louisiana Purchase	the U.S.
Hamilton,	Madison, James	Tariff
Alexander	Missouri	Tompkins,
Jackson, Andrew	Compromise	Daniel D.
Jay Treaty	National Road	War of 1812

Outline

I. Early Life
   A. Boyhood
   B. Soldier
II. Political and Public Career
   A. State Politics
   B. Monroe's Family
   C. U.S. Senator
   D. Opposition to Washington
   E. Diplomat Under Jefferson
   F. Secretary of State
III. Monroe's Administration (1817-1825)
   A. "The American System"
   B. Life in the White House
   C. Beginnings of Sectionalism
   D. War with the Seminole
   E. Diplomatic Achievements
   F. Re-election
   G. The Monroe Doctrine
IV. Later Years

Questions

What two Cabinet posts did Monroe hold at once?
Why did Monroe oppose "the American System"?
What term is often used to describe the period of Monroe's administration? Why?
How did Monroe display legislative initiative during negotiations for the purchase of Louisiana?
How did slavery become an issue during Monroe's administration?
How did Monroe meet Thomas Jefferson?
Why were Monroe and his wife unpopular during their early years in the White House?
How did Monroe arouse the hostility of George Washington while serving as minister to France?
What was the Monroe Doctrine?
In what ways did Monroe contribute to the founding of his country?

MONROE DOCTRINE was set forth by President James Monroe in a message he delivered to the Congress of the United States on Dec. 2, 1823. It practically guaranteed all the independent nations of the Western Hemisphere against European interference "for the purpose of oppressing them, or controlling in any other manner their destiny." The Doctrine said also that the American continents were "henceforth not to be considered as subjects for future colonization by any European powers." This statement meant that the United States would not allow new colonies to be created anywhere in the Americas, nor permit existing colonies to extend their boundaries.

Origins. The Monroe Doctrine grew out of conditions in Europe as well as in America. The three leading absolute monarchies of Europe were Russia, Austria, and Prussia. They had pledged themselves to "put an end to the system of representative government, in whatever country it may exist in Europe." The United States feared that these three powers (sometimes inaccurately called "The Holy Alliance") might also try to suppress representative government in the Americas.

During and after the Napoleonic Wars, most of the Spanish colonies in America had taken advantage of unsettled conditions in Europe to break away from the mother country. As they won independence, these colonies formed themselves into republics with constitutions much like that of the United States. Only Brazil chose to keep its monarchy when it declared its independence from Portugal.

After Napoleon's downfall, the monarchy was restored in Spain, and it seemed quite possible that the Holy Alliance might try to restore Spain's colonies as well. The French monarchy, which had followed the policy of the Holy Alliance to the point of actually suppressing a democratic revolution in Spain, was also suspected of intending to help Spain regain its former American possessions. A rumor that France was on the point of doing this spread over Europe during 1823.

This threat disturbed not only the United States, but Great Britain as well. As free republics, the Spanish-American colonies traded with Great Britain. If they became colonies again, whether of Spain or of France, their trade with Great Britain would certainly be cut down. Great Britain had steadily opposed the doctrine of the Holy Alliance, and had few allies in Europe. George Canning, the British foreign minister, proposed to Richard Rush, the American minister in London, that Great Britain and the United States issue a joint warning against European aggression in the Americas.

President Monroe was at first inclined to accept the British offer. Ex-Presidents Jefferson and Madison strongly favored the idea. With Great Britain "on our side," Jefferson argued, "we need not fear the whole world." But Monroe's Secretary of State, John Quincy Adams, said that the United States should not "come in as a cock-boat in the wake of the British man-of-war." He urged that the United States alone make the kind of statement Canning had in mind. He said that the British would use their sea power to prevent European intervention in America whether they had an agreement with the United States or not. Thus the United States would have all the advantages of joint action without entering into what amounted to an alliance with Great Britain. Moreover, a strictly American

declaration would clearly apply to Great Britain as well as to other European countries. Monroe finally decided to follow Adams' advice and proclaimed the Monroe Doctrine. He used practically the same words that Adams had used when he first proposed it to him.

Results. Until the late 1800's, Europe's respect for the rights of the smaller American nations rested less upon the Monroe Doctrine than upon fear of the British Navy. A possible exception to this rule occurred in the 1860's, shortly after the Civil War, while the wartime Army and Navy of the American government forced Emperor Napoleon III to give up an attempt to set up a European kingdom in Mexico. It was not again until the 1880's, when the United States began to enlarge its new Navy of steel ships, that the United States had enough power to enforce the Monroe Doctrine.

From the point of view of trade, the Monroe Doctrine probably did the United States no good whatever. Europe continued to get the larger share of Latin-American trade, most of which went to Great Britain. Nor did the Doctrine improve relations between the United States and the Latin-American countries. The nations which the Doctrine was supposed to protect resented the way the United States assumed its own superiority over them. Besides, they feared "The Colossus of the North" far more than they feared any European nation. Until the 1890's, Great Britain and other countries generally ignored the Doctrine.

The Monroe Doctrine in Action. During the 1800's, the Monroe Doctrine was seldom invoked. President James Polk referred to it in 1845 during the dispute with Great Britain over Oregon. Secretary of State William Seward referred to the Doctrine when he denounced French intervention in Mexico in the 1860's. President Grover Cleveland used it as a basis for threatening to declare war on Great Britain in 1895 if the British would not agree to arbitrate their dispute with Venezuela.

The Roosevelt Corollary. In the early 1900's, President Theodore Roosevelt gave new life and new meaning to the Monroe Doctrine. He pointed out that weakness or brutal wrongdoing on the part of any of the smaller American nations might tempt European countries to intervene. It seemed to Roosevelt that European nations might well feel justified in trying to protect the lives and property of their citizens or to collect debts justly owed to them. Roosevelt asserted that the Monroe Doctrine required the United States to prevent such justified intervention by doing the intervening itself. Under this "big stick" policy, the United States sent armed forces into the Dominican Republic in 1905, into Nicaragua in 1912, and into Haiti in 1915.

In general, President Woodrow Wilson continued Roosevelt's policy. But Wilson promised that the United States would "never again seek one additional foot of territory by conquest." He also showed restraint in dealing with the Mexican revolution that ran its course during his term in office. If he had wanted to, he could have used Roosevelt's interpretation of the Monroe Doctrine to justify a full-scale occupation of Mexico. Instead, he pursued a policy of "watchful waiting." See WILSON, WOODROW (Crisis in Mexico).

Black Star

Monrovia, the chief port and commercial center of Liberia, has one of the best-developed harbors on Africa's Atlantic coast.

The "Good Neighbor Policy." After World War I, the United States clearly recognized the need for better relations with the Latin-American countries. President Herbert Hoover made a good-will tour of South America before he took office.

President Franklin D. Roosevelt went even further and announced his Good Neighbor policy early in his administration. He took the position that all the Americas should have a share in upholding the Monroe Doctrine. Thus the defense of the Western Hemisphere became a cooperative task.

During the Hoover and Roosevelt administrations, the United States gradually withdrew its forces from the smaller American states it had occupied, and gave up the special privileges it had claimed. By a series of reciprocal trade agreements, it steadily cut down the high tariff barriers that had done so much to keep the Americas apart. Conferences on inter-American affairs were held at Montevideo in 1933, at Buenos Aires in 1936, at Lima in 1939, and at Havana in 1940. Fear of aggression brought all the American republics closer together. They met again at Rio de Janeiro in 1942, at Mexico City in 1945, and at Petropolis, Brazil, in 1947. They set up the Organization of American States at a meeting in Bogotá, Colombia, in 1948.

Misunderstandings. Many persons in the United States have often confused the Monroe Doctrine with the doctrine of *isolation*, or staying out of world affairs, which was stated by George Washington in his Farewell Address in 1796. Monroe did indeed repeat in his message the country's policy of staying out of European affairs, but he used it simply to support his argument that the European nations in turn should stay out of American affairs. Isolationism is therefore no part of the Monroe Doctrine. It simply happened to be the policy of the United States government at the time when the Monroe Doctrine was announced.

JOHN D. HICKS

See also ADAMS, JOHN QUINCY (Secretary of State); IMPERIALISM; MONROE, JAMES (The Monroe Doctrine); PAN AMERICAN CONFERENCES; PAN AMERICAN UNION.

MONRONEY, A. S. MIKE (1902-), an Oklahoma Democrat, served in the United States Senate from 1951 to 1969. He served six terms in the U.S. House of Representatives between 1939 and 1951. As a senator, he wrote the Federal Aviation Agency in 1958. This act set up the Federal Aviation Agency in 1958. ALMER STILLWELL MONRONEY was born in Oklahoma City. His father nicknamed him "Mike" after a high school teacher assigned the boy by mistake to a girls' gym class. Almer later changed his name to A. S. MIKE MONRONEY. He graduated from the University of Oklahoma, and was a reporter and political writer for the *Oklahoma News* in Oklahoma City from 1924 to 1928.

W. EUGENE HOLLON

MONROVIA, *mun ROH vee uh* (pop. 80,922; alt. 10 ft.), is the capital and chief city of Liberia. It stands on the Atlantic Coast at the mouth of the Saint Paul River, and has a modern, well-developed harbor. Monrovia is the educational and cultural center of the country. The College of West Africa is located there. The University of Liberia is 18 miles from the city.

Monrovia was named for James Monroe, President of the United States. The city was founded in 1822 by the American Colonization Society. This society bought the freedom of many American slaves, and helped them establish the Republic of Liberia.

ALAN P. MERRIAM

MONS, *mawns* or *mahnz* (pop. 27,211; alt. 85 ft.), is in western Belgium. Coal mined nearby furnishes power for many Mons factories. Important products include chemicals, cloth, and metal goods.

MONSANTO COMPANY. See CHEMICAL INDUSTRY (table).

MONSARRAT, *MAHN sah raht,* **NICHOLAS** (1910-), is an English author. He won fame for his novel *The Cruel Sea* (1951), a story of naval combat in World War II. He also wrote *The Story of Esther Costello* (1953) and *The Tribe That Lost Its Head* (1956). Monsarrat was born in Liverpool, England, was graduated from Cambridge University, and moved to Canada in 1953.

HARRY T. MOORE

MONSIGNOR, *mawn SEE nyawr,* is a title given to certain clergymen who are dignitaries of the Roman Catholic Church. The word comes from the Italian *monsignore*, meaning *My Lord*, and it is abbreviated as Msgr. Cardinals are not addressed as Monsignor. But patriarchs, archbishops, bishops, and persons attached to the papal household are given this title. In the United States it is more common to address bishops and archbishops as "Your Excellency," though an archbishop may also be called "Your Grace."

FULTON J. SHEEN

MONSOON, *mahn SOON,* is a wind that blows regularly in definite seasons. *Monsoon* comes from the Arabic word for *season*. The name was first applied to winds near Arabia that blow six months from the southwest and six months from the northeast. Monsoons also blow over India, southern Asia, northern Australia, parts of Africa, and North and South America.

Monsoons are caused by large differences in temperature between land and sea air. This difference occurs because land heats and cools faster than water. Cooler air always rushes in over warmer regions. This causes a wind. In summer, the monsoons travel from the cooler sea to the warmer land. In winter, the monsoons go from land to sea. Summer monsoons are usually accompanied by rains and are called *wet monsoons*. Winter monsoons are known as *dry monsoons*.

Engelhard, Monkmeyer

Majestic Mont Blanc in the Pennine Alps is frequently called the *monarch of mountains.* Mont Blanc has several peaks. Mountain climbers come from all parts of the world to climb its rugged slopes.

MONT BLANC, *MAWN BLAHN,* or *MAHNT BLAHNGK,* is the highest mountain in the Alps (15,781 feet), and one of the most famous peaks in Europe. It is often called the *monarch of mountains.* Its name is French for *white mountain.*

Mont Blanc rises on the border between France, Italy, and Switzerland. The base of the mountain is a huge mass of granite which extends into all three countries. Its highest peak is in southern France, in the province of Savoy. Mont Blanc is about 30 miles long and 10 miles wide. Thick woods and swift streams cover its lower slopes. But above 8,000 feet, there is always a thick blanket of snow. There are many huge glaciers on the mountain. The most famous is Mer de Glace (Sea of Ice). A scientific laboratory was built on Mont Blanc in 1893.

Jacques Balmat and Michel Paccard first climbed Mont Blanc in 1786. Today, it is easily climbed, and is a resort center. People can ride up 6,287 feet to Mer de Glace on a cog railway. For those who prefer to climb, there are shelters to aid them in their 50- to 60-hour journey. The world's highest aerial tramway goes up Aiguille du Midi, a lower peak of Mont Blanc. In 1965, the Mont Blanc tunnel, linking France and Italy, was opened for auto traffic.

EDWARD W. FOX

See also ALPS; MOUNTAIN (picture chart).

MONT CENIS TUNNEL, *MAWN suh NEE,* was the first tunnel to be cut through the Alps. It is a railroad tunnel through the mountain peak of Mont Cenis. It connects the Italian province of Turin with the French province of Savoy. The tunnel is 8.5 miles long and from 3,775 feet to 4,246 feet above sea level. Construction began in 1857. The work was finished in 1870. The power drill and the air compressor were tried out for the first time at Mont Cenis.

EDWARD W. FOX

MONT PELÉE, *MAWN puh LAY,* is an active volcano on the northern end of Martinique island in the French West Indies. It rises 4,800 feet above sea level.

The volcano erupted violently in 1902, after lying dormant since 1851. Floods of mud loosened by the eruption devastated the slopes of the mountain. A heap of lava 1,000 feet high formed in the crater. A slender spire of rock was thrust up another 1,000 feet from the crater. An avalanche of red-hot lava and clouds of hot gas swept down the mountain, destroying the city of Saint Pierre and killing about 38,000 people. Only one man, a prisoner in the city's dungeon, escaped alive, although he was seriously injured. Milder eruptions occurred between 1929 and 1932. The French government now maintains a volcano observatory on the slope of Mont Pelée.

GORDON A. MACDONALD

MONT SAINT MICHEL, *MAWN san mee SHEL,* is a large rock which juts from the waters of Mont Saint Michel Bay off the northwestern coast of France. At the top of the rock are an ancient abbey and town.

MONTAGE. See MOTION PICTURE (Terms).

MONTAIGNE, *mahn TAYN,* **MICHEL EYQUEM DE** (1533-1592), a French writer, is considered by many the creator of the personal essay. Writers up to the present time have imitated his informal, conversational style. Montaigne's essays reveal his independent mind and sound judgment, his charm and wit, and his wealth of experience in life and literature. Montaigne first began publishing his essays in 1580, adding to them as life and experience gave him new insight and understanding. He wrote a total of 107 essays.

Montaigne's best-known essays include "Of the Education of Children," "Of Cannibals," and "Of Coaches." Montaigne was a practicing Roman Catholic, but the "Apology for Raymond Sebond" and other essays show so much skepticism that some critics have questioned whether he was really a Christian.

Montaigne was born in his family's castle near Bordeaux, into a family which had recently bought its way into the nobility. His mother was of Jewish origin. Montaigne studied law, and became a minor legal official in 1554. He retired in 1570 to devote himself to writing. In 1580 and 1581 he traveled widely in Switzerland, Germany, and Italy and from 1581 to 1585 he served as mayor of Bordeaux. The most important episode in Montaigne's life was his friendship with the French writer Étienne de La Boétie from 1558 to 1563, which he immortalized in his famous essay "Of Friendship."

ABRAHAM C. KELLER

619

Grinnell Lake in Glacier National Park, Which Has 250 Lakes Within Its Boundaries

Fred Bond, Publix

MONTANA

THE TREASURE STATE

Smelter Smokestack in Anaconda, One of the World's Largest, Is 585 Feet High

Montana Highway Commission

The contributors of this article are Oscar Chaffee, State Editor of the Billings Gazette; Thomas A. Clinch, Head of the Department of History, Carroll College; and Nicholas Helburn, Professor of Geography, Western Michigan University, and former Professor of Geography, Montana State University.

Montana (blue) ranks fourth in size among all the states, and is the largest of the Rocky Mountain States (gray).

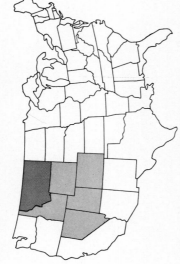

——— FACTS IN BRIEF ———

Capital: Helena.

Government: *Congress*—U.S. senators, 2; U.S. representatives, 2. *Electoral Votes*—4. *State Legislature*—senators, 55; representatives, 104. *Counties*—56.

Area: 147,138 sq. mi. (including 1,535 sq. mi. of inland water), 4th in size among the states. *Greatest Distances*—(east-west) 550 mi.; (north-south) 318 mi.

Elevation: *Highest*—Granite Peak in Park County, 12,799 feet above sea level. *Lowest*—1,800 feet above sea level, along the Kootenai River in Lincoln County.

Population: *1970 Preliminary Census*—682,133; density, 5 persons to the square mile. *1960 Census*—674,767, 41st among the states; distribution, 50 per cent urban, 50 per cent rural.

Chief Products: *Agriculture*—barley, beef cattle, eggs, hay, hogs, milk, sheep, sugar beets, wheat, wool. *Manufacturing and Processing*—food and food products; lumber and wood products; petroleum and coal products; printing and publishing; stone, clay, and glass products; *Mining*—copper, natural gas, petroleum, phosphate rock, sand and gravel, silver, talc, vermiculite.

Statehood: Nov. 8, 1889, the 41st state.

State Motto: *Oro y Plata* (Gold and Silver).

State Song: "Montana." Words by Charles C. Cohen; music by Joseph E. Howard.

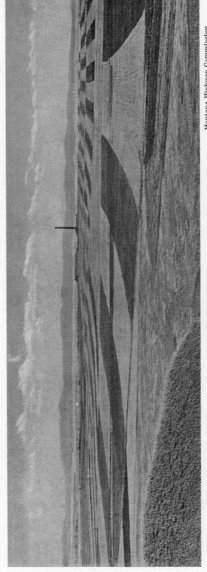

Montana Highway Commission

Strips of Wheat Farm Patterns on Farms near Great Falls

MONTANA is the fourth largest state. Only Alaska, Texas, and California have larger areas. Western Montana is a land of tall, rugged mountains. There, men dig deep into the earth to tap the state's vast deposits of copper, gold, manganese, and silver. Eastern Montana is a land of broad plains. There, vast herds of cattle graze on the prairie grasses, wheat grows in the fertile soil, and wells bring up oil from deep under the ground.

The name *Montana* comes from a Spanish word meaning *mountainous*. Early travelers, who saw the sun glistening on the lofty, snow-capped peaks, called the area the *Land of Shining Mountains*. These mountains contained a wealth of gold and silver, which gave the state another nickname, the *Treasure State*. Glacier National Park has mountain peaks so steep and remote that they have never been climbed.

Early Montana was Indian country. But gold was discovered there in 1862 and great numbers of eager prospectors rushed to the area. Mining camps sprang up overnight and wealth came to the territory. But the gold also brought problems. Outlaws spread terror in the mining camps until groups of citizens called *vigilantes* took the law into their own hands. The vigilantes hanged many of the badmen and drove others away.

Montana was also the scene of another struggle. The efforts of the Indians to keep their land reached a climax in the state. The last stand of General George A. Custer and the final battles of the Nez Percé War were fought in Montana.

The mountains, the battlefields, the old gold camps, and the vast, lonely distances still make a visitor feel close to the American frontier. In the capital, Helena (pronounced *HEHL uh nuh*), the main street is called Last Chance Gulch. The name comes from the gold camp that stood on that site. Even today, when a basement is dug for a building in Helena, the digging often produces some gold dust.

Billings is the largest city in Montana. For the relationship of Montana to the other states in its region, see the article on the ROCKY MOUNTAIN STATES.

Constitution. Montana is still governed under its original constitution, which was adopted before state-hood in 1889. But the state's basic law has been *amended* (changed) about 30 times. The legislature may propose amendments. A legislative amendment must be ap-proved by two-thirds of the members of each house of the legislature. Then it must be approved by a majority of the voters.

Amendments may also be proposed by a *constitutional convention*, a special group called to revise the basic law. A constitutional convention may be called if approved by two-thirds of the legislators, and a majority of the voters. Any amendments proposed by a constitutional convention must be approved by a majority of the citizens voting in an election.

Executive. The governor of Montana serves a four-year term, and may be re-elected any number of times. The governor, the attorney general, and the secretary of state make up the state board of examiners. This board controls the jobs and salaries of many state employees.

The governor has powers of appointment involving key officials in about 80 state agencies and institutions. He also has strong veto powers over legislation. For ex-ample, he may veto individual items in an *appropri-ation* (money) bill, and sign the rest of the bill into law. The governor is paid $22,000 a year. For a list of all the governors of Montana, see the *History* section of this article.

The lieutenant governor, attorney general, secretary of state, and treasurer are elected to four-year terms, and may be re-elected any number of times. However, the treasurer cannot serve two terms in a row.

Legislature, called the *Legislative Assembly*, consists of a 55-member Senate and a 104-member House of Representatives. Senators are elected from 31 senatorial districts. They serve four-year terms. Representatives are elected from 38 representative districts. They serve two-year terms. The legislature meets on the first Monday in January of odd-numbered years. Sessions are limited to 60 days.

In 1965, a federal court ruled that the *apportionment* (division) of the legislature did not give cities equal representation based on population. Later in 1965, the court drew up a temporary reapportionment plan. In 1967, the legislature adopted the plan permanently.

Courts. The highest court of appeals in Montana is the state Supreme Court. It consists of four associate justices and one chief justice. All are elected by the voters to six-year terms. The trial courts for major civil and criminal cases are the district courts. District judges are elected to four-year terms from each of 18 judicial districts. Municipal courts, police courts, and justice of the peace courts handle less serious cases.

Local Government. Each of the state's 56 counties elects three county commissioners to run the affairs of the county. The commissioners serve six-year terms. About 120 cities and towns operate with a mayor-council form of government. Only two cities, Bozeman and Helena, have the council-manager system. Cities and counties are allowed to combine into one govern-ment unit if the people vote for it. However, no such consolidations have taken place.

Taxation. State taxes provide about 60 per cent of the state government's income. More than two-thirds of

The Governor's Mansion Stands on a Hillside near the Capitol. The Building Was First Occupied in 1959.

Montana Highway Commission

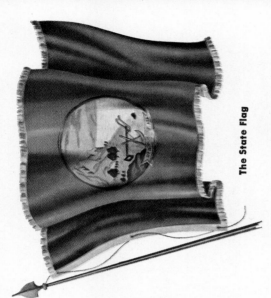

The State Flag

The State Bird
Western Meadow Lark

The State Flower
Bitterroot

The State Tree
Ponderosa Pine

The State Seal

Symbols of Montana. On the state seal, a plow, a pick, and a shovel rest on the soil to show Montana's agricultural opportunities and its mineral industries. The Great Falls of the Missouri River and the mountain scenery represent the natural beauty and resources of the state. The state motto appears on a ribbon. The seal was adopted in 1889. The state flag, adopted in 1905, bears an adaptation of the seal.

Flower illustration courtesy of Eli Lilly and Company

the revenue comes from income taxes and sales taxes on certain items. The state also taxes motor vehicles, property, and other items. Federal programs provide about 40 per cent of the state government's income.

Politics. In the early days, the Democratic party dominated Montana politics. Many people voted Democratic because they came to Montana from the traditionally Democratic South. Montanans joked that part of the Confederate army never surrendered, it just retreated to Montana.

Since 1940, Montana voters have paid more attention to individual candidates than to parties. For example, they have repeatedly elected Democrats to the U.S. Senate, but have picked only two Democratic governors since 1940. One Montana Senator, Mike Mansfield, became U.S. Senate majority leader in 1961. Usually, the eastern congressional district elects a Republican to the House of Representatives, and the western district elects a Democrat. Montana has given its electoral votes about equally to Republican and Democratic presidential candidates. For the state's voting record in presidential elections, see ELECTORAL COLLEGE (table).

State Capitol in Helena has a copper-covered dome 165 feet high. Helena has been the state capital since 1875. Earlier capitals were Bannack (1864-1865) and Virginia City (1865-1875).

Montana Highway Commission

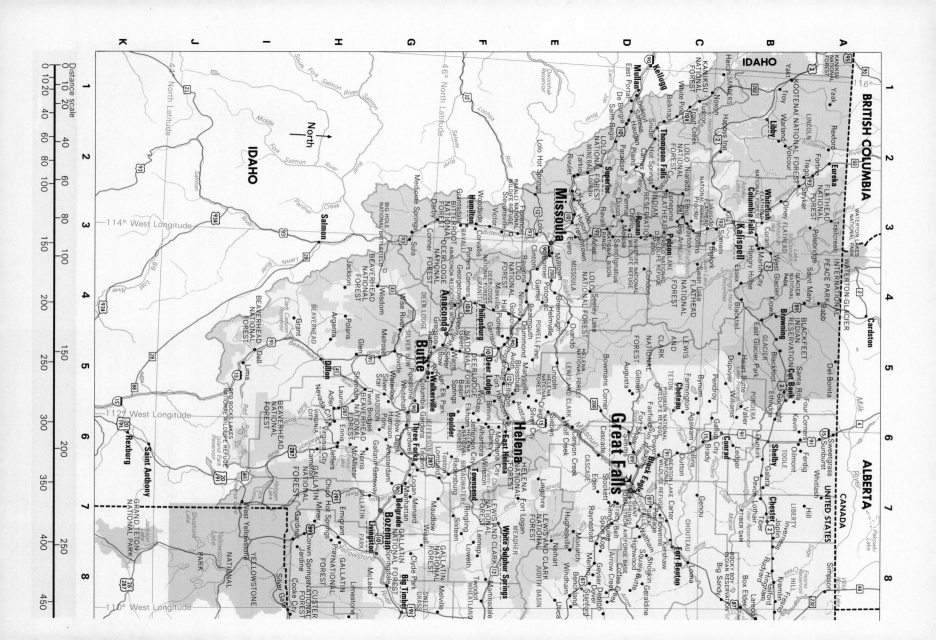

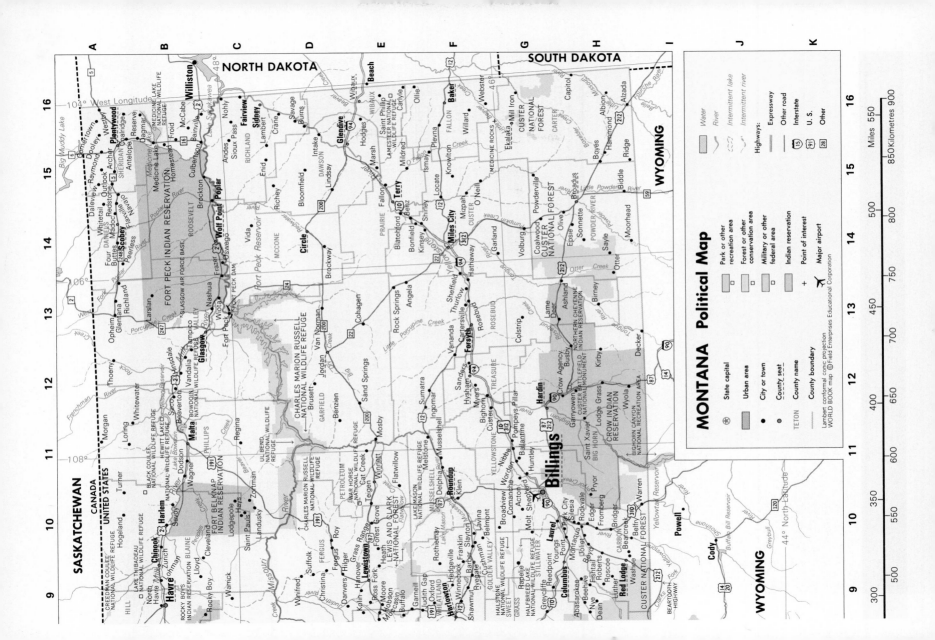

MONTANA MAP INDEX

Population

Great Falls is one of the largest cities in Montana. It lies near the falls of the Missouri River, and was named for them. The city owes its development largely to its use of the falls to furnish power for hydroelectric plants. Great Falls is a banking, industrial, wholesale, and distributing center. Its chief industries include the refining of copper, zinc, and petroleum.

Great Falls Chamber of Commerce

MONTANA — Index to political map

Name	Pop.	Loc.
Hot Springs	585.	D 2
Hughesville		B 8
Hungry Horse		B 3
Huntley		H 5
Huson		D 2
Hysham	494.°	F 12
Ingomar		F 11
Intake		D 16
Inverness		B 8
Isnay	59	H 4
Jackson		G 4
Jardine		H 8
Jeffers		H 6
Jefferson City	452.°	F 6
Joliet	557.°	H 9
Joplin	185.	B 8
Jordan	363.°	D 12
Judith Gap	185.	F 8
Kalispell	10,370.°	C 3
Kershaw		B 3
Kevin	375.	B 6
Kila		C 3
Kinsey		F 14
Kiowa		B 4
Kirby		H 12
Klein		F 10
Knowlton		F 15
Kolin		E 8
Kremlin		B 8
Lakeside		C 3
Lambert		C 15
Lame Deer		G 13
Landusky		C 10
Laredo		B 9
Larslan		B 13
Laurel	4,412.°	G 10
Laurin		H 6
Lavina	212.	F 10
Ledger		C 8
Lennep		F 8
Lewistown	6,183.°	E 9
Libby	3,241.°	B 1
Lima	397.	H 5
Limestone		H 8
Lincoln		E 5
Lindsay		D 15
Lingshire		E 7
Livingston	6,783.°	G 8
Lloyd		B 8
Locate		F 15
Lodge Grass	687.	H 12
Lodgepole		C 10
Logan		G 6
Lohman		B 9
Lolo		E 3
Lolo Hot Springs		E 3
Loma		C 7
Lombard		G 7
Lonepine		C 2
Lookout		A 1
Loring		B 11
Lothair		B 7
Loweth		F 8
Lozeau		D 2
Luther		H 9
Madoc		A 14
Malta	2,145.°	B 11
Manhattan	889.	G 7

Name	Pop.	Loc.
Marsh		E 15
Martin City		B 3
Martinsdale		F 8
Marysville		E 6
Maudlow		G 7
Maxville		F 4
McAllister		G 6
McCabe		B 16
McLeod		G 8
McQueen*	1,345.	G 5
Medicine Lake	452.	B 15
Medicine Springs		B 7
Melrose		G 5
Melstone	266.	F 11
Melville		G 8
Menard		G 7
Merino		D 8
Mildred		F 14
Miles City	8,922.°	F 13
Mill Iron		F 15
Milltown		E 3
Miner		H 8
Missoula	29,232.°	E 3
Mizpah		F 14
Moccasin		E 9
Moiese		D 3
Molt		G 10
Monarch		D 7
Montana City		F 6
Montaqua		B 8
Moore	216.	E 9
Moorhead		H 14
Morgan		A 11
Mosby		E 11
Musselshell		F 11
Myers		G 11
Nashua	796.	C 13
Navajo		F 10
Neihart	150.	D 7
Nevada City		H 6
Niarada		C 3
Nibbe		G 11
Nimrod		E 4
Nohly		C 16
Norris		G 6
North Havre	1,168.	B 9
Noxon		C 1
Nye		H 9
O'Neill		F 15
Oilmont		B 6
Olive		G 14
Ollie		E 16
Olney		B 3
Opheim	457.	A 13
Opportunity		F 5
Oswego		C 12
Otter		H 13
Outlook	226.	A 15
Ovando		E 4
Oxford		C 14
Pablo		C 3
Paradise		D 2
Park City		H 10
Peerless		B 14
Pendroy		C 6
Perma		D 2
Phillipsburg	1,112.°	F 4
Phosphate		F 5

Name	Pop.	Loc.
Pioneer		F 5
Pipestone		G 6
Plains	1,032.	D 2
Plentywood	2,228.°	A 15
Plevna	263.	F 16
Polaris		G 4
Polebridge		A 3
Polson	2,431.°	C 3
Pompeys Pillar		G 11
Pony		G 6
Poplar	1,421.	C 15
Portage		D 7
Porters Corners		E 4
Potomac		D 3
Powderville		F 14
Power		D 6
Pray		H 8
Proctor		C 3
Pryor		H 10
Radersburg		F 6
Ramsay		G 5
Rapelje		G 9
Ravalli		D 3
Ravenna		E 4
Raymond		A 15
Raynesford		D 8
Red Lodge	1,811.°	H 9
Redpoint		G 10
Redstone		B 14
Regina		C 11
Reserve		B 15
Rexford		A 2
Richey	480.	D 14
Richland		A 11
Ridge		H 13
Rimini		F 6
Ringling		F 7
Rivulet		D 3
Roberts		H 9
Rock Springs		F 12
Rockvale		H 10
Rocky Boy		C 9
Rollins		C 3
Ronan	1,367.	C 3
Roscoe		H 9
Rosebud		F 13
Ross Fork		E 8
Rothiemay		F 9
Roundup	2,072.°	F 10
Roy		D 10
Rudyard		B 8
Ryegate	314.°	F 9
Saco	490.	B 11
St. Ignatius	940.	D 3
St. Mary		B 5
St. Phillip		G 12
St. Regis		D 2
St. Xavier		H 11
Saltese		D 1
Sand Springs		E 11
Sandcoulee		D 7
Sanders		F 12
Santa Rita		B 7
Savage		D 16
Sayle		H 14

Name	Pop.	Loc.
Scobey	1,318.°	A 14
Seeley Lake		E 4
Shawmut		F 9
Sheffield		F 14
Shelby	3,106.°	B 6
Shepherd		H 5
Sheridan	539.	F 4
Shirley		D 8
Shonkin		C 7
Sidney	4,453.°	C 16
Sieben		E 10
Silesia		H 10
Silver Bow Park*	4,798.	G 5
Silver City		E 6
Silver Gate		G 5
Silver Star		G 5
Simms		D 6
Simpson		A 8
Sioux Pass		E 15
Sixteen		F 7
Slayton		F 10
Snider		D 2
Somers		C 3
Sonnette		G 14
Spion Kop		E 8
Springdale		G 8
Square Butte		D 8
Stanford	615.°	E 8
Stevensville	784.	F 3
Stockett		D 7
Stryker		B 3
Suffolk		D 9
Sula		G 3
Sumatra		F 10
Sun River		E 6
Sunburst	822.	B 6
Superior	1,242.°	C 2
Swan Lake		C 4
Sweetgrass		A 6
Tampico		B 12
Tarkio		D 2
Teigen		E 10
Terry	1,140.°	E 15
Thoeny		B 12
Thompson Falls	1,350.°	D 2
Three Forks	1,170.	G 6
Thurlow		F 13
Tiber		B 7
Toston		F 7
Townsend	1,382.°	F 7
Tracy		D 6
Trailcreek		F 2
Trego		B 2
Trident		G 6
Troy	1,018.°	B 1
Trout Creek		C 1
Turner		A 10

Name	Pop.	Loc.
Tuscor		C 1
Twin Bridges	509.	H 5
Twodot		F 8
Utica		E 8
Valier	724.	B 6
Van Norman		D 13
Vananda		F 12
Vandalia		D 11
Vaughn		D 6
Victor	539.	F 3
Vida		F 12
Virginia City	194.°	H 6
Volborg		G 14
Volcour		B 11
Wagner		B 11
Walkerville	1,074.	G 5
Waltham		D 7
Warland		B 3
Warm Springs		F 5
Warren		I 10
Warrick		C 9
Washoe		G 5
Waterloo		F 6
Webster		B 7
West Glacier		B 3
West Yellowstone		I 7
Westby	309.	C 16
White Pine		C 2
White Sulphur Springs	1,155.°	F 7
Whitefish	3,360.	B 3
Whitehall	1,031.	G 6
Whitetail		B 11
Whitewater		B 11
Whitlash		A 7
Wibaux	766.°	E 16
Wickes		F 6
Willard		F 16
Williams		B 8
Willow Creek		G 6
Windham		E 8
Winifred	220.	D 9
Winnecook		F 8
Winnett	360.°	E 11
Winston		F 7
Wiota		G 8
Wisall		G 13
Wisdom		G 4
Wise River		G 4
Wolf Creek		E 6
Wolf Point	3,107.°	C 14
Woodside		F 3
Worden		G 11
Wyola		H 12
Yaak		A 1
Yakt		B 1
Youngs Point		H 10
Zortman		C 10
Zurich		B 10

*Does not appear on map; key shows general location.
°County seat.
Sources: Latest census figures (1970 preliminary census, where available, 1960 census, or special census). Cities and towns without population information are unincorporated places under 1,000 in population and are not listed in census reports.

MONTANA/People

The 1970 preliminary United States census reported that 682,133 persons lived in Montana. The population had increased 1 per cent over the 1960 figure of 674,767. Montana's 21,200 Indians, most of whom live on reservations, make up about 3 per cent of the state's population.

About half the people live in cities and towns and about half live in farm areas. Billings is the only city of more than 60,000 population. Billings and Great Falls are the only Standard Metropolitan Statistical Areas (see METROPOLITAN AREA). For their populations, see the Index to the political map of Montana.

Most of Montana's cities began as mining towns, or as centers of trade for farm and ranch areas. For example, Butte grew from a mining camp. So did Helena, the state capital. Missoula developed as an agricultural trade center. See the separate articles on the cities of Montana listed in the Related Articles at the end of this article.

The majority of Montanans are Protestants, but Roman Catholics form the largest single religious group.

POPULATION

This map shows the *population density* of Montana, and how it varies in different parts of the state. Population density means the average number of persons who live on each square mile.

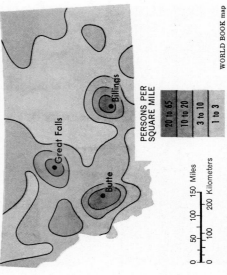

PERSONS PER SQUARE MILE
20 to 65
10 to 20
3 to 10
1 to 3

Great Falls • Butte • Billings

0 50 100 150 Miles
0 100 200 Kilometers

Schools. Montana's first schools were started in mining camps in the early 1860's. They had private teachers who charged tuition. The Roman Catholic Church organized a boarding school for Indians in the Flathead Valley in 1864. The legislature provided for free public schools in 1893, and for county high schools in 1897.

Today, the schools are supervised by an elected superintendent of public instruction and a board of education appointed by the governor. The state superintendent serves a four-year term. Each county and most school districts have a superintendent of schools.

Libraries and Museums. The library at the University of Montana in Missoula owns an outstanding collection relating to the history of the Northwest. The library of the state historical society in Helena has a collection of early Montana newspapers. Montana has more than 70 public libraries throughout the state.

The Montana Historical Society in Helena features exhibits on the development of the state. Many persons visit the museum to see its fine collection of paintings and sculpture by famous cowboy artist Charles M. Russell. Great Falls also has a Russell museum. The Montana College of Mineral Science and Technology at Butte has a museum of minerals. Other museums are at Big Hole National Battlefield, Browning, Custer Battlefield National Monument, Lewistown, and Virginia City.

Custer Hill at Custer Battlefield National Monument

Ernst Peterson, Publix

UNIVERSITIES AND COLLEGES

Montana has nine universities and colleges accredited by the Northwest Association of Secondary and Higher Schools. For enrollments and further information, see UNIVERSITIES AND COLLEGES (table).

Name	Location	Founded
Carroll College	Helena	1909
Eastern Montana College	Billings	1925
Great Falls, College of	Great Falls	1932
Montana, University of	Missoula	1893
Montana College of Mineral Science and Technology	Butte	1893
Montana State University	Bozeman	1893
Northern Montana College	Havre	1929
Rocky Mountain College	Billings	1883
Western Montana College	Dillon	1893

Few states equal Montana in attractions for outdoor recreation. Sportsmen from all over the United States travel to Montana to catch trout and other fish or to hunt deer and other big game. Lovers of the outdoors also enjoy the state's national parks, national forests, dude ranches, ski lodges, summer resorts, and other attractions. Trips to old ghost towns and to the sites of Indian battles interest tourists who like history.

PLACES TO VISIT

Following are brief descriptions of some of Montana's most interesting places to visit.

Anaconda Reduction Works, at Anaconda, is one of the world's largest copper smelters. Its smokestack—585 feet high—is one of the largest in the world. Tours are conducted twice a day during the summer.

Beartooth Highway leads from Red Lodge to the northeast entrance to Yellowstone Park. Motorists driving this scenic route see spectacular mountain views as they wind over the 11,000-foot-high Beartooth Plateau.

Giant Springs, near Great Falls, discharges 270,000 gallons of water a minute. This huge spring was discovered by Lewis and Clark in 1805.

Glacier National Park, in northwestern Montana, includes about a million acres of majestic mountain scenery. It gets its name from 60 glaciers that lie on the mountain slopes. Glacier park has several rugged peaks that have never been climbed. The park has more than 250 lakes. See GLACIER NATIONAL PARK.

Great Falls of the Missouri, near Great Falls, is the highest waterfall on the Missouri River. Its waters drop 400 feet in 8 miles.

Medicine Rocks, near Ekalaka, lie in the badlands of eastern Montana. Wind and water carved these sandstone rocks into unusual shapes.

Virginia City, near Dillon, has been restored to look the way it did in 1865, when it was one of the nation's richest gold camps.

Yellowstone National Park lies mainly in northwestern Wyoming, but three of the five park entrances are in Montana. These are near Cooke City, Gardiner, and West Yellowstone. See YELLOWSTONE NATIONAL PARK.

National Monument and Forests. The sites of two famous Indian battles have been preserved by the federal government. These are Custer Battlefield National Monument, south of Hardin, and Big Hole National Battlefield, near Hamilton.

Eleven national forests cover about 16,669,000 acres in Montana. Four extend into Idaho, South Dakota, or Washington. The largest are Beaverhead, Flathead, Gallatin, Kootenai, Lewis and Clark, and Lolo. The others are Bitterroot, Custer, Deerlodge, Helena, and Kaniksu. For areas and features, see NATIONAL FOREST (table).

In 1964, Congress set aside five national forest areas in Montana as national wildernesses. A National Bison (buffalo) Range covers 19,000 acres near Moiese. About 500 of the shaggy animals roam the area.

State Parks and Forests. Montana has 26 state parks and monuments. For further information, write the Director, State Parks Division, State Highway Commission, Helena, Mont. 59601.

Ray Atkeson
Camping in Glacier National Park

Bill Browning, Montana Chamber of Commerce
North American Indian Days in Browning

Ray Atkeson
Old West Relics in Virginia City

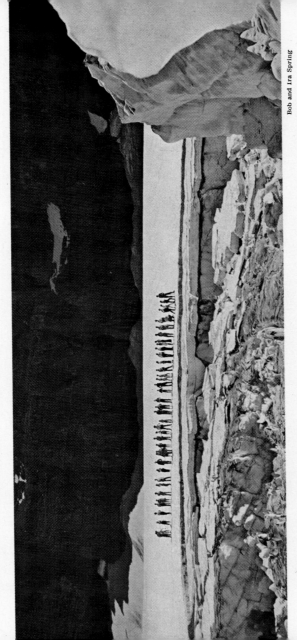
Bob and Ira Spring
Grinnell Glacier Crevasse in Glacier National Park

Montana's "Cowboy and Indian" background is reflected in the rodeos and Indian ceremonies held throughout the state. Almost every Montana town has a rodeo. National riders compete for large prizes in some rodeos. In others, hometown cowboys show their skill. Rodeo owners buy wild horses in a May Bucking Horse Sale in Miles City. Indians on Montana's reservations perform colorful dances and ceremonies.

Winter events in Montana highlight skiing and snowmobile riding. The Western Snowmobile Association Roundup is a popular event held in March. The roundup features statewide races and rallies.

ANNUAL EVENTS

Other outstanding events include the following:

January-March: Blue Jay Dance at Flathead Indian Reservation near Arlee (January); Winter Carnival in Whitefish (January); Billings Market Week in Billings (February); Mesopust Croatian celebrations in Anaconda, Butte, and Great Falls (before Lent).

April-June: Bitterroot Feast of Flathead Indians at Camas Prairie near Arlee (May); Rodeo in Hardin (June); Rocky Boy Indian ceremonial dances at Rocky Boy Indian Reservation near Box Elder (June); Re-enactment of Custer's Last Stand in Crow Agency (June).

July-September: Independence Day celebrations and rodeos in Butte, Kalispell, Lewistown, Red Lodge, and other towns (July 4); Assiniboin and Sioux ceremonial at Fort Peck Indian Reservation near Poplar (July); Rodeos in Livingston and Wolf Point (July); Piegan medicine lodge ceremonial at Blackfoot Indian Reservation near Browning (July); Crow ceremonial in Crow Agency (July); Cherry Regatta in Polson (August); Rodeo in Cooke City (August); Western Montana State Fair in Missoula and North Montana State Fair in Great Falls (August); Midland Empire Fair and Rodeo in Billings (August); Festival of Nations in Red Lodge (August); Harvest Festival in Hamilton (August); Eastern Montana Fair in Miles City (September).

629

MONTANA

ALBERTA

SASKATCHEWAN

B. C.

NORTH DAKOTA

WYO.

BOUNDARY PLATEAU

CANADA
UNITED STATES

Longitude West of Greenwich

116° 115° 114° 113° 112° 111° 110° 109° 108° 107° 106° 105° 104°

St. Mary Res.

Elzikom Coulee

WOOD MTN. 3,350 FT.

Frenchman R.

Big Muddy Cr.

MT. BLACKISTON 9,600 FT.

WATERTON LAKES NAT. PK.

6,983 FT. + WEST BUTTE

EAST BUTTE + 6,960 FT.

Milk River

West Br.

POPLAR R.

GLACIER WATERTON NATIONAL PARK
CLEVELAND 10,438 FT.
LOGAN PASS 6,654 FT.

MT. HENRY 7,235 FT. +

PURCELL MOUNTAINS

GILWRAY RANGE

MT. STIMSON 10,155 FT.

INTERNATIONAL

PEACE PARK

Medicine Lake

SNOWSHOE PK. + 8,712 FT.

Hungry Horse Res.

MARIAS PASS 5,216 FT.

Marias River

Havre

GREAT

Milk River

Glasgow

Missouri River

CABINET

Kalispell

Flathead Lake

ROCKY MTN. + 9,400 FT.

Tiber Res.

BEAR PAW + 6,906 FT.

LITTLE ROCKY MTS.

Fort Peck Res.

ROCKY

SWAN 9,255 FT.

Teton River

MOUNTAIN

Missouri

6,922 FT. BIG HOLE PK.

SILVERTIP MTN. 8,890 FT.

HIGHWOOD

River

PINEY BUTTES

River

LOOKOUT PASS

MC DONALD PK. + 10,300 FT.

SCAPEGOAT MTN. + 9,185 FT.

Great Falls

HIGHWOOD PK. + 7,678 FT.

MTS.

Big Dry Cr.

Redwater

ILLINOIS PK. 7,684 FT.

RED MTN. 9,419 FT.

Sun R.

JUDITH

Glendive

BLUE MTN. 3,076 FT.

ROGERS PASS 5,609 FT.

Smith River

LITTLE

MTS.

Judith River

PLAINS

CLEARWATER

Rhodes PK. 7,940 FT.

Missoula LOLO PASS 5,187 FT.

GARNET RANGE

Clark Fork

MC DONALD PASS 6,325 FT.

HELENA

Canyon Ferry Res.

BELT

BIG SNOW 8,800 FT. +

Musselshell River

Miles City

Powder River

SLIDEROCK MTN. 7,900 FT.

FLINT CREEK RANGE

JACK MTN. 8,789 FT.

Deer Lodge

CASTLE MTS.

MOUNTAIN

NORTHERN PACIFIC RY.

WARD MTN. 9,010 FT.

Anaconda

Butte

CRAZY

Lochsa River

EL CAPITAN 9,936 FT.

MOUNTAINS

CRAZY PK. + 11,214 FT.

Yellowstone River

Billings

NORTH POLE + 8,802 FT.

LOST TRAIL PASS 7,244 FT.

BIG HOLE NAT'L BATTLEFIELD

PIPESTONE PASS

Big Hole R.

Jefferson R.

Livingston

BOZEMAN PASS 6,002 FT.

PRYOR

Rosebud Cr.

CUSTER BATTLEFIELD N.M.

Tongue River

MT. TORREY 11,179 FT.

Madison R.

Bozeman

MT. BLACKMORE + 10,196 FT.

MTS.

Bighorn River

Little Bighorn

R. MT. MC GUIRE + 10,070 FT.

Salmon River

RUBY RANGE

Beaverhead R.

MT. WOOD + 12,661 FT.

Yellowtail Res.

GRANITE PK. 12,799 FT. HIGHEST PT. IN MONTANA

Powder River

Little Powder R.

HOGBACK MTN. 10,605 FT.

KOCH MTN. 11,293 FT.

ELECTRIC PK. 11,155 FT.

Missouri R.

SALMON RIVER

TWIN PKS. 10,328 FT.

7,672 FT. BANNOCK PASS

Red Rock River

CENTENNIAL VALLEY

YELLOWSTONE

MOUNTAINS

WHITECLOUD PKS. 11,470 FT. +

BORAH PK. 12,662 FT. +

GARFIELD MTN. 10,961 FT.

MONIDA PASS 6,823 FT.

CENTENNIAL RANGE

Hebgen Res.

TARGHEE PASS 7,028 FT.

OLD FAITHFUL GEYSER

NATIONAL

Shoshone Lake

Yellowstone Lake

PARK

10,300 FT. + MT. SHERIDAN

CM TERRAIN MONTANA
COPYRIGHT BY
RAND McNALLY & COMPANY
MADE IN U.S.A.

Legend

Barren Areas Above Timber

Deciduous Trees

Evergreen Trees

Grass

⚹ State Capital

Rail Lines

• Cities and Towns

1 inch = 64 Statute Miles

Miles 0 10 20 30 40 50 60

Lambert Conformal Conic Projection

Specially created for **World Book Encyclopedia** by Rand McNally and World Book editors

MONTANA / The Land

Land Regions. Montana has two major land regions. They are (1) the Great Plains and (2) the Rocky Mountains.

The Great Plains of Montana are part of the vast Interior Plain of North America that stretches from Canada to Mexico. In Montana, this high, gently rolling land makes up the eastern three-fifths of the state. The land is broken by hills and wide river valleys. Here and there, groups of mountains rise sharply from the plains. These ranges include the Bear Paw, Big Snowy, Judith, and Little Rocky. In southeastern Montana, wind and water have created a barren badland of gullies and colorful columns of red, yellow, brown, and white stone.

The Rocky Mountains cover the western two-fifths of Montana. This is a region of unusual beauty. The valleys have flat, grassy floors, and the mountains are forested with fir, pine, spruce, and other evergreens. In southwestern Montana, the valleys may stretch 30 to 40 miles from one mountain range to another. In the northwest, most valleys are narrow—from 1 to 5 miles wide. Snow covers the higher mountains four to six months each year. There are many permanent snowfields and a few active glaciers in the higher ranges. The glaciers that once covered this land carved the highest mountains into jagged peaks. They also left thousand of clear, cold lakes.

There are more than 50 mountain ranges or groups in this area. The most important ranges include the Absaroka, Beartooth, Beaverhead, Big Belt, Bitterroot, Bridger, Cabinet, Crazy, Flathead, Gallatin, Little Belt, Madison, Mission, Swan, and Tobacco Root. The highest peaks rise in south-central Montana just north of Yellowstone Park. Granite Peak in Park County is the state's highest mountain. It rises 12,799 feet.

Faults in the earth's crust in this region create the danger of earthquakes. The worst quake period recorded was in 1935, when more than 1,200 shocks were felt in 80 days in the Helena area.

Rivers and Lakes. Montana is the only state drained by river systems which empty into the Gulf of Mexico, Hudson Bay, and the Pacific Ocean. The Missouri River system drains into the Gulf of Mexico by way of the Mississippi River. The Columbia drains into the Pacific Ocean. The Belly, St. Mary's, and Waterton rivers reach Hudson Bay through the Nelson-Saskatchewan river system.

Headwaters of the Missouri River are in southwestern Montana near Three Forks. Three rivers join to form the Missouri: the Gallatin, *left*, the Madison, *center*, and the Jefferson, *right*.

Bill Browning, Montana Chamber of Commerce

Land Regions of Montana

Fort Peck Dam Spillway carries excess water from Fort Peck Reservoir to the Missouri River, background. Water flows down the spillway through these gates, foreground.

Montana Highway Commission

The Yellowstone River curves gently through the lush farmlands of Paradise Valley near the Absaroka Mountains. Flat, fertile valleys stretch as far as 40 miles between mountain ranges in the Rocky Mountain region of southwestern Montana.

Ray Atkeson

Montana's most important rivers are the Missouri and its branch, the Yellowstone. These rivers drain about six-sevenths of the state. The Missouri starts in western Montana, where the Jefferson, Madison, and Gallatin rivers meet near the town of Three Forks. The Missouri flows north past Helena, then through a deep scenic gorge called the Gates of the Mountains. It curves eastward. Fort Peck Dam, on the Missouri in northeastern Montana, is the world's largest earth-fill dam. The Missouri leaves Montana at the North Dakota border. The main tributaries of the Missouri in Montana are the Marias, Milk, Sun, and Teton.

The Yellowstone flows north out of Yellowstone Park and then runs east and somewhat north. It joins the Missouri in North Dakota. The chief branches of the Yellowstone—the Bighorn, Clarks Fork, Powder, and Tongue rivers—flow into it from the south.

The *Continental Divide* winds through Montana. This height of land separates the waters running west into the Pacific from those that run east to the Atlantic.

The major rivers west of the divide are the Kootenai and the Clark Fork of the Columbia. The chief branches of the Clark Fork are the Bitterroot, Blackfoot, Flathead, and Thompson rivers. These western streams drain only about one-seventh of the land, but they carry as much water as the eastern Montana rivers.

Montana has only one large natural lake. This is Flathead Lake, which covers about 189 square miles in the northwest. The rest of the large lakes are man-made. The largest is Fort Peck Reservoir, on the Missouri River, which covers 383 square miles. Other large lakes include Hungry Horse, Canyon Ferry, and Tiber reservoirs. Yellowtail Dam, which was completed in 1966, creates a 71-mile-long lake in Montana and Wyoming.

MONTANA / Climate

Montana's climate varies considerably from one area to the other because the state is so large and has such great differences in elevation. The region west of the Continental Divide has cooler summers and warmer winters than the area east of the divide. In the west, the average January temperature is about 20° F. Eastern Montana's January average is around 14° F. July temperatures average 64° F. in the west, and 71° F. in the east. The state's record high temperature of 117° F. was recorded at Glendive on July 20, 1893, and at Medicine Lake on July 5, 1937. Before Alaska became a state in 1959, Rogers Pass had the lowest temperature recorded in the United States, −70° F. on Jan. 20, 1954.

Most of Montana, except the western edge, has annual *precipitation* (rain, melted snow, and other forms of moisture) of 13 to 14 inches. Generally, about half of this comes as rain between May 1 and July 31. This rain in the growing season is important to the success of Montana's farmers. The western mountain areas receive more moisture than the plains. Heron, in the northwest, gets more than 34 inches a year. Snowfall ranges from 15 inches to as much as 300 inches a year.

One feature of the Montana winter is the occasional *chinook* wind. This warm, dry wind blows down the eastern slopes of the mountains, and melts the snow from the grazing land. Because of this, the grass is exposed temporarily and the ranchers can graze their cattle on the range for part of the winter.

Bill Browning, Montana Chamber of Commerce

Heavy Snowfall in the mountains near Whitefish makes it possible for skiers to enjoy their sport during much of the year.

AVERAGE YEARLY PRECIPITATION
(Rain, Melted Snow, and Other Moisture)

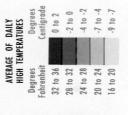

Centimeters	Inches
61 to 122	24 to 48
30 to 61	12 to 24
0 to 30	0 to 12

SEASONAL TEMPERATURES

JANUARY

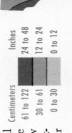

AVERAGE OF DAILY LOW TEMPERATURES

Degrees Centigrade	Degrees Fahrenheit
-9 to -4	16 to 24
-13 to -9	8 to 16
-18 to -13	0 to 8
-22 to -18	-8 to 0

AVERAGE OF DAILY HIGH TEMPERATURES

Degrees Fahrenheit	Degrees Centigrade
32 to 36	0 to 2
28 to 32	-2 to 0
24 to 28	-4 to -2
20 to 24	-7 to -4
16 to 20	-9 to -7

JULY

AVERAGE OF DAILY LOW TEMPERATURES

Degrees Centigrade	Degrees Fahrenheit
13 to 18	56 to 64
9 to 13	48 to 56
4 to 9	40 to 48
0 to 4	32 to 40

AVERAGE OF DAILY HIGH TEMPERATURES

Degrees Fahrenheit	Degrees Centigrade
84 to 92	29 to 33
76 to 84	24 to 29
68 to 76	20 to 24

MONTHLY WEATHER IN BUTTE AND GREAT FALLS

		JAN	FEB	MAR	APR	MAY	JUNE	JULY	AUG	SEPT	OCT	NOV	DEC	Average of:
BUTTE		28	33	40	51	61	69	80	78	66	55	41	31	High Temperatures
		0	5	14	26	33	42	45	42	34	27	16	6	**Low Temperatures**
		9	9	10	9	11	13	10	7	7	7	7	8	Days of Rain or Snow
GREAT FALLS		8	8	9	8	11	13	8	7	7	6	7	6	Days of Rain or Snow
		32	35	43	56	66	73	84	81	69	59	45	35	High Temperatures
		14	15	22	33	42	49	55	53	44	37	26	18	Low Temperatures

Temperatures are given in degrees Fahrenheit.

WORLD BOOK maps

Source: U.S. Weather Bureau

Montana's land features divide it into two main economic regions. On the plains, agriculture and oil production are the most important industries. In the mountains, metal mining and logging are the major activities. Both regions have manufacturing plants.

The U.S. government owns about 30 per cent of the land in Montana. Government agencies control grazing of sheep and cattle, cutting of trees, and mining in those areas. This makes the federal government an important factor in the economy of Montana.

The tourist industry also produces important income for Montana. The national parks alone attract about 4 million visitors a year.

Natural Resources. Montana is rich in natural resources. The state has swift-flowing streams, vast reserves of minerals, and millions of acres of cropland, grassland, and forestland.

Soil. The soils of the northern part of the state are a mixture of clay, sand, and gravel left by melting glaciers. Much of the soil of the southern part was formed from rocks of shallow seas that covered the area millions of years ago. Along the rivers and in the western valleys, silts deposited by water form the soils. In a few areas, fertile wind-blown dust lies in a layer several feet thick. In southwestern Montana, ash from ancient volcanic eruptions has enriched the soil.

Minerals. Montana has huge deposits of three important minerals—coal, copper, and petroleum. Reserves of coal rank among the nation's largest. More than 2 billion tons of *bituminous* (soft) coal lie under Montana. In addition, there is more than 100 times that much coal of lower quality. The reserves of copper around Butte are among the largest in the nation. Petroleum reserves exceed 450 million barrels. Natural gas is found in many oil fields.

Beneath Butte Hill and Summit Valley, in the western mountains, lie huge ore reserves. In addition to copper, this ore contains gold, lead, silver, and zinc. Smaller quantities of metals lie in other western Montana areas. Other mineral reserves include bentonite, chromite, clay, fluorspar, gemstones, gypsum, limestone, manganese, phosphate rock, pumice, sand and gravel, talc, tungsten, uranium, and vermiculite.

Grasslands. About two-thirds of Montana, or 60 million acres, was originally grassland. Of this, about 46 million acres—half the area of the state—are still used for grazing. The most important grasses are buffalo grass, blue grama, and western wheat grass.

Forests cover more than 22 million acres, or about one-fourth of Montana. About 6 million acres are available for logging. Some forests are in national parks and other reserves. Others are too poor in quality or too far from transportation to be useful. Much of the 16 million acres of commercial timber is still virgin forest. Douglas fir is the most important tree for logging. Various kinds of cedar, pine, and spruce also are important.

Wildlife. Montana has large numbers of big game animals. Deer are found both on the plains and in the mountains. Pronghorn antelope thrive on the plains. Bear, moose, mountain goats, mountain sheep, and elk live in the mountains. Small fur-bearing animals such as beaver, mink, and muskrat are also found there. Common game birds include wild ducks and geese, grouse, pheasants, and partridges. Montana's high, cold streams and lakes are famous for trout and grayling.

Agriculture. Farm products account for about $565,-100,000—more than half the value of goods produced in Montana each year. The state has about 27,000 farms. Montana farms average about 2,400 acres. But many ranches cover as much as 7,000 acres, or about 11 square miles.

Most of the farmland is used for grazing. Livestock accounts for about half of Montana's farm income. Montana supports about 3 million cattle and calves—more than four for each person in the state. There are almost twice as many sheep as people. Other leading livestock products include eggs, hogs, milk, and wool.

One-fifth of the farmland is planted in crops. Montana ranks among the leading states in wheat production. Much of Montana's wheat is the valuable durum variety, used in making macaroni and spaghetti. Montana farmers also raise large quantities of barley, hay, sugar beets, and various seeds. About 1,900,000 acres of Montana's farmland are irrigated. Sugar beets and hay are the chief irrigated crops. Farmers in irrigated areas also grow potatoes and other vegetables. The state's biggest fruit crop is sweet black cherries.

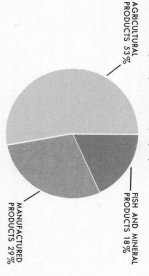

MONTANA'S PRODUCTION IN 1967

Total value of goods produced—$1,063,687,000

AGRICULTURAL PRODUCTS 53%

FISH AND MINERAL PRODUCTS 18%

MANUFACTURED PRODUCTS 29%

Note: Manufacturing percentage based on value added by manufacture. Other percentages based on value of production. Fish Products are less than 1 per cent.

Sources: U.S. Government statistics

MONTANA'S EMPLOYMENT IN 1967

Total number of persons employed—238,700

	Number of Employees
Government	52,000
Wholesale & Retail Trade	47,300
Agriculture	37,300
Services	30,600
Manufacturing	24,500
Transportation & Public Utilities	18,800
Construction	13,800
Finance, Insurance & Real Estate	7,500
Mining	6,900

Source: U.S. Department of Labor

FARM, MINERAL, AND FOREST PRODUCTS

This map shows where the state's leading farm, mineral, and forest products are produced. The major urban areas (shown on the map in red) are the state's important manufacturing centers.

WORLD BOOK map

0   50   100   150   200 Miles

0   50   100   200   300 Kilometers

Manufacturing, including processing, provides more than a quarter of the annual value of Montana's products. Goods manufactured there have a *value added by manufacture* of about $312 million a year. This figure represents the value created in products by Montana's industries, not counting such costs as materials, supplies, and fuel.

The manufacture of lumber and wood products is Montana's most important industry. The state ranks as a leading producer of *softwood* logs. Softwood comes from cone-bearing trees such as pine. Most of the logs are sent to sawmills to be cut into lumber. Montana's 200 sawmills produce more than a billion board feet of lumber a year. A mill at Missoula makes paper. Montana lumber also supplies plywood plants in Columbia Falls, Kalispell, Libby, Missoula, and Polson. Montana produces about 2,200,000 Christmas trees a year. Eureka claims the title *Christmas Tree Capital of the World.*

Much of Montana's other manufacturing consists of the refining and processing of its farm and mineral products. Billings, Hardin, and Sidney have sugar refineries. Flour is milled from Montana wheat in three locations. Meat-packing plants are located in Billings, Butte, Great Falls, and Missoula.

Anaconda, Butte, East Helena, and Great Falls lead in smelting and refining metals. Many factories make metal products. Great Falls plants manufacture copper and aluminum wire and cable, and a factory in Billings produces metal pipe. A large plant in Columbia Falls produces aluminum from imported ore.

Mining is carried on in most Montana counties. It provides nearly one-fifth of the value of all goods produced in Montana, or about $186,524,000.

Petroleum, the leading mineral product in value, is found from the Rocky Mountains east to the North Dakota border. The Williston Basin, in eastern Montana, leads in petroleum production. Other producing areas include Carbon, Musselshell, Powder River, Rose-

bud, and Sheridan counties. Oil fields in the Cut Bank area also yield much natural gas. Montana oil and gas production has a value of about $89 million a year.

Butte Hill has yielded most of the metals produced in Montana. The metals output varies widely from year to year, depending on labor conditions and prices. Copper provides from 60 to 90 per cent of the value of metal produced. The Butte ore that contains copper also contains gold, silver, and zinc. Butte area deposits are so large that Montana stands among the leaders in the production of all four metals. Montana also leads the nation in the production of manganese ore.

Sand and gravel production ranks third in value behind oil and copper. Other construction materials include gypsum, used in wallboard, and limestone for cement. Montana leads the nation in production of vermiculite, an important material for insulation.

Montana ranks high in producing phosphate rock for fertilizer. It also produces coal and talc.

Electric Power. Montana is a leading state in hydroelectric power production. In the late 1960's, two new dams were added to power sources developed in the 1950's and early 1960's. A large plant at Billings generates electricity by burning oils left from petroleum refining, or by using natural gas. Another plant that uses coal has a production capacity of 180,000 kilowatts. A large plant at Sidney burns low-grade coal. For Montana's kilowatt-hour production, see ELECTRIC POWER (table).

Transportation. Montana has about 75,000 miles of roads, with about half of them surfaced. The state has about 190 airports. Billings and Great Falls are the commercial aviation centers. Railroads use about 5,000 miles of track in Montana. The Utah & Northern, the first railroad in Montana, entered the area in 1880.

Communication. Montana has more than 90 newspapers, including 16 dailies. The largest papers are the *Billings Gazette* and the *Great Falls Tribune.* The first important newspaper, the *Montana Post,* appeared at Virginia City in August, 1864. The first radio station, KFBB, began broadcasting at Great Falls in 1922. The first television stations, KXLF-TV and KOPR-TV, began operating in Butte in 1953. Today, Montana has about 45 radio stations and 8 television stations.

Indian Days. Before the white man arrived, two groups of Indian tribes lived in the region that is now Montana. The tribes that lived on the plains were the Arapaho, Assiniboin, Atsina, Blackfoot, Cheyenne, and Crow. The mountains in the west were the home of the Bannock, Kalispel, Kutenai, Salish, and Shoshoni tribes. Other nearby tribes such as the Sioux, Mandan, and Nez Percé hunted in the Montana region.

Exploration. French trappers probably came to the Montana area as early as the 1740's. But the first white men who entered the region to explore it were members of the expedition led by Meriwether Lewis and William Clark. These two Americans led their party to the Pacific Coast in 1805, and returned in 1806. They crossed Montana both going and coming. After 1807, fur traders became active there. In 1847, the American Fur Company built the first permanent settlement in Montana at Fort Benton on the Missouri River.

The United States got most of what is now Montana as part of the Louisiana Purchase (see LOUISIANA PURCHASE). The northwestern part was gained by treaty with England in 1846. At various times, parts of Montana were in the territories of Louisiana, Missouri, Nebraska, Dakota, Oregon, Washington, and Idaho.

The Gold Rush. In 1862, prospectors found gold in Grasshopper Creek in southwestern Montana. Other gold strikes followed and wild mining camps grew around the gold fields. These included Bannack, Diamond City, Virginia City, and others.

The mining camps had almost no effective law enforcement. Finally, the citizens took the law into their own hands. One famous incident involved the two biggest gold camps—Bannack and Virginia City. The settlers learned that their sheriff, Henry Plummer, was actually an outlaw leader. The men of the two towns formed a *vigilance committee* to rid themselves of the outlaws. These vigilantes hanged Plummer in January,

IMPORTANT DATES IN MONTANA

1803 Eastern Montana became U.S. territory through the Louisiana Purchase.

1805-1806 Lewis and Clark explored part of Montana on their journey to and from the Pacific Coast.

1846 The Oregon treaty with England made northwestern Montana part of the United States.

1862 Gold was discovered on Grasshopper Creek.

1864 Congress established the Montana Territory.

1876 The Sioux and Cheyenne Indians wiped out General Custer's troops at the Battle of the Little Bighorn.

1877 Chief Joseph and the Nez Percé Indians surrendered to federal troops after several battles.

1880 The Utah & Northern Railroad entered Montana.

1883 The Northern Pacific Railroad crossed Montana.

1889 Montana became the 41st state in the Union on Nov. 8.

1910 Congress established Glacier National Park.

1940 Fort Peck Dam and Reservoir were completed.

1951 The first oil wells in the Montana section of the Williston Basin started production.

1955 The Anaconda Aluminum Company dedicated a $65 million plant at Columbia Falls.

1966 Construction of Yellowtail Dam was completed.

1967 Construction began on Libby Dam.

1864. They adopted as their symbol the numbers 3-7-77. These numbers represented the dimensions of a grave—3 feet wide, 7 feet long, and 77 inches deep. Many outlaws were hanged or driven from Montana.

Many of the early prospectors came from the South, particularly from Confederate army units that broke up early in the Civil War (1861-1865). One of the major gold fields was called Confederate Gulch, because three Southerners found the first gold there.

During the boom years, gold dust was the principal money. For example, missionaries did not pass collection plates at their services. They passed a tin cup into which the miners put gold dust. Chinese laundrymen even found gold in their wash water after they washed the miners' clothing.

Sidney Edgerton, an Idaho official, saw the need for better government of the wild mining camps. At the time, Montana was part of the Idaho territory. Edgerton wrote Washington urging the creation of a new territory. On Dec. 12, 1864, the Montana territory was created with Edgerton as governor.

Ranching began to develop on a large scale during territorial days. By 1860, cattle raising was established in the mountain valleys. In 1866, a cattleman named Nelson Story drove a herd of a thousand longhorn cattle from Texas to Montana. Story's herd started the Montana cattle industry in earnest. The coming of the

HISTORIC MONTANA

Livestock Industry began in Montana in 1853 when settler John Grant brought a large herd of cattle to the region. He had bought them while he was traveling to Montana on the Oregon Trail. ▶

Chief Joseph and his Nez Percé Indians surrendered to federal troops in 1877, after a 1,000-mile chase. This ended Indian troubles in Montana.

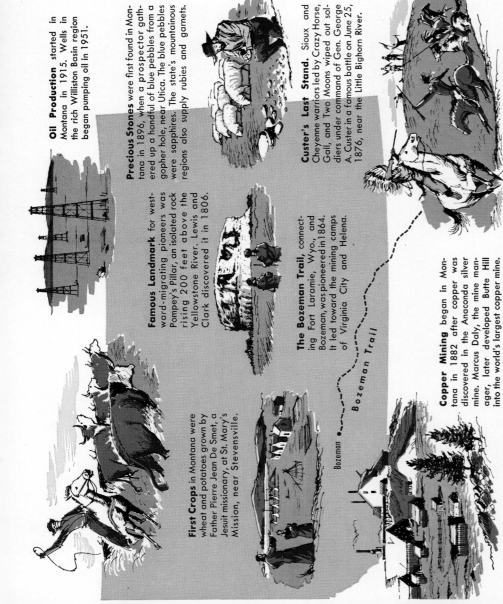

Oil Production started in Montana in 1915. Wells in the rich Williston Basin region began pumping oil in 1951.

Precious Stones were first found in Montana in 1896, when a prospector gathered up a handful of blue pebbles from a gopher hole, near Utica. The blue pebbles were sapphires. The state's mountainous regions also supply rubies and garnets.

Custer's Last Stand. Sioux and Cheyenne warriors led by Crazy Horse, Gall, and Two Moons wiped out soldiers under command of Gen. George A. Custer in a famous battle on June 25, 1876, near the Little Bighorn River.

Famous Landmark for westward-migrating pioneers was Pompey's Pillar, an isolated rock rising 200 feet above the Yellowstone River. Lewis and Clark discovered it in 1806.

The Bozeman Trail, connecting Fort Laramie, Wyo., and Bozeman, was pioneered in 1864. It led toward the mining camps of Virginia City and Helena.

Bozeman Trail

Bozeman

First Crops in Montana were wheat and potatoes grown by Father Pierre Jean De Smet, a Jesuit missionary, at St. Mary's Mission, near Stevensville.

Copper Mining began in Montana in 1882 after copper was discovered in the Anaconda silver mine. Marcus Daly, the mine manager, later developed Butte Hill into the world's largest copper mine.

Northern Pacific Railroad in 1883 opened the way to the eastern markets, and caused even more growth. But disaster struck the cattle industry in the bitterly cold winter of 1886-1887. Cattle died by the thousands in howling blizzards and temperatures far below zero. Ranching continued after this, but on a smaller scale.

Indian Fighting. Two of the most famous Indian campaigns in American history were fought in Montana during the territorial days. On June 25, 1876, Sioux and Cheyenne Indians wiped out a portion of the 7th Cavalry Regiment under General George A. Custer. This famous battle, known as "Custer's Last Stand," was fought near the Little Bighorn River in southern Montana. The last serious Indian fighting in Montana started when the U.S. government tried to move the Nez Percé Indians from their lands in Oregon. Chief Joseph of the Nez Percé decided to lead his tribe to Canada through Montana. The Indians and U.S. troops fought several small battles, and then a two-day battle at Big Hole in southwestern Montana. About 40 miles from the Canadian border, Chief Joseph's Indians were captured by troops under Colonel Nelson A. Miles. See INDIAN WARS (The Sioux Wars; The Nez Percé War).

Statehood. Between 1880 and 1890, the population of Montana grew from about 39,000 to nearly 143,000. The people of Montana first asked for statehood in 1884, but they had to wait five years. Finally, Montana

was admitted as the 41st state on Nov. 8, 1889. Joseph K. Toole of Helena became the first state governor.

Much of Montana's growth during the 1880's and 1890's came because of the mines at Butte. The earliest mines produced gold. Then silver was discovered in the rock ledges of Butte Hill. Later, the miners found rich veins of copper. Miners came to Butte from Ireland, England, and other areas of Europe. Smelters were built, and more men were hired to operate them. Butte Hill became known as the *Richest Hill on Earth.*

Marcus Daly and William A. Clark led the development of Butte copper, and controlled many of the richest mines. The two men became rivals in both business and politics. The great wealth produced by the mines gave both men great power. Daly built the town of Anaconda, and spent large sums of money in a campaign to make it the state capital. Clark opposed Daly's plan, and the voters picked Helena as the capital.

Clark wanted to be a U.S. Senator, but Daly opposed him. In the campaign of 1899, Clark was accused of bribery. He won, but resigned rather than face an investigation by a Senate committee. Two years later, Clark won his Senate seat in a second election. He was helped by F. Augustus Heinze, another mineowner. Heinze had arrived in Butte long after Daly and Clark became millionaires. But Heinze became wealthy through clever use of mining law and court suits.

First Daly, then the others sold their properties to a single corporation, which became the Anaconda Company. The company reached into many areas of Montana life. It organized an electric power company, built a railroad, and constructed dams. It also controlled forests, banks, and newspapers. Anaconda became so important in the life of the state that Montanans referred to it simply as "The Company."

Progress as a State. During the early 1900's, Montana made increasing use of its natural resources. New dams harnessed the state's rivers, providing water for irrigation and electric power for industry. The extension of the railroads assisted the processing industries. New plants refined sugar, milled flour, and processed meat. In 1910, Congress created Glacier National Park, which became an attraction for the tourists.

Jeannette Rankin of Missoula was elected to the U.S. House of Representatives in 1916. She was the first woman to serve in Congress. She won fame in 1941 as the only member of Congress to vote against U.S. entry into World War II. Miss Rankin said she did not believe in war and would not vote for it.

Depression Years. Montana suffered during the Great Depression of the 1930's. Demand for the state's metals dropped because of the nationwide lag in production. Drought contributed to the drop in farm income brought on by the depression.

However, state and federal programs continued to develop Montana's resources during the 1930's. The building of the giant Fort Peck Dam helped provide jobs. Completion of the dam in 1940 provided badly needed water for irrigation. Other projects included insect control, irrigation, rural electrification, and soil conservation. Construction of parks, recreation areas, and roads also continued under government direction. Three governors of Montana during this period also sponsored relief measures that helped the state recover. In 1940, Montana voters elected Republican Sam C. Ford of Helena as governor. He was only the third Republican governor in Montana history.

The Mid-1900's. Montana's economy boomed during World War II (1939-1945). The state's meat and grain were in great demand, and its copper and other metals were used to make war materials. After the war, lower prices for grain reduced agricultural income. Many Montanans moved from farming areas to towns and cities to find jobs. Some small farming towns were abandoned.

Montana's petroleum industry expanded rapidly in the early 1950's, when major oil fields were discovered in the Williston Basin along the Montana-North Dakota border. Wells in the new Montana fields began pumping oil in 1951. In 1955, the Anaconda Aluminum Company opened a $65-million plant in northwestern Montana, and aluminum products became important to the state's economy. During the 1960's, Anaconda spent more than $50 million to improve operations at the Butte mines and to make better use of the remaining ore there.

Tourism grew as an important source of income in Montana during the mid-1900's. The state developed more parks and historic sites, and private developers opened dude ranches, summer resorts, and skiing centers. Such ski areas as Big Mountain, near Whitefish, helped extend Montana's tourist season through the winter.

The state's irrigation and water conservation programs were also expanded. In 1966, Yellowtail Dam on the Bighorn River in southern Montana was completed. This dam provides water for electric power, irrigation, and recreation. Work began in 1967 on the $373-million Libby Dam project on the Kootenai River in northwestern Montana. Completion was scheduled for 1972.

Republicans held the governorship through most of the 1950's and 1960's. But in 1968, Republican Governor Tim M. Babcock was defeated in his bid for reelection by Forrest H. Anderson, a Democrat.

Montana Today is trying to attract new industries and to broaden its economy. Agriculture remains important to Montana's economy. In the 1970's. But the increasing use of machines and improved farming methods has reduced the need for farmworkers. More Montanans are moving to cities than the cities can supply with jobs. Thousands of workers have left the state.

A major challenge facing Montana is to attract industries that would preserve the state's famed scenic beauty and outdoor sports activities. In the late 1960's and early 1970's, citizens formed a number of groups to help prevent pollution of natural resources and recreational areas.

Several other developments offer promise for Montana's future. The Anaconda Company has increased production at its Butte copper mines and other Montana properties. Fuel needs in the United States are expected to create a great demand for Montana's huge coal reserves. To increase tourism, the state is building more roads, boating facilities, and camping sites.

OSCAR CHAFFEE, THOMAS A. CLINCH, AND NICHOLAS HELBURN

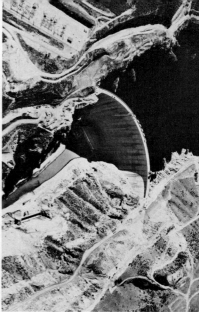

Yellowtail Dam on the Bighorn River near Hardin was completed in 1966. It provides water for irrigation, hydroelectric power, and recreation. Its reservoir is about 71 miles long.

U.S. Bureau of Reclamation, Billings

THE GOVERNORS OF MONTANA

	Party	Term
1. Joseph K. Toole	Democratic	1889-1893
2. John E. Rickards	Republican	1893-1897
3. Robert Burns Smith	Democratic	1897-1901
4. Joseph K. Toole	Democratic	1901-1908
5. Edwin L. Norris	Democratic	1908-1913
6. Sam V. Stewart	Democratic	1913-1921
7. Joseph M. Dixon	Republican	1921-1925
8. John E. Erickson	Democratic	1925-1933
9. Frank H. Cooney	Democratic	1933-1935
10. W. Elmer Holt	Democratic	1935-1937
11. Roy E. Ayers	Democratic	1937-1941
12. Sam C. Ford	Republican	1941-1949
13. John W. Bonner	Democratic	1949-1953
14. J. Hugo Aronson	Republican	1953-1961
15. Donald G. Nutter	Republican	1961-1962
16. Tim M. Babcock	Republican	1962-1969
17. Forrest H. Anderson	Democratic	1969-

MONTANA/Study Aids

Related Articles in WORLD BOOK include:

BIOGRAPHIES

Custer, George A.
Daly, Marcus
Joseph, Chief
Mansfield, Mike

Rankin, Jeannette
Russell, Charles M.
Sitting Bull
Wheeler, Burton K.

CITIES

Anaconda
Billings

Butte
Great Falls

Helena
Missoula

HISTORY

Lewis and Clark
Expedition
Louisiana Purchase

Western Frontier Life
Westward Movement

NATIONAL PARKS AND MONUMENTS

Custer Battlefield National
Monument
Glacier National Park

Yellowstone National
Park

PHYSICAL FEATURES

Bitterroot Range
Kootenay River and
District
Lewis and Clark Cavern

Missouri River
Rocky Mountains
Yellowstone River

PRODUCTS

For Montana's rank among the states in production, see the following articles:

Barley
Copper

Lead
Sheep

Silver
Sugar Beet

Wheat
Wool

OTHER RELATED ARTICLES

Assiniboin Indians
Cheyenne Indians
Crow Indians
Fort Peck Dam

Gros Ventre Indians
Indian, American
Kutenai Indians
Rocky Mountain States

Outline

I. Government
  A. Constitution
  B. Executive
  C. Legislature
  D. Courts
  E. Local Government
  F. Taxation
  G. Politics

II. People

III. Education
  A. Schools
  B. Libraries and Museums

IV. A Visitor's Guide
  A. Places to Visit
  B. Annual Events

V. The Land
  A. Land Regions
  B. Rivers and Lakes

VI. Climate

VII. Economy
  A. Natural Resources
  B. Agriculture
  C. Manufacturing
  D. Mining
  E. Electric Power
  F. Transportation
  G. Communication

VIII. History

Questions

What three great river systems drain Montana?
What minerals are most important to Montana?
What Montana artist won fame for his paintings and sculptures of the West?
What two famous Indian battles were fought in Montana during territorial days?
What two agricultural products are most important to Montana's farmers?
What did the symbol 3-7-77 mean in early Montana?
What expedition explored Montana in 1805-1806?
Why did early Montanans usually vote for Democrats?
Which two famous parks lie at least partly in Montana?
Why does Montana's climate vary so greatly?

Books for Young Readers

CALL, FLORENCE. *Rising Arrow.* Viking, 1955. Two boys spend a year on a Montana sheep ranch.
HENRY, RALPH C. *Our Land Montana.* State Publishing Co., Helena, 1962.

Books for Older Readers

DEVOTO, BERNARD. *Across the Wide Missouri.* Houghton, 1963. Rocky Mountain fur trade of the 1830's.
DIMSDALE, THOMAS J. *Vigilantes of Montana.* Univ. of Oklahoma Press, 1959.
GUTHRIE, ALFRED B., JR. *The Big Sky.* Houghton, 1949. A story of the early trappers in Montana.
HAMILTON, JAMES M. *From Wilderness to Statehood: A History of Montana, 1805-1900.* Binfords, 1957.
HOWARD, JOSEPH K. *Montana: High, Wide and Handsome.* Rev. ed. Yale Univ. Press, 1959.
HUTCHENS, JOHN K. *One Man's Montana: An Informal Portrait of a State.* Lippincott, 1964. Reminiscences of boyhood in Montana.
MCCRACKEN, HAROLD. *Charles M. Russell Book; The Life and Work of the Cowboy Artist.* Doubleday, 1957.
Montana: A State Guide Book. Rev. ed. Hastings, 1955.
RENNE, ROLAND R., and HOFFMAN, J. W. *The Montana Citizen.* State Publishing Co., Helena, Mont., 1960.
SCHULTZ, JAMES W. *My Life as an Indian.* Duell, 1957.
STEWART, EDGAR I. *Custer's Luck.* Univ. of Oklahoma Press, 1955. The story of the Indian Wars that occurred before Custer's Last Stand, and a lengthy account of that battle.
SWEETMAN, LUKE D. *Back Trailing on Open Range.* Caxton, 1951.
WALKER, MILDRED. *Winter Wheat.* Harcourt, 1944. A story about life on a Montana wheat ranch.

MONTANA, UNIVERSITY OF, is a coeducational state-supported school in Missoula, Mont. It includes the college of arts and sciences, and schools of fine arts, forestry, law, business administration, education, journalism, and pharmacy. The university awards bachelor's, master's, doctor of education, and doctor of philosophy degrees. The university also has a biological experiment station, a forest nursery, and a 22,000-acre experimental forest. In addition, it operates a bureau of business and economic research, a wildlife research unit, and a forest and conservation experiment station. The University of Montana was chartered in 1893. For enrollment, see UNIVERSITIES AND COLLEGES (table).

MONTANA COLLEGE OF MINERAL SCIENCE AND TECHNOLOGY. See UNIVERSITIES AND TECHNOLOGY (table).

MONTANA STATE UNIVERSITY is a state-supported coeducational school in Bozeman, Mont. The university offers courses in agriculture, architecture, art, commerce, education, engineering, home economics, liberal arts, and nursing. Courses lead to bachelor's, master's, and doctor's degrees. The Montana Cooperative Extension Service and the Montana Agricultural Experiment Station are connected with the university. Montana State University was founded in 1893. For the enrollment of Montana State University, see UNIVERSITIES AND COLLEGES (table).

LEON H. JOHNSON

H. K. NEWBURN

MONTAUK PENINSULA is a long strip of land at the eastern end of Long Island. Montauk Point, at the tip of the peninsula, forms the extreme eastern point of the state of New York. A United States lighthouse has stood on the point since the 1790's. Fishing is a major industry. See NEW YORK (map).   WILLIAM E. YOUNG

MONTCALM, *mänt KAHM,* or *mawn KAHLM,* **MARQUIS DE** (1712-1759), Louis Joseph de Montcalm-Gozon, a French general, was killed in one of the last great battles between the French and English in America. Montcalm was wounded on the Plains of Abraham in the battle for the city of Quebec. He died in the city a few hours later. The French-Canadians consider him a hero, although his army lost the battle to the English. The English commander, General James Wolfe, was killed in the action.

Montcalm defeated the British in the first part of the French and Indian War. He captured Oswego and Fort William Henry on Lake George.

Detail of a portrait by an unknown artist, Marquis de Montcalm, Paris (Public Archives of Canada).

Marquis de Montcalm

As the war progressed, Montcalm realized that a decisive battle would be fought between the French and English at Quebec. He gathered his main forces to defend the city, and threw back the first English attack. But Wolfe appeared with his whole force on the Plains of Abraham on Sept. 13, 1759. Montcalm led the French attack, but his troops broke under the heavy fire of the English. Montcalm was wounded and died.

Montcalm was born in France, near Nîmes. He joined the French army at the age of 12, and became a captain at 17. He won distinction in the War of the Austrian Succession. By 1756, he had become commander of the French troops in America.

See also FRENCH AND INDIAN WARS (The French and Indian War); QUEBEC, BATTLE OF; WOLFE, JAMES.   RAYMOND O. ROCKWOOD

MONTCLAIR, N.J. (pop. 43,129; alt. 240 ft.), is a residential suburb of New York City. It lies on the eastern slope of the Watchung Mountains, about 6 miles west of Newark (see NEW JERSEY [map]). Residents can commute to New York City daily over two railroads. The Montclair Art Museum was established in 1918. One of the city's most famous artists was George Inness. The city is the home of Montclair State College.

Montclair was incorporated in 1868. It has a commission government.   RICHARD P. McCORMICK

MONTCLAIR STATE COLLEGE. See UNIVERSITIES AND COLLEGES (table).

MONTE CARLO (pop. 9,516; alt. 35 ft.) is part of the principality of Monaco. It lies on the Riviera, 9 miles from Nice, France, and overlooks the Mediterranean Sea. The district near Monte Carlo is a popular resort area. Exports from the Monte Carlo region include olive oil, oranges, and perfumes.

Monte Carlo has been most famous as an international gambling center since the middle of the 1800's. The shipping magnate, Aristotle Socrates Onassis, owns the casino. Citizens of Monaco are forbidden to gamble at this club, but each year thousands of visitors come from all parts of the world to play roulette, baccarat, and other games of chance.

See also MONACO.   GEORGE KISH

MONTE CARLO OF THE FAR EAST. See MACAO.

MONTE CASSINO, *MAHN' tee kuh SEE noh,* is an abbey in Italy, located between Rome and Naples. Here St. Benedict founded the Roman Catholic Benedictine order (see BENEDICTINE). About A.D. 529, St. Benedict sought refuge from persecution inside the ruined city of Cassino. Later, St. Benedict and his followers built the monastery on a height above the town.

The Benedictine order at Monte Cassino reached the height of its influence from 1038 to 1087. Abbot Desiderius, who later became Pope Victor III, ruled it during that time. The monks of Monte Cassino produced manuscripts and paintings which became famous throughout the world. In 1071, a magnificent new abbey church was consecrated. It was named a cathedral in 1321.

In 1866, when Italy dissolved many of its monasteries, Monte Cassino became a national monument. Its buildings held a monastery, a school for laymen, and two seminaries. The abbey's library contained an excellent

Woodward, Black Star

Monte Carlo's famous casino plays host each year to thousands of vacationers. They take part in many gambling activities. Huge fortunes have been won and lost in the casino.

collection of manuscripts. During World War II, the Allied advance was held up at Cassino and the abbey was bombarded. But most of its treasures were saved. By 1952, the Italian government had rebuilt the buildings along their original lines. They put the masterpieces of the monastery on display for the public.   SHEPARD B. CLOUGH

MONTE CRISTO, *MAHN tee KRIHS toh,* or *MOHN tay KREES toh,* is a small, barren island in the Mediterranean. The island covers 4 square miles. In ancient times it was known as *Oglasa.* It became famous through Alexandre Dumas' well-known novel, *The Count of Monte Cristo.* The novel tells how the hero discovered a fabulous treasure there.

Monte Cristo lies 27 miles south of the island of Elba. Most of the island is a mountain of granite, rising 2,000 feet above sea level. Benedictine monks once had a monastery on the island, but they abandoned it after Mediterranean pirates attacked them in 1553. More than 300 years later, the Italian government tried to establish a penal colony on Monte Cristo. It soon gave up the attempt.   BENJAMIN WEBB WHEELER

MONTE ROSA, *MOHN tay ROH zah,* is a mountain with several peaks. One of these, Dufourspitze, 15,200 feet, is the highest in the Pennine Alps. All of Monte Rosa's peaks are more than 10,000 feet above sea level. The mountain stands on the border between Italy and Switzerland. See also ALPS.   FRANKLIN CARL ERICKSON

MONTENEGRO, *mahn tuh NEE groh* (pop. 472,000), is one of the six political divisions of Yugoslavia. Its name means *black mountain.* This probably refers to the appearance of Mount Lovchen in southern Montenegro.

Location and Description. Montenegro's eastern border forms a rough triangle between Serbia and Albania. Its southern coastline extends along the Adriatic Sea (see YUGOSLAVIA [color map]). Grassy mountain slopes cover most of Montenegro's 5,333 square miles. Tiny patches of poor farmland rest in the high valleys. Great cliffs rise behind the Gulf of Kotor in the south. Mount Lovchen towers at the end of the range.

History and Government. The people of Montenegro are a branch of the Serbian Slavs. They moved to the Black Mountain region in the 1300's, and settled in the upland valleys. During the Middle Ages, Montenegro was part of the Serbian kingdom. In 1389, it became an independent principality, after the Turks conquered Serbia. In 1860, Prince Nicholas became ruler of Montenegro. Later he took the title of king. He gave the country a parliament and a new criminal code.

Montenegro fought in three wars in the 1900's. It fought with Bulgaria, Greece, and Serbia against the Ottoman Empire in the First Balkan War in 1912-1913. In 1913, it fought with Greece, Serbia, and Romania against Bulgaria (see BALKANS). In World War I, it fought with the Allies. After Austria-Hungary collapsed in 1918, the National Assembly deposed King Nicholas and voted for union with Serbia. When the new kingdom adopted a constitution in 1921, it became a province (see YUGOSLAVIA [History]).   S. HARRISON THOMSON

MONTEREY, *MAHN tuh RAY,* Calif. (pop. 25,436; alt. 25 ft.), was California's capital under Spanish and Mexican rule, and under the Americans until 1850. The Presidio, founded by the Spanish in 1770, is today the home of the U.S. Army Language School. It was formerly the Capitol, and also marks the spot where Sebastián Vizcaíno, a Spanish explorer, landed in 1602.

Monterey lies on the sloping shores of the southern end of Monterey Bay (see CALIFORNIA [political map]). Tourists, conventions, and military bases provide much of the area's income. A colony of artists and writers is there. Monterey Peninsula College and the Naval Postgraduate School are in Monterey. Fort Ord, an Army training center, is nearby. The Salinas-Monterey metropolitan area has a population of 224,316. Monterey has a council-manager government.   GEORGE SHAFTEL

MONTEREY INSTITUTE OF FOREIGN STUDIES. See UNIVERSITIES AND COLLEGES (table).

MONTERREY, *MAHN teh REH ee,* or *MAHN tuh RAY* (pop. 872,578; alt. 1,624 ft.), Mexico's third largest city, lies in a fertile valley near the Texas border (see MEXICO [political map]). The Pan American Highway links Monterey with Laredo, Tex., 140 miles northeast. Many people from the United States live in Monterey. The city is known for its iron and steel foundries, and for its breweries. More than 500 factories produce textiles, cement, soap, plastics, and other products. A natural-gas pipeline between Texas and Monterrey aided the city's industrial growth. Monterrey has several old Spanish-style buildings and many modern structures. The Technological Institute, just outside the city, attracts many U.S. students in the summer. Spanish settlers founded Monterrey about 1560. It was incorporated as a city in 1596.   JOHN A. CROW

MONTERREY, BATTLE OF. See MEXICAN WAR (Taylor's Campaign).

MONTES, ISMAEL. See BOLIVIA (Wars).

MONTESQUIEU, *mahn tuls KYOO* (1689-1755), was a French philosopher. His major work, *The Spirit of the Laws* (1748), greatly influenced the writing of constitutions throughout the world, including the Constitution of the United States.

Montesquieu believed that laws underlie all things—human, natural, and divine. One of philosophy's major tasks was to discover these laws. Man was difficult to study because the laws governing his nature were highly complex. Yet Montesquieu believed that these laws could be discovered by *empirical* (experimental) methods of investigation (see EMPIRICISM). Knowledge of the laws would ease the ills of society and improve human life.

According to Montesquieu, there were three basic types of government—monarchal, republican, and despotic. A monarchal government had limited power placed in a king or queen. A republican government was either an aristocracy or a democracy. In an aristocracy, only a few people had power. In a democracy, all the people had it. A despotic government was controlled by a tyrant, who had absolute authority. Montesquieu believed that legal systems should vary according to the basic type of government.

Montesquieu supported human freedom and opposed tyranny. He believed that political liberty involved separating the legislative, executive, and judicial powers of government. He also believed that liberty and respect for properly constituted law could exist at the same time.

Montesquieu, whose real name was Charles de Secondat, was born near Bordeaux. He inherited the title Baron de la Brède et de Montesquieu. He gained fame with his *Persian Letters* (1721), which ridiculed Parisian life and many French institutions. He also criticized the church and national governments of France. Montesquieu was admitted to the French Academy in 1727. He lived in England from 1729 to 1731 and came to admire the English political system.   STEPHEN A. ERICKSON

MONTESSORI, *mohn tes SOH ree,* **MARIA** (1870-1952), an Italian educator, developed a special method of teaching young children that became known as the Montessori Method (see MONTESSORI METHOD). She believed that children should be free to find out things for themselves and to develop through individual activity. By her method, pupils were neither punished nor rewarded for things done in school.

Miss Montessori was born in Ancona, Italy, and earned a medical degree from the University of Rome. She first taught mentally defective children, but in 1907 took charge of nursery schools in a Rome slum area. Later she traveled throughout the world, writing and lecturing about her teaching method.   GALEN SAYLOR

MONTESSORI METHOD is an educational system designed to help children learn how to learn by themselves. Montessori programs aim to develop positive learning attitudes and habits in children from about 3 to 6 years of age, an age when they are best able to form them. Many experts in education believe Montessori can help a child become aware of his abilities and gain confidence in himself while making use of his abilities.

Special teaching materials and learning tasks are used for developing awareness and confidence. These materials make use of a child's desire to manipulate and discover insights on his own. They include three-dimensional geometric shapes and letters of the alphabet designed to be examined by a blindfolded child to improve his sense of touch. Devices such as a frame covered with cloth containing snaps, zippers, or buttons aim to teach the child how to perform practical, everyday tasks without the help of adults. Counting devices give the child experience in working with numbers. Other materials are designed to improve a child's language skills and acquaint him with art, music, and science.

Supporters of Montessori programs believe that the materials, used under the guidance of specially trained teachers, help children develop a lasting curiosity and positive attitudes and habits toward learning. Montessori teachers must complete a year of training at a Montessori training center after receiving a bachelor's degree from a university or college.

Maria Montessori of Italy devised the Montessori Method in the early 1900's. Montessori schools were established in many parts of the world, but their number declined in the 1930's, largely because of inadequately prepared teachers.

In the 1950's, Nancy McCormick Rambusch revived the Montessori Method in the United States. She established the American Montessori Society, which sets standards for the more than 600 Montessori schools in the United States. The society's headquarters are at 175 5th Avenue, New York, N.Y. 10010.   URBAN H. FLEEGE

See also MONTESSORI, MARIA.

MONTEUX, *MawN TUH,* **PIERRE** (1875-1964), conducted the San Francisco Symphony Orchestra from 1934 to 1952. He assisted in the premieres of many notable contemporary scores, especially those written for the Diaghilev Ballet, which he conducted.

Monteux was born in Paris. He studied at the Paris Conservatory, where he won first prize for violin playing in 1896. He joined the Paris Colonne Orchestra as a violinist and later became its conductor. In 1911, Serge Diaghilev invited Monteux to conduct his famous Ballet Russe. He conducted French operas at the Metropolitan Opera House in New York City from 1917 to 1919. Later, he conducted the Boston Symphony Orchestra. He served as a guest conductor after retiring from the San Francisco Symphony Orchestra. In 1961, he became principal conductor of the London Symphony Orchestra.   IRVING KOLODIN

MONTEVERDI, *mahn tuh VEHR dee,* **CLAUDIO** (1567-1643), was an Italian composer. His works greatly influenced the change from the strict style of Renaissance music to the emotional style of the baroque movement (see BAROQUE). Monteverdi is often considered the first important composer of opera, and his *Orfeo* (1607) the first modern opera. Only two of his other operas have survived in complete form—*The Return of Ulysses* (1641) and *The Coronation of Poppea* (1642), his masterpiece.

Monteverdi was a master of composing for orchestra. In writing for strings, he pioneered in using an agitated effect called *tremolo* and a plucking technique called *pizzicato*. He was also one of the great composers of religious music and madrigals (see MADRIGAL). Monteverdi's *Vespers* (1610) combined church chants with *secular* (nonreligious) music, using chords. These devices included *arias* (vocal solos) and *recitative* (speech recited to music).

Monteverdi was born in Cremona. From 1590 to 1612, he was employed as a musician and composer by the Duke of Mantua. From 1613 until his death, Monteverdi was choirmaster of the Cathedral of St. Mark in Venice. Beginning in 1637, he also served as composer for the first public opera house in Venice.   JAMES SYKES

MONTEVIDEO, *MAHN tuh vuh DAY oh* (pop. 1,202,-890; alt. 80 ft.), is the capital and largest city of Uruguay. According to an old legend, the city got its name from the cry of a Portuguese sailor when he first spotted the hill on which Montevideo now stands. The sailor shouted "Monte vide eu" (I see a mountain).

Location and Description. Montevideo stands on the eastern bank of the Río de la Plata (Silver River), 135 miles southeast of Buenos Aires, Argentina. It has wide, tree-lined streets, well-planned business and residential sections, and attractive suburbs. For location, see URUGUAY (color map).

The oldest part of Montevideo, called Ciudad Vieja, or *Old City,* is on a small peninsula on the west side of the city. The Plaza Constitución, the original city square, lies in the heart of this section.

The Ciudad Nueva, or *New City,* lies east of the Ciudad Vieja. The University of the Republic and the government buildings stand in this section. Montevideo has many flower-filled squares and beautiful public parks, such as the Prado with its famous rose gardens, and Rodó Park, which completely surrounds a lake. Montevideo is often called the *City of Roses,* because of the rose gardens that bloom throughout the community.

Industry and Trade. Montevideo's chief industry is meat packing. Cattlemen ship sheep and cattle to the

Plaza Independencia, in Montevideo, is often called the *Times Square* of Montevideo. The Palace of the President, *background,* is Uruguay's "White House." The statue of General Artigas, *right,* honors a hero of the fight to gain Uruguay's independence.

city from farms and ranches on the rich Uruguayan plains. Montevideo ships wool, meat, hides, and other agricultural products to all parts of the world. The city handles three-fourths of Uruguay's exports. Companies of many countries, including the United States, have offices, factories, and packing houses in Montevideo.

Transportation in Uruguay centers in the capital. Roads, railroads, and airlines connect Montevideo with other cities in the country. Airliners and ships from many countries stop regularly at Montevideo.

Activities of the People. Montevideo has a number of museums, libraries, and theaters. The government radio station sponsors a symphony orchestra, and private organizations present ballets, concerts, and operas. The city is a center of intellectual life for Uruguay and for much of South America. The University of the Republic is one of South America's best universities.

History. Spanish settlers founded Montevideo in 1726. The city suffered many sieges and invasions during Uruguay's struggle for independence, and in the early years of the republic. Commerce and industry expanded rapidly in Montevideo during the late 1800's. By 1960, the population had grown 10 times as large as it was in 1879.

JOHN TATE LANNING

MONTEZUMA, *MAHN tee ZOO muh,* or MOCTEZUMA, was the name of two Aztec rulers of Mexico (see AZTEC).

Montezuma I (1390?-1464?) became emperor in 1440. He won fame as a military leader who expanded the boundaries of the Aztec Empire to the Gulf of Mexico. He started a vast public works program. He built a huge dike that kept the waters of Lake Texcoco from flooding his capital, Tenochtitlán (now Mexico City), and built an aqueduct to bring fresh water from the springs of Chapultepec to his capital.

Montezuma II (1480?-1520), the great-grandson of Montezuma I, was Emperor of Mexico when the Spaniards came. He ruled from 1502 to 1520. During his reign, he extended the Aztec domain as far south as Honduras. Like Montezuma I, he built many temples, water conduits, and hospitals. But his people disliked him for his appointments of favorites and his heavy taxation. The last New Fire Ceremony occurred in 1507 under his reign. It was a rite designed to insure the continuance of the world for another cycle.

He and his people believed that Hernando Cortes, the leader of the Spaniards, was Quetzalcoatl, the White God of the Aztecs, who had sailed away many years before but promised to return. At first, Montezuma welcomed the Spaniards with gifts of golden ornaments. Later, he tried to keep them from entering Tenochtitlán, but it was too late. Cortes captured the city and the Emperor. The Indian people attacked the palace and Montezuma tried vainly to calm them. But he was stoned to death. Several American writers have used the dramatic meeting between Montezuma and Cortes as the theme of their books.

WILLIAM H. GILBERT

See also CORTES, HERNANDO; DOLL (Famous Collectors); MARINE CORPS, UNITED STATES (History).

MONTEZUMA CASTLE NATIONAL MONUMENT is in central Arizona. It contains a five-story cliff-dwelling ruin in a niche in the face of a cliff. The 842.09-acre monument was established in 1906. It includes Montezuma Well. For location, see ARIZONA (physical map).

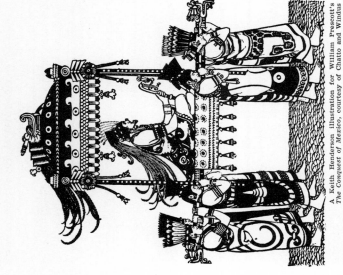

A Keith Henderson illustration for William Prescott's *The Conquest of Mexico,* courtesy of Chatto and Windus

**Montezuma II, Emperor of Mexico, rode a magnificent litter to meet the conqueror of his country, Hernando Cortes.

MONTFORT, SIMON DE

MONTFORT, SIMON DE (1208?–1265), EARL OF LEICESTER, an English statesman and soldier, contributed to the growth of parliamentary government in England. He has been called "the father of the House of Commons." But his work was rather to advance and strengthen a parliamentary system already in existence.

Montfort was a favorite of King Henry III. But he lost favor because of his zeal for political reform. Henry III wanted to rule as he pleased, and Montfort led a rebellion aimed at limiting the king's power by law. King Henry and his son (later Edward I) took up arms, but Montfort captured them both at the battle of Lewes in 1264. Shortly after, Montfort assembled the parliament that won him fame.

Parliament had been only another name for the king's Great Council of barons and prelates, although some commoners had served in the past. Montfort wished to give all the people a voice in affairs. He called to this parliament of January, 1265, two representatives from each shire and two from each town and borough.

Montfort was killed a few months later in the battle of Evesham. His tomb became an English shrine. He was born in France, a son of the Earl of Leicester, and came to England when he was 21.

PAUL M. KENDALL

MONTGOLFIER, *mônt GAHL fih er,* was the family name of two brothers, **Jacques Étienne** (1745–1799), and **Joseph Michel** (1740–1810). They invented the first balloons to carry men into the air. In June, 1783, they filled a balloon made of cloth and paper with hot air. On its first public trial, their balloon rose about 6,000 feet. Five months later, Pilâtre de Rozier became the first man to fly, going up about 80 feet in a Montgolfier balloon.

The Montgolfiers were born at Vidalon-lez-Annonay, France. They were directors of a paper factory in France. But they were poor businessmen, and had to be rescued from failure by pensions.

ROBERT E. SCHOFIELD

See also BALLOON (History of Balloons).

MONTGOMERY, Ala. (pop. 134,393; met. area 199,734; alt. 160 ft.), the capital of Alabama, is a chief agricultural market in the South. The city is often called the *Cradle of the Confederacy.* The Confederate States of America was organized here in 1861, with Montgomery as its capital.

Location, Size, and Description. Montgomery lies on a bluff of the Alabama River, about 100 miles southeast of Birmingham. Rich farm lands surround the city. For location, see ALABAMA (political map).

This attractive city has giant shade trees along its streets, and historic old homes with spacious grounds and gardens. It covers 33 square miles. The Capitol stands on landscaped Goat Hill amid giant trees at the head of Dexter Avenue, the city's main business street.

Places of interest in Montgomery include the White House of the Confederacy, a Museum of Fine Arts, and the State Department of Archives and History. The Air University, at Maxwell Air Force Base, Huntingdon College, and Alabama State College are there.

Industry and Commerce. Montgomery is the center of agricultural trade in the southeast. It serves as an important market for cotton, livestock, yellow pine and hardwood lumber.

The city is the largest dairying center in the southeast. Other chief products include cottonseed oil, sirup, pickles, truck trailers, farm machinery, furniture, and lumber.

History. In 1817, Andrew Dexter of Massachusetts and General John Scott of Georgia laid out towns called New Philadelphia and Alabama Town. These towns, along with a third settlement called East Alabama, consolidated in 1819 as Montgomery. The name honors General Richard Montgomery, a hero of the Revolutionary War.

In 1846, the city became the capital of Alabama. The city adopted the commission form of government in 1910. Montgomery is the county seat of Montgomery County. In 1956, Montgomery became one of the first Southern cities officially to abolish racial segregation on public buses.

CHARLES G. SUMMERSELL

See also ALABAMA (color picture, State Capitol).

MONTGOMERY, BERNARD LAW (1887–   ), VIS-COUNT MONTGOMERY OF ALAMEIN, was a British Army commander in World War II. His victories in North Africa and Europe made him the idol of Great Britain. Montgomery's appearance in his familiar beret in the victory parade in London in June, 1946, aroused a public demonstration greater than that given the king. Montgomery was a hard-driving, self-confident leader.

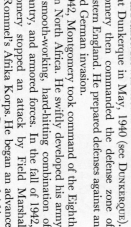

Lord Montgomery

United Press Int.

At the outbreak of World War II, Montgomery was a major general. He took command of the Third Army and led it for nine months in France. He was rescued with his men from the beach at Dunkerque in May, 1940 (see DUNKERQUE). Montgomery then commanded the defense zone of southeastern England. He prepared defenses against an expected German invasion.

In 1942, Montgomery took command of the Eighth Army in North Africa. He swiftly developed his army into a smooth-working, hard-hitting combination of air, infantry, and armored forces. In the fall of 1942, Montgomery stopped an attack by Field Marshal Erwin Rommel's Afrika Korps. He began an advance at El Alamein that drove the Germans out of Africa.

638

After the African campaign, Montgomery helped plan the invasion of France. He was promoted to field marshal. During the final Allied drive against Germany in 1944, he commanded the British forces that landed in France. After the war, he became head of the British zone of occupation in Germany. He served as chief of the British Imperial General Staff from 1946 to 1948, and chairman of the commanders-in-chief of the Western European Union from 1948 to 1951. He served as Deputy Supreme Allied Commander of the North Atlantic Treaty Organization (NATO) from 1951 to 1958.

Montgomery was born in London. His father was a Church of England clergyman who became Bishop of Tasmania. Montgomery attended the Royal Military College at Sandhurst, and became an infantry lieutenant in 1908. C. L. MOWAR

MONTGOMERY, JOHN J. See GLIDER (History).
MONTGOMERY, LUCY MAUD. See CANADIAN LITERATURE (After Confederation).
MONTGOMERY, RICHARD. See REVOLUTIONARY WAR IN AMERICA (Canada Invaded).
MONTGOMERY WARD AND CO. See MAIL-ORDER BUSINESS; WARD, AARON MONTGOMERY.

MONTH. The calendar year is divided into 12 parts, each of which is called a *month*. But the word *month* has other meanings. Several kinds of months are measured by the motion of the moon. At one point in the moon's regular path, it is closest to the earth. This point is called the *perigee*. The time the moon takes to revolve from one perigee to the next is an *anomalistic month*. This period averages 27 days, 13 hours, 18 minutes, and 33.1 seconds.

If the moon were looked at from a distant star it would seem to make a complete revolution around the earth in 27 days, 7 hours, 43 minutes, and 11.5 seconds. This period is a *sidereal month*. The *proper lunar month*, which is called the *synodical month*, is the period between one new moon and the next, an average of 29 days, 12 hours, 44 minutes, and 2.8 seconds.

The synodical month is one of three natural divisions of time. The other two are the rotation of the earth on its axis, or a day, and the revolution of the earth around the sun, or a year. Another astronomical month is the *solar month*, which is one twelfth of a solar year. The solar month is the time taken by the sun to pass through each of the 12 signs of the zodiac (see ZODIAC).

Our calendar months vary in length from 28 days to 31 days. The lengths of calendar months have been made by man, and have no relation to astronomy. At first the 12 months were 29 and 30 days alternately. Later, days were added to the months to make the year come out closer to a solar year, or the time required for the earth to go once around the sun.

In the Gregorian calendar which we use today, each day of the month is called by its number. June 1 is the "first of June," and so on. The ancient Greeks divided the month into 3 periods of 10 days, and the French Revolutionary calendar used months of equal length divided into 3 parts of 10 days each. The fifteenth day of the month was called the fifth day of the second decade.

The Roman system was even more complicated. The Roman calendar had three fixed days in each month, the *calends*, the *nones*, and the *ides*. The Romans counted backward from these fixed days. They would say something would happen, for example, three days before the nones. The calends were the first day of the month. The ides were at the middle, either the 13th or 15th of the month. The nones were the ninth day before the ides, counting both days. When the soothsayer told Julius Caesar to "beware the Ides of March," he meant a very definite day. PAUL SOLLENBERGER

See also the articles in WORLD BOOK on each month of the year. See also CALENDAR; DAY; IDES.

MONTICELLO, *MAHN tuh SELL oh*, is the home that Thomas Jefferson designed and built on a hilltop in Albemarle County, Virginia. The name means *little hill*. Jefferson said of the house, "All my wishes end where I hope my days will end, at Monticello."

Work on Monticello began in 1768. But the house was remodeled several times, and was not completed until 1809. Jefferson borrowed many ideas from classical European buildings. The columned portico idea came from the Temple of Vesta in Rome. The centralized plan came from Andrea Palladio's Villa Rotonda in Vicenza. The dome resembles the dome of the Hotel Salm in Paris. The house contains many things Jefferson invented, including a revolving desk, a dumb-waiter, and a calendar clock. Monticello belongs to the Thomas Jefferson Memorial Foundation. SIBYL MOHOLY-NAGY

See also JEFFERSON, THOMAS (picture).

MONTMORENCY RIVER, *MAHNT moh REN sih*, is a short, swift stream in Quebec. It is named for François de Laval-Montmorency, first bishop of Quebec. The Montmorency rises in Snow Lake and flows southward for about 60 miles. It empties into the Saint Lawrence River about 7 miles northeast of Quebec City. Montmorency Falls, which are about 150 feet wide and 275 feet high, lie at the mouth of the river. The Montmorency Falls furnish water power for nearby industry. M. G. BALLANTYNE

MONTPELIER, Vt. (pop. 8,782; alt. 485 ft.), is the state capital, stands along the Winooski River in the central section of the state (see VERMONT [political map]). The life insurance and granite industries employ many of the city's people. Other industries include printing and the manufacture of plastics, clothespins, machinery, and stone-finishing and sawmill equipment. Montpelier lies on an ancient Indian trade route. Founded in 1786, it became a city in 1894. It has a council-manager type of government. WALTER R. HARD, JR.

See also VERMONT (color picture: State Capitol).

Montpelier, Vt., lies on the Winooski River in the Green Mountains. The state Capitol, built in 1859, has a gold dome.
George Hunter, Shostal

639

Montreal Tourist Bureau

Montreal, Canada's Largest City, is dominated by Mount Royal. From a park on the mountain, visitors can view the city's towering office buildings, church spires, French-type stone houses, tree-lined streets, and the St. Lawrence River.

Montreal
Coat of Arms

CONCORDIA SALUS

MONTREAL, *MAHN tree ALL,* Quebec (pop. 1,293,701; met. area pop. 2,436,817), is the largest city in Canada and the seventh largest in North America. It is Canada's chief manufacturing, financial, and transportation center.

Montreal owes its economic importance to its strategic location. It lies at the entrance to the St. Lawrence Seaway, and ranks as one of the world's largest inland ports. The city's harbor, the chief port of entry to Canada, bustles with passengers and freight. More grain is shipped from the harbor in Montreal than from any other port in the world. The harbor is also the terminal of a crude oil pipeline from Portland, Me. This pipeline serves Montreal's oil refineries and petrochemical plants.

The most striking feature of Montreal is 769-foot-high Mount Royal, which rises in the center of the city. From lookout platforms on the steep slopes of the mountain, visitors can gaze over tree-lined streets, spired churches, modern office buildings, and well-planned parks.

Montreal is the second-largest French-speaking city in the world. Paris is the largest. About 63 of every 100 persons in Montreal speak French. Signs throughout the city appear in both French and English. *Old Montreal,* the waterfront district, reminds visitors of France, because of its architecture and atmosphere. Streets and buildings in this section still have their old French names. The names of most streets and buildings

north of Dorchester Boulevard, in the western part of the city called *Uptown Montreal,* are English.

Location, Size, and Description

Montreal lies on the triangular Island of Montreal, at the junction of the Ottawa and St. Lawrence rivers in southern Quebec. The island is about 32 miles long, and between 7 and 10 miles wide. Montreal covers about 65 of the island's 194 square miles. For the monthly weather in Montreal, see QUEBEC (Climate).

The backbone of the island is a 769-foot-high hill which the people call "the mountain." In 1535, the French explorer Jacques Cartier climbed to the top of it and named it *Mont Réal* (Mount Royal). The city takes its name from the mountain. Montreal surrounds the independent residential cities of Westmount and Outremont on the slopes of Mount Royal. Several nearby cities have been annexed through the years, but these two have chosen to remain independent.

Montreal was built on a series of terraces rising steeply from the banks of the St. Lawrence River to the slopes of Mount Royal. The city has many tree-lined streets and parks. St. Lawrence Boulevard (Boulevard St-Laurent) crosses the island at its widest point, dividing it into east and west sections.

Old Montreal, along the river front and around Notre Dame Church, has many reminders of its past when the city was part of New France. The Maisonneuve Monument in the Place d'Armes honors the founder of the city, Paul de Chomedey, Sieur de Maisonneuve. An obelisk in the Place Royale commemorates the establishment of Montreal. Along narrow streets, old buildings with gabled roofs, and others with Victorian façades, stand side by side with towering modern structures. Many stately buildings and historical houses have been restored, including Bonsecours Church and Bonsecours Market, which is now used as a City Hall annex. Many plaques indicate where other historical landmarks stood.

Montreal's tallest buildings line Dorchester Boulevard. Dominion Square and Place du Canada are the center of the hotel, shopping and entertainment district. From Place Ville Marie to Place Victoria, underground walks, subway stations, and shopping arcades link office buildings, hotels, and restaurants.

Notre Dame Street (Rue Notre-Dame) is the longest on the island. It winds through the west-end industrial district; the administrative center, which includes City Hall and the courthouses; and the east-end manufacturing and oil-refining area.

Nineteen rail and highway bridges and two tunnels under the St. Lawrence River link Montreal with the mainland. The largest bridge, Jacques Cartier Bridge, is 8,670 feet long. Other bridges include the Honoré Mercier, the Victoria Jubilee, and the Champlain.

The People and Their Work

The People. About 12 per cent of Canada's people live in greater Montreal. Of every 100 persons in the city, about 63 have French ancestors; 22 are of English, Scottish, or Irish descent; and the rest are of Italian, Polish, or other origin. Many residents speak both French and English. Roman Catholics make up about three-fourths of the population. Most of the Protestants belong to the Anglican, United Church of Canada, and Presbyterian faiths.

Work of the People. Montreal has developed as a leading commercial and industrial city largely because of its position as a transportation center. The city also has abundant, low-cost hydroelectric power.

More than half the workers make their living from manufacturing. The heaviest industries are located along the waterfront and along the tracks of the city's many railways. Greater Montreal has over 5,000 industrial plants, which employ more than 260,000 workers. The plants produce about $5½ billion worth of goods a year. The city's greatest industry is foods- and beverages-manufacturing. Other leading industries produce iron and steel, and clothing; and refine petroleum. Montreal plants also make aircraft, chemicals, electrical equipment, railroad cars, sheet metal and tobacco products.

The Montreal Stock Exchange, founded in 1874, is the oldest in Canada. The Bank of Montreal was established in 1817, the first of five federally chartered banks with headquarters in Montreal. Many insurance companies also have their main offices here.

Transportation and Communication

Transportation. Montreal is a natural crossroads, with air-, land-, and water-transportation routes extending inland in all directions. The St. Lawrence River links the city with the Atlantic Ocean. The St. Lawrence Seaway makes Montreal a stopover point for Atlantic-Great Lakes trade (see SAINT LAWRENCE SEAWAY). Montreal is the terminal of three canal systems—the St. Lawrence Seaway, the Ottawa River Canal, and the Hudson-Champlain-Richelieu canal system.

Montreal Harbor lies a thousand miles from the Atlantic Ocean. It is one of the largest ports in North America in volume of shipping. It stretches 12 miles along the north bank of the St. Lawrence River, with 10 miles of concrete wharves and docks. Ships dock without the delays of coastal ports, because the harbor is tideless.

A dredged 100-mile channel with a minimum depth of 35 feet provides an entrance to the harbor. Longshoremen load and unload ships at the upper harbor between the Jacques Cartier and Victoria Jubilee bridges. Almost 6,000 vessels with more than 20 million tons of cargo enter the harbor each year.

The lower harbor serves the grain elevators, oil refineries, and other industries of eastern Montreal. Five large elevators can store more than 22½ million bushels of grain. Montreal is the world's greatest grain port, shipping 2½ million tons of grain a year.

The Canada Steamship Lines operates one of the world's largest systems of inland freight, grain, and ore carriers. The line carries about 13½ million tons of cargo a year.

Aviation. About 4½ million passengers a year pass through Montreal International Airport in Dorval, southwest of Montreal. It is the largest and one of the busiest airports in Canada. Two international aviation organizations have headquarters in Montreal—the International Civil Aviation Organization, and the International Air Transport Association.

Railroads. Two great transcontinental railway systems operate from Montreal, Canada's railway center. The Canadian Pacific Railway and the Canadian National Railways travel east to the Atlantic seaboard and west to the Pacific Coast. Central Station, which serves the Canadian National Railways, handles more than 6 million passengers annually. Canadian Pacific trains enter the smaller Windsor station. Several railways have running rights to and from the United States. In 1968, North America's first turbine-powered passenger train went into service between Montreal and Toronto.

Local Transportation. The Metro, a 16-mile subway that runs on rubber tires, was opened in 1966. A bus service is operated by the Montreal Transportation Commission. Over 10 major highways enter Montreal.

Communication. Montreal has three French-language radio stations, five English-language stations, and two French and English stations. There are two French-language television stations and two English-language stations. French-speaking residents read *La Presse, Le Devoir, Montréal-Matin,* and *Le Journal de Montréal.* English-language papers are the *Gazette* and *Montreal Star.*

Education

Schools. Children attend about 400 schools supervised by Roman Catholic school boards, and 100 schools under the Protestant school board. See the Education section in the article on QUEBEC (province).

The University of Montreal, McGill University, and Sir George Williams University are privately owned. The University of Montreal is the largest university outside of France with all courses taught in French. The Provincial Department of Education maintains schools of fine arts, a music conservatory, and institutes of technical, applied, and graphic arts.

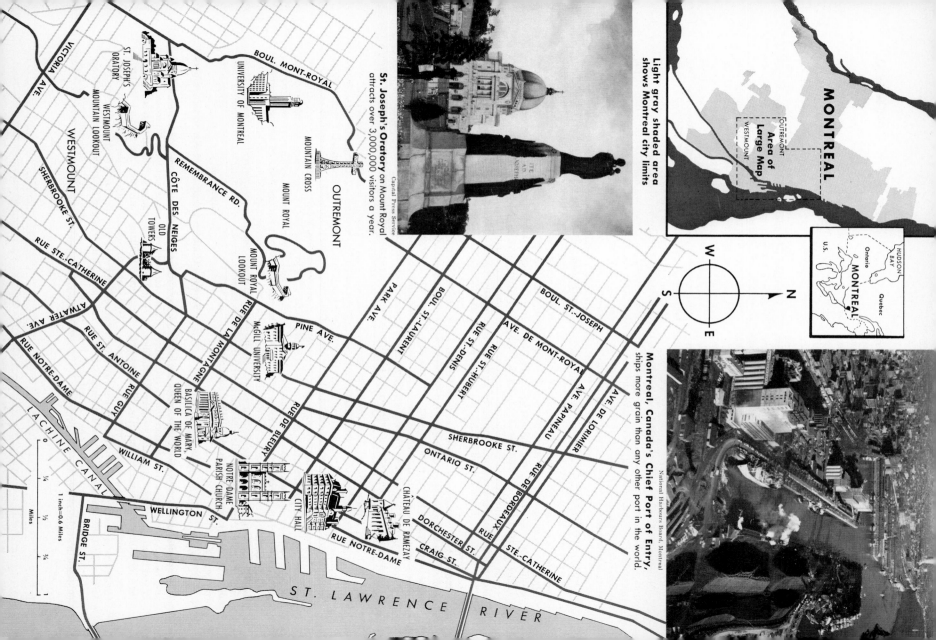

MONTREAL

Area of
Large Map

OUTREMONT
WESTMOUNT

HUDSON
BAY

Ontario

Quebec

MONTREAL

U.S.

W

S

N

E

St. Joseph's Oratory on Mount Royal
attracts over 3,000,000 visitors a year.

Capital Press Service

VICTORIA AVE.

ST. JOSEPH'S
ORATORY

WESTMOUNT
MOUNTAIN LOOKOUT

WESTMOUNT

BOUL. MONT-ROYAL

UNIVERSITY OF MONTREAL

MOUNTAIN CROSS

MOUNT ROYAL

OUTREMONT

SHERBROOKE ST.

REMEMBRANCE RD.

CÔTE DES NEIGES

OLD TOWERS

MOUNT ROYAL LOOKOUT

RUE STE.-CATHERINE

ATWATER AVE.

RUE ST. ANTOINE

RUE DE LA MONTAGNE

McGILL UNIVERSITY

PINE AVE.

PARK AVE.

BOUL. ST.-LAURENT

RUE ST.-DENIS

RUE ST.-HUBERT

AVE. DE MONT-ROYAL

BOUL. ST.-JOSEPH

AVE. PAPINEAU

AVE. DE LORIMIER

RUE NOTRE-DAME

RUE ST. GUY

BASILICA OF MARY,
QUEEN OF THE WORLD

RUE DE BLEURY

SHERBROOKE ST.

RUE DE BORDEAUX

WILLIAM ST.

NOTRE-DAME
PARISH CHURCH

ONTARIO ST.

CITY HALL

CHÂTEAU DE RAMEZAY

DORCHESTER ST.

RUE STE.-CATHERINE

WELLINGTON ST.

RUE NOTRE-DAME

CRAIG ST.

BRIDGE ST.

LACHINE CANAL

1 inch = 0.6 Miles

0   ¼   ½   ¾   1

Miles

ST.   LAWRENCE   RIVER

Montreal, Canada's Chief Port of Entry,
ships more grain than any other port in the world.

National Harbours Board, Montreal

Libraries. The Montreal Civic Library has 13 branches. It is noted for its Gagnon Collection of Canadiana. The Fraser-Hickson Library, the Quebec National (formerly Saint Sulpice) Library, and the Westmount Library are also open to the public. McGill University owns the Osler collection of medical history. The George Baby Collection of Archives and the Pariseau collection on the history of science and medicine may be seen at the University of Montreal.

What to See and Do in Montreal

Montreal has about 300 parks and playgrounds, covering more than 3,000 acres. The largest parks are Angrignon, Jarry, Lafontaine, Maisonneuve, Mount Royal, and Saint Helen's Island. Lafontaine Park has a children's zoo. Jarry Park features football and baseball fields and tennis courts. Visitors in Maisonneuve Park enjoy the Botanical Gardens, golf course, tennis courts, and sports center. Saint Helen's Island has picnic grounds, an open-air restaurant, and a swimming pool. The Metropolitan Zoo will be in Angrignon Park.

Automobiles may not enter Mount Royal Park, except by a scenic route crossing it. Visitors may ride in horse-drawn carriages in summer, or use sleighs in winter. People attend summer plays at the Mountain Playhouse, and open-air concerts elsewhere in the park. At the summit of the mountain, a 100-foot wrought-iron cross, illuminated at night, commemorates the flood that Montreal survived in 1643.

The Place des Arts in downtown Montreal has halls for concerts, opera, and ballet and drama.

Sports. Winter sports on Mount Royal are a major attraction of the city. Montreal is famous for its skiing. As many as 15,000 skiers may throng to Mount Royal after a snowfall. A ski patrol enforces safety regulations. Beaver Lake offers ice skating. There are winter carnivals and sports contests in the park. The Montreal Canadiens of the National Hockey League play at the Forum. The Montreal Alouettes of the Canadian Football League play at the Autostadium. The Montreal Expos of the National Baseball League play at Jarry Park.

Churches. Montreal is famous for its more than 300 beautiful churches. Saint Patrick's Church, of medieval Gothic architecture, is a religious center for English-speaking Roman Catholics. Many French-speaking Roman Catholics use another Gothic structure, the Notre Dame Parish Church. It has two towers called *Temperance* and *Perseverance.* The west tower, *Perseverance,* has a 12-ton bell called "Le Gros Bourdon."

Notre Dame de Bonsecours Church is also called *the Sailors' Church.* It is the oldest church in the city, built in 1771 on the foundations of an earlier building. A statue of the Virgin Mary, on the roof of the church, is said to perform miracles to help sailors.

The Basilica of Mary, Queen of the World, was patterned after Saint Peter's Cathedral in Rome, and is the seat of the Roman Catholic archdiocese of Montreal. It was called St. James Basilica until 1959. Saint Joseph's Oratory stands on the north slope of Mount Royal. Every year more than 3 million persons visit this shrine. The seat of the Anglican diocese, Christ Church Cathedral, is a decorated Gothic building.

Museums. The Château de Ramezay, built in 1705 by the second French governor of Montreal, Claude de Ramezay, is now a history museum. The Montreal Museum of Fine Arts displays excellent paintings. The Museum of Contemporary Art exhibits modern works.

History and Government

French Settlement. In 1535, the explorer Jacques Cartier sailed up the St. Lawrence River to the Lachine Rapids, directly north of Montreal. He found the Huron Indian village of Hochelaga at the base of Mount Royal. Samuel de Champlain visited the site in 1611. Montreal was founded in 1642, when Paul de Chomedey, Sieur de Maisonneuve, brought a small Roman Catholic missionary group to the island to work among the Indians. The settlement was first called Ville-Marie, dedicated to the Virgin Mary. Maisonneuve built Montreal Fort, a stockade about 320 feet long. Iroquois Indians attacked the colony, but it soon prospered as a religious center and a fur-trading post.

English Settlement. Montreal fell to British troops under General Jeffery Amherst in 1760, during the French and Indian War. The battle marked the end of the fighting in this war in North America. Canada became a British colony with the signing of the Treaty of Paris in 1763. New York traders then came to Montreal, and merchants arrived from Great Britain.

In 1775, during the Revolutionary War in America, General Richard Montgomery's forces occupied Montreal in an attempt to gain French-Canadian support against the British. The American troops were forced to withdraw, leaving Montreal a British possession.

The 1800's. Canada's first steamship, the *Accommodation,* sailed on the St. Lawrence River from Montreal to Quebec in 1809. The Lachine Canal opened in 1825, creating a navigable waterway for small vessels between Montreal and the Great Lakes. By 1832, the city had become important enough to receive a charter. From 1844 until 1849, Montreal served as the capital of the United Provinces of Canada. The construction of the transcontinental Canadian Pacific Railway from 1870 to 1885 brought new prosperity to the city.

The 1900's. The city more than tripled its population between 1900 and 1960. Construction of the St. Lawrence Seaway in the late 1950's set off a business boom. A city development program widened Dorchester Boulevard, added new buildings, and enlarged the harbor. Today, Montreal is a summit of the "golden triangle," the rich industrial area between the St. Lawrence River, the Richelieu River, and the United States border. More than 800 industrial projects were begun in the late 1950's. In 1967, over 50 million persons attended Expo 67, an international exhibition held in Montreal. Part of the exhibition reopened after the exhibition closed. In 1970, Montreal was chosen as the site of the 1976 Summer Olympics.

A mayor and a city council govern Montreal. The Metropolitan Corporation serves as an advisory commission to the city's government. Montreal's principal revenue comes from taxes on property, business, water, and sales.

LÉON LORTIE

Related Articles in WORLD BOOK include:

Botanical Garden (picture)
Expo 67
McGill University

Montreal, University of
Sir George Williams
University

The University of Montreal, the largest French-language university outside France, stands on the slopes of Mount Royal.

University of Montreal

MONTREAL, UNIVERSITY OF, is a private, coeducational university in Montreal, Que. All courses are conducted in French. They include architecture, arts and science, dentistry, economics, education, engineering, humanities, hygiene, law, library science, medicine, music, nursing, optometry, pharmacy, philosophy, political science, social work, sociology, theology, town planning, and veterinary medicine. The extension department conducts evening, summer, radio, and television courses. The university has a large computing center and an atom smasher. Research is conducted in all fields of study, especially in the medical, natural, physical, and social sciences. The university's libraries contain over a million volumes.

The University of Montreal was founded in 1876 as the Montreal branch of Laval University. It separated from Laval in 1919, and was chartered as the University of Montreal in 1920. It was controlled by the Roman Catholic Church until a lay board of trustees was appointed in 1967. For enrollment, see CANADA (table: Universities and Colleges).

MONTRÉAL-NORD, Quebec (pop. 67,806; alt. 100 ft.), lies on Montreal Isle, and adjoins the northeast section of the city of Montreal (see QUEBEC [political map]). In English, the city's name is MONTREAL NORTH. It produces transportation equipment, wood products, and electrical appliances. Founded in 1915, Montréal-Nord became a city in 1959. It has a mayor-council form of government.   DEMONTIGNY MARCHAND

MONTRESOR, BEN (1926-   ), is a stage designer and illustrator of children's books. He won the Caldecott Medal for 1965 for his illustrations in *May I Bring a Friend?* (1964). He also wrote and illustrated *House of Flowers* (1962) and *Witches of Venice* (1963). He designed sets for theater, opera, ballet, and motion pictures. Montresor was born in Verona, Italy.

He sailed for America in March, 1604, with Jean de Biencourt de Poutrincourt and Samuel de Champlain. They explored the Bay of Fundy and settled temporarily at the mouth of the Saint Croix River. In the summer of 1605, they founded Port Royal, Nova Scotia. Sieur de Monts then returned to France, leaving Poutrincourt behind as governor.

MONTS, *maun*, SIEUR DE (1560?-1630?), PIERRE DU GUAST, a French explorer and colonizer, settled the region of Acadia in Canada. He was interested in the fur trade, discovery, and navigation. He was an intimate friend of King Henry IV of France, who made him a lieutenant general and governor of Acadia.   HUBERT CHARBONNEAU

Sieur de Monts later won permission to send Champlain to explore Canada. Champlain founded Quebec in 1608, and sailed to Canada again in 1610. Sieur de Monts was born in Saintonge, France.   JEAN BRUCHÉSI

See also ACADIA; ANNAPOLIS ROYAL; CHAMPLAIN, SAMUEL DE; POUTRINCOURT, JEAN DE BIENCOURT DE.

MONTSERRAT, *MÄHNT suh RAT*, is one of the Leeward Islands in the West Indies. It is a British colony. It lies about 250 miles southeast of Puerto Rico (see WEST INDIES [map]). Montserrat has an area of 38 square miles and a population of 15,000. It has three groups of mountains. The highest group is the Soufrière Hills, which rise about 3,000 feet in the southern part of the island. Sea-island cotton and tomatoes are the chief crops. The capital is Plymouth.

Christopher Columbus discovered Montserrat in 1493 during his second voyage to the Western Hemisphere. He named it after a mountain in Spain. Irish settlers came to the island in 1632, and today many of the people speak with a *brogue* (Irish accent). The English and French fought for possession of the island for about 150 years. Britain has controlled Montserrat since 1783.

MONTSERRAT, *MÄHNT sur RAT*, is a mountain and a famous monastery near Barcelona in eastern Spain. The mountain's highest peak is 4,054 feet above sea level. Its name probably means *saw-toothed mountain*, referring to the jagged outline of its many peaks.

The monastery of Montserrat, built in the 700's or 800's, is about 20 miles northwest of Barcelona. Many pilgrims visit the restored church to see the *Black Virgin*, patron saint of Catalonia. Christopher Columbus brought Indians to pay homage there.   GEORGE KISH

MONUMENT is a structure, usually a building or statue, built in memory of a person or an event. *National monuments* are places of historic, scientific, or scenic interest set aside by the U.S. government as public property. They include natural features, such as canyons, and man-made structures, such as historic forts. For a list of national monuments that have separate articles in WORLD BOOK, see NATIONAL PARK SYSTEM (table).

See also MEMORIAL and its Related Articles.

MONUMENT VALLEY. See UTAH (color picture; Places to Visit).

MONUMENT VALLEY NAVAJO TRIBAL PARK. See ARIZONA (Places to Visit).

MOOD is a person's state of mind or outlook on life. Everyone's mood may change from day to day, or, sometimes, from hour to hour. But in certain mental illnesses, usually called *manic-depressive psychoses*, the patient's mood is obviously disturbed (see PSYCHOSIS). He may be sad, or happy and excited, for no visible reason. His mood changes often. Some psychiatrists believe that the basic trouble with such patients is a disturbance of their mood. They have suggested calling such illnesses *primary mood disturbances*. Psychoanalysts have shown that an apparently unexplainable mood can be caused by unconscious thoughts, wishes, or guilt feelings. If this is true, it is more correct to think of mood disturbances as a *secondary* cause of the symptoms of manic-depressive patients.   CHARLES BRENNER

MOOD, or MODE, is a term applied to verb forms that distinguish among certain kinds of meaning. For example, the verb *is* in "He is my brother" is an *indicative*

mood form; that is, it states a fact. But the verb *were* in "if he were my brother" is a *subjunctive* mood form; that is, it expresses a condition contrary to fact.

Some languages have elaborate mood forms, but in English not many contrasts remain between the indicative and the subjunctive mood. For the verb *be*, the indicative forms of the present tense are *I am, you are, he is, we are,* and *they are.* The subjunctive forms are *I be, you be, he be, we be,* and *they be.* In the past tense, the indicative forms are *I was, you were, he was, we were,* and *they were,* and the subjunctive forms are *I were, you were, he were, we were,* and *they were.* Other verbs have a distinction at only one point: the third person singular of the present tense. For instance, *he calls* is indicative, but *he call* is subjunctive.

Subjunctive Uses. A person who speaks English properly will use the past subjunctive of *be* after the word *if* when the clause expresses something that is not true. Examples include "If he *were* my brother, I would leave home," or "If I *were* you, I would do nothing about it."

The present subjunctive occurs most commonly in "that" clauses after verbs such as *ask, insist,* and *urge.* Appropriate examples here would be "He asked that we *be* admitted," "I insisted that he *stay*," and "We urged that he *call* home immediately."

Older English usage employed the present subjunctive frequently in clauses introduced by *if* and *though,* such as "If it *be* he, let him be admitted," and "Though he *call* repeatedly, I shall not answer."

Other examples of old uses of the subjunctive have survived in expressions such as "God bless you" or "suffice it to say." If the indicative were called for, the proper forms would be *blesses* and *suffices,* respectively.

Imperative Mood. The term *imperative mood* is commonly given to verbs that express commands or requests, such as *"Stop the music," "Leave the room,"* and *"Give* this to your mother." In English, the imperative form is the *base* (simple) form of the verb. Imperative sentences usually have no subjects, and the omission of the subject is one of the chief signals that the sentence is a command or a request. But sometimes, imperative sentences do have subjects, as in "You do it, George."

Verb Phrases. The terms *mood* and *mode* are also applied sometimes to verb phrases like *might go, should stay,* and *may try.* These are often called *modal auxiliaries.* In Latin, Greek, and some other languages, their meanings are expressed by mood endings on the verb. But, in English, modern grammar experts usually limit the term *mood* to the indicative, subjunctive, and imperative forms.   PAUL ROBERTS

MOODIE, SUSANNA (1803-1885), was a Canadian novelist and poet. She wrote *Roughing It in the Bush* (1852), a vivid account of pioneer life in Canada. She also wrote *Enthusiasm and Other Poems* (1830), *Life in the Clearings* (1853), *Mark Hurdlestone* (1853), *Flora Lindsay* (1854), *Matrimonial Speculations* (1854), *Geoffrey Moncton* (1856), and *Dorothy Chance* (1867). But these novels and poems were not equal to *Roughing It in the Bush.* She was born in Suffolk, England, and moved to Canada in 1832 with her husband, a British officer. DESMOND PACEY

MOODY, DWIGHT LYMAN (1837-1899), was an American evangelist. He founded the interdenominational Moody Memorial Church, the Moody Bible Institute, and the Moody Press in Chicago (see MOODY BIBLE INSTITUTE). He also established a pri-

vate high school for girls and another for boys near Northfield, Mass.

Moody was born in Northfield. He left a job as a clerk in a Boston shoe store to become a shoe salesman in Chicago in 1856. He devoted all his time to Sunday school and YMCA activities after 1860. He conducted great evangelistic campaigns in the United States and Britain, appearing with Ira D. Sankey, a gospel singer and hymn writer.   EARLE E. CAIRNS

MOODY, HELEN WILLS. See WILLS, HELEN N.

MOODY, PAUL. See LOWELL, FRANCIS CABOT.

MOODY, WILLIAM VAUGHN (1869-1910), was an American dramatist, poet, teacher, and literary historian. Critics hailed his play *The Great Divide* (1906) as a landmark in American drama because of its frank treatment of the collision between eastern puritanism and western frontier individualism. Moody planned a verse *trilogy* (three related plays) on the theme of "the unity of God and man." He completed *The Masque of Judgment* (1900) and *The Fire Bringer* (1904), but died before finishing the third play, *The Death of Eve.* He also wrote *The Faith Healer* (1909).

Moody's *Poems* (1901) contain the well-known lyrics "Gloucester Moors" and "The Quarry." While teaching at the University of Chicago, Moody wrote *History of English Literature* (1902) with Robert Morss Lovett. Moody was born in Spencer, Ind.   RICHARD MOODY

MOODY BIBLE INSTITUTE is a school for training workers in various fields of Christian service. Dwight L. Moody founded it in Chicago in 1886. The institute offers a 3-year program on the college level. It also reaches a wide audience through its radio station, publishing division, monthly magazine, worldwide distribution of free Christian literature, film production, and Bible conferences. Enrollment is 1,000 in day school, 1,200 in evening school, 450 in summer school, and 37,000 in correspondence school.   S. MAXWELL CODER

Moody Bible Institute offers college-level Christian service training. Its headquarters, below, are on LaSalle Street, Chicago.

Moody Bible Institute

MOON

MOON is the earth's nearest neighbor in space. In 1969, this huge ball of gray rock became the first object in space to be visited by man.

The moon is the brightest object in the night sky, but it gives off no light of its own. When the moon "shines," it is *reflecting* (casting back) light from the sun. On some nights, the moon looks like a gleaming silver globe. On other nights, it appears as a thin slice of light. But the moon does not change its size or shape. It seems to change as different parts of it are lighted by the sun.

The moon travels around the earth once about every $29\frac{1}{2}$ days and is the earth's only natural satellite. The average distance between the centers of the earth and the moon is 238,857 miles. This distance equals about 10 trips around the earth at the equator. A rocket journey to the moon and back takes about six days.

Because the moon is so near the earth, it seems much larger than the stars and about the same size as the sun. The moon measures about 2,160 miles across. This distance is about a fourth of the *diameter* (width) of the

Eugene M. Shoemaker, the contributor of this article, is Chairman of the Division of Geological Sciences at the California Institute of Technology and former chief investigator for the Apollo lunar geology experiments.

earth and 400 times smaller than the diameter of the sun. If the moon could be seen next to the earth, it would look like a tennis ball next to a basketball.

The earth is not the only planet with a moon. For example, Jupiter has 12 satellites. The earth's moon is the fifth largest of the 32 natural satellites of the planets. For more information on natural satellites, see the separate planet articles, such as SATURN.

The moon is a silent, lonely place with no life of any kind. Compared with the earth, it has changed little over billions of years. The moon has no air, no wind, and no water. On the moon, the sky is black—even during the day—and the stars are always visible. At night, the rocky surface becomes colder than any place on the earth. In the day, the rocks are too hot to touch.

Through the centuries, man has gazed at the moon, worshiped it, and studied it. Man's long-time dream of traveling to the moon became history on July 20, 1969, when astronaut Neil A. Armstrong of the United States set foot on it.

Space flights and moon landings have provided many facts about the moon. By exploring the moon, man may be able to solve mysteries about the earth, the sun, and the planets. For more information on exploring the moon, see the WORLD BOOK article on SPACE TRAVEL.

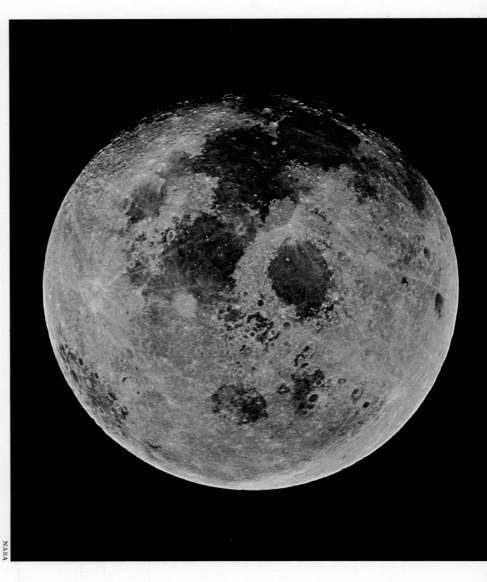

The Moon Was Photographed by the Apollo 11 Astronauts during their return trip to the earth. They had made man's first landing on the moon. The astronauts landed on the Sea of Tranquility, a large, dark-colored lava plain. The highland areas of the moon are lighter in color.

NASA

NASA

The Far Side of the Moon has many craters and a rugged surface. The large crater in the center of the photograph is International Astronomical Union Crater No. 308. It is about 50 miles wide. The lunar footprint shown at the right was made by Edwin E. Aldrin, Jr., an Apollo 11 astronaut.

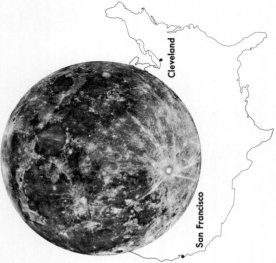

Cleveland

San Francisco

The Diameter of the Moon is 2,160 miles, or about a fourth of the earth's diameter. If the moon were placed on top of the United States, it would extend almost from San Francisco to Cleveland, a distance of 2,166 miles.

THE MOON AT A GLANCE

Age: More than 4,500,000,000 (4½ billion) years.

Distance from the Earth: *Shortest*—221,456 miles; *Greatest*—252,711 miles; *Mean*—238,857 miles.

Diameter: About 2,160 miles, about a fourth that of the earth.

Circumference: About 6,790 miles, about a fourth that of the earth.

Surface Area: About 14,650,000 square miles.

Rotation Period: 27 days, 7 hours, 43 minutes.

Revolution Period Around the Earth: 29 days, 12 hours, 44 minutes.

Average Speed Around the Earth: 2,300 miles per hour.

Length of Day and Night: About 14 earth-days each.

Temperature at Equator: *Sun at zenith over maria,* 260° F. (127° C.); *Lunar night on maria,* −280° F. (−173° C.).

Surface Gravity: About $\frac{1}{6}$ that of the earth.

Escape Velocity: About 1½ miles per second, or $\frac{1}{5}$ that of the earth.

Mass: $\frac{1}{81}$ that of the earth.

Volume: $\frac{1}{50}$ that of the earth.

Atmosphere: Little or none.

The Moon's Surface. When seen with the unaided eye from the earth, the moon looks like a smooth globe with dark and light patches of gray. Field glasses or a small telescope will bring into view the major features first seen by Galileo, the famous Italian scientist of the 1600's.

The dark patches on the moon are broad, flat plains that Galileo may have thought were covered with water. He called them *maria*, a Latin word meaning *seas*. Today, we know the maria are lowlands of rock covered by a thin layer of rocky soil. Most of the light gray parts of the moon's surface are rough and mountainous. These areas are called *highlands*. The maria occur mainly on the near side of the moon, which faces the earth. The far side is nearly all highlands.

Most of the maria were formed from 3½ to 4 billion years ago by great flows of *lava* (molten rock) that poured out and cooled on the moon's surface. The lava that formed the maria has filled in the low places on the moon. Some of the low places are giant craters. The lava filling these craters forms round maria.

Craters are the most numerous features of the moon's surface. The moon has craters within craters, craters on top of craters, and even connected craters. Scientists estimate that the moon has half a million craters that are more than a mile wide. A total of about 30 thousand billion craters are at least a foot wide.

Most of the small craters are simple bowl-shaped pits with low rims. Most craters from 5 to 10 miles wide have high walls and level floors. Many craters wider than 15 miles have hilly floors or central peaks. Large craters are rimmed by mountains and have steep, terraced walls. The largest crater, the Imbrium Basin in the Sea of Rains, is about 700 miles wide. Its floor is covered by dark lava, which forms one eye of the familiar "man in the moon."

Certain craters on the moon are called *ray craters*. These craters are surrounded by light gray streaks known as *rays*. The rays look like splashes of bright material and extend out in many directions. Around Tycho, a 54-mile-wide crater, a few rays are 10 to 15 miles wide and can be traced for nearly a thousand miles. Swarms of small *secondary craters* in the rays probably were formed by the impact of rocks thrown out of the ray craters. The rays probably are mixtures of broken rocks thrown from the ray craters and other rock fragments splashed out of the secondary craters. Scientists know that the ray craters were formed late in the history of the moon because their rays cross over maria, mountains, and other craters.

Billions of small craters on the moon have been formed by the bombardment of *meteoroids*, solid objects that travel through space in orbits around the sun. Large numbers of meteoroids also hit the earth's atmosphere each year. Most of them are melted or broken up high in the air, producing streaks of light called *meteors*. Only the largest meteoroids reach the earth's surface with enough speed to dig a crater. The moon's lack of atmosphere means that even tiny meteoroids strike its surface and form craters. Erosion on the moon takes place so slowly that craters no larger than a foot in diameter will remain there for millions of years.

Schmidt Crater, on the western edge of the Sea of Tranquility, is 7 miles wide. The moon has billions of craters, the largest of which is about 700 miles wide.

NASA

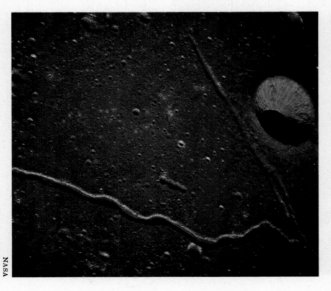

A Winding Rille, *right,* is one of several long, narrow valleys on the moon that probably were caused by flowing lava. Maskelyne G Crater, *top,* is about 4 miles wide.

NASA

Many large craters on the moon probably were formed when *comets* or *asteroids* hit the moon. These bodies also travel around the sun, but they are much larger than meteoroids. The moon's largest and oldest craters may have been created by the impact of *planetesimals*, solid objects that perhaps crashed together and formed the moon itself.

A few craters on the moon look like volcanic craters on the earth. Some of these craters are found on the tops of small mountains or in the centers of low, rounded hills. In other places, craters are lined up in a row just as volcanoes on the earth commonly are lined up. Many of the lunar craters that resemble volcanoes are found on the lava plains.

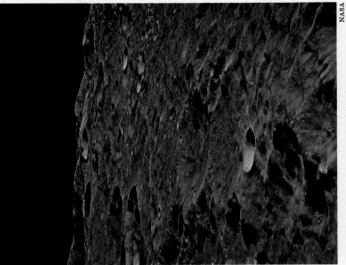

NASA

Rays of Bright Material spread from some craters across the moon's surface. This ray crater on the far side of the moon was photographed by the Apollo 13 astronauts.

NASA

A Basalt Rock returned by the Apollo 11 astronauts resembles lava rock from volcanoes on the earth. The holes were caused by gases escaping from the molten rock.

NASA

The Surface of the Moon's Far Side has more craters and mountains than that of the side that always faces the earth. The far side has fewer "seas," and its craters appear smooth and worn.

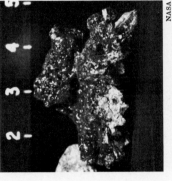

NASA

A Breccia Rock from the Apollo 12 mission consists of soil and rock pieces squeezed together. This sample is about 3½ centimeters, or 1⅜ inches, wide.

NASA

The Most Unusual Moon Rock is this lemon-sized Apollo 12 sample. It has high radioactivity and may be older than the lava flows that form the maria.

The mountainous areas of the moon are scattered with huge craters. All the major mountain ranges of the moon appear to be the broken rims of these huge craters. The rugged Apennine Mountains, near the Sea of Rains, rise about 20,000 feet. The Leibnitz Mountains, near the moon's south pole, are at least 26,000 feet high. They are about as tall as the highest mountains on the earth.

The moon also has long, narrow valleys called *rilles*. Most rilles are straight and probably were formed when the moon's outer crust was cracked, and sections of the surface dropped down. *Sinuous rilles* are winding channels that look much like dry riverbeds. They probably were formed by the flow of lava on the maria.

What the Moon Is Made Of. Scientists have learned much about the composition of the moon by studying rocks and soil brought back by U.S. astronauts. But many questions will remain unanswered until samples can be taken from a number of places on the moon.

Moon soil collected by the first Apollo astronauts was dark gray to brownish gray in color. It consisted of tiny pieces of ground-up rock, bits of glass, and scattered chunks of rock. The soil was formed by repeated grinding and churning of the moon's surface as meteoroids hit it and flying pieces of the moon knocked out craters. Soil on the maria generally is from 5 to 20 feet deep. About half of it consists of bits of glass. A microscope shows that some soil grains are glass balls.

646d

MOON MAP INDEX

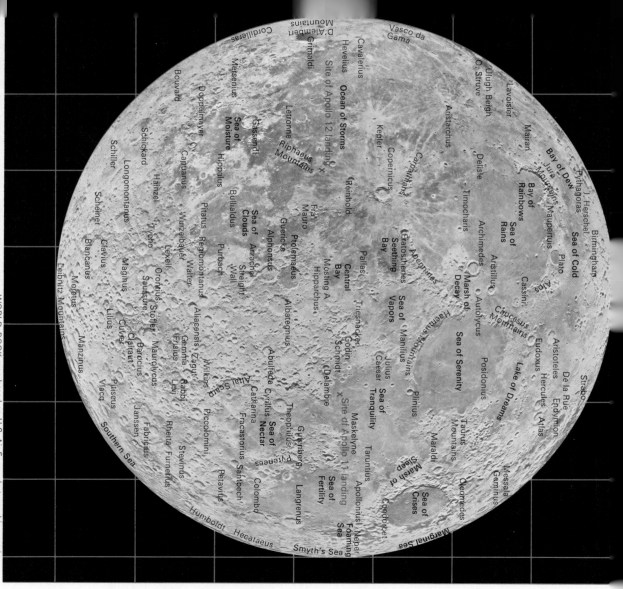

WORLD BOOK map based on U.S. Air Force photographic mosaic.

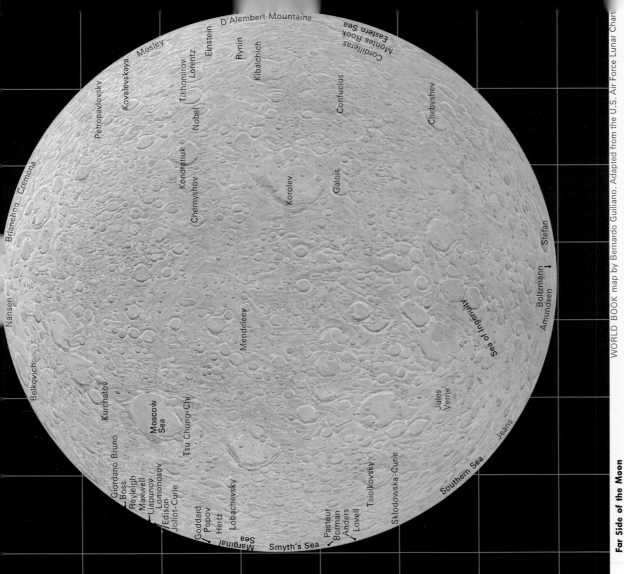

WORLD BOOK map by Bernardo Guiliano. Adapted from the U.S. Air Force Lunar Chart

Far Side of the Moon

*Name not officially recognized by the International Astronomical Union.

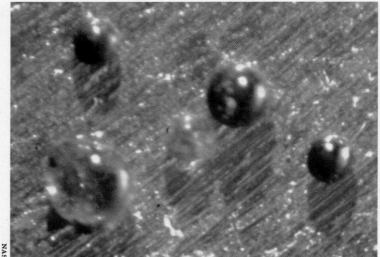

Tiny Colored Glass Balls are found in much lunar soil. The spherules shown above are about the size of a period. These samples were brought back by the Apollo 11 astronauts.

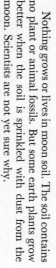

Microcraters on Some Moon Samples can be seen only with a microscope. This crater, magnified 1,700 times, was formed by the high-speed impact of cosmic dust on broken glass particles.

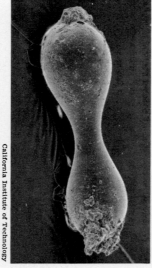

A Dumbbell-Shaped Blob is one of the glassy objects that are found in the moon's soil. Such objects probably were formed when meteorites struck the moon, splattering molten droplets.

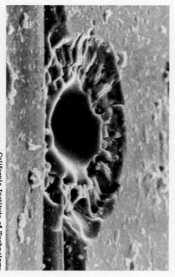

Nothing grows or lives in moon soil. The soil contains no plant or animal fossils. But some earth plants grow better when the soil is sprinkled with dust from the moon. Scientists are not yet sure why.

Moon rocks consist chiefly of minerals containing aluminum, calcium, iron, magnesium, oxygen, silicon, and titanium. Hydrogen, helium, and other gases are trapped in some of the rocks. Scientists believe some of these gases reached the moon as part of the *solar wind*, electrified gas that constantly streams from the sun. No new elements have been discovered in the moon samples. Scientists have found a few minerals not known to occur naturally on the earth, but these belong to well-known mineral families.

Two main types of rock have been collected by the astronauts. One type is *basalt*, a hardened lava and the most common volcanic rock on the earth. The lava rocks are mainly crystals of feldspar, pyroxene, and ilmenite. These minerals were formed at about 2200° F. Their presence on the moon proves that part of it was extremely hot when the maria were formed. The second type of rock, called *breccia*, is made of soil and pieces of rock squeezed together when hit by falling objects.

The moon's outer crust seems stiff and strong, but much remains to be learned about its interior. On the Apollo 13 flight, mission controllers sent part of the giant Saturn rocket crashing into the moon. The resulting *seismic* (earthquakelike) vibrations lasted about four hours. These long-lasting vibrations had not been expected by scientists.

Gravity. Astronauts walk easily on the moon, even though they wear heavy equipment. They feel light because the force of gravity on the moon's surface is six times weaker than that on the surface of the earth. A boy or girl who weighs 60 pounds on the earth would weigh only 10 pounds on the moon. Gravity is weaker on the moon because the moon's *mass* (the amount of matter a body contains) is about 81 times smaller than the earth's mass. In 1968, scientists found that the force of gravity differs slightly from place to place on the moon. They believe the slight difference is caused by large concentrations of mass in many of the round maria. Scientists have used the term *mascons* to describe these areas, but the cause of mascons is not yet known.

Atmosphere and Weather. The moon has little or no atmosphere. If the moon ever did have a surrounding layer of gases, it would have leaked away into space because of the moon's weak gravity. The moon has no weather, no clouds, no rain, and no wind. There is no water on its surface. Astronauts on the moon must carry air with them to breathe. They must talk to each other by radio because there is no air to carry sound.

Temperature. The surface of the moon gets much hotter and colder than any place on the earth. At the moon's equator, noon temperatures on the maria are as high as 260° F. Temperatures drop below −280° F. during the two-week lunar night. In some deep craters near the moon's poles, the sun never shines and the temperature is always near −400° F. Astronauts wear space suits to protect them from the heat and cold.

The Orbit of the Moon. Every 29½ days, the moon makes a trip around the earth. It follows an *elliptical* (oval shaped) path called an *orbit*. One such trip around the earth is called a *revolution*. The moon moves at an average speed of about 2,300 miles per hour along its 1.4-million-mile orbit. The moon also travels with the earth as the earth circles the sun every 365¼ days, an earth year. The moon actually moves from west to east in the sky. But it seems to move from east to west as it rises and sets because the earth spins much faster than the moon revolves around the earth.

Because the moon's orbit is oval, the moon is not always the same distance from the earth. The point where the moon comes closest to the earth is 221,456 miles away. This point is called the moon's *perigee*. The moon's farthest point from the earth is 252,711 miles away. This point is the moon's *apogee*.

Two forces hold the moon in its orbit. One of these forces is *gravity*, which tries to pull the earth and the moon toward each other. The other force is *centrifugal force*, which tries to pull the moon away from the earth and throw it farther into space. The effect of these forces can be seen by swinging a ball in a circle at the end of a string. Centrifugal force makes the ball pull outward on the string. The string keeps the ball from flying away,

much as gravity keeps the moon from escaping from the earth. Gravity and centrifugal force are never completely balanced as the moon travels around the earth. As a result, the moon's distance and speed change constantly.

Scientists measure the moon's revolution around the earth in *synodic months* and *sidereal months*. A synodic month—about 29½ days—is the period from one new moon to the next. It is the time the moon takes to revolve around the earth in relation to the sun. If the moon were to start on its orbit from a spot exactly between the earth and the sun, it would return to almost the same place about 29½ days later. A synodic month equals a full day on the moon. This *lunar day* is divided into about two weeks of light and two weeks of darkness.

A sidereal month—about 27⅓ days—is the time the moon takes to make one trip around the earth in relation to the stars. If the moon's revolution were to begin on a line with a certain star, it would return to the same position about 27⅓ days later.

Rotation. The moon rotates completely on its *axis* (an imaginary line through its north and south poles) only once during each trip around the earth. The moon rotates from west to east, the same direction that it

HOW THE MOON GETS ITS LIGHT

The moon gives off no light of its own. It shines by reflecting sunlight. Like the earth, half of the moon is always lighted by the sun's direct rays, and the other half is always in shadow. At times during the month, only a small slice of the moon's side that faces the earth is in full sunshine. The moon appears as a thin, bright crescent. *Earthshine* (sunlight reflected by the earth), dimly lights the moon's "dark" side when it faces the earth. Because the moon is made up chiefly of dark gray rocks and dust, it reflects only 10 per cent of the light it receives.

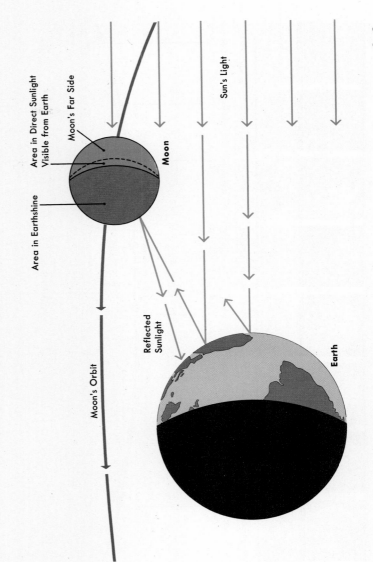

Area in Earthshine

Area in Direct Sunlight
Visible from Earth

Moon's Far Side

Moon

Sun's Light

Moon's Orbit

Reflected
Sunlight

Earth

WORLD BOOK diagram

MOON

travels around the earth. At its equator, the moon rotates at a speed of about 10 miles per hour. When you look up at the moon, you always see the same side. The moon is held in this position by gravitational forces. We know that the moon is rotating because we can see only one side of it. If the moon did not rotate, we would be able to see its entire surface.

Sometimes we can see a short distance around the *limb* (edge) of the moon. The moon seems to swing from side to side and nod up and down during each revolution. These apparent motions are called *librations*. They are caused by slight changes in the moon's speed of revolution and by a five-degree tilt of the moon's orbit to the orbit of the earth. At different times, the librations enable us to see a total of 59 per cent of the moon's surface from the earth. The other 41 per cent can never be seen from the earth. The moon's far side was a complete mystery until Oct. 7, 1959, when a Russian rocket orbited the moon and sent back a few pictures of one far side area to the earth. On Dec. 24, 1968, the Apollo 8 astronauts became the first men to see the far side.

WHY THE MOON HAS PHASES

The Phases of the Moon. During a synodic month, we can see the moon "change" from a slim crescent to a full circle and back again. These apparent changes in the moon's shape and size are actually different con-

ditions of lighting called *phases*. They are caused by changes in the amount of sunlight reflected by the moon toward the earth. The moon seems to change shape because we see different parts of its sunlit surface as it orbits the earth. Like the earth, half the moon is always lighted by the sun's rays except during eclipses. Sometimes the far side of the moon is in full sunlight even though it is out of view.

When the moon is between the sun and the earth, its sunlit side—the far side—is turned away from the earth. Astronomers call this darkened phase of the moon a *new moon*. In this phase, the side of the moon facing the earth is dimly lighted by *earthshine*, which is sunlight reflected from the earth to the moon.

A day after a new moon, a thin slice of light appears along the moon's eastern edge. The line between the sunlit part of the moon's face and its dark part is called the *terminator*. Each day, more and more of the moon's sunlit side is seen as the terminator moves from east to west. After about seven days, we can see half of a full moon. This half-circle shape is half of the moon's side that is exposed to sunlight and is the part that can be seen from the earth. This phase is called the *first quarter*. About seven days later, the moon has moved to a point where the earth is between the moon and the sun. We

The moon seems to change shape from day to day as it goes through *phases*. The moon changes from *new moon* to *full moon* and back again every 29½ days. The phases are caused by the moon's orbit around the earth as the earth and moon travel around the sun. Half of the moon is always in sunlight, but varying amounts of the lighted side are visible from the earth. As the moon and earth move along their orbits, more of the sunlit part is seen until a full moon. Then less and less of the sunlit part is seen until the dark new moon returns.

WORLD BOOK diagram

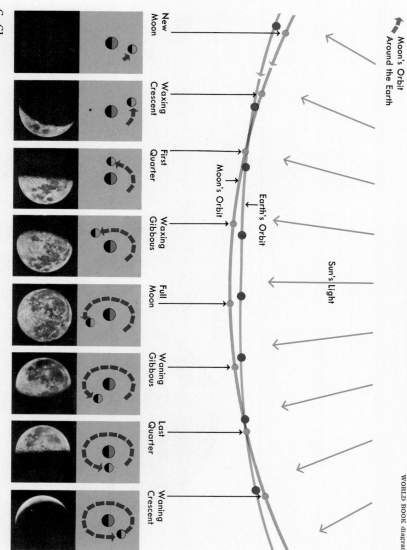

New Moon

Waxing Crescent

First Quarter

Waxing Gibbous

Full Moon

Waning Gibbous

Last Quarter

Waning Crescent

- ● Earth
- ● Moon
- ⇢ Moon's Orbit Around the Earth

Moon's Orbit

Earth's Orbit

Sun's Light

can now see the entire sunlit side. This phase is called *full moon*. A full moon seems bright on a clear night. But a whole sky of full moons would be only about a fifth as bright as the sun.

About seven days after full moon, we again see half of a full moon. This phase is called the *last quarter*, or the third quarter. After another week, the moon returns to a point between the earth and the sun for the new moon phase. As the moon changes from new moon to full moon, it is said to be *waxing*. During the period from full moon back to new moon, the moon is *waning*. When the moon appears smaller than half of a full moon, it is called *crescent*. When the moon looks larger than half of a full moon, yet is not a full moon, it is called *gibbous*.

The moon rises and sets at different times. In the new moon phase, it rises above the horizon with the sun in the east and travels close to the sun across the sky. With each passing day, the moon rises an average of about 50 minutes later and drops about 12 degrees farther behind in relation to the sun. By the end of a week—at the first quarter phase—the moon rises at about noon and sets at about midnight. In another week—at full moon—it rises as the sun sets and sets as the sun rises. At last quarter, it rises at about midnight

and sets at about noon. A week later—back at new moon—the moon and the sun rise together in the east.

Eclipses. The earth and the moon both throw shadows into space. When a full moon passes through the earth's shadow, we see an *eclipse* of the moon. During a lunar eclipse, the moon is a dark reddish color. It is faintly lighted by red rays from the sun that have been *refracted* (bent) by the earth's atmosphere. During another kind of eclipse, the new moon passes directly between the earth and the sun. When part or all of the sun is hidden by the moon, we see a *solar eclipse* (an eclipse of the sun). Solar eclipses occur where the shadow of the moon passes across the earth. See ECLIPSE.

The Moon and Tides. Since ancient times, man has watched the rising and falling of the water level along the seashore. Just as the earth's gravity pulls on the moon, the moon's gravity pulls on the earth and its large bodies of water. The moon's gravity pulls up the water directly below the moon. On the other side of the earth, the moon pulls the solid body of the earth away from the water. As a result, two bulges called *high tides* are formed on the oceans and seas. As the earth turns, these tidal bulges travel from east to west. Every place along the seashore has two high tides and two low tides daily. See TIDE.

WHY WE SEE ONLY ONE SIDE OF THE MOON

When we look at the moon, we always see the same side. This is because the moon turns once on its axis in the same time that it circles the earth. Astronomers call the moon's motion synchronous rotation. The force of gravity always keeps the same side of the moon toward the earth. This diagram shows why one side of the moon can never be seen from the earth. As the moon turns, a moon landmark such as a crater, shown as a red dot, stays in about the same position during the month. Sometimes the landmark is hidden in the dark part of the moon facing the earth. But because it does not move to the side of the moon opposite the earth, we know that we are seeing only one side of the moon. If the moon did not turn in its journey around the earth, the landmark would gradually seem to move across the visible surface of the moon. It would disappear around the moon's western edge and return to view on the moon's eastern edge about 14 days later.

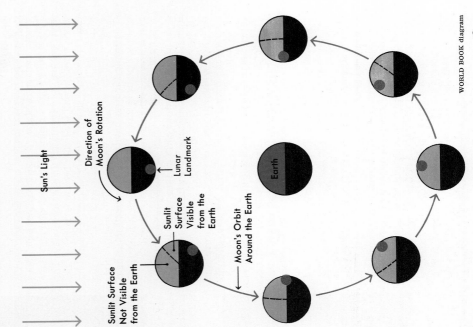

Sun's Light

Direction of Moon's Rotation

Lunar Landmark

Sunlit Surface Visible from the Earth

Sunlit Surface Not Visible from the Earth

Moon's Orbit Around the Earth

Earth

Age and History. Scientists have learned that the moon is about 4.6 billion years old by studying lunar samples brought back by the Apollo astronauts. The moon's age is determined by measuring the amounts of radioactive atoms of certain elements in the lunar soil. Each of the radioactive atoms *decays* (changes into another element) at a known rate. How long this decay has been occurring can be figured by comparing the amount of radioactive atoms of an element with the amount of the atoms of the elements into which it has decayed. The earth and meteorites that have fallen on the earth are also about 4.6 billion years old. On the basis of this evidence, scientists believe that the solar system was formed at about that same time.

The early history of the moon's surface suggests that the moon was formed partly by the falling together of large solid bodies. Chunks of hardened lava brought back by the Apollo 11 astronauts show that lava flows on the Sea of Tranquility are about 4 billion years old. These lava plains are many hundreds of millions of years younger than the moon. Most of the large craters had already been formed before the lava poured across the moon's surface. These large craters may have been formed by the impact of solid bodies from which the moon was made. But scientists do not know where this happened.

Scientific Theories have been developed to explain how the moon was formed. But more scientific exploration is needed before the mystery can be solved.

In 1879, George H. Darwin, an English mathematician, suggested that the earth and the moon were once a single body. Shortly after the earth was formed, according to his theory, a huge bulge was produced on the earth by the attraction of the sun. The earth was spinning much more rapidly than it is today, and the bulge pulled away from the earth by centrifugal force. Other scientists have pointed out that the material of the bulge probably would have become extremely hot and may have broken up into many pieces. Later, the pieces may have fallen together again to form the moon.

A second theory states that the moon was formed as a separate planet that followed its own orbit around the sun. Every few years, the moon came close to the earth because their orbits were similar. During one of these close passes, the moon was captured in the earth's gravitational field.

A third theory is that the earth and moon were formed close to each other from a disk of gas and dust around the sun. They were formed as a double-planet system, much like the systems of double stars that are common in our galaxy. The large craters created early in the moon's history may have been formed by the impact of smaller moons that were circling the earth, or by planetesimals that were orbiting the sun.

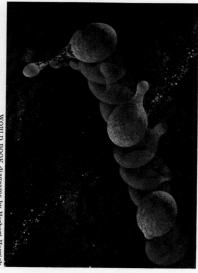

WORLD BOOK diagrams by Herbert Herrick

The "Escape" Theory of the moon's origin says that the earth and the moon were once a single body. The sun's gravity caused a bulge on one side of the fast-spinning earth. A lopsided dumbbell formed, and the small end broke away and became the moon.

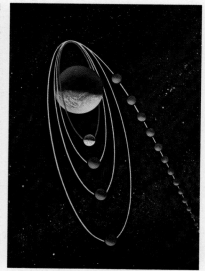

The "Capture" Theory of the moon's formation says that the moon was once a planet that traveled around the sun. At some point along its orbit, the moon was captured by the earth's gravity and became a satellite of the earth.

A Third Moon Formation Theory says that the moon was formed at about the same time as the earth and in the same region of space. The two bodies were made from huge whirlpools of gas and dust that were left over when the sun was formed.

Measuring Time. Since ancient times, man has measured time by the phases of the moon. The American Indians recorded that a harvest or a hunt took place a certain number of "moons" ago. People in Moslem countries still use a calendar with 354 days, or 12 synodic lunar months. Jews use the lunar calendar to establish the dates of religious holidays. Christians observe Easter on a date that varies each year because it is related to the full moon. The words *month* and *Monday* come from old English words related to *moon.*

Mythology. Early peoples thought the moon was a powerful god or goddess. The ancient Romans called their moon goddess Diana. She was the goddess of the hunt and the guardian of wild beasts and fertile fields. She used a moon crescent for a bow and moonbeams for arrows. The moon goddess of the ancient Greeks was Selene, and the early Egyptians honored the moon god Khonsu. The Babylonians knew the moon as Sin, sometimes called Nannar, the most powerful of the sky gods. Some American Indian tribes believed that the moon and the sun were brother and sister gods, with the moon being much more important than the sun. Today, some primitive peoples still worship the moon.

Legend and Folklore. Many peoples who did not think of the moon as sacred believed that it influenced all life on the earth. Early wise men and priests taught that the moon was related to birth, growth, and death because it waxed and waned. Some people feared eclipses as signs of famine, war, or other disasters. According to one superstition, sleeping in moonlight could make a person insane. The word *lunatic,* which means *moonstruck,* comes from *luna,* a Latin word meaning *moon.* Even today, many people believe that the moon is related to changes in the weather. Others think that seeds grow especially well when planted during a waxing moon. The moon has an important place in *astrology,* a popular *pseudo* (false) science.

Legends of various lands told how the "man in the moon" had been imprisoned there for stealing or for breaking the Sabbath. Some people saw other figures in the moon's markings—Jack and Jill, a beautiful lady, or a cat, donkey, frog, or rabbit.

Many people once believed that some form of life existed on the moon. The ancient Greek writer Plutarch told of moon demons that lived in caves. Johannes Kepler, a German astronomer of the 1600's,

An Early Moon Map was drawn in 1645 by Johann Hevelius, a city official of Danzig, Poland. Hevelius, an amateur astronomer, charted about 250 lunar formations with a telescope.

Illustration by Johann Hevelius from Selenographia, Danzig, 1647. Courtesy the John Crerar Library, Chicago

---

MILESTONES IN MOON STUDY

c. 2200 B.C. The Mesopotamians recorded lunar eclipses.

500's B.C. The Chaldeans predicted the dates of eclipses.

c. 459 B.C. Anaxagoras, a Greek philosopher, noted that the moon's light came from the sun and explained eclipses.

c. 335 B.C. Aristotle, a Greek philosopher, used lunar eclipses to prove that the earth was ball-shaped.

c. 280 B.C. Aristarchus, a Greek astronomer, found a way to measure the moon's distance from the earth.

c. 150 B.C. Hipparchus, a Greek astronomer, measured the period of the moon's revolution around the earth.

c. 74 B.C. Posidonius, a philosopher born in Syria, explained the effect of the moon and the sun on the earth's tides.

A.D. c. 150 Ptolemy, an astronomer in Egypt, discovered the irregularity of the moon's motion in its orbit. His largely incorrect writings became the chief astronomical authority for 14 centuries.

1543 Nicolaus Copernicus, a Polish astronomer, published a book reviving the idea that the earth was a moving planet. Present-day astronomy is based on his work.

c. 1588-1598 Tycho Brahe, a Danish astronomer, made observations leading to theories about the moon's motion.

c. 1600-1609 Johannes Kepler, a German astronomer, discovered the oval shaped orbits of the planets.

1609-1610 Galileo, an Italian scientist, made the first practical use of the telescope to study the moon.

c. 1645 Johann Hevelius, a Polish pioneer of moon mapping, charted more than 250 moon formations.

1687 Sir Isaac Newton explained the basis for the moon's motion and its tidal effect on the earth.

c. 1828 F. P. Gruithuisen, a German astronomer, suggested meteoroids as a cause of some lunar craters.

1850's William C. Bond and J. A. Whipple, of Harvard Observatory, took photographs of lunar features.

1920's Bernard Lyot, a French astronomer, concluded that a layer of dust covered the moon's surface.

1930 The American astronomers Edison Pettit and G. B. Nicholson obtained the first reliable lunar temperatures.

1946 The U.S. Army Signal Corps bounced radio waves from the moon's surface.

1959 Russia launched *Luna 2,* the first spaceship to hit the moon. Russia's *Luna 3* sent the first pictures of the moon's far side back to the earth.

1964-1965 U.S. spacecraft *Rangers VII, VIII,* and *IX* took the first close-up television pictures of the moon.

1966 Russia's *Luna 9* became the first spacecraft to make a soft landing on the moon.

1968 The Apollo 8 astronauts flew 10 orbits around the moon.

1969 The Apollo 11 and Apollo 12 astronauts landed on the moon. They collected samples, took photographs, set up scientific experiments, and explored the nearby area.

1970 Russia's *Luna 16* became the first unmanned spacecraft to return soil samples from the moon.

wrote that lunar craters were built by moon creatures. In 1822, F. P. Gruithuisen, another German astronomer, told of discovering a "lunar city." In the 1920's, the American astronomer W. H. Pickering declared that swarms of insects might live on the moon. Many scientists hoped that certain chemicals might be found on the moon to give clues as to how life began on the earth.

Literature and Music. Many authors and poets have written about the moon and have described its beauty. In *A Midsummer Night's Dream*, the famous English playwright William Shakespeare compared the moon to "a silver bow new-bent in heaven." In "The Cloud," the English poet Percy Bysshe Shelley described the moon as "that orbèd maiden, with white fire laden, whom mortals call the moon . . . ."

Other writers have told of imaginary space flights to the moon. During the A.D. 100's, the Greek writer Lucian described a hero who was lifted to the moon after his ship got caught in a waterspout. In 1638, Francis Godwin, an English bishop, wrote a story about a man who flew to the moon in a raft pulled by trained swans. Later in the 1600's, the French author Cyrano de Bergerac wrote of a moon ship that used a form of rocket propulsion. The French novelist Jules Verne blasted his characters to the moon from a 900-foot-long cannon in *From the Earth to the Moon*, published in 1865. In *The First Men in the Moon* (1901), the English writer H. G. Wells described an antigravity substance that sent travelers on a journey to the moon.

The moon has also been a favorite topic of musicians. One of the 14 piano sonatas written by Ludwig van Beethoven, the famous German composer, came to be

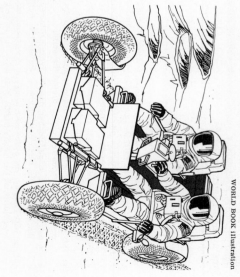

known as the *Moonlight Sonata. Clair de lune*, meaning *moonlight*, is the title of musical works by at least three French composers, including Claude Debussy. Popular songs have included "Moonlight Bay," "Moonlight and Roses," "By the Light of the Silvery Moon," and "Moon River."

Moon Study. Some ancient peoples believed that the moon was a rotating bowl of fire. Others thought it was a mirror that reflected the earth's land and seas. In spite of such beliefs, early astronomers worked out many correct ideas about the moon's size, shape,

An Apollo 12 Astronaut Explores the Moon's Surface near the lunar module, *Intrepid*. Astronauts Charles Conrad, Jr., and Alan L. Bean left the module twice to collect samples, set up scientific experiments, and take walks totaling about 1½ miles on the Ocean of Storms.

NASA

A Lunar Rover may someday carry two astronauts and their equipment. This battery-powered vehicle weighs about 400 pounds, travels 10 miles per hour, and has a range of 75 miles.

WORLD BOOK illustration

motion, and distance from the earth. An important advance came in 1609, when Galileo used a crude telescope for the first scientific study of the moon's surface.

Man's knowledge about the moon increased as *selenographers* (scientists who study moon geography) drew improved maps of the lunar surface. With the development of cameras and photography in the mid-1800's, the moon could be photographed in detail.

The space age, which began in 1957, opened a new chapter in man's study of the moon. On Sept. 12, 1959, Russia launched *Luna 2*, the first man-made object to reach the moon. Since that time, Russia and the United States have launched about 30 unmanned spacecraft that either landed on the moon or passed close enough to send back useful information. From 1966 to 1968, the United States landed five Surveyor spacecraft on the moon. These lunar probes took almost 90,000 detailed photographs and also sent back information on the moon's composition. During the same period, the United States launched five Lunar Orbiters that photographed 98 per cent of the moon's surface. These spacecraft paved the way to a manned landing by showing that the moon's surface would hold the weight of a spacecraft and by locating suitable landing sites. On July 20, 1969, Apollo 11 landed on the moon. Man's firsthand exploration and study of the moon had begun.

Man's Future on the Moon. For years to come, scientific exploration will be man's main reason for traveling to the moon. Before the mid-1970's, Apollo astronauts are expected to explore the lunar highlands, major craters, rilles, and other features. On some of these missions, men may travel across the moon's surface on small powered vehicles called *lunar rovers*.

The astronauts will gather moon rocks and soil from different sites and will take many photographs. The men also will conduct various scientific experiments. For example, they will drill holes in the moon's surface and lower instruments into them. These instruments will show how much heat is being lost from the moon and may give clues about the moon's early history. Some of the most important scientific work will continue to be the analysis of lunar samples brought back to the earth. Sometime in the future, some lunar exploration might be carried out by unmanned surface vehicles controlled from the earth.

Someday, a scientific base may be built on the moon. For short periods, teams of astronaut-scientists could explore the surrounding area and conduct experiments at a temporary base. Later, these stations might be enlarged into permanent moon colonies where 50 to 100 men could live and work for months or even longer. Some scientists believe moon bases should be built underground for protection against the sun's radiation, An-extremes of heat and cold, and falling meteoroids. Another idea is to land large roving vehicles on the moon's surface to serve as mobile laboratories.

Perhaps scientists will one day set up telescopes on the moon. The earth's atmosphere limits the study of faraway stars and galaxies. Astronomers on the moon would have a clearer view of the universe. Looking even farther into the future, some scientists think the moon could be used as a place to launch or refuel flights into deep space. Rockets could travel from the moon to the other planets on less power than is needed to travel to the planets from the earth. However, most scientists predict that earth-orbiting space stations will be better places than the moon to place telescopes and to launch deep space missions.

Today, the moon is a symbol of the peaceful exploration of space. No nation owns the moon. In 1967, more than 90 nations signed a treaty governing space exploration. This treaty declares that outer space, including the moon, cannot be claimed by any country or be used for military purposes.

EUGENE M. SHOEMAKER

MOON/Study Aids

Related Articles in WORLD BOOK include:

Astrology	Gravitation	Orbit
Astronaut	Harvest Moon	Planetarium
Astronomy	Luna	Satellite
Calendar	Meteor	Solar System
Crescent	Monday	Space Travel
Diana	Month	Tektite
Eclipse	Mythology	Telescope
Galileo	Observatory	Tide

Outline

I. **What the Moon Is Like**
  A. The Moon's Surface
  B. What the Moon Is Made Of
  C. Gravity
  D. Atmosphere and Weather
  E. Temperature

II. **How the Moon Moves**
  A. The Orbit of the Moon
  B. Rotation
  C. The Phases of the Moon
  D. Eclipses
  E. The Moon and Tides

III. **How the Moon Was Formed**
  A. Age and History
  B. Scientific Theories

IV. **The Moon in History**
  A. Measuring Time
  B. Mythology
  C. Legend and Folklore
  D. Literature and Music
  E. Moon Study
  F. Man's Future on the Moon

Questions

What causes the phases of the moon?
Why does a 180-pound man weigh only 30 pounds on the moon's surface?
What are three theories of how the moon was formed?
What are *maria?* How were they probably formed?
Why does the same side of the moon always face the earth?
How much of the moon's surface can be seen from the earth?
How does the moon's diameter compare with that of the earth?
What is a *synodic month? A sidereal month?*
When did the first man-made object reach the moon?
What makes the moon "shine"?
What is the moon's mean distance from the earth?
What is meant by the moon's *perigee* and *apogee?*

MOON, MOUNTAINS OF THE. See RUWENZORI RANGE.

MOONEY, EDWARD CARDINAL (1882-1958), was named Roman Catholic Archbishop of Detroit in 1937. Pope Pius XII appointed him a cardinal in 1946. Cardinal Mooney was born at Mount Savage, Md. He studied at St. Charles College in Baltimore, St. Mary's Seminary in Cleveland, and the North American College in Rome, Italy. He served as Bishop of Rochester, N.Y., from 1933 to 1937. His services on the executive board of the National Welfare Conference won him the unofficial title, "The dean of the American hierarchy." Cardinal Mooney died in Rome, in October, 1958, just after Pope Pius XII died. JOHN T. FARRELL and FULTON J. SHEEN

MOONEY, WILLIAM. See TAMMANY, SOCIETY OF.

MOONFLOWER is an attractive flower in the morning-glory family. It is a climbing vine that may grow 10 feet high. Its broad, heart-shaped leaves shut out sunlight and make an excellent screen for porches. Its pure white trumpet-shaped flowers may be 3 to 6 inches across. They are delicately scented, and close when exposed to strong sunlight. The moonflower grows quickly. The parts of the flower above ground die every year, but the roots remain alive. New parts grow from the roots each year.

Scientific Classification. The moonflower is a member of the morning-glory family, *Convolvulaceae*. It is genus *Calonyction*, species *C. aculeatum*.
H. D. HARRINGTON

Moonflower
W. Atlee Burpee

MOONSTONE is a whitish variety of the mineral called *feldspar* (see FELDSPAR). Moonstone can be cut and used as a gem. It is a birthstone for June. Light will shine through it, but not so clearly as through glass. The stone also reflects light with a bluish or pearly-colored sheen which comes from inside the stone. Ceylon produces many moonstones.

See also BIRTHSTONE; GEM (color picture).
FREDERICK H. POUGH

MOOR is a large area of open wasteland. A layer of peat that is usually wet covers some moors. The word is most often applied to the moors of Scotland and other parts of the British Isles, where heather grows in abundance. But there are also moors in northwest Europe and North America. Most moors, especially in North America, have sphagnum moss growing on them. Many moors have special names.

See also PEAT.

MOOR. In ancient history, the Romans called the people of northwestern Africa *Mauri* and the region they lived in *Mauretania*. These peoples belonged to a larger group, the *Berbers* (see BERBER). The Berbers became Moslems and adopted Arabic as their language. They joined the Arabs in conquering Spain during the 700's. The so-called Moorish civilization of the Middle Ages was in large part Arabic. The Moors lost much of their land in Spain by 1276. In 1492, Ferdinand and Isabella of Spain drove out the last Moors. Most of

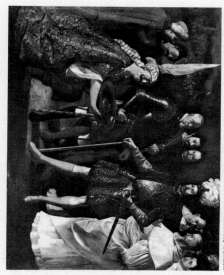

Moors Surrendered Seville after being defeated by Ferdinand III in 1248. The Moors lost much of their land in Spain by 1276.
The Surrender of Seville (1634) by Francisco Zurbarán, The Trustees of the Grosvenor Estates, London

the refugees settled in North Africa. Today, the term *Moor* may refer to all inhabitants of northwestern Africa who are Moslems and who speak Arabic. Or it can refer to Moslems of Spanish, Jewish, or Turkish descent who live in North Africa.

The term *Moor* in its French form *Maure* designates the nomads of the western Sahara in Africa. The term *Moor* also applies to the Arab-Sinhalese Moslems of Ceylon. In the form *Moro*, it refers to Moslems who live in the southern Philippines.

A common but incorrect belief that Moors are Negroes was spread by William Shakespeare's play *Othello*. Moors belong to the Mediterranean group of the Caucasoid (white) race.
VERNON ROBERT DORJAHN

See also ALHAMBRA; ARAB; BOABDIL; FERDINAND V; GRANADA.

MOOR HEN. See GALLINULE.

MOORE, ANNE CARROLL (1871-1961), was an American librarian and editor of children's books. She won the Catholic Library Association's Regina medal in 1960 for her pioneer work in children's library service, and for encouraging good writing for children. Her best-known book is *Nicholas, A Manhattan Christmas Story* (1924). She was born in Limerick, Maine.

MOORE, CLEMENT CLARKE (1779-1863), wrote the most popular of our Christmas poems, "A Visit from St. Nicholas," also known as "Twas the Night Before Christmas." He wrote the poem in 1822, for his own six children. It was published in 1823, and quickly became famous. Moore was born in New York City, and was graduated from Columbia University. He later taught there for 29 years, as a professor of Oriental and Greek literature. He published other works, including *Poems* (1844) and a Hebrew dictionary. ARVID SHULENBERGER

MOORE, COLLEEN. See DOLL (Dollhouses).

MOORE, DOUGLAS STUART (1893-1969), was an American composer, best known for his operas on American subjects. He won the 1951 Pulitzer prize for music for *Giants in the Earth*, based on Ole Rölvaag's novel about the hardships of Norwegian farmers in the Dakota Territory in the 1800's. Moore's most successful work, *The Ballad of Baby Doe* (1956), concerns a Colorado mining heiress. *The Devil and Daniel Webster*

(1939) is based on Stephen Vincent Benét's short story set in New England. Moore's other compositions include the symphonic suite *Pageant of P. T. Barnum* (1926) and the symphonic poem *Moby Dick* (1928).

Moore was born in Cutchogue, N.Y. He became a professor of music at Columbia University in 1926 and was head of the Columbia music department from 1940 to 1962. He wrote *From Madrigal to Modern Music* (1942), an analysis of musical styles.   GILBERT CHASE

MOORE, GEORGE AUGUSTUS (1852-1933), was an Irish author. His novels show the influence of Honoré de Balzac's realism and Émile Zola's naturalism. *Confessions of a Young Man* (1888) is a clever portrayal of experimental painters in Paris. *Esther Waters* (1894) is a grim story of a servant girl's misfortunes. *Héloïse and Abelard* (1921), a fictional account of a famous medieval love story, ranks as Moore's fictional masterpiece. It is one of the few great imaginative reconstructions of life in the Middle Ages.

Moore was born in County Mayo. He worked to establish a native Irish drama and helped bring about the Irish Literary Revival. He described his efforts in *Hail and Farewell* (1911-1914), a memoir. *Avowals* (1919) and *Conversations in Ebury Street* (1924) are autobiographical works in the form of dialogues. HARRY T. MOORE

MOORE, HENRY (1898-   ), is an English sculptor. His works resemble wood or stone objects that have been shaped by natural forces. Many of his works are designed to stand permanently in natural outdoor surroundings.

Moore uses holes or openings in his work to emphasize its three-dimensional quality. The holes create a sense of mass or volume. Moore has associated the openings in his sculpture with the ". . . fascination of caves in hillsides and cliffs." A good example is Moore's elmwood *Reclining Figure*, reproduced in color in SCULPTURE (Looking at Sculpture).

Moore's bronze *Family Group* (1949) shows how he simplifies his human figures, treating the proportion freely. His figures are composed of flowing *convex* (curving outward) and *concave* (curving inward) forms that create rich contrasts of light and dark. A good example is his 1955 stone *Family Group*, reproduced in WORLD (Challenge of the World).

Moore was born into a coal-mining family in Castleford, near Leeds. He attended the Leeds School of Art and the Royal College of Art in London. As a young sculptor, he was inspired by Mexican and African carvings, and his own early work reflects the simple and monumental quality of primitive sculpture. Moore's early work aroused a mixed reaction among critics. He began to attract popular interest with his drawings of people in underground shelters during World War II. His best-known sculpture includes *King and Queen* (1953) and his *Reclining Figure* (1965) at Lincoln Center in New York City.   THEODORE E. KLITZKE

See also ATOMIC ENERGY (picture: A Symbol of Atomic Power); SCULPTURE (picture: Carving in Wood).

MOORE, SIR JOHN (1761-1809), was a British soldier. In 1808, he was sent to Spain with 10,000 men to reinforce the British position. Moore heard that Napoleon was marching with a superior force to crush him. Moore retreated, but the French forced him to fight at Coruña. He was killed just as his troops were winning. Moore was born in Glasgow, Scotland.

MOORE, MARIANNE (1887-   ), ranks with Emily Dickinson among America's finest woman poets. Although some of her verse is difficult to understand, Miss Moore is a superb craftsman. She generally uses poetic forms in which the controlling element is the number and arrangement of syllables rather than conventional patterns of meter or rhyme.

Miss Moore's subjects—often birds, exotic animals, and other things in nature—may seem to limit her range, but she uses them as symbols of honesty and

Marianne Moore

steadfastness. These virtues mark her work, from *Poems* (1921) through *Complete Poems* (1967) and her critical prose collected in *Predilections* (1955). Her *Collected Poems* won the 1952 Pulitzer prize for poetry.

Marianne Moore was born in St. Louis, and became a teacher and a librarian. As the editor of *The Dial* magazine from 1925 to 1929, Miss Moore played an important part in encouraging young writers and publishing their work.   ELMER W. BORKLUND

MOORE, THOMAS (1779-1852), an Irish poet, wrote the words for some of the best-loved songs in the English language. They include "Believe Me If All Those Endearing Young Charms," "The Last Rose of Summer," and "Oft in the Stilly Night." Moore wrote much light, serious, and satirical verse, and much prose. His works were as widely read in his day as the works of Lord Byron and Sir Walter Scott. But he is remembered today mostly for his verse set to music.

Moore was born in Dublin and was graduated from Trinity College there. He studied law for a time in London. His literary works include a translation of Anacreon's poems (1800); *Lalla Rookh* (1817), a romance; and a biography of Byron (1830).   GEORGE F. SENSABAUGH

MOORE COLLEGE OF ART. See UNIVERSITIES AND COLLEGES (table).

MOORER, THOMAS HINMAN (1912-   ), an admiral in the United States Navy, became chairman of the Joint Chiefs of Staff in 1970. Moorer served as Chief of Naval Operations from 1967 until President Richard M. Nixon named him chairman of the Joint Chiefs.

Moorer was a Navy pilot during World War II (1939-1945). He became commander of the U.S. Seventh Fleet in 1962 and commander in chief of the U.S. Pacific Fleet in 1964. Moorer served as commander in chief of the U.S. Atlantic Fleet from 1965 to 1967. At the same time, he was Supreme Allied Commander in the Atlantic for the North Atlantic Treaty Organization. Moorer was born in Mount Willing, Ala. He graduated from the U.S. Naval Academy. DONALD W. MITCHELL

MOORES CREEK NATIONAL MILITARY PARK. See NATIONAL PARK SYSTEM (table).

MOORHEAD STATE COLLEGE. See UNIVERSITIES AND COLLEGES (table).

MOORISH ARCHITECTURE is a name given to the Islamic architecture of Spain. See ISLAMIC ART.

MOOSE. The moose is the largest member of the deer family. It is larger than any deer that lived in past ages. The largest kind of moose live in Alaska. Sometimes they grow $7\frac{1}{2}$ feet high at the shoulder and weigh from 1,500 to 1,800 pounds.

Moose live in northern regions throughout the world. In Europe, they live from northern Scandinavia and northern Europe to Siberia. In North America, they live from Maine to Alaska and south through the Rocky Mountains to Wyoming. Outside of America, these animals are called *elk*, not moose. But the American elk is different. Its correct name is *wapiti*.

The moose has long legs, and high shoulders that look like a hump. The upper part of the moose's muzzle hangs 3 or 4 inches over its chin. The *bell*, an unusual growth of skin covered with hair, hangs underneath its throat. Its coat is brownish black on the upper parts. This dark color fades to a grayish or grayish brown on the belly and lower parts of the legs.

The bull moose has heavy, flattened *antlers* (horns). The antlers on an unusually large moose spread 6 feet or more. Each antler has 6 to 12 short points which stick out like fingers from the palm of a huge hand. A moose sheds its antlers every year and grows a new pair. The antlers are full-grown by late August. The bull then strips off the dead skin, called "velvet," and polishes his great weapons against trees.

The mating season of the moose lasts from four to eight weeks in the fall. The bull wanders about at this time searching and calling for cows. The cows also call to bulls. A bull usually follows every sound to see if it was made by a cow or a rival bull. Moose hunters often try to lure the game within shooting range. They imitate the hoarse grunts of the bull or the love call of a cow by using a horn or by calling through cupped hands.

Baby moose are born in late May or June. The mother carries them inside her body for about seven and one-half months before they are born. A cow may have one calf, twins, or, rarely, triplets. The calf is reddish brown and has long legs. After the first few days, it can travel about with its mother. At this time, the bull stays by himself or with other males.

Moose like best to live in forest land that has willow swamps and lakes in it. There the animals spend the summer, and the cows care for their young.

Throughout this season, they often visit the water to get rid of flies and to feed on water plants. Moose are fine swimmers, and do not hesitate to cross lakes and rivers. They also like to roll in mud holes and eat the salty earth or salt licks. In the summer, their food includes leaves and tender twigs as well as grass and herbs. Moose have such short necks and long legs that they must straddle or get on their knees to eat low plants. They often push against and bend young trees to reach the tender leaves on top.

Moose remain strictly alone in summer. They stay together more in winter. Both males and females sometimes gather in small bands in swamps and woods. They find protection from the cold winds there. They browse on the twigs and shoots of trees. With their long legs, moose can walk easily in deep snow.

At one time, hunters nearly killed all the moose in the eastern United States, but today, a few of the animals live as far south as Massachusetts. Moose are protected by law in the United States and Canada.

Scientific Classification. Moose belong to the deer family, *Cervidae*. The American moose is genus *Alces*, species *A. americana*. It is *A. alces*. The European species of moose is called *elk*.

See also ANIMAL (color picture, Animals of the Woodlands); ELK.

VICTOR H. CAHALANE

D. S. Rawson

MOOSE, LOYAL ORDER OF, is a fraternal order that has branches in the United States, Canada, and Great Britain. Each of the more than 1 million members is required to have unquestionable devotion to his country's flag and loyalty to democratic government. Members of the Moose take part in many civic and philanthropic endeavors.

The Loyal Order of Moose was founded in Louisville, Ky., in 1888. Headquarters are in Mooseheart, Ill., about 40 miles west of Chicago. Here the order maintains "Child City," a home for the dependent children of Moose members who have died. It was founded in 1913, and has more than 110 fireproof buildings. The home provides academic, vocational, and spiritual training. In 1950, a $1½ million church, serving all faiths, was dedicated in Mooseheart.

Loyal Order of Moose Emblem

Moosehaven, "City of Contentment," is situated on the St. Johns River, 14 miles from Jacksonville, Fla. This model home for the dependent aged of the Moose has 18 modern buildings, including a health care center.

Critically reviewed by the LOYAL ORDER OF MOOSE

MOOSE JAW, Saskatchewan (pop. 33,417; alt. 1,798 ft.), is a manufacturing center at the meeting point of Thunder Creek and the Moose Jaw River, about 400 miles west of Winnipeg. For location, see SASKATCHEWAN (political map). Farmers and ranchers of central Saskatchewan send their products to Moose Jaw's flour mills, grain elevators, and stockyards. Other industries include oil refining and the manufacture of building insulation.

The name Moose Jaw is believed to have come from the shape of a river that flows through the city. The town was chartered in 1884 and became a city in 1903. It has a mayor-council government.   F. C. CRONKITE

MOOSE RIVER drains many of the streams of northern Ontario into the Hudson Bay. The Mattagami and Missinaibi streams join to form the Moose River. It is only 75 miles long. But the streams that empty into it drain 42,100 square miles of northeastern Ontario.

MOOSEHEAD LAKE. See MAINE (Rivers and Lakes).

MOOSEHEART, Ill. See MOOSE, LOYAL ORDER OF.

MOOT. See BOROUGH.

MORA, *MO ruh,* **JUAN RAFAEL** (1814-1860), served as president of Costa Rica from 1849 to 1859. He was called "National Hero" for defending Central America against an American adventurer, William Walker, in 1856 and 1857 (see WALKER, WILLIAM). Mora established public schools in Costa Rica and made elementary education compulsory. He encouraged the coffee industry, built public buildings, and gave Costa Rica its first national bank and its first street-lighting system.

Rebels drove Mora from Costa Rica in 1859. He returned in 1860, but was defeated in a revolt and was executed at Puntarenas. He was born in San José on Feb. 8, 1814.   DONALD E. WORCESTER

MORAINE, *moh RAYN,* is the earth and stones that a glacier carries along and deposits when the ice melts. Moraine also means a line of such material on the sur-

face of a glacier, or an uneven ridge of material deposited at the edge of the melting ice. A glacier in a mountain valley carries on each side a line of rock fragments which have rolled onto the ice from nearby slopes. Such a line is called a *lateral moraine.*

When two mountain glaciers unite, the lateral moraines between them merge into a *medial moraine* along the middle of the united glacier. A large ridge is built up when the ice melts from a mountain glacier, or in front of a continental ice sheet. This ridge has mounds and hollows and is called a *terminal moraine.* Some of the terminal moraines formed by the great ice sheets of the Ice Age are ranges of hills. Some of those built by the great mountain glaciers of the Ice Age are also hills. *Ground moraine* is the material deposited beneath the ice as the glacier melts.   ELDRED D. WILSON

See also GLACIER.

MORAL AND SPIRITUAL VALUES. See ETHICS; PHILOSOPHY (What Is Good and What Is Evil?).

MORAL RE-ARMAMENT (MRA) works to further democracy by stressing moral and spiritual values. It aims to change the motives of men and nations and so create a basis for social, racial, and international justice.

MRA centers around the beliefs of Frank Buchman, an American educator whose *Oxford Group* started in the 1920's. In 1938, it became known as Moral Re-Armament. MRA became known in the 1960's for its "Sing Out" musical demonstrations performed by youths in many countries of the world.

MRA training centers are operated in Michigan, Switzerland, Japan, India, and Brazil. Its headquarters are at 112 E. 40th Street, New York, N.Y. 10016, and 833 S. Flower Street, Los Angeles, Calif. 90017.

MORALE is the general attitude or outlook of an individual or a group toward a specific situation. It influences, and is influenced by, such factors as courage, confidence, and determination. Morale may seriously affect both well-being and performance, and is closely related to what is called *esprit de corps.* When morale is "high," the spirit and confidence of an individual or a group are generally good, resulting in a high level of performance. When morale is "low," performance is usually correspondingly poor.

Businessmen, military officers, college deans, athletic coaches, and other leaders have learned to analyze the morale in their groups. They recognize that, in any situation, the level of morale is a decisive factor in determining successful group performance and individual achievement. Psychologists and sociologists conduct research to learn what factors tend to raise or lower morale.   ALEXANDER A. SCHNEIDERS

See also ALIENATION.

MORALITY PLAY is a form of drama in which actors represent such qualities or conditions as virtue, vice, wealth, poverty, knowledge, or ignorance. Men first produced morality plays in England in the 1400's. Like the miracle and mystery plays, they developed from religious pageants. Their purpose was to teach a lesson, or to show the eternal struggle between Good and Evil fighting to gain control of man. They moved slowly, and were usually dull and undramatic. The characters of Vice and the Devil came to be somewhat like a vaudeville team in a modern revue, and helped to make the morality plays entertaining to the audience. The clowns and fools of William Shakespeare's plays were a development of the comic characters in morality plays. Other actors represented such things as Bad Habits, Colic, Pill, and even Dinner, Supper, and Banquet.

Today, these plays are little more than a literary curiosity. *Everyman*, a favorite morality play in the 1500's, was printed in several editions. People still produce this dramatic allegory occasionally. *Everyman* is performed annually at the music and drama festival in Salzburg, Austria.

See also Miracle Play.

CHARLES W. COOPER

MORATORIUM, *MOHR uh TOH ree um,* is a postponement of the time for payment of debts or financial obligations. It is accomplished by executive or legislative decree. A moratorium is often declared following a money panic, political or industrial upheaval, or national calamity, such as flood or earthquake. The moratorium delays legal action on debts. But it does not release the debtor from his obligation to pay. It merely postpones the day the debt is due.

The credit system is now widely used throughout the world, and moratorium has come to mean mostly the postponement of payment on commercial debts. Bills of exchange, drafts, and bank deposits are the kinds of things affected by a moratorium. Household and personal obligations are usually not included.

Moratoriums were used only on occasions of public disaster before World War I. The first war moratorium was decreed by England in 1914. The bills of exchange due in London were not met by payments because of the war. A one-year moratorium on intergovernmental debts was declared in 1931, to allow Germany to recover its financial stability. Franklin D. Roosevelt declared a moratorium in 1933, to save the financial system of the United States.

L. T. FEATLEY

MORAVIA, *moh RAY vee uh,* once called the Great Moravian Empire, was a province of Austria-Hungary before 1918. It is now part of Czechoslovakia. Brno, or Brünn, is the principal city.

Moravia covers an area of more than 10,000 square miles. The land is fertile and picturesque. Moravia is separated from Bohemia on the west by mountainous woods and thinly populated land, from Silesia on the north by the Sudetes Mountains, and from Slovakia on the east by the Carpathian Mountains. Small rivers flow southeast into the Morava River, which empties into the Danube. For location, see Czechoslovakia (map).

The People and Their Work. Most of the 3,719,499 people of Moravia are Czechs, and are of the Roman Catholic faith. The chief crops are rye, oats, barley, wheat, corn, flax, and sugar beets. Leather goods, yarn, silk, wine, glass, and machinery made in Moravia are well known in many parts of the world. Woolen goods and sugar are the principal exports.

History. In the 800's the Moravian and Slovak tribes united and formed the Great Moravian Empire, which included Moravia, Slovakia, Bohemia, lower Austria, and some territories in Silesia and Poland.

In the late 700's and early 800's, the Slav peoples in Moravia came under the sway of Charlemagne. In the early 900's, the Magyars invaded the Moravian Empire, and conquered it. Emperor Otto I defeated the Mag-

yars in 955, and Moravia became a *march* (frontier territory) of the Holy Roman Empire.

From 1029 on, Moravia was part of the Bohemian kingdom. Sometimes it was an essential part, sometimes a *margraviate*, or fief. In 1526, both Bohemia and Moravia passed under the rule of the Hapsburg family. The first Hapsburg ascended the Bohemian throne through the marriage of King Vladislav's daughter Anne to the Hapsburg Ferdinand. He became King of Bohemia and Hungary. In this way the foundation of the future Austro-Hungarian monarchy was laid. S. HARRISON THOMSON

MORAVIA, ALBERTO. See ITALIAN LITERATURE (The 1900's).

MORAVIAN CHURCH is a Protestant denomination that was formed after the death of religious reformer John Huss in Bohemia. In 1457, some supporters of the martyred Huss organized themselves as the *Unitas Fratrum* (Unity of Brethren). They stressed the sole authority of the Bible; simplicity in worship; receiving the Lord's Supper in faith without authoritative human explanation; and disciplined Christian living. In 1467, the group established its own ministry. Despite suppression, the Brethren flourished and were an important religious force by the time of Martin Luther. See BRETHREN; HUSS, JOHN.

The Brethren suffered great persecution during the Thirty Years' War (1618-1648). The group revived during the Pietist movement in Germany in the early 1700's. Pietists were Christians—mainly Lutherans—who wanted to return to the simple life of the early Christians. Beginning in 1722, refugees from Moravia under the leadership of Count von Zinzendorf reorganized the church. It then became known as the Moravian Church. The group built Herrnhut, a town on the count's estate in Saxony. Herrnhut became the base for missionary activity throughout the world, especially among underdeveloped countries. The church has always been noted for its missionary work.

Moravians moved to Pennsylvania in 1740 and to North Carolina in 1753. Bethlehem, Pa., is headquarters for the northern province of the church. Winston-Salem, N.C., is headquarters for the southern province. The church has three orders of the ministry—bishops, presbyters, and deacons. Provincial and district *synods* (conferences) of ministers and laymen administer the church. For membership in the United States, see RELIGION (table).

Critically reviewed by the MORAVIAN CHURCH

MORAVIAN COLLEGE. See UNIVERSITIES AND COLLEGES (table).

MORAVIANTOWN, BATTLE OF. See WAR OF 1812 (Chief Battles of the War [Thames River]).

MORAY. See EEL.

MORAY FIRTH. See SCOTLAND (Rivers and Lakes).

MORAZÁN, *MOH rah SAHN,* **FRANCISCO** (1799-1842), a Central American soldier and statesman, was elected president of the United Provinces of Central America in 1830 and served for almost 10 years. He promoted trade and education.

The federation collapsed in 1839, and Morazán was elected president of El Salvador. He was forced into exile within a year. He was elected president of Costa Rica in 1842, but his enemies killed him. Morazán was born in Tegucigalpa, Honduras. He served as secretary general of Honduras in 1824 and as president of the Council of State in 1826.

DONALD E. WORCESTER

MORDANT, *MAWR dunt.* Substances called *mordants* combine chemically with dyes to form insoluble dyes that do not dissolve easily. The dye might wash out, but the colored compound will not, so the color is permanent. Common mordants include salts of chromium, iron, aluminum, tin, or other metals. These are basic or metallic mordants, and are used with acid dyes. Tannic acid, lactic acid, and oleic acid are other common mordants. These are acid mordants, and combine with basic dyes. The compounds of basic mordants with dyes are called *lakes*. When alizarin, an acid dye, is mordanted with a basic aluminum salt, it colors cotton cloth a bright red, called *Turkey red.*

FRED FORTESS

MORDECAI. See ESTHER; HAMAN.

MORDVINOFF, *MAWRD vihn awv,* **NICOLAS** (1911-), an author, illustrator, and painter, won the Caldecott medal in 1952 for his illustrations in *Finders Keepers,* a children's book by William Lipkind. Mordvinoff was born in Petrograd (now Leningrad), Russia. He became a United States citizen in 1951.

MORE, SAINT THOMAS (1477?-1535), was a great English author, statesman, and scholar. He served as lord chancellor, the highest judicial official in England, from 1529 to 1532. But More resigned because he opposed King Henry VIII's plan to divorce his queen. He was beheaded in 1535 for refusing to accept the king as head of the English church. More has since become an example of the individual who places his own conscience above the claims of *secular* (nonreligious) authority. In 1935, he was canonized as a saint of the Roman Catholic Church.

His Life. More was born in London, probably in 1477 but perhaps late in 1478. He studied at Oxford University. More began his legal career in 1494, and became an undersheriff of London in 1510. By 1518 he had entered the service of King Henry VIII as royal councilor and ambassador. He was knighted and made undertreasurer in 1521, and was chancellor of the Duchy of Lancaster from 1525 to 1529.

More became lord chancellor after Cardinal Wolsey was dismissed late in 1529. At that time, Henry VIII was engaged in a bitter battle with the Roman Catholic Church. He wanted to divorce Catherine of Aragon so he could marry Anne Boleyn. More resigned his office because he could not support the king's policy against the pope. In April, 1534, More was imprisoned for refusing to swear to the Act of Succession, which named Henry VIII as head of the Church of England. More was convicted of high treason on *perjured* (falsely sworn) evidence at his trial on July 1, 1535. He was beheaded on July 6.

Character and Writings. More's personality combined intense concern for the problems of his day and spiritual detachment from worldly affairs. He was a devoted family man, and lived a plain, simple private life. He was famed for his merry wit. Yet to the people of his day, More was a contradictory figure—merriest when he seemed saddest and saddest when he appeared most

happy. He was a patron of the arts and his close friends included the humanist Erasmus and the artist Hans Holbein.

More's sympathetic philosophy is best reflected in *Utopia* (written in Latin in 1516). *Utopia* is an account of an ideal society, with justice and equality for all citizens. This masterpiece gave the word *utopia* to European languages. More also produced much English and Latin prose and poetry. His works include *History of King Richard III* (1513) and a long series of writings in which he defended the church against the attacks of Protestant reformers. He wrote his finest English work, *A Dialogue of Comfort Against Tribulation,* while in prison.

RICHARD S. SYLVESTER

See also UTOPIA; RENAISSANCE (England).

MOREA. See PELOPONNESUS.

MORELL, *moh REHL,* **BEN** (1892-), an American naval officer, founded the Seabees of the United States Navy. He commanded them during World War II (see SEABEES). Morell served both as chief of the bureau of yards and docks and as chief of the civil engineers of the U.S. Navy from 1937 to 1946. He retired from the Navy as an admiral in 1946. He then became president, and later chairman of the board, of Jones & Laughlin Steel Corporation. He retired in 1958. Morell was born in Salt Lake City, Utah.

ROBERT W. ABBETT

MOREHEAD STATE UNIVERSITY. See UNIVERSITIES AND COLLEGES (table).

MOREHOUSE COLLEGE. See UNIVERSITIES AND COLLEGES (table).

MORELIA, *moh RAYL yah* (pop. 133,949; alt. 6,366 ft.), is the capital of the Mexican state of Michoacán. It lies in central Mexico, about 130 miles northwest of Mexico City (see MEXICO [political map]). Its industries include flour mills, vegetable processing plants, and chemical factories. The city has a beautiful cathedral and an old stone aqueduct with 253 arches. Many of Morelia's buildings were built while Mexico was a Spanish colony. Morelia was founded as Valladolid in 1541. In 1828, the city was renamed for José María Morelos y Pavón, a leader in Mexico's fight for independence from Spain.

ROBERT C. WEST

MORELOS, *moh RAY lohs,* with an area of 1,908 square miles, is the second smallest state in Mexico. It lies in central Mexico, just south of Mexico City. Its northern section has altitudes of over 10,000 feet. Southern Morelos is lower and has many broad valleys. Cuernavaca is the capital and largest city (see CUERNAVACA). For location, see MEXICO (political map). The state has a population of 511,179. Crops include rice, corn, peanuts, and sugar cane. Morelos was founded in 1869. It was named for José María Morelos y Pavón, a Mexican hero. The revolt led by Emiliano Zapata in the early 1900's destroyed much property in the state.

CHARLES C. CUMBERLAND

MORELOS, JOSÉ MARÍA. See MEXICO (Revolt Against the Spaniards).

MORENCI, Ariz. (pop. 2,431; alt. 4,840 ft.), lies in the mountainous area of southeastern Arizona. It is about 213 miles from Phoenix, on a slope of the Gila Mountains (see ARIZONA [political map]). The city has the largest and oldest open-pit copper mine in Arizona. Mining in the area started in the early 1870's. Morenci was founded in 1871.

ALICE B. GOOD

Saint Thomas More
Detail of an oil portrait by Hans Holbein the Younger, the Frick Collection, New York

MORES

MORES, *MOH reez,* is a general word used for the most important ideas and acts of people within a society. *Mores* is a Latin word meaning *customs.* Mores represent required behavior, and are formally expressed in the morals and laws of a people. For example, American criminal laws largely incorporate the mores of our society. Another source of American mores is the Ten Commandments.

Mores differ greatly from one culture to another. In King Solomon's time, a man was permitted to have as many wives as he wanted at one time. In our society, he may legally have only one at a time. Mores also may change noticeably from time to time in the same society.

See also FOLKWAY.

JOHN F. CUBER

MORGAGNI, *mohrGAHNyee,* **GIOVANNI BATTISTA** (1682-1771), an Italian anatomist and pathologist, became known as "the father of pathologic anatomy." He became a professor of anatomy at the University of Padua in 1712. He lectured, studied, and wrote there about his post-mortem findings. He performed more than 600 autopsies himself. A statue of him stands in the Hall of Immortals of the International College of Surgeons in Chicago. Morgagni was born in Forlì, Italy, on Feb. 25, 1682.

He was graduated from the University of Bologna. He discovered and described many diseases of the heart and blood vessels. His great book, *On the Seats and Causes of Diseases* (1761), is a landmark in the history of pathology (see PATHOLOGY).

CAROLINE A. CHANDLER

MORGAN is the family name of three great American bankers.

Junius Spencer Morgan (1813-1890) founded the Morgan financial empire. As a young man, he made a fortune in the dry-goods business, and in 1854 became a member of the London banking firm of George Peabody and Company. The name later was changed to J. S. Morgan and Company, and the firm became a famous international banking house with headquarters in London. Morgan was born in what is now Holyoke, Mass.

John Pierpont Morgan (1837-1913), a son of Junius, became one of the greatest financiers in the United States. He joined his father's banking firm in 1856. Morgan was a member of the firm of Dabney, Morgan & Company from 1864 to 1871. In 1871, Morgan and the Drexel family of Philadelphia established the firm of Drexel, Morgan & Company. Morgan reorganized the firm under the name of J. P. Morgan & Company in 1895.

Morgan's firm became a leader in financing American business and in marketing bond issues of the United States government. It also sold bonds of the British government. Morgan helped organize the United States Steel Corporation in 1901. He was active in financing the International Harvester, American Telephone and Telegraph, and General Electric companies. Morgan and his associates served as directors of corporations, banks, railroads, public utility companies and insurance firms. In 1912, Morgan was investigated by a Congressional committee because of his great financial power, but nothing personally discreditable to him was revealed.

After the panic of 1893, Morgan helped reorganize many railroads, including the Northern Pacific, Erie, Southern, and the Philadelphia and Reading. In 1904, the Supreme Court of the United States dissolved the Northern Securities Company because it violated the Sherman Anti-Trust Act. Morgan and other financiers had created the company to control key railroads in the West.

In 1895, Morgan's firm sold all of a $62 million government bond issue. The sale ended a gold shortage in the U.S. Treasury. During the panic of 1907, Morgan loaned money to banks to keep them from closing.

Morgan made many gifts to education and charity. He founded the Lying-in Hospital in New York City, and gave a large sum to the Harvard Medical School. Morgan was an ardent Episcopalian, and gave a substantial share of the funds to build the Cathedral of Saint John the Divine in New York City.

He was a great art collector and gave many valuable pictures, statues, and books to American libraries and museums. Some of his most famous collections were loaned to the Metropolitan Museum of Art in New York, which he helped found. Morgan was a famous yachtsman. He was active in the defense of the America's Cup in international yachting several times.

Morgan was born in Hartford, Conn. He was educated at the University of Göttingen in Germany.

John Pierpont Morgan, Jr. (1867-1943), was the son of John Pierpont Morgan. When his father died in 1913, Morgan took over many of the financial posts J. P. Morgan had held. Morgan succeeded his father as chairman of the board of United States Steel.

Morgan's firm became an official wartime purchasing agent for Great Britain in the United States in 1914. In this position, he placed contracts for the manufacture of food and munitions. The J. P. Morgan Company handled most of the postwar international loans, including many dealing with reparations. Morgan was appointed a member of the commission to revise the Dawes Plan in 1929 (see DAWES PLAN).

Like his father, Morgan made large gifts to education and the arts. In 1923, he dedicated his father's library as an institution of research. Under the terms

Junius S. Morgan
Culver

John Pierpont Morgan
Brown Bros.

John P. Morgan, Jr.
U&U

of the gift, the library will be kept intact as a complete unit until March 31, 2013, a hundred years from the date of his father's death. In 1920, Morgan gave his house in London to the United States for use as the residence of the United States ambassador.

Morgan was born at Irvington, N.Y., and graduated from Harvard University.　W. H. BAUGHN

MORGAN, CHARLES LANGBRIDGE (1894-1958), was a British novelist, playwright, and critic. His novels are noted for their graceful prose. They include *Portrait in a Mirror* (1929), *The Fountain* (1932), *Sparkenbroke* (1936), and *The River Line* (1949). Most of his essays are found in the two volumes of *Reflections in a Mirror* (1944-1946).

Morgan was born in Kent. He entered the Royal Navy in 1907, and served on the Atlantic Ocean and in China from 1911 to 1913. After resigning in 1913, he rejoined the navy in 1914 and served during World War I. *The Fountain* is based partly on his internment in The Netherlands at that time. After the war, he received a degree from Oxford University and joined the staff of the *London Times* in 1921. He became the *Times* drama critic in 1926. Morgan married a Welsh novelist, Hilda Vaughan, in 1923. From 1954 to 1956, he served as international president of P.E.N. (Poets, Playwrights, Editors, Essayists, and Novelists).　HARRY T. MOORE

MORGAN, DANIEL (1736-1802), served as an American officer in the Revolutionary War. He joined the Revolutionary forces in 1775 as a captain. He volunteered to go with Benedict Arnold on his expedition to Quebec, and was taken prisoner there. On his release in 1776, he became a colonel in charge of a Virginia regiment. He organized a corps of sharpshooters in 1777 that helped General Horatio Gates in his battles against General John Burgoyne. Morgan resigned from the army in 1779 because of poor health, but was recalled in 1780 and became a brigadier general. He commanded the American troops at the victory at Cowpens, S.C., in 1781. He received the thanks of Congress and a gold medal for his part in the battle.

After the war, he helped put down the Whiskey Rebellion in 1794 in western Pennsylvania (see WHISKEY REBELLION). He served as a Federalist from Virginia in the U.S. House of Representatives from 1797 to 1799. Morgan was probably born in Hunterdon County, New Jersey. He ran away from home and worked for a time as a laborer and as a wagon driver.　JOHN R. ALDEN

MORGAN, EDWIN DENISON. See ARTHUR, CHESTER ALAN (Political Growth).

MORGAN, SIR HENRY (1635?-1688), the most famous English pirate, fought the Spanish fleet on the seas and robbed Spanish towns in the West Indies. He served for a time as lieutenant governor of Jamaica and commander in chief of English forces there.

Morgan's bold raids began in 1668. Thomas Modyford, the governor of Jamaica, issued Morgan a privateer's commission to cruise against the Spanish and collect information about a rumored attack on Jamaica.

His Attacks. Morgan attacked and captured the inland town of Puerto Principe (now Camagüey), Cuba. He then sailed to Portobelo, Panama, a town so well fortified that the French under his command deserted rather than risk the attack. Morgan took the city after a severe battle. He forced nuns and priests to place ladders against the city walls for his attacking force.

Etching from Alexandre Olivier Exquemelin, *Bucaniers of America.* London, 1684. Courtesy of the Rare Book Division, The New York Public Library, Astor, Lenox and Tilden Foundations.

Sir Henry Morgan, a daring English pirate, was knighted by King Charles II for his attacks on the Spanish.

Morgan's men looted the city. Governor Modyford disapproved of these attacks on Puerto Principe and Portobelo, because Morgan's orders were to attack ships, not towns. Morgan, however, celebrated his victories with a drinking party aboard his ship. The ship suddenly exploded, killing more than 300 men. But Morgan survived the explosion.

He looted Maracaibo, Venezuela, in 1669, and also captured three Spanish ships that had been sent specifically to take him. Morgan took a heavy ransom from Maracaibo and returned to Jamaica. Governor Modyford once again rebuked Morgan for the exploits, but made him commander of all the ships of war in Jamaica.

Attack on Panama. Morgan then commanded 1,400 men. In January, 1671, he attacked Panama City, Panama, and captured it in a remarkable battle. The Spaniards turned a herd of wild bulls against Morgan, but the bulls stampeded and helped rout the Spaniards. Morgan burned Panama City and took much of the city's treasures. Morgan shared some of the spoils with his men, but abandoned them and sailed away with the bulk of the loot.

His attack on Panama violated a peace treaty signed by Spain and England in 1670. England had agreed to end acts of piracy on Spanish towns in the West Indies if Spain would recognize England's rule over English West Indian colonies. Morgan was arrested for attacking Panama, and was sent to England for trial. King Charles II forgave him for his attack, and knighted him in 1674. Morgan then returned to Jamaica as lieutenant governor and commander in chief of the English forces there. He was dismissed in 1683, but served on the Jamaican council. He died in his bed in 1688.

Morgan was born in Wales and went to Jamaica as a boy.　WILLARD H. BONNER

The Morgan Raiders enter Paris, Ky., during the Civil War. Morgan led his men on many successful raids behind Union lines.

John Hunt Morgan

MORGAN, JOHN HUNT (1825-1864), a Confederate general, led the daring Morgan Raiders during the Civil War. His troops, a group of volunteer cavalrymen, raided public property, burned bridges, took horses, and captured railroad supplies. They also caused severe losses among Union troops. Morgan never commanded more than 4,000 men, but it is said he captured as many as 15,000 soldiers.

In 1863, Morgan was ordered to invade Kentucky and draw General William S. Rosecrans' army from Tennessee. Morgan went farther than he was ordered. He broke through the federal lines in Kentucky and crossed the Ohio River into Indiana. A flood caused the river to rise, and Morgan could not return to Confederate territory. He was captured in July, 1863, and was imprisoned in Columbus, Ohio.

Morgan escaped the next November and continued his raids. He was defeated in Kentucky, in June, 1864. He went to Greeneville, Tenn., where he was surrounded and shot by Union troops in September, 1864. Morgan was born in Huntsville, Ala. He spent his boyhood in Kentucky.

FRANK E. VANDIVER

MORGAN, JUSTIN (1748-1798), owned and gave his name to a horse, the original stallion of the breed of Morgan horses. The breed became famous for its strength, endurance, and speed (see Horse [Saddle Horses; color picture]). Morgan was born in West Springfield, Mass. He moved to Randolph, Vt., in 1788, and became a schoolteacher, singing master, and town clerk there. When the horse was a colt, he obtained it from a farmer in payment of a debt. This unusual stallion died at the age of 29.

CHESTER B. BAKER

MORGAN, LEWIS HENRY (1818-1881), was an American anthropologist who studied the social organization of the Iroquois Indians. His writings on the social and cultural development of peoples of the world were used widely for many years. Morgan's theory of evolution was that all races of people passed from savagery to barbarism to civilization in their development. His writings include *League of the Ho-dé-no-sau-nee or Iroquois* (1851), and *Ancient Society* (1877). He was also active in politics. He was born in Aurora, N.Y.

DAVID B. STOUT

MORGAN, THOMAS HUNT (1866-1945), an American geneticist, won the 1933 Nobel prize in physiology and medicine for his work on heredity described in *The*

Theory of the Gene (1926). He showed through his experiments that certain characteristics are transmitted from generation to generation through genes (see HEREDITY [Genetics]).

Morgan studied the laws of heredity by using the fruit fly (*Drosophila melanogaster*) for experiments in breeding. His research clarified the physical basis for the linkage and recombination of hereditary traits. He was the first to explain sex-linked inheritance, that some traits pass to only one or the other sex. Morgan and his associates proved that genes are arranged on the chromosomes in a fixed linear order (see CHROMOSOME).

He began his experiments at Columbia University, where he was professor of biology from 1904 to 1928. He was director of the William G. Kerckhoff Biology Laboratory at the California Institute of Technology from 1928 to 1941. He wrote *Evolution and Genetics* (1925), *Experimental Embryology* (1927), and was co-author of *Mendelian Heredity* (1905). Morgan was born in Lexington, Ky. He studied at the University of Kentucky, McGill University, the University of Edinburgh, and received his Ph.D. from Johns Hopkins University. His many honors included membership in the Royal Society (1919).

MORDECAI L. GABRIEL

MORGAN HORSE. See HORSE (Saddle Horses; color picture); MORGAN, JUSTIN.

MORGAN STATE COLLEGE. See UNIVERSITIES AND COLLEGES (table).

MORGANATIC MARRIAGE. See MARRIAGE.

MORGANTOWN, W.Va. (pop. 22,487; alt. 825 ft.), is the home of West Virginia University. Manufacturing plants make brass plumbing fixtures, hand-blown glass, and textiles. Limestone quarries and two of the world's largest coal mines are located near the city. Morgantown lies on the banks of the Monongahela River, 72 miles south of Pittsburgh (see WEST VIRGINIA [political map]). Colonel Zackquill Morgan founded Morgan-

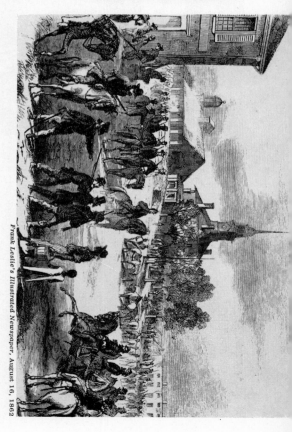

Frank Leslie's Illustrated Newspaper, August 16, 1862

Crane, Black Star

Thomas Hunt Morgan

town about 1766. The city was known as Morgan's Town when it was chartered in 1785. It has a council-manager form of government.

F. P. SUMMERS

MORGARTEN, BATTLE OF. See SWITZERLAND (The Struggle for Freedom).

MORGENTHAU, *MORE gun thau,* **HENRY, JR.** (1891-1967), served as United States secretary of the treasury from 1934 to 1945 under Presidents Franklin D. Roosevelt and Harry S. Truman. During World War II, he organized the Victory Bond campaign that raised more than $200 billion. He proved efficient in the treasury post, although he probably would have preferred the job of secretary of agriculture.

Morgenthau lived near Roosevelt's Hyde Park (N.Y.) estate, and they were close friends. When Roosevelt became governor of New York in 1929, he named Morgenthau head of his Agricultural Advisory Commission. Morgenthau served briefly in 1933 as chairman of the Federal Farm Board and then as governor of the Farm Credit Administration. He also served as undersecretary of the treasury before he was named secretary in 1934.

During World War II, he proposed the Morgenthau Plan for Germany. It would have eliminated most of Germany's heavy industries, and ended German military power. It was never adopted. Morgenthau took a leading part in the 1944 Bretton Woods (N.H.) international monetary conference. He was born in New York City.

HARVEY WISH

MORGUE, in journalism. See NEWSPAPER (Terms).

MÖRIKE, *MUHR ih kuh,* **EDUARD** (1804-1875), was a German lyric poet. He overcame the vagueness that characterizes much romantic poetry. Some of his work suggests a pleasant, untroubled atmosphere. But Mörike's most admired poems are about single objects or moments in time, such as an old lamp in a summer house, or two lovers as they disappear around a corner.

Mörike also wrote prose. *Mozart on His Journey to Prague* (1855) is considered a masterpiece of short German prose. It is a charming story about Mozart, delicately clouded by an awareness of the young composer's approaching death. Mörike also wrote *Painter Nolten* (1832), a subtle psychological novel.

Mörike was born in Ludwigsburg. He became a Protestant minister in 1834. But he retired in 1843 to devote himself to writing.

JEFFREY L. SAMMONS

MORÍNIGO, HIGINIO. See PARAGUAY (Recent Developments).

MORISON, SAMUEL ELIOT (1887-   ), is an American historian, teacher of history, and winner of two Pulitzer prizes. His *Admiral of the Ocean Sea,* a life of Columbus, won the prize in 1943, and his *John Paul Jones* received it in 1960. His other books include *History of United States Naval Operations in World War II* in 15 volumes (1947-1962), *The Intellectual Life of Colonial New England* (1960), *One Boy's Boston* (1962), and *The Oxford History of the American People* (1965).

Morison was born in Boston and was educated at Harvard University and in Paris. In 1915, he became a teacher of history at Harvard. He served in World War I and World War II. He was elected to the American Academy of Arts and Letters in 1963.

MERLE CURTI

MORLEY, CHRISTOPHER (1890-1957), was a popular American literary journalist. His greatest success was as an essayist in such collections as *Shandygaff* (1918) and

Christopher Morley

Tales from a Rolltop Desk (1921). His novels include *Parnassus on Wheels* (1917), *Where the Blue Begins* (1922), *Thunder on the Left* (1925), and *Kitty Foyle* (1939). He also wrote much entertaining light verse, such as *Mandarin in Manhattan* (1933). He wrote one of the best literary columns of his time, first for the *New York Evening Post* and later for the *Saturday Review.*

Morley was born in Haverford, Pa. He was graduated from Haverford College in 1910, and was a Rhodes Scholar at Oxford University from 1910 to 1913. He later lectured at several colleges.

ARTHUR MIZENER

MORLEY, EDWARD W. See MICHELSON, ALBERT A.

MORLEY, THOMAS (1557-1603?), was an English composer. He won fame for his light songs, which included canzonets, airs, and madrigals. Many of his *ballets,* a song form borrowed from Italy, are still sung today. "It Was a Lover and His Lass," with words from Shakespeare's *As You Like It,* is one of his best-known songs. Morley also composed some church music and music for the lute, viol, and flute. He was organist at Saint Paul's Cathedral and the Chapel Royal in London for many years.

WARREN S. FREEMAN

MORMON CRICKET is not really a cricket, but belongs to the family of katydids and long-horned grasshoppers. It can be very harmful to crops. It lives in the western United States and as far east as Kansas.

Mormon crickets are brown or black, and grow about 2 inches long. They have small wings, but cannot fly. In summer, the female lays its eggs one at a time in the ground. The young hatch the next spring, and are full-grown by summer. Farmers sometimes use poisonous dusting powder and baits to kill them.

In 1848, a swarm of Mormon crickets threatened to ruin the crops of the Mormon settlers in Utah. But flocks of gulls suddenly appeared and ate the insects (see UTAH [picture: Mormons Gather]).

Scientific Classification. The Mormon cricket belongs to the katydid family, *Tettigoniidae.* It is genus *Anabrus,* species *A. simplex.*

See also ORTHOPTERA.

URI. LANHAM

The Mormon Cricket is very destructive to crops in the western United States. It has small wings but cannot fly.

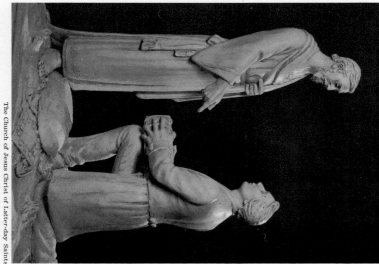

The Church of Jesus Christ of Latter-day Saints

Joseph Smith, *right,* the founder of the Mormon Church, said he received the Book of Mormon from the Angel Moroni.

MORMONS

MORMONS is the name commonly given to members of the Church of Jesus Christ of Latter-day Saints. They are so called because of their belief in the *Book of Mormon.* They claim that the Church as established by Christ did not survive in its original form, and was restored in modern times by divine means. Thus, they believe that their church is the true and complete church of Jesus Christ restored to earth. Mormons are more correctly called *Latter-day Saints,* using the word "saint" in its Biblical sense to designate any member of Christ's church.

The church has more than 2,500,000 members. Most Mormons live in the western United States, and church headquarters are in Salt Lake City, Utah. The church is also established in most other countries of the world.

Several other churches accept the *Book of Mormon,* but are not associated with the church described in this article. The largest of these is the Reorganized Church of Jesus Christ of Latter Day Saints, which has headquarters in Independence, Mo.

Church Doctrines

Mormon beliefs are based on ancient and modern revelations from God. Many of these revelations are recorded in scriptures. These scriptures include the Bible, the *Book of Mormon, Doctrine and Covenants,* and the *Pearl of Great Price.*

Mormons regard the Bible as the word of God, but they believe that it is not a complete record of all that God said and did. The *Book of Mormon* is a history of early peoples of the Western Hemisphere. Mormons teach that the *Book of Mormon* was divinely inspired, and regard it as holy scripture. The *Book of Mormon* was translated by Joseph Smith from golden plates which he said he received from the angel Moroni. *Doctrine and Covenants* contains revelations made by God to Joseph Smith. The *Pearl of Great Price* contains writings of Smith and his translation of some ancient records.

Mormons believe in a unique concept of God. They teach that this concept was revealed by God through Joseph Smith and other prophets. Mormons believe that the Supreme Being is God the Father, who is a living, eternal being having a glorified body of flesh and bone. Man's own body is made in the image of God.

Mormons teach that God the Father created all mankind as spirit children before the earth was made. They regard Jesus Christ as the first spirit-child the Supreme Being created. They believe that Christ created the world under the direction of God the Father. They also refer to Christ as the Creator. Jesus Christ came down to earth and was born of the Virgin Mary. He was the only one of God's spirit-children begotten by the Father in the flesh. He is divine.

Jesus Christ died on the cross for the sins of all mankind and brought about the resurrection of all. He lives today as a resurrected, immortal being of flesh and bone.

God the Father and Jesus Christ are two separate beings. Together with the Holy Ghost, they form a Trinity, Godhead, or governing council in the heavens. The Holy Ghost is a third personage, but is a spirit without a body of flesh and bone.

Mormons claim that their doctrine is the one which Jesus and His apostles taught. They believe that the first principles and ordinances of the gospel are faith in Jesus Christ; repentance; baptism by immersion for the remission of sins; and the laying on of hands for the gift of the Holy Ghost. They believe that a person must be called of God by prophecy and by a laying on of hands by those who have the authority to preach the gospel and to administer its ordinances.

Mormons believe in life after death, and in the physical resurrection of the body. The spirit, awaiting the resurrection of the body, continues in an intelligent existence. During this time, persons who did not know the gospel in life may accept it after death. Mormons believe, for this reason, that living persons can be baptized on behalf of the deceased. In this ceremony, a living Mormon acts as a representative of the dead person and is baptized for him. Other rites are performed for the dead.

Since Mormons believe in life after death, they believe that family life continues after death. Marriages performed in a Mormon temple are for eternity, and not just for this life. Mormons believe in a final judgment in which all men will be judged according to their faith and works. Each man will be rewarded or punished according to his own merit.

Mark E. Petersen, the contributor of this article, is a member of the Council of the Twelve Apostles of the Church of Jesus Christ of Latter-day Saints and chairman of the Church Information Service.

Some Mormons practiced *polygamy* (the practice of a man having more than one wife at the same time) as a religious principle during the mid-1800's. But the church outlawed the practice in 1890 after the Supreme Court of the United States ruled it illegal.

They believe in upholding the civil law of the country in which they are established. For example, they believe the Constitution of the United States is an inspired document. Mormons in the United States are urged by their religion to uphold its principles.

Church Organization

Mormons regard the organization plan of their church as divinely inspired. They have no professional clergy. However, all members in good standing, young and old, can participate in church government through several church organizations. A 38-man body called the General Authorities heads the church. This group consists of the president and two counselors; the Council of the Twelve Apostles; a group of assistants to the Council of the Twelve Apostles; the Patriarch to the church; the seven-man First Council of the Seventy; and the three-member Presiding Bishopric.

Under the General Authorities are regional and local organizations called *stakes* and *wards*. Each *stake* (diocese) is governed by a president and two counselors, who are assisted by an advisory council of 12 men. A stake has between 2,000 and 10,000 members. A *ward* (congregation) is governed by a bishop and two counselors. Wards have an average of 500 to 600 members.

Worthy male members of the church may enter the priesthood, which is divided into two orders. The *Aaronic* (lesser) order is for young men 12 to 20 years old. The *Melchizedek* (higher) order is for men over 20.

Mormon Pioneers Left Nauvoo, Ill., in 1846, on the way west to the valley of the Great Salt Lake in Utah. The Mormons had established the city of Nauvoo only seven years earlier. But it be-

Each order is subdivided into *quorums* (groups). Mormons believe that the priesthood provides authority to act in God's name in governing the church and in performing religious ceremonies.

Several auxiliary organizations assist the priesthood. The Sunday School, the largest auxiliary organization, provides religious education for adults and children. The Women's Relief Society helps the sick and the poor, and directs women's activities. The Young Men's and Young Women's Mutual Improvement Associations are programs for teen-agers and young adults. The Primary Association sponsors classwork and recreation for children under 12 years of age.

The church operates an extensive educational system. It provides weekday religious education for high school students in about 1,900 *seminaries* located near public high schools in 42 states and six foreign countries. The church conducts 66 weekday religious *institutes* for Mormon students near college campuses. It also maintains fully accredited colleges and universities in Utah, Idaho, and the Pacific Islands. Best known of these is Brigham Young University in Provo, Utah.

Mormons assist aged, handicapped, and unemployed members through a voluntary *welfare program.* Projects directed by the wards and stakes help the poor.

Voluntary contributions from members and income from church-operated businesses support the church. Most members contribute a *tithe* (one-tenth of their annual income) to the church. Thousands of young men and women work for 18 to 30 months in a world-wide missionary program without pay.

History

Revelations. During the early 1800's, Joseph Smith, the son of a New England farmer, received a series of

came a hotbed of anti-Mormon feeling. Many of the saints were killed and their homes and fields burned. After Joseph Smith's death, Brigham Young led the pioneers.

Mormon Temple in Utah, the magnificent six-spired granite structure of the Church of Latter-day Saints, dominates Temple Square in Salt Lake City. The domed Tabernacle, at left background, is famous for its huge organ and choir.

divine revelations. According to Smith's account, God the Father and Jesus Christ appeared to him near Palmyra, N.Y., in 1820. They advised him not to join any existing church and to prepare for an important task. Smith said he was visited by an angel named Moroni three years later. Moroni told him about golden plates on which the history of early peoples of the Western Hemisphere was engraved in an ancient language. In 1827, Smith found the plates on Cumorah, a hill near Palmyra. His translation of the plates, called the *Book of Mormon*, was published in 1830.

Joseph Smith and his associates founded the church on April 6, 1830. The church grew rapidly, and had 1,000 members by the end of the first year.

Mormons in the Middle West. Mormon communities were established at Kirtland, Ohio, and Independence, Mo., during the early 1830's. Smith moved the church headquarters to Kirtland in 1831, and the town was the

center of church for almost 10 years. He instituted the basic organization and many of the present doctrines there. The first Mormon temple was completed there in 1836.

The 1830's were years of growth, but serious problems arose at the same time. Disputes among some church members themselves, the collapse of a Mormon bank in 1837, and conflict with non-Mormon neighbors broke up the Kirtland community. In 1838, Smith and his loyal followers moved to Missouri, and joined other Mormons there. But trouble again arose. The Missouri Mormons had been driven from Independence in 1834, and had settled in a town called Far West, in northern Missouri. In the fall of 1838, mobs attacked the Mormons in several of their settlements. In the "massacre at Haun's Mill," 20 Mormons, including some children, were killed. Joseph Smith and other leaders were arrested on what Mormons believe were false charges.

The Mormon Tabernacle in Salt Lake City, Utah, has a 375-member choir. The choir has won world-wide fame through concerts. The huge organ, begun in 1866, still contains some of the original pipes. Free weekday organ concerts attract thousands of visitors to the Tabernacle.

Ordered out of Missouri, about 15,000 Mormons fled to Illinois in 1838. Smith escaped from prison a few months later and rejoined his people in Illinois.

They founded the city of Nauvoo, which soon became the largest city in the state. The rapid growth of Nauvoo, and the important part Mormons played in state politics made non-Mormons suspicious and hostile again. One faction set up a newspaper to fight Smith, who had become a candidate for President of the United States. The paper was destroyed, and Smith was blamed for it. He, his brother Hyrum, and other church leaders were arrested and jailed. On June 27, 1844, a mob attacked the jail, and Smith and his brother were shot and killed.

The Mormons in Utah. Brigham Young became the next church leader. Mobs forced the Mormons out of Illinois in 1846. Joseph Smith had planned to move his people to the Great Basin in the Rocky Mountains. This plan was now put into effect by Brigham Young. In 1847, Young led the advance party of settlers into the Great Salt Lake valley. The population grew rapidly, and by 1849, the Mormons had set up a civil government. They applied for admission to the Union as the *State of Deseret*, but Congress created the Territory of Utah in 1850 instead, and appointed Young governor.

Trouble with non-Mormons began again. It was falsely reported in Washington, D.C., that the Mormons were rebelling. Anti-Mormon public opinion caused President James Buchanan to replace Young with a non-Mormon governor and to send troops to Utah in 1857. The trouble that followed has been called the Utah War. It ended in 1858 when Young accepted the new governor and President Buchanan gave full pardon to all concerned.

The number of Utah settlements increased until the territory's population reached 140,000 in 1877. Congress continued to oppose the practice of polygamy, and the church outlawed the practice in 1890. A Mormon ambition was realized in 1896 when Utah was admitted to the Union as the 45th state.

Mormons Today have won a reputation as a temperate, industrious people who have made their churches monuments to thrift and faith. Their meeting houses are in many ways model community centers. They include facilities for worship, learning, and recreation. The great temple in Salt Lake City was built during the period from 1853 to 1893. There are 12 other temples in the world. The temples are devoted entirely to religious ceremonies, and are open only to worthy Mormons. All other Mormon meeting places, chapels, and recreation halls are open to the general public.

The promotion of music and the arts has long been important to the Latter-day Saints. The 375-voice Mormon Tabernacle Choir in Salt Lake City is famous for its broadcasts, telecasts, and concert tours. The choir, now more than a hundred years old, has been heard on U.S. radio networks since 1929.
MARK E. PETERSEN

Related Articles in WORLD BOOK include:

Cardston
Deseret
Lamanites
Latter Day Saints,
 Reorganized Church of
 Jesus Christ of
Lehi
Polygamy
Smith, Joseph
Smith, Joseph F.
Trails of Early Days (map)
Utah (history;
 pictures)
Young, Brigham

W. Atlee Burpee

MORNING-GLORY is the name of a family made up mainly of climbing plants. The *garden morning-glory* is one of the best-known plants in this group. Other common plants of this family are the *bindweed, jalap, moonflower, scammony,* and *sweet potato.* The morning-glory grows rapidly, and twines about nearby objects. It grows from 10 to 20 feet high, and is widely used as a covering for posts, fences, and porches. The garden morning-glory has dark green leaves shaped like a heart. The flowers are shaped like a funnel, and are of various shades and mixtures of purple, blue, red, pink, and white. The fragrant flowers open in the morning, but close in the sunlight later in the day. The seeds are often soaked in water overnight before planting. This softens the seed covering and makes sprouting easier. Japanese varieties have flowers 7 inches in diameter. Their flowers are mixtures of purple, blue, rose, and violet. The morning-glory is the flower for September.

Scientific Classification. Morning-glories belong to the morning-glory family, *Convolvulaceae.* The garden morning-glory is classified as genus *Ipomoea,* species *I. purpurea.*
JULIAN A. STEYERMARK

Related Articles in WORLD BOOK include:

Bindweed	Flower (color	Jalap
Convolvulus	picture: Summer	Moonflower
Dodder	Garden Flowers)	Scammony
		Sweet Potato

MORNING STAR. See EVENING STAR.

MORNINGSIDE COLLEGE. See UNIVERSITIES AND COLLEGES (table).

MORO. See PHILIPPINES (The People).

MOROCCO is a kind of leather made from the skins of goats. It was first made by the Moors of southern Spain and Morocco. Genuine morocco is soft, elastic, and has fine grain and texture. Vegetable tanning is used to prepare morocco leather (see LEATHER [Vegetable Tanning]). The leather is then dyed and used for bookbindings, upholstery, and fine shoes.

665

MOROCCO

Berber Horsemanship is a matter of great pride and importance because these people travel, herd livestock, and fight on horseback. In a mock battle, left, they show their skill as horsemen.

MOROCCO, *moh ROCK oh,* is a small, mountainous country in North Africa. It lies only 9 miles from Spain, across the Strait of Gibraltar. A strong power in Morocco could block the strait and halt any nation's ships entering the Mediterranean Sea from the Atlantic Ocean. Germany and France nearly went to war in the early 1900's over control of Morocco. Moroccans call their country EL MAGHREB-EL-AKSA in Arabic, which means *the Farthest West.* Rabat is the capital. Sometimes the government moves to Tangier for several weeks in the summer. Casablanca is Morocco's largest city.

About 70 of every 100 Moroccans grow crops in the lowlands, or herd cattle, goats, and sheep in the highlands. Southeast of the mountains, the Sahara stretches along Morocco's border with Algeria and Spanish Sahara. Almost all Moroccans are Berbers, Arabs, or of mixed Berber and Arab descent. Their ancestors—who were called *Moors*—ruled Spain, Portugal, and much of North Africa from the 700's to the 1400's. France and Spain controlled what is now Morocco from 1912 until Morocco became independent in 1956.

The Land and Its Resources

The Land. The Atlas Mountains cover most of Morocco. The country's highest peak, Jebel Toubkal, rises 13,665 feet in the west-central region. Mountains in the north and west slope down to a narrow, fertile, coastal plain along the Atlantic and the Mediterranean. In the southeast, the mountains are lower near the Sahara.

Rivers and Lakes. Small rivers, including the Guir and Ziz, rush out of the Atlas Mountains and dry up in the desert. The Sebou, Tensift, Oum er Rbia and other rivers flow from the mountains to the Atlantic. The 320-mile-long Moulouya River is the longest in Morocco. It rises in the heart of the Atlas range and empties into the Mediterranean. Small lakes often are dry up during the summer and crops are planted in the lake beds.

Natural Resources. The northwestern Atlas Mountains have large deposits of phosphates, Morocco's chief mineral resource. Morocco also has antimony, barium, coal, cobalt, copper, iron ore, lead, manganese, petro-

leum, and zinc deposits. Cedar, oak, olive, pine, and poplar trees cover the lower mountain slopes. Argan trees grow on the coastal plain.

Climate. Breezes from the Atlantic Ocean cool the coastal plain. Temperatures here average about 72° F. in summer and 60° F. in winter. Between 13 and 16 inches of rain falls on the plain every year. The northwestern Atlas Mountains have cool weather with bitter, snowy winters. About 32 inches of rain falls on the these slopes. Less than 8 inches of rain falls on the desert, where the temperature averages 130° F. in summer and about 62° F. in winter.

Life of the People

Morocco has a population of about 15,941,000. About one-third of the people speak Berber. Two-thirds speak Arabic. Most of the Berbers live in the mountains

---
FACTS IN BRIEF

Capital: Rabat.

Official Language: Arabic.

Form of Government: Constitutional monarchy.

Area: 172,414 square miles. *Greatest Distances*—(east-west) 760 miles; (north-south) 437 miles. *Coastline*—612 miles (Atlantic); 234 miles (Mediterranean).

Population: *1960 Census*—11,626,232; distribution, 71 per cent rural, 29 per cent urban. *Estimated 1971 Population*—15,941,000; density, 92 persons to the square mile. *Estimated 1976 Population*—18,385,000.

Chief Products: *Agriculture*—almonds, barley, beans, citrus fruits, corn, oats, olives, peas, wheat. *Manufacturing and Processing*—candles, cement and other building materials, foodstuffs, leather, soap, textiles. *Mining*—clay, lead, limestone, marble, phosphates.

Flag: The flag has a green star centered on a red field. See FLAG (color picture: Flags of Africa).

National Anthem: "Al Nachid Al Watani" ("The National Anthem").

National Holiday: Fête du Trône, March 3; Independence Day, November 18.

Money: *Basic Unit*—dirham. One hundred Moroccan francs equal one dirham. For the value of the dirham in dollars, see MONEY (table: Values).

(see BERBER). Most of the Arabic-speaking people live in the lowlands. About 200,000 Europeans—most of them French and Spanish—live in or near the cities. About 98 of every 100 Moroccans are Moslems. Most of the Europeans living in Morocco are Roman Catholics.

Language. Arabic is Morocco's official language, but the Berber tribes speak various Berber dialects. French and Spanish are used in business and government.

Way of Life. In the average Moroccan family, the wife cares for the home and children, and the husband earns the living. Often, a grown son or other male relative lives with the family and helps the father.

Shelter. Most city people live in small adobe houses. Some of the houses were built hundreds of years ago. Many houses have no windows in order to keep out the heat. Many Berbers come to the cities looking for jobs. They are very poor and live in huts made of canvas,

Keith G. Mather, the contributor of this article, is a British expert on Africa and the Middle East. He has lived and traveled in Africa and has written extensively on African countries.

planks, and corrugated iron on the outskirts of the cities. In mountain towns, houses rise above each other on the steep slopes. The roof of one house may be level with the foundation of another.

Most Moroccan herdsmen live in tents made of wool or goat hair, mixed with braided or woven plant fibers. These tents stand in *douaoeur* (circles). Farmers live in either *nouaiel* or *diour.* Nouaiel are round houses built of branches and roofed with straw. Adobe homes are called *diour.*

Food. Favorite Moroccan foods include lamb, chicken, fruits, and vegetables. The people enjoy *mechoui* (whole roasted lamb) and *pastilla* (salted pie containing lamb, eggs, pigeon, chicken, vegetables, and spices).

Clothing. Most Moroccans dress as their ancestors did. The men wear loose, wide trousers called *seraweel.* They also wear *kumsan* (cotton shirts that reach to their ankles). Kumsan are gathered at the waist with a wide sash. Large hooded cloaks called *djellabiat* serve as outer garments in cool weather. Men often wear turbans or tall, red, brimless hats called *tarabich.* Both men and women wear leather sandals.

Women wear linen shirts called *bloozat,* which have loose, short sleeves. Their loose trousers, also called *seraweel,* are tied at the waist with silk sashes. Outside the home, many Moroccan women follow the Moslem custom of covering their heads and their entire faces except their eyes with body-length cloaks called *haiak.*

Recreation. Moroccans enjoy hunting and trout fish-

ing. Other favorite sports include basketball, boxing, field hockey, soccer, swimming, and volleyball.

City Life. Casablanca, Fez, Marrakech, and Rabat are the only cities with more than 200,000 persons. Most large Moroccan cities have a modern section, a Jewish section called a *mellah,* and an Arab-Moorish section called a *medina.* The modern areas generally have tall apartment buildings, wide streets, and beautiful parks. In the medinas and mellahs, small, ancient adobe buildings are huddled together along winding streets. Many streets are so narrow that a man standing in the center can touch buildings on both sides. Merchants sell food, clothing, jewelry, and other items in the small crowded stalls of *souks* (open air markets). See also CASABLANCA; FEZ; MARRAKECH; RABAT.

Country Life. Most Moroccan farmhouses have two rooms, one for the father and one for the mother and children. Families sleep on mats on the floor, and eat their meals seated on the floor around a low table.

Work of the People

Agriculture. Farms near the coast and in the northwestern Atlas Mountains grow most of the country's agricultural products. Most farmers plant their crops by hand, and use horses to pull wooden plows. Wheat and barley are the main crops, but farmers also raise beans, corn, dates, grapes, nuts, oats, olives, peas, and citrus fruits. Farmers along the coast and herdsmen in the mountains raise cattle, goats, and sheep.

Fishing Industry. Fishing fleets catch anchovies, sardines, and tuna in the Atlantic and Mediterranean. The chief fisheries are in Agadir, Casablanca, and Safi.

Manufacturing and Processing. Morocco's main industries include food processing; leather tanning; the manufacture of leather goods, textiles, tiles, cement, and other building materials; and metal working. A chemical plant in Safi processes phosphates. Hydroelectric plants provide most of Morocco's power.

Skilled craftsmen pass their trades down from generation to generation. Their leather goods, woolen rugs, silver jewelry, brasswork, and pottery are world famous. See ISLAMIC ART.

Forest Products. Sawmills produce about 1,800,000 cubic feet of timber a year from Morocco's cedar forests. Woodlands also supply more than 15,000 tons of cork annually for domestic use and for export.

Trade. Morocco imports slightly more than it exports. The country imports machinery, petroleum, timber, textiles, and foods—coffee, dairy products, sugar, tea, and wheat. Its chief exports include citrus fruits, cork, fish, tomatoes, vegetables, wine, phosphates, and iron, lead, manganese, and zinc ores. Morocco trades mostly with France, West Germany, Spain, Britain, The Netherlands, and the United States. Tourism also provides revenue.

Transportation. Morocco has about 30,000 miles of

Location Map of Morocco

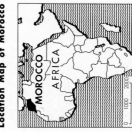

The U.S. Is More Than 20 Times the Size of Morocco.

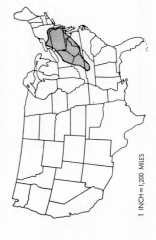

1 INCH = 1,200 MILES

roads, but less than a third of this total is paved. Most travelers ride mules or horses. Over 1,000 miles of railroads link the large cities. Ships from many countries dock in Casablanca, Tangier, Safi, Kenitra, and Mohammadia. International flights provide service to airports in Casablanca, Rabat, Oujda, and Agadir.

Communication. Morocco has about 12 daily newspapers and about 35 weekly and monthly magazines. Extensive radio networks reach the entire country. Television is available in the cities.

Education

Only about 14 of every 100 Moroccans can read and write, but the number is increasing. In 1967, about 1,014,000 children attended primary schools, and 211,000 were in secondary schools. There are 23 teachers' colleges and more than 80 vocational training centers, including an engineering school. Morocco has two universities. About 8,000 students attend institutions of higher education. Arabic is gradually replacing French as the language used in schools.

Government

Morocco is a constitutional monarchy. The king is head of state. Under the 1962 constitution, the king appoints a prime minister and other ministers to run the government. The king presides over the *Council of Ministers* (cabinet).

According to the constitution, Parliament is composed of a House of Representatives and a House of Councilors. Members of the House of Representatives are elected by the people for four-year terms. Members of the House of Councilors are elected for six-year terms by members of local councils and representatives of agriculture, business, industry, and labor. But in 1965, the king suspended Parliament and dismissed the cabinet. He assumed full legislative and executive powers. Morocco is divided into 19 provinces and two *urban*

Moorish Archways pierce the walls that formerly protected the ancient city of Fez. All traffic had to pass through these gates.

H. Armstrong Roberts

prefectures (cities). There are three main political parties. The supreme court is the high court. There are also regional courts and three courts of appeal.

History

Early Years. In ancient times, the northern part of what is now Morocco formed part of the empire of Carthage. It became the Roman province of *Mauretania* after Rome conquered Carthage in 146 B.C. Berbers lived in the area then. When Roman power declined, Vandals crossed from Europe in 429 and invaded Morocco. Byzantine forces conquered the area 100 years later.

Arab armies swept westward across North Africa in the 600's. They conquered Morocco and introduced the Moslem religion. The Moroccan Berbers helped the Arabs conquer the Iberian Peninsula (now Spain and Portugal) in the 700's. The conquerors came to be known as Moors. Many more Arabs came to Morocco from the east in the 1000's.

The Moorish empire had great military power. It extended north into part of France. But it lacked unity until the Berber chieftain Yusuf Ibn-Tashfin unified it in the 1060's. Another Berber, Abd-el-Mumin, seized control in 1147. Within a hundred years, however, local princes regained power and lawlessness returned.

Spanish and Portuguese princes finally united against the Moors. By 1492, they had ended Moorish rule in the Iberian Peninsula, and within a few years, they conquered several cities along the Atlantic and Mediterranean coasts of Morocco. The Moors defeated them near Ksar el Kebir in northern Morocco, but Spain kept Ceuta and Melilla. In the late 1500's, the Moors turned back the Turks, who had conquered much of North Africa. But the local chiefs still fought among themselves, and the sultans who ruled the country were often overthrown.

The Pirate Era. Moroccan pirates provided one of the country's main sources of income from the 1300's to the

Modern Moroccan Apartments differ greatly from the windowless homes in which most Moroccans live in the cities and towns.

Zoltan Glass, Pix

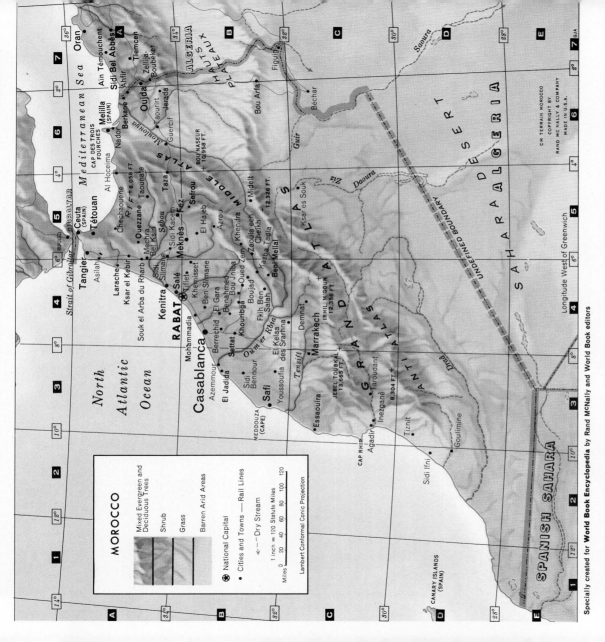

Specially created for **World Book Encyclopedia** by Rand McNally and World Book editors

MOROCCO

Mixed Evergreen and Deciduous Trees

Shrub

Grass

Barren Arid Areas

⊛ National Capital

• Cities and Towns —— Rail Lines

←-→ Dry Stream

1 inch = 120 Statute Miles

Miles 0 20 40 60 80 100 120

0 20 40 60 80 100 120 Statute Miles

Lambert Conformal Conic Projection

MOROCCO MAP INDEX

Physical Features

Anti Atlas (Mountains)	D	3
Bou Naseur (Mountain)	B	6
Cap des Trois Fourches (Cape)	A	6
Cap Rhir	C	3
Daoura River	C	5
Draâ River	D	4
Grand Atlas (Mountains)	C	4
Guir River	B	6
Hauts Plateaux (Plateau Region)	B	7
Irhil M'Goun (Mountain)	C	4
Jebel Toubkal (Mountain)	C	4
Meddouza (Cape)	B	3
Middle Atlas (Mountain)	B	5
Moulouya River	A	6
Oum er Rbia River	B	4
Rif (Mountainous Region)	A	5
Sebou River	A	5
Strait of Gibraltar	A	4
Tensift River	C	3
Ziz River	B	5

Cities and Towns

Agadir	C	4
Ahfir	A	6
Al Hoceima	A	4
Asilah	A	4
Azemmour	B	3
Azrou	B	5
Benahmed	B	4
Ben Slimane	B	4
Beni Mellal	A	6
Berkane	A	6
Berrechid	B	4
Bhalil*	B	5
Bou Arfa	B	7
Boujad	B	4
Bou Jniba	A	5
Casablanca	A	4
Ceuta (Spanish Possession)	A	5
Chechaouene	A	5
Demnat	B	4
El Gaat	B	5
El Hajeb	B	5
El Jadida	B	3
El Kelaa des Srarhna	C	3
Essaouira		

Agadir	16,695	C	4
Ahfir	10,794	A	6
Al Hoceima	11,262	A	4
Asilah	10,839	A	4
Azemmour	12,449	B	3
Azrou	14,143	B	5
Benahmed	6,650	B	4
Ben Slimane	10,305	B	4
Beni Mellal	28,933	A	6
Berkane	20,496	A	4
Berrechid	13,780	A	4
Bhalil*	5,909	B	5
Bou Arfa	8,775	B	4
Boujad	14,728	B	4
Bou Jniba	7,271	B	4
Casablanca	1,085,000	B	4
Ceuta (Spanish Possession)	82,000	A	5
Chechaouene	13,223	A	4
Demnat	5,368	C	3
El Gaat	7,817	B	5
El Hajeb	40,302	B	5
El Jadida		B	3
El Kelaa des Srarhna	10,187	B	4
Essaouira	26,392	C	3

Fez	235,000	A	5
Figuig	12,108	B	7
Fkih Ben Salah	13,484	B	4
Goulimine	8,015	D	2
Guercif	5,579	A	6
Inezgane	6,917	C	4
Jerada	18,872	A	6
Kasba Tadla	11,733	B	4
Kenitra	105,000	A	4
Khemisset	13,695	B	5
Khenifra	18,503	B	5
Khouribga	40,838	B	4
Ksar el Kebir	34,035	A	5
Ksar es Souk	6,551	B	5
Larache	30,763	A	4
Marrakech	255,000	C	3
Mechra Bel Ksiri	5,315	A	5
Meknès	185,000	B	5
Melilla (Spanish Possession)	78,000	A	6
Midelt	6,504	B	5
Mohammadia	35,010	B	4
Moulay Idriss*	8,146	A	5
Nador	17,583	A	6
Oued Zem	18,640	B	4

Ouezzane	26,203	A	5
Oujda	130,000	A	7
Rabat	266,000	A	4
Safi	100,000	B	3
Salé	89,000	A	4
Sefrou	21,478	B	5
Settat	29,617	B	4
Sidi Bennour	5,479	B	3
Sidi Bou Lanouar*	6,828	B	4
Sidi Kacem	19,478	A	5
Sidi Slimane	11,484	A	5
Souk el Arba du Rharb	11,624	A	4
Tangier	110,000	A	4
Taounate	5,442	A	5
Taourirt	17,141	C	3
Taroudant	31,667	C	4
Taza	100,000	B	5
Tétouan	7,733	A	6
Tiznit	7,284	B	3
Youssoufia	8,302	B	3
Zaouia ech Cheikh	5,211	B	5
Zellija*	8,721	A	7
Boubeker			

*Does not appear on map; key shows general location.
Source: Latest census figures.

CM TERRAIN MOROCCO
COPYRIGHT BY
RAND MCNALLY & COMPANY
MADE IN U.S.A.

668a

Map labels: MOROCCO, Oran, Mediterranean Sea, ALGERIA, HAUTS PLATEAU, North Atlantic Ocean, RIF, MIDDLE ATLAS, GRAND ATLAS, ANTI ATLAS, SAHARA ALGERIA, DESERT, SPANISH SAHARA, CANARY ISLANDS (SPAIN), Strait of Gibraltar, Ceuta (SPAIN), Tangier, Tétouan, Melilla (SPAIN), Nador, Al Hoceima, Oujda, Tiemcen, Figuig, Béchar, Saoura, Casablanca, RABAT, Salé, Fez, Meknès, Marrakech, Agadir, Essaouira, Safi, El Jadida, Kenitra, UNDEFINED BOUNDARY, Longitude West of Greenwich

The **Houses of Tétouan, Morocco**, above, are crowded together along narrow, winding streets. Tétouan lies at the foot of the Rif mountains. It is a leading industrial center.

Fritz Henle, Photo Researchers

The **Harbor at Tangier**, below, lies at the western end of the Mediterranean, facing the Strait of Gibraltar. A Moroccan guide gazes across the bay from a rooftop in the Casbah.

George Danielle, Photo Researchers

1800's. The United States struck a blow against piracy in 1801 when it fought a war with Tripoli. Tripoli—now part of Libya—was a small North African state from which pirates attacked U.S. and European shipping. Sultan Moulay Souliman of Morocco came to Tripoli's aid in 1802 and declared war on the United States. But he called the war off before the United States even knew about his action (see BARBARY STATES). In 1814, Morocco abolished the practice of capturing and enslaving Christians. It outlawed piracy in 1817.

Moroccan tribesmen attacked Melilla in 1893 and killed many Spaniards there. The sultan paid Spain $3,800,000 in payment for that attack.

French and Spanish Control. In the early 1900's, the Moroccan sultans were weak and unable to keep order. European colonial powers then became interested in Morocco. France had already occupied Algeria. When fighting broke out in Morocco near the Algerian border, France moved to take over Morocco. But Germany objected. European powers met in 1906 and agreed to respect Moroccan independence and to maintain equal trading rights there (see ALGECIRAS CONFERENCE).

France sent troops to Morocco in 1907, and Spain sent troops in 1911. Again, Germany objected, but Great Britain backed France. In 1912, the sultan signed the Treaty of Fez, giving France control over Morocco's government and finances, and authority to keep an army there. France recognized three zones of Spanish influence: (1) the port of Ifni and its surrounding area; (2) a long strip of land along the Mediterranean coast; and (3) the area between the Draâ River and the southern border. These zones were to be administered by a Spanish high commissioner in Tétouan. The rest of Morocco, except for Tangier, was administered by a French resident general in Rabat. But armed tribesmen fought against French and Spanish forces during the 1920's. France did not gain complete control of French Morocco until 1934. However, the French developed agriculture, industry, and mining, and built hydroelectric power stations, schools, and hospitals.

Tangier had long been a business and diplomatic center. Great Britain, France, and Spain made it an international zone in 1925. It was ruled jointly by them (and also by Italy after 1928). In 1956, Tangier was returned to Moroccan rule. Its special status was ended in 1960.

After France surrendered to Germany in World War II, the pro-German Vichy French government ruled French Morocco. But the Sultan and Moroccan nationalists supported the Allies. In 1942, Allied troops took French Morocco and made it a major Allied base.

Independence. After World War II, Moroccan nationalists tried to overthrow French and Spanish rule. Sultan Sidi Mohammed ben Youssef (King Mohammed V) also wanted independence for Morocco. He was forced into exile by the French in 1953 and replaced with Sidi Mohammed ben Moulay Arafa, who cooperated with the French. Moroccans greatly resented Ben Youssef's exile, and terrorism and killings flared anew.

France finally gave in to Moroccan pressure in 1955 and allowed Ben Youssef to return to Morocco and set up an independent monarchy. Ben Youssef promised to establish democratic government as soon as possible. France granted independence to French Morocco on Mar. 2, 1956. All of the northern Spanish zone except Ceuta and Melilla became part of independent Morocco.

Morocco became a member of the United Nations in November, 1956. The sultan formally became king of Morocco in 1957. He felt the new title was more in accord with his plan to establish a constitutional monarchy. In 1958, Spain turned over all of its southern holdings except Ifni to Morocco. It returned Ifni in 1969.

Recent Developments. In May, 1960, King Mohammed V assumed administrative control of the government. He appointed his son, Prince Moulay Hassan, as deputy premier. The king died on Feb. 26, 1961, and Moulay Hassan became King Hassan II.

In 1962, Morocco adopted its first constitution and became a constitutional monarchy with Islam as the state religion. King Hassan II appointed Ahmed Bahnini premier in 1963. He became the first premier in Moroccan history who was responsible to the Parliament. But the government failed to put through the king's program of administrative and economic reforms.

Hassan proclaimed a state of emergency in 1965. He dismissed the cabinet, suspended Parliament, and took over the government's lawmaking and executive powers. He appointed a new government responsible to him, and promised that new elections would be held after the constitution had been revised.

KEITH G. MATHER

Related Articles in WORLD BOOK include:

Africa (picture)	Hassan II	Olive (table)
Arab League	Larache	Rabat
Atlas Mountains	Marrakech	Rif
Caliph	Meknès	Sultan
Casablanca	Mohammed V	Tangier
Fez		

Outline

I. **The Land and Its Resources**
  A. The Land   C. Natural Resources
  B. Rivers and Lakes   D. Climate

II. **Life of the People**
  A. Language   C. City Life
  B. Way of Life   D. Country Life

III. **Work of the People**
  A. Agriculture   D. Forest Products
  B. Fishing Industry   E. Trade
  C. Manufacturing and   F. Transportation
     Processing   G. Communication

IV. **Education**

V. **Government**

VI. **History**

Questions

Why did Morocco declare war on the United States in 1802?

What is unusual about Morocco's national capital?

Why is Morocco's location important?

How does the *mellah* differ from the *medina*?

How do most of the people earn their living?

What was unusual about the government of Tangier?

Who brought the Moslem religion to Morocco? When?

How was Morocco's government modernized?

MORONI was the son of *Mormon* and the last of the prophets on the American continent, according to Mormon beliefs. See MORMONS; SMITH, JOSEPH (picture).

MORPHEUS, *MAWR fyoos* or *MAWR fee us,* was the god of dreams in Greek mythology. He was one of the sons of Somnus (Hypnos), the god of sleep. He took human form and appeared to people in their sleep. To be "in the arms of Morpheus" means to be asleep, and the drug morphine is named after him.

MORPHINE, *MAWR feen* (chemical formula, $C_{17}H_{19}NO_3$). This grayish-brown drug is obtained from the opium poppy. It is the most important alkaloid of opium, and makes up about 10 per cent of the total alkaloids found in opium. Before morphine can be sold, it is treated with dilute sulfuric acid and bleaching agents until it becomes white feathery crystals.

Morphine is used medicinally to relieve pain. When given in large doses, it will relieve acute pain and because of its narcotic action, it permits the sufferer to go to sleep. In small doses, it will reduce the feeling of pain without causing sleep. But morphine is dangerous, and doctors advise its use only to ease severe pain.

An overdose of morphine will cause death by slowing the lungs until they stop functioning. The treatment for an overdose of morphine is a prompt stomach wash and doses of potassium permanganate. Every attempt should be made to keep the patient awake, even by walking him around the room. Doctors treat morphine poisoning with a drug called *nalorphine*.

Some narcotics addicts take morphine habitually. Morphine addicts make up one of the largest groups of drug addicts in the United States. They become physical and mental wrecks. Their condition arises partly from morphine's effects and partly because they often sell all they have to pay the price charged for the drug by the criminals who sell it. Some addicts can be cured with special treatment (see DRUG ADDICTION).

Federal narcotics laws restrict the sale of morphine and other narcotics. A doctor who prescribes a narcotic must list his name and registration number, the patient's name and address, and the facts justifying its use in the treatment of the patient.

See also ALKALOID; ANALGESIC; HEROIN; MORPHEUS; OPIUM.

A. K. REYNOLDS

MORPHOLOGY, in grammar. See SYNTAX.

MORPHOLOGY, *mawr FAHL oh jih*, is the branch of biological science which deals with the form and structure of animals and plants. It covers the three main phases of animal and plant forms: (1) their development; (2) the history of an organism as a whole and of its separate parts; (3) the resemblances and differences between several forms of the same plant or animal. In the study of botany, morphology is sometimes called *structural botany*. In the study of animal structure, it is the foundation of anatomy.

In geology, morphology is the study of the external form of rocks.

The German writer Johann von Goethe made up the term *morphology* from the Greek words *morphe*, meaning *form*, and *logos*, meaning *doctrine*.

WILLIAM C. BEAVER

MORRILL, JUSTIN SMITH (1810-1898), represented Vermont in the U.S. House of Representatives from 1855 to 1867, and in the U.S. Senate from 1867 to 1898. He proposed the Morrill Act of 1862, which established the Land-Grant Colleges and Universities (see LAND-GRANT COLLEGE OR UNIVERSITY). He introduced the Morrill Tariff Act in 1861. He helped found the Republican Party, and helped pass legislation that established the present Library of Congress. Morrill was born in Strafford, Vt.

MORRILL ACTS. See LAND-GRANT COLLEGE OR UNIVERSITY.

C. B. BAKER

MORRILL TARIFF ACT OF 1861. See TARIFF (The Tariff in United States History).

MORRIS, ESTHER HOBART (1814-1902), led the fight for women's suffrage in Wyoming. Through her efforts, the territory of Wyoming passed a women's suffrage law in 1869 that became a model for later suffrage laws. When Wyoming became a state in 1890, it was the first state to permit women to vote.

Born Esther McQuigg in Tioga County, New York, she settled in the Wyoming territory in 1868. She became the first woman justice of the peace in the U.S. in 1870. A statue of her represents Wyoming in Statuary Hall in the U.S. Capitol in Washington, D.C. LOUIS FILLER

MORRIS, GOUVERNEUR (1752-1816), was an American statesman and diplomat. He headed the committee that wrote the final draft of the United States Constitution. Much of the credit for the wording in the Constitution belongs to him.

Morris was suspected of sympathies for England at the outbreak of the Revolutionary War, but he soon proved himself to be one of the most loyal American patriots. He spoke in favor of the power of the Continental Congress at the revolutionary congress of New York in 1775, and served as a leading member of the New York constitutional convention in 1776. He was a member of the Continental Congress from 1778 to 1779. Morris headed several committees, and acted as draftsman of important documents. He was one of General George Washington's most able supporters in Congress. He attracted the attention of Robert Morris, financial agent of Congress, and served brilliantly as assistant superintendent of finance from 1781 to 1785. Morris was elected Pennsylvania delegate to the Constitutional Convention in 1787. At first he favored a strong, centralized government controlled by the wealthy.

In 1789, he went to Paris as a financial agent. From 1792 to 1794, he served as minister to France. From 1800 to 1803 he was a United States senator from New York. Morris was also a key figure in promoting the Erie Canal project. Morris was born on Jan. 31, 1752, in Morrisania, N.Y.

CLINTON ROSSITER

MORRIS, LEWIS (1726-1798), was a signer of the Declaration of Independence from New York. He served in the Continental Congress from 1775 to 1777, where he worked on committees supervising supplies of ammunition and military stores. Morris later served in the New York state legislature from 1777 to 1790. He was a major general of the New York state militia during the Revolutionary War. He was born in Morrisania, N.Y., and was a half brother of Gouverneur Morris (see MORRIS, GOUVERNEUR).

MORRIS, ROBERT (1734-1806), was a Pennsylvania signer of the Declaration of Independence. He made his greatest contribution to the new republic from 1781 to 1784, as American superintendent of finance. Morris represented Pennsylvania from 1789 to 1795 as a Federalist in the first United States Senate. He also was one

Gouverneur Morris

BROWN BROS.

of the best known merchants in the United States. Morris became prominent when he served in the Continental Congress from 1776 to 1778, and headed two of its most important committees. One committee obtained war materials, and the other instructed the country's diplomats in Europe.

Morris' political and business experience led to his appointment as finance superintendent. The nation's paper currency was almost worthless when he took office in 1781. Morris established the Bank of North America to help relieve the shortage of acceptable currency. He also issued notes, based on his own credit, that served as money.

He was born in Liverpool, England. He came to America in 1747 with little money. As a result of his exceptional business and administrative ability, he built up a network of business connections in America and Europe that made him wealthy.

After leaving his government financial post in 1784, Morris became a land speculator. He lost his fortune in these operations, and was imprisoned for bankruptcy from 1798 to 1801. He spent his last years in poverty and obscurity.

CLARENCE L. VER STEEG

MORRIS, "TOM," THOMAS, SR. See GOLF (Golf Immortals).

MORRIS, WILLIAM (1834-1896), was an English poet, artist, and reformer. A man of many talents, he tried to make his vision of beauty an actual part of everyday life. In 1861, he helped found Morris & Company to produce home furnishings of good design and craftsmanship. Among them was the Morris chair. He practiced many crafts, such as wood engraving.

Morris developed a liking for the culture of the Middle Ages in his studies at Oxford. He believed that through arts and crafts he could find a way out of industrial ugliness back to the joys of creation men had experienced in the Middle Ages. All these interests came to focus in 1891, when Morris founded the Kelmscott Press. He designed three type faces, supervised the making of fine paper, and produced books. Morris was born at Walthamstow, England.

RAY NASH

See also Book (Improvements in Books).

MORRIS BROWN COLLEGE. See UNIVERSITIES AND COLLEGES (table).

MORRIS DAM forms a water-supply reservoir for Pasadena, Calif. It lies on the San Gabriel River, and is 328 feet high and 780 feet long. Engineers completed the dam in 1934.

MORRIS HARVEY COLLEGE. See UNIVERSITIES AND COLLEGES (table).

MORRIS PLAN BANK was organized to lend money to people who owned no property. These people might otherwise have had to borrow from "loan sharks" or friends. Arthur J. Morris of Norfolk, Va., founded the first Morris Plan Bank in 1900. It was patterned after thousands of similar institutions in Europe.

Loans of the type that once were made by the Morris Plan Bank are now made by many commercial banks and by personal loan companies. Only a few Morris Plan Banks still operate.

L. T. FLATLEY

See also LOAN COMPANY.

MORRISON, HERBERT STANLEY (1888-1965), BARON MORRISON OF LAMBETH, was one of the leaders of the British Labour party. He began his career as an errand boy and a telephone operator, and rose to become Foreign Secretary of his country.

Morrison served during World War II as Home Secretary and Minister of Home Security in the coalition government of 1940 to 1945. He was a powerful member of Prime Minister Winston Churchill's war cabinet, even though he had been a conscientious objector in World War I. In Prime Minister Clement Attlee's Labour government of 1945-1951, Morrison served as Lord President of the Council, leader of the Labour majority in the House of Commons, and deputy prime minister. He served briefly as Foreign Secretary in 1951. He lost his government post when the Conservative party came into power in 1951. He was made a peer in 1959. Morrison was born in Brixton, England.

C. L. MOWAT

MORRISTOWN, N.J. (pop. 17,712; alt. 405 ft.), a city in north-central New Jersey, lies about 30 miles west of New York City (see NEW JERSEY [map]). Many Morristown residents commute daily to their jobs in New York City on the Erie-Lackawanna Railroad. Morristown is headquarters for the Seeing Eye School, which trains dogs to guide blind persons (see SEEING EYE).

Morristown was an encampment for George Washington's armies for two winters during the Revolutionary War. The Jacob Ford Mansion, Washington's headquarters for seven months, is now a museum. Jockey Hollow, another section of Morristown, was the site of the crude huts where Washington's soldiers spent the winters. These historic places are preserved in Morristown National Historical Park. The city has a mayor-council government.

RICHARD P. McCORMICK

MORRISTOWN NATIONAL HISTORICAL PARK. See NATIONAL PARK (Historical Parks).

MORRO CASTLE. See HAVANA; SAN JUAN.

MORRO CASTLE DISASTER. See ASBURY PARK.

MORROW, DWIGHT WHITNEY (1873-1931), was an American lawyer, banker, and diplomat. He served brilliantly as United States Ambassador to Mexico from 1927 to 1930 during the Mexican-American diplomatic crises (see COOLIDGE, CALVIN [Foreign Affairs]).

Morrow was born in Huntington, W.Va. After practicing law in New York City, he joined the banking firm of J. P. Morgan and Company in 1914. During World War I, his outstanding work on the Military Board of Supply earned him the Distinguished Service Medal. His daughter, Anne, married Charles A. Lindbergh (see LINDBERGH, CHARLES A. [Anne Morrow]).

HARVEY WISH

MORROW, HONORÉ, AHN oh RAY', WILLSIE (1880?-1940), was an American historical novelist. She spent 10 years of research on the life of Abraham Lincoln before writing her novels about him. Her Lincoln trilogy, *Great Captain*, consists of *Forever Free* (1927), *With Malice Toward None* (1928), and *The Last Full Measure* (1930). She also wrote *Mary Todd Lincoln* (1928). Mrs. Morrow was born in Ottumwa, Iowa.

HARRY H. CLARK

MORS. See SOMNUS.

Brown Bros.

Robert Morris

MORSE, SAMUEL F. B.

MORSE, SAMUEL FINLEY BREESE (1791-1872), developed the first successful electric telegraph in the United States, and invented the Morse code, still used occasionally to send telegrams (see TELEGRAPH). Morse also became one of the best early American portrait painters. He helped found the National Academy of Design, and became its first president in 1826.

Early Life. Morse was born on April 27, 1791, in Charlestown, Mass. He was the son of a minister and author. From early childhood Morse was talented in art, and studied to be an artist. His classmates at Yale College admired his clever art, and he was known there for his miniatures in ivory. He had such teachers at Yale as Jeremiah Day, a mathematician, and Benjamin Silliman, a chemist and physicist. He found their electrical and chemical experiments "amusing and instructive." But, when he was graduated in 1810, he wanted only to study art. His father opposed Morse's desire to become a professional artist. Finally, he consented to let Morse go to England to study art.

He went to London in 1811. He evidently arrived in a gay mood, and spent too much money on new clothes. He applied for admission to the Royal Academy of Arts. The academy would not accept him until he submitted some work. Morse was advised to do a small sketch of a statue in black and white chalk. He worked hard, but each time he submitted the sketch, he was told to "finish it." He learned he must "sacrifice painting to study," Morse wrote, "I have had no new clothes for nearly a year. My best are threadbare, my shoes out at the toes, my stockings all want to see my mother."

Artistic Success. Hard work had its reward. Morse modeled a figure of Hercules in clay. A professor at the academy liked the statue so much, he advised Morse to enter it in competition for the gold medal of the Adelphi Society of Arts. One proud day in 1812, before an audience of English nobility, the Duke of Norfolk pinned the Adelphi gold medal on the young American.

Morse's painting, *The Dying Hercules*, was accepted in 1813 for the annual Royal Academy art exhibit. One British critic rated it among the nine best of a thousand paintings in the exhibit. Another painting, *The Judgment of Jupiter*, was accepted for the 1815 exhibit.

Morse came home from his London triumphs in 1815. But he went through many lean years before he became the well-known portrait painter. His portrait of Marquis de Lafayette (1825) is in the New York City Hall. The New York Public Library owns another Morse painting of Lafayette. Morse wanted to do more than paint portraits. He wanted to do vast historical pictures. The Capitol in Washington, D.C., was being built during this time. Morse heard that four huge paintings were to be in the rotunda of the Capitol. He went back to Europe in 1829 to prepare himself for this challenge. He stayed three years.

Morse and the Telegraph. Morse first became interested in the electric telegraph in 1832. He was on board the ship *Sully* on his way home from Europe. He learned during a dinner conversation at sea that men had found they could send electricity instantly over any known length of wire. From that moment on, he was on fire with the idea of an electric telegraph. He spent

the rest of the voyage making notes and drawing pictures. He said to the captain when he left the ship, "Well, captain, should you hear of the telegraph one of these days, as the wonder of the world, remember the discovery was made on the good ship *Sully*."

Morse arrived home almost penniless. He was counting on winning a commission to do a painting for the Capitol. The fee would support him while he worked on the telegraph. But John Quincy Adams, a member of the committee selecting artists, remarked that he did not think American artists were good enough. A fiery answer to Adams appeared in a New York paper. James Fenimore Cooper had written it, but people thought Morse had. Morse did not get a commission to do any of the paintings.

The Lean Years. Morse's brothers, Sidney and Richard, gave him a room on the top floor of their newspaper building. There Morse lived, cooking his own meals, and slaving over the telegraph. The new University of the City of New York offered him a position as teacher of painting and sculpturing. His salary evidently depended on fees from pupils, and every spare penny went into work on his invention. Leonard D. Gale, a professor, became interested and helped him.

There was plenty of work to do. Morse could not buy insulated wire on reels. He had to buy wire in pieces, solder the pieces together, then wrap the wire, inch by inch, foot by foot, mile by mile, with cotton thread. After he worked five years, he demonstrated the telegraph in 1837. He hoped the men who saw it would invest money to help him complete it. They found it interesting and amusing but would not invest in it.

The most valuable person watching the demonstration was Alfred Vail, a university student. Vail's father and brother owned an iron and brass works in Speedwell, N.J. Vail offered to build a sturdier model of the telegraph. Morse made him a partner, with a one-fourth interest in the telegraph. In 1838, Morse took the new machine to Washington in an effort to obtain money from Congress to test the telegraph. Congress refused. Morse made a trip to England and France, but could find no support.

Morse prepared a dramatic demonstration of the telegraph machine in 1842. He waterproofed two miles of wire with pitch, tar, and rubber, and laid it under-

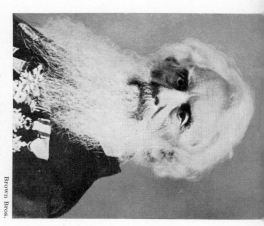

Samuel F.B. Morse

Morse Built a Notched Rod, or Port Rule, *above,* to operate the key of his telegraph sending device.

The First Public Telegraph Message, sent from Washington to Baltimore in 1844, was recorded on tape, below.

water from the Battery to Governors Island. The New York papers carried an announcement of the great demonstration. Unfortunately, a ship's anchor caught the wire. The sailors brought it up, and cut it. The crowds who had come to see the "wonder of the ages" went away later muttering about a hoax.

His Success. Morse made one more attempt in 1843 to interest Congress. The last night of the session, long after Morse had given up hope, Congress passed a bill appropriating $30,000 to test the telegraph. Morse strung the telegraph line from the United States Supreme Court room in the Capitol to Baltimore, Md. On May 24, 1844, Morse stood among a large group of spectators and tapped out on the telegraph

Samuel Morse First Won Recognition as a Painter. His portrait *Marquis de Lafayette,* below, shows his artistic skill.

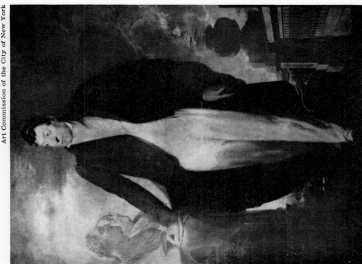

his famous message, "What hath God wrought."

Morse and his telegraph were known within 12 years throughout North America and Europe. The English telegraph companies gave a banquet in his honor in 1856. W. F. Cooke, a rival inventor, in his tribute to Morse at the banquet said, "I was consulted only a few months ago on the subject of a telegraph for a country in which no telegraph at present exists. I recommended the system of Professor Morse. I believe that system to be one of the simplest in the world."

Credit for the invention of the telegraph also should be given to Morse's partners, Gale and Vail. Many others gave substantial help in developing it.

Morse won wealth and fame. Rulers of other countries decorated him. A group of European countries united to give him a cash award of 400,000 francs. Morse became an honorary member of societies in the United States and Europe. The telegraph operators of America gave him the unusual honor of unveiling a statue to him while he was still living. It was unveiled on June 10, 1871, in New York City's Central Park. Morse died the next year in New York City.   JEAN LEE LATHAM

MORSE, WAYNE LYMAN (1900-   ), served as United States senator from Oregon, first as a Republican, then as a Democrat. He was elected in 1944 and in 1950 as a Republican. Calling himself an "independent Republican," he withdrew from the Republican Party in 1952 and supported Democratic presidential candidate Adlai E. Stevenson. Morse became a Democrat in 1955, and was re-elected to the Senate as a Democrat in 1956 and 1962. He was defeated in his bid for re-election in 1968. Morse's major interests in the Senate included labor-management relations, Latin-American affairs, and international law. In the 1960's, Morse became one of the most outspoken critics of United States involvement in the Vietnam War.

Morse was born in Madison, Wis. He was graduated from the University of Wisconsin in 1923, and earned law degrees at the University of Minnesota and at Columbia University. Morse began teaching law at the University of Oregon in 1929. He was dean of the university's law school from 1931 to 1944.   JESSE L. GILMORE

The Morse Code was once used to send telegraph messages in the United States and Canada.

		NUMERALS		PUNCTUATION
A	H	O	V	
B	I	P	W	1
C	J	Q	X	2
D	K	R	Y	3
E	L	S	Z	4
F	M	T	&	5
G	N	U	$	6
				7
				8
				9
				0

Comma   Period   Semi-Colon   Interrogation

The International Morse Code is now used chiefly to send messages by short-wave radio.

A	G	N	U	NUMERALS
B	H	O	V	1
C	I	P	W	2
D	J	Q	X	3
E	K	R	Y	4
F	L	S	Z	5
	M	T		6
				7
				8
				9

PUNCTUATION AND OTHER SIGNS

Period   Comma   Interrogation
Colon   Semicolon   Quotation Marks
S O S   Understand   Wait
End of Message   Start   Error

MORSE CODE is a system of dots, dashes, and spaces, that telegraphers in the United States and Canada once used to send messages by wire. The code was named for Samuel Morse, who patented the telegraph in 1840. The letters that occur most frequently in our language are represented by the simplest symbols.

The dot is made by quickly pressing and releasing the key of the telegraph sender. This produces a rapid *click-clack* sound in the receiver at the other end. A short dash is twice as long as a dot. A long dash, as for the capital letter *T*, is equal to four dots. The space between the dots and dashes that make up a letter is the same length as a dot. The space between the letters of a word is equal to three dots. A space which is part of a letter combination is equal to two dots.

For years, all telegraph messages and most news were transmitted by Morse code. Now, most such messages are sent by automatic facsimile and printing telegraph machines. Radio and telegraph operators in other countries once used International Morse Code, also called International and Continental Code. But facsimile and printing methods of sending messages are now more widely used.

See also TELEGRAPH; TELETYPEWRITER.

WESTERN UNION TELEGRAPH COMPANY

MORTALITY. See LIFE.

MORTAR. See BRICK AND BRICKLAYING (Mortar).

MORTAR is a short-range weapon that is used to reach nearby targets that are protected by hills or other obstacles. A mortar fires a shell on a high arc that enables it to clear obstacles. It has a higher angle of fire, shorter barrel, and lower muzzle *velocity* (speed) than a gun or a howitzer. Mortars are light, can be moved easily, and have greater firepower. For example, the 81-millimeter mortar can fire a 12-pound shell about 2,500 yards.

A mortar consists of a tube closed at the *breech* (bottom) end, that rests on a base plate. Two adjustable legs support the muzzle end. Soldiers fire the

mortar by dropping the ammunition down the muzzle of the tube. When the ammunition reaches the bottom, it strikes the firing pin, which explodes the *primer*. Most mortar shells have fins to prevent them from tumbling in the air. Artillery mortars have *bore* diameters of 105 millimeters or larger. Infantry mortars have diameters less than 105 millimeters.

Before World War II, armies used heavy, stubby mortars. Large mortars were also used to defend coastlines. But howitzers have largely replaced these heavy mortars in present-day warfare. The lightweight and easily moved infantry mortar became an important weapon during World War II.

See also CIVIL WAR (picture); GUN; HOWITZER.

JOHN D. BILLINGSLEY

MORTARBOARD. See CAPS AND GOWNS.

MORTE DARTHUR. See MALORY, SIR THOMAS.

U.S. Army

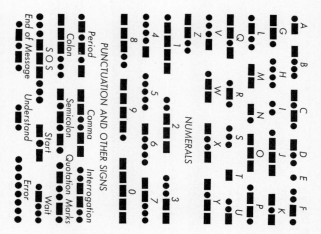

The 81-mm Mortar has a maximum firing range of 10,500 feet. It was one of the most effective weapons used in World War II.

MORTGAGE, *MAWR gihj.* A farmer wishes to increase the output of his farm by adding modern machinery, but is short of ready money. Or a husband and wife wish to buy a home of their own, but their savings are less than the cost of the house.

These persons can have what they want by arranging with a bank, building and loan association, or private investor for a loan which amounts to part of the property's value. A *mortgage* on the property is given as security for the debt. The mortgage gives to the lender the right to take over the property if the debt is not paid. The person who borrows the money is called the *mortgagor*, and the person who lends it is called the *mortgagee.* The word *mortgage* comes from two French words, and means *dead pledge*, because when the debt has been paid, the mortgage becomes void, or "dead."

The Mortgage Deed is a formal document setting forth an accurate description of the property and a clear statement of the terms of the loan. The mortgage may contain a clause declaring the entire debt payable if the mortgagor fails at any time to pay interest or taxes on the property. Unlike the ordinary real estate mortgage, which contains two parties, the corporate mortgage usually involves three parties: the corporation, the *bondholders*, or lenders, and the trustees. Where the trustee is used, the mortgage is turned over to the third party in a document called a *deed of trust.* The mortgage must be recorded in the county recorder's office. Otherwise, the mortgagee loses his rights in case an innocent third party should purchase the property for its market value, not realizing there was a mortgage against it.

Second Mortgage. A property with a mortgage against it may be mortgaged a second time. The second mortgage usually carries a higher rate of interest than the first, because it is much less safe. If a man must sell his property in order to pay off the mortgages, the holder of the second mortgage gets nothing until the claims of the first mortgage are fully satisfied.

Foreclosure. If the person who lends the money is not repaid on time, he may *foreclose* the mortgage. An officer of the court will then seize the property and transfer it to the person who lent the money. The mortgage allows the lender to take title to the property in this way as soon as the terms of the mortgage are not met. But one who forecloses a mortgage must usually put the property up for sale and give the original owner any amount received for it above the value of the mortgage. The laws of various states provide that the mortgagor may also be allowed the right to redeem the property within a stated period of time after the public sale.

In some states, the ancient idea of the mortgage has been changed. It is no longer regarded as a deed which gives the mortgagee title to the property, and which may be voided. Instead, it is considered a *lien* on the property, which gives the mortgagee the right to have the property sold in order to satisfy the mortgage debt.

Chattel Mortgage. A mortgage may be given on personal property as well as on real estate. A farmer may mortgage a crop that has been planted but has not yet ripened. A merchant may give a mortgage on the goods on his shelves, even though they are sold and replaced again and again.

See also HOUSING AND URBAN DEVELOPMENT, DEPARTMENT OF.

L. T. FLATLEY

MORTGAGE BOND. See BOND.

MORTICIAN, *mawr TISH un,* is a person who prepares the dead for burial. He is often called an *undertaker* or *funeral director.* The mortician is a necessary, respected member of every community. His job includes preservation and restoration of the bodies of the dead, sanitation in order to protect the health of the living, and consolation of the mourners.

The mortician *preserves* bodies from decay by removing the blood and body fluids, and injecting a preserving fluid into the arteries. He *restores* a body by preparing a lifelike representation of the dead person. Mortuary science has developed many skills that make it possible for morticians to re-create a natural appearance, even after accidental death or prolonged sickness. Facial treatments and natural hair styles are particularly effective.

Since early times, the mortician has had the responsibility of protecting the community from possible contamination from decaying organic matter. Finally, the mortician is usually in a position to offer experienced and sympathetic counsel to the mourners.

The mortician cares for funeral arrangements. He obtains burial permits, notifies relatives and the newspapers, and plans with the clergyman for services in the home, in the church, in the funeral home, and at the grave. The funeral home has a chapel, a preparatory laboratory, and a casket selection room. The mortician's equipment usually includes a hearse, flower-car, limousines, and an ambulance.

In Early Times. The earliest morticians were ancient Egyptian priests and their assistants, who specialized in the preservation of bodies. The Egyptians believed that the *Ka*, or soul, needed a body in order to survive in the next world. They thought that the soul visited the preserved body in the grave, and ate food that had been placed there. For this reason, the Egyptians built elaborate tombs, and furnished them with great care. They built huge tombs under the ground, and others as vast monuments, such as the Pyramids. In early Egypt, about 4000 B.C., morticians used spices, resins, gums, unguents, soda solutions, pitch, and oils to preserve bodies for burial. They sometimes separated the brain and vital organs from the body, and preserved them in earthen jars. They often wrapped the bodies of the dead in linen cloth.

The *libitanarius*, or funeral director, in ancient Rome supervised the elaborate and expensive torchlight processions and burials given to socially prominent and wealthy persons.

Barber-surgeons took care of embalming in England during the 1600's, and undertakers attended only to funeral arrangements. Later, undertakers began to serve as embalmers.

As a Career. American embalmers and funeral directors receive licenses from the individual states. Requirements vary, but most states require an applicant to complete courses in biology, anatomy, and related subjects in an accredited school of mortuary science. An applicant must usually pass a state examination and serve as an apprentice before he receives a license to practice. A college education is a decided preprofessional advantage.

CHARLES L. WALLIS

See also EMBALMING; FUNERAL CUSTOMS; MUMMY.

MORTON, JOHN

MORTON, JOHN (1724-1777), was a Pennsylvania signer of the Declaration of Independence. He served in the Continental Congress from 1774 to 1777. Morton began his political career in 1756 as a member of the Pennsylvania Assembly. He served in the assembly for nearly 20 years. He also served as an associate judge of the Pennsylvania state Supreme Court. He served as one of four Pennsylvania delegates to the Stamp Act Congress in 1765 (see STAMP ACT). Morton was born in Ridley, Pa.
ROBERT J. TAYLOR

MORTON, JULIUS STERLING (1832-1902), an American political leader and nature lover, established the first United States observance of Arbor Day (see ARBOR DAY). Morton was secretary of agriculture from 1893 to 1897 in President Grover Cleveland's Cabinet. He was secretary of the Nebraska territory from 1858 to 1861, and also served as acting governor for several months. He was born in Adams, N.Y., and received degrees from the University of Michigan and Union College. Nebraska placed a statue of Morton in the Statuary Hall Collection in 1937.
ARTHUR A. EKIRCH, JR.

Neb. State Historical Society
Julius Sterling Morton

MORTON, LEVI PARSONS (1824-1920), served as Vice-President of the United States from 1889 to 1893, under President Benjamin Harrison. He also was minister to France from 1881 to 1885, and governor of New York in 1895 and 1896. Morton was a Republican. His political success started in 1879 when he was elected to a term in the House of Representatives from New York.

He entered the banking business during the Civil War, and became a prominent New York City banker. His company, through its London branch, was fiscal agent of the United States from 1873 to 1884. He taught school and owned a dry goods firm in New Hampshire before he became a banker. Morton was born in Shoreham, Vt.
IRVING G. WILLIAMS

MORTON, OLIVER PERRY (1823-1877), served as governor of Indiana during the Civil War and as a Republican United States senator from 1867 until his death. He was elected lieutenant governor in 1860, and became governor in 1861 when Governor Henry Lane resigned to enter the Senate. As governor, Morton helped raise volunteer troops. He raised money through his own efforts to support troops when the Indiana legislature refused to grant him funds. While in the Senate, he served as an adviser to President Ulysses S. Grant. Morton was born in Wayne County, Indiana. Indiana placed a statue of Morton in the Statuary Hall Collection in 1900.
W. B. HESSELTINE

Culver
Levi Parsons Morton

MORTON, WILLIAM THOMAS GREEN (1819-1868), an American dentist, introduced ether as an anesthetic for painless dentistry. Morton made the first public demonstration of ether in 1846, and took full responsibility for its effects. Crawford W. Long used ether during surgery in 1842, but he did not make his discovery public until 1848 (see LONG, CRAWFORD W.).

Morton first used ether in extracting a tooth from a patient. He used it at the suggestion of Charles T. Jackson of the Harvard Medical School. Morton had experimented with ether on animals and on himself. He used ether a second time in 1846 in an operation performed by John C. Warren at the Massachusetts General Hospital. Morton called his anesthesia *letheon.*

The method spread rapidly to England, France, and other countries. In 1852, the French Academy of Science awarded the Montyon prize of 5,000 francs jointly to Jackson and Morton. Both men claimed sole credit for the discovery, and Morton refused to share the prize with Jackson. A bitter quarrel followed, and Morton spent much of his later life in lawsuits, which ruined him financially. Morton was born on Aug. 9, 1819, in Charlton, Mass.
GEORGE ROSEN
See also ANESTHESIA; ETHER.

Brown Bros.
William Morton

MORTON ARBORETUM. See ARBORETUM; ILLINOIS (Places to Visit).

MOSAIC, *moh ZAY ik,* is a decoration made by fitting together small pieces of colored glass, stone, or other material. The pieces are set in cement to form a pattern on some surface, usually a floor, wall, or ceiling. The colored pieces are called *tesserae.* Marble is generally used for floors, and glass for walls. A flat, decorative design is best suited for mosaics.

Mosaics were widely used during Greek, Roman, and early Christian times. Mosaic floors found in Roman ruins in Italy, Great Britain, and the Middle East give an idea of Roman luxury. Excavators found a famous mosaic, the Alexander mosaic, in the ruins of Pompeii. Mosaics served as the main decorations for floors and *apses,* or alcoves, in Byzantine buildings. Churches like Saint Sophia in Istanbul, Saint Mark's in Venice, and several in Ravenna, Italy, contain especially beautiful Byzantine mosaics. Both Byzantine and early Christian mosaics in Rome made use of flat, decorative designs.

The Indians of Latin America also knew how to make mosaics. Fine examples of stone mosaics have been found in the temples of Mitla near Oaxaca, Mexico, and the Temple of the Warriors at Chichén Itzá, in Yucatán, Mexico. Mosaics also decorate Mexico City's University City.

In the United States, the Cathedral of Saint John the Divine, in New York City, contains fine mosaics by Louis Tiffany. The work of Frederick Wilson in the Wade Memorial Chapel, in Cleveland, is also a notable example of mosaic work.

See also BYZANTINE ART (Painting and Mosaics; pictures); BRAZIL (picture: Life is Brightened).
WILLIAM M. MILLIKEN

Byzantine Mosaics decorate the upper walls and vaulted ceilings of St. Mark's Cathedral in Venice, Italy. The magnificent, colored-glass designs picture many scenes from the Bible, such as the *Drunkenness of Noah,* above.

An Italian Mosaic of an old ship and part of a lighthouse, *left,* was unearthed during the excavation of Ostia, an ancient military and commercial port of Rome. Roman architecture made much use of elaborate mosaic decorations.

MOSAICS

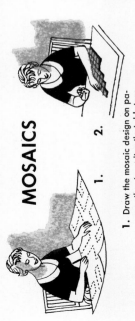

1. Draw the mosaic design on paper, then trace it on the table top.
2. Cement the tiles along the edge first, working toward the center.
3. After the cement hardens, apply grout, or filler, to fill cracks.
4. An hour later, polish the finished surface with a soft cloth.

The Finished Mosaic Design makes a handsome table top.

MOSAIC DISEASE is a plant disease caused by a virus. The leaves of affected plants become mottled with light and dark-green blotches. The disease usually stunts the growth of plants, and may cause flowers to become streaked and twisted. Plants attacked by the disease include beans, carnations, orchids, potatoes, sweet peas, tobacco, and wheat, and weeds such as burweed and milkweed. Insects, such as aphids, often transmit the virus from diseased plants to healthy ones. Gardeners protect plants by using insecticides to control insects. There is no cure for a plant that has mosaic disease, and it should be removed and burned.

Diseased plants should never be divided or used for cuttings because every part is infected. HENRY T. NORTHEN

MOSBY, *MOZE bih,* **JOHN SINGLETON** (1833-1916), was a famous Confederate ranger during the Civil War. He joined the Confederate cavalry in 1861, and served on "Jeb" Stuart's staff in 1862. He began his independent ranger activities in 1863. His raids on Union bases and camps were so effective that part of north-central Virginia soon became known as "Mosby's Confederacy." After the war, Mosby practiced law and held several public offices. He was born in Powhatan County, Virginia.

FRANK E. VANDIVER

Weston Kemp

Red Square lies in the heart of Moscow. At one end stands famous St. Basil's Church, left, near Lenin's tomb, center, Spasskaya Tower, right, rises above a gate in the Kremlin walls.

MOSCOW

MOSCOW, *MAHS koh,* is the capital and largest city of Russia. It is the fifth largest city in the world, and ranks second in size only to London among all European cities. Moscow also is the capital of the Russian Soviet Federated Socialist Republic. This state is the largest and most important of the 15 republics that make up Russia.

About a million *Muscovites* (people of Moscow) work in the city's many government offices. The Russian Communist Party, which controls the government, has its headquarters in Moscow. It influences Communists throughout the world. Many decisions made in Moscow affect millions of persons on all continents.

Moscow was once the home of Russia's czars, and the city has many old palaces and museums filled with art treasures. Today, Moscow is a crowded industrial community. A Russian must have permission from the government to live in Moscow. If he lives in Moscow and wants to move somewhere else in the city, he also must have official permission. These restrictions help keep the residential sections from becoming too crowded.

Large new factories stand near huge apartment buildings in Moscow's main residential areas. The city's chief industry is the manufacture of automobiles, buses,

and trucks. Other important products include chemicals, electrical machinery, and textiles. Moscow is also the cultural center of Russia. Its ballet performances especially are world famous.

Moscow lies in the north-central part of European Russia, about 400 miles southeast of Leningrad. The Moscow River flows through the city. Moscow is built in the shape of a huge wheel. Many wide boulevards extend from the center of the city like the spokes of a wheel. They cross two circular boulevards, which form inner and outer rims of the wheel.

Famous Landmarks. At the center of the wheel stands the Kremlin. This old fortress is the center of the Russian government. Inside its 1½-mile-long walls are beautiful cathedrals and palaces, as well as government buildings. Some of the cathedrals date from the 1400's. Many czars are buried in the Cathedral of the Archangel. The Supreme Soviet, Russia's parliament, meets in the Grand Kremlin Palace. See KREMLIN.

Red Square lies just outside the Kremlin walls. This large plaza, nearly a quarter of a mile long, took its name in Russian from an old word meaning both *beautiful* and *red.* There, huge military and civilian parades celebrate the anniversary of the Russian Revolution and other special occasions. Some of these parades include hundreds of thousands of marchers, and last several hours. Russian leaders watch the parades from atop the Lenin Mausoleum. Thousands of Russians

Richard Antony French, the contributor of this article, is Lecturer in the University College and School of Slavonic and East European Studies at the University of London.

678

line up daily at the tomb to view the preserved body of Lenin, the founder of Communist Russia.

Opposite the Kremlin on Red Square is GUM, Russia's largest department store. Famous Saint Basil's Church is also on Red Square. This 400-year-old building is part of the State Historical Museum. It has eight many-colored, onion-shaped domes. The Hotel Rossia, one of the world's largest hotels, faces the Kremlin and Red Square.

Muscovites are proud of their subway system, called the *Metro*. The city has more than 70 subway stations, which look like palace halls and are the fanciest in the world. Each is designed differently. Many are beautifully decorated with chandeliers, marble panels, paintings, stained glass, and statues.

Sports and Recreation. Muscovites have many facilities for recreation. Luzhniki, a huge sports area, includes Lenin Stadium, which can seat about 103,000 persons. The stadium is used mostly for soccer, a kind of football, the people's favorite sport, and for track events. A soccer club called Dynamo has Moscow's second largest stadium.

Every year, about seven million persons go to Gorki Park, Moscow's most popular amusement center. It has an open-air theater, various exhibits, and facilities for such sports as boating, ice skating, and tennis. Many chess champions play at the Central Chess Club. In winter, the hills near Moscow attract skiers.

Music and Art. The Bolshoi Theater presents ballets that many persons consider Russia's highest artistic achievement. Young dancers from all parts of Russia are trained at the Bolshoi Theater's school. The Symphony Orchestra of the U.S.S.R. performs at the Tchaikovsky Conservatory. Moscow also has many famous drama theaters, such as the Maly and Moscow Art theaters.

The city has about 150 museums and art galleries. The State Historical Museum attracts many students of early Russian history. The Central Lenin Museum and the Museum of the Revolution have exhibits on the Russian Revolution. Dazzling treasures of the czars are displayed in the Armory Museum in the Kremlin.

Schools. Moscow State University is the oldest and largest university in Russia. It was established in 1755, and has more than 30,000 students. The science building, 37 stories high, is Moscow's tallest skyscraper. Moscow has more than a thousand elementary schools and high schools, and over 80 colleges.

About 3,000 main and branch libraries operate throughout Moscow. The Lenin State Library, the largest library in Russia, has one of the largest collections of books and manuscripts in the world.

Economy. Moscow is the most important industrial city in Russia. Its factories produce a wide variety of products, but chiefly automobiles, buses, and trucks. Other important products include chemicals, electrical machinery, measuring instruments, steel, and textiles. About a million persons work in Moscow's factories. Moscow is the transportation center of Russia. Highways and railways extend in all directions from the city to most parts of the country. Moscow also has three

---

FACTS IN BRIEF

Population: 6,507,000.
Area: 342 square miles.
Altitude: 625 feet above sea level.
Climate: *Average temperature*—January, 14° F.; July, 66° F. *Average annual precipitation* (rainfall, melted snow, and other forms of moisture)—24 inches.
Government: City Soviet of about 1,100 deputies, headed by a chairman (two-year terms).
Founded: 1147.

MOSCOW

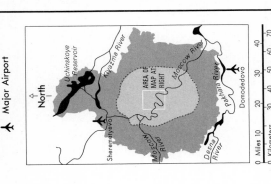

..... City Limits
▨ Forest-Park Zone
✈ Major Airport

North

Uchinskoye Reservoir
Klyazma River
Sheremetyevo
Moscow River
AREA OF MAP AT RIGHT
Moscow River
Desna River
Pakhara River
Domodedovo

0 Miles 10   20   30   40   50   60   70
0 Kilometers

INNER MOSCOW

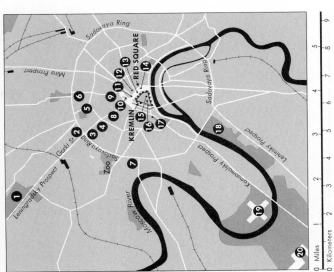

Sadovaya Ring
Mira Prospect
RED SQUARE
KREMLIN
Leningradsky Prospect
Gorki St.
Zoo
Sadovaya Ring
Sadovaya Ring
Moscow River
Komsomolsky Prospect
Leninsky Prospect

0 Miles   1   2   3   4   5
0 Kilometers   1 2 3 4 5 6 7 8 9

■ Rail Line and Station
▬ Major Street
▨ Park

WORLD BOOK map-FGA

679

major airports, the largest of which is in Domodedovo, southwest of the city. The famous subway system, the Metro, has more than 60 miles of track. More than 3½ million passengers ride it daily. The Moscow Canal links the city to the great Volga River.

More than 1,400 magazines and about 30 newspapers are published in Moscow. Some of the newspapers are among the largest in the world. They include *Pravda* (Truth), published by the Communist Party, and *Izvestia* (News), the official government paper. Radio Moscow, operated by the government, broadcasts programs on four channels. The Central Television Studios, also government operated, transmit on two channels.

Government. Moscow is governed by a *City Soviet* (City Council), elected every two years. Before an election, the city is divided into districts of 6,000 persons each. More than a thousand districts are created in this way, and each district elects one deputy to the City Soviet. Every district has only one candidate. He is nominated by the Communist Party or by such organizations as school groups, sports clubs, and trade unions. The candidate is elected unless most of the voters cross his name off the ballot.

The City Soviet elects one of its deputies as chairman. It also chooses an Executive Committee to govern Moscow between legislative sessions. All buildings and all public services such as education and transportation are managed by 30 city departments. The city government also supervises some industries. Moscow is divided into 17 wards. Each ward has its own elected soviet and executive committee.

History. Moscow was founded in 1147 by Yuri Dolgoruki, a prince of the region. The town lay on an important land and water trade routes, and it grew and prospered. During the 1200's, Tartar invaders from Asia conquered Moscow and other Russian lands. The Russian princes were forced to recognize the Tartars as their rulers, and pay them taxes.

During the 1300's, the Moscow princes collected taxes in their region for the Tartars. In exchange for increasing the taxes, the princes were granted more territory. The Moscow princes took land from rival princes with Tartar help. By the late 1400's, Moscow had become the most powerful Russian city. Moscow threw off Tartar control during the late 1400's under Ivan III, who was called Ivan the Great. His grandson, Ivan IV, later called Ivan the Terrible, was crowned czar of all Russia in 1547.

Moscow grew rapidly during the 1600's. The czars built palaces in the Kremlin, and noblemen built mansions. New churches and monasteries arose, and industries developed. Many merchants, traders, and workers settled in the city. In 1703, Peter I, called Peter the Great, began building a new capital at St. Petersburg (now Leningrad). But Moscow remained an important center of culture, industry, and trade.

In the fall of 1812, invading French troops under Napoleon entered Moscow without a struggle. Most of the people had abandoned the city. Soon afterward, a fire believed set by the Russians destroyed most of Moscow. After 35 days, the French left the city and began a disastrous retreat through the snow and cold. In 1905 and again in 1917, fierce revolutions against

the czar took place in several Russian cities, including Moscow. In the October Revolution of 1917, the government fell into the hands of the Bolsheviks (later called Communists). They moved the Russian capital back to Moscow in 1918.

Moscow grew rapidly during the 1930's. In World War II (1939-1945), German troops advanced almost to the city but never captured it. German air raids damaged Moscow, however. During the 1950's, the crowded city began a large-scale program of erecting apartment buildings. In 1960, the government more than doubled Moscow's city limits. A six-mile-wide zone of forests and parks was established around it. By the late 1960's, more than 100,000 apartments were being built in Moscow every year. RICHARD ANTONY FRENCH

See also RUSSIA (pictures); EUROPE (color pictures).

MOSCOW ART THEATER became one of the most influential theaters of the 1900's. It presents plays by major Russian authors and has made several tours of Western countries. The theater is best known for its productions of plays by the Russian authors Anton Chekhov, Maxim Gorki, and Leo Tolstoy. One of the theater's founders, Konstantin Stanislavski, developed his *Method* style of acting there. The style stresses psychological realism in the interpretation and presentation of plays. The Method technique has had great impact on Western theater.

The Moscow Art Theater was founded in 1898 by Stanislavski and Vladimir Nemirovich-Danchenko. Its production in 1898 of Chekhov's *The Seagull* started his career as a successful playwright.

See also STANISLAVSKI, KONSTANTIN; DRAMA (picture: Realism and Naturalism).

MOSELEY, HENRY GWYN-JEFFREYS (1887-1915), was a British physicist noted for his research on X rays. About 1913, he discovered a systematic relationship between X-ray spectra and the atomic number of the elements emitting the X rays. This discovery allowed scientists to determine the atomic number of unknown elements and to arrange them in the proper places in the Periodic Table (see ELEMENT, CHEMICAL).

Moseley was born in Weymouth, England, on Nov. 23, 1887. He was educated at Oxford University. He did research work there and at Manchester under Lord Rutherford, the physicist.

During World War I, Moseley was killed in the invasion of Gallipoli, in August, 1915. As a result of this loss, the British government assigned its scientists to noncombat duties during World War II. RALPH E. LAPP

MOSELLE. See WINE.

MOSELLE RIVER, *moh* ⟨ZEL, or *maw* ⟨ZEL, a branch of the Rhine River, rises in the Vosges Mountains in eastern France. It flows northeastward for 314 miles and empties into the Rhine in Koblenz, West Germany. It is called the *Mosel* in Germany. Much of the Moselle is of little use to navigation because it is very shallow. However, a 170-mile canal finished in 1964 enables barge traffic to go about 200 miles up the river. The famous Moselle wines are produced along the river's banks, especially near Trier. Major iron and steel works line the Moselle's banks in eastern France.

The Moselle was the scene of bitter fighting during World Wars I and II. Twice in World War I the Germans followed the river for nearly its whole length during the Allied drives on Paris.

ROBERT E. DICKINSON

School of St. Rocco, Venice (Anderson from Art Reference Bureau)

Moses Strikes a Rock with a rod to provide water for the Israelites wandering in the desert. God refused to permit Moses to enter the Promised Land because he hit the rock twice instead of once, thus doubting God's power. The story is told in the Book of Numbers, chapter 20. This dramatic version of the episode was painted by Tintoretto, a famous Italian painter of the 1500's.

MOSES was the great leader chosen by God to deliver the Israelites from slavery in Egypt and to give them a code of laws by which they could govern themselves in their new home, Palestine.

His Early Life. After 430 years of living in Egypt (Exodus 12:40), the Israelites had grown to a large population. The Egyptian government feared that they would become too numerous to control. And so the king (Pharaoh) of Egypt ordered that all baby boys born to Israelites be killed. Moses was born to Israelite parents during this period. They risked death by keeping him alive in their own home for three months. Then they placed him in a waterproof basket in the rushes along the Nile River.

There, the baby was discovered by a daughter of the king. She reared him in her palace as her own adopted son. His sister, who had been watching the basket, suggested his own mother as his nurse. During his childhood years, she taught him all about his own people, the Israelites.

When Moses was 40 years old, he saw an Israelite slave being brutally beaten. Moses intervened to protect the slave. In doing so, he had to kill the Egyptian doing the beating. Moses then ran away from Egypt to save his own life.

He found refuge with a Midianite priest named Jethro, who lived near Mount Sinai. Later Moses married Jethro's daughter, Zipporah. There, Moses lived the quiet life of a shepherd for about 40 years. Then one day the Lord spoke to him from a burning bush and called upon him to go back to Egypt and lead the Israelites out of the land of their enslavement. He was to bring them into Palestine, in the land of Canaan, where their ancestors had lived. Moses felt completely unable to perform this task. But God promised to help him and give him all the power he needed to persuade the people to follow him. God promised to help him force the Egyptian Pharaoh to let the Israelites go.

Moses the Leader. When Moses returned to Egypt, the former king (possibly Thutmose III) had died, and his son (probably Amenhotep II) had taken his place. But this new Pharaoh proved to be stubborn, and refused to let the Israelites leave his land. Nine times Moses directed by God (Exodus 7-11) to threaten Egypt with a terrible plague if Pharaoh would not release them. After each plague struck Egypt, the king promised to let the Israelites go. But, each time, as soon as the plague was over, he broke his promise.

Finally, in the tenth plague, the oldest son of the king and all the other first-born sons in Egypt died on the night of Passover, and only the Israelites were unharmed. This plague at last forced Pharaoh to let all the Israelites go. He let them take all their women and children, their livestock, and their property. The Lord told the Israelites to celebrate the anniversary of the Passover from then on, because that was the night the Death Angel had passed by the homes where the blood of the Passover lamb had been sprinkled on the doorway, and the Egyptians had been forced to release the Israelites from slavery (see PASSOVER).

But Pharaoh changed his mind again, and wanted his former slaves back. The slowly-moving multitude of Israelites had just come to the edge of the Red Sea when the Egyptian chariots caught up to them. God told Moses to stretch forth his rod towards the waters of the Red Sea. This miraculously parted the waters and left a dry path for the Israelites to walk across. Just as they reached the other side safely, the Egyptian chariots started across after them. But suddenly the waters swirled back into place, and all the Egyptian pursuers were drowned. See RED SEA (picture).

The Great Works of Moses. Moses then led his people over to Mount Sinai, where the Lord spoke to them directly and offered to make them His chosen people. When they promised to be true to Him, He gave them the Ten Commandments (Exodus 20:1-17), then revealed the other laws and regulations privately to Moses. Moses communed with the Lord for 40 days at the top of Mount Sinai (see SINAI; TEN COMMANDMENTS).

While Moses was on the mountain, the Israelites fell into grievous sin. They had a golden image made for themselves, consisting of a calf or young bull, such as the Egyptians worshiped. When Moses saw them sacrificing to this idol and dancing before it, he became so angry that he threw to the ground the tablets he had carried down from the mountain. These tablets contained the Ten Commandments. Many of the Israelites were killed in punishment for this sin. After they repented, Moses went back up the mountain to plead for them before the Lord. There he received a new copy of the Ten Commandments for his people.

Under God's direction, Moses also wrote the books of Exodus, Leviticus, and Numbers during his 40 years of wandering in the wilderness of Sinai. To explain the early history of the Hebrew people, he wrote Genesis, with its record of the promises God had made to Abraham and his descendants, as well as the origin of the world and of mankind.

During the last year or two of his life, Moses wrote the book of Deuteronomy. It was a convenient and practical summary of God's law and a reminder to the Hebrews always to remain faithful to the one true God. Thus, we are indebted to Moses for writing the first five books of the Bible, under God's direction and guidance. Some scholars have questioned whether Moses really wrote these books, but for the most part both Jews and Christians have always honored Moses as their author.

After receiving the plans from God for building a large tent or "tabernacle" for His worship, Moses had it built exactly as he had been told. On the great day of its dedication, the Tabernacle was set up, the sacrifices were offered on the altar, and a dazzling, bright "glory cloud" settled down over the hallowed place to show that God was present in the midst of His people, to bless and protect them (see TABERNACLE.) In order to serve in this Tabernacle, the whole tribe of Levi, to which Moses belonged, was set apart at a solemn service of consecration. His older brother, Aaron, was anointed to be chief priest, in charge of all the worship and sacrifices presented by the Israelites to God (see AARON).

Journey to Canaan. From Mount Sinai, Moses led his people to the border of Canaan, intending to lead them in and conquer the land. But the Israelites lost courage there. They heard how strong and well armed the Canaanites were, and they rebelled against Moses and the Lord Himself. Therefore, they had to spend the next 40 years wandering up and down in the wilderness, until the older generation had finally died. Their children grew up to be brave soldiers, and Moses led them against the tribes living on the east side of the River Jordan and conquered them.

God did not permit Moses to lead the Israelites across the river to Canaan, because at Kadesh he and Aaron had taken to themselves the glory that belonged to God (Num. 20). This was left to Joshua (see JOSHUA). But Moses was permitted a view of the promised land from the top of Mount Nebo before he died. Moses was mourned by his grateful people, and was honored ever afterwards as the founder of the Israelite commonwealth.

See also DEUTERONOMY; EXODUS; JEWS (Beginnings); ART AND THE ARTS (picture).

GLEASON L. ARCHER, JR.

Grandma Moses Properties, Inc., New York City

Out for the Christmas Trees by Grandma Moses shows the innocence and charm of her paintings. She began to paint when she was 76, and painted 25 pictures in the year after her 100th birthday. She took her subjects from memories of her life on farms in northern New York and Virginia.

Grandma Moses Properties, Inc.; Polaroid Land Photograph

Grandma Moses, *left,* began painting when she was 76 years old. Her gaily colored pictures of the upstate New York countryside hang in many art museums today.

MOSES, GRANDMA (1860-1961), was an American primitive painter. She started painting when she was 76 years old and remained active until near her death. She never had an art lesson. Grandma Moses painted simple but realistic scenes of rural life. These colorful and lively pictures were based on memories of her own youth in the late 1800's. Critics have praised her work for its freshness, innocence, and humanity.

Grandma Moses was born ANNA MARY ROBERTSON in Washington County, New York. She was married to Thomas Moses in 1887. For many years, she em-broidered pictures on canvas. She began to paint when arthritis made it difficult for her to hold embroidery needles. An art dealer first discovered her paintings in 1938, and she was represented in a show at the Museum of Modern Art in New York City in 1939. Her first one-man show was in 1940. Her autobiography, *My Life's History,* was published in 1952.   EDWIN L. FULWIDER

MOSHAV. See ISRAEL (Agriculture).
MOSLEM LEAGUE. See INDIA (History).

683

MOSLEMS

MOSLEMS are people who practice the religion of Islam, preached by Mohammed in the A.D. 600's. The term *Moslem* comes from the Arabic word *Muslim*, meaning *one who submits* (to God). There are about 465 million Moslems throughout the world today. They form the majority of the population in the Middle East, North Africa, and such southeast Asian nations as Pakistan, Malaysia, and Indonesia. There are about 15,000 Moslems in the United States.

The first Moslems, the Arabs, began in the 600's to establish an empire that eventually stretched from the Atlantic Ocean to the borders of China. This empire absorbed many peoples and their cultures. The Moslems have been called the standardbearers of learning during the Middle Ages. They transmitted much of the knowledge of the ancient world, and helped lay the foundations for Western culture. Arab Moslems made such an impact on the Middle East that today much of the area is known as the *Arab world*. Arabic is its major language, and Islam its chief religion.

Early Period

Before Mohammed. Islam first began in Arabia. In ancient times, the pagan Arabs were organized into tribes which formed two distinct groups. By 100 B.C., the southern tribes had become powerful enough to establish several Arab kingdoms. One of the northern tribes, the Quraysh, later gained control of Mecca. This city lay on the main trade route from Yemen to Syria and Egypt. They built the city into a powerful commercial center.

At that time, the Arabs worshiped nature and idols. Their chief gods were al-Lat, al-Uzza, and Manat. The Kaaba, the most famous shrine in Arabia, stood in Mecca. The city attracted religious pilgrims, traders, and settlers from all Arabia and neighboring countries. Jews and Christians mixed freely with the Arabs. Many Arabs were converted to Judaism and Christianity.

The Prophet. Mohammed was born about A.D. 570, and grew up in Mecca. His family belonged to the Quraysh tribe. Mohammed was disturbed by the injustices of life in Mecca and because the people worshiped idols. When he was about 40, he experienced a vision in which he was called to be a prophet of God. Mohammed began to preach the punishment of evildoers. He urged the Arabs to worship the one God and to accept him as God's prophet.

The people of Mecca were frightened and angered by Mohammed's preachings, and began to oppose him. Mohammed went secretly to Medina, a town about 200 miles from Mecca. The people there had agreed to accept him as God's messenger and ruler. Mohammed's *Hegira*, or *Emigration*, took place in A.D. 622. Moslems count that year as the beginning of the Islamic Era. Mohammed began to attack caravans from Mecca. In 630, through diplomacy, he occupied the city. See MOHAMMED.

The First Caliphs.
After Mohammed's death in 632, rulers later called *caliphs* led the Moslems (see CALIPH). The first four caliphs, called the *rightly guided*, and several famous Arab military leaders accomplished the first

The Spread of Islam

major expansion of the Moslem world. This expansion resulted from both political and religious motives. With these conquests, the Arabs took an important place in world history.

Mohammed gained control of most of Arabia when he took Mecca. But some tribes revolted after the prophet's death. Abu Bakr, the first caliph, subdued them and restored them to Islam. He also sent successful Arab forces into the Byzantine provinces of Syria and Palestine, and the Persian province of Iraq. These *holy wars* continued under the caliphs Omar, who ruled from 634 to 644, and Othman, who ruled from 644 to 656. The Moslems occupied the Persian capital of Ctesiphon. They also annexed the Byzantine provinces of Syria, Palestine, and Egypt, and part of North Africa. The Persians failed in their last attempt to regain their empire during the caliphate of Ali, who ruled from 656 to 661.

The Omayyad Caliphs,
who ruled from 661 to 750, led the Arab Moslems to new victories. The caliphate was founded by the caliph Muawiya. He was a member of the aristocratic Meccan family of Umayyah, from which the caliphate takes its name. The Omayyads established their capital at Damascus in 661. They fought the Turkish tribes in Central Asia, sent an expedition into Sindh in India, and reached the borders of China. Under these caliphs, the Moslems also fought the Byzantines in Asia Minor and around the Mediterranean Sea. They twice laid siege to Constantinople (now Istanbul), but without success. The Moslems captured Cyprus, Rhodes, and Sicily, and completed the conquest of North Africa. Many Berbers were converted to Islam.

The Omayyads then turned to Europe, and invaded Spain in 711. A Moslem army crossed the Pyrenees Mountains and marched through southern France until Charles Martel turned it back in 732 near Tours. Many historians regard this battle as one of the most important ever fought, because it determined that Christianity, rather than Islam, would dominate Europe.

Gaining Converts.
The caliphs did not conquer new lands solely to gain converts, but many conquered peoples embraced Islam. Unlike the Byzantine Christians, the Moslem conquerors granted a large measure of religious tolerance. All non-Moslems had to pay a special tax in return for not serving in the Moslem army. But many worked as officers and tax collectors in the civil administration, and as doctors and tutors at the court. At first, only a few were converted to Islam. Gradually, the Moslems produced their own administrative and professional classes. Beginning about 750, conversion to Islam increased until Islam became the predominant religion in most of the conquered lands.

Division of Islam.
From the time of Mohammed's death in 632, several separate groups competed for leadership among the Moslems. In 750, two branches of Mohammed's family, the *Abbasids* and the *Shiites*, or *Alids*, overthrew the Omayyad caliphate. Dissatisfied Persians helped them. But a youthful Omayyad prince, Abd al-Rahman, escaped and made his way across North Africa to Spain. He subdued and pacified the rival Arab and Berber factions and established the Omayyad dynasty of Spain. The dynasty lasted from 756 to 1031. It had its capital at Córdoba.

In the East, the victors quarreled among themselves. The Abbasids outwitted the Shiites and established the Abbasid caliphate, also called the Caliphate of Bagh-

Moslems in a Great Mosque in Cairo, Egypt. The people face the East and have their shoes off. Prayer starts with the cry "La ilaha illa-llahu, Muhammad rasul allahi." This means, "There is no God but God, and Mohammed is His prophet."

dad. They ruled from 750 to 1258, and built the new capital city of Baghdad. Gradually, the Abbasid empire decayed, and independent dynasties sprang up. The Abbasid empire received its death blow when Baghdad fell to the Mongols in 1258. The Shiites, driven underground, agitated as a political and religious minority. One of their religious leaders, Ubaydullah, claimed descent from Fatima, the daughter of Mohammed. He founded the Fatimite dynasty, which lasted from 909 to 1171. This dynasty ruled North Africa, Egypt, Syria, Palestine, and the Hejaz. Cairo, Egypt, was its capital. See FATIMITE DYNASTY.

Moslem Influence in Europe

The Crusades. The Moslems threatened Christian Europe, and several wars resulted. The Christians of eastern and western Europe forgot their differences, and united in a series of wars called the *Crusades*. The Christians conquered Syria and Palestine, and captured Jerusalem in 1099. But a great Moslem general, Saladin, recaptured it for the Abbasids in 1187. The crusaders gradually lost ground, and retreated from Acre, their last stronghold in Syria, in 1291. See CRUSADES.

Moslem Learning. As a result of their conquests, Moslems came into contact with Greek science and philosophy, and with Persian history and literature. The Arabs became learned in these fields, and also developed a new science and literature of their own in Arabic. Moslem geographers explored many new areas. They also spread knowledge of other discoveries, including the Chinese inventions of paper and gunpowder, and the Hindu system of numerals (see ARABIC NUMERALS).

The Moslems not only honored learning, but also developed distinctive arts (see ISLAMIC ART). They also founded many academies and universities. The most famous were at Baghdad, Cairo, and Córdoba. Moslem scholars of many nations traveled freely throughout the Moslem world. European scholars traveled to Moslem countries, especially Spain, to study Islamic philosophy, mathematics, and medicine. They translated major Arabic works into Latin, the language of learning of the West. In this way, much of the knowledge of the classical world was preserved during the Middle Ages.

The Moslem Turks

Arabs dominated the early spread of Islam, and created the Moslem empire. An alien group, the Turks, invaded Moslem lands, and built their empire on the remains of the Abbasid empire.

The Seljuk Turks. Barbarian Turks of Central Asia challenged the Abbasid Caliphate of Baghdad in the 1000's. They were first led by Seljuk, and were named for him. The weak caliph had to receive them and honor their leader Tughril as *sultan*. The Seljuk Turks gained control of the Abbasid caliphs, but the Fatimites fought the Turkish invaders. The Seljuks became *Sunnite* Moslems and were among Islam's strongest supporters. After their last strong leader, Malikshah, died in 1092, they split into rival branches. See SELJUK.

The Ottoman Turks. Various newly converted Turkish tribes served with the Seljuks. One group, the Ottoman Turks, took their name from their leader Othman. They seized Anatolia in the 1300's and established the

Ottoman dynasty. This dynasty ruled the greatest Moslem state of modern times, with 36 sultans in a direct line from Othman in the 1300's to 1922. The Ottoman Turks fought the Mongols and put an end to the Byzantine Empire when they seized Constantinople in 1453. Their empire expanded rapidly in Asia and Europe. They conquered the Mameluke dynasty in Egypt in the early 1500's (see MAMELUKE). The Turkish sultans then assumed the title of *caliph*. They fought Christian Europe successfully until halted at Vienna in 1683.

Moslems Today

Colonialism. In 1700, three great Moslem empires existed: the Mogul empire in India, the Safavid empire in Persia, and the Ottoman empire in Turkey. The Mogul and Safavid empires came under the influence of European powers such as Great Britain and Russia and gradually disappeared. European expansion and economic control seriously weakened the Ottoman empire. By 1900, European colonial powers dominated most of the Moslem world. The French established themselves in North Africa, and the Dutch took Indonesia. Britain occupied Egypt and the Sudan, set up an empire in India, and ruled Malaya. In the 1900's, Italy seized territories in North Africa and the Levant.

European ideas also penetrated into Moslem countries and brought about many changes. Modern education and economic reform spread. The Moslem peoples wanted to be up-to-date, strong, and independent of their European masters.

Independence. Most Moslem peoples gained their independence in the 1900's. They form a highly important group of nations that stretches from the Atlantic Ocean to Indonesia. Some of the world's busiest trade and communications routes cross their territories. The chief problems of the newly independent Moslem countries have been to achieve stable governments and to feed their people. Some Moslem nations, such as Egypt and Pakistan, have too many people living on too little land. Other countries lack the moisture and fertile soil needed to produce food. None is truly industrialized yet. Old quarrels and conflicting interests keep the Moslem peoples from being united. But they are bound by religious and cultural ties and a common determination to resist colonialism.

Critically reviewed by ALI H. ABDEL KADER

See articles on countries where Moslems live, such as EGYPT. See also ISLAM with its Related Articles.

MOSQUE, *mahsk*, is a Moslem house of worship. The main features of a mosque include a *mihrab* (prayer niche pointing toward Mecca), a *minaret* (tower from which the people are called to prayer.) Many mosques have pointed domes, several minarets, and open courts where worshipers gather and wash their faces and limbs before praying. Ornate pillared archways often surround the courts.

Early mosques were often little more than fenced-in yards. Later, they became elaborate. When the Moslems conquered a city, they sometimes converted churches into mosques. A beautiful modern mosque is part of the Islamic Center, Washington, D.C. ALI H. ABDEL KADER

Related Articles in WORLD BOOK include:

Iran (picture)	Islamic Art (Mosques)
Islam (The Mosque)	Jerusalem (picture)	Mecca
	Minaret

MOSQUITIA. See MOSQUITO COAST.

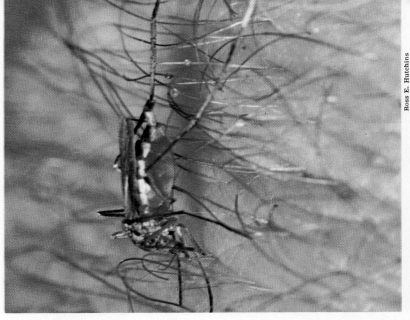

A **Culex Mosquito** plunges its sharp, needlelike mouth parts through a person's skin and sucks his blood.

Ross E. Hutchins

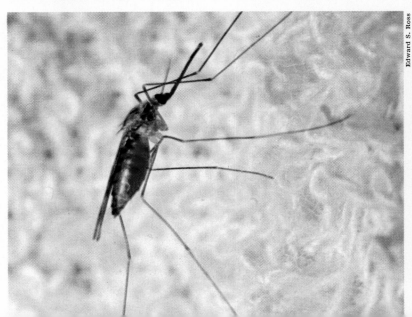

An **Anopheles Mosquito,** its abdomen swollen with a victim's blood, may rest for more than 24 hours after feeding.

Edward S. Ross

MOSQUITO is an insect that spreads some of the worst diseases of man and animals. Certain kinds of mosquitoes carry the germs that cause such serious diseases as encephalitis, malaria, and yellow fever. When a mosquito "bites," or even touches any object, it may leave germs behind. Many kinds of mosquitoes do not spread diseases, but they have painful "bites."

Mosquitoes are found in all parts of the world, even near the North Pole. Most kinds of mosquitoes that cause disease live in the hot, damp lands near the equator. Large numbers of mosquitoes are also found in the Arctic. In Alaska, northern Canada, and Siberia, mosquitoes often gather in great swarms that look like clouds. They attack men, interfering with such work as fishing, lumbering, and mining. There are more than 2,000 kinds of mosquitoes, and about 150 of them live in the United States.

Man controls mosquitoes in many ways. Scientists have developed chemicals called *insecticides*, which kill mosquitoes and other insects. Small amounts of these chemicals kill mosquitoes when sprayed in homes, garages, and other buildings. Thick mists of insecticides may be sprayed into fields, forests, and gardens.

Dale W. Jenkins, the contributor of this article, is Assistant Director of Bioscience Programs at the National Aeronautics and Space Administration.

Man also controls mosquitoes by destroying the places in which they grow. Mosquitoes lay their eggs in marshes, swamps, and other pools of quiet water. Engineers may build canals through marshes to drain off the water, and often fill small pools and swamps with soil. They also spread thin layers of oil or insecticides on top of the water.

Most kinds of mosquitoes are $\frac{1}{8}$ of an inch to $\frac{1}{4}$ of an inch long. Among the smallest is a mosquito of Formosa that measures about $\frac{1}{16}$ of an inch from the tip of one wing to the tip of the other. One of the largest is the American gallinipper. It grows about $\frac{2}{5}$ of an inch long, and is about $\frac{2}{5}$ of an inch from wing tip to wing tip.

The hum of a mosquito is the sound of its wings beating. A mosquito's wings move about 1,000 times a second. A female's wings make a higher tone than a

FACTS IN BRIEF

Names: *Male,* none; *female,* none; *young,* wrigglers or tumblers; *group,* swarm.

Number of Eggs: 100 to 300 at a time, depending on species. As many as 1,000 a year for each female.

Length of Life: 30 days or more for female; 10 to 20 days for male.

Where Found: All parts of the world.

Scientific Classification: Mosquitoes belong to the fly order *Diptera.* They make up the family *Culicidae.*

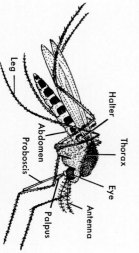
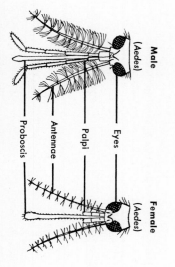
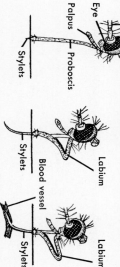
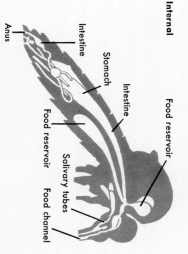

MOSQUITO

male's wings, and the sound helps males find mates. Mosquitoes are *flies* (insects with two wings). The word *mosquito* is Spanish and means *little fly*.

The Body of a Mosquito

The mosquito's slender body has three parts: (1) the head, (2) the thorax, and (3) the abdomen. A thin, elastic shell covers the body. Fine hair and thin scales grow on the shell and on the wings. Most kinds of mosquitoes are black, brown, gray, or tan. Many species have white or light colored markings on their backs, legs, or wings. A few kinds are bright blue or green, and seem to shine with coppery or golden lights.

Head. The mosquito has a large, round head that is joined to the thorax by a short, thin neck. Two huge *compound* eyes cover most of the head. These eyes, like those of most other kinds of insects, are made up of thousands of six-sided lenses. Each lens points in a slightly different direction and works independently. A mosquito cannot focus its eyes for sharp vision, but it quickly sees any movement. The eyes are always open, even when the insect sleeps.

A mosquito hears and smells with its two antennae, which grow near the center of its head between the eyes. A female mosquito's antennae are long and somewhat like threads. The male's antennae are also long, but they have many bushy hairs which give them a feathery appearance.

The mouth of a mosquito looks somewhat like a funnel. The broadest part is nearest the head, and a tubelike part called the *proboscis* extends downward. A mosquito uses its proboscis to "bite," and as a straw to sip liquids, its only food. The males and females of many species sip plant juices.

How a Mosquito "Bites." Only female mosquitoes "bite," and only the females of a few species attack man and animals. They sip the victim's blood, which they need for the development of the eggs inside their bodies.

Mosquitoes do not really bite because they cannot open their jaws. When a mosquito "bites," it stabs through the victim's skin with six needlelike parts called *stylets*, which form the center of the proboscis. The stylets are covered and protected by the insect's lower lip, called the *labium*. As the stylets enter the skin, the labium bends and slides upward out of the way. Then saliva flows into the wound through channels formed by the stylets. The mosquito can easily sip the blood because the saliva keeps it from clotting. Most persons are allergic to the saliva, and an itchy welt called a "mosquito bite" forms on the skin. After the mosquito has sipped enough blood, it slowly pulls the stylets out of the wound, and the labium slips into place over them. Then the insect flies away.

The amount of blood taken varies greatly among individual mosquitoes. Some may sip as much as 1½ times their own weight at a time.

THE BODY OF A MOSQUITO

External

Leg

Halter

Abdomen

Thorax

Proboscis

Eye

Antenna

Palpus

Internal

Intestine

Stomach

Intestine

Anus

Food reservoir

Food reservoir

Salivary tubes

Food channel

Food reservoir

THE HEADS OF MOSQUITOES

Antenna

Eyes

Palpi

Antennae

Proboscis

Male (Aedes)

Female (Aedes)

HOW A MOSQUITO "BITES"

A mosquito stabs a victim's skin with sharp stylets hidden in the proboscis. As the insect pushes the stylets down, they curve and enter a blood vessel. The *labium* (lower lip) slides out of the way.

Antenna

Eye

Palpus

Proboscis

Stylets

Stylets

Labium

Blood vessel

Stylets

Labium

Stylets

WORLD BOOK illustration by Tom Dolan

THE LIFE CYCLE OF A CULEX MOSQUITO

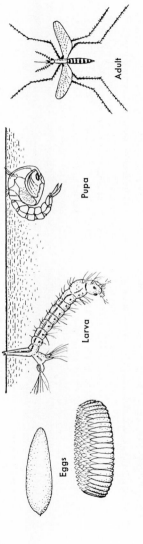

Eggs

Larva

Pupa

Adult

THE LIFE CYCLE OF AN ANOPHELES MOSQUITO

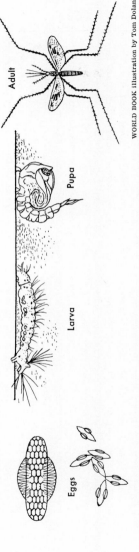

Eggs

Larva

Pupa

Adult

WORLD BOOK illustration by Tom Dolan

Thorax. The mosquito's thorax is shaped somewhat like a triangle, with the broadest part above and the narrowest part underneath. Thin, flat scales of various colors form patterns on the upper part of the thorax of certain kinds of mosquitoes. These patterns help identify different species. One kind of mosquito that spreads yellow fever has a U-shaped pattern formed by white scales on a background of dark scales.

Strong muscles are attached to the inside shell wall of the thorax. These muscles move the mosquito's legs and wings. A mosquito has six long, slender legs, and each leg has five major joints. A pair of claws on each leg helps the insect cling to such flat surfaces as walls and ceilings. The mosquito uses all its legs when it walks, but usually stands on only four of them. Many kinds of mosquitoes rest on their four front legs. Some kinds hold their two hind legs almost straight out behind them, but others curve their legs over their backs. White scales form bands on the legs of some species.

Mosquitoes have two wings, unlike most other kinds of insects which have four wings. The wings are so thin that the veins show through. The veins not only carry blood to the wings, but also help stiffen and support them. Thin scales cover the veins and the edges of the wings. These scales rub off like dust when anything touches them. Some species of mosquitoes may have scales of beautiful colors.

Instead of hind wings, which most other insects have, a mosquito has two thick, rodlike parts with knobs at the tips. These parts, called *halteres*, give the mosquito its sense of balance. The halteres vibrate at the same rate as the wings when the insect flies.

A mosquito lifts itself into the air as soon as it beats its wings. It does not have to run or jump to take off.

In the air, the mosquito can dart quickly and easily in any direction. The halteres keep the insect in balance. A mosquito must beat its wings constantly while it is in the air. It does not glide during flight or when coming in for a landing as do butterflies, moths, and most other flying insects. A mosquito beats its wings until its feet touch a landing place.

Abdomen of a mosquito is long and slender, and looks somewhat like a tube. Some kinds of mosquitoes have an abdomen with a pointed end. Other kinds have an abdomen with a rounded end. The shape of the abdomen helps scientists identify the species.

A mosquito breathes through air holes called *spiracles* along the sides of its body. The abdomen has eight pairs of spiracles, and the thorax has two pairs. Air flows into the holes, and tubes carry the air from the spiracles to all parts of the mosquito's body.

The Life of a Mosquito

A mosquito's life is divided into four stages: (1) egg, (2) larva, (3) pupa, (4) adult. At each stage the mosquito's appearance changes completely, and the insect lives a different kind of life. In warm climates, some species develop from newly hatched eggs into adults in only a week. In the cold climate of the far north, mosquito eggs may remain frozen from autumn until late spring. They hatch in May or June, and take a month or more to grow into adults.

Egg. A female mosquito lays from 100 to 300 eggs at a time, depending on the species. One female may lay as many as 3,000 eggs during her lifetime. The eggs are laid through an opening called the *ovipositor* at the tip of the female's abdomen.

The females of most species of mosquitoes lay their

eggs in water or near it, but each species has a favorite spot. Some like quiet swamps, and others prefer salt marshes. Still others lay their eggs in hidden pools that form in tin cans, garbage pails, fallen logs, or hollow tree stumps.

Among some species, the females drop their eggs one at a time. Frilly, transparent parts on the shell keep each egg afloat until it hatches. The females of other species arrange their eggs in groups that look somewhat like rafts. The female rests on the surface of the water while she lays her eggs, which are narrow at the top. With her hind legs, she carefully pushes the eggs, wide ends downward, into raftlike groups. Each group of eggs is held together by a sticky substance from the female's body. The eggs of most kinds of mosquitoes hatch in two or three days in warm weather.

All mosquito eggs must have moisture to hatch, but not all species lay their eggs in water. Certain mosquitoes, called floodwater mosquitoes, drop their eggs in mud left by a flood. The eggs hatch after another flood takes place—perhaps years later. Another species, sometimes called pond mosquitoes, lays its eggs in hollow places left by ponds that have dried up. The eggs hatch after rains fill the ponds with water. The eggs of some kinds of pond mosquitoes do not hatch after the first rain. They must be soaked by a second or even a third rain before they hatch into larva.

Larva of a mosquito is often called a *wriggler* because it is so active. The wrigglers of most species move about by jerking their bodies through the water.

A wriggler looks somewhat like a worm or a caterpillar. A thin, skinlike shell covers its body. The wriggler has a broad head, with two short, bushy antennae on each side. It has two eyes behind the antennae, near the back of the head. Its mouth is on the underside of the head, near the front. Long hairs called *mouth brushes* grow around the jaws and sweep food into the wriggler's mouth. Unlike an adult mosquito, a wriggler can open its jaws and chew its food. The wriggler eats small plants and small animals that live in the water, including other wrigglers and one-celled animals called *protozoans*.

A wriggler breathes through a tubelike *siphon* (air tube) at the rear of its body. To get air, it pushes its siphon above the surface of the water.

The larvae of certain swamp mosquitoes do not have to come to the surface for air. They get air from the leaves, stems, and roots of various underwater plants. The larva of one kind of swamp mosquito has a breathing tube with two sharp tips. It uses one tip to hold itself to the plant, and moves the other tip back and forth in the plant tissue to get the oxygen stored there.

The larvae of many species of mosquitoes grow quickly. They *molt* (shed their skins and grow new ones) four times in 4 to 10 days. After the last molt, the larvae change into pupae. The larvae of some species spend the winter at the bottom of ponds. They change into pupae early in spring.

Pupa. A mosquito pupa looks somewhat like a comma. The head and thorax are rolled into a ball, and the abdomen hangs down like a curved tail. A thin shell, like that of the larva, covers the pupa's body. The pupa breathes through trumpet-shaped tubes attached

to the top of its thorax. The pupa sticks these tubes out of the water to get air. The pupa of certain swamp mosquitoes, whose larva gets air from underwater plants, pushes its tubes into the plant. After this pupa has changed into an adult, it pulls out the tubes or breaks them off and leaves them in the plant. The pupa then swims to the surface.

The pupae of most species of insects do not move, but almost all kinds of mosquito pupae can swim. These pupae are sometimes called *tumblers* because they roll and tumble in the water.

A mosquito pupa does not eat. It changes into an adult in two to four days. The pupal shell splits down the back, and the adult mosquito pushes its head and front legs out. The insect then pulls the rest of its body from the shell.

Adult. After the adult mosquito leaves the pupal shell, its wings dry quickly and it flies a short distance away. Most species of mosquitoes spend their whole lives within a mile of the place where they hatched. A few kinds may travel as far as 20 miles away to find food or mates.

A female mosquito attracts a mate by the high-pitched sound made by her wings. The pupal shell splits down for the first 24 to 48 hours of their lives, until the hairs on their antennae are dry.

The females of some species must sip blood before they can lay eggs that will hatch. Each species of female prefers the blood of certain kinds of animals. Some feed only on frogs, snakes, or other cold-blooded animals. Others prefer birds. Still others suck the blood of cows, horses, and man.

Some male mosquitoes may live only 10 to 20 days, but a female may live 30 days or more. The females of some species live through the winter in barns, garages, houses, caves, or in the bark of logs. Some species spend the winter as eggs or as larvae. They develop into adults in spring.

Related Articles in WORLD BOOK include:

DDT	Gorgas, William C.
Dengue	Insecticide
Dragonfly	Malaria
Elephantiasis	Reed, Walter
Finlay, Carlos Juan	Sleeping Sickness
Fly	Yellow Fever

MOSQUITO BOAT. See PT BOAT.

MOSQUITO COAST, or MOSQUITIA, is a strip of land that lies along the east coast of Nicaragua and the northeast coast of Honduras. It has an area of over 30,000 square miles and extends for about 200 miles from the San Juan River in Nicaragua to the Aguan River in Honduras. The southern part makes up the department of Zelaya in Nicaragua. The northern part lies in the departments of Gracias a Dios and Colón in Honduras. The Mosquito Coast received its name from the Mosquito Indians.

See also HONDURAS; NICARAGUA.

MOSQUITO HAWK. See NIGHTHAWK.

MOSQUITO NETTING, or MOSQUITO BAR, is a rough, stiff cotton gauze made with a leno weave (see GAUZE). The best quality netting has 14 meshes to an inch while the poorer netting has 12. Mosquito netting is used to screen windows, beds, and baby carriages. It comes in white, green, and black.

DALE W. JENKINS

ROLLIN S. ATWOOD

The Sphagnum is one of the abundant members of the moss group. These mosses have considerable commercial use.

Haircap Moss develops these leafy shoots, which look like the tips of branches on some varieties of evergreen trees.

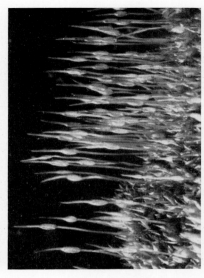

Apple Moss gets its name from its round, applelike spore capsules. It grows in damp cavities or on shady banks.

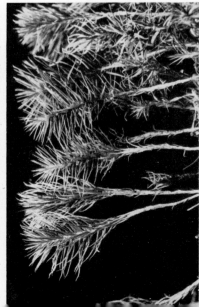

Capsules with Spores on their straight stalks look like tiny spears. This is young cord moss, a common species.

Hugh Spencer; Devereux Butcher

Aulacomnium grows in the woods where the soil is very rich. The beanlike pods on the long stalks contain the moss spores.

MOSS is made up of soft green plants growing so close together that they often form pads, or cushions. Sometimes they resemble groves of minute ferns or small trees. The mosses, together with the liverworts, are called *bryophytes* (see BRYOPHYTE; LIVERWORT).

One group of mosses grows in shallow fresh water. Another grows on land, on such places as damp banks, rocks, and trees. Mosses can live in damp climates at many different temperatures and heights. Some mosses also grow in dry, warm places. Mosses, lichens, and liverworts may have been the first plants to live on land.

A single moss plant has tiny leaves growing around a stem. The rootlets look like hairs and grow from the bottom of the stem. They are called *rhizoids*.

Growth of New Plants. New plants are formed in two stages. The first occurs when male and female plant cells join to form a new growth. This kind of reproduction is called *sexual*. Male and female cells are formed in different organs that grow from the top of the moss stem or a branch. The male sex organ is called the *antheridium*. The female organ is the *archegonium*. The antheridium bursts when it becomes ripe and damp enough and the male cells escape. Some of them may reach the archegonium, where they travel through a tube and join the egg. The two cells then grow together and form a long, erect stalk called the *seta*, with a spore case, or *capsule*, at the end.

The second, or *asexual*, stage in the growth of the new plant takes place in this capsule. Certain cells divide and form *spores*, which serve as tiny seeds (see SPORE). Most moss capsules have a mouth covered by a

lid. When the spores ripen, the lid falls off. A set of "teeth" around the mouth controls the scattering of the spores. These teeth are *hygroscopic*, which means that they take water from the air. They move as they become moistened or dried.

The spores may sprout into branching, threadlike growths called *protonema*. Buds from the protonema then grow into new moss plants with leaves and rhizoids.

Many spores are scattered far and wide, and often sprout wherever it is warm and damp enough. In the hot sun some mosses curl their leaves. The curl is

MOSS

caused by cells that change in shape as they dry. The curled mosses look brown and dead, but showers and cooler weather make them fresh and green again. Some mosses quickly show the moisture changes in the air. They turn a different shade of green with every change.

How Mosses Help Man. Mosses are soil makers. Their small rootlets, working slowly, break off tiny bits of rock. In time, they can break stone into a dust as fine as if it had been mashed with a hammer. The leaves gather dust particles from the air. These particles, with the dead tissue of the plant, make the soil deeper.

Many mosses hold the rain as it falls on the ground, instead of letting it run off. They keep the ground damp, and make it a good place for other plants to grow. They also help prevent floods by holding the water in the soil.

Peat beds are swampy places where peat moss (*sphagnum*) grows. The moss on the surface grows over layers of dead moss. The dead deposits have partly decayed through the ages and have changed to peat. People use peat as a fuel. They also grind it and mix it with the soil as a fertilizer. Peat helps the soil hold more moisture. Peat bogs lie in Ireland, Germany, Sweden, and Holland, and in parts of the United States. See PEAT MOSS.

Sphagnum moss makes an excellent packing material. It is especially useful for wrapping live plants that must be shipped. The moss has a spongy texture.

In Lapland, mothers line babies' cradles with moss, because it is soft and warm. It is also mixed with reindeer hair for stuffing mattresses. Some birds line their nests with moss. Frontiersmen used it to fill the cracks between the logs of their cabins.

Other Plants. Certain plants called moss are not true mosses. The Spanish moss which hangs from the branches of trees in the South is a flowering plant that belongs to the pineapple family (see SPANISH MOSS). Farmers of Ireland use the seaweed called Irish moss for food and medicine (see IRISH MOSS). The Icelanders and Laplanders make bread from Iceland moss, a lichen (see LICHEN). People in middle Asia eat cup moss, another lichen.

Scientific Classification. Mosses are in the phylum *Bryophyta*. They form the class *Musci*.

ROLLA M. TRYON

Motel de Ville, New Orleans

Motels stand beside American highways, offering motorists clean, comfortable, convenient lodging accommodations.

MOSSADEGH, MOHAMMED. See IRAN (The Nationalist Movement).

MÖSSBAUER, *MUHS bow uhr,* **RUDOLF LUDWIG** (1929-   ), a German physicist, shared the 1961 Nobel prize in physics for research into gamma rays. He discovered the "Mössbauer Effect," a method of producing gamma rays with a precise, predictable wave length. This enables physicists to use gamma radiation to make precise measurements. The "Mössbauer Effect" was later used to confirm some predictions made by Albert Einstein in his relativity theory. Mössbauer was born in Munich and received his Ph.D. from the technical institute there. He joined the faculty at the California Institute of Technology in 1960.

MOSSBUNKER. See MENHADEN.

MOSUL, *moh SOOL* (pop. 243,311; met. area 315,157; alt. 800 ft.), the most important city in northern Iraq, lies on the west bank of the Tigris River. In Arabic, its name is AL MAWŞIL. The ruins of ancient Nineveh lie a mile away, across the river. Mosul is an old trading city, where people buy and sell the grains, fruits, and sheep of the region. It was an ancient center for craftsmen. "Mosul bronze" pieces and muslin, a fine cotton textile, received their names from the city. The most impressive building in Mosul is the Great Mosque, formerly a Christian church.

Mosul declined in importance for many years. But it became important again after men discovered oil in the nearby hills. A railroad built in 1940 links Mosul with Baghdad and Basra in the south and with Turkey and Europe in the north.

MAJID KHADDURI

MOSZKOWSKI, *maush KAWF skee,* **MORITZ** (1854-1925), was a Polish-German pianist and composer. He became known for his piano pieces, the most popular being the *Spanish Dances;* the ballet *Laurin;* the symphony *Joan of Arc;* and orchestral suites. Moszkowski was born in Breslau, Germany (now Wrocław, Poland), and studied in Dresden and Berlin. He made his concert debut in 1873. He often toured as a pianist. He appeared in London in 1886 to play at the Philharmonic concerts, and returned there many times in later years both as pianist and conductor. Moszkowski lived in Berlin until 1897, and then he retired to Paris.

ROBERT U. NELSON

MOTEL is a group of cabins or an inn located near a highway for the convenience of travelers making overnight stops. The word was formed by combining parts of the words *motor* and *hotel.* Travelers like motels because they are easy to find and they are informal. The motorists can park their cars nearby. Some motels have space for only a few motorists, but others can house more than 200 families. Some motels provide swimming pools, children's playgrounds, restaurants, and air conditioning. The motel industry began in the 1930's. At the time, motels were called *tourist cabins.*

H. B. MEEK

See also HOTEL.

Frank Lane

The Hawk Moth looks like a hummingbird as it hovers in front of a flower. It sips the flower's nectar through its long tubelike proboscis.

MOTH

MOTH. One of the most familiar sights of summer is a group of moths fluttering around a streetlight. These soft, winged insects live almost everywhere. Moths have been found in hot deserts and on cold mountaintops, and in every country from the equator to near the Poles. North America has from 10,000 to 15,000 different *species* (kinds) of moths.

Moths are close relatives of butterflies. In fact, there is no sure, simple way to tell moths and butterflies apart. Generally, moths fly at night and butterflies fly during the day. But many moths fly by day, visiting flowers and sucking nectar as do butterflies. Most moths are colored less brightly than butterflies. But many moths have bright colors, and many butterflies are plain and dull. When a moth rests, it folds its wings back flat over its body. A butterfly usually holds its wings up over its back, or spread out at an angle. Most moths have *antennae* (feelers) that look like tapering hairs. Butterflies have knobs at the tips of their antennae. See BUTTERFLY (picture, How to Tell Butterflies from Moths).

Some moths are helpful and many are harmful to man. The valuable silkworm moth spins the silk used to make beautiful cloth. Many moths pollinate flowers as they go from blossom to blossom searching for nectar. The clothes moth is the best known harmful moth. But the most harmful moths are the ones that destroy trees, food crops, and other plants.

Life Cycle of the Moth

Moths, like butterflies, have a complicated life history. The *eggs* laid by the female moth hatch into tiny *larvae*, or *caterpillars*. The caterpillar turns into a *pupa*. The pupa changes into an *adult* moth which spreads its wings and flies away. The entire process of changes is called *metamorphosis* (see METAMORPHOSIS).

Egg. The female moth generally lays its eggs on plants. But moths also lay their eggs on other things that the larva can eat.

Larva (Caterpillar). After the larva hatches, it usually eats its eggshell. Then it begins to eat the plant or other material on which it is living. The larva is the only stage that causes damage.

As the caterpillar grows, it goes through several steps. At the end of each step, the caterpillar sheds the hard skin that covers its head and body. It immediately swells out much larger and grows another hard skin. After another period of feeding, the caterpillar again sheds its skin and increases in size. This shedding of the skin is called *molting*. The caterpillars of various kinds of moths molt from four to a dozen or more times.

Head of a Moth Caterpillar includes a mouth, 12 tiny eyes, and 2 short *antennae*. The caterpillar chews its food with strong, biting jaws called *mandibles*. It uses the antennae to feel its way along. The eyes are arranged in a curved row on each side of the head, just above the mouth. A caterpillar has a good sense of taste, but sees only enough to tell light from dark.

A short projection called the *spinneret* sticks out below the mouth. The caterpillar squeezes out an almost continuous stream of liquid silk through the spinneret. The silk quickly hardens to a slender thread that gives the caterpillar a foothold wherever it goes. Some caterpillars swing from the silk thread to escape danger as spiders do.

Body of a Moth Caterpillar is divided into 12 *segments* (parts). The first three body segments behind the head form the *thorax*. Each segment of the thorax has a pair of short, sharp-tipped, jointed legs. These are true legs that change into the legs of the adult moth. The rest of the body is the *abdomen*. The abdomen has five pairs of false legs called *prolegs*. Each of these fleshy, leglike organs has a curved row of tiny hooks at its tip. Caterpillars breathe through openings called *spiracles*.

Pupa. After a moth caterpillar molts for the last time, it becomes a *pupa*. From the outside, a pupa looks dead. But inside, the pupa is very much alive. It is changing from a caterpillar to an adult moth. In some species of moths, this dramatic change takes place in less than a week. In other species, it may take several months, or even a year or more.

MOTH

Before changing into pupae, many moth larvae spin around themselves silken cases called *cocoons.* (Only a few species of butterflies spin cocoons.) The silk in the cocoon of the silkworm moth is the kind used to make silk thread and cloth. The cocoon protects the larva from its enemies and the weather. As the larva changes into a pupa, a hard *pupal shell* develops. Thousands of species of moths do not spin cocoons. Their pupae rest in the earth or in rotting wood. See Cocoon; Silk (Raising Silkworms).

Adult. To come out of its cocoon, an adult moth first cracks the pupal shell. The moth cracks the shell by expanding its body with air and contracting its muscles. Then the moth comes out of the cocoon. Some moths have body parts that serve as "cutters" to open the cocoon. Other moths produce a liquid that dissolves the cocoon. Some moths build cocoons with "escape hatches" through which the adult comes out.

The Adult Moth

Adult moths range in size from those with wings

Alexander B. Klots
The Proboscis, a hollow tube, coils under the moth's face when not in use. The moth straightens it out to sip nectar from deep inside flowers.

$\frac{1}{16}$ of an inch long to giants with 12-inch wingspreads. Like other insects, an adult moth has three main sections: (1) the head, (2) the thorax, and (3) the abdomen. The body of a moth is covered with scales and hairs.

Head. The head of a moth includes the insect's most important sense organs. On each side is a large *compound eye,* which is made up of thousands of separate eyes. Adult moths have keen vision. They also have a good sense of smell which they use to find flowers and other sources of food. Male moths locate females chiefly by smell. The two antennae are the chief organs of smell. The antennae may also serve as organs of touch and perhaps hearing. Beneath the head are two pairs of jutting organs called the *palpi.* They serve as organs of taste, and perhaps smell.

Most adult moths cannot bite or chew. Instead of true jaws, an adult moth has a long, tubeshaped *proboscis* (a tube extending from the mouth). To get food, it thrusts the proboscis into flowers or liquids, and sucks up the food.

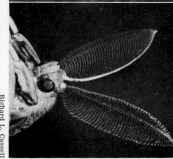

Richard L. Cassell
The Antennae of some moths look like feathery rabbit ears. They "smell" odors that help the moth find a mate.

lizards, and other insects. Few moths are able to fight their enemies. They can only fly away or hide. Some moths taste bad or are even poisonous to certain other animals. Most of these moths have bright colors that warn their enemies. Other moths have colors that blend with their surroundings and make them hard to see.

Insect enemies of moths, such as wasps and flies, lay their eggs inside the moth caterpillar's body. The eggs develop into larvae, which feed on the caterpillar and kill it. Caterpillars depend chiefly on their color for protection. Most of them are brown, green, or some other plain color. But some have bold, bright colors and patterns. These colorations help disguise a caterpillar by making it look like something else.

Harmful Caterpillars

Farm and Forest Pests. One of the most destructive moth caterpillars is the *tent* caterpillar. Its pupae live in a silken, tentlike nest on tree branches which they strip for food. Many kinds of *tussock* moths have larvae that attack trees. These include the caterpillars of

Alexander B. Klots
The Frenulum, a bristle at the base of the front wing, locks into the hind wing, and holds the wings together.

Thorax is the front section of an adult moth's body. It supports the three pairs of slender legs and the two pairs of wings. The wings of most adult moths are thickly covered with tiny, flat scales that overlap like shingles on a roof. The arrangement of the scales gives most moths distinctive wing patterns. The scales rub off as a fine, powdery dust.

Most adult moths have a special part called the *frenulum.* (No butterflies have a frenulum.) During flight, a frenulum links the front and back wings on each side. It keeps the wings working together.

Abdomen. The rear section of the adult moth's body has most of the spiracles through which it breathes. The abdomen also includes the reproductive organs.

How Moths Live

Adult moths usually sleep during the day and come out at night to search for food. Although moths see well in the dark, they find flowers chiefly by using their sharp sense of smell. Moths drink water, the sap from trees, and other liquids in addition to nectar. Enemies of moths include spiders, birds, frogs, toads,

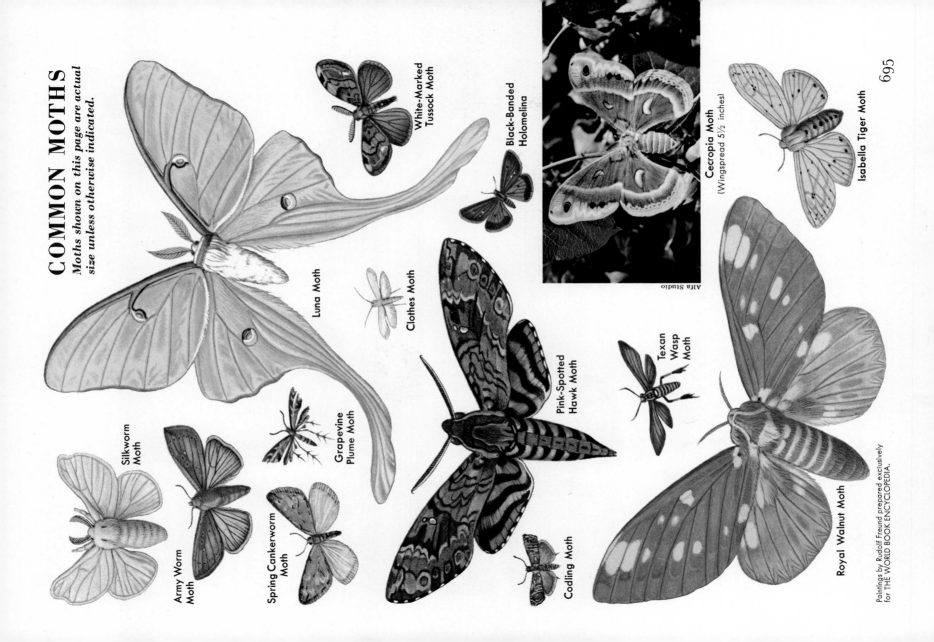

COMMON MOTHS

Moths shown on this page are actual size unless otherwise indicated.

White-Marked Tussock Moth

Black-Banded Holomelina

Cecropia Moth
(Wingspread 5½ inches)

Isabella Tiger Moth

Alfa Studio

Luna Moth

Clothes Moth

Silkworm Moth

Grapevine Plume Moth

Pink-Spotted Hawk Moth

Texan Wasp Moth

Army Worm Moth

Spring Cankerworm Moth

Codling Moth

Royal Walnut Moth

Paintings by Rudolf Freund prepared exclusively for THE WORLD BOOK ENCYCLOPEDIA.

MOTHS OF MANY LANDS

Isabella Tiger Moth

Xanthopilopteryx superba
Africa

Napata splendida
Bolivia

Chrysocale principalis
Mexico

Inma grammozona
New Guinea

The Giant Hercules Moth of New Guinea and Australia is probably the largest moth in the world. It has a wing-spread of about 10 inches, and could cover an adult robin from bill to tail.

A Nepticulid Moth of the eastern United States is one of the smallest moths known. It has a wingspan of about ⅛ inch. It is shown here in twice life size.

Erasmia pulchella
Bhutan

Josia oribia
Mexico

Euchromia formosa
Madagascar

COMMON MOTH CATERPILLARS
(Not to scale)

Isabella Tiger Moth

Codling Moth

Clothes Moth

Silk Moth

Tussock Moth

Pink Bollworm

Army Worm

Peach Moth

Tent Caterpillar

European Corn Borer

Corn Earworm

Spring Cankerworm

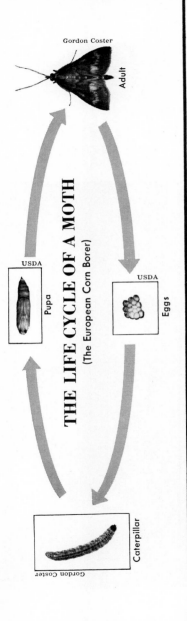

THE LIFE CYCLE OF A MOTH
(The European Corn Borer)

Adult — Gordon Coster
Pupa — USDA
Eggs — USDA
Caterpillar — Gordon Coster

the *gypsy* moth and the *brown-tail* moth.

Moth caterpillars that attack crops include the *army worm*, the *corn borer*, the *corn ear worm*, and the *cutworms*. The *codling* moth, the *peach* moth, and other moths have caterpillars that bore into apples, peaches, and other fruits. The caterpillar of the *pink bollworm* moth attacks cotton fields throughout the world.

Some moth caterpillars protect themselves with chemicals. Puss moth caterpillars can squirt acid at attackers. The caterpillars of slug moths and io moths have poisonous *spines* (needlelike growths) that cause a painful rash on the skin of persons who handle them.

Clothes Moths damage clothing, rugs and carpets, upholstery, furs, and other household items. These moths all belong to the family *Tineidae*. The females lay their eggs on woolen and silk fabrics, and on furs. The caterpillars feed on these materials, causing serious damage. The adults do no harm.

Getting rid of clothes moths can be difficult. It does no good to kill a flying clothes moth, because the eggs have already been laid. The simplest way to prevent moth damage is to buy garments that have been moth-proofed by treating them with a special chemical. Dry cleaning or laundering, especially before storage, removes larvae or eggs. Woolen garments should always be stored in tightly sealed containers. Putting moth balls or moth flakes in a garment bag provides extra protection. Spraying with an insecticide or fumigation are also good ways to kill moth larvae.

Kinds of Moths

Both moths and butterflies belong to the order *Lepidoptera*. Some of the largest families of moths are described below. The scientific name of each family is given in parenthesis.

Giant Silkworm Moths (*Saturniidae*) include most of the largest moths. (The commercial *Chinese silkworm* belongs to another family, *Bombycidae*.) Among the giant silkworm moths are the moths with the largest wing area, the *atlas* and *hercules* of Asia. Also in the family are two large North American moths, the familiar *cecropia* and *polyphemus*. They have wings up to 6 inches from tip to tip. In addition, the group includes the pale green, long-tailed *luna*.

Midget Moths (*Nepticulidae*) are tiny moths with wing spans of less than ⅛ inch.

Owlet Moths (*Noctuidae*) are the most common moths in North America. Cutworms, army worms, and bollworms belong to this family.

Prominents (*Notodontidae*) are brown or gray moths that are found almost everywhere in the world.

Slug Caterpillar Moths (*Eucleidae*) are favorites with collectors. The caterpillars have varied shapes and colors, and many adults have striking colors.

Collecting Moths

The best place to collect moths is near a light, especially a fluorescent one. Moths are strongly attracted by the ultraviolet light produced by fluorescent lamps. Adult moths seldom live long in captivity. Many kinds never eat or drink after being captured. They usually batter themselves to death. Females kept in dark containers sometimes lay eggs from which caterpillars hatch. Caterpillars can also be collected and raised on foliage.

ALEXANDER B. KLOTS

Related Articles. The article on BUTTERFLY has much information that applies to moths. See also:

Army Worm	Cutworm	Metamorphosis
Brown-Tail Moth	Death's-Head Moth	Peach Moth
Caterpillar	Gypsy Moth	Pink Bollworm
Codling Moth	Hawk Moth	Tent Caterpillar
Corn Borer	Leaf Miner	Tussock Moth
Corn Ear Worm	Measuring Worm	

Outline

I. Life Cycle of the Moth
  A. Egg   C. Pupa
  B. Larva (Caterpillar)   D. Adult
II. The Adult Moth
  A. Head   B. Thorax   C. Abdomen
III. How Moths Live
IV. Harmful Caterpillars
  A. Farm and Forest Pests   B. Clothes Moths
V. Kinds of Moths
VI. Collecting Moths

Questions

How do moths and butterflies differ?
How do moths emerge from their cocoons?
How long does it take for a pupa to become an adult?
What is the difference between the mouth of a caterpillar and the mouth of an adult moth?
What is the *frenulum*?
What kinds of moths do the most serious damage?
What plant parts do caterpillars eat?
What moths have the largest wingspread?
What moth produces silk?
What are the chief enemies of moths?

MOTH BALL is a small white or gray ball about the size of a marble, which is used to protect fabrics and furs from moths. The balls are stored with the fabrics. Moth balls are usually made of naphthalene.

MOTHER is the title often given to any source or origin, as it is the name of a female parent. For example, a person may speak of the land of his birth as his *mother-land* or *mother country*. He may call the language of his parents his *mother tongue*. The title *mother of mankind* is often given to Eve, the ancestor of all people. Roman Catholics and many other Christians use the title *Mother of God* for the Virgin Mary. The woman in charge of a convent is called *Mother* or *Mother Superior*.

In other languages, the word for mother is similar. In Latin, the term is *mater*, in French *mère*, in German *Mutter*, in Greek *mētēr*, and in Russian *mat'*.

Early peoples in ancient civilizations compared nature's creative powers with those of a mother, because a mother is the source of life. In many places, they worshiped a great mother goddess. The Assyrians called their goddess *Ishtar*. The Greeks worshiped *Demeter*, and the Romans *Ceres*. Other names for the mother goddess were *Cybele* and *Rhea*.

In the United States, the second Sunday in May of each year honors motherhood (see MOTHER'S DAY).

MOTHER CAREY'S CHICKEN is the name sailors have given to the various kinds of birds called petrels (see PETREL). The name Mother Carey is a changed form of the Latin words *Mater cara*, which means *tender mother* or *dear mother*. This refers to the Virgin, the Mother of Jesus. The sailors believe that the petrels are under her especial care, and so call them Mother Carey's chickens.

MOTHER GOOSE is the mythical little old lady who was supposed to have told the nursery stories and rhymes that children know and love so well. But whether or not she was a real person remains a mystery. In an old graveyard in Boston, Mass., there are several tombstones bearing the name of *Goose*. Some people claim that one of them marks the grave of Mother Goose. Her real name was supposed to have been

Elizabeth Vergoose. Her son-in-law, a printer named Thomas Fleet, was supposed to have published in 1719 the songs and rhymes she sang to her grandchildren. No copy of this book has ever been found, however, and most scholars doubt the truth of this story.

Mother Goose probably was not a real person. The name "Mother Goose" is the direct translation from the French *Mère l'Oye*. In 1697, the Frenchman, Charles Perrault, published the first book in which this name was used. It was called *Histoires du Temps passé*, *(Stories of Long Ago)*, or *Contes de ma Mère l'Oye*, (*Tales of Mother Goose*). It contains eight tales, but no rhymes. Among the tales were "Sleeping Beauty," "Cinderella," and "Puss in Boots." Perrault did not invent these stories. They were already quite popular in his day, and he only collected them. Some believe that these stories go back to "Goose-Footed Bertha," mother of the French ruler, Charlemagne.

In 1729, Robert Sambers translated Perrault's tales into English. Then, about 1760, John Newbery, the first English publisher of children's books, brought out *Mother Goose's Melody*, a tiny book illustrated with woodcuts. It contained 52 rhymes, such as "Ding Dong Bell," "Little Tom Tucker," and "Margery Daw," as well as 15 songs from Shakespeare's plays. This collection became very popular, and before long copies and imitations of Newbery's edition flooded the London bookstalls. Isaiah Thomas, a publisher in Worcester, Mass., republished Newbery's book in 1785.

Old King Cole. Newbery's edition was the first to associate rhymes as well as stories with Mother Goose. Many of these rhymes existed hundreds of years before they were called Mother Goose rhymes. Some of them are just jingles with no real meaning. Others seem to tell about real people and historical events. One tells about King Cole, who was supposed to have been a

Whistler's Mother is one of the world's most famous paintings. James Whistler, an American artist, painted it in Paris in 1871 to honor his mother.

E. S. Herrman

very popular king of Britain in the A.D. 200's. He seems to have loved music, and his daughter was supposedly a skilled musician. The king would have long been forgotten but for the rhyme:

> Old King Cole was a merry old soul,
> And a merry old soul was he;
> He called for his pipe, and he called for his bowl,
> And he called for his fiddlers three.

It is quite possible that court jesters made up many of these rhymes. Others may have been made up by noblemen or men in the street.

Little Jack Horner. According to legend, the Bishop of Glastonbury, England, had sent his steward, Jack Horner, to King Henry VIII with the title deeds of 12 estates. For safety, the deeds were hidden in a Christmas pie. On his way to the king, Jack Horner lifted the pie crust, pulled out a "plum," that is, the deed of an estate, and kept it. The rhyme goes:

> Little Jack Horner
> Sat in a corner
> Eating his Christmas pie.
> He put in his thumb,
> And pulled out a plum,
> And said, "What a brave boy am I."

To this day the Horner family owns the estate from that deed at Mells Park, England.

Hey Diddle Diddle. Queen Elizabeth I had a reputation for teasing her ministers the way a cat plays with mice. She loved to dance to the tune of a fiddle. One of her advisers was nicknamed "Moon," and another was known as the Queen's "Lap-Dog," She never ate without having one of her ladies in waiting, called "Spoon," taste her soup first. A gentleman of the court was called "Dish" because he carried in the food. When one day the "Dish" and the "Spoon" eloped, this jingle was invented:

> Hey, diddle, diddle,
> The cat and the fiddle,
> The cow jumped over the moon;
> The little dog laughed
> To see such sport,
> And the dish ran away with the spoon.

Many collections of Mother Goose rhymes have been published over the years in England and the United States.

ARTHUR M. SELVI

See also LITERATURE FOR CHILDREN with its Books to Read section; NURSERY RHYME; NEWBERY, JOHN; PERRAULT, CHARLES.

MOTHER OF CANADA. See SAINT LAWRENCE RIVER.

MOTHER-OF-PEARL. Certain sea animals, such as the pearl oyster, the abalone, and the nacre, line their shells with a layer of material in glowing color. This layer is called *mother-of-pearl*. It varies in color from pale grayish-blue and pink to purple and green. Shells containing mother-of-pearl are found off the coasts of tropical countries, particularly around the South Sea Islands, around the Philippine Islands, Australia, Panama, and Lower California. The finest mother-of-pearl is found in shells from Australia and Ceylon. Those from Panama are called *bullock shells* in commerce, and are small and thick.

Mollusks in many inland waters also produce mother-of-pearl. The shells of fresh-water clams in the Mississippi and other rivers are used in making buttons. The chief uses for mother-of-pearl are in pocketknife handles, buttons, and beads.

WILLIAM J. CLENCH

See also ABALONE; BUTTON; MOLLUSK; PEARL.

MOTHER OF PRESIDENTS. See OHIO; VIRGINIA.

MOTHER OF STATES. See VIRGINIA.

MOTHER OF THE WEST. See MISSOURI.

MOTHERS, NATIONAL CONGRESS OF. See PARENTS AND TEACHERS, NATIONAL CONGRESS OF (History).

MOTHER'S DAY is set apart every year in honor of motherhood. On the second Sunday in May, many families and churches make a special point of honoring mothers. Many people follow the custom of wearing a carnation on Mother's Day. If a person wears a colored carnation, it means that his mother is living. If he wears a white carnation, it indicates that his mother is dead.

A day for honoring mothers was observed many years ago in England. It was called *Mothering Sunday*, and came in mid-Lent. The Yugoslavs and people in some other countries have long observed similar days.

United Press Int.

Anna Jarvis

Julia Ward Howe made the first known suggestion for a Mother's Day in the United States in 1872. She suggested that people observe a Mother's Day on June 2 as a day dedicated to peace. For several years, she held an annual Mother's Day meeting in Boston. Mary Towles Sasseen, a Kentucky schoolteacher, started conducting Mother's Day celebrations in 1887. Frank E. Hering of South Bend, Ind., launched a campaign for the observance of Mother's Day in 1904.

Three years later, Anna Jarvis of Grafton, W.Va., and Philadelphia, began a campaign for a nationwide observance of Mother's Day. She chose the second Sunday in May, and began the custom of wearing a carnation. On May 10, 1908, churches in Grafton and Philadelphia held Mother's Day celebrations. The service at Andrews Methodist Episcopal Church in Grafton honored the memory of Anna Jarvis' own mother, Mrs. Anna Reeves Jarvis.

At the General Conference of the Methodist Episcopal Church in Minneapolis, Minn., in 1912, a delegate from Andrews Church introduced a resolution recognizing Anna Jarvis as the founder of Mother's Day. It suggested that the second Sunday in May be observed as Mother's Day.

Mother's Day received national recognition on May 9, 1914. On that day, President Woodrow Wilson signed a joint resolution of Congress recommending that Congress and the executive departments of the government observe Mother's Day. The following year, the President was authorized to proclaim Mother's Day as an annual national observance.

ELIZABETH HOUGH SECHRIST

MOTHER'S PENSION. See AID TO DEPENDENT CHILDREN.

MOTION. See PARLIAMENTARY PROCEDURE (Motions).

MOTION

MOTION occurs when an object changes its position in space. But motion is a relative rather than an absolute term. An object may be in motion in regard to another object, and yet two moving objects can be stationary in regard to each other. For example, we may go for an automobile ride and pass a man standing by the side of the road. We will be in motion as far as the man by the side of the road is concerned. We will be at rest in regard to the friend on the seat next to us.

Actually, of course, everything on earth is in motion in regard to any fixed point in space. We may think we are sitting at rest in a chair, but because of the earth's rotation we are moving very rapidly. Furthermore, we are moving with the earth as it moves on its path around the sun. The sun itself is dragging the earth with it toward a point in distant space.

If we are driving a car and pass another car on the road going in the same or the opposite direction, the apparent motion of the other car is its motion *relative* to the motion of our car.

Scientists speak of two important kinds of motion. One is called *rectilinear* motion. This is motion in a straight line. When objects are moving freely without constraint, they normally move in a straight line. Motion along a curved path is called *curvilinear* motion.

Velocity and Acceleration. Usually, when we discuss how fast an object moves we use the term *speed.* Scientists, however, are more precise and use the term *velocity.* When we say that an object is moving with a constant velocity, we mean that it is moving in a straight line at a constant speed. The velocity of an object changes if either its direction or its speed changes. If an automobile goes around a curve and the speedometer does not change, its speed does not change. But its velocity changes because of a change of direction. Velocity may be expressed in any units of measurement we are using, as long as the units tell us how far an object travels during a certain interval of time. For example, we may speak of velocity in terms of miles per hour, feet per second, or centimeters per second. When the velocity of a moving object is constant, the motion is said to be uniform.

When the velocity of an object increases, it is accelerating. Acceleration is how much the velocity has increased during a certain period of time. The acceleration of an automobile traveling along a straight road is usually expressed in miles per hour per second. If a car starts off at a speed of 2 miles an hour for the first second, and travels 4 miles an hour the second second, and 6 miles an hour the third second, we say its acceleration is uniform at 2 miles per hour. Its velocity has increased two miles per hour each second.

If the velocity of an object is decreased, this is called *negative acceleration* or *deceleration.* This occurs in an automobile when the brakes are put on. An automobile may move ten feet, eight feet, six feet, four feet, and two feet in succeeding seconds. In the case of this particular automobile, the deceleration is *uniform.* Both acceleration and deceleration can be *variable* as well as uniform.

Certain simple laws regarding velocity may be determined by rolling a ball down an inclined plane. If a ball is allowed to roll down such a plane, it will roll down at a uniformly accelerated motion. The distance the ball will roll in any length of time is directly proportionate to the square of the number of seconds it rolls. The uniform acceleration of a ball started at rest will be twice the distance the ball travels during the first second.

We can find the final velocity of the ball at any given moment if we multiply the acceleration by the time. In cases where the acceleration is constant, the distance in one half the acceleration times the square of the number of seconds it has traveled. A ball started from rest with an acceleration of two feet will travel sixteen feet in four seconds.

The formula for finding the final velocity of an object started from rest, is $v = at$, which means the final velocity equals the acceleration times the time. The formula for finding the distance the ball travels the time. The formula is $S = \frac{1}{2}at^2$. In this formula, the distance is S, the acceleration is a, and t^2 represents the square of the time spent. To find the distance traveled in any given second, we can use the formula $S = \frac{1}{2}d(2t-1)$. In other words, at any given second the ball will travel a space equal to one half of the acceleration times twice the time minus one.

The preceding formulas apply the same way to motion that is uniformly retarded. They also apply to bodies which are falling in the air. However, for freely falling bodies, in such formulas we substitute g, which equals 980 centimeters per second per second, or 32.16 feet per second per second, for the acceleration.

Momentum. The momentum of a moving object is its mass times its velocity. The momentum is the impact produced when a moving object strikes an object at rest. A very heavy object moving slowly has a large momentum, as does a very light object moving at a great speed. The impact of both of these when they strike against an object is very great. The momentum of an automobile in motion is important to every driver or pedestrian. Whenever an object has momentum, it also has *kinetic energy*, which is called the energy of motion. The kinetic energy of an object is one half of its mass multiplied by its velocity squared. This energy is given up when one object strikes another, or is responsible for what is referred to as *impact.* For example, the impact of an automobile at 60 miles an hour is nine times as large as at 20 miles an hour.

One way to increase the momentum of a moving body is to increase its velocity. A simple way of increasing its velocity is to have a force act upon it for the longest possible time. A good tennis player or golfer knows that follow-through is important in striking the ball. In following through, the club or racket acts upon the ball for the longest possible time and therefore the ball travels faster.

Newton's Laws of Motion. The great scientist Sir Isaac Newton announced three laws that govern the actions of motion. These laws, however, do not take into effect such extraneous things as air resistance or other friction. They refer only to ideal motion, removed from any friction.

Newton's first law states that any body moving uniformly in a straight line or in a state of rest will remain in uniform motion in a straight line or in a state of rest unless it is acted upon by some outside force. The property of matter that tends to keep it in motion when in motion, or at rest when at rest is called its *inertia.* Both acceleration and deceleration require overcoming the inertia of an object.

Newton's second law of motion tells what happens when a force is applied to a moving body. The change which any force makes in the motion of an object depends upon two things. One is the size of the force, and the other is the mass of the object. The greater the force, the greater the acceleration; the greater the mass of the object, the smaller the acceleration. The motion or the change of motion takes place in the direction in which a force acts.

Suppose we try to discover the path taken by a moving bullet. We can calculate easily enough the direction and velocity of the bullet as it leaves the muzzle of the gun. But the bullet is also being acted upon by the gravity of the earth. If we fired a bullet horizontally

THE PRINCIPLE OF MOTION

SPEED — Remains the same

VELOCITY — Changes as car goes around curve

from a gun, at the end of one second, no matter how far the bullet traveled, it would have dropped just as much as a freely falling body, which falls 16.08 feet during the first second after it is dropped. That is why the rear sights of rifles are adjusted so that the rifle is actually aimed higher at different targets. This takes care of the drop of the bullet as it moves from the gun.

The effects of two or more forces acting upon the path of a body are calculated by means of *vectors*. A vector is a quantity that tells how large a force is (its *magnitude*) and the direction in which it acts. Forces acting upon a single point are called *concurrent forces*. Suppose a rowboat is being pulled forward parallel to the shore of a lake by a boy walking along the shore. At the same time, another boy in the rowboat uses an oar to push the boat away from the shore, out into the lake. The boat then has two kinds of motion, one along the shore and the other out into the lake. Suppose the boy on the bank exerts a force of 10 pounds while the boy in the boat exerts 15 pounds of force. We can represent these forces by lines drawn in scale at right angles from the point where the boat started. If we construct a parallelogram from these lines, we can determine the resultant path of the boat by drawing a diagonal of the parallelogram, beginning at the point where the boat started. This diagonal also represents the magnitude of the combined forces.

Newton's third law of motion states that for every action there is an equal and opposite reaction. This is the principle behind the jet propulsion engine (see JET PROPULSION). There are many other examples of

this law. We are all familiar with rotating lawn sprinklers that spin when water squirts from their nozzles. Such sprinklers have two or four arms. As the water emerges from the nozzles, the arms are pushed around in the opposite direction, and the water sprays over the lawn.

When you shoot a rifle, there is a kick or recoil. The explosion of the powder in the rifle occurs in all directions, but the bullet is permitted to escape out of the barrel of the rifle. In the meantime, the exploding powder shoves the rifle itself back against your shoulder.

Suppose you have a line of heavy bowling balls strung from the ceiling, so that each ball just touches the next ball as it hangs down. Take two balls from one end of the line and allow them to strike the others. Two balls will fly outward from the other end of the line. If you use one ball, one ball will be moved.

There are other examples of this reaction. Drop a baseball off the edge of a table. The ball will immediately fall to the earth. But at the same time that the ball is falling to earth, the earth is moving toward the ball. Of course, this action of the earth is very small, too minute even to be measured.

Friction. Much of what has previously been discussed about motion refers to ideal motion. Motion as we see it about us, however, is always affected by a factor called friction. Friction is really the resistance to motion. One of the most common things that causes friction is the air. Automobiles and airplanes are streamlined in order to reduce some of this resistance in the air.

However, friction is also a help, because unless friction existed between our feet and the earth, we would not be able to walk. We could not nail two boards together if it were not for friction, because only friction holds the nail in place. When we apply the brakes while driving an automobile, it is friction that stops the car.

One way by which we reduce friction is by use of lubricating oil. Friction between liquid substances is much less than that between solid substances. There are many ways of combating friction. Some metals develop less friction when sliding over each other than the ordinary metals do. These are called antifriction metals and are used in many machines. Furthermore, the smoother the two surfaces that are to move against each other, the less friction there will be between them. Friction may be greatly reduced by the use of wheels, ball bearings, roller bearings, and lubricants. Because of these, one man can push an automobile, and six men can push a locomotive. Casters on a bed reduce the friction that would exist if we had to push the bed across the floor on its legs.

E. A. FESSENDEN

Related Articles in WORLD BOOK include:

Acceleration	Kinematics
Energy (Potential and Kinetic)	Lubricant
Falling Bodies, Law of	Momentum
Force	Newton, Sir Isaac
Friction	Perpetual Motion Machine
Gyroscope	Velocity
Inertia	Viscosity
	Waves

MOTION, PERPETUAL. See PERPETUAL MOTION MACHINE.

Stanley Kubrick's 2001: A Space Odyssey

John Wayne in John Ford's Stagecoach

MOTION PICTURE

MOTION PICTURE. In every country of the world, motion pictures are one of the most important ways of having fun and spreading information. "¡Vamos al cine!" says a Spaniard. "Allons au cinéma!" calls a Frenchman. "Eiga Ni Ikimasho!" exclaims a Japanese. "Let's go to the movies!" says an American.

When we see movies, we feel that we are a part of what we see and hear. We may cheer the hero and hiss the villain in a western. We laugh at talking animals in cartoons. We share the problems presented in serious motion pictures made from great books or plays. Motion pictures often open our minds to new thoughts, new ideas, and new situations.

Motion pictures provide entertainment. They are also used in science, education, industry, and many other fields. Movies in schools can help children learn. Scientists take motion pictures of their research experiments. Doctors can watch movies of operations. Sales-

Arthur Knight, the contributor of this article, is Professor of Cinema at the University of Southern California. He is the author of The Liveliest Art, a history of motion pictures.

Clark Gable and Vivien Leigh in *Gone with the Wind*

Ginger Rogers and Fred Astaire in *The Gay Divorcee*

The Beatles in *Yellow Submarine*

Marcello Mastroianni in Federico Fellini's *8½*

men learn how to sell by watching movies. And millions of persons make home movies as a hobby.

Hollywood, Calif., is considered the motion-picture capital of the world, although several nations now make more movies each year than the United States.

Importance of Motion Pictures

Entertainment is the chief use we make of motion pictures. Movies for entertainment range from long feature films to half-hour films prepared for television.

Feature Films are usually the main attraction at a movie theater. They may cover a wide range of subjects including comedy, romance, music, adventure, sports, current events, and science. Screen writers dip into all periods of history for material for their stories. They even make movies about the future. Motion pictures may tell stories from the Bible or from the biographies of famous persons. Gangster movies show the evils of crime. War movies bring the dangers and bravery of the battlefield to the screen. Motion pictures also present such social problems as alcoholism, mental illness, and racial prejudice.

KINDS OF MOTION PICTURES

Most feature pictures run nearly two hours. Pictures made for teen-age audiences or as the second film in a double feature usually run 80 to 90 minutes. Special productions, such as *Gone With the Wind*, often run over three hours and are shown with an intermission.

Short Subjects run for 7 to 20 minutes between feature films. They include cartoons, travelogues, and brief concerts of classical or popular music. Such famous characters as Mickey Mouse, Donald Duck, and Gerald McBoing-Boing are beloved by children and adults throughout the world.

Television Films cover the same range of subjects as theatrical motion pictures. But they usually run for only 30 or 60 minutes. Some of the major motion-picture companies make films especially for television. Some companies in the United States and Canada make only TV films. The TV networks also produce filmed television shows. In fact, more film is used in Hollywood to make TV movies than to make movies for theaters. Hundreds of feature pictures made by the motion-picture studios are also shown on television.

Education. Teachers sometimes use motion pictures to help students learn facts and skills quickly and easily. Educational films bring history to life. They show students how people live in other parts of the world. Films based on books help students understand and appreciate literature. Science films use slow motion, cartoons, and other special techniques to demonstrate processes that otherwise could not be seen or studied thoroughly. Business and industry use motion pictures to help

Westerns, such as *High Noon*, have been popular ever since the movies began.

Biographies, such as *The Story of Louis Pasteur*, tell the lives of famous persons.

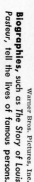

train employees, to promote sales, and to introduce new products and processes. For example, a steel company may produce a film that illustrates the many ways that steel can be used.

Athletic teams take movies of their games. Afterward, they examine the pictures to find what mistakes the players made. Boxers, golfers, and other athletes also study movies to improve their skills.

The widespread use of educational films developed during World War II. The armed forces and government agencies used films to aid in basic and technical training. Motion pictures taught soldiers such skills as how to put weapons together and how to conceal themselves and their equipment. Other films explained the causes of the war, and tried to keep up the soldiers' spirits. The government still makes and uses many training films.

Schools, universities, and commercial producers make educational films. City, county, and state education agencies, as well as colleges and universities, have film libraries. Some state university film libraries have as many as 7,000 films. In Canada, the government's National Film Board produces educational films.

Information. Travelogues and documentaries are shown in regular motion-picture theaters. Their purpose is to give the audience information.

Travelogues give the viewer a pair of "seven-league boots" in which to explore the world. The motion-picture screen can take millions of persons to any place where a camera crew can shoot pictures. Travelogues

UPA Pictures, Inc.
Animated Cartoons, such as *Gerald McBoing-Boing,* entertain and amuse millions of persons of all ages throughout the world.

may show the life of fishermen in Nova Scotia, the scenic wonders of African jungles, the pyramids and the Great Sphinx of Egypt, or the scenic splendor of the Swiss Alps.

Documentaries show people in real-life situations. They are usually short subjects, but some are of feature length. Documentaries may record great historical events. For example, *The Fighting Lady* told the story of an aircraft carrier in World War II. Some documentaries study a family, a race, or a group of people, such as the Eskimos in Robert Flaherty's *Nanook of the North.* Others show events of social or scientific importance. For example, *The River* shows how floods may be controlled. Many industries make documentaries as part of their public-relations programs. These documentaries may tell the history of the industry. Or they may explain how the industry and its products make life easier and more pleasant.

In recent years, television has surpassed theaters in bringing documentary motion pictures to viewers. Many documentary films are produced each year, generally by the networks themselves, specifically for television. Regularly scheduled newscasts use motion pictures in their daily coverage. Entertainment programs may be canceled to present films of special interest, such as an astronaut's flight or an analysis of problems of current national interest. Other programs recreate historical events by carefully re-editing old films.

Advertising. Motion pictures make effective advertisements. Many companies have motion-picture divi-

Musicals, such as *The King and I,* combine music, singing, dancing, and colorful costumes and settings to tell a story.
20th Century-Fox Film Corp.

Walt Disney Productions
Documentaries record events in an entertaining manner. Walt Disney's *White Wilderness* tells how animals live in the Arctic.

sions in their advertising departments. They produce films for use by schools, clubs, and adult groups. More than 10,000 movie theaters in the United States show *advertising trailers* (advertising messages from 40 seconds to 15 minutes long).

Sponsors often film their television advertising messages. *Fluffs* (mistakes) can be cut from filmed commercials. These films can also show characteristics of the product that could not be shown by actors in the TV studio. For example, an automobile commercial might show a car being driven over high mountains or rough roads. Cartoon commercials are popular with advertisers. They cost more to produce than regular motion-picture commercials, but they persuade more people to buy the advertisers' products.

As a Hobby. Millions of families throughout the world take their own motion pictures. These "home movies" may present a record of family activities, the growth of children, or the details of vacation trips. The development of amateur motion pictures began in 1923, when a low-cost film that could be used in small cameras was developed. Low-cost color and sound film made home movies even more popular. Most home movies are taken on either 8mm or 16mm equipment.

As Art. The motion picture can do a great many things not possible in any other art. It can show the excitement of a great cavalry charge. It can condense all the agony of war into a single close-up of the face of a dying soldier. By the use of color and costumes, motion pictures re-create the glamour of the courts of kings and

Art and Fantasy combine in such films as *Tales of Hoffmann,* an opera in which unusual photographic effects help set the mood.
Lion International Films, Ltd.

PEOPLE WHO MAKE MOTION PICTURES

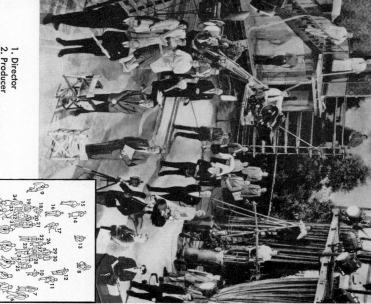

The Rank Organisation Limited

1. Director
2. Producer
3. Still Cameraman
4. Dubbing and Music Mixer
5. Secretary
6. Property Man
7. Electrician
8. Electrician
9. Electrician
10. Sound Mixer
11. Sound-Boom Operator
12. Drapes Man
13. Scenery Painter
14. Carpenter
15. Painter
16. Rigger
17. Camera Operator
18. Camera Grip Man
19. Camera Crane Operator
20. Chief Electrician
21. Director of Photography
22. Assistant Director
23. Clapper Boy
24. Actor
25. Actress
26. Fashion Designer
27. Wardrobe Assistant
28. Wardrobe Assistant
29. Art Director
30. Construction Manager
31. Continuity Girl
32. Make-up Artist
33. Actress
34. Actress
35. Hairdresser
36. Production Manager

Sica's *The Bicycle Thief*, Federico Fellini's *La Strada*, John Huston's *The Treasure of the Sierra Madre*, and Fred Zinneman's *High Noon*.

Social Influence. Motion pictures often influence the habits of audiences. Women and girls copy the dresses and hair styles of glamorous actresses. Young boys dress like the cowboy heroes who gallop across the motion-picture screen. Motion pictures even affect buying habits. When Clark Gable took off his shirt in a motion picture, he had no undershirt on. The sales of men's undershirts promptly dropped.

Motion pictures made in the United States have been exported to nearly every country in the world. They have spread the ideas of American culture. Films produced in other countries also help promote international understanding.

A Trip to a Motion-Picture Studio

A motion-picture *lot* (studio) resembles a bustling industrial community spread out over dozens of acres. A high fence surrounds the lot. Inside, dozens of buildings stand along paved streets. Some buildings are huge, barnlike *sound stages* where movies are filmed. Other buildings include offices, laboratories, and workshops.

People Who Make Motion Pictures

People Who Make Motion Pictures represent about 275 occupations. Many, such as carpenters, painters, electricians, and engineers, perform about the same jobs they would in any community. But some of the same jobs are found only inside a motion-picture studio. For example, *special-effects men* use models to create a storm in mid-ocean, to blow up a city, or to create the illusion of traveling in space—all within a studio lot. They can also make imitation snow, rain, or hail. *Powder men* produce smoke without fire. *Green men* duplicate the plant life of any region on earth. *Agers* give the appearance of wear and tear to furniture and clothes. *Make-up men* change the appearance of actors to fit their parts.

The Producer is in charge of making a movie. He selects the director and other key workers to make the picture. He also helps choose the *cast* of actors and actresses. The producer supervises everything that goes into the picture. He has charge of the budget, and plans the schedule for "shooting" the picture.

The Director controls the performance of the actors by rehearsing and instructing them. He usually helps plan the picture from the start. He attends conferences on the

emperors. By trick photography, the giants of legend appear real.

Motion pictures have another unique characteristic. They can present a series of ideas and emotions in rapid succession. The pictures on the screen follow each other in an artistic pattern. They create emotional effects, which is the objective of any fine art. Many motion pictures have ranked among the major artistic achievements of our time. Such pictures as John Ford's *The Informer*, Orson Welles' *Citizen Kane*, and Sir Laurence Olivier's *Henry V* have raised motion pictures to high levels of art. Other artistically important films include Sergei Eisenstein's *The Battleship Potemkin*, Vittorio De

— INTERESTING FACTS ABOUT MOTION PICTURES —

Admissions collected at motion-picture theaters in the United States total about $1 billion a year.

A Feature Motion Picture that runs about 2 hours uses almost 2 miles of film.

Electric Light used in a single day to produce American movies could light a town of 5,000 persons for a year.

Enough Film to Reach from the Earth to the Moon— 221,000 miles—is used in the United States each year to make motion pictures.

Motion-Picture Theaters. The United States has about 13,000 indoor theaters and 3,800 drive-ins. Canada has about 1,300 indoor theaters and more than 200 drive-ins.

Production Costs of a feature-length movie average more than $25,000 each day. Some scenes may cost as much as $25,000 an hour to shoot, although they may appear on the screen for only two minutes.

Weekly Audiences of 44 million persons in the United States and 130 million in other countries see the 160 to 165 movies that Hollywood produces yearly.

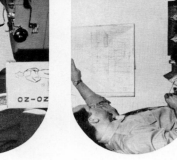

Screen Writer may adapt a book or play for the movies, or he may write an original script. *Warner Bros. Pictures, Inc.*

Set Designer plans the movie sets and builds scale models to show how they should look.

Carpenters build walls, panels, and partitions that will be used in the movie set.

Costume Designer sketches patterns of original costumes that will be used in the movie.

Musicians record background music. They synchronize their music with the action by watching the film as they play. *Warner Bros. Pictures, Inc.*

Film Editor studies the film and helps decide which scenes will appear in the finished picture.

script, sets, costumes, and editing. The director helps the producer choose the cast and plan work schedules. He arranges the scenes in the most convenient order for shooting. Scenes that take place on the same set may be shot one after another, regardless of where they will appear in the story. The director must see that each scene of the movie is filmed with the best dramatic results. He controls the pace and movement of the story. Sometimes the director also serves as producer.

Actors and Actresses. Few generals, presidents, or dictators are as well known as the leading motion-picture actors and actresses. *Stars* are performers who have achieved great fame and popularity. But only a small number of screen actors and actresses—perhaps 1 of every 100—become stars. Some actors play important "supporting" roles. Others play shorter roles, or "bit" parts. *Extras* rarely have lines. They may appear as people passing by or in crowd scenes. Movie performers work long hours to learn lines and rehearse their parts.

Writers prepare the *screenplay* (story on which the motion picture is based). Many movies are *adaptations* taken from novels, biographies, literary classics, and stage plays. When a screen writer creates his own story, it is called an *original*. The *scenario* (movie script) tells the story in detail as it will appear on film. It contains the dialogue for the actors and describes in detail the atmosphere and background of each scene. It also includes instructions about the shots that will be taken.

The Composer writes the background music for a movie. He generally begins after reviewing a rough version of the picture and consulting with the director to determine the desired mood from scene to scene. The composer must write music that will help establish emotions in the audience, fit the action, and not drown out the actors. The composer often conducts his own music when it is recorded for the film.

The Film Editor, or *Film Cutter*, works in the cutting room. The director and the producer work closely with him, because editing has much to do with the way a picture appears in its final form.

The *sound* or *effects editor* and the *music editor* assist the film editor in preparing the sound tracks for a picture.

Sound Stages are the largest and most impressive buildings on a lot. From the outside, they look like airplane hangars. These long, high, windowless buildings are called sound stages because both pictures and dialogue are recorded in them. Movie people also use *sound stage* to mean the set on which the picture is filmed.

A network of electric cables crosses the floor of the sound stage. These cables supply power for the lights and equipment used to shoot the picture. The floors are also cluttered with partitions, machinery, and wires. The set itself is carefully planned by *set designers*. Their plans allow the actors room to move about, and let the camera photograph every part of the action. For example, the set of an elegantly furnished living room of a New York City apartment may have two, three, or four walls. The walls are usually *wild*. This means they can be moved about to allow the cameras to focus on all parts of the room. The cameras are mounted on large, self-powered vehicles called *dollies*. Dozens of powerful lights shine down from above. Microphones hang down just out of range of the cameras. The view of the city's skyline showing through a rear window is either a realis-

MOTION-PICTURE CAMERA

Motion-Picture Camera takes a picture as a still camera does. A strip of unexposed film moves past the aperture. The film pauses for 1/50 of a second behind the aperture as each frame (picture) is taken. Then the film moves on to expose the next frame. The exposed film is pulled up into the rear magazine. Every second, 24 frames are exposed.

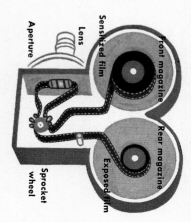

tery, American frontier towns, an English mining village, the brownstone houses of New York, the Cathedral of Notre Dame in Paris, opera houses, concert halls, and a Japanese fishing village.

Other Buildings. The *prop* (property) department has rooms filled with an amazing assortment of furniture, tapestry, and lighting fixtures from every period of history. Props also include jewelry, silverware, pottery, firearms, musical instruments, and many other items.

The *wardrobe department* contains row upon row of gowns and costumes of the past and present. Seamstresses, dressmakers, and milliners provide clothing for the cast and care for the costumes. In the *plaster shop*, talented workers use paper, plaster, and plastics to create anything from castles and cottages to cliffs and prison walls. Sets are built in the *carpenter shop*.

The studio's *research department* resembles a library. Tens of thousands of books and many rows of photograph files help producers check every fact and detail in a movie. *Technical advisers* often work with the script writers and on the set, to guard against errors. For example, a naval officer might act as technical adviser in a movie about ships.

---

tic, painted background, a greatly enlarged photograph, or a motion picture projected on a screen by projectors behind the screen.

The cameramen, technicians, and workmen make final preparations to shoot the scene. When all is ready, the director calls for silence. The stage becomes completely quiet so that no noise will be recorded along with the actors' voices. The cameras start to turn at the director's command of "Action" or "Roll it." The director may order the same scene shot many times before he is satisfied. He may spend hours shooting a scene that the audience sees for only two minutes.

Permanent Outdoor Sets are life-sized reproductions of houses, buildings, and even whole towns. The buildings usually consist only of fronts supported by wooden braces. They are used as backgrounds for outdoor scenes. Studios often use the same sets over and over again in different movies. Minor changes, such as the names of stores and the colors of buildings, are made to fit the needs of different scripts. The changes also keep the audience from recognizing that the set was used in other films. Permanent outdoor sets in Hollywood include reproductions of London streets, a Tibetan monas-

---

HOW SOUND PICTURES ARE MADE

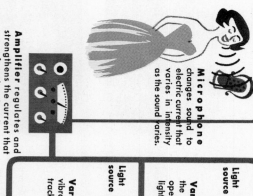

Microphone changes sound to electric current that varies in intensity as the sound varies.

Amplifier regulates and strengthens the current that comes from the microphone.

Magnetic Recording. Current from an amplifier causes changes in an electromagnet. Impulses from the electromagnet create a magnetic pattern on an iron-oxide stripe on the film.

Electromagnet

Magnetized stripe on film

Light source

Variable-Density Recording uses light shining on a shutter gate. Changes in current from the amplifier change the size of the gate opening. The stronger the current, the wider the opening and the more light gets to the film. The weaker the current, the smaller the opening. The light exposes the film sound track, recording the sound as a series of light and dark bands.

Shutter gate

Exposed sound track

Light source

Variable-Area Recording uses a light that shines on a mirror. Current from the amplifier vibrates the mirror. As the mirror vibrates, it shines the light in a wavy pattern on the film sound track. The light exposes the film, and reproduces sound as a wavy line on the film.

Mirror

Exposed sound track

MOTION-PICTURE SOUND PROJECTOR

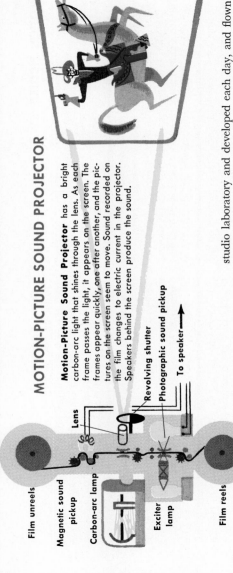

Motion-Picture Sound Projector has a bright carbon-arc light that shines through the lens. As each frame passes the light, it appears on the screen. The frames appear quickly, one after another, and the pictures on the screen seem to move. Sound recorded on the film changes to electric current in the projector. Speakers behind the screen produce the sound.

Film unreels

Lens

Magnetic sound pickup

Carbon-arc lamp

Exciter lamp

Revolving shutter

Photographic sound pickup

To speaker →

Film reels

The *music department* usually occupies a separate building. Here, composers, arrangers, conductors, and orchestras create and play the music for motion pictures. This music is recorded and later *dubbed in* (added to the picture's sound track). *Background music* helps set the mood for the action and dialogue of the scenes. Music must help the effects the film is trying to achieve.

Other structures at big studios include rehearsal rooms, offices, and laboratories where films are processed and developed.

On Location. Making pictures in a place other than the studio is called *going on location*. When a large part of a film story takes place on or near a mountain, plain, desert, lake, or ocean, the producer sometimes makes the movie outside the studio. Casts and crews may travel all over the world to shoot their pictures. Studio craftsmen can build sets that resemble African jungles or the streets of Rome. However, many producers feel that filming on the actual spot increases the realism of their pictures and gives the audience the additional pleasure of becoming tourists through the movies.

Shooting on location also has disadvantages. The cast, camera crew, technicians, and equipment must be transported to the location. Generators must be brought to provide power for lights and other apparatus. The company has to house and feed the workers. Trees or brush must often be cleared away in mountain or jungle areas, and roads must be built so trucks can carry personnel and equipment. The film must be flown to the

studio laboratory and developed each day, and flown back so that the director and others can see the results. Outside noises from birds or airplanes may spoil the sound track. But these problems can be corrected at the studio.

Filming a Picture. Every feature picture consists of hundreds, sometimes thousands, of separate shots. In the final film, the shots are all blended together so that the picture progresses smoothly. Each scene is filmed many times and from many points of view, depending on what the director wants to emphasize. He may use a *long shot* to show the outside of a drug store, a *mid-shot* to pick out a boy and girl sitting at the soda fountain, *closeups* of each of them as they talk together, and then finish with a *pan* or *dolly shot* as they walk out of the store. Each shot represents a separate camera *setup* that offers the best view for catching a particular moment in the development of the story. Generally, only a single camera is used. In spectacular scenes, such as the chariot race in *Ben Hur*, however, as many as a dozen cameras may be used at once.

In television, cost often is more important than quality. So television shows are often filmed with three cameras running at once. Each camera gives one view of the action. As in motion pictures, the film editor selects the best shots for each scene from all this footage, then pieces them together to give the correct emphasis, rhythm, and movement to the story. Even after he has completed his work, the producer or director may tell him to cut out dull spots in the story, or make further changes that will heighten the drama. Up to 40 hours of film may be shot to make a 90-minute program.

HOW SOUND IS REPRODUCED IN THEATERS

- **LIGHT RECORDING**

Sound exciter lamp

Projector

Electric eye

Film

Amplifier

Speaker

As the film runs through the projector, a light in the projector shines through the sound-track pattern to hit an electric eye. The

electric eye changes the pattern into electric current, which is strengthened by an amplifier and changed to sound by a speaker.

- **MAGNETIC RECORDING**

Projector

Electromagnet

Film

Amplifier

Speaker

An electromagnet in the projector changes impulses from the magnetized stripe into electric current. An amplifier strengthens the current and a speaker changes it into sound.

MOTION PICTURE

How Motion Pictures Work

Motion pictures are possible only because the eye does not record exactly what it sees. When the eye sees a brightly lighted object, it continues to record what it has seen for a fraction of a second after the light goes out. This action of the eye is known as persistence of vision (see EYE [Persistence of Vision]).

Projector. When you spend an evening at the movies, you see a long series of pictures in which the characters do not actually move. You actually see about 130,000 different photographs in the average feature film. A machine called a *projector* throws these pictures on the screen, one after the other, so rapidly that they do not appear as separate pictures. One photograph seems to blend continuously with the following photograph, creating the illusion of motion. The projector also has a mechanism that reproduces the sound for the movie.

In the projector, *sprocket wheels* with small teeth move the film past a powerful beam of light. The projector stops and starts the film 24 times a second. Each time the film stops, the light beam projects a picture on the screen. A revolving shutter shuts out the light from the beam while the film moves on to the next frame. The viewer's persistence of vision fills in the dark intervals, and the action appears continuous. Actually, the screen is dark for a longer period of time than it is bright!

Camera. In taking a motion picture, light from an object focuses through the lens of the camera onto film. This film moves in a similar manner and at the same speed as film in a projector. Cameras are mounted on tripods or other foundations, so that they remain steady while the picture is being taken. A special device sometimes joins the camera to its base so that the cameraman can take *panoramic shots* (shots that cover a wide range). To take a "pan" shot, he may move the camera from side to side, or he may make a "tilt" shot by moving it vertically on its axis.

Cameras usually have special lenses, so cameramen can photograph scenes in several ways. *Wide-angled* lenses take in a broad field. *Telephoto* lenses permit distant objects to be photographed as if they were near.

Special slow-motion cameras take pictures at speeds greater than 24 pictures a second. These cameras record action that is too fast for the eye to follow. A movement that takes only a fraction of a second is projected in slow motion for a longer period. Cameras of extremely slow speeds take single pictures at widely-spaced intervals. These cameras can show slow movements, such as plants growing and flowers blooming, so they seem to happen rapidly.

Film for motion pictures is a flexible strip of celluloid coated with light-sensitive chemicals. It has small, evenly-spaced holes along the edges. These holes allow the sprockets in the camera and the projector to move the film. Film for professional motion pictures is either 35 or 70 millimeters, or about 1⅜ or 2¾ inches, wide. Films for educational use in schools are usually 16 millimeters, or about ⅝ of an inch, wide. Most home movies are made on film 8 millimeters, or a little more than ¼ inch, wide. This narrow film permits the use of small cameras and projectors. It is about half as expensive as 16-millimeter film.

Color Pictures originally required a complicated camera that exposed three strips of film at the same time. But today a standard motion-picture camera of the type used for black-and-white film can also take color pictures. Some films for taking color pictures have light-sensitive dyes. Others go through a complicated process known as *color separation*. See TECHNICOLOR.

Sound. When an actor speaks on a motion-picture set, the sound waves produced by his voice strike a microphone. The microphone catches the pattern of the sound waves and changes them into a varying electric current (see MICROPHONE). This current is then *amplified* (strengthened) much as sound is amplified in a radio receiver. The sounds, which are now variations in current, are recorded along the edge of the film by either a photographic or a magnetic process. The area on which sound is recorded is called the *sound track*.

In the *magnetic* method, a magnetic iron-oxide coating is applied to the edges of the film. Impulses from the microphone move a beam of light. A narrow band on the film is exposed to this beam of light. It records the sound as a pattern of light and dark bands, or as varying areas of light against dark. When the film runs through the projector, a photoelectric cell changes the light pattern back to electric current (see ELECTRIC EYE).

In the *photographic* method, the impulses transmitted by the microphone move a beam of light. A narrow band on the film is exposed to this beam of light. It records the sound as a pattern of light and dark bands, or as varying areas of light against dark. When the film runs through the projector, a photoelectric cell changes the light pattern back to electric current (see ELECTRIC EYE).

Amplifiers strengthen the electric current from the projector. Then the speaker converts these currents into the sounds that we hear in the theater.

The *dialogue* (spoken part) of a motion picture usually is recorded at the time that the scene is filmed. Technicians then add sound effects and background music to the sound track after the picture is taken. However, the sounds of orchestras, bands, and singers appearing in the picture may be recorded before the scene is filmed. After a successful sound recording, the director shoots the scene so that the actions correspond with the sound track. In this way, he gets the best possible effect without the waste of money and time to refilm the scene.

Separate sound tracks for voice, music, and sound effects are blended into a *composite* track. This track is printed with the silent picture to make a complete sound and picture print.

Special Effects and tricks with the camera help present a story smoothly and dramatically. In a *dissolve*, one scene on the screen gradually merges with and seems to be replaced by a second scene. This can be done by printing the beginning of one scene on the end of the other. A *fade-out* can be made by passing over the lens a glass that is transparent at one end and gradually grows darker and darker until it is black at the other end. But fade-outs and dissolves are usually made in the laboratory by using chemicals. This lets the producer begin, end, or overlap scenes as he wishes. A specially-shaped *mask* placed over the camera lens may give the impression of looking through a keyhole, field glasses, or other opening. Sometimes cameramen shoot scenes in which an actor plays two parts at the same time. For this, they use a mask that covers half the lens. First the film is run through showing the actor in one pose, and

half the film is masked. Then the film is run through again with the other half masked. Cameramen produce many photographic stunts with a combination camera and projection machine called a *special-effects printer* or an *optical printer*.

Screen was once merely a square of white fabric on which pictures were projected. A modern screen has a special highly reflective surface to give a clear picture with bright colors. Its surface may be covered with small beads of glass. Or it may be painted with titanium dioxide or a mixture of white lead and white zinc.

The speaker for the sound track is placed behind the screen, so that the sounds seem to come from the picture. From 20 to 40 holes are punched into every square inch of the screen's surface to allow the sound to project through the screen.

Wide-Screen Processes were introduced in 1952, to show larger pictures. These processes use huge screens that measure 60 feet wide or more, almost twice as large as the earlier rectangular screens. They also have more

powerful projectors that improve the quality of the picture. The wide screen, combined with *stereophonic sound* (sound coming from speakers in different parts of the theater), gives a feeling of depth.

Cinerama was the first wide-screen process. It used three projectors to throw the picture onto a three-paneled curved screen. The original three strips are now combined and printed on a single 70 mm film for simpler projection. So, *Cinerama* resembles *Todd-AO*, which also uses 70mm film process, and is generally shown on a slightly curved screen. *CinemaScope*, the most common wide-screen process, appears on a flat screen 2½ times as wide as it is high. An *anamorphic lens* in the camera records a compressed picture on regular film, and a compensating lens on the projector expands the picture for the wide screen. Variations on the anamorphic principle are the basis for *Technirama* and other wide-screen processes.

The Motion-Picture Industry

In the United States, the motion-picture industry employs about 174,000 part-time and full-time technical and artistic workers. Most have never seen Hollywood. They work for the industry in more than 10,000 cities, towns, and villages. These people work on publicity, on advertising, on distribution, and in motion-picture theaters.

The major motion-picture companies have large studios in and near Hollywood. They have their main sales offices in and near New York City, where the companies' business and financial headquarters are located. They also have branch offices in 25 to 35 leading cities in the United States and Canada. Most major companies have offices in the chief cities in other countries.

Each major company produces from 20 to 30 feature films each year, as well as short subjects for theatrical or television exhibition. They may also distribute the films of independent producers. Some companies do not produce films themselves. They act as agents for independent producers, and may distribute from 40 to 50 independently produced films each year. They contract to distribute films for a percentage of the film's rentals. They also receive a percentage of the film's profit if they have financed the film. The eight major American distributing companies are Allied Artists, Columbia, Loew's (Metro-Goldwyn-Mayer), Paramount, Twentieth Century-Fox, United Artists, Universal-International, and Warner Brothers.

Independent producing companies are frequently

MOTION-PICTURE TERMS

Cut is the director's signal that a shot is finished.

Close-up is a camera shot taken at close range.

Dissolve is a film shot in which one scene slowly disappears while another moves in to take its place.

Extra is a performer hired by the day for scenes that need groups or crowds of people.

Fade-out is a scene that gradually disappears.

Flash Back is a scene that interrupts the story to tell about something that happened in the past.

Grip is a carpenter who makes emergency changes or repairs on a movie set.

Juicer is an electrician who operates the lights on a movie set.

Long Shot is a scene or subject filmed at long range.

Mixer is a machine that records sound and dialogue. The engineer responsible for recording sound is also called the *mixer*.

Montage is a series of dissolves and quick cuts used to indicate a change in time or events, or to dramatize a point in the story.

Rushes are day-to-day scenes of a picture filmed and developed for the director, producer, and film editor to examine. Rushes are also called *dailies*.

Screen Treatment is a scene-by-scene outline of a movie story. It does not contain the dialogue or technical details of a *scenario* (shooting script).

Set is a building, room, or area prepared or built for a movie scene inside or outside the studio.

Shoot means to photograph any part of a motion picture.

Take is a portion of a scene filmed and recorded without pause or interruption.

Special Effects Produce Illusions. Cobwebs, *left*, are really rubber cement. A trick set, *center*, exaggerates distance. Trick photography, *right*, can make objects appear much larger or smaller.

formed by stars, producers, and directors who have worked for the major studios. These *independents* select stories and arrange for casts and financing. They often rent studio space from major companies. Most independents produce from one to five pictures a year.

Distribution of motion pictures works somewhat like a vast circulating library. *Film exchanges* are the distribution offices of large studios and distributing companies. They supply films to theaters throughout the world. They rent films belonging to studios or independents. They usually charge the theater-owner a percentage of the total box-office receipts, but sometimes the fee is on a flat rental basis.

Organizations. Many different organizations exist within the motion-picture industry. The largest distribution companies belong to the Motion Picture Association of America and to the Motion Picture Export Association of America. The major studios are members of the Association of Motion Picture Producers. Most of the main independent producers belong to the Society of Independent Motion Picture Producers.

About 2,850 persons in Hollywood, including top-ranking actors, producers, directors, craftsmen, and technicians, belong to the Academy of Motion Picture Arts and Sciences. Each year this organization gives awards called "Oscars" for outstanding achievement in the various branches of film-making.

Most of the persons who work in film studios belong to some union or guild. Actors, writers, directors, cameramen, film editors, musicians, and even producers have their own organizations. So do carpenters, costumers, painters, plasterers, and plumbers. About 40 unions and guilds are in the motion-picture industry.

Regulation. The film industry in the United States maintains certain moral standards in movies through a voluntary system of self-regulation. In 1930, the Motion Picture Association of America adopted the Motion Picture Production Code to govern the making of motion pictures. In 1968, it set up a code that provides a film rating system. The categories are *G*—all ages admitted; *GP*—all ages admitted but parental guidance suggested; *R*—restricted to adults and persons under the age of 17 if accompanied by a parent or guardian; *X*—no one admitted under the age of 17, although the age may vary in different parts of the United States. The code also deals with film advertising and film titles.

For many years, the governments of several states and of a few cities maintained official censor boards. These boards reviewed all movies before the films could be shown in the area. The board could forbid the showing of a picture, or require certain scenes to be cut. A series of federal and state court decisions, beginning in 1952, severely restricted the legal basis for film censorship. By the late 1960's, only a few communities in the United States still had official censorship boards.

Hundreds of critics review motion pictures in newspapers and magazines. Some civic and religious groups have their own committees to rate pictures and advise their members about them.

In Other Countries. About 140 to 200 films made in other countries are shown widely in the United States each year. They come chiefly from Great Britain, France, Italy, and Germany. In addition, film ex-changes import many more films for limited audiences. For example, Mexican pictures are popular with persons of Mexican background who live in Texas and New Mexico.

The average neighborhood theater shows few pictures from other lands, because not enough persons care to see them. But in large cities, special theaters called *art houses* show mainly movies made in France, Italy, and other countries. These pictures may be in another language with English *subtitles* (translations) printed on the screen. Or they may have English *dubbed in* (substituted) for the original language.

Japan produces more movies than any other nation. In some years, Japan produces more than 500 features. The Japanese have received high international praise for their work in photography, especially in color.

India produces about 500 films a year. But this total often includes several versions of the same feature in different languages for various sections of India. The people of India especially enjoy screen stories that include songs and dances typical of the country.

Italy ranks first among the European nations in the number of pictures produced. Italians make about 130 movies each year. Many of these films are co-produced with movie-makers in other countries. Italy has produced impressive pictures filmed in such real settings as the streets of Rome and Naples.

Great Britain produces about 115 motion pictures a year. British comedies and dramas have long been popular in the United States. The techniques used by many British directors reflect their training in making documentary movies. They use natural sets and lighting whenever possible.

France produces about 100 motion pictures annually. The French have a flair for witty, sophisticated comedies. They are particularly interested in character study.

Russia produces about 85 films a year. Principal studios are located in Moscow and Leningrad. Only a few theaters in the United States show Russian films. Many Russian films are made for propaganda purposes.

Development of Motion Pictures

Early Developments. In about 65 B.C., the Roman poet Lucretius discovered the principle of the persistence of vision. About 200 years later, the Greek astronomer Ptolemy experimentally proved its existence. In 1824, Peter Mark Roget helped to spur the invention of motion pictures with a paper he read on the subject before the Royal Society in London (see ROGET, PETER M.). In 1826, Henry Fitton, an English scientist, developed a toy that made use of this principle. The toy consisted of a paper disk with a picture of a cage on one side and a picture of a bird on the other. The disk had strings fastened to opposite edges. When the card was whirled between the strings, the bird appeared to be inside the cage. John Ayrton Paris, an English physician, manufactured this toy as the *thaumatrope*.

Many other persons experimented with the idea of creating motion in pictures. In 1832, Joseph Antoine Ferdinand Plateau, a Belgian scientist, developed the *phenakistoscope*, the first device for making pictures appear to move. Plateau placed two rotating disks a few inches apart along a rod. He painted pictures of an object or a person along the edge of one disk. Each picture advanced the motion a little bit. Slots were cut in the other disk. When the two disks were rotated, the pictures seemed to move as they came into view in the slots. In 1852, Franz Uchatius, an Austrian military officer, used the principle of the phenakistoscope to project pictures on a wall. Other variations of these devices included the *zoetrope*, developed by Pierre Hubert Desvignes of France in 1860, and the *praxinoscope*, developed by Émile Reynaud of France in 1877.

In 1861, Coleman Sellers, a Philadelphia inventor, developed the *kinematoscope*. It consisted of pictures arranged around a rod, much like the paddles of a water wheel. They were viewed through an eyepiece. The pictures moved when a knob was turned rapidly, and came into view one after another.

Another early device called the *kineograph* is still used. It was patented by John Barnes Linnett in 1868. It consists of successive pictures of a single action, made up into a little book. When the edges of the book are flipped rapidly, the pictures come into view in rapid succession and seem to have motion.

The first successful photography of motion took place in 1877. Five years earlier, Ex-governor Leland Stanford of California had asked Eadweard Muybridge, a San Francisco photographer, to make instantaneous photos of running horses. After many attempts, and with the assistance of engineer John D. Isaacs, Muybridge succeeded by setting up 24 cameras in a row, with strings stretched across a racetrack to the shutter of each camera. When the horse ran by, it broke each string in succession, tripping the camera shutters.

The First Motion Pictures. In the late 1800's, inventors in the United States, France, and Great Britain tried to find ways to make and project motion pictures. These early experimenters included Thomas Armat, Thomas A. Edison, C. Francis Jenkins, and Woodville Latham of the United States; William Friese-Greene and Robert W. Paul of Great Britain; and Louis and Auguste Lumière and Etienne Jules Marey of France. After many failures, success came suddenly to a number of pioneers at the same time. No one knows who first produced and projected motion pictures.

In 1887, Edison began to work on a device to make a series of pictures appear to move. But he did not succeed until 1889, after the American inventor George Eastman developed strips of flexible celluloid camera film. A series of pictures could be photographed on this film and moved rapidly. With the assistance of William Kennedy Laurie Dickson, Edison developed two ma-

chines that made use of Eastman's film. The *kinetograph* was a device for taking a series of photographs. The *kinetoscope* was a cabinet in which 50 feet of film revolved on spools. A person could look through a peephole in the cabinet and watch the pictures move. In 1894, Edison opened the Kinetoscope Parlor in New York City. It had two rows of peep-show machines. The machines showed filmed bits of vaudeville acts and some homemade pictures, such as *Fred Ott's Sneeze*. Edison made all these films in his "Black Maria" tar-paper studio in West Orange, N.J.

In 1895, Armat and Latham successfully projected motion pictures in public demonstrations. The Lumière brothers in France and Paul in England developed successful projection methods about this time. Probably the first commercial presentation of a movie took place in Paris on Dec. 28, 1895, when the Lumière brothers demonstrated their *Cinematographe* in the Grand Café.

On April 23, 1896, Edison presented the first theatrical showing of motion pictures in the United States. His show took place at Koster and Bial's Music Hall in New York City. He used Armat's projection machine, the *vitascope*. The program included a few scenes from a prize fight, a performance by a dancer, and a scene of waves rolling in on a Manhattan beach. The waves seemed so real that they sent people in the front rows scurrying back to avoid being soaked!

French pictures, using a projector made by the Lumières, were shown in New York City in June, 1896. In October, a motion-picture program at Oscar Hammerstein's Olympia Music Hall showed William McKinley during his campaign for the presidency.

The motion picture had now become a form of public amusement. Within a few years, traveling showmen with movies entertained at street fairs, picnics, and medicine shows in one town after another. Idle storerooms were used as theaters in many cities.

An early movie, *The Life of an American Fireman*, had no real plot. It merely described an incident. But it was the first movie to show that motion pictures *could* tell a story. It was produced in 1903 by the Edison Company and directed by Edwin S. Porter. Later that year, Porter produced the ancestor of all western pictures, *The Great Train Robbery*. This movie was the screen's first effort to tell a real story in pictures. In it, Porter used new methods of effective film editing. He also showed move-

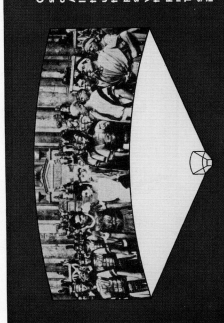

Cinemascope uses standard-sized film and one projector. A special camera lens distorts the picture so that the figures are squeezed together, top. In the projector, another special lens reverses the distortion, so that the picture appears normal, bottom. The wide screen is slightly curved to improve the focus.

The Thaumatrope, developed in 1826, was a paper disk with strings fastened to opposite ends. When the disk was whirled, the bird on one side of the card appeared in the cage on the other side.

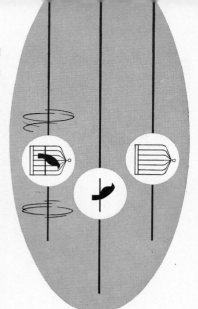

Georges Méliès of France, a former magician, discovered that he could do tricks with a camera. He was the father of special effects, of fantasy in movie-making, and of trick photography. His most famous movie, *A Trip to the Moon,* produced in 1902, was 11 minutes long (1,000 feet), about three times as long as the average motion picture at that time. Méliès used trick photography to show a rocket ship traveling to the moon.

The Nickelodeon. The first motion-picture theater, the Electric Theater in Los Angeles, opened in 1902.

ment toward and away from the camera, as well as in front of it. "Bronco Billy" Anderson, the first of the cowboy stars, appeared in it briefly. Similar pictures soon followed, including *The Great Bank Robbery* and *Trapped by Bloodhounds.*

The Phenakistoscope, developed in 1832, had two revolving disks. When the disks were whirled, an observer looking through slots in one disk saw pictures on the other disk appear to move.

The Praxinoscope, developed in 1877, had a mirror with several sides in the center of a cylinder. When the cylinder rotated, the pictures on it were reflected in the mirror and seemed to move.

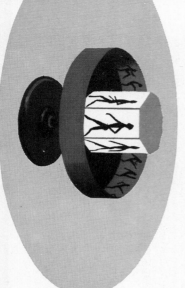

The First Successful Photographs of Motion were taken by the English photographer Eadweard Muybridge in 1877. He stretched a row of threads across a horse's path. As the horse ran by, it broke the threads and tripped the shutters of a row of cameras. Mounted in a row, the pictures showed how the horse moved. These pictures, using the same method, were taken by Muybridge in 1878.

Culver

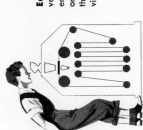

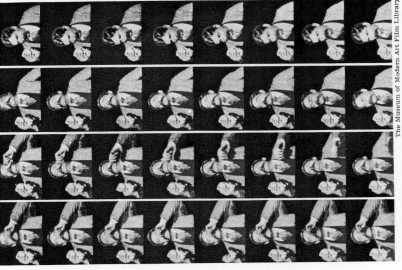

Edison's Kinetoscope, developed in the 1890's, had an endless roll of film that moved on spools. By looking through the peephole at the top, the viewer watched pictures move.

Fred Ott's Sneeze, the first motion picture close-up sequence, was photographed by Thomas A. Edison in 1893. The film strips should be read from top to bottom, beginning with the upper left frame, as you would read columns in a newspaper.

For the price of 10 cents, it offered an hour's amusement in "a vaudeville of moving pictures." By 1905, the story film had made motion pictures extremely popular. In McKeesport, Pa., a real-estate dealer named Harry Davis installed a movie projector in a vacant storeroom. The picture, accompanied by piano music, was *The Great Train Robbery.* Davis charged 5 cents for admission. This was the first "nickelodeon." It became famous overnight, and by 1907 about 5,000 nickelodeons had appeared throughout the United States.

The sudden growth of the nickelodeon increased the demand for motion pictures. Companies were formed to produce movies to satisfy the demand. By 1908, hundreds of pictures were being produced every year. Films shot in studios replaced those made in back yards and on roof tops. Many men previously engaged in other businesses turned their attention to the films, including Adolph Zukor, Carl Laemmle, Louis B. Mayer, Lewis J. Selznick, Jesse Lasky, and Samuel Goldwyn.

In 1907, the first motion-picture pioneers arrived in Los Angeles to film outdoor scenes for a one-reel version of *The Count of Monte Cristo.* This venture took advantage of the California weather and scenery, and marked the start of movie production there. William A. Selig produced and released the film.

In 1908, David W. Griffith began directing hundreds of one-reel films for the Biograph Studio in New York City. He averaged two films a week. Griffith learned to use such dramatic devices as the close-up, flash-back, fade-out, and montage. These devices made the characters seem more human, kept up suspense, and helped the audience identify itself with the action.

The Silent Era. Hollywood became the movie capital of the world between 1910 and 1920. Individual producers and then larger companies built studios there. Labor and other costs were lower than in New York City. Many pictures were shot outdoors with sunlight as the only source of light.

Few directors in this period used scripts. Instead, they worked from story outlines that they broke down into shots as they went along. Directors added the dialogue later in the form of titles printed on the film. Many directors and carpenters "doubled" as actors. The actors helped the carpenters with whatever settings appeared in the films. At first, the motion-picture performers were not identified by name. But when the films began to attract fan mail, the names of the actors were listed. The "star system" was born in 1910. By 1915, it dominated the motion-picture industry.

The Birth of a Nation, directed by D. W. Griffith in 1915, marked the beginning of modern movie-making. The Civil War battle scenes, photography, excellent editing, and suspenseful story raised the art of the motion picture to the level of literature and the theater.

Motion pictures became a big business after the success of *The Birth of a Nation.* Nickelodeons outgrew their storerooms and moved into theaters. Large producing companies established nationwide systems to distribute films to exhibitors, and purchased theaters of their own. Movies, once entertainment primarily for the poor and illiterate, had suddenly reached the hearts not only of all Americans but of all the world.

The best-known stars of this period included Mary Pickford, "America's Sweetheart," who played innocent-young-girl parts, and Charlie Chaplin, who portrayed the comedy role of "The Tramp." Other famous early actors and actresses included Theda Bara, the first vamp; and Francis X. Bushman and Beverly Bayne, the screen's first "love team." Ruth Roland and Pearl White became national favorites in serial thrillers.

The westerns galloped along with such cowboy favorites as William S. Hart and Tom Mix.

Mack Sennett, a former plumber's helper, produced and directed popular comedies. The Keystone Cops' wild chases, Ben Turpin's crossed eyes, and Mabel Normand's pixie-like athletics all became famous in Sennett's films. Charlie Chaplin made his first pictures for Sennett.

Memorable pictures of the early 1920's included *The Mark of Zorro, The Three Musketeers,* and *Robin Hood,* all swashbuckling adventure stories starring Douglas Fairbanks. Griffith directed *Orphans of the Storm* and *Way Down East. The Four Horsemen of the Apocalypse* brought fame to matinee idol Rudolph Valentino. The epic World War I picture *The Big Parade* starred John Gilbert and was directed by King Vidor. Feature-length comedies included *The Freshman* with shy Harold Lloyd, and *The Navigator* with stony-faced Buster Keaton.

Cecil B. De Mille directed a spectacular silent production of *The Ten Commandments.* Another spectacular was Fred Niblo's *Ben Hur,* known for its thrilling chariot-race scene. John Ford directed *The Iron Horse,* an epic of the building of the Union Pacific Railroad. *The Phantom of the Opera,* one of the best-remembered horror stories, starred Lon Chaney, "The Man of a Thousand Faces." Chaney was a master of make-up. He often played parts in which he appeared to be hideously

deformed. Greta Garbo became famous as a mysterious siren in *The Flesh and the Devil,* in which she played opposite John Gilbert. Jackie Coogan, a popular child star, appeared with Charlie Chaplin in *The Kid.*

In 1919, *The Cabinet of Dr. Caligari* was made in Germany. This psychological horror-fantasy became one of the most popular and influential pictures of its time, and one of the first "art films." The success of the picture encouraged Hollywood to import famous German directors and stars to make films in the United States.

Around 1910, several inventors attempted to produce motion pictures in color. But the first commercially successful color motion-picture process was developed in 1917 by Herbert T. Kalmus. He called his color process *Technicolor.* The first all-color, feature-length film, *Toll of the Sea,* was produced in 1922.

Talking Pictures developed slowly and required many new inventions and techniques. From the early days of motion pictures, men had tried to combine sound with films. Some of them tried to accompany the film with a phonograph record, so that sound would be heard at the same time that the action was seen. Others, including the inventor Lee De Forest, tried to register sound waves on the film. But, until about 1923, no one found a practical method of producing movies with sound.

In 1926, Warner Brothers produced *Don Juan,* a silent film with accompanying musical score on records. The picture used a device called the Vitaphone. But talking pictures really started in 1927, when Warner Brothers used the same device to produce *The Jazz Singer,* a feature-length film starring Al Jolson. This picture revolutionized the industry and ended the silent era.

At about the same time, William Fox produced short films and newsreels with sound. His method, called *Movietone,* had a sound track on the film.

Talkies (sound movies) became popular almost immediately. Musicals featured many established stage and operatic singers, along with dance stars and large choruses. Nelson Eddy and Jeanette MacDonald starred in several musical romances, including the popular operetta *Naughty Marietta.* The dance team of Fred Astaire and Ginger Rogers appeared in such pictures as *Carefree.* One of the first musicals made with a large cast

Bettmann Archive

THE SILENT ERA

Culver

Charlie Chaplin, a great comedian, was known for his sympathetic role of "The Tramp."

Culver

Pearl White starred in adventure serials, such as *Black Secret* and *The Perils of Pauline.*

Culver

Rudolph Valentino, "The Sheik," was famed as a lover.

The Museum of Modern Art Film Library

The First Movie Studio, "The Black Maria," was built in 1893 by Thomas A. Edison.

Mary Pickford was known as "America's Sweetheart."

Mary Pickford

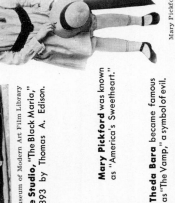

Culver

Theda Bara became famous as "The Vamp," a symbol of evil.

of singers and dancers was *Forty-Second Street*. The film was one of several in the 1930's featuring spectacular dance sequences directed by Busby Berkeley.

Many stars of the silent movies could not change to the talkies successfully. Some had poor or uneducated voices. Others, such as the German actor Emil Jannings, had heavy European accents. But others, including Greta Garbo, Gary Cooper, and Gloria Swanson, continued successfully in sound movies.

Many movies of the 1930's were based on subjects of current interest. Gangster pictures, such as *Little Caesar* with Edward G. Robinson, reflected the gangster influence of the prohibition era. *Heroes for Sale*, with Richard Barthelmess, depicted the conditions of the depression. *Dead End*, with Humphrey Bogart, showed life in the slums. Paul Muni starred in *I Am a Fugitive from a Chain Gang*, a portrayal of brutality of Southern chain gangs. *American Madness* presented the public's reaction to Franklin D. Roosevelt's "Bank Holiday."

Many realistic motion pictures told about the lives of famous persons. Muni starred in *The Story of Louis Pasteur*, *The Life of Emile Zola*, and *Juarez*. Lionel, John, and Ethel Barrymore starred in *Rasputin and the Empress*.

Supernatural horror movies, such as *Dracula* with Bela Lugosi, and *Frankenstein* with Boris Karloff, created a sensation in the early 1930's. *The Invisible Man* with Claude Rains and *King Kong* with Fay Wray used trick photography to achieve their startling effects.

Comedy of the 1930's differed from that of the silent movies. Few comedians of the silent screen succeeded in the talkies. Speech slowed down the action of their jokes, most of which depended on quick timing. W. C. Fields became one of the most successful comedians in sound pictures, starring in such comedies as *The Bank Dick* and *My Little Chickadee*. The Marx Brothers—Harpo, Groucho, and Chico—played in a series of zany comedies including *A Night at the Opera* and *A Day at the Races*. The "screwball comedies" treated daily living as a crazy adventure, where anything could happen. Films of this type included *It Happened One Night*, with Claudette Colbert and Clark Gable, and *The Thin Man*, with William Powell and Myrna Loy.

Shirley Temple became one of the best-loved child

stars of all time. She sang and danced in many films, including *Little Miss Marker* and *Poor Little Rich Girl*.

During the depression in the 1930's, theaters began to present double features. Many also gave gifts or prizes to the audience. These practices helped attract people.

In the middle and late 1930's, motion pictures matured under the guidance of such producers as Samuel Goldwyn, David O. Selznick, Irving Thalberg, and Darryl Zanuck. They made movies based on books and plays, including *Dodsworth*, *Wuthering Heights*, *Mutiny on the Bounty*, *David Copperfield*, and *The Good Earth*.

The 1930's came to a triumphant close with the historic Selznick production of *Gone With the Wind*. This Civil War drama lasted 220 minutes. It cost about $4 million, and was the longest film up to that time.

The 1940's. World War II influenced many motion pictures of the 1940's. Anti-Fascist films and war pictures included *Casablanca*, *The Best Years of Our Lives*, *Mrs. Miniver*, and *Battleground*.

Motion pictures also began to deal with social injustice and illness. *Gentleman's Agreement* and *Home of the Brave* encouraged tolerance. Robert Rossen's production of *All the King's Men* dealt with a political boss. *The Grapes of Wrath*, directed by John Ford, described the difficulties of migrant farmers during the depression. *The Lost Weekend* told of alcoholism, and *The Snake Pit* dealt with mental illness.

Alfred Hitchcock gained fame as the master director of suspense with *Rebecca* and *Suspicion*. John Huston became one of the great directors with *The Treasure of the Sierra Madre*. Orson Welles impressed the motion-picture world with his work as author, producer, director, and star of *Citizen Kane*. Charlie Chaplin wrote, produced, directed, and starred in many of his comedies. Laurence Olivier produced, directed, and acted in the productions of Shakespeare's *Henry V* and *Hamlet*. Bob Hope and Bing Crosby sang and joked their way through such musical comedies as *The Road to Morocco*. Walt Disney produced several popular full-length cartoon features, including *Pinocchio* and *Fantasia*.

During the late 1940's, drive-in theaters became popular. These theaters first appeared about 1935.

Foreign films became popular in the United States after World War II. At first, these films were shown only in small "art theaters" in large cities. But gradually they spread to smaller towns and neighborhood theaters in large cities. By the late 1950's, European directors, actors, and actresses were winning a large number of Academy Awards.

Directors from many countries became famous among motion-picture fans in the United States in the 1950's and 1960's. They included Roberto Rossellini, Vittorio De Sica, and Federico Fellini of Italy; Ingmar Bergman of Sweden; Jean-Luc Godard and François Truffaut of France; Akira Kurosawa of Japan; Satyajit Ray of India; and Tony Richardson and David Lean of England.

Competition with Television. Attendance at movies, spectator sports, and other amusements fell during the 1950's. Many persons preferred to travel, or to take part in sports. Others became interested in do-it-yourself hobbies. In this same period, the television industry developed rapidly and affected motion picture attendance. By 1958, about 42 million homes, or about 80

ACADEMY AWARDS

The "Oscar" symbolizes motion-picture excellence. The statue is 10 inches high and weighs 7 pounds. It is made of gold-plated bronze.

Statuette © by the Academy of Motion Picture Arts and Sciences

YEAR	BEST PICTURE	BEST ACTOR	BEST ACTRESS
1927-28	Wings	Emil Jannings (The Way of All Flesh, The Last Command)	Janet Gaynor (Seventh Heaven, Street Angel, Sunrise)
1928-29	The Broadway Melody	Warner Baxter (In Old Arizona)	Mary Pickford (Coquette)
1929-30	All Quiet on the Western Front	George Arliss (Disraeli)	Norma Shearer (The Divorcee)
1930-31	Cimarron	Lionel Barrymore (A Free Soul)	Marie Dressler (Min and Bill)
1931-32	Grand Hotel	Fredric March (Dr. Jekyll and Mr. Hyde), Wallace Beery (The Champ)	Helen Hayes (The Sin of Madelon Claudet)
1932-33	Cavalcade	Charles Laughton (The Private Life of Henry VIII)	Katharine Hepburn (Morning Glory)
1934	It Happened One Night	Clark Gable (It Happened One Night)	Claudette Colbert (It Happened One Night)
1935	Mutiny on the Bounty	Victor McLaglen (The Informer)	Bette Davis (Dangerous)
1936	The Great Ziegfeld	Paul Muni (The Story of Louis Pasteur)	Luise Rainer (The Great Ziegfeld)
1937	The Life of Emile Zola	Spencer Tracy (Captains Courageous)	Luise Rainer (The Good Earth)
1938	You Can't Take It With You	Spencer Tracy (Boys Town)	Bette Davis (Jezebel)
1939	Gone With the Wind	Robert Donat (Goodbye, Mr. Chips)	Vivien Leigh (Gone With the Wind)
1940	Rebecca	James Stewart (The Philadelphia Story)	Ginger Rogers (Kitty Foyle)
1941	How Green Was My Valley	Gary Cooper (Sergeant York)	Joan Fontaine (Suspicion)
1942	Mrs. Miniver	James Cagney (Yankee Doodle Dandy)	Greer Garson (Mrs. Miniver)
1943	Casablanca	Paul Lukas (Watch on the Rhine)	Jennifer Jones (The Song of Bernadette)
1944	Going My Way	Bing Crosby (Going My Way)	Ingrid Bergman (Gaslight)
1945	The Lost Weekend	Ray Milland (The Lost Weekend)	Joan Crawford (Mildred Pierce)
1946	The Best Years of Our Lives	Fredric March (The Best Years of Our Lives)	Olivia de Havilland (To Each His Own)
1947	Gentleman's Agreement	Ronald Colman (A Double Life)	Loretta Young (The Farmer's Daughter)
1948	Hamlet	Sir Laurence Olivier (Hamlet)	Jane Wyman (Johnny Belinda)
1949	All the King's Men	Broderick Crawford (All the King's Men)	Olivia de Havilland (The Heiress)
1950	All About Eve	José Ferrer (Cyrano de Bergerac)	Judy Holliday (Born Yesterday)
1951	An American in Paris	Humphrey Bogart (The African Queen)	Vivien Leigh (A Streetcar Named Desire)
1952	The Greatest Show on Earth	Gary Cooper (High Noon)	Shirley Booth (Come Back Little Sheba)
1953	From Here to Eternity	William Holden (Stalag 17)	Audrey Hepburn (Roman Holiday)
1954	On the Waterfront	Marlon Brando (On the Waterfront)	Grace Kelly (The Country Girl)
1955	Marty	Ernest Borgnine (Marty)	Anna Magnani (The Rose Tattoo)
1956	Around the World in 80 Days	Yul Brynner (The King and I)	Ingrid Bergman (Anastasia)
1957	The Bridge on the River Kwai	Alec Guinness (The Bridge on the River Kwai)	Joanne Woodward (The Three Faces of Eve)
1958	Gigi	David Niven (Separate Tables)	Susan Hayward (I Want to Live!)
1959	Ben-Hur	Charlton Heston (Ben-Hur)	Simone Signoret (Room at the Top)
1960	The Apartment	Burt Lancaster (Elmer Gantry)	Elizabeth Taylor (Butterfield 8)
1961	West Side Story	Maximilian Schell (Judgment at Nuremberg)	Sophia Loren (Two Women)
1962	Lawrence of Arabia	Gregory Peck (To Kill a Mockingbird)	Anne Bancroft (The Miracle Worker)
1963	Tom Jones	Sidney Poitier (Lilies of the Field)	Patricia Neal (Hud)
1964	My Fair Lady	Rex Harrison (My Fair Lady)	Julie Andrews (Mary Poppins)
1965	The Sound of Music	Lee Marvin (Cat Ballou)	Julie Christie (Darling)
1966	A Man for All Seasons	Paul Scofield (A Man for All Seasons)	Elizabeth Taylor (Who's Afraid of Virginia Woolf?)
1967	In the Heat of the Night	Rod Steiger (In the Heat of the Night)	Katharine Hepburn (Guess Who's Coming to Dinner)
1968	Oliver!	Cliff Robertson (Charly)	Katharine Hepburn (The Lion in Winter), Barbra Streisand (Funny Girl)
1969	Midnight Cowboy	John Wayne (True Grit)	Maggie Smith (The Prime of Miss Jean Brodie)

ACADEMY AWARDS

BEST SUPPORTING ACTOR

No Award

No Award
No Award

No Award
No Award

No Award

No Award

No Award

Walter Brennan (Come and Get It)
Joseph Schildkraut (The Life of Emile Zola)

Walter Brennan (Kentucky)

Thomas Mitchell (Stagecoach)
Walter Brennan (The Westerner)
Donald Crisp (How Green Was My Valley)

Van Heflin (Johnny Eager)
Charles Coburn (The More the Merrier)
Barry Fitzgerald (Going My Way)

James Dunn (A Tree Grows in Brooklyn)
Harold Russell (The Best Years of Our Lives)
Edmund Gwenn (Miracle on 34th Street)
Walter Huston (Treasure of Sierra Madre)
Dean Jagger (Twelve O'Clock High)

George Sanders (All About Eve)
Karl Malden (A Streetcar Named Desire)
Anthony Quinn (Viva Zapata)

Frank Sinatra (From Here to Eternity)
Edmond O'Brien (The Barefoot Contessa)
Jack Lemmon (Mister Roberts)
Anthony Quinn (Lust for Life)

Red Buttons (Sayonara)

Burl Ives (The Big Country)
Hugh Griffith (Ben-Hur)
Peter Ustinov (Spartacus)
George Chakiris (West Side Story)

Ed Begley (Sweet Bird of Youth)
Melvyn Douglas (Hud)
Peter Ustinov (Topkapi)
Martin Balsam (A Thousand Clowns)
Walter Matthau (The Fortune Cookie)

George Kennedy (Cool Hand Luke)

Jack Albertson (The Subject Was Roses)

Gig Young (They Shoot Horses, Don't They?)

BEST SUPPORTING ACTRESS

No Award

No Award
No Award

No Award
No Award

No Award

No Award

No Award

Gale Sondergaard (Anthony Adverse)
Alice Brady (In Old Chicago)

Fay Bainter (Jezebel)

Hattie McDaniel (Gone With the Wind)
Jane Darwell (The Grapes of Wrath)
Mary Astor (The Great Lie)

Teresa Wright (Mrs. Miniver)
Katina Paxinou (For Whom the Bell Tolls)
Ethel Barrymore (None But the Lonely Heart)

Anne Revere (National Velvet)
Anne Baxter (The Razor's Edge)

Celeste Holm (Gentleman's Agreement)
Claire Trevor (Key Largo)
Mercedes McCambridge (All the King's Men)

Josephine Hull (Harvey)
Kim Hunter (A Streetcar Named Desire)
Gloria Grahame (The Bad and the Beautiful)

Donna Reed (From Here to Eternity)
Eva Marie Saint (On the Waterfront)
Jo Van Fleet (East of Eden)
Dorothy Malone (Written on the Wind)

Miyoshi Umeki (Sayonara)

Wendy Hiller (Separate Tables)
Shelley Winters (The Diary of Anne Frank)
Shirley Jones (Elmer Gantry)
Rita Moreno (West Side Story)

Patty Duke (The Miracle Worker)
Margaret Rutherford (The V.I.P.'s)
Lila Kedrova (Zorba the Greek)
Shelley Winters (A Patch of Blue)
Sandy Dennis (Who's Afraid of Virginia Woolf?)

Estelle Parsons (Bonnie and Clyde)

Ruth Gordon (Rosemary's Baby)

Goldie Hawn (Cactus Flower)

BEST DIRECTOR

Frank Borzage (Seventh Heaven), Lewis Milestone (Two Arabian Knights)
Frank Lloyd (The Divine Lady)
Lewis Milestone (All Quiet on the Western Front)

Norman Taurog (Skippy)
Frank Borzage (Bad Girl)

Frank Lloyd (Cavalcade)

Frank Capra (It Happened One Night)

John Ford (The Informer)
Frank Capra (Mr. Deeds Goes to Town)
Leo McCarey (The Awful Truth)

Frank Capra (You Can't Take It With You)

Victor Fleming (Gone With the Wind)
John Ford (The Grapes of Wrath)
John Ford (How Green Was My Valley)

William Wyler (Mrs. Miniver)
Michael Curtiz (Casablanca)
Leo McCarey (Going My Way)

Billy Wilder (The Lost Weekend)
William Wyler (The Best Years of Our Lives)
Elia Kazan (Gentleman's Agreement)
John Huston (Treasure of Sierra Madre)
Joseph L. Mankiewicz (A Letter to Three Wives)

Joseph L. Mankiewicz (All About Eve)
George Stevens (A Place in the Sun)
John Ford (The Quiet Man)

Fred Zinnemann (From Here to Eternity)
Elia Kazan (On the Waterfront)
Delbert Mann (Marty)
George Stevens (Giant)

David Lean (The Bridge on the River Kwai)

Vincente Minelli (Gigi)
William Wyler (Ben-Hur)
Billy Wilder (The Apartment)
Robert Wise and Jerome Robbins (West Side Story)

David Lean (Lawrence of Arabia)
Tony Richardson (Tom Jones)
George Cukor (My Fair Lady)
Robert Wise (The Sound of Music)
Fred Zinnemann (A Man for All Seasons)

Mike Nichols (The Graduate)

Sir Carol Reed (Oliver!)

John Schlesinger (Midnight Cowboy)

of every 100 in the United States, had television sets. Motion pictures became more and more of a financial risk as theatrical attendance declined and production costs rose. To meet the competition, movie-makers experimented with new ways to project motion pictures. They even tried to use the stereoscopic technique for full-length pictures. But the need for special glasses kept this method from becoming widely used (see STEREOSCOPE). Producers established trends toward better color, longer pictures, and more films shot in authentic settings.

During the 1950's, television began to search for inexpensive and popular program material. Stations showed their viewers old motion pictures. The first of these films were released to television in 1951. More people see motion pictures today than ever before, chiefly because of television.

In the 1950's and early 1960's, many motion pictures were made with wide-screen processes, and *The Robe* established the success of CinemaScope, and *Around the World in 80 Days* scored a triumph for Todd-AO. Cinerama's huge curved screen became immensely popular. The new screen processes were often used for musicals and historical spectacles, including *The Greatest Show on Earth*, *The Ten Commandments*, and *West Side Story*. Outstanding motion pictures of the 1950's included *All About Eve* with Bette Davis, *Sunset Boulevard* starring Gloria Swanson, *On the Waterfront* with Marlon Brando, and *From Here to Eternity* with Frank Sinatra. Adult westerns, or westerns that were also serious motion pictures, included *High Noon*, *Shane*, and *Hud*. Several original television plays were made into motion pictures in the mid-1950's and early 1960's. They included *Requiem for a Heavyweight*, *Twelve Angry Men*, and *Marty*. *Tom Jones*, based on a novel by Henry Fielding, became one of the most successful motion pictures of the 1960's. A series of films based on the James Bond novels by Ian Fleming also were popular in the 1960's. Movie musicals returned to popularity with the success of such films as *My Fair Lady*, *The Sound of Music*, and *Mary Poppins*.

Motion-Picture Careers

Young people who consider the movies as a career usually think mainly of acting. But few would-be actors and actresses succeed in Hollywood, especially if they have had little professional training or experience. A screen career requires more than good looks. Dramatic ability, training, personality, poise, imagination, and an expressive voice are also important. Talent scouts and producers turn more and more to Broadway plays, television, summer and stock theaters, college drama schools, and actors' studios to select motion-picture actors and actresses.

Positions in other movie-making arts and crafts are usually filled by persons who have demonstrated their ability before going to Hollywood. They receive further training in the studios. Screen writers, for example, are usually authors who have published stories, or had their plays produced. Art directors often have backgrounds in art, architecture, and design. Composers and musicians provide musical scores for motion pictures.

More than 100 colleges and universities offer courses in film production and related subjects. These courses do not guarantee jobs in film production or the allied fields. But the training and preparation that they provide help increase job opportunities. ARTHUR KNIGHT

Related Articles in WORLD BOOK include:

ACTORS AND ACTRESSES

Astaire, Fred	Gish (family)	Lloyd, Harold C.
Barrymore (family)	Guinness, Sir Alec	Marx Brothers
Bogart, Humphrey	Hope, Bob	Mix, Tom
Brando, Marlon	Ives, Burl	Murphy, George
Chaplin, Charlie	Jolson, Al	Olivier, Sir Laurence
Chevalier, Maurice	Kaye, Danny	Pickford, Mary
Crosby, Bing	Keaton, Buster	Reagan, Ronald
Davis, Bette	Kelly, Grace P.	Rogers, Will
Dietrich, Marlene	Laughton, Charles	Temple, Shirley
Fairbanks (family)	Laurel and	Valentino, Rudolph
Fields, W. C.	Hardy	Welles, Orson
Gable, Clark		
Garbo, Greta		

DIRECTORS AND PRODUCERS

Antonioni, Michelangelo	Griffith, D. W.	
Bunuel, Luis	Hitchcock, Alfred	
Capra, Frank	Huston (family)	
Clair, René	Kazan, Elia	
De Mille, Cecil B.	Kubrick, Stanley	
De Sica, Vittorio	Kurosawa, Akira	
Disney, Walt	Lubitsch, Ernst	
Eisenstein, Sergei M.	Sennett, Mack	
Fellini, Federico	Sturges, Preston	
Flaherty, Robert Joseph	Wilder, Billy	
Ford, John	Wyler, William	
Goldwyn, Samuel	Zinnemann, Fred	

OTHER BIOGRAPHIES

Edison, Thomas A.	Jenkins, Charles	Lumière (family)
Hays, Will	Johnston, Eric	

OTHER RELATED ARTICLES

Arc Light (picture)	Hollywood	Television
Camera	Photography	Theater
Cartoon	Sound	Western Frontier Life
Drama	Technicolor	(Entertainment)

Outline

I. Importance of Motion Pictures
A. Entertainment
B. Education
C. Information
D. Advertising
E. As a Hobby
F. As Art
G. Social Influence

II. A Trip to a Motion-Picture Studio
A. People Who Make Motion Pictures
B. Sound Stages
C. Permanent Outdoor Sets
D. Other Buildings
E. On Location

III. How Motion Pictures Work
A. Projector
B. Camera
C. Film
D. Color Pictures
E. Sound
F. Special Effects
G. Screen
H. Wide-Screen Processes

IV. The Motion-Picture Industry
A. In the United States
B. In Other Countries

V. Development of Motion Pictures

VI. Motion-Picture Careers

Questions

What is persistence of vision? How does it make motion pictures possible?
Why are motion pictures useful as teaching aids?
What unusual problems occur on location?
How is sound recorded for motion pictures?
How have motion-picture producers tried to meet the competition from television?
Who was the first "star"?
What country makes the most movies?
What great movie marked the beginning of modern movie-making?

MOTION SICKNESS. See AIRSICKNESS; SEASICKNESS.

MOTIVATION is a word that is popularly used to explain why people behave as they do. In psychology and the other behavioral sciences, the word has a more limited use. Some scientists view motivation as the factor that determines behavior, as expressed in the phrase "All behavior is motivated." This usage expresses a general attitude or conviction, and is similar to the popular usage. However, when studying motivation, other scientists focus on two specific aspects of motivated behavior—the energization or arousal of behavior, and the direction of behavior.

Some scientists view motivation as the factor that energizes behavior. That is, motivation arouses an organism and causes it to act. According to this viewpoint, motivation provides the energy in behavior, but habits, abilities, skills, and structural features of organisms give direction or guidance to what they do. Other scientists, however, say that motivation serves some direction-giving function. Thus, in the behavioral sciences, motivation can mean energization or direction of behavior or both.

Energization is like arousal or activation, and means being "stirred up" or "ready for action." Energization can take place in several ways. An organism can be aroused by stimuli from outside or inside its body. If you touch a hot burner, pain from the external stimulus arouses behavior. A new or unexpected stimulus can arouse fear in some cases, and curiosity in other cases. Stomach contractions that produce hunger pangs are an internal stimulus. Thirst, which is often said to consist of dryness in the mouth and throat, is another internal stimulus.

Physiological conditions can make organisms sensitive to stimuli from the environment. For example, when hormones, the chemical secretions of the endocrine glands, reach a certain level in many species of birds, the birds begin nest-building activities.

After an organism has been aroused, its actions depend on the external or internal stimuli that call forth habits or other dispositions to respond in particular ways. An aroused organism with no habits or dispositions, or with no stimuli available to evoke habits or dispositions, acts aimlessly or restlessly. With such stimuli and habits present, the aroused organism acts purposefully and effectively.

Motivational conditions themselves may provide stimuli that direct behavior. For example, hunger or some other internal motive may direct an organism toward food. Or a motive state such as sex may make the organism sensitive to external stimuli, including a mate. But the directing function of the stimulation arising from motives differs from the arousal function of motives.

Kinds of Motives suggested by behavioral scientists usually include four groups: (1) homeostatic motives, (2) non-homeostatic motives, (3) learned motives, and (4) incentive-like motives.

Homeostatic Motives include hunger, thirst, respiration, and excretion. Just as a thermostat works to maintain a balanced temperature in a room, homeostatic motives work to keep the body in a balanced internal state. (The term *homeostasis* refers to the body's tendency to maintain such a balanced internal state.) Homeostatic motives are set in motion either by bodily deficits or by bodily excesses. When a person's

body needs water, for example, bodily changes occur that make the individual thirsty and motivate him to seek something to drink.

Non-homeostatic Motives, like homeostatic ones, are biological in character, but they do not function homeostatically. Non-homeostatic motives include sex, such maternal activity as nest-building, and motives dealing with curiosity about the environment.

Learned Motives are acquired through reward and punishment in social situations, especially those of early childhood. These motives include anxiety, dependency, aggression, and a desire for social approval.

Incentive-like Motives include such incentives as money, prizes, status, and other goals. Through learning, we come to value these incentives so that the possibility of attaining them is motivating. Many homeostatic, non-homeostatic, and learned motives may also function through incentive-like processes. Food, for example, can arouse an animal because a hungry animal has learned that obtaining and eating food will reduce its hunger. In animals, also, a learned motive such as fear is usually associated with and aroused by a specific place where the animal experienced fear previously.

Theories of Motivation. Most general theories of motivation identify important sources of motives and describe their operation. Some theories stress sex and aggression, and others emphasize a variety of homeostatic, biological motives. Both groups of theories state that the organism seeks to remove a state of tension or arousal.

Still other theories emphasize such motives as curiosity, information-seeking, and interest in problem-solving. These theories indicate that organisms seek an intermediate level of arousal rather than the complete reduction of tension.

Some psychologists believe organisms tend to seek pleasure and avoid pain or unpleasantness. Other students of motivation say that realization of one's potentialities is the basic motivational factor.

In addition to general theories of motivation, there are theoretical descriptions of specific motivated behavior including sex, aggression, hunger, thirst, achievement, and dependency. A complete theory of motivation has not yet been formulated.   CHARLES N. COFER

See also DEVELOPMENTAL PSYCHOLOGY (Psychoanalytic Theory; Cognitive Theory); LEARNING (How We Learn; Efficient Learning); PERCEPTION (Factors Affecting Perception); PSYCHOLOGY.

MOTIVATION RESEARCH tries to learn how people choose things they buy. It also seeks to find out what people learn from advertising. Motivation researchers explore the feelings and points of view of consumers. They use knowledge from psychology, sociology, and other social sciences to interpret these emotions and attitudes. Motivation researchers interview people in a conversational way, and sometimes give them tests that must be analyzed by psychologists and sociologists. This type of research has shown that people do not shop with only price and quality in mind. They may buy something to impress others, or to keep up with their group. A person may also buy something to imitate someone he admires.   BURLEIGH B. GARDNER

See also ADVERTISING (Research).

MOTLEY, JOHN LOTHROP

MOTLEY, JOHN LOTHROP (1814-1877), an American historian and diplomat, won recognition chiefly for his historical writings on The Netherlands. He wrote *The Rise of the Dutch Republic* (1856) and *History of the United Netherlands* (1860-1867). Motley was U.S. minister to Austria from 1861 to 1867, and minister to England from 1869 to 1870. He was elected to the Hall of Fame in 1910. Motley was born in Dorchester, Mass. He was graduated from Harvard College, and later studied at universities in Germany.

The Beautiful Motmot is known for its oddly shaped tail.

MOTMOT is one of a group of South and Central American birds with oddly shaped tails. The tail feathers are long, and spread out at the tip like a tennis racket. The barbs on the bird's two middle tail feathers wear off. This gives the motmot's tail its unusual shape.

Motmots have handsome feathers colored blue, black, green, and cinnamon. They range from 6½ to 20 inches long. Motmots like to live alone, usually in gloomy forests. They sometimes build their nests in holes in trees. But some motmots build their nests in tunnels that they bore in river banks. The female lays three or four glossy white or cream-colored eggs. Motmots eat insects, reptiles, and fruit. The motmot has a *serrated* (saw-edged) bill.

Scientific Classification. Motmots belong to the motmot family, *Momotidae*.

MERLE CURTI

MOTON, MOH *tun*, **ROBERT RUSSA** (1867-1940), was an American Negro educator. He succeeded his close friend, Booker T. Washington, as president of Tuskegee Institute in 1915 (see TUSKEGEE INSTITUTE). Moton did much to promote racial good will. He served in 1930 as chairman of the Commission on Interracial Cooperation, and received the Spingarn Medal in 1932.

At the request of President Woodrow Wilson, Moton went to France in 1918 to study conditions affecting Negro soldiers in World War I. He served in 1930 as chairman of the United States Commission on Education in Haiti. Moton wrote several books, including *Racial Good Will* (1916), *What the Negro Thinks* (1929), and his autobiography, *Finding a Way Out* (1920).

He was born in Amelia County, Virginia, a descendant of an African tribal chief. Moton was taught by his mother, who worked as a cook for a planter's family. He was graduated from Hampton Institute, and served as commandant there.

GEORGE E. HUDSON

MOTOR. See ENGINE; ELECTRIC MOTOR; ROCKET (Kinds of Rockets).

MOTOR, ELECTRIC. See ELECTRIC MOTOR.
MOTOR CAR. See AUTOMOBILE.
MOTOR SCOOTER. See MOTORCYCLE.

CLAUDE A. EGGERTSEN

MOTORBOAT

MOTORBOAT is a boat driven by any kind of engine except a steam engine. Motorboats range in size from 10-foot open runabouts to luxurious yachts that may be more than 100 feet long. In addition to pleasure craft, they include diesel tugs, power barges, fishing trawlers, police launches, and patrol boats. Many types of motorboats are used by naval and coast guard services in all parts of the world. One of the most famous of these boats was the swift-striking PT (patrol torpedo) boat of the United States Navy in World War II (see PT BOAT).

Each year, thousands of vacationers enjoy motorboating in the inland or coastal waters of the United States and Canada. They use special trailers to carry smaller boats from their garages or back yards to lakes, bays, or oceans that may be hundreds of miles away. Boats as long as 25 feet can be carried behind family automobiles.

Thousands of boating enthusiasts build their own motorboats. Some of them, using only a set of plans, buy their own materials and assemble their boats from start to finish. But most home boatbuilders buy kits that have all the parts cut out and ready to assemble. They follow instructions supplied with the kit that tell them how to put the parts together. They build boats ranging from small, open runabouts to cabin cruisers that can sleep several persons.

There are two general types of motorboats: (1) outboard motorboats and (2) inboard motorboats. An *outboard* motorboat has one or more motors on the outside of the hull, usually at the *stern* (rear). An *inboard* motorboat has the motor inside the hull.

Outboard Motorboats are the most popular type of motorboat for sportsmen. They include small, open craft about the size and design of rowboats, as well as *outboard cruisers* more than 20 feet long. These boats have cabins equipped with bunks, stoves, refrigerators, and radios. Outboard hulls may be made of wooden planks, fiber glass, aluminum, molded plywood, or sheet plywood. The most popular outboard motorboats measure from 10 to 18 feet long, and serve for cruising, fishing, and water skiing. Outboard motors are made of light aluminum alloys that can remain in salt water without rusting. They range from less than 10 horsepower to as much as 100 horsepower. Some outboard motorboats are powered by two engines that run side by side at the stern.

Inboard Motorboats range from small launches to ocean-going yachts. Many vacationers enjoy speeding over lakes and towing water skiers with open inboard motorboats. These boats are generally from 17 to 25 feet long and have shiny paint or natural varnish finishes. They are particularly popular on fresh-water lakes. Boatmen in coastal areas often use more rugged cabin boats for fishing in rough seas. Many of these boats, called *sea skiffs*, have hulls made with overlapping planks, like those of a clapboard house. This kind of construction, called *lapstrake* or *clinker planking*, makes the hull extremely sturdy.

A flat-bottomed inboard motorboat, called a *hydroplane*, has a light hull and a powerful motor designed especially for racing. It does not slice through the water like other motorboats. Instead, it lifts up and skims over the water's surface. Many small motorboats used for utility or cruising also have the shallow, hydroplane-type hull. But a narrower, deeper hull, called a *displacement* hull, is used on larger boats, including cabin cruisers, motor yachts, and work launches.

MOTORBOAT

The engine of an inboard motorboat may be in the back of the boat and connected to the propeller with gears. Or, it may be in the center of the boat and connected to the propeller by a long propeller shaft. Gears and clutches transmit the power from an inboard motor to the propeller so that the propeller does not turn as fast as the engine. In this way, both the engine and the propeller can turn at the most efficient speeds. Most inboard motors are cooled by water pumped in from the outside, run through the cooling system of the engine, then pumped out again. Other engines have separate, self-contained cooling systems, some air-cooled.

Boat engines, like those used in automobiles, use light materials, operate at high speeds, and often have cylinders aligned in a V shape. In fact, many inboard motorboats use automobile engines that have been converted for use in boats.

Development of the Motorboat. Historians are not sure who invented the first motorboat. Probably the first motorboat designed for pleasure use was developed by F. W. Ofeldt of the United States in 1885. This craft was powered by a two-horsepower engine which used naphtha for fuel. Gottlieb Daimler of Germany used a gasoline engine in a boat in 1887. A motorboat powered by an electric storage battery was exhibited at the Paris Exposition in 1889. But motorboating did not become practical or popular until the gasoline engine was perfected in the early 1900's.

The first motorboats had long, narrow hulls. Their engines had to be large and heavy if they were to produce much speed. Early motorboats seldom achieved speeds faster than 30 miles an hour. But the speed record for an inboard motorboat gradually exceeded the 100-miles-an-hour mark. In 1939, Sir Malcolm Campbell of Great Britain set a record of 141.74 miles an hour, which lasted for many years. In 1952, Stanley Sayres of Seattle, Wash., set the record for propeller-driven inboard motorboats. His 3,000-horsepower hydroplane sped 178.497 miles an hour. Donald Campbell, the son of Sir Malcolm Campbell, set records in 1957, 1958 and 1959 in a jet motorboat. In 1964, he smashed all previous records with a mark of 276.34 miles an hour (see CAMPBELL, DONALD). But jet motorboats cannot be used for most boating because of the danger of their exhausts to nearby persons and boats. The Gold Cup race is perhaps the leading national motorboat race. It was first run on the Hudson River in New York in 1904.

Outboard motorboats began to gain wide popularity in the 1940's. Before 1941, some special racing motors capable of developing 50 horsepower had been built, but the average outboard motor in the United States had only 3.6 horsepower. Motor sizes expanded in the late 1940's, after light motors could be built of aluminum alloys. By the late 1950's, manufacturers were making outboard motors with as much as 70 horsepower. In 1960, Burt Ross, Jr., of Spokane, Wash., set an outboard-motorboat speed record of 115.547 miles an hour. In the early 1960's, manufacturers began producing jet turbine inboard boats, diesel outboard motors, and hydrofoils.

WILLIAM W. ROBINSON

See also BOATS AND BOATING; HYDROFOIL; HYDRO-PLANE; OUTBOARD MOTOR; YACHT.

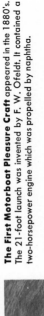

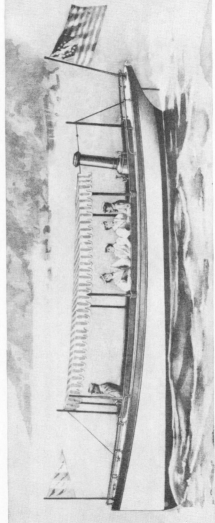

Consolidated Shipbuilding Corp.

The First Motorboat Pleasure Craft appeared in the 1880's. The 21-foot launch was invented by F. W. Ofeldt. It contained a two-horsepower engine which was propelled by naphtha.

Chris Craft

A Powerful Speedboat, *left,* skims the water at speeds of nearly 50 miles an hour. Racing models go much faster. **A Big Cabin Cruiser,** *below,* is the "flagship" of the motorboat fleet. This ocean-going boat has sleeping space for 10.

Chris Craft

MOTORCYCLE

Harley-Davidson Motor Co.

Steam-Powered Bicycle—About 1869

Smithsonian Institution

Steam-Powered Tricycle—About 1888

Gasoline-Powered Motorcycle—1902

Motorcycles, invented in the 1860's, provide fun and transportation. They are widely used by sportsmen, police departments, and delivery services.

MOTORCYCLE is a type of two- or three-wheeled vehicle driven by a gasoline engine. The motorcycle has a much heavier *frame,* or body, than its forerunner, the bicycle. But the rider sits in about the same position on both vehicles. The engine is mounted midway between the wheels of the motorcycle. It is placed low in order to keep the vehicle from being top-heavy, which would make it hard to handle.

Thousands of persons in the United States and Canada use motorcycles for vacation trips, pleasure rides, sport, and transportation to work and school. But motorcycles have many other uses. Police departments depend on motorcycles for pursuit and traffic patrol. Police officers send and receive instructions on radios installed on their motorcycles. In many U.S. cities, the three-wheeled motorcycles have replaced the two-wheeled motorcycles. Garages, automobile dealers, and messenger services have also found many commercial uses for three-wheeled motorcycles.

Motor scooters are small motorcycles with the engine mounted over or directly in front of the rear wheel. The motor scooter does not have a bicycle-type frame. Instead, the driver sits with both feet on a floor board.

The motorcycle solved many transportation problems during World Wars I and II. Military officers found that motorcycles were extremely maneuverable, and well suited to dispatch and messenger work. Men on motorcycles could carry vital messages and supplies from the battle front to the rear lines in the shortest possible time. Troop convoys and military police also used motorcycles extensively.

Operating a Motorcycle. Motorcycles have all the equipment needed to operate easily and safely. Most of them have front- and rear-wheel brakes. The front-wheel brake works from a lever on the handlebar. A foot pedal controls the rear-wheel brake. Kick starters turn over the motor with little effort, and twist-grip controls on the right handlebar regulate the motor speed. A simple foot lever shifts the gears. The clutch operates from a lever on the handlebar in the same way that an automobile clutch operates from the floorboard. Most persons find a motorcycle easier to drive than a bicycle.

Motorcycle Engines. The first motorcycles were not much more than engine-driven bicycles. A belt running from the engine to the rear wheel supplied the power. Gradually, these vehicles became heavier and larger. Finally a chain, which is stronger than a belt, replaced the belt. The chain drive also enabled motorcycles to have three- or four-gear transmissions. This made possible a greater range of speeds.

Some motorcycles have shaft drives such as those on automobiles. But most have chain drives. The front, or *primary,* chain is enclosed in a dustproof guard. The ignition system operates from either a magnet or a battery and generator (see IGNITION). Motorcycle engines have one, two, or four cylinders. They are usually air-cooled. Many motorcycles travel from 50 to 100 miles on a gallon of gasoline.

Motorcycles may have either two- or four-cycle engines (see GASOLINE ENGINE [Kinds]). Two-cycle engines run like most lawnmower or outboard engines, and need oil in the gasoline to insure proper lubrication of the motor. Despite this slight disadvantage, two-cycle

Parts of a Motorcycle

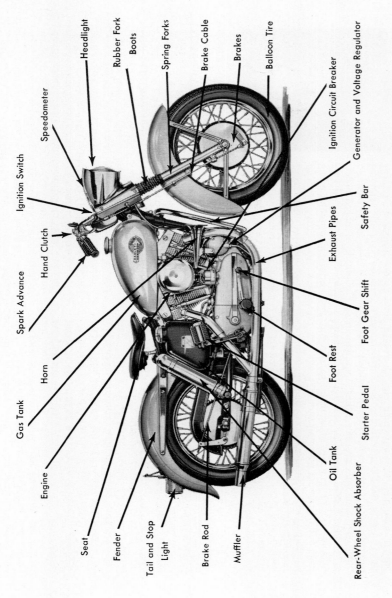

Parts of a Motorcycle — Gas Tank, Spark Advance, Ignition Switch, Speedometer, Headlight, Rubber Fork, Boots, Spring Forks, Brake Cable, Brakes, Balloon Tire, Ignition Circuit Breaker, Generator and Voltage Regulator, Horn, Hand Clutch, Engine, Seat, Fender, Tail and Stop Light, Brake Rod, Muffler, Rear-Wheel Shock Absorber, Starter Pedal, Oil Tank, Foot Rest, Foot Gear Shift, Exhaust Pipes, Safety Bar

engines are easier to service and repair than four-cycle engines. They provide a smooth, steady source of power, because the engine fires every time the piston reaches the top of the cylinder.

Four-cycle engines fire on every other stroke of the piston. They are usually much larger than two-cycle engines, and deliver more speed and power. They also get more power than a two-cycle engine from the same amount of fuel.

Rider Comfort has increased in motorcycles just as it has in automobiles, trains, and airplanes. Hydraulic springs have replaced old-fashioned coil springs to help eliminate jars and road shocks. The front wheel has *helical*, or spiral, springs that are hydraulically controlled by a special oil. The rear wheel has hydraulic suspension that works like the shock absorbers on an automobile.

The hydraulic rear-brake system provides uniform brake pressure and helps prevent skidding and sliding on quick stops. Large, foam-rubber seats not only make riding more comfortable, but are big enough to seat two passengers instead of one. If more passenger space is needed, a sidecar may be attached to most motorcycles.

The Sport of Motorcycling is more than a mere pastime for young people. This growing, well-organized sport is governed by the American Motorcycle Association (A.M.A.), with headquarters in Columbus, Ohio. The association provides a complete set of regulations that govern every phase of motorcycle activity in the United States, including safety.

The A.M.A. approves all racing and motorcycle club activity. One of the most important races is the 200-mile event held annually at Daytona Beach, Fla. Other outstanding events include the 100- and 50-mile motorcycle races.

The A.M.A. has established a point system to determine the Grand National Champion racer for each year. The winner of each of the various national championship races receives 9 points. Second place earns 7 points, third place, 5; fourth place, 3; fifth place, 2; and sixth place, 1. The racer who earns the most points in a year is Grand National Champion and can carry the "Number 1" plate on his motorcycle during the next racing season.

The A.M.A. also supervises and approves the *clocking*, or timing, of all speed events. In 1958, Jess Thomas set the world straightaway speed record for motorcycles. He sped across the salt flats at Bonneville, Utah, at 214.47 miles an hour.

Many sports enthusiasts enjoy the activities provided by motorcycle clubs. Most motorcycle clubs in the United States belong to the A.M.A. To receive a charter in the A.M.A., a club must have at least 12 members in good standing with the organization.

History. One of the first motorcycles was the steam-driven velocipede invented in 1866 by W. W. Austin of Winthrop, Mass. The boiler was suspended back of the seat, and the piston rods were connected directly to the rear wheel. Gottlieb Daimler of Germany invented the first real motorcycle. He attached a four-cycle piston engine to a bicycle frame about 1885. This invention provided the basis for the well-constructed, powerful motorcycles of today.

See also BICYCLE.

GLENN O. MITTELSTADT

MOTT, JOHN RALEIGH

MOTT, JOHN RALEIGH (1865-1955), was an international religious leader. He became secretary of the International Committee of the Young Men's Christian Association in 1888. He served as chairman of the Student Volunteer Movement from 1888 to 1920, and later founded the World's Student Christian Federation.

In the interests of a world-wide Christian endeavor, he traveled nearly two million miles. He stimulated national student movements and brought countries and denominations together. A brilliant organizer and evangelist, he shared the 1946 Nobel peace prize, and received the Distinguished Service Medal for his work in World War I. He has been described as truly a "world citizen." Mott was born in Livingston Manor, N.Y. He spent much of his early life in Iowa, and was graduated from Cornell University.

ALAN KEITH-LUCAS

MOTT, LUCRETIA COFFIN (1793-1880), an American reformer, worked for woman's rights and the abolition

Detail of a portrait by Joseph Kyle, from the collection of Mrs. Alan Valentine. (R. E. Condit)

Lucretia Mott

of slavery. In 1848, she and Elizabeth Cady Stanton called the first woman's rights convention, at Seneca Falls, N.Y. (see STANTON, ELIZABETH; WOMAN SUFFRAGE). Mrs. Mott was also a supporter of temperance and peace movements.

She began to speak at meetings of the Society of Friends (Quakers) about 1817, and became noted for her eloquence and leadership. Her husband, James Mott, a Philadelphia businessman who was also interested in reforms, supported her right to speak publicly.

Mrs. Mott helped found the American Anti-Slavery Society and the Philadelphia female anti-slavery society in 1833. She went as a delegate to the World Anti-Slavery Convention in London in 1840. She and other women were refused seats there, because they were women. This incident helped begin the woman's-rights movement. Mrs. Mott was born on Jan. 3, 1793, on Nantucket Island, Mass.

LOUIS FILLER

MOTTO is a word, phrase, or sentence that expresses an attitude or a principle. Some mottoes are personal. Davy Crockett's motto was *Be Sure You're Right, Then Go Ahead*. Other mottoes are used by groups, states, or nations. The Boy Scouts' motto is *Be Prepared*. The motto of the United States is *In God We Trust*. Each state, except Alaska, has its own motto.

People have used mottoes since the beginning of civilization. Archaeologists have found them on the oldest monuments. Many mottoes are in Latin. It was the custom to use Latin mottoes in the Middle Ages, because Latin was the formal written language. The custom persisted even after Latin was no longer used.

For the mottoes of the states, see the Facts in Brief tables in the state articles, see the Facts in Brief). See also E PLURIBUS UNUM.

MOUFLON. See SHEEP (Wild Sheep).

MOULD. See MOLD (plant); CAST AND CASTING with its list of related articles.

MOULMEIN, *mool MAYN* (pop. 108,020; alt. 130 ft.), Burma's third largest city, is one of the country's chief ports. It lies on the Gulf of Martaban in southeastern Burma. The British founded the city in 1827 when they took southern Burma. For location, see BURMA (color map).

MOULTING. See MOLTING.

MOULTON, FOREST RAY, helped develop geologic theories. See EARTH (How the Earth Began).

MOULTRIE, *MOO trih,* or *MOOL trih,* **WILLIAM** (1730-1805), was an American military leader in the Revolutionary War. Fort Moultrie in the Charleston (S.C.) harbor was named for him (see FORT MOULTRIE).

He entered the Continental Army at the start of the war, and became a brigadier general after his brave defense of Charleston harbor against the British fleet in 1776. He defeated the British again at Beaufort in 1779. Moultrie was captured when Charleston surrendered in 1780. He was set free in a prisoner exchange in 1782, became a major general, and served until the end of the war. Moultrie was governor of South Carolina from 1785 to 1787 and 1792 to 1794. His *Memoirs of the American Revolution* was published in two volumes in 1802. He was born in Charleston.

JOHN R. ALDEN

MOUND BIRD makes its home from the Nicobar Islands in the Indian Ocean eastward to the Philippines and Australia. It usually lives near the sea. Mound birds are dull-colored, and most are about the size of a chicken.

Mound birds lay 8 to 10 pinkish eggs in mounds of earth that they scrape together with their large feet. They mix leaves and other plant material with the earth. This material gives off heat as it decays. The heat of the sun hatch the eggs. The birds use the same mounds for many years, adding to them each season. Some mounds become more than 14 feet high and 70 feet around. The female places each egg in a hole ½ to 5 inches deep which she digs in the top of the mound. The young birds hatch in six weeks.

Scientific Classification. Mound birds make up the megapode family, *Megapodiidae.*

RODOLPHE MEYER DE SCHAUENSEE

See also BIRD (Building the Nest).

Mound Birds heap earth and decaying plants over their eggs. The decaying material gives off heat, which hatches the eggs.

CSIRO, AUSTRALIA

MOUND BUILDERS

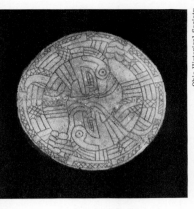

A Brown Sandstone Disk found in a temple mound has a design of two rattlesnakes. The 8½-inch disk may have served as a palette.

An Effigy Mound near Lake Koshkonong, Wisconsin, has the stylized shape of a turtle.

A Flat Pyramid Mound that stood at Aztalan village, near Lakemills, Wis., is shown in this artist's drawing. A stockade set with blockhouses surrounded the village.

Twin Burial Mounds stand at Fort Ancient State Memorial, near Lebanon, Ohio. Indians built the mounds in the A.D. 1100's or 1200s.

MOUND BUILDERS. Many mounds and earthworks made by early American Indians lie scattered throughout the central and eastern United States. Some are square, and others are round or oval. Effigy mounds have the shape of animals. Some mounds were burial places for the dead. Others, with flat tops, had lodges or temples on top. The valleys of the Mississippi and Ohio rivers contain an especially large number of mounds. Ohio and Illinois each have more than 10,000.

The Mound Builders were various groups of prehistoric American Indians who lived at different times and had various cultures. We do not know what these early Indians called themselves. Archaeologists, who study ancient times, have given the groups such names as Hopewell and Mississippian.

The Mound Builders used countless baskets of earth to make the mounds. This amount of labor indicates a well-developed social organization. The sharp flint axes and hatchets tell us that the Mound Builders could cut down trees and shape the wood. The arrowheads, knives, and sharp bone needles prove that they killed and skinned wild animals, ate their flesh, and used their pelts for clothing. Hoes and spades show that their owners knew how to farm. We know that corn ranked as one of their main crops. The Mound Builders also raised tobacco, and smoked it in beautiful stone pipes. Many mounds contain objects that come from faraway places, so we know that the Mound Builders traded a great deal. For example, Ohio mounds have contained black volcanic glass called *obsidian* and grizzly-bear teeth from the Rocky Mountains, copper from the

Robert S. Peabody
Foundation for Archaeology
Stone Image of a Chief came from Etowah Mounds, Georgia. It measures 25 inches.
Ohio Historical Society

Thin Mica Hand was found in a Hopewell grave mound in south-central Ohio.

Objects Found in Mounds help scientists learn how early Indians lived. Mounds have yielded pottery, tools, pipes, stone sculptures, wood and shell masks, and ornaments made from shell, copper, and mica.

Copper Duck Hawk adorned a chief.

Ohio Historical Society
An Otter Holding a Fish decorates a carved stone pipe.

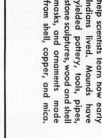

Lake Superior region, mica from New England, and shells from the Gulf of Mexico.

Archaeologists have divided the mounds and their builders into two main groups: (1) burial mounds, and (2) temple mounds.

Burial Mounds. Indians of the Ohio River Valley began building large mounds of earth around A.D. 600. They used the mounds as tombs, sometimes burying as many as a thousand people in one mound. Many scholars believe that the Indians may have learned about building such mounds from Asian peoples. One of the best-known groups of burial mound Indians belonged to the *Hopewell* culture. They formed an alliance of tribes that stretched from Kansas to New York, and from the Gulf of Mexico to Wisconsin. Hopewell people lived by hunting, fishing, and farming. They built round lodges covered with skins or bark. The men wore simple breechcloths but painted their bodies with white and purple dye. Women wore wrap-around skirts. Both men and women liked jewelry of shells, copper, and mica. Hopewell Indians produced some of the finest arts and crafts of the eastern United States. Their carvings in wood and stone often represented realistic men and animals. Their work in copper probably excelled that of all other Indians north of the Rio Grande River.

Temple Mounds became widespread about the year 1000. Indians who built these mounds lived mainly along the Mississippi River and its branches, and their culture is often called *Mississippian.* Temple mound culture reached its peak in the area that now includes Arkansas, Kentucky, Tennessee, and the southeastern states. It also extended northward into Illinois, Wisconsin, and Minnesota. These Indians lived mainly by farming. They organized complicated village-states and religious cults. Their flat-topped mounds served as bases

for temples and chiefs' houses, and probably originated in Mexico. Mississippian peoples built square or rectangular houses and temples of poles covered with matting or thatch. Carvings and paintings decorated the temples, and a sacred fire burned inside. Mississippian Indians ranked among the best potters of eastern North America. Many Mississippian arts and crafts have curious decorations of crosses, spiders, snakes, weeping eyes, and other symbols. Scholars believe that these symbols represent a *Southern Death Cult,* which may have started in Mexico after the white men came.

Hernando de Soto saw temple mound peoples when his expedition traveled through southern North America in 1539-1542. Indians living in this way included the early Cherokee, Chickasaw, Creek, and Natchez. But, by the time white settlers arrived in greater numbers about 125 years later, the Indians had abandoned many of their old ways, and they no longer built such mounds.

Some Famous Mounds. One of the best-known effigy mounds is the *Great Serpent Mound,* near Hillsboro, Ohio. It has the shape of a serpent, and is more than 1,300 feet long. Temple mound sites include *Aztalan,* near Madison, Wis., a village with stockaded walls; and *Etowah Mounds,* near Cartersville, Ga. The *Cahokia Mounds,* near East St. Louis, Ill., include *Monk's Mound,* the largest earthwork in the world.

See also the articles on the various states where the mounds are located, such as Ohio (Places to Visit).

WAYNE C. TEMPLE

MOUND CITY GROUP NATIONAL MONUMENT, near Chillicothe, Ohio, contains a large group of prehistoric mounds. Historians believe the mounds were built by the Indian tribes who first inhabited the state. The monument covers 67½ acres. It was established in 1923. See also MOUND BUILDERS.

MOUNT, in palmistry. See PALMISTRY.

MOUNT ALLISON UNIVERSITY is a coeducational university at Sackville, New Brunswick, Canada. It is under the auspices of the United Church of Canada, but students of all faiths are admitted. The university offers degree courses in arts, sciences, fine arts, music, education, commerce, home economics, and secretarial work. It was chartered in 1858. For enrollment, see CANADA (table, Universities and Colleges). L. H. CRAGG

MOUNT ANGEL COLLEGE is a coeducational liberal arts college at Mount Angel, Ore. It is operated by the Roman Catholic Church. Mount Angel grants B.A. and B.S. degrees. It was founded in 1887 as Mount Angel Normal School, a women's college. Men students were first admitted in 1958. For enrollment, see UNIVERSITIES AND COLLEGES (table).

MOUNT ANGEL SEMINARY is a men's school operated by the Roman Catholic Church at St. Benedict, Ore. It was founded in 1889. It has major and minor seminary departments. The college of liberal arts has departments of philosophy and religion, language and literature, social science, and natural science. For enrollment, see UNIVERSITIES AND COLLEGES (table).

MOUNT APO, AH poh, is an extinct volcano on the island of Mindanao in the Philippines. It is nearly 10,000 feet tall, the highest mountain in the Philippines. Mount Apo forms part of a mountain ridge near Davao Gulf.

MOUNT ASSINIBOINE, uh SIN uh boin, rises on the boundary between the Canadian provinces of British Columbia and Alberta. It forms part of the Continental Divide. The peak lies 20 miles south of Banff and stands 11,870 feet high. Men first climbed the mountain in 1903.

MOUNT BAKER. See WASHINGTON (Land Regions).

Mount Assiniboine is one of the highest peaks in the Canadian Rockies. It rises 11,870 feet above sea level.
Engelhard, Monkmeyer

MOUNT CARMEL extends 13 miles in northwestern Israel from the Esdraelon Valley to the south coast of the Bay of Acre. It rises 1,791 feet above sea level.

MOUNT COOK is the highest peak (12,349 feet) in New Zealand. It is in the Southern Alps in Tasman National Park, in the west-central part of New Zealand's South Island. The Maoris called it Aorangi. It was named Mount Cook for Captain James Cook, the English navigator who first saw it.

MOUNT DEMAVEND. See MOUNTAIN (color picture, Mountains of the World).

MOUNT DESERT (pop. 8,000) is an island off the coast of Maine, about halfway between Portland and the Canadian border. For location, see MAINE (physical map). It covers about 100 square miles. Cadillac Mountain, the island's highest peak, rises 1,530 feet above sea level. Acadia National Park, established there in 1919, was the first national park east of the Mississippi River. French explorer Samuel de Champlain (1567?-1635) discovered Mount Desert in 1604. ROBERT M. YORK

See also ACADIA NATIONAL PARK; CHAMPLAIN, SAMUEL, DE; BAR HARBOR.

MOUNT ELBERT. See COLORADO (Land Regions).

MOUNT ELBRUS, the highest mountain in Europe, rises 18,481 feet in the Caucasus Mountains. Mount Elbrus lies about 150 miles from Tiflis in the Georgian Soviet Socialist Republic in southwestern Russia. Over 20 glaciers, covering about 55 square miles, descend from the mountain. THEODORE SHABAD

See also MOUNTAIN (color picture).

MOUNT EREBUS. See ANTARCTICA (West Antarctica); MOUNTAIN (table); BAR HARBOR.

MOUNT ETNA is one of the most famous volcanoes in the world. It rises 11,122 feet on the eastern coast of the island of Sicily. Part of its base, which is about 100 miles around, lies on the Mediterranean Sea.

Mount Etna (sometimes spelled Aetna) makes a colorful picture with its snow-covered peaks, the forests growing on its slopes, and the orchards, vineyards, and orange groves about its base. The region around the slopes of Etna is the most thickly populated area of Sicily. Nearby are the cities of Catania and Acireale, and 63 villages.

The first recorded eruption of Mount Etna occurred about 700 B.C. There have been more than 80 eruptions since then, some extremely violent. About 20,000 persons were killed in an earthquake that accompanied a 1669 eruption. Several towns were destroyed in 1950 and 1951 eruptions. Violent eruptions in 1960 ripped a new hole in the mountain's east side. GORDON A. MACDONALD

See also MOUNTAIN (color picture); VOLCANO.

Wide World

Craters of Mount Etna in Sicily belch smoke after the violent eruption of 1928. Hot lava flowed from the craters and caused death and destruction in the densely populated areas nearby. Two towns were completely destroyed by lava.

MOUNT EVEREST
WORLD'S HIGHEST MOUNTAIN

Sir Edmund Hillary and Tenzing Norgay, a Nepalese tribesman, *right*, became the first men to climb the 29,028-foot Mount Everest. They scaled the southern face of the mountain on May 29, 1953, after more than two months of climbing. The snow-covered western face of the great peak, below, is seen from the Khumbu Glacier, about four miles away.

MOUNT EVANS is a Rocky Mountain peak in north-central Colorado. It is the highest point (14,264 feet) in the United States that can be reached by automobile.

MOUNT EVEREST is the highest mountain in the world. It rises to a height of about 5½ miles above sea level. The mountain is in the Himalaya range, on the frontiers of Tibet and Nepal, north of India. For location, see INDIA (color map). Surveyors agree that Mount Everest is over 29,000 feet tall, but disagree on its exact height. A British government survey in the middle 1800's set the height at 29,002 feet. The 1954 Indian government survey set the present official height at 29,141 feet. But a widely used unofficial figure is 29,028 feet. Mount Everest was named for Sir George Everest (1790-1866), a British surveyor-general of India. Tibetans call it *Chomolungma*. Nepalese call it *Sagarmatha*.

Many climbers have tried to scale Mount Everest since the British first saw the mountain in the 1850's. Avalanches, crevasses, and strong winds have combined with extreme steepness and thin air to make Mount Everest difficult to climb. Sir Edmund Hillary of New Zealand and Tenzing Norgay, a Nepalese Sherpa tribesman, reached the top on May 29, 1953, the first men to do so. They were members of a British expedition led by Sir John Hunt. The expedition left Katmandu, Nepal, on March 10, 1953. It approached the mountain from its south side—which most earlier parties had called unclimbable. As the climbers advanced up the slopes, they set up a series of camps, each with fewer members. The last camp, one small tent at an altitude of 27,900 feet, was established by Hillary and Norgay, who reached the summit alone. See HILLARY, SIR EDMUND P.

In 1956, a Swiss expedition climbed Mount Everest twice. It also became the first group to scale Lhotse, the fourth highest peak in the world and one of the several summits of the Mount Everest massif.

In 1963, Norman G. Dyhrenfurth led a U.S. expedition that climbed Mount Everest. On May 1, James W. Whittaker, accompanied by Nepalese guide Nawang Gombu, became the first American to reach the top of the mountain. He climbed to the summit from the south. Barry C. Bishop, Luther G. Jerstad, Thomas F. Hornbein, and William F. Unsoeld, members of the same expedition, reached the top on May 22. Bishop and Jerstad approached from the south. Hornbein and Unsoeld became the first climbers to scale the difficult west ridge. The four Americans met near the top of the mountain. Indian expeditions reached the summit on May 20, 22, 24, and 29, 1965.

Some Sherpa tribesmen claim a creature they call the *Yeti*, or *Abominable Snowman*, lives around Mount Everest. But climbers have not seen it. SIR EDMUND P. HILLARY

See also ABOMINABLE SNOWMAN; MOUNTAIN (picture chart); DYHRENFURTH, NORMAN G.; WHITTAKER, JAMES W.

MOUNT FORAKER, *FOR uh ker*, is the sixth highest mountain in North America. It towers 17,395 feet in Mount McKinley National Park in south-central Alaska. Mount Foraker is one of the peaks of the Alaska Range. It was first climbed in 1934. See also ALASKA RANGE; MOUNT McKINLEY NATIONAL PARK.

MOUNT FUJI, *FOO jih*, or *FOO jee*, is the highest mountain in Japan (12,388 feet). It lies on the island of Honshu, about 60 miles west of Tokyo. For years, visitors have called the mountain *Fujiyama*. The Japanese call it *Fuji-san*. Fuji has long, symmetrical slopes. Its top often is hidden by clouds. Its crown of snow melts in summer. The Japanese have long considered it a sacred mountain, and more than 50,000 pilgrims climb to its summit every year. The top contains an inactive volcano crater. HUGH BORTON

See also ASIA (color picture); MOUNTAIN (picture chart); VOLCANO.

MOUNT GODWIN AUSTEN, also called DAPSANG, or K2, is the world's second highest mountain. It is located in the Karakoram range of the Himalaya in northern Kashmir. The peak of Godwin Austen, which reaches 28,250 feet, is snow-covered and usually hidden in clouds. There are glaciers 30 and 40 miles long on its flanks. The mountain was named for Henry Haversham Godwin Austen (1834-1923), an Englishman who surveyed it in the late 1850's. He referred to the peak as K2 in his reports. See INDIA (color map). An Italian expedition reached the top of the mountain for the first time in July, 1954. It was led by Ardito Desio. See also MOUNTAIN (picture chart). J. E. SPENCER

MOUNT HAMILTON. See LICK OBSERVATORY.

MOUNT HERMON. See SYRIA (Location).

MOUNT HOLYOKE COLLEGE. See UNIVERSITIES AND COLLEGES (table); LYON, MARY.

Mount Fuji rises 12,388 feet on the Japanese island of Honshu. It has been considered sacred since ancient times. Each summer, thousands of Japanese make a pilgrimage to the top.

MOUNT HOOD is an inactive volcano in the Cascade Mountain Range of northern Oregon. It rises about 30 miles south of the Columbia River. The mountain is 11,245 feet high. There are many glaciers on its slopes. See also MOUNTAIN (picture chart).

MOUNT JEFFERSON. See OREGON (Land Regions).

MOUNT KAILAS. See HIMALAYA.

MOUNT KAMET. See HIMALAYA.

MOUNT KANCHENJUNGA, *KAHN chen JOONG gah,* or KINCHINJUNGA, *KIN chin JANG gah,* is the third highest mountain (28,168 feet) in the world. It is part of the Himalaya, and rises about 100 miles east of Mount Everest, between Nepal and Sikkim. A British expedition climbed it for the first time in 1955. See also MOUNTAIN (picture chart).

MOUNT KATAHDIN. See MAINE (color picture).

MOUNT KATMAI. See ALASKA (Land Regions).

MOUNT KENNEDY. See CANADA (physical map). See also MOUNTAIN (table; picture chart).

MOUNT KENYA is an extinct volcanic cone in central Kenya, East Africa, 70 miles from Nairobi. It is 17,058 feet high, the second tallest mountain in Africa. Mount Kenya has permanent glaciers on its slopes. Sir Halford Mackinder, an Englishman, first climbed it in 1899. See also MOUNTAIN (table; picture chart).

MOUNT KILIMANJARO. See KILIMANJARO.

MOUNT KINABALU. See BORNEO (The Land).

MOUNT KOSCIUSKO, *KAHZ ih US koh,* is the highest peak in Australia (7,316 feet). It is in the Muniong Range of the Australian Alps, in southeastern New South Wales. Mount Kosciusko is 240 miles southwest of Sydney.

See also MOUNTAIN (picture chart).

MOUNT LOGAN is the highest peak in Canada. It ranks also as the second highest peak in North America. It rises 19,850 feet and lies in the Saint Elias Range in the southwest corner of the Yukon Territory, near the Alaska boundary. The peak was named for Sir William E. Logan, director of the Canadian Geological Survey from 1842 to 1869. Until 1898, Mount Logan was believed to be the highest peak in North America. Then surveyors measured Mount McKinley in Alaska (see Mount McKinley).

See also MOUNTAIN (picture chart); YUKON.

MOUNT LUCANIA, *lyoo KAY' nih uh,* is the ninth highest mountain in North America. It rises 17,150 feet in the southwestern corner of the Yukon Territory of Canada. Mount Lucania is one of the peaks of the Saint Elias Range. See also SAINT ELIAS RANGE.

MOUNT MAKALU, *MUH kuh loo,* is the fourth highest mountain in the world. Makalu stands in the Himalaya about 10 miles southeast of Mount Everest, near the border between Nepal and Tibet. Its highest peak, Makalu I, rises 27,824 feet. Makalu II is 25,130 feet high. In 1955, French mountaineers led by Jean Franco became the first men to climb to the top of Makalu. See also MOUNTAIN (picture chart).

MOUNT MANSFIELD. See GREEN MOUNTAINS.

MOUNT MARCY. See ADIRONDACK MOUNTAINS.

MOUNT MARTY COLLEGE. See UNIVERSITIES AND COLLEGES (table).

MOUNT MARY COLLEGE. See UNIVERSITIES AND COLLEGES (table).

MOUNT MAYON. See PHILIPPINES (Mountains).

the *top of the continent* because it has the highest summit in North America. Mount McKinley has two ice-covered peaks, the South Peak (20,320 feet), and the North Peak (19,470 feet). The height of the South Peak was believed to be 20,269 feet for many years. But in 1956, after 10 years of surveys, the U.S. Geological Survey established the height as 20,320 feet. The mountain is part of the Alaska Range. It was named for William McKinley, the twenty-fifth president of the United States. It is the chief scenic attraction of Mount McKinley National Park. Its north side is one of the world's greatest unbroken precipices.

In 1906, Dr. Frederick A. Cook, a reputable American explorer, claimed to have been the first man to reach the summit. But in 1910 his claim was proved to be a fraud (see Cook, FREDERICK ALBERT). That same year, a party of miners from Fairbanks, led by Peter Anderson and William Taylor, said they had reached the top. They claimed that they erected a flagpole that could be seen with binoculars from Fairbanks.

In 1913, Archdeacon Hudson Stuck, Harry P. Karstens, and two companions climbed to the summit of the South Peak, the first persons to attain that goal. From there, they sighted the miners' flagpole planted on the slightly lower North Peak. In 1932, Alfred D. Lindley, Harry J. Liek, Erling Strom, and Grant Pearson reached the top of the South Peak and two days later climbed the North Peak. This made them the first persons to ascend both peaks.

See also MOUNT McKINLEY NATIONAL PARK; ALASKA (picture); MOUNTAIN (picture chart).

JAMES J. CULLINANE

MOUNT McKINLEY NATIONAL PARK was established in February, 1917, to protect the herds of wild animals that roam the finest game region in North America. The park is in south-central Alaska, about 120 miles southwest of Fairbanks and about 340 miles north of Seward. It has an area of 1,939,493 acres.

Mount McKinley, in the southwestern end of the park, is the chief attraction. It is the highest peak in North America, and towers to 20,320 feet. Mount Foraker, near McKinley, has an elevation of 17,395 feet. More than 300 other peaks of the Alaska Range rise along the southern border of the park.

About thirty kinds of animals live in this rich game region. There are moose, caribou, mountain sheep, red and silver foxes, squirrels, and rabbits. More than eighty kinds of birds nest in the park. It is the only place in the world where the nests of the surfbird and the wandering tattler have been found. Other birds found in Mount McKinley National Park include the golden eagle, golden plover, jaeger, raven, robin, Alaska jay, and white-crowned sparrow.

The park season lasts from June 1 to Sept. 15. The park may be reached by rail or highway. JAMES J. CULLINANE

See also ALASKA RANGE; MOUNT McKINLEY; MOUNT FORAKER.

MOUNT MERCY COLLEGE. See UNIVERSITIES AND COLLEGES (table).

MOUNT MITCHELL, in western North Carolina, is the highest point east of the Mississippi River. It is 6,684 feet high and is located in Mount Mitchell State Park, 20 miles northeast of Asheville. The peak is part of the Black Mountains. See also BLACK MOUNTAINS; MOUN-

MOUNT MAZAMA. See CRATER LAKE.

MOUNT McKINLEY, in central Alaska, is often called

TAIN (table: Famous Mountains of the World); NORTH CAROLINA (color picture).

MOUNT NEBO, *NEE boh,* was the peak in the Mount Pisgah range from which Moses saw the Promised Land. According to the Bible (Deut. 34:5), he died there. Mount Nebo is probably Jabal an Naba, in present-day Jordan. A shrine to the Babylonian god Nebo may have stood on the mountain. See also MOUNT PISGAH.

MOUNT OF OLIVES is a low range of hills about half a mile east of Jerusalem. It is also called MOUNT OLIVET. According to the Bible, Jesus went down from Olivet to make His triumphal entry into Jerusalem. Each night of His last week, He returned to Mount Olivet (Luke 21:37) until the night of His betrayal. Acts 1 names Olivet as the place from which He rose into Heaven. The Church of the Ascension stands on Mount Olivet where the Ascension is supposed to have occurred.

See also GETHSEMANE; JERUSALEM (Jerusalem at the Time of Jesus Christ [picture; map]); JESUS CHRIST (The Trial).

MOUNT OF THE HOLY CROSS is a peak in the Sawatch Mountains of west-central Colorado. It is 13,986 feet high. The peak is called Mount of the Holy Cross because two snow-filled crevasses once formed a large cross at the top of the mountain. In 1929, President Herbert C. Hoover made the peak a national monument. But one crevasse later crumbled away, and, by 1950, the cross no longer was apparent. The mountain then was removed from the list of national monuments.

MOUNT PALOMAR OBSERVATORY. See PALOMAR OBSERVATORY.

MOUNT PISGAH, *PIHZ guh,* is a small mountain range in central Jordan. According to the Bible (Deut. 34:1), Moses saw the Promised Land from its highest peak, Mount Nebo. The mountain towers 2,631 feet. The Pisgah range rises east of the River Jordan. The northern half of the Dead Sea lies southwest of the range. This range was part of the ancient kingdom of Moab in Palestine. Balak, a king of Moab, built his seven altars for the prophet Balaam on Mount Pisgah, offered sacrifices, and asked Balaam to curse the people of Israel. CHRISTINA PHELPS HARRIS

See also MOUNT NEBO.

MOUNT RAINIER, in Mount Rainier National Park, near Seattle, is the highest mountain in the state of Washington. Gassy fumes still rise from its great volcanic cone, but its deeply cut slopes show that the volcano was largely formed long ago. The peak is 14,410 feet above sea level. Automobile roads lead through fine cedar and fir forests to the mountain. Mountain torrents, patches of red heather, and white avalanche lilies line the routes. Indians of the Northwest called Rainier the *Mountain that was God.*

Hazard Stevens and P. B. Van Trump were the first to climb to the top of the mountain. They climbed it by way of the Gibraltar Route in 1870. The climb to the top is a real test of endurance. Deep crevasses, ice caves,

Majestic Mount Rainier, an extinct volcano, rises 14,410 feet high in Mount Rainier National Park in west-central Washington. Emmons Glacier covers the northeast slope.

MOUNT RAINIER NATIONAL PARK

and steep cliffs make the shorter climbs exciting and colorful. With experienced guides, such climbing is not dangerous.

Paradise Valley, with hotel accommodations, perches at 5,400 feet on the slope near the timber line on Mount Rainier. Paradise Valley lies between the Nisqually and Paradise glaciers. Twenty-six glaciers feed the swift streams and tumbling waterfalls which roar through the glacial valleys. Wild flowers of every color border the glaciers. The Nisqually and the Cowlitz glaciers are the most often explored of the ice regions in the park. The Wonderland Trail encircles the mountain. Its 90-mile length can be covered in about a week to 10 days.

Mount Rushmore is a national memorial to four great Americans. It has the largest figures of any statue in the world. The head of George Washington, *left*, is as high as a five-story building. The other heads, *left to right*, are Thomas Jefferson, Theodore Roosevelt, and Abraham Lincoln.

South Dakota Dept. of Highways

See also SEATTLE (picture); WASHINGTON (picture); MOUNTAIN (picture chart).

MOUNT RAINIER NATIONAL PARK is in west-central Washington, near Seattle. The park was established in 1899 to preserve the natural beauty of majestic, ice-clad Mount Rainier. It covers 241,992 acres.

An old volcanic cone, 14,410-foot-high Mount Rainier bears upon its slopes a glacier system more than 40 square miles in extent. Twenty-six "rivers of ice" originate at or near its summit.

Covering the mountain's lower slopes are magnificent forests of Douglas fir, western hemlock, and western red cedar. Blacktail deer and mountain goats are among the many animals that are found in the national park.

To enjoy fully the park's spectacular scenery and interesting natural phenomena, visitors must hike or ride horseback. One park trail—the 90-mile Wonderland Trail—circles the peak and enters remote areas. Overnight shelters are provided for visitors. In winter, mile-high Paradise Valley on the south side of Mount Rainier is popular for skiing.

See also FAIRY FALLS; MOUNT RAINIER.

JAMES J. CULLINANE

MOUNT REVELSTOKE. See CANADA (National Parks).

MOUNT ROBSON is the highest point in the Canadian Rockies. Mount Robson is 12,972 feet high, and rises on the east-central border of British Columbia. For location, see BRITISH COLUMBIA (physical map). Mount Robson Provincial Park surrounds the snow-capped peak.

MOUNT ROGERS. See VIRGINIA (Land Regions); MOUNTAIN (picture chart: Mountains of the World).

MOUNT ROYAL. See MONTREAL.

MOUNT ROYAL PARK. See QUEBEC (Places to Visit).

MOUNT RUSHMORE NATIONAL MEMORIAL is a huge carving on a granite cliff called Mount Rushmore in the Black Hills of South Dakota. It shows the faces of four American Presidents: George Washington, Thomas Jefferson, Theodore Roosevelt, and Abraham Lincoln. The head of Washington is as high as a five-story building (about 60 feet). This is to the scale of a man 465 feet tall.

Gutzon Borglum designed the memorial and supervised most of its work. Workmen used models on the scale of one inch equaling one foot to obtain measurements for the figures. The models were lifted to the edge of the cliff to guide the workmen. The men cut the figures from Mount Rushmore's granite cliff with drills and dynamite.

Work on the memorial began in 1927 and continued, with lapses, for over 14 years. Borglum died in 1941, before the memorial was completed, and his son Lincoln finished the work. Gilbert C. Fife described it in his book *Mount Rushmore.*

Mount Rushmore stands in the mountains 25 miles from Rapid City. It rises 5,725 feet above sea level, and more than 500 feet above the valley. Thus, the memorial stands taller than the Great Pyramid of Egypt (see PYRAMIDS). The memorial is part of the National Park System.

See also BORGLUM, GUTZON; MOUNTAIN (picture chart: Mountains of the World); SOUTH DAKOTA (color picture).

JAMES J. CULLINANE

MOUNT SAINT AGNES COLLEGE. See UNIVERSITIES AND COLLEGES (table).

MOUNT SAINT ELIAS. See SAINT ELIAS MOUNTAINS.

MOUNT SAINT JOSEPH-ON-THE-OHIO, COLLEGE OF. See UNIVERSITIES AND COLLEGES (table).

MOUNT SAINT MARY COLLEGE. See UNIVERSITIES AND COLLEGES (table).

MOUNT SAINT MARY'S COLLEGE, Calif. See UNIVERSITIES AND COLLEGES (table).

MOUNT SAINT MARY'S COLLEGE is a Roman Catholic liberal arts college for men at Emmitsburg,

Md. Mount Saint Mary's offers courses in the sciences, humanities, education, social studies, and business administration. The college grants A.B. and B.S. degrees. Founded in 1808, it is the second oldest Catholic college in the United States. For enrollment, see UNIVERSITIES AND COLLEGES (table). JOHN J. DILLON, JR.

MOUNT SAINT SCHOLASTICA COLLEGE. See UNIVERSITIES AND COLLEGES (table).

MOUNT SAINT VINCENT, COLLEGE OF, is a Roman Catholic college for women in New York City. It was organized as an academy in 1847, and became a college in 1910. Courses are offered in liberal arts, commerce, education, and nursing. For enrollment, see UNIVERSITIES AND COLLEGES (table).

MOUNT SAINT VINCENT UNIVERSITY, a Roman Catholic school in Halifax, N.S., is the only women's university in Canada that grants its own degrees. It offers courses in business education, education, home economics, liberal arts, nursing, and pure science, leading to bachelor's and master's degrees.

Mount Saint Vincent University was founded in 1873. For enrollment, see CANADA (table: Universities and Colleges). SISTER CATHERINE WALLACE

MOUNT SHASTA towers 14,162 feet above sea level in northern California. It rises almost two miles above the low mountains on which it rests. It is one of the southernmost of the great volcanoes in the Cascade Range between northern California and the Canadian border. For location, see CALIFORNIA (physical map). Successive lava flows over thousands of years made Mount Shasta. It is not considered an active volcano. But the mountain has a hot spring near its summit.

A second volcano called *Shastina* lies on the western slope of Mount Shasta, about 2,500 feet below the main peak. Shastina's crater is almost perfect, but the crater of Mount Shasta is badly scarred. Five small glaciers still exist on the mountain. JOHN W. REITH

MOUNT SINAI. See SINAI.
MOUNT STEPHEN, BARON. See STEPHEN, GEORGE.
MOUNT TAAL. See PHILIPPINES (Rivers and Lakes).
MOUNT TABOR, *TA bur,* stands in northern Israel between Nazareth and Tiberias. The mountain rises 1,880 feet above the Plain of Esdraelon. It offers a beautiful view of the surrounding area. Walnut and oak trees once covered the slopes of Mount Tabor. Today, only a few trees grow on the mountain.

The Old Testament refers to Mount Tabor as the place where Barak fought Sisera (Judges 4). In 218 B.C., King Antiochus III of Syria founded a city at the summit of Mount Tabor. The early Christians believed the mountain was the scene of Christ's Transfiguration (see TRANSFIGURATION). The Crusaders built a church on the top of Mount Tabor. In 1212, the Arabs fortified the site, and called it Jabal al-Tor. SYDNEY N. FISHER

MOUNT TAMBORA. See VOLCANO (table).

MOUNT UNION COLLEGE is a coeducational liberal arts school in Alliance, Ohio. It is controlled by the Methodist Church. Mount Union was the first college in the United States to offer summer courses. It was founded in 1846. For enrollment, see UNIVERSITIES AND COLLEGES (table).

MOUNT VERNON was the home of George Washington. It lies in Fairfax County, Virginia, about 15 miles south of Washington, D.C. The tomb of George and Martha Washington is also at Mount Vernon. More than a million tourists visit this national shrine each year.

Washington lived at Mount Vernon as a farmer before he was called upon in 1775 to take command of the Continental Army in the Revolutionary War. When the war ended, he came back to Mount Vernon to retire. But his service to his country was not finished. In 1789, he was elected as the first President of the United States. At the end of his second term, he returned to the estate to live in quiet and peace until his death two years later.

The Buildings. The mansion is a large, comfortable building with white pillars. It stands on a high bluff overlooking the Potomac River. There are 19 large rooms in the two-and-a-half story building. The attic has dormer windows. The mansion is built of wood, but the board siding on the outside is arranged to look like stone. The house has great dignity and beauty. See VIRGINIA (color picture).

Washington's half brother, Lawrence, built the main section of the house in 1743. He first called the beautiful country estate the Little Hunting Creek Plantation. Later, he named it for Admiral Edward Vernon, his former commander in the British Navy. George Washington added the *piazza,* a two-story porch along the river side of the house, after returning from the Revolutionary War. See VIRGINIA (color picture).

The inside of the house has been restored as nearly as possible to its original state. Many of Washington's books are still in the south study, and his harpsichord is in the music room. The beds upstairs are so high that persons used a stool or stepladder to get into them.

Nearly 20 smaller buildings stand at the sides and behind the mansion. Some were living quarters for the servants and craftsmen. Others housed farm implements and animals. Nearly everything Washington and his family needed was grown or made on the 8,000-acre plantation. Mount Vernon shows the way in which wealthy Southern planters used to live.

The Grounds and the Tomb. The grounds around the mansion add to the beauty of the estate. A wide, green lawn sweeps away from the east porch, and ends in a park at the foot of the hill. Flower gardens, and fruit and shade trees surround the buildings on the estate. Washington himself planted many of the trees which still flourish.

The simple ivy-covered tomb where George and Martha Washington are buried stands at the foot of a hill, south of the house.

A National Shrine. By 1853, the estate was in a run-down condition because it could not be maintained as a self-supporting farm. Then a group of women formed the Mount Vernon Ladies' Association to save the grounds and buildings. These women aroused public interest in the project. Gifts of money from people in all parts of the country enabled them to buy the estate. They restored buildings which had fallen into ruin, and repaired the mansion. They recovered many of the original articles of furniture and decoration. John Augustine Washington, Jr., the last private owner of Mount Vernon, presented the key of the Bastille, which is exhibited in the central hall. Lafayette gave the key to Washington in 1790, during the French Revolution. Other valuable personal articles of the family were also placed in the house. Thus this peaceful, lovely spot

A View of Mount Vernon on the west side. The historic home of George Washington stands on high ground overlooking the Potomac River near Washington, D.C.

Mount Vernon Ladies' Association

Washington Sat Here. This secretary-desk was purchased by Washington at the close of his Presidency. Visitors can see the rooms much as they were at the time Washington lived there.

The Washington Dining Room at Mount Vernon was the scene of many formal dinner parties during the late 1700's.

Pickow; Three Lions, Inc.

A Telescope Washington Used to gaze at the sky now stands on a table in the library of his mansion at Mount Vernon.

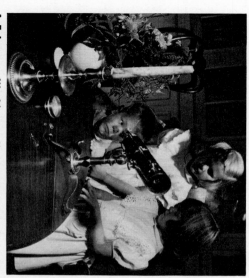

The Ivy-Covered Tomb of George and Martha Washington is south of the house on the Mount Vernon estate.

was saved to become a national memorial. The Mount Vernon Ladies' Association of the Union now cares for the estate.

In 1931, the United States government completed the scenic Memorial Highway from Washington, D.C., to Mount Vernon. The road follows the banks of the Potomac River.   CHARLES C. WALL

See also MOUNT VERNON LADIES' ASSOCIATION OF THE UNION; WASHINGTON, GEORGE.

MOUNT VERNON, N.Y. (pop. 72,918; alt. 115 ft.), is a suburb of New York City. It lies about 14 miles north of New York City's Grand Central Station. Its products include chemicals, clothing, decals, electrical equipment, paints, pharmaceuticals, wire from precious metals, and X-ray equipment.

The Mount Vernon area was first settled in 1664, and called *Hutchinson's*. Later, it was renamed Eastchester. In 1851, the Home Industrial Association of New York incorporated Mount Vernon as a community of homes for workers. It was chartered as a city in 1892. Old St. Paul's Church, seized by Hessian troops as a barracks during the Revolutionary War, still stands in Mount Vernon.

John Peter Zenger, a New York newspaper editor, was arrested for his story of the election of an assemblyman. The election was held in Mount Vernon. His release helped to establish the American principle of freedom of the press. Mount Vernon has a mayor-council government.   WILLIAM E. YOUNG

MOUNT VERNON, Ohio (pop. 13,284; alt. 990 ft.), lies along the Kokosing River, about 40 miles northeast of Columbus. For location, see OHIO (political map). Mount Vernon resembles early American towns. All the public buildings, and many schools and stores, are built in the colonial style of architecture.

Mount Vernon was the birthplace of Daniel Decatur Emmett, who wrote "Dixie" while playing with a minstrel group in New York City in 1859. A loyal Unionist, Emmett made little effort to claim authorship of the song adopted by the Confederacy during the Civil War.

Mount Vernon is the trading center for a rich farming and livestock-raising region. Its factories make engines, machine tools, and paperboard and glass products.

Mount Vernon was founded in 1805 and incorporated as a city in 1853. It is the seat of Knox County. It has a mayor-council government.   JAMES H. RODABAUGH

MOUNT VERNON LADIES' ASSOCIATION OF THE UNION is a national organization that owns and cares for the estate of Mount Vernon, the home and burial place of George Washington. The association maintains the house and grounds as a national shrine. Everything is kept as nearly as possible the way it was when George Washington was alive.

The Mount Vernon Ladies' Association began for the sole purpose of preserving Mount Vernon for the people of the United States. When George Washington died, he left Mount Vernon to his nephew, Bushrod Washington. In 1853, John A. Washington, the great grandnephew of George Washington, offered to sell Mount Vernon to the United States government, or to the state of Virginia. Both Congress and the Virginia legislature refused to buy it. There was danger that the estate would be destroyed.

Ann Pamela Cunningham started the Mount Vernon Ladies' Association. She decided to raise $200,000 to buy Mount Vernon. She succeeded, and became the organization's first regent. Today, the association is made up of a regent and vice-regents. The regent is elected by the vice-regents. Each vice-regent represents a state that has taken part in the movement to preserve Mount Vernon. By the terms of its charter and title, the association has full ownership of Mount Vernon as long as the group exists and keeps its trust. Otherwise, the ownership of Mount Vernon will pass to the state of Virginia. The association maintains the estate with fees people pay for admission. The headquarters of the Mount Vernon Ladies' Association are in Mount Vernon, Va.   Critically reviewed by the MOUNT VERNON LADIES' ASSOCIATION OF THE UNION

See also CUNNINGHAM, ANN PAMELA; MOUNT VERNON.

MOUNT VESUVIUS. See VESUVIUS.

MOUNT WASHINGTON is the highest peak in New Hampshire, and in the northeastern United States. It rises 6,288 feet in the Presidential Range of the White Mountains (see WHITE MOUNTAINS). Mount Washington is the center of a summer and winter resort area. See also NEW HAMPSHIRE (color picture).

MOUNT WASHINGTON COG RAILWAY. See NEW HAMPSHIRE (Places to Visit; color picture).

MOUNT WHITNEY, one of the highest mountains in the United States, rises 14,495 feet. Snow-capped Mount Whitney lies in the southern part of the Sierra Nevada Range of California. Its cluster of granite pinnacles and domes rises sharply to more than 10,000 feet above the valley below. Mount Whitney was named for Josiah Dwight Whitney (1819-1896), state geologist of California. See also MOUNTAIN.   WALLACE E. AKIN

MOUNT WILSON OBSERVATORY is an astronomical observatory on Mount Wilson in California, 5,700 feet above sea level. About 10 miles northeast of Pasadena, it is part of the Mount Wilson-Palomar Observatories operated by the Carnegie Institution of Washington, D.C., and the California Institute of Technology. Mount Wilson Observatory maintains offices, laboratories, and workshops in Pasadena.

This observatory has a 100-inch reflector telescope, which was the most powerful in the world for many years. It was completed in 1918, and has been used to make remarkable studies of remote stars and nebulae.

The studies by the observatory have included the measurement of diameters of stars by Albert A. Michelson; studies of the expanding motions of remote galaxies by Edwin Hubble and Milton L. Humason; and the invention by Walter S. Adams of a spectrographic method for determining stellar distances. Mount Wilson also specializes in astrophysical studies of the sun, recording daily the magnetic properties of sunspots.

The 100-inch reflector was polished in the observatory's own shop. The moving parts of this telescope weigh about 100 tons. The observatory has a 60-inch reflecting telescope and several tower telescopes.

Mount Wilson Observatory was founded in 1904 by George E. Hale, who also organized the Yerkes Observatory in Williams Bay, Wis.   Critically reviewed by MOUNT WILSON OBSERVATORY

See also HALE, GEORGE E.; HUBBLE, EDWIN POWELL; MICHELSON, ALBERT A.; OBSERVATORY.

MOUNTAIN

MOUNTAIN. The word *mountain* means different things to different persons. People who live in a vast, nearly level plain, such as the steppes of Russia, might call even a small hill a mountain. But those who live in an area similar to Colorado would not call a region mountainous unless it were very high and rugged.

By general agreement, geographers and geologists define a mountainous area as one that lies at least 2,000 feet above its surroundings. Its land surface consists of long slopes, deep canyons or valleys, and high, narrow ridges. The region also includes two or more zones of climate and plant life. See CLIMATE.

Mountains cover about a fifth of the land surface of the world. Some continents, such as Africa and Australia, have only a few mountains. Others, especially Asia, have vast areas that are high and rugged. *Submarine mountains* lie under water and help form the floors of seas and oceans. Some of them rise above the water to form groups of islands, such as the West Indies.

Through thousands of years, man has gradually explored most of the earth's surface. As unexplored regions have become fewer, mountain climbers today often defy death to be the first to scale a lofty peak. See MOUNTAIN CLIMBING.

Types of Mountains. Mountainous regions are created by movements of the earth's crust. These movements occur very slowly, but on a large scale. Different parts of the earth's crust react in different ways to these movements, and form four basic types of mountains.

In some places, the earth's crust folds into great waves, somewhat like the "upfolds" and "downfolds" of a washboard. An example of such *folded mountains* is the Jura range on the French-Swiss border.

In other places, the earth's crust breaks into huge blocks, some of which move upward and some downward. These are *faultblock mountains*, or *block mountains*, such as the Sierra Nevada in California.

The earth's crust may also change without folding or breaking into blocks. Instead, the top section of the crust rises into domes that look like great blisters. The Black Hills of South Dakota are examples of these *dome mountains*.

In some places, the crust cracks and *lava* (molten rock) and rock ashes and gases move up through the cracks and pipelike vents. The lava and ashes pile up, layer on layer, building the land higher and higher. *Volcanic mountains* such as the Cascade Mountains of Washington and Oregon may result from such pile-ups. Individual volcanic peaks, such as Vesuvius in Italy, often rise on top of these volcanic masses. At times, the volcanic masses build up from the bottom of the sea, creating such islands as the Hawaiian group. See VOLCANO.

How Mountains Are Measured. Surveyors usually measure the height of land surface, including mountains, by determining the distance of the land above sea level. When we say that the height, or altitude, of Pikes Peak in Colorado is 14,110 feet, we mean that its

FAMOUS MOUNTAINS OF THE WORLD

NAME	HEIGHT (ft.)	RANGE	LOCATION	INTERESTING FACTS
Aconcagua	22,834	Andes	Argentina	Highest peak in the Western Hemisphere.
Annapurna	26,504	Himalaya	Nepal	Eleventh highest peak in the world.
Ararat	17,011	Armenian Plateau	Turkey	Noah's ark is supposed to have rested on Ararat after the Deluge.
Cayambe	18,996	Andes	Ecuador	An extinct volcano with a square-topped crater.
Chimborazo	20,561	Andes	Ecuador	For many years thought to be the highest mountain in the Western Hemisphere.
Cho Oyu	26,867	Himalaya	Nepal-Tibet border	Seventh highest peak in the world (subpeak of Everest)
Communism Peak	24,590	Pamir-Alai	Russia	Highest peak in Russia.
Cook	12,349	Southern Alps	New Zealand	Highest peak in New Zealand.
Cotopaxi	19,347	Andes	Ecuador	Highest active volcano in the world.
Dhaulagiri	26,810	Himalaya	Nepal	Fifth highest mountain in the world.
Elbert	14,431	Sawatch	Colorado	Highest peak of Rocky Mountains.
Elbrus or Elbruz	18,481	Caucasus	Russia	Highest mountain of the Caucasus.
Erebus	12,448	Ross Barrier	Ross Island	Active volcano in the Antarctic.
Everest	29,028	Himalaya	Nepal-Tibet border	Highest mountain in the world.
Fuji	12,388	On volcanic island	Japan	Considered sacred by many Japanese.
Godwin Austen, or K2, or Dapsang	28,250	Karakorum	Kashmir	Second highest mountain in the world.
Hood	11,245	Cascade	Oregon	Inactive volcano.
Ixtacihuatl	17,343	Sierra Madre	Mexico	Name is Aztec for white woman.
Jungfrau	13,668	Alps	Switzerland	An electric railroad runs part way up the mountain.
Kanchenjunga or Kinchinjunga	28,168	Himalaya	Nepal-Sikkim border	Third highest mountain in the world.
Kenya	17,058	Isolated peak	Kenya	About 20 miles south of the equator.
Kilimanjaro	19,340	Isolated peak	Tanzania	Highest mountain in Africa.
Kosciusko	7,316	Australian Alps	New S. Wales	Highest peak in Australia.
Lassen Peak	10,466	Cascade	California	Only active volcano in the United States outside Alaska and Hawaii.
Lhotse I	27,890	Himalaya	Nepal-Tibet border	Fourth highest peak in the world (subpeak of Everest).
Lhotse II	27,560	Himalaya	Nepal-Tibet border	Sixth highest peak in the world (subpeak of Everest).

summit (highest peak) rises 14,110 feet above the level of the sea. Actually, the mountain is far inland and its top rises only about 9,000 feet above the surface of the nearby Great Plains.

A barometer is an instrument that records air pressure (see BAROMETER). The barometer and the barometric altimeter, an instrument based on the barometer, are used to measure heights. Altimeters give quick, easy altitude readings. An accurate altimeter can determine altitudes to within a few feet. Most of our figures for mountain heights were obtained with altimeters.

For more accurate readings, surveyors use complicated instruments and techniques based on geometry and trigonometry. With these methods, they can measure a mountain without actually climbing it. They do need to see the peak, however.

No completely foolproof method of measuring land height has been developed. Climatic and other conditions affect all instrument readings, so that results vary regardless of the method used. For example, different surveys have reported the height of Mount Everest as 29,002, 29,141, and 29,028 feet. The last figure is the one most commonly accepted.

Man and Mountains. Man has always been interested in mountains, either because he finds them a barrier to travel and communication, or because they are useful or attractive. When mountains stand in his way, man seeks ways to cross them or go around them. In Europe, the snow-capped Alps hinder land travel from Italy to countries in the north and west. The high-ways and railroads that cross the Alps include tunnels, trestles, and looping curves that follow mountainsides.

Mountains have influenced history in many ways. Primitive man often stood in awe of mountains, because he believed that gods lived among the high peaks. The beginnings of modern religions, such as Judaism and Christianity, are connected with mountains. For example, Jehovah gave Moses the tablets bearing the Ten Commandments on Mount Sinai. Roman soldiers crucified Jesus Christ on Mount Calvary. Mountains have determined settlement patterns when great numbers of people migrated in search of new lands. The Appalachians limited settlement to the eastern seaboard of the United States for many years. Many conquering armies have been forced to retreat when they reached mountain areas. People familiar with the rugged terrain defeated the intruders who did not know how to do mountain fighting. Basque mountaineers, for example, trapped Charlemagne's army in the Pyrenees.

People who live in mountains or mountain valleys use the natural resources of their regions. The high, grass-covered slopes provide pastures for grazing animals. The thick forests that grow on mountain land too rugged for cultivation provide wood for fuel and lumber. Swift mountain streams turn turbines that generate electric energy. Mines yield valuable minerals. Beautiful mountain scenery attracts vacationers for hiking, camping, hunting, and skiing.   ROBERT M. GLENDINNING

FAMOUS MOUNTAINS OF THE WORLD

NAME	HEIGHT (ft.)	RANGE	LOCATION	INTERESTING FACTS
Logan	19,850	Saint Elias	Canada	Highest peak in Canada.
Longs Peak	14,256	Rocky Mountains	Colorado	In Rocky Mountain National Park.
Maipu or Maipo	17,464	Andes	Chile-Argentina border	Active volcano.
Makalu	27,824	Himalaya	Nepal-Tibet border	Fourth highest mountain in the world.
Manaslu	26,658	Himalaya	Nepal	Tenth highest peak in the world.
Matterhorn	14,685	Pennine Alps	Switzerland-Italy border	Favorite for daring mountain climbers.
Mauna Kea	13,796	On volcanic island	Hawaii	Highest peak on these islands.
Mauna Loa	13,680	On volcanic island	Hawaii	Kilauea, world's largest active crater, is on the side of Mauna Loa.
McKinley	20,320	Alaska	Alaska	Highest peak in North America and in the United States.
Mitchell	6,684	Appalachian	North Carolina	Highest peak in the Appalachians.
Mont Blanc	15,781	Pennine Alps	France	Highest mountain in the Alps.
Monte Rosa	15,200	Pennine Alps	Switzerland-Italy border	Iron, copper, and gold are mined from its slopes.
Nanga Parbat	26,660	Himalaya	Kashmir	Sixth highest mountain in the world.
Orizaba	18,701	Mexican Plateau	Mexico	Highest peak in Mexico.
Pikes Peak	14,110	Rampart	Colorado	Most famous of the Rocky Mountains.
Popocatepetl	17,887	Mexican Plateau	Mexico	Name is Aztec for *Smoking Mountain.* Volcano now inactive.
Rainier	14,410	Cascade	Washington	Highest peak in Washington.
Saint Elias	18,008	Saint Elias	Canada-Alaska border	Second highest peak in this range.
Shasta	14,162	Cascade	California	Famous for its twin peaks.
Tolima	17,110	Cordillera Occidental	Colombia	Active volcano.
Vesuvius	3,842	—	Italy	Only active volcano on the mainland of Europe.
Vinson Massif	16,864	Sentinel Mountains	Antarctica	Highest peak in Antarctica.
Whitney	14,495	Sierra Nevada	California	Highest mountain in California.

739

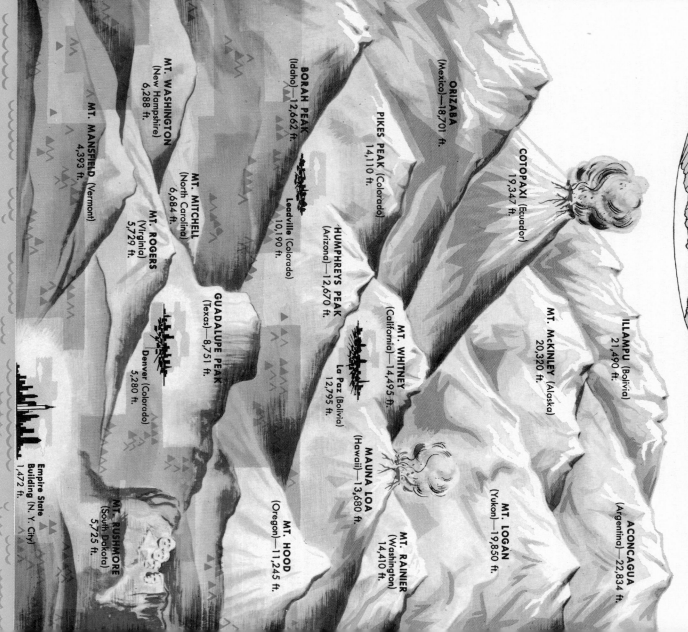

MOUNTAINS OF THE WORLD

Leading mountain ranges appear on the world map at the left. Famous mountains shown below and to the right are drawn to scale in their true shapes. For height comparison, five cities and a mountain pass are shown at their correct altitudes.

ROCKIES
ALASKA MTS.
ANDES
APPALACHIANS
URALS
ATLAS MTS.
ALPS
HIMALAYA

MT. MANSFIELD (Vermont) 4,393 ft.

MT. WASHINGTON (New Hampshire) 6,288 ft.

BORAH PEAK (Idaho)—12,662 ft.

MT. MITCHELL (North Carolina) 6,684 ft.

PIKES PEAK (Colorado) 14,110 ft.

ORIZABA (Mexico)—18,701 ft.

Leadville (Colorado) 10,190 ft.

MT. ROGERS (Virginia) 5,729 ft.

HUMPHREYS PEAK (Arizona)—12,670 ft.

COTOPAXI (Ecuador) 19,347 ft.

GUADALUPE PEAK (Texas)—8,751 ft.

Denver (Colorado) 5,280 ft.

MT. WHITNEY (California)—14,495 ft.

La Paz (Bolivia) 12,795 ft.

MT. McKINLEY (Alaska) 20,320 ft.

ILLAMPU (Bolivia) 21,490 ft.

Empire State Building (N. Y. City) 1,472 ft.

MT. RUSHMORE (South Dakota) 5,725 ft.

MT. HOOD (Oregon)—11,245 ft.

MAUNA LOA (Hawaii)—13,680 ft.

MT. RAINIER (Washington) 14,410 ft.

MT. LOGAN (Yukon)—19,850 ft.

ACONCAGUA (Argentina)—22,834 ft.

MT. EVEREST (Nepal-Tibet)
29,028 ft.

MT. GODWIN AUSTEN (K-2)
(Kashmir)—28,250 ft.

MT. MAKALU
(Nepal-Tibet)—27,824 ft.

ANNAPURNA
(Nepal)—26,504 ft.

KANCHENJUNGA
(Nepal-Sikkim)—28,168 ft.

LENIN (Russia)—23,382 ft.

KILIMANJARO
(Tanzania)
19,340 ft.

MT. DEMAVEND (Iran)
18,934 ft.

MT. ELBRUS (Russia)
18,481 ft.

MT. KENYA (Kenya)
17,058 ft.

ARARAT
(Turkey)—17,011 ft.

MONT BLANC
(France)
15,781 ft.

MATTERHORN
(Switzerland)
14,685 ft.

JUNGFRAU
(Switzerland)
13,668 ft.

MT. EREBUS
(Antarctica)
12,448 ft.

MT. FUJI (Japan)—12,388 ft.

Lhasa (Tibet)
11,800 ft.

MT. ETNA (Sicily) 11,122 ft.

Great St. Bernard Pass
(Switzerland and Italy)
about 8,100 ft.

OLYMPUS (Greece)
9,550 ft.

Simla (India)
7,186 ft.

MT. KOSCIUSKO (Australia)
7,316 ft.

PARNASSUS (Greece)
8,061 ft.

BEN NEVIS
(Scotland)—4,406 ft.

KRAKATOA
(Indonesia)—2,667 ft.

VESUVIUS (Italy)
3,842 ft.

30,000 ft.

25,000 ft.

20,000 ft.

15,000 ft.

10,000 ft.

5,000 ft.

Sea Level

MOUNTAIN

Related Articles. See the various continent, country, state, and province articles where mountains are discussed, and related articles are discussed, such as ASIA (Natural Features); ARGENTINA (Land Regions); ALABAMA (The Land). See VOLCANO with its list of Related Articles. See also the following:

AFRICA

Atlas Mountains
Kilimanjaro
Mount Kenya
Ruwenzori Range

ASIA

Altai Mountains
Annapurna
Ararat
Elburz Mountains
Ghats
Himalaya
Hindu Kush
Khyber Pass
Kunlun Mountains
Lebanon Mountains
Mount Carmel
Mount Cook
Mount Everest
Mount Fuji
Mount Godwin Austen
Mount Kanchenjunga
Mount Kosciusko
Mount Makalu
Mount Nebo
Mount of Olives
Mount Pisgah
Mount Tabor
Owen-Stanley Mountains
Pamirs, The
Stanovoy Mountains
Tien Shan Mountains
Ural Mountains
Yablonovyy Mountains

CANADA

Canadian Shield
Coast Range
King Mountain
Mount Assiniboine
Mount Logan
Mount Lucania
Rocky Mountains
Saint Elias Mountains
Selkirk Mountains

EUROPE

Alps
Apennines
Ardennes
Belfort Gap
Ben Nevis
Black Forest
Brenner Pass
Carpathian Mountains
Caucasus Mountains
Dartmoor
Dolomites
Harz Mountains
Jungfrau
Jura
Matterhorn
Mont Blanc
Monte Rosa
Montserrat
Mount Elbrus
Olympus
Parnassus
Pelion
Pennine Chain
Pyrenees
Saint Bernard, Great and Saint Bernard, Little
Saint Gotthard Pass
Simplon Pass and Tunnel
Snowdon
Sudetes Mountains
Vosges Mountains

MEXICO

Ixtacihuatl
Orizaba
Paricutín
Popocatepetl
Sierra Madre

SOUTH AMERICA

Aconcagua
Andes Mountains
Chimborazo
Cotopaxi
El Misti
Huascarán
Illampu
Illimani
Ojos del Salado
Pichincha
Tupungato

UNITED STATES

Adirondack Mountains
Alaska Range
Allegheny Mountains
Appalachian Mountains
Berkshire Hills
Bitterroot Range
Black Hills
Black Mountains
Blue Ridge Mountains
Boundary Peak
Cascade Range
Catskill Mountains
Clingmans Dome
Coast Range
Cumberland Gap
Cumberland Mountains
Gannett Peak
Great Divide
Great Smoky Mountains
Green Mountains
Mesabi Range
Mount Evans
Mount Foraker
Mount Hood
Mount McKinley
Mount Mitchell
Mount of the Holy Cross
Mount Rainier
Mount Rushmore
Mount Shasta
Mount Washington
Mount Whitney
Olympic Mountains
Ozark Mountains
Piedmont Region
Pikes Peak
Rocky Mountains
Sangre de Cristo Mountains
Sierra Madre
Sierra Nevada
Stone Mountain
Teton Range
Wasatch Range
White Mountains

Outline

I. Types of Mountains
II. How Mountains Are Measured
III. Man and Mountains

Questions

What are the four main types of mountains? How are they formed?

What kind of mountain formations created the Hawaiian Islands?

How do geographers define a mountainous area?

About how much of the earth's surface is mountainous?

In what ways do people use mountainous regions?

What instruments do surveyors use to obtain most of the mountain heights we know?

MOUNTAIN ASH is the name for a group of trees and shrubs that grow in the Northern Hemisphere. They grow chiefly in high places. *American mountain ash* grows from Newfoundland south to northern Georgia. The leaves of the mountain ash are compound, made up of several separate leaflets. The white flowers grow in

The American Mountain Ash, *below,* grows to be about 30 feet tall. The tree is common in eastern North America. A sprig from a mountain ash, *right,* has clustered red berries and compound leaves like the leaves of roses.

Devereux Butcher

U.S. Forest Service

Mountain Climbers use ropes, ice axes, spiked boots, and snow glasses when scaling icy slopes or vertical rock faces.

Photo by George Burns, reprinted courtesy of *The Saturday Evening Post*, © 1956, by Curtis Publishing Co.

large, flattened clusters. The orange-to-red fruits are clusters of berrylike *pomes*.

Mountain ash is valuable as wildlife food and as an ornamental tree for lawns and gardens. The wood from the *European mountain ash*, or *rowan tree*, may be used for making tool handles. Superstitious people once believed the rowan tree would drive away evil spirits.

Scientific Classification. The mountain ash belongs to the rose family, *Rosaceae*. The American mountain ash is genus *Sorbus*, species *S. americana*. The rowan tree is *S. aucuparia*.   T. EWALD MAKI

MOUNTAIN AVENS is a small, hardy plant that grows wild in the northern and arctic regions. It is the floral emblem of Canada's Northwest Territories. The plant has small, saucer-shaped, yellow or white flowers. It grows on high ledges and rocky slopes in North America, Europe, and Asia.

Scientific Classification. The mountain avens belongs to the rose family, *Rosaceae*. It is genus *Dryas*. The yellow mountain avens of the Canadian Rockies is *D. tomentosa*.

MOUNTAIN BEAVER has lived on earth longer than any other rodent. Mountain beavers lived in North America at least 60 million years ago. Today, they live along the Pacific coast and in nearby mountains. Mountain beavers are also called *boomers*, *sewellels*, and *whistlers*, but all these names are misleading. They are not related to beavers and they do not make booming or whistling noises. *Sewellel* is an Indian word meaning *robe*.

Mountain beavers are about a foot long and look like large voles rather than like beavers (see VOLE). They have short, thick bodies, short legs and small eyes and ears. Their fur is thick and short. Mountain beavers live in groups called *colonies*. They make their homes in tunnels they dig in the banks of streams.

Scientific Classification. Mountain beavers are the only surviving members of the mountain beaver family, *Aplodontiidae*. They make up the genus *Aplodontia*, species *A. rufa*.   DANIEL H. BRANT

MOUNTAIN CLIMBING, or **MOUNTAINEERING,** is a difficult, adventurous sport. It requires special knowledge, skills, and equipment. Mountain climbers must be in good physical condition and have good judgment. Mountain climbing can be dangerous to an untrained person. Even many skilled climbers have lost their lives trying to conquer challenging peaks.

Making a Climb. A climb usually begins early in the day, perhaps before dawn. The climbers may plan to return before dusk, so they allow extra daylight time in case they meet unexpected delays. On low, easy mountains, climbers may go up more than a mile in vertical height in one day. On difficult peaks, they may be able to clamber only a few hundred feet. Climbers slow down at high altitudes, because the air has less oxygen the higher one goes. This makes breathing difficult and tires climbers more quickly. Climbers sometimes use special oxygen equipment at high altitudes.

Mountaineers must know how to use maps and compasses, because they often must find their way where there are no trails. They may travel through dense woods as they approach a mountain, and then cross steep slopes and rock slides above the tree line on the mountain. Climbers may move up steep rock faces and over snow fields and glaciers filled with crevasses.

In dangerous areas, climbers rope themselves together in groups of two, three, or occasionally more persons. Sometimes, only one climber may move at a time. The others brace themselves to tighten the rope and stop the climber's fall if he should slip.

Climbing Equipment. Climbers carry packsacks loaded with first-aid supplies, food, and extra clothing for sudden changes in weather. If the climb requires more than one day, they also carry cooking gear, sleeping bags, and perhaps a tent. It is important for climbers to wear boots that help them avoid slipping. They may wear boots which have rubber soles with lugs, leather soles with nails, or a combination of these. Climbers may also strap *crampons* on their boots for climbing on ice or hard snow. Crampons are metal frames with 8 to 12 spikes. In addition, a climber may carry an *ice ax* to aid in keeping his balance, to cut steps in snow and ice, and to stop himself from falling. These axes have a 3-foot wooden shaft tipped on one end with a metal point. The other end has a metal head pointed on one side and *adz*-shaped on the other.

Climbing Areas. Most mountains in the United States can be climbed safely by parties of three or more persons over a weekend or a week's vacation. Every summer, professional and amateur climbers scale such famous American peaks as Mount Rainier and the Grand Teton. The leading climbing areas in the United States include the Rocky Mountains, the Cascade Range, and the Sierra Madre Mountains. The larger cities near mountains in the United States have mountaineering clubs.

World interest in mountain climbing began in the 1800's, and the Alps have always been Europe's most popular climbing area. Almost none of the world's famous peaks were climbed until the 1800's. Other famed climbing areas include the Andes Mountains in South America, and the Himalaya (mountains) and the Karakoram Range in Asia. Large expeditions must be organized to climb the highest peaks in Asia. These mountains are far from roads, and an expedition must carry enough supplies to last several weeks.

Perhaps the best-known climb was the 1953 conquest of 29,028-foot Mount Everest, the world's highest peak. A British expedition, which included 10 climbers, established camps on the mountain's slopes. Sir Edmund P. Hillary of New Zealand and Tenzing Norgay, a Sherpa guide, reached the summit.

Critically reviewed by Sir Edmund P. Hillary

PAUL W. WISEMAN

See also Mountain; Mount Everest.

MOUNTAIN FLOWERS. See Flower (color picture: Mountain Flowers).

MOUNTAIN GOAT. See Chamois; Ibex; Cashmere Goat; Rocky Mountain Goat.

MOUNTAIN LAUREL is an evergreen plant that grows from New Brunswick to the Gulf States and west to Arkansas. As a shrub it grows 5 to 10 feet high. As a tree, it grows as high as 30 feet. Mountain laurel has pink, white, or purple flowers. Its glossy dark leaves are oblong and pointed at the ends. Mountain laurel is also called *kalmia*. This evergreen is sometimes used in landscaping.

Scientific Classification. Mountain laurel is a member of the heath family, *Ericaceae*. It is genus *Kalmia*, species *K. latifolia*.

J.-J. Levison

MOUNTAIN LION is a large wild animal of the cat family. Mountain lions once lived throughout the forests of the United States and southern Canada. When settlers moved in, they drove this animal from large areas.

Mountain lions now live in the western states from

eastern New Mexico and Wyoming to the Pacific Coast, and in a few places in Louisiana and Florida. They are also found in Alberta and British Columbia, and throughout much of Mexico, Central America, and to the tip of South America.

Early settlers gave the animal the name of *cougar*, or mountain lion. They thought it was a female lion. Other names for this animal are *catamount* and *puma*. Especially in the eastern states, it is known as *panther*, a name also given to several other kinds of cat.

An adult mountain lion may be either a gray color or a reddish or yellowish color called *tawny*. Its hairs are fawn-gray tipped with reddish brown or grayish. This animal has no spots, and in this way it is different from the jaguar. The throat, the insides of the legs, and the belly are white, and the tip of the tail is black. Some mountain lions are solid black. A full-grown animal may be 4 to 5 feet long or even more, not counting the heavy tail, which is 2 to 3 feet long. The heaviest mountain lion on record weighed 227 pounds. The body is slender, and the legs are long. The head is round and rather small.

Mountain lions have from one to five cubs at a time, generally two years apart. The average number is three. The cubs weigh about 1 pound at birth. They are covered with fur, but they are lighter brown than their parents. The cubs have large brownish-black spots on the body and dark rings on the short tail. Adults care for their young until they are able to survive alone. Young lions need about two years to develop enough skill in hunting to find their own food. They may live to be 10 or 12 years old.

The cry of the mountain lion is wild and terrifying. It sounds like a woman screaming in pain. The animal also has a soft whistle call.

The mountain lion usually hunts at night. It will travel many miles after game in a single night. Its chief prey is deer, with elk the second choice. Occasionally it kills a bighorn. In case of need it will feed on small mammals—even skunks and porcupines. The mountain lion keeps under cover while stalking its prey. Then suddenly the lion leaps out upon the animal, breaking

A Mountain Lion often crouches in the branches of a tree, lying in wait for its prey. It can leap on an animal and kill it.

Tom Lark, Western Ways

the animal's neck or dragging it down to the ground. Ranchers regard mountain lions as pests. But the big cats seldom kill calves or other domestic animals. Biologists believe that mountain lions should be controlled but not killed off, because these big cats play an important part in the animal world. They feed mainly on old and diseased deer.

Mountain lions are not usually dangerous to man. They actually are timid toward man, and are less likely to attack him than other wild cats. According to Latin-American legend, the mountain lion has a playful nature, and seems to want to make friends with man.

Scientific Classification. The mountain lion is a mammal that belongs to the cat family, *Felidae*. It is genus *Felis*, species *F. concolor*.

See also PANTHER.

MOUNTAIN MEN. See MISSOURI RIVER (History); WESTWARD MOVEMENT (Exploration).

MOUNTAIN NESTOR. See KEA.

MOUNTAIN PASS is a passageway over a mountain barrier. Passes generally occur at low points on mountain watersheds, or in valleys between mountain ridges. The importance of a pass depends on the need for communication between the people living on each side.

Well-known passes include Donner (7,088 ft.) in California; Brenner (4,498 ft.) between Italy and Austria; and Khyber (3,370 ft.) between Pakistan and Afghanistan.   ROBERT M. GLENDINNING

MOUNTAIN STATE. See WEST VIRGINIA.
MOUNTAIN STATES. See ROCKY MOUNTAIN STATES.
MOUNTAIN TIME. See TIME.
MOUNTAIN VIEW, Calif. (pop. 30,889; alt. 95 ft.), lies about 40 miles southeast of San Francisco, near the southwest shore of San Francisco Bay. For location, see CALIFORNIA (political map). The city got its name for the beautiful view it offers of the Santa Cruz Mountains. Mountain View industries produce electronic equipment. The city also has fruit and vegetable canneries, and an olive oil mill. Moffett Field, a U.S. Naval Air Station, is nearby. The city is the home of St. Patrick's College. Mountain View was incorporated in 1902. It has a council-manager government.

MOUNTAINEERING. See MOUNTAIN CLIMBING.
MOUNTAINS OF THE MOON. See RUWENZORI RANGE.

MOUNTBATTEN, LOUIS (1900-   ), EARL MOUNTBATTEN OF BURMA, is a British naval leader. He became first sea lord of Great Britain in 1955, and received the rank of admiral of the fleet in 1956. He served as chief of the defense staff from 1959 to 1965, when he became governor of the Isle of Wight.

Mountbatten became a lieutenant in the British Navy in 1920. He later served as personal aide-de-camp to his cousin, the prince of Wales, later King Edward VIII. At the outbreak of World War II, he was a captain and the personal aide-de-camp to King George VI.

Mountbatten command-

Louis Mountbatten
Radio Times Hutton Picture Library

ed the destroyer *Kelly*, which was sunk in the Battle of Crete in May, 1941. He was then given command of the aircraft carrier *Illustrious*, until he became chief of combined operations in March, 1942. In this position he helped plan commando raids against St. Nazaire and Dieppe in France. In 1943, he became supreme allied commander of the Southeast Asia Command.

After the war, Mountbatten became viceroy of India. In 1947, he supervised the creation of the dominions of Pakistan and India, and then stayed on as the first governor-general of India. In 1948, Mountbatten resigned and returned to navy duty. He became a lord commissioner of the admiralty, fourth sea lord, and chief of supplies and transport in 1950. He served in the North Atlantic Treaty Organization (NATO) from 1952 to 1954 as commander in chief of all allied forces in the Mediterranean except the U.S. Sixth Fleet.

Mountbatten was born June 25, 1900, in Windsor, England. He was the son of Prince Louis Alexander, a cousin of King George V of England. Mountbatten was educated at the Royal Naval Academy, Dartmouth. He entered the British Navy in 1913. He is the uncle of Prince Philip (see PHILIP, PRINCE).   C. L. MOWAT

MOUNTBATTEN-WINDSOR. See WINDSOR (family).
MOUNTED POLICE. See ROYAL CANADIAN MOUNTED POLICE.

MOURNING is the term which refers to outward signs of grief for the dead or some calamity. Almost every nation has special mourning customs and costumes. These include special colors and types of garments, as well as special ceremonies. See FUNERAL CUSTOMS.

MOURNING DOVE is an American bird with a sad, cooing call. It breeds from southern Canada through Mexico, and winters as far south as Panama. The bird is about 12 inches long. It is mostly grayish-brown, with a tinge of pink on its breast. The tail has a white border and black spots. This bird is a swift flier.

It places its nest, built loosely of twigs, in a tree or bush, or on the ground. The bird lays two white eggs. The young hatch in about two weeks, and there may be three or four families in a season. Very young birds put their beaks in the parents' throats and feed on partly digested food, mixed with a fluid that is called *pigeon's milk*. The mourning dove eats many weed seeds, as well as some insects.

Scientific Classification. The mourning dove belongs to the pigeon and dove family, *Columbidae*. It is genus *Zenaidura*, species *Z. macroura*.   HERBERT FRIEDMANN

See also DOVE; TURTLEDOVE.

The Soft-Voiced, Gentle Mourning Dove makes a flimsy nest of twigs. Since the passenger pigeon became extinct, this has been the best-known wild pigeon of North America.
Charles W. Schwartz

Cy La Tour

A House Mouse Stuffs Itself with Stolen Grain.

MOUSE is a small animal with soft fur, a pointed snout, round black eyes, rounded ears, and a thin tail. The word *mouse* is not the name of any one kind of animal or family of animals. Many kinds of *rodents* (gnawing animals) are called mice. They include small rats, small hamsters, gerbils, jerboas, lemmings, voles, harvest mice, deer mice, and grasshopper mice. All these animals have chisel-like front teeth that are useful for gnawing. A rodent's front teeth grow throughout the animal's life.

There are hundreds of kinds of mice, and they live in most parts of the world. They can be found in the mountains, in fields and woodlands, in swamps, near streams, and in deserts.

Probably the best known kind of mouse is the house mouse. It lives wherever people live, and often builds its nest in homes, garages, or barns. Some kinds of white house mice are raised as pets. Other kinds of house mice are used by scientists to learn about sickness, to test new drugs, and to study behavior.

House Mice

House mice probably lived in the homes of ancient man and stole his food, just as mice do today. The word *mouse* comes from an old Sanskrit word meaning *thief*. Sanskrit is an ancient language of Asia, where scientists believe house mice originated. House mice spread from Asia throughout Europe. The ancestors of the house mice that now live in North and South America were brought there by English, French, and Spanish ships during the 1500's.

House mice always seem to be busy. Those that live in buildings may scamper about at any time of day or night. House mice that live in fields and forests usually come out only at night. All house mice climb well, and can often be heard running between the walls of houses.

746

Daniel Brant, the contributor of this article, is Professor of Biology at Humboldt State College.

FACTS IN BRIEF

Common Name	Scientific Name	Gestation Period	Number of Young	Where Found
*House Mouse	*Mus musculus*	18-21 days	4-7	Worldwide
American Harvest Mouse	*Reithrodontomys fulvescens*	21-24 days	1-7	North and South America
Grasshopper Mouse	*Onychomys leucogaster*	29-38 days	3-4	North America
Deer Mouse	*Peromyscus maniculatus*	21-27 days	1-9	North and South America

*The house mouse belongs to the family of Old World rats and mice, *Muridae*. The American harvest, grasshopper, and deer mice belong to the family of New World rats and mice, *Cricetidae*.

J. M. Conrader

White-Footed Mouse and Her Young

Jane Burton, Photo Researchers

Harvest Mouse

Cordell Andersen, NAS

Grasshopper Mouse

Body of a house mouse is 2½ to 3½ inches long without the tail. The tail is the same length or a little shorter. Most house mice weigh ½ to 1 ounce. Their size and weight, and the length of their tails, differ greatly among the many varieties, and even among individual animals of the same variety.

The fur of most house mice is soft, but it may be stiff and wiry. It is grayish brown on the animal's back and sides, and yellowish white underneath. House mice raised as pets or for use in laboratories may have pure white fur, black or brown spots, or other combinations of colors. The house mouse's tail is covered by scaly skin or by short, fine hair.

A house mouse has a small head and a long, narrow snout. Several long, thin whiskers grow from the sides of the snout. These whiskers, like those of a cat, help the mouse feel its way in the dark. The animal has rounded ears, and its eyes look somewhat like round black beads. A mouse can hear well, but it has poor sight. Probably because house mice cannot see well, they may enter a lighted room even if people are there.

Like beavers, muskrats, rats, and other rodents, all mice have strong, sharp front teeth that grow throughout the animal's life. With these chisel-like teeth, mice can gnaw holes in wood, tear apart packages to get at food inside, and damage books, clothing, and furniture.

Food. A house mouse eats almost anything that human beings eat. It feasts on any grain, meat, or vegetable that it can find. Mice also eat such household items as glue, leather, paste, and soap. House mice that live out of doors eat insects, and the leaves, roots, seeds, and stems of plants. Mice always seem to be looking for something to eat, but they need little food. They damage much more food than they eat.

Homes. House mice live wherever they can find food and shelter. Any dark place that is warm and quiet makes an excellent home for mice. A mouse may build its nest in a warm corner of a barn, on a beam under the roof of a garage, or in a box stored in an attic or basement. The animal may tear strips of clothing or upholstery to get materials for its nest. It may line the nest with feathers or cotton stolen from pillows. House mice that live in fields or woodlands dig holes in the ground and build nests of grass inside. They may line the nests with feathers or pieces of fur.

Young. A female house mouse may give birth every 20 to 30 days. She carries her young in her body for 18 to 21 days before they are born. She has four to seven young at a time. Newborn mice have pink skin and no fur, and their eyes are closed. They are completely helpless. Soft fur covers their bodies by the time the mice are 10 days old. When they are 14 days old, their eyes open. The young mice stay near the nest for about three weeks after birth. Then they leave to build their own nests, and soon start raising families. Most female house mice begin to have young when they are about 45 days old.

Enemies. Man is probably the worst enemy of the house mouse. People set traps and place poisons where mice can easily find them. Almost every meat-eating animal is an enemy of house mice. Cats and dogs hunt mice in houses and barns. Coyotes, foxes, snakes, and other animals capture them in forests and woodlands.

MOUSE

Owls, hawks, and other large birds swoop down on them in fields and prairies. Rats and even other mice are also enemies. House mice may live as long as a year in a hidden corner of an attic or basement. But they have so many enemies that few wild mice survive more than two or three months. Some mice kept as pets or in laboratories may live six years.

House mice avoid their enemies by hiding. A mouse seldom wanders far from its nest. It spends most of its time within an area of about 200 feet in diameter. Wherever possible, the mouse moves along paths protected by furniture, boxes, or other objects. The mouse scampers as fast as it can across the open spaces between the objects. House mice do not like water and try to avoid it, but they can swim.

Some Other Kinds of Mice

American Harvest Mice look like house mice, but are smaller and have more hair on their tails. Most American harvest mice also have much larger ears. Harvest mice live near the Pacific Ocean, from southwestern Canada to Ecuador. They also live in the eastern United States south of the Potomac and Ohio rivers. Some kinds of harvest mice live in salt marshes or in tropical forests, but most species prefer open grassy regions.

Harvest mice build their nests in places where tall grass grows. They weave leaves of grass into ball-shaped nests that are 6 to 7 inches in diameter. The mice build their nests 6 to 12 inches above the ground in branches of bushes or on stems of grass. Harvest mice are excellent climbers, and use the plant stems as ladders to reach their nests. They grasp the plant stems with their tails as they climb. Harvest mice also make nests in the ground.

These mice eat green plant sprouts, but they prefer seeds. They pick seeds off the ground, or they "harvest" seeds from plants by bending the plant stems to the ground where they bite off the seeds.

A female harvest mouse has one to seven young at a time. She carries the young mice in her body for 21 to 24 days before they are born. When the young are about 2 months old, they may start their own families.

Grasshopper Mice are about the same size as house mice, but they look fatter and have stubby tails. Their fur is brown or gray above and white underneath. They probably got their name because they eat grasshoppers.

THE SKELETON OF A MOUSE

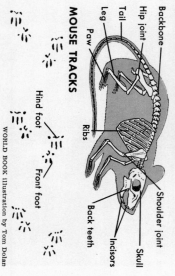

Backbone
Hip joint
Leg
Tail
Paw
Ribs
Shoulder joint
Skull
Incisors
Back teeth

MOUSE TRACKS

Hind foot
Front foot

WORLD BOOK illustration by Tom Dolan

A Laboratory Mouse gets food when it presses a button on a wall with vertical stripes. The mouse has learned to avoid the wall with horizontal stripes because it gets no reward there. Scientists study mice to find out about their ability to learn.

George McKay, The Jackson Laboratory

These mice are found in the dry regions and deserts of the western and southwestern United States, and in northern Mexico. Grasshopper mice live wherever they can find shelter in the ground. They often use burrows abandoned by such rodents as gophers, ground squirrels, and deer mice.

The female grasshopper mouse carries her young inside her body for 29 to 38 days. Usually three or four young are born at a time. The young mice become adults when they are about three months old.

Grasshopper mice are most active at night, when they come out of their burrows to hunt. Unlike most other kinds of mice, grasshopper mice prefer to eat meat rather than plants. They eat any animal they can overpower, including insects, worms, and other grasshopper mice. Their favorite foods are grasshoppers and scorpions. Grasshopper mice hunt their prey much as cats do. They quietly creep up to their victims and attack quickly.

Deer Mice, sometimes called *white-footed mice,* are 6 to 8 inches long. Their tails are 2½ to 4 inches long. The fur on their upper parts is gray, and the belly fur is white. The ears of these mice are large compared to the size of their bodies.

There are more than 50 species of deer mice. They are found from northern Colombia throughout North America as far north as Alaska and Labrador. They live in every kind of region—mountains, plains, deserts, and swamps.

Deer mice build their nests in tunnels they dig, or in hollow logs, tree stumps, or cracks in rocks. The mice may go into houses to find soft materials such as cloth or cotton for their nests. They usually build several nests a year because they move out as soon as a nest gets soiled.

A female deer mouse gives birth to one to nine young at a time. She carries them in her body for 21 to 27 days before birth. The young live in the nest for three to six weeks, and then leave to build nests of their own.

Deer mice usually rest during the day and look for food at night. They eat berries, fruits, leaves, nuts, seeds, and insects. When excited, these mice thump their front feet rapidly on the ground, making a drumming noise.

See also RAT; RODENT; JUMPING MOUSE.

DANIEL BRANT

MOUSE DEER. See PHILIPPINES (Natural Resources).

MOUSE TOWER (in German, DER MÄUSETURM) is a tower on a small island in the Rhine River near Bingen, Germany. A famous legend tells about the tower and the cruel Bishop Hatto of Bingen who built it. According to the legend, the bishop fled there to escape a horde of mice. The mice came to avenge the deaths of peasants whom the cruel bishop had burned alive. The horde of mice attacked the tower and devoured the wicked tyrant.

Experts have identified several historical characters with this story, including two Archbishop Hattos of Mainz. Robert Southey wrote a ballad about the tale, and it appears in a collection of folk tales gathered by Jakob and Wilhelm Grimm.

In reality, *Mäuseturm* appears to be a corruption of *mautturm*, meaning *toll tower*. The tower was probably built in the 1200's as a place for collecting tolls from boats on the Rhine.

ARTHUR M. SELVI

MOUSORGSKI, MODEST. See MUSSORGSKY, MODEST.

MOUTH is the part of the body which is adapted for taking in food. The lips at the mouth opening help us drink and pick up our food. Inside, we have two rows of teeth, one above the other, to grind and crush food into pulp that can be digested. Salivary glands in the walls of the mouth give off saliva which becomes mixed with our food as we chew it, and also helps digestion (see SALIVA).

The entire mouth cavity is lined with mucous membrane. The top of the mouth (the roof) consists of a bony front part, called the *hard palate*, and a soft part in the rear, called the *soft palate*. The hard palate forms a partition between the mouth and the nose. The soft palate arches down at the back of the mouth to form a curtain between the mouth and the *pharynx*. The pharynx is the back part of the throat. It connects the mouth and the nose with both the *esophagus* (the tube that carries food to the stomach), and with the *trachea* (the windpipe that carries air to the lungs). A flexible bundle of muscles extends from the floor of the mouth to form the *tongue*, one of the most useful organs in the body. The tongue not only helps us to eat, swallow, and talk, but it contains almost all the sense organs of taste (see TASTE).

Harmful germs enter the body through both the mouth and nose. Both these openings should be kept clean to help ward off disease. The mouth cavity is an excellent breeding place for germs because it is warm and moist all the time.

The teeth should be scrubbed thoroughly at least twice a day, and the mouth should be rinsed out after every meal. The teeth should be brushed lengthwise as well as crosswise, to remove particles of food. Jagged teeth can infect the mouth through irritation and may even cause cancer. Diseased gums cause loss of teeth from pyorrhea. Disease of the teeth may cause the body to become infected by bacteria. Trench mouth, or Vincent's angina, is one of the most common infections of the mouth. Painful cankers may also attack the mucous membrane which lines the mouth.

ARTHUR C. GUYTON

Related Articles in WORLD BOOK include:

Canker	Palate	Tongue
Cold Sore	Pyorrhea	Trench Mouth
Dentistry	Teeth	

MOUTH ORGAN. See HARMONICA.

MOUTHBREEDER. See FISH (Reproduction).

MOUTON. See FUR (Lamb and Sheep).

MOVABLE FEAST. See FEASTS AND FESTIVALS.

MOVIE. See MOTION PICTURE.

MOWAT, SIR OLIVER (1820-1903), a Canadian statesman, served as prime minister and attorney general of Ontario from 1872 to 1896. His term was one of the longest in British parliamentary history. During his administration, Mowat introduced the ballot in municipal and provincial elections and extended the voting franchise. He fought the national government to obtain more political rights for the provinces. Before the provinces were united, he served as chancellor of Upper Canada (now Ontario). He was lieutenant governor of Ontario from 1897 until his death. He was born in what is now Kingston, Ont.

WILLIAM R. WILLOUGHBY

Sir Oliver Mowat

MOYNIHAN, DANIEL PATRICK

MOYNIHAN, DANIEL PATRICK (1927-   ), was named counsellor to the President and given Cabinet status by Richard M. Nixon in November, 1969. From January to November, 1969, Moynihan had headed the staff of the federal Council for Urban Affairs.

An authority on the problems of cities and of minority groups, Moynihan became known for his books and articles on immigration, the anti-poverty program, and Negro family life. He served as an assistant to Governor Averell Harriman of New York in the 1950's and served in the U.S. Department of Labor from 1961 to 1965.

Moynihan was born in Tulsa, Okla., but grew up in the slums of New York City. He graduated from Tuft's Fletcher University and received a doctorate from Tuft's Fletcher Institute of International Law and Diplomacy. In 1966, he became head of the Joint Center for Urban Studies at Harvard University and Massachusetts Institute of Technology.

DAVID S. BRODER

PARTS OF THE MOUTH

Hard Palate
Mouth Cavity
Soft Palate
Uvula
Tongue Muscles
Hyoid Bone
Upper Teeth
Lips
Tongue
Lower Teeth
Jawbone
Salivary Glands

MOZAMBIQUE

⊛ Capital

● Other City or Town

⊢⊣ Road

⊢⊢ Rail Line

▲ MOUNTAIN

~ River

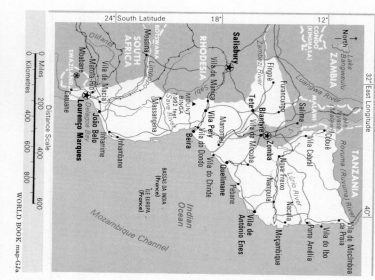

WORLD BOOK map-GJa

MOZAMBIQUE, *MOH zam BEEK,* also called PORTU-GUESE EAST AFRICA, is a Portuguese overseas province on the southeast coast of Africa. Mozambique plays a strategic role in the economies of its neighboring territories. It provides unskilled labor and access to the sea for its neighbors, South Africa, Malawi, Zambia, and Rhodesia. It also helps Portugal maintain a balanced economy by supplying needed raw materials. Lourenço Marques is the capital and chief port (see LOURENÇO MARQUES).

Location, Size, and Description. Mozambique is a long, narrow strip of fertile land which stretches about 1,500 miles north and south along the Indian Ocean. With its 302,330 square miles, Mozambique is eight times larger than Portugal and slightly larger than Texas. Mozambique is bordered by Tanzania on the north, Malawi on the northwest, Zambia and Rhodesia on the west, and by South Africa on the south. Swaziland lies at the southwestern corner of Mozambique. On the eastern coast, the Mozambique Channel separates Mozambique from the island of Madagascar (see MOZAMBIQUE CHANNEL).

Most of Mozambique lies in a low coastal plain. The

colony has some mountains, especially near the western border, where they rise to more than 5,000 feet above sea level. Several large rivers flow eastward across the territory through fertile valleys. Fifty thousand acres of irrigated land have been prepared for settlement by Portuguese colonists in the Limpopo Valley as part of a six-year project launched in 1953. The Limpopo River flows through southern Mozambique. The Zambezi River flows through the center of the province.

Mozambique is not rich in mineral resources. However, there may be substantial uranium deposits in the Tete region. The province also has deposits of gold and silver. Much of the land in Mozambique is suitable for farming.

The province has a wet and a dry season. Heavy, irregular rains fall from November to April. The average annual rainfall ranges between 30 inches in the south and 56 inches in the north. The humidity is high even during the dry season, averaging between 70 and 80 per cent. Annual temperatures in Mozambique average between 72° F. in the south and 80° F. in the central Zambezi region.

The People. About 7,584,000 people live in Mozambique. About 67,000 of the inhabitants are Europeans, and 17,000 are of Asiatic descent. Most of the rest are Africans who speak Bantu languages.

The Europeans in Mozambique live almost exclusively in Lourenço Marques and Beira. The European quarters of these cities are clean and spacious, and have modern stores and buildings. Other cities include João Belo, Quelimane, Tete, Vila Cabral, Vila de An-

Food Merchants of Lourenço Marques, Mozambique, display fresh tropical fruits and vegetables in an open-air market. Women take care of most of the displays.

Weldon King

Weldon King

A Gleaming White Apartment Building stands out against the sky in Lourenço Marques, the capital of Mozambique. The mosaic sidewalk is typical of cities built by the Portuguese.

tonio Enes, Vila do Chinde, Vila de Mocímboa da Praia, and Vila Pery. Africans in the cities live in cane houses with sheet-metal roofs. Outside the cities, they live in thatched huts. Four or five huts arranged in a circle make up a typical African homestead.

The Portuguese government compels African men in the southern districts of Mozambique to work for wages at least six months of each year. Thousands of African men work in the mines and on farms in South Africa and other neighboring countries. An estimated 500,000 Africans work outside Mozambique each year. In the northern districts, companies from outside the province are not permitted to hire Mozambique laborers. A program begun in 1947 requires about a million men, women, and children a year to plant cotton for Portugal's textile industry.

Important products exported from Mozambique include cashew nuts, copra, sisal, sugar, and tea (see COCONUT PALM [table]). The chief food crops are corn, manioc, millet, peanuts, and sweet potatoes.

Education. The Portuguese government has been slow to provide social services for the non-European population. Portuguese children must attend school, but not African children. Only one of every 100 Africans can read. Africans attend special schools run by religious missions. But much of the school day is spent working on mission farms, and only about 2,000 Africans advance beyond the third grade each year.

Transportation and Trade. Mozambique's most important sources of wealth are its government-owned railroads and harbors. More than 80 per cent of the Rhodesian overseas trade passes through the ports of Lourenço Marques and Beira. Under the terms of a treaty with South Africa, at least 47.5 per cent of the seaborne trade enroute to the industrial heartland around Johannesburg must pass through the port of Lourenço Marques. In return, Mozambique furnishes up to 100,000 African miners a year for South Africa's gold and coal mines.

Mozambique's railway system consists of 12 lines connecting the ports with the interior. The lines run for a total of 1,464 miles and carry about 3½ million tons of freight and a million passengers a year. Mozambique has few paved roads, but a network of second-class roads permits travel by automobile into almost all districts.

Government. Seven elected delegates represent Mozambique in Portugal's national assembly. Most major legislation and administrative policy is determined by the Overseas Ministry. The highest administrative authority in Mozambique is the governor general. Mozambique also has a provincial legislative council composed of 16 elected and 8 nominated members. Citizens of Mozambique enjoy the same political rights as Portuguese citizens. However, only 5,000 of Mozambique's Africans are considered citizens. All other Africans have the status of *natives*, or *indigenas*, which places them under special laws and regulations. Portuguese policy provides for a change of status from native to *citizen*, but it is difficult for the Africans to acquire the education necessary for the change. Mozambique is divided into nine districts: Cabo Delgado, Gaza, Inhambane, Lourenço Marques, Manica and Sofala, Moçambique, Niassa, Tete, and Zambézia.

History. The Portuguese explorer, Vasco da Gama, visited Mozambique in 1498. Arabs lived in the area at that time. The Portuguese established forts and trading posts at Sofala in the southeastern section and on the island of Mozambique in the early 1500's. The earliest penetration of the interior was along the Zambezi Valley. In 1632, a military post was established at Tete, on the Zambezi River. Mozambique soon became a center of the Portuguese slave trade. The Delagoa Bay area, claimed by both Britain and Portugal, became a Portuguese possession in 1875 (see DELAGOA BAY).

Large parts of Mozambique were once controlled and governed by private companies. The Mozambique Company received a charter from Portugal in 1891 for the administration of what is now Manica and Sofala district. This area reverted to Portuguese authority in 1942 when the charter of the Mozambique Company expired.

After World War I, part of German East Africa was added to Mozambique. This region, known as the Kionga Triangle, lies south of the Ruvuma River. The African tribes in the southern area of Mozambique were not brought under control until 1895. Occasional uprisings in the northern part of the country continued until 1917.

During the 1950's, Portugal began a series of six-year plans to speed the economic development of Mozambique. But the African residents rebelled, and demanded self-government. Uprisings began in 1961, and Portugal rushed troops into Mozambique. Rebels from Mozambique were trained in nearby African countries. Guerrilla raids against the Portuguese forces increased in 1964. MARVIN HARRIS

MOZAMBIQUE CHANNEL separates the Malagasy Republic from Mozambique, a Portuguese province on the southeastern coast of Africa (see MOZAMBIQUE [map]). The channel is more than 1,000 miles long and from 250 to 600 miles wide. The Comoro Islands lie at the northern entrance. It is an important shipping lane. Important ports include Lourenço Marques, Beira, and Moçambique in Mozambique, and Tuléar and Majunga in the Malagasy Republic. F. G. WALTON SMITH

MOZART, WOLFGANG AMADEUS

MOZART, WOLFGANG AMADEUS (1756-1791), was one of the world's great composers. With Joseph Haydn, he was the leading composer of what historians of music call the *classical period*. Mozart died before his 36th birthday, but he still left over 600 works. Many consider his *Don Giovanni* the world's greatest opera.

His Life

Mozart was born on Jan. 27, 1756, in Salzburg, Austria, son of a respected musician. His father, Leopold, was the leader of the local orchestra, and also wrote the first important book about violin playing. At the age of three, Wolfgang showed signs of remarkable musical talent. He learned to play the harpsichord, a keyboard instrument related to the piano, at the age of 4. He was composing music at 5. When he was 6, he played for the Austrian empress at her court in Vienna.

Before he was 14, Mozart had composed many works called *sonatas* for the harpsichord, piano, or the violin, as well as orchestral and other works. His father recognized Wolfgang's amazing talent and devoted most of his time to his son's general and musical education. Wolfgang never attended school. Leopold took him on concert tours through much of Europe. Wolfgang composed, gave public performances, met many musicians, and played the organ in many churches. In 1769, like his father before him, he began working for the archbishop of Salzburg, who also ruled the province. The Mozarts often quarreled with the archbishop, partly because

Mozart composed the opera *The Magic Flute* the year he died. In this scene, Prince Tamino and Pamino, daughter of the Queen of the Night, prepare for initiation rites to prove themselves worthy of each other.

Unfinished portrait (1789) by Joseph Lange, Mozart Museum, Salzburg; from Art Reference Bureau; Fred Fehl

Wolfgang was often absent from Salzburg. Finally, the archbishop dismissed the young Mozart in 1781.

Mozart was actually glad to leave Salzburg, a small town, and seek his fortune in Vienna, one of the music capitals of Europe. By this time people took less notice of him, because he was no longer a child prodigy. However, he was a brilliant performer and active as a composer. Mozart married in 1782. He did not have a regular job in Vienna and tried to earn a living by selling his compositions, giving public performances, and giving music lessons. None of these activities produced enough income to support his family. He even traveled to Germany for the coronation of a new emperor, but his concerts there did not attract as much attention as he hoped. He died in poverty on Dec. 27, 1791.

His Works

Operas. Mozart excelled in almost every kind of musical composition. Several of his 22 operas gained wide recognition soon after his death, and they still please audiences all over the world. *The Marriage of Figaro* (1786) and *Don Giovanni* (1787) are operas he composed with words in Italian. *The Magic Flute* (1791) has German words. Each of these contains *arias* (beautiful melodies for singers), *recitative* (rapidly sung dialogue), *ensembles* in which several people sing at the same time, and choruses. The orchestra provides an ever-changing expressive accompaniment. The drama ranges from slapstick and other forms of comedy to tragedy.

Symphonies. Mozart wrote over 40 symphonies, many of which are performed today. Some originally were *overtures* (orchestral introductions) for operas, and last only a few minutes. His later symphonies, which are the most popular today, are full-length orchestral compositions that last 20 to 30 minutes. Most consist of four *movements* (sections). His last and most famous symphony, Number 41 (1788), is nicknamed the *Jupiter*.

Church Music. Mozart composed a great amount of church music, most of it for performance at the Salzburg Cathedral. He wrote Masses and shorter pieces called *motets*; and he set psalms to music, especially for the *vesper* (afternoon or evening) service. The music is beautiful and varied. It includes choral and solo parts, usually with accompaniment by organ and orchestra. Mozart's best-known sacred work is the *Requiem* (Mass for the Dead), which he began in the last year of his life. While writing it, Mozart is said to have thought a great deal about his own death. Parts of the *Requiem* were composed during his final illness. He died before the work was finished.

Other Works. Mozart wrote other orchestral works, generally of a somewhat lighter nature, called *serenades*. Some were intended for outdoor performance. One has become well-known under the title *Eine kleine Nachtmusik* (*A Little Night Music*, 1787). Mozart also wrote many compositions called *concertos* for a solo instrument such as violin or piano, with orchestral accompaniment. He often played the solo part.

Throughout his life Mozart composed *chamber music*—works for a small number of instruments in which only one musician plays each part. Mozart concentrated on string quartets (two violins, viola, and cello). He was influenced in this by Haydn, whose quartets he admired. He dedicated six quartets to Haydn. Mozart's sonatas for piano and for violin and piano are outstanding. The piano was then still fairly new and was widely played by amateurs. More than any other composer, Mozart helped to make the instrument popular. His melodies for piano had a "singing," sustained quality, with gradual changes between soft and loud.

His Style. In spite of the hardships and disappointments he suffered as a composer, much of Mozart's music is cheerful and vigorous. Mozart had a good sense of humor, and liked puns and practical jokes. He composed many lighter works. These include the opera *Così Fan Tutte* (*All Women Are Like That*, 1790), much of his early instrumental music, and *canons* (rounds) with nonsense words.

Mozart also produced deeply serious music. His most profound works include the piano concerto in D minor, several string quartets, the string quintet in G minor, and his last three symphonies—E flat major, G minor, and the *Jupiter*. Larger works may contain both serious and light elements, as does *Don Giovanni*.

Mozart belonged to the Order of Freemasons and wrote several compositions for their meetings. Some scenes from his fairy-tale opera *The Magic Flute* were inspired by Masonic traditions and beliefs.

A catalog of Mozart's works was first prepared by Ludwig Köchel (1800-1877), a German music lover. Today, Mozart's works are still identified by the numbers Köchel assigned to them.

Today Mozart's music is known and admired throughout the world. A famous music festival held each summer in Salzburg features his works. REINHARD G. PAULY

M.R.A. See MORAL RE-ARMAMENT.

MUCH ADO ABOUT NOTHING. See SHAKESPEARE, WILLIAM (tables).

MUCILAGE, *MYOO suh lij*, is a thick, sticky substance which is usually made by dissolving gum in water, or in some other liquid. The purpose of mucilage is to cause two substances to *adhere* (stick together). Therefore, mucilage is classified as an *adhesive*. The exact ingredients of mucilage vary with the uses to which the adhesive is to be put. Gum arabic dissolved in hot water makes gum-arabic mucilage. When aluminum sulfate is added to the solution, the adhesive may be used to make paper stick to glass. Glycerin or sugar may be added to mucilage to keep it moist until it is used.

Dextrin is dissolved in cold water to make a mucilage which is used on the back of postage stamps. Glue and gelatin also are used to make mucilage, but these substances also need vinegar, glycerin, or acid in order to keep them in a fluid state. CHARLES L. MANTELL

See also GLUE; GUM ARABIC.

MUCK, KARL (1859-1940), a German conductor, was principal conductor of the Boston Symphony Orchestra in 1906 and 1907, and again from 1912 to 1918. His second term in Boston ended when he was falsely accused of being a German spy, and was interned. In 1892, Muck was appointed *Kapellmeister* (conductor), and in 1908, musical director of the Berlin Royal Opera. From 1922 to 1933 he led the Hamburg Philharmonic Orchestra. He conducted outstanding performances of Wagner's *Parsifal* at the Bayreuth Festival from 1901 to 1932. He was born in Darmstadt. DAVID EWEN

MUCKRAKING is a term applied to writings by American reformers of the early 1900's who exposed social and political evils. President Theodore Roosevelt in 1906 first used the word *muckraking* to condemn sen-

sational and untruthful writers. The first muckraker was Josiah Flynt Willard. His series, *The World of Graft*, appeared in 1901 in *McClure's Magazine*. Later, articles by Lincoln Steffens, Ray Stannard Baker, Ida M. Tarbell, and Upton Sinclair dealt with city government, labor unions, and business. LOUIS FILLER

See also AMERICAN LITERATURE (Social Critics); LLOYD, HENRY DEMAREST.

MUCUS, *MYOO kus*, is a thick, clear, slimy fluid found in the nose, mouth, and other organs and passages that open to the outside of the body. It is made up mostly of a gluco-protein compound, that is, a compound of protein and sugar. This fluid is produced by cells in the mucous membranes, and covers the surfaces of the membranes.

Mucus performs two principal duties. It provides lubrication for material which must pass over the membranes, such as food passing down the gullet, or food tube. It also catches foreign matter and keeps it from entering the body. The mucous membranes of the nose, sinuses, and *trachea* (windpipe) are covered with fine hairlike structures known as *cilia*. The motions of the cilia cause the mucus to carry bacteria and dust up the windpipe to the nose and throat where it can be swallowed or blown out. Infection of the mucous membrane is known as a "cold." WILLIAM V. MAYER

See also COLD, COMMON; MEMBRANE; MOUTH; NOSE.

MUD DAUBER. See WASP (Solitary Wasps).

MUD HEN. See COOT.

MUD MOUNTAIN DAM, formerly called STEVENS DAM, is a large rock-fill dam on the White River in Washington. It stands about 30 miles east of Tacoma. The dam is 425 feet high, and 700 feet long at the top. It has a volume of 2,360,000 cubic yards. The reservoir holds 106,000 acre-feet of water. T. W. MERMEL

MUD PUDDLE CLUB. See BUTTERFLY (Assemblies).

MUD PUPPY is a rather large salamander which lives in American ponds and streams. Mud puppies may grow as much as 17 inches long, but an 8-inch animal

New York Zoological Society

The Mud Puppy Looks Sluggish but it darts very quickly from the mud to catch and swallow its prey.

may be full-grown. The mud puppy has a slimy body. It may be dark brown, gray-brown, or black, usually with darker spots. It has a powerful flat tail, four weak

MUDD, SAMUEL ALEXANDER

legs, and a short flat head. It has deep purplish-red external gills on each side behind its head. The mud puppy is also called the *water dog*.

Mud puppies live in the Great Lakes, the Mississippi River, and ponds and streams as far south as Georgia and as far west as Texas. Mud puppies usually stay in 2 to 8 feet of fresh water, especially among water plants. They attach their yellow eggs to some object lying under about 4 feet of sunny water. The young are about three-fourths of an inch long when they hatch.

Mud puppies eat crayfish, fish eggs, and other water animals. They usually hunt during the hours of dawn or dusk. They may remain active throughout the year.

Scientific Classification. The mud puppy belongs to the mud puppy family, *Proteidae*. The most common species of the mud puppy is classified as genus *Necturus*, species *N. maculosus*.

W. FRANK BLAIR

MUDD, SAMUEL ALEXANDER (1833-1883), was the doctor who set John Wilkes Booth's leg after President Abraham Lincoln's assassination. Mudd did not recognize Booth. A military court tried the doctor as a "conspirator" and found him guilty as an accessory after the fact in the assassination. Sentenced to life imprisonment, Mudd saved many prisoners and guards in a yellow fever epidemic. He was freed in 1869, after nearly four years in prison. Mudd was born in Charles County, Maryland.

MUDFLOWS. See VOLCANO (Products of Volcanic Eruption).

MUELLER, PAUL (1899-1965), a Swiss chemist, won the 1948 Nobel prize for physiology and medicine for discovering the insect-killing properties of DDT. The drug first was produced in Austria in 1873, but Muel-

ler discovered its value as an insect-killer in 1939 while searching for a plant contact insecticide. DDT was used widely during World War II. It suppressed typhus in Italy and Japan (see DDT). Mueller was born in Olten, Switzerland, and was graduated from the University of Basel.

HENRY H. FERTIG

MUENCH, ALOISIUS J. CARDINAL (1889-1962), became a cardinal of the Roman Catholic Church in 1959. He became bishop of Fargo, N.Dak in 1935 and the papal *nuncio* (ambassador) to West Germany in 1951. Cardinal Muench was born in Milwaukee, and was ordained a priest in 1913. He was elevated to archbishop in 1950.

THOMAS P. NEILL

MUEZZIN. See MINARET; ISLAM (Duties).

MUFFLER is a device that silences the noise of an engine. The mufflers on most automobiles look like long metal cans that are connected to the exhaust pipes. The heat and pressure inside the cylinders, where exhaust gases' originate, are much greater than the heat and pressure of the outside air (see GASOLINE ENGINE). If the exhaust gases went directly into the outside air, the sudden change would create a loud, sharp noise. Mufflers reduce the noise by forcing the exhaust gases through a series of *perforations* (small holes) before they reach the open air. The gases expand and cool as they pass through the perforations.

MUGGER. See CROCODILE.

MUGWORT. See WORMWOOD.

MUGWUMP is an Indian word meaning *chief*. People used the term sarcastically in 1884 to describe a group of Republicans who refused to support their party's presidential candidate, James G. Blaine. These men did not trust Blaine, and believed he was opposed to reforms in government. They worked and voted for the Democratic candidate, Grover Cleveland, who had a reputa-

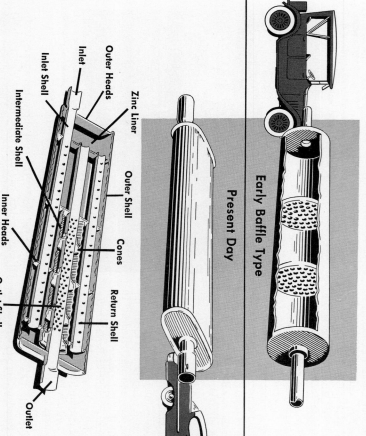

Inlet

Outer Heads

Inlet Shell

Zinc Liner

Intermediate Shell

Inner Heads

Outlet Shell

Outer Shell

Inner Shell

Cones

Return Shell

Outlet

Early Baffle Type

Present Day

MUFFLER

Early Mufflers sent exhaust through perforated baffles. This method slowed exhaust and lowered engine efficiency.

Mufflers Today route exhaust through a series of perforated pipes. They silence noise better and reduce engine power less than the older type.

tion for stubborn honesty. The Mugwumps were men of considerable influence. HAROLD W. BRADLEY

See also CLEVELAND, GROVER (Election of 1884).

MUHAMMAD. See MOHAMMED.

MUHAMMAD, ELIJAH (1897-), is the head of the Black Muslim movement, a Negro organization that combines religious beliefs with strong social protest. He favors complete separation of Negroes and whites, and formation of an all-Negro state or territory somewhere in the United States.

He taught his followers to make themselves self-sufficient by establishing their own schools and businesses. He preached that Negroes should be thrifty, clean, and hardworking, and should abstain from pork, drugs, tobacco, and alcoholic drinks.

Elijah Muhammad was born ELIJAH POOLE in Sandersville, Ga., and moved to Detroit in the 1920's. He met Wali Farad, founder of the movement there, and changed his name to Elijah Muhammad. He became leader of the movement and moved its headquarters to Chicago when Farad disappeared in 1934. RICHARD BARDOLPH

See also BLACK MUSLIMS.

MUHAMMAD ALI. See CLAY, CASSIUS.

MUHLENBERG, MYOO lun burg, is the family name of four outstanding American religious leaders.

Henry Melchior Muhlenberg (1711-1787) helped found the Lutheran Church in the United States. He accepted an appointment as pastor to Lutherans in Pennsylvania in 1742. When he arrived from Germany in Philadelphia in 1742, he found weak, divided, and confused congregations. Within a month Muhlenberg had gained control, and began establishing the Lutheran Church. Muhlenberg was born in Einbeck, Hanover, Germany.

John Peter Gabriel Muhlenberg (1746-1807), the oldest son of Henry Melchior Muhlenberg, was an American Lutheran minister. He served churches in New Jersey from 1769 to 1771, then became a minister in Woodstock, Va., in 1771. There, on a Sunday in 1775, after conducting church service, Muhlenberg removed his robe to reveal a military uniform. He enrolled men in his parish into a regiment, and became its colonel. Muhlenberg commanded troops at the Revolutionary War battles of Brandywine, Germantown, Monmouth, and Yorktown, and rose to the rank of major general. He served as a Democratic-Republican representative from Pennsylvania in the United States Congress from 1789 to 1791, 1793 to 1795, and 1799 to 1801. He was born in Trappe, Pa. A statue of Muhlenberg represents Pennsylvania in the United States Capitol in Washington, D.C.

Frederick Augustus Conrad Muhlenberg (1750-1801), the second son of Henry Melchior Muhlenberg, was a Lutheran minister and American statesman. He served as a minister in Pennsylvania and New York from 1770 until 1779. He represented Pennsylvania as a Federalist in the first four U.S. Congresses, and served as speaker

Wide World

Elijah Muhammad

of the House of Representatives in the first (1789-1791) and third (1793-1795) Congresses. He was born in Trappe, Pa.

William Augustus Muhlenberg (1796-1877), grandson of Frederick Augustus Conrad Muhlenberg, was an Episcopal clergyman. In 1828, he established Flushing Institute, a boys' boarding school on Long Island. This was one of the first church-sponsored schools in the United States. William Muhlenberg was born in Philadelphia. F. A. NORWOOD

MUHLENBERG COLLEGE. See UNIVERSITIES AND COLLEGES (table).

MUIR, myoor, **JOHN** (1838-1914), an explorer, naturalist, and writer, campaigned for forest conservation in the United States. His efforts influenced the U.S. Congress to pass the Yosemite National Park Bill in 1890, establishing both Yosemite and Sequoia National Parks. He persuaded President Theodore Roosevelt to set aside 148,000,000 acres of forest reserves. A redwood forest in California's Coast Range near San Francisco was named Muir Woods in 1908 to honor his contributions to forest conservation.

Muir tramped through many regions of the United States, Europe, Asia, Africa, and the Arctic. He spent six years in the area of Yosemite Valley and was the first man to explain the glacial origin of Yosemite Valley. In 1879, he discovered a glacier in Alaska which now bears his name. He called California "the grand side of the mountain," and owned a large fruit ranch in that state.

Muir kept notebooks during his travels, to use in his writings. He wrote *The Mountains of California* (1894), *Our National Parks* (1901), and *The Yosemite* (1912).

Muir was born in Dunbar, Scotland. His family moved to Wisconsin when he was 11. He grew up on a farm and developed a great love of nature. As a boy, he attracted attention with his inventions. He entered the University of Wisconsin at the age of 22. He supported himself by teaching, and by summer farm work. His interests included botany. CHESTER B. BAKER

United Press Int.

John Muir

MUIR WOODS NATIONAL MONUMENT, near San Francisco, Calif., contains one of the most famous redwood groves in the state. William Kent, a California statesman, donated the grove to the United States. The 503-acre monument was established in 1908. See also MUIR, JOHN.

MUKDEN, MOOK den (pop. 2,411,000; alt. 200 ft.), also called SHEN-YANG, is the capital of Liaoning province in China. It lies in Manchuria, on the bank of the Hun River. Five railroads meet at Mukden. The city is in the center of the most thickly populated part of Manchuria. It has three airports, and hundreds of factories which produce metal products, machine tools, and airplanes.

The center and oldest part of Mukden was built during the Middle Ages. It has narrow streets and ancient buildings, and is surrounded by high stone walls. Outside this section lies the Russian quarter, which the Russians built in the early 1900's, when they occupied Mukden. The Japanese developed many suburbs of Mukden when they invaded Manchuria in 1931. A few miles north of Mukden is a beautiful park which contains the tombs of the Manchu emperors who once ruled the vast Chinese Empire.

An important battle of the Russo-Japanese War (1905) took place in Mukden. The Japanese invasion of Manchuria (1931) began with a clash between Japanese and Chinese forces near Mukden.

THEODORE H. E. CHEN

MUKDEN, BATTLE OF. See RUSSO-JAPANESE WAR (Last Battles).

MUKERJI, *MOO ker JEE,* **DHAN GOPAL** (1890-1936), is best known for his books which interpret India for children. His mother told him fables and old religious tales of India when he was a boy. In his stories, he used these and childhood memories of life in the jungle. In 1928, he won the Newbery medal for *Gay-Neck* (1928), the story of a carrier pigeon. Mukerji was born near Calcutta, the son of Brahmin parents. He attended the universities of Calcutta and Tokyo. He came to America in 1910 and was graduated from Stanford University in 1914.

EVELYN RAY SICKELS

MULATTO, *myoo LAT oh,* is a person of mixed white and Negro descent. The term *mulatto* is applied correctly to those who have one white and one Negro parent. Mulattoes are often called *half-breeds.* The child of a white person and a mulatto is a *quadroon.* Mulattoes vary in appearance. Some have dark skins and kinky hair and some do not. The word *creole* is often confused with *mulatto.* In the United States, a creole is a white Southerner of French or Spanish ancestry. See also CREOLE; MESTIZO.

VERNON R. DORJAHN

MULBERRY is any one of a group of trees with small edible fruits resembling blackberries. The fruits have many tiny seeds. The oval or heart-shaped leaves are toothed and often divided into lobes. The trees in the mulberry family have milky juice.

The *white mulberry* from China provides food for the silkworm, and has been grown since ancient times. After the silkworm eats the bright green leaves, it spins a cocoon of fine silky fibers. The silk industry then weaves these fibers into silken fabrics. The white mulberry has been planted in the United States, but the silkworm industry has never been successful in America. See SILK.

The *red mulberry* is a medium-sized tree that grows in the eastern half of the United States. It has

Ralph Crane, *Life* © Time, Inc.

A 20-Mule Team used to haul borax from a mine and refinery in Boron, Calif. Mules have great strength and endurance.

large, dark green leaves. Birds and other wildlife eagerly eat the purplish fruits. Mulberry wood is used for fence posts, furniture, and the interiors of homes. The Indians made cloth from the fibrous bark. In Europe, people use the dark, juicy fruits of the *black mulberry* as dessert, and to make preserves and wine. *Paper mulberry* from eastern Asia has been planted for shade in the eastern part of the United States. Its leaves are gray. Paper has been made from its bark.

Scientific Classification. Mulberries belong to the mulberry family, *Moraceae.* The white mulberry is genus *Morus,* species *M. alba.* The red mulberry is *M. rubra,* and the black is *M. nigra.*

ELBERT L. LITTLE, JR.

See also BANYAN TREE; BREADFRUIT.

MUCH is any material that is spread over soil so that air can get through, but so that water in the soil cannot evaporate. Mulch may be made of manure, straw, hay, clover, chaff, alfalfa, corncobs, leaves, sawdust, wood chips, and many other substances. It is often applied about two or three inches thick. It helps keep water in the soil by reducing evaporation, and it also decays and enriches the soil. It also keeps down the number of weeds that would otherwise grow up to com-

The Mulberry Tree thrives in almost any kind of soil. Its fruit has tiny seeds, and may be white, violet, or black.

J. Horace McFarland

pete with plant crops. Mulch is valuable to home gardeners, but it often costs more than commercial fertilizers.

William R. Van Dersal

MULE, *myool*, is a domestic animal and beast of burden. It is the offspring of a *mare* (female horse) and a *jackass* (male donkey). The offspring of a male horse (stallion) and a female ass (jenny) is called a *hinny*. Mules are used in all parts of the world.

A mule looks somewhat like both its parents. Like the jackass, a mule has long ears, short mane, small feet, and a tail with a tuft of long hairs at the end. From the mother it gets a large, well-shaped body and strong muscles. She also gives it a horse's ease in getting used to harness. The father gives the mule a braying voice, sure-footedness, and endurance. An important quality from the jackass is the way a mule saves its strength when it is forced to work hard and for a long time. It is less likely to suffer from overwork than a horse.

Mules resist disease well. It is sometimes said that they do not catch diseases, but experts have found that this is not true. Unfortunately, mules do not have offspring of their own, except in extremely rare cases. Animals which cannot have offspring are said to be

sterile. All male mules and most female mules are sterile. But a few female mules have produced young when bred to male asses or to stallions. These rare offspring are either three-fourths ass or three-fourths horse.

Mules can remain strong under much harsh treatment and work, but they work better if they are treated with kindness. When owners take proper care of their mules, they will do as much work as horses, and will do it under harder conditions. The way mules can bear rough treatment makes them suitable for work in construction camps, mines, and military zones.

In the United States, over nine-tenths of all the mules work on farms and plantations. Most of them are used in the South.

E. Lendell Cockrum

See also Donkey; Glanders; Hinny.

MULE DEER is a beautiful deer that has large, furry ears similar to those of a mule. This grayish- to brownish-colored deer stands about 3 to 3½ feet high, and has large, branching antlers. It has a peculiar stiff-legged gait, but it can bound swiftly over the roughest trail. It lives from northern Mexico north to southern Yukon and Alaska, and from northern Texas and eastern North Dakota west to the Pacific Coast. The mule deer eats grass during the spring, but lives on buds, leaves, and twigs of shrubs the rest of the year. It is also called the *blacktail*, but this name usually applies to the type of mule deer that lives in the forests near the northwestern Pacific Coast.

Scientific Classification. Mule deers belong to the deer family, *Cervidae*. They are classified as genus *Odocoileus*, species *O. hemionus*.

See also ANIMAL (color picture: Animals of the Deserts).

VICTOR H. CAHALANE

MULHACÉN. See ISLAM (The Structure of Islam).

MULLAH. See SPAIN (Land Regions).

MULLEIN, *MUL in,* or *MULLEN,* is the name of a group of woolly biennial plants that belong to the fig-wort family. There are over 100 kinds of mullein. Three grow in the United States and southern Canada. The *common mullein* grows in rocky pastures, along roadsides, and in waste places. A tall plant with a thick, woolly stem, it has thick, velvety leaves. Yellow flowers grow in clusters in the form of a spike at the top of the stalk. The *moth mullein* is smaller. It has smooth, lobed, and deeply-veined leaves.

Both the stem and leaves of the mullein irritate the skin when touched. The leaves of the mullein were formerly used to make a tea for treating coughs, nervous disorders, and inflammations.

The *white mullein* is a less common mullein which grows in the eastern United States. A thin, powdery down covers the plant. The mullein may be controlled

J. Horace McFarland; L. W. Brownell

Common Mullein plants begin to grow in early spring, *left.* Their tall stems bloom with yellow flowers in the summer, *right.*

by cutting the flower stalks before the seed forms or by spraying with a *herbicide* (chemical weed killer).

Scientific Classification. Mulleins belong to the figwort family, *Scrophulariaceae.* The common mullein is genus *Verbascum,* species *V. thapsus.* The white mullein is *V. lychnitis;* the moth, *V. blattaria.*

LOUIS PYENSON

MULLENS, PRISCILLA. See ALDEN.

MÜLLER, ERWIN W. See ION MICROSCOPE.

MÜLLER, FRIEDRICH MAX. See LINGUISTICS (The Comparativists).

MULLER, HERMANN JOSEPH (1890-1967), was an American geneticist. He received the 1946 Nobel prize in physiology and medicine for discovering that X rays

can produce *mutations* (sudden changes in genes). Studying the breeding of fruit flies, Muller and geneticist Thomas Hunt Morgan made important discoveries in heredity while Muller was a student at Columbia University. Muller later made further experiments in producing mutations artificially in fruit flies. The results of these experiments, published in 1927, brought him the Nobel prize. Muller was born in New York City. He became a professor of zoology at Indiana University in 1945. See also HEREDITY (Genetics).

HENRY H. FERTIG

MULLET, *MUL et.* Two different families of fish are called mullets. *Gray mullets* are bluish-silvery fish with stout bodies. They are from 1 to 2 feet long, and have blunt heads and small mouths. The teeth, if any, are very weak. Great numbers of these fish live close to the shore in nearly all temperate and tropical waters. Their

State of Calif. Dept. of Fish and Game

The Striped Mullet Thrives in Shallow Coastal Waters.

flesh is wholesome and has a good flavor. The *common,* or *striped,* mullet is the largest and best of all the species. It weighs from 10 to 12 pounds. Striped mullets are plentiful around the Florida Keys and on the Gulf Coast.

Surmullets, or *red mullets,* are small, brightly colored fish that live chiefly in warm seas. Like the gray mullets, they have small mouths and weak teeth. Two long feelers called *barbels* hang like strings from the chin.

Scientific Classification. The gray mullets make up the mullet family, *Mugilidae.* The common mullet is genus *Mugil,* species *M. cephalus.* Red mullets belong to the goatfish family, *Mullidae.* The red mullet of Europe is genus *Mullus,* species *M. barbatus.*

LEONARD P. SCHULTZ

MULLIKEN, ROBERT S. See NOBEL PRIZES (table [1966]).

MULLION. See ARCHITECTURE (Architectural Terms).

MULOCK, SIR WILLIAM (1844-1944), the *Grand Old Man of Canada,* was a leader in law, politics, and education for more than 60 years. A Liberal, he represented York County in the House of Commons from 1882 to 1905. In 1896, Mulock became postmaster general. He introduced the two-cent postage rate from Canada to all parts of the British Empire. He served as Canada's first minister of labor, from 1900 to 1905. In 1905, he was appointed chief justice of the Exchequer Court of Ontario, and in 1923 he became chief justice of Ontario. He attended the University of Toronto, and served as chancellor of the university from 1924 to 1944. Mulock was born at Bondhead, in what is now Ontario.

JOHN T. SAYWELL

MULTĀN, *mool TAHN* (pop. 358,201; alt. 400 ft.), is one of the oldest cities of West Pakistan, dating back to the 300's B.C. Multān lies near the left bank of the Chenāb River, southwest of Lahore. It is a manufacturing center for surgical instruments and steel furniture.

ROBERT I. CRANE

MULTIGRAPH. See DUPLICATOR.

Multiple Births Usually Occur Among Small Animals, but Chihuahuas Rarely Have Litters This Big.

MULTIPLE BIRTH is the birth of more than one baby at a time. Twins, triplets, quadruplets, and quintuplets are all examples of multiple birth. Human beings rarely have more than one child at a time. The smaller animals often have large litters. The opossum, for example, has up to 18 young in its litter. Dogs, cats, rabbits, and pigs all give birth to more than one offspring. Cows, horses, camels, and other large mammals usually have only one at a time.

Human twins are born about once in every 96 births. The estimate for triplets is one set in every 9,216 births, and for quadruplets only one set in every 884,736 births. The odds in favor of quintuplets are only one set in about 85 million births. Some scientists believe that the tendency to have more than one child at a time is hereditary. Twins, for example, seem to run in some families.

Some twins come from two different eggs which merely happen to be fertilized and develop at the same time. Such twins are called *fraternal twins. Identical twins* are born from the cell mass originating from a single egg which has become divided. If the cell mass separates before it begins to take shape, the identical twins will be almost exactly alike in every respect. But the split may come after the cell mass has begun to take shape. The cell mass has already developed a right and left side. In that case, one twin may be left-handed, while the other is right-handed.

Before the development of modern medicine, the children in multiple births had little chance to survive. The children often had less care and less food than they would have had if they had been born alone. Even twins suffered. Modern care and medical knowledge have increased the survival of multiple-birth children. The famous Dionne quintuplets, born near Callander, Ont., Canada, in 1934, were the first quintuplets known to survive for more than a few hours after birth. Since the Dionnes, other sets of quintuplets have survived the period of early infancy. GEORGE W. BEADLE

See also DIONNE QUINTUPLETS; QUADRUPLETS; QUINTUPLETS; TRIPLETS; TWINS.

MULTIPLE SCLEROSIS, *skle ROH sis,* sometimes called MS, is a disease that attacks the brain and the spinal cord. *Sclerosis* comes from the Greek word meaning *hard.* In multiple sclerosis, many small hard areas appear scattered throughout the white substance of the brain and spinal cord. These patches interfere with the normal functions of the nerve pathways. As a result, the patient may show such symptoms as sudden blindness in one eye, and fleeting tingling, prickly sensations in the legs. These symptoms may be accompanied by an unsteady walk or balance, and stiff muscles. The muscle movements are more obvious when the patient stands, balances, or walks. But *intention tremor* (jerky movements of the arms) and *ataxia* (jerky movements of the legs) can also be seen in a resting position. The illness may begin with all the acute signs and symptoms, as in any infection of the central nervous system. This acute phase usually results in scattered hard areas in the brain and spinal cord, that is, *multiple* sclerosis.

MS may last many years. Periods of normal health or less severe symptoms may be followed by unpredictable symptoms that get progressively worse. During the first years, MS responds somewhat to treatment, such as rest and physical therapy. Most patients feel that they are in good health and are unusually cheerful. They seem to accept their disabilities in walking and in muscle coordination. But the disease gradually worsens. Sometimes after five to ten years, MS results in paralysis of the legs, blindness, and loss of urinary and rectal control. The cause of the disease is not known. No cure for it has been found. HANS H. REESE

MULTIPLEX STEREO. See HIGH FIDELITY (Development).

759

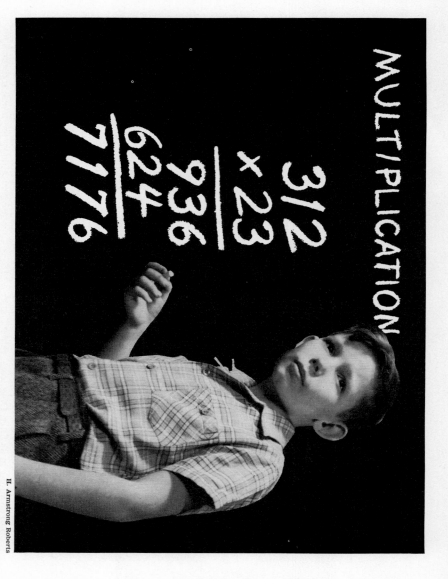

H. Armstrong Roberts

MULTIPLICATION

$$\begin{array}{r} 312 \\ \times\,23 \\ \hline 936 \\ 624 \\ \hline 7176 \end{array}$$

MULTIPLICATION is a short way of adding or counting equal numbers. It is one of the four basic operations in arithmetic along with addition, subtraction, and division.

Suppose you want to know how much five candy bars will cost. The candy bars are 6¢ each. You can find the answer by addition: 6+6+6+6+6=30. But it is easier to learn that five 6's are always 30. Learning facts like this is the basis of multiplication.

Learning To Multiply

Many persons learn multiplication only by memorizing its facts and rules. Often they do not understand the methods that they are using. The best way for a person

to learn multiplication is to find out how it works.

Writing Multiplication. The different operations in arithmetic are shown by special symbols. The symbol of multiplication is ×. The statement 5×6=30 means "five 6's are 30." People also read this as "6 multiplied by 5 is 30" or "5 times 6 is 30."

The number that is being multiplied, or added together a number of times, is called the *multiplicand*. The number that does the multiplying, or the number of times the multiplicand is to be added, is called the *multiplier*. The result, or answer, is called the *product*. A multiplication problem is usually written like this:

$$\begin{array}{r} 6 \\ \times 5 \\ \hline 30 \end{array}$$

Multiplicand
Multiplier
Product

You do not need to write the names every time, but it is important to keep the columns straight when multiplying larger numbers. An understanding of place value is important in learning multiplication. See DECIMAL NUMERAL SYSTEM (Learning the Decimal System).

Multiplication Facts. A statement such as 5×6=30 is a *multiplication fact*. It consists of a multiplier, a multiplicand, and a product. You should use addition to discover the multiplication facts. For example, 6+6+6+6+6=30. After discovering a multiplication fact, you should memorize it. By knowing the 100 multiplication facts, you can learn to multiply any numbers,

——— MULTIPLICATION TERMS ———

Annexing Zeros is a quick way of multiplying by 10, 100, 1,000, and so on. It means placing zeros at the end of the number being multiplied.

Carry, in multiplication, means to change a number from one place in the product to the next. A 10 in the 1's place is carried to the 10's place.

Multiplicand is the number that is multiplied. In 4×8=32, 8 is the multiplicand.

Multiplication Fact is a basic statement in multiplication, such as 6×3=18.

Multiplier is the number that does the multiplying. In 4×8=32, 4 is the multiplier. It is used when the multiplier has two or more digits.

Partial Product is the result of multiplying a number by one digit of the multiplier. It is used when the multiplier has two or more digits.

Product is the answer or result of multiplication. In 4×8=32, 32 is the product.

The 100 Multiplication Facts

	0	1	2	3	4	5	6	7	8	9
×0	0	0	0	0	0	0	0	0	0	0
×1	0	1	2	3	4	5	6	7	8	9
×2	0	2	4	6	8	10	12	14	16	18
×3	0	3	6	9	12	15	18	21	24	27
×4	0	4	8	12	16	20	24	28	32	36
×5	0	5	10	15	20	25	30	35	40	45
×6	0	6	12	18	24	30	36	42	48	54
×7	0	7	14	21	28	35	42	49	56	63
×8	0	8	16	24	32	40	48	56	64	72
×9	0	9	18	27	36	45	54	63	72	81

Most of the multiplication facts are easy to learn. If you play a game and make a score of 0 four times, your score is 0, because $4 \times 0 = 0$. Similarly, $5 \times 0 = 0$, $6 \times 0 = 0$ and $8 \times 0 = 0$. Zero multiplied by any number is zero. Any number multiplied by zero is also zero. You

have now learned 19 of the multiplication facts!

If you make a score of 1 four times, your score is 4, because $4 \times 1 = 4$. Similarly, $5 \times 1 = 5$, $6 \times 1 = 6$, and $8 \times 1 = 8$. One multiplied by any number is that number. Any number multiplied by one is also that same number. You now know 17 more multiplication facts.

The two boxes of eggs shown below illustrate an important rule in multiplication.

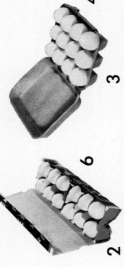

Each box contains 12 eggs. You can look at the box of eggs at the left in two ways. You might say that there are six rows of eggs with two eggs in each row. Or, you could say that there are two rows of eggs with six eggs in each row. You can also look at the box of eggs at the right in two ways. You might say that there are four rows of eggs with three eggs in each row. Or, you could say that there are three rows of eggs, with four eggs in each row. The multiplication facts that show this are:

$6 \times 2 = 12$ $\quad$ $4 \times 3 = 12$
$2 \times 6 = 12$ $\quad$ $3 \times 4 = 12$

This example shows that *numbers can be multiplied in any order.* The products will always be the same. Knowing this rule cuts down the number of multiplication facts to be learned from 100 to 55.

Knowing the *squares* is helpful in learning the multiplication facts. A square is a number multiplied by itself. Here are the squares that help to learn the facts:

$2 \times 2 = 4$	$5 \times 5 = 25$	$8 \times 8 = 64$
$3 \times 3 = 9$	$6 \times 6 = 36$	$9 \times 9 = 81$
$4 \times 4 = 16$	$7 \times 7 = 49$	

$$5 \times 3 = 15$$

Multiplication Facts Can Be Learned From Play. Toy soldiers on parade show a multiplication fact. The soldiers march forward in three straight lines. Five soldiers march in each line. How many soldiers are there all together? Adding the lines shows that there are $5 + 5 + 5$, or 15 soldiers all together. Three 5's, or 5×3, are always 15. And $5 \times 3 = 15$ is one of the 100 multiplication facts.

MULTIPLICATION

You can make pictures of the squares with dots. Here are the dot pictures of the squares of six and seven:

If you add a row of six dots to the first picture, you will have seven 6's. This shows that 36+6=42 or 7×6=42. If you take away a row of dots from the second picture, you will have six 7's. This shows that 49−7=42 or 6×7=42. Making dot pictures can help you learn the multiplication facts. For example, you can make a square containing four dots to show 2×2. Another square containing nine dots shows 3×3. A third square could show 4×4, and so on.

Learning the multiplication facts takes time and study. But knowing these facts is necessary to become skilled at multiplying. You can become even better at arithmetic if you learn the division facts as you learn the multiplication facts. The division facts are the opposite of the multiplication facts. See Division (Division Facts).

Multiplying by One Digit

Any number from 0 to 9 is called a *digit*. The number 26 is a two-digit number. The number 514 is a three-digit number. A digit gets its value from the place it occupies in a number. The first place on the right is for 1's, the next to the left is for 10's, the next for 100's, and so on. For example, in the number 347, the 3 means three 100's, the 4 means four 10's, and the 7 means seven 1's. Depending on its place, the digit 2 may mean two 1's, (2), two 10's (20), two 100's (200), or two 1,000's (2,000). You combine the idea of place value with the multiplication facts to multiply large numbers.

Here is an example of the steps needed to work a multiplication problem using more than one multiplication fact. There are 32 students in a class. Each student uses one sheet of paper a day. How many sheets of paper will be needed for three days? We could solve the problem by using addition: 32+32+32=96. The class will need 96 sheets of paper for three days. Multiplication is quicker and easier. The number 32 is three 10's and two 1's. The basic idea is to multiply first the 1's by 3 and then the 10's.

First, you multiply the two 1's by 3. This is 3×2=6. You write the 6 in the 1's place in the product. Next, you multiply the three 10's by 3. This is 3×30=90. The 90 is nine 10's, and you write the 9 in the 10's place in the product. The answer is 96.

$$\begin{array}{r} 32 \\ \times\,3 \\ \hline 96 \end{array}$$

You multiply a larger number by one digit in much the same way:

$$\begin{array}{r} 302 \\ \times\,4 \\ \hline 1208 \end{array}$$

First, you multiply the two 1's by 4. This is 4×2=8. You write the 8 in the 1's place in the product. Next, you multiply the 0 or "no" 10's by 4. This is 4×0=0. You write the 0 in the 10's place in the product. Then you multiply the three 100's. This is 4×300=1,200. You write the 12 in the 100's and 1,000's place in the product. The answer is 1,208.

When you multiply a large number by one digit, you must multiply each digit of the larger number—the 1's, 10's, 100's, and so on—one at a time. As you do each of these multiplications, you must write down the products of each of these multiplications—the 1's, 10's, 100's, and so on.

How To Carry in Multiplication

Students learn how to "carry" when they learn addition. When you add several numbers, there may be a 10 in the sum of the 1's column. You carry or add this 10 to the 10's column, usually by writing a small 1 above the 10's column. Carrying in multiplication is similar:

Addition	Multiplication
¹12	¹12
12	×8
12	96
12	
12	
12	
96	

When you add the eight 12's, the eight 2's total 16, or one 10 and six 1's. You write the six 1's in the 1's place in the sum. You add the 10 to the 10's place by writing a 1 at the top of that column. Adding the 1's column gives you nine 10's. You write nine 10's in the 10's place in the sum. To multiply 8×12, you multiply the eight 2's. 8×2=16. You write the six 1's in the 1's place in the product. You write a 1 to be added to the product of 8×1 in the 10's place. This is 8×1=8 and 8+1=9. You write the nine 10's in the 10's place in the product. This is 8×1=8 and 8+1=9.

$$\begin{array}{r} {}^{1}12 \\ \times\,8 \\ \hline 96 \end{array}$$

Be sure to multiply first. Then add the "carry number" to the product.

Multiplying by Large Numbers

A multiplier that has more than one digit introduces a new idea in multiplication. This is the use of the *partial product*. You can learn this idea best from an example.

Jim wants to know how many cartons of milk his school used last month. It used 312 cartons each day for 23 days.

The multiplier, 23, has two digits. It has two 10's and three 1's. You must use these as separate parts. First, you multiply 312 by the three 1's. This is 3×2=6. You write the 6 in the 1's place in the product. Then, 3×1=3 and 3×3=9. You write the 3 and the 9 in

$$\begin{array}{r} 312 \\ \times\,23 \\ \hline 936 \\ 624 \\ \hline 7176 \end{array}$$

Partial Product
Partial Product
Product

the 10's and 100's places in the product. This product of 3×312 is a partial product. Next, you multiply 312 by the two 10's. You write the product of this multiplication below the first product. You start this new partial product one place to the left, in the 10's place, because 312 is now being multiplied by 10's, not by 1's. First, 2×2=4. This is four 10's. You write the 4 below the 10's place in the first product. Next, 2×1=2 and 2×3=6. You write the 2 and the 6 in the 10's and 1,000's places of the second partial product. Now, the two partial products must be added together. The first partial product is 3×312 or 936. The second partial product is 20×312 or 6,240. Thus, 936+6,240=7,176. The answer is that the school uses 7,176 cartons of milk in 23 days.

Multiplying by a three-digit multiplier is the same as by a two-digit multiplier. But there are three partial products instead of two. When you use the 100's part of the multiplier in this kind of problem, remember to write this product beginning in the 100's place.

```
  123
×234
  492
 369
246
28782
```

First Partial Product
Second Partial Product
Third Partial Product
Product

Notice that the partial product of 2×123 is started in the 100's column directly under the 2.

You do not write "carry numbers" when you are multiplying by larger numbers. You must carry in your mind. If you wrote in carry numbers, you could easily confuse them with the carry numbers from another part of the multiplier.

Multiplying by Zero

Zeros in combination with other digits represent 10's, 100's, 1,000's, and so on. When there are zeros in a multiplier, you can shorten the work of multiplication.

```
 14        14
×20       ×20
 00       280
28
280
```

In the example at the right, you can see that there will be no 1's in the 1's place. So you can write a 0 to show the 1's place, and write the product of the two 10's on the same line. This shortens the work.

You must be careful when you use this method with a three-digit multiplier that ends in zero. The difficulty comes in placing the second partial product:

```
  214
×320
 4280
642
68480
```

You begin the second partial product in the 100's place, because 3, the part of the multiplier being used, represents 100's. You should always check the place of the

multiplier when you write its partial product.

An easy way to multiply by 10, 100, 1,000, and other multiples of 10 is to *annex zeros*. This means to place zeros at the end of a number.

10×2=20   100×2=200   1,000×2=2,000

Stated as a rule, this means that *to multiply by 10, annex a zero to the multiplicand. To multiply by 100, annex two zeros to the multiplicand. To multiply by 1,000, annex three zeros to the multiplicand.*

You can extend this method:

400×12=4,800

You multiply 12 by 4, and annex two 0's.

When you multiply larger numbers, there may be a zero in the 10's place of the multiplier.

```
  423
×302
  846
12690
127746
```

In this case, you write a zero in the 10's place of the second partial product. This is to make sure you start the next partial product in the 100's place.

How To Check Multiplication

You should always check the answer in multiplication to be sure you have solved the problem correctly. You have seen that numbers can be multiplied in any order and the product remains the same. For example, 2×4=8 and 4×2=8. The best way to check a product is to change the places of the multiplier and multiplicand and do the multiplication again.

```
  15        12        342        153
×12       ×15      ×153       ×342
  30        60      1026        306
15        12      1710        612
180       180       342        459
                  52326      52326
```

The products are the same, but the partial products are different. If you make a mistake one way, you probably will not make it the other way. If your answers are different, you can locate your mistake.

When you multiply a large number by one digit, you can check it easily by dividing the product by the single digit. See Division (Short Division).

```
3425        3425
 ×5        5/17125
17125
```

Multiplication Rules

These five rules will help you solve problems in multiplication.

1. Remember that multiplication is a short way of adding equal numbers. The multiplier tells you how many times a number is to be multiplied.

2. Learn the meaning of the multiplication facts and learn to recall the facts quickly. Remember that a number multiplied by zero is zero and that a number multi-

MULTIPLICATION

plied by one is the same number. Also remember that zero multiplied by any number is zero.

3. Remember the methods for multiplying by one or more digits. You multiply the 1's, 10's, 100's, and 1,000's of the multiplicand one after the other and write the result in the product. When the multiplier has two or more digits, you must use partial products.

4. Place value has great importance in multiplication. Always keep the columns straight, and start the product under the digit you are using in the multiplier.

5. Learn to check the answer after working a problem in multiplication. You can do this by changing the places of the multiplier and multiplicand, and doing the multiplication again.

Fun with Multiplication

Many of the games that can be played using the addition, subtraction, and division facts can be changed a little for the use of multiplication facts.

Product! is played by a group of children sitting in a circle. The leader selects a number, such as 5. The player next to the leader begins with 1, and the group counts around to the left. When the counting comes to a product of 5, the player calls "Product!" instead of the number. The counting goes like this: "1, 2, 3, 4, Product!, 6, 7, 8, 9, Product!", and so on. A player who forgets to say "Product!" is out, and the winner is the last player left in the game.

Finger Multiplying can be fun for one person. By using fingers, you can multiply 5, 6, 7, 8, or 9 by 5, 6, 7, 8, or 9.

Suppose you want to multiply 8×6. Close the fingers of both hands. Open 3 fingers on the left hand. The 5 closed on the right hand and the 3 open stand for 8. Now open 1 finger on the right hand. The 5 that were closed and the 1 now open on the right hand stand for 6. Now 3 fingers should be open on the left hand and 1 finger open on the right. This is the 10's digit of the answer. Add the fingers open: 3+1=4. There are four 10's in the answer. The closed fingers give the 1's digit. There are 2 fingers closed on the left hand and 4 fingers

closed on the right hand. Multiply these to get the 1's digit. This is 2×4=8. Add the 10's and the 1's. Four 10's and eight 1's are 48. This shows that 8×6=48.

$$8 \times 6 = ?$$
$$30 + 10 = 40$$
$$2 \times 4 = \frac{8}{48}$$

Richard Madden

Another example is 9×7. Start with the fingers closed. Open 4 fingers on the left hand for 9 (4+5=9). Open 2 fingers on the right hand for 7 (5+2=7). Add the fingers open: 4+2=6. This is the 10's digit. There is 1 finger closed on the left hand and 3 fingers closed on the right hand. Multiply these for the 1's digit. 1×3=3. Add the six 10's and the three 1's: 60+3=63. This shows that 9×7=63.

Outline

I.	**Learning To Multiply**
	A. Writing Multiplication B. Multiplication Facts
II.	**Multiplying by One Digit**
III.	**How To Carry in Multiplication**
IV.	**Multiplying by Large Numbers**
V.	**Multiplying by Zero**
VI.	**How To Check Multiplication**
VII.	**Multiplication Rules**
VIII.	**Fun with Multiplication**

Related Articles in World Book include:

Addition	Division
Arithmetic	Factor
Decimal Numeral	Fraction
System	Mathematics
	Numeration
	Systems
	Subtraction

PRACTICE MULTIPLICATION EXAMPLES

1.	275 ×608	4.	840 ×364	7.	804 ×708	10.	307 ×400	13.	479 ×900	16.	358 ×679
2.	790 ×200	5.	300 ×705	8.	700 ×700	11.	906 ×368	14.	680 ×509	17.	478 ×297
3.	600 ×320	6.	500 ×457	9.	305 ×930	12.	947 ×350	15.	960 ×470	18.	689 ×698

19. How many stamps does Jim have in his stamp book? The book has 5 pages with 48 stamps on each page.

20. How much will 5 books cost at $2.25 each?

21. Several boys ride their bicycles at a speed of 5 miles per hour for 3 hours. How far will they ride?

22. How far will Mr. Scott's automobile go on 10 gallons of gasoline? It goes 16 miles on 1 gallon.

23. Eggs cost 60¢ a dozen. How much will 6 dozen cost?

24. Four mothers plan to bring a dozen cookies each for a picnic. How many cookies will there be?

ANSWERS TO THE PRACTICE EXAMPLES

1.	167,200	5.	211,500	9.	283,650	13.	431,100	17.	141,966	21.	15 miles
2.	158,000	6.	228,500	10.	122,800	14.	346,120	18.	480,922	22.	160 miles
3.	192,000	7.	569,232	11.	333,408	15.	451,200	19.	240 stamps	23.	$3.60
4.	305,760	8.	490,000	12.	331,450	16.	243,082	20.	$11.25	24.	48 cookies

MULTNOMAH FALLS, *mult NOH muh,* occur on Multnomah Creek as it tumbles down from the Cascade Mountains. The creek empties into the Columbia River in northwest Oregon. The falls are northeast of the Bridal Veil Falls, and are about 620 feet high.

See also WATERFALL (picture chart).

MUMFORD, LEWIS (1895-   ), is an American social critic, philosopher, and historian. Many of his books explore the relation between modern man and his environment. Several of his books deal with city planning. *The City in History* won the National Book Award for 1961. The book describes how man's civilization is expressed in the development of cities.

Mumford wrote a four-volume philosophy of civilization called *The Renewal of Life.* The series included *Technics and Civilization* (1934), *The Culture of Cities* (1938), *The Condition of Man* (1944), and *The Conduct of Life* (1951). He also wrote several histories of architecture and studies of American culture. He was born in Flushing, N.Y.

MUMMER'S PARADE. See PENNSYLVANIA (Annual Events; color picture); FEASTS AND FESTIVALS (picture).

MUMMY is an embalmed body that has been preserved for thousands of years. The ancient Egyptians believed that the dead lived on in the next world, and that their bodies had to be preserved forever as they were in life. They believed that the body would serve a person after it was projected into the next world. So they spent much effort in developing methods of embalming. Thousands of years later, archaeologists found the preserved bodies in tombs. Many museums have one or more Egyptian mummies. The most famous are

probably those of Ramses II and Tutankhamon, who were *pharaohs* (rulers) of Egypt.

Scientists now know what materials and processes the Egyptians used to mummify bodies. The process was simple when mummifying began, and gradually became more elaborate. Wealthy persons could afford a more expensive treatment than the poor. Ancient texts state that a complete treatment required 70 days. Embalmers removed the brain through a nostril. They removed the internal organs, except the heart and kidneys, through an incision such as a surgeon makes. They usually filled the empty abdomen with linen pads, and sometimes with sawdust. Then they placed the body in natron (sodium carbonate) until the tissues were dried out. Finally, they wrapped the body carefully in many layers of linen bandages and placed it in a coffin. Sometimes there were two or more coffins, one inside the other. The coffins were made of wood or stone, and were either rectangular or shaped like the wrapped mummy. The mummy in its coffin was then placed in a tomb, along with many objects of daily use. The ancient Egyptians believed that the dead would need this equipment in the next world.

The dry climate in some parts of the world, such as Peru, Mexico, and Egypt, preserves dead bodies almost as well as Egyptian embalming methods did. Such naturally preserved bodies are sometimes called mummies also.

See also EMBALMING; PYRAMIDS; RAMSES II; TUTANKHAMON.   GEORGE R. HUGHES

Egyptian Funerary Customs XXII-XXIII Dynasty From Sheik Abd El Kurna
Mummy of Kharu-shery, The Metropolitan Museum of Art, New York

Mummy Case of a Woman Named Tinto, Field Museum of Natural History

American Museum of Natural History

Ancient Mummies of Peru and Egypt show the burial customs of these lands. The Peruvian mummy, *left,* was buried in a sitting position. It was wrapped in cloth, with silver ornaments on the face. Dolls, cloth bags, and sticks wound with colored yarn surround the body. Egyptian mummies, *center* and *right,* were wrapped, and then stretched out full length in decorated coffins.

MUMPS is a contagious disease. It is caused by a *virus* (an extremely small germ) that chiefly attacks glandular and nervous tissue. Its effects are most obvious in the *parotid* (salivary) glands just below and in front of the ears. The main characteristic is the glandular swelling that becomes apparent within 14 to 21 days after the patient has been exposed to mumps.

The first symptom of mumps is a pain below and in front of the ear. This is followed by considerable difficulty in chewing and swallowing. Then the parotid gland usually begins to swell rapidly. Mumps may attack the parotid glands on both sides of the neck at the same time, or may occur on one side only. Often, mumps attack other glands of the neck. The glands remain swollen for about one week. Mumps can most easily be caught from a sick person from seven days before he shows symptoms until nine days after.

Nearly every case of mumps ends in recovery, and the disease is not considered a serious one. But it may be accompanied by other diseases or complications with long-lasting aftereffects. To ward off complications, persons with mumps are usually kept in bed until they are entirely well. Sometimes, to prevent or treat complications, doctors prescribe antibiotic drugs to keep other infections from setting in on the already weakened areas. The patient must also be careful to keep his mouth clean by gargling and rinsing.

Little can be done to hasten recovery from the mumps. But warmth or cold applied to the swollen glands helps relieve pain, and most doctors advise the patient to drink lots of liquids.

Edvard Munch's Lithograph The Cry illustrates the feeling of anguish and inner torment that appears in many of his works.

The Art Institute of Chicago,
The Kate S. Buckingham Fund

In teen-age children and adults, complications are likely to go along with mumps. Usually the complications are the appearance of the disease in other parts of the body besides the glands of the neck.

Persons who have had mumps in both parotid glands are not likely to get the disease again. Those who have had mumps on only one side may have a recurrence following another exposure. Persons who receive an injection of mumps vaccine are protected against infection, but it is not certain how long this protection lasts. Persons also may avoid infection if inoculated within a week after exposure with serum that contains the antibodies of mumps (see SERUM).   AUSTIN EDWARD SMITH

See also DISEASE (table).

MUNCH, EDVARD (1863-1944), was a Norwegian painter and printmaker. He used intense colors and body attitudes to show love, sickness, anxiety, and death. He planned much of his work as a "frieze of life," on the theme of "the joys and sorrows of the individual human seen close...." His exhibitions greatly influenced the German expressionist movement of the early 1900's. His paintings include *Spring, The Sick Child,* and *The Death of Marat.* He also was famous for a number of the lithographs he produced, such as *The Cry, Melancholy,* and *Death Room.* Munch was born in Löten, near Hamar, Norway.
GEORGE D. CULLER

MUNCHAUSEN, *mun CHAW zun,* **BARON,** was the name given to the narrator and central figure in an anonymous booklet of tall tales, *Baron Munchausen's Narrative of His Marvellous Travels and Campaigns in Russia.* It was first published in England in 1785. The booklet sold so widely that enlarged editions began to pour from the printing presses. These used extravagant boasts. The German translation appeared in 1786. The author is assumed to have been a German exile living in London named Rudolph Erich Raspe (1737-1794).

A real Baron Hieronymus Karl Friedrich Munchausen lived in Germany in the 1700's. Raspe may have known him. Although Munchausen may have told some good stories, he disapproved of the great lies the book attributed to him. Munchausen tried in vain to escape the swarm of visitors that the publication brought to him. He died in grief at being named the world's biggest boaster. His name is still used to describe an exaggerator or boaster.
FRANK GOODWYN

MUNCIE, Ind. (pop. 68,603; met. area 110,938; alt. 950 ft.), is a major producer of glass fruit jars and other glass food containers. It lies on the West Fork of the White River 50 miles northeast of Indianapolis (see INDIANA [political map]). Muncie also produces automobile parts, meat products, and wire fencing.

Muncie is the home of Ball State University.

Muncie was named for the Munsee Indians. The first white settlement was established about 1833. Muncie was chartered as a city in 1865. It has a mayor-council form of government. Muncie gained widespread attention when sociologists Robert S. and Helen M. Lynd studied social and economic conditions in the city. They reported their findings in *Middletown* (1929), and *Middletown in Transition* (1937).
PAUL E. MILLON, JR.

MUNDELEIN, *MUN duh line,* **GEORGE WILLIAM CARDINAL** (1872-1939), became Roman Catholic Archbishop of Chicago in 1915, and a cardinal of the Roman Catholic Church in 1924. As archbishop, he was faced with the problems of administering Church affairs in Chicago, the jurisdiction that probably had the greatest variety of nationalities as well as the most people. His declared objective was to make all of these Catholics aware of their need to become good American citizens.

He built a magnificent seminary for the education of priests at Mundelein, Ill. Cardinal Mundelein was born in New York City, and served in Brooklyn before going to Chicago.　JOHN T. FARRELL and FULTON J. SHEEN

MUNDELEIN COLLEGE. See UNIVERSITIES AND COLLEGES (table).

MUNDT, MUNT, KARL EARL (1900–), a South Dakota Republican, has served in the United States Senate since 1948. He also served five terms in the U.S. House of Representatives between 1939 and 1948. Mundt and Richard M. Nixon wrote the Mundt-Nixon Anti-Communist Bill of 1948 requiring Communist party members to register with the U.S. Department of Justice. The Mundt-Nixon bill did not become law, but its provisions were included in the *Internal Security Act* (1950). Mundt introduced legislation to provide money for Voice of America radio broadcasts after World War II (see VOICE OF AMERICA). He also introduced legislation authorizing educational exchange programs between the United States and other countries.

Mundt was born in Humboldt, S.Dak. He was graduated from Carleton College and from Columbia University.　EVERETT W. STERLING

MUNG BEAN. See Bean (Kinds of Beans).

MUNICH, *MI'OO nik* (pop. 1,210,465; alt. 1,699 ft.), is Germany's third largest city. It ranks next in population to Berlin and Hamburg. Munich lies 310 miles southwest of Berlin on the Bavarian plain. For location, see GERMANY (political map). It is the capital of Bavaria.

The German name for Munich is *München*, which means *Place of the Monks*. Tradition says that this name goes back to the 700's, when an outpost of the rich abbey of Tegernsee was stationed there.

Munich is well remembered today for its connection with the Nazi party, which was founded in 1918. Munich was the scene of Adolf Hitler's "Beer Hall Putsch" of 1923. Hitler held a mass meeting in a beer hall and attempted a revolution to seize power (see HITLER, ADOLF [The Beer Hall Putsch]). In 1938, Great Britain, Italy, France, and Germany signed an agreement at Munich to hand Czechoslovakia's Sudetenland over to Germany (see MUNICH AGREEMENT).

Before the rise of the Nazi party, Munich was as peaceful as a village and as rich in opportunities as a great metropolis. The Isar River rolled rapidly from a spring under blue glacier ice toward the Danube River. Along the banks of the Isar were many gardens with waterfalls, brooks, and miniature lakes.

Munich lies less than 100 miles from the Brenner Pass on the border between Austria and Italy. The snowy peaks of the Alps can be seen from the city. The location of Munich has made the city a meeting place of northern and southern Europe.

Industries. Munich has long been famous for the production of stained glass for church windows. The city also makes bells, chiefly for churches. Bells cast in the foundries of Munich have been sent to many lands.

Munich has been successful in the production of lithographing and engraving work. Other important manufactures include chinaware, delicate optical instru-

ments, and mechanical-drawing tools. Beer is the city's most important export.

Important Buildings. The three most famous buildings in Munich are the Cathedral, the Palace, and the German Museum. But beautiful palaces, churches, and public buildings can be found throughout the city. The German Museum is one of the most famous museums in the world for exhibits in technology and science. The imposing State Library contains over a million books and more than 50,000 manuscripts. The National Theater, one of the largest theaters in Germany, was bombed and destroyed during World War II. It was completely restored after five years of labor. The $15 million building was reopened officially in 1963.

Three famous museums were almost destroyed by World War II bombings. They were the old Pinakothek, the new Pinakothek, and the Glyptothek. Some of the valuable collections of paintings and sculptures housed in these museums were saved, reassembled, and exhibited after the war.

Munich has a university which was founded in 1472. This university was moved from Landshut to Munich in 1826. It has about 20,000 students, and a library of over 700,000 volumes.

History. Munich was founded in 1158 by Duke Henry the Lion. In 1181, the Emperor Frederick Barbarossa deposed Prince Henry and gave the city to a prince of the House of Wittelsbach. The Wittelsbachs ruled Munich and the surrounding country from that day to the end of World War I. From 1919 to the end of World War II, the history of Munich was the story of how the Nazi party grew and rose to power (see NAZISM). The Allies bombed much of the city during the war. After the war, Munich was the largest city in the United States zone of occupation.　JAMES K. POLLOCK

Stachus Square in Munich, Germany, leads to the *Karlstor,* a stone archway which dates from the 1300's, *background.*
German Tourist Information Office

MUNICH AGREEMENT

MUNICH AGREEMENT forced Czechoslovakia to give up the Sudetenland, part of its territory, to Nazi Germany. As a result, Germany got a fifth of Czechoslovakia's land, 800,000 Czechs, over 3 million persons of German descent, and most of the country's industries. The agreement was signed in Munich, Germany, on Sept. 30, 1938, by Adolf Hitler of Germany, Neville Chamberlain of Great Britain, Edouard Daladier of France, and Benito Mussolini of Italy.

The Munich Agreement set up an international commission to mark off the new boundaries. People in some of the disputed areas were given the right to choose between the Czechoslovakian and German governments. When the commission drew the frontiers, more land passed into Germany's hands than the agreement provided. Germany soon took over all Czechoslovakia.

Britain and France believed that the Munich Agreement would keep Europe at peace. Neville Chamberlain, the Prime Minister of Britain, declared that the Munich Agreement had brought "peace for our time." Hitler said that the Sudetenland was "the last territorial claim I have to make in Europe." He had made it a point to "repatriate" all German-speaking people. There seemed to be some hope that Hitler's claims might end at this point. But German troops invaded Poland on Sept. 1, 1939, starting World War II.

The Munich Agreement was one of the worst of the tragic blunders that led up to the war. British and American cartoonists made Chamberlain, with his everpresent umbrella, the symbol of the Munich Agreement and of appeasement.   NORMAN D. PALMER

MUNICIPAL GOVERNMENT. See CITY GOVERNMENT.

MUNITIONS. See AMMUNITION; KRUPP.

MUÑOZ MARÍN, LUIS (1898-   ), served from 1948 until 1964 as the first elected governor of Puerto Rico. He refused to run for governor in 1964. He was elected to the Senate in 1964 and in 1968. He founded the Popular Democratic Party, and was its leader until he resigned in 1968 (see PUERTO RICO [History]).

Muñoz Marín was born in San Juan, and educated in the United States. He was elected to the Puerto Rican legislature in 1932. Muñoz Marín won popularity for his support of social and economic reform. He promoted low-cost housing and land reform, and brought industries to the island. In 1952, he helped make Puerto Rico a commonwealth of the United States.   JAIME BENÍTEZ

MUNRO, HECTOR HUGH (1870-1916), was a British writer who wrote under the pen name SAKI. Munro is best known for his witty short stories. Many of the stories satirize British society of the early 1900's. Munro's stories were published in *Reginald* (1904), *The Chronicles of Clovis* (1911), *Beasts and Super-Beasts* (1914), and *The Square Egg* (published in 1924, after his death). Munro also wrote two novels. *The Unbearable Bassington* (1912) is an entertaining satire on British society. In *When William Came* (1913), Munro predicted with remarkable accuracy the coming of World War I and English reactions to it.

Munro was born in Akyab, Burma. He was taken to England when he was two years old, and became a well-known London journalist. Munro was killed in battle in France during World War I.   JOHN ESPEY

Queensbridge Housing Project, New York, WORLD BOOK photo by Robert Crandall; New York Graphic Society

MUNSEE INDIANS, *MUN see*, were a division of the Delaware Indian tribe. They lived around the headwaters of the Delaware River and along the western bank of the Hudson River. White settlers drove them from the Delaware River region about 1740, and the Munsee settled along the Susquehanna River. They later scattered throughout parts of the United States and Canada.

See also DELAWARE INDIANS.

MUNSELL COLOR SYSTEM. See COLOR (diagram; Color Systems).

MUNSEY, *MUN see*, **FRANK ANDREW** (1854-1925), was a pioneer publisher of low-priced magazines and newspapers. He had very little education or financial backing, but made a fortune of nearly $20 million. He started *Munsey's Magazine* in 1889. The magazine's circulation reached 650,000 by 1900. Munsey built a successful grocery chain and used his profits to buy 17 newspapers. He was feared by newspapermen because he often bought competing newspapers and then combined them into one. Munsey was born in Mercer, Me.   JOHN ELDRIDGE DREWRY

MUNTJAC. See DEER (Asian and European Deer).

MUNTZ METAL. See BRASS.

MUON. See MESON.

MURAL PAINTING is a painting on a wall, usually the inside wall of a building. Sometimes murals also adorn outside walls. Some murals are painted on ceilings. Artists may use *fresco* or *oil* paint in creating a mural. In a fresco, they apply water-color paints directly on wet plaster. They may paint murals in oils on the wall itself, or on canvas, metal, or wood. Oil paintings often have greater detail than frescoes.

In the earliest murals, men of the Stone Age painted hunting scenes on the walls of their caves. The Egyptians and other peoples often painted designs and pictures on their walls. Many have been preserved.

The great period of mural painting came during the Italian Renaissance, which began in the early 1300's. Scholars regard Giotto, one of the early artists of the Renaissance, as the first great mural painter of this period. Many of the greatest mural painters lived during this time. Michelangelo painted the famous frescoes on the walls and ceiling of the Sistine Chapel in the Vatican. Raphael painted many frescoes in other rooms of the same palace. Two paintings from the Vati-

can, Michelangelo's *The Creation of Adam* and Raphael's *The School of Athens*, appear in WORLD BOOK in color in the PAINTING article. Probably the most popular mural painter of the 1800's was Pierre Puvis de Chavannes.

Since 1900, there has been a widespread revival of mural painting. Under the public works program in the United States in the 1930's, artists decorated many post offices and other public buildings with murals (see ANTIRENTER [picture]). Famous recent mural painters include Thomas Hart Benton, John Steuart Curry, José Clemente Orozco, and Diego Rivera.   THOMAS MUNRO

Related Articles in WORLD BOOK include:

Africa (color picture)	Giotto	Raphael
Benton, Thomas H.	La Farge, John	Rivera, Diego
Curry, John S.	Latin America (picture)	Sistine Chapel
Fra Angelico	Michelangelo	Tintoretto
Fresco	Orozco, José C.	Titian
		Vatican City

MURANO. See GLASS (The Middle Ages).

United Nations

Housing Project Mural, *left,* was painted by Philip Guston in 1940 and 1941. Guston later became famous for his abstract paintings. The mural, called *Martial Memory,* is in the Queensbridge Housing Project in New York City.

United Nations Mural called *Peace, right,* was painted in 1957 by the Brazilian artist Cândido Portinari. The mural can be seen in the General Assembly building of the UN in New York City.

"X Ray" Mural, *left,* was painted by a native in a cave in northwestern Australia. In addition to the external view of the subject, "X ray" art reveals what the artist cannot see but knows is there, such as the internal organs of this large fish.

MURAT, *myoo RAH,* **JOACHIM** (1771?-1815), the most famous French cavalry commander under Napoleon I, ruled Naples as King Joachim I from 1808 to 1814. He served with Napoleon Bonaparte, and distinguished himself in Italy in 1796. Napoleon made him a general in 1799 for defeating the Turks in Egypt. Murat's cavalry attacks played an important part in Napoleon's victories at Austerlitz, Jena, and Friedland (see NEY, MICHEL).

He shared the misfortunes of the 1812 Russian campaign with Napoleon. Murat deserted Napoleon when he was defeated at Leipzig in 1813. But, when Napoleon escaped from his prison on the island of Elba in 1815, Murat tried to win all Italy for him. The Austrians, however, defeated him. After the Battle of Waterloo in 1815, Murat tried to recover his kingdom of Naples, but he was quickly captured, condemned, and executed. Murat was born in Bastide, Lot, France. In 1800, he married Napoleon's sister, Caroline.   VERNON J. PURYEAR

MURDER. When one person willfully kills another without legal justification, the crime is called a *murder.* The clearest example of this is a case where one person deliberately kills another because of hatred, envy, or greed. But there are also situations where a killing is considered murder even when no specific intent to kill exists. For example, if a criminal commits a robbery and accidentally kills someone, he is guilty of murder. The fact that he is committing a serious crime indicates that he has a reckless disregard for human life and safety. This takes the place of actual intent to kill.

The law punishes murder by long prison sentences or by death. Some states permit the jury or the judge to select the penalty. Other states have no death penalty, and the court must decide the sentence. Prison sentences may range from 14 years to life.

Every murder is a homicide, but the law does not call all homicides murders. A killing that is accidental or that has legal justification may be called a *homicide.* For example, if a police officer kills an escaping burglar or convict, the act of killing is a homicide. But the court may not consider the officer guilty of murder or of any other crime. The same is true of a person who kills another person in self-defense. But it is up to the court to decide whether the killing was in self-defense.

When a killing occurs during a fit of anger, the law may deal less harshly with the killer than when the killing was deliberate. If a person is highly insulted and then kills the person who insulted him, the law may consider the killing *manslaughter.* Punishments for manslaughter are less severe than for murder.   FRED E. INBAU

See also CAPITAL PUNISHMENT; CRIME; HOMICIDE; MANSLAUGHTER.

MURDOCH, IRIS (1919-   ), is a British author of witty and complex novels. The meanings of her symbolic situations and dialogue are often difficult to understand. Miss Murdoch lectured in philosophy at Oxford University from 1948 to 1962, and her interest in philosophic issues is apparent in all her works.

Jean Iris Murdoch was born in Dublin. Her first book was *Sartre, Romantic Rationalist* (1953), a study of the French philosopher Jean-Paul Sartre. In her first novel, *Under the Net* (1954), the leading character has a series of encounters and adventures during which he

tries to discover some meaning in his life. Miss Murdoch's other novels include *The Flight from the Enchanter* (1955), *The Sandcastle* (1957), *The Bell* (1958), *A Severed Head* (1961), *The Italian Girl* (1964), and *The Red and the Green* (1965).   JOHN ESPEY

MURFREESBORO, BATTLE OF. See CIVIL WAR (The War in the West; table: Major Battles).

MURIATIC ACID. See HYDROCHLORIC ACID.

MURILLO, BARTOLOMÉ ESTEBAN (1618-1682), was an important Spanish painter of the 1600's. He is considered the best interpreter of the gentle, optimistic side of Christianity. Murillo is known for the warmth and humanity of his religious paintings, especially those of the Holy Family and the Immaculate Conception.

Murillo's painting *The Immaculate Conception* is reproduced on the opposite page. It shows the delicate beauty and fine shadings of light and atmosphere that characterize his work. Like many of Murillo's paintings, this work has a gentleness that borders on sentimentality. The picture's complex spiraling composition and careful detail are typical of Murillo's work. Murillo also painted dignified and flattering portraits, and scenes of daily life, especially scenes showing children.

Murillo was born in Seville. His paintings before 1645 were influenced by the realism and dark coloring found in the work of the Spanish artists Jusepe de Ribera and Francisco Zurbarán. Later, influenced by Flemish and Venetian masters, Murillo became more concerned with problems of light, color, and atmosphere. In 1645, the Franciscan order in Seville gave Murillo his first important commission. Within 15 years, he was Spain's most important painter.   MARILYN STOKSTAD

MURMANSK, *moor MAHNSK* (pop. 287,000; alt. 85 ft.) is Russia's chief port on the Arctic Ocean. It is the world's largest city north of the Arctic Circle. The warm Gulf Stream keeps the harbor free of ice the year round. Murmansk stands on the far-northern Kola Peninsula. For location, see RUSSIA (political map).

The city is a fishing and shipbuilding center. It has fish canneries, metal and woodworking factories, net and barrel factories, and refrigerating plants. Exporters ship fish, lumber, and minerals from the city. A polar research station is located there. A railroad links Murmansk with Leningrad.

Murmansk was founded in 1915, and developed rapidly in the 1930's.   THEODORE SHABAD

MURPHY, AUDIE. See TEXAS (The Early 1900's).

MURPHY, FRANK (1890-1949), of the United States, was a statesman and jurist noted for his liberal views. He served as a Detroit municipal court judge from 1922 to 1930 and as mayor of Detroit from 1930 to 1933. He was governor general of the Philippines from 1933 to 1935, U.S. high commissioner to the Philippines from 1935 to 1936, and governor of Michigan in 1937 and 1938. President Franklin D. Roosevelt made Murphy, a Democrat, U.S. attorney general in 1939. In 1940, the President appointed Murphy to the Supreme Court of the United States. Murphy was born in Harbor Beach, Mich.

MURPHY, GEORGE LLOYD (1902-   ), a one-time motion picture and Broadway star, became a United States senator from California in 1964. As an actor, Murphy was probably best known for his dancing roles. In politics, he became identified with the conservative wing of the Republican Party.   SIDNEY GLAZER

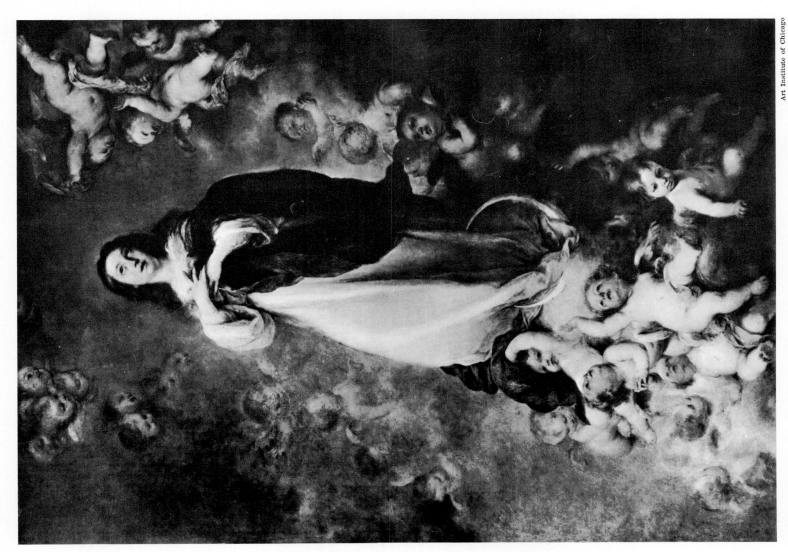

Murillo's Painting *The Immaculate Conception* is one of the best examples of the spiritual quality of much of his work. The picture also shows how Murillo sometimes emphasized sentimentality in his paintings. This picture was painted for the Seville Cathedral in Spain to honor the Roman Catholic doctrine of the Virgin Mary's freedom from the stain of original sin.

MURPHY, JOHN BENJAMIN

Murphy was born in New Haven, Conn., and attended Yale University for two years. He started in show business as a dancer in the 1920's, and made his first motion picture in 1934. In the 1940's, he served as president of the Screen Actors Guild. In 1952, he went into public relations and became increasingly active in politics. He helped plan the 1956 and 1960 Republican National Conventions.

CAROL L. THOMPSON

MURPHY, JOHN BENJAMIN (1857-1916), an American surgeon, was internationally famous as a teacher and a doctor. Dr. William Mayo once described him as "the surgical genius of our generation." Murphy's battle to establish appendicitis as a surgical disease contributed greatly to surgical progress. He developed new techniques in surgery of the blood vessels, joints, and tendons. He invented the "Murphy button" in 1892, a device that linked together the severed ends of intestines. It led to important advances in intestinal surgery.

From 1895 to 1916, he was chief surgeon at Mercy Hospital, Chicago. He was a professor of surgery at Rush Medical College and Northwestern University. He was born in Appleton, Wis.

NOAH D. FABRICANT

MURPHY, WILLIAM P. See MINOT, GEORGE.

MURRAY, ALFALFA BILL. See OKLAHOMA (The 1930's).

MURRAY, GILBERT (1866-1957), a British classical scholar, gained fame for his translations of Greek plays. He wrote poetry and plays of his own, and books on the Greek dramatists Aeschylus, Euripides, and Aristophanes. His works include *The Classical Tradition in Poetry* (1927) and *Hellenism and the Modern World* (1953). Murray was born in Sydney, Australia. He studied in London and at Oxford, and became a professor of Greek at Glasgow University, and later at Oxford. He was a leader in movements supporting the League of Nations.

MURRAY, JAMES (1719?-1794), was a British soldier who became the first British governor of Canada. He was born in Sussex, England, and went to America in 1757. He fought against the French at Louisbourg in 1758.

Murray served as one of the three brigadiers under General James Wolfe in the successful battle against the French at Quebec. After the British victory, Murray was left in command of the city, which he later defended against a French Army that was led by General François de Lévis.

Murray was made governor of Quebec in 1760. Three years later, when French rule was ended, he became governor of all Canada. He had to face many difficult problems in the relations between the English and the Indians and also between the French Canadians and the English officers and merchants. Some of the men working under him accused him of favoring the French. He was recalled to England in 1766, but was cleared of all charges by the House of Lords.

JOSEPH E. BAKER

MURRAY, SIR JOHN (1841-1914), was a British naturalist, oceanographer, and deep-sea explorer. He specialized in studying the ocean bottom. He was one of the naturalists on the expedition of H.M.S. *Challenger*, which made a scientific study of oceans and ocean bottoms from 1872 to 1876. Afterward, Murray edited the expedition's 50 volumes of scientific reports. He also

wrote *The Depths of the Ocean* (1912) and *The Ocean* (1913), considered a classic in its field.

Murray was born in Cobourg, Ontario. He was graduated from the University of Edinburgh, and spent most of his life in Great Britain. He made a notable study of Scottish *lochs* (lakes).

JOHN E. CASWELL

MURRAY, PHILIP (1886-1952), succeeded John L. Lewis as president of the Congress of Industrial Organizations (CIO) in 1940, and held that post until his death. He played an important part in setting World War II government labor policies. He saw to it that the CIO unions kept their "no-strike" pledge during the war. He also served on the National Defense Mediation Board.

Murray rose to his CIO position after 36 years as a labor union organizer and leader. He advanced in the United Mine Workers to the post of vice-president, which he held from 1920 to 1942. Murray ended a long friendship with John L. Lewis soon after he succeeded him as president of the CIO.

When the CIO began organizing the steel industry in 1935, Murray became chairman of the organizing committee. He served as the first president of the United Steelworkers of America from 1942 to 1952. In the late 1940's, he led a successful fight to oust Communist-dominated unions from the CIO. He led the steelworkers in three national strikes after World War II.

Murray was born in Blantyre, Scotland, the son of a coal miner. In 1902, he moved to the United States with his family, and began working in the mines at the age of 10. He got into an argument with a mine foreman soon after he started, and lost his job. The other miners went on strike in sympathy with Murray, but lost the strike. Murray served as a member of Woodrow Wilson's War Labor Board and on the National Bituminous Coal Production Committee during World War I. He was the co-author, with Morris L. Cooke, of *Organized Labor and Production* (1940).

JACK BARBASH

MURRAY RIVER is the largest waterway in Australia. It is also one of the most important sources of irrigation in the country. The Murray River system includes the Darling, Lachlan, and Murrumbidgee rivers, and drains an area larger than that of France and Spain combined. For location, see AUSTRALIA (physical map).

The Murray rises in the Australian Alps near the eastern boundary of Victoria. It flows northwestward and forms the boundary between Victoria and New South Wales. It then crosses eastern South Australia and empties into the Indian Ocean through Encounter Bay. The Murray River is 1,600 miles long. With the Darling River, it forms a system 2,310 miles long.

A system of dams irrigates about 1½ million acres of land. The dams were built under the Murray River Agreement made in 1915 by New South Wales, South Australia, and Victoria. The dam system, which includes the Hume Dam, also permits ships to sail 1,000 miles up the river. The Snowy Mountains Scheme was begun in 1949. Scheduled for completion in 1975, this project will include 17 large dams and several small ones. It will direct water into the Murray and Murrumbidgee rivers. It will provide hydroelectric power for Victoria and New South Wales, and enough water to irrigate about 1,000 square miles.

See also RIVER (chart: Longest Rivers).

C. M. H. CLARK

MURRAY STATE UNIVERSITY. See UNIVERSITIES AND COLLEGES (table).

MURRE, *mur,* is the name of a group of sea birds in the auk family, related to the guillemot. Great colonies of murres live on rocky coasts of the North Atlantic and North Pacific. Thousands of the birds crowd the rock ledges during the breeding season. The female murre hatches a single egg, which it lays on the bare stone. The murre is between 16 and 17 inches long. Its body is heavy and its head large. It has short wings. The bird is brownish-black above, and white on the breast and throat.

The large eggs vary from white to blue and green. Black, brown, or lavender spots usually mark them. The eggs are pointed, and roll in a small circle when moved.

Scientific Classification. Murres are members of the auk family, *Alcidae.* The common murre is genus *Uria,* species *U. aalge.*

ALEXANDER WETMORE

MURRUMBIDGEE RIVER, *mur um BIJ ee,* is an Australian stream that flows into the Murray River, north of the Victoria border. The stream rises in the Australian Alps and flows northwest for about 1,350 miles across the southern part of New South Wales. A system of dams, built under the Murray River Agreement in 1915, increased the importance of the Murrumbidgee River.

C. M. H. CLARK

See also AUSTRALIA (Rivers); MURRAY RIVER.

MUSCAT, *MUS kat,* or MASQAT (pop. 5,080; alt. 65 ft.), is the capital of Muscat and Oman, a country in Arabia. The city lies on the Muscat Bay of the Gulf of Oman. Rugged mountains separate it from the interior of the peninsula. The city is the country's administrative center. Muscat is important because of its location at the entrance to the Persian Gulf. For location, see MUSCAT AND OMAN (map).

DOUGLAS D. CRARY

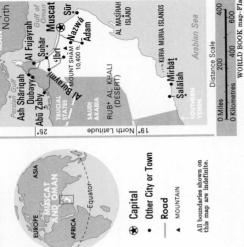

Capital
● **Other City or Town**
— **Road**
▲ MOUNTAIN

All boundaries shown on this map are indefinite.

WORLD BOOK map—FIa

MUSCAT AND OMAN, *MUS cat and oh MAN,* is a small country on the southeastern tip of the Arabian peninsula. It is about as big as Kansas, but it has only about one-fourth as many people as that state.

Muscat and Oman is one of the hottest countries in the world. Temperatures there sometimes reach 130° F. Only a few places get more than six inches of rain a year. Much of the inland part of the country is desolate land where nothing grows. The border with Saudi Arabia, in the region of the *Rubʿ Al Khali* (Empty Quarter) desert, never has been officially agreed upon.

The country has little industry, no railroads, few roads, and only one important airport. Muscat is the capital and leading port (see MUSCAT).

Government. A *sultan* (ruler) governs the country with the aid of a five-man council he appoints. But some people living in the mountains and other inland areas support the *imam,* their Islamic religious leader, rather than the sultan. *Walis* (governors) are in charge of local government units.

People. Most of the people are Arabs who belong to the Ibadite sect of Islam. Some are members of the Sunni Moslem sect. Many Negroes, Indians, and *Baluchis* (people whose ancestors came from Baluchistan, Pakistan) live in the coastal towns. Members of the primitive Shuḥūḥ tribe occupy the Musandam Peninsula.

── **FACTS IN BRIEF** ──

Capital: Muscat.

Official Language: Arabic.

Form of Government: Sultanate.

Area: 82,000 square miles. *Greatest Distances*—(north-south) 500 miles; (east-west) 400 miles. *Coastline*—about 1,200 miles.

Population: No census. *Estimated 1971 Population*—570,000; density, 7 persons to the square mile. *Estimated 1976 Population*—579,000.

Chief Products: Coconuts, dates, hides, limes.

Flag: Solid red flag stands for the Moslem religion. See FLAG (color picture: Flags of Asia and the Pacific).

A Fledgling Murre nestles between its mother's feet on a rocky nesting place where the sea birds gather.

Fish and Wildlife Service

insula at the northern tip of the country. They live in caves and exist mainly on fish from the Gulf of Oman.

Most of the people are poor and cannot read or write. They farm or work on the large date and coconut plantations. A few are fishermen, or work for cattle and camel breeders. The people live in tents, or in houses that have mud and stone walls and flat roofs. The men wear flowing white robes and headdresses to shield them from the sun and sand. Many of them carry knives or guns. Most of the women wear long, black dresses. They also wear masks that cover most of their faces to keep them from being seen by strange men.

Land. The northernmost part of the country, the barren, rocky Musandam Peninsula, is separated from the rest of the country by the Trucial States. Southeast of there, a low coastal plain stretches for about 1,000 miles along the Gulf of Oman and Arabian Sea. It rises to a plateau about 1,000 feet above sea level. Most farming is done in the fertile Al Bāṭinah area which stretches about 200 miles along the Gulf of Oman.

The mountain range of Al Hajar stands south of Al Bāṭinah. Mount Shām (10,400 ft.), part of Al Hajar, is the country's highest point. The central Az Zāhirah plateau is dry and mostly uncultivated. The fertile Dhofar region lies in the southwest corner of the country.

Economy. Oases along the northern coast produce dates, limes, and pomegranates. Coconuts grow on the southern coast. Oman camels are bred throughout the country. The most important exports are dates and hides. Oil was discovered in the country in 1963, but production did not start until 1967.

History. Portuguese forces captured Muscat and Oman in the early 1500's. But local Arabs expelled them in the mid-1600's and later took over other Portuguese possessions in East Africa. The present sultan's family came to power in 1743. In 1798, the British signed an agreement with the sultan and have maintained close relations ever since. In the 1800's, heirs to the sultanate formed Muscat and Oman as it is known today. In 1913, a newly elected imam acquired governing powers in the interior. The present imam headed resistance against the sultan in 1955 and 1957. When the sultan's forces defeated those of the imam in 1959, the imam fled into exile.

GEORGE RENTZ

MUSCATEL. See WINE.

MUSCLE is the tissue that makes it possible for a person or animal to move from place to place. Muscles make the heart beat, force blood to circulate, and push food through the digestive system.

The human body has more than 600 muscles. These muscles are usually grouped into two main types—*skeletal* and *smooth*. Skeletal muscles are attached to the skeleton, causing the bones to move. For example, several groups of skeletal muscles move the arm bones. Smooth muscles are found in the blood vessels, digestive system, and other internal organs. A third type of muscle, called *cardiac* (heart) muscle, resembles both skeletal and smooth muscles.

Skeletal Muscles make up a large part of the arms, legs, chest, abdomen, neck, and face. They vary greatly in size, depending on the type of job they do. For example, eye muscles are small and fairly weak, but thigh muscles are large and strong.

All muscles are made up of cells called *muscle fibers*. Skeletal muscle fibers differ in appearance from smooth muscle fibers. A fiber of skeletal muscle is long and slender. It may have many *nuclei* (structures that direct the fiber's activities). The fibers lie parallel to each other in bundles. Under a microscope, they show alternating light and dark bands called *striations*. For this reason, skeletal muscles are also called *striated muscles*.

Skeletal muscles are attached to bones in different ways. For example, the ends of face muscles are attached directly to bones. But the ends of other skeletal muscles have white, tough, flexible cords of tissue, called *tendons*, that attach the muscles to bones.

To do its job, both ends of a skeletal muscle must be attached to the skeleton. The end of the muscle that normally does not move and is closest to the central part of the body is called the *origin*. The other end, called the *insertion*, is attached to the bone it moves. A *flexor* is a muscle that bends a joint and brings a limb closer to the body. An *extensor* muscle does the opposite. For example, flexor muscles of the upper arm bend the elbow, and extensors straighten the arm.

Skeletal muscles contract rapidly when a nerve or spinal cord injury *stimu-lates* them (causes them to react). Skeletal muscles usually move *voluntarily* (under conscious control), but they also may move *involuntarily* (without conscious control). For example, involuntary movement occurs when a person jerks his hand away from a hot object before he can think about doing so.

Skeletal muscles must be stimulated by a nerve or they will not operate. When a person suffers a nerve or spinal cord injury, paralysis may result.

Through exercise, a person can make his muscle fibers grow bigger, making an entire muscle larger. For example, the biceps of the upper arm can be enlarged by exercise. Too much exercise may *strain* (stretch or tear) the muscle fibers. That is why many persons may experience soreness after physical activities such as gardening or playing baseball or tennis.

Smooth Muscles differ from skeletal muscles in structure, location, and the way they contract. A smooth muscle fiber contains only one nucleus, and contracts more slowly and rhythmically than a skeletal muscle fiber. The walls of the stomach and intestines have sheets of smooth muscles arranged in circular and lengthwise patterns. These muscles contract slowly and rhythmically to move food along for digestion. The smooth muscles in blood vessels can relax to make the vessel openings wide, or contract to make them narrow.

Smooth muscles do not always have to be stimulated directly by a nerve to work. Certain body chemicals, called *hormones*, can make smooth muscles contract. For example, fear or excitement causes special nerve fibers to release hormones called *epinephrine* (adrenalin) and *norepinephrine* (noradrenalin). These hormones reduce the number of contractions of intestinal muscles until the movements finally stop. At the same time, they cause smooth muscles in the arteries of the intestines and skin to contract, reducing the flow of blood to those parts. As a result, more blood flows to the brain and skeletal muscles. Smooth muscles cannot be controlled voluntarily. Because of this, they sometimes are called *involuntary muscles*.

Cardiac Muscle (heart muscle) has striations like skeletal muscles, but it cannot be controlled voluntarily.

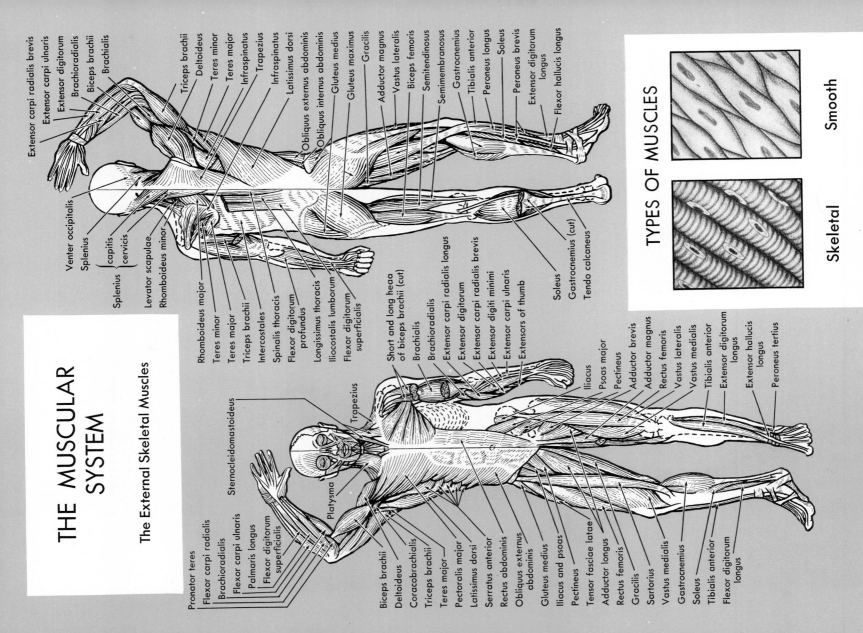

MUSCLE SENSE

A special regulator in the heart, called the *sinoatrial node* (*S-A node*), gives off rhythmic stimulations that cause heart muscle to contract, or beat. For further information on the heart, its parts, and how they work, see HEART.

How Muscles Work. Skeletal muscles must be stimulated by nerves. Smooth muscles are stimulated by a special set of nerves that belong to the *autonomic nervous system*, and by hormones (see NERVOUS SYSTEM). A person usually is unaware of the normal contractions of smooth and skeletal muscles. But when these contractions become severe or prolonged, a condition called *cramps* results.

Many scientific studies have been made to determine why muscles contract. According to the *sliding filament* theory, muscle cells are made up of long, parallel chains of protein molecules that can slide over each other. If the muscle cell is stimulated, the molecular chains slide over one another and the cell contracts.

Like all living cells, muscle fibers need energy to work. They get the energy from food. Special structures in the cell, called *enzymes*, break down the food to release the energy. The most important food sources for energy are fats and *carbohydrates* (sugars and starches). Some of the energy escapes as heat, but the rest is captured to make a special "high energy" substance called *ATP* (adenosine triphosphate). This compound stores the energy and releases it when the fiber needs energy to do work.

All muscle fibers produce wastes, such as *lactic acid*, as they work. If a muscle works very hard, these wastes collect in the muscle. As a result, the fibers lose some of their ability to contract, and the muscle *fatigues* (becomes tired). Then the muscle must rest so that the body can remove the wastes.

GORDON FARRELL.

Related Articles in WORLD BOOK include:

Convulsions	Human Body
Cramp	(Trans-Vision)
Diaphragm	Sphincter
Heart	
	Tendon
	Tetany
	Tongue

MUSCLE SENSE, or CONSCIOUS PROPRIOCEPTION, is one of two senses that tells a person what position parts of his body are in. The other sense is sight. As a person walks down the street, he knows the position of his legs without looking at them. *Proprioceptors* (nerves) in the joints, muscles, and tendons of his legs are sensitive to pressure and tension. The proprioceptors send information about the state of the joints, muscles, and tendons to the brain. The brain combines the information, enabling the person to sense the position of his body and to influence movement. There are proprioceptors for most parts of the body.

W. B. YOUMANS.

MUSCLE SHOALS is an area on the Tennessee River in northwestern Alabama. The Muscle Shoals rapids lie between the cities of Florence, Tuscumbia, and Sheffield. The town of Muscle Shoals lies east of the rapids. Congress created the Tennessee Valley Authority in 1933. The TVA controls two dams at Muscle Shoals. Wilson lies at the west end of the area, and Wheeler, about 15 miles east. The dams raise the water level above the rapids to form lakes which hold the season's rainfall. The dams have improved river navigation because the water held in the lakes insures a more nearly

uniform depth of water during wet and dry weather. Wilson and Wheeler provide hydroelectric power. Wheeler Dam serves also to control floods.

Two nitrate plants were completed at Muscle Shoals in 1918. The plants were constructed under the National Defense Act of 1916. They were built because it was feared World War I might cut off nitrate supplies from Chile.

CHARLES G. SUMMERSELL.

See also DAM; TENNESSEE VALLEY AUTHORITY.

MUSCOVITE. See MICA; MINERAL (color picture).

MUSCULAR DYSTROPHY, *DIS troh fee,* is any one of several serious muscle diseases that are *inherited* (passed on from parents to children). Muscular dystrophy causes muscles to become weak and waste away. It usually affects *skeletal muscles* (muscles that move bones), such as those of the arms and legs.

Muscular dystrophy is caused by *genes* that do not work normally. Genes are the tiny, basic units of heredity. They are located in cells, where they direct the development of living things. Scientists do not completely understand the changes produced in the muscles by the abnormal genes. As a result, no effective treatment has yet been developed for muscular dystrophy.

Doctors recognize various kinds of muscular dystrophy. The classifications are based on (1) the way the disease was inherited; (2) the age of the patient when the disease began; (3) the muscles most badly damaged; (4) the rate at which the disease develops; and (5) other disorders that develop during the disease.

Pseudohypertrophic muscular dystrophy is the most common kind in childhood. The word *pseudohypertrophic* means *false enlargement*. The name refers to the way the patient's calf muscles seem to get bigger. The muscles actually waste away, but they seem to grow because of the fat that collects in them. Pseudohypertrophic muscular dystrophy usually begins before the age of 5. It eventually affects most body muscles, including those that make the heart and lungs function. A patient usually is confined to a wheelchair by the age of 12 and dies before the age of 20. This form of muscular dystrophy is inherited as a *sex-linked recessive* disease. This means it usually develops only in the boys of a family. It is passed on by females, although females seldom develop it. It is the only one of the four main kinds of muscular dystrophy that is sex-linked.

Facio-scapulo-humeral muscular dystrophy first affects the face, shoulder, and upper arm muscles. Later, it affects almost all the muscles, but it does not progress as rapidly as the pseudohypertrophic type. It begins at about 13 or 14 years of age, but patients may be able to work for 30 or more years afterwards.

Limb-girdle muscular dystrophy first affects the muscles of the hips and shoulders. It also begins at about the age of 13 or 14, and develops at about the same rate as the facio-scapulo-humeral type.

Myotonic muscular dystrophy causes muscles to waste away and prevents them from relaxing normally. For example, after shaking hands, a patient may not be able to loosen his grip right away. Myotonic muscular dystrophy differs from the other forms in another way. That is, the patient may develop certain nonmuscular disorders—such as diabetes mellitus and cataracts—as the muscular disease gets worse. Patients with the myotonic form often do not become disabled until they are 30, 40, or even older.

VICTOR A. McKUSICK

MUSE, *myooz.* The Muses were the nine goddesses of the arts and sciences in Greek mythology. They were the daughters of Zeus and Mnemosyne, goddess of memory. They lived on Mount Helicon. The Muses were the attendants of Apollo, the god of poetry. They sang in chorus at all the feasts of the gods on Mount Olympus. Ancient writers always called on one of the Muses before beginning to write.

The names of the Muses, the art or science they represented, and their symbols are:

NAME	ART OR SCIENCE	SYMBOL
Calliope	Epic poetry	Tablet and stylus
Clio	History	Laurel wreath; scroll
Euterpe	Lyric poetry	Flute
Thalia	Comedy; pastoral poetry	Comic mask; shepherd's staff
Melpomene	Tragedy	Tragic mask; sword
Terpsichore	Dancing	Lyre
Erato	Love poetry	Lyre
Polyhymnia	Sacred song	Veil
Urania	Astronomy	Globe

Giulio Romano did a well-known painting called *Apollo and the Muses.* Edmund Spenser wrote a long poem called "The Tears of the Muses." PADRAIC COLUM

MUSEUM, *myoo ZEE um,* is an institution that collects and preserves original objects. This is its chief purpose. For example, some museums collect and show masterpieces of art. Others tell the exciting story of mankind through relics of past ages. A museum may show old-time automobiles, important industrial processes, or the bones of giant prehistoric animals. Museums use their collections for scholarly research

and public education. Some museums serve a whole nation. Others serve a small community or a single school. Many museums have special facilities and activities for children. Thousands of school classes visit museums every year. The word *museum* comes from the Greek word *mouseion,* meaning *temple of the Muses,* or *a place to study* (see MUSE).

Kinds of Museums include history, art, natural history, and applied science museums. *General museums* combine some or all of these fields in one institution. There are also children's museums, site museums, and folk museums. Museums may be operated by national, state, or local governments, or by private organizations or individuals.

History Museums outnumber all other kinds, but many are small institutions. They may tell the story of a nation, a city, a man, an event, or an industry.

Art Museums may cover periods and kinds of art. Or they may specialize in art of one period, one country, one artist, or one medium. See ART MUSEUM.

Natural History Museums bring together collections of animals, plants, and objects used by people throughout the world. Some specialize in a small area or branch of natural history, such as minerals.

Applied Science Museums show industrial and scientific equipment and processes. Health museums are a form of applied science museum.

Children's Museums design their exhibits and plan their programs for children. They offer games, hobby

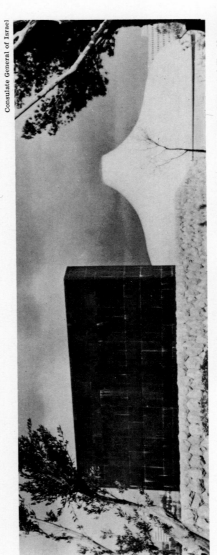

Consulate General of Israel

Archaeological Museum, *above,* called the Shrine of the Book, houses the famous Dead Sea Scrolls in Jerusalem, Israel. The white cupola and the black basalt wall represent the war of the Sons of Light against the Sons of Darkness. The war is described in one of the Scrolls.

National Historical Wax Museum

Wax Museum, *right,* in Washington, D.C., re-creates scenes from American history with lifelike realism. One exhibit shows life-sized figures of famous western characters in a typical frontier saloon.

clubs, and other activities that interest young persons.

Site Museums interpret the story of the particular places where they are located. The site may be a battlefield, the home of a famous man, or a geographical feature of scenic or scientific importance. Most site museums are small and are located in national or state parks. Some are called *trailside museums*.

Folk Museums consist of groups of old buildings carefully restored to re-create the way people once lived. These museums developed in northern Europe. In the United States, such museums include Colonial Williamsburg, Va., and Old Sturbridge Village, Mass.

How Museums Function. Museums gain their collections through gifts, by buying or trading with other museums, and by sending out collecting expeditions. Museum staffs maintain complete records of every object in the museum. They clean and restore damaged objects and protect collections from decay. Most museums systematically arrange and store the bulk of their objects in *study collections* for scholars to use. They usually exhibit only their choicest objects to the public. In addition to a museum's permanent exhibits, it may also arrange special temporary exhibitions. Museums also offer guide service, lectures, courses of study, publications, and other educational activities.

History. The first institution called a museum was actually a university. It was founded at Alexandria, Egypt, by Ptolemy I, a Macedonian general who seized Egypt in the 300's B.C. Museums as we know them today developed hundreds of years later. They grew out of private collections started by noblemen and wealthy individuals during the Renaissance (see RENAISSANCE). The Ashmolean Museum at Oxford University in Great Britain was probably the first such museum. The university founded it in 1683 with a collection donated by Elias Ashmole (1617-1692), an English collector. The British Museum, the oldest of the great national museums, contained the collections of three scholars when it opened in 1759. The Charles Town Library Society founded the first public museum in the United States in 1773 in Charleston, S.C. At first, museums concentrated on building up their collections. Since the late 1800's, museums have devoted increasing attention to public education.

RALPH H. LEWIS

Related Articles. See ART MUSEUM and its list of Related Articles. See also the following articles:

Academy of Natural Sciences of Philadelphia
American Museum of Natural History
Armed Forces Institute of Pathology
British Museum

Field Museum of Natural History
National Air Museum
Smithsonian Institution
Taxidermy (picture)
United States National Museum

MUSEUM OF MODERN ART in New York City is one of the world's leading museums devoted to the collection and exhibition of modern art. Its permanent collection includes almost 2,000 paintings and works of sculpture from the 1880's to the present. The collection covers the major revolutionary modern art movements, including impressionism, postimpressionism, cubism, surrealism, abstract expressionism, and the assemblages and constructions of today.

The museum collections also include about 8,000 prints; about 1,000 drawings; a representative selection of furniture and other manufactured objects; posters and typographical design; and architectural models and drawings. Every day the museum shows motion pictures from its library of commercial, documentary, educational, and experimental films. It also has a collection of photography from the 1840's to today.

The museum presents about 25 exhibitions each year taken from public and private collections in the United States and other countries. It also organizes about 60 shows each year that tour other museums and educational institutions throughout the world.

The museum's art center offers about 100 classes to child and adult amateurs and helps train teachers in new methods of art education. The museum also publishes several books each year. Its library has almost 25,000 books, periodicals, and catalogs, and about 100,000 clippings for research and reference.

The museum was founded in 1929 and is located at 11 West 53rd Street. It is supported by membership dues, private contributions, admissions, and the sale of books and other services.

ELIZABETH SHAW

MUSEUM OF SCIENCE AND INDUSTRY is an educational institution in Chicago designed to acquaint the public with the basic principles of science, and the uses of science in industry. Its exhibits emphasize current developments in science and industry. They use some historical material to provide a suitable background.

The museum uses no uniform method of display. Each exhibit is designed individually, and is presented with variations in architectural design, color, light, and all other aspects of display. Each exhibit tells its story simply, logically, and fully. To make understanding easier, the exhibits emphasize audience participation. Visitors may push a button or turn a crank, or walk into a life-size display and become part of the exhibit. Among the exhibits, visitors may see themselves in color television, take a trip through a life-size coal mine, go aboard a full-sized submarine, stroll down a 1910 street, watch chicks hatch, see the latest developments in agriculture, and learn the fundamentals of atomic energy.

The museum is located at 57th Street and Lake Michigan in Chicago's Jackson Park. It is housed in the Fine Arts Building of the World's Columbian Exposition of 1893. This outstanding example of classical architecture was reconstructed at a cost of $8 million to serve its present purpose. The building contains 600,000 square feet of floor space. A small portion of the museum was opened in 1933. The major areas were opened in 1940. Julius Rosenwald founded the museum (see ROSENWALD, JULIUS).

D. M. MACMASTER

MUSHET, MUSH et, ROBERT FORESTER (1811-1891), was an English metallurgist. In 1870, he patented a special tungsten steel that had remarkable self-hardening qualities. It was especially suitable for machine tools, because it retained its cutting edge, even when red-hot from friction.

Mushet helped improve the Bessemer process of steelmaking when he discovered that the addition to the molten steel of an iron-manganese alloy called *spiegeleisen* would help recarburize it. This led to an improvement in the strength of the steel (see IRON AND STEEL [The Bessemer Converter]).

Mushet was born in Coleford, England. Between 1858 and 1861, he took out about 20 patents on alloys of iron and steel.

RICHARD D. HUMPHREY

MUSHROOM

U.S.D.A.

The Deadly Destroying-Angel Mushroom grows in woods. It looks safe, but there is no known remedy for its fatal poison.

MUSHROOM. Mushrooms, or toadstools, which often grow from the ground like small umbrellas, are among the best-known of the plants called *fungi*. They grow in decaying vegetable matter, sometimes hidden under leaves or moss. The name *mushroom*, as well as the old-fashioned term *mushromp*, may come from the French word for moss.

Mushrooms and Toadstools. Botanists do not separate mushrooms and toadstools into two different groups. People generally give the name *mushroom* to the kinds that can be eaten, and *toadstool* to those that are poisonous. An edible kind may have poisonous relatives which belong to the same genus. Children usually think all mushrooms are toadstools, and avoid them all as poisonous. It is probably fortunate that they do. Children are not taught to recognize the different mushrooms, the way they are taught to recognize the common birds. Only a skilled person can tell which mushrooms are safe and which contain deadly poisons.

There are about 38,000 known species of mushrooms. Different mushrooms have many different shapes, from the ordinary umbrella to the less familiar coral, or branching, shape. They may also be shaped like shelves. Their colors range from pure white to pastel pinks and lavenders, from pale yellow to flaming orange and brilliant red, from dull gray to velvety brown.

Parts of the Mushroom

The main part of the mushroom plant is underground. It looks like a web of fine threads, sometimes packed close together like a mass of felt. This part of the plant is called the *mycelium*. The umbrella growth, which most people call a mushroom, is really a stalk that grows up from the mycelium. It may be compared with a fruit of other plants, for its work is to scatter the cells

from which new mushroom plants grow. The umbrella is called a *sporophore*, which means the *part that bears the spores*.

In sporophores that are just beginning to grow, the top of the stalk forms a small knob, called a button. The button spreads out until it has the full umbrella shape. This wide top is the crown. If a person examines a full-grown mushroom, he will see many thin ridges on the underside of the crown. These thin growths are the *gills*, which bear the spores. They grow out all around the center stalk toward the edge of the crown.

The spores are cells that are specially suited for growing new mushroom plants. They are carried on tiny stalks that grow out from the surface of the gills. There may be millions of them on a single sporophore. Single spores are so small that they can be seen only through a microscope. A mass of spores sometimes looks like powder. Frequently, but not always, the mass has the same color as the gills. A mushroom crown laid with its gills down on a piece of paper will leave a spore print which shows a definite pattern. This print is made up of thousands of the spores.

The Life Story of the Mushroom

How the Mushroom Gets Its Food. Fungi have none of the green plant material called *chlorophyll*. Green plants with chlorophyll can use sunlight to prepare carbohydrates, a type of food they need. They manufacture it from water and carbon dioxide, one of the gases in the air. Mushrooms have no "leaf green" and must use food that has already been prepared by some green plant. They may be found growing on old stumps or logs, decaying twigs or leaves, or even on rich soil. In this way they are able to get their food. Here and there is found a species which grows on the trunks or branches of living trees. Mushrooms which grow on living plants are called *parasites*.

The main part of the mushroom plant, the mycelium, lives entirely inside the material that gives it nourishment. When the mycelium grows in a log or tree it causes the wood to decay or rot. The decay makes more material for the mushroom to live on.

Mushrooms need a great deal of moisture. After a spell of wet weather in spring, summer, or fall many of these fungi spring up suddenly.

How a Mushroom Grows. The story of the common table mushroom will give a good idea of the way other mushrooms grow. This is the mushroom that is often raised for food. It is grown in a specially prepared mixture of well-fermented stable manure. The mixture, called a *compost*, is arranged on benches or in boxes. When the temperature is right, pieces of mushroom spawn are placed just below the surface of the compost, and about one foot apart.

The spawn is really the *mycelium*, the part of the mushroom plant that grows underground.

The mushroom spawn grows out like threads through the whole bed of compost. Meanwhile, a layer of soil about an inch deep has been placed over the compost. In seven or eight weeks, mushrooms begin to appear on the surface of the soil. They come up first in the so-called *pinhead* stage. The pinhead is really a little knot or head of new growth, shaped more or less like a ball.

Jar

Common Field

Jack O'lantern

Chestnut

Bird's Nest

Naucoria

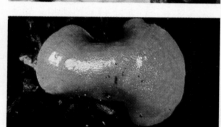

Rough-Stemmed

MUSHROOMS WITH STRANGE AND UNUSUAL SHAPES

MUSHROOMS THAT GROW IN THE SUNLIGHT

TREE-STUMP MUSHROOMS THRIVE ON DEAD WOOD

BOLETUS MUSHROOMS HAVE NO GILLS

Club

Paneolus

Beefsteak

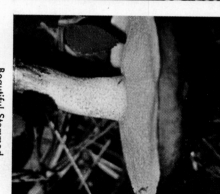
Beautiful-Stemmed

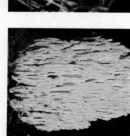
Coral

Puffball

Little Helmet

Clitopilus

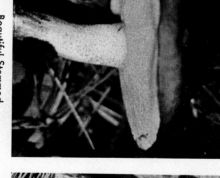

Granular

MUSHROOMS

Russula

Destroying Angel

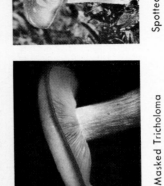

Spotted Cortinarius

Mahogany

Rutherford Platt

Hygrophorus

BRIGHT-COLORED MUSHROOMS THAT GROW IN SHADY PLACES

Fly Amanita

THE DEADLY AMANITAS ARE DISTINCTIVE AND WIDESPREAD

Masked Tricholoma

Zoned

THE SHELFLIKE BRACKETS GROW ON TREES

Amanitopsis

Blushing Amanita

Violet Cortinarius

RARE-COLORED BLUE AND PURPLE MUSHROOMS

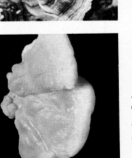

Sulfur Polypore

Honey

Caesar's Amanita

Milky Blue

Drawing Pad

In a few days the pinhead has grown into a tiny button. If the air is dry, the pinhead may form below the surface of the soil. As it continues to grow, the button may then push up through the earth. These buttons seem to shoot up very quickly. Actually, it often takes a week for a pinhead to reach the "small button" stage of development. The button then will measure about half an inch across.

As the young button grows larger, the upper part, or cap, develops more rapidly. The gills grow underneath this cap, but are hidden by a curtain, or veil. As the cap grows wider and the stem grows longer, the veil covering the gills breaks away. Then the pink gills are easy to see. The broken veil remains attached to the stem and forms a ring called the *annulus*. The annulus stays on the stem for some time. The whole plant continues to grow larger, and soon looks like an open umbrella. When the mushroom is mature, the gills become brownish-black.

Different species and genera of mushrooms have very different kinds of veils and gill colors. In the genus *Amanita*, which contains several very poisonous species, there is sort of an envelope that covers the entire plant. This envelope breaks near the base as the mushroom expands, and leaves a kind of cup at the base of the stem. The envelope sometimes remains on the surface of the cap, where it breaks up into squares or large patches. In this case there is also an inner veil that forms a ring on the stem. Amanitas can be recognized by this ring. The table mushroom has no membrane covering it all over, so no cup will be formed at the base of the table mushroom's stem.

The gills of Amanita may be white or slightly colored. The gills of young common table mushrooms are pink, changing to brown or brown-black as they mature.

Fairy Rings. Sometimes a person sees circles of lighter grass growing on a lawn or meadow. These are the rings that the fairies are supposed to leave behind in the morning after they have danced at night.

In spite of this pretty story, the real cause of fairy rings is the growing habits of mushrooms. The mushroom spawn does not seem to be able to grow in the same place for a long time. The spot where it is growing spreads out, and the mushrooms grow in wider and wider rings. At first the grass above the spawn is thinner. But once the mushroom spawn has decayed, it fertilizes the soil and makes it richer. Then the grass in the circle is even thicker than that found in the rest of the lawn.

Kinds of Mushrooms

It would be impossible in this article to describe or even list all the kinds of mushrooms. Botanists have given each one a Latin name which tells what group it belongs to. Many also have familiar names.

Harmless Varieties. There are a thousand or more varieties of mushrooms that are good to eat. Many of these belong to the group called the *agarics*. This name

The spores growing in the gills may be carried off by the wind. They find their way to the ground or to leaves which later may be eaten by animals. When they sprout, they send off tiny threads. The threads can be seen by the naked eye only after they have grown and branched a great deal.

comes from the Latin word for *field*. All the mushrooms of this kind grow in pastures, lawns, and open fields.

The common table mushroom belongs to the agarics. It is the only mushroom cultivated on a large scale and sold on the market. In France it is called the *champignon*, from the French word *champ*, meaning *field*. This mushroom never grows very large. Its spores are brown, and it has no cup. Its gills are a delicate pink when the plant is young. As it grows older they turn to dark brown. These are important points for the mushroom picker to remember. Wild common table mushrooms grow thickest in the fall or late summer.

The *horse mushroom* is another kind that is good to eat. It is similar to the common mushroom, but is very much larger and coarser.

The *parasol mushroom* is taller and more graceful. It looks like a small white or delicate tan umbrella on a slender handle.

The edible *Amanitopsis* should never be confused with its relative, the deadly poisonous *Amanita*, or death cup. The two plants look almost alike, but the dangerous one has a frill that the wholesome mushroom does not have.

The *oyster mushroom* grows in clusters on stumps or partly decayed trees. It has white gills and one-sided stalks.

One of the most delicious of the mushrooms is the *morel*. Its cups look like cone-shaped sponges, pitted like a honeycomb. The morel grows best among leaves or wood ashes.

The *chanterelle* or *little goblet*, is a dainty, reddish-yellow mushroom. It has this name because it is shaped like a cup.

The *coral mushroom* has a branching form of beautiful pink, lavender, or amber. This species is most common in Sweden. Another branching variety is the *golden Clavaria*, which is a beautiful honey color. It is also delicious to eat.

Fairy-ring mushrooms have a flavor like nuts. They are often dried and preserved for eating. Other familiar

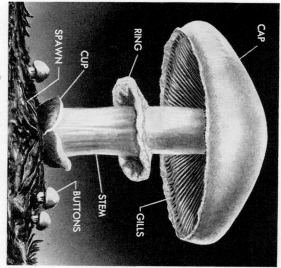

Parts of the Mushroom

CAP

RING

SPAWN

CUP

GILLS

STEM

BUTTONS

types are the *inkcap* or *shaggy mane*, the *bear's head*, and the *hedgehog* mushrooms. The inkcap first grows underneath the sod. When there is a warm rain, it pushes up overnight, and by the close of day has dripped away in an inky liquid.

Many tasty kinds of mushrooms are not so well-known. One of these is the *Jew's ear*. The Chinese are so fond of this type that they import it from the South Sea Islands. Another is the *green Russula*, which looks like the trumpet of a gray-green morning-glory. The *golden Peziza* is shaped like a cup and lined with orange-red. Still others are the *trembling mushrooms*, a quivering mass like jelly, and the *liver fungus*, which is sometimes called *vegetable beefsteak*.

The familiar *puffballs* are also called *smoke balls* and *devil's snuffboxes*. If a person strikes a puffball with a twig he can see it give off a tiny puff of "smoke." It is really scattering its dusty spores to the wind. Some puffballs grow to be more than two feet across.

One species harmful to timber is the curious *bracket mushroom*. It looks like a small shelf that grows partly around the tree trunk. Its colors are brown above and white below.

Poisonous Mushrooms. The most dreaded of the poisonous mushrooms are two members of the Amanita group, the *death cup* and the *fly Amanita*.

The death cup grows in the woods from June until fall. Its poison acts like the venom of a rattlesnake, as it separates the corpuscles in the blood from the serum. No antidote is known for the poison of the death cup. The only hope for anyone who has eaten it is to clean out his stomach promptly with a stomach pump. One variety is known as the *destroying angel*.

The death cup has often been mistaken for the common mushroom. A person can avoid this mistake if he observes carefully. The poisonous plant has white gills, white spores, and the fatal poison cup around its stem. The plant that is safe to eat has brown or brown-black gills, brown spores, and no cup. Many of the mistakes come from picking it in the button stage, for it does not show all these differences until it is larger.

The fly mushroom grows in the woods or along the roadside. It looks good enough to eat with its bright red, yellow, or orange cup. But it paralyzes the nerves which control the heart action.

History tells us that Czar Alexis of Russia died from eating the fly mushroom. Yet it is not quite so deadly as the death cup. When a person has eaten a fly mushroom, it is necessary to empty his stomach promptly and give him injections of atropine. The fly mushroom can be recognized by its scaly cap and stem, a deep frill at the top, white spores, and a bulblike base.

Satan's mushroom, the *emetic Russula*, and the *verdigris mushroom* are all poisonous to some people and not to others. A very unpleasant smelling mushroom is the *stinkhorn*, sometimes called the *fetid wood witch*. It often grows in backyards or under open stairways.

Doctors are able to recognize slightly different effects from the different kinds of poisonous mushrooms. But the symptoms are very similar in all cases of mushroom poisoning. There are always severe pains in the abdomen, followed by a bluish appearance of the skin. After these symptoms, the patient collapses. He is almost certain to die, unless a doctor can treat him promptly. See FIRST AID (table, Antidotes).

Mushrooms must be fresh when eaten. None should be eaten if it shows the least sign of decay, or if insects have been feeding on it. It is also dangerous to eat most that have a milky juice.

Some people believe any mushroom is poisonous if it has bright colors. This notion is not correct, for some of the most brilliant are also among the most wholesome. Another false notion is that only poisonous mushrooms will turn a silver spoon black when they are being cooked. Many safe kinds will also turn table silver black, after they have been cooked.

Mushrooms as a Food

Men have eaten mushrooms since very early times. The Greeks and Romans were fond of them. Today they are the chief food of the natives on Tierra del Fuego at the tip of South America, and of natives in some parts of Australia. More people in Europe than in America eat mushrooms.

In most countries, people consider mushrooms a table delicacy rather than a main food. These fungi are about 88 per cent water and almost half the rest is bulk that the body cannot digest. Experts on food say that mushrooms are not any more nourishing than juicy cabbage leaves.

Mushrooms can be eaten creamed, baked, fried, broiled, stewed, or served in salad. Stores now sell many of the edible varieties at all seasons—fresh, dried, or canned.

Mushroom Culture. The business of raising mushrooms has become more and more popular around large cities. Growers find that it pays well. They can carry on a small business in cellars, caves, or old quarries. Almost any place where the temperature can be kept steady will do. Mushroom growing as an industry is something different. Today, a large plant must have specially designed mushroom houses, and standard methods of business. Still, it is not unusual for boys and girls to raise small crops for market. Many have earned money for a college education this way. Many books on mushrooms tell how to grow the crops. The United States Department of Agriculture will also send helpful bulletins on the subject.

Scientific Classification. Mushrooms are fungi that belong to many different families of the division *Thallophyta* in the plant kingdom. These families belong to the class *Basidiomycetes*. The commonly cultivated field mushroom belongs to the family *Agaricaceae*. It is genus *Agaricus*, species *A. campestris*.

WILLIAM F. HANNA

See also FUNGI; PUFFBALL.

MUSIAL, STANLEY FRANK (1920-), ranks as one of the greatest baseball players of all time. Nicknamed *Stan the Man*, he was a star outfielder and first baseman for the St. Louis Cardinals between 1941 and 1963. He won seven National League batting titles, and had a .331 lifetime batting average. Musial played more games (3,026), made more hits (3,630), and batted in more runs (1,951) than any other National League player. He became a Cardinal vice-president in 1963. President Lyndon B. Johnson named him director of the President's Council on Physical Fitness in 1964. Musial was born in Donora, Pa. See also BASEBALL (Recent Developments; picture).

ED FITZGERALD

MUSIC

MUSIC is a basic social and cultural activity of mankind. Music has probably existed in some form from the earliest days of man. Man was born with a great musical instrument, his voice. He undoubtedly used his voice to express himself through music long before he thought of making music with instruments. For thousands of years in man's early history, music existed only as simple and natural voice sounds. Then man began making music with a wide variety of musical instruments. Today, composers write their music down using special symbols, and performers can record their music permanently on records or tape.

Music takes many forms and reflects many different ways of life. But all types of music have one basic quality in common. That is, all music is a form of communication in which sounds are deliberately organized in some manner for an artistic purpose.

Robert C. Marsh, the contributor of this article, is the music critic of The Chicago Sun-Times. Halsey Stevens, one critical reviewer, is a composer and Chairman of the Department of Composition at the University of Southern California. James Sykes, the other critical reviewer, is a musician and a professor of music at Dartmouth College.

The Chicago Symphony Orchestra and Chorus Perform the Music of Bach.

WORLD BOOK photo

Ravi Shankar Plays the Music of India.

Capitol Records

Arthur Rubinstein and Quartet Play Chamber Music.

RCA Records

article. This article deals primarily with what is commonly called *classical* music. Classical music may also be called *serious* music. But this term is inaccurate because jazz and folk music are serious forms of music, even though they are often performed in informal surroundings.

Enjoying Music

The way to enjoy music is to find music that interests you and listen to it. By listening repeatedly to music, you become familiar with the way composers and performers use music to communicate with an audience. If the music says nothing to you at first, try again, until you think you understand it. It is possible to enjoy music without understanding it fully. But the greatest enjoyment comes with the greatest understanding.

After listening to music, try to make some music yourself. You may want to play the piano, the violin, the clarinet, or some other instrument. If you cannot play, you can sing—either alone or with others. Even if you do not want anyone to hear the results, you may find pleasure in making music. You may discover that making music is a natural way to express yourself.

Understanding Music. It is easy to accept music as a quiet background sound that helps provide a pleasant atmosphere. But if you want to understand serious music, you must listen to it as an example of artistic communication. Music for listening must be loud enough for you to follow all that is being played or sung. Intelligent listening is an active process. When you listen to a familiar work of music, you can anticipate what comes next with the same pleasure you find in rereading a favorite story or poem. As you learn more about the music, you form ideas about how it should be performed. When you hear it again, you can judge whether the performance pleases or disappoints you.

If the music is unfamiliar, but in a musical style you know, you will find pleasure as it brings forth unexpected melodies and harmonies. You may also find a sense of challenge, because you may not fully understand the significance of some part of the music, and must wait for more than one hearing. If the style is also unfamiliar, you have an even greater challenge. You must learn not only what the composer is saying, but also how he says it. You will probably have to listen to the work several times before you fully understand its significance.

Only persons who know many styles of the musical language can enjoy the fullest pleasures of music. Instead of limiting yourself to the music you find familiar and enjoyable, give yourself a chance to explore new kinds as well. If you do not enjoy a piece of music the first time you hear it, go back to it later. You may be surprised at how much more you hear in it after a few months.

Judging Music. We appreciate music because it communicates something to us in which we find momentary or enduring satisfaction. We judge music by the success with which it communicates, and by the length of time in which we retain interest in what it has to say. If a specific work of music communicates nothing to us, then it means nothing to us—and what it means to others is unimportant. But if it is an acknowledged

Jack Stager, Globe Photos

Ray Charles Plays the Blues.

Simon and Garfunkel Play Folk Music.

Bob Bonis

A musical performance is often called *re-creative* because it evolves from a previous creative work of art written down by the composer. Composers write music in a symbolic form called *notation.* Usually, notation provides only an outline of a performance, and the musicians, singers, and conductors must interpret the notes. Thus, a musical performance is really a partnership between composer and performer.

WORLD BOOK has separate articles on different types of music, including BALLET, FOLK MUSIC, JAZZ, and OPERA. A complete list of WORLD BOOK articles on music appears in the *Related Articles* section at the end of this

masterpiece, such as a Beethoven symphony, we owe it to ourselves to go back to it from time to time and try to understand it. We can study such music for years without exhausting the possibilities for discovery.

A person with limited musical experience can judge only his own responses. When he speaks, he is really talking only about himself. But a person who has learned many kinds of musical styles feels that he can talk about music itself. He thinks that if the music has any meaning, he will be able to grasp it.

Musical Instruments

Almost all the instruments that produce music can be grouped in three major classes: string, wind, and percussion. They make sounds in three different ways. Vibrating strings produce the musical tones in the first group. Wind blown into or through a tube produces the tones in the second group. Something struck produces the sounds in the third group. But, because of the way musical instruments are made, most experts divide them into six major groups: (1) stringed, (2) wood wind, (3) brass, (4) percussion, (5) keyboard, and (6) others.

Stringed Instruments are of four basic types—bowed, plucked, struck, and wind. In the first type, the string is bowed (rubbed with a bow) to produce sounds. The important bowed strings are the *violin* family, which includes the *violin, viola, cello* (or *violoncello*), and *bass* (or double bass). Other bowed strings include the older *viol* family.

In the second type of stringed instrument, the player *plucks* the strings to produce tones. He may use his fingers, as in playing a harp. Or he may use a *plectrum*, a small piece of ivory, wood, or metal. The most important plucked-string instrument in an orchestra is the *harp*. Other plucked strings, usually played by themselves rather than with an orchestra, include the *banjo, guitar, lute, lyre, mandolin, sitar, ukulele,* and *zither*. The *harpsichord* has plucked strings, but it is often classed with keyboard instruments.

In the third type, the string is *hammered* to produce a tone. Two older instruments, the *clavichord* and the *dulcimer,* or *cimbalom,* have hammered strings. The most important hammered-string instrument, the *piano,* is usually classed with keyboard instruments. In an orchestra, the piano may also be used for percussion.

In the fourth type of stringed instrument, the strings vibrate in the wind. The only instrument of this type is the *aeolian harp*. It is never used in orchestral music.

Wood-Wind Instruments are grouped together because at one time they were all made of wood. Today, they may be made of metal or plastic. Wood winds produce tones when the musician blows air into or through a tube, either directly or past a vibrating *reed*. He covers holes in the tube to play various tones. In the *flute* family, he blows across a hole in the tube. Two thin pieces of reed, vibrating together, produce the sound in the *bassoon, oboe,* and *English horn*. A single reed, vibrating against a slot in the mouthpiece, produces the sound in the *clarinet* and *saxophone* families.

Brass Instruments all have rather long *bores* (tubes) with mouthpieces at one end and flaring *bells* (openings) at the other. Many brass instruments have *valves* that serve to lengthen or shorten the tube, lowering or raising the pitch. The *horn* family has a narrow, conical bore, with a funnel-shaped mouthpiece and a large bell. The *trumpet* family has a narrow, cylindrical bore, a cup-shaped mouthpiece, and a moderate-sized bell. The *cornet* has a cup mouthpiece and a bore that is partly conical and partly cylindrical. The *bugle* has a cup mouthpiece, a wide, conical bore, and a moderate bell. The *trombone* family has a larger mouthpiece than the trumpets, and usually has a slide instead of valves to lengthen the bore. The *tuba* family has a wide, conical bore and a cup mouthpiece, as do the *flügelhorns*.

Percussion Instruments include two basic types: those that play definite pitches and those that produce indefinite pitches. *Kettledrums* or *timpani* can be tuned to specific pitches, and are grouped with *chimes, glockenspiels, marimbas, tubular bells,* and *xylophones*. Indefinite-pitch instruments include the *drum* family (except kettledrums) and *castanets, cymbals, gongs, tambourines, triangles,* and many others.

Keyboard Instruments include all instruments that have keyboards connected with a mechanism for producing tones. The *piano,* hammered strings; the *harpsichord* has plucked strings; the *celesta,* hammered metal bars; and the *organ,* pipes. Unlike other keyboard instruments, the organ can sustain a tone indefinitely. The *carillon* is often played from a keyboardlike console, and many others.

Other Instruments. Some reed instruments have *free reeds* that vibrate back and forth in a slot. They include the *accordion, concertina, harmonica,* and *harmonium*. *Bagpipes* have both double reeds (like the oboe) and single reeds (like the clarinet). The *flageolet,* the *ocarina,* and the *recorder* are flutes with a whistle mouthpiece.

Since the late 1800's, various new instruments have been invented. Some produce sound by electronic means. The *Theremin* and the *Ondes Martenot* are probably the most significant in the electronic group. Electric organs and pianos today substitute electronic tone generators for the more conventional pipes and strings. Electronic amplification has also been added to older instruments, chiefly the guitar and double bass. Other older instruments have undergone extensive technical improvements. Since 1945, composers have been able to use electronic tone generators to produce sounds without using regular orchestral instruments.

Instrumental Music

Music written for instruments is classified according to the number of performers who play it. One musician plays a solo, a small number play chamber music, and many—as many as a hundred—play orchestral music.

Instrumental Solos. Some instruments, such as the piano, violin, and harp, are excellent for solo performances. The musician can play more than one tone at a time, giving his music richness and depth. Other instruments, for example the flute and clarinet, can play only one tone at a time. However, composers have written important solo parts for them. These instruments are often accompanied by a piano, although the performance then technically becomes a duo.

Composers have written vast amounts of music for solo piano. This music ranges from simple pieces to the 32 complex piano sonatas by Beethoven. After a few

GROUPS OF INSTRUMENTS

Shown here and on the following three pages are 44 instruments, divided into the six major groups of instruments: stringed, woodwind, brass, percussion, keyboard, and other instruments.

STRINGED INSTRUMENTS

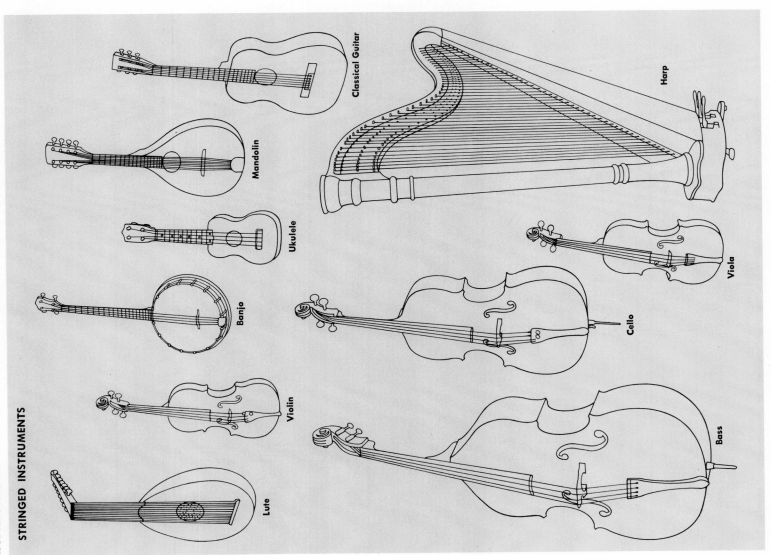

Classical Guitar

Harp

Mandolin

Ukulele

Viola

Banjo

Cello

Violin

Bass

Lute

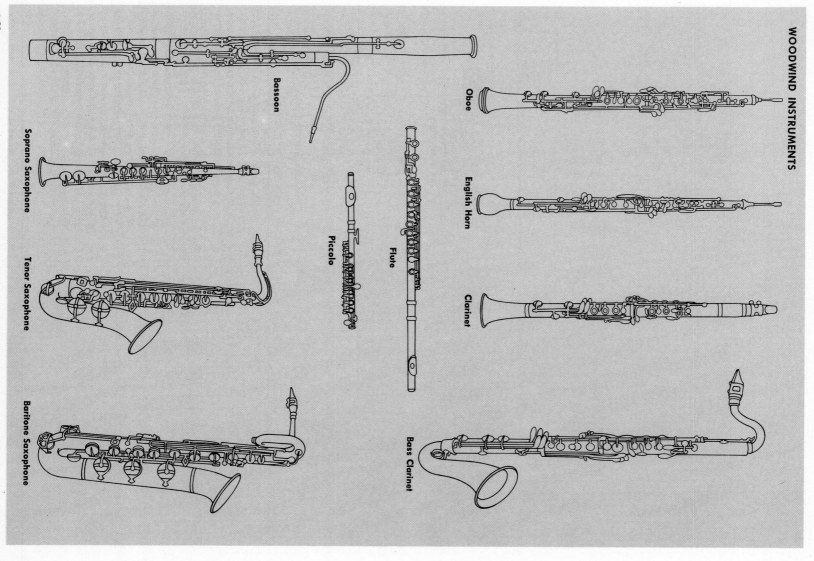

Bassoon

Oboe

Soprano Saxophone

English Horn

Piccolo

Flute

Tenor Saxophone

Clarinet

Baritone Saxophone

Bass Clarinet

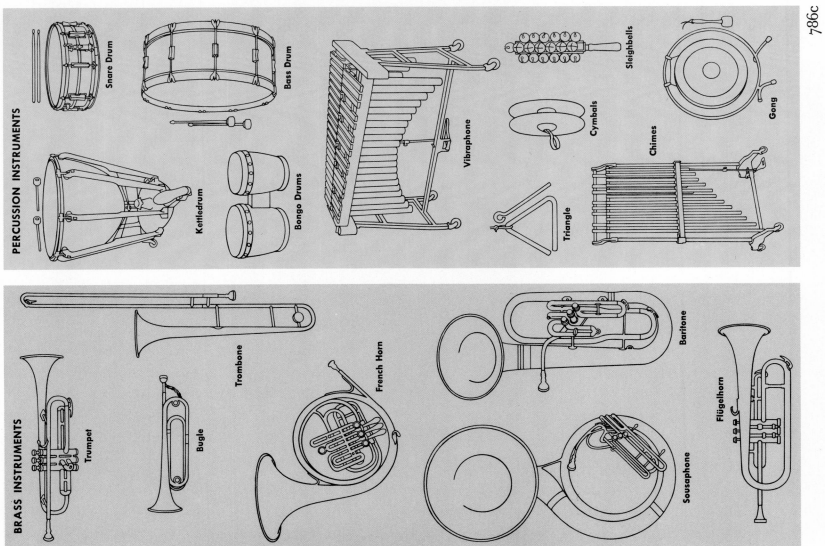

PERCUSSION INSTRUMENTS

Snare Drum

Bass Drum

Sleighbells

Gong

Kettledrum

Bongo Drums

Vibraphone

Cymbals

Chimes

Triangle

BRASS INSTRUMENTS

Trombone

Bugle

Trumpet

French Horn

Baritone

Sousaphone

Flügelhorn

KEYBOARD INSTRUMENTS

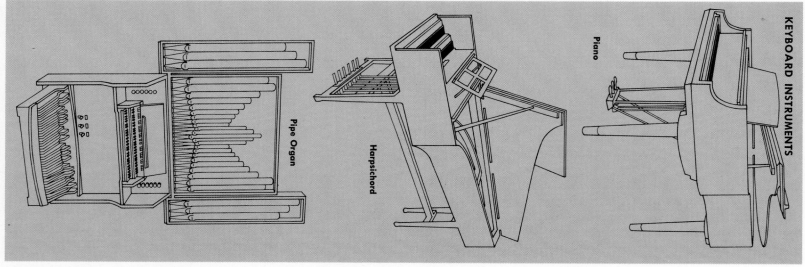

Pipe Organ

Harpsichord

Piano

OTHER INSTRUMENTS

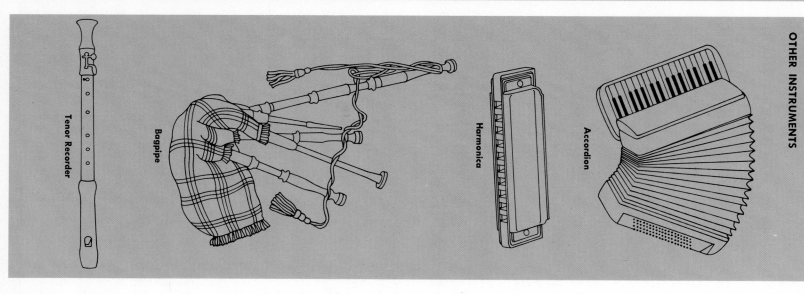

Tenor Recorder

Bagpipe

Harmonica

Accordion

lessons, almost anyone can play easy piano music. Concert pianists may spend years studying difficult music. Bach wrote the most famous works for violin and cello solo. The greatest composers have written little music for the solo harp, but skilled harpists can play much music that was written for piano.

Chamber Music is written for small combinations of instruments in a number of musical forms. It was originally played in *chambers* (private rooms), rather than in churches or public halls. Musicians played chamber music for the musical satisfaction it provided themselves and small groups of music lovers. It was not originally intended for public performance before large audiences.

The most important literature of chamber music is for a *string quartet*. This group has two violins, a viola, and a cello. In a *piano quartet*, the piano replaces one violin, although the term has also been used to mean a group of four pianos. The *duet sonata* has a piano and one other instrument such as a violin. The *string trio* consists of a violin, a viola, and a cello. The *piano trio* has a violin, a cello, and a piano. Mozart's *viola quintets* are written for two violins, two violas, and a cello. A *piano quintet* often has a piano and four members of the string quartet, but Schubert's "Trout" quintet uses a piano, a violin, a viola, a cello, and a double bass. A *wood-wind quintet* consists of flute, oboe, clarinet, bassoon, and French horn. The French horn is technically a brass instrument.

Sextets have six musicians, *septets* seven, and *octets* eight. Aaron Copland and a few other composers have produced *nonets* with nine players. There is also a great deal of musical literature which calls for groups of stringed, wind, and brass instruments ranging in size from 10 to 30 or more. Such a group is called a *chamber orchestra* today.

Orchestral Music, like chamber music, has been written in a variety of forms. It may be divided into two groups: works for soloist and orchestra, and works for orchestra alone.

Soloists and Orchestra together play several kinds of works. A vocal soloist sometimes sings with the orchestra in a *song cycle*, or in a work such as Brahms's *Alto Rhapsody*. An instrumental soloist performs with the orchestra in such works as Johannes Brahms's piano concerto in B♭ for piano and orchestra. In its early development, a *concerto* was understood as a "friendly rivalry" between two groups of performers. But it has come to mean an extended work in which the "rivalry" is expressed by a solo instrument and the orchestra, contrasting the individuality and resources of the two. Most concertos have three *movements* (sections) with a *cadenza* (a long passage for the soloist) near the end of the first movement. A *double* or *triple* concerto has two or three soloists. In a *concerto grosso*, a small group plays solo parts and is contrasted with a larger orchestra. See CONCERTO.

The Orchestra Alone plays many kinds of works, including overtures, suites, and symphonies. An *overture* may be a separate work, or it may be a short introductory work for a stage performance, such as an opera, a ballet, or a play. A *suite* is usually a group of short pieces, often in dance forms, as in Bach's four suites for orchestra, and Bartók's *Dance Suite*. A *symphonic* poem, also known as a *tone poem*, is a work for orchestra based on a nonmusical idea, such as a work of literature or a painting. The *symphony* is the most highly developed form of orchestral music. It is a work of large scope in which the composer expresses his most highly organized musical ideas. See SYMPHONY; SUITE.

Vocal Music

Singing Voices are grouped according to the ranges in which they sing and the color and quality of the voice itself. In terms of range, a *soprano* sings the highest woman's part. A *mezzo-soprano* sings a little below her, and a *contralto* or *alto* has the lowest woman's voice. A *tenor* sings the highest man's part, a *baritone* the middle range, and a *bass* the lowest part. In terms of *timbre* (tone color), a *coloratura* soprano has a light, sparkling, brilliant tone. The *lyric* soprano has a warmer, darker voice than the *coloratura*. The *dramatic soprano* makes an impact less by the high range of her voice than by the force with which she projects and the majesty of her tone. The highest male voices were once those of the *castrato* singers. Castrati were highly regarded in the 1600's and 1700's. The highest male voice heard today is the *countertenor*, whose range is approximately that of a contralto. The *Heldentenor* (heroic tenor) is a vocal type developed in the mid-1800's and characterized by robust brilliance. The *basso profundo* sings the lowest bass notes. A *basso cantante* or *bass-baritone* is a baritone with a well-developed lower range. A *basso buffo* sings comic roles.

Songs can be divided into two groups: those by composers whose names we know, and those of unknown origin. We know that "Sophisticated Lady" was written by Duke Ellington, and "The Erl King" by Schubert. But no one knows who composed the beautiful English folk song "Greensleeves." Songs can also be divided into *popular* and *art* songs. The few popular songs that last for many years usually have greater musical interest, or say something more, than the hundreds that fade away. Art songs are serious music, and the best ones may remain fresh for hundreds of years. The composer usually chooses a poem with some literary merit of its own, and sets it to music. He uses music to strengthen and amplify the meaning of the words. See FOLK MUSIC; POPULAR MUSIC.

Choral Music. The earliest choral music was sung in unison, with each person singing the same note. Choruses may have sung *a cappella* (without accompaniment) or with instruments playing the same melodies that were sung. In the Middle Ages, singers began combining two or more melodies, and by the 1500's and 1600's the practice of *part-singing* was highly developed. Instead of everyone singing the same notes, each voice or section had an individual part. Informal choral singing has long been a popular form of recreation. Amateur choral societies developed in Europe in the 1800's. At the same time, the barbershop quartet became popular in the United States (see BARBERSHOP QUARTET SINGING).

Opera was first written just before 1600. The first operas used simple *chords* (harmony). These chords allowed the solo voice to sing the words of the text clearly in a kind of simplified musical speech called *recitative*.

MUSIC

Operas combine music and stage action. A good opera is an exciting or moving stage performance and has music that emphasizes the dramatic or comic values of the story.

The cast of an opera may include a chorus of persons suitable to the story—villagers, soldiers, gypsies, or others. A soprano generally sings the part of the heroine. The leading male role is usually given to the tenor. Occasionally, when the composer is portraying a hero who is an older man or a man with flaws of character, the leading singer is a baritone. The most important female role, after the heroine, generally goes to a mezzo-soprano or a contralto, depending on the type of character to be portrayed. Contraltos make the best evil characters, just as baritones and basses are usually chosen for male roles of this type. But the baritone is often the hero's best friend, and the bass may be a king or other person of great dignity. A large orchestra usually accompanies the singers.

In *light opera* and *musical comedies*, the story almost always has a happy ending. The music is immediately appealing, and the purpose is as much to entertain as to transmit any artistic message. But these forms can comment effectively on the times. Sir Arthur Sullivan, Jacques Offenbach, Johann Strauss, Jr., Victor Herbert, Richard Rodgers, Frederick Loewe, and Leonard Bernstein won popularity and respect in these fields. See MUSICAL COMEDY; OPERA.

Oratorios use choruses, soloists, and instruments to tell a story in music without the theatrical action seen in an opera. Some, such as Handel's *Messiah*, are performed year after year. A well-known short oratorio is *Belshazzar's Feast* by Sir William Walton. An uncut performance of *Messiah* lasts more than three hours. The Walton oratorio lasts less than an hour. Most oratorios have religious subjects. They involve soloists (usually soprano, contralto, tenor, and bass), at least one chorus, often a supplementary chorus (such as one of children), and an orchestra. The narration in oratorio, as in certain types of opera, is done by the use of recitative. The oratorio form won wide popularity in the 1700's and 1800's. See ORATORIO.

The Elements of Music

Sound in Music usually has a definite *pitch* that we describe as "high" or "low." A musical sound, called a *tone*, is produced when something causes a series of vibrations that recur a certain number of times each second. For example, heavy wires that vibrate slowly, only 32.7 times a second, produce the lowest C on the piano. The thin wires that produce the highest C on the piano vibrate more than 4,000 times a second, or almost 130 times as fast as the lowest.

Musical tones also have other characteristics. For example, some tones are long and some short. We call this the *duration*. The same tone, played on different instruments, has different tone colors. This is the *quality* of the tone. Some tones are loud and others soft. We call this the *intensity* of the tone. A tone often has other tones that support and accompany it. They form its *harmony*. If a series of tones make up a tune, we may call it a *melody*. For other information on sound, see SOUND.

A *scale* is a series of tones arranged according to rising or falling pitch. The piano keyboard has a regular pattern of white and black keys. The distance from one key to the next, whether black or white, is always a half step. The half step above any white key is called its *sharp*, and the half step below any white key is called its *flat*. Composers use many kinds of scales. Most scales are based on the octave, except in Oriental music. An *octave* (named for the Latin word for eight) is the interval between two tones of the same name. The higher tone has twice as many vibrations per second as the lower, so the relationship is based as much on physics as on art.

In the illustrations on the opposite page we use the piano, an instrument which is tuned to *equal temperament*. This means that the intervals between tones have been made uniform. Each black key stands for two notes, such as C♯ or D♭. Actually, these notes are not precisely the same. Equal temperament permits a keyboard instrument to be of practical size and still play in reasonably accurate tune in all keys. A stringed instrument without a fretted fingerboard, such as the violin, permits the player to produce C♯ and D♭ as separate tones. A singer with a good ear can also make these distinctions. The notes from C to C on the piano comprise an octave. The octave may be divided into 12 equal parts, each of which is a half step. These 12 half steps make up the *chromatic scale*. You hear the chromatic scale when you play all the white and black keys from C to C on the piano.

Until about a hundred years ago, most western music was not based on the full chromatic scale, but on 7 tones taken from it. This seven-tone scale with its *octave* (eighth) tone is called the *diatonic scale*. The tones of the diatonic scale are not an equal distance apart. You hear the diatonic major scale when you play all the white keys from C to C on the piano, or when you sing *do-re-mi-fa-sol-la-ti-do*. The tones make up a specific pattern of whole steps and half steps, in this order: two whole steps; half step; three whole steps; half step.

Because of this pattern of whole steps and half steps, the seven tones of the diatonic major scale vary in importance. The strongest tone is the *tonic*, the first tone of the scale. The tonic serves as the central point for the organization of the other tones. The tonic also gives the scale its name. For example, in the D major scale, D is the tonic. Any of the 12 half steps within an octave may serve as the tonic in a diatonic major scale. This means that there are 12 different diatonic major scales. There are also 12 different diatonic minor scales, although most minor scales, as used by composers, are not completely diatonic in character. Different locations of the half steps are the chief distinction between major and minor scales.

Next to the tonic, the most important tones of the diatonic scale are the fifth, called the *dominant*, and the fourth, called the *subdominant*. In terms of melody, the seventh tone is important because it usually leads to the tonic. The seventh is called the *leading tone*. Many composers of the last hundred years, and especially composers since the end of World War II, have preferred to use the chromatic rather than the diatonic scale.

Melody is a succession of musical tones—in its simplest form, a tune. We remember a beautiful song more for its melody than for its words. We can enjoy

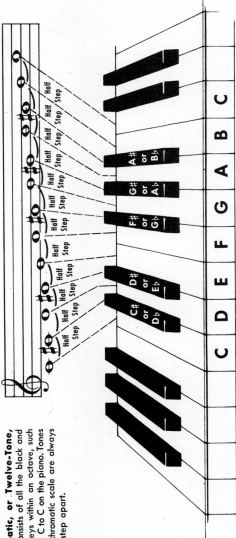

Chromatic, or Twelve-Tone, scale consists of all the black and white keys within an octave, such as from C to C on the piano. Tones in the chromatic scale are always a half step apart.

the flowing, attractive melodies in the symphonies of Brahms or Tchaikovsky long before we know much about the other elements of music. A melody consists of a series of tones played in a fixed pattern of pitches and rhythms. It may be repeated, expanded, or varied, according to the composer's wishes. But not all music has long, tuneful melodies. Composers often use a short series of notes, called a *motive*, as the basis for the development of their musical ideas. The first four notes of Beethoven's *Fifth Symphony* form such a motive. The theme of the first movement grows out of repetition and variation of this motive.

Harmony. The tones heard with a tone strengthen it and often help set its mood. Composers harmonize music in *chords*, which are groups of three or more related tones sounded at the same time. Chords are built on the scale and the physical properties of the tones themselves (see HARMONICS). If you play C, E, G, and the C at the octave, you will hear the basic C major chord.

The chords and harmonies in a piece of music are usually based on the same scale. We can say that they are in the same *tonality* (sometimes called *key*). The name of the scale on which the work is based is drawn from the tone on which the scale starts (such as C or F),

and also from whether the chords are major or minor. For the last 500 years, composers have usually used a harmonic system based on the tonic and dominant tones of the scale. After fixing the tonic tone and home key firmly in the listener's mind, the composer may *modulate* (shift) into the key in which the dominant of the "home" key becomes the new tonic. Modulation adds variety and may emphasize a contrasting section of his work. After the composer finishes the contrasting section, he usually returns to the "home" key.

Rhythm may be considered as everything that has to do with the duration of the musical sounds. Accent is an important factor in musical rhythm. The composer usually builds his music on a pattern of regularly recurring strong and weak accents. This pattern of accents permits the music to be divided into units of time called *measures* or *bars*. Weak accents help build the rhythm by creating anticipation for the strong ones. We can easily recognize the difference between a waltz rhythm of *ONE two three ONE two three* and a march rhythm of *ONE two ONE two*.

Tempo is the rate of speed at which music is played. It is related to, but not a part of, rhythm. A change in tempo can often change the meaning of music.

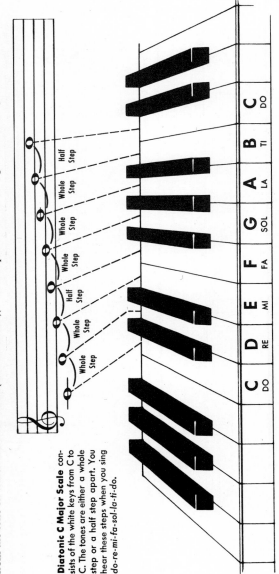

Diatonic C Major Scale consists of the white keys from C to C. The tones are either a whole step or a half step apart. You hear these steps when you sing do-re-mi-fa-sol-la-ti-do.

MUSIC

Tone Color is one of the most elusive qualities in music. Human voices may sing the same range of notes, yet produce widely different sounds. Different choices of chords give varying colors. Various instruments affect the tone color of the music they play. A melody may seem dark and mournful when played on the English horn. The same melody may sound bright and gay when played on the flute or violin. Tempo and rhythm are also factors in the effect a melody has on us.

In *orchestrating* his music, a composer takes advantage of differences in tone color. He may introduce the melody with one instrument, then have various other instruments play it, and finally have the entire orchestra play it. He may vary the groups that play the melody and its harmony. The strings are the foundation of the orchestra, and are often given the most important melodies. Wood winds have distinctive tones, and they, too, are given prominent melodies. Brass instruments provide rich sounds that may be massive, solemn, or brilliant. Percussion instruments emphasize the rhythmic elements. Special instruments, such as the saxophone or the mandolin, are sometimes introduced for special effects. Prokofiev, in his *Peter and the Wolf*, had instruments represent specific characters in the story —a flute for the bird, a bassoon for Peter's grandfather, an oboe for the duck, three horns for the wolf, and a string quartet for Peter himself.

MUSICAL NOTES

Notation. Music is written and printed in a picture language of its own called *notation*. Notation indicates (1) the pitch of the tones, (2) their place in a sequence of tones, (3) their *duration* (the length of time a tone is held), and (4) the composer's ideas about how they should be performed. *Notes* are written signs that represent *tones* (musical sounds). The notes appear on a *staff*, a set of five horizontal lines. The higher the composer places the note, the higher its pitch. The order in which he places it, from left to right, indicates its place in a sequence of notes. Notes are symbols in black and white. Different symbolic forms are used to show how long a time the sound is intended to last.

Medieval composers faced one of their main problems in finding a way to write music so that persons who had never heard a work could sing or play it. Guido d'Arezzo (995?-1050?), a monk, was probably the first to use parallel lines in the form of a staff and to name the notes of the scale (see GUIDO D'AREZZO). Churchmen now had a way to preserve religious music in writing. No one tried to preserve the secular music of the times.

A *clef sign* at the left end of a staff determines the position of notes on the staff. The *treble clef* is often called the *G clef* because its sign fixes the G above middle C on the second line from the bottom of the staff. The *bass clef*, often called the *F clef*, fixes the F below middle C on the second line from the top. Higher notes, such as those for the right end of the piano, appear in the treble clef. Lower notes appear in the bass clef. Music for the viola is written in the *alto C clef*, which fixes middle C on the third line. Music for the trombone, bassoon, and cello sometimes appears in the *tenor C clef*, where middle C is on the second line from the top.

A *key signature* appears at the right of the clef sign. By using sharp signs or flat signs, the composer indicates that certain notes should always be played sharp or flat. In this way, he shows the key of his work. Key signatures take from one to seven sharp or flat signs.

The composer may place an *accidental* in front of a certain note. *Accidentals* are the signs for sharp, flat, or

The Language of Music

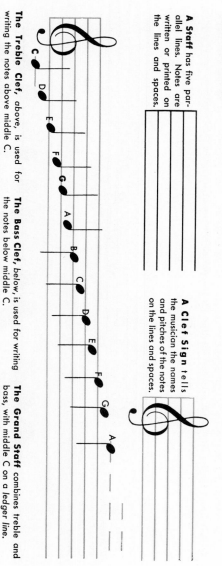

A **Clef Sign** tells the musician the names and pitches of the notes on the lines and spaces.

A **Staff** has five parallel lines. Notes are written or printed on the lines and spaces.

The Treble Clef, above, is used for writing the notes above middle C.

The Bass Clef, below, is used for writing the notes below middle C.

The Grand Staff combines treble and bass, with middle C on a ledger line.

The Position of Each Note on a Staff Indicates Its Pitch.

natural that show a change from the key signature. Any note not marked sharp or flat is called *natural*. The natural sign cancels a sharp or flat. There are also double sharps and double flats.

A *time signature* appears at the right of the key signature. It is shown as a fraction, such as $\frac{4}{4}$, $\frac{3}{4}$, $\frac{5}{4}$, $\frac{12}{8}$, $\frac{6}{8}$, or $\frac{2}{2}$. The denominator shows what kind of note—quarter, eighth, or half—is the unit of measurement and receives one beat. The numerator shows how many beats there are to a measure. In a song marked $\frac{4}{4}$, the composer shows that four quarter notes should receive one beat each. One measure of $\frac{4}{4}$ may have a whole note worth four beats, or eight eighth notes worth half a beat each, or two quarter notes and a half note, or some other combination totaling four beats.

A given time unit may vary widely in its clock-time duration. If a beat of a quarter note lasts a long time, such as $1\frac{1}{2}$ seconds, the *tempo* (speed) is very slow. But if it lasts a short time, such as $\frac{1}{2}$ second, the tempo is fast.

Duration, or Time Values. The shape of a note indicates its duration, just as its position on the staff shows its pitch. Whole notes have open oval shapes. Half notes look like whole notes, but have *stems*. Quarter notes have solid oval shapes with stems. Eighth, sixteenth, thirty-second, and sixty-fourth notes have one, two, three, or four *flags* on their stems.

Rests indicate silence, or no sound. They have various shapes, and have the same time values as the notes they replace. In the orchestra, a musician may have many measures of rests in between the music he plays. *Bar lines* separate one measure from another. *Repeat signs* next to the bar lines at the beginning and end of a section show that the section is to be repeated.

Dynamics, or loudness and softness, are indicated by a set of abbreviations for Italian words. For example, *p* or *piano* means *soft*, *pp* or *pianissimo* means *very soft*,

and *f* or *forte* means *loud*. These and other terms appear in the list *Terms Used in Music* in this article.

Expression. When a composer wants a group of notes to be played smoothly as a unit, he marks them as a *phrase*. When he wants two tones of the same pitch to be played as a continuous sound, he *ties* them with a curved line over the notes. He may put abbreviations for dynamics next to certain notes, or he can mark volume changes with *crescendo* and *decrescendo* signs. Or he may write instructions for the musicians.

Scores contain music written for several instruments, or for instruments and voices. In a typical orchestral and vocal score, music for the wood-wind instruments appears at the top. Parts for the brass and percussion instruments are just below. Then comes the music for the soloists, either vocal or instrumental, followed by that for the chorus, if there is one. The music for strings appears at the bottom.

Each performer reads from a *part* that contains only the music he plays or sings. He follows the directions of the conductor. The performer keeps track of the bars during which he is silent, so he can make his entrances correctly. The conductor uses the full score. He must glance down the entire length of the page to read the notes for each part in any one measure, so he will know what each performer should be playing.

Names of Compositions. Musical works have various names, official and unofficial. The official name may identify the form of the work and indicate its home key, as in *Symphony No. 9 in D minor*. This name often includes an *opus* (work) *number* that tells where the composition comes in the composer's life work. He may have written other works between his eighth and ninth symphonies. For example, Beethoven's *Symphony*

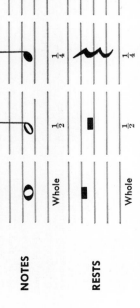

Notes and Rests, *above*, have shapes that show how long they last. The notes and rests shown from *left to right* are whole, half, quarter, eighth, sixteenth, thirty-second, and sixty-fourth.

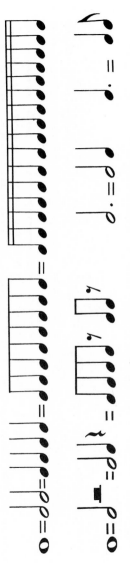

Note Equivalents, *below.* Two half notes or four quarter rests equal a whole note. A dotted note has one and a half times its value. That is, a dotted half note equals a half and a quarter.

The Shape of Each Note or Rest Shows Its Time Value.

791

No. 8 in F major is opus 93, and his *Symphony No. 9 in D minor* is opus 125. Opus numbers usually indicate the order of publication, rather than of composition.

Some composers never use opus numbers. Others keep this added identification for the music they consider most important. Mozart wrote so much music that he never tried to keep track of it all. We identify his works by *Köchel numbers*, such as *K. 550*, which show their places in the catalog published by a music scholar, Ludwig von Köchel, in 1862. Some works are identified by their places in a famous edition of music issued by a well-known publisher. For many years, Haydn's last symphonies had such numbers as *B.&H. No. 13*, that showed their places in a set of scores issued by Breitkopf and Härtel, a famous publisher in Leipzig. We now use numbers and keys to identify his works, and *B.&H. No. 13* is called *Symphony No. 88 in G major*.

Unofficial names have come from composers and audiences alike. Tchaikovsky named his mournful sixth symphony *Pathétique*, meaning *pathetic*. Its official name is *Symphony No. 6 in B minor, op. 74*. Other works have unofficial names given them by the public. Beethoven's *Sonata in C sharp minor, op. 27, No. 2*, is commonly called the "Moonlight Sonata." Beethoven gave it an entirely different name, *sonata quasi una fantasia*, which means "sonata in the manner of a fantasy."

Some works have unofficial names taken from the persons to whom they were dedicated. Bach wrote six concertos for the ruler of Brandenburg, and we call them the *Brandenburg Concertos*. Other works are named for the places where they were composed (for example Mozart's "Linz" symphony, K. 425), or where they were first performed (such as Haydn's "Paris" symphonies, numbers 82 through 87). Still others are named for distinctive melodies or orchestrations, such as Haydn's "Drum Roll" symphony, number 103.

Many composers identify their works with titles that provide imaginative descriptions of what their music says, such as Debussy's *La Mer (The Sea)*.

Musical Forms

The elements of music must take some form in order to be music, just as lines and colors must be arranged together to create a painting. Composers use various forms to organize these elements into works of art.

Song Form, usually a two-part song or three-part song, is one of the simplest types of musical form. A two-part form may be represented by A for the first theme and B for the second theme. Often a two-part song consists of two treatments of one theme, A, A'. More advanced is the three-part song (A-B-A) in which the first theme returns again to complete the form.

Sonata Form. The most important large form in serious music for the last 200 years has been the classical sonata form as written by Mozart and Beethoven. It originated in the 1700's and developed in the next century. We call a sonata for orchestra a *symphony*, a sonata for a small instrumental group and orchestra a *concerto*, and a sonata for a small instrumental group a *duet, trio, quartet,* or *quintet*. These works have more similarities as sonatas than they have differences in size or orchestration.

A sonata is usually divided into major sections called *movements*, somewhat like chapters in a book or acts in

a play. In most sonatas, the longest movement opens the work and sets its character. This movement involves the most complex musical writing. A slower, more lyric section may come next to provide contrast. Then comes a fast, short section in contrast to both the movements before it. The *finale* (last movement) usually returns to the feeling of the opening. It sums up the composer's ideas, sometimes quoting some of the themes heard earlier. Some sonatas have only one movement, and others may have five or six.

The first movement of most sonatas is usually written in *sonata form*. This means that the movement itself has four parts, played without pauses in between. The first part, called the *exposition*, states the main theme, or group of themes, in a *home tonality* (sometimes named in the title of the work). It also states a contrasting theme, or group of themes, in a different tonality. After fixing those themes in our minds, the composer introduces the second part of the movement, the *development*. Here he uses his themes or fragments of themes in many different ways and he often employs many changes of tonality. In this way, the music builds to a climax of expressive force. In the third section, the *recapitulation*, the composer restates the themes more or less as we first heard them. The fourth section, the *coda*, brings the movement to an end. The coda may be considered as part of the recapitulation, and the sonata form as having only three parts.

Variation Form consists of a series of different treatments of a theme. The theme itself is usually stated fully at the opening or close of the work. The composer may base his variations on the whole theme, or on only part of it, or even on part of its accompaniment. He usually changes key for some of his variations.

Canon and Fugue are *polyphonic* (many-voiced) forms in which one instrument or singer states a theme and the other performers then play or sing it in regular order. Such a repetition of a theme in succession in voice parts is called *imitation*. Imitation can be defined as the repetition of a melodic phrase or theme modified in some way but still resembling the original.

In a *canon*, all the voices have the same theme throughout the work. *Rounds* follow the imitation form, as in the works "Row, Row, Row Your Boat" and "Frère Jacques." In a *fugue*, the composer may vary the different parts by imitating the theme with slight variations. He may also break off the theme entirely and introduce a second theme, or write a contrasting *episode* to give variety.

Free Form, as its name implies, gives the composer the greatest freedom of all. He may introduce two themes, the development of a third, then the third one itself. Or he may not use any conventional succession of themes. His problems in achieving unity become great, and he must make his harmonization and orchestration so unified that they give the sense of unity the form lacks. Debussy used free form in *Jeux (Games)*.

History

Ancient Civilization. Many ancient works of art show musicians and their instruments. Unfortunately, we have little detailed knowledge of how men made or played these instruments. Only five or six complete pieces of music from the ancient world still exist, all of them Greek.

Egypt. Early in Egyptian history, during the 4000's B.C., people clapped disks and sticks together, jingled metal rods, and sang songs. Later, in the great temples of the gods, priests trained choirs in singing ritual music. Court musicians sang and played several types of harps and wind and percussion instruments. Military bands used trumpets and drums.

Palestine. The people of Bible lands probably did not develop as much music as the Egyptians did. The Bible contains the words of many Hebrew songs and chants, such as the Psalms. It mentions harps, drums, trumpets, cymbals, and other instruments. The music in Solomon's temple at Jerusalem in the 900's B.C. probably included trumpets and choral singing to the accompaniment of stringed instruments.

China. The early Chinese believed that music had magic powers, as well as the power to please, because they thought it reflected the order in the universe. They were great systematizers, and set up an imperial bureau about 200 B.C. to establish an absolute system of pitch. Chinese music used a *pentatonic* (five-tone) scale. It had no half steps, and sounded somewhat like the five black keys of the piano. Chinese musicians played the zither, various flutes, and percussion instruments.

India. Musical traditions in India go back to the 1200's B.C. The people believed that music was directly related to the fundamental processes of human life. They developed religious music in ancient times, and worked out music theories by about 300 B.C. Musicians

Key Signatures tell what key the music is written in. If it has no flats or sharps, the music may be in the key of C major or its relative minor, A minor. Each major key has a relative minor.

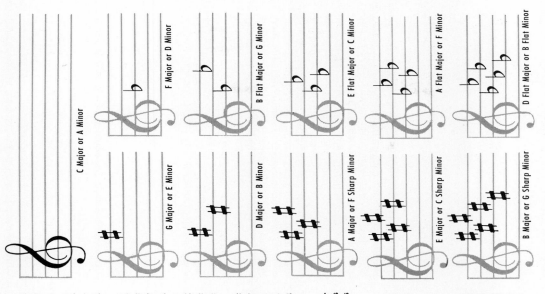

C Major or A Minor

G Major or E Minor

F Major or D Minor

D Major or B Minor

B Flat Major or G Minor

A Major or F Sharp Minor

E Flat Major or C Minor

E Major or C Sharp Minor

A Flat Major or F Minor

B Major or G Sharp Minor

D Flat Major or B Flat Minor

F Sharp Major or D Sharp Minor

G Flat Major or E Flat Minor

C Sharp Major or A Sharp Minor

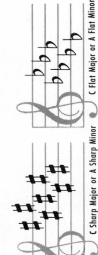

C Flat Major or A Flat Minor

A Measure contains a set number of beats. Its *time signature* appears as a fraction, showing how many beats each measure has (four or three in the examples below) and what kind of note gets one beat (quarter notes in both examples illustrated below).

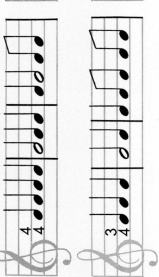

Accidentals are signs for sharp (♯), flat (♭), and natural (♮). They appear with the notes and make them higher or lower.

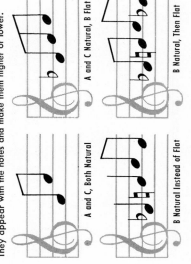

A and C, Both Natural

A and C Natural, B Flat

B Natural Instead of Flat

B Natural, Then Flat

played wind, stringed, and percussion instruments. Indian music was not based on a system of whole steps and half steps, like the diatonic scale. Instead of using specific notes, Indian composers followed a complicated set of formulas called *ragas*. Ragas permitted the choice between certain notes but required the omission of other notes. They set the emotional mood and even the philosophic meaning of the performance.

Greece. The Greeks used letters of the alphabet to represent musical tones. They grouped these tones in *tetrachords* (successions of four tones). The first and fourth tones have a relationship somewhat like that between C on the piano and the next F above. By combining these tetrachords in various ways, the Greeks created groups of tones called *modes*. Modes were the forerunners of more modern major and minor scales.

Greek thinkers worked out music theories more thoroughly than any other ancient people. In the 1800's, composers became interested in modes again. They felt that major and minor scales had lost their freshness.

Pythagoras, a Greek who lived in the 500's B.C., thought that music and mathematics provided keys to the secrets of the world. He believed that the planets produce different tones in harmony, so that the universe itself sings. This belief shows the importance of music in Greek worship, as well as in dance and drama. The Greeks wrote music for chorus and for instruments of the harp and wind families.

Rome. The Romans copied Greek music theory and performing techniques, but also invented such new instruments as the straight trumpet, which they called the *tuba*. They often used the *hydraulis*, the first pipe organ, in the sports arena. Water pressure maintained an even flow of air for the pipes. Regardless of legend,

University Museum, University
of Pennsylvania, Philadelphia

In Babylonia, court musicians played ornate instruments. This lyre, probably made at Ur in the 2600's B.C., was covered with gold and shell.

Musicians at a Banquet from the tomb of Djeserkara' somb in Thebes. The Oriental Institute, Chicago

In Egypt, musicians played reed pipes, and stringed instruments such as lyres, lutes, and harps. This wall painting was made in the 1400's B.C.

794

the emperor Nero could not have fiddled while Rome burned. The violin had not yet been invented, and he probably played a hydraulis or a lyre.

The Middle Ages. Chanting was part of Christian worship from early times. It gradually developed into a type of melody called *plain song*. St. Ambrose (A.D. 340?-397) helped work out a set of rules to maintain an appropriate style in singing hymns. Music that follows these rules is called *Ambrosian chant*. It was the first systematically composed form of plain song. Under Pope Gregory the Great, who died in 604, churchmen developed the *Gregorian chant*, which is more important today.

Plain song did not use the kind of musical scale we use today. It was built on a series of *modes* similar to those of Greek music. The diatonic scale of today fixes the pitches of certain notes and indicates the relationship between notes. Plain song did not always set the relationships of specific notes, but only set the relationships between notes. Plain song has no harmony or accompaniment. The music of antiquity and the early medieval period is often called *monophony*. It has a single melodic line which all performers played or sang. In the early Middle Ages, the people sang both religious and *secular* (nonreligious) music in the monophonic manner.

Later, they wanted to sing and play more interesting and complicated music than monophony. They put two or more melodies together, creating a type of music called *polyphony*, which means "many sounds." Early polyphony, sometimes called *organum*, appeared in Europe about 800. *Counterpoint* (polyphonic writing) developed in the next few hundred years.

The Renaissance in music dates from the 1300's in southern Europe and from somewhat later in northern Europe. Composers wished to write music on secular themes without regard to the practices of the church. Composers were attracted to the possibilities of polyphonic writing, in which each voice could be assigned its own line of melody. Polyphonic writing provided technical opportunities for effects of great brilliance not previously possible. A secular form of composition, the *madrigal*, appeared in Italy during the 1300's. Composers wrote madrigals in their own language, rather than in Latin. Madrigal singing spread northward. Such Flemish composers as Guillaume Dufay (1400?-1474), Josquin des Prés (1445?-1521), and Orlando di Lasso (1532?-1594) wrote some works in this style. Most of their writing was religious, however.

In Italy, Giovanni Palestrina (1525?-1594) developed the most important systematic approach to polyphonic writing before Bach. During the Renaissance, English music reached heights it has never surpassed. Thomas Tallis (1505?-1585) was the first great English composer. He was closely rivaled by William Byrd (1543?-1623). Thomas Morley (1557-1603?), John Dowland (1563-1626), and Orlando Gibbons (1583-1625) set poetry of the period to music.

Baroque Music replaced the Renaissance style after 1600 and dominated European music until about 1750. Baroque music was elaborate and emotional. It was ideally suited to the treatment of dramatic subjects. The important new form was opera, closely followed by the oratorio, which also drew upon devices used in the theater.

Claudio Monteverdi (1567-1643) of Italy was the first major composer of opera. Jean Baptiste Lully (1632-1687), an Italian by birth, became the first master of operatic writing in France. Heinrich Schütz (1585-1672) wrote the first German opera and much sacred music. Alessandro Scarlatti (1659-1725) was the greatest Italian operatic composer of his era. His son Domenico (1685-1757) was one of a group of masters of secular instrumental music. Arcangelo Corelli (1653-1713) was another important figure in the group. Italian baroque music reached its height with the

works of Antonio Vivaldi (1677?-1741). French composers who wrote in a similar style include François Couperin (1668-1733) and Jean Philippe Rameau (1683-1764). Henry Purcell (1659?-1695) was the major English composer in this period.

The Early 1700's: Bach. Johann Sebastian Bach (1685-1750) was the greatest member of the most important musical family in history. From the 1500's through the 1700's, more than 50 members of Bach's family gained recognition as musicians. Bach wrote music in nearly every form and style known in northern Europe during his lifetime. But, in his own time, he was most famous as the organist and choirmaster of various churches in Germany. Part of his job was to write music for religious services. He had little of it published and none was played more than a few times in public.

Bach gave methodical expression to the tonic-dominant system of harmony (explained in the *Harmony* section of this article). Musicians still study Bach's use of this harmony in such works as *The Well-Tempered Clavier*, a collection of 48 preludes and fugues that use all the major and minor keys. Other important composers of Bach's time include Dietrich Buxtehude (1637-1707) and Georg Philipp Telemann (1681-1767).

The Later 1700's: Classicism. Three composers dominated the music of the times. They were George Frideric Handel (1685-1759), Joseph Haydn (1732-1809), and Wolfgang Amadeus Mozart (1756-1791). As *classical* composers, they believed that music should be polished and gallant in manner. They wanted to express emotions only in a refined and elegant way. Their works sparkle with brilliance and gaiety and all three wrote huge amounts of music. Handel wrote over 40 operas and more than 20 oratorios. Haydn wrote more than 100 symphonies. As for Mozart, most people could not

Palace Musicians (Sung Dynasty). The Art Institute of Chicago, Kate S. Buckingham Fund

Figurines de Tanagre, The Louvre, Paris (Alinari from Art Reference Bureau)

In Greece, many people enjoyed playing such stringed instruments as the harp and the lyre. This statue was found in the ruins of Tanagra.

In China, palace musicians played instruments that resemble the lute, harp, xylophone, cymbals, and flute.

even copy in 35 years the more than 600 works he wrote in that time. The public demanded this great output.

Haydn and Mozart, during their later years, wrote the first real symphonic masterworks. As a result, some persons think of them only in terms of their contributions to the symphony. But both composers also played an important part in developing the piano sonata, the string quartet, and other musical forms. Mozart also led in developing the opera. He surpassed his predecessor Christoph Willibald Gluck (1714-1787). Mozart produced works that have the universal quality of Shakespeare's greatest plays and that appear to speak directly to men of every era.

The Early 1800's: Romanticism. Classical composers felt the deepest emotions. But their musical works are composed in an artistic language that required a good deal of reserve. They emphasized elegance and form as tests of artistic discipline and taste. The romantics believed such conventions were artificial. They felt music should be fanciful and emotional, with the imagination providing the means, and sentiment sustaining the mood. Force of expression was intended to make up for any lack of polish in their work.

Ludwig van Beethoven (1770-1827) was a master of classical forms. But he departed from them whenever he felt it necessary to achieve his artistic goals. He was fundamentally a classicist, but wrote works that fully anticipated the romantic spirit. He specialized in piano music, string quartets, and orchestral works. The great German composer expected his works to be performed repeatedly and to live beyond his lifetime. Beethoven wrote only nine symphonies—less than a fourth as many as Mozart, and less than a tenth as many as Haydn. But Beethoven's symphonies are far more complex than any earlier ones.

An outstanding early romantic composer, Franz Schubert (1797-1828), wrote symphonies, piano music, string quartets, and more than 600 of the most beautiful songs ever composed. Another German romantic, Carl Maria von Weber (1786-1826), provided the first important example of national feeling in opera. In Der Freischütz, he began the practice of selecting story and music that reflected national character, instead of simply following classical models.

Felix Mendelssohn (1809-1847), also of Germany, won lasting fame for his instrumental music. His works include the Overture he wrote at the age of 17 for Shakespeare's A Midsummer Night's Dream. Mendelssohn was largely responsible for reviving interest in Bach's music. As a performer, he began the practice of stressing older music, rather than the latest works by living composers. Another German composer, Robert Schumann (1810-1856), composed four symphonies and much beautiful piano and vocal music. Frédéric Chopin (1810?-1849), born in Poland, spent most of his life in France. He wrote nothing for the orchestra alone, but his many works for the piano keep his name alive.

The Later 1800's: Nationalism. One of the outgrowths of romanticism was that many composers began searching for ways to express the feelings of their peoples in music. Musical nationalism developed in many ways in various countries. Some composers studied folk music, and used folk melodies in their works.

In France, nationalism took the form of a distinctive new tradition in opera and in dramatic symphonic works. Hector Berlioz (1803-1869) was the first composer to appreciate the tonal resources of the new instruments, such as the valve horn, that were developed during his lifetime. He also made new use of symphonic music to express vivid pictures, as in his Fantastic Symphony and Harold in Italy.

Giacomo Meyerbeer (1791-1864), although a German by birth, dominated French opera. His grandiose works are mostly forgotten, but we still enjoy those of his successors, including Ambroise Thomas (1811-1896), Charles Gounod (1818-1893), Léo Delibes (1836-1891), Jules Massenet (1842-1912), and Gustave Charpentier (1860-1956), Georges Bizet (1838-1875) wrote the ever-popular Carmen. Jacques Offenbach (1819-1880), also of German birth, created the French light opera.

In instrumental music, Belgian-born César Franck (1822-1890) wrote only one symphony, but influenced symphonic form. The same motifs dominate all three movements of his cyclic work. Vincent d'Indy (1851-1931) and Ernest Chausson (1855-1899) followed the cyclic form. Other French composers in the years after Berlioz included Camille Saint-Saëns (1835-1921), Gabriel Fauré (1845-1924), and Paul Dukas (1865-1935).

Franz Liszt (1811-1886), born in Hungary but active in both France and Germany, represents a tie between

Medieval Music was not usually written with notes, but with neumes, signs above the words that showed whether the melody should go up or down. This page was written in the A.D. 1000's.

The Newberry Library, Chicago

French and German music. His piano compositions and symphonic poems have never lost their popularity. His *Hungarian Rhapsodies* are based on gypsy tunes rather than Hungarian folk tunes.

In Germany, Richard Wagner (1813-1883) dominated operatic music with his revolutionary music dramas. Anton Bruckner (1824-1896) wrote vast symphonies based on Wagner's principles. The last half of the 1800's saw sharp debates between Wagnerians and the followers of Johannes Brahms (1833-1897). Brahms rejected the influence of the theater, and tried to continue the tradition of Beethoven. His followers preferred "pure" or nondescriptive music to the scene-painting of Berlioz or the dramatizations of Wagner. The two groups often clashed at concerts, shouting boos and catcalls.

Gustav Mahler (1860-1911) was strongly influenced by Wagner, but developed a highly individual style in his symphonies and songs. Hugo Wolf (1860-1903) ranks with Schubert as a composer of music for voice. The Viennese style of waltz music and light opera began with Johann Strauss (1804-1849) and reached its height with his son Johann Jr., "the waltz king" (1825-1899).

In Italy, Gioacchino Rossini (1792-1868), Gaetano Donizetti (1797-1848), and Vincenzo Bellini (1801-1835) developed the opera. Italian opera reached its highest level in the works of Giuseppe Verdi (1813-1901). Giacomo Puccini (1858-1924) continued the tradition with emphasis on beautiful melodies. Other operatic composers included Ruggiero Leoncavallo (1858-1919) and Pietro Mascagni (1863-1945).

In Russia, serious music began with the operas of Mikhail Glinka (1804-1857). He was not a professional composer, and his most important followers also had other careers. Alexander Borodin (1833-1887) was a celebrated chemist, Modest Mussorgsky (1839-1881) was a government official, and Nicholas Rimsky-Korsakov (1844-1908) was a naval officer. These three joined Mily Balakirev (1837-1910) and César Cui (1835-1918) to form a group called *the Five*. Mussorgsky had the greatest musical ability of the group.

The most popular Russian composer was Peter Ilich Tchaikovsky (1840-1893). His last three symphonies remain the most widely admired Russian works in this form. Sergei Rachmaninoff (1873-1943) concentrated chiefly on piano works.

In the English-Speaking Countries, little music of international significance appeared during the 1800's. Sir Arthur Sullivan (1842-1900) began an English light-opera tradition in his famous partnership with Sir W. S. Gilbert, who wrote the words for Sullivan's music. Sir Edward Elgar (1857-1934) was the first important English symphonist, and Frederick Delius (1862-1934) developed an individual approach to the symphonic poem. Edward MacDowell (1861-1908), an American, wrote many beautiful piano works. Victor Herbert (1859-1924) began an American tradition of light opera.

In Other Parts of Europe. Nationalism flourished in the music of three Czech composers, Bedřich Smetana (1824-1884), Antonín Dvořák (1841-1904), and Leoš Janáček (1854-1928). Scandinavian composers included Edvard Grieg (1843-1907) of Norway, Carl Nielsen (1865-1931) of Denmark, and Jan Sibelius (1865-1957) of Finland.

The 1900's have seen four major developments in the history of music: (1) the continued growth of nationalism; (2) the appearance of major American and Latin-American composers; (3) the rise of international styles in music for the first time since the classical period of the 1700's; and (4) the search for new harmonic principles to replace tonic-dominant harmony.

Nationalism became a force in Spanish music with the works of Manuel de Falla (1876-1946). Russian composers, ruled by their Communist government, developed an officially anti-romantic outlook known as *socialist realism*, but it often showed strong romantic sympathies. Major exponents of this style included Sergei Prokofiev (1891-1953), Aram Khachaturian (1903-   ), Dimitri Kabalevsky (1906-   ), and Dimitri Shostakovich (1906-   ). In England, Ralph Vaughan Williams (1872-1958), Sir William Walton (1902-   ), and Benjamin Britten (1913-   ) usually followed fairly conservative practices.

Richard Strauss (1864-1949), the dominant figure in German music for more than 50 years, wrote for the theater or the concert hall with equal mastery. The Hungarian masters Béla Bartók (1881-1945) and Zoltán Kodály (1882-1967) discovered individual musical styles based upon Hungarian folk songs. Paul Hindemith (1895-1963) and Carl Orff (1895-   ) also developed strong personal styles in German music.

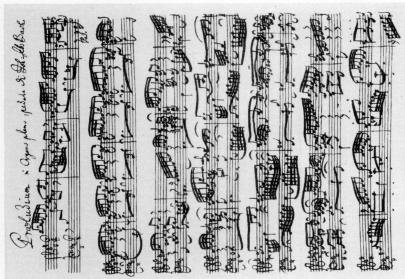

A Bach Manuscript, for the *Prelude and Fugue in B minor* for organ, shows the great care the composer used in putting his notes on paper. Bach wrote and signed this page about 1740.
The New York Public Library

MUSIC

New American Composers began expressing vital new ideas in music during the 1900's. Charles Ives (1874-1954) wrote advanced and technically unorthodox music, and had to wait years before his major works were even performed. John Alden Carpenter (1876-1951), less extreme in his musical ideas, won earlier recognition. Many American composers studied in Paris with Nadia Boulanger (1887-), a great French music teacher. They included Walter Piston (1894-), Virgil Thomson (1896-), Roy Harris (1898-), and Aaron Copland (1900-). Three younger composers —Elliott Carter (1908-), Samuel Barber (1910-), and William Schuman (1910-)—reveal more distinctively American influences. Howard Hanson (1896-) presented conservative musical ideas, and Roger Sessions (1896-) became an advanced harmonic innovator. Latin America produced such important composers as Carlos Chávez (1899-) of Mexico, Heitor Villa-Lobos (1887-1959) of Brazil, and Alberto Ginastera (1916-) of Argentina.

International Styles of the 1900's began with the "impressionism" developed in France by Claude Debussy (1862-1918). His works influenced Alexander Scriabin (1872-1915) in Russia and Charles Griffes (1884-1920) in America. Two Italian composers, Ottorino Respighi (1879-1936) and Ildebrando Pizzetti (1880-1968), also followed Debussy's example. In France, Maurice Ravel (1875-1937) won the widest acceptance in the years after Debussy, although some critics believe that Erik Satie (1866-1925) made more original contributions. Olivier Messiaen (1908-), a French composer, became noted for his rhythmic complexity and original harmonic style.

Melodic emphasis appeared in the works of a French group called *Les Six,* led by Arthur Honegger (1892-1955), Darius Milhaud (1892-), and Francis Poulenc (1899-1963). Czech-born Bohuslav Martinů (1890-1959) agreed with *Les Six* on the importance of melody. Ernest Bloch (1880-1959), born in Switzerland, also emphasized melodic content. Another Swiss composer, Frank Martin (1890-), combined melodic and rhythmic drive in his works.

Igor Stravinsky (1882-) led in developing many new musical styles. Born in Russia, he lived in France and Switzerland before settling in the United States. His musical development led him through nationalism and neoclassicism to composition in the 12-tone system which Arnold Schönberg had advocated in his most influential years. Stravinsky's early ballets, especially *The Rite of Spring* (which caused fist fights at its premiere in 1913), were quickly accepted as contemporary classics. In fact, the continued popularity of his early ballets sometimes obscured the merits of his later work. Another composer whose technique developed enormously through his lifetime was Edgard Varèse (1883-1965). Varèse was born in Paris but spent his most important years in the United States. He has been called the father of electronic music.

New Harmonic Principles appeared to Arnold Schönberg (1874-1951) to be the only way to keep music alive. The Austrian-born composer believed that musicians had exhausted the tonic-dominant system, and felt that music needed an entirely new harmonic structure. In Schönberg's *twelve-tone* technique, all 12 notes in the chromatic scale have equal value. There are no key signatures or scales. Instead, his works have *tone rows* in which all 12 tones are arranged in a predetermined order. All the melodies and harmonies are drawn from the tone row, which does not change within a composition. At first these innovations aroused storms of protest from audiences and from conservative composers and critics. Schönberg's most important disciples were two other Austrians, Anton Webern (1883-1945) and Alban Berg (1885-1935). Others experimented with various forms of *atonality* (writing in the chromatic scale without a conventional tonal center) and *polytonality* (writing in two or more keys at one time).

In the 1960's, nationalism apparently had ceased to function as a genuine force in serious music. The music world presented a situation similar to the 1600's, when international styles dominated the scene and composers of widely different backgrounds could share the same artistic viewpoint. In Communist countries, socialist realism was the official style. Other approaches to composition were condemned as lacking in emotional appeal. There were, however, signs of composition in styles other than socialist realism.

GREAT COMPOSERS

This table includes the world's great composers of symphonies, operas, and concertos from 1650 to the present. Two important Italian composers before 1650 were Claudio Monteverdi (1567-1643) and Giovanni Palestrina (1525?-1594).

Each composer has a separate biography in WORLD BOOK.

1650

1700

1750

1800

PURCELL (1659?-1695) BRIT.

VIVALDI (1677?-1741) ITAL.

BACH (1685-1750) GER.

HANDEL (1685-1759) GER.

HAYDN (1732-1809) AUS.

MOZART (1756-1791) AUS.

BEETHOVEN (1770-1827) GER.

SCHUBERT (1797-1828) AUS.

ROSSINI (1792-1868) ITAL.

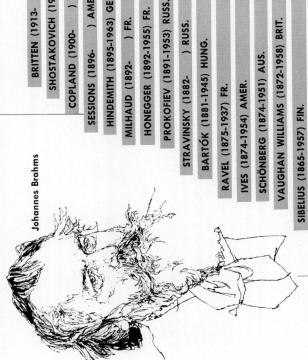

2000

1950

1900

1850

Ludwig van Beethoven

Johann Sebastian Bach

Johannes Brahms

BRITTEN (1913-) BRIT.
SHOSTAKOVICH (1906-) RUSS.
COPLAND (1900-) AMER.
SESSIONS (1896-) AMER.
HINDEMITH (1895-1963) GER.
MILHAUD (1892-) FR.
HONEGGER (1892-1955) FR.
PROKOFIEV (1891-1953) RUSS.
STRAVINSKY (1882-) RUSS.
BARTÓK (1881-1945) HUNG.
RAVEL (1875-1937) FR.
IVES (1874-1954) AMER.
SCHÖNBERG (1874-1951) AUS.
VAUGHAN WILLIAMS (1872-1958) BRIT.
SIBELIUS (1865-1957) FIN.
R. STRAUSS (1864-1949) GER.
DEBUSSY (1862-1918) FR.
MAHLER (1860-1911) AUS.
PUCCINI (1858-1924) ITAL.
RIMSKY-KORSAKOV (1844-1908) RUSS.
DVOŘÁK (1841-1904) CZECH.
TCHAIKOVSKY (1840-1893) RUSS.
MUSSORGSKY (1839-1881) RUSS.
BIZET (1838-1875) FR.
BRAHMS (1833-1897) GER.
BRUCKNER (1824-1896) AUS.
FRANCK (1822-1890) BELG.
VERDI (1813-1901) ITAL.
WAGNER (1813-1883) GER.
LISZT (1811-1886) HUNG.
SCHUMANN (1810-1856) GER.
CHOPIN (1810?-1849) POL.
MENDELSSOHN (1809-1847) GER.
BERLIOZ (1803-1869) FR.

Some composers continued to write in diatonic or, more commonly, chromatic harmonies. They extended the limits of the tonic-dominant system of harmony without destroying it. Although frequently attacked by critics and other composers for their conservatism, these composers nevertheless managed to retain a large portion of music audiences. The most fashionable and important international style was 12-tone music as defined by Schönberg and his disciples. Important figures in this style include Ernst Křenek (1900–) of Austria, Luigi Dallapiccola (1904–) of Italy, Ben Weber (1916–) of the United States, and Pierre Boulez (1925–) of France. An American, Gunther Schuller (1925–), tried to combine jazz with the 12-tone technique. The German Karlheinz Stockhausen (1928–) was one of several composers to occasionally omit live performers in favor of purely electronic music.

The acceptance of the tape recorder after World War II made direct composition on tape possible. Composers used both natural sounds and electronically produced sounds in taped music. They altered the result in the laboratory, producing a synthesis of tones which cannot be performed except by tape playback. Electronic techniques have greatly extended the technical possibilities open to the composer and the range of musical expression.

Stockhausen and John Cage (1912–) of the United States became important figures in the development of *chance* or *aleatory* music. Unlike electronic music, aleatory music depends mainly upon live performance. But the composer does not specify all the pitches and rhythms of his compositions. Performers introduce random elements, and no two performances of a given work are the same.

Careers in Music

Serious music is one of the most difficult professions in which to achieve a high level of success. Many fully qualified candidates compete keenly for almost every desirable position. The most successful concert artists and operatic celebrities may earn several thousand dollars for a single performance. But many excellent musicians receive less for a whole year's work.

A person should have exceptional musical ability before he seriously considers a musical career. Mere interest and skill are not enough. To attain even minimum success, he needs absolute dedication—the conviction that music is the most important thing in life. He should become a musician only if he cannot imagine himself doing anything else.

Training for any career in music includes systematic groundwork in the principles of harmony and music theory. The would-be musician must know the music written for his instrument, and how to play the instrument.

TERMS USED IN MUSIC

*A cappella, *ah kah PEL uh*, is singing without accompaniment.

Accelerando, *ah chel er AHN doh*, means speeding up the tempo.

Accidentals, *ak sih DEN tulz*, are sharps, flats, and naturals not included in a key signature.

Adagio, *ah DAH joh*, means slow, but not as slow as largo.

Ad libitum, *ad LIHB ih tum*, allows the musician to play the written notes with great freedom.

Agitato, *ah jee TAH toh*, means restless or excited.

Allegretto, *al uh GRET oh*, means brisk and light, but not as fast as allegro.

Allegro, *uh LAY groh*, means fast and lively.

Andante, *ahn DAHN tay*, means smooth and flowing, at a moderate speed.

Andantino, *ahn dahn TEE noh*, means not quite andante. It usually means a little faster, but once meant a little slower.

Animato, *ah nee MAH toh*, means lively or animated.

Appassionato, *ah PAHS syo NAH tah*, means with great feeling.

*Canon is a strict form in which several voices sing or play the same tune one after another, overlapping, without variation.

Arpeggio, *ahr PEHJ oh*, is a series of tones played quickly, one right after another.

Brillante, *bree LAHN tay*, means bright or sparkling.

Cadenza, *kah DEN zuh*, is a solo passage where the performer displays his virtuosity.

*Cantata, *kahn TAH tah*, is a fairly short work for one or more soloists and orchestra, often with chorus.

Cantabile, *kahn TAH bee lay*, means songlike.

Chord is a group of related tones played together.

Clef is a sign that fixes the positions of certain notes on the lines and spaces of the staff.

Coda is the ending of a movement or other work.

Con brio, *kohn BREE oh*, means with liveliness and great spirit.

Con moto, *kohn MOH toh*, means with strong feeling of motion.

Crescendo, *kruh SHEN doh*, means growing louder.

Decrescendo, *day kruh SHEN doh*, means growing softer.

Diminuendo, *duh MIHN oo EHN doh*, means gradually growing softer.

Enharmonic keys are those that can be written in two different ways, but are played with exactly the same notes on a piano. Composers may write in F sharp major, rather than in G flat major, although the sound as played is identical.

*Espressivo, *ehs press SEE voh*, means with expression.

*Fantasia, *fan TAY zhuh*, is a fantasy—a work in no specific form, or in a free form.

Fifth is an interval of five steps between tones.

Figured bass is a system of figures attached to a bass melody that continues throughout a composition. The figures, which the composer writes under the melody, indicate successive harmonies of the composition. Figured bass is usually played on a keyboard instrument with a cello reinforcing the bass melody. The practice of figured bass began with opera about 1600 and lasted into the 1700's. It is a central element in baroque music. It is also called *basso continuo* or *thoroughbass*.

Finale, *fuh NAH lee*, is the ending—the last act or scene of an opera or the last movement in a symphony, concerto, or other work.

Flat is the half step below a given tone, bearing the same letter name as that tone.

Forte, *FAWR tay*, means strong and loud.

Fortissimo, *fawr TISS ih moh*, means as loud as possible.

Glissando, *glih SAHN doh*, means sliding.

Grace note is a single note or part of a group used in a melody. It is printed in small type and subtracts its time value from the note which follows.

Interval is the difference in pitch between two tones, expressed in the steps of the scale.

*Key is the "home" center of a musical work.

Larghetto, *lahr GET oh*, means slower than adagio, but not as slow as largo.

Largo, *LAHR go*, means extremely slow.

Ledger line is a short line drawn above or below the

ment itself. He should complete at least a general high school course, taking private music lessons at the same time. He should then study music in a college or conservatory, or with private teachers. While he studies formally, he must also study and practice independently. He will soon discover that, in the final analysis, the greatest musicians are those who continue to learn.

Opportunities. Most persons who study music would like to become recognized performers or composers. But teaching music in public and private schools offers the largest number of career opportunities. Many composers earn their living by teaching, or by arranging or orchestrating the works of others. Musicians perform in symphony orchestras or dance bands, or in the small groups that play in theaters, on television or radio programs, or at public affairs. A few exceptionally talented musicians perform as soloists with orchestras or opera companies, or give solo concerts.

Several career fields combine musical talent with other interests. Concert management is a specialized field requiring a knowledge of both music and business. Music critics and historians must have the special abilities of both musicians and writers. The recording industry has openings for knowledgeable persons.

International cultural exchange programs and the role of the performing arts as an element in national prestige have grown in importance. Therefore, jobs have opened in arts programs with major foundations and with government information services. *Ethnomusicology,* which studies music as a key to understanding a society, is an important new field combining the arts and social studies. The field of serious jazz study is also gaining acceptance. The increase in community orchestras and choral groups provides additional opportunities for employment.

Before a student can enter any of these careers, he must spend much time in preparation. But even a little success justifies a great deal of hardship and effort. Few successful professional musicians regret their choice of a way of life.

ROBERT C. MARSH

Critically reviewed by HALSEY STEVENS and JAMES SYKES

Related Articles. See the Arts section of the articles on various countries, such as Mexico (Arts). See also the following articles:

BIOGRAPHIES

For biographies of other persons relating to Music, see the lists of Related Articles at the end of HYMN; MUSICAL COMEDY; ORCHESTRA; ORGAN; PIANO; POPULAR MUSIC; SINGING; and VIOLIN. See also:

AMERICAN COMPOSERS

Barber, Samuel	Cadman, Charles W.
Bernstein, Leonard	Copland, Aaron
Blitzstein, Marc	Cowell, Henry
Bloch, Ernest	Damrosch (Walter J.)

─ TERMS USED IN MUSIC ─

staff. It is used for any note that is too high or too low to be drawn on the staff.

Legato, *lay GAH toh,* means graceful and smooth.

Maestoso, *mah es TOH zoh,* means majestic.

Major scale is one of the two basic modes of music. A major scale has two *tetrachords* (half scales), each rising two whole steps and then a half step. All major scales follow a set pattern which contains whole step and half step intervals as follows: two wholes, one half, three wholes, one half. On any of the *chromatic* half steps within a given octave, a major scale may be built, using this pattern.

***Measure** or **Bar** is a unit of musical time containing an indicated number of beats.

Mezzo, *MED zoh,* means medium. It modifies other terms, as in **mezzo forte** (fairly loud).

Minor scale is one of the two basic modes of music. There are three forms of minor scales starting on any given tone. They are *harmonic minor scale,* the most frequently used form of minor; *natural minor scale;* and *melodic minor scale.*

Moderato, *MAHD uh RAH toh,* means playing in moderate tempo.

Modulation, *mahd you LAY shun,* is moving from one key to another. This may involve a change in the key signature.

Molto, *MOHL toh,* means a great deal or very much. It modifies other terms, as in **molto allegro** (very fast).

Natural is a note that is neither sharp nor flat.

Non troppo, *nohn TROHP oh,* means not too much or not exaggerated.

Obbligato, *ahb luh GAH toh,* is an accompanying part.

Octave, *AHK tihv,* is an interval of eight notes.

Pianissimo, *pee uh NISS ih moh,* means as soft as possible.

Piano, *pee AH noh,* means soft.

Pitch is the highness or lowness of a tone, depending on the number of times that its sound waves vibrate in a second.

Più, *pyoo,* means more. It modifies other terms, as in **più presto** (faster than presto).

Pizzicato, *pit suh KAH toh,* means plucking the strings of a violin or other bowed instrument.

Poco, *POH koh,* means little.

***Polyphony,** *puh LIHF uh nee,* means having several voices sing or play several melodies at the same time.

Prestissimo, *press TIHS uh moh,* means fast as possible.

Presto, *PRESS toh,* means very fast.

Rallentando, *RAHL len TAHN doh,* means gradually slowing the tempo.

***Round** is a short form in which several voices sing the same theme, overlapping, one after another.

Scale is a series of tones or steps leading from one tone to its octave.

***Scherzo,** *SKEHR tso,* is a whimsical movement or work, often highly rhythmic.

Sforzando, *sfaor TSAHN doh,* means with a sudden, strong accent.

Sharp is the half step above a given tone, bearing the same letter name as that tone.

Song cycle is a group of poems set to music as a unit.

Sostenuto, *sahs tuh NOO toh,* means sustaining the tone.

Sotto voce, *soht toh* or *SAHT oh VOH chay,* means in a low, soft voice, almost a whisper.

Staccato, *stuh KAH toh,* means with clearly distinct tones, sharply separated from one another.

Staff consists of five horizontal lines and the spaces between them. Notes are written on the lines and spaces.

Tetrachord, is a four-note half scale, rising two and a half steps. Differences in the location of the half steps are the chief difference between major and minor modes.

Third is an interval whose tones are written on adjacent lines or adjacent spaces of the staff, such as C-E or G♯-B.

Tremolo, *TREHM uh toh,* means quivering or trembling.

Triad is a chord made up of a *root* note and the notes a third and a fifth above it.

Vibrante, *vee BRAHN tay,* means pulsing or vigorous.

Vivace, *vee VAH chay,* means lively or played with great speed.

*Has an article in WORLD BOOK.

De Koven, Reginald
Dello Joio, Norman
Ganz, Rudolph
Gershwin, George
Gould, Morton
Grainger, Percy A.
Grofé, Ferde
Hanson, Howard H.
Harris, Roy
Hindemith, Paul

AUSTRIAN COMPOSERS

Berg, Alban
Bruckner, Anton
Czerny, Karl
Haydn, Joseph
Mahler, Gustav
Mozart, Wolfgang Amadeus
Schnabel, Artur
Schönberg, Arnold
Schubert, Franz P.
Strauss, Oscar
Strauss (family)

BRITISH COMPOSERS

Britten, Benjamin
Byrd, William
Delius, Frederick
Dowland, John
Elgar, Sir Edward W.
Gibbons, Orlando
Gilbert and Sullivan
Goossens, Sir Eugene
Morley, Thomas
Purcell, Henry
Tallis, Thomas
Vaughan Williams, Ralph
Walton, Sir William

FRENCH COMPOSERS

Berlioz, Louis Hector
Bizet, Georges
Couperin, François
Debussy, Claude
Delibes, Léo
D'Indy, Vincent
Dukas, Paul A.
Fauré, Gabriel U.
Franck, César A.
Gounod, Charles F.
Honegger, Arthur
Ibert, Jacques
Lalo, Édouard
Lully, Jean B.
Massenet, Jules É. F.
Milhaud, Darius
Offenbach, Jacques
Poulenc, Francis
Rameau, Jean Philippe
Ravel, Maurice
Saint-Saëns, Camille
Satie, Erik
Thomas, Ambroise

GERMAN COMPOSERS

Bach (family)
Beethoven, Ludwig van
Brahms, Johannes
Bruch, Max
Buxtehude, Dietrich
Gluck, Christoph W.
Handel, George F.
Humperdinck, Engelbert
Mendelssohn, Felix
Meyerbeer, Giacomo
Praetorius, Michael
Reger, Max
Schumann, Robert; (Clara)
Spohr, Louis
Strauss, Richard
Wagner, Richard
Weber, Carl Maria von

ITALIAN COMPOSERS

Bellini, Vincenzo
Boccherini, Luigi
Busoni, Ferruccio B.
Cherubini, Luigi
Clementi, Muzio
Corelli, Arcangelo
Dallapiccola, Luigi
Donizetti, Gaetano
Leoncavallo, Ruggiero
Mascagni, Pietro
Monteverdi, Claudio
Paganini, Niccolò
Palestrina, Giovanni
Pergolesi, Giovanni B.
Puccini, Giacomo
Respighi, Ottorino
Rossini, Gioacchino A.
Scarlatti (family)
Tartini, Giuseppe
Verdi, Giuseppe
Vivaldi, Antonio

RUSSIAN COMPOSERS

Arensky, Anton
Borodin, Alexander
Glinka, Mikhail I.
Khachaturian, Aram I.
Mussorgsky, Modest
Prokofiev, Sergei S.
Rachmaninoff, Sergei V.
Rimsky-Korsakov, Nicholas
Rubinstein, Anton G.
Scriabin, Alexander
Shostakovich, Dimitri
Stravinsky, Igor F.
Tchaikovsky, Peter I.

OTHER COMPOSERS

Albéniz, Isaac
Bartók, Béla
Chávez, Carlos
Chopin, Frédéric F.
Dohnányi, Ernst von
Dvořák, Antonin
Falla, Manuel de
Garcia, Manuel [1775; 1805])
Ginastera, Alberto
Grieg, Edvard
Janáček, Leoš
Kodály, Zoltán
Kubelík (Jan)
Lehár, Franz
Liszt, Franz
Moszkowski, Moritz
Nielsen, Carl A.
Paderewski, Ignace J.
Sibelius, Jan
Smetana, Bedřich
Villa-Lobos, Heitor
Wieniawski, Henri

KINDS OF MUSIC

Ballet
Chamber Music
Folk Music
Hymn
Jazz
Musical Comedy
Opera
Operetta
Oratorio
Popular Music
Program Music
Sacred Music

ELEMENTS OF MUSIC

Cadence
Counterpoint
Dynamics
Harmonics
Harmony
Homophony
Key
Measure
Melody
Natural Key
Pitch
Polyphony
Rhythm
Sound
Tempo
Tie
Timbre
Tonality
Tone
Treble
Triplet

INSTRUMENTAL MUSICAL FORMS

Binary Forms
Concerto
Étude
Fantasia
Fugue
Gigue
Intermezzo
March
Overture
Rhapsody
Rondo
Round
Scherzo
Serenade
Sonata
Suite
Symphonic Poem
Symphony
Variations

MUSICAL INSTRUMENTS

Accordion
Bagpipe
Balalaika
Banjo
Bass
Bassoon
Bell
Bugle
Calliope
Castanets
Celesta
Cello
Cembalo
Chimes
Clarinet
Clavichord
Clavilux
Concertina
Cornet
Cymbal
Drum
Dulcimer
English Horn
Fife
Flageolet
Flute
Flügelhorn
French Horn
Glocken-spiel
Gong
Guitar
Hand Organ
Harmonica
Harmonium
Harp
Harpsichord
Horn
Hornpipe
Jew's-Harp
Lute
Lyre
Mandolin
Marimba
Mellophone
Oboe
Ocarina
Orchestra
Organ
Piano
Piccolo
Pipe
Recorder
Saxophone
Spinet
Tambourine
Theremin
Timbrel
Tom-Tom
Triangle
Trombone
Trumpet
Tuba
Ukulele
Viol
Viola
Violin
Virginal
Xylophone
Zither

VOCAL MUSIC

A Cappella
Alto
Aria
Ave Maria
Ballad
Barbershop
Bard
Barcarole
Baritone
Bass
Berceuse
Calypso
Canon
Cantata
Carol
Chantey
Chorale
Chorus
Contralto
Libretto
Lieder
Lullaby
Madrigal
Mastersinger
Meistersinger
Minnesinger
Minstrel
Monophony
Music
Passion
Recitative
Singing
Skald
Song
Soprano
Spiritual
Tenor
Troubadour
Trouvère
Voice
Yodel

OTHER RELATED ARTICLES

American Guild of Organists
American Society of Composers, Authors and Publishers
Band
Baton
Carillon
Cecilia, Saint
Conducting
Cossacks, Don

Folk Music
Greece, Ancient
(The Arts)
Indian, American (Music)
Metronome
Metropolitan Opera
Association
Muse
Music Clubs, National
Federation of
National Anthems
National Music Camp
Orchestra
Pulitzer Prizes
(Music)
Ragtime
Tin Pan Alley
Tuning Fork
Western Frontier Life
(Music)
Westminster Choir

Outline

I. Enjoying Music
A. Understanding Music
B. Judging Music

II. Musical Instruments
A. Stringed Instruments
B. Wood-Wind Instruments
C. Brass Instruments
D. Percussion Instruments
E. Keyboard Instruments
F. Other Instruments

III. Instrumental Music
A. Instrumental Solos
B. Chamber Music
C. Orchestral Music

IV. Vocal Music
A. Singing Voices
B. Songs
C. Choral Music
D. Opera
E. Oratorios

V. The Elements of Music
A. Sound in Music
B. Melody
C. Harmony
D. Rhythm
E. Tempo
F. Tone Color

VI. The Language of Music
A. Notation
B. Scores
C. Names of Compositions

VII. Musical Forms
A. Song Form
B. Sonata Form
C. Variation Form
D. Canon and Fugue
E. Free Form

VIII. History

IX. Careers in Music

Questions

How can we learn to enjoy music? To judge it?
What career opportunities await music students?
What is the distance between tones in the chromatic scale? How does the diatonic scale differ?
What is the difference between a note and a tone?
How do *art* songs differ from *popular* songs?
Who is generally credited with devising the musical staff? Why was this development important?
How are a concerto and a symphony similar?
What is the basis for the harmonic relationships in music?
Why did romantic composers disagree with the rules followed by classical composers?
How does a composer indicate the pitch of a tone?

Books for Young Readers

BALET, JAN B. *What Makes an Orchestra.* Oxford, 1951.
BRITTEN, BENJAMIN, and HOLST, IMOGEN. *The Wonderful World of Music.* Doubleday, 1958.
BULLA, CLYDE R. *Stories of Favorite Operas.* Crowell, 1959. This illustrated book presents the stories of 23 of the most popular operas.
DONIACH, SHULA. *Every Child's Book of Music and Musicians.* Ambassador, 1961.
HUGHES, LANGSTON. *The First Book of Jazz.* Watts, 1954.
KAUFMANN, HELEN L. *History's 100 Greatest Composers.* Grosset, 1957.
MONTGOMERY, ELIZABETH R. *The Story Behind Musical Instruments.* Dodd, 1953.
NORMAN, GERTRUDE. *The First Book of Music.* Watts, 1954. This brief history of music has descriptions of musical instruments, short biographical sketches of some of the composers, and other information.

Books for Older Readers

BERNSTEIN, LEONARD. *Leonard Bernstein's Young People's Concerts for Reading and Listening.* Simon & Schuster, 1962.
COMMINS, DOROTHY. *All About the Symphony Orchestra and What It Plays.* Random House, 1961. Thumbnail sketches of 46 important composers are included.
GROUT, DONALD J. *A History of Opera.* 2nd ed. Columbia, 1965.
GROVE, GEORGE, ed. *Dictionary of Music and Musicians.* 5th ed. Edited by Eric Blom. 9 vols. St. Martin's, 1954. Vol. 10, Supplementary vol. to the 5th ed., 1961.
HJELMERVIK, KENNETH, and BERG, RICHARD C. *Marching Bands.* Ronald, 1953.
HOWARD, JOHN TASKER, and BELLOWS, GEORGE K. *A Short History of Music in America.* Crowell, 1957.
LANG, PAUL HENRY. *Music in Western Civilization.* Norton, 1941.
MARSH, ROBERT C. *Toscanini and the Art of Conducting.* New rev. ed. Collier, 1962.
SHIPPEN, KATHERINE B., and SEIDLOVA, ANCA. *The Heritage of Music.* Viking, 1963.

Books of Music

BERTAIL, INEZ, ed. *Complete Nursery Song Book.* Rev. ed. Lothrop, 1954. This book contains 150 nursery songs.
BONI, MARGARET B., ed. *Fireside Book of Favorite American Songs.* Arranged for the piano by Norman Lloyd. Simon & Schuster, 1956. *The Fireside Book of Folk Songs.* Arranged for the piano by Norman Lloyd. 1947.
GLAZER, TOM, comp. *Tom Glazer's Treasury of Folk Songs.* Grosset, 1964.
LYONS, JOHN H. *Stories of Our American Patriotic Songs.* Vanguard, 1942.

MUSIC BOX is an instrument that plays tunes automatically. Steel pins protrude from a rotating cylinder driven by clockwork or a spring. The pins pluck metal teeth of various lengths, producing soft, high-pitched sounds of great delicacy. Several teeth may be tuned to the same note, so the box can repeat notes rapidly. Music boxes may be connected with clocks, and play certain tunes on the hour.

Early music boxes had tiny flute pipes instead of teeth, and gave an organlike sound. Joseph Haydn wrote many charming pieces for the instrument. In the 1800's, some inventors developed music boxes that had as many as 400 teeth. Small music-box movements are often built into powder boxes, cigarette boxes, bracelets, and other everyday objects.   KARL GEIRINGER

MUSIC CLUBS, NATIONAL FEDERATION OF, is the largest music organization in the world. It is devoted to developing and maintaining high music standards in the United States and its possessions.

The federation has about 600,000 members. Persons may join as individuals or through local music clubs, school clubs, choirs, choruses, conservatories, dance groups, or symphony orchestras.

The federation offers many awards and scholarships. Winners of the "Young Artist Auditions" receive $1,500 awards. The federation also sponsors "Cavalcade for Creative Youth," an annual contest for young composers, and it commissions works by American composers. It sponsors American Music Month and Parade of American Music in February and National Music Week in May. It publishes *Music Clubs Magazine* and *Junior Keynotes.* The federation was founded in 1898. The federation's headquarters are at 600 S. Michigan Avenue, Chicago, Ill. 60605.

Critically reviewed by the NATIONAL FEDERATION OF MUSIC CLUBS

MUSIC DRAMA. See MUSICAL COMEDY; OPERA; OPERETTA.

MUSICAL COMEDY

MUSICAL COMEDY is an entertainment written for the stage. It consists of a story, spoken in dialogue form, with songs, choruses, dances, and incidental music. *Musicals* are the unique contribution of the United States to world theater.

Nearly all well-known musical comedies originate on the Broadway stage in New York City, where they often play for several years to large audiences. The music is usually recorded and heard on radio and television by millions of people throughout the entire world. Many of our most popular and best-loved songs have originated in musical comedies.

Elements of Musical Comedy

The Story, called the *book*, is the most important thing in any musical comedy. It must be interesting and dramatic, and is usually amusing. The story must explain the characters and hold the interest of the audience throughout the *show*. It also connects the 20 or more musical numbers in the show.

The story may be original. But most musicals are based on older well-known novels, plays, or motion pictures. These include *The Three Musketeers*, *The Wizard of Oz*, *My Fair Lady* (based on George Bernard Shaw's *Pygmalion*), and *Oklahoma!* (based on the play *Green Grow the Lilacs*).

Music adds romantic color, humor, or drama to the story, particularly through the *lyrics*, or words, of the songs. Composers usually write original music, but may adapt classical or other music. For example, many of the musical themes for *Kismet* came from the music of Alexander Borodin.

Dancing provides variety, with colorful costumes and interesting patterns of steps, leaps, whirls, and general movement. Sometimes the dances merely entertain the audience. But they may also help tell the story with gestures and movements, as in Jerome Robbins' dances for *West Side Story* by Leonard Bernstein.

Staging a Musical Comedy

Writing. The writer, composer, and *lyricist*, or lyric writer, usually *collaborate*, or work together. Generally, the writer first works out a rough version of the story. The composer and lyricist locate places in the story where they want to write songs. At this point, all three begin working together to make a whole show out of the separate elements.

Sometimes the composer has an idea for a melody which he gives the lyricist, who then writes the words. Each one makes changes in order to accommodate the other.

Producing. When all the writing is completed, a producer or manager raises the money to put the musical on the stage. He tries to raise between $250,000 and $500,000 from various *angels*, or investors, who buy shares in the show. In return, they receive their investment and a certain percentage of the profits. The producer then selects a director to supervise the entire production. A scene-designer and a costume-designer prepare sketches from which the construction crew and

costumes can work. In a musical, there may be 10 or 12 different stage sets, compared to one or two for a "straight" play. Elaborate production details may include revolving stages and many special effects. A conductor joins the staff to direct the singers and the orchestra, and a *choreographer*, or dance director, plans and rehearses the movements of dancers and singers. A press agent writes publicity and advertising.

The producers and directors hold many auditions to select the *principals*, or stars, and the supporting players, chorus, and dancers. They usually look for versatile performers who combine acting with singing and dancing. Usually they hear from 2,000 to 3,000 singers in order to select 12 to 16 men and women for the chorus. From about 1,000 dancers tested, they select 16 or 20.

Rehearsals take place daily, for four or five weeks.

Performing. All musical comedies play six to ten weeks in cities outside New York in order to change, cut, and improve the show. They also hold daytime rehearsals during these *out-of-town tryouts*.

Opening night on Broadway may make the difference between a *hit* and a failure. If the newspaper critics and the first-night audience like the musical, it will probably enjoy a long *run*. *Road companies* of the show may play in American cities, while other companies perform abroad.

History

Beginnings. The first musical comedy is generally considered to be an English work, John Gay's *The*

Musical Comedies draw large audiences to theaters in all parts of the world. They are among the most popular forms of stage entertainment. The "hit" musical *My Fair Lady*, with words by Alan Jay Lerner and music by Frederick Loewe, won immediate popularity on stage and on records.

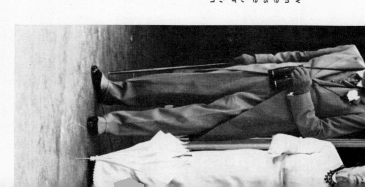

Friedman-Abeles

Beggars' Opera, written in 1728. But the musical-comedy form has had its widest development in the United States. It developed largely out of German operettas of the late 1800's and early 1900's. The most famous of these included Franz Lehár's *The Merry Widow; The Gypsy Baron* by Johann Strauss, Jr.; and Oscar Straus' *The Chocolate Soldier*. Operettas contained semiclassical music derived partly from grand opera and partly from folk songs. The stories dealt largely with romantic, somewhat improbable situations. American composers such as Victor Herbert, Rudolf Friml, and Sigmund Romberg also wrote operettas. See OPERETTA.

The 1900's have seen a great variety of more solid and original musical comedies. In the 1920's, Vincent Youmans wrote scores for such shows as *No, No Nanette* (1924), and *Hit The Deck* (1927). The books he used seem out of style today, but songs like "Tea for Two" and "Hallelujah" are still popular.

Composers soon began to choose more realistic books and to write more varied music—gay, lyrical, and even serious. These trends resulted in such musical comedies as Jerome Kern's *Show Boat* (1927) and *Roberta* (1933), Cole Porter's *Kiss Me, Kate* (1948), Irving Berlin's *Annie Get Your Gun* (1946), and George Gershwin's *Of Thee I Sing*, which won the 1932 Pulitzer prize.

The trend to collaboration began in the 1930's. Composers and lyricists worked together to produce musical comedies which have enjoyed great popularity. The team of Richard Rodgers and Lorenz Hart wrote many shows, including *A Connecticut Yankee* (1927) and *By*

Jupiter (1942). After Hart died, Rodgers teamed with Oscar Hammerstein II to write some of the most successful musical comedies in stage history. These include *Oklahoma!* (1943), *Carousel* (1945), and *South Pacific* (1949). Frederick Loewe and Alan Jay Lerner collaborated on *Brigadoon* (1947) and *My Fair Lady* (1956).   LEHMAN ENGEL

Related Articles in WORLD BOOK include:

Berlin, Irving	Lehár, Franz
Friml, Rudolf	Porter, Cole
Gershwin, George	Rodgers, Richard
Hammerstein (Oscar II)	Romberg, Sigmund
Herbert, Victor	Straus, Oscar
Kern, Jerome	Strauss, Johann (1825-1899)

MUSICAL INSTRUMENT. See MUSIC (Musical Instruments).

MUSICAL NOTATION. See MUSIC (Notation).

MUSICIAN. See the Careers section in MUSIC; RADIO; TELEVISION.

MUSICIANS, AMERICAN FEDERATION OF, is a labor union affiliated with the American Federation of Labor and Congress of Industrial Organizations. It has local unions in the United States and Canada.

The Federation claims jurisdiction over nearly all workers in the field of music. These include instrumental performers, arrangers, copyists, orchestra librarians, conductors, and music machine operators.

The union was founded in 1896 in Indianapolis, Ind. It has headquarters at 425 Park Ave., New York 22, N.Y. It publishes the monthly *International Musician*. For membership, see LABOR (table).   HERMAN D. KENIN

See also PETRILLO, JAMES CAESAR.

803

MUSICK, EDWIN C.

MUSICK, EDWIN C. See AVIATION (Red-Letter Dates [1935]).

MUSK is an ingredient in many expensive perfumes. It is used to preserve the fragrance—or add to the fragrance—of perfumes, and sometimes to add to the fragrance—of perfumes. Musk is formed as a liquid in a gland of the male musk deer, an animal that lives in the mountains of China and India. The gland lies under the skin of the male's abdomen. When the gland is removed and dried, the musk forms into grains. The grains are extracted with alcohol to produce the perfume ingredient.

MUSK DEER is a small, clumsy-looking deer. It roams the mountainous forests of central, eastern, and northeastern Asia. It gets its name from a globe-shaped musk gland in the skin of the male's abdomen. Musk from this gland is used in making perfume. The musk in one gland weighs about an ounce when dried. Because of the value of musk, the deer has been hunted, trapped, and snared until it is nearly extinct.

The musk deer has no antlers. It stands from 20 to 24 inches tall at the shoulders, and about 2 inches higher at the rump. Its hind legs are longer and heavier than the front legs. The deer's coarse, brittle hair is yellowish-brown to dark brown. The male deer has a pair of long canine teeth it uses for fighting.

The musk deer roams about alone instead of ranging in herds like other deer. It comes out only at night, to feed on lichens, grass, roots, and twigs of shrubs. Musk deer mate in January, and the doe bears a single spotted fawn the following June.

Scientific Classification. The musk deer belongs to the deer family, *Cervidae*. It forms the subfamily *Moschinae*. The musk deer is classified as genus *Moschus*, species *M. moschiferus*.

VICTOR H. CAHALANE

MUSK HOG. See PECCARY.

MUSK OX is a shaggy, slow, clumsy-looking animal that lives in the far north. The *bull* (male) gives off a musklike odor during its breeding season. Adult bulls are about 7 to 8 feet long, 4 to 5 feet high, and weigh as much as 900 pounds. The cows are smaller. Musk oxen are covered with long, shaggy, dark-brown hair—curly and matted over the humped shoulders, and straight on the rest of the body. Musk oxen are agile even though their short, stocky legs make them look awkward. The animals have short tails and hoofs like those of cattle. The bull has massive, sharp-pointed horns that curve down, outward, and up. A pair of horns may measure 29 inches across.

Musk oxen feed on grass, willows, lichens, and other small plants. They once roamed in large numbers throughout the American arctic regions. But they have been almost wiped out by hunters. Musk oxen live along the arctic coast of the Northwest Territories of Canada, on some of the islands to the north and east, and in Greenland. A few musk oxen also live on Nunivak Island in Alaska.

Scientific Classification. The musk ox belongs to the bovid family, *Bovidae*. The musk ox is genus *Ovibos*, species *O. moschatus*.

See also ANIMAL (color picture: Polar Regions).

DONALD F. HOFFMEISTER

MUSKEGON, *mus KEE gun*, Mich. (pop. 46,485; met. area 149,943; alt. 620 ft.), lies on the east shore of Lake Michigan, 110 miles northeast of Chicago. Its location

has made it a thriving industrial center. For location, see MICHIGAN (political map).

Industries. Factories in Muskegon produce machinery, motors, billiard and bowling equipment, electric cranes, chemicals, gasoline pumps, knit goods, office and school furniture, paper, and wire products. The city also has metal refining and molding plants, oil refineries, and furnaces and foundries for gray iron, alloy iron, and steel, brass, and aluminum castings.

Transportation. The natural landlocked harbor, formed by the mouth of the Muskegon River, makes the city one of the largest ports in Michigan in tonnage handled. In the early 1960's, it handled more than 3,225,000 tons a year, 121,000 tons of which was in overseas trade. Ferries carry railroad cars, automobiles, and passengers across Lake Michigan to Wisconsin ports.

History. In 1812, Jean Baptiste Recollet set up a trading post on the site of Muskegon. The city derives its name from a Chippewa Indian word meaning *river with marshes*. Muskegon was once a center of the Michigan lumber industry. During the 1880's, it had 47 sawmills. The lumber industry declined after 1890 when the supply of lumber began to dwindle, and a number of mills burned. But the city industrialized rapidly and now has about 175 manufacturing plants. Muskegon was incorporated as a village in 1860, and received its city charter in 1869. It has a council-manager form of government.

WILLIS F. DUNBAR

Cultural Institutions. Muskegon is the home of an art gallery, donated by Charles H. Hackley. The city also has a community college, a museum, a manual training school, and a vocational school.

MUSKELLUNGE, *MUS kuh lunj*. There are more than 20 ways to spell the name *muskellunge*. This famous game fish is the largest species of the pike family. It sometimes reaches a length of nearly 8 feet and a weight of about 70 pounds. The muskellunge looks much like the common pike. But it does not have the dusky bars or spots of varying size on its olive to silvery-gray skin.

The muskellunge lives in the lakes and quiet rivers of southern Canada. It is also found in the upper Mississippi Valley, the Great Lakes, and the Saint Lawrence and Ohio rivers. People consider it among the best of food fishes, equal to the black and striped bass.

The "muskie" is a prize among fishermen, who troll to catch it. The tremendous size and strength of the muskellunge makes a stout line and a heavy hook necessary. Fishermen use live bait to lure the fish. For many years, the state of New York has hatched and stocked a kind of muskellunge known as *Chautauqua muskellunge*. This type reaches a length of 5 feet. It is also called *salmon pike* or *white pickerel*. The Chautauqua muskellunge has white, delicious flesh.

Scientific Classification. The muskellunge belongs to the pike family, *Esocidae*. It is genus *Esox*, species *E. masquinongy*. The Chautauqua muskellunge is *Esox masquinongy*; subspecies *ohiensis*; the northern, *E. masquinongy immaculatus*; and the Great Lakes muskellunge, *E. masquinongy masquinongy*.

See also FISH (color picture: Fresh-Water Fishes); FISHING (table: Game-Fishing World Records).

CARL L. HUBBS

MUSKET was the firearm that infantry soldiers used before the perfection of the rifle. The name was first used in Italy in the 1500's to describe heavy hand guns.

It may have come from the Italian word *moschetto*, meaning *young sparrow hawk*, or from the name of an Italian inventor, Moschetta of Feltro. Some people believe the musket originated in Russia and that the name comes from *Muscovy*, which was the early name for Russia.

Early muskets were 6 or 7 feet long, and weighed 40 pounds or more. They fired either single round balls or round balls with smaller lead balls called *buckshot*. They were loaded from the muzzle. The first muskets were *matchlocks*, guns in which a cord match set off the powder charge. They were followed by flintlocks, *wheel locks*, in which a revolving wheel set off sparks, and *caplocks*, in which a paper held the explosive charge. Muskets were so inaccurate that men found it difficult to hit a target more than 100 yards away. But they continued in military use long after the invention of the rifle. A man could slip a round musket ball easily down the barrel, but he had to pound rifle bullets down.

Muskets were used extensively in the Revolutionary War and the Napoleonic wars. The infantrymen stood in parallel lines and fired at each other. Today, a few squads with rifles and machine guns could defeat a regiment of men with muskets.   JACK O'CONNOR

See also BLUNDERBUSS; FLINTLOCK; HARQUEBUS; POWDER HORN.

MUSKHOGEAN. See INDIAN, AMERICAN (North American Indian Languages [Hokan-Siouan]).

MUSKIE, EDMUND SIXTUS (1914-   ), was the Democratic candidate for Vice-President of the United States in 1968. Vice-President Hubert H. Humphrey and Muskie were defeated by their Republican opponents, Richard M. Nixon and Governor Spiro T. Agnew of Maryland.

Early Life. Muskie was born on March 28, 1914, in Rumford, Me. His father, a tailor, had come to the United States from Poland in 1903. He changed the family name from Marcisczweski. Edmund's mother, who came from Buffalo, N.Y., recalled that he was a quiet boy who "wouldn't even play with other children, he was so bashful."

Edmund worked his way through Bates College in Lewiston, Me. He was elected to Phi Beta Kappa, and graduated in 1936. He graduated from Cornell University Law School in 1939, and started to practice law in Waterville, Me. Muskie served as a naval officer during World War II.

In 1948, Muskie married Jane Gray (1927-   ) of Waterville. The Muskies had five children, Stephen (1949-   ), Ellen (1951-   ), Melinda (1956-   ), Martha (1958-   ), and Edmund, Jr. (1961-   ).

Political Career. Muskie began his political career in 1946, when he was elected to the Maine House of Representatives.

He was re-elected in 1948 and 1950, and became minority leader of the few Democrats in the House of Representatives.

Muskie not only was elected governor of a heavily Republican state in 1954, but he was re-elected two years later. He was the first Democratic governor of Maine to be re-elected since the Civil War. As governor, Muskie promoted economic and educational improvements, and stepped up control of water pollution.

Muskie was elected to the U.S. Senate in 1958, and won re-election in 1964.   CARROLL KILPATRICK

See also HUMPHREY, HUBERT H.

MUSKINGUM COLLEGE. See UNIVERSITIES AND COLLEGES (table).

MUSKMELON is the fruit of a plant that belongs to the gourd family. Muskmelons grow on vines that are sometimes nearly 7 feet long. Two or three melons grow on each vine. They are closely related to Persian melons and cucumbers. Muskmelons may vary greatly in the size and color of the rind and flesh. The *honeydew* melon has a green, smooth rind and green flesh; the *cantaloupe* has a yellowish-brown and yellow-orange

United Fresh Fruit, Vegetable Assn.

J. Horace McFarland

Muskmelons grow on long, leafy vines and may vary greatly in skin texture. Tip Tops, *above left*, have a smooth skin with evenly spaced ridges. The cantaloupe, *above*, has a coarse, fibrous skin.

Edmund S. Muskie

LEADING MUSKMELON GROWING STATES

Tons of muskmelons grown in 1967

State	Tons
California	389,100 tons
Texas	96,700 tons
Arizona	77,350 tons
Georgia	16,500 tons
Indiana	13,750 tons
Michigan	9,350 tons

Source: *Vegetables—Fresh Market, 1967 Annual Summary,* U.S. Department of Agriculture

flesh. The seeds of all varieties attach to a netlike fiber in a central hollow of the melon. Ripe muskmelons have a distinctive, sweet flavor, and give off an odor which is much like that of musk. The outer shell or rind of muskmelons is fairly hard. The thick inner layer of juicy pulp is the portion of the melon eaten.

Muskmelons can be grown only during the warm season. High quality muskmelons grow in nearly every state. In the United States, more than 80 per cent of the commercial crop grows in Arizona, California, and Texas. In late spring, farmers plant from 5 to 8 muskmelon seeds in hills which are spaced 5 feet apart each way. The plants spread their vines in all directions. As the fruits become mature, they take on a rich color and begin to separate from the stem. The cells which connect the fruit to the plant break down and pull away from the stems. A fruit which is partly separated from the stem is ripe and ready to be harvested.

Until recently, people thought that muskmelons had little food value. But today, we know that the yellow pulp of the muskmelon is a rich source of vitamins A and C. Melons have a fuel value of 185 calories per pound. They are made up of about 89.5 parts water, 9.3 parts carbohydrates, 0.6 parts ash, and 0.6 parts protein. Muskmelons are also a mild laxative.

Experts believe that muskmelons were grown first in India. But, by very early times, people in Asia and in Egypt also grew them. The ancient Romans and Greeks ate muskmelons. In America, muskmelons have been cultivated since colonial days.

Muskmelons were first grown commercially about 1890. At that time, the small hard-shelled type of melon, which we call cantaloupe, was brought to America from the town of Cantalupo, Italy. Unlike older types, this kind of muskmelon can be shipped across the country.

See also MELON; GOURD.

Scientific Classification. Muskmelons belong to the gourd family, *Cucurbitaceae*. The muskmelon is genus *Cucumis*, species *C. Melo*. The cantaloupe is *C. melo*, variety *cantalupensis*.

ARTHUR J. PRATT

MUSKOGEE, *mus KOH gee,* Okla. (pop. 38,059; alt. 602 ft.), lies in rich farming country in the eastern part of the state (see OKLAHOMA [political map]). Industry in Muskogee centers around the processing of poultry, and the manufacture of glassware, clothing, corrugated boxes, steel products, and tire patches. Many of the city's residents work in government institutions located in Muskogee. These government institutions include the regional offices of the Veterans Administration, a veterans' hospital, the Five Civilized Tribes Indian Agency, the Eastern District Federal Court, and the Oklahoma State School for the Blind. Muskogee is also the home of Bacone College, a junior college for Indians.

Muskogee developed in the 1870's. But long before that, the Creek Indians settled in the area. Their language, Muskogee, gave the town its name. The city is the county seat of Muskogee County, and has a council-manager type of government.   JOHN W. MORRIS

MUSKOKA LAKES, *mus KOH kuh,* are a group of scenic lakes in the rocky uplands of southern Ontario. The swift-flowing Muskoka River drains the Muskoka Lakes into Georgian Bay. The lakes lie from 125 to 150

miles north of Toronto, Lake Muskoka, the largest of the group, covers 54 square miles. Lake Joseph, Lake of Bays, Rosseau Lake, and hundreds of smaller lakes lie nearby. There are many beautiful streams and waterfalls in the area surrounding the Muskoka Lakes.

The lake district is one of the most famous summer-resort regions in North America. Well-known resort centers in the area include Bala, Baysville, Bracebridge, Dorset, Gravenhurst, and Port Sydney. The area has extensive forests of balsam fir, pine, and spruce. The leaves of the birch and maple trees add vivid colors to the region each autumn.

D. F. PUTNAM

MUSKRAT is an animal that lives in swampy places near streams and rivers. Muskrats get their name from their unpleasant musklike odor. They live in many parts of North America, and in parts of Europe.

Muskrats are suited to life in the water. They have scaly, somewhat flattened tails that they use to steer themselves in the water. The webbed toes on their hind feet help them swim. Muskrats grow about a foot long and have a 10-inch tail. Their light-brown fur is sold as "Hudson seal" after it has been dyed and the longer, coarser hairs have been removed. Muskrat meat is tasty, and is sold as "marsh rabbit."

Most muskrats live in *burrows* (tunnels) that they

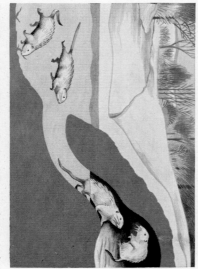
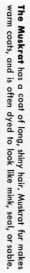

Cross-Section of a Muskrat Burrow. The tunnel opens under water, so that the animals can swim in and out under the ice,

R. M. Cady, Courtesy Pennsylvania Game Commission

The Muskrat has a coat of long, shiny hair, Muskrat fur makes warm coats, and is often dyed to look like mink, seal, or sable.

dig in the banks of streams. They often damage dikes and levees as they dig. They also make houses by plastering water plants such as cattails and reeds together with mud. Muskrat houses usually have more than one underwater entrance. There may also be an entrance above water.

Muskrats eat a variety of foods. They eat green vegetation, berries, twigs, and corn and other farm crops. They even eat snails, the meat from *carcasses* (dead animals), and the plants that make up the insides of their own houses.

Muskrats increase rapidly after they move into a region. Female muskrats give birth to as many as three litters of three to eight young each year. As a result, the muskrat population often increases rapidly and the animals may soon become overcrowded. Also, muskrats fight a great deal among themselves. Many of them travel as much as 20 miles to find peaceful homes away from other muskrats.

Muskrats are rodents. They are related to lemmings and voles, but are somewhat larger than these animals.

Scientific Classification. The muskrat belongs to the subfamily *Microtinae*, of the New World rat and mouse family *Cricetidae*. The muskrat is genus *Ondatra*, species *O. zibethicus*. DANIEL H. BRANT

See also FUR; TRAPPING.

MUSLEM, or **MUSLIM.** See MOSLEMS.

MUSLIN, *MUZ lin,* is a closely woven white or unbleached cotton cloth. It is named for the city of Mosul, in Iraq, where it was first made. The British use the word *muslin* to mean sheer cotton fabrics, but in the United States, muslin means a firm cloth for everyday use. Wide muslin is called *sheeting*.

MUSSEL, *MUS'l,* is an animal that lives in water. Its body is covered with a protective shell made up of two similar pieces called *valves.* The valves are joined at one point by a hinge, and can be opened and closed somewhat like a lady's compact. The mussel's body lies inside the shell, and consists of various organs including the foot, gills, stomach, and heart. *Fresh-water mussels* live in streams and lakes. *Sea mussels* live in ocean water.

Several kinds of sea mussels can be eaten. The common blue mussel, which is from 3 to 6 inches long, is a popular food in Europe. Its shell is bluish black on the outside and pearly-blue on the inside. The sea mussels use the *foot* to spin long, silky threads called a *byssus.* The byssus anchors the mussel to a rock, where it may spend the rest of its life.

Fresh-water mussels are a valuable source of *mother-of-pearl,* which lines the inside of their shells. Mother-of-pearl is used to make pearl buttons.

Scientific Classification. Mussels are in the phylum *Mollusca.* Sea mussels belong to the family *Mytilidae.* The common mussel is in the genus *Mytilus,* and is species *M. edulis.* Fresh-water mussels are in the fresh-water mussel family, *Unionidae.* There are many genera, including *Anodonta* and *Elliptio.* R. TUCKER ABBOTT

See also BUTTON; MOTHER-OF-PEARL; PEARL; SHELL.

MUSSET, *myoo SAY,* **ALFRED DE** (1810-1857), was a French poet, dramatist, and novelist. He is remembered chiefly for his plays, *Comédies et Proverbes* (1840). He wrote these in a witty, poetic style, and they reveal a deep understanding of the inner motives of the characters. Musset believed that a writer should experience suffering to create good literature. He published his first book of poems, *Tales of Spain and Italy,* in 1829. He wrote his best poems in memory of his love for the famous woman writer George Sand (see SAND, GEORGE). Musset was born in Paris. He spent most of his adolescence among writers. WALLACE FOWLIE

MUSSOLINI, *moos soh LEE nee,* **BENITO** (1883-1945), founded Fascism and ruled as dictator of Italy for almost 21 years. He tried to build Italy into a great empire. Instead, he left it occupied by the armies of other nations.

As dictator, Mussolini took the title *Il Duce,* the leader. He reduced unemployment, and improved the railway service. But the price of his reforms was the enslavement of the Italian people. He kept control by such methods as murder, exile, and the prison camp. He was a strong man, who gloried in his strength. He wanted the men of Italy to be soldiers, and the women to be mothers of soldiers. He loved to hear the acclaiming shouts of "Duce! Duce!" from his people.

Mussolini was not a religious or a moral man. He abolished the Roman Catholic youth organizations, and fought church influence in state affairs. But in 1929 he improved relations with the Roman Catholic Church by signing an agreement with Pope Pius XI. This gave the pope temporal powers in Vatican City.

Early Life. Mussolini was born on July 29, 1883, in Dovia, Italy. His mother was the village schoolmistress, and his father, a blacksmith. After attending school at Predappio, Mussolini was sent at the age of 14 to a school at Faenza operated by the Salesian Friars. But he rebelled against the strict discipline of the school, and was expelled for bad conduct. He then went to a normal school at Forlì and earned a degree.

Mussolini taught in an elementary school for a short time. In 1902 he went to Switzerland, and earned his living as a workman. During his stay there, he often

The Black, Ridged Shells of these fresh-water mussels have a pearly lining which makes them valuable for the manufacture of pearl buttons. The shells are hinged at the back.
Cornelia Clarke

United Press Int.

Benito Mussolini Loved Dramatic Poses. Clenched fist, jutting jaw, and theatrical actions were all part of his fiery speeches. Millions of Italians followed him blindly.

got into trouble with the police for vagrancy and fighting. He returned to Italy in 1904 to perform his required military service, then taught school in 1907 and 1908.

Mussolini went to Trent, Austria (now Trento, Italy), in 1909. He worked there for a socialist newspaper, and wrote several literary works. Again he got into trouble, this time for publicly supporting Italian claims to Trent, and was expelled from Austrian territory. Upon returning to Italy, he edited a socialist newspaper at Forlì. He became editor of *Avanti*, the leading socialist newspaper in Italy, in 1912.

Quarrels with Socialists. When World War I broke out, Mussolini aroused the anger of Socialist party leaders because he urged that Italy enter the war immediately against Germany. As a result, he was expelled from the Socialist party on Nov. 25, 1914.

Mussolini immediately founded his own newspaper, *Il Popolo d'Italia*. He wrote violent editorials trying to drive Italy into the war. When Italy did enter the war, he enlisted in the army and became a corporal. He served in the trenches from September, 1915, until he was wounded in February, 1917.

Fascist Dictator. In March, 1919, Mussolini founded in Milan the first political group to be called fascist (see FASCISM). At first, its program was strongly nationalistic, intended to appeal to discontented war veterans. Mussolini urged the Italian people to rebuild the glories of ancient Rome. Later, he drafted a program to win property-owning Italians to his cause. By October, 1922, his Fascist party was powerful enough to force the weak King Victor Emmanuel III to call on Mussolini to head the government.

His Conquests. In 1935 and 1936, he invaded and conquered Ethiopia. There, with machine-gun fire, his soldiers mowed down peaceful people who still used bows and arrows.

When the Spanish Civil War broke out in 1936, both Mussolini and Adolf Hitler decided to support the rebel leader, General Francisco Franco. They sent military forces to fight in Spain.

World War II. After Germany had almost completely conquered France in 1940, Mussolini entered World War II and invaded southern France. A few days later, France surrendered, but disaster after disaster followed elsewhere for the Italian armies. In Africa, Greece, and finally in Italy itself, Mussolini's armies met defeat. German forces kept Italy from total collapse for a time, but Mussolini had lost his cause.

The Fascist Grand Council turned against him in July, 1943, and he was overthrown and imprisoned. But German parachutists rescued him, and took him to Milan. He became the head of a puppet government there.

See also ITALY (History).

His Death. In the spring of 1945, the German forces in northern Italy collapsed. With his mistress Clara Petacci and 16 followers, Mussolini fled towards Switzerland. The Italian underground discovered them at Lake Como. After a brief trial, they shot Mussolini and Clara Petacci. Their bodies were taken to Milan, and hung by the heels in front of a garage. Later, his body was hidden to prevent demonstrations by his followers. In August, 1957, at the request of his widow, he was buried near Predappio.

R. JOHN RATH

MUSSORGSKY, *moo SAWRG skih,* or **MOUSORGSKI, MODEST** (1839-1881), a Russian composer, wrote the great opera, *Boris Godunov* (1874). It is considered a landmark, pointing a way toward realism in music for present-day composers. Mussorgsky wrote the words and the music for *Boris Godunov* from a play by Alexander Pushkin and from Nikolai Karamzin's *History of the Russian State* (1819-1826).

He conceived a musical setting that would be "true" rather than "beautiful." His "truth" involved realism in which speech is made more poignant by the accompanying music. Mussorgsky was influenced by Russian church services in which speech and music are combined. He also used rhythms and melodies of Russian folk songs. Stark harmonic and orchestral sounds emphasize the opera's drama.

Bettmann Archive

Modest Mussorgsky

Mussorgsky left much of his music unfinished and in a confused condition. His works include *St. John's Night on Bare Mountain* (1867) for orchestra; *Pictures from an Exhibition* (1874), a suite for piano, orchestrated in 1922 by Maurice Ravel; and the opera *Khovanthina*, completed in 1883 by Nicholas Rimsky-Korsakov. He was born in Karevo, Russia.

THEODORE M. FINNEY

MUSTACHE. See BEARD.

MUSTAFA, or **MUSTAPHA, KEMAL PASHA.** See KEMAL ATATÜRK.

MUSTAGH, or **KARAKORAM, RANGE.** See HIMALAYA.

MUSTANG is the name of the small, hardy wild horse that once roamed the American Southwest. It descended from the Spanish horses brought to America by Hernando Cortes. *Mustang* perhaps came from the Spanish word *mesteño,* meaning *strayed,* or *ownerless, horses.*

MUSTANG. See AIR FORCE (color picture, Fighting Planes of Three Wars).

MUTATION is a change in a *gene*, the part of a cell that determines the characteristics living things inherit from their parents. The changed gene produces a different inherited trait than it did before. The changed gene is then *transmitted* (passed on) to the generations that follow. Mutations may produce only a slight change, such as a change in the color of eyes, or they may produce great changes, such as new types or severe diseases. See GENE.

The new type of plant or animal produced by mutation is called a *mutant* or *sport*. Examples are the short-legged Ancon sheep, the white turkey, the platinum fox, and the pink grapefruit.

Mutations occur rarely. The rate of change varies among different kinds of plants and animals. Most mutant genes are *recessive* (remain undeveloped in the organism's cell). But a few are *dominant*, and take effect immediately. Most mutations cause harmful effects, such as the reduction in size of wings on a fly. However, sometimes a mutation is beneficial to an animal or plant, or is useful to man. Mutations have improved several farm crops.

Mutations are caused by a change in the order of units in a material called *deoxyribonucleic acid* (DNA). DNA makes up genes. DNA contains coded "instructions," on how the cell should duplicate and divide. Scientists can change the order of DNA units in the cell with radiation and chemical treatments. X ray, a kind of radiation, has been used in many experiments to cause mutations. However, scientists cannot tell in advance which genes will mutate. The way people inherit mutations is an important study in the science of *genetics*.

J. HERBERT TAYLOR

Related Articles in WORLD BOOK include:

Breeding	Heredity
Cell	Mink (picture: The White Mink)
De Vries, Hugo	Radiation (How Radiation
Evolution (Variation	Can Change Living Things)
and Change)	Sport

MUTE. See DEAF-MUTE.

MUTINY is a revolt against authority. The term has been popularly confined to an unlawful attempt by a crew to take command of a naval ship. But it applies to any concerted resistance by military personnel to lawful military authority. Mutiny is one of the gravest military offenses, and it may be punished by death. In 1842, Midshipman Philip Spencer, son of Secretary of War John C. Spencer, was hanged for mutiny, along with two seamen, on the U.S.S. *Somers*.   JOHN W. WADE

See also BLIGH, WILLIAM; PITCAIRN ISLAND; SEPOY REBELLION.

MUTSUHITO, *moo tsoo hee toh* (1852-1912), reigned as emperor of Japan from 1867 to 1912. Japan developed from a feudal state into an industrial and military power during his reign. He introduced Western ideas into the Japanese way of life.

He began his reign in a period of confusion. Japan had been ruled by shoguns, or ruling lords, for hundreds of years (see SHOGUN). Japanese noblemen persuaded the shogun to resign in 1867, and restored the ruling power to Emperor Mutsuhito. He adopted as his title *Meiji* (enlightened rule). He is known as the *Meiji emperor* (see JAPAN [History; picture]).

J. Horace McFarland

Lush Green Leaves of the Potherb Mustard Plant make an excellent summer vegetable that is high in vitamin content.

MUSTARD is the name of a family of leafy, annual plants that grow in temperate regions, such as the United States and Canada. People use a powder made from the seeds of certain kinds of mustard plants in salad dressing, to flavor meat, and in preparing pickles and some kinds of fish.

The leaves of mustard are large, thick, and rather jagged in shape. They have a deep green color. The leaves may be harvested while still tender, and eaten as *potherb* (greens). If the leaves are not harvested, the plant soon sends up a strong seed stalk and becomes unfit to eat.

Mustard is an easy crop to grow. Farmers sow the seeds for the spring crop about two weeks before the last frosts of spring. The seeds for fall crops should be sown about 50 days before the first autumn frosts. Popular varieties include black and white mustard. Both are annual plants, and grow from seeds.

White Mustard grows only about 2 or 3 feet in height. It has stiff branching stems, hairy leaves, bristly pods, and small brilliant yellow flowers. The seeds of the white mustard plant are yellowish.

Black Mustard grows to a height of 6 feet or more. Black mustard plants have bright yellow flowers, with smooth pods that lie close to the stem. Manufacturers use their dark brown seeds in commercial mustard products.

Mustard greens are an excellent source of vitamins A, B, and C. In addition, their bulk and fiber tend to have a mildly laxative effect. The oil which mustard seeds contain gives the substance its high flavor. It also makes mustard a valuable household remedy. Mixed with warm water, mustard can be used to cause vomiting. It can also be used in a plaster to relieve pain.

Many flowers of the mustard family have separate articles in WORLD BOOK. For a list of these flowers, see FLOWER (table: Families [Mustard]).

Scientific Classification. Mustards belong to the mustard family, *Cruciferae*. The common white mustard is genus *Brassica*, species *B. hirta*. Black mustard is *B. nigra*. Most mustards used for greens are *B. juncea*. S. H. WITTWER

MUSTARD GAS. See CHEMICAL-BIOLOGICAL-RADIOLOGICAL WARFARE.

MUT. See AMON (picture).

Mutsuhito set out to equal the military and economic power of the West. His government sponsored industries, gave the farmers title to their land, instituted education for all his people, and developed up-to-date military forces. He introduced a strong, Prussian-style constitution. Japan defeated China in 1895, and Russia in 1905. Mutsuhito made an alliance with England in 1902, and added Korea to Japan's territory in 1910. These developments established Japan as a great power.

Mutsuhito was born in Kyoto, a year before Commodore Matthew Perry arrived in Japan. He was enshrined as a god after his death.

MARIUS B. JANSEN

MUTTON is the flesh of grown sheep. The meat of young sheep is called *lamb*. The meat of a sheep becomes mutton when the animal is about a year old. Mutton is dark pink and has white fat. It is stronger in flavor and rougher than lamb. Americans eat less than a half pound of mutton and only about 4 pounds of lamb per person in a year. See also LAMB.

JOHN C. AYRES

MUTUAL BROADCASTING SYSTEM (MBS) is a radio network with outlets throughout the United States. The network has more than 470 affiliated stations from coast to coast. All MBS stations are independently owned and operated.

Four independent radio stations formed the network in 1934 as the Quality Group. These stations were WOR of New York City, WGN of Chicago, WLW of Cincinnati, and WXYZ of Detroit. Later in 1934, the name was changed to the Mutual Broadcasting System. In 1936, MBS became a coast-to-coast network. The Minnesota Mining and Manufacturing Company bought MBS in 1960. The network maintains its headquarters in New York City.

See also RADIO (The Radio Industry).

HAROLD GOLD

MUTUAL COMPANIES are businesses that are owned and operated by the users of the services they provide. Mutual companies include many insurance companies, banks, savings and loan associations, cooperatives, and credit unions. The government gives mutual companies special tax treatment because they do not seek *profit* in the usual sense. Instead, they pass on any *profits* to their members in the form of lower costs or insurance premiums, or higher interest paid on savings deposits.

See also CREDIT UNION; SAVINGS AND LOAN ASSOCIATION.

LEONARD C. R. LANGER

MUTUAL FUND is an investment company that is formed by a large number of persons who pool their money to invest in stocks and other securities. Unlike other types of investment companies, a mutual fund does not have a fixed amount of capital stock. Instead, investors may buy additional shares in the company at any time. For this reason, mutual funds are also called *open-end investment companies*.

Mutual fund shares are never bought or sold on stock exchanges. An investor can buy shares from an investment broker authorized by the fund. A few funds sell shares directly to investors. The purchaser pays the net asset value of the share plus an *acquisition cost* that covers selling and administrative expenses. A fund shareholder must sell his stock to the fund when he wants to dispose of it. The fund must buy back its shares at any time for their approximate net asset value.

Some mutual funds invest in only one type of security, such as common stocks. *Balanced funds* invest in a mixture of securities, including common stocks, preferred stocks, and bonds.

NICHOLAS ROTH

MUTUALISM. See SYMBIOSIS.

MUUMUU. See HAWAII (Clothing).

MVD, the Ministry of Internal Affairs, together with the KGB, the Committee of State Security, made up the police force in Russia. The MVD was responsible for conventional police protection and border police activities. The KGB is the secret police agency. Secret police have been a feature of Russian life under the czars and Communists. They were once called Cheka, GPU, OGPU, and then NKVD. The MVD and KGB were set up in 1946, when police powers in Russia were reorganized. In 1960, the MVD was abolished as a national organization. Some of its functions had already been transferred to the KGB. Each of the 15 Soviet republics have its own MVD.

WILLIAM B. BALLIS

MWANAMUTAPA EMPIRE. See ZIMBABWE.

MWERU, LAKE. See the map with the CONGO (KINSHASA) article.

MYCELIUM. See MUSHROOM (Parts of the Mushroom).

MYCENAE, *my SEE nee,* was a city in ancient Greece, located six miles north of Argos in the southern peninsula. German archaeologist Heinrich Schliemann uncovered five royal graves at the site of Mycenae in 1876. This discovery started the study of the Bronze Age on the Greek mainland. These graves, known as the *Shaft Graves,* contained jewels, bronze weapons, and other objects made of bronze, gold, and silver.

Mycenae was the leading political and cultural center on mainland Greece from about 1450 to 1100 B.C., and its influence spread as far east as Cyprus. The Late Bronze Age on the Greek mainland from 1580 to 1100 B.C. is often called the *Mycenaean* period, because of Mycenae's prominence. The city became famous for its royal palace, walled fortress, and beehive-shaped tombs for kings. The tombs can still be seen at the site. Dorians sacked the city in the late 1100's B.C., and Mycenae never regained its power.

See also ARCHITECTURE (Greek [picture: Lion Gate]).

NORMAN A. DOENGES

MYCOLOGY, *my KAHL oh jih,* is the study of fungi. *Field mycologists* specialize in the fungi found in fields and woods. *Medical mycology* deals with the fungi that cause human and animal diseases. *Industrial mycology* concerns the activities of fungi in rotting or spoiling raw materials and manufactured goods, and the uses of fungi in industrial fermentations. See also FUNGI.

MYELITIS, *MY uh LY tis,* means inflammation of the spinal cord or of the bone marrow. It is a general term, and does not tell the cause or location of the inflammation or injury. Poliomyelitis is one form of myelitis (see POLIOMYELITIS). Other forms include multiple sclerosis and rabies (see MULTIPLE SCLEROSIS; RABIES). Symptoms of myelitis diseases often include backache and paralysis.

IRVIN STEIN

MYLAR is the DuPont Company trademark for a transparent *polyester* film. It is durable and exceptionally strong, and can withstand corrosive materials and rough handling. It is an excellent electrical insulator, and industries use it to insulate wires, cables, and electronic parts. Mylar also is used to make metallic yarns, decorative materials, and magnetic tape.

See also PLASTICS.

CLIFFORD L. MILLER

Democracy (1944) is considered an outstanding study of race relations in the United States. Myrdal's studies of the economic and social development of underdeveloped nations led him to write *Asian Drama: An Inquiry into the Poverty of Nations* (1968). This book tries to tell why so many people of southern Asia are poor, and what, if anything, can be done about it.

Myrdal was born in Gustafs, near Sandviken, Sweden. His full name is KARL GUNNAR MYRDAL. He received a law degree and a doctor of laws in economics degree from the University of Stockholm. He was minister of commerce in the Swedish Cabinet from 1945 to 1947. He served as executive secretary of the United Nations Economic Commission for Europe from 1947 to 1957. In 1960, Myrdal became director of the Institute of International Economic Studies in Stockholm.

JAMES W. VANDER ZANDEN

MYRIAMETER. See METRIC SYSTEM (Tables of the Metric System).

MYRON. See DISCUS THROW.

MYRRH, *mur,* is a fragrant gum resin that is used in making perfume and incense. It comes from the trunks of certain small trees of the genus *Commiphora* that grow in eastern Africa and southern Arabia. Myrrh is sold to manufacturers in the form of *tears* (drops). The tears range in color from yellow to brown-red. Alcohol is added to the tears to dissolve the resin and leave the gum behind. The resin hardens, forming a hard, brown, resinlike substance that gives perfume and incense a spicy, heavy-oriental odor. When steam is passed through myrrh, a fragrant oil used in perfume and incense is produced.

Myrrh has been used in making incense and perfumes since ancient times. One of the Wise Men brought the infant Jesus a gift of myrrh (Matt. 2). PAUL Z. BEDOUKIAN

MYRTLE, *MUR t'l,* is an attractive evergreen shrub or small tree. It grows wild in regions along the Mediterranean Sea and temperate regions of Asia. Some persons in the United States cultivate it as an ornamental plant. The myrtle has shining blue-green leaves and fragrant white flowers. The leaves, bark, and berries are also fragrant. Manufacturers use them in making perfume. The bark is used in tanning industries of southern Eu-

Myrtle Blooms with Many Pretty Flat, White Flowers.

J. Horace McFarland

Santa Catalina Island Co.

The Myna Bird is often kept as a pet because of its ability to talk. These mynas rival parrots in their power to mimic human speech. Some of them can talk with amazing distinctness.

MYNA is the name given to several kinds of birds in the starling family. Myna birds are native to India, Burma, and other parts of Asia. The common *house myna* is a bold, fearless bird somewhat larger than a robin. Its handsome colors range from rich wine-brown on the lower breast to deep black on the head, neck, and upper breast. It has a prominent splash of white on the lower edge of its wings, and its bill and legs are a bright yellow. The myna feeds on plants, insects, and worms. It often builds its nest in crevices of buildings. The myna is a noisy, sociable bird that is common about yards and buildings. It is often seen strutting among chickens or perched on the backs of cattle.

The *crested myna* has long feathers on its forehead that form a permanent bushy crest. It lives in cultivated fields and pastures. The crested myna is sometimes so fearless that a person may approach within a few feet of one before it becomes alarmed. It has been brought to the Philippines, Japan, and British Columbia.

Talking mynas are sometimes kept as pets. Many learn to imitate the human voice, and can talk, sing, and whistle. They sometimes perform on television.

Scientific Classification. Mynas are in the starling family, *Sturnidae.* The common house myna is genus *Acridotheres,* species *A. tristis.* The crested myna is *A. cristatellus.* The talking myna is *Gracula religiosa.* GEORGE E. HUDSON

MYOCARDITIS, *MY oh kahr DIE tis,* is an inflammation of the myocardium, the muscular part of the heart. *Acute bacterial myocarditis* is caused by bacterial infection. *Toxic myocarditis* is due to poisons or drugs which reach the heart through the blood system.

MYOGLOBIN. See KENDREW, JOHN COWDERY.

MYOPIA. See NEARSIGHTEDNESS.

MYRDAL, *MIHR dahl,* **GUNNAR** (1898-   ), is a Swedish sociologist and economist. He gained fame for his thorough studies of major world problems. His book *An American Dilemma: The Negro Problem and Modern*

rope. Ancient Greeks thought myrtle was sacred to the goddess of love, Aphrodite. They used it in festivals.

The common periwinkle is often called *running myrtle*. It has creeping stems and attractive blue flowers.

Scientific Classification. Common myrtles belong to the myrtle family, *Myrtaceae*. They are classified as genus *Myrtus*, species *M. communis*. The common periwinkle is in the dogbane family, *Apocynaceae*. It is genus *Vinca*, species *V. minor*.

THEODORE W. BRETZ

See also BAYBERRY; GUAVA; PIMENTO.

MYRTLEWOOD. See LAUREL; WOOD.

MYSTERIES, *MIHS tur ihz,* were religious ceremonies held in ancient Greece and Rome. In these ceremonies, people worshiped certain gods and goddesses, especially Demeter (Ceres), Persephone (Proserpina), and Dionysus (Bacchus).

The word *mystery* comes from a Greek word meaning *one who keeps quiet,* indicating an *initiate,* or person introduced to the secret rites of a mystery. The initiates were sworn to silence, and they often were put to death if they revealed the secrets of the mysteries. Because most of the initiates did keep silent, scholars know little about the initiations, which were a central part of the mysteries.

The *Eleusinian Mysteries* were the greatest of all Greek mysteries. They were connected with the worship of Demeter, Persephone, and Pluto. These rites began in Athens, where the initiates first bathed in the sea. Then they marched to Eleusis in a religious procession. In the evening, certain ceremonies were spoken, revealed, and performed in the hall of mysteries at Eleusis. During the preliminary rites, initiates had to fast and partake of a sacred drink. The chief rites may have included a dramatic performance of the story of Pluto and Persephone, a symbolic descent into the underworld, and a revelation of Demeter, the grain goddess. The initiates were promised happiness in the next world.

The followers of Orpheus conducted the *Orphic Mysteries.* Orpheus is supposed to have founded these rites in honor of Dionysus. Those who believed in the Orphic religion also claimed to know the secret of happiness after death.

Mystic cults in the Roman world included those of Cybele (Rhea), Isis, and Mithras. These cults practiced magic rites, sacraments, purifications, and baptisms in their mysteries.

VAN JOHNSON

Related Articles in WORLD BOOK include:

Bacchus	Mithras	Proserpina
Ceres	Orpheus	Rhea
Isis	Pluto	

MYSTERY PLAY. See ENGLISH LITERATURE (The Age of Chaucer); MIRACLE PLAY; MORALITY PLAY; PASSION PLAY.

MYSTERY STORY is a term applied to two related types of prose fiction. One type presents the mystery of a crime and its solution. The other suggests the mystery of supernatural events. But the crime story may also suggest unnatural or devilish doings.

Mystery stories about crime are also known as *detective stories.* They are among the most popular works of contemporary fiction. Characteristically, they are carefully plotted schemes of crime and detection, clues and suspense, and sometimes pursuit and violence. Many readers gain enjoyment by trying to outguess the criminal in the story. Most stories of this type do not stress characterization, social scene, or serious comments on life. The Sherlock Holmes stories of Arthur Conan Doyle and the novels of Dorothy L. Sayers, Agatha Christie, Mary Roberts Rinehart, and Georges Simenon are famous examples of mystery stories about crime.

The term *mystery story* was formerly applied to tales of the supernatural such as Frank Stockton's *The Lady, or the Tiger* and Edgar Allan Poe's *The Gold Bug,* and to riddle stories.

CHARLES W. COOPER

MYSTIC SEAPORT, a reconstructed water-front village, is a reminder of maritime life in the days of the great sailing ships. It lies on the Mystic River in Mystic, Conn. For location, see CONNECTICUT (political map). Waterfront buildings and shops typical of the mid-1800's stand along Mystic Seaport's cobblestone streets. The *Charles W. Morgan,* New England's last wooden whaleship, are moored at the Seaport's docks. Sea Scouts and other youths learn seamanship aboard these famous old sailing ships. The Marine Historical Museum here has one of the finest collections of clipper ship models in America. The *Australia,* the oldest American schooner afloat, and the Marine Historical Association established Mystic Seaport in 1929. Each year, hundreds of tourists visit the water-front village and the Marine Historical Museum.

ALBERT E. VAN DUSEN

See also CONNECTICUT (color picture).

MYSTIC SHRINE. See MASONRY.

MYSTICISM, *MIHS tuh sihz'm,* is the teaching or belief that a person achieves knowledge of God through direct awareness or personal intuition, rather than through logic and reasoning. A person who accepts mysticism is called a *mystic.* He wants to realize truth or ultimate meaning, not just think it.

The mystic feels that all attempts to prove the existence of God by logic end in questions that cannot be answered. He believes that all the truths discovered by science lead finally to objects in time and space. The mystic believes that, following certain preparations, the heart can understand in a flash of insight what the mind may not be able to understand logically. He feels that intuition is the basis of religion.

Since mysticism seeks to go beyond the limits of logic and reasoning, it has some dangerous aspects. In religion, it has sometimes been associated with unstable personality. St. John of the Cross, a great Christian mystic, speaking of a nun who claimed to have held conversations with God, said: "All this that she says, 'God spoke to me; I spoke to God,' seems nonsense. She has only been speaking to herself." But mysticism still remains an expression of man's desire to have first-hand experience of meaning, reality, or God.

Mysticism plays a prominent part in Hinduism, Buddhism, Taoism, and Shinto. Quakers (The Society of Friends) also stress the mystical element in religion. Judaism, Christianity, and Islam have produced many mystics. Famous Roman Catholic mystics include St. Bernard, Meister Eckhart, Jan van Ruysbroeck, St. Theresa, St. Francis of Assisi, and St. John of the Cross. Among Protestant mystics are Jacob Boehme, George Fox, and Rufus Jones. Some mystics believed that the ordinary experience of life should be blended with the higher spiritual life. Then the spirit can achieve happiness in spite of worldly difficulties.

FLOYD H. ROSS

MYTHOLOGY

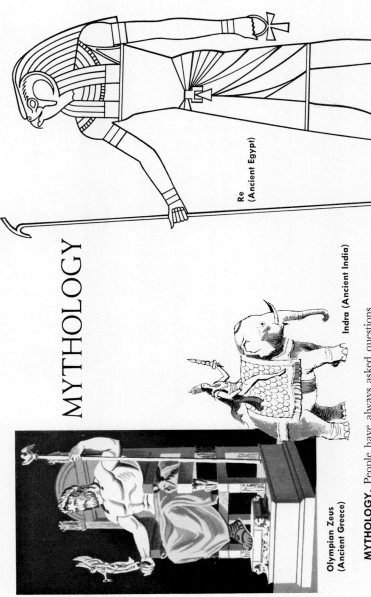

Re (Ancient Egypt)

Indra (Ancient India)

Olympian Zeus (Ancient Greece)

Odin (Scandinavia)

Nasjonalgalleriet, Oslo

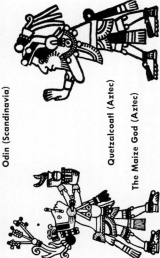

Quetzalcoatl (Aztec)

The Maize God (Aztec)

MYTHOLOGY. People have always asked questions about things around them. They have always wanted to know why the sun seems to rise in the morning and set in the evening. They have always wanted to know why land is sometimes flat, sometimes hilly, sometimes rich, and sometimes poor. They have always wanted to know what makes an echo call back to them.

Today we have books on astronomy to teach us that the sunrise is not a real rising of the sun, but is caused by the turning of the earth on its axis. We have books on geology to teach us how mountains and deserts were formed. We have books on physics to teach us that an echo is not an answering voice, but merely the same sound thrown back to us.

The people of long ago did not have scientists to tell them what they wanted to know. They had no books in which to search for answers. So the people made up their own answers to the questions and wove them into some of the most beautiful stories and fancies the world has ever known.

This does not mean that some wise man simply invented, all at once, the answer to such a question as why the sun rises. The explanation developed gradually. So wonderful an object as the sun must be more than human. And thus there grew up the idea that the sun was a god—one of the strongest of the gods. But even a god could not walk across the great stretch of sky between morning and evening. So legend gave him a chariot drawn by magnificent white horses. In time such stories grew up about almost every object in nature. The rustling of the leaves was supposed to be the murmuring voice of the goddess who lived in the tree. The hurrying stream was a nymph rushing to join her lover, the sea. The stars were good people whom the gods had placed in the sky, so that their virtues might never be forgotten. Thus the belief called *anthropomorphism* was born, in which the gods were thought of as being like human beings in form and action.

The stories which the people made up are called *myths*. The whole system of such stories form what is called *mythology*. There are two kinds of myths. The *explanatory* myth is described above. It answers natural questions about natural objects. The *aesthetic* myth seems to have no object except to entertain.

How Myths Began. There are four general beliefs about how gods and myths about them were invented. Each of these theories gives us a reason why it is important, as well as interesting, to study mythology.

An ancient Greek writer, Euhemerus (300's B.C.), believed that the ancient gods were patterned after heroes who actually lived at one time. His theory is called *Euhemerism*.

A second theory was put forth by philologists, or people who study the growth of language. This theory claims that men repeating things their grandfathers said understood them in a different sense and out of that misunderstanding created myths. A grandfather said, "Time eats up everything." Generations later "everything" might mean "all children." The word for "time" might not be the word then used; it might sound very solemn, and seem as if a god was being spoken about—'Chronos (or Saturn) devours his children.' So a myth would arise about the primeval god devouring his children until his wife gave him a stone wrapped in swaddling clothes.

The third theory, that of personifying the things of nature to explain their causes, is supported by many anthropologists, or people who study the history of the human race.

A French sociologist, Émile Durkheim, explained myths from the fourth viewpoint, that of society as a whole. He said that ancient peoples got so excited during their tribal festivities that they thought a great power was coming to them from some object in their camps. This emblem, then, would be sacred to them. Soon other objects connected with this one would also be sacred. Perhaps the sun shining on the sacred object in the camp would become the most sacred of all objects, and thus the greatest god of all.

We study mythology because it is the religion of a primitive people. And it is their science and literature as well. It is their religion because it tells what the gods do and what the people should do to please the gods. It is their science because it explains natural events by making up supernatural causes for them. It is their literature, containing their favorite tales.

Some Interesting Questions. It is often found that a myth which grew up in Greece or in Egypt is very much like one woven by the faraway Norsemen, or even than some American Indian tale is strangely like one that the Romans made. Even the wisest scholars have not been able to explain exactly how this likeness between myths happened. Some declare that long, long ago all these people must have had common ancestors. They say the myths must have been invented before people became separated and moved to different parts of the world. But most scholars have another explanation. They say that the different peoples found themselves in the same world, with the same things going on around them. Thus the peoples naturally asked the same questions, and made up similar answers.

A second question arises about the character of the mythological gods. Some of the ancient gods were not only jealous and cruel and vengeful, but actually immoral as well. It would seem that they set very poor examples for the people to follow. Indeed, there was one powerful god, Mercury, who had special charge of thieves and helped them out of their troubles. Some students of mythology believe that wise men invented good and kindly gods, thinking that they might be helpful to the people. Then other storytellers came along later and made up the others in a spirit of daring and irreverence. Another explanation is that all the myths are only legends about human heroes with human failings, as Euhemerus believed.

The Greeks and Romans, the Norsemen, the Egyptians, the Aztecs, and the Hindus are the peoples whose mythologies have been most studied. Only the first two will be treated here in detail. The Egyptian and Hindu myths have not been woven into our literature and so they do not have a wide appeal. Some of the Egyptian and Hindu gods are described in separate articles in THE WORLD BOOK ENCYCLOPEDIA.

Myths Concerning the Creation of the World

Greek and Roman. The Romans had some gods of their own, but they also adopted most of those of the Greeks. They also took over the Greek story of the creation. First of all, said the Greeks, there was just a vast hole, known as Chaos. From this there rose Love, which created the goddess Gaea, or Terra (Earth). From these two came the sky and the mountains, the sea, and the animals. Chaos also brought forth two beings, Erebus (Darkness) and Nox (Night). And from these gloomy creatures, strangely enough, sprang two beautiful beings, Light and Day.

Gaea and Uranus (Heaven) were mother and father to twelve children who grew to gigantic size and were

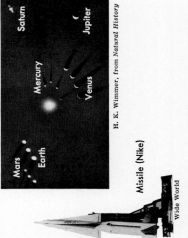

Saturn Jupiter Mercury Venus Mars Earth

H. K. Wimmer, from Natural History

Ford Motor Co.
Automobile (Mercury)

Missile (Thor)

United Press Int.

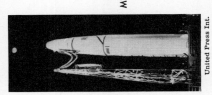

Names from Mythology have been given to countless objects, such as the planets, and to many products in everyday use. Recently, they have been given to missiles for defense.

Missile (Nike)

Wide World

called Titans. Uranus, the first ruler of all things, proved to be very cruel. At length Gaea helped one of the Titans, Saturn, to overthrow Uranus, and Saturn became king. His period of rule was called the Golden Age, because everyone on earth was good and happy. But this ended when one of Saturn's sons, Jupiter, overthrew Saturn and made himself king of the universe. He gave the sea to his brother Neptune, and gave the underworld, or Hades, to his brother Pluto.

Norse. In the beginning, the Norse myths say, there was no world, but just a great formless hole, or abyss. To the north were mist and darkness and to the south were fire and light. Out of the mist world there flowed twelve rivers which emptied into the abyss and were frozen there. Fiery blasts from the fire world melted this ice, and a vapor arose. The vapor condensed, came to life, and became the giant Ymir, father of all the giants. From the same source was formed the huge cow, Adhumbla, whose milk fed the giant. Adhumbla in turn fed herself by licking the salt from the ice. As she licked, she uncovered Bori, the first of the gods, from whom all the other gods were descended. Bori's grandsons, Odin, Vili, and Ve, fought and slew the wicked Ymir, and formed the world from his body. His flesh became the dry land, his blood the seas, his skull the overarching heavens, his bones the rocks, his hair the forests, and his scattered brains the clouds. Then light was needed. So the three gods placed sparks from the fire world in the heavens as sun, moon, and stars.

Myths Explaining the Making of Man

Greek and Roman. For a time the gods had the earth to themselves, according to Greek and Roman myths, but it was a lonesome place. Then the Titan Prometheus molded a clay figure in the image of the gods and breathed life into it. Prometheus wanted to bestow some helpful gift upon this creature of his skill because he was very proud of it. But his brother Epimetheus had given all the good qualities to the animals. He had given a hard shell to the tortoise, swiftness to the hare, slyness to the fox, strength to the bear, and fierceness to the tiger. What remained for man? Prometheus knew of something more valuable than any of these. So from the home of the gods he brought back a tube of that wonderful thing, fire. The gods were very angry and severely punished Prometheus and the race of men.

Norse. The Norse myths say that one day Odin was walking near the seashore with two other gods. They were talking sadly about the fact that there was no one to enjoy the beautiful world they had made. Their own home was far above the earth. All at once Odin saw two shapely trees, an ash (Ask) and an elm (Embla). "From these," he declared, "I shall make creatures that shall live in this world we have fashioned—bask in its warmth, drink of its waters, force its soil to bear; and they shall give us homage which will be sweet to us." Then of the ash he made a man, of the elm a woman. And from these two sprang all the race of men.

Myths of Sin and Punishment

Greek and Roman. In the Golden Age, all men were innocent. But the gods were still angry because man had learned to use the most wonderful thing the gods themselves possessed—fire. Pandora was sent to earth with a box of evils. As a result, the world became so wicked that Jupiter saw that he must sweep it clean of its people and give it a new start. He caused a great rain to fall and a flood to cover the earth. When it passed, only virtuous Deucalion and Pyrrha were left. They repeopled the earth by casting over their shoulders the stones which lay about them on the mountain top. It is strange and interesting to find in the Greek mythology a story so very like the Biblical account of the flood and the saving of Noah. It is like meeting one's next-door neighbor in a faraway land.

Norse. Most of the Norse gods were very good and kindly. But there was one, Loki, who took delight in mischief and wickedness. It was he and the evil giants who first taught men to sin. Men learned quickly, and soon the age of innocence passed away. Gods and men had to fight for their very existence against the powers of evil. Some time, the Norse people believed, there should come a dreadful time known as the Twilight of the Gods (Ragnarök). Then the evil forces would triumph over the good, and the rule of Odin would come to an end. A new world was to arise out of this destruction. Innocence and happiness were to prevail again under the rule of new gods.

The Gods

Greek and Roman. The great gods, according to the Greek poets, had their home on Mount Olympus. Zeus (Jupiter) was their king. Hera (Juno), his sister and wife, was their queen. Others who lived on Mount Olympus (in Roman names) were Apollo, Mars, Mercury, Vulcan, Diana, Minerva, Venus, and Vesta. Ceres, goddess of agriculture and a sister of Jupiter, had a home on Olympus, but she preferred to live on earth, close to her work. Neptune lived in the sea. There were

MYTHOLOGY

Nasjonalgalleriet, Oslo; Alinari

thousands of other deities. Some had great power, but others ruled only the particular stream, tree, wind, or mountain that was their dwelling place. The Greeks held a yearly "Festival to the Unknown Gods" to make sure they worshiped all the gods.

Norse. There were, according to the Norse myths, twelve great gods and twenty-four goddesses. They had their home in a wonderful region above the earth, called *Asgard*. A rainbow bridge led from Asgard to earth. The gods often crossed the rainbow to take part in the affairs of men. The Norse deities seem to have behaved far better than the Greek gods. Besides Odin and Loki, the chief Norse gods and goddesses were

───── GREEK AND ROMAN GODS ─────

Position	Roman Name	Greek Name
King of the Gods	Jupiter	Zeus
God of the Sun and Youth	Apollo	Apollo
God of War	Mars	Ares
God of the Sea	Neptune	Poseidon
Messenger of the Gods	Mercury	Hermes
Blacksmith for the Gods	Vulcan	Hephaestus
God of Wine	Bacchus	Dionysus
God of Love	Cupid	Eros
God of the Underworld	Pluto	Pluto
God of Time	Saturn	Kronos
Queen of the Gods	Juno	Hera
Goddess of Agriculture	Ceres	Demeter
Goddess of the Moon and		
of Hunting	Diana	Artemis
Goddess of Wisdom	Minerva	Athena
Goddess of Love and Beauty	Venus	Aphrodite
Goddess of the Home	Vesta	Hestia

Balder, Freya, Frigg, Heimdall, Thor, and Tyr. There are individual articles in THE WORLD BOOK ENCYCLOPEDIA that describe most of these gods.

Explanatory Myths

The change from summer to winter was one of the common happenings which puzzled the ancient peoples. The following stories give very interesting explanations for the change. The first one, *The Underground Queen*, was invented by the Greeks. The second, *The Death of Balder*, came from the Norse peoples. To each is added a brief paragraph pointing out the part it had in the "science" of the ancients. But the stories are worth while just as stories, without any such explanation.

The Underground Queen

Ceres, the goddess of agriculture, was one of the busiest of the goddesses. In the springtime she had to go from field to field throughout the earth, attending to the sowing of the seeds. In the summer she watched grains and fruits grow. In the autumn she went about blessing the harvests. She loved the work, but was always glad to come back to her home and to her beautiful daughter, Proserpina, whom the Greeks called Persephone. Ceres loved Proserpina very dearly.

Proserpina also had her duties. She had charge of all the flowers. In the springtime violets and daisies and buttercups sprang up in her footsteps as she walked across the meadows. Naturally, she loved the flowers and spent much of her time in the fields with her companions, tending the flowers and gathering them for wreaths.

One day the girls were playing in the meadows when they heard a strange, rumbling sound. A huge, dark chariot, with a handsome but gloomy-looking driver, was coming toward them. The girls screamed in terror and started to run. But the driver stopped his chariot, and seizing Proserpina, he bore her away with him in his chariot. The frightened girl called to her companions and to her mother. But the black horses carried her on too swiftly for any help to follow. Meanwhile, the stern-looking man explained to Proserpina that he was Pluto,

In Battle, the Norse Valkyries swept down to select the heroes destined to die in combat, *left.* Greek myths also included stories of a race of warlike women, the Amazons, *right.*

king of all the regions below the earth. He explained that he loved her and wanted her for his wife. Proserpina answered:

"I must tell my mother. She will be wild with grief when she finds that I am gone and knows not where to look for me."

But Pluto shook his head.

"She would never let you go with me," he declared.

While they were talking thus, they had come to the bank of the River Cyane, which stood in their way. Angrily, Pluto struck the ground with his great three-pronged spear, or trident. The earth opened and made him a passage to his underground kingdom. The darkness in which they found themselves was delightful to Pluto. But to Proserpina it was nothing less than horrible.

"You will like it when you become accustomed to it," said Pluto.

Gradually the way grew lighter, though the light was white and ghostly—not like the beautiful golden light of the upper world.

They came at length to the huge palace of Pluto. He expected Proserpina to exclaim with delight over its gorgeousness. Pluto owned all the gold and silver and gems that lay hidden in the earth, and had used them to decorate his palace. But Proserpina was not used to gorgeousness. She and her mother had always lived simply, and the rich gems were less to her than a handful of fragrant flowers would have been. And she would gladly have exchanged all the jewel-studded lights for one look at the stars.

It was the same way with the food. All her life she had eaten only the plainest dishes—simple grains, fruits, bread, and milk. And the rich food which Pluto ordered to be placed before her seemed so strange to her that she would not even taste it.

Meanwhile, Proserpina's mother was almost distracted with fear and grief. The girl's companions could tell her nothing except that a man in a black chariot had carried her daughter off. She could have no idea who the man was. She sought day and night through one country after another for her daughter. But it was all in vain.

Finally, Ceres became angry with the earth which had failed to aid her in her search, and laid a curse upon it.

Drought and famine, she declared, should extend over the whole earth. Nothing green should grow. There should be no seedtime and no harvest until her daughter should come back to her. In vain, the people implored her; in vain, tales of their suffering reached her. The gracious and kindly goddess was cruel enough now.

At length she found a clue. The river Arethusa, which comes up from the Lower World, had seen in the kingdom of the underworld a queen who looked like Proserpina. She was pale and sad, and the white poppies in her hair were very different from the bright flowers she had been so fond of wearing. But the river thought that beyond a doubt it was Proserpina. Ceres knew not whether to be glad or sorry. Her daughter was found, but found where? She went to the meeting place of the gods on Olympus and implored Jupiter to have her daughter brought to her. All the gods felt sorry for Ceres. They also felt sorry for the suffering people on earth. At length Jupiter summoned Mercury, the messenger of the gods, and sent him to the regions of the underworld.

"I will do my best," said the king of gods, "but the Fates are even stronger than I. They have declared that if your daughter has eaten anything while in Pluto's realm, she may not again come back to the light of day."

When Mercury (Hermes in Greek) reached the kingdom of Pluto and stood before the king and the sad-eyed queen, he himself felt sorry for her. He hoped that he could take her back with him. But alas! He found that Proserpina had eaten a few of the seeds of a pomegranate.

"It cannot be," Mercury said, and he went sadly back to the assembly of the gods.

At length, the Fates agreed to be less severe. They declared that Proserpina must spend six months of every year with Pluto in the dark kingdom, because of the seeds she had eaten. She might spend the remaining six months with her mother on the earth.

You may imagine the delight of Ceres when it came time for her daughter to return to her. She stood anxiously at the door of her cottage, waiting, watching. Suddenly there seemed to be a new freshness in the air.

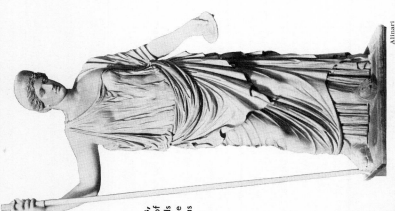

In the Home of the Gods, Juno, *right,* was the wife of Jupiter and queen of the gods in Roman mythology. Her Norse counterpart, Frigg, *left,* was the wife of Odin.

Alinari

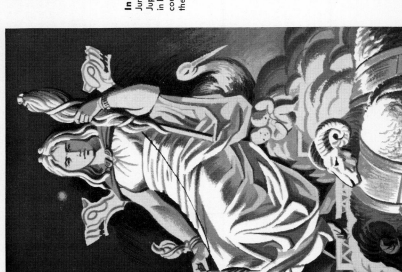

The dry grass in the meadows grew green before her eyes. Purple violets and yellow buttercups started up all about her.

"She is come!" she cried. And sure enough, Proserpina was advancing toward her across the meadows, her hands outstretched, her garments blowing in the breeze. No longer was she the sad, white-faced queen of the underworld. This was the old, glad Proserpina who had left her long before.

Ceres was one of the kindest of the goddesses, and the Greeks felt she would not make her people suffer by taking away her warmth all through the winter months without a good reason. So they made this beautiful tale of the loss of Proserpina. Ceres mourned when Proserpina descended to the underworld each year. No flowers bloomed and no seeds sprouted, because it was winter. But when she returned to the upper world, spring came with all its gladness.

The Death of Balder

Balder the Beautiful was the center of all brightness and cheer in Asgard, home of the gods. Everybody loved him except Lok, or Loki, who was so wicked that he could not love anybody who was good and happy. He let himself brood upon his hatred for Balder until it seemed that the only thing in life he cared for was to injure Balder. And Balder seemed to feel his danger, for he had most terrible dreams of unknown woe to come. Finally Balder spoke of his fears to his father and mother, Odin and Frigg.

"Do not fear, my son," said Frigg comfortingly, "I shall visit everything on earth—every beast and bird, every treacherous poison and every lurking disease, every stone and tree and creeping thing, and even the flaming fire—and make them promise not to harm Balder."

Feeling much safer, Balder went home to his shining palace and his beloved wife, Nanna. A smile again shone from his eyes.

Frigg's journey about the earth made her heart very proud, for every object and living thing on earth gladly vowed not to injure Balder.

"Why should we hurt the one whom most we love?" they questioned—"the one without whose presence the earth would be a gloomy place?"

The happy Frigg went back to Asgard, wearied with her journeyings. Just as she was about to enter Valhalla,

she saw a tiny mistletoe plant on the branches of a strong oak. For an instant she stopped, because she had exacted no promise from the little shrub. But finally she passed on without speaking, thinking the mistletoe was too young and weak to do any harm.

When the gods heard of her success, they hit upon a new way of amusing themselves. Balder stood upon their playground and allowed them to hurl their weapons at him. The sharpest spears, the most jagged stones harmed Balder no more than a shower of rose petals. They turned aside just as they came to him.

But there was one god who had had no invitation to this sport—Loki. When he passed by and saw it, he was furiously angry. Did all things love Balder? He hastily disguised himself as a poor old woman and went to Frigg's palace.

"Mother of the gods," said this old woman, "your son Balder will be killed, for the gods are hurling at him their sharpest darts."

"Ah," said the happy mother, "they cannot harm him, for all things in heaven and earth have taken an oath not to injure him."

"Marvelous!" said the visitor. "You must be a proud mother to have such an honor shown your son. Did you really mean everything?"

"Yes," answered Frigg. "Oh, no," she added carelessly, "I did not trouble to ask the little shrub on the oak eastward of Valhalla. It could do no one any harm."

With more flattering words, Loki slipped away and resumed his own shape. He hastened to the Valhalla oak. He cut off the mistletoe, now grown larger and stronger, and fashioned a dart from it. Then he joined the other gods at the sporting ground. He approached Hoder, Balder's blind brother, who stood apart with no weapon in his hand, and asked him why he did not join in the game.

"Gladly would I do honor to Balder," said Hoder, "but I cannot tell in which direction to throw, nor have I anything to hurl."

"That I can remedy," said Loki. "I will direct your aim, and I will give you the dart."

Gladly Hoder agreed. Under Loki's guidance, he threw the mistletoe dart. But instead of falling harmless at Balder's feet, it pierced him through and through, and he fell down dead. For a moment there was a horror-stricken silence. Then a wail of anguish went up, and the gods rushed toward Hoder and demanded his life. But Heimdall, wisest of the gods, persuaded them that it was not the fault of the blind Hoder, but of the treach-

GOD AND HEROES

THOR

ZEUS

MERCURY

HERCULES

Bettmann Archive; Alinari; Newark Public Library

erous Loki, who had now vanished. He persuaded them to make plans for bringing Balder back.

Hermod, called the Nimble, mounted Odin's eight-footed steed Sleipnir, and rode away to the abode of Hela, goddess of the dead. It was a long, cold, and dark journey. At last he came to Hela's realm and pleaded with her to return Balder. But the dark goddess was the daughter of Loki, and remained unmoved at the sad tale.

"Let us see," she said coldly, "whether it is true that everything loved and mourns for him. If all things in the world weep for him, he shall go back. But if one person or one thing refuse to weep, here he shall stay."

Somewhat cheered, Hermod rode back to Asgard and told this tale. Messengers were sent out through all the world to beg everything to weep for Balder. Only success greeted them, until at length they found an old hag sitting at the mouth of a cave.

"With dry tears will I weep," she scoffed. "Hela shall keep her prey."

"It is Loki in disguise," they whispered as they made their way sorrowfully back to Asgard.

Then they carried the beautiful body of Balder to the seashore and laid it upon his great ship, on which a funeral pile had been raised. Each god cast into the pile his chief treasure, and then the fire was lighted. At the last moment, Balder's wife Nanna hurled herself upon the pile, because she could not live without her husband. All ablaze, the ship was launched for the open sea. Silently the gods stood and watched it as it drifted on and on, burning ever higher and higher. And when the night was almost gone, the distant flame flickered out, and the gods knew that Balder was gone forever.

In this myth, Balder represents the summer, all too fleeting in the northern lands. Hoder, blind and grim, is the winter with its bitter strength. And the death of Balder is the slaying of the summer by winter.

Aesthetic Myths

The ancients had no novels or short stories such as we have today. But they did have their myths, which must have answered the same purpose. The aesthetic myths seem to have had no teaching purpose, except as any good story teaches its own lesson. The story of Atalanta is one of the most pleasing of the Greek myths.

The Story of Atalanta's Race

Schoeneus, king of Boeotia, had one daughter, Atalanta. Although she was the most beautiful girl in the kingdom, she remained a maiden in her father's house long after all her companions were married. And this was not because she lacked suitors. Young men, handsome, strong, rich, fearless, came constantly to her father's palace seeking her in marriage. They all went away unhappy.

For Atalanta had made a vow that she would not marry, but would devote her life to the chase, like the goddess Diana. But it was hard to refuse so many fine men without having a very good reason. So she made up her mind to give a different answer to her suitors. Accordingly, when the next youth presented himself, she replied:

"I shall marry the man who can defeat me in a race, but everyone who tries and fails shall be put to death."

Atalanta was not really cruel. She simply wanted to keep people from bothering her about marriage.

Now, Atalanta could run as swiftly as the deer she hunted in the forests. A number of suitors raced with her, but lost, and met their deaths by reason of their love for her. The people of her father's kingdom were beginning to murmur among themselves at her cruelty. One day a youth, Hippomenes by name, who had never before seen Atalanta, acted as judge in one of the races. As he took his place in the judge's seat, he said to himself: "How can any man be so foolish as to risk his life for

Arriving in the Underworld, according to Greek mythology, the dead were ferried across the River Styx to Pluto's kingdom.

Bettmann Archive

Arriving in Valhalla, according to Norse mythology, heroes slain in battle were welcomed to a feast by the Valkyries.

Bettmann Archive

the sake of this one girl, when there are so many beautiful girls to choose from?"

But when he saw Atalanta step forward, he changed his mind. Never had he looked upon anything so beautiful. He found himself hoping that the youths who ran with her would be defeated.

And as she ran, she looked even more beautiful. Her bright hair blew backward in the breeze, a lovely color flushed her face, and her gracefulness was wonderful to look upon. She won as she always did, and the youths who had made trial of their skill were mercilessly put to death. But even this did not frighten Hippomenes.

"What glory," he said to her, "can there be in defeating weaklings like those who just ran with you? Tomorrow, if you will, I shall try my speed and endurance against yours."

Atalanta felt that she would scarcely wish to defeat this young man, so handsome did he look, so brave, so worthy to be her partner. Still she only nodded her head, and made up her mind to give him as hard a trial as she had given the others.

Now, Hippomenes knew that he could never hope to conquer her in a fair race, but he thought:

"There are ways in which it can be managed. Every girl is curious, and every girl likes beautiful things."

Accordingly, when he took his place beside Atalanta the next day, he had in the front of his robe three beautiful golden apples. As the starting signal was given, the two sped forward, side by side. For a moment it seemed as if he would actually outrun her, but with a fleet step she passed him. Instantly, he seized one of his golden apples and tossed it a little ahead of her. She caught her breath and almost stopped, but her desire to win was strong. But the beautiful golden apple looked so tempting that she hastily stooped to grasp it. Running with all his might, Hippomenes threw a second apple, and again Atalanta slowed to seize it, yet keeping fairly ahead of the youth. Almost despairing, Hippomenes tossed the third apple, and most beautiful of all. It was the largest, ruddiest, and most beautiful of all.

This was too much for the princess. She stopped suddenly, stooped, and seized the apple. The delay was but for a second, but it was all Hippomenes needed. He passed her, and with a final rush, reached forward and touched the maple goal. He had won! And the cheers of the people told that they were glad that at last their beautiful, haughty princess had been conquered.

And as Atalanta came toward Hippomenes, all could see that she looked far more happy in her defeat than she had looked before in all her victories.

PADRAIC COLUM

Alinari

The Sun God, Apollo, *above,* was also god of music and poetry in Greek mythology. In Norse mythology, Frey, *right,* was the god of peace and prosperity and of crops.

Related Articles in World Book include:

EGYPTIAN GODS AND GODDESSES

Amon	Horus	Re	Set
Anubis	Isis	Serapis	Thoth
Hathor	Osiris		

GREEK AND ROMAN GODS AND GODDESSES

Aeolus	Furies	Lares and	Prometheus
Aesculapius	Graces	Penates	Proteus
Apollo	Hades	Luna	Rhea
Atlas	Hebe	Mars	Saturn
Aurora	Hecate	Mercury	Satyr
Bacchus	Helios	Minerva	Somnus
Calliope	Hygeia	Morpheus	Terra
Ceres	Hymen	Muse	Thanatos
Cupid	Hyperion	Nemesis	Titan
Diana	Iris	Neptune	Triton
Fates	Janus	Pan	Uranus
Faun	Juno	Pluto	Venus
Flora	Jupiter	Plutus	Vesta
Fortuna		Pomona	Vulcan

MYTHS AND MYTHOLOGICAL CHARACTERS

Achates	Cecrops	Hero and	Orion
Achilles	Charon	Leander	Orpheus
Actaeon	Circe	Hesperides	Pandora
Adonis	Clytemnestra	Io	Paris
Agamemnon	Daedalus	Iphigenia	Penelope
Ajax	Daphne	Jason	Perseus
Alcestis	Deucalion	Laocoön	Phaedra
Amphitryon	Dido	Lotus-	Phaëthon
Andromache	Egeria	Eater	Priam
Antigone	Electra	Medea	Proserpina
Arachne	Endymion	Memnon	Protesilaus
Arethusa	Erebus	Menelaus	Psyche
Argonauts	Europa	Mentor	Pygmalion
Ariadne	Eurydice	Midas	Rhada-
Baucis and	Galatea	Minos	manthus
Philemon	Ganymede	Narcissus	Semele
Boreas	Hector	Nausicaa	Sisyphus
Cadmus	Hecuba	Neoptolemus	Tantalus
Calypso	Helen of	Nestor	Theseus
Cassandra	Troy	Niobe	Troy
Castor and	Hercules	Oedipus	Ulysses
Pollux	Hermione	Orestes	

MYTHOLOGICAL CREATURES

Apis	Fafnir	Minotaur	Roc
Argus	Genii	Nereid	Scylla
Centaur	Giant	Nix	Sea Ser-
Cerberus	Gorgon	Nymph	pent
Chimaera	Harpy	Pegasus	Siren
Chiron	Hydra	Phoenix	Unicorn
Cyclops	Medusa	Polyphemus	Troy
Dryad	Mermaid	Python	Werewolf
Elf			

MYTHOLOGICAL PLACES AND EVENTS

Abydos	Elysian Fields	Olympus
Acheron	Etna	Parnassus
Aganippe	Hellespont	Pelion
Arcadia	Hephaestus,	Pillars of Hercules
Asgard	Temple of	Quirinal
Atlantis	Hesperia	Styx
Augean Stables	Ionian Sea	Tartarus
Cyclades	Labyrinth	Thebes
Delphi	Lethe	Troy
Dodona	Niflheim	Valhalla

OTHER RELATED ARTICLES

Augur	Golden Fleece
Bulfinch (Thomas)	Gordian Knot
Cornucopia	Hecatomb
Folklore	Lorelei

NORSE GODS AND GODDESSES

Balder	Frigg	Loki	Thor
Frey	Heimdall	Norns	Valkyrie
Freyja	Hel	Odin	

Lupercalia   Nectar   Sibyl
Marduk   Oracles   Trojan Horse
Mysteries   Saturnalia   Tuesday
Nebo

Outline

I. **Introduction**
  A. How Myths Began
  B. Some Interesting Questions
II. **Myths Concerning the Creation of the World**
  A. Greek and Roman   B. Norse
III. **Myths Explaining the Making of Man**
  A. Greek and Roman   B. Norse
IV. **Myths of Sin and Punishment**
  A. Greek and Roman   B. Norse
V. **The Gods**
  A. Greek and Roman   B. Norse
VI. **Explanatory Myths**
VII. **The Underground Queen**
VIII. **The Death of Balder**
IX. **Aesthetic Myths**
X. **The Story of Atalanta's Race**

Questions

Why do people study mythology today?
How do *explanatory* myths differ from *aesthetic* myths?
Who were Balder? Atalanta? Ceres? Loki? Jupiter? Why were they important?
What explanations are given for the origins of many myths? Which seems the most probable?
Why did the Greeks consider Prometheus so important? What story did they tell about him?
How did the Norse myths explain the existence of sin and punishment?
What peoples created the mythologies most often studied today?
What reasons can be given for the remarkable similarities among the myths of different peoples?

Books to Read

BULFINCH, THOMAS. *Book of Myths.* Macmillan, 1964. This book contains selections from the author's *The Age of Fable.* A fuller edition, suitable for older readers, is *Mythology: The Age of Fable; The Age of Chivalry; Legends of Charlemagne.* New ed. Crowell, 1962.

COLUM, PADRAIC. *The Golden Fleece and the Heroes Who Lived Before Achilles.* Macmillan, 1959. Myths retold for young readers.

COOLIDGE, OLIVIA E. *Greek Myths.* Houghton, 1949. *Legends of the North.* 1951.

FRAZER, JAMES G. *New Golden Bough.* Abridged ed. by Theodore H. Gaster. Criterion, 1959.

GAYLEY, CHARLES M. *Classic Myths in English Literature and in Art.* Rev. ed. Ginn, 1939.

GRAVES, ROBERT. *The Greek Myths.* 2 vols. Penguin, 1955. This collection of the myths of Greece shows their many variations and reinterprets them in the light of modern discoveries. *Greek Gods and Heroes.* Doubleday, 1960. Retells 27 classic legends in stimulating and colloquial language.

GREEN, ROGER L. *Heroes of Greece and Troy.* Retold from the ancient authors. Walck, 1961.

GRIMAL, PIERRE, ed. *Larousse World Mythology.* Putnam, 1965. This book contains up-to-date descriptions of the origins of myths.

HAMILTON, EDITH. *Mythology.* Little, Brown, 1942. A vivid account of the Greek, Roman, and Norse myths.

HOSFORD, DOROTHY G. *Thunder of the Gods.* Holt, Rinehart, & Winston, 1952. The author describes the adventures of Odin, Thor, Balder, and Loki.

KERÉNYI, CARL. *The Gods of the Greeks.* Grove Press, 1960. Stories of the Greek myths by an authority on Greek philosophy and ancient history.

Larousse Encyclopedia of Mythology. Ed. by Felix Guirand. Prometheus Press, 1959. Articles on the mythologies of all the major cultures, with extensive coverage of the Greek myths.

ROSE, HERBERT J. *A Handbook of Greek Mythology.* Dutton, 1959.

SABIN, FRANCES ELLIS. *Classical Myths That Live Today.* Ralph V.D. Magoffin, classical ed. Silver Burdett, 1958.

SELLEW, CATHERINE F. *Adventures with the Heroes.* Little, Brown, 1954. Stories of the Volsungs and Nibelungs.

MYXEDEMA. See GOITER.